STATUTES AND ORDINANCES OF THE UNIVERSITY OF CAMBRIDGE

STATUTES AND ORDINANCES OF THE UNIVERSITY OF CAMBRIDGE

AND

PASSAGES FROM ACTS OF PARLIAMENT RELATING TO THE UNIVERSITY

PUBLISHED BY AUTHORITY

CAMBRIDGE UNIVERSITY PRESS

2014

CAMBRIDGE
UNIVERSITY PRESS

University Printing House, Cambridge CB2 8BS, United Kingdom

Cambridge University Press is part of the University of Cambridge.

It furthers the University's mission by disseminating knowledge in the pursuit of education, learning and research at the highest international levels of excellence.

www.cambridge.org

Revised edition 2014

Printed in the United Kingdom by the Linney Group, Mansfield

ISBN 978-1-107-42837-9

CONTENTS

STATUTES OF THE UNIVERSITY OF CAMBRIDGE

Approved by Her Majesty in Council on 11 February 2014 (Reporter, *6338, 2013–14, p. 371*)

Statute A

The Chancellor and the Government of the University

Statute B

Membership of the University and Degrees

Statute C

University Offices and Employment in the University

Schedule

Academic Staff

Statute D

Discipline and the University Courts

Statute E

Trusts

SPECIAL ORDINANCES OF THE UNIVERSITY OF CAMBRIDGE

Approved by Grace 2 of 3 July 2013

Special Ordinances under Statute A

The Chancellor and the Government of the University

Special Ordinance

Special Ordinances under Statute B

Membership of the University and Degrees

Special Ordinance

Special Ordinances under Statute C

University Offices and Employment in the University

Special Ordinance

Special Ordinances under Statute D

Discipline and the University Courts

Special Ordinance to Statute G

Colleges and Collegiate Foundations

ORDINANCES OF THE UNIVERSITY OF CAMBRIDGE

Chapter I

The Chancellor and the Government of the University

Chapter II

Matriculation, Residence, Admission to Degrees, Discipline

CHAPTER III

EXAMINATIONS

CHAPTER IV

PRELIMINARY EXAMINATIONS AND TRIPOS EXAMINATIONS

CHAPTER V

B.A. DEGREE AND M.A. DEGREE

CHAPTER VI

GRADUATE STUDENTS

CHAPTER VII

DEGREES, DIPLOMAS, AND OTHER QUALIFICATIONS

CHAPTER VIII

CHAPTER IX

FACULTIES, DEPARTMENTS, AND OTHER INSTITUTIONS UNDER THE SUPERVISION OF THE GENERAL BOARD

CHAPTER X

CHAPTER XI

UNIVERSITY OFFICES AND GRANTS OF TITLE

CHAPTER XII

TRUSTS

CHAPTER XIII

FINANCE AND PROPERTY

CHAPTER XIV

COLLEGES

CHAPTER XV

APPENDIX I: PROCEDURES AND GUIDELINES

HISTORICAL NOTE

The University of Cambridge is thought to have originated in the early thirteenth century, and there is no doubt that by about 1250 it was a recognized centre of study. It was not, however, until 1318 that Cambridge received from Pope John XXII formal recognition as a *Studium Generale* or *Universitas*.

The University is a common law corporation, being a corporation by prescription consisting of a Chancellor, Masters, and Scholars who from time out of mind have had the government of their members and enjoyed the privileges of such a corporation. By Act of Parliament *13 Elizabeth Cap. 29* passed in the year 1571 the incorporation of the University and all privileges then held under charter or by prescription were duly confirmed. The University is now authorized by the Lord Chancellor to act in relation to charitable, ecclesiastical, and public trusts as a trust corporation.

The corporate title of the University is *The Chancellor, Masters, and Scholars of the University of Cambridge*.

ARMS OF THE UNIVERSITY

The arms now borne by the University of Cambridge, *gules a cross ermine and four gold leopards with a book gules upon the cross*, were granted by Robert Cooke, Clarencieux King of Arms, on 9 June 1573.

REDUCED DRAWING OF THE COMMON SEAL

The Common Seal now in use was made in 1580 and on the reverse bears the inscription *Matthaeus Stokis Bedellus dedit formam 1580 Guilielmus Farrand Procurator dedit materiam.*

PREFACE

Following the enactment of the Universities of Oxford and Cambridge Act 1923, a body of Commissioners styled the University of Cambridge Commissioners was appointed to make new Statutes for the University, superseding the Statutes of 1882. Statutes were made by the Commissioners and approved by His Majesty in Council during 1926–28. For particulars of these new Statutes, see the Preface to the edition of 1928; and for amending Statutes approved since that date, see the prefaces to subsequent editions. For the final form of the Statutes which were in force immediately before 1 October 1926, see p. 136 of the edition of 1928.

During 2012–13, new Statutes were approved by the Regent House. The new Statutes were not incorporated into the 2013 edition but are included in the present edition, following their approval by Her Majesty in Council as follows:

Grace	*Approved by Order in Council*	*Published in* Reporter, *2013–14*	*Statutes affected*
2 of 3 July 2013	11 February 2014	p. 371	Statutes A–U rescinded and replaced by new Statutes A–J

During 2013–14, further amending Statutes have been made as shown below; these have been incorporated into the present edition, although they had not received the approval of Her Majesty in Council at the time when the volume was passed for press.

Grace	*Passages affected*
1 of 30 April 2014	A IV 2, A V 2
1 of 4 June 2014	C III 16

STATUTES OF THE UNIVERSITY OF CAMBRIDGE

Deum timeto: regem honorato: virtutem colito:
disciplinis bonis operam dato

Statute A

THE CHANCELLOR AND THE GOVERNMENT OF THE UNIVERSITY

CHAPTER I

THE CHANCELLOR, THE SENATE, THE HIGH STEWARD, THE DEPUTY HIGH STEWARD, AND THE COMMISSARY

1. The Chancellor of the University shall be elected by the members of the Senate voting in person and shall hold office, in accordance with the laws and customs of the University, until he or she voluntarily resigns or until the Senate otherwise determines.

2. The manner of nominating candidates, of taking votes in an election, and of determining the result of the election may be prescribed by Ordinance from time to time and unless so prescribed shall be as has been customary heretofore. When an election has taken place, an instrument of election shall be sealed as soon as conveniently may be, and shall be delivered to the person elected without delay.

3. The Chancellor shall have power to call Congregations of the Regent House, and to admit candidates to degrees and titles of degrees.

4. The Chancellor shall have power to see that all officers of the University duly perform their duties.

5. The Chancellor shall perform such other duties as may be prescribed by Statute or Ordinance.

6. If the office of Chancellor is vacant, the duties and powers of the Chancellor which are not otherwise allocated by Statute or Special Ordinance to the Vice-Chancellor shall be discharged by the High Steward (or the Deputy High Steward).

7. The following shall be members of the Senate:

(*a*) the Chancellor and the Vice-Chancellor;

(*b*) all persons whose names were inscribed on the Roll of the Regent House at the time of the last promulgation;

(*c*) all persons who hold any of these complete degrees of the University: any Doctor's degree of the University, any Master's degree of the University, or the degree of Bachelor of Divinity of the University;

provided always that

(i) if any member of the Senate wishes to resign her or his membership and so informs the Registrary, and if the Council deems the reasons given sufficient and permits the resignation, that person shall cease forthwith to be a member of the Senate, and shall not be reinstated except by a subsequent decision of the Council which shall not be taken until a period of five years has elapsed from the date of removal;

(ii) any person who suffers suspension or deprivation of her or his degree shall not be a member of the Senate during the continuance of such suspension or deprivation.

8. It shall be the duty of the Senate to enact Ordinances regulating its own procedure.

The High Steward, the Deputy High Steward, and the Commissary

9. The High Steward shall be elected by the members of the Senate voting in person. The arrangements prescribed by Statute and Ordinance for the election of the Chancellor shall apply also to the election of the High Steward.

10. The Deputy High Steward shall be appointed by the High Steward by Letters Patent.

11. The High Steward and the Deputy High Steward shall perform such duties as have heretofore been customary and any duties prescribed by Statute or Ordinance. When the office of High Steward is vacant the duties of that office shall be performed by the Deputy High Steward.

12. The Commissary shall be appointed by Letters Patent by the Chancellor or, if the office of Chancellor is vacant, by the High Steward. The Commissary shall have judicial or quasi-judicial experience or be legally qualified, and shall not hold any other office in the University or a College. In the event of a vacancy in the office of Commissary the Chancellor (or the High Steward if the office of Chancellor is vacant) shall appoint an Acting Commissary who shall have the full powers of the Commissary to act under the provisions of this chapter until a newly appointed Commissary takes office.

13. The Commissary shall perform such duties as have heretofore been customary and any duties prescribed by Statute or Ordinance. In the discharge of her or his duties under this chapter the Commissary shall not be under the direction of the Council or of any other authority in the University.

14. Each of the officers of High Steward, Deputy High Steward, and Commissary shall hold office until he or she voluntarily resigns or until the Senate otherwise determines.

CHAPTER II

POWERS OF THE UNIVERSITY

1. The University shall have power, for the encouragement of learning, the maintenance of good order and discipline, and the management of its affairs, to enact Ordinances and to issue Orders (whether by way of exception to an Ordinance or otherwise); provided always that no such Ordinance or Order shall contravene any provision of the Statutes.

2. The University may admit to any of the several degrees listed in or established pursuant to Statute B II a matriculated person who has done all that is required by the Statutes or Ordinances. Admission to a degree shall take place when a candidate is admitted to it in person at a Congregation of the Regent House; provided that the University may prescribe conditions under which a candidate may be admitted to a degree in absence.

3. The University shall have all the powers of a natural person to acquire, manage, charge, deal with, and dispose of property, both real and personal, and to enter into and carry out any transaction relating to its property or otherwise in connection with the management of its affairs, so that it may exercise any power and may enter into and carry out any kind of transaction without limitation.

4. The powers in Section 3 of this chapter may be exercised at the absolute discretion of the University and shall apply to investment as well as to any other activity or function of the University.

5. The powers in Section 3 of this chapter shall apply to property, both real and personal, of which the University is trustee, save that, in the case of a trust of which the University is not sole trustee, where the trust instrument creating the trust expressly provides to the contrary and less than sixty years have elapsed since that instrument came into operation, the powers shall not so apply without the consent of the other trustees.

6. The University may enact Ordinances providing for:

(*a*) the exercise and delegation of the powers in Section 3 of this chapter; and/or

(*b*) the collective investment of any property, real or personal, held by or for the University, with or without any other property.

7. Such Ordinances shall be read with, and shall have the same force as, these Statutes to the extent that they are consistent with these Statutes, Ordinances, and any Act of Parliament.

8. In favour of any person having dealings with the University, a certificate signed by the Registrary that any Ordinances enacted under Section 6 of this chapter have been complied with shall be conclusive.

9. The University shall have power to levy fees and other charges for any purpose or purposes connected with the University.

10. The University shall have power to accept benefactions, and shall not be prevented from accepting a benefaction even if the conditions attached thereto are at variance with the Statutes.

11. Subject to the provisions of the Statutes, the University may delegate the exercise of any of the powers specified in Sections 9 and 10 above.

12. The University shall have power to make Ordinances under which fines may be imposed by a University authority. Any such Ordinance shall state the classes of cases in which the fine may be imposed and the maximum amount which may be imposed in any one case.

13. (*a*) The University shall have a Great Common Seal and a Common Seal, and shall have power to give authority or to make Ordinances giving authority for either of the seals to be affixed to a document or to a class of documents. Neither seal shall be affixed without such authority, except when authority has been given in some other manner for which provision is made by Statute.

(*b*) The Great Common Seal shall be kept in some secure place, in a chest fastened with three locks, the keys of which shall be severally kept by the Vice-Chancellor and the Proctors; it shall not be affixed to any document except in the presence of the Vice-Chancellor or a duly appointed deputy and the Proctors or their deputies.

(*c*) The Common Seal shall be kept in some secure place, and shall be fastened with two keys, which shall be severally kept by the Vice-Chancellor, or by a Pro-Vice-Chancellor designated from time to time by the Vice-Chancellor, such designation to be published, and by the Registrary; it shall not be affixed to any document except in the presence of those officers or deputies appointed by them.

14. Titles of degrees may be granted *honoris causa* to members of the Royal Family, to British subjects who are of conspicuous merit or have done good service to the State or to the University, and to foreigners of distinction.

CHAPTER III

THE REGENT HOUSE

1. The Regent House shall be the governing body of the University.

2. Any power of making, altering, or repealing Statutes which is assigned to the University by the Universities of Oxford and Cambridge Act 1923, or by any other Act of Parliament, shall be exercised by the Regent House.

3. The powers of enacting, issuing and amending Special Ordinances, Ordinances and Orders, shall be exercised by Grace of the Regent House except so far as such powers are assigned by Statute to any other authority.

4. Special Ordinances shall be made (or amended) by Grace of the Regent House, in all cases after the issue of a Report to the University by the Council, the General Board, or jointly by the Council and the General Board. The Report shall state the main purpose of the proposed Special Ordinance (or amendment).

5. Any matter which under Statute, Special Ordinance or Ordinance shall be regulated or determined by Special Ordinance, may only be so regulated or determined.

6. A Special Ordinance (not being a Special Ordinance prescribing the scale or basis of assessment of the contributions to be made by the Colleges to University purposes), which affects any College, shall not be subject to alteration without the consent of that College.

7. Whenever it is provided that an act or thing shall or may be done or determined by the University, it shall be done or determined by Grace of the Regent House unless it is expressly stated that it is to be done or determined otherwise, provided that the Regent House may delegate by Grace to the Council or to another University body or authority to act on its behalf in such matters as it may from time to time determine.

8. The members of the Regent House at any time shall be those persons whose names were on the Roll of the Regent House at the time of the last promulgation.

9. The Registrary shall promulgate the Roll of the Regent House in each year on a day appointed by Ordinance. Promulgation shall be by publication in the *Cambridge University Reporter.*

10. The Registrary shall inscribe on the Roll of the Regent House the names of the following persons:

(*a*) (i) the Chancellor, the High Steward, the Deputy High Steward, the Commissary, and (ii) the members of the Council in class (*e*),

(*b*) other University officers and persons treated as such under Statute J 7;

(*c*) Heads of Colleges;

(*d*) Fellows of Colleges, provided that they conform to such conditions of residence as may be determined by Ordinance;

(*e*) such other persons holding appointments in the University or a College in such categories and subject to such qualifying periods of service as shall be determined from time to time by Ordinance;

provided always that any person who is qualified for membership in class (*b*), class (*d*), or class (*e*) shall cease to be so qualified at the next promulgation after he or she attains the age of seventy years.

Chapter IV

THE COUNCIL AND ITS COMMITTEES

1. (*a*) The Council shall be the principal executive and policy-making body of the University. The Council shall have general responsibility for the administration of the University, for the planning of its work, and for the management of its resources; it shall have power to take such action as is necessary for it to discharge these responsibilities. It shall also perform such other executive and administrative duties as may be delegated to it by the Regent House or assigned to it by Statute or Ordinance.

(*b*) The Council shall have the right of reporting to the University. It shall advise the Regent House on matters of general concern to the University.

(*c*) The Council shall make an Annual Report to the University, and shall initiate and submit a Grace for the approval of the Report by the Regent House.

(*d*) The Council shall have the power of initiating and submitting Graces to the Regent House and to the Senate. The procedure for the submission of Graces shall be prescribed by Special Ordinance.

(*e*) The Council shall oversee the work of all those institutions in the University which are placed under its supervision, and shall ensure that the University officers assigned to those institutions are satisfactorily performing the duties and fulfilling the conditions of tenure of their offices.

[**2.** The Council shall consist of the Chancellor, the Vice-Chancellor, nineteen elected members, and four appointed members in the following classes:

Members elected by the Regent House

(*a*) four from among the Heads of Colleges;

(*b*) four from among the Professors and Readers;

(*c*) eight from among the other members of the Regent House.

Members in each of classes (*a*), (*b*), and (*c*) shall be elected by the Regent House for a period and in a manner determined by Special Ordinance.

Elected student members

(*d*) three from among the students in the University, of whom at least one shall be from among those certified by the Registrary to be graduate students.

Members in class (*d*) shall be elected by the students in the University for a period and in a manner determined by Special Ordinance.

Appointed members

(*e*) four persons appointed by Grace of the Regent House who at the time of appointment are not qualified to be members of the Regent House except under Statute A III 10(*a*)(ii) nor are employees of the University or a College, one of whom shall be designated by the Council to chair the Audit Committee of the Council.

Members in class (*e*) shall be appointed by Grace of the Regent House on the nomination of the Council; the arrangements for nomination shall be prescribed by Ordinance.

For the purpose of this Statute the terms 'student in the University' and 'graduate student' shall be defined by Ordinance.][1]

⟨**2.** The Council shall consist of the Chancellor, the Vice-Chancellor, and twenty-three members in the following classes:

[1] The section in angular brackets will replace the section in square brackets subject to the approval by Her Majesty in Council of the amendments of Statute approved by Grace 1 of 30 April 2014.

Members elected by the Regent House

(*a*) four from among the Heads of Colleges;
(*b*) four from among the Professors and Readers;
(*c*) eight from among the other members of the Regent House.
Members in each of classes (*a*), (*b*), and (*c*) shall be elected by the Regent House for a period and in a manner determined by Special Ordinance.

Student members

(*d*) three student members.
Members in class (*d*) shall be such persons as shall be prescribed by Special Ordinance and shall serve for a period determined by Special Ordinance.

Appointed members

(*e*) four persons appointed by Grace of the Regent House who at the time of appointment are not qualified to be members of the Regent House except under Statute A III 10 (*a*)(ii) nor are employees of the University or a College, one of whom shall be designated by the Council to chair the Audit Committee of the Council.
Members in class (*e*) shall be appointed by Grace of the Regent House on the nomination of the Council; the arrangements for nomination shall be prescribed by Ordinance.〉[1]

3. Detailed provision for periods of service, nomination, election (or appointment), tenure and continuing eligibility of members of Council shall be made by Ordinance. Provision shall be made by Ordinance for the filling of casual vacancies by resignation, death, disqualifications or otherwise and for bye-elections.

4. No person shall be elected a member of the Council after attaining the age of seventy years.

The Chair and the Deputy Chair

5. (*a*) The Chair of the Council shall be the Vice-Chancellor, provided that the Chancellor shall have the right to take the chair at any meeting of the Council at which he or she is present. If neither the Chancellor nor the Vice-Chancellor is present, the Chair shall be a member of the Council appointed by the Vice-Chancellor to act as her or his deputy, or in the absence of such deputy some other member of the Council chosen by the members present.

(*b*) Notwithstanding the provisions of Section 5(*a*), the Council shall from time to time designate a member of the Council in class (*a*), (*b*), (*c*), or (*e*), as Deputy Chair of the Council, who shall take the chair at such proceedings of the Council as the Council may determine from time to time, notwithstanding the fact that the Chancellor or the Vice-Chancellor is present.

Frequency of meetings and quorum

6. The Council shall meet at least twice in each term. No business shall be transacted at a meeting unless nine members at least are present.

Committees of the Council

7. There shall be
(*a*) the following standing committees of the Council: the Finance Committee and the Audit Committee;
(*b*) such other committees, whether standing or occasional, as may be appointed by the Council from time to time.

8. The Finance Committee shall consist of:
(*a*) the Vice-Chancellor, or a duly appointed deputy, who shall be Chair;
(*b*) such number of persons as shall be determined by Ordinance, elected or appointed in a manner prescribed by Special Ordinance; provided that
(i) the membership of the Committee shall include three persons elected by representatives of the Colleges; and
(ii) not less than three members of the Committee (including the Vice-Chancellor) shall be members of the Council.

[1] The section in angular brackets will replace the section in square brackets subject to the approval by Her Majesty in Council of the amendments of Statute approved by Grace 1 of 30 April 2014.

9. It shall be the duty of the Finance Committee

(*a*) to advise the Council on the management of the University's assets, including real property, moneys, and securities, investments, reserves, income and expenditure;

(*b*) to perform such other duties as may be assigned to it by Statute or Ordinance or by the Council.

10. Subject to the provisions of Statute A IV 2(*e*), the composition of the Audit Committee shall be determined by Special Ordinance. The Audit Committee shall perform such duties as may be assigned to it by Statute or Ordinance.

CHAPTER V

THE GENERAL BOARD, THE SCHOOLS, FACULTIES, AND DEPARTMENTS

The General Board of the Faculties

1. (*a*) Subject to the powers of the Regent House, and subject to the responsibilities of the Council under Statute A IV 1, the General Board of the Faculties ('the General Board') shall be responsible for the academic and educational policy of the University, and shall advise the University on questions relating to such policy. The General Board is accountable to the Council for its management of the University's academic and educational affairs. It shall make an Annual Report to the Council on the discharge of its duties. It shall fulfil the duties placed on it by Statute or Ordinance.

(*b*) The General Board shall consider the estimates of annual expenditure submitted by Faculty Boards and other authorities and, if it approves them, shall transmit them to the Council. The Board shall allocate the funds made available to it for the support of teaching and research.

(*c*) The General Board shall oversee the teaching and research work undertaken by the Schools, Faculties, Departments, and other institutions placed under its supervision; it shall ensure, in respect of those institutions,

(i) that the University officers assigned to those institutions are satisfactorily performing the duties and fulfilling the conditions of tenure of their offices;

(ii) that adequate facilities for teaching and research are available;

(iii) that appropriate courses of study and instruction are provided and that the teaching given is of the highest standard;

(iv) that research of the highest quality is conducted.

(*d*) The General Board shall have the power to make regulations about any matters within its responsibility, such regulations not to be inconsistent with the provisions of any Statute, Ordinance or Order, and to be published. In particular the Board may make regulations relating to:

(i) the administration and management of the institutions under its supervision other than Schools and the Councils of the Schools; and

(ii) University courses and examinations, degrees, diplomas, and other qualifications in accordance with Statute B (except the degree of Master of Arts).

[**2.** The General Board shall consist of the following members:

(*a*) the Vice-Chancellor, as Chair;

(*b*) eight members of the Regent House appointed by the Councils of the Schools to serve for four years in accordance with arrangements determined by Special Ordinance;

(*c*) four members of the Regent House appointed by the Council, to serve for four years, subject to the requirement that not fewer than three members of the Board (including the Vice-Chancellor) shall be members of the Council. If a member of the Board ceases to be a member of the Council he or she shall not thereby cease to be a member of the Board;

(*d*) two members elected by and from among the students of the University to serve for one year, of whom one shall be from among those certified by the Registrary to be undergraduate students, and one from among those certified by the Registrary to be graduate students. For the purpose of this Statute the terms 'student in the University' and 'graduate student' shall be defined by Ordinance.][1]

⟨**2.** The General Board shall consist of the following members:

(*a*) the Vice-Chancellor, as Chair;

[1] The section in angular brackets will replace the section in square brackets subject to the approval by Her Majesty in Council of the amendments of Statute approved by Grace 1 of 30 April 2014.

(*b*) eight members of the Regent House appointed by the Councils of the Schools to serve for four years in accordance with arrangements determined by Special Ordinance;

(*c*) four members of the Regent House appointed by the Council, to serve for four years, subject to the requirement that not fewer than three members of the Board (including the Vice-Chancellor) shall be members of the Council. If a member of the Board ceases to be a member of the Council he or she shall not thereby cease to be a member of the Board;

(*d*) two student members, who shall be such persons as shall be prescribed by Special Ordinance and shall serve for a period determined by Special Ordinance.〉[1]

3. If any member of the General Board becomes Vice-Chancellor, her or his seat shall thereupon become vacant.

4. The General Board shall meet at least twice in each term, provided that the Chair shall have power to cancel any meeting if there is insufficient business. No business shall be transacted at a meeting unless five members at least are present.

5. The Registrary or a University officer designated from time to time by the Council after consultation with the General Board shall be Secretary of the Board.

The Schools

6. On the recommendation of the General Board the University may at any time by Special Ordinance institute one or more Schools. There shall be placed in each School such Faculties, Departments, and other institutions as the University may from time to time determine by Ordinance.

7. There shall be a Council of each School. The composition of such a Council, the number and manner of appointment of its members, and, subject to the provisions of Section 8 below, its powers and duties shall be determined by Ordinance.

8. Subject to the provisions of Section 7, the duties of the Council of a School shall include:

(*a*) the preparation of such academic and financial plans, and reports as the General Board shall determine;

(*b*) the allocation of the funds made available to it by the General Board amongst the institutions comprising the School;

(*c*) working with the institutions which comprise the School to ensure institutional and School academic plans are consistent, realistic, and affordable;

(*d*) consideration of any matter referred to it by the General Board.

9. There shall be a Head of each School who shall be appointed and hold office on such terms as may be determined by Ordinance.

10. The Head shall be Chair of the Council of the School and the principal academic officer of the School. The Head of School shall be responsible to the Council of the School, the General Board, and the Vice-Chancellor for the overall running of the School, including the use of the funds specified under 8(*b*) and the implementation of the approved plans referred to in 8(*a*).

11. The Council of each School shall have the right of reporting to the University.

The Faculties

12. The term 'Faculty' shall denote a body of persons associated in accordance with the Statutes for the purpose of furthering the study of a subject or subjects.

13. On the recommendation of the General Board the University may at any time by Ordinance institute one or more Faculties. Each Faculty shall be assigned to one or other of the Schools.

14. There shall be a Board of each Faculty, which shall oversee the work of the Faculty. Provision shall be made by Ordinance for the membership of Faculties and for the composition of Faculty Boards.

Departments

15. On the recommendation of the General Board, the University may at any time constitute one or more Departments within any Faculty, may constitute Departments independent of any Faculty but under the supervision of the General Board, or may suppress any Department.

16. There shall be a Head of each Department appointed in accordance with Regulations made by the General Board.

[1] The section in angular brackets will replace the section in square brackets subject to the approval by Her Majesty in Council of the amendments of Statute approved by Grace 1 of 30 April 2014.

17. Subject to the powers of the Council of School, the Faculty Board or comparable authority and subject to the Ordinances and such Regulations as the General Board may make from time to time, it shall be the duty of the Head of a Department:

(*a*) to organize the teaching and research of the Department;

(*b*) to prepare and submit to the General Board, in accordance with arrangements determined by Ordinance, the annual estimates of the Department for consideration by the Board in accordance with Statute A V 1(*b*);

(*c*) to be responsible for the proper application of the funds available to the Department, and to ensure that the approved estimate of expenditure is not exceeded and that the accounts are correctly maintained;

provided that the duties specified under Subsections (*b*) and (*c*) may be assigned by the Head of a Department to some other person approved by the General Board.

Degree Committees

18. There shall be Degree Committees for such Faculties and other institutions as may be determined by the General Board after consultation with the Board of Graduate Studies. Each Degree Committee shall be constituted in accordance with Regulations made by the General Board.

19. Subject to the powers of the Board of Graduate Studies, it shall be the duty of each Degree Committee to exercise such functions as may be prescribed by Regulation of the General Board in respect of the approval of students as Graduate Students and the supervision of their work, the award of degrees, diplomas, and certificates in respect of graduate study or contributions to learning, and other cognate matters.

CHAPTER VI

BOARDS, SYNDICATES, AND COMMITTEES

1. There shall be in the University

(*a*) such Boards, Syndicates, and Committees as may by any other provision of the Statutes be required to be maintained;

(*b*) any other Boards, Syndicates, or Committees established by Ordinance.

2. Any Board or Syndicate constituted by Statute or Ordinance or by Grace of the Regent House shall have the right of reporting to the University.

3. No person shall be appointed or reappointed a member of any Board, or of any body of Electors or Managers even though it be not expressly called a Board, or of any Syndicate other than an occasional Syndicate, who at the commencement of her or his period of service or further period of service, as the case may be, would have attained the age of seventy years.

CHAPTER VII

THE BOARD OF SCRUTINY

1. There shall be in the University a Board of Scrutiny, which shall in each year scrutinize on behalf of the Regent House the Annual Report of the Council, the abstract of the accounts of the University, the allocations Report of the Council required by Statute F I 1(*b*), and any other Report of the Council proposing allocations from the Chest. In addition the Board shall perform such other duties, and shall have such powers, as may be specified by Ordinance or Order.

2. The Board of Scrutiny shall have the right of reporting to the University on any matters falling within the scope of Section 1 above which in the Board's opinion should be drawn to the attention of the University.

3. Subject to the provisions of Section 4 below, the Board of Scrutiny shall consist of

(*a*) the Proctors;

(*b*) the two Pro-Proctors who are nominated by the Colleges;

(*c*) eight members of the Regent House elected by the Regent House, as follows:

- (i) two persons who have been members of the Regent House for not more than ten years on 1 October next following their election;

(ii) six persons who are members of the Regent House.
Arrangements for election shall be made by Ordinance.

4. No person may be a member of the Board of Scrutiny who is a member of the Council, the General Board, or the Finance Committee of the Council, or who holds any of the University offices of Chancellor, Vice-Chancellor, Pro-Vice-Chancellor, University Advocate, Deputy University Advocate, Registrary, Assistant Registrary, or Secretary of a School. The University may by Ordinance make provision from time to time to designate University offices which are established by Ordinance and which have primarily administrative duties, the holders of which shall be prohibited from membership of the Board as though they were listed in this Statute. If any member of the Board of Scrutiny becomes a member of any of the aforementioned bodies or is appointed or elected to any of the aforementioned offices or ceases to be a member of the Regent House, her or his seat shall thereupon become vacant. The Chair and Secretary of the Board shall be elected annually.

5. The Board of Scrutiny shall have power

(*a*) to consult any official documents or accounts (other than those of the University Press) which may be relevant to any enquiry;

(*b*) to consult such official documents or accounts of the University Press as may be specified by Ordinance;

(*c*) to make enquiry, whether in person or in writing, of the officers of any authority on matters pertaining to a subject of enquiry;

(*d*) to request that a matter be put down for discussion by the Regent House, which request the Council shall not unreasonably refuse.

No documents or accounts requested by the Board under Subsection (*a*) or Subsection (*b*) above shall be withheld except on the ground of their irrelevance. Such withholding shall require the written sanction of the Vice-Chancellor.

CHAPTER VIII

CONDUCT OF BUSINESS

Provision shall be made by Special Ordinance for

(*a*) calling Congregations;

(*b*) preparation and submission of Reports to the Regent House and the Senate; and their Discussion;

(*c*) submission of Graces (that is, resolutions) to the Regent House and the Senate; arrangements for voting and amendments. All Graces submitted require the authorization of the Council;

(*d*) elections by the Regent House and the Senate, and other elections.

CHAPTER IX

REVIEW

Compliance with the Statutes and Ordinances

1. (*a*) If, within thirty days after the doing of any act by any person or body having power to act under the Statutes, or in the event of failure or omission to act as required by Statute, Ordinance, or Order within thirty days after the date specified for the performance of that act, it is represented in writing to the Vice-Chancellor by a member of the University that there has been a contravention of the Statutes, Ordinances, or any Order in the doing of such act, or in such failure or omission, the Vice-Chancellor shall inquire into the matter and shall declare either that there has been no such contravention, or that the said act or matter is of no effect, or, if the Vice-Chancellor is of the opinion that the contravention has not affected the result, that in her or his opinion the validity of the act or matter is not affected by the circumstances represented. Where the Vice-Chancellor finds that there has been a failure or omission to act he or she may give such directions in the matter as shall seem to him or her to be appropriate. The person making the representation shall state in writing the act or matter to which he or she refers, and with full detail of the contravention of Statute, Ordinance, or Order which he or she represents has taken place. The Vice-Chancellor shall give her or his decision promptly but in any event within three months, unless the person making the representation has agreed in writing to an extension of time.

(*b*) If the person making the representation is dissatisfied with the Vice-Chancellor's decision, or if he or she believes that there has been unreasonable delay, he or she may make a representation to the Commissary in the manner prescribed in this chapter. The decision of the Commissary shall be final. If there is no representation to the Commissary, the decision of the Vice-Chancellor shall be final.

(*c*) No act shall be invalid by reason of the fact that there has been a contravention of the Statutes, Ordinances, or Order unless there has been a representation in writing under Section 1(*a*) of this chapter within thirty days after the doing thereof.

(*d*) No act shall be invalid by reason of the fact that any person taking part in the act, and chosen in the manner prescribed or authorized by the Statutes, Ordinances, or Order to be the person or a member of the body authorized to act, was not qualified to be so chosen.

Declaration of the meaning of a Statute

2. If any doubt arises as to the true meaning of any Statute of the University, or of any Statute for the University and any one or more of the Colleges in common, the Council may apply to the Chancellor, who shall then declare in writing the meaning of the Statute in question, and such declaration shall be registered by the Registrary of the University, and the meaning of the Statute as therein declared shall be deemed the true meaning thereof. The University shall defray the cost of any legal advice obtained by the Chancellor for the performance of her or his duty under this section.

Review by the Commissary

3. The Commissary shall have full power to determine all questions referred to her or his decision by a member of the University under the provisions of this chapter. The Commissary shall have the power to review, amend, or quash the decision of any University authority on the ground that the decision, or some aspect of the decision, was *ultra vires*, illegal, irrational, procedurally irregular or incorrect in fact, and to make such order (including an order to amend, quash, or refer back the decision) as seems to her or him to be justified. The Commissary's powers under the provisions of this chapter shall not extend to:

(*a*) any matter still subject to further review by or appeal to any University authority, or which would otherwise be capable of review by any independent adjudicator for student complaints in higher education, as established by or pursuant to Act of Parliament;

(*b*) the merits or substance of a decision made by:

(i) a University Court;

(ii) a Board of Examiners, a Degree Committee, the Board of Graduate Studies, a Review Committee or similar authority, in relation to the result of a University examination;

(*c*) any decision by a University authority concerning the appointment of an individual or individuals to employment in the University, or concerning promotion in such employment;

(*d*) any matter under the responsibility of the Press Syndicate or the Local Examinations Syndicate.

4. In any particular case or cases the Commissary may appoint a person to act as her or his deputy, and may delegate to such a deputy her or his powers under the provisions of this chapter in respect of the case or cases concerned.

5. The Commissary or a deputy so appointed shall have the power to strike out a case which in her or his opinion is vexatious, frivolous, or out of time.

6. In relation to any case (not being a case struck out as vexatious, frivolous, or out of time) the Commissary shall direct that the matter shall be dealt with by oral or written representations, or both. Such representations shall be made:

(*a*) on behalf of the University by a person or persons appointed by the Council; and

(*b*) by any other party or parties to the proceedings either in person or through a representative.

7. The Commissary shall make general rules of procedure which shall bind the parties in any particular case. The rules of procedure shall make provision for a time limit or time limits within which a matter shall be raised with the Commissary. In any particular case the decision of the Commissary (or a duly appointed deputy) on any procedural matters shall be final, and the provisions of Statute A IX 1 shall not apply to it.

8. The Council shall consult the Commissary before proposing any Ordinance concerning matters regulated by Sections 3–9 of this chapter. The Commissary shall have the right to publish a statement for the guidance of the University about any such proposed Ordinance.

9. The University shall defray the cost of any legal advice obtained by the Commissary for the performance of her or his duties under this chapter.

Temporary Statute

10. (*a*) Nothing in this chapter enables or requires the Commissary to hear any appeal or to determine any dispute regulated under the provisions of the Education Reform Act 1988 about a member of the academic staff of the University as defined in the Statutes, which, being a matter regulated under the said Act, concerns the member's appointment or employment, or the termination of that appointment or employment. The Commissary has no power to disallow or annul any Ordinance made under or having effect for the purposes of the Statutes in relation to matters regulated under the said Act.

(*b*) When (*a*) is no longer needed, this section may be repealed by Grace.

CHAPTER X

MISCELLANEOUS

Commencement and transitional provisions

1. Repeal of a Statute does not invalidate any order, election or appointment made or thing done under a Statute repealed, nor revive nor restore any Statute, order, or trust, or any power or provision repealed or abrogated by a repealed Statute.

Interpretation

2. In any Statute, Special Ordinance or Ordinance,

(*a*) the term 'Ordinance' means a Special Ordinance made under Statute A III 3 or an Ordinance;

(*b*) the term '*in statu pupillari*' shall mean a member of the University (in which term shall be included a member of a College, or of an Approved Society, resident in the University with a view to matriculation) who has not been admitted to an office in the University (or to a post in the University Press specially designated under Statute J 7 or to an appointment approved by the University for the purpose of Statute A III 10(*e*)), or to a Fellowship or office of a College, or to a degree which qualifies the holder for membership of the Senate under Statute A I 7(*c*), and is of less than three and a half years' standing from admission to her or his first degree (if any);

(*c*) words of the masculine gender import the feminine unless this interpretation is excluded expressly or by necessary implication;

(*d*) the term 'degree' means degree of the University unless in any Statute or Ordinance that meaning is expressly or by necessary implication excluded; a complete degree is a degree other than a title of degree.

(*e*) whenever it is required that any matter be published, an announcement in the *Cambridge University Reporter* shall be sufficient publication.

(*f*) The term 'Grace' shall mean an act, vote or decree of the Regent House or the Senate, the procedure for which shall be prescribed by Ordinance.

3. Subject to the provisions of the amendments of Statutes made by Grace 1 of 26 January 1994, a reference to the Council of the Senate in any Act of Parliament, Order in Council, Statute, Ordinance, or other instrument binding on the University shall be construed as a reference to the Council, and a reference to the Financial Board shall be construed as a reference to the Finance Committee of the Council.

Signature of Reports

4. A Report of the Council, or of any other body that has the right of reporting to the University, shall be signed by those members of the reporting body who agree with the Report; provided that no person *in statu pupillari* shall sign a Report if he or she has been excluded, under the provisions of any Statute or Ordinance for reserved business, from any part of the discussion of the Report.

Casting vote in elections

5. If in an election for which votes have been taken by poll there is an equality of votes between two or more candidates, the Vice-Chancellor or other returning officer, whether or not he or she has previously voted or been entitled to vote, may, unless it is otherwise expressly provided by Ordinance, give a casting vote.

Sermons

6. Sermons shall be preached in the University Church during Full Term on such days as may be appointed by the Chancellor or by the University. No one shall be allowed in any sermon before the University to impugn the doctrine or discipline of the Church of England as established by law. A Commemoration of Benefactors shall be held every year in the University Church, at such time and in such manner as the University prescribes.

Provision for certain former offices

7. When in any Statute, Ordinance, contract, document, instrument of any description or any statement reference is made to the Treasurer or to the Secretary General of the Faculties after 14 December 2005 such reference shall be construed as a reference to the Registrary, or a duly appointed deputy, unless different provision is made by Statute or Ordinance.

Special Ordinances required

8. Provision may be made by Special Ordinance for:

(*a*) filling casual vacancies on University bodies;

(*b*) termination of membership of University bodies on account of failure to attend meetings;

(*c*) the majority necessary for a decision of a University body, and, if necessary, for the quorum necessary for business to be transacted; and for comparable matters;

(*d*) the appointment of committees by University bodies, and delegation of decision to such committees or to a University officer; provided such delegation does not relieve the delegating body of responsibility for the matter delegated;

(*e*) exclusion of members *in statu pupillari* from the proceedings of a University body or bodies about particular classes of business.

Ordinances required

9. Provision shall be made by Ordinance for the academical year, the dates of the Michaelmas, Lent, and Easter Terms in each academical year, for the dates of Full Term in each term, for residence, and for the Precincts of the University.

Statute B

MEMBERSHIP OF THE UNIVERSITY AND DEGREES

CHAPTER I

MEMBERSHIP OF THE UNIVERSITY, ADMISSION, AND MATRICULATION

1. The University shall, by Ordinance, state the conditions on which persons may matriculate as a member of the University, as

(*a*) an undergraduate student;

(*b*) a student pursuing a course for a degree specified in Statute B II 1(*c*) or research, or a course of study and training for research, intended for a degree specified in Statute B II 1(*d*);

(*c*) a University officer;

(*d*) an affiliated student;

(*e*) a person falling within the terms of Statute A III 10(*e*);

(*f*) a person in any other category determined by Statute or Ordinance.

2. Membership of the University is for life, or until resignation, or deprivation by decision of a University court. Resignation entails cancellation of any degree. Renunciation of a degree entails resignation of membership of the University. Detailed provision for resignation of membership and renunciation of degrees shall be made by Ordinance. Provision for reinstatement after resignation or renunciation may be made by Ordinance.

3. Admission to courses and candidature for a qualification shall be *either*

(*a*) by College, in the case of a Tripos, and other courses or qualifications determined by Ordinance; *or*

(*b*) by a University authority, and by a College, in the case of other courses or qualifications leading to a degree so identified by Ordinance; *or*

(*c*) by a University authority, in the case of other courses or qualifications so identified by Ordinance.

Any admission by Colleges and any candidature for a qualification is subject to the requirements of the Statutes and Ordinances of the University.

CHAPTER II

DEGREES

1. The degrees in the University are:

(*a*) Bachelor of Arts, and such other Bachelor's degrees as may be established by Special Ordinance;

(*b*) Master of Arts;

(*c*) Such other Master's degrees as may be established by Special Ordinance;

(*d*) Doctor of Philosophy, and such other Doctor's degrees as may be established by Special Ordinance;

(*e*) Bachelor of Divinity;

(*f*) Master of Surgery; and

(*g*) Doctor of Divinity, Doctor of Law, Doctor of Medicine, Doctor of Science, Doctor of Letters, and Doctor of Music.

2. Provision may be made by Ordinance

(*a*) for admission to the degree of Master of Arts on the recommendation of the Council;

(*b*) for admission to degrees by incorporation of graduates of the University of Oxford or the University of Dublin (Trinity College);

(*c*) for a candidate for a degree who has kept a term or terms by residence at either of the University of Oxford or the University of Dublin (Trinity College) to receive an allowance of not more than the same number of terms towards the terms required to be kept in this University; and

(*d*) prescribing conditions under which the status of Bachelor of Arts and or Master of Arts may be held or may be granted by the Council.

3. Eligibility under Section 2(*a*) or (*b*) above may be made by Ordinance to include holders of office elect or designate. Provision may be made by Ordinance for the admission under Section 2(*a*) and (*b*) above of persons holding posts designated by the Council in University institutions.

4. Degrees shall rank in such order of precedence as may be determined by Ordinance, and in the absence of such Ordinance, in such order as has previously been customary.

Chapter III

COURSES AND EXAMINATIONS, ALLOWANCES

1. The General Board shall by Regulation, make provision for courses, and examinations, in these categories:

Courses for matriculated students

(*a*) courses leading to the Bachelor of Arts and other Bachelor's degrees established by Special Ordinance;
(*b*) courses leading to Master's degrees established by Special Ordinance;
(*c*) courses of study and training for research, and research, intended for the Doctor of Philosophy or other Doctor's degree established by Special Ordinance;
(*d*) other courses or qualifications to be offered by the University including those leading to certificates or diplomas;

Courses not limited to matriculated students, including certificates and diplomas

(*e*) other courses or qualifications to be offered by the University;

Higher degrees

(*f*) candidature and examination for the degrees of Bachelor of Divinity, Master of Surgery, and Doctors degrees listed in Statute B II 1(*g*).

2. Such regulations shall specify
(*a*) the University authority primarily responsible for the course or examination,
(*b*) for courses and qualifications in Section 1(*a*)–(*d*) above, normal residence requirements, the length of courses and arrangements for examination, and
(*c*) for courses and qualifications in Section 1(*e*) above, attendance requirements (if any), the length of courses and arrangements for examinations.

3. The General Board may make additional detailed provision for the above matters by Regulation.

4. The University shall make Ordinances on the recommendation of the General Board:
(*a*) for the grant of allowances to individual students in respect of courses and examinations in Section 1(*a*)–(*e*) above; and for arrangements for the review of such decisions about allowances;
(*b*) for arrangements for appeal or review of matters within the responsibility of the University about a course or examination in Section 1(*a*)–(*e*) above, raised by the student concerned.

Statute C

UNIVERSITY OFFICES AND EMPLOYMENT IN THE UNIVERSITY

CHAPTER I

UNIVERSITY OFFICES: GENERAL

University Officers

1. (*a*) The University officers shall be those persons only who hold any of the University offices of Chancellor, Vice-Chancellor, Pro-Vice-Chancellor, High Steward, Deputy High Steward, Commissary, Proctor, Orator, Registrary, Librarian, Director of the Fitzwilliam Museum, Esquire Bedell, University Advocate, and Deputy University Advocate, or any other University office established or specified by Statute or Ordinance. Provision shall be made by Special Ordinance made on the recommendation of the General Board for a scheme of leave of absence or dispensation from duty applying to holders of specified offices.

The competent authorities

(*b*) In any Statute or Ordinance the term 'competent authority' in relation to a University institution or a University officer shall mean either the Council or the General Board, according as the institution concerned is under the supervision of the Council or the General Board.

(*c*) The institutions under the supervision of the General Board shall be the Schools, Faculties, Departments, and any other institution placed under the supervision of the General Board by Statute, by Ordinance, or otherwise. All other institutions in the University, except the University Press, shall be under the supervision of the Council.

(*d*) In any Statute or Ordinance the term 'authority comparable with a Faculty Board' or the term 'comparable authority' shall mean the Board or Syndicate constituted by Statute or Ordinance for the management of a Department or other institution which is independent of any Faculty but under the supervision of the General Board.

(*e*) Offices established either by the University or by the competent authority may be established by these authorities on a part-time basis.

Detailed provisions for University Officers

2. Under this section, provision shall be made by Special Ordinance on the recommendation of the competent authorities for the following in respect of University officers (other than those whose offices are named specifically in Section 1(*a*) above):

(*a*) procedures for grievance, discipline, accountability and assessment of capability, redundancy, and removal from office on medical grounds or grounds of incapacity;
(*b*) appointment or election if not provided for by Statute or Special Ordinance;
(*c*) remuneration;
(*d*) superannuation;
(*e*) tenure and retirement; admission to University office;
(*f*) determination of duties and residence and accountability for residence;
(*g*) dispensation from discharge of duties on account of illness or other sufficient cause;
(*h*) other conditions of service.

3. This Statute and any Ordinance made under this Statute shall be construed in every case to give effect to the following guiding principles, that is to say:

(*a*) to ensure that members of the academic staff have freedom within the law to question and test received wisdom, and to put forward new ideas and controversial or unpopular opinions, without placing themselves in jeopardy of losing their jobs or privileges;
(*b*) to enable the University to provide education, promote learning, and engage in research efficiently and economically;
(*c*) to apply the principles of justice and fairness.

Duties of University Teaching Officers

4. It shall be the duty of all holders of University offices entitled to leave under a Special Ordinance made under Statute C I 1(*a*) to devote themselves to the advancement of knowledge in their subject, to give instruction therein to students, to undertake from time to time such examining of students as may be required by the Board, Syndicate, or other body which is chiefly concerned with their duties, and to promote the interests of the University as a place of education, religion, learning, and research. The duty to examine students shall be restricted by Ordinance to the examining of candidates for such examinations for degrees and other qualifications of the University as the University may from time to time determine.

Deputies and substitutes

5. The competent authority may appoint a deputy to act for a University officer, upon such terms of remuneration as it thinks fit,

(*a*) during any period of the officer's absence from duty in accordance with any Special Ordinance made under Statute C I 1(*a*), or during any term when in accordance with Ordinances the officer is not required to reside;
(*b*) during any vacancy in the office;
(*c*) in any emergency.

A deputy appointed under this section shall exercise the powers and shall perform the duties of the officer for whom he or she deputizes and shall have the right to attend and vote in that officer's absence at meetings of any body of which the officer is a member *ex officio*.

Limitation

6. The University shall have power, or may delegate the power, to preclude a University officer from undertaking any work outside the scope of her or his office or to limit the amount of such work.

Concurrent appointments

7. No University office shall be tenable concurrently with any other University office except in cases in which it may be determined otherwise

(*a*) by the University, if it is proposed that a University officer should hold more than one of the offices specified in any Special Ordinance made under Statute C I 1(*a*) regarding special leave or dispensation from duties; or
(*b*) by the competent authority or authorities, if none or only one of the offices to be held is so specified.

Temporary and transitional provision for the Schedule

8. (*a*) The Schedule to this Statute has effect.

(*b*) The whole or any part of the Schedule may be rescinded by Grace, following a Report to the Regent House. Any cross-references to the Schedule in Statute or Special Ordinance which require amendment as a result of such rescission may be amended by Grace.

(*c*) Provision may be made by Special Ordinance for transitional provisions, which may make necessary modification to any unrescinded portions of the Schedule and cross-references in Statutes and Special Ordinances so that they may continue to operate.

(*d*) When the Schedule is completely rescinded under (*b*) above this section may be repealed by Grace.

CHAPTER II

EMPLOYMENT IN THE UNIVERSITY

1. Subject to the provisions of the Statutes and Ordinances regarding University officers, the University may engage persons for employment in the service of the University, may determine their salaries and pensions (if any), and may prescribe the conditions of their service. The University may delegate the exercise of any of these powers.

2. The competent authorities shall establish committees and processes for the management of employment by the University. Regulations for the establishment of such committees may be made by Ordinance.

Chapter III

THE VICE-CHANCELLOR AND THE PRO-VICE-CHANCELLORS

1. The Vice-Chancellor shall be appointed by the Regent House on the nomination of the Council, who may nominate any person of their choice. The person appointed shall enter upon office on a day determined by the University. As soon as conveniently may be thereafter, he or she shall be formally admitted to the office at a Congregation of the Regent House called by the Chancellor or, if the Chancellor is absent or the office of Chancellor is vacant, by the Proctors. The procedures for nomination and admission shall be prescribed by Ordinance.

2. The Vice-Chancellor shall be appointed in the first instance for five years or, in exceptional circumstances, for such other period as the University may determine. He or she may be reappointed for a further period or periods, provided that no one shall hold the office of Vice-Chancellor for a total period of more than seven years. The procedure for reappointment shall be prescribed by Ordinance.

3. The Vice-Chancellor shall enjoy the customary rights and perform the customary duties of the office. He or she shall have power to ensure that all University officers duly perform their duties, and shall have such other powers and duties as may be prescribed by Statute or Ordinance.

4. The Vice-Chancellor shall have power, after her or his formal admission, but not before, to call Congregations of the Regent House and to admit candidates to degrees or titles of degrees.

5. Except as provided in Section 6 below,

(*a*) the Vice-Chancellor shall be Chair of the Council and the General Board, and of any other body of which he or she is *ex officio* a member, provided that the Chancellor shall have the right to take the chair at any meeting of the Council at which he or she is present;

(*b*) the Vice-Chancellor may attend a meeting of any body constituted in the University by or under Statute or Ordinance, or of any body appointed by such a body, save that this provision shall not apply to meetings of any of the following bodies:

(i) the Board of Scrutiny;
(ii) a University court constituted by or under Statute D;
(iii) a Board of Examiners for a University examination;
(iv) a Degree Committee for a Faculty or other institution;
(v) any other body which the University may specify by Grace.

6. The Vice-Chancellor shall not be present at any meeting of the Council or of any other body when the body is considering her or his reappointment or the appointment of her or his successor as Vice-Chancellor.

7. Provided always that he or she shall in general take the chair in person at meetings of the Council and the General Board, the Vice-Chancellor shall have power to appoint persons to act on her or his behalf as follows:

(*a*) The Vice-Chancellor may appoint, from among the Heads of Colleges or other members of the Regent House, one or more persons to be designated Deputy Vice-Chancellors, to whom he or she may delegate any of the duties assigned by Statute or Ordinance to the Vice-Chancellor. The name of any person so appointed shall be published forthwith.

(*b*) The Vice-Chancellor may appoint a member of the Regent House to act as her or his deputy in any matter, including attendance at a meeting under Section 5(*b*) above, or to perform any duty assigned by Statute or Ordinance to the Vice-Chancellor.

8. During her or his tenure of office, the Vice-Chancellor shall not undertake the duties of any other University office or any College office, or any duties inconsistent with the performance of the duties of the Vice-Chancellorship.

9. In the event of incapacity or prolonged absence from Cambridge of the Vice-Chancellor, or of suspension of the Vice-Chancellor under the Schedule to Statute C, or in the event of a vacancy in the Vice-Chancellorship, the Council shall if necessary appoint a member of the Regent House to serve as Acting Vice-Chancellor and shall publish such person's name forthwith. A person so appointed shall perform the duties, and shall exercise all the powers, of the Vice-Chancellor during the period of her or his appointment.

10. If for any reason the Vice-Chancellorship falls vacant before the expiry of the holder's term of office, a new Vice-Chancellor shall be appointed as soon as conveniently may be, in accordance with the provisions of Sections 1 and 2 above.

Removal of the Vice-Chancellor from office

11. Any three members of the Council may make a complaint to the Chancellor seeking the removal of the Vice-Chancellor from the office of Vice-Chancellor for good cause.

12. If it appears to the Chancellor that the complaint is trivial or invalid or unjustified, he or she may determine that no further action shall be taken upon it.

13. If it appears to the Chancellor, on the evidence presented, that the case alleged could, if proved, constitute good cause for dismissal or removal of the Vice-Chancellor from office, he or she shall direct the University Advocate to prefer a charge or charges to be considered by the University Tribunal. Such a charge or charges shall be dealt with in accordance with the provisions made under Chapter III and Chapter V of the Schedule to Statute C, provided that the Chancellor shall perform any duty and exercise any power there assigned to the Vice-Chancellor.

14. For the purpose of the removal of the Vice-Chancellor for incapacity on medical grounds, the provisions made under Chapters IV and V of the Schedule to Statute C, shall have effect, provided that the Chancellor shall perform any duty or exercise any power there assigned to the Vice-Chancellor.

Pro-Vice-Chancellors

15. There shall be such number of offices of Pro-Vice-Chancellor as shall be determined by the Council subject to a maximum determined by Ordinance. The Pro-Vice-Chancellors shall report to the Council through the Vice-Chancellor.

[**16.** Each appointment or reappointment to an office of Pro-Vice-Chancellor shall be made by the Council after consultation with the General Board, on the recommendation of a Nominating Committee constituted by Ordinance. A Pro-Vice-Chancellor shall hold office for not more than three years and shall be eligible for reappointment, provided that no person shall hold the office of Pro-Vice-Chancellor for a total period of more than six years.][1]

⟨**16.** Each appointment or reappointment to an office of Pro-Vice-Chancellor shall be made by the Council after consultation with the General Board, on the recommendation of a Nominating Committee constituted by Ordinance. A Pro-Vice-Chancellor shall hold office for not more than three years at a time and shall be eligible for reappointment, provided that no person shall hold the office of Pro-Vice-Chancellor for a total period of more than six, or in exceptional circumstances eight, years, whether consecutively or otherwise.⟩[1]

17. A Pro-Vice-Chancellor shall perform such duties as may be prescribed by Statute or Ordinance, and such other duties as may be determined by the Council, or the Vice-Chancellor.

CHAPTER IV

THE PROCTORS

1. The Proctors and Pro-Proctors shall be elected by the Regent House. They shall be nominated for election by such of the Colleges as may be prescribed by Special Ordinance, in turn, two for every year, according to the Cycle prescribed in that Special Ordinance; provided that the University shall have power to amend the Cycle from time to time. The persons nominated for election shall be members of the Senate of at least three years' standing. Further provisions for nomination and appointment may be made by Ordinance.

2. If the College whose turn it is fails to make a nomination, or if the Regent House declines to elect the person nominated, the Council shall nominate a person for election by Grace of the Regent House.

3. Each Proctor and each deputy Proctor shall by public declaration give an undertaking that he or she will faithfully discharge the duties of the office.

4. If the office of Proctor becomes vacant after the election by death, resignation, deprivation, or any other cause, Trinity Hall shall nominate and present a person for election, in manner as nearly similar as possible to that described above, and the person elected shall hold office until the first weekday of the Michaelmas Term next ensuing.

[1] The section in angular brackets will replace the section in square brackets subject to the approval by Her Majesty in Council of the amendments of Statute approved by Grace 1 of 4 June 2014.

Chapter V

THE ORATOR

1. The Orator is placed under the direction of the Council. It shall be the duty of the Orator

(*a*) to write addresses for presentation to other universities and institutions;

(*b*) to present to the University persons on whom titles of degrees are to be conferred *honoris causa*.

2. The Orator shall be appointed by Grace of the Regent House on the nomination of the Council.

Chapter VI

THE REGISTRARY

1. The Registrary is placed under the direction of the Council. It shall be the duty of the Registrary

(*a*) to act as the principal administrative officer of the University, and as the head of the University's administrative staff;

(*b*) to keep a record of the proceedings of the University, and to attend for that purpose all Congregations of the Regent House and such other public proceedings of the University as may be specified by Statute or Ordinance or by the Council;

(*c*) to act as Secretary to the Council;

(*d*) to receive reports of Boards, Syndicates, and other bodies, and to deal with them as required by Statute or Ordinance;

(*e*) to be responsible for maintaining a register of members of the University, and keeping records of matriculations and class-lists, and of degrees, diplomas, and other qualifications;

(*f*) to edit *Statutes and Ordinances* and the *Cambridge University Reporter*;

(*g*) to perform such other duties as may be prescribed by Statute or Ordinance or by the Council.

2. The Registrary shall be appointed by the Council.

3. The Registrary shall not be a member of the Council.

4. There shall be under the direction of the Council administrative officers in categories determined by Special Ordinance. So far as the Council may allow or direct, any duty of the Registrary may be performed by such an officer.

5. During a vacancy in the office of Registrary, the Council may appoint an Acting Registrary upon such terms of remuneration as it thinks fit.

Chapter VII

THE LIBRARIAN

Provision shall be made by Special Ordinance for the appointment of the Librarian and for the determination of the duties and responsibilities of the Librarian.

Chapter VIII

THE DIRECTOR OF THE FITZWILLIAM MUSEUM

The Director of the Fitzwilliam Museum has charge of all the objects in the Museum and in the Marlay Collection. Provision shall be made by Special Ordinance for the appointment of the Director, and for the further determination of the duties and responsibilities of the office.

Chapter IX

THE ESQUIRE BEDELLS

1. There shall be two Esquire Bedells who shall be members of the Senate appointed by the Council. They shall be equal in rank, shall attend the Chancellor and the Vice-Chancellor on public occasions, and shall perform such other duties as may be prescribed by Ordinance or Order.

2. The Esquire Bedells are placed under the direction of the Council.

Chapter X

THE UNIVERSITY ADVOCATE, THE DEPUTY UNIVERSITY ADVOCATES

1. The University Advocate shall be a member of the Regent House appointed by Grace on the nomination of the Council. The University Advocate shall not as such be under the direction of any Board, Syndicate, or other body. The duties of the office of University Advocate shall be as specified by Statute or Ordinance.

2. There shall be one or more Deputy University Advocates, each of whom shall be a member of the Regent House appointed by Grace on the nomination of the Council after consultation with the Advocate. A Deputy University Advocate shall carry out any of the duties of the Advocate when requested to do so by the Advocate or when the Advocate is unable to act, and also during any vacancy in the office of Advocate.

3. Subject to the provisions of the Schedule to Statute C, the tenure of the office of University Advocate and the tenure of the office of Deputy University Advocate shall be prescribed by Ordinance.

Chapter XI

PROFESSORS

1. There shall be in the University the Regius Professorships of Divinity, Civil Law, Physic, Hebrew, Greek, History, Engineering and Botany; and such other Professorships as may be specified by or in accordance with Special Ordinance.

2. Professorships are to be established in institutions under the supervision of the General Board either by Statute, or by Grace of the Regent House after consideration of a Report of the General Board.

3. Detailed provision for the procedure for election or appointment to Professorships shall be made by Special Ordinance, made on the recommendation of the General Board.

Chapter XII

READERS

Readerships are to be established in institutions under the supervision of the General Board. Provision shall be made by Ordinance made on the recommendation of the General Board for the procedure for the appointment of Readers.

Chapter XIII

UNIVERSITY SENIOR LECTURERS AND LECTURERS

1. University Senior Lectureships and University Lectureships are to be held in institutions under the supervision of the General Board.

2. Provision shall be made by Special Ordinance for the method of appointment of University Senior Lecturers and related matters.

3. University Lecturers shall be appointed by Appointments Committees. Provision shall be made by Special Ordinance for Appointments Committees, which may be established individually, jointly, or for part of a School, a Faculty, a Department, or other institution under the supervision of the General Board.

4. Provision may be made by Special Ordinance for the appointment of Associate Lecturers.

SCHEDULE

ACADEMIC STAFF

CHAPTER I

CONSTRUCTION, APPLICATION, AND INTERPRETATION

1. No provision of this schedule shall enable any member of the academic staff to be dismissed unless the reason for the dismissalmay in the circumstances (including the size and the administrative resources of the University) reasonably be treated as a sufficient reason for dismissing the member concerned.

2. This schedule shall apply to every person who holds any of the University offices specified or referred to in Statute C I 1(*a*), except the offices of Vice-Chancellor, Chancellor, High Steward, Deputy High Steward, and Commissary.

In this schedule any reference to academic staff is a reference to the persons to whom this schedule applies.

3. In this schedule the terms 'dismiss' and 'dismissal' refer to the dismissal of a member of the academic staff, and include remove or, as the case may be, removal from office, and, in relation to employment under a contract, shall be construed in accordance with Section 55 of the Employment Protection (Consolidation) Act 1978.

4. For the purposes of this schedule the term 'good cause' in relation to the dismissal of a member of the academic staff, being in any case a reason which is related to conduct or capability or qualifications for performing work of the kind which the person concerned was appointed or employed to do, shall mean:

(*a*) conviction for an offence which may be deemed by a Tribunal appointed under the provisions of Chapter III of this schedule to be such as to render the person convicted unfit for the performance of the duties of her or his office or for employment as a member of the academic staff; *or*

(*b*) conduct of an immoral, scandalous, or disgraceful nature incompatible with the duties of the office or employment; *or*

(*c*) conduct constituting failure or persistent refusal or neglect or inability to perform the duties or comply with the conditions of the office; *or*

(*d*) physical or mental incapacity established under the provisions of Chapter IV of this schedule.

In relation to a member of the academic staff, the term 'capability' shall mean capability assessed by reference to skill, aptitude, health, or any other physical or mental quality, and the term 'qualifications' shall mean any degree, diploma, or other academic, technical, or professional qualification relevant to her or his office or position.

5. For the purposes of this schedule dismissal shall be taken to be dismissal by reason of redundancy if it is attributable wholly or mainly to:

(*a*) the fact that the University has ceased, or intends to cease, to carry on the activity for the purposes of which the member of the academic staff concerned was elected or appointed, or has ceased, or intends to cease, to carry on that activity in the place in which the member concerned works or worked; *or*

(*b*) the fact that the requirements of that activity for members of the academic staff to carry out work of a particular kind, or for members of the academic staff to carry out work of a particular kind in that place, have ceased or diminished or are expected to cease or diminish.

6. (*a*) In any case of conflict, the provisions of this schedule shall prevail over those of any other Statute, Special Ordinance and over those of any Ordinance, and the provisions of any Ordinance made under this schedule shall prevail over those of any other Ordinance; provided that Chapter III and Chapter IV, of this schedule shall not apply in relation to anything done or omitted to be done before the date[1] on which the instrument making these modifications was approved under Subsection (9) of Section 204 of the Education Reform Act 1988.

[1] This date was 15 July 1993; see the preface to the 1995 edition of *Statutes and Ordinances*.

(*b*) Nothing in any appointment made, or contract entered into, shall be construed as overriding or excluding any provision made by this schedule concerning the dismissal of a member of the academic staff by reason of redundancy or for good cause; provided that nothing in this subsection shall invalidate any waiver made under Section 142 of the Employment Protection (Consolidation) Act 1978.

(*c*) No one shall sit as a member of any of the bodies established under this schedule, and no one shall be present at a meeting of such a body when the body is considering its decision or discussing a point of procedure, except as provided by this schedule or by Ordinances made under this schedule.

(*d*) The provisions of Section 2 of Special Ordinance D (iii) shall apply to any notice required by this schedule, or by Ordinance made thereunder, and the provisions of Statute D II 6 and 22 and Sections 1, 3 and 4 of Special Ordinance D (iii) shall apply to any proceedings before the University Tribunal or the Septemviri.

(*e*) In this schedule references to numbered chapters, sections, and subsections are references to chapters, sections, and subsections so numbered in this schedule.

CHAPTER II

REDUNDANCY

1. This chapter enables the appropriate body to dismiss any member of the academic staff by reason of redundancy. For the purposes of this chapter the appropriate body shall be either the Council or the General Board, as the case may be, acting in its capacity as the competent authority.

2. Nothing in this chapter shall prejudice, alter, or affect any rights, powers, or duties of the University or apply in relation to a person unless

(*a*) her or his appointment was made, or contract of employment was entered into, on or after 20 November 1987; *or*

(*b*) he or she was promoted on or after that date.

3. For the purposes of Section 2 above in relation to a person, a reference to an appointment made or a contract entered into on or after 20 November 1987 or to promotion on or after that date shall be construed in accordance with subsections (3) to (6) of Section 204 of the Education Reform Act 1988.

4. The Regent House shall have power to decide:

either (*a*) on the recommendation of the Council, that there should be a reduction in the academic staff of the University as a whole;

or (*b*) on the recommendation of the competent authority concerned, that there should be a reduction in the academic staff of any School, Faculty, Department, or other institution,

by way of redundancy. Neither the Council nor the competent authority may delegate the power to make recommendations pursuant to this section.

5. Where the Regent House has reached a decision under Section 4 the competent authority concerned shall appoint a Redundancy Committee to be constituted in accordance with Section 6 below, whose duties shall be:

(*a*) to select the requisite members of the academic staff and recommend them for dismissal by reason of redundancy;

(*b*) to report its recommendations to the competent authority by such date as the latter may specify.

6. A Redundancy Committee shall comprise:

(*a*) a Chair;

(*b*) two members of the Council;

(*c*) two members of the General Board, not being members of the Council.

7. The competent authority shall either approve any selection recommended under Section 5 above or remit it to the Redundancy Committee for further consideration in accordance with any further directions that the competent authority may give. A selection shall not be approved under this section unless the member of the academic staff concerned has been afforded a reasonable opportunity to make representations to the competent authority.

8. If the competent authority has approved a selection recommended by the Redundancy Committee, it shall publish the recommendation in a Report to the University. No member of the academic staff shall be dismissed by reason of redundancy except after the approval by Grace of the recommendations of such a Report.

9. If, following a Report of the competent authority, a recommendation for the dismissal of a member of the academic staff has been approved by Grace, the competent authority may direct an appropriate officer as its delegate to dismiss the member concerned.

10. Each member of the academic staff selected for dismissal shall be given separate notice of such selection. The notice shall sufficiently identify the circumstances which have satisfied the competent authority that the intended dismissal is reasonable, and in particular shall include:

(*a*) a summary of the action taken by the competent authority under the provisions of this chapter;

(*b*) an account of the selection procedure used by the Redundancy Committee;

(*c*) a reference to the rights of the person notified to appeal against the notice and to the time within which any such appeal is to be instituted under Chapter V of this schedule;

(*d*) a statement indicating when the intended dismissal is to take effect.

CHAPTER III

DISCIPLINE, DISMISSAL, AND REMOVAL FROM OFFICE

1. For the purpose of any disciplinary procedures under Sections 2–4 below the responsible person in relation to any particular member of the academic staff shall be the Head of the appropriate Department or other institution, or the Chair of the Board, Syndicate, or other body which is chiefly concerned with the member's duties.

2. If it appears to the responsible person that there are grounds for believing that the conduct or performance of a member of the academic staff is or has been unsatisfactory, he or she shall inquire into the matter. If the responsible person concludes after investigation that the member is at fault, he or she may issue an oral warning to the member. The responsible person shall specify the reason for the warning, shall indicate that it constitutes the first stage of the University's disciplinary procedure, and shall advise the member that he or she may appeal against the warning by following the procedure laid down in pursuant to Chapter VI for the redress of a grievance.

3. If the responsible person concludes after investigation that the fault is sufficiently serious to justify it, or if a further offence occurs, he or she may issue a written warning to the member. Such a warning shall specify the complaint made against the member, the improvements required in the member's conduct or performance, and the period of time within which such improvements are to be made. The responsible person shall advise the member that he or she may appeal against the warning by following the procedure laid down in pursuant to Chapter VI for the redress of a grievance, and shall indicate that, if no satisfactory improvement takes place within the stated time, a complaint may be made to the Vice-Chancellor under Section 5 below.

4. The responsible person shall keep a written record of any warning issued under Section 2 or Section 3 above. No further account shall be taken of an oral warning when one year has elapsed after the date of its issue, and no further account shall be taken of a written warning when two years have elapsed after the date of its issue.

5. If a complaint is made to the Vice-Chancellor concerning the conduct or performance of a member of the academic staff, and if it appears to the Vice-Chancellor that there are grounds for believing that the conduct or performance to which the complaint relates could constitute good cause for dismissal, the Vice-Chancellor shall institute such investigations or inquiries (if any) as appear to her or him to be necessary.

6. If in a particular case it appears to the Vice-Chancellor that a complaint concerning a member of the academic staff is trivial or unjustified, or that it relates to an alleged infringement of Statutes or Ordinances, or of rules made under any Ordinance, for which a standard penalty is normally imposed in the University or within the School, Faculty, Department, or other institution, the Vice-Chancellor may dismiss the complaint summarily, or decide not to proceed further under this chapter.

7. In the case of a complaint not disposed of under Section 6 above, the Vice-Chancellor shall treat the complaint as disclosing a sufficient reason for proceeding further under this chapter and shall write to the member of the academic staff concerned inviting comment in writing. The Vice-Chancellor shall have discretion:

(*a*) to suspend the member without loss of stipend, and

(*b*) to exclude the member from all University premises or any part thereof, pending a final decision.

8. As soon as may be following the receipt of any comments, or after twenty-eight days if no comment is received within that period, the Vice-Chancellor shall consider the matter in the light of all the evidence then available. If no comment is received within twenty-eight days, the Vice-Chancellor may proceed as if the member of the academic staff had denied the complaint in its entirety. The Vice-Chancellor may:

(*a*) dismiss the matter; *or*

(*b*) refer the matter for consideration under Sections 2 and 3 of this chapter or under Statute D II 2; *or*

(*c*) deal with it informally if it appears to the Vice-Chancellor appropriate to do so and if the member of the academic staff agrees in writing that the matter should be dealt with in that way; *or*

(*d*) direct the University Advocate to prefer a charge or charges to be considered by the University Tribunal.

9. If the Vice-Chancellor has directed the University Advocate to prefer a charge or charges, the Clerk of the Tribunal shall notify the member concerned of the date, time, and place to attend the Tribunal, and of the charge or charges, and shall send the member any documents specified therein. The University Advocate shall present the charge or charges to the Tribunal, shall make any necessary administrative arrangements for the summoning of witnesses and the production of documents, and shall be generally responsible for the proper presentation of the case to the Tribunal.

10. The procedure to be followed in respect of the preparation, hearing, and determination of charges by the Tribunal shall be prescribed by Ordinances made under this section.

11. Without prejudice to the generality of the foregoing, such Ordinances shall ensure:

(*a*) that the member of the academic staff concerned is entitled to be represented by another person, whether such person is legally qualified or not, in connection with and at any hearing by the Tribunal;

(*b*) that a charge shall not be determined without an oral hearing at which the member concerned and any person appointed by the member to represent him or her are entitled to be present;

(*c*) that witnesses may be called, both on behalf of the member and by the University Advocate, and that such witnesses may be questioned concerning any relevant evidence;

(*d*) that full and sufficient provision is made for postponements, adjournments, dismissal of the charge or charges for want of prosecution, remission of the charge or charges to the Vice-Chancellor for further consideration, and for the correction of accidental errors;

(*e*) that appropriate time limits are set for each stage of the proceedings (including the hearing) to the intent that the charge shall be heard and determined by the Tribunal as expeditiously as is reasonably practicable.

12. If the charge or charges are upheld, the Tribunal shall determine the appropriate penalty (if any), which may be:

(*a*) if the Tribunal finds that the conduct or performance of the member of the academic staff concerned constitutes good cause for dismissal, the removal of the member from office; *or*

(*b*) such lesser penalty under the member's contract of employment or terms of appointment, including any penalty specified in Statute D II 3, as appears to the Tribunal fair and reasonable in all the circumstances of the case.

If the Tribunal determines that dismissal is the appropriate penalty, the Chair of the Tribunal shall have power to impose that penalty. If the Chair does not impose the penalty of dismissal, or if the Tribunal has determined that some lesser penalty is appropriate, the Tribunal may impose a sentence in accordance with the provisions of Statute D II 3.

13. The Clerk of the Tribunal shall notify the Vice-Chancellor, the University Advocate, and the member concerned of the Tribunal's decision on any charge referred to it. Such notification shall include the Tribunal's findings of fact regarding the charge, the reasons for its decision, the penalty (if any) determined by the Tribunal, and the penalty (if any) imposed by the Tribunal or the Chair. The Clerk of the Tribunal shall draw attention to the period of time within which any appeal should be instituted by ensuring that a copy of Chapter V of this schedule is sent to the member concerned.

Chapter IV

REMOVAL FOR INCAPACITY ON MEDICAL GROUNDS

1. This chapter makes separate provision for the dismissal or removal from office of a member of the academic staff by reason of incapacity on medical grounds.

2. In this chapter

(*a*) references to medical grounds are references to capability assessed by reference to health or any other physical or mental quality;

(*b*) references to the appropriate officer are references to the Vice-Chancellor or an officer acting as the Vice-Chancellor's delegate;

(*c*) references to a member of the academic staff include, in cases where the nature of the alleged disability so requires, a responsible relative or friend or other person having authority to act on behalf of that member in addition to (or instead of) the member.

3. If it appears to the competent authority that the removal from office of a member of the academic staff on medical grounds should be considered, the secretary of the competent authority

(*a*) shall inform the member accordingly, giving notice of the reasons;

(*b*) shall notify the member in writing that it is proposed to make an application to the member's medical practitioner for a medical report and shall seek the member's consent in writing in accordance with the requirements of the Access to Medical Reports Act 1988;

(*c*) may suspend the member from the performance of her or his duties without loss of stipend.

4. If in the light of any medical report obtained under Section 3 above the competent authority is satisfied that a member of the academic staff should be required to retire on medical grounds, and if the member accepts the opinion of the competent authority, the appropriate officer shall terminate the member's employment on those grounds.

5. If the member does not agree that her or his removal from office on medical grounds should be considered, or if after a medical report has been obtained the member declines to retire on medical grounds, the competent authority may refer the case in confidence, with all relevant medical and other evidence (including any such evidence submitted by the member), to a Medical Board comprising:

(*a*) a medically qualified chair appointed by the Council with the agreement of the member concerned or, in default of such agreement, on the nomination of the President of the Royal College of Physicians of London;

(*b*) one person appointed by the competent authority;

(*c*) one person appointed by the member concerned or, in default of such appointment, a second person appointed by the competent authority.

6. The procedure to be followed in respect of the preparation, hearing, and determination of a case by a Medical Board shall be prescribed by Ordinances made under this section. Such Ordinances shall ensure:

(*a*) that the member concerned is entitled to be represented by another person, whether such person is legally qualified or not, in connection with and at any hearing by the Board;

(*b*) that a case shall not be determined without an oral hearing at which the member concerned is entitled to be represented;

(*c*) that witnesses may be called and may be questioned concerning any relevant evidence;

(*d*) that the case is heard and determined as expeditiously as is reasonably practicable.

The Board may require the member concerned to undergo medical examination.

7. The University shall meet the reasonable costs of any medical report or medical examination required under Section 3 or Section 6 above.

8. If a Medical Board determines that a member's removal from office would be justified on medical grounds, the appropriate officer may terminate the employment of the member on those grounds.

Chapter V

APPEALS

1. This chapter establishes procedures for hearing and determining appeals by members of the academic staff who are dismissed or under notice of dismissal or who are otherwise disciplined.

2. This chapter applies to appeals against, or arising from,

(*a*) any decision of a competent authority (or of a delegate of such a body) to dismiss in the exercise of its powers under Chapter II of this schedule;

(*b*) any proceedings, or any decision reached, under Chapter III;

(*c*) any dismissal otherwise than in pursuance of Chapter II or Chapter III;

(*d*) any disciplinary decision of a University authority otherwise than in pursuance of Chapter III;

(*e*) any decision reached under Chapter IV;

(*f*) any proceedings, or any decision reached, under Statute C III 11–14 including any decision reached in pursuance of Statute C III 14;

and 'appeal' and 'appellant' shall be construed accordingly; provided that the following shall not be subject to appeal:

(i) a decision of the Regent House under Chapter II, Section 4;

(ii) any finding of fact by the Tribunal under Chapter III or Statute C III, or any medical finding by a Medical Board under Chapter IV; save where, with the consent of the Septemviri, fresh evidence is called on behalf of the appellant at the hearing of the appeal.

3. A member of the academic staff may institute an appeal in accordance with Statute D II 4.

4. The Septemviri may allow or dismiss an appeal in whole or in part and, without prejudice to the foregoing, may:

(*a*) remit an appeal from a decision under Chapter II (or any issue arising in the course of such an appeal), to the competent authority for further consideration as they may direct;

(*b*) remit an appeal from a decision under Chapter III to be heard again either by the same Tribunal or by a differently constituted Tribunal to be appointed under the provisions of that Chapter;

(*c*) substitute any lesser alternative penalty that might have been imposed in respect of the original charge or charges under the provisions of Chapter III;

(*d*) remit an appeal arising under Chapter IV to be heard again either by the same Medical Board or by a differently constituted Medical Board to be appointed under the provisions of that Chapter.

5. The Clerk of the Septemviri shall notify the decision of the Septemviri on any appeal, including any decision reached in the exercise of their powers under Section 4 above, together with any findings of fact different from those reached by the competent authority under Chapter II or by a Tribunal under Chapter III, as the case may be, to the Vice-Chancellor, to the University Advocate, and to the appellant.

Chapter VI

GRIEVANCE

1. Every University officer has a right to raise any concerns, problems, or complaints relating to her or his appointment or employment, not being matters for which express provision is made elsewhere in Statutes and Ordinances.

2. The University shall establish by Special Ordinance, and may vary from time to time, procedures for the redress of any grievance by a University officer concerning her or his appointment or employment.

Statute D

DISCIPLINE AND THE UNIVERSITY COURTS

Chapter I

DISCIPLINE

For the due maintenance of good order and discipline within the University, the University shall from time to time prescribe such regulations as may be thought expedient in regard to the wearing of academical dress, the rendering of assistance and obedience to all persons in authority in the University and the definition and determination of offences and penalties.

Chapter II

THE UNIVERSITY COURTS

1. There shall be a court called the University Tribunal, and a court called the Septemviri, which shall be constituted by Special Ordinance. These courts shall have no jurisdiction over the Chancellor, the High Steward, the Deputy High Steward, or the Commissary.

2. The University Tribunal shall adjudicate, in accordance with the provisions of this Statute, when a University officer, a member of the Senate, or a person not *in statu pupillari* who holds either a degree or the title of a degree is charged with an offence against the discipline of the University, or with grave misconduct.

3. The University Tribunal may impose any of the following sentences either singly or in combination:

(*a*) deprivation or suspension of membership of the University;

(*b*) deprivation or suspension of degree or title of degree, or postponement of, or disqualification from, admission to degree;

(*c*) deprivation or suspension of the status of Master or Bachelor of Arts;

(*d*) a fine;

(*e*) an order to pay compensation;

(*f*) deprivation or suspension of the right to use University premises or facilities;

(*g*) any sentence considered by the Tribunal to be lighter;

or may, notwithstanding that a person charged has been found to have committed an offence, resolve not to impose any sentence; provided that any person who is deprived of membership of the University or whose membership of the University is suspended shall thereby suffer deprivation or suspension of degrees and titles of degrees during the continuance of such deprivation or suspension.

4. Any person sentenced by the University Tribunal or the Court of Discipline (see Section 10 below) may appeal to the Septemviri within twenty-eight days after notice of the Tribunal's decision. Such an appeal shall be subject to such conditions as are determined by Special Ordinance.

5. The Septemviri shall act as a court of appeal and

(*a*) shall hear appeals by persons holding any of the University offices specified or referred to in Statute C I 1(*a*), except the offices of Chancellor, High Steward, Deputy High Steward, and Commissary in accordance with the provisions of Chapter V of the Schedule to Statute C and such other provisions as may be determined by Special Ordinance;

(*b*) shall hear appeals by other persons charged before the University Tribunal from findings or sentences of the Tribunal, and shall have power to quash a finding or to vary a sentence to any sentence within the limits of the power of the Tribunal;

(*c*) shall hear appeals by persons charged before the Court of Discipline from findings or sentences of that court and shall have power to quash a finding or to vary a sentence to any sentence within the limits of the power of the Court of Discipline.

6. Subject to the provisions of the Schedule to Statute C, the University Tribunal and the Septemviri shall have power to make rules of procedure except in so far as such rules may have been determined by Statute or Ordinance; provided that, if any question of law or of interpretation or application of any of the rules of procedure arises during the course of a hearing, or if a question of procedure arises which cannot be resolved by reference to those rules, the matter shall be decided by the Chair, whose decision shall, for the case which is being heard, be final. The Chair of the Septemviri may issue supplementary practice directions in respect of the Septemviri or any other University court, and the Chair of each other court may issue supplementary practice directions in respect of that court.

7. Every finding or sentence of a University court and every determination of an appeal by the Septemviri shall require the concurrence of a majority of the members present.

8. The Septemviri is to consist of a legally qualified member of the University appointed by Grace as Chair and six members of the Regent House, each appointed by Grace. Detailed provision for these appointments shall be made by Special Ordinance.

9. The University Tribunal is to consist of a legally qualified member of the University as Chair and four members of the Regent House, each appointed by Grace. Provision for the appointment of the Chair and members shall be made by Special Ordinance.

10. There shall be a court, called the Court of Discipline, which shall consist of a Chair, who shall be legally qualified or shall have had experience of acting in a judicial capacity, and four members of the University, not more than two of whom may be persons *in statu pupillari*. Provision for the appointment of the Chair and members shall be made by Special Ordinance.

11. As a court of appeal, the Court of Discipline shall hear appeals from findings of any court established under the provisions of Section 17 of this chapter and shall have power to quash the finding. The decision of the Court on an appeal shall be final.

12. As a court of first instance the Court of Discipline shall, subject to the provisions of this Statute, adjudicate when any person *in statu pupillari* and any person resident in the University with a view to matriculation is charged with an offence against the discipline of the University.

The procedure for the initiation of proceedings before the Court shall be prescribed by Ordinance. The Court may impose the following sentences, either singly or in combination:

(*a*) deprivation or suspension of membership of the University;
(*b*) deprivation or suspension of degree, or postponement of, or disqualification from, admission to degree;
(*c*) deprivation or suspension of the status of Bachelor of Arts;
(*d*) rustication which is exclusion from residence in the Precincts of the University;
(*e*) an order to pay compensation;
(*f*) deprivation or suspension of the right to use University premises or facilities;
(*g*) any sentence considered by the Court to be lighter;

or may, notwithstanding that a person charged has been found to have committed an offence, resolve not to impose any sentence; provided that any person who is deprived of membership of the University or whose membership of the University is suspended shall thereby suffer deprivation or suspension of all degrees during the continuance of such deprivation or suspension.

13. The Registrary or a deputy appointed by the Registrary shall be Clerk of the University Courts.

14. Notice of a meeting of a University Court shall be given to the Head of the College of which the person charged or making an appeal is a member.

Notice of a meeting of a University Court shall be given to the Head of the College of which the person charged or making an appeal is a member.

15. The Court of Discipline and a court of summary jurisdiction established under Section 17 below shall have power to make rules of procedure except in so far as such rules may have been determined by Statute or Ordinance; provided that, if any question of law or interpretation or application of any of the rules of procedure arises during the course of a hearing, or if a question of procedure arises which cannot be resolved by reference to those rules, the matter shall be decided by the Chair, whose decision shall, for the case which is being heard, be final.

16. If a charge of misconduct in an examination has been brought against any person before a University Court and if such person's qualification for the award of a degree, diploma, or certificate is or includes success in that examination, he or she shall not be admitted to the degree, or receive the diploma or certificate, until the charge has been finally disposed of, notwithstanding that he or she may have done all that is required by Statute or Ordinance for the award of the degree, diploma, or certificate. If the Court finds that a person so charged has committed an offence, it may advise the Vice-Chancellor to issue a notice amending the class-list for the examination or other list of approved candidates, or to issue an amended list superseding the original list; and, if no appeal is made to the Septemviri, the Vice-Chancellor shall act in accordance with the advice of the Court or, if an appeal is made to the Septemviri, in accordance with the decision of that court.

17. The University may by Ordinance establish a court of summary jurisdiction ('the Summary Court') and make provision whereby, notwithstanding the provisions of Section 12 of this chapter, such court as a court of first instance may adjudicate when any person is charged with an offence against the discipline of the University who comes within the jurisdiction of the Court of Discipline. Such a court may award the following sentences either singly or in combination:

(*a*) a fine not exceeding such sum as shall be determined by Ordinance;

(*b*) any order to pay compensation not exceeding such sum as shall be determined by Ordinance;

(*c*) deprivation or suspension of the right to use University premises or facilities;

(*d*) any sentence considered by the court to be lighter;

or may, notwithstanding that a person has been found to have committed an offence or such an act, resolve not to impose any sentence. Any person sentenced by a court established under this section may, if he or she obtains leave either from the Chair of the court or from the Chair of the Court of Discipline, appeal in accordance with a procedure determined by Ordinance to the Court of Discipline from the finding of the court but no person shall be given leave to appeal against sentence. The composition of such a court, its method of appointment and rules of procedure, and the procedure for the initiation of proceedings before the court shall be determined by Ordinance. A court established under this section shall have such functions and powers as a court of appeal as may be determined by Ordinance.

18. The Summary Court is to consist of a legally qualified member of the University as Chair, one member of the Regent House and one member *in statu pupillari*. Provision for the appointment of the Chair and members shall be made by Ordinance.

19. Subject to the provisions of Section 20 of this chapter, any person whose case is being heard or adjudicated upon by any of the aforesaid courts

Subject to the provisions of Section 20 of this chapter, any person whose case is being heard or adjudicated upon by any of the aforesaid courts

(*a*) shall be given a reasonable opportunity of being heard by such court; *and*

(*b*) shall have the right to call witnesses and to question witnesses upon whose evidence the case against her or him is based; provided that in the case of an appeal neither party to the case shall recall witnesses examined at first instance or introduce additional evidence except with the leave of the Chair of the court, which shall be given only if the Chair is satisfied that to do so is necessary or expedient in the interests of justice.

20. Notwithstanding the provisions of Section 19 of this chapter, any court established under Section 17 may conduct the whole or part of its proceedings on the basis of written statements submitted by the parties and any other of the aforesaid courts may, if or to the extent that it appears to the Chair to be impracticable to conduct an oral hearing, proceed likewise.

21. If any person *in statu pupillari* intentionally or recklessly disrupts or impedes the proceedings of any of the aforesaid courts, the Chair of the court shall have power, either singly or in combination:

(*a*) to impose a fine not exceeding such sum as shall be determined from time to time by Ordinance;

(*b*) to exclude such person from the court;

(*c*) to rusticate such person for a period not longer than the duration of the proceedings before the court;

and the decision of the Chair shall be final; provided that a person rusticated under this section may, through her or his Tutor, apply to the Chair who imposed the sentence for a review of the sentence on grounds of undue hardship and the Chair shall have power to revoke or vary the sentence. An order of rustication shall take effect notwithstanding that such an application may have been made.

22. Subject to any limitations that may be imposed by Ordinance, the fact that any person has been or is liable to be prosecuted in a court of law in respect of an act or conduct which is the subject of the proceedings before them shall not affect the jurisdiction and powers of the aforesaid courts under this Statute.

Statute E

TRUSTS

Chapter I

GENERAL PROVISIONS

1. The University shall maintain those lectureships, scholarships, prizes, and other emoluments for which provision is made by any trust for the time being binding on the University, in addition to those mentioned by name in this Statute.

2. When in any regulations governing a trust, which is more than sixty years old at the date of the original making of this Statute,[1] it is directed that any act shall or may be done by the Senate, the direction is hereby altered so that the act shall or may be done by the University (that is to say, by Grace of the Regent House).

3. When in any regulations governing a trust, which is less than sixty years old at the date of the original making of this Statute,[1] it is directed that any act shall or may be done by the Senate, the direction is hereby altered so that the act shall or may be done by the University (that is to say, by Grace of the Regent House); provided that if the trust has a trustee or governing body other than the University such alteration shall take effect only if the consent of such trustee or governing body is obtained.

4. When in any regulations governing a trust it is directed that any act shall or may be done by the General Board of Studies or a Special Board of Studies or a Board of Studies, the direction is hereby altered so that the said act shall or may be done by the General Board or the appropriate Board representing for the time being the branch of studies concerned.

5. The regulations concerning any endowment mentioned by name in Chapters II to XXXII (inclusive) of this Statute, which are contained in any instrument of foundation, Act of Parliament, Order in Council, decree, order, statute or other instrument operative before the original commencement of this Statute,[1] are rescinded, save in so far as any of the said regulations may be embodied in this Statute.

6. The name of the founder (or of the person commemorated by the fund) shall be attached to any emolument charged upon any of the said endowments and shall appear in any announcement of the award.

7. The following provisions of this section shall govern existing and future trust funds save in so far as it may be provided otherwise in any instrument of foundation or Statute for the time being governing a particular trust fund.

(i) The awarders of a scholarship, prize, or other emolument charged upon a trust shall not award the whole or any part of the income at their disposal on any occasion when there is no candidate of sufficient merit.

(ii) The University may from time to time direct whether the awarders of a scholarship, prize, or other emolument charged upon a trust fund are to take into consideration the financial circumstances of candidates, and in the absence of any directions such circumstances shall not be taken into consideration.

(iii) When the income of a trust fund is insufficient for the effective maintenance of a lectureship, scholarship, prize, or other emolument charged upon the fund, the University shall have power to suspend such emolument.

(iv) Any part of the income of a trust fund not expended in any year shall be accumulated by investment or otherwise, and any accumulation shall at the discretion of the Council either be applied as income in any one or more subsequent years or be added to the capital of the fund.

(v) When two or more candidates for a scholarship, prize, or other emolument are of equal merit, the awarders may divide between them the income then at their disposal.

(vi) When it is provided that the income of a trust fund shall be used for the award of scholarships, prizes, or other emoluments, it shall be lawful to charge upon the income of the fund the expenses connected with the making of the award, including the remuneration of the awarders.

[1] 14 January 1927.

(vii) Candidature for scholarships, prizes, and other emoluments charged upon a trust fund shall be invited on such occasions (not necessarily annual) as the University may from time to time determine.

(viii) The University may make Ordinances from time to time regarding the nature, amounts, conditions of tenure, duration, and payment of any emoluments charged upon the fund, the eligibility of candidates, the persons by whom, the subjects for which, and the manner in which awards are to be made, and any other matters relating to the administration of the fund.

(ix) When a prize is to be awarded for an essay, dissertation, poem, or the like, the University may make payment of the prize money conditional on the prize-winner's work being printed (or printed and published) in an approved manner.

8. Notwithstanding the provisions of any instrument of foundation governing a particular trust, the University shall have the power to make Ordinances so as to apply part of the income of the fund for the purpose of increasing the value of an emolument or the remuneration of the awarders, or maintaining additional emoluments of the same character, or for another purpose or other purposes; provided that such application is consonant with the original purpose of the endowment and that no such application shall be made during the life of the founder of the trust without her or his consent, and that if the trust is less than sixty years old, and has a trustee or governing body other than the University, no such application shall be made without the consent of such trustee or governing body.

CHAPTER II

THE BELL, ABBOTT, AND BARNES FUNDS

1. The investments from time to time representing the endowment given by deed of foundation executed on 18 July 1810 by William Bell shall constitute a trust fund called the Bell Fund.

2. The investments from time to time representing the endowment given by the will of John Abbott, who died on 13 May 1870, shall constitute a trust fund called the Abbott Fund.

3. The investments from time to time representing the endowment given by deed of trust executed on 19 February 1844 by John Barnes shall constitute a trust fund called the Barnes Fund.

4. The first charge on the income of the Bell, Abbott, and Barnes Funds shall be the provision of exhibitions or grants (or both) for students for proficiency in some branch or branches of University studies. The University shall have power to determine the eligibility of candidates. Any part of the income of any of the funds that is not expended in any year as aforesaid may, at the discretion of the electors, be used to enable awards to be made to students who are in need of financial assistance by the governing bodies of such Colleges and such institutions recognized under Statute G I as may from time to time be determined by Grace or Ordinance.

5. No award shall be made by the electors which is not in their opinion justified by the financial circumstances of the candidate.

6. In the case of each of the Bell and Abbott Funds, if the electors are of opinion that one or more of the candidates, being children of clergymen of the Church of England, show adequate proficiency, they shall make provision for the needs of such candidates before they may make any award from the fund to any other candidate.

7. In the case of the Barnes Fund, if the electors are of opinion that one or more of the candidates, having been educated at Christ's Hospital, now at Horsham in the County of Sussex, St Paul's School, now in the County of London, or the Merchant Taylors' School, now in the County of Hertfordshire, show sufficient proficiency, they shall make provision for the needs of such candidates before they may make any award from the fund to any other candidate.

8. In the case of the Abbott Fund, if two or more candidates show equal proficiency preference shall be given to candidates born in the West Riding of Yorkshire.

CHAPTER III

THE JOHN STEWART OF RANNOCH FUNDS

1. The investments representing the endowment given by the will of John Stewart of Rannoch, who died on 19 July 1884, shall constitute three trust funds called the John Stewart of Rannoch Hebrew Fund, the John Stewart of Rannoch Greek and Latin Fund, and the John Stewart of Rannoch Sacred Music Fund, the primary use of which shall be to provide scholarships in one or more of the subjects of Hebrew, Greek and Latin, and Sacred Music respectively. If two or more candidates for a scholarship show equal proficiency preference shall be given to candidates who are natives of the counties of Wilts, Somerset, or Gloucester, including the city and county of Bristol.

2. After provision has been made for the scholarships in accordance with Section 1 any unexpended income accumulated in the funds may be used for making grants to scholars or to other persons engaged in the study of any of the subjects with which the funds are associated; for purchasing books, musical instruments, or other material for the Faculties concerned; or for any other purpose for the promotion of the study of the aforesaid subjects in the University.

3. The University may from time to time make regulations governing the application of the funds.

CHAPTER IV

THE TYSON FUND

1. The investments from time to time representing the endowment given by the will of Henry Tyson, who died on 27 March 1852, shall constitute a trust fund called the Tyson Fund.

2. The income of the fund shall be used to provide medals, and prizes for the winners of the medals, to be awarded for proficiency in a prescribed branch, or one or more prescribed branches, of mathematical study.

3. Regulations prescribing a branch or branches of study, regarding the form and substance and number of the medals, and regarding any other matters relating to the administration of the fund, shall be made in such manner as the University may determine from time to time: provided that astronomy shall always be a prescribed branch of study.

CHAPTER V

THE HARE FUND

1. The investments from time to time representing the benefaction given to the University in 1861 by the friends of Julius Charles Hare shall constitute a trust fund called the Hare Fund.

2. The income of the Hare Fund shall be used to provide one or more prizes for dissertations in English on subjects falling within the scope of the Faculty of Classics.

CHAPTER VI

THE HULSEAN FUND

1. The investments from time to time representing the endowment given by the will of John Hulse, who died on 14 December 1790, shall constitute a trust fund called the Hulsean Fund.

2. There shall be paid out of the income of the fund (*a*) to the Master, Fellows and Scholars of St John's College, for the maintenance of scholarships in the College, one-third part of the net income arising from the property in Sandbach and Bradwell (forming part of the original endowment) or from any property from time to time representing the same; (*b*) to the Chest such sum for defraying expenses connected with the administration of the fund as the Finance Committee of the Council may think fit.

3. The remainder of the income of the fund shall be used to provide a Hulsean Preachership, a Hulsean Prize, and, if the University from time to time so determines, a Hulsean Lectureship, and, after such provision has been made, towards providing the stipend of the Norris-Hulse Professor.

4. A Hulsean Preacher shall be elected in every year, whose duty it shall be to deliver in the University one or more sermons.

5. When a Hulsean Lecturer is appointed it shall be her or his duty to deliver lectures on some branch of Christian Theology.

6. The electors to the Preachership and Lectureship shall be the Vice-Chancellor, the Masters of Trinity and St John's Colleges, and the Professors of Divinity; provided that the Vice-Chancellor, the Master of Trinity, and the Master of St John's shall each have power to appoint a deputy to act on her or his behalf, and that the Professors of Divinity shall each have power to appoint a deputy who is another Professor in the Faculty of Divinity to act on her or his behalf.

7. Subject to this Statute the University may from time to time make regulations regarding the time and manner of elections to the Preachership and Lectureship, the conditions and duration of their tenure, the remuneration of the Preacher and the Lecturer, and any other matters relating to the administration of the fund.

8. The Hulsean Prize shall be awarded for a dissertation on a subject pertaining to some branch of Christian Theology.

9. A winner of the prize shall not again be a candidate.

CHAPTER VII

THE CRAVEN FUND

1. That part of the annual income of the foundation established by the will of John first Baron Craven of Ryton, who died in 1649, which is appropriated to the University of Cambridge shall constitute a trust fund called the Craven Fund.

2. The fund shall be used to provide one or more scholarships for knowledge of the languages and civilizations of ancient Greece and Rome, to provide one or more studentships, the holders of which shall engage in advanced study or research in the languages, literature, history, philosophy, archaeology, or art of ancient Greece or Rome, or the comparative philology of the Indo-European languages, and otherwise for the furtherance by means of grants of research in the said subjects.

3. The administration of the fund shall be entrusted to a Board of Managers constituted in such manner as the University may determine from time to time.

4. It shall be the duty of the Managers to elect the Craven Student or Students, without holding a competitive examination for the purpose, and to decide what grants (if any) are to be made for the furtherance of research. They shall perform their duties in accordance with regulations made by the University from time to time.

5. A Craven Student shall pursue her or his study or research (according to a scheme to be approved by the Managers) away from Cambridge, unless the Managers at their discretion waive this requirement.

6. In the election to any Craven Studentship or Craven Scholarship the Managers or Electors shall not take into consideration the financial circumstances of the candidates.

CHAPTER VIII

THE BATTIE, BROWNE, DAVIES, PITT, PORSON, AND WADDINGTON FUNDS

1. The investments from time to time representing the endowment given by William Battie by deed of gift dated 30 September 1747 shall constitute a trust fund called the Battie Fund.

2. The investments from time to time representing the endowment given by the will of Sir William Browne, who died on 10 March 1774, shall constitute a trust fund called the Browne Fund.

3. The investments from time to time representing the endowment given by the will of Jonathan Davies, who died on 5 December 1809, shall constitute a trust fund called the Davies Fund.

4. The investments from time to time representing the benefaction given to the University in 1813 by a Committee of Members of the Senate and the Pitt Club in London in memory of the Right Honourable William Pitt shall constitute a trust fund called the Pitt Fund.

5. The investments from time to time representing the benefaction given to the University in 1808 by the friends of Richard Porson shall constitute a trust fund called the Porson Fund.

6. The investments from time to time representing the benefaction given in 1870 by Anne and Clara Waddington in memory of their brothers shall constitute a trust fund called the Waddington Fund.

7. The several incomes of the Battie, Davies, Pitt, and Waddington Funds shall be used to provide one or more scholarships for knowledge of the languages and civilizations of ancient Greece and Rome, and otherwise to provide grants for the furtherance of such knowledge.

8. The income of the Browne Fund shall be used to provide medals for Greek and Latin verse, to provide one or more scholarships for knowledge of the languages and civilizations of ancient Greece and Rome, and otherwise to provide grants for the furtherance of such knowledge.

9. The income of the Porson Fund shall be used to provide a prize for the best translation of a set passage from an English poet in Greek verse, to provide one or more scholarships for knowledge of the languages and civilizations of ancient Greece and Rome, and otherwise to provide grants for the furtherance of such knowledge.

10. Subject to this Statute the University may make regulations from time to time as to number, form and substance of Sir William Browne's medals, as to prescribing the subjects of exercises to be submitted and the metres in which they are severally to be written, the eligibility of candidates, and any other matters regarding the award of the medals.

11. In the election to any emolument mentioned in this chapter the electors shall not take into consideration the financial circumstances of the candidates.

CHAPTER IX

THE JOHN LUCAS WALKER FUND

1. The investments from time to time representing the sum appointed by Sir Richard Webster, Attorney-General, in favour of the University, under the will of John Lucas Walker, who died in 1886, shall constitute a trust fund called the John Lucas Walker Fund.

2. The income of the fund shall be used to provide one or more studentships, called John Lucas Walker Studentships, the holders of which shall devote themselves to original research or to whole time study and training for research in Pathology, and, after provision has been made for at least one such studentship, to the furtherance of original research in that subject by exhibitions, prizes, grants, or otherwise.

CHAPTER X

THE CROSSE FUND

1. The investments from time to time representing the fund created by deed of trust dated 14 August 1833 out of the estate of John Crosse, who died on 17 June 1816, shall constitute a trust fund called the Crosse Fund.

2. The income of the fund shall be used to provide scholarships, studentships, prizes, or grants (or any one or more of such emoluments) for the furtherance of the knowledge of the Holy Scriptures in Hebrew and Greek, Ecclesiastical History, and Christian Theology.

CHAPTER XI

THE SEATONIAN FUND

1. The investments from time to time representing the estate given by the will of Thomas Seaton, who died on 18 August 1741, shall constitute a trust fund called the Seatonian Fund.

2. The income of the fund shall be used to provide one or more Seatonian Prizes for poems in English on a subject set by the adjudicators which shall be deemed by them to conform to the condition imposed by the founder, namely that it shall be conducive to the honour of the Supreme Being and the recommendation of virtue.

Chapter XII

THE RUSTAT FUND

1. The investments from time to time representing the endowment given in January 1666–67 by deed of gift by Tobias Rustat shall constitute a trust fund called the Rustat Fund.

2. The income of the fund shall be used for the purchase of books and manuscripts for the University Library.

3. Any books bought out of the said income shall be impressed with the Rustat arms, unless on account of the nature of the book this course is undesirable.

4. The University may make regulations as to the persons by whose advice purchases are to be made, as to the conditions under which books or manuscripts purchased may be taken out of the Library, and otherwise as to the administration of the fund.

Chapter XIII

THE WORTS FUND

1. The investments from time to time representing the endowment created by the will of William Worts dated 21 June 1709 shall constitute a trust fund called the Worts Fund.

2. The income of the Worts Fund shall be subject in the first instance to the following charges, namely,

(i) a charge of £30 a year in favour of the Old Schools of Cambridge, so long as the said schools shall be maintained as schools for poor children;

(ii) a charge of £40 a year to be laid aside, as the founder directed, for the maintenance and repairs of the road from Emmanuel College to the Gogmagog Hills, and for the maintenance of the galleries in Great St Mary's Church (for both of which objects the founder provided in his will); such sum to be expended from time to time as there shall be occasion, in such proportions to each object as the Finance Committee of the Council shall think fit;

(iii) a further charge of £40 a year to be applied in accordance with an order of the Court of Chancery dated 27 March 1742 towards the repairs of the said road;

(iv) a charge of such sum, for defraying expenses connected with the administration of the fund, as the Finance Committee of the Council may think fit.

3. After the aforesaid charges have been met the income of the fund shall be applied as follows, namely,

(i) the University may in any year place at the disposal of the General Board from the income of the fund a sum not exceeding £400, which may be applied in accordance with regulations made by the University from time to time to the making of grants for the promotion or encouragement of investigations in countries outside Great Britain respecting the religion, learning, law, politics, customs, manners, and rarities, natural or artificial, of those countries, or for purposes of geographical discovery or of antiquarian or scientific research in such countries, subject to any conditions as to publication of the results of investigations which may be laid down at the time of the making of the grant;

(ii) the remaining income of the Worts Fund shall be applied to the use of the University Library in such manner as the University may from time to time determine.

Chapter XIV

THE REDE FOUNDATION

1. The rent-charge received under the foundation of the executors of Sir Robert Rede, who died on 8 January 1518–19, shall be used for the payment of a Lecturer, whose duty it shall be to deliver in term time one lecture in every year, called the Rede, Sir Robert, Lectureship.

2. The University may from time to time make regulations regarding the appointment of the Lecturer, the tenure of the office, the subjects of the lectures, and the times and places of delivery.

Chapter XV

THE PREACHER ON THE FOUNDATION OF THE LADY MARGARET

1. There shall be a preacher on the foundation of the Lady Margaret. The preacher shall be appointed by the Vice-Chancellor and shall hold office for one year.

2. The University may from time to time make regulations for the preachership.

Chapter XVI

THE LE BAS FUND

1. The investments from time to time representing the endowment given in 1848 by subscribers in memory of Charles Webb Le Bas shall constitute a trust fund called the Le Bas Fund.

2. The income of the fund shall be used for the furtherance of the study of Literature by the provision of any one or more emoluments (whether scholarships, studentships, prizes, or grants for research) or otherwise.

Chapter XVII

THE PEREGRINE MAITLAND FUND

1. The investments from time to time representing the endowment given in 1844 by subscribers in memory of Sir Peregrine Maitland shall constitute a trust fund called the Peregrine Maitland Fund.

2. The income of the fund shall be used to advance the study of subjects arising from or affecting the spread of the Christian religion, the comparison of the Christian religion with other religions, and the contact of Christian and other civilizations, by the provision of any one or more emoluments (whether scholarships, studentships, prizes, or grants for research) or otherwise.

Chapter XVIII

THE BURNEY FUND

1. The investments from time to time representing the endowment given by deed of trust dated 19 January 1847 by Jane Caroline Burney in pursuance of the wish of her brother Richard Burney shall constitute a trust fund called the Burney Fund.

2. The income of the fund shall be used for the furtherance of the study of the Philosophy of Religion (these words being interpreted so that they may include Christian Ethics and questions relating to the truth and evidence of the Christian Religion) by the provision of any one or more emoluments (whether scholarships, studentships, prizes, or grants for research) or otherwise.

Chapter XIX

THE NORRISIAN FUND

1. The investments from time to time representing the endowment given by John Norris, who died on 5 January 1777, shall constitute a trust fund called the Norrisian Fund.

2. The income of the fund shall be used to provide a prize to be awarded for an essay on a subject pertaining to some branch of Christian Theology.

3. After provision has been made for the prize the remainder of the income or any part thereof may be applied towards the stipend of the Norris-Hulse Professor.

CHAPTER XX

THE WHEWELL BENEFACTION

1. The rents of the chambers in the buildings known as Whewell's Courts, which rents are part of the income of the trust created by the will of William Whewell, who died on 6 March 1866, shall be subject to the deduction by Trinity College of the amount of all rates, taxes, cost of repairs and other outgoings (including wages of porters and other servants of the College employed in or about the said buildings).

2. The net income of the trust shall be applied annually as follows, namely,

(*a*) £150 shall be applied to the maintenance of scholarships in Trinity College;

(*b*) the remainder shall be paid to the University and shall constitute a trust fund, which shall be used for one or more of the following purposes, namely, the remuneration of the Whewell Professor of International Law, the provision of Whewell Scholarships in International Law, and the furtherance in any other manner of the study of International Law.

3. The election to and tenure of the Whewell Professorship shall be governed by Statute C.

4. A Whewell Professor or Whewell Scholar shall have the right to be admitted a member of Trinity College on payment of the fees fixed for the time being for admission.

5. The Whewell Professor and any Whewell Scholar shall so long as he or she is a member of Trinity College have the right to be assigned a set of chambers in Whewell's Courts on the terms of paying such rent and charges for services as are prescribed by the Council of the College from time to time and generally upon the like terms (as nearly as may be) and under the same rules as other chambers in the College are assigned to members thereof.

CHAPTER XXI

THE YORKE FUND

1. The investments from time to time representing the endowments given by the will of Edmund Yorke, who died on 29 November 1871, shall constitute a trust fund called the Yorke Fund.

2. The income shall be used to provide one or more prizes for essays on subjects pertaining to some branch of law or legal history, or otherwise for the furtherance of research in law or legal history.

CHAPTER XXII

THE GEORGE LONG FUND

1. The investments from time to time representing the endowments given by the friends of George Long, who died on 10 August 1869, shall constitute a trust fund called the George Long Fund.

2. The income of the fund shall be used to provide one or more prizes for distinguished proficiency in one or both of the subjects of Roman law and jurisprudence.

CHAPTER XXIII

THE STANTON FUND

1. The investments from time to time representing the endowments given by Vincent Henry Stanton in pursuance of a letter addressed to the Vice-Chancellor on 15 January 1904 shall constitute a trust fund called the Stanton Fund.

2. The income of the fund shall be used for the furtherance of the teaching of the Philosophy of Religion in the University either by the payment of the stipend or part of the stipend of a University Lecturer in that subject, or by the provision of special lectures, or otherwise.

Chapter XXIV

THE HARDING FUND

1. The investments from time to time representing the endowment given by Colonel Harding, which was accepted on 22 November 1912, shall constitute a trust fund called the Harding Fund.

2. The income of the fund shall be applied towards the payment of a University Lectureship in a branch or branches of Zoology.

Chapter XXV

THE ISAAC NEWTON FUND

1. The income of investments representing for the time being the fund given by Frank McClean and accepted on 5 March 1891 shall be used for the furtherance of advanced study and research in the subjects of Astronomy (especially Gravitational Astronomy but also including the other branches of Astronomy and Astronomical Physics) and Physical Optics by the maintenance of one or more studentships called Isaac Newton Studentships.

2. The Master, Fellows, and Scholars of Trinity College may at any time transfer to the University the investments and other assets representing the fund for the time being, and upon so doing shall be discharged from the trust.

3. The following expenses may be charged upon the fund on the recommendation of the electors:

(*a*) the purchase of instruments or apparatus required by an Isaac Newton Student for the purpose of her or his study or research: provided that such instruments or apparatus shall be the property of the trust,

(*b*) extraordinary expenses connected with the course of study or research of a Student.

Chapter XXVI

THE ARNOLD GERSTENBERG FUND

1. The income of the fund given by Leonora Philipps by deed executed on 15 December 1892 in accordance with the wish of her brother Arnold Gerstenberg shall be used for the promotion of the study of Moral Philosophy and Metaphysics among students (men and women alike) of Natural Science.

2. The Master, Fellows, and Scholars of Trinity College may at any time transfer to the University the investments and other assets representing the fund for the time being, and upon so doing shall be discharged from the trust.

Chapter XXVII

THE PRENDERGAST FUND

1. The income of the Prendergast Fund created in memory of Guy Lushington Prendergast by deed executed on 8 June 1888 by Elizabeth Sophia Prendergast shall be used for the furtherance of advanced study and research in the language, literature, history, philosophy, archaeology, and art of ancient Greece, by the maintenance of one or more studentships, or by the provision of grants for research in the said subjects.

2. The Master, Fellows, and Scholars of Trinity College may at any time transfer to the University the investments and other assets representing the fund for the time being, and upon so doing shall be discharged from the trust.

Chapter XXVIII

THE SMITH FUND

1. The investments from time to time representing the endowments given by the will of Robert Smith, who died on 2 February 1768, shall constitute a trust fund called the Smith Fund.

2. The net income of the fund shall be applied annually as follows, namely,

(*a*) one-half shall be applied towards the payment of the stipend of the Plumian Professor;

(*b*) one-half shall be used to provide one or more prizes for original work in any subject in Mathematics and its applications.

Chapter XXIX

THE RAYLEIGH PRIZES

The income of the benefaction given in 1909 by friends of John third Baron Rayleigh shall be used to provide one or more prizes for original work in any subject in Mathematics and its applications.

Chapter XXX

THE CARUS, SCHOLEFIELD, KAYE, HEBREW, EVANS PRIZE, JEREMIE, AND GEORGE WILLIAMS FUNDS, AND THE THEOLOGICAL STUDIES FUND

1. The investments from time to time representing the benefactions accepted from William Carus and his friends in 1853 and augmented by an anonymous donor in 1894 shall constitute a trust fund called the Carus Fund, the income of which shall be used in the first place to provide a prize or prizes for the encouragement of the accurate study of the New Testament in Greek.

2. The investments from time to time representing the benefaction given in 1856 by subscribers in memory of James Scholefield shall constitute a trust fund called the Scholefield Fund, the income of which shall be used in the first place to provide a prize or prizes for the encouragement of the critical study of the Holy Scriptures.

3. The investments from time to time representing the benefaction given in memory of John Kaye, who died on 18 February 1853, shall constitute a trust fund called the Kaye Fund, the income of which shall be used in the first place to provide a prize or prizes for a dissertation upon a subject pertaining to ancient ecclesiastical history, the canon of Scripture, or Biblical criticism.

4. The investments from time to time representing the benefaction given by members of the University in 1865 and augmented by Joshua Nussey in 1867 shall constitute a trust fund called the Hebrew Fund, the income of which shall be used in the first place to provide a prize or prizes for the encouragement of the study of Hebrew in the University.

5. The investments from time to time representing the benefaction given in memory of Robert Wilson Evans, who died on 10 March 1866, shall constitute a trust fund called the Evans Prize Fund, the income of which shall be used in the first place to provide a prize or prizes for proficiency in a branch or branches of Christian Theology.

6. The investments from time to time representing the benefaction given by James Amiraux Jeremie in 1870 shall constitute a trust fund called the Jeremie Fund, the income of which shall be used in the first place to provide a prize or prizes for the encouragement of a critical study of the Septuagint Version of the Old Testament and such other Hellenistic literature as may serve to illustrate the New Testament.

7. The investments from time to time representing the benefaction given in memory of George Williams, who died on 26 January 1878, shall constitute a trust fund called the George Williams Fund, the income of which shall be used in the first place to provide one or more prizes for proficiency in a branch or branches of Christian Theology.

8. Subject to this Statute the University may make from time to time regulations regarding the number and value of the prizes to be awarded under this Statute, and any other matters relating to the administration of the funds.

9. There shall be established a trust fund called the Theological Studies Fund, to which at the discretion of the Finance Committee of the Council may be transferred from time to time any surplus income or accumulated balance of surplus income of the Carus Fund, the Scholefield Fund, the Kaye Fund, the Hebrew Fund, the Evans Prize Fund, the Jeremie Fund, or the George Williams Fund. The income of the Theological Studies Fund shall be administered in such manner and for such purposes as may be prescribed from time to time by Ordinance, for the encouragement of theological study by members of the University.

Chapter XXXI

THE WILTSHIRE PRIZE

The income of the benefaction given in 1900 by Thomas Wiltshire shall be used to provide one or more prizes for proficiency in either or both of the subjects of Geology and Mineralogy.

Chapter XXXII

ENDOWED PROFESSORSHIPS AND READERSHIPS

The provisions of any instrument of foundation, Act of Parliament, Order in Council, decree, order, statute, or other instrument (other than those of any Statute made by the University Commissioners) regarding any Professorship or Readership founded before 14 January 1927 shall cease to have effect from 13 May 1927. Each such Professorship and Readership shall thenceforth be governed by Statute C, and the University shall have power to determine from time to time the scope of the subject specified in the statutable title of the office.

Provided always that (*a*) if on 30 September 1926 provisions were in force for the election to a Professorship otherwise than in accordance with Statute B Chapter IX of the Old Statutes such provisions shall remain in force but be subject to alteration by the University from time to time, and (*b*) nothing in this section shall invalidate any Statute made by the Commissioners regarding any particular Professorship or affect the right of the Crown to appoint to the Regius Professorships of Civil Law, Physic, and History, and to the King Edward VII Professorship of English Literature.

Provided also that the investments from time to time constituting the endowment of any Professorship or Readership founded before 14 January 1927 shall continue to be treated as a separate trust fund and the income thereof shall be applied towards the stipend of the Professorship and any pension contribution payable by the University in respect of it.

Chapter XXXIII

THE PROFESSORSHIPS OF DIVINITY AND HEBREW

1. Notwithstanding the provisions of the preceding chapter, if the income from the endowments attached to any of the Professorships of Divinity is more than is required to pay the stipend of the Professor and the pension contribution payable in respect of the Professor by the University, the excess, or such part of the excess as may be required, shall be used towards making good any deficiency in the income from the endowments attached to any other Professorship of Divinity, and the remaining excess, if any, after all such deficiencies have been made good, shall be used towards providing the stipend of the Regius Professor of Hebrew.

2. If a Professor of Divinity or the Regius Professor of Hebrew is admitted to a Bishopric or Deanery or any benefice with cure of souls, the Professorship shall *ipso facto* become vacant.

Chapter XXXIV

THE DIXIE PROFESSORSHIP OF ECCLESIASTICAL HISTORY

1. This Statute shall be for the University of Cambridge and for Emmanuel College in common.

2. There shall be established as heretofore in the University of Cambridge a Professorship to be called the Dixie Professorship of Ecclesiastical History.

3. The Professor shall comply with the provisions of the Statutes of the University relating to the duties of Professors.

4. The election to the Professorship shall be in accordance with the provisions of University Statute C XI 3, the Master of Emmanuel College being added to the Board of Electors as therein defined; provided that if the Mastership of Emmanuel College be vacant, or if the Master be also a candidate for the Professorship, the senior member of the Governing Body of Emmanuel College who is not a candidate shall take the Master's place on the Board; provided also that if the Master of Emmanuel College or the senior member of the Governing Body as aforesaid at any time be in any other capacity a member of the Board, such person shall not on that ground have two votes.

5. The Dixie Professor of Ecclesiastical History shall by virtue of admission to the Professorship, without need of any further election, be entitled to admission to the Professorial Fellowship permanently associated under the provisions of Statute XIX, Section 5 [of the College Statutes] with the tenure of the Dixie Professorship at Emmanuel College (except during any period for which the said Professorship shall be held by the Head of any College in Cambridge) upon making the declaration required under the provisions of Statute XXII [of the College Statutes] to be made by other Fellows of the College, and shall be entitled (subject to the provisions of Statute XXV [of the College Statutes]) to hold the said Fellowship while continuing to hold the office of Dixie Professor, but no longer.

6. In respect of the Professorial stipend of the Dixie Professor of Ecclesiastical History the College shall pay to the University in each quarter of the financial year the sum of one hundred and ninety-two pounds and fifty pence (which sum shall include the contribution due in respect of superannuation) out of the general revenue of the College.

7. From such sum as shall in each year be authorized to be levied by the University from the College in accordance with the Statutes of the University for contributions of Colleges for University purposes, the College shall be entitled to deduct annually the sum of three hundred and fifty pounds on account of the payment made by the College in respect of the Dixie Professor.

8. For any period during which this Professorship shall be vacant there shall be a *pro rata* diminution of the amount payable under Section 6 of this Statute, and also a *pro rata* diminution of the deduction made under Section 7 of this Statute from the College's contribution to the University.

Chapter XXXV

THE LOWNDEAN PROFESSORSHIP OF ASTRONOMY AND GEOMETRY

Notwithstanding the title of the Lowndean Professorship of Astronomy and Geometry it shall be competent for the electors on each occasion to elect a Professor who proposes to profess solely or chiefly Astronomy, or one who proposes to profess solely or chiefly Geometry. This Statute shall not imply any limitation of the power of the University or of the General Board under Statute C or any Special Ordinance made under it. In particular, it shall be competent for the University in exercising its powers of making regulations under Statute C to provide that for the time being at successive elections to the Professorship candidature may be limited, or preference may be given by the electors, to candidates who propose to profess only one of the subjects Astronomy and Geometry, or some particular subject or subjects falling within the scope of one of them.

Chapter XXXVI

THE VERE HARMSWORTH PROFESSORSHIP OF IMPERIAL AND NAVAL HISTORY

Notwithstanding the title of the Vere Harmsworth Professorship of Imperial and Naval History it shall be competent for the electors on each occasion to elect a Professor who proposes to profess solely or chiefly the History of the British Empire, or one who proposes to profess solely or chiefly Naval History. This Statute shall not imply any limitation of the power of the University or of the General Board under Statute C or any Special Ordinance made under it.

CHAPTER XXXVII

THE CROTCH FUND

1. The investments from time to time representing the endowments given to the University under the will of George Robert Crotch dated 22 June 1872 and the will of William Duppa Duppa Crotch dated 15 August 1903 shall together constitute a trust fund called the Crotch Fund.

2. The income of the Crotch Fund shall be used for the purchase of books and specimens for the Museum of Zoology or otherwise for the general purposes of that Museum as may be provided by Ordinance.

CHAPTER XXXVIII

THE BENN W. LEVY FUND

1. The investments from time to time representing the benefaction given in 1910 by the Committee of the Benn W. Levy Memorial Fund shall constitute a trust fund called the Benn W. Levy Fund, the income of which shall be devoted to the furtherance of original research in Biochemistry by the establishment of a Studentship to be called the Benn W. Levy Studentship, the holder of which shall undertake original research in Biochemistry.

2. Notwithstanding any provision of the trust to the contrary, any part of the income of the fund not expended in any year may be applied at the discretion of the Managers of the fund as income in any subsequent year.

CHAPTER XXXIX

THE CLERK MAXWELL FUND

1. The investments from time to time representing the endowment created by the will of Mrs Clerk Maxwell, who died on 5 November 1879, shall constitute a trust fund called the Clerk Maxwell Fund.

2. The income of the fund shall be used to provide one or more Scholarships, called Clerk Maxwell Scholarships, for the advancement by original research of Experimental Physics, especially Electricity, Magnetism, and Heat, and, after provision has been made for at least one such Scholarship, to further original research in those subjects by any other means.

3. The University may from time to time make regulations governing the administration and application of the fund.

CHAPTER XL

THE ARTHUR BALFOUR FUND

1. The investments from time to time representing

(*a*) the benefaction accepted by Grace 1 of 23 May 1912 of £20,000 for the endowment of a Professorship of Genetics to be called the Arthur Balfour Professorship of Genetics and

(*b*) the benefaction conveyed to the University by the Right Honourable Arthur James Balfour and the Right Honourable Reginald Baliol, Viscount Esher, in a Trust Deed dated the tenth of December nineteen hundred and thirteen

shall together constitute a trust fund called the Arthur Balfour Fund. The first charge on the income of the Arthur Balfour Fund shall be the cost of the stipend, national insurance, pension contributions, and family allowances, if any, of the Arthur Balfour Professor of Genetics.

2. Notwithstanding any provision of the Trust Deed referred to in subparagraph (*b*) of the foregoing Section 1 to the contrary the whole of the property described therein as Whittingehame Lodge shall be available for the Department of Genetics and if that Department shall at any time not have need of the whole or any part of the property the income deriving from it or from capital sums accruing from its disposal shall be credited to the Arthur Balfour Fund.

Chapter XLI

THE HARNESS FUND

1. The investments from time to time representing the endowment created by the benefaction conveyed to the University in 1871 by the Executive Committee of subscribers to a memorial of the late Reverend William Harness, M.A., Prebendary of St Paul's and Incumbent of All Saints', Knightsbridge, and formerly of Christ's College, shall constitute a trust fund called the Harness Fund.

2. The income of the fund shall be used to provide a prize called the Harness Prize for the best English essay upon some subject connected with Shakespearian Literature.

3. The University may from time to time make regulations for the prize.

Chapter XLII

THE ELLEN McARTHUR FUND

1. The investments from time to time representing the endowment created by the will of Miss Ellen McArthur which were accepted by Grace 1 of 25 November 1927 shall constitute a trust fund called the Ellen McArthur Fund.

2. The income of the fund shall be used for the encouragement of the study of Economic History.

3. The University may from time to time make regulations governing the application of the fund.

Chapter XLIII

THE REBECCA FLOWER SQUIRE FUND

1. The investments from time to time representing the endowment for the foundation and support of scholarships in Law created by the will of Miss Rebecca Flower Squire, who died on 26 November 1898, shall constitute a trust fund called the Rebecca Flower Squire Fund, the income of which shall be used to provide scholarships in Law in accordance with Section 2 of this Statute and to make grants to persons engaged in the study of Law in accordance with Section 3 of this Statute.

2. The University may from time to time make regulations governing the application of the fund provided that

(*a*) no person shall be elected into a scholarship unless

(i) he or she is a British citizen or a citizen of a country of the Commonwealth,

(ii) he or she has declared in writing the sincere intention of qualifying as a barrister or a solicitor or as a teacher of law, and of practising or teaching law accordingly;

(*b*) in making an election preference shall be given to the Founder's kin and to candidates born within the parish of St Mary Newington, London, in accordance with clause 6 of the Scheme of Management and Regulation of the Squire Scholarships in Law set out in the Schedule to the Declaration of Trust dated the eighth day of August nineteen hundred and two by which the endowment was created;

(*c*) the tenure of a scholarship shall be subject to the scholar becoming or continuing to be a resident member of the University.

3. The income of the fund may also be used to make grants on grounds of financial hardship to any resident member of the University engaged in the study of law who is qualified in accordance with Section 2(*a*) above.

Chapter XLIV

THE R. A. NICHOLSON FUND

1. The investments from time to time representing the endowment created in 1955 by the will of Mrs Cecilia Nicholson, widow of Professor R. A. Nicholson, sometime Sir Thomas Adams's Professor of Arabic, shall constitute a trust fund called the R. A. Nicholson Fund.

2. The first charge on the income of the Fund shall be the provision of a prize or prizes for distinction in the study of Arabic and Persian, or of one of those languages, to be called the R. A. Nicholson Prize or Prizes.

3. The University may from time to time make regulations for the Fund and the Prize or Prizes. Such regulations may provide for income not expended on the Prizes to be used for the support of study or research in the University in the field of Arabic or Persian or both those languages.

Chapter XLV

THE F. E. ELMORE FUND

1. The investments from time to time representing the endowment created in 1932 by the will of Frank Edward Elmore shall constitute a trust fund called the F. E. Elmore Fund.

2. The first charge on the income of the Fund shall be the provision of one or more studentships to be known as Elmore Medical Research Studentships, the holders of which shall devote themselves to research in medicine or in some branch of the medical sciences at or from the University.

3. The University may from time to time make regulations for the Fund and the Studentships. Such regulations may provide for income not expended on Studentships to be used for the support of study or research in the University in the field of medical education or research.

Chapter XLVI

THE SANDYS FUND AND STUDENTSHIP

1. The income of the fund created by the will of Sir John Edwin Sandys, Litt.D., Orator Emeritus, shall be used primarily for the furtherance of study and research in the languages, literature, history, archaeology, and art of ancient Greece and Rome and the comparative philology of the Indo-European languages.

2. The Trustees of the Fund shall be the Master, Fellows, and Scholars of St John's College.

3. The first charge on the income of the Fund shall be the maintenance of a studentship called the Sandys Studentship, which shall be open to graduates of the University and persons who are registered as Graduate Students in the University. The holder of the Studentship shall undertake advanced study or research in one or more of the subjects specified in Section 1 above, and for this purpose shall spend a large part of the year at a university or other place of learning outside the British Isles.

4. The Studentship shall be tenable for one year, but a Student may be re-elected on not more than two occasions.

5. The Electors to the Studentship shall include the Classical Lecturers of St John's College and the holders of such University offices as may be specified by the University from time to time.

6. After provision has been made for the Studentship, the remainder of the income of the Fund shall be applied by the Trustees for the benefit of the Library of St John's College.

7. Subject to the above provisions, the University, after consulting the Council of St John's College, may from time to time make regulations for the Fund and the Studentship.

Chapter XLVII

MEDIEVAL SCANDINAVIAN HISTORY FUND

The income of the Tennant Fund that has been accrued up to 31 July 2007, together with any interest earned on such income after 31 July 2007, shall be used to establish a separate fund to support a Lectureship in Medieval Scandinavian History in the University (the accrued income up to 31 July 2007 constituting permanent endowment and the interest earned after 31 July 2007 constituting expendable income within the new fund).

Statute F

FINANCE, AUDIT, PLANNING AND RESOURCE ALLOCATION, PROPERTY AND BUILDINGS

CHAPTER I

FINANCE, THE CHEST, AND AUDIT

Financial matters

1. It shall be the duty of the Council
(*a*) to exercise general supervision over the finances of the University including reserves and investments and the income and expenditure of the Chest and over the finances of all institutions in the University;
(*b*) to keep under review the University's financial position and to make a Report thereon to the University at least once in each year, recommending allocations from the Chest;
(*c*) under arrangements made by Ordinance, to appoint or recommend Bankers to the University;
(*d*) to prepare and to publish the annual accounts of the University in accordance with UK applicable accounting standards such that the accounts give a true and fair view of the state of affairs of the University;
(*e*) to perform such other duties relating to financial management as may be assigned to it by Statute or Ordinance.

The Chest and accounts

2. Save as is otherwise provided in Statutes or Ordinances, all income accruing to the University shall be credited to the account of the Chest.

3. Separate accounts shall be kept in such form as the Council may direct for all trust funds, for such funds as may be created special funds by the Council or the University, and for the funds arising from grants from external sources or from grants or gifts from other bodies or persons for special work carried out under the direction of the University.

4. Any money received by any University body or officer for the purpose of any Faculty or Department or other institution, or for any other University purpose, shall be included in the appropriate account.

Audit

5. Except as may be provided otherwise by Statute J and by Section 6 below, the accounts of the University shall be audited annually by external auditors appointed by Grace on the nomination of the Council.

6. The accounts of the Local Examinations Syndicate shall be audited annually by external auditors appointed by the Council. The requirements of Section 1(*d*) of this chapter shall apply to these accounts. The Council shall in every year appoint one or more persons from among the members of the Finance Committee, who shall examine these accounts, confer with the auditor or auditors, and report to the Council.

CHAPTER II

PLANNING AND RESOURCE ALLOCATION, BUILDINGS

1. The Council shall establish committees and processes for planning and resource allocation within the University and for the management, maintenance, and development of University buildings, and may do so jointly with the General Board. Regulations for the establishment of such committees may be made by Ordinance.

2. The Council shall be responsible for the care, management, and maintenance of all property, both real and personal, which is either owned by the University or held in trust for University purposes, except such as may be committed by Statute or Ordinance to the care and management of some other University body.

3. Approval by Grace of the Regent House shall be required for the erection of a new University building or for the demolition or substantial alteration of an existing University building.

Statute G

COLLEGES AND COLLEGIATE FOUNDATIONS

Chapter I

THE COLLEGES AND COLLEGIATE FOUNDATIONS

Colleges

1. The Colleges in the University are:
Peterhouse, Clare College, Pembroke College, Gonville and Caius College, Trinity Hall, Corpus Christi College, King's College, Queens' College, St Catharine's College, Jesus College, Christ's College, St John's College, Magdalene College, Trinity College, Emmanuel College, Sidney Sussex College, Downing College, Girton College, Newnham College, Selwyn College, Fitzwilliam College, Churchill College, Murray Edwards College, Darwin College, Wolfson College, Clare Hall, Robinson College, Lucy Cavendish College, St Edmund's College, Hughes Hall, and Homerton College.

Approved Foundations

2. The University shall have power to recognize by Grace as an Approved Foundation any institution which is maintained within the Precincts of the University for the advancement of education, learning, and research and which

(*a*) is incorporated or subsists under a trust instrument;

(*b*) has provision in its charter, articles of association, memorandum of association, or trust instrument, as the case may be, for its government through a Committee of Management, Board of Trustees, Council, or similar body;

(*c*) if it proposes to admit students or does admit students, has suitable provision for their education and discipline.

3. Further conditions under which an institution may receive and continue to enjoy recognition as an Approved Foundation shall be determined by Ordinance from time to time; provided that (*a*) no Approved Foundation shall without its consent become subject to any conditions other than those under which recognition was first granted to it *and* (*b*) no Approved Foundation shall alter any provision in its charter, articles of association, memorandum of association, or trust instrument, as the case may be, unless it has given to the Council notice of the proposed alteration and either the University has granted its consent or the Council has announced that the proposed alteration does not affect the University or prejudice the interests of the University.

4. Any provision in any Statute or Ordinance affecting Colleges (unless excluded by Special Ordinance) applies to Approved Foundations.

5. The Council may refer any cause of concern or complaint relating to an Approved Foundation to the governing body of the Approved Foundation. If (in the opinion of the Council) the governing body of the Foundation refuses to take or fails to take within reasonable time such measures as the Council requires, the Council shall refer the matter to the Chancellor. A court composed of the Chancellor, or a deputy appointed by the Chancellor, and two assessors appointed by the Chancellor, shall then inquire into the matter may by the unanimous votes of all its members declare that recognition as an Approved Foundation is withdrawn from the institution concerned permanently or for a period.

Approved Societies

6. The University shall have power to recognize by Grace as an Approved Society any society which is maintained within the Precincts of the University for the advancement of education, learning, and research.

7. The conditions under which a society may receive, and continue to enjoy, recognition as an Approved Society shall be determined from time to time by Special Ordinance, provided that (*a*) no society which proposes to admit or does admit students shall receive or continue to enjoy such recognition unless it makes suitable provision for their education and discipline *and* (*b*) no Approved Society shall alter any provision in its charter, articles of association, memorandum of association, trust instrument, scheme of government, or any other instrument prescribing the form of constitution of the society, unless it has given to the Council notice of the proposed alteration and either the

University has approved it by Grace or the Council have announced that the proposed alteration does not affect the University or prejudice the interests of the University.

8. Any provision of Statutes or Ordinance concerning Fellowship of a College, some office in a College, membership of a College, matriculation, residence, admission to and presentation for degrees, discipline, teaching or instruction on behalf of a College, and the obligations of Colleges in respect of Fellowships, shall be applicable as if the term 'College' included any Approved Society. Further such application may be made by Special Ordinance.

Chapter II

COLLEGE CONTRIBUTIONS AND THE COLLEGES FUND

1. Every College in the University shall make a yearly contribution, which shall be applied to the purposes hereinafter prescribed.

2. The following items shall constitute the assets of a College:

(*a*) all property, real and personal of whatsoever nature, held by the College, or held in trust for the College;

(*b*) all property held by the College or by or with any other trustee or trustees on trusts any of the purposes of which concerns the College;

(*c*) all property held by a subsidiary of the College;

(*d*) any business of the College, as defined in Section 4; and

(*e*) (considered as assets of negative value) all liabilities of the College or of a subsidiary of the College,

but the assets and liabilities relating to any occupational pension scheme registered for income tax purposes shall not be included in the assets of the College.

3. (*a*) The following assets of a College shall constitute its operational assets:

(i) all interests in land within the precincts of the University held mainly for Collegiate purposes by the College;

(ii) all tangible personal property held mainly for Collegiate purposes within that land; and

(iii) any asset approved as an operational asset by the Finance Committee, having regard to the use of the asset for Collegiate purposes.

(*b*) With the approval of the Finance Committee,

(i) a vacancy or temporary use of an asset shall be disregarded; and

(ii) a College may declare an asset to be non-operational.

(*c*) For the purpose of this section,

(i) a purpose is to be treated as beneficial notwithstanding that the beneficiary may make payment or give any other consideration for the benefit received;

(ii) any matter ancillary to a Collegiate purpose shall be treated as included within that purpose; and

(iii) where different parts of an asset are held for different purposes, those parts shall be treated as separate assets; and

(iv) subject to the approval of the Finance Committee, a right held by a College to repayment of a loan made by it in connection with an interest in land may be treated as an interest in land within the scope of Subsection 3(*a*)(i); and

(v) for the purpose of Subsection 3(*a*)(ii), the term 'Collegiate purposes' shall include purposes associated with a business of the College.

4. A business of a College shall mean any activity that involves the use of the operational assets of the College conducted or permitted by the College or by a subsidiary of the College with a view to deriving income other than from the College or its members, whether or not that activity falls within the charitable purposes of the College.

5. The assessable assets of a College shall comprise all of its assets except

(*a*) its operational assets; and

(*b*) assets held by the College or by or with any other trustee or trustees on trusts approved by the Finance Committee as being exclusively for non-Collegiate purposes.

6. The assessable amount of a College, in respect of any year, shall be the value of its assessable assets on the valuation date. The valuation date shall be the last day of the accounting period for the preceding year. A change in the accounting period for a College shall require the approval of the Finance Committee.

7. In the case of a trust partly for Collegiate and partly for non-Collegiate purposes, the value of the assets of the trust in respect of any year shall be taken to be the value at the valuation date of the whole assets of the trust multiplied by the Collegiate distribution for the accounting period for that year divided by the income for that accounting period. For the purpose of this section, in relation to a trust,

(*a*) the Collegiate distribution for an accounting period means the amount applied from the trust during that period for Collegiate purposes or transferred from the trust to the College during that period, not including any amount approved as a capital distribution by the Finance Committee for the purpose of this section; and

(*b*) the income for an accounting period shall not include any additions to the trust during that period, and shall not include any gain of a capital nature during that period except to the extent that the computation of income of the trust is in accordance with a rule approved by the Finance Committee for the purpose of this section.

8. The value of a business of a College in respect of any year shall be derived from a notional operating surplus equal to the turnover of the business during the accounting period for that year multiplied by a defined percentage, which notional operating surplus is then capitalized for a yield of four per cent (or such other figure as may be determined by Ordinance). For the purpose of this section,

(*a*) turnover shall mean total revenue after deduction of Value Added Tax (or any similar deduction approved by the Finance Committee) and before any other deduction therefrom, but shall not include any revenue derived from the College or its members;

(*b*) the defined percentage shall be determined according to the nature of the business concerned and shall be such figure as the Finance Committee consider to be an appropriate estimate of the profit normally to be expected from a business of that nature, where profit means the turnover less the costs of the operation of the business, not including any costs relating to the operational assets of the College; and

(*c*) where a business involves the use of both operational assets and other assets of the College, an apportionment shall be made, by a method approved by the Finance Committee, to determine its value in relation to the use of operational assets only.

9. The Finance Committee shall make, and may vary from time to time, rules for the purposes of this chapter. Without prejudice to the generality of the foregoing, such rules may include provision for

(*a*) the valuation of assessable assets that are in use in part only as operational assets;

(*b*) the valuation of assets that are owned jointly by the College and some other person or persons;

(*c*) the submission of information and evidence by Colleges in connection with any matters concerning this chapter;

(*d*) the disregard of businesses of a specified nature and the reduction (whether for business of a specified nature, or in relation to income, or otherwise) of the profit percentage defined under Section 8;

(*e*) the set off of assets and liabilities between the College and a subsidiary of the College;

(*f*) the variation of the valuation date for certain classes of assets; and

(*g*) the certification of the value of assessable assets.

Such rules shall include provision for the disregard of a business established as a school for the supply of Choristers to the College.

10. The Finance Committee may obtain professional advice in connection with any matter concerning this chapter. The cost of such advice shall be paid from the Colleges Fund.

11. The Finance Committee may give written notice to a College of its intention to review the contribution payable by the College in respect of any year. Such notice shall specify the year in respect of which it is given, and shall be given not later than the end of the accounting year sixth after the accounting year for the year in respect of which it is given. But later notice may be given where the intention of the Finance Committee is based on facts of which it was previously unaware and could not reasonably have been aware. Any such later notice shall specify the facts on which it is based and shall be given not later than three months after the Finance Committee first became aware of those facts. No notice shall be given later than the end of the accounting year twelfth after the accounting year for the year in respect of which it is given. A notice given under this section may require the submission of such information and evidence as is specified in the notice in connection with any matter concerning this chapter. A notice shall state a time by which any information and evidence specified in it, and any representations in relation to it, shall be received from the College.

12. After considering the information, evidence, and representations received from the College within the time stated in the notice (or within any extension of time allowed), the Finance Committee shall conduct its review and shall determine the contribution due from the College in respect of the year concerned. Such determination shall be binding and effectual for the purposes of this chapter, but may be varied by the Finance Committee after further review made on the application of the College. After conducting a review, the Finance Committee may require payment by the College to the Colleges Fund of all or any part of the costs incurred by the University in the review.

13. The Finance Committee may agree with a College the nature, valuation date or value of any of its assets. Such agreement may be unconditional or subject to such conditions as the Finance Committee may determine. Such agreement shall be terminable at will by the Finance Committee, provided that such termination shall not affect the contribution payable by a College in respect of any year the accounting period for which has then passed. An agreement may be made notwithstanding any conflict with rules made by the Finance Committee under this chapter.

14. In making rules under this chapter, and in agreeing with a College under Section 13 the nature, valuation date or value of any of its assets, the Finance Committee shall have regard to the desirability of achieving fair, reasonable, and administratively simple outcomes.

15. Any approval by the Finance Committee under this chapter may be given unconditionally or subject to such conditions as the Finance Committee may determine.

16. The contribution of a College shall be calculated in accordance with the provisions of the Schedule to this chapter.

17. Every College shall pay to the University on or before 31 December following the end of the accounting period for a year one-half of the contribution calculated for that year, and the remaining one-half on or before 30 June next following.

18. The contributions of the Colleges shall be paid into a Colleges Fund. Payments from the Colleges Fund shall be made in accordance with the provisions of this chapter and, in accordance with Ordinances enacted by the University, for grants to the Colleges. Such grants may include investment for the benefit of a College in an amalgamated fund constituted under Statute A II 6(*b*) subject to such restrictions as may be prescribed by Ordinance.

19. If in the opinion of the Finance Committee inequity or hardship owing to exceptional circumstances would be inflicted upon a College by the enforcement of the provisions of this chapter, the University shall have power to remit or defer payment of the whole or part of the contribution of the College in respect of any year.

20. If there is any dispute between the Finance Committee and a College concerning any matter in relation to this chapter, the question shall be decided by the Council. Any College affected by the decision of the Council may, within six months after notice of the decision, appeal to the Chancellor or, if the office of Chancellor is vacant, the High Steward, who may affirm, reverse, or vary the decision.

21. Where a College becomes aware of any error in the calculation of its contribution, it shall notify the Finance Committee, who shall determine what correction (if any) should be made.

22. Where a correction or other adjustment is made to the assessable amount of a College in respect of any past year, the Finance Committee shall notify all of the Colleges of the changes to be made in relation to that year. Each College shall account for such changes in the accounting period in which notification is given.

23. In the interpretation of this chapter:

(*a*) holding, as regards property, means having (whether alone or with others) a legal or equitable interest in, possession of, or (where appropriate) occupation of the property, and held shall be interpreted accordingly;

(*b*) the assets of a College shall have the meaning given by Section 2, and ownership by the College shall be interpreted accordingly;

(*c*) Collegiate purposes shall include

(i) any purpose beneficial to the Head, Fellows, officers or employees of the College (whether currently or formerly) as such;

(ii) any purpose beneficial to resident members of the College as such;

(iii) any purpose directly conducive to operation of the College as a place of education, religion, learning, and research (or of any of those things);

but shall not include

(iv) subject to the approval of the Finance Committee, any provision of benefits which are not granted by the College or by a subsidiary of the College; or

(v) any provision of benefits to persons not within the scope of (i) or (ii) above;

and non-Collegiate purposes shall be construed accordingly;

(*d*) a subsidiary of a College shall include any company, trust or other corporate or unincorporated body which is owned or controlled by or on behalf of the College, and for this purpose ownership shall include entitlement, directly or indirectly, to the benefit of at least one-half of the property of the subsidiary and control shall include entitlement, directly or indirectly, to appoint, control or influence at least one-half of the persons having the general control and management of the administration of the subsidiary, but shall not include any company, trust or other body excluded from this definition with the approval of the Finance Committee;

(*e*) the accounting period for any year shall be the accounting period the last day of which falls in that year; and

(*f*) the Finance Committee shall mean the Finance Committee of the Council.

SCHEDULE TO STATUTE G II

The contributions of a College under Statute G II 16 shall be calculated according to the following rules:

Each year the total of the contributions of the Colleges shall equal the sum of the net payment for the year, as notified by the Finance Committee, from the Colleges Fund of the costs of the University under Statute G II 10 and 11 and £3,000,000 multiplied by the multiplier for that year.

The multiplier shall be equal to the ratio of the value of an index six months immediately preceding the valuation date to its value in July 2005, that index to be determined by the University reflecting general economic circumstances.

In each year the assessable amount of a College shall be divided into bands. The first band shall comprise the assessable amount of the College up to 1.25% of the sum of the assessable amounts of all the Colleges for that year. The second band shall comprise the assessable amount of the College between 1.25% of that sum and the average assessable amount of all the Colleges. The third band shall comprise the assessable amount of the College in excess of that average.

No contribution shall be payable on the first band. The rate of contribution payable on the third band shall be twice that payable on the second band.

Chapter III

ACCOUNTS

1. Every College shall close its accounts in each year on a day not earlier than 30 June and not later than 30 September, and shall have them audited by a qualified Auditor not being a member of the Governing Body.

2. There shall be an inter-Collegiate Committee on College Accounts composed of representatives of the several Colleges, to which each College shall be entitled to appoint one member.

It shall be the duty of the Committee

(*a*) to meet at least once a year;

(*b*) to consider the form of the Recommended Cambridge College Accounts, having regard to developments in accounting practice generally; *and*

(*c*) to make recommendations to the Finance Committee of the Council as it deems necessary for the amendment of the Recommended Cambridge College Accounts.

3. Except as provided by Section 6, every College shall when preparing its accounts:

(*a*) have regard to the Recommended Cambridge College Accounts as determined from time to time by the University on the recommendation of the Finance Committee of the Council, made after considering the advice of the Inter-Collegiate Committee on College Accounts; *and*

(*b*) give a true and fair view of the state of affairs of the College at the end of the financial year and of the income and expenditure of the College for the financial year.

4. Every College shall ensure:

(*a*) that the report of its Auditor includes an opinion that the accounts comply with Section 3 of this Statute and that the payment due under Statute G II has been calculated in accordance with the provisions therein; *and*

(*b*) that its accounts are submitted, together with the report of its Auditor, to the Registrary not later than 31 December next after their closing.

If an Auditor is unable to report that the accounts comply with Section 3 of this Statute and that the payment due under Statute G II has been calculated in accordance with the provisions therein, he or she shall state in writing the reasons for that, and the College shall send the statement to the Registrary.

5. Every College shall submit each year to the Registrary a return signed by its Auditor, in such form as shall be prescribed by the Finance Committee after consultation with the Inter-Collegiate Committee on College Accounts, showing the calculation of the payment due under Statute G II. The University shall publish annually the returns of the several Colleges and financial statements for the Colleges Fund.

6. The amendments of Statute G III and the repeal of Schedules D and E made by Grace 1 of 6 August 2003 shall have effect in respect of the accounts of each College for such year as the College shall specify by notice addressed to the Registrary and for each year thereafter; provided that a College which has not given such notice shall prepare its accounts in the form that was required by Statute G III on 1 October 2002, with such modifications relating to University contribution as may be approved by the Finance Committee. Such a College shall additionally submit to the Registrary a return signed by its Auditor, in such form as shall be prescribed by the Finance Committee, showing the calculation of the payment due under Statute G II.

CHAPTER IV

ACADEMIC OBLIGATIONS

Membership of a College

1. Save as may be determined by the Council in respect of a person or a class of persons, no College shall allow any person admitted for the purpose of study or research to remain a resident member of the College after the division of her or his first term of residence[1] who is not *either*

(*a*) matriculated; *or*

(*b*) permitted by the Council, under such conditions (if any) as the Council may impose, to be matriculated in the latter half of that term, or in a later term; provided always that King's College may as heretofore allow their Lay Clerks, Choristers, and Master over the Choristers to be members of the College although not matriculated or qualified to be matriculated.

2. The University may, in accordance with Statute E I 1 of the Statutes of Wolfson College, make Ordinances prescribing conditions subject to which the College may admit and present for degrees candidates for the degrees of Bachelor of Arts, Bachelor of Music, Bachelor of Education, and Bachelor of Theology for Ministry.

3. The University may, in accordance with Statute F I 1 of the Statutes of St Edmund's College, make Ordinances prescribing conditions subject to which the College may admit and present for degrees candidates for the degrees of Bachelor of Arts, Bachelor of Music, and Bachelor of Theology for Ministry.

4. The University may, in accordance with Statute 39 of the Statutes of Lucy Cavendish College, make Ordinances prescribing conditions subject to which the College may admit and present for degrees candidates for the degrees of Bachelor of Arts, Bachelor of Music, Bachelor of Education, and Bachelor of Theology for Ministry.

5. The University may, in accordance with Statute IX 1 of the Statutes of Hughes Hall, make Ordinances prescribing conditions subject to which the College may admit and present for degrees candidates for the degrees of Bachelor of Arts, Bachelor of Music, Bachelor of Education, and Bachelor of Theology for Ministry.

Fellowships

6. Every College shall maintain Fellowships. Further provision may be made by Special Ordinance.

[1] The words 'first term of residence' in this section shall, in their application to a woman, mean her first term of residence subsequent to 27 April 1948.

Statute J

THE UNIVERSITY PRESS

1. There shall be in the University a University Press which shall be devoted to printing and publishing in the furtherance of the acquisition, advancement, conservation, and dissemination of knowledge in all subjects; to the advancement of education, religion, learning, and research; and to the advancement of literature and good letters.

2. There shall be in the University a Press Syndicate. The management of the finance, property, and affairs generally of the University Press shall be the responsibility of the Press Syndicate which shall exercise in relation thereto all the powers of the University except in so far as the Statutes and Ordinances expressly or by necessary implication provide otherwise. The Press Syndicate shall consist of the Vice-Chancellor or a duly appointed deputy as Chair and such number of members of the Senate appointed in such manner as shall be determined from time to time by Ordinance.

3. The Press Syndicate shall have power in the name of the University and for the purposes of the University Press to exercise the powers in Statute A II 3–8. These powers shall apply to investment as well as to any other activity or function of the University Press. Save only insofar as the Statutes, Ordinances or regulations enacted under Statute J 5 expressly or by necessary implication provide otherwise, these powers may be exercised at the absolute discretion of the Press Syndicate.

4. All income accruing to the University Press shall be credited to the accounts of the Press Syndicate and all University Press capital and income shall be controlled by the Press Syndicate and applied by them at their sole discretion for the purposes of the University Press.

5. The Council shall have authority to impose limitations on the power of the Press Syndicate to enter into any financial commitments or to grant security on the property of the University Press.

6. The Press Syndicate shall have power in the name of the University to engage persons for employment in the service of the University Press, determine their salaries and pensions, and prescribe the conditions of their service.

7. Persons holding certain posts in the University Press which have been specially designated under this section by the Council on the recommendation of the Press Syndicate shall be treated as University officers for the purposes of Statute A III 10(*b*), Statute B I 1, Statute B II 2, and Statute A X 2(*b*).[1]

8. The accounts of the University Press shall be audited annually by one or more qualified accountants appointed by the Council. The Council shall in every year appoint one or more persons from among the members of the Finance Committee, who shall examine these accounts, confer with the auditor or auditors, and report to the Council.

9. There shall be a Press Seal, as a seal of the University to be used on the directions of the Press Syndicate in matters relating to the affairs of the University Press; but the existence of the Press Seal shall not invalidate the use in connection with such matters of any other seal of the University. The University shall have power to make Ordinances concerning the custody and affixing of the Press Seal.

10. The Press Syndicate shall have power to delegate any of their powers under this Statute subject to any limitations imposed by Ordinance.

11. The term 'property of the University Press' here and elsewhere in Statutes and Ordinances shall refer to property of the University, both real and personal, held or used for the purposes of the University Press. In favour of any person having dealings with the University Press a certificate signed by the Registrary that any particular property is the property of the University Press, or that any limitations imposed under Statute J 5 have been complied with, shall be conclusive.

12. The Press Syndicate shall make an Annual Report to the Council, which shall be published to the University either as a whole or in summary.

13. Notwithstanding the provisions of the foregoing sections, the Council shall have power in circumstances which the Council deems to be exceptional, on the advice of its Finance Committee, to discharge the Press Syndicate, and to assume full responsibility itself for the management of the Press for the time being. If the Council has occasion to exercise the powers available under this section, the Council shall make a full report to the University on the circumstances necessitating such action.

[1] The following have been specially designated under this section: the Secretary of the Press Syndicate, Directors, Associate Directors, Senior Editors and Senior Managers of the Press.

PASSAGES FROM ACTS OF PARLIAMENT RELATING TO THE UNIVERSITY OF CAMBRIDGE

From the Universities of Oxford and Cambridge Act 1923

An Act to make further provision with respect to the Universities of Oxford and Cambridge and the Colleges therein. [31st July 1923.]

1. (1) There shall be two bodies of Commissioners to be styled respectively "the University of Oxford Commissioners" and "the University of Cambridge Commissioners"............ Establishment of Commissions.

5. The powers of the Commissioners shall continue in force until the end of the year nineteen hundred and twenty-five and no longer: Duration of Commissions.

Provided that His Majesty in Council may, on the application of the Commissioners, continue their powers for such further period as His Majesty may think fit, but not beyond the end of the year nineteen hundred and twenty-seven.

6. (1) Subject to the provisions of this Act, the Commissioners shall, from and after the first day of January, nineteen hundred and twenty-five, make statutes and regulations for the University, its colleges and halls, and any emoluments, endowments, trusts, foundations, gifts, offices, or institutions in or connected with the University in general accordance with the recommendations contained in the Report of the Royal Commission, but with such modifications (not being modifications directly dealing with the curriculum or course of study in the University) as may, after the consideration of any representations made to them, appear to them expedient. Duties of Commissioners.

(2) In making any statutes or regulations under this Act, the Commissioners shall have regard to the need of facilitating the admission of poorer students to the Universities and colleges.

7. (1) A statute affecting the University made by the Commissioners or by any other authority, not being a statute made for a college, shall be subject to alteration from time to time by statute made by the University under this Act, but, if and in so far as any such statute (not being a statute prescribing the scale or basis of assessment of the contributions to be made by the colleges to University purposes) affects a college, it shall not be subject to alteration except with the consent of the college. Power of Universities and colleges to alter statutes.

(2) A statute for a college made by the Commissioners, and any statute, ordinance or regulation made by or in relation to a college under any authority other than that of this Act, shall be subject to alteration from time to time by statute made by the college under this Act and passed at a general meeting of the governing body of the college specially summoned for the purpose by the votes of not less than two-thirds of the number of persons present and voting:

Provided that –

(*a*) notice of any proposed statute for a college shall be given to the University before the statute is submitted to His Majesty in Council; and

(*b*) a statute made for a college which affects the University shall not be altered except with the consent of the University.

(3) The provisions contained in this Act (including the provisions of the Schedule to this Act) with respect to the making of statutes by the Commissioners and to the proceedings to be taken after the making thereof in connection with statutes made by the Commissioners, and to the effect thereof after approval, shall, with the necessary substitutions, apply to the making of statutes by the University or by a college and to the proceedings to be taken in connection with statutes made by the University or a college, and to the effect of such statutes.

8. (1) No statute shall be made under any of the provisions of this Act for altering a trust, except with the consent of the trustees or governing body of the trust, unless sixty years have elapsed since the date on which the instrument creating the trust came into operation, but nothing in this subsection shall prevent the making of a statute increasing the endowment of any emolument or otherwise improving the position of the holder thereof. Statutes relating to trusts and college contributions to University purposes.

(2) In the making of any statute by the University, prescribing or altering the scale or basis of assessment of contributions to be made by the colleges to University purposes, regard shall be had in the first place to the needs of the several colleges in themselves for educational and other collegiate purposes.

10. The provisions of the Universities of Oxford and Cambridge Act 1877 shall, as set out with modifications in the Schedule to this Act, apply to the Commissioners appointed under this Act and to their procedure, powers and duties and to any statutes made by them as if they were re-enacted with the said modifications in this Act. Application for purposes of the Act of certain provisions of 40 & 41 Vict. c. 48.

Power to establish superannuation funds for certain university and college employees.

11. (1) It shall be lawful for the University to make a scheme for establishing a superannuation fund for the benefit of persons in the employment of the University, not being members of its administrative or teaching staff, and for a college to adopt in relation to persons in the employment of the college, not being members of its administrative or teaching staff, any scheme so made.

(2) The provisions of this Act relating to the making of statutes, ordinances and regulations by the University or a college shall not apply to any statutes, ordinances or regulations made for the purposes of this section.

(3) Nothing in this section shall be taken to be in derogation of or to affect the duties of the Commissioners or the powers of the University or a college under the foregoing provisions of this Act.

Short title.

12. This Act may be cited as the Universities of Oxford and Cambridge Act 1923.

SCHEDULE

Provisions of the Universities of Oxford and Cambridge Act 1877, applied for purposes of this Act[1]

2. In this Act –

Interpretation.

"The University" means the University of Oxford and the University of Cambridge respectively, or one of them separately (as the case may require):

"The Senate" means the Senate of the University of Cambridge:

"College" means a College in the University, and includes the Cathedral or House of Christ Church in Oxford:

"Hall" means St Edmund Hall, in the University of Oxford:…………

"The Governing Body" of a College means, as regards the Colleges in the University of Cambridge, except Downing College, the head and all actual fellows of the College, bye-fellows excepted, being graduates, and as regards Downing College, the head, professors, and all actual fellows thereof, bye-fellows excepted, being graduates:

"Emolument" includes –

(1) A headship, professorship, lectureship, readership, prælectorship, fellowship, bye-fellowship, tutorship, studentship, scholarship, exhibition, demyship, postmastership, taberdarship, Bible clerkship, servitorship, sizarship, subsizarship, or other place in the University or a College or the Hall, having attached thereto an income payable out of the revenues of the University or of a College or the Hall, or being a place to be held and enjoyed by a head or other member of a College or the Hall as such, or having attached thereto an income to be so held and enjoyed, arising wholly or in part from an endowment, benefaction, or trust; and

(2) The income aforesaid, and all benefits and advantages of every nature and kind belonging to the place, and any endowment belonging to, or held by, or for the benefit of, or enjoyed by, a head or other member of a College or the Hall as such, and any fund, endowment, or property held by or on behalf of the University or a College or the Hall, for the purpose of advancing, rewarding, or otherwise providing for any member of the University or College or Hall, or of purchasing any advowson, benefice, or property to be held for the like purpose, or to be in any manner applied for the promotion of any such member;…………

"School" means a school or other place of education beyond the precincts of the University, and includes a College in Scotland:

"Advowson" includes right of patronage, exclusive or alternate.

Regard to main design of founder.

14. The Commissioners, in exercising their power to make a statute, shall have regard to the main design of the founder of any institution or emolument which will be affected by the statute, except where that design has ceased to be observed before the passing of this Act, or where the trusts, conditions, or directions affecting the institution or emolument have been altered in substance by or under any other Act.

Provision for education, religion, &c.

15. The Commissioners, in making a statute, shall have regard to the interests of education, religion, learning and research, and in the case of a statute which affects a College or the Hall shall have regard, in the first instance, to the maintenance of the College or Hall for those purposes.

Power to allow continuance of voluntary payments.

20. Nothing in or done under this Act shall prevent the Commissioners from making in any statute made by them for a College such provisions as they think expedient for the voluntary continuance of

[1] As amended by the Selwyn College Cambridge Act 1988 and the Keble College Oxford Act 1988.

any voluntary payment that has been used to be made out of the revenues of the College in connection with the College estates or property.

30. A statute made by the Commissioners may, if the Commissioners think fit, be in part a statute for the University, and in part a statute for a College or the Hall. Distinction of University and College Statutes.

The Commissioners shall in each statute made by them declare whether the same is a statute, wholly or in any and what part, for the University or for a College or the Hall therein named; and the declaration in that behalf of the Commissioners shall be conclusive, to all intents.

If any statute is in part a statute for a College or the Hall, it shall, for the purposes of the provisions of this Act relative to the representation of Colleges and the Hall, and of the other provisions of this Act regulating proceedings on the statute, be proceeded on as a statute for the College or Hall.

31. Where the Commissioners contemplate making a statute for the University or a statute for a College or the Hall containing a provision for any purpose relative to the University, or a statute otherwise affecting the interests of the University, they shall, one month at least (exclusive of any University vacation) before adopting any final resolution in that behalf, communicate the proposed statute in the University of Oxford to the Hebdomadal Council, and to the Head and to the Visitor of the College affected thereby, or to the Principal of the Hall, and in the University of Cambridge to the Council of the Senate and to the Governing Body of the College affected thereby. Communication of proposed statutes for University, &c. to Council, &c.

The Commissioners shall take into consideration any representation made to them by the Council, College, Visitor, Principal, or Governing Body respecting the proposed statute.

Within seven days after receipt of such communication by the Council, the Vice-Chancellor of the University shall give public notice thereof in the University.

32. Where the Commissioners contemplate making a statute for a College or the Hall, they shall, one month at least (exclusive of any University vacation) before adopting any final resolution in that behalf, communicate the proposed statute to the Vice-Chancellor of the University and to the Head, and in the University of Oxford the Visitor, of the College, and to the Principal of the Hall. Publication of proposed statutes for Colleges and Halls

Within seven days after receipt of such communication the Vice-Chancellor shall give public notice thereof in the University.

34. Any statute made by the Commissioners shall operate without prejudice to any interest possessed by any person by virtue of his having, before the statute comes into operation, become a member of a College or the Hall, or been elected or appointed to a University or College emolument, or acquired a vested right to be elected or appointed thereto............ Saving for existing interest.

45. The Commissioners, within one month after making a statute, shall cause it to be submitted to His Majesty in Council, and notice of it having been so submitted shall be published in the London Gazette (in this Act referred to as the gazetting of a statute)............ Submission of statutes to His Majesty in Council.

46. At any time within eight weeks (exclusive of any University vacation) after the gazetting of a statute, the University or the Governing Body of a College, or the trustees, governors, or patron of a University or College emolument, or the Principal of the Hall, or the Governing Body of a school, or any other person or body, in case the University, College, emolument, Hall, school, person, or body, is directly affected by the statute, may petition His Majesty in Council for disallowance of the statute, or of any part thereof. Petition against statute.

47. It shall be lawful for His Majesty in Council to refer any statute petitioned against under this Act to the Universities Committee. Reference to Committee.

The petitioners shall be entitled to be heard by themselves or counsel in support of their petition.

It shall be lawful for His Majesty in Council to make, from time to time, rules of procedure and practice for regulating proceedings on such petitions.

The costs of all parties of and incident to such proceedings shall be in the discretion of the Universities Committee; and the orders of the Committee respecting costs shall be enforceable as if they were orders of a Division of the High Court of Justice.

48. If the Universities Committee report their opinion that a statute referred to them, or any part thereof, ought to be disallowed, it shall be lawful for His Majesty in Council to disallow the statute or that part, and thereupon the statute or that part shall be of no effect............ Disallowance by Order in Council.

49. If a statute is not referred to the Universities Committee, then, within one month after the expiration of the time for petitioning against it, the statute shall be laid before both Houses of Parliament, if Parliament is then sitting, and if not, then within fourteen days after the next meeting of Parliament. Statutes not referred, or not disallowed, to be laid before Houses of Parliament.

If a statute is referred to the Universities Committee, and the Committee do not report that the same ought to be wholly disallowed or to be remitted to the Commissioners, then as soon as conveniently may be after the report of the Universities Committee thereon, the statute, or such part thereof as is not disallowed by Order in Council, shall be laid before both Houses of Parliament.

Approval of statutes by Order in Council.

50. If neither House of Parliament, within four weeks (exclusive of any period of prorogation) after a statute or part of a statute is laid before it, presents an address praying His Majesty to withhold his consent thereto, it shall be lawful for His Majesty in Council by Order to approve the same.

Statutes to be binding and effectual.

51. Every statute or part of a statute made by the Commissioners, and approved by Order in Council, shall be binding on the University and on every College and on the Hall, and shall be effectual notwithstanding any instrument of foundation or any Act of Parliament, Order in Council, decree, order, statute, or other instrument, or thing constituting wholly or in part an instrument of foundation, or confirming or varying a foundation, or endowment, or otherwise regulating the University or a College or the Hall.

Power in Cambridge for Chancellor to settle doubts as to meaning of University statutes.

52. If after the cesser of the powers of the Commissioners any doubt arises with respect to the true meaning of any statute made by the Commissioners for the University of Cambridge, the Council of the Senate may apply to the Chancellor of the University for the time being, and he may declare in writing the meaning of the statute on the matter submitted to him, and his declaration shall be registered by the Registrary of the University, and the meaning of the statute as therein declared shall be deemed to be the true meaning thereof.

Saving for Tests Act, 34 & 35 Vict. c. 26.

57. Nothing in this Act shall be construed to repeal any provision of the Universities Tests Act 1871.

From the Education Reform Act 1988

The University Commissioners.

202.—(1) There shall be a body of Commissioners known as the University Commissioners (in this section and sections 203 to 207 of this Act referred to as ''the Commissioners'') who shall exercise, in accordance with subsection (2) below, in relation to qualifying institutions, the functions assigned to them by those sections.

(2) In exercising those functions, the Commissioners shall have regard to the need—

(*a*) to ensure that academic staff have freedom within the law to question and test received wisdom, and to put forward new ideas and controversial or unpopular opinions, without placing themselves in jeopardy of losing their jobs or privileges they may have at their institutions;

(*b*) to enable qualifying institutions to provide education, promote learning and engage in research efficiently and economically; and

(*c*) to apply the principles of justice and fairness.

(3) The following are qualifying institutions for the purposes of this section and sections 203 to 206 of this Act, namely—

(*a*) any university or other institution to which, during the period of three years beginning 1st August 1987, grants in aid are or have been made by the Universities Funding Council, or by the Secretary of State acting on the advice of the University Grants Committee;

(*b*) any constituent college, school or hall or other institution of a university falling within paragraph (*a*) above; and

(*c*) any institution not falling within paragraph (*a*) above which is authorised by charter to grant degrees and to which, during the period of three years beginning 1st August 1987, grants are or have been made by the Secretary of State.

(4) Schedule 11 to this Act shall have effect with respect to the Commissioners.

Duty of Commissioners.

203.—(1) The Commissioners shall exercise the powers conferred by section 204 of this Act with a view to securing that the statutes of each qualifying institution include—

(*a*) provision enabling an appropriate body, or any delegate of such a body, to dismiss any member of the academic staff by reason of redundancy;

(*b*) provision enabling an appropriate officer, or any delegate of such an officer, acting in accordance with procedures determined by the Commissioners, to dismiss any member of the academic staff for good cause;

(*c*) provision establishing disciplinary procedures determined by the Commissioners for dealing with any complaints made against any member of the academic staff relating to his appointment or employment;

(*d*) provision establishing procedures determined by the Commissioners for hearing and determining appeals by any members of the academic staff who are dismissed or under notice of dismissal (whether or not in pursuance of such provision as is mentioned in paragraph (*a*) or (*b*) above) or who are otherwise disciplined; and

(*e*) provision establishing procedures determined by the Commissioners for affording to any member of the academic staff opportunities for seeking redress for any grievances relating to his appointment or employment.

(2) No provision such as is mentioned in subsection (1)(*a*) or (*b*) above which is included in the statutes of a qualifying institution by virtue of section 204 of this Act shall enable any member of the academic staff to be dismissed unless the reason for his dismissal may in the circumstances (including the size and administrative resources of the institution) reasonably be treated as a sufficient reason for dismissing him.

(3) Where any such provision as is mentioned in subsection (1) above is included in the statutes of a qualifying institution (whether by virtue of section 204 of this Act or otherwise) and—

(*a*) there is no requirement for any instrument which would have the effect of modifying the provision to be approved by Her Majesty in Council or to be laid before both Houses of Parliament; and

(*b*) but for this subsection, there would be no requirement for such an instrument to be approved by the Privy Council;

the Commissioners shall exercise the powers conferred by that section with a view to securing that no instrument which would have the effect of modifying the provision shall have that effect unless it has been approved by the Privy Council;

(4) Any reference in this section to academic staff includes a reference to persons whose terms of appointment or contracts of employment are, in the opinion of the Commissioners, so similar to those of academic staff as to justify their being treated as academic staff for the purposes of this section.

(5) For the purposes of this section the dismissal of a member of staff shall be taken to be a dismissal by reason of redundancy if it is attributable wholly or mainly to —

(*a*) the fact that the institution has ceased, or intends to cease, to carry on the activity for the purposes of which he was appointed or employed by the institution, or has ceased, or intends to cease, to carry on that activity in the place in which he carried out his work; or

(*b*) the fact that the requirements of that activity for members of staff to carry out work of a particular kind in that place, have ceased or diminished or are expected to cease or diminish.

(6) For the purposes of this section ''good cause'', in relation to a member of the academic staff of a qualifying institution, means a reason which is related to his conduct or to his capability or qualifications for performing work of the kind which he was appointed or employed to do; and in this subsection—

(*a*) "capability", in relation to such a member, means capability assessed by reference to skill, aptitude, health or any other physical or mental quality; and

(*b*) "qualifications", in relation to such a member, means any degree, diploma or other academic, technical or professional qualification relevant to the office or position held by him.

(7) In this section—

"appropriate", in relation to a body or officer of a qualifying institution, means appearing to the Commissioners to be appropriate having regard to the nature and circumstances of the institution;

"dismiss" and "dismissal"—

(*a*) include remove or, as the case may be, removal from office; and

(*b*) in relation to employment under a contract, shall be construed in accordance with section 55 of the Employment Protection (Consolidation) Act 1978.

(8) In this section and sections 204 to 206 of this Act "statutes", in relation to an institution, includes any regulations, ordinances or other instruments which, in the opinion of the Commissioners, serve as statutes for the purposes of that institution and are designated as such by the Commissioners.

204.—(1) For the purpose of performing the duty imposed on them by section 203 of this Act, the Commissioners may make such modifications of the statutes of any qualifying institution as they consider necessary or expedient. Powers of Commissioners.

(2) Modifications made for the purpose of securing that the statutes of a qualifying institution comply with the requirements of section 203(1)(*a*) of this Act shall not apply in relation to a person unless—

(*a*) his appointment is made, or his contract of employment is entered into, on or after 20th November 1987; or (*b*) he is promoted on or after that date.

(3) For the purposes of this section a person shall be taken to be promoted on or after 20th November 1987 if (and only if) immediately before that date he is paid on a scale which provides for a maximum rate of remuneration (his former pay scale) and on or after that date the terms of his appointment, or of his contract of employment, are varied (whether with effect before or after that date) so that—

(*a*) his rate of remuneration is increased to a rate which exceeds the highest point on his former pay scale at the date on which the increase takes effect; or

(*b*) he is paid on another scale on which the highest point at the date the variation takes effect exceeds the highest point on his former pay scale at that date; or

(*c*) he is paid on a basis which does not provide for a maximum rate of remuneration.

(4) For the purposes of subsection (3) above references, in relation to a pay scale, to the highest point on the scale at any date are references to the maximum rate of remuneration payable at that date in accordance with the scale whether on a regular or a discretionary basis.

(5) For the purposes of this section a person holding an office or position of any description shall not be taken to be promoted by reason only of any general variation of the terms of appointment or of contracts of employment of persons holding offices or positions of that description.

(6) Modifications such as are mentioned in subsection (2) above shall not apply in relation to a person who held an office or position at the institution in question immediately before 20th November 1987 by reason only of the fact that—

(*a*) he is appointed to, or employed in, a different office or position at the institution instead of his former office or position if the terms of his appointment or of his contract of employment which relate to remuneration are the same as those of his former appointment or contract of employment;

(*b*) he is appointed to, or employed in, an additional office or position at the institution which carries no remuneration; or

(*c*) he is promoted or is appointed to, or employed in, a different office or position at the institution if he is so promoted, appointed or employed only on a temporary basis for a particular purpose with an expectation that the promotion will cease to have effect, or that he will resume his former office or position, when that purpose is accomplished.

(7) Modifications made for the purpose of securing that the statutes of a qualifying institution comply with the requirements of section 203(1)(*b*) of this Act shall not apply in relation to anything done or omitted to be done before the date on which the instrument making the modifications is approved under subsection (9) below.

(8) Subject to subsections (2) to (7) above, the Commissioners' powers under this section include power to make such incidental, supplementary and transitional provision as they consider necessary or expedient.

(9) No instrument made in the exercise of the Commissioners' powers under this section shall have effect unless it has been approved by Her Majesty in Council.

PROCEDURE FOR MAKING A STATUTE FOR A COLLEGE[1]

The procedure for making a College Statute is prescribed by the Universities of Oxford and Cambridge Act 1923. The following provides information on the steps to be taken in assessing whether a proposed College Statute affects the University.

(1) Proposed College Statutes should be sent to the Vice-Chancellor, who within seven days of receipt shall give public notice of the proposed Statute by publishing a notice in the *Reporter* or by posting a notice outside the Senate-House, describing where the text of it may be seen.

(2) When the Vice-Chancellor has given public notice of a proposed Statute, the Council will consider it, and will then announce:

either (*a*) that in their opinion the proposed Statute alters a Statute which affects the University, and may not be made without the consent of the University; but that the interests of the University are not prejudiced by it, and that they will bring before the Regent House a Grace for the grant of the necessary consent;

or (*b*) that in their opinion the proposed Statute alters a Statute which affects the University, and may not be made without the consent of the University; that the interests of the University are prejudiced by it and that they will bring before the Regent House a Grace for the refusal of the necessary consent;

or (*c*) that in their opinion the proposed Statute makes no alteration of any Statute which affects the University, and does not require the consent of the University; that the interests of the University are not prejudiced by it, and that they have resolved to take no action upon it;

or (*d*) that in their opinion the proposed Statute makes no alteration of any Statute which affects the University, and does not require the consent of the University; but that the interests of the University are prejudiced by it, and that they have accordingly resolved to petition Her Majesty in Council for its disallowance, or for the disallowance of part of it.

(3) When the Vice-Chancellor makes an announcement under sub-paragraph (*a*) or sub-paragraph (*c*) above, the Grace seeking the consent of the Regent House or the resolve of the Council to take no action, as the case may be, must be subject to a time limit, and the Council has determined that this limit shall be one year. Any such Grace or announcement will include a statement that it is subject to the proviso that the proposed Statute be submitted to the Privy Council by a specified date (that is to say a date one year later than the date of the announcement) after which date the Council will wish to reconsider the proposed Statute.

(4) If, after a proposed Statute has been submitted to the Privy Council, the Vice-Chancellor is informed that the Governing Body of a College wish to make further alterations of it, the procedure set out above should be followed afresh in its entirety, except in the following case. After giving public notice in accordance with sub-paragraph (3) above of receipt of the further alterations, the Vice-Chancellor may, if it is clear that the alterations are of a minor character and will not render the Statute substantially different from the Statute which was the subject of the earlier announcement under sub-paragraph (*a*) or sub-paragraph (*c*), in due course and after consultation with the Privy Council, as appropriate, give notice that no further statement on behalf of the University is required.

[1] Amended by Notice (*Reporter*, 6340, 2013–14, pp. 377–8).

RULES OF PROCEDURE MADE BY THE COMMISSARY UNDER STATUTE A IX 7

1. The review jurisdiction of the Commissary is established by the Statutes of the University. These rules of procedure bind the parties in any particular case. They are subject to the provisions of Statute A I 13 and A IX 3–10.

2. The Commissary will not consider applications about matters excluded under the provisions of Statute A IX 3.

3. A member of the University submitting a matter to the Commissary must do so in writing, using the approved application form. The applicant shall send three copies of the form and of the accompanying material to the Commissary at the specified address.

4. An application for review by the Commissary shall not, without the leave of the Commissary, which will only be given in exceptional circumstances, be made later than three months after the date of the matter in respect of which review is requested.

5. The applicant must, in the application and accompanying material, make a full declaration of the material facts and circumstances, and may not introduce new material thereafter without the leave of the Commissary.

6. All material submitted in a particular case will be disclosed by the Commissary to the parties and to the person or persons nominated by the Council to make representations for the University.

7. The Commissary will refer an application (other than one rejected as vexatious, frivolous, or out of time) to any other party and to the University representative nominated by the University Council. These persons will be asked to make a written response. The Commissary will refer these responses to the applicant, who may make a written statement about them. This statement will be sent by the Commissary to the other parties and to the University representative.

8. Upon receipt of the statements referred to in rule 7 the Commissary will direct whether the matter will be dealt with on the basis of written representations or at an oral hearing. The Commissary's direction in this regard will be communicated in writing.

9. The procedure for any oral hearing will be determined by the Commissary in any particular case.

10. Any power or function of the Commissary under these rules may be exercised or discharged by a duly appointed Deputy.

SPECIAL ORDINANCES OF THE UNIVERSITY OF CAMBRIDGE

SPECIAL ORDINANCES UNDER STATUTE A

THE CHANCELLOR AND THE GOVERNMENT OF THE UNIVERSITY

SPECIAL ORDINANCE A (i):

Submission of Graces (Special Ordinance under Statute A IV 1(d)) Conduct of business (in the Regent House) (Special Ordinance under Statute A VIII)

1. Reports of the Council, or of any Board, Syndicate, or other body that has the right of reporting to the University, shall be submitted to the University by being published in the *Cambridge University Reporter*. A Report of any body other than the Council shall be sent to the Registrary for communication to the Council, who may refer it to the General Board and to any other body or person whom it wishes to consult. Such a Report shall be published not later than six months after the date on which it was first sent to the Registrary, unless the reporting body agrees to postpone its publication until a later date. Any comments on the Report which the Council or the General Board may wish to publish to the University shall be published with the Report.

2. Congregations of the Regent House, for the transaction of University business, and meetings of the Regent House, for the discussion of Reports and other matters, shall be held in the Senate-House or elsewhere within the Precincts of the University on such dates and at such times as may be appointed by the Chancellor, Vice-Chancellor or the Council. The manner of holding a Congregation and of transacting business at a Congregation shall be prescribed by Ordinance from time to time.

3. Members of the Senate shall have the right to attend and to speak at Discussions of the Regent House. The University may specify by Ordinance other persons or classes of persons, in addition to members of the Regent House and the Senate, who shall be entitled to speak at such Discussions. At the Vice-Chancellor's discretion other persons not so specified may be invited to attend or to speak at any particular Discussion.

4. The Council shall ensure that any remarks made at a Discussion are considered by the appropriate University authority. After any necessary consultation the Council shall publish such response to the remarks as it sees fit.

5. Any fifty members of the Regent House may initiate a Grace for submission to the Regent House, and any twenty-five members may initiate a proposal for the amendment of a Grace already submitted to the Regent House but not yet approved.

6. In respect of Graces and amendments of Graces initiated under Section 5, the Vice-Chancellor shall have power to rule inadmissible any Grace or amendment which directly concerns a particular person, and shall have such further powers as may be specified by Ordinance.

7. (*a*) Subject to the exercise by the Vice-Chancellor of the powers conferred by Section 6 or by Ordinances made under that Section, the Council shall consider any Grace or amendment initiated under Section 5, and either (i) shall authorize the submission of the Grace or amendment to the Regent House or (ii) shall publish a Report giving reasons for its decision to withhold authorization and recommending the Regent House to approve that decision. If such approval is not given, the Council shall, not later than the end of the term next following, submit the Grace or amendment to the Regent House.

(*b*) If a Grace or amendment initiated under Section 5 involves expenditure from University funds additional to that already authorized, the Council shall refer the Grace or amendment to the Finance Committee, and to the General Board or another body as appropriate, for their advice; in submitting such Grace or amendment to the Regent House, the Council shall at the same time publish a statement indicating how it is intended to make financial provision for the proposed expenditure.

8. Any proposal to be placed before the Regent House or the Senate for approval shall be in the form of a Grace. Further detailed provision for the initiation, submission and amendment of Graces shall be made by Ordinance.

SPECIAL ORDINANCE A (ii):

Membership of the Council: detailed provisions (Special Ordinance under Statute A IV 3)

[References in this Special Ordinance to Classes shall be to the classes prescribed in Statute A IV 2.

1. (*a*) Members of the Council in classes (*a*), (*b*), and (*c*) shall be elected to serve for four years, an election of half the members in each class being held during Full Michaelmas Term in each alternate year.

(*b*) Members of the Council in class (*d*) shall be elected in each academical year on a date to be determined by or under Ordinance to serve for one year from a date to be determined by Ordinance.

(*c*) Members of the Council in class (*e*) shall be appointed to serve for four years from 1 January in a year when the calendar year is odd; the appointment of half the members in this class shall take place in each alternate year.

2. (*a*) If a member of the Council in any of classes (*a*), (*b*), and (*c*), or any person nominated for election as a member in one of those classes, ceases to be a member of the Regent House, or suffers suspension or deprivation of her or his University office, degrees, or membership of the University, that member's seat shall thereupon become vacant, or the nomination shall thereupon become invalid, as the case may be.

(*b*) If a member of the Council becomes Chancellor or Vice-Chancellor, her or his seat shall thereupon become vacant.

(*c*) If a member of the Council in class (*a*) or class (*b*) ceases to be the Head of a College or a Professor or Reader, as the case may be, that member's seat shall not thereby become vacant.

(*d*) If a member of the Council in class (*d*), or any person nominated for election as a member in that class, ceases to be a student in the University as defined in accordance with Statute A IV 2, or suffers deprivation or suspension of her or his degree or membership of the University, or suffers rustication by a University Court or by a College, that member's seat shall thereupon become vacant, or the nomination shall thereupon become invalid, as the case may be.

3. (*a*) If any casual vacancy occurs by death, by resignation, or otherwise, among the elected members of the Council during their period of service, or if it is known that such a vacancy will occur by reason of a member's resignation, or if any person elected dies, resigns, or is otherwise disabled from beginning service between the publication of the result of the election and the day upon which such a person is due to begin service, the vacancy shall be filled by the holding of a bye-election; provided that no bye-election shall be held to fill a vacancy that occurs less than sixty days of full term before the end of tenure of the member whose death, resignation, or disablement has created the vacancy.

(*b*) If at any election the total number of vacancies is not filled, the Vice-Chancellor shall arrange a further election to fill such vacancies as are unfilled.

(*c*) If, after the last date for sending in nominations and before the result of the election has been decided, a person nominated for election in any class dies, or is disabled from serving as a member, or if such a person's nomination becomes invalid under the provisions of Section 2(*a*) or 2(*d*) above, all nominations for that class shall be deemed to be void, and the Vice-Chancellor shall give notice thereof and shall arrange a new election.

(*d*) Any bye-election, further election, or new election held under subsection (*a*), (*b*), or (*c*) above shall take place as soon as conveniently may be; the arrangements for the election shall be determined and published by the Vice-Chancellor.

(*e*) If any casual vacancy occurs by death, by resignation, or otherwise, among the members in class (*e*), the casual vacancy shall be filled in accordance with the procedure for the appointment of members in class (*e*) in Statute A IV 2(*e*).

4. (*a*) The period of service of members in classes (*a*), (*b*), and (*c*) shall be as follows:

(i) A person elected during the Michaelmas Term (otherwise than to fill a casual vacancy) shall begin service on the first day of January next following the election.

(ii) A person elected in any term other than a Michaelmas Term or elected to fill a casual vacancy which has already occurred shall begin service on the day next following the publication of the result of the election; provided that, if at an election of either such kind the number of persons nominated in any class does not exceed the number of vacancies in that class, the person or persons nominated shall be deemed to be elected and shall begin service on the day following the last day for the receipt of nominations.

(iii) A person elected in any term other than a Michaelmas Term (otherwise than to fill a casual vacancy) shall serve, notwithstanding the provisions of Section 1(*a*) above, until the end of the calendar year next but two following the year in which the election takes place.

(*b*) Any person elected a member in class (*d*) at a bye-election to fill a casual vacancy which has already occurred shall begin service on the day next following the publication of the result of the bye-election, provided, that, if the number of persons nominated in a bye-election does not exceed the number of vacancies, the person or persons nominated shall be deemed to be elected and shall begin service on the day following the last day for the receipt of nominations.][1]

⟨References in this Special Ordinance to classes are to the classes prescribed in Statute A IV 2.

1. (*a*) Members of the Council in classes (*a*), (*b*), and (*c*) shall be elected to serve for four years, an election of half the members in each class being held during Full Michaelmas Term in each alternate year.

(*b*) Members of the Council in class (*d*) shall be

(i) the President of Cambridge University Students Union;

(ii) the President of the Graduate Union;

(iii) one student elected by and from among the students in the University.

Members in categories (i) and (ii) of class (*d*) shall serve for one year from the commencement of their term of office as President. The member in category (iii) of class (*d*) shall be elected in each academical year on a date and in a manner determined by or under Ordinance and shall serve for one year from 1 July next following her or his election.

(*c*) Members of the Council in class (*e*) shall be appointed to serve for four years from 1 January in a year when the calendar year is odd; the appointment of half the members in this class shall take place in each alternate year.

2. (*a*) If a member of the Council in any of classes (*a*), (*b*), and (*c*), or any person nominated for election as a member in one of those classes, ceases to be a member of the Regent House, or suffers suspension or deprivation of her or his University office, degrees, or membership of the University, that member's seat shall thereupon become vacant, or the nomination shall thereupon become invalid, as the case may be.

(*b*) If a member of the Council becomes Chancellor or Vice-Chancellor, her or his seat shall thereupon become vacant.

(*c*) If a member of the Council in class (*a*) or class (*b*) ceases to be the Head of a College or a Professor or Reader, as the case may be, that member's seat shall not thereby become vacant.

(*d*) If the member of the Council in category (i) of class (*d*) ceases to be President of Cambridge University Students Union or if the member of the Council in category (ii) of class (*d*) ceases to be President of the Graduate Union, that member's seat shall thereupon become vacant.

(*e*) If the member of the Council in category (iii) of class (*d*), or any person nominated for election as the member in that class, ceases to be a student in the University, or suffers deprivation or suspension of her or his degree or membership of the University, or suffers rustication by a University Court or by a College, that member's seat shall thereupon become vacant, or the nomination shall thereupon become invalid, as the case may be.

3. (*a*) If any casual vacancy occurs by death, by resignation, or otherwise, among the elected members of the Council during their period of service, or if it is known that such a vacancy will occur by reason of a member's resignation, or if any person elected dies, resigns, or is otherwise disabled from beginning service between the publication of the result of the election and the day upon which such a person is due to begin service, the vacancy shall be filled by the holding of a bye-election; provided that no bye-election shall be held to fill a vacancy that occurs less than sixty days of full term before the end of tenure of the member whose death, resignation, or disablement has created the vacancy.

(*b*) If at any election the total number of vacancies is not filled, the Vice-Chancellor shall arrange a further election to fill such vacancies as are unfilled.

(*c*) If, after the last date for sending in nominations and before the result of the election has been decided, a person nominated for election in any class dies, or is disabled from serving as a member, or if such a person's nomination becomes invalid under the provisions of Section 2(*a*) or 2(*d*) above, all nominations for that class shall be deemed to be void, and the Vice-Chancellor shall give notice thereof and shall arrange a new election.

(*d*) Any bye-election, further election, or new election held under subsection (*a*), (*b*), or (*c*) above shall take place as soon as conveniently may be; the arrangements for the election shall be determined and published by the Vice-Chancellor.

[1] Subject to the approval by Her Majesty in Council of the amendments of Statute approved by Grace 1 of 30 April 2014 the Special Ordinance in square brackets will be replaced by the Special Ordinance in angular brackets with effect from the date on which the amendments of Statute take effect.

(*e*) If any casual vacancy occurs by death, by resignation, or otherwise, among the members in class (*e*), the casual vacancy shall be filled in accordance with the procedure for the appointment of members in class (e) in Statute A IV 2(*e*).

4. (*a*) The period of service of members in classes (*a*), (*b*), and (*c*) shall be as follows:

(i) A person elected during the Michaelmas Term (otherwise than to fill a casual vacancy) shall begin service on the first day of January next following the election.

(ii) A person elected in any term other than a Michaelmas Term or elected to fill a casual vacancy which has already occurred shall begin service on the day next following the publication of the result of the election; provided that, if at an election of either such kind the number of persons nominated in any class does not exceed the number of vacancies in that class, the person or persons nominated shall be deemed to be elected and shall begin service on the day following the last day for the receipt of nominations.

(iii) A person elected in any term other than a Michaelmas Term (otherwise than to fill a casual vacancy) shall serve, notwithstanding the provisions of Section 1(*a*) above, until the end of the calendar year next but two following the year in which the election takes place.

(*b*) Any person elected a member in class (*d*) at a bye-election to fill a casual vacancy which has already occurred shall begin service on the day next following the publication of the result of the bye-election, provided, that, if the number of persons nominated in a bye-election does not exceed the number of vacancies, the person or persons nominated shall be deemed to be elected and shall begin service on the day following the last day for the receipt of nominations.

5. For the purpose of this Special Ordinance the term 'student in the University' shall be defined by Ordinance.〉[1]

SPECIAL ORDINANCE A (iii):

Finance Committee of the Council (Special Ordinance under Statute A IV 8)

1. The Finance Committee of the Council shall consist of:

(*a*) the Vice-Chancellor, or a duly appointed deputy, who shall be Chair;

(*b*) three members of the Regent House elected by representatives of the Colleges;

(*c*) four persons appointed by the Council, at least two of whom shall be members of the Regent House;

(*d*) one member of the General Board appointed by the General Board;

(*e*) three members of the Regent House appointed by Grace of the Regent House;

(*f*) not more than two persons co-opted by the Committee, provided that it shall not be obligatory for the Committee to co-opt any person or persons;

subject always to the requirement that not less than three members of the Committee (including the Vice-Chancellor) shall be members of the Council.

2. Members in classes (*b*)–(*e*) shall be appointed or elected in the Michaelmas Term, and shall serve from 1 January next following. Members in classes (*b*) and (*e*) shall serve for three years, and members in classes (*c*) and (*d*) for four years. Co-opted members shall serve until 31 December of the year in which they are co-opted, or of the year next following, as the Committee shall determine at the time of their co-optation. If a member in class (*b*) or class (*e*) ceases to be a member of the Regent House, or if the member in class (*d*) ceases to be a member of the General Board, such a member's seat shall thereupon become vacant.

3. For the purpose of the election of members of the Committee in class (*b*), each College shall appoint one representative, whose name shall be communicated to the Registrary. The election shall be conducted in accordance with the Single Transferable Vote regulations; voting shall be by ballot. The arrangements for the election shall be determined by the Registrary.

4. The Registrary or a University officer designated from time to time by the Council shall act as Secretary of the Committee.

5. No business shall be conducted at a meeting of the Finance Committee unless five members at least are present.

[1] Subject to the approval by Her Majesty in Council of the amendments of Statute approved by Grace 1 of 30 April 2014 the Special Ordinance in square brackets will be replaced by the Special Ordinance in angular brackets with effect from the date on which the amendments of Statute take effect.

SPECIAL ORDINANCE A (iv):
Audit Committee of the Council (Special Ordinance under Statute A IV 10)

1. There shall be a standing committee of the Council, called the Audit Committee, which shall consist of:

(*a*) a member of the Council in class (*e*) (as referred to in Statute A IV 2(*e*)) appointed by the Council to serve as Chair of the Committee,

(*b*) two members of the Council appointed by the Council from among its members who are members of the Regent House, provided that neither the Vice-Chancellor, a Pro-Vice-Chancellor, nor the Chair of a Council of a School shall be eligible to serve,

(*c*) four persons, not being members of the Regent House or employees of the University, appointed by the Council with regard to their professional expertise and experience in comparable roles in corporate life, including at least two members with experience of finance, accounting, or auditing,

(*d*) not more than three persons co-opted by the Committee, of whom

(i) the first person co-opted shall be a member of the Regent House, such person not being a member of the Council;

(ii) not more than two co-opted persons shall be members of the Regent House, such persons not being members of the Council;

(iii) not more than two co-opted persons shall be external members, one but not more than one of whom may be a member of the Council in class (*e*) (as referred to in Statute A IV 2(*e*)),

provided that it shall not be obligatory for the Committee to co-opt any person or persons.

For the purpose of these regulations, external members are defined as the following members of the Audit Committee:

(*a*) persons who are members of the Council in class (*e*) (as referred to in Statute A IV 2(*e*),

(*b*) persons who are not employees of the University or any of its companies or of a College, and who do not hold College Fellowships which qualify them for membership of the Regent House.

2. Members in classes (*a*), (*b*), and (*c*) shall be appointed in the Michaelmas Term to serve for three years from 1 January next following their appointment. No member in class (*a*), (*b*), and (*c*) may serve for more than eight consecutive years. Co-opted members shall serve until 31 December of the year in which they are co-opted or of the following year, as the Committee shall decide at the time of their co-optation.

3. No person may be a member of the Audit Committee who is a member of the Finance Committee. If a member of the Audit Committee becomes a member of the Finance Committee, her or his place shall thereupon become vacant.

4. No decision of the Audit Committee shall have any binding effect unless there are at least five members, three at least of these being external members, present at a meeting of the Audit Committee. If a decision is the subject of a vote and there is an equality of votes cast, the Chair, or Acting Chair, as the case may be, shall be entitled to give a second or casting vote.

5. In the absence of the Chair of the Committee, the Audit Committee shall elect an acting Chair from the external members present.

SPECIAL ORDINANCE A (v):
The General Board, the Schools, and the assignment of Faculties, Departments etc. (Special Ordinance under Statute A V)

Amended by Grace 1 of 19 March 2014

[**1.** Members of the General Board in classes (*b*) and (*c*) pursuant to Statute A V 2 shall serve for four years, half the members in each class being appointed at the same time as, or shortly after, each biennial election of members of the Council. Changes of membership shall take effect from 1 January next following. Further arrangements for the election of Members in class (*b*) shall be made by Ordinance. Members of the General Board in class (*d*) shall serve for one year and shall be elected by students in the University in accordance with Statute A V 2(*d*) and in a manner determined by Ordinance, in each academical year on a date determined by or under Ordinance.][1]

[1] Subject to the approval by Her Majesty in Council of the amendments of Statute approved by Grace 1 of 30 April 2014 the regulation in square brackets will be replaced by the regulations in angular brackets and the following regulation renumbered with effect from the date on which the amendments of Statute take effect.

⟨**1.** Members of the General Board in classes (*b*) and (*c*) pursuant to Statute A V 2 shall serve for four years, half the members in each class being appointed at the same time as, or shortly after, each biennial election of members of the Council. Changes of membership shall take effect from 1 January next following. Further arrangements for the election of members in class (*b*) shall be made by Ordinance.

2. The members of the General Board in class (*d*) shall be

(i) the Education Officer of Cambridge University Students Union;

(ii) the President of the Graduate Union.

The members in class (*d*) shall serve for one year from the commencement of their term of office as Education Officer or President, as the case may be. If the member in category (i) of class (*d*) ceases to be the Education Officer of Cambridge University Students Union or if the member in category (ii) of class (*d*) ceases to be President of the Graduate Union, that member's seat shall thereupon become vacant.⟩[1]

2. These Schools are established by this Special Ordinance. They comprise the following faculties (and the departments contained in them) and other institutions, which are assigned by Ordinance:

ARTS AND HUMANITIES: Faculties of Architecture and History of Art, of Asian and Middle Eastern Studies, of Classics, of Divinity, of English, of Modern and Medieval Languages, of Music, and of Philosophy, the Centre for Research in the Arts, Social Sciences, and Humanities, and the Language Centre.

HUMANITIES AND SOCIAL SCIENCES: Faculties of Economics, of Education, of History, of Human, Social, and Political Science, and of Law, the Departments of History and Philosophy of Science and of Land Economy, and the Centres of African Studies, of Latin-American Studies, and of South Asian Studies.

BIOLOGICAL SCIENCES: Faculties of Biology, and of Veterinary Medicine, the Wellcome Trust/Cancer Research UK Gurdon Institute, and the Sainsbury Laboratory.

CLINICAL MEDICINE: Faculty of Clinical Medicine.

PHYSICAL SCIENCES: Faculties of Earth Sciences and Geography, of Mathematics, and of Physics and Chemistry, and the Isaac Newton Institute for Mathematical Sciences.

TECHNOLOGY: Faculties of Business and Management, of Computer Science and Technology, and of Engineering, the Department of Chemical Engineering and Biotechnology, and the University of Cambridge Institute for Sustainability Leadership.

SPECIAL ORDINANCE A (vi):
Boards and Syndicates (Special Ordinance under Statute A VI 1(a))

The following Boards and Syndicates are established by this Special Ordinance. The composition and responsibilities of each are to be determined by Ordinance:

(i) the Board of Graduate Studies;

(ii) the Board of Examinations;

(iii) the Local Examinations Syndicate;

(iv) Fitzwilliam Museum Syndicate;

(v) Library Syndicate.

SPECIAL ORDINANCE A (vii):
University bodies; miscellaneous provisions; delegation (Special Ordinance under Statute A X 8)

1. Whenever in any Statute or Ordinance provision is made for the election or appointment of members of any Board, Syndicate, or other body, in such case unless it is otherwise expressly provided by Statute or Ordinance as the case may be

(*a*) a retiring member shall, if in all respects qualified, be able to be re-elected or reappointed;

[1] Subject to the approval by Her Majesty in Council of the amendments of Statute approved by Grace 1 of 30 April 2014 the regulation in square brackets will be replaced by the regulations in angular brackets and the following regulation renumbered with effect from the date on which the amendments of Statute take effect.

(*b*) any casual vacancy shall be filled by the election or appointment of a member to serve for the unexpired portion of the period of service of her or his predecessor; such an election or appointment shall be made in accordance with the provisions of any Statute or Ordinance prescribing arrangements for elections or appointments to the body concerned, provided that the University or the General Board, as appropriate, may make Ordinances, or regulations, respectively, permitting the filling of a casual vacancy by co-optation.

2. The University may make Ordinances in pursuance of which a member of the Council, of any Board, Syndicate, or Committee, or of the Council of a School, shall, if not a member *ex officio*, vacate her or his membership on account of failure to attend meetings.

3. The University may by Ordinance make regulations as to the number of members which shall constitute a quorum, as to the majority necessary for the decision of certain questions, and for the procedure of every University body generally, and subject thereto the body may itself make such regulations. Subject to any Ordinance and to any regulation made by the body, elections or decisions shall be made by a majority of the members present and voting, but only if there is a quorum; provided that the Chair of a meeting shall be entitled when there is an equality of votes to give a second or casting vote. When there is not present at a meeting the Chair of the body, or any person otherwise entitled to preside, the members present shall appoint a chair of the meeting.

4. A University body may appoint committees for any such general or special business as in the opinion of the body may be better regulated or managed by means of a committee, and may delegate to any committee so appointed, or to any University officer, with or without restrictions or conditions, the exercise of any functions proper to the body, provided that

(*a*) such delegation shall not relieve the delegating body of responsibility for the matter delegated;

(*b*) members of the delegating body shall have the right of access to all papers considered by such committees or persons;

(*c*) subject to any contrary provision of Statutes or Ordinances, such delegation shall not extend

(i) to any election or appointment to a University office;

(ii) to any decision of a University Court established by Statute D II;

(iii) to any resolution concerning the award of a degree, diploma, certificate, or other qualification; or

(iv) to any other matter specified by Ordinance; and

(*d*) such delegation may be withdrawn (either generally or in respect of a specific matter) at any time.

5. No person *in statu pupillari* shall be present, whether as a member or otherwise, at a meeting of any body constituted in the University by Statute, or of any other body appointed by such a statutory body, for the discussion of, or decision on, any matter which the Chair of the meeting declares to be reserved. The following matters shall be reserved:

(i) the employment or promotion, or any matter relating to the employment or promotion, of individuals by the University;

(ii) the admission and academic assessment of individuals;

(iii) such other matters as may be specified by Statute or Ordinance in respect of any particular body or class of bodies; and

(iv) any other matter at the discretion of the Chair;

provided that none of the provisions of this section shall apply to meetings of the Regent House for discussion, to Congregations of the Regent House, or to meetings of any court constituted by or under Statute D.

Service as a member of a Board, Syndicate, or other body shall be deemed not to be employment for the purpose of (i) above; nevertheless, appointments, nominations for appointment, or co-optations of persons to serve as members of Boards, Syndicates, or other bodies may be reserved under (iii) or (iv) above.

In any case of doubt, the Chair shall decide whether an item of business is reserved and the Chair's decision shall be final. No person *in statu pupillari* shall receive papers relating to any item of reserved business, except that members of any body constituted by Statute, or of any body appointed by such a statutory body, who are *in statu pupillari* may, if the statutory body so decides, receive minutes of the decisions taken on reserved business.

SPECIAL ORDINANCES UNDER STATUTE B

MEMBERSHIP OF THE UNIVERSITY AND DEGREES

SPECIAL ORDINANCE B (i)

Degrees (Special Ordinance under Statute B II)

1. Degrees additional to those named in Statute B II 1

Primary Degree
Bachelor of Medicine
Bachelor of Music
Bachelor of Surgery
Bachelor of Theology for Ministry
Bachelor of Veterinary Medicine
Master of Advanced Study
Master of Business Administration
Master of Corporate Law
Master of Education
Master of Engineering
Master of Finance
Master of Law
Master of Letters
Master of Mathematics
Master of Music
Master of Natural Sciences
Master of Philosophy
Master of Research
Master of Science
Master of Studies
Doctor of Education
Doctor of Engineering
Doctor of Veterinary Medicine

2. Students may be admitted to a primary degree (as listed above or otherwise designated by Ordinance) without having previously been admitted to any degree in the University. Save as otherwise provided by Statute or Special Ordinance no one shall be admitted to any degree other than the primary degree without having previously been admitted to a degree in the University.

3. Save as otherwise provided by Statute or Special Ordinance no one shall be admitted to any degree of the University unless he or she has complied with such conditions of residence as shall have been approved by Ordinance.

SPECIAL ORDINANCES UNDER STATUTE C

UNIVERSITY OFFICES AND EMPLOYMENT IN THE UNIVERSITY

SPECIAL ORDINANCE C (i):

University Teaching Officers: sabbatical leave, dispensation, duty to examine (Special Ordinance under Statute C I 1)

1. Every office specified in Schedule C (i) 1 shall be a University office and the holder shall be entitled to be dispensed from discharging the duties of her or his office during one term for every six terms of service as hereinafter defined; provided always that

(*a*) the officer shall obtain the consent of the General Board, which consent shall not be unreasonably withheld;

(*b*) in estimating the amount of leave of absence due under this section at any time account shall not be taken of any service done by the officer more than six years before;

(*c*) an officer shall not necessarily receive any stipend in respect of any period of absence under this section, but the General Board may fix the amount (if any) of the stipend payable in respect of such period.

For the purposes of this section the General Board shall have power to determine whether a term or part of a term is to be reckoned as a term of service in any case where the holder of an office specified in the Schedule has been excused compliance with any or all of the conditions of the office under Statute C and the Ordinances or has been dispensed from discharging all or part of the duties of the office under Section 2 below; and for the same purposes a term of service shall be defined as any term during which or during part of which a University officer has held such an office, except

(i) any term for which or for part of which the General Board has excused the officer from compliance with any or all of the conditions of her or his office under Statute C and the Ordinances but has not allowed the term to be reckoned as a term of service;

(ii) any term for which or for part of which the General Board has dispensed the officer from discharging all or part of the duties of her or his office under Section 2 below but has not allowed the term to be reckoned as a term of service;

(iii) any term for which the officer has been dispensed from discharging the duties of her or his office under this section.

2. The competent authority may for sufficient cause dispense a University officer from discharging all or part of the duties of her or his office, as follows:

(*a*) The competent authority may dispense an officer, on account of her or his illness, from discharging the duties of her or his office for a period not exceeding six months, without loss of stipend. The competent authority may extend such dispensation and if it does so shall fix the amount (if any) of the stipend payable to the officer.

(*b*) The competent authority may dispense an officer, for sufficient cause other than illness, from discharging the duties of her or his office for a period not exceeding five years. In exceptional circumstances the competent authority, with the concurrence of the votes of not less than two-thirds of the whole number of its members, may grant such a dispensation for a period longer than five years, or may extend beyond five years a dispensation already granted, provided always that such a dispensation or extension shall not be valid without the concurrence of the Board, Syndicate, or other body chiefly concerned with the duties of the officer. No stipend shall be payable to the officer during any such dispensation (whether or not the period of dispensation exceeds five years) unless at the time of giving it or at the time or times of extending it the competent authority, having regard to all the circumstances of the case, including the nature of the sufficient cause and the question whether the officer is receiving or will receive payment from some source other than the University during the period of the dispensation, shall determine that the whole or part of the normal stipend is to be payable.

(*c*) The competent authority may dispense an officer, for sufficient cause other than illness, from discharging part of the duties of her or his office for a period not exceeding five years in the first instance, and may extend beyond five years a dispensation already granted, provided always that such a dispensation or extension shall not be valid without the concurrence of the Board, Syndicate, or other body chiefly concerned with the duties of the officer. A reduced stipend, as determined by the competent authority, shall be payable during such a dispensation.

3. The competent authority shall have power to determine whether any period, or part thereof, of an officer's dispensation or partial dispensation from duty under this Special Ordinance shall be omitted in reckoning the limit of tenure fixed at the time of the officer's appointment or reappointment to her or his office.

SCHEDULE C (i) 1

University offices whose holders are entitled to leave under Special Ordinance C (i)

Amended by Grace 3 of 12 March 2014

Professors
Readers
University Senior Lecturers
University Lecturers
Assistant Directors of Research
Senior Assistants in Research
University Pathologist in the Department of Veterinary Medicine
Assistant Directors of Development Studies

Director of the Melville Laboratory for Polymer Synthesis
Director of the Institute of Criminology
Director of the Scott Polar Research Institute
Director of the Botanic Garden
Executive Director of Research in the Faculty of Economics
Deputy Director of the McDonald Institute for Archaeological Research

SPECIAL ORDINANCE C (ii)

University Officers (Special Ordinance under Statute C I 2)

1. Certain matters which may be regulated in future by Special Ordinances under Statute C I 2 are at present provided for by the Schedule to Statute C (formerly Statute U).[1]

2. The competent authority shall decide, after hearing the opinion of the Faculty Board or other authority concerned, whether a University office that is vacant or is expected to become vacant shall be filled or left vacant; provided that this shall not apply to

(*a*) any of the offices specified individually in Statute C I 1;

(*b*) any Professorship;

(*c*) any office which is required to be filled under the terms of a trust subsisting at the time.

An election or appointment to an office may be made by anticipation as from a future date if it is known that the office will then be established, or will then be vacant and may be filled.

3. (*a*) The tenure of a University officer other than an officer specified in Schedule C (vii) 1 shall begin on such date as may at the time of the election or appointment be specified by the electing or appointing body; or, if no such date is specified, then

(i) if the office is already vacant or is newly established, the officer's tenure shall begin on the day of the election or appointment,

(ii) if the office is not yet vacant, the officer's tenure shall begin on the day after that on which the retiring officer vacates the office;

provided that no such body shall specify a date, or shall make an election or an appointment without specifying a date, so that the tenure of the officer elected or appointed begins on a date that is either earlier than the day on which the office fell vacant, or more than six months earlier than the day of the election or appointment, or more than eighteen months later than that day.

(*b*) Wherever in respect of a University office or category of University office provision is made by Statute or Ordinance or has been made by Grace for reappointment, and reappointment has not been precluded by the conditions upon which a particular office was established or re-established, no holder of such office or of an office in such category shall be reappointed more than one year before the date on which her or his present tenure of the office is due to expire.

(*c*) Where any Statute or Ordinance provides that a University office shall be divided into grades, whether identified by a number or by a specific title, each grade shall, unless otherwise specified in the relevant Statute or Ordinance, be regarded as a separate University office, and promotion from a lower grade to a higher grade within an office which is so divided shall be regarded as appointment to a different office.

4. Unless it is otherwise provided by Statute or Ordinance, every officer shall be admitted to her or his office as soon as may be after the commencement of tenure by subscribing, in a book kept at the Registry, a declaration that the officer will well and faithfully discharge all the duties of the office, and by entering in the book the date of entering upon the office.

5. The stipend of an office shall accrue due to an officer from the commencement of tenure unless he or she fails to enter upon the duties of the office on or before the required date as hereinafter defined. The required date shall be that specified by the electing or appointing body at the time of the election or appointment, or, if no such date is specified, it shall be that of the commencement of tenure if the commencement is not on the day of the officer's election or appointment, or the first day of the next term if the commencement is on the day of the officer's election or appointment.

6. An officer who fails to enter upon the duties of her or his office on or before the required date shall report the fact to the competent authority. The competent authority shall then determine the date from which the officer's stipend is due to accrue, and may excuse the officer from compliance with

[1] Cross-reference may be amended by Grace pursuant to Statute C I 8(*c*).

any or all of the conditions of the office during a period of not more than one year after the required date, subject to any deduction of stipend which the competent authority may determine.

7. Except where it is otherwise determined by the University, stipends shall be considered as accruing from day to day and shall be apportionable in respect of time accordingly.

8. The University shall have power to prescribe by Ordinance that the stipend attached to any office shall be subject to deduction on account of emoluments received by the holder from a College or Colleges.

9. No person or body shall have authority to make any representation or contract on behalf of the University, except in the performance of duties assigned to such person or body by or under Statute or Ordinance, or by consent of the University authority concerned. Such consent may be given either with regard to a particular transaction or generally with regard to a class or classes of transaction, and shall be subject to any restrictions which may be imposed by the authority concerned.

10. The University shall join in the Universities Superannuation Scheme and shall pay the pension contributions due thereunder in respect of the pensionable salaries of those officers who become members of the Scheme.

11. Every University officer (other than the Chancellor, the High Steward, the Deputy High Steward, the Commissary, and any University officer who is exempted under any Statute from the provisions of this section) shall comply with such regulations concerning residence and accessibility as may be made by the University.

12. Subject to the provisions of Statute C and any Special Ordinance made under Statute C, a University officer shall be entitled, unless the tenure of her or his office is limited in accordance with the provisions of any other Statute or Ordinance or by Grace, to hold office until the retiring age so long as he or she satisfactorily performs the duties of the office. All University officers (other than the Chancellor, the High Steward, the Deputy High Steward, the Commissary, and any University officer who is exempted under any Statute or Special Ordinance from the provisions of this section) shall vacate their offices not later than the end of the academical year in which they attain the age of sixty-seven years.

13. Every University officer shall send to the secretary of the competent authority and of the Board, Syndicate, or other body which is chiefly concerned with the officer's duties, such returns as the competent authority and the other body may respectively direct.

14. The duty to undertake examining which is imposed by Statute C I 4 shall not apply to any University officer who was appointed to her or his current office with effect from a date earlier than 1 October 1994.

SPECIAL ORDINANCE C (iii)

The Proctors (Special Ordinance under Statute C IV)

1. The election of the Proctors shall be held on the first weekday of the Michaelmas Term each year at 10 o'clock in the morning, the Proctors for the previous year vacating their offices immediately beforehand. At the election the two Esquire Bedells shall stand in scrutiny and shall take their own votes and those of other voters by the words *placet* or *non placet*. If each of the persons nominated is approved by a majority of those voting, the Esquire Bedells shall declare her or him to be elected. When the Proctors have been elected, the election of the deputy Proctors shall be held without delay. If after the election a Proctor desires to nominate an additional person for election as deputy Proctor, he or she shall request the Council to submit a Grace to the Regent House for the approval of the person nominated.

2. The Cycle of Nominations shall be as set out in Schedule C (iii) 1. When the series of years specified in the Cycle is ended, the order of nomination shall proceed as in the beginning of the Cycle and until the end of it, and so on continually.

3. In the Easter Term of each year the Head of each College whose turn it is to nominate a Proctor for the ensuing academical year shall, either in person or through a deputy, present to the Vice-Chancellor, in the presence of the Registrary, the person nominated by the College, and shall certify in writing that during the past two years the person nominated has resided in the University for the greater part of each of three terms at least. Before the end of the academical year each of the two persons nominated Proctor shall nominate either one or two persons for election as deputy Proctors.

4. If the nomination of a Proctor, having been duly made by a College, becomes void or is withdrawn before the election for some cause deemed sufficient by the Council, the College shall make a further nomination.

SCHEDULE C (iii) 1

Cycle for the nomination of Proctors[1]

1999–2000	Jesus New Hall	2016–17	Trinity Hall St Edmund's
2000–01	Downing Magdalene	2017–18	Newnham Darwin
2001–02	Christ's Selwyn	2018–19	St Catharine's Lucy Cavendish
2002–03	King's Gonville and Caius	2019–20	Fitzwilliam Peterhouse
2003–04	Robinson Darwin	2020–21	Emmanuel Clare Hall
2004–05	Peterhouse Newnham	2021–22	Churchill Clare
2005–06	St Catharine's Fitzwilliam	2022–23	Pembroke Girton
2006–07	Churchill Pembroke	2023–24	St John's Corpus Christi
2007–08	Trinity Clare	2024–25	King's Hughes Hall
2008–09	Girton Corpus Christi	2025–26	Trinity Sidney Sussex
2009–10	Emmanuel St John's	2026–27	Homerton Queens'
2010–11	King's Sidney Sussex	2027–28	Jesus Murray Edwards
2011–12	Christ's Jesus	2028–29	Downing Magdalene
2012–13	Murray Edwards Magdalene	2029–30	Christ's Selwyn
2013–14	Downing Queens'	2030–31	Robinson Darwin
2014–15	Robinson Selwyn	2031–32	Gonville and Caius Wolfson
2015–16	Gonville and Caius Wolfson		

SPECIAL ORDINANCE C (iv):
Administrative Officers (Special Ordinance under Statute C VI 4)

There shall be administrative officers under the direction of the Council in categories to be determined by Ordinance.

SPECIAL ORDINANCE C (v):
The Librarian (Special Ordinance under Statute C VII)

1. There shall be in the University a Library Syndicate which shall have power to make rules for the management of the University Library, provided that such rules shall not be inconsistent with any Ordinance. The composition of the Library Syndicate and the manner of its appointment shall be determined by Ordinance from time to time.

[1] The present cycle was approved by Grace 7 of 26 May 1999 and amended by Grace 4 of 3 November 2010.

2. The Librarian is placed under the direction of the Library Syndicate and shall act as Secretary to it. It shall be the duty of the Librarian

(*a*) to be responsible for the management of the University Library in all respects as determined by Ordinance and by the rules made by the Library Syndicate;

(*b*) to act as the General Board's principal adviser on matters relating to libraries;

(*c*) to be responsible, in consultation with the Registrary where appropriate, for the custody and arrangement in the Library of the University archives and of documents that are added thereto at the request of the Registrary or otherwise, provided that the Registrary shall be entitled to require the temporary deposit in the Registry of any document to which he or she may need to refer.

3. The Librarian shall be elected by a Board of Electors consisting of the Vice-Chancellor, or a duly appointed deputy, two persons appointed by the Council, three persons appointed by the General Board, and five persons appointed by the Library Syndicate. One at least of the Electors appointed by the General Board and one at least of those appointed by the Library Syndicate shall be persons who at the time of their appointment are not resident in the University nor officially connected with it, and three at least of the Electors appointed by the Library Syndicate shall be appointed from among the members of that Syndicate. The Secretary of the General Board, or a duly appointed deputy, shall be Secretary to the Board of Electors.

4. Electors shall be appointed in the Michaelmas Term to serve for four years from 1 January following their appointment.

5. If an Elector is or becomes a candidate for the office of Librarian he or she shall be disqualified from acting thereafter in the matter of that election, and the other Electors shall have power to act.

6. If an appointment to the Board of Electors is made after the Electors have first met to consider a vacancy in the office of Librarian, the Elector so appointed shall not have any vote in the election of the Librarian, but that Elector's predecessor, if not a candidate for the office of Librarian, shall retain her or his right to vote in the election.

7. (*a*) When the Librarian is due under the Statutes to retire, the Vice-Chancellor shall report the fact to the Council and to the General Board in the Michaelmas Term, but not later than the division of that term, of the academical year next before the year at the end of which the retirement is due to take place.

(*b*) When it becomes known to the Vice-Chancellor that a vacancy has occurred or will occur in the Librarianship otherwise than by the holder's becoming due under the Statutes to retire, the Vice-Chancellor shall report the fact to the Council and to the General Board at their next meetings.

8. Not later than the thirtieth day after reporting a vacancy or an expected vacancy in the Librarianship the Vice-Chancellor shall publish a Notice inviting applications to fill the vacancy; provided that the General Board shall have power to suspend the publication of such a Notice for any period not exceeding one year.

9. The Board of Electors shall have power to act notwithstanding one or more vacancies in the number of its members and shall have power to adjourn and generally to regulate its own procedure, provided that

(*a*) no election shall be made earlier than the day following that on which the qualifications of the candidates have been considered in the first instance at a meeting of the Board;

(*b*) no election shall be made unless two-thirds at least of the members of the Board (exclusive of any member disqualified by being a candidate) are present at the time of voting and a majority of the members present vote in favour.

10. The Board of Electors shall have power (*a*) to offer the Librarianship to a person who has not submitted an application for the office, provided that such a person's qualifications have been considered at two meetings held on different days, and (*b*) to enquire whether any person or persons other than those who have submitted applications would accept the office if offered.

11. If at the end of two years from the date of publication under Section 8 of the Notice inviting applications for the Librarianship the Electors have been unable to make an election, the Librarian shall be appointed by the Chancellor or, if the office of Chancellor is vacant, by the High Steward.

SPECIAL ORDINANCE C (vi):
The Director of the Fitzwilliam Museum (Special Ordinance under Statute C VIII)

1. The Director of the Fitzwilliam Museum (who shall also be Marlay Curator) shall, subject to the direction of the Fitzwilliam Museum Syndicate, have charge of all the objects in the Museum and in the Marlay Collection and shall perform such other duties as may be prescribed by Ordinance.

2. The manner of appointment and, subject to the provisions of Statute C and any Special Ordinance made under it, the conditions of tenure of office of the Director and the manner of appointment of the Syndicate shall be determined by Ordinance from time to time.

SPECIAL ORDINANCE C (vii)
Professors (Special Ordinance under Statute C XI 3)

Amended by Grace 5 of 16 July 2014

Part A: Professors

1. In addition to the Regius Professorships specified in Statute C XI, there shall be in the University such Professorships as by any trust for the time being binding on the University are required to be maintained; such Professorships as are for the time being included in Schedule C (vii) 1 and such Professorships as are for the time being established by Ordinance.

2. Subject to the provisions of any trust for the time being binding on the University,

(*a*) the University may make regulations for a Professorship under which candidature for that Professorship at any election thereto may be limited, or preference may be given by the Board of Electors, to candidates whose work is connected with a particular area of study within the general field of the title of the Professorship;

(*b*) either before or after the occurrence of a vacancy in a Professorship to which no such regulations apply, the General Board may determine that candidature for the Professorship at the next election thereto shall be limited, or preference shall be given, as aforesaid.

Notice of any such limitation or preference shall be published to the University forthwith.

3. No Professorship shall be established in the University except by Grace of the Regent House after the publication of a Report of the General Board. The Report shall state whether or not it is recommended that the Professorship be placed in Schedule C (vii) 1. If the Report recommends inclusion in Schedule C (vii) 1, it may also recommend inclusion in Schedule G (i) 2.

4. (*a*) When a Professorship becomes vacant or is due shortly to become vacant, the University may, on the recommendation of the General Board, terminate or temporarily discontinue it as from the date of the vacancy or modify the conditions relating to it, unless such termination or temporary discontinuance or modification can only be effected by Statute or by an authority other than the University.

(*b*) If it is reported to the General Board that a Board of Electors has been unable to make an election to a Professorship, the General Board may publish a Notice temporarily discontinuing the Professorship for a specified period determined under the provisions of Section 20 of Part B below, unless such temporary discontinuance can only be effected by Statute or by an authority other than the University.

5. If a Professorship is one which cannot be temporarily discontinued or the conditions of which cannot be modified otherwise than by making a Statute or by submitting an application for the alteration of a trust to an authority other than the University, and if the University has approved such a Statute or has submitted such an application, the election shall remain suspended until the result of the submission of the Statute to Her Majesty in Council or of the application to the other authority is known.

6. Subject to the provisions of Statute C and this Special Ordinance regarding the age of retirement, the University shall have power to establish a Professorship limited to a fixed term of years or to the tenure of one Professor only, or to direct that election to a Professorship (being neither a Professorship to which appointments are made by the Crown nor a Professorship governed for the time being by a trust expressly providing otherwise) shall be for a prescribed term of years or until a prescribed date.

7. The University shall assign each Professorship to a Faculty or Department or other institution under the supervision of the General Board, as appropriate, and may change the assignment from time to time. Subject to the concurrence of the authorities concerned, the duties of a particular Professorship may concern such institutions as the General Board shall determine.

8. Professorial stipends shall be determined from time to time by the University, provided that a Professor shall always receive any emolument to which he or she is entitled under the terms of any trust for the time being binding on the University.

9. The University may from time to time prescribe the minimum amount of instruction to be given by a Professor and the character of such instruction.

10. The University may from time to time by Ordinance impose restrictions on the nature of College offices that may be held by Professors and on the teaching which Professors may give otherwise than on behalf of the University.

11. If the University alters either the title of a Professorship or the definition of the scope of a Professorship, such alteration shall not have effect during the tenure of the person then holding the office except with her or his consent; but if the person concerned consents to the alteration he or she shall be entitled to hold the office under the same conditions as if the alteration had been made before her or his election to the office.

12. The University shall have power to add or remove Professorships to or from the list of those specified in Schedule C (vii) 1.

13. Any person who has not previously held the Slade Professorship of Fine Art may be elected to that Professorship for a period not exceeding three years notwithstanding that he or she has attained the age of sixty-seven years; but no one shall be re-elected to the Professorship for a period such that the tenure of the office will continue beyond the end of the academical year in which he or she will attain the age of sixty-seven years.

14. Any person may be elected or re-elected to one of the following Professorships, notwithstanding that he or she has attained, or will attain during the tenure of the office, the age of sixty-seven years: the John Wilfrid Linnett Visiting Professorship of Chemistry, the Alexander Todd Visiting Professorship of Chemistry, the Arthur Goodhart Visiting Professorship in Legal Science, the Pitt Professorship of American History and Institutions, the Simón Bolívar Professorship of Latin-American Studies, and the Diane Middlebrook and Carl Djerassi Visiting Professorship of Gender Studies.

Part B: Elections to Professorships

1. Elections to all Professorships shall be governed by the provisions of this Special Ordinance (Parts A and B) except for

(*a*) the Regius Professorships of Civil Law, Physic, and History, and the King Edward VII Professorship of English Literature, to which appointments are made by the Crown;

(*b*) a Professorship limited to the tenure of one Professor only, if established for a particular person by Grace;

(*c*) the following Professorships, to which elections are made by the General Board:

(i) any Professorships on the John Humphrey Plummer Foundation;

(ii) the Quick Professorship of Biology;

(iii) any Professorship the tenure of which is less than a year or is limited to a specified number of years;

provided that

(i) any Professorship to which the appointment is to be made under the terms of any trust binding for the time being on the University shall be governed by this Special Ordinance only so far as this Special Ordinance is compatible with the terms of the trust;

(ii) elections to the Dixie Professorship of Ecclesiastical History shall be made in accordance with the provisions of the Statute relating thereto for the University and for Emmanuel College in common.

2. Except as otherwise prescribed in Section 1 above, the election to a Professorship shall be made by a Board of Electors constituted in accordance with either Section 4 or Section 5 below. Subject to the provisions of Section 3, such a Board of Electors may be *either*

(*a*) a standing Board, of which the appointed members shall be appointed to serve for four years, *or* (*b*) an *ad hoc* Board, of which the appointed members shall be appointed to serve until the election has been made and the Professor has entered upon the duties of the office, or until the General Board has published a Notice of temporary discontinuance under Part A Section 4(*b*) above.

3. A Board constituted in accordance with Section 4 may be either a standing Board or an *ad hoc* Board, as determined by the General Board under Section 6 below. A Board constituted in accordance with Section 5 shall be an *ad hoc* Board. The Registrary or a University officer designated by the Council (or a duly appointed deputy appointed by the Registrary or such University officer) shall act as Secretary to a Board of Electors. The membership of a standing Board shall be published at least once in each year. The membership of an *ad hoc* Board shall be published as soon as conveniently may be after the members have been appointed.

4. If a Professorship has been assigned to a Faculty or Department, or other institution under the supervision of the General Board, the election shall be made by a Board of Electors consisting of

(*a*) the Vice-Chancellor or a duly appointed deputy;

(*b*) eight persons appointed by the Council, two on the nomination of the Council itself, three on the nomination of the General Board, and three on the nomination of the Faculty Board concerned in the case of a Professorship assigned to a Faculty or to a Department within a Faculty, or on the nomination of the comparable authority in the case of a Professorship assigned to a Department independent of any Faculty or other institution under the supervision of the General Board.

5. If the General Board considers it desirable that the assignment of a Professorship should be deferred until the election has been made to that Professorship, the election shall be made by a specially constituted Board consisting of

(*a*) the Vice-Chancellor or a duly appointed deputy;

(*b*) five persons appointed by the Council, two on the nomination of the Council itself and three on the nomination of the General Board;

(*c*) such number of additional persons representing the branches of the subject included in the scope of the Professorship as the General Board shall determine, appointed by the Council on the nomination of the bodies deemed by the General Board to be concerned.

6. When a Professorship is first established, the General Board shall determine, after consulting such Faculty Boards or comparable authorities as are deemed by the General Board to be concerned, whether elections to the Professorship are to be made by a standing Board of Electors or by an *ad hoc* Board. The General Board shall subsequently have power to review its decision at any time and, after consulting the Faculty Boards or comparable authorities concerned, to reverse its previous decision; such reversal shall take effect from the first day of October next following.

7. Nominations for any Board of Electors shall be made on such dates as will enable the General Board to nominate with knowledge of the nominations of the Faculty Boards or comparable authorities concerned.

8. When a standing Board of Electors is constituted for the first time the members shall be appointed for periods so determined by the Council that in the year next but one and in every subsequent year (*a*) two of the eight appointed Electors shall retire on the thirtieth day of September, and (*b*) none of the nominating bodies shall nominate more than one Elector save when a casual vacancy is to be filled.

9. No person shall be appointed or reappointed a member of a standing Board of Electors who at the commencement of her or his period of service or further period of service, as the case may be, would have attained the age of sixty-seven years; and no person shall be appointed a member of an *ad hoc* Board of Electors who at the commencement of her or his period of service would have attained the age of seventy years.

10. To ensure the representation of opinion outside the University, every Board of Electors shall include at least two persons who are not the holders of any University office as defined in Statute C I 1(*a*) and are not habitually resident within twenty miles of the University Church. At least one such person shall be included among those nominated by the General Board, and at least one among those nominated by the Faculty Board or comparable authority (in the case of a Board constituted in accordance with Section 4) or among those nominated by the bodies deemed by the General Board to be concerned (in the case of a Board constituted in accordance with Section 5).

11. If a member of a Board of Electors who has been nominated as a representative of opinion outside the University subsequently becomes the holder of a University office as defined in Statute C I 1(*a*) or becomes habitually resident within twenty miles of the University Church, her or his place on the Board shall not thereby become vacant; but when next the body which nominated that person is to nominate a member of the Board it shall nominate a person qualified as in Section 10, unless there is already such a person among its nominees.

12. Whenever a vacancy from any cause other than lapse of time occurs on a Board of Electors (other than on an *ad hoc* Board after the Electors have first met to consider a vacancy in the Professorship), a new Elector shall be appointed to fill the vacant place. If an appointment to a standing Board of Electors is made after the Electors have first met to consider a vacancy in the Professorship, the Elector so appointed shall not take part in that election, and her or his predecessor shall retain the right, subject to the provisions of Section 13 below, to take part in the election. If the General Board publishes a Notice under Part A, Section 4(*b*) above temporarily discontinuing the Professorship, the publication of the Notice shall have the same effect for the purposes of this section as if an election had been made.

13. If an Elector is or becomes a candidate for a Professorship, he or she shall be disqualified from acting thereafter in the matter of that election, and the remaining Electors shall have power to act.

14. A Board of Electors shall have power to act notwithstanding one or more vacancies in the number of its members, and shall have power to adjourn and generally to regulate its own procedure, provided that

(*a*) no election shall be made earlier than the day following that on which the qualifications of the candidates have been considered in the first instance at a meeting of the Board;

(*b*) no election shall be made unless two-thirds at least of the members of the Board (exclusive of any member disqualified by being a candidate) are present at the time of voting and a majority of the members present vote in favour.

15. A Board of Electors shall have power (*a*) to enquire whether any person or persons other than those who have submitted applications would accept the Professorship if offered, and (*b*) to offer the Professorship to a person who has not submitted an application, provided that such a person's qualifications have been considered at two meetings held on different days.

16. The following provisions shall apply to all Professorships other than those limited to the tenure of a single holder:

(*a*) When a Professor is due under Statutes or Ordinances to retire, the Vice-Chancellor shall report the fact to the General Board not later than the division of the Michaelmas Term of the academical year next but one preceding the year at the end of which the retirement is due to take place.

(*b*) When it becomes known to the Vice-Chancellor that a vacancy has occurred or will occur in a Professorship otherwise than by the holder's becoming due to retire or by the expiry of the period for which he or she was elected, the Vice-Chancellor shall report the fact to the General Board at the next opportunity.

(*c*) If a vacancy is due to occur in a Professorship by the expiry of a period of discontinuance of more than three years, action shall be taken in accordance with subsection (*a*) above as if the end of that period were the end of the year in which a holder of the Professorship is due to retire. If a period of discontinuance is three years or less, action shall be taken in accordance with subsection (*b*) above.

17. When the Vice-Chancellor has reported under Section 16 above that a vacancy has occurred or is expected to occur in a Professorship, the General Board shall consider whether the conditions relating to the Professorship should be modified, or whether the Professorship should be terminated or temporarily discontinued. For this purpose the General Board shall consult such Faculty Boards or comparable authorities as are concerned, and also the Council of the relevant School, and shall ask whether they recommend that the vacancy should be filled, and if so whether they recommend (*a*) that candidature for the Professorship should be limited, or alternatively that preference should be given by the Electors, to persons whose work is connected with a particular area of study within the general field of the title of the office, or (*b*) that candidature should be open without limitation or preference to all persons whose work falls within that general field. In reaching a decision on these questions the General Board shall take into account, but shall not be bound by, the recommendations of the authorities consulted under this section.

18. (*a*) Not later than the end of the eighteenth month after the Vice-Chancellor's report under Section 16 of a vacancy or an expected vacancy in a Professorship, the General Board shall *either*

(i) agree that the vacancy shall be filled; *or*

(ii) ask the Council to promote a Grace for the termination or temporary discontinuance of the Professorship from the date of the vacancy; *or*

(iii) ask the Council to promote a Grace extending by a specified amount the period prescribed by this subsection within which the General Board is required to act under sub-subsection (i) or (ii) above.

(*b*) Not later than the date specified by subsection (*a*) above if the Board agrees that the vacancy shall be filled or if the Professorship is one that the University is required by any Statute or trust to maintain, *or* not later than the end of the term next following the term in which a Grace under subsection (*a*)(ii) above has been rejected, the Board

(i) may ask the Council to promote a Grace for the amendment of the Statute or Ordinances prescribing the conditions relating to the Professorship; and

(ii) if the Professorship is one to which no such Statute or Ordinances apply, shall determine the conditions which shall relate to the Professorship at the next election.

19. Not later than the end of the twelfth month after

(*a*) the General Board has agreed under Section 18(*a*)(i) that a vacancy shall be filled without the need for approval by Grace under Section 18(*b*)(i) of any modification of the conditions relating to the Professorship, or

(*b*) the University has approved or rejected any Grace submitted under Section 18(*b*)(i) or has rejected any Grace submitted under Section 18(*a*)(ii),

the Vice-Chancellor shall publish a Notice inviting applications to fill the vacancy.

20. (*a*) If at the end of two years from the date of publication of the Notice inviting applications for a Professorship the Electors have been unable to make an election they shall report this fact and the reasons for it to the General Board. The General Board shall then *either*

(i) grant the Electors a further period of not more than two years in which to make an election; *or*

(ii) publish a Notice discontinuing the Professorship for a specified period which shall not extend beyond the end of the seventh academical year following the date of publication under Section 19 of the Notice inviting applications.

(*b*) If the Electors have been granted a further period of two years under Section 20(*a*)(i) and within that further period have again been unable to make an election they shall report this fact and the reasons for it to the General Board. The General Board shall then *either*

(i) recommend the Council to ask the Chancellor, or, if the office of Chancellor is vacant, the High Steward, to appoint the Professor; *or*

(ii) publish a Notice discontinuing the Professorship for a specified period which shall neither be less than one year nor extend beyond the end of the seventh academical year following the date of publication under Section 19 of the Notice inviting applications.

SCHEDULE C (vii) 1:
Professorships

Amendment of this schedule is made by Grace. Professorships are assigned to this schedule by Ordinance or Grace.

This schedule lists University officers whose offices qualify them to hold Professorial Fellowships.

Administrative officers

The Vice-Chancellor
The Registrary
The Librarian
The Director of the Fitzwilliam Museum

Professors

Abrahamic Faiths and Shared Values (Sultan Qaboos)
Accounting
Active Tectonics
Aerodynamics

Aeronautical Engineering (Francis Mond)
Aerothermal Technology
Algebra
Algebraic Geometry
American History (Paul Mellon)
American History and Institutions (Pitt)
American Intellectual History
Anaesthesia
Analytical Biotechnology
Analytical Physics
Anatomy
Ancient History
Ancient Philosophy (Laurence)
Anglo-Saxon (Elrington and Bosworth)
Animal Embryology (Charles Darwin)
Applied Mathematics (1964)
Applied Mathematics (2003)
Applied Mathematics (2006)
Applied Mathematics (2013)
Applied Statistics and Signal Processing
Applied Thermodynamics (Hopkinson and Imperial Chemical Industries)
Applied Thermodynamics
Arabic (Sir Thomas Adams's)
Archaeological Science (George Pitt-Rivers)
Archaeology (Disney)
Architecture (1970)
Architecture and the Moving Image
Arts, Humanities, and Social Sciences (John Harvard)
Astronomy
Astronomy (Royal Society)
Astronomy and Experimental Philosophy (Plumian)
Astronomy and Geometry (Lowndean)
Astrophysical Fluid Dynamics
Astrophysics (1909)
Astrophysics (2009)
Astrophysics (2011)
Astrophysics and Cosmology
Atmospheric Science
Behavioural Ecology
Behavioural Neuroscience (2009)
Behavioural Neuroscience (2013)
Behavioural Science
Biochemical Engineering
Biochemistry (Sir William Dunn)
Biochemistry (Herchel Smith)
Biological Chemistry
Biology (Quick)
Biomedical Magnetic Resonance
Biophysical Chemistry
Biophysics
Biostatistics (MRC Research)
Botany (Regius)
Brain Physics
Cancer Biology (Royal Society Napier Research)
Cancer Epidemiology
Cancer Research (Ursula Zoëllner)

Cancer Research (2001, Grace 10 of 13 December 2000)
Cancer Therapeutics
Cardiopulmonary Medicine
Cardiothoracic Surgery
Cardiovascular Medicine (British Heart Foundation)
Cardiovascular Sciences (British Heart Foundation)
Cell and Cancer Biology
Cell Physiology
Cellular Biochemistry
Cellular Dynamics
Cellular Neuroscience
Cellular Pathophysiology and Clinical Biochemistry
Cellular Pharmacology
Celtic
Chemical and Structural Biology (John Humphrey Plummer)
Chemical Engineering (Shell)
Chemical Engineering (1999)
Chemical Engineering (2009)
Chemical Physics (1999)
Chemical Physics (2008)
Chemical Physics (2011)
Chemical Reaction Engineering
Chemistry (BP) (1702)
Chemistry (Geoffrey Moorhouse Gibson)
Chemistry (1968)
Chemistry (1996)
Chemistry (2012)
Chemistry and Chemical Biology (2012)
Chemistry and Chemical Biology (2013)
Child and Adolescent Psychiatry
Children's Poetry
Chinese Development (Chong Hua)
Chinese History, Science, and Civilization (Joseph Needham)
Chinese Management (Sinyi)
Civil Engineering (2007)
Civil Engineering (2013)
Civil Engineering (Sir Kirby Laing)
Civil Justice and Private Law
Civil Law (Regius)
Classical Archaeology (Laurence)
Classics
Climate Change Economics and Policy
Clinical Biochemistry and Medicine
Clinical Gerontology
Clinical Magnetic Resonance Imaging
Clinical Microbiology
Clinical Neuropsychology
Clinical Neuroscience
Clinical Nursing Research (Florence Nightingale Foundation)
Clinical Oncology
Clinical Pharmacology
Cognitive Developmental Neuroscience
Cognitive Psychology (MRC Research)
Combinatorial Mathematics
Commonwealth History (Smuts)
Communications Systems (Marconi)

Company and Securities Law
Comparative and Developmental Criminology
Comparative Cognition
Comparative Immunogenetics
Comparative Pathology
Comparative Philology
Complex Physical Systems (Schlumberger)
Computational Engineering
Computational Linguistics (2004)
Computational Linguistics (2011)
Computational Logic
Computational Physics
Computer Assisted Reasoning
Computer Science (1994)
Computer Science (2012)
Computer Science (Robert Sansom)
Computer Technology (1997)
Computer Technology (2005)
Computer Vision and Pattern Recognition
Computing
Conservation and Development (Moran)
Conservation Biology (Miriam Rothschild)
Conservation Science
Construction Engineering (Laing O'Rourke)
Control Engineering (2002)
Control Engineering (2006)
Corporate Governance (Adam Smith)
Corporate Law (S. J. Berwin)
Cosmology
Cosmology (Stephen W. Hawking)
Cosmology and Astrophysics
Criminology (Wolfson)
Criminology and Criminal Justice (2006)
Criminology and Criminal Justice (2010)
Cultural History and Aesthetics
Cymatogeny
Demography
Developmental Biology (John Humphrey Plummer)
Developmental Biology (2008)
Developmental Cardiovascular Physiology and Medicine
Developmental Genetics
Developmental Mechanick
Developmental Neuroscience
Developmental Psychology
Developmental Psychopathology
Device Materials
Divinity (Lady Margaret's)
Divinity (Norris-Hulse)
Divinity (Regius)
Early Modern European History
Early Modern French Literature and Culture
Earth Sciences (BP Foundation McKenzie)
Earth Sciences (Royal Society Research)
Ecclesiastical History (Dixie)
Ecological and Developmental Criminology
Ecology and Evolutionary Biology (Prince Philip)

Econometric Theory and Economic Statistics
Econometrics
Economic Geography
Economic History (1928)
Economic History (2004)
Economic Theory
Economics (Frank Ramsey)
Economics (1970)
Economics (2007)
Economics (2013)
Economics and Game Theory
Economics and Organization
Education (1938)
Education (2000)
Education (2000)
Education (2002)
Education (2004)
Education (2004)
Education (2005)
Education (2008)
Education (2011)
Electrical Engineering
Electron Device Physics (Hitachi)
Electronics
Empirical Macroeconomics
Empirical Sociology
Endocrine Physiology
Endocrinology
Energy and Materials Science
Energy Technologies
Engineering (1875)
Engineering (1966, Grace 5 of 1 December 1965)
Engineering (2008)
Engineering (2012)
Engineering (Rank)
Engineering (Regius)
Engineering (Van Eck)
Engineering Design
Engineering Tribology
English (1966, Grace 2 of 1 December 1965)
English (2001)
English (2001, Grace 1 of 21 November 2001)
English and Applied Linguistics
English Law (Rouse Ball)
English Literature (King Edward VII)
English Literature (2004)
English Private Law
Enterprise Studies (Margaret Thatcher)
Environment and Policy
Environmental Systems Analysis
Epidemiology (MRC Research)
Epidemiology and Medicine
Equine and Farm Animal Science (Alborada)
European Law
European Union and Employment Law
Evolution and Behaviour

Evolutionary Biology
Evolutionary Genetics
Evolutionary Palaeobiology
Experimental Astrophysics
Experimental Combustion
Experimental Haematology
Experimental Medicine (Genzyme)
Experimental Neurology (Merck Company Foundation)
Experimental Neuroscience
Experimental Particle Physics
Experimental Philosophy
Experimental Physics (1998)
Experimental Physics (2002)
Experimental Psychology (1931)
Experimental Psychology (2013)
Experimental Quantum Physics
Family Research
Farm Animal Health, Food Science, and Food Safety (Marks & Spencer)
Finance
Finance (Sir Evelyn de Rothschild)
Fluid Dynamics
Fluid Mechanics (Dyson)
Fluid Mechanics (G. I. Taylor)
Fluid Mechanics (1998)
Fluid Mechanics (2006)
Fluid Mechanics (2006)
Fluid Mechanics (2007)
Foundations of Mathematics
French (Drapers)
French Government (Visiting)
French History
French Literature and the Visual Arts
French Philology and Linguistics
Gastroenterology
General Practice
Genetic Epidemiology
Genetics
Genetics (Arthur Balfour)
Genome Biology
Geoarchaeology
Geography (1931)
Geography (1993)
Geology (Woodwardian)
Geometry
Geophysics
German (Schröder)
German History and Thought
German Literature and Intellectual History
Graphics and Imaging
Greek (Regius)
Greek (2002)
Greek Culture (A. G. Leventis)
Haemato-oncology
Haematology
Health Management (Dennis Gillings)
Health Neuroscience (Bernard Wolfe)

Health Services Research (RAND)
Hebrew (Regius)
High Energy Physics (2003)
High Energy Physics (2009)
Histopathology
Historical Anthropology
Historical Musicology
History (Regius)
History and Philosophy of Science (2002)
History and Philosophy of Science (2010)
History and Philosophy of Science (Hans Rausing)
History and Philosophy of the Sciences (2000)
History and Public Policy
History of Art (2004)
History of Art (2015)
History of Christianity
History of European International Relations
History of International Relations
History of Medieval Art
History of Political Thought
History of Science
Human Evolution (Leverhulme)
Human Genetics
Human Geography
Human Population Biology and Health
Hypoxia Signalling and Cell Biology
Immunogenetics
Immunology
Immunology (Sheila Joan Smith)
Immunology and Cell Biology
Immunology and Infectious Diseases
Immunology and Medicine
Imperial and Naval History (Vere Harmsworth)
Indian Business and Enterprise (Jawaharlal Nehru)
Industrial Information Engineering
Industrial Relations and Labour Economics (Montague Burton)
Infectious Disease Informatics
Infectious Diseases
Information Engineering (1994)
Information Engineering (2000)
Information Engineering (2002)
Information Engineering (2004)
Information Engineering (2012)
Information Engineering (2013)
Information Systems and Innovation Studies
Innate Immunity
Innovation and Organization
Inorganic Chemistry
Intellectual History and English Literature
Intellectual Property Law (Herchel Smith)
International Education
International Finance (Pembroke Visiting)
International History
International Law
International Law (Whewell)
International Law and International Constitutional Studies

International Relations (Sir Patrick Sheehy)
Italian (Serena)
Italian and Romance Linguistics
Japanese Studies
Land Economy
Laser Engineering
Latin (Kennedy)
Latin American Geography
Latin-American Literature
Latin-American Studies (Simón Bolívar)
Law (1973)
Law (2006)
Law and Environmental Policy (Harold Samuel)
Law and Legal History
Laws of England (Downing)
Learning Disability Psychiatry
Legal and Political Philosophy
Legal Science (Arthur Goodhart Visiting)
Linguistics
Linguistics and Philosophy of Language
Logic
Logic and Algorithms
Macroeconomics
Mammalian Development and Stem Cell Biology
Management Studies
Management Studies (Beckwith)
Management Studies (Diageo)
Management Studies (KPMG)
Manufacturing Engineering
Manufacturing Engineering (GKN)
Materials Chemistry
Materials Engineering
Materials Physics
Materials Science (2001)
Materials Science (2007)
Materials Science (2008)
Materials Science (2009)
Materials Science (2009)
Materials Science (Sir Alan Cottrell)
Materials Science (Goldsmiths')
Materials Science and Metallurgy
Mathematical Astrophysics
Mathematical Biology
Mathematical Foundations of Computer Science
Mathematical Logic
Mathematical Physics (1967)
Mathematical Physics (1978)
Mathematical Physics (1998)
Mathematical Physics (2011)
Mathematical Sciences (2001)
Mathematical Sciences (2013)
Mathematical Sciences (N. M. Rothschild & Sons)
Mathematical Statistics
Mathematics
Mathematics (Lucasian)
Mathematics (Rouse Ball)

Mathematics for Operational Research (Churchill)
Mathematics of Systems
Matrix Biochemistry
Mechanical Engineering (1993)
Mechanical Engineering (1997)
Mechanical Engineering (2006)
Mechanical Engineering (2013)
Mechanics of Materials (1997)
Mechanics of Materials (1999)
Medical Genetics (1997)
Medical Genetics (2007)
Medical Genetics and Genomic Medicine
Medical Oncology
Medical Physics
Medicinal Chemistry (Herchel Smith)
Medicine (1962)
Medicine (1987)
Medicine (2010)
Medieval and Renaissance English
Medieval English History
Medieval English Literature and Palaeography
Medieval French and Occitan
Medieval French Literature
Medieval History
Medieval Music
Medieval Music and Literature
Mediterranean History
Metabolic Medicine
Metabolism and Medicine
Metallurgy (Tata Steel)
Microbial Pathogenesis (GlaxoSmithKline)
Microbiology
Mineral Physics
Mineralogy and Mineral Physics
Mineralogy and Petrology
Mitochondrial Medicine (MRC Research)
Modern and Contemporary History
Modern and Medieval German Studies
Modern Arabic Studies (His Majesty Sultan Qaboos Bin Said)
Modern British History
Modern Chinese History
Modern Cultural History
Modern European History
Modern German and Comparative Culture
Modern History
Modern Languages
Modern Spanish Literature and Intellectual History
Molecular and Cellular Biochemistry
Molecular Biology (2004)
Molecular Biology (2011)
Molecular Biology (Herchel Smith)
Molecular Biophysics
Molecular Biotechnology
Molecular Cancer Biology (Royal Society Research)
Molecular Cell Biology
Molecular Endocrinology (Serono)

Molecular Genetics (Herchel Smith)
Molecular Genetics and Genomics
Molecular Haematology
Molecular Haemostasis
Molecular Immunology
Molecular Membrane Biology
Molecular Microbiology
Molecular Neurobiology
Molecular Neurogenetics
Molecular Neurology
Molecular Nutrition and Metabolism
Molecular Pathology (2009)
Molecular Pathology (2011)
Molecular Pharmacology
Molecular Pharmacology (Royal Society)
Molecular Physiology and Pathology
Molecular Sciences Informatics (Unilever)
Molecular Virology
Music
Music and Science
Musical Performance Studies
Nanotechnology (1999)
Nanotechnology (2011)
Natural Philosophy (Jacksonian)
Nephrology
Neurobiology (2004)
Neurobiology (2009)
Neurological Genetics
Neurology
Neurophysiology
Neuroradiology
Neurorehabilitation
Neuroscience
Neurosurgery
Neurotechnology
Nonlinear Mathematical Science
Nuclear Medicine
Number Theory and Algebra (Kuwait)
Numerical Analysis of Differential Equations
Observational Astronomy
Observational Cosmology and Astrophysics
Obstetrics and Gynaecology (1975)
Obstetrics and Gynaecology (2000)
Ocean Physics
Old Age Psychiatry
Oncological Pathology
Oncology (Li Ka Shing)
Operations Research
Ophthalmology
Organic Chemistry (Herchel Smith)
Organic Chemistry (2001)
Orthopaedic Surgery
Pacific Geography
Paediatrics (1978)
Paediatrics (1998)
Parasitology

Particle Physics
Pathology
Perinatal Physiology
Persian History
Petroleum Science (BP)
Petrology
Pharmacology (Sheild)
Philosophical Theology
Philosophy (Knightbridge)
Philosophy (Bertrand Russell)
Philosophy (2007)
Philosophy (2012)
Philosophy (2013)
Philosophy (2013)
Philosophy of Science
Phonetics
Photonic Engineering
Photonic Systems and Displays
Photonics
Physic (Regius)
Physical Chemistry
Physical Geography
Physical Metallurgy
Physics (Cavendish)
Physics (Herchel Smith)
Physics (1966, Grace 7 of 1 December 1965)
Physics (2002)
Physics (2005)
Physics (2006)
Physics (2009)
Physics of Materials (John Humphrey Plummer)
Physiology
Physiology of Reproduction (Mary Marshall and Arthur Walton)
Plant and Microbial Biochemistry
Plant Biochemistry
Plant Biochemistry and Cell Biology
Plant Development (2011)
Plant Development (2013)
Plant Ecology
Plant Systematics and Evolution
Poetry and Poetics (Gorley Putt)
Political Economy
Politics (2007)
Politics (2012)
Polymer Physics
Polymeric Materials Chemistry and Physics
Portuguese Literature and Culture
Primary Care Research
Private International Law
Protein Crystallography
Psychiatry (1998)
Psychiatry (2000)
Psychology (2007)
Psychology in the Social Sciences
Public Health Medicine
Public Law and Jurisprudence

Public Law and Private International Law
Public Understanding of Risk (Winton)
Pure Mathematics (2005)
Pure Mathematics (2009)
Pure Mathematics (Herchel Smith)
Pure Mathematics (Sadleirian)
Quantum Electronics
Quantum Physics
Quantum Physics (Leigh Trapnell)
Quaternary Palaeoenvironments
Radiation Oncology
Radio Astronomy
Radiology
Real Estate Finance (Grosvenor)
Regional and Applied Economics
Representation Theory
Reproductive Biology
Reproductive Immunology
Reproductive Physiology
Respiratory Biology
Respiratory Medicine
Rheumatology
RNA Molecular Biology
Rural Economy
Russian Literature and Cultural History
Security Engineering
Semiconductor Engineering
Signal Processing
Signalling Pharmacology
Slavonic Studies
Small Animal Medicine
Small Animal Surgery
Social Anthropology (Sigrid Rausing)
Social Anthropology (William Wyse)
Social Theory
Sociology (1985)
Sociology (2001)
Sociology and Political Economy
Sociology of Education
Spanish
Statistical Science
Statistical Signal Processing
Statistics (2012)
Statistics (2013)
Statistics in Biomedicine
Stem Cell Biology
Stem Cell Medicine
Stochastic Analysis
Stroke Medicine
Structural and Molecular Biology
Structural Biology (2000)
Structural Biology (2010)
Structural Dynamics
Superconducting Engineering
Surgery
Sustainable Design

Sustainable Reaction Engineering
Systems Biology and Biochemistry
Technology (Prince Philip)
Tectonics
Theoretical and Computational Physics
Theoretical and Mathematical Physics
Theoretical Astrophysics
Theoretical Chemistry (2004)
Theoretical Chemistry (2011)
Theoretical Chemistry (2013)
Theoretical Computer Science
Theoretical Geophysics
Theoretical Mineral Physics
Theoretical Physics (John Humphrey Plummer)
Theoretical Physics (1998)
Theoretical Physics (2001)
Theoretical Physics (2003)
Theoretical Physics (2005)
Theoretical Physics (2007)
Theoretical Physics (2007)
Theoretical Physics (2010)
Theoretical Physics (2011)
Theoretical Physics (2013)
Therapeutics
Transfusion Medicine
Transplantation
Urban and Regional Economics
Vertebrate Palaeontology
Veterinary Diagnostic Pathology
Virology
Virus Pathogenesis
Volcanology
Zoology (1866)
Zoology (2010)

Professors (subject specified on the occasion of an election)

BBV Foundation Visiting Professor
Humanitas Visiting Professors
Jawaharlal Nehru Visiting Professor

Other University officers specified in Schedule C (i) 1

Amended by Grace 3 of 12 March 2014

Director of the Botanic Garden
Director of the Institute of Criminology
Director of the Melville Laboratory for Polymer Synthesis
Executive Director of Research in the Faculty of Economics

Other University officers

Director of the M.B.A. course
Director of the Cambridge Endowment for Research in Finance
Director of the University Computing Service

SPECIAL ORDINANCE C (viii):
Readers (Special Ordinance under Statute C XII)

1. The University may from time to time prescribe the minimum amount of instruction to be given by a Reader and the character of such instruction.

2. The stipend of a Reader shall be determined by the University from time to time.

3. The University may from time to time by Ordinance impose restrictions on the nature of College offices that may be held by Readers and on the teaching which Readers may give otherwise than on behalf of the University.

SPECIAL ORDINANCE C (ix):
Senior Lecturers (Special Ordinance under Statute C XIII 2)

1. Appointment to a University Senior Lectureship shall be made in such manner as the University shall from time to time determine. Such appointment shall be subject to the satisfactory completion of a period of probation under arrangements approved from time to time by the University unless the waiver of this requirement is recommended by the Appointments Committee and approved by the General Board. On confirmation of an appointment, a University Senior Lecturer shall hold office, subject to the provisions of the Schedule to Statute C,[1] until the retiring age, so long as he or she satisfactorily performs the duties of the office.

2. The teaching to be given by University Senior Lecturers and their stipends shall be determined in the same manner as for University Lecturers.

3. The restrictions imposed by Statute on the teaching which may be given by University Lecturers otherwise than on behalf of the University shall apply also to University Senior Lecturers.

4. When there is an incremental scale of prime stipends the General Board shall determine a University Senior Lecturer's place on the scale on appointment. If a revised scale of stipends is approved by the University, it shall be competent for the General Board to alter a University Senior Lecturer's place on the scale in accordance with the objects and conditions of the revision.

SPECIAL ORDINANCE C (x):
Appointments Committees (Special Ordinance under Statute C XIII 3)

1. Every appointment or reappointment to an office of University Lecturer shall be made by the Appointments Committee constituted in accordance with Section 2 below for the Faculty or Department or other institution in which the Lectureship is established or, if the General Board decides that the duties of a particular Lectureship concerned more than one institution, by a special Appointments Committee constituted in accordance with either Section 3(*a*) or Section 3(*b*) below, as the case may be. Every appointment or reappointment to an office of University Lecturer shall be made by the Appointments Committee with the concurrence of the votes (which shall be given in person at a meeting) of at least five members of the Appointments Committee, or of at least two-thirds of the number of members present, whichever is the greater number.

2. The Appointments Committee for a Faculty or Department or other institution under the supervision of the General Board, as the case may be, shall consist of:

(*a*) the Vice-Chancellor (or a duly appointed deputy) as Chair;

(*b*) *either*

(i) when the Lectureship is established in a Faculty, the Chair of the Faculty Board;

or (ii) when the Lectureship is established in a Department, the Head of that Department;

or (iii) when the Lectureship is established in an institution independent of a Faculty or Department, the Head of the institution;

(*c*) three persons appointed by the Faculty Board or, in the case of a Lectureship established in a Department independent of any Faculty or an institution independent of any Department or Faculty, three persons appointed by the comparable authority concerned;

(*d*) two persons appointed by the General Board;

provided that the General Board shall have power to prescribe by Ordinance an alternative constitution for the Appointments Committee for a Department independent of any Faculty or for an institution independent of any Department or Faculty.

[1] Cross-reference may be amended by Grace pursuant to Statute C I 8(*c*).

3. When the General Board decides that the duties of a particular University Lectureship concern more than one institution and specifies the institution concerned, the appointment or reappointment to such an office shall be made by a special Appointments Committee constituted as follows:

(*a*) if the duties concern more than one Department in a single Faculty but not the Faculty as a whole, the Appointments Committee constituted as in Section 2 above but excluding the Chair of the Faculty Board and including the Heads of such Departments as may be specified by the General Board;

(*b*) if the duties concern more than one institution, or any combination of these other than as provided for in subsection (*a*) above, an Appointments Committee consisting of:

(i) the Vice-Chancellor (or a duly appointed deputy) as Chair;

(ii) the Chair of the Board of each Faculty which is specified by the General Board as concerned;

(iii) the Head of each Department or other institution which is specified by the General Board as concerned;

(iv) for each institution specified as concerned, a number of persons appointed by the appropriate Faculty Board or Boards, or by the comparable authority or authorities, to be determined as follows:

either (1) for each of two institutions, two persons;

or (2) for each of more than two institutions, one person;

(v) two persons appointed by the General Board.

4. The following provisions shall apply to appointed members of any Appointments Committee constituted in accordance with Section 2 or Section 3 above:

(*a*) members shall be appointed in the Michaelmas Term of each calendar year of which the number is even, to serve during the two calendar years next ensuing; provided that when an Appointments Committee is newly constituted in accordance with Section 2 or Section 3 above, or is reconstituted in accordance with Section 3 in view of a change in the institutions specified by the General Board as concerned in the duties of the office, the appointed members of the new Appointments Committee shall be appointed forthwith and shall serve until the end of the next calendar year of which the number is even;

(*b*) no person shall be appointed or reappointed a member of an Appointments Committee who at the commencement of her or his period of service or further period of service, as the case may be, would have attained the age of seventy years.

5. (*a*) The appointment to a University Lectureship shall be subject to the satisfactory completion of a period of probation under arrangements approved from time to time by the University unless the waiver of this requirement is recommended by the Appointments Committee and approved by the General Board.

(*b*) On confirmation of an appointment, a University Lecturer shall hold office, subject to the provisions of Statute C or any Special Ordinance made under it, until the retiring age, so long as he or she satisfactorily performs the duties of the office.

6. The General Board shall have power to direct, either of its own motion or on the recommendation of the Faculty Board, comparable authority, or Appointments Committee concerned, or in order to comply with a trust binding on the University for the time being, that in a special case an appointment or a reappointment to be made by an Appointments Committee shall be for a fixed term, which shall be prescribed by the General Board and which may be shorter than the period specified in Section 5(*b*) above.

7. The General Board, after consulting the Faculty Board or other authority concerned, shall fix for each institution the limits within which the amounts of teaching to be given by all University Lecturers in the institution shall be determined. The lower limit of such teaching shall not be less than thirty hours' lectures a year; provided that

(*a*) an equivalent amount of other teaching may be substituted for lectures, the equivalence of such teaching being determined by the General Board;

(*b*) the General Board shall have power, in exceptional circumstances and on the recommendation of the Faculty Board or comparable authority concerned, to prescribe for a Lecturer, for periods not exceeding three years at a time, and under such conditions as the General Board may specify, an amount of teaching which is less than that specified above.

8. The amount of teaching to be undertaken by a University Lecturer shall be determined by the Faculty Board or comparable authority concerned within the limits fixed by the General Board in accordance with Section 7 above. Such teaching shall normally be given during full term, but the Faculty Board or comparable authority, with the approval of the General Board and with the officer's consent, may prescribe that some of it shall be given during the Long Vacation.

9. If a University Lecturer undertakes administrative work in connection with a Faculty, Department, or other institution, the General Board shall have power, on the recommendation of the Faculty Board or comparable authority concerned, to allow the Lecturer to count such administrative work as part of the duties for which he or she receives a pensionable stipend as a Lecturer.

10. In prescribing the amount of teaching to be given by a University Lecturer in any year the Faculty Board or comparable authority shall have regard to the character of the subject-matter of the lectures or other teaching, to the time which will be involved in preparation therefor, to any University administrative work approved by the General Board under Section 9 above, and to any College administrative work. If a Lecturer considers that the amount of teaching prescribed is unreasonable he or she may appeal to the General Board, whose decision shall be final.

11. A University Lecturer shall not undertake for remuneration during full term without the consent of the General Board any teaching other than teaching given on behalf of the University or a College or Colleges or the delivery of occasional lectures. The amount of teaching given by a University Lecturer on behalf of a College or Colleges shall not, except with the consent of the General Board, exceed twelve hours a week, or, if the Lecturer is a Tutor or Bursar, eight hours a week. The General Board may on account of the nature of the subject or the circumstances of the particular case extend the maximum number of hours a week to fifteen, or if the Lecturer is a Tutor or Bursar to ten. For the purposes of this section the terms Tutor and Bursar shall include Assistant Tutors and Assistant Bursars unless in a particular case the General Board shall decide otherwise.

12. The prime stipends or scales of stipends for University Lecturers shall be determined by the University on the recommendation of the General Board.

13. When there is an incremental scale of prime stipends the General Board shall determine a University Lecturer's place on the scale on appointment. If a revised scale of stipends is approved by the University, it shall be competent for the General Board to alter a University Lecturer's place on the scale in accordance with the objects and conditions of the revision.

14. The prime stipend of a University Lecturer shall be subject, in respect of payments received from a College or Colleges other than payments for teaching and the direction of studies and such occasional payments as may be exempted by the General Board, to deductions to be determined by Ordinance.

SPECIAL ORDINANCE C (xi):

Associate Lecturers (Special Ordinance under Statute C XIII 4)

1. The General Board may create Associate Lectureships and assign each Associate Lectureship to a Faculty or Department, as appropriate. The Board shall have power to direct an Appointments Committee to make an appointment or reappointment to a particular Associate Lectureship conditional on the holding of a post specified by the Board in an institution connected with the University.

2. Every appointment or reappointment to a University office of Associate Lecturer shall be made by the Appointments Committee for the Faculty or Department constituted in accordance with Section 2 of Special Ordinance C (x), or, if the General Board decides that the duties of a particular Associate Lectureship concern more than one Faculty or Department and specifies those Faculties or Departments, by a special Appointments Committee constituted in accordance with Section 3 of that Special Ordinance. Every appointment or reappointment to an office of Associate Lecturer shall be made by the Appointments Committee with the concurrence of the votes (which shall be given in person at a meeting) of at least five members of the Appointments Committee, or of at least two-thirds of the number of members present, whichever is the greater number. An Associate Lecturer shall be appointed and may thereafter be reappointed for such periods not exceeding five years at a time as the Appointments Committee shall determine; provided that if an Associate Lecturer ceases to hold the post in an institution connected with the University which has been specified by the General Board in accordance with Section 1 he or she shall thereupon vacate the Associate Lectureship.

3. All Associate Lecturers shall be required to devote themselves to the advancement of knowledge in their subject, to give instruction therein to students, and to promote the interests of the University as a place of education, religion, learning, and research. Every Associate Lecturer shall be required in each academical year to deliver a course or courses of lectures during a number of hours prescribed by the Faculty Board or comparable authority concerned, which shall be not less than sixteen, or to do such amount of other teaching as the General Board on the recommendation of the Faculty Board or comparable authority shall determine to be equivalent thereto, in a subject or subjects prescribed annually by the Faculty Board or comparable authority.

4. Associate Lecturers shall be subject to such conditions of residence as may be imposed from time to time by Ordinance. They shall not be subject to any of the restrictions imposed by Statute on the teaching which may be given by University Lecturers otherwise than on behalf of the University.

5. No Associate Lecturer shall be paid a stipend by the University unless for a particular Associate Lecturer, after consultation with the Faculty Board or comparable authority concerned and with the approval of the Council, the General Board decides otherwise and determines the stipend to be paid and whether it shall be pensionable.

SPECIAL ORDINANCE C (xii):
Redress of Grievances (Special Ordinance under Schedule to Statute C Chapter VI 2)

General

1. Every University officer has a right to raise any concerns, problems, or complaints relating to her or his appointment or employment, not being matters for which express provision is made elsewhere in Statutes and Ordinances.

2. The purpose of this Ordinance is to provide an appropriate means for University officers to seek redress of workplace concerns as informally, fairly and speedily as possible. Where after investigation a grievance is found to be vexatious or malicious, and without any reasonable foundation, disciplinary action may follow.

3. An officer may at any time withdraw a grievance or may agree that it has been resolved.

4. The 'Responsible Person' in relation to any particular officer shall for the purposes of this Ordinance be either (i) the Head or Director of the appropriate Department, Division of the Unified Administrative Service or other institution or the Chair of the Board, Syndicate, or other body which is chiefly concerned with the officer's duties; or (ii) such other University officer as the secretary of the competent authority (as determined by Statute D I 1(*b*)) may determine. In cases of doubt, the secretary of the competent authority shall determine who is the Responsible Person.

Unless otherwise specified, the Responsible Person may delegate any duty prescribed by Ordinance or under any rule, code of practice, guidance or other provision made under Statute or Ordinance to a named person, provided that the written permission of the secretary of the competent authority to such delegation is obtained in each case, and references to the Responsible Person shall include reference to such other person as appropriate.

5. The expression 'working day' shall exclude weekends, public holidays, or any other day when the University Offices are closed.

6. If at any time during the Formal or Appeal Stage of this Grievance Procedure the aggrieved officer considers that any aspect of the process is subject to unreasonable delay, he or she may make a complaint in writing:

(*a*) at the Formal Stage, to the Director of the Human Resources Division or, if he or she is the Responsible Person, the Chair of the Human Resources Committee, and

(*b*) at the Appeal Stage, to the Chair of the Human Resources Committee

who shall investigate the alleged delay and respond in writing within five working days of receipt of the complaint. In exceptional circumstances where a complaint has been received, the person to whom the complaint is made may determine that another officer shall act as the Responsible Person or that an officer appointed to inquire into a grievance at the Appeal Stage shall be removed or replaced.

Mediation

7. At the Informal and Formal stages of the Grievance Procedure the aggrieved officer and the person responsible for considering the grievance shall consider whether to refer the matter to mediation. The University's internal mediation service may be used if desired. Participation in mediation is voluntary. Anything said or produced by either party to any mediation will be considered to be confidential and without prejudice.

Informal Stage

8. Grievances should first be raised informally by the officer with the person to whom the officer is immediately responsible. Where the conduct of that person is the subject of the grievance, the aggrieved officer should raise the matter informally with a University officer senior to that person. It is expected that most grievances will be resolved at or before this stage.

Formal Stage

9. If the grievance cannot be resolved by informal discussions, then the officer may make a written complaint to the Responsible Person. Where bullying or harassment is the subject matter of the grievance, the Responsible Person may, after consultation with the Human Resources Division, determine that the complaint be regarded as a complaint under the Dignity at Work Procedure if it is considered that this will offer a more appropriate means of addressing the officer's concerns. Where such a determination is made, the officer may subsequently make a further written complaint to the Responsible Person if he or she is dissatisfied with the outcome of the Dignity at Work Procedure. A grievance cannot be considered under this procedure while a complaint is being considered under the Dignity at Work procedure in respect of the same subject matter.

10. If the grievance directly concerns the Responsible Person, the officer should write to the Director of Human Resources who, in consultation with the Chair of the Human Resources Committee (or, if the Director of Human Resources is the Responsible Person, the Chair of the Human Resources Committee), will appoint a person to act in place of the Responsible Person in the Formal Stage of the Grievance Procedure. Where such an appointment is to be made by the Director of Human Resources, he or she will act in consultation with the Chair of the Human Resources Committee.

11. On receipt of a written grievance the Responsible Person should notify the Human Resources Division without delay. The Human Resources Division will inform the secretary of the competent authority, as determined by Statute C I 1(*b*), and advise on the requirements of fair and correct practice and procedure, to ensure that these are applied consistently across the University.

12. The Responsible Person will arrange a meeting with the officer, if possible within five working days after receipt of the complaint, and will inform the officer of her or his right to be accompanied, confirming that information in writing. The Responsible Person may, if the subject matter of the grievance requires particular knowledge or expertise, or involves another part of the University, invite to the meeting such other officer or officers as may be of assistance in hearing the grievance and advising the Responsible Person, and will inform the officer that they will be attending the meeting.

13. The officer has the right to be accompanied by a colleague or by a trade union representative. For a person to qualify as a trade union representative, he or she must be certified in writing by the union as having experience of, or having received training in, acting as a worker's companion at disciplinary or grievance meetings. The officer has no right to insist on being accompanied by a particular person against that person's will.

14. Before the meeting takes place, the officer shall propose to the Responsible Person whom he or she has chosen as a companion, if any. The Responsible Person shall accept the companion chosen by the officer unless their choice is unreasonable, for example if the companion has a conflict of interest or might prejudice a fair discussion of the grievance, when the Responsible Person may ask them to choose a different companion.

15. Where possible, the timing and location of the meeting should be agreed with the officer. If the officer's companion cannot attend on the proposed date, the officer can suggest another date as long as it is reasonable and is not more than five working days after the date originally proposed by the responsible person. That five day time limit may be extended by mutual agreement. The meeting should be held in a private location and there should be no interruptions.

16. At the meeting, the officer shall be allowed to explain the complaint and say how he or she thinks it should be settled. If a point in the meeting is reached where the Responsible Person is not sure how to deal with the grievance or believes that further investigation is necessary, he or she should adjourn the meeting to get advice or to investigate further.

17. The officer's companion shall be allowed to participate fully in the meeting, to confer with the officer during the course of the meeting and if necessary to request an adjournment to confer privately with the officer. The companion may not answer questions on the officer's behalf, nor address the meeting if the officer does not wish it, nor prevent the Responsible Person from conducting the proceedings in any way.

18. The Responsible Person should give the grievance careful consideration before responding.

19. The Responsible Person should write to the officer within a reasonable time, and normally not more than five working days after the meeting (including any adjournment) has concluded, responding to the grievance and referring to the officer's right of appeal. Where it is not possible to respond within five working days the officer should be given an explanation for the delay and told when a response can be expected. The response shall be sent by recorded delivery to the officer's home address as notified to the University by the officer.

Appeal Stage

20. If the officer wishes to appeal, he or she may, within ten working days after the date of the letter of response, write to the Director of Human Resources asking that the grievance be referred to the Human Resources Committee. The Director of Human Resources shall have discretion to accept a later appeal where he or she is satisfied that there was good reason why that appeal could not be submitted within ten working days.

21. On receipt of such a request, the Human Resources Committee will appoint one or more persons to inquire into the grievance with a view to resolving it, and to report. The inquiry shall be subject to the Rules of inquiry contained in paragraph 26.

22. If at any time the grievance is withdrawn, or agreed to have been resolved, by the officer who made it, then the person or persons inquiring into the grievance shall not be obliged to proceed further or to report.

23. The Human Resources Committee will decide, after consideration of any report, what action (if any) to take. The Secretary of the Committee shall promptly notify the aggrieved officer in writing of its decision by recorded delivery to the officer's home address as notified to the University by the officer.

24. The Human Resources Committee and the person or persons appointed to inquire into the grievance shall proceed with all reasonable speed.

25. This is the end of the procedure and there is no further appeal.

Rules of inquiry

26. The following rules shall apply as regards an inquiry under the Appeal Stage of the grievance procedure:

(i) Before any report is made, the aggrieved officer shall be heard. Such a meeting need not be by all of the persons (if more than one) inquiring into the grievance.

(ii) The aggrieved officer shall be entitled to be represented or accompanied for that purpose by a trade union officer or a colleague, on the same basis as described in paragraphs 12–16 above.

(iii) Subject to the above rules, the person or persons conducting the enquiry shall use all reasonable endeavours to ensure that the conduct of the inquiry is just and fair.

27. This procedure is established pursuant to the Schedule to Statute C, Chapter VI 2.

Transitional provision

28. This Ordinance shall apply to all grievances submitted in writing by officers on or after 13 March 2013. The former arrangements contained in former Statute U, VI shall be deemed to apply to all grievances submitted in writing prior to that date, together with the former Regulations relating to Grievance Committees in Ordinances, Chapter II.[1] When no longer required this provision may be repealed by Grace.

[1] The regulations were last published in *Statutes and Ordinances* 2012, p. 212.

SPECIAL ORDINANCES UNDER STATUTE D

DISCIPLINE AND THE UNIVERSITY COURTS

SPECIAL ORDINANCE D (i):
Appointment of Chairs and members of University Courts (Special Ordinance under Statute D II 8–10)

1. The Septemviri shall consist of a Chair, who shall be a legally qualified member of the University appointed by Grace for four years, and six members of the Regent House appointed singly by Grace for two years; provided that:

(i) a member of the Septemviri who is appointed after the commencement of proceedings before the Septemviri shall take no part in those proceedings;

(ii) a member of the Septemviri whose membership would otherwise terminate during any such proceedings shall remain a member in respect of those proceedings until they are concluded;

(iii) no person shall be a member of the Septemviri during any period in which he or she is a member, or has been elected or appointed but not yet become a member, of the Council or the General Board, save as provided in (ii) above; and in that case such a person shall not attend a meeting or receive papers for a meeting of the Council or of the General Board, and such continued membership of the Septemviri shall constitute a sufficient cause of absence from meetings of either of those bodies.

2. Five members of the Septemviri shall constitute a quorum.

3. The University Tribunal shall consist of a Chair, who shall be a legally qualified member of the University, and four members of the Regent House. The method and period of appointment of the Chair and of the other members shall be prescribed by Ordinances made under this section. The Registrary, or a deputy appointed by the Registrary, shall be Clerk of the University Tribunal.

4. The Court of Discipline shall consist of a Chair, who shall be legally qualified or shall have had experience of acting in a judicial capacity, and four members of the University, not more than two of whom may be persons *in statu pupillari*. The method and period of appointment of the members of the Court shall be determined by Ordinance; provided that

(i) no member of the Council or of the Septemviri and no person who has been elected or appointed but not yet become a member of either of those bodies shall be a member of the Court;

(ii) a member of the Court who becomes a member of the Council shall nevertheless remain a member of the Court until the conclusion of the proceedings for which he or she has been appointed but shall not attend a meeting or receive papers for a meeting of the Council, and such continued membership of the Court shall constitute a sufficient cause for absence from meetings of the Council.

Three members of the Court shall constitute a quorum and every finding or sentence shall require the concurrence of the votes of a majority of the members present. If any member of the Court is unable or unwilling to act in connection with a particular charge or appeal, he or she shall be replaced by an alternate who shall be appointed in a manner prescribed by Ordinance.

SPECIAL ORDINANCE D (ii):
Appeal to the Septemviri (Special Ordinance under Statute D II 4)

1. An appeal to the Septemviri may be instituted by serving on the Registrary notice in writing setting out the grounds of the appeal. A notice of appeal shall be served within twenty-eight days of the date on which the document notifying the decision appealed from was sent to the appellant, provided that the Septemviri shall have power to hear an appeal submitted after that date if they consider that justice and fairness so require in the circumstances of the case.

2. The Registrary shall inform the Septemviri of any notice of appeal received and of the date when it was served, and shall inform the appellant that this has been done.

3. The procedure to be followed in respect of the preparation, consolidation, hearing, and determination of appeals shall be prescribed by Ordinances made under this section.

4. Without prejudice to the generality of the foregoing, such Ordinances shall ensure:

(*a*) that an appellant is entitled to be represented by another person, whether such person is legally qualified or not, in connection with and at any hearing of an appeal;

(*b*) that an appeal shall not be determined without an oral hearing at which, in addition to the University Advocate, the appellant and any person appointed to represent the appellant are entitled to be present and, with the consent of the Septemviri, to call witnesses;

(*c*) that full and sufficient provision is made for postponements, adjournments, dismissal of the appeal for want of prosecution, and the correction of accidental errors;

(*d*) that the Septemviri may set appropriate time limits for each stage of the proceedings (including the hearing itself) to the intent that any appeal shall be heard and determined as expeditiously as is reasonably practicable.

5. The Clerk of the Septemviri shall notify the decision of the Septemviri on any appeal, to the Vice-Chancellor, to the University Advocate, and to the appellant.

6. (*a*) A person sentenced by the Court of Discipline to deprivation or suspension of membership of the University, to deprivation or suspension of degree, or to rustication, may appeal to the Septemviri.

(*b*) A person on whom the Court of Discipline has imposed some other sentence may appeal to the Septemviri if he or she obtains leave either from the Chair of the Court or from the Chair of the Septemviri.

(*c*) An appeal under this section shall be instituted within twenty-eight days after the decision of the Court.

SPECIAL ORDINANCE D (iii):
The University Advocate; miscellaneous provisions (Special Ordinance under Statute D)

1. Evidence that a person has been convicted of an offence by or before any court of law, or that any court of law has found proved an offence with which a person was charged, shall, for the purpose of proving that he or she committed the offence or was guilty of any act or conduct in respect of which he or she was so charged or convicted, be admissible in any proceedings before any court established by Statute D or any Special Ordinance under Statute D.

2. Any notice required by Statute D, or by Ordinance or regulation made under it, to be sent to any person may be sent to the address supplied to the Registrary by that person's College as her or his usual or last known address.

3. If the time for which any member of one of the aforesaid courts has been appointed expires after a charge or appeal has been brought before the court but before it has been disposed of, such member shall (and her or his successor shall not) be a member of the court for the purpose of hearing and determining that charge or appeal.

4. If, after a charge or appeal has been brought before any of the aforesaid courts but before it has been disposed of, one or more members of the court become unable or unwilling to act, the remaining members of the court may continue the hearing and determine the case notwithstanding that they do not constitute a quorum for that court.

5. Any person whose case is adjudicated upon by the Court of Discipline shall be given a reasoned decision in writing.

6. Any person who is deprived of membership of the University or whose membership of the University is suspended shall not, during the continuance of such deprivation or suspension, be eligible to be admitted to any degree, or to receive any diploma or certificate, or to be a candidate for any examination; and any person upon whom a sentence other than deprivation or suspension of membership of the University is imposed under any of the provisions of Statute D or any Special Ordinance made under it and who fails to comply with such sentence shall not be eligible to be admitted to any degree, or to receive any diploma or certificate, or, except with the consent of the Council, to be a candidate for any examination.

7. Every complaint against a person who comes within the jurisdiction of the University Tribunal or the Court of Discipline (other than a complaint against a University officer under the Schedule to Statute C)[1] which requests that a matter be made the subject of proceedings before either of those courts shall be considered by the University Advocate, provided that only a member of the Regent House shall be entitled to make a complaint alleging that a person who comes within the jurisdiction of the University Tribunal has committed grave misconduct, and that only a member or an employee of the University shall be entitled to make a complaint alleging that a person who comes within the

[1] Cross-reference may be amended by Grace pursuant to Statute C I 8(*c*).

jurisdiction of either of those courts has committed an offence under the general regulations for discipline. It shall be the duty of the Advocate to determine whether the person against whom the complaint is made shall be charged and if so before which court; provided that the Advocate shall reject any complaint

(*a*) if it does not specify the name, and College (if any), of the person against whom it is made; *or*

(*b*) if in the Advocate's opinion the evidence presented is not sufficient to enable her or him to decide whether the person should be so charged; *or*

(*c*) if in the Advocate's opinion a complaint is vexatious, frivolous, or trivial; *or*

(*d*) if in the Advocate's opinion a complaint of grave misconduct is not of sufficiently direct concern to the University to justify its being brought before the University Tribunal.

No proceedings shall be initiated before any of the University courts established by this Statute or any Special Ordinance under this Statute, other than proceedings under the provisions of the Schedule to Statute C,[1] unless the Advocate has so determined in accordance with this section and with any Ordinance made under Statute D.

SPECIAL ORDINANCES UNDER STATUTE G

COLLEGES AND COLLEGIATE FOUNDATIONS

SPECIAL ORDINANCE G (i):

Professorial Fellowships: the obligations of Colleges in respect of Fellowships
(Special Ordinance under Statute G IV 6)

1. Every College shall maintain the number of Fellowships without dividend allotted to it in Schedule G (i) 1 for such Professors or other University officers as are specified Schedule C (vii) 1. The Fellowships required to be maintained as aforesaid are hereinafter termed Professorial Fellowships, and the number of such Fellowships allotted to a College is hereinafter termed the quota. A person holding or appointed or elected to hold an office placed in Schedule C (vii) 1 shall not be elected at a College to any Fellowship other than a Professorial Fellowship. An officer specified Schedule C (vii) 1 who is the Head of a College shall be deemed to be the holder of a Professorial Fellowship in that College.

2. The Council shall in the year 2016 and in every tenth year thereafter consider Schedule G (i) 1 and may in that year, or, if they think fit, in any intermediary year propose a revision thereof. The Council shall publish any proposed revision to the University and, save as hereinafter provided, the proposed revision shall become effective when thirty days of full term have elapsed after its publication. At any time within that period any College affected by the proposed revision may make representations to the Chancellor. Thereafter the Chancellor shall have power to make the proposed revision or any modification thereof approved by the Council or to make no revision.

3. The University may make alterations in Schedule G (i) 1 from time to time by Grace.

4. A College shall not have power to elect to a Professorial Fellowship a person holding, or appointed or elected to hold an office placed in Schedule C (vii) 1, unless at the time of the election to such a Fellowship *either*

(i) it has among its Fellows a number competent to hold Professorial Fellowships less than its quota of such Fellowships; *or*

(ii) at each College among its Fellows the number competent to hold Professorial Fellowships is not less than its quota of such Fellowships; *or*

(iii) he or she has held the office for two years and throughout that time it has been placed in Schedule C (vii) 1:

provided that

(*a*) this section shall not debar a College or other competent authority from appointing to the Headship of the College a person holding or appointed or elected to hold an office placed in Schedule C (vii) 1, nor shall it debar a College from electing to a Professorial Fellowship a person holding such an office who at the time of her or his appointment or election to the office (even if the office was not then Schedule C (vii) 1) was or had previously been a Fellow of the College;

[1] Cross-reference may be amended by Grace pursuant to Statute C I 8(*c*).

(*b*) this section shall not debar a College from electing to a Professorial Fellowship a person holding, or appointed to hold, the office of Vice-Chancellor;

(*c*) this section shall not debar the Dixie Professor of Ecclesiastical History from becoming a Professorial Fellow of Emmanuel College, or the Regius Professor of Greek from becoming a Professorial Fellow of Trinity College, or the Downing Professor of the Laws of England from becoming a Professorial Fellow of Downing College, or the Churchill Professor of Mathematics for Operational Research from becoming a Professorial Fellow of Churchill College;

(*d*) this section shall not debar a College from electing to a Professorial Fellowship, with effect from a date not later than a date in the academical year next but one following, a person holding, or appointed or elected to hold an office placed in Schedule C (vii) 1, if it appears to the University Registrary that on the day from which such election is to take effect the College would, unless the election were made, have among its Fellows a number of such persons less than its quota of Professorial Fellowships;

(*e*) for the purposes of the conditions numbered (i) and (ii) in this section a person elected to a Professorial Fellowship with effect from a future date shall from the day on which such election is made be reckoned as if he or she were already a Fellow competent to hold a Professorial Fellowship;

(*f*) in the application of this section to a College of which only men may be Fellows, Colleges of which only women may be Fellows shall be disregarded and *vice versa*;

(*g*) in the application of this section to Colleges of which both men and women may be Fellows, Colleges of which only men may be Fellows shall be disregarded if the person to be elected is a woman and *vice versa*;

(*h*) during the year in which a quota is first allotted to a College and during the five years next following that year, the College shall be deemed to have satisfied the condition numbered (ii) in this section when it has among its Fellows a number competent to hold Professorial Fellowships which is less by one than its quota of such Fellowships;

(*i*) if among the Fellows of any College the total number[1] of persons competent to hold Professorial Fellowships has for a continuous period of nine months been less than the quota of such Fellowships for that College, and if the College certifies to the Registrary that during such period it has been unable to elect to Professorial Fellowships a sufficient number of persons to satisfy the condition numbered (ii) in this section, the College may, if it so consents, be deemed for a period not exceeding one year (calculated from the date on which the College's certificate is received by the Registrary) to have satisfied that condition.

5. If among the Fellows of any College the actual number of persons competent to hold Professorial Fellowships is less than the quota of such Fellowships for that College, and if there are in the University five or more persons competent to hold Professorial Fellowships but not holding Fellowships at any College, that College shall take steps to ensure that the vacancy is filled not later than one year after its occurrence, provided that

(*a*) in the application of this section to a College of which only men may be Fellows, five or more persons shall mean five or more men, and in the application of this section to a College of which only women may be Fellows, five or more persons shall mean five or more women;

(*b*) if a College shall have offered a Professorial Fellowship to a competent person, and if that person shall have declined the offer, the College shall be entitled to reckon her or him, for the purposes of its obligations under this chapter, as not competent to hold a Professorial Fellowship.

6. A Fellowship with dividend shall not be tenable by an officer specified in Schedule C (vii) 1, provided that this section shall not debar such an officer from receiving from a College as dividend the whole or part of the remuneration due to her or him as Head of the College.

7. Any dispute between the University and a College regarding the obligations of the College under this Special Ordinance shall be referred to the Council, from which an appeal shall lie to the Chancellor.

8. In the application of this Special Ordinance to a College which is able under its Statutes to elect men or women to Fellowships but which, if previously a College of which only men might be Fellows has never elected a woman (other than a bursar) to a Fellowship, or if previously a College of which only women might be Fellows has never elected a man (other than a bursar) to a Fellowship, that College shall be deemed to be a College of which only men may be Fellows or of which only women

[1] Calculated in accordance with the provisions of Section 4(*d*).

may be Fellows as the case may be; provided that in either case for the purpose of the first election of a Professorial Fellow of the opposite sex Section 4 of this Special Ordinance shall apply as if the College were one of which both men and women may be Fellows.

9. A Professorship placed in Schedule C (vii) 1 may be specified by Grace as a Professorship which, for the purpose of this Special Ordinance, shall also be placed in Schedule G (i) 2. A Professorship placed in Schedule G (i) 2 shall be governed by the following special provisions notwithstanding anything contained in Sections 4 and 5 of this Special Ordinance

(*a*) a College may elect a person or persons holding a Professorship so specified to a Professorial Fellowship although the College has at the time a number of Professorial Fellows not less than its quota of Professorial Fellowships;

(*b*) a College which shall elect a person or persons holding a Professorship so specified to a Professorial Fellowship may include that Fellowship, or those Fellowships, among its Professorial Fellowships for the purpose of satisfying its obligations under Section 1 of this Special Ordinance;

(*c*) a College which has elected a person or persons holding a Professorship so specified to a Professorial Fellowship may exclude that Fellowship, or those Fellowships, from its Professorial Fellowships for the purpose of determining whether the College is entitled to make a further election.

10. For the purposes of this Special Ordinance:

(*a*) a Fellow of a College with dividend shall mean a Fellow who is entitled to a share of the divisible balance of the corporate revenue of the College in each year, or of any other funds applicable to the payment of the emolument of a Fellowship, and a Fellowship with dividend means a Fellowship held by a Fellow with dividend;

(*b*) a Fellow of a College without dividend shall mean a Fellow who is not entitled as aforesaid, although entitled to the same commons and allowances as Fellows with dividend, and a Fellowship without dividend means a Fellowship held by a Fellow without dividend.

Schedule G (i) 1

Quotas of Professorial Fellowships for the several Colleges and Approved Societies

(This schedule is amended by Grace)

Christ's	5
Churchill	7
Clare	3
Clare Hall	2
Corpus Christi	3
Darwin	3
Downing	4
Emmanuel	4
Fitzwilliam	3
Girton	4
Gonville and Caius	8
Homerton	0
Hughes Hall	2
Jesus	4
King's	8
Lucy Cavendish	0
Magdalene	2
Murray Edwards	1
Newnham	1
Pembroke	3
Peterhouse	3
Queens'	3
Robinson	2
St Catharine's	3
St Edmund's	1
St John's	10
Selwyn	3
Sidney Sussex	3
Trinity	13
Trinity Hall	3
Wolfson	3

Schedule G (i) 2

Professorships subject to Section 9

(This schedule is amended by Grace)

BBV Foundation Visiting Professor
Simón Bolívar Professorship of Latin-American Studies
Arthur Goodhart Visiting Professorship in Legal Science
Jawaharlal Nehru Visiting Professorship
Pitt Professorship of American History and Institutions
French Government Visiting Professor
Pembroke Visiting Professor of International Finance
Humanitas Visiting Professorships

ORDINANCES OF THE UNIVERSITY OF CAMBRIDGE

CHAPTER I

THE CHANCELLOR AND THE GOVERNMENT OF THE UNIVERSITY

CAMBRIDGE UNIVERSITY REPORTER

1. The *Cambridge University Reporter* shall contain Contents.

(*a*) in its official part, University Notices issued by authority;

(*b*) in its unofficial part, reports of Discussions held under Special Ordinance A (i) 2; notices of *non placet* of Graces, without comment (other than references to the Reports discussed), signed by persons entitled to vote; notices, not authorized for inclusion in the official part, of lectures and other instruction; notices sent by Colleges; notices and reports of learned societies connected with the University; and such advertisements as the Registrary may think fit to insert.

2. Numbers of the *Reporter* shall be published at the discretion of the Registrary. Publication in the *Reporter* shall include publication on the *Reporter* website (http://www.admin.cam.ac.uk/reporter/). This publication shall include from time to time, and at least weekly during term, a consolidated issue of all new Notices, Reports, Graces, and other items which have appeared on the website. If publication in the *Reporter* of a Report, Grace, Notice, or other matter as required by any Statute or Ordinance is not possible for a period or by a specified date, it shall be sufficient publication for the purpose of the Statute or Ordinance if the Registrary causes it to be posted outside the Senate-House and a copy of it to be sent to the Head of each College and Approved Society, the Chair of each Faculty, the Head of each Department, and the Director or corresponding officer responsible for every other institution of the University, with a request for its publication within the institution; in such circumstances the Report, Grace, Notice, or other matter shall be published also in the *Reporter* as soon as it becomes possible. Publication.

NOMINATION AND ELECTION OF THE CHANCELLOR

1. There shall be a Nomination Board which shall consist of Nomination Board.

(*a*) the members for the time being of the Council;

(*b*) sixteen members of the Senate, four appointed each year by Grace of the Senate on the nomination of the Council to serve for four years, provided that of these four at least one shall be a person who is not resident in the University and at least one other shall be a person who has been a member of the Senate for not more than fifteen years on the date of appointment.

2. The Registrary shall be Secretary of the Nomination Board.

3. When it is known that the office of Chancellor is vacant or, if the vacancy has not yet occurred, that the Chancellor has determined the date on which he or she will resign, the Vice-Chancellor shall give public notice of the matter and of the prescribed date for the purpose of these regulations. If there is a vacancy in the office the date of such notice shall be the prescribed date. If the vacancy has not yet occurred, the prescribed date shall be either the date of such notice or seventy days of term before the vacancy is due to occur, whichever is later. In such notice the Vice-Chancellor shall also invite members of the Senate to submit, within twenty-one days of term after the prescribed date, the names of any persons whom they wish the Nomination Board to consider. Procedure for election.

4. Not more than seventy days of term after the prescribed date the Nomination Board shall give public notice of the name of a candidate whom they nominate, and shall certify that they have obtained the candidate's consent in writing to be so nominated; provided that in exceptional circumstances the Council may permit such a nomination to be published at a later date than is here specified.

5. In addition to the candidate nominated by the Nomination Board, any other person shall be eligible whose nomination has been received by the Vice-Chancellor not earlier than the date of publication of the Board's nomination and not later than twenty-eight days of term after that date. Such a nomination shall be signed by not less than fifty members of the Senate, and shall be accompanied by a statement, signed by the nominee, consenting to be so nominated.

6. A candidate who has been duly nominated may withdraw from the election by lodging notice in writing to that effect with the Vice-Chancellor not later than seven days before the first of the days appointed for voting under Regulation 8(*b*).

7. On receipt of a valid notice of the withdrawal of a candidate the Vice-Chancellor shall give public notice of such withdrawal; and notwithstanding any preceding provision of these regulations, the period within which nominations may be received shall continue for twenty-eight days of term after the day on which such notice is given, and if days for voting have been appointed under Regulation 8(*b*) their appointment shall be deemed to be rescinded. If the candidate of whose withdrawal the Vice-Chancellor gives notice has been nominated by the Nomination Board, that body shall within twenty-one days of term after the day on which the Vice-Chancellor gives such notice either

(*a*) give public notice of the name of a further candidate whom they nominate, and certify that they have obtained that candidate's consent in writing to such nomination; or

(*b*) give public notice that they do not intend to make a further nomination.

8. On the day following the last day on which nominations may be received

(*a*) if there is one candidate only, the Vice-Chancellor shall give public notice that that candidate is elected;

(*b*) if there are two or more candidates, the Vice-Chancellor shall give public notice appointing two days of term, which need not be consecutive, for voting; provided that neither of those days shall be less than twenty-one or more than thirty-five days of term after the day on which such notice is given, and that one of them shall be a Saturday.

9. Voting shall take place between the hours of 10 a.m. and 8 p.m. on each of the appointed days, provided that, where necessary to allow for all persons who were present before 8 p.m. to cast their vote, the returning officer may announce an extension to these hours. Voting shall be in person, and the method of voting and of counting the votes shall be that provided for in the Single Transferable Vote regulations.

10. If information is received at any time before the completion of the election of the death of any candidate the Vice-Chancellor shall forthwith give public notice of it. All proceedings taken under these regulations before the date of that notice shall be treated as ineffectual, and the provisions of the preceding regulations shall apply as if the date of the notice were the prescribed date.

High Steward. **11.** These regulations shall apply to the election of the High Steward in the same way as to the election of the Chancellor.

No act on Sunday. **12.** If any day fixed by the application of these regulations is a Sunday, any action to be taken on or by that day shall be taken on or by the following Monday.

ROLL OF THE REGENT HOUSE

Amended by Grace 1 of 27 November 2013

1. On the first weekday in October the Registrary shall publish a list of the names which it is proposed to place on the Roll of the Regent House for the ensuing year. At the time of publication of the list the Vice-Chancellor shall fix a time and place for publicly hearing objections which any member of the University may make to the inclusion or omission of any name. The decision of the Vice-Chancellor regarding any such objection shall be final.

2. No person shall qualify for membership of the Regent House by virtue of holding a Fellowship of a College unless he or she is ordinarily resident within twenty miles of the University Church.

3. The Roll of the Regent House shall be promulgated on the fifth weekday in November.

Membership under Statute A III 10(e)

The categories of membership of the Regent House under Statute A III 10(*e*) shall be:

(i) holders of the appointments of Senior Research Associate, Research Associate, Lecturer (unestablished), and Assistant Lecturer (unestablished);

(ii) in any College: persons holding the office of Tutor, Assistant Tutor, Steward or Bursar or Assistant Bursar; or College Lecturer (if held full time in a College or Colleges). The Head of any College shall certify in writing to the Registrary by 1 October each year the names of such persons;

(iii) Computer Associates, Grades I, II, and III;

(iv) Affiliated Lecturers;

(v) holders of appointments on the staff of the Local Examination Syndicate as Group Chief Executive, Chief Executive, Deputy Chief Executive, Director, Assistant Director, and Senior Manager;

provided that no person shall qualify for membership in categories (i), (iii), or (iv) unless he or she is also a member of a Faculty, or holds an appointment listed in those categories in a Department or other University institution which is independent of a Faculty.

CONDUCT OF BUSINESS

Discussions

1. (*a*) Every Report submitted to the University shall be brought forward for consideration by the Regent House at a Discussion.

(*b*) If ten members of the Regent House submit a request on paper, by fax or by electronic mail from addresses within the cam.ac.uk domain to the Registrary that a topic of concern to the University should be brought forward for discussion, the Registrary shall report the request to the Council, and shall include the topic among the matters for consideration at an early Discussion.

2. When a Discussion is to be held, either of a Report or of any other matter, the Vice-Chancellor shall invite members of the Regent House to attend by means of a Notice published in the *Reporter*.

3. The following may also attend Discussions and take part:

(*a*) graduates of the University;

(*b*) members of Faculties;

(*c*) persons *in statu pupillari*;

(*d*) other persons authorized by the Vice-Chancellor to attend a particular Discussion.

4. The Vice-Chancellor or a duly appointed deputy shall preside at a Discussion.

5. The person presiding at a Discussion shall have power to impose a general limit on the length of speeches or to rule out of order particular remarks in a speech on the grounds that they are irrelevant or defamatory or to terminate the discussion of a particular topic.

6. Remarks made at a Discussion shall normally be published in the *Reporter*, provided that the Registrary, as editor of the *Reporter*, shall have discretion to omit or, with the agreement of the author, to amend any remarks which in his or her opinion are likely to be held to be defamatory. The Registrary shall not include in the formal record any remarks which are ruled out of order or which are otherwise in breach of a procedural ruling by the Vice-Chancellor or other person presiding. If any remarks are so omitted or amended, the Registrary shall include a note of the fact with the remarks as published.

Graces and Congregations of the Regent House

1. No Grace shall be submitted to the Regent House except with the authorization of the Council. Every Grace, other than a Supplicat for a degree or degrees, whether the Grace is initiated by the Council, or by some other University body, or by individual members of the Regent House under Special Ordinance A (i) 5, shall be put before the Council for authorization at a meeting, provided that a Grace shall be deemed to have been duly authorized if a copy of the Grace has been sent by the Registrary to every member of the Council so as to reach the member's address not later than the fifth day before the day specified for publication, and if no member has informed the Registrary of an objection to the Grace by 10 a.m. on the day next but one before the day of publication. The submission of Supplicats for degrees may be authorized by the Council in accordance with the procedure prescribed in the regulations for admission to degrees. Authorization.

2. Graces shall be submitted to the Regent House either by being published in the *Reporter* or by being read by the Senior Proctor at a Congregation. The procedure in connection with Graces submitted by publication shall be as prescribed in Regulations 4–15 below; the procedure in connection with Graces submitted at a Congregation shall be as prescribed in Regulations 16–30. Submission.

3. For the purpose of these regulations the expression 'term' shall be deemed to include that part of the Long Vacation during which it is provided by Ordinance that courses of instruction may be given within the Precincts of the University. Definition of term.

Graces submitted by publication

4. Except as provided in Regulations 16 and 21, every Grace relating to a matter which under Statute or Ordinance is to be determined by the Regent House shall be submitted to the Regent House by being published in the *Reporter*.

Approval. **5.** A Grace shall be deemed to have been approved by the Regent House at 4 p.m. on the Friday next but one after the day of its submission unless before that hour

either (*a*) the Grace has been withdrawn by the Vice-Chancellor in accordance with Regulation 6;

or (*b*) the Council have given notice in accordance with Regulation 7 that a vote is to be taken on the Grace;

or (*c*) a request has been received by the Vice-Chancellor for a vote to be taken on the Grace in accordance with Regulation 8;

or (*d*) a proposal has been received by the Vice-Chancellor for the amendment of the Grace in accordance with Regulation 9.

Withdrawal. **6.** A Grace may be withdrawn by the Vice-Chancellor (i) at any time before the hour specified in Regulation 5 for its approval, and (ii) if voting is requested (Regulation 5(*c*)) or (iii) if amendment is proposed (Regulation 5(*d*)), within three weeks after the day of its submission. Withdrawal of a Grace under this regulation shall be announced by means of a Notice posted outside the Senate-House and subsequently published. If the Council decide to resubmit such a Grace in its original form they shall either (*a*) call a ballot or (*b*) publish an explanatory Notice explaining why in their opinion a ballot is not necessary.

Ballots. **7.** The Council shall have power to determine that a vote shall be taken by ballot on any Grace. Notice of such a ballot shall be published in the *Reporter* when the Grace is submitted.

8. Any twenty-five members of the Regent House may submit a written request to the Vice-Chancellor for a vote to be taken on a Grace by ballot. If such a request is received by the Vice-Chancellor before the hour specified in Regulation 5 for the approval of the Grace, a ballot shall be held in accordance with the provisions of Regulation 13, unless the Grace is withdrawn under Regulation 6.

Amendments. **9.** A written proposal for the amendment of a Grace which has been submitted to the Regent House may be initiated by members of the Regent House in accordance with Special Ordinance A (i) 5, provided that the proposal is received by the Vice-Chancellor before the hour specified in Regulation 5 for the approval of the Grace or, if a request for a ballot on the Grace has been received, within one week of the date on which a Notice of the request has been published under Regulation 10 below. In that event, (unless the Grace is withdrawn under Regulation 6), and subject to the provisions of Special Ordinance A (i) 7 and of Regulation 11 below, a vote shall be taken by ballot, using the procedure prescribed in the Single Transferable Vote regulations; the options to be voted on shall include (*a*) approval of the proposal contained in the Grace as submitted to the Regent House, (*b*) rejection of the proposal, (*c*) approval of alternative proposals formulated in accordance with the amendment or amendments proposed, and may include (*d*) any further alternative proposal which may be formulated by the Council; provided that the Vice-Chancellor may instead decide that a vote shall be taken by ballot, using the procedure prescribed in the Single Transferable Vote regulations, between propositions that the Grace be left unamended or that it be substituted by one of such one or more alternative forms as may be determined by the Vice-Chancellor to reflect the amendment or amendments proposed. If an alternative form is approved, then that alternative form shall be substituted for the Grace as originally submitted, and shall be treated for all purposes as if it were that Grace. A ballot shall then be taken for the approval of the Grace, in accordance with Regulation 13 below.

Notice. **10.** If a request for voting is received under Regulation 8, or if a proposal for the amendment of a Grace is received under Regulation 9, the Vice-Chancellor shall give notice accordingly by means of a Notice posted outside the Senate-House and subsequently published. The Notice shall include the names of the persons who have requested the ballot or who have proposed the amendment, as the case may be.

11. The Vice-Chancellor shall have the following powers in respect of proposals initiated under Regulation 9 for the amendment of a Grace:

(*a*) If in the opinion of the Vice-Chancellor a proposed amendment is in substance and effect incompatible with the main purpose of the Grace to which it refers, or immaterial to that purpose, the Vice-Chancellor may rule the amendment inadmissible, or may refer it to the Council for subsequent separate submission as a Grace. The proposers of such an amendment shall be deemed to have requested that a vote be taken on the Grace in accordance with Regulation 8 above.

(*b*) If two or more amendments have been proposed which in the opinion of the Vice-Chancellor are substantially similar in effect the Vice-Chancellor may select one of the amendments for submission to the Regent House and may rule the other or others inadmissible.

(*c*) The Vice-Chancellor shall have authority to determine the form in which the various propositions are set out in the voting papers; without prejudice to the generality of that power (i) if in the opinion of the Vice-Chancellor a proposed amendment comprises two or more separable propositions, the Vice-Chancellor may treat the amendment as if it were a number of amendments, each comprising one or more of those propositions as the Vice-Chancellor may determine; and (ii) the Vice-Chancellor may determine that votes shall be taken on propositions as if they were separate Graces, each such Grace being treated for all purposes as if it were the Grace as originally submitted. The Vice-Chancellor shall if necessary indicate in the voting papers (i) whether the result of voting is effective without a further Grace (by rescinding or amending a Statute, Ordinance or Order, or otherwise) or (ii) whether a further Grace would be needed to implement the result of voting.

12. If a ballot is to be held under any of Regulations 7–9, the arrangements for voting shall be determined by the Vice-Chancellor, subject to the provisions of Regulation 13, and shall be published in the *Reporter*.

13. For a ballot on a Grace of the Regent House, or a ballot held under the provisions of Regulation 9 above, the period during which votes may be cast by all members of the Regent House shall commence not later than a day appointed by the Vice-Chancellor, which shall be neither less than fourteen days nor normally more than twenty-eight days of term after the publication of the Notice announcing the ballot; provided that the Vice-Chancellor shall have power to postpone the commencement of voting until a date not later than eighty days of term after the publication of the Notice. The Vice-Chancellor shall give public notice of the period during which votes may be cast. The latest time for casting a vote shall be not earlier than the tenth day after the day appointed for the commencement of voting. Ballot.

14. When a ballot is held in accordance with the preceding regulations, the presiding officer shall be the Vice-Chancellor or a duly appointed deputy. The presiding officer shall

(*a*) arrange for the counting of the votes as soon as possible after the conclusion of the voting;
(*b*) decide upon the validity of any doubtful vote;
(*c*) declare the result as soon as the counting of the votes is completed.

If there is an equality of votes, the Grace or amendment shall be deemed not to be approved. The result of a ballot shall be announced by means of a Notice posted outside the Senate-House and subsequently published.

15. If an obvious or immaterial error occurs in the published form of a Grace or amendment, the Vice-Chancellor may announce a correction by means of a Notice published in the *Reporter* and for the purpose of Regulation 5 or Regulation 9, as the case may be, the Grace or amendment shall be deemed to have been submitted in its corrected form. Correction of errors.

Graces submitted at a Congregation

16. The Council shall have power at their discretion to submit Graces on the following matters to the Regent House at a Congregation:

(*a*) Graces for the conferment of a degree or degrees;
(*b*) Graces concerning any matter on which in the opinion of the Council or the Vice-Chancellor a decision must be taken urgently.

17. Except as provided in Regulation 21, Congregations of the Regent House shall be held in the Senate-House or elsewhere within the Precincts of the University at such times as may be appointed by the Vice-Chancellor by means of a Notice published in the *Reporter*. If in the opinion of the Vice-Chancellor a Congregation cannot be held at the place announced, the Vice-Chancellor may determine that the Congregation shall be held elsewhere within the Precincts of the University; provided that Notice.

(*a*) such notice as may be practicable shall be given beforehand;
(*b*) no Grace shall be submitted at the Congregation unless there are at least twenty members of the Regent House present.

If the Vice-Chancellor is not available, the powers of the Vice-Chancellor under this regulation may be exercised by one of the Pro-Vice-Chancellors or by a Deputy Vice-Chancellor.

Constitution. **18.** In order to constitute a Congregation the presence of the following officers, or of deputies for them appointed in accordance with the several provisions of the Statutes, shall be necessary: the Chancellor or the Vice-Chancellor, the two Proctors, and the Registrary; provided that, in respect of a Congregation held before the Vice-Chancellor has been formally admitted to office,

(*a*) the presence of the Chancellor or the Vice-Chancellor shall not be necessary;

(*b*) if the Chancellor is absent, the Proctors shall exercise the powers and perform the duties of the Vice-Chancellor.

19. The two Pro-Proctors who have been nominated by Colleges shall either in person or by deputies approved by the Vice-Chancellor attend all Congregations; the other Pro-Proctors shall attend all such Congregations as the Vice-Chancellor may request them to attend.

Publication of Graces. **20.** Except as provided in Regulation 21, every Grace to be submitted at a Congregation, other than a formal Supplicat for a degree or degrees, shall be published in the *Reporter* before 4 p.m. on the day next but one preceding the Congregation at which the Grace is to be submitted.

Cases of urgency. **21.** If any matter should arise at any time upon which in the opinion of the Vice-Chancellor it is desirable that a decision should be taken at once, a Grace relating to such matter may be submitted, without being previously published in the *Reporter*, at a Congregation held at such time and place within the Precincts of the University as the Vice-Chancellor shall determine; provided that

(*a*) such notice as may be practicable is given beforehand,

(*b*) there are at least twenty members of the Regent House present at the Congregation when the Grace is submitted,

(*c*) when a Grace is brought forward of which notice has not been given beforehand in accordance with Regulation 20, the attention of the Congregation shall be formally and distinctly called to the fact,

(*d*) the Grace and the decision on the Grace shall be published subsequently in the *Reporter*.

If the Vice-Chancellor is not available, the powers of the Vice-Chancellor under this regulation may be exercised by one of the Pro-Vice-Chancellors or by a Deputy Vice-Chancellor.

Withdrawal. **22.** A Grace of which notice of submission at a Congregation has been given may be withdrawn by the Vice-Chancellor at any time before it is submitted; provided that

(*a*) the attention of the Congregation shall be formally and distinctly called by the Vice-Chancellor to the withdrawal;

(*b*) the Vice-Chancellor shall subsequently explain the reasons for the withdrawal to the Council.

Correction of errors. **23.** If an obvious or immaterial error occurs in the published form of a Grace it may be corrected at the Congregation by the Vice-Chancellor, provided that the attention of the Congregation shall be formally and distinctly called by the Vice-Chancellor to any such correction.

Submission. *Non placet.* **24.** All Graces submitted to the Regent House at a Congregation shall be read audibly at the Congregation by the Senior Proctor. Any member of the Regent House who wishes to oppose a Grace may do so by calling *Non placet* immediately after the Grace has been read. If *Non placet* is called, a vote shall be taken on the Grace; provided that, if written notice of intention to oppose the Grace has not been received by the Registrary and published in the *Reporter* before the Congregation, the Vice-Chancellor shall have power to withdraw the Grace. A Grace so withdrawn shall be resubmitted, either at a Congregation or by publication, as soon as convenient thereafter.

Voting. **25.** When in accordance with Regulation 24 a vote is to be taken on a Grace submitted at a Congregation, voting shall take place forthwith in accordance with the procedure prescribed in Regulations 26–29; provided that the Vice-Chancellor shall have power to determine that the vote shall be taken at a later date by ballot.

26. If a vote on a Grace submitted at a Congregation is to be taken forthwith, the Senior Esquire Bedell shall once or oftener, as necessary, call in an audible voice *Ad scrutinium.* Members of the Regent House who desire to vote shall assemble, if they are in favour of the Grace, on the south side of the Senate-House and, if they are opposed to it, on the north side.

27. If in the opinion of both Proctors the result of such a division is obvious, the Senior Proctor shall forthwith declare the result without taking the votes singly; but any two members of the Regent House may in such a case request the Vice-Chancellor to direct that the votes shall be taken singly, and the Vice-Chancellor shall thereupon so direct.

28. Whenever the votes are taken singly, either in consequence of the Vice-Chancellor's direction or because the Proctors do not regard the result of the division as obvious, those members of the Regent House who are in favour of the Grace shall vote on the south side of the Senate-House and those who are opposed to it on the north side. The votes of those who are on the south side shall be taken singly by the Senior Proctor and one of the two Pro-Proctors; the votes of those who are on the north side shall be taken singly at the same time by the Junior Proctor and the other of the two Pro-Proctors.

Each voter shall vote by delivering to a Proctor (or to a Pro-Proctor) a card on which shall be inscribed

(*a*) the voter's name, degree, and College,

(*b*) the word *Placet* or the words *Non placet* (as the case may be),

(*c*) the number of the Grace to which the card applies (if more than one Grace is opposed at the Congregation).

29. The Vice-Chancellor shall have power to determine whether the votes shall be counted forthwith or whether the counting shall be deferred until the end of the Congregation. If the results of the voting are ascertained forthwith, the Senior Proctor, after communicating the number of votes on each side to the Vice-Chancellor, shall declare them publicly to the Congregation. If the votes are counted after the end of the Congregation the results shall be published by a Notice posted outside the Senate-House as soon as they have been ascertained.

30. If the Vice-Chancellor determines under the provisions of Regulation 25 that voting on any Grace is to be by postal ballot, the Senior Proctor shall make an announcement to that effect at the Congregation. Such a ballot shall be conducted in accordance with Regulations 12–14 above.

GRACES OF THE SENATE

1. In the following regulations the term Grace shall mean Grace of the Senate.

2. No Grace shall be submitted to the Senate except with the authorization of the Council. Every Grace shall be put before the Council for authorization at a meeting, provided that a Grace may be deemed to have been duly authorized under the alternative procedure specified in Regulation 1 of the regulations for Graces of the Regent House. Authorization.

3. Graces shall be submitted to the Senate by being published in the *Reporter*. Submission.

4. A Grace shall be deemed to have been approved by the Senate at 4 p.m. on the Friday next but one after the day of its submission unless before that hour Approval.

either (*a*) the Grace has been withdrawn by the Vice-Chancellor in accordance with Regulation 5;

or (*b*) the Council have given notice in accordance with Regulation 6 that a vote is to be taken on the Grace;

or (*c*) a request has been received by the Vice-Chancellor for a vote to be taken on the Grace in accordance with Regulation 7.

5. A Grace may be withdrawn by the Vice-Chancellor at any time before the hour specified in Regulation 4 for its approval, provided that the Vice-Chancellor shall not have power to withdraw any Grace in respect of which a vote has been requested under Regulation 4(*c*). Withdrawal of a Grace under this regulation shall be announced by means of a Notice posted outside the Senate-House and subsequently published. Withdrawal.

6. The Council shall have power to determine that a vote shall be taken by ballot on any Grace. Notice of such a ballot shall be published in the *Reporter* when the Grace is submitted. Ballots.

7. Any ten members of the Senate may submit a written request to the Vice-Chancellor for a vote to be taken on a Grace by ballot. If such a request is received by the Vice-Chancellor before the hour specified in Regulation 4 for the approval of the Grace, a ballot shall be held in accordance with the provisions of Regulation 10.

8. If a request for voting is received under Regulation 7, the Vice-Chancellor shall give notice accordingly by means of a Notice posted outside the Senate-House and subsequently published. The Notice shall include the names of the persons who have requested the ballot.

9. If a ballot is to be held under Regulation 6 or Regulation 7, the arrangements for voting shall be determined by the Vice-Chancellor, subject to the provisions of Regulation 10, and shall be published in the *Reporter*.

10. In a ballot of the Senate voters shall give their votes in person. The Vice-Chancellor shall appoint two days, which need not be consecutive, for voting; provided that

(*a*) neither of the days appointed shall be less than fourteen days or normally more than twenty-eight days of term after the publication of the Notice announcing the ballot;

(*b*) one of the days appointed shall be a Saturday;

(*c*) the Vice-Chancellor shall have power to postpone the holding of the ballot until a date not later than eighty days of term after the publication of the Notice.

Voting shall take place between the hours of 10 a.m. and 4 p.m. on each of the appointed days.

11. The arrangements for presiding over a ballot of the Senate, for counting the votes, and for announcing the result shall be as prescribed in Regulation 14 of the regulations for Graces of the Regent House.

Correction of errors.

12. The arrangements for the correction of obvious or immaterial errors in Graces of the Senate shall be as prescribed in Regulation 15 of the regulations for Graces of the Regent House.

Notice by the Council

Discussions and Fly-sheets

Discussions

1. The Council are of the view that a Discussion is likely to be more representative of different points of view, and hence more fruitful, if speakers will regard fifteen minutes as the normal maximum duration of a speech.

2. The Council consider it inappropriate for a speaker at a Discussion to include in his or her remarks a list of the names of persons who support the speaker's views. They have requested the Vice-Chancellor or other person presiding at a Discussion to rule out of order any speaker who attempts to read out such a list.

3. The Council wish to remind those attending Discussions that the Vice-Chancellor or other person presiding at a Discussion has authority to make procedural rulings which must be observed by those present.

4. Remarks should be germane to the topic under discussion. Irrelevant remarks may be ruled out of order by the Vice-Chancellor or other person presiding at a Discussion. A person whose remarks are ruled out of order is expected to respect such ruling and to restrict further remarks to the topic under discussion, or to terminate his or her remarks. Remarks which are ruled out of order, or which are otherwise in breach of a procedural ruling by the Vice-Chancellor or other person presiding do not form part of the Discussion and will not be published.

5. The Council believe that members of the Regent House and others qualified or invited to speak in Discussions will wish ordinary standards of courtesy and restraint to be observed in remarks made in Discussions.

Fly-sheets and other statements

Statements issued by members of the Regent House

6. To enable members of the Regent House to make known their views on questions which are to be the subject of a ballot, the Council have authorized the Registrary to arrange for the circulation of statements on such issues, provided that any such statement is signed by at least ten members of the Regent House. The University will bear the cost of reproducing and circulating such a statement if it reaches the Registrary by 1 p.m. on a day specified by the Council; each statement must bear the names and initials (in block capital letters) of the signatories. The specified day will be not earlier than the eighth day (or exceptionally the seventh day) following the publication of the Council's Notice announcing a ballot; provided that the Registrary may accept up to twenty-four hours later a statement signed by a representative of the body whose proposal is to be voted on. In order that they may be readily available for reference, all statements which have been issued as fly-sheets will be published in the *Reporter* after the proposals to which they relate have been voted on. In relation to any statements made in a fly-sheet which may be held to be defamatory, the Council have agreed that the Registrary, after consultation with the Vice-Chancellor, shall have discretion to decide whether such statements are to be included in the fly-sheet as published in the *Reporter*. The Registrary will inform the Council of any amendment made to a fly-sheet in this way.

Statements issued by members of the Senate

7. Arrangements similar to those described in paragraph 6 will apply *mutatis mutandis* to statements issued by members of the Senate in connection with ballots of the Senate. Such statements will not be circulated as fly-sheets, but will be published in the *Reporter* before the ballot.

Statements issued by persons in statu pupillari

8. The procedure described in paragraph 6 above for the issue of fly-sheets by members of the Regent House will apply *mutatis mutandis* to fly-sheets issued in connection with ballots of the Regent House by members of the University *in statu pupillari*. The Vice-Chancellor may, however, determine on a particular occasion that such members may not submit fly-sheets. Fly-sheets must be signed by at least five of the following: the President, the Deputy Presidents, and the Women's Officer of Cambridge University Students Union, the President of the Graduate Union, the three student members of the Council, the Presidents of College Junior Combination Rooms and Middle Combination Rooms (or their equivalents) and, in the case of a proposal from a Faculty Board or similar body, the student members of the body concerned. The Council have agreed that the Vice-Chancellor may, for reasons of economy, limit the number of such fly-sheets to be published on any occasion and that such a limitation may be announced at the outset or when the total number of fly-sheets is known. Fly-sheets signed by persons *in statu pupillari* will be circulated to members of the Regent House only.

THE COUNCIL

Legal Powers

The Council shall have authority to take legal advice, retain solicitors, and bring, defend, or conduct legal proceedings on behalf of the University as they may think necessary or desirable in the interests of the University.

Appeals to the Council

Subject to the provisions of the Schedule to Statute C, the Council shall hear appeals from any person who comes within the jurisdiction of the University Tribunal under Statute D II 2 and upon whom a University authority has, under Statute A II 12 and in accordance with an Ordinance or with a rule made under Ordinance, imposed a sentence, provided that such a person has delivered to the Registrary, within twenty-eight days after notice of the sentence imposed by the University authority concerned, written notice of his or her appeal to the Council. The Council shall have power to quash the finding or to vary the sentence within the limits of the power of that authority, and the decision of the Council shall be final.

Reserved Business

Under the provisions of Special Ordinance A (vii) 5(iii) proposals for the conferment of degrees or titles of degrees, and any matter which would for a Faculty Board be reserved business under the provisions of Regulation 11 of the General Regulations for the Constitution of the Faculty Boards, shall be reserved business for the Council.

Review of Decisions of the Applications Committee

The Council shall establish a procedure for the review of decisions taken by it in respect of individuals in exercise of its powers in respect of allowances of terms under the regulations for Residence and the Precincts of the University and its powers under the regulations for allowances to candidates for examinations. No person who applies for review under the procedure so established shall be entitled to apply also for review of the same matter under the procedure for determining complaints by members of the University *in statu pupillari* established under the regulation for complaints by students (p. 220).

APPENDIX

Review of decisions of the Applications Committee of the Council: procedure

1. A student, or her or his Tutor with the student's consent, may seek review of a decision in relation to that student made by the Applications Committee.

2. A request for review shall be made in writing, stating the grounds of review, normally within three weeks of written notification of the Committee's decision (unless, in exceptional circumstances, the Registrary or a deputy permits a longer period). If the request includes, in the opinion of the Chair of the Committee, relevant additional information not previously available, the Committee will reconsider its decision at its next meeting following receipt of the request. If no such additional information is included or if, on reconsideration, the decision is reaffirmed by the Committee, the procedure described in the following paragraphs shall apply.

3. The Registrary or a deputy will appoint a reviewer chosen from a panel of potential reviewers maintained by the Council. Exceptionally, a panel of three reviewers may be appointed. If so, references below to 'the reviewer' shall be construed accordingly.

4. The reviewer will consider the request, the documentation available to the Committee (less any confidential medical information), the Ordinances which apply to the Committee's decision, and the Committee's Notes of Guidance. He or she will obtain an opinion from the Committee, seek such other information as he or she may require and, at her or his discretion, may hold a hearing (but there is no obligation to hold a hearing). The reviewer will issue an adjudication in writing as soon as possible, stating findings of fact, conclusions, and, if any, recommendations, for consideration by the Committee. The reviewer shall be concerned with determining whether there is evidence of: inadequate consideration of the matter by the Committee; the Committee having made a decision, to the detriment of the student, which is inconsistent with the relevant Ordinances or its own Notes of Guidance; or material circumstances of which the Committee was unaware and which were of such a nature as, had the Committee been so aware, to have been likely to cause the Committee to have reached a different decision.

5. The Committee shall normally accept the recommendation of the reviewer. If, exceptionally, the reviewer's recommendation is not accepted, a written explanation shall be provided to the reviewer, the student, and her or his Tutor and shall be submitted to the Council. The Committee may decide not to accept a recommendation in any instance in which: (i) the reviewer has sought to make a decision replacing that of the Committee; (ii) the reviewer's recommendation is inconsistent with the Ordinances governing Allowances; or (iii) the reviewer's recommendation is such that, were it to be accepted, it would set a precedent which would not be in the interests of the proper conduct of Committee's business or in the wider interests of the University. The Council (or an officer appointed by it) should be satisfied that the Committee's written explanation is consistent with one or more of these instances.

6. The conclusion of the Committee's consideration of any recommendation of a review is the normal final point of decision within the University. Any subsequent review would normally be by the national Office of the Independent Adjudicator for Higher Education, or exceptionally, if relevant, some other University review (for example by the Commissary under Statute A I 13 and A IX 3–10 and the rules of procedure (p. 61) or under Statute A IX 1.

7. A reviewer may summarily dismiss an application which seems to her or him to be vexatious or frivolous.

Notice by the Council

Statement of intention

In carrying out their functions as the principal executive and policy-making body of the University the Council will consult the Regent House on questions of policy which in the Council's judgement are likely to prove controversial. They will do this by submitting a Grace to the Regent House for the approval of a provisional decision or statement of intention; where appropriate, such a Grace will allow for the expression of a preference between alternative options. The Council will give consideration to remarks made at any Discussion of such matters and to the outcome of any vote on them.

Election of Members of the Council

Members in classes (a)–(c)

Ballot. **1.** At each election of a member or members of the Council in any of classes (*a*), (*b*), and (*c*) voting shall be as set out in Regulations 2–7 below.

2. The election shall be conducted in accordance with the Single Transferable Vote regulations.

3. The period during which votes may be cast by all members of the Regent House shall be determined by the Vice-Chancellor, who shall give public notice of that period, provided that, for an election held in the Michaelmas Term, voting shall commence at least ten days after the promulgation of the Roll of the Regent House and the latest time for casting a vote shall not be earlier than the tenth day after the day appointed for the commencement of voting.

Nominations. **4.** In order to be eligible in any class a candidate must be nominated on a paper sent to the Vice-Chancellor so as to arrive not later than noon on the tenth day before the date appointed for the commencement of voting. The paper must contain (*a*) a statement signed by two members of the Regent House, certifying that they nominate the candidate for election as a member in that class, and (*b*) a statement signed by the candidate certifying that he or she consents to be so nominated. No person shall be nominated for election in more than one class. On the receipt of each nomination the Vice-Chancellor shall forthwith publish it by causing it to be posted outside the Senate-House. A nomination may not be withdrawn after such publication.

5. Not later than the last day for the receipt of nominations each person nominated for election shall send to the Registrary a *curriculum vitae*, details of which shall be published for the information of members of the Regent House.

6. There shall be a separate vote for each class of members to be elected.

7. An election shall not be deemed invalid owing to the misdirection, late arrival, or non-arrival of any material relating to the election.

[*Members in class (d)*

8. The members of the Council in class (*d*) shall be in two categories as follows:

(i) two students elected by and from among all the students in the University,

(ii) one graduate student elected by and from among all the graduate students in the University.

Members in class (*d*) shall serve for one year from 1 July next following the election.

9. The annual election of members in class (*d*) shall be held in Full Lent Term. The date and place or places of the election, the last date for the receipt of nominations, and the procedures for voting shall be determined by the Vice-Chancellor, subject to any conditions approved by the Council; provided that the last date for the receipt of nominations shall be not later than the seventh day of Full Term before the day appointed for the election.

10. Not later than thirty-five days of term before the date appointed for the election, the Vice-Chancellor shall give public notice of the date appointed for the election and the final date for the receipt of nominations.

11. Not later than twenty-eight days of term before the date appointed for the election, the Registrary shall make public electoral rolls of all the persons who on the preceding 31 October were eligible, under the provisions of Statute A IV and of these regulations and of the rules made under these regulations to vote and to stand as candidates in the election of members in categories (i) and (ii) of class (*d*). Any person may within seven days of the publication of the rolls send to the Registrary a written objection to the inclusion of any name in, or the omission of any name from, either roll. The decision of the Registrary on any such objection shall be final. Unless otherwise determined by the Vice-Chancellor, the electoral rolls or, if amended by the Registrary, the electoral rolls so amended, shall be the rolls for any election in class (*d*) held at any time in the calendar year in which the electoral rolls were first published. Electoral rolls.

12. In order to be eligible a candidate must issue notice of their intention to stand not later than the last date for nominations determined under Regulation 7 above. A candidate may only stand in one category. A notice of intention to stand once received by the Vice-Chancellor may not be withdrawn. The Vice-Chancellor shall subsequently publish a complete list of persons intending to stand in the *Reporter*. Nominations.

13. The nomination of any candidate who has suffered suspension or deprivation of her or his degree or membership of the University, or who is suffering a sentence of rustication by a University Court or by a College, or whose name, or the name of any of whose nominators, is not included in the roll for the category in which the candidate has been nominated, or in that roll as amended by the Registrary, shall be invalid.

14. The Council shall from time to time make rules in accordance with which the Registrary shall certify persons as students in the University or as graduate students for the purpose of Statute A IV 2. Any question of interpretation of the rules shall be decided by the Registrary, whose decision shall be final.][1] Rules.

⟨*Members in class* (*d*)(*iii*)

8. The annual election of the member in category (iii) of class (*d*) shall be held jointly by Cambridge University Students Union and the Graduate Union in accordance with an electoral scheme for the conduct of such election which shall be submitted to the Council jointly by the President of the Cambridge University Students Union and the President of the Graduate Union each year.

9. For the purposes of Special Ordinance A (ii), the term 'student in the University' shall mean any person eligible to vote in elections for the office of President as governed by the constitutions of the Cambridge University Students Union and the Graduate Union as determined from time to time, or who would be so eligible but who has resigned his or her membership of the Union.⟩[1]

Members in classes (*a*)–(*d*)

15. After an election the Vice-Chancellor shall arrange for the counting of the votes and shall publish the result of the election as soon as conveniently possible.

[*APPENDIX*

Rules made by the Council in accordance with Regulation 14 for the election of members of the Council

1. These rules shall apply to the compilation of electoral rolls for the election of members of the Council in categories (i) and (ii) of class (*d*).

[1] Subject to the approval by Her Majesty in Council of the amendments of Statute approved by Grace 1 of 30 April 2014 the regulations in square brackets will be replaced by the regulations in angular brackets and the following regulation renumbered with effect from the date on which the amendments of Statute take effect.

2. The term student in the University shall mean a matriculated person certified by the Registrary to be pursuing a course of study leading to a Tripos examination, or a course of study or research leading to a degree, diploma, or certificate of the University.

3. The term undergraduate shall mean a student in the University whose course of study is one leading to any of the following degrees: B.A., M.Eng., M.Math., M.Sci., M.A.St., B.Th. The term graduate student shall mean a student in the University who is not an undergraduate so defined.

4. The Registrary shall include in the electoral roll for category (i) the name of any sabbatical officer of CUSU or GU.

5. The Registrary shall include in the electoral roll for category (ii) the name of any sabbatical officer of CUSU or GU but shall not include in the roll of candidates qualified to stand for election in this category any student who qualifies as an undergraduate student under rule 3.

6. A person whose name is on the Register of Graduate Students shall be eligible for inclusion in the appropriate roll whether or not registered as a candidate for a particular degree, diploma, or certificate.

7. The Registrary shall not include in either roll the name of any Graduate Student who, on 31 October next preceding the election, had been registered for her or his current course of study or research for more than four calendar years, or the name of any Graduate Student holding a Fellowship of any College on 31 October next preceding the election.][1]

Nomination of Members of the Council in Class (e) (External Members)

Nominating Committee.

1. The Council shall discharge its duty of making nominations for appointment by Grace of members of the Council in class (*e*) on the recommendation of a Nominating Committee which shall consist of:

(*a*) a member appointed by the Council on the nomination of the Proctors and Deputy Proctors either (i) from among those current members of the Council in class (*e*) or (ii) from among former members of the Council in class (*e*);

(*b*) the Vice-Chancellor;

(*c*) two members elected by the Regent House from among those who at the time of election are current members of Council in classes (*a*), (*b*), and (*c*);

(*d*) four members of the Senate elected by the Regent House.

2. The member in class (*a*) shall be appointed to serve for two years starting from 1 October in a year when the calendar year is odd, and shall be in the chair. No member of the Council in class (*e*) shall serve on the Nominating Committee when his/her own reappointment to the Council is being considered.

3. An election of one member in class (*c*) and two members in class (*d*) of the Nominating Committee shall be held during Full Easter Term when the calendar year is odd. Members in classes (*c*) and (*d*) shall be elected to serve for four years from 1 October next following the aforementioned election. The election shall be conducted in accordance with Regulations 1–7 and 15 of the regulations for the election of members of the Council. If at any election the total number of vacancies is not filled, the Vice-Chancellor shall arrange a further election to fill such vacancies as are unfilled.

4. No person may be a member of the Nominating Committee in class (*d*) who is a member of the Council, or who holds the University office of Pro-Vice-Chancellor, Registrary, or Director or Deputy Director in the University Offices.

5. If a member in class (*d*) of the Nominating Committee, or any person nominated for election as a member in that class, becomes a member of Council, or is appointed to any of the offices in Regulation 4, or ceases to be a member of the Senate, that member's seat shall thereupon become vacant, or the nomination shall thereupon become invalid, as the case may be.

6. The provisions of Special Ordinance A (vii) 1(*b*) shall apply to the initial appointment of a member in class (*a*) and to the filling of a casual vacancy in class (*a*), save that no Ordinance may be made permitting the filling of a casual vacancy by co-option. The provisions of Special Ordinance A (ii) 3 regarding the filling of casual vacancies in the membership of the Council shall apply to the initial elections of members in classes (*c*) and (*d*) and to the filling of casual vacancies in classes (*c*) and (*d*).

7. A retiring member of the Nominating Committee in classes (*a*), (*c*), or (*d*) who has served for four or more consecutive years shall not be eligible to serve again as a member of the Nominating Committee in classes (*a*), (*c*), or (*d*) until one year has elapsed after the end of his or her previous period of service.

[1] Subject to the approval by Her Majesty in Council of the amendments of Statute approved by Grace 1 of 30 April 2014 the rules in square brackets will be rescinded from the date on which the amendments of Statute take effect.

8. The Registrary shall be Secretary of the Nominating Committee. Secretary.

9. The Nominating Committee shall make arrangements for:

(*a*) public advertisement of the intention to make a nomination;

(*b*) consultation with the Audit Committee about the requirements for the chairing of that committee, having regard to the need for compliance with any relevant requirements of the Financial Memorandum with the Higher Education Funding Council for England as to the chairing of the Audit Committee.

10. The Nominating Committee shall submit a recommended name to the Council for each vacancy, together with a statement by the person so recommended that he or she consents to nomination and consents to serve, if appointed by Grace, for the period and in the role concerned. Nominations.

THE BOARD OF SCRUTINY

Amended by Grace 1 of 27 November 2013

1. It shall be the duty of the Board of Scrutiny to scrutinize on behalf of the Regent House each year the Annual Report of the Council (including the Annual Report of the General Board to the Council), the accounts of the University, and any Report of the Council proposing allocations from the Chest.

2. In carrying out their scrutiny of the documents specified in Regulation 1, the Board shall have the right to examine the policies of the University and the arrangements made for the implementation of those policies, and to report thereon to the Regent House.

3. The Board shall have power, in accordance with Statute A VII 5(*a*), to consult any official documents or accounts (other than those of the University Press) which are relevant to any enquiry that they may conduct under the provisions of Regulation 2; they shall also have power, under the provisions of Statute A VII 5(*b*), to consult such documents or accounts relating to the University Press as have been submitted by the Press Syndicate or by officers of the Press to the Council or to the Finance Committee of the Council.

4. (*a*) At its first meeting in each academical year the Board shall elect a chair and a secretary to hold office until the end of that academical year. No person may be re-elected as chair at the end of her or his period of service in that office.

(*b*) The chair shall call a meeting of the Board as soon as may be convenient following the publication of the matter to be considered.

(*c*) The secretary shall allow any member of the Regent House to consult the minutes of the Board.

5. Under Statute A VII 4, holders of the following University offices established by Ordinance, which have primarily administrative duties, may not be elected as members of the Board:

Director and Deputy Director in the University Offices (Unified Administrative Service)
Assistant Treasurer

ELECTION OF MEMBERS OF THE BOARD OF SCRUTINY

Amended by Grace 1 of 27 November 2013

1. The election of members of the Board of Scrutiny in class (*c*) shall be conducted in accordance with Regulations 1–7 and 15 of the regulations for the election of members of the Council.

2. An election of one member in class (*c*)(i) and of three members in class (*c*)(ii) shall be held during Full Easter Term in each alternate year; the arrangements for the election shall be determined by the Vice-Chancellor. The members so elected shall serve for four years from 1 October next following their election. The University may make regulations specifying the procedure to be followed if at any election insufficient nominations are received to fill the vacant places in class (*c*).

3. If at any election insufficient nominations are received to fill the vacant places either in class (*c*)(i) or in class (*c*)(ii), the Council shall appoint as many members as may be necessary.

4. The provisions of Special Ordinance A (ii) 3 regarding the filling of casual vacancies in the membership of the Council shall apply to the filling of casual vacancies in the elected membership of the Board of Scrutiny. A retiring member of the Board who has served for four or more consecutive years shall not be eligible to serve again as a member in class (*c*) until one year has elapsed after the end of her or his previous period of service.

THE GENERAL BOARD

Amended by Grace 1 of 27 November 2013

Appointment of members.

1. Members of the General Board in class (*b*) shall be appointed in the Michaelmas Term to serve for four years from 1 January next following. Two members shall be appointed by the Council of the School of Arts and Humanities, two by the Council of the School of the Humanities and Social Sciences, one by the Council of the School of the Biological Sciences, one by the Council of the School of Clinical Medicine, one by the Council of the School of the Physical Sciences, and one by the Council of the School of Technology.

Election of student members.

[**2.** The members of the General Board in class (*d*) shall be in two categories as follows:

(i) one student elected by and from among all undergraduate students in the University;

(ii) one graduate student elected by and from among all graduate students in the University.

Members in class (*d*) shall serve for one year from 1 July next following the election.

3. The arrangements for the election shall be governed *mutatis mutandis* by the arrangements set out in Regulations 8–15 of the regulations for the election of members of the Council.[1]][2]

Chair.

4. If the Vice-Chancellor is unable to be present at any meeting, the Chair for that meeting shall be a member of the Board appointed by the Vice-Chancellor to act as her or his deputy, or in the absence of such deputy some other member of the Board chosen by the members present.

Representatives.

5. When the General Board intends to discuss a proposal put forward by any Faculty Board or other body, it shall give that body an opportunity, if in the General Board's opinion it would assist the conduct of business, to send a representative to attend the meeting at which the proposal is to be discussed and to take part in the discussion.

6. The teaching programmes proposed by Faculty Boards and comparable authorities shall be submitted to the General Board. The Board shall either approve them or remit them for further consideration, and shall publish them to the University when approved.

Reserved business.

7. Under the provisions of Special Ordinance A (vii) 5(iii) the appointment (or nomination for appointment) of Examiners, Electors to Professorships, members of Appointments Committees, and members of Degree Committees shall be reserved business; and the provisions of Special Ordinance A (vii) 5 concerning reserved business shall apply to any member of the General Board in class (*d*) who is not *in statu pupillari* as if he or she were *in statu pupillari*.

NOTICE BY THE GENERAL BOARD

Statement of intention

In considering any proposal for enacting or amending an Ordinance in pursuance of their powers under Statute A V 1(*d*), the General Board will consult other University bodies as appropriate. If in the course of such consultation the Board become aware that the matter is likely to prove controversial, they will also consult the Regent House by initiating a Grace enabling the Regent House to express an opinion on the proposed change. The Board will give consideration to remarks made at any Discussion of such matters and to the outcome of any vote on them.

SINGLE TRANSFERABLE VOTE REGULATIONS

Elections to which applicable.

1. These regulations may be applied by Grace to the election of persons for membership of bodies within the University or for other purposes. Any election to which they have been so applied shall be conducted in accordance with the following provisions. For voting other than by paper ballot, the regulations shall be construed accordingly.

Method of voting.

2. Every elector in giving his or her vote:

(*a*) must enter on the voting-paper (*see* diagram below), against the figure 1, the name of the candidate to whom he or she gives first preference;

(*b*) may in addition enter on the voting-paper, against the figures 2, 3, and so on, the names of any other candidates in order of preference.

[1] See p. 118.

[2] Subject to the approval by Her Majesty in Council of the amendments of Statute approved by Grace 1 of 30 April 2014 the regulations in square brackets will be rescinded and the following regulations renumbered with effect from the date on which the amendments of Statute take effect.

Order of preference	List the candidates in order of preference
1	
2	
3	
4	
5	
6	
7	
8	

3. A voting-paper shall not be valid unless the elector's first preference is legibly and unambiguously expressed.

4. There shall be appended to each voting-paper the following instructions:

Enter against the figure 1 the name of the candidate to whom you give first preference.

You may also enter, against the figures 2, 3, and so on, the names of other candidates in the order of your preference for them, continuing until you are indifferent. The order of your preferences is crucial. A later preference can be considered only if an earlier preference has received sufficient votes to qualify for election or has been excluded because of insufficient support. Under no circumstances can a later preference count against an earlier preference.

5. *Counting of votes: the first stage*

Counting of votes.

(*a*) The voting-papers shall be sorted into parcels according to the first preferences recorded for each candidate, any invalid papers being set aside.

(*b*) The number of first preference votes for each candidate and the total number of valid votes (i.e. voting-papers) shall be determined.

(*c*) The returning officer shall then determine the number of votes sufficient to secure the election of a candidate (the 'quota'), by dividing the total number of valid votes by (n + 1), where n represents the number of places to be filled, the result

(i) being rounded up to the next whole number above, if it is greater than 100 and is not an exact whole number,

or (ii) being rounded up in the second decimal place, if it is less than 100 and is not exact to two decimal places.

6. *Election of a candidate*

If at any stage of the count a candidate is credited with a number of votes equal to or exceeding the quota he or she shall be deemed to be elected, except that, if the number of candidates attaining the quota is greater than the number of places to be filled, the two or more candidates who attained the quota at the most recent stage of the count shall be deemed not to be elected, and the returning officer shall proceed to the next stage of the count.

7. *Counting the votes: subsequent stages*

Subsequent stages of the count shall be conducted as follows. When a candidate is deemed to be elected, the surplus of his or her votes (if any) above the quota shall be transferred[1] to the continuing candidates next in order of the voters' preference, in accordance with the provisions of Regulations 8 and 9. If two or more candidates have surpluses, the returning officer shall transfer[1] all such surpluses, beginning with the largest. When all surpluses have been transferred,[1] including any consequential surplus that arises as a result of the transfer of other surpluses, the candidate with the smallest number of votes shall be excluded from the poll, and his or her votes shall similarly be transferred to the continuing candidates next in order of the voters' preference, in accordance with the provisions of Regulations 10 and 11. If such a transfer creates a surplus, that surplus shall in turn be transferred,[1] and so on until the required number of candidates has been elected. Each transfer, whether of the

[1] But see Regulation 8(*d*). The transfer of a surplus shall be deferred until a later stage of the count if it would not affect the order of the two (or, in certain circumstances, more than two) candidates lowest on the poll.

surplus votes of an elected candidate or of the total votes of an excluded candidate, shall be deemed to constitute a further stage of the count.

8. *The transfer of a surplus*

When a candidate is deemed to be elected, the returning officer shall calculate the surplus of that candidate's votes above the quota, and shall apply the following provisions:

(*a*) If the number of votes credited to any candidate is greater than the quota and one or more vacancies remain, the surplus of that candidate's votes shall be transferred in accordance with the provisions of Regulation 9, except as provided under Regulation 8(*d*) below.

(*b*) If two or more candidates have a surplus, the largest of these surpluses shall be transferred.

(*c*) If two or more candidates have equal surpluses, the surplus of the candidate who was credited with the largest number of votes at the earliest stage at which they had an unequal number of votes shall be transferred first; if such two or more candidates have been credited with an equal number of votes at all stages of the count, the returning officer shall determine by lot which surplus to transfer.

(*d*) If the surplus of an elected candidate, together with any other surplus not yet transferred, does not exceed

either (i) the difference between the numbers of the votes credited to the two continuing candidates lowest on the poll,

or (ii) the difference between the total number of votes credited to the two or more candidates lowest on the poll and the number of votes credited to the candidate next above them on the poll,

the transfer of such a surplus shall be deferred and shall be reconsidered at the next stage of the count.

9. A surplus shall be transferred in the following manner:

(*a*) In the case of a surplus arising at the first stage, the returning officer shall examine all the voting-papers in the parcel of the elected candidate whose surplus is to be transferred.

(*b*) In the case of a surplus arising at a later stage, which results from the transfer of another surplus or from the exclusion of a candidate or candidates, the returning officer shall examine only the papers which are contained in the sub-parcel last received by the elected candidate, which gave rise to the surplus.

(*c*) The voting-papers to be examined shall be sorted into sub-parcels according to the next available preferences for continuing candidates, any papers on which no next available preference is expressed being set aside.

(*d*) The number of papers in each sub-parcel, the total number of transferable papers, and the number of non-transferable papers shall be determined.

(*e*) The returning officer shall determine the value of the papers to be transferred in the following manner:

(i) If the present total value of the transferable papers exceeds the surplus, the transferable papers shall be transferred at a fractional transfer value, which shall be determined by dividing the surplus by the number of transferable papers to two decimal places, ignoring any remainder. The papers shall be marked with their new transfer value.

(ii) If the present total value of the transferable papers does not exceed the surplus, the transfer value of each paper shall be its present value.

(*f*) Each continuing candidate shall be credited with the value of any papers transferred to him or her, and any non-transferable differences between the total value of such papers and the surplus shall be added to the previous non-transferable total.

(*g*) When a surplus has been transferred under this regulation, the returning officer shall ascertain which candidates (if any) are deemed to be elected in accordance with the provisions of Regulation 6.

10. *The exclusion of a candidate*

If, when all surpluses have been transferred (or when their transfer has been deferred under Regulation 8(*d*)), one or more vacancies remain unfilled, the candidate or candidates credited with the smallest number or numbers of votes shall be excluded from the poll, as follows:

(*a*) The two or more candidates credited with the smallest number of votes shall be excluded together if the total number of votes of such two or more candidates together with the total of any surpluses not transferred under Regulation 8(*d*) does not exceed the number of votes credited to the candidate with the next smallest number of votes.

(*b*) Otherwise, the candidate credited with the smallest number of votes shall be excluded if the number of votes of such a candidate together with the total of any surpluses not transferred under Regulation 8(*d*) does not exceed the number of votes credited to the candidate with the next smallest number of votes.

(*c*) If the two or more candidates credited with the smallest number of votes have each the same number of votes, the candidate who had the smallest number at the earliest stage at which they had an unequal number shall be excluded. If such two or more candidates have been credited with the same number of votes at all stages of the count, the returning officer shall determine by lot which candidate to exclude.

11. The exclusion of a candidate or candidates from the poll shall be effected in the following manner:

(*a*) The voting-papers of the candidate or candidates to be excluded shall be arranged in parcels in descending order of their transfer value.

(*b*) The parcel of papers of the highest transfer value shall be sorted into sub-parcels according to the next available preferences for continuing candidates, any papers on which no next available preference is expressed being set aside.

(*c*) The returning officer shall determine the number and value of the papers in each sub-parcel, and the number and value of the non-transferable papers.

(*d*) Each continuing candidate shall be credited with the value of any papers transferred to him or her, and the value of any non-transferable papers shall be added to the previous non-transferable total.

(*e*) After the transfer of a parcel of papers of any one transfer value, the returning officer shall ascertain which candidates (if any) are deemed to be elected in accordance with the provisions of Regulation 6.

(*f*) Any remaining parcels of papers shall be sorted and transferred in turn in descending order of their transfer value in the same way; after each such transfer the returning officer shall ascertain which candidates (if any) are deemed to be elected in accordance with the provisions of Regulation 6.

12. *The final stages*

(*a*) When the proposed exclusion of a candidate or candidates would reduce the number of continuing candidates to the number of vacancies remaining unfilled, such continuing candidates shall be deemed to be elected.

(*b*) When the last vacancies can be filled under this regulation, no further transfers of votes shall be made, and the remaining continuing candidate or candidates shall be formally excluded from the poll.

13. In publishing the result of the election the returning officer shall include a notification of any transfer of votes made under these regulations, and of the total number of votes credited to each candidate after any such transfer. Publication of results.

14. Any candidate or any candidate's representative may, at any time during the counting of the votes, either before the commencement or after the completion of any transfer of votes, request the returning officer to re-examine and recount the papers of any or all candidates (not being papers set aside at a previous transfer as finally dealt with), and the returning officer shall forthwith re-examine and recount the same accordingly; the returning officer shall also have discretion to recount votes either once or more often in any case in which he or she is not satisfied as to the accuracy of any previous count; provided that nothing contained in this regulation shall make it obligatory for the returning officer to recount the same votes more than once. Recounts.

15. If any question shall arise in relation to any transfer of votes, the decision of the returning officer, whether expressed or implied by his or her acts, shall be final. Queries.

16. For the purposes of these regulations the Vice-Chancellor or a duly appointed deputy shall be the returning officer. Returning officer.

17. In these regulations: Definitions.

(*a*) 'valid voting-paper' means a voting-paper on which a first or an only preference is legibly and unambiguously expressed;

(*b*) 'invalid voting-paper' means a voting-paper on which no first preference is expressed, or on which any first preference is void for uncertainty;

(*c*) 'continuing candidate' means a candidate not yet elected and not excluded from the poll;

(*d*) 'next available preference' means the next preference in order, passing over any earlier preferences for candidates who have already been elected or excluded;

(*e*) 'transferable paper' means a voting-paper on which a next available preference for a continuing candidate is legibly and unambiguously expressed;

(*f*) 'non-transferable paper' means a voting-paper on which no next available preference for a continuing candidate is expressed, or on which any next available preference is void for uncertainty;

(*g*) 'transfer value' means the value, being unity or less, at which a voting-paper is transferred from an elected or an excluded candidate to a continuing candidate.

BOARDS, SYNDICATES, ETC.

GENERAL REGULATIONS

Appointment, Attendance, and Retirement of Members

Amended by Grace 1 of 27 November 2013

Period of appointment.

1. Unless it is otherwise provided by Statute or Ordinance, members of permanent Boards, Syndicates, and other bodies constituted by Statute or Ordinance shall be appointed for such periods that one or more members shall retire annually.

Periods of appointment when body first constituted.

2. When such a Board, Syndicate, or other body is first constituted the Council shall, unless it is otherwise provided by Grace or by the regulations for the body concerned, determine the periods for which each of the members first elected or appointed shall serve, and the Registrary shall publish a notice of the Council's determination.

Appointment of successors.

3. If a member of any body constituted in the University by or under Statute or Ordinance has declared an intention to resign her or his membership of the body on a specified date, a successor may be elected or appointed, as the case may be, to fill the forthcoming vacancy not more than forty-two days of term before the expected date of the vacancy.

Late appointments.

4. The Council shall be empowered to make an appointment, or to approve an appointment to a particular body made by the authority specified in the regulations for that body, on a date later than the regulations prescribe when the appointing body have been unable to make an appointment by the prescribed date.

Chair's casting vote.

5. If at a meeting of an electing or appointing body it should appear upon a vote being taken that an election or appointment would be decided by the Chair's casting vote, and the Chair should desire to postpone the giving of such vote, a majority of the members present at the meeting may authorize the Chair to give that vote, and so to decide the election or appointment, without a further meeting of the body, at any time within six weeks of the day on which such authority is given.

Members *in statu pupillari*.

6. The members of any body constituted in the University by Statute or Ordinance shall not include persons *in statu pupillari* except in so far as it is expressly provided (whether by the use of the phrase *in statu pupillari* or by the use of some other phrase) in the Statute or Ordinance which determines the composition of that body.

Absence from meetings.

7. If a member of such a Board, Syndicate, or other body is absent from three successive meetings of which due notice has been given, that member's seat shall become vacant at the end of the third of such meetings, unless at that or an earlier meeting the cause of the absence has been declared sufficient by the body of which the person concerned is a member; provided that *ex officio* members, members in class (*e*) of Faculty Boards, and any member appointed when not normally resident within ten miles of the University Church, shall be exempted from the operation of this regulation. Any vacancy caused under this regulation shall be reported to the Registrary by the Secretary of the body concerned.

Expenses of non-resident members.

8. A non-resident member of such a Board, Syndicate, or other body shall be entitled to reimbursement of his or her expenses in respect of attendance at a meeting of the body concerned up to a sum not exceeding the return railway fare between Cambridge and the member's normal place of residence or other place approved by the Finance Committee of the Council, together with a subsistence allowance, in accordance with rates to be determined from time to time by the Finance Committee.

'Co-opted' included in 'appointed'.

9. In any Statute or Ordinance, unless that meaning is expressly or by necessary implication excluded, the term 'appointed' shall include the meaning 'co-opted'.

Annual Reports

The Council or the General Board may require that the Annual Report of any Board, Syndicate, or other body which is responsible to them, or of the Head of any Department which is under their supervision, shall conform to such conditions as they may consider desirable. The Report may be published in the *Reporter* if the Council or the General Board, as the case may be, are of the opinion, after consulting the body or the Head of the Department concerned, that there are special reasons justifying such publication.

SPECIAL REGULATIONS

Board of Electors to Livings

1. The selection for presentation to a vacant benefice shall be made by a Board of Electors which shall be constituted for the occasion and which shall consist of the Vice-Chancellor (or a duly appointed deputy) and eight members of the Senate appointed by the Council (four on the nomination of the Faculty Board of Divinity). The selection made shall require the approval of the Council. Board of Electors, to select for approval by Council.

2. In general, when any benefice, the presentation to which is to be made by the University, shall become vacant, the Board shall give public notice of the vacancy and of the date by which applications for the benefice shall be made, provided that the Board may in exceptional circumstances determine that no such notice should be given. If no public notice is given the Board shall indicate the fact to the Council when communicating their selection. Notice of vacancy in a benefice.

3. If the Electors shall be unable to select a clerk for any vacant benefice the selection shall be made by the Vice-Chancellor. If the Vice-Chancellor shall be unable to select a clerk, he or she shall report to the Council to that effect. Failure to select.

4. When a clerk has been selected, the Council shall be empowered to order that the Common Seal of the University be affixed to the deed of presentation. Sealing of deed of presentation.

5. If an Elector shall be a candidate for a vacant benefice, he or she shall be thereby disqualified from acting in the selection of a clerk for such benefice. Candidature of an Elector.

6. The Registrary or a deputy appointed by the Registrary shall be Secretary of the Board of Electors. Secretary of Board.

Board of Examinations

1. The Board of Examinations shall consist of: Constitution.

(*a*) a Pro-Vice-Chancellor, appointed by the General Board, as Chair;

(*b*) the Proctors;

(*c*) three persons appointed by the Council;

(*d*) three persons appointed by the General Board, one of whom shall be a member of that Board's Education Committee and one of whom shall be a person *in statu pupillari* appointed on the recommendation of Cambridge University Students Union;

(*e*) one Senior Tutor appointed by the Senior Tutors' Committee.

Except for the member in class (*d*) *in statu pupillari*, the members in classes (*c*), (*d*), and (*e*) shall be appointed in the Michaelmas Term to serve for four years from 1 January following their appointment, save that membership of the member in class (*d*) who is a member of the General Board's Education Committee and of the member in class (*e*) shall lapse if the person ceases to be a member of the Education Committee or a Senior Tutor, as the case may be.

The member in class (*d*) *in statu pupillari* shall be appointed in the Easter Term to serve for one year from 1 July next following her or his appointment.

2. The Registrary, or a duly appointed deputy, shall be Secretary of the Board. The Board shall meet at least once in each term. Secretary.

3. The Board shall have the duty of assigning lecture-rooms so far as that duty may be delegated to them by the Council. Lecture-rooms.

4. The Board shall be charged with arrangements for the conduct of all University examinations, other than those for which the Board of Graduate Studies are responsible, as follows: Examinations.

(*a*) The Board shall provide and prepare suitable rooms for all University examinations. Examination rooms.

(*b*) The Board shall draw up an order for each examination in consultation with the Examiners, and shall publish it at least a fortnight before the examination begins. The order of examination shall be prefixed to the final list of candidates for each examination. Orders of Examinations.

Special arrangements.

(*c*) The Board shall consider the cases of candidates who for special reasons apply to be examined under other than the ordinary conditions, or at other times than those previously advertised, and shall give or withhold permission for them to be examined otherwise. They shall also determine the conditions under which such permission may be given. Applications shall be sent by Tutors to the Secretary of the Board.

Supervisors and Invigilators.

(*d*) The Board shall appoint a Supervisor and one or more Invigilators for each session of a University examination held within the Precincts of the University. Supervisors shall be responsible for the general arrangements in the examination room; they shall prepare a report on the candidates' attendance, and shall despatch the candidates' scripts at the end of the session in accordance with instructions issued by the Secretary of the Board. Invigilators shall be present throughout the session and shall be responsible for the surveillance of the candidates.

(*e*) The Board shall instruct Supervisors and Invigilators in their duties, and may make rules (see the Appendix to these regulations) for the guidance of candidates and for the prevention of misconduct. The Board shall have power to impose on a person infringing one or more of those rules a fine not exceeding £175.

(*f*) When the Supervisor or Invigilator is not an Examiner it shall be the duty of the Chair of Examiners or the Senior Examiner to arrange for one at least of the Examiners to be present for the first twenty minutes of each session.

Payment of Examiners.

(*g*) The Board shall be charged with the payment of all Examiners and Assessors in accordance with the relevant Ordinances; and they shall pay the expenses of all practical examinations. Before making such payments they shall obtain from the Chair of Examiners or the Senior Examiner, or from the individual Examiners, statements of the work done by and the payments due to each Examiner and Assessor, and shall see that these statements are in conformity with the Ordinances. The Board shall also determine the rates of payments to be made to Supervisors and Invigilators.

Room attendants.

(*h*) In addition to Supervisors and Invigilators, it shall be the duty of the Board to provide a suitable number of attendants at each examination room. The Board shall have power to employ additional staff in this capacity when necessary.

Recording of candidates' attendance.

(*i*) It shall be the duty of the staff of the Board's Office to record the attendance of candidates for all University examinations. An amended copy of the final list of candidates shall be prepared after the beginning of every examination, and retained as part of the University's official record.

5. The Board shall make such reports to the Council and to the General Board as they deem necessary or as those bodies may require.

APPENDIX

Rules for the Guidance of Candidates and for the Prevention of Misconduct in Examinations

1. Candidates shall not commence writing at the start of an examination session until authorized to do so by the Supervisor or Senior Invigilator. Candidates shall stop writing at the end of an examination session when similarly instructed.

2. Except with the consent of the Supervisor or Senior Invigilator, no candidate shall be allowed to enter an examination room later or to leave an examination room earlier than thirty minutes after the beginning of a session.

3. A candidate may take a small screw-top bottle of water to her or his desk for consumption during an examination session provided that no disturbance is thereby caused to other candidates. Except with the written consent of the Secretary of the Board of Examinations no other items of food or drink may be taken into an examination room. A Supervisor, Invigilator, or Examiner has authority to deprive a candidate of unauthorized items until the examination session is ended.

4. No candidate shall take into an examination room or have in her or his possession during an examination any book or paper relevant to the examination unless specifically authorized. A Supervisor, Invigilator, or Examiner has authority to confiscate such documents.

5. No candidate shall take into an examination room any electronic calculator or other means of data storage or retrieval unless specifically authorized. A Supervisor, Invigilator, or Examiner has authority to confiscate unauthorized items. If a candidate is suspected of unfair means, the item will be confiscated until the Advocate has authorized its return. Where also specified, an electronic calculator must carry an official mark indicating that it has been approved for use in University examinations.

6. No candidate shall have in her or his possession during an examination any electronic communication or audio device. A Supervisor, Invigilator, or Examiner has authority to deprive a candidate of such equipment until the examination session is ended.

7. Candidates shall not remove from an examination room any paper except the question paper and such books or papers, if any, as they were authorized to take into the room. Until the time at which candidates are allowed to leave the examination room, no copy of any examination paper shall be taken from the room without the consent of the Supervisor or Invigilator.

8. No candidate shall communicate with any other candidate during an examination session.

9. Candidates shall not leave their places during a session except with the consent of the Supervisor or an Invigilator.

10. Candidates shall be dressed decently and not in a manner that is likely to create a disturbance in the examination room, or to distract the attention of other candidates.

11. A Supervisor, Invigilator, or Examiner shall report to the Board of Examinations any breach of these rules and shall inform the candidate concerned that such a report is to be made. A candidate shall not be dismissed from a session except as provided in Rule 12.

12. A candidate who acts in such a way as to disturb or inconvenience other candidates shall be warned and may, at the discretion of the Supervisor, Invigilator, or Examiner, either be required to change seat or be dismissed from the session.

13. Candidates attending a practical examination must comply with the safety requirements of the laboratory in which the examination is held.

14. Candidates shall have regard for the welfare of others, including the general public, at the end of examination sessions (both their own sessions and those of others). In particular they should avoid: noise that might disturb active examinations or other work nearby; littering or damage, especially with food or drink; and obstructing highways or thoroughfares. Candidates shall comply with instructions given by University staff performing their duties.

Board of Graduate Studies

1. The Board of Graduate Studies shall consist of

(*a*) one member appointed by the General Board as Chair, who shall also be a member of the Education Committee; Constitution.

(*b*) two members of the Regent House appointed by the Council;

(*c*) four members of the Regent House appointed by the General Board;

(*d*) two members of the Regent House appointed by the Senior Tutors' Committee, one of whom shall normally be a Graduate Tutor;

(*e*) up to four members of the Regent House co-opted by the Board.

Members in classes (*a*), (*b*), and (*c*) shall be appointed in the Michaelmas Term to serve for four years from 1 January next following their appointment. Members in classes (*d*) and (*e*) shall be appointed in the Easter Term to serve for three years from 1 October.

2. It shall be the duty of the Board: Duties.

(*a*) to decide on applications for admission as Graduate Students from persons who have been recommended for admission by a Degree Committee, and to exercise a general superintendence over Graduate Students;

(*b*) to exercise such functions as may be assigned to the Board by Ordinance in the admission to the University of such other categories of graduate students, who do not seek admission under (*a*) above, and to record their subsequent progress; excluding Affiliated Students;

(*c*) to consider and decide upon all applications of Graduate Students for such allowances under the regulations for the degrees of Doctor of Philosophy, Doctor of Engineering, Master of Science, Master of Letters, and Master of Philosophy, as may be prescribed by Ordinance;

(*d*) to consider and decide upon all applications of candidates for special allowances under the special regulations for the degree of Doctor of Philosophy;

(*e*) to consider and decide upon applications from candidates for special allowances under the regulations for the Diplomas in Economics, in International Law, and in Legal Studies, and Certificates of Postgraduate Study;

(*f*) to receive the reports, recommendations or resolutions of the Degree Committees on the work of candidates for the degrees of D.D., LL.D., Sc.D., Litt.D., Mus.D., Ph.D., Eng.D., Ed.D., M.Sc., M.Litt., M.Res., M.Phil., M.St., and Vet.M.D. who have been recommended by the Degree Committee concerned, and to publish the names of those candidates on whom, in the opinion of the Board or of the Degree Committee concerned, the degrees should be conferred;

(*g*) to receive the reports, recommendations, and resolutions of the Degree Committees on the work of candidates for the qualifications listed in (*e*) above who have been recommended or approved by the Degree Committee concerned, and to publish the names of those candidates to whom, in the opinion of the Board, or of the Degree Committee concerned, the qualifications should be awarded;

(*h*) to award studentships or scholarships from funds under the Board's control and to make nominations for national postgraduate awards to the appropriate awarding body;

(*i*) to supervise the Board of Graduate Studies General Fund;

(*j*) to circulate to other universities information as to conditions of research and to correspond with candidates and other persons concerned;

(*k*) to make an Annual Report to the Council and such other reports to the University as they think fit;

(*l*) to undertake such other functions as may from time to time be assigned to them by the University.

Finance. **3.** The balance of the annual income of the Board of Graduate Studies General Fund shall be invested, and held at the disposal of the Board of Graduate Studies for the furtherance of postgraduate study and research in the University.

Secretary. **4.** The duties of the Secretary shall be:

(*a*) to receive all applications for admission, allowances, and examination;

(*b*) to conduct the correspondence of the Board;

(*c*) to give information and advice to students;

(*d*) to undertake any other duties assigned to the Secretary by the Board.

University and Assistants Joint Board

Constitution. **1.** The University and Assistants Joint Board shall consist of members in the following classes:

(*a*) the Vice-Chancellor (or a duly appointed deputy) as Chair;

(*b*) (i) eight members of the Senate, four of whom at least shall be either Heads of institutions or other persons concerned with the administration of assistant staff therein, appointed as follows:

(1) four persons, of whom one at least shall be a member of the Council, appointed by the Council;

(2) four persons appointed by the General Board;

(ii) the Registrary, the Director of the Finance Division, and the Academic Secretary, and the Head of the Human Resources Division of the University Offices (or their deputies) who shall be members *ex officio*;

(*c*) such number of University assistants representing bargaining units as the Council shall determine after discussion with those organizations to which the Council have granted negotiating rights. The Council shall from time to time announce in a Notice published in the *Reporter*:

(i) a definition of each bargaining unit;

(ii) the number of members of the Board in class (*c*) representing each organization to which negotiating rights have been granted for that bargaining unit.

Members of the Board in class (*b*)(i) shall be appointed in the Michaelmas Term to serve for four years from 1 January following their appointment; provided that, if at any time among the members in sub-class (1) there has ceased for any reason to be at least one member who is also a member of the Council, the Council shall have power to replace, if necessary, one of the members in that sub-class so as to satisfy that requirement for the remainder of the tenure of the person so replaced. Members of the Board in class (*c*) shall serve for such length of time as may be decided by the organization that they represent.

Joint Secretaries. **2.** The Council shall appoint a University officer to be Joint Secretary of the Board. The members of the Board in class (*c*) shall appoint one of their own number to be Joint Secretary of the Board.

3. The method of appointment of members in class (*c*) shall be decided by the organizations that they represent. The organizations concerned shall inform both Joint Secretaries of the names of the representatives whom they have appointed before those representatives take their place on the Board.

Duties of the Board. **4.** The duties of the Board shall be:

(*a*) to keep under review the terms and conditions of employment of the assistant staff of the University;

(*b*) to consider any matter that is referred to them by the Council or by the General Board, or any matter relating to the terms and conditions of employment of the assistant staff which they are requested to consider by the members of the Joint Board in class (*b*) or class (*c*);

(*c*) to form Special Joint Negotiating Committees to consider all matters which affect more than one bargaining unit; representation on such Special Joint Negotiating Committees shall be subject to agreement between members of the Board in classes (*b*) and (*c*) provided that the Head of the Human Resources Division of the University Offices shall be one member from class (*b*) and there shall be at least one member in class (*c*) from each organization representing the bargaining units affected;

(*d*) to form for each bargaining unit a Standing Joint Negotiating Committee consisting of:

(i) (1) the Head of the Human Resources Division of the University Offices;

(2) three members appointed from among the members of the Board in class (*b*) by the members of the Board in class (*b*)(i);

(ii) the members of the Board in class (*c*) representing that bargaining unit.

5. The duties of each Standing Joint Negotiating Committee shall be: Duties of Standing Joint Negotiating Committees.

(*a*) subject to the provisions of Regulation 4(*c*), to keep under review the terms and conditions of employment of the assistant staff of the bargaining unit concerned, including in particular matters relating to salaries and wages; allowances; hours of work, holidays, and compensation for overtime; payments during absence through sickness; training; recruitment; welfare; recognition of long service; and pensions (other than matters relating to the operation or management of the Pension Scheme);

(*b*) to consider any matter that is referred to them by the Joint Board or any matter relating to the terms and conditions of employment of the assistant staff which they are requested to consider by members of the Committee in either class (*b*) or class (*c*) of the Board. When the members of a Committee in both classes (*b*) and (*c*) of the Board agree to recommend amendment of any regulation, supplementary regulation, schedule, or instruction concerning the conditions of employment of University assistants within the bargaining unit concerned, the Committee shall report thereon to the Board.

6. No business shall be transacted by any Joint Negotiating Committee, whether Special or Standing, unless there is present a majority of the members of the Committee in each of classes (*b*) and (*c*) of the Board.

7. Each Joint Negotiating Committee shall mutually agree on the choice of a person to act as Chair. The Chair need not be a member of the Joint Board. Unless the Chair is a member of the Committee, he or she shall not have a vote.

8. The Chair shall adjourn or intermit any meeting of a Joint Negotiating Committee if members of the Committee in either class (*b*) or (*c*) of the Board so request.

9. A Joint Negotiating Committee shall allow officials from an organization represented on that Joint Negotiating Committee, who need not be University assistants, to attend and take part in the meetings of the Committee if this is requested by those members of the Committee in class (*c*) of the Board who represent that organization.

10. The rules of procedure of each Joint Negotiating Committee shall be subject to agreements on procedure that may be negotiated from time to time between the Council and the General Board, acting on behalf of the University as employer, and the Trade Unions or other organizations represented on that Committee, provided that Procedure.

(*a*) no details of voting shall be recorded at any meeting of a Joint Negotiating Committee, and reports of a Joint Negotiating Committee shall not be signed by members;

(*b*) no resolution of a Joint Negotiating Committee shall be valid unless agreed by a majority of the members of the Committee in each of classes (*b*) and (*c*) of the Board.

11. Resolutions of a Joint Negotiating Committee shall be transmitted to the Joint Board for submission to the Council before publication. No amendment proposed by the Council or the Joint Board shall be made unless it is agreed by a majority of the members of the appropriate Joint Negotiating Committee in each of classes (*b*) and (*c*) of the Board.

12. If there is a failure to agree within a Joint Negotiating Committee the substance of the failure shall be reported to the Board for discussion. If there is still failure to agree after discussion within the Board, the matter shall be referred to the Council, in which case, if the Council are unable to put forward a proposal acceptable to a majority of the members of the Joint Negotiating Committee concerned in each of classes (*b*) and (*c*) of the Board, the Council shall then request the members of the Joint Negotiating Committee to reach agreement on the machinery to be used for settlement.

Accommodation Syndicate

Constitution. **1.** There shall be an Accommodation Syndicate, which shall consist of:

(*a*) the Vice-Chancellor (or a duly appointed deputy) as Chair;

(*b*) three persons appointed by the Council, one of whom shall be a research worker employed by the University in an unestablished capacity;

(*c*) one person appointed by the Senior Tutors' Committee;

(*d*) one person appointed by the Committee of Graduate Tutors;

(*e*) one person appointed by the Bursars' Committee;

(*f*) one member of the assistant staff appointed by the University and Assistants Joint Board;

(*g*) two members of the University *in statu pupillari* appointed by the Graduate Union;

(*h*) one member of the University *in statu pupillari* appointed by Cambridge University Students Union;

(*i*) not more than two persons co-opted by the Syndicate, provided that it shall not be obligatory for the Syndicate to co-opt any person or persons.

Members in classes (*b*), (*c*), (*d*), (*e*), and (*f*) shall be appointed in the Michaelmas Term to serve for four years from 1 January following their appointment. Members in classes (*g*) and (*h*) shall be appointed in the Easter Term to serve for the academical year next following their appointment. Any member in class (*i*) shall serve until the end of the calendar year in which he or she is co-opted.

Duties. **2.** The duties of the Syndicate shall be:

(*a*) to keep under review the accommodation (other than accommodation provided by Colleges) available for members of the University *in statu pupillari*, persons employed by the University,[1] and academic visitors;

(*b*) to maintain a register of such accommodation and to provide an advisory service relating to it;

(*c*) to ensure as far as possible an adequate supply of such accommodation;

(*d*) to supervise the work of the Accommodation Office.

Secretary of the Syndicate. **3.** There shall be a University office of Secretary of the Accommodation Syndicate, appointments and reappointments to which shall be made by an Appointments Committee consisting of the members of the Syndicate in classes (*a*), (*b*), (*c*), (*d*), and (*e*).

Duties. **4.** The duties of the Secretary shall be:

(*a*) to attend the meetings of the Syndicate;

(*b*) to be responsible to the Syndicate for the work of the Accommodation Office;

(*c*) to report periodically to the Syndicate on the availability of accommodation;

(*d*) generally to assist the Syndicate in all matters connected with the work of the Syndicate.

Quorum. **5.** No business shall be transacted at any meeting of the Syndicate unless the Chair and four other members at least are present.

Reserved business. **6.** The provisions of Special Ordinance A (vii) 5 concerning reserved business shall apply to the Syndicate and to the Appointments Committee prescribed in Regulation 3 as if they were bodies constituted by Statute. These provisions shall apply also to any member of the Syndicate in class (*i*) who is not *in statu pupillari* as if he or she were a person *in statu pupillari*.

Reports. **7.** The Syndicate shall make such reports to the Council as the Council may require.

Careers Service Syndicate

Constitution. **1.** There shall be a Careers Service Syndicate which shall be responsible for the administration of the University Careers Service. The Syndicate shall consist of:

(*a*) the Vice-Chancellor (or a duly appointed deputy) as Chair;

(*b*) four members of the Regent House appointed by the Council;

(*c*) twelve members of the Regent House nominated by the Colleges, Approved Foundations, and Approved Societies, in sequential rotation;

(*d*) two members of the University *in statu pupillari* appointed by the Council;

(*e*) not more than twelve persons co-opted by the Syndicate.

Members in class (*b*) shall be appointed in the Michaelmas Term to serve for four years from 1 January following their appointment. Members in class (*c*) shall be appointed in the Michaelmas Term to serve

[1] Including research workers employed by the University in an unestablished capacity, postdoctoral research workers, and University assistants.

for three years from 1 January following their appointment, four being appointed each year. The order of rotation of Colleges for the nomination of members in class (*c*) shall be as follows:

Christ's College, Churchill College, Clare Hall, Clare College, Corpus Christi College, Lucy Cavendish College, Downing College, Emmanuel College, Darwin College, Fitzwilliam College, Gonville and Caius College, Girton College, Jesus College, King's College, Hughes Hall, Magdalene College, Pembroke College, Murray Edwards College, Peterhouse, Queens' College, St Edmund's College, Robinson College, St Catharine's College, Newnham College, St John's College, Selwyn College, Wolfson College, Sidney Sussex College, Trinity College, Trinity Hall, Homerton College.

Members in class (*d*) shall be appointed in the Easter Term to serve for the academical year following that in which they are appointed. Members in class (*e*) shall be appointed in the Lent Term to serve for four years from 1 October following their appointment.

Meetings.

2. All meetings of the Syndicate shall be summoned by the Vice-Chancellor (or a duly appointed deputy); there shall be at least one meeting in each academical year.

Quorum.

3. The Chair and four other members shall constitute a quorum of the Syndicate.

Duties.

4. The duties of the Syndicate shall include the following:

(*a*) to determine the policy for the University Careers Service;

(*b*) to provide information and advice about careers for all members of the University;

(*c*) to establish and organize means of communication between members of the University who are seeking employment and employers, and in particular to keep registers of those seeking employment;

(*d*) to administer the funds of the Syndicate and to approve the annual estimates, and to prepare and keep accounts, which shall be audited annually and published with the University Accounts;

(*e*) to perform such other functions as may from time to time be assigned to the Syndicate by the University;

(*f*) to make an Annual Report to the Council, and such other reports to the University as they think fit;

(*g*) to promote the exchange of ideas between members of the University and representatives of other organizations on matters affecting the employment of graduate members of the University, in particular by holding seminars and other informal meetings from time to time.

Executive Committee.

5. The Syndicate shall appoint from their members an Executive Committee and shall delegate thereto such of their functions as they may deem expedient. The Executive Committee shall consist of the Chair of the Syndicate *ex officio* and four members of the Syndicate chosen from among those in classes (*b*) and (*c*).

Secretary of the Syndicate and Director of the Careers Service.

6. There shall be the University office of Secretary of the Syndicate, the holder of which shall be designated Director of the Careers Service, and such number of University offices of Careers Adviser as may be determined from time to time by the Council on the recommendation of the Syndicate. Appointments and reappointments to the office of Secretary and to an office of Careers Adviser shall be made by an Appointments Committee consisting of:

Appointments Committee.

(*a*) the Vice-Chancellor (or a duly appointed deputy) as Chair;

(*b*) the Chair of the Syndicate;

(*c*) three members of the Syndicate appointed by the Syndicate;

(*d*) two persons appointed by the Council,

(*e*) (except for the appointment of the Secretary of the Syndicate) the Secretary of the Syndicate.

Members in classes (*c*) and (*d*) shall be appointed in the Michaelmas Term of each calendar year of which the number is even, to serve for the two calendar years next ensuing. A member in class (*c*) who ceases to be a member of the Syndicate shall thereupon cease to be a member of the Appointments Committee.

7. For the appointment or reappointment of the Secretary of the Syndicate, the Registrary, or his or her deputy, shall act as Secretary of the Appointments Committee. For any other appointment, the Secretary of the Syndicate concerned shall act as Secretary.

8. The duties of the Secretary or Careers Advisers shall be determined by the Syndicate.

Deputy Director.

9. The Syndicate shall designate one of the Careers Advisers as Deputy Director.

10. There shall be such number of University offices of Assistant to the Careers Advisers in Grade I and of such offices in Grades II and III as shall be determined from time to time by the Council on the recommendation of the Syndicate. Appointment and reappointment to the office of Assistant to the

Careers Advisers shall be made by the Secretary of the Syndicate under procedures to be determined from time to time by the Council after consultation with the Syndicate.

11. The duties of an Assistant to the Careers Advisers shall be determined by the Syndicate and the scale of stipends of each grade of the office shall be determined by the Council, after consultation with the Syndicate.

Residence of officers.

12. The Secretary and any other University officer on the staff of the University Careers Service shall be resident in the University during term and for four weeks in the Long Vacation.

Income.

13. The following shall be paid to the funds of the Syndicate:

(*a*) an annual grant, to be continued until the University shall decide otherwise;

(*b*) annual and other grants from Colleges, Approved Foundations, and Approved Societies in Cambridge;

(*c*) contributions from public bodies and individuals in aid of the purposes of the Syndicate;

(*d*) payments made in respect of publications issued by the Syndicate.

Reserved business.

14. The provisions of Special Ordinance A (vii) 5 concerning reserved business shall apply to the Syndicate and to the Executive Committee as if they were bodies constituted by Statute.

Information Strategy and Services Syndicate

Rescinded by Grace 1 of 22 May 2013

Local Examinations Syndicate

Amended by Grace 1 of 27 November 2013

Constitution.

1. The Local Examinations Syndicate shall consist of:

(*a*) the Vice-Chancellor (or a duly appointed deputy) as Chair;

(*b*) a University officer appointed by the Council;

(*c*) six members of the Regent House appointed by the Council;

(*d*) six members appointed by the Council on the nomination of the Syndicate who shall include persons with experience and expertise in education, training, and business matters relevant to the work of the Syndicate;

Members in classes (*c*) and (*d*) shall be appointed in the Michaelmas Term to serve for four years from 1 January following their appointment.

Chief Executive of the Syndicate.

2. There shall be the post of Chief Executive of the Syndicate. The Chief Executive shall act as Secretary of the Syndicate. The duties of the Chief Executive shall be determined by the Syndicate.

Quorum.

3. No business shall be transacted at any meeting of the Syndicate unless five members are present, of whom at least three are members in classes (*a*), (*b*), and (*c*).

Advisory Councils.

4. There shall be such number of Advisory Councils as the Council may from time to time approve on the advice of the Syndicate. The function of an Advisory Council shall be to advise and assist the Syndicate in their work. The membership of each Advisory Council shall consist of:

(*a*) a Chair who shall be the Chair of the Syndicate or a deputy appointed by the Chair;

(*b*) three members of the Regent House appointed by the Syndicate from among the members of the Syndicate in class (*c*);

(*c*) not more than four other members of the Regent House appointed by the Syndicate;

(*d*) not more than twenty persons appointed by the Syndicate, who shall include persons with experience relevant to the work of the Advisory Council concerned.

Members in classes (*b*), (*c*), and (*d*) shall be appointed in the Michaelmas Term to serve for two years from 1 January following their appointment.

5. If a member of an Advisory Council in class (*b*) ceases to be a member of the Syndicate he or she shall thereupon cease to be a member of the Advisory Council concerned.

6. The Secretary of the Syndicate or a deputy appointed by the Secretary shall act as Secretary of each Advisory Council established under Regulation 4.

7. There shall also be a University office of Principal Assistant Secretary. The office shall be suppressed when it next falls vacant. The duties of the office shall be determined by the Syndicate.

8. Appointments and reappointments to the post of Chief Executive of the Syndicate shall be made by a Committee specially constituted on the occasion of each appointment or reappointment. Such a Committee shall consist of: Appointments Committee.

(*a*) the Vice-Chancellor or a duly appointed deputy;

(*b*) the Chair of the Syndicate;

(*c*) three persons appointed by the Council;

(*d*) three persons appointed by the Syndicate;

The Registrary shall act as Secretary of the Committee.

9. The primary work of the Syndicate shall be the conduct and administration of examinations in schools and other institutions and for persons who are not members of the University, including the fixing of fees, the issue of syllabuses, and the appointment and payment of Examiners.

10. Subject to the approval of the Council, the Syndicate shall be authorized to establish one or more companies registered under the Companies Acts with limited liability, either wholly-owned by the University or, if charitable, of which the University is the sole member, and to transfer part of its work to such company or companies. The Syndicate shall act on behalf of the University in relation to the affairs of such company or companies, except that those members of the board or governing body of each company whose appointment is the responsibility of the University shall be appointed by the Council on the nomination of the Syndicate.

11. Without prejudice to the generality of Regulation 9, the Local Examinations Syndicate shall be authorized to exercise in the name of the University in relation to the affairs of the Syndicate the following powers (being powers which for the avoidance of doubt it is desirable to mention expressly) namely: Powers.

(*a*) to co-operate with the Department for Children, Schools and Families, associations of teachers, and other bodies in Great Britain in the provision of examinations, and to issue certificates to successful candidates;

(*b*) to co-operate with educational authorities and other bodies overseas in the provision of examinations and to issue special certificates;

(*c*) to make arrangements for the inspection of schools on application by the school authorities;

(*d*) to conduct special scholarship and other examinations, primarily intended for persons who are not members of the University, such as examinations for Certificates of Proficiency in English and other modern languages, and to co-operate with other bodies for such purposes;

(*e*) to administer under Ordinance or Grace or when requested by the Council such scholarship and prize funds as may be or have been established from benefactions to the University and to award any such scholarship or prize;

(*f*) to make donations from time to time, subject to the approval of the Council, to the Cambridge Commonwealth, European and International Trust, and other trusts established by the University to raise funds for the support of students from overseas studying in the University;

(*g*) to bring, defend, and conduct on behalf of the University any legal proceedings in connection with the affairs of the Syndicate, provided that before instituting such proceedings they shall notify the Vice-Chancellor of their intention so to do; and they shall also notify the Vice-Chancellor, as soon as circumstances permit, of any legal proceedings threatened or brought against the University in connection with the affairs of the Syndicate;

(*h*) in the name of the University to engage persons for employment in the service of the Syndicate, to determine their salaries and pensions, and to prescribe the conditions of their service, provided that the scheme for the structure of salaries, for pension arrangements, and for conditions of service of staff shall be subject to the general approval of the Council;

(*i*) to do anything, subject to the provisions of Ordinances, which is calculated to facilitate, or is conducive to or incidental to, the discharge of any of their functions prescribed by these regulations.

12. The Syndicate shall make an Annual Report to the Council to which shall be appended the audited Annual Accounts of the Syndicate. Annual Report.

13. In any year in which the audited accounts show a sufficient balance the Syndicate shall pay over to the University Chest such a proportion of the balance as shall be agreed upon between the Syndicate and the Council.

Press Syndicate

Constitution. **1.** The Press Syndicate shall consist of:

(*a*) the Vice-Chancellor (or a duly appointed deputy) as Chair;

(*b*) a University officer appointed by the Council;

(*c*) sixteen members of the Senate appointed by the Council in the Michaelmas Term to serve for four years from 1 January following their appointment.

The Press Syndicate shall appoint a Secretary of the Press Syndicate who shall be the Chief Executive of the University Press.

Quorum. **2.** No business shall be transacted at any meeting of the Press Syndicate unless five members at least are present.

Powers. **3.** Without prejudice to the generality of the powers conferred by Statute on the Press Syndicate for the management of the affairs of the University Press, the Press Syndicate shall be authorized in the name of the University to exercise in relation to the affairs of the University Press the following powers (being powers which for the avoidance of doubt it is desirable to mention expressly) namely:

(*a*) to engage such persons for employment in the service of the University Press as they in their sole discretion shall from time to time decide, and to determine their salaries and conditions of their service, including notice of termination of employment and retiring age;

(*b*) to bring, defend, and conduct on behalf of the University any legal proceedings in connection with the affairs of the University Press, provided that before instituting such proceedings they shall notify the Vice-Chancellor of their intention so to do; and they shall also notify the Vice-Chancellor, as soon as circumstances permit, of any legal proceedings threatened or brought against the University in connection with the affairs of the University Press;

(*c*) to acquire for the purposes of the University Press any property real or personal and whether in the United Kingdom or elsewhere or any estate or interest therein; and to dispose in any manner of any such property, being property of the University Press; but subject always to the provisions of the general regulations for University property (sites and buildings) insofar as they shall be expressly stated to apply to the University Press, and, as regards land in the United Kingdom, to any restrictions for the time being imposed by law on the acquisition or disposal of land by the University;[1]

(*d*) to establish and maintain branches of the University Press in any part of the world and if they think fit to cause companies or other bodies approved by them to be incorporated for the holding or management of any such branches;

(*e*) to establish reserve funds when in their opinion such funds are necessary to make provision for the future continuance of the University Press or for its prospective liabilities;

(*f*) to cause the Press Seal to be affixed to any document in accordance with the provisions of Regulation 7 of these regulations;

(*g*) to delegate any of their powers to a committee of the Press Syndicate or, except in the case of their power under sub-paragraph (*f*) of this regulation, to any officer of the University Press.

Property of the University Press. **4.** All property of the University Press the title of which is capable of registration shall be registered in the name of the Chancellor, Masters, and Scholars of the University of Cambridge, or of nominees approved by the Finance Committee of the Council.

Financial year. **5.** The financial year of the University Press shall end on 30 April.

6. The Press Syndicate shall prepare, and shall publish an abstract of, the annual accounts of the University Press.

Press Seal. **7.** The Press Syndicate shall provide for the safe custody of the Press Seal, which shall be used only by the authority of the Press Syndicate or of a committee of the Press Syndicate authorized by the Press Syndicate in that behalf, and every instrument to which the Press Seal shall be affixed shall be signed by a member of the Press Syndicate and countersigned by the Secretary of the Press Syndicate or by some other employee of the University Press who has been designated by the Press Syndicate for that purpose.

[1] The Press Syndicate have undertaken not to dispose, without the approval of the University, of the Pitt Building or of any property acquired from the University and specially designated by agreement between the Press Syndicate and the Council at the time of acquisition. The Syndicate have also undertaken to offer the Council the first option to acquire, at prevailing market price, any property in Cambridge which is to be disposed of by the Syndicate, such option if not taken up to lapse fourteen days after the offer.

SELECT PREACHERS SYNDICATE

1. There shall be a Select Preachers Syndicate consisting of the Vice-Chancellor, the Regius, the Lady Margaret's, and the Norris-Hulse Professors of Divinity, the Vicar of Great St Mary's Church, the two Proctors, and four members of the Senate appointed by the Council in the Michaelmas Term to serve for four years from 1 January following their appointment. The Syndicate shall make such reports to the Council as the Council may require. Constitution.

2. The Syndicate shall exercise the power of the University under Statute A X 6 to appoint the days during Full Term on which sermons shall be preached in the University Church. The Syndicate shall in every year not later than the end of the Lent Term publish the days that they have appointed for sermons (including the Hulsean Sermon) to be preached in the University Church during the following year. They shall at the same time submit to the Vice-Chancellor the names of the persons whom they recommend for appointment as Lady Margaret's Preacher and as preacher of the Ramsden Sermon, together with a list of persons (other than the Hulsean Preacher) to be invited to accept appointment as Select Preachers for the remaining days which they have appointed. The allocation of days to the several preachers shall be made by the Vice-Chancellor. If any preacher be prevented from preaching on the day assigned, the Syndicate shall submit to the Vice-Chancellor an alternative name. Powers and duties.

3. In addition to the Select Preachers who have been appointed in any year under Regulation 2, the Vice-Chancellor may on the recommendation of the Select Preachers Syndicate appoint a person or persons to preach in the University Church on another day or other days in that year. Other sermons.

4. For every sermon the Select Preacher shall be paid a fee at a rate to be determined from time to time by the Council, on the recommendation of the Select Preachers Syndicate. A non-resident Select Preacher shall be entitled to receive, in addition to the fee, the return railway fare between Cambridge and his or her normal place of residence or other place approved by the Finance Committee of the Council, together with a subsistence allowance in accordance with rates to be determined from time to time by the Finance Committee. Select Preacher's fee.

5. The Select Preachers Syndicate, in drawing up the list of preachers before the University, may use such liberty in the choice of preachers as is exercised by Diocesan Bishops in accordance with resolutions of the Convocations of the Church of England.

SENATE-HOUSE SYNDICATE

1. The Senate-House Syndicate shall consist of the Vice-Chancellor as Chair, the Registrary, the Esquire Bedells, the Proctors, the two Pro-Proctors who are nominated by the Colleges, and eight members of the Senate appointed by the Council in the Michaelmas Term to serve for four years from 1 January following their appointment. Constitution.

2. The Syndicate shall be responsible for the management and regulation of public ceremonials taking place in the Senate-House. They shall be empowered to make arrangements for admission to the Senate-House, for its proper preparation on occasions of public ceremonial, for issuing tickets when they think proper, for providing and assigning seats, and for assisting the University officers in the maintenance of order. The Syndicate shall have full control of the Senate-House Yard on occasions of public ceremonial in the Senate-House. Duties and powers.

3. The Syndicate shall make such reports to the Council as the Council may require.

SOCIETIES SYNDICATE

1. The Societies Syndicate shall consist of: Constitution.

(*a*) the Vice-Chancellor (or a deputy), who shall be the Chair;

(*b*) the Junior Proctor (or a deputy);

(*c*) the Chair of the Committee of Senior Treasurers of College Amalgamated Clubs;

(*d*) two members of the Regent House appointed by the Council, of whom at least one shall be a Bursar or a Senior Tutor;

(*e*) three members of the University *in statu pupillari* appointed by the Technical Committee of the Syndicate from among the members of that Committee, provided that, when the Committee has among its members one or more graduate students, one member should be a graduate student;

(*f*) two members of the University *in statu pupillari* appointed by the College delegates who serve on the Cambridge University Students Union Council;

(*g*) the Cambridge University Students Union Services Officer and the Graduate Union President, *ex officio*.

2. Members in class (*d*) shall be appointed in the Michaelmas Term to serve for four years from 1 January following their appointment. Members in classes (*e*), (*f*), and (*g*) shall be appointed for one year from 1 October.

Duties. **3.** It shall be the duty of the Syndics:

(*a*) to meet at least once in each academical year;

(*b*) to manage any funds that may be made available to them, and to keep the accounts thereof;

(*c*) to consider applications for financial assistance from societies, and to make grants to those societies which in their opinion are most deserving of such assistance; provided that if, in the opinion of the Registrary, an application has serious legal or financial implications for the University, no grant shall be made in respect of that application without the concurrence of the Council;

(*d*) to give particular consideration to applications from societies judged by Faculty Boards to have special educational merits;

(*e*) to report annually to the Council in the Michaelmas Term on the financial assistance provided to societies during the previous academical year.

Powers. **4.** The Syndics shall have power:

(*a*) to require every society which applies for financial assistance:

(i) to demonstrate that membership of the society is open in principle and in practice to all resident members of the University, irrespective of political, religious, or social considerations;

(ii) to submit to the Syndics, in a form approved by them, a copy of its accounts, correctly audited, and countersigned by its Senior Treasurer;

(iii) to state the use which it intends to make of a grant or loan, and to report within an agreed period of time on the use made of each grant or loan;

(iv) to present evidence that it is not able to improve its immediate financial condition by raising membership fees, by improving management, by eliminating wasteful expenditure, or by recruiting more effectively;

(*b*) to delegate to the Technical Committee constituted in accordance with Regulation 5 any part of their duties and powers that they may think fit.

Technical Committee

Constitution. **5.** There shall be a Technical Committee of the Societies Syndicate which shall consist of:

(*a*) the Junior Proctor (or a deputy), who shall be Chair;

(*b*) twelve members of the University *in statu pupillari*, one appointed by each of twelve societies nominated annually by the Syndics;

(*c*) the members of the Societies Syndicate appointed in class (*f*);

(*d*) the Cambridge University Students Union Services Officer and the Graduate Union President, *ex officio*.

Members in classes (*b*) and (*d*) shall be appointed in the Easter Term to serve for one year from 1 October following their appointment.

Duties. **6.** It shall be the duty of the Technical Committee:

(*a*) to meet at least once in each term;

(*b*) to consider applications for financial assistance from societies, and to make grants to societies not exceeding an amount to be determined by the Syndics; provided that if, in the opinion of the Registrary, an application has serious legal or financial implications for the University, no grant shall be made in respect of that application without the concurrence of the Council;

(*c*) to submit annually to the Syndics an audited copy of any accounts which the Syndics may require the Committee to keep.

Sports Syndicate

Constitution. **1.** The Sports Syndicate shall consist of:

(*a*) the Vice-Chancellor or a duly appointed deputy as Chair;

(*b*) five members of the Senate appointed by the Council;

(*c*) one member of the Finance Committee of the Council, appointed by the Council on the nomination of the Committee;
(*d*) the Chair of the Committee of Senior Treasurers of College Amalgamated Clubs or a representative appointed by the Chair;
(*e*) the Director of Physical Education;
(*f*) two Senior Treasurers of University sports clubs co-opted by the Syndicate;
(*g*) not more than two other persons co-opted by the Syndicate;
(*h*) one person *in statu pupillari* appointed by a special meeting of delegates of the Colleges, each College deciding for itself how its delegate shall be appointed;
(*i*) six persons *in statu pupillari*, four appointed by the Blues Committee and two appointed by the Women's Blues Committee.

2. Members in classes (*b*) and (*c*) shall be appointed in the Michaelmas Term to serve for four years from 1 January next following their appointment. Co-opted members shall serve until 31 December of the year in which they are co-opted or of the following year as the Syndicate shall determine at the time of their co-optation. Members in classes (*h*) and (*i*) shall be appointed in the Michaelmas Term to serve for the remainder of the current academical year.

3. There shall be at least one meeting of the Syndicate in each academical year. Meetings.

4. The Director of Physical Education shall serve as Secretary of the Syndicate.

5. The Syndicate shall advise the Council and the University about policy, facilities, and arrangements for sport in the University. The Syndicate shall seek to ensure that the University's needs in the field of sport are properly provided for by the University sports clubs; for that purpose the Syndicate shall exercise general control and supervision over the clubs which have been approved by them and which appear in the list maintained under Regulation 7(*c*) of these regulations.

6. The Syndicate shall have general responsibility for the management of the Physical Education Centre, Fenner's cricket and tennis grounds, the Wilberforce Road sports ground, and such other University premises, facilities, and services for sport and physical recreation as the Council shall from time to time assign to the Syndicate. The Syndicate shall make rules for these premises, facilities, and services, shall make such arrangements for their day-to-day running as they consider appropriate, shall appoint a Fenner's Committee and such other committees or sub-syndicates as they consider necessary for effective management, shall exercise general supervision over the work of the staff assigned to the Syndicate, shall advise the Council on the number of staff required, and shall prepare annual estimates for submission to the Council. Management of facilities for sport.

7. The Syndicate shall have power: Powers.
(*a*) to inspect the accounts of the Central Athletics Committee;
(*b*) to approve the object, constitution, and rules of the University sports clubs;
(*c*) to maintain a list of approved University sports clubs and to add to that list any sports clubs which in the opinion of the Syndicate are providing for the University's needs in the field of sport, and to remove from it any clubs which in their opinion are failing to do so;
(*d*) to invite representations, whether by attendance at its meetings or otherwise, from the officers of any sports club when an item of business before the Syndicate affects the interests of the particular club.

8. The Syndicate shall make an Annual Report to the Council and such other reports as the Council may require.

9. The provisions of Special Ordinance A (vii) 5 concerning reserved business shall apply to the Syndicate as if it were a body constituted by Statute.

10. There shall be the University offices of Director of Physical Education and Assistant Director of Physical Education and such number of University offices of Physical Education Officer as the Council shall from time to time determine.

11. Under the general control of the Syndicate, the Director of Physical Education shall be the professional and administrative head of the premises, facilities, and services specified in Regulation 6 and, subject to the powers of the Syndicate and of the Fenner's Committee, shall be responsible for their day-to-day management.

12. Appointments and reappointments to the University office of Director of Physical Education, to the University office of Assistant Director of Physical Education, and to a University office of Physical

Education Officer shall be made by an Appointments Committee of which the Registrary, or a deputy appointed by the Registrary, shall act as Secretary and which shall consist of:

(*a*) the Vice-Chancellor (or a duly appointed deputy) who shall be Chair;
(*b*) the Chair of the Sports Syndicate;
(*c*) two members of the Regent House appointed by the Council;
(*d*) two members of the Regent House appointed by the Sports Syndicate;
(*e*) the Director of Physical Education, when an appointment or reappointment is to be made to the office of Assistant Director of Physical Education or to an office of Physical Education Officer.

Members in classes (*c*) and (*d*) shall be appointed in the Michaelmas Term to serve for two years from 1 January following their appointment.

13. Every appointment or reappointment to a University office by the Committee shall be made with the concurrence of the votes (which shall be given in person at a meeting) of not fewer than four members of the Committee. Special Ordinance C (x) 4 shall apply to the Committee as if it were an Appointments Committee for a Faculty.

Fenner's Committee.

14. There shall be a Fenner's Committee, which shall be responsible to the Sports Syndicate. The Committee shall consist of:

(*a*) one member of the Sports Syndicate, appointed by the Syndicate, who shall be Chair of the Committee;
(*b*) three members of the Senate, appointed by the Sports Syndicate, one on the nomination of each of the following bodies: the Cambridge University Cricket Club, the Cambridge University Lawn Tennis Club, the Cambridge University Cricket and Athletics Club Ltd;
(*c*) the Director of Physical Education.

Members in classes (*a*) and (*b*) shall be appointed in the Michaelmas Term to serve for four years from 1 January next following their appointment. The Director of Physical Education shall act as Secretary of the Committee.

15. The Committee shall have the following duties in relation to Fenner's cricket and tennis grounds:

(*a*) to make recommendations to the Sports Syndicate for the management of the grounds;
(*b*) to exercise general oversight over the administration and maintenance of the grounds and the work of the staff;
(*c*) to administer such funds as may be made available to them;
(*d*) to prepare annual estimates for submission to the Sports Syndicate;
(*e*) to make an Annual Report to the Sports Syndicate.

University Theatre Syndicate

Constitution.

1. There shall be a University Theatre Syndicate which shall consist of:

(*a*) the Vice-Chancellor (or a duly appointed deputy) as Chair;
(*b*) two Trustees of the Amateur Dramatic Club, appointed by the Council;
(*c*) one member of the Senate, appointed by the Council;
(*d*) one member of the Finance Committee of the Council, appointed by the Council on the nomination of the Committee;
(*e*) one person appointed by the Societies Syndicate;
(*f*) one person appointed by the Faculty Board of English;
(*g*) the President and the Senior Treasurer, for the time being, of the Amateur Dramatic Club;
(*h*) one member of the Amateur Dramatic Club, appointed by the Committee of the Club, who shall be a technician working in the ADC Theatre;
(*i*) one member of the Technical Committee of the Societies Syndicate appointed by that Syndicate;
(*j*) one person appointed by the Cambridge Arts Theatre Trust;
(*k*) the Chair of the Executive Committee, *ex officio*;
(*l*) not more than two persons, who may include persons *in statu pupillari*, co-opted by the Syndicate; one of these persons shall be chosen specifically to represent the interests of music and opera.

Members in classes (*b*), (*c*), (*d*), (*e*), (*f*), and (*j*) shall be appointed in the Michaelmas Term to serve for four years from 1 January following their appointment. Members in classes (*h*) and (*i*) shall be appointed to serve for the remainder of the academical year in which they are appointed. Co-opted members shall serve for the remainder of the academical year in which they are co-opted. The Secretary shall be appointed by the Registrary.

2. It shall be the main purpose of the University Theatre Syndicate to endeavour to ensure that the ADC Theatre is available for use and enjoyment as a University theatre, primarily for the production by University and College societies of plays, operas, and concerts, and the showing of films. Subject to any directions made by the Council or the Finance Committee, it shall be the duty of the Syndicate, in consultation with the Societies Syndicate, to determine the general policy of the ADC Theatre, particularly its administration and finance. The Syndicate shall keep under review the other theatrical facilities available in Cambridge, and shall take account of them in determining that policy each year. The Syndicate shall report annually to the Council in the Michaelmas Term on the affairs of the ADC Theatre, and shall in particular report the productions that have taken place there and indicate those produced by University and College societies. Duties.

3. There shall be an Executive Committee for the ADC Theatre which shall consist of: Executive Committee.

(*a*) a member of the Regent House as Chair, appointed by the Council on the nomination of the Finance Committee;

(*b*) a University officer appointed by the Council;

(*c*) the members of the University Theatre Syndicate in classes (*c*), (*g*), and (*h*).

The Chair shall be appointed in the Michaelmas Term to serve for four years from 1 January following his or her appointment. The Secretary shall be appointed by the Registrary.

4. Subject to any directions made by the Council or the Finance Committee, it shall be the duty of the Executive Committee: Duties.

(*a*) to meet at least three times each term;

(*b*) to administer the ADC Theatre, and to make and publish rules and procedures for its use;

(*c*) to determine for each user the period for which the facilities of the Theatre shall be available, and to fix the contract terms applicable to each user;

(*d*) to establish and keep under review the financial procedures for the Theatre, to prepare and approve annual estimates of receipts and expenditure, to administer the Theatre's funds, and to receive at each meeting a report of its receipts and attendance;

(*e*) to authorize the appointment of staff, other than the Manager, and to supervise their work;

(*f*) to report termly to the Registrary the productions that have taken place in the Theatre, with their financial results, and to report annually to the Finance Committee on the overall financial performance of the Theatre.

5. Appointments and reappointments to the University office of Manager of the ADC Theatre shall be made by the Council on the recommendation of the University Theatre Syndicate. The stipend of the holder of the office shall be determined by the Council on the advice of the Finance Committee. The duties of the office shall be determined by the University Theatre Syndicate. Manager.

West and North West Cambridge Estates Syndicate

1. The West and North West Cambridge Estates Syndicate shall consist of: Constitution.

(*a*) a person appointed by the Council as Chair who shall be a person with experience and expertise in matters relevant to the affairs of the Syndicate;

(*b*) a University officer appointed by the Council; and

(*c*) nine members appointed by the Council who shall be persons with experience and expertise in matters relevant to the affairs of the Syndicate (at least five of whom shall be members of the Regent House).

Subject to Regulation 12 below and the General Regulations for Boards, Syndicates, etc., members in classes (*a*) and (*c*) shall be appointed for four years from 1 January following their appointment.

2. The Registrary shall appoint the Secretary of the Syndicate.

3. No business shall be transacted at any meeting of the Syndicate unless at least five members are present, of whom at least three are members of the Regent House. Quorum.

4. Within the strategic and financial framework and any other limitations set by the Council or the University, as amended from time to time, the Syndicate shall be responsible for: Responsibilities

(i) the management, development, and stewardship of the North West Cambridge Estate (being the University's land and property holdings in the area between Madingley Road, Huntingdon Road, and the M11 motorway); and

(ii) the development and stewardship of the West Cambridge Estate (being the University's land and property holdings in the area bounded by Madingley Road, Clerk Maxwell Road, the Coton Footpath, and the M11).

5. Subject to the restrictions set out in Regulations 4, 6, and 7, the Syndicate shall be authorized to exercise in the name of the University in relation to the affairs of the Syndicate all the powers of the University, except in so far as the Statutes and Ordinances expressly or by necessary implication provide otherwise.

6. The approval of the Finance Committee shall be required for any proposal to borrow money or to establish or acquire an interest in any company registered under the Companies Acts or otherwise.

7. For the avoidance of doubt, no proposal relating to the erection, demolition or substantial alteration of any building for academic or (non-commercial) research purposes shall be implemented unless it has been specifically approved by Grace of the Regent House.

Annual Report. **8.** The Syndicate shall make an Annual Report to the Council, which shall include a budget and audited accounts and which shall be published to the University either as a whole or in summary. The Syndicate shall make such other reports and take such other steps as the Council may require from time to time.

Declaration of personal and business interests. **9.** Members of the Syndicate shall register and declare all personal and business interests which may, or may be perceived to, influence their judgement in connection with the affairs of the Syndicate and, where appropriate, shall withdraw from related business and discussions. The Council may from time to time determine procedures for the financial regulation and conduct of the affairs of the Syndicate after consultation with the Chair of the Syndicate.

Project Director. **10.** There shall be the post of a Project Director for the North West Cambridge project. The duties of the Project Director shall be determined by the Syndicate. Appointments and reappointments to the post of Project Director shall be made by the Syndicate.

11. The Council shall have the power in exceptional circumstances to discharge the Syndicate and to assume full responsibility itself for the management, development, and stewardship of the West and North West Cambridge Estates for the time being.

12. The Council shall have the power at any time to revise the period of a person's appointment as a member of the Syndicate.

Undergraduate Admissions Committee

Constitution. **1.** There shall be an Undergraduate Admissions Committee which shall consist of:

(*a*) the Pro-Vice-Chancellor with special responsibility for educational matters;

(*b*) the Secretary or an Associate Secretary of the Senior Tutors' Committee;

(*c*) the intercollegiate Director of Admissions;

(*d*) three persons appointed by the Senior Tutors' Committee;

(*e*) one person appointed by the Admissions Forum;

(*f*) one person appointed by the Bursars' Committee;

(*g*) four members of the Regent House, being three representatives of the Councils of the Schools, appointed by the Council on the nomination of the General Board and one further member appointed by the Council on its own nomination;

(*h*) the Access Officer of Cambridge University Students Union;

(*i*) not more than three persons co-opted by the Committee, provided that it shall not be obligatory for the Committee to co-opt any person or persons.

Tenure. **2.** The members of the Committee other than those in classes (*a*), (*b*), (*c*), (*h*), and (*i*) shall be appointed in the Michaelmas Term to serve for three years from the date of their appointment. Members in class (*i*) shall serve until the end of the calendar year in which they are co-opted.

3. Members in classes (*a*) and (*b*) shall jointly chair the Committee.

Duties. **4.** It shall be the duty of the Committee:

(*a*) to keep under review undergraduate admissions policy and practice, including matters related to widening access and participation and the funds associated with such activities, and to student numbers, and to make recommendations accordingly to the appropriate University or intercollegiate bodies;

(*b*) to promote fairness and consistency in the Colleges' admissions policies.

Management Group. **5.** The Committee shall establish a Management Group, not necessarily consisting wholly of members of the Committee, for the Cambridge Admissions Office.

Restrictions. **6.** The Committee shall have no authority in the consideration of, or decision on, the applications of individual candidates for admission, and they shall so discharge their duties as in no way to diminish the freedom or the responsibility of the Colleges in the admission of members of the University *in statu pupillari*.

7. The provision of Special Ordinance A (vii) 5 concerning reserved business shall apply to the Committee as if it were a body constituted by Statute. Reserved business.

Joint Committee on Development

Amended by Graces 2 of 27 November and 3 of 18 December 2013

1. The Joint Committee on Development shall be a joint Committee of the Council and the Colleges and shall consist of: Constitution.

(*a*) the Vice-Chancellor and the Chair of the Colleges Committee (*ex officio*) who shall be co-Chairs;
(*b*) a member of the Council appointed by the Council;
(*c*) three members of the Regent House appointed by the Council, on the nomination of the General Board, who shall normally be persons having experience of fund-raising at the University level, one of whom shall be a Head of School;
(*d*) a Head of House appointed by the Colleges' Standing Committee;
(*e*) four persons appointed by the Colleges' Standing Committee having regard to their experience of fund-raising for the Colleges;
(*f*) the Executive Director of Development and Alumni Relations;
(*g*) the Executive Director of Cambridge in America.

Members in classes (*b*) to (*e*) shall be appointed in the Michaelmas Term to serve for three years from 1 January next following their appointment. The Pro-Vice-Chancellor (Planning and Resources), the Registrary, the Academic Secretary, the Director of the Finance Division, and the Chief Operating Officer of Development and Alumni Relations of the University Offices shall have the right to attend meetings of the Committee.

2. The Registrary shall designate a University officer to act as Secretary to the Joint Committee. Secretary.

3. The duties of the Joint Committee shall be: Duties.

(*a*) to monitor the performance of, and recommend revisions to, the overall strategy for fund-raising on behalf of the University and the Colleges;
(*b*) to keep under review and facilitate the relationships and links between the University and the Colleges and their members;
(*c*) to receive and approve nominations to the Guild of Benefactors;
(*d*) to facilitate and support effective collaboration between the University and the Colleges;
(*e*) to establish, implement, and ensure the effectiveness of codes of practice and policies in support of its remit;
(*f*) to receive and review the budget and work plan for collaborative activity in fund-raising undertaken through the office of Cambridge in America in the USA, and any such similar bodies that may be established in future on a jointly funded basis elsewhere in the world, and to recommend them to the Planning and Resources Committee for approval.

Health and Safety Executive Committee

1. The Health and Safety Executive Committee shall be a committee jointly of the Council and the General Board and shall consist of: Constitution.

(*a*) the Vice-Chancellor (or a duly appointed deputy) as Chair;
(*b*) three members of the Regent House appointed by the Council on the recommendation of the General Board of whom one shall be from an institution within the Schools of Arts and Humanities or the Humanities and Social Sciences and one from an institution within the Schools of the Biological Sciences, Clinical Medicine, Physical Sciences, or Technology;
(*c*) the Chair of the Consultative Committee for Safety;
(*d*) not more than two persons co-opted by the Committee, provided that it shall not be obligatory for the Committee to co-opt any person or persons.

2. Members in class (*b*) shall be appointed in the Michaelmas Term to serve for four years from 1 January next following their appointment. Co-opted members shall serve until 31 December of the year in which they are co-opted or of the following year, as the Committee shall determine at the time of their co-optation. The Director of Health and Safety, the Director of Human Resources, and the

Director of the Estate Management and Building Service shall have the right to attend meetings of the Committee. The Secretary of the Committee shall be appointed by the Registrary.

Secretary.

Duties of the Committee.

3. The Committee shall:

(*a*) ensure the necessary management actions are taken to give effect to University health and safety policy;

(*b*) review the effectiveness of the University health and safety policy at intervals agreed by the Committee, but not exceeding two years;

(*c*) review University strategy on health and safety at intervals not exceeding two years;

(*d*) ensure that information about decisions on health and safety is communicated from the Committee to staff of the University;

(*e*) receive annual reports on health and safety;

(*f*) receive regular summary reports from the Consultative Committee for Safety and the Occupational Health Committee, and receive information from other sources where appropriate to health and safety;

(*g*) oversee and, where appropriate, approve the development of University health and safety policy.

Annual Report.

4. The Committee shall make an Annual Report to the Council and the General Board.

5. The Committee shall meet at least once in each term.

Information Services Committee

Constitution.

1. The Information Services Committee shall be a Committee of the Council and the General Board, and shall consist of:

(*a*) the Vice-Chancellor (or a duly appointed deputy) as Chair;

(*b*) three persons appointed by the Council after consultation with the General Board;

(*c*) one person appointed by the Council who is not a member of the Regent House;

(*d*) three persons appointed from among the Heads of the Schools by the General Board;

(*e*) two persons appointed by the Colleges' Committee;

(*f*) one person appointed by the Library Syndicate;

(*g*) the Registrary;

(*h*) two members of the University in *statu pupillari*, co-opted by the Committee, one of whom shall be a graduate student;

(*i*) one person co-opted by the Committee, although it shall not be obligatory for the Committee to exercise this power.

2. The Director of Information Services shall be the executive officer of the Committee.

3. The appointment of members in classes (*b*), (*c*), (*d*), (*e*) and (*f*) shall be made in the Michaelmas Term for periods of four years from 1 January following. Two members in class (*b*), the member in class (*c*), one member in class (*d*) and one member in class (*e*) shall be appointed to serve in a year when the calendar year is odd; one member in class (*b*), two members in class (*d*), one member in class (*e*) and the member in class (*f*) shall be appointed to serve in a year when the calendar year is even. Co-opted members in classes (*h*) and (*i*) shall serve until 31 December of the year following that in which they are co-opted, provided that if a member in class (*h*) ceases to be in *statu pupillari* he or she shall thereupon cease to be a member in that class.

Secretary.

4. The Registrary shall appoint the Secretary of the Committee, in consultation with the Chair.

Duties.

5. It shall be the duty of the Committee:

(*a*) to establish and keep under review, subject to the approval of the Council and the General Board and, where appropriate, the Colleges, a strategy for information services, and staffing requirements, across the University and Colleges in support of research, teaching and administration;

(*b*) to promote the effective and efficient implementation of the information strategy where appropriate throughout the University and the Colleges, to advise on developments in information technology and its implementation, including the sharing of experience and solutions;

(*c*) to establish mechanisms to ascertain information requirements of users across the University and the Colleges, and ensure that these requirements inform the strategy under (*a*) above;

(*d*) to ensure, through the Director of Information Services, that any such information policies, facilities, and services provided by the University Information Services are operating effectively and are fit for purpose, and to approve general principles for the allocation of resources and priorities in the use of information technology facilities;

(*e*) to review and propose the budget for the University Information Services, on advice from the Director of Information Services;

(*f*) to be responsible for ensuring that appropriate project and budgetary management and control mechanisms are in place for such major information systems and technology projects as the Council or the General Board may from time to time determine, and to be accountable for the funds allocated for such projects;

(*g*) to ensure that all centrally provided systems and services provide value for money;

(*h*) to set, consulting the Councils of the Schools, Colleges and other institutions as necessary, minimum standards of service to be provided;

(*i*) to be responsible for the regulation and security of the use of information technology facilities within the University, and of such computing facilities in College institutions as may be designated for this purpose from time to time by the appropriate College authorities concerned, and for this purpose to make, or amend, and publish rules, subject to approval by the competent authority, and to impose on a person infringing one or more of those rules either or both of the following penalties:

(i) the suspension of authorization to use computing resources for such a period as the Information Services Committee shall determine;

(ii) a fine not exceeding £175.

(*j*) to make an annual report to the Council and the General Board and to the Senior Tutors' and Bursars' Committees, that report to include a review of the strategy for information services.

6. The Committee shall establish such sub-committees, or other bodies reporting to it, as it considers necessary effectively to discharge its duties.

RULES MADE BY THE INFORMATION SERVICES COMMITTEE

In these rules the following definitions shall apply. The term IT facilities shall mean the facilities of the University Information Services, and all other information technology facilities provided by the University, and any in College institutions designated by the appropriate College authority concerned as facilities to which these rules shall apply. The term Authorized Officer shall mean the Director of Information Services in the case of services under the supervision of the Information Services Committee, or in other cases the relevant University or College officer (in the case of University institutions, the Chair of the Council of the School, the Chair of the Faculty Board, or the Head of the Department; in the case of Colleges, a person appointed by the College for the purpose).

IT facilities are provided for use only in accordance with the aims of the University and the Colleges as promulgated from time to time, unless stated otherwise by the appropriate Authorized Officer.

1. No person shall use IT facilities, or allow them to be used by others, without due authorization given by the Information Services Committee or by the appropriate Authorized Officer, who may impose conditions of use to ensure efficient operation.

2. By means of published documentation an Authorized Officer may designate an IT facility as authorized for use by specified classes of persons and for specified purposes. In the case of facilities not so designated, resources are allocated individually; every such allocation of IT resources shall be used only for the designated purpose and only by the person to whom the allocation was made. Use shall not be made of IT resources allocated to another person or group of persons unless such use has been specifically authorized by the Information Services Committee or by the appropriate Authorized Officer.

3. No person shall by any wilful, deliberate, reckless, or unlawful act or omission interfere with the work of another user or jeopardize the integrity of data networks, computing equipment, systems programs, or other stored information.

4. All persons authorized to use IT facilities shall be expected to treat as privileged any information which may become available to them through the use of such facilities and which is not obviously intended for unrestricted dissemination; such information shall not be copied, modified, disseminated, or used, either in whole or in part, without the permission of the appropriate person or body.

5. In the case of any information which is designated in a Notice issued by or on behalf of the Information Services Committee as proprietary or otherwise confidential, every person using IT facilities shall be required:

(*a*) to observe any instructions that may be issued specifying ways in which the information may be used;

(*b*) not to copy, modify, disseminate, or make use of it in any way not specified in those instructions, without first obtaining permission from the appropriate Authorized Officer.

6. No person shall use IT facilities to process personal data except in accordance with the provisions of relevant legislation, including the Data Protection Act 1998. Any person wishing to use IT facilities for such a purpose shall be required to inform the Authorized Officer in advance and to comply with any restrictions that may be imposed concerning the manner in which the data may be processed.

7. No person shall use IT facilities for private financial gain or for commercial purposes, including consultancy or any other work outside the scope of official duties or functions for the time being, without specific authorization to do so.

8. Any person who misuses IT facilities or who uses IT facilities for private financial gain or for commercial purposes, with or without specific authorization to do so, may be charged with the cost of such use or misuse at a rate determined from time to time by the appropriate Authorized Officer. If any person who has been so charged with the cost of IT resources fails to make reimbursement, any authorization to use IT facilities shall be suspended automatically until reimbursement is made in full, and the matter shall be reported by the Committee to the appropriate University or College financial authority.

9. No person shall use IT facilities for unlawful activities.

10. Any person believed to be in breach of one or more of these rules shall be reported by the Authorized Officer to the Committee who may at their discretion, after considering the Officer's report and any other relevant matters, impose a penalty or penalties in accordance with Regulation 5(*i*) for the Committee. The Committee may also recommend to the appropriate University or College authority that proceedings be initiated under either or both of the University and College disciplinary procedures and any appropriate legislation.

University Software Policy

Under UK Copyright Law, the illegal reproduction of software can be subject to civil damages without financial limit and to criminal penalties including fines and imprisonment. Both the person who made the illegal copy and the relevant University authorities would be liable to prosecution for each illegal copy found. The Council and the General Board have accordingly approved the following Software Policy in regard to computer software licensed by the University of Cambridge and its Colleges with which all members of the University are expected to comply:

1. The University of Cambridge and its Colleges use under licence computer software (both programs and data) from a variety of outside companies. The University does not own this software or its related documentation and, unless authorized by the licence, does not have the right to copy it in any way.

2. Whenever and however such software is used (including software mounted on Local Area Networks and multiple machines) University and College staff and students must comply with the licence agreement.

3. The condition in 2 above shall apply not only to software on computers owned by the University and its Colleges but also to software on personal machines owned by individual University and College staff and students insofar as the software is being used for University or College purposes, including student course-work.

Procedures for managing software licences

4. *Responsibility.* Heads of institutions are responsible for ensuring that all software used within the institution and stored on computers for which the institution is responsible has been properly obtained and is being used within the terms of the software licence. The following paragraphs recommend the steps which need to be taken to ensure that any reasonable legal challenge can be met.

5. *Appointment of a responsible officer.* The Head of the institution should appoint a member of staff (the Software Licence Manager) to be formally responsible to the Head of the institution for software licence management and compliance.

6. *Software licence inventory.* The Software Licence Manager should maintain an inventory of software licences held by the institution. The following information should be recorded for each item of licensed software:

the name, platform, and version number of the software,
the number of copies purchased,
the date purchased and purchase order reference,
the location of the software licence (if a paper licence was issued),
the location (or IP address) of the system or systems on which the software is stored,
any restrictions on the licensed use of the software.

7. *Software licence storage.* As far as is practical, software licences should be stored in one place in the institution.

8. *Software procurement.* Institutional purchasing procedures should ensure that the software licence inventory is updated accordingly whenever licensed software is purchased. In a small Faculty or Department or other institution this might be accomplished by requiring all software purchases to be made by the Software Licence Manager. In a large Faculty, Department, or other institution, more flexible procedures may be necessary.

9. *Disciplinary procedures.* Use of licensed software without a licence or use of software outside the terms of the licence is illegal and must be treated as a disciplinary offence. The Head of the institution is responsible firstly for ensuring that corrective action is taken as soon as an offence comes to light and then for ensuring that appropriate disciplinary action is taken.

10. All users who obtain software from Information Services are required to sign a statement which says that they are fully aware of the University Software Policy and agree to uphold it.

Software obtained privately by individuals

11. Users of software for University or College purposes, including student course-work, which has been obtained privately from other sources must also comply with the terms of the agreement under which that software has been obtained. It is the responsibility of such users to ensure that the necessary authorizations for the software are readily available.

12. All users of University computers must comply with the conditions under which they are permitted access to the computers. Where the access conditions prohibit installation of privately obtained software, this condition must be strictly adhered to.

Medical Education Committee

1. The Medical Education Committee shall consist of: Constitution.

(*a*) the Regius Professor of Physic as Chair;
(*b*) the Director of Education (Biological Sciences) in the Faculty of Biology;
(*c*) the Director of Medical Education in the Faculty of Clinical Medicine;
(*d*) the Chair of the Council of the School of the Biological Sciences;
(*e*) the Chair of the Faculty Board of Biology;
(*f*) two persons appointed by the Senior Tutors' Committee;
(*g*) one person appointed by the Faculty Board of Biology from among the members of that Board in class (*f*);
(*h*) one person appointed by the Faculty Board of Clinical Medicine;
(*i*) one person appointed by the Faculty Board of Clinical Medicine from among the members of that Board in class (*f*);
(*j*) one person appointed by the Faculty Board of Clinical Medicine who shall be a Pre-Registration House Officer.

2. Members in class (*f*) shall be appointed in the Michaelmas Term to serve for four years from 1 January following their appointment. Members in classes (*g*) and (*i*) shall be appointed in the Michaelmas Term and the Lent Term respectively, and shall serve until they cease to be members of the Faculty Board by which they are appointed. The member in class (*j*) shall be appointed in the Lent Term, and shall serve for one year from the date of his or her appointment. Appointments.

3. The Secretary of the Committee shall be appointed by the Secretary General of the Faculties. Secretary.

4. It shall be the duty of the Committee to keep under review the provision of medical education in the University, with a view to ensuring consistency of standards in different subjects, the integration of core elements of the medical curriculum, and the introduction of appropriate innovations in the curriculum. The Committee shall advise the Faculty Boards of Biology and Clinical Medicine on the following matters: Duties.

(*a*) matters relating to the education of medical students, including admissions policies, student statistics, and examination results;
(*b*) matters relating to resources needed for the provision of medical education;
(*c*) proposals for changes in the medical curriculum and in the relevant examinations.

5. The Committee shall meet at least once each term. No business shall be transacted at any meeting of the Committee unless at least five members are present. Quorum.

6. The Committee shall make such reports to the General Board as the Board may require. Reports.

7. The provisions of Special Ordinance A (vii) 5 concerning reserved business shall apply to the Medical Education Committee as if it were a body constituted by Statute. Reserved business.

Military Education Committee

1. There shall be a Military Education Committee which shall consist of: Constitution.

(*a*) the Vice-Chancellor (or a duly appointed deputy) as Chair;
(*b*) four members of the Senate appointed by the Council;
(*c*) two members of the Senate appointed by the Senior Tutors' Committee;
(*d*) one person appointed by the Ministry of Defence (Navy), one by the Ministry of Defence (Army), and one by the Ministry of Defence (Air Force);
(*e*) the Commanding Officer for the time being or, in the Commanding Officer's absence, the Adjutant, of the Officers Training Corps;
(*f*) the Commanding Officer for the time being or, in the Commanding Officer's absence, the Adjutant, of the Air Squadron;
(*g*) the Commanding Officer for the time being or, in the Commanding Officer's absence, the Coxswain, of the Royal Naval Unit;
(*h*) the Secretary of the Careers Service Syndicate or a deputy, who shall be a member of the staff of the Careers Service Syndicate, appointed by the Secretary;
(*i*) two persons appointed by the University of East Anglia, one by Anglia Ruskin University, and one by the University of Essex;

(*j*) not more than two persons co-opted by the Committee, provided that it shall not be obligatory for the Committee to co-opt any person or persons.

2. Members in classes (*b*) and (*c*) shall be appointed in the Michaelmas Term to serve for four years from 1 January following their appointment. Co-opted members shall serve until the end of the calendar year following that in which they are co-opted.

Secretary. **3.** The Secretary of the Committee shall be appointed by the Registrary.

Duties. **4.** It shall be the duty of the Committee:

(*a*) to encourage co-operation and to act as a link between the University and the staffs of the Officers Training Corps, the Air Squadron, and the Royal Naval Unit;

(*b*) to correspond from time to time with the Ministry of Defence (Navy, Army, and Air Force), and the authorities at other universities on Service matters.

5. The Committee shall make such reports to the Council as the Council may require.

No cost to University. **6.** The University shall incur no financial responsibility for the maintenance of the Officers Training Corps, the Air Squadron, or the Royal Naval Unit.

Committee of Management for the Natural Sciences Tripos

1. There shall be a Committee of Management for the Natural Sciences Tripos, which shall be responsible, in consultation with the Faculty Boards and other authorities concerned, for co-ordinating the administration of the Natural Sciences Tripos.

Constitution. **2.** The Committee of Management shall consist of:

(*a*) two persons appointed by the General Board, one on the nomination of the Council of the School of the Biological Sciences, and one on the nomination of the Council of the School of the Physical Sciences;

(*b*) eleven persons appointed by the General Board, four on the nomination of the Council of the School of the Physical Sciences in consultation with the Faculty Boards of Earth Sciences and Geography, Mathematics, and Physics and Chemistry, four on the nomination of the Faculty Board of Biology, one on the nomination of the Board of History and Philosophy of Science, one on the nomination of the Faculty Board of Computer Science and Technology, and one on the nomination of the Chemical Engineering and Biotechnology Syndicate;

(*c*) the Chairs of Examiners for the Natural Sciences Tripos for the current academical year;

(*d*) two members of the University *in statu pupillari* appointed by the Committee of Management from among those students who are candidates for any Part of the Natural Sciences Tripos;

(*e*) not more than three persons co-opted by the Committee, provided that it shall not be obligatory for the Committee to co-opt any person or persons.

Appointments. **3.** Members in classes (*a*) and (*b*) shall be appointed in the Michaelmas Term to serve for three years from 1 January following their appointment. Members in class (*d*) shall be appointed in the Michaelmas Term to serve for one year from 1 January following their appointment. Members in class (*e*) shall serve until 31 December of the year in which they are co-opted or of the year next following, as the Committee shall determine at the time of their co-optation.

Chair. **4.** The Committee shall elect a Chair, who shall be a member of the Committee in class (*a*) or (*b*). The Secretary of the Committee shall be a University officer designated by the General Board.

Meetings. **5.** The Committee shall meet at least once in each term.

Quorum. **6.** Eight members of the Committee shall form a quorum.

Duties. **7.** The duties of the Committee of Management for the Natural Sciences Tripos shall be:

(*a*) to keep under review all student-related administration for the several Parts of the Tripos;

(*b*) to supervise policies and guidance relating to examinations for the Tripos, and to provide relevant information to the Examiners for the several Parts of the Tripos;

(*c*) to obtain reports from the Examiners for the several Parts of the Tripos, and to ensure that Chairs of Faculty Boards and Heads of Departments are informed, as may be appropriate, about matters arising from such reports;

(*d*) to keep under review the regulations for the several Parts of the Tripos and, in consultation with the Faculty Boards and other authorities concerned, what amendments of the regulations for the Tripos are desirable, and to report to the General Board or the University, as appropriate, concerning proposals for such amendments;

(*e*) to make, after consulting the Faculty Boards and other authorities concerned, supplementary regulations for the Tripos;

(*f*) subject to any powers which the General Board may wish to exercise under Regulation 6 of the General Regulations for the General Board, to determine, after consulting the authorities concerned, the time-table of teaching for the Natural Sciences Tripos;

(*g*) to exercise with respect to any Preliminary Examination pertaining to the Natural Sciences Tripos, except so far as regards the nomination of Examiners, the powers and duties assigned to Faculty Boards by the regulations for Preliminary Examinations;

(*h*) to disseminate information about the Tripos within the University and to promote awareness and understanding of the Tripos in schools and other institutions outside the University;

(*i*) to consider matters referred to the Committee by the General Board, the Councils of the Schools, and the Faculty Boards and other authorities concerned;

(*j*) to make an Annual Report to the General Board, the Councils of the Schools and the Faculty Boards, and other authorities concerned with the Natural Sciences Tripos.

8. The provisions of Special Ordinance A (vii) 5 concerning reserved business shall apply to the Committee of Management as if it were a body constituted by Statute. Reserved business.

Cambridge Committee for Russian and East European Studies

1. The Cambridge Committee for Russian and East European Studies shall consist of: Constitution.

(*a*) the Head of the Department of Slavonic Studies;

(*b*) two persons appointed by the General Board, one on the nomination of the Head of the Department of Slavonic Studies;

(*c*) eight members of the Regent House, one appointed by each of the Faculty Boards of Asian and Middle Eastern Studies, Earth Sciences and Geography, Economics, History, and Modern and Medieval Languages, two appointed by the Faculty Board of Human, Social, and Political Science, and one by the Library Syndicate;

(*d*) not more than three persons co-opted by the Committee, provided that it shall not be obligatory for the Committee to co-opt any person or persons.

Members in classes (*b*) and (*c*) shall be appointed in the Michaelmas Term to serve for three years from 1 January next following their appointment. Co-opted members shall serve until the end of the calendar year in which they are co-opted.

2. The Committee shall elect annually one of their number as Chair and one as Secretary. Chair and Secretary.

3. The Committee shall have the following duties: Duties.

(*a*) in collaboration with the Faculty Boards concerned, to promote teaching and research in Russian and East European Studies;

(*b*) to co-operate with outside bodies in the encouragement of research in these subjects;

(*c*) to administer funds allocated to them for the purposes specified in (*a*) and (*b*) above;

(*d*) to perform such other duties as may be assigned to them from time to time by the General Board.

4. The Committee shall make such reports to the General Board as the Board may require. Reports.

Consultative Committee for Safety

1. The Consultative Committee for Safety shall consist of: Constitution.

(*a*) the Vice-Chancellor (or duly appointed deputy), as Chair;

(*b*) one person appointed by the Council in respect of the non-School institutions;

(*c*) six members of the Senate appointed by the General Board of whom one each shall be nominated by the Council of the School of Arts and Humanities, the Council of the School of the Humanities and Social Sciences, the Council of the School of the Physical Sciences, the Council of the School of the Biological Sciences, the Council of the School of Technology, the Faculty Board of Clinical Medicine;

(*d*) one person appointed from each of the unions formally recognized by the University, as nominated by the relevant association, provided that each member in this class shall have power to appoint a deputy to take her or his place at a particular meeting;

(*e*) one member of the Cambridge University and College Union appointed from that body;

(*f*) four persons appointed by the Consultative Committee's Sub-committees of whom one shall be nominated by each Sub-committee;
(*g*) two persons *in statu pupillari*, of whom one at least shall be nominated by the Graduate Union and one by Cambridge University Students Union, appointed by the Council;
(*h*) two persons appointed on the nomination of the Forum of Professional Safety Advisers from among their number;
(*i*) the Director of the Estate Management and Building Service or a duly appointed deputy, *ex officio*;
(*j*) the Director of the Human Resources Division, *ex officio*;
(*k*) not more than three members co-opted by the Committee, provided that it shall not be obligatory for the Committee to co-opt any person or persons.

Members in classes (*b*), (*c*), (*d*), and (*e*) shall be appointed in the Michaelmas Term to serve for four years from 1 January following their appointment. Members in classes (*f*), (*g*), and (*h*) shall be appointed to serve for one year from 1 October. Members in class (*k*) shall serve until 31 December of the year in which they are co-opted, or of the following year, as the Committee shall determine at the time of their co-optation. A person appointed in class (*d*) or class (*e*) shall cease to be a member if the Chair is notified in writing that the appointment has been terminated by the trade union which appointed her or him. The Secretary of the Committee, who shall normally be the Director of Health and Safety, shall be appointed by the Registrary.

Secretary.

The following persons shall attend: the Occupational Health Manager, the Director of University Biomedical Support Services, the University Security Adviser, the University Fire Safety Manager, staff of the Occupational Health and Safety Service as required.

Duties of the Committee.

2. The Committee shall be responsible for advising the Health and Safety Executive Committee on all matters concerning safety in the University.

Sub-committees.

3. The Committee shall establish the following standing Sub-committees: one for Ionizing and Non-Ionizing Radiations, one for Biological Safety, one for Chemical Safety, and one for Physical Safety. The Committee shall determine the duties and powers of each standing sub-committee and may amend those duties and powers from time to time. The Chair and Secretary of the Consultative Committee for Safety shall have the right to attend any meeting of a sub-committee.

University Radiation Officer and Departmental records.

4. The University officer designated as University Radiation Officer shall have access to the records maintained in Departments of the kinds and amounts of radioactive substances used, the methods used for their disposal, and the lists of persons working on radioactive substances, ionizing and non-ionizing radiations, or laser beams.

Staff Childcare Committee

Constitution.

1. The Staff Childcare Committee shall consist of:
(*a*) one person appointed by the Council, who shall be Chair;
(*b*) one person appointed by the General Board;
(*c*) one person appointed by the Local Examinations Syndicate;
(*d*) one person with experience of assistant staff matters appointed by the Council;
(*e*) one person appointed by the Council on the nomination of the Finance Committee;
(*f*) one person, who shall act as Secretary, appointed by the Registrary;
(*g*) not more than two persons co-opted by the Committee, provided that it shall not be obligatory for the Committee to co-opt any person or persons.

2. Members in classes (*a*)–(*e*) shall be appointed in the Michaelmas Term to serve for three years from 1 January following their appointment. Co-opted members shall serve until 31 December of the year in which they are co-opted or of the following year, as the Committee shall determine at the time of their co-optation.

Duties.

3. The duties of the Committee shall be:
(*a*) to advise the Council on all matters relating to childcare for University staff;
(*b*) to oversee the management of the University childcare facilities for University staff;
(*c*) to administer funds allocated to them for these purposes.

University Combination Room

Committee.

1. The University Combination Room shall be managed by a Committee of the Council which shall consist of
(*a*) four persons appointed by the Council;

(*b*) four members of the Regent House elected by the Regent House.

Members shall be appointed or elected, as the case may be, in the Michaelmas Term to serve for four years from 1 January following their appointment.

2. The election of members in class (*b*) shall be conducted by postal ballot, and shall be held at the same time as the biennial election of members of the Council. The arrangements for the election shall be those prescribed in Regulations 1 and 2 of the regulations for the election of members of the Council. If insufficient nominations are received to fill the number of vacancies the Council shall appoint as many members as may be necessary. Election.

3. If a casual vacancy occurs in class (*b*), the Committee shall have power to co-opt a member to fill it for the unexpired portion of the tenure. The name of any person so co-opted shall be published by Notice. Casual vacancies.

Veterinary Education Committee

1. The Veterinary Education Committee shall consist of: Constitution.

(*a*) the Head of the Department of Veterinary Medicine, or a person appointed by the Head of the Department, who shall be Chair;

(*b*) the Director of Education (Biological Sciences) in the Faculty of Biology;

(*c*) the Secretary of the Faculty Board of Veterinary Medicine, who shall be Secretary of the Committee;

(*d*) four persons appointed by the Faculty Board of Biology;

(*e*) four persons appointed by the Faculty Board of Veterinary Medicine;

(*f*) one person appointed by the Senior Tutors' Committee;

(*g*) the members of the Faculty Board of Veterinary Medicine in class (*f*).

The Secretary of the School of the Biological Sciences and the Secretary of the Faculty Board of Biology shall have the right to attend meetings of the Committee.

2. Members in classes (*d*), (*e*), and (*f*) shall be appointed in the Michaelmas Term to serve for four years from 1 January following their appointment. Appointments.

3. It shall be the duty of the Committee to keep under review the provision of veterinary education in the University, with a view to ensuring that the preclinical and clinical parts of the course leading to the Vet.M.B. Degree form a coherent whole, that the balance of elements in the curriculum is appropriate, and that standards in different subjects are consistent. The Committee shall advise the Faculty Boards of Biology and Veterinary Medicine on the following matters: Duties.

(*a*) matters relating to the education of veterinary students, including admissions policies, student statistics, and examination results;

(*b*) matters relating to resources needed for the provision of veterinary education;

(*c*) proposals for changes in the veterinary curriculum and in the relevant examinations.

The Committee shall advise the Faculty Board of Clinical Medicine on any matters relating to veterinary education which are relevant to that Faculty Board.

4. The Committee shall meet at least twice in each academical year. No business shall be transacted at any meeting of the Committee unless at least five members are present. Quorum.

5. The Committee shall make such reports to the General Board as the Board may require. Reports.

6. The provisions of Special Ordinance A (vii) 5 concerning reserved business shall apply to the Veterinary Education Committee as if it were a body constituted by Statute. Reserved business.

Conservators of the River Cam

Under the River Cam Conservancy Act 1922 three of the thirteen Conservators are appointed by the Council in the Michaelmas Term of every third year to hold office for three years from 1 January following their appointment.[1]

Association of Commonwealth Universities

The representative of the University in its capacity of Ordinary Member of the Association of Commonwealth Universities shall be the Vice-Chancellor, *ex officio*.

[1] The next year of appointment is 2017.

Marine Biological Association

Endowments, 1904, p. 579

Member of the Council.

1. In accordance with By-law 17 of the Marine Biological Association the University of Cambridge shall become a Governor of the said Association, and shall acquire the perpetual right of nominating annually one member of the Council of the Association to serve for one year, from the annual meeting in one year to that in the following year.

Appointment of member of Council.

2. The representative of the University of Cambridge on the Council of the Marine Biological Association shall be appointed by the Council of the University on the nomination of the Faculty Board of Biology in the Lent Term to serve for one year from the date of the annual meeting of the Association next following; but it shall be open to the University at any time to modify this arrangement.

Nomination to table.

3. The University's right of nomination to a table at the Laboratory of the Marine Biological Association at Plymouth shall be exercised by the Faculty Board of Biology, who may nominate either a member of the University or, if no suitable member of the University has applied, some other suitable person.

Cambridge University Hospitals and Papworth Hospital NHS Foundation Trusts, West Suffolk NHS Trust, and Cambridgeshire and Peterborough Mental Health Partnership NHS Trust

These Trusts are established under the terms of the National Health Service and Community Care Act 1990, which has now been superseded by the Health and Social Care (Community Health and Standards) Act 2003, and came into existence on or after 1 April 1993. The Trusts have a significant teaching commitment within the meaning of paragraph 3(1)(*d*) of Schedule 2 to the Act as a result of which one of the non-executive Directors of each Trust is appointed from the University.

National Health Service Advisory Appointments Committees

Where there is provision in regulations made by the Department of Health in the exercise of powers under the National Health Service Act 1977, as amended by the Health Services Act 1980, for the nomination by the University of members of Advisory Appointments Committees for appointments in the National Health Service, such nominations shall be made by the Regius Professor of Physic or a deputy appointed by the Professor.

Royal College of Veterinary Surgeons

Two members of the Council of the Royal College of Veterinary Surgeons who may in accordance with the provisions of the Veterinary Surgeons Act 1948 be appointed by the University shall be appointed by the Council of the University. One of the two members shall be appointed on the nomination of the Faculty Board of Veterinary Medicine.

SUPERANNUATION SCHEMES

GENERAL REGULATION

There shall be two Superannuation Schemes: the Universities Superannuation Scheme as provided in the special regulations for the Scheme and as detailed in the rules of the Scheme,[1] and the Federated Superannuation System for Universities Superannuation Scheme as provided in the special regulations for the Scheme.[2]

[1] The rules of USS were last published in *Ordinances*, 1985, p. 72. Up-to-date copies of the rules may be obtained from the Head of the Pensions Section or from the Pensions web page at http://www.admin.cam.ac.uk/offices/pensions/.

[2] The regulations for FSSU were last published in *Ordinances*, 1979, p. 108. The scheme for supplementation of superannuation benefits under FSSU was last published in *Ordinances*, 1985, p. 124.

SPECIAL REGULATIONS

UNIVERSITIES SUPERANNUATION SCHEME

1. Subject to the provisions of Rule 5 of the Scheme, the following shall be eligible for membership of the Universities Superannuation Scheme (USS): Who are eligible.

(*a*) all University officers (other than the holders of particular offices exempt by Statute or officers or classes of officers specified in Regulation 2) who have been

(i) elected or appointed to office on or after 1 April 1975, unless as members previously of the Staff of an Institution in the Federated Superannuation System for Universities they have not elected to transfer to the USS,

(ii) elected or appointed to office before 1 April 1975 and have elected to transfer to the USS;

(*b*) other persons or classes of persons taking part in University teaching, research, or administration who on or after 1 April 1975 have been approved for the purpose by the former Financial Board or by the Finance Committee of the Council, subject in the case of persons or classes of persons attached to an institution under the supervision of the General Board to a recommendation from that Board, or who having been so approved before 1 April 1975 have elected to transfer to the USS.

2. The following shall not normally be eligible for membership of the Universities Superannuation Scheme:

(*a*) the holder of any particular University office exempt by Statute;

(*b*) any person engaged by the Press Syndicate in the service of the University Press;

(*c*) any University officer who on appointment to his or her office is, and elects to remain, a member of the National Health Service Superannuation Scheme;

(*d*) any person who on first appointment to a University office was aged 60 years or over;

(*e*) the holder of any particular office the stipend of which, in view of the nature and extent of the duties and in view of the length of tenure of the office, has been determined by Ordinance or by Grace on the recommendation of the competent authority to be non-pensionable.

3. Contributions to be paid by members of the Scheme shall be deducted from their stipends.

4. The Scheme may be so altered from time to time, without the authority of a Grace, as to keep it in harmony with the Scheme as amended from time to time by Universities Superannuation Scheme Limited. Amendment of Scheme.

LATHAM PENSION FUND

1. The sum bequeathed to the University by the late Reverend Henry Latham, Master of Trinity Hall, shall form a fund to be called the Latham Pension Fund, hereinafter referred to as the Fund.

2. The capital of the Fund shall be invested in the names of the Chancellor, Masters, and Scholars of the University of Cambridge in such manner as the Finance Committee of the Council may from time to time direct.

3. Occasional or annual grants may from time to time be made from the Fund by the Council to members of the University who have been engaged in University or College work and have become incapacitated by age or infirmity, or to wives and children of members of the University who have been so engaged and have died without making sufficient provision for their families. Applications for such grants should be sent to the Vice-Chancellor.

4. The accounts of the Fund shall be published annually in the University Accounts.

5. If in any year the whole income of the Fund is not expended the excess of income over expenditure may at the discretion of the Finance Committee of the Council either be carried on to the next year or be invested as an increase of the capital of the Fund.

6. Any sums of money bequeathed or given for the augmentation of the Fund shall be added to the capital of the Fund.

7. These regulations shall be subject to alteration by Ordinance provided that the regulations shall always be in accordance with the provisions of Mr Latham's will.[1]

[1] *Endowments*, 1904, p. 570.

UNIVERSITY MARSHAL

Appointment. **1.** The University Marshal shall be appointed by the Council in accordance with the regulations for employment by the University.

Duties. **2.** It shall be the duty of the University Marshal to attend on the Vice-Chancellor on ceremonial occasions and to carry out the Vice-Chancellor's orders.

EQUAL OPPORTUNITIES POLICY

Policy statement. The University of Cambridge is committed in its pursuit of academic excellence to equality of opportunity and to a pro-active and inclusive approach to equality, which supports and encourages all under-represented groups, promotes an inclusive culture, and values diversity. This commitment is underpinned by the University's core values, expressed in its mission statement:

- freedom of thought and expression,
- freedom from discrimination.

The University is therefore committed to a policy and practice which require that, for students, admission to the University and progression within undergraduate and graduate studies will be determined only by personal merit and by performance. For staff, entry into employment with the University and progression within employment will be determined only by personal merit and by the application of criteria which are related to the duties and conditions of each particular post and the needs of the institution concerned.

Subject to statutory provisions, no student, member of staff, applicant for admission as a student, or applicant for appointment as a member of staff will be treated less favourably than another because of her or his belonging to a protected group. This commitment applies to a former student, alumnus or alumna, or former employee where the alleged unlawful conduct arises out of and is closely connected to the former student's or former staff member's previous relationship with the University.

Protected groups are defined in the Equality Act 2010 as Sex, Gender Reassignment, Marriage or Civil Partnership, Pregnancy or Maternity, Race (including Ethnic or National Origin, Nationality or Colour), Disability, Sexual Orientation, Age, or Religion or Belief. The University respects all religious and philosophical beliefs, as well as the lack of religion or belief, and the right of all members of its community to discuss and debate these issues freely.

If any person admitted as a student or appointed as a member of staff considers that he or she is suffering from unlawful discrimination, harassment, or victimization in her or his admission, appointment, or progression through the University because of belonging to any of the above protected groups, he or she may make a complaint, which will be dealt with through the agreed procedures for complaints or grievances or the procedures for dealing with bullying and harassment, as appropriate.

Good practice definitions. The University will take active steps to promote good practice. In particular it will:

(*a*) work towards the elimination of unlawful discrimination, harassment, and victimization based on a protected characteristic, whether actual, perceptive, or associative;

(*b*) advance equality of opportunity between persons who share a protected characteristic and persons who do not share it;

(*c*) foster good relations between persons who share a protected characteristic and persons who do not share it;

(*d*) subject its policies to continuous assessment in order to examine how they affect protected groups and to identify whether its policies help to achieve equality of opportunity for all these groups, or whether they have an adverse impact;

(*e*) monitor the recruitment and progress of all students and staff, collecting and collating equalities information and data as required by law or for the furtherance of University equalities objectives;

(*f*) promote an inclusive culture, good practice in teaching, learning, and assessment, and good management practice, through the development of codes of best practice, policies, and training;

(*g*) take positive action wherever possible to support this policy and its aims, and

(*h*) publish this policy widely amongst staff and students, together with policy assessments, equality analysis and results of monitoring.

The Equal Opportunities Policy will be enacted through by the University's Equality Objectives, associated implementation plans, and the Combined Equality Scheme.[1] The Combined Equality Scheme explains how the University will fulfil its statutory obligations in relation to equalities legislation.

It considers:

- Governance and Policy Development, including relevant committees, compliance, equal pay, assessing the impact of policies and practices and reporting;
- Developing and Implementing Best Practice;
- Inclusive Practice for Students and Staff – including the University's Diversity Networks, Dignity at Work, and Dignity at Study procedures;
- Promotion of Equality and Diversity, including relevant diversity events, training, and guidance, and
- Data and Information Provision, including appropriate monitoring and compliance reporting.

Progress against actions and objectives will be reported in the Equality and Diversity Annual Reviews and Data Reports.[2]

The University will meet all statutory obligations under relevant legislation and, where appropriate, anticipate future legal requirements. This will be informed by: Statutory obligations.

- The Equality Act (2010) and associated secondary legislation
- Criminal Justice and Immigration Act (2008)
- The Racial and Religious Hatred Act (2006)
- The Civil Partnership Act (2004)
- The Gender Recognition Act (2004)
- Criminal Justice Act (2003)
- The Human Rights Act (1998)
- The Protection from Harassment Act (1997)
- Special Education Needs and Disability Act (2001).

In addition, this will be informed by the Codes of Practice or Guidance issued by the Equality and Human Rights Commission and other relevant bodies. These Codes are not legally binding (though they are admissible as evidence in Employment Tribunals) and the University supports them fully.

This policy will be amended as appropriate to meet the demands of future legislation.

EMPLOYMENT BY THE UNIVERSITY

Flexible Working Policy

(Covering flexible working arrangements for periods of more than three months)

Introduction

1. This policy on flexible working arrangements for University staff has been developed bearing in mind the University's commitment to equality of opportunity (in particular that of appointment on the basis of merit) and with the intention of helping members of staff to balance their commitments and interests outside work with their contractual duties and responsibilities. It is recognized that being able to offer flexibility in working arrangements may assist members of staff to return to work after a period of absence or to continue in work or to adjust to retirement.

2. This policy complies with national legislation, including the Part-time Workers (Prevention of Less Favourable Treatment) Regulations 2000, the Fixed-term Employees (Prevention of Less Favourable Treatment) Regulations 2002, and the Flexible Working Regulations 2002. Staff working flexibly will be valued and respected in the same way as full-time staff. In addition, their contractual benefits will be the same, on a *pro rata* basis if working less than full-time, as full-time staff engaged on the same type of contract and performing the same or similar work, unless objectively justifiable.

3. Flexible arrangements offered to members of staff under this policy cover a wide range of different arrangements including part time or term-time working, job share, compressed or annual hours, staggered hours or flexitime. At all times, the arrangements that are agreed will attempt to balance the needs of the member of staff with the work to be carried out and should be in the interests of the institution[3] concerned. Some of these arrangements will be of a permanent nature and, where

[1] http://www.admin.cam.ac.uk/offices/hr/equality/cambridge/scheme/

[2] http://www.admin.cam.ac.uk/offices/hr/equality/reports/

[3] 'Institution' means all academic and academic-related departments, including administrative units, libraries, museums, and any other individual sections or units of the University.

appropriate, will fulfil the University's obligations under the Flexible Working Regulations. Others will be of a temporary nature, to accommodate a member of staff's need for an adjustment of their working arrangements to balance commitments outside work. However, flexible working arrangements will not be agreed where a member of staff wishes to 'try out' employment offers outside the University. In addition, applications to work flexibly will not normally be considered where the member of staff would be undertaking other remunerative employment outside the University.

4. This policy also applies to staff wishing to apply to work flexibly for a limited period in certain circumstances such as:

- career break (for officers and comparable appointments) and family leave (for assistant staff);
- graduated return from maternity or sick leave.

(Study and research leave are covered by separate arrangements outside the scope of this policy.)

5. Details of these schemes are given in the *Staff Guide for Academic and Academic-Related Staff* and the *Assistant Staff Handbook*, which can be found, together with more detailed procedural information on these schemes, on the Human Resources Division website (www.admin.cam.ac.uk/offices/hr/). In all cases, the temporary arrangements must be to the institution's as well as the individual's benefit and the timescales must be clearly defined.

6. Statutory rights to temporary leave, such as maternity, parental, emergency, paternity, and adoption are covered by separate arrangements outside the scope of this policy. Details of relevant policies, notes of guidance, and forms are available on the Human Resources Division website (www.admin.cam.ac.uk/offices/hr/policy/).

7. In addition to giving serious consideration to any request to work flexibly, Heads of institutions[1] and all those responsible for appointing staff are encouraged to consider routinely how certain duties in their department could be covered on a part-time basis, or divided up in different ways when reviewing a job vacancy or assessing the workload of the department or of an individual job.

Eligibility

1. This policy applies to all staff, regardless of length of service, who request flexibility in their working arrangements for a period of time of longer than three months.

2. Requests to work flexibly for periods of less than three months, for example for compassionate reasons or as a graduated return from sick leave, should be reviewed with the member of staff and agreed locally by the Head of institution or comparable authority, in accordance with guidance given by the Human Resources Division.

Notices by the Council and the General Board

University flexible working policy

In the light of the new right from 6 April 2007 under the Work and Families Act 2006 for adult carers to make requests to work flexibly under the Flexible Working (Amendment) Regulations 2006, the Council and the General Board give notice of the existing, more favourable University flexible working policy applicable to all employees (http://www.admin.cam.ac.uk/offices/hr/policy/flexible/policy/).

Further details on other family-related leave provisions, including paternity, adoption, parental, and emergency leave, are available on the University's website (http://www.admin.cam.ac.uk/offices/hr/policy/).

Staff Review and Development Scheme: arrangements for appraisal

The Council and the General Board have approved the framework Staff Review and Development Scheme covering all staff which is set out below. Guidance on aspects of the Scheme is issued by the Human Resources Division, who will periodically review the effectiveness of these arrangements, in consultation with the Heads of institutions.

1. The purpose of the Scheme shall be to enhance work effectiveness and facilitate career development. The framework gives institutions the flexibility to adapt their own local schemes.

2. The underlying objectives of the process shall be as set out below. The Scheme involves discussing ways in which the member of staff's work can be developed and ways in which any difficulties or obstacles to progress can be removed. It will ensure that staff are clear about their responsibilities and have a formal regular opportunity (at least every two years) to discuss any help they may need in meeting them.

[1] 'Head of institution' means the Head of a Department, Chair of a Board of a Faculty not organized into Departments, Director or the authorized deputy or designated nominee, as appropriate within that institution.

3. Institutions shall specify in their schemes the preparatory documentation to be supplied by a member of staff being reviewed, how both parties should prepare for the meeting, and how the action plan is recorded afterwards. Their scheme should cover the key stages in the Staff Review and Development process of planning, discussion, and recording, as set out below, and be submitted through the Human Resources Division for approval on behalf of the competent authority.

4. Accountability and responsibility for the operation of the Scheme will rest with each institution. The Head of each institution shall be responsible for co-ordinating the procedure before and after each cycle of reviews.

5. The competent authority shall make such changes in the procedure as they consider necessary in the interest of efficient operation.

Purposes of Staff Review and Development (SRD)

The University SRD Scheme is designed to incorporate and extend the objectives set out in the CVCP/AUT agreement of 1987 and the subsequent agreements between the CVCP and MSF and Unison. It is intended to:

- provide an opportunity for reviewing in a positive and constructive way the work of an individual member of staff and how this has been carried out;
- ensure that the individual's contribution to the institution is recognized and to agree specific objectives for the forthcoming review period;
- provide a means of balancing the ambitions and personal needs of the individual with the overall objectives of the institution and university as a whole;
- provide opportunities for the discussion of training needs for the current role and any development for future career opportunities;
- allow for the identification and discussion of difficulties or obstacles which hamper effectiveness.

At the University of Cambridge we aim through the process to:

- provide an opportunity for positive and constructive two-way review of work progress;
- allow agreement of an action plan;
- provide for discussion of training needs for the member of staff's current role and career development;
- allow for identification and discussion of difficulties or obstacles to effectiveness;
- provide a way of balancing personal needs and ambitions with the University's overall objectives.

Stages in the Staff Review and Development process

Stage	*Content*	*Process*
STAGE ONE: PREPARATION		
(*a*) *Planning* Preparing for the discussion	A confidential review of the previous period and planning for the next period of review.	The member of staff concerned completes a preparatory review of progress. The reviewer plans for the discussion by completing a similar review of the member of staff's progress. Also, the reviewer specifies what documents the member of staff needs to bring to the review meeting and gathers together information on the University's and institution's objectives.
(*b*) *Agenda* Setting the agenda for the meeting	Both the reviewer and member of staff list what they would like to discuss at the meeting.	The member of staff identifies issues that he or she would like to discuss with the reviewer and lists them. This list may be passed to the reviewer to add additional items that he/she would like to raise, photocopy, and return it to the member of staff.
STAGE TWO: DISCUSSION		
A review meeting takes place	Reviewer and member of staff discuss the member of staff's progress over the review period, training and development needs, and agree on action plan for the future.	(1) The formal framework for the meeting is in accordance with the institution's scheme. (2) A constructive, two-way open discussion takes place. (3) Actions resulting from the review are agreed, to be recorded after the meeting
STAGE THREE: RECORDING		
(*a*) *Outcomes* Recording the decisions and outcomes from the meeting	The discussion and/or the decisions are recorded, including action plans and training needs. These remain confidential to the member of staff concerned and reviewer (and the Head of institution if specified in the institution's scheme).	(1) The documents may be completed by either party so long as they are seen and signed by both. They may be signed by the Head of institution (or his/her nominated representative if the Head is not the reviewer) if this is specified in the institution's scheme. (2) Both the member of staff and the reviewer are given copies of the completed documents. (3) Staff Development Unit may be given a copy of the individual statement of agreed training and development outcomes, if this has been agreed with the member of staff.

Stage	*Content*	*Process*
There are additional processes which may take place at institutional level:		
(*b*) *Summary* Listing and analysing the overall institutional needs	Reviewers draw together the issues identified in individual reviews.	Each reviewer produces a summary of the generic issues identified in the review he or she has completed, and passes them to the Head of institution or his/her nominated representative, with suggestions for overcoming them. (This summary **must** be anonymous and **must not** refer explicitly or implicitly to any members of staff.)
(*c*) *Institutional response* Producing an institutional summary	The Head of institution confirms that the process is completed and identifies any training needs requiring central action.	Head or designated person co-ordinates all reviewer summaries to produce an overall institutional summary. This may be discussed at a meeting of all reviewers and fed back to staff generally to let them know in summary what issues have emerged and what steps are being taken to address them. Staff Development Unit may be informed of some generic training needs so that it can assist in meeting them and also so that the Unit can plan future University training activity appropriately.

Assistant Staff

Definitions.

1. In the regulations for employment by the University unless the context shall require otherwise:

(*a*) the term *competent authority* shall mean

(i) the General Board, for persons or classes of persons employed in institutions under the supervision of the General Board,

(ii) the Council, for all other persons or classes of persons;

(*b*) the term *institution* shall mean any Faculty, Department, or other institution in which the employment of persons or classes of persons to whom the following regulations apply has been authorized by the competent authority.

Status of University assistant.

2. Every person employed by the University, unless he or she is a University officer or belongs to one of the classes of persons specified in the Schedule to these general regulations, shall have the status of University assistant. The Council, after consultation with the University and Assistants Joint Board, shall have power to amend the Schedule of classes of persons excluded from the status of University assistant.

3. The Council, after consultation with the University and Assistants Joint Board, shall from time to time publish Rules[1] governing the terms and conditions of employment of University assistants.

4. The terms and conditions of employment of University assistants published under Regulation 3 shall be administered by the Council in consultation with the General Board. The terms and conditions of employment of a person excluded from the status of University assistant[2] shall be determined by the authority under whose supervision the institution in which he or she is employed is placed.

Establishments.

5. The competent authority shall, after consultation with the Head of the institution concerned, prescribe for each institution in which University assistants are employed a maximum number of assistants who may be employed in each of the several categories specified in the Schedule published in accordance with Regulation 3; and they shall be empowered to specify conditions relating to the continuance, amendment, or administration of any such establishment so prescribed.

Appointments.

6. Any proposal relating to the appointment, within the limits of the establishment prescribed under Regulation 5, of a person as a University assistant, shall be made by the Head of the institution concerned. Every appointment, together with the terms and conditions proposed for that appointment by the Head of the institution concerned, shall be in accordance with the provisions of the Rules and Schedules published under Regulation 3 and shall require the approval of the competent authority.

[1] Rules governing the terms and conditions of employment of University assistants published under Regulation 3 are not published in the *Reporter*, but the Council will publish a Notice in the *Reporter* on each occasion when the Rules have been substantially changed. Copies of the Rules and amendments will be distributed to all concerned by the Human Resources Division, from where additional copies may be obtained on request.

[2] See Regulation 2 and the Schedule appended to these general regulations.

Every person to be appointed as a University assistant shall be informed in writing of the terms and conditions of appointment as so approved. No such appointment shall be valid until the appointment has been approved by the competent authority and until the terms and conditions of the appointment have been accepted in writing by the person to whom the appointment is offered.

7. The Council in consultation with the General Board shall have power to arrange or approve schemes or courses of training for University assistants and to determine, in consultation with Heads of institutions, conditions governing the release of assistants from duty in order to undertake training. The competent authorities shall also have power to meet, in whole or in part, expenses incurred by assistants in connection with their training. Training schemes.

8. If an assistant is required to occupy an official residence, his or her occupancy shall be in accordance with the provisions of the regulation for official residences and shall be subject to terms and conditions determined thereunder in consultation with the competent authority. Official residences.

Schedule of Classes of Persons Excluded from the Status of University Assistant

(*a*) University officers,
(*b*) Departmental Demonstrators,
(*c*) persons receiving non-pensionable payments for occasional or temporary duties in connection with teaching, demonstrating, or examinations,
(*d*) persons engaged in a temporary pensionable or non-pensionable capacity to take part in research work upon terms and conditions not applicable to University assistants,
(*e*) persons engaged by the Press Syndicate,
(*f*) persons engaged in the Estate Management and Building Service in a non-pensionable capacity while undertaking professional training,
(*g*) persons other than University officers, engaged in work at the University Farm, either as agricultural workers or as clerical, secretarial, or technical workers,
(*h*) persons engaged as estate workers on the Madingley Estate,
(*i*) persons engaged by the Local Examinations Syndicate, other than University officers,
(*j*) the staff of the ADC Theatre,
(*k*) the staff of the University Centre,
(*l*) persons engaged in a temporary pensionable or non-pensionable capacity to undertake administrative or technical work upon terms and conditions not applicable to University assistants, who have been placed in this category after consultation with the Assistant Staff Committee,
(*m*) any person engaged as Occupational Nurse to assist the Consultant Occupational Physician.

CONTRIBUTORY PENSION SCHEME

1. There is and shall be a fund established under the authority of the Oxford and Cambridge Act 1923 under the name of the Contributory Pension Scheme for the purpose of providing, under the rules of the Scheme,[1] pensions, grants, and allowances to such assistants and other persons employed by the University of Cambridge, or by an associated Employer, as are members of the Scheme. Preamble.

2. The Trustee of the Scheme shall be C U Pension Trustee Limited (Company No. 6600561) the registered office of which is at The Old Schools, Trinity Lane, Cambridge, CB2 1TS or another person or persons appointed by the University under Rule 8 {appointment and removal of trustee} and shall hold the Fund on trust to apply it in accordance with the provisions of the Scheme. Trustee.

3. Subject to the provisions of Rule 43 {eligibility and admission} of the Scheme, the following shall be eligible for membership of the Contributory Pension Scheme: Who is to join.

(*a*) all University assistants;
(*b*) such other employees of the University as are ineligible to join the Universities Superannuation Scheme;
(*c*) permanent employees of any Employer.

4. Contributions to be paid by members of the Scheme shall be deducted from their salaries.

5. Subject to the restrictions contained in Rule 5 {amendment} and in Schedule 2 to the Rules {contracting-out}, the Scheme may be altered from time to time without the authority of a Grace in order to ensure its continued approval by the Pension Schemes Office and by the National Insurance Alterations of Scheme.

[1] Revised rules for the Contributory Pension Scheme were approved by Grace 1 of 24 October 2012 (amended by Grace 1 of 30 July 2014). Up-to-date copies of the rules may be obtained from the Head of the Pensions Section or from the Pensions web page at http://www.admin.cam.ac.uk/offices/pensions/.

Contributions Office of the Inland Revenue or any bodies which succeed either of them. Such alterations shall be published in the *Reporter*.

FEES

GENERAL

Degrees.

1. The fee for each degree, other than degrees for which the fees are included in a University Composition Fee, is specified in the regulations for the particular degree.

2. The fee for admission to any degree by incorporation shall be £5.

Examinations.

3. The fee for any examination not included in a University Composition Fee shall be as specified in the regulations for the particular examination.

An unmatriculated student who takes any University examination before coming into residence shall pay a fee of £3 in respect of each such examination.

Fines.

4. A fine of £5 shall be incurred by a candidate whose entry for any University Studentship, Scholarship, Exhibition, Prize, or Medal is received late, but who is nevertheless admitted to the examination or competition.

Payment of fees and fines.

5. The Registrary shall inform the several Colleges of any fees and fines that may be due in respect of their members under these regulations. Candidates for any examination who are not entered by a College shall themselves send any fee that may be due to the Registrary when sending in their names; they shall not be admitted to the examination unless the fee and any fine or fines that they may have incurred have been paid.

Remission of fees and fines.

6. The proper fee, if any, and any fine or fines that may have been incurred must be paid in respect of every candidate whose name has been entered for an examination and whose withdrawal has not been received at the Registry by the latest day prescribed for the receipt of entries. Nevertheless, the Council may in case of hardship remit the whole or part of any fee or fine incurred in connection with candidature for an examination or competition or degree. Applications for such remission must be sent to the Registrary without delay. An application made on grounds of illness should be accompanied, if possible, by a certificate signed by a medical practitioner.

Payment.

7. Except where it is otherwise provided in any particular regulations all fees and fines payable under Ordinance shall be paid to the Treasurer.

UNIVERSITY COMPOSITION FEES

Liability to pay a University Composition Fee.

1. Except as provided otherwise in the general regulations for admission as a Graduate Student, a matriculated student who is pursuing a course leading to a qualification specified in the following regulations or a Graduate Student not registered as a candidate for any qualification shall pay a University Composition Fee, at the rate specified in Regulation 10, as follows:

(*a*) Students taking the following courses shall pay a fee for each year of the course:

The course leading to the M.B.A. Examination.

The course leading to an examination for the M.St. Degree.

(*b*) Students undertaking research leading to the M.D. Degree shall pay a fee for the course.

(*c*) Any other student shall pay a fee at one third of the annual fee:

(i) for each term which the student has kept by residence;

(ii) for each term in which the student has been in residence, or has been engaged in a course of study in the University, for twenty-one days or more;

(iii) for each term allowed by the Council as a term of residence.

(*d*) Notwithstanding sub-paragraph (*c*) above,

(i) in the case of a student in receipt of university fee loan support from the Student Loans Company, University Composition Fee liability shall arise on certification of attendance at each liability date for the proportion of the annual amount relating to that liability date, as determined by the Student Loans Company; and

(ii) in the case of a student who is a qualifying person under the Student Fees (Qualifying Courses and Persons) (England) Regulations, but not in receipt of university fee loan support from the Student Loans Company, University Composition Fee liability shall arise on attendance at each liability date for the relevant proportion of the annual amount.

2. In addition to the requirements of Regulation 1, a matriculated student pursuing a course leading to one of the following examinations or qualifications shall pay the University Composition Fee at the appropriate rate prescribed for any term or terms in which, as part of the arrangements for the course, he or she has not been in residence:

Asian and Middle Eastern Studies Tripos
Chemical Engineering Tripos
Education Tripos
Engineering Tripos
Manufacturing Engineering Tripos
Mathematical Tripos
Modern and Medieval Languages Tripos
Natural Sciences Tripos
Postgraduate Certificate in Education
Final M.B. Examination for the M.B., B.Chir. Degrees (if a student pursues his or her clinical studies in the University)
Bachelor of Theology for Ministry
Doctor of Education
Doctor of Engineering

For students commencing the following courses, or commencing a course of research or study as a Graduate Student with a view to registration for one of the following courses, on or after 1 October 2010:

Doctor of Philosophy
Master of Science
Master of Letters
Master of Philosophy
Certificate of Postgraduate Study

3. Payment of a University Composition Fee under these regulations shall entitle a matriculated student without additional fee What the fee covers.

(*a*) to attend any course within the University which is listed in the table of fees attached to these regulations save for the following courses which, except with the special permission of the General Board, are open only to candidates for the examinations to which they lead, that is to say

(i) courses of class work or practical instruction,

(ii) any other course notified as being specially restricted,

provided that, if a student wishes to attend a course of instruction in any subject listed in the table of fees without subsequently taking an examination in that subject, he or she shall be permitted to do so only if accommodation is available after provision has been made for all those students for whom the course is primarily intended;

(*b*) to be admitted or readmitted to any University examination, unless the regulations for the particular examination provide otherwise;

(*c*) to be admitted to any primary degree or to receive any diploma or certificate which is listed in the table of fees for which he or she has become qualified;

(*d*) to be admitted to the M.A. Degree on becoming qualified therefor.

4. In addition to paying a University Composition Fee a student shall be liable to pay Additional payments.

(*a*) any fines that he or she may incur under Ordinance;

(*b*) any deposit or charge required by a Faculty Board or the Head of a Department to cover the cost of breakages, loss of equipment on loan, or abnormal supplies of material.

5. A member of the University who is not liable to pay a University Composition Fee under Regulation 1 or 2 of these regulations and for whom no provision is made in any other regulation, but who has been given permission by the General Board to attend a course of instruction, shall pay a fee of such amount for each term or year as shall be determined by the General Board from time to time; provided that a graduate of the University who is not reading for a University examination may attend without payment any lectures announced in the *Reporter* by a Faculty Board with the approval of the General Board as being available to such a person. Other students.

6. A candidate who has at no time paid one of the University Composition Fees prescribed in these regulations or in any other regulations for University Composition Fees shall pay a fee of £5 for admission to each degree.

Powers of the Council.

7. The Council shall have power

(*a*) to determine the appropriate fee for a student other than a Graduate Student in cases of doubt;

(*b*) to reduce or remit fees in cases of hardship, provided that no student shall be entitled to a remission of part of a University Composition Fee for any term on the ground that he or she has not made use of any of the facilities provided by the University.

Powers of the Board of Graduate Studies.

8. The Board of Graduate Studies shall have power

(*a*) to determine the appropriate fee for a Graduate Student in cases of doubt;

(*b*) to reduce or remit fees in accordance with the general regulations for admission as a Graduate Student.

Definitions.

9. Overseas students shall be as defined in the Appendix to these regulations, and all students thereby excluded from that category shall be home students.

10. Subject to the provisions of Regulations 11 and 12, University Composition Fees shall be payable at the rates shown in the tables to these regulations, according to students' status as home or overseas students[1] and according to their subject of study and prior qualifications. A student who is dissatisfied with her or his categorization for the purposes of University Composition Fees shall proceed under the Student Complaints Procedure[2] and, for the purpose of that Procedure, the matter complained of shall be taken to have occurred at the time of commencement of the course of study.

11. The Board of Graduate Studies shall have power to vary the category of a particular Graduate Student in consideration of the facilities required by the student in pursuing her or his course of study.

12. The University Composition Fees charged to Home and EU undergraduate students shall be subject to approval by Grace of the Regent House. These fees shall be subject to the following conditions:

(i) the recommendation for the fees to be charged shall be accompanied by an analysis of the costs of an undergraduate education agreed by the General Board and the Council following consultation with the Colleges;

(ii) the fees to be charged shall not exceed any limit prescribed by law;

(iii) for such students who are undertaking a required period abroad the rate shall be half the full amount or such other amount that may be determined by the Secretary of State for this category;

(iv) for such students beginning courses on or after 1 August 2009 which lead to a qualification (other than courses in Medical and Veterinary Sciences leading to the B.A. Degree or courses in Architecture or for the Postgraduate Certificate in Education) which is equivalent to, or at a lower level than, a qualification they possessed when they began their course (ELQ students) the rate shall be the fee determined by the University for ELQ students.[3]

[1] Table 5D shows the rates of fees for students admitted before 1 September 2013 and to whom the Island rate of fees applies. The Island rate has been abolished for students admitted on and after 1 September 2013.

[2] See p. 220.

[3] Students who have proceeded to the B.A. Degree but have been given leave to read for another Tripos 'not for honours' are deemed to be ELQ students for the purpose of their fee liability (see Table 5B).

TABLE OF FEES, 2014–15

Graces 2 of 18 December 2013, 1 of 12 March, 7 of 16 July, and 3 of 30 July 2014

Table 1[1]

Annual Fee (£)

Qualification	Home and EU 2014–15 Old Regime: H/EU students who commenced before 2012–13 (except those to whom the old system fee applies)	Home and EU 2014–15 New Regime: H/EU students who commenced in 2012–13 or later years	Overseas 2014–15 A: Overseas students who commenced in or before 2010–11	Overseas 2014–15 B: Overseas students who commenced in 2011–12	Overseas 2014–15 C: Overseas students who commenced in 2012–13 or later years
B.A. Degree[2] *Courses leading to Tripos, Preliminary, or Ordinary Examinations in*					
Group 1					
Anglo-Saxon, Norse, and Celtic	3,465	9,000	13,020	13,668	14,346
Archaeology and Anthropology (final intake October 2012)	3,465	9,000	13,020	13,668	14,346
Asian and Middle Eastern Studies	3,465	9,000	13,020	13,668	14,346
Classics	3,465	9,000	13,020	13,668	14,346
Economics	3,465	9,000	13,020	13,668	14,346
Education	3,465	9,000	13,020	13,668	14,346
English	3,465	9,000	13,020	13,668	14,346
History	3,465	9,000	13,020	13,668	14,346
History of Art	3,465	9,000	13,020	13,668	14,346
Human, Social, and Political Sciences	3,465	9,000	13,020	13,668	14,346
Land Economy	3,465	9,000	13,020	13,668	14,346
Law	3,465	9,000	13,020	13,668	14,346
Linguistics	3,465	9,000	13,020	13,668	14,346
Modern and Medieval Languages	3,465	9,000	13,020	13,668	14,346
Philosophy	3,465	9,000	13,020	13,668	14,346
Politics, Psychology, and Sociology (final intake October 2012)	3,465	9,000	13,020	13,668	14,346
Theological and Religious Studies	3,465	9,000	13,020	13,668	14,346
Group 2					
Mathematics	3,465	9,000	13,020	13,668	15,999
Group 3					
Architecture	3,465	9,000	17,043	17,889	18,774
Geography	3,465	9,000	17,043	17,889	18,774
Music	3,465	9,000	17,043	17,889	18,774
Group 4					
Chemical Engineering	3,465	9,000	17,043	20,799	21,831
Computer Science	3,465	9,000	17,043	20,799	21,831
Engineering	3,465	9,000	17,043	20,799	21,831
Management Studies	3,465	9,000	17,043	20,799	21,831
Manufacturing Engineering	3,465	9,000	17,043	20,799	21,831
Natural Sciences	3,465	9,000	17,043	20,799	21,831
Psychological and Behavioural Sciences	3,465	9,000	17,043	20,799	21,831

[1] See Tables 5A–5C for fee rates for continuing 'Old system' students, certain students taking equivalent or lower qualifications, and students for whom the Island rate of fees applies. The Island rate has been abolished for students admitted on and after 1 September 2013.

[2] Students who have proceeded to the B.A. Degree but have been given leave to read for another Tripos 'not for honours' are deemed to be ELQ students for the purpose of their fee liability (see Table 5B).

Annual Fee (£)

	Home and EU		Overseas		
	2014–15		2014–15		
	Old Regime	New Regime	A	B	C
Qualification	H/EU students who commenced before 2012–13 (except those to whom the old system fee applies)	H/EU students who commenced in 2012–13 or later years	Overseas students who commenced in or before 2010–11	Overseas students who commenced in 2011–12	Overseas students who commenced in 2012–13 or later years
Group 5					
Medical and Veterinary Sciences (including for this purpose the Second M.B. and Second Vet.M.B. Examinations)[1]	3,465	9,000	17,043	33,075	34,722
Year Abroad[2]	1,725	1,350	1,725	50% full fee	50% full fee
B.Th. Degree	3,465	9,000	13,020	13,668	14,346
Medical and Veterinary Degrees: M.B., B.Chir. Degrees, Vet.M.B. Degree[3]	3,465	9,000	31,521	33,075	34,722
M.Eng. Degree and M.Sci. Degree	3,465	9,000	17,043	20,799	21,831
M.Math. Degree	3,465	9,000	13,020	13,668	15,999
Certificates					
Certificate in Humanities Computing for Languages	3,465	9,000	17,043	17,889	18,774
Certificate in Modern Languages	3,465	9,000	13,020	13,668	14,346
Postgraduate Certificate in Education (P.G.C.E.)	3,465	9,000	17,043	17,889	18,774
M.A.St. Degree:					
Courses leading to examinations in					
Astrophysics	3,465	3,465	17,043	20,799	21,831
Materials Science	3,465	3,465	17,043	20,799	21,831
Mathematics	3,465	3,465	13,020	13,668	15,999
Physics	3,465	3,465	17,043	20,799	21,831

[1] Parts IA and IB. The fee payable by a student who is reading for another Tripos in order to satisfy the requirements for the B.A. Degree is the fee set out for that Tripos.

[2] The Year abroad fee applies to students undertaking a full year course of study abroad or working away (see Regulation 6 for the Law Tripos, Regulation 23 for the Asian and Middle Eastern Studies Tripos, Regulation 28 for the Modern and Medieval Languages Tripos, Regulation 23 for the Engineering Tripos). The special fee arrangements applying to students on a year abroad under the Erasmus Scheme are changing in 2014–15 for students admitted in and after 2012, and the fee liability is as above.

[3] Payable only if a student pursues her or his clinical studies in the University.

Table 2[1]

Qualification	Annual Fee (£) Home/EU 2014–15	Annual Fee (£) Overseas 2014–15
LL.M. Degree	8,250	19,446
M.C.L. Degree	22,050	22,050
M.Ed. Degree: (*two-year part-time course*)		
Students who commenced before 2014–15	2,571	7,908
Students who commence in 2014–15	3,300	8,166
Ed.D. Degree: (*five-year part-time course*)		
Home/EU students who commenced before 2014–15	2,397	
Home/EU students who commence in 2014–15	3,300	
M.Mus. Degree	6,207	16,911
M.Phil. Degree:[2]		
Courses leading to examinations in		
Advanced Chemical Engineering	8,046	22,776
Advanced Computer Science	8,046	22,776
African Studies	6,000	15,807
American Literature	5,160	15,807
Anglo-Saxon, Norse, and Celtic	5,160	15,807
Applied Biological Anthropology	6,000	18,774
Archaeological Research	6,000	15,807
Archaeology	6,000	15,807
Architecture	5,160	15,807
Architecture and Urban Design Year 1	3,465	19,824
Architecture and Urban Design Year 2	1,725	9,912
Architecture and Urban Studies	5,160	19,824
Asian and Middle Eastern Studies	5,160	15,807
Assyriology	6,000	15,807
Astronomy	3,996	18,774
Biological Anthropological Science	6,000	18,774
Biological Science	3,996	18,774
Bioscience Enterprise	8,046	18,774
Chemical Engineering and Biotechnology	3,996	18,774
Chemistry	3,996	18,774
Classics	5,160	15,807
Clinical Science (Rare Diseases)	3,996	23,649
Clinical Science (Translational Medicine and Therapeutics)	3,996	23,649
Computational Biology	3,996	18,774
Conservation Leadership	3,996	18,774
Criminological Research	6,000	15,807
Criminology	6,000	15,807
Development Studies	10,440	19,446
Developmental Biology	3,996	18,774
Early Modern History	6,000	15,807
Earth Sciences	3,996	18,774
Economic and Social History	6,000	15,807
Economic Research	11,640	18,948
Economics	11,640	18,948
Education	6,600	16,332
Egyptology	6,000	15,807
Energy Technologies	4,644	20,013
Engineering	3,996	18,774
Engineering for Sustainable Development	3,996	18,774
English Studies	5,160	15,807
Environmental Policy	8,250	15,807
Epidemiology	3,996	18,774
European Literature and Culture	5,160	15,807
Finance	9,363	18,774
Finance and Economics	11,640	18,948
Financial Research	3,996	18,774
Fluid Flow in Industry and the Environment	3,996	18,774
Geographical Research	3,996	14,346
Geography (Arts)	3,996	14,346

[1] Island students who commenced in or after 2013–14 pay the Overseas rate of fee.

[2] Where an M.Phil. course is taken on a part-time basis over two years the fee payable each year is half that shown in the table.

	Annual Fee (£)	
	Home/EU	**Overseas**
Qualification	**2014–15**	**2014–15**
Geography (Science)	3,996	18,774
Historical Studies	6,000	15,807
History of Art and Architecture	5,160	15,807
History, Philosophy, and Sociology of Science, Technology, and Medicine	6,000	17,550
Human Evolutionary Studies	6,000	18,774
Industrial Systems, Manufacturing, and Management	6,315	19,446
Innovation, Strategy, and Organization	3,996	18,774
International Relations and Politics	9,000	18,948
Land Economy	6,000	15,807
Land Economy Research	6,000	15,807
Latin-American Studies	6,000	15,807
Management	18,774	18,774
Management Science and Operations	3,996	18,774
Materials Science and Metallurgy	3,996	18,774
Medical Science	3,996	18,774
Medieval and Renaissance Literature	5,160	15,807
Medieval History	6,000	15,807
Micro- and Nanotechnology Enterprise	3,996	18,774
Modern European History	6,000	15,807
Modern Society and Global Transformations	6,000	17,025
Modern South Asian Studies	6,000	15,807
Multi-disciplinary Gender Studies	5,412	15,807
Music Studies	5,160	15,807
Nuclear Energy	6,000	21,201
Philosophy	5,160	15,807
Physics	3,996	18,774
Planning, Growth, and Regeneration	8,250	15,807
Polar Studies	3,996	14,346
Political Thought and Intellectual History	6,000	15,807
Primary Care Research	3,996	18,774
Public Health	3,996	18,774
Public Policy	22,050	22,050
Real Estate Finance	11,640	18,948
Scientific Computing	3,996	18,774
Screen Media and Cultures	5,160	15,807
Social and Developmental Psychology	5,160	15,807
Social Anthropology	9,000	18,948
Technology Policy	18,774	18,774
Theology and Religious Studies	5,160	15,807
Theoretical and Applied Linguistics	5,160	15,807
Veterinary Science	3,996	18,774
M.Res. Degree:		
Courses leading to examinations in		
Biological Science	3,996	18,774
Future Infrastructure and Built Environment	3,996	18,774
Gas Turbine Aerodynamics	3,996	18,774
Graphene Technology	3,996	18,774
Integrated Photonic and Electronic Systems	3,996	18,774
Medical Science	3,996	18,774
Physical Sciences	3,996	18,774
Sensor Technologies and Applications	3,996	18,774
Social Anthropology	9,000	18,948
Ultra Precision Engineering	3,996	18,774
Diplomas		
Courses leading to examinations in		
Conservation of Easel Paintings	3,996	18,774
Economics (Advanced Diploma)	6,600	15,807
International Law	6,000	15,807
Legal Studies	6,000	15,807
Theology and Religious Studies	3,996	14,346

Table 3[1]

Annual Fee (£)

Qualification	Home/EU 2014–15: Home/EU students	Overseas 2014–15 A: Overseas students who commenced in or before 2010–11	B: Overseas students who commenced in 2011–12	C: Overseas students who commenced in 2012–13 and 2013–14	D: Overseas students who commence in 2014–15
Eng.D. Degree	3,996	17,043	17,889	18,732	19,671
Ph.D., M.Sc., and M.Litt. Degrees, and Certificates of Postgraduate Study (C.P.G.S.):[2,3]					
Group 1 Arts	3,996	13,020	13,668	14,313	15,030
Group 2 Science	3,996	17,043	17,889	18,732	19,671
Group 3 Clinical	3,996	31,521	33,075	34,644	36,378

Group 1 Arts: Anglo-Saxon, Norse, and Celtic; Archaeology; Architecture; Asian and Middle Eastern Studies; Classics; Criminology; Development Studies; Divinity; Economics; Education; English, Geography, History; History of Art; History and Philosophy of Science; Land Economy; Law; Mathematics; Modern and Medieval Languages; Music; Philosophy; Politics & International Studies; Sociology; Social Anthropology; Theoretical & Applied Linguistics
Group 2 Science: Architecture; Astronomy; Biochemistry; Biological Anthropology; Biological Science; Chemistry; Chemical Engineering; Computer Science; Earth Sciences; Engineering; Geography; Management Studies; Materials Science; Pathology; Physics; Physiology, Development & Neuroscience; Plant Sciences; Psychiatry; Psychology; Public Health & Primary Care; Zoology
Group 3 Clinical: Clinical Medicine; Veterinary Medicine

Table 4A

Fee for the course (£) (for all students)

Qualification	2014–15
M.B.A. Degree (*one-year course*)	40,500
Executive M.B.A. (*two-year part-time course*)	
2014 intake	58,000
M.Fin. Degree (*one-year full-time course*)	36,570
M.D.Degree (*fee for the course*)	3,996

Table 4B[4]

Annual fee (£)

Qualification	Home/EU 2014–15	Overseas 2014–15
M.St. Degree: *two-year part-time courses in*		
Advanced Subject Teaching		
Course commencing August 2014	5,000	10,000
Applied Criminology, Penology, and Management		
Course commencing in March 2014	3,750	3,750
Applied Criminology and Police Management		
Course commencing in March 2014	3,750	3,750
Building History		
Course commencing in October 2014	5,460	7,875
Construction Engineering		
Course commencing in September 2014	10,000 incl. College fee	10,000 incl. College fee

[1] Island students who commenced in or after 2013–14 pay the Overseas rate of fee.
[2] For students following a part-time course the fee payable each term is 60% of the termly fee of a full-time student (i.e. 60% of one-third of the annual fee).
[3] Please note that Architecture and Geography appear in both Groups 1 and 2.
[4] Island students who commenced on or after 1 September 2013 pay the Overseas rate of fee.

	Annual fee (£)	
	Home/EU	**Overseas**
Qualification	**2014–15**	**2014–15**
Creative Writing Course commencing in October 2014	5,000	10,000
History (starts September 2014) Course commencing in September 2014	5,000	10,000
Interdisciplinary Design for the Built Environment Course commencing in September 2014	5,600	5,600
International Relations *No course commencing in September 2014*		
Sustainability Leadership Course commencing in September 2014	8,750	8,750

Table 5A: *Continuing 'Old system' Home/EU students*
Home/EU undergraduate students who commenced before 1 September 2006, or who commenced before 1 September 2007 having deferred entry from an earlier year, are classified as continuing 'Old system' students. This table is no longer published as there should be no 'Old system' students in 2014–15 (if there are, fees will be at the same rates as in 2013–14).

Table 5B: *Home/EU ELQ students*
The following rates shall apply to Home/EU students commencing a course in 2009–10 or later years leading to a qualification which is equivalent to, or at a lower level than, a qualification they possessed when they began their course (ELQ students).[1]
ELQ students on courses in Medical and Veterinary Sciences leading to the B.A. Degree, as defined in the Regulations, to the M.B. or B.Chir. Degrees, the Vet.M.B. Degree, on courses in Architecture, or the Postgraduate Certificate in Education, are exempt from the ELQ policy and pay the Regulated fees set out below.

	Annual Fee (£)	
	Continuing Home/EU ELQ students	**New Regime Home/EU ELQ students**
	Continuing students who commenced before 1 September 2012	Students who commenced on or after 1 September 2012
Qualification	**2014–15**	**2014–15**
B.A. Degree:		
Groups 1–5 (except Architecture and Medical and Veterinary Sciences)	7,731	9,000
Architecture	3,465	9,000
Medical and Veterinary Sciences	3,465	9,000
B.Th. Degree	7,731	9,000
Medical and Veterinary Degrees: M.B., B.Chir., Vet.M.B.	3,465	9,000
M.Eng. Degree, M.Sci. Degree, and M.Math. Degree	7,731	9,000
M.A.St. Degree	n/a	9,000
Certificates (excluding P.G.C.E.)	7,731	9,000
Postgraduate Certificate in Education (P.G.C.E.)	3,465	9,000
Year abroad[2]	3,864	4,500
Year abroad (ELQ exempt)[2]	1,725	1,350

[1] Students who have proceeded to the B.A. Degree but have been given leave to read for another Tripos 'not for honours' are deemed to be ELQ students for the purpose of their fee liability.

[2] The Year abroad fee applies to students undertaking a full year course of study abroad or working away (see Regulation 6 for the Law Tripos, Regulation 23 for the Asian and Middle Eastern Studies Tripos, Regulation 28 for the Modern and Medieval Languages Tripos, Regulation 23 for the Engineering Tripos). The special fee arrangements applying to students on a year abroad under the Erasmus Scheme are changing in 2014–15 for students admitted in and after 2012, and the fee liability is as above.

Table 5C: *Continuing Island Students (Channel Islands and Isle of Man)*
The following rates shall apply to undergraduate student members of the University for whom the Continuing Island student rate of fees applies.
The separate Island rates of fee have been discontinued for students who commenced a course in 2013–14 or later. See Table 1 for Overseas rates.

Annual Fee (£)

	Continuing Island Students	
	Other Island students who commenced before 1 September 2012	Island students who commenced on or after 1 September 2012 and before 1 September 2013
Qualification	**2014–15**	**2014–15**
B.A. Degree:		
Group 1	6,834	9,000
Group 2 and 3	8,571	9,000
Group 4 and 5	10,500	10,500
B.Th. Degree	6,834	9,000
Medical and Veterinary Degrees: M.B., B.Chir. Degrees, Vet.M.B. Degree	24,000	24,000
M.Eng. Degree and M.Sci. Degree	10,500	10,500
Certificates (excluding P.G.C.E.)	10,500	10,500
Postgraduate Certificate in Education (P.G.C.E.)	n/a	9,000
M.A.St.		
Astrophyics	10,500	10,500
Materials Science	10,500	10,500
Mathematics	8,571	9,000
Physics	10,500	10,500
Year abroad[1]	3,417	4,500

[1] The Year abroad fee applies to students undertaking a full year course of study abroad or working away (see Regulation 6 for the Law Tripos, Regulation 23 for the Asian and Middle Eastern Studies Tripos, Regulation 28 for the Modern and Medieval Languages Tripos, Regulation 23 for the Engineering Tripos). The special fee arrangements applying to students on a year abroad under the Erasmus Scheme are changing in 2014–15 for students admitted in and after 2012, and the fee liability is as above.

TABLE OF FEES, 2015–16

Table 1[1]

Annual Fee (£)

Qualification	Home and EU 2015–16 Old Regime: H/EU students who commenced before 2012–13 (except those to whom the old system fee applies)	Home and EU 2015–16 New Regime: H/EU students who commenced in 2012–13 or later years	Overseas 2015–16 A: Overseas students who commenced in or before 2010–11	Overseas 2015–16 B: Overseas students who commenced in 2011–12	Overseas 2015–16 C: Overseas students who commenced in 2012–13 or later years
B.A. Degree:[2] *Courses leading to Tripos, Preliminary, or Ordinary Examinations in*					
Group 1					
Anglo-Saxon, Norse, and Celtic	3,465	9,000	13,671	14,352	15,063
Archaeology and Anthropology (final intake October 2012)	3,465	9,000	13,671	14,352	15,063
Asian and Middle Eastern Studies	3,465	9,000	13,671	14,352	15,063
Classics	3,465	9,000	13,671	14,352	15,063
Economics	3,465	9,000	13,671	14,352	15,063
Education	3,465	9,000	13,671	14,352	15,063
English	3,465	9,000	13,671	14,352	15,063
History	3,465	9,000	13,671	14,352	15,063
History of Art	3,465	9,000	13,671	14,352	15,063
Human, Social, and Political Sciences	3,465	9,000	13,671	14,352	15,063
Land Economy	3,465	9,000	13,671	14,352	15,063
Law	3,465	9,000	13,671	14,352	15,063
Linguistics	3,465	9,000	13,671	14,352	15,063
Modern and Medieval Languages	3,465	9,000	13,671	14,352	15,063
Philosophy	3,465	9,000	13,671	14,352	15,063
Politics, Psychology, and Sociology (final intake October 2012)	3,465	9,000	13,671	14,352	15,063
Theological and Religious Studies	3,465	9,000	13,671	14,352	15,063
Group 2					
Mathematics	3,465	9,000	13,671	14,352	16,800
Group 3					
Architecture	3,465	9,000	17,895	18,783	19,713
Geography	3,465	9,000	17,895	18,783	19,713
Music	3,465	9,000	17,895	18,783	19,713
Group 4					
Chemical Engineering	3,465	9,000	17,895	21,840	22,923
Computer Science	3,465	9,000	17,895	21,840	22,923
Engineering	3,465	9,000	17,895	21,840	22,923
Management Studies	3,465	9,000	17,895	21,840	22,923
Manufacturing Engineering	3,465	9,000	17,895	21,840	22,923
Natural Sciences	3,465	9,000	17,895	21,840	22,923
Psychological and Behavioural Sciences	3,465	9,000	17,895	21,840	22,923
Group 5					
Medical and Veterinary Sciences (including for this purpose the Second M.B. and Second Vet.M.B. Examinations)[3]	3,465	9,000	17,895	34,728	36,459

[1] See Tables 5A and 5B for fee rates for certain students taking equivalent or lower qualifications (ELQ) and for continuing Island students. The Island rate has been abolished for students admitted on and after 1 September 2013.

[2] Students who have proceeded to the B.A. Degree but have been given leave to read for another Tripos 'not for honours' are deemed to be ELQ students for the purpose of their fee liability (see Table 5A).

[3] Parts IA and IB. The fee payable by a student who is reading for another Tripos in order to satisfy the requirements for the B.A. Degree is the fee set out for that Tripos.

Annual Fee (£)

	Home and EU		Overseas		
	2015–16		2015–16		
	Old Regime	New Regime	A	B	C
Qualification	H/EU students who commenced before 2012–13 (except those to whom the old system fee applies)	H/EU students who commenced in 2012–13 or later years	Overseas students who commenced in or before 2010–11	Overseas students who commenced in 2011–12	Overseas students who commenced in 2012–13 or later years
Year Abroad[1]	1,725	1,350	n/a	50% full fee	50% full fee
B.Th. Degree	3,465	9,000	13,671	14,352	15,063
Medical and Veterinary Degrees: M.B., B.Chir. Degrees, Vet.M.B. Degree[2]	3,465	9,000	33,096	34,728	36,459
M.Eng. Degree and M.Sci. Degree	3,465	9,000	17,895	21,840	22,923
M.Math. Degree	3,465	9,000	13,671	14,352	16,800
Certificates					
Certificate in Humanities Computing for Languages	3,465	9,000	17,895	18,783	19,713
Certificate in Modern Languages	3,465	9,000	13,671	14,352	15,063
Postgraduate Certificate in Education (P.G.C.E.)			*Moved to Table 2*		
M.A.St. Degree: *Courses leading to examinations in*					
Astrophysics	3,465	9,300	17,895	21,840	22,923
Materials Science	3,465	9,300	17,895	21,840	22,923
Mathematics	3,465	9,300	13,671	14,352	16,800
Physics	3,465	9,300	17,895	21,840	22,923

[1] The Year abroad fee applies to students undertaking a full year course of study abroad or working away (see Regulation 6 for the Law Tripos, Regulation 23 for the Asian and Middle Eastern Studies Tripos, Regulation 28 for the Modern and Medieval Languages Tripos, Regulation 23 for the Engineering Tripos). The special fee arrangements applying to students on a year abroad under the Erasmus Scheme are changing in 2014–15 for students admitted in and after 2012, and the fee liability is as above.

[2] Payable only if a student pursues her or his clinical studies in the University.

Table 2[1]

	Annual Fee (£)	
	Home/EU students	**Overseas students**
Qualification	**2015–16**	**2015–16**
LL.M. Degree	14,361	23,379
M.C.L. Degree	25,959	25,959
M.Ed. Degree: (*two-year part-time course*)[2]		
Students who commenced before 2014–15	4,050	9,387
Students who commenced in or after 2014–15	4,980	10,053
Ed.D. Degree: (*five-year part-time course*)[2]		
Home/EU students who commenced before 2014–15	4,221	–
Home/EU students who commenced in or after 2014–15	4,980	–
Overseas students who commenced in or after 2014–15	–	10,053
Postgraduate Certificate in Education (P.G.C.E.)		
Home/EU students who commenced before 2012–13	3,465	–
Home/EU students who commenced in or after 2012–13	9,000	–
Overseas students who commenced in or after 2012–13	–	22,674
M.Mus. Degree	9,291	20,718
M.Phil. Degree:[3]		
Courses leading to examinations in		
Advanced Chemical Engineering	11,037	26,877
Advanced Computer Science	11,037	26,877
African Studies	9,960	19,557
American History [starts MT 2015]	9,960	19,557
American Literature	8,223	19,557
Anglo-Saxon, Norse, and Celtic	8,223	19,557
Applied Biological Anthropology	9,960	22,674
Archaeological Research	9,960	19,557
Archaeology	9,960	19,557
Architecture	8,223	19,557
Architecture and Urban Design		
Old Regime Home/EU students Year 1	3,465	–
Old Regime Home/EU students Year 2	1,725	–
New Regime Home/EU students Year 1	9,000	–
New Regime Home/EU students Year 2	4,500	–
Overseas students Year 1	–	20,814
Overseas students Year 2	–	10,407
Architecture and Urban Studies	8,223	23,775
Asian and Middle Eastern Studies	8,223	19,557
Asian and Middle Eastern Studies (Research) [starts MT 2015]	8,223	19,557
Assyriology	9,960	19,557
Astronomy	7,035	22,674
Biological Anthropological Science	9,960	22,674
Biological Science	7,035	22,674
Bioscience Enterprise	11,037	22,674
Chemical Engineering and Biotechnology	7,035	22,674
Chemistry	7,035	22,674
Classics	8,223	19,557
Clinical Science (Translational Medicine and Therapeutics)	7,035	27,792
Clinical Science (Rare Diseases)	7,035	27,792
Comparative European Literatures and Cultures [name change MT 2015]	8,223	19,557
Computational Biology	7,035	22,674
Conservation Leadership	7,035	22,674
Criminological Research	9,960	19,557
Criminology	9,960	19,557
Development Studies	13,608	23,379
Developmental Biology	7,035	22,674
Early Modern History	9,960	19,557
Earth Sciences	7,035	22,674
Economic and Social History	9,960	19,557

[1] Island students who commenced in or after 2013–14 pay the Overseas rate of fee.

[2] The fees are the annual fee.

[3] The fees in this table for one-year full-time courses are the fees for the course for part-time students studying for the same qualification. The fee payable in each of two part-time years is half the full-time fee chargeable in the year of entry.

Qualification	Annual Fee (£) Home/EU students 2015–16	Overseas students 2015–16
Economic Research	14,832	22,857
Economics	14,832	22,857
Education	9,960	20,109
Egyptology	9,960	19,557
Energy Technologies	7,695	23,976
Engineering	7,035	22,674
Engineering for Sustainable Development	7,035	22,674
English Studies	8,223	19,557
Environmental Policy	11,376	19,557
Epidemiology	7,035	22,674
Finance	12,036	22,674
Finance and Economics	14,832	22,857
Financial Research	7,035	22,674
Fluid Flow in Industry and the Environment	7,035	22,674
Geographical Research	7,035	17,991
Geography (Arts)	7,035	17,991
Geography (Science)	7,035	22,674
Historical Studies	9,960	19,557
History of Art and Architecture	8,223	19,557
History, Philosophy, and Sociology of Science, Technology, and Medicine	9,960	21,390
Human Evolutionary Studies	9,960	22,674
Industrial Systems, Manufacturing, and Management	9,402	25,002
Innovation, Strategy, and Organization	7,035	22,674
International Relations and Politics	12,141	22,857
Land Economy	9,960	19,557
Land Economy Research	9,960	19,557
Latin-American Studies	9,960	19,557
Machine Learning, Speech, and Language Technology [starts MT 2015]	11,211	24,960
Management	22,674	22,674
Management Science and Operations	7,035	22,674
Materials Science and Metallurgy	7,035	22,674
Mathematics [starts MT 2015]	7,035	17,991
Medical Science	7,035	22,674
Medieval and Renaissance Literature	8,223	19,557
Medieval History	9,960	19,557
Micro- and Nanotechnology Enterprise	7,035	22,674
Modern British History [starts MT 2015]	9,960	19,557
Modern European History	9,960	19,557
Modern South Asian Studies	9,960	19,557
Multi-disciplinary Gender Studies	9,960	19,557
Music Studies	8,223	19,557
Nuclear Energy	9,081	25,221
Philosophy	8,223	19,557
Physics	7,035	22,674
Planning, Growth, and Regeneration	11,376	19,557
Polar Studies	7,035	17,991
Political Thought and Intellectual History	9,960	19,557
Primary Care Research	7,035	22,674
Public Health	7,035	22,674
Public Policy	26,115	26,115
Real Estate Finance	14,832	22,857
Scientific Computing	7,035	22,674
Screen Media and Cultures	8,223	19,557
Social and Developmental Psychology	8,223	19,557
Social Anthropology	12,141	22,857
Sociology [starts MT 2015]	9,960	20,856
Technology Policy	22,674	22,674
Theology and Religious Studies	8,223	19,557
Theoretical and Applied Linguistics	8,223	19,557
Veterinary Science	7,035	22,674
World History [starts MT 2015]	9,960	19,557
M.Res. Degree:		
Courses leading to examinations in		
Biological Science	7,035	22,674
Future Infrastructure and Built Environment	7,035	22,674
Gas Turbine Aerodynamics	7,035	22,674

Annual Fee (£)

Qualification	Home/EU students 2015–16	Overseas students 2015–16
Graphene Technology	7,035	22,674
Integrated Photonic and Electronic Systems	7,035	22,674
Medical Science	7,035	22,674
Physical Sciences	7,035	22,674
Sensor Technologies and Applications	7,035	22,674
Social Anthropology	12,141	22,857
Ultra Precision Engineering	7,035	22,674
Diplomas:		
Courses leading to examinations in		
Conservation of Easel Paintings	7,035	22,674
Economics (Advanced Diploma)	9,960	19,557
International Law	9,960	19,557
Legal Studies	9,960	19,557
Theology and Religious Studies	7,035	17,991

Table 3[1,2]

Annual Fee (£)

	Home/EU students		**Overseas students**			
	2015–16		**2015–16**			
	A	**B**	**A**	**B**	**C**	**D**
Qualification	Home/EU students who commenced before 2015–16	Home/EU students who commence in 2015–16	Overseas students who commenced in or before 2010–11	Overseas students who commenced in 2011–12, 2012–13, and 2013–14	Overseas students who commenced in 2014–15	Overseas students who commence in 2015–16
Eng.D. Degree	7,035	7,362	20,856	21,693	22,632	23,889
Ph.D., M.Sc., and M.Litt. Degrees, and Certificates of Postgraduate Study (C.P.G.S.): [3,4]						
Group 1 Arts	7,035	7,362	16,632	17,274	17,991	19,017
Group 2 Science	7,035	7,362	20,856	21,693	22,632	23,889
Group 3 Clinical	7,035	7,362	36,057	37,605	39,339	41,430

Group 1 Arts: Anglo-Saxon, Norse, and Celtic; Archaeology; Architecture; Asian and Middle Eastern Studies; Classics; Criminology; Development Studies; Divinity; Economics; Education; English, Geography, History; History of Art; History and Philosophy of Science; Land Economy; Law; Mathematics; Modern and Medieval Languages; Music; Philosophy; Politics and International Studies; Sociology; Social Anthropology; Theoretical and Applied Linguistics.
Group 2 Science: Architecture; Astronomy; Biochemistry; Biological Anthropology; Biological Science; Chemistry; Chemical Engineering; Computer Science; Earth Sciences; Engineering; Geography; Management Studies; Materials Science; Pathology; Physics; Physiology, Development and Neuroscience; Plant Sciences; Psychiatry; Psychology; Public Health and Primary Care; Zoology.
Group 3 Clinical: Clinical Medicine; Veterinary Medicine.

[1] For students commencing in 2015–16 and later years the fee will be fixed for the duration of their course (i.e. fees in each year of their course will be the same as the fee in their year of entry).

[2] Island students commencing in 2013–14 and later years pay the Overseas rate of fee.

[3] For part-time students who commenced before 2015 the fee payable is 60% of the full-time rate applicable to the year they commenced; for part-time students who commence in and after 2015 the fee payable is 60% of the full-time fee charged in their year of entry.

[4] Please note that Architecture and Geography appear in both Groups 1 and 2.

Table 4A

Qualification	*Fee for the course (£) for all students)* 2015–16
M.B.A. Degree (*one-year course*)	44,960
Executive M.B.A. (*two-year part-time course*)	
2015 intake	63,960
M.Fin. Degree (*one-year full-time course*)	40,625
M.D. Degree (*fee for the course*)	7,035

Table 4B

	Annual Fee (£)	
	Home/EU students	**Overseas students**
Qualification	**2015–16**	**2015–16**
M.St. Degree: *two-year part-time courses in*		
Advanced Subject Teaching		
Course commencing in August 2014	6,480	11,480
Course commencing in September 2015	6,530	12,200
Applied Criminology, Penology, and Management		
Course commencing in March 2014	5,230	5,230
Course commencing in March 2015	5,230	5,230
Applied Criminology and Police Management		
Course commencing in March 2014	5,230	5,230
Course commencing in March 2015	5,230	5,230
Building History		
Course commencing in October 2014	6,940	9,355
Course commencing in October 2015	7,250	10,250
Construction Engineering		
Course commencing in September 2014	10,000	10,000
Course commencing in September 2015	10,845	10,845
Creative Writing		
Course commencing in October 2014	6,480	11,480
Course commencing in October 2015	6,530	12,200
History		
Course commencing in September 2014	6,480	11,480
Course commencing in September 2015	6,530	12,200
Interdisciplinary Design for the Built Environment		
Course commencing in September 2014	6,873	6,873
Course commencing in September 2015	7,080	7,080
International Relations		
No course commencing in September 2014	–	–
Course commencing in September 2015	6,530	10,700
Sustainability Leadership		
Course commencing in September 2014	10,023	10,023
Course commencing in September 2015	10,230	10,230

Table 5A: *Home/EU ELQ students*

The following rates shall apply to Home/EU students commencing a course in 2009–10 or later years leading to a qualification which is equivalent to, or at a lower level than, a qualification they possessed when they began their course (ELQ students).[1]

ELQ students on courses in Medical and Veterinary Sciences leading to the B.A. Degree, as defined in the Regulations, to the M.B. or B.Chir. Degrees, the Vet.M.B. Degree, on courses in Architecture, or the Postgraduate Certificate in Education, are exempt from the ELQ policy and pay the Regulated fees set out below.

Annual Fee (£)

	Continuing Home/EU ELQ students	**New Regime Home/EU ELQ students**
	Continuing students who commenced before 1 September 2012	Students who commenced on or after 1 September 2012
Qualification	**2015–16**	**2015–16**
B.A. Degree:		
Groups 1–5 (except Architecture and Medical and Veterinary Sciences)	7,923	9,300
Architecture	3,465	9,000
Medical and Veterinary Sciences	3,465	9,000
B.Th. Degree	7,923	9,300
Medical and Veterinary Degrees: M.B., B.Chir., Vet.M.B.	3,465	9,000
M.Eng. Degree, M.Sci. Degree, and M.Math. Degree	7,923	9,300
M.A.St. Degree	n/a	9,300
Certificates (excluding P.G.C.E.)	7,923	9,300
Postgraduate Certificate in Education (P.G.C.E.)	3,465	9,000
Year abroad[2]	3,960	4,650
Year abroad (ELQ exempt)	1,725	1,350

Table 5B: *Continuing Island Students (Channel Islands and Isle of Man)*

The following rates shall apply to undergraduate student members of the University for whom the Continuing Island student rate of fees applies.

The separate Island rates of fee have been discontinued for students who commenced a course in 2013–14 or later. See Table 1 for Overseas rates.

Annual Fee (£)

	Continuing Island Students	
	Other Island students who commenced before 1 September 2012	Island students who commenced on or after 1 September 2012 and before 1 September 2013
Qualification	**2015–16**	**2015–16**
B.A. Degree:		
Group 1	7,005	9,000
Group 2 and 3	8,786	9,000
Group 4 and 5	10,500	10,500
B.Th. Degree	7,005	9,000
Medical and Veterinary Degrees: M.B., B.Chir., Vet.M.B.	24,000	24,000
M.Eng. Degree and M.Sci. Degree	10,500	10,500
Certificates (excluding P.G.C.E.)	10,500	10,500
Year abroad[2]	3,501	4,500

[1] Students who have proceeded to the B.A. Degree but have been given leave to read for another Tripos 'not for honours' are deemed to be ELQ students for the purpose of their fee liability.

[2] The Year abroad fee applies to students undertaking a full-year course of study abroad or working away (see Regulation 6 for the Law Tripos, Regulation 23 for the Asian and Middle Eastern Studies Tripos, Regulation 28 for the Modern and Medieval Languages Tripos, Regulation 23 for the Engineering Tripos). The special fee arrangements applying to students on a year abroad under the Erasmus Scheme are changing in 2014–15 for students admitted in and after 2012, and the fee liability is as above.

APPENDIX

Definition of an overseas student for the purposes of University Composition Fees

An overseas student is a person to whom the University may lawfully charge higher fees than persons not so categorized by virtue of the provisions of the Education (Fees and Awards) (England) Regulations, as they may be amended from time to time.[1]

CERTIFICATES OF DEGREES AND EXAMINATIONS AND MATRICULATION

1. The Registrary shall issue a certificate free of charge to every person proceeding to a University award, but a fee shall be charged for issuing a copy of a certificate.

2. The Registrary may issue on request a degree certificate of an alternative design, bearing the arms of the University printed in colour; a fee shall be charged for such a certificate.

3. The Registrary may issue a statement of verification attesting matriculation, or the passing of any examination, or the class obtained by a candidate in a Tripos Examination or the degrees or University awards held by the candidate. A fee may be charged for each such statement.

4. In addition to statements of verification supplied under Regulation 4 of the regulations for the disclosure of examination marks, the Registrary may issue more detailed transcripts[2] than the statements of verification specified in Regulation 3 above to the candidate to whom the information relates. A person who has proceeded to a degree or who has completed a course leading to a University award shall receive such a transcript relating to the examination or examinations for that degree or award free of charge; a fee shall be charged for issuing a copy of the transcript or for issuing a transcript to a person who has not proceeded to a degree or completed a course leading to an award.

5. The fees charged under Regulations 1–4 shall be determined from time to time by the General Board. A Schedule of the fees charged shall be published in the *Reporter* from time to time.

PAYMENTS

PAYMENTS TO COLLEGES FOR THE USE OF LECTURE-ROOMS

The Finance Committee of the Council shall be authorized to approve payments to Colleges for the use of lecture-rooms or other accommodation placed at the disposal of the University for use for University teaching.

PAYMENTS AND VALUE ADDED TAX

All sums, specified in or determined under Ordinances by way of a payment by the University, which might be liable to Value Added Tax shall be inclusive of Value Added Tax and no further payment by reason of that tax shall be made.

ADMISSION TO LECTURES AND LABORATORIES BY SPECIAL LEAVE

1. If a member of the University or an applicant for admission under Regulation 2 desires to pursue research in the interests of a commercial or industrial undertaking or association, or is not at liberty to publish the results of the research, facilities may be granted by the Head of the Department concerned, with the concurrence of the Council. The fees to be charged in such a case shall be subject to the approval of the General Board. Facilities for research.

2. Except as provided in Regulation 1, teachers from other universities, university colleges, or comparable institutions, of subjects pertaining to a Faculty or Department, or persons pursuing research Teachers from other institutions.

[1] The current regulations are the Education (Fees and Awards) (England) Regulations 2007 (Statutory Instruments 2007, No. 779) as amended by the Education (Student Fees, Awards and Support) (Amendment) (No. 2) Regulations 2007 (Statutory Instruments 2007, No. 2263), the Education (Student Fees, Awards and Support) (Amendment) Regulation 2011 (Statutory Instruments 2011, No. 87), the Education (Fees and Awards) (England) Regulations 2007 (Amendment) Regulations 2011 (Statutory Instruments 2011, No. 1987), and the Education (Student Fees, Awards and Support) (Amendment) Regulations 2012 (Statutory Instruments 2012, No. 1653). The category of persons who are not overseas students is defined in Schedule 1 to the principal Regulations (as amended).

[2] A transcript is a formal, verifiable, and comprehensive record of an individual student's learning. It will normally include information about the nature, level, content, and status of the studies undertaken by the individual named on the original qualification document, in addition to recording the outcomes.

upon such subjects, who are neither members of the University nor employed by the University may be admitted by the Chair of a Faculty not organized in Departments, or by the Head of a Department, to courses of instructions in that Faculty or Department, or to work in the laboratory of that Department, for a period not exceeding one year from the date of their first admission under this regulation to courses or laboratory work in any Faculty or Department in the University. This period may be extended by the Council.[1] Persons so admitted shall be charged such fees, if any, as the Faculty Board or the Head of the Department may determine in each case.

Special circumstances. **3.** In special circumstances persons not coming under Regulation 1 or 2 may, if they could not reasonably be expected to become members of the University, be admitted to courses of instruction organized by a Faculty or Department, or to work in a laboratory. It shall be for the Council to grant or to refuse admission to such persons. Application should be made to the Registrary, specifying the special circumstances.

Register. **4.** Secretaries of the Boards of Faculties not organized in Departments, Heads of Departments, or the authorities responsible for admitting candidates to courses for Diplomas or Certificates, shall send to the Registrary, by the division of each term and before 20 July, the names of all persons receiving instruction in their Faculties or Departments, or working in a laboratory under Regulations 1–3, and the Registrary shall enter the names in an official Register, from which the Council shall have power at any time, without assigning reasons, to remove any name.

Fees. **5.** A person admitted under Regulation 3 to a course of instruction which consists of or includes work in a laboratory shall pay a fee the same in amount as the undergraduate rate of University Composition Fee (for home students or for overseas students as may be appropriate) for each term or vacation for which he or she is so admitted. A person admitted under Regulation 3 to any other course of instruction shall pay a fee which is one-third of that amount.

6. A lecture or course of lectures announced as free to all members of the University, even if it is not announced as free to other persons also, may be attended without fee by persons who have leave under these regulations, and by other persons also to whom the lecturer gives leave to attend.

7. The Council may for special reason reduce or waive any fee payable under Regulation 5.[2]

Prohibition. **8.** A member of the University who has been forbidden by the authorities of his or her College to reside in the University as a member of that College shall not during the continuance of such prohibition attend University lectures or laboratories without the leave of the Council unless he or she has been admitted to another College.

ADMISSION TO LECTURES AND LABORATORIES BY SPECIAL LEAVE: NOTICE

The Council have announced (*Reporter*, 1930–31, p. 394) that with reference to Regulation 3:

(1) Applicants should mention all the Faculties or Departments in which they wish to attend instruction.

(2) Leave will not ordinarily be given for more than two terms.

(3) Leave to attend instruction in the Long Vacation may be given to persons not yet admitted, but already approved for admission, to a College of the University, if it is certified that during the period of instruction they will reside either at their homes, or in accordance with the regulations for the residence of persons *in statu pupillari* and under the discipline of their College.

The Council have announced (*Reporter*, 1951–52, p. 894) that under Regulations 4 and 7 they will give leave to a University assistant to attend courses of instruction, and will remit all the fees incurred, if

(*a*) the assistant's application is supported by the Head of his or her Department, or, if the Faculty concerned is not organized in Departments, by the Chair of the Faculty Board, and

(*b*) if the course of instruction that the assistant wishes to attend is one in which accommodation is in any way limited, the application also has the support of the Head of the Department, or, if the Faculty concerned is not organized in Departments, the Chair of the Faculty Board, under the auspices of which the instruction is to be given.

Applications for such leave should be addressed to the Registrary.

RESEARCH IN UNIVERSITY LABORATORIES IN THE INTEREST OF OUTSIDE BODIES: NOTICE

In accordance with Grace 4 of 18 March 1950, the Council announced (*Reporter*, 1949–50, p. 1191) that from 1 October 1950 they would not grant facilities in University laboratories for pursuing research financed from outside the University unless the arrangements had been approved in advance by the Council; and that they would

[1] The Council give notice that only in very exceptional circumstances will they extend this period by more than a year.

[2] The Council give notice that no fee will be charged under Regulation 5 to full-time Student Gardeners, whether paid or unpaid, who are recommended for this exemption by the Regius Professor of Botany.

not, in general, give such approval unless those arrangements provided that all financial transactions, including any payments that might be proposed by the outside body to a University teaching officer in connection with such research, were made through the University Treasurer in consultation with the Head of the Department concerned. In view of the arrangements for stipends under the Statutes approved by His Majesty in Council on 30 June 1949, the Council gave further notice that any such payments would be subject to the approval of the General Board.

The General Board have agreed that they will be willing to consider a proposal for a non-pensionable payment to a University officer for work in connection with a contract between the University and an authority outside the University, if such a payment is recommended by the Head of the Department concerned and is provided for in the contract.

POWER TO AFFIX THE SEALS OF THE UNIVERSITY

1. The Great Common Seal of the University shall not be affixed to any document unless authority has been given by Grace of the Regent House.

2. The Common Seal may be affixed to any document within the following classes of documents either in pursuance of an order of the Council or, if the Council have delegated authority to the Finance Committee in relation to any of the following classes, in pursuance of an order of the Finance Committee:

(*a*) documents authorizing or enabling the University Bankers to receive dividends and interest payable on all stocks, shares, and securities standing in the corporate name of the University;

(*b*) documents necessary for effecting the sale of real and personal property and of stocks, shares, and securities standing in the corporate name of the University;

(*c*) documents necessary for effecting the transfer of real and personal property and of stocks, shares, and securities which may be purchased in the corporate name of the University;

(*d*) documents necessary for effecting the transfer of real and personal property and of stocks, shares, and securities which may be transferred to the University in pursuance of any gift or bequest which may have been accepted by the University;

(*e*) documents necessary for obtaining registration in the corporate name of the University of real and personal property and for obtaining inscription or registration in the corporate name of the University of bearer bonds or other stocks, shares, and securities belonging to the University;

(*f*) assignments of assurance policies made under the regulations for the Superannuation Scheme;

(*g*) forms of appointment of proxy or proxies to vote at meetings of stockholders or shareholders;

(*h*) documents of consent to loans from the Church Commissioners for purposes relating to ecclesiastical benefices of which the University is patron;

(*i*) leases, licences, and other documents relating to property;

(*j*) documents necessary for transactions relating to Loan Fund II;

(*k*) documents giving the consent of the University to alterations in or transactions affecting parsonage-houses, church-yards, or glebe-lands of benefices of which the University acts as patron;

(*l*) documents relating to any contract which has been duly approved by the appropriate University body responsible under Statute or Ordinance;

(*m*) deeds of presentation and deeds of nomination to vacant benefices.

3. The Vice-Chancellor (or a Pro-Vice-Chancellor designated by the Vice-Chancellor, under Statute A II 13) and the Registrary, or deputies appointed by them under Statute A II 13(*c*) to be present at the sealing, shall attest under their hands the affixing of the Common Seal. The Registrary shall keep a record of all documents to which the Common Seal has been affixed.

CHAPTER II

MATRICULATION, RESIDENCE, ADMISSION TO DEGREES, DISCIPLINE

MATRICULATION

How it is effected.

1. A person shall be deemed to be matriculated from the beginning of the term in which a completed Matriculation Registration Form and satisfactory evidence of his or her qualification to matriculate are received by the Registrary.

Matriculation Registration Form.

2. Every candidate for matriculation shall subscribe to the following declaration by signing the Matriculation Registration Form:

'I promise to observe the Statutes and Ordinances of the University as far as they concern me, and to pay due respect and obedience to the Chancellor and other officers of the University.'

Submission of Form.

3. The Matriculation Registration Form when completed, together with any necessary evidence of matriculability, shall be submitted to the Registrary by the proper authority of the College to which the candidate belongs or, if the candidate is not a member of a College, by the Head of the Department or other person who would be qualified to present the candidate for a degree under Regulation 9 for admission to degrees. For a candidate *in statu pupillari*, other than a Graduate Student, the completed Matriculation Registration Form and evidence of matriculability must be sent to the Registrary so as to arrive not later than the division of the candidate's first term of residence; provided that the Registrary shall have power to accept such form and evidence at a later date, subject to the payment of a fine of £1 in respect of each candidate unless the Tutor concerned has adduced reasons for delay which are regarded as adequate by the Council.

CLASSES OF PERSONS QUALIFIED TO MATRICULATE

In addition to the persons qualified under Statute B I 1, the Council have approved the following classes of persons as qualified for matriculation:

(*a*) persons to whom the Council have granted the status of Master of Arts;
(*b*) persons who have been granted leave by the Degree Committee for the Faculty of Law to present themselves as candidates for the degree of Master of Law;
(*c*) persons who have been approved by a Faculty Board, Degree Committee, or other body concerned as candidates for any one of the following University awards:
  (i) Diplomas in the Conservation of Easel Paintings, Modern Languages, and Theology and Religious Studies;
  (ii) Certificates in Humanities Computing for Languages and Modern Languages;
(*d*) persons who have been approved by the Head of the Department of Education for admission to the course of study leading to the Postgraduate Certificate in Education;
(*e*) persons employed by the University or by a College who hold appointments approved by the University for the purpose of Statute A III 10(*e*).[1]
(*f*) persons approved as clinical students by the authorities of the School of Clinical Medicine for admission to courses leading to the degrees of Bachelor of Medicine and Bachelor of Surgery;
(*g*) members of an institution within the Cambridge Theological Federation who at the end of their first year of studying in an institution with the Federation have passed the Qualifying Examination in Theology for Ministry (with a view to becoming candidates for the B.Th. Degree).

EXAMINATION REQUIREMENTS FOR MATRICULATION

Scheme.

1. A student shall satisfy the examination requirements for matriculation if satisfying the requirements set out in Schedule I for the course for which he or she has been offered admission or the same subjects in other qualifications judged by the admitting College to be equivalent; in taking each decision a College shall have regard to the schedule of qualifications attached to these regulations (Schedule II) and to such advice as may be issued from time to time by the General Board.

Exceptions.

2. If a candidate is not in the judgement of his or her admitting College completely qualified as above, but the College believes that the candidate is fit to be admitted as a candidate for honours, the

[1] See p. 110.

College may deem the candidate to be qualified. In taking such a decision a College shall have regard to such advice as is issued from time to time by the General Board.

3. A College shall supply such information about compliance with the examination requirements for matriculation or about a decision taken under Regulation 2 in the report of a student or students admitted as the General Board shall require in any particular instance or generally.

4. The General Board shall have the authority to amend the Schedules to these regulations. Amendment of Schedules.

SCHEDULE I

EXAMINATION REQUIREMENTS FOR MATRICULATION

(subject to amendment by the General Board under Regulation 4)

1. In order to be admitted, candidates must show evidence of a broad educational background and good standards of literacy and numeracy.[1] A high standard of performance in three General Certificate of Education (GCE) A level subjects (or equivalent) is normally required. The University does not have any formal requirement for any particular subjects in the General Certificate of Secondary Education (GCSE), save for those indicated in section 2 below.

2. Eligibility to matriculate for admission to the following Triposes shall require a pass in the subject(s) specified:

Tripos	*Subject*
	GCE A Level (or equivalent) unless otherwise indicated
Classical (direct entry to Part IA)	Greek or Latin
Computer Science	Mathematics
Economics	Mathematics
Education	The subject within the Tripos in which the candidate intends to specialize
Engineering	Physics and Mathematics (and Chemistry for those intending to take the Chemical Engineering Tripos via the Engineering Tripos); or Mathematics and a suitable vocational qualification in an engineering discipline; or Physics and the Level 3 Certificate in Mathematics for Engineering as part of the Advanced Diploma in Engineering
English	English Literature or combined English Language/Literature
Mathematical	Mathematics and (at least at AS Level) Further Mathematics
Medical and Veterinary Sciences	GCSEs – Double Award Science and Mathematics or single award Biology and Physics and Mathematics AS and A Levels – Chemistry and two of Biology, Physics, and Mathematics, including at least one at A Level
Modern and Medieval Languages	At least one of the two languages intended in the Tripos
Music	Music or an appropriate alternative qualification such as Associated Board Grade VIII Theory
Natural Sciences	Two from Biology, Physics, Chemistry, and Mathematics

SCHEDULE II

EXAMINATION REQUIREMENTS FOR MATRICULATION: QUALIFYING AWARDS

(subject to amendment by the General Board under Regulation 4)

Qualifications awarded by UK public examining bodies

GCE: A level (and AS)
GCSE
Advanced Diploma
Higher Diploma
Scottish Certificate of Education
Welsh Baccalaureate
Cambridge Pre-U
Other qualifications of comparable standard awarded by UK public examination bodies (e.g. IGCSE; vocational A levels)

[1] GCSE passes at grade C and above in English Language and in a Mathematics or Science Subject would normally satisfy these requirements, as would an appropriate level of attainment in other qualifications such as the Scottish Certificate of Education or the European and International Baccalaureates.

Other qualifications issued by UK public examining bodies (e.g. Certificate of Proficiency in English (Cambridge Assessment), IELTS

Other Member States of the European Union

Normal secondary leaving examination and awards, qualifying the holder for admission to university in the country of issue (e.g. French Baccalaureate, German Abitur)
European Baccalaureate

Other European countries

Equivalent qualifications to the above

International qualifications

International Baccalaureate

Other countries

Qualifications judged by the admitting College to be substantially equivalent to the above (e.g. US Scholastic Aptitude Test, including Advanced Placement)

RESIGNATION OF MEMBERSHIP OF THE UNIVERSITY

Grace 1 of 27 November 2013

If any matriculated person wishes to resign her or his membership of the University in accordance with Statute B I 2 and so informs the Registrary, and if the Council deems the reasons given sufficient and decides to allow such resignation, that person's name shall be removed from the list of members of the University at the next publication of the list, and any name so removed shall be reinstated only in accordance with a subsequent decision of the Council which shall not be taken until a period of five years has elapsed from the date of removal. The name of any matriculated person which under this section is removed from the list of members of the University shall if such person is a member of the Senate be removed also from the register of the Senate in accordance with the provisions of Statute A I 7.

Stat. B I.

AFFILIATED STUDENTS

Amended by Graces 1 of 6 and 27 November 2013, and 4 of 30 July 2014

1. Any person who before matriculation in the University of Cambridge has received or become qualified to receive a degree from another institution of higher education shall be entitled, on or after matriculation, to be approved as an Affiliated Student, provided that

(*a*) on becoming qualified for the degree he or she had been a member of one or more such institutions for not less than three academical years;

(*b*) the degree has been approved for the purpose by the Council of the University.

2. In particular cases the Council may approve as an Affiliated Student

(*a*) a member or former member of an institution of higher education who does not fulfil the requirements of Regulation 1;

or (*b*) an adult student of exceptional qualifications who is specially recommended by the Strategic Committee of the Institute of Continuing Education, provided that the student has followed courses of study in adult education classes for at least four years, of which three years shall have been spent in University extra-mural classes, or distributed between such classes and an institution of full-time higher education.

3. Application for approval as an Affiliated Student shall be made on a student's behalf by his or her Tutor to the Registrary, and shall be accompanied by evidence of the student's qualification for such approval. Such application may be made at any time after the student has been provisionally accepted for admission to a College but not later than the end of the student's first term of residence. Approval of a student as an Affiliated Student shall have effect from the beginning of his or her first term of residence.

4. A person approved as an Affiliated Student shall be deemed to have satisfied the examination requirements for matriculation. For the purposes of the regulations for Triposes and the regulations for degrees other than the Ph.D., M.Sc., M.Litt., M.Phil., M.Eng., M.A.St., M.Res., M.Fin., and M.B.A. Degrees, an Affiliated Student's first term of actual residence shall be reckoned as his or her fourth term of residence and he or she shall be deemed to have kept by residence the three terms preceding the first term of actual residence.

5. In the application of the regulations for Ordinary B.A. Degree an Affiliated Student shall be deemed to have the equivalent of one Part I Honours Examination.

6. Provided always that (unless otherwise prescribed below for a particular Tripos) no student shall take Part II of any Tripos as his or her first Honours Examination later than the sixth term after the first term of actual residence, an Affiliated Student shall have the following privileges:

Anglo-Saxon, Norse, and Celtic

If the Faculty Board of English allow it in a particular case, leave to take Part II of the Anglo-Saxon, Norse, and Celtic Tripos under the same conditions as if he or she had previously obtained honours in another Honours Examination, with or without the further privilege of taking the examination in the second term after the student's first term of actual residence.

Archaeology and Anthropology[1]

Asian and Middle Eastern Studies

If the Faculty Board of Asian and Middle Eastern Studies allow it in a particular case, *either*

(i) leave to take Part IB of the Asian and Middle Eastern Studies Tripos in the second term after the student's first term of residence, *or*

(ii) leave to take Part II of the Asian and Middle Eastern Studies Tripos in the eighth term after the student's first term of residence.

Chemical Engineering

If the Chemical Engineering and Biotechnology Syndicate allow it in a particular case, *either*

(i) leave to take Part I of the Chemical Engineering Tripos in the second term after the student's first term of actual residence without having previously obtained honours in an Honours Examination, *or*

(ii) leave to take Part IIA of the Chemical Engineering Tripos under the same conditions as if the student had previously obtained honours in Part I of that Tripos, with or without the further privilege of taking the examination in the second term after his or her first term of actual residence.

Classics

Either

(i) the right to take Part II of the Classical Tripos under Regulation 24 not earlier than the fifth term after the student's first term of actual residence without having previously obtained honours in an Honours Examination, *or*

(ii) if the Faculty Board of Classics allow it in a particular case, leave to take Part II of the Classical Tripos under Regulation 23 in the second term after the student's first term of actual residence without having previously obtained honours in an Honours Examination.

Computer Science

If the Faculty Board of Computer Science and Technology allow it in a particular case, leave to take Part IB of the Computer Science Tripos in the second term after the student's first term of actual residence or Part II of the Computer Science Tripos in the second term after the student's first term of actual residence without having previously obtained honours in an Honours Examination.

Economics

If the Faculty Board of Economics allow it in a particular case, leave to take Part IIA of the Economics Tripos not earlier than the second term after the student's first term of actual residence under the same conditions as if he or she had previously obtained honours in Part I of the Tripos.

Education

If the Faculty Board of Education allow it in a particular case, leave to take Part II of the Education Tripos not earlier than the fifth term after the student's first term of actual residence without having previously obtained honours in an Honours Examination.

[1] Rescinded with effect from 1 October 2014.

Engineering

If the Faculty Board of Engineering allow it in a particular case, *either*

(i) leave to take Part IIA of the Engineering Tripos in the second term after the student's first term of actual residence without having previously obtained honours in an Honours Examination, *or*

(ii) leave to take Part IIB of the Engineering Tripos under the same conditions as if the student had previously obtained honours in Part IIA of that Tripos, with or without the further privilege of taking the examination in the second term after his or her first term of actual residence.

English

The right to take in the second term after the student's first term of actual residence the Preliminary Examination for Part II of the English Tripos; and the right to take in the fifth term after the student's first term of actual residence Part II of the English Tripos, subject to the regulations for that Part which apply to Affiliated Students.

Geography

If the Faculty Board of Earth Sciences and Geography allow it in a particular case, *either*

(i) leave to take Part IB of the Geographical Tripos in the second term after the student's first term of actual residence without having previously obtained honours in an Honours Examination, *or*

(ii) leave to take Part II of the Geographical Tripos under the same conditions as if he or she had previously obtained honours in another Honours Examination, with or without the further privilege of taking the examination in the second term after the student's first term of actual residence.

History

If the Faculty Board of History allow it in a particular case, *either*

(i) leave to take Part I of the Historical Tripos in the fifth term after his or her first term of actual residence, *or*

(ii) leave to take Part II of the Historical Tripos under the same conditions as if he or she had previously obtained honours in another Honours Examination, with or without the further privilege of taking the examination in the second term after the student's first term of actual residence,

save that the Faculty Board, when granting leave either under (i) or under (ii), may require the student to take one or more additional papers prescribed by the Board from the papers for either Part of that Tripos.

History of Art

The right to take Part IIA of the History of Art Tripos in the second term after the student's first term of actual residence and to take Part IIB of the Tripos in the fifth term after the student's first term of actual residence, under the same conditions as if he or she had previously obtained Honours in another Honours Examination.

Human, Social, and Political Sciences

If the Faculty Board of Human, Social, and Political Sciences allow it in a particular case, leave to take Part IIA of the Human, Social, and Political Sciences Tripos in the second term after the student's first term of actual residence.

Land Economy

If the Board of Land Economy allow it in a particular case, *either*

(i) leave to take Part IB of the Land Economy Tripos in the second term after the student's first term of actual residence without having previously obtained honours in an Honours Examination, *or*

(ii) leave to take Part II of the Land Economy Tripos in the fifth term after the student's first term of actual residence without having previously obtained honours in another Honours Examination.

Law

If the Faculty Board of Law allow it in a particular case, leave to take Part II of the Law Tripos under the same conditions as if he or she had previously obtained honours in Part IB of that Tripos, with or without the further privilege of taking the examination in the second term after the student's first term of actual residence.

Linguistics

The right to take Part IIA of the Linguistics Tripos in the second term after the student's first term of actual residence and to take Part IIB not earlier than the fifth term after the student's first term of actual residence, under the same conditions as if he or she had previously obtained honours in another Honours Examination.

Management Studies

If the Faculty Board of Business and Management allow it in a particular case, leave to take the Management Studies Tripos under the same conditions as if he or she had previously obtained honours in another Honours Examination, with or without the further privilege of taking the examination in the second term after the student's first term of actual residence.

Mathematics

Either

(i) the right to take Part IB of the Mathematical Tripos in the second term after the student's first term of actual residence without having previously obtained honours in an Honours Examination, *or*

(ii) if the Faculty Board of Mathematics allow it in a particular case, leave to take Part II of the Mathematical Tripos in the second term after the student's first term of actual residence without having previously obtained honours in an Honours Examination.

Modern and Medieval Languages

(*a*) The right to take Part II of the Modern and Medieval Languages Tripos under Regulation 24(*d*) not earlier than the fifth term after the student's first term of actual residence.

(*b*) If the Faculty Board of Modern and Medieval Languages allow it in a particular case, leave to take Part II of the Modern and Medieval Languages Tripos under Regulation 24(*e*) in the second term after the student's first term of actual residence.

Music

The right to take Part IB of the Music Tripos in the second term after the student's first term of actual residence without having previously obtained honours in an Honours Examination.

Natural Sciences

Either

(i) the right to take Part IB of the Natural Sciences Tripos in the second term after the student's first term of actual residence without having previously obtained honours in an Honours Examination, *or*

(ii) if the Faculty Board or comparable authority concerned with the subject that the student desires to offer allow it in a particular case, leave to take Part II of the Natural Sciences Tripos under the same conditions as if the student had previously obtained honours in Part IB of that Tripos, with or without the further privilege of taking the examination in the second term after his or her first term of actual residence.

Philosophy

Either

(i) the right to take Part IB of the Philosophy Tripos in the second term after the student's first term of actual residence, *or*

(ii) the right to take Part II of the Philosophy Tripos either in the second term or in the fifth term after the student's first term of actual residence under the same conditions as if he or she had previously obtained honours in another Honours Examination.

Politics, Psychology, and Sociology[1]

Theological and Religious Studies

The right to take Part IIA of the Theological and Religious Studies Tripos under Regulation 24 in the second term after the student's first term of actual residence and to take Part IIB of the Theological and Religious Studies Tripos under Regulation 27 in the fifth term after the student's first term of actual residence without having previously obtained honours in an Honours Examination.

[1] Rescinded with effect from 1 October 2014.

7. Any application for leave which a student may wish to seek under the provisions of Regulation 6 shall be made, not later than the end of the student's first term of residence, through a Tutor to the Registrary, who shall transmit it to the Faculty Board or Syndicate concerned.

A Faculty Board may delegate its functions under Regulation 6 to the Degree Committee for the Faculty, and shall inform the Registrary of the period of any such delegation.

8. All or any of the privileges of Affiliation (that is to say, the privileges which under this Ordinance may be granted to Affiliated Students) may be granted by the Council to any particular applicant who is a member or former member of an institution engaged in the education of adult students, although the requirements of this Ordinance have not been fulfilled.

STATUS OF BACHELOR OF ARTS

1. A Graduate Student who is not a graduate of the University and has not the status of Master of Arts shall, so long as he or she is registered as a Graduate Student, have the status of Bachelor of Arts.

2. The Council may grant the status of Bachelor of Arts to a person resident in the University who does not qualify for that status under Regulation 1 and who

(*a*) holds a degree of another university, or a qualification deemed by the Council to be equivalent to a degree, and

(*b*) has attained the age of twenty-one years, and

(*c*) has been recommended by the Head of a College or a Tutor of a College and is certified to have been admitted to the College;

provided that

(i) such a person, if not already matriculated as a member of the University, shall be so matriculated at the first opportunity after the grant of that status;

(ii) the grant shall be for a period specified in each case, and may be revoked by the Council at any time.

3. A possessor of the status of Bachelor of Arts

(*a*) shall have the same privileges as a Bachelor of Arts with regard to the Libraries and Museums of the University, and the Botanic Garden;

(*b*) shall be entitled to wear the B.A. gown without strings, but not the hood.

4. A possessor of the status of Bachelor of Arts shall not be a candidate for any examination leading to the degree of Bachelor of Arts or Bachelor of Music.

STATUS OF MASTER OF ARTS

1. A Graduate Student or other person who has previously had the status of Bachelor of Arts shall, on attaining the age of twenty-four years, have the status of Master of Arts for so long as he or she is not of standing to proceed to the degree of Master of Arts.

2. The Council may grant the status of Master of Arts to any of the following if they have attained the age of twenty-four years and have not proceeded to the degree of Master of Arts or any higher degree:

(*a*) a University officer during his or her tenure of office, or a person holding a post in the University Press specially designated under Statute J 7;

(*b*) a Fellow of a College during his or her tenure of a Fellowship;

(*c*) a person employed by the University who holds an appointment approved by the University for the purpose of Statute A III 10(*e*) during his or her tenure of the appointment;[1]

(*d*) the Commandant and the Adjutant for the time being of the University Air Squadron, the University Officers Training Corps, and the University Royal Naval Unit;

(*e*) a person who holds a degree of another university, or a qualification deemed by the Council to be equivalent to a degree, and who has been recommended by the Head of a College or a Tutor of a College and is certified to have been appointed to a College office, or admitted to the College;

[1] See p. 110.

(*f*) a graduate of another university or a visiting scholar working in the University, or in an institution connected with the University recognized for this purpose by the Council, who is recommended by the Chair of a Faculty Board or the Head of a Department as an appropriate person for the grant of this status;[1]

provided that

(i) such a person, if not already matriculated as a member of the University, shall be so matriculated at the first opportunity after the grant of this status;

(ii) a grant made under subsection (*e*) or subsection (*f*) above shall be for a period specified in each case, and may be revoked by the Council at any time.

3. A possessor of the status of Master of Arts:

(*a*) shall have the same privileges as a Master of Arts with regard to the Libraries (other than the University Library), the Museums, and the Botanic Garden of the University;

(*b*) shall be entitled to wear the M.A. gown without strings, but not the hood;

(*c*) for the purpose of keeping terms by residence, may certify his or her own residence;

(*d*) shall not be subject to the regulations for motor vehicles or the regulations for bicycles and boats.

4. A possessor of the status of Master of Arts shall not be a candidate for any examination leading to the degree of Bachelor of Arts or Bachelor of Music.

INCORPORATION

1. A person who is a graduate of the University of Oxford or the University of Dublin (Trinity College) may be admitted by incorporation to a degree which in the opinion of the Council is equivalent to the highest degree which either of those Universities has conferred upon him or her, provided that the person concerned: Conditions.

(*a*) has been matriculated as a member of the University;

(*b*) has attained the age of twenty-four years (unless in a particular case the Council see fit to grant exemption from this provision);

(*c*) has satisfied the Council that the qualifications required for the Oxford or Dublin degree in question included residence as well as the passing of examinations or the performance of other exercises;

(*d*) has been admitted to a University office or a Headship or a Fellowship (other than an Honorary Fellowship) of a College, or holds a post in the University Press specially designated under Statute J 7 or is a Head-elect or designate of a College,

provided also that if the person concerned holds a University office or a designated post in the University Press or a Fellowship of a College, which on initial appointment or election did not carry tenure to the retiring age, he or she already has held a University office or offices, or such a post or posts in the University Press, or a Fellowship or Fellowships (other than an Honorary Fellowship) of a College or of different Colleges, or any combination of these, for a total period, which need not be continuous, of at least three years.

2. Each application by or on behalf of a candidate for admission to a degree by incorporation shall state: Applications.

(*a*) the candidate's full name and date of birth;

(*b*) the name of the College, if any, to which he or she has been admitted or approved for admission;

(*c*) the University office, College Headship, or College Fellowship that he or she holds;

(*d*) evidence of the degree conferred by the University of Oxford or Dublin in respect of which application is made;

and shall be sent to the Registrary.

3. The standing of a person admitted to a degree by incorporation shall be reckoned from the date of his or her corresponding Oxford or Dublin degree. Standing.

[1] For the purpose of this regulation the term 'Chair of a Faculty Board' shall be taken to include the Chair of a Board, Syndicate, or other body responsible for a University institution, and the term 'Head of a Department' shall be taken to include the Director of a Sub-department or a Centre of Studies. The Council have agreed that the institutions recognized for the purpose of granting M.A. status under Regulation 2(*f*) shall include all the institutions recognized from time to time by the General Board for the purpose of Regulation 5(4)(*a*) of the regulations for the use of the University Library (see p. 670).

Allowance of terms.

4. A candidate for a degree who has kept one or more terms by residence at the University of Oxford or the University of Dublin (Trinity College) shall be allowed not more than the same number of terms towards the terms required to be kept for the Cambridge degree, if the Council are satisfied that for each term so allowed he or she has resided, according to the requirements of the University of Oxford or Dublin, for not less than fifty-six days of term.

5. If a student is so allowed a term or terms previous to the term in which he or she became a member of the University, that student's standing shall be reckoned from the beginning of the first term in which he or she was a member of the University of Oxford or of Dublin (Trinity College).

TERMS AND LONG VACATION

Grace 1 of 27 November 2013

1. There shall be three terms in the year, called respectively the Michaelmas Term, the Lent Term, and the Easter Term. The University shall determine the days on which each term shall begin and end, provided that the three terms shall together include two hundred and twenty-seven days at least.

2. The University libraries, laboratories, and museums shall be closed, and lectures shall not be given, on Good Friday.

3. The University shall determine from time to time by Ordinance what portion of each term, being not less than three-fourths, shall constitute full term.

4. The term 'academical year' shall mean the year beginning on the first day of the Michaelmas Term.

DATES OF TERM AND FULL TERM

Amended by Grace 1 of 27 November 2013

1. The Michaelmas Term shall begin on 1 October and shall consist of eighty days, ending on 19 December. The Lent Term shall begin on 5 January and shall consist of eighty days, ending on 25 March or in any leap year on 24 March. The Easter Term shall begin on 10 April and shall consist of seventy days ending on 18 June, provided that in any year in which Full Easter Term begins on or after 22 April the Easter Term shall begin on 17 April and end on 25 June.

2. Full Term shall consist of three-fourths of the whole term reckoned from the first day of Full Term as hereinafter determined.

3. The dates on which Full Terms begin and end shall be as shown in the table appended to these regulations.

Portion of term to be kept.

4. The portion of each term during which students shall be required to reside in order to keep the term shall be three-fourths.

First term of residence.

5. Except as may be provided by the Ordinances relating to a particular institution, the term in which a person who is required to keep certain terms by residence first resides in accordance with Regulation 3 or 4 for the Residence and Precincts of the University, as the case may be, shall be accounted that person's first term of residence whether he or she keeps the term, or is allowed it, or not.

Allowance of terms not kept by residence.

6. For the purposes of admissibility to examinations or competitions, or of the payment of emoluments of Studentships, Scholarships, and the like, a term allowed by the Council shall be reckoned as a term kept.

7. The Council shall have the same power to allow terms of residence to candidates for Diplomas and Certificates as they have under Regulation 10 of the regulations for Residence and Precincts of the University in respect of candidates for degrees.

8. A course of instruction given during the Long Vacation shall not occupy more than four weeks. Except with the approval of the Council on the recommendation of the General Board, no such course given within the Precincts of the University shall begin earlier than the second Monday after General Admission or end later than the sixth Saturday after the Saturday of General Admission.

Year	Full Mich. Term begins Oct. Tu.	Full Mich. Term ends Dec. Fri.	Full Lent Term begins Jan. Tu.	Full Lent Term ends March Fri.	Easter Day	Full Easter Term begins Apr. Tu.	Full Easter Term ends June Fri.	General Admission June Wed.–Sat.
2013–14	8	6	14	14	20 Apr.	22	13	25/26/27/28
2014–15	7	5	13	13	5 Apr.	21	12	24/25/26/27
2015–16	6	4	12	11	27 Mar.	19	10	22/23/24/25
2016–17	4	2	17	17	16 Apr.	25	16	28/29/30/1 July
2017–18	3	1	16	16	1 Apr.	24	15	27/28/29/30
2018–19	2	30 Nov.	15	15	21 Apr.	23	14	26/27/28/29
2019–20	8	6	14	13	12 Apr.	21	12	24/25/26/27
2020–21	6	4	19	19	4 Apr.	27	18	30/1/2/3 July
2021–22	5	3	18	18	17 Apr.	26	17	29/30/1/2 July
2022–23	4	2	17	17	9 Apr.	25	16	28/29/30/1 July
2023–24	3	1	16	15	31 Mar.	23	14	26/27/28/29
2024–25	8	6	21	21	20 Apr.	29	20	2/3/4/5 July
2025–26	7	5	20	20	5 Apr.	28	19	1/2/3/4 July
2026–27	6	4	19	19	28 Mar.	27	18	30/1/2/3 July
2027–28	5	3	18	17	16 Apr.	25	16	28/29/30/1 July
2028–29	3	1	16	16	1 Apr.	24	15	27/28/29/30
2029–30	2	30 Nov.	15	15	21 Apr.	23	14	26/27/28/29

NOTICE

When application is made for the allowance of a single term the Council will require to be satisfied that the applicant has kept by actual residence as much as practicable of Full Term in the term applied for.

If the student commenced residence later than the commencement of Full Term in the term applied for, the reason must be stated in the application.

The Council request that any application for the allowance of a second term may be accompanied by a repetition of particulars concerning the term previously allowed. Apart from very exceptional circumstances the Council will not allow a second term unless a good part of the two terms has been kept.

RESIDENCE AND PRECINCTS OF THE UNIVERSITY

Amended by Grace 1 of 27 November 2013

1. A person who is required by Statute, Ordinance or Regulation to keep certain terms by Residence shall be deemed to have kept a term by residence if he or she has resided within the University Precincts during such part (being not less than three-fourths) of that term, and in such manner, as the University may prescribe by Ordinance. The University may prescribe by Ordinance areas in and about Cambridge (not necessarily within the University Precincts) within which terms of residence may be kept by specified classes of person, and the University may delegate the power to determine that terms of residence may be kept in exceptional cases elsewhere than within the University Precincts or the prescribed areas. The terms 'reside', 'residence', and 'University Precincts' shall have the meanings ascribed to them in this Ordinance. Terms of residence.

2. The Precincts of the University shall be the area within a boundary defined as extending three miles from Great St Mary's Church, measured in a straight line, and as including Madingley Hall and such other places about Cambridge as may from time to time be determined by Grace, or by such authority as may be provided by Grace, whether generally or with respect to particular persons or classes of persons. Boundaries for keeping terms.

3. A person keeping terms by residence who is pursuing a course leading to the LL.M., M.A.St., M.C.L., M.Eng., M.Sci., M.Math., Vet.M.B., Mus.B., B.A., or B.Th. Degree, or the M.B., B.Chir.

Degrees (if pursuing his or her clinical studies in the University) shall reside within the Precincts of the University

(*a*) in the College[1] of which he or she is a member, or in a building provided and controlled by that College as a hostel;

or (*b*) in any of the following places which shall be recognized as houses of residence for such number of students in each case as the Council, after consultation with the Accommodation Syndicate, may from time to time determine: Margaret Beaufort Institute, Institute for Orthodox Christian Studies, Ridley Hall, Wesley House, Westcott House, and Westminster College;

or (*c*) with the permission of his or her College,[1] in other accommodation within the Precincts of the University, not being part of any College; provided that, before granting such permission, the College authorities must be satisfied with the arrangements for observing the normal conditions of residence;

or (*d*) in any hospital or nursing home within the precincts of the University, or in any University Hospital, Associate Teaching Hospital or Associate Teaching General Practice;

or (*e*) in exceptional circumstances, and for grave cause approved by the student's College, in some other place outside the Precincts of the University.

4. A person keeping terms by residence who is pursuing a course leading to a qualification of the University other than a degree or degrees specified in Regulation 3, or who is a registered Graduate Student pursuing a course that is not leading to a qualification of the University, or who is the possessor of the status of Master of Arts, shall not be subject to the conditions of place prescribed by that regulation but shall reside in the area within a boundary defined as extending ten miles from Great St Mary's Church, measured in a straight line; provided that in exceptional circumstances, and for grave cause approved by the Board of Graduate Studies in the case of a Graduate Student or otherwise by the student's College, such a person may be granted permission to reside outside that area.

Days of residence.

5. Residence shall be reckoned by days. No person keeping terms by residence shall be considered to have resided during any day unless he or she has resided during some part of such day and of the following night and has complied with such other conditions of residence, if any, as may be required by the authorities of his or her College; provided that a part of the day on which such a person completes his or her residence for the term may be counted as a day of residence.

6. For the purpose of reckoning residence the day shall be held to extend from 6 a.m. to midnight.

Certificate of residence.

7. Residence shall be certified to the University under the hand of the Head of the College to which the student belongs.

8. Save as may otherwise be provided for,[2]

(*a*) no one shall be admitted to the degree of Bachelor of Medicine or Surgery, or Master of Advanced Study or Business Administration (having followed a one-year or two-year integrated course of study prescribed by Ordinance) or Finance or Law or Research, or to the degrees of Master of Letters or Science or Philosophy, or Doctor of Philosophy having followed a full-time course, or to the degree of Doctor of Engineering, unless he or she has kept three terms at least by residence;

(*b*) no one shall be admitted to the degree of Bachelor of Theology for Ministry unless he or she has kept five terms at least by residence;

(*c*) no one shall be admitted to the degree of Bachelor of Arts or Music or Veterinary Medicine unless he or she has kept nine terms at least by residence;

(*d*) no one shall be admitted to the degree of Master of Engineering or Mathematics or Natural Sciences unless he or she has kept twelve terms at least by residence.

9. A Graduate Student may be granted in respect of work done in the University before matriculation an allowance of not more than three terms towards the three terms required to be kept under paragraph 7(*a*) above for any of the degrees of Master of Letters or Master of Science or Doctor of Engineering or Doctor of Philosophy, and an allowance of not more than one term towards the number of terms required to be kept for the degree of Master of Philosophy which requires a two-year course of study.

10. The Council may grant allowances of terms as follows:

(*a*) On account of illness or other grave cause, the Council may grant (i) one or two terms to any candidate for a degree who but for such allowance would be required to keep more than six terms by actual residence, (ii) one term to any candidate for a degree who but for such allowance would be required to keep six or fewer terms by actual residence.

[1] Or Approved Society.
[2] See also the regulations for Affiliated Students.

(*b*) On the recommendation of the Faculty Board or comparable authority concerned, the Council may allow not more than three terms to any candidate for a degree who but for such allowance would be required to keep six or more terms by actual residence and who since matriculation has pursued a course or courses of study outside the University under the direction of that Faculty Board or comparable authority.

(*c*) In circumstances which interfere with the normal tenor of residence of a large number of students, the Council may grant allowances of terms, in addition to the allowances hereinbefore provided, to students who fulfil such conditions as the Council may specify.

ADMISSION TO DEGREES

Supplicats

Amended by Grace 1 of 27 November 2013

1. Every Supplicat, that is to say, every Grace for a complete degree not conferred under Statute B II 2, shall be in the form prescribed from time to time by the Council, and shall be signed by the Head or Praelector or the deputy for the Head or Praelector of the applicant's College; provided that, if the applicant is a University officer who is not a member of any College, the Supplicat shall be signed by the Chair of the Faculty Board or the Head of the Department or other institution to which the applicant's office is assigned. Form of Supplicats.

2. Except as hereinafter provided no degree shall be conferred unless a Supplicat and certificate of terms (if necessary) have been sent to the Registrary so as to arrive not later than 10 a.m. on the morning of the day next but seven before that on which the degree is to be conferred, or, if a degree is to be conferred on a day of General Admission, not later than 10 a.m. on the morning of the day next but ten before that day. Submission of Supplicats and certificates of terms.

3. Notwithstanding that the provisions of Regulation 2 have not been satisfied, a degree may be conferred at any Congregation provided that the necessary documents have been received by the Registrary in time for proper consideration, and provided that a fine of £1 shall be paid in addition to the degree fee, if any. A fine shall not be charged in respect of a candidate who needs to keep the current term in order to qualify for the degree but has not done so on the day preceding the day on which the Supplicat is due to be received by the Registrary; provided that the Supplicat has been received at the proper time together with a statement of the reason for the delay in submitting the certificate of terms.

4. No degree shall be conferred upon any person unless *either* Submission of Graces and Supplicats to the Regent House.

(*a*) a Grace has been approved by the Regent House authorizing the conferment of the degree, of which due notice has been given in accordance with Regulation 20 of the regulations for Graces and Congregations of the Regent House; *or*

(*b*) a Supplicat in the prescribed form has been sent to the Registrary in accordance with Regulation 2 or 3 of these regulations and the conferment of the degree has been approved in the manner hereinafter provided.

No person shall be admitted in absence to the title of a degree, nor shall any person be admitted to a complete degree in absence unless this has been requested in the Supplicat or in the application for a degree conferred under Statute B II 2.

5. No degree for which residence is required as a qualification shall be conferred on any person unless the Head of the person's College or the deputy for the Head has certified to the Registrary that that person has kept the residence required. Certificate of terms.

6. No Grace for a degree or for the title of a degree shall be in force longer than one calendar year from the date of its approval. Time limit.

7. One hour and a half before the time appointed for each Congregation at which any degree is to be conferred (other than a degree for whose conferment a Grace has been approved by, or will at that Congregation be submitted to, the Regent House) the Registrary shall cause to be posted on a board in the Schools Arcade a list of names of persons whose Supplicats have been received and who are certified by the Registrary to have done all that is required of them by the Statutes and Ordinances and to be qualified to proceed on that day to the degrees for which they have applied. If any member of the Regent House informs the Vice-Chancellor in writing, not later than an hour after the posting of the list, that he or she intends to *non placet* the conferment of a degree upon any person named in the list, the Vice-Chancellor shall cause that person's name to be struck out from the list. At the Congregation the conferment of the degrees set out in the Registrary's list upon the persons named therein shall be proposed to the Regent House in the following collective formula:

Supplicant reverentiis vestris viri mulieresque ——[1] *quorum nomina juxta senaculum in porticu proposuit hodie Registrarius nec delevit Procancellarius* (or *Procancellaria*) *ut gradum quisque quem rite petivit assequatur.*

8. Where the Vice-Chancellor, having received written notice of *non placet*, has, in accordance with Regulation 7 above, caused the name of the person in respect of whom that notice is given to be struck out from the Registrary's list, the degree in respect of which notice of *non placet* has been given shall not be conferred upon that person unless a Grace to that effect has been submitted to and approved by the Regent House after the giving of due notice in accordance with Regulation 20 of the regulations for Graces and Congregations of the Regent House.

Exceptions.

9. The following are exceptions, in whole or in part, to the above regulations:

(*a*) (i) Women upon whom, before 27 April 1948 the title of a degree has been conferred shall be deemed to have been admitted to the corresponding degree on the date of the diploma conferring the title of the degree, provided always that any such woman who shall apply through her College to the Registrary to be admitted to the degree in person shall be so admitted on payment of a fee to be determined by the University.

(ii) Any woman qualified before 27 April 1948 to receive the title of a degree who has not received it shall be entitled to be admitted to the corresponding degree.

(iii) Residence kept by members of Girton College or of Newnham College before 27 April 1948 shall be deemed to be residence kept for the purposes of Statute or Ordinance.

(*b*) Any person who satisfied the Examiners for the LL.B. Examination before 1 October 1982 may,

(i) if he or she has already proceeded to the degree of Bachelor of Law, apply to the Registrary through her or his College for the redesignation of the degree as Master of Law,

or

(ii) if he or she has not already proceeded to the degree of Bachelor of Law, supplicate instead for the degree of Master of Law.

On receipt of an application under (i) above the Registrary shall issue a certificate of redesignation and shall amend the University's records accordingly.

Presentation and Admission of Candidates for Degrees

Amended by Grace 2 of 5 February 2014

By whom candidates are to be presented.

10. Recipients of titular degrees conferred under Statute A II 14 and candidates for complete degrees, if they are admitted to their degrees after presentation in person, shall be presented in the order prescribed in Regulations 11–13 by the persons specified in the following sub-paragraphs (*a*)–(*g*); provided that

(i) no one shall be presented by a person who is not a member of the Senate;

(ii) in exceptional circumstances the Vice-Chancellor or other person presiding at the Congregation may authorize presentation by a deputy for the person specified in the appropriate sub-paragraph below.

(*a*) Recipients of titular degrees shall be presented by the Orator, who shall make a speech in presenting each person.

(*b*) Candidates for the degree of M.A. conferred under Statute B II 2(*a*), or for the degrees of Ph.D. or M.A. by incorporation, who are not members of Colleges, and candidates for the degrees of Sc.D. or Litt.D. by incorporation, shall be presented by the Head of the Department or by the Chair or Secretary of the Board, Syndicate, Faculty Board, or other body under whose supervision they are working, or, if they hold a University office assigned to one of the central administrative offices, by the Registrary.

(*c*) Candidates for the degrees of D.D. or B.D., LL.D., Med.Sc.D., and Mus.D., shall be presented by the Regius Professors of Divinity, Law, and Physic, and the Professor of Music, respectively,

[1] When this formula is used at each Congregation on the days of General Admission, at this point of the formula will be inserted the name of the College or names of the group of Colleges (e.g. '*Collegii Regalis et Collegii Sanctae et Individuae Trinitatis*') whose candidates are about to be presented, and the words '*viri mulieresque*' and '*quorum*' will be adapted as necessary.

or by their deputies, the deputy being required to be a Doctor in the same Faculty as the Professor, or, for the degree of Mus.D., the Chair of the Faculty Board of Music.

(*d*) Candidates for the degrees of Sc.D. or Litt.D. (other than candidates for those degrees by incorporation) shall be presented by the Chair of the Degree Committee which has recommended them for the degree, or by a Doctor of Science or of Letters (as the case may be) deputed by the Chair.

(*e*) Candidates for the degree of M.Chir. shall be presented by the Regius Professor of Physic, or by a Doctor of Medicine or Master of Surgery deputed by the Professor.

(*f*) Candidates for the degrees of M.D. and Vet.M.D. shall be presented by the Chair of the Degree Committee for the Faculties of Clinical Medicine and Veterinary Medicine, or by a Doctor of Medicine, Science, or Veterinary Medicine deputed by the Chair.

(*g*) Candidates for other degrees shall be presented by the Praelectors of their Colleges.

In any case of doubt the Vice-Chancellor shall decide by whom a candidate is to be presented.

11. At each Congregation for the conferment of degrees the various degrees shall be conferred, subject to the provisions of Regulation 15, in an order corresponding to the order of seniority of graduates; provided that *Order of presentation and conferment.*

(*a*) every titular degree shall be conferred before any complete degree is conferred;

(*b*) all degrees for which candidates are presented under Regulation 10(*b*)–(*f*) shall be conferred before any candidates are presented by Praelectors of Colleges under Regulation 10(*g*);

(*c*) candidates for the degree of M.A. under Statute B II 2(*a*) or for any degree by incorporation under Statute B II 2(*b*), whether they are presented under Regulation 10(*b*) or under Regulation 10(*g*), shall be presented before other candidates are presented under the same regulations for the same degree; *M.A. under Statute B II 2.*

(*d*) the approval at a Congregation of the collective formula prescribed in Regulation 7 shall, in the case of each person referred to in the formula who is not presented in person at that Congregation, constitute the conferment of the degree and admission to the degree for which he or she is a candidate (other than a title of a degree).

12. All the candidates to be presented for degrees under Regulation 10(*g*) who are members of the same College shall be presented by the Praelector of that College before any candidate for a degree is presented by the Praelector of any College which follows it in the order of Colleges prescribed in Regulation 13; provided that the Vice-Chancellor shall have power to order that, at any Congregation other than a Congregation for General Admission to Degrees, all the candidates for the same degree shall be presented by the Praelector of each College in turn before any candidate is presented for the degree which next follows it in the order of seniority of graduates. *Presentation by Praelectors.*

13. Except as provided by Regulation 16, the order of Colleges shall be King's College, Trinity College, St John's College, followed by the other Colleges specified in Statute G I 1 in order of their foundation, followed by the Colleges recognized under Statute G in order of their recognition. *Order of Colleges.*

14. Every year the Wednesday, Thursday, Friday, and Saturday in the week next but one following the last week of Full Easter Term shall be days of General Admission to Degrees. On each day of General Admission there shall be one or more Congregations for General Admission to Degrees at such hours as the Vice-Chancellor shall appoint. *General Admission.*

15. The following provisions shall apply to Congregations for General Admission to Degrees:

(*a*) except with the approval of the Vice-Chancellor, no degree other than that of LL.M., M.Eng., M.Sci., M.Math., B.A., Mus.B., Vet.M.B., or B.Th. may be conferred at a Congregation for General Admission to Degrees;[1,2]

(*b*) a candidate proceeding to the degree of M.Eng. or M.Sci. or M.Math., and to the degree of B.A. at the same Congregation shall be presented for the two degrees together.

16. The assignment of Colleges to each of the several Congregations for General Admission shall be determined by the Council from time to time in consultation with the Colleges; provided that, except with the consent of the Colleges concerned, the assignment shall not be such as to change the order of Colleges which is prescribed in Regulation 13.

[1] No person qualifying for the M.Eng. Degree on the basis of performance in an examination taken in 1989 or an earlier year may proceed to the degree, either in person or in absence, at a Congregation for General Admission to Degrees (see Grace 31 of 11 December 1991).

[2] No person qualifying for either the M.Math. Degree or the M.A.St. Degree on the basis of examination performance before 2011 shall be permitted to proceed to the degree, either in person or in absence, at a Congregation for General Admission to Degrees.

Forms of Presentation for Degrees

1. Subject to the provisions of Regulation 2 concerning shortened forms of presentation, the following formulae shall be used by Praelectors and other persons in presenting candidates for degrees:

B.A. etc. *For the degree of Bachelor of Arts, Medicine, Music, Surgery, Theology for Ministry, or Veterinary Medicine*

Dignissime domine, Domine Procancellarie,[1] et tota Academia, praesento vobis

(for a man) hunc virum, quem scio tam moribus quam doctrina esse idoneum[2]

or

(for a woman) hanc mulierem, quam scio tam moribus quam doctrina esse idoneam[2]

ad gradum assequendum...;[3] idque tibi fide mea praesto totique Academiae.

M.A. etc. *For the degree of Master of Arts, Advanced Study, Business Administration, Corporate Law, Education, Engineering, Finance, Law, Letters, Mathematics, Music, Natural Sciences, Philosophy, Research, Science, Studies, or Surgery*

Dignissime domine, Domine Procancellarie,[1] et tota Academia, praesento vobis

(for a man) hunc virum, quem scio tam moribus quam doctrina esse idoneum[2]

or

(for a woman) hanc mulierem, quam scio tam moribus quam doctrina esse idoneam[2]

ad gradum assequendum...;[3] idque tibi fide mea praesto totique Academiae.

M.Eng. or M.Sci. or M.Math. with B.A. Degree. *For the degrees of Master of Engineering or Natural Sciences or Mathematics and Bachelor of Arts when candidates are presented for the two degrees together*

Dignissime domine, Domine Procancellarie,[1] et tota Academia, praesento vobis

(for a man) hunc virum, quem scio tam moribus quam doctrina esse idoneum[2]

or

(for a woman) hanc mulierem, quam scio tam moribus quam doctrina esse idoneam[2]

ad gradus assequendos Magistri in Ingeniaria (*or* Scientiis Naturalibus *or* Mathematica) necnon Baccalaurei in Artibus; idque tibi fide mea praesto totique Academiae.

M.A. under Stat. B II 2. *For the degree of Master of Arts under Statute B II 2*

Dignissime domine, Domine Procancellarie,[1] et tota Academia, praesento vobis

(for a man) hunc virum, ut, habita officii ad quod admissus est ratione, co-optetur in ordinem Magistrorum in Artibus.

or

(for a woman) hanc mulierem, ut habita officii ad quod admissa est ratione, co-optetur in ordinem Magistrorum in Artibus.

[1] This form of words is to be used when the person presiding at the Congregation (the Vice-Chancellor or duly appointed deputy) is a man. Other forms of words are to be used as follows:

When the person presiding at the Congregation (the Vice-Chancellor or duly appointed deputy) is a woman:

Dignissima domina, Domina Procancellaria,...

When the Chancellor is presiding the word 'Cancellarie' (for a man) or 'Cancellaria' (for a woman) is used instead of 'Procancellarie'.

[2] Other forms of words are to be used as follows:

(for two or more men)		hos viros, quos scio tam moribus quam doctrina esse idoneos
(for two or more women)		has mulieres, quas scio tam moribus quam doctrina esse idoneas
(for a group consisting of men and women)		hos viros et has mulieres, quos scio tam moribus quam doctrina esse idoneos
	or	hos viros et hanc mulierem, quos scio tam moribus quam doctrina esse idoneos
	or	hunc virum et has mulieres, quos scio tam moribus quam doctrina esse idoneos
	or	hunc virum et hanc mulierem, quos scio tam moribus quam doctrina esse idoneos

[3] The words appropriate to the particular degree are to be inserted here. See the Schedule to these regulations.

For the degree of Bachelor or Doctor of Divinity B.D. D.D.

Dignissime domine, Domine Procancellarie,[1] et tota Academia, praesento vobis

(for a man) reverendum hunc virum, quem scio tam moribus quam doctrina esse idoneum
or
(for a woman) reverendam hanc mulierem, quam scio tam moribus quam doctrina esse idoneam

ad gradum assequendum...;[2] idque tibi fide mea praesto totique Academiae.

For the degree of Doctor of Education, Engineering, Law, Letters, Medical Science, Medicine, Music, Philosophy, Science, or Veterinary Medicine Ed.D. Eng.D. LL.D. Litt.D. M.D. Med.Sc.D. Mus.D. Ph.D. Sc.D. Vet.M.D.

Dignissime domine, Domine Procancellarie,[1] et tota Academia, praesento vobis

(for a man) hunc virum, quem scio tam moribus quam doctrina esse idoneum
or
(for a woman) hanc mulierem, quam scio tam moribus quam doctrina esse idoneam

ad gradum assequendum...;[2] idque tibi fide mea praesto totique Academiae.

For a degree by incorporation Degree by incorporation.

Dignissime domine, Domine Procancellarie,[1] et tota Academia, praesento vobis

(for a man) hunc virum, ut in nostra Academia incorporetur et sit eodem gradu quo est apud suos...[3]
or
(for a woman) hanc mulierem, ut in nostra Academia incorporetur et sit eodem gradu quo est apud suos...[3]

For the title of a degree, *honoris causa* Titular degree.

Dignissime domine, Domine Procancellarie,[1] et tota Academia, praesento vobis

(for a man) egregium hunc virum, ut honoris causa habeat titulum gradus...[2]
or
(for a woman) egregiam hanc mulierem, ut honoris causa habeat titulum gradus...[2]

2. When presenting two or more groups of candidates for the same degree, a Praelector shall use one of the following formulae for each group after the first:

(for a man)	Hunc etiam praesento et de hoc idem vobis praesto.
(for two or more men)	Hos etiam praesento et de his idem vobis praesto.
(for a woman)	Hanc etiam praesento et de hac idem vobis praesto.
(for two or more women)	Has etiam praesento et de his idem vobis praesto.

Forms of Admission to Degrees

1. Subject to the provisions of Regulation 2, the following formulae shall be used by the Chancellor, or by the Vice-Chancellor, or by a duly appointed deputy, in admitting candidates to degrees or to the titles of degrees:

For the degree of Master of Arts under Statute B II 2 M.A. under Stat. B II 2.

Auctoritate mihi commissa admitto te in ordinem Magistrorum in Artibus, in nomine Patris et Filii et Spiritus Sancti.

[1] This form of words is to be used when the person presiding at the Congregation (the Vice-Chancellor or duly appointed deputy) is a man. Other forms of words are to be used as follows:

When the person presiding at the Congregation (the Vice-Chancellor or duly appointed deputy) is a woman:

Dignissima domina, Domina Procancellaria,...

When the Chancellor is presiding the word 'Cancellarie' (for a man) or 'Cancellaria' (for a woman) is used instead of 'Procancellarie'.

[2] The words appropriate to the particular degree are to be inserted here. See the Schedule to these regulations.

[3] The word appropriate to the candidate's previous degree is to be inserted here, as follows:

For a graduate of the University of Oxford	Oxonienses
For a graduate of Trinity College, Dublin	Dublinenses

Degree by incorporation.

For a degree by incorporation

Auctoritate mihi commissa admitto te ad gradum...[1] ut in nostra Academia incorporeris et sis eodem gradu quo es apud tuos...,[2] in nomine Patris et Filii et Spiritus Sancti.

Titular degree.

For the title of a degree honoris causa

Auctoritate mihi commissa admitto te honoris causa ad titulum gradus...,[1] in nomine Patris et Filii et Spiritus Sancti.

M.Eng. or M.Sci. or M.Math. with B.A. Degree

For the degrees of Master of Engineering or Natural Sciences or Mathematics and Bachelor of Arts when the two degrees are conferred together

Auctoritate mihi commissa admitto te ad gradus Magistri in Ingeniaria (*or* Scientiis Naturalibus *or* Mathematica) necnon Baccalaurei in Artibus, in nomine Patris et Filii et Spiritus Sancti.

All other degrees.

For all other degrees

Auctoritate mihi commissa admitto te ad gradum...,[1] in nomine Patris et Filii et Spiritus Sancti.

2. The person conferring degrees is authorized, at his or her discretion,

(*a*) to vary the formulae given in Regulation 1 by omitting the words ‘in nomine Patris et Filii et Spiritus Sancti’ or replacing them with the words ‘in nomine Dei’;

(*b*) in admitting candidates to any degree, except for a doctoral degree or the degrees of B.D., M.Chir. or the M.A. under Statute B II 2, to use one of the following shortened formulae, as appropriate:

In eodem nomine te etiam admitto ad gradum (*or* gradus)...[1]

Te etiam admitto ad gradum (*or* gradus)...[1]

Te etiam admitto ad eundem gradum (*or* ad eosdem gradus)

SCHEDULE

The words appropriate to the particular degree are to be inserted in the formulae for presentation for degrees and admission to degrees, as follows:

For the B.D. Degree	Baccalaurei in Sacra Theologia
For the M.B. Degree	Baccalaurei in Medicina
For the Vet.M.B. Degree	Baccalaurei in Veterinaria Medicina
For the Mus.B. Degree	Baccalaurei in Musica
For the B.A. Degree	Baccalaurei in Artibus
For the B.Th. Degree	Baccalaurei in Theologia Pastorali
For the M.Chir. Degree	Magistri in Chirurgia
For the M.A. Degree	Magistri in Artibus
For the LL.M. Degree	Magistri in Jure
For the M.Sc. Degree	Magistri in Scientiis
For the M.Litt. Degree	Magistri in Litteris
For the M.Phil. Degree	Magistri in Philosophia
For the M.Eng. Degree	Magistri in Ingeniaria
For the M.B.A. Degree	Magistri in Negotiis Administrandis
For the M.Fin. Degree	Magistri in Re Pecuniaria
For the M.Ed. Degree	Magistri in Educatione
For the M.Sci. Degree	Magistri in Scientiis Naturalibus
For the M.St. Degree	Magistri in Studiis
For the M.Res. Degree	Magistri in Arte Vestigandi
For the M.Math. Degree	Magistri in Mathematica
For the M.A.St. Degree	Magistri in Studio Ampliore
For the M.Mus. Degree	Magistri in Musica
For the M.C.L. Degree	Magistri in Jure Negotiationis Societatum
For the D.D. Degree	Doctoris in Sacra Theologia
For the LL.D. Degree	Doctoris in Jure
For the M.D. Degree	Doctoris in Medicina
For the Sc.D. Degree	Doctoris in Scientiis
For the Litt.D. Degree	Doctoris in Litteris

[1] The words appropriate to the particular degree are to be inserted here. See the Schedule to these regulations.

[2] The word appropriate to the candidate’s previous degree is to be inserted here, as follows:

For a graduate of the University of Oxford	Oxonienses
For a graduate of Trinity College, Dublin	Dublinenses

For the Mus.D. Degree	Doctoris in Musica
For the Vet.M.D. Degree	Doctoris in Veterinaria Medicina
For the Ph.D. Degree	Doctoris in Philosophia
For the Eng.D. Degree	Doctoris in Ingeniaria
For the Ed.D. Degree	Doctoris in Educatione
For the Med.Sc.D. Degree	Doctoris in Scientiis Medicinis

ORDER OF SENIORITY OF GRADUATES

1. The order of seniority of graduates shall be as follows

The Chancellor
The Vice-Chancellor
The High Steward
The Deputy High Steward
The Commissary
The Pro-Vice-Chancellors
Heads of Colleges
The Regius Professor of Divinity
The Regius Professor of Civil Law
The Regius Professor of Physic
The Regius Professor of Hebrew
The Regius Professor of Greek
The Regius Professor of History
The Regius Professor of Botany
The Regius Professor of Engineering
Professors, the Orator, the Registrary, the Librarian, the Director of the Fitzwilliam Museum, if Doctors, in the order of their complete degrees
Doctors of Divinity
Doctors of Law
Doctors of Medicine[1]
Doctors of Medical Science
Doctors of Science and Doctors of Letters
Doctors of Music
The Orator
The Registrary
The Librarian
Professors, the Director of the Fitzwilliam Museum, if not Doctors, in the order of their appointment
Members of the Council
Bachelors of Divinity
Doctors of Medicine[2]
Doctors of Veterinary Medicine
Doctors of Philosophy
Doctors of Engineering
Doctors of Education
Masters of Surgery
Masters of Arts
Masters of Law
Masters of Corporate Law
Masters of Science and Masters of Letters
Masters of Research
Masters of Philosophy
Masters of Music
Masters of Mathematics
Masters of Advanced Study
Masters of Engineering
Masters of Business Administration
Masters of Finance
Masters of Education
Masters of Natural Sciences
Masters of Studies
Bachelors of Medicine
Bachelors of Surgery
Bachelors of Law
Bachelors of Veterinary Medicine
Bachelors of Music
Bachelors of Arts
Bachelors of Education
Bachelors of Theology for Ministry

2. Of two persons holding the same or an equal degree, he or she shall be the senior who was admitted to the degree on the earlier day.[3]

3. Of two persons admitted to the same or an equal degree on the same day, he or she shall be the senior who was the senior in virtue of any degree previously held; or, if neither of them was previously senior to the other, he or she whose surname comes before the other's in alphabetical order.[3]

4. For the purpose of determining seniority among Bachelors of Arts, the days of General Admission in the Easter Term shall be counted as one and the same day.

5. In processions the following conventions shall be observed: Processions.

(*a*) the Esquire Bedells precede the Chancellor and the Vice-Chancellor;

(*b*) the Vice-Chancellor is accompanied by the Registrary and followed immediately by the Proctors;

[1] Persons who proceeded to this degree before 1 March 2014.

[2] Persons who proceeded to this degree after 1 March 2014.

[3] For the purpose of determining the seniority of a woman upon whom the title of a degree was conferred before women became eligible for complete degrees of the University, the date of the Diploma conferring the title of the degree is deemed to be the day on which she was admitted to that degree.

(*c*) in a procession before the conferment of honorary degrees the Vice-Chancellor is accompanied also by the Orator;

provided that the Vice-Chancellor, after consulting the Proctors, shall have power to vary the order of any procession, subject to giving notice on each occasion of any intended variation in the normal order.

ACADEMICAL DRESS

General

Wearing of academical dress by those *in statu pupillari*.

1. Members of the University *in statu pupillari* shall be required to wear the academical dress appropriate to their status in this University when attending University ceremonies in the University Church or in the Senate-House, and at all other times at which the Vice-Chancellor may by public notice direct that academical dress be worn.

Wearing of academical dress by those not *in statu pupillari*.

2. Members of the University not *in statu pupillari* shall wear the academical dress appropriate to their respective degrees of this University in the University Church, the Senate-House, and the Schools, and generally on public occasions and at official meetings, and on all other occasions on which the Vice-Chancellor may by public notice request that academical dress be worn.

Scarlet days.

3. The Doctors in the several Faculties shall wear their festal gowns in public on Christmas Day, Easter Day, Ascension Day, Whitsunday, Trinity Sunday, All Saints' Day, on the day appointed for the Commemoration of Benefactors, on the days of General Admission to Degrees, and on all other occasions on which the Vice-Chancellor may by public notice request that festal gowns be worn.

4. Notwithstanding the foregoing regulations, on the occasions specified in Regulation 3 any member of the University who holds a degree of another university or degree-awarding institution may wear the academical dress appropriate to that degree; save that this provision shall not apply to the Chancellor, the Vice-Chancellor, the High Steward, the Deputy High Steward, the Commissary, the Proctors, the Registrary, or the Esquire Bedells, or to a deputy for any of those officers, or to any person presenting or being presented for a degree of the University.

The Proctors and Esquire Bedells.

5. A Proctor or a deputy for a Proctor or an Esquire Bedell, when carrying out the duties of his or her office, shall wear the academical dress of a Master of Arts.

6. The senior Esquire Bedell shall be familiar with all details of academical dress of the University and shall draw the Vice-Chancellor's attention to unauthorized variations.

7. Drawings of hoods and gowns of the University, and specimens of the proper materials and colours, shall be kept by the Registrary.

8. Notwithstanding the regulations for academical dress which follow, a member of the University, other than a Proctor or a deputy for a Proctor or an Esquire Bedell when carrying out the duties of his or her office, may continue to wear any academical dress of the University which when he or she first wore it conformed to the practice of the time.

Black Gowns

D.D.: a full-sleeved gown, or alternatively the M.A. gown, either of which should have a looped cord and a button at the back and should be worn with a black silk scarf;

LL.D.: a gown with square-ended sleeves slit vertically above the arm-slits and sewn across below them, wings on the shoulders, and a flap-collar at the back;

M.D.[1] or Med.Sc.D.: a gown with square-ended sleeves sewn across below the arm-slits and a flap-collar at the back, trimmed with a single row of Doctors' lace down each front and round the collar, across each sleeve at the bottom and above the arm-slit, and with two vertical rows from the centre of the arm-slit to the shoulder;

Sc.D.: the M.A. gown but with a single row of Doctors' lace placed horizontally above each arm-slit;

Litt.D.: the M.A. gown but with a single row of Doctors' lace placed vertically above each arm-slit;

Mus.D.: the M.D. gown but with a double row of Doctors' lace on the lower part of the collar;

B.D.: the M.A. gown but with a looped cord and a button on the back as on the D.D. gown;

M.D.[2]: the Ph.D. gown;

[1] For persons awarded the degree before 1 March 2014.

[2] For persons awarded the degree after 1 March 2014.

Vet.M.D.: the Ph.D. gown;

Ph.D.: the M.A. gown but with Doctors' lace, four inches (10 cm) in length, placed horizontally above each arm-slit, the bottom edge of the lace being three inches (7.5 cm) from the edge of the opening;

Eng.D.: the Ph.D. gown;

Ed.D.: the Ph.D. gown but with four buttons placed in a horizontal row above the Doctors lace;

M.Chir.: the M.A. gown but with three rows of single black silk cord across the sleeve above each arm-slit, showing a space of half an inch (1.25 cm) between row and row, the first row being three-eighths of an inch (1 cm) above the opening;

M.A.: a silk or stuff gown with glove sleeves, having horizontal slits to free the arm, and with strings;

LL.M.: the M.Chir. gown but with two rows of single cord across the sleeve;

M.C.L.: the LL.M. gown;

M.Mus.: the M.A. gown but with three buttons joined by cords forming a triangle, two buttons on the upper edge of each arm-slit, five inches (12.5 cm) apart, the third in the middle five inches (12.5 cm) above the slit;

M.Sc.: the M.A. gown but with three buttons placed horizontally, two-and-a-half inches (6.25 cm) apart and joined by a cord, along each arm-slit;

M.Litt.: the M.Sc. gown but with the buttons and cord placed vertically;

M.Res.: the M.Phil. gown but with the buttons joined by two vertical cords;

M.Phil.: the M.A. gown but with a vertical cord from the centre of the arm-slit to the shoulder and with one button at the top of the cord and one button at the bottom of the cord on each sleeve;

M.Math.: the M.A. gown but with a circle of cord on the sleeve with a button in the centre;

M.A.St.: the M.A. gown but with a double circle of cord on the sleeve with a button in the centre;

M.Eng.: the M.A. gown but with a circle of cord on the sleeve with a button in the centre;

M.B.A.: the M.A. gown but with four buttons joined by cords forming a square on the upper edge of each arm-slit;

M.Fin.: the M.A. gown but with four buttons joined by cords forming a diamond on the upper edge of each arm slit;

M.Ed.: the M.A. gown but with five buttons joined by cords forming a cross on the upper edge of each arm-slit;

M.Sci.: the M.A. gown but with a circle of cord on the sleeve with a button in the centre;

M.St.: the M.A. gown but with five buttons joined by cords forming a cross on the upper edge of each arm-slit;

M.B.: a gown of black silk or stuff, shorter than the M.A. gown, with open sleeves, not slit but turned back to form a triangle bisected by one black cord about five inches (12.5 cm) long with a button at the top of the cord, and with strings;

B.Chir.: the M.B. gown but having on each sleeve three parallel cords half an inch (1.25 cm) apart, with a button at the top of each cord;

B.A.: a stuff gown like the M.B. gown, with open sleeves not turned up with a cord but slit vertically from the shoulders and caught together at the bottom of the slit;

LL.B.: the M.B. gown but having on each sleeve two parallel cords, with a button at the top of each cord;

Mus.B.: the M.B. gown but on each sleeve one cord and button, with another button on each side of the sleeve at the corner of the triangle formed by the turned-back piece of sleeve;

Vet.M.B.: the M.B. gown but with two buttons placed vertically one at the top and one at the bottom of the cord on each sleeve;

B.Ed.: the B.A. gown but having on each sleeve four parallel cords about one inch (2.5 cm) apart and five inches (12.5 cm) long with a button at the top of each cord;

B.Th.: the B.A. gown but with a looped cord and a button on the back as on the B.D. gown;

Possessor of the status of Master of Arts: the M.A. gown but without the strings;

Possessor of the status of Bachelor of Arts: the B.A. gown but without the strings.

Undergraduates' gowns shall reach to the knees.

The buttons of black gowns are of 26-line flat black twill-mohair; the cords are of $\frac{1}{8}$ black 'silk', and twisted double except in the M.Chir. and LL.M. gowns.

HOODS[1]

Doctor, other than M.D.,[2] Vet.M.D., Ph.D., Eng.D. or Ed.D.: of the same material as the festal gown, lined with the same material as the lining of the gown;

B.D.: of black corded silk lined with black silk;

M.D.[2]: the Ph.D. hood but with a part lining of mid-cherry silk four inches (10 cm) deep;

Vet.M.D.: of black corded silk lined with scarlet cloth, the hood part lined with mid-cherry silk, four inches (10 cm) deep;

Ph.D.: of black corded silk lined with scarlet cloth;

Eng.D.: of black corded silk lined with bronze silk, the hood part lined with scarlet cloth, four inches (10 cm) deep;

Ed.D.: of black corded silk lined with light blue silk, the hood part-lined with scarlet cloth, four inches (10 cm) deep;

M.Chir.: of black corded silk lined with mid-cherry silk;

M.A.: of black corded silk lined with white silk;

LL.M.: of black corded silk lined with light-cherry silk;

M.C.L.: the LL.M. hood but with a part lining of white silk four inches (10 cm) deep;

M.Mus.: of black corded silk lined with dark-cherry satin;

M.Sc.: of black cloth lined with pink silk shot with light blue;

M.Litt.: of black cloth lined with scarlet silk;

M.Res.: of black cloth lined with dark plum red silk;

M.Phil.: of black cloth lined with blue silk;

M.Math.: of black cloth lined with slate blue silk;

M.A.St.: of black cloth lined with gold silk;

M.Eng.: of black cloth lined with bronze silk;

M.B.A.: of black cloth lined with dark green silk;

M.Fin.: of black cloth lined with light green silk;

M.Ed.: of black corded silk lined with light blue silk;

M.Sci.: of black corded silk lined with pink silk shot with light blue;

M.St.: of black corded silk lined with yellow silk;

M.B.: the hood and tippet of mid-cherry silk, the hood part-lined with white fur and the tippet edged with white fur;

B.Chir.: the M.B. hood but with no fur edging to the tippet;

B.A.: of black stuff, part-lined with white fur, the tippet edged with white fur; *or, until further order*, of black stuff, part-lined with white, the tippet edged with white;

LL.B.: the M.B. hood and tippet but of light-cherry silk;

Mus.B.: the M.B. hood and tippet, but of dark-cherry satin;

Vet.M.B.: the M.B. hood but with an edging of white fur, two inches wide (5 cm), to the tippet;

B.Ed.: of black stuff, part-lined with blue silk and an edging of white fur, the tippet edged with white fur;

B.Th.: of black stuff, lined with black silk, the tippet edged with white fur.

The neckband of a hood is of the outer colour, with no edging of the lining material. The corners of tippets are square.

FESTAL GOWNS

D.D.: a gown of scarlet cloth lined with dove-coloured silk, that is silk of a turquoise-blue shot with rose-pink; at the back and on each sleeve a black button (22-line flat silk) and $\frac{1}{8}$ black twisted cord; black strings: under this gown a black silk cassock should be worn;

LL.D.: a gown of scarlet cloth lined with light-cherry silk; scarlet buttons and cords and strings;

M.D.[3] or Med.Sc.D.: a similar gown lined with mid-cherry silk;

Sc.D.: a similar gown lined with pink silk shot with light blue;

Litt.D.: a similar gown lined with scarlet silk to match the cloth;

[1] The fur used for Bachelors' hoods is artificial fur.
[2] For persons awarded the degree after 1 March 2014.
[3] For persons awarded the degree before 1 March 2014.

Mus.D.: a gown of cream damask, lined with dark-cherry satin, having short wide sleeves; the buttons, cords, and strings to match the satin;

M.D.[1]: the Ph.D. festal gown;

Vet.M.D.: the Ph.D. festal gown;

Ph.D.: the silk M.A. gown but with a facing of scarlet cloth, four inches (10 cm) wide, the full length of the front or the Ph.D. black gown but with a facing of scarlet cloth, four inches (10 cm) wide, the full length of the front;

Eng.D.: the Ph.D. festal gown.

Ed.D.: the Ed.D. black gown but with a facing of scarlet cloth, four inches (10 cm) wide the full length of the front.

Headdresses

With a festal gown, for a Doctor of Divinity a black velvet cap, for a Doctor in another Faculty a wide-brimmed round velvet bonnet with gold string and tassels: provided that a Doctor, when taking part in ceremonial in the Senate-House, may with the festal gown wear the square cap;

with all other gowns, for residents the square cap: provided that an undergraduate shall wear either the square cap or no headdress.

Dress at Graduation

1. Any person presenting a candidate for a doctorate other than the M.D., Vet.M.D., Ph.D., Eng.D., or for the degree of B.D., wears a cope.[2]

2. All persons presenting for degrees wear dark clothes with their academical dress.

3. A person being admitted to the title of a degree *honoris causa* wears the gown of the degree without a hood.

4. A person being admitted to a degree by incorporation or to the degree of M.A. under Statute B II 2 wears the gown and hood of the degree that he or she is to receive.

5. A graduate of the University being admitted to a degree wears the gown and hood of the highest degree that he or she has received from the University.

6. A possessor of the status of B.A. or M.A. who is not a graduate of the University and who is being admitted to a degree, other than the degree of M.A. under Statute B II 2 or a degree by incorporation, shall wear the gown appropriate to his or her status, and the hood of the degree, or of the higher of the two degrees, that he or she is to receive.

7. An undergraduate being admitted to a degree wears an undergraduate gown, and the hood of the degree, or of the higher of the two degrees, that he or she is to receive.

8. All persons being admitted to degrees wear dark clothes with their academical dress. Persons wearing a dinner jacket or lounge suit wear white ties and bands.

9. The Proctors shall have power, on request from a person who is to present a graduand for a degree, to grant the presenter or the graduand dispensation from Regulation 2 or 8 concerning dress at graduation as appropriate, and also, if necessary, to grant such a person dispensation from the regulations concerning headdresses; provided that the Proctors shall be satisfied in every case that there are reasonable grounds for granting such dispensation.

ADDRESSES TO THE SOVEREIGN AND FORMAL LETTERS TO OTHER UNIVERSITIES

1. The presentation of an address to the Sovereign shall require approval by the University. The text of such an address shall be approved by the Council.

2. An address to the Sovereign shall be presented by the Chancellor, provided that, if the Chancellor is absent, or if the office of Chancellor is vacant, it shall be presented by the Vice-Chancellor.

3. The Chancellor shall be accompanied in the presentation of an address by the Esquire Bedells and by a deputation consisting of the Vice-Chancellor, the Orator, the Proctors, and the Registrary,

[1] For persons awarded the degree after 1 March 2014.

[2] Three copes of different lengths are kept in the Senate-House for the use of persons presenting for degrees.

together with not more than six other members of the University nominated by the Vice-Chancellor; provided that the Vice-Chancellor shall not be required to nominate additional members to the deputation on a particular occasion.

4. The presentation of a formal letter to another university or similar institution shall require approval by the University. The text of such a letter shall also be approved by the University.

SERMONS AND COMMEMORATIONS

Commemoration of Benefactors.

1. The service for the Commemoration of Benefactors[1] shall be held each year on the first Sunday in November, except in any year in which this day is appointed as Remembrance Sunday when the Service shall be held on either the preceding or the following Sunday as determined by the Select Preachers Syndicate.

Preacher.

2. It shall be the duty of the Lady Margaret's Preacher to preach at the service.

Ramsden Sermon.

3. The annual Ramsden Sermon, founded by Mrs Ramsden through J. H. Markland, Esq., is to be delivered on such Sunday of Full Term and by such preacher as the Vice-Chancellor for the time being shall appoint, upon the subject of Church Extension overseas, especially within the Commonwealth of Nations.

Mere's Commemoration.

4. The sermon at Mere's Commemoration[2] shall be preached on the first Tuesday in Full Easter Term.

Great St Mary's Church.

5. The arrangement of the seats in the University Church at all University services shall be entrusted to the Vice-Chancellor.

CAMBRIDGE UNIVERSITY STUDENTS UNION

1. There shall be a Cambridge University Students Union, which shall be an association of members of the University who are pursuing a course of study or research in the University.

Objects of CUSU.

2. The constitution of Cambridge University Students Union shall provide for the objects of the Union to be:

(i) to advance the education of its members;

(ii) to provide, in the interests of the social welfare of its members, facilities for recreation or other leisure-time activity, being facilities:

(*a*) that will improve their conditions of life by enabling and assisting them to participate in the intellectual, social, and other activities of or connected with the University; or

(*b*) of which they have need by reason of their being students;

(iii) to promote equal opportunity for access to Cambridge and its affiliated institutions for all applicants, and furthermore to encourage access to the University for applicants from backgrounds under-represented in the University;

(iv) in furtherance of the objects specified above, to act as a channel of communication between its members and Cambridge University and other bodies.

Amendments.

3. No amendment of the constitution of Cambridge University Students Union to give effect to a change in the objects of the Union shall have effect unless Regulation 2 has been amended by the University. No other amendment of the constitution of Cambridge University Students Union shall have effect unless approval has been given by the Council.

Financial assistance.

4. The Council shall have discretion to provide financial assistance to Cambridge University Students Union.

Estimates of income and expenditure.

5. The President of Cambridge University Students Union shall be the principal financial officer of the Union and shall be accountable to the Council for the financial management of the Union (in addition to his or her accountability and responsibility under the provisions of the constitution of the Union). In the Michaelmas Term of each academical year the President shall submit to the Council estimates of the Union's income and expenditure for the Union's next financial year.

[1] The Form of Service for the Commemoration of Benefactors is published by the University Press. Copies are available in Great St Mary's Church on the day of the Commemoration.

[2] See *Endowments*, 1904, pp. 19, 20. This sermon is preached either by the Vice-Chancellor or by a preacher nominated by the Vice-Chancellor.

6. Before the division of the Lent Term in each academical year the President of Cambridge University Students Union shall provide the Council with the audited accounts of the Union for the Union's previous financial year. Accounts.

7. The offices of President shall be defined, and not more than four other officers of Cambridge University Students Union designated for the purpose by the Council may be defined, as major offices for the purposes of Section 22(2)(*d*) of the Education Act 1994; the office of Women's Officer shall not be so defined. The Council shall have discretion to make an allowance under Regulation 1(*b*) or 3(*a*)(i) for Allowances to Candidates for Examinations, where necessary, for the President, all or any of the four designated officers, and the Women's Officer, of Cambridge University Students Union, on the application of a Tutor of the respective College. Offices.

8. The Council shall have discretion to maintain a working relationship with Cambridge University Students Union in the manner described in their Notice dated 26 November 1979.[1] Relations with Council.

9. Cambridge University Students Union shall be recognized by the Council as an organization representing junior members of the University, in University as distinct from College matters, subject to the conditions set out in these regulations.

10. Any member of the Union who wishes to resign membership in a particular academical year shall be entitled to do so by giving notice in writing, on a prescribed form, to the Registrary. The Registrary shall inform the President of the resignation, and the President shall forthwith delete the name of the person from any electoral roll or register of the Union, with immediate effect. Such resignation shall be effective for the remainder of the academical year, and such person shall not be regarded as represented by the Union under the provisions of these regulations. A person who has exercised this right, and who holds an office of the Union, or membership of any committee or other body in the Union, shall thereby vacate it. Resignation.

11. If a complaint by a member of the Union, or a person who would be entitled to be a member if he or she had not exercised the right of resignation under Regulation 10, cannot be satisfactorily resolved by the officers of the Union, the complainant may refer the complaint to the Junior Proctor, who shall seek the opinion of the appropriate officer or officers of the Union, shall investigate the matter, and shall report on it in writing in such terms as he or she considers appropriate, indicating his or her finding as to whether or not the complaint is upheld, giving such reasons as he or she thinks fit, and stating provisionally what remedy, if any, he or she proposes. Notice of such findings and of any provisional remedy shall be sent by the Junior Proctor to the President or other appropriate officer of the Union, to the complainant, and to the Registrary. The Junior Proctor shall consider any representations made by these persons and shall then confirm, modify, or withdraw his or her findings and provisional remedy. Any remedy so confirmed, whether or not after modification, shall be executed without delay. The final decision of the Junior Proctor shall be notified to the Vice-Chancellor and those to whom the provisional decision was notified. Any functions of the Junior Proctor under this regulation may be delegated by that officer to another Proctor or Pro-Proctor. Complaints.

12. The President of the Union shall submit to the Council each year in the Michaelmas Term an electoral scheme for the conduct of elections in the Union in the remainder of the academical year. The scheme shall provide for the appointment, subject to confirmation by the Council, of returning officers, and for the Council to receive from the returning officers a report on the conduct of each election. Elections.

GRADUATE UNION

Amended by Grace 1 of 19 February 2014

1. There shall be a Graduate Union, which shall be an association of members of the University who are pursuing in the University a course of graduate study or research, as defined by the constitution of the Union.

2. The constitution of the Graduate Union shall provide for the objects of the Union to be: Objects of Graduate Union.

the advancement of education of graduate students at the University and any other persons who are members of the Union by:

(*a*) promoting the interests and welfare of graduate students and other members of the Union, and providing support and advice to them;

[1] See *Reporter*, 1979–80, p. 146.

(*b*) being a recognized representative channel between graduate students (other than those who are not members of the Union) and the University and bodies external to the University; and

(*c*) providing social, cultural, sporting, and recreational activities and forums for discussions and debate for the personal development of graduate students and any other persons who are members of the Union,

and 'graduate students' shall mean any individual who is formally matriculated and registered for an approved graduate or postgraduate programme provided by the University, all undergraduates of the University who are in their fourth or higher year of residence, or who are formally registered for an approved programme of study provided by the University and are 21 years of age or over at the commencement of their course of study, and any student who is a member of the institutions belonging to the Cambridge Theological Federation or any successor body.

Amendments. **3.** No amendment of the constitution of the Graduate Union to give effect to a change in the objects of the Union shall have effect unless Regulation 2 has been amended by the University. No other amendment of the constitution of the Union shall have effect unless approval has been given by the Council.

Financial assistance. **4.** The Council shall have discretion to provide financial assistance to the Graduate Union.

Estimates of income and expenditure. **5.** The President of the Graduate Union shall be the principal financial officer of the Union and shall be accountable to the Council for the financial management of the Union (in addition to his or her accountability and responsibility under the provisions of the constitution of the Union). In the Michaelmas Term of each academical year the President shall submit to the Council estimates of the Union's income and expenditure for the Union's next financial year.

Accounts. **6.** Before the division of the Lent Term in each academical year the President of the Graduate Union shall provide the Council with the audited accounts of the Union for the Union's previous financial year.

President. **7.** The office of President of the Graduate Union shall be defined as a major office for the purposes of Section 22(2)(*d*) of the Education Act 1994.

Relations with Council. **8.** The Council shall have discretion to maintain a working relationship with the Graduate Union in the manner described in their Notice dated 26 November 1979.[1]

9. The Graduate Union shall be recognized by the Council as an organization representing junior members of the University who are graduate students, in University as distinct from College matters, subject to the conditions set out in these regulations.

Resignation. **10.** Any member of the Union who wishes to resign membership in a particular academical year shall be entitled to do so by giving notice in writing, on a prescribed form, to the Registrary. The Registrary shall inform the President of the resignation, and the President shall forthwith delete the name of the person from any electoral roll or register of the Union, with immediate effect. Such resignation shall be effective for the remainder of the academical year, and such person shall not be regarded as represented by the Union under the provisions of these regulations. A person who has exercised this right, and who holds an office of the Union, or membership of any committee or other body in the Union, shall thereby vacate it.

Complaints. **11.** If a complaint by a member of the Union, or a person who would be entitled to be a member if he or she had not exercised the right of resignation under Regulation 10, cannot be satisfactorily resolved by the officers of the Union, the complainant may refer the complaint to the Junior Proctor, who shall seek the opinion of the appropriate officer or officers of the Union, shall investigate the matter, and shall report on it in writing in such terms as he or she considers appropriate, indicating his or her finding as to whether or not the complaint is upheld, giving such reasons as he or she thinks fit, and stating provisionally what remedy, if any, he or she proposes. Notice of such findings and of any provisional remedy shall be sent by the Junior Proctor to the President or other appropriate officer of the Union, to the complainant, and to the Registrary. The Junior Proctor shall consider any representations made by these persons and shall then confirm, modify, or withdraw his or her findings and provisional remedy. Any remedy so confirmed, whether or not after modification, shall be executed without delay. The final decision of the Junior Proctor shall be notified to the Vice-Chancellor and those to whom the provisional decision was notified. Any functions of the Junior Proctor under this regulation may be delegated by that officer to another Proctor or Pro-Proctor.

[1] See *Reporter*, 1979–80, p. 146.

12. The President of the Union shall submit to the Council each year in the Michaelmas Term an electoral scheme for the conduct of elections in the Union in the remainder of the academical year. The scheme shall provide for the appointment, subject to confirmation by the Council, of returning officers, and for the Council to receive from the returning officers a report on the conduct of each election. Elections.

Code of practice in respect of student unions issued under section 22 of the Education Act 1994

1. Section 22 of the Education Act 1994 places a number of responsibilities on governing bodies of universities (as defined by section 21, sub-section 5). Sub-section 3 of that section provides that every governing body shall prepare and issue, and where necessary revise, a code of practice as to the manner in which the requirements of sub-sections 1 and 2 are to be carried into effect in relation to any students' union for students of the establishment, setting out in relation to each of the requirements details of the arrangements made to secure its observance. The present code of practice is issued by the Council in respect of Cambridge University Students Union (CUSU) and Cambridge University Graduate Union.

General duty of governing bodies

2. Sub-section 1 requires the governing body to take 'such steps as are reasonably practicable to secure that any students' union for students of the establishment operates in a fair and democratic manner and is accountable for its finances'. This requirement is fulfilled through compliance with the requirements of the Ordinances for each union, with the provisions of the present code of practice, and with the constitutions of the two unions.

Particular requirements of the Act

3. Sub-section 2 requires governing bodies to take 'such steps as are reasonably practicable to secure that the following requirements are observed by or in relation to any students' union for students of the establishment'. These detailed requirements are dealt with below.

(*a*) *Written constitution*: Unions should have a written constitution.

Both CUSU and the Graduate Union have written constitutions.

(*b*) *Constitutions to be approved by the governing body and to be reviewed by it.* The provisions of unions' constitutions are to be subject to the approval of the governing body of the university and to review by it at intervals of not more than five years.

The constitutions of CUSU and the Graduate Union have been reviewed on their recognition by the University; the regulations for each union require amendments of the objects clause to be approved by Grace, and require the Council to approve other amendments to the constitutions. The constitutions of the two unions are reviewed in the Easter Term each year by the Council, acting through their Committee for the Supervision of the Student Unions (CCSSU).

(*c*) *Opting out.* A student should have the right not to be a member of a union or in the case of a representative body which is not an association to signify that he or she does not wish to be represented by it and students who exercise that right should not be unfairly disadvantaged with regard to the provision of services or otherwise by reason of their having done so.

The regulations for each union include provision for resignation; a form for this purpose may be obtained from the University Offices, The Old Schools, or from the officers of either union. The Council have been informed that the unions would nevertheless wish to continue to make their services available to students who choose not formally to be members and the Council have made it a condition of University funding of the two unions that this should be so. Payments should normally continue to be made by College student unions to CUSU or the Graduate Union as the case may be in relation to any student who has opted out of membership.

(*d*) *Election to major union offices.* The Act provides that appointment to major union offices should be by election in a secret ballot in which all members are entitled to vote.

The regulations for each union indicate which sabbatical offices are to be regarded as major union offices. Election to these offices is by secret ballot.

(*e*) *Union elections.* Governing bodies are required to satisfy themselves that union elections are fairly and properly conducted.

The regulations for the two unions require them to submit to the Council electoral schemes for the conduct of elections. There is provision for the Council to be informed of the appointment of returning officers, to confirm their appointment, and to receive from the returning officers a report on the conduct of elections. The CCSSU deal with this business on behalf of the Council.

(*f*) *Sabbatical or paid elected offices.* A person is not to hold sabbatical union office, or paid elected union office, for more than two years in total at the establishment.
A provision to this effect is included in the constitution of each union.

(*g*) *Financial management.* The financial affairs of unions are to be properly conducted and appropriate arrangements are to exist for the approval of unions' budgets, and the monitoring of expenditure by the governing body.

The regulations require the estimates and accounts of the two unions to be submitted to the Council. The regulations also provide for the President to be financially responsible and to be accountable to the Council for the financial management of each union. Under the HEFCE Audit Code of Practice, the two unions are within the scope of the University's internal audit service and of the Audit Committee of the Council. It is a condition of University grant to both unions that interim half-yearly reports on expenditure should be made to the Council, and the Council will invite the CCSSU, and if necessary the Finance Committee, to consider these reports, and the accounts and estimates of the two unions.

(*h*) *Financial reports.* Financial reports of unions are to be published annually or more frequently, and are to be made available to the governing body and to all students; each report is in particular to contain a list of external organizations to which the union has made donations in the period to which the report relates and details of these donations.

Compliance with these requirements is a condition of grant from the University. The unions will circulate their accounts annually to JCR and MCR presidents and equivalent, who will make them available for reference in Colleges by junior members. The accounts will also be available for reference by junior members in the University Offices, The Old Schools, and, in respect of each union, at its own offices.

(*i*) *Groups or clubs.* The procedure for student unions to allocate resources to groups or clubs is to be fair and is to be set down in writing and freely accessible to all students.

In Cambridge the principal allocations to University clubs and societies are made not by the unions, but by two University bodies, the Societies Syndicate and the Sports Syndicate. To the limited extent that the two unions make allocations to groups, clubs, or societies, they are required to operate fairly and to approve a written procedure, to be approved by the Council through the CCSSU.

(*j*) *Affiliation to external organizations.* If a union decides to affiliate to an external organization it must publish notice of its decision stating the name of the organization and details of any subscription or similar fee paid or proposed to be paid and of any donation made or proposed to be made to the organization, and such notice is to be made available to the governing body and to all students.

The constitutions of the two unions make provision for these procedures. Notice to the governing body is to be given to the CCSSU on the Council's behalf, and notice to students is by circulation of notices for display in Colleges.

(*k*) *Report on affiliation.* When a union is affiliated to any external organization a report is to be published annually or more frequently containing a list of external organizations to which the union is currently affiliated and details of subscriptions or similar fees paid or donations made to such organizations in the past year or since the last report, and such reports are to be made available to the governing body and to all students.

The constitutions of the two unions contain provision for these procedures.

(*l*) *Review of affiliations.* There are to be procedures for the review of affiliations to external organizations under which the current list of affiliations is submitted for approval by members annually or more frequently, and at such intervals of not more than a year as the governing body may determine and under which a requisition may be made by such proportion of members, not exceeding five per cent., as the governing body may determine, that the question of continued affiliation to any particular organization be decided upon by a secret ballot in which all members are entitled to vote.

Appropriate constitutional provision has been made in the constitutions of both unions. The Council have determined that the proportion of members seeking a requisition for a secret ballot shall be two per cent, and that such a requisition may be made once a year, in the Lent Term.

(*m*) *Complaints procedures for students.* There is to be a complaints procedure to be available to all students or groups of students who are dissatisfied in their dealings with a union or who claim to have been unfairly disadvantaged by reason of their having exercised the opt-out right referred to in paragraph (*c*) above, and this complaints procedure is to include provision for an independent person appointed by the governing body to investigate and report on complaints.

The regulations for each union include provision for a complaints procedure, the Junior Proctor being the independent person to investigate complaints. If the Junior Proctor believes that he or she cannot properly act independently in a particular case he or she will delegate the matter to another Proctor or Pro-Proctor, as provided for in the University regulations.

(*n*) *Remedies.* Complaints are to be dealt with promptly and fairly and where a complaint is upheld there should be an effective remedy.

University regulations for the unions require any remedy confirmed after an investigation under 3(*m*) to be executed by the union without delay. The union is required to notify the Secretary of the CCSSU confirming that the remedy has been implemented. Compliance with these remedies is a condition of University grant to the unions. If a remedy is not implemented, the matter will be referred to the CCSSU so that abatement or termination of University grant, or other measures, can be considered.

Sub-section 4

5. Governing bodies are to bring to the attention of all students at least once a year the code of practice; any restrictions imposed on the activities of student unions by the law relating to charities; and where applicable, the provisions of section 43 of the Education (No. 2) Act 1986 about freedom of speech in universities and colleges, and of any code of practice issued under it relevant to the activities or conduct of unions.

These matters are brought to the attention of students by the publication annually of Proctorial notices; by the publication of the present code of practice in *Statutes and Ordinances,* and information provided on the University's online student gateway. An account of the restrictions on the activities of unions, together with information on charity law, and the provisions of Section 43 of the 1986 Act and the University's code of practice under that section are included on the student gateway at http://www.cam.ac.uk/current-students/cambridge-life/student-unions.

Sub-section 5

6. Governing bodies are to bring to the attention of all students at least once a year and to include in any information generally made available to persons considering whether to become students of the establishment information about the right of opt-out from union membership (paragraph (*c*) above) and about arrangements made for services for students who have opted out.

This information is given by Proctorial notice and by information for applicants included in prospectuses.

DISCIPLINE

General

Whereas it is the duty of the University to maintain good order and discipline within the University:

1. No member of the University shall intentionally or recklessly disrupt or impede or attempt to disrupt or impede the activities and functions of the University, or any part thereof, or of any College.

2. No member of the University shall intentionally or recklessly impede freedom of speech or lawful assembly within the Precincts of the University. No member of the University shall intentionally or recklessly fail to give any notice which is required to be given to a University officer or a University authority under the terms of a code of practice issued under the provisions of section 43 of the Education (No. 2) Act 1986.

3. No member of the University shall intentionally occupy or use any property of the University or of any College except as may be expressly or by implication authorized by the University or College authorities concerned.

4. No member of the University shall intentionally or recklessly damage or deface or knowingly misappropriate any property of the University or of any College.

5. No member of the University shall intentionally or recklessly endanger the safety, health, or property of any member, officer, or employee of the University within the Precincts of the University.

6. No candidate shall make use of unfair means in any University examination. Unfair means shall include plagiarism[1] and, unless such possession is specifically authorized, the possession of any book, paper or other material relevant to the examination. No member of the University shall assist a candidate to make use of such unfair means.

7. No member of the University shall forge or falsify or knowingly make improper use of any degree certificate or other document attesting to academic achievement, or knowingly make false statements concerning standing or concerning results in examinations.

8. All members of the University shall comply with any instruction given by a University officer, or by any other person authorized to act on behalf of the University, in the proper discharge of his or her duties.

9. All members of the University shall state their names and the Colleges to which they belong when asked by a Proctor or Pro-Proctor, or by any other person in authority in the University or in any of the Colleges in the University.

10. Regulations 1–9 above, the regulations for the initiation of proceedings under these regulations, the regulations for motor vehicles, and the regulations for bicycles and boats, shall apply to persons *in statu pupillari* who have not matriculated as if such persons were members of the University.

Notice by the General Board

University-wide statement on plagiarism

The General Board, with the agreement of the Board of Examinations and the Board of Graduate Studies, has issued this guidance for the information of candidates, Examiners, and Supervisors. It may be supplemented by course-specific guidance from Faculties and Departments.

[1] Plagiarism is defined as submitting as one's own work, irrespective of intent to deceive, that which derives in part or in its entirety from the work of others without due acknowledgement.

Plagiarism is defined as submitting as one's own work, irrespective of intent to deceive, that which derives in part or in its entirety from the work of others without due acknowledgement. It is both poor scholarship and a breach of academic integrity.

Examples of plagiarism include **copying** (using another person's language and/or ideas as if they are a candidate's own), by:

- **quoting verbatim** another person's work without due acknowledgement of the source;
- **paraphrasing** another person's work by changing some of the words, or the order of the words, without due acknowledgement of the source;
- **using ideas** taken from someone else without reference to the originator;
- **cutting and pasting** from the Internet to make a pastiche of online sources;
- **submitting someone else's work** as part of a candidate's own without identifying clearly who did the work. For example, buying or commissioning work via professional agencies such as 'essay banks' or 'paper mills', or not attributing research contributed by others to a joint project.

Plagiarism might also arise from **colluding** with another person, including another candidate, other than as permitted for joint project work (i.e. where collaboration is concealed or has been forbidden). A candidate should include a general acknowledgement where he or she has received substantial help, for example with the language and style of a piece of written work.

Plagiarism can occur in respect to all types of sources and media:

- text, illustrations, musical quotations, mathematical derivations, computer code, etc.;
- material downloaded from websites or drawn from manuscripts or other media;
- published and unpublished material, including lecture handouts and other students' work.

Acceptable means of acknowledging the work of others (by referencing, in footnotes, or otherwise) vary according to the subject matter and mode of assessment. Faculties or Departments should issue written guidance on the relevant scholarly conventions for submitted work, and also make it clear to candidates what level of acknowledgement might be expected in written examinations. Candidates are required to familiarize themselves with this guidance, to follow it in all work submitted for assessment, and may be required to sign a declaration to that effect. If a candidate has any outstanding queries, clarification should be sought from her or his Director of Studies, Course Director or Supervisor as appropriate.

Failure to conform to the expected standards of scholarship (e.g. by not referencing sources) in examinations may affect the mark given to the candidate's work. In addition, suspected cases of the use of unfair means (of which plagiarism is one form) will be investigated and may be brought to one of the University's Courts. The Courts have wide powers to discipline those found guilty of using unfair means in an examination, including depriving such persons of membership of the University, and deprivation of a degree.

Fines

The Board of Examinations, the Information Services Committee and the Library Syndicate shall have power to impose a fine not exceeding £175 on any person who infringes the regulations for those bodies or the rules made by them under those regulations.

Motor Vehicles

1. A member of the University *in statu pupillari* shall not keep, use, or cause to be kept for his or her use any motor vehicle other than a moped within ten miles of Great St Mary's Church while in residence in term or in the Long Vacation period of residence, unless he or she shall have obtained, on his or her Tutor's written recommendation, a licence for that vehicle signed by the Special Pro-Proctor for motor vehicles. The Special Pro-Proctor may issue such a licence to any member of the University *in statu pupillari* who is a graduate of a university, or who has the status of Bachelor of Arts, or who has kept (or been allowed) nine terms by residence, or to whom the Proctors decide that its issue is warranted by exceptional individual circumstances.

2. A member of the University *in statu pupillari* who is not qualified to hold a licence under Regulation 1 may, on the written recommendation of his or her Tutor, be granted a licence to keep a motor vehicle to be used for the purposes of a University Department or of a University or College club or society, or for any other purpose approved by the Special Pro-Proctor, provided that the application be supported in writing, in the case of a University Department by the Head of the Department, and in the case of a University or College club or society, by the committee of the club or society.

3. A licence shall normally be valid until the end of the academical year in which it is issued but it may be suspended or revoked at any time by the Special Pro-Proctor, subject to an appeal to the Summary Court.

4. An application for a licence must be made within seven days of the vehicle being brought within a ten-mile radius of Great St Mary's Church, or, if it is already within that radius, within seven days of its coming into the possession of the applicant, or within the first seven days of Full Michaelmas Term if the application is for a renewal.

5. A licence shall at all times be prominently displayed on the vehicle for which it is issued.

6. The issue of a licence may be conditional upon the person to whom it is issued being covered by insurance on behalf of passengers, and upon restrictions on the garaging and parking of a vehicle for which it is issued.

7. These regulations for motor vehicles shall not apply to

(*a*) the use of motor vehicles licensed by the Cambridgeshire Police Authority, or in charge of or driven by tradesmen or their employees,

(*b*) the hiring of motor vehicles, or the receiving of driving instruction, from firms appearing on lists maintained by the Special Pro-Proctor.

8. The Special Pro-Proctor shall have power to impose a fine not exceeding £175 for an offence against any of these regulations or for a breach of any condition made by the Special Pro-Proctor under Regulation 6.

Bicycles and Boats

1. A member of the University *in statu pupillari* shall not keep, or cause to be kept for his or her use, a bicycle within the Precincts of the University, unless it bears a distinguishing mark in accordance with instructions to be issued from time to time by the Proctors.

2. A member of the University *in statu pupillari* shall not keep, or cause to be kept for his or her use, a boat to be used within the Precincts of the University, unless it is registered annually with the Conservators of the River Cam and bears a distinguishing mark in accordance with instructions to be issued from time to time by the Proctors.

Clubs and Societies

1. Any club or society consisting wholly or partly of members of the University *in statu pupillari* may apply to the Junior Proctor for registration as a University society. A club or society applying for registration shall submit to the Junior Proctor a statement of its current financial position and a copy of its constitution. The Junior Proctor may refer such an application to the Societies Syndicate. If the Junior Proctor refuses to register a club or society the club or society may appeal to the Societies Syndicate, who may if they think fit register the club or society.

2. All registered clubs or societies shall deposit any changes in their constitution with the Junior Proctor, and shall notify him or her of any change of officers.

3. Every registered club or society shall deposit by 31 December each year with the Junior Proctor a copy of its accounts for the previous academical year audited either professionally or by a resident member of the Senate or by a person approved for this purpose by the Junior Proctor.

4. A club or society whose constitution requires it to have a Senior Treasurer shall not amend its constitution so as to remove this requirement without obtaining the prior approval of the Junior Proctor and submitting to the Junior Proctor a statement of its current financial position.

5. Any club or society sanctioned by the Proctors before these regulations take effect shall be deemed to have been registered in accordance with these regulations.

6. Any registration granted or deemed to have been granted under these regulations may be withdrawn at the discretion of the Junior Proctor, subject to a right of appeal by the club or society to the Societies Syndicate.

7. No club or society consisting wholly or partly of members of the University *in statu pupillari*, whether registered under the provisions of these regulations or not, shall, while occupying University premises, engage in trade without the permission of the Finance Committee of the Council. The Finance Committee may make such permission conditional on the submission to them of annual audited accounts or subject to such other conditions (including the condition that the club or society shall be registered as a limited liability company) as the Finance Committee may deem desirable in the interests of the University or of its members. For the purpose of this regulation

(*a*) the term 'trade' shall include the buying or selling of goods or services, whether for profit or otherwise, but shall not include the sale of tickets for admission to a public performance given by a club or society, or the sale of any paper, magazine, or journal published by a club or society or of advertising space in such a publication;

(*b*) the term 'occupying' shall not include the occasional hiring of University premises.

Meetings and Public Gatherings on University Premises

Code of practice issued under section 43 of the Education (No 2) Act 1986[1]

1. Section 43 of the Education (No 2) Act 1986, referring to freedom of speech in universities, polytechnics, and colleges, requires the Council to issue and keep up to date a code of practice to be followed by members, students, and employees of the University for the organization of meetings, etc., which are to be held on University premises, and for the conduct required of members, students, and employees of the University in connection with meetings, etc. This code of practice therefore applies to all members, students, and employees of the University, in respect of all University premises, which for the purposes of this code includes the Union Society. Outdoor, as well as indoor, meetings, etc., on University premises are included.

2. Members of the University are reminded that alleged offences under the general regulations for discipline may be brought by the University Advocate before the University Tribunal, the Court of Discipline, or the Summary Court, as appropriate.

Organization of meetings, etc., on University premises

3. Authority is required for meetings and public gatherings to be held on University premises, whether indoors or out of doors. In the case of accommodation assigned to a single Faculty or Department, the permission of the relevant Faculty or Departmental authorities is required. In the case of accommodation not so assigned, permission must be obtained from the central University authorities and, if a room is to be reserved, a booking must be made through the relevant office. The organizers of meetings, etc., must comply with any conditions set by the University authorities concerned for the organization of the meeting or other activity and the arrangements to be made. Such conditions may include the requirement that tickets should be issued for public meetings, that an adequate number of stewards should be available, that the police should be consulted about the arrangements, and that the time and place of the meeting should be changed. The cost of meeting the requirements, and the responsibility for fulfilling them, rests with the organizers.

4. In addition to seeking the permission referred to in paragraph 3, the organizers of all meetings, etc., to be held on University premises which are to be addressed or attended by persons who are not resident members of the University (except for academic meetings organized by the authorities of a Faculty or Department, or for any meetings or classes of meetings approved for the purpose by the Senior Proctor as being commonly or customarily held on University premises) are required to give notice to the Senior Proctor. This notice may be given on the form used to book University premises, a copy of which will be sent by the University authority concerned to the Senior Proctor. The organizers may also, if they wish, communicate directly with the Proctors to give further details. Information is required at least five clear days in advance (although the Senior Proctor may, at his or her discretion, agree to receive information closer to the time of the meeting than this). The information needed is the date and time of the meeting, the place, the names, addresses, and Colleges (if any) of the organizers, the name of the organization making the arrangements, and the name of any expected speaker, whether or not a member of the University.

5. The organizers of any meeting must comply with instructions given by a Proctor, by any other University officer, or by any other person authorized to act on behalf of the University, in the proper discharge of his or her duties. The attention of members of the University is drawn to Regulations 8 and 9 of the general regulations for discipline.

Colleges

6. The provisions of section 43 of the Education (No 2) Act 1986 apply also to the Colleges in respect of their own members, students, and employees, and in respect of visiting speakers. Each College is requested by the University to name a senior member who will be responsible for enforcing the provisions of the Act in that College and will co-operate as necessary with the Proctors. Members of the University are reminded that University disciplinary regulations apply on College premises as elsewhere in the Precincts of the University. A College may invite the Proctors to enter its premises.

Other legal requirements

7. The attention of organizers of public meetings and assemblies is drawn to sections 11 and 14 of the Public Order Act 1986, concerning processions and assemblies. Other legal requirements may affect the conduct of meetings, etc. A speaker, for example, who incites an audience to violence or to a breach of the peace or to racial hatred transgresses the bounds of lawful speech. Equally, assemblies of persons, even if directed to lawful

[1] Section 43 of the Education (No 2) Act 1986 was reproduced in *Reporter*, 1986–87, p. 578.

purposes, cease to be lawful if they cause serious public disorder or breaches of the peace. Attention is also drawn to the provisions of the Licensing Acts, which apply to certain University premises, including the University Centre. These Acts require the licensee to maintain good order on licensed premises, and give the licensee the power to expel persons from the premises if he or she considers it necessary.

Application of the code

8. Any person who is in any doubt about the application of this code of practice to any meeting or public gathering in the University is under an obligation to consult the Senior Proctor, who will determine whether the provisions of the code apply.

UNIVERSITY COURTS

Initiation of proceedings before the University Tribunal, the Court of Discipline, or the Summary Court

1. Any proceedings against a person to whom the Schedule to Statute C applies shall be subject to the provisions of Chapter III of that Schedule. Proceedings against any other member of the University shall be subject to the provisions of Special Ordinance D (iii) 7.

2. (*a*) If the Vice-Chancellor has directed under the Schedule to Statute C, Chapter III 8, that a charge is to be preferred against a person to whom the Schedule to Statute C applies, the case shall be presented by the University Advocate.

(*b*) If in response to a complaint made under Special Ordinance D (iii) 7 the University Advocate determines that proceedings shall be brought against a member of the University before the University Tribunal or the Court of Discipline or the Summary Court, the case shall be presented either by the Advocate or by the complainant, as may be decided by the Advocate; provided that, if a charge arises from a complaint made by the Proctors, the Advocate shall be responsible for presenting the case on behalf of the University.

3. The Advocate shall give written notice to the Registrary and to the complainant of the decisions taken in accordance with Special Ordinance D (iii) 7 and Regulation 2(*b*) above; if the Advocate decides that a person is to be charged, written notice shall be given to the Clerk of the appropriate court.

4. If a member of the University commits an act or engages in conduct for which he or she is liable to be prosecuted in a court of law and which is also an offence under the general regulations for Discipline, such member shall not be charged with an offence unless the Advocate is satisfied either that any proceedings against the member in a court of law in respect of that act or conduct have been completed and that he or she has been convicted of an offence or that the member is unlikely to be prosecuted in a court of law in respect of that act or conduct.

5. If a member of the University *in statu pupillari* is charged with an offence under the general regulations for discipline in respect of an act or conduct for which he or she has been convicted of an offence in a court of law, such member may on proof of such conviction be sentenced to deprivation or suspension of membership of the University, or may be rusticated, or deprived of any particular privileges or facilities in the University, provided that such action is in the opinion of the Court of Discipline necessary for the protection of the interests of the University; but he or she shall not be liable to any other sentence.

6. If a member of the University *in statu pupillari* commits an act which is an offence under the general regulations for discipline and also an offence against the discipline of his or her College, such member shall be charged before a University court only if the Advocate is satisfied either

(*a*) that such member will not be subject to disciplinary proceedings in respect of that act by his or her College, or

(*b*) that the general interest of the University in the maintenance of good order and discipline in the University is not likely otherwise to be sufficiently protected.

7. In these regulations all references to conviction in a court of law shall mean that the court has found that the offence charged has been proved and that the person so charged has not been acquitted either upon trial or upon appeal.

UNIVERSITY TRIBUNAL

Appointment of members of the University Tribunal

Panels.

1. The Council shall maintain a panel, hereinafter referred to as panel (*a*), of persons who are eligible under Special Ordinance D (i) 3 to serve as Chair of the University Tribunal and who are willing to do so, and shall appoint in the Michaelmas Term each year such number of persons as the Council may think fit, to serve as members of the panel for one year from 1 January following their appointment. No member of the Council or of the Septemviri shall be a member of panel (*a*).

2. The Council shall maintain a panel, hereinafter referred to as panel (*b*), of members of the Regent House who are willing to serve as members of the University Tribunal, and shall appoint ten persons to the panel in the Michaelmas Term each year, to serve for one year from 1 January following their appointment. No member of the Council or of the Septemviri shall be a member of panel (*b*).

Chair.

3. Not later than 31 December in each year the Vice-Chancellor shall appoint a member of panel (*a*) to serve as Chair of the University Tribunal for one year from 1 January next following; in making the appointment the Vice-Chancellor shall, if possible, select a person who is not a member of the Regent House. If the person appointed is unable or unwilling to act as Chair for a particular case, the Vice-Chancellor shall appoint another member of panel (*a*) to act as Chair for that case.

4. When a member of the University is to be charged before the University Tribunal, the Chair of the Tribunal shall appoint a date, time, and place for a hearing. The Chair shall have power, if the circumstances require it, to cancel a hearing so arranged at any time before the commencement of the hearing, and to appoint a different date, time, and place.

Appointment of Tribunal.

5. When a hearing has been arranged, the Clerk of the Tribunal shall forthwith send written notice to all members of panel (*b*), informing them of the date, time, and place appointed, and requiring them to indicate, not later than 5 p.m. on the fourth day after the day on which the notice is despatched, whether they are able and willing to serve. The Chair shall then appoint the other members of the Tribunal by causing lots to be drawn from among those members of panel (*b*) who have informed the Clerk of the Tribunal that they are able and willing to serve; and the Clerk shall thereupon inform the persons appointed of the charge or charges to be heard and the name of the person charged. The Chair shall in like manner appoint three reserve members of the Tribunal from panel (*b*) who shall be required to attend the Tribunal at the commencement of the proceedings so that lots may be drawn from among them if it becomes necessary to replace any member or members of the Tribunal who have failed to attend or who have otherwise become unable or unwilling to serve or against whose membership the Chair has under Regulation 6 allowed an objection. No member of the Tribunal shall be replaced after the commencement of the hearing.

6. A person charged before the Tribunal shall be entitled to object for good cause to any member appointed to serve on the Tribunal for those proceedings. The Chair alone shall rule on any such objection and his or her decision shall be final.

7. If at the commencement of the proceedings the Chair is unable, using the procedure prescribed in Regulation 5, to appoint the appropriate number of members of the Tribunal from panel (*b*), he or she shall appoint such number of members from the panel as may be needed to fill the vacant place or places.

8. If on any occasion there are insufficient members of panel (*b*) who are able and willing to serve as members of the Tribunal, the Vice-Chancellor shall appoint the appropriate number of members of the Regent House to fill the vacant places.

9. If after the commencement of proceedings the Chair becomes unable or unwilling to act, the Vice-Chancellor shall discharge the Tribunal and a new Tribunal shall be appointed in accordance with the provisions of Regulations 3–8. If after the commencement of proceedings any other member of the Tribunal becomes unable or unwilling to act, the remaining members shall continue to act, so long as there remain two members in addition to the Chair who are able and willing to act, but not otherwise. If more than two members become unable or unwilling to act, the Vice-Chancellor shall discharge the Tribunal and a new Tribunal shall be appointed in accordance with the provisions of Regulations 3–8.

Rules of Procedure

Notice.

1. When a member of the University is to be charged before the University Tribunal, the University Advocate, or other person responsible for presenting the case, shall send written notice to the Clerk of the Tribunal of the charge or charges to be brought before the Tribunal and the particulars thereof, and shall send with the notice any documents which it is proposed to produce and a list of all witnesses whom it is proposed to call, together with statements of the evidence that they are expected to give.

2. The parties to a hearing by the Tribunal shall be: Parties.

(*a*) the person charged;

(*b*) the University Advocate or other person responsible for presenting the case;

(*c*) any person who may be added as a party by the Tribunal, either on application or of their own motion.

3. The person charged and any person added as a party by the Tribunal shall be entitled to be represented by another person, whether such person is legally qualified or not, in connection with or at any hearing by the Tribunal.

4. The Clerk of the Tribunal shall not less than fourteen days (or such shorter period as may be agreed by the Clerk with the parties) before the date appointed for the hearing send to each party (*a*) a notice of the hearing, which shall contain information and guidance concerning attendance at the hearing, the calling of witnesses and the bringing of documents, representation by another person, and written submissions, and (*b*) a copy of the charge or charges, together with the other information specified in Regulation 1. Summons.

5. It shall be the duty of the person presenting the case to make any necessary arrangements for the summoning of witnesses and the production of documents, and generally for the proper presentation of the case to the Tribunal.

6. No additional witness or documentary evidence may be introduced by the person presenting the case, beyond those of which notice has been given under Regulation 1, without the consent of the Tribunal, and such consent shall not be given save for good reason; if such late introduction is permitted, the person charged shall be allowed an adjournment sufficient to enable him or her to consider the additional evidence and respond to it, and to introduce further evidence as appropriate.

7. A charge shall not be determined without an oral hearing at which the person charged and any other parties to the hearing are entitled to be present together with their representatives, if any.

8. The Tribunal may sit either in public or *in camera* at the discretion of the Chair, provided that if the person charged so requests they shall normally sit *in camera*. The Tribunal shall have power, if they think it appropriate in the circumstances, to hear charges against two or more persons at the same hearing. Admission to hearing.

9. The Tribunal shall have power to proceed with a hearing in the absence of any of the persons entitled to be present and, notwithstanding the provisions of Regulation 7, the Chair shall have power to exclude any person from a hearing if in the opinion of the Chair such exclusion is necessary for the maintenance of order.

10. (*a*) The fact that any person has been, or is liable to be, prosecuted in a court of law in respect of an act or conduct which is the subject of proceedings before the University Tribunal shall not affect the jurisdiction or the powers of the Tribunal under Chapter III of the Schedule to Statute C; but the Tribunal shall consider the advisability of referring the matter to the police and, if they so refer the matter, shall adjourn their proceedings for such time as is reasonable in the circumstances to enable a prosecution to be undertaken.

(*b*) Evidence that a person has been convicted of an offence by or before any court of law, or that any court of law has found proved an offence with which a person was charged, shall, for the purpose of proving that the person committed the offence or was guilty of any act or conduct in respect of which he or she was so charged or convicted, be admissible in any proceedings before the University Tribunal.

11. Each party to a hearing before the Tribunal, or his or her representative, shall be entitled to make an opening statement, to give evidence, to call witnesses, to question any witness concerning any relevant evidence, and to address the Tribunal after the evidence has been heard. Conduct of hearing.

12. Subject to the provisions of the Schedule to Statute C and of these Ordinances, the Tribunal shall have power to regulate their own procedure. The Chair may set time-limits for each stage of the proceedings, and any meeting of the Tribunal may be postponed or adjourned at the discretion of the Chair. It shall be the duty of the Tribunal and of the Chair to ensure that a charge is heard and determined as expeditiously as is reasonably practicable.

13. The Tribunal shall have power to dismiss a charge for want of prosecution, or, in the case of a charge brought under Chapter III of the Schedule to Statute C, to remit the charge to the Vice-Chancellor for further consideration.

14. The Tribunal shall not find a charge proved unless they are satisfied that it has been proved beyond reasonable doubt.

Penalty.

15. If the Tribunal find a charge proved, they shall, after giving the parties an opportunity to address them concerning the penalty to be imposed, determine the appropriate penalty (if any) in accordance with the provisions of Statute D II 3 or, in the case of a person charged under the Schedule to Statute C, in accordance with the provisions of Chapter III 12 of the Schedule to Statute C; and the Tribunal or the Chair, as appropriate, shall have power to impose such penalty.

16. The Clerk of the Tribunal shall be entitled to be present throughout the hearing and at any meeting of the Tribunal, and shall keep a sufficient record of the proceedings of the Tribunal.

Decision.

17. The Tribunal's decision shall be recorded in a document signed by the Chair which shall contain:

(*a*) the Tribunal's findings of fact regarding the charge;

(*b*) the reasons for the Tribunal's decision;

(*c*) the penalty (if any) determined by the Tribunal;

(*d*) the penalty (if any) imposed by the Tribunal or the Chair, as appropriate.

18. The Clerk of the Tribunal shall send a copy of the document specified in Regulation 17 to the Vice-Chancellor, the person charged, and the other parties to the hearing, and shall also send to the person charged a copy of Chapter V of the Schedule to Statute C and Special Ordinance D (ii) 1–5 concerning appeals.

19. The Chair shall have power by certificate under his or her hand to correct in documents recording the decisions of the Tribunal any clerical errors arising therein from accidental mistakes or omissions.

COURT OF DISCIPLINE

Appointment of members of the Court of Discipline

Composition of Court.

1. Any person against whom the University Advocate has determined that a charge shall be brought before the Court of Discipline shall be entitled, subject to the provisions of Regulations 8 and 9, to choose whether, for those proceedings, the Court shall consist, in addition to the Chair, of two members of the Regent House and two persons *in statu pupillari* or of four members of the Regent House; provided that if, within seven days after notice of the charge, such person fails to notify his or her choice to the Clerk of the Court, the Court shall, subject to the provisions of Regulations 8 and 9, consist of the Chair, two members of the Regent House, and two persons *in statu pupillari*.

Panels.

2. The Council shall maintain a panel, hereinafter referred to as panel (*a*), of persons who are eligible under Special Ordinance D (i) 4 to serve as Chair of the Court of Discipline and who are willing to do so, and shall appoint in the Michaelmas Term in each year such number of persons as the Council may think fit, to serve as members of the panel for one year from 1 January following their appointment. No member of the Council shall be a member of panel (*a*).

3. The Council shall maintain a panel, hereinafter referred to as panel (*b*), of members of the Regent House who are prepared to serve as members of the Court of Discipline and the Summary Court, and shall appoint ten persons to the panel in the Michaelmas Term of each year, to serve for one year from 1 January following their appointment. No member of the Council or of the Septemviri shall be a member of panel (*b*).

4. The Council shall invite the Junior Combination Room Committee of each College, or if in any College there is no such Committee such other body as in the Council's opinion is the nearest equivalent to a Junior Combination Room Committee, to nominate, not later than the division of the Michaelmas Term in each year, one eligible member of the College for appointment by the Council to a panel, hereinafter referred to as panel (*c*), of members of the University *in statu pupillari* to serve as members of the Court of Discipline and the Summary Court. An eligible member of the College shall be a member of the College *in statu pupillari* who is willing to serve on panel (*c*) and who is keeping terms by residence or, having kept the number of terms required, is pursuing a course of study or research in the University. Not later than the last day of the Michaelmas Term in each year the Council shall announce the names of the persons whom they have appointed members of panel (*c*). The persons appointed shall serve for one year from 1 January following their appointment; provided that if a member ceases to be an eligible member of a College as defined in this regulation, he or she shall cease to be a member of panel (*c*).

5. The Vice-Chancellor shall not later than 31 December in each year appoint a member of panel (*a*) to serve as Chair for one year from 1 January next following and shall seek to appoint as Chair a member of the panel who is not a member of the Regent House. If the Chair is unable or unwilling to act as Chair for a particular case, the Vice-Chancellor shall appoint another member of panel (*a*) to act as Chair for that case. Chair.

6. The Clerk of the Court shall, on the instructions of the Chair for the particular case, send written notice to all members of panel (*b*) and, when appropriate, of panel (*c*), informing them of the date, time, and place at which the Court is to assemble, and requiring them to indicate, not later than 5 p.m. on the fourth day after the day on which the notice is despatched, whether they are able and willing to serve. The Chair shall then appoint the other members of the Court in accordance with the provisions of Regulation 1 by causing lots to be drawn from among those members of panel (*b*) and, when appropriate, of panel (*c*) who have informed the Clerk of the Court that they are able and willing to serve; and the Clerk of the Court shall thereupon inform the persons appointed of the charge or charges to be heard and the name and College of the person charged. The Chair shall in like manner appoint three reserve members of the Court from panel (*b*) and, when appropriate, three from panel (*c*) who shall be required to attend the Court at the commencement of the proceedings so that lots may be drawn from among them if it becomes necessary to replace any member or members of the Court who have failed to attend or who have otherwise become unable or unwilling to serve or against whose membership the Chair has under Regulation 7 allowed an objection. No member of the Court shall be replaced after the commencement of the proceedings. Appointment of the Court.

7. A person charged before the Court shall be entitled to object for good cause to any member appointed to serve on the Court for those proceedings. The Chair alone shall rule on any such objection and his or her decision shall be final.

8. If at the commencement of the hearing the Chair is unable under the provisions of Regulation 6 to appoint the appropriate number of members of the Court from panel (*b*) or panel (*c*), he or she shall appoint such number of members from the appropriate panel as may be needed to fill the vacant place or places; provided that, if in the Chair's judgement the appointment of a member or members from panel (*c*) cannot be achieved without undue delay, the Chair shall be empowered to appoint a member or members from panel (*b*) to fill the vacant place or places.

9. If on any occasion there are insufficient members of panel (*b*) or panel (*c*) who are able and willing to serve as members of the Court, the Vice-Chancellor shall appoint the appropriate number of members of the Regent House to fill the vacant places on the Court.

Rules of Procedure[1]

1. The Clerk of the Court shall send to any person charged before the Court written notice of (*a*) the complaint against him or her, and (*b*) the date, time, and place to attend the Court, and shall draw attention to the provisions of the regulations for the appointment of members of the Court whereby the person charged is entitled to choose the composition of the Court. Copies of such notice shall be sent to the complainant and to the Head of the College of the person charged. Summons.

2. The Court may sit either in public or *in camera* at the discretion of the Chair except that, when the defendant requests that it shall sit *in camera*, the Chair shall normally so decide. If the Court sits *in camera*, the following shall be entitled to be present: the defendant, the defendant's Tutor (or a deputy appointed by the Tutor), the Head of the defendant's College (or a deputy appointed by the Head), the University Advocate, the complainant, and any person appointed to represent the defendant, the complainant, or the University Advocate. Admission to hearing.

3. Whether the Court sits in public or *in camera*, it may proceed in the absence of any of the persons entitled to be present and, notwithstanding Regulation 2, the Chair shall have power to exclude any person if in the opinion of the Chair such exclusion is necessary for the maintenance of order. Conduct of hearing.

4. The Chair shall not impose under Statute D II 21 any fine exceeding £175.

5. The Court shall not find a charge proved unless it is satisfied that the charge has been proved beyond reasonable doubt.

[1] See the Registrary's Notice on the operation, procedures, and practice of the Court of Discipline (*Reporter*, 2010–11, p. 411).

Sentence to have immediate effect.

6. Any sentence imposed by the Court shall have immediate effect; provided that the Chair of the Court and the Chair of the Septemviri shall each have power to suspend a sentence until the conclusion of the proceedings by the Septemviri of any appeal against a decision of the Court.

Appeal.

7. Any person who appeals to the Court of Discipline shall notify the Registrary in writing. Such notice shall specify the grounds of the appeal and shall state whether the appeal is in respect of the whole or in respect of any specified part of the finding of the Summary Court. Except with the leave of the Court of Discipline, the appellant shall not be entitled in the proceedings of an appeal to rely on any grounds of appeal not specified in the notice of appeal.

SUMMARY COURT

Composition of Court.

1. A court, called the Summary Court, shall be established under the provisions of Statute D II 17 and shall, except as provided in Regulations 6 and 7, consist of a Chair, one member of the Regent House, and one member of the University *in statu pupillari*. Two members of the Court shall constitute a quorum. Every finding of the Court and every decision on sentence shall require the concurrence of at least two members of the Court.

Chair and Deputy Chair.

2. The Chair and a Deputy Chair, both of whom shall be legally qualified members of the Senate, shall be appointed by the Vice-Chancellor in the Michaelmas Term in each year to serve for one year from 1 January following their appointment.

Appointment of Court.

3. The Chair of the Summary Court shall as soon as may be convenient in the Lent Term appoint the other two members of the Summary Court to serve until 31 December following their appointment by causing lots to be drawn from among the members of panel (*b*) and panel (*c*) for the Court of Discipline.

4. A person charged before the Court shall be entitled to object for good cause to any member of the Court. The Chair alone shall rule on any such objection and his or her decision shall be final.

5. The Deputy Chair shall act in place of the Chair on any occasion when the Chair is unable or unwilling to act. If any member of the Court other than the Chair is unable or unwilling to serve for the proceedings of a particular case, or if the Chair allows an objection under Regulation 4 to a member of the Court other than the Chair, the Chair shall appoint by lot a member of the appropriate panel to replace such member.

6. If the Chair is able to appoint only one of the other members of the Court in accordance with these regulations, the Court shall proceed as a Court of two members.

7. If the Chair is unable to appoint any other member of the Court in accordance with these regulations the Chair alone shall constitute the Court and shall, notwithstanding the provisions of Regulation 1, have power to exercise any of the powers of the Court.

Clerk.

8. The Registrary, or a duly appointed deputy, shall be Clerk of the Summary Court.

Summons.

9. When the University Advocate determines that a charge shall be heard by the Summary Court, he or she shall send to the Clerk of the Court, for service on the person charged,

(*a*) a notice informing the person charged of the offence he or she is alleged to have committed and stating the amount of any fine (not exceeding £175) and of any order for compensation (not exceeding £250) which the University Advocate would consider appropriate if the offence were proved,

(*b*) a statement of the facts which would be placed before the Summary Court by or on behalf of the Advocate if the person charged did not appear before the Court.

10. The Clerk of the Court shall thereupon serve on the person charged copies of the notice and the statement sent by the University Advocate and shall in writing inform him or her of

(*a*) the date, time, and place fixed for the hearing;

(*b*) the powers of the Court, under Regulation 11 below, to adjudicate in the absence of the person charged.

The Clerk shall invite the person charged to state in writing

(i) whether he or she admits the offence alleged;

(ii) whether he or she disputes the amount of the fine or compensation specified in the University Advocate's notice;

(iii) whether he or she proposes to attend the hearing;

and, if the person charged does not propose to attend the hearing, shall invite him or her to submit in writing any facts which it is desired to draw to the attention of the Court.

11. If the Court is satisfied that the procedures prescribed in Regulations 9 and 10 have been carried out, it may proceed to hear and dispose of the case in the absence of the person charged, whether or not the Advocate is also absent; provided that Conduct of hearing.

(*a*) the Court shall not allow any statement of the facts to be made by or on behalf of the University Advocate other than the statement served on the person charged in accordance with Regulations 9 and 10;

(*b*) the Court shall not impose a fine or order compensation exceeding the amounts specified by the University Advocate under Regulation 9(*a*);

(*c*) the Court may adjourn the proceedings at any time and require the person charged to attend.

12. The Court may sit either in public or *in camera* at the discretion of the Chair.

13. The Court shall have power when hearing a case as a court of first instance to determine at any time, subject to the consent of the person charged, not to proceed with the hearing and to require the University Advocate to bring the charge and present the case before the Court of Discipline. Reference to Court of Discipline.

14. The Court shall not in respect of a single offence impose on any person a fine exceeding £175 or order compensation exceeding £250. Maximum fine.

15. Any person found by the Court sitting as a court of first instance to have committed an offence shall, if he or she wishes to appeal under Statute D II 17 to the Court of Discipline, deliver to the Clerk of the Summary Court, within twenty-eight days after notice of the decision of the Court, written application for leave to appeal. Appeals from decisions of the Court.

16. Any sentence imposed by the Court shall have immediate effect; provided that the Chair of the Court and the Chair of the Court of Discipline shall each have power to suspend a sentence until the conclusion of the proceedings by the Court of Discipline of any appeal against a finding of the Summary Court. Sentence to have immediate effect.

17. As a court of appeal, the Summary Court shall hear appeals by persons who come within the jurisdiction of the Court of Discipline under Statute D II 12 and upon whom a University authority (other than the Court of Discipline) has, under Statute, or in accordance with an Ordinance or with a rule made under an Ordinance, imposed a sentence, provided that such a person has delivered to the Clerk of the Summary Court, within twenty-eight days after notice of the sentence imposed by the University authority concerned, written notice of appeal to the Court; and the Court shall have power to quash the finding or to vary the sentence within the limits of the power of the authority in question, and its decision shall be final. Appeals to the Court.

18. If a person charged or an appellant appears before the Court, he or she may be represented at the proceedings only by a resident member of the Regent House or by a resident member of the University *in statu pupillari*.

19. Except in so far as the procedure of the Court is determined under the provisions of Statute D II and of these regulations, it shall be determined by the Chair.

MEDICAL BOARDS

1. When a Medical Board is appointed to hear a case under Chapter IV 5 of the Schedule to Statute C,

(*a*) the competent authority concerned shall appoint a person to present the case to the Board,

(*b*) the Chair of the Board shall appoint a person to act as Secretary of the Board.

2. If after the commencement of proceedings a member of the Board becomes unable or unwilling to act, the Vice-Chancellor shall discharge the Board and a new Board shall be appointed in accordance with the provisions of Chapter IV 5 of the Schedule to Statute C.

3. The parties to a hearing before a Medical Board shall be: Parties.

(*a*) the person whose possible retirement on medical grounds is under consideration by the Board, hereinafter referred to as the person concerned;

(*b*) the person appointed to present the case to the Board.

4. The person concerned shall be entitled to be represented by another person, whether such person is legally qualified or not, in connection with and at any hearing by the Board.

5. The person appointed to present the case to the Board shall send to the Secretary of the Board a written statement of the case and any relevant medical evidence, and shall send with the statement any documents which it is proposed to produce and a list of all witnesses whom it is proposed to call, together with statements of the evidence that they are expected to give.

6. The Chair of the Board shall appoint a date, time, and place for a hearing by the Board. The Chair shall have power, if the circumstances require it, to cancel a hearing so arranged at any time before the commencement of the hearing, and to appoint a different date, time, and place.

Summons. **7.** When a hearing has been arranged, the Secretary of the Board shall not less than fourteen days (or such shorter period as may be agreed by the Secretary with the parties) before the date appointed for the hearing send notice of the hearing to the person concerned and to any representative appointed under Regulation 4. Such notice shall include:

(*a*) information and guidance concerning attendance at the hearing, the calling of witnesses and the bringing of documents, representation by another person, and written submissions;

(*b*) a statement of the case, together with the other information specified in Regulation 5.

8. It shall be the duty of the person presenting the case to make any necessary arrangements for the summoning of witnesses and the production of documents, and generally for the proper presentation of the case to the Board.

9. No additional witness or documentary evidence may be introduced by the person presenting the case, beyond those of which notice has been given under Regulation 5, without the consent of the Board, and such consent shall not be given save for good reason; if such late introduction is permitted, the person concerned shall be allowed an adjournment sufficient to enable him or her to consider the additional evidence and respond to it, and to introduce further evidence as appropriate.

10. A case shall not be determined without an oral hearing at which the person concerned is entitled to be represented. Any hearing of or in connection with a case by a Medical Board shall take place *in camera*.

Conduct of hearing. **11.** A Medical Board shall have power to proceed with a hearing in the absence of the person concerned or of his or her representative and, notwithstanding the provisions of Regulation 10, the Chair shall have power to exclude any person from a hearing if in the opinion of the Chair such exclusion is necessary for the maintenance of order.

12. Each party to a hearing before a Medical Board, or his or her representative, shall be entitled to make an opening statement, to give evidence, to call witnesses, to question any witness concerning any relevant evidence, and to address the Board after the evidence has been heard.

13. Subject to the provisions of the Schedule to Statute C and of these Ordinances, a Medical Board shall have power to regulate their own procedure, and any meeting of the Board may be postponed or adjourned at the discretion of the Chair. It shall be the duty of the Board and of the Chair to ensure that a case is heard and determined as expeditiously as is reasonably practicable.

14. A Medical Board shall not determine that any person's removal from office would be justified by reason of incapacity on medical grounds unless they are satisfied that the incapacity has been proved beyond reasonable doubt.

15. The Secretary of the Board shall be entitled to be present throughout the hearing and at any meeting of the Board, and shall keep a sufficient record of the proceedings of the Board.

Decision. **16.** The Board's decision shall be recorded in a document signed by the Chair which shall contain:

(*a*) the Board's medical findings;

(*b*) the Board's other findings of fact;

(*c*) the reasons for the Board's decision.

17. The Secretary of the Board shall send a copy of the document specified in Regulation 16 to the person concerned, to his or her representative (if any), and to the person responsible for presenting the case to the Board, and shall also send to the person concerned a copy of Chapter V of the Schedule to Statute C and Special Ordinance D (ii) 1–5 concerning appeals.

18. The Chair shall have power by certificate under his or her hand to correct in documents recording the decisions of the Board any clerical errors arising therein from accidental mistakes or omissions.

SEPTEMVIRI

Appointment. **1.** Except as provided by Special Ordinance D (i) 1–2 members of the Court of the Septemviri shall be appointed as follows:

(*a*) the Chair shall be appointed in the Michaelmas Term to serve for four years from 1 January following his or her appointment;

(*b*) in each year three Septemviri shall be appointed in the Michaelmas Term to serve for two years from 1 January following their appointment.

2. The Registrary, or a deputy appointed by the Registrary, shall act as Clerk of the Septemviri.

3. Any person who wishes to institute an appeal to the Septemviri under the provisions of Statute D or Chapter V of the Schedule to Statute C shall send to the Clerk of the Septemviri a notice in writing setting out the grounds of appeal and stating whether the appeal is in respect of the whole or in respect of any specified part of any finding of fact, decision, or sentence. In the proceedings of an appeal the appellant shall not be entitled, except with the leave of the Septemviri, to rely on any grounds of appeal not specified in the notice of appeal. Notice of appeal.

4. When an appeal to the Septemviri is instituted, the Chair of the Septemviri shall appoint a date, time, and place for the hearing of the appeal. The Chair shall have power, if the circumstances require it, to cancel a hearing so arranged at any time before the commencement of the hearing, and to appoint a different date, time, and place.

5. The parties to an appeal shall be: Parties.

(*a*) the appellant;

(*b*) (i) in the case of an appeal against a decision of a competent authority under Chapter II of the Schedule to Statute C, the competent authority;

(ii) in the case of an appeal against a decision of the University Tribunal or any other University court, or of a Medical Board, or an appeal arising from proceedings before such a body, the University Advocate or other person who was responsible for presenting the case to the Tribunal or other body;

(iii) in the case of an appeal against a disciplinary decision of any other University authority, the authority concerned;

(iv) in the case of an appeal against any dismissal of a University officer otherwise than in pursuance of Chapters II, III, or IV of the Schedule to Statute C, the competent authority concerned;

(*c*) any other person added as a party by the Septemviri or by the Chair of the Septemviri, either on application or otherwise.

6. When a hearing has been arranged, the Clerk shall send to each party

(*a*) a notice of the hearing which shall contain information and guidance concerning attendance at the hearing, the bringing of documents, representation by another person, and the calling of fresh evidence;

(*b*) a copy of the notice provided by the appellant under Regulation 3.

7. Any party to an appeal shall be entitled to be represented by another person, whether such person is legally qualified or not, in connection with and at the hearing of the appeal.

8. An appeal shall not be determined without an oral hearing at which the appellant and his or her representative, if any, are entitled to be present.

9. The Septemviri may sit either in public or *in camera* at the discretion of the Chair, provided that if the appellant so requests they shall normally sit *in camera*. The Septemviri shall have power, if they think it appropriate in the circumstances, to hear appeals by two or more parties at the same hearing. Admission to hearing.

10. The Septemviri shall have power to proceed with a hearing in the absence of any of the persons entitled to be present and, notwithstanding the provisions of Regulation 8, the Chair shall have power to exclude any person from a hearing if in the opinion of the Chair such exclusion is necessary for the maintenance of order.

11. Each party to a hearing before the Septemviri shall be entitled to make a statement and to address the Septemviri; but witnesses may not be called save with the consent of the Septemviri. Leave to adduce fresh evidence, or to recall witnesses examined at first instance, shall be given only if the Septemviri are satisfied that it is necessary or expedient in the interests of justice. Conduct of hearing.

12. Subject to the provisions of Statute D II, and Chapter V of the Schedule to Statute C and Special Ordinance D (ii), and of these Ordinances, the Septemviri shall have power to regulate their own procedure. The Chair may set time-limits for each stage of the proceedings, and any meeting of the Septemviri may be postponed or adjourned at the discretion of the Chair. It shall be the duty of the Septemviri and of the Chair to ensure that any appeal is heard and determined as expeditiously as is reasonably practicable.

13. The Chair of the Septemviri shall not impose under Statute D II 21 any fine exceeding £175.

14. The Septemviri shall have power to allow or dismiss an appeal, or to dismiss an appeal for want of prosecution, or to remit an appeal for further consideration in accordance with the provisions of Chapter V 4 of the Schedule to Statute C.

15. The Clerk of the Septemviri shall be entitled to be present throughout the hearing and at any meeting of the Septemviri, and shall keep a sufficient record of the proceedings.

Decision. **16.** The decision of the Septemviri shall be recorded in a document signed by the Chair which shall contain:

(*a*) any findings of fact which differ from those reached by any other University authority which has previously considered the case;

(*b*) the reasons for the decision of the Septemviri;

(*c*) any penalty determined by them.

17. The Clerk of the Septemviri shall send a copy of the document specified in Regulation 16 to the Vice-Chancellor, the appellant, and the other parties to the appeal.

18. The Chair shall have power by certificate under his or her hand to correct in documents recording the decisions of the Septemviri any clerical errors arising therein from accidental mistakes or omissions.

COMPLAINTS BY STUDENTS

The Council shall publish and keep under review a procedure for determining complaints by members of the University *in statu pupillari*.

Student Complaints Procedure Approved by the Council

The University is committed to high quality of educational and other provision for students, and encourages students to say where there is cause for concern in individual or general matters. It undertakes to take such representation seriously. In raising possible issues of complaint students will themselves be aware of and have observed their obligations as members of the University.

The University aims to handle complaints in a way which is sympathetic, fair, and efficient, which encourages informal conciliation, facilitates early resolution, maintains individual privacy and confidentiality, and permits useful feedback.

This procedure is for all people matriculated as students in the University, undergraduate and postgraduate. Non-matriculated students have their own procedures (for example under the Board of Continuing Education).

A complaint will normally be about a problem encountered by a student in connection with educational or other activities or services provided by the University. It will not necessarily be *against* anybody, whether a person or an institution, although some complaints may be against individuals or University institutions. Complaints principally arising about matters covered by other specific procedures (such as those for the review of graduate or undergraduate examination results, or the codes of practice about racial and sexual harassment) should be raised under those procedures.

Because the purpose of the complaints procedure is, if possible, to resolve problems, a complaint should be made promptly, in an attempt to resolve them quickly and informally. The procedure, therefore, has three stages, and the Council hope that most problems will be solved in the first two stages of advice, and informal process. The three stages are:

(i) Discussion and Advice
(ii) Informal Process
(iii) Formal Process

Each stage is described in a later section.

There is also a system of formal quasi-visitatorial review by the Commissary.

Some general points about the procedure

The student is entitled to fair and independent consideration of a complaint. The rights of the student and the rights of any person complained against are both important and must be kept in balance. Every effort will be made to ensure that both are treated with fairness and dignity. Complaints will not be treated as though lodged against the University unless that is stated to be the case. There will be separation between the provision for advice and provision for dealing with or adjudicating on a complaint. The student should not suffer retaliation for making a complaint in good faith and a student who believes that he or she has suffered a reprisal should raise the matter. If a complaint which is not upheld is found to have been made maliciously, the student may be subject to disciplinary procedure.

The student may withdraw a complaint or stop the process at any time in Stage 1 or 2 and, in Stage 3, with the consent of the Chair of the panel. Personal privacy will be respected. Confidential information will not be communicated without the consent of the student, other than in exceptional circumstances (for example in reporting an alleged criminal offence to the Police). The student has a free choice of adviser and of representative, who need not be the same person. Normally this would be a College Tutor, but students are free to go to someone else if they prefer.

Complaints will be dealt with promptly to ensure that delay does not hinder fair resolution. Minor complaints will normally be resolved at an early stage.

A complaint can only be brought by a student affected, although several affected students may act together. A particular complaint cannot normally be pursued under both University and College procedures.

If a complaint is upheld there should be a satisfactory remedy or outcome, which may include:

- a full explanation;
- an apology (which is not an admission of liability);
- the matter put right if possible;
- if appropriate, some kind of financial recompense (for example if the student had paid for something which he or she did not receive);
- if appropriate, disciplinary action may be taken.

Written records will be kept of complaints. The student will have access to the documents submitted about his or her case, and those taking part in the complaint will be informed that this is so. Otherwise the records will be confidential. An annual report will be made to the Council and the General Board, in which references to individual cases will be made anonymously.

Stage 1: Discussion and Advice

1.1. It is very important to get early advice about problems. Often, this can resolve the matter quickly and informally.

1.2. Normally, a student would seek the advice of a College officer such as a Tutor, or Director of Studies, or if a graduate student their University Supervisor.

Other possibilities include:

- other relevant members of the academic staff of the University;
- the University Counselling Service;
- the Disability Resource Centre;
- appropriate advisers or mentors in University Faculties or Departments;
- officers of CUSU (e.g. the welfare officer, the academic affairs officer, or the women's officer) or the President of the Graduate Union
- administrative staff of Faculties and Departments;
- appropriate officers of the Central Administration (e.g. for graduate students, officers in the office of the Board of Graduate Studies).

1.3. The student can expect to be given advice on how to proceed and on an appropriate course of action, advice about what would constitute an appropriate remedy, and an opportunity to consider whether there is indeed a complaint to be addressed. The student will then be in a position to decide whether to proceed further, and how.

Stage 2: Informal Process

2.1. It is in the interest of the students that a complaint to be dealt with informally should be raised at the 'local' level (in the Faculty, Department, or relevant University service) as soon as possible. If there has been a delay the student should explain the reason. The student should if possible record the complaint in writing (the advice about a written statement in Stage 3 may be helpful).

2.2. The student should if possible raise the complaint directly with the person responsible for the matter. It may not always be easy to do this if the complaint is about the conduct of this person: if for some reason the student cannot go direct to the person alone he or she should ask for someone else to be present, or should raise the matter with another person in the organization concerned (the Head, Deputy Head, or Secretary of the organization, or a person or persons nominated for the purpose).

2.3. If possible a suitable solution will be agreed and implemented, to solve the problem.

2.4. If the student is dissatisfied with the outcome of such an informal process, he or she may consider whether to raise the matter formally through Stage 3.

Stage 3: Formal Process

3.1. Students must exhaust informal routes before making a formal complaint, or give a good reason for not doing so. A good reason might be that the problem is particularly serious, or that when it was raised informally there was refusal to deal with it. Informal processes are suitable for dealing with many problems, but if a complaint includes very serious allegations, and especially where a person complained against must have an opportunity to give his or her side of the matter, it may be necessary to refer straight to Stage 3. If informal routes seem not to have been exhausted a formal complaint may be referred to informal resolution.

3.2. A student wishing to make a formal complaint must do so in writing. The written statement initiates the formal process and must include a description of what has happened to give rise to the complaint including dates, times, and other details. It is necessary to show that something has gone wrong in the discharge of a University duty towards the student, and that the student has suffered as a result. The statement should include:

- the name of the person or University institution about whom/which the complaint is made (but a complaint need not necessarily be against a person or institution);
- the name of any witnesses who will corroborate the complaint, including a written statement from each to say that they have given their consent;
- documentary evidence, together with a list of contents and numbered pages;
- an outline of what action a student would like to be taken or what remedy he or she is seeking;

- if desired, the name of the person who has agreed to accompany, support, or represent the student at any meeting or hearing.
- It would be almost always sensible for the student to discuss the written statement of the complaint with an appropriate adviser (for example those named in paragraph 1.2). The complaint should be addressed to The Registrary at the University Offices, The Old Schools, Cambridge.

3.3. A complaint will be referred to a Reviewer, not connected with the College or Department of the student, for consideration. If the student wishes, the Reviewer will act with a student assessor, also not connected with the College or Department of the student.

3.4. The University Council will maintain a panel of potential Reviewers and a panel of potential student assessors. The Reviewer, and if necessary the student assessor, for a particular complaint will be designated by the Registrary, or a deputy. The student will have an opportunity to object, for good cause, to a person designated and the Registrary, or the deputy, will rule on the objection.

3.5. The written statement of complaint will also be referred to any person or University institution concerned, so that they can, if they wish, make a written response, to be considered by the Reviewer and the assessor.

3.6. The Reviewer will normally hear the representations about the complaint in person, but the Reviewer may also determine that the complaint should be dealt with on the basis of written submissions without a hearing. If a hearing takes place the student may be accompanied by an adviser or friend.

3.7. The Reviewer will issue a report, to which the student assessor, if any, may append any comments. The report will contain findings about the complaint, and may make recommendations as to remedies, if any, to be adopted, or other action recommended to be taken.

3.8. The Reviewer may terminate the proceedings, determine that a complaint is rejected as vexatious or frivolous, or refer the complaint for informal resolution as in Stage 2.

3.9. Legal representation and legal advice are not necessary in Stage 3.

3.10. The Reviewer will not (without agreement by those concerned) take into consideration documents or information which are not available to the student, the Reviewer, and to any person or University institution concerned. The Reviewer may request disclosure of documents requested by the student or any person or institution concerned. The Reviewer will seek to ensure that appropriate safeguards are made for the confidentiality of disclosed documents.

3.11. The Registrary, or the deputy, will nominate an administrative officer to assist the Reviewer. This officer has the right to be present throughout the whole proceedings of any hearing, and will prepare the draft report. The officer will also issue the 'completion of proceedings' letter for the purposes of possible further application to the Office of the Independent Adjudicator (OIA), if review or complaint procedures within the University are then believed to be completed.

Timing

A complaint under Stage 2 or 3 shall be made within three months of the occurrence of the matter complained about; a complaint under Stage 3 following from one under Stage 2 shall be made within three months of the completion of Stage 2; unless, exceptionally, the Reviewer allows a longer time, for exceptional good cause.

PROCEDURES TO DETERMINE FITNESS TO PRACTISE OF PRECLINICAL AND CLINICAL MEDICAL STUDENTS

Introduction

1. The General Medical Council (GMC) has a duty, as a matter of public safety under the Medical Act 1983, to ensure that medical students are fit to practise medicine when they apply to the GMC for provisional registration. The following regulations shall govern the procedures in the University to ensure that preclinical and clinical medical students are fit to practise medicine as defined in guidance issued by the Medical Schools Council and General Medical Council.

Medical Students Register.

2. There shall be a Medical Students Register which shall be maintained by the Faculty Boards of Biology and Clinical Medicine through a Fitness to Practise Committee (FTP Committee).

3. Any person or body may refer any matter which gives a cause for concern about a medical student's fitness to practise to the FTP Committee in accordance with these procedures.

Adjudication Panel.

4. Where the FTP Committee considers that there is a question to be determined concerning the fitness to practise of a medical student, the FTP Committee shall appoint an Investigator who shall report to the FTP Committee. Having considered the Investigator's report, the FTP Committee may refer the matter to a Fitness to Practise Adjudication Panel (FTP Adjudication Panel) to consider whether the student is fit to practise medicine or whether to impose sanctions (which include formal warnings, conditions, and suspension or removal from the Medical Students Register).

Appeal.

5. A medical student shall, if required to do so, attend meetings and/or hearings with the FTP Committee, an Investigator, and a FTP Adjudication Panel. A medical student and the FTP Committee may appeal to a Fitness to Practise Appeal Panel (FTP Appeal Panel) on grounds specified in these procedures.

6. Fitness to practise issues can arise from a student's conduct, health, or performance. Medical students have a responsibility to report any illness or disability that may affect their fitness to practise to their Senior Tutor or Director of Studies and, as appropriate, to the Director of Medical Education in the Faculty of Clinical Medicine or the Director of Education (Biological Sciences) in the Faculty of Biology.

7. The University also has a duty to support its medical students. The Medical and Veterinary Student Progress Panel (MVSPP) monitors the academic performance and progress of preclinical and clinical medical students, including issues relating to ill health and any other cause for concern which does not merit a referral to the FTP Committee. Medical and Veterinary Student Progress Panel.

8. A student who wishes to remain on the Medical Students Register will be expected to co-operate with obtaining such reports from the University's Occupational Health and Safety Service and/or other experts as may be deemed necessary.

9. When applying for provisional registration with the General Medical Council, medical students are required to inform the GMC of the details of any referral to the FTP Committee and any and all matters that might have a bearing on her or his fitness to practise.

The composition, roles, and duties of the Fitness to Practise bodies

Fitness to Practise Committee (FTP Committee)

10. The FTP Committee shall comprise a minimum of three members: Membership.

(*a*) a Chair appointed by the Faculty Board of Clinical Medicine who shall be a member of the Regent House and a practising GMC-registered medical practitioner;

(*b*) one member appointed by the Faculty Board of Clinical Medicine who shall be a member of the Regent House and a practising GMC registered medical practitioner; and

(*c*) one member appointed by the Faculty Board of Biology who shall be a member of the Regent House and not a GMC-registered medical practitioner.

11. No member of the FTP Committee shall have had any material involvement or interest in respect of each individual case before the FTP Committee. All members of the FTP Committee shall be required to make a declaration of interest in the case.

12. Members of the FTP Committee shall be appointed in the Michaelmas Term to serve for three years from 1 January following their appointment.

13. The Faculty Boards of Clinical Medicine and Biology shall in addition jointly maintain a Fitness to Practise Panel (FTP Panel). Every three years in the Michaelmas Term, or as necessary: Fitness to Practise Panel.

(*a*) the Faculty Board of Clinical Medicine shall appoint to the FTP Panel at least six members of the Regent House qualifying for appointment to the FTP Committee under Regulation 10(*b*);

(*b*) the Faculty Board of Biology shall appoint to the FTP Panel at least six members of the Regent House qualifying for appointment to the FTP Committee under Regulation 10(*c*).

14. In the event of a member of the FTP Committee appointed under Regulations 10(*a*) or 10(*b*) having a conflict of interest in any case, a replacement member qualifying for appointment to the FTP Committee under those regulations shall be appointed from the FTP Panel for the purposes of the case in question by the Chair of the Faculty Board of Clinical Medicine.

15. In the event of a member of the FTP Committee appointed under Regulation 10(*c*) having a conflict of interest in any case, a replacement member qualifying for appointment to the FTP Committee under that regulation shall be appointed from the FTP Panel for the purposes of the case in question by the Chair of the Faculty Board of Biology

16. The Faculty Board of Clinical Medicine shall appoint a person to be Secretary to the FTP Committee. Secretary.

17. The FTP Committee may co-opt a maximum of two members to the FTP Committee from the FTP Panel or elsewhere and may require such reports to be prepared as it considers necessary. Co-opted members.

18. The duties of the FTP Committee shall be: Duties of the Committee.

(*a*) to maintain the Medical Students Register on behalf of the Faculty Boards of Biology and of Clinical Medicine;

(*b*) to produce and keep under review a code of conduct to be observed by medical students;

(*c*) to consider all expressions of concern about a medical student's fitness to practise and, if appropriate, to appoint an Investigator from the FTP Panel who shall have discretion to investigate any issues relating to the student's fitness to practise medicine;

(*d*) to consider an Investigator's report, make recommendations and, if appropriate, refer a medical student to a FTP Adjudication Panel;

(*e*) to keep under review these Fitness to Practise procedures and to recommend changes to the Faculty Boards of Biology and Clinical Medicine, who shall report such changes to the University for approval.

Meetings. **19.** The FTP Committee shall meet at least once a year in the Michaelmas Term and whenever there is any business to consider. Three members shall constitute a quorum. The Chair shall have a casting vote, if necessary. In the absence of the Chair for a meeting of the FTP Committee, the member appointed under Regulation 10(*b*) may become Chair for that meeting, or the meeting may be adjourned.

20. The FTP Committee shall submit the minutes of its meetings to the Faculty Boards of Biology and of Clinical Medicine and to the Medical Education Committee.

Fitness to Practise Adjudication Panel (FTP Adjudication Panel)

Chair and members. **21.** A FTP Adjudication Panel shall comprise a Chair and two other members, all of whom shall be appointed by the Registrary from the FTP Panel as soon as practicable after he or she has been notified (by the Secretary to the FTP Committee) that a case has been referred to a FTP Adjudication Panel. The Chair shall be a practising GMC-registered medical practitioner.

Quorum. **22.** The three members of a FTP Adjudication Panel shall constitute the quorum for a hearing of the FTP Adjudication Panel at which a medical student's fitness to practise is determined. The Chair shall have a casting vote, if necessary.

23. A FTP Adjudication Panel shall decide whether a medical student is fit to practise medicine and should remain on the Medical Students Register and/or should be subject to sanctions.

24. No member of a FTP Adjudication Panel shall have had any material involvement or interest in the case. All members of a FTP Adjudication Panel shall be required to make a declaration of interest in respect of the case. A replacement member shall be appointed by the Registrary from the FTP Support Panel in the event of a conflict of interest.

25. A FTP Adjudication Panel may require such reports to be prepared as it considers necessary.

Secretary. **26.** The Secretary of the medical student's Faculty Board, or her or his nominated deputy, shall serve as Secretary to a FTP Adjudication Panel. For the purpose of these regulations, preclinical students are assigned to the Faculty of Biology and clinical students to the Faculty of Clinical Medicine.

Fitness to Practise Appeal Panel (FTP Appeal Panel)

27. An Appeal Panel shall be appointed to consider an appeal which is made by a medical student or by the FTP Committee in respect of a decision of a FTP Adjudication Panel.

Panels. **28.** The Council of the University shall maintain three panels, panel (*a*), panel (*b*), and panel (*c*), from which members of an Appeal Panel shall be appointed as follows:

panel (*a*): persons who are legally qualified or who have had experience of acting in a judicial capacity, not being members of the Council;

panel (*b*): members of the Regent House not being members of the FTP Committee, FTP Panel, or FTP Adjudication Panel or of the Faculties of Biology or Clinical Medicine;

panel (*c*): members of the academic staff of a UK Medical School, being practising GMC-registered medical practitioners, who are not members of the Regent House.

29. The Council shall appoint in the Michaelmas Term each year such number of persons as they shall see fit to serve as members of each panel for three years from 1 January following their appointment.

Members. **30.** An Appeal Panel shall consist of three members:

(*a*) one person designated by the Vice-Chancellor from panel (*a*), who shall be the Chair of the Appeal Panel;

(*b*) one drawn by lot from panel (*b*);

(*c*) one drawn by lot from panel (*c*).

31. No member of an Appeal Panel shall have had any material involvement or interest in the case. All members of the Appeal Panel shall be required to make a declaration of interest in respect of the case. In the event of a conflict of interest, an alternative member shall be appointed by the Vice-Chancellor or by lot, as appropriate.

32. The Registrary, or a person nominated by the Registrary, shall act as Clerk of the Appeal Panel. Clerk.

33. The three members of the Appeal Panel shall constitute the quorum. The Chair shall have a casting vote, if necessary. Quorum.

Fitness to Practise Procedures

34. The consideration of whether or not a medical student is fit to practise medicine shall take place in accordance with the following procedures which may comprise of at least three stages, a preliminary consideration by the FTP Committee, an investigation, and an adjudication by a FTP Adjudication Panel, and may be followed by a final appeal stage.

35. If at any stage the Chair of any of the bodies involved considers that the medical student may have committed an offence under the criminal law or against the discipline of the University, the Chair shall suspend proceedings and refer the circumstances for consideration by the police or to the University Advocate under Statute D, as appropriate. In such instances, the body or bodies shall not normally reach a decision on the student's fitness to practise until either the police or University Advocate (as appropriate) has confirmed that it is not intended to institute proceedings against the medical student, or, if proceedings are taken, until the criminal courts or University Courts (as appropriate) have ruled finally on the matter. Pending the outcome of any consideration by the police and the criminal courts and/or the University Advocate and the University Courts, the FTP Committee and its Chair shall review the student's status and take any measures under these procedures which are considered necessary.

36. The FTP Committee, the Investigator, a FTP Adjudication Panel, and the Appeal Panel may obtain legal advice through the Registrary to assist with the performance of their duties under these procedures.

37. Any notification to a medical student under these procedures may be sent to the medical student's University email address.

Preliminary stage involving the Fitness to Practise Committee

38. Any expression of concern that a medical student may not be fit to practise medicine shall be made in writing to the Secretary of the FTP Committee; it shall show clearly the author's name and address. Anonymous referrals shall only be acted upon in exceptional circumstances as the FTP Committee sees fit, having regard to the seriousness of the issues raised and the fairness to any individuals mentioned in the referral. The FTP Committee may also consider that the identity of individuals, although known to the FTP Committee, may need to be withheld or protected in exceptional circumstances.

39. The Secretary of the FTP Committee shall communicate the expression of concern to the Chair of the FTP Committee who may take Chair's action in respect of any measures which are considered necessary or appropriate pending consideration by the FTP Committee.

40. The Secretary of the FTP Committee shall inform the medical student of the details of any expression of concern and, at the discretion of the Chair of the FTP Committee, arrange for the student to attend a meeting of the FTP Committee. During any meeting with the FTP Committee, the medical student may be accompanied by a member of the University or other representative chosen by the medical student who shall notify the Secretary of the FTP Committee two days in advance of any meeting if he/she will be accompanied and by whom.

41. The Secretary of the FTP Committee shall inform the medical student of the persons appointed to be members of the FTP Committee. If the medical student has good cause to object to the membership of the FTP Committee, he or she shall provide grounds to the Secretary of the FTP Committee in writing within seven days. In the case of a member appointed under Regulation 10(*a*) or (*b*), the Chair of the Faculty Board of Clinical Medicine shall decide whether to replace that member of the FTP Committee and shall appoint an alternative member as considered appropriate. In the case of a member appointed under Regulation 10(*c*), the Chair of the Faculty Board of Biology shall decide whether to replace that member of the FTP Committee and shall appoint an alternative member as considered appropriate. The Secretary of the FTP Committee shall inform the medical student accordingly. The decision of the Chair of the Faculty Board of Clinical Medicine or of the Chair of the Faculty Board of Biology shall be final.

42. The FTP Committee shall decide whether the medical student shall during the course of any fitness to practise procedures:

(*a*) continue her or his studies without limitation;

(*b*) continue her or his studies under specified conditions;

(*c*) be prohibited from entering specified clinical facilities as a medical student; and/or

(*d*) be provisionally suspended from the Medical Students Register and therefore from the clinical components of the course.

43. The FTP Committee may, pending the outcome of any fitness to practise procedures, review and change a decision regarding a medical student's status and any measures which are considered necessary.

44. The FTP Committee shall determine whether the matter can and should be dealt with informally, whether the matter should be referred back to the Student Progress Panel (MVSPP), or whether an Investigator should be appointed to investigate the student's conduct, health, and/or performance. The FTP Committee shall normally take this initial decision within one month from the date of receipt of the expression of concern.

Procedures under Statute D.

45. If the University Advocate institutes proceedings against the medical student under Statute D any subsequent judgement of a University Court may be considered as evidence within any fitness to practise procedures. If a University Court finds that a charge is proven against the student then that finding shall be conclusive evidence that the medical student in question has committed the offence against the discipline of the University with which he or she was charged.

Investigation

46. If the FTP Committee decides to commence an investigation, the Secretary of the FTP Committee shall write to the medical student concerned and to the Senior Tutor of the student's College stating that an investigation of the medical student's fitness to practise is going to take place. The letter to the medical student shall state the nature of the expression of concern and the grounds for commencing the investigation.

Investigator.

47. The FTP Committee shall appoint an Investigator from the FTP Panel who has had no material involvement or interest in this case. The Investigator shall interview the medical student concerned, the maker of the allegation (unless an anonymous concern has been permitted), and any other relevant persons. A formal note of each interview shall be prepared by the Investigator and, if possible, agreed with the person who has been interviewed. A written report shall be prepared and submitted by the Investigator to the FTP Committee.

48. The FTP Committee, an Investigator and a FTP Adjudication Panel may, at any stage, require reports to be prepared by the Occupational Health and Safety Service and/or other experts as to the student's fitness to practise and will expect the student to co-operate with obtaining such reports in order for those bodies to discharge their duties to consider the student's fitness to practise. All such reports shall be co-ordinated through the FTP Committee.

49. During any interview with the Investigator, the medical student may be accompanied by a member of the University or other representative chosen by the medical student who shall notify the Investigator two days in advance of any meeting if he/she will be accompanied and by whom.

50. On receipt of the Investigator's report, the FTP Committee shall take one of the following decisions:

(*a*) that no further action be taken;

(*b*) that there is no serious issue to be determined with regard to the medical student's fitness to practise, but that the medical student would benefit from remedial measures being put in place; the Chair of the FTP Committee shall on behalf of the FTP Committee (i) agree such measures with the medical student, the student's Senior Tutor, and the Director of Medical Education in the Faculty of Clinical Medicine or the Director of Education (School of the Biological Sciences) in the Faculty of Biology as appropriate, and then so inform the Secretary of the FTP Committee in writing, or (ii) in the event of failure to agree such measures, the FTP Committee shall refer the matter to a FTP Adjudication Panel; or

(*c*) that there may be a serious issue to be determined concerning the medical student's fitness to practise and shall refer the matter to a FTP Adjudication Panel.

Decision.

51. The Secretary of the FTP Committee shall inform the medical student, the MVSPP, and the student's Senior Tutor in writing of the FTP Committee's decision and of any agreed measures normally within seven days. Where the FTP Committee decide that a matter shall be referred to a FTP Adjudication Panel, the Secretary of the FTP Committee shall notify the Registrary and the student's Faculty Board Secretary. Correspondence from the Secretary informing the student shall be submitted to the next full meeting of the FTP Committee.

Adjudication by FTP Adjudication Panel

52. If a medical student is referred by the FTP Committee to a FTP Adjudication Panel, the Chair of the FTP Adjudication Panel shall determine the procedure to be adopted by the FTP Adjudication Panel which shall normally include:

(*a*) informing the medical student of the persons appointed to be members of the FTP Adjudication Panel;

(*b*) providing the medical student with copies of the documents provided by the FTP Committee to the FTP Adjudication Panel, including the Investigator's report;

(*c*) informing the medical student of the names of any persons who may be asked to attend a FTP Adjudication Panel to give evidence and setting out the basis upon which the medical student may call persons who may have information relevant to the case to give evidence (whether they are members of the University or not) either orally at the hearing or in writing;

(*d*) setting a timetable for the progress of the proceedings, including time limits for each step of the proceedings and a date, time and place for the hearing.

53. The Secretary of the FTP Adjudication Panel shall inform the medical student and the Chair of the FTP Committee of the procedure to be followed. The Chair of the FTP Adjudication Panel may at any stage of the proceedings hold a case management meeting at which she or he may (i) review the progress of the proceedings, and in particular the extent to which any timetable previously set by the Chair has been complied with, (ii) issue or vary directions or time limits for the further conduct of the proceedings, and/or (iii) set or vary a date, time, or place for the hearing. The Secretary of the FTP Adjudication Panel shall inform the medical student and the Secretary of the FTP Committee of the date, time, and place of a case management meeting at least seven days in advance of such meeting.

54. If the medical student has good cause to object to the membership of a FTP Adjudication Panel, he or she shall provide grounds to the Secretary of the FTP Adjudication Panel in writing within seven days of being notified of the membership of the FTP Adjudication Panel. The Registrary shall decide whether to replace that member of the FTP Adjudication Panel and shall appoint an alternative member from the FTP Panel as considered appropriate. The Secretary of a FTP Adjudication Panel shall inform the medical student accordingly. The decision of the Registrary shall be final. Objection to members of the Panel.

55. The medical student shall attend all case management meetings and hearings of a FTP Adjudication Panel in person, unless prevented by exceptional circumstances. If the medical student fails to attend any case management meeting or any hearing without reasonable explanation, a FTP Adjudication Panel may, at its discretion, consider the case in the medical student's absence.

56. The medical student may choose to be accompanied by a member of the University or other representative chosen by the medical student who must inform the Secretary of the FTP Adjudication Panel of the identity of the individual and the capacity in which he or she is attending as soon as practicable and at least four days in advance of the case management meeting or hearing.

57. The medical student's Senior Tutor (or a deputy appointed by the Senior Tutor), if not nominated by the student, shall be entitled, with the student's consent, to be present at any case management meeting or hearing.

58. Case management meetings and hearings of the FTP Adjudication Panel shall be conducted in private unless the Chair of a FTP Adjudication Panel agrees to a request from the student for any case management meeting or hearing to be held in public. Private hearing.

59. A Chair of the FTP Adjudication Panel shall determine the procedure for the conduct of a FTP Adjudication Panel hearing to consider a medical student's fitness to practise. The procedure shall normally be as follows: Procedure for conduct of the hearing.

(*a*) The Chair shall introduce all those present at the hearing and explain the powers of a FTP Adjudication Panel.

(*b*) The Chair shall invite the Chair of a FTP Committee (or a person appointed by her or him) to make an opening statement and shall then invite FTP Adjudication Panel members to ask questions.

(*c*) The Chair shall invite the medical student or her or his representative to make a statement and shall then invite FTP Adjudication Panel members to question the student.

(*d*) The Chair shall invite any other persons called upon to attend the hearing (normally to include the Chair of a FTP Committee and Investigator) to make a brief statement and shall then invite FTP Adjudication Panel members to ask questions.

(*e*) At each stage, the Chair shall have discretion to allow reciprocal questioning by all parties.

(*f*) When the Chair is satisfied that a FTP Adjudication Panel has completed its questioning and that the medical student and other persons present have had a full opportunity to convey information to a FTP Adjudication Panel, the student and all other persons not on a FTP Adjudication Panel except the Secretary of a FTP Adjudication Panel shall withdraw. The Secretary of a FTP Adjudication Panel shall remain to provide advice on procedure but shall take no part in a FTP Adjudication Panel reaching its decision on the case itself.

(*g*) A FTP Adjudication Panel shall then discuss the case.

(*h*) Those attending the first part of the hearing shall all be invited back into the hearing once a FTP Adjudication Panel has concluded its discussions. A FTP Adjudication Panel shall seek any further clarification which it requires, and may at its discretion call for a further adjournment or adjournments. The Chair shall then outline to the medical student a FTP Adjudication Panel's decision.

60. A FTP Adjudication Panel, following consideration of the case, may make one of the following decisions on the balance of probabilities and by a simple majority (the Chair having a casting vote if necessary):

(*a*) declare that the medical student is fit to practise and that he or she may continue on the course with no conditions or other sanctions;

(*b*) declare that the student is fit to practise but provide a formal warning which should be added to the medical student's record;

(*c*) declare that there are grounds for concern as to the student's fitness to practise and impose other sanctions in respect of the student's continuation with her or his course of study for the Second or Final M.B. Examinations which may include

(i) that the student be temporarily suspended from the Medical Students Register, specifying the arrangements for monitoring by the FTP Committee of the suspension (including a minimum period if appropriate) and the arrangements for the termination of suspension, or

(ii) that the student be subject to other conditions.

(*d*) declare that the medical student is unfit to practise, that the medical student be removed from the Medical Students Register and that the General Medical Council be informed of this sanction.

Decision. **61.** The Secretary of a FTP Adjudication Panel shall confirm the decision of a FTP Adjudication Panel and the reasons for the decision in writing normally within seven days, specifying any time period or sanction that may apply, to the medical student and also to the Chair of the FTP Committee, the MVSPP, the Senior Tutor of the student's College, the Director of Medical Education in the School of Clinical Medicine and, as appropriate, the Director of Education in the School of Biological Sciences.

Appeal

62. A medical student and the FTP Committee shall have the right of appeal to an Appeal Panel in respect of a decision of a FTP Adjudication Panel as set out in these procedures.

63. A medical student and the FTP Committee may give notice of appeal in respect of a decision of a FTP Adjudication Panel on only one or more of the following grounds:

(*a*) irregularity in process;

(*b*) the coming to light of fresh evidence, which was not available and/or presented for a good reason; and/or

(*c*) the proportionality of a sanction imposed by the FTP Adjudication Panel.

64. A notice of appeal shall be in writing and shall be received by the Registrary within twenty-eight days of the date of notification of a FTP Adjudication Panel decision. The notice of appeal shall state the grounds on which the appeal is made and provide all material relied upon for the appeal. On receipt of the notice of appeal, and if the Registrary considers that there are grounds for an appeal as set out within these procedures, the Registrary shall appoint an Appeal Panel to hear the appeal. The parties shall not be entitled to rely during the appeal hearing, without the permission of the Appeal Panel, on any grounds other than those set out in the notice of appeal.

65. During the consideration of the appeal, the decision of a FTP Adjudication Panel shall remain in force.

66. An Appeal Panel hearing shall be arranged as soon as possible, and normally within three months of the date of the Registrary receiving the notice of appeal, in accordance with the following procedures: Appeal Panel hearing procedures.

(*a*) The Clerk of the Appeal Panel shall inform the medical student and the Chair of the FTP Committee of the persons appointed to be members of the Appeal Panel. If the medical student or the Chair of the FTP Committee has good cause to object to the membership of the Appeal Panel, he or she shall provide grounds to the Clerk of the Appeal Panel in writing within seven days or as determined by the Chair of the Appeal Panel. The Vice-Chancellor shall decide whether that member of the Appeal Panel should be replaced and, if the Vice-Chancellor decides that the member should be replaced, a replacement member shall be designated by the Vice-Chancellor (in the case of the Chair) or drawn by lot (in the case of any other member). The Clerk of the Appeal Panel shall inform the parties accordingly. The decision of the Vice-Chancellor shall be final.

(*b*) Any documentation to be considered by the Appeal Panel shall be sent to the parties and the members of the Appeal Panel at least fourteen days before the hearing.

(*c*) The medical student may be accompanied by a member of the University or other representative chosen by the medical student who must inform the Secretary to the Appeal Panel of the identity of the person and the capacity in which he or she is attending seven days in advance of the hearing. The medical student's Senior Tutor (or a deputy appointed by the Senior Tutor), if not nominated by the student, shall, with the agreement of the student, be entitled to be present.

(*d*) The hearing shall be held in private unless the Chair of the Appeal Panel agrees to a request from the student that the hearing be held in public.

(*e*) The Chair of the FTP Adjudication Panel, or a person appointed by her or him, shall represent the FTP Adjudication Panel at the Appeal Panel hearing. The Chair of the FTP Committee, or a person appointed by her or him, shall represent the FTP Committee at the Appeal Panel hearing.

67. The Appeal Panel shall consider its decision in private. The Clerk of the Appeal Panel shall be present throughout the hearing and throughout consideration by the Appeal Panel of its decision.

68. The Appeal Panel may confirm, quash, amend, or refer back the decision to the same, or a newly constituted, FTP Adjudication Panel.

69. As soon as possible, normally within seven days from the Appeal Panel hearing, the Clerk of the Appeal Panel shall inform the medical student in writing of the decision and the reasons for the decision. That notification shall specify whether the case is to be referred back to a FTP Panel or, if not, the notification should be a Completion of Procedures letter and inform the medical student that she or he may refer the matter to the Office of the Independent Adjudicator for Higher Education. The Secretary to the Appeal Panel shall also inform the Chair of the FTP Adjudication Panel, the Chair of the FTP Committee, the MVSPP, the Senior Tutor of the student's College, the Director of Medical Education in the School of Clinical Medicine and, as appropriate, the Director of Education in the School of Biological Sciences. Decision.

Record and declaration

70. The FTP Committee and the Faculty Boards of Biology or Clinical Medicine, as appropriate, shall make a record of any sanctions imposed (including a formal warning, a suspension or removal from the Medical Students Register, or other conditions) or undertakings provided by a medical student relating to arrangements for the monitoring or supervision of her or his conduct, health, or performance. The FTP Committee shall determine whether the information is to be kept permanently on the medical student's record, until a further review or until one year after the student has obtained full registration with the General Medical Council.

71. A medical student upon whom conditions have been imposed shall be required to confirm in writing that he or she shall comply with such conditions.

72. A medical student who has undertaken to comply with arrangements for the management and supervision of her or his conduct, health, or performance shall be required to confirm in writing that he or she will comply with the arrangements.

73. When applying to the General Medical Council for provisional registration, a student shall inform the General Medical Council of the details of any referral to the Fitness to Practise Committee and any and all matters that might have a bearing on her or his fitness to practise.

PROCEDURES TO DETERMINE FITNESS TO PRACTISE OF PRECLINICAL AND CLINICAL VETERINARY STUDENTS

Grace 1 of 29 January 2014

Introduction

1. The Royal College of Veterinary Surgeons (RCVS) has a duty to ensure that veterinary students are fit to practise veterinary medicine when they apply for registration. The following regulations shall govern the procedures in the University to ensure that preclinical and clinical veterinary students are fit to practise veterinary medicine.

Veterinary Students Register.

2. There shall be a Veterinary Students Register, which shall be maintained by the Faculty Boards of Biology and Veterinary Medicine through a Veterinary Fitness to Practise Committee (VFTP Committee).

3. Any person or body may refer any matter which gives a cause for concern about a veterinary student's fitness to practise to the VFTP Committee in accordance with these procedures.

Adjudication Panel.

4. Where the VFTP Committee considers that there is a question to be determined concerning the fitness to practise of a veterinary student, the VFTP Committee shall appoint an Investigator who shall report to the VFTP Committee. Having considered the Investigator's report, the VFTP Committee may refer the matter to a Fitness to Practise Adjudication Panel (VFTP Adjudication Panel) to consider whether the student is fit to practise veterinary medicine or whether to impose sanctions (which include formal warnings, conditions and suspension, or removal from the Veterinary Students Register).

Appeal.

5. A veterinary student shall, if required to do so, attend meetings and/or hearings with the VFTP Committee, an Investigator, and a VFTP Adjudication Panel. A veterinary student and the VFTP Committee may appeal to a Fitness to Practise Appeal Panel (VFTP Appeal Panel) on grounds specified in these procedures.

6. Fitness to practise issues can arise from a student's conduct, health, or performance. Veterinary students have a responsibility to report any illness or disability that may affect their fitness to practise to their Senior Tutor or Director of Studies and, as appropriate, to the Director of Teaching in the Faculty of Veterinary Medicine or the Director of Education (Biological Sciences) in the Faculty of Biology.

Medical and Veterinary Student Progress Panel.

7. The University also has a duty to support its veterinary students. The Medical and Veterinary Student Progress Panel (MVSPP) monitors the academic performance and progress of preclinical and clinical veterinary students, including issues relating to ill health and any other cause for concern which does not merit a referral to the VFTP Committee.

8. A student who wishes to remain on the Veterinary Students Register will be expected to co-operate with obtaining such reports from the University's Occupational Health Service and/or other experts as may be deemed necessary.

9. When applying for registration with the Royal College of Veterinary Surgeons (RCVS) veterinary students will be required to inform the RCVS of the details of any referral to the VFTP Committee and any and all matters that might have a bearing on his or her fitness to practise.

The Composition, Roles, and Duties of the Fitness to Practise Bodies

Fitness to Practise Committee (VFTP Committee)

Membership.

10. The VFTP Committee shall comprise a minimum of three members:

(*a*) a Chair appointed by the Faculty Board of Veterinary Medicine who shall be a practising veterinary surgeon;

(*b*) one member appointed by the Faculty Board of Veterinary Medicine who shall be a practising veterinary surgeon; and (*c*) one member appointed by the Faculty Board of Biology who shall be a member of the Regent House and not normally a registered veterinary surgeon.

11. No member of the VFTP Committee shall have had any material involvement or interest in respect of each individual case before the VFTP Committee. All members of the VFTP Committee shall be required to make a declaration of interest in the case.

12. Members of the VFTP Committee shall be appointed in the Michaelmas Term to serve for three years from 1 January following their appointment.

13. The Faculty Boards of Veterinary Medicine and Biology shall in addition jointly maintain a Veterinary Fitness to Practise Support Panel (VFTP Support Panel). Every three years in the Michaelmas Term, or as necessary: Veterinary Fitness to Practise Support Panel.

(*a*) the Faculty Board of Veterinary Medicine shall appoint to the VFTP Support Panel at least six members qualifying for appointment to the VFTP Committee under Regulation 10(*b*);

(*b*) the Faculty Board of Biology shall appoint to the VFTP Support Panel at least six members of the Regent House qualifying for appointment to the VFTP Committee under Regulation 10(*c*).

14. In the event of a member of the VFTP Committee appointed under Regulations 10(*a*) or 10(*b*) having a conflict of interest in any case, a replacement member qualifying for appointment to the VFTP Committee under those regulations shall be appointed from the VFTP Support Panel for the purposes of the case in question by the Chair of the Faculty Board of Veterinary Medicine.

15. In the event of a member of the VFTP Committee appointed under Regulation 10(*c*) having a conflict of interest in any case, a replacement member qualifying for appointment to the VFTP Committee under that regulation shall be appointed from the VFTP Support Panel for the purposes of the case in question by the Chair of the Faculty Board of Biology.

16. The Faculty Board of Veterinary Medicine shall appoint a person to be Secretary to the VFTP Committee. Secretary.

17. The VFTP Committee may co-opt a maximum of two members to the VFTP Committee from the VFTP Support Panel or elsewhere and may require such reports to be prepared as it considers necessary. Co-opted members.

18. The duties of the VFTP Committee shall be: Duties of the Committee.

(*a*) to maintain the Veterinary Students Register on behalf of the Faculty Boards of Biology and of Veterinary Medicine;

(*b*) to produce and keep under review a code of conduct to be observed by veterinary students;

(*c*) to consider all expressions of concern about a veterinary student's fitness to practise and, if appropriate, to appoint an Investigator from the VFTP Support Panel who shall have discretion to investigate any issues relating to the student's fitness to practise medicine;

(*d*) to consider an Investigator's report, make recommendations and, if appropriate, refer a veterinary student to a VFTP Adjudication Panel;

(*e*) to keep under review these Fitness to Practise procedures and to recommend changes to the Faculty Boards of Biology and Veterinary Medicine, who shall report such changes to the University for approval.

19. The VFTP Committee shall meet at least once a year in the Michaelmas Term and whenever there is any business to consider. Three members shall constitute a quorum. The Chair shall have a casting vote, if necessary. In the absence of the Chair for a meeting of the VFTP Committee, the member appointed under Regulation 10(*b*) may become Chair for that meeting, or the meeting may be adjourned. Meetings.

20. The VFTP Committee shall submit the minutes of its meetings to the Faculty Boards of Biology and of Veterinary Medicine and to the Veterinary Education Committee.

Fitness to Practise Adjudication Panel (VFTP Adjudication Panel)

21. A VFTP Adjudication Panel shall comprise a Chair and two other members, all of whom shall be appointed by the Registrary from the VFTP Support Panel as soon as practicable after she or he has been notified (by the Secretary to the VFTP Committee) that a case has been referred to a VFTP Adjudication Panel. The Chair shall be a practising registered veterinary practitioner. Chair and members.

22. The three members of a VFTP Adjudication Panel shall constitute the quorum for a hearing of the VFTP Adjudication Panel at which a veterinary student's fitness to practise is determined. The Chair shall have a casting vote, if necessary. Quorum.

23. A VFTP Adjudication Panel shall decide whether a veterinary student is fit to practise medicine and should remain on the Veterinary Students Register and/or should be subject to sanctions.

24. No member of a VFTP Adjudication Panel shall have had any material involvement or interest in the case. All members of a VFTP Adjudication Panel shall be required to make a declaration of interest in respect of the case. A replacement member shall be appointed by the Registrary from the VFTP Support Panel in the event of a conflict of interest.

25. A VFTP Adjudication Panel may require such reports to be prepared as it considers necessary.

Secretary. **26.** The Secretary of the veterinary student's Faculty Board, or his or her nominated deputy, shall serve as Secretary to a VFTP Adjudication Panel. For the purpose of these regulations, preclinical students are assigned to the Faculty of Biology and clinical students to the Faculty of Veterinary Medicine.

Fitness to Practise Appeal Panel (VFTP Appeal Panel)

27. An Appeal Panel shall be appointed to consider an appeal which is made by a veterinary student or by the VFTP Committee in respect of a decision of a VFTP Adjudication Panel.

Panels. **28.** The Council of the University shall maintain three panels, panel (*a*), panel (*b*), and panel (*c*), from which members of an Appeal Panel shall be appointed as follows:

panel (*a*): persons who are legally qualified or who have had experience of acting in a judicial capacity, not being members of the Council;

panel (*b*): members of the Regent House not being members of the VFTP Committee, VFTP Support Panel, or VFTP Adjudication Panel, or of the Faculties of Biology or Veterinary Medicine;

panel (*c*): members of the academic staff of a UK Veterinary School, being practising RCVS-registered veterinary practitioners, who are not members of the Regent House.

29. The Council shall appoint in the Michaelmas Term each year such number of persons as they shall see fit to serve as members of each panel for three years from 1 January following their appointment.

Members. **30.** An Appeal Panel shall consist of three members:

(*a*) one person designated by the Vice-Chancellor from panel (*a*), who shall be the Chair of the Appeal Panel;

(*b*) one drawn by lot from panel (*b*);

(*c*) one drawn by lot from panel (*c*).

31. No member of an Appeal Panel shall have had any material involvement or interest in the case. All members of the Appeal Panel shall be required to make a declaration of interest in respect of the case. In the event of a conflict of interest, an alternative member shall be appointed by the Vice-Chancellor or by lot, as appropriate.

Clerk. **32.** The Registrary, or a person nominated by the Registrary, shall act as Clerk of the Appeal Panel.

Quorum. **33.** The three members of the Appeal Panel shall constitute the quorum. The Chair shall have a casting vote, if necessary.

Fitness to Practise Procedures

34. The consideration of whether or not a veterinary student is fit to practise medicine shall take place in accordance with the following procedures which may comprise of at least three stages, a preliminary consideration by the VFTP Committee, an investigation, and an adjudication by a VFTP Adjudication Panel, and may be followed by a final appeal stage.

35. If at any stage the Chair of any of the bodies involved considers that the veterinary student may have committed an offence under the criminal law or against the discipline of the University, the Chair shall suspend proceedings and refer the circumstances for consideration by the police or to the University Advocate under Statute D, as appropriate. In such instances, the body or bodies shall not normally reach a decision on the student's fitness to practise until either the police or University Advocate (as appropriate) has confirmed that it is not intended to institute proceedings against the veterinary student, or, if proceedings are taken, until the criminal courts or University Courts (as appropriate) have ruled finally on the matter. Pending the outcome of any consideration by the police and the criminal courts and/or the University Advocate and the University Courts, the VFTP Committee and its Chair shall review the student's status and take any measures under these procedures which are considered necessary.

36. The VFTP Committee, the Investigator, a VFTP Adjudication Panel, and the Appeal Panel may obtain legal advice through the Registrary to assist with the performance of their duties under these procedures.

37. Any notification to a veterinary student under these procedures may be sent to the veterinary student's University email address.

Preliminary stage involving the Fitness to Practise Committee

38. Any expression of concern that a veterinary student may not be fit to practise medicine shall be made in writing to the Secretary of the VFTP Committee; it shall show clearly the author's name and address. Anonymous referrals shall only be acted upon in exceptional circumstances as the VFTP Committee sees fit, having regard to the seriousness of the issues raised and the fairness to any individuals mentioned in the referral. The VFTP Committee may also consider that the identity of individuals, although known to the VFTP Committee, may need to be withheld or protected in exceptional circumstances.

39. The Secretary of the VFTP Committee shall communicate the expression of concern to the Chair of the VFTP Committee who may take Chair's action in respect of any measures which are considered necessary or appropriate pending consideration by the VFTP Committee.

40. The Secretary of the VFTP Committee shall inform the veterinary student of the details of any expression of concern and, at the discretion of the Chair of the VFTP Committee, arrange for the student to attend a meeting of the VFTP Committee. During any meeting with the VFTP Committee, the veterinary student may be accompanied by a member of the University or other representative chosen by the veterinary student who shall notify the Secretary of the VFTP Committee two days in advance of any meeting if he/she will be accompanied and by whom.

41. The Secretary of the VFTP Committee shall inform the veterinary student of the persons appointed to be members of the VFTP Committee. If the veterinary student has good cause to object to the membership of the VFTP Committee, he or she shall provide grounds to the Secretary of the VFTP Committee in writing within seven days. In the case of a member appointed under Regulation 10(*a*) or (*b*), the Chair of the Faculty Board of Veterinary Medicine shall decide whether to replace that member of the VFTP Committee and shall appoint an alternative member as considered appropriate. In the case of a member appointed under Regulation 10(*c*), the Chair of the Faculty Board of Biology shall decide whether to replace that member of the VFTP Committee and shall appoint an alternative member as considered appropriate. The Secretary of the VFTP Committee shall inform the veterinary student accordingly. The decision of the Chair of the Faculty Board of Veterinary Medicine or of the Chair of the Faculty Board of Biology shall be final.

42. The VFTP Committee shall decide whether the veterinary student shall during the course of any fitness to practise procedures:

(*a*) continue her or his studies without limitation;

(*b*) continue her or his studies under specified conditions;

(*c*) be prohibited from entering specified clinical facilities as a veterinary student; and/or

(*d*) be provisionally suspended from the Veterinary Students Register and therefore from the clinical components of the course.

43. The VFTP Committee may, pending the outcome of any fitness to practise procedures, review and change a decision regarding a veterinary student's status and any measures which are considered necessary.

44. The VFTP Committee shall determine whether the matter can and should be dealt with informally, whether the matter should be referred back to the Student Progress Panel (MVSPP), or whether an Investigator should be appointed to investigate the student's conduct, health, and/or performance. The VFTP Committee shall normally take this initial decision within one month from the date of receipt of the expression of concern.

45. If the University Advocate institutes proceedings against the veterinary student under Statute D, any subsequent judgement of a University Court may be considered as evidence within any fitness to practise procedures. If a University Court finds that a charge is proven against the student then that Procedures under Statute D.

finding shall be conclusive evidence that the veterinary student in question has committed the offence against the discipline of the University with which he or she was charged.

Investigation

46. If the VFTP Committee decides to commence an investigation, the Secretary of the VFTP Committee shall write to the veterinary student concerned and to the Senior Tutor of the student's College stating that an investigation of the veterinary student's fitness to practise is going to take place. The letter to the veterinary student shall state the nature of the expression of concern and the grounds for commencing the investigation.

Investigator. **47.** The VFTP Committee shall appoint an Investigator from the VFTP Support Panel who has had no material involvement or interest in this case. The Investigator shall interview the veterinary student concerned, the maker of the allegation (unless an anonymous concern has been permitted), and any other relevant persons. A formal note of each interview shall be prepared by the Investigator and, if possible, agreed with the person who has been interviewed. A written report shall be prepared and submitted by the Investigator to the VFTP Committee.

48. The VFTP Committee, an Investigator, and a VFTP Adjudication Panel may, at any stage, require reports to be prepared by the Occupational Health Service and/or other experts as to the student's fitness to practise and will expect the student to co-operate with obtaining such reports in order for those bodies to discharge their duties to consider the student's fitness to practise. All such reports shall be co-ordinated through the VFTP Committee.

49. During any interview with the Investigator, the veterinary student may be accompanied by a member of the University or other representative chosen by the veterinary student who shall notify the Investigator two days in advance of any meeting if he/she will be accompanied and by whom.

50. On receipt of the Investigator's report, the VFTP Committee shall take one of the following decisions:

(*a*) that no further action be taken;

(*b*) that there is no serious issue to be determined with regard to the veterinary student's fitness to practise, but that the veterinary student would benefit from remedial measures being put in place; the Chair of the VFTP Committee shall on behalf of the VFTP Committee (i) agree such measures with the veterinary student, the student's Senior Tutor, and the Director of Teaching in the Department of Veterinary Medicine or the Director of Education in the Faculty of Biology as appropriate, and then so inform the Secretary of the VFTP Committee in writing, or (ii) in the event of failure to agree such measures, the VFTP Committee shall refer the matter to the VFTP Adjudication Panel; or

(*c*) that there may be a serious issue to be determined concerning the veterinary student's fitness to practise and shall refer the matter to the VFTP Adjudication Panel.

Decision. **51.** The Secretary of the VFTP Committee shall inform the veterinary student, the MVSPP, and the student's Senior Tutor in writing of the VFTP Committee's decision and of any agreed measures normally within seven days. Correspondence from the Secretary informing the student shall be submitted to the next full meeting of the VFTP Committee.

Adjudication by VFTP Adjudication Panel

52. If a veterinary student is referred by the VFTP Committee to a VFTP Adjudication Panel, the Chair of the VFTP Adjudication Panel shall determine the procedure to be adopted by the VFTP Adjudication Panel which shall normally include:

(*a*) informing the veterinary student of the persons appointed to be members of a VFTP Adjudication Panel;

(*b*) providing the veterinary student with copies of the documents provided by the VFTP Committee to a VFTP Adjudication Panel, including the Investigator's report;

(*c*) informing the veterinary student of the names of any persons who may be asked to attend a VFTP Adjudication Panel to give evidence and setting out the basis upon which the veterinary student may call persons who may have information relevant to the case to give evidence (whether they are members of the University or not) either orally at the hearing or in writing;

(*d*) setting a timetable for the progress of the proceedings, including time limits for each step of the proceedings and a date, time, and place for the hearing.

53. The Secretary of the VFTP Adjudication Panel shall inform the veterinary student and the Chair of the VFTP Committee of the procedure to be followed. The Chair of the VFTP Adjudication Panel may at any stage of the proceedings hold a case management meeting at which she or he may (i) review the progress of the proceedings, and in particular the extent to which any timetable previously set by the Chair has been complied with, (ii) issue or vary directions or time limits for the further conduct of the proceedings, and/or (iii) set or vary a date, time, or place for the hearing. The Secretary of the VFTP Adjudication Panel shall inform the veterinary student and the Secretary of the VFTP Committee of the date, time and place of a case management meeting at least seven days in advance of such meeting.

Objection to members of the Panel.

54. If the veterinary student has good cause to object to the membership of a VFTP Adjudication Panel, he or she shall provide grounds to the Secretary of a VFTP Adjudication Panel in writing within seven days of being notified of the membership of the VFTP Adjudication Panel. The Registrary shall decide whether to replace that member of a VFTP Adjudication Panel and shall appoint an alternative member from the VFTP Support Panel as considered appropriate. The Secretary of a VFTP Adjudication Panel shall inform the veterinary student accordingly. The decision of the Registrary shall be final.

55. The veterinary student shall attend all case management meetings and hearings of a VFTP Adjudication Panel in person, unless prevented by exceptional circumstances. If the veterinary student fails to attend any case management meeting or any hearing without reasonable explanation, a VFTP Adjudication Panel may, at its discretion, consider the case in the veterinary student's absence.

56. The veterinary student may choose to be accompanied by a member of the University or other representative chosen by the veterinary student who must inform the Secretary of the VFTP Adjudication Panel of the identity of the individual and the capacity in which he or she is attending as soon as practicable and at least four days in advance of the case management meeting or hearing.

57. The veterinary student's Senior Tutor (or a deputy appointed by the Senior Tutor), if not nominated by the student, shall be entitled, with the student's consent, to be present at any case management meeting or hearing.

Private hearing.

58. Case management meetings and hearings of the VFTP Adjudication Panel shall be conducted in private unless the Chair of a VFTP Adjudication Panel agrees to a request from the student for any case management meeting or hearing to be held in public.

Procedure for conduct of the hearing.

59. A Chair of the VFTP Adjudication Panel shall determine the procedure for the conduct of a VFTP Adjudication Panel hearing to consider a veterinary student's fitness to practise. The procedure shall normally be as follows:

(*a*) The Chair shall introduce all those present at the hearing and explain the powers of a VFTP Adjudication Panel.

(*b*) The Chair shall invite the Chair of a VFTP Committee (or a person appointed by him or her) to make an opening statement and shall then invite VFTP Adjudication Panel members to ask questions.

(*c*) The Chair shall invite the veterinary student or her or his representative to make a statement and shall then invite VFTP Adjudication Panel members to question the student.

(*d*) The Chair shall invite any other persons called upon to attend the hearing (normally to include the Chair of a VFTP Committee and Investigator) to make a brief statement and shall then invite VFTP Adjudication Panel members to ask questions.

(*e*) At each stage, the Chair shall have discretion to allow reciprocal questioning by all parties.

(*f*) When the Chair is satisfied that a VFTP Adjudication Panel has completed its questioning and that the veterinary student and other persons present have had a full opportunity to convey information to a VFTP Adjudication Panel, the student and all other persons not on a VFTP Adjudication Panel except the Secretary of a VFTP Adjudication Panel shall withdraw. The Secretary of a VFTP Adjudication Panel shall remain to provide advice on procedure but shall take no part in a VFTP Adjudication Panel reaching its decision on the case itself.

(*g*) A VFTP Adjudication Panel shall then discuss the case.

(*h*) Those attending the first part of the hearing shall all be invited back into the hearing once a VFTP Adjudication Panel has concluded its discussions. A VFTP Adjudication Panel shall seek any further clarification which it requires, and may at its discretion call for a further adjournment or adjournments. The Chair shall then outline to the veterinary student a VFTP Adjudication Panel's decision.

60. A VFTP Adjudication Panel, following consideration of the case, may make one of the following decisions on the balance of probabilities and by a simple majority (the Chair having a casting vote if necessary):

(*a*) declare that the veterinary student is fit to practise and that he or she may continue on the course with no conditions or other sanctions;

(*b*) declare that the student is fit to practise but provide a formal warning which should be added to the veterinary student's record;

(*c*) declare that there are grounds for concern as to the student's fitness to practise and impose other sanctions in respect of the student's continuation with her or his course of study for the Second or Final Vet. M.B. Examinations which may include

(i) that the student be temporarily suspended from the Veterinary Students Register, specifying the arrangements for monitoring by the VFTP Committee of the suspension (including a minimum period if appropriate) and the arrangements for the termination of suspension, or

(ii) that the student be subject to other conditions.

(*d*) declare that the veterinary student is unfit to practise, that the veterinary student be removed from the Veterinary Students Register, and that the Royal College of Veterinary Surgeons be informed of this sanction.

Decision.

61. The Secretary of a VFTP Adjudication Panel shall confirm the decision of a VFTP Adjudication Panel and the reasons for the decision in writing normally within seven days, specifying any time period or sanction that may apply, to the veterinary student and also to the Chair of the VFTP Committee, the MVSPP, the Senior Tutor of the student's College, the Director of Teaching in the Department of Veterinary Medicine and, as appropriate, the Director of Education in the School of the Biological Sciences.

Appeal

62. A veterinary student and the VFTP Committee shall have the right of appeal to an Appeal Panel in respect of a decision of a VFTP Adjudication Panel as set out in these procedures.

63. A veterinary student and the VFTP Committee may give notice of appeal in respect of a decision of a VFTP Adjudication Panel on only one or more of the following grounds:

(*a*) irregularity in process;

(*b*) the coming to light of fresh evidence, which was not available and/or presented for a good reason; and/or

(*c*) the proportionality of a sanction imposed by the VFTP Adjudication Panel.

64. A notice of appeal shall be in writing and shall be received by the Registrary within twenty-eight days of the date of notification of a VFTP Adjudication Panel decision. The notice of appeal shall state the grounds on which the appeal is made and provide all material relied upon for the appeal. On receipt of the notice of appeal, and if the Registrary considers that there are grounds for an appeal as set out within these procedures, the Registrary shall appoint an Appeal Panel to hear the appeal. The parties shall not be entitled to rely during the appeal hearing, without the permission of the Appeal Panel, on any grounds other than those set out in the notice of appeal.

65. During the consideration of the appeal, the decision of a VFTP Adjudication Panel shall remain in force.

Appeal Panel hearing procedures.

66. An Appeal Panel hearing shall be arranged as soon as possible, and normally within three months of the date of the Registrary receiving the notice of appeal, in accordance with the following procedures:

(*a*) The Clerk of the Appeal Panel shall inform the veterinary student and the Chair of the VFTP Committee of the persons appointed to be members of the Appeal Panel. If the veterinary student or the Chair of the VFTP Committee has good cause to object to the membership of the Appeal Panel, he or she shall provide grounds to the Clerk of the Appeal Panel in writing within seven days or as determined by the Chair of the Appeal Panel. The Vice-Chancellor shall decide whether that member of the Appeal Panel should be replaced and, if the Vice-Chancellor decides that the member should be replaced, a replacement member shall be designated by the Vice-Chancellor (in the case of the Chair) or drawn by lot (in the case of any other member). The

Clerk of the Appeal Panel shall inform the parties accordingly. The decision of the Vice-Chancellor shall be final.

(*b*) Any documentation to be considered by the Appeal Panel shall be sent to the parties and the members of the Appeal Panel at least fourteen days before the hearing.

(*c*) The veterinary student may be accompanied by a member of the University or other representative chosen by the veterinary student who must inform the Secretary to the Appeal Panel of the identity of the person and the capacity in which he or she is attending seven days in advance of the hearing. The veterinary student's Senior Tutor (or a deputy appointed by the Senior Tutor), if not nominated by the student, shall, with the agreement of the student, be entitled to be present.

(*d*) The hearing shall be held in private unless the Chair of the Appeal Panel agrees to a request from the student that the hearing be held in public.

(*e*) The Chair of the VFTP Adjudication Panel, or a person appointed by her or him, shall represent the VFTP Adjudication Panel at the Appeal Panel hearing. The Chair of the VFTP Committee, or a person appointed by her or him, shall represent the VFTP Committee at the Appeal Panel hearing.

67. The Appeal Panel shall consider its decision in private. The Clerk of the Appeal Panel shall be present throughout the hearing and throughout consideration by the Appeal Panel of its decision.

68. The Appeal Panel may confirm, quash, amend, or refer back the decision to the same, or a newly constituted, VFTP Adjudication Panel.

69. As soon as possible, normally within seven days from the Appeal Panel hearing, the Clerk of the Appeal Panel shall inform the veterinary student in writing of the decision and the reasons for the decision. That notification shall specify whether the case is to be referred back to a VFTP Panel or, if not, the notification should be a Completion of Procedures letter and inform the veterinary student that she or he may refer the matter to the Office of the Independent Adjudicator for Higher Education. The Secretary to the Appeal Panel shall also inform the Chair of the VFTP Adjudication Panel, the Chair of the VFTP Committee, the MVSPP, the Senior Tutor of the student's College, the Director of Teaching in the Department of Veterinary Medicine and, as appropriate, the Director of Education in the School of the Biological Sciences. Decision.

Record and declaration

70. The VFTP Committee and the Faculty Boards of Biology or Veterinary Medicine, as appropriate, shall make a record of any sanctions imposed (including a formal warning, a suspension or removal from the Veterinary Students Register, or other conditions) or undertakings provided by a veterinary student relating to arrangements for the monitoring or supervision of her or his conduct, health, or performance. The VFTP Committee shall determine whether the information is to be kept permanently on the veterinary student's record, until a further review, or until one year after the student has obtained full registration with the Royal College of Veterinary Surgeons.

71. A veterinary student upon whom conditions have been imposed shall be required to confirm in writing that he or she shall comply with such conditions.

72. A veterinary student who has undertaken to comply with arrangements for the management and supervision of her or his conduct, health, or performance shall be required to confirm in writing that he or she will comply with the arrangements.

73. When applying to the Royal College of Veterinary Surgeons for registration, a student shall inform the Royal College of Veterinary Surgeons of the details of any referral to the Fitness to Practise Committee and any and all matters that might have a bearing on his or her fitness to practise.

PROCEDURES TO DETERMINE THE PROGRESS OF PRECLINICAL AND CLINICAL MEDICAL STUDENTS AND PRECLINICAL AND CLINICAL VETERINARY STUDENTS

Amended by Grace 1 of 29 January 2014

Introduction

1. The Medical and Veterinary Student Progress Panel (MVSPP) shall be a joint body of the Faculty Boards of Biology, Clinical Medicine, and Veterinary Medicine in consultation with the Colleges.

2. The MVSPP shall review or advise on the progress of a student having regard to:

(i) academic performance including failure in M.B. or Vet.M.B. examinations;

(ii) ill health.

Additionally, the advice of the MVSPP may be sought as a result of:

(iii) cause for concern about the student's conduct but not meriting immediate referral to the Fitness to Practise Committee or Veterinary Fitness to Practise Committee.

The Roles, Duties, and Composition of the Medical and Veterinary Student Progress Panel (MVSPP)

3. The MVSPP shall consist of:

(*a*) the Director of Medical Education in the Clinical School (who shall chair the MVSPP);

(*b*) the Director of Education (Biological Sciences) in the Faculty of Biology;

(*c*) the Director of Teaching in the Veterinary School;

(*d*) the Associate Clinical Dean, West Suffolk Hospital;

(*e*) three members appointed by the Senior Tutors' Committee;

(*f*) one member appointed by the Faculty Board of Biology;

(*g*) one member appointed by the Faculty Board of Clinical Medicine;

(*h*) one member appointed by the Faculty Board of Veterinary Medicine;

(*i*) an administrative officer appointed by the Faculty Board of Clinical Medicine and an administrative officer appointed by the Faculty Board of Veterinary Medicine (who shall act as joint secretaries to the MVSPP).

4. In respect of each individual case before the MVSPP, all members of the MVSPP shall be required to make a declaration of interest in the case.

5. Members in classes (*e*)–(*h*) shall be appointed in the Michaelmas Term to serve for three years from 1 January following their appointment.

6. The duties of the MVSPP shall include:

(*a*) to meet termly, and whenever there is any business to consider, to provide expert advice to the Colleges, and to work with Colleges to ensure that students who have not achieved the required academic standard or are experiencing health or other personal problems receive appropriate support;

(*b*) to review the progression of all students annually in the Michaelmas Term;

(*c*) to review all requests made on behalf of medical and veterinary students for additional attempts in exceptional circumstances at M.B. and Vet.M.B. examinations, and to give advice to the relevant Faculty Board;

(*d*) to prepare an annual summary report on any issues arising for the attention of Senior Tutors and Faculty Boards.

7. Five members shall constitute a quorum. The MVSPP shall report to the Faculty Boards of Biology, Clinical Medicine, and Veterinary Medicine.

Appeal Process for F1 Doctors

Introduction

1. A holder of the degree of M.B.B.Chir. from the University who seeks full registration with the General Medical Council (GMC) and who satisfies the requirements of the Medical Act 1983 as to experience, may apply to the University for a Certificate of Experience under Section 10 of that Act following satisfactory completion of an approved Foundation Year Programme (F1 Programme) of placements in a formal employment setting. In these procedures, a doctor with a degree of M.B.B.Chir. from the University on an approved F1 Programme is referred to as a 'F1 doctor'.

2. The initial decision to provide a Certificate of Experience to a F1 doctor who holds a M.B.B.Chir. from the University, is taken, on behalf of the University, by Health Education East of England (HEEoE) which is the Local Education and Training Board (LETB) linked to the University. This decision is based on evidence, collated for the Annual Review of Competency Progression (ARCP), that the F1 doctor has completed the requirements of the Foundation Programme Curriculum for Foundation Year 1. This evidence is collated by the LETB (or equivalent body) linked to the F1 doctor's Foundation School.

3. In these procedures, the LETB (or equivalent body) linked to the F1 doctor's Foundation School is referred to as 'the LETS'. The LETS makes a recommendation to HEEoE on whether the F1 doctor has completed the requirements of the Foundation Programme Curriculum for Foundation Year 1 (approved by the GMC). In any case in which the LETB recommends that the F1 doctor has not completed the requirements of the Foundation

Programme Curriculum and that the F1 doctor be released from the Foundation Programme, HEEoE will decline to issue a Certificate of Experience and the F1 doctor may appeal to the University under these procedures.

4. Such appeals will normally only be heard after the initial period of F1 training has been extended by the LETS due to the F1 doctor concerned being unable to provide evidence of the acquisition of competences and performance in practice in accordance with the requirements of the Foundation Programme curriculum.

5. Appeals with respect to a decision to extend the F1 year of training will normally be heard by the LETS.

The composition, roles, and duties of the F1 Doctor Appeal Panel

6. A F1 Doctor Appeal Panel shall be appointed to consider an appeal which is made by a F1 doctor in respect of a decision by the LETS to recommend the F1 doctor is released from the Foundation Programme (ARCP Outcome 4). A F1 Doctor Appeal Panel shall be appointed by the Registrary, following consultation with the Director of Medical Education of the Clinical School of the University, as soon as practicable after receiving the notice of the appeal. The F1 Doctor Appeal Panel shall comprise the Director of Medical Education of the Clinical School of the University as Chair (or a nominated deputy) and a minimum of four other members, one of whom shall not be a GMC-registered medical practitioner.

7. The Secretary of the Faculty Board of Clinical Medicine, or her or his nominated deputy, shall serve as Clerk to the F1 Doctor Appeal Panel.

8. No member of the F1 Doctor Appeal Panel shall have had any material involvement or interest in respect of the individual case before the panel. All members of the F1 Doctor Appeal Panel shall be required to make a declaration of interest in the case.

F1 Doctor Appeal Panel procedures

9. A F1 doctor may appeal on one or more of the following grounds:

(i) irregularity in the process followed by the LETS;

(ii) the coming to light of fresh evidence, which was not available and/or presented to the LETS for a good reason;

(iii) the recommendation of the LETS was manifestly unreasonable.

10. A notice of appeal shall be in writing and shall be received by the LETS within twenty-one days of the F1 doctor being notified of the decision.

11. The notice of appeal shall state the grounds on which the appeal is made. The F1 doctor shall not be entitled to rely, during the appeal, without the permission of the F1 Doctor Appeal Panel, on any grounds other than those set out in the notice of appeal.

12. On receipt of the notice of appeal, the LETB shall inform the Registrary and the Director of Medical Education of the Clinical School of the University. The Registrary shall then appoint a F1 Doctor Appeal Panel to determine the appeal.

13. If the F1 doctor formally withdraws, in writing, from the F1 Programme at this stage, the LETB shall confirm the position in writing with the F1 doctor and shall inform the Registrary and the Director of Medical Education. The Clerk of the F1 Doctor Appeal Panel shall write to the F1 doctor to confirm that no further action will be taken on the appeal.

14. The Chair of the F1 Doctor Appeal Panel shall determine the procedure to be adopted by the F1 Doctor Appeal Panel which shall normally include:

(*a*) informing the F1 doctor of the persons appointed to be members of the F1 Doctor Appeal Panel;

(*b*) informing the F1 doctor and the LETB of the evidence required for consideration by the F1 Doctor Appeal Panel;

(*c*) informing the F1 doctor and the LETB of the names of any persons who may be asked to attend a F1 Doctor Appeal Panel hearing to give evidence and setting out the basis upon which the F1 doctor may call persons who may have information relevant to the case to give evidence either orally at the hearing or in writing;

(*d*) setting a timetable for the progress of the proceedings, including time limits for each step of the proceedings and making arrangements for any hearing.

15. The Clerk of the Appeal Panel shall inform the F1 doctor of the procedure to be followed and whether he or she is required to attend any appeal hearing.

16. If the F1 doctor has good cause to object to the membership of a F1 Doctor Appeal Panel, he or she shall provide grounds to the Clerk of the F1 Doctor Appeal Panel in writing within seven days of being notified of the membership of the panel. The Registrary shall decide whether to replace that member of the panel and shall appoint an alternative member as considered appropriate. The Clerk of the F1 Doctor Appeal Panel shall inform the F1 doctor accordingly. The decision of the Registrary shall be final.

17. The F1 doctor may choose to be accompanied by another person chosen by her or him. The F1 doctor shall, at least seven days in advance of any hearing, inform the Clerk of the F1 Doctor Appeal Panel of the identity and contact details of any such person, her or his relationship to the F1 doctor (if any) and the capacity in which he or she is attending.

18. The hearing shall be held in private unless the Chair of the F1 Doctor Appeal Panel agrees to a request from the F1 doctor that the hearing be held in public.

19. The Chair of the F1 Doctor Appeal Panel shall determine the procedure for the conduct of any hearing. The Clerk of the F1 Doctor Appeal Panel shall notify the F1 doctor and the members of the panel of the procedure to be followed.

20. The F1 Doctor Appeal Panel shall consider its decision in private. The Clerk of the F1 Doctor Appeal Panel shall be present throughout the hearing and throughout consideration by the panel of its decision.

21. The F1 Doctor Appeal Panel shall normally make a decision on the day of the hearing. If this is not possible the panel shall reserve its decision for a later date to be notified to the parties. The decision of the F1 Doctor Appeal Panel shall be by a simple majority and the Chair shall have a casting vote.

22. The F1 Doctor Appeal Panel may confirm the original decision, or may substitute the previous decision with the recommendation of an alternative course of action in accordance with the options available under F1 Programme guidance.

23. As soon as possible, normally within seven days from the F1 Doctor Appeal Panel hearing, the Clerk of the F1 Doctor Appeal Panel shall inform the F1 doctor in writing of the decision.

24. The decision of the F1 Doctor Appeal Panel is final and there is no further right of appeal within the University.

25. The Faculty Board of Clinical Medicine and the LETS shall make a record of the decision and any recommendations or actions to be taken.

26. The Faculty Board of Clinical Medicine shall send a copy of the record to the LETB, HEEoE, and the General Medical Council.

CHAPTER III

EXAMINATIONS

HONOURS EXAMINATIONS

1. The Honours Examinations of the University shall be the examinations for any undivided Tripos, and the examinations for the several Parts and Sections of Triposes which are divided into Parts or Sections or into Parts and Sections. The term Honours Examination shall not include a Qualifying Examination or Preliminary Examination connected with any Tripos. Honours Examinations.

2. No one who is, or is qualified to be, a member of the Senate, or is, or has been, registered as a Graduate Student shall be a candidate for honours in any Honours Examination.

3. No person shall be a candidate for honours in more than one Honours Examination in the same term.

ALLOWANCES TO CANDIDATES FOR EXAMINATIONS

1. The Council shall have power:

(*a*) to admit to candidature for an examination or for a University Studentship, Scholarship, Exhibition, Prize, or Medal, a person who is not qualified by Ordinance to be a candidate, and Candidature despite Ordinance.

(*b*) to determine that for the purposes of candidature for an examination or competition one or more terms may be disregarded in reckoning the standing of a particular candidate. Leave to intermit.

2. No person who is not qualified by Ordinance, or under the foregoing regulation, or by special Grace, shall be admitted to an examination leading to a degree, diploma, or certificate, except with the approval of the Council who shall have power to determine the conditions of such admission and the fee, if any, to be paid for such admission. The name of a candidate admitted under this regulation to an Honours Examination shall, if he or she satisfies the Examiners, be published in a separate list under the heading: Anomalous candidature.

The following, who are not candidates for honours, have satisfied the Examiners.

3. The Council, on satisfactory evidence supplied by a candidate's Tutor that the candidate has been hindered by illness or other grave cause in preparing for or taking any University examination, except one for which candidates are required to be Graduate Students or one leading to the M.B., B.Chir. Degrees, or the Vet.M.B. Degree, shall have power, when they think fit. Powers of the Council;

(*a*) *If the candidate has been absent from the whole examination*

(i) allow the candidate leave to have disregarded such terms as are necessary in order to put the candidate in standing to take the same examination on a future occasion, as specified by the Council; to give leave to intermit,

or (ii) to make the candidate whichever of the following allowances they may consider appropriate: to make allowances,
allow the candidate the examination;
declare the candidate to have attained the honours standard;

or (iii) if the candidate is a candidate for Part II, Part IIA or Part IIB of a Tripos, to declare the candidate to have deserved the Ordinary B.A. Degree.

or (iv) to put the candidate in standing to proceed as a candidate for another examination, where the candidate would not otherwise be of such standing.

(*b*) *If the candidate has been absent from part of the examination*

(i) to authorize the Examiners to declare the candidate to have deserved honours or to have deserved to have passed the examination, whichever is appropriate; provided that the Examiners shall not make that declaration unless they judge the candidate to have performed with credit in a substantial part of the examination and unless they either are unable to include the candidate in the list of successful candidates or would otherwise have to award the candidate a class that would in their opinion misrepresent his or her abilities; to delegate decisions to Examiners,

or (ii) to make the candidate whichever of the allowances specified in (*a*) they may consider appropriate. to make allowances.

(*c*) *If the candidate has attended the whole of the examination and has failed*

to make the candidate whichever of the allowances specified in (*a*) they may consider appropriate.

(*d*) *If the candidate has attended the whole or part of the examination and has obtained honours by the inclusion of his or her name in one of the classes*

(i) to remove the candidate's name from the class concerned and to declare the candidate to have deserved honours;

or (ii) to authorize the Chair of Examiners, or a deputy appointed by the Chair from among the Examiners, to move the candidate's name to a higher class, provided that such an amendment shall not be made unless the Chair of Examiners or deputy, after consulting at least two other Examiners, is satisfied that the candidate has performed at the standard of the higher class in all but a relatively small part of the examination.

(*e*) *If the candidate has attended part of the examination and has been declared to have deserved honours in accordance with* (*b*)(*i*)

to authorize the Chair of Examiners, or a deputy appointed by the Chair from among the Examiners, to include the candidate's name in one of the classes, provided that such an amendment shall not be made unless the Chair of Examiners or deputy, after consulting at least two other Examiners, is satisfied that the candidate has performed at the standard of the class concerned in all but a relatively small part of the examination.

Honours by allowance.

4. When the Council allow a candidate an examination which is an Honours Examination, such a candidate shall thereby have obtained honours therein.

5. The Council shall not, save in exceptional circumstances, normally make an allowance to a candidate for the B.A. Degree of an examination under Regulation 3 on more than one occasion, save that, for the purpose of this regulation, an allowance under Regulation 3(*a*)(i) shall not be regarded as such an allowance.

Publication of allowances.

6. The names of students to whom the Council make allowances under Regulation 3 (other than under sub-paragraph (*b*)(i)) shall not be appended to the lists of successful candidates for the examinations for which they were severally entered, but shall be published by the Registrary.

Deferment of essays, etc.

7. Where the regulations for an Honours Examination or for a Preliminary Examination provide for a candidate to submit by a specified date a dissertation, thesis, or essay, either in addition to the written papers or in substitution for one or more of them, the Chair of Examiners or the Senior Examiner may on the application of the candidate's Tutor grant a brief extension to a specified date by which the work shall be submitted. A dissertation, thesis, or essay submitted later than the date specified by the Chair of Examiners or the Senior Examiner, or in the regulation concerned if no extension has been granted, shall not be accepted.

8. In the case of a candidate who has been declared to have deserved honours under Regulation 3(*b*)(i) or 3(*d*)(i), the following statement shall be appended to any certificate issued by the Registrary relating to that examination:

This candidate, who was absent from part of the examination for good cause, performed with credit in a substantial part of it. In accordance with the University's regulations the authorities concerned are of the opinion that it would be unfair to classify the candidate on the basis of the incomplete performance since they believe that this would not adequately represent the candidate's attainment. They have accordingly agreed to declare the candidate to have deserved honours in this examination.

Leave for Allowances to Candidates for Examinations: Notice

The Council has given notice (*Reporter*, 2010–11, p. 903)[1] of the procedure required by it when dealing with applications under these regulations:

(i) No application is considered unless it is submitted by the candidate's Tutor.

(ii) An application must state under which regulation or regulations it is made.

(iii) An allowance made under Regulation 1(*b*) or 3(*a*)(i) is normally granted in respect of the three terms of an academical year. Exceptionally it may be granted in respect of the terms of more than one academical year.

(iv) An application made on medical grounds must be supported by a certificate, preferably given by a doctor practising in or near Cambridge or by a counsellor from the University Counselling Service. The Council's Standing Committee on Applications may determine which type of certificate it requires in relation to applications under particular regulations.

(v) An application must include a detailed statement of reasons and be accompanied by copies of all supervision reports.

[1] Amended by Notice (*Reporter*, 2012–13, p. 194).

(vi) An application for exemption from an *academic* condition for taking a particular examination is not normally approved unless the Faculty Board or similar body concerned have given their concurrence, and that concurrence is indispensable in the case of examinations forming part of the requirements for a professional qualification.

(vii) The Council is not empowered to give permission for a candidate to offer a combination of papers, whether within one examination or from more than one examination, which is not provided for by Ordinance or by regulations made under Ordinance. Permission to offer a non-standard combination of papers can be given only by the General Board; such permission will not be granted unless the Faculty Board or other authority concerned are in agreement.

(viii) The Council shall authorize its Standing Committee on Applications to issue notes on the procedures adopted by that Committee in its consideration, on behalf of the Council, of applications for allowances under these regulations.

ENTRIES AND LISTS OF CANDIDATES FOR EXAMINATIONS

Amended by Grace 2 of 11 December 2013

1. These regulations shall apply to all Honours Examinations, Preliminary Examinations, and to any other examinations for which written papers are set (except those covered by the regulations for the Ph.D., M.Sc., and M.Litt. Degrees, and for the M.Phil. Degree), and to the examination for the Postgraduate Certificate in Education. Scope of regulations.

2. In September of each year the Secretary of the Board of Examinations shall circulate to Senior Tutors a Table of Dates giving the dates of the examinations to be held in the following academical year and the dates by which entries of candidates and corrections of those entries are to be submitted. Registrary's Notice.

3. Candidates *in statu pupillari* shall enrol for the examinations listed in Regulation 11 by entering the details, as approved by each student's Director of Studies, into the University's on-line student record database during the period 1 October to 8 November each year. Entries.

4. Entries of candidates *in statu pupillari* into the examinations listed in Regulations 12–15 shall be signed by the candidates concerned and sent to the Board of Examinations by Senior Tutors of Colleges by the date specified by the Board under those regulations.

5. Any entry of a candidate who proposes to offer less than is required by the regulations for the examination concerned shall, unless the entry has been prescribed by a Degree Committee under the general regulations for admission as a Graduate Student, require the sanction of the Council. The name of any such candidate shall not be included in the class-list for the examination concerned.

6. Entries and corrections shall be deemed to have been sent to the Board of Examinations on the day on which they were received at the Board.

7. If the latest date for the submission of entries or corrections falls on a Saturday or Sunday, they shall be due on the previous Friday. If the day for the issue of a list of candidates falls on a Saturday or a Sunday, the list shall be issued on the previous Friday.

8. For every examination a first list of candidates shall be issued, followed by a final, corrected list. The first list and the final list for each examination shall be sent by the Secretary of the Board of Examinations List of candidates.

(*a*) to the Chair of Examiners concerned, or, if there is no Chair, to the senior resident Examiner;

(*b*) to the Head of the Faculty or the Department concerned or, in the case of Faculties not organized in Departments, to the Secretary of the Faculty Board;

(*c*) to the Senior Tutor of each College.[1]

9. For the examinations specified in Regulations 11–15 the Secretary of the Board of Examinations shall send to Colleges, for transmission to individual candidates, an entry verification form showing the details of each candidate's entry; each candidate shall either sign the form as correct or indicate what amendments of the entry are required, and shall return the form to the Senior Tutor, who shall inform the Secretary of the Board of any amendments required. The Secretary of the Board shall subsequently send to Colleges for each candidate an entry confirmation form giving details of the candidate's entry, the time and place of each written paper for which the candidate is entered, and any identification number allocated to the candidate. Verification of entries.

10. The latest dates for the submission of entries and corrections of entries, and for the issue of lists of candidates and of entry verification and confirmation forms, shall be as shown in Regulations 11– Timetables of entries and lists.

[1] For the examinations specified in Regulations 11–15 the lists shall be divided by College, and the list sent to each College shall comprise the members of that College who are entered for the examination in question.

15, provided that the Board of Examinations shall have authority to amend those dates in respect of any Tripos, Preliminary, or other examinations held before the division of the Easter Term.

11. For the examinations specified below the procedures shall be as shown in the following table in accordance with Regulation 3:

	Not later than
Entries received via the on-line student record database in the Board of Examinations	8 November
First lists of candidates to be issued	End of third quarter of Michaelmas Term
Entry verification forms to be issued	Division of Lent Term
Corrections of entries to be sent to Board of Examinations by Colleges	Last day of Full Lent Term
Final lists of candidates and entry confirmation forms to be issued	First day of Full Easter Term

Anglo-Saxon, Norse, and Celtic Tripos, Parts I and II, and Preliminary Examination for Part I
Archaeological and Anthropological Tripos, Part IIB
Architecture Tripos, Parts IA, IB, and II
Asian and Middle Eastern Studies Tripos, Parts IA and IB
Chemical Engineering Tripos, Parts I, IIA, and IIB
Classical Tripos, Parts IA, IB, and II, and Preliminary Examinations for Parts IA and II
Computer Science Tripos, Parts IA, IB, and II
Economics Tripos, Parts I, IIA, and IIB
Economics, Advanced Diploma in
Education Tripos, Parts I and II, and Preliminary Examinations for Parts I and II
Education, Postgraduate Certificate in
Engineering Tripos, Parts IA and IB
English Tripos, Parts I and II, and Preliminary Examinations for Parts I and II
Geographical Tripos, Parts IA, IB, and II, and Preliminary Examination for Part II
History of Art Tripos, Parts I, IIA, and IIB
Conservation of Easel Paintings, Diploma in
Historical Tripos, Parts I and II, and Preliminary Examinations for Parts I and II
Human, Social, and Political Sciences Tripos, Parts I, IIA, and IIB
Land Economy Tripos, Parts IA, IB, and II
Law Tripos, Parts IA, IB, and II
Law for European students, Examination in
LL.M. Examination
M.C.L. Examination
Linguistics Tripos
Management Studies Tripos
Manufacturing Engineering Tripos, Parts IIA and IIB
Mathematical Tripos, Parts IA, IB, and II
[Medical and Veterinary Sciences Tripos, Parts IA and IB (from these entries, entries for the various Easter Term Second M.B. and Second Veterinary M.B. Examinations are created)][1]
⟨Medical and Veterinary Sciences Tripos, Parts IA and IB (except IB Lent Term Examination in Head and Neck Anatomy; from these entries, entries for the various Easter Term Second M.B. and Second Veterinary M.B. Examinations are created)⟩[1]
Modern and Medieval Languages Tripos, Parts IA, IB, and II[2]
Modern Languages, Diploma and Certificate in
Music Tripos, Parts IA, IB, and II
Mus.B. Examination
Natural Sciences Tripos, Parts IA, IB, II, and III (excluding Astrophysics and Physics), and Preliminary Examination for Part II
Philosophy Tripos, Parts IA, IB, and II
Politics, Psychology, and Sociology Tripos, Parts IIA and IIB[3]
Psychological and Behavioural Sciences Tripos, Parts I, IIA, and IIB
Theological and Religious Studies Tripos, Parts I, IIA, and IIB
Theology and Religious Studies, Advanced Diploma in

12. For the examinations specified below the procedures shall be as shown in the following table in accordance with Regulation 4:

[1] The entry in angular brackets will replace the entry in square brackets with effect from the 2015 examinations.
[2] Except for the oral examinations for Part II, for which the procedure shall be as specified in Regulation 13.
[3] The examinations for Parts IIA and IIB will be held for the last time in 2014 and 2015 respectively.

	Not later than
Entries received in the Board of Examinations	8 November
First lists of candidates to be issued	End of third quarter Michaelmas Term
Entry verification forms to be issued	Division of Lent Term
Corrections of entries to be sent to Board of Examinations by Colleges	Last day of Full Lent Term
Final lists of candidates and entry confirmation forms to be issued	First day of Full Easter Term

Asian and Middle Eastern Studies Tripos, Part II[1] and the Preliminary Examination for Part II
Theology for Ministry, First and Second Examination

13. For the examinations specified below the procedures shall be as shown in the following table in accordance with Regulation 4:

	Not later than
Entries received in the Board of Examinations	Eight weeks before the beginning of the examination
First lists of candidates and entry verification forms to be issued	Six weeks before the beginning of the examination
Corrections of entries to be sent to Board of Examinations by Colleges	Four weeks before the beginning of the examination
Final lists of candidates and entry confirmation forms to be issued	Two weeks before the beginning of the examination

Oral Examinations in Arabic, Hebrew, and Persian for Part II of the Asian and Middle Eastern Studies Tripos
Oral Examinations for Part II of the Modern and Medieval Languages Tripos
⟨Medical and Veterinary Sciences Tripos, Part IB (Lent Term examination)⟩[2]
Second M.B. Examination (Lent Term and September examinations)
Second Vet.M.B. Examination (Lent Term and September examinations)
Final M.B. Examination
Final Veterinary Examination

14. For the examinations specified below the procedure for submission of entries (in accordance with Regulation 4) and for the circulation of lists of candidates shall be as shown:

	Not later than
Entries received in the Board of Examinations (names only)	8 November
First lists of candidates to be issued (names only)	End of the third quarter of Michaelmas Term
Entries received from the Secretary of the Faculty Board (details)	End of the sixth week of Full Lent Term
Final lists of candidates and entry confirmation forms issued	Beginning of the last week of Full Lent Term

Engineering Tripos, Parts IIA and IIB
Natural Sciences Tripos, Part III, Physics

15. For the examinations specified below the procedure for submission of entries (in accordance with Regulation 4) and for the circulation of lists of candidates shall be as shown:

	Not later than
Entries received in the Board of Examinations (names only)	8 November
First list of candidates to be issued (names only)	End of the third quarter of Michaelmas Term
Entries received in the Board of Examinations from the Secretary of the Faculty Board (details)	End of second week of Full Easter Term
Final lists of candidates and entry confirmation forms to be issued	Beginning of the third week of Full Easter Term

Mathematical Tripos, Part III
Natural Sciences Tripos, Part III, Astrophysics

16. No alteration of an entry, other than a withdrawal of it, and no additional entry shall be accepted after the latest date specified for the submission of corrections. No amendments after latest date.

17. In accordance with the general regulations for admission as a Graduate Student, the Examiners for any Tripos or for the LL.M. Examination shall have power at the request of a Degree Committee to arrange for the examination of Graduate Students and to report the result of such examination direct Graduate Students.

[1] Except for the oral examinations in Arabic, Hebrew, and Persian for which the procedure shall be as specified in Regulation 13.
[2] The entry in angular brackets will be inserted with effect from the 2015 examinations.

to the Secretary of the Degree Committee. The names of such students shall not appear in any class-list.

Matriculation. **18.** No student shall be admitted to an examination leading to the degree of M.Phil., M.B., B.Chir., LL.M., B.A., Mus.B., or Vet.M.B., except, in the case of a student holding a degree of another university, the Second M.B. Examination, unless (*a*) the student has satisfied the examination requirements for matriculation or (*b*) the student belongs to one of the classes of persons whom the Council have approved as qualified for matriculation.

DATES OF EXAMINATIONS AND PUBLICATION OF CLASS-LISTS

Amended by Grace 2 of 11 December 2013, and Grace 5 of 30 July 2014

Board of Examinations. **1.** The dates on which the Qualifying Examination in Theology for Ministry, the First and Second Examinations for the B.Th. Degree, all examinations for the M.Phil. Degree, and all Preliminary Examinations shall begin shall be determined by the Board of Examinations in consultation with the Faculty Boards and other similar bodies concerned.

Easter Term examinations. **2.** The dates on which all other examinations held in the Easter Term shall begin (except for examinations for the M.B., B.Chir., and Vet.M.B. Degrees, and for Certificates of Postgraduate Study, which shall begin on dates determined in accordance with the regulations for those examinations) shall be as set out in the table below, provided that

(*a*) in any year in which candidates for an examination are permitted to offer a paper or subject included in another examination, the time-tables of the examinations shall be arranged accordingly;

(*b*) in any year in which Full Easter Term begins on or after 22 April, all examinations held in that term which are specified in the table below as beginning on or after the Monday before the last Sunday but one in May shall begin one week later than the dates specified in the table;

(*c*) it shall be competent for the Board of Examinations, on the recommendation of the Committee for the Natural Sciences Tripos, to determine that practical examinations for Part IA of that Tripos be held on up to four of the weekdays immediately preceding the date specified for the beginning of examinations for that Part, and that the practical examination for the subject Physiology, Development, and Neuroscience in Part II of that Tripos be held at any time after the first day of Full Easter Term;

(*d*) subject to the agreement of the Faculty Board or other comparable body concerned, it shall be competent for the Board of Examinations to determine that any particular paper of an examination in the following list shall be held up to three days (Saturdays and Sundays not being counted) before the date specified for the beginning of that examination.

Monday before first day of Full Easter Term	Classical Tripos, Part IA Engineering Tripos, Parts IIA and IIB Natural Sciences Tripos, Part III[1] (Easter Term examination)
Second day of Full Easter Term	Manufacturing Engineering Tripos, Part IIB
First Monday of Full Easter Term	Chemical Engineering Tripos, Part IIA
First Friday of Full Easter Term	Manufacturing Engineering Tripos, Part IIA
Second Tuesday of Full Easter Term	Management Studies Tripos
Wednesday before last Sunday but one in May	Education Tripos, Parts I and II Diplomas and Certificates in Modern Languages[2]
Thursday before last Sunday but one in May	English Tripos, Part II Geographical Tripos, Part II

[1] Examination in Physics only. See also Regulation 3.

[2] Except for the oral examinations, which shall begin on the following dates: oral examination for the Diploma, the Monday before the first day of Full Easter Term; oral examination for the Certificate, the fourth Friday of Full Easter Term.

Friday before last Sunday but one in May	English Tripos, Part I Land Economy Tripos Linguistics Tripos Modern and Medieval Languages Tripos, Parts IA, IB[1], and II[2] Philosophy Tripos
Saturday before last Sunday but one in May	Medical and Veterinary Sciences Tripos, Part IB[3] Natural Sciences Tripos, Part IB
Monday before last Sunday in May	Chemical Engineering Tripos, Part IIB Economics Tripos, Part IIB Law Tripos LL.M. Examination M.C.L. Examination Music Tripos, Parts IB and II Mus.B. Examination
Tuesday before last Sunday in May	Architecture Tripos, Parts IA and IB Theological and Religious Studies Tripos Advanced Diploma in Theology and Religious Studies
Wednesday before last Sunday in May	Classical Tripos, Part II Advanced Diploma in Economics Geographical Tripos, Part IA Historical Tripos, Part I Music Tripos, Part IA Natural Sciences Tripos, Part II
Thursday before last Sunday in May	History of Art Tripos, Part I Mathematical Tripos, Parts IA and III Politics, Psychology, and Sociology Tripos, Parts IIA and IIB[4] Psychological and Behavioural Sciences Tripos, Parts IIA and IIB
Friday before last Sunday in May	Asian and Middle Eastern Studies Tripos[5] Historical Tripos, Part II
Monday before first Sunday in June	Anglo-Saxon, Norse, and Celtic Tripos Architecture Tripos, Part II Archaeological and Anthropological Tripos, Part IIB Chemical Engineering Tripos, Part I Computer Science Tripos, Parts IA and IB Economics Tripos, Part IIA Engineering Tripos, Part IB Mathematical Tripos, Part II Medical and Veterinary Sciences Tripos, Part IA Natural Sciences Tripos, Part III
Tuesday before first Sunday in June	Computer Science Tripos, Part II Mathematical Tripos, Part IB

[1] Except for the following examinations, which shall begin on the dates specified.
(i) Oral examination A, the fourth Friday of Full Easter Term;
(ii) Oral examination B, the Monday before the first day of Full Easter Term;
(iii) Section (*b*) (listening comprehension test) of Paper B3 in the several languages, the Monday before the last Sunday but one in May.

[2] Except for the oral examinations, which shall begin not earlier than the eighth day before the first day of Full Michaelmas Term.

[3] Except the *viva voce* examination in Comparative Vertebrate Biology, which shall begin on the first day of Full Easter Term.

[4] The examinations for Parts IIA and IIB will be held for the last time in 2014 and 2015 respectively.

[5] Except for the following oral examinations:
(i) for Part II in Arabic, Hebrew, and Persian, which shall be held not earlier than the eighth day before the first day of Full Michaelmas Term;
(ii) Part II in all other languages, which shall be held not earlier than the third Monday of Full Easter Term;
(iii) for Part IA and IB of the Asian and Middle Eastern Studies Tripos, which shall be held not earlier than the third Monday of Full Easter Term.

Wednesday before first Sunday in June	Classical Tripos, Part IB[1] Engineering Tripos, Part IA Geographical Tripos, Part IB
Thursday before first Sunday in June	Human, Social, and Political Sciences Tripos, Parts I, IIA, and IIB Psychological and Behavioural Sciences Tripos, Part I
Friday before first Sunday in June	Natural Sciences Tripos, Part IA History of Art Tripos, Parts IIA and IIB
Monday after first Sunday in June	Economics Tripos, Part I

Examinations not in Easter Term.

3. The dates on which all examinations not held in the Easter Term shall begin (except for the examinations for the M.B., B.Chir., and Vet.M.B. Degrees, which shall begin on dates determined in accordance with the regulations for those examinations) shall be as follows:

⟨Medical and Veterinary Tripos, Part IB[2] (Lent Term examination)
The last day of Full Lent term⟩[3]

Natural Sciences Tripos, Part III[4] (Lent Term examination)
The Monday that next precedes the first day of Full Lent Term.

Change of date.

4. If it is necessary, from whatever cause, to begin an examination on a date other than that specified by Ordinance and there is not time to obtain approval by Grace for the change, the Council, or if a meeting of the Council cannot conveniently be convened, the Registrary or a deputy, shall have power to approve the change, on the recommendation of the Chair of Examiners, provided that the change shall be announced in the *Reporter* as soon as possible.

Publication of class-lists.

5. The latest dates for publication, where applicable, of class-lists of Preliminary Examinations and of examinations the dates of which are specified in Regulation 2 shall be as follows:

The Monday before the days of General Admission:
The class-lists for undivided Triposes, Part II examinations for Triposes, Part IIA of the Chemical Engineering Tripos, Part IB of the Medical and Veterinary Sciences Tripos, Part IB of the Natural Sciences Tripos, Part IIA of the Manufacturing Engineering Tripos, and the Second Examination for the B.Th. Degree.

The Friday after the days of General Admission:
The class-lists for all other Honours Examinations, for the LL.M. Examination and the Mus.B. Examination, for the Preliminary Examinations, Qualifying Examinations, Certificate Examinations, and the First Examination for the B.Th. Degree.

FORM AND CONDUCT OF EXAMINATIONS

1. For any examination or part of an examination no change in the form and conduct of the examination, by comparison with the form and conduct of that examination in the previous year, shall be made if it would affect the preparation of candidates, unless

either (*a*) the Ordinances governing the examination have been amended with effect from a date later than that of the examination in the previous year;

or (*b*) any supplementary regulations defining or limiting the scope of the examination have been published or amended not later than the date specified in the Schedule to these regulations;

or (*c*) the Faculty Board or other body concerned have published, not later than the date specified in the Schedule, a Notice of the changes of form and conduct, not governed by the regulations or supplementary regulations, that will be made.

2. For any examination or part of an examination held for the first time, the Faculty Board or other body concerned shall publish by the first day of the Full Term preceding that in which the examination takes place, a Notice specifying in as much detail as possible the form and conduct of that examination or part of an examination.

3. In these regulations the term *examination* in Regulations 1 and 2 shall include any course-work, essay, or other exercise specified in the Ordinances governing that examination.

[1] Except for Papers 11 and 12, the examinations for which shall be held on the first and second days of Full Easter Term.
[2] Examination in Head and Neck Anatomy only.
[3] The entry in angular brackets will be inserted with effect from the 2015 examinations.
[4] Examination in Physics only.

SCHEDULE

	Not later than
For any examination or part of an examination held between the beginning of the Easter Term and the beginning of the following Michaelmas Term	Last day of Full Michaelmas Term preceding the examination
For any examination or part of an examination held between the beginning of the Michaelmas Term and the beginning of the following Lent Term	Last day of Full Easter Term preceding the examination
For any examination or part of an examination held between the beginning of the Lent Term and the beginning of the following Easter Term	14 October in the academical year in which the examination takes place

Duration of Written Examination Papers

Unless prescribed otherwise in the regulations for a particular Preliminary, Qualifying, or Tripos Examination, or an examination for a Diploma or Certificate, all written papers in those examinations (other than written papers or similar exercises which constitute the whole or part of a practical examination) shall each be of three hours' duration.

Interviews

Notwithstanding the provisions of any other Ordinance, the Examiners for any Tripos Examination, Qualifying Examination, or Preliminary Examination, or for any examination for a Diploma or Certificate for which candidates are not required to be Graduate Students, shall have discretion, after consultation with the Board of Examinations, to summon a particular candidate or particular candidates for interview on any aspect of the written work of the candidate or candidates not produced in an examination room which in the opinion of the Examiners requires elucidation.

Marking and classing conventions and criteria

Faculty Boards and comparable authorities shall be entitled to issue to the Examiners and Assessors appointed for the examination concerned details of the conventions and criteria to be applied in marking written papers and other work and, where applicable, in determining class-lists. Such details and any changes to them shall be issued not later than the end of the Full Michaelmas Term preceding the examination.

PUBLICATION OF LISTS OF SUCCESSFUL CANDIDATES IN EXAMINATIONS

1. Save in so far as the General Board shall allow otherwise, every Examiner who has taken part in an examination shall be present, unless prevented by grave cause approved before the meeting by the Vice-Chancellor, at the final meeting of the Examiners, which shall be defined as follows: Meetings of Examiners.

(*a*) Each Examiner for any Part of the Medical and Veterinary Sciences Tripos, or for Part IA or Part IB of the Natural Sciences Tripos, shall be present at the meeting of the Examiners at which the marks of the candidates in his or her particular subject are finally approved.

(*b*) Each Examiner for any other examination for which a class-list is published shall be present at the meeting of the Examiners at which that list is finally approved.

2. For each of the examinations specified in Regulation 1(*a*) there shall be held, in addition to the final meetings of Examiners in particular subjects, a subsequent meeting of the Chair and the Senior Examiners, at which the class-list for the whole examination shall be finally approved, and at which the following shall be present:

(*a*) the Chair of Examiners or, in the absence of the Chair, an Assistant Chair of Examiners;

(*b*) the Senior Examiner (or a designated deputy) for each particular subject of the examination.

3. At the final meeting of the Examiners held under Regulation 1(*b*), or at the meeting of the Chair and the Senior Examiners held under Regulation 2, two copies of the class-list, as finally approved, shall be signed by all those present. These copies shall be sent without delay to the Registrary by the Lists to be sent to the Registrary.

Chair of Examiners. One of the two copies, if they are in print, or, if they are not in print, a printed copy subsequently signed by the Chair of Examiners, shall be preserved in the Registry as the authoritative list.

Time of publication.

4. All class-lists shall be published by the Registrary and subsequently printed in the *Reporter*. A list shall be deemed to have been published as soon as either (*a*) the Registrary has caused a copy of it to be posted outside the Senate-House or (*b*) a copy of it has been read in the Senate-House. Any copy of a list read in the Senate-House shall immediately thereafter be posted outside the Senate-House. Until printing of a class-list in the *Reporter*, a copy of the class-list issued for posting outside the Senate-House or in any Faculty, Department, or other institution in the University or a College, or read in the Senate-House shall exclude the name of any candidate where such exclusion has been determined by the Council for good cause.

Distribution of copies.

5. The Registrary shall arrange for copies of each complete list to be sent to each College, Approved Foundation, and Approved Society as soon as possible after publication.

Notice of probable date of publication of lists.

6. The Chair of Examiners shall communicate to the Registrary as soon as practicable a statement of the day on which the Registrary may expect to receive the list and whether the list is to be read in the Senate-House; and the Registrary shall cause to be posted outside the Senate-House, or shall insert in the *Reporter*, a notice of the expected date of publication.

Amended lists.

7. In any case in which the Chair of Examiners satisfies the Vice-Chancellor that a list published in accordance with the foregoing regulations needs amendment, the Vice-Chancellor may authorize the issue of a Notice amending the list, or of an amended list to supersede the original list.

DISCLOSURE OF EXAMINATION MARKS

1. Regulations 2–5 below shall apply to the following University examinations:

All Tripos, Preliminary, and Qualifying Examinations
The Examination in Law for European students
The LL.M. Examination
The Second M.B., and Final M.B. Examinations
The Mus.B. Examination
The Second Veterinary M.B. Examination and the Final Veterinary Examination
The examinations for Diplomas in Modern Languages
The examination for Certificates in Modern Languages
The examination for the Postgraduate Certificate in Education
The Qualifying Examination in Theology for Ministry and the First and Second Examinations for the B.Th. Degree.

2. The Examiners for each of the examinations specified in Regulation 1 above shall communicate to the Registrary and to Tutors or other designated College officers, or officers of institutions within the Cambridge Theological Federation, for transmission to their pupils, the marks of their pupils and such other information as may be considered advisable; provided that, in the case of examinations leading to the degrees of M.B., B.Chir., and Vet.M.B., such communication shall be in accordance with the regulations for those degrees.

3. Marks and other information shall also be communicated on request to bodies responsible for making University or College awards, to bodies responsible for awarding postgraduate studentships, to the Board of Graduate Studies, and to Heads of Departments, Chairs of the Boards of Faculties not organized in Departments, and Secretaries of Degree Committees, and, in the case of marks obtained in the Final M.B. Examination, to the Director of Medical Education in the Clinical School.

4. Marks and other information may also be provided in a statement of verification by the Registrary, on evidence supplied by the Examiners, to examining bodies external to the University, for the purpose of exemption from their examinations. The fee to be charged for such a certificate shall be determined by the General Board from time to time.

5. The nature of the marks and other information to be communicated under Regulations 2–4 above shall be determined from time to time by the Faculty Board or comparable authority concerned, or by the Committee of Management for the Natural Sciences Tripos in the case of that Tripos, and shall be notified to the General Board for their approval.

6. Except as may be otherwise required by law, marks and other information communicated under Regulations 2–4 shall not be disclosed to any person or body except (i) those specified in those regulations and (ii) the individual candidate to whom the marks relate.

REVIEW PROCEDURE FOR EXAMINATIONS FOR UNDERGRADUATE AND CERTAIN OTHER QUALIFICATIONS

1. The following regulations shall apply to any University examination listed in the Schedule to these regulations.

2. No representations under these regulations shall be considered unless they relate to

(*a*) the conduct of the examination or;

(*b*) a decision by a Faculty Board or comparable authority not to allow a student who has completed the requirement for the B.A. Degree to progress to that Part of a Tripos required for the M.Eng. or the M.Math. or the M.Sci. Degree.

3. No representations under Regulation 5 shall be considered if they reach the Registrary later than 4 p.m. on the third day (excluding Saturday and Sunday) after the candidate concerned has completed all parts of his or her examination. In exceptional circumstances the Registrary may allow a short extension of this deadline.

4. No representations under Regulation 6 shall be considered if (*a*) for those relating to 2(*a*) above, they reach the Registrary later than one month after the date upon which the list of successful candidates is signed or (*b*) for those relating to 2(*b*) above, they reach the Registrary later than one month after the date upon which the Faculty Board or comparable authority reaches its decision. In exceptional circumstances the Registrary may allow an extension of these deadlines.

5. Representations concerning the conduct of an examination arising before the list of successful candidates is signed shall be submitted to the Registrary by the candidate or by a Tutor on the candidate's behalf. The Registrary shall thereupon refer the representations to the Chair of Examiners for consideration by the Examiners at their final meeting. The Examiners shall take whatever action they think fit in the light of the representations. Within one week of the signing of the list of successful candidates, the Chair shall submit a report to the Registrary including an explanation of the action taken by the Examiners on the representations. The Registrary shall thereupon send a copy of that report to the candidate, to the Tutor (if any) submitting the representations, and to the Senior Tutor of the candidate's College. If the representations reach the Chair of Examiners after the final meeting they shall be considered in accordance with the provisions of Regulation 6.

6. Representations concerning the conduct of an examination arising after the list of successful candidates is signed shall be submitted to the Registrary by the candidate or by a Tutor on the candidate's behalf. The Registrary shall thereupon refer the representations to the Chair of Examiners. The representations shall be considered by the Chair and at least two other Examiners. Within one month of receiving the representations the Chair shall submit a report to the Registrary including an explanation of any action which the Chair has taken on the representations. The Registrary shall thereupon send a copy of that report to the candidate, to the Tutor (if any) submitting the representations, and to the Senior Tutor of the candidate's College. The same procedures shall apply to representations falling within Regulation 2(*b*) above, save that the Chair of the Faculty Board or comparable body shall consider the representations with at least two other members and report to the Registrary accordingly.

7. If the candidate concerned is dissatisfied with the response from the Chair of Examiners (or the Chair of the Faculty Board or comparable body as the case may be), the candidate may apply to the Registrary for the matter to be considered by an Examinations Review Committee constituted in accordance with Regulation 8, provided that such an application shall not normally be considered unless it is received by the Registrary within three months of the date on which the report from the Chair of Examiners (or the Chair of the Faculty Board or comparable body as the case may be) is communicated in accordance with Regulation 5 or 6, as appropriate. In exceptional circumstances the Registrary may allow an extension of this deadline. The candidate shall, in the application, provide a full statement of his or her complaint. Examinations Review Committee.

8. A Review Committee appointed under these regulations shall consist of three members as follows: Membership.

(*a*) one member, who shall have appropriate experience in matters of procedure, appointed by the Council, as Chair;

(*b*) one member who is external to the University appointed by the General Board;

(*c*) one member of the Regent House appointed by the General Board.

In the event that the Chair declares an interest or is otherwise unable to act, the member under category (*b*) shall act as Chair, and two members of the Regent House shall be appointed to act. In the event that the member under category (*b*) declares an interest or is otherwise unable to act, two members of the Regent House shall be appointed to act.

9. The General Board shall maintain a panel of members of the Regent House who are willing to serve as members of a Review Committee in class (*c*), and shall appoint twelve persons to the panel, four persons being appointed in the Michaelmas Term of each year to serve for three years from 1 January following their appointment. When any representations are to be referred to a Review Committee, the General Board shall nominate one member of the panel for appointment as a member of the Review Committee for the particular case. In selecting a member of the panel for appointment as a member of a Review Committee, the Board shall exclude any person who has been involved in the particular case at an earlier stage. A person appointed a member of a Review Committee shall serve until the conclusion of the particular case for which he or she was appointed. In the event that the person so appointed is unable to do so, the General Board shall appoint a replacement member from the panel.

10. The Registrary, or a deputy appointed by the Registrary, shall act as Secretary to a Review Committee.

11. The Secretary to the Review Committee shall notify the candidate of the persons appointed to be members of the Review Committee. The candidate shall be entitled to object for good cause to any member so appointed. The Vice-Chancellor shall rule on any such objection, and his or her decision shall be final. If the Vice-Chancellor allows such an objection, another member shall be appointed to replace the person who was the subject of the objection.

Grounds for complaint.

12. A Review Committee shall consider any representations which are referred to them under Regulation 7 which in the judgement of the Committee constitutes a complaint on one or more of the following grounds:

(*a*) that there existed material circumstances relating to the conduct of the examination (excluding circumstances relating to the candidate's course of study) of which the Examiners were unaware;

(*b*) that procedural irregularities occurred in the conduct of the examination, which were of such a nature as to cause reasonable doubt as to whether the Examiners would have reached the same conclusion had the irregularities not occurred;

(*c*) that there is demonstrable evidence of prejudice, bias, or inadequate assessment in the examination process;

(*d*) that, with regard to representations falling within Regulation 2(*b*), there existed material circumstances (excluding circumstances relating to the candidate's course of study) of which the Faculty Board or comparable body were unaware, or that procedural irregularities occurred in the Faculty Board's or comparable body's decision which were of such a nature as to cause reasonable doubt as to whether that body would have reached the same decision had the irregularities not occurred, or that there is demonstrable evidence of prejudice, bias or inadequate assessment in that body's decision.

In considering the representations at this stage the Committee shall have power to seek statements from other persons or bodies, as they think fit. If the Committee are of the view that the case does not fall within any of the grounds specified above, they shall dismiss the complaint and shall inform the candidate accordingly.

13. Subject to the provisions of Regulation 12, any statement of complaint received by the Review Committee shall be made available to each of the following:

(*a*) the Chair of Examiners (or the Chair of the Faculty Board or comparable authority if the complaint relates to Regulation 2(*b*));

(*b*) any person against whom a complaint is laid;

(*c*) any other person specified by the Review Committee.

Each of these persons shall be given an opportunity to submit a written statement to the Committee in response to the complaint. The Committee shall have power to seek statements from other persons or bodies, as they think fit.

14. Any statement submitted to the Review Committee under Regulation 13 shall be made available to the candidate who shall be afforded an opportunity to comment upon it.

15. The Committee shall appoint a day and time for a hearing at which the candidate shall be entitled to be present and to be accompanied by a Tutor or other adviser being either a junior member of the University, an officer of Cambridge University Students Union, or a member of the Regent House; any person accompanying the candidate shall be permitted to act as the candidate's representative and to speak on his or her behalf. Any person or persons against whom a complaint is laid shall also be entitled to be present (and to be accompanied by a member of the Regent House). The Committee may also, at their discretion, invite other parties to attend.

16. A Review Committee shall consider any complaint referred to them under Regulation 7 and shall have power to dismiss the complaint or, if they consider it justified: Decision of Review Committee.

(*a*) to require the Chair of Examiners to re-convene as many of the original Examiners as can conveniently be assembled for the purpose of reconsidering their earlier decisions on the particular case, no fewer than three Examiners inclusive of the Chair to constitute a quorum; *or*

(*b*) to require the General Board to appoint one or more additional Examiners to make an independent report or reports on the work presented by the candidate, and to require the Chair of Examiners to convene a meeting of as many of the original Examiners as can conveniently be assembled together with the additional Examiner or Examiners to reconsider the earlier decisions on the particular case, no fewer than three of the original Examiners inclusive of the Chair, and the additional Examiner or Examiners, to constitute a quorum; *or*

(*c*) to require the candidate, or the candidate's work, to be re-examined under whatever arrangements may be specified by the Review Committee, after consultation with the Chair of Examiners;

(*d*) to require (if the complaint relates to Regulation 2(*b*)) the Faculty Board or comparable body to reconsider their decision.

17. The Secretary of the Review Committee shall send written notification of the Committee's decision and the reasons for it to the candidate, the Chair of Examiners (or the Chair of the Faculty Board or comparable body if the complaint falls within Regulation 2(*b*)), and to the other parties specified in Regulation 13.

18. Subject to any other provisions of the Statutes and Ordinances, the decision of a Review Committee on a particular case shall be final.

19. The Chair of Examiners may appoint a deputy or deputies from among the Examiners to act on his or her behalf in relation to the foregoing regulations during the Chair's absence from Cambridge or for other good cause. The same power of delegation may be exercised by a Faculty Board or comparable authority or its Chair for complaints falling within Regulation 2(*b*).

20. A Review Committee shall, if they so wish, be entitled to make general recommendations about examination procedures to the General Board, irrespective of the outcome of their consideration of a complaint.

SCHEDULE

EXAMINATIONS FOR WHICH THE FOREGOING REGULATIONS APPLY

Examinations, including where appropriate Preliminary, Ordinary, and Qualifying examinations, taken by matriculated students and leading to the following qualifications:

B.A. Degree
B.Th. Degree
M.B., B.Chir. Degrees
Mus.B. Degree
Vet.M.B. Degree
LL.M. Degree
M.C.L. Degree
M.Eng. Degree
M.Sci. Degree
M.B.A. Degree
M.Ed. Degree[1]
M.Fin. Degree
M.Mus. Degree
M.Math. Degree
M.A.St. Degree

Diplomas in:
Conservation of Easel Paintings
Modern Languages
Theology and Religious Studies

Certificate in Humanities Computing for Languages
Certificate in Modern Languages
Postgraduate Certificate in Education
Examination in Law for European Students

[1] Candidates admitted prior to 1 October 2013.

GENERAL REGULATIONS FOR EXAMINERS AND ASSESSORS

Appointment procedure.

1. Examiners, Chairs of Examiners, and Assessors shall be appointed in accordance with the provisions of Regulations 2–3 below, provided always that the General Board shall have power, after consulting the Faculty Board or other authority concerned, and subject to the provisions of Statute B III 1, to authorize an alternative procedure, or to vary the timetable set out in Regulation 3, in the case of a particular examination.

Nomination and appointment.

2. Examiners and Assessors for the examinations specified in the Schedule to these regulations shall be appointed by the General Board on the nomination of the body specified in the special regulations for each examination. For each board of Examiners the General Board shall also appoint, on the nomination of the same body, a resident member of the Regent House as Chair of Examiners.

Timetable.

3. Nominations shall be made in accordance with the following timetable:

Chairs of Examiners and Senior Examiners: not later than the first day of the Michaelmas Term in the academical year in which the examination is to be held.

Other Examiners: not later than the division of the Michaelmas Term in the academical year in which the examination is to be held.

Assessors: not later than four weeks before the beginning of the examination concerned.

Late appointments.

4. If it is necessary from whatever cause for an Examiner or Assessor to be nominated after the normal date, the General Board or (if the nomination cannot be considered by the General Board without undue delay) the Secretary of the General Board or a deputy appointed by the Secretary shall have power, on the recommendation of the Chair of Examiners, to approve such a nomination and to make the appointment.

5. The Chair of Examiners shall call such meetings as may be necessary for considering the papers proposed to be set and settling them in common, and for drawing up the list of successful candidates, and generally shall see that the regulations for the examination are observed.

Voting.

6. In an equality of votes a Chair of Examiners shall have a second or casting vote.

Scheme for Examiners.

7. Each body of Examiners shall draw up, and the Chair of Examiners shall send to the Secretary of the Board of Examinations, a scheme showing which of the Examiners is to attend at the beginning of each session with which they are concerned.

8. Except as may be provided otherwise in the regulations for a particular examination, in a year in which a candidate for any examination ('Examination A') offers a paper from another examination ('Examination B'), any Examiner or Assessor responsible for that paper in Examination B shall act as Assessor to the Examiners for Examination A and shall advise them on the candidate's performance; provided that, if no candidate for Examination B has entered for that paper, the body responsible for nominating Examiners for Examination B shall nominate for appointment in the Lent Term an Assessor or Assessors to set the paper and advise the Examiners for Examination A on the performance of the candidate. Assessors so acting or appointed under this regulation may be summoned to meetings of the Examiners for the purpose of consultation and advice, but shall not be entitled to vote.

9. The duty to examine students which is imposed by Statute C I 4 on every University officer specified in the Schedule to Special Ordinance C (i) 1 shall be restricted to the examining of candidates for any of the degrees of Master of Advanced Study, Business Administration, Engineering, Finance, Law, Corporate Law, Mathematics, Music, Natural Sciences, Philosophy, and Research, or Bachelor of Arts, Medicine, Music, Surgery, and Veterinary Medicine, or for any Certificate or Diploma of the University listed in the Table of Fees under University Composition Fees.

SCHEDULE

(*a*) Preliminary and Qualifying Examinations.
(*b*) Honours Examinations.
(*c*) The examinations for the degrees of LL.M., M.C.L., M.B.A., M.Ed., M.Fin., M.B., B.Chir., Vet.M.B., and Mus.B.
(*d*) Examinations for all Diplomas except those in International Law and Legal Studies.
(*e*) The examination for the Postgraduate Certificate in Education.
(*f*) The Examination in Law for European students.
(*g*) The Qualifying Examination in Theology for Ministry, and the First and Second Examinations for the degree of B.Th.
(*h*) The examinations for the Certificates in Humanities Computing for Languages and in Modern Languages.

PAYMENTS TO EXAMINERS AND ASSESSORS

Amended by Grace 8 of 16 July 2014

1. (*a*) No payment shall be made to any University officer, other than an Associate Lecturer who receives no stipend from the University, in respect of any of the examining duties specified in these regulations. Restrictions.

(*b*) No payment shall be made to any member of the staff of an institution within the Cambridge Theological Federation in respect of such duties undertaken in connection with any of the following examinations: the Qualifying Examination in Theology for Ministry; the First Examination and the Second Examination for the B.Th. Degree.

2. Any person appointed to be an Examiner who does not hold a University office, or a Fellowship or some other office or post in a College, and who does not teach any course of instruction which forms part of the teaching programme for the examination concerned, may be appointed as an External Examiner by the General Board, or other authority as appropriate, on the nomination of the body specified in the regulations for the examination concerned. Any payment to an External Examiner shall be conditional on him or her meeting the requirements of an External Examiner as laid out by the General Board from time to time. External Examiners.

3. Subject to the provisions of Regulation 1, payment for acting as an Examiner or an Assessor in any of the examinations specified in this regulation shall be made at the rates shown below, subject to the following provisions: Payments.

(i) the payment for examining or assessing components of an examination other than those specified below shall be determined by the General Board, having regard to the nature of the examining or assessment;

(ii) except by special permission of the General Board, no one shall receive more than one additional payment for acting as an External Examiner or Assessor under any of subsections (*a*)–(*d*) below;

(iii) if a person examines for a written paper or other component part of an examination which is offered in more than one examination, he or she shall not thereby be qualified to receive more than one payment for acting as Examiner or Assessor.

(*a*) *Preliminary, Qualifying, and Honours Examinations*
Examination in Law for European students
Examinations for the LL.M., M.C.L., M.B.A., M.Ed., M.Fin., M.A.St., and Mus.B. Degrees
Qualifying Examination in Theology for Ministry, First Examination, and Second Examination for the B.Th. Degree
Examinations for the Diploma in Conservation of Easel Painting, and Advanced Diplomas in Economics and Theology and Religious Studies
Examinations for Certificates of Postgraduate Study, for Diplomas and Certificates in Modern Languages, and for the Certificate in Humanities Computing for Languages
Examination for the Postgraduate Certificate in Education

For acting as an Examiner	£110
For acting as an Assessor	£55
For acting as an External Examiner	£600
For marking answers to a complete written paper of at least three hours	£9
For marking answers to a complete written paper of two hours	£5
For marking answers to a complete written paper of less than two hours	£4
For assessing a dissertation or thesis	£20

(*b*) *Oral Examinations*

(i) Oral Examinations for Parts IA and IB of the Modern and Medieval Languages Tripos, Part IA and IB of the Asian and Middle Eastern Studies Tripos, Part IA of the Law Tripos, the Preliminary Examination for Part I of the Education Tripos, and for Diplomas and Certificates in Modern Languages

For acting as an Examiner in a language	£55
For acting as an External Examiner (additional payment)	£55
For each candidate examined	£5

(ii) Oral Examinations for Part II of the Modern and Medieval Languages Tripos and Part II of the Asian and Middle Eastern Studies Tripos, and Part II of the Education Tripos

For acting as an Examiner in a language	£55

For acting as an External Examiner (additional payment) £55
For each candidate examined £17

(*c*) *Practical examinations of the Music Tripos and the Education Tripos*

(i) Aural tests and keyboard tests for Part IA of the Music Tripos
For each candidate examined £5

(ii) Performance tests and keyboards tests for Part IB of the Music Tripos, the Preliminary Examinations in Education, and Parts I and II of the Education Tripos
For each candidate examined £6

(iii) Practical rehearsal and practical examination for the Preliminary Examinations in Education and Part I of the Education Tripos
For each candidate examined £6

(iv) Performance tests for Part II of the Music Tripos and Part II of the Education Tripos
For each half day spent acting as an Assessor £75
For each half day spent acting as an External Assessor (additional payment) £75

(*d*) *Examinations for the M.B., B.Chir. Degrees and the Vet.M.B. Degree*

(i) *Second M.B. Examination*
For acting as an Examiner
(1) in Introduction to the Scientific Basis of Medicine and in Social Context of Health and Illness £55
(2) in any other subject £145
For acting as an Assessor or External Assessor in Preparing for Patients £145
For acting as an External Examiner (additional payment)
(1) in Introduction to the Scientific Basis of Medicine and in Social Context of Health and Illness £80
(2) in any other subject £220
For marking answers to a complete written paper of at least three hours £9
For marking answers to a complete written paper of two hours £5
For marking answers to a complete written paper of less than two hours £4
For marking a report submitted as part of Preparing for Patients £5

(ii) *Second Veterinary M.B. Examination*
For acting as an Examiner
(1) in Comparative Vertebrate Biology, Preparing for the Veterinary Profession, and Principles of Animal Management £55
(2) in any other subject £145
For acting as an Assessor
(1) in Preparing for the Veterinary Profession and Principles of Animal Management £30
(2) in any other subject £75
For acting as an External Examiner (additional payment)
(1) in Comparative Vertebrate Biology, Preparing for the Veterinary Profession, and Principles of Animal Management £80
(2) in any other subject £220
For marking answers to a complete written paper of at least three hours £9
For marking answers to a complete written paper of two hours £5
For marking answers to a complete written paper of less than two hours £4

(iii) *Final M.B. Examination, each Part*
For acting as an Examiner £145
For acting as an External Examiner (additional payment) £145
For each half day after the first day spent
(1) as an Examiner in clinical, oral, or practical examinations £70
(2) as an External Examiner in examining in Cambridge £145

(iv) *Final Veterinary Examination, each Part*
For acting as an Examiner £130
For acting as an External Examiner (additional payment) £130
For each half day after the first day spent

(1) as an Examiner in clinical, oral, or practical examinations	£70
(2) as an External Examiner in examining in Cambridge	£130
(*e*) *Examinations for Postgraduate Diplomas in Legal Studies or International Law*	
For assessing a thesis	£70
(*f*) *Examinations for the M.Phil. Degree*	
For acting as an Examiner or Assessor	£110
For acting as an External Examiner	£600
For marking answers to a written paper or other written work prescribed by the regulations for a particular subject	£10
For assessing a dissertation or thesis	£70
(*g*) *Examinations for the M.Res. Degree*	
For acting as an Examiner or Assessor	£110
For acting as an External Examiner	£600
For marking answers to a complete written paper or other written work prescribed by the regulations for a particular subject	£10
For assessing a dissertation or thesis	£70
(*h*) *Examinations for the M.Mus. Degree*	
For acting as an Examiner or Assessor	£110
For acting as an External Examiner	£600
For marking answers to a complete written paper or other written work prescribed by the regulations for a particular subject	£10
For assessing a dissertation or thesis	£70
For acting as an Examiner of a compulsory practical component	£150
For acting as an Assessor of an optional practical component	£75

4. Payment to any person for acting as Examiner, Assessor, or referee in any examination leading to one of the degrees of Master of Surgery, Science, Letters, or Studies, or to the degree of Doctor of Engineering or Philosophy or to any higher degree shall be made in accordance with the regulations for the degree concerned.

5. The Chair of Examiners or the Senior Examiner shall be responsible for notifying the Secretary of the Board of Examinations of the details of the payments to be made to those Examiners and Assessors, if any, who are qualified to receive payment.

6. An External Examiner or Assessor appointed to examine within the University shall be entitled to receive travelling expenses and a subsistence allowance, as follows: External Examiners.

(*a*) For the examinations specified in subsections (*a*)–(*e*) of Regulation 3, travelling expenses shall normally be equal to the return rail fare between Cambridge and the Examiner's usual place of residence or other place approved by the General Board, provided that the Board of Examinations may approve payment of a mileage allowance for travel by car or payment for alternative means of travel when travel by train is inconvenient. Travelling expenses shall not normally be paid for more than three visits in connection with any single examination; but the General Board may waive this restriction on the recommendation of the Chair of Examiners concerned.

Subsistence allowance may be claimed at rates determined from time to time by the Finance Committee of the Council, provided that no payment shall be made in respect of a day or a night when the Examiner's attendance in Cambridge in connection with the examination is unnecessary.

Claims for travelling expenses and subsistence allowance must be made through, and be approved by, the Chair of Examiners concerned. In addition to payment for the expenses provided for in this regulation, the Board of Examinations may approve payment of other reasonable expenses incurred by an Examiner or Assessor, whether internal or external, in connection with the execution of his or her duties.

(*b*) Examiners for other examinations may claim payment of travelling expenses and a subsistence allowance in accordance with Regulation 11 of the regulations for the Ph.D., M.Sc., and M.Litt. Degrees.

CHAPTER IV

PRELIMINARY EXAMINATIONS AND TRIPOS EXAMINATIONS

The provisions contained in this Chapter are Regulations of the General Board

PRELIMINARY EXAMINATIONS

GENERAL REGULATIONS

Purpose of examinations.

1. The Faculty Boards or other bodies responsible for the teaching for Honours Examinations shall be authorized to hold examinations preliminary to the Tripos with which they are concerned, or to a Part or Section of it, for the purpose of testing the progress of honours students, and their fitness for honours work. The Preliminary Examinations shall not be deemed Honours Examinations of the University.

Authority of Faculty Boards.

2. Subject to the powers of the General Board and the Board of Examinations, the Faculty Boards and comparable authorities shall have power to determine the standard, scope, management, and conduct of the Preliminary Examinations with which they are concerned, and shall make special regulations for those examinations, subject to the approval of the General Board. Not later than the end of the Easter Term each year a Notice shall be published giving details of any amendments of the special regulations which have been made by the authorities concerned, to have effect for the examinations to be held in the following year; after the publication of that Notice, no further amendments shall be made of the special regulations for any Preliminary Examination save in exceptional circumstances and by special permission of the General Board. A Faculty Board or other body shall have power to make supplementary regulations defining all or any of the subjects of the examinations with which they are concerned and to amend or withdraw such regulations as they think fit, provided that due notice is given of any change.

Subjects of examinations.

3. The variable subjects for all the Easter Term Preliminary Examinations shall be published by the Faculty Board or other body concerned in the Easter Term next before that in which the examination is held; provided that the Board or other body concerned shall have the power of subsequently issuing amendments if they are satisfied that no student's preparation for the examination is adversely affected.

Requirements.

4. A Faculty Board may prescribe requirements for candidates to take and pass the Preliminary Examination to the corresponding Tripos.

Standing of candidates.

5. No student may take a Preliminary Examination unless he or she has kept one term.

Examiners and Assessors.

6. The Faculty Boards or other bodies concerned shall nominate such number of Examiners and Assessors as they think fit for each Preliminary Examination, except in so far as the regulations for an examination provide for papers to be the responsibility of the Examiners for a particular Tripos examination.

Class-lists.

7. The names of candidates who pass a Preliminary Examination, other than the Preliminary Examinations for Parts IA and II of the Classical Tripos, for Parts I and II of the Education Tripos, for Parts I and II of the English Tripos, for Part I of the Historical Tripos, and for the Linguistics Tripos, shall be arranged in three classes, and the Examiners, if they think fit, may divide any class; the names in each class or division of a class shall be arranged in alphabetical order. The names of candidates who pass the Preliminary Examination for either Part of the Classical Tripos, for either Part of the Education Tripos, for either Part of the English Tripos, and for Part I of the Historical Tripos, shall be arranged in alphabetical order in one class. The general regulations regarding the publication and correction of class-lists shall apply to these examinations also.

Committee of Management for the Natural Sciences Tripos.

8. Except so far as regards the nomination of Examiners the powers and duties assigned to Faculty Boards in these regulations shall be performed with respect to any Preliminary Examination pertaining to the Natural Sciences Tripos by the Committee of Management for the Natural Sciences Tripos.

SPECIAL REGULATIONS

ANGLO-SAXON, NORSE, AND CELTIC

1. There shall be a Preliminary Examination for Part I and for Part II of the Anglo-Saxon, Norse, and Celtic Tripos.

Part I

2. The examination shall consist of Papers 1–10 of Part I of the Anglo-Saxon, Norse, and Celtic Tripos, as follows:

Paper 1. England before the Norman Conquest
Paper 2. Scandinavian history in the Viking Age
Paper 3. The Brittonic-speaking peoples from the fourth century to the twelfth
Paper 4. The Gaelic-speaking peoples from the fourth century to the twelfth
Paper 5. Old English language and literature
Paper 6. Old Norse language and literature
Paper 7. Medieval Welsh language and literature
Paper 8. Medieval Irish language and literature
Paper 9. Insular Latin language and literature
Paper 10. Palaeography and codicology

3. In order to be classed, a candidate shall offer any four papers.

Part II

4. The examination shall consist of papers 1–10 of Part I of the Anglo-Saxon, Norse, and Celtic Tripos, as listed above.

5. In order to be classed, a candidate shall offer any four papers.

ASIAN AND MIDDLE EASTERN STUDIES

1. There shall be a Preliminary Examination for Part II of the Asian and Middle Eastern Studies Tripos.

2. The subjects of examination shall be as follows:

Chinese with Japanese
Japanese with Chinese

Each candidate shall offer one subject.

3. There shall be separate examinations for each subject, as specified below:

(*a*) Chinese with Japanese

Candidates shall offer:

(i) Papers J.1–3 from the Asian and Middle Eastern Studies Tripos;
(ii) one paper chosen from Papers J.6, J.9–10, AMES.1, and C.7–8 from the Asian and Middle Eastern Studies Tripos;
(iii) an oral examination in Japanese, under conditions set out by the Faculty Board from time to time.

(*b*) Japanese with Chinese

Candidates shall offer:

(i) Papers C.1–3 from the Asian and Middle Eastern Studies Tripos;
(ii) one paper chosen from Papers C.7–8, AMES.1, and J.7–10, from the Asian and Middle Eastern Studies Tripos;
(iii) an oral examination in Chinese, under conditions set out by the Faculty Board from time to time.

4. No candidate shall offer a paper he or she has previously offered in any Honours Examination.

5. The Examiners shall be the Examiners for Part IA and Part IB of the Asian and Middle Eastern Studies Tripos.

CLASSICS

1. There shall be Preliminary Examinations for Part IA, and for Part II of the Classical Tripos.

Part IA

2. Candidates wishing to present themselves for Part IA of the Classical Tripos under Regulation 2(*b*) of the General Regulations for the Classical Tripos should successfully complete the Preliminary Examination for Part IA.

3. The examination shall consist of:

(*a*) Two written papers, each of three hours:

Paper 1. Latin texts
Paper 2. Latin questions

(*b*) A portfolio of two essays each of no more than 4,000 words in length, including notes but excluding bibliography, and on a topic approved by the Faculty Board of Classics. Candidates should submit the titles of their essays through their Directors of Studies to the Academic Secretary of the Faculty in time to be considered by the third Monday of Full Easter Term. The essays shall be typewritten, in English, and shall be submitted through the candidate's Director of Studies to the Academic Secretary, in accordance with detailed arrangements approved by the Board, so as to arrive not later than the seventh Tuesday of the Full Easter Term in which the examination takes place. Candidates will be required to declare that the essays are their own work and that they do not contain material already used to any substantial extent for a comparable purpose. Where appropriate full and proper acknowledgement must be given to the work of others.

4. In the class-list a mark of distinction may be attached to the name of any candidate whose work in the examination shows special merit.

Part II

5. The papers for this examination shall be taken from among the papers for Part II of the Classical Tripos, and the Examiners shall be the Examiners for that examination. Every candidate shall offer two papers, of which not more than one may be taken from the Schedule of Optional Papers.

SUPPLEMENTARY REGULATIONS

PART IA

Paper 1. Latin texts

This paper will contain passages in Latin for seen translation and for critical discussion.

Paper 2. Latin questions

This paper will contain passages in Latin for unseen translation, and exercises on the Latin language.

EDUCATION

Part I. 1. There shall be a Preliminary Examination for Part I of the Education Tripos.

2. The Examination shall comprise two sections as set out below. Each candidate shall offer the examination requirements set out in Section I and the examination requirements for a single subject area as set out in Section II. At the discretion of the Examiners the examination may include an oral examination on the course-work submitted under Section I.

Section I. Education studies

Section I consists of two written papers, one of three hours' duration and one of two hours' duration, and the submission of course-work, as prescribed by the Faculty Board of Education not later than the beginning of the Michaelmas Term preceding the examination.

Paper 1	Foundation course in the disciplines of education
Paper 2	Language, communication, and literacy (also serves as Paper 11 of Part I of the Politics, Psychology, and Sociology Tripos)
Course-work	

Section II. Subject studies

Candidates may offer papers from only one subject area. Where stated, some papers are examined by means other than a single written paper. For papers offered by the Faculty of Education, the Faculty

Board of Education shall specify arrangements for the submission of course-work, the sitting of practical examinations, or performances or workshops not later than the beginning of the Michaelmas Term preceding the examination. Some subject areas may restrict the combinations of papers that may be offered.

Biological Sciences

All candidates shall offer:

either Elementary Mathematics for Biologists (the examination requirements for this subject as set out in the regulations for Part IA of the Natural Sciences Tripos)

or Mathematical Biology (the examination requirements for this subject as set out in the regulations for Part IA of the Natural Sciences Tripos)

and

either Biology of Cells (the examination requirements for this subject as set out in the regulations for Part IA of the Natural Sciences Tripos)

or Evolution and Behaviour (the examination requirements for this subject as set out in the regulations for Part IA of the Natural Sciences Tripos)

or Physiology of Organisms (the examination requirements for this subject as set out in the regulations for Part IA of the Natural Sciences Tripos)

Classics

All candidates shall offer:

Latin language and texts (Paper 3 from Part IA of the Classical Tripos)

and Classical questions (Paper 5 from Part IA of the Classical Tripos)

English

All candidates shall offer:

Paper Ed.E1 Literature, drama, film

and Paper Ed.E2 Literary criticism

English and Drama

All candidates shall offer:

Paper Ed.E1 Literature, drama, film

and Paper Ed.D1 Drama production I (performance or workshop and submission of a note-book)

Geography

All candidates shall offer:

either Human geography (Paper 1 from Part IA of the Geographical Tripos)

or Physical geography (Paper 2 from Part IA of the Geographical Tripos)

Each paper from Part IA of the Geographical Tripos shall count as two papers.

History

All candidates shall offer:

Historical argument and practice (Paper 1 of the Preliminary Examination for Part I of the Historical Tripos)

and one of Papers 2–19 from the Preliminary Examination for Part I of the Historical Tripos.

Modern and Medieval Languages

All candidates shall offer:

Use of the foreign language (Paper B1 from Part IA of the Modern and Medieval Languages Tripos)

and Translation from the foreign language (Paper B2 from Part IA of the Modern and Medieval Languages Tripos)

and oral examination B in the foreign language, providing that both papers and the oral examination are all offered from the same language

and one paper taken from Schedule IA of the regulations of the Modern and Medieval Languages Tripos.

Music

All candidates shall offer two of the following papers from Part IA of the Music Tripos.

Paper 1	Music and musicology today
Paper 2	Music history I
Paper 3	Music history II
Paper 4	Introduction to music analysis
Paper 5	Tonal skills I
Paper 6	Tonal skills II

Physical Sciences

All candidates shall offer:

Mathematics (the examination requirements for this subject as set out in the regulations for Part IA of the Natural Sciences Tripos)

and

either Chemistry (the examination requirements for this subject as set out in the regulations for Part IA of the Natural Sciences Tripos)

or Physics (the examination requirements for this subject as set out in the regulations for Part IA of the Natural Sciences Tripos)

Religious Studies

All candidates shall offer:

either World religions in comparative perspective (Paper A7 from the Theological and Religious Studies Tripos)

or Philosophy of religion and ethics (Paper A8 from the Theological and Religious Studies Tripos)

and

either Jesus and the origins of the Gospel (Paper A3 from the Theological and Religious Studies Tripos)

or Christianity and the transformation of culture (Paper A4 from the Theological and Religious Studies Tripos)

Where, under the regulations for the Theological and Religious Studies Tripos, a paper may be offered in a form of assessment other than a written paper, the paper offered shall be submitted under conditions specified in the regulations for that Tripos.

Part II.

3. There shall be a Preliminary Examination for Part II of the Education Tripos.

4. The Examination shall comprise four sections, as set out below. Candidates shall offer:

either (*a*) the examination requirements set out in Section I and Section II;

(*b*) two further papers taken from the examination requirements set out in Section III, provided that, with the permission of the Faculty Board, a candidate may offer in place of one paper a dissertation, under conditions set out in Regulation 6;

or (*a*) the examination requirements set out in Section I;

(*b*) three further papers taken from the examination requirements from Section II, Section III, and Section IV, providing that candidates shall offer no fewer than two papers from Section IV.

Section I. Education studies

Section I consists of two written papers, each of three hours' duration.

Paper 1 Disciplines of education I

Paper 2 Disciplines of education II

Section II. Globalization, modernity, and education

Section II consists of one written paper of three hours' duration.

Paper 3 Globalization, modernity, and education

Section III. Special subjects in education

Candidates may offer one special subject in education, which shall count as one paper. The special subjects, and the examination requirements for each special subject, shall be announced by the Faculty Board from time to time, providing that due care is taken to give sufficient notice to all candidates.

Section IV. Subject studies

Candidates may offer two or three papers from only one subject area specified in Schedule 1 to the Education Tripos.[1] Where stated, some papers are examined by means other than a single written paper. Some subject areas may restrict the combinations of papers that may be offered.

5. For either Preliminary Examination, no candidate shall offer any paper, dissertation, or other exercise that he or she has previously offered in any University examination.

6. A candidate who intends to submit a dissertation under Regulation 4 shall submit the proposed topic to the Secretary of the Faculty Board through her or his Director of Studies, by a date announced by the Faculty Board not later than the beginning of the Michaelmas Term preceding the examination. The Secretary shall communicate the approval or rejection of the proposed topic to the candidate no later than the beginning of the Lent Term preceding the examination.

The submitted dissertation shall be of not less than 8,000 words and not more than 10,000 words, inclusive of notes and appendices. Dissertations shall be submitted by candidates through the Undergraduate Office to the Secretary of the Faculty Board by a date specified by the Faculty Board not later than the beginning of the Michaelmas Term preceding the examination. Each dissertation shall be in typescript, unless previous permission has been obtained from the Faculty Board to present it in manuscript; it shall bear the candidate's examination number and shall be accompanied by a brief synopsis.

[1] See p. 321.

Candidates will be required to declare that the dissertation is their own work and that it does not contain material already used to any substantial extent for a comparable purpose. At the discretion of the Examiners, a candidate may be examined *viva voce* on her or his dissertation.

ENGLISH

1. There shall be a Preliminary Examination for Part I, and for Part II, of the English Tripos.

2. The Examiners shall be the Examiners for Parts I and II of the Tripos.

3. (*a*) For the purposes of the Regulations and any Supplementary Regulations, the study of 'English literature' shall be understood to mean, in the Preliminary Examination to both Parts of the Tripos, the study of literary works written in the English language (including Old English); of literary works of the British Isles including Ireland (whether written in English, or in other languages such as Latin or French); and of literary works written in Old Norse and the Medieval Celtic languages. It shall be understood to embrace the study of the English language.

(*b*) The study of 'English literature' shall normally also embrace, in the Preliminary Examination to both Parts of the Tripos, English literary translations of works originally written in other languages, so long as due consideration is given to the fact of translation.

(*c*) For the Preliminary Examination to Part I of the English Tripos, the study of 'English literature' shall also embrace such philosophical, historical and other writing as normally comes within the scope of Papers 3, 4, 6 and 7 of Part I of the Tripos as illustrated by reading lists announced by the Faculty Board.

(*d*) For the Preliminary Examination to Part II of the English Tripos, the study of 'English literature' shall also embrace such philosophical, historical and other writing, and such products of non-literary media and expressive forms, as normally come within the scope of Papers 1, 2, and 20 to 25 of Part II of the Tripos as illustrated by reading lists announced by the Faculty Board.

(*e*) In the Preliminary Examination to both Parts of the Tripos, relevant comparisons with other materials that fall outside the scope of 'English literature' thus defined shall be accepted; but only so long as greater weight falls, in each answer offered, on materials that come within the aforementioned scope.

4. Candidates must not use the same material twice, either within any given paper or across either examination as a whole.

Part I

5. The papers in the Preliminary Examination for Part I shall be as follows:

Paper A.	English literature and its contexts, 1300–1550
Paper B.	English literature and its contexts, 1500–1700
Paper C.	English literature and its contexts, 1660–1870
Paper D1.	English literature and its contexts, 1830–1945
Paper D2.	English literature and its contexts, 1870–present

A candidate shall offer *either* Paper A *or* Paper D, and *either* Paper B *or* Paper C. Every paper shall be set for three hours. Candidates offering Paper D may do so by offering either Paper D1 or Paper D2 but not both. Candidates offering any of Papers B, C, D1, and D2 shall be required to demonstrate, in each such paper offered, substantial knowledge of English literature before and after the medial date specified for the paper in question.

Part II

6. The papers in the Preliminary Examination for Part II shall be as follows: Papers 1, 2, and 20 to 25 of Part II of the English Tripos. A candidate shall offer any two papers. Every paper shall be set for three hours except Papers 1 and 21 which shall be set for three and a half hours. In Papers 21 to 25 candidates shall be required to demonstrate substantial knowledge of the literature of the British Isles (which may include Ireland). Candidates offering any of Papers 22, 24, 25A, and 25B shall be required to demonstrate, in each such paper offered, substantial knowledge of English literature before and after the medial date specified for the paper in question.

GEOGRAPHY

1. There shall be a Preliminary Examination for Part II of the Geographical Tripos.

2. The papers for this examination shall be taken from among the papers for Part IB of the Geographical Tripos and the Examiners shall be the Examiners for that examination.

3. Each candidate shall

(*a*) offer Paper 1 from Group A of Part IB of the Geographical Tripos and

(*b*) offer three papers from Group B of Part IB of the Geographical Tripos; and

(*c*) submit to the Examiners, in accordance with arrangements to be specified by the Head of Department of Geography and, by a date or dates to be announced not later than the first quarter of Michaelmas Term, a record of a practical exercise or exercises undertaken by the candidate. All items in section (*c*) shall be submitted together with a declaration as specified in Regulation 25 of the Geographical Tripos.

HISTORY

1. There shall be Preliminary Examinations for Part I and for Part II of the Historical Tripos.

Part I

2. The examination shall consist of nineteen papers as follows:

Section A

Paper 1. Historical argument and practice

Section B

British Political History

Paper 2. British political history, 380–1100
Paper 3. British political history, 1050–1509
Paper 4. British political history, 1485–1714
Paper 5. British political history, 1688–1886
Paper 6. British political history, since 1880

Section C

British Economic and Social History

Paper 7. British economic and social history, 380–1100
Paper 8. British economic and social history, 1050–*c*. 1500
Paper 9. British economic and social history, *c*. 1500–1750
Paper 10. British economic and social history, 1700–1880
Paper 11. British economic and social history, since *c*. 1880

Section D

European History

Paper 12. European history, 776 BC–AD 69
Paper 13. European history, 31 BC–AD 900
Paper 14. European history, 900–*c*. 1215
Paper 15. European history, 1200–1520
Paper 16. European history, 1450–1760
Paper 17. European history, 1715–1890
Paper 18. European history, since 1890

Section E

World History

Paper 19. World history, from 1400

3. In order to be included in the list of successful candidates, a candidate shall offer Paper 1 and two papers from Sections B–E. Only one paper may be offered from each section.

Part II

4. The examination shall consist of Papers 1 and 4–30 of Part II of the Historical Tripos. In order to be classed a candidate shall offer Paper 1 and either two or three papers, provided that no candidate shall offer a paper which he or she would not be permitted to offer as a candidate for the Tripos. A candidate who offers four papers shall be classed on the basis of the best three of those papers. The Examiners shall be the Examiners for Part II of the Tripos.

SUPPLEMENTARY REGULATIONS

PART I

Paper 1. Historical argument and practice

This paper aims to provide an opportunity for candidates to reflect on broad issues of historical argument and practice. The paper is a means of enabling candidates to raise and discuss fundamental questions which relate their specialist knowledge to more general themes of historical inquiry and explanation. The paper will offer a choice of questions, from which candidates will be required to answer one.

Papers 2–19. British, European, and world history

The scope of Papers 2–18 shall be that of the corresponding papers in Part I of the Tripos. The scope of Paper 19 shall be that of Papers 21 and 23 in Part I.

Three questions must be answered but no question shall be specified as compulsory, except that in Paper 4 (British political history, 1485–1714) and in Paper 18 (European history, since 1890) candidates will be required to answer at least one question from each of sections A and B.

NATURAL SCIENCES

Amended by Notice (Reporter, *2013–14, p. 718*)

1. There shall be a Preliminary Examination for Part II of the Natural Sciences Tripos. The subjects of the examination shall be as follows:

Chemistry	Materials Science
[Geological Sciences] ⟨Earth Sciences⟩[1]	Physics
History and Philosophy of Science	Psychology

2. Each candidate for the examination shall offer one of these subjects and shall satisfy the requirements set out in the regulations below. No candidate may offer a paper which they have previously offered in Part IB of the Natural Sciences Tripos.

3. The examination in Chemistry shall consist of the examination requirements for the subjects Chemistry A and Chemistry B in Part IB of the Tripos. The Examiners in Chemistry A and Chemistry B in Part IB shall be the Examiners in Chemistry in the Preliminary Examination.

4. The examination in Physics shall consist of:

either (i) the examination requirements for the subjects Physics A and Physics B in Part IB of the Tripos

or (ii) the examination requirements for the subjects Physics A and Physics B and Mathematics in Part IB of the Tripos.

The Examiners in the subjects Physics A and Physics B and Mathematics in Part IB shall, as appropriate, be the Examiners in Physics in the Preliminary Examination.

5. The examination in [Geological Sciences] ⟨Earth Sciences⟩[1] shall consist of the examination requirements for the subjects [Geological Sciences A and Geological Sciences B] ⟨Earth Sciences A and Earth Sciences B⟩[1] in Part IB of the Tripos. The Examiners in [Geological Sciences A and Geological Sciences B] ⟨Earth Sciences A and Earth Sciences B⟩[1] in Part IB shall, as appropriate, be the Examiners in [Geological Sciences] ⟨Earth Sciences⟩[1] in the Preliminary Examination.

6. The examination in History and Philosophy of Science shall consist of:

(*a*) the papers in History and Philosophy of Science set for Part IB of the Tripos;

and

(*b*) three essays, each of not more than 5,000 words in length and on three separate topics approved by the Board of History and Philosophy of Science. Not more than one topic may be chosen from any one field.

The Examiners in History and Philosophy of Science in Part IB shall be the Examiners in History and Philosophy of Science in the Preliminary Examination.

7. The examination in Materials Science shall consist of the examination requirements for Materials Science in Part IB of the Tripos and two subjects selected from Chemistry A, Mathematics, Physics A, and Physics B, in Part IB of the Tripos. The Examiners in Materials Science in Part IB shall be the Examiners in Materials Science in the Preliminary Examination.

8. The examination in Psychology shall consist of the examination requirements for Experimental Psychology in Part IB of the Tripos. The Examiners in Experimental Psychology in Part IB shall be the Examiners in Psychology in the Preliminary Examination.

9. For each subject there shall be published a separate class-list, which shall be signed by the Examiners in that subject. In each list the names of the successful candidates shall be arranged in three classes, of which the second shall be divided into two divisions.

[1] The subject(s) in angular brackets will replace the subject(s) in square brackets with effect from 1 October 2015.

TRIPOS EXAMINATIONS

ANGLO-SAXON, NORSE, AND CELTIC TRIPOS

Amended by Notices (Reporter, *2013–14, pp. 528 and 718*)

Two Parts. **1.** The Anglo-Saxon, Norse, and Celtic Tripos shall consist of two Parts. A separate class-list shall be published for each Part.

Standing of candidates. **2.** The following may present themselves as candidates for honours in Part I:

(*a*) a student who has not obtained honours in an Honours Examination provided that he or she has kept one term and that six complete terms have not passed after his or her first term of residence;

(*b*) a student who has obtained honours in an Honours Examination, in the year after or next but one after so obtaining honours, provided that twelve complete terms have not passed after his or her first term of residence.

3. The following may present themselves as candidates for honours in Part II:

(*a*) a student who has obtained honours in Part I of the Anglo Saxon, Norse, and Celtic Tripos in the year after so obtaining honours, provided that twelve complete terms have not passed after her or his first term of residence;[1]

(*b*) a student who has obtained honours in another Honours Examination in the year next after or next but one after so obtaining honours, provided that twelve complete terms have not passed after her or his first term of residence;

(*c*) an Affiliated Student as allowed by the Faculty Board of English in accordance with the regulations for Affiliated Students.

4. No student shall be a candidate for both Parts, or for either Part and also for another Honours Examination, in the same term.

5. No student who has been a candidate for either Part shall again be a candidate for the same Part.

Supplementary regulations. **6.** The Faculty Board of English may from time to time make supplementary regulations defining all or any of the subjects set out in the following regulations, and may modify, alter, or withdraw such supplementary regulations as they think fit, due care being taken that sufficient notice is given of any change.

Variable subjects. **7.** The Faculty Board of English shall give notice before the end of the Easter Term in every academical year of the variable subjects for the examinations to be held in the academical year next but one following; provided that the Board shall have the power of subsequently issuing amendments if they have due reason for doing so and if they are satisfied that no student's preparation for the examination is adversely affected.

Examiners and Assessors. **8.** The Faculty Board of English shall nominate such number of Examiners as they may deem sufficient for each Part of the Tripos, and shall have the power to nominate Assessors for any papers.

9. The questions proposed by each Examiner and Assessor shall be submitted for approval to the whole body of Examiners.

10. The answers to each question shall be read by at least two Examiners or Assessors.

Class-lists. **11.** In the class-list for each Part of the Tripos, the names of the candidates who obtain honours shall be arranged in three classes, of which the second shall be divided into two divisions. The names in the first and third classes and in each division of the second class shall be arranged in alphabetical order. A mark of distinction shall be affixed to the names of those candidates placed in the first class whose work either in a part or in the whole of the examination is of special merit.

Part I. **12.** The papers in Part I shall be as follows:

Paper 1. England before the Norman Conquest.
Paper 2. Scandinavian history in the Viking Age.[2]
Paper 3. The Brittonic-speaking peoples from the fourth century to the twelfth.
Paper 4. The Gaelic-speaking peoples from the fourth century to the twelfth.
Paper 5. Old English language and literature (also serves as Paper 26 of Part II of the English Tripos (New Regulations)).[2]
Paper 6. Old Norse language and literature (also serves as Paper 27A of Part II of the English Tripos (New Regulations)).[2]

[1] See also the regulations for Affiliated Students.
[2] This paper is also available to candidates for Part II of the Modern and Medieval Languages Tripos; see p. 395.

Paper 7. Medieval Welsh language and literature (also serves as Paper 28A of Part II of the English Tripos (New Regulations)).[1]

Paper 8. Medieval Irish language and literature (also serves as Paper 29A of Part II of the English Tripos (New Regulations)).[1]

Paper 9. Insular Latin language and literature (also serves as Paper 8E of Part I and Paper 30 of Part II of the English Tripos (New Regulations)).

Paper 10. Palaeography and codicology.

Paper 11. Early medieval literature and its contexts (also serves as Paper 20 of Part II of the English Tripos (New Regulations)).

Paper 12. Love, violence, and power in France 1100–1500 (Paper Fr. 3 of the Modern and Medieval Languages Tripos).

Paper 13. Medieval Latin literature, from 650 to 1300 (Paper ML 2 of the Modern and Medieval Languages Tripos).[2]

Paper 14. The North Sea in the early Middle Ages (Paper A25 of Part IIB of the Archaeological and Anthropological Tripos and Paper ARC26 of Parts IIA and IIB of the Human, Social, and Political Sciences Tripos).

Paper 15. Europe in late Antiquity and the migration period (Paper A27 of Part IIB of the Archaeological and Anthropological Tripos and Paper ARC27 of Parts IIA and IIB of the Human, Social, and Political Sciences Tripos).

13. A candidate for Part I shall offer six of the papers specified in Regulation 12, provided that — Scheme of papers.

(*a*) no candidate shall offer more than two papers chosen from among Papers 11–15;

(*b*) no candidate shall offer both Paper 14 and Paper 15;

(*c*) a candidate may submit in place of any one of the papers required under this regulation a dissertation on a topic approved by the Head of the Department of Anglo-Saxon, Norse, and Celtic which falls within the scope of one or more of Papers 1–10.

14. The papers in Part II shall be as follows: — Part II.

Paper 1. A subject in Anglo-Saxon history specified by the Faculty Board of English.

Paper 2. A subject in Scandinavian history of the Viking Age specified by the Faculty Board of English.

Paper 3. A subject in Celtic history specified by the Faculty Board of English.

Paper 4. A subject in Anglo-Saxon, Norse, and Celtic history specified by the Faculty Board of English.

Paper 5. A subject in Old English literature specified by the Faculty Board of English.[1]

Paper 6. Advanced medieval Scandinavian language and literature (also serves as Paper 27B of Part II of the English Tripos (New Regulations)).[1]

Paper 7. Advanced medieval Welsh language and literature (also serves as Paper 28B of Part II of the English Tripos (New Regulations)).[1]

Paper 8. Advanced medieval Irish language and literature (also serves as Paper 29B of Part II of the English Tripos (New Regulations)).[1]

Paper 9. A subject in Insular Latin literature specified by the Faculty Board of English.

Paper 10. Textual criticism.

Paper 11. Germanic philology (also serves as Paper 31 of the Linguistics Tripos).[1]

Paper 12. Celtic philology (also serves as Paper 27 of the Linguistics Tripos).[1]

Paper 13. Medieval English literature, 1066–1500 (Paper 6 of Part II of the English Tripos (New Regulations)).

Paper 14. A subject in medieval European history (a paper on a subject announced for a paper of Part II of the Historical Tripos which in any year has been approved for the purpose of this regulation by the Faculty Board of English).

Paper 15(*a*). Historical linguistics (Paper 11 of the Linguistics Tripos).[3]

Paper 15(*b*). History of the English language (Paper 13 of the Linguistics Tripos).[4]

Paper 16. The North Sea in the early Middle Ages (Paper A25 of Part IIB of the Archaeological and Anthropological Tripos and Paper ARC26 of Parts IIA and IIB of the Human, Social, and Political Sciences Tripos).

Paper 17. Europe in late Antiquity and the migration period (Paper A27 of Part IIB of the Archaeological and Anthropological Tripos and Paper ARC27 of Parts IIA and IIB of the Human, Social, and Political Sciences Tripos).

Paper 18. Topics in medieval studies: to be specified by the Faculty Board from time to time (Paper Fr.7 of the Modern and Medieval Languages Tripos).

Paper 19. England before the Norman Conquest (Paper 1 of Part I of the Anglo-Saxon, Norse, and Celtic Tripos).

Paper 20. Scandinavian History in the Viking Age (Paper 2 of Part I of the Anglo- Saxon, Norse, and Celtic Tripos).

[1] This paper is also available to candidates for Part II of the Modern and Medieval Languages Tripos; see p. 395.

[2] This paper is suspended until further notice.

[3] This paper will be suspended in 2015–16 and in each alternate year thereafter.

[4] This paper will be suspended in 2014–15 and in each alternate year thereafter.

Paper 21. The Brittonic-speaking peoples from the fourth century to the twelfth (Paper 3 of Part I of the Anglo-Saxon, Norse, and Celtic Tripos).

Paper 22. The Gaelic-speaking peoples from the fourth century to the twelfth (Paper 4 of Part I of the Anglo-Saxon, Norse, and Celtic Tripos).

Paper 23. Old English language and literature (Paper 5 of Part I of the Anglo-Saxon, Norse, and Celtic Tripos. Also serves as Paper 8A of Part I of the English Tripos and Paper 26 of Part II of the English Tripos (New Regulations)).

Paper 24. Old Norse language and literature (Paper 6 of Part I of the Anglo-Saxon, Norse, and Celtic Tripos. Also serves as Paper 8B of Part I and Paper 27A of Part II of the English Tripos (New Regulations)).

Paper 25. Medieval Welsh language and literature (Paper 7 of Part I of the Anglo-Saxon, Norse, and Celtic Tripos. Also serves as Paper 8C of Part I and Paper 28A of Part II of the English Tripos (New Regulations)).

Paper 26. Medieval Irish language and literature (Paper 8 of Part I of the Anglo-Saxon, Norse, and Celtic Tripos. Also serves as Paper 8D of Part I and Paper 29A of Part II of the English Tripos (New Regulations)).

Paper 27. Insular Latin language and literature (Paper 9 of Part I of the Anglo-Saxon, Norse, and Celtic Tripos. Also serves as Paper 8E of Part I and Paper 30 of Part II of the English Tripos (New Regulations)).

Paper 28. Palaeography and codicology (Paper 10 of Part I of the Anglo-Saxon, Norse, and Celtic Tripos).

Scheme of papers.

15. Except as provided in Regulation 16, a candidate for Part II shall offer

(*a*) four of papers 1–18, provided that:

(i) a candidate may not offer more than one paper chosen from among Papers 13–18;

(ii) no candidate who has previously offered Paper 14 in Part I of the Anglo-Saxon, Norse, and Celtic Tripos shall offer Paper 16;

(iii) no candidate who has previously offered Paper 15 in Part I of the Anglo-Saxon, Norse, and Celtic Tripos shall offer Paper 17;

(iv) no candidate shall offer a subject which he or she has previously offered in any other Honours examination;

(*b*) a dissertation on a topic, approved by the Head of the Department of Anglo-Saxon, Norse, and Celtic, which falls within the scope of one or more of Papers 1–10 of Part I and Papers 1–12 of Part II.

16. (*a*) A candidate for Part II who takes the examination in the year next after obtaining honours in Part I of the Anglo-Saxon, Norse, and Celtic Tripos or in another Honours Examination may offer in place of one of the papers required under Regulation 15(*a*) one paper chosen from among Papers 19–28;

(*b*) candidates for Part II who take the examination in the year next but one after obtaining honours in another Honours Examination may offer in place of up to two of the papers required under Regulation 15(*a*) papers chosen from among Papers 23–27;

provided that:

(i) a candidate may not offer a paper that he or she has previously offered in another Honours Examination;

(ii) a candidate may not offer any of the following combinations of papers:

Paper 5 together with Paper 23;
Paper 6 together with Paper 24;
Paper 7 together with Paper 25;
Paper 8 together with Paper 26;
Paper 9 together with Paper 27.

Dissertation.

17. (*a*) A candidate for Part I who wishes to offer a dissertation under Regulation 13(*c*), or a candidate for Part II who is required to offer a dissertation under Regulation 15(*b*), shall submit an application, including the title of the proposed dissertation, a brief account of its scope, and a statement of the scheme of papers to be offered in the examination. Applications shall be submitted to the Head of the Department, so as to arrive not later than the division of the Michaelmas Term next preceding the examination.

(*b*) Each candidate must obtain the approval of the proposed title by the Faculty Board not later than the last day of the Full Michaelmas Term next preceding the examination. When the Faculty Board have approved a title, no change shall be made to it or to the candidate's scheme of papers, without the further approval of the Faculty Board.

(*c*) A Part I dissertation shall be of not fewer than 7,000 and not more than 10,000 words in length, and a Part II dissertation shall be of not fewer than 9,000 and not more than 12,000 words in length, including appendices but excluding bibliography. Candidates will be required to declare that the dissertation is their own work and that it does not contain material already used to any substantial extent for a comparable purpose. Every dissertation shall be typewritten.

(*d*) A dissertation shall be submitted to the Head of the Department, so as to arrive not later than the first day of the Full Easter Term in which the examination is to be held.

(*e*) The Examiners shall have power to examine a candidate *viva voce* on his or her dissertation and on the general field of knowledge within which it falls.

SUPPLEMENTARY REGULATIONS

Part I

Paper 1. England before the Norman Conquest

An introduction to the history and civilization of England from the age of the Anglo-Saxon settlements to the Norman Conquest. Candidates will be required to use primary sources in the original languages or in translation.

Paper 2. Scandinavian history in the Viking Age

An introduction to the history and culture of Denmark, Norway, and Sweden in the Viking Age, including the westward expansion to the North Atlantic and the eastward expansion to Russia and Ukraine. Candidates will be required to use primary sources in the original languages or in translation.

Paper 3. The Brittonic-speaking peoples from the fourth century to the twelfth

An introduction to the history and culture of the Brittonic-speaking peoples from the collapse of the Roman Empire to the Anglo-Norman invasions. Candidates will be required to use primary sources in the original languages or in translation.

Paper 4. The Gaelic-speaking peoples from the fourth century to the twelfth

An introduction to the history and culture of the Gaelic-speaking peoples from the fourth century to the twelfth. Candidates will be required to use primary sources in the original languages or in translation.

Paper 5. Old English language and literature (also serves as Paper 26 of Part II of the English Tripos (New Regulations))

An introduction to the language and literary characteristics of Old English prose and poetry. There will be set texts in the original language; candidates will be required to translate passages from the set texts and an unseen passage of Old English, and to write essays on selected topics.

Paper 6. Old Norse language and literature (also serves as Paper 27A of Part II of the English Tripos (New Regulations))

An introduction to the language and literary characteristics of Old Norse prose and poetry. There will be set texts in the original language; candidates will be required to translate passages from the set texts and an unseen passage of Old Norse, and to write essays on selected topics.

Paper 7. Medieval Welsh language and literature (also serves as Paper 28A of Part II of the English Tripos (New Regulations))

An introduction to the language and literature of Wales from the beginnings to the end of the Middle Ages. There will be set texts in the original language; candidates will be required to translate, and to comment on the linguistic characteristics of, passages from the set texts, to translate an unseen passage of Middle Welsh, and to write essays on selected topics.

Paper 8. Medieval Irish language and literature (also serves as Paper 29A of Part II of the English Tripos (New Regulations))

An introduction to the language and literature of early medieval Ireland, in particular until the end of the tenth century. There will be set texts in the original language; candidates will be required to translate, and to comment on the linguistic characteristics of, passages from the set texts, to translate an unseen passage of Old Irish, and to write essays on selected topics.

Paper 9. Insular Latin language and literature (also serves as Paper 8E of Part I and Paper 30 of Part II of the English Tripos (New Regulations))

An introduction to the Latin literature of England and the Celtic-speaking countries from the fourth century to the twelfth. An advanced knowledge of Latin is not expected when preparation is begun, although some knowledge of the language is desirable. There will be set texts in the original language; candidates will be required to show detailed knowledge of these and to write essays on selected topics.

Paper 10. Palaeography and codicology

An introduction to the manuscript as a physical object and the history of scripts used in the manuscript sources studied in Papers 1–9. Candidates will be required to answer compulsory practical questions, and to write essays on selected topics.

PART II

Paper 1. A subject in Anglo-Saxon history specified by the Faculty Board of English

An advanced topic in the history and civilization of England from the age of the Anglo-Saxon settlements to the Norman Conquest. Candidates will be required to use primary sources in the original languages or in translation.

Paper 2. A subject in Scandinavian history of the Viking Age specified by the Faculty Board of English

An advanced topic in the history and culture of Denmark, Norway, and Sweden in the Viking Age, including the westward expansion to the North Atlantic and the eastward expansion to Russia and Ukraine. Candidates will be required to use primary sources in the original languages or in translation.

Paper 3. A subject in Celtic history specified by the Faculty Board of English

An advanced topic in the history and culture of the Celtic-speaking peoples from the fourth century to the twelfth. Candidates will be required to use primary sources in the original languages or in translation.

Paper 4. A subject in Anglo-Saxon, Norse, and Celtic history specified by the Faculty Board of English

An advanced topic in the history and culture of Anglo-Saxon England, medieval Scandinavia, and the medieval Celtic-speaking peoples. Candidates will be required to use primary sources in the original languages or in translation.

Paper 5. A subject in Old English literature specified by the Faculty Board of English

The work of an author or a group of authors, or a group of texts, or a literary topic or genre within the field of Old English literature, will be prescribed for special study. Candidates will be required to use primary sources in the original language.

Paper 6. Advanced medieval Scandinavian language and literature (also serves as Paper 27B of Part II of the English Tripos (New Regulations))

Scandinavian languages and literatures from the medieval period are studied. There will be set texts in the original language. Candidates will be required to translate and comment on extracts from these set texts and to translate unseen passages, and also to write essays on selected topics in medieval Scandinavian literature.

Paper 7. Advanced medieval Welsh language and literature (also serves as Paper 28B of Part II of the English Tripos (New Regulations))

Welsh language and literature from the beginnings to the end of the Middle Ages are studied. There will be set texts in Old and Middle Welsh. Candidates will be required to translate and comment on extracts from these set texts and to translate unseen passages from Middle Welsh. There will be a further group of set texts, in medieval Breton and Cornish. Candidates will be required to translate and comment on extracts from these set texts. They will also be required to write essays on selected topics in medieval Welsh, Breton, and Cornish language and literature.

Paper 8. Advanced medieval Irish language and literature (also serves as Paper 29B of Part II of the English Tripos (New Regulations))

Irish language and literature from the beginnings to the end of the Middle Ages are studied. There will be set texts in the original language. Candidates will be required to translate extracts from these set texts and to translate unseen passages, and also to write essays on selected topics in medieval Irish language and literature.

Paper 9. A subject in Insular Latin literature specified by the Faculty Board of English

The work of an author or a group of authors, or a group of texts, or a literary topic or genre within the field of Insular Latin literature, will be prescribed for special study. Candidates will be required to use primary sources in the original language.

Paper 10. Textual criticism

An introduction to the processes by which extant sources written in the languages studied for Papers 5–9 have been transmitted, and of the scholarly methods by which these sources are converted into a usable form. The various editorial and diplomatic approaches and techniques are studied. Candidates will be required to answer a compulsory practical question and to write essays on selected topics.

Paper 11. Germanic philology (also serves as Paper 31 of the Linguistics Tripos)

The history and grammar of the Germanic languages will be studied in relation to one another and to their Indo-European background. Candidates will be required to comment on passages and to write essays on selected topics.

Paper 12. Celtic philology (also serves as Paper 27 of the Linguistics Tripos)
The history and grammar of the Celtic languages will be studied in relation to one another and to their Indo-European background. Candidates will be required to comment on passages and to write essays on selected topics.

ARCHAEOLOGICAL AND ANTHROPOLOGICAL TRIPOS

Amended by Notices (Reporter, *2013–14, pp. 529 and 719*)

General

1. The Archaeological and Anthropological Tripos shall consist of three Parts, Part I, Part IIA, and Part IIB. In Part IIA and Part IIB there shall be an examination in each of the following three subjects: Archaeology (including Assyriology and Egyptology), Biological Anthropology, Social Anthropology. For Part I there shall be a single class-list; for Part IIA and Part IIB there shall be a separate class-list for each of the three subjects of the examination. Three Parts.

2. The Faculty Board of Human, Social, and Political Science shall nominate such number of Examiners to conduct the examination for Part I of the Tripos, and a Senior Examiner and such number of Examiners to conduct the examination in each subject for Part IIA and Part IIB, as they shall deem sufficient. The Faculty Board shall have power to nominate such number of Assessors as they shall deem sufficient to assist the Examiners for each Part. If required to do so, Assessors shall set papers in the subject or subjects assigned to them, shall mark the answers of the candidates in those papers, shall assess dissertations, and shall advise the Examiners on the performance of candidates in the examination. Assessors may be summoned to meetings of the Examiners for the purpose of consultation and advice, but shall not be entitled to vote. Examiners and Assessors.

3. The Faculty Board may from time to time make supplementary regulations defining all or any of the subjects and specified texts of examination and may modify, alter, or withdraw such supplementary regulations as they think fit, due care being taken that sufficient notice is given of any change. Supplementary regulations.

4. Before the end of the Easter Term each year the Faculty Board shall give notice of the variable subjects for the examinations to be held in the academical year next following; provided that the Board shall have the power of subsequently issuing amendments if they have due reason for doing so and if they are satisfied that no student's preparation for the examination is adversely affected. The Board shall have power when they give notice of variable subjects to announce any consequential restriction on the combination of papers that a candidate may choose to offer. Variable subjects.

5. The questions proposed by each Examiner and Assessor shall be submitted for approval to the whole body of Examiners for Part I or to the Examiners in the particular subject for Part IIA or Part IIB.

6. The answers to each question shall be read by at least two Examiners or Assessors.

7. Separate meetings shall be held of all the Examiners for Part I and of the three bodies of Examiners for Part IIA and Part IIB, at which the respective class-lists shall be drawn up. In each class-list the names of the candidates who deserve honours shall be placed in three classes, of which the second shall be divided into two divisions. The names in the first and third classes, and in each division of the second class, shall be arranged in alphabetical order. For special excellence a mark of distinction may be awarded. The class-lists for Part IIA and Part IIB shall indicate whether a candidate has offered in the examination the Assyriology and/or Egyptology option.

8. No student shall be a candidate for more than one Part, or for any Part and also for another Honours Examination in the same term.

9. No student who has been a candidate for any Part shall again be a candidate for the same Part.

10. A candidate shall not offer in any Part of the Tripos a paper that he or she has previously offered in another University examination.

Part I

11. The following may present themselves as candidates for honours in Part I: Standing of candidates.

(*a*) a student who has not obtained honours in another Honours Examination, provided that he or she has kept one term and that three complete terms have not passed after the student's first term of residence;

(*b*) a student who has obtained honours in another Honours Examination, in the year after so obtaining honours, provided that he or she has kept seven terms and that nine complete terms have not passed after the student's first term of residence.

12. The scheme of examination for Part I shall be as follows:

Paper 1. The development of human society (also serves as Paper 6 of Part I of the Politics, Psychology, and Sociology Tripos).
Paper 2. Humans in biological perspective (also serves as Paper 7 of Part I of the Politics, Psychology, and Sociology Tripos).
Paper 3. Human societies: the comparative perspective (also serves as Paper 8 of Part I of the Politics, Psychology, and Sociology Tripos).
Paper 4A. Being human: an interdisciplinary approach.
Paper 4B. Introduction to sociology: modern societies (Paper 2 of Part I of the Politics, Psychology, and Sociology Tripos).
Paper 4C. The analysis of modern politics I (Paper 1 of Part I of the Politics, Psychology, and Sociology Tripos).
Paper 4D. Introduction to psychology (Paper 3 of Part I of the Politics, Psychology, and Sociology Tripos).
Paper 5. Introduction to the cultures of Egypt and Mesopotamia.
Paper 6. Akkadian language I (also serves as Paper X.1 of Part IA of the Asian and Middle Eastern Studies Tripos).
Paper 7. Egyptian language I (also serves as Paper X.2 of Part IA of the Asian and Middle Eastern Studies Tripos).

A candidate for Part I shall offer one of the following:

Either (i) Papers 1, 2, and 3, and one of Papers 4A, 4B, 4C, 4D, and 5;
or (ii) Paper 5; Papers 6 or 7; two further papers chosen from Papers 1, 2, and 3;
or (iii) Paper 5; Papers 6 and 7; and one further paper chosen from Papers 1, 2, and 3.

Part IIA and Part IIB

Standing of candidates.

13. A student who has obtained honours in Part I of the Archaeological and Anthropological Tripos or in another Honours Examination may be a candidate for honours in Part IIA in the year next after so obtaining honours.

14. (*a*) A student who has obtained honours in any Honours Examination other than Part I of the Archaeological and Anthropological Tripos may be a candidate for honours in Part IIB in the year next after so obtaining honours, provided that

(i) the student has kept seven terms and twelve complete terms have not passed after his or her first term of residence;

(ii) candidature in Archaeology shall be subject to the requirement of sub-paragraph (*b*) below.

(*b*) No student shall be a candidate for Part IIB in Archaeology unless the Head of the Department of Archaeology and Anthropology is satisfied that the student has, since matriculation, undertaken at least six weeks of archaeological excavation or fieldwork[1] on a project or projects (or in the case of candidates for Assyriology or Egyptology on a study visit to Egypt or the Middle East and/or study in a museum) approved by the Head of the Department, provided that the Head of the Department shall have power to grant exemption from this requirement to a candidate who has obtained an equivalent amount of appropriate experience in some other way. Before the division of the Lent Term each year the Head of the Department shall draw up a list of those candidates who have satisfied this requirement or have been granted exemption from it, and shall communicate this information to the Registrary.

Papers in Part IIA and Part IIB.

15. The scheme of examination for Part IIA and Part IIB[2] shall be as follows:

Archaeology

A1. Archaeological thought I
A2. Archaeology in action I
A3. Archaeological thought II
A4. Archaeology in action II
A10. Archaeological practice

Special areas

A5. The archaeology of early human development[3]
A6. The Palaeolithic of the Old World

[1] Students will normally be required to spend two weeks on a training excavation arranged by the Head of the Department and four weeks on some other approved excavation or fieldwork.

[2] For further information on the papers offered for Part IIB in 2014–15, see Notice (*Reporter*, 6354, 2013–14, p 667).

[3] These papers will be available in alternate years, see the supplementary regulations.

A7. Topics in Palaeolithic archaeology[1]
A8. European prehistory
A9. Special topics in European prehistory
A13. Aegean prehistory (Paper D1 of Part II of the Classical Tripos)
A14. A topic within classical archaeology and/or art (Paper D2 of Part II of the Classical Tripos)
A15. A topic within classical archaeology and/or art (Paper D3 of Part II of the Classical Tripos)
A16. A topic within classical archaeology and/or art (Paper D4 of Part II of the Classical Tripos)
A17. The historical archaeology of Ancient Egypt I[1]
A18. The historical archaeology of Ancient Egypt II[1]
A19. Ancient Egyptian religion I[1]
A20. Ancient Egyptian religion II[1]
A21. Mesopotamian culture I: literature[1]
A22. Mesopotamian culture II: religion and scholarship[1]
A23. Mesopotamian archaeology I: prehistory and early states[1]
A24. Mesopotamian archaeology II: territorial states to empires[1]
A25. The North Sea in the early Middle Ages (also serves as Paper 14 of Part I and Paper 16 of Part II of the Anglo-Saxon, Norse, and Celtic Tripos)
A26. The Long Viking Age
A27. Europe in Late Antiquity and the Migration Period (also serves as Paper 15 of Part I and Paper 17 of Part II of the Anglo-Saxon, Norse, and Celtic Tripos)
A28. The archaeology of medieval Britain
A29. Ancient India I: prehistory of India[1]
A30. Ancient India I: the Indus civilization and beyond[1]
A31. Ancient India II: early historic cities of South Asia[1]
A32. Ancient India II: art and architecture of ancient India[1]
A33. Ancient South America[1]
A34. The archaeology of Mesoamerica and North America[1]
A36. The late prehistoric and historical archaeology of sub-Saharan Africa
A37. Introduction to scientific approaches in archaeology
A38. Archaeological science

Assyriology

M1. Akkadian language II (also serves as Paper X.6 of Part IB of the Asian and Middle Eastern Studies Tripos)
M2. Akkadian language III
M3. Sumerian
M4. Mesopotamian history I: states and structures[1]
M5. Mesopotamian history II: empires and systems[1]

Egyptology

E1. Egyptian language II (also serves as Paper X.7 of Part IB of the Asian and Middle Eastern Studies Tripos)
E2. Egyptian language III

The Faculty Board shall announce before the end of the Easter Term the papers that will be available in the examinations to be held in the next academical year.

Biological Anthropology

BA1. Foundations in biological anthropology: the human animal
BA2. Foundations in biological anthropology: the human journey
BA3. Foundations in biological anthropology: the human lifespan
BA4. Theory and practice in anthropology
BA5–17. Not more than thirteen papers, each on a special subject in biological anthropology prescribed by the Faculty Board. In announcing the special subjects available the Faculty Board shall also announce the form of the examination which shall be either a written examination of two hours' duration or the submission of an essay or other exercise in accordance with the provisions of Regulation 19 and which may also include practical work to be submitted in accordance with the provisions of Regulation 18.

Social Anthropology

S1. Foundations of social anthropology I
S2. Foundations of social anthropology II
S3. Theory, methods, and enquiry in social anthropology

[1] These papers will be available in alternate years, see the supplementary regulations.

S4. Thought, belief, and ethics
S5. Political economy and social transformations
S6. Ethnographic areas

Special subjects in social anthropology

S7–11. Not more than five papers, each on a special subject in social anthropology prescribed by the Faculty Board. Each paper shall be of three hours' duration, provided that the Faculty Board may announce an alternative mode of assessment for any of the special subjects which shall consist of the submission of two essays in accordance with the provisions of Regulation 19(*b*).

Part IIA.

16. Subject to the provisions of Regulation 10, candidates for Part IIA shall offer papers and other exercises as follows:

(*a*) *Candidates in Archaeology*

Option 1 (Archaeology)

(i) Papers A1, A2, and A10;
(ii) one paper chosen from Papers A5–A37;
(iii) *either* one further paper chosen from Papers A5–A37,
or one paper chosen from the following: Papers S7–S11;
or two papers chosen from Papers BA5–17;
(iv) the submission of records of practical work, in accordance with the provisions of Regulation 18.

Option 2 (Assyriology)

(i) Paper M1[1] or Paper ARC4 of Part I of the Human, Social, and Political Sciences Tripos;
(ii) Paper A23 or A24;
(iii) two papers from Papers A1 or A2, A21–22, M4–5.

Option 3 (Egyptology)

(i) Paper E1[2] or Paper ARC5 of Part I of the Human, Social, and Political Sciences Tripos;
(ii) Paper A1 or A2;
(iii) Paper A17 or A18;
(iv) Paper A19 or A20.

Option 4 (Assyriology and Egyptology)

(i) Paper M1[1] or Paper ARC4 of Part I of the Human, Social, and Political Sciences Tripos;
(ii) Paper E1[2] or Paper ARC5 of Part I of the Human, Social, and Political Sciences Tripos;
(iii) Paper A17 or A18;
(iv) one paper from Paper A21–24.

(*b*) *Candidates in Biological Anthropology*

(i) Papers BA1, BA2, and BA3;
(ii) two papers chosen from BA5–17 or one paper chosen from Papers A5–A37, S7–S11.

(*c*) *Candidates in Social Anthropology*

(i) Papers S1–S3;
(ii) *either* one paper chosen from Papers S7–S11,
or one paper chosen from Papers A5–A37,
or two papers chosen from Papers BA5–17,
or one paper chosen from the following:

Historical Tripos, Part I
Paper 21. Empires and world history from the fifteenth century to the First World War.

Politics, Psychology, and Sociology Tripos, Part IIA
Paper Pol. 3. The analysis of modern politics II.
Paper Psy. 1. Social psychology.
Paper Soc. 1. Social theory.
Paper Soc. 2. Contemporary societies and global transformations.

[1] Paper M1 can only be taken at Part IIA if a candidate has taken Paper 6 at Part I.
[2] Paper E1 can only be taken at Part IIA if a candidate has taken Paper 7 at Part I.

17. Subject to the provisions of Regulation 10, candidates for Part IIB shall offer papers and other exercises as follows: Part IIB.

(*a*) *Candidates in Archaeology*

Option 1 (Archaeology)

(i) Papers A3 and A4;

(ii) *either* two papers chosen from the following: Papers A5–A38,

or one paper chosen from Papers A5–A38 and one paper chosen from Papers S7–S11, BA1–3 (subject to the approval of the Head of the Department of Archaeology and Anthropology for students choosing a paper from S7–S11 and BA1–3),

or one paper chosen from Papers A5–A38 and two papers chosen from Papers BA5–17 (subject to the approval of the Head of the Department of Archaeology and Anthropology);

(iii) *either* one further paper chosen from Papers A5–A38,

or a dissertation on a subject in archaeology approved by the Faculty Board, which shall be submitted in accordance with the provisions of Regulation 20;

(iv) the submission of records of practical work, in accordance with the provisions of Regulation 18,

provided that a candidate may not offer (i) Paper A22 unless he or she has previously taken either Paper A21 or Papers A23 or A24, and (ii) Paper A38 unless he or she has previously taken Paper A37.

Option 2 (Assyriology)

(i) Paper M2[1] or M1;

(ii) Paper A23 or A24;

(iii) two papers chosen from A4, A21–22, M3,[2] M4–5;

(iv) either one further paper chosen from A4, A21–22, M3,[2] M4–5, or a dissertation on a subject approved by the Faculty Board, which shall be submitted in accordance with the provisions of Regulation 20.

Option 3 (Egyptology)

(i) Paper E2[3] or E1;

(ii) Paper A17 or A18;

(iii) Paper A19 or A20;

(iv) Paper A4;

(v) a dissertation on a subject approved by the Faculty Board, which shall be submitted in accordance with the provisions of Regulation 20.

Option 4 (Assyriology and Egyptology)

(i) Paper M2[1] or M1;

(ii) Paper E2[3] or E1;

(iii) Paper A17 or A18;

(iv) one paper from Papers A21–24;

(v) either one further paper chosen from A19–24, M3,[2] M4–5, or a dissertation on a subject approved by the Faculty Board, which shall be submitted in accordance with the provisions of Regulation 20.

(*b*) *Candidates in Biological Anthropology*

(i) if a candidate took Part IIA of the Archaeological and Anthropological Tripos:

(1) Paper BA4;

(2) two papers chosen from Papers BA5–17;

(3) *either* two further papers chosen from Papers BA5–BA17,

or one paper chosen from Papers A5–38, S7–S11 (subject to the approval of the Head of the Department of Archaeology and Anthropology for students choosing a paper from A5–A38, and S7–S11),

[1] Paper M2 can only be taken at Part IIB if a candidate has taken Paper M1 at Part IIA.
[2] Paper M3 can only be taken if a candidate is also taking Paper M2.
[3] Paper E2 can only be taken at Part IIB if a candidate has taken Paper E1 at Part IIA.

(4) *either* two further papers chosen from Papers BA5–17,
or a dissertation on a subject in Biological Anthropology approved by the Faculty Board, which shall be submitted in accordance with the provisions of Regulation 20;

(ii) if a candidate did not take Part IIA of the Archaeological and Anthropological Tripos:
(1) Papers BAN2–4 of the Human, Social, and Political Sciences Tripos;
(2) *either* two papers chosen from Papers BA5–17, subject to restrictions of paper combinations to be announced by the Faculty Board
or a dissertation which shall be submitted in accordance with the provisions of Regulation 20.

(*c*) *Candidates in Social Anthropology*

(i) Papers S4–S6;
(ii) *either* one paper chosen from Papers S7–S11,
or one paper chosen from Papers A5–A38, BA1–3 (subject to the approval of the Head of the Department of Archaeology and Anthropology for students choosing a paper from A5–A38, and BA1–3),
or two papers chosen from Papers BA5–17 (subject to the approval of the Head of the Department of Archaeology and Anthropology);
(iii) *either* one further paper chosen from Papers S7–S11,
or a dissertation on a subject in social anthropology approved by the Faculty Board, which shall be submitted in accordance with the provisions of Regulation 20.

Practical work. **18.** Candidates for Part IIA and Part IIB in Archaeology (and where appropriate in Biological Anthropology) shall present for the inspection of the Examiners, by a date which the Head of the Department shall announce not later than the division of the Michaelmas Term, records of such practical work done during the courses leading to the examination as shall be determined from time to time by the Faculty Board. The Examiners shall be provided by the Head of the Department with assessments of candidates' practical work, and shall take these assessments into account in assigning marks for the examination.

Seminar courses. **19.** (*a*) The arrangements for the submission of essays or other exercises by candidates for Part IIA and Part IIB in Biological Anthropology who choose a paper from Papers BA5–17 for which the Faculty Board have announced that the examination shall be by one of these alternative means shall be as follows:

Essays shall not exceed 4,000 words in length, excluding footnotes, figures, tables, appendices, and bibliography. Candidates shall be required to state in the bibliography the sources that they have used and to declare that the essay represents their own work unaided except as may be specified in the declaration. Detailed instructions about other exercises shall be issued by the Head of the Department together with the announcements of variable subjects by the Faculty Board. Each essay or other exercise shall be typewritten, unless a candidate has obtained previous permission from the Faculty Board to present it in manuscript; essays or other exercises shall be submitted to the Head of the Department so as to arrive not later than the third Monday of the Full Easter Term in which the examination is to be held. A candidate who submits an essay or other exercise after that date may be penalized.

(*b*) The arrangements for the submission of essays by candidates for Part IIB in Social Anthropology who choose a paper from S7–11, for which the Faculty Board have announced that the examination may be by this form of assessment, shall be as follows:

Two essays shall be submitted, each not exceeding 5,000 words in length, excluding footnotes, figures, tables, appendices, and bibliography. Candidates shall be required to state in the bibliography the sources that they have used and to declare that the essay represents their own work unaided except as may be specified in the declaration. Each essay shall be typewritten, unless a candidate has obtained previous permission from the Faculty Board to present it in manuscript; essays shall be submitted to the Administration Office in the Department of Archaeology and Anthropology, one to arrive not later than the first Friday of Full Lent Term and one to arrive by the first Friday of Full Easter Term. A candidate who submits an essay after the required date may be penalized. A candidate who submits an essay or other exercise in place of the written examination may not also submit a dissertation.

(*c*) The arrangements for the submission of essays by candidates taking paper A21 for Part IIA and Part IIB in Archaeology shall be as follows:

Three essays shall be submitted, each not exceeding 2,000 words in length, excluding footnotes, figures, tables, appendices and bibliography. Candidates shall be required to state in the bibliography the sources that they have used and to declare that the essay represents their own work unaided, except as may be specified in the declaration. Each essay shall be typewritten, unless a candidate has obtained previous permission from the Faculty Board to present it in manuscript. Essays shall be submitted to the Administration Office in the Division of Archaeology, the first to arrive not later than the last Monday of Full Michaelmas Term, the second to arrive not later than the fifth Monday of Full Lent Term, and the third not later than the third Monday of Full Easter Term. A candidate who submits an essay after the required date may be penalized. The submitted essays shall form 40% of the assessment for this paper; the remainder of the assessment (60%) shall be by an examination of two hours' duration.

20. (*a*) A candidate for Part IIB who wishes to offer a dissertation under Regulation 17 shall submit an application, including the title of the proposed dissertation, a brief account of its scope, and a statement of the scheme of papers to be offered in the examination. A candidate who so wishes may request permission to include a film or filmed material, amounting to not more than twenty minutes in length, as a component part of the dissertation. Applications shall be submitted to the Head of the Department so as to arrive not later than the last day of the Full Michaelmas Term next preceding the examination. Dissertations.

(*b*) Each candidate must obtain the approval of the Faculty Board for the proposed title not later than the division of the Lent Term. When the Faculty Board have approved a title, no change shall be made to it, or to the candidate's scheme of papers, without the further approval of the Faculty Board.

(*c*) A dissertation shall be of not more than 10,000 words in length, excluding footnotes, figures, tables, appendices, and bibliography. Each dissertation shall be typewritten, unless a candidate has obtained previous permission from the Faculty Board to present it in manuscript.

(*d*) A dissertation shall be submitted to the Senior Examiner in the Department not later than the following dates:

(i) for a dissertation submitted under Regulation 17(*a*)(iii) or 17(*c*)(iii),[1] the division of the Easter Term in which the examination is held;

(ii) for a dissertation submitted under Regulation 17(*b*)(ii),[2] the third Monday of the Full Easter Term in which the examination is held.

A dissertation shall be accompanied by (i) a brief synopsis on a separate sheet of paper of the contents of the dissertation, and (ii) a certificate signed by the candidate that it is his or her own original work, and that it does not contain material that has already been used to any substantial extent for a comparable purpose.

21. At the discretion of the Examiners, a candidate for Part IIB may be examined *viva voce*.

Temporary Regulation

22. Examinations for the Archaeological and Anthropological Tripos will be held for the last time as follows:

Part I in 2013
Part IIA in 2014
Part IIB in 2015

SUPPLEMENTARY REGULATIONS

Amended by Notice (Reporter, *2013–14, p. 637*)

Part I

Paper 1. The development of human society (also serves as Paper 6 of Part I of the Politics, Psychology, and Sociology Tripos)

This paper serves as an introduction to the collection, analysis, and interpretation of archaeological data, and focuses on major issues in the development of human societies. Examples are drawn from the entire span of the human career, from the initial evolution of hominid behaviour patterns to the emergence of historically documented

[1] That is a dissertation submitted by candidates for Part IIB in Archaeology or Social Anthropology.
[2] That is a dissertation submitted by candidates for Part IIB in Biological Anthropology.

states and empires. Issues are explored in terms of the principal archaeological methods and theories which contribute to our current understanding of past societies.

Paper 2. Humans in biological perspective (also serves as Paper 7 of Part I of the Politics, Psychology, and Sociology Tripos)

This paper provides an introduction to biological anthropology. The syllabus covers the genetic basis of life; evolutionary theory; primate biology, ecology, and behaviour; human evolution; human diversity, geographical patterns of variation and its genetic basis; human ecology, including disease, nutrition, energetics, and behaviour; problems in gene-environment interactions and behavioural genetics. Two special subjects will be prescribed from time to time by the Faculty Board.

Paper 3. Human societies: the comparative perspective (also serves as Paper 8 of Part I of the Politics, Psychology, and Sociology Tripos)

This paper provides an introduction to the aims, scope, and methods of social anthropology. It covers the whole range of human societies, past and present, with a view to understanding them both individually in depth and within a broad comparative perspective. It approaches social life from a number of different angles, focusing on the ideas that people hold, their forms of organization, the way they interact, and the things they produce.

Paper 4A. Being human: an interdisciplinary approach

This paper combines approaches from archaeology, biological anthropology, and social anthropology to study the human condition. Questions addressed will concern: the origins and evolution of human society; symbols, communication, and culture; problems of human ecology and adaptation. Special topics may include sex and gender; sociality and social inequality; art and material culture; technology; language; health and illness; nutrition and development.

Paper 4B. Introduction to sociology: modern societies (also serves as Paper 2 of Part I of the Politics, Psychology, and Sociology Tripos)

The origins and institutional features of modern societies. Social change and global interconnections in the modern world. Selected aspects of modern societies including work, stratification, and inequality; gender and sexual divisions; race and ethnicity; political organization and the modern state; culture and mass communication; deviance and social control.

Paper 5. Introduction to the cultures of Egypt and Mesopotamia

This paper introduces the cultures of Egypt and Mesopotamia and is taught through lectures in each subject area and comparative seminars. The paper is in two parts: section A consists of five comparative questions; section B consists of ten subject specific questions, five related to Egypt and five to Mesopotamia. Students are required to answer one question from each section and a third question from either section.

Paper 6. Akkadian language I (also serves as Paper X.1 of Part IA of the Asian and Middle Eastern Studies Tripos)

This paper consists of passages for transliteration from cuneiform and translation from Akkadian taken from the texts read in class and specified from time to time in the *Reporter*, a passage for translation from English into transliterated Akkadian, and questions on grammar.

Paper 7. Egyptian language I (also serves as Paper X.2 of Part IA of the Asian and Middle Eastern Studies Tripos)

This paper covers the study of hieroglyphic texts in Middle Egyptian, the classic form of the language. Students will be expected to transliterate and translate into English passages from the specified texts, and comment where appropriate. They will also be given a passage from an unspecified text for transliteration and translation into English.

PARTS IIA AND IIB

ARCHAEOLOGY

Paper A1. Archaeological thought I

Why study archaeology, when did people start studying archaeology, and what role does archaeology play in contemporary society? Answers to such questions are discussed in the course for this paper, which reviews the history of archaeological thought. The main issues in archaeology, as they have been seen since the early nineteenth century, are covered, with emphasis placed on the rise of a scientific archaeology in the mid-twentieth century and reactions to it.

Paper A2. Archaeology in action I

The course for this paper shows how the sciences and the humanities are integrated in the practice of archaeology over a broad range of topics concerned with the nature of past societies. The interdisciplinary character of archaeology is explored through consideration of a range of thematic issues, such as material culture; the study of landscapes and settlements; the establishment and study of temporal sequences, and archaeological field methods.

Paper A3. Archaeological thought II

The course for this paper provides an opportunity to extend the depth and range of theoretical issues introduced in Paper A1. In terms of depth, there is fuller coverage of modes of explanation and interpretation in archaeology and discussion of how they are situated within wider debates in the sciences and the humanities. In terms of range, the scope of archaeological awareness is extended to global issues, drawing on a variety of themes in world archaeology.

Paper A4. Archaeology in action II

This paper expands on the range of themes covered in Paper A2, exploring ways in which a wide range of scientific approaches and techniques can be integrated with humanistic and social science perspectives in studying and interpreting the nature of past societies. The interdisciplinary character of archaeology is explored through consideration of a range of thematic issues, such as human impact on the environment; the study of households and communities; the archaeology of death and the body; the archaeology of 'art'; categorization and style; symbols and power; production and exchange, and contemporary notions of heritage.

Paper A10. Archaeological practice

The course for this paper provides an introduction to the practical methods and approaches used by archaeologists to create and analyse archaeological data. It covers the ways in which archaeological theories are applied in practice, through data recovery, analysis, and interpretation. Much of the instruction is provided through hands-on practicals, field trips, and fieldwork.

Special areas

Papers A5/A7, A17/A18, A19/A20, A23/A24, A26/A27, A29/A30, A31/A32, and A33/A34

These papers are paired. Courses are taught over a two-year cycle and are examined in alternate years, so that in any particular year one paper of each pair will be set, corresponding to the subject that has been taught in that year.

Papers A5, A6, and A7. Palaeolithic and Mesolithic archaeology

This course surveys the development of human societies from their primate origins 2–3 million years ago to the emergence of food production in the early postglacial period. The scope of the course is world-wide; it puts special emphasis on the processes of population dispersal (of both the earliest hominids and biologically modern humans) and the processes of technological and social adaptation to the changing environmental conditions of the Pleistocene period. Special emphasis is placed on the patterns of human social and cognitive development, and on the inevitably close inter-relationships between the parallel processes of biological and cultural evolution throughout the course of human development. One of Papers A5 and A7 is taught in alternate years.

Paper A8. European prehistory

This course presents a broad general introduction to later European prehistory from the beginning of the Holocene through the earliest historical societies. Coverage includes the Mesolithic, the Neolithic, the Copper and Bronze Ages, and the Iron Age.

Paper A9. Special topics in European prehistory

This course presents advanced discussion of special topics in European prehistory. Each year's topics are drawn from a rotating list of regional, thematic, and/or theoretical subjects relevant to Later European Prehistory (Mesolithic through Iron Age). It is normally expected that students will have taken or be taking Paper A8 (Later European prehistory) currently.

Papers A13–A16. Classical archaeology

Within Classical archaeology, four different papers are available, concerning which information is available from the Faculty of Classics.

Papers A17/18. The historical archaeology of Ancient Egypt I and II

The course reviews the historical archaeology of ancient Egypt from its origins to the Roman conquest and integrates archaeological, textual, and artistic evidence. Emphasis is placed on examining the nature of society, urbanism, kingship and political power, ideology, and interactions between Egypt and its neighbours. The course is taught over a two-year cycle: A17 covers the unification of Egypt to the end of the Second Intermediate Period (*c.* 3000–1550 BC); A18 covers the New Kingdom and up to the Roman conquest (*c.* 1550–30 BC).

Papers A19/20. Ancient Egyptian religion I and II

This course examines archaeological, textual, and artistic evidence for ancient Egyptian religious practices and beliefs. The course is taught over a two-year cycle: A19 covers the period from the unification of Egypt to the end of the Second Intermediate Period (*c.* 3000–1550 BC); A20 covers the New Kingdom and up to the Roman conquest (*c.* 1550–30 BC).

Paper A21. Mesopotamian culture I: literature

This paper will cover both Sumerian and Akkadian literary texts in translation, and thus be open to candidates not studying either language. It will cover myths and epics, including Gilgamesh and the Epic of Creation, as well as political and 'Wisdom' literature. Assessment will be by one examination of two hours' duration in which candidates must answer two questions (60% of the final mark for the paper), and by the submission of three essays of 2,000 words each, which together make up 40% of the final mark for the paper.

Paper A22. Mesopotamian culture II: religion and scholarship

This paper will deal with literacy and numeracy in ancient Mesopotamia; science and scholarship, including divination; religious beliefs as expressed in both the textual and the archaeological sources. Knowledge of the languages will not be required.

Papers A23/24. Mesopotamian archaeology I and II

This course covers the archaeology of modern Iraq and Syria. Subjects addressed include the development of agriculture and urbanism, the relationship of the environment to the rise of complex society, the interplay of textual and archaeological data, propaganda and the presentation of kingship and power, symbolism in art and architecture, and the archaeological evidence for religious ritual. The course covers the archaeology of Mesopotamia in two periods (6000–2000 BC and 2000–539 BC), is taught over a two-year cycle and examined in Papers A23 and A24 in alternate years.

Paper A25. The North Sea in the early Middle Ages and Paper A26. The Long Viking Age

This course surveys the period which saw the rise, development, and fall of the Roman Empire, and the emergence of the early medieval states which were the foundation of modern Europe; it relates mainly to the northern and western parts of Europe (including Scandinavia). The course includes two papers which are both normally taught every year.

Paper A28. The archaeology of medieval Britain

This course covers the archaeology of post-conquest Britain, approximately AD 1050 to 1500. This was the period when the 'historic' landscape of Britain took on its pre-industrial form, and the history of landscape and villages, castles, towns, and the church is still visible in the material remains of this period. Since East Anglia is particularly rich in such evidence, lectures are complemented by field trips or museum sessions for almost every topic.

Papers A29/A30 and A31/A32. Ancient India

This course surveys the archaeology and art of ancient India extending from the prehistoric periods up to the fifth century AD. In one year the main emphasis is on the earlier prehistoric periods (up to the emergence of agriculture), together with a survey of the principal excavated historical sites (*c.* 600 BC to *c.* AD 400). In the other year the emphasis is placed on the later prehistoric and proto-historic periods, and on the major features of Indian art, architecture, inscriptions, and coins. The course also surveys the geographical and environmental features of ancient India, and the history of archaeological research in the subcontinent. Four modules are taught over a two-year cycle, two being available each year: Prehistory of India; The Indus civilization and beyond; Early historic cities of South Asia; Art and architecture of ancient India.

Paper A33/A34. Archaeology of the Americas

The course covers major developments in the region, from the peopling of the New World and the origins of agriculture to the rise of complex societies that culminated in the late pre-Hispanic empires (Inka and Aztec). Emphasis is placed on theoretical approaches to understanding the long-term development of social inequality and the rise of complex societies, and attention is given to the interactions of human populations with their environments. Two modules (Ancient South America, and Archaeology of Mesoamerica and North America) are taught over a two-year cycle and are examined in alternate years.

Paper A36. The late prehistoric and historical archaeology of sub-Saharan Africa

The course provides a broad overview of the prehistory of the African continent from the earliest times, together with the historical archaeology of sub-Saharan Africa. Emphasis is placed upon the study of Post-Pleistocene times and upon the relationship between archaeology and other sources of information about the African past. The subject is viewed from an essentially African perspective, although due attention is paid to external connections. Students are encouraged to view African prehistory as an essential and central part of human development.

Papers A37 and A38. Introduction to scientific approaches in archaeology; Archaeological science

The courses for these papers allow students to explore a range of scientific approaches in archaeology in depth. Consideration is given to the geo-archaeological context of our evidence, and the dynamics of preservation and transformation of archaeological materials. From this foundation students can select from a range of bio-archaeological and environmental options, e.g. in archaeobotany or zoo-archaeology, backed up by laboratory practicals. These papers can be taken with, and are designed to complement, any of the papers on special areas, for those candidates who wish to put a greater emphasis on scientific method in the course as a whole.

Assyriology

Paper M1. Akkadian language II (also serves as Paper X.6 of Part IB of the Asian and Middle Eastern Studies Tripos)

This paper is for candidates in their second year of study of Akkadian, and will test candidates' knowledge of the Old Babylonian and Standard Babylonian dialects of Akkadian as used in literary and historical texts. They will be required to transliterate from cuneiform and translate passages from both seen and unseen texts. Comment may be required on points of grammar and/or content.

Paper M2. Akkadian language III

This paper is for candidates in their third year of study of Akkadian. It will include transliteration and translation from unseen texts and from a range of Akkadian texts studied during the year including letters and legal documents, some in Assyrian dialect. Comment may be required on points of grammar and/or content.

Paper M3. Sumerian

This paper is only offered to candidates taking Paper M2 in Part IIB. It will consist of passages from Sumerian texts studied during the year for transliteration and translation, together with questions on Sumerian grammar.

Papers M4/M5. Mesopotamian History I and II

These papers are taught through the same lecture course as Mesopotamian archaeology (Papers M4/5 are the same as Papers A23/24), in the same two-year cycle. In year I the course covers the early history of Sumer and Akkad, through the Old Babylonian period in Mesopotamia and Syria. In year II it covers the 'Amarna Period' or later 2nd millennium BC, and the Assyrian and Babylonian empires down to the fall of Babylon to Cyrus in 539 BC. A balance is maintained between the narrative of political events and social and economic history.

Egyptology

Paper E1. Egyptian language II (also serves as Paper X.7 of Part IB of the Asian and Middle Eastern Studies Tripos)

This paper contains passages from specified and unspecified texts for transliteration and translation into English. The passages are taken from Middle Egyptian texts.

Paper E2. Egyptian language III

This paper contains passages from specified and unspecified texts for transliteration and translation into English. The passages are taken from Old and Middle and Late Egyptian texts.

Biological Anthropology

BA1. Foundations in biological anthropology: the human animal

This paper examines the human species in a broad comparative perspective, with two themes. The first is the extent to which humans share their biology and behaviour with other animals, especially primates. The second perspective is concerned with comparisons between humans and the rest of the biological world in terms of similarities, differences, and uniqueness. Material will be drawn from genetics, morphology, and behaviour.

BA2. Foundations in biological anthropology: the human journey

This paper will look at the evolution of the human species, from its origins among the great apes, to the evolution of modern humans, and the diversity that has taken place in the course of the last 10,000 years, leading to the processes of modernization. Material will be drawn from the fossil record, archaeology, genetics, and human population biology and ecology.

BA3. Foundations in biological anthropology: the human lifespan

This paper looks at human biology and behaviour from the perspective of development and ontogeny. From conception to death, humans undergo a process of development that is shaped by both genes and environment. The patterns of such development can be framed in terms of life history theory, the role of nutrition, and the interactions between demography and threats to life such as disease, and the way in which reproduction is integrated into the lifespan.

BA4. Theory and practice in anthropology

This paper explores current developments in the discipline, and how advances in theory and method in anthropology and related disciplines are having an impact on anthropology and the understanding of the human species and its diversity. Emphasis is on the understanding of analytical methods and assessment of hypotheses to tackle problems in biological anthropology.

BA5–BA17. Special subjects

The aim of these papers is to examine in detail particular subjects in biological anthropology and related disciplines. Topics for special subjects will be announced by the Faculty Board, and details of the syllabus will be provided in the course handbook.

Social Anthropology

Paper S1. Foundations of social anthropology I

Kinship and economics have been linked in the major theories of production, reproduction, and exchange. The course for this paper considers the conditions under which kinship becomes an organizing template for economic relations, and its bearing on group dynamics and gender relations. New patterns of marriage, conjugality, sexuality, and procreation throw into relief the continuing relevance of classic kinship theory. Under the rubric of economics, the course treats the nature and interaction of different systems of production, distribution, and exchange, and historical processes of economic transformation; it reviews different ways of conceptualizing the economy, the works of major theorists, and key contemporary debates in economic anthropology.

Paper S2. Foundations of social anthropology II

The course for this paper brings together politics and religion. Under politics, it deals with theories of the state; inequality; war and violence; law and dispute-settlement; political action, strategy, and tactics; 'fourth-world' political action and resistance; social movements; the role of ideology and theories of governance. Under religion, the course deals with the major anthropological theories of religion and their relation to systems of knowledge and ideology. Specific fields covered include ritual and sacrifice; spirit possession and shamanism; forms of traditional knowledge and classification; world religions; the transformation of religion in the contemporary world. Emphasis will be given to the many links between politics and religion.

Paper S3. Theory, methods, and enquiry in social anthropology

This course provides a grounding in sociological theories and discusses their relation to more recent anthropological theory and methods. Topics to be discussed include: eighteenth and nineteenth century social theory; Marx, Durkheim, Simmel, Weber, Mauss; functionalism, structural-functionalism; structuralism; cultural materialism and neo-Marxism; interpretative anthropology, semiology, and symbolic anthropology. These theories are seen in the context of anthropological field research and the various types of anthropological writing.

Paper S4. Thought, belief, and ethics

The courses for this paper will normally cover anthropological perspectives on mind, thought, and belief. Particular concerns may be expected to include the anthropology of cognition, knowledge, and belief systems, and the anthropological study of ethics and moral economy.

Paper S5. Political economy and social transformations

The courses for this paper will normally cover anthropological perspectives on political economy and processes of social transformation. Particular concerns may be expected to include anthropological contributions to the study of value, property, and domination, and the growth and legacy of modern social forms including capitalism and socialism.

Paper S6. Ethnographic areas

Candidates will be required to offer one ethnographic area from a choice of three, which will be specified by the Faculty Board each year and will be taken from the following list: Europe, Latin America, Inner Asia, South Asia, Southeast Asia, the Pacific, Africa.

Papers S7–S11. Special subjects in social anthropology

Up to five papers will be available each year. These are currently drawn from the following list:

(a) Medical anthropology

This course is concerned with illness and healing in comparative perspective. It discusses ideas of health and illness, causation and healing, how they are constructed and how they change. A wide range of societies provides the examples of different approaches, from urban and industrialized contexts to relatively isolated, self-sufficient settings. Alternative systems of medicine and local regional systems, as well as the impact of western biomedicine on local regional systems, are considered in relation to medical pluralism and contexts of practice. Attention is also given to the cultural understanding of the body in illness, and to the management of childbirth and reproduction in different societies. Teaching for the course is by lecture and seminar.

(b) The anthropology of cities and space

While a primary objective of this paper is to examine the processes of city transformation in recent times, attention is also paid to pre-twentieth century and non-European cities. Processes of urbanization bring out the political, economic, and cultural complexities of city social organization. Images of the city are approached through examining utopian thought and experimentation, social engineering, urban planning, and forms of architecture. The city as a symbolic form and as a centre of power is addressed through studies of urban rituals, processions, commemorations, buildings, and through consideration of the relationships between space, the body, and gender. The paper also includes an examination of the ways in which the city has been theorized, and the problems of reconciling the distinctive method of fieldwork-based anthropology when applied to the large-scale organizational complexity of urban life.

(c) Gender, kinship, and care

This paper aims to use a variety of disciplinary perspectives to explore powerful new developments in the experience and understandings of gender and kinship in the context of the emergent field of 'care'. The course addresses recent developments in gender theory and global changes in the nature of intimacy. It examines anthropological evidence of the re-emergence of more traditional kinship and gender relations in new forms. Cross-cultural studies of same-sex and heterosexual relationships and especially friendships will be examined so as to better theorize the ways in which care is being reconfigured both within and outside normative kinship configurations. The new theorization of care builds upon the new ways of caring for the sick, frail, and elderly as well as the young and examines policy concerns about the failures of parents in the care of children. It also examines care as a form of governance and identifies the ways in which the multiple and culturally specific ways of 'caring' are often not recognized by the state which increasingly seeks to standardize practices of care and divest them of their socio-cultural meanings and significances. Themes to be addressed include: gender and work/family balance, migration and the international division of reproductive labour (employed care givers and global 'care-chains'), 'caring capitalism', new models and practices of parenting, domestic and state coercions, public planning, and state policy in the realm of care.

(*d*) *Anthropology beyond professional texts*

The professionalization of anthropology as a social science resulted among other things in the definition of the discipline through a specific kind of empirical research (fieldwork) and a specific narrative form (ethnography). There are of course other professionals who address issues central to anthropological concerns: other social scientists, philosophers, historians, novelists, and poets – many of whom borrow from anthropological works and whose works are borrowed as well. This paper seeks to broaden the basis on which anthropological texts may be analysed as well as to broaden critical awareness of anthropological inquiry beyond textual form. Both the bases on which anthropological knowledge came to be defined and the grounds on which these bases may be re-evaluated critically are presented, including an examination of the professionalization of anthropology, and the intellectual traditions influential in this process; the theoretical question of 'representation', and how 'others' represent themselves to themselves. In collaboration with the Faculty of English, the paper addresses aspects of literary theory through the consideration of specific texts and literary techniques, poetics, the use of 'multimedia', and what one may learn from the parallel examinations of anthropological and non-anthropological texts.

(*e*) *Anthropology, communication, and the arts*

This paper draws attention to the aesthetic and performative aspects of human communication. It provides an introduction to the main perspectives anthropologists have brought to an understanding of the visual and performing arts. While the paper provides a broad cross-cultural overview of distinctive artistic practices and productions, each year a section of the course focuses in some detail on a particular cultural area. Where appropriate the course will draw on the extensive collections of the Museum of Archaeology and Anthropology and the video library held within the Department of Archaeology and Anthropology. Topics for study are drawn from the following areas: theories of non-western art and aesthetics; social and technical aspects of artistic production and consumption; the use of different media in anthropological analysis; the poetics and politics of representation; museology; masking and body decoration; the anthropology of dance; aspects of ethnomusicology; and analyses of film and advertising.

(*f*) *Anthropology and development*

This paper covers social, economic, and political aspects of 'development', with particular reference to the experience of the poorer countries since World War II and to the theories and practical involvement of anthropologists. Case studies of development projects of rural and urban areas are analysed, with particular attention being paid to indigenous knowledge, and the participation of local people in projects which transform their lives. Other themes include socialist development, the demise of 'peasant economy', and the emergence of new social movements in Third World cities. Anthropological approaches to the study of policy, planning, and development organizations are also considered and throughout the course students are encouraged to maintain a critical stance towards the very concept of 'development'.

(*g*) *The anthropology of post-socialist transformations*

The paper aims to examine the societies of the former Soviet Union and Eastern and Central Europe as they are currently undergoing transformation. Virtually all of them have abandoned socialism for different political and economic paths. The aim of this paper is to understand (*a*) what actually existing socialism was, (*b*) the causes and consequences of its collapse, and (*c*) what heritage or residue of socialism remains in the post-socialist societies. We examine the processes of transformation, in political, economic, social, and cultural terms. The paper focuses particularly on ways in which we can analyse the experience of sudden change, the associated phenomena labelled as 'development' or 'regression', emerging social and familial forms, new attitudes to history and memory, and changes in 'high' and popular culture, ideology, and values.

(*h*) *Nationalism, race, and ethnicity*

The aim of this paper is to offer a critical introduction to the literature on nationalism, race, and ethnicity both in and outside anthropology, and to explore the ideas advanced in that literature in relation to material drawn from specific historical and cultural contexts. This includes the intellectual history of the concepts of, respectively, nation and race, to be examined through the main relevant theoretical literature. Historical, anthropological, and sociological approaches are covered. Specific case material, drawn from a range of geographical and historical contexts, will address issues such as the politics of identity in Britain; thinking about conflict in Northern Ireland; 'tribalism' and the culture of post-colonial states in sub-Saharan Africa; communal identities and violence in South Asia; religion and communal mobilization; Diaspora communities and transnationalism; gendering the nation. The examples vary from time to time.

(*i*) *The anthropology of colonialism and empire*

Focusing on a wide range of regional case studies, this paper explores the emergence of colonial politics, cultures, and imperial systems of power as objects of anthropological analysis, and considers the ways in which both the making and unmaking of Western as well as non-Western imperial systems have had ramifications for the societies and cultures studied by anthropologists. A variety of theoretical and interpretive approaches will be discussed, but the main emphasis will be on ethnographic accounts, and on the anthropological implications of historical studies. A wide range of examples may be covered, including social, cultural, and political transformations arising from Western colonial conquest and rule in Asia, Africa, and the Americas, and aspects of empire as conceptualized and experienced under Chinese, Ottoman, and/or Russian/Soviet rule.

(*j*) *Anthropology and law*

Legal frameworks have re-emerged, in the contemporary period, as ways to justify social and political action. The language of 'the law' pervades a multiplicity of arenas, both local and global, implicating experience, personhood, and subjectivity. The aim of this paper is to show the way the law is used as a vehicle to structure relations, whether between states, between colonized and colonizer, or between special interest groups (as in the case of new technologies). Legal systems acquire a social and cultural character of their own, appearing to be departments of modern life and thus potential ethnographic objects. If such systems represent themselves as normative and rational, from an anthropological view they are contextualized by other phenomena. The course explores what it means to study legal systems, and in doing so opens up questions about organizing concepts (such as 'rights') of major contemporary importance.

(*k*) *Science and society*

The aim of this paper is to offer a critical exploration of recent developments and debates in the anthropology of science in a wide range of social and regional settings, as well as across diverse traditions of thought. The course explores what it means to study societal, institutional, and epistemic conditions of science and scientific knowledge production through a comparative frame. From an anthropological view the critical study of 'cross-cultural science' *as* ethnographic object puts into political relief the way that encounters between 'parallel worlds', 'purity', 'hybridity', 'reliability', 'evidence', 'verification', and so on are justified as particular social forms and moral action claims.

ARCHITECTURE TRIPOS

Three Parts.

1. The Architecture Tripos shall consist of three Parts: Part IA, Part IB, and Part II. A separate class-list shall be published for each Part.

Standing of candidates.

2. The following may present themselves as candidates for honours in Part IA:

(*a*) a student who has kept one term, provided that three complete terms have not passed after her or his first term of residence;

(*b*) a student who has obtained honours in another Honours Examination in the year next after so obtaining honours, provided that the student has kept four terms and that nine complete terms have not passed after her or his first term of residence.

3. A student who has obtained honours in Part IA of the Architecture Tripos may be a candidate for honours in Part IB in the year next after so obtaining honours, provided that he or she has kept four terms, and has satisfied the Examiners in studio-work in the examination for Part IA.

4. A student who has obtained honours in Part IB of the Architecture Tripos may be a candidate for honours in Part II in the year after so obtaining honours, provided that

(*a*) the student has kept seven terms and twelve complete terms have not passed after her or his first term of residence, and

(*b*) the student has satisfied the Examiners in studio-work in the examination for Part IB.

5. No student shall be a candidate for more than one Part, or for any Part and also for another Honours Examination, in the same term; and no student who has been a candidate for honours in any Part shall again be a candidate for honours in the same Part.

Professional qualification.

6. Subject to the provisions of Regulation 5, a student who is not eligible to be a candidate for honours shall be entitled to take the examination for any Part of the Architecture Tripos as a candidate not for honours for the purpose of qualifying for exemption from professional examinations, provided that he or she has obtained honours in another Honours Examination and, if a candidate for Part IB or Part II, has satisfied the requirements of these regulations in so far as they relate to studio-work.

Examiners and Assessors.

7. To conduct the examination in each Part the Faculty Board shall nominate such number of Examiners as they shall deem sufficient. The Board shall have power to nominate Assessors to the Examiners for any of the papers. The Assessors shall be responsible for setting the questions in the subject or subjects assigned to them and for advising the Examiners on the candidates' performance in those questions.

Class-lists.

8. In each Part the names of the candidates who obtain honours shall be arranged in three classes, of which the second shall be divided into two divisions. The names in the first and third classes and in each division of the second class shall be arranged in alphabetical order. A mark of distinction may be affixed to the names of those candidates placed in the first class whose work either in a part or in the whole of the examination is of special merit. In the class-lists for Part IA and Part IB, a mark *s* shall be attached to the names of those candidates who have satisfied the Examiners in studio-work.

9. The names of candidates who, having presented themselves under the provisions of Regulation 6, attain the honours standard shall be published in a list headed 'The following who are not candidates for honours have attained the honours standard'.

10. The Faculty Board shall have power to make supplementary regulations defining all or any of the subjects set out in the following regulations as they think fit. Supplementary regulations.

11. Public notice of subjects, special periods, and books prescribed under the following regulations or under any supplementary regulations shall be given by the Faculty Board (*a*) for Part IA and for Part IB of the Tripos, not later than the Easter Term next preceding the examination to which they apply, and (*b*) for Part II of the Tripos, not later than the Easter Term next but one preceding the examination to which they apply; provided that the Board shall have the power of subsequently issuing amendments if they have due reason for doing so and if they are satisfied that no student's preparation for the examination is adversely affected. Notice of books and subjects.

PART IA

12. The examination for Part IA of the Architecture Tripos shall consist of three sections: Scheme of examination for Part IA.

Section A. Five papers as follows:

Paper 1. An introduction to the histories and theories of architecture to 1800.
Paper 2. An introduction to the histories and theories of architecture from 1800 to the present.
Paper 3. Fundamental principles of construction.
Paper 4. Fundamental principles of structural design.
Paper 5. Fundamental principles of environmental design.

Section B. Studio-work.
Section C. Course-work.

13. A candidate for Part IA shall be required:

(*a*) to offer all five papers in Section A;
(*b*) for Section B, to present for the inspection of the Examiners, not later than the Friday before the first day of the written examination, a portfolio of studio-work carried out during the current academical year and attested by satisfactory evidence;
(*c*) for Section C, to present for the inspection of the Examiners, by the same day, records in an appropriate form of course-work done by the candidate, and bearing, as an indication of the good faith of the record, the signatures of the teachers under whose direction the work was performed.

The Examiners shall be provided by the Head of the Department with assessments of all the course-work carried out by candidates of which records have been presented under (*c*).

PART IB

14. The examination for Part IB of the Architecture Tripos shall consist of three sections: Scheme of examination for Part IB.

Section A. (i) Two papers (Papers 1 and 2) on historical and theoretical topics concerning architecture and its setting. For Paper 1 candidates will be required to submit two essays of 2,000 words. Paper 2 shall be assessed by a three-hour written examination.
(ii) Three introductory papers (Papers 3–5) on technical topics concerning the theory and practice of construction and of structural and environmental design.

Section B. Studio-work.
Section C. Course-work.

15. A candidate for Part IB shall be required:

(*a*) to offer Papers 1–5, subject to the qualifications that candidates cannot address in Paper 2 a topic chosen for an essay in Paper 1, and each essay must be on a separate topic.
(*b*) for Section B, to present for the inspection of the Examiners, not later than the Friday before the first day of the written examination, a portfolio of studio-work carried out during the current academical year and attested by satisfactory evidence;
(*c*) for Section C, to present for the inspection of the Examiners, by the same day, records in an appropriate form of course-work done by the candidate, and bearing, as an indication of the

good faith of the record, the signatures of the teachers under whose direction the work was performed.

Detailed instructions will be issued by the Department, by the division of the Michaelmas Term preceding the examination, regarding the coverage of prescribed texts and topics and any other requirements for the portfolio as a whole. Candidates will be required to declare that the essays are their own work. The essays shall consist of work done for supervisions and shall be in English and submitted with supervisors' comments but without revision of any kind by the candidate. They shall be submitted by the candidate to the Secretary of the Faculty Board, in accordance with detailed arrangements approved by the Board, so as to arrive not later than the first Friday of the Full Easter Term in which the examination takes place. Candidates may be called for *viva voce* examination in connection with their portfolios.

The Examiners shall be provided by the Head of the Department with assessments of all the course-work carried out by candidates of which records have been presented under (*c*).

Part II

Scheme of examination for Part II.

16. The examination for Part II of the Architecture Tripos shall consist of four sections:

Section A. (i) One paper on the theoretical and historical aspects of architecture and urbanism (Paper 1).

(ii) Three papers (Papers 2–4) on the technical aspects of the theory and practice of construction and of structural and environmental design.

Section B. Studio-work.

Section C. Course-work.

Section D. A thesis, or an alternative exercise approved by the Faculty Board, on a subject approved by the Faculty Board.

Papers 1–3 in Section A shall be examined by written papers, each of which shall be of three hours' duration. Paper 4 shall be examined by the submission of course-work.

17. A candidate for Part II shall be required:

(*a*) for Section A, to offer Papers 1–4;

(*b*) for Section B, to present for the inspection of the Examiners, not later than the Friday before the first day of the written examination, a portfolio of studio-work carried out during the current academical year and attested by satisfactory evidence;

(*c*) for Section C, to present for the inspection of the Examiners, by the same day, records in an appropriate form of course-work done by the candidate;

(*d*) for Section D, to submit a thesis, or an alternative exercise approved by the Faculty Board, in accordance with the provisions of Regulations 18 and 19.

The Examiners shall be provided by the Head of the Department with assessments of all the course-work carried out by candidates of which records have been presented under (*c*).

Thesis.

18. (*a*) Not later than 1 June each year the Faculty Board shall publish by Notice in the Department of Architecture a list of subject areas for the thesis or other exercise required for Section D in the examination to be held in the following academical year. In publishing the list the Faculty Board shall specify what types of exercise (if any) are permitted as alternatives to a thesis.

(*b*) Each candidate shall submit the proposed subject of his or her thesis or other exercise to the Secretary of the Faculty Board not later than the end of the third quarter of the Michaelmas Term next preceding the examination. A candidate may propose *either* (i) a subject that falls within one of the subject areas in the list published by the Faculty Board under sub-paragraph (*a*) above, *or* (ii) a subject of the candidate's own choice.

(*c*) Each candidate shall obtain the approval of the proposed subject by the Faculty Board not later than the last day of the Michaelmas Term.

(*d*) The Secretary of the Faculty Board shall notify the Examiners of candidates' subjects; the Examiners shall have power to impose restrictions on the questions that a candidate may offer in Paper 1, and shall inform candidates of any such restrictions not later than the end of the first quarter of the Easter Term.

19. A thesis presented under Regulation 17(*d*) shall be of not less than 7,000 words and not more than 9,000 words in length, including notes, appendices, and bibliography; an alternative exercise shall be of comparable substance. Each thesis shall be printed or typewritten, and shall be submitted through the candidate's Tutor to the Head of the Department of Architecture so as to arrive not later than the first day of Full Easter Term. Each candidate will be required to sign a declaration that the thesis is his or her own work, unaided except as may be specified in the declaration, and that it does not contain material that has already been used to any substantial extent for a comparable purpose.

20. In each Part the Examiners may impose such oral and practical tests as they think fit, and in drawing up the class-list they shall take into account the candidates' performance in all such tests, and in the studio-work and course-work, as well as in the written papers and theses or alternative exercises, together with the assessment of course-work presented by the Head of the Department. A candidate for Part II may be examined *viva voce*, at the discretion of the Examiners, on the subject of his or her thesis or alternative exercise. Oral and practical tests.

SUPPLEMENTARY REGULATIONS

Part Ia

Section A

Paper 1. An introduction to the histories and theories of architecture to 1800

The paper deals with a selective introduction to the histories of architecture and the city in Western Europe and to theoretical writings on architecture and the role of the architect from classical antiquity to the start of the nineteenth century.

Paper 2. An introduction to the histories and theories of architecture from 1800 to the present

The paper deals with a selective introduction to the histories of architecture and the city in Western Europe and to theoretical writings on architecture and the role of the architect from the nineteenth century to the present.

Paper 3. Fundamental principles of construction

The paper may include questions on the development of construction methods, the elementary principles of construction of small buildings, and the basic properties of construction materials.

Paper 4. Fundamental principles of structural design

The paper may include questions on the elementary principles of structural design of buildings, on simple statics, stress analysis, and strength of structural materials.

Paper 5. Fundamental principles of environmental design

The paper may include questions on the elementary principles of environmental control in buildings and servicing of buildings.

Part Ib

Section A

Paper 1. Essays on the history of architecture, urbanism, and design

The essays submitted for this paper must relate to the subject matter of the history and theory lecture courses given for Paper 2 in the Michaelmas and Lent Terms.

Paper 2. The history and theory of architecture, urbanism, and design

The courses of lectures for this paper will be specified from time to time by the Faculty Board of Architecture and History of Art and will cover topics from the history and theory of architecture, urbanism, and design.

Paper 3. Principles of construction

This paper may include questions on the principles governing the use of constructional elements in complex building types, properties of materials, dimensional co-ordination, analysis of simple methods of enveloping space.

Paper 4. Principles of structural design

This paper may include questions on the structural aspects of architectural design, the behaviour of structural elements under load, the use of load-bearing brickwork, steel, and reinforced concrete, systems of roof spanning and their calculation, the mathematical and graphical determination of simple structural systems.

Paper 5. Principles of environmental design

This paper may include questions on the principles of environmental control and functional design, the practical applications of the principles of thermal response, of acoustics, and of lighting in buildings, micro-climate, planning and designing for user needs.

PART II

SECTION A

Paper 1. Advanced studies in the theoretical and historical aspects of architecture and urbanism

The paper will be divided into a number of sections corresponding to the topics or periods in the theory and history of architecture and urbanism announced by the Faculty Board under the provisions of Regulation 18(*a*). Under the provisions of Regulation 18(*b*) the Faculty Board shall have power to debar a candidate from attempting a specified section or sections.

Paper 2. Management, practice, and law

Paper 3. Advanced studies in structural analysis, construction technology, and environmental design related to case studies

Paper 4. Architectural engineering

ASIAN AND MIDDLE EASTERN STUDIES TRIPOS

Amended by Notices (Reporter, *2013–14, pp. 56, 330, and 719*)

GENERAL

Three Parts.

1. The Asian and Middle Eastern Studies Tripos shall consist of three Parts: Part IA, Part IB, and Part II.

Standing of candidates.

2. The following may present themselves as candidates for honours in Part IA:

(*a*) a student who has not obtained honours in an Honours Examination, provided that he or she has kept one term and that three complete terms have not passed after his or her first term of residence;

(*b*) a student who has obtained honours in an Honours Examination, in the year next after so obtaining honours, provided that twelve complete terms have not passed after his or her first term of residence.

3. The following may present themselves as candidates for honours in Part IB:[1]

(*a*) a student who has obtained honours in Part IA of the Asian and Middle Eastern Studies Tripos, in the year after so obtaining honours;

(*b*) any other student, provided that he or she has kept one term and that twelve complete terms have not passed after his or her first term of residence, and subject to the prior approval of the Faculty Board of Asian and Middle Eastern Studies.

4. The following may present themselves as candidates for honours in Part II:[1]

(*a*) a student who has previously obtained honours in Part IB of the Asian and Middle Eastern Studies Tripos under Regulation 3(*a*), in the year next but one after so obtaining honours, provided that he or she has kept seven terms and that fifteen complete terms have not passed after his or her first term of residence;

(*b*) a student who has previously obtained honours in Part IB of the Asian and Middle Eastern Studies Tripos under Regulation 3(*b*), in the year next but one after so obtaining honours, provided that he or she has kept five terms and that fifteen complete terms have not passed after his or her first term of residence;

(*c*) a student who has previously obtained honours in any Honours Examination, other than Part IA or Part IB of the Asian and Middle Eastern Studies Tripos, in the year next but one after so obtaining honours, provided that he or she has kept seven terms and that fifteen complete terms have not passed after his or her first term of residence, and subject to the prior approval of the Faculty Board.

5. No student shall be a candidate for more than one Part, or for any Part and also for another Honours Examination, in the same term.

6. No student who has been a candidate for any Part shall again be a candidate for the same Part. No candidate shall offer a paper he or she has previously offered in any other Honours Examination.

Supplementary regulations.

7. The Faculty Board shall have the power to issue from time to time supplementary regulations defining or limiting all or any of the subjects of the examination, and to modify, alter or withdraw such supplementary regulations, provided that due care is taken to give sufficient notice of any change.

[1] See also the regulations for Affiliated Students.

8. The Faculty Board shall have the power to prescribe, not later than the end of the Easter Term in the year next before the examination to which they apply, a number of additional papers to be offered to candidates in each subject of both Part IB and Part II of the examination, providing that (i) the Faculty Board are not required to offer additional papers in Part IB and (ii) at least two papers shall be prescribed in each subject in Part II. When giving notice of the additional papers, the Faculty Board shall prescribe the mode of examination for each paper and any restrictions on the combination of papers that any candidate may offer. The Faculty Board shall have the power of subsequently issuing amendments if they have due reason for so doing and if they are satisfied that no student's preparation for the examination is adversely affected. Additional papers.

9. There shall be a separate body of Examiners for each Part. The Faculty Board shall nominate such number of Examiners for each Part as they may deem sufficient. For each body of Examiners, the Faculty Board shall also have power to nominate one or more Assessors to assist the Examiners. Examiners and Assessors.

10. The Examiners shall set, and shall be responsible for marking, all written papers except papers from another Tripos, and shall also mark dissertations submitted under Regulations 22 and 23. If required to do so, Assessors shall propose questions in the subject or subjects assigned to them, shall review the answers of candidates to those questions, and shall report as required to the Examiners. An Assessor may be summoned, for the purpose of consultation and advice, to meetings of the relevant body of Examiners, but shall not be entitled to vote.

11. The subject matter for each oral examination shall be approved by the body of Examiners for the corresponding Part. Two Examiners or Assessors shall conduct the oral examination of each candidate.

12. The Examiners shall have regard to the style and method of candidates' answers and shall give credit for excellence in these respects. They shall give due credit for the performance of candidates in the oral examinations. The Examiners shall be empowered to examine any candidate *viva voce*.

13. The names of those candidates who deserve honours in each Part shall be placed in three classes, of which the second shall be divided into two divisions. The names in the first and third classes and in each division of the second class shall be arranged in alphabetical order. Each class-list shall also indicate the subject or subjects which each candidate has offered in the examination. A mark of distinction may be awarded for special excellence. Class-lists.

PART IA

14. The subjects of examination in Part IA shall be as follows: Scheme of examination for Part IA.

East Asian Studies
Middle Eastern Studies
Middle Eastern Studies with a Modern Language

Each candidate shall offer one subject.

15. The papers for the examination in Part IA shall be as follows:

EAS.1	Introduction to East Asian history
C.1	Modern Chinese translation and writing 1
C.2	Modern Chinese texts 1
C.3	Literary Chinese 1
J.1	Modern Japanese 1
J.2	Japanese grammar and translation
J.3	Modern Japanese texts 1
MES.1	Elementary Arabic language A
MES.2	Elementary Arabic language B (one and a half hour written examination)
MES.3	Elementary Persian language
MES.4	Elementary Hebrew language A
MES.5	Elementary Hebrew language B
MES.6	Introduction to the history and culture of the Middle East
MES.7	Introduction to the contemporary Middle East
X.1	Akkadian I (Paper ARC4 of Part I of the Human, Social, and Political Sciences Tripos)
X.2	Egyptian language I (Paper ARC5 of Part I of the Human, Social, and Political Sciences Tripos)

Unless otherwise specified, all papers consist of a three-hour written examination.

16. There shall be separate examinations for each subject, as specified below:

(*a*) *East Asian Studies*

Candidates shall offer:

(i) Paper EAS.1;
(ii) *either* Papers C.1–3 and an oral examination in Chinese;
or Papers J.1–3 and an oral examination in Japanese.

The oral examination shall be offered under conditions set out by the Faculty Board from time to time.

(*b*) *Middle Eastern Studies*

Candidates shall offer:

either (i) Papers MES.1 and MES.2;
(ii) one paper chosen from MES.6–7;
(iii) one further paper chosen from MES.3–7 and X.1–2;

or (i) two papers chosen from MES.3–5;
(ii) one paper chosen from MES.6–7;
(iii) one further paper chosen from MES.6–7 and X.1–2.

Candidates offering any of Papers MES.2, MES.3, and MES.5 shall also offer an oral examination associated with that paper and under conditions set out by the Faculty Board from time to time. Candidates offering two of these papers shall offer two oral examinations.

(*c*) *Middle Eastern Studies with a Modern Language*

Candidates shall offer:

(i) *either* Papers MES.1 and MES.2;
or one paper chosen from MES.3–5, and one paper chosen from MES.6–7;
(ii) Papers B1 and B2 and oral examination B in *one* of the modern languages set for Part IA of the Modern and Medieval Languages Tripos;
(iii) one paper chosen from among the papers in Schedule IA of the Modern and Medieval Languages Tripos.

Candidates offering any of Papers MES.2, MES.3, and MES.5 shall also offer an oral examination associated with that paper and under conditions set out by the Faculty Board from time to time.

PART IB

Scheme of examination for Part IB.

17. The subjects of examination in Part IB shall be as follows:

East Asian Studies
Middle Eastern Studies
Middle Eastern Studies with a Modern Language

Each candidate shall offer one subject.

18. The papers for the examination in Part IB shall be as follows:

AMES.1	Cinema East
C.4	Modern Chinese translation and writing 2
C.5	Modern Chinese texts 2
C.6	Literary Chinese 2
C.7	History of dynastic China
C.8	Globalization in China, 1850 to the present (an essay of 8,000 words, to be submitted not later than the first day of Full Easter Term)
J.4	Modern Japanese 2
J.5	Modern Japanese texts 2
J.6	Japanese history
J.7	Literary Japanese
J.8	Japanese literary modernity
J.9	Japanese society
J.10	Japanese politics
MES.11	Intermediate Arabic language
MES.12	Intermediate Persian language
MES.13	Intermediate Hebrew language
MES.14	Intermediate literary Arabic
MES.15	Intermediate literary Persian
MES.16	Intermediate literary Hebrew
MES.17	The formation of Islam
MES.18	Topics in Hebrew studies
MES.19	The formation of the modern Middle East
MES.20	Themes in the anthropology of Islam

X.3 Structures and meanings (Paper 2 of the Linguistics Tripos)
X.4 Life, thought, and worship of modern Judaism (Paper B14 of the Theological and Religious Studies Tripos)
X.5 Introduction to Islam (Paper B15 of the Theological and Religious Studies Tripos)
X.6 Akkadian language II (Paper M1 of Parts IIA and IIB of the Archaeological and Anthropological Tripos)[1]
X.7 Egyptian language II (Paper E1 of Parts IIA and IIB of the Archaeological and Anthropological Tripos)[2]
X.8 Sounds and words (Paper 1 of the Linguistics Tripos)
X.13 Language, brain, and society (Paper 3 of the Linguistics Tripos)

Unless otherwise specified, all papers consist of a three-hour written examination.

19. There shall be separate examinations for each subject, as specified below:

(*a*) *East Asian Studies*

Candidates shall offer:

either (i) Papers C.4–6;
(ii) one paper chosen from C.7–8;
(iii) one further paper chosen from C.7–8, J.6, J.8–10, AMES.1, X.3, and the additional papers announced by the Faculty Board under Regulation 8;
(iv) an oral examination in Chinese;

or (i) Papers J.4–6;
(ii) one paper chosen from J.7–10;
(iii) one further paper chosen from J.7–10, C.7–8, AMES.1, X.3, and the additional papers announced by the Faculty Board under Regulation 8;
(iv) an oral examination in Japanese.

The oral examination shall be offered under conditions set out by the Faculty Board from time to time.

(*b*) *Middle Eastern Studies*

Candidates shall offer:

(i) one paper chosen from Papers MES.11–13;
(ii) *either* (*a*) four further papers chosen from MES.11–20, AMES.1, X.3–8, and X.13, and the additional papers announced by the Faculty Board under Regulation 8, providing that no more than two papers may be chosen (i) from Papers MES.11–13 or (ii) from Papers X.3–8 and X.13 and that no candidate may offer both Papers X.6 and X.7;
or (*b*) one paper from MES.1, 3–5, and three further papers chosen from MES.14–20, AMES.1, and X.3–5, 8, 13 and the additional papers announced by the Faculty Board under Regulation 8, providing that no more than two papers may be chosen from Papers X.3–5, X.8, and X.13 and that no paper previously offered in Part IA may be offered in Part IB.

Candidates offering any of Papers MES.3, 5, 11–13 shall also offer an oral examination associated with that paper and under conditions set out by the Faculty Board from time to time. Candidates offering two of the papers shall offer two oral examinations.

(*c*) *Middle Eastern Studies with a Modern Language*

Candidates shall offer:

(i) one paper chosen from Papers MES.11–13;
(ii) one paper chosen from MES.14–20, AMES.1, and any additional papers announced by the Faculty Board under Regulation 8,
(iii) three further papers chosen from: MES.14–20, AMES.1, X.3–5, X.8, X.13, Paper B3 in one of the modern languages set for Part IB of the Modern and Medieval Languages Tripos, and any papers not marked with an asterisk in Schedule IB of the Modern and Medieval Languages Tripos, providing that no more than one paper may be chosen from X.3–5, X8, X13.[3]

[1] Paper X.6 can only be taken at Part IB if a candidate has taken Paper X.1 at Part IA.
[2] Paper X.7 can only be taken at Part IB if a candidate has taken Paper X.2 at Part IA.
[3] With the approval of the Faculty Board of Asian and Middle Eastern Studies, a candidate who takes a paper listed in the Schedule which is marked with a dagger may submit a portfolio of essays under the conditions set out in Regulation 23 of the Modern and Medieval Languages Tripos.

Candidates offering any of Papers MES.11–13 shall also offer an oral examination associated with that paper and under conditions set out by the Faculty Board from time to time.

PART II

Scheme of examination for Part II.

20. The subjects of examination in Part II shall be as follows:
Chinese
Chinese with Japanese
Japanese
Japanese with Chinese
Middle Eastern Studies
Middle Eastern Studies with a Modern Language

Each candidate shall offer one subject.

21. The papers for the examination in Part II shall be as follows:

C.11	Modern Chinese translation and writing 3
C.12	Modern Chinese texts 3
C.13	Literary Chinese 3
J.11	Modern Japanese 3
J.12	Modern Japanese texts 3
MES.31	Advanced Arabic language
MES.32	Advanced Persian language
MES.33	Advanced Hebrew language
MES.34	Advanced literary Arabic
MES.35	Advanced literary Persian
MES.36	Advanced literary Hebrew

Unless otherwise specified, all papers consist of a three-hour written examination.

22. There shall be separate examinations for each subject, as specified below:

(*a*) *Chinese*

Candidates shall offer:

(i) Papers C.11–13;
(ii) two papers chosen from the papers announced by the Faculty Board under Regulation 8;
(iii) a dissertation, under conditions set out in Regulation 23.

Candidates shall also offer an oral examination, under conditions set out by the Faculty Board from time to time.

(*b*) *Chinese with Japanese*

Candidates shall offer:

(i) Papers J.4–5 from Part IB of the Tripos;
(ii) Paper C.12;
(iii) *either* Paper C.11;
or Paper C.13;
(iv) two papers chosen from the papers announced by the Faculty Board under Regulation 8, provided that only papers prefixed with C. may be chosen.

Candidates shall also offer a Japanese oral examination, under conditions set out by the Faculty Board from time to time.

This option may only be taken with the permission of the Faculty Board, such permission to be granted no later than the division of the Lent Term of the year next preceding the examination.

(*c*) *Japanese*

Candidates shall offer:

(i) Papers J.11–12;
(ii) two papers chosen from the papers announced by the Faculty Board under Regulation 8;
(iii) a dissertation, under conditions set out in Regulation 23.

Candidates shall also offer an oral examination, under conditions set out by the Faculty Board from time to time.

(*d*) *Japanese with Chinese*

Candidates shall offer:

(i) Papers C.4–5 from Part IB of the Tripos;
(ii) Paper J.12;

(iii) three papers chosen from the papers announced by the Faculty Board under Regulation 8, provided that only papers prefixed with J., EAS., or K. may be chosen.

Candidates shall also offer a Chinese oral examination, under conditions set out by the Faculty Board from time to time.

(*e*) *Middle Eastern Studies*

Candidates shall offer:

(i) one paper chosen from Papers MES.31–33;

(ii) *either* (*a*) three further papers chosen from MES.31–36 and the additional papers announced by the Faculty Board under Regulation 8, providing that no more than two papers may be chosen (i) from Papers MES.31–33 or (ii) from those papers offered by other Faculties;

or (*b*) one paper chosen from MES.11–13 and two papers chosen from MES.34–36 and the additional papers announced by the Faculty Board under Regulation 8, providing that no more than two papers may be chosen from those papers offered by other Faculties, and that no paper previously offered in Part IB may be offered in Part II.

(iii) a dissertation, under conditions set out in Regulation 23.

Candidates offering any of Papers MES.11–13, 31–33 shall also offer an oral examination associated with that paper and under conditions set out by the Faculty Board from time to time. Candidates offering two of the papers shall offer two oral examinations.

(*f*) *Middle Eastern Studies with a Modern Language*

Provided that no more than two languages may be offered in total,[1] candidates shall offer:

(i) one paper chosen from Papers MES.31–33;

(ii) three papers chosen from: MES.34–36, the additional papers announced by the Faculty Board under Regulation 8, Paper C1 or C2 in one of the modern languages set for Part II of the Modern and Medieval Languages Tripos, and papers from Schedule II of the Modern and Medieval Languages Tripos;

(iii) *either* a dissertation on a topic in Asian and Middle Eastern Studies, approved and supervised by the Faculty Board of Asian and Middle Eastern Studies under conditions set out in Regulation 23;

or a dissertation on a topic in Modern and Medieval Languages, approved and supervised by the Faculty Board of Modern and Medieval Languages under conditions set out for the optional dissertation in Regulation 27(i) of the Modern and Medieval Languages Tripos.

Candidates offering any of Papers MES.31–33 shall also offer an oral examination associated with that paper and under conditions set out by the Faculty Board from time to time.

23. Any candidate submitting a dissertation under Regulation 22 shall be required to have spent a period of at least eight months, since matriculation, in a country or countries deemed appropriate by the Faculty Board and under conditions approved for this purpose by the Faculty Board,[2] providing that the Faculty Board may waive this requirement under exceptional circumstances. Period abroad.

A candidate who is required to submit a dissertation under Regulation 22 shall submit the proposed title, together with a statement of the papers to be offered in the examination, to the Secretary of the Faculty Board so as to arrive not later than the division of the Michaelmas Term next preceding the examination. Each candidate must obtain the approval of the proposed title by the Faculty Board not later than the end of that term. A dissertation, which shall be of not more than 12,000 words in length (inclusive of notes and appendices), should show evidence of reading, judgement, and power of exposition, but not necessarily evidence of original research, and must give full references to the sources used. One electronic and two paper copies of each dissertation, marked with the candidate's examination number, shall be submitted in a format specified by the Faculty Board from time to time to the Secretary of the Faculty Board so as to arrive not later than the third day of the Full Easter Term in which the examination is to be held.

[1] Including those languages offered under Schedule II of the Modern and Medieval Languages Tripos.

[2] During the period spent abroad students will normally be required either to follow an appropriate course of study or to undertake some suitable form of employment; in either case the Faculty Board's approval will be required.

Each candidate will be required to sign a declaration that the dissertation is his or her own work, unaided except as may be specified in the declaration, and that it does not contain material that has already been used to any substantial extent for a comparable purpose. Each copy of the dissertation shall be accompanied by a summary of not more than 300 words in English, except that a candidate offering a dissertation under Regulation 22(*a*) (Chinese) shall furnish instead a summary in Chinese of not less than 600 characters. The maximum marks allocated to the dissertation shall be one quarter of the maximum marks for the examination as a whole.

PARTS IA, IB, AND II

Other subjects. **24.** The Faculty Board shall have power to grant permission to a candidate for any Part of the Tripos to offer in the examination a subject or language other than those specified in Regulations 14, 17, and 20, provided that the Board are satisfied:

(*a*) that any language which is thus offered possesses a literature adequate for the purposes of examination;

(*b*) that the general scope of a subject which is thus offered is similar to that of the subjects specified in Regulations 14, 17, and 20;

(*c*) that the requisite teaching can be provided.

Applications for such permission shall be made through the candidate's Tutor to the Secretary of the Faculty Board at the earliest possible date and in no circumstances later than the following dates:

the division of the Easter Term in the year next preceding the examination, for a candidate taking Part IA or Part IB;

the division of the Easter Term in the year next but one preceding the examination, for a candidate taking Part II.

For subjects offered under this regulation the Faculty Board shall have power to determine the papers to be set, in general conformity with the provisions of Regulations 16, 19, and 22.

25. Not later than the division of Full Michaelmas Term each year the Secretary of the Faculty Board shall inform the Registrary of any subjects for which permission has been granted under Regulation 24, together with the names of the candidates to whom such permission has been granted.

SUPPLEMENTARY REGULATIONS

Amended by Notices (Reporter, *2013–14, pp. 243, 244, 449, 721, and 735*)

PART IA

EAS.1. Introduction to East Asian history

The course covers the history of East Asia thematically from the earliest times to the present, focusing on China, Japan, and Korea. Students will read literature, historical monographs, and primary sources to familiarize themselves with various types of historical evidence.

C.1. Modern Chinese translation and writing 1

This course is to enable students to use basic elements of Chinese grammar correctly, use Chinese over a range of everyday situations, write basic Chinese and translate English into Chinese at the sentence level, and write simple essays in Chinese.

C.2. Modern Chinese texts 1

Modern Chinese is taught intensively throughout the year, and in this paper students are required to translate passages in modern Chinese into English. This paper is mainly designed to assess the student's ability in understanding and translating simple Chinese texts.

C.3. Literary Chinese 1

An introduction to the literary Chinese language. The course introduces students to basic vocabulary, syntax, and grammar of the classical period. Excursions are made into the etymology of graphs, the origins of common proverbs and set phrases as well as the intellectual world behind the selected text passages.

J.1. Modern Japanese 1

The course aims to teach students modern Japanese with primary emphasis on reading and writing. The textbook used for this purpose is Bowring and Laurie, *Introduction to Modern Japanese*. In the Michaelmas and Lent Terms students undergo an intensive study of the grammar of modern Japanese. In the Easter Term the course focuses on the development of students' listening and speaking skills.

J.2. Japanese grammar and translation

This paper is taught in conjunction with J.1 in the Michaelmas and Lent Terms and separately in the Easter Term. It also draws upon skills learned in tackling the texts in J.3, both in terms of ability to construe Japanese texts and in terms of understanding of grammatical patterns.

J.3. Modern Japanese texts 1

The reading of one or two short stories in order to put into practice the skills and knowledge learned in the Michaelmas and Lent Terms.

MES.1. Elementary Arabic language A

MES.2. Elementary Arabic language B

These two papers are taught as a single course. The aim is to equip students to read and write Modern Standard Arabic, and cover all the basic grammar, and to hold simple conversations in one particular Arabic dialect.

MES.3. Elementary Persian language

This paper introduces students to Persian grammar and the written and oral use of the language (listening and comprehension practice in the language laboratory). Reading classes expose students to the language in action and to a variety of usages of the grammatical rules.

MES.4. Elementary Hebrew language A

In this course students are introduced to the language of the Hebrew Bible. In Michaelmas Term students will concentrate on working through the textbook *Introduction to Biblical Hebrew* by T. Lambdin. In Lent Term the focus will be on a philologically and linguistically oriented reading of Genesis 1–4 (and possibly related texts) along with the integration of secondary literature dealing with pertinent issues of both a linguistic and non-linguistic nature.

MES.5. Elementary Hebrew language B

In this course, students acquire competence in spoken and written Modern Hebrew. Classes will cover Modern Hebrew grammar and representative texts from Modern Hebrew literature. All students taking this course also take an introductory course on Biblical Hebrew grammar in the Michaelmas Term and are required to answer one question on Biblical Hebrew in the examination.

MES.6. Introduction to the history and culture of the Middle East

This paper provides an introduction to the history of the Middle East and the political, religious, and cultural developments of the different regions and periods. It aims to familiarize the student with the sources of information available and with the main themes that will arise in studying Middle Eastern societies in subsequent years of the Tripos.

MES.7. Introduction to the contemporary Middle East

This paper provides a critical introduction to the languages, cultures, and literatures of the Middle East.

PART ID

AMES.1. Cinema East

The course provides students with the opportunity to explore the film traditions of East Asia through a number of possible themes, including modernity, identity and nation, and genre. These broad concerns encompass common themes of comparative significance, such as gender, city and countryside, love, marriage, and family and violence and are expressed in genres such as melodrama. Each student will give two presentations and write two essays (1,500–2,000 words) each term, one on each of the four sections of the course; feedback on these will be given in supervisions or in group discussions.

C.4. Modern Chinese translation and writing 2

This course aims to develop the students' ability to translate English texts into Chinese and to write Chinese compositions of various styles, such as letters, messages, notices, narration.

C.5. Modern Chinese texts 2

This course enables students to read modern Chinese writings, both literary and non-literary. Information about authors, the background, and the linguistic and stylistic features of the texts is provided as appropriate. The purpose is to give students experience of intensive and extensive reading. Students read unabridged texts from beginning to end, thus increasing their vocabulary and familiarity with modern written Chinese and advancing their understanding of aspects of Chinese historical and cultural experience in 20th-century and contemporary China.

C.6. Literary Chinese 2

An introduction to selected works of poetry, prose, and fiction in literary Chinese. The course draws on texts ranging from early medieval to late imperial times. Students are introduced to the basic features of grammar and genre and the intellectual and historical background of the readings in question.

C.7. History of dynastic China

The history of dynastic China from the Qin through Qing periods. The course, consisting of lectures and essay seminars, introduces students to the formative political, social, economic, religious, and cultural features that defined the Chinese empire.

C.8. Globalization in China, 1850 to the present

The history of globalization in China from the Taiping Rebellion in the mid nineteenth century until today. For the century after 1850, it will examine the rise of the large vibrant port cities that resulted from the rapid expansion of foreign trade and became centres of social, political, and cultural change. It will also analyse Chinese migration, the emergence of Chinese forms of modernity, the rise of resistance movements to Western financial imperialism, and the effects of revolution and warfare. China's current phase of globalization will be placed against the background of this earlier phase of globalization.

J.4. Modern Japanese 2

The main aims of this course are that students: (*a*) acquire the ability to understand intermediate written and spoken Japanese; (*b*) acquire the ability to express themselves in Japanese in a limited range of topics; (*c*) increase competence in written skills.

J.5. Modern Japanese texts 2

Reading selected twentieth-century Japanese literary and non-literary texts, with attention to style and content, the aim being to gain proficiency in reading, pronouncing, translating, and interpreting modern prose.

J.6. Japanese history

Topics in the history of Japan in the 19th and 20th centuries. In order to analyse Japan's current relations with its Asian counterparts, the course also examines Japan's shifting self-image and foreign relations over the centuries, with particular focus on China.

J.7. Literary Japanese

An introduction to the grammar of literary, pre-modern Japanese, followed by readings of simple prose and poetry. Some essay work on aspects of classical literature is also required.

J.8. Japanese literary modernity

An introduction to modern and contemporary Japanese fiction. The course covers a number of topics, including the aesthetics and politics of literary modernity, colonial writing, the development of women's fiction, or Japanese postmodernity, while studying in some detail works of representative writers from the late Meiji era to recent decades.

J.9. Japanese society

An introduction to Japanese society, its current phenomena and their historical and cultural background. Starting from our own images and influential descriptions of Japanese society, this course will investigate family, demography, education, work, and leisure, as well as life stages and different aspects of daily (and nightly) life of the various social groups.

J.10. Japanese politics

An introduction to post-1945 Japanese politics examining Japan's political parties and institutions from a comparative perspective. In considering the distinctiveness of the Japanese political system, it addresses a number of central issues including Japan's economic growth, central-local government relations, the legal system, and the politics of defence and foreign policy. The paper pays particular attention to the nature of domestic political change since the mid 1990s as well as the economic and security policy challenges for a country that is increasingly active both globally and regionally. In analysing Japan's politics comparatively, the paper also addresses the issues of authorization and democratization in Korea, Korea's post-1945 political economy, and the security aspects of the Korean peninsula.

MES.11. Intermediate Arabic language

The aim of this course is to consolidate students' understanding of Arabic grammar and expand their vocabulary so that they can confidently read a range of Arabic materials such as newspaper and magazine articles, and to develop their speaking and listening skills and their speaking in one particular dialect of Arabic.

MES.12. Intermediate Persian language

This paper consists of language work, building on the four major language skills of reading, listening, writing, and speaking. In addition, the students read a variety of texts in modern Persian as language exercises, for translation, and vocabulary build-up.

MES.13. Intermediate Hebrew language

This paper enables students to deepen their knowledge of Hebrew. There will be two sections containing questions on classical Hebrew and Modern Hebrew respectively. Candidates taking the Modern Hebrew option will have an oral as part of their paper.

MES.14. Intermediate literary Arabic

This paper introduces students to a variety of Arabic literary texts to enhance their understanding of textual analysis and linguistic expression.

MES.15. Intermediate literary Persian

This paper provides an introduction to Persian literary texts, using a selection of readings from classical prose writers and poets. The objective is both to introduce major classical Persian authors and to see the written language in action as a vehicle for literary expression.

MES.16. Intermediate literary Hebrew

In this course students have the opportunity to study modern and medieval literary texts. The focus will be on the literary analysis and the historical contextualization of selected texts.

MES.17. The formation of Islam

A thematic survey of Islamic history in the first four centuries dealing with key aspects of the religious, political, social, and cultural evolution of classical Muslim societies. The course will include introductions to the Qur'an, Hadith, and Islamic law as well as a variety of historical texts reflecting the world view of Muslims of this era.

MES.18. Topics in Hebrew studies

This course will enable students to study the special topics of (i) the history of the Hebrew language and (ii) modern Hebrew culture (literature, film, history).

MES.19. The formation of the modern Middle East

This paper examines key moments in the formation of the modern Middle East and North Africa with an emphasis on developing an understanding of the periods of transition and conflict that have shaped and defined modern societies in the region since the nineteenth century. The course is divided into three sections: the Ottoman empire and the Arab world, Iran, and Israel.

MES.20. Themes in the anthropology of Islam

This course introduces anthropological approaches to the Middle East and Islam, and examines the relationship between different forms of knowledge about the Middle East and the modern political history of the region.

PART II

C.11. Modern Chinese translation and writing 3

This course enables students (*a*) to use an extensive range of Chinese vocabulary, idioms, and expressions in translation into Chinese and in Chinese essay writing, (*b*) to produce appropriate degrees of formality in translating and writing, and (*c*) to write in Chinese on various topics and in different styles.

C.12. Modern Chinese texts 3

The course continues the work done in the acquisition of the modern Chinese language in previous years. Students will be presented with various types of texts, ranging from modern and contemporary fiction, newspapers, and articles on contemporary China, to scholarly writings and government documents.

C.13. Literary Chinese 3

This course introduces advanced selections of poetry, prose, and fiction in literary Chinese. The course draws on texts ranging from early medieval to late imperial times. Students will be introduced to features of grammar and genre as well as the intellectual and historical background of the readings in question.

J.11. Modern Japanese 3

The main aims of the course are that students: (*a*) acquire the ability to understand advanced written and spoken Japanese; (*b*) acquire the ability to discuss, in Japanese, a wide range of topics; (*c*) increase competence in written skills.

J.12. Modern Japanese texts 3

This course consists of reading texts in advanced modern Japanese with much attention given not only to grammar and syntax but also to context. Supplementary reading will also be expected.

MES.31. Advanced Arabic language

This paper aims to develop students' reading and writing skills in Modern Standard Arabic. Students are introduced to a range of academic and literary texts in order to develop their ability to follow complex discussions and improve their understanding of linguistic structures. Classes run completely in Arabic.

MES.32. Advanced Persian language

This paper aims to develop students' reading, writing, speaking, and listening skills. The students will write essays and prepare presentations in Persian.

MES.33. Advanced Hebrew language

This paper enables students to develop their skills in writing and translating Hebrew and in critically assessing passages of Hebrew literature. There will be two sections containing questions on classical Hebrew and Modern Hebrew respectively. Candidates taking the Modern Hebrew option will have an oral as part of their paper.

MES.34. Advanced literary Arabic

This paper introduces students to a selection of advanced texts to enhance their understanding of textual analysis and linguistic expression and to develop their knowledge of literary historical and critical approaches. One or more types of Arabic writing from one or more periods will be the focus of sustained study.

MES.35. Advanced literary Persian

This paper uses a selection of either classical or contemporary Persian poetry and prose, to study the treatment of particular themes and rhetoric techniques.

MES.36. Advanced literary Hebrew

This paper focuses on themes of interest and importance in Modern and Medieval Hebrew literature.

Additional papers available for examination under Regulation 8

The papers available will be drawn from the following lists:

EAS.2. The East Asian region

A seminar-based course that extends the comparative approach adopted in EAS.1. It concentrates on thematic and policy issues relevant to understanding Japan, the Korean peninsula, China (broadly defined), and also Southeast Asia, as well as the role of the United States in East Asia. The course runs over two terms and draws explicitly on historical research and social science methodology in addressing how best to conceptualize 'East Asia' as a region. Topics addressed will vary from year to year, depending on the research interests of the teaching officers involved, but an indicative list of subjects covered in the course would include some, but not necessarily all of the following issues: the Cold War as a historical phenomenon; conflict and war in East Asia and contemporary security challenges; comparative models of economic development in East Asia and the role of 'plan-rational' policy-making; the role of the nation-state and competing models of historical identity; multilateralism, the emergence of trans-national actors and economic integration in East Asia; political legitimacy, contrasting models of authoritarian rule, and democratization as a political movement; demographic change; energy and environmental policy and technological change.

EAS.3. The Korean wave[1]

This course examines the contemporary form of East Asian cultural production known as the 'Korean wave.' Since the mid-1990s, South Korean pop culture has enjoyed tremendous popularity throughout Asia. This phenomenon marks an unusual moment in East Asian history as the economic rise of China has not led to Chinese cultural hegemony. By studying the Korean wave, it is possible to come to a better understanding of the dynamics of East Asia in the era of globalization and the possibility of the emergence of a pan-Asian identity. This paper focuses on two of the principal genres of the Korean wave, television dramas and cinema. Through a detailed study of representative works, it will examine issues such as Korean national identity, collective memory, melodrama, the Confucian family in the modern world, and the globalization of media cultures. Social and historical contexts, changes in film production and patterns of consumption, and the development of the Korean film industry on the global stage will be considered, as well as the key aspects of genre and film style.

C.14. Advanced Chinese texts

This course involves the intensive study of texts that are specifically linked to the special subject that the student has chosen.

C.15. The Chinese tradition[2]

While never constant and always debated, in the course of Chinese history certain fundamental approaches emerged toward government, organizing society, prosecuting warfare, communicating, pursuing personal profit, and thinking about the supernatural. This lecture course will examine these approaches, discuss their historical development, and analyse how they still impact on China today. Topics may include the role of Confucianism in traditional China and its revival today, Chinese attitudes towards human and natural environments, aesthetics and the arts, religious practices, popular mobilizations against authority, attitudes toward poverty, wealth, redistribution and consumption, the organization of commerce, and governmentality.

C.16. Early and imperial China

This is an advanced, seminar-based, course with alternate modules on early and medieval China and late imperial China. The paper engages students in an in-depth study of the central socio-religious, philosophical, and socio-economic paradigms that shaped early and dynastic Chinese society. Students are asked to work with key primary sources of the period concerned and examine related secondary scholarship. The paper seeks to identify the origins of ideas, social practices, and institutions that have permeated traditional Chinese society and have shaped the Chinese tradition up to the present day. Thematic rubrics explored in this paper may vary and cover topics such

[1] This paper will not be offered in 2014–15.
[2] This paper is suspended until further notice.

as cosmology and correlative thought, the Confucian classics, the Buddhist and the Daoist traditions, sacrificial religion, food culture, ritual and law, perceptions of the body and medicine, writing and print culture, agriculture and mercantile culture, urban and local culture.

C.17. Modern Chinese literature[1]

The course aims to introduce undergraduates to the field of modern Chinese literature as it evolved through the 20th century and up to the present. Literature, whether popular or elite, has had a vital place in modern experience. In the first term students become familiar with some of the major canonical writers and issues. Teaching in the second term is organized around a particular topic: possible examples are post-Mao and contemporary fiction; fiction and film in Republican popular culture; Chinese modernism.

C.18. China and warfare

The Taiping Rebellion, the Sino-Japanese War of 1894–95, the Allied Invasion of 1900, the warlord wars of the 1910 and 1920s, the War of Resistance against Japan from 1931 to 1945, the Chinese-Communist Civil War of 1945 to 1946, and the Korean War from 1950 to 1953 all have impacted on China's historical development in modern times. This course will examine these wars themselves, but will focus on their cultural, social, and political effects. It will also analyse their impact on dominant ideas Chinese have about themselves, their relations with other countries, and their position in the world.

C.19. Chinese linguistics

This course is designed to acquaint students with the nature and workings of the Chinese language and to help them establish a linguistic framework for the description and analysis of Chinese. It will enable students to understand and explain typological and syntactic differences between Chinese and English on the basis of linguistic theories, and to introduce them to some contentious issues in the study of the Chinese language.

C.20. Contemporary Chinese society

An introduction to key socio-political and cultural developments in reform-era China (from the early 1980s to the present), while situating them in the historical contexts of the late Imperial and Maoist periods. Topics covered will include Chinese political culture, kinship and marriage, reproduction and family planning, gender and sexuality, urban and rural lives, ethnic minorities, religion, state and society, nationalism, migration, the Chinese diaspora, etc. The analytical approaches are drawn from anthropology, political science, sociology, and cultural studies.

J.13. Advanced Japanese texts

This course involves the intensive study of texts that are specifically linked to the special subject that the student has chosen.

J.14. Classical Japanese texts

The course focuses on texts of the Tokugawa period and requires previous knowledge of classical Japanese (J.7).

J.15. Modern Japanese cultural history

This seminar-style course will explore a range of topics in the sociology, history, and cultural representation of Japan's minority communities. Particular attention will be paid to Burakumin and Zainichi Korean communities, and to the forms of cultural expression developed by their writers. The seminars will be supplemented by screening and study of both documentary and narrative films. The course may include an optional component covering readings in Japanese.

J.16. Tokugawa Japan

This paper focuses on early-modern Japanese cultural history. It offers insights on key-aspects of Edo-period visual and literary culture and allows reflections upon aspects of Japanese contemporary society which have roots in early-modern times. The paper does not require any knowledge of classical Japanese, as primary sources available either in modern Japanese or in English translation are selected. Students who know classical Japanese can choose to work on the original texts in critical edition. Secondary sources include materials both in Japanese and in English. The specific topic of the paper may change from year to year, including a vast range of themes such as education, family, leisure, gender, disaster, news, etc.

J.17. Modern Japanese history[1]

This course will be run in seminar style with weekly discussions and student presentations. Topics will vary depending on the year but may include: propaganda and social mobilization, Sino-Japanese relations, post-War Japanese political and social development, food and culture, as well as comedy and Japan's relations within East Asia. The focus will be on primary text readings in English and Japanese.

J.18. Japanese politics and international relations[1]

This is an advanced seminar-based course focusing on Japan's 20th-century international relations. The precise focus will vary from year to year, but in each instance the emphasis will be on situating the study of Japan within the disciplinary context of International Relations and Diplomatic History, and will involve working with both secondary and primary source material. The course will consider aspects of Japan's key bilateral relations in East

[1] This paper will not be offered in 2014–15.

Asia and globally, as well as a number of important thematic issues, including, but not necessarily limited to regional security, alliance relations, political economy, resource and trade policy, and debates over national identity.

J.19. Contemporary Japanese society[1]

This is an advanced seminar-based course focusing on contemporary Japanese society. The focus will vary from year to year, such as questions of learning and education, family, time, space, gender or the like, investigating these topics from a wide range of angles. In each instance the emphasis will be on situating the study of Japan within the disciplinary context of Social Anthropology and Sociology. The course is aimed at deepening students' understanding of (selected aspects of) Japanese society as well as developing research and writing skills. It will involve working with both secondary and primary source material.

K.1. Readings in elementary Korean

This course will cover the basic grammar of modern written Korean with a view to developing reading fluency. Students will mainly be reading materials in hangul script, but some texts in mixed script (with Chinese characters) will also be used.

MES.37. History of the pre-modern Middle East[2]

This paper examines in some detail aspects of the history of Middle East, either in a particular region and period, or addressing particular themes, with an emphasis on developing an understanding of the evolution of Middle East history and the periods of transition that have shaped and defined the pre-modern societies in the region.

MES.38. History of the modern Middle East: language, national identity, and conflict

The paper investigates the role language plays in articulating national identity and conflict in the Middle East. The main focus of the paper will be on Arabic, but consideration will also be given to Hebrew, Persian, and Turkish.

MES.39. Special subject in the pre-modern Middle East[2]

This paper provides a focused analysis of a particular subject relating to the pre-modern Middle East.

MES.40. Special subject in the contemporary Middle East[2]

This paper provides a focused analysis of a particular subject relating to the contemporary Middle East. Students may choose one of two subjects which will be announced by the Faculty Board.

MES.41. Comparative Semitic linguistics[1,2,3]

This paper offers the opportunity for students of the Semitic languages to contextualize their language work within the larger field of comparative Semitic linguistics.

MES.42. Elementary Sanskrit

The course aims to cover the whole of Sanskrit grammar and introduce the students to some of the essential features and concepts of pre-modern South Asian civilisation and literary culture.

MES.43. Elementary Hindi language

This paper introduces students to contemporary Hindi language through a series of exercises testing grammar, reading, writing, speaking, and listening.

X.9. Judaism II (Paper C8 of the Theological and Religious Studies Tripos)

This paper will consider the life, thought, and worship of medieval and modern Judaism. The Faculty Board of Divinity may from time to time prescribe subjects and texts for special study.

X.10. Islam II (Paper C9 of the Theological and Religious Studies Tripos)

This paper will deal with two advanced topics in Islamic studies specified from time to time by the Faculty Board of Divinity. The Board may also from time to time prescribe texts for special study.

X.11. Judaism and philosophy (Paper D2(*c*) of the Theological and Religious Studies Tripos)

The Faculty Board of Divinity may from time to time prescribe texts for special study.

X.14. The Jewish presence in medieval society (Paper 9 of Part II of the Historical Tripos)

This paper consists of a three-hour examination. Candidates answer three questions out of a choice of at least eleven questions.

[1] This paper will not be offered in 2014–15.

[2] This paper is also available to candidates for Part II of the Modern and Medieval Languages Tripos; see p. 395.

[3] This paper is also available to candidates for the Linguistics Tripos; see p. 373.

CHEMICAL ENGINEERING TRIPOS

1. The Chemical Engineering Tripos shall consist of three Parts, Part I, Part IIA, and Part IIB. There shall be a separate class-list for each Part. Three Parts.

2. A student who has obtained honours in Standing of candidates.

either (*a*) Part IA of the Natural Sciences Tripos, having offered Chemistry *or* Physics *or* Biology of Cells and *either* Mathematics *or* Mathematical Biology in that examination,

or (*b*) Part IA of the Computer Science Tripos, having offered Chemistry *or* Physics *or* Biology of Cells from Part IA of the Natural Sciences Tripos in that examination,

or (*c*) Part IA of the Engineering Tripos,

may be a candidate for honours in Part I of the Chemical Engineering Tripos in the year after so obtaining honours, provided that nine complete terms have not passed after the student's first term of residence.

3. The Chemical Engineering and Biotechnology Syndicate may in special circumstances, which they shall themselves determine, give leave to a student who has obtained honours in any Honours Examination to be a candidate for honours in Part I of the Chemical Engineering Tripos in the year after so obtaining honours, provided that the student has kept four terms and that nine complete terms have not passed after his or her first term of residence.

4. A student who has obtained honours in Part I of the Chemical Engineering Tripos may be a candidate for honours in Part IIA in the year after so obtaining honours, provided that twelve complete terms have not passed after his or her first term of residence.[1]

5. A candidate who, under arrangements approved by the Chemical Engineering and Biotechnology Syndicate, has spent not less than three terms studying at the Massachusetts Institute of Technology and has been certified by the President of the Institute after consultation with the Chair of Examiners for Part I of the Chemical Engineering Tripos to have studied diligently during that period, shall be deemed thereby to have obtained honours in that Part of the Tripos. A list containing the names of persons so qualified shall be certified by the Chair of the Chemical Engineering and Biotechnology Syndicate and published in the *Reporter*. Period of study at Massachusetts Institute of Technology.

6. The Chemical Engineering and Biotechnology Syndicate may in special circumstances, which they shall themselves determine, give leave to a student who has obtained honours in any Honours Examination to be a candidate for honours in Part IIA of the Chemical Engineering Tripos in the year after so obtaining honours, provided that the student has kept seven terms and that twelve complete terms have not passed after his or her first term of residence.

[**7.** A student who has obtained honours in Part IIA of the Chemical Engineering Tripos may be a candidate for honours in Part IIB in the year after so obtaining honours, provided that he or she has not proceeded to the B.A. Degree, and provided also that fifteen complete terms have not passed after the student's first term of residence.][2]

⟨**7.** A student who has obtained honours in Part IIA of the Chemical Engineering Tripos may be a candidate for honours in Part IIB of the Chemical Engineering Tripos in the year after so obtaining honours, provided that he or she:

(*a*) has attained a satisfactory standard, as defined by the Chemical Engineering and Biotechnology Syndicate, in previous Honours Examinations;

(*b*) has not proceeded to the B.A. Degree;

provided that fifteen complete terms have not passed after the student's first term of residence.⟩[2]

8. No student shall be a candidate for any Part and also for another Honours Examination in the same term.

9. No student who has been a candidate for any Part shall again be a candidate for the same Part.

10. The Chemical Engineering and Biotechnology Syndicate shall nominate such number of Examiners as they think sufficient for each Part of the Tripos, and shall also have power to nominate one or more Assessors for each Part. If required to do so, Assessors shall propose questions in the papers or parts of papers assigned to them by the Examiners, shall mark the answers of the candidates in those papers or parts of papers, and shall advise the Examiners on the performance of candidates in the examination. Assessors may be summoned to meetings of the Examiners for the purpose of consultation and advice, but shall not be entitled to vote. Examiners and Assessors.

[1] See also the regulations for Affiliated Students.
[2] The regulation in angular brackets will replace the regulation in square brackets with effect from 1 October 2015.

11. In each Part of the Tripos, the questions proposed by each Examiner or Assessor shall be submitted for approval to the whole body of Examiners for that Part. The answers to each question shall, as far as possible, be examined by two at least of the Examiners or Assessors.

12. In each Part the names of the candidates who obtain honours shall be arranged in three classes, of which the second class shall be divided into two divisions. The names of those in the first and third classes and in each division of the second class shall be arranged in alphabetical order. For special excellence in Part IIA or Part IIB a mark of distinction may be awarded.

Supplementary regulations.

13. The Chemical Engineering and Biotechnology Syndicate shall have power to publish supplementary regulations defining the scope and character of each of the examination papers and to amend such supplementary regulations from time to time as they may think fit. Any alteration of supplementary regulations shall be published before the division of the Easter Term in the academical year before that in which it is to have effect.

Scheme of examination for Part I.

14. (*a*) The examination for Part I shall consist of four written papers, each of which shall be of three hours' duration. A candidate for Part I shall offer Papers 1, 2, and 3, and either Paper 4(1) or Paper 4(2) as detailed in the supplementary regulations.

(*b*) The Examiners for Part I shall take into account course-work prescribed by the Chemical Engineering and Biotechnology Syndicate. Details of the work required shall be published by Notice in the Department of Chemical Engineering and Biotechnology no later than the beginning of the Full Michaelmas Term preceding the examination. The Examiners may require each candidate to submit reports on the course-work undertaken. The Examiners may impose such oral or practical tests as they think fit.

Scheme of examination for Part IIA.

15. (*a*) The examination for Part IIA shall consist of four written papers, each of which shall be of three hours' duration.

(*b*) The Examiners for Part IIA shall take into account course-work prescribed by the Chemical Engineering and Biotechnology Syndicate. Details of the work required shall be published by Notice in the Department of Chemical Engineering and Biotechnology no later than the beginning of the Full Michaelmas Term preceding the examination. The Examiners may require each candidate to submit reports on the course-work undertaken. The Examiners may impose such oral or practical tests as they think fit.

Scheme of examination for Part IIB.

16. (*a*) The scheme of the examination for Part IIB shall be as follows:

Group A:	Compulsory topics
Group B:	Advanced chemical engineering topics
Group C:	Broadening material topics
Group D:	Research project

Each candidate shall be required to take all Group A topics, to take a total of eight modules from Group B and Group C topics, and to take a Group D project. The Chemical Engineering and Biotechnology Syndicate shall have power to announce restrictions on the combination of modules that a candidate may choose to offer.

(*b*) The examination paper on Group A compulsory topics shall be of two hours' duration.

(*c*) Each Group B module on an advanced chemical engineering topic shall be examined either by a written paper of one and a half hours' duration or by course-work or by a combination of the two. Not later than the end of the Full Easter Term each year, the Chemical Engineering and Biotechnology Syndicate shall give notice of the modules prescribed for the following academical year, and shall specify the mode of examination for each module. For modules to be examined by course-work, details of the work required shall be published by the Syndicate by Notice in the Department of Chemical Engineering and Biotechnology not later than the beginning of the Full Michaelmas Term preceding the examination.

(*d*) Each Group C module on a broadening material topic shall be examined by course-work. Not later than the end of the Full Easter Term each year, the Syndicate shall give notice of the broadening material topics prescribed for the following academical year. The Examiners may require each candidate to submit reports on the course-work undertaken. The Examiners may impose such oral or practical tests as they think fit.

(*e*) Each candidate shall undertake a Group D project, in which they perform original work in one or more of the following forms: a theoretical investigation, an experimental investigation, an essay, a design project. The Examiners shall require each candidate to submit one or more written reports on the work undertaken. The Examiners may impose such oral or practical tests as they think fit.

17. Each candidate for any Part of the Chemical Engineering Tripos shall be required to sign a declaration that the candidate has read and understood the policies and procedures of the Department of Chemical Engineering and Biotechnology and the University on plagiarism. Each candidate submitting a report under Regulation 16(*e*) shall be required to sign a declaration that the work submitted is her or his own work, unaided except as specified in the text, and that it does not contain material that has already been used to any substantial extent for a comparable purpose. If two or more candidates have undertaken work in collaboration, they will each be required to indicate the extent of their contribution.

SUPPLEMENTARY REGULATIONS

Part I

Papers 1, 2, and 3

These papers will each be on Chemical Engineering principles. They may, for example, include questions on fluid mechanics, process calculations (including thermodynamics), heat and mass transfer, equilibrium staged processes, reactor theory, biotechnology, process systems (including economics and safety, health, and the environment), computer aided process engineering, and mathematical methods.

Paper 4(1)

This paper is to be taken by candidates who have previously obtained honours in the Natural Sciences Tripos or the Computer Science Tripos. In addition to a section on Chemical Engineering principles, it will include questions on General Engineering.

Paper 4(2)

This paper is to be taken by candidates who have previously obtained honours in the Engineering Tripos. In addition to a section on Chemical Engineering principles, it will include questions on Chemistry.

An Affiliated Student or a student admitted to the examination for Part I under the provisions of Regulation 3 will take the section prescribed for him or her by the Chemical Engineering and Biotechnology Syndicate.

CLASSICAL TRIPOS

Amended by Notices (Reporter, *2013–14, pp. 637 and 723*)

General

1. The Classical Tripos shall consist of three Parts: Part IA, Part IB, and Part II. A separate class-list shall be published for each Part. Three Parts.

2. The following may present themselves as candidates for honours in Part IA: Standing of candidates.

(*a*) a student who has kept one term, provided that three complete terms have not passed after her or his first term of residence;

(*b*) a student who has successfully completed the Preliminary Examination to Part IA, provided that six complete terms have not passed after her or his first term of residence;

(*c*) a student who has obtained honours in another Honours Examination, in the year next after or next but one after so obtaining honours, provided that nine complete terms have not passed after her or his first term of residence.

3. A student who has obtained honours in Part IA or, at the discretion of the Faculty Board, in another Honours Examination, may be a candidate for honours in Part IB in the year next after so obtaining honours, provided that at the time of the examination he or she has kept four terms and that twelve complete terms have not passed after his or her first term of residence.

4. The following may present themselves as candidates for honours in Part II:

(*a*) a student who has obtained honours in Part IA and Part IB of the Classical Tripos in the year next after so obtaining honours, provided that at the time of the examination he or she has kept seven terms and that twelve complete terms have not passed after her or his first term of residence. In exceptional circumstances a candidate who has obtained honours in Part IA, but not in Part IB of the Classical Tripos, may be a candidate for honours in Part II of the Classical Tripos, subject to approval by the Faculty Board;

(*b*) a student who has obtained honours in another Honours Examination in the year next after or next but one after so obtaining honours, provided that at the time of the examination he or she has kept seven terms and that twelve complete terms have not passed after her or his first term of residence;[1]

[1] See also the regulations for Affiliated Students.

(*c*) an Affiliated Student as allowed by the Faculty Board in accordance with the regulations for Affiliated Students.

5. No student who has been a candidate for any Part shall again be a candidate for the same Part.

6. No student who has obtained honours in Part IA or Part IB of the Modern and Medieval Languages Tripos, having offered classical Greek or classical Latin in the examination, shall be a candidate for Part IA or Part IB of the Classical Tripos.

Examiners. Assessors.

7. For each Part of the Tripos the Faculty Board of Classics shall nominate such number of Examiners as they shall deem sufficient. The Faculty Board shall have power to nominate one or more Assessors to the Examiners for each Part. The Assessors shall, if required, propose questions in the papers or parts of papers assigned to them by the Examiners, shall mark the answers of the candidates in those papers or parts of papers, shall read theses and participate in the *viva voce* examinations thereon, and shall report as required to the Examiners.

8. Assessors appointed under Regulation 7 may be summoned to meetings of the Examiners for the purpose of consultation and advice, but shall not be entitled to vote. Every paper in Part II of the Classical Tripos shall be examined by at least two of the whole body of Examiners and Assessors.

Meetings of Examiners.

9. Before the examination there shall be general meetings of the Examiners for Part IA, Part IB, and Part II, when the papers set by each Examiner or Assessor shall be submitted to the whole body of Examiners for their approval.

Style and method.

10. The Examiners shall have regard to the style and method of the candidates' answers and shall give credit for excellence in these respects.

Supplementary regulations.

11. The Faculty Board shall have power to make supplementary regulations defining all or any of the subjects set out in the following regulations and to modify, alter, or withdraw such supplementary regulations as they think fit.

Notice of books and subjects.

12. Public notice of books or subjects prescribed under the following regulations or under any supplementary regulations shall be given by the Faculty Board

(*a*) for Part IA and Part IB of the Tripos, not later than the Easter Term preceding the examination to which they apply,

(*b*) for Part II of the Tripos, not later than the Easter Term next but one preceding the examination to which they apply,

provided that the Board shall have the power of subsequently issuing amendments if they have due reason for doing so and if they are satisfied that no student's preparation for the examination is adversely affected. The Board shall also have the power when they first give notice of the books or subjects prescribed for a particular examination to announce any consequential restriction on the combination of papers that a candidate may choose to offer.

PART IA

Papers in Part IA.

13. The examination shall consist of seven papers, each to be set for three hours, as follows:

Paper 1. Greek language and texts (also serves as Paper GL 1 of Part IA of the Modern and Medieval Languages Tripos)

Paper 2. Alternative Greek language and texts (also serves as Paper GL 2 of Part IA of the Modern and Medieval Languages Tripos)

Paper 3. Latin language and texts (also serves as Paper GL 3 of Part IA of the Modern and Medieval Languages Tripos)

Paper 4. Alternative Latin language and texts

Paper 5. Classical questions (also serves as Paper GL 5 of Part IA of the Modern and Medieval Languages Tripos)

Paper 6. Greek prose and verse composition (also serves as Paper GL 6 of Part IA of the Modern and Medieval Languages Tripos)

Paper 7. Latin prose and verse composition (also serves as Paper GL 7 of Part IA of the Modern and Medieval Languages Tripos)

14. Every candidate shall offer either Paper 1 or Paper 2, either Paper 3 or Paper 4, and Paper 5. Paper 2 is intended for candidates who had little or no knowledge of Greek before entry to the University, and Paper 4 is intended for candidates who had little or no knowledge of Latin before doing so and who have not successfully completed the Preliminary Examination to Part IA. No candidate may offer Paper 2 and Paper 4. In addition, a candidate may offer one or both of Papers 6 and 7; the Examiners shall give credit for proficiency in these papers.

15. The names of candidates who obtain honours shall be placed by the Examiners in three classes. The names in each class shall be in alphabetical order. In the class-list a mark of distinction may be attached to the name of any candidate whose work in the examination shows special merit. A mark of distinction, *G* or *L* respectively, shall be attached to the names of those candidates who, in offering either Paper 6 or Paper 7 acquit themselves with credit in that paper. A mark, *g* or *l* respectively, shall be attached to the names of those candidates who, in offering either Paper 6 or Paper 7 satisfy the Examiners in that paper. Class-list for Part IA.

16. In arranging the class-list the Examiners shall take into account the standard attained by candidates in each paper as well as the aggregate of marks obtained by them.

PART IB

17. The examination shall consist of the following papers, each to be set for three hours: Papers in Part IB.

Paper 1. Passages for translation from Greek authors (also serves as Paper GL 11 of the Modern and Medieval Languages Tripos).
Paper 2. Alternative passages for translation from Greek authors (also serves as Paper GL 12 of the Modern and Medieval Languages Tripos).
Paper 3. Passages for translation from Latin authors (also serves as Paper GL 13 of the Modern and Medieval Languages Tripos).
Paper 4. Alternative passages for translation from Latin authors.
Paper 5. Greek literature (also serves as Paper GL 15 of the Modern and Medieval Languages Tripos).
Paper 6. Latin literature (also serves as Paper GL 16 of the Modern and Medieval Languages Tripos).
Paper 7. Greek and Roman history (also serves as Paper GL 17 of the Modern and Medieval Languages Tripos).
Paper 8. Greek and Roman philosophy (also serves as Paper GL 18 of the Modern and Medieval Languages Tripos and as Paper 4 of Part IB of the Philosophy Tripos).
Paper 9. Greek and Roman art and archaeology (also serves as Paper GL 19 of the Modern and Medieval Languages Tripos).
Paper 10. Greek and Latin philology and linguistics (also serves as Paper GL 20 of the Modern and Medieval Languages Tripos).
Paper 11. Translation from English into Greek prose and verse (also serves as Paper GL 21 of the Modern and Medieval Languages Tripos).
Paper 12. Translation from English into Latin prose and verse (also serves as Paper GL 22 of the Modern and Medieval Languages Tripos).

18. A candidate shall be required to offer six papers as follows:
Paper 1 or Paper 2; Paper 3 or Paper 4; Papers 5 and 6; and two papers chosen from among Papers 7–10.

19. In addition to the papers to be offered under Regulation 18, a candidate may offer Paper 11 or Paper 12 or both these papers.

20. The names of candidates who obtain honours shall be placed by the Examiners in three classes, of which the second shall be divided into two divisions. The names in the first and third classes and in each division of the second class shall be in alphabetical order. In drawing up the class-list the Examiners shall have regard in the first place to the work done by the candidates in the six papers which they are required to offer, and no candidate shall be excluded from any class on the ground that he or she has not offered either or both of Papers 11 and 12 in addition. A mark of distinction, an asterisk, shall be attached to the names of candidates whose work in those six papers shows special merit. In determining the place in the class-list of any candidate who has offered either or both the Papers 11 and 12 in addition, the Examiners shall give credit for proficiency in these papers. A mark of distinction, G or L respectively, shall be attached to the names of those candidates who, in offering either Paper 11 or Paper 12, acquit themselves with credit in that paper. A mark, g or l respectively, shall be attached to the names of those candidates who, in offering either Paper 11 or Paper 12, satisfy the Examiners in that paper. Class-list for Part IB.

21. In arranging the class-list the Examiners shall take into account the standard attained by candidates in each paper as well as the aggregate of marks obtained by them.

PART II

22. The examination shall consist of papers assigned to five groups, A, B, C, D, E, representing five fields of study, and to a sixth group, X, representing a combination of two or more of these fields of study, and certain papers from other Triposes, as set out below. Papers in Part II.

Group A (Literature)

A1. A prescribed Greek author or authors, and a prescribed Latin author or authors (also serves as Paper 31 of Part II of the English Tripos (New Regulations)).[1]
A2. Prescribed Greek texts (also serves as Paper 32 of Part II of the English Tripos (New Regulations)).[1]
A3. Prescribed Latin texts (also serves as Paper 33 of Part II of the English Tripos (New Regulations)).[1]
A4. Greek and Latin textual criticism and transmission of texts.

Group B (Philosophy)

B1. Plato.[1,2]
B2. Aristotle.[1,2]
B3. A prescribed subject or period in Greek and Roman philosophy.[2]

Group C (History)

C1. A prescribed period or subject of Greek history (may also serve as a paper in Part II of the Historical Tripos).
C2. A prescribed period or subject of Roman history.
C3. A prescribed subject taken from ancient history.
C4. A subject in ancient or medieval European history (may also be the same, in whole or in part, as a paper in Part II of the Historical Tripos).[1]

Group D (Archaeology)[3]

D1. Aegean prehistory.
D2. A topic within classical archaeology and/or art.
D3. A topic within classical archaeology and/or art.[1]
D4. A topic within classical archaeology and/or art.

Group E (Language)

E1. Elements of comparative linguistics (also serves as Paper 28 of the Linguistics Tripos).
E2. The Greek language (also serves as Paper 29 of the Linguistics Tripos).[1]
E3. The Latin language (also serves as Paper 30 of the Linguistics Tripos).[1]

Group X

X1. A subject specified by the Faculty Board from time to time.[1]
X2. A subject specified by the Faculty Board from time to time.[1]
X3. A subject specified by the Faculty Board from time to time.

Schedule of Optional Papers

Amended by Notices (Reporter, *2013–14, pp. 40, 447, 637, and 723*)

Paper O1. History of ideas on language (Paper 12 of the Linguistics Tripos).[4]
Paper O2. Introduction to modern Greek language and culture (Paper Gr. 3 of the Modern and Medieval Languages Tripos).
Paper O3. Tragedy (Paper 2 of Part II of the English Tripos (New Regulations)).
Paper O4. History and theory of literary criticism (Paper 16 of Part II of the English Tripos (New Regulations)).
Paper O5. Philosophy of mind (Paper 2 of Part II of the Philosophy Tripos).

[1] This paper is also available to candidates for Part II of the Modern and Medieval Languages Tripos; see p. 395.
[2] This paper is also available to candidates for Part II of the Philosophy Tripos; see p. 423.
[3] The papers in this group also serve as papers in Archaeology in Part IIA and Part IIB of the Archaeological and Anthropological Tripos, see p. 272
[4] This paper is suspended in 2014–15 and in each alternate year thereafter.

Paper O6. History of political thought to *c.* 1700 (Paper 19 of Part I of the Historical Tripos).
Paper O7. A special subject in Neo-Latin literature: selected authors (Paper NL 2 of the Modern and Medieval Languages Tripos).
Paper O8. Judaism and Hellenism (Paper D2(*d*) of the Theological and Religious Studies Tripos).
Paper O9. Early medieval literature and its contexts (Paper 2 of Part I of the English Tripos (New Regulations)).
Paper O10. The Romance languages (Paper CS 1 of the Modern and Medieval Languages Tripos).
Paper O11. Ancients and Moderns (Paper 1 set for the subject History and Philosophy of Science in Part II of the Natural Sciences Tripos).
Paper O12. Archaeology in action (Paper ARC2 of Part I of the Human, Social, and Political Sciences Tripos).

23. A student who is a candidate for Part II in the year next after obtaining honours in Part IB or in another Honours Examination shall offer

(*a*) *either* (i) two papers belonging to a single Group, chosen from among the six Groups A, B, C, D, E, X;
or (ii) one paper chosen from one of the six Groups A, B, C, D, E, X, together with a thesis, as prescribed in Regulation 26, on a topic (proposed by the candidate and approved by the Faculty Board) which falls wholly within the area of that Group;

and

(*b*) *either* (i) two additional papers chosen from Groups A, B, C, D, E, X, and from the Schedule of Optional Papers;
or (ii) one additional paper chosen from Groups A, B, C, D, E, X, and from the Schedule of Optional Papers, together with a thesis, as prescribed in Regulation 26 on a topic (proposed by the candidate and approved by the Faculty Board) which falls within the field of Classics;

provided that

(1) no candidate shall offer a thesis on a topic that coincides substantially with the subject of any of the papers that he or she is offering in the examination;
(2) no candidate shall offer more than one thesis, or more than two papers from Group X, or more than one paper from the Schedule of Optional Papers.

24. A student who is a candidate for Part II in the year next but one after obtaining honours in Part IB or in another Honours Examination shall offer

(*a*) *either* (i) two papers belonging to a single Group, chosen from among the six Groups A, B, C, D, E, X;
or (ii) one paper chosen from one of the six Groups A, B, C, D, E, X, together with a thesis, as prescribed in Regulation 26, on a topic (proposed by the candidate and approved by the Faculty Board) which falls wholly within the area of that Group;

and

(*b*) *either* (i) three additional papers chosen from Groups A, B, C, D, E, X, and from the Schedule of Optional Papers;
or (ii) two additional papers chosen from Groups A, B, C, D, E, X, and from the Schedule of Optional Papers, together with a thesis, as prescribed in Regulation 26, on a topic (proposed by the candidate and approved by the Faculty Board) which falls within the field of Classics;

provided that

(1) no candidate shall offer a thesis on a topic that coincides substantially with the subject of any of the papers that he or she is offering in the examination;
(2) no candidate shall offer more than one thesis, or more than two papers from Group X, or more than one paper from the Schedule of Optional Papers.

25. A candidate may be examined *viva voce* on the field of study of a Group from which he or she offers two or more papers, provided that the scope of such an examination shall be restricted to the subjects of the papers which the candidate has offered. *Viva voce* examinations shall be held at such times as the Examiners may appoint, and the times appointed shall be announced not later than the second day after the beginning of the examination.

26. (*a*) A candidate who wishes to offer a thesis under Regulation 23 or Regulation 24 shall submit an application, including the title of the proposed thesis, a brief account of its scope, and a statement of the scheme of papers to be offered in the examination. Applications shall be submitted through Thesis.

candidates' Directors of Studies to the Academic Secretary (Undergraduate) of the Faculty, so as to arrive not later than the second Monday of the Full Michaelmas Term next preceding the examination.

(*b*) Each candidate must obtain the approval of the proposed title by the Faculty Board not later than the last day of the Full Michaelmas Term next preceding the examination. When the Faculty Board have approved a title, no change shall be made to it or to the candidate's scheme of papers, without the further approval of the Faculty Board. Any application for a change in title or scheme of papers must be submitted through the candidate's Director of Studies to the Academic Secretary (Undergraduate) as soon as possible, and in any case no later than ten days before the last Faculty Board meeting of the Lent Term. If a candidate decides to offer a paper in place of a thesis, this is deemed to be a change in the scheme of papers and must be notified to the Faculty Board in accordance with the same timetable.

(*c*) A thesis shall not exceed 10,000 words in length, including notes but excluding bibliography. Candidates will be required to declare that the thesis is their own work and that it does not contain material already used to any substantial extent for a comparable purpose.

(*d*) A thesis shall be submitted in accordance with the detailed arrangements approved by the Faculty Board, to the Academic Secretary (Undergraduate) so as to arrive not later than the first Monday of the Full Easter Term in which the examination is to be held.

(*e*) Each thesis shall be examined by two Examiners or by an Examiner and an Assessor, and the candidate shall be examined by them upon it *viva voce*.

Class-list for Part II.

27. The names of the candidates who obtain honours shall be placed by the Examiners in three classes, of which the second shall be divided into two divisions. The names in the first and third classes and in each division of the second class shall be arranged in alphabetical order. A mark of distinction shall be awarded for special excellence.

SUPPLEMENTARY REGULATIONS

Part IA

Paper 1. Greek language and texts

This paper will contain passages for unseen translation and seen passages for analysis and appreciation from prescribed texts.

Paper 2. Alternative Greek language and texts

This paper will contain passages for unseen translation appropriate for candidates who had little or no knowledge of Greek before entry to the University and seen passages for analysis and appreciation from prescribed texts.

Paper 3. Latin language and texts

This paper will contain passages for unseen translation and seen passages for analysis and appreciation from prescribed texts.

Paper 4. Alternative Latin language and texts

This paper will contain passages for unseen translation appropriate for candidates who had little or no knowledge of Latin before entry to the University and seen passages for analysis and appreciation from prescribed texts.

Paper 5. Classical questions

This paper will contain questions on:

(*a*) Greek and Latin literature;
(*b*) Greek and Roman philosophy;
(*c*) Greek and Roman history;
(*d*) Greek and Roman art and archaeology;
(*e*) Classical philology and linguistics.

Paper 6. Greek prose and verse composition

This paper will contain passages for translation into Greek prose and verse, with some specified passages which may be attempted by candidates for Paper 2.

Paper 7. Latin prose and verse composition

This paper will contain passages for translation into Latin prose or verse, with some specified passages which may be attempted by candidates for Paper 4.

PART IB

Paper 1. Passages for translation from Greek authors

This paper will contain passages for translation, both seen and unseen.

Paper 2. Alternative passages for translation from Greek authors

This paper will contain passages for translation, both seen and unseen, and is appropriate for candidates who had little or no knowledge of Greek before entry to the University.

Paper 3. Passages for translation from Latin authors

This paper will contain passages for translation, both seen and unseen.

Paper 4. Alternative passages for translation from Latin authors

This paper will contain passages for translation, both seen and unseen, and is appropriate for candidates who had a limited knowledge of Latin before entry to the University.

Paper 5. Greek literature
and
Paper 6. Latin literature

Each of these papers will contain seen passages for analysis and appreciation from prescribed texts, and essay and other questions on these and other prescribed works.

Paper 7. Greek and Roman history

The paper will contain questions on topics in Greek and Roman history to be specified from time to time.

Candidates for the Classical Tripos will be given credit for knowledge of both Greek and Roman history. Candidates for the Modern and Medieval Languages Tripos will not be expected to show knowledge of both Greek and Roman history.

Paper 8. Greek and Roman philosophy

A text or texts will be prescribed. The paper will contain questions on the prescribed text or texts, and questions on ancient philosophers and philosophical systems.

Paper 9. Greek and Roman art and archaeology

The paper will contain questions relating to the Aegean world, Italy and the Roman Empire: questions may require comments on images.

Paper 10. Greek and Latin philology and linguistics

This paper will contain questions on topics in Greek, Latin, and comparative Greek/Latin philology and linguistics to be specified from time to time. Candidates for the Modern and Medieval Languages Tripos will not be expected to show knowledge of both Greek and Latin philology and linguistics.

Paper 11. Translation from English into Greek prose and verse

This paper will contain passages for translation into Greek prose or verse, with some specified passages which may be attempted only by candidates taking Paper 2.

Paper 12. Translation from English into Latin prose and verse

This paper will contain passages for translation into Latin prose or verse, with some specified passages which may be attempted only by candidates taking Paper 4.

PART II

GROUP A (LITERATURE)

Paper A1. A prescribed Greek author or authors, and a prescribed Latin author or authors

This paper will contain questions on a Greek author or authors and on a Latin author or authors. The works prescribed here will be taken from among the major works of Greek and Latin literature.

Paper A2. Prescribed Greek texts

This paper will contain passages for literary comment and essay questions.

Paper A3. Prescribed Latin texts

This paper will contain passages for literary comment and essay questions.

Paper A4. Greek and Latin textual criticism and transmission of texts

This paper will contain passages for textual comment, questions on palaeography and essay questions: candidates will be required to answer questions on passages in each of the two languages.

Group B (Philosophy)

Paper B1. Plato

In any year, a text and/or subject for study will be prescribed.

Paper B2. Aristotle

In any year, a text and/or subject for study will be prescribed.

Group C (History)

Paper C3. A prescribed subject taken from ancient history

These papers may contain questions on the literary, epigraphical, and archaeological sources for the period or subject prescribed, and questions that involve a knowledge of geography and topography and of the political, legal, and social antiquities of the period or subject prescribed; such questions will not require a technical knowledge of archaeology.

Group D (Archaeology)

Paper D2. A topic within classical archaeology and/or art

Paper D3. A topic within classical archaeology and/or art

If, in any year, the subject prescribed for Paper D2 is connected with early Hellenic archaeology, the subject prescribed for Paper D3 will be connected with classical (Greco-Roman) art; if the subject prescribed for Paper D2 is connected with early Greek art, the subject prescribed for Paper D3 will be connected with the archaeology of the Greek and Hellenistic world.

Group E (Language)

Paper E1. Elements of comparative linguistics

This paper will cover the principles of the comparative method and of historical reconstruction and their applications to Indo-European phonology, morphology, syntax, and lexicon. A knowledge of the relevant phenomena in Vedic will be required.

Paper E2. The Greek language

A prescribed subject in the history of the Greek language.

Paper E3. The Latin language

A prescribed subject in the history of the Latin language.

For each of Papers E2 and E3 the Faculty Board will prescribe texts for special study. Each paper will include a compulsory question on the prescribed texts.

Group X

There will be not more than three papers in this group, X1, X2, X3, whose subjects will be prescribed from time to time by the Faculty Board of Classics. The subjects will be of an inter-disciplinary nature, requiring knowledge related to more than one of the fields of study represented by Groups A, B, C, D, and E.

COMPUTER SCIENCE TRIPOS

Amended by Notice (Reporter, *2013–14, p. 222)*

General

Four Parts. **1.** The Computer Science Tripos shall consist of four Parts: Part IA, Part IB, Part II, and Part III.

2. No student may be a candidate for more than one Part, or for any Part and also for another Honours Examination, in the same term.

3. No student who has been a candidate for any Part shall again be a candidate for the same Part.

Supplementary regulations. **4.** The Faculty Board of Computer Science and Technology shall have power to issue from time to time supplementary regulations defining or limiting all or any of the papers for examination. Due care shall be taken that sufficient notice is given of any alteration of such supplementary regulations.

Examiners and Assessors. **5.** For each Part of the Tripos the Faculty Board shall nominate such number of Examiners as they shall deem sufficient. They may also nominate for appointment one or more Assessors to the Examiners in such subjects as they consider desirable, and the Assessors so appointed shall, if required to do so, set papers or parts of papers and shall advise the Examiners on the performance of candidates in such subjects. The Assessors, when summoned by the Chair, shall attend meetings of the Examiners for the purpose of consultation and advice, but shall not be entitled to vote.

6. The questions proposed by each Examiner or Assessor shall be submitted to, and approved by, the Examiners collectively.

7. The names of the candidates who obtain honours in each of Parts IA, IB, and II shall be arranged in three classes, of which the second shall be divided into two divisions. The names in the first and third classes, and in each division of the second class, shall be arranged in alphabetical order. Class-lists.

8. The papers for Parts IA, IB, and II of the Computer Science Tripos shall be as follows: Scheme of examination.

Paper 1. Computer science 1.[1]
Paper 2. Computer science 2.
Paper 3. Computer science 3.
Paper 4. Computer science 4.
Paper 5. Computer science 5.
Paper 6. Computer science 6.
Paper 7. Computer science 7.
Paper 8. Computer science 8.
Paper 9. Computer science 9.

PART IA

9. A student may be a candidate for honours in Part IA if he or she has kept one term, provided that three complete terms have not passed after his or her first term of residence. Standing of candidates.

10. A candidate for Part IA shall submit a portfolio of assessed laboratory work as prescribed in Regulation 11, and shall offer: Requirements.

either (*a*) (i) Papers 1 and 2 of the Computer Science Tripos; and
(ii) Papers 1 and 2 from Part IA of the Mathematical Tripos;
or (*b*) (i) Papers 1 and 2 of the Computer Science Tripos; and
(ii) the examination requirements for the subject Mathematics, as set out in the regulations for Part IA of the Natural Sciences Tripos; and
(iii) *either* Introduction to psychology (Paper PBS 1 of Part I of the Psychological and Behavioural Sciences Tripos) *or* the examination requirements for one subject chosen from the list below and as set out in the regulations for Part IA of the Natural Sciences Tripos:

Chemistry
Earth Sciences
Evolution and Behaviour
Physics
Physiology of Organisms

11. A candidate for Part IA shall submit to the Head of the Department a portfolio of assessed laboratory work. The Head of the Department shall announce not later than the division of the Michaelmas Term next preceding the examination the nature of the laboratory work to be undertaken and the dates by which, and the manner in which, the results of such work are to be presented. The Examiners shall be provided by the Head of the Department with assessments of the work submitted by each candidate, and shall take these assessments into account when assigning marks for the examination. Laboratory work.

PART IB

12. A student who has obtained honours in Part IA of the Computer Science Tripos or in another Honours Examination may be a candidate for honours in Part IB in the year after so obtaining honours, provided that he or she has kept four terms and that nine complete terms have not passed after her or his first term of residence.[2] Standing of candidates.

13. A candidate for Part IB shall offer Papers 3, 4, 5, and 6, and shall submit a portfolio of assessed laboratory work as prescribed in Regulation 14. Requirements.

14. A candidate for Part IB shall submit to the Head of the Department a portfolio of assessed laboratory work. The Head of the Department shall announce not later than the division of the Michaelmas Term next preceding the examination the nature of the laboratory work to be undertaken Laboratory work.

[1] This paper is available to candidates for the Natural Sciences Tripos and the Psychological and Behavioural Sciences Tripos.
[2] See also the regulations for Affiliated Students.

and the dates by which, and the manner in which, the results of such work are to be presented. The Examiners shall be provided by the Head of the Department with assessments of the work submitted by each candidate, and shall take these assessments into account when assigning marks for the examination.

Part II

Standing of candidates.

15. A student who has obtained honours in Part IB of the Computer Science Tripos may be a candidate for honours in Part II in the year after so obtaining honours, provided that he or she has kept seven terms and that twelve complete terms have not passed after her or his first term of residence.[1]

Requirements.

16. A candidate for Part II shall offer Papers 7, 8, and 9, and shall submit a dissertation as prescribed in Regulation 17.

Dissertation.

17. A candidate for Part II shall submit the proposed title of her or his dissertation to the Head of the Department by the end of the first quarter of the Michaelmas Term next preceding the examination, and shall obtain the approval of the Head of the Department for the title by the division of the Michaelmas Term. Two copies of the dissertation, which shall be computer-printed and shall not exceed 12,000 words in length, excluding appendices, footnotes, and bibliography, shall be submitted by the candidate to the Head of the Department so as to arrive not later than noon on the third Friday before the first day of the examination. Each candidate will be required to sign a declaration that the dissertation is his or her own work, unaided except as may be specified in the declaration, and that it does not contain material that has already been used to any substantial extent for a comparable purpose; if two or more candidates have undertaken a dissertation in collaboration, they will each be required to indicate the extent of their contribution. The Examiners shall have power to examine any candidate *viva voce* on the subject of her or his dissertation and on the general field of knowledge within which it falls.

Period of study at Massachusetts Institute of Technology.

18. A student who, under arrangements approved by the Faculty Board of Computer Science and Technology, has spent not less than three terms studying at the Massachusetts Institute of Technology and has been certified by the President of the Institute after consultation with the Chair of Examiners for Part II of the Computer Science Tripos to have studied diligently during that period, shall be deemed thereby to have obtained honours in that Part of the Tripos. A list containing the names of persons so qualified shall be certified by the Chair of the Faculty Board and published in the *Reporter*.

Part III

Standing of candidates.

19. A student who has obtained honours in Part II of the Computer Science Tripos may be a candidate for honours in Part III in the year after so obtaining honours, provided that he or she:

(*a*) has kept ten terms and that fifteen complete terms have not passed after her or his first term of residence;[1]

(*b*) has attained a satisfactory standard, as defined by the Faculty Board, in previous honours examinations;

(*c*) has not proceeded to the B.A. Degree.

Requirements.

20. A candidate for Part III shall offer a combination of written papers, project dissertations, essays, and demonstrations of research training as duly specified by the notice of the Head of the Department not later than the end of the Easter Term next preceding the examination.

Other than for written papers, each candidate will be required to sign a declaration that each unit of assessment is her or his own work, unaided except as may be specified in the declaration, and that it does not contain material that has already been used to any substantial extent for a comparable purpose; if two or more candidates have undertaken a dissertation in collaboration, they will each be required to indicate the extent of their contribution. The Examiners shall have power to examine any candidate *viva voce* on the subject of such work and on the general field of knowledge within which it falls.

21. The names of the candidates who obtain honours in Part III shall be arranged in alphabetical order in a single class, with distinctive marks attached to the names of those candidates who in the opinion of the Examiners deserve special credit, (*d*) for a distinguished performance, (*m*) for a meritorious performance.

[1] See also the regulations for Affiliated Students.

ECONOMICS TRIPOS

1. The Economics Tripos shall consist of three Parts: Part I, Part IIA, and Part IIB. A separate class-list shall be published for each Part. Three Parts.

2. The scheme of the examination for Part I of the Tripos shall be that defined in Regulations 14 and 15 and for Part IIA of the Tripos that defined in Regulations 16–18 and for Part IIB of the Tripos that defined in Regulations 19–25.

3. The Faculty Board of Economics shall have power to make from time to time supplementary regulations further defining all or any of the subjects of the examination and regulations determining the credit that shall be assigned to such subjects respectively and marking out the lines of study that are to be pursued by the candidates, and to publish lists of books recommended to the candidates and to modify or alter any such supplementary regulations or lists as occasion may require. Sufficient notice of any such modifications or alterations shall be given to avoid hardship to candidates. The Faculty Board shall summon every year a conference of Lecturers on the subjects included in the Tripos, at which these supplementary regulations and lists shall be considered and suggestions for their revision received. Supplementary regulations.

4. A student may be a candidate for honours in Part I if at the time of the examination he or she has kept one term, provided that three complete terms have not passed after his or her first term of residence. Standing of candidates.

5. The following may present themselves as candidates for honours in Part IIA, if they have kept four terms:

(*a*) a student who has obtained honours in Part I of the Economics Tripos and has not subsequently obtained honours in any other Honours Examination, provided that six complete terms have not passed after his or her first term of residence;[1]

(*b*) a student who has obtained honours in any other Honours Examination, in the year after so obtaining honours, provided that nine complete terms have not passed after his or her first term of residence.

A student who, under arrangements approved by the Faculty Board, has spent not less than three terms studying at the Massachusetts Institute of Technology and has been certified by the President of the Institute after consultation with the Chair of Examiners for Part IIA of the Economics Tripos to have studied diligently during that period, shall be deemed thereby to have obtained honours in that Part of the Tripos. A list containing the names of persons so qualified shall be certified by the Chair of the Faculty Board and published in the *Reporter*. Period of study at Massachusetts Institute of Technology.

6. A student who has obtained honours in any other Honours Examination other than Part I of the Economics Tripos or has been deemed to have obtained Honours in Part IIA of the Economics Tripos under Regulation 5 may be a candidate for honours in Part IIB in the year after so obtaining honours, provided that the student has kept seven terms and that twelve complete terms have not passed after his or her first term of residence.[1]

7. No student shall be a candidate for more than one Part, or for any Part and also for another Honours Examination, in the same term.

8. No student who has been a candidate for any Part shall again be a candidate for the same Part.

9. A candidate shall not offer in any Part of the Tripos a paper that he or she has previously offered in another University examination.

10. In each Part the names of the students who obtain honours shall be arranged in three classes, of which the second shall be divided into two divisions. The names in the first and third classes and in each division of the second class shall be arranged in alphabetical order.

11. The Faculty Board shall nominate such number of Examiners as they may deem sufficient for each Part of the Tripos. Examiners.

12. The Faculty Board shall have power to nominate one or more Assessors to assist the Examiners in any Part of the Tripos. Assessors shall be responsible for setting the paper or papers in the subject or subjects assigned to them, and for looking over the work of the candidates therein, and shall present a written report to the Examiners. Assessors shall have a right to attend the meetings of the Examiners, but shall not have a vote in determining the class-list. Assessors.

[1] See also the regulations for Affiliated Students.

13. In each Part the questions proposed by the Examiners or Assessors shall be submitted to and approved by the Examiners for that Part collectively.

Part I

Scheme of examination for Part I.

14. The scheme of examination for Part I of the Tripos shall be as follows:

Paper 1. Microeconomics
Paper 2. Macroeconomics
Paper 3. Quantitative methods in economics
Paper 4. Political and sociological aspects of economics
Paper 5. British economic history

15. In Part I every candidate shall offer all the papers specified in Regulation 14.

Part IIA

Scheme of examination for Part IIA.

16. The scheme of examination for Part IIA of the Tripos shall be as follows:

Paper 1. Microeconomics
Paper 2. Macroeconomics
Paper 3. Theory and practice of econometrics I
Paper 4. Economic development
Paper 5. *either* (*a*) Analysis of politics (Paper POL1 of Part I of the Human, Social, and Political Sciences Tripos),
or (*b*) Introduction to sociology: modern societies (Paper SOC1 of Part I of the Human, Social, and Political Sciences Tripos),
or (*c*) International relations I (Paper POL2 of Part I of the Human, Social, and Political Sciences Tripos).
Paper 6. Mathematics for economists and statisticians
Paper 7. Labour

Each paper shall be set for three hours except Paper 3. The examination for Paper 3 shall consist of a written paper of three hours' duration and the submission of project work undertaken by the candidate; details of the project work required and the arrangements for its submission shall be prescribed from time to time by the Faculty Board.

17. A candidate for Part IIA shall offer

(*a*) Papers 1, 2, and 3

and (*b*) one or two papers chosen from among Papers 4–7.

18. If under Regulation 17(*b*) a candidate offers two papers, the paper of these two on which the Examiners judge the candidate's performance to be least good shall be taken into account only if that would be to the candidate's advantage.

Part IIB

Scheme of examination for Part IIB.

19. The scheme of the examination for Part IIB of the Tripos shall be as follows:

Papers 1, 2. Economic principles and problems
Paper 3. A subject in economics[1]
Paper 4. Economic theory and analysis
Paper 5. Mathematical economics[1]
Paper 6. Banking, money, and finance
Paper 7. Public economics
Paper 8. The economics of developing countries
Paper 9. Industry
Paper 10. Theory and practice of econometrics II
Paper 11. Time series and financial econometrics[1]
Paper 12. A subject in economics[1]
Paper 13. A subject in economics[1]
Paper 14. A subject in economic history
Paper 15. A subject in economic history[2]

[1] This paper is suspended until further notice.
[2] Paper 15 will not be available for examination in 2015.

Paper 16. A subject in sociology II (Paper Soc. 5 of the Politics, Psychology, and Sociology Tripos in any year that the subject of that paper is 'Modern Britain')

Paper 17. A subject in the field of sociology and politics

Each paper shall be of three hours' duration.

20. Except as provided in Regulation 22 a candidate for Part IIB shall offer

(*a*) Papers 1 and 2

and (*b*) two or three papers chosen from among Papers 3–17, provided that a candidate must offer at least one paper chosen from Papers 3–15;

and (*c*) a dissertation, submitted in accordance with the provisions of Regulation 25, within the field of any one of Papers 1–4, 6–15, or within a field from among other fields which the Faculty Board shall specify from time to time.

21. If under Regulation 20(*b*) a candidate offers three papers, the paper of these three on which the Examiners judge the candidate's performance to be least good shall be taken into account only if that would be to the candidate's advantage, provided that at least one of Papers 3–15 shall always be taken into account.

22. A candidate who takes the examination in the year next after obtaining honours in any Tripos examination other than Part IIA of the Economics Tripos shall offer Papers 1 and 2 and not less than two nor more than three papers chosen from among Papers 3–17, provided that a candidate must offer at least one paper chosen from Papers 3–15. If a candidate offers three such papers, that paper from among the three in which the Examiners judge the candidate's work to be least good shall be taken into account only if that would be to the candidate's advantage, provided that at least one of Papers 3–15 shall always be taken into account.

23. For Papers 12, 13, and 15 the Faculty Board shall announce by the division of the Lent Term of the year preceding the examination a total of not more than three subjects for each paper. In any case where the Faculty Board announce more than one such subject for a paper, a candidate may offer not more than one of the subjects announced. For Paper 17 a candidate may not offer more than one of the subjects specified in the supplementary regulations for this paper.

24. Some choice of questions shall be allowed in all papers.

25. (*a*) A candidate for Part IIB under Regulation 20 shall submit an application to the Secretary of the Faculty Board, specifying the proposed topic of the dissertation, and the paper or field within which it falls. Applications shall be considered by the Examiners; the approval or rejection of a candidate's proposed topic shall be communicated to the candidate. A candidate whose proposed topic is rejected may submit a revised application. Dissertation.

(*b*) When a candidate's proposed topic has been approved by the Examiners, no change shall be made in it, except that a candidate may subsequently apply for permission to revise the topic.

(*c*) The timetable for the submission and the approval of applications under sub-paragraphs (*a*) and (*b*) shall be announced by the Faculty Board not later than the end of the Michaelmas Term. All applications shall be submitted in accordance with detailed instructions issued by the Board.

(*d*) A dissertation shall be in English, and shall be of not less than 6,000 words and not more than 7,500 words in length,[1] including notes and appendices but excluding bibliography. Candidates will be required to give full references to sources used.

(*e*) Two copies of the dissertation, in typewritten or computer-printed form, shall be submitted, in accordance with detailed arrangements approved by the Faculty Board, so as to reach the Secretary of the Faculty Board not later than the first day of the Full Easter Term in which the examination is to be held. Together with the dissertation each candidate shall submit

(i) two copies of a brief synopsis of the contents of the dissertation, and

(ii) a declaration signed by the candidate that the dissertation is his or her own work, unaided except as may be specified in the declaration, that it does not contain material which has already been used to any substantial extent for a comparable purpose, and that it does not exceed the maximum permitted length.

26. The Examiners shall have power to examine a candidate *viva voce* on the subject of her or his project submitted under Regulations 14 or 16, or on her or his dissertation submitted under Regulation 25.

[1] One A4 page consisting largely of charts, statistics, or symbols shall be regarded as the equivalent of 250 words; the contents of such pages must be presented so as to be readily legible.

SUPPLEMENTARY REGULATIONS

Part I

Papers 1 and 2

Both papers will emphasize theoretical issues (some questions may also be set which require knowledge of the history of economic thought).

Paper 1. Microeconomics

This paper will deal with the following: the theory of the consumer: choice and demand; the theory of the producer; costs and supply; supply, demand, and market equilibrium; partial and general equilibrium analysis; demand and supply in factor markets; market equilibrium under various forms of industrial structure; market failure and the role of the state; elementary game theory and bargaining.

Paper 2. Macroeconomics

The paper will provide an introduction to the following topics. National income accounting. Classical theory of output and employment. Elementary neoclassical growth theory. Quantity theory of money. Economic fluctuations and short-run equilibrium. Interaction between goods and financial markets: the IS-LM model; Simple open economy macroeconomics; Aggregate supply and the labour market; Stabilization policy.

Paper 3. Quantitative methods in economics

This paper will cover the application of simple statistical and mathematical techniques to a range of problems in economics. The written examination for the paper will be set in four sections.

Candidates are required to answer questions from all four sections of the written paper: the marks attached to each section, and the number of questions to be answered, will be shown on the question paper. Sections A and B of the paper will comprise a number of questions on mathematical techniques, and the application of these techniques to simple problems in economic theory. Sections C and D of the paper will deal with the manner in which statistics contributes to the study of economic problems and to the discussion of issues of public policy. The questions in these sections will test candidates' ability to perform relatively simple statistical derivations, to analyse problems in applied economics, and their knowledge of statistical sources. Sections A and C will each contain four short questions: students will be required to answer all questions in these sections. Sections B and D will each contain two long questions of which students will be required to answer one. The paper will be of three hours' duration with an additional fifteen-minute reading time prior to the beginning of the examination.

Paper 4. Political and sociological aspects of economics

This paper considers the influence of political and sociological factors on economic affairs. It reviews the history of economic and social policy-making in the post-war period in Britain. It examines a variety of influences on policy: the political ideologies that inform the conduct of policy; the domestic and international institutions that provide the context within which policy is formed; the nature of power in government; and the broader social and economic processes that shape the environment in which economic policy is conducted. The paper examines the changing nature of institutions that have regulated the employment relationship and shaped labour standards with the decline of trade unions and the increased role of the law. As background to a wider understanding of the global economy, it introduces the economic analysis of property rights, civil liberties, social capital, income inequality, the family, religion, and terrorism.

Paper 5. British economic history

This paper will be concerned with three main themes in the industrial development of Britain between 1750 and 1939: the industrial revolution, problems of growth and trade in the mature economy up to 1914, and the inter-war years; it will also cover some of the demographic and social changes associated with this industrial development. The specific topics which will be covered in the course of the analysis of the main themes include the long-run growth of output, productivity, and the standard of living; the costs of growth; demographic changes; capital accumulation and technical progress; entrepreneurship; foreign trade, the export of capital, and the role of the Empire; changes in the industrial structure; the labour market; government economic policies.

Part IIa

Paper 1. Microeconomic principles

The paper covers the following topics in economic theory: consumer theory; producer theory; equilibrium and markets; welfare economics; game theory and industrial organization; introduction to decision-making under uncertainty; asymmetric information; financial markets.

Paper 2. Macroeconomic principles

The paper aims to develop a good understanding of macroeconomics at the intermediate level, and to provide a rigorous framework for macroeconomic analysis. The paper covers topics from five areas: intertemporal macroeconomics including the behaviour of consumption, investment, and labour supply; labour markets, unemployment, and inflation; monetary economics, interest rates, and the role of the banking system; open economy macroeconomics including foreign exchange rate fluctuations; macroeconomic policy.

Papers 1 and 2 will contain a number of questions that will involve candidates in manipulating simple mathematical models at a level of mathematical competence no higher than that required in Paper 3 in Part I of the Economics Tripos.

Paper 3. Theory and practice of econometrics I

This paper deals with the manner in which statistics contributes to the study of economic and social problems and to the discussion of issues of public policy. Its main purpose is to test candidates' understanding of the intuition and concepts which underlie elementary statistical techniques, and their ability to analyse problems in applied economics, by bringing to bear on them relevant economic theory, knowledge of statistical sources, and relatively simple statistical derivations. A detailed schedule of the specific statistical techniques covered in this paper will be published by the Faculty Board not later than the start of the Michaelmas Term of the academic year in which the examination is to be held.

The examination for Paper 3 will consist of two components, as follows:

(*a*) A three-hour written paper which tests candidates' understanding of the logic of the methods covered in the course.

(*b*) Project work, involving use of the Faculty's computing facilities, on topics chosen by the candidate from a list of topics specified by the Examiners. Candidates will be required to select one topic, involving the application of data sources and statistical methods to economic problems.

The written paper will carry 60% of the weight for the examination as a whole, and the project 40%.

Paper 4. Economic development

The paper introduces concepts and theories in development economics and applies them to the comparative development experiences of selected countries or regions. It is designed to provide a useful foundation for candidates proposing to take Part IIB specialist options in development economics or economic history. It also constitutes a self-contained one-year course for those interested in this field but not planning to pursue it further. The concepts and theories covered are: the concept and measurement of 'development'; models of growth and development, population growth, human and physical capital investment dual economy models; coordination failure and the big push; factor market failures in developing economies including insurance and credit; trade policy issues; inequality and growth; the political economy of development.

The examination will be in two sections. Section (1) will include purely analytical questions. Section (2) will require candidates to relate their analysis of theoretical issues to comparative historical evidence from a small number of countries, the current choice of which will be announced by the Faculty Board early in the academical year. Candidates will be required to answer one question from Section (1) and two questions from Section (2). Each answer will carry equal weight.

Paper 5.

either (*a*) *Analysis of politics* (Paper POL1 of Part I of the Human, Social, and Political Sciences Tripos)

or (*b*) *Introduction to sociology: modern societies* (Paper SOC1 of Part I of the Human, Social, and Political Sciences Tripos)

or (*c*) *International relations I* (Paper POL2 of Part I of the Human, Social, and Political Sciences Tripos)

Paper 6. Mathematics for economists and statisticians

The paper covers those aspects of linear algebra, differential and integral calculus, differential and difference equations, probability theory, and statistical theory that are used in various parts of the Tripos. This paper is a pre-requisite for Paper 11 (*Time series and financial econometrics*) of Part IIB of the Economics Tripos and is recommended for those who plan to take Paper 6 (*Banking, money, and finance*) of Part IIB of the Economics Tripos.

Paper 7. Labour

The paper has the following subject matter: the determination of (the level and structure of) wages and employment by employer demand and household supply; theories of compensating differentials, human capital, internal labour markets, asymmetric information, labour mobility, industrial conflict, discrimination, and collective organization and activity; current issues in industrial relations and the management of the employment relationship; gender issues in, and public policies towards, the labour market. Candidates will be expected to know the main empirical characteristics of the British labour market, and some comparative attributes to other advanced economies. They should be familiar with the main sources of data on the British labour market and modern approaches to the analysis of such data. They should also be able to draw selectively on contributions from sociology and political science.

PART IIB

Papers 1 and 2. Economic principles and problems

These papers will deal with the scope and method of economics, with fundamental ideas, and with the application of the methods of economic analysis to economic problems. The papers will be designed to afford scope for the exercise of analytical power in abstract reasoning and in interpreting economic data. A few questions of a more advanced analytical character may be set, but the papers as a whole will be so framed as to be within the competence of those who have not made a study of advanced methods of analysis. A main object will be to test the power of candidates to apply their theoretical reasoning to actual problems. Candidates will, therefore, be expected to show a general knowledge and understanding of the role of the Government in economic affairs and of the working and effects of the principal economic institutions in the fields of production and distribution, of money and banking, of international economics, of employment, labour, and wage determination. Knowledge of the British economy is a basic requirement. Candidates should be able to analyse British problems in their international setting. Some questions will be asked about international economic problems and institutions, and about the problems of different types of economy. The questions set will not require such detailed knowledge as may be appropriate in Papers 3–9, but an understanding of general principles.

Paper 3. A subject in economics[1]

Paper 4. Economic theory and analysis

In this paper questions will be set of a more advanced character than in Papers 1 and 2, and the emphasis will rest on the theoretical aspects of economics. The paper will provide opportunity for the use of analytical methods including mathematics.

Paper 5. Mathematical economics[1]

Paper 6. Banking, money, and finance

This paper provides an introduction to advanced topics regarding the economic functions of money, credit, banking, financial asset markets, and monetary policy.

The topics to be covered in the paper will include: portfolio theory; valuation of financial assets and options; coordination of monetary and fiscal policy; bank risk management and regulation; and the design and transmission of monetary policy. Questions for this paper will assume knowledge of analytical models, relevant empirical evidence, and recent significant events regarding banking, financial markets, and monetary policy in developed and emerging economies.

Paper 7. Public economics

The paper studies the following subject matter: optimal taxation, externalities, and environmental policy; empirical evaluation of the effects of taxation and benefits on economic behaviour; social security; political decision-making and political economics; public expenditure and tax systems in practice. The paper will require knowledge of the relevant theories and institutions.

Paper 8. The economics of developing countries

The paper deals with the problems of growth and development in developing countries. Standard analytical tools, microeconomic and macroeconomic, are used to analyse key economic problems. The paper provides a framework for the understanding of how market failures and institutional failures affect economic and institutional development. Candidates are expected to show familiarity with the theoretical issues, to apply theory to the experience of a number of developing countries, and to use basic econometric knowledge to assess empirical evidence.

Paper 9. Industry

This paper will have the following subject matter: The modern business enterprise: its internal organization and functioning and their implications for its economic performance; competition, selection, and external constraints on corporate behaviour; law and the corporation; alternative theories of the firm; financial systems, capital structure, and corporate financial choices; multinational corporations; the market for corporate control. The evolution of firms, markets, and industries; standard models of imperfect competition, strategic behaviour; the relationship between industrial structure, behaviour, and performance; information technology and networks; technical change. Deindustrialization and structural changes in UK industry; issues of competition and industrial policies in the context of the international economy.

The Faculty Board will publish a list of prescribed readings for this paper at the beginning of the Michaelmas Term of the academic year in which the examination will be held. Students will be expected to be familiar with these readings, and to develop an understanding of the relevant literature which lies beyond them. The examination for this paper will be set in two sections. Section A will contain not less than three questions which relate closely to the topics covered in the prescribed readings, while Section B will contain not less than eight questions on more general topics associated with the subject matter of the paper. Candidates will be required to answer one question from Section A, and three questions from Section B.

Paper 10. Theory and practice of econometrics II

This paper develops and extends the econometric techniques beyond those covered in Paper 3 in Part IIA. It will involve discussion of the empirical application of these techniques to economic problems using examples from the econometric literature. Technical derivations will be kept to a minimum. The examination for this paper consists of a written paper of three hours' duration.

[1] This paper is suspended until further notice.

Paper 11. Time series and financial econometrics[1]

The paper provides a grounding in econometric theory, particularly as it relates to time series. Proofs and derivations play a more important role than in Paper 10. Candidates will be expected to show an understanding of both the statistical theory and the way in which statistical methods can be used in economics and finance.

Questions may be posed on regression, estimation procedures such as maximum likelihood and generalized methods of moments, test statistics, model selection, simultaneous equations, the properties of time series models and the way in which they are fitted and selected, dynamic models, and cointegration. Financial topics may include predictability of asset returns, volatility, portfolio analysis, CAPM model, factor model, and option pricing.

The use of approved calculators and statistical tables is permitted in the examination. The examination paper will consist of two sections, and students will be required to answer six questions from Section A, and two questions from Section B. Each section will carry equal weight.

Paper 12. A subject in economics[1]

Paper 13. A subject in economics[1]

Paper 14. A subject in economic history

This paper will, until further notice, be a paper entitled 'World Depression in the interwar years'. Its main focus will be on the causes and courses of the Great Depression of the 1930s, but the events of the 1920s including the inflation and deflation of 1919–21 will also receive attention. Topics covered will include the transfer problem and international monetary arrangements, the growth of protection and the development of trading blocs, monopolistic tendencies and changes in income distribution, technology and structural changes, the agrarian depression, and the comparative experience of different countries with regard to unemployment, especially following the trough of the cycle.

The main countries considered will be Britain, France, Germany, the USA, and Japan, but the paper will not be exclusively confined to these, and, in particular, the experience of some of the main primary producing countries will also be studied.

Paper 15. A subject in economic history[2]

Paper 16. A subject in sociology II (Paper Soc. 5 of the Politics, Psychology, and Sociology Tripos in any year that the subject of that paper is 'Modern Britain')

Candidates for this paper who are taking the Economics Tripos shall be examined by written examination.

Paper 17. A subject in the field of sociology and politics

Until further notice the subjects specified for this paper, from which candidates are required to select one, will be

(*a*) *A specified subject in South Asian Studies: the history and politics of South Asia* (Paper Int. 8 of the Politics, Psychology, and Sociology Tripos),

(*b*) *Society, politics, and culture in Latin America* (Paper Int. 7 of the Politics, Psychology, and Sociology Tripos),[1]

(*c*) *A subject in sociology IV* (Paper Soc. 7 of the Politics, Psychology, and Sociology Tripos in any year that the subject of that paper is 'The political economy of capitalism'),

(*d*) *An interdisciplinary subject IV* (Paper Int. 9 of the Politics, Psychology, and Sociology Tripos).

EDUCATION TRIPOS

1. The Education Tripos shall consist of two Parts; a separate class-list shall be published for each Part. Two Parts.

2. The following may present themselves as candidates for Part I: Standing of candidates.

(*a*) a student who has kept one term, provided that six complete terms have not passed after her or his first term of residence;

(*b*) a student who has obtained honours in another Honours Examination in the year next after or next but one after so obtaining honours, provided that twelve complete terms have not passed after her or his first term of residence.

3. The following may present themselves as candidates for honours in Part II provided[3] that they have kept seven terms and that twelve complete terms have not passed after their first term of residence:

(*a*) a student who has obtained honours in Part I of the Education Tripos, in the year next after so obtaining honours;

[1] This paper is suspended until further notice.
[2] Paper 15 will not be available for examination in 2015.
[3] See also the regulations for Affiliated Students.

(*b*) a student who has obtained honours in any Honours Examination other than Part I of the Education Tripos, in the year next or next but one after so obtaining honours.

4. No student shall be a candidate for both Parts, or for either Part and also for another Honours Examination, in the same term.

5. No student who has been a candidate for either Part shall again be a candidate for the same Part.

Supplementary regulations. **6.** The Faculty Board of Education shall have power to issue from time to time supplementary regulations defining or limiting all or any of the subjects of examination, and to modify, alter, or withdraw such supplementary regulations as occasion may require, provided that due care is taken to give sufficient notice of any change.

Variable subjects. **7.** Public notice of any variable subjects for the examinations in any year shall be given by the Faculty Board before the end of the Easter Term in the year next but one preceding the examination to which they apply; provided that the Board shall have the power of subsequently issuing amendments if they have due reason for doing so, and if they are satisfied that no student's preparation for the examination is adversely affected.

8. Not later than the first day of Full Michaelmas Term each year the Faculty Board shall publish, by Notice in the Faculty of Education, details of the course-work, performances, workshops, and practical examinations to be undertaken by candidates for each Part of the Tripos during the ensuing academical year.

Examiners. **9.** There shall be two separate bodies of Examiners, one for Part I and one for Part II. The Faculty Board shall nominate such number of Examiners as they deem sufficient to conduct the examinations. Assessors. The Faculty Board shall also have power to nominate one or more Assessors to assist the Examiners in any subject of the Tripos. Assessors shall propose questions in the papers or parts of papers assigned to them by the Examiners, shall mark the answers of the candidates in those papers or parts of papers, and shall advise the Examiners on the performance of candidates in the examination. Assessors may be summoned to meetings of the Examiners for the purpose of consultation and advice.

Class-lists. **10.** In the class-lists for each Part of the Tripos, the names of the candidates who obtain honours shall be arranged in three classes, of which the second shall be divided into two divisions. In addition the Examiners may affix a mark of distinction to the names of candidates placed in the first class whose work is of special merit. The names in the first and third classes and each division of the second class shall be arranged in alphabetical order.

Part I. **11.** The examination for Part I shall comprise three sections, as set out below. Candidates shall offer:

(*a*) the examination requirements set out in Section I;

(*b*) three further papers taken from the examination requirements set out in Section II and Section III, providing that candidates shall offer no fewer than two papers from Section III.

Section I. Education studies

Section I consists of two written papers, each of three hours' duration.

Paper 1 Disciplines of education
Paper 2 Disciplines of education II

Section II. Globalization, modernity, and education

Section II consists of one written paper of three hours' duration.

Paper 3 Globalization, modernity, and education

Section III. Subject studies

Candidates may offer two or three papers from one subject area only, as outlined in Schedule 1.

Part II. **12.** The examination for Part II shall comprise four sections, as set out below. Candidates shall offer:

(*a*) the examination requirements set out in Section I;

(*b*) four further papers taken from the examination requirements set out in Sections II–IV, providing that candidates shall offer at least one paper from Section II and no more than two papers from Section IV.

Candidates may not offer more than one dissertation in total under Sections II, III, and IV. Unless otherwise stated in Schedule 2, any dissertation shall be submitted under the conditions set out in Regulation 14.

Section I. Research and investigation in education

Candidates shall submit a dissertation on a topic related to the investigation and analysis of an educational problem. The dissertation shall be submitted under the conditions set out in Regulation 14. At the discretion of the Examiners, the examination may include an oral examination on the dissertation.

Section II. Advanced topics in education studies

Section II consists of three written papers, each of three hours' duration, and a dissertation.

Paper 1 Disciplines of education I
Paper 2 Disciplines of education II
Paper 3 Disciplines of education III (also serves as Paper Soc. 8 of the Politics, Psychology, and Sociology Tripos)
Paper 4 Dissertation in an education discipline

Section III. Special subjects in education

Candidates may offer one or more special subjects in education, which shall each count as one paper. The special subjects, and the examination requirements for each special subject, shall be announced by the Faculty Board from time to time, providing that due care is taken to give sufficient notice to all candidates.

Section IV. Subject studies

Candidates may offer up to two papers from one subject area only, as outlined in Schedule 2.

13. For both Parts, no candidate shall offer any paper, dissertation, or other exercise that he or she has previously offered in any University examination.

14. A candidate who intends to submit a dissertation under Section II of Part I, or under Sections I, II, III, and IV of Part II, shall submit the proposed topic to the Secretary of the Faculty Board through her or his Director of Studies, by a date announced by the Faculty Board not later than the beginning of the Michaelmas Term preceding the examination. The Secretary shall communicate the approval or rejection of the proposed topic to the candidate no later than the beginning of the Lent Term preceding the examination. Dissertations.

The submitted dissertation shall be of not less than 8,000 words and not more than 10,000 words, inclusive of notes and appendices. Dissertations shall be submitted by candidates through the Undergraduate Office to the Secretary of the Faculty Board by a date specified by the Faculty Board not later than the beginning of the Michaelmas Term preceding the examination. Each dissertation shall be in typescript, unless previous permission has been obtained from the Faculty Board to present it in manuscript; it shall bear the candidate's examination number and shall be accompanied by a brief synopsis.

Candidates will be required to declare that the dissertation is their own work and that it does not contain material already used to any substantial extent for a comparable purpose. At the discretion of the Examiners, a candidate may be examined *viva voce* on his or her dissertation.

15. Candidates intending to offer papers in Modern and Medieval Languages at Part II shall during the academical year next before the year of the examination be required to spend a period studying abroad under the conditions specified for the year abroad in the regulations of Part II of the Modern and Medieval Languages Tripos, including all conditions relating to the submission of evidence of, and reports on, the period of study abroad and applications for the approval of the candidates' plans.

SCHEDULE 1

SUBJECTS AND PAPERS FOR SECTION III OF PART I OF THE EDUCATION TRIPOS

Candidates may offer two or three papers chosen from only one subject area, as outlined in the Schedule. Where stated, some papers are examined by means other than a single written paper. Some subject areas may restrict the combinations of papers that may be offered.

Biological Sciences

All candidates shall offer the equivalent of two or three papers.

The following options shall count as one paper:

Biology of Cells (the examination requirements for this subject as set out in the regulations for Part IA of the Natural Sciences Tripos)

Evolution and Behaviour (the examination requirements for this subject as set out in the regulations for Part IA of the Natural Sciences Tripos)

Physiology of Organisms (the examination requirements for this subject as set out in the regulations for Part IA of the Natural Sciences Tripos)

The following options shall count as two papers:

Animal Biology (the examination requirements for this subject as set out in the regulations for Part IB of the Natural Sciences Tripos)

Cell and Developmental Biology (the examination requirements for this subject as set out in the regulations for Part IB of the Natural Sciences Tripos)

Ecology (the examination requirements for this subject as set out in the regulations for Part IB of the Natural Sciences Tripos)

Physiology (the examination requirements for this subject as set out in the regulations for Part IB of the Natural Sciences Tripos)

Plant and Microbial Sciences (the examination requirements for this subject as set out in the regulations for Part IB of the Natural Sciences Tripos)

Classics

All candidates shall offer the following two papers:

Passages for translation from Latin authors (Paper 3 of Part IB of the Classical Tripos)
Latin literature (Paper 6 of Part IB of the Classical Tripos)

A candidate who wishes to offer three papers may additionally offer one of Papers 7–10 from Part IB of the Classical Tripos.

English

English and Drama

Candidates may offer two or three of the following papers:

Paper Ed.D2 Film, culture, and identity
Paper Ed.D3 Drama production II (performance or workshop and submission of a note-book)
Paper Ed.E3 Shakespeare
English literature and its contexts, 1300–1550 (Paper 3 of Part I of the English Tripos (New Regulations))
English literature and its contexts, 1500–1700 (Paper 4 of Part I of the English Tripos (New Regulations))
English literature and its contexts, 1660–1870 (Paper 6 of Part I of the English Tripos (New Regulations))
English literature and its contexts, 1870 to the present (Paper 7B of Part I of the English Tripos (New Regulations))
Practical criticism and critical practice (Paper 6 of Part I of the English Tripos (Old Regulations))

A candidate may offer a dissertation in place of any of these papers, provided that only one dissertation is offered in total. Any dissertation shall be offered under the conditions specified in Regulation 14.

Geography

Candidates may offer two or three papers from Part IA or Part IB of the Geographical Tripos, in accordance with the examination requirements as set out in the regulations for that Tripos.

'Human geography' (Paper 1) and 'Physical geography' (Paper 2) from Part IA of the Geographical Tripos shall each count as two papers.

Candidates offering two papers shall offer:

either Human geography (Paper 1 from Part IA of the Geographical Tripos)
or Physical geography (Paper 2 from Part IA of the Geographical Tripos)
or two papers from Section B of Part IB of the Geographical Tripos in the area (human or physical geography) previously offered in the Preliminary Examination.

Candidates may not offer a paper previously offered in the Preliminary Examination.

Candidates offering three papers shall offer:

either (i) Human geography (Paper 1 from Part IA of the Geographical Tripos) *or* Physical geography (Paper 2 from Part IA of the Geographical Tripos)
and one paper from Section B of Part IB of the Geographical Tripos in the area (human or physical geography) previously offered in the Preliminary Examination
or (ii) three papers from Section B of Part IB of the Geographical Tripos in the area (human or physical geography) previously offered in the Preliminary Examination.

Candidates may not offer a paper previously offered in the Preliminary Examination.

Candidates taking papers from Part IB of the Geographical Tripos will be required to submit a portfolio of course-work under conditions specified by the Faculty Board of Earth Sciences and Geography not later than the division of the Easter Term next preceding the examination.

History

Candidates may offer two or three of any of the following papers:

Paper ARC1 of Part I of the Human, Social, and Political Sciences Tripos
Any of Papers 2–24 of Part I of the Historical Tripos

Modern and Medieval Languages

All candidates shall offer the following paper:

Translation into the foreign language, and test in the foreign language through audio-visual media (Paper B3 from Part IB of the Modern and Medieval Languages Tripos), all in the language which he or she has previously offered in the Preliminary Examination for Part I of the Education Tripos

and

one or two additional papers taken from Schedule IB to the regulations for the Modern and Medieval Languages Tripos

Music

Candidates may offer two or three of any of the following papers:
Music analysis (Paper 2 of Part IB of the Music Tripos)
Composition portfolio (Paper 5 of Part IB of the Music Tripos), which shall be submitted under conditions specified in the regulations of the Music Tripos
Any of the additional papers from Part IB of the Music Tripos announced by the Faculty Board of Music, which shall be undertaken under any conditions specified by the Faculty Board of Music when they are announced.
Dissertation (Paper 6 of Part IB of the Music Tripos) in accordance with Regulation 15 of the Music Tripos.

Physical Sciences

All candidates shall offer the equivalent of two or three papers.
The following options shall count as one paper:
Chemistry (the examination requirements for this subject as set out in the regulations for Part IA of the Natural Sciences Tripos)
Earth Sciences (the examination requirements for this subject as set out in the regulations for Part IA of the Natural Sciences Tripos)
Materials Science (the examination requirements for this subject as set out in the regulations for Part IA of the Natural Sciences Tripos)
Physics (the examination requirements for this subject as set out in the regulations for Part IA of the Natural Sciences Tripos)

The following options shall count as two papers:
Chemistry A (the examination requirements for this subject as set out in the regulations for Part IB of the Natural Sciences Tripos)
Chemistry B (the examination requirements for this subject as set out in the regulations for Part IB of the Natural Sciences Tripos)
Physics A (the examination requirements for this subject as set out in the regulations for Part IB of the Natural Sciences Tripos)

Religious Studies

Candidates may offer two or three papers chosen from Group B in Regulation 18 of the Theological and Religious Studies Tripos. Where, under the regulations for that Tripos, a paper may be offered in a form of assessment other than a written paper, the paper offered shall be submitted under conditions specified in the regulations for the Theological and Religious Studies Tripos.

SCHEDULE 2

SUBJECTS AND PAPERS FOR SECTION IV OF PART II OF THE EDUCATION TRIPOS

Candidates may offer up to two papers from only one subject area, as outlined in the Schedule. Where stated, some papers are examined by means other than a single written paper. Some subject areas may restrict the combinations of papers that may be offered.

Biological Sciences

A candidate who wishes to offer one paper may offer either of the two written papers from the subject History and Philosophy of Science from Part IB of the Natural Sciences Tripos.

A candidate who wishes to offer two papers may offer one of the following options, which shall count as two papers:
Animal Biology (the examination requirements for this subject as set out in the regulations for Part IB of the Natural Sciences Tripos)
Cell and Developmental Biology (the examination requirements for this subject as set out in the regulations for Part IB of the Natural Sciences Tripos)
Ecology (the examination requirements for this subject as set out in the regulations for Part IB of the Natural Sciences Tripos)
Experimental Psychology (the examination requirements for this subject as set out in the regulations for Part IB of the Natural Sciences Tripos)
History and Philosophy of Science (the examination requirements for this subject as set out in the regulations for Part IB of the Natural Sciences Tripos)
Physiology (the examination requirements for this subject as set out in the regulations for Part IB of the Natural Sciences Tripos)
Plant and Microbial Sciences (the examination requirements for this subject as set out in the regulations for Part IB of the Natural Sciences Tripos)

Classics

Candidates may offer one or two of the papers from Part II of the Classical Tripos.

English

English and Drama

Candidates may offer one or two of the following papers:

A paper from a list of Part II papers of the English Tripos announced by the Faculty Board of Education at the start of the Michaelmas Term.

Paper Ed.D4 Modern drama and theatre

Paper Ed.A1 Arts and performance (written paper and submission of course-work)

A candidate may offer a dissertation in place of any of the papers above, providing that the candidate may offer only one dissertation in total. Any other dissertation shall be offered under the conditions specified in Regulation 14.

Geography

Candidates may offer one or two papers from Part II of the Geographical Tripos, in accordance with the examination requirements as set out in the regulations for the Geographical Tripos.

History

Candidates may offer one or two of Papers 4–30 of Part II of the Historical Tripos.

Modern and Medieval Languages

Students who have completed the course in Modern and Medieval Languages in Part I of the Education Tripos shall have the following choices for Part II:

(A) A one-year Part II, the equivalent of five papers in Education Studies as set out in Regulation 12.

(B) A two-year Part II, the equivalent of five papers in Education Studies including a period spent abroad as detailed in Regulation 15.

Option A

The student having undertaken an intensive study course or similar and gained an acceptable form of certification in a further language (in the country of that language) which shall be one of those normally available within the Education with Modern and Medieval Languages Tripos, other than French:

1. Three Education papers as set out in Regulation 12
2. *and* translation from and into the foreign language offered at Part I (Paper C1 from Part II of the Modern and Medieval Languages Tripos)
3. *and* oral examination C from Part II of the Modern and Medieval Languages Tripos in the foreign language offered at Part I
4. *and* papers in a new language as follows: Papers A1 and A2 from Part IA of the Modern and Medieval Languages Tripos, together with Oral examination A in the same language in place of a Year Abroad Project, provided that both papers shall be in the same language, which the student shall not have offered in any previous examination.

For the purposes of marking 2 and 3 shall together be considered equivalent to one paper; 4 shall be considered equivalent to one paper.

Option B

1. Year Abroad Project in accordance with the regulations for Part II of the Modern and Medieval Languages Tripos
2. *and* three Education papers as set out in Regulation 12
3. *and* translation from and into the foreign language (Paper C1 from Part II of the Modern and Medieval Languages Tripos)
4. *and* oral examination C from Part II of the Modern and Medieval Languages Tripos

For the purposes of marking 1, 3, and 4 shall together be considered equivalent to one paper.

And either:

5. an additional paper taken from Schedule II of the regulations for the Modern and Medieval Languages Tripos
6. *or* use of the foreign language (Paper B1 from Part IA of the Modern and Medieval Languages Tripos) in a post A-level language not studied at Part I, which shall be one of those normally available within the Education with Modern and Medieval Languages Tripos
7. *or* a further Education paper.

Music

Candidates may offer one or two of the following papers:

Paper 1 of Part II of the Music Tripos, a dissertation which shall be submitted under the regulations of the Music Tripos

Any of Papers 3–6 of Part II of the Music Tripos, all of which shall be submitted or undertaken under the conditions specified in the regulations for the Music Tripos

Any of the additional papers from Part II of the Music Tripos announced by the Faculty Board of Music, which shall be undertaken under any conditions specified by the Faculty Board of Music when they are announced

Paper Ed.A1 Arts and performance (written paper and submission of course-work)

Physical Sciences

A candidate who wishes to offer one paper may offer either of the two written papers from the subject History and Philosophy of Science from Part IB of the Natural Sciences Tripos.

A candidate who wishes to offer two papers may offer one of the following options, which shall count as two papers:

Chemistry A (the examination requirements for this subject as set out in the regulations for Part IB of the Natural Sciences Tripos)

Chemistry B (the examination requirements for this subject as set out in the regulations for Part IB of the Natural Sciences Tripos)

[Geological Sciences A] ⟨Earth Sciences A⟩[1] (the examination requirements for this subject as set out in the regulations for Part IB of the Natural Sciences Tripos)

[Geological Sciences B] ⟨Earth Sciences B⟩[1] (the examination requirements for this subject as set out in the regulations for Part IB of the Natural Sciences Tripos)

History and Philosophy of Science (the examination requirements for this subject as set out in the regulations for Part IB of the Natural Sciences Tripos)

Materials Science (the examination requirements for this subject as set out in the regulations for Part IB of the Natural Sciences Tripos)

Physics A (the examination requirements for this subject as set out in the regulations for Part IB of the Natural Sciences Tripos)

Physics B (the examination requirements for this subject as set out in the regulations for Part IB of the Natural Sciences Tripos)

Religious Studies

Candidates may offer one or two papers from Group C in Regulation 18 of the Theological and Religious Studies Tripos. Where, under the regulations for that Tripos, a paper may be offered in a form of assessment other than a written paper, the paper offered shall be submitted under conditions specified in the regulations for the Theological and Religious Studies Tripos.

ENGINEERING TRIPOS

Amended by Notice (Reporter, *2013–14, p. 117*)

GENERAL

1. The Engineering Tripos shall consist of four Parts, Part IA, Part IB, Part IIA, and Part IIB.

2. No student who has been a candidate for any Part of the Engineering Tripos shall again be a candidate for the same Part.

3. The Faculty Board of Engineering shall nominate such number of Examiners as they think sufficient for each Part of the Engineering Tripos. They may also nominate for appointment one or more Assessors to the Examiners in such subjects as they consider desirable; the Assessors so appointed shall set papers or parts of papers and shall advise the Examiners on the performance of candidates in their subjects. The Assessors, when summoned by the Chair, shall attend meetings of the Examiners for the purpose of consultation and advice, but shall not be entitled to vote. Examiners and Assessors.

4. In each Part of the Engineering Tripos the questions proposed by each Examiner or Assessor shall be approved by the body of Examiners, or by a sub-group of those Examiners as nominated by the Chair of Examiners.

5. The Faculty Board shall have power to define or limit by supplementary regulations all or any of the subjects of examination, to determine the credit that shall be assigned to each subject, and to mark out the lines of study that are to be pursued by candidates. They shall also have power to modify or alter any such supplementary regulations as occasion may require, due care being taken that sufficient notice is given of any change. Supplementary regulations.

PART IA

6. The following may present themselves as candidates for honours in Part IA: Standing of candidates.

(*a*) a student who has kept one term, provided that three complete terms have not passed after his or her first term of residence;

[1] The subject in angular brackets will replace the subject in square brackets with effect from 1 October 2015.

(*b*) a student who has obtained honours in another Honours Examination in the year after so obtaining honours, provided that nine complete terms have not passed after the student's first term of residence.

Papers in Part IA.

7. The following papers shall be set in Part IA:

1. Mechanical engineering
2. Structures and materials
3. Electrical and information engineering
4. Mathematical methods

Every candidate shall offer all four papers. Each paper shall be of three hours' duration.

Course-work.

8. The Examiners shall take into account such course-work done by candidates as shall from time to time be determined by the Faculty Board. For this purpose the Head of the Department of Engineering shall present to the Examiners detailed reports on the performance of each candidate in this course-work. Details of the work required of candidates shall be published by the Faculty Board by Notice in the Department of Engineering not later than the beginning of the Full Michaelmas Term next preceding the examination.

Class-lists for Part IA.

9. The names of the candidates who obtain honours in Part IA shall be arranged in three classes, of which the second shall be divided into two divisions. The names in the first and third classes, and in each division of the second class, shall be arranged in alphabetical order.

PART IB

Standing of candidates.

10. The following may present themselves as candidates for honours in Part IB:

(*a*) a student who has obtained honours in Part IA of the Engineering Tripos, in the year after so obtaining honours;

(*b*) a student who has obtained honours in any Honours Examination, other than Part IA of the Engineering Tripos, in the year after so obtaining honours, provided that he or she has attained a satisfactory standard, as defined by the Faculty Board of Engineering, in his or her last Honours Examination; provided always that the student has kept four terms and that nine complete terms have not passed after his or her first term of residence.

Papers in Part IB.

11. The following papers shall be set in Part IB:

1. Mechanics
2. Structures
3. Materials
4. Thermofluid mechanics
5. Electrical engineering
6. Information engineering
7. Mathematical methods
8. Selected topics

Each paper in Part IB shall be of two hours' duration, except Paper 8. The examination for Paper 8 shall consist of *either* a written paper of two and a half hours' duration, *or* a written paper of one and a half hours' duration and the submission of course-work in one foreign language. Every candidate shall offer all eight papers.

Course-work.

12. The Examiners shall take into account such course-work done by candidates as shall from time to time be determined by the Faculty Board. For this purpose the Head of the Department of Engineering shall present to the Examiners detailed reports on the performance of each candidate in this course-work. Details of the work required of candidates shall be published by the Faculty Board by Notice in the Department of Engineering not later than the beginning of the Full Michaelmas Term next preceding the examination.

13. In order to obtain honours in Part IB a candidate must satisfy the Examiners that he or she has such industrial or equivalent experience as shall be determined from time to time by the Faculty Board.

Class-lists for Part IB.

14. The names of the candidates who obtain honours in Part IB shall be arranged in three classes, of which the second shall be divided into two divisions. The names in the first and third classes, and in each division of the second class, shall be arranged in alphabetical order.

PART IIA

Standing of candidates.

15. The following may present themselves as candidates for honours in Part IIA of the Engineering Tripos:

(*a*) a student who has obtained honours in Part IB of the Engineering Tripos, in the year after so obtaining honours;

(*b*) a student who has obtained honours in any Honours Examination other than Part IA or Part IB of the Engineering Tripos, in the year after so obtaining honours, provided that he or she has attained a satisfactory standard, as defined by the Faculty Board of Engineering, in his or her last Honours Examination; provided always that the student has kept seven terms and that twelve complete terms have not passed after his or her first term of residence.

16. The scheme of examination for Part IIA of the Engineering Tripos shall be as follows: Scheme of examination for Part IIA.

Group A: Energy, fluid mechanics, and turbomachinery
Group B: Electrical engineering
Group C: Mechanics, materials, and design
Group D: Civil, structural, and environmental engineering
Group E: Management and manufacturing
Group F: Information engineering
Group G: Bioengineering
Group I: Imported modules from other courses
Group M: Multidisciplinary modules
Group S: Modules shared with Part IIB of the Engineering Tripos

In each of Groups A, B, E, and F the Faculty Board shall prescribe modules whose total duration for written papers shall be nine hours. In each of Groups C and D the Faculty Board shall prescribe modules whose total duration for written papers shall be ten and a half hours. In Group G the Faculty Board shall prescribe modules whose total duration for written papers shall be no more than nine hours. Not later than the end of the Easter Term each year the Faculty Board shall give notice of the modules prescribed for the examination to be held in the academical year next following, and shall specify the mode of examination for each module. In giving such notice the Faculty Board shall announce combinations of modules which satisfy the qualifying conditions for each engineering area specified by the Board and shall have power to announce restrictions on the combination of modules that a candidate may choose to offer.

17. Each module in Groups A, B, C, D, E, F, and G shall be examined *either* by a written paper of one and a half hours *or* by a written paper of three hours. Each module in Groups I, M, and S shall be examined *either* by a written paper of one and a half hours *or* by a written paper of one and a half hours, and course-work.

18. Each candidate shall offer modules whose total duration for written papers amounts to fifteen hours, chosen subject to any restrictions announced by the Faculty Board under Regulation 16.

19. The Examiners shall take into account such course-work done by candidates as shall from time to time be determined by the Faculty Board. For this purpose the Head of the Department of Engineering shall present to the Examiners detailed reports on the performance of each candidate in this course-work. Details of the work required of candidates shall be published by the Faculty Board by Notice in the Department of Engineering not later than the beginning of the Michaelmas Term next preceding the examination. Course-work.

20. Every candidate submitting course-work under Regulations 18 or 19 shall be required to sign a declaration that the work submitted is his or her own work, unaided except as may be specified in the declaration; if two or more candidates have undertaken work in collaboration, they shall be required to indicate the extent of their collaboration.

21. In order to obtain honours in Part IIA of the Engineering Tripos a candidate must satisfy the Examiners that he or she has such industrial or equivalent experience as shall be determined from time to time by the Faculty Board; a statement of each candidate's experience shall be certified by the Head of the Department of Engineering. Industrial experience.

22. For each combination of subjects in Part IIA, announced by the Faculty Board under Regulation 16 as an engineering area, there shall be a separate class-list. The names of the candidates who obtain honours in each engineering area shall be arranged in three classes, the second of which shall be divided into two divisions. The names in the first and third classes and in each division of the second class shall be arranged in alphabetical order. For special excellence in Part IIA a mark of distinction may be awarded. Class-lists for Part IIA.

23. A candidate who, under arrangements approved by the Faculty Board of Engineering, has spent not less than three terms studying at an institution listed in the Schedule to these regulations and who has been certified by the head of that institution, after consultation with the Chair of Examiners for Part IIA of the Engineering Tripos, to have studied diligently during that period, shall be deemed thereby to have obtained honours in Part IIA of the Engineering Tripos. A list containing the names Period of study at an institution listed in the Schedule.

of persons so qualified shall be certified by the Chair of the Faculty Board of Engineering and published in the *Reporter*.

PART IIB

Standing of candidates.

24. A student who has obtained honours in Part IIA of the Engineering Tripos or has been deemed to have obtained honours in Part IIA of the Engineering Tripos under Regulation 23 may, in the year after or next but one after so obtaining honours, be a candidate for honours in Part IIB of the Engineering Tripos, provided that he or she

(*a*) has attained a satisfactory standard, as defined by the Faculty Board, in previous Honours Examinations;

(*b*) has not proceeded to the B.A. Degree;

provided always that fifteen complete terms have not passed after the student's first term of residence.[1]

Scheme of examination for Part IIB.

25. The scheme of examination for Part IIB of the Engineering Tripos shall be as follows:

Group A: Energy, fluid mechanics, and turbomachinery
Group B: Electrical engineering
Group C: Mechanics, materials, and design
Group D: Civil, structural, and environmental engineering
Group E: Management and manufacturing
Group F: Information engineering
Group G: Bioengineering
Group I: Imported modules from other courses
Group M: Multidisciplinary modules
Group R: Research modules

In each group except Groups G, I, M, and R the Faculty Board shall prescribe not fewer than six and not more than twelve modules for examination; each module shall be examined *either* by a written paper which shall normally be of one and a half hours' duration *or* by course-work *or* by a combination of the two. Not later than the end of the Easter Term each year the Faculty Board shall give notice of the modules prescribed for the examination to be held in the academical year next following, and shall specify the mode of examination for each module. In giving such notice the Faculty Board shall announce combinations of modules which satisfy the qualifying conditions for each engineering area specified by the Board and shall have power to announce restrictions on the combination of modules that a candidate may choose to offer. For modules to be examined by course-work, an outline of the work required of candidates shall be published by the Faculty Board by Notice in the Department of Engineering not later than the beginning of the Full Michaelmas Term next preceding the examination.

26. Each candidate

Project.

(*a*) shall be required to undertake a project. Details of all elements of the project work, and the requirements of submission for their assessment, shall be published by the Faculty Board by Notice in the Department of Engineering not later than the first Friday of Full Michaelmas Term in the year of candidature.

and

(*b*) except as provided in Regulation 27, shall offer eight modules, subject to any restrictions announced by the Faculty Board under Regulation 25.

Dissertation.

27. With the permission of the Faculty Board, a candidate for Part IIB may submit, in place of any one of the modules which he or she would otherwise be required to offer under Regulation 26(*b*) a dissertation on a subject approved by the Faculty Board which falls within the field of the module concerned.

28. A candidate who wishes to offer a dissertation under Regulation 27 shall submit a statement of the modules that he or she intends to offer under Regulation 26(*b*), together with details of the project to be undertaken under Regulation 26(*a*) and the title of the proposed dissertation, to the Secretary of the Faculty Board, in accordance with any instructions issued by the Faculty Board, not later than the fourth Wednesday of Full Michaelmas Term in the year of candidature. A candidate shall obtain the approval of his or her proposed scheme of examination, and of the title of the dissertation, by the Faculty Board not later than the end of the third quarter of the Michaelmas Term.

29. A dissertation offered under Regulation 27 shall contain full references to any sources used in its composition, and shall be of not less than 4,000 words and not more than 5,000 words in length,

[1] See also the regulations for Affiliated Students.

including footnotes and appendices. Candidates shall submit their dissertations to the Chair of Examiners not later than the end of the first week of Full Easter Term in the year of candidature. Each dissertation shall be in typewritten form (unless previous permission has been obtained from the Faculty Board through a candidate's Tutor to present the dissertation in manuscript).

30. Every candidate submitting project work under Regulation 26(*a*) or course-work under Regulation 26(*b*) shall be required to sign a declaration that the work submitted is his or her own work, unaided except as may be specified in the declaration; if two or more candidates have undertaken work in collaboration, they shall be required to indicate the extent of their collaboration. Every candidate submitting a dissertation under Regulation 27 shall be required to sign a declaration that the work submitted is his or her own work and that it does not contain material already used to any substantial extent for a comparable purpose.

31. For each combination of subjects in Part IIB, announced by the Faculty Board under Regulation 25 as an engineering area, there shall be a separate class-list. The names of the candidates who obtain honours in each engineering area shall be arranged in alphabetical order in a single class, with distinctive marks attached to the names of those candidates who in the opinion of the Examiners deserve special credit, (d) for a distinguished performance, (m) for a meritorious performance. Class-lists for Part IIB.

SCHEDULE

Institutions approved for the purpose of Regulation 23 (Exchange Programmes)

Massachusetts Institute of Technology	Ecole Centrale Paris
Technical University of Munich	National University of Singapore

SUPPLEMENTARY REGULATIONS

PART IA

Paper 1. Mechanical engineering

The paper shall consist mainly of questions on: kinematics of particles and rigid bodies, and dynamics of particles, in two dimensions; mechanical vibrations; basic concepts of thermodynamics, fluid mechanics, and their applications.

Paper 2. Structures and materials

The paper shall consist mainly of questions on: equilibrium, compatibility and elasticity of structures; buckling phenomena in simple structures; properties and applications of engineering materials; the physical origins of the properties.

Paper 3. Electrical and information engineering

The paper shall consist mainly of questions on: linear circuits and devices; electromagnetics; digital circuits and information processing.

Paper 4. Mathematical methods

The paper shall consist mainly of questions on: vectors, functions, and complex numbers; ordinary differential equations; Fourier series, matrices; functions of several variables; probability; computing.

PART IB

Paper 1. Mechanics

The paper shall consist mainly of questions on: kinematics and dynamics of particles and rigid bodies; moment of momentum, D'Alembert's principle; accelerations and dynamic stresses in mechanisms; applications to machinery.

Paper 2. Structures

The paper shall consist mainly of questions on: elastic analysis of statically indeterminate beams and frames; stress and strain in thin-walled structures; analysis of stress and strain; the Tresca and von Mises yield criteria; plastic theory of structures.

Paper 3. Materials

The paper shall consist mainly of questions on: the thermal and thermomechanical behaviour of engineering materials; the forming, joining, and heat treatment of engineering materials, and the control of microstructure and properties; the influence of manufacturing processes on design and material selection.

Paper 4. Thermofluid mechanics

The paper shall consist mainly of questions on: fluid dynamics, including boundary layers and internal flows: heat transfer by convection; heat exchangers; thermodynamics, including irreversibility, properties of working fluids, non-ideal cycles, and power generation.

Paper 5. Electrical engineering

The paper shall consist mainly of questions on: transistors; operational amplifiers with feedback; power in AC circuits; electrical machines; electromagnetic waves.

Paper 6. Information engineering

The paper shall consist mainly of questions on: control systems; transfer functions; feedback; stability; signal and data analysis; communications; signal and transmission path characteristics; modulation; digitizations of signals.

Paper 7. Mathematical methods

The paper shall consist mainly of questions on: vector calculus and PDEs; probability; linear algebra.

Paper 8. Selected topics

The paper shall consist mainly of questions on topics in professional engineering activities as shall from time to time be determined by the Faculty Board, and divided into sections corresponding to those activities. Candidates will be required to answer questions from two sections or, in the case of candidates offering a foreign language, one section. In addition there will be a section on Introductory Business Economics, from which candidates will be required to answer one question.

(Old Regulations)

ENGLISH TRIPOS

OLD REGULATIONS[1]

GENERAL

Two Parts.

1. The English Tripos shall consist of two Parts.

2. The scheme of the examination shall be as defined in Regulations 15–18.

Notice of variable subjects, etc.

3. Public notice of all the variable subjects and of the texts or portions of subjects specified for special study shall be given by the Faculty Board of English before the end of the Easter Term in the year next but one preceding the examination to which they apply; provided that the Board shall have the power of subsequently issuing amendments if they have due reason for doing so and if they are satisfied that no student's preparation for the examination is adversely affected. The Board shall have power when they give notice of the variable subjects selected for a particular examination to announce any consequential restriction on the combination of papers that a candidate may choose to offer.

The Board shall have power to define or limit by supplementary regulations all or any of the subjects of examination, and to modify or alter such supplementary regulations as occasion may require.

Standing of candidates.

4. The following may present themselves for examination in Part I:

(*a*) a student who has not obtained honours in an Honours Examination and has kept one term, provided that six complete terms have not passed after his or her first term of residence;

(*b*) a student who has obtained honours in an Honours Examination, in the year next after or next but one after so obtaining honours; provided that twelve complete terms have not passed after his or her first term of residence.

5. A student who has obtained honours in Part I of the English Tripos or in another Honours Examination may be a candidate for Part II in the year after or next but one after so obtaining honours, provided that twelve complete terms have not passed after his or her first term of residence.[2]

6. No student shall be a candidate for both Parts, or for either Part and also for another Honours Examination, in the same term.

7. No student who has been a candidate for either Part shall again be a candidate for the same Part.

8. No student who has failed to attain the standard for honours in Part I shall be a candidate for Part II.

Examiners and Assessors.

9. (*a*) To conduct the examination in each Part of the Tripos the Faculty Board shall nominate such number of Examiners as they deem appropriate.

[1] These regulations will be replaced by New Regulations in accordance with the timetable in Temporary Regulation 22 of the New Regulations, p. 344.

[2] See also the regulations for Affiliated Students.

(*b*) The Faculty Board shall have power to nominate Assessors to assist the Examiners for each Part of the Tripos. Assessors may be summoned to meetings of the Examiners for the purpose of consultation and advice, but shall not be entitled to vote. **(Old Regulations)**

10. Before the examination there shall be general meetings of the Examiners for Part I and of the Examiners for Part II, when the papers set by each Examiner or Assessor shall be submitted to the whole body of Examiners for their approval, and shall be settled by the Examiners for each Part in common. Meetings of Examiners.

11. In each Part the answers to the questions in each paper shall be read by two of the whole body of Examiners and Assessors for that Part.

12. The style and method of the candidates' answers shall be taken into account.

13. The Examiners for Part I and the Examiners for Part II shall hold separate meetings, at which the class-list for each Part shall be drawn up. In each of these lists the names of the candidates who deserve honours shall be placed in three classes, of which the second shall be divided into two divisions. The names in the first and third classes, and in each division of the second class, shall be arranged in alphabetical order. Class-lists.

14. For special excellence in either Part a mark of distinction may be awarded.

PART I

15. The papers in Part I shall be as follows:

Paper 1. English literature and its contexts, 1300–1550 (also serves as Paper 21 in Part II of the English Tripos (New Regulations))
Paper 2. English literature and its contexts, 1500–1700 (also serves as Paper 22 in Part II of the English Tripos (New Regulations))
Paper 3. English literature and its contexts, 1688–1847 (also serves as Paper 24 in Part II of the English Tripos (New Regulations))
Paper 4. English literature and its contexts, 1830 to the present (also serves as Paper 25 in Part II of the English Tripos (New Regulations))
Paper 5. Shakespeare (also serves as Paper 23 in Part II of the English Tripos (New Regulations))
Paper 6. Practical criticism and critical practice
Paper 7. European languages and literatures
Paper 8. English language for literature, 1300 to the present
Paper 9. English literature and its contexts, 1300 to the present (open dissertation)
Paper 10. Early medieval literature and its contexts (also serves as Paper 20 of Part II of the English Tripos (New Regulations), as Paper O9 of Part II of the Classical Tripos, and as Paper 11 of Part I of the Anglo-Saxon, Norse, and Celtic Tripos)
Paper 11. Insular Latin language and literature (Paper 9 of Part I of the Anglo-Saxon, Norse, and Celtic Tripos)
Paper 12. Old Norse language and literature (Paper 6 of Part I of the Anglo-Saxon, Norse, and Celtic Tripos)
Paper 13. Medieval Welsh language and literature (Paper 7 of Part I of the Anglo-Saxon, Norse, and Celtic Tripos)
Paper 14. Medieval Irish language and literature (Paper 8 of Part I of the Anglo-Saxon, Norse, and Celtic Tripos)

Every paper shall be set for three hours except Papers 1, 6, 7, and 8 which shall be set for three and a half hours, and Paper 9 which shall comprise a dissertation, to be submitted in accordance with the provisions of Regulation 20, the topic of which must fall within the scope of Papers 1–5 but may range across the chronological boundaries of individual papers within this group.

16. Every candidate for Part I shall offer Papers 1 and 5 and

either (*a*) Papers 2–4; and two papers from among Papers 6, 7, 8, 9, and 10;

or (*b*) Papers 2–4; one paper from among Papers 6, 7, 8, 9, and 10; and one paper from among Papers 11–14;

or (*c*) two papers from among Papers 2–4; two papers from among Papers 6–10; and one paper from among Papers 11–14.

or (*d*) two papers from among Papers 2–4; three papers from among Papers 6, 7, 8, and 10;

(Old Regulations)

provided that

(i) in substitution for one of Papers 2–4, a candidate who has not offered Paper 9 may offer a dissertation, to be submitted in accordance with the provisions of Regulation 20, on a topic falling within the scope of that paper, except that (1) no candidate shall submit a dissertation of which the main emphasis is on literature written in a foreign language[1] and (2) if a candidate submits a dissertation in substitution for Paper 2 it shall not be wholly or largely on Shakespeare;

(ii) in substitution for one of Papers 2–4, a candidate may offer a portfolio of essays, to be submitted in accordance with the provisions of Regulation 17, on topics falling within the scope of that paper, except that (1) if a candidate submits a portfolio in substitution for Paper 2 it shall not be wholly or largely on Shakespeare, (2) a candidate who submits a portfolio may not offer a dissertation on a topic which falls principally within the scope of the paper for which the portfolio is substituted.

Portfolio.

17. (*a*) A candidate who intends to offer a portfolio under Regulation 16(ii) shall notify the Director of Undergraduate Studies through his or her Director of Studies, in accordance with detailed arrangements approved by the Board. Such notification shall be not later than a date in the Full Lent Term to be promulgated by the Board in the Michaelmas Term.

(*b*) A portfolio submitted under Regulation 16(ii) shall consist of three essays, each of not fewer than 1,500 words and not more than 2,000 words in length. Portfolio essays must be on subjects of literary interest which fall within the scope of the paper for which they are substituted. The portfolio of essays as a whole should exhibit a range and substance comparable with that required by the examination paper for which it is substituted. It should show knowledge of work before and after the date specified in the rubric for the paper for which it was substituted. Candidates will be required to declare that the essays are their own work and that they do not contain material already used to any substantial extent for a comparable purpose. Where appropriate full and proper acknowledgement must be given to the work of others.

(*c*) The essays shall be typewritten, in English, with proper attention to style and presentation; they shall be submitted through the candidate's Director of Studies to the Director of Undergraduate Studies, in accordance with detailed arrangements approved by the Board, so as to arrive not later than the last Thursday of the Full Lent Term next preceding the examination. Candidates may be called for *viva voce* examination in connection with their portfolios.

Part II

18. The papers in Part II shall be as follows:

Group A (compulsory papers)

Paper 1.	Practical criticism
Paper 2.	Tragedy (also serves as Paper O3 of Part II of the Classical Tripos)

Group B(i)

Paper 3.	Chaucer
Paper 4.	Medieval English literature, 1066–1500 (also serves as Paper 13 of Part II of the Anglo-Saxon, Norse, and Celtic Tripos)
Paper 5.	Special period of English literature (taken from the period after 1500 and before 1700)
Paper 6.	Special period of English literature (taken from the period after 1700)
Paper 7.	Special subject I

Group B(ii)

Paper 8.	English moralists
Paper 9.	History and theory of literary criticism (also serves as Paper O4 of Part II of the Classical Tripos)
Paper 10.	Postcolonial and related literatures
Paper 11.	American literature
Paper 12.	Special subject II

[1] See further the supplementary regulations, p. 335.

(Old Regulations)

Group C(i)

Paper 13. History of the English language[1]
Paper 14. Early medieval literature and its contexts (Paper 10 of Part I of the English Tripos)
Paper 15. Old English language and literature (Paper 5 of Part I of the Anglo-Saxon, Norse, and Celtic Tripos)

Group C(ii)

Paper 16. Insular Latin language and literature (Paper 9 of Part I of the Anglo-Saxon, Norse, and Celtic Tripos)
Paper 17A. Old Norse language and literature (Paper 6 of Part I of the Anglo-Saxon, Norse, and Celtic Tripos)
Paper 17B. Advanced medieval Scandinavian language and literature (Paper 6 of Part II of the Anglo-Saxon, Norse, and Celtic Tripos)
Paper 18A. Medieval Welsh language and literature (Paper 7 of Part I of the Anglo-Saxon, Norse, and Celtic Tripos)
Paper 18B. Advanced medieval Welsh language and literature (Paper 7 of Part II of the Anglo-Saxon, Norse, and Celtic Tripos)
Paper 19A. Medieval Irish language and literature (Paper 8 of Part I of the Anglo-Saxon, Norse, and Celtic Tripos)
Paper 19B. Advanced medieval Irish language and literature (Paper 8 of Part II of the Anglo-Saxon, Norse, and Celtic Tripos)
Paper 20. Topics in medieval studies: to be specified by the Faculty Board from time to time (Paper Fr. 7 of the Modern and Medieval Languages Tripos)
Paper 21. Living, loving, and dying in Renaissance France (Paper Fr. 8 of the Modern and Medieval Languages Tripos)
Paper 22. Reason, experience, and authority: French literature, thought, and history, 1594–1700 (Paper Fr. 9 of the Modern and Medieval Languages Tripos)
Paper 23. French literature, thought, and history, from 1690 to 1799 (Paper Fr. 10 of the Modern and Medieval Languages Tripos)
Paper 24. Gender, desire, and power in 19th century French culture (Paper Fr. 11 of the Modern and Medieval Languages Tripos)
Paper 25. Ethics and experience: literature, thought, and visual culture of the French-speaking world (1900 to the present) (Paper Fr. 12 of the Modern and Medieval Languages Tripos)
Paper 26. Dante and the culture of his age (Paper It. 7 of the Modern and Medieval Languages Tripos)
Paper 27A. Introduction to Neo-Latin literature, from 1350 to 1700 (Paper NL 1 of the Modern and Medieval Languages Tripos)
Paper 27B. A special subject in Neo-Latin literature: selected authors (Paper NL 2 of the Modern and Medieval Languages Tripos)
Paper 28. A special subject in comparative literature (i) and (ii) (Papers CS 4[1] and 5 of the Modern and Medieval Languages Tripos)
Paper 29. A paper in linguistics (Paper 11 or Paper 13 of Parts IIA and Parts IIB of the Linguistics Tripos)[2]
Paper 30. A prescribed Greek author or authors, and a prescribed Latin author or authors (Paper A1 of Part II of the Classical Tripos)
Paper 31. Prescribed Greek texts (Paper A2 of Part II of the Classical Tripos)[1]
Paper 32. Prescribed Latin texts (Paper A3 of Part II of the Classical Tripos)

Group D

Paper 33. English literature and its contexts, 1300–1550 (Paper 1 of Part I of the English Tripos)
Paper 34. English literature and its contexts, 1500–1700 (Paper 2 of Part I of the English Tripos)
Paper 35. English literature and its contexts, 1688–1847 (Paper 3 of Part I of the English Tripos)
Paper 36. English literature and its contexts, 1830 to the present (Paper 4 of Part I of the English Tripos)
Paper 37. Shakespeare (Paper 5 of Part I of the English Tripos)

Each paper shall be set for three hours except Papers 1 and 33 which shall be set for three and a half hours. The Faculty Board shall announce in every year, subject to the provisions of Regulation 3, not more than four special subjects for Paper 7, and may in addition announce not more than three special subjects for Paper 12; in each case a candidate may offer not more than one of these subjects. A question paper shall be set for each subject so announced and for which there is a candidate. Every

[1] This paper is suspended until further notice.
[2] This paper will be *either* Paper 11 or Paper 13 of Parts IIA and IIB of the Linguistics Tripos, whichever of those papers is offered.

(Old Regulations) candidate who offers a paper in which there is a choice of subjects shall take only one of these question papers; the candidate's examination entry shall state which subject he or she intends to offer.

19. Every candidate for Part II shall offer:

(*a*) a dissertation on a subject in English literature;

(*b*) both papers from Group A;

(*c*) *either* (i) if the candidate takes the examination in the year next after obtaining honours in another Honours Examination, one of the following combinations:

either two papers chosen from Groups B and C

or one paper chosen from Groups B and C and a second dissertation on a topic in English literature;

or (ii) if the candidate takes the examination in the year next but one after obtaining honours in another Honours Examination, or if the candidate is an Affiliated Student, one of the following combinations:

either three papers chosen from Groups B and C

or two papers chosen from Groups B and C and a second dissertation on a topic in English literature;

provided that:

(i) a candidate shall not offer any paper that he or she has previously offered in another Honours Examination;

(ii) a candidate shall not offer both Paper 9 and one of the special subjects for Paper 12 if the Faculty Board in announcing that special subject have specified that it may not be so combined; nor more than one of the papers from Group C(ii); nor both Papers 17A and 17B; nor both Papers 18A and 18B; nor both Papers 19A and 19B;

(iii) a candidate who has obtained honours in Part I of the English Tripos or any allowance on that examination towards a degree shall not offer both Paper 5 and Paper 6;

(iv) in choosing a topic for a dissertation to be offered under this regulation a candidate shall not be precluded from proposing a topic in the same field as that of any of the papers that he or she is offering in the examination, save that, if the dissertation required under sub-paragraph (*a*) above is in the field of one of the candidate's papers, the Faculty Board may at their discretion decline to allow the candidate to offer a second dissertation in the field of one of his or her papers;

(v) a dissertation offered under this regulation shall be submitted in accordance with the provisions of Regulation 20;

(vi) every candidate who has not previously obtained honours in Part I of the English Tripos shall offer *either* at least one paper from among Papers 3–7 *or*, subject to the approval of the Faculty Board, and in substitution for one such paper, one paper from among Papers 33–37, except that a candidate who offers a special subject which is a Shakespearian subject announced by the Faculty Board for Paper 7 shall not also offer Paper 37. An application for leave to offer one of Papers 33–37 shall be sent through the candidate's Director of Studies to the Director of Undergraduate Studies so as to arrive not later than the penultimate Friday of the Michaelmas Term next preceding the examination and shall state the scheme of papers that the candidate proposes to offer, together with the topic of the dissertation required under sub-paragraph (*a*) above and of any dissertation offered under sub-paragraph (*c*) above. In determining whether to approve such an application the Faculty Board shall take into consideration both the overall balance of the proposed scheme and the potential overlap between the papers to be offered under it. After the Faculty Board have approved such a candidate's proposed scheme, no change may be made in the scheme without the further approval of the Faculty Board.

Parts I and II

Dissertations. **20.** (*a*) A candidate who intends to offer either a compulsory dissertation in Part II under Regulation 19(*a*), or Paper 9, or an optional dissertation in either Part under Regulation 16(i) or Regulation 19(*c*), shall submit the proposed topic of the dissertation through his or her Director of Studies to the Director of Undergraduate Studies, in accordance with detailed arrangements approved by the Board, so as to arrive not later than the penultimate Friday of the Full Michaelmas Term next preceding the examination.

(*b*) The Director of Undergraduate Studies shall communicate the Board's approval or rejection of the proposed topic to the candidate's Director of Studies. When the Board have approved a topic, no change shall be made in it or in a scheme of work approved by the Board without the further approval of the Board. A candidate may submit a revised topic so as to reach the Director of Undergraduate Studies not later than a date in the Full Lent Term to be promulgated by the Board in the Michaelmas Term; topics submitted after that date will be considered by the Board only in the most exceptional circumstances. **(Old Regulations)**

(*c*) The length of a dissertation shall be as follows:

for Part I, not more than 5,000 words in length;

for Part II, not fewer than 6,000 words and not more than 7,500 words in length.

In each case the prescribed length shall include notes and appendices, although appendices beyond the prescribed limit may be allowed in special circumstances, subject to the approval of the Faculty Board given not later than the division of the Lent Term next preceding the examination. Candidates will be required to declare that the dissertation is their own work and that it does not contain material already used to any substantial extent for a comparable purpose.

(*d*) Every dissertation shall be typewritten, in English, with proper attention to style and presentation in accordance with detailed guidelines issued by the Faculty Board; it shall be sent through the candidate's Director of Studies to the Director of Undergraduate Studies, accompanied by a brief synopsis of its contents and a list of the books and articles used in its preparation, and in accordance with detailed arrangements approved by the Board, so as to arrive not later than the first Tuesday of the Full Easter Term in which the examination is to be held.

(*e*) A candidate may be called for *viva voce* examination in connection with his or her dissertation.

21. At the same time as dissertation topics are submitted through candidates' Directors of Studies to the Director of Undergraduate Studies, each candidate shall submit the whole scheme of work to be offered in the examination. The Director of Undergraduate Studies shall communicate the Board's approval or rejection of the proposed scheme of work to the candidate's Director of Studies. Schemes of work.

SUPPLEMENTARY REGULATIONS

Part I

For the purpose of the regulations and supplementary regulations for Part I of the English Tripos, 'English literature' shall be understood to mean the literature in English of the British Isles including Ireland. In Papers 1–5 candidates must answer primarily in relation to English literature thus defined, and questions will not be asked, nor may answers be primarily written, on authors other than those who were born, or have spent a substantial part of their lives working, in the British Isles. This will not however preclude the possibility of comparison, where appropriate, with other literature in English (such as American or Commonwealth), provided that greater weight falls on English literature than on other literature. These rules shall also govern the acceptability of topics for period dissertations substituted for Papers 2, 3, and 4 but not the open dissertation under Paper 9, in which candidates may write on any literature(s) in English irrespective of country of origin. No more than one dissertation may be submitted. Candidates submitting a dissertation under Paper 9 are permitted to offer an examination paper which covers the same period as the topic for the dissertation. Candidates substituting a portfolio for Papers 2–4 may not offer a dissertation under Paper 9 on a topic which falls principally within the scope of the paper for which the portfolio is substituted. More detailed guidance about the acceptability of specific authors as the subjects of examination answers or as the topics of dissertations may be given in a document issued by the Faculty Board of English and revised as necessary from time to time.

Paper 1. English literature and its contexts, 1300–1550

Medieval texts shall be prescribed for special study; and passages shall be set from them for translation or comment, or both. The Faculty Board may give notice from time to time of a list of topics on which optional questions will be set. Questions shall be set both on the literature and on the life and thought of the period.

Paper 2. English literature and its contexts, 1500–1700

Questions shall be set both on the literature and on the life and thought of the period.[1]

Paper 3. English literature and its contexts, 1688–1847

Questions shall be set both on the literature and on the life and thought of the period.[1]

Paper 4. English literature and its contexts, 1830 to the present

Questions shall be set both on the literature and on the life and thought of the period.[1]

[1] The Faculty Board may from time to time give notice of a prescribed text or texts or of a specified topic for special study in this paper.

(Old Regulations)

Paper 5. Shakespeare

Questions shall be set requiring explanation and discussion of a specified work or specified works. Questions shall also be set on other works of Shakespeare and matters of historical and critical interest relevant to his works.

Paper 6. Practical criticism and critical practice

The paper, which will be set for three and a half hours (including half an hour's reading time), will consist of questions offering passages of English verse or prose from various periods for critical comment. The passages set may also include extracts from works of literary criticism and theory, some of which may be in translation. The questions will require close critical analysis of the given passages. They will also allow for the raising of general critical and theoretical issues appropriate to the reading of those extracts. Candidates will be required to answer three questions.

Paper 7. European languages and literatures

The languages within the scope of this paper are: classical Greek; classical Latin; French; German; Italian; Old English. Candidates will not be required to show knowledge of more than one of these languages, though they may do so if they wish. In each language, except in the case of Old English, two texts (or collections of texts) will be prescribed for study. Candidates will be required to show knowledge of two such texts (except in the case of Old English, where only one text is set).

Paper 8. English language for literature, 1300 to the present

This paper requires candidates to recognize and describe in English writing from 1300 to the present day; linguistic features (such as syntax, lexis, register, elementary phonetics, rhetoric); the relations between spoken and written Englishes; the historical development and study of the language, in its literary and other varieties; contact between English and other languages. The Faculty Board shall, from time to time, prescribe specified topics, with lists of relevant reading. Candidates will be required to answer on at least one of the specified topics.

Paper 9. English literature and its contexts, 1300 to the present: Open dissertation

The topic of a dissertation to be submitted under this paper must fall within the scope of Papers 1–5. It may be comparative across the period boundaries of the individual papers. The dissertation shall be prepared and submitted in accordance with Regulation 20.

Paper 10. Early medieval literature and its contexts (also serves as Paper 20 of Part II of the English Tripos (New Regulations), as Paper O9 of Part II of the Classical Tripos, and as Paper 11 of Part I of the Anglo-Saxon, Norse, and Celtic Tripos).

The period covered by this paper is 1066–*c.* 1350. English, French, and Latin texts shall be prescribed for special study, and passages set from them for translation or explanation or both. Questions shall also be set on English, French, and Latin texts of the period. Candidates will be required to show knowledge of *one* of these three languages, and of work in at least one other of them, which they may, if they wish, have studied in translation. Candidates are expected to show such knowledge of the life and thought of the period as is necessary for the understanding of its literature.

Part II

Paper 1. Practical criticism

Passages of English prose and verse for critical comment.

Paper 2. Tragedy (also serves as Paper O3 of Part II of the Classical Tripos)

Tragedy ancient and modern in connection and comparison with English Tragedy.

Paper 3. Chaucer

Candidates will be expected to show a full and detailed knowledge of the works of Chaucer. Questions shall be set on those works and on Chaucer's relationship to his contemporaries and to the life and thought of his age.

Paper 4. Medieval English literature, 1066–1500 (also serves as Paper 13 of Part II of the Anglo-Saxon, Norse, and Celtic Tripos)

A specific literary subject shall be prescribed for special study. It shall be of a kind to require reading in early as well as in late medieval English literature and may involve the study of related texts from other languages.

Paper 5. Special period of English literature (taken from the period after 1500 and before 1700)

Candidates will be required to show a substantial knowledge of the literature of whatever period is prescribed together with its life and thought.

Paper 6. Special period of English literature (taken from the period after 1700)

Candidates will be required to show a substantial knowledge of the literature of whatever period is prescribed together with its life and thought.

(Old Regulations)

Paper 7. Special subject I

The work of an author or of a group of authors, or a literary topic or genre, or a period not already prescribed for Paper 5 or Paper 6, within the field of English literature, shall be prescribed for special study. Relevant texts may be recommended for study from time to time. In accordance with Regulation 18 the Faculty Board may from time to time prescribe a number of such special subjects of which one may be offered by candidates for this paper.

Paper 8. English moralists

Questions will be set on the history and nature of moral thought, broadly interpreted. Candidates will be invited to show knowledge of a range of literary, philosophical, social, and political writings by authors from Plato to the present, but the paper will normally permit concentration on a particular chronological period or selection of authors. Candidates will also be given opportunities to relate the themes of this paper to their existing interests in poetry, drama, and the novel. From time to time a special topic may be specified for study.

Paper 9. History and theory of literary criticism (also serves as Paper O4 of Part II of the Classical Tripos)

The paper shall comprise historical, critical, and comparative questions on works and problems in the history of literary criticism and also of literary theory from the fourth century BC to the present day. A sufficient number of questions will be set to enable candidates to choose questions on a limited chronological period (including the modern period).

Paper 10. Postcolonial and related literature

The scope of the paper is, subject to the following qualifications, literature in English outside the British Isles and the United States of America. It includes expatriate nationals publishing in those countries (e.g. Rushdie, d'Aguiar, Lessing). Comparative and incidental reference to British, Irish, American, and foreign language texts is welcome but should not form the greater part of any single answer. Answering on texts in translation is permitted but should not constitute the greater part of answers to the paper as a whole.

The paper will be divided into two sections. Section A will consist of passages for comment; Section B will consist of essay questions, enabling comparison between texts from different regions.

Paper 11. American literature

The subject covered by this paper is American literature, life, and thought, with special reference to the period from 1820 to the present day. A list of books may be recommended from time to time for special study. All candidates will be expected to show such knowledge of the life and thought of the period as is necessary for understanding its literature.

Paper 12. Special subject II

For a year for which a subject is announced for this paper under Regulation 18, the work of an author or of a group of authors, or a literary topic or genre, or a period not already prescribed for Paper 5, or 6, or 7, shall be prescribed for special study. Relevant foreign texts as well as English texts may be recommended for study from time to time. In accordance with Regulation 18 the Faculty Board may from time to time prescribe a number of such special subjects of which one may be offered by candidates for this paper.

Paper 13. History of the English language

This paper will be concerned with the historical development and structure of the English language and of its internal and extra-territorial varieties. A specified topic will be prescribed for special study.

The paper will be divided into two sections. Section A will contain questions pertaining to the specified topic; Section B will contain essay questions of a more general nature. Candidates will be required to answer one question from Section A and two questions from Section B.

Dissertations

For the purpose of Regulations 19(*a*) and 19(*c*) governing the submission of dissertations in Part II of the Tripos, 'English literature' shall be understood to mean literature written in the English language (including Old English), works written by authors of the British Isles in other languages, such as Latin or French, and works written in Old Norse and the Medieval Celtic languages. It shall be understood to embrace the English language and such philosophical, historical, and other writing as normally comes within the scope of the English Tripos.

Where a topic is chosen involving comparison with a foreign literature, the dissertation should be primarily on an English literary topic, though there is no objection to comparison with other literature where this is relevant. Where a topic involves comparison between literature and another medium such as music or the visual arts, the weight of the dissertation should likewise fall on literature (which may, for example, include libretti). Discussion of work produced in a medium other than literature is not admissible as the exclusive topic of a dissertation.

More detailed guidance about the acceptability of specific writings as the topic of a dissertation may be given in a document issued by the Faculty Board of English and revised as necessary from time to time.

(New Regulations)

ENGLISH TRIPOS

NEW REGULATIONS[1]

Amended by Notice (Reporter, *2013–14, p. 529)*

GENERAL

Two Parts.

1. The English Tripos shall consist of two Parts.

2. (*a*) For the purposes of the Regulations and any Supplementary Regulations, the study of 'English literature' shall be understood to mean, in both Parts of the Tripos, the study of literary works written in the English language (including Old English); of literary works of the British Isles including Ireland (whether written in English, or in other languages such as Latin or French); and of literary works written in Old Norse and the Medieval Celtic languages. It shall be understood to embrace the study of the English language.

(*b*) The study of 'English literature' shall normally also embrace, in both Parts of the Tripos, English literary translations of works originally written in other languages, so long as due consideration is given to the fact of translation.

(*c*) For Part I of the English Tripos, the study of 'English literature' shall also embrace such philosophical, historical and other writing as normally comes within the scope of Papers 1 to 8E of that Part as illustrated by reading lists announced by the Faculty Board.

(*d*) For Part II of the English Tripos, the study of 'English literature' shall also embrace such philosophical, historical and other writing, and such products of non-literary media and expressive forms, as normally come within the scope of Papers 1 to 30 of that Part as illustrated by reading lists announced by the Faculty Board.

(*e*) In both Parts of the Tripos, relevant comparisons with other materials that fall outside the scope of 'English literature' thus defined shall be accepted, both in written papers that focus on the study of 'English literature' and in dissertations and portfolios of essays that focus on the same; but only so long as greater weight falls, in each answer, dissertation or essay offered in this context, on materials that come within the aforementioned scope.

(*f*) In addition, in both Parts of the Tripos, the English Tripos shall include certain papers which concentrate on the study of literatures other than 'English literature' thus defined. However, it shall not be permissible to make this material the principal basis of any dissertation, any essay within a portfolio of essays, or any answer to a written paper primarily concerned with 'English literature'.

3. The scheme of the examination shall be as defined in Regulations 14 to 21.

Notice of variable subjects, etc.

4. Notice of all the variable papers available for examination, and of the variable subjects, texts, or portions of subjects specified for special study, shall be given by the Faculty Board of English before the end of the Easter Term (i) two years prior to the examination in the case of Part I of the Tripos, (ii) one year prior to the examination in the case of Part II of the Tripos; provided that, in both cases, the Board shall have the power of subsequently issuing amendments if they have due reason for doing so and if they are satisfied that no student's preparation for her or his examination will be adversely affected. The Board shall have power when they give notice of the variable subjects selected for a particular examination to announce any consequential restriction on the combination of papers that a candidate may offer. The Board shall have power to define or limit by supplementary regulations all or any of the subjects of examination, and to modify or alter such supplementary regulations as occasion may require.

Standing of candidates.

5. The following may present themselves as candidates for honours in Part I:

(*a*) a student who has not obtained honours in an Honours Examination and has kept four terms, provided that six complete terms have not passed after her or his first term of residence;

(*b*) a student who has obtained honours in an Honours Examination, in the year next but one after so obtaining honours; provided that nine complete terms have not passed after her or his first term of residence.

6. The following may present themselves as candidates for honours in Part II:

(*a*) a student who has obtained honours in Part I of the English Tripos, in the year after so obtaining honours; provided that twelve complete terms have not passed after her or his first term of residence;

[1] These regulations will come into effect in accordance with the timetable in Temporary Regulation 22, p. 344.

(*b*) a student who has obtained honours in another Honours Examination, in the year after or next but one after so obtaining honours; provided that twelve complete terms have not passed after her or his first term of residence; (New Regulations)

(*c*) a student who has obtained honours in Part I of the English Tripos or any other Honours Examination and who has spent the intervening year undertaking legitimate study in another University, in the year next but one after so obtaining honours; provided that twelve complete terms have not passed after her or his first term of residence, and subject to the provision in Regulation 19(*c*)(i);

(*d*) an Affiliated Student, in accordance with the General Regulations for Affiliated Students, and subject to the terms of Regulation 19 of the English Tripos that pertain to Affiliated Students.

7. No student shall be a candidate for both Parts, or for either Part and also for another Honours Examination, in the same term.

8. No student who has been a candidate for either Part shall again be a candidate for the same Part.

9. (*a*) To conduct the examination in each Part of the Tripos the Faculty Board shall nominate such number of Examiners as they deem appropriate. Examiners and Assessors.

(*b*) The Faculty Board shall have power to nominate Assessors to assist the Examiners for each Part of the Tripos. Assessors may be summoned to meetings of the Examiners for the purpose of consultation and advice, but shall not be entitled to vote.

10. Before the examination there shall be general meetings of the Examiners for Part I and of the Examiners for Part II, when the papers set by each Examiner or Assessor shall be submitted to the whole body of each Part's Examiners for their approval and shall be settled by the Examiners for each Part. Meetings of Examiners.

11. The Examiners for Part I and the Examiners for Part II shall hold separate meetings, at which the class-list for each Part shall be drawn up. In each of these lists the names of the candidates who deserve honours shall be placed in three classes, of which the second shall be divided into two divisions. The names in the first and third classes, and in each division of the second class, shall be arranged in alphabetical order. Class-lists.

12. For special excellence in either Part a mark of distinction may be awarded.

13. In each examination, candidates must not use the same material twice, either within any given paper or across the examination as a whole. Nor should material be repeated from one examination to the next.

Part I

14. The papers in Part I shall be as follows.

Paper 1.	Practical criticism and critical practice
Paper 2.	Early medieval literature and its contexts, 1066–1350 (also serves as Paper 20 of Part II of the English Tripos, as Paper O9 of Part II of the Classical Tripos, and as Paper 11 of Part I of the Anglo-Saxon, Norse, and Celtic Tripos)
Paper 3.	English literature and its contexts, 1300–1550 (also serves as Paper 21 of Part II of the English Tripos)
Paper 4.	English literature and its contexts, 1500–1700 (also serves as Paper 22 of Part II of the English Tripos)
Paper 5.	Shakespeare (also serves as Paper 23 of Part II of the English Tripos)
Paper 6.	English literature and its contexts, 1660–1870 (also serves as Paper 24 of Part II of the English Tripos)
Paper 7A.	English literature and its contexts, 1830–1945 (also serves as Paper 25A of Part II of the English Tripos)
Paper 7B.	English literature and its contexts, 1870–present (also serves as Paper 25B of Part II of the English Tripos)
Paper 8A.	Old English language and literature (Paper 5 of Part I of the Anglo-Saxon, Norse, and Celtic Tripos. Also serves as Paper 26 of Part II of the English Tripos)
Paper 8B.	Old Norse language and literature (Paper 6 of Part I of the Anglo-Saxon, Norse, and Celtic Tripos. Also serves as Paper 27A of Part II of the English Tripos)
Paper 8C.	Medieval Welsh language and literature (Paper 7 of Part I of the Anglo-Saxon, Norse, and Celtic Tripos. Also serves as Paper 28A of Part II of the English Tripos)
Paper 8D.	Medieval Irish language and literature (Paper 8 of Part I of the Anglo-Saxon, Norse, and Celtic Tripos. Also serves as Paper 29A of Part II of the English Tripos)
Paper 8E.	Insular Latin language and literature (Paper 9 of Part I of the Anglo-Saxon, Norse, and Celtic Tripos. Also serves as Paper 30 of Part II of the English Tripos)

(New Regulations)

Paper 9A. Greek literature (Paper 5 of Part IB of the Classical Tripos)
Paper 9B. Latin literature (Paper 6 of Part IB of the Classical Tripos)
Paper 10A. Introduction to French literature, linguistics, film, and thought (Paper Fr.1 of the Modern and Medieval Languages Tripos)
Paper 10B. Love, violence, and power in France 1100–1500 (Paper Fr.3 of the Modern and Medieval Languages Tripos)
Paper 10C. Rethinking the human: French literature, thought, and culture 1500–1700 (Paper Fr.4 of the Modern and Medieval Languages Tripos)
Paper 10D. Revolutions in writing, 1700–1900 (Paper Fr.5 of the Modern and Medieval Languages Tripos)
Paper 10E. Innovation and upheaval: deformation and reformulation in the 20th and 21st centuries (Paper Fr.6 of the Modern and Medieval Languages Tripos)
Paper 10F. Texts and contexts (Paper A3 in Italian of the Modern and Medieval Languages Tripos)
Paper 10G. Introduction to German studies (Paper Ge.1 of the Modern and Medieval Languages Tripos)
Paper 10H. The making of German culture, I (Paper Ge.4 of the Modern and Medieval Languages Tripos)
Paper 10I. Modern German culture, I (Paper Ge.5 of the Modern and Medieval Languages Tripos)
Paper 10J. Modern German culture, II (Paper Ge.6 of the Modern and Medieval Languages Tripos)
Paper 10K. Introduction to the language, literatures, and cultures of the Spanish-speaking world (Paper Sp.1 of the Modern and Medieval Languages Tripos)
Paper 10L. Introduction to the language, literatures, and cultures of Portuguese-speaking countries (Paper Pg.1 of the Modern and Medieval Languages Tripos)
Paper 10M. Introduction to Russian culture (Paper Sl.1 of the Modern and Medieval Languages Tripos)
Paper 10N. Russian culture from the Golden Age to the Silver Age (Paper Sl.4 of the Modern and Medieval Languages Tripos)
Paper 10O. Russian culture after 1880 (Paper Sl.5 of the Modern and Medieval Languages Tripos)
Paper 10P. Introduction to the language, literature, and culture of Ukraine (Paper Sl.9 of the Modern and Medieval Languages Tripos)

Every paper shall be set for three hours except Papers 1 and 3 which shall be set for three and a half hours.

15. Every candidate for Part I shall offer Papers 3 and 5 and any four papers from among Papers 1, 2, 4, 6, 7, 8, 9, and 10, provided that

(i) a candidate may offer only one of *either* Paper 8, *or* Paper 9, *or* Paper 10;

(ii) only one option may be offered from amongst the list of options available for Paper 7, and likewise for each of Papers 8, 9, and 10;

(iii) in substitution for one of Papers 4, 6, and 7 not substituted by a portfolio of essays under proviso (iv) below, a candidate may offer a dissertation, to be submitted in accordance with the provisions of Regulation 16, on a topic falling within the scope of that paper; except that if a candidate submits a dissertation in substitution for Paper 4 it shall not be wholly or largely on the subject of Shakespeare and his writings;

(iv) additionally or alternatively, in substitution for one of Papers 4, 6, and 7 not substituted by a dissertation under proviso (iii) above, a candidate may offer a portfolio of essays, to be submitted in accordance with the provisions of Regulation 17, on topics falling within the scope of that paper; except that if a candidate submits a portfolio in substitution for Paper 4 it shall not be wholly or largely on the subject of Shakespeare and his writings;

(v) a candidate for the English Tripos offering an option under Paper 8, or Paper 9, or Paper 10 shall be required to offer this option as a written paper, and may not substitute it with any form of course-work, albeit that such substitutions may be available to candidates who are offering the same papers for the Anglo-Saxon, Norse, and Celtic Tripos, or the Classical Tripos, or the Modern and Medieval Languages Tripos;

(vi) a candidate offering any of Papers 3 to 7 either as a written paper or substituted by a portfolio of essays, shall be required to demonstrate, in each such paper offered, substantial knowledge of the literature of the British Isles (which may include Ireland);

(vii) a candidate offering any of Papers 4, 6, 7A, and 7B either as a written paper or substituted by a portfolio of essays, shall be required to demonstrate, in each such paper offered, substantial knowledge of English literature before and after the medial date specified for the paper in question.

Dissertations. **16.** (*a*) A candidate who intends to offer a dissertation under Regulation 15(iii) shall submit the proposed topic of the dissertation for formal approval to the Director of Undergraduate Studies of the Faculty Board through her or his Director of Studies in accordance with the arrangements for such notification approved by the Board. Such proposals must be made by the penultimate Friday of the Full Michaelmas Term preceding the examination. Once a topic has been approved on behalf of the

(New Regulations)

Faculty Board, no change shall be made to it without further formal approval. A candidate may, however, submit a revised topic for approval so as to reach the Director of Undergraduate Studies at any time up until the sixth Wednesday of the Full Lent Term preceding the examination.

(*b*) The dissertation must be on a topic of 'English literature' (as defined by Regulation 2) falling within the scope of the paper for which the dissertation is substituted. Relevant comparisons may be made with other materials, whether those be drawn from elsewhere in Part I or (in accordance with Regulation 2(*e*)) from beyond Part I, so long as greater weight falls on materials that come within the scope of the relevant paper.

(*c*) The length of a dissertation shall be not fewer than 4,000 words and not more than 5,000 words. The prescribed length shall include notes and appendices, although appendices beyond the prescribed limit may be allowed in special circumstances, subject to formal approval given on behalf of the Faculty Board not later than the sixth Wednesday of the Full Lent Term preceding the examination. Every dissertation shall be typewritten, in English, paying proper attention to style and presentation.

(*d*) Candidates shall be required to declare that the dissertation is their own work and that it does not contain material used to any substantial extent for a comparable purpose prior to the date of its submission. Where appropriate, full and proper acknowledgement must be given to the work of others via footnotes. The dissertation must be accompanied by a synopsis of its contents of not fewer than 100 words and not more than 150 words, and by a bibliography of the books, articles, and electronic and online resources used in its preparation. The prescribed length detailed under sub-paragraph (*c*) above shall include neither the synopsis nor the bibliography.

(*e*) The dissertation shall be submitted to the Director of Undergraduate Studies through the candidate's Director of Studies, in accordance with arrangements approved by the Faculty Board, so as to arrive at the Faculty not later than 5 p.m. on the first Tuesday of the Full Easter Term in which the examination is to be held.

(*f*) Candidates may be called for *viva voce* examination in connection with their dissertations.

17. (*a*) A candidate who intends to offer a portfolio of essays under Regulation 15(iv) shall notify the Director of Undergraduate Studies of the Faculty Board through her or his Director of Studies in accordance with the arrangements for such notification approved by the Board. Initial such notification must be made by the penultimate Friday of the Full Michaelmas Term preceding the examination. Notification of any change of intention thereafter must be made no later than the sixth Wednesday of the Full Lent Term preceding the examination. Portfolio.

(*b*) A portfolio shall consist of three essays. All of the essays must be on topics of 'English literature' (as defined by Regulation 2) falling within the scope of the paper for which the portfolio is substituted. Relevant comparisons may be made with other materials, whether those be drawn from elsewhere in Part I or (in accordance with Regulation 2(*e*)) from beyond Part I, so long as greater weight falls, in each essay, on materials that come within the scope of the relevant paper. It must also demonstrate substantial knowledge of English literature before and after the medial date specified for the paper for which it stands in substitution.

(*c*) Each essay shall be not fewer than 1,500 words and not more than 2,000 words in length. The prescribed length shall include any notes. The essays shall be typewritten, in English, paying proper attention to style and presentation.

(*d*) Candidates shall be required to declare that the essays are their own work and that they do not contain material used to any substantial extent for a comparable purpose prior to the date of their submission. Where appropriate, full and proper acknowledgement must be given to the work of others, although formal footnoting shall not be a requirement. Each essay must be accompanied by a bibliography of the books, articles, and electronic and online resources used in its preparation. The prescribed length shall exclude these bibliographies.

(*e*) The portfolio shall be submitted to the Director of Undergraduate Studies through the candidate's Director of Studies, in accordance with arrangements approved by the Faculty Board, so as to arrive at the Faculty not later than 5 p.m. on the last Thursday of the Full Lent Term preceding the examination.

(*f*) Candidates may be called for *viva voce* examination in connection with their portfolios.

(New Regulations)

Part II

18. The papers in Part II shall be as follows:

Group A

Paper 1. Practical criticism
Paper 2. Tragedy (also serves as Paper O3 of Part II of the Classical Tripos)[1]
Paper 3. Compulsory dissertation

Group B

Paper 4. Optional dissertation
Paper 5. Chaucer[1]
Paper 6. Medieval English literature, 1066–1500 (also serves as Paper 13 of Part II of the Anglo-Saxon, Norse, and Celtic Tripos)
Paper 7. Early modern drama, 1588–1642
Paper 8. Material Renaissance
Paper 9. Lyric
Paper 10. English literature, 1847–1872
Paper 11. Modernism and the short story
Paper 12. Contemporary writing in English
Paper 13. Postcolonial and related literatures[1]
Paper 14. American literature
Paper 15. English moralists
Paper 16. History and theory of literary criticism (also serves as Paper O4 of Part II of the Classical Tripos)
Paper 17. Shakespeare in performance
Paper 18. Literature and visual culture[1]
Paper 19. A paper or papers in English literature announced by the Faculty Board from time to time.

Group C

Paper 20. Early medieval literature and its contexts, 1066–1350 (Paper 2 of Part I of the English Tripos; also serves as Paper O9 of Part II of the Classical Tripos, and as Paper 11 of Part I of the Anglo-Saxon, Norse, and Celtic Tripos)
Paper 21. English literature and its contexts, 1300–1550 (Paper 3 of Part I of the English Tripos)
Paper 22. English literature and its contexts, 1500–1700 (Paper 4 of Part I of the English Tripos)
Paper 23. Shakespeare (Paper 5 of Part I of the English Tripos)
Paper 24. English literature and its contexts, 1660–1870 (Paper 6 of Part I of the English Tripos)
Paper 25A. English literature and its contexts, 1830–1945 (Paper 7A of Part I of the English Tripos)
Paper 25B. English literature and its contexts, 1870–present (Paper 7B of Part I of the English Tripos)
Paper 26. Old English language and literature (Paper 5 of Part I of the Anglo-Saxon, Norse, and Celtic Tripos. Also serves as Paper 8A of Part I of the English Tripos (New Regulations))
Paper 27A. Old Norse language and literature (Paper 6 of Part I of the Anglo-Saxon, Norse, and Celtic Tripos. Also serves as Paper 8B of Part I of the English Tripos (New Regulations))
Paper 27B. Advanced medieval Scandinavian language and literature (Paper 6 of Part II of the Anglo-Saxon, Norse, and Celtic Tripos)
Paper 28A. Medieval Welsh language and literature (Paper 7 of Part I of the Anglo-Saxon, Norse, and Celtic Tripos. Also serves as Paper 8C of Part I of the English Tripos (New Regulations))
Paper 28B. Advanced medieval Welsh language and literature (Paper 7 of Part II of the Anglo-Saxon, Norse, and Celtic Tripos)
Paper 29A. Medieval Irish language and literature (Paper 8 of Part I of the Anglo-Saxon, Norse, and Celtic Tripos. Also serves as Paper 8D of Part I of the English Tripos (New Regulations))
Paper 29B. Advanced medieval Irish language and literature (Paper 8 of Part II of the Anglo-Saxon, Norse, and Celtic Tripos)
Paper 30. Insular Latin language and literature (Paper 9 of Part I of the Anglo-Saxon, Norse, and Celtic Tripos. Also serves as Paper 8E of Part I of the English Tripos (New Regulations))
Paper 31. A prescribed Greek author or authors, and a prescribed Latin author or authors (Paper A1 of Part II of the Classical Tripos)
Paper 32. Prescribed Greek texts (Paper A2 of Part II of the Classical Tripos)
Paper 33. Prescribed Latin texts (Paper A3 of Part II of the Classical Tripos)

[1] This paper is also available to candidates for Part II of the Modern and Medieval Languages Tripos; see p. 395.

(New Regulations)

Paper 34. Topics in medieval studies to be specified by the Faculty Board from time to time (Paper Fr.7 of the Modern and Medieval Languages Tripos)
Paper 35. Living, loving, and dying in Renaissance France (Paper Fr.8 of the Modern and Medieval Languages Tripos)
Paper 36. Reason, experience, and authority: French literature, thought, and history, 1594–1700 (Paper Fr.9 of the Modern and Medieval Languages Tripos)
Paper 37. French literature, thought, and history, from 1690–1799 (Paper Fr.10 of the Modern and Medieval Languages Tripos)
Paper 38. Gender, desire, and power in 19th century French culture (Paper Fr.11 of the Modern and Medieval Languages Tripos)
Paper 39. Ethics and experience: literature, thought, and visual culture of the French-speaking world (1900–present) (Paper Fr.12 of the Modern and Medieval Languages Tripos)
Paper 40. Dante and the culture of his age (Paper It.7 of the Modern and Medieval Languages Tripos)
Paper 41A. Introduction to Neo-Latin literature, from 1350 to 1700 (Paper NL.1 of the Modern and Medieval Languages Tripos)
Paper 41B. A special subject in Neo-Latin literature (Paper NL.2 of the Modern and Medieval Languages Tripos)
Paper 42A. A special subject in comparative literature (i) (Paper CS.4 of the Modern and Medieval Languages Tripos)
Paper 42B. A special subject in comparative literature (ii) (Paper CS.5 of the Modern and Medieval Languages Tripos)
Paper 43A. Historical linguistics (Paper 11 of the Linguistics Tripos)[1]
Paper 43B. History of the English language (Paper 13 of the Linguistics Tripos)[2]

Every paper shall be set for three hours except Papers 1 and 21 which shall be set for three and a half hours. Under the provisions of Regulation 4, the Faculty Board shall announce, each year, the variable papers in Group B (Papers 5 to 19) and Group C (Papers 26 to 43) that shall be available for examination in the following year. A question paper shall be set for every paper in the given year's schedule (other than Papers 3 and 4) for which there is a candidate.

19. Every candidate for Part II shall offer:

(*a*) Papers 1, 2, and 3;

(*b*) *either* (i) if the candidate takes the examination in the year after obtaining honours in another Honours Examination, *two* papers chosen from amongst Papers 4 to 43;

or (ii) if the candidate takes the examination in the year next but one after obtaining honours in another Honours Examination, or if the candidate is an Affiliated Student, *three* papers chosen from amongst Papers 4 to 43; provided that since the availability of each of Papers 5 to 19 and Papers 26 to 43 for examination in any given year will not be confirmed until the Easter Term of the preceding year, these papers should not be selected for study until the year of actual examination, and then only in accordance with the list of papers announced as available that year.

(*c*) In offering papers for examination, the candidate's choices shall be further governed by the following provisions:

(i) if a candidate takes the examination in the year next but one after obtaining honours in any Honours examination but has spent the intervening year undertaking legitimate study in another University, the candidate shall offer only *two* papers chosen from amongst Papers 4 to 43, sub-paragraph (b)(ii) above notwithstanding;

(ii) no candidate shall offer both Papers 17 and 23, or both Papers 25A and 25B, or both Papers 27A and 27B, or both Papers 28A and 28B, or both Papers 29A and 29B, or both Papers 41A and 41B, or both Papers 42A and 42B, or both Papers 43A and 43B;

(iii) a candidate who has obtained honours in Part I of the English Tripos or any allowance on that examination towards a degree shall not offer any of Papers 21 to 25;

(iv) if a candidate has not previously obtained honours in Part I of the English Tripos and either takes the Part II examination in the year next but one after obtaining honours in another Honours examination or is an Affiliated Student, the candidate shall offer at least one paper from among Papers 20 to 25;

(v) a candidate shall not offer any paper that he or she has previously offered in another Honours Examination;

[1] This paper is suspended in 2015–16 and each alternate year thereafter.
[2] This paper is suspended in 2014–15 and each alternate year thereafter.

(New Regulations)

(vi) a candidate offering any of Papers 21 to 25 shall be required to demonstrate, in each such paper offered, substantial knowledge of the literature of the British Isles (which may include Ireland);

(vii) a candidate offering any of Papers 22, 24, 25A, or 25B shall be required to demonstrate, in each such paper offered, substantial knowledge of English literature before and after the medial date specified for the paper in question;

(viii) a candidate for the English Tripos offering any of Papers 26 to 43 shall be required to offer them as written papers, and may not substitute them with any form of course-work, albeit that such substitutions may be available to candidates who are offering the same papers for the Anglo-Saxon, Norse, and Celtic Tripos, or the Classical Tripos, or the Modern and Medieval Languages Tripos, or the Linguistics Tripos;

(ix) a candidate for Part II of the English Tripos offering any of Papers 22, 24, or 25 shall be required to offer them as written papers, and may not substitute them with any form of course-work, albeit that such substitutions may be available to candidates who are offering the same papers for Part I of the English Tripos;

(x) dissertations offered under this Regulation, whether for Paper 3 or Paper 4, shall be submitted in accordance with the provisions of Regulation 21.

Schemes of work.

20. (*a*) Every candidate shall submit her or his scheme of work (a list of papers to be offered for examination), together with the proposed topic(s) of her or his dissertation(s), for formal approval to the Director of Undergraduate Studies of the Faculty Board through her or his Director of Studies in accordance with the arrangements for such notification approved by the Board. Submissions must be made by the penultimate Friday of the Full Michaelmas Term preceding the examination.

(*b*) The Director of Undergraduate Studies and the Undergraduate Submissions Committee, acting on behalf of the Faculty Board, shall consider each such submission with respect to two considerations:

(i) where a candidate offers both Papers 3 and 4, if one of the dissertations so offered is in the same field as one of the candidate's papers, these parties may decline to allow the candidate to offer the second dissertation in the field of that same or any other of her or his papers;

(ii) where a candidate offers six papers, these parties shall consider the overall balance of the candidate's scheme of work and the potential for overlap, whether between papers or between papers and the dissertation(s), and may reject such proposals as they judge fail to demonstrate sufficient breadth.

(*c*) Once a scheme of work and topic(s) have been approved on behalf of the Faculty Board, no change shall be made to them without further formal approval. A candidate may, however, submit a revised scheme and/or topic(s) for approval so as to reach the Director of Undergraduate Studies at any time up until the sixth Wednesday of the Full Lent Term preceding the examination.

Dissertations.

21. (*a*) Every candidate, in offering one or more dissertations under Regulation 19, shall submit the proposed topic(s) thereof for formal approval in accordance with the provisions of Regulation 20.

(*b*) Dissertations must be on topics of 'English literature' as defined under Regulation 2, save that (Regulation 2(*b*) notwithstanding) where Part II 'English literature' papers such as Papers 2, 9, 15, and 16 encompass the study of specified musical or foreign-language materials, permission to make these latter materials the primary focus of a dissertation shall be at the discretion of the Undergraduate Submissions Committee, acting on behalf of the Faculty Board. Relevant comparisons may always be made with any foreign-language materials or materials that fall outside the scope of 'English literature' without obtaining prior permission, so long as those comparisons are made subject to the terms of Regulation 2(*e*).

Temporary Regulation

22. (i) The examinations for Part I of the English Tripos shall be held under the Old Regulations for the last time in 2014. They shall be held under the New Regulations for the first time in 2015.

(ii) The examinations for Part II of the English Tripos shall be held under the Old Regulations for the last time in 2013. They shall be held under the New Regulations for the first time in 2014.

GEOGRAPHICAL TRIPOS

1. The Geographical Tripos shall consist of three Parts: Part IA, Part IB, and Part II. Three Parts.

2. The following may present themselves as candidates for honours in Part IA: Standing of candidates.

(*a*) a student who has not obtained honours in another Honours Examination, provided that he or she has kept one term and that three complete terms have not passed after his or her first term of residence;

(*b*) a student who has obtained honours in another Honours Examination, in the year after so obtaining honours, provided that he or she has kept four terms and that nine complete terms have not passed after his or her first term of residence.

3. A student may be a candidate for honours in Part IB in the year after obtaining honours either in Part IA or in another Honours Examination, provided that he or she has kept four terms and that twelve complete terms have not passed after his or her first term of residence.

4. A student may be a candidate for honours in Part II:

either (*a*) in the year next after obtaining honours in Part IB of the Geographical Tripos,

or (*b*) in the year next or next but one after obtaining honours in another Honours Examination, other than Part IA of the Geographical Tripos;

provided that he or she has kept seven terms and that twelve complete terms have not passed after his or her first term of residence.[1]

5. No student shall be a candidate for more than one Part, or for any Part and also for another Honours Examination, in the same term.

6. No student who has been a candidate for any Part shall again be a candidate for the same Part.

7. The Faculty Board of Earth Sciences and Geography shall have power to issue from time to time supplementary regulations defining or limiting all or any of the subjects of examination. Due care shall be taken that sufficient notice is given of any alterations of such supplementary regulations. Supplementary regulations.

8. The Faculty Board shall nominate for each Part of the Tripos such number of Examiners as they shall deem sufficient. There shall be two separate bodies of Examiners, one for Part IA and Part IB, and one for Part II. There shall be a separate Chair of Examiners for each body of Examiners. Examiners.

9. The Faculty Board shall have power to nominate one or more Assessors to assist each body of Examiners. An Assessor may be summoned to meetings of the Examiners for the purpose of consultation and advice, but shall not be entitled to vote. Assessors.

10. The questions proposed by each Examiner and Assessor shall be submitted to the whole body of Examiners for approval.

11. The Examiners shall have regard to the style and method of candidates' answers, and shall give credit for excellence in these respects.

12. In the class-list for each Part of the Tripos the names of those who obtain honours shall be arranged in three classes, of which the second shall be divided into two divisions. Class-lists.

13. For special excellence in each Part of the Tripos a mark of distinction may be awarded.

14. In the examination for each Part of the Tripos the Examiners may take account of the laboratory and field work done by candidates during the courses leading to the examination.

15. Notice of prescribed areas shall be published by the Faculty Board in the *Reporter* before the end of the Easter Term next preceding the examination to which they apply; provided that the Board shall have the power of subsequently issuing amendments if they have due reason for doing so and if they are satisfied that no student's preparation for the examination would be adversely affected. Notice of subjects.

PART IA

16. The examination shall consist of two papers as follows: Scheme of examination for Part IA.

Paper 1. Human geography
Paper 2. Physical geography

17. Each paper shall be set for three hours. A candidate for Part IA shall

(*a*) offer both papers; and

(*b*) submit to the Examiners, in accordance with arrangements to be specified by the Head of the Department of Geography and by a date or dates to be announced not later than the end of the first quarter of the Michaelmas Term, records of five practical exercises undertaken by the candidate, together with a declaration as specified in Regulation 25.

The Examiners shall have power to examine candidates *viva voce* on their submitted work.

[1] See also the regulations for Affiliated Students.

PART IB

18. The papers for Part IB shall be as follows:

Section A

Paper 1. Living with global change

Section B

Paper 2. Human geography I
Paper 3. Human geography II
Paper 4. Human geography III
Paper 5. Physical and environmental geography I
Paper 6. Physical and environmental geography II
Paper 7. Physical and environmental geography III

The paper in Section A and each paper in Section B shall consist of a written paper of two hours' duration together with the submission of course-work; details of the course-work required of candidates, and the arrangements for the submission of the course-work shall be published by the Faculty Board not later than the division of the Easter Term next preceding the examination.

19. A candidate for Part IB shall offer:

(*a*) Paper 1,

(*b*) three papers from Section B, and

(*c*) submit to the Examiners, in accordance with arrangements to be specified by the Head of the Department of Geography and by a date or dates to be announced not later than the end of the first quarter of the Michaelmas Term,

(i) a record of a practical exercise or exercises undertaken by the candidate, and

(ii) a record of a practical exercise undertaken by the candidate and based on a residential field class.

All items of submitted work in sections (*a*), (*b*), and (*c*) shall be accompanied by a declaration as specified in Regulation 25.

PART II

Scheme of examination for Part II.

20. The papers for Part II shall be as follows:

Paper 1. A prescribed topic or topics in human geography I
Paper 2. A prescribed topic or topics in human geography II
Paper 3. A prescribed topic or topics in human geography III
Paper 4. A prescribed topic or topics in human geography IV
Paper 5. A prescribed topic or topics in physical geography I
Paper 6. A prescribed topic or topics in physical geography II
Paper 7. A prescribed topic or topics in physical geography III
Paper 8. A prescribed topic or topics in physical geography IV
Paper 9. A prescribed topic or topics in geography I
Paper 10. A prescribed topic or topics in geography II
Paper 11. A prescribed topic or topics in geography III
Paper 12. A prescribed topic or topics in geography IV

Each paper shall consist of *either* a written paper of three hours' duration *or* a written paper of two hours' duration together with the submission of course-work; the mode of examination of each paper, details of the course-work required of candidates, and the arrangements for the submission of the course-work shall be published by the Faculty Board not later than the division of the Easter Term next preceding the examination.

21. A candidate for Part II shall offer any four papers from the papers specified in Regulation 20.

Dissertation.

22. Except as provided in (*a*) and (*b*) below, every candidate for Part II shall send to the Chair of Examiners so as to arrive not later than the first Tuesday of the Full Term in which the examination is to be held, for submission to the Examiners, a dissertation on some geographical subject. This regulation shall not apply to:

(*a*) an Affiliated Student who is a candidate for Part II in the first, second, or third term after his or her first term kept;

or (*b*) a student who has not obtained honours in either Part IA or Part IB of the Geographical Tripos and who is a candidate for Part II in the year next after obtaining honours in another Honours Examination; such a student shall submit in place of the dissertation a critical review essay of dissertation length.

23. Every candidate submitting a dissertation or a critical review essay under Regulation 22(*b*) shall obtain the approval of the Head of the Department for the subject of the proposed dissertation not later than the end of the Michaelmas Term next preceding the examination.

24. A dissertation shall be of not less than 8,000 words and not more than 10,000 words in length, shall be word-processed, unless previous permission has been obtained from the Chair of Examiners through a candidate's Tutor to present the dissertation in manuscript, and shall be accompanied by a declaration as specified in Regulation 25. The dissertation shall be taken into consideration by the Examiners, who shall have power to examine a candidate upon it *viva voce*.

25. When submitting records of practical exercises for Part IA (Regulation 17(*b*)), or course-work, essays and records of practical exercises, and dissertation proposals for Part IB (Regulations 18 and 19(*b*)), or course-work or a dissertation for Part II (Regulations 20 and 24), or a critical review essay for Part II (Regulation 22(*b*)), a candidate will be required to sign a declaration that the work submitted is his or her own work, unaided except as may be specified in the declaration (full and proper acknowledgement being given of the work of others), and that it does not contain material that has already been used to any substantial extent for a comparable purpose; if two or more candidates have undertaken practical exercises in collaboration, they will each be required to indicate the extent of their contribution.

HISTORICAL TRIPOS

Amended by Notice (Reporter, *2013–14, p. 529*)

1. The Historical Tripos shall consist of two Parts. A separate class-list shall be published for each Part. Two Parts.

2. The Faculty Board of History shall have power to define or limit by supplementary regulations all or any of the subjects of the examination; to determine the credit that shall be assigned to such subjects respectively; to mark out the lines of study that are to be pursued by candidates; and to modify or alter any such supplementary regulations as occasion may require. They shall also have power to publish from time to time lists of books recommended to the candidates. Supplementary regulations.

3. Before the end of the Easter Term each year the Faculty Board shall give notice of the variable subjects for the examinations to be held in the academical year next but one following; provided that

(*a*) the Faculty Board shall have the power of subsequently issuing amendments if they have due reason for doing so and if they are satisfied that no student's preparation for the examination is adversely affected;

(*b*) a subject prescribed for Paper 1 of Part I may be withdrawn by the Faculty Board upon notice given in the *Reporter* not later than the end of the Full Michaelmas Term next but one preceding the examination concerned.

4. The following may present themselves as candidates for honours in Part I: Standing of candidates.

(*a*) a student who has kept four terms; provided that six complete terms have not passed after his or her first term of residence;

(*b*) a student who has obtained honours in another Honours Examination in the year next after or next but one after so obtaining honours; provided that the student has kept seven terms and that twelve complete terms have not passed after his or her first term of residence.

5. A student who has obtained honours in another Honours Examination may be a candidate for honours in Part II in the year next after or next but one after so obtaining honours; provided that the student has kept seven terms and that twelve complete terms have not passed after his or her first term of residence.

6. An Affiliated Student may be a candidate for honours either in Part I or in Part II as allowed by the Faculty Board in accordance with the regulations for Affiliated Students.

7. No student shall be a candidate for both Parts, or for either Part and also for another Honours Examination, in the same term.

8. No student who has been a candidate for either Part shall again be a candidate for the same Part.

9. The Faculty Board shall nominate such number of Examiners as they may deem sufficient for each Part of the Tripos. Examiners.

10. The Faculty Board shall have power to nominate one or more Assessors to assist the Examiners in either Part of the Tripos. Assessors shall, if required, set the paper or papers assigned to them, shall look over the work of the candidates therein, and shall present a report to the Examiners. They may Assessors.

be summoned to meetings of the Examiners for the purpose of consultation and advice, but shall not be entitled to vote.

11. The Examiners shall have regard to the style and method of the candidates' answers and shall give credit for excellence in these respects.

Class-lists.

12. In each Part, the names of the candidates who obtain honours shall be arranged in three classes, of which the second shall be divided into two divisions. The names in the first and third classes and in each division of the second class shall be arranged in alphabetical order. A mark of distinction shall be affixed to the names of those candidates placed in the first class whose work either in a part or in the whole of the examination is of special merit. Explanation of the mark shall be limited to the words 'With distinction'.

Scheme of examination for Part I.

13. The scheme of examination for Part I shall be:

Section A

Themes and Sources

Paper 1. Themes and sources

Section B

British Political History

Paper 2. British political history, 380–1100
Paper 3. British political history, 1050–1509
Paper 4. British political history, 1485–1714
Paper 5. British political history, 1688–1886
Paper 6. British political history, since 1880

Section C

British Economic and Social History

Paper 7. British economic and social history, 380–1100
Paper 8. British economic and social history, 1050–*c.* 1500
Paper 9. British economic and social history, *c.* 1500–1750
Paper 10. British economic and social history, 1700–1880
Paper 11. British economic and social history, since *c.* 1880

Section D

European History

Paper 12. European history, 776 BC–AD 69
Paper 13. European history, 31 BC–AD 900
Paper 14. European history, 900–*c.* 1215
Paper 15. European history, 1200–1520
Paper 16. European history, 1450–1760
Paper 17. European history, 1715–1890
Paper 18. European history, since 1890[1]

Section E

Political Thought

Paper 19. History of political thought to *c.* 1700 (also serves as Paper O6 of Part II of the Classical Tripos and Paper POL7 of the Human, Social, and Political Sciences Tripos)
Paper 20. History of political thought from *c.* 1700 to *c.* 1890 (also serves as Paper POL8 of the Human, Social, and Political Sciences Tripos)

Section F

World History

Paper 21. Empires and world history from the fifteenth century to the First World War[2]
Paper 23. World history since 1914

Section G

American History

Paper 22. North American History, *c.* 1500 to 1865
Paper 24. The history of the United States from 1865

[1] This paper is also available to candidates for Part II of the Modern and Medieval Languages Tripos; see p. 395.
[2] This paper is also available to candidates for Part IIA of the Archaeological and Anthropological Tripos.

Each paper shall be of three hours' duration, except Paper 1. The examination for Paper 1 shall consist of the submission of an essay, on a topic chosen from a list of topics announced by the Faculty Board; the length of the essay and the arrangements for its submission shall be prescribed by the Faculty Board from time to time.

14. Candidates for Part I shall offer papers as follows:

(*a*) a candidate who takes the examination in the fourth, fifth, or sixth term after the first term of residence, or in the year next but one after obtaining honours in another Honours Examination, or a candidate who is an Affiliated Student and has been given leave by the Faculty Board to take Part I in the fourth, fifth, or sixth term after the first term kept, shall offer Paper 1 and five other papers;

(*b*) a candidate who takes the examination in the year next after obtaining honours in another Honours Examination shall offer Paper 1 and four other papers;

provided that

(i) every candidate shall offer at least one paper from Section B, at least one paper from Section C, and at least one paper from Sections D–G;

(ii) no candidate who has obtained honours in either Part of the Classical Tripos shall offer Paper 12 or Paper 13;

(iii) the Faculty Board may specify from among Papers 2–24 a paper or papers which an Affiliated Student who is a candidate under this regulation shall or shall not offer.

PART II

15. The scheme of examination for Part II shall be:

Scheme of examination for Part II.

Section A

Paper 1. Historical argument and practice

Section B

Special Subject[1]

Paper 2. Essay Paper
Paper 3. Sources Paper

Section C

Political Thought

Paper 4. The history of political thought from *c.* 1700 to *c.* 1890 (also serves as Paper Pol. 15 of the Politics, Psychology, and Sociology Tripos)[2]

Paper 5. Political philosophy and the history of political thought since *c.* 1890 (also serves as Paper Pol. 6 of the Politics, Psychology, and Sociology Tripos)

Paper 6. States between states: The history of international political thought from the Roman empire to the early nineteenth century

Section D

Specified Subjects

Papers 7–30. A variable number of papers on topics or comparative themes in history specified by the Faculty Board,[3]

provided that within the range of papers listed in Sections B and D, a minimum of one paper in each of the following subject areas shall be offered:

(i) ancient history;[1]
(ii) medieval history;
(iii) early modern history;
(iv) economic and/or social history;
(v) modern British and/or Irish history;
(vi) modern European history;
(vii) American history;

[1] One or more subjects specified in Sections B and D may also serve as Group C papers of Part II of the Classical Tripos.

[2] This paper is also available, in certain years, to candidates for Part II of the Modern and Medieval Languages Tripos; see p. 395

[3] One or more subjects specified in Section D may also be available to candidates for Part II of the Modern and Medieval Languages Tripos; see p. 395.

(viii) African, Asian or Latin-American history;

and that no fewer than twelve specified subjects shall be offered in Section D.

16. Candidates for Part II shall offer papers, or papers and a dissertation, as follows:

(*a*) a candidate who takes the examination in the year next after obtaining honours in Part I of the Historical Tripos or in another Honours Examination, or a candidate who is an Affiliated Student and has been given leave by the Faculty Board to take Part II in the first, second, or third term after the first term kept, shall offer Papers 1, 2, and 3, and

either two papers from Sections C–D

or one paper from Sections C–D and a dissertation as prescribed in Regulation 17 on a topic, the title of which has been approved by the Faculty Board, within the range of the Historical Tripos as a whole, provided that a candidate shall not submit a dissertation on a topic falling within the scope of any of the papers that he or she is offering in the examination;

(*b*) a candidate who takes the examination in the year next but one after obtaining honours in Part I of the Historical Tripos or in another Honours Examination, or a candidate who is an Affiliated Student and has been given leave by the Faculty Board to take Part II in the fourth, fifth, or sixth term after the first term kept, shall offer Papers 1, 2, and 3, and

either four papers from Sections C–D

or three papers from Sections C–D and a dissertation as prescribed in Regulation 17 on a topic, the title of which has been approved by the Faculty Board, within the range of the Historical Tripos as a whole, provided that a candidate shall not submit a dissertation on a topic falling within the scope of any of the papers that he or she is offering in the examination;

provided that

(i) no candidate shall offer any paper that he or she has previously offered as a candidate for another Honours Examination;

(ii) the Faculty Board may give notice before the end of the Easter Term in the academical year next but one preceding the examination that a candidate who offered a particular paper or combination of papers in Part I of the Historical Tripos may not offer a particular paper or papers from Section D of Part II;

(iii) no candidate who has obtained honours in Part II of the Classical Tripos shall offer the paper which serves as the subject for Paper C4 of Part II of the Classical Tripos;

(iv) no candidate shall offer in Papers 2 and 3, a subject which he or she has already offered in Group C of Part II of the Classical Tripos;

(v) no candidate who has previously offered Paper 20 in Part I of the Historical Tripos shall offer Paper 4;

(vi) the Faculty Board may specify from among Papers 4–30 a paper or papers which an Affiliated Student who is a candidate under this regulation shall or shall not offer;

(vii) a candidate who has previously obtained honours in Part I of the Historical Tripos, but who did not offer in that Part a paper from among

either Paper 1 (Themes and Sources) provided that the option selected by the candidate is one which has been announced by the Faculty Board as a subject falling mainly in the period before 1750;

or Papers 2–4, 7–9, 12–16, and 19,

or Papers 23 and 24 (if the subject specified for the paper fell mainly in the period before 1750),

shall offer in Part II

either Papers 2 and 3, provided that the special subject selected by the candidate is one which has been announced by the Faculty Board as a subject falling mainly in the period before 1750,

or one of the following papers, provided that the subject specified for the paper is a subject falling mainly in the period before 1750:

Papers 7–30;

or a dissertation as prescribed in Regulation 17, provided that its subject falls mainly in the period before 1750;

(viii) a candidate who has previously obtained honours in Part I of the Historical Tripos but who did not offer in that Part a paper from among Papers 12–18 shall offer in Part II a paper from Section D on a subject in European history specified by the Faculty Board.

17. (*a*) A candidate for Part II who wishes to offer a dissertation under Regulation 16 shall submit an application, including the title of the proposed dissertation and a statement of the scheme of papers to be offered in the examination. Applications, signed by the candidate's Director of Studies, shall be submitted to the Academic Secretary of the Faculty so as to arrive not later than the division of the Easter Term next preceding the examination. Applications submitted after that date will be considered by the Board only in the most exceptional circumstances. Dissertation.

(*b*) Each candidate shall obtain the approval of the proposed title by the Faculty Board not later than the last day of August preceding the examination. When the Faculty Board have approved a title, no change shall be made to it without the further approval of the Board. A candidate may submit a revised title so as to reach the Academic Secretary of the Faculty not later than the division of the Lent Term; titles submitted after that date will be considered by the Board only in the most exceptional circumstances.

(*c*) A dissertation shall be not less than 10,000 words and not more than 15,000 words in length, shall show knowledge of primary sources, and shall give full reference to all sources used. Each dissertation shall be typewritten, with proper attention to style and presentation in accordance with detailed guidelines issued by the Faculty Board. Candidates will be required to provide a brief synopsis of the contents of the dissertation, and to declare that the dissertation is their own original work and that it does not contain material already used to any substantial extent for a comparable purpose.

(*d*) A dissertation shall be submitted through the candidate's Director of Studies to the Academic Secretary of the Faculty, in accordance with arrangements approved by the Board, so as to arrive not later than the first Friday of the Full Easter Term in which the examination is to be held.

(*e*) A candidate may be called for *viva voce* examination on his or her dissertation and on the general field of knowledge within which it falls.

SUPPLEMENTARY REGULATIONS

Amended by Notice (Reporter, *2013–14, p. 530*)

PART I

Paper 1. Themes and sources

The purpose of this paper is to give candidates experience of problems in the interpretation of historical sources within a thematic framework. Each candidate will be required to select an option from a list of options announced by the Faculty Board, and each option will include a number of essay topics. An essay on a topic chosen from a list announced by the Faculty Board will be submitted. Some of the topics may involve the use of sources in a foreign language.

Papers 2–6. British political history, from AD *380 to the present day*

In these papers candidates will be required to show knowledge of political aspects and also of general aspects of English, Irish, Scottish, and Welsh history where relevant to the period studied. Candidates will be expected to show evidence of their ability to use and interpret contemporary documents. In each paper three questions must be answered, but no question will be specified as compulsory.

Papers 7–11. British economic and social history, from AD *380 to the present day*

In these papers candidates will be required to show knowledge of economic, social, and cultural aspects and also of general aspects of English, Irish, Scottish, and Welsh history where relevant to the period studied. Candidates will be expected to show evidence of their ability to use and interpret contemporary documents. In each paper three questions must be answered, but no question will be specified as compulsory.

Papers 12–18. European history, from 776 BC *to the present day*

These papers will survey European history in the periods concerned, in its political, constitutional, cultural, economic, and social aspects. Candidates will also be required to show knowledge of general aspects of European history. In each paper candidates will be required to answer three questions.

Paper 18 will be set in two sections. In one section the major emphasis will be on political and constitutional history; in the other section the major emphasis will be on economic, social, intellectual, and cultural history. Candidates will be required to answer three questions, at least one question to be taken from each section.

Paper 19. History of political thought to c. *1700* (also serves as Paper O6 of Part II of the Classical Tripos and Paper POL7 of the Human, Social, and Political Sciences Tripos)

Paper 20. History of political thought from c. *1700 to* c. *1890* (also serves as Paper POL8 of the Human, Social, and Political Sciences Tripos)

These papers will deal with political ideas and arguments in relation to the general historical contexts in which they arose. Each paper will be divided into two sections. Section A will consist of questions on prescribed texts. Section B will be designed to test knowledge of a series of themes of importance in the history of political thought in the period covered by the paper. Candidates will be required to answer three questions, at least one question to be taken from each section.

Paper 21. Empires and world history from the fifteenth century to the First World War

This paper will deal comparatively with the growth of political, economic, and cultural relations between Europe and the rest of the world since 1400; and with their effects in world history. Candidates will be required to answer three questions.

Paper 22. North American history, c. *1500 to 1865*

This paper will concentrate on the history of those parts of North America which now form the United States. Candidates will be required to answer three questions.

Paper 23. World history since 1914

The paper will explore the climax and decline of Europe's older imperial systems during the first half of the twentieth century, the emergence of new forms of imperial power, and the making of the modern 'postcolonial' world in the context of world war and global economic shifts. Candidates will be required to answer three questions.

Paper 24. The history of the United States from 1865

The paper will concentrate on the history of those parts of North America which now form the United States. The paper will be set in two sections. Section A will consist of thematic questions; in Section B questions will be arranged chronologically. Three questions must be answered; one from Section A, two from Section B.

Part II

Paper 1. Historical argument and practice

This paper aims to provide an opportunity for candidates to reflect on broad issues of historical argument and practice arising out of their work for all three years of the Historical Tripos, but especially Part II. The paper is a means of enabling candidates to raise and discuss fundamental questions which relate their specialist knowledge to more general themes of historical inquiry and explanation. The focus of this paper, as distinct from other Part II papers, is on understanding the conceptual, historiographical, and methodological dimensions of historical argument and practice. However, the paper also fundamentally requires candidates to develop their understanding of these conceptual, historiographical, and methodological issues in relation to their work for their other Part II papers, for example by critically evaluating the merits of different approaches in relation to the more specific and empirical material that they encounter elsewhere in the Tripos. The questions will be designed to encourage broad discussion of issues derived from, and relevant to, papers set in Part II, and will also allow candidates to draw upon their wider reading, done within and outside Parts I and II. The paper will offer a choice of questions, from which candidates will be required to answer one.

Papers 2 and 3. Special Subject: sources and long essay

Each candidate shall choose one special subject from a list of special subjects published by the Faculty Board. For each of the subjects primary sources will be specified, some of which may be in a foreign language. A candidate will be required to take one three-hour examination paper and to submit an essay of 6,000 to 7,000 words. The examination paper will include extracts from the specified primary sources and will require commentary by the candidate. For the essay candidates will be required to select an option from a list of options announced by the Faculty Board and to discuss an historical issue with reference to the primary sources, including those specified for the special subject.

Paper 4. The history of political thought from c. *1700 to* c. *1890* (also serves as Paper Pol. 15 of the Politics, Psychology, and Sociology Tripos)

This paper will deal with political ideas and arguments in relation to the general historical contexts in which they arose. The paper will be divided into two sections. Section A will consist of questions on prescribed texts. Section B will be designed to test knowledge of a series of themes of importance in the history of political thought in the period covered by the paper. Candidates will be required to answer three questions, at least one question to be taken from each section.

Paper 5. Political philosophy and the history of political thought since c. *1890* (also serves as Paper Pol. 6 of the Politics, Psychology, and Sociology Tripos)

This paper will explore the central texts and key ideas of twentieth-century political thought, looking at both analytical concepts and historical context. It is divided into two parts, Section A which covers historical topics organized around authors and their texts, and Section B which covers a variety of themes in contemporary political philosophy. Students are required to answer three questions, taking at least one from each section.

Paper 6. States between states: The history of international political thought from the Roman empire to the early nineteenth century

This paper will explore the history of European thinking about polities in relation to other polities from the Roman empire to the early nineteenth century. It considers a wide range of source texts from different historical contexts and examines the manifold and complex ways in which the 'international' arena of politics was theorized in different periods. Candidates will be required to answer three questions.

HISTORY OF ART TRIPOS

1. The History of Art Tripos shall consist of three Parts, Part I, Part IIA, and Part IIB. Three Parts.

2. The following may present themselves as candidates for honours in Part I: Standing of candidates.

(*a*) a student who has not obtained honours in an Honours Examination, provided that he or she has kept one term and that three complete terms have not passed after his or her first term of residence;

(*b*) a student who has obtained honours in an Honours Examination in the year next after so obtaining honours, provided that he or she has kept four terms and that twelve complete terms have not passed after his or her first term of residence.

3. A student who has obtained honours in Part I of the History of Art Tripos or in another Honours Examination may be a candidate for honours in Part IIA in the year after so obtaining honours, provided that he or she has kept four terms and that nine complete terms have not passed after his or her first term of residence.[1]

4. A student who has obtained honours in an Honours Examination other than Part I of the History of Art Tripos may be a candidate for honours in Part IIB in the year after so obtaining honours, provided that he or she has kept seven terms and that twelve complete terms have not passed after his or her first term of residence.[1]

5. No student shall be a candidate for more than one Part, or for any Part and also for another Honours Examination, in the same term.

6. No student who has been a candidate for any Part shall again be a candidate for the same Part.

7. The Faculty Board of Architecture and History of Art shall nominate such number of Examiners as they deem sufficient for each Part of the Tripos. Examiners.

8. The Faculty Board shall have power to nominate one or more Assessors to assist the Examiners in any of the subjects in each Part of the Tripos. If required to do so, Assessors shall set papers in the subject or subjects assigned to them, shall mark the answers of the candidates in those papers, shall assess essays and dissertations, and shall advise the Examiners on the performance of candidates in the examination. Assessors may be summoned to meetings of the Examiners for the purpose of consultation and advice, but shall not be entitled to vote. Assessors.

9. The questions proposed by each Examiner and Assessor shall be submitted to the whole body of Examiners for approval.

10. The Faculty Board shall have power:

(*a*) to issue from time to time supplementary regulations defining or limiting all or any of the subjects of examination and determining the scope and character of the papers, and to amend or withdraw such supplementary regulations as occasion may require, due care being taken that sufficient notice is given of any change; Supplementary regulations.

(*b*) to determine the credit to be assigned to each paper, and to establish guidelines to be followed by the Examiners for assessing candidates' work in the examination and for drawing up the class-lists.

11. Public notice of subjects, special periods, and books prescribed under the following regulations or under any supplementary regulations for the Tripos shall be given by the Faculty Board (*a*) for Part I, before the end of the Easter Term of the year next preceding the examination to which they apply, and (*b*) for Part IIA and Part IIB, before the end of the Easter Term next but one preceding the examination to which they apply; provided that the Board shall have the power of subsequently issuing amendments if they have due reason for doing so and if they are satisfied that no student's preparation for the examination is adversely affected. Notice of books and subjects.

12. There shall be a separate class-list for each Part. In each list the names of candidates who deserve honours shall be placed in three classes, of which the second shall be divided into two divisions. The names in the first and third classes, and in each division of the second class, shall be arranged in alphabetical order. A mark of distinction may be awarded for special excellence. Class-lists.

[1] See also the regulations for Affiliated Students.

Part I

Scheme of examination for Part I.

13. The scheme of examination for Part I shall be:

Paper 1.	The objects of art history.
Papers 2 and 3.	The making of art.
Papers 4 and 5.	The meaning of architecture and art.

Papers 3 and 5 shall each consist of reproductions of works of art requiring comment and interpretation.

Each candidate shall offer all five papers and shall submit a Part I short dissertation, as prescribed in Regulation 18, on a subject approved by the Faculty Board relating to some aspect of art or architecture in or around Cambridge.

Parts IIA and IIB

Scheme of examination for Parts IIA and IIB.

14. The scheme of examination for Part IIA and Part IIB shall be:

Paper 1.	Approaches to the history of art, with reference to works of criticism.
Paper 2.	The display of art.
Papers 3–24.	Such number of pairs of papers on special subjects as the Faculty Board shall announce from time to time in accordance with Regulation 10. There shall be not less than eight and not more than eleven pairs of such papers on special subjects. Each pair of papers shall deal with a particular person, subject, or period in the history of art. In each pair of papers, the second paper shall consist of reproductions of works of art requiring comment and interpretation.

15. A candidate for Part IIA shall offer Paper 1 and two pairs of papers on special subjects.

16. A candidate for Part IIB

(*a*) who has obtained honours in Part IIA of the History of Art Tripos shall offer Paper 2; two pairs of papers on special subjects; and a Part IIB dissertation of between 7,000 and 9,000 words on a subject approved by the Faculty Board dealing with a particular person, work of art, subject, or period in the history of art;

(*b*) who takes the examination in the year after obtaining honours in another Tripos shall offer *either* Paper 1 *or* Paper 2; two pairs of papers on special subjects; and a Part IIB dissertation of between 7,000 and 9,000 words on a subject approved by the Faculty Board dealing with a particular person, work of art, subject, or period in the history of art.

Parts I, IIA, and IIB

17. A candidate shall not offer in any Part of the Tripos a paper that he or she has previously offered in another University examination.

Dissertation title.

18. (*a*) Each candidate for Part I shall submit the proposed title of his or her Part I short dissertation for approval by the Faculty Board. Titles shall be submitted to the Secretary of the Department of History of Art so as to arrive not later than the division of the Lent Term next preceding the examination.

(*b*) Each candidate for Part IIA shall submit a statement of the scheme of papers to be offered in the examination to the Secretary of the Department of History of Art, so as to arrive not later than the second Monday of the Full Michaelmas Term next preceding the examination.

(*c*) Each candidate for Part IIB shall submit the proposed title of his or her Part IIB dissertation for approval by the Faculty Board. Titles shall be submitted to the Secretary of the Department of History of Art, so as to arrive not later than the last day of the Full Michaelmas Term next preceding the examination.

(*d*) The Secretary of the Faculty Board shall communicate the Board's approval or rejection of a proposed dissertation title to each candidate. When the Board have approved a title, no change shall be made to it or, in the case of Part IIA or Part IIB, to the candidate's scheme of papers, without the further approval of the Board.

(*e*) The length of a Part I short dissertation or a Part II dissertation shall be as follows:

A short dissertation submitted by a candidate for Part I shall be of not more than 5,000 words in length. A dissertation submitted by a candidate for Part IIB shall be of not less than 7,000 words and not more than 9,000 words in length.

In each case the prescribed length shall include notes and appendices, but not bibliography. Each dissertation shall be printed or typewritten.

(*f*) (i) Part I short dissertations shall be submitted to the Secretary of the Department of History of Art, in accordance with detailed arrangements approved by the Faculty Board, so as to arrive not later than the Friday after the division of the Easter Term in which the examination is to be held.

(ii) Two copies of the Part IIB dissertation shall be submitted to the Secretary of the Department of History of Art, in accordance with detailed arrangements approved by the Faculty Board, so as to arrive not later than the first day of the Full Easter Term in which the examination is to be held.

Each candidate submitting a dissertation will be required to sign a declaration that the work submitted is his or her own work, unaided except as may be specified in the declaration, and that it does not contain material that has already been used to any substantial extent for a comparable purpose.

SUPPLEMENTARY REGULATIONS

Part I

Paper 1. The objects of art history

The course for this paper consists of a survey of Western (and some non-Western) art, which introduces students to the development of the visual arts. It provides an opportunity to study the material covered at first hand, by using the resources of the Fitzwilliam Museum and other Cambridge collections, and in relation to its historical and artistic background.

Papers 2 and 3. The making of art

These papers are concerned with painting and sculpture; the Faculty Board may prescribe specified artists, or specified subjects or periods, for special study. The first half of the course deals with the processes and attitudes which have shaped the world of images, such as methods and materials, the creative process, and notions of quality and taste, as well as the reproduction of images. The course introduces students to such questions, and focuses on specific artists, periods, and traditions. The second half of the course deals with sculpture; it covers various topics, such as techniques and materials, classical sculpture and its legacy, and more modern developments.

Papers 4 and 5. The meaning of architecture and art

The course for these papers is divided into two halves, dealing respectively with traditions of representation and architectural meaning; the Faculty Board may prescribe specified artists or periods for special study. The course aims to provide an awareness of changing attitudes to architecture and art in Western Europe. Emphasis is placed on close critical study of a range of key examples, as well as their context. The first part of the course covers various topics in the study of the visual arts, focusing on the content and interpretation of the figurative arts. The second part covers areas such as the theory and use of classical orders, building typology, and the relationship between design and construction.

Part IIB

Paper 1. Approaches to the history of art, with reference to works of criticism

This paper will deal with the influence of writers of classical antiquity upon the Renaissance approach to art and architecture; with changing attitudes towards both antiquity and the Middle Ages in the eighteenth century; with nineteenth-century and twentieth-century theoretical and critical approaches to art and architecture; and with recent developments in art historical methods, the growth of connoisseurship, formal and stylistic criticism, and sociological and iconographical interpretations of works of art and architecture.

HUMAN, SOCIAL, AND POLITICAL SCIENCES TRIPOS[1]

Amended by Notices (Reporter, *2013–14, pp. 530 and 724*)

General

1. The Human, Social, and Political Sciences Tripos shall consist of three Parts, Part I, Part IIA, and Part IIB. In Part IIA and Part IIB there shall be an examination in each of the following five subjects: Archaeology (including Assyriology and Egyptology), Biological Anthropology, Politics and International Relations, Social Anthropology, Sociology, and there shall be a joint examination in each of the following six pairs of subjects: Archaeology and Social Anthropology, Biological Anthropology and Archaeology, Politics and Sociology, Social and Biological Anthropology, Sociology and Social Anthropology, Social Anthropology and Politics. For Part I there shall be a single class-list; for Part Three parts.

[1] These regulations will come into effect in accordance with the timetable in Temporary Regulation 22.

IIA and Part IIB there shall be a separate class-list for each of the five subjects of the examination and for each joint examination.

Examiners and Assessors.

2. The Faculty Board of Human, Social, and Political Science shall nominate a Senior Examiner and such number of Examiners to conduct the examination for Part I of the Tripos, and a Senior Examiner and such number of Examiners to conduct the examination in each subject for Part IIA and Part IIB, as they shall deem sufficient. The Faculty Board shall have power to nominate such number of Assessors as they shall deem sufficient to assist the Examiners for each Part. If required to do so, Assessors shall set papers in the subject or subjects assigned to them, shall mark the answers of the candidates in those papers, shall assess dissertations, and shall advise the Examiners on the performance of candidates in the examination. Assessors may be summoned to meetings of the Examiners for the purpose of consultation and advice, but shall not be entitled to vote.

Supplementary Regulations.

3. The Faculty Board may from time to time make supplementary regulations defining all or any of the subjects and specified texts of examination and may modify, alter, or withdraw such supplementary regulations as they see fit, due care being taken that sufficient notice is given of any change.

Variable subjects.

4. Before the end of the Easter Term each year the Faculty Board shall give notice of the variable subjects for the examinations to be held in the academical year next following; provided that the Board shall have the power of subsequently issuing amendments if they have due reason for doing so and if they are satisfied that no student's preparation for the examination is adversely affected. The Board shall have power when they give notice of variable subjects to announce any consequential restriction on the combination of papers that a candidate may choose to offer.

5. The questions proposed by each Examiner and Assessor shall be submitted for approval to the whole body of Examiners for Part I or to the Examiners in the particular subject for Part IIA or Part IIB.

6. Separate meetings shall be held of all the Examiners for Part I and of the five bodies of Examiners for Part IIA and Part IIB, at which the respective class-lists shall be drawn up. The five bodies of Examiners for Part IIA and Part IIB shall also draw up class-lists for the following subjects: Archaeology and Social Anthropology (the Examiners for Archaeology), Biological Anthropology and Archaeology (the Examiners for Biological Anthropology), Politics and Sociology (the Examiners for Politics and International Relations), Social and Biological Anthropology (the Examiners for Social Anthropology), Sociology and Social Anthropology (the Examiners for Sociology), and Social Anthropology and Politics (the Examiners for Social Anthropology). In each class-list the names of the candidates who deserve honours shall be placed in three classes, of which the second shall be divided into two divisions. The names in the first and third classes, and in each division of the second class, shall be arranged in alphabetical order. For special excellence a mark of distinction may be awarded. The class-lists for the subject Archaeology in Part IIA and Part IIB shall indicate whether a candidate has offered in the examination the Assyriology and/or Egyptology option.

7. No student shall be a candidate for more than one Part, or any Part and also for another Honours Examination in the same term.

8. No student who has been a candidate for any Part shall again be a candidate for the same Part.

9. A candidate shall not offer in any Part of the Tripos a paper that he or she has previously offered in another University examination.

PART I

Standing of candidates.

10. The following may present themselves as candidates for honours in Part I:

(*a*) a student who has not obtained honours in another Honours Examination, provided that he or she has kept one term and that three complete terms have not passed after the student's first term of residence;

(*b*) a student who has obtained honours in another Honours Examination, in the year after so obtaining honours, provided that he or she has kept seven terms and that nine complete terms have not passed after the student's first term of residence.

11. The scheme of examination for Part I shall be as follows:

Section A

ARC1.	Introduction to archaeology
ARC2.	Archaeology in action (also serves as Paper O12 in Part II of the Classical Tripos)
ARC3.	Introduction to the cultures of Egypt and Mesopotamia

ARC4.	Akkadian language I (also serves as Paper X.1 of Part IA of the Asian and Middle Eastern Studies Tripos)
ARC5.	Egyptian language I (also serves as Paper X.2 of Part IA of the Asian and Middle Eastern Studies Tripos)
BAN1.	Humans in biological perspective
POL1.	Analysis of politics (also serves as an optional paper for Paper 5 of Part IIA of the Economics Tripos)
POL2.	International relations I (also serves as an optional paper for Paper 5 of Part IIA of the Economics Tripos)
SOC1.	Modern societies I: introduction to sociology (also serves as an optional paper for Paper 5 of Part IIA of the Economics Tripos)
SAN1.	Social anthropology: the comparative perspective

Section B

PBS1.	Introduction to psychology

A candidate for Part I shall be required to offer four papers as follows:

(*a*) three papers from Section A;

(*b*) one further paper from Section A or a paper from Section B.

Part IIA and Part IIB

12. The following may present themselves as candidates for honours in Part IIA: Standing of candidates.

(*a*) a student who has obtained honours in Part I of the Human, Social, and Political Sciences Tripos in the year next after so obtaining honours, provided that six complete terms have not passed after her or his first term of residence;

(*b*) a student who has obtained honours in any other Honours Examination, in the year next after or next but one after so obtaining honours, provided that twelve complete terms have not passed after her or his first term of residence.[1]

13. A student who has obtained honours in Part IIA of the Human, Social, and Political Sciences Tripos may be a candidate for honours in Part IIB in the year next after so obtaining honours, provided that:

(i) the student has kept seven terms and twelve complete terms have not passed after her or his first term of residence;[1]

(ii) no student shall be a candidate for Part IIB in Archaeology unless the Head of the Department of Archaeology and Anthropology is satisfied that the student has, since matriculation, undertaken at least one week of study visit and six weeks of archaeological excavation or fieldwork on a project or projects (or in the case of candidates for Assyriology or Egyptology, an equivalent study visit to Egypt or the Middle East and/or study in a museum) approved by the Head of the Department, provided that the Head of the Department shall have power to grant exemption from this requirement to a candidate who has obtained an equivalent amount of appropriate experience in some other way. Before the division of the Lent Term each year the Head of the Department shall draw up a list of those candidates who have satisfied this requirement or have been granted exemption from it, and shall communicate this information to the Registrary.

14. A student who has obtained honours in another Honours Examination other than Part IIA of the Human, Social, and Political Sciences Tripos may be a candidate for honours in either Part IIA or Part IIB in the year after so obtaining honours, provided that the student has kept seven terms and that twelve complete terms have not passed after her or his first term of residence. Such students shall offer, subject to the provisions of Regulation 9, four papers chosen from those available in Part IIA and Part IIB, in accordance with the guidelines issued by the Faculty Board, and conditional upon written permission from the relevant Head of Department obtained not later than the division of the Michaelmas Term next preceding the examination.

15. The scheme of examination for Part IIA and Part IIB shall be as follows:[2]

[1] See also the regulations for Affiliated Students.

[2] For further information on the papers offered for Part II in 2014–15, see Notice (*Reporter*, 6354, 2013–14, p. 667).

Archaeology

ARC6. Archaeological theory and practice I
ARC7. Archaeological theory and practice II
ARC8. Archaeological science I
ARC9. Archaeological science II
ARC10. The Palaeolithic of the Old World
ARC11. Topics in Palaeolithic archaeology
ARC12. European prehistory
ARC13. Special topics in European prehistory
ARC14. Aegean prehistory (Paper D1 from the Classical Tripos)
ARC15. A topic within classical archaeology and/or art (Paper D2 from the Classical Tripos)
ARC16. A topic within classical archaeology and/or art (Paper D3 from the Classical Tripos)
ARC17. A topic within classical archaeology and/or art (Paper D4 from the Classical Tripos)
ARC18. The historical archaeology of Ancient Egypt I[1]
ARC19. The historical archaeology of Ancient Egypt II[2]
ARC20. Ancient Egyptian religion I[1]
ARC21. Ancient Egyptian religion II[2]
ARC22. Mesopotamian archaeology I: prehistory and early states[1]
ARC23. Mesopotamian archaeology II: territorial states to empires[2]
ARC24. Mesopotamian culture I: literature[2]
ARC25. Mesopotamian culture II: religion and scholarship[1]
ARC26. The North Sea in the Early Middle Ages
ARC27. Europe in Late Antiquity and the Migration Period
ARC28. The archaeology of medieval Britain (also serves as Paper 11 of Part II of the History Tripos)
ARC29. Ancient India I: the Indus civilization and beyond[1]
ARC30. Ancient India II: Early historic cities of South Asia[2]
ARC31. Ancient South America[2]
ARC32. The archaeology of Mesoamerica and North America[1]
ARC33. The archaeology of Africa
ARC34. Akkadian language II (also serves as Paper X.6 of Part IB of the Asian and Middle Eastern Studies Tripos)
ARC35. Akkadian language III
ARC36. Sumerian language
ARC37. Egyptian language II (also serves as Paper X.7 of Part IB of the Asian and Middle Eastern Studies Tripos)
ARC38. Egyptian language III
ARC39. Mesopotamian history I: states and structures[1]
ARC40. Mesopotamian history II: empires and systems[2]

The Faculty Board shall announce before the end of the Easter Term the papers that will be available in the examinations to be held in the next academical year.

Biological Anthropology

BAN2. A subject in biological anthropology I
BAN3. A subject in biological anthropology II
BAN4. A subject in biological anthropology III
BAN5. Theory and practice in biological anthropology
BAN6. A subject in biological anthropology IV
BAN7. A subject in biological anthropology V
BAN8. A subject in biological anthropology VI
BAN9. A subject in biological anthropology VII

Politics and International Relations

POL3. International relations II
POL4. Comparative politics
POL5. Conceptual issues in politics and international relations
POL6. Statistics and methods[3]
POL7. The history of political thought to *c.* 1700 (Paper 19 of Part I of the Historical Tripos)

[1] This paper will be available, in alternate years, from 1 Oct 2014.
[2] This paper will be available, in alternate years, from 1 Oct 2015.
[3] This paper is suspended until further notice.

POL8.	The history of political thought from *c.* 1700 to *c.* 1890 (Paper 20 of Part I of the Historical Tripos)
POL9.	Conceptual issues and texts in politics and international relations
POL10.	The history of political thought from *c.*1700 to *c.*1890 (Paper 4 of Part II of the Historical Tripos)
POL11.	Political philosophy and the history of political thought since *c.* 1890 (Paper 5 of Part II of the Historical Tripos)
POL12.	A subject in politics and international relations I
POL13.	A subject in politics and international relations II[1]
POL14.	A subject in politics and international relations III
POL15.	A subject in politics and international relations IV
POL16.	A subject in politics and international relations V
POL17.	A subject in politics and international relations VI
POL18.	A subject in politics and international relations VII
POL19.	A subject in politics and international relations VIII

Social Anthropology

SAN2.	Kinship and economic anthropology
SAN3.	The anthropology of politics and religion
SAN4.	Theory, methods, and enquiry in social anthropology
SAN5.	Thought, belief, and ethics
SAN6.	Political economy and social transformation
SAN7.	The anthropology of an ethnographic area

Special subjects in social anthropology

SAN8.	A subject in social anthropology I
SAN9.	A subject in social anthropology II
SAN10.	A subject in social anthropology III
SAN11.	A subject in social anthropology IV
SAN12.	A subject in social anthropology V

Sociology

SOC2.	Social theory
SOC3.	Modern societies II
SOC4.	Concepts and arguments in sociology
SOC5.	Statistics and methods
SOC6.	A subject in sociology I
SOC7.	A subject in sociology II
SOC8.	A subject in sociology III
SOC9.	A subject in sociology IV
SOC10.	A subject in sociology V
SOC11.	A subject in sociology VI
SOC12.	A subject in sociology VII
SOC13.	A subject in sociology VIII
SOC14.	Disciplines of education III (Paper 3 of Part II of the Education Tripos)
SOC15.	Criminology, sentencing, and the penal system (Paper 23 of the Law Tripos)

16. Each paper shall be of three hours' duration except POL5, SOC4, ARC6–13, and ARC18–33. The examination for Papers POL5 and SOC4 shall consist of the submission of two essays each of not more than 5,000 words. The Faculty Board shall publish by notice in each Department of the Faculty of Human, Social, and Political Science prescribed titles or subjects for essays by the beginning of the Michaelmas Term next preceding the examination concerned. The essays for POL5 and SOC4 shall be submitted in printed or typewritten form to the Senior Examiner in the relevant subject as follows: one essay no later than the end of the first week of Full Lent Term, and one essay no later than the end of the first week of Full Easter Term. Papers ARC6–13 and ARC18–33 will be assessed by a three-hour written examination plus mandatory course-work elements, prescribed titles or details of which will be published by the Faculty Board by the end of the Easter Term of the year preceding the examination concerned.

[1] This paper will also be available, in certain years, to candidates for the Economics Tripos.

Part IIA. **17.** Subject to the provisions of Regulation 9, candidates for Part IIA shall offer papers and other exercises as follows:

(*a*) *Candidates in Archaeology*

Option 1 (*Archaeology*)

(i) ARC6;
(ii) two papers chosen from Papers ARC2[1], ARC8, ARC10–33;
(iii) one paper chosen from BAN2–4, POL3–4, SAN8–12, SOC2–3, and Paper 1 *or* Paper 2 for the subject History and Philosophy in Part IB of the Natural Sciences Tripos, or one further paper chosen from ARC8, ARC10–33, or *either* Paper 7 *or* Paper 8 borrowed from Part I of the Historical Tripos, or one paper chosen from PBS3–4 borrowed from Part IIA of the Psychological and Behavioural Science Tripos.

Option 2 (*Assyriology*)

(i) ARC34[2] or ARC4;
(ii) ARC22 or ARC23;
(iii) one paper chosen from ARC24–25 and ARC39–40;
(iv) one paper chosen from ARC2, ARC6, ARC8, ARC10–21, ARC24–33, or ARC39–40.

Option 3 (*Egyptology*)

(i) ARC37[3] or ARC5;
(ii) ARC2 or ARC6;
(iii) ARC18 or ARC19;
(iv) ARC20 or ARC21.

Option 4 (*Assyriology and Egyptology*)

(i) ARC34[2] or ARC4;
(ii) ARC37[3] or ARC5;
(iii) one paper from ARC18–21;
(iv) one paper from ARC22–25.

(*b*) *Candidates in Biological Anthropology*

(i) Papers BAN2–4;
(ii) one paper chosen from ARC8, ARC10–33, BAN6–9, POL3–4, SAN8–12, SOC2–3, and Paper 1 *or* Paper 2 for the subject History and Philosophy in Part IB of the Natural Sciences Tripos, or one paper chosen from PBS3–4 borrowed from Part IIA of the Psychological and Behavioural Science Tripos.

(*c*) *Candidates in Politics and International Relations*

(i) POL3;
(ii) POL4;
(iii) *either* POL7 *or* POL8;
(iv) one paper chosen from ARC8, ARC10–33, BAN2–4, SAN8–12, SOC2–3, SOC5, Paper 1 *or* Paper 2 for the subject History and Philosophy in Part IB of the Natural Sciences Tripos, POL5–6, or *either* Paper 10 *or* Paper 11 borrowed from Part I of the Historical Tripos, or one paper chosen from PBS3–4 borrowed from Part IIA of the Psychological and Behavioural Science Tripos.

(*d*) *Candidates in Social Anthropology*

(i) Papers SAN2–4;
(ii) one paper chosen from SAN8–12, ARC8, ARC10–33, BAN2–4, POL3–4, SOC2–3, and Paper 1 *or* Paper 2 for the subject History and Philosophy in Part IB of the Natural Sciences Tripos, or Paper PBS3 borrowed from Part IIA of the Psychological and Behavioural Science Tripos.

[1] Paper ARC2 is required if a candidate has not taken it at Part I.
[2] Paper ARC34 can only be taken at Part IIA if a candidate has taken Paper ARC4 at Part I.
[3] Paper ARC37 can only be taken at Part IIA if a candidate has taken Paper ARC5 at Part I.

(*e*) *Candidates in Sociology*

(i) SOC2;

(ii) SOC3;

(iii) *either* SOC4 *or* SOC5;

(iv) one paper chosen from ARC8, ARC10–33, BAN2–4, POL3–4, SAN8–12, SOC4–5, Papers PBS3–4 of the Psychological and Behavioural Sciences Tripos, and Paper 1 *or* Paper 2 for the subject History and Philosophy in Part IB of the Natural Sciences Tripos, or *either* Paper 10 *or* Paper 11 borrowed from Part I of the Historical Tripos.

(*f*) *Candidates in Archaeology and Social Anthropology*

(i) one paper chosen from ARC2 and ARC6, and one paper chosen from ARC2, ARC6, ARC8, and ARC10–33;

(ii) two papers chosen from SAN2–4.

(*g*) *Candidates in Biological Anthropology and Archaeology*

(i) one paper chosen from ARC2 and ARC6, and one paper chosen from ARC2, ARC6, ARC8, and ARC10–33;

(ii) two papers chosen from BAN2–4.

(*h*) *Candidates in Politics and Sociology*

(i) one paper chosen from POL3–4;

(ii) one paper chosen from POL7–8;

(iii) SOC2 and SOC3.

(*i*) *Candidates in Social and Biological Anthropology*

(i) two papers chosen from SAN2–4;

(ii) two papers chosen from BAN2–4.

(*j*) *Candidates in Sociology and Social Anthropology*

(i) SAN2 and SAN3;

(ii) SOC2 and SOC3.

(*k*) *Candidates in Social Anthropology and Politics*

(i) POL3 or POL4;

(ii) POL7 or POL8;

(iii) one paper chosen from SAN2–3, and one paper chosen from SAN2–4 and SAN8–12.

18. Candidates for Part IIB who have taken Part IIA in the Human, Social, and Political Sciences Tripos may not change their subject track between Parts IIA and IIB, unless changing from a joint track to one of the single subjects within it. Subject to the provisions of Regulation 9, candidates for Part IIB shall offer papers and other exercises as follows: Part IIB.

(*a*) *Candidates in Archaeology*

Option 1 (*Archaeology*)

(i) ARC7;

(ii) two papers chosen from Papers ARC8–33[1], one of which may be substituted by a dissertation on a subject approved by the Head of the Department of Archaeology and Anthropology, which shall be submitted in accordance with the provisions of Regulation 20;

(iii) one further paper chosen from Papers ARC8–33, BAN2–4, BAN6–9, POL13–14[2], SAN8–12, SOC6–15[3].

Option 2 (*Assyriology*)

(i) ARC35[4] or ARC34;

(ii) ARC22 or ARC23;

[1] Paper ARC9 can only be taken if a candidate has taken Paper ARC8 at Part IIA.
[2] Papers POL13–14 can only be taken if POL3 or POL4 was taken at Part IIA.
[3] Paper SOC6 can only be taken if SOC2 was taken at Part IIA.
[4] Paper ARC35 can only be taken at Part IIB if a candidate has taken Paper ARC34 at Part IIA.

(iii) one paper chosen from ARC24–25, ARC36[1], or ARC39–40;
(iv) *either* one further paper chosen from ARC7, ARC8–21[2], ARC26–33, ARC36[1], ARC39–40, *or* a dissertation on a subject approved by the Head of the Department of Archaeology and Anthropology, which shall be submitted in accordance with the provisions of Regulation 20.

Option 3 (*Egyptology*)
(i) ARC38[3] or ARC37;
(ii) ARC18 or ARC19;
(iii) ARC20 or ARC21;
(iv) *either* one further paper chosen from ARC7, ARC8, ARC10–17, ARC22–33, *or* a dissertation on a subject approved by the Head of the Department of Archaeology and Anthropology, which shall be submitted in accordance with the provisions of Regulation 20.

Option 4 (*Assyriology and Egyptology*)
(i) ARC35[4] or ARC34;
(ii) ARC38[3] or ARC37;
(iii) one paper from ARC18–25;
(iv) *either* one further paper chosen from ARC18–25, ARC36[1], *or* a dissertation on a subject approved by the Head of the Department of Archaeology and Anthropology, which shall be submitted in accordance with the provisions of Regulation 20.

(*b*) *Candidates in Biological Anthropology*
(i) BAN5;
(ii) two papers chosen from Papers BAN6–9, one of which may be substituted by a dissertation on a subject approved by the Head of the Department of Archaeology and Anthropology, which shall be submitted in accordance with the provisions of Regulation 20;
(iii) *either* one paper chosen from ARC8–33[2], POL13–14[5], SAN8–12, SOC6–15[6], *or* a further paper chosen from BAN6–9.

(*c*) *Candidates in Politics and International Relations*
(i) POL9;
(ii) two papers chosen from POL10–19[7], one of which may be substituted by a dissertation on a subject approved by the Head of the Department of Politics and International Studies, which shall be submitted in accordance with the provisions of Regulation 20;
(iii) *either* one paper chosen from ARC8–33[2], BAN2–4, BAN6–9, SAN8–12, SOC6–15[6], *or* a further paper chosen from POL10–19[7].

(*d*) *Candidates in Social Anthropology*
(i) Papers SAN5, SAN6, and SAN7;
(ii) *either* one paper chosen from Papers SAN8–12, ARC8–33[2], BAN2–4, BAN6–9, POL13–14[5], SOC6–15[6], *or* a dissertation on a subject approved by the Head of the Department of Archaeology and Anthropology, which shall be submitted in accordance with the provisions of Regulation 20.

(*e*) *Candidates in Sociology*
(i) one paper chosen from SOC6–13;
(ii) two further papers chosen from SOC6–15, one of which may be substituted by a dissertation on a subject approved by the Head of the Department of Sociology, which shall be submitted in accordance with the provisions of Regulation 20;
(iii) one paper chosen from ARC8–33[2], BAN2–4, BAN6–9, POL13–14[5], SAN8–12, Papers PBS9–12 of the Psychological and Behavioural Sciences Tripos or a further paper chosen from SOC6–15.

(*f*) *Candidates in Archaeology and Social Anthropology*

[1] Paper ARC36 can only be taken if a candidate is also taking Paper ARC35.
[2] Paper ARC9 can only be taken if a candidate has taken Paper ARC8 at Part IIA.
[3] Paper ARC38 can only be taken at Part IIB if a candidate has taken Paper ARC37 at Part IIA.
[4] Paper ARC35 can only be taken at Part IIB if a candidate has taken Paper ARC34 at Part IIA.
[5] Papers POL13–14 can only be taken if POL3 or POL4 was taken at Part IIA.
[6] Paper SOC6 can only be taken if SOC2 was taken at Part IIA.
[7] Paper POL10 cannot be taken if POL8 was taken in Part IIA.

(i) Paper ARC6 or ARC7;
(ii) one paper chosen from SAN5 and SAN6;
(iii) one paper chosen from ARC8–33[1] and one paper chosen from SAN5–12; one of these papers may be substituted by a dissertation on a subject approved by the Head of the Department of Archaeology and Anthropology, which shall be submitted in accordance with the provisions of Regulation 20.

(*g*) *Candidates in Biological Anthropology and Archaeology*
(i) Paper ARC6 or ARC7;
(ii) one paper chosen from BAN6–9;
(iii) one paper chosen from ARC8–33[1] and a further paper chosen from BAN6–9; one of these papers may be substituted by a dissertation on a subject approved by the Head of the Department of Archaeology and Anthropology, which shall be submitted in accordance with the provisions of Regulation 20.

(*h*) *Candidates in Politics and Sociology*
(i) two papers chosen from POL6, POL10–19[2];
(ii) two papers chosen from SOC5–15[3];
(iii) a candidate may substitute for one paper a dissertation on a subject approved by the Head of the Department of Politics and International Studies, which shall be submitted in accordance with the provisions of Regulation 20.

(*i*) *Candidates in Social and Biological Anthropology*
(i) one paper chosen from SAN5 and SAN6;
(ii) one paper chosen from BAN6–9;
(iii) one paper chosen from SAN5–12 and a further paper chosen from BAN6–9; one of these papers may be substituted by a dissertation on a subject approved by the Head of the Department of Archaeology and Anthropology, which shall be submitted in accordance with the provisions of Regulation 20.

(*j*) *Candidates in Sociology and Social Anthropology*
(i) two papers chosen from SOC5–15;
(ii) one paper chosen from SAN5 and SAN6, and one paper chosen from SAN5–SAN12[4];
(iii) a candidate may substitute for one paper a dissertation on a subject approved by the Head of the Department of Sociology, which shall be submitted in accordance with the provisions of Regulation 20.

(*k*) *Candidates in Social Anthropology and Politics*
(i) two papers from POL10–19[2];
(ii) one paper chosen from SAN5 and SAN6, and one paper chosen from SAN5–SAN12[4];
(iii) a candidate may substitute for one paper a dissertation on a subject approved by the Head of the Department of Archaeology and Anthropology, which shall be submitted in accordance with the provisions of Regulation 20.

19. Candidates for Part IIA and Part IIB in Archaeology and Biological Anthropology shall present for the inspection of the Examiners, by a date which the Head of the Department of Archaeology and Anthropology shall announce not later than the division of Michaelmas Term, records of such practical work done during the courses leading to the examination as shall be determined from time to time by the Faculty Board. The Examiners shall be provided by the Head of Department with assessments of the candidates' practical work, and shall take these assignments into account in assigning marks for the examination. Practical work.

20. (*a*) A candidate for Part IIB who wishes to offer a dissertation shall submit an application, including the title of the proposed dissertation, a brief account of its scope, and a statement of the scheme of papers to be offered in the examination. A candidate who so wishes may request permission to include a film or filmed material, amounting to not more than twenty minutes in length, as a component part of the dissertation. Applications shall be submitted to the Head of the relevant Dissertations.

[1] Paper ARC9 can only be taken if a candidate has taken Paper ARC8 at Part IIA.
[2] Paper POL10 cannot be taken if POL8 was taken in Part IIA.
[3] Paper SOC5 cannot be taken if a candidate is also taking POL6.
[4] Paper SAN7 cannot be taken unless the candidate is also taking SAN5 or SAN6.

Department so as to arrive not later than the division of the Full Michaelmas Term next preceding the examination.

(*b*) Each candidate must obtain the approval of the Head of Department for the proposed title not later than the division of the Lent Term. When the Head of Department has approved a title, no change shall be made to it, or to the candidate's scheme of papers, without the further approval of the Head of Department.

(*c*) A dissertation shall be of not more than 10,000 words in length. The inclusion of footnotes, figures, tables, appendices, and bibliography in the word count will be specified by each department. Each dissertation shall be typewritten, with two printed copies submitted in addition to a copy in an approved electronic format.

(*d*) A dissertation shall be submitted to the Senior Examiner in the relevant subject not later than the second Friday of the Full Easter Term in which the examination is held.

A dissertation shall be accompanied by (i) a brief synopsis on a separate sheet of paper of the contents of the dissertation, and (ii) a certificate signed by the candidate stating the word count of the dissertation, that it is her or his own original work, and that it does not contain material that has already been used to any substantial extent for a comparable purpose.

21. At the discretion of the Examiners, a candidate for Part IIB may be examined *viva voce*.

Temporary Regulation

22. The examinations for the Human, Social, and Political Sciences Tripos shall be held for the first time as follows:

Part I in 2014
Part IIA in 2015
Part IIB in 2016

LAND ECONOMY TRIPOS

Amended by Notice (Reporter, *2013–14, p. 243*)

Three Parts.

1. The Land Economy Tripos shall consist of three Parts: Part IA, Part IB, and Part II.

Standing of candidates.

2. A student may be a candidate for honours in Part IA if he or she has kept one term, provided that three complete terms have not passed after the student's first term of residence.

3. A student who has obtained honours in Part IA or in another Honours Examination may be a candidate for honours in Part IB in the year after so obtaining honours, provided that he or she has kept four terms and that nine complete terms have not passed after the student's first term of residence.[1]

4. A student who has obtained honours in Part IB or in another Honours Examination may be a candidate for honours in Part II in the year after so obtaining honours, provided that he or she has kept seven terms and that twelve complete terms have not passed after the student's first term of residence.[1]

5. No student shall be a candidate for more than one Part, or for any Part and also for another Honours Examination, in the same term.

6. No student who has been a candidate for honours in any Part shall again be a candidate for honours in the same Part.

Examiners.

7. There shall be two separate bodies of Examiners, one for Part IA, and one for Part IB and Part II. In each case, the Board of Land Economy shall nominate such number of Examiners as they shall deem sufficient.

Assessors.

8. The Board of Land Economy shall have power to nominate one or more Assessors to assist the Examiners in any of the subjects of the Tripos. Each Assessor shall propose questions in the papers assigned to him or her by the Examiners, shall look over the answers of the candidates to those questions, and shall report thereon to the Examiners. An Assessor may be summoned to meetings of the Examiners for the purpose of consultation and advice, but shall not be entitled to vote.

9. Each body of Examiners shall elect one of their number to act as Chair.

10. The questions proposed by each Examiner or Assessor shall be submitted to the whole body of Examiners for approval.

[1] See also the regulations for Affiliated Students.

11. There shall be a separate class-list for each Part of the Tripos. In each list the names of those who obtain honours shall be arranged in three classes, of which the second shall be divided into two divisions. The names in the first and third classes, and in each division of the second class, shall be arranged in alphabetical order. For special excellence a mark of distinction may be awarded. Class-lists.

12. The papers for the Land Economy Tripos, which shall be divided into Groups I–III, shall be as follows: Scheme of examination.

GROUP I

Paper 1A. Economics I
Paper 1B. Economics II
Paper 2. The public sector: institutional and legal frameworks
Paper 3. Quantitative and legal methods for land economists
Paper 4. Land economy, development, and sustainability

GROUP II

Paper 5. Environmental economics and law
Paper 6. Fundamentals of finance and investment
Paper 7. Regional economics and policy
Paper 8. The law of real property: principles, policy, and economic implications
Paper 9. Private law
Paper 10. The built environment
Paper 11. Land and urban economics

GROUP III

Paper 12. Law and economics
Paper 13. Landlord and tenant law
Paper 14. Planning policy and practice
Paper 15. Advanced techniques in finance and investment for real estate
Paper 16. Land, food, and ecosystem services
Paper 17. Land policy and development economics

The subject of each paper shall be examined by means of a paper of three hours' duration, except Papers 1A, 1B, and 4 which shall each be examined by means of a paper of two hours' duration. Additionally, the examination for each of Papers 4 and 6 shall include submission of a report on a project undertaken by the candidate; the work to be undertaken for the project, its length, and the arrangements for the submission of the report, shall be prescribed from time to time by the Board of Land Economy.

13. A candidate for honours in Part IA shall offer all four papers from Group I.

14. A candidate for honours in Part IB shall offer papers as follows:

(*a*) a candidate who has previously obtained honours in Part IA of the Land Economy Tripos shall offer five papers chosen from Group II, including Paper 8 or Paper 9 or both;

(*b*) a candidate who has not previously obtained honours in Part IA of the Land Economy Tripos shall offer:

(i) Paper 3;

(ii) four papers chosen from Group II, including Paper 8 or Paper 9 or both;

provided that

(1) a candidate who has been granted exemption under Regulation 15 shall not offer Paper 3 but shall instead offer a further paper chosen from Groups II–III;

(2) a candidate who has previously offered Paper 11 of the Law Tripos shall not offer Paper 8 of the Land Economy Tripos;

(3) a candidate who has previously offered both Paper 4 and Paper 10 of the Law Tripos shall not offer Paper 9 of the Land Economy Tripos.

15. The Board of Land Economy shall have power to grant exemption from the requirement to offer Paper 3 to any candidate for honours in Part IB under Regulation 14(*b*) who satisfies the Board that he or she has passed an examination of an acceptable standard in statistics or quantitative methods. Application for such exemption shall be made in writing through the candidate's Tutor to the Secretary of the Board of Land Economy not later than the end of the second week of the Full Michaelmas

Term preceding the examination; the candidate shall be notified of the Board's decision not later than the division of the Michaelmas Term.

16. Candidates for honours in Part II shall offer papers and a dissertation as follows:

(*a*) A candidate who has previously obtained honours in Part IB of the Land Economy Tripos shall offer

(i) four papers chosen from Groups II and III, including at least three papers from Group III; provided that a candidate shall not offer any paper that he or she has previously offered in another Honours Examination, and provided also that a candidate shall not, without leave of the Board of Land Economy, offer Paper 15 unless that candidate has attained a satisfactory standard in Paper 6 in Part IB;

(ii) a dissertation, which shall be submitted in accordance with the requirements of Regulation 17.

(*b*) A candidate who has not previously obtained honours in Part IB of the Land Economy Tripos shall offer

(i) four papers chosen from Groups II and III, including at least two papers from Group III; provided that a candidate shall not offer any paper that he or she has previously offered in another Honours examination;

(ii) a dissertation, which shall be submitted in accordance with the requirements of Regulation 17.

Dissertation.

17. A dissertation offered under Regulation 16 shall be submitted in accordance with the following provisions:

(*a*) Every dissertation shall be on a topic falling within the area of Land Economy.

(*b*) Each candidate taking the examination under Regulation 16(*a*) shall submit an application to the Board of Land Economy, giving the title of the proposed dissertation, a brief account of its scope, and a statement of the scheme of papers to be offered in the examination. Applications shall be submitted to the Secretary of the Department of Land Economy so as to arrive not later than the division of the Michaelmas Term.

(*c*) Each candidate must obtain the approval of the proposed title by the Board not later than the last day of Full Michaelmas Term. When the Board have approved a title, no change may be made in it or in the candidate's scheme of papers without the further approval of the Board.

(*d*) During Full Lent Term, on a day or days specified by the Head of the Department of Land Economy, each candidate shall give a brief oral presentation of the subject matter of his or her dissertation to two Examiners (who may include an Assessor). In assigning marks for the examination the Examiners shall take account of a candidate's oral presentation.

(*e*) A dissertation shall not exceed 10,000 words in length, including footnotes, tables, and appendices.[1] Each candidate will be required to sign a declaration that the dissertation is his or her own work, unaided except as may be specified in the declaration, and that it does not contain material that has already been used to any substantial extent for a comparable purpose. Every dissertation shall be typewritten or computer-printed, unless the candidate has obtained permission from the Board to present it in manuscript.

(*f*) Dissertations shall be submitted so as to reach the Secretary of the Department not later than the seventh day of the Full Easter Term in which the examination is to be held. A candidate who submits a dissertation after this date may be penalized.

Supplementary regulations.

18. The Board of Land Economy shall have power to make supplementary regulations defining all or any of the subjects of examination, and to modify, alter, or withdraw such supplementary regulations as they see fit, due care being taken that sufficient notice is given of any change.

SUPPLEMENTARY REGULATIONS

Amended by Notices (Reporter, *2013–14, pp. 243, and 424*)

GROUP I

Paper 1A. Economics I

An introduction to microeconomics and welfare economics.

Paper 1B. Economics II

An introduction to macroeconomics and macroeconomic policy.

[1] One A4 page consisting largely of tables, statistics, or symbols shall be regarded as the equivalent of 250 words.

Paper 2. The public sector: institutional and legal frameworks

A study of constitutional and administrative law, including the European Union, Parliament, the Executive, next step agencies, quangos and other government agencies, local government, and judicial review.

Paper 3. Quantitative and legal methods for land economists

An introduction to relevant skills required for successful study on the Land Economy Tripos. These include legal skills, mathematics (including refreshing mathematical skills), statistics, and qualitative policy analysis.

Paper 4. Land economy, development, and sustainability

Major economic, demographic, institutional, and technological changes and their impact upon the natural and built environments of the United Kingdom. The examination for this paper includes the submission of a report on a project (see below).

GROUP II

Paper 5. Environmental economics and law

Principles of environmental economics and law, environmental policy and policy analysis, urban and rural environmental management.

Paper 6. Fundamentals of finance and investment

An introduction to the analytical techniques for identifying risk/return opportunities in real estate and other financial markets, and the different types of funding/investment strategies available to real estate professionals.

The examination for this paper includes the submission of a report on a project (see below).

Paper 7. Regional economics and policy

Theories relating to regional growth and the economic analysis of regional development and policies designed to influence patterns of growth and development. The term 'region' is defined broadly to include international trading blocs, nations, and regions within a particular country.

Paper 8. The law of real property: principles, policy, and economic implications

An introduction to land law in England and Wales, including estates, tenure, title, registration systems, mortgages, and other interests in land.

Paper 9. Private law

Principles of contract and tort, introduction to company law.

Paper 10. The built environment

Elements of building design and construction and the impact of social, economic, legal, and technological factors on the built environment.

Paper 11. Land and urban economics

The economics of land markets and policies for public intervention in land markets, urban economics, the economics of housing and housing policy, and commercial property.

GROUP III

Paper 12. Law and economics

The relationship between the disciplines of law and economics, including economic theories and analysis of law, the part played by economic theory in legal reasoning, the role of law in allocating resources and in correcting market failures, and economic and legal theories of value and of compensation.

Paper 13. Landlord and tenant law

The land law of England and Wales of particular relevance to the relationship of landlord and tenant: common law of leases and of the rights and obligations of the parties to leases; the statutory regulation of residential, business, and agricultural tenancies; and homelessness.

Paper 14. Planning policy and practice

The law, administration, practice, and theory of land use planning in Great Britain.

Paper 15. Advanced techniques in finance and investment for real estate

An introduction to advanced methods in the valuation and financing of real estate, mixed asset portfolio allocation, and risk management.

Paper 16. Land, food, and ecosystem services

The ownership and use of land for primary production in the United Kingdom and other developed countries. Food production and consumption. Land uses and the provision of ecosystem services. Public policies towards rural land and ecosystem services.

Paper 17. Land policy and development economics

The role of land, agriculture, and natural resources in the growth and development of low income countries and their relationships to richer countries.

Groups I and II

Papers 4 and 6: project reports

The project to be undertaken for each of these papers and the word length shall be specified by the Board of Land Economy and announced not later than the division of the Lent Term. Candidates will be required to submit in typescript, by a date to be announced by the Board, an account of the project in the form of an extended essay. The account should be in English. It should report the statistical and other sources and techniques used by the candidate as well as presenting the candidate's results and conclusions. Each candidate will be required to sign a declaration that the project and the report on it are his or her own work, unaided except as may be specified in the declaration, and that the report does not contain material that has already been used to any substantial extent for a comparable purpose; if two or more candidates have undertaken a project in collaboration, they will each be required to indicate the extent of their contribution.

LAW TRIPOS

Amended by Notices (Reporter, *2013–14, pp. 117, 243, and 531*)

Three Parts.

1. The Law Tripos shall consist of three Parts: Part IA, Part IB, and Part II.

Standing of candidates.

2. A student may be a candidate for honours in Part IA if he or she has kept one term, provided that three complete terms have not passed after his or her first term of residence.

3. The following may be candidates for honours in Part IB:

(*a*) a student who has not obtained honours in an Honours Examination, provided that he or she has kept four terms and that six complete terms have not passed after his or her first term of residence;

(*b*) a student who has obtained honours in Part IA of the Law Tripos or in another Honours Examination, in the year next after so obtaining honours, provided that twelve complete terms have not passed after his or her first term of residence.

4. The Faculty Board of Law may grant to a student, who has passed with sufficient credit before coming into residence an examination in law the standard and scope of which are approved by the Faculty Board, the privilege of being a candidate for honours in Part IB earlier than as aforesaid, provided that the student has kept one term.

5. Students who have obtained honours in Part IB of the Law Tripos and have kept seven terms may be candidates for honours in Part II as follows:

(*a*) A student who has spent a period studying at a European university in accordance with the provisions of Regulation 6, and who has satisfied the requirements of that regulation, may be a candidate for Part II in the year next but one after obtaining honours in Part IB, provided that fifteen complete terms have not passed after her or his first term of residence.

(*b*) Any other student having obtained honours in Part IB of the Law Tripos may be a candidate for Part II in the year next after obtaining honours in Part IB, provided that twelve complete terms have not passed after her or his first term of residence.

6. In order to be a candidate for Part II under Regulation 5(*a*) a student shall produce evidence to the Secretary of the Faculty Board to demonstrate that during the academical year next before the year of candidature he or she satisfactorily completed a course of study in a member country of the European Community at a university approved for this purpose by the Faculty Board.

7. A student who wishes to study abroad in accordance with the provisions of Regulation 6 shall make application on a form approved by the Faculty Board and obtainable from the Faculty Office. An application shall be submitted through the student's Tutor to the Secretary of the Faculty Board so as to arrive not later than the end of the first quarter of the Michaelmas Term of the academical year next preceding that which the student proposes to spend abroad. The Secretary shall inform each student as soon as possible whether his or her application is approved.

8. A student who has obtained honours in Part IB under Regulation 4 may be a candidate for honours in Part II,[1] provided that he or she has kept four terms.

[1] See also the regulations for Affiliated Students.

The Faculty Board may grant to a student, who has passed with sufficient credit before coming into residence an examination in law the standard and scope of which are approved by the Faculty Board, the privilege of being a candidate for honours in Part II earlier than as aforesaid and without having passed any examination after coming into residence, provided that the student has kept one term.

A student who has obtained honours in Part II under this regulation shall be qualified to proceed to the B.A. Degree when he or she has kept six terms, provided that a student who satisfies the Examiners for the LL.M. Examination before completing six terms' residence, and who elects to proceed to the LL.M. Degree, shall not also be entitled to proceed to the B.A. Degree.

9. No student shall be a candidate for more than one Part, or for any Part and also for another Honours Examination, in the same term.

10. No student who has been a candidate for honours in any Part shall again be a candidate for honours in the same Part.

11. Subject to the provisions of Regulation 9, a student who is not eligible to be a candidate for honours shall be entitled, provided that he or she has kept four terms at least, to take the examination for either Part IB or Part II as a candidate not for honours. Candidates not for honours.

12. There shall be three separate bodies of Examiners, one for Part IA, one for Part IB, and one for Part II. For each Part, the Faculty Board shall nominate such number of Examiners as they shall deem sufficient to conduct the examination. Examiners.

13. The Faculty Board shall have power to nominate one or more Assessors to examine in any of the subjects of the Tripos. Assessors shall be required to set the paper or papers in the subjects assigned to them and to present such written reports to the Examiners as may be required. Assessors may be summoned to meetings of the Examiners for the purpose of consultation and advice, but shall not be entitled to vote.

14. There shall be a separate class-list for each Part of the Tripos. In each list the names of the successful candidates shall be arranged in three classes, of which the second shall be divided into two divisions. The names in the first and third classes, and in each division of the second class, shall be arranged in alphabetical order. In each class-list a mark of distinction shall be affixed to the names of those candidates placed in the first class whose work is of special merit. In the class-list for Part II the symbol (*e*) shall be placed against the names of those candidates who have taken the examination under Regulation 5(*a*).

15. The papers for the Law Tripos which shall be divided into Groups I–IV shall be as follows: Scheme of Examination.

GROUP I

Paper 1.	Civil law I.
Paper 2.	Constitutional law.
Paper 3.	Criminal law.
Paper 4.	Law of tort.
Paper 5.	Legal skills and methodology (half-paper).

GROUP II

Paper 10.	Law of contract.
Paper 11.	Land law.
Paper 12.	International law.

GROUP III

Paper 13.	Civil law II.
Paper 20.	Administrative law.
Paper 21.	Family law.
Paper 22.	Legal history.
Paper 23.	Criminology, sentencing, and the penal system (also serves as Paper Int. 6 of the Politics, Psychology, and Sociology Tripos).
Paper 25.	Criminal procedure and criminal evidence.
Paper 46.	Comparative law.
Paper 47.	Jurisprudence.

GROUP IV

Paper 24. Equity.
Paper 26. European Union law.
Paper 27. Competition law.
Paper 40. Commercial law.
Paper 41. Labour law.
Paper 42. Intellectual property.
Paper 43. Company law.
Paper 44. Aspects of obligations.
Paper 45. Conflict of laws.
Paper 48. Prescribed subjects (half-papers).

The Faculty Board shall have power, not later than the end of the Easter Term in the year preceding the examination to which they apply, to prescribe not more than twelve subjects for Paper 48, or to transfer any paper from Group II to Group III. Each paper shall be of three hours' duration, except Paper 48, for each subject of which the examination shall consist of a half-paper of two hours' duration.

16. A candidate for honours in Part IA of the Tripos shall offer Papers 1–5 from Group I.

17. A candidate for honours in Part IB shall offer five papers chosen from among Papers 1, 2, and 4 and Groups II and III, provided that

(i) a candidate who has not offered successfully Paper 5 in Part IA shall also offer Paper 5 in Part IB;[1]

(ii) a candidate who was not a candidate for honours in Part IA shall also offer Paper 5 in Part IB;

(iii) a candidate shall not offer any paper which he or she has previously offered in another University examination.

18. A candidate for honours in Part II shall

either (*a*) offer five papers chosen from among Paper 3 (Criminal law) and Groups III and IV,

or (*b*) offer four papers chosen from among Paper 3 (Criminal law) and Groups III and IV and in addition participate in a seminar course and submit an essay on a subject prescribed by the Faculty Board or chosen by the candidate from a number of subjects so prescribed,

provided that

(i) a candidate shall not offer any paper which he or she has previously offered in another University examination;

(ii) a candidate who has not previously offered Paper 1 (Civil law I) may not offer Paper 13 (Civil law II).

Seminar course.

19. A candidate who under Regulation 18 chooses to substitute for one paper of Part IB or Part II, respectively, participation in a seminar course together with submission of an essay on a prescribed subject, as provided in those regulations, shall be assessed by the Examiners for Part IB or Part II, as applicable, after they have considered a report from the lecturer or lecturers appointed by the Faculty Board to conduct the seminar course. Candidates may be called for *viva voce* examination on the subject or subjects of any seminar course in which they have participated.

The procedure for prescribing the subject or subjects of a seminar course, for notifying a candidate's intention to participate in such a course, and for assessing that participation and the essay submitted in connection with the course, shall be as follows:

(*a*) Subjects which may be prescribed shall be provisionally notified to Directors of Studies by the Faculty Board and shall be published in the *Reporter* not later than the division of the Easter Term next preceding the academical year in which the seminar courses are to be conducted.

(*b*) A candidate wishing to take part in a seminar course shall make written application to the Secretary of the Faculty Board before the end of the Easter Term next preceding the academical year in which he or she wishes to take part. The Board shall have power to accept or reject applications, having regard to the number of candidates who apply to take part in each course, and the Secretary of the Faculty Board shall notify each candidate, before 31 July, of the acceptance or rejection of his or her application. Later applications, provided that they are submitted not later than the end of the first week of Full Michaelmas Term in the academical year in which the seminar course is to be conducted, may be accepted at the discretion of the Board; if such an application is accepted, the candidate shall be notified before the division of the Michaelmas Term.

[1] Regulation 17(i) is applicable with effect from 1 October 2015.

(*c*) Subjects shall be prescribed by the Faculty Board and published in the *Reporter* before the end of the Long Vacation period of residence next preceding the academical year in which seminar courses are to be conducted. Any subject prescribed by the Faculty Board may be withdrawn by the Board upon notice given in the *Reporter* within the first three weeks of Full Michaelmas Term in the academical year in which the seminar course was to have been conducted. Each candidate who has applied to take part in such a seminar course shall be informed of its withdrawal by the Secretary of the Faculty Board.

(*d*) A lecturer conducting a seminar course shall set each candidate an essay on a prescribed subject. An essay shall not without leave of the Faculty Board exceed 12,000 words including footnotes and appendices, but excluding bibliography. Such leave may be sought no later than fourteen days before the date, specified below, by which essays must be received by the Secretary of the Faculty Board. Candidates shall be required to state in a preface the sources that they have used and to declare that the essay represents their own work unaided except as may be specified in the declaration. Essays shall be sent to the Secretary of the Faculty Board so as to arrive not later than the seventh day of Full Easter Term in the year in which the examination is to be held. A candidate who submits an essay after this date may be penalized. The essay shall be computer- or type-written.

(*e*) A lecturer conducting a seminar course shall, if not an Examiner, be an Assessor for Part IB or Part II, as applicable and shall report to the Examiners a mark for each candidate (equivalent to the mark for a paper in the examination) based upon the assessment of the candidate's essay and performance in class.

20. The Faculty Board of Law shall have power to issue from time to time supplementary regulations defining or limiting all or any of the subjects of examination, and determining the scope, character, and conditions of the papers and the credit that shall be assigned to each, and to amend or withdraw such regulations; provided that due care is taken to give sufficient notice of any supplementary regulation or of any amendment of an existing supplementary regulation. Supplementary regulations.

EXAMINATION IN LAW FOR EUROPEAN STUDENTS

1. The papers for the examination in Law for European Students shall be the papers set in Groups I–IV of the Law Tripos. Each candidate shall Papers.

either (*a*) offer three papers;

or (*b*) offer two papers and in addition participate in a seminar course and submit an essay on a subject prescribed by the Faculty Board of Law or chosen by the candidate from a number of subjects so prescribed, in accordance with the provisions of Regulation 20 for the Law Tripos.

2. A student may be a candidate for the Examination if he or she Standing of candidates.

(*a*) has been approved by the Faculty Board of Law and

(*b*) has kept one term under an exchange scheme agreed between the Faculty Board and a university of a member country of the European Community,

provided that three complete terms have not passed after the student's first term of residence.

3. The Faculty Board shall nominate such number of Examiners as they shall deem sufficient, and shall have power to nominate one or more Assessors to the Examiners. Examiners and Assessors.

4. The names of candidates who have satisfied the Examiners shall be arranged in alphabetical order in a single class. Class-list.

LINGUISTICS TRIPOS

Amended by Notice (Reporter, *2013–14, p. 531*)

1. The Linguistics Tripos shall consist of three Parts: Part I, Part IIA, and Part IIB. There shall be a separate class-list for each Part. Three Parts.

2. A student who has not obtained honours in an Honours Examination may be a candidate for honours in Part I, provided that he or she has kept one term and that three complete terms have not passed after his or her first term of residence. Standing of candidates.

3. A student who has obtained honours in another Honours Examination may be a candidate for honours in Part IIA,[1] in the year after so obtaining honours, provided that he or she has kept four terms and that twelve complete terms have not passed after his or her first term of residence.

4. A student who has obtained honours in Part IIA of the Linguistics Tripos may be a candidate for honours in Part IIB,[1] in the year after so obtaining honours, provided that he or she has kept seven terms and that fifteen terms have not passed after his or her first term of residence.

5. No student shall be a candidate for more than one Part, or for one Part and also for another Honours Examination, in the same term.

6. No student who has been a candidate for any Part shall again be a candidate for the same Part.

Examiners and Assessors.

7. For each Part of the Tripos, the Faculty Board of Modern and Medieval Languages shall nominate such number of Examiners as they think sufficient to conduct the examination, and shall have power to nominate one or more Assessors to assist the Examiners in any of the subjects of the examination. If required to do so, Assessors shall set papers in the subject or subjects assigned to them, shall mark the answers of the candidates in those papers, shall assess dissertations, and shall advise the Examiners on the performance of candidates in the examination. Assessors may be summoned to meetings of the Examiners for the purpose of consultation and advice, but shall not be entitled to vote.

8. The papers set by each Examiner or Assessor shall be submitted to the Chair of the Examiners and one other Examiner for their approval.

Supplementary regulations.

9. The Faculty Board shall have power:

(*a*) to issue from time to time supplementary regulations defining or limiting all or any of the subjects of examination and determining the scope and character of the papers, and to amend or withdraw such supplementary regulations as occasion may require, due care being taken that sufficient notice is given of any change;

(*b*) to determine the credit to be assigned to each paper, and to establish guidelines to be followed by the Examiners for assessing candidates' work in the examination and for drawing up the class-list;

(*c*) to specify papers which shall include course-work or other exercises in addition to the written paper. The details of the course-work or other exercises required of candidates and the arrangements for the submission of such course-work or other exercises shall be prescribed by the Faculty Board from time to time. Each candidate will be required to sign a declaration that the course-work or other written exercises are her or his own work, unaided except as may be specified in the declaration, and that they do not contain material that has already been used to any substantial extent for a comparable purpose.

Variable subjects.

10. Before the end of the Easter Term each year the Faculty Board shall give notice of any variable subjects for the examination to be held in the academical year next following; provided that the Board shall have the power of subsequently issuing amendments if they have due reason for doing so and if they are satisfied that no student's preparation for the examination is adversely affected.

11. In the class-lists for each Part of the Tripos the names of the candidates who obtain honours shall be placed in three classes, of which the second shall be divided into two divisions. The names in the first and third classes, and in each division of the second class, shall be arranged in alphabetical order. For special excellence a mark of distinction may be awarded.

Scheme of examination.

12. The papers set for the Linguistics Tripos shall be as follows:

Section A

Paper 1. Sounds and words (also serves as Paper X.8 of Part IB of the Asian and Middle Eastern Studies Tripos and Paper Li. 1 of the Modern and Medieval Languages Tripos)

Paper 2. Structures and meanings (also serves as Paper X.3 of Part IB of the Asian and Middle Eastern Studies Tripos and as Paper Li. 2 of the Modern and Medieval Languages Tripos)

Paper 3. Language, brain, and society (also serves as Paper X.13 of Part IB of the Asian and Middle Eastern Studies Tripos and Paper Li. 3 of the Modern and Medieval Languages Tripos)

Paper 4. History and varieties of English (also serves as Paper Li. 4 of the Modern and Medieval Languages Tripos)

Section B

Paper 5. Linguistic theory

[1] See also the regulations for Affiliated Students.

Section C

Paper 6. Phonetics (also serves as Paper Li. 6 of the Modern and Medieval Languages Tripos)
Paper 7. Phonological theory (also serves as Paper Li. 7 of the Modern and Medieval Languages Tripos)[1]
Paper 8. Morphology (also serves as Paper Li. 8 of the Modern and Medieval Languages Tripos)[1]
Paper 9. Syntax (also serves as Paper Li. 9 of the Modern and Medieval Languages Tripos)
Paper 10. Semantics and pragmatics (also serves as Paper Li. 10 of the Modern and Medieval Languages Tripos)
Paper 11. Historical linguistics (also serves as Paper 15(*a*) of Part II of the Anglo-Saxon, Norse, and Celtic Tripos, as Paper 43A of Part II of the English Tripos (New Regulations), and as Paper Li. 11 of the Modern and Medieval Languages Tripos)[2]
Paper 12. History of ideas on language (also serves as Paper O1 of Part II of the Classical Tripos and Paper Li. 12 of the Modern and Medieval Languages Tripos)[3]
Paper 13. History of the English language (also serves as Paper 15(*b*) of Part II of the Anglo-Saxon, Norse, and Celtic Tripos, Paper Li. 13 of the Modern and Medieval Languages Tripos and as Paper 43B of Part II of the English Tripos (New Regulations))[3]
Paper 14. History of the French language (also serves as Paper Li.14 of the Modern and Medieval Languages Tripos)[4]
Paper 15. First and second language acquisition (also serves as Paper Li.15 of the Modern and Medieval Languages Tripos)
Paper 16. Psychology of language processing and learning (also serves as Paper Li.16 of the Modern and Medieval Languages Tripos)
Paper 17. A subject in linguistics to be specified by the Faculty Board from time to time (also serves as Paper Li. 17 of the Modern and Medieval Languages Tripos)
Paper 18. Computational linguistics (also serves as Paper Li.18 of the Modern and Medieval Languages Tripos)
Paper 19. A subject in linguistics to be specified by the Faculty Board from time to time[5]

Section D

Paper 20. The language of Italy (Paper It. 10 of the Modern and Medieval Languages Tripos)
Paper 21. The Hispanic languages (Paper Sp. 11 of the Modern and Medieval Languages Tripos)
Paper 22. Aspects of the history of the German language (Paper Ge. 11 of the Modern and Medieval Languages Tripos)
Paper 23. The history of the Russian language (Paper Sl. 8 of the Modern and Medieval Languages Tripos)
Paper 24. The history and structure of modern Greek (Paper Gr. 7 of the Modern and Medieval Languages Tripos)
Paper 25. The Romance languages (Paper CS 1 of the Modern and Medieval Languages Tripos)
Paper 26. The Slavonic languages (Paper CS 3 of the Modern and Medieval Languages Tripos)
Paper 27. Celtic philology (Paper 12 of Part II of the Anglo-Saxon, Norse, and Celtic Tripos)
Paper 28. Elements of comparative linguistics (Paper E1 of Part II of the Classical Tripos)
Paper 29. The Greek language (Paper E2 of Part II of the Classical Tripos)
Paper 30. The Latin language (Paper E3 of Part II of the Classical Tripos)
Paper 31. Germanic philology (Paper 11 of Part II of the Anglo-Saxon, Norse, and Celtic Tripos)
Paper 32. Comparative Semitic linguistics (Paper MES.41 of Part II of the Asian and Middle Eastern Studies Tripos)
Paper 33. The French language: variation and change (Paper Fr.13 of the Modern and Medieval Languages Tripos)

13. A candidate for Part I of the Linguistics Tripos shall offer Papers 1–4.

14. (i) A candidate who takes the examination for Part IIA after obtaining honours in Part I of the Linguistics Tripos shall offer four papers chosen from Sections C and D.

(ii) A candidate who takes the examination for Part IIA in the year next after obtaining honours in another Honours Examination shall offer:

(*a*) Papers 1 and 2;

(*b*) two papers chosen from Sections C and D;

provided that a candidate who has previously offered one or both of Papers 1 and 2 in a previous Honours Examination shall substitute that paper or both papers by either one further paper or two further papers, respectively, chosen from Sections C and D.

[1] No candidate who offered Paper 8 ‘Phonology and morphology’ for examination in the Linguistics Tripos, Part IIA, in 2014 shall offer either Paper 7 or Paper 8 for examination in Part IIB in 2015.
[2] This paper will be suspended in 2015–16 and in each alternate year thereafter until further notice.
[3] This paper will be suspended in 2014–15 and in each alternate year thereafter until further notice.
[4] This paper will be suspended in both 2014–15 and 2015–16; and in each alternate year thereafter.
[5] Not available for examination in 2014–15.

15. A candidate who takes the examination for Part IIB shall offer:

(*a*) Paper 5;

(*b*) two papers chosen from Sections C and D, provided that a candidate shall not offer a paper that he or she has previously offered in another Honours Examination;

(*c*) a dissertation submitted under the provisions of Regulation 16.

Dissertation.

16. The following provisions shall apply to a dissertation offered under Regulation 15:

(*a*) Every dissertation shall be on a subject that falls within the scope of papers from Section C. A candidate shall not offer a dissertation on a subject that falls substantially within the scope of any paper that he or she intends to offer in the examination.

(*b*) A candidate shall submit the proposed title of the dissertation, together with a statement of the scheme of papers to be offered in the examination, through her or his Tutor to the Secretary of the Faculty Board so as to arrive not later than the third Friday of the Full Michaelmas Term next preceding the examination. A candidate shall obtain the approval of the proposed title by the Faculty Board not later than the last day of that Full Term.

(*c*) When the Faculty Board have approved a title, no change may subsequently be made in it, except that a candidate may apply to the Faculty Board for permission to revise the title of that dissertation; such an application shall be submitted not later than the second Friday of the Full Lent Term next preceding the examination.

(*d*) A dissertation shall be in English, but quotations from primary sources may be given in the language of the original provided an English translation is also given. A dissertation shall be typewritten, except where a non-Roman or symbolic typeface is necessary and cannot be provided; in such a case hand-written or photocopied extracts may be inserted. A dissertation shall normally be of not less than 8,000 words and in any case not more than 10,000 words in length (including notes but excluding appendices and bibliography).

(*e*) Two copies of the dissertation shall be submitted, in accordance with detailed arrangements approved by the Faculty Board, so as to reach the Secretary of the Faculty Board not later than the Monday of the last week of the Full Lent Term next preceding the examination. Each candidate will be required to sign a declaration that the dissertation is her or his own work, unaided except as may be specified in the declaration, and that it does not contain material that has already been used to any substantial extent for a comparable purpose.

(*f*) A candidate may be called for *viva voce* examination on the subject of her or his dissertation.

SUPPLEMENTARY REGULATION

Paper 6. Phonetics

The examination for this paper will consist of a written paper and a practical component. The practical component will assess competence in impressionistic and quantitative phonetic methods.

MANAGEMENT STUDIES TRIPOS

One Part.

1. The Management Studies Tripos shall consist of one Part only.

Standing of candidates.

2. The following may present themselves as candidates for honours in the Management Studies Tripos if twelve terms have not passed after their first term of residence:

(*a*) a student who has obtained honours in an Honours Examination in the first, second, or third term after his or her first term of residence, and has subsequently been successful in a Preliminary Examination;

(*b*) a student who has obtained honours in an Honours Examination in the fourth, fifth, or sixth term after his or her first term of residence.[1]

3. No student shall be a candidate for the Management Studies Tripos and also for another Tripos Examination in the same term, and no student shall be a candidate for the Management Studies Tripos on more than one occasion.

Examiners and Assessors.

4. The Faculty Board of Business and Management shall nominate such number of Examiners as they think sufficient. They may also nominate for appointment one or more Assessors to the Examiners in such subjects as they consider desirable, and the Assessors so appointed shall set papers or parts of

[1] See also the regulations for Affiliated Students.

papers and shall advise the Examiners on the performance of candidates in those subjects. The Assessors, when summoned by the Chair, shall attend meetings of the Examiners for the purpose of consultation and advice, but shall not be entitled to vote.

5. The questions proposed by each Examiner or Assessor shall be submitted to the whole body of Examiners for approval. Questions.

6. The names of the candidates who obtain honours shall be arranged in three classes of which the second shall be divided into two divisions. The names in the first and third classes and in each division of the second class shall be arranged in alphabetical order. For special excellence a mark of distinction may be awarded. Class-list.

7. The Faculty Board of Business and Management shall have power to define or limit by supplementary regulations all or any of the subjects of examination, and to modify or alter any such supplementary regulations as occasion may require. They shall also have power to determine the credit that shall be assigned to each subject of examination, and to mark out the lines of study that are to be pursued by candidates. Supplementary regulations.

8. The following papers shall be set: Scheme of examination.

M1. Marketing and organizational behaviour.
M2. Quantitative methods and operations management.
M3. Economics and finance.

9. Each candidate shall offer all three papers, and shall submit to the Examiners, not later than the last Monday of Full Easter Term, a report, of not more than 6,000 words, excluding footnotes and bibliography, on a project designed to give evidence of the candidate's industrial, commercial, or equivalent experience. The subject of the project shall be chosen from a list of approved subjects which shall be announced by the Director of Judge Business School not later than the last day of Full Lent Term. Reports shall be in typewritten form (unless a candidate has obtained previous permission from the Faculty Board of Business and Management to present a report in manuscript). Each candidate will be required to sign a declaration that the project and the report on it are his or her own work, unaided except as may be specified in the declaration, and that the report does not contain material that has already been used to any substantial extent for a comparable purpose; if two or more candidates have undertaken a project in collaboration, they will each be required to indicate the extent of their contribution.

10. Candidates shall complete course-work for two elective courses, which shall be chosen from a list published by the Faculty Board of Business and Management. For this purpose the internal Examiner for the course-work shall present to the Examiners a report on the performance of each candidate in this coursework. Details of the work required of candidates shall be published by the Faculty Board by notice not later than the beginning of the Full Michaelmas Term preceding the examination. Course-work.

SUPPLEMENTARY REGULATIONS

M1. Marketing and organizational behaviour

The paper will consist mainly of questions on the theory and practice of marketing and the organization and behaviour of people at work.

M2. Quantitative methods and operations management

The paper will consist mainly of questions on the quantitative methods used in management and operations management.

M3. Economics and finance

The paper will consist mainly of questions on the economics of firms and markets, the theory of finance, and financial accounting.

MANUFACTURING ENGINEERING TRIPOS

Amended by Notice (Reporter, *2013–14, p. 56*)

1. The Manufacturing Engineering Tripos shall consist of two Parts: Parts IIA and IIB. There shall be a separate class-list for each Part. Two Parts.

2. A student who has obtained honours in Part IB of the Engineering Tripos or in Part I of the Chemical Engineering Tripos may be a candidate for honours in Part IIA of the Manufacturing Standing of candidates.

Engineering Tripos in the year after so obtaining honours, provided that the student has kept seven terms and that twelve complete terms have not passed after his or her first term of residence.

3. The Faculty Board of Engineering may in special circumstances, which they shall themselves determine, give leave to a student who has obtained honours in any Honours Examination to be a candidate for honours in Part IIA of the Manufacturing Engineering Tripos in the year after so obtaining honours, provided that he or she has attained a satisfactory standard, as defined by the Faculty Board, in his or her last Honours Examination, and provided also that the student has kept seven terms and that twelve complete terms have not passed after his or her first term of residence.

Period of study at Massachusetts Institute of Technology.

4. A student who, under arrangements approved by the Faculty Board of Engineering, has spent not less than three terms studying at the Massachusetts Institute of Technology and has been certified by the President of the Institute after consultation with the Chair of Examiners for Part IIA of the Manufacturing Engineering Tripos to have studied diligently during that period, shall be deemed thereby to have obtained honours in that Part of the Tripos. A list containing the names of persons so qualified shall be certified by the Chair of the Faculty Board of Engineering and published in the *Reporter*.

5. A student who has obtained honours in Part IIA of the Manufacturing Engineering Tripos or has been deemed to have obtained honours in Part IIA of the Manufacturing Engineering Tripos under Regulation 4 may be a candidate for honours in Part IIB in the year next after or next but one after so obtaining honours, provided that he or she

(*a*) has attained a satisfactory standard, as defined by the Faculty Board, in previous Honours Examinations;

(*b*) has not proceeded to the B.A. Degree;

(*c*) presents a reasoned case to the Faculty Board by the Division of Easter Term of the year in which Part IIA is taken should he or she wish to proceed to Part IIB in the year next but one after obtaining honours in Part IIA;

provided always that fifteen complete terms have not passed after the student's first term of residence.

6. No student shall be a candidate for either Part and also for another Honours Examination in the same term.

Examiners and Assessors.

7. The Faculty Board of Engineering shall nominate such number of Examiners for each Part of the Tripos as they shall consider sufficient. The Examiners for each Part shall elect one of their number to act as Chair. The Faculty Board may nominate one or more Assessors to the Examiners in each Part of the Tripos. Assessors shall be responsible *either* for setting the paper or papers or questions assigned to them *or* for looking over the work of the candidates therein and presenting a report to the Examiners *or* both, as the Examiners may decide. The Assessors, when summoned by the Chair, shall attend meetings of the Examiners for the purpose of consultation and advice, but shall not be entitled to vote.

Questions.

8. In each Part of the Tripos the questions proposed by each Examiner or Assessor shall be submitted to the whole body of Examiners for approval.

Course-work.

9. The Examiners for each Part of the Tripos shall take into account such course-work done by candidates as shall from time to time be determined by the Faculty Board of Engineering. For this purpose the Head of the Department of Engineering shall present to the Examiners a detailed report on the performance of each candidate in this course-work. Details of the work required of candidates for each Part shall be published by the Faculty Board of Engineering by Notice in the Department of Engineering not later than the beginning of the Full Michaelmas Term preceding the examination. Every candidate submitting course-work under this regulation shall be required to sign a declaration that the work submitted is her or his own work, unaided except as may be specified in the declaration; if two or more candidates have undertaken work in collaboration, they shall be required to indicate the extent of their collaboration.

Class-lists.

10. In Part IIA the names of the candidates who obtain honours shall be arranged in three classes of which the second shall be divided into two divisions. The names of those in the first and third classes and in each division of the second class shall be arranged in alphabetical order. For special excellence in Part IIA a mark of distinction may be awarded. In Part IIB the names of the candidates who obtain honours shall be arranged in alphabetical order in a single class and distinctive marks shall be attached to the names of those candidates who in the opinion of the Examiners deserve special credit. The mark (*d*) shall be used to denote a distinguished performance, and the mark (*m*) a meritorious performance.

11. The Faculty Board of Engineering shall have power to publish supplementary regulations defining the scope and character of each of the examination papers and to amend such supplementary regulations from time to time as they may think fit. Any alteration of supplementary regulations shall be published before the division of the Easter Term in the academical year before that in which it is to have effect. Supplementary regulations

PART IIA

12. The examination for Part IIA of the Manufacturing Engineering Tripos shall consist of ten modules which shall be examined by either written examination, essays or course-work as specified by the Faculty Board of Engineering. Scheme of examination for Part IIA.

Not later than the end of the Easter Term each year the Faculty Board shall give notice of the modules prescribed for the examination to be held in the academical year next following, and shall specify the mode of examination for each module. In giving such notice the Faculty Board shall ensure that the examination shall provide for written papers whose total duration shall be at least twelve hours.

13. In order to obtain honours in Part IIA, a candidate must satisfy the Examiners that he or she has such industrial or equivalent experience as shall be determined from time to time by the Faculty Board; a statement of each candidate's experience shall be certified by the Head of the Department of Engineering.

PART IIB

14. The examination for Part IIB shall consist of two written papers. Part IIB.

SUPPLEMENTARY REGULATIONS

PART IIB

Paper 1 shall consist mainly of questions on technological aspects of manufacturing.
Paper 2 shall consist mainly of questions on managerial aspects of manufacturing.

MATHEMATICAL TRIPOS

GENERAL

1. The Mathematical Tripos shall consist of four Parts, Part IA, Part IB, Part II, and Part III. Four Parts.

2. The Faculty Board shall nominate such number of Examiners as they think sufficient for each Part of the Tripos, and shall also have power to nominate one or more Assessors for each Part. Assessors shall propose questions in the papers or parts of papers assigned to them by the Examiners, shall mark the answers of the candidates in those papers or parts of papers, and shall advise the Examiners on the performance of candidates in the examination. Assessors may be summoned to meetings of the Examiners for the purpose of consultation and advice, but shall not be entitled to vote. Examiners and Assessors

PART IA

3. A candidate shall offer one of the following options: Scheme of examination for Part IA.

(*a*) Pure and Applied Mathematics

(*b*) Mathematics with Physics.

The examination for Part IA shall consist of five papers. The Faculty Board of Mathematics shall determine how the questions on the various subjects shall be distributed among the papers.

4. Every candidate shall offer Papers 1, 2, and 3, and one additional paper as follows:

(*a*) A candidate offering Option (*a*) shall offer Paper 4.

(*b*) A candidate offering Option (*b*) shall offer the subject Physics from Part IA of the Natural Sciences Tripos (the written paper and the submission of note-books).

5. The following may present themselves as candidates for honours in Part IA: Standing of candidates.

(*a*) a student who has kept one term, provided that three complete terms have not passed after his or her first term of residence;

(*b*) a student who has obtained honours in another Honours Examination in the year next after so obtaining honours, provided that nine complete terms have not passed after his or her first term of residence.

No student shall be a candidate for Part IA on more than one occasion.

Class-list.

6. The names of the candidates who have obtained honours shall be placed in three classes, of which the second shall be divided into two divisions. The names in the first and third classes and in each division of the second class shall be arranged in alphabetical order. The symbol (*p*) shall be placed against the names of those candidates who have satisfied the Examiners in the option Mathematics with Physics.

PART IB

Scheme of examination for Part IB.

7. The examination for Part IB shall consist of four papers. The Faculty Board shall determine how the questions on the various subjects shall be distributed among the papers.

Standing of candidates.

8. A student who has obtained honours in an Honours Examination may be a candidate for honours in Part IB in the year next after so obtaining honours, provided that twelve complete terms have not passed after his or her first term of residence.[1] No student shall be a candidate for Part IB on more than one occasion.

9. Candidates for Part IB may submit note-books containing records of practical work done by them. Such practical work shall be prescribed from time to time by the Faculty Board of Mathematics, and shall be carried out in accordance with instructions which shall be announced not later than the division of the Michaelmas Term next preceding the examination by the Head of the Department in which the work is to be performed. As an indication of good faith, each candidate shall submit, with the records of his or her work, a declaration that these instructions have been observed. The Head of the Department shall present an assessment of this work to the Examiners, and the Examiners shall take account of this assessment in drawing up the class-list. Candidates may be examined *viva voce* on their submitted work.

Class-list.

10. The names of the candidates who have obtained honours shall be placed in three classes, of which the second shall be divided into two divisions. The names in the first and third classes and in each division of the second class shall be arranged in alphabetical order.

Period of study at Massachusetts Institute of Technology.

11. A candidate who, under arrangements approved by the Faculty Board of Mathematics, has spent not less than three terms studying at the Massachusetts Institute of Technology and has been certified by the President of the Institute after consultation with the Chair of Examiners for Part IB of the Mathematical Tripos to have studied diligently during that period, shall be deemed thereby to have obtained honours in Part IB of the Mathematical Tripos. A list containing the names of persons so qualified shall be certified by the Chair of the Faculty Board of Mathematics and published in the *Reporter*.

PART II

Schemes of examination for Part II.

12. The examination for Part II shall consist of four papers. The Faculty Board shall determine how the questions on the various subjects shall be distributed among the papers.

Standing of candidates.

13. A student who has obtained honours in an Honours Examination other than Part IA of the Mathematical Tripos may be a candidate for honours in Part II in the year next or next but one after so obtaining honours, provided that he or she has kept four terms and that twelve complete terms have not passed after his or her first term of residence.[1] No student shall be a candidate for Part II on more than one occasion.

Records of practical work.

14. Candidates for Part II may submit note-books containing records of practical work done by them. Such practical work shall be prescribed from time to time by the Faculty Board of Mathematics, and shall be carried out in accordance with instructions which shall be announced not later than the division of the Michaelmas Term next preceding the examination by the Head of the Department in which the work is to be performed. As an indication of good faith, each candidate shall submit, with the records of his or her work, a declaration that these instructions have been observed. The Head of the Department shall present an assessment of this work to the Examiners, and the Examiners shall

[1] See also the regulations for Affiliated Students.

take account of this assessment in drawing up the class-list. Candidates may be examined *viva voce* on their submitted work.

15. The names of the candidates who have obtained honours shall be placed in three classes: Wranglers, Senior Optimes, and Junior Optimes, of which the Senior Optimes shall be divided into two divisions. The names of the Wranglers and of the Junior Optimes and of those in each division of the Senior Optimes shall be arranged in alphabetical order. Class-list.

PART III

16. The examination for Part III shall comprise written papers, each of which shall be set for either two hours or three hours, and topics for an optional essay. The number of papers that the Faculty Board intend to set and the subject and duration of each paper shall be announced by the Board not later than 1 November next preceding the examination. A member of the Faculty may request that a paper or papers be set additional to those announced, provided that such a request is made to the Secretary of the Faculty Board no later than the division of the Michaelmas Term next preceding the examination. The member of the Faculty shall take responsibility for preparing a proposal that will contain an outline syllabus and shall agree to set and assess the examination if so requested by the Examiners. The subject and duration of each additional paper that the Faculty Board agree to set shall be announced by them not later than the last day of the Full Michaelmas Term next preceding the examination. Scheme of examination for Part III.

17. Each candidate shall send, through his or her Director of Studies, to the Chair of Examiners, so as to arrive before the end of the second Friday of the Full Easter Term in which the examination is to be held, the titles of the papers that he or she wishes to offer. No candidate shall offer papers whose total duration amounts to more than nineteen hours or, if the candidate has submitted an essay in accordance with the provisions of Regulation 19, papers whose total duration amounts to more than sixteen hours.

18. Before the last day of the Full Michaelmas Term next preceding the examination the Examiners shall announce a number of topics for an essay. A candidate may request that an essay may be submitted on a topic other than those announced, provided that the request is made, through the candidate's Director of Studies, so as to reach the Secretary of the Faculty Board not later than 1 February next preceding the examination. Any additional topics approved by the Examiners shall be announced by them not later than 1 March next preceding the examination. Essay.

19. Each candidate may submit an essay on any one topic that has been announced. A candidate who desires to do so shall, through his or her Director of Studies, so inform the Chair of Examiners before the end of the first quarter of the Easter Term in which the examination is to be held, and shall submit the essay, through his or her Director of Studies, so as to reach the Chair of Examiners not later than the end of the second Friday of the Full Easter Term. Each essay shall state the sources consulted; it shall be prefaced by a declaration signed by the candidate that it represents the candidate's own work unaided except as may be specified in the declaration, and that it does not contain material that the candidate has already used to any substantial extent for a comparable purpose. The Examiners shall have power at their discretion, to examine a candidate *viva voce* on the subject of his or her essay.

20. The following may be a candidate for honours in Part III: Standing of candidates.

(*a*) a student who has obtained honours in Part II of the Mathematical Tripos, in the year next after so obtaining honours, provided that he or she has attained a satisfactory standard as prescribed by the Faculty Board of Mathematics in previous Honours Examinations;

(*b*) a student who has obtained honours or who has been deemed to have obtained honours in any Honours Examination other than Part II of the Mathematical Tripos, in the year next after so obtaining honours, provided that he or she has been given leave to do so by the Faculty Board of Mathematics;

always provided that he or she has not proceeded to the B.A. Degree.

21. No student shall be a candidate for Part III on more than one occasion, or for Part III and for another Honours Examination in the same term.

22. The names of the candidates who have obtained honours in the examination for Part III shall be arranged in alphabetical order in one class. Distinctive marks shall be attached to the names of those candidates who in the opinion of the Examiners deserve special credit. The mark (*d*) shall be used to denote a distinguished performance, and the mark (*m*) a meritorious performance. Class-list.

MEDICAL AND VETERINARY SCIENCES TRIPOS

Amended by Notices (Reporter, *2013–14, pp. 251 and 665*)

General

Two Parts.

1. The Medical and Veterinary Sciences Tripos shall consist of two Parts: Part IA and Part IB.

Standing of candidates.

2. The following may present themselves as candidates for honours in Part IA:

(*a*) a student who has not obtained honours in another Honours Examination, provided that he or she has kept one term and that three complete terms have not passed after his or her first term of residence,[1]

(*b*) a student who has obtained honours in another Honours Examination, in the year after so obtaining honours, provided that nine complete terms have not passed after his or her first term of residence.

3. A student who has obtained honours in Part IA of the Medical and Veterinary Sciences Tripos may be a candidate for honours in Part IB in the year after so obtaining honours, provided that twelve complete terms have not passed after his or her first term of residence.

4. Notwithstanding the provisions of Regulations 2 and 3, a student who is above the standing for honours may be a candidate not for honours in Part IA and Part IB for the purpose of becoming qualified to be a candidate subsequently for the Final M.B. Examination or for Part I of the Final Veterinary Examination.

5. No student shall be a candidate for more than one Part, or for any Part and another Honours Examination, in the same term.

6. No student who has been a candidate for any Part shall again be a candidate for the same Part.

7. The Faculty Board of Biology shall have power to issue from time to time supplementary regulations defining or limiting all or any of the subjects of the examinations for Part IA and Part IB. Due care shall be taken that sufficient notice is given of any alteration of such supplementary regulations.

Examiners and Assessors.

8. There shall be two bodies of Examiners, one for each Part of the Tripos. For each of the two bodies there shall be a Chair of Examiners and an Assistant Chair, appointed on the nomination of the Faculty Board of Biology.

9. In each Part of the Tripos there shall be appointed for each subject a Senior Examiner and such number of Examiners and Assessors as are required to conduct the examination.

The Examiners shall be nominated by the Faculty Board of Biology.

Duties of Examiners.

10. The Examiners in each subject shall be jointly responsible for all the questions set in that subject. The work of each candidate in any subject shall be tested by at least two Examiners in the subject, and the Examiners in each subject shall be jointly responsible for the marks in that subject. At least two Examiners or one Examiner and one Assessor shall set and conduct every oral and practical examination. The Examiners shall have regard to the style and method of candidates' answers, and shall give credit for excellence in these respects.

Duties of Assessors.

11. The Assessors shall propose questions in the parts of the subjects assigned to them by the Examiners, shall look over the answers of the candidates to those questions, and shall report thereon to the Examiners. The Assessors may be required to assist the Examiners in setting and conducting every oral and practical examination. The Assessors may be summoned to meetings of the Examiners for the purpose of consultation and advice, but shall not be entitled to vote.

Communication of marks.

12. The Chair shall communicate the marks of all candidates to the Registrary.

13. The names of candidates who, having presented themselves under Regulation 4, attain the prescribed standard shall be published by the Examiners in lists headed 'The following (who are not candidates for honours) have attained the honours standard'.

Part IA

Scheme of examination for Part IA.

14. In Part IA the examination shall consist of the following subjects:

Functional Architecture of the Body (FAB)
Homeostasis (HOM)
Molecules in Medical Science (MIMS)
Veterinary Anatomy and Physiology (VAP)

[1] See also the regulations for Affiliated Students.

15. The examination in each subject shall consist of *either* two written papers *or* one written paper and a practical examination, covering three sections numbered I–III, as specified below. In addition, the examination in Homeostasis shall include the submission of reports of practical work.

(*a*) The examination in Homeostasis shall consist of:

(i) one written paper of three hours, which shall contain compulsory short-answer questions (Section I)[1] and essay questions (Section III); candidates will be allowed one hour to complete Section I;

(ii) a practical examination of two hours (Section II);[1]

(iii) reports of practical work which shall be submitted to the Examiners by the dates published in the practical handbook. In assigning marks for the examination, the Examiners may take account of the reports.

(*b*) The examination in Molecules in Medical Science shall consist of:

(i) one written paper of three hours, which shall contain compulsory short-answer questions (Section I) and practical questions (Section II);[1] candidates will be allowed one hour to complete Section I;

(ii) one written paper of two hours (Section III).

(*c*) The examination in Functional Architecture of the Body shall consist of:

(i) one written paper of two hours and 45 minutes, which shall contain compulsory short-answer questions (Section I)[1] and essay questions (Section III); candidates will be allowed 45 minutes to complete Section I;

(ii) a practical examination of one and a half hours (Section II)[1].

(*d*) The examination in Veterinary Anatomy and Physiology shall consist of:

(i) one written paper of three hours, which shall contain compulsory short-answer questions (Section I)[1] and essay questions (Section III); candidates will be allowed one hour to complete Section I;

(ii) a practical examination of two hours (Section II)[1].

16. In each subject the examination shall carry the same maximum marks; the maximum marks allocated to Sections I and II together shall be equal to the maximum marks allocated to the remaining parts of the examination in that subject.

17. Every candidate shall offer the subjects Homeostasis and Molecules in Medical Science, and *either* Functional Architecture of the Body *or* Veterinary Anatomy and Physiology.

18. The names of the candidates who obtain honours in Part IA shall be arranged in three classes, of which the second shall be divided into two divisions. The names in the first and third classes, and in each division of the second class, shall be arranged in alphabetical order.

PART IB

19. In Part IB the examination shall consist of the following subjects:

Biology of Disease (BOD)
Comparative Vertebrate Biology (CVB)
⟨Head and Neck Anatomy (HNA)⟩[2]
Human Reproduction (HR)
Mechanisms of Drug Action (MODA)
Neurobiology with Animal Behaviour (NAB)
Neurobiology with Human Behaviour (NHB)
Veterinary Reproductive Biology (VRB)

20. The examination in each subject shall consist of one written paper and a practical examination, covering three sections numbered (I)–(III) as specified below. Scheme of examination for Part IB.

(*a*) The examinations in Biology of Disease and in Mechanisms of Drug Action shall each consist of:

(i) one written paper of three hours, which shall contain compulsory short-answer questions (Section I)[3] and essay questions (Section III); candidates will be allowed one hour to complete Section I;

[1] In each subject of Part IA Sections I and II of the examination also serve as the examination in the corresponding subject of the Second M.B. Examination or the Second Vet.M.B. Examination.

[2] The subject in angular brackets will be inserted with effect from the 2015 examinations.

[3] In each subject of Part IB Sections I and II of the examination also serve as the examination in the corresponding subject of the Second M.B. Examination or the Second Vet.M.B. Examination.

(ii) a practical examination of two hours (Section II).[1]

[(*b*) The examinations in Neurobiology with Human Behaviour, and in Neurobiology with Animal Behaviour shall each consist of:

(i) one written paper of three hours, which shall contain compulsory short-answer questions (Section I)[1] and essay questions (Section III); candidates will be allowed one hour to complete Section I;

(ii) a practical examination of one hour (Section II).[1]][2]

⟨(*b*) The examination in Neurobiology with Animal Behaviour shall consist of:

(i) one written paper of three hours, which shall contain compulsory short-answer questions (Section I) and essay questions (Section III); candidates will be allowed one hour to complete Section I;

(ii) a practical examination of one hour (Section II).

(*c*) The examination in Neurobiology with Human Behaviour shall consist of:

(i) one written paper of one and a half hours which shall contain compulsory short-answer questions (Section I);

(ii) a practical examination of one hour (Section II);

(iii) one written paper of three hours (Section III) which shall contain essay questions on Neurobiology and Psychology of Medicine⟩[2]

(*c*) The examinations in Human Reproduction and in Veterinary Reproductive Biology shall each consist of:

(i) one written paper of two-and-a-half hours, which shall contain compulsory short-answer questions (Section I)[1] and essay questions (Section III); candidates will be allowed one hour to complete Section I;

(ii) a practical examination of one hour (Section II).[1]

(*d*) The examination in Comparative Vertebrate Biology shall consist of:

(i) a combined written and practical paper of an hour and a half, which shall contain short answer questions (Section I) and a practical examination (Section II)[1]; candidates will be allowed forty-five minutes to complete each section;

(ii) one written paper of one-and-a-half hours, which shall contain essay questions (Section III).

⟨(*f*) The examination in Head and Neck Anatomy shall consist of combined written and practical papers totalling an hour and a half, which shall contain a practical paper (Sections I and II) and short answer questions (Section III).⟩[3]

21. Every candidate shall offer the following for the examination:

[*either* (*a*) the written papers and practical examinations for each subject in Scheme A and a further written paper (Special Options) of three hours' duration, which shall contain questions on topics offered in each of the subjects in Scheme A;

or (*b*) the written papers and practical examinations for each subject in Scheme B.][4]

⟨*either* (*a*) the written papers and practical examinations for each subject in Scheme A;

or (*b*) the written papers and practical examinations for each subject in Scheme B.⟩[4]

Scheme A

Biology of Disease (BOD)
⟨Head and Neck Anatomy (HNA)⟩[5]
Human Reproduction (HR)
Mechanisms of Drug Action (MODA)
Neurobiology with Human Behaviour (NHB)

[1] In each subject of Part IB Sections I and II of the examination also serve as the examination in the corresponding subject of the Second M.B. Examination or the Second Vet.M.B. Examination.

[2] The paragraph in square brackets will be replaced by the paragraphs in angular brackets and the subsequent paragraphs accordingly renumbered with effect from the 2015 examinations.

[3] The paragraph in angular brackets will be inserted with effect from the 2015 examinations.

[4] The paragraphs in square brackets will be replaced by the paragraphs in angular brackets with effect from the 2015 examinations.

[5] The subject in angular brackets will be inserted with effect from the 2015 examinations.

SCHEME B

Biology of Disease (BOD)
Veterinary Reproductive Biology (VRB)
Mechanisms of Drug Action (MODA)
Neurobiology with Animal Behaviour (NAB)
Comparative Vertebrate Biology (CVB)

22. The maximum marks allocated to the examination in each subject or paper shall be in the following proportions:

Biology of Disease (BOD)	10
Comparative Vertebrate Biology (CVB)	8
⟨Head and Neck Anatomy (HNA)	4⟩[1]
Human Reproduction (HR)	8
Mechanisms of Drug Action (MODA)	10
Neurobiology with Animal Behaviour (NAB)	10
[Neurobiology with Human Behaviour (NHB)	10][2]
⟨Neurobiology with Human Behaviour (NHB)	14⟩[2]
Veterinary Reproductive Biology (VRB)	8
Special Options paper	8

For the examinations in each subject, the maximum marks for Sections I and II together shall be equal to the maximum marks allocated to Section III.

[**23.** Public notice of the topics covered in the Special Options paper shall be given by the Faculty Board not later than the division of the Easter Term of the year next preceding the examination concerned, provided that the Board shall have the power of subsequently issuing amendments if they have due reason for doing so and if they are satisfied that no student's preparation for the examination is adversely affected. The Faculty Board shall have power:

(*a*) in giving notice of Special Options, to announce restrictions on the number of candidates who may be permitted to offer a particular Special Option;

(*b*) if a particular Special Option is over-subscribed, to allocate candidates to other Special Options, using a procedure which takes account of their expressed preferences as far as is practicable.][3]

24. The names of the candidates who obtain honours in Part IB shall be arranged in three classes, of which the second shall be divided into two divisions. The names in the first and third classes, and in each division of the second class, shall be arranged in alphabetical order. Class-list for Part IB.

SUPPLEMENTARY REGULATIONS

PART IA

Functional Architecture of the Body (FAB)

Section I will consist of compulsory short-answer questions on tissue anatomy, aspects of organogenesis, the topographical, functional, and applied anatomy of the human body. Section II will consist of a practical examination and will cover similar aspects. In Section III, candidates will be required to write essays.

Homeostasis (HOM)

Section I will contain computer-marked and short-answer questions on nerve and neuromuscular transmission, muscle, autonomic nervous system, cardiovascular system, respiration, kidney, salt and water balance, digestion, absorption, and temperature regulation. Section II will contain questions on the practical work in experimental physiology and histology. Section III will contain essay questions. Candidates will also be required to submit note-books containing records of practical work (see Regulation 15(*a*)(iii)).

Molecules in Medical Science (MIMS)

The examination will test knowledge and understanding of the material contained in the MIMS course. Section I will consist of short-answer questions on the lecture material. Section II will consist of questions on practical aspects, including interpretation and handling of data. Section III will contain essay questions and will consist of three subsections, A, B, and C, each containing a choice of questions. Candidates will be required to answer one question from each subsection. Subsection A will relate principally to the lectures given in the Michaelmas Term, subsection B principally to the lectures given in the Lent and Easter Terms, and subsection C to the entire course of lectures and practicals. The nature of the questions in Section III will be to test integrated understanding rather than detailed factual knowledge.

[1] The subject in angular brackets will be inserted with effect from the 2015 examinations.
[2] The entry in angular brackets will replace the entry in square brackets with effect from the 2015 examinations.
[3] The regulation in square brackets will be rescinded and the following regulation renumbered with effect from the 2015 examinations.

Veterinary Anatomy and Physiology (*VAP*)

Section I will consist of computer-marked and short-answer questions on the anatomy of domestic mammals and on the structure and function of the gastrointestinal systems of herbivorous mammals. Section II will consist of questions on associated practical work. In Section III, candidates will be required to write two or three essays chosen from not fewer than eight.

PART IB

Biology of Disease (*BOD*)

The examination in BOD will be treated from the standpoint of abnormal biology. It will include the variations that may occur in the structure and functions of living cells, tissues, and organs, together with the biology of parasites, bacteria, and viruses. Section I will consist of compulsory short-answer questions on the lecture material. Section III will consist of essay questions. Section II will consist of a two-hour practical examination which will include laboratory work and questions on practical aspects and problem solving.

Comparative Vertebrate Biology (*CVB*)

The examination will require knowledge of the structure and function of birds, fish, amphibians and reptiles, and certain species of laboratory animal.

⟨*Head and Neck Anatomy* (*HNA*)

The examination will require knowledge of the structure and function of the human head and neck.⟩[1]

Human Reproduction (*HR*)

Section I will consist of compulsory short-answer questions and Section II will consist of practical questions. Section III will consist of a written paper that will contain essay questions on reproductive biology and the social and ethical aspects of reproduction and the effects of reproductive activity on populations.

Mechanisms of Drug Action (*MODA*)

Sections I and III of the examination in MODA will require knowledge of the actions of drugs on whole organisms and mammalian systems, and also of the mode of drug action at the cellular, sub-cellular, and molecular levels. Section I will include compulsory short-answer questions and Section III will include essay questions. Section II will consist of a practical examination and will include questions on data handling and problem solving; laboratory work will not be involved. Questions that require an elementary knowledge of statistical procedures may be included in all three sections of the examination.

Neurobiology with Animal Behaviour (*NAB*)

The examination in NAB will require knowledge of the structure and functions of the central nervous system, the special sense organs, neuropharmacology and animal behaviour, with particular reference to domestic animals. Section I will include or consist entirely of compulsory short-answer questions. Section III will consist of essay questions. In Section II, candidates will be examined on practical aspects of neuroanatomy and in experimental neurophysiology; questions may be included which require an elementary knowledge of statistical procedures.

Neurobiology with Human Behaviour (*NHB*)

The examination in NHB will require knowledge of the structure and functions of the central nervous system and the special sense organs, neuroanatomy, experimental psychology and some of its applications to medicine. Particular topics will include neuropharmacology; learning and memory; perception and information processing; intelligence and development; emotion and its physiological basis; and social psychology. Section I will include or consist entirely of compulsory short-answer questions. Section III will consist of essay questions. In Section II, candidates will be examined on practical aspects of neuroanatomy and in experimental neurophysiology; questions may be included which require an elementary knowledge of statistical procedures.

Veterinary Reproductive Biology (*VRB*)

Section I of the examination will consist of computer-marked and short-answer questions on the structure and function of the reproductive systems of mammals, with particular reference to domestic mammals. Section II will consist of questions on associated practical work and may include a data-handling exercise. Section III will consist of essay questions.

[1] The subject in angular brackets will be inserted with effect from the 2015 examinations.

MODERN AND MEDIEVAL LANGUAGES TRIPOS

Amended by Notices (Reporter, *2013–14, pp. 532 and 638*)

General

1. The Modern and Medieval Languages Tripos shall consist of three Parts, Part IA, Part IB and Part II. Three Parts.

2. The following may present themselves as candidates for honours in Part IA: Standing of candidates.

(*a*) a student who has not obtained honours in another Honours Examination, provided that he or she has kept one term and that three complete terms have not passed after his or her first term of residence;

(*b*) a student who has obtained honours in another Honours Examination, in the year after so obtaining honours, provided that he or she has kept four terms and that nine complete terms have not passed after his or her first term of residence.

3. The following may present themselves as candidates for honours in Part IB:

(*a*) a student who has obtained honours in Part IA of the Modern and Medieval Languages Tripos, in the year after so obtaining honours;

(*b*) a student who has obtained honours in another Honours Examination, in the year after so obtaining honours, provided that he or she has kept four terms and that nine complete terms have not passed after his or her first term of residence, and subject to the prior approval of the Faculty Board of Modern and Medieval Languages.

4. The following may present themselves as candidates for honours in Part II:[1]

(*a*) A student who has obtained honours either in Part IB of the Modern and Medieval Languages Tripos or in another Honours Examination, and has subsequently spent a period abroad in accordance with the requirements of Regulations 28 and 29, may be a candidate in the year next but one after last obtaining honours, provided that he or she has kept seven terms and that fifteen complete terms have not passed after his or her first term of residence

(*b*) A student who has obtained honours in another Honours Examination may be a candidate in the year after so obtaining honours, provided that he or she has kept seven terms and that twelve complete terms have not passed after his or her first term of residence

(*c*) A student who has obtained honours in Part IB of the Modern and Medieval Languages Tripos may, in exceptional circumstances, be a candidate for Part II in the year after so obtaining honours, by seeking special permission to do so from the Faculty Board by the division of the Lent Term preceding the year in which he or she wishes to take Part II. Such a candidate shall offer the papers currently listed in Regulation 24(*b*).

(*d*) An Affiliated Student may be a candidate under Regulation 24(*d*) or, with leave of the Faculty Board of Modern and Medieval Languages, under Regulation 24(*e*), in accordance with the regulations for Affiliated Students.

5. No student shall be a candidate for more than one Part, or for any Part and also for another Honours Examination, in the same term.

6. No student who has been a candidate for any Part shall again be a candidate for the same Part.

7. Except as otherwise specified in Schedule A, the written papers in each Part shall be of three hours' duration.

8. There shall be a separate body of Examiners for each Part, provided that the Faculty Board of Modern and Medieval Languages shall have power to nominate an Examiner to examine in more than one Part. From among the resident Examiners for each Part the Faculty Board shall appoint such number of Senior Examiners as they may deem sufficient. Examiners and Assessors.

9. The Faculty Board shall have power to nominate one or more Assessors to assist the Examiners in any of the subjects in any Part of the Tripos. If required to do so, Assessors shall set papers in the subject or subjects assigned to them, shall mark the answers of the candidates in those papers, shall assess dissertations, projects, and course-work, shall set and conduct oral examinations, and shall advise the Examiners on the performance of candidates in the examination. Assessors may be summoned to meetings of the Examiners for the purpose of consultation and advice, but shall not be entitled to vote.

10. To conduct the examination in each Part, the Faculty Board shall nominate at least two Examiners for each modern language in which candidates desire to present themselves. The Faculty Board shall have power to nominate any Examiner to examine in more than one language.

[1] See also the regulations for Affiliated Students.

11. The Faculty Board shall nominate such number of Examiners for the papers in classical Latin and classical Greek in Part IA and Part IB as they shall deem sufficient.

12. For each Part of the Tripos the Chair and Senior Examiners, in consultation, shall approve the questions proposed for each written paper and the subject matter proposed for each oral examination.

13. (*a*) The Examiners or Assessors shall assess any course-work submitted by the candidate under Regulation 16. Except where otherwise specified a candidate's answers to the questions in each written paper and other submitted work shall be written in English.

(*b*) Two Examiners or Assessors shall conduct the oral examination of each candidate in each language.

Class-lists.

14. For Part IA there shall be a separate class-list for each language, which shall be drawn up at a meeting attended by the Examiners (including the Senior Examiner) responsible for that language and by the Chair of Examiners; each list shall indicate whether a candidate has offered Option A or Option B. For each of the other Parts there shall be a single class-list, which shall be drawn up at a meeting attended by all the Examiners for that Part.

15. In each class-list the names of the candidates who have obtained honours shall be arranged in three classes, of which the second shall be divided into two divisions. The names in the first and third classes and in each division of the second class shall be arranged in alphabetical order. Marks of distinction may be awarded as follows:

In Part IA, for special excellence in any language.

In Part IB or Part II, for special excellence in the examination as a whole.

In Part II, for special excellence in the oral examination.[1]

In determining the place in the class-list of any candidate who has offered one of Papers GL 6, GL 7, GL 21, or GL 22 in addition, the Examiners shall give credit for proficiency in these papers. A mark of distinction, *G* or *L* respectively, shall be attached to the names of those candidates who, in offering one of Papers GL 6, GL 7, GL 21, or GL 22 acquit themselves with credit in that paper. A mark, *g* or *l* respectively, shall be attached to the names of those candidates who, in offering one of Papers GL 6, GL 7, GL 21, or GL 22 satisfy the Examiners in that paper.

Supplementary regulations.

16. The Faculty Board shall have power:

(*a*) to issue from time to time supplementary regulations defining or limiting all or any of the subjects of examination and determining the scope and character of the papers, and to amend or withdraw such supplementary regulations as occasion may require, due care being taken that sufficient notice is given of any change;

(*b*) to determine the credit to be assigned to each paper, and to establish guidelines to be followed by the Examiners for assessing candidates' work in the examination and for drawing up the class-lists.

(*c*) to specify papers which shall include course-work in addition to the written paper. The details of the course-work required of candidates and the arrangements for the submission of such course-work shall be published by the Faculty Board not later than the division of the Easter Term next preceding the examination. Each candidate will be required to sign a declaration that the course-work is his or her own work, unaided except as may be specified in the declaration, and that it does not contain material that has already been used to any substantial extent for a comparable purpose.

Variable subjects.

17. The Faculty Board shall give public notice of all the variable subjects selected for the examinations in any year as follows:

(*a*) for the written examinations for Part IA and Part IB: before the end of the Easter Term of the year next preceding the examination concerned;

(*b*) for the written examinations for Part II: before the division of the Easter Term of the year next preceding the examination concerned;

provided that the Board shall have the power of subsequently issuing amendments if they have due reason for doing so, and if they are satisfied that no student's preparation for the examination is adversely affected. The Board shall have power when they give notice of the variable subjects selected for a particular examination to announce any consequential restriction on the combination of papers that a candidate may choose to offer, or on the subject areas in which a candidate may offer a dissertation.

[1] Such a mark shall indicate the language offered in the oral examination.

18. Examinations shall be held in the following languages:

(*a*) In each Part of the Tripos papers shall be set and oral examinations shall be held, as specified in Schedule A, in the following modern languages: Dutch[1], French, German, Italian, modern Greek[2], Polish, Portuguese, Russian, Spanish, and Ukrainian. In Part II Papers C1 and C2[3] shall be set in medieval Latin.[4]

(*b*) In Part IB and Part II papers shall be set in medieval Latin,[4] Neo-Latin, in linguistics, and in comparative studies, as specified in Schedule B.

(*c*) In Part IA and Part IB papers shall be set in classical Greek and classical Latin, as specified in Schedule C.

(*d*) In Part II papers from other Triposes shall be available to candidates, as specified in Schedule D.

19. A candidate shall not offer in any Part of the Tripos a paper that he or she has previously offered in another University examination.

Part IA

20. (*a*) In each of the modern languages specified in Regulation 18(*a*) other than French, the examination for Part IA shall consist of either Option A or Option B, as set out below. In French the examination shall consist of Option B only. Scheme of examination.

Option A. Papers A1, A2, and A3.
Oral examination A.

Option B. Papers B1 and B2.
Oral examination B.
One paper from Schedule IA relating to the language concerned.

(*b*) In classical Greek or Latin the examination for Part IA shall consist of either Option A (in Greek only) or Option B (in either Greek or Latin) as follows:

Option A. Papers GL 2 and GL 5.

Option B. Papers GL 1 or GL 3 and GL 5.

In Greek a candidate may additionally offer Paper GL 6; in Latin, Paper GL 7.

21. Subject to the provisions of Regulation 19, every candidate for Part IA shall offer:

either two modern languages

or one modern language together with either classical Greek or classical Latin.

A candidate shall offer *either* Option A in one language and Option B in the other, *or* Option B in both languages.

22. In order to obtain honours in Part IA a candidate shall be required to attain the honours standard in each of two languages.

Part IB

23. Subject to the provisions of Regulation 19, candidates for Part IB shall offer written papers and other exercises as follows:

(*a*) a candidate who offered two modern languages in Part IA, choosing Option A in one and Option B in the other, shall offer in Part IB:

(i) Papers B1 and B2, together with oral examination B, in the language in which he or she previously offered Option A;

(ii) one paper from Schedule IB relating to that language;[5]

(iii) a second paper from Schedule IB;

(iv) *either* a third paper from Schedule IB
or Paper B3 in the language in which he or she previously offered Option B;

[1] Papers in Dutch for Part IA and Part IB except Du. 5 are suspended until further notice.

[2] All papers in Modern Greek except Gr. 3 are suspended until further notice. All papers in Modern Greek as specified in Schedule A are suspended until further notice.

[3] See Schedule A.

[4] These papers will not be available until further notice.

[5] See the notes to Schedule IB, p. 394

(*b*) a candidate who offered two modern languages in Part IA, choosing Option B in each, shall offer in Part IB Paper B3 in each of the two languages, and three papers chosen from Schedule IB;

(*c*) a candidate who offered one modern language and either classical Greek or classical Latin in Part IA shall offer papers in Part IB as prescribed in the supplementary regulations;

(*d*) for a candidate for Part IB under Regulation 3(*b*)[1] the Faculty Board shall have power to determine the papers that the candidate shall offer, in general conformity with the provisions of either (*a*) or (*b*) above.

provided that a candidate may offer, in place of one of the designated papers from Schedule IB,[2] two long essays, each of not fewer than 3,500 words and not more than 4,000 words in length including footnotes but excluding bibliography. Both essays must be in answer to questions prescribed by the examiners for the paper and advertised by the division of term preceding the submission deadline. The two essays shall be submitted to the Secretary of the Faculty Board, in accordance with detailed arrangements approved by the Board, so as to arrive not later than 12 noon on the first Friday of the Full Lent Term and Full Easter Term respectively. Candidates may receive one hour's supervision devoted to discussion of a plan of each essay but shall receive no further assistance in the writing of the essays. Detailed instructions will be issued by the Faculty and Departments regarding any other requirements for the essays as a whole. Candidates will be required to declare that the essays are their own work, and that they do not overlap in content with material submitted for supervisions. Candidates may be called for *viva voce* examination in connection with their essays.

PART II

24. Subject to the provisions of Regulation 19, candidates for Part II shall offer written papers and other exercises as follows:

(*a*) A student who is a candidate for Part II under Regulation 4(*a*)[3] shall offer:

(i) Papers C1 and C2 in any language, provided that a candidate shall not be required to offer both papers in the same language;

(ii) a year abroad project, which shall be offered in accordance with the provisions of Regulation 27;

(iii) *either* three papers chosen from Schedule II and Schedule D, not more than two of which shall be taken from Schedule D,

or two papers chosen from Schedule II and Schedule D, together with a dissertation offered in accordance with the provisions of Regulation 27;

(iv) oral examination C in a language in which the candidate offers one or both of Papers C1 and C2, provided that, if the candidate has obtained honours in Part IB of the Modern and Medieval Languages Tripos, the language shall be a language offered as a language paper as listed in Schedule A by the candidate in Part IA and/or Part IB. The Faculty Board have agreed that the following papers shall constitute a language for the purposes of this regulation: Du. 5, Gr. 3, and Pg. 3.

(*b*) A student who is a candidate for Part II under Regulation 4(*c*)[4] shall offer:

(i) Papers C1 and C2 in any language, provided that a candidate shall not be required to offer both papers in the same language;

(ii) *either* three papers chosen from Schedule II and Schedule D, not more than two of which shall be taken from Schedule D,

or two papers chosen from Schedule II and Schedule D, together with a dissertation offered in accordance with the provisions of Regulation 27;

[1] That is a candidate who has obtained honours in an Honours Examination other than Part IA of the Modern and Medieval Languages Tripos.

[2] See the notes to Schedule IB, p. 394

[3] That is, a student who takes Part II in the year next but one after last obtaining honours (*either* in Part IB of the Modern and Medieval Languages Tripos *or* in another Honours Examination), having subsequently spent a year abroad in accordance with the requirements of Regulations 28 and 29.

[4] That is, a student who takes Part II in the year after obtaining honours in Part IB of the Modern and Medieval Languages Tripos.

(iii) oral examination C in a language in which the candidate offers one or both of Papers C1 and C2, provided that, if the candidate has obtained honours in Part IB of the Modern and Medieval Languages Tripos, the language shall be a language offered as a language paper as listed in Schedule A by the candidate in Part IA and/or Part IB. The Faculty Board have agreed that the following papers shall constitute a language for the purposes of the regulation: Du. 5, Gr. 3, and Pg. 3.

(*c*) A student who is a candidate for Part II under Regulation 4(*b*)[1] shall offer:

(i) Papers C1 and C2 in any language, provided that a candidate shall not be required to offer both papers in the same language;

(ii) *either* three papers chosen from Schedule II and Schedule D, not more than two of which shall be chosen from Schedule D,

or two papers chosen from Schedule II and Schedule D, together with a dissertation offered in accordance with the provisions of Regulation 27.

(*d*) An Affiliated Student who takes the examination in the fifth term after his or her first term of actual residence shall offer:

(i) Papers C1 and C2 in any language, provided that a candidate shall not be required to offer both papers in the same language;

(ii) a project, which shall be offered in accordance with the provisions of Regulation 27;

(iii) *either* four papers chosen from Schedule II and Schedule D, not more than two of which shall be taken from Schedule D,

or three papers chosen from Schedule II and Schedule D, not more than two of which shall be taken from Schedule D, together with a dissertation offered in accordance with the provisions of Regulation 27;

(iv) oral examination C in a language in which the candidate offers one or both of Papers C1 and C2.

(*e*) An Affiliated Student who has been given leave to take Part II in the second term after his or her first term of actual residence shall offer papers and other exercises as under sub-paragraph (*b*) above, except that oral examination C must be in a language approved by the Faculty Board at such time as that leave has been given.

provided that a candidate who offers a dissertation under (*a*)(iii), (*b*)(ii), (*c*)(ii), or (*d*)(iii) may not also offer two papers from Schedule D that are assessed by means other than a written examination, unless the Faculty Board has given special permission for the candidate to do so.

25. A student who is a candidate for Part II under Regulations 4(*a*) or 4(*c*) who has not achieved a satisfactory standard, as defined by the Faculty Board, either in Paper B3 or in the aggregated marks of Papers B1 and B2 in any language in the examination for Part IB, may not offer Papers C1 or C2 in that language.

26. The Faculty Board shall have discretion in exceptional circumstances to grant exemption from the oral examination specified in Regulation 24(*a*), (*b*), or (*d*) to any candidate on the application of his or her Tutor. The Secretary of the Faculty Board shall send to the Registrary, not later than the first day of the Easter Term in which the written examination is to be held, a list of candidates to whom the Faculty Board have granted exemption from the oral examination under this regulation. Exemption from oral examination.

27. (i) A year abroad project or dissertation offered under Regulation 24 shall be submitted in accordance with the provisions set out in sub-paragraphs (*a*)–(*h*) below. Year abroad project and dissertations.

(*a*) Every year abroad project offered under Regulation 24(*a*)(ii) shall be on a subject that falls within the field of modern and medieval languages, including linguistics and comparative studies. A dissertation offered under Regulation 24(*a*)(iii), (*b*)(ii), (*c*)(ii), or (*d*)(iii) (henceforward termed an optional dissertation) shall be on a subject that falls within the scope of a paper from Schedule II.

(*b*) *Year abroad project*

A candidate who is required to offer a year abroad project under Regulation 24(*a*) shall give notice to the Secretary of the Faculty Board of the subject of the proposed project and the general area within which it will fall by a date announced by the Faculty Board, which shall be not later than the third Friday of the Full Easter Term in the year next but one preceding the

[1] That is, a student who takes Part II in the year after obtaining honours in an Honours Examination other than Part IB of the Modern and Medieval Languages Tripos.

examination. If, after giving such notice, a candidate subsequently wishes to revise his or her choice of subject and to offer a project on a subject that falls within a general area different from that notified, he or she must seek the permission of the Faculty Board not later than the division of the Full Lent Term in the year next preceding the examination.

After giving notice as required above, a candidate shall submit the proposed title of the project to the Secretary of the Faculty Board, in accordance with any instructions issued by the Board and according to the timetable set out in Schedule E.

(*c*) *Optional dissertations*[1]
Every candidate who wishes to offer such a dissertation shall submit the proposed title to the Secretary of the Faculty Board, in accordance with any instructions issued by the Board and according to the timetable set out in Schedule E. A candidate shall obtain the approval of the proposed title by the Faculty Board according to the timetable set out in Schedule E. When the Faculty Board have approved a title, no change may subsequently be made in it, except that a candidate who has elected to offer an optional dissertation may apply to the Faculty Board for permission to revise the title of that dissertation; such an application shall be submitted not later than the second Friday of the Full Lent Term next preceding the examination. A candidate who has elected to offer two papers and a dissertation, rather than three papers, under Regulation 24(*a*), (*b*), or (*c*), or three papers and a dissertation, rather than four papers, under Regulation 24(*d*), and who subsequently fails to obtain the approval of the title of the proposed dissertation by the due date, or who fails to submit the dissertation by the due date, shall be required to offer in the examination either three papers or four papers, as the case may be.

(*d*) A year abroad project shall be written in English, except that quotations from primary sources must be in the language of the original. An optional dissertation may be written in a modern foreign language instead of English if the Faculty Board so agree.

(*e*) A year abroad project may take three forms. If in the form of a dissertation, it shall normally be of not less than 7,000 words and in any case not more than 8,000 words in length. If in the form of a translation project, it shall normally be of not less than 6,000 words and in any case not more than 7,000 words in length. If in the form of a linguistics project it shall normally consist of a set of linguistic data of not less than 2,000 words and not more than 3,000 words in length, accompanied by an appropriate transcription or morpheme-by-morpheme gloss, a translation, and a formal analysis. The formal analysis shall normally be not more than 4,000 words in length. An optional dissertation shall normally be of not less than 8,000 words and in any case not more than 10,000 words in length.

(*f*) The word limits specified in sub-paragraph (*e*) above include notes and appendices but exclude bibliography. A project or dissertation shall be typewritten, except where a non-Roman or symbolic typeface is necessary and cannot be provided; in such a case hand-written or photocopied extracts may be inserted. A project or dissertation within the field of comparative studies shall relate to at least two languages. Each candidate will be required to sign a declaration that the project or dissertation is her or his own work, unaided except as may be specified in the declaration, and that it does not contain material that has already been used to any substantial extent for a comparable purpose.

(*g*) Two copies of the year abroad project or optional dissertation shall be submitted, in accordance with detailed arrangements approved by the Faculty Board, so as to reach the Secretary of the Faculty Board by the date specified in Schedule E.

(*h*) A candidate may be called for *viva voce* examination on the subject of his or her year abroad project or optional dissertation; the *viva voce* examination shall be conducted in English, or, in the case of a optional dissertation which is written in a foreign language, in the language in which the dissertation is written.

(ii) (*a*) A project offered under Regulation 24(*d*)(ii) shall be submitted in accordance with the provisions set out for year abroad projects in sub-paragraphs (*a*) and (*d*)–(*h*) above.

[1] The Faculty Board have agreed that any student who wishes to submit an optional dissertation in Part II, in place of a Part II Schedule paper that has been suspended, shall be allowed to do so, assuming that teaching by supervision is available. Students and Directors of Studies will be required to confirm in writing, that they understand that failure to submit the dissertation and to sit a Part II Schedule paper in its place, will result in zero marks for this option. Certain papers in Part II may not be replaced by an optional dissertation, see Schedule II.

(*b*) A student who is required to offer a project under Regulation 24(*d*) shall give notice to the Secretary of the Faculty Board of the subject of the proposed project and the general area within which it will fall by a date announced by the Faculty Board, which shall be not later than the third Friday of the Full Easter Term in the year next preceding the examination.

After giving notice as required above, a candidate shall submit the proposed title of the project to the Secretary of the Faculty Board, in accordance with any instructions issued by the Board and according to the timetable set out in Schedule E.

28. No student shall be a candidate for Part II under Regulation 4(*a*) unless evidence has been produced to the Secretary of the Faculty Board that during the academical year next before the year of the examination he or she has spent a period studying abroad under conditions approved by the Faculty Board in a country or countries relevant to the papers to be offered in the examination.[1] Such evidence will normally consist of a certificate from a university or employer confirming dates of attendance. Every student shall submit a report on their year abroad to the Faculty Board in the manner prescribed from time to time by the Board. Students shall keep the Secretary of the Faculty Board informed of their address abroad at all times. Year abroad.

29. A candidate proposing to study abroad in accordance with the provisions of Regulation 28 shall apply to the Faculty Board for the approval of his or her plans, using a form issued by the Faculty Board and available in the Year Abroad Office. The application shall be submitted through the candidate's Director of Studies to the Secretary of the Faculty Board so as to arrive not later than the last day of Full Michaelmas Term in the academical year next preceding that which the candidate proposes to spend abroad, and shall indicate the country or countries that the student intends to visit and the way in which he or she will be occupied while abroad.[1] If a student subsequently changes his or her plans, he or she must inform the Secretary of the Faculty Board and seek permission afresh.

SCHEDULE A

In each language specified in Regulation 18(*a*) the following papers and other exercises shall be set:

Paper A1. Introduction to the foreign language, 1.
Paper A2. Introduction to the foreign language, 2. (Two hours)
Paper A3. Introduction to the foreign language, 3.
Oral examination A.
Paper B1. Use of the foreign language.
Paper B2. Translation from the foreign language. (Two hours)
Paper B3. Translation into the foreign language, and test in the foreign language through audio-visual media.
Oral examination B.
Paper C1. Translation from and into the foreign language. (Two hours)
Paper C2. Foreign language: text and culture. (Two hours)
Oral examination C.

SCHEDULE B

Amended by Notice (Reporter, *2013–14, p. 532*)

Dutch

Du.	1.	Introduction to Dutch literature.[2]
Du.	2.	The medieval and sixteenth-century literature and history of the Low Countries, *c.* 1170 to *c.* 1585.[2]
Du.	3.	The literature, history, and culture of the Republic of the United Netherlands, 1585 to 1700.[2]
Du.	4.	Literature, history, and culture of Belgium and the Netherlands from 1830 to the present day.[2]
Du.	5.	Introduction to the language and literature of the Low Countries.

French

Fr.	1.	Introduction to French literature, linguistics, film, and thought.
Fr.	2.	Structures and varieties of French.

[1] The Faculty Board shall normally require a student to reside abroad for a period of at least eight months and to undertake during that time *either* a course of study approved by them at a university, *or* an assistantship at a school, *or* some other form of employment approved by them. The period of residence abroad in a location or locations under conditions approved by the Faculty Board shall normally coincide with the academic year in Cambridge, beginning in October; the Year Abroad Project shall normally be completed during a student's Year Abroad and shall not be worked on for any period of term-time residence in Cambridge during the Year Abroad, although some face-to-face supervision might take place

[2] This paper is suspended until further notice.

Fr.	3.	Love, violence, and power in France, 1100–1500 (also serves as Paper 12 of Part I of the Anglo-Saxon, Norse, and Celtic Tripos).
Fr.	4.	Rethinking the human: French literature, thought, and culture, 1500–1700.
Fr.	5.	Revolutions in writing, 1700–1900.
Fr.	6.	Innovation and upheaval: deformation and reformulation in the 20th and 21st centuries.
Fr.	7.	Topics in medieval studies to be specified by the Faculty Board from time to time (also serves as Paper 18 of Part II of the Anglo-Saxon, Norse, and Celtic Tripos and as Paper 34 of Part II of the English Tripos (New Regulations)).
Fr.	8.	Living, loving, and dying in Renaissance France (also serves as Paper 35 of Part II of the English Tripos (New Regulations)).
Fr.	9.	Reason, experience, and authority: French literature, thought, and history, 1594–1700 (also serves as Paper 36 of Part II of the English Tripos (New Regulations)).
Fr.	10.	French literature, thought, and history, from 1690 to 1799 (also serves as Paper 37 of Part II of the English Tripos (New Regulations)).
Fr.	11.	Gender, desire, and power in 19th century French culture (also serves as Paper 38 of Part II of the English Tripos (New Regulations)).
Fr.	12.	Ethics and experience: literature, thought, and visual culture of the French-speaking world (1900 to the present) (also serves as Paper 39 of Part II of the English Tripos (New Regulations)).
Fr.	13.	The French language: variation and change (also serves as Paper 33 of the Linguistics Tripos).
Fr.	14.	A special topic in French studies (A) to be specified by the Faculty Board from time to time.
Fr.	15.	A special topic in French studies (B) to be specified by the Faculty Board from time to time.
Fr.	16.	A special topic in French studies (C) to be specified by the Faculty Board from time to time.

German

Ge.	1.	Introduction to German studies.
Ge.	2.	German history and thought since 1750.
Ge.	3.	Introduction to German literary texts.[1]
Ge.	4.	The making of German culture, I.
Ge.	5.	Modern German culture I, 1750 to 1914.
Ge.	6.	Modern German culture, II.
Ge.	7.	German: a linguistic introduction.
Ge.	8.	German literature, thought, and history, from 1700 to 1815, including Goethe works to 1832.
Ge.	9.	German literature, thought, and history, from 1815 to 1914.
Ge.	10.	German literature, thought, and history, since 1910.
Ge.	11.	Aspects of the history of the German language (also serves as Paper 22 of the Linguistics Tripos).
Ge.	12.	A special period or subject in German literature, thought, or history (i).
Ge.	13.	A special period or subject in German literature, thought, or history (ii).
Ge.	14.	The making of German culture, II.
Ge.	15.	Modern German cultures of performance.

Modern Greek

Gr.	1.	Greek literature, thought, and history, since 1880.[1]
Gr.	2.	Introduction to the Cretan Renaissance.[1]
Gr.	3.	Introduction to modern Greek language and culture (also serves as Paper O2 of Part II of the Classical Tripos).
Gr.	4.	Crete and Cyprus in the Renaissance period.[1]
Gr.	5.	Greek literature, thought, and history, from 1700 to 1900.[1]
Gr.	6.	Greek literature, thought, and history, since 1900.[1]
Gr.	7.	The history and structure of modern Greek (also serves as Paper 24 of the Linguistics Tripos).[1]

Ibero-Lusophone Studies

IL.	1.	Ibero-American cinema.

Italian

It.	1.	Italian texts and contexts.
It.	2.	Structure and varieties of Italian.
It.	3.	Italian modernism.[1]
It.	4.	Autobiography and self-representation in Italian culture.
It.	5.	Italian identities: place, language, and culture.
It.	6.	Modern Italian culture.
It.	7.	Dante and the culture of his age (also serves as Paper 40 of Part II of the English Tripos (New Regulations)).
It.	8.	Italian literature, thought, and culture, 1500–1650.
It.	9.	Text and image.
It.	10.	The language of Italy (also serves as Paper 20 of the Linguistics Tripos).

[1] This paper is suspended until further notice.

Medieval Latin

ML 1. Continuity and change in Latin literature, from 200 to 650.[1]
ML 2. Medieval Latin literature, from 650 to 1300 (also serves as Paper 13 of Part I of the Anglo-Saxon, Norse, and Celtic Tripos).[1]

Neo-Latin

NL 1. Introduction to Neo-Latin literature, from 1350 to 1700 (also serves as Paper 41A of Part II of the English Tripos (New Regulations)).
NL 2. A special subject in Neo-Latin literature: selected authors (also serves as Paper O7 of the Classical Tripos and as Paper 41B of Part II of the English Tripos (New Regulations))

Portuguese

Pg. 1. Introduction to the language, literatures, and cultures of Portuguese speaking countries
Pg. 2. Introduction to Lusophone literature.[1]
Pg. 3. Introduction to the language and literature of Portugal, Brazil, and Portuguese-speaking Africa.
Pg. 4. Self, family, nation, and Empire in Lusophone culture.
Pg. 5. Literature and culture of Portugal and Brazil from 1595.[2]

Slavonic Studies

Sl. 1. Introduction to Russian culture.
Sl. 2. The history and culture of Early Rus.
Sl. 3. Early modern Russia: literature, history, and visual culture from 1300 to 1725.[1]
Sl. 4. Russian culture from the Golden Age to the Silver Age.
Sl. 5. Russian culture after 1880.[3]
Sl. 6. Russian culture after 1953.
Sl. 7. Soviet and Russian cinema.
Sl. 8. The history of the Russian language (also serves as Paper 23 of the Linguistics Tripos).
Sl. 9. Introduction to the language, literature, and culture of Ukraine.
Sl. 10. Studies in twentieth-century Ukrainian literature and film.
Sl. 11. Russia in revolution, from 1861 to 1917.
Sl. 12. Socialist Russia 1917–1991.
Sl. 13. Introduction to the language, literature, and culture of Poland.

Spanish

Sp. 1. Introduction to the language, literatures, and cultures of the Spanish speaking world.
Sp. 2. Introduction to Hispanic texts.[1]
Sp. 3. Medieval Iberian and Spanish Golden Age culture.
Sp. 4. Modern Spanish culture and history.
Sp. 5. Spanish-American culture and history.
Sp. 6. Topics in medieval Iberian culture.[1]
Sp. 7. Spanish literature, thought, and history, from 1492 to 1700.
Sp. 8. Spanish cinema and television.[4]
Sp. 9. Spanish literature, thought, and history, after 1820.
Sp. 10. Introduction to Catalan language and culture.
Sp. 11. The Hispanic languages (also serves as Paper 21 of the Linguistics Tripos).
Sp. 12. Latin-American culture.
Sp. 13. Contemporary Latin-American culture.
Sp. 14. Spanish literature, life, and history, before 1492.

Linguistics

Li. 1. Sounds and words (Paper 1 of the Linguistics Tripos).
Li. 2. Structures and meanings (Paper 2 of the Linguistics Tripos).
Li. 3. Language, brain, and society (Paper 3 of the Linguistics Tripos).
Li. 4. History and varieties of English (Paper 4 of the Linguistics Tripos).
Li. 6. Phonetics (Paper 6 of the Linguistics Tripos).
Li. 7. Phonological theory (Paper 7 of the Linguistics Tripos).
Li. 8. Morphology (Paper 8 of the Linguistics Tripos).
Li. 9. Syntax (Paper 9 of the Linguistics Tripos).
Li. 10. Semantics and pragmatics (Paper 10 of the Linguistics Tripos).
Li. 11. Historical linguistics (Paper 11 of the Linguistics Tripos).[5]
Li. 12. History of ideas on language (Paper 12 of the Linguistics Tripos).[6]

[1] This paper is suspended until further notice.
[2] This paper is suspended until further notice. It will, however, be available to be offered as an optional dissertation
[3] This paper is suspended until 1 October 2015.
[4] This paper is suspended until further notice, and will not be available to be offered as an optional dissertation.
[5] This paper is suspended in 2015–16 and each alternate year thereafter until further notice.
[6] This paper is suspended in 2014–15 and each alternate year thereafter until further notice.

Li.	13.	History of the English language (Paper 13 of the Linguistics Tripos).[1]
Li.	14.	History of the French language (Paper 14 of the Linguistics Tripos).[2]
Li.	15.	First and second language acquisition (Paper 15 of the Linguistics Tripos).
Li.	16.	Psychology of language processing and learning (Paper 16 of the Linguistics Tripos).
Li.	17.	A subject in Linguistics to be specified by the Faculty Board from time to time (Paper 17 of the Linguistics Tripos).
Li.	18.	Computational linguistics (Paper 18 of the Linguistics Tripos).

Comparative Studies

CS	1.	The Romance languages (also serves as Paper 25 of the Linguistics Tripos, and as Paper O10 of Part II of the Classical Tripos).
CS	2.	The Germanic languages.[3]
CS	3.	The Slavonic languages (also serves as Paper 26 of the Linguistics Tripos).
CS	4.	A special subject in comparative literature (i) (also serves as part of Paper 42A of Part II of the English Tripos (New Regulations)).[3,4]
CS	5.	A special subject in comparative literature (ii) (also serves as part of Paper 42B of Part II of the English Tripos (New Regulations)).[4]
CS	6.	European film.[4]

SCHEDULE IA

Amended by Notice (Reporter, *2013–14, p. 532*)

Papers available in Part IA

Dutch:	Du.	1[3].
French:	Fr.	1.
German:	Ge.	1.
Modern Greek:	Gr.	1[3].
Italian:	It.	1.
Portuguese:	Pg.	1.
Slavonic Studies:	Sl.	1.
Spanish:	Sp.	1.

SCHEDULE IB[5,6]

Amended by Notices (Reporter, *2013–14, pp. 532 and 638*)

Papers available in Part IB

Dutch	Du.	2[3], 3[3], 4[3], 5[7,8].
French	Fr.	2, 3†, 4†, 5†, 6†.
German	Ge.	1, 2†, 3*[3], 4, 5†, 6†, 7.
Modern Greek	Gr.	1*[3], 2†[3], 3[8,9], 4[3], 5[3], 6[3], 7[3].
Italian	It.	2, 3[3], 4†, 5†.
Medieval Latin	ML	1[3], 2.[3]
Neo-Latin	NL	1†.
Portuguese	Pg.	1, 2†[3], 3[8,10], 4†.
Slavonic Studies	Sl.	2, 3[3], 4†, 5[11], 6†, 7†, 8, 9[8], 11, 12, 13[8].
Spanish	Sp.	1, 2†[3], 3†, 4†, 5†, 6[3], 10[8], 11.
Linguistics	Li.	1, 2, 3, 4.
Comparative Studies	CS	1.

[1] This paper is suspended in 2014–15 and each alternate year thereafter until further notice.
[2] This paper is suspended in both 2014–15 and 2015–16; and in each alternate year thereafter until further notice.
[3] This paper is suspended until further notice.
[4] No candidate may offer more than one paper from among Papers CS 4–6.
[5] Asterisked papers in Schedule IB may be taken only by candidates who offered Option A in the language concerned in Part IA. Such a candidate must offer at least one asterisked paper in that language in Part IB.
[6] Papers marked with a dagger may be replaced by two long essays under Regulation 23.
[7] This paper is not available to candidates who offered Dutch as a language in Part IA or for a Certificate or Diploma.
[8] No candidate may offer more than one of Papers Du. 5, Gr. 3, Pg. 3, Sl. 9, Sl. 13, or Sp. 10 in any one year.
[9] This paper is not available to candidates who offered Modern Greek as a language in any Part of the Modern and Medieval Languages Tripos or for a Certificate or Diploma.
[10] This paper is not available to candidates who offer or offered Portuguese as a language in any Part of the Modern and Medieval Languages Tripos or for a Certificate or Diploma.
[11] This paper is suspended until 1 October 2015.

SCHEDULE II

Amended by Notices (Reporter, *2013–14, pp. 532 and 638*)

Papers available in Part II

Dutch:	Du.	2[1], 3[1], 4[1].
French:	Fr.	7, 8, 9, 10, 11, 12, 13, 14, 15, 16.
German:	Ge.	8, 9, 10, 11, 12, 13, 14, 15.
Modern Greek:	Gr.	3[2,3,4], 4[1], 5[1], 6[1], 7[1].
Ibero-Lusophone Studies:	IL.	1.
Italian:	It.	6, 7, 8, 9, 10.
Medieval Latin:	ML	1[1], 2[1].
Neo-Latin:	NL	1, 2.
Portuguese:	Pg.	3[2,3,5], 4, 5[1].
Slavonic Studies:	Sl.	2, 3[1], 4, 5[6], 6, 7, 8, 9[2,3,7], 10[7], 11, 12, 13[2,3].
Spanish:	Sp.	7, 8[1,3], 9, 10[2,3], 11, 12, 13, 14.
Linguistics:	Li.	6, 7, 8, 9, 10, 11[8], 12[9], 13[9], 14[10], 15, 16, 17, 18.
Comparative Studies:	CS	1, 2[1], 3, 4[1], 5, 6.[11]

SCHEDULE C

GL 1.	Greek language and texts (Paper 1 of Part IA of the Classical Tripos)
GL 2.	Alternative Greek language and texts (Paper 2 of Part IA of the Classical Tripos)
GL 3.	Latin language and texts (Paper 3 of Part IA of the Classical Tripos)
GL 5.	Classical questions (a modified version of Paper 5 of Part IA of the Classical Tripos)
GL 6.	Greek prose and verse composition (Paper 6 of Part IA of the Classical Tripos)
GL 7.	Latin prose and verse composition (Paper 7 of Part IA of the Classical Tripos)
GL 11.	Passages for translation from Greek authors (Paper 1 of Part IB of the Classical Tripos).
GL 12.	Alternative passages for translation from Greek authors (Paper 2 of Part IB of the Classical Tripos).
GL 13.	Passages for translation from Latin authors (Paper 3 of Part IB of the Classical Tripos).
GL 15.	Greek literature (Paper 5 of Part IB of the Classical Tripos).
GL 16.	Latin literature (Paper 6 of Part IB of the Classical Tripos).
GL 17.	Greek and Roman history (Paper 7 of Part IB of the Classical Tripos).
GL 18.	Greek and Roman philosophy (Paper 8 of Part IB of the Classical Tripos).
GL 19.	Greek and Roman art and archaeology (Paper 9 of Part IB of the Classical Tripos).
GL 20.	Greek and Latin philology and linguistics (Paper 10 of Part IB of the Classical Tripos).
GL 21.	Translation from English into Greek prose and verse (Paper 11 of Part IB of the Classical Tripos).
GL 22.	Translation from English into Latin prose and verse (Paper 12 of Part IB of the Classical Tripos).

SCHEDULE D

Papers from other Triposes that may be taken in Part II

Subject to the provisions of Regulation 24, candidates for the Modern and Medieval Languages Tripos who take any of the papers in this schedule may submit the alternative exercises permitted for those papers.

[1] This paper is suspended until further notice.
[2] No candidate may offer more than one of Papers Du. 5, Gr. 3, Pg. 3, Sl. 9, Sl. 13, or Sp. 10 in any one year.
[3] This paper may not be replaced by an optional dissertation.
[4] This paper is not available to candidates who offered Modern Greek as a language in any Part of the Modern and Medieval Languages Tripos or for a Certificate or Diploma.
[5] This paper is not available to candidates who offer or offered Portuguese as a language in any Part of the Modern and Medieval Languages Tripos or for a Certificate or Diploma.
[6] This paper is suspended until 1 October 2015.
[7] No candidate may offer more than one of Papers Sl. 9 or Sl. 10 in any one year.
[8] This paper is suspended in 2015–16 and in each alternate year thereafter.
[9] This paper is suspended in 2014–15 and in each alternate year thereafter.
[10] This paper is suspended in both 2014–15 and 2015–16; and in each alternate year thereafter until further notice.
[11] No candidate may offer more than one paper from among Papers CS 4–6.

Anglo-Saxon, Norse, and Celtic Tripos, Part I

Paper 2. Scandinavian history in the Viking Age
Paper 5. Old English language and literature
Paper 6. Old Norse language and literature
Paper 7. Medieval Welsh language and literature
Paper 8. Medieval Irish language and literature

Anglo-Saxon, Norse, and Celtic Tripos, Part II

Paper 5. A subject in Old English literature specified by the Faculty Board of English
Paper 6. Advanced medieval Scandinavian language and literature
Paper 7. Advanced medieval Welsh language and literature
Paper 8. Advanced medieval Irish language and literature
Paper 11. Germanic philology
Paper 12. Celtic philology

Asian and Middle Eastern Studies Tripos, Part II

Paper MES.37. History of the pre-modern Middle East
Paper MES.39. Special subject in the pre-modern Middle East
Paper MES.40. Special subject in the contemporary Middle East: political anthropology of Islam and the Middle East
Paper MES.41. Comparative Semitic linguistics

Classical Tripos, Part II

Paper A1. A prescribed Greek author or authors, and a prescribed Latin author or authors
Paper A2. Prescribed Greek texts
Paper A3. Prescribed Latin texts
Paper B1. Plato
Paper B2. Aristotle
Paper C4. A subject in ancient or medieval European history
Paper D3. A topic within classical archaeology and/or art
Paper E2. The Greek language
Paper E3. The Latin language
Paper X1. A subject specified by the Faculty Board from time to time
Paper X2. A subject specified by the Faculty Board from time to time

English Tripos, Part II (New Regulations)

Paper 2. Tragedy
Paper 5. Chaucer
Paper 13. Postcolonial and related literatures
Paper 18. Literature and visual culture

Historical Tripos, Part I

Paper 18. European history, since 1890

Historical Tripos, Part II

Paper 4. History of political thought from *c.* 1700 to *c.* 1890

Papers in European history announced by the Faculty Board of Modern and Medieval Languages from among Papers 7–30 of Part II of the Historical Tripos, in accordance with the provisions of Regulation 17(*b*).

Philosophy Tripos, Part II

Paper 11. Aesthetics

Politics, Psychology, and Sociology Tripos, Parts IIA and IIB

Paper Int. 7. Society, politics, and culture in Latin America[1]

SCHEDULE E

Requirements for projects and optional dissertations in Part II

	Date by which titles are to be submitted	*Date by which approval is to be obtained*	*Date by which projects and dissertations are to be submitted*
Projects	Third Friday of Full Easter Term next preceding the examination	End of Easter Term	First Friday of Full Michaelmas Term
Optional dissertations	Third Friday of Full Michaelmas Term next preceding the examination	Last day of Full Michaelmas Term	Monday of the last week of Full Lent Term

[1] This paper is suspended until further notice.

SUPPLEMENTARY REGULATIONS

Parts Ia and Ib

Papers A1, A2, and A3, and Oral Examination A

These papers and the corresponding Oral Examination (Oral Examination A) will be of a standard of difficulty appropriate for candidates who had no knowledge, or relatively little knowledge, of the foreign language before entry to the University.

Papers A1, A2, and A3. Introduction to the foreign language

Papers A1 and A2 (two hours) will consist of exercises designed to test candidates' knowledge of essential vocabulary and grammatical structures, their ability to comprehend (and in certain cases to translate) authentic material in the foreign language, and their skill in the active use of the foreign language. The exercises set for Papers A1 and A2 in each language will be specified by the Faculty Board from time to time; they will not necessarily be identical in all languages.

The maximum mark allocated to Paper A2 will be two-thirds of the maximum mark allocated to a three-hour paper.

Paper A3 may include questions on literary, cultural, linguistic, or historical topics, some of which may be based on more extensive material in the foreign language, as specified by the Faculty Board from time to time.

Oral examination A

The examination will consist of (*a*) reading aloud a passage taken from a text chosen by the Examiners, and (*b*) a conversation based either on the subject-matter of the text or on a prescribed topic, as specified by the Faculty Board from time to time.

A copy of the chosen text will be made available to each candidate not less than fifteen minutes before the beginning of his or her examination.

The maximum mark allocated to the oral examination will be one-third of the maximum mark allocated to a three-hour written paper.

Papers B1, B2, and B3, and Oral Examination B

Paper B1. Use of the foreign language

This paper will consist of one or more passages in the foreign language. Exercises on the passage(s) may include questions of a grammatical and lexical nature, critical response, précis, and guided writing. Candidates will normally be required to answer in the foreign language. Candidates may be required to translate a passage or passages of continuous prose into the foreign language.

Paper B2. Translation from the foreign language

This paper (two hours) will contain exercises in translation from the foreign language, of which one may be a commentary on a passage in the foreign language or a commentary on a translation or an exercise in comparative translation. In Portuguese and in Spanish four questions will be set, of which candidates will be required to attempt two; in all other languages three questions will be set, of which candidates will be required to attempt two. In French, Italian, Portuguese, and Spanish the passages set will be chosen from material in the foreign language not earlier than 1500, in Russian from material not earlier than 1700, and in German from material not earlier than 1800.

The maximum mark allocated to this paper will be two-thirds of the maximum mark allocated to a three-hour paper.

Paper B3. Translation into the foreign language, and test in the foreign language through audio-visual media

The examination for this paper will consist of two exercises, (*a*) translation from English into the foreign language (two hours), and (*b*) test in the foreign language through audio-visual media (one and a half hours).

Section (*a*) will consist of one or more passages of English prose, amounting to not more than 400 words in total, for translation into the foreign language.

Section (*b*). In the comprehension test, candidates will be required to watch and listen to prepared audio-visual material in the foreign language, of not less than seven minutes and not more than ten minutes in length, during which they will be allowed to make notes. After an interval during which candidates will be allowed to read the exam questions, the passage will be repeated. Candidates will be required to answer questions in writing on the material presented. This will include comprehension questions, as well as a written summary, a response, or a commentary based on the passage. The questions will be posed, and answers will be required, in the foreign language.

Oral examination B

The examination will consist of (*a*) reading aloud a passage taken from a text chosen by the Examiners, and (*b*) conversation on the subject-matter of the text. The examination may also include conversation on general topics.

A copy of the chosen text will be made available to each candidate not less than fifteen minutes before the beginning of his or her examination.

The maximum mark allocated to the oral examination will be one-third of the maximum mark allocated to a three-hour written paper.

PART II

Papers C1 and C2, and Oral Examination C

Paper C1. Translation from and into the foreign language

This paper (two hours) will consist of two exercises: (*a*) will consist of one passage of English prose, amounting to 250 words in total, for translation into the foreign language; (*b*) will consist of one passage in the foreign language, amounting to not more than 250 words in total, for translation into English. Both exercises must be attempted.

The maximum mark allocated to this paper will be 70% of the maximum mark allocated to a three-hour written paper.

Paper C2. Foreign language: text and culture

This paper (two hours) will consist of two passages in the foreign language. Candidates will be required to answer on one passage. Answers must be in the foreign language, showing knowledge of wider contexts as well as responding to the specific text. Passages will relate to a prescribed topic as specified by the Faculty Board from time to time.

Oral examination C

The examination will consist of a five-minute presentation and ten-minute conversation between the candidate and the Examiners: the subject of discussion shall be the candidate's Year Abroad Project. The maximum mark allocated to the oral examination will be 60% of the maximum mark allocated to a three-hour written paper.

PART IB

Candidates who in Part IA offered Option A in a modern language and Option B in classical Greek or Latin

A candidate who offered one modern language and one classical language in Part IA, choosing Option A in the modern language and Option B in the classical language, shall offer in Part IB:

(i) Papers B1 and B2, together with oral examination B, in the modern language;
(ii) one paper from Schedule IB relating to that language;
(iii) Paper GL 15 or GL 16;
(iv) one further paper from among Paper GL 11 or GL 13, Papers GL 17–20, and the papers in Schedule IB.

In Greek a candidate may additionally offer Paper GL 21; in Latin, Paper GL 22.

Candidates who in Part IA offered Option B in a modern language and Option A in classical Greek

A candidate who offered one modern language and classical Greek in Part IA, choosing Option A in classical Greek and Option B in the modern language, shall offer in Part IB:

(i) Papers GL 12 and GL 15;
(ii) one paper chosen from among Papers GL 17–20;
(iii) two papers chosen from among the following: one further paper from among Papers GL 17–20; the papers in Schedule IB; and Paper B3 in the modern language.

A candidate may additionally offer Paper GL 21.

Candidates who in Part IA offered Option B in a modern language and Option B in classical Greek or Latin

A candidate who offered one modern language and one classical language in Part IA, choosing Option B in both, shall offer in Part IB:

(i) Paper B3 in the modern language;
(ii) either Paper GL 15 or Paper GL 16;
(iii) three papers chosen from Paper GL 11 or GL 13, Papers GL 17–20, and the papers in Schedule IB.

In Greek a candidate may additionally offer Paper GL 21; in Latin, Paper GL 22.

(Old Regulations)

MUSIC TRIPOS

OLD REGULATIONS[1]

Three Parts.

1. The Music Tripos shall consist of three Parts: Part IA, Part IB, and Part II.

Standing of candidates.

2. A student may be a candidate for honours in Part IA if he or she has kept one term, provided that three complete terms have not passed after his or her first term of residence.

3. A student who has obtained honours in Part IA of the Music Tripos or in another Honours Examination may be a candidate for honours in Part IB[2] in the year next after so obtaining honours, provided that twelve complete terms have not passed after his or her first term of residence.

[1] These regulations will be replaced by New Regulations in accordance with the timetable in Temporary Regulation 24 of the Old Regulations and Regulation 22 of the New Regulations, pp. 401 and 405.

[2] See also the regulations for Affiliated Students.

(Old Regulations)

4. A student who has obtained honours in Part IB of the Music Tripos may be a candidate for honours in Part II in the year next after so obtaining honours, provided that twelve complete terms have not passed after his or her first term of residence.

5. No student shall be a candidate for more than one Part, or for any Part and also for another Honours Examination or the Mus.B. Examination, in the same term.

6. No student who has been a candidate for honours in any Part shall again be a candidate for honours in the same Part.

7. Subject to the provisions of Regulation 5, a student who is not eligible to be a candidate for honours may be a candidate for any Part of the Tripos so as to qualify as a candidate for the Mus.B. Examination, provided that he or she has kept four terms at least.

Examiners.

8. There shall be three separate bodies of Examiners, one for Part IA, one for Part IB, and one for Part II. The Faculty Board of Music shall nominate such number of Examiners as they shall deem sufficient to conduct the examinations.

Assessors.

9. The Faculty Board shall have power to nominate one or more Assessors to assist the Examiners in any of the subjects of the Tripos. Assessors shall be responsible for setting the paper or papers or other tests in the subjects assigned to them, and shall present to the Examiners such written reports as the Examiners may require. Assessors may be summoned, for the purpose of consultation and advice, to meetings of the Examiners, but shall not be entitled to vote.

Class-lists.

10. There shall be a separate class-list for each Part of the Tripos. In each list the names of the successful candidates shall be arranged in three classes, of which the second shall be divided into two divisions. The names in each of the first and third classes and in each division of the second class shall be arranged in alphabetical order. In each class-list a mark of distinction may be awarded for special excellence.

11. The names of candidates who have satisfied the Examiners under Regulation 7 shall be placed in an alphabetical list headed 'The following (who are not candidates for honours) have attained the honours standard'.

Scheme of examination.

12. The scheme of examination for Part IA shall be:

Paper 1. Harmony and counterpoint I.
Paper 2. Harmony and counterpoint II.
Paper 3. Historical subjects.
Paper 4. Historical and cultural studies.
Paper 5. Analysis.
Paper 6. Practical musicianship.

Papers 1 and 3–5 shall be of three hours' duration. Paper 2 shall consist of a portfolio of written work; the arrangements for submission of the portfolio shall be prescribed by the Faculty Board. Paper 6 shall consist of an aural test of not more than three hours' duration, together with a separate keyboard test. A candidate for Part IA shall offer all the papers for that Part.

13. The scheme of examination for Part IB shall be:

Paper 1. Portfolio of tonal compositions.
Paper 2. Analysis.
Paper 3. Portfolio of free compositions.
Paper 4. Dissertation.
Paper 5. Advanced keyboard skills.

The Faculty Board shall have the power to prescribe, not later than the division of the Easter Term in the year next before the examination to which they apply, not more than seven additional papers, which will be divided into two sections: (A) Historical topics and (B) Other topics.

Each paper shall be of three hours' duration, with the following exceptions:

(*a*) Papers 1 and 3, which shall be submitted in accordance with Regulation 18;

(*b*) Paper 4, which shall be submitted in accordance with Regulation 19;

(*c*) Paper 5, which shall consist of a practical test of keyboard skills, candidates being required to play on a variety of keyboard instruments;

(*d*) in announcing additional papers, the Faculty Board shall have the power, subject to the approval of the General Board, to specify an alternative mode of examination for one or more of those papers.

14. A candidate for Part IB shall offer five papers in all: Papers 1 and 2; and three other papers chosen from Papers 3–5 and from the additional papers prescribed by the Faculty Board, provided that

(Old Regulations)

at least one paper shall be from Section A of the additional papers. At least two of the papers must be from among those examined by a three-hour written examination.

15. A candidate for Part IB shall be allowed to present a recital either on an instrument or of singing. Such a recital, if of sufficient merit, may be taken into account by the Examiners.

16. The scheme of the examination for Part II shall be:

Paper 1. Dissertation.
Paper 2. Advanced tonal composition.
Paper 3. Portfolio of free compositions.
Paper 4. Analysis portfolio.
Paper 5. Notation portfolio.
Paper 6. Test of performance.
Paper 7. Fugue.

The Faculty Board shall have the power to prescribe, not later than the division of the Easter Term in the year next before the examination to which they apply, not more than ten additional papers.

Each paper shall be of three hours' duration, with the following exceptions:

(*a*) Paper 1, which shall be submitted in accordance with Regulation 19;

(*b*) Papers 2–5, which shall be submitted in accordance with Regulation 18;

(*c*) the examination for Paper 6 which shall consist of a recital *either* on an instrument *or* of singing;

(*d*) Paper 7, which shall be of four hours' duration;

(*e*) in announcing additional papers, the Faculty Board shall have the power, subject to the approval of the General Board, to specify an alternative mode of examination for one or more of those papers.

17. A candidate for Part II shall offer six papers in all: these shall include at least one and not more than four from Papers 1–5, and at least two from Papers 6–7 and the additional papers announced by the Faculty Board under Regulation 16. A candidate must offer a combination of papers that is examined by at least six hours of written examination.

Portfolio of compositions.

18. A candidate who offers either Paper 1 or Paper 3 in Part IB, or Papers 2–5 in Part II, shall submit a portfolio to the Chair of Examiners so as to arrive not later than the following dates: for Paper 3 in Part IB or Paper 3 in Part II, the fourth day of Full Easter Term in which the examination is held; for Paper 4 in Part II, the eleventh day of Full Easter Term in which the examination is held; for Paper 1 in Part IB or Papers 2 and 5 in Part II, the fifteenth day of Full Easter Term in which the examination is held. The compositions, analyses, or transcriptions contained in such a portfolio shall be written by the candidate during the current academical year; each separate item shall be initialled by the teacher under whose direction it was written, as an indication that the teacher approves the submission. Candidates will be required to declare that the contents of the portfolio are their own work and that they do not contain material already used to any substantial extent for a comparable purpose.

Dissertation.

19. (*a*) The examination for Paper 4 in Part IB and Paper 1 in Part II shall consist of a dissertation on a musical subject of the candidate's own choice approved by the Faculty Board which falls wholly or substantially outside the subject or subjects chosen by the candidate for any other papers. A candidate who wishes to offer such a dissertation shall submit the proposed title to the relevant Chair of Examiners so as to arrive not later than the division of Michaelmas Term preceding the examination.

(*b*) Each candidate must obtain the approval of the proposed subject by the Teaching Committee of the Faculty Board not later than the division of the Lent Term.

(*c*) A dissertation for Part IB shall be of not less than 5,000 words and not more than 7,000 words (excluding bibliography and appendices but including footnotes). A dissertation for Part II shall be of not less than 7,000 words and not more than 10,000 words (excluding bibliography and appendices but including footnotes). Dissertations shall be in typewritten form, unless previous permission has been obtained from the Chair of Examiners to present the dissertation in manuscript.

(*d*) Each candidate shall submit two copies of her or his dissertation to the appropriate Chair of Examiners so as to arrive not later than the eighth day of the Full Easter Term in which the examination is to be held. The Examiners shall have power to request an electronic copy of the dissertation in addition.

20. Each candidate will be expected to sign a declaration indicating that the work submitted for Paper 2 of Part IA, a dissertation under Regulation 19, or an essay for any other paper, is her or his own work, unaided except as may be specified in the declaration, and that it does not contain material that has already been used to any substantial extent for a comparable purpose.

21. For the purpose of drawing up the class-list the Examiners for Part II shall have the power to call a candidate for interview on matters arising from the examination, but they shall take account of such an interview only if it would be to the candidate's advantage. (Old Regulations) Interview.

22. The Faculty Board may issue from time to time supplementary regulations defining all or any of the subjects of the examination, and may modify or alter such supplementary regulations as occasion may require, due care being taken that sufficient notice is given of any alteration. Supplementary regulations.

23. Before the division of the Easter Term in each year the Faculty Board shall give notice of the subjects to be set for Papers 3 and 4 of Part IA for the examination to be held in the academical year next following, provided that the Board shall have the power of subsequently issuing amendments if they have due reason for doing so and if they are satisfied that no student's preparation for the examination is adversely affected. Notice of variable subjects.

Not less than two weeks before the start of the examination by written papers, the Board shall notify candidates of the works prescribed for Paper 5 of Part IA and Paper 2 of Part IB.

TEMPORARY REGULATION

24. The examination for the Music Tripos shall be held under the old regulations for the last time
for Part IA in 2012
for Part IB in 2013
for Part II in 2014

SUPPLEMENTARY REGULATIONS

PART IA

Paper 1. Harmony and counterpoint I

The paper will consist of an exercise on sixteenth-century counterpoint and the completion of a song accompaniment.

Paper 2. Harmony and counterpoint II

Candidates will be required to prepare a fugal exposition, a set of variations (either for piano or on a ground) and complete a passage for string quartet from a given opening. The paper will be made available between 10 a.m. and noon on the fourth Monday of Full Easter Term and is to be returned by noon on the following day (i.e. after a period of 24 hours).

Paper 3. Historical subjects

The paper will be divided into two sections. The first will contain questions on a subject in Western music; candidates will be required to answer two questions. The second will include questions on the principles of editing, using materials related to the period or repertory prescribed for the first section; candidates will be required to answer one question.

Paper 4. Historical and cultural studies

The paper will be divided into two sections. The first will contain questions on a subject in Western music. The second will include questions on Western music, ethnomusicology, music and science, or notation. Candidates will be required to answer three questions, at least one from each section.

Paper 5. Analysis

The paper will be divided into two sections. In the first section, compositions, or extracts from compositions, either from the period 1700–1780 or from the period 1780–1830 will be provided for analysis. In the second section, compositions or extracts from compositions from the period not represented in the first section will be provided for analysis. The compositions or extracts examined in the second section will be drawn from a repertoire prescribed by the Faculty Board at the beginning of the academical year in which the examination takes place. Candidates will be required to answer two questions, one from each section.

Paper 6. Practical musicianship

Aural tests will include: a memorization test (rhythms); dictation exercises (melodies and three-part counterpoint); a mistake-spotting test; timbre recognition and scoring exercises; recognition of set pieces; and aural analysis.

Keyboard tests will include: reading the score of a string quartet; transposition of a chorale; harmonization of a melody (in a style from the period before 1830); realization of a figured bass at the keyboard; and reading three-part sixteenth-century counterpoint using C3, C4, and F4 clefs.

PART IB

Paper 1. Portfolio of tonal compositions

Candidates will be required to submit a portfolio comprising two tonal compositions and a fugue in three or four parts, together with a recording, on conventional instruments, of one of the two compositions. The compositions shall be in different forms chosen from the following: binary, ternary, scherzo and trio, ritornello, rondo, theme

(Old Regulations)

and variations, sonata. The fugue must demonstrate knowledge of invertible counterpoint, and may be scored for any traditional combination of instruments; it should not exceed seventy bars in length.

In place of one of the two compositions, candidates may submit a through-composed song or group of songs, each of which must possess a clear and appropriate formal structure, for solo voice and piano accompaniment, or for solo voice and accompaniment by a group of instruments. One of the two non-fugal compositions shall be of not more than about eight minutes' duration, excluding repeats, and the other two compositions shall be of not more than about five minutes' duration, excluding repeats. Each composition or group of songs shall be for an ensemble of not more than five players. One composition may be for solo keyboard (including organ) or other polyphonic instrument, but melody instruments may be used only in ensemble. The fugue may also be for a keyboard instrument. Candidates will be responsible for providing a recording of an acceptable quality, but the quality of recorded sound will not contribute to the final mark.

Paper 2. Analysis

The paper will be divided into two sections. In the first, compositions, or extracts from compositions, either from the period 1830–1914 or from the period 1914 to the present day will be prescribed not less than two weeks before the start of the examination by written papers. The choice of period for the prescribed works will be at the Examiners' discretion. Candidates will be permitted to bring unmarked copies of the relevant scores into the examination, and will be required to answer questions on the works. In the second section, compositions or extracts from compositions from the period not represented by the prescribed works will be provided for analysis. Candidates will be required to answer two questions, one from each section.

Paper 3. Portfolio of free compositions

Candidates will be required to submit a portfolio of three compositions. One should be a setting of words, and one should include either fugal elements or incorporate the techniques of groundbass and/or chaconne. Normal staff notation will usually be expected, but electro-acoustic submissions are also acceptable. In addition, each candidate must submit a recording of at least one of the three pieces.

Paper 5. Advanced keyboard skills

The examination will consist of five components. Three will be examined after a total of ten minutes' preparation by the candidate: (i) harmonization of a melody; (ii) orchestral score-reading; and (iii) vocal score-reading (C1, C3, C4, and F4 clefs). The other two components – (iv) figured bass and (v) transposition of a song accompaniment – will be given out two days before the examination. The instrumentalist and singer with whom to perform, respectively, (iv) and (v) will be supplied by the Examiners.

Recital

The examination will consist of a recital of not more than ten minutes' duration either on an instrument or of singing. Candidates should inform the Chair of Examiners not later than the division of the Michaelmas Term next preceding the examination of the instrument chosen or the type of voice (this information must be supplied in written form, and initialled by the candidate's Director of Studies). Candidates must provide an accompanist or page turner (or both) if required.

Part II

Paper 2. Advanced tonal composition

Candidates will be required to submit a portfolio comprising one substantial composition, which should be either an instrumental work in four movements or an extended song cycle. The tonal idiom should be appropriate to a period and place in Europe between 1780 and 1900; the duration of the composition should be between twenty-five and thirty-five minutes. Candidates will be required to submit a recording of the composition on conventional instruments. The composition should be scored for a maximum of five performers (including a singer, in the case of a song cycle). The instruments are to be chosen from the following: flute, oboe, clarinet, bassoon, French horn, piano, violin, viola, cello, double bass. Melody instruments may be used either in a duo with piano or in an ensemble of at least three instruments; the piano may be used on its own.

Paper 3. Portfolio of free compositions

Candidates will be required to submit a portfolio of three compositions. One should be a setting of words, and one should include fugal elements and/or incorporate the techniques of ground bass and/or chaconne. One piece should be for orchestra (with or without voices) or ensemble of no fewer than ten players. One piece should be no shorter than eight minutes in duration. Normal staff notation will usually be expected, but electro-acoustic submissions are also acceptable. In addition, each candidate must submit a recording of at least one of the three pieces.

Paper 4. Analysis portfolio

Candidates will be required to submit two essays involving the use of analytical techniques, to a maximum total length of 8,000 words.

Paper 5. Notation portfolio

Candidates will be required to submit three projects involving the study of notations and of original source material, to a maximum total length of 6,000 words in addition to transcriptions.

(Old Regulations)

Paper 6. Test of performance

The examination for this paper will consist of a test of performance.

The test of performance, which may take place before an audience consisting of staff, students, and others, including External and Internal Examiners, will consist of a recital of not more than twenty-three minutes' playing time, on an instrument or in accompaniment of an instrument or of singing. Details of the complete programme must be sent to the Secretary of the Faculty Board for approval by the Faculty Board so as to arrive not later than the fourth day of Full Lent Term next preceding the examination. Candidates must provide an accompanist or page turner (or both) if required. Candidates must provide the Examiners with two copies of each piece they are performing, in the edition being used. In addition candidates should provide the Examiners with two copies of a programme setting out the pieces in the order in which they are to be performed.

Paper 7. Fugue

Candidates will be required to compose a fugue in not more than four parts from a choice of subjects.

MUSIC TRIPOS

(New Regulations)

NEW REGULATIONS[1]

Amended by Notice (Reporter, *2013–14, p. 118*)

1. The Music Tripos shall consist of three Parts: Part IA, Part IB, and Part II. Three Parts.

2. A student may be a candidate for honours in Part IA if he or she has kept one term, provided that three complete terms have not passed after her or his first term of residence. Standing of candidates.

3. A student who has obtained honours in Part IA of the Music Tripos or in another Honours Examination may be a candidate for honours in Part IB in the year next after so obtaining honours, provided that twelve complete terms have not passed after her or his first term of residence.

4. A student who has obtained honours in Part IB of the Music Tripos may be a candidate for honours in Part II in the year next after so obtaining honours, provided that twelve complete terms have not passed after her or his first term of residence.

5. No student shall be a candidate for more than one Part, or for any Part and also for another Honours Examination, in the same term. No student who has been a candidate for honours in any Part shall again be a candidate for honours in the same Part.

6. There shall be three separate bodies of Examiners, one for Part IA, one for Part IB, and one for Part II. The Faculty Board of Music shall nominate such number of Examiners as they shall deem sufficient to conduct the examinations. Examiners.

7. The Faculty Board shall have power to nominate one or more Assessors to assist the Examiners in any of the subjects of the Tripos. Assessors shall be responsible for setting the paper or papers or other tests in the subjects assigned to them, and shall present to the Examiners such written reports as the Examiners may require. Assessors may be summoned, for the purpose of consultation and advice, to meetings of the Examiners, but shall not be entitled to vote. Assessors.

8. There shall be a separate class-list for each Part of the Tripos. In each list the names of the successful candidates shall be arranged in three classes, of which the second shall be divided into two divisions. The names in each of the first and third classes and in each division of the second class shall be arranged in alphabetical order. In each class-list a mark of distinction may be awarded for special excellence. Class-lists.

9. The scheme of examination for Part IA shall be: Scheme of examination.

Paper 1. Music and musicology today
Paper 2. Music history 1
Paper 3. Music history 2
Paper 4. Introduction to music analysis
Paper 5. Tonal skills 1
Paper 6. Tonal skills 2

Paper 1 will consist of a two-hour examination and the submission of an extended essay or equivalent exercise to be chosen from a specified list, or a composition in accordance with Regulation 17, or an instrumental or vocal recital in accordance with Regulation 18; each element will attract equal weighting. Papers 2–4 will each consist of a three-hour examination. Papers 5 and 6 will be examined through a three-hour examination (counting for two-thirds of the marks for Paper 5), a 28-hour takeaway paper (counting for one-third of the marks for each of Papers 5 and 6), and a practical examination comprising

[1] These regulations will come into effect in accordance with the timetable in Temporary Regulation 22, p. 405.

(New Regulations)

an aural test and keyboard test (each counting for one-third of the marks for Paper 6). A candidate for Part IA shall offer all the papers for that Part.

10. The scheme of examination for Part IB shall be:

Paper 1. Historical studies
Paper 2. Music analysis
Paper 3. Applied tonal skills
Paper 4. Introduction to performance studies
Paper 5. Composition portfolio
Paper 6. Dissertation

The Faculty Board shall have the power to prescribe, not later than the division of the Easter Term in the year next before the examination to which they apply, not more than six additional papers. Each paper shall be of three hours' duration, with the following exceptions:

(*a*) Paper 3 will consist of three submitted elements (which may include composition in specified styles, orchestration, arrangement, and/or film scoring) in accordance with Regulation 14; each element will attract equal weighting;

(*b*) Paper 4 will consist of a three-hour examination plus either an essay in accordance with Regulation 17 or a recital in accordance with Regulation 18; each element will attract equal weighting;

(*c*) Paper 5 will be submitted in accordance with Regulation 14;

(*d*) Paper 6 will be submitted in accordance with Regulation 15.

(*e*) In announcing additional papers, the Faculty Board shall have the power, subject to the approval of the General Board, to specify an alternative mode of examination for one or more of those papers.

11. A candidate for Part IB shall offer six papers in all: Papers 1, 2, and 3; and three other papers. Subject to the approval of the Faculty Board, a candidate at Part IB may be permitted by the Faculty Board to offer not more than one Part II paper.

12. The scheme of the examination for Part II shall be:

Paper 1. Analysis portfolio
Paper 2. Composition portfolio
Paper 3. Notation portfolio
Paper 4. Advanced performance
Paper 5. Dissertation

The Faculty Board shall have the power to prescribe, not later than the division of the Easter Term in the year next before the examination to which they apply, not more than twelve additional papers. Each paper shall be of three hours' duration, with the following exceptions:

(*a*) Papers 1–3 will be submitted in accordance with Regulation 14;

(*b*) Paper 4 will consist of a recital in accordance with Regulation 18;

(*c*) Paper 5 will be submitted in accordance with Regulation 15.

(*d*) In announcing additional papers, the Faculty Board shall have the power, subject to the approval of the General Board, to specify an alternative mode of examination for one or more of those papers.

13. A candidate for Part II shall offer six papers in all. A candidate must offer a combination of papers that is examined by at least six hours of written examination. Subject to the approval of the Faculty Board, a candidate for Part II may be permitted by the Faculty Board to offer not more than one Part IB paper.

Portfolio of compositions.

14. A candidate who offers either Papers 3 or 5 in Part IB, or Papers 1–3 in Part II, shall submit a portfolio to the Chair of Examiners so as to arrive not later than the following dates: for Paper 5 in Part IB or Paper 2 in Part II, the fourth day of Full Easter Term in which the examination is held; for Paper 1 in Part II, the eleventh day of Full Easter Term in which the examination is held; for Paper 3 in Part IB or Paper 3 in Part II, the fifteenth day of Full Easter Term in which the examination is held. The compositions, analyses, or transcriptions contained in such a portfolio shall be written by the candidate during the current academical year; each separate item shall be initialled by the teacher under whose direction it was written, as an indication that the teacher approves the submission. Candidates will be required to declare that the contents of the portfolio are their own work and that they do not contain material already used to any substantial extent for a comparable purpose.

Dissertation.

15. (*a*) The examination for Paper 6 in Part IB and Paper 5 in Part II shall consist of a dissertation on a musical subject of the candidate's own choice approved by the Faculty Board which falls wholly or substantially outside the subject or subjects chosen by the candidate for any other papers. A candidate who wishes to offer such a dissertation shall submit the proposed title to the relevant Chair of Examiners so as to arrive not later than the division of Michaelmas Term preceding the examination. (New Regulations)

(*b*) Each candidate must obtain the approval of the proposed subject by the Faculty Board not later than the division of the Lent Term.

(*c*) A dissertation for Part IB shall be of not less than 5,000 words and not more than 7,000 words (excluding bibliography and appendices but including footnotes). A dissertation for Part II shall be of not less than 7,000 words and not more than 10,000 words (excluding bibliography and appendices but including footnotes). Dissertations shall be in typewritten form.

(*d*) Each candidate shall submit an electronic copy and two hard (paper) copies of her or his dissertation to the appropriate Chair of Examiners so as to arrive not later than the eighth day of the Full Easter Term in which the examination is to be held.

16. Each candidate will be required to sign a declaration indicating that the work submitted for Paper 1 in Part IA, Papers 3–6 in Part IB, or Papers 1–3 or 5 in Part II, is her or his own work, unaided except as may be specified in the declaration, and that it does not contain material that has already been used to any substantial extent for a comparable purpose.

17. A candidate who offers Paper 1 in Part IA, or Paper 4 in Part IB, shall submit the following materials to the Chair of Examiners so as to arrive not later than the following dates: for Paper 1 in Part IA, an essay, extended exercise or composition by the fourth day of Full Easter Term in which the examination is held; for Paper 4 in Part IB, an essay by the eleventh day of Full Easter Term in which the examination is held.

18. A candidate who offers the recital option of Paper 1 in Part IA, the recital option of Paper 4 in Part IB, or Paper 4 in Part II shall give a recital of a length specified by Faculty Board. Each candidate must obtain the approval of the proposed programme by the Teaching Committee of the Faculty Board not later than the end of Michaelmas Term (for Parts IA and IB) or the division of the Lent Term (for Part II).

19. For the purpose of drawing up the class-list the Examiners for Part II shall have the power to call a candidate for interview on matters arising from the examination, but they shall take account of such an interview only if it would be to the candidate's advantage. Interview.

20. The Faculty Board may issue from time to time supplementary regulations defining all or any of the subjects of the examination, and may modify or alter such supplementary regulations as occasion may require, due care being taken that sufficient notice is given of any alteration. Supplementary regulations.

21. The Board shall notify candidates of the work or works prescribed for Paper 4 of Part IA not later than the first day of Full Michaelmas Term preceding the examination, and for Paper 2 of Part IB not less than two weeks before the start of the examination by written papers. Notice of prescribed papers.

TEMPORARY REGULATION

22. The examination for the Music Tripos shall be held under the new regulations for the first time
for Part IA in 2013
for Part IB in 2014
for Part II in 2015

NATURAL SCIENCES TRIPOS

Amended by Notices (Reporter, *2013–14, pp. 41, 244, 252, 596, and 724*)

GENERAL

1. The Natural Sciences Tripos shall consist of four Parts: Part IA, Part IB, Part II, and Part III. Four Parts.

2. The following may present themselves as a candidate for honours in Part IA: Standing of candidates.

(*a*) a student who has not obtained honours in another Honours Examination, provided that he or she has kept one term and that three complete terms have not passed after her or his first term of residence;

(*b*) a student who has obtained honours in another Honours Examination in the year next after so obtaining honours, provided that the student has kept seven terms and that nine complete terms have not passed after her or his first term of residence.

3. A student who has obtained honours in another Honours Examination may be a candidate for honours in Part IB in the year next after so obtaining honours, provided that the student has kept four terms and that six complete terms have not passed after her or his first term of residence.[1]

4. A student who not earlier than the fourth term after her or his first term of residence has obtained honours in an Honours Examination other than Part IA of the Natural Sciences Tripos or Part IA of the Medical and Veterinary Sciences Tripos, may be a candidate for honours in Part II after so obtaining honours[2]; provided that the student has kept seven terms and that twelve complete terms have not passed after her or his first term of residence.[1]

Period of study at Massachusetts Institute of Technology.

A student who, under arrangements approved by the Committee of Management for the Natural Sciences Tripos, has spent not less than three terms studying at the Massachusetts Institute of Technology and has been certified by the President of the Institute after consultation with the Chair of Examiners for Part II of the Natural Sciences Tripos to have studied diligently during that period, shall be deemed thereby to have obtained honours in that Part of the Tripos. A list containing the names of persons so qualified shall be certified by the Chair of the Committee of Management and published in the *Reporter*.

5. The following may present themselves as a candidate for honours in Part III, provided that he or she has not proceeded to the B.A. Degree:

(*a*) a student who has obtained honours in Part II of the Natural Sciences Tripos or has been deemed to have obtained honours in Part II of the Tripos under Regulation 4, in the year next after so obtaining honours, provided that he or she has attained a satisfactory standard, as prescribed by the relevant authority,[3] in previous Honours Examinations;

(*b*) a student who has obtained honours or has been deemed to have obtained honours in any honours examination, other than Part II of the Natural Sciences Tripos, provided that he or she has been given leave to do so by the relevant authority,[3] in special circumstances, which they shall themselves determine.

6. No student shall be a candidate for more than one Part, or for any Part and also for another Honours Examination, in the same term.

7. No student who has been a candidate for any Part shall again be a candidate for the same Part.

Supplementary regulations.

8. The Committee of Management for the Natural Sciences Tripos in consultation with the Faculty Board or comparable authority concerned shall have power to issue from time to time supplementary regulations defining or limiting all or any of the subjects of the examination. Due care shall be taken that sufficient notice is given of any alteration of such supplementary regulations.

Examiners and Assessors.

9. Faculty Boards or comparable authorities shall be identified as nominating bodies, as specified below, and shall be responsible for nominating a Senior Examiner and such number of Examiners and Assessors as they may deem sufficient. An Examiner may be appointed to examine in more than one Part of the Tripos in any year.

Nominating bodies	*Subjects*
PART IA	
Faculty Board of Biology	Biology of Cells
	Elementary Mathematics for Biologists
	Evolution and Behaviour
	Physiology of Organisms
	Mathematical Biology
Faculty Board of Earth Sciences and Geography	Earth Sciences
Faculty Board of Mathematics	Mathematics
Faculty Board of Physics and Chemistry	Chemistry
	Physics
Faculty Board of Physics and Chemistry	Materials Science

[1] See also the regulations for Affiliated Students.

[2] In the year next but one after so obtaining honours in the case of successful candidates in the Preliminary Examinations for Part II of the Natural Sciences Tripos.

[3] The relevant authority for this purpose shall be the Faculty Board or comparable authority within whose scope the proposed Part III subject of examination falls, as specified in Regulation 9.

Part Ib

Faculty Board of Biology	Animal Biology Biochemistry and Molecular Biology Cell and Developmental Biology Ecology Experimental Psychology Neurobiology Pathology Pharmacology Physiology Plant and Microbial Sciences
Faculty Board of Earth Sciences and Geography	[Geological Sciences A] ⟨Earth Sciences A⟩[1] [Geological Sciences B] ⟨Earth Sciences B⟩[1]
Board of History and Philosophy of Science	History and Philosophy of Science
Faculty Board of Mathematics	Mathematics
Faculty Board of Physics and Chemistry	Chemistry A Chemistry B Materials Science Physics A Physics B

Part II

Faculty Board of Biology	Biochemistry Biological and Biomedical Sciences Genetics Neuroscience Pathology Pharmacology Physiology, Development, and Neuroscience Physiology and Psychology Plant Sciences Psychology Zoology
Faculty Board of Earth Sciences and Geography	[Geological Sciences] ⟨Earth Sciences⟩[1]
Board of History and Philosophy of Science	History and Philosophy of Science
Faculty Board of Physics and Chemistry	Astrophysics Chemistry Materials Science Physics
Faculty Boards of Earth Sciences and Geography, and Physics and Chemistry, jointly	Physical Sciences

Part III

Faculty Board of Biology	Biochemistry Systems Biology
Faculty Board of Earth Sciences and Geography	[Geological Sciences] ⟨Earth Sciences⟩[2]
Board of History and Philosophy of Science	History and Philosophy of Science
Faculty Board of Physics and Chemistry	Astrophysics Chemistry Materials Science Physics

10. There shall be three bodies of Examiners, one for Part IA, one for Part IB, and one for Part II and Part III. For each of the three bodies there shall be a Chair of Examiners, provided that the same person may be appointed Chair for two or more of the bodies. For each body there may also be one or more Assistant Chairs of Examiners. Chairs and Assistant Chairs of Examiners shall be appointed on the nomination of the Committee of Management for the Natural Sciences Tripos; nominations shall be made not later than the last day of Full Easter Term in the calendar year next preceding that in which the examination is to be held. Examiners.

[1] The subject in angular brackets will replace the subject in square brackets with effect from 1 October 2015.
[2] The subject in angular brackets will replace the subject in square brackets with effect from 1 October 2016.

Duties of Examiners.

11. The Examiners in each subject shall be jointly responsible for all the questions set and for the marks awarded in that subject. At least two Examiners or one Examiner and one Assessor shall set and conduct every oral and practical examination.

12. The Examiners shall have regard to the style and method of candidates' answers, and shall give credit for excellence in these respects.

Duties of Assessors.

13. The Assessors shall propose questions in the parts of the subjects assigned to them by the Examiners, shall look over the answers of the candidates to these questions, and shall report thereon to the Examiners. The Assessors may be required to assist the Examiners in setting and conducting every oral and practical examination. The Assessors may be summoned to meetings of the Examiners for the purpose of consultation and advice, but shall not be entitled to vote.

Communication of marks.

14. The Chairs of Examiners shall communicate the marks of all candidates to the Registrary.

PART IA

Scheme of examination for Part IA.

15. The subjects of examination in Part IA, which shall be divided into two groups, A and B, shall be as follows:

GROUP A

Biology of Cells	Evolution and Behaviour
Chemistry	Materials Science
Computer Science[1]	Physics
Earth Sciences	Physiology of Organisms

GROUP B

Elementary Mathematics for Biologists	Mathematical Biology
Mathematics	

The maximum marks allocated to each subject shall be:

Each subject in Group A	100
Elementary Mathematics for Biologists	70
Mathematics	75
Mathematical Biology	75

16. Each candidate shall offer three subjects from Group A and one subject from Group B providing that no candidate shall offer both Biology of Cells and Computer Science. A candidate taking the examination under the provisions of Regulation 2(*b*) shall not offer Biology of Cells, Evolution and Behaviour, or Physiology of Organisms, if he or she has previously obtained honours in the Medical and Veterinary Sciences Tripos.

17. (*a*) There shall be separate examinations set for each subject, as specified below:

(i) one written paper of three hours:

Chemistry	Materials Science
Computer Science[1]	Physics
Elementary Mathematics for Biologists	Mathematical Biology
Evolution and Behaviour	

(ii) two written papers of three hours:

Mathematics

(iii) one written paper of three hours and a practical examination:

Biology of Cells	Physiology of Organisms
Earth Sciences	

The practical examination (where such exists) may include a *viva voce* examination.

(*b*) In addition to the written and practical examinations, for all subjects except Biology of Cells and Physiology of Organisms, candidates shall be required to submit records of practical work and/or fieldwork for each subject. Such records shall be presented for inspection on the request of the Examiners as follows: in Computer Science, on a date or dates announced by the Head of the Computer Laboratory no later than the division of Michaelmas Term; in Materials Science, on a date or dates announced by the Head of the Department of Materials Science and Metallurgy not later than the beginning of the Michaelmas Term; in Mathematics, on a date or dates to be announced by the Examiners not later than the beginning of the Michaelmas Term; in other subjects, on the day after

[1] This subject is Paper 1 of the Computer Science Tripos.

the last written examination in that subject. The records shall bear the signatures of the teachers under whose direction the work was performed.

(*c*) In assigning marks for the examination in Earth Sciences, the Examiners may, at their discretion, take account of the note-books submitted by candidates. In assigning marks for the examination in all other subjects, except Biology of Cells and Physiology of Organisms, the Examiners shall take account of the records of practical work and/or fieldwork submitted by candidates. Assessment shall be undertaken by the Examiners or, for the following subjects, be provided to the Examiners from the following persons:

Subject	*Provider of assessment*
Chemistry	Head of the Department of Chemistry
Computer Science	Head of the Computer Laboratory
Elementary Mathematics for Biologists	Chair of the Faculty Board of Biology
Evolution and Behaviour	Chair of the Faculty Board of Biology
Materials Science	Head of the Department of Materials Science and Metallurgy
Physics	Head of the Department of Physics
Mathematical Biology	Chair of the Faculty Board of Biology

18. The names of the candidates who obtain honours in Part IA shall be arranged in three classes. The names in each class shall be arranged in alphabetical order. Class-list for Part IA.

19. In arranging the class-list the Examiners shall take into account the absolute number of aggregate marks obtained and may further take into account the standard obtained by candidates in each subject.[1]

Part IB

20. The subjects of examination in Part IB shall be as follows: Scheme of examination for Part IB.

Animal Biology
Biochemistry and Molecular Biology
Cell and Developmental Biology
Chemistry A
Chemistry B
Ecology
Experimental Psychology
[Geological Sciences A] ⟨Earth Sciences A⟩[2]
[Geological Sciences B] ⟨Earth Sciences B⟩[2]
History and Philosophy of Science
Materials Science
Mathematics
Neurobiology
Pathology
Pharmacology
Physics A
Physics B
Physiology
Plant and Microbial Sciences

21. Each candidate shall offer three subjects, provided that:

(*a*) no candidate may offer Physics B with either Animal Biology or Pharmacology;

(*b*) not more than one subject shall be chosen from any one of the groups numbered (i) to (ix) below:

(i) Chemistry A; Neurobiology;
(ii) Ecology; Pathology; Physics A;
(iii) Cell and Developmental Biology; Materials Science;
(iv) [Geological Sciences B] ⟨Earth Sciences B⟩[2]; Physics B;
(v) Biochemistry and Molecular Biology; [Geological Sciences A] ⟨Earth Sciences A⟩[2];
(vi) Experimental Psychology; Plant and Microbial Sciences;
(vii) Animal Biology; Mathematics; Pharmacology;
(viii) Chemistry B; Physiology;
(ix) History and Philosophy of Science.

22. No candidate shall offer Mathematics if he or she has previously obtained honours in Part IB of the Mathematical Tripos, or unless he or she:

either (i) has previously offered Mathematics in Part IA of the Natural Sciences Tripos,

or (ii) has obtained honours in Part IA of the Mathematical Tripos, or in Part IA of the Computer Science Tripos, or in Part IA of the Engineering Tripos,

[1] The maximum number of aggregate marks shall be 375 for those candidates who take Mathematical Biology or Mathematics and 370 for those candidates who take Elementary Mathematics for Biologists. Candidates taking Elementary Mathematics for Biologists will consequently have a 5 mark penalty for taking this mathematical option.

[2] The subject(s) in angular brackets will replace the subject(s) in square brackets with effect from 1 October 2015.

or (iii) is an Affiliated Student.

23. (*a*) There shall be separate examinations set for each subject, as specified below:

(i) two written papers of three hours:

*Animal Biology
*Chemistry A
*Chemistry B
*Ecology
*History and Philosophy of Science
*Materials Science
*Mathematics
*Physics A
*Physics B

(ii) two written papers, one of two hours and one of three hours and a practical examination:

Physiology

(iii) two written papers of three hours and a practical examination:

Biochemistry and Molecular Biology
Cell and Developmental Biology
*Experimental Psychology
*[Geological Sciences A] ⟨Earth Sciences A⟩[1]
*[Geological Sciences B] ⟨Earth Sciences B⟩[1]
*Plant and Microbial Sciences

(iv) two written papers, one of one hour and one of three hours, and a practical examination:

Neurobiology
*Pharmacology

(v) two written papers, one of one and a half hours and one of three hours, and a practical examination:

Pathology

The practical examination (where such exists) shall be as follows: in Plant and Microbial Sciences it shall be of one and a half hours' duration; in Physiology it shall be of one hour and twenty minutes' duration; in Experimental Psychology and Neurobiology, it shall be of one and a half hours' duration; in [Geological Sciences A and Geological Sciences B] ⟨Earth Sciences A and Earth Sciences B⟩[1], it shall be in two parts, one of three hours' duration and one of one and a half hours' duration; in all other subjects, it shall be of three hours' duration.

(*b*) A candidate who offers one or more of the subjects marked with an asterisk shall, in addition to the written and practical examinations, be required to submit records of practical work and/or fieldwork for each subject. Such records shall be presented for the inspection of the Examiners on a date or dates to be announced by the Head of the Department concerned; they shall bear the signatures of the teachers under whose direction the work was carried out.

(*c*) In assigning marks for the examinations in [Geological Sciences A and Geological Sciences B] ⟨Earth Sciences A and Earth Sciences B⟩[1], the Examiners may, at their discretion, take account of the records of practical work and/or fieldwork (where such exist) submitted by candidates. In assigning marks for the examination in all other subjects, the Examiners shall take account of the records submitted by candidates (where such exist). Assessment shall be undertaken by the Examiners or, for the following subjects, be provided to the Examiners from the following persons:

Subject	*Provider of assessment*
Animal Biology	Head of the Department of Zoology
Chemistry A	Head of the Department of Chemistry
Chemistry B	Head of the Department of Chemistry
Experimental Psychology	Head of the Department of Psychology
Materials Science	Head of the Department of Materials Science and Metallurgy
Physics A	Head of the Department of Physics
Physics B	Head of the Department of Physics

Class-list for Part IB.

24. The names of the candidates who obtain honours in Part IB shall be arranged in three classes, of which the second shall be divided into two divisions. The names in the first and third classes, and in each division of the second class, shall be arranged in alphabetical order.

25. In arranging the class-list the Examiners may take into account the standard attained by candidates in each subject as well as the aggregate of marks obtained by them.

PART II

Scheme of examination for Part II.

26. The subjects of examination in Part II shall be as follows:

Astrophysics
Biochemistry
Biological and Biomedical Sciences
Pathology
Pharmacology
Physical Sciences

[1] The subject(s) in angular brackets will replace the subject(s) in square brackets with effect from 1 October 2015.

Chemistry
Genetics
[Geological Sciences] ⟨Earth Sciences⟩[1]
History and Philosophy of Science
Materials Science
Neuroscience
Physics
Physiology, Development, and Neuroscience
Physiology and Psychology
Plant Sciences
Psychology
Zoology

27. Each candidate for Part II shall offer one of these subjects, and shall satisfy the requirements set out in Regulation 30 for the subject offered.

28. Each candidate submitting a dissertation, essay, critical review, thesis, project report, or similar exercise under Regulation 30 shall be required to sign a declaration that the exercise submitted is her or his own work, unaided except as may be specified in the declaration, and that it does not contain material that has already been used to any substantial extent for a comparable purpose; if two or more candidates have undertaken work in collaboration, they shall each be required to indicate the extent of their contribution. The Examiners shall have power if they consider that a piece of work submitted for the examination is not sufficiently legible, to require that it be resubmitted in typescript.

29. For each subject in Part II the Examiners may, at their discretion, examine a candidate *viva voce*.

30. Examination requirements for the particular subjects shall be as follows: Subject requirements.

Astrophysics. Each candidate shall offer

(*a*) four written papers of three hours each;
(*b*) records of practical, project, or other work.

The practical, project, or other work and their examination requirements shall be prescribed from time to time by the Director of the Institute of Astronomy, and shall be carried out in accordance with instructions which shall be announced not later than the division of the Michaelmas Term next preceding the examination. As an indication of good faith, each candidate shall submit, with the records of her or his work, a declaration that these instructions have been observed. The records of practical, project, or other work shall be submitted to the Director of the Institute of Astronomy not later than a date announced by the Director not later than the division of the Michaelmas Term next preceding the examination.

The Examiners shall be provided by the Director with assessments of the work submitted by the candidates, and shall take account of this work in drawing up the class-list.

Biochemistry. Each candidate shall offer

(*a*) five written papers, four papers (Papers 1, 2, 3, and 4) of three hours each and one paper (Paper 5) of three and a quarter hours (the first quarter of an hour of which shall not be used for writing answers to questions);
(*b*) one essay of not more than 3,000 words, excluding footnotes and bibliography
(*c*) a thesis of not more than 5,000 words, excluding footnotes and bibliography.

The essay shall be on a subject chosen by the candidate from a list of approved subjects announced by the Head of the Department of Biochemistry not later than the division of the Michaelmas Term. The essay shall be submitted to the Examiners not later than the eighth day of Full Lent Term.

The thesis shall give an account of an investigation undertaken by the candidate, the subject of which shall be chosen by the candidate in consultation with staff of the Department of Biochemistry. Each candidate shall inform the Head of the Department of Biochemistry of the subject chosen before the end of Full Michaelmas Term. The thesis shall be submitted to the Examiners not later than the ninth day of Full Easter Term.

In assigning marks for the examination the Examiners shall take account of candidates' essays and theses.

Biological and Biomedical Sciences. Each candidate shall offer

(*a*) the examination requirements of one Major Subject;
(*b*) the examination requirements of one Minor Subject;
(*c*) a dissertation of not more than 6,000 words, excluding tables, figures, and references.

The Major and Minor Subjects and their examination requirements shall be announced by the Faculty Board of Biology not later than the division of the Lent Term in the year next preceding the examination. When giving notice of the Subjects to be offered, the Faculty Board of Biology shall have power, in consultation with the Board of Examinations, to announce restrictions on the combinations of subjects that any candidate may offer in the examination.

The subject of the dissertation shall be on a topic related to either the Major or Minor Subject offered by the candidate. The subject shall be either proposed by the candidate and approved by the Chair of the Faculty Board of Biology, or chosen by the candidate from a list of subjects announced by the Chair of the Faculty Board. Each candidate shall obtain the approval for her or his subject not later than the division of Michaelmas Term. Dissertations shall be prepared in accordance with guidelines which shall be issued by the Faculty Board of Biology not later than the division of the Michaelmas Term. The dissertation shall be submitted to the Examiners not later than the first Friday of Full Easter Term.

[1] The subject(s) in angular brackets will replace the subject(s) in square brackets with effect from 1 October 2015.

Chemistry. Each candidate shall offer:

(*a*) four written papers of three hours each;
(*b*) records of further work.

The types of further work and their examination requirements shall be announced by the Head of the Department of Chemistry not later than the division of the Easter Term in the year next preceding the examination. The records of further work shall be submitted to the Head of the Department not later than the first Monday of Full Easter Term and shall bear the signatures of the teachers under whose direction the work was performed. The Examiners shall be provided by the Head of the Department with assessments of the work submitted by candidates, and shall take these assessments into account in assigning marks for the examination.

In drawing up the class-list the Examiners shall take account of the standard attained by a candidate in each part of the examination as well as the aggregate of marks obtained.

⟨*Earth Sciences.* Each candidate shall offer:

(*a*) three courses, chosen from a list of five, to be assessed by
  (i) two written papers of three hours each;
  (ii) three practical examinations or continuously assessed practical work, one associated with each of the three courses offered;
  (iii) a written paper of three hours' duration, consisting of three essays, each essay chosen from topics related to the seminars in each of the three courses offered;
(*b*) a report of a research project of not more than 5,000 words, excluding footnotes;
(*c*) records of classwork and fieldwork.

At the discretion of the Examiners a candidate may be called for a *viva voce* examination on the candidate's project work and on general aspects of the Earth Sciences.

The practical work and examination requirements associated with each course shall be announced by the Head of the Department of Earth Sciences not later than the beginning of the Michaelmas Term.

The report of a research project shall be on a subject which may be either proposed by the candidate and approved by the Head of the Department of Earth Sciences or chosen by the candidate from a list of approved subjects announced by the Head of the Department by the beginning of the Easter Term in the year next preceding the examination. Each candidate shall either obtain the approval of the Head of the Department for the subject proposed or notify the Head of the Department of the subject chosen from the list not later than 30 June in the year next preceding the examination. The report shall be submitted to the Examiners not later than the second day of Full Lent Term.

The records of classwork and fieldwork shall be submitted to the Examiners through the Head of the Department of Earth Sciences not later than the last day of the written examinations and shall bear the signatures of the teachers under whose direction the work was performed. The types of classwork and fieldwork shall be announced by the Head of the Department not later than the beginning of the Michaelmas Term.⟩[1]

Genetics. Each candidate shall offer:

(*a*) five written papers of three hours each;
(*b*) an essay of between 3,000 and 5,000 words;
(*c*) a thesis of not more than 3,500 words, excluding tables, figures, and references.

The subject of the essay shall be either proposed by the candidate and approved by the Examiners, or chosen by the candidate from a list of approved subjects announced by the Examiners. Each candidate shall either obtain the approval of the Examiners for the subject proposed or notify the Examiners of the subject chosen from the list not later than the end of Full Michaelmas Term. The essay shall be submitted to the Examiners not later than the first day of Full Lent Term and shall contain a critical review of an area of genetics or related to genetics.

The subject of the thesis shall be either proposed by the candidate and approved by the Examiners, or chosen by the candidate, subject to the approval of the Examiners, from a list of subjects announced by the Examiners. Each candidate shall obtain the approval of the Examiners for her or his subject not later than the end of Full Michaelmas Term. The thesis shall be submitted to the Examiners not later than the seventh day after the last day of Full Lent Term.

In assigning marks for the examination the Examiners shall take account of the submitted essay and thesis.

[*Geological Sciences.* Each candidate shall offer:

(*a*) three written papers of three hours each, and shall take practical examinations or offer continuously assessed practical work associated with each of the papers offered;
(*b*) a written paper of three hours' duration, consisting of an essay chosen from a list of topics having reference to general aspects of the Natural Sciences;
(*c*) a report of a research project of not more than 5,000 words, excluding footnotes;
(*d*) records of classwork and fieldwork.

The practical work and examination requirements associated with each paper shall be announced by the Head of the Department of Earth Sciences not later than the beginning of the Michaelmas Term. The Examiners shall be provided by the Head of the Department with assessments of the continually assessed practicals; in assigning marks for the examination the Examiners shall take account of the assessments.

[1] The subject 'Earth Sciences' will replace the subject 'Geological Sciences' with effect from 1 October 2015.

The report of a research project shall be on a subject which may be either proposed by the candidate and approved by the Head of the Department of Earth Sciences or chosen by the candidate from a list of approved subjects announced by the Head of the Department by the beginning of the Easter Term in the year next preceding the examination. Each candidate shall either obtain the approval of the Head of the Department for the subject proposed or notify the Head of the Department of the subject chosen from the list not later than 30 June in the year next preceding the examination. The report shall be submitted to the Examiners not later than the second day of Full Lent Term.

The records of classwork and fieldwork shall be submitted to the Examiners through the Head of the Department of Earth Sciences not later than the last day of the written examinations and shall bear the signatures of the teachers under whose direction the work was performed. The types of classwork and fieldwork shall be announced by the Head of the Department not later than the beginning of the Michaelmas Term. [1]

History and Philosophy of Science. The examination shall comprise two alternative options, (A) and (B). Option A is normally the choice of students who intend to graduate after taking Part II; option B is normally the choice of those who plan to proceed to Part III. Students are free to choose either option.

A candidate who chooses option (A) shall offer

(*a*) three written papers of three hours each, to be chosen by the candidate from a list of not more than ten papers;

(*b*) a dissertation of between 5,000 and 12,000 words, inclusive of notes;

(*c*) two essays, each of not more than 3,000 words in length.

A candidate who chooses option (B) shall offer

(*a*) four written papers of three hours each, to be chosen by the candidate from a list of not more than ten papers;

(*b*) two essays, each of not more than 3,000 words in length.

The written papers shall be chosen from a list published by the Board of History and Philosophy of Science not later than the end of Full Easter Term in the year preceding the examination.

The two essays shall each be on a source chosen from a list of prescribed sources which shall be published by the Board of History and Philosophy of Science not later than the end of Full Easter Term in the year next preceding the examination. A candidate shall obtain the approval of the Board for the subjects proposed for the essays not later than the last day of Full Michaelmas Term. The essays shall be submitted to the Examiners not later than the division of the Lent Term.

The dissertation shall be on a topic proposed by the candidate and approved by the Board of History and Philosophy of Science not later than the division of the Lent Term. The dissertation shall show evidence of reading, judgement, criticism, and power of exposition, and shall give full references to sources used. The dissertation shall be submitted to the Examiners not later than the first Monday of Full Easter Term.

Materials Science. Each candidate shall offer:

(*a*) four written papers of three hours each;

(*b*) further work.

The further work and its examination requirements and submission arrangements shall be announced by the Head of the Department of Materials Science and Metallurgy not later than the beginning of the Michaelmas Term and shall comprise course-work and practical work. Records of further work shall be submitted to the Examiners through the Head of the Department and shall bear the signatures of the teachers under whose direction the work was performed.

The Examiners shall be provided by the Head of the Department with assessments of the work submitted by candidates, and shall take the assessments into account in assigning marks for the examination.

Neuroscience. Each candidate shall offer

(*a*) four written papers of three hours each;

(*b*) a critical review, in printed or typewritten form, of not more than 2,000 words, excluding tables, figures, and bibliography;

(*c*) a report of a research project, in printed or typewritten form, of not more than 5,000 words, excluding tables, appendices, footnotes, and bibliography.

The critical review shall be on a published scientific paper chosen from a list of papers announced by the Chair of the Faculty Board of Biology not later than the second Friday of Full Michaelmas Term. Each candidate shall notify the Chair of the paper that he or she has chosen for review not later than the end of Full Michaelmas Term. The review shall be submitted to the Examiners not later than the second Friday of Full Lent Term.

The report of a research project shall be on a subject either proposed by the candidate and approved by the Chair of the Faculty Board of Biology, or chosen by the candidate from a list of approved subjects announced by the Chair, not later than the division of the Michaelmas Term. Each candidate shall either obtain the approval of the Chair for the subject proposed, or notify the Chair of the subject chosen from the list, not later than the end of Full Michaelmas Term. The report shall be submitted to the Examiners not later than the fifth day of the Full Easter Term in which the examination is to be held.

During Full Easter Term, on a day specified by the Chair of the Faculty Board of Biology, each candidate shall be required to give a brief oral presentation of her or his project to an audience consisting of staff and students and including internal Examiners.

[1] The subject 'Earth Sciences' will replace the subject 'Geological Sciences' with effect from 1 October 2015.

In assigning marks for the examination the Examiners shall take account of the candidates' research projects (both the report and the presentation).

Pathology. Each candidate shall offer

(*a*) four written papers of three hours each, and a practical examination of two and a half hours;

(*b*) a project report.

The project report shall be on a subject either proposed by the candidate and approved by the Head of the Department of Pathology, or chosen by the candidate from a list of approved subjects announced by the Head of the Department not later than the beginning of the Michaelmas Term. Each candidate shall either obtain the approval of the Head of the Department for the subject proposed, or notify the Head of the Department of the subject chosen from the list, not later than the second Friday of Full Michaelmas Term. The report or essay shall be submitted to the Examiners not later than the end of Full Lent Term, in a format specified by the Head of the Department not later than the beginning of the Michaelmas Term.

Pharmacology. Each candidate shall offer

(*a*) four written papers of three hours each;

(*b*) a report of a research project.

The report of the research project shall be on a subject chosen from a list of approved subjects announced by the Head of the Department of Pharmacology not later than the division of the Michaelmas Term. Each candidate shall notify the Head of the Department of the subject chosen from the list not later than the end of Full Michaelmas Term. The report shall be submitted to the Examiners not later than the tenth day of Full Easter Term.

During the second or third week of Full Easter Term, each candidate is required to give a brief oral communication to an audience consisting of staff and students of the Department and including the internal Examiners.

In assigning marks for the examination the Examiners shall take account of the written and oral reports of the research projects.

Physical Sciences. Each candidate shall offer

(*a*) the examination requirements of one Half Subject, chosen from Chemistry, [Geological Sciences] ⟨Earth Sciences⟩[1], Physics;

(*b*) the examination requirements of a subject from Part IB of the Tripos, as specified in Regulation 23, subject to any restrictions outlined below;

(*c*) a dissertation of 5,000 words, inclusive of notes, but excluding tables, figures, and references. The subject of the dissertation shall be on a topic approved by the Head of the Department in which the candidate is offering the Half Subject. Each candidate shall obtain the approval for her or his subject not later than the division of the Michaelmas Term. Dissertations shall be prepared in accordance with guidelines which shall be issued by the Faculty Boards of Earth Sciences and Geography, and Physics and Chemistry, jointly, not later than the division of the Michaelmas Term. The dissertation shall be submitted to the Head of the Department in which the candidate is offering the Half Subject not later than the first Friday of Full Easter Term and shall bear the signatures of the teacher under whose direction the work was performed.

(i) The examination requirements for Half Subject Chemistry shall consist of three written papers, each of one and a half hours' duration, and the submission of note-books of further work. The types of further work and their examination requirements shall be announced by the Head of the Department of Chemistry not later than the division of the Easter Term in the year next preceding the examination. The records of further work shall be submitted to the Head of the Department not later than the first Monday of Full Easter Term and shall bear the signatures of the teachers under whose direction the work was performed. The Examiners shall be provided by the Head of the Department with assessments of the work submitted by candidates, and shall take these assessments into account in assigning marks for the examination.

Half Subject Chemistry may not be offered unless the candidate has previously offered either Chemistry A or Chemistry B in Part IB of the Tripos.

(ii) The examination requirements for Half Subject Physics shall consist of:

(1) two papers drawn from Papers 1, 2, 3, and 4 of the papers in Physics for Part II of the Natural Sciences Tripos;

(2) one paper drawn from Papers 5, 6, 7, and 8 of the papers in Physics in Part II of the Natural Sciences Tripos;

(3) two units of further work not to include the research review;

(4) a computing exercise.

Each paper shall be of two hours' duration.

The types of further work and their examination requirements shall be announced by the Head of the Department of Physics not later than the beginning of the Michaelmas Term. Records of further work shall be submitted to the Head of the Department not later than the fourth Monday of Full Easter Term and shall bear the signatures of the teachers under whose direction the work was performed. The Examiners shall be provided by the Head of the Department with assessments of the work submitted by candidates, and shall take these assessments into account in assigning marks for the examination.

[1] The subject in angular brackets will replace the subject in square brackets with effect from 1 October 2015.

Half Subject Physics may not be offered unless the candidate has previously offered Physics A or Physics B in Part IB of the Tripos.

(iii) The examination requirements for Half Subject [Geological Sciences] ⟨Earth Sciences⟩[1] shall consist of:

(1) one written paper of one and a half hours' duration and two written papers of two hours' duration each, and practical examinations or continually assessed practical work associated with each paper offered;

(2) a written paper of three hours' duration, consisting of an essay chosen from a list of topics having reference to general aspects of the Natural Sciences;

(3) records of practical work and fieldwork.

The practical work and examination requirements associated with each paper shall be announced by the Head of the Department of Earth Sciences not later than the beginning of the Michaelmas Term. The Examiners shall be provided by the Head of the Department with assessments of the continually assessed practicals; in assigning marks for the examination the Examiners shall take account of the assessments.

The records of classwork and fieldwork shall be submitted to the Examiners through the Head of the Department of Earth Sciences not later than the last day of the written examinations and shall bear the signatures of the teachers under whose direction the work was performed. The types of classwork and fieldwork shall be announced by the Head of the Department not later than the beginning of the Michaelmas Term.

Half Subject [Geological Sciences] ⟨Earth Sciences⟩[1] may not be offered unless the candidate has previously offered *either* [Geological Sciences A *or* Geological Sciences B] ⟨Earth Sciences A *or* Earth Sciences B⟩[2] in Part IB of the Tripos.

Physics. Each candidate shall offer:

(*a*) Papers 1, 2, 3, and 4;
(*b*) a minimum of three and a maximum of four from Papers 5, 6, 7, and 8;
(*c*) three or more units of further work;
(*d*) a computing exercise.

Each paper shall be of two hours' duration.

The types of further work and their examination requirements shall be announced by the Head of the Department of Physics not later than the beginning of the Michaelmas Term. The records of further work shall be submitted to the Head of the Department not later than the fourth Monday of Full Easter Term and shall bear the signatures of the teachers under whose direction the work was performed. The Examiners shall be provided by the Head of the Department with assessments of the work submitted by candidates, and shall take these assessments into account in assigning marks for the examination.

If a candidate offers four papers in (*b*) the Examiners will take into account the three components which they judge to be the best.

If a candidate offers more than three units of further work in (*c*) the Examiners will take into account the three components which they judge to be the best.

In drawing up the class-list the Examiners shall take account of the standard attained by a candidate in each part of the examination as well as the aggregate of marks obtained.

Physiology, Development, and Neuroscience. Each candidate shall offer

(*a*) four written papers of three hours each;
(*b*) a report of a research project.

The report of a research project shall be on a subject which may be either proposed by the candidate and approved by the Head of the Department of Physiology, Development, and Neuroscience or chosen by the candidate from a list of approved subjects announced by the Head of the Department not later than the end of the Easter Term in the year preceding the examination. Each candidate shall either obtain the approval of the Head of Department for the subject proposed, or notify the Head of the Department of the subject chosen from the list, not later than the beginning of the Michaelmas Term. The report shall be submitted to the Examiners not later than the third day of the Full Easter Term in which the examination is to be held.

Physiology and Psychology. Each candidate shall offer

(*a*) four written papers of three hours, two in Physiology and two in Psychology;
(*b*) two printed or typewritten copies of a report of a project, of not more than 5,000 words in length, excluding tables, appendices, footnotes, and bibliography, on a subject in the field of Physiology or Psychology.

A candidate who offers a project in the field of Physiology shall submit a report on a subject which may be either proposed by the candidate and approved by the Head of the Department of Physiology, Development, and Neuroscience or chosen by the candidate from a list of approved subjects announced by the Head of the Department by the beginning of the Michaelmas Term. Each candidate shall either obtain the approval of the Head of the Department for the subject proposed or notify the Head of the Department of the subject chosen from the list not later than the end of the Michaelmas Term. The two copies of the report shall be submitted to the Examiners not later than the third day of the Full Easter Term in which the examination is to be held.

A candidate who offers a project in the field of Psychology shall submit a report on a subject chosen by the candidate from a list of approved subjects announced by the Head of the Department of Psychology by the beginning of the Michaelmas Term. Each candidate shall obtain the approval of the Head of the Department for

[1] The subject in angular brackets will replace the subject in square brackets with effect from 1 October 2015.
[2] The subjects in angular brackets will replace the subjects in square brackets with effect from 1 October 2016.

the subject chosen from the list not later than the division of the Michaelmas Term. The two copies of the report shall be submitted to the Examiners not later than the tenth day of Full Easter Term.

Plant Sciences. Each candidate shall offer

(*a*) four written papers of three hours each;
(*b*) an essay of not more than 2,500 words, excluding tables, figure legends, and bibliography;
(*c*) a report of a research project, of not more than 5,000 words, excluding tables, figure legends, appendices, and bibliography.

The essay shall be on a subject chosen by the candidate from a list of approved subjects announced by the Head of the Department of Plant Sciences and shall be submitted to the Examiners. The dates of announcement of subjects and submission of essays shall be announced by the Head of the Department not later than the second Friday of Full Michaelmas Term.

The report of a research subject shall be on a subject chosen by the candidate from a list of approved subjects announced by the Head of the Department of Plant Sciences and shall be submitted to the Examiners. The dates of announcement of subjects and submission of essays shall be announced by the Head of the Department not later than the second Friday of Full Michaelmas Term.

Psychology. The examination shall comprise two alternative options, (A) and (B). For both options, each candidate shall offer

(*a*) four written papers, Papers 1–4, of three hours each, provided that a candidate may submit, in addition to those papers, two copies of an original dissertation of not more than 8,000 words, excluding appendices, footnotes, and bibliography;
(*b*) two copies of a report of a research project not exceeding 5,000 words, exclusive of tables, appendices, footnotes, and bibliography.

The title of the dissertation shall be on a subject chosen by the candidate and approved by the Senior Examiner not later than the end of the Michaelmas Term next preceding the examination. Two copies of the original dissertation, if it is offered, shall be submitted to the Senior Examiner not later than the fifth Monday of Full Lent Term.

The report of a research project shall be on a subject either proposed by the candidate and approved by the Head of Department of Psychology or chosen by the candidate from a list of approved subjects announced by the Head of the Department at the beginning of the Michaelmas Term. Each candidate shall obtain the approval of the Head of the Department for the subject chosen not later than the division of the Michaelmas Term. The report shall be submitted to the Examiners not later than the tenth day of Full Easter Term.

If a candidate offers four papers and a dissertation, the Examiners shall assess her or his performance on (i) Paper 1 and (ii) three of the following: Papers 2, 3, 4, or the dissertation, discounting the one component out of the four in which they judge the candidate's work to be least good, providing that no component out of Papers 2, 3, or 4 shall be discounted if it is not of at least second-class standard.

Zoology. Each candidate shall offer

(*a*) four written papers of three hours each;
(*b*) a written paper of two hours' duration, consisting of an essay chosen from a list of topics having reference to general aspects of the Natural Sciences;
(*c*) a critical review of not more than 2,000 words, excluding tables and bibliography;
(*d*) records of project work or practical work, or both.

The critical review shall be on a subject chosen by the candidate from a list of approved subjects announced by the Head of the Department of Zoology not later than the end of the first quarter of the Michaelmas Term. The critical review shall be submitted to the Examiners on a date which the Head of the Department shall announce not later than the end of the first quarter of the Michaelmas Term.

The records of project work, or practical work, or both may be either chosen by the candidate from a list of approved subjects announced by the Head of the Department of Zoology not later than the end of the first quarter of the Michaelmas Term, or proposed by the candidate and approved by the Head of the Department by not later than the end of the first quarter of the Michaelmas Term. The records shall be submitted to the Examiners on the first day of the written examination and shall bear the signatures of the teachers under whose direction the work was performed.

The Examiners shall be provided by the Head of the Department of Zoology with assessments of the work submitted by candidates under (*c*) and (*d*), and shall take the assessments into account in assigning marks for the examination.

Class-lists for Part II.

31. For each subject in Part II there shall be published a separate class-list, which shall be signed by the Examiners in that subject, provided that the class-list for the subject Physiology and Psychology shall be signed by the Examiners in both those subjects.

The names of the candidates who obtain honours in each subject or combination of subjects shall be arranged in three classes, of which the second shall be divided into two divisions. The names in the first and third classes, and in each division of the second class, shall be arranged in alphabetical order.

PART III

Scheme of examination for Part III.

32. The subjects of examination in Part III shall be as follows:

Astrophysics	History and Philosophy of Science
Biochemistry	Materials Science
Chemistry	Physics
[Geological Sciences] ⟨Earth Sciences⟩[1]	Systems Biology

33. Every candidate for Part III shall offer one of these subjects, and shall satisfy the requirements set out in Regulation 36 for the subject offered. In addition to the requirements set out in Regulation 36, the Committee of Management for the Natural Sciences Tripos may authorize no more than ten additional interdisciplinary papers which shall be included in the examination requirements of one or more subjects. Public notice of the interdisciplinary papers shall be given not later than the end of the Easter Term in the year next preceding the examination, provided that the Committee of Management shall have the power of subsequently issuing amendments if they have due reason for doing so and if they are satisfied that no candidate's preparation for the examination is adversely affected. The Committee of Management shall have power:

(i) in giving notice of the papers, to limit the subjects in which each paper is to be offered;
(ii) to specify the mode of assessment for each paper;
(iii) for each subject, to define or otherwise modify the duration of each examination paper outlined in Regulation 36 for candidates who choose to offer one or more of the interdisciplinary papers.

34. Every candidate submitting a dissertation, essay, thesis, project report, or similar exercise under Regulation 36 shall be required to sign a declaration that the exercise submitted is her or his own work, unaided except as may be specified in the declaration, and that it does not contain material that has already been used to any substantial extent for a comparable purpose; if two or more candidates have undertaken work in collaboration, they shall each be required to indicate the extent of their contribution. The Examiners shall have power if they consider that a piece of work submitted for the examination is not sufficiently legible, to require that it be resubmitted in typescript.

35. For each subject in Part III the Examiners may, at their discretion, examine a candidate *viva voce*.

Subject requirements.

36. Examination requirements for the particular subjects shall be as follows:

Astrophysics. Each candidate shall offer

(*a*) a number of written papers;
(*b*) submit a report of a research project of not more than 8,000 words, excluding figures, tables, captions, references, and appendices.

The number of written papers to be set and the subject and duration of each paper shall be announced by the Director of the Institute of Astronomy not later than 1 November next preceding the examination.

The subject of the research project shall be chosen by the candidate from a list of approved subjects announced by the Director of the Institute of Astronomy not later than the end of the Easter Term in the year next preceding the examination. Each candidate shall notify the Director of the subject chosen from the list not later than the second Friday of Full Michaelmas Term. The report of a research project shall be submitted to the Examiners not later than the second Monday of Full Easter Term.

Biochemistry. Each candidate shall offer

(*a*) two written papers, Paper 1 of three hours and Paper 2 of three and a quarter hours (the first quarter of an hour of which shall not be used for writing answers to questions);
(*b*) a report of a research project of not more than 8,000 words, excluding footnotes and bibliography.

The subject of the research project may be either proposed by the candidate and approved by the Head of the Department of Biochemistry, or chosen by the candidate from a list of approved subjects, which shall be announced by the Head of the Department not later than the end of the Easter Term in the year next preceding the examination. Each candidate shall either obtain the approval of the Head of the Department for the subject proposed, or notify the Head of the Department of the subject chosen from the list, not later than 31 August next preceding the examination. The report of a research project shall be submitted to the Examiners not later than the ninth day of Full Easter Term.

In assigning marks for the examination the Examiners shall take account of candidates' research reports.

Chemistry. Each candidate shall offer

(*a*) three written papers of three hours each;
(*b*) a report of a research project of not more than 5,000 words, excluding footnotes.

The subject of the research project may be either proposed by the candidate and approved by the Head of the Department of Chemistry, or chosen by the candidate from a list of approved subjects announced by the Head of

[1] The subject in angular brackets will replace the subject in square brackets with effect from 1 October 2016.

the Department not later than the division of the Easter Term in the year next preceding the examination. Each candidate shall either obtain the approval of the Head of the Department for the subject proposed, or notify the Head of the Department of the subject chosen from the list, not later than the end of the Full Easter Term in the academical year preceding the examination. The report of a research project shall be submitted to the Examiners through the Head of the Department not later than the Friday following the last day of Full Lent Term.

In assigning marks for the examination the Examiners shall take account of the written reports of the research projects.

⟨*Earth Sciences.* Each candidate shall offer

(*a*) six written papers, each of one and a half hours' duration and shall offer any assessed practical work associated with each of those papers;

(*b*) a written paper of three hours' duration, consisting of two essays chosen from a list of topics having reference to general aspects of the Natural Sciences;

(*c*) a report of a research project of not more than 7,500 words, excluding footnotes;

(*d*) records of classwork and fieldwork.

At the discretion of the Examiners a candidate may be called for a *viva voce* examination on the candidate's project work and on general aspects of the Earth Sciences.

The examination requirements and any practical work associated with each paper shall be announced by the Head of the Department of Earth Sciences not later than the beginning of the Michaelmas Term. The Examiners shall be provided by the Head of the Department of Earth Sciences with assessments of any assessed practicals; in assigning marks for the examination the Examiners shall take account of the assessments.

The report of a research project shall be on a subject which may be either proposed by the candidate and approved by the Head of the Department of Earth Sciences or chosen by the candidate from a list of approved subjects announced by the Head of the Department by the beginning of the Lent Term in the year next preceding the examination. Each candidate shall either obtain the approval of the Head of the Department for the subject proposed or notify the Head of the Department of the subject chosen from the list not later than the division of the Lent Term next preceding the examination. The report shall be submitted to the Examiners not later than the first Friday of Full Lent Term.

The records of classwork and fieldwork shall be submitted to the Examiners through the Head of the Department of Earth Sciences not later than the last day of the written examinations and shall bear the signatures of the teachers under whose direction the work was performed. The types of classwork and fieldwork shall be announced by the Head of the Department not later than the beginning of the Michaelmas Term.⟩[1]

[*Geological Sciences.* Each candidate shall offer

(*a*) three written papers (Papers 1–3), each of three hours' duration, and shall take practical examinations or offer continuously assessed practical work associated with Papers 2 and 3;

(*b*) a report of a research project of not more than 7,500 words, excluding footnotes;

(*c*) records of classwork and fieldwork.

The practical work and examination requirements associated with each paper shall be announced by the Head of the Department of Earth Sciences not later than the beginning of the Michaelmas Term. The Examiners shall be provided by the Head of the Department of Earth Sciences with assessments of the continually assessed practicals; in assigning marks for the examination the Examiners shall take account of the assessments.

The report of a research project shall be on a subject which may be either proposed by the candidate and approved by the Head of the Department of Earth Sciences or chosen by the candidate from a list of approved subjects announced by the Head of the Department by the beginning of the Lent Term in the year next preceding the examination. Each candidate shall either obtain the approval of the Head of the Department for the subject proposed or notify the Head of the Department of the subject chosen from the list not later than the division of the Lent Term next preceding the examination. The report shall be submitted to the Examiners not later than the first Friday of Full Lent Term.

The records of classwork and fieldwork shall be submitted to the Examiners through the Head of the Department of Earth Sciences not later than the last day of the written examinations and shall bear the signatures of the teachers under whose direction the work was performed. The types of classwork and fieldwork shall be announced by the Head of the Department not later than the beginning of the Michaelmas Term.][1]

History and Philosophy of Science. Each candidate shall offer

(*a*) a literature review of between 3,000 and 5,000 words;

(*b*) two short essays, each of not more than 2,500 words, excluding bibliography, each from a list of topics drawn from those covered by the Advanced Seminar;

(*c*) a research paper of not more than 5,000 words including footnotes but excluding bibliography;

(*d*) a dissertation, of not more than 15,000 words including footnotes but excluding appendices and bibliography.

All pieces of work must be approved by the Board of History and Philosophy of Science.

The literature review shall be submitted on the last day of Michaelmas Full Term. The list of short essay titles, from which candidates will choose two titles from eight, shall be issued by the Head of the Department of History and Philosophy of Science shortly after the division of Lent Term and students will have one week in which to prepare the two essays for submission to the Examiners. The title of each candidate's research paper, which must be on a different topic from all other pieces of work, shall be approved by the Board of History and Philosophy

[1] The subject 'Earth Sciences' will replace the subject 'Geological Sciences' with effect from 1 October 2016.

of Science at its meeting in the second half of Lent Term. The research paper shall be submitted on the last day of Lent Full Term. The title of the dissertation and supervisor shall be approved by the Board of History and Philosophy of Science at its meeting in the second half of Lent Term. The dissertation shall be submitted at the beginning of the final week of Easter Full Term.

Materials Science. Each candidate shall offer

(*a*) three written papers of three hours each;
(*b*) a report of a research project of not more than 7,000 words, including footnotes, but excluding appendices and bibliography;
(*c*) records of course-work and associated exercises.

The subject of the research project may be either proposed by the candidate and approved by the Head of the Department of Materials Science and Metallurgy, or chosen by the candidate from a list of approved subjects announced by the Head of the Department not later than the end of the Easter Term in the year next preceding the examination. Each candidate shall either obtain the approval of the Head of the Department for the subject proposed, or notify the Head of the Department of the subject chosen from the list, not later than the beginning of the Michaelmas Term.

Details of the course-work and other exercises and their examination requirements shall be announced by the Head of the Department not later than the beginning of Michaelmas Term. The records of course-work and associated exercises shall be submitted to the Examiners through the Head of the Department on a date to be announced by the Head of the Department not later than the division of the Michaelmas Term.

The Examiners shall be provided by the Head of the Department with assessments of the course-work and other exercises, and shall take the assessments into account in assigning marks for the examination.

Physics. Each candidate shall offer

(*a*) one written paper of three hours in general physics;
(*b*) at least three major topics and at least three minor topics, provided that in place of one or more of the minor topics a candidate may submit *either* units of further work (comprising classwork and/or practical work) *and/or* a report of a project, undertaken during the previous Long Vacation, of not more than 5,000 words excluding footnotes;
(*c*) a report of a research project of not more than 5,000 words, excluding footnotes.

The Head of the Department of Physics shall announce not less than five major topics and ten minor topics, and the types of further work for the examination, including the form of assessment for each topic or piece of further work, not later than the beginning of the Michaelmas Term.

Records of further work shall be submitted to the Examiners through the Head of Department not later than the fifth Monday of the Full Easter Term in which the examination is to be held: they shall bear the signatures of the teachers under whose direction the work was performed.

The report of a project undertaken in the Long Vacation, if it is offered, shall be submitted not later than the first Monday of Full Michaelmas Term. Such a project shall be on a subject proposed by the candidate and approved by the Head of the Department of Physics; candidates shall submit proposals to the Head of the Department during the preceding Easter Term, and shall obtain the approval of the Head of the Department for the subject proposed not later than the last day of that term.

The subject of the research project may be either proposed by the candidate and approved by the Head of the Department of Physics, or chosen by the candidate from a list of approved subjects announced by the Head of the Department not later than the division of the Michaelmas Term. Each candidate shall either obtain the approval of the Head of the Department for the subject proposed, or notify the Head of the Department of the subject chosen from the list, not later than the end of Full Michaelmas Term. The report of a research project shall be submitted to the Head of the Department not later than the third Monday of Full Easter Term.

The Examiners shall be provided by the Head of the Department of Physics with assessments of the reports or further work submitted by candidates under (*b*) and (*c*), and shall take the assessments into account in assigning marks for the examination.

Systems Biology. Each candidate shall offer

(*a*) three written papers; one paper of two hours, one paper of three hours, and one paper of three and a quarter hours (the first quarter of an hour of which shall not be used for writing answers to questions);
(*b*) a computer-based practical examination of three hours;
(*c*) a practical report of a design project;
(*d*) a report of a research project of not more than 6,000 words, excluding footnotes and bibliography.

The subject of the research project may be either proposed by the candidate and approved by the Chair of the Course Management Committee, or chosen by the candidate from a list of approved subjects, which shall be announced by the Chair of the Course Management Committee not later than the end of the Easter Term in the year next preceding the examination.

Each candidate shall either obtain the approval of the Chair of the Course Management Committee for the subject proposed, or notify the Chair of the Course Management Committee of the subject chosen from the list, not later than the first Friday of Full Michaelmas Term. The report of a research project shall be submitted to the Examiners not later than the ninth day of Full Easter Term.

In assigning marks for the examination the Examiners shall take account of project reports.

Class-lists for Part III.

37. For each subject in Part III there shall be published a separate class-list, which shall be signed by the Examiners in that subject. The names of the candidates who obtain honours in each subject shall be arranged in three classes, of which the second shall be divided into two divisions. The names in the first and third classes, and in each division of the second class, shall be arranged in alphabetical order. In arranging the class-list the Examiners for the subject Chemistry in Part III shall take into account the candidate's performance in Part II, where that candidate has been classed in that examination.

SUPPLEMENTARY REGULATIONS

Amended by Notice (Reporter, *2013–14, p. 41*)

Unless otherwise stated, the written papers and practical examinations in a subject shall cover all aspects of the course.

Part IA

Elementary Mathematics for Biologists

This paper is appropriate for candidates who do not have an advanced qualification in Mathematics before entry to the University.

Part IB

Physics B

All candidates will offer Paper 1. Paper 2A is to be offered by candidates not offering Mathematics in Part IB of the Natural Sciences Tripos. Paper 2B is to be taken by candidates offering Mathematics in Part IB of the Natural Sciences Tripos.

Part II

Biological and Biomedical Sciences

The maximum marks allocated to each component shall be as follows:

Major Subject	65
Minor Subject	15
Dissertation	20

Chemistry

All candidates shall offer Paper 2 and Paper 3. Candidates who have previously offered Chemistry A *and* Chemistry B in Part IB of the Natural Sciences Tripos shall also offer Paper 1A and Paper 4A; candidates who have previously offered *only one* out of Chemistry A and Chemistry B in that examination shall also offer *either* Paper 1A and Paper 4A *or* Paper 1B and Paper 4B.

Physical Sciences

The papers set for the Half Subjects shall either be those set for the Part II subject of the same name, or contain a subset of questions from those papers. The maximum marks allocated to each component shall be as follows:

Half Subject	60
Part IB Subject	25
Dissertation	15

Physiology and Psychology

Candidates will offer two psychology papers from Papers 2, 3, and 4, taken by candidates offering the subject Psychology Option A (Psychology).

Psychology

The examination shall comprise two alternative options, (A) and (B). Option (A) is for students wishing to obtain accreditation with the British Psychological Society, and will be known as Psychology (Psychology); option (B) is for students who do not require accreditation with the Society, and will be known as Psychology (Cognitive Neuroscience).

PHILOSOPHY TRIPOS

Amended by Notice (Reporter, *2013–14, p. 638*)

1. The Philosophy Tripos shall consist of three Parts: Part IA, Part IB, and Part II. A separate class-list shall be published for each Part. Three Parts.

2. The Faculty Board shall nominate such number of Examiners as they may deem sufficient to examine in each Part of the Tripos. The Faculty Board may also nominate one or more Assessors for each Part of the Tripos. Assessors shall be responsible for setting the questions in the subjects assigned to them by the Examiners, and for advising the Examiners on the performance of candidates in those questions. An Assessor may be summoned to meetings of the Examiners for the purpose of consultation and advice, but shall not be entitled to vote. Examiners and Assessors.

3. The questions proposed for each Part by each Examiner or Assessor for that Part shall be submitted to and approved by the Examiners for that Part collectively; and the answers to each question shall be examined, as far as possible, by two at least of the Examiners or Assessors. The Examiners and Assessors shall take account of the style and method of the candidates' answers and shall give credit for excellence in these respects.

4. The papers for Part IA shall be as follows: Part IA.

Paper 1. Metaphysics
Paper 2. Ethics and political philosophy
Paper 3. Logic[1]
Paper 4. Set texts
Paper 5. General paper

Every candidate shall offer Papers 1–5.

5. (*a*) The papers for Part IB shall be as follows: Part IB.

Paper 1. Metaphysics and epistemology
Paper 2. Logic
Paper 3. Ethics
Paper 4. Greek and Roman philosophy (Paper 8 of Part IB of the Classical Tripos)
Paper 5. Early modern philosophy
Paper 6. Philosophy of science
Paper 7. Political philosophy
Paper 8. Experimental psychology (the subject Experimental Psychology in Part IB of the Natural Sciences Tripos)
Paper 9. General paper

(*b*) Subject to the provision of sub-paragraphs (*c*) and (*d*) of this regulation, a candidate for Part IB shall offer papers as follows:

either (i) Papers 1, 2, and 9, and two papers from Papers 3–7;
or (ii) Papers 1, 2, and 8, and one paper from Papers 3–7.

The weighting of Paper 8, for those who offer it, shall be double that of other papers.

(*c*) No candidate who has previously offered Experimental psychology in Part IB of the Natural Sciences Tripos shall offer Paper 8.

(*d*) In place of any one of the Papers 1–3, and 5–7 a candidate may submit two essays, each of not less than 3,000 words and not more than 4,000 words in length, including footnotes and appendices but excluding bibliography, on two topics approved by the Chair of Examiners, which shall both fall within the syllabus of that paper; provided that a candidate who chooses to submit essays under the provisions of this sub-paragraph shall not write in Paper 9 an essay on a subject that overlaps significantly with either of the submitted essays.

6. The papers for Part II shall be as follows: Part II.

Paper 1. Metaphysics
Paper 2. Philosophy of mind (also serves as Paper O5 of Part II of the Classical Tripos)
Paper 3. Ethics
Paper 4. European philosophy from Kant
Paper 5. Philosophy in the Long Middle Ages[2]
Paper 6. Philosophy of science
Paper 7. Mathematical logic
Paper 8. Philosophical logic
Paper 9. Special subject specified by the Faculty Board from time to time

[1] This paper is also available to up to six candidates for Paper B17 in Part IIA of the Theological and Religious Studies Tripos.
[2] This paper is also available to candidates for Part IIB of the Theological and Religious Studies Tripos.

Paper 10. Political philosophy
Paper 11. Aesthetics[1]
Paper 12. General paper

7. Except as provided in Regulation 8 below, a candidate for Part II shall offer papers as follows:

either (*a*) four papers from among Papers 1–11 and the papers specified in the Schedule to these regulations, and (*b*) a dissertation offered in accordance with Regulation 9

or (*a*) four papers from among Papers 1–11 and the papers specified in the Schedule to these regulations, and (*b*) Paper 12;

provided that a candidate who has previously obtained honours in Part II of the Classical Tripos or Part IIB of the Theological and Religious Studies Tripos shall not offer any paper that he or she offered in that examination.

(*c*) a candidate who takes the examination in the year next but one after last obtaining honours in any examination shall offer

either (i) four papers from among Papers 1–11 and the papers specified in the Schedule to these regulations, and (ii) a dissertation offered in accordance with Regulation 9

or (i) four papers from among Papers 1–11 and the papers specified in the Schedule to these regulations, and (ii) Paper 12;

provided that a candidate who has previously obtained honours in Part II of the Classical Tripos or Part IIB of the Theological and Religious Studies Tripos shall not offer any paper that he or she offered in that examination.

Essays.

8. In place of any one of Papers 1–11 and the papers from the Classical Tripos specified in the Schedule to these regulations, a candidate for Part II of the Philosophy Tripos may submit two essays, each of not less than 3,000 words and not more than 4,000 words in length, including footnotes and appendices but excluding bibliography, on two topics approved by the Chair of Examiners, which shall both fall within the syllabus of that paper, provided that

(i) a candidate who chooses to submit essays under the provisions of this paragraph shall not write in Paper 12 an essay on a subject that overlaps significantly with either of the submitted essays;

(ii) a candidate who chooses to submit essays shall not write in place of Paper 12 a dissertation on a subject that overlaps significantly with either of the submitted essays.

(iii) a candidate for Part II under Regulation 7(*b*) may not offer both two submitted essays in accordance with this regulation and a dissertation in accordance with Regulation 9.

Dissertation or essays.

9. (*a*) A candidate for Part IB who chooses to offer two submitted essays under the provisions of Regulation 5(*d*), or a candidate for Part II who chooses to offer a dissertation under the provisions of Regulation 7 and/or two submitted essays under the provisions of Regulation 8 shall submit the proposed title of the dissertation or the proposed titles of the essays, together with a statement of the papers to be offered in the examination, and in the case of essays a statement of the paper which they are intended to replace, to the Chair of Examiners so as to arrive not later than two weeks before the last day of Full Michaelmas Term. A candidate must obtain the approval of the Chair of Examiners for the proposed title or titles not later than the last day of Full Michaelmas Term.

(*b*) Essays shall be submitted to the Chair of Examiners, in accordance with detailed arrangements approved by the Faculty Board, so as to arrive not later than the last day of the Lent Term next preceding the examination.

(*c*) Dissertations shall be submitted to the Chair of Examiners, in accordance with detailed arrangements approved by the Faculty Board, so as to arrive not later than the second Friday of the Easter Term in which the examination is to be held.

(*d*) Every candidate submitting a dissertation or a pair of essays will be required to sign a declaration that the work submitted is her or his own work, unaided except as may be specified in the declaration, and that it does not contain material that has already been used to any substantial extent for a comparable purpose. The Examiners shall have power to examine any candidate *viva voce* on the dissertation or the essays.

(*e*) A dissertation, which shall be on a topic of philosophical interest approved by the Chair of Examiners, shall be of not more than 8,000 words and (except with the permission of the Chair of Examiners) not less than 6,000 words in length, including footnotes and appendices but excluding bibliography.

[1] This paper is also available to candidates for Part II of the Modern and Medieval Languages Tripos; see p. 395.

10. The Faculty Board shall have power to publish supplementary regulations for the topics included in the several subjects before mentioned, and to issue a list of books in relation to which questions shall be set. They shall also have power to modify or alter the supplementary regulations and the list from time to time as they see fit, due care being taken that sufficient notice is given of any change. Public notice of all the variable subjects and texts prescribed for special study shall be given by the Faculty Board before the end of the Easter Term in the year next preceding the examination to which they apply; provided that the Board shall have the power of subsequently issuing amendments if they have due reason for doing so and if they are satisfied that no student's preparation for the examination is adversely affected. Supplementary regulations and notice of variable subjects.

11. A student may be a candidate for honours in Part IA if at the time of the examination he or she has kept one term, provided that three complete terms have not passed after his or her first term of residence. Standing of candidates.

12. The following may present themselves as candidates for honours in Part IB:

(*a*) a student who has not obtained honours in an Honours Examination, provided that he or she has kept four terms and that six complete terms have not passed after his or her first term of residence;

(*b*) a student who has obtained honours in Part IA of the Philosophy Tripos or in another Honours Examination, in the year next after so obtaining honours, provided that twelve complete terms have not passed after his or her first term of residence.

13. The following may present themselves as candidates for honours in Part II:

(*a*) a student who has obtained honours in Part IB of the Philosophy Tripos in the year after so obtaining honours, provided that at the time of the examination the student has kept seven terms, and that twelve complete terms have not passed after her or his first term of residence;[1]

(*b*) a student who has obtained honours in another Honours Examination in the year next after or next but one after so obtaining honours, provided that at the time of the examination the student has kept seven terms, and that fifteen complete terms have not passed after her or his first term of residence;

(*c*) an Affiliated Student as allowed by the Faculty Board of Philosophy in accordance with the regulations for Affiliated Students.

14. No student shall be a candidate for more than one Part in the same year. No student who has been a candidate for any Part shall again be a candidate for the same Part.

15. In each Part, the names of the candidates who obtain honours shall be arranged in three classes, of which the second shall be divided into two divisions. The names in the first and third classes, and in each division of the second class, shall be arranged in alphabetical order. Each class-list may show, by some convenient mark, whether a candidate has passed with special distinction. Class-lists

SCHEDULE

Papers from other Triposes that may be taken in Part II

A candidate for Part II of the Philosophy Tripos may take one or two of the following papers:

Classical Tripos, Part II
Group B (*Philosophy*)

B1. Plato
B2. Aristotle
B3. A prescribed subject or period in Greek and Roman philosophy

Theological and Religious Studies Tripos, Part IIB
Group C

C11. Metaphysics

[1] See also the regulations for Affiliated Students.

POLITICS, PSYCHOLOGY, AND SOCIOLOGY (SOCIAL AND POLITICAL SCIENCES) TRIPOS[1]

Amended by Notices (Reporter, *2013–14, pp. 534 and 726*)

General

Three Parts.

1. The Politics, Psychology, and Sociology Tripos (Social and Political Sciences Tripos)[1] shall consist of three Parts: Part I, Part IIA, and Part IIB. A separate class-list shall be published for each Part.

Standing of candidates.

2. A student may be a candidate for honours in Part I if at the time of the examination he or she has kept one term, provided that three complete terms have not passed after the student's first term of residence.

3. The following may present themselves as candidates for honours in Part IIA;

(*a*) a student who has obtained honours in Part I of the Politics, Psychology, and Sociology (Social and Political Sciences) Tripos and has not subsequently obtained honours in any other Honours Examination, provided that six complete terms have not passed after his or her first term of residence;[2]

(*b*) a student who has obtained honours in another Honours Examination, in the year after so obtaining honours, provided that nine complete terms have not passed after his or her first term of residence.

4. A student who has obtained honours in any other Honours Examination other than Part I of the Politics, Psychology, and Sociology (Social and Political Sciences) Tripos may be a candidate for honours in Part IIB in the year after so obtaining honours, provided that the student has kept seven terms and that twelve complete terms have not passed after his or her first term of residence.[2]

5. No student shall be a candidate for any Part and also for another Honours Examination in the same term.

6. No student shall be a candidate for any Part on more than one occasion.

Supplementary regulations.

7. The Faculty Board of Human, Social, and Political Science shall have power to issue from time to time supplementary regulations defining or limiting all or any of the subjects of examination. Due care shall be taken that sufficient notice is given of any alteration of such supplementary regulations. The Faculty Board shall also have power to publish from time to time lists of books recommended to the candidates.

Notice of variable subjects.

8. The Faculty Board shall give notice of any variable subjects for Parts IIA and IIB of the Tripos, before the division of the Easter Term of the year next but one preceding the examination concerned, provided that the Faculty Board shall have the power of subsequently issuing amendments if they have due reason for so doing and if they are satisfied that no student's preparation for the examination is adversely affected.

Examiners and Assessors.

9. The Faculty Board shall nominate such number of Examiners as they deem sufficient for each Part of the Tripos. The Faculty Board shall also have power to nominate one or more Assessors to assist the Examiners in any Part of the Tripos. The Assessors shall propose questions in the parts of the examination assigned to them by the Examiners, shall look over the answers of the candidates to these questions, and shall report thereon to the Examiners. The Assessors may be summoned to meetings of the Examiners for the purposes of consultation and advice, but shall not be entitled to vote.

10. In each Part of the Tripos, the questions proposed by each Examiner and Assessor shall be submitted for approval to the whole body of Examiners.

11. A candidate shall not offer in any Part of the Tripos a paper that he or she has previously offered in another University examination.

[1] The title of the Social and Political Sciences Tripos has been amended to Politics, Psychology, and Sociology. Candidates who started the course before 1 October 2008 will continue to take papers under the title of the Social and Political Sciences Tripos, while candidates starting on or after 1 October 2008 will take papers under the title of the Politics, Psychology, and Sociology Tripos.

[2] See also the regulations for Affiliated Students.

PART I

Scheme of examination for Part I.

12. The scheme of examination for Part I shall be as follows:

Section A

Paper 1.	Analysis of politics I (also serves as Paper 4C of Part I of the Archaeological and Anthropological Tripos and as Paper 5(*a*) of Part IIA of the Economics Tripos)
Paper 2.	Introduction to sociology: modern societies I (also serves as Paper 4B of Part I of the Archaeological and Anthropological Tripos and as Paper 5(*b*) of Part IIA of the Economics Tripos)
Paper 3.	Introduction to psychology (also serves as Paper 4D of Part I of the Archaeological and Anthropological Tripos and as a paper in Part IA of the Computer Science Tripos)

Section B

Paper 4.	Introduction to research methods and statistics for social scientists[1]
Paper 5.	International relations I (also serves as Paper 5(*c*) of Part IIA of the Economics Tripos)
Paper 6.	The development of human society (Paper 1 of Part I of the Archaeological and Anthropological Tripos)
Paper 7.	Humans in biological perspective (Paper 2 of Part I of the Archaeological and Anthropological Tripos)
Paper 8.	Human societies: the comparative perspective (Paper 3 of Part I of the Archaeological and Anthropological Tripos)
Paper 9.	Computer Science 1: Introduction to computer science (Paper 1 of Part IA of the Computer Science Tripos)
Paper 10.	British economic history (Paper 5 of Part I of the Economics Tripos)
Paper 11.	Language, communication, and literacy (Paper 2 of the preliminary examination for Part I of the Education Tripos)

A candidate for Part I shall be required to offer four papers as follows:

(*a*) two papers from Section A;

(*b*) two further papers, *either* one from section A and one from section B, *or* two from section B.

13. The names of the candidates who obtain honours in Part I shall be placed by the Examiners in three classes, of which the second shall be divided into two divisions. The names in the first and third classes and in each division of the second class shall be arranged in alphabetical order.

PARTS IIA AND IIB

Scheme of examination for Parts IIA and IIB.

14. The scheme of examination for Parts IIA and IIB[2] shall be as follows:

Politics and International Studies

Pol. 1.	The history of political thought to *c.* 1700 (Paper 19 of Part I of the Historical Tripos)
Pol. 2.	The history of political thought from *c.* 1700 to *c.* 1890 (Paper 20 of Part I of the Historical Tripos)
Pol. 3.	The analysis of modern politics II[3]
Pol. 4.	The analysis of modern politics III
Pol. 6.	Political philosophy and the history of political thought since *c.* 1890 (Paper 5 of Part II of the Historical Tripos)
Pol. 7.	A subject in politics and international studies II
Pol. 8.	A subject in politics and international studies III
Pol. 9.	A subject in politics and international studies IV
Pol. 10.	A subject in politics and international studies VII[4]
Pol. 11.	A subject in politics and international studies V[5]
Pol. 12.	A subject in politics and international studies VI
Pol. 13.	Conceptual issues and texts in politics and international studies
Pol. 14.	The history of political thought to *c.* 1700[4]
Pol. 15.	The history of political thought from *c.* 1700 to *c.* 1890 (Paper 4 of Part II of the Historical Tripos)

Psychology within the Social Sciences

Psy. 1.	Social psychology[3]
Psy. 2.	Experimental psychology (the subject Experimental Psychology in Part IB of the Natural Sciences Tripos)
Psy. 3.	Biological and cognitive psychology
Psy. 4.	Development and psychopathology

[1] This paper is suspended until further notice.
[2] For further information on the papers offered for Part IIB in 2014–15, see Notice (*Reporter*, 6354, 2013–14, p. 667).
[3] This paper is also available to candidates for Part IIA of the Archaeological and Anthropological Tripos.
[4] This paper will not be available in Part IIB in 2014–15.
[5] This paper will also be available, in certain years, to candidates for the Asian and Middle Eastern Studies Tripos.

Psy. 5. A subject in psychology I[1]
Psy. 6. A subject in psychology II
Psy. 7. A subject in psychology III

Sociology

Soc. 1. Social theory[2]
Soc. 2. Contemporary societies and global transformations[2]
Soc. 3. Concepts and arguments in sociology[3]
Soc. 4. A subject in sociology I
Soc. 5. A subject in sociology II[4]
Soc. 6. A subject in sociology III
Soc. 7. A subject in sociology IV[4]
Soc. 8. Disciplines of education III (Paper 3 of Part II of the Education Tripos)
Soc. 9. A subject in sociology V
Soc. 10. A subject in sociology VI

Interdisciplinary papers

Int. 1A. Inquiry and analysis I[3]
Int. 1B. Inquiry and analysis I[3]
Int. 2. Inquiry and analysis II
Int. 3. An interdisciplinary subject I
Int. 4. An interdisciplinary subject II
Int. 5. An interdisciplinary subject III[1]
Int. 6. Criminology, sentencing, and the penal system (Paper 23 of the Law Tripos)
Int. 7. Society, politics, and culture in Latin America[1, 4, 5]
Int. 8. A specified subject in South Asian Studies[4]
Int. 9. An interdisciplinary subject IV[4]
Int. 10. An interdisciplinary subject V[1]

Not more than one subject shall be specified for each of Pol. 4, 7–9, 11, 12, Psy. 5–7, Soc. 4–7, 9, 10, and Int. 3–5, 9, 10.

15. (*a*) Each paper shall be of three hours' duration, except Psy. 2, Soc. 3, and Int. 1A and Int. 1B, provided that Pol. 7–9, 11, Soc. 4–7, 9, 10, and Int. 3–9 may be examined by an alternative mode of assessment, which shall consist of the submission of two essays, each of not more than 5,000 words. The examination for Soc. 3 shall consist of the submission of two essays, each of not more than 5,000 words. The examination for Int. 1A and Int. 1B shall consist of the submission of a research project, a statistical assignment, and one methodological essay.

(*b*) The Faculty Board shall publish by notice in each Department of the Faculty of Human, Social, and Political Science prescribed titles or subjects for essays by the division of the Michaelmas Term next preceding the examination concerned. The work to be undertaken for the research project shall be prescribed from time to time by the Faculty Board.

(*c*) The essays, the statistical assignment, and the report of the research project, shall be submitted in printed or typewritten form to the Secretary of the Faculty Board as follows: essays for all papers except Int. 1A and Int. 1B (that is, Pol. 7–9, Pol. 11, Soc. 3–7, Soc. 9–10, Int. 3–9), one essay no later than the end of the first week of Full Lent Term, and one essay no later than the end of the first week of Full Easter Term; for Int. 1A and Int. 1B the statistical assignment shall be submitted before the division of the Lent Term, the methodological essay before the end of the Lent Term, and the report before the division of the Easter Term. Each essay, the assignment, and the report shall bear the candidate's examination number but not the candidate's name. Candidates may be called for *viva voce* examination in connection with their essays, statistical assignment, or research project.

16. Subject to the provisions of Regulation 11 a candidate for Part IIA shall offer one of the following options:

(*a*) *either* Pol. 1 *or* Pol. 2, Pol. 3, and Pol.4;

(*b*) Psy. 1, *either* Psy. 2 *or* Psy. 3, and Int. 1A;

(*c*) Soc. 1, *either* Soc. 2 *or* Pol. 3 *or* Pol. 4, and *either* Soc. 3 *or* Int. 1B;

[1] This paper is suspended until further notice.
[2] This paper is also available to candidates for Part IIA of the Archaeological and Anthropological Tripos.
[3] This paper will not be available in Part IIB in 2014–15.
[4] This paper will also be available, in certain years, to candidates for the Economics Tripos.
[5] This paper will also be available, in certain years, to candidates for Part II of the Modern and Medieval Languages Tripos; see p 395.

(*d*) Psy. 1, *either* Soc. 1 *or* Soc. 2, and Int. 1A;

17. Subject to the provision of Regulation 11, a candidate for Part IIB who has taken option (*a*) in Part IIA shall offer:

(*a*) one paper chosen from Pol. 6–12, 14, 15[1];

(*b*) Pol. 13;

(*c*) *either* (i) two further papers chosen from Pol. 6–12, Int. 3–10, Psy. 1, Soc. 1, 4, 5, 7, or 9, or paper SOC5 from the Human, Social, and Political Sciences Tripos;

or (ii) one further paper chosen from Pol. 6–12, Int. 3–10, Psy. 1, Soc. 1, 4, 5, 7, 9, and a dissertation.

A candidate who chooses any of Papers Pol. 7–9, 11, Soc. 4, 5, 7, 9, Int. 3–9 under (*a*) or (*c*) option (i), and who does not include Paper SOC5 from the Human, Social, and Political Sciences Tripos among the papers offered, may offer two essays in place of one of those papers, in accordance with the provisions of Regulation 15.

18. Subject to the provisions of Regulation 11 a candidate for Part IIB who has taken option (*b*) in Part IIA shall offer:

(*a*) Psy. 4;

(*b*) one paper chosen from Psy. 5–7;

(*c*) one further paper chosen from Psy. 5–7, Pol. 1–4, Soc. 1, Soc. 2, Soc. 4, Soc. 8, Soc. 10, Int. 2–10, and a dissertation, as prescribed in Regulation 22.

Candidates may not offer extended essays in place of any of these papers.

19. Subject to the provisions of Regulation 11 a candidate for Part IIB who has taken option (*c*) in Part IIA shall offer:

(*a*) one paper chosen from Soc. 4–10;

(*b*) *either* (i) three further papers chosen from Soc. 4–10, Pol. 1–2, Psy. 1, Int. 2–10, two of which may also be chosen from Pol. 7–8, Pol. 10–11;

or (ii) two further papers chosen from Soc. 4–10, Pol. 1–2, Pol. 7–8, Pol. 10–11, Psy 1, Int. 2–10, and a dissertation as prescribed in Regulation 22.

A candidate who chooses any of Papers Soc. 4–7, 9, 10, Pol. 7, 8, 11, Int. 3–9 under (*a*) or (*b*) option (i) may offer two essays in place of one of those papers, in accordance with the provisions of Regulation 15.

20. Subject to the provisions of Regulation 11 a candidate for Part IIB who has taken option (*d*) in Part IIA shall offer:

(*a*) two papers chosen from Psy. 2–7, Soc. 4–10, Int. 3, Int.4;

(*b*) *either* (i) two further papers chosen from Psy. 2–7, Soc. 1, 2, 4–10, Pol. 1–4, Int. 2–10;

or (ii) one further paper chosen from Psy. 2–7, Soc. 1, 2, 4–10, Pol. 1–4, Int. 2–10, and a dissertation as prescribed in Regulation 22.

A candidate who chooses any of Papers Soc. 4–7, 9, 10, Int. 3–9 under (*a*) or (*b*) option (i) may offer two essays in place of one of those papers, in accordance with the provisions of Regulation 15.

21. Subject to the provisions of Regulation 11 a candidate for Part IIB who has not previously obtained honours in Part IIA shall offer, with the approval of the Faculty Board, on application by the candidate's Tutor not later than the division of the Michaelmas Term next preceding the examination, four papers chosen from the papers available in Part IIA and Part IIB; provided that a candidate who does not include Int. 1 among the papers chosen may offer two essays of not more than 5,000 words in place of one of Pol. 7–9, 11, Soc. 4–7, 9–10, Int. 3–9 in accordance with the provisions of Regulation 15. Candidates taking a paper from among Psy. 1–7 may substitute one Part II paper with Paper PBS2 from Part I of the Psychological and Behavioural Sciences Tripos, subject to the approval of the Faculty Board.

22. (*a*) A candidate who wishes to offer a dissertation under Regulations 17–20 shall submit an application, including the topic of the proposed dissertation, a brief account of its scope, and a statement of the scheme of papers to be offered in the examination. A candidate may not choose for the dissertation a topic in the same field as that of Pol. 1 or Pol. 2, or Pol. 14 or Pol. 15. Applications shall be submitted to the Secretary of the Faculty Board, in accordance with any instructions issued by the Faculty Board, so as to arrive not later than the second Friday of Full Michaelmas Term next preceding the examination. Dissertation.

[1] Pol. 15 may not be taken if a candidate took Pol. 2 at Part IIA.

(*b*) Each candidate must obtain the approval of the Faculty Board for the proposed topic not later than the last day of the Michaelmas Term. After the Faculty Board have approved a topic no substantial change may be made in it without the further approval of the Faculty Board.

(*c*) A dissertation shall contain full references to any sources used in its composition, and shall be of not less than 6,000 words and not more than 10,000 words in length, including footnotes and appendices but excluding any bibliography.

(*d*) A dissertation shall be submitted in printed or typewritten form to the Secretary of the Faculty Board not later than the end of the second week of the Full Easter Term in which the examination is to be held. Each dissertation shall bear the candidate's examination number but not the candidate's name and shall be accompanied by a certificate signed by the candidate that it is his or her own original work, and that it does not contain material that has already been used to any substantial extent for a comparable purpose.

(*e*) The Examiners shall have power to examine a candidate *viva voce* on the subject of the dissertation and in the general field of knowledge within which it falls.

Class-lists. **23.** There shall be separate class-lists for Parts IIA and IIB of the Tripos. The names of the candidates in each class-list shall be arranged in three classes, of which the second shall be divided into two divisions. The names in the first and third classes, and in each division of the second class, shall be arranged in alphabetical order. In each class-list a mark of distinction may be attached to the name of any candidate whose work in the examination shows special merit.

Temporary Regulation

24. Examinations for the Politics, Psychology, and Sociology (Social and Political Sciences) Tripos will be held for the last time as follows:

Part I in 2013
Part IIA in 2014
Part IIB in 2015

SUPPLEMENTARY REGULATIONS

Amended by Notice (Reporter, *2013–14, p. 726*)

Part I

Paper 1. Analysis of modern politics (also serves as Paper 4C of Part I of the Archaeological and Anthropological Tripos and as Paper 5(*a*) of Part IIA of the Economics Tripos)

The course for this paper provides an introduction to some central questions about the nature of modern politics through an examination of a set of political thinkers and some consideration of their work in relation to a range of examples from practical politics.

Paper 2. Introduction to sociology: modern societies (also serves as Paper 4B of Part I of the Archaeological and Anthropological Tripos and Paper 5(*b*) of Part IIA of the Economics Tripos).

An introduction, through the work of Marx, Weber, and Durkheim, to key concepts and theories in sociology. An examination of core institutions and characteristics of modern societies including power and the modern state; the rise of nationalism; citizenship and social welfare; culture and the media; class and inequality; gender and the family; globalization and social change.

Paper 3. Introduction to psychology (also serves as Paper 4D of Part I of the Archaeological and Anthropological Tripos)

The scope of social psychology. Methods and levels of analysis. Selected topics from the following:

The self in social context. Personality and personality traits. Nature-nurture issues in socialization. Cognitive and affective bases of social behaviour. Parent–child relationships. The family, marriage, and divorce. Gender and gender roles. Social interaction processes. Small group processes. Attitudes and ideologies. Learning about society. The social psychology of work. Social aspects of mental illness. Cross-cultural variations in perception, thinking, and social behaviour.

Paper 5. International relations I (also serves as Paper 5(*c*) of Part IIA of the Economics Tripos)

The course for this paper provides an introduction to the subject of International Relations, whose main focus is the nature of politics at the international level. It does so by focusing on the concept of the 'international society' of states, which refers to the set of institutions and common procedures generated over the last three and a half centuries in various attempts to manage co-existence, but which now includes many non-state actors and a number of different levels of interaction. The four principal themes of the course are: the *historical evolution* of the international system; the causes and consequences of *war*; the sources of such *order* as exists in international life; and the *ethical dilemmas* arising from the interaction of competing political systems.

Parts IIa and IIb

Paper Pol. 1. The history of political thought to c. 1700 (Paper 19 of Part I of the Historical Tripos)

Paper Pol. 2. The history of political thought from c. 1700 to c. 1890 (Paper 20 of Part I of the Historical Tripos)

Paper Pol. 3. The analysis of modern politics II[1]

This paper examines questions about ethics and world politics normatively and in a variety of concrete political contexts. The examination will be divided into two sections. Candidates will be required to answer two questions from the first section of the examination and one from the second.

Paper Pol. 4. The analysis of modern politics III

The paper examines a range of issues, substantive and methodological, in comparative politics. A candidate will be required to take a two-hour written examination and to submit an essay of not more than 5,000 words. The examination will require the candidate to answer two questions, taking each question on a different region or case study. For the essay, a candidate will be required to select an option from a list of questions announced by the Faculty Board. The essay and the examination will each carry 50% of the mark for the paper.

Paper Pol. 5. Conceptual issues in modern politics

Conceptual questions that arise in the study of modern politics. This paper is examined by two 5,000-word essays.

Paper Pol. 6. Political philosophy and the history of political thought since c. 1890 (Paper 5 of Part II of the Historical Tripos)

The course for this paper explores the central texts and key ideas of twentieth-century political thought, looking at both analytical concepts and historical context. It is divided into two parts, Section A covers historical topics organized around authors and their texts, and Section B which covers a variety of themes in contemporary political philosophy.

Paper Pol. 7. A subject in modern politics and international studies II

A subject in modern politics and international studies specified by the Faculty Board from time to time.

Paper Pol. 8. A subject in modern politics and international studies III

A subject in modern politics and international studies specified by the Faculty Board from time to time.

Paper Pol. 9. A subject in modern politics and international studies IV

A subject in modern politics and international studies specified by the Faculty Board from time to time.

Paper Pol. 10. A subject in politics and international studies VII[2]

Paper Pol. 11 A subject in modern politics and international studies V[3]

A subject in modern politics and international studies specified by the Faculty Board from time to time.

Paper Pol. 12. A subject in modern politics and international studies VI

A subject in modern politics and international studies specified by the Faculty Board from time to time.

Paper Pol. 13. Conceptual issues and texts in politics and international studies

General issues, theoretical, conceptual and practical, in modern politics.

Paper Pol. 14. The history of political thought to c. *1700*[2]

Paper Pol. 15. The history of political thought from c. *1700 to* c. *1890* (Paper 4 of Part II of the Historical Tripos).

Paper Psy. 1. Social psychology[1]

The scope of this paper will include all those aspects of psychology which are relevant to an understanding of human social behaviour and its development. In any single year the paper will offer students the opportunity to study a number of individual and interpersonal processes from within this range (e.g. aggression, altruism, applied social psychology, attitudes, attribution theory, communication, conflict, conformity co-operation, emotion, group processes, identity, impression formation, inter-group relations, interpersonal attraction, personality, prejudice, pro-social behaviour, relationships, social cognition, social influence, social psychiatry, stereotyping, trust), and alternative frameworks within which the study of human social behaviour has been conceptualized (e.g. discursive psychology, experimental social psychology, psychoanalysis, social representations theory). The relationship between social psychology and other parts of psychology will also be addressed.

[1] This paper is also available to candidates for Part IIa of the Archaeological and Anthropological Tripos.
[2] This paper will not be available in Part IIb in 2014–15.
[3] This paper will also be available, in certain years, to candidates for the Asian and Middle Eastern Studies Tripos.

Paper Psy. 2. Experimental psychology (the subject Experimental Psychology in Part IB of the Natural Sciences Tripos)

The paper is assessed by two three-hour papers, a written practical of an hour-and-a-half, and practical reports.

Paper Psy 3. Biological and cognitive psychology

This paper covers biological and cognitive topics involving the connection of brain, body, and behaviour, and will do so from a social sciences perspective. Specific content includes neuroanatomy, neuroendocrinology, and neurophysiology, as well as learning, memory, judgement, decision making, intelligence, and cognition and emotion. Topics are presented in the context of the complete individual, and in interaction with the social environment. Lectures include relevant methodologies and methodological issues, and integrative examples will be provided on topics such as executive function, sex differences in the brain, social neuroscience, and autism. Practicals will serve to further illustrate the links between theoretical foundations and experimental methods. Students are expected to read in depth, as well as broadly, and to bring their independent perspective and insight to the material at hand.

Paper Psy. 4. Development and psychopathology

The course for this paper considers children's development from infancy to adolescence, with a focus on the interface between typical and atypical development. Topics considered include infancy, prematurity, early theory of mind and autism, early executive function and conduct disorder, the transition to school, adolescence and associated problems (e.g. self-harming), parenthood, and abuse.

Paper Psy. 5. A subject in psychology I[1]

A subject in psychology specified by the Faculty Board from time to time.

Paper Psy. 6. A subject in psychology II

A subject in psychology specified by the Faculty Board from time to time.

Paper Psy. 7. A subject in psychology III

A subject in psychology specified by the Faculty Board from time to time.

Paper Soc. 1. Social theory[2]

This paper provides an account of the main intellectual traditions and key contributions of contemporary social theory. The time period extends from *c.* 1920 to the present day, but the paper concentrates on recent (post-1960) literature and developments. A limited number of traditions and orientations are selected for detailed discussion; these traditions and orientations are situated in their social and intellectual contexts, and the writings of key thinkers are examined in some depth.

Paper Soc. 2. Contemporary societies and global transformation[2]

Theories of global scale, political and economic transformation: Marxist theories of capitalism and imperialism; world systems theory; development theory; modernity; globalization. The evolution of a global economy: Fordism and post-Fordism; multi- and trans-national corporations: the information and knowledge economy; convergence and diversity in capitalism; global finance. The development of the modern state: the interstate system and new forms of 'geo-governance'; economic globalization and state power. Post-communist societies and the problem of 'transition'. Global communication and information networks: communication and development; cultural identity and the information age. Globalization and social change: health, the family.

Paper Soc. 3. Concepts and arguments in sociology[3]

Conceptual and explanatory issues that arise in the study of modern societies. The paper is examined by two 5,000-word essays.

Paper Soc. 4. A subject in sociology I

A subject in sociology specified by the Faculty Board from time to time.

Paper Soc. 5. A subject in sociology II[4]

A subject in sociology specified by the Faculty Board from time to time.

Paper Soc. 6. A subject in sociology III

A subject in sociology specified by the Faculty Board from time to time.

Paper Soc. 7. A subject in sociology IV[4]

A subject in sociology specified by the Faculty Board from time to time.

Paper Soc. 8. Disciplines of education III (Paper 3 of Part II of the Education Tripos).

Paper Soc. 9. A subject in sociology V

A subject in sociology specified by the Faculty Board from time to time.

[1] This paper is suspended until further notice.
[2] This paper is also available to candidates for Part IIA of the Archaeological and Anthropological Tripos.
[3] This paper will not be available in Part IIB in 2014–15.
[4] This paper will also be available, in certain years, to candidates for the Economics Tripos.

Paper Soc. 10. A subject in sociology VI

A subject in sociology specified by the Faculty Board from time to time.

Paper Int. 1. Inquiry and analysis I[1]

This paper introduces candidates to the concepts and methods of social research. It will give candidates the conceptual and methodological knowledge to evaluate different styles of social inquiry and provide the necessary skills to design and implement an empirical inquiry. Candidates will be introduced to the basic philosophical ideas that underpin social research and will be instructed in the appropriate use of basic descriptive and inferential statistical techniques. The paper will be examined by one 2,500-word methodological essay, one 3,500-word statistical assignment, and a project report of 5,000 words.

Paper Int. 2. Inquiry and analysis II

This course extends students' understanding of the theory and practice of social inquiry and analysis. Students will be encouraged to tackle the challenges posed by combining quantitative and qualitative approaches. Students will also be introduced to the various approaches used in studies of social and individual change, including advanced multivariate techniques and longitudinal design and analysis.

Paper Int. 3. An interdisciplinary subject I

An interdisciplinary subject specified by the Faculty Board from time to time.

Paper Int. 4. An interdisciplinary subject II: Racism, race, and ethnicity

This course explores the emergence of modern notions of race and ethnicity, contemporary forms of racism, processes of racialization, and the social and political forces that have shaped them. Key questions will include: How are racial ideas conceptualized and justified through a variety of biological, social, and cultural discourses? How did race and ethnicity come to be defined and embedded in the context of colonial and post-colonial rule? What are the often complex relations between ideas of race, the production of difference and identity, and the pervasiveness of social exclusion? Why does race remain such a powerful determinant of individual and collective identities? What is the specificity of ethnicity in contemporary society? Why and how does race and ethnicity matter?

Paper Int. 5. An interdisciplinary subject III[2, 3]

An interdisciplinary subject specified by the Faculty Board from time to time.

Paper Int. 6. Criminology, sentencing, and the penal system (Paper 23 of the Law Tripos)

A key aim of this paper is to allow students to gain a critical and informed understanding of patterns of crime, pathways into and out of crime, and critical issues regarding law, policy and practice in relation to criminal justice and sentencing. The first section will look at the social construction of criminal statistics and the influence of the media in shaping popular understandings of crime, individual, family and situational factors in relation to pathways into crime as well as resilience and desistance and offender rehabilitation in regard to pathways out of crime. The second section involves a focus on theories of punishment and the part that different forms of punishment can play in reducing crime. The third part turns to sentencing issues, the legal framework, and dilemmas in theory and practice, whilst the fourth part concentrates on specific groups of offenders: young offenders, sex offenders, dangerous offenders, and women, for example, and the particular challenges in dealing with those groups of offenders. The final element turns to community penalties, prisons, parole, and to the broad issues of fairness, discretion, gender, and race in late modern criminal justice. The paper will be examined by *either* (*a*) a three-hour paper consisting of 4 questions, *or* (*b*) two long essays of 5,000 words each.

Paper Int. 7. Society, politics, and culture in Latin America[3]

Using a range of approaches drawn from sociology, political science, political economy, social anthropology, and cultural studies, the course for this paper covers the history of Latin America in the period since the Second World War. Particular attention is paid to structural change in the region's economy and its relationship with the international economy, to the resulting transition from a state-led inward-looking model of development to the more outward-looking neo-liberal model adopted at the end of the century, and to variations in the concomitant process of democratization. The consequences and corollaries of these changes are traced in the fields of culture and religion, in the changing patterns of popular mobilization, and in the proliferation of 'informal' economic activities.

Paper Int. 8. A specified subject in South Asian Studies[2]

Paper Int. 9. An interdisciplinary subject IV[2]

An interdisciplinary subject specified by the Faculty Board from time to time.

Paper Int. 10. An interdisciplinary subject V[3]

An interdisciplinary subject specified by the Faculty Board from time to time.

[1] This paper will not be available in Part IIB in 2014–15.
[2] This paper will also be available, in certain years, to candidates for the Economics Tripos.
[3] This paper is suspended until further notice.

PSYCHOLOGICAL AND BEHAVIOURAL SCIENCES TRIPOS[1]

Amended by Notice (Reporter, *2013–14, p. 447*)

General

Three parts.

1. The Psychological and Behavioural Sciences Tripos shall consist of three Parts: Part I, Part IIA, and Part IIB.

2. No student shall be a candidate for more than one Part, or for any Part and also for another Honours Examination, in the same term.

3. No student shall be a candidate for any Part on more than one occasion.

4. No student shall offer any paper which he or she has previously offered in another University examination.

Examiners and Assessors.

5. There shall be three separate bodies of Examiners, one for Part I, one for Part IIA, and one for Part IIB. For each of the three bodies there shall be a Chair of Examiners, provided that the same person may be appointed Chair for two or more bodies. For each body there might also be one or more Assistant Chairs of Examiners. Chairs and Assistant Chairs of Examiners shall be appointed on the nomination of the Committee of Management of the Psychological and Behavioural Sciences Tripos; nominations shall be made not later than the last day of Full Easter Term in the calendar year next preceding that in which the examination is to be held. For each of the three bodies, the Committee of Management shall, in consultation with Faculty Boards or comparable authorities, nominate such number of Examiners as they shall deem sufficient to conduct the examination. An Examiner may be appointed to examine in more than one Part of the Tripos in any year.

6. The Chairs of Examiners shall communicate the marks of all candidates to the Registrary.

7. The Committee of Management shall have power to nominate one or more Assessors to examine in any of the subjects of the Tripos. Assessors shall be required to set the paper or papers in the subjects assigned to them and to present such written reports to the Examiners as may be required. Assessors may be summoned to meetings of the Examiners for the purpose of consultation and advice, but shall not be entitled to vote.

Class-lists.

8. There shall be a separate class-list for each Part of the Tripos. In each list the names of the successful candidates shall be arranged in three classes, of which the second shall be divided into two divisions. The names in the first and third classes, and in each division of the second class, shall be arranged in alphabetical order. In each class-list a mark of distinction shall be affixed to the names of those candidates placed in the first class whose work is of special merit.

9. Before the end of the Easter Term the Committee of Management shall give notice of the Optional Papers for the examinations to be held in the next academical year provided that the Committee shall have the power of subsequently issuing amendments if they have due reason for doing so and if they are satisfied that no student's preparation for the examination is adversely affected. The Committee shall have power when they give notice of Optional Papers to announce any consequential restriction on the combination of papers that a candidate may choose to offer.

Supplementary regulations.

10. The Committee of Management in consultation with a Faculty Board or comparable authority concerned shall have power to issue from time to time supplementary regulations or Notices defining or limiting all or any of the subjects of examination, and determining the scope, character, and conditions of the papers and the credit that shall be assigned to each, and to amend or withdraw such regulations and Notices; provided that due care is taken to give sufficient notice of any supplementary regulation or of any amendment of an existing supplementary regulation.

Part I

Scheme of Examination.

11. The scheme of examination for Part I shall be as follows.

Section A

PBS 1. Introduction to psychology (also serves as a paper in Part IA of the Computer Science Tripos)
PBS 2. Psychological enquiry and methods

[1] These regulations will come into effect in accordance with the timetable in Temporary Regulation 25.

Section B

Optional Papers announced by the Faculty Board in accordance with Regulation 9.

12. A student may be a candidate for honours in Part I if he or she has kept one term, provided that three complete terms have not passed after his or her first term of residence.

13. A candidate for honours in Part I of the Tripos shall offer four written papers as follows:

(*a*) the two papers in Section A, *plus*

(*b*) two papers from Section B.

14. There shall be separate examinations of three hours' duration set for each paper specified in Section A. Papers in Section B will be examined in accordance with the regulations set down by the Faculty or comparable authority concerned.

PART IIA

15. A student who has obtained honours in Part I of the Tripos or in another Honours Examination, in the year next after so obtaining honours, provided that twelve complete terms have not passed after her or his first term of residence, may be a candidate for honours in Part IIA. Standing of Candidates

16. The scheme of examination for Part IIA shall be as follows:

PBS 3.	Social psychology (also serves as a paper in Part II of the Human, Social, and Political Sciences Tripos)
PBS 4.	Biological and cognitive psychology (also serves as a paper in Part II of the Human, Social, and Political Sciences Tripos)
PBS 5.	Experimental psychology (the subject Experimental Psychology in Part IB of the Natural Sciences Tripos)
PBS 6.	Research project, as prescribed in Regulation 19
PBS 1.	Introduction to psychology (Paper PBS 1 from Part I of the Tripos)
PBS 2.	Psychological enquiry and methods (Paper PBS 2 from Part I of the Tripos)

Optional Papers from the list published in accordance with Regulation 9.

17. A candidate for Part IIA shall offer four papers as follows:

(*a*) PBS 3;

(*b*) *either* (i) PBS 4 and two further papers chosen from the list of Optional Papers published in accordance with Regulation 9,[2]

or (ii) PBS 5, PBS 6, and one further paper chosen from the list of Optional Papers published in accordance with Regulation 9,[2]

subject to Regulation 4, and provided that any candidate who has not previously completed Part I of the Tripos must, except with the permission of the Committee of Management, offer PBS 1 and PBS 2 if he or she has not previously offered either paper within another Tripos.

18. There shall be separate examinations of three hours' duration set for Papers PBS 3 and PBS 4. Other papers will be examined in accordance with the regulations set down by the Faculty or comparable authority concerned.

19. Candidates offering PBS 6 shall submit a research project of not more than 5,000 words including footnotes and appendices but excluding any bibliography, in an area approved by the Committee of Management not later than the division of the Michaelmas Term, in printed or typewritten form to the Secretary of the Committee of Management not later than the end of the second week of the Full Easter Term in which the examination is to be held.

PART IIB

20. A student who has obtained honours in Part IIA of the Tripos and has kept seven terms may be a candidate for honours in Part IIB provided that twelve complete terms have not passed after her or his first term of residence.[1]

21. The scheme of examination for Part IIB shall be as follows.

PBS 7.	Research dissertation as prescribed in Regulation 24
PBS 8.	Development and psychopathology
PBS 9.	Cognitive psychology (Paper 2 for the subject Psychology in Part II of the Natural Sciences Tripos)

[1] See also the regulations for Affiliated Students.

[2] Provided that no pair of papers from the Optional Papers list with the same number, a and b are offered (e.g. HPS1a or HPS1b).

PBS 10. Behavioural and clinical neuroscience (Paper 3 for the subject Psychology in Part II of the Natural Sciences Tripos)
PBS 11. Social and developmental psychology, and individual differences (Paper 4 for the subject Psychology in Part II of the Natural Sciences Tripos)
PBS 12. A paper in psychology 1
PBS 13. A paper in psychology 2
PBS 14. A paper in psychology 3

Optional Papers from the list published in accordance with Regulation 9.

22. A candidate for honours in Part IIB shall be required to offer PBS 7, the research dissertation, and three further papers, provided that no candidate shall offer more than two papers out of PBS 9, PBS 10, and PBS 11.

23. There shall be separate examinations of three hours' duration for each paper specified. Candidates may be called for *viva voce* examination.

Dissertations. **24.** Candidates for Part IIB shall submit a research dissertation in an area of Psychology.

(*a*) Each candidate must obtain the approval of the Committee of Management for the proposed topic not later than the division of the Michaelmas Term. The application shall be in accordance with any instructions issued by the Committee of Management and will include the topic of the proposed dissertation and a brief account of its scope. After the Committee of Management have approved a topic no substantial change may be made in it without the further approval of the Committee of Management.

(*b*) The research dissertation shall contain full references to any sources used in its composition, and shall be of not less than 6,000 words and not more than 10,000 words in length, including footnotes and appendices but excluding any bibliography.

(*c*) The research dissertation shall be submitted in electronic or printed form to the Secretary of the Committee of Management not later than the end of the second week of the Full Easter Term in which the examination is to be held. Each dissertation shall bear the candidate's examination number but not the candidate's name and shall be accompanied by (i) a brief synopsis on a separate sheet of paper of the contents of the dissertation, and (ii) a certificate signed by the candidate that it is her or his own original work, and that it does not contain material that has already been used to any substantial extent for a comparable purpose.

Temporary Regulation

25. The examinations for the Psychological and Behavioural Sciences Tripos shall be held for the first time as follows:

Part I in 2014
Part IIA in 2015
Part IIB in 2016

THEOLOGICAL AND RELIGIOUS STUDIES TRIPOS

Amended by Notices (Reporter, *2013–14, pp. 448, 639, and 727*)

Three Parts. **1.** The Theological and Religious Studies Tripos shall consist of three Parts, Part I, Part IIA, and Part IIB.

Timetables. **2.** In any year in which candidates for honours in the Theological and Religious Studies Tripos and candidates for honours in some other Tripos desire to offer papers common to both Triposes, the timetables for the examinations shall be arranged accordingly.

Notice of subjects. **3.** Public notice of all the variable subjects selected for the examinations in any year shall be given by the Faculty Board of Divinity before the end of the Easter Term of the year next preceding the examination concerned; provided that the Board shall have the power of subsequently issuing amendments if they have due reason for doing so and if they are satisfied that no student's preparation for the examination is adversely affected.

Supplementary regulations. **4.** The Faculty Board of Divinity shall have power to issue supplementary regulations defining or limiting all or any of the subjects of the examinations and to publish lists of books or of documents. Such lists of books or documents and other reading lists for papers shall be made available in the Faculty Library by the end of the Full Easter Term of the year next preceding the examination. The

Faculty Board shall also have power to alter such supplementary regulations and such lists, due care being taken that sufficient notice is given of any change.

Standing of candidates.

5. The following may present themselves as candidates for honours in Part I:

(*a*) a student who has not obtained honours in an Honours Examination, provided that he or she has kept one term and that three complete terms have not passed after his or her first term of residence;

(*b*) a student who has obtained honours in an Honours Examination in the year next after so obtaining honours, provided that he or she has kept four terms and that twelve complete terms have not passed after his or her first term of residence.

6. A student who has obtained honours in another Honours Examination may be a candidate for honours in Part IIA,[1] in the year after so obtaining honours, provided that he or she has kept four terms and that twelve complete terms have not passed after his or her first term of residence.

7. A student who has obtained honours in any Honours Examination other than Part I of the Theological and Religious Studies Tripos may be a candidate for honours in Part IIB,[1] in the year after so obtaining honours, provided that he or she has kept seven terms and that fifteen terms have not passed after his or her first term of residence.

8. No student shall be a candidate for more than one Part, or for one Part and also for another Honours Examination, in the same term.

9. No student who has been a candidate for any Part shall again be a candidate for the same Part.

10. A candidate shall not offer in any Part of the Tripos a paper that he or she has previously offered in another University Examination.

Examiners.

11. The Faculty Board shall nominate such number of Examiners as they may deem sufficient for each Part of the Tripos.

Assessors.

12. The Faculty Board may also nominate such number of Assessors as they may deem necessary for either Part of the Tripos. Assessors shall be responsible for setting the paper or papers in the subjects assigned to them by the Examiners, for looking over the work of the candidates therein, and for presenting such reports to the Examiners as may be required by them. Assessors may be summoned to meetings of the Examiners for the purpose of consultation and advice, but shall not be entitled to vote.

13. The questions proposed by each Examiner and Assessor shall be submitted to the whole body of Examiners for approval.

14. The Examiners and Assessors shall have regard to the style and method of a candidate's answers, and shall give credit for excellence in these respects.

15. The Examiners shall take account of a candidate's performance in an additional paper, or in the weaker of two papers either of which may be deemed to have been taken as an additional paper, only in so far as it is to the candidate's advantage. They shall not exclude a candidate from any class on the ground that he or she has not offered an additional paper.

Dissertation.

16. (*a*) A candidate who, in accordance with Regulation 26(*b*) or Regulation 27(*b*), wishes to offer a dissertation shall apply, giving the title of the proposed topic, to the Secretary of the Faculty Board not earlier than the beginning of the Easter Term and not later than the first Monday of the Full Michaelmas Term in the calendar year next preceding the examination. A dissertation may be on any topic relating to the subject of any paper in the Tripos, but the Board may, when giving approval for a particular topic, impose the condition that a candidate who offers a dissertation on that topic may not offer a particular paper or a particular prescribed subject in a paper. The Secretary shall inform the candidate as soon as possible, and in any case before the end of Full Michaelmas Term, whether the topic has been approved by the Faculty Board.

(*b*) No change shall be made in the topic of a candidate's dissertation after the end of Full Michaelmas Term, but the Faculty Board shall have power to approve minor changes of wording in the title which clarify or define more precisely the scope of a topic previously approved, provided that such changes are submitted to the Secretary of the Faculty Board by the division of the Lent Term.

(*c*) A dissertation, which shall be of not more than 10,000 words (inclusive of notes and footnotes used to convey information, comment, or analysis, but exclusive of bibliography and footnotes which act simply as references), shall be sent to the Secretary of the Faculty Board so as to arrive not later than the third Monday of the Full Easter Term in which the examination is to be held, together with

[1] See also the regulations for Affiliated Students.

a written declaration that it is the candidate's own original work and that it does not contain material already used to any substantial extent for a comparable purpose. A dissertation should show evidence of reading, judgement, and criticism, and of a power of exposition, but not necessarily of original research, and should give full references to sources used. It must be written in English unless the candidate has received permission from the Board to use some other specified language; a request for such permission must be made when the original application is submitted.

(*d*) The dissertation shall be submitted under detailed arrangements approved by the Faculty Board. The Examiners shall have power to examine a candidate *viva voce* on his or her dissertation and on the general field of knowledge in which it falls.

Class-lists.

17. There shall be separate class-lists for each Part. In each list the names of the candidates who obtain honours shall be arranged in three classes, of which the second shall be divided into two divisions. The names in the first and third classes and in each division of the second class shall be arranged in alphabetical order. The Examiners may affix a special mark to the names of those candidates whose work is in their opinion of special distinction.

Scheme of examination.

18. The papers for the Theological and Religious Studies Tripos, which shall be divided into Groups A–D, shall be as follows:

Group A

Paper A1. Scriptural languages and texts:
- A. Hebrew I (Elementary Hebrew)
- B. New Testament Greek
- C. Sanskrit
- D. Qur'anic Arabic

Paper A2. David: Israel's greatest hero?
Paper A3. Jesus and the origins of the Gospel
Paper A4. Christianity and the transformation of culture
Paper A5. Who is Jesus Christ?
Paper A6. Understanding contemporary religion
Paper A7. World religions in comparative perspective
Paper A8. Philosophy of religion and ethics

Group B

Paper B1. Intermediate languages and texts:
- A. Hebrew
- B. New Testament Greek
- C. Sanskrit
- D. Qur'anic Arabic

Paper B2. The literature, history, and theology of the exilic age
Paper B3. Judaism in the Greek and Roman periods
Paper B4. The letters of Paul
Paper B5. The Johannine tradition
Paper B6. Christianity in Late Antiquity (to *circa* 600)
Paper B7. Themes in world Christianities: context, theology, and power
Paper B8. Study of theology I
Paper B9. God and the *imago Dei*[1]
Paper B10. Philosophy of religion: God, freedom, and the soul
Paper B11. Ethics and faith
Paper B12. Theology and the natural sciences I
Paper B13 Religious themes in literature
Paper B14. Life, thought, and worship of modern Judaism (also serves as Paper X.4 of Part IB of the Asian and Middle Eastern Studies Tripos)
Paper B15. Introduction to Islam (also serves as Paper X.5 of Part IB of the Asian and Middle Eastern Studies Tripos)
Paper B16. Life and thought of religious Hinduism and of Buddhism
Paper B17. Logic (Paper 3 of Part IA of the Philosophy Tripos)

[1] This paper is suspended until 1 October 2015.

GROUP C

Paper C1. Advanced language and texts:
A. Hebrew
B. Greek
C. Sanskrit
D. Arabic
Paper C2. Creation and covenant
Paper C3. New Testament Christology
Paper C4. Topic in the history of Christianity[1]
Paper C5. Study of theology II
Paper C6. Disputed questions in the Christian tradition
Paper C7. Topics in the study of religion
Paper C8. Judaism II (also serves as Paper X.9 of the Asian and Middle Eastern Studies Tripos)
Paper C9. Islam II (also serves as Paper X.10 of the Asian and Middle Eastern Studies Tripos)
Paper C10. Hinduism and Buddhism II
Paper C11. Metaphysics[2]
Paper C12. Theology and the natural sciences II

GROUP D

Paper D1. Special subjects, specified by the Faculty Board
Paper D2. Interdisciplinary subjects, specified by the Faculty Board

19. Each paper shall be of three hours' duration, provided that the Faculty Board shall have power to specify by supplementary regulation a paper or papers from any group which shall be examined by an alternative mode of assessment, in accordance with the provisions of Regulation 20.

20. The alternative mode of assessment for any paper specified by the Faculty Board under Regulation 19 shall consist of *either* (*a*) the submission of two essays *or* (*b*) the submission of a portfolio of six essays on topics chosen by the candidate from a list of topics published by the Faculty Board not later than the first Friday of the Full Michaelmas Term next preceding the examination. Where two essays are submitted under (*a*), the length of each essay shall be, for a candidate in Part I, not more than 3,000 words in length and, for candidates in Parts IIA and IIB, not more than 5,000 words in length. Where a portfolio of six essays is submitted under (*b*), the length of each essay shall be not fewer than 1,500 words and not more than 2,000 words in length. In all cases, word limits shall include notes and footnotes used to convey information, comment, or analysis, but exclude bibliography and footnotes which act simply as references. Candidates shall be required to declare that the essays are their own work. The essays shall be typewritten, in English, and shall be submitted through the candidate's Director of Studies to the Secretary of the Faculty Board in accordance with detailed arrangements approved by the Board, so that the first essay submitted under (*a*) or the portfolio of essays submitted under (*b*) arrive not later than 1 p.m. on the first Monday of Full Easter Term and the second essay under (*a*) not later than 1 p.m. on the third Monday of Full Easter Term.

21. (*a*) Every candidate who offers a paper in which there is a choice of subject shall take only one of these question papers (except as provided for in Regulations 23(i) 24(i), 24(ii), 26(i), and 27(ii)); the candidate's examination entry shall state which subject he or she intends to offer.

(*b*) For Papers D1 and D2 the Faculty Board shall from time to time prescribe subjects as follows:

For Paper D1, not more than seven subjects.

For Paper D2, not more than seven subjects.

A separate question paper shall be set for each subject so prescribed for which there is a candidate.

(*c*) The Board may also prescribe that a candidate who offers a particular subject in one of Papers D1 and D2 may not also offer another particular paper.

22. A candidate for Part I shall offer: Papers to be offered in Part I.

(*a*) one language from Paper A1;

(*b*) *either* Paper A2 *or* Paper A3;

(*c*) three other papers chosen from Papers A2–A8;

provided that

[1] This paper is suspended until 1 October 2015.
[2] This paper is also available to candidates for Part II of the Philosophy Tripos, see p. 423.

(i) a candidate who has previously obtained honours in the Classical Tripos or the Asian and Middle Eastern Studies Tripos may not offer in Paper A1 a language in which he or she has previously offered a paper in an Honours Examination;

(ii) a candidate may not offer more than two papers which have been specified by the Faculty Board under Regulation 19.

Papers to be offered in Part IIA.

23. A student who is a candidate for Part IIA in the year next after obtaining honours in Part I of the Theological and Religious Studies Tripos shall offer four papers chosen from Group B, provided that

(i) a candidate who so wishes may offer as an additional paper *either* a second language from Paper A1 other than the one he or she has offered in Part I *or* a second language from Paper B1, if he or she is offering that Paper;

(ii) a candidate may not offer more than two papers which have been specified by the Faculty Board under Regulation 19;

(iii) a candidate may only offer one of Papers B13(*a*) and B13(*b*);

(iv) not more than one paper in the same language may be offered.

24. A student who is a candidate for Part IIA in the year next after obtaining honours in an Honours Examination other than Part I of the Theological and Religious Studies Tripos or who is an Affiliated Student[1] shall offer four papers, including:

(*a*) Paper A1, unless he or she *either* (i) is exempted from this requirement under the provisions of Regulation 28, *or* (ii) offers Paper B1 under section (*c*) of this regulation;

(*b*) one paper chosen from among Papers B2–B5;

and

(*c*) *either* (1) two other papers chosen from Group B, if he or she offers Paper A1,
or (2) three other papers chosen from Group B;

provided that

(i) a candidate who so wishes may offer as an additional paper
either (1) another Paper chosen from Group B,
or (2) if he or she is exempt from the requirement to offer Paper A1, a language from Paper A1 other than that for which exemption has been granted;
or (3) if he or she offers Paper B1, a second language from Paper B1;

(ii) a candidate who has previously obtained honours in the Classical Tripos or the Asian and Middle Eastern Studies Tripos may not offer in Paper A1 a language in which he or she has previously offered a paper in an Honours Examination;

(iii) a candidate may not offer more than two papers which have been specified by the Faculty Board under Regulation 19;

(iv) a candidate may only offer one of Papers B13(*a*) and B13(*b*);

(v) not more than one paper in the same language may be offered.

25. A student who is a candidate for Part IIA in the year next after obtaining honours in an Honours Examination other than Part I of the Theological and Religious Studies Tripos and who has kept seven terms shall offer four papers chosen from Group B, provided that

(i) a candidate who so wishes may offer as an additional paper another paper chosen from Group B;

(ii) a candidate who so wishes may offer Paper A1 instead of Paper B1;

(iii) a candidate who has previously obtained honours in the Classical Tripos or the Asian and Middle Eastern Studies Tripos may not offer in Paper A1 a language in which he or she has previously offered a paper in an Honours Examination;

(iv) a candidate may not offer more than two papers which have been specified by the Faculty Board under Regulation 19;

(v) a candidate may only offer one of Papers B13(*a*) and B13(*b*);

(vi) not more than one paper in the same language may be offered.

Papers to be offered in Part IIB.

26. A student who is a candidate for Part IIB in the year next after obtaining honours in Part IIA under Regulations 23 or 24 shall offer:

either (*a*) two papers chosen from Group C; *and* both Papers D1 and D2

[1] See also the regulations for Affiliated Students.

or (*b*) three papers chosen from Group C; *and* one paper chosen from Group D
provided that

(i) a candidate who offered paper A1 in Part IIA may offer Paper B1 in the same language instead of Paper C1 as one of the papers chosen from Group C;
(ii) a candidate may offer as an additional paper, *either* a language from Papers A1 or B1 which he or she has not previously offered, *or* a second language from Paper C1, if he or she is offering that paper, *or* one further paper chosen from Group C;
(iii) no candidate may offer more than two papers which have been specified by the Faculty Board under Regulation 19;
(iv) a candidate may offer a dissertation on a topic approved by the Faculty Board in place of one paper chosen from Group D. Such a candidate may not offer more than one paper which has been specified by the Faculty Board under Regulation 19;
(v) not more than one paper in the same language may be offered.

27. A student who is a candidate for Part IIB in the year next after obtaining honours in an Honours Examination other than Part I or Part IIA of the Theological and Religious Studies Tripos or who is an Affiliated Student[1] shall offer:

either (*a*) two papers chosen from Group C; *and* both Papers D1 and D2
or (*b*) three papers chosen from Group C; *and* one paper chosen from Group D
provided that

(i) a candidate may offer Paper B1 in the same language instead of Paper C1 as one of the papers chosen from Group C;
(ii) a candidate may offer as an additional paper, *either* a language from Papers A1 or B1 which he or she has not previously offered, *or* a second language from Paper C1, if he or she is offering that paper, *or* one further paper chosen from Group C;
(iii) a candidate who has previously obtained honours in the Classical Tripos or the Asian and Middle Eastern Studies Tripos may not offer in Paper A1 a language in which he or she has previously offered a paper in an Honours Examination;
(iv) no candidate may offer more than two papers which have been specified by the Faculty Board under Regulation 19;
(v) a candidate may offer a dissertation on a topic approved by the Faculty Board in place of one paper chosen from Group D. Such a candidate may not offer more than one paper which has been specified by the Faculty Board under Regulation 19;
(vi) not more than one paper in the same language may be offered.

28. The Faculty Board shall have power to exempt from the requirement to offer a language from Paper A1 any candidate for Part IIA under Regulation 24 who produces evidence that he or she has done work of a satisfactory standard in Greek or in Hebrew or in Sanskrit or in Arabic, whether in Cambridge or elsewhere. Such a candidate shall not offer in Part IIA Paper A1 in the language in which he or she has gained exemption. Any application for exemption shall be sent through the candidate's Director of Studies to the Secretary of the Faculty Board so as to arrive not later than the first Monday of the Full Michaelmas Term next preceding the examination, and shall include details of the applicant's qualifications. The Secretary shall inform the candidate's Director of Studies as soon as possible, and in any case by the division of the Michaelmas Term, whether the application has been approved. Exemption

SUPPLEMENTARY REGULATIONS

Amended by Notices (Reporter, *2013–14, pp. 448, 464, and 639*)

Paper A1. Scriptural languages and texts

This paper will comprise four sections, Section A, Hebrew I (Elementary Hebrew), Section B, New Testament Greek, Section C, Sanskrit, and Section D, Qur'anic Arabic; candidates will be required to confine their answers to a single section. Section A will contain (i) questions on Hebrew grammar, and (ii) passages for translation, linguistic comment, pointing, and retranslation from a portion or portions of the Old Testament prescribed by the Faculty Board. Section B will contain passages for translation, and for exegetical and grammatical comment, from one or more portions of the New Testament which the Board shall from time to time prescribe. Copies of a Greek lexicon will be available in the examination for those who wish to make use of them. Section C will contain (i)

[1] See also the regulations for Affiliated Students.

questions on Sanskrit grammar, and (ii) passages for translation, linguistic and exegetical comment, from a portion or portions of the Hindu and Buddhist scriptures prescribed by the Board. Section D will contain (i) questions on Arabic grammar, and (ii) passages for translation, linguistic and exegetical comment from a portion or portions of the Qur'an, the Hadith, and early Islamic theological literature prescribed by the Board.

Paper A2. David: Israel's greatest hero?

This paper will provide an introduction to the critical study of the Old Testament literature, history, and religion, focussing on the figure of David. Texts for special study will be prescribed by the Faculty Board.

Paper A3. Jesus and the origins of the Gospel

This paper will, until further notice, be entitled 'Jesus and the origins of the Gospel'. It will be concerned with central issues (arising from the primary sources and critical scholarship) in the study of the Gospels and the Historical Jesus. The Board may also prescribe a particular text or texts for special study.

Paper A4. Christianity and the transformation of culture

This paper will introduce students to the history of Christianity by considering key periods and issues in the interaction of Christianity with the culture in which it is set. The topic of the paper will be announced annually by the Faculty Board.

Paper A5. Who is Jesus Christ?

This paper will introduce some of the major themes and disciplines of Christian theology through a focus on Jesus Christ. The Faculty Board may from time to time prescribe texts for special study.

Paper A6. Understanding contemporary religion

This paper will offer a broad introduction to the sociological study of religion with a particular focus on understanding developments in Britain since 1945 including secularization, charismatic religion, the New Age, new religious movements, and multiculturalism.

Paper A7. World religions in comparative perspective

This paper will approach at least two religions through the study of a topic or topics specified annually by the Faculty Board, in the context of the history, beliefs, and practices of the main religions of the world. This paper shall be examined by the submission of two essays in accordance with the provisions of Regulation 20.

Paper A8. Philosophy of religion and ethics

This paper will introduce students to the philosophy of religion and to ethics. The Faculty Board may from time to time prescribe texts for special study.

Paper B1. Intermediate language and texts

A. *Hebrew*

This paper will contain (i) passages for translation, linguistic, and exegetical comment, and retranslation from portions of text which the Faculty Board will from time to time prescribe, and (ii) essay questions on literary and theological aspects of the prescribed texts. Candidates may not offer in this paper any prescribed text which they have previously offered in Paper A1.

B. *New Testament Greek*

This paper will contain passages for translation, textual, exegetical, and theological comment from such portions of text as the Faculty Board will from time to time prescribe.

C. *Sanskrit*

This paper will contain passages for translation from a number of texts which the Faculty Board shall from time to time prescribe, together with questions on the language and content of those texts.

D. *Qur'anic Arabic*

This paper will contain passages for pointing, for translation, and for linguistic and exegetical comment from portions of the Qur'an, Qur'anic commentaries, and other Islamic literature which the Faculty Board shall from time to time prescribe. The paper will also contain a passage for translation from English into Arabic.

Paper B2. The literature, history, and theology of the exilic age

This paper will be concerned with Old Testament history from the reign of Hezekiah to the conquest of Babylon by Cyrus and with theological and literary responses to the Babylonian invasions and their consequences in the literature of the time, with particular reference to relevant sections of Genesis-Numbers; Deuteronomy; Joshua-2 Kings; Job; exilic elements in the Psalter; Isaiah 40–55; Jeremiah; Lamentations; Ezekiel. The Faculty Board will prescribe a portion of the Old Testament for special study.

Paper B3. Judaism in the Greek and Roman periods

This paper will be concerned with an essential period for our understanding of the formation of Judaism (and of nascent Christianity). It will examine the social, historical, and political contexts in which ancient Jews shaped their identity from the rise, after Persian rule, of Alexander the Great (332 BCE) up to and including the series of Roman revolts that culminated in the one named after Bar-Kokhba (132–5 CE).

Paper B4. The letters of Paul

This paper will study the Pauline 'corpus', including Ephesians and the Pastoral epistles. There will be questions on historical, literary, and critical problems, but the emphasis will be on the theological thought and practice of the apostle Paul. The Faculty Board may also prescribe a particular text or texts for special study.

Paper B5. The Johannine tradition

This paper will be concerned with central issues (arising from the primary sources and critical scholarship) in the study of the Fourth Gospel and Johannine Epistles. Although students will be expected to read the full text of the Gospels and Epistles, specific texts for more detailed study will be announced by the Faculty Board.

Paper B6. Christianity in Late Antiquity (to circa *600)*

This paper is concerned with the main historical and theological developments in Christianity in Antiquity set within the social, historical, political, and cultural contexts of the Roman Empire and its immediate successors.

Paper B7. Themes in world Christianities: context, theology, and power

This paper will be concerned with both the common themes and the diversity of contemporary Christianity in its global setting. Particular emphasis will be given to the contextual character of Christian theological reflection outside Europe and the USA since 1914 in relation both to indigenous cultures and to structures of global political and economic power.

Paper B8. Study of theology I

This paper is concerned with the Christian understanding of God and humanity. The course aims to study this through classic texts from different periods, understood in the context of their time and in relation to current theological discussions. The Faculty Board may from time to time prescribe topics and texts for special study.

Paper B9. God and the imago Dei[1]

This paper is concerned with three central loci of Christian systematic theology: the doctrine of the Trinity, the doctrine of God and the *imago Dei*, as well as the way in which these doctrines intersect.

Paper B10. Philosophy of religion: God, freedom, and the soul

This paper will explore some classical themes in the philosophy of religion. These will include attributes of God, issues of the relationships between God and the world, and issues of God and 'the soul'.

Paper B11. Ethics and faith

The paper will study questions concerning the nature and form of moral judgment, as treated in the history of Western philosophy.

Paper B12. Theology and the natural sciences I

This paper will cover (*a*) topics in contemporary natural science that bear upon theology, and theological responses to these proposals and (*b*) historical, philosophical, and methodological perspectives on the dialogue between theology and science.

Paper B13. Religious themes in literature

This paper will consider religious themes in literature connected to a set topic, to be announced by the Faculty Board at the end of the Easter Term preceding the year in which the paper is taught. This paper shall be examined by a portfolio of six essays in accordance with the provisions of Regulation 20.

Paper B14. Life, thought, and worship of modern Judaism (also serves as Paper X.4 of Part IB of the Asian and Middle Eastern Studies Tripos)

This paper will be concerned with the life, thought, and worship of modern Judaism. The Faculty Board may from time to time prescribe texts for special study.

Paper B15. Introduction to Islam (also serves as Paper X.5 of Part IB of the Asian and Middle Eastern Studies Tripos)

This paper will cover the origins, development, and contemporary situation of the theology, law, and mysticism of Islam. It will deal with literary-critical and interpretative problems relating to the founding documents of the religion, and with contemporary methodologies in philosophy of religion, gender studies, and comparative jurisprudence as applied to Islam. References to Christianity may be included. The Faculty Board may from time to time prescribe texts for special study.

Paper B16. Life and thought of religious Hinduism and of Buddhism

The paper will consider the origins and development up to contemporary times of the beliefs and practices of the Hindu and Buddhist traditions. It will deal with problems of interpretation relating to the formation and understanding of founding texts, and with relevant issues in such areas as gender studies and the functioning of élite and colonial influences. The Faculty Board may from time to time prescribe texts for special study.

[1] This paper is suspended until 1 October 2015.

Paper C1. Advanced languages and texts

A. *Hebrew*

This paper will be concerned with the exegesis of prescribed text or texts in Hebrew. It will involve translation from and linguistic, text-critical, and exegetical comment on texts which the Faculty Board will from time to time prescribe, including some parts of the prophetic and poetic books of the Old Testament; passages for unseen translation from Hebrew into English; a passage for translation from English into Hebrew; and essay questions on literary and theological aspects of the prescribed texts.

B. *Greek*

This paper will contain (i) passages for translation, and for textual, grammatical, exegetical, and theological comment from such portions of text as the Faculty Board will from time to time prescribe, and (ii) passages for unseen translation from texts of similar provenance.

C. *Sanskrit*

This paper will contain passages for translation and comment from a number of texts which the Faculty Board shall from time to time prescribe, together with questions on the language and content of those texts.

D. *Arabic*

This paper will be concerned with the translation of, and linguistic and exegetical comment on portions of the Qur'an, Qur'anic commentaries, and other Islamic literature which the Faculty Board shall from time to time prescribe.

Paper C2. Creation and covenant

This paper will examine from the perspective of biblical theology, as well as a historical perspective, the twin themes of creation and covenant in the Hebrew Bible. Through close textual analysis the relationship between these themes will be studied, and their role in contemporary biblical theologies, both Jewish and Christian, will be explored.

Paper C3. New Testament Christology

This paper will be concerned with central issues, arising from the primary sources and critical scholarship, in the study of Christology within the New Testament.

Paper C4. Topic in the history of Christianity[1]

This paper will be concerned with a topic in the history of Christianity, as specified by the Faculty Board from time to time. This paper shall be examined by the submission of two essays in accordance with the provisions of Regulation 20.

Paper C5. Study of theology II

This paper will be concerned with an advanced topic in the study of theology. The topic will be prescribed by the Faculty Board.

Paper C6. Disputed questions in the Christian tradition

The paper will examine theological problems arising within 'classical' Christian theology, in the context of major theological loci. The Faculty Board may from time to time prescribe topics and texts for special study.

Paper C7. Topic in the study of religion

This paper will be concerned with an aspect of the study of religion, as specified by the Faculty Board from time to time.

Paper C8. Judaism II (also serves as Paper X.9 of the Asian and Middle Eastern Studies Tripos)

This paper will consider the life, thought, and worship of medieval and modern Judaism. The Faculty Board may from time to time prescribe subjects and texts for special study.

Paper C9. Islam II (also serves as Paper X.10 of the Asian and Middle Eastern Studies Tripos)

This paper will deal with two advanced topics in Islamic studies specified from time to time by the Faculty Board. The Board may also from time to time prescribe texts for special study.

Paper C10. Hinduism and Buddhism II

This paper will be concerned with two advanced topics in the Hindu and Buddhist traditions prescribed from time to time by the Faculty Board. The Board may also from time to time prescribe texts for special study.

Paper C11. Metaphysics[2]

This paper studies the major problems of (religious) metaphysics that have been handed down to contemporary philosophy of religion from the Enlightenment period. Taking Kant's *Critique of Pure Reason* as its starting point, it first provides a close, critical examination of Kant's own reworking of the notions of 'God' and 'soul', and of his rejection of the classical arguments for God's existence. It then provides a systematic account of the

[1] This paper is suspended until 1 October 2015.

[2] This paper is also available to candidates for Part II of the Philosophy Tripos, see p. 423.

major responses to, or evasions of, Kant's challenge in the 20th and 21st centuries amongst those philosophers of religion who have sought either to repristinate theological metaphysics, or to give philosophical credence to God-talk by means of other, 'post-metaphysical', strategies of defence. Once this map of current philosophical alternatives is outlined, the lectures turn to re-examine four classic problems of theological metaphysics in the light of them: 'natural theology' and its current possibilities; the problem of evil; the soul and immortality; and God and time.

Paper C12. Theology and the natural sciences II

This paper will cover a focused range of topics in the relation of contemporary natural sciences with theology.

Paper D1.

Papers in this group except D1(*a*), (*b*), and (*f*) shall be examined by the submission of two essays in accordance with the provisions of Regulation 20.

(*a*) *Old Testament*

This paper will examine some of the central critical and theological issues in the Pentateuch. The Faculty Board will prescribe a text for special study.

(*b*) *New Testament special subject*

This paper will explore in detail a topic of particular interest to students of Christianity in the first two centuries. The topic will be prescribed by the Faculty Board.

(*c*) *A topic in the history of Christianity*

This paper will study in detail a topic in the history of Christianity. The topic will be prescribed by the Faculty Board.

(*d*) *The doctrine of God*

This paper will study the doctrine of God through classic texts from several periods. The Faculty Board may from time to time prescribe topics and texts for special study.

(*e*) *Philosophy in the Long Middle Ages* (Paper 5 of Part II of the Philosophy Tripos)

(*f*) *Jews, Christians, and Muslims before and after Muhammad*

This paper proposes a new historical framework for the study of the history and interaction of rabbinic Judaism, patristic Christianity, and early Islam.

(*g*) *The self and salvation in Indian and Western thought*

This topic will be studied from a comparative point of view. The Faculty Board may from time to time prescribe texts for special study.

Paper D2.

Papers in this group except D2(*c*) shall be examined by the submission of two essays in accordance with the provisions of Regulation 20.

(*a*) *Body, self, and society*[1]

This paper is concerned with the Christian doctrine of human nature. It is studied in relation to a dossier of primary texts from the patristic to the Renaissance period, arranged round four topics

(*b*) *Theological interpretation of the Gospel of John*

This paper will be concerned with the theological interpretation of a basic Christian text, the Gospel of John. It will explore the practice of theological interpretation of scripture with reference to this Gospel, drawing on modern and premodern theologians and commentators.

(*c*) *Judaism and philosophy* (also serves as Paper X 11 of the Asian and Middle Eastern Studies Tripos)

The Faculty Board may from time to time prescribe texts for special study.

(*d*) *Judaism and Hellenism* (also serves as Paper O8 of Part II of the Classical Tripos)

This paper will be concerned with the interaction between Jewish and Hellenistic traditions from the time of Alexander the Great until the early rabbis. It will examine the conceptual problems of 'Hebraism and Hellenism' through an examination of the literature, history, and religious life of Jews in the period.

(*e*) *The rise of Pentecostalism, 1900 to the present day*

This paper will be concerned with the transregional history of Pentecostalism, from 1900 to the present day.

(*f*) *Topics in Christian ethics*

This paper is concerned with topics in applied Christian ethics, as specified from time to time by the Faculty Board.

(*g*) *Imagination*

This paper is concerned with the role of imagination in religious belief and explores the philosophical and theological problems involved in representing the divine presence through images, symbols, or imaginary narratives.

[1] This paper will not be available in 2014–15.

CHAPTER V

B.A. DEGREE AND M.A. DEGREE

BACHELOR OF ARTS

BY HONOURS

How obtained.

1. A candidate shall obtain honours in an Honours Examination by the inclusion of his or her name in one of the classes, or under the heading 'Declared to have deserved honours', in the class-list of that examination, or by being allowed the examination by the Council; provided that honours in Part IA of the Modern and Medieval Languages Tripos, if not obtained by an allowance from the Council, shall be obtained only as is laid down in the regulations for that Tripos.

2. On completing the requisite number of terms, a student shall be qualified to proceed to the degree of Bachelor of Arts by Honours if not earlier than the last but one of the terms that the student needs for that degree he or she has obtained honours as follows:

(*a*) in Part II or Part III of any Tripos;

or (*b*) in Part IIA or Part IIB of any Tripos;

or (*c*) in the Linguistics Tripos (Old Regulations), or the Management Studies Tripos;

provided that a student who matriculated before 1 January 2010 shall be qualified to proceed to the degree of Bachelor of Arts by Honours under the regulations for the degree of Bachelor of Arts by Honours in force on that date.

3. On completing the requisite number of terms,[1] a student who has obtained honours as prescribed in Regulation 2 earlier than the last but one of the terms needed for the degree of Bachelor of Arts shall be qualified to proceed to that degree

(*a*) if not earlier than the last but one of the terms needed for the degree he or she has passed one of the following examinations:

(i) the LL.M. Examination, provided that a student who elects to proceed to the LL.M. Degree shall not also be entitled to proceed to the B.A. Degree;

(ii) the Mus.B. Examination, provided that a student who elects to proceed to the Mus.B. Degree shall not also be entitled to proceed to the B.A. Degree;

(iii) an examination for the M.Phil. Degree (one-year course), provided that a student who elects to proceed to the M.Phil. Degree shall not also be entitled to proceed to the B.A. Degree;

Certificate of diligent study.

or (*b*) if it is certified by the Head of the student's College and by her or his Tutor that they have satisfied themselves, on the evidence of one or more University or College teachers who have had direct knowledge of the student's work during the time in question, that he or she has been engaged in appropriate academic studies, and has been regular and diligent therein during all the terms kept since he or she last obtained honours; provided that such a certificate shall not apply to more than four terms, and that it shall not be valid if it is signed earlier than the tenth day before the end of Full Term in the last term which the student must keep for the degree.

4. For the purpose of Regulation 2, notwithstanding that the class-list for the examination in which a student needs to obtain honours in order to complete the qualifications for the B.A. Degree has not been published before the first day of General Admission to Degrees, he or she shall be deemed to be qualified to proceed to that degree at the appropriate Congregation if the Chair of the Examiners for that examination, after consulting the Examiners concerned, has informed the Registrary sufficiently in advance of the Congregation that it is certain that the name of the student will be included in the class-list either in one of the classes or under the heading 'Declared to have deserved honours'.

5. A certificate submitted for the purpose of Regulation 3(*b*) shall be sent to the Registrary so as to arrive not later than the end of Full Term in the last term to which it relates. A student whose certificate reaches the Registrary later than the last day of Full Term shall, if the certificate is accepted, incur a fine of £1.

[1] See the regulations for the Residence and Precincts of the University (p. 189).

Ordinary B.A. Degree[1]

1. No student shall be a candidate for the Ordinary B.A. Degree without having first been a candidate for an Honours Examination. Primary condition.

2. On completing the requisite number of terms, a student shall be entitled to supplicate for the Ordinary B.A. Degree if he or she has obtained two honours examinations in Part I, Part IA or Part IB of any Tripos, provided that: Requirements for degree.

(i) the two honours examinations shall not be in the same Tripos; and

(ii) the second of these honours examinations shall be attained not earlier than the last but one of the terms that the student needed for the degree.

MASTER OF ARTS

1. A Bachelor of Arts may be admitted Master of Arts not less than six years from the end of his or her first term of residence if two years have elapsed since he or she was admitted Bachelor of Arts.

2. The degree of Master of Arts may be conferred upon a person who has been admitted to the office of Vice-Chancellor.

3. The degree of Master of Arts may be conferred on any other person qualified under Statute B II 2, provided that he or she

(*a*) has been matriculated as a member of the University;

(*b*) has attained the age of twenty-four years (unless in a particular case the Council see fit to grant exemption from this provision);

(*c*) holds one or more of the following positions:

(i) the Headship of a College, or being a Head-elect or designate of a College;

(ii) a Fellowship (other than an Honorary Fellowship) of a College;

(iii) a University office;

(iv) a post in the University Press specially designated under Statute J 7;

(v) an appointment approved by the University for the purpose of Statute A III 10(*e*) in a University institution designated by the University for the purpose of Statute B II 2;[2]

provided also that, if the person concerned holds one of the positions specified in sub-paragraphs (*c*)(ii)–(v) which on initial appointment or election did not carry tenure to the retiring age, he or she has already held such a position, or any combination of such positions, for a total period, which need not be continuous, of at least three years.

4. Each application by or on behalf of a candidate for the degree of Master of Arts under Statute B II 2 shall state:

(*a*) the candidate's full name and date of birth;

(*b*) the name of the College, if any, to which he or she has been admitted or approved for admission;

(*c*) the University office, College Headship, College Fellowship, or other post or appointment that the candidate holds;

and shall be sent to the Registrary.

[1] The Council has agreed, with the concurrence of the General Board, that any student who matriculated before 1 October 2011, and who may have been adversely affected by these changes to the regulations for the Ordinary Degree through, for example, intermitting, may apply to the Applications Committee to be considered for the award of the degree under the regulations current before 1 October 2011; see *Statutes and Ordinances*, 2010, p. 431.

[2] The Local Examinations Syndicate has been designated for the purpose of Statute B II 2.

CHAPTER VI

GRADUATE STUDENTS

GENERAL REGULATIONS FOR ADMISSION AS A GRADUATE STUDENT

Amended by Graces 4 of 25 June and 9 of 16 July 2014

Applications for admission.

1. Applications for admission as a Graduate Student shall be sent to the Secretary of the Board of Graduate Studies.

2. Each application shall include:

(*a*) a statement of the course of research or study which the applicant wishes to pursue, the date from which he or she wishes to begin the course, and the degree or other qualification, if any, for which he or she wishes to become a candidate;

(*b*) a completed graduate application form together with such other statements and evidence as the Board of Graduate Studies may require;

(*c*) such payment of a fee in respect of admission charges as the Council and the General Board, on the recommendation of the Board of Graduate Studies, may determine from time to time.

3. Exceptionally, a person who is not a graduate of a university or similar institution may be admitted as a Graduate Student if he or she submits evidence of general educational qualification satisfactory to the Board.

4. The Secretary of the Board shall communicate each application for admission as a Graduate Student to the Secretary of the Degree Committee for the Faculty or other approved institution with which the proposed course of research or study appears to be most nearly connected, subject to the approval of the Board in cases coming under Regulation 3. The Degree Committee shall consider the application and shall communicate their opinion thereon to the Secretary of the Board. If the Degree Committee agree to decline the application it shall fail, and the Secretary shall so inform the applicant. If the Degree Committee agree to recommend approval of the application, and confirm that appropriate facilities are available for the applicant's proposed course of research or study, their recommendation shall be considered by the Board, who shall decide upon the application. If the Board approve an applicant for admission as a Graduate Student the applicant's name shall be entered on the Register of Graduate Students.

5. The Board shall determine the conditions of each applicant's admission as a Graduate Student, the term from which he or she is admitted, and the conditions of his or her registration as a candidate for a degree or other qualification, if any, after considering recommendations by the Degree Committee. Before declining a recommendation that a student be registered as a candidate for a particular degree or other qualification the Board shall give a representative appointed by the Degree Committee an opportunity of explaining the Committee's reasons for their recommendation. The Board shall have power after considering a recommendation by the Degree Committee:

(*a*) to vary the conditions of a particular student's admission and of his or her registration as a candidate for a degree or other qualification;

(*b*) to register as a candidate for the M.Sc. or M.Litt. Degree a candidate previously registered for the M.D. degree, or the Ph.D. Degree or Eng.D. Degree or Ed.D. Degree, or to register as a candidate for the Ph.D. Degree a candidate previously registered for the Eng.D. Degree or Ed.D. Degree;

(*c*) to register as a candidate for the M.Phil. Degree or M.Res. Degree a candidate previously registered for the Ph.D. Degree, or for the M.Sc. or M.Litt. Degree, who has not submitted a dissertation in candidature for one of those degrees, and to allow such a student to count towards his or her course of study for the M.Phil. Degree or M.Res. Degree not more than three terms during which he or she was a candidate for the Ph.D. Degree, or for the M.Sc. or M.Litt. Degree;

(*d*) to register as a candidate for the Ph.D. Degree, or for the M.Sc. or the M.Litt. Degree, a Graduate Student who has been approved for the M.Phil. Degree or M.Res. Degree and to allow such a student to count towards his or her course of research as a candidate for the Ph.D. Degree, or for the M.Sc. or M.Litt. Degree, such terms as the Board may determine in accordance with the regulations for the Ph.D., M.Sc., and M.Litt. Degrees;

(*e*) to register as a candidate for the Ph.D. Degree, or for the M.Sc. or M.Litt. Degree, a Graduate Student who has been approved for the M.St. Degree or M.Ed. Degree, and who may have proceeded to that degree, and to allow such a student to count towards his or her course of research as a candidate for the Ph.D. Degree, or for the M.Sc. or M.Litt. Degree, not more than three terms of the period during which he or she was a candidate for the M.St. Degree or M.Ed. Degree or up to five terms where the candidate registers for the part-time Ph.D., M.Sc., or M.Litt. Degree;

(*f*) to register a student for a course of research or of study as a candidate for a particular degree or other qualification from the term of his or her admission as a Graduate Student or from any subsequent term; and

(*g*) to determine that any particular term of a student's course of research or of study shall not count towards the requirements for the M.D. degree, or the Ph.D. Degree, or Eng.D. Degree, or Ed.D. Degree, or M.Sc. Degree, or M.Litt. Degree, or M.Phil. Degree, or M.Res. Degree, or other qualification;

provided that, before exercising any of the powers conferred by clauses (*a*)–(*g*) above in a manner contrary to the Degree Committee's recommendation, the Board shall give a representative appointed by the Degree Committee an opportunity of explaining the Committee's reasons for their recommendation.

Matriculation.

6. Admission as a Graduate Student shall not have effect in respect of any period before the term in which the student was admitted to a College and was matriculated, except as provided in Regulations 1(*d*) and 2 of the regulations for the Ph.D., Eng.D., Ed.D., M.Sc., and M.Litt. Degrees.

Prizes or Scholarships.

7. A Graduate Student shall not be admitted as a candidate for any University Studentship, Scholarship, Exhibition, Prize, Medal, or other such emolument, which is open only to undergraduates. For the purpose of any regulation respecting the standing of candidates for any other emolument, the term from which a student not a graduate of the University is admitted as a Graduate Student shall be counted as his or her tenth term, and an allowance of terms made by the Council under Regulation 2 of the regulations for the Ph.D., M.Sc., and M.Litt. Degrees, and Ed.D. Degree or under Regulation 3 of the regulations for the Eng.D. Degree, shall count in calculating such a student's standing for the purpose of this regulation. Any term during which a student had leave to intermit his or her course of research or study under Regulation 1(*c*) of the regulations for the Ph.D., M.Sc., and M.Litt. Degrees, or any period of intermission allowed under Regulation 5 of the regulations for the M.Phil. Degree or under Regulation 5 for the regulations for the M.Res. Degree, shall not count unless the Board shall have decided otherwise.

Conditions for pursuing course.

8. Each Graduate Student shall pursue *either*

(*a*) a course of research approved by the Board and by the Degree Committee who recommended his or her admission, or, with the consent of the Board and the Degree Committees concerned, by some other Degree Committee, under the direction of a Supervisor appointed by the Degree Committee concerned, and shall comply with any special conditions that the Degree Committee or the Board may lay down in his or her case, *or*

(*b*) a course of advanced study and research, as prescribed in the regulations for the Eng.D. Degree or Ed.D. Degree, *or*

(*c*) a course of advanced study, as prescribed in the appropriate special regulations for the M.Ed. Degree or M.Phil. Degree and approved by the Board and the Degree Committee concerned, under the direction of a Supervisor appointed by the Degree Committee concerned, and shall comply with any special conditions that the Degree Committee or the Board may lay down in his or her case, *or*

(*d*) a course of training in research, as prescribed in the appropriate special regulations for the M.Res. Degree and approved by the Board and the Degree Committee concerned, under the direction of a Supervisor appointed by the Degree Committee concerned, and shall comply with any special conditions that the Degree Committee or the Board may lay down in her or his case, *or*

(*e*) a course of study or of research as prescribed in the regulations for a University Diploma or Certificate, or in partial fulfilment of the requirements for a degree or other qualification of another university or similar institution.

A Degree Committee shall be responsible to the Board for the general supervision of the work of each Graduate Student under their care, and shall appoint a Supervisor for each such student. The Degree Committee shall, for such courses of research or training as the Board shall determine, also appoint an

Adviser. The Board shall prescribe such duties of the Supervisor and Adviser as it deems necessary for the supervision of Graduate Students. All appointments of Supervisors and Advisers shall be communicated by the Degree Committee to the Secretary of the Board and to the Supervisor or Adviser, and the Board shall have power to make representations to the Degree Committee about any particular appointment.

Each Supervisor shall send to the Secretary of the Board, for communication to the Degree Committee concerned, a written report on the work of each Graduate Student under her or his charge. Such a report shall be sent

(i) once each term,[1]

(ii) at any time when in the Supervisor's opinion a Graduate Student is not making satisfactory progress in her or his work, is otherwise not fulfilling the conditions that have been laid down in her or his case, or appears unlikely to reach the standard of the degree or other qualification for which he or she is registered as a candidate.

Progress examination.

9. The Degree Committee concerned shall have power to require a Graduate Student to take a progress examination. The form of the examination shall be subject to approval by the Board. Any such examination shall be held not later than the end of the vacation following the second term after the term of the student's admission as a Graduate Student or at a time to be determined by the Board. For Graduate Students registered for the part-time Ph.D., Ed.D., M.Litt., or M.Sc. Degrees the progress examination shall be not later than the fourth term after the term of the student's admission. The Board, after considering a recommendation by the Degree Committee, shall determine how many, if any, of the terms previous to an examination under this regulation shall be counted for the purpose of Regulation 1 of the regulations for the Ph.D., M.Sc., and M.Litt. Degrees, and Regulation 4 of the regulations for the M.Phil. Degree, and Regulation 4 of the regulations for the M.Res. Degree.

It shall be the duty of the Examiners for the examination so approved to report in writing to the Degree Committee. The Degree Committee shall forward such reports to the Secretary of the Board.

The payment to any Examiner who is not a University officer (other than an Associate Lecturer who receives no stipend from the University) shall be fixed by the Board after considering a recommendation by the Degree Committee.

10. The Board shall have the power to remove any Graduate Student from the Register of Graduate Students:

(*a*) if he or she is no longer a member of a College;

(*b*) if he or she has failed to pay the fees due from a Graduate Student;

(*c*) if he or she has completed twelve terms of research as a full-time Graduate Student registered for the Ph.D., M.Sc., M.Litt. or M.D. or Eng.D. Degree or a proportionately longer period if registered as a part-time Graduate Student. In such a case the Board shall consult the Degree Committee before depriving the person of the status of Graduate Student;

(*d*) if, in the opinion of the Degree Committee and the Board, the report on the examination prescribed under Regulation 9 is such as to show that the candidate is not qualified to continue in his or her course;

(*e*) if, after completing three terms (if registered for a full-time course) or five terms (if registered for a part-time course) he or she is not registered as a candidate for any degree, provided that in such a case the Board shall have obtained the concurrence of the Degree Committee in the deprivation;

(*f*) if the Degree Committee have satisfied the Board

  (i) that the student has not been working to their satisfaction; *or*

  (ii) that the student has not complied with the conditions laid down in his or her case; *or*

  (iii) that, in their opinion, the student is not likely to reach the standard of the M.Sc. or M.Litt. Degree, or M.Phil. or M.Ed. or M.Res. Degree, or of any other qualification for which he or she might be registered as a candidate.

Fees.

11. (*a*) A Graduate Student who is registered as a candidate for the Ph.D., M.Litt. or M.Sc. Degree shall pay the University Composition Fee as determined by Regulation 10 of the regulations for University Composition Fees for each term up to and including the term in which he or she submits a dissertation or a revised dissertation for the Ph.D., M.Litt. or M.Sc. Degree, up to a maximum of nine

[1] At least three times over the duration of the course for a candidate for the M.Ed. Degree.

terms if a candidate for the Ph.D. Degree or six terms if a candidate for the M.Litt. or M.Sc. Degree. The maximum number of terms shall not include any term allowed to be counted under Regulation 5(*a*).

(*b*) A Graduate Student who is registered as a candidate for the M.D. Degree shall pay the University Composition Fee as determined by Regulation 10 of the regulations for University Composition Fees for the course.

(*c*) A Graduate Student who is registered as a candidate for a qualification other than the Ph.D., M.Litt. or M.Sc. or M.D. Degree shall pay the University Composition Fee as determined by Regulation 10 of the regulations for University Composition Fees for each term up to and including the term in which he or she completes the requirements for the qualification, up to the maximum specified in the regulations for the qualification.

(*d*) A Graduate Student shall pay the same total fee whether registered for a part-time course or for a full-time course leading to the same qualification, and the maximum number of terms specified in clause (*a*) shall be increased accordingly.[1]

(*e*) A person employed in a University institution[2] at least 40% full-time who has been accepted for admission as a Graduate Student, and who is registered as a candidate for the Ph.D., M.Litt, or M.Sc. Degree, or for an M.Phil. Degree examined by thesis and oral only, or for a Certificate of Postgraduate Studies, shall pay a University Composition Fee of one-third the Home and EU postgraduate Fee for any term in which that person continues in employment by the University.

(*f*) The Board, in cases of hardship or for any other cause which they may deem sufficient and on the recommendation of the Degree Committee concerned, may remit or reduce the fee payable under clause (*a*) in respect of a particular Graduate Student.

(*g*) In the case of a Graduate Student following a course of study that requires a period of instruction in an approved institution, the Board may, on the recommendation of the Degree Committee concerned, remit or reduce payments under clause (*a*) of this regulation.

12. If the Tutor of a candidate for the M.Phil. or M.Res. or M.Ed. Degree, or for any Diploma or Certificate for which candidates are required to be Graduate Students, supplies the Board of Graduate Studies with satisfactory evidence that the candidate has been hindered by illness or other grave cause in preparing for or taking the examination or any part of the examination for the degree or other qualification concerned, and such representations are received by the Secretary of the Board not later than three months after the date on which the result of the examination was communicated, the Board shall have power, notwithstanding any provision to the contrary in the relevant regulations, Allowances for illness, etc.

either (*a*) to approve the candidate for the degree or other qualification without further examination, provided that no candidate shall be so approved unless the Degree Committee concerned judge him or her to have performed with credit in a substantial part of the examination,

or (*b*) to allow the candidate to be examined or re-examined under such conditions and at such time as may be determined by the Board after consultation with the Degree Committee concerned;

provided that a candidate may reject the offer of an allowance by writing to the Secretary of the Board within one month of the date on which the allowance was offered. Representations received after the prescribed time limit shall not be considered.

A student, or her or his Tutor with the student's consent, may seek review of a decision in relation to that student made by the Board of Graduate Studies. A request for review shall be made in writing, stating the grounds of review, normally within one month of written notification of the Board's decision (unless, in exceptional circumstances, the Registrary or a deputy permits a longer period). If the request includes, in the opinion of the Chair of the Board, relevant additional information not previously available, the Board will reconsider its decision at its next meeting following receipt of the request. If no such additional information is included or if, on reconsideration, the decision is reaffirmed by the Board, the procedure described in the following paragraphs shall apply.

[1] For a Graduate Student who completes the part-time course leading to a Ph.D. Degree in five years or an M.Litt. or M.Sc. Degree in ten terms the fee will be 60% of the full-time fee each term. For a Graduate Student who completes the course leading to the M.Phil. Degree through Route C, the fee will be determined at the date of admission and will be payable in two annual instalments.

[2] That is, an institution that is under the supervision of the Council or the General Board. A candidate must hold a contract of employment with the University to be eligible for payment of a reduced fee. He or she will become liable to pay the full Composition Fee at the appropriate rate for the remainder of the course of research if he or she ceases to be employed by the University before qualifying for the degree for which he or she was registered as a candidate. The Staff Fee is not currently available to employees of the Colleges, the University Press, or Cambridge Assessment.

The Registrary or a deputy shall appoint a reviewer. Exceptionally, a panel of three reviewers may be appointed. If so, references below to 'the reviewer' shall be construed accordingly.

The reviewer will consider the request, the documentation available to the Board (less any confidential medical information), the Ordinances which apply to the Board's decision, and the Board's Notes of Guidance. He or she will obtain an opinion from the Board, seek such other information as he or she may require and, at her or his discretion, may hold a hearing (but there is no obligation to hold a hearing). The reviewer will issue an adjudication in writing as soon as possible, stating findings of fact, conclusions, and, if any, recommendations, for consideration by the Board. The reviewer shall be concerned with determining whether there is evidence of: inadequate consideration of the matter by the Board; the Board having made a decision, to the detriment of the student, which is inconsistent with the relevant Ordinances or its own Notes of Guidance; or material circumstances of which the Board was unaware and which were of such a nature as, had the Board been so aware, to have been likely to cause the Board to have reached a different decision.

The Board shall normally accept the recommendation of the reviewer. If, exceptionally, the reviewer's recommendation is not accepted a written explanation shall be provided to the reviewer, the student, and her or his Tutor. The Board may decide not to accept a recommendation in any instance in which: (i) the reviewer has sought to make a decision replacing that of the Board; (ii) the reviewer's recommendation is inconsistent with the Ordinances governing Allowances; or (iii) the reviewer's recommendation is such that, were it to be accepted, it would set a precedent which would not be in the interests of the proper conduct of the Board's business or in the wider interests of the University.

The conclusion of the consideration by the Board of Graduate Studies of any recommendation by a review shall be the normal final point of decision within the University. A reviewer may summarily dismiss an application which seems to her or him to be vexatious or frivolous.

Certificates.

13. A Graduate Student who wishes to be a candidate for a degree or other qualification at some other university or similar institution, shall receive, on application to the Secretary of the Board, for any period of study in the University of not less than two terms, a certificate that he or she has pursued his or her studies during that period with regularity and industry, if, in the opinion of the Supervisor concerned, a course record statement can properly be given. The certificate shall be signed by the Secretary of the Board. A fee of £7 shall be charged for each such certificate and for any similar certificate, letter, statement, or document that may be issued by the Secretary of the Board on application by a Graduate Student.

14. Fees shall be payable to Supervisors of Graduate Students as follows:

(*a*) No fee shall be payable to the holder of a University office specified in the Schedule to Special Ordinance C (i) 1. No fee shall be payable to the holder of an office in an institution which maintains a formal University Partner Institute agreement with the University for any supervision undertaken during the duration of that agreement.[1]

(*b*) Subject to the provisions of clause (*a*),

(i) a fee of not less than £55 a term shall be paid to a Supervisor for each Graduate Student under his or her supervision who falls under Regulation 11 on receipt by the Board of Graduate Studies of the report specified in Regulation 8;

(ii) at the request of the Schools Degree Committee concerned, the Board may pay a fee of not less than £55 a term to the Supervisor of a Graduate Student who has leave under either Regulation 1(*b*) of the regulations for the Ph.D., M.Sc., and M.Litt. Degrees, and for the Ed.D. Degree, or Regulation 2(*a*) of the regulations for the Eng.D. Degree, or Regulation 4 of the regulations for the M.Phil. Degree or Regulation 4 of the regulations for the M.Res. Degree to work outside the University;

(iii) when a remission or reduction is made under Regulation 11(*f*) in respect of a Graduate Student who has not completed the requirements for the degree or other qualification for which he or she is registered or has applied to become registered, the Supervisor shall be paid a fee of not less than £55 a term;

[1] The Institutions which currently maintain a formal University Partner Institute agreement are as follows: Animal Health Trust; BBSRC Babraham Institute; British Antarctic Survey; Cambridge Crystallographic Data Centre; European Bioinformatics Institute – European Molecular Biology Laboratory; MRC Biostatistics Unit; MRC Cognition and Brain Sciences Unit; MRC Mitochondrial Biology Unit; MRC Human Nutrition Research Unit; National Institute of Agricultural Botany; Wellcome Trust Sanger Institute.

(iv) when a remission or reduction is made under Regulation 11(*f*) in respect of a Graduate Student who has completed the number of terms of research or study and residence required for the degree or other qualification for which he or she is registered, the Board School in which the student is registered shall decide whether the Supervisor is to be paid a fee in respect of that student.

TEMPORARY REGULATION

15. The amendments to Regulations 10 and 11 approved by Grace 3 of 10 March 2010 shall apply to students commencing a course of research or study as a Graduate Student, or with a view to registration as a Graduate Student following such a course, on or after 1 October 2010.

REVIEW OF THE RESULTS OF EXAMINATIONS FOR POSTGRADUATE QUALIFICATIONS

Amended by Grace 8 of 21 May 2014

1. The following regulations shall apply to any University examination listed in the Schedule to these regulations. Powers of the Board.

2. The Board of Graduate Studies shall have power, in connection with any examination for a degree or other qualification, to remit a recommendation or resolution received from a Degree Committee concerning a particular candidate to the Degree Committee for further consideration. The Degree Committee may recommend a course of action as a consequence of any such remission but the power to determine the action to be taken lies with the Board of Graduate Studies and not with the Degree Committee

3. The Board shall consider any representations made by or on behalf of a candidate which constitute a complaint about the conduct of the examination in that candidate's case, provided that such representations shall not be considered unless they are received by the Secretary of the Board not later than three months after the date on which the result of the examination was communicated to the candidate. The Board shall consider the representations which in the judgment of the Board constitute a complaint on one or more of the following grounds:

(*a*) that there existed material circumstances relating directly to the examination (excluding circumstances relating to the candidate's course of research or course of study) of which the Examiners were not aware;

(*b*) that procedural irregularities occurred in the conduct of the examination, which were of such a nature as to cause reasonable doubt as to whether the Examiners would have reached the same conclusion had the irregularities not occurred;

(*c*) that there is demonstrable evidence of prejudice, bias, or inadequate assessment in the examination process.

If the Board are of the view that a complaint does not fall within any of the grounds specified above, they shall dismiss the complaint and shall inform the complainant accordingly

The Board shall consult the Degree Committee concerned under Regulation 2 about any representations made under this regulation.

4. If after considering any views expressed by the relevant Degree Committee under Regulation 2 and any representations made by or on behalf of a candidate under Regulation 3:

(*a*) the Board are satisfied that the examination of that candidate was properly conducted and that the complaint is unjustified, the Board shall so inform the candidate; or

(*b*) if the Board are satisfied that the examination of that candidate was not properly conducted and that the complaint is justified, they shall have power, after consulting the Degree Committee concerned, the Examiners concerned, and any other persons or body specified by the Board:

(i) to require the Examiners to re-examine the candidate;

(ii) if the candidate has not been examined orally, to require the Examiners to hold an oral examination;

(iii) if the candidate has been examined orally, to require the Examiners to hold a further oral examination;

(iv) to permit the candidate to submit a revised dissertation, thesis, or other exercise, to be examined by the same Examiners;

(v) to require the Degree Committee to appoint one or more additional Examiners to make an independent report or reports on the work submitted by the candidate;

(vi) to require the Degree Committee to appoint new Examiners to replace the Examiners previously appointed, and to permit the candidate

either (A) to be re-examined by the new Examiners,

or (B) to submit a revised dissertation, thesis, or other exercise, to be examined by the new Examiners;

(vii) to require the Examiners (either the Examiners previously appointed or new Examiners appointed under sub-paragraph (vi), as the case may be) to set fresh examination papers or other exercises, as appropriate, to be taken by the candidate under arrangements specified by the Board.

Review Committee.

5. If, after the candidate has been informed of a decision taken by the Board of Graduate Studies the candidate, or a person acting on the candidate's behalf, makes representations challenging the Board's decision under Regulation 4(*a*) or rejecting one or more of the remedial steps determined by the Board under Regulation 4(*b*)(i) to (vii), then the Board shall refer such representations to a Review Committee constituted in accordance with Regulation 6, provided that those representations are received by the Secretary of the Board within three months of the date on which the Board's decision was communicated by the Secretary to the candidate. For the avoidance of doubt representations received after this period has expired shall not be considered.

Membership.

6. A Review Committee appointed under these regulations shall consist of

(*a*) the Vice-Chancellor, or a duly appointed deputy, as Chair;

(*b*) two persons appointed by the General Board.

The General Board shall maintain a panel of members of the Regent House who are willing to serve as members of a Review Committee, and shall appoint twelve persons to the panel, four persons being appointed in the Michaelmas Term of each year to serve for three years from 1 January following their appointment. When any representations are to be referred by the Board of Graduate Studies to a Review Committee, the General Board shall appoint two members of the panel to serve as members of the Review Committee for the particular case. In selecting members of the panel for appointment as members of a Review Committee, the Board shall exclude any person who has been involved in the particular case at an earlier stage. A person appointed a member of a Review Committee shall serve until the conclusion of the particular case for which he or she was appointed.

Secretary.

7. The Academic Secretary, or a deputy appointed by the Academic Secretary, shall act as Secretary to a Review Committee.

8. For the purpose of these regulations the term 'complainant' shall mean the student making a complaint, or on whose behalf a complaint is made.

9. The Secretary to the Review Committee shall notify the complainant of the persons appointed to be members of the Committee. The complainant shall be entitled to object for good cause to any member so appointed. The Vice-Chancellor shall rule on any such objection, and her or his decision shall be final. If the Vice-Chancellor allows such an objection, the General Board shall appoint another member of the panel to serve as a member of the Committee.

Grounds for complaint.

10. The Review Committee shall consider the representations made or referred to them under these regulations which in the judgement of the Committee constitute a complaint on one or more of the following grounds:

(*a*) that there existed material circumstances relating directly to the examination (excluding circumstances relating to the candidate's course of research or course of study) of which the Examiners were not aware;

(*b*) that procedural irregularities occurred in the conduct of the examination, which were of such a nature as to cause reasonable doubt as to whether the Examiners would have reached the same conclusion had the irregularities not occurred;

(*c*) that there is demonstrable evidence of prejudice, bias, or inadequate assessment in the examination process.

If the Committee are of the view that a complaint does not fall within any of the grounds specified above, they shall dismiss the complaint and shall inform the complainant and the Board of Graduate Studies accordingly. For the purposes of these regulations the term 'examination' relates to the assessment of the candidate's performance by the original or any subsequently appointed Examiners and not to any consideration of the case by the relevant Degree Committee or the Board of Graduate Studies.

11. Any representation considered by a Review Committee to fall within any of the grounds specified in Regulation 10 shall be made available to each of the following:

(*a*) the Board of Graduate Studies;

(*b*) the Degree Committee concerned;

(*c*) the Examiners concerned;

(*d*) any other person or body specified by the Review Committee.

Each of these parties shall be given an opportunity to submit a written statement to the Committee in response to the complaint. Such a statement may include reports of the Examiners or extracts from those reports. The Committee shall have power to seek statements from other persons or bodies, as they think fit.

12. Any statement submitted to the Review Committee under Regulation 11 shall be made available to the complainant and to the other parties specified in that regulation, each of whom shall be afforded an opportunity to comment on it.

13. Once the Review Committee have received the comments specified in Regulation 12, they shall appoint a day and time for a hearing at which the complainant shall be entitled to be present and to be accompanied by not more than two advisers, each of whom shall be either an officer of the Graduate Union, a sabbatical officer of Cambridge University Students' Union, or a member of the Regent House; one of these advisers shall be permitted to act as the complainant's representative and to speak on her or his behalf. The Committee may, at their discretion, invite the Examiners concerned to the hearing.

Decision of Review Committee.

14. A Review Committee shall consider any complaint or any representations referred to them under Regulation 5 and shall have power to dismiss the complaint or, if they consider it justified:

(*a*) to require the Board of Graduate Studies or the Degree Committee concerned to reconsider their earlier decisions on the particular case;

(*b*) to require the Examiners to re-examine the candidate;

(*c*) if the candidate has not been examined orally, to require the Examiners to hold an oral examination;

(*d*) if the candidate has been examined orally, to require the Examiners to hold a further oral examination;

(*e*) to permit the candidate to submit a revised dissertation, thesis, or other exercise, to be examined by the same Examiners;

(*f*) to require the Degree Committee to appoint one or more additional Examiners to make an independent report or reports on the work submitted by the candidate;

(*g*) to require the Degree Committee to appoint new Examiners to replace the Examiners previously appointed, and to permit the candidate

either (i) to be re-examined by the new Examiners,

or (ii) to submit a revised dissertation, thesis, or other exercise, to be examined by the new Examiners;

(*h*) to require the Examiners (either the Examiners previously appointed or new Examiners appointed under sub-paragraph (*g*), as the case may be) to set fresh examination papers or other exercises, as appropriate, to be taken by the candidate under arrangements specified by the Review Committee.

15. The Secretary to the Review Committee shall send written notification of the Committee's decision and the reasons for it to the complainant and to the other parties specified in Regulation 11.

16. The decision of a Review Committee on any particular case shall be final. No person who applies for a review under the review procedure established by these regulations shall be entitled also for review of the same matter under the procedure for determining complaints by members of the University *in statu pupillari* established under the regulation for complaints by students[1].

[1] See p. 220.

SCHEDULE

Examinations for which the foregoing regulations apply

Examinations, including progress examinations approved under Regulation 9 of the General Regulations for Admission as a Graduate Student, leading to the following qualifications:

B.D. Degree
M.D. Degree
Vet.M.D. Degree
Ph.D. Degree
Ph.D. Degree by special regulations
Eng.D. Degree
Ed.D. Degree
M.Sc. Degree
M.Litt. Degree
M.Res. Degree
M.Phil. Degree
M.Ed. Degree[1]
M.St. Degree
Certificate of Postgraduate Study
Diplomas in:
  Economics
  Legal Studies
  International Law

[1] Candidates admitted from 1 October 2013.

CHAPTER VII

DEGREES, DIPLOMAS, AND OTHER QUALIFICATIONS

The provisions contained in this Chapter are Regulations of the General Board

MASTER OF ADVANCED STUDY

GENERAL REGULATIONS

1. The M.A.St. Degree shall be awarded on completion of a course of advanced study. A subject of such study, together with the programme aims, learning outcomes, and syllabus for the course, and the special regulations for the examination and any subsequent amendments thereof, shall be approved by the General Board on the recommendation of the Faculty Board or other body concerned, after consultation with the appropriate Degree Committee. M.A.St. Degree.

2. A candidate for the M.A.St. Degree must be approved by the Degree Committee concerned and shall comply with any special conditions that the Degree Committee may lay down in a particular case. Candidature. The course shall extend over one academical year. A candidate shall be required to attend in all three terms of the year, beginning from the date announced by the Degree Committee for the start of lectures, classes, or other formal instruction. Attendance.

3. The Faculty Board or other body concerned shall have power to issue supplementary regulations determining the scope and manner of assessment of the examination, and shall be empowered to amend such supplementary regulations from time to time as they may think fit, due care being taken that sufficient notice is given of any change.

4. The Faculty Board or other body concerned shall appoint such number of Examiners and Assessors as they shall deem sufficient to conduct the examination for the M.A.St. Degree and to report on the performance of a candidate. The Examiners and Assessors shall undertake such duties as the Faculty Board or other body may decide. Examiners and Assessors.

5. On completing the requisite number of terms a student who has satisfied the Examiners in the examination for the M.A.St. Degree shall be entitled to proceed to the degree. Approval for degree.

6. A candidate who has failed to satisfy the Examiners shall not be eligible to take the examination for the degree again.

7. No student shall be a candidate for the M.A.St. Degree on more than one occasion or for the M.A.St. Degree and for another University examination in the same term.

8. For each subject, the names of the candidates who satisfy the Examiners shall appear in alphabetical order in a single class. In each class-list distinctive marks may be attached to the names of those candidates who in the opinion of the Examiners deserve special credit. The Chair of Examiners shall communicate the marks of all candidates to the Registrary.

9. While following the course of study leading to the examination for the M.A.St. a student shall pay the appropriate University Composition Fee for the course. Fees payable.

10. A student who has taken the examination for the M.A.St. Degree shall not be entitled to count the period or any part of the period during which he or she has been a candidate for that examination towards a course of research for the degree of Ph.D., M.Sc., or M.Litt.

SPECIAL REGULATIONS

Amended by Notice (Reporter, *2013–14, p. 358*)

ASTROPHYSICS

The examination in Astrophysics for the Master of Advanced Studies Degree shall comprise written papers, and a report of a research project, as set out in the regulations for the subject Astrophysics in Part III of the Natural Sciences Tripos. The conduct of the examination shall be governed for the regulations for that part, provided that a candidate shall be a candidate not for honours and the candidate's name shall not appear in the class-list for the Tripos. Distinctive marks may be attached to the names of those candidates who in the opinion of the Examiners deserve special credit: the mark (*d*) being used to denote a distinguished performance and the mark (*m*) a meritorious performance.

Materials Science

The examination in Materials Science for the M.A.St. Degree shall comprise the examination requirements as set out in the regulations for the subject Materials Science in Part III of the Natural Sciences Tripos. The conduct of the examination shall be governed for the regulations for that part, provided that a candidate shall be a candidate not for honours and the candidate's name shall not appear in the class-list for the Tripos. Distinctive marks may be attached to the names of those candidates who in the opinion of the Examiners deserve special credit: the mark (*d*) being used to denote a distinguished performance and the mark (*c*) a commendable performance.

Mathematics

The examination in Mathematics for the M.A.St. Degree shall comprise written papers, and topics for an optional essay as set out in the regulations for Part III of the Mathematical Tripos. The conduct of the examination shall be governed for the regulations for that part, provided that a candidate shall be a candidate not for honours and the candidate's name shall not appear in the class-list for the Tripos. Distinctive marks may be attached to the names of those candidates who in the opinion of the Examiners deserve special credit: the mark (*d*) being used to denote a distinguished performance and the mark (*m*) a meritorious performance.

Physics

The examination in Physics for the M.A.St. Degree shall comprise the examination requirements as set out in the regulations for the subject Physics in Part III of the Natural Sciences Tripos. The conduct of the examination shall be governed for the regulations for that part, provided that a candidate shall be a candidate not for honours and the candidate's name shall not appear in the class-list for the Tripos. Distinctive marks may be attached to the names of those candidates who in the opinion of the Examiners deserve special credit: the mark (*d*) being used to denote a distinguished performance and the mark (*c*) a commendable performance.

MASTER OF BUSINESS ADMINISTRATION

Candidature.

1. A candidate for the M.B.A. Examination must be approved by the Degree Committee for the Faculty of Business and Management, who shall assign to each candidate a date of commencement of candidature.

2. The Degree Committee may approve as a candidate for the M.B.A. Examination any student who has satisfied the Committee that by reason of previous study he or she is qualified to engage in postgraduate work in Management Studies.

3. Applications for approval under Regulation 2 shall be sent to the Secretary of the Degree Committee so as to arrive not later than 31 March next preceding the date on which the applicant wishes his or her candidature to begin, provided that the Committee shall have power to consider applications submitted after that date.

Course of study.

4. The course of study leading to the M.B.A. Examination shall cover the following aspects of business administration: basic skills and functional knowledge, organizational integration, the organization in its environment. The course of study shall consist, at the choice of the candidate, of one of the following:

(*a*) *One-year course*
A course extending over one academical year, including three terms' residence in the University.

(*b*) *Two-year integrated course*
A course extending over two academical years, including three terms' residence in the University, and not less than one year of supervised study and employment in one or more participating organizations approved for this purpose by the Faculty Board of Business and Management.

(*c*) *Executive M.B.A. course*
A course extending over a period of two years comprising a number of course units and project work, which shall include not less than 300 hours of formal instruction in the University and not less than 120 hours of open study prescribed by the Faculty Board.

No student's name shall appear on the list of successful candidates for the M.B.A. Examination unless the Director of the Judge Institute of Management is satisfied that the student has diligently attended the course.

5. No student shall be a candidate for the M.B.A. Examination or for any part thereof on more than one occasion.

6. The M.B.A. Examination shall consist of compulsory modules, elective modules, and project work. Examination of the modules may be by written paper, essay, coursework, or another mode of assessment announced by the Faculty Board. Each candidate will have to complete a minimum of three written papers, the duration of which will be announced by the Faculty Board. Examination.

(*a*) *Compulsory modules*

The Faculty Board shall give notice of the topics and form of assessment for each compulsory module by the end of the term immediately preceding the start of the course (provided that the Board shall have the power of subsequently issuing amendments if they have due reason for doing so and they are satisfied that no student's preparation for the examination is adversely affected.)

(*b*) *Elective modules*

The Faculty Board shall give notice of the topics and form of assessment for each elective module by the end of the term immediately preceding the term in which the work is to be completed.

(*c*) *Project work*

(i) *One-year course* (Regulation 4(*a*)):

The Faculty Board shall give notice of the list of summer activities and the format for submission by the end of the Lent Term, provided that the Board shall have the power of subsequently issuing amendments if they have due reason for doing so and they are satisfied that no student's preparation for the examination is adversely affected.

(ii) *Two-year integrated course* (Regulation 4(*b*)):[1]

One or more reports on project work, which shall be submitted in such form and assessed in such manner as the Faculty Board may determine, provided that the Board shall have the power of subsequently issuing amendments if they have due reason for doing so and they are satisfied that no student's preparation for the examination is adversely affected

(iii) *Executive M.B.A. course* (Regulation 4(*c*)):

The Faculty Board shall give notice of the format and length for submission of project work by the end of the Lent Term provided that the Board shall have the power of subsequently issuing amendments if they have due reason for doing so and they are satisfied that no student's preparation for the examination is adversely affected.

The Examiners shall have power to examine a candidate *viva voce* on any or all of the three sections of the examination (*a*)–(*c*).

7. The Faculty Board of Business and Management shall have power to issue supplementary regulations determining the scope and manner of assessment of the examination, and shall be empowered to amend such supplementary regulations from time to time as they may think fit, due care being taken that sufficient notice is given of any change. Supplementary regulations.

8. The Faculty Board shall nominate such number of Examiners and Assessors as they may deem sufficient, including a resident member of the Senate as Chair of Examiners. Examiners and Assessors.

9. The names of the candidates who satisfy the Examiners shall appear in separate class-lists headed 'One-year candidates' or 'Two-year integrated candidates' or 'Executive M.B.A. candidates', according to the course of study that they have followed. The names of the candidates in each class-list shall be arranged in alphabetical order in a single class. The Chair of Examiners shall communicate the marks of all candidates to the Registrary. Class-lists.

10. While following the course of study leading to the M.B.A. Examination a student shall pay the appropriate University Composition Fee for each year of the course (including periods spent away from Cambridge). Fee.

11. On completing the requisite number of terms,[2] or hours of study, as set out in Regulation 4 a student who has satisfied the Examiners in the M.B.A. Examination shall be entitled to proceed to the degree of M.B.A.

[1] This course is currently suspended.

[2] See the regulations for Residence and Precincts of the University (p. 189).

Relation to courses of research.

12. A student who has taken the M.B.A. Examination shall not be entitled to count the period or any part of the period during which he or she has been a candidate for that examination towards a course of research for the degree of Ph.D., M.Sc., or M.Litt.

DEGREES IN DIVINITY

Bachelor of Theology for Ministry

Amended by Notice (Reporter, *2013–14, p. 727*)

1. The degree of Bachelor of Theology for Ministry may be awarded to a candidate who:

(*a*) has satisfied Examiners in the First and Second Examinations for the degree;

(*b*) has completed five terms at least by residence,[1]

(*c*) has submitted to the Examiners a satisfactory portfolio in Pastoral Studies under the provisions of Regulations 19 and 25.

Restrictions.

2. A student who has proceeded, or who is qualified to proceed, to the B.Th. Degree shall not be a candidate for any Honours Examination except by special permission of the Council, on the application of the student's Tutor. In considering applications the Council shall have regard to the privileges granted to Affiliated Students. A student who has been granted permission under this regulation shall not offer in any Honours Examination a paper which is the same as, or which substantially overlaps with, a paper which he or she has offered in the First or Second Examination for the B.Th. Degree.

Examinations.

3. There shall be a First Examination and a Second Examination for the B.Th. Degree. The names of successful candidates in both the First and Second Examinations shall be arranged in alphabetical order in three classes, with the second class being divided.

Standing of candidates.

4. Subject to the provisions of Regulation 6, a student may be a candidate for the First Examination if he or she

(*a*) has been proposed for the degree by a House of the Cambridge Theological Federation[2], and admitted by the Faculty Board of Divinity; and

(*b*) has been matriculated and has kept two terms as a member of the University; provided that three complete terms have not passed after the student's first term of residence reading for the B.Th. Degree.

5. Subject to the provisions of Regulation 6, a student may be a candidate for the Second Examination if he or she

(*a*) has satisfied the Examiners in the First Examination; and

(*b*) has kept five terms as a member of the University;

provided that nine complete terms have not passed after the student's first term of residence as a member of the University reading for the B.Th. Degree.

6. (*a*) The Faculty Board of Divinity shall have power to grant an allowance of not more than one term to a student who has spent a period of not less than eight weeks working under supervision outside the University under conditions approved by the Faculty Board, provided that no student shall be granted such an allowance on more than one occasion.

(*b*) A student who wishes to spend a period away from Cambridge under the provisions of this regulation shall apply to the Faculty Board for the approval of his or her plans. Such an application shall be submitted to the Secretary of the Faculty Board so as to arrive not later than the first day of the Full Easter Term in the academical year next preceding that in which the student's proposed absence is to fall.

(*c*) A term allowed under this regulation may be counted for the purposes of satisfying the requirements of Regulation 4 or Regulation 5 above, but may not be counted for the purpose of satisfying the requirements for residence for the degree of Bachelor of Theology.

7. No student shall be a candidate for both the First and Second Examinations, or for either of those examinations and also for an Honours Examination of the University, in the same term. No student who has been a candidate for either the First or the Second Examination shall again be a candidate for the same examination.

[1] See the regulations for Residence and Precincts of the University (p. 189).

[2] The following institutions are members of the Cambridge Theological Federation: Ridley Hall, Wesley House, Westcott House, Westminster College, the Margaret Beaufort Institute, the Institute for Orthodox Christian Studies, and the Eastern Region Ministry Course.

8. The Faculty Board shall nominate such number of Examiners for each of the three examinations as they deem sufficient, and shall have power to nominate one or more Assessors to assist the Examiners in any subject. Assessors shall propose questions in the papers or parts of papers assigned to them by the Examiners, shall mark the answers of the candidates in those papers or parts of papers, and shall advise the Examiners on the performance of candidates in the examination. Assessors may be summoned to meetings of the Examiners for the purpose of consultation and advice, but shall not be entitled to vote. Examiners and Assessors.

9. The Examiners shall take account of a candidate's performance in an additional paper, or in the weaker of two papers either of which may be deemed to have been taken as an additional paper, only in so far as it is to the candidate's advantage. They shall not exclude a candidate from any class on the ground that he or she has not offered an additional paper.

10. The Faculty Board of Divinity shall have power to issue from time to time supplementary regulations defining or limiting all or any of the subjects of examination, and to modify, alter, or withdraw such supplementary regulations as occasion may require, provided that due care is taken to give sufficient notice of any change. Supplementary regulations.

11. Public notice of any variable subjects for the examinations in any year shall be given by the Faculty Board before the end of the academical year next but one preceding the examination concerned, provided that the Board shall have the power of subsequently issuing amendments if they have due reason for doing so and if they are satisfied that no student's preparation for the examination is adversely affected. Variable subjects.

12. Not later than the first day of Full Michaelmas Term each year the Faculty Board shall publish, by Notice in the Faculty of Divinity and in the Member Institutions of the Cambridge Theological Federation, details of the course-work to be undertaken by candidates for the examinations to be held during the ensuing academic year. Course-work.

13. The papers for the First and Second Examinations for the degree of B.Th. shall be divided into Groups A–E and shall be as set out below. Each paper shall be designated as either a full paper or a half-paper; in the following list the papers marked with an asterisk shall be half-papers. Scheme of examination.

Group A

B.Th.1.	Introduction to Biblical Hebrew
B.Th.2.	Elementary Hebrew (Paper A1A of the Theological and Religious Studies Tripos)
B.Th.3.	Introduction to New Testament Greek
B.Th.4.	New Testament Greek (Paper A1B of the Theological and Religious Studies Tripos)

Group B

B.Th.11.	Reading the Christian Bible
B.Th.12.	Christian doctrine
B.Th.13.	Belief and practice in the early church
B.Th.14.	Reform and renewal in Christian history[1]
B.Th.15.	Special subject in Christian history
B.Th.16.	Special subject in the study of religion[1]

Group C

B.Th.21.	Intermediate Hebrew
B.Th.22.	Intermediate Greek[1]
B.Th.23.	Old Testament studies
B.Th.24.	New Testament studies
*B.Th.25.	Old Testament exegesis
*B.Th.26.	New Testament exegesis
*B.Th.27.	Biblical themes in Christian doctrine
*B.Th.28.	The study of Christian mission[1]
*B.Th.29.	The Gospel and western culture
B.Th.30.	Philosophy of religion
*B.Th.31.	Church and sacraments[1]
*B.Th.32.	Patterns of Christian worship
*B.Th.33.	Subjects specified by the Faculty Board
*B.Th.34.	Special study

[1] This paper is suspended in 2014–15.

GROUP D

B.Th.41.	Further studies in Christian doctrine
B.Th.42.	Topics in church history
B.Th.43.	Judaism, Christianity, and Islam in encounter
B.Th.44.	Christian ethics
*B.Th.45.	Advanced subjects specified by the Faculty Board
*B.Th.46.	Further advanced subjects specified by the Faculty Board
B.Th.47.	Special study

GROUP E

B.Th.51.	Pastoral portfolio A
B.Th.52.	Pastoral portfolio B

14. (*a*) Each full paper shall consist of *either* an examination of three hours' duration, *or* an examination of two hours' duration plus one essay (mixed mode), *or* two essays. The Faculty Board shall specify by supplementary regulation which one of these modes of assessment shall apply in the case of each paper.

(*b*) Each half-paper shall consist of *either* an examination of two hours' duration, *or* one essay. The Faculty Board shall specify by supplementary regulation which one of these modes of assessment shall apply in the case of each half-paper.

(*c*) Candidates for the First Examination and the Second Examination may not offer for each examination more than two full papers (or the equivalent number of full papers and half-papers) whose assessment is wholly by essay.

(*d*) All essays offered under the alternative modes of assessment specified under (*a*) or (*b*) above shall be of not more than 3,000 words in length, on a topic chosen by the candidate from a list of topics published by the Faculty Board not later than the first day of Full Michaelmas Term. Essays shall be typewritten, in English, and shall be submitted to the Secretary of the Faculty Board in accordance with detailed arrangements approved by the Board, so as to arrive not later than the third Tuesday of Full Easter Term. Candidates who submit essays of more than 3,000 words in length shall be liable to be penalized by the Examiners.

15. (*a*) Every candidate who offers a paper in which there is a choice of subject shall specify on his or her examination entry which subject he or she intends to offer.

(*b*) In approving a particular subject for study in any of Papers B.Th.34 and B.Th.47 the Faculty Board may stipulate that the candidate concerned may not offer (or have already offered) another particular paper whose content is deemed to overlap with that subject.

First Examination.

16. A candidate for the First Examination shall offer

(*a*) four full papers (or the equivalent number of full papers and half-papers) chosen from Groups B and C;

(*b*) a language paper chosen from papers B.Th.1 to B.Th.4 unless the candidate has previously passed a biblical language course which is deemed by the Faculty Board to be of equivalent standard;

(*c*) Paper B.Th.51; provided that

(i) a candidate may not offer the same set texts for Papers B.Th.23 or B.Th.24 as for Papers B.Th.25 or B.Th.26;

(ii) a candidate who so wishes may offer as an additional paper a language paper chosen from Papers B.Th.1–B.Th.4 in a language from which he or she has not been exempted by the Faculty Board.

Second Examination.

17. A candidate for the Second Examination shall offer

(*a*) either four full papers (or the equivalent number of full papers and half-papers) chosen from Groups C and D, or three full papers (or the equivalent number of full papers and half-papers) chosen from Groups C and D plus a dissertation, as specified in Regulations 21 and 22; a candidate who so wishes may offer as an additional paper a language paper chosen from Papers B.Th.1–B.Th.4 in a language which he or she has not previously offered;

(*b*) Paper B.Th.52;

provided that:

(i) a candidate shall not offer any paper or half-paper that he or she has previously offered in the First Examination;

(ii) a candidate may not offer the same set texts for Papers B.Th.23 or B.Th.24 as for Papers B.Th.25 or B.Th.26 (whether taken as part of the First or Second Examination).

18. A candidate may not offer B.Th.34 and B.Th.47 in the same examination. The special study may be on any topic relating to theology for ministry, but in approving a particular topic the Faculty Board may stipulate that the candidate concerned may not offer (or have already offered) a particular paper or a particular prescribed subject within a paper.

19. (*a*) A candidate who wishes to offer papers B.Th.34 or B.Th.47 under Regulations 16 or 17 shall submit an application, including the title of the proposed special study and a statement of the scheme of papers to be offered in the examination. Applications shall be submitted to the Secretary of the Faculty Board so as to arrive not later than the division of the Michaelmas Term next preceding the examination concerned.

(*b*) Each candidate must obtain the approval of the proposed title by the Faculty Board not later than the last day of each Full Michaelmas Term. When the Faculty Board have approved a title, no change shall be made to it or to the candidate's scheme of papers without the further approval of the Faculty Board.

Dissertation.

20. A candidate for the Second Examination may, with the permission of the Faculty Board, submit in place of any full paper which he or she would otherwise offer under Regulation 17, a dissertation on a topic approved by the Faculty Board. A dissertation may be on any topic relating to the subject of any full or half-paper in Groups B, C, or D, but in approving a particular topic the Faculty Board may stipulate that the candidate concerned may not offer (or have already offered) a particular paper or a particular prescribed subject within a paper; provided that no candidate shall offer more than one dissertation.

21. (*a*) A candidate who wishes to offer a dissertation under Regulation 17 shall submit an application, including the title of the proposed dissertation and a statement of the scheme of papers to be offered in the examination. Applications shall be submitted to the Secretary of the Faculty Board so as to arrive not later than the division of the Michaelmas Term next preceding the examination concerned.

(*b*) Each candidate must obtain the approval of the proposed title by the Faculty Board not later than the last day of each Full Michaelmas Term. When the Faculty Board have approved a title, no change shall be made to it or to the candidate's scheme of papers without the further approval of the Faculty Board.

(*c*) A dissertation shall be typewritten and shall be of not less than 8,000 words and not more than 10,000 words in length, including footnotes, but excluding bibliography. Candidates will be required to declare that the dissertation is their own work and that it does not contain material already used to any substantial extent for a comparable purpose. Candidates who submit dissertations of more than 10,000 words in length shall be liable to be penalized by the Examiners.

(*d*) A dissertation shall be submitted to the Secretary of the Faculty Board, in accordance with detailed arrangements approved by the Board, so as to arrive not later than the third Tuesday of the Full Easter Term in which the examination is to be held.

Pastoral Studies.

22. (*a*) Course-work presented for Papers B.Th.51 and B.Th.52 shall be submitted to the Secretary of the Faculty Board in accordance with detailed arrangements approved by the Board, so as to arrive not later than the third Tuesday of Full Easter Term. Candidates who submit work in excess of the stated maximum lengths shall be liable to be penalized by the Examiners.

(*b*) A candidate who fails to satisfy the Examiners in Paper B.Th.52 at the end of the Second Examination year may apply to the Faculty Board to be reassessed in the examination. Such permission shall be granted on not more than one occasion. If any candidate is given permission to be reassessed under this regulation, the assessment shall be concluded on the basis of such additional work as the Examiners may require and shall be completed in the academical year next following the first assessment, except by special permission of the Faculty Board granted in exceptional circumstances.

SUPPLEMENTARY REGULATIONS[1]

Group A

B.Th.1. Introduction to Biblical Hebrew

This paper will contain (i) questions on the principles of Hebrew grammar and syntax, and (ii) passages for translation from Hebrew into English, taken from a text prescribed by the Faculty Board.

The examination will take the form of a three-hour written paper.

B.Th.2. Elementary Hebrew

This paper will make use of the teaching for Tripos Paper A1A.This paper will contain (i) questions on Hebrew grammar, and (ii) passages for translation, linguistic comment, pointing, and retranslation from a portion or portions of the Old Testament prescribed by the Faculty Board.

The examination will take the form of a three-hour written paper.

B.Th.3. Introduction to New Testament Greek

This paper will contain (i) questions on the principles of New Testament Greek grammar and syntax, and (ii) passages for translation from Greek into English, taken from a text prescribed by the Faculty Board.

The examination will take the form of a three-hour written paper.

B.Th.4. New Testament Greek

This paper will make use of the teaching for Tripos Paper A1B.This paper will contain passages for translation, and for exegetical and grammatical comment, from one or more portions of the New Testament which the Faculty Board shall from time to time prescribe. Copies of a Greek lexicon will be available in the examination for those who wish to make use of them.

The examination will take the form of a three-hour written paper.

Group B

B.Th.11. Reading the Christian Bible

This paper introduces students to critical study of the Old and New Testaments. It places selected biblical writings in their historical and cultural contexts while focusing on their thematic and theological concerns.

The examination will take the form of a three-hour written paper.

B.Th.12. Christian doctrine

This paper will introduce some of the major themes and disciplines of Christian theology through a focus on Jesus Christ. The Faculty Board may from time to time prescribe texts for special study.

This paper will be examined by the mixed mode of assessment specified in Regulation 14(*a*).

B.Th.13. Belief and practice in the early church

This paper will be concerned with the development of Christian life, thought, pastoral practice and prayer in the first six centuries of the Church's existence. The course aims to introduce students to the importance of understanding the historical, political, philosophical, and social context in which Christianity developed in order to enhance their critical awareness of context in pastoral ministry and mission.

This paper will be examined by the mixed mode of assessment specified in Regulation 14(*a*).

B.Th.14. Reform and renewal in Christian history

This paper is concerned with the themes of Reform and renewal in the Christian tradition, taking the lenses of the Protestant and Catholic Reformations to deepen understanding of how these relate to the institutions of Church and State, society and culture, and the individual.

This paper will be examined by the mixed mode of assessment specified in Regulation 14(*a*).

B.Th.15. Special subject in Christian history

This paper will be concerned with the study of an aspect of the cultural formation and impact of Christian belief and practice, as specified by the Faculty Board.

This paper will be examined by the submission of two 3,000-word essays.

B.Th.16. Special subject in the study of religion

This paper will be concerned with the study of religion in one or more of the human and social sciences, as specified by the Faculty Board.

This paper will be examined by the mixed mode of assessment specified in Regulation 14(*a*).

[1] Papers marked with an asterisk are half-papers.

Group C

B.Th.21. Intermediate Hebrew

This paper will use the classes for Tripos Paper B1A. This paper will contain (i) passages for translation, linguistic and exegetical comment and retranslation from portions of text which the Faculty Board will from time to time prescribe, and (ii) essay questions on literary and theological aspects of the prescribed texts. Candidates may not offer in this paper any prescribed text which they have previously offered in Paper A1.

The examination will take the form of a three-hour written paper.

B.Th.22. Intermediate Greek

This paper will use the classes for Tripos paper B1B. This paper will contain passages for translation, textual, exegetical and theological comment from such portions of text as the Faculty Board will from time to time prescribe.

The examination will take the form of a three-hour written paper.

B.Th.23. Old Testament studies

This paper will provide for the study of a particular theme within the Old Testament prescribed by the Faculty Board. It will be concerned with the range of biblical texts, their theology, and with questions regarding the use of the texts in Christian faith and practice. A set text may be specified for more detailed study.

This paper will be examined by the mixed mode of assessment specified in Regulation 14(*a*).

B.Th.24. New Testament studies

This paper will provide for the close study of a particular theme within the New Testament from a selection prescribed by the Faculty Board. It will be concerned with the range of biblical texts, their theology, and with questions regarding the use of the texts in Christian faith and practice. A set text may be specified for more detailed study.

This paper will be examined by the mixed mode of assessment specified in Regulation 14(*a*).

**B.Th.25. Old Testament exegesis*

This paper will provide for the close study of one or more Old Testament texts or themes from a selection prescribed by the Faculty Board. It will be concerned with the background, content, theology, and interpretation of the relevant Old Testament material, and with questions regarding the use of the material in Christian faith and practice.

The examination will take the form of a two-hour written examination.

**B.Th.26. New Testament exegesis*

This paper will provide for the close study of one or more New Testament texts or themes from a selection prescribed by the Faculty Board. It will be concerned with the background, content, theology, and interpretation of the relevant New Testament material, and with questions regarding the use of the material in Christian faith and practice.

The examination will take the form of a two-hour written examination.

**B.Th.27. Biblical themes in Christian doctrine*

This paper will introduce students to the discipline of biblical theology, by exploring a number of pivotal theological themes as they are discernible in specific Scriptural texts, and as they relate to the doctrines and practices of the Church.

The examination will take the form of a two-hour written paper.

**B.Th.28. The study of Christian mission*

This paper will help students relate some of the central issues and debates in the study of Christian mission to their own context and future ministry. Particular emphasis will be given to questions of Christianity and culture and to learning from the experience of the world church.

This paper will be examined by the submission of one 3,000-word essay.

**B.Th.29. The Gospel and Western culture*

This paper will examine theologically the relationship between the gospel and Western culture, including the intellectual, social, and religious trends in both modernity and postmodernity that help to shape people's thinking in the 21st century, and exploring their impact on contemporary church life and practice.

This paper will be examined by the submission of one 3,000-word essay.

B.Th.30. Philosophy of religion

This paper will explore some classical themes in the philosophy of religion. These will include attributes of God, issues of the relationships between God and the world, and issues of God and 'the soul'.

This paper will be examined by the mixed mode of assessment specified in Regulation 14(*a*).

**B.Th.31. Church and sacraments*

This paper will explore critically the theological roots and pastoral implications of a variety of approaches to the subject, with particular reference to contemporary ecclesiological questions.

The examination will take the form of a two-hour written paper.

**B.Th.32. Patterns of Christian worship*

This paper will explore how God is encountered and believers are formed in worship, by considering the Eucharist, Christian initiation, and services of the word from historical, theological, and phenomenological perspectives.

The examination will take the form of a two-hour written paper.

**B.Th.33. Subjects specified by the Faculty Board*

This paper will be concerned with a special subject as specified by the Faculty Board from time to time. Candidates may choose one special subject from a maximum of four in any one year.

This paper will be examined by the submission of one 3,000-word essay.

**B.Th.34. Special study*

This paper will be concerned with a special study in an aspect of theology, as approved by the Faculty Board.

This paper will be examined by the submission of one 3,000-word essay.

Group D

B.Th.41. Further studies in Christian doctrine

This paper will provide for the close study of one specialist area in Christian theology, chosen from the subjects prescribed by the Faculty Board. Candidates may choose one specialist area from a maximum of four in any one year.

The examination will take the form of a three-hour written paper.

B.Th.42. Further church history

This paper will provide for the close study of one specialist area in Church history, chosen from the subjects prescribed by the Faculty Board. Candidates may choose one specialist area from a maximum of four in any one year.

This paper will be examined by the mixed-mode of assessment specified in Regulation 14(*a*).

B.Th.43. Judaism, Christianity and Islam in encounter

This paper will be concerned with an introduction to the study of Judaism and Islam, whereby students will be encouraged both to understand these faiths in their own terms and also to reflect on Christian relations with Jews and Muslims and the theological issues involved.

This paper will be examined by the mixed mode of assessment specified in Regulation 14(*a*).

B.Th.44. Christian ethics

This paper will be concerned with the theory and practice of Christian ethics and with developing in candidates mature, well-informed habits in moral thinking, appreciation and judgment appropriate to a Christian teaching and pastoral ministry, and Christian living.

This paper will be examined by the mixed-mode of assessment specified in Regulation 14(*a*).

**B.Th.45. Advanced subjects specified by the Faculty Board*

This paper will be concerned with a special subject as specified by the Faculty Board from time to time. Candidates may choose one special subject from a maximum of four in any one year.

This paper will be examined by the submission of one 3,000-word essay.

**B.Th.46. Further advanced subjects specified by the Faculty Board*

This paper will be concerned with a special subject as specified by the Faculty Board from time to time. Candidates may choose one special subject from a maximum of four in any one year.

This paper will be examined by the submission of one 3,000-word essay.

B.Th.47. Special study

This paper will be concerned with a special study in an aspect of theology as approved by the Faculty Board.

This paper will be examined by the submission of two 3,000-word essays.

Group E

B.Th.51. Pastoral portfolio A

This paper will test a candidate's development as a practical theologian who reflects on their own engagement with the church and the world.

This paper will be examined by the submission of one piece of course-work.

B.Th.52. Pastoral portfolio B

This paper will test a candidate's further development as a practical theologian who reflects on their own engagement with the church and the world.

This paper will be examined by the submission of two pieces of course-work.

Bachelor of Divinity

1. In order to qualify for the degree of Bachelor of Divinity a candidate shall be required to give proof of a significant contribution to the knowledge of one or more of the following subjects: Biblical exegesis, criticism, or history; the nature and grounds of Christian belief; dogmatic theology; the study of other religions in relation to the Christian religion; ecclesiastical history, antiquities, or literature; the philosophy of religion; or such other subject connected with Christian theology as may from time to time be approved by the Degree Committee for the Faculty of Divinity.

2. Any person may be a candidate for the degree of Bachelor of Divinity who is a graduate of the University and who Standing of candidates.

either (*a*) is of not less than five years' standing from admission to his or her first degree of the University,

or (*b*) is of not less than five years' standing from admission to his or her first degree of some other university and has been admitted (i) to some office in the University or to a Headship or a Fellowship of a College, and (ii) to the degree of Master of Arts under Statute B II 2 or to a degree of the University by incorporation.

3. A candidate for the degree shall apply in writing to the Secretary of the Board of Graduate Studies, and shall specify the work or works on which his or her claim to the degree is based, which may be either (*a*) one or more published works or (*b*) a dissertation specially composed for the purpose or (*c*) a combination of the two. A candidate shall send with the application a fee of £360 for the Chest, and two copies of each of the works specified under (*a*), (*b*), or (*c*), provided that the Board of Graduate Studies may, subject to the concurrence of the Degree Committee, allow a candidate to submit only one copy. All work submitted shall be accompanied by a declaration stating to what extent, if any, it is substantially the same as work that the candidate may have submitted, or is currently submitting, for a degree or diploma or other qualification of this or any other university or similar institution; and shall, apart from quotations, be written in English unless in a particular case the Degree Committee have allowed a candidate to submit material in some other language. Method of application.

4. Each application shall be forwarded by the Secretary of the Board of Graduate Studies to the Degree Committee, who shall give preliminary consideration to the application and shall determine whether the works submitted constitute *prima facie* a qualification for the degree; the Committee may appoint an Assessor to assist them in the matter. The Committee shall also satisfy themselves that the candidate possesses a competent knowledge of Christian theology. Preliminary consideration.

5. If the Committee decide that the work or works submitted do not constitute *prima facie* a qualification for the degree, a resolution of the Committee to that effect, with the names of those present and voting on either side, shall be communicated to the Secretary of the Board of Graduate Studies, who shall communicate the decision to the candidate. In such a case £288 out of the fee of £360 paid by the candidate under Regulation 3 shall be returned.

6. If the Committee decide that the work or works submitted do constitute *prima facie* a qualification for the degree, they shall appoint not less than two persons to act as Referees. Each Referee shall submit an independent written report on the works specified in the candidate's application; these reports shall be treated as confidential documents. Referees.

7. A candidate who submits a dissertation may, at the discretion of the Degree Committee, be called for *viva voce* examination.

8. If after considering the reports of the Referees the Degree Committee are satisfied that the candidate's work is of the requisite standard for the degree, a resolution of the Committee to that effect, with the names of those present and voting on either side, shall be communicated to the Board of Graduate Studies together with the reports of the Referees. The Chair of the Degree Committee shall publish the name of the candidate as approved for the degree of Bachelor of Divinity. Approval for degree.

9. If after considering the reports of the Referees the Degree Committee are of the opinion that the candidate's work is not of the requisite standard for the degree, a resolution of the Committee to that effect, with the names of those present and voting on either side, shall be communicated to the Board of Graduate Studies together with the reports of the Referees. The Secretary of the Board shall communicate this decision to the candidate.

10. No candidate for a degree shall be present at the deliberations either of the Committee or of the Board of Graduate Studies respecting his or her own case. Candidate not to be present.

11. If a candidate has based his or her claim to the degree either wholly or in a part on a dissertation not previously printed, the degree shall not be granted until the dissertation has been printed; provided Printing of dissertation.

that the Degree Committee shall be empowered, subject to the provisions of Regulation 12, to exempt a candidate from this requirement. A candidate who submits a printed dissertation shall not be at liberty to make any alteration or addition without the leave of the Chair of the Degree Committee.

Copy for Library.

12. Every candidate whose claim to the degree is based either wholly or in part on a dissertation shall ensure that a printed or typewritten copy of the dissertation is deposited in the University Library. The degree shall in no case be conferred until this requirement has been satisfied.[1]

Payments.

13. Each Referee shall receive a fee of £135. An Assessor appointed under Regulation 4 shall receive a fee of £42. If an Assessor is subsequently appointed a Referee the fee of £42 shall form part of the fee of £135 due to him or her as a Referee. The Board of Graduate Studies may approve the payment of reasonable expenses incurred by Referees in the execution of their duties.

14. No fee shall be payable on admission to the degree.

Doctor of Divinity

1. In order to qualify for the degree of Doctor of Divinity a candidate shall be required to give proof of distinction by some original contribution to the knowledge of one or more of the following subjects: Biblical exegesis, criticism, or history; the nature and grounds of Christian belief; dogmatic theology; the study of other religions in relation to the Christian religion; ecclesiastical history, antiquities, or literature; the philosophy of religion; or such other subject connected with Christian theology as may from time to time be approved by the Degree Committee for the Faculty of Divinity.

Standing of candidates.

2. Any person may be a candidate for the degree of Doctor of Divinity who is a graduate of the University and who

either (*a*) is a Bachelor of Divinity of not less than three years' standing,

or (*b*) is of not less than twelve years' standing from admission to his or her first degree of the University,

or (*c*) is of not less than twelve years' standing from admission to his or her first degree of some other university and has been admitted (i) to some office in the University or to a Headship or a Fellowship of a College, and (ii) to the degree of Master of Arts under Statute B II 2 or to a degree of the University by incorporation.

Method of application.

3. A candidate for the degree shall apply in writing to the Secretary of the Board of Graduate Studies, and shall specify the published works on which her or his claim to the degree is based, providing a summary in not more than five hundred words of the field of research covered by these works. A candidate shall send with the application a fee of £582 for the Chest, and two copies of each of the works specified, provided that the Board of Graduate Studies may, subject to the concurrence of the Degree Committee, allow a candidate to submit only one copy. All the works submitted shall, apart from quotations, be written in English unless in a particular case the Degree Committee have allowed a candidate to submit material in some other language.

4. Each application shall be forwarded by the Secretary of the Board of Graduate Studies to the Degree Committee, who shall give preliminary consideration to the application and shall determine whether the works submitted constitute *prima facie* a qualification for the degree; the Committee may appoint an Assessor to assist them in the matter.

5. In considering an application from a candidate under Regulation 2(*b*) or 2(*c*), the Committee shall satisfy themselves

(*a*) that the candidate possesses a competent knowledge of Christian theology;

(*b*) that the quality and quantity of the work submitted are not less than would have been required from a candidate under Regulation 2(*a*) in respect of the consecutive submissions for the B.D. and D.D. Degrees.

Referees.

6. If the Committee decide that the work or works submitted do not constitute *prima facie* a qualification for the degree, a resolution of the Committee to that effect, with the names of those present and voting on either side, shall be communicated to the Secretary of the Board of Graduate Studies, who shall communicate the decision to the candidate. In such a case £510 out of the fee of £582 paid by the candidate under Regulation 3 shall be returned.

[1] Evidence that this requirement has been satisfied should be sent to the Registrary, so as to arrive not later than the day preceding the day of graduation.

7. If the Committee decide that the work or works submitted do constitute *prima facie* a qualification for the degree, they shall appoint not less than two persons to act as Referees. Each Referee shall submit an independent written report on the works specified in the candidate's application; these reports shall be treated as confidential documents.

8. If after considering the reports of the Referees the Degree Committee are satisfied that the candidate's work is of the requisite standard for the degree, a resolution of the Committee to that effect, with the names of those present and voting on either side, shall be communicated to the Board of Graduate Studies together with the reports of the Referees. Approval for degree.

9. If the Board of Graduate Studies after receiving such a communication resolve that the degree should be conferred, the Secretary of the Board shall publish the name of the candidate as approved for the degree of Doctor of Divinity. Such a resolution shall not be valid unless passed with the concurrence of the votes, cast at a meeting, of five members of the Board.

10. If after considering the reports of the Referees the Degree Committee are of the opinion that the candidate's work is not of the requisite standard for the degree, a resolution of the Committee to that effect, with the names of those present and voting on either side, shall be communicated to the Board of Graduate Studies together with the reports of the Referees. The Secretary of the Board shall communicate this decision to the candidate.

11. No candidate for a degree shall be present at the deliberations either of the Committee or of the Board of Graduate Studies respecting his or her own case. Candidate not to be present.

12. Each Referee shall receive a fee of £175. An Assessor appointed under Regulation 4 shall receive a fee of £42. If an Assessor is subsequently appointed a Referee the fee of £42 shall form part of the fee of £175 due to him or her as a Referee. The Board of Graduate Studies may approve the payment of reasonable expenses incurred by Referees in the execution of their duties. Payments.

13. No fee shall be payable on admission to the degree.

DEGREES IN EDUCATION

Master of Education

1. The M.Ed. Degree (part-time course) shall be awarded for advanced study. A candidate for the M.Ed. Examination must be approved by the Degree Committee for the Faculty of Education and the Board of Graduate Studies, who shall assign to each candidate a date of commencement of candidature. Candidature.

2. Applications for admission as an M.Ed. student shall be sent to the Secretary of the Board of Graduate Studies.

3. The Board of Graduate Studies may approve as a candidate for the M.Ed. Examination any student who has satisfied the Board that by reason of previous study he or she is qualified to engage in graduate work in Education.

4. Applications for approval under Regulation 2 shall be sent to the Board of Graduate Studies so as to arrive not later than 30 June next preceding the date on which the applicant wishes her or his candidature to begin, provided that the Board shall have power to consider applications submitted after that date.

5. A candidate for the M.Ed. Degree (part-time course) shall be a registered Graduate Student who shall pursue in the University or similar institution approved by the Degree Committee concerned and by the Board of Graduate Studies a course of advanced study under the direction of a Supervisor appointed by the Degree Committee concerned and shall comply with any special conditions that the Degree Committee or the Board may lay down in a particular case. The course shall extend over two academical years; students are required to attend in all six terms of the year, beginning from the date announced by the Degree Committee for the start of lectures, classes, or other formal instruction. Conditions for pursuing course.

6. The Board of Graduate Studies, on the recommendation of the Degree Committee, may allow a candidate to intermit her or his course for not more than six terms, except in exceptional circumstances, which terms shall not count for any purpose of these regulations. No student's name shall appear on the list of successful candidates for the M.Ed. Examination unless the Degree Committee is satisfied that the student has diligently attended the course.

7. Every Supervisor shall send to the Degree Committee at least three times during the course a written report on the work of each student who is studying for the M.Ed. Examination under her or his direction. Supervisor's reports.

Notice of subjects.

8. The Faculty Board of Education shall announce not later than the end of the Easter Term each year the subjects to be covered in the course during the academical year next but one following; provided that the Board shall have the power of subsequently issuing amendments if they have due reason for doing so and if they are satisfied that no student's preparation for the examination is adversely affected.

Supplementary regulations.

9. The Faculty Board of Education shall have power to issue supplementary regulations determining the scope and manner of assessment of the examination, and shall be empowered to amend such supplementary regulations from time to time as they may think fit, due care being taken that sufficient notice is given of any change.

Examiners and Assessors.

10. The Degree Committee shall nominate for each academical year such number of Examiners and Assessors as they may deem sufficient, including a resident member of the Senate as Chair of Examiners.

M.Ed. Examination.

11. The M.Ed. Examination shall consist, at the choice of the candidate, of either Option A or Option B, as follows:

Option A

The examination shall consist of a thesis, of not more than 30,000 words in length, excluding footnotes, tables, appendices, and bibliography, on a subject approved by the Degree Committee.

The examination shall include an oral examination on the thesis and on the general field of knowledge within which it falls.

Option B

The examination shall consist of:

(i) a thesis of not more than 20,000 words in length excluding footnotes, tables, appendices, and bibliography, on a subject approved by the Degree Committee;

(ii) two essays each of at least 6,000 and not more than 6,500 words in length (or the equivalent thereof), on topics approved by the Degree Committee.

The examination shall include an oral examination on the thesis and the essays, and on the general field of knowledge within which they fall, save that the Examiners may, at their discretion, waive the requirement for an oral examination.

Fee.

12. While studying in the University for the M.Ed. Examination, a candidate shall pay the appropriate University Composition Fee for each term of such study.

13. A student who has satisfactorily completed the course and has satisfied the Degree Committee in the M.Ed. Examination shall be entitled to proceed to the degree of Master of Education.

Relation to courses of research.

14. A student who has taken the M.Ed. Examination, and who is subsequently admitted as a Graduate Student registered for the degree of Ph.D., Ed.D., M.Sc., or M.Litt., may be permitted to seek exemption from terms of research for that degree under the provisions of Regulation 1(*a*) of the regulations for those degrees.

15. Notwithstanding the provision of Regulation 4, the Degree Committee of Education and the Board of Graduate Studies shall have power to permit a candidate who has attained an appropriate standard of postgraduate study to follow a course of study leading to the award of the Master of Education extending over a period of one academical year.

Doctor of Education

1. In order to qualify for the degree of Doctor of Education a candidate shall be required satisfactorily to complete a course of training prescribed for that degree and provide evidence of a significant original contribution to study in the field of education.

Conditions of pursuing course.

2. Subject to clauses (*a*)–(*c*) below, a Graduate Student registered for the degree of Doctor of Education (Ed.D.) shall pursue in the University, and such other places as the Board of Graduate Studies and the Degree Committee for the Faculty of Education shall determine, a part-time course of training and research under supervision for not less than fifteen terms.

The number of terms shall begin with the term from which the student is registered as a candidate for the degree and shall be consecutive except in so far as the student may have been allowed to intermit her or his course under clause (*a*) below, or except in so far as the Board may have determined that he or she shall not be allowed to count any particular term towards the requirements for the Degree.

(*a*) The Board, after considering a recommendation by the Degree Committee for the Faculty of Education, may exempt from up to five terms of her or his course a student who is registered as a candidate for the Ed.D. Degree, provided that before admission as a Graduate Student he or she had been engaged

either (i) in full-time or part-time research

or (ii) in other work done after graduation deemed by the Degree Committee and the Board to have provided satisfactory training for the course of research in question.

(*b*) On account of illness or other sufficient cause, the Board, after considering a recommendation by the Degree Committee, may allow a student to intermit her or his course for one or more terms. Such terms shall not count for any purpose of these regulations except as provided in Regulation 7 of the general regulations for admission as a Graduate Student.

(*c*) On the recommendation of the Degree Committee, the Board may allow a student who has been approved for, and may have proceeded to, the M.Ed. Degree, or the M.Phil., or M.St., or M.Res. Degree in an appropriate subject to count not more than five terms towards her or his course.

Every application for a dispensation under clauses (*a*)–(*c*) shall be made in writing to the Secretary of the Board, and shall be accompanied by a written opinion from the applicant's Supervisor. Application for dispensation.

3. On the recommendation of the Board, the Council may grant to a Graduate Student in respect of work done in the University before matriculation, if the student's matriculation was delayed for sufficient cause, an allowance of terms not exceeding five in number, towards the minimum of fifteen terms required to be kept under Regulation 2.

4. The Board may grant to a Graduate Student, after considering an application supported by the student's Tutor, up to five terms of research towards satisfying the requirements of Regulation 2, on account of illness or other grave cause. For every term so allowed the student shall pay the appropriate fee as prescribed in Regulation 11 of the general regulations for admission as a Graduate Student.

5. In order to be registered as a candidate for the degree, a Graduate Student must have completed, to the satisfaction of the Board and the Degree Committee, such course-work, undertaken either in the University or at such other place as may have been approved for this purpose, as the Board and Degree Committee may have specified. Requirements.

6. The course of training and research shall be conducted under such supervisory arrangements as the Board and the Degree Committee shall specify. The Board and the Degree Committee shall satisfy themselves that, during the periods when a student is working outside the University, appropriate arrangements for supervision and for reporting on the student's progress are in place. Supervision.

7. The examination for the degree of Ed.D. shall consist of: Ed.D. examination.

(*a*) the submission of a dissertation embodying the results of the candidate's approved course of research, which shall be submitted in accordance with the provisions of Regulations 8–10,

(*b*) an examination, conducted orally or in writing, on the subject of the dissertation and on the general field of knowledge within which it falls, provided that in exceptional circumstances, and on the recommendation of the Degree Committee, the Board may dispense with such an examination.

8. A candidate may submit her or his dissertation not earlier than the first day of the term during which he or she expects to complete the requirements of Regulation 2, provided that, and not later than the last day of the seventh year after he or she was registered, with the permission of the Board, a dissertation may be submitted later than that day. An allowance of terms made by the Council under Regulation 3 shall count in calculating the standing of a student for the purpose of this regulation. Dissertation.

9. In submitting their dissertations, candidates shall state, generally in a preface and specifically in notes or in a bibliography, the sources from which their information is derived, the extent to which they have availed themselves of the work of others, and the portions of the dissertation which are claimed as original. They shall also be required to declare that the dissertation submitted is not substantially the same as any that they may have submitted for a degree or diploma or similar qualification. The work, apart from quotations, shall be written in English. Candidates shall also submit a statement by those responsible for their supervision certifying the conditions under which each candidate's work was undertaken.

10. Two copies of each candidate's dissertation, accompanied by the statement referred to in Regulation 9 and three copies of a summary of about 300 words in length, shall be sent to the Secretary of the Board, who shall forward the copies and two copies of the summary to the Secretary of the Degree Committee. In special circumstances the Board, after consulting the Degree Committee, may allow a candidate to submit one copy only of the dissertation. The dissertation shall be referred to two Examiners, appointed by the Degree Committee. Neither of the Examiners shall have been the candidate's Supervisor. Each Examiner shall make an independent report on the dissertation to the Degree Committee. The two Examiners shall jointly conduct the oral examination specified for the dissertation under Regulation 7(*b*), and shall sign a joint certificate of the result. If the Examiners do not agree in their recommendations or if for any other reason the Degree Committee or the Board need a further opinion or opinions on the merit of the work submitted, the Degree Committee may appoint an additional Examiner or additional Examiners, provided that not more than one additional Examiner shall be appointed without leave of the Board. Each additional Examiner so appointed shall make an independent report on the dissertation to the Degree Committee.

11. If a candidate fails to satisfy the Examiners in the oral examination specified for the dissertation under Regulation 7(*b*), the Degree Committee may permit the candidate to be re-examined by the same Examiners. Permission so given shall be communicated to the Secretary of the Board and shall not be given on more than one occasion. Each Examiner who takes part in an examination under this regulation shall be paid a fee of £42 in addition to any fees to which he or she may be entitled under Regulation 12, and may also claim travelling expenses in accordance with the provisions of that regulation.

Payments to Examiners.

12. Each Examiner shall receive a fee from the Chest. Such a fee shall be £135 if the Examiner takes part in the oral examination specified for the dissertation under Regulation 7(*b*), or £100 if the Examiner does not so take part, either because the Board, on the recommendation of the Degree Committee, have dispensed with the oral examination or for any other reason. Examiners may claim travelling expenses, on terms and conditions specified by the Board if their place of residence is more than ten miles from Great St Mary's Church or if an oral examination or a consultation between the Examiners is for good reason held outside Cambridge. The Board may also approve payment of other reasonable expenses incurred by an Examiner in connection with the execution of her or his duties. A subsistence allowance may be claimed by Examiners at rates determined from time to time by the Finance Committee of the Council, provided that payment may be made only in respect of a day or a night on which the Examiner's absence from her or his normal place of residence in connection with the execution of her or his duties is necessary. The travelling expenses of a candidate who is required to travel to an oral examination outside Cambridge may be paid in whole or in part, at rates determined by the Board; such a candidate may also claim a subsistence allowance at rates determined from time to time by the Finance Committee, under the same conditions as apply to the Examiners.

Approval for Ed.D. Degree.

13. If, after considering the reports of the Examiners, the Degree Committee are satisfied that the candidate's work is of the requisite standard for the degree, a recommendation of the Committee to that effect, with the names of those present and voting on either side, shall be communicated to the Board, together with the reports of the Examiners. If the Board, after receiving such communication, at a meeting at which not less than five members are present, resolve that the candidate be approved for the Ed.D. Degree, the Secretary of the Board shall publish a notice of the candidate's approval for the award of the Degree.

Revised dissertation.

14. If, after considering the reports of the Examiners, the Degree Committee consider that the candidate's dissertation is not of the requisite standard for the degree, the Board may, at a meeting at which no less than five members are present, permit the candidate to submit a revised dissertation, but they shall not do so unless the Degree Committee have expressly recommended that such permission be given. The communication conveying such a recommendation by a Degree Committee shall contain the names of those present and voting on either side, and shall be accompanied by the reports of the Examiners. A candidate shall not be allowed to submit a revised dissertation on more than one occasion.

Approval for M.Litt. Degree in lieu.

15. If, after considering the reports of the Examiners, the Degree Committee consider that the candidate's work is not of the standard requisite for the Ed.D. Degree, but that it is of the standard requisite for the M.Litt. Degree, their recommendation to that effect, with the names of those present and voting on either side, shall be communicated to the Board, together with the reports of the Examiners. If after receiving such communication the Board decide, at a meeting at which not less than five members are present, that the candidate could properly be approved for the award of the lower degree, the Secretary of the Board shall ask the candidate whether he or she is willing to be approved for the award of the M.Litt. Degree. Subject to the candidate's agreement being received by the Secretary not later than the last day of the term following the term or vacation in which the decision on her or his candidature was made, the Board shall approve the candidate for the award of that degree and the Secretary shall publish a notice of such approval. The Board may, in exceptional circumstances, which they shall themselves determine, accept a candidate's agreement at a later date.

16. The Board shall be the deciding authority on all recommendations communicated to them by Degree Committees that candidates be approved for the award of the Ed.D. or M.Litt. Degree or that they be allowed to submit revised dissertations. The Board shall not approve a candidate for the award of a degree unless the Degree Committee have recommended the award of that degree; before refusing an award so recommended they shall give a representative appointed by the Degree Committee an opportunity of explaining the Committee's reasons for their recommendation. Deciding authority.

17. If after considering the reports of the Examiners the Degree Committee resolve that a candidate's work is not of the requisite standard for any degree, and if they do not recommend that the candidate be allowed to submit a revised dissertation, their resolution to that effect with the names of those present and voting on either side, shall be communicated to the Board, together with the reports of the Examiners. The Secretary of the Board shall communicate this decision to the candidate. Unsuccessful candidate to be informed.

18. Before being admitted to a degree, a student shall deposit with the Secretary of the Board one copy of her or his dissertation and two copies of the summary, in a form approved by the Board. The Secretary shall deposit the copy of the dissertation together with one copy of the summary in the University Library, where they shall be available for consultation and for the making of copies for inter-library loan purposes, unless the Board determine that they shall, for a period specified by the Board, be available only to the author or to those who have the author's written permission to consult the material. The summary shall be available for copying and publication at the discretion of the Board. Copy of dissertation for Library.

DEGREES IN ENGINEERING

MASTER OF ENGINEERING

On completing the requisite number of terms,[1] a student who has obtained honours in Part IIB of the Chemical Engineering Tripos or in Part IIB of the Engineering Tripos or in Part II of the Manufacturing Engineering Tripos or in Part III of the Computer Science Tripos shall be entitled to proceed to the M.Eng. Degree.

DOCTOR OF ENGINEERING

1. In order to qualify for the degree of Doctor of Engineering a candidate shall be required satisfactorily to complete a course of training prescribed for that degree and provide evidence of a significant original contribution to study in the field of engineering.

2. Subject to clauses (*a*)–(*c*) below, a Graduate Student registered for the degree of Doctor of Engineering (Eng.D.) shall pursue in the University, and such other places as the Board of Graduate Studies and the Degree Committee concerned shall determine, a course of training and research under supervision for not less than twelve terms. Conditions for pursuing course.

The number of terms shall begin with the term from which the student is registered as a candidate for the degree and shall be consecutive except in so far as the student may have been allowed to intermit his or her course under clause (*b*) below, or except in so far as the Board may have determined that he or she shall not be allowed to count any particular term towards the requirements for the degree.

(*a*) The Board, after considering a recommendation by the Degree Committee concerned, may allow a Graduate Student to spend all but three terms of his or her course as a candidate for a degree, or any lesser number of terms, working under supervision outside the University under conditions approved by the Degree Committee and the Board.

(*b*) On account of illness or other sufficient cause, the Board, after considering a recommendation by the Degree Committee concerned, may allow a Graduate Student to intermit his or her course of research for one or more terms. Such terms shall not count for any purpose of these regulations except as provided in Regulation 7 of the general regulations for admission as a Graduate Student.

[1] See the regulations for Residence and Precincts of the University (p. 189).

(*c*) A student who is qualified to receive, but who has not received, a Certificate of Postgraduate Study in a subject intended as preparation for the Eng.D. Degree may be allowed to count not more than three terms of the period during which he or she was a candidate for the Certificate concerned towards the Degree.

Application for dispensation. Every application for a dispensation under clauses (*a*)–(*c*) shall be made in writing to the Secretary of the Board, and shall be accompanied by a written opinion from the applicant's Supervisor.

3. On the recommendation of the Board, the Council may grant to a Graduate Student in respect of work done in the University before matriculation, if the student's matriculation was delayed for sufficient cause, an allowance of terms not exceeding three in number, towards the minimum of three terms required to be kept under Regulation 8 for Residence and Precincts of the University for full-time study leading to the Eng.D. Degree.

4. The Board may grant to a Graduate Student, after considering an application supported by the student's Tutor, one or two terms of research towards satisfying the requirements of Regulation 2, on account of illness or other grave cause. For every term so allowed the student shall pay the appropriate fee as prescribed in Regulation 11 of the general regulations for admission as a Graduate Student.

Requirements. **5.** In order to be registered as a candidate for the Degree, a Graduate Student must have completed, to the satisfaction of the Board and the Degree Committee concerned, such course-work, undertaken either in the University or at such other place as may have been approved for this purpose, as the Board and Degree Committee may have specified.

Supervision. **6.** The course of training and research shall be conducted under such supervisory arrangements as the Board and the Degree Committee concerned shall specify. The Board and the Degree Committee shall satisfy themselves that, during the periods when a student is working outside the University, appropriate arrangements for supervision and for reporting on the student's progress are in place.

Eng.D. examination. **7.** The examination for the degree of Eng.D. shall consist of:

(*a*) such course-work as the Board and the Degree Committee concerned shall specify;

(*b*) the submission of a dissertation embodying the results of the candidate's approved course of research, which shall be submitted in accordance with the provisions of Regulations 8–9; in place of a dissertation, a candidate may, by special permission of the Board and the Degree Committee concerned, submit a portfolio of work of equivalent length;

(*c*) an examination, conducted orally, on the subject of the dissertation, and the general field of knowledge within which it falls, provided that in exceptional circumstances, and on the recommendation of the Degree Committee concerned, the Board may dispense with such an examination.

Dissertation. **8.** A candidate may submit his or her dissertation not earlier than the first day of the term during which he or she expects to complete the requirements of Regulation 2 and not later than the last day of the vacation following the twelfth term after that in which the student was registered as a candidate for the degree, provided that, with the permission of the Board, a dissertation may be submitted later than that day. An allowance of terms made by the Council under Regulation 3 shall count in calculating the standing of a student for the purpose of this regulation.

9. In submitting their dissertations, candidates shall state, generally in a preface and specifically in notes or in a bibliography, the sources from which their information is derived, the extent to which they have availed themselves of the work of others, and the portions of the dissertation which are claimed as original. They shall also be required to declare that the dissertation submitted is not substantially the same as any that they may have submitted for a degree or diploma or similar qualification. The work, apart from quotations, shall be written in English. Each Degree Committee shall have power to specify a maximum length for dissertations submitted by students working under its supervision. Candidates will also submit a statement by those responsible for their supervision certifying the conditions under which each candidate's work was undertaken.

10. Two copies of each candidate's dissertation, accompanied by the statement referred to in Regulation 9 and three copies of a summary of about 300 words in length, shall be sent to the Secretary of the Board, who shall forward the copies and two copies of the summary to the Secretary of the Degree Committee concerned. In special circumstances the Board, after consulting the Degree Committee, may allow a candidate to submit one copy only of the dissertation. The dissertation shall be referred to two Examiners, appointed by the Degree Committee. Neither of the Examiners shall have been the candidate's Supervisor. Each Examiner shall make an independent report on it to the Degree Committee. The two Examiners shall jointly conduct the oral examination specified in Regulation 7(*c*), and shall sign a joint certificate of the result. If the Examiners do not agree in their recommendations or if for any other reason the Degree Committee or the Board need a further opinion or opinions on the merit of the work submitted, the Degree Committee may appoint an additional Examiner or additional Examiners, provided that not more than one additional Examiner shall be appointed without leave of the Board. Each additional Examiner so appointed shall make an independent report on the dissertation to the Degree Committee.

11. If a candidate fails to satisfy the Examiners in the oral examination specified in Regulation 7(*c*), the Degree Committee may permit the candidate to be re-examined by the same Examiners. Permission so given shall be communicated to the Secretary of the Board and shall not be given on more than one occasion. Each Examiner who takes part in an examination under this regulation shall be paid a fee of £42 in addition to any fees to which he or she may be entitled under Regulation 12, and may also claim travelling expenses in accordance with the provisions of that regulation.

Payments to Examiners.

12. Each Examiner shall receive a fee from the Chest. Such a fee shall be £135 if the Examiner takes part in the oral examination specified in Regulation 7(*c*), or £100 if the Examiner does not so take part, either because the Board, on the recommendation of the Degree Committee, have dispensed with the oral examination or for any other reason. Examiners may claim travelling expenses, on terms and conditions specified by the Board if their place of residence is more than ten miles from Great St Mary's Church or if an oral examination or a consultation between the Examiners is for good reason held outside Cambridge. The Board may also approve payment of other reasonable expenses incurred by an Examiner in connection with the execution of his or her duties. A subsistence allowance may be claimed by Examiners at rates determined from time to time by the Finance Committee of the Council, provided that payment may be made only in respect of a day or a night on which the Examiner's absence from his or her normal place of residence in connection with the execution of his or her duties is necessary. The travelling expenses of a candidate who is required to travel to an oral examination outside Cambridge may be paid in whole or in part, at rates determined by the Board; such a candidate may also claim a subsistence allowance at rates determined from time to time by the Finance Committee, under the same conditions as apply to the Examiners.

Approval for Eng.D. Degree.

13. If, after considering the reports of the Examiners on the examinations specified in Regulation 7, the Degree Committee are satisfied that the student's work is of the requisite standard for the degree, a recommendation of the Committee to that effect, with the names of those present and voting on either side, shall be communicated to the Board, together with the reports of the Examiners. If the Board, after receiving such communication, at a meeting at which not less than five members are present, resolve that the candidate be approved for the Eng.D. Degree, the Secretary of the Board shall publish a notice of the candidate's approval for the award of the Degree.

Revised dissertation.

14. If, after considering the reports of the Examiners, the Degree Committee consider that a student's dissertation is not of the requisite standard for the degree, the Board may, at a meeting at which no less than five members are present, permit the student to submit a revised dissertation, but they shall not do so unless the Degree Committee have expressly recommended that such permission be given. The communication conveying such a recommendation by a Degree Committee shall contain the names of those present and voting on either side, and shall be accompanied by the reports of the Examiners. A student shall not be allowed to submit a revised dissertation on more than one occasion.

Approval for M.Sc. Degree in lieu.

15. If, after considering the reports of the Examiners, the Degree Committee consider that a student's work is not of the standard requisite for the Eng.D. Degree, but that it is of the standard requisite for the M.Sc. Degree, their recommendation to that effect, with the names of those present and voting on either side, shall be communicated to the Board, together with the reports of the Examiners. If after receiving such communication the Board decide, at a meeting at which not less than five members are present, that the candidate could properly be approved for the award of the lower degree, the Secretary of the Board shall ask the candidate whether he or she is willing to be approved for the award of the M.Sc. Degree. Subject to the candidate's agreement being received by the Secretary not later than the last day of the term following the term or vacation in which the decision on his or her candidature was made, the Board shall approve the candidate for the award of that degree and the Secretary shall publish a notice of such approval. The Board may, in exceptional circumstances, which they shall themselves determine, accept a candidate's agreement at a later date.

Deciding authority.

16. The Board shall be the deciding authority on all recommendations communicated to them by Degree Committees that candidates be approved for the award of the Eng.D. or M.Sc. Degree or that they be allowed to submit revised dissertations. The Board shall not approve a candidate for the award of a degree unless the Degree Committee have recommended the award of that degree; before refusing an award so recommended they shall give a representative appointed by the Degree Committee an opportunity of explaining the Committee's reasons for their recommendation.

Unsuccessful candidate to be informed.

17. If after considering the reports of the Examiners the Degree Committee resolve that a candidate's work is not of the requisite standard for any degree, and if they do not recommend that the candidate be allowed to submit a revised dissertation, their resolution to that effect, with the names of those present and voting on either side, shall be communicated to the Board, together with the reports of the Examiners. The Secretary of the Board shall communicate this decision to the candidate.

Copy of dissertation for Library.

18. Before being admitted to a degree, a student shall deposit with the Secretary of the Board one copy of his or her dissertation and two copies of the summary, in a form approved by the Board. The Secretary shall deposit the copy of the dissertation together with one copy of the summary in the University Library, where they shall be available for consultation and for the making of copies for inter-library loan purposes, unless the Board determine that they shall, for a period specified by the Board, be available only to the author or to those who have the author's written permission to consult the material. The summary shall be available for copying and publication at the discretion of the Board.

MASTER OF FINANCE

Candidature.

1. A candidate for the Master of Finance Examination must be approved by the Degree Committee for the Faculty of Business and Management.

2. The Degree Committee may approve as a candidate for the Master of Finance Examination any student who has satisfied the Committee that by reason of previous study he or she is qualified to engage in postgraduate work in Finance.

3. Applications for approval under Regulation 2 shall be sent to the Secretary of the Degree Committee so as to arrive not later than 31 March next preceding the date on which the applicant wishes his or her candidature to begin, provided that the Committee shall have power to consider applications submitted after that date.

4. A candidate for the Master of Finance Examination shall pursue in the University a course of study extending over three terms.

5. The Degree Committee for the Faculty of Business and Management shall publish, not later than the end of the Easter Term each year, a list of subjects in Finance for the academical year next following. The list shall be divided into two groups, Group 1 (core subjects) and Group 2 (specialist subjects).

6. No student shall be a candidate for the M.Fin. Examination or for any part thereof on more than one occasion.

Examination.

7. The Master of Finance Examination shall consist of three sections, as follows:

(*a*) *Written papers*

Three written papers as prescribed by the Faculty Board. Each candidate will be required to take no fewer than two written papers on subjects from Group 1.

(*b*) *Course-work*

The Faculty Board shall give notice of the topics and format for submission of course-work by the end of the term immediately preceding the term in which the work is to be completed.

(*c*) *Project work*

The Faculty Board shall give notice on project work and format for submission by the end of the Lent Term provided that the Board shall have the power of subsequently issuing amendments if they have due reason for doing so and they are satisfied that no student's preparation for the examination is adversely affected.

The Examiners shall have power to examine a candidate *viva voce* on any or all of the three sections of the examination (*a*)–(*c*).

Supplementary regulations.

8. The Faculty Board shall have power to issue supplementary regulations determining the scope and manner of assessment of the examination, and shall be empowered to amend such supplementary regulations from time to time as they may think fit, due care being taken that sufficient notice is given of any change.

Examiners and Assessors.

9. The Faculty Board shall nominate such number of Examiners and Assessors as they may deem sufficient, including a resident member of the Senate as Chair of Examiners.

10. The names of candidates who satisfy the Examiners shall be arranged in alphabetical order in a single class. The Chair of Examiners shall communicate the marks of all candidates to the Registrary. Class-list.

11. While following the course of study leading to the Master of Finance Examination a student shall pay the appropriate University Composition Fee. Fee.

12. A student who has completed the course of study and has satisfied the Examiners in the Master of Finance Examination shall be entitled to proceed to the Master of Finance Degree.

13. A student who has taken the Master of Finance Examination shall not be entitled to count any part of the period during which he or she has been a candidate for that examination towards a course of research for the degree of Ph.D., M.Sc., or M.Litt. Relation to courses of research.

DEGREES IN LAW

Master of Corporate Law

1. A candidate for the Master of Corporate Law (M.C.L.) Examination: Candidature.

(*a*) must be approved by the Faculty Board of Law, who shall assign to each candidate a date of commencement of candidature; and

(*b*) shall pursue in the University a course of study prescribed by the Faculty Board of Law, which shall extend over three terms.

2. The Faculty Board may approve as a candidate for the M.C.L. Examination any student who has satisfied the Faculty Board that by reason of previous study or practice of law he or she is qualified to engage in postgraduate study of law at an advanced level.

In giving approval the Faculty Board may require a student:

(*a*) to obtain such class or grade as they may think fit in any examination taken or to be taken by the student;

(*b*) to be a candidate for the M.C.L. Examination in a particular year specified by the Faculty Board.

3. A student whose candidature has been approved under Regulation 2 may be a candidate for the M.C.L. Examination provided that he or she has kept at least two terms at the time of the examination.

4. No student shall be a candidate for the M.C.L. Examination on more than one occasion, or for the M.C.L. Examination and another University examination in the same term.

5. The course of study leading to the M.C.L. Examination shall provide students with an advanced understanding of the law and regulation which governs the operation of business corporations in the UK. No student's name shall appear on the list of successful candidates for the M.C.L. Examination unless the Chair of the Faculty Board of Law is satisfied that the student has diligently attended the course. Course of study.

6. The M.C.L. Examination shall consist of two sections as follows: M.C.L. Examination.

(*a*) *Written papers*

Not more than fifteen subjects, prescribed by the Faculty Board of Law. Each paper shall be designated as either a full paper or a half-paper. Before the end of the Easter Term each year the Faculty Board shall announce the subjects prescribed for the examination to be held in the academical year next following, and shall give notice of the form of the examination for each subject, which shall be:

(i) for each full paper, a written paper of three hours' duration,

(ii) for each half-paper, a written paper of two hours' duration.

(*b*) *Course-work*

Such course-work as may be prescribed by the Faculty Board from time to time.

7. The Faculty Board shall have power to restrict candidates' choice of subjects, and their choice of questions within a written paper; any such restriction shall be announced not later than the second Friday of the Full Michaelmas Term next preceding the examination. Restriction.

8. Courses prescribed by the Faculty Board under Regulation 6(*a*) shall be published in the *Reporter* by the first Monday in the August next preceding the academical year in which those courses are to be conducted. Any such course prescribed by the Faculty Board may be withdrawn by the Board upon notice given in the *Reporter* within the first three weeks of Full Michaelmas Term in the academical year in which the course was to have been conducted. Each candidate who has applied to take part in a course so withdrawn shall be informed of its withdrawal by the Secretary of the Faculty Board.

9. Each candidate shall offer:

(i) one full paper prescribed for examination under Regulation 6(*a*)(i); and
(ii) four half-papers prescribed for examination under Regulation 6(*a*)(ii), and
(iii) course-work prescribed under Regulation 6(*b*).

Class-lists. **10.** The names of the candidates who satisfy the Examiners for the M.C.L. Examination shall be arranged in three classes, of which the second shall be divided into two divisions. The names in the first and third classes and in each division of the second class shall be arranged in alphabetical order. A mark of distinction shall be affixed to the names of those students placed in the first class whose work is of special merit.

Examiners. **11.** Examiners for the M.C.L. Examination shall be nominated by the Faculty Board of Law. The Faculty Board shall nominate such number of Examiners as they shall deem sufficient. The provisions of the regulations for the Law Tripos relating to the appointment and duties of Assessors shall apply *mutatis mutandis* to the M.C.L. Examination.

12. On completing the requisite number of terms, a student who has satisfied the Examiners for the M.C.L. Examination and has met the requirements of Regulation 5 shall be entitled to proceed to the M.C.L. Degree.

Fee. **13.** A student who is a candidate for the M.C.L. Examination shall pay the appropriate University Composition Fee.

Master of Law

LL.M. Examination

Amended by Notice (Reporter, *2013–14, p. 464*)

Scheme of examination. **1.** The LL.M. Examination shall comprise not more than thirty-five subjects, prescribed by the Faculty Board of Law, which may include a seminar paper, to be assessed by thesis only, and which shall include not less than four subjects that fall within each of the following fields:

Commercial law
European law
Intellectual property
International law.

2. (*a*) Before the end of the Easter Term each year the Faculty Board shall announce the subjects prescribed for the examination to be held in the academical year next following, and shall give notice of the form of the examination for each subject, which shall be:

either (i) a written paper of three hours' duration,
or (ii) a written paper of two hours' duration together with the submission of an essay of not more than 7,000 words, including footnotes and appendices but excluding bibliography, on a topic approved by the Faculty Board which falls within the field of the subject;

provided that in any subject specified by the Faculty Board candidates shall have a free choice between the two forms of examination (i) and (ii).

(*b*) At the same time, the Faculty Board shall prescribe and give notice of those subjects, if any, which will be assessed by examination only.

(*c*) At the same time, if a seminar paper is one of the subjects prescribed under Regulation 1 for the academical year next following, the Faculty Board shall prescribe and give notice of those courses (not exceeding six in number) in which seminars are to be held that year.

3. (*a*) The Faculty Board shall have power to restrict candidates' choice of subjects, and their choice of questions within a written paper; any such restriction shall be announced not later than the second Friday of the Full Michaelmas Term next preceding the examination.

(*b*) Courses prescribed by the Faculty Board under Regulation 2(*c*) shall be published in the *Reporter* before the end of the Long Vacation period of residence next preceding the academical year in which those courses are to be conducted. Any such course prescribed by the Faculty Board may be withdrawn by the Board upon notice given in the *Reporter* within the first three weeks of Full Michaelmas Term in the academical year in which the course was to have been conducted. Each candidate who has applied to take part in a course so withdrawn shall be informed of its withdrawal by the Secretary of the Faculty Board.

4. (*a*) Each candidate shall offer:

(i) four subjects prescribed for examination under Regulation 2(*a*), or

(ii) three subjects prescribed for examination under Regulation 2(*a*) and a thesis in lieu of another subject which is prescribed under Regulation 2(*a*), but not prescribed under Regulation 2(*b*), provided that the title of the thesis has been approved in accordance with the provisions of Regulation 9; or

(iii) in a year where the seminar paper is offered, three subjects prescribed for examination under Regulation 2(*a*) and the seminar paper, provided the title of the thesis by which the seminar paper is to be assessed has been approved in accordance with the provisions of Regulation 9.

(*b*) A thesis offered under Regulation 4(*a*)(ii) or (*a*)(iii) shall be submitted in accordance with the provisions of Regulations 9 and 10.

5. A candidate for the LL.M. Examination Requirements.

(*a*) must be approved by the Degree Committee for the Faculty of Law, who shall assign to each candidate a date of commencement of candidature;

and

(*b*) shall pursue in the University a course of study prescribed by the Degree Committee, which shall extend over three terms;

provided that a student shall be entitled to be a candidate for the LL.M. Examination without satisfying requirements (*a*) and (*b*) of this regulation if he or she has proceeded to the B.A. Degree and

either (i) obtained honours, or attained the honours standard, in Part I of the Law Tripos before 1980 or in Part IB or Part II before 1989,

or (ii) was before 1 October 1987 called to the Bar or admitted as a solicitor in England and Wales or in Ireland, or admitted as an advocate or a law agent in Scotland.

6. The Degree Committee may approve as a candidate for the LL.M. Examination any student who has satisfied the Committee that by reason of previous study of law he or she is qualified to engage in postgraduate study of law at an advanced level.

In giving approval the Committee may require a student

(*a*) to obtain such class or grade as they may think fit in any examination taken or to be taken by the student;

(*b*) to be a candidate for the LL.M. Examination in a particular year specified by the Committee

7. A student whose candidature has been approved under Regulation 6 may be a candidate for the LL.M. Examination provided that he or she has kept two terms at least at the time of the examination.

8. No student shall be a candidate for the LL.M. Examination on more than one occasion, or for the LL.M. Examination and another University examination in the same term. Restrictions.

9. (*a*) A candidate who intends to offer an essay under Regulation 2(*a*)(ii) or a thesis under Regulation 4(*a*)(ii) or (iii) shall submit the title of the proposed essay or thesis, together with a statement of the subjects he or she intends to offer in the LL.M. Examination, to the Secretary of the Faculty Board no later than the third Friday of the Full Michaelmas Term next preceding the examination. Essay or thesis

(*b*) A candidate may only offer such an essay or thesis if the Faculty Board has approved its title. The Faculty Board shall approve such a title, or reject the candidate's application to offer such an essay or thesis, as soon as practicable following the third Friday of the Full Michaelmas Term next preceding the examination, and in any event no later than the end of that Full Term. The Faculty Board shall promptly communicate to a candidate any decision made under this paragraph.

(*c*) The Faculty Board shall only approve the proposed title for a thesis under Regulation 4(*a*)(ii) if it is, in the opinion of the Board, within the scope of a subject prescribed for examination under Regulation 2(*a*) for the academical year in question.

(*d*) The Faculty Board shall only approve the proposed title for a thesis under Regulation 4(*a*)(iii) if it is, in the opinion of the Board, within the scope of a seminar course prescribed under Regulation 2(*c*) for the academical year in question.

(*e*) Without prejudice to any other power of the Faculty Board, it may reject a candidate's application to offer a thesis under Regulation 4(*a*)(ii) or (*a*)(iii) having regard respectively to the number of candidates who have applied to offer a thesis in lieu of a particular paper, or to the number of candidates on a particular seminar course.

(*f*) The Faculty Board shall not, save in exceptional circumstances, approve a title for a thesis under Regulation 4(*a*)(ii) or (*a*)(iii) if the proposed title falls within the scope of any of the subjects which the candidate in question is offering for the LL.M. Examination.

(*g*) When the Faculty Board has approved the title of an essay or thesis, no change shall be made to it, or to the candidate's scheme of subjects offered, without the further approval of the Board.

(*h*) A candidate for the LL.M. Examination shall submit any essay or thesis he or she is offering to the Secretary of the Faculty Board no later than 1 May next preceding that examination. A candidate who submits an essay or thesis to the Secretary of the Faculty Board after this date may be penalized by the Examiners of the LL.M. Examination.

(*i*) Any essay or thesis submitted shall be computer- or type-written.

10. A thesis offered under Regulation 4(*a*)(ii) or (*a*)(iii)

(*a*) shall be prefaced by a declaration signed by the candidate that it represents his or her own work unaided except as may be specified in the declaration, and that the work has been done during the current academical year, and

(*b*) shall contain a statement of, or notes on, the sources from which the thesis is derived, including any written work which the candidate has previously submitted or is concurrently submitting for any other degree, diploma, or similar qualification at any university or similar institution.

A thesis shall not without leave of the Faculty Board exceed 18,000 words including footnotes and appendices, but excluding bibliography. Such leave may be sought no later than fourteen days before the date specified in Regulation 9(*h*). The Faculty Board shall have power to designate the subject of a thesis as a subject in one of the fields specified in Regulation 1.

11. A candidate who offers an essay under Regulation 2(*a*)(ii) or a thesis under Regulation 4(*a*)(ii) or (*a*)(iii) may be called for *viva voce* examination in connection with such essay or thesis.

Class-list. **12.** The names of the candidates who satisfy the Examiners for the LL.M. Examination shall be arranged in three classes, of which the second shall be divided into two divisions. The names in the first and third classes and in each division of the second class shall be arranged in alphabetical order. A mark of distinction shall be affixed to the names of those students placed in the first class whose work is of special merit. The class-list shall indicate those candidates who have satisfied the Examiners in not less than three subjects, or two subjects and a thesis, in one of the fields specified in Regulation 1 In any case where a candidate offers a combination of papers (including any thesis designated as falling within a particular field under Regulation 10 above) whereby, under the foregoing provision, the class-list could indicate that the candidate has satisfied the Examiners in one of two or more of the fields specified in Regulation 1, that candidate may give notice that he or she wishes the Examiners to indicate that he or she has satisfied them in a stated field only. Any such notice shall be given by letter to the Secretary of the Faculty Board no later than 1 May of the Easter Term in which the candidate concerned takes the LL.M. Examination. If a candidate gives notice pursuant to the preceding provisions, and satisfies the Examiners in a sufficient number of papers (including any thesis) falling within the field indicated by the candidate, the class-list shall indicate that he or she has so satisfied the Examiners. If a candidate who is eligible to do so does not give notice in accordance with the preceding provisions, the class-list shall (*a*) if the candidate is classed and satisfies the Examiners in one field under Regulation 1, indicate that he or she has so satisfied the Examiners; or (*b*) if the candidate is classed and satisfies them in two or more fields under Regulation 1, indicate that he or she has satisfied them in whichever of those fields is indicated by a letter earlier in the alphabet than any other such letter. A candidate may request that the designation of any subject specialism be removed from the class-list and consequently from their examination transcript, with permanent effect.

Examiners. **13.** Examiners for the LL.M. Examination shall be nominated by the Faculty Board of Law; provided that if there is any candidate in International Law one of the Examiners shall be the Whewell Professor or a deputy nominated by the Whewell Professor. The Faculty Board shall nominate such number of Examiners as they shall deem sufficient. A lecturer conducting a seminar course prescribed under Regulation 2(*c*) shall, if not an Examiner, be an Assessor for the LL.M. and shall report to the Examiners a mark for each candidate in that course (equivalent to the mark for a paper in the examination) based upon his or her assessment of the candidate's thesis. The provisions of the

Assessors. regulations for the Law Tripos relating to the appointment and duties of Assessors shall apply *mutatis mutandis* to the LL.M. Examination.

LL.M. Degree

14. On completing the requisite number of terms,[1] a student who has satisfied the Examiners for the LL.M. Examination shall be entitled to proceed to the LL.M. Degree; provided that, if the student's course of study for the LL.M. Examination has included any term needed for the B.A. Degree, and if the student elects to proceed to the latter degree, he or she shall not be eligible also to proceed to the LL.M. Degree. Conditions.

15. A student who is a candidate for the LL.M. Examination after having been admitted to the B.A. Degree but who has not paid a University Composition Fee for any term since completing the requirements for that degree shall pay a fee of £60 on entering for the LL.M. Examination, but no further fee shall be payable by such a student for admission to the LL.M. Degree or to the M.A. Degree. Fee.

Doctor of Law

1. In order to qualify for the degree of Doctor of Law a candidate shall be required to give proof of distinction by some original contribution to the advancement of the science or study of law.

2. Any person may be a candidate for the degree of Doctor of Law who is a graduate of the University and who Standing of candidates.

either (*a*) is of not less than eight years' standing from admission to his or her first degree of the University,

or (*b*) is of not less than eight years' standing from admission to his or her first degree of some other university and has been admitted (i) to some office in the University or to a Headship or a Fellowship of a College, and (ii) to the degree of Master of Arts under Statute B II 2 or to a degree of the University by incorporation.

3. A candidate for the degree shall apply in writing to the Secretary of the Board of Graduate Studies, specifying the works on which his or her claim to the degree is based and providing a summary in not more than 500 words of the field of research covered by these works. A candidate shall send with the application a fee of £582 for the Chest, and two copies of each of the works specified, provided that the Board of Graduate Studies may, subject to the concurrence of the Degree Committee, allow a candidate to submit only one copy. All the works submitted shall, apart from quotations, be written in English unless in a particular case the Degree Committee for the Faculty of Law have allowed a candidate to submit material in some other language. A substantial part of the material submitted must have been published and the remainder must be printed or typewritten. Method of application.

4. Each application shall be forwarded by the Secretary of the Board of Graduate Studies to the Degree Committee for the Faculty of Law, who shall give preliminary consideration to the application and shall determine whether the works submitted constitute *prima facie* a qualification for the degree; the Committee may appoint an Assessor to assist them in the matter. Preliminary consideration.

5. If the Committee decide that the works submitted do not constitute *prima facie* a qualification for the degree, a resolution of the Committee to that effect, with the names of those present and voting on either side, shall be communicated to the Secretary of the Board of Graduate Studies, who shall communicate the decision to the candidate. In such a case £510 out of the fee of £582 paid by the candidate under Regulation 3 shall be returned.

6. If the Committee decide that the works submitted do constitute *prima facie* a qualification for the degree, they shall appoint not less than two persons to act as Referees. Each Referee shall submit an independent written report on the works specified in the candidate's application; these reports shall be treated as confidential documents. Referees.

7. If after considering the reports of the Referees the Degree Committee are satisfied that the candidate's work is of the requisite standard for the degree, a resolution of the Committee to that effect, with the names of those present and voting on either side, shall be communicated to the Board of Graduate Studies together with the reports of the Referees.

8. If the Board of Graduate Studies after receiving such a communication resolve that the degree should be conferred, the Secretary of the Board of Graduate Studies shall publish the name of the candidate as approved for the degree of Doctor of Law. Such a resolution shall not be valid unless passed with the concurrence of the votes, cast at a meeting, of five members of the Board. Approval for degree.

[1] See the regulations for Residence and Precincts of the University (p. 189).

9. If after considering the reports of the Referees the Degree Committee are of the opinion that the candidate's work is not of the requisite standard for the degree, a resolution of the Committee to that effect, with the names of those present and voting on either side, shall be communicated to the Board of Graduate Studies together with the reports of the Referees. The Secretary of the Board shall communicate this decision to the candidate.

Candidate not to be present.

10. No candidate for the degree shall be present at the deliberations either of the Committee or of the Board of Graduate Studies respecting his or her own case.

Payments.

11. Each Referee shall receive a fee of £175. An Assessor appointed under Regulation 4 shall receive a fee of £42. If an Assessor is subsequently appointed a Referee the fee of £42 shall form part of the fee of £175 due to him or her as a Referee. The Board of Graduate Studies may approve the payment of reasonable expenses incurred by Referees in the execution of their duties.

12. No fee shall be payable on admission to the degree.

MASTER OF MATHEMATICS (M.MATH.)

A student who has obtained honours in Part III of the Mathematical Tripos shall be entitled to proceed to the M.Math. Degree.

DEGREES IN MEDICINE AND SURGERY

(New Curriculum Regulations)

BACHELOR OF MEDICINE AND BACHELOR OF SURGERY

NEW CURRICULUM REGULATIONS

Amended by Notice (Reporter, *2013–14, p. 252*)

1. These regulations, which shall be known as the New Curriculum Regulations for the degrees of Bachelor of Medicine and Bachelor of Surgery, shall apply to those students who begin their clinical course on or after 1 September 2005.

2. On completing the requisite number of terms,[1] a student who has passed in Parts I, II, and III of the Final M.B. Examination as prescribed in these regulations shall be qualified to supplicate for the degrees of Bachelor of Medicine and Bachelor of Surgery. The short titles of these degrees shall be M.B., B.Chir.

Definitions.

3. In these regulations unless the context shall require otherwise:

(*a*) the term *Faculty Board* shall mean the Faculty Board of Clinical Medicine;

(*b*) the term *Regius Professor* shall mean the Regius Professor of Physic;

(*c*) the term *Associate Teaching Hospital* or *Associate Teaching General Practice* shall mean a hospital or health-care provider, or other institution associated with the University, which has been approved by the Faculty Board of Clinical Medicine to provide clinical placements for medical students;

(*d*) the term *instruction* shall mean instruction given in the University or elsewhere and may include practical instruction;

(*e*) the term *approved course* shall mean a course approved for the purpose of these regulations by the Faculty Board of Clinical Medicine;

(*f*) the term *approved courses of clinical instruction* shall mean courses or placements in the subjects specified below which are held in the University, University Hospital, Associate Teaching Hospital, or Associate Teaching General Practice, or other institution associated with the University as the Faculty Board may approve for the purpose of these regulations, and which have been approved by the Faculty Board as courses appropriate to a Part of the Final M.B. Examination:

for Part I: Pathology
for Part II: Clinical Paediatrics and Clinical Obstetrics and Gynaecology
for Part III: Medicine and Surgery with Clinical Pharmacology, Pathology, Psychiatry, General Practice, Public Health Medicine, Paediatrics, Obstetrics and Gynaecology, and other medical and surgical specialities covered in the curriculum.

[1] See the regulations for Residence and Precincts of the University (p. 189); terms kept or allowed before beginning the years of clinical study shall count for this purpose.

(New Curriculum Regulations)

(*g*) the term *year of clinical study* shall mean a period of twelve consecutive months (including not more than seven weeks' vacation) during which a student has attended full-time approved courses of clinical instruction as defined in Regulation 3(*f*);

(*h*) the term *evidence* shall mean:

(i) in the case of study in another university, evidence signed by a responsible officer of the university concerned;

(ii) during the period of clinical study defined in Regulation 3(*g*), evidence signed by the Director of Medical Education or another officer authorized by the Director;

(*i*) the term *satisfactory completion* shall mean that the student has performed appropriately in an examination or submitted work which satisfies the Faculty Board of Clinical Medicine which shall publish annually in the Michaelmas Term a statement in the *Reporter* outlining the requirements for satisfactory completion.

(*j*) the term *satisfactory performance* shall mean performance which satisfies the Director of Medical Education or another officer or officers authorized by the Director;

(*k*) the term *M.B./Ph.D. Programme student* shall mean a student who, having been approved by the Faculty Board for admission to a course combining research and clinical instruction in the University, has subsequently been admitted as a Graduate Student by the Board of Graduate Studies;

(*l*) the term *Cambridge Graduate Course student* shall mean a student who holds an Honours Degree of this or a recognized university and has been approved by the Faculty Board for admission to a four-year course in medicine (Cambridge Graduate Course in Medicine);

(*m*) the term *Medical Students Register* shall mean a register of students who are deemed fit to practise medicine. A student may be removed temporarily or permanently from the Register if he or she is deemed no longer a fit person to have the privilege of access to patients. Subject to the powers of the Council and of the General Board and of a Fitness to Practise Appeal Panel, the Register shall be maintained by the Faculty Boards of Biology and Clinical Medicine through the Fitness to Practise Committee.

4. There shall be a Second Examination and a Final Examination for the degrees of Bachelor of Medicine and Bachelor of Surgery, referred to in these regulations as the Second M.B. Examination and the Final M.B. Examination. Examinations.

5. The Faculty Board, after consulting other bodies concerned, shall have power to issue from time to time supplementary regulations defining or limiting all or any of the Parts, subjects, papers, or sections of the Second M.B. Examination or the Final M.B. Examination. Due care shall be taken that sufficient notice is given of any alteration of such supplementary regulations. Supplementary regulations.

6. Where a candidate for any of the examinations prescribed in these regulations is required by them to produce evidence of instruction or of any other matter, the candidate's entry shall not be considered to have been made earlier than the day on which the Registrary receives that evidence or the last part of it to be submitted. Evidence of instruction.

7. No student shall be a candidate for any subject of the Second M.B. Examination unless he or she has previously satisfied the University's premedical requirements. The premedical requirements, which shall be determined by the Faculty Board, shall be specified in Schedule A to these regulations; the Faculty Board shall have power to amend that Schedule from time to time as they think fit. Premedical requirements.

8. The Faculty Board shall have power to grant exemption from all or part of the premedical requirements to a student who is deemed by the Board to have attained a satisfactory standard in an examination or examinations approved by the Board for this purpose in an appropriate subject or subjects.

9. The subjects of the Second M.B. Examination shall be as follows: Second M.B. Examination.

Biology of Disease (BOD)
Functional Architecture of the Body (FAB)
⟨Head and Neck Anatomy (HNA)⟩[1]
Homeostasis (HOM)
Human Reproduction (HR)
Introduction to the Scientific Basis of Medicine (ISBM)
Mechanisms of Drug Action (MODA)
Molecules in Medical Science (MIMS)

[1] The subject in angular brackets will be inserted with effect from the 2015 examinations.

(New Curriculum Regulations)

Neurobiology with Human Behaviour (NHB)
Preparing for Patients (PFP)
Social Context of Health and Illness (SCHI)

provided that a candidate taking the Cambridge Graduate Course in Medicine shall not be examined in the subject PFP.

(*a*) The examinations in BOD, HOM, MIMS, and MODA shall each consist of a written paper of one hour, which shall contain compulsory short-answer questions (Section I), and a practical examination of two hours (Section II).

[(*b*) The examinations in HR and NHB shall consist of a written paper of one hour, which shall contain compulsory short-answer questions (Section I), and a practical examination of one hour (Section II).][1]

⟨(*b*) The examination in HR shall consist of a written paper of one hour, which shall contain compulsory short-answer questions (Section I), and a practical examination of one hour (Section II).

(*c*) The examination in NHB shall consist of a written paper of one and a half hours, which shall contain compulsory short-answer questions (Section I), and a practical examination of one hour (Section II).⟩[1]

(*c*) The examination in SCHI shall consist of a written paper of ninety minutes.

(*d*) The examination in ISBM shall consist of a written paper of forty-five minutes.

(*e*) The examinations in PFP shall each consist of the submission of records of such course-work done by candidates as shall be specified from time to time by the Faculty Board of Clinical Medicine after consultation with the Faculty Board of Biology.

⟨(*g*) The examination in HNA shall consist of a practical paper of one hour consisting of two sections (Section I) and (Section II).⟩[2]

(*h*) The examination in FAB shall consist of a written paper of forty-five minutes, which shall contain compulsory short-answer questions (Section I), and a practical examination of one and a half hours (Section II).

10. The Second M.B. Examination shall be held as follows:

(*a*) The examinations in BOD, FAB, HOM, HR, MIMS, MODA, and NHB shall be held twice a year, as follows:

- (i) in the Easter Term, on the dates prescribed for Part IA and Part IB of the Medical and Veterinary Sciences Tripos[3];
- (ii) in September, beginning on the Monday next but one before the first day of the Michaelmas Term.

[(*b*) The examinations in ISBM and SCHI shall be held twice a year on the last day of Full Lent Term and in the week beginning on the Monday next but one before the first day of the Michaelmas Term.][4]

⟨(*b*) The examinations in ISBM, HNA, and SCHI shall be held twice a year on the last day of Full Lent Term and in the week beginning on the Monday next but one before the first day of the Michaelmas Term.⟩[4]

(*c*) Records of course-work for PFP shall be submitted, in accordance with detailed arrangements approved by the Faculty Board after consultation with the Faculty Board of Biology.

11. A candidate for the Second M.B. Examination shall be required to have diligently attended approved courses of instruction appropriate to the subject or subjects to be offered in the examination. Approved courses recognized for this purpose shall be listed in Schedule B to these regulations; the Faculty Board shall have power to amend this Schedule from time to time as they think fit. The Faculty Board shall have authority to approve for this purpose additional courses offered by a university other than Cambridge, or, in exceptional circumstances, to waive the requirement. The Second M.B. Examination may be taken by an unmatriculated student who has satisfied this requirement and who is certified on behalf of a College to the Registrary to be a *bona fide* candidate for admission to the College.

[1] The paragraphs in angular brackets will replace the paragraph in square brackets and subsequent paragraphs will be renumbered with effect from the 2015 examinations.

[2] The paragraph in angular brackets will be inserted with effect from the 2015 examinations.

[3] In this sitting of the Second M.B. Examination the papers set are Sections I and II of the papers set in the corresponding subjects of Part IA and Part IB of the Medical and Veterinary Sciences Tripos. See Regulations 15 and 20 for that Tripos.

[4] The paragraph in angular brackets will replace the paragraph in square brackets with effect from the 2015 examinations.

[New Curriculum Regulations)

No student whose name does not appear on the Medical Students Register shall be a candidate for any subject of the Second M.B. Examination.

Exemption.

12. (*a*) The Faculty Board shall have power to grant exemption from any subject or subjects of the Second M.B. Examination to a candidate for admission as a clinical student from a university other than Cambridge, provided that the student has satisfied the conditions of Regulation 11 and has attained a satisfactory standard, as prescribed by the Faculty Board, in corresponding subjects taken in an examination for a degree of a university other than Cambridge.

(*b*) The Faculty Board shall inform the Registrary as early as possible of the names of those candidates who have been granted exemption from any subject or subjects of the Second M.B. Examination and who have satisfied the requirements in Regulation 12(*a*).

13. A candidate who is unsuccessful in the examination in any subject of the Second M.B. Examination shall be eligible for re-examination, provided that, except by special permission of the Faculty Board granted in exceptional circumstances,

(*a*) a student who fails to satisfy the Examiners in any subject other than PFP shall not be a candidate for re-examination in that subject later than nine months after his or her first attempt in that subject;

(*b*) a student whose submission for any course of PFP fails to satisfy the Examiners shall be required to submit a revised report for that course not later than the end of the current academical year;

(*c*) subject to Regulation 28, no student shall be a candidate in any subject on more than two occasions in total.

Final M.B. Examination.

14. The Final M.B. Examination shall consist of three Parts, Parts I, II, and III; Part II shall be divided into two components, Part III shall be divided into four components. All Parts shall be held in the Easter Term. Part I and Part II shall also be held in the following Michaelmas Term; the written paper components of Part III shall also be held in July. A timetable for each sitting of the examinations shall be published by the Board of Examinations after consultation with the Faculty Board, before the division of the Easter Term each year for the calendar year next following.

15. The Parts of the Final M.B. Examination shall consist of the following elements:

Part I: one written paper and a practical examination (which shall form one component). The Examiners at their discretion may examine any candidate for distinction *viva voce*.

Part II: two clinical examinations (which shall form two clinical components).

Part III: three written papers (which shall form two written components), and two clinical examinations (which shall form two clinical components).

Candidature for the Final M.B. Examination shall be subject to the restrictions and conditions specified in Regulations 16–21 below.

16. Before taking any Part of the Final M.B. Examination a student shall

(*a*) have completed the Second M.B. Examination by having passed all the subjects thereof; and

(*b*) have obtained a degree deemed appropriate by the Faculty Board.

No student whose name does not appear on the Medical Students Register shall be a candidate for any Part of the Final M.B. Examination.

17. A student who proposes to be a candidate for any Part of the Final M.B. Examination shall produce evidence of having satisfactorily completed the approved courses of clinical instruction appropriate to that Part. Except by permission of the Faculty Board in exceptional circumstances, and subject to any conditions determined by them, a course of clinical instruction shall not count towards the requirements of the Final M.B. Examination:

(*a*) if it began before the student's completion of the Second M.B. Examination;

or (*b*) if it began before the student obtained the degree required under Regulation 16(*b*) above.

18. A student who has failed to complete satisfactorily any part of the approved courses of clinical instruction, including permitted reassessments as specified by the Faculty Board of Clinical Medicine, shall not be permitted to progress to the next course of clinical instruction.

19. (*a*) Subject to the provisions of sub-paragraph (*d*)(ii) and Regulation 21 below, Parts I and II of the Final M.B. Examination shall be taken concurrently except by permission of the Faculty Board in exceptional circumstances.

(*b*) A student shall not be a candidate for the first time for Part I or Part II until at least eighteen months have elapsed since the beginning of the student's course of clinical study.

(*c*) A student who is a candidate for the first time for Part II or Part III shall offer all components.

(New Curriculum Regulations)

(*d*) A student shall not be a candidate for the first time for Part III unless

(i) he or she has completed two years and eight months of clinical study in the University, and unless

(ii) the student either has previously passed in Part I and Part II or in exceptional circumstances has been granted permission by the Faculty Board to be a candidate for Parts I, II, and III on the same occasion.

(*e*) Except by special permission of the Faculty Board in exceptional circumstances, no student shall be a candidate for the first time for Part I and Part II later than three years after beginning his or her course of clinical study and no student shall be a candidate for the first time for Part III later than five years after beginning his or her course of clinical study.

(*f*) Except by special permission of the Faculty Board in exceptional circumstances, no student shall be a candidate for the first time for Part I later than eight years after the student first took any subject in the Second M.B. Examination or an examination leading to exemption from any subject.

M.B./Ph.D. Programme.

20. The following provision shall apply to M.B./Ph.D. Programme students:

except by special permission of the Faculty Board in exceptional circumstances, such a student shall not be a candidate for the first time for Part III later than eight years after beginning his or her course of clinical study.

Re-examination.

21. If at the first attempt a student fails to satisfy the Examiners in Part I, Part II, or Part III or in a component of Part II or Part III he or she shall be eligible for re-examination in the relevant Part or component under conditions set by the Faculty Board, taking them separately or together, provided that

(*a*) a candidate for re-examination in Part II shall offer both components of Part II unless he or she has already satisfied the Examiners in one component;

(*b*) a candidate for re-examination in Part III in July shall already have passed in Part I, in both components of Part II, in the clinical components of Part III, and in such written components as required by the Examiners;

(*c*) a candidate for re-examination in Part III in any year following that in which he or she first took the examination

(i) shall already have passed in Part I and both components of Part II,

(ii) shall offer all components of Part III;

(*d*) a candidate shall not be re-examined in either Part I, or in any component of Part II or Part III later than two years after his or her first candidature for that Part or that component, except by special permission of the Faculty Board in exceptional circumstances;

(*e*) subject to Regulation 28, if a candidate fails to satisfy the Examiners in either Part or in any component of Part II or Part III on one occasion subsequent to his or her first candidature for that Part or that component, he or she shall not be re-examined in that Part or that component again except by special permission of the Faculty Board in exceptional circumstances.

22. For grave cause a student may be required by the Faculty Board to defer taking a Part of the Final Examination until he or she has received the permission of the Faculty Board to do so.

Examiners.

23. The arrangements for the appointment of Examiners shall be as follows:

(*a*) The Faculty Board shall nominate for each subject of the Second M.B. Examination a Senior Examiner and such number of other Examiners and Assessors as are required to conduct the examination; provided that for sittings of subjects of the Second M.B. Examination held under Regulation 10(*a*)(i) the Examiners shall be the Examiners appointed for those subjects in the Medical and Veterinary Sciences Tripos.

(*b*) The Regius Professor shall be an Examiner and Chair of Examiners for all Parts of the Final M.B. Examination, provided that, on the nomination of the Regius Professor, any Professor who is medically qualified, or any Doctor of Medicine who is a member of the Regent House, may be appointed to deputize for the Regius Professor for the purpose of this regulation. In addition, the Faculty Board shall nominate for Part I and for each specialty of Part II and Part III of the Final M.B. Examination, a Senior Examiner and such number of other Examiners as the Faculty Board may deem sufficient. Such Examiners shall be appointed to serve for the calendar year next following their appointment.

24. The Faculty Board shall appoint for each calendar year such number of persons as they may deem sufficient to act as Collectors and Assistant Collectors of Cases, provided that the persons so appointed shall be not less than three in number and shall include one Physician, and one Surgeon.

The Collectors and Assistant Collectors of Cases shall invite such patients and shall make such arrangements as may be required for the clinical examinations in Part II and Part III of the Final M.B. Examination. The Faculty Board shall appoint for each clinical examination such numbers of persons as they deem sufficient to act as Clinical Assessors, who shall provide marks and comments to the appointed Examiners. (New Curriculum Regulations)

25. The Examiners and Assessors in each subject or component of each examination shall observe the following requirements:

(*a*) the Examiners shall be jointly responsible for all the questions set in the written paper and the practical examination (if any) of that subject or component;

(*b*) no candidate shall be judged to have failed in any subject unless his or her work has been assessed by at least two Examiners or Assessors.

26. Separate class-lists shall be published for each subject of the Second M.B. Examination and for each Part of the Final M.B. Examination. The names of successful candidates in the several lists shall be arranged in alphabetical order. The list for Part II and Part III of the Final M.B. Examination shall indicate the components of the examination in which the candidate has passed. On the occasion of a candidate's first attempt at Part I or Part III of the Final M.B. Examination, but not on any subsequent occasion, special merit may be recognized by the award of a mark of distinction. Class-lists.

27. The Chair of Examiners shall communicate to the Registrary the marks of all the candidates for the Part, or component of a Part, or subject, of the examination with which he or she is concerned. The Registrary shall communicate to Tutors or other designated College officers, for transmission to their pupils, the marks of their pupils and such other information as may be considered advisable.[1]

28. The Faculty Board of Clinical Medicine shall establish a procedure[2] for the review of decisions taken by them in respect of students who have applied exceptionally for an additional attempt at a Second M.B., or Final M.B. examination under Regulations 13 and 21(*e*). No person who applies for review under the procedure so established shall be entitled to apply also for review of the same matter under the procedure for determining complaints by members of the University *in statu pupillari* established under the Regulation for complaints by students.[3]

TEMPORARY REGULATION

29. Notwithstanding the provisions of Regulations 1 and 14, candidates who began their clinical course before 1 September 2006 under the New Curriculum Regulations shall be examined under the regulations current in September 2007.

SCHEDULE A

PREMEDICAL REQUIREMENTS

GCE A level and GCSE

1. In this Schedule the Advanced level and AS (Advanced Subsidiary) level passes referred to are passes at those levels in a General Certificate of Education (GCE) issued by an awarding body approved by the relevant regulatory authority in England (QCA), Wales (ACCAC), and Northern Ireland (CCEA). The General Certificate of Secondary Education (GCSE) passes referred to are passes in that Certificate, at Grade A, B, or C, issued by an awarding body approved by the relevant regulatory authority in England (QCA), Wales (ACCAC), and Northern Ireland (CCEA).

Approved equivalents

2. For the purposes of this Schedule, the following shall be regarded as the equivalent of a pass at (Advanced) level:

(*a*) a pass in the Scottish Qualifications Authority National Course Advanced Higher examination at Grade A, B, C, or D;

(*b*) a pass in the Scottish Qualifications Authority National Course Higher examination at Grade A, B, or C;

(*c*) a pass at Grade 5 or above in a subject taken at the Higher level of the International Baccalaureate Diploma Programme;

(*d*) a pass in a General Certificate of Education (GCE) Advanced level within the Advanced Diploma of the Welsh Baccalaureate.

[1] See also the regulations for the disclosure of examination marks, p. 250.
[2] See the Appendix to these regulations.
[3] *Statutes and Ordinances*, p. 220.

(New Curriculum Regulations)

3. For the purpose of this Schedule, the following shall be regarded as the equivalent of a pass at AS (Advanced Subsidiary) level:

(*a*) a pass at Level 5 or above in a subject taken at the Standard level of the International Baccalaureate Diploma Programme.

4. For the purposes of this Schedule, the following shall be regarded as the equivalent of a pass in the GCSE:

(*a*) a pass at Ordinary level (Grade A, B, or C) in a GCE issued by an examining body approved by the Department for Children, Schools and Families;

(*b*) a pass in the Scottish Qualifications Authority Standard Grade examination at Grade 1, 2, or 3;

(*c*) a pass in the International GCSE at Grade A, B, or C;

(*d*) a pass at Grade 5 or above in a subject taken at Standard level of the International Baccalaureate Diploma Programme.

5. Passes in subjects of examinations for certificates conducted overseas by the Local Examinations Syndicate shall be considered for equivalence according to the level attained, provided always that the examination is conducted in the medium of English.

Premedical requirements

6. The premedical requirements shall consist of two Parts, A and B.

(*a*) A student shall be deemed to have completed Part A if he or she has *either* achieved the required standard in an admissions test approved by the Faculty Board of Clinical Medicine *or* obtained GCSE passes in the following subjects or equivalents approved by the Faculty Board:

(i) Physics;

(ii) Biology;

(iii) Mathematics;

provided that

(1) a pass in double-award science may be substituted for the passes required under (i) and (ii) above;

(2) passes at Advanced level or AS (Advanced Subsidiary) level may be substituted for the GCSE passes required under (i), (ii), and (iii) above;

(3) a credit in the Science Foundation Course of the Open University may be substituted for the GCSE passes required under (i) and (ii) above.

(*b*) A student shall be deemed to have completed Part B if he or she has obtained Advanced level or AS (Advanced Subsidiary) level passes in the following subjects or equivalents approved by the Faculty Board:

(i) Chemistry;

(ii) at least two of the following: Physics, Biology, Mathematics;

provided that

(1) at least one of these subjects must be passed at Advanced level;

(2) the examination requirements for matriculation are complied with.[1]

(*c*) A student shall be deemed to have completed Part B if he or she has obtained honours or has achieved the honours standard in Part IA of the Natural Sciences Tripos.

(*d*) For the purposes of the premedical requirements, a student who has obtained an honours degree of this or a recognized university shall be deemed to have satisfied the requirements by passing an admissions test approved by the Faculty Board of Clinical Medicine.

SCHEDULE B

APPROVED COURSES OF INSTRUCTION FOR THE SECOND M.B. EXAMINATION

In addition to the courses offered as specific preparation for the subjects for the Second M.B. Examination, the following courses have been approved by the Faculty Board of Clinical Medicine as appropriate courses of instruction for certain subjects of the Second M.B. Examination.

Subjects in the Second M.B. Examination	*Subject in Natural Sciences Tripos Examinations*	
Biology of Disease		NST IB Pathology
	or	NST II Pathology
Mechanisms of Drug Action		NST IB Pharmacology
	or	NST II Pharmacology
Molecules in Medical Science		NST IB Biochemistry and Molecular Biology
	or	NST II Biochemistry
Homeostasis		NST IA Physiology of Organisms
	and	NST IB Physiology

[1] See p. 180.

SUPPLEMENTARY REGULATIONS

Second M.B. Examination

Biology of Disease (BOD)

The examination in BOD will be treated from the standpoint of abnormal biology. It will include the variations that may occur in the structure and functions of living cells, tissues, and organs together with the biology of parasites, bacteria, and viruses. Section I will consist of compulsory short-answer questions on the lecture material. Section II will consist of a two-hour practical examination which will include laboratory work and questions on practical aspects and problem solving.

Functional Architecture of the Body (FAB)

Section I will consist of compulsory short-answer questions on tissue anatomy, aspects of organogenesis, the topographical, functional, and applied anatomy of the human body. Section II will consist of a practical examination and will cover similar aspects.

⟨*Head and Neck Anatomy (HNA)*

The examination will require knowledge of the structure and function of the human head and neck.⟩[1]

Homeostasis (HOM)

Section I will consist of computer-marked and short-answer questions on nerve and neuromuscular transmission, muscle, autonomic nervous system, cardiovascular system, respiration, kidney, salt and water balance, digestion, absorption, and temperature regulation. Section II will consist of questions on the practical work in experimental physiology and histology.

Human Reproduction (HR)

Section I will consist of compulsory short-answer questions and Section II will consist of practical questions.

Introduction to the Scientific Basis of Medicine (ISBM)

The examination will consist of compulsory short-answer or computer-marked questions on the ISBM course

Mechanisms of Drug Action (MODA)

Section I, which will include or consist entirely of short-answer questions, will require knowledge of the actions of drugs on whole organisms and mammalian systems, and also of the mode of drug action at the cellular, subcellular, and molecular levels. Section II will consist of a practical examination, which will include questions on data handling and problem solving; laboratory work will not be involved. Questions that require an elementary knowledge of statistical procedures may be included in both sections of the examination.

Molecules in Medical Science (MIMS)

The examination will test knowledge and understanding of the material contained in the MIMS course. Section I will consist of short-answer questions on the lectures. Section II will consist of questions on practical aspects, including interpretation and handling of data.

Neurobiology with Human Behaviour (NHB)

The examination in NHB will require knowledge of the structure and functions of the central nervous system and the special sense organs, neuroanatomy, experimental psychology and some of its applications to medicine. Particular topics will include neuropharmacology; learning and memory; perception and information processing; intelligence and development; emotion and its physiological basis; and social psychology. Section I will include or consist entirely of compulsory short-answer questions. In Section II, candidates will be examined on practical aspects of neuroanatomy and in experimental neurophysiology; questions may be included which require an elementary knowledge of statistical procedures.

Preparing for Patients (PFP)

Each candidate shall submit to the Examiners such written work for each strand of Preparing for Patients as shall be required by the Faculty Board of Clinical Medicine.

Social Context of Health and Illness (SCHI)

The written paper will require knowledge of social science perspectives that relate to medicine.

APPENDIX

Review of Decisions of the Faculty Board of Clinical Medicine under Regulation 28

1. A student, or her or his Tutor with the student's consent, may seek review of a decision in relation to that student made by the Faculty Board of Clinical Medicine.
2. A request for review shall be made in writing, stating the grounds of review, and be sent to the Registrary, normally within three weeks of written notification of the decision of the Faculty Board of Clinical Medicine

[1] The subject in angular brackets will be inserted with effect from the 2015 examinations.

(New Curriculum Regulations)

(unless, in exceptional circumstances, the Registrary or a deputy permits a longer period). The Registrary shall communicate the request for review to the Secretary of the Faculty Board.
3. If the request includes, in the opinion of the Chair of the Faculty Board, relevant additional information not previously available, the Faculty Board will reconsider its decision at its next meeting following receipt of the request. If no such additional information is included or if, on reconsideration, the decision is reaffirmed by the Faculty Board, the procedure described in the following paragraphs shall apply.
4. The Registrary or a deputy will appoint a reviewer chosen from a panel of potential reviewers maintained by the Council.
5. The reviewer will consider the request, the documentation available to the Faculty Board (less any confidential medical information), the Ordinances which apply to the Faculty Board's decision, and the Faculty Board's Notes of Guidance. He or she will obtain an opinion from the Faculty Board, seek such other information as he or she may require and, at her or his discretion, may hold a hearing (but there is no obligation to hold a hearing). The reviewer will issue an adjudication in writing as soon as possible, stating findings of fact, conclusions, and, if any, recommendations, for consideration by the Faculty Board. The reviewer shall be concerned with determining whether there is evidence of: the Faculty Board having made a decision, to the detriment of the student, which is inconsistent with the relevant Ordinances or its own Notes of Guidance; or material circumstances of which the Faculty Board was unaware and which were of such a nature as, had the Faculty Board been so aware, to have been likely to cause the Faculty Board to have reached a different decision.
6. The Faculty Board of Clinical Medicine shall normally accept the recommendation of the reviewer. If, exceptionally, the reviewer's recommendation is not accepted, a written explanation shall be provided to the reviewer, the student, and her or his Tutor, and shall be submitted to the Council. The Faculty Board may decide not to accept a recommendation in any instance in which: (i) the reviewer has sought to make a decision replacing that of the Faculty Board; (ii) the reviewer's recommendation is inconsistent with the relevant Ordinances; or (iii) the reviewer's recommendation is such that, were it to be accepted, it would set a precedent which would not be in the interests of the proper conduct of Faculty Board's business or in the wider interests of the University or the General Medical Council. The Council (or an officer appointed by it) should be satisfied that the Faculty Board's written explanation is consistent with one or more of these instances.
7. The conclusion of the consideration by the Faculty Board of Clinical Medicine of any recommendation of a review shall be the normal final point of decision within the University. Any subsequent review would normally be by the Office of the Independent Adjudicator (OIA).
8. The reviewer may summarily dismiss an application which seems to her or him to be vexatious or frivolous.

Special Regulations for the Conferment of the Degrees of Bachelor of Medicine and Bachelor of Surgery

Persons entitled to supplicate.

1. Notwithstanding any other provision of the Ordinances, candidates for the degrees of Bachelor of Medicine and Bachelor of Surgery, of which the short titles are M.B. and B.Chir., shall be entitled to supplicate for and to receive those degrees in the manner provided for by the following regulations.

2. A candidate for the Final M.B. Examination may supplicate for the degrees of M.B. and B.Chir. by causing a Supplicat in the form shown in Schedule A to these regulations to be delivered to the Registrary by the authorities of his or her College in the manner prescribed in Regulation 1 for admission to degrees not later than the first day of the examination. Degrees may be conferred under these regulations, notwithstanding late delivery of a supplicat, provided that the necessary documents have been sent to the Registrary in time for proper consideration and for the completion of the list referred to in Regulation 3, but the candidate shall incur a fine of £1.

List of names.

3. Not later than the third day of the examination the Registrary shall sign and cause to be posted on a board in the Schools Arcade a list of names of persons whose supplicats have been received, and who have completed the requirements of the Statutes and Ordinances for proceeding to the degrees of Bachelor of Medicine and Bachelor of Surgery, save for the completion of the Final M.B. Examination, for which they are candidates. The list shall be headed as shown in Schedule B to these regulations.

Non placet.

4. If any member of the Regent House informs the Vice-Chancellor in writing, not later than the day following the posting of the list referred to in Regulation 3, that he or she intends to *non placet* the conferment of a degree upon any person named in the list, the Vice-Chancellor shall cause that person's name to be struck out from the list and that person shall not be entitled to proceed to a degree under these regulations but may supplicate for a degree under the regulations for admission to degrees.

List of successful candidates.

5. Not later than the day next but one following that on which the publication of the lists of successful candidates for the Final M.B. Examination is completed, the Registrary shall sign and cause to be posted on a board in the Schools Arcade a list of those persons named in the list referred to in Regulation 3 whose names have not been struck out in pursuance of Regulation 4 and who have completed the Final M.B. Examination. The list shall be headed as shown in Schedule C to these regulations.

6. The posting of the list referred to in Regulation 5 shall constitute the conferment of the degree of B.Chir. upon each of the persons named in it. The names of the persons upon whom the degree has been conferred under this regulation shall be published in the *Reporter* as soon as is convenient after the posting of the list.

7. Any person who has received the degree of B.Chir. in accordance with these regulations may, not later than twelve calendar months after receiving that degree, supplicate for the degree of M.B. in the manner provided for in the regulations for admission to degrees. M.B. Degree

8. If at the expiry of twelve months from the conferment of the degree of B.Chir. upon any person in the manner provided for by these regulations no Supplicat in the prescribed form has been received by the Registrary for that person to be admitted at a Congregation to the degree of M.B., his or her name shall be included in a list, headed as shown in Schedule D to these regulations, which the Registrary shall sign and cause to be posted on a board in the Schools Arcade.

9. The posting of the list referred to in Regulation 8 shall constitute the conferment of the degree of M.B. upon each of the persons named in it The names of such persons shall be published in the *Reporter* as soon as is convenient after the posting of the list.

10. There shall be no additional fees for the conferment of the degrees of M.B. and B.Chir. under these regulations. Fees.

SCHEDULE A

DEGREES OF BACHELOR OF MEDICINE AND BACHELOR OF SURGERY

To be conferred in accordance with the special regulations for the conferment of the degrees of Bachelor of Medicine and Bachelor of Surgery.

Supplicat reverentiis vestris
ut gradus assequatur Baccalaurei in Medicina et Baccalaurei in Chirurgia. Eundem (Eandem) confirmamus tam moribus quam doctrina idoneum (idoneam) esse ad hos gradus assequendos.

SCHEDULE B

DEGREES OF BACHELOR OF MEDICINE AND BACHELOR OF SURGERY

To be conferred in accordance with the special regulations for the conferment of the degrees of Bachelor of Medicine and Bachelor of Surgery.

I hereby certify that the following persons have completed the requirements of the Statutes and Ordinances for proceeding to the degrees of Bachelor of Medicine and Bachelor of Surgery, save for completion of the Final M.B. Examination, for which they are candidates:

SCHEDULE C

DEGREE OF BACHELOR OF SURGERY

I hereby certify that the following persons have completed the requirements of the Statutes and Ordinances for proceeding to the degrees of Bachelor of Medicine and Bachelor of Surgery, that their names have been posted in accordance with the special regulations for the conferment of those degrees and have not been struck out by the Vice-Chancellor, and that in pursuance of those regulations the degree of Bachelor of Surgery is hereby conferred upon them:

SCHEDULE D

DEGREE OF BACHELOR OF MEDICINE

In pursuance of the special regulations for the conferment of the degrees of Bachelor of Medicine and Bachelor of Surgery, the degree of Bachelor of Medicine is hereby conferred upon the following persons who received the degree of Bachelor of Surgery on (*date*):

DOCTOR OF MEDICINE

1. In order to qualify for the degree of Doctor of Medicine a candidate shall be required to give proof, in accordance with the provisions of these regulations, of a significant original contribution in the science, art, or history of medicine Qualifications required.

Standing of candidates.

2. Any person may apply in accordance with Regulation 6 of these regulations to become a candidate for the degree of Doctor of Medicine who

either (*a*) holds a primary degree of the University,

or (*b*) has been admitted

(i) to some office in the University or to a Headship or a Fellowship of a College, and

(ii) to the degree of Master of Arts under Statute B II 2 or to a degree of the University by incorporation,

or (*c*) holds a medical appointment approved from time to time by the Faculty Board for Clinical Medicine for the purpose,

and also holds

either a medical degree giving entitlement to provisional or full registration with the General Medical Council,

or a degree recognized by that Council for the purpose of full registration,

or a medical degree approved by the M.D. Committee for the purpose of candidature.

No person whose candidature has been approved under Regulation 6 shall submit a dissertation or any other work until four years have elapsed since he or she was admitted

either to the degrees of Bachelor of Medicine and Bachelor of Surgery,

or to the degree of Bachelor of Surgery under Regulation 5 of the special regulations for the conferment of the degrees of Bachelor of Medicine and Bachelor of Surgery,

or to a medical degree of another university as defined above.

M.D. Committee.

3. There shall be an M.D. Committee which shall consist of:

(*a*) the Regius Professor of Physic or a deputy appointed by the Regius Professor;

(*b*) the Assessor to the Regius Professor of Physic, appointed in accordance with the provisions of Regulation 4;

(*c*) eight members of the Faculty of Clinical Medicine;

(*d*) not more than six persons co-opted by the Committee.

Members in class (*c*) shall be appointed annually by the Faculty Board of Clinical Medicine in the Michaelmas Term to serve for one year from 1 January following their appointment. Members in class (*d*) shall serve until the end of the calendar year in which they are co-opted. The Committee shall elect annually one of their own number as Chair. Six members of the Committee shall constitute a quorum.

Quorum.

Assessor to the Regius Professor.

4. The Assessor to the Regius Professor of Physic, who must be a member of the Senate and a graduate in Medicine, shall be appointed not later than the division of the Michaelmas Term in each year by the General Board on the nomination of the Faculty Board to act for one year from 1 January following the date of appointment. The Assessor shall be Secretary of the Committee, for which duty the Faculty Board may, subject to the approval of the General Board, pay a stipend.

5. If either the Chair of the M.D. Committee or the Assessor is prevented at any time by illness or other cause from performing any of the duties prescribed in these regulations, the General Board, on the nomination of the Faculty Board of Clinical Medicine, shall appoint a member of the Senate who is a graduate in Medicine to act as a deputy.

Applications.

6. A person who wishes to become a candidate for the M.D. Degree shall submit an application to the M.D. Committee. The application shall specify:

(*a*) the applicant's proposed subject of study or research, including a plan of the work to be undertaken and an account of the methods to be used;

(*b*) the place where the work is to be undertaken;

(*c*) the name of a member of the Faculty of Medicine who has agreed to act as the candidate's Supervisor for the research project specified;

(*d*) the method of financing the work;

(*e*) a letter of support for the application from the intended Supervisor and Head of the Department;

(*f*) a fee in respect of an admissions charge as recommended by the Board of Graduate Studies for an application for admission as a Graduate Student.

The M.D. Committee shall make recommendations on the admission of the candidate to the Degree Committee for the Faculty of Clinical Medicine and the Board of Graduate Studies.

If the Degree Committee and the Board of Graduate Studies approve an applicant for admission to the programme, the applicant's name shall be entered on the Register of Graduate Students.

The Degree Committee shall determine the conditions, if any, of an applicant's registration and shall assign the term from which he or she is to be admitted.

7. A candidate whose application has been approved shall pay the University Composition Fee for the course. Fee.

8. The examination for the degree of M.D. shall consist of: Examination.

(*a*) the submission of a dissertation embodying the results of the candidate's study or research, which shall be submitted in accordance with the provisions of Regulations 9 and 10;

(*b*) an oral examination ('the Act') on the subject of the dissertation and the general field of knowledge within which it falls.

By special permission of the Degree Committee, candidates may submit with the dissertation published work which they wish the Examiners to consider; such work may be considered by the Examiners at their discretion.

9. A candidate who has paid the relevant fee due under Regulation 7 shall submit to the Degree Committee, not earlier than the end of the second year after approval of the application under Regulation 6 and not later than six years after the date of such approval, unless given special permission by the Degree Committee to delay submission until a later date:

(*a*) three copies of the dissertation, in a form recommended by the M.D. Committee and approved by the Degree Committee;

(*b*) two copies of a summary of about 300 words in length;

(*c*) two copies of any published work which the candidate wishes to submit under Regulation 8.

10. In submitting their dissertations, candidates shall state, generally in a preface and specifically in notes or in a bibliography, the sources from which their information is derived, the extent to which they have availed themselves of the work of others, and the portions of the dissertation which are claimed as original. They shall also be required to declare that the dissertation submitted is not substantially the same as any that they may have submitted for another degree or for a diploma or similar qualification at this or any other university. A dissertation, apart from quotations, shall be written in English. The Degree Committee shall have power to specify a maximum length for dissertations, in consultation with the M.D. Committee.

11. Each dissertation shall be referred to two Examiners, appointed by the Degree Committee on the recommendation of the M.D. Committee. Each Examiner shall make an independent report to the Degree Committee on the dissertation. If the Examiners do not agree in their recommendations or if for any other reason the Degree Committee or the Board of Graduate Studies need a further opinion or opinions on the merit of the work submitted, the Degree Committee may appoint an additional Examiner or additional Examiners, provided that not more than one additional Examiner shall be appointed without leave of the Board of Graduate Studies. Each additional Examiner so appointed shall make an independent report on the dissertation to the Degree Committee. Each Examiner shall receive a fee and shall, if appropriate, be entitled to claim travelling expenses and a subsistence allowance as specified in the Schedule. Consideration of work submitted.

12. The Act shall be conducted by the two Examiners appointed under Regulation 11 and chaired by the Assessor, or her or his deputy. The Examiners shall jointly examine the candidate *viva voce* on questions connected with the work submitted as well as on other medical subjects and sign a joint certificate of the result. If the Examiners do not agree in their recommendations or if for any other reason the Degree Committee or the Board need a further opinion or opinions on the merit of the work submitted, the Degree Committee may appoint an additional Examiner or additional Examiners, provided that not more than one additional Examiner shall be appointed without leave of the Board. Each additional Examiner so appointed shall make an independent report on the dissertation to the Degree Committee. Conduct of the Act.

13. If a candidate fails to satisfy the Examiners in the oral examination, the Degree Committee may permit the candidate to be re-examined by the same Examiners. Permission so given shall be communicated to the Secretary of the Board of Graduate Studies and shall not be given on more than one occasion. Each Examiner who takes part in an examination under this regulation shall be paid an additional fee as specified in the Schedule in addition to any fees to which he or she may be entitled under Regulation 11, and may also claim travelling expenses in accordance with the provisions of that regulation. Re-examination.

14. The Board of Graduate Studies shall be the deciding authority on all recommendations for the award of the degree. If, after considering the reports of the Examiners on a candidate's dissertation Approval for degree.

and on her or his performance in the oral examination, the Degree Committee are satisfied that the candidate's work is of the requisite standard for the degree, showing evidence of significant original contribution to the advancement of the science, art, or history of medicine, a resolution of the Committee to that effect, with the names of those present and voting on either side, shall be communicated to the Board of Graduate Studies, together with the reports of the Examiners. If the Board, after receiving such communication, at a meeting at which not less than five members of the Board are present, resolve that the candidate be approved for the degree, the Secretary of the Board shall publish a notice of the candidate's approval for the award of the degree.

15. If, after considering the reports of the Examiners of a dissertation, the Degree Committee are of the opinion that a candidate's dissertation is not of the requisite standard for the degree, they may recommend to the Board of Graduate Studies that the candidate be permitted to submit a revised dissertation. The communication conveying such a recommendation shall contain the names of those present and voting on either side, and shall be accompanied by the reports of the Examiners. The Board may permit a candidate to submit a revised dissertation on not more than one occasion.

16. If, after considering the reports of the Examiners, the Degree Committee are of the opinion that a candidate's work is not of the requisite standard for the degree (and if they do not recommend that the candidate be allowed to submit a revised dissertation) their resolution to that effect, with the names of those present and voting on either side, shall be communicated to the Board of Graduate Studies, together with the reports of the Examiners. The Secretary of the Board shall communicate this decision to the candidate.

17. A candidate who is not approved for the M.D. degree under Regulation 16

(*a*) shall be eligible to submit a dissertation which is substantially the same in candidature for the M.Sc. Degree; or

(*b*) providing the candidate meets the eligibility requirements, may apply to be a candidate for the M.D. degree by the Special Regulations; such application may be made on not more than one occasion, after a period of not less than five years from the date of the applicant's original examination for the Degree.

Work to be deposited in the Library.

18. Before being admitted to the degree, a successful candidate examined by dissertation shall deposit with the Secretary of the M.D. Committee two copies of the dissertation and of the summary, both the dissertation and the summary being in a form approved by the M.D. Committee. The Secretary of the M.D. Committee shall deposit copies of the dissertation and the summary in the University Library and in the Medical Library, where they shall be available for consultation and for making copies for interlibrary loan purposes.

Prizes.

19. All the dissertations submitted by candidates under these regulations who have been approved for the M.D. Degree in each academical year shall be considered by the M.D. Committee for any Prize, Medal, or other emolument that is awarded for work done by a candidate for the degree; the Committee may be advised by the Assessor in this matter.

Temporary Regulation

20. These regulations shall apply for candidates whose registration as a candidate for the degree commences on or after 1 March 2012.

SCHEDULE

Payments to Examiners

To an Examiner for examining and reporting on a dissertation and for taking part in the conduct of an oral examination: £135.

To an additional Examiner not participating in an oral examination: £100.

To the Assessor: £45.

To an Examiner conducting an additional oral examination (Regulation 13): £42.

Each External Examiner shall receive in addition travelling expenses, in accordance with Regulation 12 of the regulations for the Ph.D., M.Sc., and M.Litt. Degrees.

DOCTOR OF MEDICINE (M.D.): SPECIAL REGULATIONS

Qualifications required.

1. In order to qualify for the degree of Doctor of Medicine a candidate shall be required to give proof, in accordance with the provisions of these regulations, of a significant original contribution in the science, art, or history of medicine.

2. Any person may apply in accordance with Regulation 5 of these regulations to become a candidate for the degree of Doctor of Medicine who *Standing of candidates.*

either (*a*) holds a primary degree of the University,

or (*b*) has been admitted to

(i) some office in the University or to a Headship or a Fellowship of a College, *and*

(ii) to the degree of Master of Arts under Statute B II 2 or to a degree of the University by incorporation,

and also holds

either a medical degree giving entitlement to provisional or full registration with the General Medical Council,

or a degree recognized by that Council for the purpose of full registration,

or a medical degree approved by the M.D. Committee for the purpose of candidature.

No person whose candidature has been approved under Regulation 5 shall submit a dissertation or any other work until four years have elapsed since he or she was admitted

either to the degrees of Bachelor of Medicine and Bachelor of Surgery,

or to the degree of Bachelor of Surgery under Regulation 5 of the special regulations for the conferment of the degrees of Bachelor of Medicine and Bachelor of Surgery,

or to a medical degree of another university as defined above.

3. A person shall not be eligible to proceed to the M.D. Degree under these regulations if he or she has been approved for the M.D. Degree under the regulations requiring registration as a Graduate Student.

4. A graduate of the University who has been examined for the M.D. Degree under the regulations requiring registration as a Graduate Student, but has not been approved for the M.D. Degree, may become a candidate under these regulations after a period of not less than five years from the date of submitting a dissertation or a revised dissertation, as the case may be, for the M.D. Degree.

5. A person who wishes to become a candidate for the M.D. Degree under these regulations shall submit an application to the M.D. Committee. The application shall specify *Applications.*

(*a*) the applicant's proposed subject of study or research, including a plan of the work to be undertaken and an account of the methods to be used;

(*b*) the place where the work is to be undertaken;

(*c*) the name of a member of the Faculty in which the research is to be carried out who has agreed to advise the candidate on the research project specified;

(*d*) the method of financing the work;

(*e*) a letter of support for the application from the intended adviser and Head of her or his Department;

(*f*) an application fee as specified in the Schedule to these regulations.

6. The M.D. Committee may refer the proposal to one or more referees for their opinion before deciding to approve, reject, or suggest some modification to the applicant's proposal. A referee appointed for this purpose will receive a fee as set out in the Schedule. The Assessor shall communicate the decision of the M.D. Committee to the applicant. If the proposal is rejected, all but £500 of the application fee shall be returned to the candidate.

7. The examination for the degree of M.D. under the Special Regulations shall consist of: *Examination.*

(*a*) the submission of a dissertation embodying the results of the candidate's study or research, which shall be submitted in accordance with the provisions of Regulations 8 and 9;

(*b*) an oral examination ('the Act') on the subject of the dissertation and the general field of knowledge within which it falls.

By special permission of the M.D. Committee, candidates may submit with the dissertation published work which they wish the Examiners to consider; such work may be considered by the Examiners at their discretion.

8. A candidate shall submit to the Degree Committee for the Faculty of Clinical Medicine, not later than six years after the date of such approval under Regulation 6, unless given special permission by the Degree Committee to delay submission until a later date:

(*a*) three copies of the dissertation, in a form recommended by the M.D. Committee and approved by the Degree Committee;

(*b*) two copies of a summary of about 300 words in length;

(*c*) two copies of any published work which the candidate wishes to submit under Regulation 7.

9. In submitting their dissertations, candidates shall state, generally in a preface and specifically in notes or in a bibliography, the sources from which their information is derived, the extent to which they have availed themselves of the work of others, and the portions of the dissertation which are claimed as original. They shall also be required to declare that the dissertation submitted is not substantially the same as any that they may have submitted for another degree or for a diploma or similar qualification at this or any other university. A dissertation, apart from quotations, shall be written in English. The Degree Committee shall have power to specify a maximum length for dissertations, in consultation with the M.D. Committee.

Consideration of work submitted.

10. The Degree Committee shall refer each application to the M.D. Committee, who may refer it to one or more referees for their opinion and advice before deciding that the dissertation constitutes *prima facie* a qualification for the degree. A referee so appointed shall receive a fee as specified in the Schedule to these regulations. If such a person is subsequently appointed an Examiner, the fee shall form part of the fee due to her or him as an Examiner.

11. If the Degree Committee, having been advised by the M.D. Committee, decide that the work submitted does not constitute *prima facie* a qualification for the degree, and no Examiners are to be appointed, a resolution of the Committee to that effect, with the names of those present and voting on either side, shall be communicated to the Secretary of the Board of Graduate Studies, who shall communicate the decision to the candidate. In such a case all but £600 out of the fee paid by the applicant under Regulation 5 shall be returned.

12. Each dissertation judged under Regulation 10 to constitute *prima facie* a qualification for the degree shall be referred to two Examiners, appointed by the Degree Committee on the recommendation of the M.D. Committee. Each Examiner shall make an independent report to the Degree Committee on the dissertation. If the Examiners do not agree in their recommendations or if for any other reason the Degree Committee or the Board of Graduate Studies need a further opinion or opinions on the merit of the work submitted, the Degree Committee may appoint an additional Examiner or additional Examiners, provided that not more than one additional Examiner shall be appointed without leave of the Board of Graduate Studies. Each additional Examiner so appointed shall make an independent report on the dissertation to the Degree Committee. Each Examiner shall receive a fee and shall, if appropriate, be entitled to claim travelling expenses and a subsistence allowance as specified in the Schedule.

Conduct of the Act.

13. The Act shall be conducted by the two Examiners appointed under Regulation 12 and chaired by the Assessor, or her or his deputy. The Examiners shall jointly examine the candidate *viva voce* on questions connected with the work submitted as well as on other medical subjects and sign a joint certificate of the result. If the Examiners do not agree in their recommendations or if for any other reason the Degree Committee or the Board need a further opinion or opinions on the merit of the work submitted, the Degree Committee may appoint an additional Examiner or additional Examiners, provided that not more than one additional Examiner shall be appointed without leave of the Board. Each additional Examiner so appointed shall make an independent report on the dissertation to the Degree Committee.

14. If a candidate fails to satisfy the Examiners in the oral examination, the Degree Committee may permit the candidate to be re-examined by the same Examiners. Permission so given shall be communicated to the Secretary of the Board of Graduate Studies and shall not be given on more than one occasion. Each Examiner who takes part in an examination under this regulation shall be paid an additional fee as specified in the Schedule in addition to any fees to which he or she may be entitled under Regulation 12, and may also claim travelling expenses in accordance with the provisions of that regulation.

15. The Board of Graduate Studies shall be the deciding authority on all recommendations for the award of the degree. If, after considering the reports of the Examiners on a candidate's dissertation and on her or his performance in the oral examination, the Degree Committee are satisfied that the work submitted by the candidate and her or his performance in the Act are of the requisite standard for the degree, a resolution of the Committee to that effect, with the names of those present and voting on either side, shall be communicated to the Board of Graduate Studies, together with the reports of the Examiners. If the Board, after receiving such communication, at a meeting at which not less than five members of the Board are present, resolve that the candidate be approved for the degree, the Secretary of the Board shall publish a notice of the candidate's approval for the award of the degree.

16. If, after considering the reports of the Examiners of a dissertation, the Degree Committee are of the opinion that a candidate's dissertation is not of the requisite standard for the degree, they may recommend to the Board of Graduate Studies that the candidate be permitted to submit a revised dissertation. The communication conveying such a recommendation shall contain the names of those present and voting on either side, and shall be accompanied by the reports of the Examiners. The Board may permit a candidate to submit a revised dissertation on not more than one occasion.

17. If, after considering the reports of the Examiners, the Degree Committee are of the opinion that a candidate's work is not of the requisite standard for the degree (and if they do not recommend that the candidate be allowed to submit a revised dissertation) their resolution to that effect, with the names of those present and voting on either side, shall be communicated to the Board of Graduate Studies, together with the reports of the Examiners. The Secretary of the Board shall communicate this decision to the candidate.

18. If a candidate's application for the degree under these regulations fails, he or she may reapply on one occasion only, after a period of not less than five years from the date of the original application.

19. A candidate whose application for the M.D. Degree under these regulations is not approved shall not be eligible to be approved for the M.Sc. Degree.

20. No candidate for the degree shall be present at the deliberations either of the Degree Committee or of the Board of Graduate Studies in respect of her or his own candidature.

21. No fee shall be payable on admission to the degree.

22. Before being admitted to the degree, a successful candidate examined by dissertation shall deposit with the Secretary of the M.D. Committee two copies of the dissertation and of the summary, both the dissertation and the summary being in a form approved by the M.D. Committee. The Secretary of the M.D. Committee shall deposit copies of the dissertation and the summary in the University Library and in the Medical Library, where they shall be available for consultation and for making copies for interlibrary loan purposes. *Work to be deposited in the Library.*

23. All the dissertations submitted by candidates under these regulations who have been approved for the M.D. Degree in each academical year shall be considered by the M.D. Committee for any Prize, Medal, or other emolument that is awarded for work done by a candidate for the degree; the Committee may be advised by the Assessor in this matter. *Prizes.*

TEMPORARY REGULATION

24. These regulations shall apply to all candidates whose proposal is submitted as a candidate for the degree on or after 1 March 2012.

SCHEDULE

Payments to Examiners

To a referee whose opinion is sought on the proposal (Regulation 6) or on a dissertation (Regulation 10): £45.

To an Examiner for examining and reporting on a dissertation and for taking part in the conduct of an oral examination (Regulation 12): £135.

To an additional Examiner not participating in an oral examination (Regulation 13 or 16): £100.

To the Assessor: £45.

To an Examiner conducting an additional oral examination (Regulation 14): £42.

Each External Examiner shall receive in addition travelling expenses, in accordance with Regulation 12 of the regulations for the Ph.D., M.Sc., and M.Litt. Degrees.

Application fee (Regulation 5): £1,866.

DOCTOR OF MEDICAL SCIENCE (MED.SC.D.)

1. In order to qualify for the degree of Doctor of Medical Science a candidate shall be required to give proof, in accordance with the provisions of these regulations, of distinction in the science, art or history of medicine. *Qualifications required.*

2. Any person may apply in accordance with Regulation 6 of these regulations to become a candidate for the degree of Doctor of Medical Science who *Standing of candidates.*

either (*a*) is of not less than eight years' standing from admission to her or his first degree of the University, *or* (*b*) is of not less than eight years' standing from admission to her or his first degree of some other university and has been admitted

(i) to some office in the University or to a Headship or a Fellowship of a College, *and*

(ii) to the degree of Master of Arts under Statute B II 2 or to a degree of the University by incorporation,

and also holds

either a medical degree giving entitlement to provisional or full registration with the General Medical Council,

or a degree recognized by that Council for the purpose of full registration,

or a medical degree approved by the M.D. Committee for the purpose of candidature.

No person whose candidature has been approved under Regulations 3–6 shall submit any work until five years have elapsed since he or she was admitted

either to the degrees of Bachelor of Medicine and Bachelor of Surgery,

or to the degree of Bachelor of Surgery under Regulation 5 of the special regulations for the conferment of the degrees of Bachelor of Medicine and Bachelor of Surgery,

or to a medical degree of another university as defined above.

Applications. **3.** A candidate for the degree by publication shall apply in writing to the Degree Committee for the Faculty of Clinical Medicine, specifying the published works on which her or his claim to the degree is based. He or she shall also submit:

(*a*) a summary in not more than 500 words of the field of research covered by these works;

(*b*) an application fee, as specified in the Schedule to these regulations;

(*c*) a statement that the work to be submitted is not substantially the same as any work that the candidate may have submitted for a degree, diploma, or other qualification at this or any other university.

Consideration of work submitted. **4.** The Degree Committee shall refer each application to the M.D. Committee, who may refer it to one or more assessors for their opinion and advice before deciding that the published work is of outstanding quality and constitutes *prima facie* evidence of distinction through a substantial and original contribution to the advancement of the science, art, or history of medicine. An assessor so appointed shall receive a fee as specified in the Schedule to these regulations.

5. If the Degree Committee, having been advised by the M.D. Committee, decide that the works submitted do not constitute *prima facie* a qualification for the degree, a resolution of the Committee to that effect, with the names of those present and voting on either side, shall be communicated to the Secretary of the Board of Graduate Studies, who shall communicate the decision to the candidate. In such a case, £510 out of the fee paid by the candidate under Regulation 3 shall be returned.

6. A candidate whose work has been judged to constitute *prima facie* a qualification for the degree, shall submit to the Degree Committee, not later than six years after the date of such approval, unless given special permission by the Committee to delay submission until a later date, two copies of the published works on which her or his claim to the degree is based.

7. The Degree Committee shall, on the recommendation of the M.D. Committee, appoint not less than two persons to act as Referees. Each Referee shall submit an independent written report on the works specified in the candidate's application; these reports shall be treated as confidential documents. Each Referee shall receive a fee, as specified in the Schedule.

Approval for degree. **8.** If after considering the reports of the Referees the Degree Committee are satisfied that the candidate's work is of the requisite standard for the degree, a resolution of the Committee to that effect, with the names of those present and voting on either side, shall be communicated to the Board of Graduate Studies together with the reports of the Referees.

9. The Board of Graduate Studies shall be the deciding authority on all recommendations for the award of the degree. If the Board of Graduate Studies after receiving such a communication resolve that the degree should be conferred, the Secretary of the Board of Graduate Studies shall publish the name of the candidate as approved for the degree of Doctor of Medical Science. Such a resolution shall not be valid unless passed with the concurrence of the votes, cast at a meeting, of five members of the Board.

10. If after considering the reports of the Referees the Degree Committee are of the opinion that the candidate's work is not of the requisite standard for the degree, a resolution of the Committee to that effect, with the names of those present and voting on either side, shall be communicated to the

Board of Graduate Studies together with the reports of the Referees. The Secretary of the Board shall communicate this decision to the candidate.

11. No candidate for a degree shall be present at the deliberations of the Degree Committee, the M.D. Committee or the Board of Graduate Studies respecting her or his own case.

SCHEDULE

Payments to Examiners

To an assessor (Regulation 4): £42.

To a Referee (Regulation 7): £175.

The Board of Graduate Studies may approve the payment of reasonable expenses incurred by Referees in the execution of their duties.

Application fee (Regulation 3(*b*)): £582.

MASTER OF SURGERY

1. Any person may apply, in accordance with Regulation 4 below, to become a candidate for the degree of Master of Surgery who Standing of candidates.

either (*a*) holds a primary degree of the University,

or (*b*) has been admitted (i) to some office in the University or to a Headship or a Fellowship of a College, and (ii) to the degree of Master of Arts under Statute B II 2 or to a degree of the University by incorporation,

and also holds

either a medical degree giving entitlement to provisional or full registration with the General Medical Council,

or a degree recognized by that Council for the purpose of full registration,

or a medical degree approved by the M.Chir. Committee for the purpose of candidature.

No person whose candidature has been approved under Regulation 4 shall submit a thesis, or other work approved under Regulation 6, until five years have elapsed since he or she was admitted

either to the degrees of Bachelor of Medicine and Bachelor of Surgery,

or to the degree of Bachelor of Surgery under Regulation 5 of the special regulations for the conferment of the degrees of Bachelor of Medicine and Bachelor of Surgery,

or to a medical degree of another university as defined above.

2. There shall be an M.Chir. Committee which shall consist of: M.Chir. Committee.

(*a*) the Professor of Surgery, or a deputy appointed by the Professor, as Chair;

(*b*) the Secretary of the Committee (see Regulation 3);

(*c*) five members of the Faculty of Clinical Medicine, at least two of whom shall be persons holding Professorships or Readerships in the Faculty;

(*d*) five practising surgeons, at least one of whom shall be a Consultant Surgeon to the Cambridge University Hospitals NHS Foundation Trust and at least two of whom shall be persons not resident in the University.

Members in classes (*c*) and (*d*) shall be appointed by the Faculty Board of Clinical Medicine in the Michaelmas Term to serve for two years from 1 January following their appointment. Five members of the Committee shall constitute a quorum.

3. In the Michaelmas Term of every second year the Faculty Board of Clinical Medicine shall appoint a member of the Faculty to act as Secretary of the M.Chir. Committee for two years from 1 January following the date of appointment. Subject to the approval of the General Board, the Faculty Board may pay the Secretary a stipend. If the Secretary is prevented by illness or other cause from performing any of the duties prescribed in these regulations, the Faculty Board on the nomination of the Professor of Surgery shall appoint some other member of the Faculty of Clinical Medicine to act as a deputy. Secretary.

4. A person who wishes to become a candidate for the degree shall send to the Secretary of the M.Chir. Committee Applications.

(*a*) an application on a form obtainable from the Secretary;

(*b*) details of the applicant's postgraduate appointments and surgical experience;

(*c*) one copy of any published work that the applicant wishes the Committee to consider;

(*d*) an application fee of £220.

The Committee shall decide whether or not to approve the applicant as a candidate for the degree, and the Secretary shall inform the applicant accordingly.

Thesis.

5. Except as provided in Regulation 6, a person approved as a candidate for the degree shall submit a thesis specially composed for the purpose,[1] containing original observations which may be based on clinical work or laboratory work or a combination of the two. Each candidate shall send to the Secretary of the Committee, on a form obtainable from the Secretary, an application for approval of the proposed title of the thesis; such an application shall include an outline of the work on which the thesis will be based, and shall specify the nature of any special branch of surgery in which the candidate is interested. The Secretary shall submit each application to the Committee, who may refer it to one or more referees for their opinion and advice before deciding whether to approve, reject, or suggest some modification of the candidate's proposal. The Secretary shall communicate the Committee's decision to the candidate.

Previously published work.

6. In exceptional circumstances a candidate may apply to the Committee for permission to submit instead of a thesis work which has been previously published. Such an application shall be accompanied by a declaration that the work in question is not substantially the same as any work that the candidate may have submitted for a degree, diploma, or other qualification at this or any other university. The Secretary shall communicate to the candidate the Committee's approval or rejection of the application.

Submission of thesis.

7. A candidate who has obtained the approval of the Committee under Regulation 5(*b*) or Regulation 6 shall submit to the Secretary of the Committee, not later than six years after the date of such approval, unless given special permission by the Committee to delay submission until a later date:

(*a*) three copies of the thesis, in a form approved by the Committee,[2] or of published work which the Committee have given the candidate leave to submit under Regulation 6;

(*b*) if the thesis is based wholly or partly on work already published, three copies of such work;

(*c*) a submission fee of £500.

Examiners.

8. After preliminary consideration by the M.Chir. Committee the thesis or published work shall be sent to two or more Examiners appointed by the Committee who need not be members of the Committee. The Examiners shall be required to submit independent written reports to the Committee.

Viva voce examination.

9. A candidate may be examined *viva voce* by the two Examiners appointed under Regulation 8; the Chair or the Secretary of the M.Chir. Committee, or another member of the Committee, shall preside at such an examination. The two Examiners shall sign a joint report on the candidate's performance in the examination.

Reports.

10. The M.Chir. Committee shall consider a candidate's thesis or published work and the reports of the Examiners thereon at a meeting at which not less than five members are present. If in their opinion the thesis is not of a sufficiently high standard the Committee may, on the recommendation of the Examiners, allow the candidate to submit a revised thesis on one occasion only without being required to pay any additional fee.

Approval for degree.

11. If the Committee are satisfied that a candidate's work is of the requisite standard, they shall resolve that the candidate be approved for the degree and the Secretary shall send a certificate to that effect to the Registrary. This certificate and the title of the candidate's thesis or published work shall be published in the *Reporter*.

Payments.

12. The payments to be made to the Secretary of the M.Chir. Committee, and to referees and Examiners, shall be as prescribed in the Schedule to these regulations.

13. A candidate who has been approved for the degree of M.Chir. shall be qualified to proceed to the degree. No fee shall be payable on admission to the degree.

Deposit in Libraries.

14. A successful candidate shall deposit in the University Library and the Medical Library a copy of the thesis or other work submitted in a form approved by the M.Chir. Committee.

SCHEDULE

Payments to Examiners

To the person presiding at a *viva voce* examination: £45.

To a referee (Regulation 5): £45.

To an Examiner (Regulation 8) for examining and reporting on a thesis and for taking part in a *viva voce* examination if required to do so: £135.

[1] The M.Chir. Committee will not normally accept a thesis which is mainly a reprint, copy, or reproduction of work which has already been published, but there is no objection to the incorporation and use within a thesis of the basic results of work which the candidate has already published, provided that reference to such publications is made or reprints supplied or both.

[2] A successful candidate may apply for the return of one of the copies of the thesis.

To an external Examiner who is required to take part in a *viva voce* examination an additional: £90.

Each external Examiner shall also receive railway fares to and from the place of each examination at which he or she is required to be present together with a subsistence allowance in accordance with Regulation 6 for payments to Examiners and Assessors.

REVIEW OF THE RESULTS OF EXAMINATIONS FOR THE DEGREE OF MASTER OF SURGERY

1. The M.Chir. Committee shall consider any representations made by or on behalf of a candidate which constitute a complaint about the conduct of the examination in that candidate's case for the degree of Master of Surgery provided that such representations shall not be considered unless they are received by the Secretary of the M.Chir. Committee not later than six months after the date on which the result of the examination was communicated by the Secretary to the candidate. In exceptional circumstances the Committee may allow an extension of this deadline of up to three months.

2. If after considering any representations made by or on behalf of a candidate under Regulation 1 the Committee are satisfied that the examination of that candidate was properly conducted and that the complaint is unjustified, the Committee shall so inform the candidate. If they are not so satisfied, they shall have power to reconsider their earlier decision or to refer the representations to a Review Committee constituted in accordance with Regulation 4. The Committee shall inform the candidate of their decision not more than three months following receipt of the representations.

3. The Committee shall refer to a Review Committee constituted in accordance with Regulation 4 any representations which may be made by or on behalf of a candidate after he or she has been informed of a decision taken by the Committee under Regulation 2 above, provided that such representations shall not be considered unless they are received by the Secretary within six months of the date on which the decision taken under Regulation 2 was communicated by the Secretary to the candidate. In exceptional circumstances the Review Committee may allow an extension of this deadline of up to three months. Review Committee.

4. A Review Committee appointed under these regulations shall consist of: Membership.

(*a*) the Vice-Chancellor, or a duly appointed deputy, as Chair;

(*b*) two persons appointed by the General Board from the panel of members maintained by the Board under Regulation 6 of the regulations for the review of the results of examinations for postgraduate qualifications.[1]

In selecting members of the panel for appointment as members of the Review Committee, the General Board shall exclude any person who has been involved in the particular case at an earlier stage. A person appointed a member of a Review Committee shall serve until the conclusion of the particular case for which he or she was appointed.

5. A person appointed by the Academic Secretary, shall act as Secretary to the Review Committee. Secretary.

6. For the purpose of these regulations the term 'complainant' shall mean the student making a complaint, or on whose behalf a complaint is made.

7. The Secretary to the Review Committee shall notify the complainant of the persons appointed to be members of the Review Committee. The complainant shall be entitled to object for good cause to any member so appointed. The Vice-Chancellor shall rule on any such objection, and his or her decision shall be final. If the Vice-Chancellor allows such an objection, another person shall be appointed to replace the person who was the subject of the objection.

8. The Review Committee shall consider any representations referred to them under Regulation 2 or Regulation 3 which in the judgement of the Review Committee constitute a complaint on one or more of the following grounds: Grounds for complaint.

(*a*) that there existed material circumstances relating directly to the examination of which the Examiners were not aware;

(*b*) that procedural irregularities occurred in the conduct of the examination which were of such a nature as to cause reasonable doubt as to whether the Examiners would have reached the same conclusion had the irregularities not occurred;

(*c*) that there is demonstrable evidence of prejudice, bias, or inadequate assessment in the examination process.

[1] See p. 451.

If the Review Committee are of the view that a complaint does not fall within any of the grounds specified above, they shall dismiss the complaint and shall inform the complainant and the M.Chir. Committee accordingly.

Statement of complaint.

9. When a representation is to be considered by a Review Committee the complainant shall furnish a full statement of the complaint and of the grounds on which the complaint is based, which shall be submitted to the Review Committee not later than a date to be determined by them. The Review Committee shall appoint a day and time for a hearing at which the complainant shall be entitled to be present and to be accompanied by an adviser or a representative who may speak on his or her behalf.

10. Any statement of a complaint received by the Review Committee under Regulation 9 shall be made available to each of the following:

(*a*) the M.Chir. Committee;

(*b*) the Examiners concerned;

(*c*) any other person or body specified by the Review Committee.

Each of these parties shall be given an opportunity to submit a written statement to the Review Committee in response to the complaint. Such a statement may include the reports of the Examiners or extracts from those reports. The Review Committee shall have power to seek statements from other persons or bodies, as they think fit.

11. Any statement submitted to the Review Committee under Regulation 10 shall be made available to the complainant and to the other parties specified in that regulation, each of whom shall be afforded an opportunity to comment on it.

Decision of Review Committee.

12. A Review Committee shall consider any complaint or any representations referred to them under Regulation 2 or Regulation 3 and shall have power to dismiss the complaint or, if they consider it justified:

(*a*) to require the M.Chir. Committee to reconsider their earlier decisions on the particular case;

(*b*) to require the Examiners to re-consider the candidate's submitted work;

(*c*) to require the Examiners to hold a further oral examination;

(*d*) to permit the candidate to submit a revised dissertation or thesis, or additional published work, to be examined by the same Examiners;

(*e*) to require the M.Chir. Committee to appoint one or more additional Examiners to make an independent report or reports on the work submitted by the candidate;

(*f*) to require the M.Chir. Committee to appoint new Examiners to replace the Examiners previously appointed, and to permit the candidate

either (i) to be re-examined by the new Examiners,

or (ii) to submit a revised dissertation, thesis, or additional published work, to be examined by the new Examiners;

Notification of decision.

13. The Secretary to the Review Committee shall send written notification of the Committee's decision and the reasons for it to the complainant and to the other parties specified in Regulation 10.

14. The decision of a Review Committee on any particular case shall be final.

Temporary Regulation

15. These regulations shall apply to all examinations held on or after 1 October 2003. For the purpose of this regulation an examination shall be deemed to be held on the day on which the candidate's dissertation, thesis, or other submitted work is received by the Secretary.

DEGREES IN MUSIC

Bachelor of Music[1]

Scheme of examination.

1. The examination for the degree of Bachelor of Music shall consist of two sections, as follows:

Section I.

An instrumental or vocal recital lasting not less than forty minutes.

Section II.

(*a*) A dissertation of not less than 10,000 words and not more than 15,000 words (excluding appendices) on a subject proposed by the candidate and approved by the Faculty Board of Music.

[1] This degree is suspended from 1 October 2011 (*Reporter*, 2010–11, p. 468)

(*b*) A paper of three hours' duration on the background of the subject of the candidate's dissertation. A candidate may be examined orally on questions arising from the recital or the dissertation.

Supplementary regulations.

2. The Faculty Board of Music shall have power to define or limit by supplementary regulations all or any of the subjects of the examination; to determine the credit that shall be assigned to such subjects respectively; and to make, amend, or withdraw any such supplementary regulation as occasion may require; provided that the Faculty Board shall give public notice of any new supplementary regulation or alteration of the supplementary regulations not later than the Easter Term next but one before the term in which the first examination to be affected is to be held.

Who may be a candidate.

3. Any student may be a candidate for the Mus.B. Examination who at the time of the examination (*a*) has kept seven terms and (*b*) has obtained honours, or attained the honours standard, in any Part of the Music Tripos; provided that no student shall in the same term be a candidate for the Mus.B. Examination and for any other University examination except the examination for the Diploma or Certificate in Modern Languages.

4. No student shall be a candidate for the Mus.B. Examination on more than one occasion except as provided in Regulation 5.

Re-examination.

5. The two sections of the examination shall be taken together, except that a candidate who has satisfied the Examiners at the first attempt in only one section may be re-examined in the other section alone on not more than one occasion.

6. A candidate shall send to the Secretary of the Faculty Board of Music, not later than the division of the Michaelmas Term next preceding the examination,

(*a*) a list of the works that he or she proposes to perform, and

(*b*) the proposed subject of his or her dissertation.

Candidates must obtain the approval of their proposed subjects by the Faculty Board not later than the last day of Full Michaelmas Term. Dissertations shall be submitted to the Secretary of the Faculty Board not later than the eighth day of Full Easter Term.

Class-lists.

7. The names of the candidates who have satisfied the Examiners in one or both sections of the examination shall be arranged in alphabetical order in a single class. The class-list shall indicate the section or sections of the examination in which each candidate has satisfied the Examiners. A mark of distinction may be attached to the name of any candidate whose work in either section of the examination is of special merit provided that he or she has satisfied the Examiners in both sections on the same occasion.

Qualification for proceeding to the degree.

8. A student who has satisfied the Examiners in both sections of the examination, whether taken together or on different occasions, shall be qualified to proceed to the degree of Bachelor of Music as soon as he or she has kept nine terms, provided that a student who has thus satisfied the Examiners before completing nine terms' residence, and who elects to proceed to the B.A. Degree, shall not also be entitled to proceed to the Mus.B. Degree.

Examiners and Assessors.

9. The Faculty Board shall nominate not more than three Examiners for the Mus.B. Examination. In addition the Faculty Board may nominate such number of Assessors as they shall deem sufficient.

Fee for a graduate.

10. A student who takes the Mus.B. Examination after having been admitted to the B.A. Degree, but who has not paid a University Composition Fee for any term since completing the requirements for that degree, shall pay a fee of £60 on first taking the Mus.B. Examination no further fee shall be payable by such a candidate on re-examination under Regulation 5 or on admission to the Mus.B. Degree.

SUPPLEMENTARY REGULATION

Section I

Candidates shall submit a programme lasting approximately ninety minutes of instrumental or vocal music. From this the Examiners will hear a recital of at least forty minutes' music. Each candidate shall be responsible for providing an accompanist and a page turner, where required, and shall provide an additional copy of the works for the Examiners.

Master of Music

Amended by Notice (Reporter, 2013–14, p. 639)

Candidature

1. A candidate for the M.Mus. Examination must be approved by the Degree Committee for the Faculty of Music.

2. The Degree Committee may approve as a candidate for the M.Mus. Examination any candidate who has satisfied the Committee that by reason of previous study he or she is qualified to engage in postgraduate work in Choral Studies.

Method of application.

3. Applications for approval under Regulation 2 shall be sent to the Secretary of the Degree Committee so as to arrive not later than 31 March next preceding the date on which the applicant wishes her or his candidature to begin, provided that the Committee shall have power to consider applications submitted after that date.

4. No student shall be a candidate for the M.Mus. Examination, or for any part thereof, on more than one occasion, or for the M.Mus. Examination and another University examination in the same term.

5. A candidate for the M.Mus. Examination shall pursue in the University, under the direction of a Supervisor appointed by the Degree Committee, a course of study extending over three terms.

6. The Faculty Board of Music shall announce not later than the end of the Easter Term each year the list of variable topics and set works to be covered in the course during the following academical year.

M.Mus. Examination.

7. The M.Mus. Examination shall consist of four elements, divided into [three]⟨four⟩[1] sections as follows:

Section 1: Choral conducting

The examination shall consist of the rehearsal and direction, over a period of thirty minutes, of performances of two pieces chosen by the Examiners on the day of the examination from a list of five announced by the Faculty Board.

Section 2: Seminar course

[The examination shall consist of a written paper of three hours' duration, prescribed by the Examiners. Candidates shall answer three questions from at least five topics announced by the Faculty Board; each answer shall relate to a different topic.][1]
⟨Each candidate shall write two essays of not more than 3,500 words, on topics agreed between the candidates and the Supervisor.⟩[1]

[*Section 3: Options*

Each candidate shall choose two options from three: (i) an extended essay of not more than 6,000 words, including notes but excluding appendices; (ii) *either* a critical edition of a single choral work or group of choral works unavailable in a modern scholarly edition, *or* a comparative study of particular editions of a single choral work or group of choral works, *or* a study of editorial practice in relation to choral music; (iii) *either* a choral recital of thirty minutes in length with a choir assembled by the candidate, *or* an organ recital of thirty minutes in length, for which a set work will be announced by the Faculty Board, *or* a performance as continuo accompanist, for which scores will be provided for the candidates in advance of the examination.][1]

⟨*Section 3: Choral project*

Each candidate will form an ensemble with which to offer a choral recital of thirty minutes, of which not more than five minutes will be devoted to the presentation of oral programme notes. The programme for the recital will reflect scholarly research undertaken by the candidate into repertoire and/or performance practice; and is expected to form the basis for an extended essay or editorial submission (see Section 4 below).⟩[1]

⟨*Section 4: Options*

Each candidate shall choose one option from three: (i) an extended essay of not more than 7,000 words, including notes but excluding appendices; (ii) a critical edition of a single choral work or group of choral works unavailable in a modern scholarly edition, *or* a comparative study of particular editions of a single choral work or group of choral works, *or* a study of editorial practice in relation to choral music; (iii) *either* an organ recital of thirty minutes in length, for which a set work will be announced by the Faculty Board, *or* a performance as continuo accompanist, for which scores will be provided for the candidates in advance of the examination.⟩[2]

[1] The text in angular brackets will replace the text in square brackets with effect from 1 October 2015.
[2] The section in angular brackets will be inserted with effect from 1 October 2015.

The Examiners shall have power to examine a candidate *viva voce* on any or all of the elements contained within Sections 1–[3]⟨4⟩[1] of the examination.

8. In order to satisfy the Examiners, candidates must achieve a pass mark in all three sections of the Examination.

9. The Faculty Board shall have power to issue supplementary regulations determining the scope and manner of assessment of the examination, and shall be empowered to amend such supplementary regulations from time to time as they may think fit, due care being taken that sufficient notice is given of any change. Supplementary regulations.

10. The Faculty Board shall nominate for each academical year such number of Examiners and Assessors as they may deem sufficient, including a resident member of the Senate as Chair of Examiners, and a Specialist External Examiner. Examiners and Assessors.

11. The names of the candidates who have satisfied the Examiners shall be arranged in alphabetical order in a single class. A mark of distinction shall be affixed to the names of those students whose work is considered by the Examiners to be of special merit. The Chair of Examiners shall communicate the marks of all candidates to the Registrary. Class-list.

12. While studying in the University for the M.Mus. Examination, a candidate shall pay the appropriate University Composition Fee for each term of such study. Fee.

13. A student who has satisfactorily completed the course and has satisfied the Examiners in the M.Mus. Examination shall be entitled to proceed to the degree of M.Mus.

14. A student who has taken the M.Mus. Examination shall not be entitled to count any part of the period during which he or she has been a candidate for that examination towards a course of research for the degree of Ph.D., or M.Litt. Relation to courses of research.

Doctor of Music

1. A student proceeding to the degree of Doctor of Music shall be required to give proof of distinction in musical composition.

2. Any person may be a candidate for the degree of Doctor of Music who is a graduate of the University and who Standing of candidates.

either (*a*) is of not less than eight years' standing from admission to his or her first degree of the University,

or (*b*) is of not less than eight years' standing from admission to his or her first degree of some other university and has been admitted (i) to some office in the University or to a Headship or a Fellowship of a College, and (ii) to the degree of Master of Arts under Statute B II 2 or to a degree of the University by incorporation.

3. Such candidate shall apply in writing to the Secretary of the Board of Graduate Studies and shall send with the application: Method of application.

(*a*) not more than three works composed by the candidate (printed or otherwise) upon which his or her claim to the degree is based, such works to include either an oratorio, an opera, a cantata, a symphony for orchestra, a concerto, or an extended piece of chamber music;

(*b*) a summary of not more than 500 words relating to the candidate's style and ideology as a composer;

(*c*) a fee of £582 for the Chest, which must be paid at each application made by a candidate

4. Such applications shall be referred to the Degree Committee for the Faculty of Music.

5. If such Committee shall be of opinion that these compositions constitute *prima facie* a qualification for the degree, they shall obtain separate reports upon them from the Professor of Music and from not less than two additional persons, who may be members of the Committee or not. These reports shall be treated as confidential documents. If referees are not appointed, £510 out of the fee of £582 paid by the applicant under Regulation 3 shall be returned. Reports on works sent in to be obtained.

6. Each referee shall receive a fee of £175 from the Chest. A fee of £42 may be paid to an Assessor appointed by the Degree Committee to establish whether an application under Regulation 3 constitutes *prima facie* a qualification for the degree. If an Assessor is subsequently appointed a referee the fee of £42 shall form part of the fee of £175 due to him or her as a referee. The Board of Graduate Studies Fees for referees, and an Assessor.

[1] The number in angular brackets will replace the number in square brackets with effect from 1 October 2015.

may approve the payment of reasonable expenses incurred by referees in connection with the execution of their duties.

Approval for degree.

7. If it be decided to grant the degree, a resolution of the Degree Committee to that effect, with the names of those present and voting on either side, shall be communicated to the Board of Graduate Studies together with the reports of the referees.

Publication of name of successful candidate.

If the Board of Graduate Studies after receiving such a communication resolve that the degree should be conferred, the Secretary of the Board of Graduate Studies shall publish the name of the candidate as approved for the degree of Doctor of Music. Such a resolution shall not be valid unless passed with the concurrence of the votes, cast at a meeting, of five members of the Board.

Unsuccessful candidate to be informed.

8. If the Degree Committee, either without obtaining a report or after receiving the reports of the referees, are of the opinion that the work submitted by the candidate is not of the requisite standard for the degree, a resolution to that effect shall be passed, and a copy of the resolution, with the numbers of those present and voting on either side, shall be sent to the Secretary of the Board of Graduate Studies, together with the reports of the referees if these have been obtained. The Secretary of the Board of Graduate Studies shall communicate this decision of the Degree Committee to the candidate. This information shall not be communicated to the Board of Graduate Studies except with the approval of the Chair.

Candidate not to be present.

9. No candidate for a degree shall be present at the deliberations either of the Committee or of the Board of Graduate Studies respecting his or her own case.

Case of unpublished works.

10. Should none of the works approved have been published, the Committee may require the candidate either to publish, or to deposit in the University Library, one of them, before being admitted to the degree.

11. No fee shall be payable on admission to the degree.

MASTER OF NATURAL SCIENCES (M.Sci.)

On completing the requisite number of terms,[1] a student who has obtained honours in Part III of the Natural Sciences Tripos shall be entitled to proceed to the M.Sci. Degree.

DOCTOR OF PHILOSOPHY, MASTER OF SCIENCE, AND MASTER OF LETTERS[2]

Requirements for degrees and dispensations.

1. Subject to clauses (*a*)–(*e*) below, a Graduate Student shall pursue in the University, or such other place as the Board and the Degree Committee concerned shall determine, under supervision a course of research

(i) if the student seeks the M.Sc. or M.Litt. Degree by full-time study, for not less than six terms;
(ii) if the student seeks the M.Sc. or M.Litt. Degree by part-time study, for not less than ten terms;
(iii) if the student seeks the Ph.D. Degree by full-time study, for not less than nine terms;
(iv) if the student seeks the Ph.D. Degree by part-time study, for not less than fifteen terms.

The number of terms referred to shall begin with the term from which the student is registered for a course of research as a candidate for the particular degree and shall be consecutive except in so far as the student may have been allowed to intermit his or her course under clause (*c*) below, or except in so far as the Board may have determined that he or she shall not be allowed to count any particular term towards the requirements for a degree.

(*a*) The Board, after considering a recommendation by the Degree Committee concerned, may exempt from up to three terms of his or her full-time course or from up to five terms of his or her part-time course a Graduate Student who is registered as a candidate for the Ph.D., M.Sc., or M.Litt. Degree, provided that before admission as a Graduate Student he or she had been engaged

either (i) in full-time or part-time research

or (ii) in other work done after graduation deemed by the Degree Committee and the Board to have provided satisfactory training for the course of research in question.

[1] See the regulations for Residence and Precincts of the University (p. 189).
[2] See also the special regulations for the degree of Doctor of Philosophy, p. 508.

(*b*) The Board, after considering a recommendation by the Degree Committee concerned, may allow a Graduate Student to spend all but three terms of his or her full-time course of research or five terms of a part-time course of research as a candidate for a degree, or any lesser number of terms, working under supervision outside the University under conditions approved by the Degree Committee and the Board.

(*c*) On account of illness or other sufficient cause, the Board, after considering a recommendation by the Degree Committee concerned, may allow a Graduate Student to intermit his or her course of research for one or more terms. Such terms shall not count for any purpose of these regulations except as provided in Regulation 7 of the general regulations for admission as a Graduate Student.

(*d*) If the Council have granted a student registered for a full-time course an allowance of terms of residence under Regulation 2 in respect of work done by the student in the University before matriculation, the Board, after considering a recommendation by the Degree Committee concerned, may grant the student an allowance in respect of such work towards the period during which he or she is required to pursue a course of research in the University under this regulation, provided that the number of terms so allowed shall not exceed the number of terms allowed by the Council in respect of such work. For every term so allowed the student shall pay the appropriate fee as prescribed in Regulation 11 of the general regulations for admission as a Graduate Student.

(*e*) On the recommendation of the Degree Committee concerned, the Board may allow a Graduate Student to count towards his or her course of research as a candidate for a degree a period during which he or she was a candidate for another qualification as set out in Regulation 5(*c*), 5(*e*), or 5(*f*) of the general regulations for admission as a Graduate Students or for the following Diplomas or Certificates:

(i) a student who is qualified to receive, or who has received, the Advanced Diploma in Economics, or the Postgraduate Diplomas in International Law, or in Legal Studies, as the case may be, may be allowed to count not more than three terms of the period during which he or she was a candidate for the Diploma concerned towards a full-time course or not more than five terms towards a part-time course;

(ii) a student who is qualified to receive, but who has not received, a Certificate of Postgraduate Study may be allowed to count not more than three terms of the period during which he or she was a candidate for the Certificate concerned towards a full-time course or not more than five terms towards a part-time course.

Every application for dispensation under clauses (*a*)–(*e*) shall be made in writing to the Secretary of the Board, and shall be accompanied by a written opinion from the applicant's Supervisor.

2. On the recommendation of the Board, the Council may grant to a Graduate Student in respect of work done in the University before matriculation, if the student's matriculation was delayed for sufficient cause, an allowance of terms, not exceeding three in number, towards the minimum of three terms required to be kept under Regulation 8 for Residence and Precincts of the University for full-time study leading to the M.Sc., M.Litt., or Ph.D. Degree.

3. The Board may grant to a Graduate Student, after considering an application supported by the student's Tutor, the following allowance of terms of research towards satisfying the requirements of Regulation 1, on account of illness or other grave cause:

(*a*) one or two terms of research to a candidate for the Ph.D. Degree who would otherwise be required to complete nine terms of research;

(*b*) up to three terms of research to a candidate for the Ph.D. Degree who would otherwise be required to complete fifteen terms of research;

(*c*) one term of research to a candidate for a degree who would otherwise be required to complete five terms of research;

(*d*) one or two terms of research to a candidate for a degree who would otherwise be required to complete ten terms of research.

For every term so allowed the student shall pay the appropriate fee as prescribed in Regulation 11 of the general regulations for admission as a Graduate Student.

4. Notwithstanding the provisions of Regulation 1 of these regulations and Regulation 4 of the general regulations for admission as a Graduate Student, the Board shall have power, on the recommendation of the Degree Committee concerned, to permit a Graduate Student to pursue a course of research, as a candidate for the Ph.D., M.Sc., or M.Litt. Degree, in a particular institution outside the University, under such conditions as may be prescribed by the Degree Committee and the Board. Exceptional dispensations.

Applications under this regulation shall be made in writing to the Secretary of the Board, and shall be accompanied by a written opinion from the applicant's Supervisor.

Conditions for proceeding to the Ph.D. after M.Sc. or M.Litt.

5. A Graduate Student who, having pursued a course of research registered as a candidate for the M.Sc. or M.Litt. Degree, has been approved for the award of one of those degrees, may be registered as a candidate for the Ph.D. Degree. The Board shall determine the conditions of candidature for a student so registered, after considering recommendations by the Degree Committee, provided that:

(*a*) a student shall not submit a dissertation in candidature for the Ph.D. Degree until he or she has completed at least five terms of full-time research or nine terms of part-time research under supervision subsequent to the term or vacation in which he or she submitted a dissertation for the M.Sc. or M.Litt. Degree;

(*b*) a student shall spend at least three of the five terms pursuing full-time research or five of the nine terms pursuing part-time research in the University, or at a particular institution as provided under Regulation 4; and

(*c*) if a student has proceeded to the M.Sc. or M.Litt. Degree, the Examiners conducting the examination for the Ph.D. Degree shall not take account of any work that was included in the dissertation submitted by the student in candidature for the M.Sc. or M.Litt. Degree.

A student who has been approved for the M.Sc. or M.Litt. Degree under Regulation 14 shall not be registered as a candidate for the Ph.D. Degree.

Submission of dissertation.

6. The examination for the degrees of Ph.D., M.Sc., and M.Litt. shall consist of

(*a*) the submission of a dissertation embodying the results of the candidate's approved course of research, which shall be submitted in accordance with the provisions of Regulations 7–9;

(*b*) an examination, conducted orally or in writing, on the subject of the dissertation and on the general field of knowledge within which it falls, provided that in exceptional circumstances, and on the recommendation of the Degree Committee concerned, the Board may dispense with such an examination.

By special permission of the Degree Committee, a candidate may submit other work to be considered by the Examiners together with the dissertation, the whole forming an integrated submission.

7. A candidate may submit her or his dissertation not earlier than the first day of the term during which he or she expects to complete the requirements of Regulation 1 and not later than the last day of the fourth year after the student was registered as a full-time candidate for the degree or the last day of the seventh year after the student was registered as a part-time candidate for the degree, provided that, with the permission of the Board, a dissertation may be submitted later than that day. An allowance of terms made by the Council under Regulation 2 and by the Board under Regulation 1(*d*) shall count in calculating the standing of a student for the purpose of this regulation as shall an exemption under Regulation 1(*a*).

8. In submitting their dissertations, candidates shall state, generally in a preface and specifically in notes or in a bibliography, the sources from which their information is derived, the extent to which they have availed themselves of the work of others, and the portions of the dissertation which are claimed as original. They shall also be required to declare that the dissertation submitted is not substantially the same as any that they may have submitted for a degree or diploma or similar qualification; save that the Board shall have power to allow a candidate to submit a dissertation that he or she has already submitted for a qualification other than a degree or diploma or similar qualification at any university or similar institution. A dissertation, apart from quotations, shall be written in English. Each Degree Committee shall have power to specify a maximum length for dissertations submitted by students working under its supervision.

9. Two copies of each candidate's dissertation, accompanied by three copies of a summary of about 300 words in length, shall be sent to the Secretary of the Board, who shall forward the two copies of the dissertation and two copies of the summary to the Secretary of the Degree Committee concerned. In special circumstances the Board, after consulting the Degree Committee, may allow a candidate to submit one copy only of the dissertation. The dissertation shall be referred to two Examiners, appointed by the Degree Committee. Each Examiner shall make an independent report to the Degree Committee on the dissertation. The two Examiners shall jointly conduct the oral or written examination specified in Regulation 6(*b*), and shall sign a joint certificate of the result; if the examination is conducted orally, both Examiners shall be present, provided that the Board of Graduate Studies in exceptional circumstances may permit the Examiners to conduct the oral examination by video-conference or other remote means. If the Examiners do not agree in their recommendations or if for any other reason the Degree Committee or the Board need a further opinion or opinions on the merit of the work submitted the Degree Committee may appoint an additional Examiner or additional Examiners, provided that not more than one additional Examiner shall be appointed without leave of the Board. Each additional Examiner so appointed shall make an independent report on the dissertation to the Degree Committee.

10. If a candidate fails to satisfy the Examiners in the oral or other examination specified in Regulation 6(*b*), the Degree Committee may permit the candidate to be re-examined by the same Examiners. Permission so given shall be communicated to the Secretary of the Board and shall not be given on more than one occasion. Each Examiner who takes part in an examination under this regulation shall be paid a fee of £42 in addition to any fees to which he or she may be entitled under Regulation 11, and may also claim travelling expenses in accordance with the provisions of that regulation.

11. Each Examiner shall receive a fee from the Chest. Such a fee shall be £135 if the Examiner takes part in the oral or other examination specified in Regulation 6(*b*), or £100 if the Examiner does not so take part, either because the Board, on the recommendation of the Degree Committee, have dispensed with the oral or other examination or for any other reason. Examiners may claim travelling expenses, on terms and conditions specified by the Board of Graduate Studies, if their place of residence is more than ten miles from Great St Mary's Church or if an oral examination or a consultation between the Examiners is for good reason held outside Cambridge. The Board may also approve payment of other reasonable expenses incurred by an Examiner in connection with the execution of his or her duties. A subsistence allowance may be claimed by Examiners at rates determined from time to time by the Finance Committee of the Council, provided that payment may be made only in respect of a day or a night on which the Examiner's absence from his or her normal place of residence in connection with the execution of his or her duties is necessary. The travelling expenses of a candidate who is required to travel to an oral or other examination outside Cambridge may be paid in whole or in part, at rates determined by the Board of Graduate Studies; such a candidate may also claim a subsistence allowance at rates determined from time to time by the Finance Committee, under the same conditions as apply to the Examiners. Payments to Examiners.

12. If, after considering the reports of the Examiners on a student's dissertation and on his or her performance in the oral or other examination, the Degree Committee are satisfied that the student's work is of the requisite standard for the degree for which he or she is a candidate, a resolution of the Committee to that effect, with the names of those present and voting on either side, shall be communicated to the Board, together with the reports of the Examiners. If the Board, after receiving such communication, at a meeting at which not less than five members of the Board are present, resolve that the candidate be approved for the degree sought, the Secretary of the Board shall publish a notice of the candidate's approval for the award of the Ph.D., M.Sc., or M.Litt. Degree, as the case may be. Approval for degree.

13. If, after considering the reports of the Examiners, the Degree Committee consider that a student's dissertation is not of the requisite standard for the degree for which he or she is a candidate, the Board may permit the student to submit a revised dissertation, but they shall not do so unless the Degree Committee have expressly recommended that such permission be given. The communication conveying such a recommendation by a Degree Committee shall contain the names of those present and voting on either side, and shall be accompanied by the reports of the Examiners. A student shall not be allowed to submit a revised dissertation on more than one occasion. Revised dissertation.

14. If, after considering the reports of the Examiners, the Degree Committee consider that a student's work is not of the standard requisite for the Ph.D. Degree, but that it is of the standard requisite for the M.Sc. or M.Litt. Degree, as the case may be, their resolution to that effect, with the names of those present and voting on either side, shall be communicated to the Board, together with the reports of the Examiners. If after receiving such communication the Board decide, at a meeting at which not less than five members of the Board are present, that the candidate could properly be approved for the award of a lower degree, the Secretary of the Board shall ask the candidate whether he or she is willing to be approved for the award of the M.Sc. or M.Litt. Degree, as appropriate. Subject to the candidate's agreement being received by the Secretary not later than the last day of the term following the term or vacation in which the decision on his or her candidature was made, the Board shall approve the candidate for the award of that degree and the Secretary shall publish a notice of such approval. The Board may, in exceptional circumstances, which they shall themselves determine, accept a candidate's agreement at a later date. Approval for a lower degree in lieu of Ph.D.

15. The Board shall be the deciding authority on all recommendations communicated to them by Degree Committees that candidates be approved for the award of degrees or that they be allowed to submit revised dissertations. The Board shall not approve a candidate for the award of a degree unless the Degree Committee have recommended the award of that degree; before refusing an award so recommended they shall give a representative appointed by the Degree Committee an opportunity of explaining the Committee's reasons for their recommendation.

Failure.

16. If after considering the reports of the Examiners the Degree Committee resolve that a candidate's work is not of the requisite standard for any degree, and if they do not recommend that the candidate be allowed to submit a revised dissertation, their resolution to that effect, with the names of those present and voting on either side, shall be communicated to the Board, together with the reports of the Examiners. The Secretary of the Board shall communicate this decision to the candidate.

17. Before being admitted to a degree, a student shall deposit with the Secretary of the Board one copy of her or his dissertation and one copy of the summary, both the dissertation and the summary being in a form approved by the Board. The Secretary shall deposit the copy of the dissertation together with the copy of the summary in the University Library where, subject to restricted access to the dissertation for a specified period of time having been granted by the Board of Graduate Studies, they shall be made available for consultation by readers in accordance with University Library regulations and copies of the dissertation provided to readers in accordance with applicable legislation.

Doctor of Philosophy:[1] Special Regulations

Eligibility of candidates.

1. A candidate wishing to proceed to the Ph.D. Degree under these regulations shall be required to give proof of a significant contribution to scholarship.

2. Except as provided in Regulations 3 and 4 below any person may be a candidate for the degree of Doctor of Philosophy who is a graduate of the University and who

either (*a*) is of not less than six years' standing from admission to his or her first degree of the University,

or (*b*) is of not less than six years' standing from admission to his or her first degree of some other university and has been admitted (i) to some office in the University or to a Headship or a Fellowship of a College, and (ii) to the degree of Master of Arts under Statute B II 2 or to a degree of the University by incorporation.

3. A person shall not be eligible to proceed to the Ph.D. Degree under these regulations if he or she has been approved for the Ph.D. Degree under the regulations for Research Students,[2] or under the regulations for the Ph.D., M.Sc., and M.Litt. Degrees.

4. A graduate of the University who has been examined for the Ph.D. Degree under the regulations for Research Students,[2] or under the regulations for the Ph.D., M.Sc., and M.Litt. Degrees, but has not been approved for the Ph.D. Degree, may become a candidate under these regulations after a period of not less than five years from the date of submitting a dissertation or a revised dissertation, as the case may be, for the Ph.D. Degree, provided that he or she is of standing in accordance with Regulation 2 above.

Application.

5. A candidate for the Ph.D. Degree under these regulations shall apply in writing to the Secretary of the Board of Graduate Studies, specifying the published work or works on which his or her claim to the degree is based, and naming the Faculty or other approved institution within whose scope these works fall. A candidate shall send with the application a fee of £462 for the Chest, and two copies of each of the works specified; a candidate shall also submit an introductory summary in the form of a statement of between 1,000 and 5,000 words summarizing the rationale behind the works submitted, the extent to which the works represent a consistent body of research, and the original contribution to knowledge they make. All the works submitted, apart from quotations, shall be written in English, unless in a particular case the Degree Committee have allowed a candidate to submit material in some other language.

6. A candidate, in submitting an application, shall be required (*a*) to declare that the submission as a whole is not substantially the same as any that he or she has previously made or is currently making,

[1] See also the regulations for the degrees of Doctor of Philosophy, Master of Science, and Master of Letters, p. 504.

[2] The regulations for Research Students, which were replaced on 1 October 1977 by the present general regulations for admission as a Graduate Student and for the degrees of Ph.D., M.Sc., and M.Litt., were last published in *Ordinances*, 1976, pp. 460–70.

whether in published or in unpublished form, for a degree, diploma, or similar qualification at any university or similar institution, (*b*) to state what parts if any of the work or works now submitted have previously been submitted for any such qualification, and (*c*) to declare that, until the outcome of the current application to this University is known, the work or works submitted will not be submitted for any such qualification at another university or similar institution; save that the Board shall have power to allow a candidate to submit certain works that he or she may have already submitted unsuccessfully for any such qualification, or that he or she may have already submitted or is concurrently submitting for some other purpose at any university or similar institution. A candidate who submits work published jointly with others shall submit such evidence as to the extent of his or her own contribution to that work as the Board may require.

7. The Secretary of the Board shall forward to the Secretary of the relevant Degree Committee two copies of the published work or works submitted by the candidate, together with copies of the following: the candidate's application, the candidate's introductory summary, and any evidence submitted by the candidate concerning the extent of his or her contribution to work published jointly with others. If the Degree Committee concerned are of the opinion that the published work or works submitted constitute *prima facie* a qualification for the degree, they shall appoint not less than two Examiners and shall refer the application to them. If Examiners are not appointed, £396 out of the fee of £462 paid by the applicant under Regulation 5 shall be returned.

8. The examination for the Ph.D. Degree under these regulations shall consist of the submission of published work, and of an oral examination on the work submitted and on the general field of knowledge within which it falls. The oral examination shall be held in the United Kingdom with both Examiners present unless permission to hold it elsewhere or, in exceptional circumstances, by video-conference or other remote means has been granted by the Board of Graduate Studies. Examination.

9. Each Examiner shall make an independent report on the published work or works before the oral examination and shall sign a joint certificate of the result of the oral examination.

10. If the Examiners are not satisfied with the candidate's performance in the oral examination, the Degree Committee may allow the candidate to be examined orally on one more occasion at a time to be appointed by the Examiners. Permission so given shall be communicated to the Secretary of the Board. Each Examiner who takes part in an examination under this regulation shall be paid a fee of £42 in addition to any fees to which he or she may be entitled in respect of the examination of the candidate, and may also claim travelling expenses in accordance with Regulation 12.

11. If the Examiners do not agree in their recommendations or if for any other reason the Degree Committee or the Board need a further opinion or opinions on the merit of the work submitted, the Degree Committee may appoint an additional Examiner or additional Examiners, provided that not more than one additional Examiner shall be appointed without the leave of the Board. Any additional Examiner or Examiners thus appointed shall make an independent report on the work submitted by the candidate, and may, at the discretion of such Examiner or Examiners, conduct an oral examination on that work and on the general field of knowledge within which it falls.

12. Each Examiner shall receive a fee of £135 from the Chest. A fee of £42 shall be paid to any person appointed by the Degree Committee to establish whether an application under Regulation 5 constitutes *prima facie* a qualification for the degree. If such a person is subsequently appointed an Examiner the fee of £42 shall form part of the fee of £135 due to him or her as an Examiner. When external Examiners are employed, or when an oral examination or consultation between the Examiners is held away from Cambridge, an Examiner may claim travelling expenses not exceeding the return railway-fare in the United Kingdom between the Examiner's place of residence or other place approved by the Board of Graduate Studies and the place of the oral examination or consultation. For the purpose of this regulation return railway-fare shall be taken to include boat-fare between any two ports of the United Kingdom. The Board may also (*a*) approve payment of travelling expenses not exceeding return rail- and boat-fare between the Examiner's place of residence and the place of examination or consultation, when one or both of those places is outside the United Kingdom, (*b*) approve payment of travelling expenses incurred by Examiners in travelling by air, (*c*) approve payment, at rates prescribed from time to time by the Finance Committee of the Council, of travelling expenses other than those provided for in (*a*) and (*b*) above, and (*d*) approve payment of reasonable expenses incurred by Examiners in connection with the execution of their duties.

Subsistence allowance may be claimed by Examiners, at rates to be determined from time to time by the Finance Committee, provided that payment may be made only in respect of a day or a night on which the Examiner's absence from his or her normal place of residence in connection with the execution of his or her duties is necessary.

Publication of award.

13. If the Degree Committee, on the reports of the Examiners, approve the work submitted by a candidate and his or her performance in the oral examination as of the requisite standard for the degree, their recommendation to that effect, with the names of those present and of those voting on either side, together with the reports of the Examiners, shall be communicated to the Board.

If the Board, after receiving such a communication, at a meeting at which not less than five members of the Board are present, are of the opinion that the degree should be conferred, the Secretary of the Board shall publish a notice of the candidate's approval for the award of the Ph.D. Degree.

14. If the Degree Committee, either without obtaining a report or after receiving the reports of the Examiners, are of the opinion that the work submitted by the candidate is not of the requisite standard for the degree, a resolution to that effect shall be passed, and a copy of the resolution with the numbers of those present and voting on either side, together with the reports of the Examiners, if these have been obtained, shall be communicated to the Board. The Secretary of the Board shall communicate this decision to the candidate.

15. The Board shall be the deciding authority on all recommendations communicated to them by Degree Committees that candidates be approved for the award of the degree. The Board shall not approve a candidate for the award of the degree unless the Degree Committee have recommended that it be awarded, and before refusing an award so recommended they shall give a representative appointed by the Degree Committee an opportunity of explaining the Committee's reasons for their recommendation.

Second application.

16. If a candidate's application for the degree fails, he or she may reapply on one occasion only, after a period of not less than five years from the date of the original application.

17. A candidate whose application for the Ph.D. Degree is not approved shall not be eligible to be approved for the M.Sc. Degree or M.Litt. Degree.

18. No candidate for the degree shall be present at the deliberations either of the Degree Committee or of the Board of Graduate Studies in respect of his or her own candidature.

19. No fee shall be payable on admission to the degree.

MASTER OF PHILOSOPHY

Residence for the Degree of Master of Philosophy

Save as otherwise provided in the Statutes or Ordinances, no-one shall be admitted to the degree of Master of Philosophy having followed a full-time course of advanced study prescribed by Ordinance, unless he or she has kept three terms at least by residence.

Master of Philosophy

GENERAL REGULATIONS

M.Phil. Degree routes.

1. The M.Phil. Degree shall be awarded for advanced study. Candidature for the degree shall be through one of the following routes:

Route A – one year of full-time study;

Route B – two years of full-time study, including a prescribed period of study (of not more than three terms) outside Cambridge; and

Route C – two years of part-time study.

Each subject of study, through whichever route, together with the syllabus for the course, the special regulations for the examination, and any subsequent amendments thereof, shall be approved by the General Board on the recommendation of the Faculty Board or other body concerned, after consultation with the appropriate Degree Committee.

Conduct of examination.

2. The scheme of examination for the M.Phil. Degree, including provision for an oral examination, shall be as prescribed in the appropriate special regulations for the subject as appended to these regulations. Any such prescribed scheme may require candidates also to submit a piece or pieces of written work in accordance with arrangements made by the Board of Graduate Studies on the recommendation of the appropriate Degree Committee. The examination shall be held before the end of the course, except as provided under Regulation 7, and at such time or times as may be determined by the Degree Committee concerned, subject in the case of written papers to the approval of the Board of Examinations. Each written paper shall be of three hours' duration, unless prescribed otherwise in the regulations that apply to the examination concerned.

3. No student shall be a candidate for the M.Phil. Degree and for another University examination in the same term. No student shall be a candidate for the degree on more than one occasion.

4. A candidate for the M.Phil. Degree shall be a registered Graduate Student who, subject to the provisions of Regulation 5, shall pursue in the University or similar institution approved by the Degree Committee concerned and by the Board of Graduate Studies, the specified course under the direction of a Supervisor appointed by the Degree Committee concerned, and shall comply with any special conditions that the Degree Committee or the Board may lay down in a particular case. The course under Route A shall extend over one academical year; candidates under this Route are required to reside in Cambridge for all three terms of the year, beginning from the date announced by the Degree Committee for the start of lectures, classes, or other formal instruction.[1] The courses under Routes B and C shall extend over two academical years. Students under Route B shall spend a minimum of three terms in residence in Cambridge. Students under Route C are required to attend classes or other formal instruction during the six terms of the course, beginning from the date announced by the Degree Committee. Conditions for pursuing course.

5. The Board of Graduate Studies, after considering a recommendation by the Degree Committee concerned, may allow a candidate for the M.Phil. Degree, on account of illness or other sufficient cause, to intermit his or her course of study. This period of intermission shall not count for any purpose of these regulations except as provided in Regulation 7 of the general regulations for admission as a Graduate Student. Dispensation.

6. Details of each candidate's examination entry and subsequent corrections thereof shall be submitted by the candidate to the Secretary of the Degree Committee concerned, and by the latter to the Secretary of the Board of Graduate Studies, who shall transmit them to the Registrary, in accordance with the timetables set out in the Schedule appended to the regulations. Candidate's examination entry.

7. Each candidate who is required to submit a thesis under the special regulations for the subject concerned shall submit two copies of the thesis in accordance with detailed arrangements approved by the Board, so as to arrive by a date which shall be determined by the Degree Committee, and which shall, for Route A, be not later than the last day of August in the academical year of the course and, for Routes B and C, the last day of August in the second academical year of the course, provided that a candidate may be permitted to submit her or his thesis at such later date as may be determined by the Degree Committee. Submission of thesis.

8. In submitting a thesis a candidate shall state, generally in a preface and specifically in notes or in a bibliography, the sources from which information has been derived, the extent to which use has been made of the work of others, and the portions of the thesis which are claimed as original. A thesis shall not be accepted if it is substantially the same as one that the candidate has submitted or is concurrently submitting, for any other degree, diploma, or similar qualification at any university or similar institution, but a thesis which the candidate has submitted or is concurrently submitting for some other purpose may be accepted. In submitting a thesis the candidate shall declare for what purpose, if any, other than for the M.Phil. Degree, the whole or part of it has already been or is concurrently being submitted. The thesis, apart from quotations, shall be written in English. In special circumstances the Degree Committee concerned may allow a candidate to submit only one copy of the thesis. The Examiners and the Degree Committee may take into consideration any memoir or work published by the candidate which is submitted with the thesis.

9. Every Supervisor shall send to the Secretary of the Board of Graduate Studies reports on the work of each candidate under his or her charge, in accordance with the provisions of Regulation 8 of the general regulations for admission as a Graduate Student. Supervisor's reports.

10. The Degree Committee concerned shall appoint such number of Examiners and Assessors as they shall deem sufficient to conduct the examination for the M.Phil. and to report on the performance of a candidate to the Degree Committee. The Assessors shall undertake such duties as the Degree Committee may decide. Examiners and Assessors.

[1] Exceptionally, and subject to the special permission of the Board of Graduate Studies, a candidate under Route A may be admitted from the beginning of either the Lent Term or the Easter Term if the Board are satisfied that the approved course of study for the subject concerned can be provided from that date.

(*a*) There shall be at least one External Examiner appointed for each examination. Except in the cases of examinations which consist solely of the examination of a thesis, at least one External Examiner shall be appointed as a Moderating External Examiner, who shall have responsibilities extending across a significant part of the examination in question.

(*b*) Where the scheme of examination includes written papers, the Degree Committee shall appoint a Senior Examiner; not later than the end of the Michaelmas Term the Secretary of the Degree Committee shall communicate to the Registrary the name of the Senior Examiner and the names of the Examiners and Assessors for those papers.

(*c*) Where the scheme of examination includes or comprises a thesis, each candidate's thesis shall be referred to two Examiners each of whom shall make an independent report thereon. The special regulations for the examination may provide for an oral examination on the thesis and, if so specified, on the other parts of the examination. When the oral examination relates to the thesis both Examiners of the thesis shall be among the Examiners present at the oral examination. The Degree Committee in exceptional circumstances may permit the Examiners to conduct the oral examination by video-conference or other remote means. The Examiners participating in the oral examination shall sign a joint certificate of the result, including any marks assigned thereto, of that examination. If the Examiners do not agree in their recommendation, or if for any other reason the Degree Committee need a further opinion or opinions on the merit of the work submitted, the Degree Committee may appoint additional Examiners, provided that not more than one additional Examiner may be appointed without the leave of the Board of Graduate Studies. Each additional Examiner so appointed shall make an independent report to the Degree Committee.

Approval for degree.

11. If the Degree Committee, at a meeting held to consider the reports of the Examiners, approve the candidate's performance as of the requisite standard for the M.Phil. Degree and are of the opinion that the degree should be conferred, the Degree Committee shall communicate their resolution to the candidate and to the Secretary of the Board of Graduate Studies who shall publish a notice of the candidate's approval for the award of the degree of Master of Philosophy, specifying the subject of the examination and the route of candidature.

Failure.

12. If the Degree Committee, after consideration of a candidate's marks and the reports of the Examiners in the prescribed examination, are of the opinion that the candidate's work is not of the requisite standard for the degree, the Degree Committee shall communicate their resolution to the candidate and to the Secretary of the Board of Graduate Studies. After such a resolution has been made the student concerned shall not be eligible to take the examination for the degree again.

Expenses of Examiners.

13. Payment of travelling expenses and a subsistence allowance may be claimed by Examiners in accordance with Regulation 11 of the regulations for the Ph.D., M.Sc., and M.Litt. Degrees.

Restriction.

14. A Graduate Student whose course of study for the M.Phil. Degree has included any term needed for the B.A. Degree and who elects to proceed to the B.A. Degree shall not be entitled to proceed to the M.Phil. Degree.

SCHEDULE

In accordance with Regulation 6, details of each candidate's examinations entry shall be as set out in the following time table:

Route A candidates

Entries to be submitted	*Details of written papers etc.*	*Corrections*	*Title of thesis etc.*
By candidates to Secretaries of Degree Committees	By end of Full Michaelmas Term		By division of Lent Term
By Secretaries of Degree Committees to Board of Graduate Studies	By end of Michaelmas Term	By end of third week of Full Lent Term	By end of Lent Term
By Board of Graduate Studies to Registrary	By end of first week of Full Lent Term	By division of Lent Term	

Lists of candidates for each examination shall be circulated by the Registrary to Colleges as follows:

List of entries:	By the end of the second week of Full Lent Term.
Final list of entries:	Not less than four weeks before the beginning of the examination concerned.

Route B candidates

Entries to be submitted	*Details of written examinations*	*Corrections*	*Title of thesis*
By candidates to Secretaries of Degree Committees	By end of Full Michaelmas Term of the year in which the examination is to be held	By end of second week of Full Lent Term of the year in which the examination is to be held	By end of Full Michaelmas Term of the second year of study
By Secretaries of Degree Committees to Board of Graduate Studies	By end of Michaelmas Term of the year in which the examination is to be held	By end of third week of Full Lent Term of the year in which the examination is to be held	By end of Michaelmas Term of the second year of study
By Board of Graduate Studies to Registrary	By end of first week of Full Lent Term of the year in which the examination is to be held	By division of Lent Term of the year in which the examination is to be held	

Lists of candidates for each examination shall be circulated by the Registrary to Colleges as follows:

List of entries:	By the end of the second week of Full Lent Term of the year in which the examination is to be held.
Final list of entries:	Not less than four weeks before the beginning of the written examination.

Route C candidates

Entries to be submitted	*Details of written papers etc.*	*Corrections*	*Title of thesis etc.*
By candidates to Secretaries of Degree Committees	By end of Full Michaelmas Term in first year of study		By division of Easter Term of first year of study
By Secretaries of Degree Committees to Board of Graduate Studies	By end of Michaelmas Term in first year of study	By end of third week of Full Lent Term in first year of study	By end of Easter Term in first year of study
By Board of Graduate Studies to Registrary	By end of first week of Lent Term in first year of study	By division of Lent Term in first year of study	

Lists of candidates for each examination shall be circulated by the Registrary to Colleges as follows:

List of entries:	By the end of the second week of Full Lent Term in the first year of study.
Final list of entries:	Not less than four weeks before the beginning of the examination concerned.

SPECIAL REGULATIONS

ADVANCED CHEMICAL ENGINEERING

1. The scheme of examination for the one-year course of study in Advanced Chemical Engineering for the degree of Master of Philosophy shall consist of:

(*a*) at least ten modules selected from a list of mandatory and optional modules published by the Degree Committee for the Faculty of Engineering not later than the end of the Easter Term of the academical year preceding that in which the examination is to be held, provided that the Degree Committee shall have power to give notice of additional optional modules not later than the end of the Michaelmas Term;

(*b*) a thesis of not more than 10,000 words in length, on a topic approved by the Degree Committee.

2. In publishing the list of modules and additional modules the Degree Committee shall announce the form of examination for each module, which shall be either a written paper, or one or more essays or other exercises, or a combination of these, and shall specify the duration of any written paper and the limit to be placed on the length of any essay or other exercise. A candidate may not offer a module that he or she has taken in any other University examination.

3. The examination may include, at the discretion of the Examiners, an oral examination on the work submitted by the candidate under Regulation 1, and on the general field of knowledge within which such work falls.

Advanced Computer Science

Amended by Notice (Reporter, *2013–14, p. 727*)

[**1.** The scheme of examination for the one-year course of study in Advanced Computer Science for the degree of Master of Philosophy shall consist, at the choice of the candidate, of *either* Option A *or* Option B as follows:

Option A

At least twelve modules selected from a list of mandatory and optional modules published by the Degree Committee for the Faculty of Computer Science and Technology.

Option B

(*a*) At least six modules selected from a list of mandatory and optional modules published by the Degree Committee for the Faculty of Computer Science and Technology;

and

(*b*) a thesis of not more than 15,000 words in length, on a subject approved by the Degree Committee.

2. The list of modules shall be published by the Degree Committee not later than the end of the Easter Term of the academical year preceding that in which the examination is to be held, provided that the Degree Committee shall have power to give notice of additional optional modules not later than the end of the Michaelmas Term. In publishing the list of modules and additional modules, the Degree Committee shall announce the form of examination for each module, which shall be either a written paper, or course-work, or equivalent alternative exercises approved by the Degree Committee, or a combination of these. A candidate may not offer a module that he or she has taken in any other University examination.

3. The examination may include, at the discretion of the Examiners, an oral examination on the work submitted by the candidate under Regulation 1, and on the general field of knowledge within which such work falls.][1]

⟨**1.** The scheme of examination for the one-year course of study in Advanced Computer Science for the degree of Master of Philosophy is as follows:

(*a*) at least five modules selected from a list published by the Degree Committee for the Faculty of Computer Science and Technology;

(*b*) a thesis of not more than 15,000 words in length, on a subject approved by the Degree Committee;

(*c*) course-work prescribed by the Degree Committee (which may include written work, group work, and class participation).

2. The list of modules shall be published by the Degree Committee not later than the end of the Easter Term of the academical year preceding that in which the examination is to be held, provided that the Degree Committee shall have power to give notice of additional optional modules not later than the end of the Michaelmas Term. In publishing the list of modules and additional modules, the Degree Committee shall announce the form of examination for each module, which shall be either a written paper, or course-work, or equivalent alternative exercises approved by the Degree Committee, or a combination of these. A candidate may not offer a module that he or she has taken in any other University examination.

3. The examination may include, at the discretion of the Examiners, an oral examination on the work submitted by the candidate under Regulation 1, and on the general field of knowledge within which such work falls.⟩[1]

African Studies

Amended by Notice (Reporter, *2013–14, p. 404*)

1. The scheme of examination for the one-year course of study in African Studies for the degree of Master of Philosophy shall consist of:

(*a*) an essay, either thematic or bibliographical, of not more than 5,000 words, on a topic approved by the Degree Committee for the Faculty of Human, Social, and Political Science, which is related to the topic of the candidate's thesis to be submitted under (*b*) below;

[1] The regulations in angular brackets will replace the regulations in square brackets with effect from 1 October 2015.

(*b*) a thesis of between 15,000 and 20,000 words including tables, footnotes, and appendices, but excluding bibliography, on a topic approved by the Degree Committee;

(*c*) two essays, each of not more than 5,000 words and on a topic chosen from a list of topics prescribed or approved by the Degree Committee;

(*d*) a certificate of proficiency awarded by the University of Cambridge Language Centre in Swahili or another language that has been approved by the Degree Committee, or a certificate of attendance awarded by the University of Cambridge Language Centre for training in an African language that has been approved by the Degree Committee.

The Degree Committee shall give notice of the topics specified under (*c*) above not later than the division of Lent Term each year.

2. The examination may include, at the discretion of the Examiners, an oral examination on the thesis and on the general field of knowledge within which it falls, and on the other work submitted by the candidate under Regulation 1.

AMERICAN HISTORY[1]

Notice (Reporter, *2013–14, p. 778*)

1. The scheme of examination for the one-year course of study in American History for the degree of Master of Philosophy shall consist of:

(*a*) a thesis of not less than 15,000 words and not more than 20,000 words in length, including notes and appendices, but excluding bibliography, on a topic approved by the Degree Committee for the Faculty of History;

(*b*) one essay of not more than 4,000 words in length, on a topic chosen by the candidate from a list of topics approved by the Degree Committee and falling within the following fields covered by the core course: Readings in American History and Historiography

(*c*) two essays, of not more than 4,000 words in length, on topics approved by the Degree Committee and falling within the fields covered by the following courses:

1. Politics and society in twentieth-century America
2. The history of immigration, ethnicity, and nationality in the United States
3. War and society in the United States since 1917
4. Atlantic worlds, *c.* 1500–1800

A candidate's choice of essay topic shall be associated with their course selections.

The Degree Committee shall publish the topics under Regulation 1(*b*) and (*c*) no later than the end of Easter Term in the academical year preceding the examination.

2. At the discretion of the Examiners the examination may include an oral examination on the thesis and on the general field of knowledge within which it falls.

AMERICAN LITERATURE

1. The scheme of examination for the one-year course of study in American Literature for the degree of Master of Philosophy shall consist of:

(*a*) such bibliographical, textual, critical, or methodological exercises as the Degree Committee for the Faculty of English shall from time to time determine;

(*b*) two essays, each of not less than 4,000 and not more than 5,000 words in length, on a topic approved by the Degree Committee;

(*c*) a thesis, of not less than 12,000 words and not more than 15,000 words in length (including footnotes and appendices, but excluding bibliography), on a subject approved by the Degree Committee.

2. The examination may include, at the discretion of the Examiners, an oral examination on the thesis and on the general field of knowledge within which it falls; such an oral examination may include questions relating to the other work submitted by the candidate under (*a*) and (*b*) above.

[1] This course will be available with effect from 1 October 2015.

Anglo-Saxon, Norse, and Celtic

1. The scheme of examination for the one-year course of study in Anglo-Saxon, Norse, and Celtic for the degree of Master of Philosophy shall consist of:

(*a*) such bibliographical, textual, or methodological exercises as the Degree Committee for the Faculty of English shall from time to time determine;

(*b*) two written exercises in scholarly skill, one of which may be an essay not exceeding 4,000 words in length, on topics approved or prescribed by the Degree Committee;

(*c*) a thesis, of not less than 10,000 words and not more than 15,000 words in length (including tables, footnotes, and appendices, but excluding bibliography), on a subject approved by the Degree Committee.

2. The examination shall include an oral examination on the thesis and on the general field of knowledge within which it falls, and, at the discretion of the Examiners, on the work submitted by the candidate under Regulation 1(*a*) and (*b*) above; save that the Examiners may, at their discretion, waive the requirement for an oral examination.

Applied Biological Anthropology

1. The scheme of examination for the one-year course of study in Applied Biological Anthropology for the degree of Master of Philosophy shall consist of:

(i) a thesis of not more than 20,000 words in length, excluding tables, appendices, and references, on a subject approved by the Degree Committee for the Faculty of Human, Social, and Political Science;

(ii) a quantitative exercise on statistical analysis and interpretation;

(iii) two essays each of not more than 2,500 words in length excluding tables and references based upon material from the core courses;

(iv) two written assignments (either two essays or one essay and one laboratory report) based upon material from the option courses.

2. At the discretion of the Examiners, the examination may include an oral examination on the thesis, the general field of knowledge within which it falls, and on the other work submitted as part of the examination.

Archaeological Research

1. The scheme of examination for the one-year course of study in Archaeological Research for the degree of Master of Philosophy shall consist of:

(*a*) a thesis of not more than 25,000 words in length, including footnotes, but excluding appendices and bibliography, on a topic approved by the Degree Committee for the Faculty of Human, Social, and Political Science;

(*b*) the presentation of a seminar on the topic of the candidate's thesis research and a written report of the presentation;

(*c*) one essay or project of not more than 6,000 words in length, on a subject or subjects relating to archaeological research design chosen by the candidate in consultation with her or his supervisor.

2. The examination may include, at the discretion of the Examiners, an oral examination on the thesis and on the general field of knowledge within which it falls, and on the other work submitted as part of the examination.

Archaeology

1. The one-year course of study in Archaeology for the degree of Master of Philosophy shall consist, at the choice of the candidate, of one of the following options:

Option A.	Archaeological Heritage and Museums
Option B.	Archaeological Science
Option C.	Archaeology
Option D.	Archaeology of the Americas
Option E.	Egyptian Archaeology
Option F.	European Prehistory
Option G.	Medieval Archaeology
Option H.	Mesopotamian Archaeology
Option I.	Palaeolithic and Mesolithic Archaeology
Option J.	South Asian Archaeology

provided that the Degree Committee for the Faculty of Human, Social, and Political Science shall have power to announce that a particular option is not available in any one year

2. The scheme of examination for each option shall be as follows:

(*a*) a thesis of not more than 15,000 words in length, including footnotes, but excluding appendices and bibliography, on a topic approved by the Degree Committee;

(*b*) the presentation of a seminar on the topic of the candidate's thesis research and a written report of the presentation;

(*c*) three modules selected from a list of mandatory and optional modules published by the Degree Committee.

3. In publishing the list of modules, the Degree Committee shall announce for each option which modules are mandatory, and the form of examination for each module, which shall be either a written paper, or course-work, or a combination of these, and shall specify the duration of any written paper and the limit to be placed on the length of any essay or other exercise.

4. The examination may include, at the discretion of the Examiners, an oral examination on the thesis and on the general field of knowledge within which it falls, and on the other work submitted as part of the examination.

Architecture

The scheme of examination for the one-year course of study in Architecture for the degree of Master of Philosophy shall consist of a thesis, of not less than 20,000 words and not more than 30,000 words in length, exclusive of tables, footnotes, bibliography, and appendices, on a subject approved by the Degree Committee for the Faculty of Architecture and History of Art. The examination shall include an oral examination on the thesis and on the general field of knowledge within which it falls.

Architecture and Urban Design

Amended by Notice (Reporter, *2013–14, p. 728*)

1. Candidates for the two-year course of study in Architecture and Urban Design for the degree of Master of Philosophy shall be required to undertake a placement of nine months' duration in an architectural practice or a similar alternative arrangement approved by the Degree Committee for the Faculty of Architecture and History of Art.

2. The scheme of examination shall consist of:

(*a*) a design thesis, consisting of a written dissertation and a design project on a topic approved by the Degree Committee for the Faculty of Architecture and History of Art. The written dissertation shall be of not more than 15,000 words in length, including footnotes/endnotes but excluding bibliography, acknowledgements, table of contents, list of illustrations, and appendices;

(*b*) four essays or other exercises, each of between 3,000 and 5,000 words, on topics specified by the Degree Committee;

(*c*) a logbook of a case study carried out during the placement.

3. The examination may, at the discretion of the Examiners, include an oral examination on the design thesis or on the general field of knowledge within which it falls.

Architecture and Urban Studies

Amended by Notice (Reporter, *2013–14, p. 728*)

1. The scheme of examination for the one-year course of study in Architecture and Urban Studies for the degree of Master of Philosophy shall consist of:

(*a*) a thesis, of not more than 20,000 words in length, excluding appendices and bibliography, on a topic approved by the Degree Committee for the Faculty of Architecture and History of Art;

(*b*) three essays or other exercises, each of between 3,000 and 5,000 words, on topics specified by the Degree Committee.

2. The examination may, at the discretion of the Examiners, include an oral examination on the thesis or on the general field of knowledge within which it falls.

Asian and Middle Eastern Studies

Amended by Notice (Reporter, *2013–14, p. 729*)

[**1.** The scheme of examination for the one-year course of study in Asian and Middle Eastern Studies for the degree of Master of Philosophy shall consist of:

(*a*) *either* (i) three written papers on subjects approved by the Degree Committee for the Faculty of Asian and Middle Eastern Studies, which shall fall within one of the fields specified in the Schedule to these regulations; provided that, with the approval of the Degree Committee, a candidate may offer, in place of one or more of those papers, the same number of essays, each of not more than 5,000 words, or equivalent alternative exercises approved by the Degree Committee;

or (ii) subject to the approval of the Degree Committee, two essays, each of not more than 7,500 words;

(*b*) a thesis of not more than 15,000 words, including footnotes and appendices but excluding bibliography, on a subject approved by the Degree Committee.

The papers to be set under sub-paragraph (*a*) above shall be specified by the Degree Committee not later than the end of the first quarter of the Michaelmas Term each year.

2. In place of the examination prescribed in Regulation 1, a candidate may, by special permission of the Degree Committee, granted after considering his or her experience, qualifications, and proposed subject, offer a thesis of not more than 25,000 words in length, including footnotes and appendices but excluding bibliography, on a subject approved by the Degree Committee.

3. The examination shall include an oral examination on the thesis and on the general field of knowledge within which it falls; save that, in the case of a candidate who takes the examination prescribed under Regulation 1, the Examiners may, at their discretion, waive the requirement for an oral examination.

SCHEDULE

Chinese Studies
East Asian Studies
Hebrew Studies
Japanese Studies
Middle Eastern and Islamic Studies
Sanskrit and South Asian Studies][1]

⟨The scheme of examination for the one-year course of study in Asian and Middle Eastern Studies for the degree of Master of Philosophy shall consist of:

(*a*) three written papers on subjects approved by the Degree Committee for the Faculty of Asian and Middle Eastern Studies, which shall fall within one of the pathways specified at the end of this regulation: provided that, with the approval of the Degree Committee, a candidate may offer, in place of one or more of those papers, the same number of essays, each of not more than 5,000 words, or equivalent alternative exercises approved by the Degree Committee. The papers to be set shall be specified by the Degree Committee not later than the end of the first quarter of the Michaelmas Term each year;

(*b*) a thesis of not more than 15,000 words, including footnotes and appendices but excluding bibliography, on a subject approved by the Degree Committee;

(*c*) an oral examination on the thesis and on the general field of knowledge within which it falls, but at the Degree Committee's discretion the requirement for an oral examination may be waived.

PATHWAYS

Arabic Studies
Chinese Studies
East Asian Studies
Hebrew Studies
Middle Eastern and Islamic Studies⟩[1]

[1] The regulations in angular brackets will replace the regulations in square brackets with effect from 1 October 2015.

Asian and Middle Eastern Studies (Research)[1]

Notice (*Reporter*, *2013–14, p. 729*)

The scheme of examination for the one-year course of study in Asian and Middle Eastern Studies (Research) for the degree of Master of Philosophy shall consist of a thesis of not more than 25,000 words in length, including footnotes and appendices but excluding bibliography, on a subject approved by the Degree Committee for the Faculty of Asian and Middle Eastern Studies falling within the pathways specified at the end of this regulation. The examination shall include an oral examination on the thesis and on the general field of knowledge within which it falls.

PATHWAYS

Arabic Studies	Hebrew Studies
Aramaic Studies	Japanese Studies
Chinese Studies	Middle Eastern and Islamic Studies
East Asian Studies	South Asian Studies

Assyriology

1. The scheme of examination for the one-year course of study in Assyriology for the degree of Master of Philosophy shall consist of the following:

(*a*) a thesis of not more than 15,000 words in length, including footnotes, but excluding appendices and bibliography, on a topic approved by the Degree Committee for the Faculty of Human, Social, and Political Science;

(*b*) the presentation of a seminar on the topic of the candidate's thesis research and a written report of the presentation;

(*c*) three modules selected from a list of mandatory and optional modules published by the Degree Committee.

2. In publishing the list of modules, the Degree Committee shall announce which modules are mandatory, and the form of examination for each module, which shall be either a written paper, or course-work or a combination of these, and shall specify the duration of any written paper and the limit to be placed on the length of any essay or other exercise.

3. The examination may include, at the discretion of the Examiners, an oral examination on the thesis and on the general field of knowledge within which it falls, and on the other work submitted as part of the examination.

Astronomy

1. The scheme of examination for the one-year course of study in Astronomy for the degree of Master of Philosophy shall consist of a thesis of not more than 15,000 words in length, exclusive of tables, footnotes, bibliography, and appendices, on a subject approved by the Degree Committee for the Faculty of Physics and Chemistry.

2. The examination shall include an oral examination on the thesis and on the general field of knowledge within which it falls. The thesis shall provide evidence to satisfy the Examiners that the candidate can design and carry out investigations, assess and interpret the results obtained, and place the work in the wider perspective of the subject.

Biological Anthropological Science

The scheme of examination for the one-year course of study in Biological Anthropological Science for the degree of Master of Philosophy shall consist of a thesis, of not more than 35,000 words in length, exclusive of tables, footnotes, bibliography, and appendices, on a subject approved by the Degree Committee for the Faculty of Human, Social, and Political Science. The examination shall include an oral examination on the thesis and on the general field of knowledge within which it falls. The thesis

[1] This course will be available with effect from 1 October 2015.

shall provide evidence to satisfy the Examiners that a candidate can design and carry out investigations, assess and interpret the results obtained, and place the work in the wider perspectives of the subject.

Biological Science

The scheme of examination for the one-year full-time or two-year part-time course of study in Biological Science for the degree of Master of Philosophy shall consist of a thesis, of not more than 20,000 words in length, exclusive of tables, footnotes, bibliography, and appendices, on a subject approved by the Degree Committee for the Faculty of Biology. The examination shall include an oral examination on the thesis and on the general field of knowledge within which it falls. The thesis shall provide evidence to satisfy the Examiners that a candidate can design and carry out an original investigation, assess and interpret the results obtained, and place the work in the wider perspective of the subject.

Bioscience Enterprise

The scheme of examination for the one-year course of study in Bioscience Enterprise for the degree of Master of Philosophy shall be as follows:

1. The Degree Committee for the Faculty of Engineering shall publish, not later than the end of the Easter Term each year, a list of not more than twenty mandatory modules in Bioscience Enterprise for the examination to be held in the following academical year. In publishing the list of modules the Degree Committee shall announce the form of examination for each module, which shall be either an essay or course-work, or a combination of these.

2. The examination shall consist of:

(*a*) a thesis of not more than 10,000 words in length, on a topic at the interface of bioscience and business enterprise approved by the Degree Committee, and based on work carried out by the candidate in a relevant commercial environment at one or more institutions approved by the Degree Committee. With the permission of the Examiners the internship may occasionally be replaced by a business-focused research project conducted within the University;

(*b*) no more than ten essays, each of not more than 4,000 words in length, covering the fields of science, ethics, law, and policy, and the interface of bioscience and business as specified by the Degree Committee, provided that, in place of one of these essays a candidate may submit a critical appraisal;

(*c*) course-work prescribed by the Degree Committee (which may include written work, group work, and class participation). All Bioscience Enterprise modules, components, and lectures are mandatory.

3. At the discretion of the Examiners, the examination may include an oral examination on the thesis or other work submitted by the candidate under Regulation 2 and on the general field of knowledge within which they fall.

Chemical Engineering and Biotechnology

The scheme of examination for the one-year course of study in Chemical Engineering and Biotechnology for the degree of Master of Philosophy shall consist of a thesis, of not more than 15,000 words in length, exclusive of tables, footnotes, bibliography, and appendices, on a subject approved by the Degree Committee for the Faculty of Engineering. The examination shall include an oral examination on the thesis and on the general field of knowledge within which it falls. The thesis shall provide evidence to satisfy the Examiners that a candidate can design and carry out investigations, assess and interpret the results obtained, and place the work in the wider perspectives of the subject.

Chemistry

The scheme of examination for the one-year course of study in Chemistry for the degree of Master of Philosophy shall consist of a thesis, of not more than 15,000 words in length, exclusive of tables, footnotes, bibliography, and appendices, on a subject approved by the Degree Committee for the Faculty of Physics and Chemistry. The examination shall include an oral examination on the thesis and on the general field of knowledge within which it falls. The thesis shall provide evidence to satisfy the Examiners that the candidate can design and carry out investigations, assess and interpret the results obtained, and place the work in the wider perspective of the subject.

CLASSICS

Amended by Notice (Reporter, *2013–14, p. 730*)

1. The scheme of examination for the one-year course of study in Classics for the degree of Master of Philosophy shall consist of:

(*a*) a thesis of not less than 8,000 words and not more than 12,000 words in length, including footnotes and appendices but excluding bibliography, on a topic approved by the Degree Committee for the Faculty of Classics;

and

(*b*) two pieces of submitted work, each of which may be, subject to the approval of the Degree Committee, *either* an essay of about 4,000 words *or* an exercise of comparable substance, each on a topic approved by the Degree Committee and falling within the same general area as the candidate's thesis or otherwise suitably related to it. The Degree Committee may require a candidate to offer instead of one of the essays a language examination consisting of an exercise in alternative Greek or Latin translation in one of the following written papers taken from Part IA of the Classical Tripos:

Paper 2. Alternative Greek language and texts
Paper 4. Alternative Latin language and texts;

and

(*c*) one further essay of circa 4,000 words on a topic approved by the Degree Committee. The marks for this essay shall be taken into consideration only if it has been judged to be at least of High Pass level and the candidate's other marks are borderline.

2. The examination shall include an oral examination on the thesis and on the general field of knowledge within which it falls and, at the discretion of the Examiners, on the essays or other exercises submitted by the candidate; save that the Examiners may, at their discretion, waive the requirement for an oral examination.

3. Attendance at, and participation in, relevant seminars is required.

CLINICAL SCIENCE

Amended by Notice (Reporter, *2013–14, p. 465*)

1. The scheme of examination for the one-year full-time or two-year part-time course of study in Clinical Science for the degree of Master of Philosophy shall consist of:

(*a*) a thesis not exceeding 15,000 words in length, including footnotes but excluding tables, appendices, and bibliography, on a subject approved by the Degree Committee for the Faculties of Clinical Medicine and Veterinary Medicine;

(*b*) two written examinations which may cover all core subjects prescribed in the syllabus.

2. Each candidate shall pursue research training in one of the themes approved from time to time by the General Board on the recommendation of the Degree Committee.[1]

3. The examination may include, at the discretion of the Examiners, an oral examination on the thesis and on the general field of knowledge within which it falls, and on the other work submitted by the candidate under Regulation 1.

COMPUTATIONAL BIOLOGY

The scheme of examination for the one-year course of study in Computational Biology for the degree of Master of Philosophy shall be as follows:

1. The Degree Committee for the Faculty of Mathematics shall publish, not later than the end of the Easter Term each year, a list of not more than nine modules for the examination to be held in the academical year next following. In publishing the list the Degree Committee shall announce the method of examination of each module which may include a written examination, a long essay, shorter essays,

[1] The following themes have been approved: Rare Diseases; Translational Medicine and Therapeutics.

project work, or a combination of these; they shall specify the limits to be placed on the length of any essays and project work.

2. Each candidate shall offer:

(*a*) the written examinations or other exercises specified for all the modules published under Regulation 1;

(*b*) a report of not more than 18,000 words in length and an oral presentation based on a laboratory project carried out by the candidate in one or more institutions approved by the Degree Committee.

3. The examination may include, at the discretion of the Examiners, an oral examination on the work submitted by the candidate under Regulation 2, and on the general field of knowledge within which such work falls.

Conservation Leadership

The scheme of examination for the one-year course of study in Conservation Leadership for the degree of Master of Philosophy shall consist of:

(*a*) four submitted essays, each of 4,000 words in length, or alternative exercises on a subject chosen by the candidate from a list of subjects announced by the Degree Committee for the Faculty of Earth Sciences and Geography, which shall be concerned with topics in conservation leadership;

(*b*) a placement report of not more than 10,000 words in length, on a topic approved by the Degree Committee, and based on work carried out by the candidate in one or more institutions approved by the Degree Committee;

(*c*) course-work prescribed by the Degree Committee (which may include written work, group work and class participation).

Conservation of Natural Science Materials

1. The scheme of examination for the one-year course of study in Conservation of Natural Science Materials for the degree of Master of Philosophy shall consist of:

(*a*) three written papers, as follows:

Paper 1. Preservation and museology.
Paper 2. Materials analysis and decay of materials.
Paper 3. Theory and practice of conservation.

(*b*) a thesis, of not more than 15,000 words in length, including appendices and bibliography, on a subject approved by the Degree Committee for the Faculty of Earth Sciences and Geography, which shall be submitted at the end of the period of practical experience prescribed in Regulation 3.

2. Each candidate shall undertake practical work during the course, as prescribed by the Degree Committee, and shall present for the inspection of the Examiners a record of such practical work.

3. After the completion of the course each candidate shall undertake practical conservation work during a period of twelve months spent in a museum housing collections of natural science materials, the nature of the practical work being determined by the Degree Committee. A candidate shall present for the inspection of the Examiners a record of this practical work bearing, as an indication of the good faith of the record, the signature of the museum curator under whose supervision it was performed. A statement concerning the candidate's period of experience, certified by the Head of the Department of Earth Sciences, shall be submitted to the Examiners.

4. The examination shall include an oral examination on the thesis and on the general field of knowledge within which it falls.

Criminological Research

1. Subject to the provisions of Regulation 2 below, the scheme of examination for the one-year course of study in Criminological Research for the degree of Master of Philosophy shall consist of:

(*a*) three essays, each of not more than 3,000 words, including notes and appendices, on topics chosen by the candidate from lists of topics announced by the Examiners, provided that one such essay shall be on a topic chosen by the candidate from among the topics announced by the Examiners as relating to the core course in Criminology;

and

(*b*) one essay in criminological methods of not more than 3,000 words, including notes and appendices, chosen by the candidate from a list announced by the Examiners relating to the course on Criminological Research Methods;

and

(*c*) one methodological essay of not more than 4,000 words and one work-book of assessment of materials on research methods on topics announced by the Examiners relating to the course on Research Methods;

and

(*d*) a thesis of not more than 18,000 words, including notes and appendices, on a criminological topic approved by the Degree Committee for the Faculty of Law.

At the discretion of the Examiners the examination may include an oral examination on the thesis and on the general field of knowledge within which it falls; such an oral examination may include questions relating to one or more of the other pieces of work submitted by the candidate under (*a*), (*b*), and (*c*) above.

2. In place of the scheme of examination prescribed in Regulation 1 above, a candidate may, by special permission of the Degree Committee for the Faculty of Law, granted after considering the candidate's experience and special qualifications and the proposed topic of his or her thesis, offer the following scheme of examination:

(*a*) one essay in criminological methods of not more than 3,000 words, including notes and appendices, chosen by the candidate from a list announced by the Examiners relating to the course on Criminological Research Methods;

and

(*b*) one methodological essay of not more than 4,000 words and one work-book of assessment of materials on research methods on topics announced by the Examiners relating to the course on Research Methods;

and

(*c*) a thesis of not more than 35,000 words, including notes and appendices, on a criminological topic approved by the Degree Committee for the Faculty of Law.

The examination shall include an oral examination on the thesis and on the general field of knowledge within which it falls; such an oral examination may include questions relating to one or more of the other pieces of work submitted by the candidate under (*a*) and (*b*) above.

Criminology

The scheme of examination for the one-year course of study in Criminology for the degree of Master of Philosophy shall consist of:

(*a*) four essays, each of not more than 3,000 words, including notes and appendices, on topics chosen by the candidate from lists of topics announced by the Examiners, provided that one such essay shall be on a topic chosen by the candidate from among the topics announced by the Examiners as relating to the core course in Criminology;

and

(*b*) a methodological essay of not more than 3,000 words, including notes and appendices, chosen by the candidate from a list announced by the Examiners relating to the course on Criminological Research Methods;

and

(*c*) a thesis of not more than 18,000 words, including notes and appendices, on a criminological topic approved by the Degree Committee for the Faculty of Law.

At the discretion of the Examiners the examination may include an oral examination on the thesis and on the general field of knowledge within which it falls; such an oral examination may include questions relating to one or more of the other pieces of work submitted by the candidate under (*a*) and (*b*) above.

Development Studies

The scheme of examination for the one-year course of study in Development Studies for the degree of Master of Philosophy shall be as follows:

1. For the purpose of the general regulations for the degree, the Degree Committee concerned with this examination shall be the Degree Committee for the Faculty of Human, Social, and Political Science.

2. The Development Studies Committee shall publish, not later than the end of the Easter Term each year, a list of subjects for the examination to be held in the academical year next following. The list shall be divided into two groups, Groups 1 and 2. Group 1 shall comprise the following subjects:

1. Development economics.
2. Institutions and development.
3. Sociology and politics of development.
4. Globalization, business, and development.

Group 2 shall contain not more than a total of fifteen other subjects made up of either full or half-subjects which, with the approval of the General Board and of the Degree Committee responsible for the other examination concerned, may include subjects taken from any of the examinations for the degree specified in the Schedule to these regulations. The Development Studies Committee shall have power to give notice of additional subjects not later than the end of the Michaelmas Term, provided that the total number of subjects in Group 2 in any year shall not exceed fifteen full subjects. In publishing the list and any additions to it, the Committee shall announce whether a subject is a full or half-subject and the form of examination for that subject.

The Development Studies Committee shall have power to withdraw any subject of Group 2 upon notice given in the *Reporter*, not later than the end of the Michaelmas Term; the Secretary of the Committee shall notify candidates of the withdrawal of any subject for which they have entered.

3. The examination shall consist of:

(*a*) two subjects chosen by the candidate, with the approval of the Development Studies Committee, from Group 1;

and

(*b*) *either* one full subject or two half-subjects chosen by the candidate, with the approval of the Development Studies Committee, from Group 2,

or a dissertation of not more than 12,000 words, including footnotes and appendices, on a topic approved by the Development Studies Committee;

and

(*c*) one further full subject or two further half-subjects chosen by the candidate, with the approval of the Development Studies Committee, which may be taken *either* from Group 1 *or* from Group 2.

4. The examination shall include an oral examination on the work submitted by the candidate under Regulation 3, and on the general field of knowledge within which it falls; save that the Examiners may, at their discretion, waive the requirement for an oral examination.

SCHEDULE

Subjects from the following examinations:

Economic and Social History
Economics
Environment, Society, and Development
Environmental Policy
Finance
Financial Research
Latin-American Studies
Management
Modern Society and Global Transformations
Planning, Growth, and Regeneration
Politics
Social Anthropology

DEVELOPMENTAL BIOLOGY

Amended by Notice (Reporter, *2013–14, p. 730*)

1. The scheme of examination for the one-year course of study in Developmental Biology for the degree of Master of Philosophy shall consist of:

(*a*) one essay, not exceeding 4,000 words in length, on a topic approved by the Degree Committee for the Faculty of Biology;

(*b*) a critical appraisal, not exceeding 8,000 words in length, including tables, figure legends, and appendices, but excluding bibliography, of a research project approved or prescribed by the Degree Committee;

(*c*) a report on each research placement, not exceeding 7,000 words in length, including figure legends, but excluding words in tables and bibliography.

2. Each candidate shall undertake practical work as prescribed by the Degree Committee and shall present for the inspection of the Examiners records of such practical work.

3. The examination shall include an oral examination on the work submitted by the candidate under Regulation 1 above and on the general field of knowledge within which such work falls.

Early Modern History

Amended by Notice (Reporter, *2013–14, p. 730*)

1. The scheme of examination for the one-year course of study in Early Modern History for the degree of Master of Philosophy shall consist of:

(*a*) a thesis of not less than 20,000 words and not more than 25,000 words in length, including notes and appendices, but excluding bibliography, on a topic approved by the Degree Committee for the Faculty of History;

(*b*) course-work, as prescribed by the Degree Committee;

(*c*) written exercises on three subjects chosen from the following list:

1. Palaeography
2. Language training
3. Visual and material culture
4. The book
5. Absolutism, monarchism, and state formation in early modern Britain and Europe
6. Space, place, and landscape in early modern history
7. Approaches to the long eighteenth century (this subject is shared with Modern European History)
8. Poverty, disease, and medicine in Britain, 1500–1800.

2. At the discretion of the Examiners the examination may include an oral examination on the thesis and on the general field of knowledge within which it falls.

Earth Sciences

The scheme of examination for the one-year course of study in Earth Sciences for the degree of Master of Philosophy shall consist of a thesis, of not more than 15,000 words in length, exclusive of tables, footnotes, bibliography, and appendices, on a subject approved by the Degree Committee for the Faculty of Earth Sciences and Geography. The examination shall include an oral examination on the thesis and on the general field of knowledge within which it falls. The thesis shall provide evidence to satisfy the Examiners that the candidate can design and carry out investigations, assess and interpret the results obtained, and place the work in the wider perspective of the subject. The student will also be required to take taught courses as directed.

Economic and Social History

1. The scheme of examination for the one-year course of study in Economic and Social History for the degree of Master of Philosophy shall consist of:

(*a*) an essay of not more than 3,000 words on a topic approved by the Degree Committee for the Faculty of History which falls within the field of the central concepts and problems of economic and social history and theory;

(*b*) course-work, as prescribed by the Degree Committee, on subjects falling within the fields of survey methods, statistical methods, and ethnographic methods for economic and social historians;

(*c*) two written exercises, to be undertaken under conditions specified by the Degree Committee, on each of two subjects on topics chosen from a list of options announced by the Degree Committee;

(*d*) a methodological introduction, of not more than 4,000 words, to the thesis which is to be submitted by the candidate under (*e*) below;

(*e*) a thesis, of not more than 20,000 words, on a subject approved by the Degree Committee in Economic and/or Social History.

2. At the discretion of the Examiners the examination may include an oral examination on the thesis and on the general field of knowledge within which it falls.

Economic Research

1. The scheme of examination for the one-year course of study in Economic Research for the degree of Master of Philosophy shall consist of:

(*a*) six compulsory and two additional modules, selected from a list of core and optional modules published by the Degree Committee for the Faculty of Economics, which shall each be examined by a written paper of two hours' duration;

and

(*b*) a thesis of not more than 10,000 words in length, on a subject approved by the Degree Committee.

2. The list of modules shall be published by the Degree Committee not later than the end of the Easter Term of the academical year preceding that in which the examination is to be held, provided that the Degree Committee shall have power to give notice of additional optional modules not later than the end of the Michaelmas Term. A candidate may not offer a module that he or she has taken in any other University examination.

3. The examination may include, at the discretion of the Examiners, an oral and/or written examination on the work submitted by the candidate under Regulation 1, and on the general field of knowledge within which such work falls.

Economics

1. The scheme of examination for the one-year course of study in Economics for the degree of Master of Philosophy shall consist of:

(*a*) three compulsory and five additional modules, selected from a list of core and optional modules published by the Degree Committee for the Faculty of Economics, which shall each be examined by a written paper of two hours' duration;

and

(*b*) a thesis of not more than 10,000 words in length, on a subject approved by the Degree Committee.

2. The list of modules shall be published by the Degree Committee not later than the end of the Easter Term of the academical year preceding that in which the examination is to be held, provided that the Degree Committee shall have power to give notice of additional optional modules not later than the end of the Michaelmas Term. A candidate may not offer a module that he or she has taken in any other University examination.

3. The examination may include, at the discretion of the Examiners, an oral examination on the work submitted by the candidate under Regulation 1, and on the general field of knowledge within which such work falls.

Education

The scheme of examination for the one-year course of study in Education for the degree of Master of Philosophy shall consist, at the choice of the candidate, of *either* Option A *or* Option B, as follows:

Option A

The examination shall consist of a thesis, of not more than 30,000 words in length, excluding footnotes, tables, appendices, and bibliography, on a subject approved by the Degree Committee for the Faculty of Education. The examination shall include an oral examination on the thesis and on the general field of knowledge within which it falls.

Option B

The examination shall consist of:

(*a*) a thesis of not more than 20,000 words in length, excluding footnotes, tables, appendices, and bibliography, on a subject approved by the Degree Committee for the Faculty of Education;

and

(*b*) two essays, each of at least 6,000 and not more than 6,500 words in length, on topics specified or approved by the Degree Committee.

The examination shall include an oral examination on the thesis and the essays and on the general field of knowledge within which they fall; save that the Examiners may, at their discretion, waive the requirement for an oral examination.

Egyptology

1. The scheme of examination for the one-year course of study in Egyptology for the degree of Master of Philosophy shall consist of the following:

(*a*) a thesis of not more than 15,000 words in length, including footnotes, but excluding appendices and bibliography, on a topic approved by the Degree Committee for the Faculty of Human, Social, and Political Science;

(*b*) the presentation of a seminar on the topic of the candidate's thesis research and a written report of the presentation;

(*c*) three modules selected from a list of mandatory and optional modules published by the Degree Committee.

2. In publishing the list of modules, the Degree Committee shall announce which modules are mandatory, and the form of examination for each module, which shall be either a written paper, or course-work or a combination of these, and shall specify the duration of any written paper and the limit to be placed on the length of any essay or other exercise.

3. The examination may include, at the discretion of the Examiners, an oral examination on the thesis and on the general field of knowledge within which it falls, and on the other work submitted as part of the examination.

Energy Technologies

The scheme of examination for the one-year course of study in Energy Technologies for the degree of Master of Philosophy shall consist of:

either (*a*) twelve modules selected from a set of mandatory and optional modules;

and

(*b*) a thesis, of not more than 10,000 words in length, including footnotes, appendices, and bibliography, on a topic approved by the Degree Committee for the Faculty of Engineering;

or (*c*) ten modules selected from a set of mandatory and optional modules;

and

(*d*) a thesis, of not more than 20,000 words in length, including footnotes, appendices, and bibliography, on a topic approved by the Degree Committee.

Each module shall be examined either by a written paper of ninety minutes or by course-work, or by a combination of the two. The assessment of the thesis shall include an oral presentation of the project work on which the thesis is based.

The examination may include, at the discretion of the Examiners, an oral examination on the work submitted by the candidate under (*a*)–(*d*) above, and on the general field of the knowledge within which such work falls.

Engineering

The scheme of examination for the one-year course of study in Engineering for the degree of Master of Philosophy shall consist of a thesis, of not more than 15,000 words in length, exclusive of tables, footnotes, bibliography, and appendices, on a subject approved by the Degree Committee for the Faculty of Engineering. The examination shall include an oral examination on the thesis and on the general field of knowledge within which it falls. The thesis shall provide evidence to satisfy the Examiners that a candidate can design and carry out investigations, assess and interpret the results obtained, and place the work in the wider perspective of the subject.

Engineering for Sustainable Development

The scheme of examination for the course of study in Engineering for Sustainable Development for the degree of Master of Philosophy shall consist of:

(*a*) at least eight modules selected from a set of mandatory and optional modules; each module shall be examined *either* by a written paper of ninety minutes *or* by course-work, *or* by a combination of the two;

and

(*b*) not less than two and not more than eight exercises of a form and on topics approved by the Degree Committee for the Faculty of Engineering;

and

(*c*) a thesis, of not more than 15,000 words in length, including footnotes, appendices, and bibliography, on a topic approved by the Degree Committee. Its assessment shall include an oral presentation of the project work on which the thesis is based.

The examination may include, at the discretion of the Examiners, an oral examination on the work submitted by the candidate under (*a*), (*b*), and (*c*) above, and on the general field of the knowledge within which such work falls.

English Studies

1. The scheme of examination for the one-year course of study in English Studies for the degree of Master of Philosophy shall consist of:

(*a*) such bibliographical, textual, critical, or methodological exercises as the Degree Committee for the Faculty of English shall from time to time determine;

(*b*) two essays, each of not less than 4,000 and not more than 5,000 words in length, on topics approved by the Degree Committee;

(*c*) a thesis, of not less than 12,000 words and not more than 15,000 words in length (including footnotes and appendices, but excluding bibliography), on a subject approved by the Degree Committee.

2. The examination may include, at the discretion of the Examiners, an oral examination on the thesis and on the general field of knowledge within which it falls; such an oral examination may include questions relating to the other work submitted by the candidate under (*a*) and (*b*) above.

Environment, Society, and Development[1]

1. The scheme of examination for the one-year course of study in Environment, Society, and Development for the degree of Master of Philosophy shall consist of:

(*a*) three essays or other exercises, each of not more than 4,000 words in length, on subjects chosen by the candidate from a list of subjects announced by the Degree Committee for the Faculty of Earth Sciences and Geography;

(*b*) two book reviews, each not exceeding 2,000 words in length;

(*c*) an oral presentation;

(*d*) a thesis, of not more than 10,000 words in length, excluding footnotes, tables, appendices, and bibliography, on a subject approved by the Degree Committee.

2. At the discretion of the Examiners the examination may include an oral examination on any or all of the components of the examination specified in Regulation 1, and on the general field of knowledge within which they fall.

Environmental Policy

The scheme of examination for the one-year course of study in Environmental Policy for the degree of Master of Philosophy shall be as follows:

1. The Degree Committee for the Department of Land Economy shall publish, not later than the end of the Easter Term each year, a list of subjects for the examination to be held in the academical year next following. The list shall include a core methodology subject, four other core subjects, and no fewer than four optional subjects (of which the Degree Committee may specify that a candidate shall offer one or more within any group of subjects). In publishing the list the Degree Committee shall announce whether each subject is to be examined by a written paper, by an essay or project, or by a combination of these; they shall specify the limits to be placed on the length of any essays or projects.

2. Except as provided by Regulations 3 and 4 each candidate shall offer:

(*a*) the core methodology subject;

[1] This course is suspended for 2014–15 and 2015–16.

(*b*) the four other subjects specified by the Degree Committee as core subjects;
(*c*) three optional subjects;
(*d*) a thesis, of not more than 12,000 words in length, including diagrams, footnotes, tables, and appendices, but excluding bibliography, on a topic approved by the Degree Committee.

3. In place of the core methodology subject a candidate may, by special permission of the Degree Committee, granted after considering the candidate's experience and special qualifications, offer another optional subject chosen from the list of subjects published under Regulation 1.

4. In place of any two subjects offered under Regulation 2(*b*) or (*c*), a candidate may offer studio work relating to a topic approved by the Degree Committee, and undertaken in accordance with a scheme approved by the Degree Committee.

5. At the discretion of the Examiners, the examination may include an oral examination on the work submitted by the candidate under Regulation 2 and on the general field of knowledge within which it falls.

Environmental Science[1]

1. The scheme of examination for the one-year course of study in Environmental Science for the degree of Master of Philosophy shall consist of:
(*a*) four essays or other exercises, each of not more than 4,000 words in length, on a subject chosen by the candidate from a list of subjects announced by the Degree Committee for the Faculty of Earth Sciences and Geography, which shall be concerned with research methods in environmental science; in publishing the list of subjects the Degree Committee shall announce the form of the examination for each subject, which shall be one or more essays or other exercises, or a combination of these;
(*b*) a thesis, of not more than 15,000 words in length, excluding footnotes, tables, appendices, and bibliography, on a subject approved by the Degree Committee.

2. At the discretion of the Examiners the examination may include an oral examination on any or all of the components of the examination specified in Regulation 1, and on the general field of knowledge within which they fall.

Epidemiology

1. The scheme of examination for the one-year course of study in Epidemiology for the degree of Master of Philosophy shall consist of:
(*a*) a thesis not exceeding 20,000 words in length, including footnotes, but excluding tables, appendices, and bibliography, on a subject approved by the Degree Committee for the Faculties of Clinical Medicine and Veterinary Medicine;
(*b*) two written papers, each of which may cover all the areas of study prescribed in the syllabus;
(*c*) two essays, each not exceeding 3,000 words in length, on subjects approved by the Degree Committee.

2. The examination shall include an oral examination on the thesis and on the general field of knowledge within which it falls, and, at the discretion of the Examiners, on any other component of the examination submitted by the candidate; save that the Examiners may, at their discretion, waive the requirement for an oral examination.

European Literature and Culture[2]

Amended by Notice (Reporter, *2013–14, p. 731*)

1. The scheme of examination for the one-year course of study in European Literature and Culture[2] for the degree of Master of Philosophy shall consist of:
(*a*) a thesis, of not more than 15,000 words in length, including footnotes and appendices, but excluding bibliography, on a subject approved by the Degree Committee for the Faculty of Modern and Medieval Languages;

[1] This course is suspended for 2014–15 and 2015–16.
[2] This course will be retitled Comparative European Literatures and Cultures with effect from 1 October 2015.

and

(*b*) three essays, each of not more than 4,500 words, on topics falling within areas of study to be prescribed by the Degree Committee. The Degree Committee shall publish, not later than the end of the Easter Term each year, a list of areas of study for the examination to be held in the academical year next following.

2. The examination shall include an oral examination on the thesis and on the general field of knowledge within which it falls; save that the Examiners may, at their discretion, waive the requirement for an oral examination.

FINANCE

1. The scheme of examination for the one-year course of study in Finance for the degree of Master of Philosophy shall consist of nine modules selected from a list of mandatory and optional modules published by the Degree Committee for the Faculty of Business and Management not later than the end of the Michaelmas Term next preceding the examination.

2. In publishing the list of modules the Degree Committee shall announce the form of the examination for each module, which shall be either a written paper, or one or more essays or other exercises, or a combination of these, and shall specify the duration of any written paper and the limit to be placed on the length of any essay or other exercise.

3. In place of the examination prescribed for three of the modules specified in Regulation 1, the Degree Committee may permit a particular candidate to offer a dissertation of not more than 12,000 words in length, on a topic approved by the Degree Committee.

4. The examination may include, at the discretion of the Examiners, an oral examination on the work specified in Regulations 1 and 3 and on the general field of knowledge within which it falls.

FINANCE AND ECONOMICS

1. The scheme of examination for the one-year course of study in Finance and Economics for the degree of Master of Philosophy shall consist of:

(*a*) six compulsory and two additional modules, selected from a list of core and optional modules published by the Degree Committee for the Faculty of Economics, which shall each be examined by a written paper of two hours' duration;

and

(*b*) a thesis of not more than 10,000 words in length, on a subject approved by the Degree Committee.

2. The list of modules shall be published by the Degree Committee not later than the end of the Easter Term of the academical year preceding that in which the examination is to be held, provided that the Degree Committee shall have power to give notice of additional optional modules not later than the end of the Michaelmas Term. A candidate may not offer a module that he or she has taken in any other University examination.

3. The examination may include, at the discretion of the Examiners, an oral and/or written examination on the work submitted by the candidate under Regulation 1, and on the general field of knowledge within which such work falls.

FINANCIAL RESEARCH

1. The scheme of examination for the one-year course of study in Financial Research for the degree of Master of Philosophy shall consist of:

(*a*) a thesis of not more than 12,000 words in length, including diagrams and footnotes, but excluding bibliography and appendices, on a subject approved by the Degree Committee for the Faculty of Business and Management;

and

(*b*) six modules selected from a list of mandatory and optional modules published by the Degree Committee not later than the end of the Michaelmas Term next preceding the examination.

2. In publishing the list of modules the Degree Committee shall announce the form of the examination for each module, which shall be either a written paper, or one or more essays or other exercises, or a combination of these, and shall specify the duration of any written paper and the limit to be placed on the length of any essay or other exercise.

3. The examination may include, at the discretion of the Examiners, an oral examination on the work specified in Regulation 1 and on the general field of knowledge within which it falls.

Fluid Flow in Industry and the Environment

1. The scheme of examination for the one-year course of study in Fluid Flow in Industry and the Environment for the degree of Master of Philosophy shall consist of:

(*a*) two written papers, each of three hours' duration, on subjects approved by the Degree Committee for the Faculty of Earth Sciences and Geography;

(*b*) a thesis, not exceeding 15,000 words in length, including tables, figure legends, and appendices, but excluding bibliography, on a research project approved or prescribed by the Degree Committee;

2. The examination may include, at the discretion of the Examiners, an oral examination on the thesis and on the general field of knowledge within which it falls.

Geographical Research

1. The scheme of examination for the one-year course of study in Geographical Research for the degree of Master of Philosophy shall consist of:

(*a*) two essays, each of not more than 4,000 words in length, on subjects of Geographical Research chosen by the candidate, subject to the approval of the Head of the Department of Geography, from a list announced by the Degree Committee for the Faculty of Earth Sciences and Geography;

(*b*) one essay of not more than 4,000 words and one workbook of assessment of materials on research methods on topics announced by the Degree Committee;

(*c*) a thesis of not more than 20,000 words in length, including footnotes, but excluding tables, appendices and bibliography, on a subject approved by the Degree Committee.

2. The examination may include, at the discretion of the Examiners, an oral examination on the thesis and on the general field of knowledge within which it falls.

Geography

Notice (Reporter, *2013–14, p. 253*)

The scheme of examination for the one-year course of study for the degree of Master of Philosophy shall consist of a thesis, of not more than 25,000 words in length, excluding footnotes, tables, diagrams, appendices, and bibliography, on a subject approved by the Degree Committee for the Faculty of Earth Sciences and Geography. The examination shall include an oral examination on the thesis, and on the general field of knowledge within which it falls. The thesis shall provide evidence to satisfy the Examiners that the candidate can design and carry out investigations, assess and interpret results obtained, and place the work in the wider perspective of the subject. The student may be required to take taught courses as directed.

Historical Studies

1. The scheme of examination for the one-year course of study in Historical Studies for the degree of Master of Philosophy shall consist of:

(*a*) an essay, either thematic or bibliographical, of not less than 2,000 words and not more than 5,000 words in length, on a topic approved by the Degree Committee for the Faculty of History which is related to the subject of the candidate's thesis to be submitted under (*b*) below;

and

(*b*) a thesis, of not less than 20,000 words and not more than 30,000 words in length, excluding footnotes and bibliography, on a subject approved by the Degree Committee.

2. The examination shall include an oral examination on the thesis and on the general field of knowledge within which it falls; save that the Examiners may, at their discretion, waive the requirement for an oral examination.

History, Philosophy, and Sociology of Science, Technology, and Medicine

1. The scheme of examination for the one-year course of study in History, Philosophy, and Sociology of Science, Technology, and Medicine for the degree of Master of Philosophy shall consist of:

(*a*) a thesis, of not more than 15,000 words in length, including footnotes but excluding appendices and bibliography, on a subject approved by the Degree Committee for the Department of History and Philosophy of Science;

and

(*b*) three essays, each of not more than 5,000 words, including footnotes but excluding bibliography, and, except as provided below, each on a subject approved by the Degree Committee which is related to one or more of the following areas:

1. General philosophy of science
2. History of ancient and medieval science, technology, and medicine
3. History of early modern science, technology, and medicine
4. History of modern science, technology, and medicine
5. History, philosophy, and sociology of the life sciences
6. History, philosophy, and sociology of the physical and mathematical sciences
7. History, philosophy, and sociology of the social and psychological sciences
8. History, philosophy, and sociology of medicine
9. Ethics and politics of science
10. History and methodology of history, philosophy, and sociology of science, technology, and medicine

Not more than one essay shall be chosen from any one area, except with the permission of the Degree Committee, who may allow two essays to be offered in one area, or one of the three essays to be offered in an area which is not listed above but is related to History, Philosophy, Sociology of Science, Technology, and Medicine.

2. The examination shall include an oral examination on the thesis and on the general field of knowledge within which it falls; save that the Examiners may, at their discretion, waive the requirement for an oral examination.

History of Art and Architecture

1. The scheme of examination for the one-year course of study in History of Art and Architecture for the degree of Master of Philosophy shall consist of:

(i) a thesis of not more than 15,000 words in length, including footnotes, but excluding appendices and bibliography, on a subject approved by the Degree Committee for the Faculty of Architecture and History of Art;

and

(ii) two essays, each not exceeding 4,000 words in length on topics approved by the Degree Committee;

and

(iii) two presentations, each not exceeding 3,000 words in length, on topics approved by the Degree Committee falling within the following fields:

Architectural history
Text and image

2. At the discretion of the Examiners, the examination may include an oral examination on the thesis and the essays submitted by the candidate and on the general field of knowledge within which they fall.

Human Evolutionary Studies

1. The scheme of examination for the one-year course of study in Human Evolutionary Studies for the degree of Master of Philosophy shall consist of:

(i) a thesis of not more than 20,000 words in length, excluding tables, appendices, and references, on a subject approved by the Degree Committee for the Faculty of Human, Social, and Political Science;

(ii) a quantitative exercise on statistical analysis and interpretation;

(iii) two essays each of not more than 2,500 words in length excluding tables and references based upon material from the core courses;

(iv) two written assignments (either two essays or one essay and one laboratory report) based upon material from the option courses.

2. At the discretion of the Examiners, the examination may include an oral examination on the thesis, the general field of knowledge within which it falls, and on the other work submitted as part of the examination.

Industrial Systems, Manufacturing, and Management

1. The scheme of examination for the one-year course of study in Industrial Systems, Manufacturing, and Management for the degree of Master of Philosophy shall consist of:

(*a*) reports on such course-work undertaken by the candidate as shall be prescribed from time to time by the Degree Committee for the Faculty of Engineering. The reports shall be of such number, and shall be presented in such form and assessed in such manner, as the Degree Committee may determine;

and

(*b*) a thesis of not more than 15,000 words in length including footnotes, appendices, and bibliography, on a subject approved by the Degree Committee.

2. The course-work shall include industrial investigations in one or more institutions approved by the Degree Committee, the nature and duration of the investigations being determined by the Degree Committee.

3. The examination may include, at the discretion of the Examiners, an oral examination on the work submitted under (*a*) above on the general field of industrial systems, manufacture, and management; the examination may also include, at the discretion of the Examiners, an oral examination on the work submitted under (*b*) above.

Innovation, Strategy, and Organization

1. The scheme of examination for the one-year course of study in Innovation, Strategy, and Organization for the degree of Master of Philosophy shall consist of:

(*a*) a thesis of not more than 12,000 words in length, including diagrams and footnotes, but excluding bibliography and appendices, on a subject approved by the Degree Committee for the Faculty of Business and Management;

and

(*b*) six modules selected from a list of mandatory and optional modules published by the Degree Committee not later than the end of the Michaelmas Term next preceding the examination.

2. In publishing the list of modules the Degree Committee shall announce the form of the examination for each module, which shall be either a written paper, or one or more essays or other exercises, or a combination of these, and shall specify the duration of any written paper and the limit to be placed on the length of any essay or other exercise.

3. In place of the examination prescribed for thesis specified in Regulation 1(*a*), the Degree Committee may permit a particular candidate to take three prescribed modules from a list approved by the Degree Committee.

4. The examination may include, at the discretion of the Examiners, an oral examination on work submitted under Regulation 1 and on the general field of knowledge within which it falls.

International Relations and Politics

1. The scheme of examination for the one-year course of study for the degree of Master of Philosophy in International Relations and Politics shall consist of:

(*a*) three examined courses from a list prescribed by the Degree Committee for the Faculty of Human, Social, and Political Science;

(*b*) a thesis of not less than 20,000 words and not more than 25,000 words in length, including tables, footnotes, and appendices, but excluding bibliography, on a subject approved by the Degree Committee;

(*c*) the successful completion of a research methods and thesis writing course.

2. In accordance with the general regulations for the degree of Master of Philosophy and at the discretion of the Examiners, an oral examination may be held in relation to any of the elements enumerated under Regulation 1 above.

3. A candidate who successfully passes at least two examined courses in a field of study that may be designated by the Degree Committee, and who successfully presents a thesis deemed by the Degree Committee to fall within that designated field of study, may apply to have the designation of that field of study awarded for the degree of Master of Philosophy in International Relations and Politics.

Land Economy

The scheme of examination for the one-year course of study in Land Economy for the degree of Master of Philosophy shall consist of a thesis, of not more than 30,000 words[1] in length, including diagrams, footnotes, and appendices, but excluding bibliography, on a subject approved by the Degree Committee for the Department of Land Economy. The examination shall include an oral examination on the thesis, and on the general field of knowledge within which it falls.

Land Economy Research

The scheme of examination for the one-year course of study in Land Economy Research for the degree of Master of Philosophy shall be as follows:

1. The Degree Committee for Land Economy shall publish, not later than the end of the Easter Term each year, a list of modules for the examination to be held in the academical year next following. In publishing the list the Degree Committee shall announce the method of examination of each module which may include a written examination, a long essay, shorter essays, project work, or a combination of these; they shall specify the limits to be placed on the length of any essays and project work.

2. Each candidate shall offer:

(*a*) one essay of not more than 4,000 words and one workbook of assessment of materials on research methods on topics announced by the Degree Committee;

(*b*) two modules chosen by the candidate with the approval of the Degree Committee from the list of modules published under Regulation 1;

(*c*) a thesis of not more than 20,000 words[1] in length, including diagrams, footnotes, and appendices, but excluding bibliography, on a topic approved by the Degree Committee.

3. The examination shall include an oral examination on the work submitted by the candidate under Regulation 2 and on the more general field of knowledge within which it falls; save that the Examiners may, at their discretion, waive the requirements for an oral examination.

Latin-American Studies

1. The scheme of examination for the one-year full-time or two-year part-time course of study in Latin-American Studies for the degree of Master of Philosophy shall, subject to the provisions of Regulation 2 below, consist of:

(*a*) a thesis, not exceeding 15,000 words in length, including footnotes, tables, and appendices, but excluding bibliography, on a subject approved by the Degree Committee for the Faculty of Human, Social, and Political Science;

and

(*b*) three essays, each not exceeding 5,000 words in length, including footnotes, but excluding tables, appendices, and bibliography, on subjects chosen by the candidate, subject to the approval of the Degree Committee, from the following list:

1. Latin-American history
2. Anthropology of Latin America
3. Topics in Latin-American culture
4. Economic issues in contemporary Latin America
5. Sociology and politics of Latin America
6. Latin-American film and visual arts

[1] One A4 page consisting largely of statistics or symbols shall be regarded as the equivalent of 250 words.

7. Core course in Latin-American studies
8. A subject or subjects in Latin-American studies specified from time to time by the Degree Committee

2. In place of the examination prescribed under Regulation 1 above, a candidate may, by special permission of the Degree Committee, granted after considering the candidate's experience, special qualifications, and proposed topic, offer a thesis of not more than 30,000 words in length, including footnotes, tables, appendices, and bibliography, on a topic approved by the Degree Committee.

3. The examination shall include an oral examination on the thesis submitted and on the general field of knowledge within which it falls; save that the Examiners may, at their discretion, waive the requirement for an oral examination. In the case of a candidate taking the examination under Regulation 1, such an oral examination may include questions relating to the essays offered by the candidate.

Machine Learning, Speech, and Language Technology[1]

Notice (Reporter, *2013–14, p. 666*)

1. The scheme of examination for the one-year course of study in Machine Learning, Speech, and Language Technology for the degree of Master of Philosophy shall consist of:

(*a*) at least ten modules selected from a list of mandatory and optional modules published by the Degree Committee for the Faculty of Engineering not later than the end of the Easter Term preceding the commencement of the course of study;

and

(*b*) a thesis, of not more than 20,000 words in length, including footnotes, appendices, and bibliography, on a topic approved by the Degree Committee for the Faculty of Engineering. Its assessment shall include an oral presentation of the project work on which the thesis is based.

2. The Degree Committee shall announce how modules will be examined not later than the division of Lent Term preceding the examination. Examinations shall be through written papers, or one or more pieces of course-work or other exercises, or a combination of these. The Degree Committee shall specify the duration of any written paper and the limit to be placed on the length of any piece of course-work or other exercise.

3. The examination may include, at the discretion of the Examiners, an oral examination on the work submitted by the candidate under (*a*) and (*b*) above and on the general field of knowledge within which such work falls.

Management

1. The scheme of examination for the one-year course of study in Management for the degree of Master of Philosophy shall consist of eleven modules selected from a list of mandatory and optional modules published by the Degree Committee for the Faculty of Business and Management not later than the end of the Michaelmas Term next preceding the examination.

2. In publishing the list of modules the Degree Committee shall announce the form of the examination for each module, which shall be either a written paper, or one or more essays or other exercises, or a combination of these, and shall specify the duration of any written paper and the limit to be placed on the length of any essay or other exercise.

3. The examination may include, at the discretion of the Examiners, an oral examination on the work specified under Regulation 1.

Management Science and Operations

1. The scheme of examination for the one-year course of study in Management Science and Operations for the degree of Master of Philosophy shall consist of:

(*a*) a thesis of not more than 12,000 words in length, including diagrams and footnotes, but excluding bibliography and appendices, on a subject approved by the Degree Committee for the Faculty of Business and Management;

and

[1] This course will be available with effect from 1 October 2015.

(*b*) six modules selected from a list of mandatory and optional modules published by the Degree Committee not later than the end of the Michaelmas Term next preceding the examination.

2. In publishing the list of modules the Degree Committee shall announce the form of the examination for each module, which shall be either a written paper, or one or more essays or other exercises, or a combination of these, and shall specify the duration of any written paper and the limit to be placed on the length of any essay or other exercise.

3. In place of the examination prescribed for thesis specified in Regulation 1(*a*), the Degree Committee may permit a particular candidate to take three prescribed modules from a list approved by the Degree Committee.

4. The examination may include, at the discretion of the Examiners, an oral examination on the work submitted under Regulations 1 and 3 and on the general field of knowledge within which it falls.

Materials Science and Metallurgy

1. The scheme of examination for the one-year course of study in Materials Science and Metallurgy for the degree of Master of Philosophy shall consist of a thesis of not more than 15,000 words in length, exclusive of tables, footnotes, bibliography, and appendices, on a subject approved by the Degree Committee for the Faculty of Physics and Chemistry.

2. The examination shall include an oral examination on the thesis and on the general field of knowledge within which it falls. The thesis shall provide evidence to satisfy the Examiners that the candidate can design and carry out investigations, assess and interpret the results obtained, and place the work in the wider perspective of the subject.

Mathematics[1]

Notice (Reporter, *2013–14, p. 666*)

1. The scheme of examination for the one-year course of study for the degree of Master of Philosophy shall consist of a thesis, of a length and form appropriate to the topic, on a subject approved by the Degree Committee not later than the division of the term preceding the one in which the examination is to take place.

2. The examination shall include an oral examination on the thesis and on the general field of knowledge within which it falls. The student may be required to take taught courses as directed and announced by the Degree Committee not later than the Easter Term preceding the commencement of the course of study.

Medical Science

The scheme of examination for the one-year full-time or two-year part-time course of study in Medical Science for the degree of Master of Philosophy shall consist of a thesis, of not more than 20,000 words in length, exclusive of tables, footnotes, bibliography, and appendices, on a subject approved by the Degree Committee for the Faculties of Clinical Medicine and Veterinary Medicine. The examination shall include an oral examination on the thesis and on the general field of knowledge within which it falls. The thesis shall provide evidence to satisfy the Examiners that a candidate can design and carry out an original investigation, assess and interpret the results obtained, and place the work in the wider perspective of the subject.

Medieval and Renaissance Literature

The scheme of examination for the one-year course of study in Medieval and Renaissance Literature for the degree of Master of Philosophy shall consist of:

(*a*) a thesis of between 12,000 and 15,000 words in length, including footnotes and appendices but excluding bibliography, or some equivalent submission, on a subject approved by the Degree

[1] This course will be available with effect from 1 October 2015.

Committee for the Faculty of English, which shall fall within one of the following areas of study:

Medieval literature;
Renaissance literature;
Medieval and Renaissance literature;

and

(*b*) two essays, each of not more than 4,000 words, on topics approved by the Degree Committee;

and

(*c*) one or more written exercises, approved by the Degree Committee, in the field of textual and related studies in either the medieval period or the Renaissance or both.

The examination may include, at the discretion of the Examiners, an oral examination on the thesis or the essays and on the general field of knowledge within which the work submitted falls; such an oral examination may include questions relating to the written papers and to the other exercises submitted by the candidate under (*b*) and (*c*) above.

Medieval History

Amended by Notice (Reporter, *2013–14, p. 731*)

1. The scheme of examination for the one-year course of study in Medieval History for the degree of Master of Philosophy shall consist of:

(*a*) one essay, not exceeding 5,000 words in length, or two essays, each not exceeding 3,000 words in length, as prescribed by the Degree Committee for the Faculty of History, on a topic or topics falling within a field of study chosen by the candidate from the following list:

1. The Carolingian Empire and its neighbours
2. The worlds of medieval Europe *c.* 1000–1400
3. England in the later Middle Ages *c.* 1200–1500
4. The Byzantine Empire: continuity and crisis from Justinian I to Basil II (*c.* 500–1500);

(*b*) one or more exercises in palaeography approved by the Degree Committee, related to the field of study chosen by the candidate under (*a*) above;

(*c*) a bibliography related to the subject of the thesis to be submitted under (*e*) below, containing between seventy-five and one hundred and fifty items;

(*d*) a bibliographical and historiographical essay, between 2,000 and 3,000 words in length, on the subject of the thesis;

(*e*) a thesis, between 20,000 and 25,000 words in length, including tables, footnotes, and appendices, but excluding bibliography, on a subject approved by the Degree Committee.

2. The examination shall include an oral examination on the thesis and on the general field of knowledge within which it falls; save that the Examiners may, at their discretion, waive the requirement for an oral examination.

Micro- and Nanotechnology Enterprise

The scheme of examination for the one-year course of study in Micro- and Nanotechnology Enterprise for the degree of Master of Philosophy shall be as follows:

1. The Degree Committee for the Faculty of Physics and Chemistry shall publish, not later than the end of the Easter Term each year, a list of not more than fifteen mandatory modules in Micro- and Nanotechnology Enterprise for the examination to be held in the following academical year. In publishing the list of modules the Degree Committee shall announce the form of examination for each module, which shall be an exam, an essay, course-work, or a combination of these.

2. The examination shall consist of:

(*a*) two unseen written examination papers, which may cover all core scientific projects prescribed in the syllabus;

(*b*) no more than eight essays, each of not more than 3,000 words in length, covering the fields of science, ethics, law, and policy, and the interface of micro- and nanoscience and business as specified by the Degree Committee;

(*c*) course-work prescribed by the Degree Committee (which may include written work, group work and class participation);

(*d*) a literature survey report of not more than 5,000 words in length on a scientific topic, to be followed by either a major research project in the same field (see (*e*) below), or a business-, ethics-, law-, or policy-related case study, concerning the scientific topic (see (*e*) below);

(*e*) a thesis of not more than 15,000 words in length (including tables, figure legends, and appendices, but excluding bibliography) on a major project, involving (i) in-depth scientific research (following a literature survey in the same scientific field submitted under (*d*) above), or (ii) an in-depth case study concerned with a topic in science, business, ethics, law, or policy (related to the topic covered during the literature survey submitted under (*d*) above), approved by the Degree Committee.

The work submitted under (*d*) and (*e*) shall be on a topic or project, respectively, approved by the Degree Committee.

3. The examination shall include an oral examination on the thesis or other work submitted by the candidate under Regulation 2(*e*) and on the general field of knowledge within which they fall.

MODERN BRITISH HISTORY[1]

Notice (Reporter, *2013–14, p. 779*)

1. The scheme of examination for the one-year course of study in Modern British History for the degree of Master of Philosophy shall consist of:

(*a*) a thesis of not less than 15,000 words and not more than 20,000 words in length, including notes and appendices, but excluding bibliography, on a topic approved by the Degree Committee for the Faculty of History;

(*b*) one essay of not more than 4,000 words in length, on a topic chosen by the candidate from a list of topics approved by the Degree Committee and falling within the following fields covered by the core course:

1. The first industrial nation
2. The language of the social order
3. Liberalism and its limits
4. The impact of empire
5. The rise and fall of 'separate spheres'
6. The intellectuals and the masses
7. Democracy and its limits

(*c*) two essays, of not more than 4,000 words in length, on topics approved by the Degree Committee and falling within the fields covered by the following courses:

1. The long 18th century
2. Cold War Europe and the USA
3. Class and social militancy in the long 20th century
4. History and public policy
5. Options included in the programme from year to year

A candidate's choice of essay topic shall be associated with their course selections.

The Degree Committee shall have power to give notice of any addition or variation to the list of options announced in Regulation 1(*c*) where it is satisfied that no candidate's preparation for the examination will be affected. The Degree Committee for History shall publish the list of topics under Regulation 1(*b*) and (*c*) no later than the end of Easter Term in the academical year preceding the examination.

2. At the discretion of the Examiners the examination may include an oral examination on the thesis and on the general field of knowledge within which it falls.

[1] This course will be available with effect from 1 October 2015.

Modern European History

Amended by Notice (Reporter, *2013–14, p. 731*)

1. The scheme of examination for the one-year course of study in Modern European History for the degree of Master of Philosophy shall consist of:

(*a*) a thesis of not less than 15,000 words and not more than 20,000 words in length, including notes and appendices, but excluding bibliography, on a topic approved by the Degree Committee for the Faculty of History;

(*b*) one essay of not more than 4,000 words in length, on a topic chosen by the candidate from a list of topics specified by the Degree Committee and falling within the following fields covered in the core course:

Controversies in modern European history;

(*c*) two essays, of not more than 4,000 words in length, on topics chosen from the following list

1. Russia and the West in the 18th and 19th centuries
2. Popular politics and barricades in Britain and France
3. Cold War Europe and America
4. Art and politics in interwar Europe
5. Approaches to the long eighteenth century (this topic is shared with Early Modern History).

2. At the discretion of the Examiners the examination may include an oral examination on the thesis and on the general field of knowledge within which it falls.

Modern Society and Global Transformations[1]

Amended by Notice (Reporter, *2013–14, p. 780*)

The scheme of examination for the one-year course of study in Modern Society and Global Transformations for the degree of Master of Philosophy shall be as follows:

1. The Degree Committee for the Faculty of Human, Social, and Political Science shall publish, not later than the end of the Easter Term each year, a list of not less than four and not more than seven subjects in Modern Society and Global Transformations for the examination to be held in the academical year next following.

2. The examination shall consist of:

(*a*) *either* one essay, of not less than 2,500 words and not more than 3,000 words in length,[2] on topics approved by the Degree Committee in the methodology of the social sciences;

or course-work as prescribed by the Degree Committee on subjects falling within the fields of statistical methods, survey methods, and ethnographic research methods;

(*b*) two essays, each of not less than 4,000 words and not more than 5,000 words,[2] on topics approved by the Degree Committee, and each falling within the field of one of the subjects published by the Degree Committee under Regulation 1;

(*c*) a thesis, of not less than 15,000 and not more than 20,000 words,[2] on a subject approved by the Degree Committee.

3. The examination shall include an oral examination on the essays and the thesis and on the general field of knowledge within which they fall; save that the Examiners may, at their discretion, waive the requirement for an oral examination.

Modern South Asian Studies

Amended by Notice (Reporter, *2013–14, p. 780*)

1. The scheme of examination for the one-year course of study in Modern South Asian Studies for the degree of Master of Philosophy shall consist of:

(*a*) a thesis of not less than 15,000 words and not more than 20,000 words in length, including notes and appendices, but excluding bibliography, on a topic approved by the Degree Committee for the Faculty of Human, Social, and Political Science;

(*b*) an essay of not more than 3,000 words on a topic chosen from a list of topics prescribed by the Degree Committee which are related to the core course; *and* a book review of not more than 2,000 words on a book chosen by the candidate within the remit of the core course;

[1] This course will be replaced by the course in Sociology with effect from 1 October 2015 (p. 546).
[2] Including footnotes, tables, and appendices.

(*c*) one further essay of not more than 5,000 words on a topic chosen by the candidate from a list of topics prescribed by the Degree Committee;

(*d*) a written examination of three hours' duration on a South Asian language specified by the Degree Committee *and* an oral examination of one hour's duration in that language.

The Degree Committee shall give notice of the topics specified under (*b*) and (*c*) above not later than the end of Full Michaelmas Term each year.

2. The examination may include, at the discretion of the Examiners, an oral examination on the thesis and on the general field of knowledge within which it falls, and on the essays submitted by the candidate.

Multi-Disciplinary Gender Studies

Amended by Grace 6 of 30 July 2014

1. The scheme of examination for the one-year course of study in Multi-Disciplinary Gender Studies for the degree of Master of Philosophy shall consist of:

(*a*) two essays each of not more than 5,000 words in length, on a subject chosen by the candidate from a list of subjects announced by the Degree Committee for the Faculty of Human, Social, and Political Science, which shall be concerned with research topics in gender studies;

(*b*) a thesis, of not more than 20,000 words in length, excluding footnotes, tables, appendices, and bibliography, on a subject approved by the Degree Committee.

2. At the discretion of the Examiners the examination may include an oral examination on any or all of the components of the examination specified in Regulation 1, and on the general field of knowledge within which they fall.

Music Studies

1. The scheme of examination for the one-year course of study in Music Studies for the degree of Master of Philosophy shall consist of either Option A or Option B or Option C. The Degree Committee for the Faculty of Music shall assign each candidate to a specified option.

2. *Option A – All subjects except Composition and Performance Studies*

(*a*) ten short abstracts of not more than 250 words each and an essay of not more than 3,500 words[1] on issues in musical studies;

and

(*b*) two essays, each of not more than 3,500 words,[1] on subjects specified by the Degree Committee, provided that with the permission of the Degree Committee, a candidate may substitute comparable exercises for either one or both of these essays;

and

(*c*) a thesis of not more than 15,000 words,[1] on a subject approved by the Degree Committee;

provided that with the permission of the Degree Committee a suitably qualified candidate may, in place of 2(*a*) and 2(*c*) above, submit a thesis of not more than 25,000 words[1] on a subject approved by the Degree Committee.

3. *Option B – Composition*

(*a*) ten short abstracts of not more than 250 words each and an essay of not more than 3,500 words[1] on issues in musical studies;

and

(*b*) four compositions in any idiom of the candidate's choice; the compositions should require 30–45 minutes in total to perform. Scores and recordings should be included as appropriate to the nature of the music; the submission should also be accompanied by an explanatory essay of not more than 5,000 words[1] on issues in composition as approved by the Degree Committee;

provided that with the permission of the Degree Committee a suitably qualified candidate may, in place of 3(*a*) and 3(*b*) above, submit

[1] Including tables and footnotes but excluding appendices, bibliography, musical examples, and transcriptions.

(*c*) four compositions in any idiom of the candidate's choice; the compositions should require 45–60 minutes in total to perform. Scores and recordings should be included as appropriate to the nature of the music; the submission should also be accompanied by an explanatory essay of not more than 7,500 words[1] on issues in composition as approved by the Degree Committee.

4. *Option C – Performance Studies*

(*a*) ten short abstracts of not more than 250 words each and an essay of not more than 3,500 words[1] on issues in musical studies;

and

(*b*) two essays of not more than 3,500 words,[1] on subjects specified by the Degree Committee, provided that with the permission of the Degree Committee a candidate may substitute comparable exercises for either one or both of these essays;

and

(*c*) a 15,000-word[1] thesis or a recital taking between 50 and 60 minutes to perform together with an essay on a related topic of not more than 7,500 words;[1]

provided that with the permission of the Degree Committee a suitably qualified candidate may, in place of 4(*a*) and 4(*c*) above, present a recital taking between 50 and 60 minutes to perform and submit an essay on a related topic of not more than 12,500 words.[1]

5. The examination in all Options shall include an oral examination on any aspect of the work submitted or, where applicable, performed; save that the Examiners may, at their discretion, waive the requirement for an oral examination.

NUCLEAR ENERGY

Amended by Notice (Reporter, *2013–14, p. 781*)

1. The scheme of examination for the one-year course of study in Nuclear Energy for the degree of Master of Philosophy shall consist of:

(*a*) ten modules selected from a list of mandatory and optional modules published by the Degree Committee for the Faculty of Engineering not later than the end of the Easter Term of the academical year preceding that in which the examination is to be held;

and

(*b*) an individual research project, on a topic approved by the Degree Committee, comprising

(i) a reading and planning stage, delivering a report of up to 4,000 words and an oral presentation, *and*

(ii) a research and write-up stage, delivering a dissertation of up to 15,000 words and an oral presentation.

Word counts shall include figures, but not the title page, appendices, or bibliography.

2. In publishing the list of modules and additional modules, the Degree Committee shall announce the form of examination for each module, which shall be either a written paper, or one or more pieces of course-work or other exercises, or a combination of these, and shall specify the duration of any written paper and the limit to be placed on the length of any piece of course-work or other exercise. The Degree Committee may announce limitations on the combinations of optional modules allowed. The Degree Committee shall have the power to give notice of additional optional modules not later than the end of the Michaelmas Term of the academical year of the examination.

3. The assessment of the thesis shall include an oral presentation of the project work on which the thesis is based.

4. The examination may include, at the discretion of the Examiners, an oral examination on the thesis and on the general field of knowledge within which it falls.

PHILOSOPHY

1. The scheme of examination for the one-year course of study in Philosophy for the degree of Master of Philosophy shall consist of:

(*a*) a thesis of not more than 15,000 words in length, including footnotes and appendices but excluding bibliography, on a subject approved by the Degree Committee for the Faculty of Philosophy;

[1] Including tables and footnotes but excluding appendices, bibliography, musical examples, and transcriptions.

and

(*b*) three essays, each of between 3,000 and 5,000 words in length, including footnotes, and, except as provided below, each on a subject approved by the Degree Committee which is related to one or more of the following areas of Philosophy (including in each case the history of philosophy):

Metaphysics	Ethics
Philosophy of mind	Aesthetics
Logic	Political and legal philosophy
Philosophy of science	

Not more than two essays shall be chosen from any one area. With the permission of the Degree Committee, one of the three essays may be offered in an area which is not listed above but is related to Philosophy.

2. The examination shall include an oral examination on the thesis and on the general field of knowledge within which it falls, and, at the discretion of the Examiners, on the essays submitted by the candidate; save that the Examiners may, at their discretion, waive the requirement for an oral examination.

Physics

The scheme of examination for the one-year course of study in Physics for the degree of Master of Philosophy shall consist of a thesis of not more than 15,000 words in length, exclusive of tables, footnotes, bibliography, and appendices, on a subject approved by the Degree Committee for the Faculty of Physics and Chemistry. The examination shall include an oral examination on the thesis and on the general field of knowledge within which it falls. The thesis shall provide evidence to satisfy the Examiners that the candidate can design and carry out investigations, assess and interpret the results obtained, and place the work in the wider perspective of the subject.

Planning, Growth, and Regeneration

The scheme of examination for the one-year course of study in Planning, Growth, and Regeneration for the degree of Master of Philosophy shall be as follows:

1. The Degree Committee for the Department of Land Economy shall publish, not later than the end of the Easter Term each year, a list of subjects for the examination to be held in the academical year next following. The list shall include a core methodology subject, four other core subjects, and no fewer than four optional subjects (of which the Degree Committee may specify that a candidate shall offer one or more within any group of subjects). In publishing the list the Degree Committee shall announce whether each subject is to be examined by a written paper, by an essay or project, or by a combination of these; they shall specify the limits to be placed on the length of any essays or projects.

2. Except as provided by Regulations 3 and 4 each candidate shall offer:

(*a*) the core methodology subject;

(*b*) the four other subjects specified by the Degree Committee as core subjects;

(*c*) three optional subjects;

(*d*) a thesis, of not more than 12,000 words in length, including diagrams, footnotes, tables, and appendices, but excluding bibliography, on a topic approved by the Degree Committee.

3. In place of the core methodology subject a candidate may, by special permission of the Degree Committee, granted after considering the candidate's experience and special qualifications, offer another optional subject chosen from the list of subjects published under Regulation 1.

4. In place of any two subjects offered under Regulation 2(*b*) or (*c*), a candidate may offer studio work relating to a topic approved by the Degree Committee, and undertaken in accordance with a scheme approved by the Degree Committee.

5. At the discretion of the Examiners, the examination may include an oral examination on the work submitted by the candidate under Regulation 2 and on the general field of knowledge within which it falls.

Polar Studies

The scheme of examination for the one-year course of study in Polar Studies for the degree of Master of Philosophy shall consist of:

(*a*) a thesis, of not more than 20,000 words in length, excluding footnotes, tables, appendices, and list of references, on a subject approved by the Degree Committee for the Faculty of Earth Sciences and Geography, and to be submitted at a date to be determined by them;

and

(*b*) three essays, each of about 4,000 words in length, on topics chosen by the candidate with the approval of the Degree Committee.

The examination may include, at the discretion of the Examiners, an oral examination on the thesis and the essays and on the general field of knowledge within which they fall.

Political Thought and Intellectual History

1. The scheme of examination for the one-year course of study in Political Thought and Intellectual History for the degree of Master of Philosophy shall consist of:

(*a*) a thesis of between 15,000 and 20,000 words in length, excluding footnotes, tables, appendices, and bibliography, on a topic approved by the Degree Committee for the Faculty of History;

and

(*b*) two essays, each of not more than 6,000 words, on topics approved by the Sub-committee for the M.Phil. course in Political Thought and Intellectual History, which fall within the following fields:

1. History of political thought.
2. Political theory.
3. Intellectual history.

2. The examination shall include an oral examination on the essays and the thesis and on the general field of knowledge within which they fall; save that the Examiners may, at their discretion, waive the requirement for an oral examination.

Primary Care Research

1. The scheme of examination for the course of study in Primary Care Research for the degree of Master of Philosophy shall consist of:

(*a*) a thesis not exceeding 20,000 words in length, including footnotes, but excluding tables, appendices, and bibliography, on a subject approved by the Degree Committee for the Faculties of Clinical Medicine and Veterinary Medicine;

(*b*) two written papers, each of which may cover all areas of study prescribed in the syllabus;

(*c*) two essays, each not exceeding 3,000 words in length, on subjects approved by the Degree Committee.

2. The examination may include, at the discretion of the Examiners, an oral examination on the thesis and on the general knowledge within which it falls, and on the other work submitted by the candidate.

Public Health

1. The scheme of examination for the one-year course of study in Public Health for the degree of Master of Philosophy shall consist of:

(*a*) a thesis, not exceeding 20,000 words in length, including footnotes, but excluding tables, appendices, and bibliography, on a subject approved by the Joint Degree Committee for the Faculties of Clinical Medicine and Veterinary Medicine;

(*b*) two written papers of three hours in length which may cover all the areas of study prescribed in the syllabus;

(*c*) two essays, each not exceeding 3,000 words in length, on subjects approved by the Degree Committee.

2. The examination shall include an oral examination on the thesis and on the general field of knowledge within which it falls, and, at the discretion of the Examiners, on any other component of the examination submitted by the candidate; save that the Examiners may, at their discretion, waive the requirement for an oral examination.

Public Policy

Amended by Notice (Reporter, *2013–14, p. 731*)

1. The scheme of examination for the one-year course of study in Public Policy for the degree of Master of Philosophy shall consist of:

(*a*) three case studies on topics announced by the Degree Committee for the Faculty of Human, Social, and Political Science; each case study shall be examined by an essay of no more than 3,000 words in length or by any other method considered by the Degree Committee to be equivalent. The methods of assessment shall be published by the Division of the Easter term preceding the examination;

and

(*b*) seven modules (up to two of which may be divided into half modules) to be prescribed by the Degree Committee, each module to be assessed by a method prescribed by that Committee. The modules and methods of assessment will be published by the Division of the Easter term preceding the examination;

and

(*c*) two essays of no more than 3,000 words on additional topics, to be agreed by the Degree Committee, and a report of no more than 5,000 words related to work placement.

2. The examination shall include an oral examination on the work submitted by the candidate under Regulation 1 above, save that the examiners, may at their discretion, waive the requirement for an oral examination

Real Estate Finance

The scheme of examination for the one-year course of study in Real Estate Finance for the degree of Master of Philosophy shall be as follows:

1. The Degree Committee for the Department of Land Economy shall publish, not later than the end of the Easter Term each year, a list of subjects for the examination to be held in the academical year next following. The list shall include a core methodology subject, four other core subjects, and no fewer than four optional subjects (of which the Degree Committee may specify that a candidate shall offer one or more within any group of subjects). In publishing the list the Degree Committee shall announce whether each subject is to be examined by a written paper, by an essay or project, or by a combination of these; they shall specify the limits to be placed on the length of any essays or projects.

2. Except as provided by Regulations 3 and 4 each candidate shall offer:

(*a*) the core methodology subject;

(*b*) the four other subjects specified by the Degree Committee as core subjects;

(*c*) three optional subjects;

(*d*) a thesis, of not more than 12,000 words in length, including diagrams, footnotes, tables, and appendices, but excluding bibliography, on a topic approved by the Degree Committee.

3. In place of the core methodology subject a candidate may, by special permission of the Degree Committee, granted after considering the candidate's experience and special qualifications, offer another optional subject chosen from the list of subjects published under Regulation 1.

4. In place of any two subjects offered under Regulation 2(*b*) or (*c*), a candidate may offer studio work relating to a topic approved by the Degree Committee, and undertaken in accordance with a scheme approved by the Degree Committee.

5. At the discretion of the Examiners, the examination may include an oral examination on the work submitted by the candidate under Regulation 2 and on the general field of knowledge within which it falls.

Scientific Computing

Amended by Notice (Reporter, *2013–14, p. 252*)

The scheme of examination for the one-year course of study in Scientific Computing for the degree of Master of Philosophy shall be as follows:

1. The Degree Committee for the Faculty of Physics and Chemistry shall publish, not later than the end of the Easter Term of the academical year preceding that in which the examination is to be held, a list of modules in 'Scientific Computing', provided that the Degree Committee shall have power to give notice of additional elective modules not later than the start of the Michaelmas Term. The list will include core courses in scientific computing and may include elective courses from Master's-level courses offered by the Departments of the Schools of the Physical Sciences, Technology, and Biological Sciences. In publishing the list of modules, the Degree Committee shall announce the form of examination for each module.

2. The examination shall consist of:

(*a*) a thesis of not more than 15,000 words in length (including tables, figure legends, and appendices, but excluding bibliography) on a major project, involving in-depth original scientific research and a literature survey of the topic. The topic of the project shall be approved by the Degree Committee;

(*b*) two written assignments on two of the core-course options in scientific computing. The topic of the assignments shall be approved by the Degree Committee;

(*c*) written examination papers. The form of the examination of these papers shall be dictated by the regulations of the donor Department.

3. The examination shall include an oral examination of the thesis or other work submitted by the candidate under Regulation 2(*b*), and on the general field of knowledge within which they fall.

Screen Media and Cultures

1. The scheme of examination for the one-year course of study in Screen Media and Cultures for the degree of Master of Philosophy shall consist of:

(*a*) a thesis, of not more than 15,000 words in length, including footnotes and appendices, but excluding bibliography, on a subject approved by the Degree Committee for the Faculty of Modern and Medieval Languages;

and

(*b*) three essays, each of not more than 4,500 words, on subjects either prescribed or approved by the Degree Committee.

2. The examination shall include an oral examination on the thesis and on the general field of knowledge within which it falls; save that the Examiners may, at their discretion, waive the requirement for an oral examination.

Social and Developmental Psychology

Amended by Notice (Reporter, *2013–14, p. 449*)

1. The scheme of examination for the one-year course of study in Social and Developmental Psychology for the degree of Master of Philosophy shall consist of:

(*a*) two essays, one of not more than 5,000 words and one of not more than 4,000 words in length, on topics falling within areas of study to be prescribed by the Degree Committee for the Faculty of Biology;

(*b*) an exercise of not more than 3,000 words in length, consisting of a critical appraisal of a research paper specified by the Degree Committee;

(*c*) course-work as prescribed by the Degree Committee on subjects falling within the fields of statistical methods, survey methods, and ethnographic research methods;

(*d*) a thesis, of not more than 15,000 words in length, on a subject approved by the Degree Committee.

The Degree Committee shall publish, not later than the end of the Easter Term in the year preceding the examination, a list of topics for the essays to be submitted under (*a*) above.

2. The examination shall include an oral examination on the thesis and on the general field of knowledge within which it falls and, at the discretion of the Examiners, on the other exercises submitted by the candidate; save that the Examiners may, at their discretion, waive the requirement for an oral examination.

Social Anthropology

1. The scheme of examination for the one-year course of study in Social Anthropology for the degree of Master of Philosophy shall consist of:

(*a*) a thesis, of not more than 12,000 words in length, excluding footnotes, tables, appendices, and bibliography, on a subject approved by the Degree Committee for the Faculty of Human, Social, and Political Science, which shall not fall within the field of any paper or essay offered by the candidate;

(*b*) an essay, of not more than 6,000 words in length, on a subject chosen by the candidate from a list of subjects published by the Degree Committee, which shall not fall within the field of the candidate's thesis;

(*c*) subject to the provisions of Regulation 2, two written papers, to be chosen by the candidate, subject to the approval of the Degree Committee, from among the following papers:

Paper 1. The scope of social anthropology I: production and reproduction.
Paper 2. The scope of social anthropology II: systems of power and knowledge.
Paper 3. Social anthropology and the professional process.

2. In place of any one of the papers chosen from among Papers 1–3 which a candidate would otherwise be required to offer under Regulation 1 a candidate may, by special permission of the Degree Committee, granted after considering the candidate's experience and special qualifications, offer an essay of not more than 6,000 words in length, exclusive of footnotes, appendices, and bibliography, on a subject approved by the Degree Committee.

3. The examination may, at the discretion of the Examiners, include an oral examination on the thesis and on the essay or essays offered by the candidate, and on the general field of knowledge within which they fall.

Sociology[1]

Notice (Reporter, *2013–14, p. 780*)

1. Each candidate shall, at the commencement of study, select one of the pathways specified at the end of these regulations.

2. The Degree Committee for the Faculty of Human, Social, and Political Science shall have power to withdraw any of the pathways prescribed at the end of these regulations upon Notice given in the *Reporter* not later than the end of the Full Easter Term next but one preceding the examination in question.

3. The scheme of examination for the one-year course of study in Sociology for the degree of Master of Philosophy shall consist of:

(*a*) *either* (i) one essay, of not less than 2,500 words and not more than 3,000 words,[2] on topics approved by the Degree Committee, which fall within the pathway chosen in accordance with Regulation 1;

or (ii) course-work as prescribed by the Degree Committee on subjects falling within the fields of statistical methods, survey methods, and ethnographic research methods;

(*b*) two essays, each of not less than 4,000 words and not more than 5,000 words,[2] on topics approved by the Degree Committee, with at least one essay falling within the pathway chosen in accordance with Regulation 1;

(*c*) a thesis, of not less than 15,000 and not more than 20,000 words,[2] on a subject approved by the Degree Committee, falling within the field of the pathway chosen in accordance with Regulation 1.

The topics approved by the Degree Committee under Regulation 3(*a*) and 3(*b*) shall be published not later than the Easter Term in the academical year preceding the examination.

[1] This course replaces the course in Modern Society and Global Transformations and will be available with effect from 1 October 2015.

[2] Including footnotes, tables, and appendices.

4. The examination shall include an oral examination on the essays and the thesis and on the general field of knowledge within which they fall; save that the Examiners may, at their discretion, waive the requirement for an oral examination.

PATHWAYS

Modern society and global transformations
Political and economic sociology
The sociology of media and culture
The sociology of reproduction[1]

Technology Policy

1. The scheme of examination for the one-year course of study in Technology Policy for the degree of Master of Philosophy shall consist, at the choice of the candidate, of *either* Option A *or* Option B as follows:

Option A

The examination shall consist of:

(*a*) at least nine modules selected from a list of mandatory and optional modules published by the Degree Committee for the Faculty of Business and Management not later than the end of the Michaelmas Term preceding the examination. Subject to a minimum number of nine, the Degree Committee shall specify the precise number of mandatory and optional modules required;

(*b*) a project report of not more than 12,000 words in length, including diagrams and footnotes, but excluding bibliography and appendices on a subject approved by the Degree Committee.

Option B

The examination shall consist of:

(*a*) at least six modules selected from a list of mandatory and optional modules published by the Degree Committee for the Faculty of Business and Management not later than the end of the Michaelmas Term preceding the examination;

(*b*) a thesis of not more than 12,000 words in length, including diagrams and footnotes, but excluding bibliography and appendices on a subject approved by the Degree Committee.

2. In publishing the list of modules and additional modules the Degree Committee shall announce the form of examination for each module, which shall be either a written paper, or one or more essays or other exercises, or a combination of these, and shall specify the duration of any written paper and the limit to be placed on the length of any essay or other exercise.

3. At the discretion of the Examiners, the examination may include an oral examination on the work submitted by the candidate under Regulation 1 and on the general field of knowledge within which it falls.

Theology and Religious Studies

1. The scheme of examination for the one-year course of study in Theology and Religious Studies for the degree of Master of Philosophy shall consist of:

(*a*) a thesis, of between 15,000 and 20,000 words in length, including footnotes and appendices but excluding bibliography, on a subject approved by the Degree Committee for the Faculty of Divinity;

and

(*b*) two pieces of submitted work, each of which shall be an essay of not more than 5,000 words in length, or an equivalent exercise, at least one of which must fall within the same subject area as the candidate's thesis or otherwise suitably related to it;

and

(*c*) *either* (i) one paper of three hours' duration on a language chosen from a list of languages published by the Degree Committee,

or (ii) one exercise on a subject chosen from a list of subjects for exercises approved by the Degree Committee,

[1] This pathway will not be offered in 2015–16.

or (iii) an alternative exercise within the candidate's chosen subject area, if one has not already been taken under (*b*).

The mode of examination for (ii) and (iii) shall be approved by the Degree Committee.

2. A candidate's choice of written work shall be made with the approval of the Degree Committee and in the light of the prerequisites for a thesis in the primary area and of the coherence of the candidate's programme, by the end of the Michaelmas Term.

3. The subject areas available for examination and the dates for submission of the written work shall be announced by the Degree Committee no later than the end of the Easter Term preceding the academical year next following.

4. The examiners may at their discretion request an oral examination in any aspect of the work submitted by the candidate.

Theoretical and Applied Linguistics

1. The scheme of examination for the one-year course of study in Theoretical and Applied Linguistics for the degree of Master of Philosophy shall consist of:

(*a*) a thesis not exceeding 20,000 words in length, including footnotes, but excluding tables, appendices, and bibliography, on a subject approved by the Degree Committee for the Faculty of Modern and Medieval Languages;

(*b*) four essays, of which three shall be no more than 2,000 words in length and one shall be no more than 4,000 words in length, each including footnotes, but excluding tables, appendices, and bibliography, on subjects either approved or prescribed by the Degree Committee;

(*c*) an oral presentation on a topic falling in one of the areas of study prescribed by the Degree Committee not later than the end of the Full Michaelmas Term preceding the examination.

2. The examination shall include an oral examination on the thesis and on the general field of knowledge within which it falls, and, at the discretion of the Examiners, on the essays submitted by the candidate; save that the Examiners may, at their discretion, waive the requirement for an oral examination.

Veterinary Science

The scheme of examination for the one-year full-time and two-year part-time course of study in Veterinary Science for the degree of Master of Philosophy shall consist of a thesis, of not more than 20,000 words in length, exclusive of tables, footnotes, bibliography, and appendices, on a subject approved by the Degree Committee for the Faculties of Clinical Medicine and Veterinary Medicine. The examination shall include an oral examination on the thesis and on the general field of knowledge within which it falls. The thesis shall provide evidence to satisfy the Examiners that a candidate can design and carry out an original investigation, assess and interpret the results obtained, and place the work in the wider perspective of the subject.

World History[1]

Notice (Reporter, *2013–14, p. 779*)

1. The scheme of examination for the one-year course of study in World History for the degree of Master of Philosophy shall consist of:

(*a*) a thesis of not less than 15,000 words and not more than 20,000 words in length, including notes and appendices, but excluding bibliography, on a topic approved by the Degree Committee for the Faculty of History;

(*b*) one essay of not more than 4,000 words in length, on a topic chosen by the candidate from a list of topics approved by the Degree Committee and falling within the following fields covered by the core course:

Debates in world history;

[1] This course will be available with effect from 1 October 2015.

The Degree Committee for History shall publish the topics under Regulation 1(*b*) no later than the end of Easter Term in the academical year preceding the examination.

(*c*) two essays, of not more than 4,000 words in length, on topics chosen from the following list of course options:

1. Global thinkers
2. Global China
3. Inequality: a global history
4. Print cultures in African history: publics, politics, and identities
5. Options as included in the programme from year to year

The Degree Committee shall have power to give notice of any addition or variation to the list of options announced in Regulation 1(*c*) where it is satisfied that no candidate's preparation for the examination will be affected.

2. At the discretion of the Examiners the examination may include an oral examination on the thesis and on the general field of knowledge within which it falls.

MASTER OF RESEARCH

GENERAL REGULATIONS

1. The M.Res. Degree shall be awarded for training in research. A subject of such study, together with the programme aims, learning outcomes, and syllabus for the course, and the special regulations for the examination and any subsequent amendments thereof, shall be approved by the General Board on the recommendation of the Faculty Board or other body concerned, after consultation with the appropriate Degree Committee.

2. The scheme of examination for the M.Res. Degree shall consist of written work or other exercises and the submission of a thesis (which terms shall include one or more equivalent pieces of extended research work such as an appraisal or a report), as prescribed in the appropriate special regulations for the subject as appended to these regulations. Any such prescribed scheme may require candidates also to take written papers in accordance with arrangements made by the Board of Graduate Studies on the recommendation of the appropriate Degree Committee. The examination for the Degree shall be held before the end of the course, except as provided under Regulation 7, and at such time or times as may be determined by the Degree Committee concerned, subject in the case of written papers to the approval of the Board of Examinations. Each written paper shall be of three hours' duration unless prescribed otherwise in the regulations that apply to the examination concerned. Scheme of examination.

3. No student shall be a candidate for the M.Res. Degree on more than one occasion or for the M.Res. Degree and for another University examination in the same term.

4. A candidate for the M.Res. Degree shall be a registered Graduate Student who, subject to the provisions of Regulation 5, shall pursue a course of training in research under the direction of a Supervisor appointed by the Degree Committee concerned and shall comply with any special conditions that the Degree Committee or the Board may lay down in a particular case. The course shall extend over one academical year. Students are required to attend in all three terms of the year, beginning from the date announced by the Degree Committee for the start of lectures, classes, or other formal instruction.

5. The Board of Graduate Studies, after considering a recommendation by the Degree Committee concerned,

(*a*) may allow a candidate for the M.Res. Degree to spend up to one term working under supervision outside the University under conditions approved by the Degree Committee;

(*b*) may allow a candidate for the M.Res. Degree on account of illness or other sufficient cause to intermit his or her course of study for one or more terms, which terms shall not count for any purpose of these regulations except as provided in Regulation 7 of the general regulations for admission as a Graduate Student.

Every application for dispensation under sub-paragraphs (*a*)–(*b*) shall be made to the Secretary of the Board of Graduate Studies and shall be accompanied by an opinion from the applicant's Supervisor.

6. Details of each candidate's examination entry (including the candidate's choice of written papers or other exercises, as appropriate, and the proposed subject of the thesis and subsequent corrections thereof), shall be submitted by the candidate to the Secretary of the Degree Committee concerned, and by the latter to the Secretary of the Board of Graduate Studies, who shall transmit them to the Registrary in accordance with the following timetable:

	Entries to be submitted	*Details of written papers etc.*	*Corrections*	*Title of thesis etc.*
By candidates to Secretaries of Degree Committees	By end of Full Michaelmas Term			By division of Lent Term
By Secretaries of Degree Committees to Board of Graduate Studies	By end of Michaelmas Term		By end of third week of Full Lent Term	By end of Lent Term
By Board of Graduate Studies to Registrary	By end of first week of Full Lent Term		By division of Lent Term	

Lists of candidates for each examination shall be circulated by the Registrary to Colleges as follows:

List of entries: By the end of the second week of Full Lent Term.

Final list of entries: Not less than four weeks before the beginning of the examination concerned.

Thesis.

7. Each candidate shall submit two copies of the thesis in accordance with detailed arrangements approved by the Board, so as to arrive by a date which shall be determined by the Degree Committee, and which shall not be later than the last day of August in the academical year of the course, provided that a candidate may be permitted to submit her or his thesis at such later date as may be determined by the Degree Committee. In special circumstances the Degree Committee may allow a candidate to submit only one copy of the thesis. The Examiners and the Degree Committee may take into consideration any work published by the candidate which is submitted with the thesis.

8. In submitting a thesis a candidate shall state, generally in a preface and specifically in notes or in a bibliography, the sources from which information has been derived, the extent to which use has been made of the work of others, and the portions of the thesis which are claimed as original. A thesis shall not be accepted if it is substantially the same as one that the candidate has submitted, or is concurrently submitting, for any other degree, diploma, or similar qualification at any university or similar institution, but a thesis which the candidate has submitted or is concurrently submitting for some other purpose may be accepted. In submitting a thesis the candidate shall declare for what purpose, if any, other than for the M.Res. Degree, the whole or part of it has already been or is concurrently being submitted. The thesis, apart from quotations, shall be written in English.

9. Every Supervisor shall send to the Secretary of the Board of Graduate Studies reports on the work of each candidate under his or her charge, in accordance with the provisions of Regulation 8 of the general regulations for admission as a Graduate Student.

Examiners and Assessors.

10. The Degree Committee concerned shall appoint such number of Examiners and Assessors as they shall deem sufficient to conduct the examination for the M.Res. Degree and to report on the performance of a candidate. The Examiners and Assessors shall undertake such duties as the Degree Committee may decide.

(*a*) The Degree Committee shall appoint an External Examiner and a Senior Examiner; not later than the end of the Michaelmas Term the Secretary of the Degree Committee shall communicate to the Secretary of the Board of Graduate Studies the name of these Examiners and the names of the other Examiners and Assessors.

(*b*) Each candidate's thesis shall be referred to two Examiners each of whom shall make an independent report thereon. The special regulations for the examination may provide for an oral examination on the thesis and, if so specified, on the other parts of the examination. When the oral examination relates to the thesis both Examiners of the thesis shall be among the Examiners present at the oral examination. The Degree Committee in exceptional circumstances may permit the Examiners to conduct the oral examination by video-conference or other remote means. The Examiners participating in the oral examination shall sign a joint certificate of the result, including any marks assigned thereto, of that examination. If the Examiners do not agree in their recommendation, or if for any other reason the Degree Committee need a further opinion or opinions on the merit of the thesis submitted, the Degree Committee may appoint additional Examiners, provided that not more than one additional Examiner may be appointed without the leave of the Board of Graduate Studies. Each additional Examiner so appointed shall make an independent report on the thesis to the Degree Committee.

Approval for degree.

11. If the Degree Committee at a meeting held to consider the reports of the Examiners, approve the candidate's marks in the written papers or other exercises, the thesis submitted, and her or his performance in the oral examination (where held) as of the requisite standard for the M.Res. Degree and are of the opinion that the degree should be conferred, the Degree Committee shall communicate their resolution to the candidate and to the Secretary of the Board of Graduate Studies who shall publish a notice of the candidate's approval for the award of the degree of Master of Research.

12. If the Degree Committee, after consideration of a candidate's marks and the reports of the Examiners in the prescribed examination, are of the opinion that the candidate's work is not of the requisite standard for the degree, the Degree Committee shall communicate their resolution to the candidate and to the Secretary of the Board of Graduate Studies. After such a resolution has been made the student concerned shall not be eligible to take the examination for the degree again. If not approved for degree.

13. Payment of travelling expenses and a subsistence allowance may be claimed by Examiners in accordance with Regulation 11 of the regulations for the Ph.D., M.Sc., and M.Litt. Degrees.

14. A Graduate Student whose course of study for the M.Res. Degree has included any term needed for the B.A. Degree and who elects to proceed to the B.A. Degree shall not be entitled to proceed to the M.Res. Degree.

SPECIAL REGULATIONS

BIOLOGICAL SCIENCE

The scheme of examination for the one-year course of study in Biological Science for the degree of Master of Research shall consist of a portfolio of research reports, of not more than 20,000 words in total, exclusive of tables, footnotes, bibliography, and appendices, on a theme and of a form approved and published annually in the Easter Term before the commencement of the course by the Degree Committee for the Faculty of Biology. The Degree Committee shall, at the same time, specify any other exercises which form part of the examination for candidates in particular subjects. The examination shall include an oral examination on the work submitted by the candidate and on the general field of knowledge within which such work falls. The portfolio shall provide evidence to satisfy the Examiners that a candidate can design and carry out an original investigation, assess and interpret the results obtained, and place the work in the wider perspective of the subject.

FUTURE INFRASTRUCTURE AND BUILT ENVIRONMENT

Notices (Reporter, *2013–14, pp. 306 and 781*)

1. The scheme of examination for the one-year course of study in Future Infrastructure and Built Environment for the degree of Master of Research shall consist of:

(*a*) six modules selected from a list of mandatory and optional modules published by the Degree Committee for the Faculty of Engineering not later than the end of the Easter Term of the academical year preceding that in which the examination is to be held: each module shall be examined either by a written paper, or by course-work, or by a combination of the two;

(*b*) three reports – one of up to 2,000 words; one of up to 3,000 words; one of up to 5,000 words – on projects approved by the Degree Committee; words counts are inclusive of diagrams and footnotes, but exclude bibliography and appendices;

(*c*) a thesis, of no more than 12,000 words in length, including diagrams and footnotes, but excluding bibliography and appendices, on a subject approved by the Degree Committee; its assessment shall include an oral presentation of the project work on which the thesis is based.

2. The Degree Committee shall have the power to give notice of additional modules not later than the end of the Michaelmas Term of the academical year of the examination.

3. The examination may include, at the discretion of the Examiners, an oral examination on the reports and on the general field of knowledge within which they fall, and on the other work submitted by the candidate under Regulation 1.

GAS TURBINE AERODYNAMICS

Notices (Reporter, *2013–14, pp. 306 and 781*)

1. The scheme of examination for the one-year course of study in Gas Turbine Aerodynamics for the degree of Master of Research shall consist of:

(*a*) six modules selected from a list of mandatory and optional modules published by the Degree Committee for the Faculty of Engineering not later than the end of the Easter Term of the academical year preceding that in which the examination is to be held;

(*b*) three reports, each of not more than 4,000 words in length, including diagrams and footnotes, but excluding bibliography and appendices, on projects approved by the Degree Committee;

(*c*) two industry courses to be assessed in such manner as the Degree Committee shall determine. The Degree Committee shall announce the form of assessment not later than the end of the Michaelmas Term of the academical year in which the examination takes place;

(*d*) a thesis, of no more than 12,000 words in length, including diagrams and footnotes, but excluding bibliography and appendices, on a subject approved by the Degree Committee; its assessment shall include an oral presentation of the project work on which the thesis is based.

2. Students who have taken papers from Part IIB of the Engineering Tripos prior to starting the course may, with the permission of the Degree Committee, substitute one elective module under Regulation 1(*a*) above for a technical report on an extension of one of those papers.

3. The Degree Committee shall have the power to give notice of additional modules not later than the end of the Michaelmas Term of the academical year of the examination.

4. The examination may include, at the discretion of the Examiners, an oral examination on the reports and on the general field of knowledge within which they fall, and on the other work submitted by the candidate under Regulation 1.

GRAPHENE TECHNOLOGY

Notices (Reporter, *2013–14, pp. 305 and 781*)

1. The scheme of examination for the one-year course of study in Graphene Technology for the degree of Master of Research shall consist of:

(*a*) six modules, assessed by written examination, given on a list of mandatory modules published by the Degree Committee for the Faculty of Engineering not later than the end of the Easter Term of the academical year preceding that in which the examination is to be held;

(*b*) research skills sessions of such number, and to be assessed in such manner, as the Degree Committee shall determine. The Degree Committee shall announce the form of assessment not later than the end of the Michaelmas Term of the academical year in which the examination takes place;

(*c*) two reports, each of not more than 12,000 words in length, including diagrams and footnotes, but excluding bibliography and appendices, on projects approved by the Degree Committee.

2. The Degree Committee shall have the power to give notice of additional modules not later than the end of the Michaelmas Term of the academical year of the examination.

3. The examination may include, at the discretion of the Examiners, an oral examination on the reports and on the general field of knowledge within which they fall, and on the other work submitted by the candidate under Regulation 1.

INTEGRATED PHOTONIC AND ELECTRONIC SYSTEMS

Amended by Notice (Reporter, *2013–14, p. 465*)

1. The scheme of examination for the one-year course of study in Integrated Photonic and Electronic Systems for the degree of Master of Research shall consist of:

(*a*) at least five modules selected from a list of mandatory and optional modules published by the Degree Committee for the Faculty of Engineering not later than the end of the Easter Term of the academical year preceding that in which the examination is to be held;

(*b*) two reports, each of not more than 12,000 words in length, including diagrams and footnotes, but excluding bibliography and appendices on projects approved by the Degree Committee.

2. In publishing the list of modules and additional modules the Degree Committee shall announce the form of examination for each module, which shall be either a written paper, or one or more pieces of course-work or other exercises, or a combination of these, and shall specify the duration of any written paper and the limit to be placed on the length of any piece of course-work or other exercise. The Degree Committee shall have the power to give notice of additional optional modules not later than the end of the Michaelmas Term of the academical year of the examination.

3. The examination may include, at the discretion of the Examiners, an oral examination on the reports and on the general field of knowledge within which they fall, and on the other work submitted by the candidate under Regulation 1.

Medical Science

The scheme of examination for the one-year course of study in Medical Science for the degree of Master of Research shall consist of a portfolio of research reports, of not more than 20,000 words in total, exclusive of tables, footnotes, bibliography, and appendices, on a theme and of a form approved and published annually in the Easter Term before the commencement of the course by the Degree Committee for the Faculties of Clinical Medicine and Veterinary Medicine. The examination shall include an oral examination on the work submitted by the candidate and on the general field of knowledge within which such work falls. The portfolio shall provide evidence to satisfy the Examiners that a candidate can design and carry out an original investigation, assess and interpret the results obtained, and place the work in the wider perspective of the subject.

Physical Sciences

Notice (Reporter, *2013–14, p. 253*)

1. The scheme of examination for the one-year course of study for the Degree of Master of Research in Physical Sciences shall consist of a portfolio of research reports of not more than 20,000 words in total, exclusive of tables, footnotes, bibliography, and appendices, on a theme approved by the Degree Committee for the Faculty concerned and specified in the schedule to these regulations.

2. The Degree Committee shall publish before the end of the Easter Term before the commencement of the course requirements for the form of the portfolio of research reports, and any other exercises which shall form part of the examination for candidates in the theme concerned. The Degree Committee may publish amendments to these requirements not later than the first day of the Michaelmas Term.

3. The examination shall include an oral examination on the work submitted by the candidate and on the general field of knowledge within which such work falls.

4. The portfolio shall provide evidence to satisfy the Examiners that a candidate can design and carry out an original investigation, assess and interpret the results obtained, and place the work in the wider perspective of the subject.

SCHEDULE

Nanoscience and Nanotechnology

Sensor Technologies and Applications

Notice (Reporter, *2013–14, p. 666*)

1. The scheme of examination for the one-year course of study in Sensor Technologies and Applications for the degree of Master of Research shall consist of:

(*a*) at least six modules selected from a list of mandatory and optional modules published by the Degree Committee for the Faculty of Engineering not later than the end of the Easter Term of the academical year preceding that in which the examination is to be held; *and*

(*b*) two reports, each of not more than 7,000 words in length, including diagrams and footnotes but excluding bibliography and appendices, on projects approved by the Degree Committee.

2. In publishing the list of modules and additional modules the Degree Committee shall announce the form of examination for each module, which shall be either a written paper, or one or more pieces of course-work or other exercises, or a combination of these, and shall specify the duration of any written paper and the limit to be placed on the length of any piece of course-work or other exercise. The Degree Committee shall have the power to give notice of additional optional modules not later than the end of the Michaelmas Term of the academical year of the examination.

3. The examination may include, at the discretion of the Examiners, an oral examination on the reports and on the general field of knowledge within which they fall, and on the other work submitted by the candidate under Regulation 1.

Social Anthropology

1. The scheme of examination for the one-year course of study in Social Anthropology for the degree of Master of Research shall consist of:

(*a*) two essays, each of not more than 4,000 words in length, on subjects of Social Anthropology chosen by the candidate, subject to the approval of the Head of the Department of Archaeology and Anthropology, from a list announced by the Degree Committee for the Faculty of Human, Social, and Political Science;

(*b*) one essay of not more than 4,000 words in length and one work-book of assessment of materials on research methods on topics announced by the Degree Committee;

(*c*) a thesis of not more than 15,000 words in length, including footnotes, but excluding tables, appendices, and bibliography, on a subject approved by the Degree Committee.

2. The examination may include, at the discretion of the Examiners, an oral examination on the thesis and on the general field of knowledge within which it falls.

Ultra Precision Engineering

Amended by Notice (Reporter, *2013–14, p. 465*)

1. The scheme of examination for the one-year course of study in Ultra Precision Engineering for the degree of Master of Research shall consist of:

(*a*) at least five modules selected from a list of mandatory and optional modules published by the Degree Committee for the Faculty of Engineering not later than the end of the Easter Term of the academical year preceding that in which the examination is to be held;

(*b*) two reports, each of not more than 10,000 words in length, including diagrams and footnotes, but excluding bibliography and appendices, on projects approved by the Degree Committee.

2. In publishing the list of modules and additional modules the Degree Committee shall announce the form of examination for each module, which shall be either a written paper, or one or more pieces of course-work or other exercises, or a combination of these, and shall specify the duration of any written paper and the limit to be placed on the length of any piece of course-work or other exercise. The Degree Committee shall have the power to give notice of additional optional modules not later than the end of the Michaelmas Term of the academical year of the examination.

3. The examination may include, at the discretion of the Examiners, an oral examination on the thesis and on the general field of knowledge within which it falls, and on the other work submitted by the candidate under Regulation 1.

DOCTOR OF SCIENCE AND DOCTOR OF LETTERS

1. In order to qualify for the degree of Doctor of Science or Doctor of Letters a candidate shall be required to give proof of distinction by some original contribution to the advancement of science or of learning.

Standing of candidates.

2. Any person may be a candidate for the degree of Doctor of Science or Doctor of Letters who is a graduate of the University and who

either (*a*) is of not less than eight years' standing from admission to his or her first degree of the University,

or (*b*) is of not less than eight years' standing from admission to his or her first degree of some other university and has been admitted (i) to some office in the University or to a Headship or a Fellowship of a College, and (ii) to the degree of Master of Arts under Statute B II 2 or to a degree of the University by incorporation.

Method of application.

3. A candidate for the degree shall apply in writing to the Secretary of the Board of Graduate Studies, specifying the published works on which his or her claim to the degree is based, providing a summary in not more than 500 words of the field of research covered by these works, and naming the Faculty or other approved institution within whose scope the works fall. A candidate shall send with the application a fee of £582 for the Chest, and two copies of each of the works specified, provided that the Board of Graduate Studies may, subject to the concurrence of the Degree Committee concerned, allow a candidate to submit only one copy. All the works submitted shall, apart from quotations, be written in English unless in a particular case the Degree Committee concerned have allowed a candidate to submit material in some other language.

4. Each application shall be forwarded by the Secretary of the Board of Graduate Studies to the Degree Committee concerned, who shall give preliminary consideration to the application and shall determine whether the works submitted constitute *prima facie* a qualification for the degree; the Committee may appoint an Assessor to assist them in the matter. Preliminary consideration.

5. If the Committee decide that the works submitted do not constitute *prima facie* a qualification for the degree, a resolution of the Committee to that effect, with the names of those present and voting on either side, shall be communicated to the Secretary of the Board of Graduate Studies, who shall communicate the decision to the candidate. In such a case £510 out of the fee of £582 paid by the candidate under Regulation 3 shall be returned.

6. If the Committee decide that the works submitted do constitute *prima facie* a qualification for the degree, they shall appoint not less than two persons to act as Referees. Each Referee shall submit an independent written report on the works specified in the candidate's application; these reports shall be treated as confidential documents. References.

7. If after considering the reports of the Referees the Degree Committee are satisfied that the candidate's work is of the requisite standard for the degree, a resolution of the Committee to that effect, with the names of those present and voting on either side, shall be communicated to the Board of Graduate Studies together with the reports of the Referees.

8. If the Board of Graduate Studies after receiving such a communication resolve that the degree should be conferred, the Secretary of the Board of Graduate Studies shall publish the name of the candidate as approved for the degree of Doctor of Science or Doctor of Letters, as the case may be. Such a resolution shall not be valid unless passed with the concurrence of the votes, cast at a meeting, of five members of the Board. Approval for degree.

9. If after considering the reports of the Referees the Degree Committee are of the opinion that the candidate's work is not of the requisite standard for the degree, a resolution of the Committee to that effect, with the names of those present and voting on either side, shall be communicated to the Board of Graduate Studies together with the reports of the Referees. The Secretary of the Board shall communicate this decision to the candidate.

10. No candidate for a degree shall be present at the deliberations either of the Committee or of the Board of Graduate Studies respecting his or her own case. Candidate not to be present.

11. Each Referee shall receive a fee of £175. An Assessor appointed under Regulation 4 shall receive a fee of £42. If an Assessor is subsequently appointed a Referee the fee of £42 shall form part of the fee of £175 due to him or her as a Referee. The Board of Graduate Studies may approve the payment of reasonable expenses incurred by Referees in the execution of their duties. Payments.

12. No fee shall be payable on admission to the degree.

MASTER OF STUDIES

GENERAL REGULATIONS

Amended by Notice (Reporter, *2013–14, p. 534*)

1. The M.St. Degree shall be awarded for postgraduate study. A subject of such study, and the special regulations for each subject, shall be approved by the General Board on the recommendation of the Faculty Board or other body concerned, after consultation with the appropriate Degree Committee and after submission to, and approval by, the Strategic Committee of the Institute of Continuing Education. M.St. Degree.

2. Applications for admission to a course of study leading to the M.St. Degree shall be sent to the Director of Continuing Education. The Director shall communicate each application for admission to the Secretary of the Degree Committee concerned with the applicant's proposed course, having first ascertained that appropriate accommodation, if required, is available in a laboratory or elsewhere. The Degree Committee shall consider the application and shall communicate their opinion thereon to the Director. If the Degree Committee decline the application it shall fail, and the Director shall so inform the applicant. If the Degree Committee agree to recommend approval of the application, their recommendation shall be considered by the Strategic Committee of the Institute who shall decide upon the application. Before declining an application recommended by a Degree Committee for approval Application for admission.

the Strategic Committee shall give a representative appointed by the Degree Committee an opportunity of explaining the Committee's reasons for their recommendation.

3. Any person may be approved for admission to a course leading to the M.St. Degree who has satisfied the Strategic Committee of the Institute, and the relevant Degree Committee that by reason of previous study he or she is qualified to engage in postgraduate work for the degree. The Strategic Committee shall determine the conditions, if any, of each applicant's admission and shall assign to him or her a date of commencement of candidature. The Director of Continuing Education shall maintain a register of persons who have been approved as candidates for the M.St. Degree; when an applicant has been approved for admission, his or her name shall be entered on the Register. No student shall be a candidate for the M.St. Degree on more than one occasion.

Approved course.

4. A candidate for the M.St. Degree shall pursue an approved course of postgraduate study over a period of two years. Every course of study for the degree, and any amendments of it, shall be approved by the Strategic Committee, and the General Board, on the recommendation of the Faculty Board or other body concerned.

Intermission.

5. After considering a recommendation by the Degree Committee concerned, the Strategic Committee may allow a candidate for the degree on account of illness or other sufficient cause to intermit his or her course of study for such period as they may think fit.

Supervisors.

6. For each course unit the Degree Committee concerned shall appoint a Supervisor for every student. Each Supervisor shall send to the Director of Continuing Education, at such intervals as may be specified by the Strategic Committee, a written report on the work of each student who is studying for the M.St. Degree under his or her direction; such reports shall be communicated to the Degree Committee concerned, to the Board of Graduate Studies, and to the student's Tutor.

Prizes or Scholarships.

7. A student who is registered as a candidate for the M.St. Degree shall not be admitted as a candidate for any University Studentship, Scholarship, Exhibition, Prize, Medal, or other such award, which is open only to undergraduates. For the purpose of any regulation which governs the standing of candidates for any other emolument, a candidate for the M.St. Degree who is not a graduate of the University shall be deemed to have kept by residence the nine terms next preceding the first term of his or her candidature for the M.St. Degree.

Fees.

8. While following a course of study leading to an examination for the M.St. Degree, a student shall pay the appropriate University Composition Fee for each year of such study.

Examination.

9. The examination for the M.St. Degree shall include

(*a*) the submission of a thesis, of such length as shall be prescribed in the appropriate special regulations for the subject as appended to these regulations;

and

(*b*) *either* (i) written examination papers *or* (ii) the submission of essays, project reports, or other exercises, *or* (iii) any combination of these, as prescribed in the special regulations.

The special regulations for the subject may make provision for the Degree Committee to award a Postgraduate Diploma or Postgraduate Certificate to candidates who do not complete the full requirements for the Degree.

At the discretion of the Examiners the examination may include an oral examination on the thesis and on the general field of knowledge within which it falls as prescribed in the appropriate special regulations. Each candidate shall submit two copies of his or her thesis accompanied by two copies of a summary in accordance with detailed arrangements approved by the Strategic Committee of the Institute. In special circumstances the Degree Committee concerned may allow a candidate to submit only one copy of the thesis.

Submission of thesis.

10. In submitting a thesis a candidate shall state, generally in a preface and specifically in notes or in a bibliography, the sources from which information has been derived, the extent to which use has been made of the work of others, and the portions of the thesis which are claimed as original.

A thesis shall not be accepted that is substantially the same as one that the candidate has submitted, or is concurrently submitting, for any other degree, diploma, or similar qualification at any university or similar institution, but they may accept a thesis which the candidate has submitted or is concurrently submitting for some other purpose. In submitting a thesis the candidate shall declare for what purpose, if any, other than for the M.St. Degree, the whole or part of it has already been or is concurrently being submitted. The thesis, apart from quotations, shall be written in English.

Examiners and Assessors.

11. The Degree Committee concerned shall appoint such number of Examiners and Assessors as they shall deem sufficient to conduct the examination. The Assessors shall undertake such duties as the Degree Committee may decide. The Secretary of the Degree Committee shall communicate to the Director of Continuing Education the name of the Senior Examiner and the names of the Examiners and Assessors.

12. Each candidate's thesis shall be referred by the Degree Committee to two of the Examiners, each of whom shall make an independent report thereon to the Degree Committee. Where the examination includes an oral examination, the two Examiners shall both be present at the oral examination, and shall sign a joint certificate of the result of that examination. The Degree Committee in exceptional circumstances may permit the Examiners to conduct the oral examination by video-conference or other remote means. If the Examiners do not agree in their recommendations, or if for any other reason the Degree Committee need a further opinion on the merit of a candidate's thesis, the Degree Committee may appoint additional Examiners, provided that not more than one additional Examiner shall be appointed without the leave of the Board of Graduate Studies. Each additional Examiner so appointed shall make an independent report on the thesis to the Degree Committee.

13. If the Degree Committee, at a meeting held to consider the reports of the Examiners, approve the candidate's performance as of the requisite standard for the M.St. Degree and are of the opinion that the degree should be conferred, the Degree Committee shall communicate their resolution to the candidate, to the Strategic Committee of the Institute, and to the Secretary of the Board of Graduate Studies who shall publish a notice of the candidate's approval for the award of the degree of Master of Studies. Approval for degree.

14. If the Degree Committee, after consideration of a candidate's marks and the reports of the Examiners in the prescribed examination, are of the opinion that the candidate's work is not of the requisite standard for the degree, the Degree Committee shall communicate their resolution to the candidate, to the Secretary of the Board of Graduate Studies, and to the Strategic Committee of the Institute of Continuing Education. That resolution may include award of a Postgraduate Diploma or Postgraduate Certificate under regulation 9, if so permitted under the special regulations for the subject. After such a resolution has been passed, the student shall not be eligible to take the examination for the degree again. Failure.

15. If the Tutor of a candidate for the degree supplies the Board of Graduate Studies with satisfactory evidence that the candidate has been hindered by illness or other grave cause in preparing for or taking the examination or any part of the examination for the degree, and such representations are received by the Secretary of the Board not later than three months after the date on which the result of the examination was communicated, the Board shall have power, notwithstanding any provision to the contrary in the relevant regulations,

either (*a*) to approve the candidate for the degree or other qualification without further examination, provided that no candidate shall be so approved unless the Degree Committee concerned judge her or him to have performed with credit in a substantial part of the examination,

or (*b*) to allow the candidate to be examined or re-examined under such conditions and at such time as may be determined by the Board after consultation with the Degree Committee concerned.

Representations received after the prescribed time limit shall not be considered. The Secretary of the Board shall communicate any decision by the Board under this regulation to the Strategic Committee of the Institute of Continuing Education.

A student, or her or his Tutor with the student's consent, may seek review of a decision in relation to that student made by the Board of Graduate Studies. A request for review shall be made in writing, stating the grounds of review, normally within one month of written notification of the Board's decision (unless, in exceptional circumstances, the Registrary or a deputy permits a longer period). If the request includes, in the opinion of the Chair of the Board, relevant additional information not previously available, the Board will reconsider its decision at its next meeting following receipt of the request. If no such additional information is included or if, on reconsideration, the decision is reaffirmed by the Board, the procedure described in the following paragraphs shall apply.

The Registrary or a deputy shall appoint a reviewer. Exceptionally, a panel of three reviewers may be appointed. If so, references below to 'the reviewer' shall be construed accordingly.

The reviewer will consider the request, the documentation available to the Board (less any confidential medical information), the Ordinances which apply to the Board's decision, and the Board's Notes of Guidance. He or she will obtain an opinion from the Board, seek such other information as he or she may require and, at her or his discretion, may hold a hearing (but there is no obligation to hold a hearing). The reviewer will issue an adjudication in writing as soon as possible, stating findings of fact, conclusions, and, if any, recommendations, for consideration by the Board. The reviewer shall be concerned with determining whether there is evidence of: inadequate consideration of the matter by the Board; the Board having made a decision, to the detriment of the student, which is inconsistent with the relevant Ordinances or its own Notes of Guidance; or material circumstances of which the Board was unaware and which were of such a nature as, had the Board been so aware, to have been likely to cause the Board to have reached a different decision.

The Board shall normally accept the recommendation of the reviewer. If, exceptionally, the reviewer's recommendation is not accepted a written explanation shall be provided to the reviewer, the student, and her or his Tutor. The Board may decide not to accept a recommendation in any instance in which: (i) the reviewer has sought to make a decision replacing that of the Board; (ii) the reviewer's recommendation is inconsistent with the Ordinances governing Allowances; or (iii) the reviewer's recommendation is such that, were it to be accepted, it would set a precedent which would not be in the interests of the proper conduct of the Board's business or in the wider interests of the University.

The conclusion of the consideration by the Board of Graduate Studies of any recommendation by a review shall be the normal final point of decision within the University. A reviewer may summarily dismiss an application which seems to her or him to be vexatious or frivolous.

Payments to Examiners.

16. The fees payable to Supervisors (Regulation 6) and to Examiners and Assessors (Regulation 11) shall be determined from time to time by the General Board on the recommendation of the Strategic Committee of the Institute of Continuing Education, who shall consult the Board of Graduate Studies before making such a recommendation.

Expenses of Examiners.

17. Payment of travelling expenses and a subsistence allowance may be claimed by Examiners in accordance with Regulation 11 of the regulations for the Ph.D., M.Sc., and M.Litt. Degrees.

SPECIAL REGULATIONS

Advanced Subject Teaching

The scheme of examination for the course of study in Advanced Subject Teaching for the degree of Master of Studies shall be as follows:

(*a*) two essays, each of between 3,000 and 4,000 words in length, and one essay of between 6,000 and 8,000 words in length, each on a topic approved by the Degree Committee for the Faculty of Education;

(*b*) a thesis of between 15,000 and 18,000 words in length including footnotes and appendices, but excluding bibliography, on a subject approved by the Degree Committee.

At the discretion of the Examiners the examination shall include an oral examination on the thesis and on the general field of knowledge within which it falls; such an oral examination may include questions relating to one or more of the other pieces of work submitted by the candidate under (*a*) and (*b*) above.

Applied Criminology and Police Management

[The scheme of examination for the course of study in Applied Criminology and Police Management for the degree of Master of Studies shall be as follows:

(*a*) four essays, each of not more than 3,000 words in length, which shall be chosen by the candidate from a list of topics announced by the Examiners;

(*b*) an exercise setting out a research proposal for the thesis on a topic suggested by the candidate and agreed with the Examiners; a candidate's report on such a research exercise shall not exceed 4,000 words in length, including notes and appendices;

(*c*) an oral presentation on the subject of the thesis, methods being used, preliminary results of data analysis, interpretations, and conclusions;

(*d*) a thesis of not more than 18,000 words in length, including notes and appendices, on a subject proposed by the candidate and approved by the Degree Committee for the Faculty of Law.

At the discretion of the Examiners the examination shall include an oral examination on the thesis and on the general field of knowledge within which it falls; such an oral examination may include questions relating to one or more of the other pieces of work submitted by the candidate under (*a*) and (*b*) above.][1]

[1] The regulations in angular brackets will replace the regulations in square brackets with effect from 1 January 2015.

⟨**1.** The scheme of examination for the course of study in Applied Criminology and Police Management for the degree of Master of Studies shall consist of:

(*a*) four essays, each of not more than 3,000 words in length, which shall be chosen by the candidate from a list of topics announced by the Degree Committee for the Faculty of Law;

(*b*) an exercise setting out a research proposal for the thesis on a topic suggested by the candidate and agreed with the Examiners; a candidate's report on such a research exercise shall not exceed 4,000 words in length, including notes and appendices;

(*c*) an oral presentation on the subject of the thesis, methods being used, preliminary results of data analysis, interpretations, and conclusions;

(*d*) a thesis, of not more than 18,000 words in length, including footnotes and appendices but excluding bibliography, on a subject approved by the Degree Committee.

2. At the discretion of the Examiners the examination shall include an oral examination on the thesis and on the general field of knowledge within which it falls; such an oral examination may include questions relating to one or more of the other pieces of work submitted by the candidate under 1(*a*) or 1(*b*) above.

3. The Examiners may recommend to the Degree Committee that it recommends to the Institute of Continuing Education the award of the Postgraduate Certificate to a candidate who has satisfactorily completed three of the four essays specified in 1(*a*), and to a candidate who has not completed, or fails to reach the required standard in, the fourth essay and the work required under 1(*b*) and 1(*d*).⟩[1]

Applied Criminology, Penology, and Management

[The scheme of examination for the course of study in Applied Criminology, Penology, and Management for the degree of Master of Studies shall consist of:

(*a*) four essays, each of not more than 3,000 words in length and each on a topic approved by the Degree Committee for the Faculty of Law;

(*b*) an exercise setting out a research proposal for the thesis on a topic suggested by the candidate and agreed with the Examiners; a candidate's report on such a research exercise shall not exceed 4,000 words in length, including notes and appendices;

(*c*) a thesis, of not more than 18,000 words in length, including footnotes and appendices but excluding bibliography, on a subject approved by the Degree Committee.

At the discretion of the Examiners the examination shall include an oral examination on the thesis and on the general field of knowledge within which it falls; such an oral examination may include questions relating to one or more of the other pieces of work submitted by the candidate under (*a*) and (*b*) above.][1]

⟨**1.** The scheme of examination for the course of study in Applied Criminology, Penology, and Management for the degree of Master of Studies shall consist of:

(*a*) four essays, each of not more than 3,000 words in length and each on a topic approved by the Degree Committee for the Faculty of Law;

(*b*) an exercise setting out a research proposal for the thesis on a topic suggested by the candidate and agreed with the Examiners; a candidate's report on such a research exercise shall not exceed 4,000 words in length, including notes and appendices;

(*c*) a thesis, of not more than 18,000 words in length, including footnotes and appendices but excluding bibliography, on a subject approved by the Degree Committee.

2. At the discretion of the Examiners the examination shall include an oral examination on the thesis and on the general field of knowledge within which it falls; such an oral examination may include questions relating to one or more of the other pieces of work submitted by the candidate under 1(*a*) or 1(*b*) above.

3. The Examiners may recommend to the Degree Committee that it recommends to the Institute of Continuing Education the award of the Postgraduate Certificate to a candidate who has satisfactorily completed three of the four essays specified in 1(*a*), and to a candidate who has not completed, or fails to reach the required standard in, the fourth essay and the work required under 1(*b*) and 1(*c*).⟩[1]

[1] The regulations in angular brackets will replace the regulations in square brackets with effect from 1 January 2015.

Building History

1. The scheme of examination for the course of study in Building History for the degree of Master of Studies shall consist of:

(*a*) three written papers each of three hours' duration or other exercises specified by the Degree Committee for the Faculty of Architecture and History of Art;

(*b*) a field test of one hour;

(*c*) the submission of a report of between 3,000 and 5,000 words in length on a building or building element, to include record drawings and photographs together with relevant historical maps and illustrations;

(*d*) a research proposal of between 2,000 and 3,000 words in length;

(*e*) the submission of a portfolio/log book and report of not more than 3,000 words on the required placement or guided research project, together with a fifteen-minute presentation on the placement or guided research project;

(*f*) a thesis of not more than 25,000 words in length, including footnotes and appendices, but excluding bibliography, on a subject approved by the Degree Committee.

2. The examination shall include an oral examination on the thesis and on the general field of knowledge within which it falls.

Construction Engineering

The scheme of examination for the course of study in Construction Engineering for the degree of Master of Studies shall consist of:

(*a*) a case study, of no more than 5,000 words in length, on a topic approved by the Degree Committee for the Faculty of Engineering;

(*b*) two essays, each of no more than 3,000 words in length, on a topic approved by the Degree Committee;

(*c*) a thesis of not more than 15,000 words in length, including footnotes and appendices, but excluding bibliography, on a subject approved by the Degree Committee.

At the discretion of the Examiners the examination may include an oral examination on any or all of the components of the examination specified under (*a*) to (*c*) above, and on the general field of knowledge within which they fall.

Creative Writing

1. The scheme of examination for the course of study in Creative Writing for the degree of Master of Studies shall consist of:

(*a*) four essays or compositions, up to 3,000 words each, on a topic to be approved by the Degree Committee for the Faculty of English;

(*b*) a thesis in the form of a portfolio of creative and critical writing on a subject and form approved by the Degree Committee, comprising a 3,000-word critical essay (including footnotes and appendices), and 12,000 to 15,000 words of creative prose. If the portfolio is comprised of poetry, an equivalent quantity of poems will be submitted, subject to consultation with the dissertation supervisor, plus a critical essay of 3,000 words, including footnotes and appendices.

2. At the discretion of the Examiners the examination may include an oral examination; such an oral examination may include questions relating to one or more of the other pieces of work submitted by the candidate under (*a*) and (*b*) above.

3. The Examiners may recommend to the Degree Committee that it recommends to the Strategic Committee of the Institute of Continuing Education the award of the Postgraduate Certificate to a candidate who has satisfactorily completed the requirements specified in Regulation 1(*a*) and who does not complete, or fails to reach the required standard, in the requirements set out under Regulation 1(*b*).

Historic Environment[1]

1. The scheme of examination for the course of study in Historic Environment for the degree of Master of Studies shall consist of:

(*a*) four essays, each of no more than 4,000 words in length, and each on a topic approved by the Degree Committee for the Faculty of Human, Social, and Political Science;

(*b*) a thesis of not more than 15,000 words in length, including footnotes and appendices, but excluding bibliography, on a subject approved by the Degree Committee.

2. At the discretion of the Examiners the examination shall include an oral examination on the thesis and on the general field of knowledge within which it falls.

History

Amended by Notice (Reporter, *2013–14, p. 405*)

1. The scheme of examination for the course of study in History for the degree of Master of Studies shall be as follows:

(*a*) four essays, each of up to 4,000 words in length on a topic approved by the Degree Committee for the Faculty of History;

(*b*) a thesis of between 16,000 and 20,000 words in length including footnotes and appendices, but excluding bibliography, on a subject approved by the Degree Committee.

2. At the discretion of the Examiners the examination shall include an oral examination in the thesis and on the general field of knowledge within which it falls.

3. The Examiners may recommend that the Degree Committee recommend to the Strategic Committee of the Institute of Continuing Education award of a Postgraduate Diploma to candidates who have satisfactorily completed requirements specified in 1(*a*), and to candidates who have not completed, or fail to reach the standard, in the thesis

Interdisciplinary Design for the Built Environment

Amended by Notice (Reporter, *2013–14, p. 405*)

The scheme of examination for the course of study in Interdisciplinary Design for the Built Environment for the degree of Master of Studies shall be as follows:

1. For the purpose of the general regulations for the degree, the Degree Committee concerned with this examination shall be the Degree Committee for the Faculty of Architecture and History of Art.

2. The examination shall consist of:

(*a*) a thesis, of not more than 15,000 words in length, including footnotes and appendices but excluding bibliography, on a subject approved by the Degree Committee;

(*b*) a case study, of not more than 5,000 words in length, of a project approved by the Degree Committee concerning design for the built environment;

(*c*) two essays, each of not more than 3,000 words in length, on topics approved by the Degree Committee;

(*d*) studio design work as approved by the Degree Committee.

3. At the discretion of the Examiners the examination shall include an oral examination on the thesis and on the general field of knowledge within which it falls.

4. The Examiners may recommend to the Degree Committee that it recommends to the Institute of Continuing Education the award of the Postgraduate Diploma to a candidate who has satisfactorily completed the requirements specified in Regulation 2(*b*)–(*d*), and to a candidate who has not completed, or fails to reach the required standard in, the thesis.

International Relations

1. The scheme of examination for the course of study in International Relations for the degree of Master of Studies shall consist of:

(*a*) a thesis of not more than 25,000 words in length, including tables, footnotes, and appendices, but excluding bibliography, on a subject approved by the Degree Committee for the Faculty of Human, Social, and Political Science;

[1] This course is suspended until further notice.

and

(*b*) an examination paper written under examination conditions of three hours' duration on a compulsory core course;

and

(*c*) an assessed course of study on each of six topics from a list of no fewer than eight and no more than fifteen fields to be set by the Degree Committee. The form of examination shall be determined by the Degree Committee on the recommendation of the Course Directors in advance of the course. Provided that candidates for each field shall be examined in the same way, the form of examination for any field may be:

(i) two essays not exceeding 2,000 words in length and on set topics falling within a field designated by the Degree Committee;

(ii) one essay not exceeding 4,000 words in length and on set topics falling within a field designated by the Degree Committee;

(iii) an examination paper written under examination conditions of three hours' duration on set topics falling within a field designated by the Degree Committee.

2. The arrangements for announcing the set topics for essays shall be made by the Degree Committee.

3. The examination may include, at the discretion of the Examiners, an oral examination on the thesis, or on the general field of knowledge within which this falls, or both.

4. The Examiners may recommend to the Degree Committee that it recommends to the Institute of Continuing Education the award of the Postgraduate Diploma to a candidate who has satisfactorily completed the requirements specified in Regulation 1(*c*), and to a candidate who has not completed, or fails to reach the required standard in, the thesis.

JEWISH-CHRISTIAN RELATIONS

Rescinded by Notice (Reporter, *2013–14, p. 534*)

MANUFACTURING[1]

The scheme of examination for the course of study in Manufacturing for the degree of Master of Studies shall consist of:

(*a*) course-work, as prescribed by the Degree Committee for the Faculty of Engineering;

(*b*) three case studies, each of not more than 5,000 words in length and each on a project approved by the Degree Committee;

(*c*) a thesis, of not more than 15,000 words in length, including footnotes and appendices but excluding bibliography, on a subject approved by the Degree Committee.

At the discretion of the Examiners the examination shall include an oral examination on the thesis and on the general field of knowledge within which it falls.

SUSTAINABILITY LEADERSHIP

The scheme of examination for the course of study in Sustainability Leadership for the degree of Master of Studies shall be as follows:

1. For the purpose of the general regulations for the degree, the Degree Committee concerned with the examination shall be the Degree Committee for the Faculty of Business and Management.

2. The examination shall consist of:

(*a*) two essays (a case review and a strategy paper), each of no more than 3,000 words in length, and each on a topic approved by the Degree Committee;

(*b*) an essay (a group project) of no more than 7,000 words in length on a topic approved by the Degree Committee;

(*c*) an action research project, with a ten minute oral presentation of findings, on a topic approved by the Degree Committee;

(*d*) a thesis of not more than 15,000 words in length, including footnotes and appendices, but excluding bibliography, on a subject approved by the Degree Committee.

3. At the discretion of the Examiners the examination shall include an oral examination on the thesis and on the general field of knowledge within which it falls.

[1] This course is suspended until further notice.

DEGREES IN VETERINARY MEDICINE

BACHELOR OF VETERINARY MEDICINE

REVISED REGULATIONS

1. These regulations, which shall be known as the Revised Regulations for the degree of Bachelor of Veterinary Medicine, shall apply to

(*a*) those students who begin their clinical course on or after 1 September 2003, and

(*b*) those students who begin their clinical course on or after 1 September 2002, having undertaken not more than two years of preclinical medical study in the University.[1]

2. There shall be a Second Examination and a Final Examination for the degree of Bachelor of Veterinary Medicine, referred to in these regulations as the Second Vet.M.B. Examination and the Final Veterinary Examination.

3. A student who has kept nine terms and passed Part III of the Final Veterinary Examination shall be qualified to proceed to the degree of Bachelor of Veterinary Medicine, the short title of which shall be Vet.M.B. Qualifications for Degree.

4. The Faculty Board of Veterinary Medicine shall be empowered, after consultation with the Faculty Board of Biology, to delegate to the Veterinary Education Committee from time to time all or any of the Faculty Board's powers and duties under these regulations. In these regulations unless the context shall require otherwise: Definitions.

(*a*) the term *Faculty Board* shall mean the Faculty Board of Veterinary Medicine;

(*b*) the terms *prescribed standard* and *prescribed course* shall mean respectively standard prescribed by the Faculty Board of Veterinary Medicine and course prescribed by the Faculty Board of Veterinary Medicine;

(*c*) the term *course of instruction* shall mean course of instruction given in the University or elsewhere and may include practical instruction.

(*d*) the term *Veterinary Students Register* shall mean a register of students who are deemed fit to practise veterinary medicine. A student may be removed temporarily or permanently from the Register if he or she is deemed no longer a fit person to have the privilege of access to patients. Subject to the powers of the Council and of the General Board and of a Fitness for Veterinary Practice Appeal Tribunal, the Register shall be maintained by the Faculty Boards of Biology and Veterinary Medicine through the Fitness for Veterinary Practice Committee.

5. Where these regulations require a candidate for any of the examinations prescribed therein to produce evidence of instruction or of any other matter Evidence of instruction, etc.

(*a*) the candidate's entry for the examination shall not be considered to have been made earlier than the day on which the Registrary receives that evidence or the last part of it;

(*b*) the Faculty Board of Veterinary Medicine shall have power to require that evidence of having attended a course of instruction shall be evidence of having attended a prescribed course.

6. The Faculty Board, after consulting other bodies concerned, shall have power to define or limit by supplementary regulations all or any of the subjects of the Second Vet.M.B. Examination and all or any of the Parts or sections of a Part of the Final Veterinary Examination. Supplementary regulations.

7. The subjects of the Second Vet.M.B. Examination shall be as follows: Second Vet.M.B. Examination.

Biology of Disease (BOD)
Comparative Vertebrate Biology (CVB)
Homeostasis (HOM)
Introduction to the Scientific Basis of Medicine (ISBM)
Mechanisms of Drug Action (MODA)
Molecules in Medical Science (MIMS)
Neurobiology with Animal Behaviour (NAB)
Preparing for the Veterinary Profession (PFVP)
Principles of Animal Management (PAM)
Veterinary Anatomy and Physiology (VAP)
Veterinary Reproductive Biology (VRB)

[1] That is, having taken Part IA and Part IB of the Medical and Veterinary Sciences Tripos as Affiliated Students. See Regulation 3(*e*) of the Revised Regulations for the degrees of M.B., B.Chir. (last printed in *Statutes and Ordinances*, 2011, p. 447).

(*a*) The examinations in BOD, HOM, MIMS, MODA, and VAP shall each consist of a written paper of one hour, which shall contain compulsory short-answer questions (Section I), and a practical examination of two hours (Section II).

(*b*) The examinations in VRB and NAB shall consist of a written paper of one hour, which shall contain compulsory short-answer questions (Section I), and a practical examination of one hour (Section II).

(*c*) The examination in PAM shall consist of a written paper of one hour, which shall contain compulsory short-answer questions.

(*d*) The examination in CVB shall consist of a combined written and practical paper of an hour and a half, which shall contain short answer questions (Section I), and a practical examination (Section II); candidates will be allowed forty-five minutes to complete each part.

(*e*) The examinations in ISBM and PFVP shall each consist of a written paper of forty-five minutes.

8. The Second Vet.M.B. Examination shall be held as follows:

(*a*) The examinations in BOD, CVB, HOM, MIMS, MODA, NAB, VAP, and VRB shall be held twice a year, as follows:

(i) in the Easter Term, on the dates prescribed for Part IA and Part IB of the Medical and Veterinary Sciences Tripos;[1]

(ii) in September, beginning on the Monday next but one before the first day of the Michaelmas Term.

(*b*) The examinations in ISBM, PAM, and PFVP shall be held twice a year on the last day of Full Lent Term and in the week beginning on the Monday next but one before the first day of the Michaelmas Term.

Standing of candidates.

9. A candidate for the Second Vet.M.B. shall be required:

(*a*) to have satisfied the University's premedical requirements for the Vet.M.B. The premedical requirements, which shall be determined by the Faculty Board of Veterinary Medicine, shall be specified in Schedule A to these regulations; the Faculty Board shall have power to amend that schedule from time to time as they think fit;

(*b*) to have diligently attended approved courses of instruction appropriate to the subject or subjects to be offered in the examination. Approved courses recognized for this purpose shall be listed in Schedule B to these regulations; the Faculty Board shall have power to amend that schedule from time to time as they think fit. The Faculty Board shall have authority to approve for this purpose additional courses offered by a university other than Cambridge, or, in exceptional circumstances to waive the requirement.

The Second Vet.M.B. Examination may be taken by an unmatriculated student who has satisfied these requirements and who is certified on behalf of a College to the Registrary to be a *bona fide* candidate for admission to the College. A student whose name does not appear on the Veterinary Students Register shall not be a candidate for any subject of the Second Vet.M.B. Examination.

Exemption.

10. (*a*) The Faculty Board shall have power to grant exemption from any subject or subjects of the Second Vet.M.B. Examination to a candidate for admission as a veterinary student from a university other than Cambridge, provided that the student has satisfied the conditions of Regulation 9 and has attained a satisfactory standard, as prescribed by the Faculty Board, in corresponding subjects taken in an examination for a degree of a university other than Cambridge.

(*b*) The Faculty Board shall inform the Registrary as early as possible of the names of those candidates who have been granted exemption from any subject or subjects of the Second Vet.M.B. Examination and who have satisfied the requirements in Regulation 10(*a*). The Registrary shall thereupon post a list of the names outside the Senate-House.

11. A candidate who is unsuccessful in the examination in any subject of the Second Vet.M.B. Examination shall be eligible for re-examination, provided that, except by special permission of the Faculty Board granted in exceptional circumstances,

(i) a student who fails to satisfy the Examiners in any subject other than ISBM or PAM shall not be a candidate for re-examination in that subject later than five months after his or her first attempt in that subject;

[1] In this sitting of the Second Vet.M.B. Examination the papers set are Sections I and II of the papers set in the corresponding subjects of Part IA of the Medical and Veterinary Sciences Tripos. See Regulations 15 and 20 of that Tripos.

(ii) a student who fails to satisfy the Examiners in ISBM or PAM shall not be a candidate for re-examination in that subject later than thirteen months after his or her first attempt in that subject;

(iii) subject to Regulation 26, no student shall be a candidate in any subject on more than two occasions in total.

12. The Final Veterinary Examination shall consist of three Parts. Except by permission of the Faculty Board of Veterinary Medicine in exceptional circumstances, no student shall be a candidate for the first time for any Part later than four years after the beginning of his or her course of clinical study. Final Vet. Examination.

13. The examinations for Part I of the Final Veterinary Examination shall be held on dates determined by the Faculty Board, and shall consist of written papers and practical examinations, as prescribed by the Faculty Board from time to time. The subjects of examination shall be specified by supplementary regulation. All candidates shall make their first attempt at the examination on the first published date for that examination provided that, in exceptional circumstances and for good cause, the Faculty Board may permit a candidate to defer taking the examination until the next timetabled sitting of that examination. Part I.

14. Before taking the examination in any subject of Part I, a student must have

(*a*) completed the Second Veterinary M.B. Examination by having passed all the subjects thereof,

(*b*) obtained a degree deemed appropriate by the Faculty Board, which shall be a degree of this University if the student has undertaken preclinical veterinary study in the University, and which may otherwise be a degree of a university other than Cambridge, and

(*c*) produced evidence of having, since the date of his or her matriculation, satisfactorily carried out twelve weeks of extra-mural studies in a form prescribed by the Faculty Board of Veterinary Medicine. A student may exceptionally apply, through his or her College, to the Faculty Board of Veterinary Medicine for permission to carry out these extra-mural studies while he or she is a candidate for Part I of the Final Veterinary Examination. No student may be a candidate for Part II of the Final Veterinary Examination until he or she has satisfactorily completed these extra-mural studies.

Subject to the provisions of Regulation 19(*b*) and (*c*), candidates who fail to satisfy the Examiners in any subject of Part I may present themselves for re-examination, under arrangements approved by the Faculty Board. A student whose name does not appear on the Veterinary Students Register shall not be a candidate for any subject of the Final Vet.M.B. Examination.

15. Two sittings of Part II of the Final Veterinary Examination shall be held each year, beginning on the sixth Wednesday of Full Easter Term and on the Monday that next precedes the first day of the Michaelmas Term. All candidates shall make their first attempt at the examination in the Easter Term provided that, in exceptional circumstances and for good cause, the Faculty Board may permit a candidate to defer taking the examination until the following September. The examination shall consist of two written papers and a practical examination. The two written papers and the practical examination shall each be of two hours' duration. Questions in the two written papers will cover the following areas: Part II.

1. Parasitic diseases
2. Biology of infectious disease
3. Basic clinical pharmacology, toxicology, and systems pathology
4. Animal health, animal breeding, and nutrition

16. No student may be a candidate for Part II until at least eighteen months have elapsed after the beginning of his or her course of clinical study. A candidate must have passed Part I and must have

(*a*) produced certificates of diligent attendance at courses of instruction in the following subjects:

(i) the diseases of poultry, including legislation concerned with their control;

(ii) the aetiology, epidemiology, pathology, and prophylaxis of infectious diseases of domestic animals;

(iii) helminthology, protozoology, and entomology, relevant to parasitic disease of domestic animals, and the prevention and treatment of such disease;

(iv) the husbandry, nutrition, and practical breeding of domestic animals in relation to health, welfare, and production; pastoral botany; genetics; veterinary hygiene;

(v) clinical veterinary pharmacology and toxicology;

(vi) animal management and elementary clinical methods;

(vii) pathology, pathophysiology, diagnosis, and therapeutics;
(viii) reproduction, infertility, and obstetrics;
(ix) veterinary public health, including practical instruction in the inspection and control of meat and milk;
(x) state veterinary medicine and jurisprudence;

(*b*) satisfactorily completed the clinical tests which form part of the courses specified in this regulation.

(*c*) successfully completed project work for the course of clinical study, as defined by the Faculty Board from time to time.

A candidate for Part II shall take both papers and the practical examination at the same sitting. Subject to the provisions of Regulation 19(*b*) and (*c*), candidates who fail to satisfy the Examiners may present themselves for re-examination, taking both papers and the practical examination at the same sitting.

Part III.

17. Part III of the Final Veterinary Examination shall be held twice a year beginning on the Friday of the second week of Full Easter Term and on the Monday next preceding the first day of Michaelmas Term. All candidates shall make their first attempt at the examination in the Easter Term provided that, in exceptional circumstances and for good cause, the Faculty Board may permit a candidate to defer taking the examination until the following September. Part III shall consist of four sections, each consisting of a written paper and a practical/oral examination:

1. Equine studies
2. Small animal studies
3. Farm animal studies
4. Veterinary public health

The written papers for sections 1 to 3 shall be of three hours' duration and for section 4 shall be of two hours' duration.

The Examiners shall take into account such course-work done by candidates, including practical work, as shall from time to time be determined by the Faculty Board of Veterinary Medicine. For this purpose the Head of the Department of Veterinary Medicine shall present to the Examiners a detailed assessment of the performance of each candidate in this course-work. The Examiners shall take the assessments into account in assigning marks for the examination; the maximum percentage of the total marks that may be awarded for course-work shall be determined from time to time by the Faculty Board.

A candidate attempting Part III for the first time shall be required to take a written paper in each of the four sections at the same sitting and a practical/oral examination corresponding to the written paper of each of the four sections of the examination. Subject to the provisions of Regulation 19(*b*) and (*c*), candidates who fail to satisfy the Examiners in any subject of Part III may present themselves for re-examination, under arrangements approved by the Faculty Board, in September beginning on the Monday next preceding the first day of the Michaelmas Term. The Examiners may, at their discretion, require any candidate who fails to attain the prescribed standard for any section to take a *viva voce* examination.

Candidates for Part III shall also be required to undertake an eight-week elective study period, four weeks of which shall take place following the Easter Term sitting of the written examinations. The elective shall be on a subject chosen by the candidate from a list of topics announced by the Faculty Board from time to time, or on a topic proposed by the candidate and approved by the Faculty Board. Candidates shall be required to submit a dissertation of not more than 3,000 words, give an oral presentation of their work of not more than fifteen minutes, and submit a certificate of diligent attendance signed by the elective supervisor. A satisfactory standard must be attained in the dissertation, oral presentation, and certificate of diligent attendance before the degree of Bachelor of Veterinary Medicine can be awarded. In the case of an unsatisfactory standard being achieved in any of the three elements resubmission will be required at the time of the September examination for Part III.

Standing of candidates for Part III.

18. No student may be a candidate for Part III until at least thirty-two months have elapsed after the beginning of his or her course of clinical study. No student may be a candidate for Part III if more than ninety-two months have elapsed since he or she began the preclinical veterinary medicine course, providing that the Faculty Board may waive this condition in exceptional circumstances. A candidate must have passed Part II and

(*a*) must have produced evidence of having

(i) subsequently attended further courses of instruction in clinical veterinary medicine as concerned in particular with the various species of domestic animals, including satisfactory completion of the clinical tests which form part of these courses;
(ii) attended a course of instruction in applied anatomy, surgical pathology, operative technique, anaesthesia, general and regional surgery, including satisfactory completion of the clinical tests which form part of the course;
(iii) attended a course of instruction in jurisprudence;
(iv) satisfactorily carried out work in the Clinical Pathology Laboratories and the Post Mortem Room of the Veterinary Hospital;

(*b*) must have had, since the beginning of his or her course of clinical study, at least twenty-six weeks' practical experience of veterinary work approved for this purpose by the Faculty Board of Veterinary Medicine in addition to the twelve weeks of extra-mural studies required by Regulation 15 to have been carried out since matriculation; for this purpose each candidate shall be required to submit for the inspection of the Examiners, not later than the first day of the examination, records of his or her extra-mural studies in a form prescribed by the Faculty Board from time to time.

19. Except by permission of the Faculty Board in exceptional circumstances, and subject to any conditions determined by them, Restrictions.

(*a*) no certificate or other evidence produced under Regulation 16(*a*) shall be accepted if it relates to a course of instruction that began *either* (i) before the candidate's completion of the Second Veterinary M.B. Examination, *or* (ii) before the beginning of the candidate's course of clinical study, *or* (iii) more than eight years after the candidate first took any subject of the Second Veterinary M.B. Examination or an examination leading to exemption from such a subject;

(*b*) no student shall be re-examined in any Part, or in any subject, paper, or section of a Part later than two years after his or her first candidature for that Part, subject, paper, or section;

(*c*) subject to Regulation 26, no student shall be a candidate for any Part, or for any subject, paper, or section of a Part on more than three occasions.

20. The arrangements for the appointment of Examiners for the Second Vet.M.B. Examination shall be as follows: Examiners for the Second Vet.M.B. Examination.

(*a*) For BOD, HOM, ISBM, MIMS, and MODA the Examiners shall be the Examiners appointed for those subjects in the Second M.B. Examination,

(*b*) For each of the subjects CVB, NAB, PAM, PFVP, VAP, and VRB the Faculty Board shall nominate a Senior Examiner and such number of other Examiners as are required to conduct the examination; provided that for sittings of subjects of the Second Vet.M.B. Examination held under Regulation 8(*a*)(i)[1] the Examiners shall be the Examiners appointed for those subjects in the Medical and Veterinary Sciences Tripos.

21. The Faculty Board of Veterinary Medicine shall nominate in each calendar year such number of Examiners for each Part of the Final Veterinary Examination as the General Board on the recommendation of the Faculty Board may determine. The Faculty Board shall also have power to nominate one or more Assessors to assist the Examiners in any Part of the Examination. If required to do so, Assessors shall propose questions in the subject or subjects assigned to them, shall look over the answers of candidates to those questions, shall set and conduct practical, clinical, and oral examinations, and shall report as required to the Examiners. An Assessor may be summoned, for the purpose of consultation and advice, to meetings of the relevant body of Examiners, but shall not be entitled to vote. for the Final Veterinary Examination.

22. The Examiners and Assessors shall observe the following provisions:

(*a*) the Examiners and Assessors in each subject, paper, or section shall be jointly responsible for all the questions set in that subject, paper, or section in the several examinations in which they take part;

(*b*) at least two Examiners or Assessors shall read the papers and test the practical work of each candidate;

(*c*) at least two Examiners or Assessors shall be present at, and shall participate in, the *viva voce* examination of any candidate;

[1] That is when the papers of the Second Vet.M.B. Examination are the papers set for the corresponding subjects of the Medical and Veterinary Sciences Tripos.

(*d*) in Part I, in Part II, and in each section of Part III, at least two Examiners shall be present at the meeting at which the list of successful candidates is drawn up.

Class-lists.

23. Separate class-lists shall be published for each subject of the Second Veterinary M.B. Examination, and for each Part of the Final Veterinary Examination. The names of the successful candidates in the several lists shall be arranged in alphabetical order. The lists for Part III of the Final Veterinary Examination shall indicate the sections of the examination in which the candidate has passed. In Part I, in Part II, and in each section of Part III, of the Final Veterinary Examination, a mark of distinction may be affixed to the names of the candidates whose work is of special merit.

Duties of Chairs of Examiners.

24. The Senior Examiner for each subject of the Second Vet.M.B. Examination and the Chair of Examiners for each Part of the Final Veterinary Examination shall communicate the marks of all the candidates to the Registrary, and shall communicate to Tutors or other designated College officers, for transmission to their pupils, the marks of their pupils and such other information as may be considered advisable.[1]

Candidates fees.

25. A candidate for the Vet.M.B. Degree shall pay the appropriate University Composition Fee for each term of clinical study for the degree. This fee covers admission and readmission to the Veterinary Examinations and admission to the Vet.M.B. Degree.

26. The Faculty Board of Veterinary Medicine shall establish a procedure[2] for the review of decisions taken by them in respect of students who have applied exceptionally for an additional attempt at any Part of the Vet.M.B. examination under Regulations 11 or 19(*c*). No person who applies for review under the procedure so established shall be entitled to apply also for review of the same matter under the procedure for determining complaints by members of the University *in statu pupillari* established under the Regulation for complaints by students.[3]

SCHEDULE A

PREMEDICAL REQUIREMENTS FOR THE VET.M.B.

GCE A level and GCSE

1. In this Schedule the Advanced level and AS (Advanced Subsidiary) level passes referred to are passes at those levels in a General Certificate of Education (GCE) issued by an awarding body approved by the relevant regulatory authority in England (QCA), Wales (ACCAC), and Northern Ireland (CCEA). The General Certificate of Secondary Education (GCSE) passes referred to are passes in that Certificate, at Grade A, B, or C, issued by an awarding body approved by the relevant regulatory authority in England (QCA), Wales (ACCAC), and Northern Ireland (CCEA).

Approved equivalents

2. For the purposes of this Schedule, the following shall be regarded as the equivalent of a pass at (Advanced) level:

(*a*) a pass in the Scottish Qualifications Authority National Course Advanced Higher examination at Grade A, B, C, or D;

(*b*) a pass in the Scottish Qualifications Authority National Course Higher examination at Grade A, B, or C;

(*c*) a pass at Grade 5 or above in a subject taken at the Higher level of the International Baccalaureate Diploma Programme;

(*d*) a pass in a General Certificate of Education (GCE) Advanced level within the Advanced Diploma of the Welsh Baccalaureate.

3. For the purpose of this Schedule, the following shall be regarded as the equivalent of a pass at AS (Advanced Subsidiary) level:

(*a*) a pass at Level 5 or above in a subject taken at the Standard level of the International Baccalaureate Diploma Programme.

4. For the purposes of this Schedule, the following shall be regarded as the equivalent of a pass in the GCSE:

(*a*) a pass at Ordinary level (Grade A, B, or C) in a GCE issued by an examining body approved by the Department for Children, Schools and Families;

(*b*) a pass in the Scottish Qualifications Authority Standard Grade examination at Grade 1, 2, or 3;

(*c*) a pass in the International GCSE at Grade A, B, or C;

(*d*) a pass at Grade 5 or above in a subject taken at Standard level of the International Baccalaureate Diploma Programme.

5. Passes in subjects of examinations for certificates conducted overseas by the Local Examinations Syndicate shall be considered for equivalence according to the level attained, provided always that the examination is conducted in the medium of English.

[1] See also the regulations for the disclosure of examination marks, p. 250.

[2] See the Appendix to these regulations.

[3] See p. 220.

Premedical requirements

6. The premedical requirements for the Vet.M.B. shall consist of two Parts, A and B.

(*a*) A student shall be deemed to have completed Part A if he or she has *either* achieved the required standard in an admissions test approved by the Faculty Board of Veterinary Medicine *or* obtained GCSE passes in the following subjects or equivalents approved by the Faculty Board:

(i) Physics;
(ii) Biology;
(iii) Mathematics;

provided that

(1) a pass in double-award science may be substituted for the passes required under (i) and (ii) above;
(2) passes at Advanced level or AS (Advanced Subsidiary) level may be substituted for the GCSE passes required under (i), (ii), and (iii) above;
(3) a credit in the Science Foundation Course of the Open University may be substituted for the GCSE passes required under (i) and (ii) above.

(*b*) A student shall be deemed to have completed Part B if he or she has obtained Advanced level or AS (Advanced Subsidiary) level passes in the following subjects or equivalents approved by the Faculty Board:

(i) Chemistry;
(ii) at least two of the following: Physics, Biology, Mathematics;

provided that

(1) at least one of these subjects must be passed at Advanced level;
(2) the examination requirements for matriculation are complied with.

(*c*) A student shall be deemed to have completed Part B if he or she has obtained honours or has achieved the honours standard in Part IA of the Natural Sciences Tripos.

(*d*) For the purposes of the premedical requirements for the Vet.M.B., a student who has obtained an honours degree of this or a recognized university shall be deemed to have satisfied the requirements by passing an admissions test approved by the Faculty Board of Veterinary Medicine.

SCHEDULE B

Approved courses of instruction for the Second Vet.M.B. Examination

In addition to the courses offered as specific preparation for the subjects for the Second Vet.M.B. Examination, the following courses have been approved by the Faculty Board of Veterinary Medicine as appropriate courses of instruction for certain subjects of the Second Vet.M.B. Examination.

Subjects in the Second Vet.M.B. Examination		*Subject in Tripos Examinations*
Biology of Disease		NST IB Pathology
	or	NST II Pathology
Mechanisms of Drug Action		NST IB Pharmacology
	or	NST II Pharmacology
Molecules in Medical Science	*or*	NST IB Biochemistry and Molecular Biology
		NST II Biochemistry
Homeostasis		NST IA Physiology of Organisms
	and	NST IB Physiology

SUPPLEMENTARY REGULATIONS

Second Veterinary M.B. Examination

Biology of Disease (*BOD*)

The examination in BOD will be treated from the standpoint of abnormal biology. It will include the variations that may occur in the structure and functions of living cells, tissues, and organs, together with the biology of parasites, bacteria, and viruses. Section I will consist of compulsory short-answer questions on the lecture material. Section II will consist of a two-hour practical examination which will include laboratory work and questions on practical aspects and problem solving.

Comparative Vertebrate Biology (*CVB*)

The written examination will require knowledge of the structure and function of birds, fish, and certain species of laboratory animal.

Homeostasis (*HOM*)

Section I will consist of computer-marked and short-answer questions on nerve and neuromuscular transmission, muscle, autonomic nervous system, cardiovascular system, respiration, kidney, salt and water balance, digestion, absorption, and temperature regulation. Section II will consist of questions on the practical work in experimental physiology and histology.

Introduction to the Scientific Basis of Medicine (*ISBM*)

The examination will consist of compulsory short-answer or computer-marked questions on the ISBM course.

Molecules in Medical Science (*MIMS*)

The examination will test knowledge and understanding of the material contained in the MIMS course. Section I will consist of short-answer questions on the lectures. Section II will consist of questions on practical aspects, including interpretation and handling of data.

Mechanisms of Drug Action (*MODA*)

Section I, which will include or consist entirely of short-answer questions, will require knowledge of the actions of drugs on whole organisms and mammalian systems, and also of the mode of drug action at the cellular, sub-cellular, and molecular levels. Section II will consist of a practical examination, which will include questions on data handling and problem solving; laboratory work will not be involved. Questions that require an elementary knowledge of statistical procedures may be included in both sections of the examination.

Neurobiology with Animal Behaviour (*NAB*)

The examination in NAB will require knowledge of the structure and functions of the central nervous system, the special sense organs, neuropharmacology and animal behaviour, with particular reference to domestic animals. Section I will include or consist entirely of compulsory short-answer questions. In Section II, candidates will be examined on practical aspects of neuroanatomy and in experimental neurophysiology; questions may be included which require an elementary knowledge of statistical procedures.

Principles of Animal Management (*PAM*)

The written examination will require knowledge of agriculture, animal husbandry, and farm health and safety issues.

Preparing for the Veterinary Profession (*PFVP*)

The examination will test knowledge of the material presented in the PFVP course.

Veterinary Anatomy and Physiology (*VAP*)

Section I will consist of computer-marked and short-answer questions on the anatomy of domestic mammals and, on the structure and function of the gastrointestinal systems of herbivorous mammals. Section II will consist of questions on associated practical work.

Veterinary Reproductive Biology (*VRB*)

Section I of the examination will consist of computer-marked and short-answer questions on the structure and function of the reproductive systems of mammals, with particular reference to domestic mammals. Section II will consist of questions on associated practical work and may include a data-handling exercise.

FINAL VETERINARY EXAMINATION

Amended by Notice (Reporter, *2013–14, p. 782*)

PART I

The papers and practical components of the examination shall be as follows:

Paper 1. Respiratory system
Paper 2. Principles of clinical practice
Paper 3. Dermatology
Paper 4. Principles of infectious diseases
Paper 5. Clinical pathology
Paper 6. Alimentary system
Paper 7. Integrated animal management
Paper 8. Urology
Paper 9. Animal breeding
Paper 10. Neurology
Paper 11. Endocrinology and metabolic diseases
Paper 12. Cardiology
Paper 13. Veterinary public health

The written papers will each be of one hour's duration, excepting Papers 1 (which will have a practical component), 2, and 13, which will each be of 90 minutes' duration, and Paper 6, which will be of two hours' duration and have a practical component.

PART III

The examination will consist of four sections. In three of the sections there will be a three-hour written paper and a practical/oral examination. In the fourth section there will be a two-hour written examination and a practical/oral examination. In order to satisfy the Examiners in each section candidates will be required to attain a prescribed standard in the written paper before proceeding to the practical/oral examination.

APPENDIX

Review of Decisions of the Faculty Board of Veterinary Medicine under Regulation 26

1. A student, or her or his Tutor with the student's consent, may seek review of a decision in relation to that student made by the Faculty Board of Veterinary Medicine.
2. A request for review shall be made in writing, stating the grounds of review, and be sent to the Registrary, normally within three weeks of written notification of the decision of the Faculty Board of Veterinary Medicine (unless, in exceptional circumstances, the Registrary or a deputy permits a longer period). The Registrary shall communicate the request for review to the Secretary of the Faculty Board.
3. If the request includes, in the opinion of the Chair of the Faculty Board, relevant additional information not previously available, the Faculty Board will reconsider its decision at its next meeting following receipt of the request. If no such additional information is included or if, on reconsideration, the decision is reaffirmed by the Faculty Board, the procedure described in the following paragraphs shall apply.
4. The Registrary or a deputy will appoint a reviewer chosen from a panel of potential reviewers maintained by the Council.
5. The reviewer will consider the request, the documentation available to the Faculty Board (less any confidential medical information), the Ordinances which apply to the Faculty Board's decision, and the Faculty Board's Notes of Guidance. He or she will obtain an opinion from the Faculty Board, seek such other information as he or she may require and, at her or his discretion, may hold a hearing (but there is no obligation to hold a hearing). The reviewer will issue an adjudication in writing as soon as possible, stating findings of fact, conclusions, and, if any, recommendations, for consideration by the Faculty Board. The reviewer shall be concerned with determining whether there is evidence of: the Faculty Board having made a decision, to the detriment of the student, which is inconsistent with the relevant Ordinances or its own Notes of Guidance; or material circumstances of which the Faculty Board was unaware and which were of such a nature as, had the Faculty Board been so aware, to have been likely to cause the Faculty Board to have reached a different decision.
6. The Faculty Board of Veterinary Medicine shall normally accept the recommendation of the reviewer. If, exceptionally, the reviewer's recommendation is not accepted, a written explanation shall be provided to the reviewer, the student, and her or his Tutor, and shall be submitted to the Council. The Faculty Board may decide not to accept a recommendation in any instance in which: (i) the reviewer has sought to make a decision replacing that of the Faculty Board; (ii) the reviewer's recommendation is inconsistent with the relevant Ordinances; or (iii) the reviewer's recommendation is such that, were it to be accepted, it would set a precedent which would not be in the interests of the proper conduct of the Faculty Board's business or in the wider interests of the University or the Royal College of Veterinary Medicine. The Council (or an officer appointed by it) should be satisfied that the Faculty Board's written explanation is consistent with one or more of these instances.
7. The conclusion of the consideration by the Faculty Board of Veterinary Medicine of any recommendation of a review shall be the normal final point of decision within the University. Any subsequent review would normally be by the Office of the Independent Adjudicator (OIA).
8. The reviewer may summarily dismiss an application which seems to her or him to be vexatious or frivolous.

Doctor of Veterinary Medicine

1. In order to qualify for the degree of Doctor of Veterinary Medicine a candidate shall be required to provide evidence of a significant original contribution to the study of Veterinary Medicine. Qualifications required.

2. Any person may apply to be registered as a candidate for the degree who Standing of candidates.

either (*a*) holds a degree of the University,

or (*b*) holds a University office or an unestablished appointment on the staff of the Veterinary School,

and also holds one of the following qualifications:

either (i) a veterinary degree giving entitlement to provisional or full registration with the Royal College of Veterinary Surgeons,

or (ii) a degree recognized by the Council of the Royal College of Veterinary Surgeons for the purpose of full registration,

or (iii) a veterinary degree approved by the Vet.M.D. Committee for the purpose of candidature.

No one shall be registered as a candidate for the degree until five years have elapsed since the date of his or her admission to a veterinary degree as specified above.

3. There shall be a Vet.M.D. Committee, which shall consist of: Vet.M.D. Committee.

(*a*) the Head of the Department of Veterinary Medicine or a deputy appointed by the Head of the Department, who shall be Chair;

(*b*) six persons appointed by the Degree Committee for the Faculties of Clinical Medicine and Veterinary Medicine;

(*c*) not more than six persons co-opted by the Committee.

Members in class (*b*) shall be appointed in the Michaelmas Term to serve for three years from 1 January following their appointment. Members in class (*c*) shall serve for such period as the Committee shall determine at the time of their co-optation.

Quorum. **4.** No business shall be transacted at a meeting of the Committee unless four of the members in classes (*a*) and (*b*) are present.

Applications. **5.** Any person who wishes to be registered as a candidate for the degree shall submit an application to the Secretary of the Vet.M.D. Committee. The application shall specify:

(*a*) the applicant's proposed subject of study or research, including a plan of the work to be undertaken and an account of the methods to be used;

(*b*) the place where the work is to be undertaken;

(*c*) the method of financing the work;

(*d*) the name of a suitably qualified person who is proposed as supervisor of the work.

Each application shall be accompanied by an application fee.[1]

6. Each application shall be submitted to the Vet.M.D. Committee, who may refer it to one or more referees for their opinion and advice before deciding whether to approve or reject the application or to suggest some modification of the applicant's proposals. Each referee appointed under this regulation shall receive a fee.[1] The Secretary of the Vet.M.D. Committee shall maintain a record of persons who are registered as candidates for the degree; when an application has been approved, the applicant's name shall be entered on the record. The Committee shall determine the conditions, if any, of an applicant's registration and shall assign to him or her a date of commencement of candidature.

Examination. **7.** The examination for the degree of Vet.M.D. shall consist of:

(*a*) the submission of a dissertation embodying the results of the candidate's study or research, which shall be submitted in accordance with the provisions of Regulations 9 and 10;

(*b*) an oral examination on the subject of the dissertation and the general field of knowledge within which it falls.

By special permission of the Vet.M.D. Committee, candidates may submit with the dissertation published work which they wish the Examiners to consider; such work may be considered by the Examiners at their discretion.

8. A candidate may submit his or her dissertation not earlier than two years and not later than six years after the date of registration for the degree, provided that the Vet.M.D. Committee may give a candidate special permission to delay submission until a later date. When submitting a dissertation a candidate shall pay a submission fee.[1]

9. In submitting their dissertations, candidates shall state, generally in a preface and specifically in notes or in a bibliography, the sources from which their information is derived, the extent to which they have availed themselves of the work of others, and the portions of the dissertation which are claimed as original. They shall also be required to declare that the dissertation submitted is not substantially the same as any that they may have submitted for another degree or for a diploma or similar qualification. A dissertation, apart from quotations, shall be written in English. The Degree Committee for the Faculties of Clinical Medicine and Veterinary Medicine shall have power to specify a maximum length for dissertations.

10. Two copies of each candidate's dissertation, accompanied by two copies of a summary of about 300 words in length, shall be sent to the Secretary of the Degree Committee for the Faculties of Clinical Medicine and Veterinary Medicine. Each dissertation shall be referred to two Examiners, appointed by the Degree Committee. Each Examiner shall make an independent report to the Degree Committee on the dissertation. The two Examiners shall jointly conduct the oral examination specified in Regulation 7(*b*), and shall sign a joint certificate of the result. If the Examiners do not agree in their recommendations or if for any other reason the Degree Committee or the Board of Graduate Studies need a further opinion or opinions on the merit of the work submitted, the Degree Committee may appoint an additional Examiner or additional Examiners, provided that not more than one additional Examiner shall be appointed without leave of the Board of Graduate Studies. Each additional Examiner so appointed shall make an independent report on the dissertation to the Degree Committee. Each Examiner shall receive a fee, and shall be entitled to claim travelling expenses and a subsistence allowance as appropriate.[1]

[1] See the Schedule to these regulations.

11. If a candidate fails to satisfy the Examiners in the oral examination specified in Regulation 7(*b*), the Degree Committee may permit the candidate to be re-examined by the same Examiners on payment of an additional fee.[1] Permission so given shall be communicated to the Secretary of the Board of Graduate Studies and shall not be given on more than one occasion. Each Examiner who takes part in an examination under this regulation shall be paid an additional fee, in addition to any fees to which he or she may be entitled under Regulation 10, and may also claim travelling expenses in accordance with the provisions of that regulation. Re-examination.

12. The Board of Graduate Studies shall be the deciding authority on all recommendations for the award of the degree. If, after considering the reports of the Examiners on a candidate's dissertation and on his or her performance in the oral examination, the Degree Committee are satisfied that the candidate's work is of the requisite standard for the degree, a resolution of the Committee to that effect, with the names of those present and voting on either side, shall be communicated to the Board of Graduate Studies, together with the reports of the Examiners. If the Board, after receiving such communication, at a meeting at which not less than five members of the Board are present, resolve that the candidate be approved for the degree, the Secretary of the Board shall publish a notice of the candidate's approval for the award of the degree.

13. If, after considering the reports of the Examiners, the Degree Committee are of the opinion that a candidate's dissertation is not of the requisite standard for the degree, they may recommend to the Board of Graduate Studies that the candidate be permitted to submit a revised dissertation. The communication conveying such a recommendation shall contain the names of those present and voting on either side, and shall be accompanied by the reports of the Examiners. The Board may permit a candidate to submit a revised dissertation on not more than one occasion. Failure.

14. If, after considering the reports of the Examiners, the Degree Committee are of the opinion that a candidate's work is not of the requisite standard for the degree, and if they do not recommend that the candidate be allowed to submit a revised dissertation, their resolution to that effect, with the names of those present and voting on either side, shall be communicated to the Board of Graduate Studies, together with the reports of the Examiners. The Secretary of the Board shall communicate this decision to the candidate.

15. A candidate who is not approved for the degree

(*a*) shall not be eligible to submit a dissertation which is substantially the same in candidature for the Ph.D. or M.Sc. Degree;

(*b*) may apply to be registered again as a candidate for the degree; such application may be made on not more than one occasion, after a period of not less than five years from the date of the applicant's original registration.

16. Before being admitted to the degree, a successful candidate shall deposit with the Secretary of the Vet.M.D. Committee two copies of the dissertation and of the summary, both the dissertation and the summary being in a form approved by the Committee. The Secretary of the Committee shall deposit copies of the dissertation and the summary in the University Library and in the library of the Department of Veterinary Medicine, where they shall be available for consultation and for making copies for inter-library loan purposes. Work to be deposited in Library.

17. No fee shall be payable on admission to the degree.

SCHEDULE

Fees to be paid by candidates and payments to Examiners

Application fee (Regulation 5): £220.

Payment to a referee (Regulation 6): £45.

Submission fee (Regulation 8): £500.

Payment to each Examiner taking part in the oral examination (Regulation 10): £135.

Payment to an additional Examiner (Regulation 10): £90.

Additional fee to be paid by a candidate on re-examination (Regulation 11): £135.

Additional payment to each Examiner taking part in a second examination under Regulation 11: £45.

An Examiner may claim travelling and other expenses in accordance with Regulation 12 of the regulations for the Ph.D., M.Sc., and M.Litt. Degrees.

[1] See the Schedule to these regulations.

DIPLOMA IN THE CONSERVATION OF EASEL PAINTINGS

Conditions of award.

1. The Diploma in the Conservation of Easel Paintings shall be awarded to a member of the University who has diligently attended a three-year course of instruction prescribed by the Faculty Board of Architecture and History of Art in consultation with the Director of the Hamilton Kerr Institute and has satisfied the Examiners in the examination for the Diploma as defined in the following regulations; provided that he or she has kept at least three terms. For the purpose of this regulation graduates of the University may count previous residence *in statu pupillari*.

Standing of candidates.

2. A candidate for the Diploma must be approved by the Degree Committee of the Faculty of Architecture and History of Art, who shall assign to each candidate a date of commencement of candidature. A candidate must also have:

(i) obtained honours in a first degree, normally in one or more subjects relevant to the course;

(ii) produced other evidence to satisfy the Degree Committee of his or her fitness to study for the Diploma.

3. Applications for approval must be sent, together with evidence of the qualifications required under Regulation 2, to the Administrator of the Hamilton Kerr Institute so as to arrive not later than the last day of February in the academical year next before that in which candidature is to begin.

First-year qualifying examination.

4. The qualifying examination for the Diploma at the end of the first year shall consist of:

(i) three written papers:

Practical conservation,
Science of materials,
Theory of conservation;

and

(ii) three areas of studio-work:

Laboratory practical,
Examination of painting,
Photography practical.

A candidate whose studio-work throughout the first year is successful, but whose written work fails to satisfy the Examiners, may apply to the Degree Committee for permission to take the written examinations on one more occasion within six months of his or her first attempt. A candidate whose studio-work is deemed by the Examiners to be below standard will not be allowed to continue the course.

Second-year examination.

5. The examination for the second year of the Diploma shall consist of:

(i) a portfolio of studio-work which shall be examined by continuous assessment;

(ii) written work, consisting of four essays of not less than 3,000 words and not more than 5,000 words in length, on four topics of the candidate's choice and approved by the Degree Committee, selected from the following subject areas:

(*a*) historical aspects,
(*b*) technical aspects,
(*c*) environmental impact,
(*d*) material behaviour,
(*e*) studio practices,
(*f*) ethical issues,
(*g*) treatment report and technical examination;

and (iii) two seminar presentations, each of 30 minutes' duration and of comparable substance to the written essays on topics selected from (*a*)–(*g*) above.

One of the essays *or* one of the seminar presentations must be selected from area (*g*).

Third-year examination.

6. The examination for the third year of the Diploma shall consist of:

(i) a Project, of no less than 5,000 words and no more than 10,000 words in length, to include a practical component, on a subject area of interest to the student and approved by the Degree Committee which shall be submitted in typewritten form by 7 July;

(ii) a Copy, i.e. the examination of a painting and the reproduction of the artist's technique, accompanied by documentation of no less than 5,000 words in length and no more than 10,000 words in length, which shall be submitted by 7 July;

(iii) studio-work which shall be reviewed at the end of the year;

and (iv) a *viva voce* examination in connection with the studio-work and other written work submitted by the student.

Examiners and Assessors.

7. The Degree Committee shall nominate such number of Examiners and Assessors for each examination as they deem sufficient.

8. A candidate who has satisfied the Examiners in the examination as a whole shall be entitled to a Diploma.

9. The Diploma shall be in the following form: Diploma.

THIS IS TO CERTIFY THAT having satisfied the preliminary conditions and having been admitted to the examinations appointed by the University of Cambridge has been approved by the Examiners and has been awarded the Diploma in the Conservation of Easel Painting.

10. While studying in the University for the Diploma a candidate shall pay the appropriate University Composition Fee for each term of such study. Fees.

11. A student who has qualified to receive the Diploma shall not be entitled to count the period or any part of the period during which he or she was a candidate for the Diploma towards a course of research for the degree of Ph.D., M.Sc., or M.Litt. Relation to courses of research.

ADVANCED DIPLOMA IN ECONOMICS

Amended by Notice (Reporter, *2013–14, p. 56*)

1. The Advanced Diploma in Economics shall be awarded to a member of the University, qualified under Regulation 2, who has diligently attended the course of instruction prescribed by the Faculty Board of Economics, and who has satisfied the Examiners in the examination for the Diploma as defined in the following regulations; provided that he or she has kept three terms. For the purpose of this regulation graduates of the University may count previous residence *in statu pupillari*. Conditions of award.

2. A candidate for the Diploma must be admitted as a Graduate Student by the Board of Graduate Studies, on the recommendation of the Degree Committee for the Faculty of Economics. The Board shall assign to each candidate a date of commencement of candidature. Each candidate shall pursue in the University a course of study extending over one academical year under the direction of a Supervisor appointed by the Degree Committee, and shall comply with any special conditions that the Degree Committee and the Board may prescribe.

3. Every Supervisor shall send to the Secretary of the Board of Graduate Studies reports on the work of each candidate under her or his charge, in accordance with the provisions of Regulation 8 of the general regulations for admission as a Graduate Student. Supervisors' reports.

4. Notwithstanding the provisions of Regulation 11 of the general regulations for admission as a Graduate Student, the Board of Graduate Studies, after consultation with the Degree Committee for the Faculty of Economics, shall have power to determine the payments to be made to Supervisors who are not University officers in respect of candidates for the Diploma. Payments to Supervisors.

5. No one shall be a candidate in the same year both for the Advanced Diploma in Economics and for another University examination, and no one shall be a candidate for the Advanced Diploma in Economics on more than one occasion.

6. The examination shall consist of three papers, as follows: Scheme of examination.

Paper 1. Microeconomics.
Paper 2. Macroeconomics.
Paper 3. Econometrics.

Not later than the end of the Easter Term each year the Degree Committee shall announce, for the examination to be held in the academical year next following, the form of examination for each of Papers 1 and 2, which shall be either (*a*) a written paper of three hours' duration, or (*b*) a written paper of three hours' duration together with the submission of an essay, of not more than 3,000 words[1] in length, dealing with a single topic within the field of the paper. The examination for Paper 3 shall consist of a written paper of three hours' duration together with the submission of an account of an econometric project undertaken by the candidate.

7. The Degree Committee shall have power to issue supplementary regulations defining or limiting the scope of the papers, and to modify or alter such supplementary regulations as occasion may require. Supplementary regulations.

8. The Degree Committee shall nominate such number of Examiners and Assessors as they shall deem sufficient and shall nominate one of the Examiners to be Chair. The Chair shall send a written report on each candidate's performance in the examination to the Secretary of the Degree Committee. Examiners and Assessors.

9. If the Degree Committee, after considering the report from the Chair of Examiners, resolve that a candidate is entitled to a Diploma, their resolution to that effect shall be sent to the candidate and to the Secretary of the Board of Graduate Studies. A candidate who in the opinion of the Degree Award.

[1] One A4 page consisting largely of statistics or symbols shall be regarded as the equivalent of 250 words.

Committee deserves special credit shall be entitled to a Diploma with distinction. The award of a Diploma shall be published by the Board of Graduate Studies.

Failure. **10.** If the Degree Committee are of the opinion that a candidate's performance in the examination is of insufficient merit to entitle her or him to the Diploma, their resolution to that effect shall be communicated to the candidate and to the Secretary of the Board of Graduate Studies.

11. The Advanced Diploma shall be in the following form:

THIS IS TO CERTIFY THAT having satisfied the preliminary conditions and having been admitted to the examination appointed by the University of Cambridge has been approved[1] by the Examiners and has been awarded the Advanced Diploma in Economics.

Candidate's fees. **12.** While studying in the University for the Diploma a candidate shall pay the appropriate University Composition Fee for each term of such study.

SUPPLEMENTARY REGULATIONS

Paper 1. Microeconomics

This paper offers a basic grounding in microeconomic analysis with applications to economic problems. The aim of the paper is to develop the theoretical framework, and to provide an opportunity to apply principles to practical problems.

Paper 2. Macroeconomics

This paper deals with the analysis of economies treated as complete systems and is concerned with problems of fluctuations in economic activity, employment and unemployment, inflation, economic growth, international economics and the balance of payments, the aggregate distribution of income and wealth. The paper covers analytic methods and models which provide a framework for the analysis of macroeconomic problems.

Paper 3. Econometrics

This paper deals with the statistical analysis of microeconomic and macroeconomic data as a basis for empirical studies in economics. The paper assumes a background knowledge of statistical methods as a descriptive and summarizing device and an elementary knowledge of probability theory and statistical inference.

The examination for Paper 3 consists of a written examination of three hours' duration and the submission of an account of a project undertaken by the candidate. The written examination will contribute a weight of two-thirds, and the project a weight of one-third, towards the marks for this paper. In the written paper, candidates will be expected to answer questions on statistical and econometric methods and their applications. The project will be set by the Examiners and will enable candidates to apply their economic and statistical knowledge to an empirical problem.

POSTGRADUATE DIPLOMA IN LEGAL STUDIES AND POSTGRADUATE DIPLOMA IN INTERNATIONAL LAW

Conditions of award. **1.** A Postgraduate Diploma in Legal Studies, or a Postgraduate Diploma in International Law, may be awarded by the Degree Committee for the Faculty of Law to a member of the University who has satisfied the requirements of the following regulations. For the purposes of this regulation graduates of the University may count previous residence *in statu pupillari*.

2. A candidate for the Diploma must be admitted as a Graduate Student, on the recommendation of the Degree Committee, by the Board of Graduate Studies, who shall assign to each candidate a date of commencement of candidature.

Candidate must be under supervision. **3.** A candidate for a Diploma shall pursue in the University *either* (i) a course of full-time study for at least consecutive three terms *or* (ii) a course of part-time study for at least six consecutive terms. Every candidate, whether studying in Cambridge or elsewhere, shall be placed under the direction of a Supervisor appointed by the Degree Committee and shall be subject to any special conditions that the Committee may prescribe in her or his case.

Supervisor's reports. **4.** Every Supervisor shall send to the Secretary of the Board of Graduate Studies reports on the work of each candidate under her or his charge, in accordance with the provisions of Regulation 8 of the general regulations for admission as a Graduate Student.

Thesis. **5.** The exercise for the Diploma shall be a thesis on a subject, approved by the Degree Committee, which falls within the field of Law or of International Law. The thesis, which shall not without the leave of the Degree Committee exceed 30,000 words in length, including footnotes, but excluding

[1] Insert with *Distinction* if the candidate deserves special credit.

appendices and bibliography, must afford evidence of serious study by the candidate and of ability to discuss a difficult problem critically.

6. Each candidate shall submit two copies of her or his thesis in accordance with detailed arrangements approved by the Board of Graduate Studies (i) not earlier than the end of the second term, nor later than the end of the fifth term (for a full-time student) or (ii) not earlier than the end of the fifth term, nor later than the eighth term (for a part-time student), after the term in which her or his candidature commenced, provided that the Degree Committee may allow a candidate to submit it at a later date. Each candidate will be required to sign a declaration that the thesis is his or her own work, unaided except as may be specified in the declaration, and that it does not contain material that has already been used to any substantial extent for a comparable purpose.

7. Each thesis shall be referred to two Examiners, appointed by the Degree Committee, who may at their discretion, examine the candidate orally on the thesis and on the general field of knowledge within which it falls. The Degree Committee in exceptional circumstances may permit the Examiners to conduct the oral examination by video-conference or other remote means. Each Examiner shall submit a separate report to the Degree Committee on the candidate's thesis, and the Examiners shall submit a joint report on the candidate's performance in the oral examination if such is held. Examiners.

8. If the Degree Committee require a further opinion or opinions on the merits of a candidate's thesis, they may appoint additional Examiners, provided that not more than one additional Examiner may be appointed without the leave of the Board of Graduate Studies.

9. The Degree Committee, after considering the reports of the Examiners, shall resolve whether or not the candidate is entitled to be awarded a Diploma, and shall inform the candidate and the Secretary of the Board of Graduate Studies accordingly. The award of a Diploma shall be published by the Board of Graduate Studies. The Degree Committee may allow an unsuccessful candidate to resubmit her or his thesis within a time limit fixed by them, which will normally not extend beyond the end of the term next following that in which the candidate is notified of the Degree Committee's decision to allow resubmission. The Degree Committee shall inform the Secretary of the Board of Graduate Studies of any such allowance. Awards.

10. A Postgraduate Diploma shall be in the following form, the subject being specified as 'Legal Studies' or 'International Law'. Form of Diploma.

THIS IS TO CERTIFY THAT having satisfied the preliminary conditions and having presented a thesis approved by the Degree Committee for the Faculty of Law has been awarded the Postgraduate Diploma in Legal Studies (International Law).

11. While studying for the Diploma a candidate shall pay a University Composition Fee as prescribed in Regulation 11 of the general regulations for admission as a Graduate Student. Fees.

12. Payment of a fee to a Supervisor who is not a University officer (other than an Associate Lecturer who receives no stipend from the University) shall be as prescribed in the general regulations for admission as a Graduate Student. Payments to Supervisors.

DIPLOMAS IN MODERN LANGUAGES[1]

1. A Diploma in a Modern Language shall be awarded to any person whose candidature has been approved by the Faculty Board of Modern and Medieval Languages and who has attended a course of instruction prescribed by the Faculty Board, and has satisfied the Examiners in the examination for the Diploma. Standing of candidates.

2. The Faculty Board shall announce from time to time the languages in which Diplomas may be awarded, provided that no student shall be a candidate for a Diploma in a language in which he or she is in the same term offering as a candidate for honours in the Tripos.

3. In each language the examination shall consist of an oral examination and two written papers as follows: Scheme of examination.

Paper 1. Use of the foreign language.
Paper 2. Translation from the foreign language. (Two hours)

The form, scope, and standard of the written papers and the oral examination shall be the same as that of Papers B1 and B2 and Oral Examination B of the Modern and Medieval Languages Tripos.

A candidate for a Diploma in any language shall take the oral examination and the written papers in that language in the same term.

[1] The examinations in the Diplomas in Modern Languages are suspended until further notice.

4. The maximum marks allocated to each component of the examination shall be in the following proportions:

Paper 1	3
Paper 2	2
Oral examination	1

Examiners and Assessors.

5. The Examiners in any language shall be the Examiners for that language in Part IA of the Modern and Medieval Languages Tripos. The Faculty Board shall have power to nominate one or more Assessors to assist the Examiners.

Class-lists.

6. The list of successful candidates, which shall be published at the same time as the class-list for Part IA of the Modern and Medieval Languages Tripos, shall specify the language in which each candidate has satisfied the Examiners. The symbol (*d*) shall be placed against the names of candidates who acquit themselves with distinction in the examination, and the symbol (*c*) against the names of those who acquit themselves with credit.

7. The Diploma shall be in the following form:

Form of Diploma.

THIS IS TO CERTIFY THAT having satisfied the preliminary conditions has been admitted to the examination appointed by the University of Cambridge and has been approved[1] by the Examiners and has been awarded the Diploma in[2]

Fees.

8. Any candidate studying in the University for a Diploma, if not already paying University Composition Fees, shall pay the appropriate Composition Fee for each term of such study. A candidate for the Diploma who has not paid a University Composition Fee for the term in which the examination is held shall pay an examination fee of £60.

ADVANCED DIPLOMA IN THEOLOGY AND RELIGIOUS STUDIES

Conditions of award.

1. The Advanced Diploma in Theology and Religious Studies shall be awarded to a member of the University, qualified under Regulation 2, who has diligently attended the course of instruction prescribed by the Faculty Board of Divinity, which shall extend over one academical year, and who has satisfied the Examiners in the examination for the Diploma as defined in the following regulations; provided that he or she has kept three terms. For the purpose of this regulation graduates of the University may count previous residence *in statu pupillari.*

Standing of candidates.

2. A candidate for the Diploma must be approved by the Degree Committee for the Faculty of Divinity, who shall assign to each candidate a date of commencement of candidature. No one shall be a candidate for the Diploma who has been a candidate for Parts IIA or IIB of the Theological and Religious Studies Tripos; no one shall be a candidate in the same year both for the Advanced Diploma in Theology and Religious Studies and for another Diploma or for any Honours Examination, and no one shall be a candidate for the Advanced Diploma in Theology and Religious Studies on more than one occasion.

Scheme of examination.

3. The examination for the Diploma shall consist of two Parts, as follows:

Part A

Written papers. Each candidate shall offer three papers chosen from Paper A1 and any of the papers in Groups of B, C, and D of the Theological and Religious Studies Tripos, provided that

(*a*) each candidate's choice of papers shall be subject to approval by the Degree Committee;
(*b*) a candidate shall offer at least one paper from Group C or Group D;
(*c*) a candidate shall offer only one paper from Papers A1, B1, and C1;
(*d*) a candidate shall not offer a paper which he or she has previously offered in an Honours Examination;
(*e*) subject to the approval of the Degree Committee, a candidate may elect to offer four papers, in which case the candidate's performance in the paper in which the Examiners judge his or her work to be least good shall be taken into account only if that would be to the candidate's advantage;
(*f*) no candidate shall offer more than one paper examined by an alternative mode of assessment.

Part B

A dissertation of not more than 10,000 words in length, including footnotes but not bibliography,

[1] Insert *with Distinction* or *with Credit* if appropriate.
[2] Insert the language in which the candidate has satisfied the Examiners.

on a subject approved by the Degree Committee. Candidates shall submit their dissertations to the Secretary of the Degree Committee by the third Monday of Full Easter Term of the year in which they are examined. Each candidate will be required to sign a declaration that the dissertation is his or her own work, unaided except as may be specified in the declaration, and that it does not contain material that has already been used to any substantial extent for a comparable purpose. The Examiners shall have power to examine a candidate *viva voce* on the subject of his or her dissertation and on the general field of knowledge within which it falls.

4. The Degree Committee shall nominate such number of Examiners as they deem sufficient; they shall also have power to nominate one or more Assessors to the Examiners. Examiners and Assessors.

5. A candidate who has satisfied the Examiners in both Parts of the examination shall be entitled to a Diploma.

6. In the list of successful candidates special excellence in the examination shall be recognized by the award of a mark of distinction.

7. The Advanced Diploma shall be in the following form: Form of Diploma.

THIS IS TO CERTIFY THAT having satisfied the preliminary conditions and having been admitted to the examination appointed by the University of Cambridge has been approved[1] by the Examiners and has been awarded the Advanced Diploma in Theology and Religious Studies.

8. While studying in the University for the Diploma a candidate shall pay the appropriate University Composition Fee for each term of such study. Fees.

9. A student who has taken the examination for the Diploma shall not be entitled to count the period or any part of the period during which he or she has been a candidate for the Diploma towards a course of research for the degree of Ph.D., M.Sc., or M.Litt. Relation to courses of research.

CERTIFICATE IN HUMANITIES COMPUTING FOR LANGUAGES

1. A Certificate in Humanities Computing for Languages shall be awarded to any person whose candidature has been approved by the Faculty Board of Modern and Medieval Languages and who has attended a course of lectures and classes prescribed by the Faculty Board, has satisfactorily completed the assignments for the course, and has also satisfied the Examiners in the examination for the Certificate. Standing of candidates.

2. The examination for the Certificate shall consist of: Scheme of examination.

(*a*) the creation of an academic-related website, which in the case of candidates studying for the Modern and Medieval Languages Tripos, shall be produced in a language other than English, which meets the requirements set out by the Faculty Board from time to time;

(*b*) a project in any field of humanities computing approved by the Faculty Board accompanied by a report of not more than 2,000 words.

3. The Faculty Board shall have power to define or limit the languages available for the requirements of the examination.

4. The Faculty Board shall nominate such number of Examiners and Assessors as they deem sufficient. Examiners and Assessors.

5. In the list of successful candidates the symbol (*d*) shall be placed against the names of candidates who acquit themselves with distinction in the examination, and the symbol (*c*) against the names of those who acquit themselves with credit. Class-list.

6. The Certificate shall be in the following form: Form of Certificate.

THIS IS TO CERTIFY THAT having satisfied the preliminary conditions has been admitted to the examination appointed by the University of Cambridge and has been approved[2] by the Examiners and has been awarded the Certificate in Humanities Computing for Languages.

7. Any candidate studying in the University for the Certificate, if not already paying a University Composition Fee, shall pay the appropriate Composition Fee for each term of such study. A candidate for the Certificate who has not paid a University Composition Fee for the term in which the examination is held shall pay an examination fee of £45. Fees.

[1] Insert *with Distinction* if the candidate has been awarded a mark of distinction.
[2] Insert *with Distinction* or *with Credit* if appropriate.

CERTIFICATES IN MODERN LANGUAGES

Standing of candidates.

1. A Certificate in a Modern Language shall be awarded to any person whose candidature has been approved by the Faculty Board of Modern and Medieval Languages and who has attended a course of instruction prescribed by the Faculty Board, and has satisfied the Examiners in the examination for the Certificate.

2. The Faculty Board shall announce from time to time the languages in which Certificates may be awarded. A student may be a candidate for examination in any of the languages specified by the Faculty Board, provided that no student shall be a candidate for a Certificate in a language which he or she is in the same term offering as a candidate for honours in the Tripos.

Scheme of examination.

3. In each language the examination shall consist of an oral examination and two written papers as follows:

Paper 1. Introduction to the foreign language, 1.
Paper 2. Introduction to the foreign language, 2. (Two hours)

The form, scope, and standard of the written papers and the oral examination shall be the same as that of Papers A1 and A2 and Oral Examination A of the Modern and Medieval Languages Tripos.

A candidate for a Certificate in any language shall take the oral examination and the written papers in that language in the same term.

Supplementary regulations.

4. The Faculty Board shall have power to define or limit by supplementary regulations all or any of the subjects of the examination, and to modify or alter any such supplementary regulations as occasion may require, due care being taken that sufficient notice is given of any change.

5. The maximum marks allocated to each component of the examination shall be in the following proportions:

Paper 1	3
Paper 2	2
Oral examination	1

Examiners and Assessors.

6. The Faculty Board shall nominate such number of Examiners and Assessors as they deem sufficient.

Class-list.

7. The list of successful candidates shall specify the language in which each candidate has satisfied the Examiners. The symbol (*d*) shall be placed against the names of candidates who acquit themselves with distinction in the examination, and the symbol (*c*) against the names of those who acquit themselves with credit.

Form of Certificate.

8. The Certificate shall be in the following form:

THIS IS TO CERTIFY THAT having satisfied the preliminary conditions has been admitted to the examination appointed by the University of Cambridge and has been approved[1] by the Examiners and has been awarded the Certificate in[2]

Fees.

9. Any candidate studying in the University for a Certificate, if not already paying a University Composition Fee, shall pay the appropriate Composition Fee for each term of such study. A candidate for the Certificate who has not paid a University Composition Fee for the term in which the examination is held shall pay an examination fee of £45.

CERTIFICATES OF POSTGRADUATE STUDY

GENERAL REGULATIONS

Subjects of study.

1. Certificates of Postgraduate Study shall be awarded for advanced study and training in research. A subject of such study, and the special regulations for each subject, shall be approved by the General Board on the recommendation of the Faculty Board or other body concerned after consultation with the appropriate Degree Committee, who shall satisfy themselves that candidates for the Certificate who may wish to become candidates for the degree of Ph.D., Eng.D., M.Sc., or M.Litt. will receive sufficient training in research to justify the granting of leave to count a whole or some part of the period of candidature for the Certificate towards a full-time or a part-time course of research for one of these degrees.

Course of instruction.

2. The full-time course of instruction for the Certificate shall normally extend over three consecutive terms and the part-time course of instruction shall normally extend over six consecutive terms. The

[1] Insert *with Distinction* or *with Credit* if appropriate.
[2] Insert the language in which the candidate has satisfied the Examiners.

Board of Graduate Studies, on the recommendation of the Degree Committee concerned, may agree that, for some specified courses, the full-time course of instruction may extend beyond three terms. The Board may also permit a candidate in exceptional circumstances to spend up to two years from the date of commencement of candidature in study for the Certificate.

3. A candidate for the Certificate must have been granted admission as a Graduate Student, on the recommendation of the Degree Committee concerned, by the Board of Graduate Studies, who shall assign a date of commencement of candidature. A candidate for the Certificate must also Standing of candidates.

either (*a*) if a member of the University, have completed the examination and residence requirements for the B.A. Degree;

or (*b*) if not a member of the University, produce such evidence of fitness to study for the Certificate as may be approved by the Degree Committee concerned.

Each application for admission to the status of Graduate Student must contain a statement of the course of study which the applicant desires to pursue and a statement of qualification, attainments, and previous study, and shall be sent to the Board of Graduate Studies, who shall forward it to the Degree Committee concerned.

4. A candidate shall study for the Certificate in Cambridge, or such other place as the Board and the Degree Committee concerned shall determine, under the direction of a Supervisor appointed by the Degree Committee concerned, and under any special conditions that the Committee may lay down in his or her case. All appointments of Supervisors shall be communicated by the Degree Committee to the Board of Graduate Studies, who shall be competent to make representations to the Committee about any particular appointment. Supervisor.

Every Supervisor shall send to the Secretary of the Board of Graduate Studies reports on the work of each candidate under her or his charge, in accordance with the provisions of Regulation 8 of the general regulations for admission as a Graduate Student.

5. Each candidate shall be required to submit a dissertation, unless otherwise prescribed in the Special Regulations for the subject for which he or she is registered, and to undertake an oral examination and to undergo such other forms of examination as are prescribed in the Special Regulations for that subject. Dissertation and oral examination.

6. The names of candidates who are to be examined in written papers shall be sent by the Degree Committee to the Secretary of the Board of Graduate Studies on or before 1 December next preceding the examination, together with a statement of the approved field of study in which each candidate is to be examined.

7. Each candidate shall propose, on the advice of her or his Supervisor, a title for a dissertation, and shall submit the proposal, not later than the end of the second term of candidature for full-time students or the third term of candidature for a part-time student, to the Board of Graduate Studies, in accordance with detailed arrangements specified by the Board, for approval by the Board on the recommendation of the Degree Committee concerned. Selection of course of study.

8. Each candidate shall submit two copies of her or his dissertation, in accordance with detailed arrangements specified by the Board of Graduate Studies, so as to arrive by a date which shall be determined by the Degree Committee, and which shall be not later than the last day of the student's third term of full-time candidature (fifth term of part-time candidature) unless the Board, on the recommendation of the Degree Committee, have allowed an extension of time under Regulation 2. Each candidate shall state generally in a preface to the dissertation and specifically in notes the sources from which information has been derived.

9. Each candidate's dissertation shall be referred to two Examiners appointed by the Degree Committee concerned.

10. The Examiners shall jointly examine the candidate orally upon the subject of her or his dissertation and on the general field of knowledge within which it falls. The Degree Committee in exceptional circumstances may permit the Examiners to conduct the oral examination by video-conference or other means. If the candidate is required in addition to satisfy the Examiners in a written examination, the arrangements for such an examination shall be made by the Degree Committee concerned, and the Examiners shall be the Examiners appointed to examine the dissertation. The Examiners shall report to the Degree Committee and shall at the same time return to them the two copies of the dissertation. Examiners.

11. If the Degree Committee, after consideration of the Examiners' reports, approve the candidate's performance as of the requisite standard for the award of the Certificate, the Degree Committee shall Award.

communicate their resolution to that effect to the candidate and to the Secretary of the Board of Graduate Studies.

12. The awards of Certificates shall be published by the Board of Graduate Studies, but no publication shall be made of an award to a Graduate Student who has been given leave by the Board of Graduate Studies to count the period or any part of it during which he or she has been a candidate for the Certificate towards a course of research for the degree of Ph.D., Eng.D., M.Sc., or M.Litt. No such Graduate Student shall be entitled to receive the Certificate so long as he or she remains on the Register of Graduate Studies, nor subsequently if he or she should submit a dissertation for the degree of Ph.D., Eng.D., M.Sc., or M.Litt. Nothing in this regulation shall prevent a person who has been awarded the Certificate, and whose name has been removed from the Register of Graduate Students, from being restored to that register as a candidate for the degree of Ph.D., Eng.D., M.Sc., or M.Litt., and, if the Board of Graduate Studies think fit, from being granted leave to count the whole or some part of the period of candidature for the Certificate towards a course of research for one of the aforementioned degrees. No candidate shall be entitled to receive the Certificate unless he or she has attended the prescribed course of instruction.

Form of Certificate.

13. The Certificate shall be in the following form:

THIS IS TO CERTIFY THAT having diligently attended a course of postgraduate instruction in[1] and having been admitted to the examination appointed by the University of Cambridge has been approved by the Examiners and has been awarded the Certificate of Postgraduate Study in[1]

Remuneration of Supervisors.

14. Payment of a fee to a Supervisor who is not a University officer (other than an Associate Lecturer who receives no stipend from the University) shall be made in accordance with the provisions of Regulation 14 of the general regulations for admission as a Graduate Student.

Candidate's fees.

15. While studying for the Certificate, a candidate shall pay a University Composition Fee as prescribed in Regulation 11 of the general regulations for admission as a Graduate Student.

16. A candidate who is not awarded a Certificate may not be a candidate again either in the same or in any other field, save as provided under Regulation 12.

SPECIAL REGULATIONS

Anglo-Saxon, Norse, and Celtic

1. Certificates of Postgraduate Study shall be awarded for advanced study and training in research in Anglo-Saxon, Norse, and Celtic.

2. The study and training shall include:

(*a*) attendance at courses of seminars and classes approved by the Degree Committee for the Faculty of English;

(*b*) research on a topic approved by the Degree Committee pursued under the guidance of a Supervisor appointed under Regulation 4 of the General Regulations;

(*c*) completion of the registration procedure prescribed by the Degree Committee.

3. The dissertation shall take the form of *either* a substantive essay on the topic approved under Regulation 2(*b*) *or* a specimen of written work having an evident and central relation to the larger dissertation which the student intends to submit in candidature for the M.Litt. or the Ph.D. Degree. A dissertation shall be between 8,000 and 10,000 words in length, and shall have been composed wholly or largely in the period since the student's admission as a Graduate Student.

Chemical Engineering

1. Certificates of Postgraduate Study shall be awarded for advanced study and training in research in Chemical Engineering.

2. The study and training shall include:

(*a*) courses of lectures proposed by the Chemical Engineering and Biotechnology Syndicate and approved by the Degree Committee concerned;

(*b*) practical work carried out in one or more of the following ways:

(i) experimental or theoretical exercises of an advanced type,

(ii) training in research by means of assistance with a piece of research,

[1] Insert the subject offered by the candidate (e.g. English, Natural Science (Biological Science)).

(iii) training in research by means of an original research investigation,
(iv) training in some technique.

Computer Science

1. Certificates of Postgraduate Study shall be awarded for advanced study and training in research in Computer Science.

2. The study and training shall include:

(*a*) courses of lectures approved by the Degree Committee for the Faculty of Computer Science and Technology;

(*b*) practical work carried out in one or more of the following ways:
(i) organized experiments or theoretical exercises of an advanced type,
(ii) assistance with a piece of research,
(iii) a small research investigation,
(iv) training in some technique.

3. At the discretion of the Examiners the examination for the Certificate may include (in addition to the submission of a dissertation and an oral examination as laid down in General Regulation 5) one or two written papers on subjects cognate to the lectures attended by the candidate.

4. The dissertation shall be of not more than 10,000 words in length, exclusive of tables, bibliography, and appendices.

Economics

1. Certificates of Postgraduate Study shall be awarded for advanced study and training in research in Economics.

2. The study and training shall include:

(*a*) attendance at courses of lectures, seminars, and classes approved by the Degree Committee for the Faculty of Economics;

(*b*) research on a topic approved by the Degree Committee pursued under the guidance of a Supervisor appointed under Regulation 4 of the General Regulations.

3. The dissertation shall take the form of a research proposal having an evident and central relation to the larger dissertation which the student intends to submit in candidature for the M.Litt., the M.Sc or the Ph.D. Degree. The research proposal shall be of not more than 10,000 words in length and shall include a review of the relevant literature, a research question, and an outline of a research design and methods.

4. At the discretion of the Examiners the examination may include (in addition to the submission of a dissertation and an oral examination as laid down in General Regulation 5) written papers or other exercises on subjects cognate to the lectures, seminars, and classes attended by the candidate.

Engineering

1. Certificates of Postgraduate Study shall be awarded for advanced study and training in research in Engineering.

2. The study and training shall include:

(*a*) courses of lectures approved by the Degree Committee for the Faculty of Engineering;

(*b*) practical work carried out in one or more of the following ways:
(i) experimental or theoretical exercises of an advanced type,
(ii) training in research by means of assistance with a piece of research,
(iii) training in research by means of an original research investigation.

English

1. Certificates of Postgraduate Study shall be awarded for advanced study and training in research in English.

2. The study and training shall include:

(*a*) attendance at courses of seminars and classes approved by the Degree Committee for the Faculty of English;

(*b*) research on a topic approved by the Degree Committee pursued under the guidance of a Supervisor appointed under Regulation 4 of the General Regulations;

(*c*) completion of the registration procedure prescribed by the Degree Committee.

3. The dissertation shall take the form of *either* a substantive essay on the topic approved under Regulation 2(*b*) *or* a specimen of written work having an evident and central relation to the larger dissertation which the student intends to submit in candidature for the M.Litt. or the Ph.D. Degree. A dissertation shall be between 8,000 and 10,000 words in length, and shall have been composed wholly or largely in the period since the student's admission as a Graduate Student.

Geography

1. Certificates of Postgraduate Study shall be awarded for advanced study and training in research in Geography.

2. The study and training shall include practical work carried out in one or more of the following ways:

(i) organized experiments or theoretical exercises of an advanced type approved by the Degree Committee for the Faculty of Earth Sciences and Geography,

(ii) assistance with a piece of research,

(iii) a small research investigation,

(iv) training in some technique.

3. The dissertation shall be of not more than 10,000 words in length.

History

1. Certificates of Postgraduate Study shall be awarded for advanced study and training in research in History.

2. The study and training shall include:

(*a*) attendance at courses of seminars and classes approved by the Degree Committee for the Faculty of History;

(*b*) research on a topic approved by the Degree Committee pursued under the guidance of a Supervisor appointed under Regulation 4 of the General Regulations;

(*c*) completion of the registration procedure prescribed by the Degree Committee.

3. The dissertation shall take the form of *either* a substantive essay on the topic approved under Regulation 2(*b*) *or* a specimen of written work having an evident and central relation to the larger dissertation which the student intends to submit in candidature for the M.Litt. or the Ph.D. Degree. A dissertation shall be between 8,000 and 10,000 words in length, and shall have been composed wholly or largely in the period since the student's admission as a Graduate Student.

International Relations

1. Certificates of Postgraduate Study shall be awarded for advanced study and training in research in International Relations.

2. The study and training shall include:

(*a*) attendance at courses of lectures, seminars, and classes approved by the Degree Committee for the Faculty of Human, Social, and Political Science;

(*b*) research on a topic approved by the Degree Committee pursued under the guidance of a Supervisor appointed under Regulation 4 of the General Regulations.

3. At the discretion of the Examiners the examination may include written papers or other exercises on subjects cognate to the lectures, seminars, and classes attended by the candidate.

Legal Studies

1. Certificates of Postgraduate Study shall be awarded for advanced study and training in research in Legal Studies.

2. The study and training shall include:

(*a*) attendance at courses of seminars and classes approved by the Degree Committee for the Faculty of Law;

(*b*) research on a topic approved by the Degree Committee pursued under the guidance of a Supervisor appointed under Regulation 4 of the General Regulations;

(*c*) completion of the registration procedure prescribed by the Degree Committee.

3. The dissertation shall take the form of *either* a substantive essay on the topic approved under Regulation 2(*b*) *or* a specimen of written work having an evident and central relation to the larger dissertation which the student intends to submit in candidature for the M.Litt. or the Ph.D. Degree. A dissertation shall be of not more than 15,000 words in length, inclusive of footnotes but exclusive of appendices and bibliography, and shall have been composed wholly or largely in the period since the student's admission as a Graduate Student.

Music

1. Certificates of Postgraduate Study shall be awarded for advanced study and training in research in Music.

2. The study and training shall include:

(*a*) attendance at courses of seminars and classes approved by the Degree Committee for the Faculty of Music;

(*b*) research on a topic approved by the Degree Committee pursued under the guidance of a Supervisor appointed under Regulation 4 of the General Regulations;

(*c*) completion of the registration procedure prescribed by the Degree Committee.

3. The dissertation shall take the form of *either* a substantive essay on the topic approved under Regulation 2(*b*) *or* a specimen of written work having an evident and central relation to the larger dissertation which the student intends to submit in candidature for the M.Litt or the Ph.D. Degree. A dissertation shall be of not more than 10,000 words in length, and shall have been composed wholly or largely in the period since the student's admission as a Graduate Student

Natural Science (Astronomy)

1. Certificates of Postgraduate Study shall be awarded for advanced study and training in research in Astronomy.

2. The study and training shall include:

(*a*) courses of lectures approved by the Degree Committee for the Faculty of Physics and Chemistry;

(*b*) practical work carried out in one or more of the following ways:

(i) organized experiments or theoretical exercises of an advanced type,

(ii) assistance with a piece of research,

(iii) a small research investigation,

(iv) training in some technique.

3. At the discretion of the Examiners the examination for the Certificate may include (in addition to the submission of a dissertation and an oral examination as laid down in General Regulation 5) one or two written papers on subjects cognate to the lectures attended by the candidate.

4. The dissertation shall be of not more than 12,000 words in length, inclusive of tables, bibliography, and appendices.

Natural Science (Biological Science)

1. Certificates of Postgraduate Study in Natural Science shall be awarded for advanced study and training in research in Biological Science.

2. The study and training shall include:

(*a*) a course of lectures proposed by the Head of the relevant Department or other institution and approved by the Degree Committee for the Faculty of Biology;

(*b*) one or more original research investigations.

3. The dissertation shall be of not more than 15,000 words in length, exclusive of tables, footnotes, bibliography, and appendices. In it the candidate shall provide evidence to satisfy the Examiners that he or she can design and carry out investigations, assess and interpret the results obtained, and place the work in the wider perspective of the subject.

Natural Science (Chemistry)

1. Certificates of Postgraduate Study shall be awarded for advanced study and training in research in Chemistry.

2. The study and training shall include:

(*a*) courses of lectures and research seminars approved by the Degree Committee for the Faculty of Physics and Chemistry;

(*b*) practical work carried out in one or more of the following ways:

(i) organized experiments or theoretical exercises of an advanced type,

(ii) assistance with a piece of research,

(iii) a small research investigation,

(iv) training in some technique.

3. At the discretion of the Examiners the examination may include (in addition to the submission of a dissertation and an oral examination as laid down in General Regulation 5) one or two written papers on subjects cognate to the lectures and seminars attended by the candidate.

4. The dissertation shall be of not more 12,000 words in length, inclusive of tables, bibliography, and appendices.

Natural Science (Earth Sciences)

1. Certificates of Postgraduate Study shall be awarded for advanced study and training in research in Earth Sciences.

2. The study and training shall include:

(*a*) courses of lectures approved by the Degree Committee for the Faculty of Earth Sciences and Geography;

(*b*) practical work carried out in one or more of the following ways:

(i) organized experiments or theoretical exercises of an advanced type,

(ii) assistance with a piece of research,

(iii) a small research investigation,

(iv) training in some technique.

3. At the discretion of the Examiners the examination for the Certificate may include (in addition to the submission of a dissertation and an oral examination as laid down in General Regulation 5) not more than two written papers on subjects cognate to the lectures attended by the candidate.

4. The dissertation shall be of not more than 10,000 words in length.

Natural Science (Materials Science and Metallurgy)

1. Certificates of Postgraduate Study shall be awarded for advanced study and training in research in Materials Science and Metallurgy.

2. The study and training shall include:

(*a*) courses of lectures approved by the Degree Committee for the Faculty of Physics and Chemistry;

(*b*) practical work carried out in one or more of the following ways:

(i) organized experiments or theoretical exercises of an advanced type,

(ii) assistance with a piece of research,

(iii) a small research investigation,

(iv) training in some technique.

3. At the discretion of the Examiners the examination may include (in addition to the submission of a dissertation and an oral examination as laid down in General Regulation 5) one or two written papers on subjects cognate to the lectures attended by the candidate.

4. The dissertation shall be of not more than 15,000 words in length, inclusive of tables, figure legends, and appendices, but exclusive of bibliography.

Natural Science (Materials Science and Metallurgy: High Performance Structural Metallics)

1. Certificates of Postgraduate Study shall be awarded for advanced study and training in research in Materials Science and Metallurgy in High Performance Structural Metallics.

2. The study and training shall include:

(*a*) successful completion of a minimum of eight courses of training approved by the Degree Committee for the Faculty of Physics and Chemistry;

(*b*) practical work carried out in one or more of the following ways:
- (i) organized experiments or theoretical exercises of an advanced type,
- (ii) assistance with a piece of research,
- (iii) a small research investigation,
- (iv) training in some technique,
- (v) devising and commissioning experimental work and analysing the output of this work.

3. The dissertation shall be of not more than 15,000 words in length, inclusive of tables, figures, legends, and appendices, but exclusive of bibliography.

Natural Science (Physics)

1. Certificates of Postgraduate Study shall be awarded for advanced study and training in research in Physics.

2. The study and training shall include:

(*a*) courses of lectures approved by the Degree Committee for the Faculty of Physics and Chemistry.

(*b*) practical work carried out in one or more of the following ways:
- (i) organized experiments or theoretical exercises of an advanced type,
- (ii) assistance with a piece of research,
- (iii) a small research investigation,
- (iv) training in some technique.

3. At the discretion of the Examiners the examination for the Certificate may include (in addition to the submission of a dissertation and an oral examination as laid down in General Regulation 5) one or two written papers on subjects cognate to the lectures attended by the candidate.

4. The dissertation shall be of not more than 12,000 words in length, inclusive of tables, bibliography, and appendices.

Theology and Religious Studies

1. Certificates of Postgraduate Study shall be awarded for advanced study and training in research in Theology and Religious Studies.

2. The study and training shall include:

(*a*) attendance at lectures, seminars, or classes approved by the Degree Committee for the Faculty of Divinity;

(*b*) research on a topic approved by the Degree Committee pursued under the guidance of a Supervisor appointed under Regulation 4 of the General Regulations;

(*c*) completion of the registration procedure prescribed by the Degree Committee.

3. The dissertation shall take the form of *either* a substantive essay on the topic approved under Regulation 2(*b*) *or* a specimen of written work having an evident and central relation to the larger dissertation which the student intends to submit in candidature for the M.Litt. or the Ph.D. Degree. A dissertation shall be of not more than 10,000 words in length, and shall have been composed wholly or largely in the period since the student's admission as a Graduate Student.

4. At the discretion of the Degree Committee the examination may include not more than two written papers on subjects cognate to the lectures or classes attended by the candidate; such papers may include passages for translation and comment in one or more languages relevant to the candidate's original research.

POSTGRADUATE CERTIFICATE IN EDUCATION

1. The Postgraduate Certificate in Education shall be awarded to a member of the University who has satisfactorily completed a course of study in Education prescribed by the Faculty Board of Education and has passed an examination in Education as defined in Regulations 7 and 8. No one shall be a candidate for the examination unless the Head of the Department of Education is satisfied that he or she has diligently attended the course and has undertaken the required amount of supervised work in a school or schools, as specified in Regulation 3, under arrangements approved by the Head of the Department. Conditions of award.

Standing of candidates.

2. A candidate for the Certificate must have

(*a*) *either* proceeded to a first degree in this or another university,

or attained by examination such other educational qualifications as may be accepted by the Head of the Department of Education as the equivalent of a degree of a university,

and

(*b*) been approved for admission to the course of study for the Certificate by the Head of the Department.

Course of study.

3. Subject to the provisions of Regulation 4, the course of study for the Certificate shall consist of a course extending over one academical year, including not less than ninety days of supervised work in a school or schools.

4. If a student is allowed, under Regulation 11, to be a candidate for examination or re-examination after the completion of the period specified for the course in Regulation 3, the additional period during which such a student is preparing for examination or re-examination shall be deemed to form part of the course.

5. Except with the permission of the Faculty Board no student shall be a candidate for the Certificate and for any other University examination in the same academical year.

Examiners and Assessors.

6. The Faculty Board of Education shall nominate for each academical year such number of Examiners and Assessors as they may deem sufficient, including a resident member of the Senate as Chair of Examiners.

Scheme of examination.

7. The scheme of examination for the Certificate shall be as follows:

SECTION I. The study of teaching and learning.

This section shall consist of course-work on the principles and practice of teaching in one or more subjects and the general professional role of the teacher, which shall be related to a specific age range of pupils, and may also be related to a specific area of the school curriculum.

SECTION II. Professional performance in the school and the class-room.

A candidate's professional performance shall be assessed on such evidence as the Examiners shall require the Head of the Department to provide.

The course-work for Section I, which shall be undertaken during the period of candidature, shall consist of such essays, exercises, investigations, projects, and reports, shall be submitted in such written, practical, or other form, and shall be assessed in such manner, as the Faculty Board may determine under the provisions of Regulations 9 and 10.

8. All candidates shall take Sections I and II. No candidate shall qualify for the award of a Certificate unless he or she has satisfied the Examiners in each of the sections taken.

Supplementary regulations.

9. The Faculty Board shall have power to issue supplementary regulations determining the scope and manner of assessment of the examination and shall be empowered to amend such supplementary regulations from time to time as they may think fit, due care being taken that sufficient notice is given of any change.

Submission of course-work.

10. At the beginning of each academical year, not later than the end of the first week of Full Michaelmas Term, the Faculty Board shall publish by Notice in the School of Education and in Homerton College details of the requirements for each section of the examination. The Notice shall give details of all course-work to be submitted during the current academical year, including topics prescribed, arrangements for the submission and approval of proposed subjects, and arrangements for the submission of completed course-work.

Re-examination.

11. A candidate who has failed to satisfy the Examiners in Section II at the first attempt may apply to the Faculty Board for permission to be re-examined in that section. Permission will be granted only if the application expressly has the support of the Examiners. Such permission shall not be granted on more than one occasion, nor shall a student, except by special permission of the Faculty Board granted in exceptional circumstances, be a candidate for re-examination more than two years after first taking the examination. The general conditions for re-examination shall be determined by the Faculty Board; the Examiners shall inform a candidate who fails whether he or she is required to be re-examined in order to qualify for the award of a Certificate.

12. If any student is given permission under Regulation 11 to be a candidate for examination or re-examination in Section II, the assessment shall be concluded after the completion of such period or periods of supervised work in a school or schools as the Examiners may require.

Class-lists.

13. The names of candidates who satisfy the Examiners shall be arranged in alphabetical order in a single class. The Chair of Examiners for the time being (or a deputy) shall have power to send to the

Registrary for publication at any time a Notice signed by not less than three of the Examiners containing the names of any candidates who, having previously failed to satisfy the Examiners and having been given permission to present themselves again for re-examination under Regulation 11, have subsequently qualified for the award of a Certificate.

14. A candidate who has satisfied the Examiners shall be awarded a Certificate in the following form: Form of Certificate.

THIS IS TO CERTIFY THAT

having satisfied the preliminary conditions and having diligently followed a course of study in the principles and practice of Education including class-room teaching and having been admitted to the examination appointed by the University of Cambridge has been approved by the Examiners and has been awarded the Postgraduate Certificate in Education.

15. A student who has taken the examination for the Certificate shall not be entitled to count the period or any part of the period during which he or she has been a candidate for the Certificate towards a course of research for the degree of Ph.D., M.Sc., or M.Litt. or a course of training and research for the degree of Ed.D. Relation to courses of research.

16. While studying for the Certificate a candidate shall pay the appropriate University Composition Fee for each term of such study. Fees.

SUPPLEMENTARY REGULATIONS

Section I. The study of teaching and learning

For this section each candidate will be required to submit course-work on the teaching of his or her subject or subjects, in relation to one of the following: (*a*) the education of children of early years (3–7) or (5–11) primary school age; (*b*) the education of children of middle school age (7–14); (*c*) secondary education.

DIPLOMAS AND CERTIFICATES OPEN TO NON-MEMBERS OF THE UNIVERSITY

Amended by Notices (Reporter, *2013–14, pp 405 and 447*)

1. The following regulations shall apply to any University examination for Diplomas and Certificates open to non-members of the University listed in the Schedule to these regulations.

2. A subject for any Diploma or Certificate under these regulations and listed in the Schedule, together with a syllabus for the course, the special regulations for the examination, and any subsequent amendments thereof, shall be approved by the General Board. Approval of subjects.

3. Any person may be approved for admission to a course of study leading to the award of a Diploma or a Certificate granted under the provisions of these regulations who has satisfied the relevant body[1] administering the Diploma or a Certificate as qualified to engage in study for the qualification. A register shall be kept by the Registrary of all persons who are studying with a view to obtaining such a qualification. Admission to a course.

4. A date shall be agreed between the administering body and the Registrary by which the head of the body administering the Diploma or Certificate shall send to the Registrary a list of all the students who have been newly admitted by that body and who are studying towards a Diploma or Certificate listed in the Schedule to these regulations.

5. The length of candidature for each award shall be determined by the General Board on the recommendation of the administering body. Length of candidature.

6. While studying for a Diploma or a Certificate under these regulations a candidate shall pay the appropriate fee for the course as determined by the General Board from time to time on the recommendation of the administering body. Fees.

7. No person who has not paid the appropriate fee shall be entitled to attend any lectures related to a course or any course of instruction for a Diploma or Certificate under these regulations. Non-payment of fees.

8. No person shall be permitted to be a candidate in the examination, or any part of the examination, for any Diploma or Certificate under these regulations unless the person's name is on the register and he or she has met the relevant course requirements.

[1] The bodies approved by the General Board to administer the qualifications under these regulations are: the Strategic Committee of the Institute of Continuing Education and the Management Board of the University of Cambridge Institute for Sustainability Leadership, the Committee of Management of the Language Centre, and the Faculty Boards of Business and Management, Divinity, and Education.

Lists of candidates.

9. Lists of candidates for any written papers in the examinations or any other parts of examinations for any Diploma or Certificate under these regulations shall be sent by the head of the administering body to the Registrary at least three weeks before the first assignment is due to be submitted or, in the case of written papers, before the examination starts.

Periods of previous study.

10. The General Board, on the recommendation of the administering body, shall have powers to recognize periods of previous successful study as meeting part of the requirements for the award.

11. A candidate shall study for a Diploma or Certificate under these regulations in Cambridge, or such other place as the administering body concerned, with the approval of the General Board, shall determine, under the direction of a Course Director appointed by that body and under any special conditions that that body may lay down in each case.

Examiners.

12. The administering body for a Diploma or Certificate shall appoint such number of Examiners as necessary to conduct the examination.

Awards.

13. A Diploma or Certificate under these regulations shall be awarded to any person who has attended a course of lectures and classes prescribed by the administering body, has satisfactorily completed the assignments for the course, and has also satisfied the Examiners in the examination for the Diploma or the Certificate. The list of successful candidates shall specify the subject in which each candidate has satisfied the Examiners. The symbol (*d*) may be placed against the names of candidates who acquit themselves with distinction, and the symbol (*c*) against the names of those who acquit themselves with credit.

Form of Diploma or Certificate.

14. The Diploma or Certificate shall be in the following form:

THIS IS TO CERTIFY THAT having attended a course of instruction in and having been admitted to the examination appointed by the University of Cambridge has been approved[1] by the Examiners and has been awarded the Diploma [Certificate][2] in[3]

15. The General Board, on the recommendation of the administering body, shall determine, for each award, whether a candidate who is not awarded a Diploma or Certificate may be a candidate again in either the same or in any other field.

Examiners' fees.

16. Fees to Examiners shall be as determined from time to time by the General Board on the recommendation of the administering body.

Review procedures.

17. Review procedures for examination results and student complaints shall be approved from time to time by the General Board on the recommendation of the administering body.

SCHEDULE

Examinations for which the foregoing regulations apply

Amended by Notices (Reporter, *2013–14, pp. 118, 141, 253, 405, 406, 447, and 732*)

Diplomas

Faculty of Business and Management
Postgraduate Diploma in Entrepreneurship

Faculty of Divinity
Diploma in Theology for Ministry

Faculty of Education
Postgraduate Diploma in Educational Studies

Institute of Continuing Education
Diploma in Archaeology I
Diploma in Archaeology II
Diploma in Archaeology III
Diploma in Coaching
Diploma in English Literature I
Diploma in English Literature II
Diploma in Evolutionary Biology
Diploma in Historic Environment I
Diploma in Historic Environment II
Diploma in Historic Environment III
Diploma in History of Art I
Diploma in History of Art II
Diploma in Local History I
Diploma in Local History II

Diploma of Higher Education in Archaeology
Diploma of Higher Education in Historic Environment
Diploma of Higher Education in History of Art
Diploma of Higher Education in Local History
Diploma of Higher Education in English Literature

[1] Insert *with Distinction* or *with Credit* if appropriate.
[2] Delete as appropriate.
[3] Insert the appropriate title of award and the subject in which the candidate has satisfied the Examiners.

Advanced Diploma in Archaeology
Advanced Diploma in Ecological Monitoring and Conservation
Advanced Diploma in English Literature
Advanced Diploma in Historic Environment
Advanced Diploma in History of Art
Advanced Diploma in International Development
Advanced Diploma in Local History
Advanced Diploma in Philosophy
Advanced Diploma in the Study of Religion

[Postgraduate Diploma in Applied Criminology and Police Management][1]
[Postgraduate Diploma in Applied Criminology, Penology, and Management][1]
Postgraduate Diploma in Building History
Postgraduate Diploma in Historic Environment[2]
Postgraduate Diploma in History
Postgraduate Diploma in Interdisciplinary Design for the Built Environment
Postgraduate Diploma in International Relations

Certificates

Faculty of Education
Postgraduate Certificate in Educational Research
Postgraduate Certificate of Educational Enquiry
Postgraduate Certificate of Professional Study
Postgraduate Certificate of Staff Development

Institute of Continuing Education
Certificate in Archaeology I
Certificate in Archaeology II
Certificate in Astronomy
Certificate in Coaching
Certificate in Creative Writing I
Certificate in Creative Writing II
Certificate in English Literature I
Certificate in English Literature II
Certificate in Evolutionary Biology
Certificate in Genetics
Certificate in Historic Environment I
Certificate in Historic Environment II
Certificate in Historic Environment III
Certificate in History of Art I
Certificate in History of Art II
Certificate in International Development I
Certificate in International Development II
Certificate in Local History I
Certificate in Local History II
Certificate in Philosophy I
Certificate in Philosophy II
Certificate in Physical Sciences
Certificate in Principles and Practice of Assessment
Certificate in Social Sciences

Certificate of Higher Education in Archaeology
Certificate of Higher Education in Creative Writing
Certificate of Higher Education in English Literature
Certificate of Higher Education in Genetics and Evolution
Certificate of Higher Education in Historic Building Conservation
Certificate of Higher Education in Historic Environment
Certificate of Higher Education in History of Art
Certificate of Higher Education in International Development
Certificate of Higher Education in Local History
Certificate of Higher Education in Philosophy
Certificate of Higher Education in Practical Horticulture and Plantsmanship

⟨Postgraduate Certificate in Applied Criminology and Police Management⟩[3]
⟨Postgraduate Certificate in Applied Criminology, Penology, and Management⟩[3]
Postgraduate Certificate in Building History
Postgraduate Certificate in Creative Writing
Postgraduate Certificate in Medical Education
Postgraduate Certificate in Professional Practice in Architecture

Cambridge Institute for Sustainability Leadership
Postgraduate Certificate in Sustainable Business
Postgraduate Certificate in Sustainable Value Chains

Language Centre
CULP Award in French
CULP Award in German
CULP Award in Italian
CULP Award in Spanish

Postgraduate Diploma in Entrepreneurship

Business and Management.

For the Postgraduate Diploma in Entrepreneurship administered by the Faculty Board of Business and Management, examination shall be by tasks prescribed by the Degree Committee. The volume of work required to complete the award shall be 15,000–20,000 words or equivalent.

[1] The Postgraduate Diploma in square brackets will be rescinded with effect from 1 January 2015.
[2] This Postgraduate Diploma is suspended until further notice.
[3] The Postgraduate Certificate in angular brackets will be inserted with effect from 1 January 2015.

Divinity.

Diploma in Theology for Ministry

Notice (Reporter, *2013–14, p. 406*)

1. The Faculty Board of Divinity shall be the administering body for the Diploma in Theology for Ministry, but they may delegate the detailed administration of the Diploma to their Committee for the Management of the B.Th. Degree.

2. A student may be a candidate for the Diploma of Theology for Ministry if he or she has been proposed by a Member Institution of the Cambridge Theological Federation and admitted by the Faculty Board. The course of study shall be either for one-year (full-time) or for two-years (part-time).

3. Candidates shall be required to offer five papers, or the equivalent combination of papers and half-papers, comprising:

(*a*) a total of three papers drawn from those specified for the B.Th. Degree in Groups A, B, C, and D;

(*b*) Paper B.Th. 51;

(*c*) a reflective report of no more than 3,000 words on a placement, which shall count as one half-paper; and

(*d*) a dissertation on any topic, approved by the Faculty Board, relating to the subject of any full or half-paper from among those specified for the B.Th. Degree, as specified under Regulation 21 for the Bachelor of Theology Degree, which shall count as one paper.

Education.

Postgraduate Diploma in Educational Studies

1. The Postgraduate Diploma in Educational Studies shall be administered by the Faculty of Education.

2. The Postgraduate Diploma in Educational Studies shall be awarded on the basis of the completion of 120 credits from practitioner professional development courses. The volume of work required to complete the award shall be at least 16,000 words.

Postgraduate Awards of Practitioner Professional Development

1. The postgraduate awards of Practitioner Professional Development shall be administered by the Faculty Board of Education.

2. The Postgraduate Advanced Certificate in Educational Studies shall be awarded on the basis of the completion of 90 credits from practitioner professional development courses. The volume of work required to complete the award shall be at least 12,000 words.

3. The Postgraduate Certificate in Educational Studies shall be awarded on the basis of the completion of 60 credits from practitioner professional development courses. The volume of work required to complete the award shall be at least 8,000 words.

4. The Postgraduate Award in Educational Studies shall be awarded on the basis of the completion of 30 credits from practitioner professional development courses. The volume of work required to complete the award shall be at least 4,000 words.

Continuing Education.

Diploma

For the Diplomas (60 credits) administered by the Institute of Continuing Education examination shall be by such tasks appropriate to the discipline as prescribed by the Strategic Committee for the Institute. The volume of work required to complete the award shall be 9,000–12,000 words or the equivalent.

Diploma of Higher Education

Diplomas of Higher Education (120 credits) administered by the Institute of Continuing Education shall be awarded on successful completion of two (60 credit) Diplomas.

Advanced Diploma

For the Advanced Diplomas administered by the Institute of Continuing Education examination shall be by tasks appropriate to the discipline as prescribed by the Strategic Committee for the Institute. The volume of work required to complete the award shall be 16,000–20,000 words or the equivalent.

Postgraduate Diploma

Continuing Education.

For the Postgraduate Diplomas administered by the Institute of Continuing Education examination shall be by tasks appropriate to the discipline as prescribed by the Strategic Committee for the Institute. The volume of work required to complete the award shall be 15,000–24,000 words or the equivalent.

Certificate

For the Certificates (60 credits) administered by the Institute of Continuing Education examination shall be by tasks appropriate to the discipline as prescribed by the Strategic Committee for the Institute. The volume of work required to complete the award shall be 9,000–12,000 words or the equivalent.

Certificate of Higher Education

The Certificates of Higher Education (120 credits) administered by the Institute of Continuing Education shall be awarded on successful completion of two (60-credit) Certificates.

Postgraduate Certificate

Amended by Notice (Reporter, *2013–14, p. 405*)

The scheme of examination for the Postgraduate Certificates administered by the Institute of Continuing Education shall be prescribed by the Strategic Committee for the Institute and shall require submission of work of 9,000–15,000 words or the equivalent.

Postgraduate Certificate in Sustainable Business

Amended by Notice (Reporter, *2013–14, p. 447*)

1. The Postgraduate Certificate in Sustainable Business shall be administered by the Cambridge Institute for Sustainability Leadership. CISL.

2. The scheme of examination for the Postgraduate Certificate in Sustainable Business shall be as follows:

(*a*) two essays (a case review and a strategy paper), each of not more than 3,000 words in length, and each on a topic approved by the Degree Committee,

(*b*) an essay (a group project) of not more than 7,000 words in length on a topic approved by the Degree Committee.

Postgraduate Certificate in Sustainable Value Chains

Amended by Notice (Reporter, *2013–14, p. 447*)

1. The Postgraduate Certificate in Sustainable Value Chains shall be administered by the Cambridge Institute for Sustainability Leadership.

2. The scheme of examination for the Postgraduate Certificate in Sustainable Value Chains shall be as follows:

(*a*) two assignments, each of not more than 3,000 words in length, each on a topic to be agreed with the Degree Committee;

(*b*) an assignment (a group project) of not more than 7,000 words in length on a topic to be agreed with the Degree Committee.

CULP Awards in French, German, Italian, and Spanish

Amended by Notice (Reporter, *2013–14, p. 732*)

1. The CULP Awards in French, German, Italian, and Spanish shall be administered by the Committee of Management of the Language Centre. Language Centre.

2. The scheme of examination shall consist of two examinations, each of which shall last for one hour: an examination for aural proficiency and an examination for reading and writing proficiency; there will also be an oral presentation.

CHAPTER VIII

SCHOOLS AND COUNCILS OF THE SCHOOLS

Amended by Grace 3 of 15 January 2014

Constitution of the Council of a School.

Except as provided in the regulations for any particular School, the Council of a School shall be constituted in accordance with the following provisions:

(*a*) The Board of each of the Faculties comprised in the School shall appoint annually in the Michaelmas Term one person to serve for four years from 1 January.

(*b*) The General Board shall appoint annually in the Michaelmas Term one person to serve for four years from 1 January.

(*c*) At least one member of the Council of a School shall be a member of the General Board, and that Board shall have regard to this requirement when making appointments.

(*d*) One undergraduate student member and one graduate student member of the Council of a School shall be elected by the undergraduate and graduate students respectively under the constituent Faculties, Syndicates, or other Boards or Committees of Management in each School. The student members of each Council shall be elected by ballot in each academical year. The electoral roll will be of all the persons who on 8 November were eligible, under the provisions of Election of Student Members of Faculty Boards and Other Bodies, Schedule IV, to vote and to stand as candidates in the election. The date and procedure for the election shall be determined by the Council of the School concerned, provided that the election shall not be held later than the division of the Lent Term. Students elected shall serve from the date of their election until such date in the following year as shall be determined as the day for the election of new student members, or until such earlier date as they may cease to qualify for membership of the constituent institution. The returning officer shall be the Head of the School or a member of the Regent House appointed by the Council of the School. If at an election of a student member or members the total number of vacancies is not filled, the Council of the School may fix a date for the holding of a further election to fill such vacancies as are unfilled. The persons eligible to vote and to stand as candidates in such an election shall be those persons who were so eligible in the preceding election.

School of Arts and Humanities

Amended by Graces 1 of 27 November 2013 and 10 of 16 July 2014

Membership.

1. The Council of the School of Arts and Humanities shall consist of the following members:

(*a*) one person appointed by each of the Faculty Boards of Architecture and History of Art, Asian and Middle Eastern Studies, Classics, Divinity, English, Modern and Medieval Languages, Music, and Philosophy to serve for one or two years, either from 1 October or from 1 January, as determined by the Faculty Board concerned;

(*b*) the Director of the Centre for Research in the Arts, Social Sciences, and Humanities;

(*c*) the Director of the Language Centre;

(*d*) not more than two persons co-opted by the Council of the School to serve until 30 September or 31 December either of the year in which they are co-opted or of the following year, as the Council shall determine at the time of co-optation, provided that it shall not be obligatory for the Council to co-opt any person or persons;

(*e*) one person elected from among their number by the undergraduate student members of the constituent institutions of the School;

(*f*) one person elected from among their number by the graduate student members of the constituent institutions of the School.

Meetings and quorum.

2. The Council of the School shall meet at least once in each academical year. No business shall be transacted at any meeting unless five of the members in classes (*a*) and (*b*) at least are present.

Head of the School.

3. The Head of the School shall be appointed by the Council of the School, subject to the approval of the General Board, to serve for a period of four years from 1 January following the appointment.

Duties and powers.

4. The Council of the School shall perform such duties as are specified in Statute A V 8(*a*)–(*c*) and such other duties as may be delegated to them by the General Board under Statute A V 8(*d*).

5. The provisions of Special Ordinance A (vii) 5 concerning reserved business shall apply to any member of the Council of the School in class (*c*) or (*d*) who is not *in statu pupillari* as if he or she were a person *in statu pupillari*. Reserved business.

School of the Biological Sciences

Amended by Grace 1 of 27 November 2013

1. The Council of the School of the Biological Sciences shall consist of the following members: Membership.

(*a*) the Head of each of the Departments in the Faculties of Biology and Veterinary Medicine, all of whom shall be members *ex officio*;

(*b*) the Director of the Wellcome Trust/Cancer Research UK Gurdon Institute;

(*c*) one person appointed by each of the Faculty Boards of Biology, Clinical Medicine, and Veterinary Medicine, who shall be appointed in the Michaelmas Term to serve for one year from 1 January next following;

(*d*) any member of the General Board who holds a University office in any of the Faculties or other institutions comprising the School, for so long as he or she remains a member of the General Board;

(*e*) persons co-opted by the Council of the School to serve until 31 December either of the year in which they are co-opted or of the following year, as the Council shall determine at the time of their co-optation, provided that it shall not be obligatory for the Council to co-opt any person or persons;

(*f*) one person elected from among their number by the undergraduate student members of the constituent institutions of the School;

(*g*) one person elected from among their number by the graduate student members of the constituent institutions of the School.

2. The Council of the School shall arrange to meet at least once in each academical year. No business shall be transacted at any meeting unless five of the members in classes (*a*)–(*e*) at least are present. Meetings and quorum.

3. The Head of the School shall be appointed by the Council of the School, subject to the approval of the General Board, to serve for a period of four years from 1 January following the appointment. Head of the School.

4. The Council of the School shall perform such duties as are specified in Statute A V 8(*a*)–(*c*) and such other duties as may be delegated to them by the General Board under Statute A V 8(*d*). Duties and powers.

5. The provisions of Special Ordinance A (vii) 5 concerning reserved business shall apply to any member of the Council of the School in class (*f*) or (*g*) who is not *in statu pupillari* as if he or she were a person *in statu pupillari*. Reserved business.

Secretary of the School

1. Appointments and reappointments to the University office of Secretary of the School of the Biological Sciences shall be made by an Appointments Committee consisting of the following: Appointments.

(*a*) the Vice-Chancellor (or a duly appointed deputy) as Chair;

(*b*) the Chair of the Council of the School of the Biological Sciences;

(*c*) three persons appointed by the Council of the School;

(*d*) two persons appointed by the General Board.

2. The Secretary shall act as Secretary of the Council of the School of the Biological Sciences and of Committees of the Council of the School, and shall perform such other duties as may be determined from time to time by the Council of the School with the approval of the General Board. Duties.

School of Clinical Medicine

Amended by Grace 1 of 27 November 2013

1. The Regius Professor of Physic shall be the Head of the School. Academic head.

2. The Council of the School of Clinical Medicine shall consist of the following members: Membership.

(*a*) the Regius Professor of Physic, who shall be Chair;

(*b*) the Head of each of the Departments in the Faculty of Clinical Medicine

(*c*) the Head of each Institute recognized by the Council of the School within the Faculty of Clinical Medicine;
(*d*) the Chair of the Faculty Board of Clinical Medicine;
(*e*) the Director of Medical Education in the Clinical School;
(*f*) the Head of the School of Biological Sciences;
(*g*) the Head of the Department of Pathology;
(*h*) the Director of the Academic Health Sciences System, Cambridge University Health Partners;
(*i*) the members in class (*f*) of the Faculty Board of Clinical Medicine.

3. The following shall have the right of attendance at the Council of the School of Clinical Medicine:
(*a*) the Chief Executive of Cambridge University Hospitals NHS Foundation Trust;
(*b*) the Chief Executive of Papworth NHS Foundation Trust;
(*c*) the Chief Executive of Cambridge and Peterborough Mental Health Partnership NHS Trust;
(*d*) a representative of the MRC Centre in Cambridge.

Meetings and quorum. **4.** The Council of the School shall meet at least once in each academical year. No business shall be transacted at any meeting unless five members in classes (*a*)–(*h*) at least are present.

Duties and powers. **5.** The Council of the School shall perform such duties as are specified in Statute A V 8(*a*)–(*c*) and such other duties as may be delegated to them by the General Board under Statute A V 8(*d*).

Reserved business. **6.** The provisions of Special Ordinance A (vii) 5 concerning reserved business shall apply to any member of the Council of the School in class (*i*) who is not *in statu pupillari* as if he or she were a person *in statu pupillari*.

Secretary of the School

Appointments. **1.** Appointments and reappointments to the University office of Secretary of the Clinical School shall be made by an Appointments Committee consisting of the following persons:
(*a*) the Vice-Chancellor (or a duly appointed deputy) as Chair;
(*b*) the Regius Professor of Physic;
(*c*) three persons appointed by the Faculty Board of Clinical Medicine;
(*d*) two persons appointed by the General Board.

Duties. **2.** The Secretary shall act as Secretary to the Council of the School and the Faculty Board of Clinical Medicine, and of Committees of the Faculty Board. He or she shall perform such other duties as may be determined from time to time by the Council of the School and the Faculty Board with the approval of the General Board.

School of the Humanities and Social Sciences

Amended by Grace 1 of 27 November 2013

Membership. **1.** The Council of the School of the Humanities and Social Sciences shall consist of the following members:
(*a*) the Heads of the Departments of History and Philosophy of Science and of Land Economy, the Heads of the three Departments within the Faculty of Human, Social, and Political Science, and one person appointed by each of the Faculty Boards of Economics, Education, History, and Law.
(*b*) one person appointed by the General Board, who shall be one of the two persons appointed by the Council of the School as a member of the General Board;
(*c*) persons co-opted by the Council of the School, provided that it shall not be obligatory for the Council to co-opt any person or persons;
(*d*) one person elected from among their number by the undergraduate student members of the constituent institutions of the School;
(*e*) one person elected from among their number by the graduate student members of the constituent institutions of the School.

Members in classes (*a*) and (*b*) shall be appointed in the Michaelmas Term to serve from 1 January next following. Members in class (*a*) shall serve for two years; the member in class (*b*) shall serve for two years or for so long as he or she remains a member of the General Board, whichever shall be the shorter period. Members in class (*c*) shall serve until 31 December either of the year in which they are co-opted or of the following year, as the Council shall determine at the time of their co-optation.

Meetings and quorum.

2. The Council of the School shall meet at least once in each academical year. No business shall be transacted at any meeting unless five of the members in classes (*a*)–(*c*) at least are present.

Head of the School.

3. The Head of the School shall be appointed by the Council of the School, subject to the approval of the General Board, to serve for a period of four years from 1 January following the appointment.

Duties and powers.

4. The Council of the School shall perform such duties as are specified in Statute A V 8(*a*)–(*c*) and such other duties as may be delegated to them by the General Board under Statute A V 8(*d*).

Reserved business.

5. The provisions of Special Ordinance A (vii) 5 concerning reserved business shall apply to any member of the Council of the School in class (*d*) or (*e*) who is not *in statu pupillari* as if he or she were a person *in statu pupillari*.

SCHOOL OF THE PHYSICAL SCIENCES

Amended by Grace 1 of 27 November 2013

Membership.

1. The Council of the School of the Physical Sciences shall consist of the following members:

(*a*) the Heads of the Departments in the Faculties of Earth Sciences and Geography, Mathematics and Physics and Chemistry, and the Director of the Isaac Newton Institute for Mathematical Sciences, all of whom shall be members *ex officio*;

(*b*) one person appointed by each of the Faculty Boards of Earth Sciences and Geography, Mathematics, and Physics and Chemistry, who shall be appointed in the Michaelmas Term to serve for one year from 1 January next following;

(*c*) any member of the General Board who holds a University office in any of the Faculties or other institutions comprising the School, for so long as he or she remains a member of the General Board;

(*d*) persons co-opted by the Council of the School to serve until 31 December either of the year in which they are co-opted or of the following year, as the Council shall determine at the time of their co-optation, provided that it shall not be obligatory for the Council to co-opt any person or persons;

(*e*) one person elected from among their number by the undergraduate student members of the constituent institutions of the School;

(*f*) one person elected from among their number by the graduate student members of the constituent institutions of the School.

Meetings and quorum.

2. The Council of the School shall arrange to meet at least once in each academical year. No business shall be transacted at any meeting unless five of the members in classes (*a*)–(*d*) at least are present.

Head of the School.

3. The Head of the School shall be appointed by the Council of the School, subject to the approval of the General Board, to serve for a period of four years from 1 January following the appointment.

Duties and powers.

4. The Council of the School shall perform such duties as are specified in Statute A V 8(*a*)–(*c*) and such other duties as may be delegated to them by the General Board under Statute A V 8(*d*).

Reserved business.

5. The provisions of Special Ordinance A (vii) 5 concerning reserved business shall apply to any member of the Council of the School in class (*e*) or (*f*) who is not *in statu pupillari* as if he or she were a person *in statu pupillari*.

Secretary of the School

Appointments.

1. Appointments and reappointments to the University office of Secretary of the School of the Physical Sciences shall be made by an Appointments Committee consisting of the following persons:

(*a*) the Vice-Chancellor, or a duly appointed deputy, as Chair;

(*b*) the Chair of the Council of the School of the Physical Sciences;

(*c*) three persons appointed by the Council of the School;

(*d*) two persons appointed by the General Board.

Members in classes (*c*) and (*d*) shall be appointed in the Michaelmas Term of each calendar year of which the number is even to serve for the two calendar years next ensuing.

Duties.

2. The Secretary shall act as Secretary of the Council of the School of the Physical Sciences, and of Committees of the Council of the School; and shall perform such other duties as may be determined from time to time by the Council of the School with the approval of the General Board.

School of Technology

Amended by Graces 1 of 27 November 2013, 3 of 12 March, and 1 of 19 March 2014

Membership.

1. The Council of the School of Technology shall consist of the following persons:

(*a*) the Heads of the Departments of Chemical Engineering and Biotechnology and of Engineering, the Head of the Computer Laboratory, the Director of Judge Business School, and the Director of the University of Cambridge Institute for Sustainability Leadership, all of whom shall be members *ex officio*;

(*b*) one person appointed by each of the Faculty Boards of Business and Management, of Computer Science and Technology, and of Engineering, and one by the Chemical Engineering and Biotechnology Syndicate, who shall be appointed in the Michaelmas Term to serve for one year from 1 January next following;

(*c*) any member of the General Board who holds a University office in any of the institutions comprising the School, for so long as he or she remains a member of the General Board;

(*d*) persons co-opted by the Council of the School to serve until 31 December either of the year in which they are co-opted or of the following year, as the Council shall determine at the time of their co-optation, provided that it shall not be obligatory for the Council to co-opt any persons or persons;

(*e*) one person elected from among their number by the undergraduate student members of the constituent institutions of the School;

(*f*) one person elected from among their number by the graduate student members of the constituent institutions of the School.

Meetings and quorum.

2. The Council of the School shall arrange to meet at least once in each academical year. No business shall be transacted at any meeting unless five of the members in classes (*a*)–(*d*) at least are present.

Head of the School.

3. The Head of the School shall be appointed by the Council of the School, subject to the approval of the General Board, to serve for a period of four years from 1 January following the appointment.

Duties and powers.

4. The Council of the School shall perform such duties as are specified in Statute A V 8(*a*)–(*c*) and such other duties as may be delegated to them by the General Board under Statute A V 8(*d*).

Reserved business.

5. The provisions of Special Ordinance A (vii) 5 concerning reserved business shall apply to any member of the Council of the School in class (*e*) or (*f*) who is not *in statu pupillari* as if he or she were a person *in statu pupillari*.

Secretary of the School

Appointments.

1. Appointments and reappointments to the University office of Secretary of the School of the Technology shall be made by an Appointments Committee consisting of the following persons:

(*a*) the Vice-Chancellor, or a duly appointed deputy, as Chair;

(*b*) the Chair of the Council of the School of Technology;

(*c*) three persons appointed by the Council of the School;

(*d*) two persons appointed by the General Board.

Members in classes (*c*) and (*d*) shall be appointed in the Michaelmas Term of each calendar year of which the number is even to serve for the two calendar years next ensuing.

Duties.

2. The Secretary shall act as Secretary of the Council of the School of Technology, and of Committees of the Council of the School; and shall perform such other duties as may be determined from time to time by the Council of the School with the approval of the General Board.

CHAPTER IX

FACULTIES, DEPARTMENTS, AND OTHER INSTITUTIONS UNDER THE SUPERVISION OF THE GENERAL BOARD

The provisions contained in this Chapter are Regulations of the General Board

GENERAL REGULATIONS FOR FACULTIES

1. There shall be a Faculty in respect of each of the subjects enumerated in the Schedule appended to these regulations.

2. In October of every year, not later than the first day of Full Term, the Registrary shall publish a preliminary list of the members of each Faculty. Preliminary lists.

3. Objections to the inclusion or omission of any name may be addressed to the Secretary of the Board of the Faculty concerned, and shall be decided by that Board subject to an appeal to the General Board. Any such decision of a Faculty Board or the General Board shall be communicated to the objector and to the Registrary forthwith. Objections.

4. As early as possible in the Michaelmas Term each year, and in any case not later than 28 October, the Secretary of the Board of each Faculty shall send to the Registrary the names of persons who are members of the Faculty under Regulation 1(*c*) of the Regulations for Faculty Membership. Corrected lists.

5. On the fifth weekday of November the Registrary shall promulgate the lists of the Faculties, and the lists so promulgated shall constitute the several Faculties for the purpose of the annual meetings of the Faculties. Those meetings shall be held after the sixth day and before the twenty-fifth day of November. Between the promulgation of the lists and the end of the academical year the Registrary shall not be required to ascertain or to notify any change that may occur in the membership of a Faculty. Promulgation of lists. Annual meetings.

6. In each year elections shall be held as necessary of members of Faculty Boards in category (ii) of class (*a*) and in classes (*c*) and (*f*), in accordance with the regulations for Classes of Faculty Board Membership, Elections, and Periods of Office. The names of the members elected shall be reported to the Registrary forthwith. Election of members of Faculty Boards.

7. In the exercise of their responsibility under Regulation 7 of the General Regulations for the Constitution of the Faculty Boards for preparing the teaching programme of the Faculty each Faculty Board shall Teaching programme.

either (*a*) invite to a conference at least once in each academical year the University officers and Affiliated Lecturers in the Faculty, and, if they think fit, the lecturers whose lectures have in the previous academical year been included in the scheme of lectures under Regulation 8;

or (*b*) delegate to Heads of Departments in the Faculty the responsibility for arranging similar conferences of Lecturers within their Departments. If this alternative is followed, the Faculty Board shall at least once a year receive reports from Heads of Departments on the outcome of these conferences and shall decide whether they give rise to any questions which should be considered by a conference of lecturers in the Faculty as a whole.

8. Each Faculty Board shall be authorized to invite College teaching officers or other persons to give lectures or other instruction on subjects which fall within the province of the Board, and to include such lectures or other instruction in the teaching programme of the Faculty.

9. The General Board are authorized to sanction the announcement of lectures by Professors and Readers in subjects which do not come within the scope of any Faculty Board. Lectures not within scope of Faculty Board.

SCHEDULE

Architecture and History of Art
Asian and Middle Eastern Studies
Biology
Business and Management
Classics
Clinical Medicine
Computer Science and Technology
Divinity
Earth Sciences and Geography
Economics
Education
Engineering
English
History
Human, Social, and Political Science
Law
Mathematics
Modern and Medieval Languages
Music
Philosophy
Physics and Chemistry
Veterinary Medicine

FACULTY MEMBERSHIP

Amended by Grace 1 of 27 November 2013

Faculty members.

1. The members of each Faculty in any year shall be

(*a*) those persons, giving instruction in a subject falling within the scope of the Faculty, who belong to any of the following classes, namely,

(i) University officers;

(ii) persons whose lectures or other instruction the Faculty Board has approved as part of the teaching programme of the Faculty for the current academical year, if they are (1) Heads or Fellows of Colleges or (2) persons employed by the University to undertake teaching or research;

(iii) persons who occupy in a College or in an Approved Society, as teachers of subjects falling within the scope of the Faculty, the position of Praelector, Lecturer, Assistant Lecturer, or Director of Studies;

(*b*) other persons or members of classes of persons approved for this purpose by Ordinance; and

(*c*) any other persons who may be appointed by the Faculty Board to be members of the Faculty until the next promulgation, or the next promulgation but one, of the list of the members of the Faculty.

The Faculty Board concerned shall have power to decide whether a subject falls within the scope of the Faculty for the purpose of subsection (*a*) above, and whether the instruction given by a person is of such nature and quantity as to entitle him or her to be included as a member of the Faculty under that subsection. An appeal on any such question shall lie from the Faculty Board to the General Board, from whose decision there shall be no further appeal.

Promulgation of lists.

2. A list of the members of each Faculty shall be promulgated in each year on a day prescribed by Ordinance of the General Board. Objections to the inclusion or omission of any name shall be decided in such manner as may be prescribed by Ordinance of the General Board.

3. A person may be a member of more than one Faculty.

Chair.

4. The Chair of each Faculty shall be the person elected Chair of the Faculty Board.

Election of members of Faculty Boards.

5. There shall be an annual meeting of the members of each Faculty for the election of a member or members of the Faculty Board.

6. In addition to the annual meeting, the Chair may summon a meeting of the Faculty whenever he or she thinks it desirable to do so. The Chair shall summon a meeting without delay upon receiving a written request signed by at least ten members of the Faculty.

7. At any election by a Faculty of a member of the Faculty Board nominations shall be made in writing and votes shall be taken by ballot.

8. At the annual meeting, and at any other meeting, of a Faculty there may be a discussion of any matter connected with the work of the Faculty that may be raised by any member of the Faculty after notice given to the members, or at the discretion of the Chair without notice. No resolution of a Faculty shall be binding on the Faculty Board.

CONSTITUTION OF THE FACULTY BOARDS

GENERAL REGULATIONS

Amended by Grace 1 of 27 November 2013

Classes of Faculty Board membership.

1. Every Faculty Board shall include members in each of the following classes (*a*), (*b*), and (*c*):

(*a*) members in one or both of the following categories:

(i) Heads of Departments within the Faculty;

(ii) holders of Professorships assigned to the Faculty or to a Department within the Faculty and of other offices specified in the Schedule to Special Ordinance C (vii) 1 which have been approved by Grace as qualifying their holders for membership in this category of a particular Faculty Board;

(*b*) members appointed by the Council after consultation with the General Board;

(*c*) members elected by the Faculty.

The General Board may make provision by Ordinance, on the recommendation of the Faculty Board, for the addition of members in the following classes:

(*d*) members co-opted by the Faculty Board;
(*e*) representatives of cognate studies and holders of specified offices;
(*f*) members elected by and from among the students in the Faculty in a manner to be determined by Ordinance of the General Board; provided that a member in class (*f*) shall cease to be a member if he or she ceases to be a student in the Faculty.

2. For every Faculty Board the number of members in each category of class (*a*) and the number of members in classes (*b*), (*c*), (*d*), (*e*), and (*f*) shall be determined by Ordinance of the General Board on the recommendation of the Faculty Board; provided that Number of members in classes.
(*a*) the number of members in class (*f*) shall not be more than three, and
(*b*) if there are three, at least one shall be a graduate student.

3. For every Faculty Board the General Board shall determine by Ordinance the period of membership of members in category (ii) of class (*a*) and of members in classes (*b*), (*c*), (*d*), and (*f*) and of representatives of cognate studies in class (*e*).

4. Each Faculty Board shall elect annually one of its members as Chair and, unless for a particular Faculty Board it is provided otherwise by Ordinance of the General Board, a Secretary; provided that no Board shall elect either as Chair or as Secretary a person who is a student in any Faculty. Chair and Secretary.

5. A Faculty Board may make recommendations to the General Board for any changes which it considers desirable in the Ordinances for those examinations with which it is concerned. Powers and duties.

6. Each Faculty Board shall submit to the General Board nominations of such examiners as it is required by Ordinance of the General Board to nominate.

7. Each Faculty Board shall be responsible to the General Board for ensuring the provision of appropriate instruction and adequate facilities for research in the subjects of the Faculty, for preparing the teaching programme of the Faculty, and for ensuring that the teaching given is of a high standard. For the discharge of these duties it shall be empowered:
(*a*) to make representations to the General Board concerning the resources needed by the Faculty for the support of its activities in teaching and research;
(*b*) to prescribe the subjects in which instruction is to be given in the teaching programme of the Faculty;
(*c*) to authorize courses of lectures and other instruction to be given by persons not holding University offices, under such conditions of remuneration as may be approved by the General Board;
(*d*) to report to the General Board if any University officer in the Faculty is not performing satisfactorily the duties of her or his office or is not fulfilling the conditions attaching to it.

8. The Secretary of each Faculty Board shall be responsible for the proper application of the funds available to the Faculty, other than those for which Heads of Departments are responsible under the provisions of Statute A V 17(*c*), for ensuring that the approved estimate of expenditure is not exceeded, and that the accounts are correctly maintained; provided always that if the General Board so requires these duties shall be assigned by the Faculty Board to some other person approved by the General Board. Application of funds.

9. Each Faculty Board shall submit to the General Board, in accordance with arrangements determined by Ordinance, estimates of annual expenditure for consideration by the Board in accordance with Statute A V 1(*b*).

10. A Faculty Board shall prepare any reports on the work of the Faculty which the General Board may require. Reports.

11. Under the provisions of Special Ordinance A (vii) 5(iii), the election of the Chairs and Secretaries of Faculty Boards, the co-optation of members of Faculty Boards, and the appointment (or nomination for appointment) of examiners, electors to Professorships, members of Faculties, members of Appointments Committees, and members of Degree Committees shall be reserved business; and the provisions of Special Ordinance A (vii) 5 concerning reserved business shall apply to any member of a Faculty Board in class (*f*) who is not *in statu pupillari* as if he or she were a person *in statu pupillari*. Reserved business.

Classes of Faculty Board Membership, Elections, and Periods of Office

Amended by Grace 1 of 27 November 2013

1. Subject to the provisions of Regulations 2 and 3, the number of members in each category of class (*a*) and in classes (*b*), (*c*), (*d*), (*e*), and (*f*) of each Faculty Board shall be that specified in Schedule I appended to these regulations. Numbers of members in classes.

Class (*a*). **2.** The number of members in each category of class (*a*) of each Faculty Board shall be determined as follows:

(*a*) all Heads of Departments (if any) within a Faculty shall be members in category (i) of class (*a*);

(*b*) unless there are more than five Departments within a Faculty, the total number of members in class (*a*) shall not exceed five;

(*c*) when there are five or more than five Departments within a Faculty, there shall be no members in category (ii) of class (*a*);

(*d*) when there are less than five Departments within a Faculty, the members in category (ii) shall be:

either all the persons eligible for membership of the Faculty Board in category (ii), provided that this would not increase the total number of members in class (*a*) to more than five;

or such number of persons as will bring that total number up to five, elected from among all the persons who are eligible for membership of the Faculty Board in that category by all those eligible persons, or in such other manner as may be approved by the General Board on the recommendation of the Faculty Board.

Offices (other than Professorships) specified in the Schedule to Special Ordinance C (vii) 1 which qualify their holders for membership in category (ii) of class (*a*) of a particular Faculty Board shall be those specified in Schedule II appended to these regulations.

Class (*b*). **3.** The number of members in class (*b*) of each Faculty Board shall be two.

Class (*e*). **4.** The General Board shall determine for each Faculty Board, in consultation with any other Faculty Board or other body concerned, the cognate studies to be represented by members in class (*e*) and the method of appointment of those representatives, and shall specify the offices by virtue of which the holders shall be members in class (*e*). Details of the membership of Faculty Boards in class (*e*) shall be appended to these regulations as Schedule III.

Periods of membership. **5.** The elected members of each Faculty Board in category (ii) of class (*a*) shall serve for two years or four years, as the Faculty Board shall determine, from 1 January following their election.

Members in class (*b*) shall serve for two years from 1 January following their appointment.

Members in class (*c*) shall serve for four years from 1 January following their election.

Members in class (*d*) shall serve for one year from 1 January following the date of their co-optation or for the remainder of the calendar year in which they are co-opted, as the Faculty Board shall determine.

Members in class (*e*) who are appointed as representatives of cognate studies shall serve for two years from 1 January following their appointment.

Members in class (*f*) shall serve from the date of their election until such date in the following year as shall be determined, in accordance with the regulations for the election of student members of Faculty Boards, as the day for the election of members in class (*f*), or until such earlier date as they may, under the provisions of Regulation 1 of the General Regulations for the Constitution of the Faculty Boards, cease to qualify for membership in class (*f*).

Election of members in class (*a*)(ii), **6.** For each Faculty Board which includes members in category (ii) of class (*a*), an election of such members shall be held each year, if necessary, on a date between the sixth and the twenty-fifth day of November. Such an election shall be conducted in accordance with the provisions of Regulation 2(*d*) above.

in class (*c*). **7.** For each Faculty Board an election of members in class (*c*) shall be held each year at the annual meeting of the Faculty. The procedure for the election of members in class (*c*) shall be that prescribed in the Single Transferable Vote Regulations, except that the returning officer shall be the Chair of the Faculty or in the Chair's absence a deputy appointed by the Chair subject to the approval of the General Board; provided that, in order to secure the representation of Departments within the Faculty or of institutions associated with the Faculty, the Faculty may from time to time determine that some or all of the candidates for election shall be nominated in accordance with a procedure approved by the General Board on the recommendation of the Faculty.

Casual vacancies. **8.** If a casual vacancy occurs in class (*c*), the Faculty Board shall be empowered to co-opt a member to fill the vacancy from the date of its occurrence until the end of the calendar year or, if the vacancy occurs between the annual meeting of the Faculty and 31 December, until the end of the following calendar year; and at the next annual meeting of the Faculty a member shall be elected to serve for the remaining complete years (if any) of the period of tenure of his or her predecessor.

9. For each Faculty Board an election of members in class (*f*) shall be held each year. Such an election shall be conducted in accordance with the regulations for the election of student members of Faculty Boards and other bodies.

Election of student members of Faculty Boards and other bodies

1. These regulations shall apply to each Faculty Board or other University body whose membership includes student members, except in so far as may be provided otherwise in the special regulations for a particular Faculty Board or other body. Application of regulations.

2. A Faculty Board or other University body shall adopt for the election of its student members one of the schemes listed in Schedule IV below. A body which intends to hold an election of student members for the first time shall notify the Registrary not later than 1 October in the academical year in which the election is to be held. A body may subsequently alter its choice of scheme, provided that it notifies the Registrary not later than 1 October in the academical year in which the change is to take effect. Schemes of election.

3. If the scheme adopted provides for the electors to be divided into categories according to their course of study or their year of study, the Registrary shall be notified accordingly.

4. For each Faculty Board or other body to which these regulations apply an election of student members shall be held in each academical year on a day in Full Term not earlier than the division of the Michaelmas Term and not later than the last day of Full Lent Term. The persons eligible to vote and to stand as candidates shall be those persons who are certified by the Registrary to be students in the Faculty concerned or, in an election of members of a body other than a Faculty Board, those persons whose course of study or research is similarly certified by the Registrary to be in a subject falling within the scope of the body concerned. Voting shall be by ballot. The date and procedure of the election, the final date for the receipt of nominations, and the hours of voting shall be determined by the Faculty Board or other body concerned; provided that the final date for the receipt of nominations shall not be later than the seventh day of Full Term before the day appointed for the election. Date of election and procedure.

5. The returning officer shall be the Chair of the body concerned or a member of the Regent House appointed by the body.

6. Not later than the fourteenth day of Full Term before the day appointed for the election, the returning officer shall give public notice of the date and place appointed for the election, the hours of voting, and the final date for the receipt of nominations. Notice of election.

7. Nominations shall be in writing. Each nomination shall be signed by two persons proposing and seconding the nomination and shall be accompanied by a statement signed by the candidate, consenting to be nominated. Nominations.

8. Not later than the tenth day after the division of the Michaelmas Term, the Registrary shall send to the returning officer for each body to which these regulations apply an electoral roll of all the persons who on 8 November were eligible, under the provisions of Regulation 1 of the General Regulations for the Constitution of the Faculty Boards and of these regulations, to vote and to stand as candidates in the election. The roll shall be undivided, or divided into sections corresponding to categories determined in accordance with Regulation 3. The returning officer shall make the roll public forthwith and voting shall not commence earlier than the second day after the roll is published. The Registrary shall have power, on the recommendation of the returning officer, to amend the roll at any time before the time fixed for the start of voting. The nomination of any candidate whose name, or the name of whose proposer or seconder, is not included in the roll (or, if the roll is divided into categories, in the section of the roll for the category for which the candidate has been nominated), or in the roll (or the appropriate section of the roll) as amended by the Registrary, shall be declared by the returning officer to be invalid. Electoral rolls.

9. If at any election of a student member or members the total number of vacancies is not filled, the Faculty Board or other body may fix a date for the holding of a further election to fill such vacancies as are unfilled. Unless the body concerned determines otherwise, the persons eligible to vote and to stand as candidates in such an election shall be those persons who were so eligible in the preceding election; provided that no such person may vote or be a candidate in a further election if the Registrary certifies that he or she is no longer entitled to be included in the relevant electoral roll. Unfilled vacancies.

10. If a casual vacancy occurs, the body concerned shall determine whether a bye-election shall be held to fill the vacancy and shall determine the date on which any such election is to be held. Unless Casual vacancies.

the body concerned determines otherwise, the persons eligible to vote and to stand as candidates in a bye-election shall be those persons who were eligible at the time of the last preceding annual election to vote and to stand as candidates in the election to the place which has been vacated, provided that no such person may vote or be a candidate in a bye-election if the Registrary certifies that he or she is no longer entitled to be included in the relevant electoral roll.

11. The General Board, after consulting the Council, shall from time to time make rules in accordance with which:

(*a*) the Registrary shall certify persons as students in a Faculty for the purpose of Regulation 1 of the General Regulations for the Constitution of the Faculty Boards, and as persons entitled to be included in the electoral roll for the purpose of an election to any body other than a Faculty Board; and

(*b*) the terms graduate student and undergraduate shall be defined for the purpose of the schemes listed in Schedule IV to these regulations.

Subject to such rules, any question of interpretation of these regulations shall be decided by the Registrary, whose decision shall be final.

SCHEDULE I

Amended by Notices (Reporter, *2013–14, pp. 251, 305, and 357*)

The composition of the Faculty Boards[1]

Faculty Board	*Classes*							*Total*
	(*a*)(i)	(*a*)(ii)	(*b*)	(*c*)	(*d*)	(*e*)	(*f*)	
Architecture and History of Art	2	3	2	5	2	2	3	19
Asian and Middle Eastern Studies	2	3	2	6	2	5	3	23
Biology	8	0	2	8	6	7	3	34
Business and Management	1	4	2	10	5	1	3	26
Classics	0	5	2	8	4	0	3	22
Clinical Medicine	12	0	2	10	3	8	3	38
Computer Science and Technology	1	4	2	4	2	1	3	17
Divinity	0	5	2	8	6	2	3	26
Earth Sciences and Geography	2	3	2	10	2	2	3	24
Economics	1	4	2	8	3	1	3	22
Education	1	4	2	8	4	0	3	22
Engineering	1	4	2	10	3	3	3	26
English	1	4	2	11	3	2	3	26
History	0	5	2	9	4	1	3	24
Human, Social, and Political Science	3	2	2	9	3	6	3	28
Law	1	4	2	8	3	0	3	21
Mathematics	2	3	2	10	4	0	3	24
Modern and Medieval Languages	6	0	2	12	3	3	3	29
Music	0	2	2	6	4	1	3	18
Philosophy	0	3	2	6	3	3	3	20
Physics and Chemistry	4	1	2	8	3	0	3	21
Veterinary Medicine	1	4	2	4	4	4	2	21

SCHEDULE II

Offices (other than Professorships) specified in the Schedule to Special Ordinance C (vii) 1 which qualify their holders for membership in category (ii) of class (a) of particular Faculty Boards

Offices	*Faculty Boards for which the holders are eligible as members in category (ii) of class (a)*
Directorship of the Fitzwilliam Museum	Architecture and History of Art
Executive Directorship of Research in the Faculty of Economics	Economics

[1] See Regulation 1 of the General Regulations for the Constitution of the Faculty Boards for the definition of the classes of membership.

SCHEDULE III

Amended by Notices (Reporter, *2013–14, pp. 305, and 357*)

Membership of Faculty Boards in class (e)

(Representatives of cognate studies and holders of specified offices)

Faculty Board	*Representatives of cognate studies and method of appointment*	*Holders of specified offices*
Architecture and History of Art	—	The Director of Kettle's Yard; the Director of the Hamilton Kerr Institute
Asian and Middle Eastern Studies	One person appointed by the Faculty Board of History; one person appointed by the Faculty Board of Modern and Medieval Languages; two persons appointed by the Faculty Board of Human, Social, and Political Science	The Director of the Language Centre
Biology	One person appointed by each of the Faculty Boards of Earth Sciences and Geography, Human, Social and Political Science, Physics and Chemistry, and Veterinary Medicine	The Director of the Centre for Family Research; the Director of Education (Biological Sciences) in the Faculty of Biology; the Director of Medical Education in the Faculty of Clinical Medicine
Business and Management	—	The Director of the M.B.A. course
Classics	—	—
Clinical Medicine	One person appointed by the Faculty Board of Biology; one person appointed by the University officers in the Department of Pathology	The Regius Professor of Physic; the Chair of the Consultant Staff Council in Cambridge; the Director of Medical Education; the Regional Postgraduate Dean; the Associate Deans with responsibility for undergraduate clinical medical education; the Professor of Pathology
Computer Science and Technology	—	The Departmental Secretary of the Computer Laboratory
Divinity	One person appointed by the Faculty Board to represent Hebrew; one person appointed by the Faculty Board to represent Ecclesiastical History	—
Earth Sciences and Geography	One person appointed by the Faculty Board of Biology	The Director of the Scott Polar Institute
Economics	—	The Professor of Economic History
Education	—	—
Engineering	—	The Head of the Department of Chemical Engineering and Biotechnology; the Head of the Department of Materials Science and Metallurgy; the Head of the Computer Laboratory
English	One person appointed by the Faculty Board of Modern and Medieval Languages	—
History	—	The Professor of Ancient History
Human, Social, and Political Science	One person appointed by each of the Faculty Boards of Biology, Economics, Education, and History	The Director of the Museum of Archaeology and Anthropology, the Director of the McDonald Institute for Archaeological Research

Faculty Board	*Representatives of cognate studies and method of appointment*	*Holders of specified offices*
Law	—	—
Mathematics	—	—
Modern and Medieval Languages	One person appointed by the Faculty Board of Asian and Middle Eastern Studies; one person appointed by the Faculty Board of English	The Director of the Language Centre
Music	One person appointed by the Faculty Board of an appropriate discipline as determined by the General Board on the recommendation of the Faculty Board of Music	—
Philosophy	One person appointed by the Faculty Board of Classics; one person appointed by the University officers in the Department of Psychology; one person appointed by the Board of History and Philosophy of Science	—
Physics and Chemistry	—	—
Veterinary Medicine	Two persons appointed by the Faculty Board of Biology; one person appointed by the Faculty Board of Clinical Medicine	The Director of Education (Biological Sciences) in the Faculty of Biology

SCHEDULE IV

Under the several schemes for the election of student members of Faculty Boards and other bodies, the student members shall be as set out below. For bodies other than Faculty Boards the terms 'student in the Faculty' and 'undergraduate in the Faculty' shall be understood to mean appropriately qualified persons as certified by the Registrary in accordance with Regulation 4 above.

Scheme A. Two students elected in a single constituency by all the students in the Faculty.

Scheme C. Two students, as follows: (i) one graduate student elected by all the graduate students in the Faculty, and (ii) one undergraduate elected by all the undergraduates in the Faculty.

Scheme C. Three students, as follows: (i) one graduate student elected by all the graduate students in the Faculty, and (ii) two undergraduates elected by all the undergraduates in the Faculty.

Scheme D. Three students, as follows: (i) one graduate student elected by all the graduate students in the Faculty; (ii) one undergraduate elected by and from a class of undergraduates in the Faculty defined by reference to a specified year or years of study; and (iii) one undergraduate elected by and from among all the undergraduates in the Faculty who are not eligible to be members in category (ii).

Scheme E. Three students, as follows: (i) one graduate student elected by all the graduate students in the Faculty; (ii) one undergraduate elected by and from among all the undergraduates in the Faculty pursuing a course of study appropriate to a specified Tripos or a specified degree; and (iii) one undergraduate elected by and from among all the undergraduates in the Faculty who are not eligible to be members in category (ii).

Scheme F. Three students, as follows: (i) one undergraduate elected by all the undergraduates in the Faculty; (ii) one graduate student elected by and from among the graduate students in the Faculty pursuing a course of study appropriate to a specified degree or other qualification; and (iii) one graduate student elected by and from among all the graduate students in the Faculty who are not eligible to be members in category (ii).

Scheme H. Two students, as follows: (i) one student elected by and from among all the students in the Faculty pursuing a course of study appropriate to a specified Tripos or a specified degree or other qualification; and (ii) one student elected by and from among all the students in the Faculty who are not eligible to be members in category (i).

Scheme J. See p. 637.

Scheme K. Three students, as follows: (i) two students elected by and from among the students in the Faculty pursuing a course of study appropriate to a specified degree or other qualification; and (ii) one student elected by and from among all the students in the Faculty who are not eligible to be members in category (i).

Rules made by the General Board in accordance with Regulation 11 for the election of student members of Faculty Boards and other bodies

1. These rules shall apply to the compilation of electoral rolls for the election of student members of Faculty Boards and other University bodies.

2. The term student in the Faculty shall mean a matriculated person certified by the Registrary to be pursuing a course of study leading to a Tripos examination, or a course of study or research leading to a degree, diploma, or certificate of the University, in a subject falling within the scope of the Faculty.

3. The Registrary shall not at any time include the name of any person in the electoral roll for the election of student members of more than one Faculty Board, or in such an electoral roll and also in an electoral roll for the election of student members of any of the following bodies: the Chemical Engineering and Biotechnology Syndicate, the Board of History and Philosophy of Science, the Board of Land Economy.

4. Notwithstanding that a Graduate Student may be under the supervision of the Degree Committee for a Faculty, the Registrary may include his or her name in the electoral roll for the election of students to serve on one of the bodies specified in Rule 1 other than a Faculty Board if satisfactory evidence is provided by the Secretary of the Degree Committee or otherwise, showing that it is appropriate to do so.

5. A person whose name is on the Register of Graduate Students shall be eligible for inclusion in the appropriate electoral roll, whether or not registered as a candidate for a particular degree, diploma, or certificate.

6. The Registrary shall include in the appropriate electoral roll the name of any sabbatical officer of CUSU who has, before completing a course of study leading to the degree for which he or she intends to be a candidate been given an allowance under Regulation 1(*b*) or 3(*a*)(i) for Allowances to Candidates for Examinations for the purpose of holding such office, but shall not include any such sabbatical officer who has completed a course of study for any of the degrees specified in Rule 9(*a*) below and has not commenced any further course of study.

7. The Registrary shall not include in any electoral roll the name of any Graduate Student who

either (*a*) on 31 October next preceding the election had been registered for his or her current course of study or research for more than four calendar years,

or (*b*) held a Fellowship of a College on 31 October next preceding the election,

or (*c*) was a member of a Faculty at the most recent promulgation of the lists of the Faculties.

8. The Registrary shall assign candidates for the Natural Sciences Tripos and the Medical and Veterinary Sciences Tripos to electoral rolls in accordance with the procedure prescribed below.

9. For the purpose of the schemes listed in Schedule IV to the regulations for Classes of Faculty Board Membership, Elections, and Periods of Office,

(*a*) the term undergraduate shall mean a student whose course of study is one leading to any of the following degrees: B.A., M.A.St., M.Eng., M.Math., M.Sci., B.Th.;

(*b*) the term graduate student shall mean a student who is not an undergraduate so defined;

(*c*) Affiliated Students whose course of study is one leading to the B.A. Degree shall, in their first year of study, be deemed to be in their second year and, in their second year, shall be deemed to be in their third year.

Procedure for the allocation to electoral rolls of candidates for the Natural Sciences Tripos and the Medical and Veterinary Sciences Tripos

1. Candidates for the Natural Sciences Tripos and the Medical and Veterinary Sciences Tripos shall, subject to the rules set out in paragraphs 2 and 3 below, be eligible for inclusion in the electoral rolls of such of the following Faculty Boards and other bodies as include a class of members elected by students:

A. The Faculty Board of Earth Sciences and Geography.
B. The Faculty Board of Mathematics.
C. The Faculty Board of Physics and Chemistry.
D. The Faculty Board of Biology.
H. The Board of History and Philosophy of Science.

2. Subject to paragraph 1 and the rules set out in paragraph 3 below, candidature for the following subjects or Parts shall confer eligibility for inclusion in the electoral rolls of the bodies specified in paragraph 1 as follows:

Natural Sciences Tripos

Part IA

Biology of Cells	D
Chemistry	C
Evolution and Behaviour	D
Earth Sciences	A
Materials Science	C
Physics	C
Physiology of Organisms	D

The subjects Computer Science, Mathematical Biology, Elementary Mathematics for Biologists, and Mathematics shall not confer eligibility for an electoral roll.

Part IB

Animal Biology	D
Biochemistry and Molecular Biology	D
Cell and Developmental Biology	D

Chemistry A	C
Chemistry B	C
Ecology	D
Experimental Psychology	D
Geological Sciences A	A
Geological Sciences B	A
History and Philosophy of Science	H
Mathematics	B
Materials Science	C
Neurobiology	D
Pathology	D
Pharmacology	D
Physics A	C
Physics B	C
Physiology	D
Plant and Microbial Sciences	D
Part II	
Astrophysics	C
Biochemistry	D
Biological and Biomedical Sciences	D
Chemistry	C
Experimental and Theoretical Physics	C
Genetics	D
Geological Sciences	A
History and Philosophy of Science	H
Materials Science	C
Neuroscience	D
Pathology	D
Pharmacology	D
Physical Sciences	C
Physiology, Development, and Neuroscience	D
Physiology and Psychology	D
Plant Sciences	D
Psychology	D
Zoology	D
Part III	
Astrophysics	C
Biochemistry	D
Chemistry	C
Experimental and Theoretical Physics	C
Geological Sciences	A
Materials Science	C
Systems Biology	D
Medical and Veterinary Sciences Tripos	
Part IA	D
Part IB	D

3. Candidates for Part II and Part III of the Natural Sciences Tripos and for Part IA and Part IB of the Medical and Veterinary Sciences Tripos shall be allocated to electoral rolls in accordance with paragraph 2. Candidates for the remaining examinations shall be allocated to electoral rolls as follows, provided that any candidate offering two or more subjects of which only one confers eligibility for inclusion in the electoral roll of a Faculty Board (or other body) which includes a class of a members elected by students shall be allocated to that roll:

Part IA and Part IB of the Natural Sciences Tripos. Candidates offering two subjects conferring eligibility for the same electoral roll shall be allocated to that roll. Other candidates shall be allocated at their choice to any one of the electoral rolls for which they are eligible.

4. Any candidates who, in accordance with paragraph 3 above, are eligible for inclusion in more than one electoral roll shall, through their Tutors, communicate their choice of electoral roll to the Registrary not later than the last day of Full Michaelmas Term. The Registrary may exclude from any electoral roll the name of any such candidate who fails to send notification of his or her choice of electoral roll by that date.

DEGREE COMMITTEES

Constitution. **1.** There shall be a Degree Committee for each Faculty, and for each of the institutions specified in the Schedule to these regulations. The constitution of such a Degree Committee shall be determined by the General Board on the recommendation of the Faculty Board or other comparable authority and after consultation with the Board of Graduate Studies, provided that no person shall be a member of a Degree Committee who has been admitted as a Graduate Student or who is a candidate for a Diploma or a Certificate or comparable qualification, the regulations for which do not require him or her to be admitted as a Graduate Student.

2. If the constitution of a Degree Committee that has been approved by the General Board under Regulation 1 includes provision for members co-opted by the Committee, the co-opted members of the Committee shall serve for one year from 1 January following the date of their co-optation or for the remainder of the calendar year in which they are co-opted, as the Faculty Board or comparable authority shall determine.

3. Each Degree Committee shall elect one of its members as Chair of the Committee, and a Secretary. Chair and Secretary.

4. The Secretary of the Committee shall inform the Registrary of any change in its membership.

5. Subject to the approval of the General Board, after consultation with the Board of Graduate Studies, each Degree Committee may determine from time to time how many members shall form a quorum; provided that a resolution that a person be recommended or approved for the award of a degree, or that a person be not so recommended or approved, shall not be valid unless passed with the concurrence of the votes, cast at a meeting, of one-half of the whole number of members of the Committee. Quorum.

SCHEDULE

Department of Land Economy
Department of History and Philosophy of Science

DEPARTMENTS AND HEADS OF DEPARTMENTS

1. There shall be Departments within the several Faculties, and Departments independent of any Faculty, as specified in Regulation 3.

2. Subject to the provisions of Regulation 3, the Head of each Department, who shall be a University officer engaged in teaching and research in the Department, shall be appointed by the General Board, on the recommendation of the Faculty Board or other authority concerned, for a period not exceeding five years at a time, save that in a particular case the General Board shall have power, after consultation with the Faculty Board or other authority concerned, to make an appointment for a period not exceeding ten years at a time.

3. The Heads of the several Departments shall be as follows:

Departments within Faculties

Faculty of Architecture and History of Art.

Architecture A person appointed in accordance with Regulation 2.

History of Art A person appointed in accordance with Regulation 2.

Faculty of Asian and Middle Eastern Studies.

Department of East Asian Studies A person appointed in accordance with Regulation 2.

Department of Middle Eastern Studies A person appointed in accordance with Regulation 2.

Faculty of Biology.

Biochemistry

A person appointed in accordance with Regulation 2, provided that the General Board may, on the recommendation of the Faculty Board of Biology, require the Head of the Department to resign the Headship with effect from the date on which a newly-elected holder of the Sir William Dunn Professorship of Biochemistry takes up the duties of the office, so that the latter may be appointed Head of the Department for a period not exceeding five years in the first instance.

Psychology

A person appointed in accordance with Regulation 2, provided that the General Board may, on the recommendation of the Faculty Board of Biology, require the Head of the Department to resign the Headship with effect from the date on which a newly-elected holder of the Professorship of Experimental Psychology takes up the duties of the office, so that the latter may be appointed Head of the Department for a period not exceeding five years in the first instance.

Genetics

A person appointed in accordance with Regulation 2, provided that the General Board may, on the recommendation of the Faculty Board of Biology, require the Head of the Department to resign the Headship with effect from the date on which a newly-elected holder of the Arthur Balfour Professorship of Genetics takes up the duties of the office, so that the latter may be appointed Head of the Department for a period not exceeding five years in the first instance.

Pathology

A person appointed in accordance with Regulation 2, provided that the General Board may, on the recommendation of the Faculty Board of Biology, require the Head of the Department to resign the Headship with effect from the date on which a newly-elected holder of the Professorship of Pathology takes up the duties of the office, so that the latter may be appointed Head of the Department for a period not exceeding five years in the first instance.

Pharmacology

A person appointed in accordance with Regulation 2, provided that the General Board may, on the recommendation of the Faculty Board of Biology, require the Head of the Department to resign the Headship with effect from the date on which a newly-elected holder of the Sheild Professorship of Pharmacology takes up the duties of the office, so that the latter may be appointed Head of the Department for a period not exceeding five years in the first instance.

Physiology, Development, and Neuroscience

A person appointed in accordance with Regulation 2.

Plant Sciences

A person appointed in accordance with Regulation 2, provided that the General Board may, on the recommendation of the Faculty Board of Biology, require the Head of the Department to resign the Headship with effect from the date on which a newly-elected holder of the Regius Professorship of Botany takes up the duties of the office, so that the latter may be appointed Head of the Department for a period not exceeding five years in the first instance.

Zoology

A person appointed in accordance with Regulation 2, provided that the General Board may, on the recommendation of the Faculty Board of Biology, require the Head of the Department to resign the Headship with effect from the date on which a newly-elected holder of the Professorship of Zoology (1866) takes up the duties of the office, so that the latter may be appointed Head of the Department for a period not exceeding five years in the first instance.

Faculty of Business and Management.

Judge Institute of Management (Judge Business School) The Director of Judge Business School.

Faculty of Clinical Medicine.

Clinical Biochemistry

A person appointed in accordance with Regulation 2, provided that the General Board may, on the recommendation of the Faculty Board of Clinical Medicine, require the Head of the Department to resign the Headship with effect from the date on which a newly-elected holder of the Professorship of Clinical Biochemistry and Medicine takes up the duties of the office, so that the latter may be appointed Head of the Department for a period not exceeding five years in the first instance.

Clinical Neurosciences A person appointed in accordance with Regulation 2.

Haematology

A person appointed in accordance with Regulation 2, provided that the General Board may, on the recommendation of the Faculty Board of Clinical Medicine, require the Head of the Department to resign the Headship with effect from the date on which a newly-elected holder of the Professorship of Haematology takes up the duties of the office, so that the latter may be appointed Head of the Department for a period not exceeding five years in the first instance.

Medical Genetics

A person appointed in accordance with Regulation 2, provided that the General Board may, on the recommendation of the Faculty Board of Clinical Medicine, require the Head of the Department to resign the Headship with effect from the date on which a newly-elected holder of the Professorship of

Medical Genetics (1995) takes up the duties of the office, so that the latter may be appointed Head of the Department for a period not exceeding five years in the first instance.

Medicine A person appointed in accordance with Regulation 2.

Obstetrics and Gynaecology

A person appointed in accordance with Regulation 2, provided that the General Board may, on the recommendation of the Faculty Board of Clinical Medicine, require the Head of the Department to resign the Headship with effect from the date on which a newly-elected holder of the Professorship of Obstetrics and Gynaecology (1975) takes up the duties of the office, so that the latter may be appointed Head of the Department for a period not exceeding five years in the first instance.

Oncology

A person appointed in accordance with Regulation 2, provided that the General Board may, on the recommendation of the Faculty Board of Clinical Medicine, require the Head of the Department to resign the Headship with effect from the date on which a newly-elected holder of the Cancer Research UK Professorship of Oncology takes up the duties of the office, so that the latter may be appointed Head of the Department for a period not exceeding five years in the first instance.

Paediatrics

A person appointed in accordance with Regulation 2, provided that the General Board may, on the recommendation of the Faculty Board of Clinical Medicine, require the Head of the Department to resign the Headship with effect from the date on which a newly-elected holder of the Professorship of Paediatrics (1978) takes up the duties of the office, so that the latter may be appointed Head of the Department for a period not exceeding five years in the first instance.

Psychiatry

A person appointed in accordance with Regulation 2, provided that the General Board may, on the recommendation of the Faculty Board of Clinical Medicine, require the Head of the Department to resign the Headship with effect from the date on which a newly-elected holder of the Professorship of Psychiatry (1976) takes up the duties of the office, so that the latter may be appointed Head of the Department for a period not exceeding five years in the first instance.

Public Health and Primary Care

A person appointed in accordance with Regulation 2, provided that the General Board may, on the recommendation of the Faculty Board of Clinical Medicine, require the Head of the Department to resign the Headship with effect from the date on which a newly-elected holder of the Professorship of Epidemiology and Medicine takes up the duties of the office, so that the latter may be appointed Head of the Department for a period not exceeding five years in the first instance.

Radiology

A person appointed in accordance with Regulation 2, provided that the General Board may, on the recommendation of the Faculty Board of Clinical Medicine, require the Head of the Department to resign the Headship with effect from the date on which a newly-elected holder of the Professorship of Radiology takes up the duties of the office, so that the latter may be appointed Head of the Department for a period not exceeding five years in the first instance.

Surgery

A person appointed in accordance with Regulation 2, provided that the General Board may, on the recommendation of the Faculty Board of Clinical Medicine, require the Head of the Department to resign the Headship with effect from the date on which a newly-elected holder of the Professorship of

Surgery takes up the duties of the office, so that the latter may be appointed Head of the Department for a period not exceeding five years in the first instance.

Faculty of Computer Science and Technology.

Computer Laboratory A person appointed in accordance with Regulation 2.

Faculty of Earth Sciences and Geography.

Earth Sciences A person appointed in accordance with Regulation 2.

Geography A person appointed in accordance with Regulation 2.

Faculty of Education.

Education A person appointed in accordance with Regulation 2.

Faculty of Engineering.

Engineering A person appointed in accordance with Regulation 2.

Faculty of English.

Anglo-Saxon, Norse, and Celtic

A person appointed in accordance with Regulation 2, provided that the General Board may, on the recommendation of the Faculty Board of English, require the Head of the Department to resign the Headship with effect from the date on which a newly-elected holder of the Elrington and Bosworth Professorship of Anglo-Saxon takes up the duties of the office, so that the latter may be appointed Head of the Department for a period not exceeding five years in the first instance.

Faculty of Human, Social, and Political Science.

Archaeology and Anthropology A person appointed in accordance with Regulation 2.

Sociology A person appointed in accordance with Regulation 2.

Politics and International Studies A person appointed in accordance with Regulation 2.

Faculty of Law.

Institute of Criminology The Director of the Institute of Criminology.

Faculty of Mathematics.

Applied Mathematics and Theoretical Physics A person appointed in accordance with Regulation 2.

Pure Mathematics and Mathematical Statistics A person appointed in accordance with Regulation 2.

Faculty of Modern and Medieval Languages.

French

A person appointed in accordance with Regulation 2, provided that the General Board may, on the recommendation of the Faculty Board of Modern and Medieval Languages, require the Head of the Department to resign the Headship with effect from the date on which a newly-elected holder of the Drapers Professorship of French takes up the duties of the office, so that the latter may be appointed Head of the Department for a period not exceeding five years in the first instance.

German and Dutch

A person appointed in accordance with Regulation 2, provided that the General Board may, on the recommendation of the Faculty Board of Modern and Medieval Languages, require the Head of the Department to resign the Headship with effect from the date on which a newly-elected holder of the Schröder Professorship of German takes up the duties of the office, so that the latter may be appointed Head of the Department for a period not exceeding five years in the first instance.

Italian

A person appointed in accordance with Regulation 2, provided that the General Board may, on the recommendation of the Faculty Board of Modern and Medieval Languages, require the Head of the Department to resign the Headship with effect from the date on which a newly-elected holder of the Serena Professorship of Italian takes up the duties of the office, so that the latter may be appointed Head of the Department for a period not exceeding five years in the first instance.

Slavonic Studies

A person appointed in accordance with Regulation 2, provided that the General Board may, on the recommendation of the Faculty Board of Modern and Medieval Languages, require the Head of the Department to resign the Headship with effect from the date on which a newly-elected holder of the Professorship of Slavonic Studies takes up the duties of the office, so that the latter may be appointed Head of the Department for a period not exceeding five years in the first instance.

Spanish and Portuguese

A person appointed in accordance with Regulation 2, provided that the General Board may, on the recommendation of the Faculty Board of Modern and Medieval Languages, require the Head of the Department to resign the Headship with effect from the date on which a newly-elected holder of the

Professorship of Spanish takes up the duties of the office, so that the latter may be appointed Head of the Department for a period not exceeding five years in the first instance.

Theoretical and Applied Linguistics A person appointed in accordance with Regulation 2.

Institute of Astronomy The Director of the Institute of Astronomy.

Faculty of Physics and Chemistry.

Materials Science and Metallurgy A person appointed in accordance with Regulation 2.

Chemistry A person appointed in accordance with Regulation 2.

Physics A person appointed in accordance with Regulation 2.

Veterinary Medicine A person appointed in accordance with Regulation 2.

Faculty of Veterinary Medicine.

Departments independent of any Faculty

Departments independent of any Faculty.

Chemical Engineering and Biotechnology A person appointed in accordance with Regulation 2.

History and Philosophy of Science A person appointed in accordance with Regulation 2.

Land Economy A person appointed in accordance with Regulation 2.

Acting Heads of Departments.

4. The General Board, on the recommendation of the Faculty Board or other authority concerned, shall appoint a person to be Acting Head of a Department during any period of absence from duty of the Head of that Department, or during any period when there is a vacancy in an office whose holder is *ex officio* Head of the Department. A person so appointed shall be recognized as Head of the Department for all purposes.

Deputy Heads of Departments.

5. The General Board shall have power to establish one or more Deputy Headships in any Department specified by them and, at the request of the Head of such a Department and after consultation with the relevant Faculty Board or other authority, to appoint one or more Deputy Heads of that Department. A person appointed Deputy Head shall hold office for a period of not more than three years at a time, and shall be eligible for reappointment. The duties and powers of each Deputy Head appointed under this regulation shall be determined by the General Board after consultation with the Head of the Department.

SPECIAL REGULATIONS FOR FACULTIES AND DEPARTMENTS

Institute of Astronomy

Astronomy.

1. The Institute of Astronomy, incorporating the Newall Observatory and the Solar Physics Observatory, shall be a Department within the Faculty of Physics and Chemistry.

Director and Head.

2. Appointments and reappointments to the University office of Director of the Institute of Astronomy shall be made by the General Board, on the recommendation of the Faculty Board of Physics and Chemistry, from among the University officers engaged in teaching and research in the Institute. Appointments and reappointments shall be for periods not exceeding five years at a time, save that in a particular case the General Board shall have power, after consulting the Faculty Board, to make an appointment for a period not exceeding ten years at a time. The Director shall be the Head of the Department *ex officio*.

3. The Professor of Astrophysics shall be Director of the Solar Physics Observatory *ex officio*.

Advisory Committee.

4. There shall be a Departmental Advisory Committee of the Institute consisting of:

(*a*) the Head of the Department, who shall be the Chair;

(*b*) the Plumian Professor of Astronomy and Experimental Philosophy, and the Professor of Astrophysics, who shall be members *ex officio*;

(*c*) three University officers in the Institute elected by a body consisting of all the members of the Faculty of Physics and Chemistry who have been designated for the purpose by the Board of that Faculty on the nomination of the Departmental Advisory Committee.

Elections of members in class (*c*) shall be held annually before the end of the Michaelmas Term and shall be in accordance with a procedure determined from time to time by a meeting of those entitled to vote. One member shall be elected in every calendar year of which the number is odd, and

Astronomy. two members in every calendar year of which the number is even. A member elected shall serve for the two calendar years next ensuing, provided that if he or she ceases to be a member of the Faculty he or she shall thereupon cease to be a member of the Departmental Advisory Committee.

Duties. **5.** The Committee shall advise the Head of the Department at least once a term on matters concerning the teaching, research, and administration within the Institute.

6. The Secretary of the Institute of Astronomy shall act as Secretary of the Committee and as Secretary of the Faculty Board of Physics and Chemistry.

Visiting Fellowships

Purpose. **1.** In order to enable scholars from outside Cambridge to take part in and contribute to the work of the Institute of Astronomy, there shall be Visiting Fellowships for persons who have made important contributions to the study of astronomy.

Number. The maximum number of Visiting Fellows that there may be in the Institute at any one time shall be determined by the General Board. A Visiting Fellowship shall not be filled, either by appointment or by reappointment, without the permission of the General Board.

Appointments and tenure. **2.** Appointments and reappointments to Visiting Fellowships shall be made by the Faculty Board of Physics and Chemistry on the recommendation of the Head of the Department for periods not exceeding one year at a time.

Duties. **3.** A Visiting Fellow shall be required to take part in the teaching and research programme of the Institute.

Restrictions. **4.** Visiting Fellows shall not hold any University office during the tenure of their Fellowships. A Visiting Fellow who is not a member of the University at the time of appointment shall be required to become a member as soon as is conveniently possible thereafter.

Stipend. **5.** The stipend, if any, of a Visiting Fellow shall be determined by the Faculty Board of Physics and Chemistry with the approval of the General Board on the occasion of each appointment or reappointment.

Grants. **6.** Subject to the approval of the General Board the Departmental Advisory Committee of the Institute may make grants to Visiting Fellows to meet travelling or other expenses incurred in connection with their Fellowships.

The McClean Fund

Name. **1.** The sum bequeathed to the University by the late Frank McClean, M.A., of Trinity College, shall form a fund called the McClean Fund.

Purpose. **2.** The annual income and capital of the McClean Fund shall be applied for the purpose of providing improved instrumental equipment for the Newall Observatory, in such manner as may be approved by the Faculty Board of Physics and Chemistry.

Payments. **3.** Applications made by the Professor of Astrophysics and approved by the Faculty Board of Physics and Chemistry shall be sufficient authority for payments to be made from the income or capital of the McClean Fund, it being understood that in any question of proposed expenditure which in the opinion of the Faculty Board will involve increased charges for maintenance, application shall be made to the University for its sanction.

4. The foregoing regulations shall be subject to alteration by Ordinance provided that the regulations shall always be in accordance with the provisions of Mr McClean's will.

Institute of Astronomy Flower Fund

Title. **1.** The sum received from Professor Donald Lynden-Bell, Emeritus Professor of Astrophysics in the University, shall form a fund called the Institute of Astronomy Flower Fund.

Application. **2.** The income of the Fund shall be applied by the Secretary of the Institute of Astronomy to purchase bulbs, Cambridgeshire wild flowers, and/or trees to enhance the beauty of the grounds and especially Adams Walk at the Institute.

Sheepshanks Benefaction Fund

Astronomy.

Endowments, 1904, p. 131, Grace 1 of 7 July 2010

The sums available under the Sheepshanks Benefaction shall be administered by the Departmental Advisory Committee of the Institute of Astronomy and shall be applied to support the work of the Institute.

The John Couch Adams Astronomership[1]

1. Appointments and reappointments to the University office of John Couch Adams Astronomer shall be made by the General Board, subject to the concurrence of the Faculty Board of Physics and Chemistry, for such periods not exceeding five years at a time as the General Board shall determine. Before the appointment is made the General Board shall confer with the Director of the Institute of Astronomy, and the appointment may be cancelled at any time by the General Board with the concurrence of the Faculty Board of Physics and Chemistry. (Appointments and tenure.)

2. The stipend of the John Couch Adams Astronomer shall be the income of the John Couch Adams Astronomership Fund, and shall be paid by quarterly instalments. (Stipend.)

3. The duties of the John Couch Adams Astronomer shall be determined by the General Board after consultation with the Faculty Board of Physics and Chemistry. (Duties.)

4. The John Couch Adams Astronomer shall be or become a member of the staff of the Institute of Astronomy and, if not Director of the Institute, shall be responsible to the Director. (To whom responsible.)

DEPARTMENT OF BIOCHEMISTRY

Biochemistry.

School of Biochemistry

The offer of £165,000 for the endowment of a School of Biochemistry, conveyed in a scheme received from the Trustees of the late Sir William Dunn, Bart. (*Reporter*, 1919–20, p. 1094), was accepted by Grace 1 of 22 June 1920 upon terms which were last published in *Ordinances*, 1967, pp. 427–8.

Colman Library

Of the sum of £2,000 given to the University by Sir Jeremiah Colman, Bart., M.A., of St John's College, for a library for the School of Biochemistry, £500 shall be expended in the purchase of the existing library books, the balance being invested in Trustee Securities and kept intact, the income therefrom being held available for the maintenance of the library in perpetuity, the provision of scientific journals and their binding, or for any incidental requirement in the upkeep of the library.

The library shall be called the Colman Library.

FACULTY OF BIOLOGY

Biology.

Director of Education (Biological Sciences)

1. Appointments and reappointments to the University office of Director of Education (Biological Sciences) in the Faculty of Biology shall be made by an Appointments Committee consisting of the following persons: (Appointments Committee.)

(*a*) the Vice-Chancellor (or a duly appointed deputy) as Chair;
(*b*) the Regius Professor of Physic;
(*c*) the Chair of the Faculty Board of Biology;
(*d*) the Head of the Council of the School of the Biological Sciences;
(*e*) one person appointed by the General Board.

2. The Directorship shall be held concurrently with a University office. (Director.)

3. The duties of the Director shall be determined by the General Board after consultation with the Faculty Board of Biology. (Duties.)

[1] The John Couch Adams Astronomership is supported by a trust fund of which the trustees are the Master, Fellows, and Scholars of St John's College; see *Reporter*, 1919–20, pp. 563 and 665.

Biology.

Residence. **4.** The Director shall conform to such conditions of residence as may be determined by the Faculty Board of Biology subject to the approval of the General Board.

Tenure. **5.** Appointments shall be for a period of up to five years at a time.

Medical Students Register

The Faculty Board and the Faculty Board of Clinical Medicine shall maintain jointly through a Fitness to Practise Committee a register of students who are deemed fit to practise medicine and consequently to be admitted as candidates for the Second Examination and the Final Examination for the degrees of Bachelor of Medicine and Bachelor of Surgery. A Fitness to Practise Appeal Panel shall have the power on appeal from a student affected by a decision of the Fitness to Practise Adjudication Panel to confirm, quash, amend, or refer back to the same, or a newly constituted, Fitness to Practise Adjudication Panel the decision in question.

Veterinary Students Register

Amended by Grace 1 of 29 January 2014

The Faculty Board and the Faculty Board of Veterinary Medicine shall maintain jointly through a Veterinary Fitness to Practise Committee a register of students who are deemed fit to practise veterinary medicine and consequently to be admitted as candidates for the Second Examination and the Final Examination for the degree of Bachelor of Veterinary Medicine. A Veterinary Fitness to Practise Appeal Panel shall have the power on appeal from a student affected by a decision of the Veterinary Fitness to Practise Adjudication Panel to confirm, quash, amend, or refer back to the same, or a newly constituted, Veterinary Fitness to Practise Adjudication Panel the decision in question.

CENTRE FOR FAMILY RESEARCH

Management

Committee of Management. **1.** The Centre for Family Research shall be an institution within the Faculty of Biology and shall be under the general control of a Committee of Management which shall consist of:

(*a*) the Director of the Centre;
(*b*) the Deputy Director of the Centre;
(*c*) one person appointed by the General Board;
(*d*) three persons appointed by the Faculty Board of Biology;
(*e*) not more than two persons co-opted at the discretion of the Committee.

2. Members in classes (*c*) and (*d*) shall be appointed in the Michaelmas Term to serve for four years from 1 January following their appointment. Co-opted members in class (*e*) shall serve until 31 December of the year in which they are co-opted or of the year next following, as the Committee shall determine at the time of their co-optation.

Chair and Secretary. **3.** The Committee shall elect one of their members other than the Director to be their Chair, to serve for three years from 1 January following his or her election. The Secretary of the Committee shall be appointed by the Secretary of the Department of Psychology.

Duties. **4.** Subject to the powers of the Council, the General Board, and the Faculty Board of Biology, the duties of the Committee shall be as follows:

(*a*) to promote study and research in family life and kinship, and to co-operate with outside bodies in the encouragement of such study and research;
(*b*) to administer funds allocated to them for the purposes specified in (*a*) above;
(*c*) to supervise the work of staff of the Centre.

5. Five members of the Committee shall form a quorum.

Staff of the Centre

Director and Deputy Director. **1.** The Directorship and the Deputy Directorship of the Centre shall each be held concurrently with a University office in the Faculty of Biology.

2. The Director and the Deputy Director shall be appointed by the General Board on the recommendation of the Faculty Board of Biology. They shall each hold office for four years, and shall be eligible for reappointment.

3. Under the general control of the Committee of Management, the Director shall be the administrative head of the Centre and shall be responsible for the direction of study and research in the Centre. Biology. Duties of the Director.

4. Under the general control of the Committee of Management, the Deputy Director shall deputize for the Director of the Centre as required and shall carry out such other duties as the Director shall determine.

5. The Director and the Deputy Director of the Centre shall conform to such conditions of residence as may be determined by the Committee of Management with the approval of the General Board.

DEPARTMENT OF CHEMICAL ENGINEERING AND BIOTECHNOLOGY

Chemical Engineering and Biotechnology. Management.

1. The Department of Chemical Engineering and Biotechnology shall be a Department independent of any Faculty. The Department shall be managed by the Chemical Engineering and Biotechnology Syndicate under the supervision of the General Board.

2. Appointments and reappointments to a University office in the Department of Chemical Engineering and Biotechnology other than an office of Technical Officer shall be made by an Appointments Committee for the Department consisting of the following persons: Appointments Committee.

(*a*) the Vice-Chancellor (or a duly appointed deputy) as Chair;

(*b*) (i) the Chair of the Chemical Engineering and Biotechnology Syndicate;

(ii) the Head of the Department;

(*c*) three University officers appointed by the Syndicate;

(*d*) two persons appointed by the General Board.

The Appointments Committee shall have the same powers and duties in respect of the Department as the Appointments Committee for a Faculty has or shall have by Statute or Ordinance in respect of a Faculty; and Special Ordinance C (x) 4 shall apply to the Committee as if it were the Appointments Committee for a Faculty.

3. University officers in the Department of Chemical Engineering and Biotechnology shall be members both of the Faculty of Physics and Chemistry and of the Faculty of Engineering. Officers in the Department.

Chemical Engineering and Biotechnology Syndicate

Amended by Grace 3 of 12 March 2014

1. The Chemical Engineering and Biotechnology Syndicate shall consist of Constitution.

(*a*) the Heads of the Departments of Chemical Engineering and Biotechnology, Chemistry, and Engineering;

(*b*) two persons appointed by the Council;

(*c*) two persons appointed by the General Board;

(*d*) one person appointed each by the Councils of the Schools of the Biological Sciences, Clinical Medicine, the Physical Sciences, and Technology;

(*e*) three persons elected from amongst their own number by the Professors of the Department of Chemical Engineering and Biotechnology, except for any Professor who is the Head of the Department;

(*f*) three persons elected from amongst their own number by the University officers of the Department of Chemical Engineering and Biotechnology, except for the Professors and the Head of the Department;

(*g*) not more than two persons co-opted by the Syndicate;

(*h*) two persons elected in accordance with Regulation 3.

2. Members in classes (*b*)–(*d*) shall be appointed in the Michaelmas Term to serve for four years from 1 January following their appointment. Members in classes (*e*) and (*f*) shall be elected in the Michaelmas Term to serve for two years from 1 January following their election. The procedure for such elections shall be that prescribed in the Single Transferable Vote regulations, except that the Returning Officer shall be the Chair of the Syndicate or a Deputy appointed by the Chair subject to the approval of the General Board. If a casual vacancy occurs in class (*e*) or (*f*) the Syndicate shall co-opt a member to fill the vacancy; a member so appointed and any member co-opted in class (*g*) shall serve until the end of the calendar year in which they are co-opted. Appointments.

3. The provisions for the election of members of Faculty Boards in class (*f*) and for the period for which such members shall serve, which are contained in the regulations for the constitution of the Student members of the Syndicate.

Faculty Boards and for the Classes of Faculty Board Membership, Elections, and Periods of Office, and in the rules made under those regulations, shall apply, *mutatis mutandis*, to the election and period of membership of members of the Syndicate in class (*h*).

Chair and Secretary. **4.** The Syndicate shall elect annually a Chair and a Secretary, each of whom shall be a member of the Syndicate in a class other than class (*h*).

Powers and duties. **5.** Except so far as may be determined otherwise by Ordinance the Syndicate shall have the same powers and duties as are assigned by the General Regulations for the Constitution of the Faculty Boards to the Board of a Faculty organized in Departments.

Reserved business. **6.** The provisions of Special Ordinance A (vii) 5 concerning reserved business shall apply as if the Syndicate were a body constituted by Statute and any matter which would, if the Syndicate were a Faculty Board, be reserved business under Regulation 11 of the General Regulations for the Constitution of the Faculty Boards shall also be reserved. These provisions shall apply to any members of the Syndicate in class (*h*) who are not *in statu pupillari* as if they were *in statu pupillari.*

Director of Biotechnology

Rescinded by Grace 3 of 12 March 2014

Chemistry.

Department of Chemistry

Departmental Committee

Departmental Committee. **1.** There shall be a Departmental Committee of the Department of Chemistry consisting of:

(*a*) the Head of the Department who shall be Chair;

(*b*) not more than four persons holding Professorships assigned to the Department of Chemistry; provided that

(i) when the Head of the Department is a Professor, the number of persons in this class shall be three;

(ii) when the number of Professorships assigned to the Department exceeds four the Professors shall elect from among themselves members to serve in this class for periods of two years at a time;

(*c*) four University officers in the Department elected in accordance with Regulation 2 by a body comprising all University officers whose offices are assigned to, or established in, the Department and those other members of the Faculty of Physics and Chemistry who have been designated for the purpose by the Board of that Faculty on the nomination of the Departmental Committee;

(*d*) persons co-opted by the Committee to serve until the end of the academical year in which they are co-opted or of the following academical year as the Committee may determine at the time of their co-optation, provided that it shall not be obligatory for the Committee to co-opt any person or persons;

(*e*) the Secretary of the Department, who shall be Secretary of the Committee.

2. Elections of members in class (*c*) shall be held annually before the end of the Easter Term and shall be in accordance with a procedure determined from time to time by a meeting of those entitled to vote. A member elected in this class shall serve for a period of two years from 1 October following his or her election and shall at the end of that period be eligible for re-election for one further period of two years, after which two years shall elapse before he or she shall again be eligible for re-election.

Duties. **3.** The Committee shall meet at least once a term and shall advise the Head of the Department on matters concerning teaching, research, staffing, resources, and administration within the Department.

Classics.

Faculty of Classics

Museum of Classical Archaeology

1. The Museum of Classical Archaeology shall be an institution within the Faculty of Classics.

Curator and Committee. **2.** The administration of the Museum of Classical Archaeology shall be entrusted to a Curator under the direction of a Committee consisting of six members of the Regent House, three appointed by the General Board and three appointed by the Faculty Board of Classics.

Classics.

3. Members of the Committee shall be appointed in the Michaelmas Term to serve for three years from 1 January following their appointment.

Dame Mary Grainger Sandys bequest.

4. The bequest of Dame Mary Grainger Sandys shall form a fund called the Museum of Classical Archaeology Endowment Fund the income of which shall be applied for the benefit of the Museum of Classical Archaeology in such manner as the Committee for the Museum may from time to time direct.

Jocelyn Toynbee Library Fund.

5. The moneys subscribed in honour of Professor Jocelyn Toynbee shall form a fund called the Jocelyn Toynbee Library Fund, the income of which shall be used at the discretion of the Committee for the Museum to purchase, for the Museum or for the Library of the Faculty of Classics, books and other materials on subjects connected with the art or archaeology of the Roman world.

Annual Report and Accounts.

6. It shall be the duty of the Committee to present a report every year to the Faculty Board of Classics. The accounts of the Committee shall be audited annually and shall be published with the University Accounts.

7. The Committee shall be empowered to frame and submit to the University for approval further regulations for admission to the Museum.

Director and Curator of the Museum of Classical Archaeology

Director.

1. There shall be a University office of Director of the Museum of Classical Archaeology, which shall be held in conjunction with another University office.

Curator.

2. There shall be a University office of Curator of the Museum of Classical Archaeology who shall act under the Director as the executive officer of the Museum. The office of Curator shall not normally be held concurrently with any other University office.

Appointments and tenure.

3. Appointments and reappointments to the Director and Curator of the Museum of Classical Archaeology shall be determined by the Committee for the Museum, subject to the approval of the General Board. Appointments to the Directorship shall be for such periods not exceeding three years at a time as the Committee shall determine.

Duties.

4. The duties of the Director and Curator of the Museum of Classical Archaeology shall be determined by the Committee for the Museum, subject to the approval of the General Board.

5. The Curator shall act as Secretary to the Committee for the Museum.

6. Under the direction of the Committee, the Director shall exercise a general superintendence over the Museum and its collections and over the staff of the Museum.

7. The Director shall be responsible for the maintenance of the catalogues, published and unpublished, of the Museum's collections, and shall undertake such other duties in connection with the administration of the Museum as the Committee shall from time to time direct.

Members of Faculty.

8. The Director and Curator shall be members of the Faculty of Classics under Regulation 1(*b*) of the Regulations for Faculty Membership.

FACULTY OF CLINICAL MEDICINE

Clinical Medicine.

Amended by Notice (Reporter, *2013–14, p. 140*)

Submission of Departmental estimates.

1. The Heads of Departments in the Faculty of Clinical Medicine shall submit the annual estimates of their Departments to the Faculty Board of Clinical Medicine. The Faculty Board shall be responsible for scrutinizing the estimates, revising them where necessary, and submitting them in a consolidated form to the General Board for their approval.

Accommodation.

2. The Faculty Board shall be responsible for allocating to Departments the accommodation assigned to the School of Clinical Medicine by the General Board.

Register of students.

3. The Faculty Board and the Faculty Board of Biology shall maintain jointly through a Fitness to Practise Committee a register of students who are deemed fit to practise medicine and consequently to be admitted as candidates for the Second Examination and the Final Examination for the degrees of Bachelor of Medicine and Bachelor of Surgery. A Fitness to Practise Appeal Panel shall have the power on appeal from a student affected by a decision of the Fitness to Practise Adjudication Panel to confirm, quash, amend, or refer back to the same, or a newly constituted, Fitness to Practise Adjudication Panel the decision in question.

Establishments.

4. The Faculty Board shall be responsible for recommending to the General Board the number and categories of University offices to be established in each Department, and, notwithstanding Regulation 5

Clinical Medicine. for employment by the University, the number and grades of University assistants to be established in each Department.

Recognition of clinical tutors. **5.** The General Board shall be authorized to grant, on the recommendation of the Faculty Board of Clinical Medicine, the title of University of Cambridge Senior Clinical Tutor to any person, other than a University officer, who in the University, or in such University Hospital, Associate Teaching Hospital, or Associate Teaching General Practice or other institution associated with the University as the Faculty Board may have approved for the purposes of the regulations for the degrees of Bachelor of Medicine and Bachelor of Surgery, makes a regular and sufficient contribution throughout a year of clinical study to the teaching of candidates for those degrees by means of lectures, seminars, or other kinds of demonstration, supervision, or instruction approved by the Faculty Board. The recognition shall be for not more than three years at a time and shall be renewable.

Resources and Planning Committee of the Faculty Board of Clinical Medicine

Rescinded by Notice (Reporter, *2013–14, p. 140*)

Director of Medical Education

Appointments. **1.** Appointments and reappointments to the University office of Director of Medical Education in the Faculty of Clinical Medicine shall be made by the General Board, on the advice of a Committee specially constituted for the particular occasion.

Tenure. **2.** Appointment shall be for an initial period of five years. On reappointment, the Director shall hold office, subject to the provisions of Statute C, until the retiring age, so long as he or she satisfactorily performs the duties of the office.

Duties. **3.** The duties of the Director of Medical Education shall be determined by the General Board after consultation with the Faculty Board of Clinical Medicine.

Regional Postgraduate Dean

Appointments. **1.** Appointments and reappointments to the University office of Regional Postgraduate Dean in the Faculty of Clinical Medicine shall be made by an Appointments Committee consisting of the following persons:

(*a*) the Vice-Chancellor (or a duly appointed deputy) as Chair;
(*b*) the Regius Professor of Physic;
(*c*) the Regional Director of Public Health (East of England);
(*d*) the Director of Medical Education.

The Committee shall have power to make an appointment or reappointment to the office of Regional Postgraduate Dean conditional on the holding of a post specified by the Faculty Board of Clinical Medicine in an institution connected with the University. If the Regional Postgraduate Dean ceases to hold such a post he or she shall thereupon vacate the Deanship.

Duties. The duties of the Regional Postgraduate Dean shall be determined by the General Board after consultation with the Faculty Board of Clinical Medicine who shall consult the Directorate of Health and Social Care, Midlands and East of England.

2. No stipend shall be attached to the office of Regional Postgraduate Dean

Directors and Assistant Directors of Studies in General Practice

Number. **1.** There shall be such number of University offices of Director and Assistant Director of Studies. in General Practice (including not more than two offices of Director) as the General Board may from time to time determine on the recommendation of the Faculty Board of Clinical Medicine.

Appointments. **2.** Appointments and reappointments to a University office of Director or Assistant Director of Studies in General Practice shall be made by an Appointments Committee consisting of the following persons:

(*a*) the Vice-Chancellor (or a duly appointed deputy) as Chair;
(*b*) the Regius Professor of Physic;
(*c*) the Director of Medical Education;
(*d*) three persons appointed by the Faculty Board of Clinical Medicine;

(*e*) two persons appointed by the General Board. **Clinical Medicine.**

3. Appointments and reappointments to a University office of Director of Studies in General Practice shall be for periods not exceeding five years at a time. Appointments and reappointments to a University office of Assistant Director of Studies in General Practice shall be for periods not exceeding three years at a time. Tenure.

4. The duties of a Director or an Assistant Director of Studies in General Practice shall be determined by the General Board after consultation with the Faculty Board of Clinical Medicine. Duties.

Associate Deans

1. There shall be such number of University offices of Associate Dean in the Faculty of Clinical Medicine as the General Board may from time to time determine on the recommendation of the Faculty Board of Clinical Medicine. Number.

2. Appointments and reappointments to a University office of Associate Dean shall be for periods not exceeding five years at a time and shall be made by an Appointments Committee consisting of the following persons: Appointments.

(*a*) the Vice-Chancellor (or a duly appointed deputy) as Chair;
(*b*) the Regius Professor of Physic;
(*c*) the Regional Director of Public Health (East of England);
(*d*) the Director of Medical Education;
(*e*) the Regional Postgraduate Dean;
(*f*) one person appointed by the Faculty Board of Clinical Medicine;
(*g*) three persons appointed by the General Board, of whom two shall be appointed on the nomination of the Directorate of Health and Social Care, Midlands and East of England.

3. The duties of an Associate Dean shall be determined by the General Board after consultation with the Faculty Board of Clinical Medicine who shall consult the Directorate of Health and Social Care, Midlands and East of England. Duties.

4. An Associate Dean shall conform to such conditions of residence as may be determined by the Faculty Board of Clinical Medicine subject to the approval of the General Board. Residence.

Certain University offices whose holders have clinical responsibilities in the National Health Service

1. No Professor, Reader, University Senior Lecturer, University Lecturer, Assistant Director of Research, or Clinical Lecturer, who holds an honorary clinical contract in the National Health Service, nor the Consultant Occupational Physician, shall engage in private medical practice for more than one NHS session (one half-day) each working week. All payments for private practice work shall be administered by the Cambridge University Technical Services Ltd. The officer concerned may elect to receive a fee for such private practice which will be calculated after the deduction of administrative and overhead costs. Income remaining after this fee has been paid shall be placed in a fund or funds to be used for medical education or research administered according to arrangements approved by the Faculty Board of Clinical Medicine.

2. No University officer who receives additional payments for clinical responsibility under the regulations for those payments, nor the Consultant Occupational Physician, shall be a Tutor, Assistant Tutor, Steward, Bursar, or Assistant Bursar of a College, nor shall he or she give instruction on behalf of a College or Colleges for more than six hours a week, or, if a Professor, four hours a week.

Arrangement with the United Cambridge Hospitals[1]

CENTRE FOR MEDICAL GENETICS AND POLICY

Management

1. The Centre for Medical Genetics and Policy shall be an institution within the Faculty of Clinical Medicine and shall be under the general control of a Committee of Management, which shall consist of: Committee of Management.

(*a*) the Director;

[1] These regulations were last printed in *Statutes and Ordinances*, 1988, p. 731.

Clinical Medicine.

(*b*) one person appointed by each of the following:
the General Board,
the Faculty Board of Clinical Medicine,
the Council of the School of Biological Sciences,
the Council of the School of the Arts and Humanities,
the Council of the School of the Humanities and Social Sciences, and
the Council of the School of Technology,
provided that a person appointed by any one of the Faculty Board of Clinical Medicine or the Councils of the Schools may also be the person appointed by the General Board;
(*c*) one person appointed by the Directorate of Health and Social Care, Midlands and East of England (or its successor body);
(*d*) not more than four persons co-opted at the discretion of the Committee.

2. Members in classes (*b*) and (*c*) shall be appointed in the Michaelmas Term to serve for four years from 1 January following their appointment. Members in class (*d*) shall serve until 31 December of the year in which they are co-opted or of the year next following, as the Committee shall determine at the time of their co-optation.

Chair and Secretary.

3. The Committee shall elect one of their members other than the Director to be their Chair, to serve for three years from 1 January following his or her election. The Director of the Centre shall serve as Secretary of the Committee.

Duties.

4. Subject to the powers of the Council, the General Board, and the Faculty Board of Clinical Medicine, the duties of the Committee shall be as follows:
(*a*) to promote teaching in the field of policy in Medical Genetics and in its public health, ethical, legal, and social implications, and to promote research in those fields and the publication of the results of such research;
(*b*) to co-operate with outside bodies in the encouragement of research in the policy, public health, ethical, legal, and social implications of Medical Genetics;
(*c*) to establish policies and procedures for the administration of grants, endowments, and other resources received for the benefit of the Centre and to determine and agree the respective responsibilities of the various Faculty Boards and University institutions participating in the Centre;
(*d*) to administer funds allocated to them for the purposes set out in (*a*) and (*b*) above;
(*e*) to supervise the work of staff at the Centre;
(*f*) to prepare annual estimates for submission to the General Board.

Reports.

5. The Committee shall have the right of reporting to the University.

Director of the Centre

Director.

1. The Directorship of the Centre may be held concurrently with another University Office.

2. The Director shall be appointed by the General Board on the recommendation of the Committee of Management. He or she shall hold office for five years, and shall be eligible for reappointment.

Duties.

3. Under the general control of the Committee of Management, the Director shall be the administrative head of the Centre and shall be responsible for the promotion of the subject generally.

4. The Director shall be responsible for ensuring appropriate direction of the research in the Centre.

Institute of Public Health

Amended by Notice (Reporter, *2013–14, p. 95*)

Management

Committee of Management.

1. The Institute of Public Health shall be an institution within the Faculty of Clinical Medicine, and shall be under the general control of a Committee of Management, which shall consist of:
(*a*) the Director;
(*b*) the Regius Professor of Physic;
(*c*) one person appointed by the General Board;
(*d*) one person appointed by the Faculty Board of Clinical Medicine;
(*e*) one person appointed by the Medical Research Council;
(*f*) one person appointed by the Secretary of State for Health;

Clinical Medicine.

(*g*) not more than five persons co-opted at the discretion of the Committee

2. Members in classes (*c*), (*d*), (*e*), and (*f*) shall be appointed in the Michaelmas Term to serve for four years from 1 January following their appointment. Co-opted members in class (*g*) shall serve until 31 December of the year in which they are co-opted or of the year next following, as the Committee shall determine at the time of their co-optation.

Chair and Secretary.

3. The Committee shall elect one of their members other than the Director to be their Chair and to serve for three years from 1 January following her or his election. The Director of the Institute shall serve as Secretary of the Committee.

Duties.

4. Subject to the powers of the Council, the General Board, and the Faculty Boards concerned, the duties of the Committee shall be as follows:

(*a*) in collaboration with the Faculty Board of Clinical Medicine, and with any other Faculty Boards concerned, to promote teaching in the field of public health, and to promote research in that field and the publication of the results of such research;

(*b*) to collaborate with outside bodies in the encouragement of teaching and research in public health;

(*c*) to administer funds allocated to them for the purposes specified in (*a*) and (*b*) above;

(*d*) to establish such advisory bodies, representing interests and activities associated with public health as it sees fit;

(*e*) to approve annual estimates prepared by the Executive Committee for submission to the General Board;

(*f*) to make an Annual Report to the Faculty Board of Clinical Medicine on the affairs of the Institute;

(*g*) the Committee of Management may designate, for a period not exceeding five years at a time, one of the Executive Committee of the Institute to act as Deputy Director.

Executive Committee.

5. The Institute shall have an Executive Committee, the membership of which shall be:

(*a*) the Director of the Institute;

(*b*) the Head of the Department of Public Health and Primary Care;

(*c*) the Director of the MRC Epidemiology Unit;

(*d*) the Director of the MRC Biostatistics Unit;

(*e*) the Heads of any Public Health England Units based at the Institute;

(*f*) other persons co-opted at the discretion of the Committee.

Duties.

6. The Executive Committee shall:

(*a*) promote and enable research and teaching in the field of public health and the publication of the results of such research;

(*b*) administer funds allocated to the Institute to support its mission;

(*c*) prepare annual estimates for submission to the Committee of Management.

Director of the Institute

Director.

1. There shall be a University office of Director of the Institute, which may be held in conjunction with another University office.

2. The Director shall be appointed by the General Board on the recommendation of the Committee of Management. He or she shall hold office for five years, and shall be eligible for reappointment.

Duties.

3. Under the general control of the Committee of Management, the Director shall be the administrative Head of the Institute, and shall be responsible for the direction of study and research in public health in the Institute and the promotion of the subject generally.

Consultant Occupational Physician[1]

Appointments and tenure.

1. Appointments and reappointments to the University office of Consultant Occupational Physician in the Faculty of Clinical Medicine shall be made by an Appointments Committee consisting of the following persons:

(*a*) the Vice-Chancellor (or a duly appointed deputy) as Chair;

(*b*) three persons appointed by the General Board, one on the nomination of the Faculty Board of Clinical Medicine;

[1] See also the regulations for certain University offices whose holders have clinical responsibilities in the National Health Service (p. 621).

Clinical Medicine.

(*c*) three persons appointed by the Cambridge University Hospitals NHS Foundation Trust;

(*d*) one person appointed by the Committee of Management of the University Health Services.

The tenure of the Consultant Occupational Physician shall be the same as that prescribed for a University Lecturer by Special Ordinance C (x) 5 and 6.

Duties of Physician.

2. The duties of the Consultant Occupational Physician shall be:

(i) to act as medical adviser to the General Board of the Faculties and the Council as appropriate on the hazards to health which arise in the course of work in the University, to arrange and maintain a surveillance system of the health of persons who may be at special risk, and to keep such records and to maintain such liaison with medical practitioners, local authorities, health authorities, and government agencies as may be appropriate;

(ii) to engage in research, and to undertake such amount of teaching as may be determined by the General Board on the recommendation of the Faculty Board of Clinical Medicine;

(iii) to act as Director of Occupational Health Services to the Cambridge University Hospitals NHS Foundation Trust.

For these duties the Consultant Occupational Physician shall be responsible

(*a*) as they concern the University, to the Head of the Human Resources Division of the University Offices,

(*b*) as they concern the Cambridge University Hospitals NHS Foundation Trust, to that Trust.

3. The Consultant Occupational Physician shall be required to discharge these duties throughout the year save for a period not exceeding seven weeks, including public holidays, in any one academical year.

Payments for clinical responsibility.

4. The Consultant Occupational Physician shall be eligible to receive payments for clinical responsibility under the terms of Regulation 5 of the regulations governing payments additional to stipend.

Positron Emission Tomography (PET) Scientific Services

Director

Appointment.

1. Appointments and reappointments to the University office of Director of PET Scientific Services in the Faculty of Clinical Medicine shall be made by an Appointments Committee constituted as follows:

(*a*) the Vice-Chancellor (or a duly appointed deputy) as Chair;

(*b*) the Regius Professor of Physic;

(*c*) three persons appointed by the Faculty Board of Clinical Medicine;

(*d*) two persons appointed by the General Board.

Members in classes (*c*) and (*d*) shall be appointed in the Michaelmas Term of each calendar year of which the number is even to serve for the two calendar years next following.

Duties.

2. The Director shall be responsible to the Faculty Board of Clinical Medicine for the scientific and technical management of the PET component of the Brain Imaging Centre; and shall undertake such other duties as the Faculty Board may from time to time determine, subject to the approval of the General Board.

Residence.

3. The Director shall conform to such conditions of residence as may be determined by the General Board, after consultation with the Faculty Board of Clinical Medicine.

Divinity.

Faculty of Divinity

A University officer who is a member of the Faculty of Divinity and who under the provisions of the Regulations for a University officer holding a Residentiary Canonry of Ely Cathedral holds a residentiary Canonry of Ely Cathedral shall not be a Tutor, Assistant Tutor, Bursar, Assistant Bursar, or Steward of a College.

Committee of Management for the degree of Bachelor of Theology for Ministry

Amended by Notice (Reporter, *2013–14, p. 406*)

Committee of Management.

1. There shall be a Committee of Management for the B.Th. Degree, responsible to the Faculty Board of Divinity for the detailed administration of the Degree, which shall consist of:

(*a*) three members of the Regent House appointed by the Faculty Board of Divinity;

Divinity.

(*b*) two persons appointed by the Council of the Cambridge Theological Federation;[1]
(*c*) not more than two persons co-opted by the Committee, provided that it shall not be obligatory for the Committee to co-opt any person or persons;
(*d*) two members who are candidates for the B.Th. Degree, elected by all the students who are pursuing the course of study for that degree.

Members in classes (*a*) and (*b*) shall be appointed in the Michaelmas Term to serve for three years from 1 January next following their appointment. Members in class (*c*) shall serve until 31 December of the year in which they are co-opted, or of the following year, as the Committee shall determine at the time of their co-optation. Regulations 4–7 and 9–10 for the selection of student members of Faculty Boards and other bodies shall apply to the election of members in class (*a*) as if all members were matriculated students. One member in class (*d*) shall be elected in the Michaelmas Term to serve for one year from 1 January next following their election, and one member in class (*d*) shall be elected in the Lent Term to serve for one academic year from 1 October next following their election.

Chair and Secretary.

2. The Faculty Board shall appoint annually one of the members in class (*a*) to be Chair, and the Secretary shall be the Registrar of the Cambridge Theological Federation *ex officio*.

3. The Committee may also have responsibility for the detailed administration of the Diploma in Theology for Ministry, if the Faculty Board of Divinity so decide.

DEPARTMENT OF EARTH SCIENCES

Earth Sciences.

Departmental Committee

Departmental Committee.

1. There shall be a Departmental Committee of the Department of Earth Sciences consisting of:
(*a*) the Head of the Department who shall be Chair;
(*b*) not more than three persons holding Professorships assigned to the Department of Earth Sciences: provided that
  (i) when the Head of the Department is a Professor, the number of places in this class, subject to a maximum of two, shall be one less than the number of Professorships assigned to the Department;
  (ii) when the number of such Professorships exceeds the number of places the Professors shall elect from among themselves members to serve in this class for periods of two years at a time;
(*c*) such number of University officers in the Department as will bring the total number of members in classes (*a*), (*b*), and (*c*) to six, elected in accordance with Regulation 2 by a body comprising all University officers whose offices are assigned to the Department and those members of the Faculty of Earth Sciences and Geography who have been designated for the purpose by the Board of that Faculty on the nomination of the Departmental Committee;
(*d*) persons co-opted by the Committee to serve until the end of the academical year in which they are co-opted or of the following academical year as the Committee shall determine at the time of their co-optation, provided that it shall not be obligatory for the Committee to co-opt any person or persons.

2. Elections of members in class (*c*) shall be held annually before the end of the Easter Term and shall be in accordance with a procedure determined from time to time by a meeting of those entitled to vote. A member elected in this class shall serve for a period of two years from 1 October following his or her election and shall at the end of that period be eligible for re-election for one further period of two years, after which two years shall elapse before he or she shall again be eligible for re-election.

Duties.

3. The Committee shall meet at least once a term and shall advise the Head of the Department on matters concerning the teaching, research, staffing, resources, and administration within the Department.

SEDGWICK MUSEUM OF EARTH SCIENCES

Staff.

1. There shall be the following University offices on the staff of the Museum:
(*a*) the office of Director of the Museum;

[1] Ridley Hall, Wesley House, Westcott House, Westminster College, the Margaret Beaufort Institute of Theology, the Institute for Orthodox Christian Studies, and the Eastern Region Ministry Course.

Earth Sciences.

(*b*) the office of Curator of the Museum or Senior Assistant Curator of the Museum or Assistant Curator of the Museum, as the General Board shall from time to time determine;

(*c*) such other offices of Curator, designated Curator of a specified collection, as the General Board shall from time to time determine.

2. (*a*) The office of Director of the Museum shall be held in conjunction with another University office in the Department of Earth Sciences.

(*b*) The office of Curator of the Museum may be held in conjunction with the office of Director, but shall not be held in conjunction with any other University office. The office of Senior Assistant Curator or Assistant Curator of the Museum shall not be held in conjunction with any other University office.

(*c*) Any office of Curator of a specified collection shall be held in conjunction with another University office in the Department of Earth Sciences.

Appointments and tenure.

3. (*a*) Appointments and reappointments to the office of Director of the Museum shall be made by the Appointments Committee for the Faculty of Earth Sciences and Geography, and shall be for such periods not exceeding five years at a time as the Appointments Committee shall determine.

(*b*) Appointments and reappointments to the office of Curator, Senior Assistant Curator, or Assistant Curator of the Museum or to any office of Curator of a specified collection shall be made by the Appointments Committee for the Faculty of Earth Sciences and Geography with the Director as an additional member for this purpose.

Duties.

4. The Director shall be responsible to the Head of the Department of Earth Sciences for the management of the Museum and for such other duties relating to the Museum as shall be determined by the Head of the Department from time to time.

5. The Curator, Senior Assistant Curator, or Assistant Curator of the Museum shall be responsible through the Director to the Head of the Department for the cataloguing, maintenance, and conservation of the collections of the Museum, for making arrangements for their display, and for making them available for study and research. The holders of other offices on the staff of the Museum shall assist in these duties.

Teaching.

6. If the holder of a University office on the staff of the Museum is a University Lecturer, the performance of the officer's duties in the Museum shall be taken into account by the Faculty Board of Earth Sciences and Geography in determining the amount of the officer's teaching work so that the total of that work, together with work in the Museum, is within the limits fixed by the General Board under Special Ordinance C (x) 7.

7. The holder of an office of Curator or Senior Assistant Curator or Assistant Curator of the Museum shall undertake at the request of the Faculty Board of Earth Sciences and Geography, without additional payment, such teaching as the Faculty Board may consider desirable, having regard to the due performance of the officer's duties in the Museum. The amount of teaching given by such an officer on behalf of a College or Colleges shall not exceed six hours a week.

Hours of attendance.

8. The hours of attendance in the Museum of members of the staff shall be determined by the Faculty Board of Earth Sciences and Geography on the recommendation of the Head of the Department of Earth Sciences.

Members of Faculty.

9. The holders of University offices on the staff of the Museum shall be members of the Faculty of Earth Sciences and Geography under Regulation 1(*b*) of the Regulations for Faculty Membership.

Economics.

Faculty of Economics

Executive Director of Research

1. There shall be an office[1] of Executive Director of Research in the Faculty of Economics, which may be held on such terms and conditions as the General Board shall determine. The office may be tenable concurrently with another University office.

2. Appointments and reappointments to the University office of Director shall be made by the Appointments Committee for the Faculty of Economics and two persons appointed by the General Board for the particular occasion.

3. The duties of the Director shall be to advance knowledge and to promote and direct research in Economics, to give instruction to students, and to facilitate the research of University officers in the

[1] This office is an office specified in the Schedules to Special Ordinances C (i) 1 and C (vii) 1.

Faculty, subject to the powers of the Faculty Board of Economics. Such teaching as the Director may give on behalf of the University, including the supervision of Graduate Students, shall be given without additional remuneration as part of the duties of the office. Economics

4. The Director shall conform to such conditions of residence as may be determined by the Board with the approval of the General Board.

5. The Director shall not be a Tutor, Assistant Tutor, Bursar, Assistant Bursar, or Steward of a College.

Marshall Library Fund

1. The Marshall Library Fund shall be divided into two accounts of which one shall be called the Marshall Library Fund I and shall consist of the capital and income of Mrs Marshall's benefaction,[1] and the other shall be called the Marshall Library Fund II and shall consist of the capital and income of Mrs Marshall's bequest. Two accounts.

2. The Faculty Board of Economics shall be authorized to make supplementary payments into the Marshall Library Fund I out of the Faculty Fund. Fund I.

3. The Faculty Board shall be authorized to provide out of the Marshall Library Fund I the expenses of rent, equipment, purchase of books, attendance, etc., of a research library for the use of students of Economics, to be called the Marshall Library.

4. Payments from the Marshall Library Fund II shall be made by resolution of the Faculty Board, subject to the approval of the General Board, with the exception that the reinvestment of the income of the Fund be conducted as at present. Fund II.

FACULTY OF EDUCATION

Education.

DEPARTMENT OF EDUCATION

1. The Department of Education shall have the title 'The School of Education', and the Head of the Department shall be the academic head of the School and shall be designated Dean of Educational Studies. Title and Head of Department.

2. The Secretary of the Department of Education shall act as Secretary of the Faculty Board of Education. Secretary.

CENTRE FOR COMMONWEALTH EDUCATION

Constitution

The Centre for Commonwealth Education shall be an institution within the Faculty of Education.

Management

1. The Centre shall be under the general control of a Committee of Management which shall consist of: Committee of Management.

(*a*) three members appointed by the General Board, on the recommendation of the Commonwealth Institute, of whom one shall be appointed as Chair;

(*b*) the Head of the School of Education and the Director of the Centre *ex officio*;

(*c*) two members appointed by the General Board, of whom one shall be appointed on the recommendation of the Faculty Board of Education.

The Secretary of the Centre shall serve as Secretary of the Management Committee. Secretary.

2. Members in classes (*a*) and (*c*) shall be appointed in the Michaelmas Term to serve for four years from 1 January following their appointment. No member of the Management Committee, other than members in class (*b*), shall serve on the Committee for more than eight consecutive years.

3. Subject to the powers of the Council, the General Board, and the Faculty Board of Education, the duties of the Committee shall be: Duties.

(*a*) to promote research, scholarship, and teaching in Commonwealth Education;

[1] See *Reporter*, 1924–25, p. 122, and Grace 1 of 29 May 1925.

Education.

(*b*) to determine the policies, priorities, and strategic plans of the Centre, in consultation with the Director;

(*c*) to review and approve the operational and business plans of the Centre and the annual budget of the Centre prepared by the Director;

(*d*) to receive annual financial reports and audited accounts of the Centre;

(*e*) to transmit documents and decisions on the above matters including an Annual Report to the Institute and the General Board and, where appropriate, to the Advisory Board;

(*f*) to take such other actions as may be conducive or necessary to the furtherance of the purpose of the Centre.

Quorum. **4.** The Management Committee shall meet at least once each term. The Chair and three other members present at a meeting shall constitute a quorum.

Advisory Board

Advisory Board. **1.** There shall be an Advisory Board, which shall consist of:

(*a*) four members appointed by the General Board, on the recommendation of the Institute, of whom one shall be appointed Chair;

(*b*) three members appointed by the General Board on the recommendation of the Faculty Board of Education;

(*c*) five members, one from each region of the Commonwealth, appointed by the General Board on the recommendation of the Institute;

(*d*) up to two persons co-opted for specific purposes at the discretion of the Advisory Board; and

(*e*) the Director *ex officio*.

Secretary. The Secretary of the Centre shall serve as Secretary of the Advisory Board.

2. Members of the Advisory Board in classes (*a*), (*b*), and (*c*) shall be appointed for a term of four years and shall be eligible for reappointment; provided that no member of the Advisory Board shall serve on the Board for more than eight consecutive years. Members in class (*d*) shall serve for such specific periods as the Advisory Board may at their discretion determine to be necessary to fulfil the specific purpose for which they are appointed.

Quorum. **3.** The Advisory Board shall meet at least once in each academical year. The Chair and six other members (excluding any co-opted members) present at a meeting shall constitute a quorum.

4. Members of the Advisory Board shall serve as such without remuneration from the Centre, but the Centre may pay them a *per diem* fee and reasonable expenses incurred in attending meetings.

Duties. **5.** The duties of the Advisory Board shall be:

(*a*) to advise the Director of the Centre on ways in which the Centre may efficiently and effectively undertake its purpose and functions;

(*b*) to advise the Director on the financial implications of such activities and potential sources of funding;

(*c*) to assist the Director in furthering the Centre's programmes by promoting co-operation with other bodies concerned with educational research in Commonwealth countries;

(*d*) to receive reports on the policies, operations, and activities of the Centre.

Staff of the Centre

Director. **1.** There shall be a University Office of Director of the Centre which may be held concurrently with another University office.

2. The Director shall be appointed by the General Board on the recommendation of a committee which shall consist of:

(*a*) the Vice-Chancellor, or a duly appointed Deputy, as Chair; and

(*b*) eight members appointed by the General Board, after consultation with the Faculty Board of Education and the Commonwealth Institute, of whom three should not be resident members of the University.

Tenure. The Director shall hold office for ten years and shall be eligible for reappointment for further periods of five years, as determined by the General Board on the advice of a Committee specially constituted for the occasion.

3. Subject to the duties of the Committee of Management, the Director shall be the administrative head of the Centre, and shall be responsible to the Committee of Management for the proper operation and management of the Centre and for ensuring the effective carrying out of the Centre's purpose and functions, including the direction of teaching and research in the Centre. The Director shall: **Education.** Duties of Director.

(*a*) develop and submit to the Management Committee plans for the implementation of the research programmes and operational activities of the Centre;
(*b*) prepare the Annual Report of the Centre;
(*c*) prepare the annual budget of the Centre for submission to the Management Committee for approval;
(*d*) prepare the annual accounts of the Centre for submission, after audit, to the Management Committee; and
(*e*) keep and have available for review by the Management Committee and other appropriate parties financial accounts and other records on a current basis.

4. There shall be two offices of Assistant Director of the Centre, which may be held concurrently with another University office. Appointments to the office of Assistant Director shall be made by an Appointments Committee consisting of: Assistant Directors.

(*a*) the Vice-Chancellor, or Deputy, as Chair;
(*b*) the Director;
(*c*) two members appointed by the General Board;
(*d*) three members appointed by the Management Committee.

Appointments and reappointments shall be made for periods not exceeding five years to be determined by the Appointments Committee, subject to the approval of the General Board. Tenure.

The duties of the Assistant Directors shall be to assist the Director in all matters concerned with the work of the Centre. In the absence from duty of the Director, an Assistant Director designated by the General Board shall exercise the authority and perform the functions of the Director. Duties of Assistant Directors.

5. There shall be an office of Secretary of the Centre to which appointment shall be made as prescribed in Regulation 1 of the regulations for Secretaries and Superintendents of Faculties, Departments, and other institutions under the supervision of the General Board. Appointments and reappointments shall be made for periods of up to five years, as determined by the Appointments Committee, subject to the approval of the General Board. Secretary.

Visiting Fellowships

1. In order to enable scholars from outside Cambridge to take part in and contribute to the work of the Centre there shall be Visiting Fellowships for persons who have made or are making important contributions to research, or who are pursuing advanced work in the subject. Purpose and definitions.

2. Appointments and reappointments to Visiting Fellowships shall be made by the Director of the Centre for periods not exceeding one year at a time. Appointments and tenure.

3. The stipend, if any, of a Visiting Fellow shall be determined by the Director with the approval of the General Board on the occasion of each appointment or reappointment. Stipend.

Research Affiliates

The Director may from time to time grant the status of Research Affiliate to persons (other than the salaried research staff of the Centre) who contribute to the Centre's work.

DEPARTMENT OF ENGINEERING

Engineering.

Director of Research (Administration and Development)

1. Appointments and reappointments to the University office of Director of Research (Administration and Development) shall be made in accordance with arrangements agreed from time to time by the competent authority.

2. The duties of the Director shall be determined by the General Board after consultation with the Faculty Board of Engineering.

3. The Director shall be a member of the Faculty of Engineering under Regulation 1 (*b*) of the Regulations for Faculty Membership.

Engineering.

Superintendent of the Engineering Workshops

1. Appointments and reappointments to the University office of Superintendent of the Engineering Workshops shall be made by the Appointments Committee for the Faculty of Engineering.

2. The duties of the Superintendent shall be determined by the General Board after consultation with the Faculty Board of Engineering.

3. The Superintendent shall be a member of the Faculty of Engineering under Regulation 1 (*b*) of the Regulations for Faculty Membership.

Senior Design Engineers, Design Engineers, and Electronic Design Engineers in the Department of Engineering

Appointments. **1.** Appointments and reappointments to a University office of Senior Design Engineer and to a University office of Design Engineer and to a University office of Electronic Design Engineer shall be made by the Appointments Committee for the Faculty of Engineering. The number of offices of Senior Design Engineer, Design Engineer, and Electronic Design Engineer in the Department of Engineering shall be determined by the Faculty Board of Engineering, on the recommendation of the Head of the Department of Engineering, subject to the approval of the General Board.

Duties. **2.** The duties of a Senior Design Engineer, of a Design Engineer, and of an Electronic Design Engineer shall be determined by the Faculty Board of Engineering, subject to the approval of the General Board.

Members of Faculty. **3.** The Senior Design Engineers, Design Engineers, and Electronic Design Engineers shall be members of the Faculty of Engineering under Regulation 1 (*b*) of the Regulations for Faculty Membership.

HPS.

Department of History and Philosophy of Science

Management. **1.** The Department of History and Philosophy of Science shall be a Department independent of any Faculty. The Department shall be managed by the Board of History and Philosophy of Science under the supervision of the General Board.

Appointments Committee. **2.** Appointments and reappointments to a University office in the Department of History and Philosophy of Science shall be made by an Appointments Committee for the Department consisting of the following persons:

(*a*) the Vice-Chancellor (or a duly appointed deputy) as Chair;

(*b*) (i) the Chair of the Board of History and Philosophy of Science,

(ii) the Head of the Department and the Professor of History and Philosophy of Science;

(*c*) three members of the Board of History and Philosophy of Science appointed by the Board;

(*d*) two persons appointed by the General Board.

The Appointments Committee shall have the same powers and duties in respect of the Department as the Appointments Committee for a Faculty has or shall have by Statute or Ordinance in respect of a Faculty; and Special Ordinance C (x) 4 shall apply to the Committee as if it were the Appointments Committee for a Faculty.

Duties. **3.** The Head of the Department shall be responsible to the Board of History and Philosophy of Science for the preservation, augmentation, and display of the collections in the Whipple Museum of the History of Science and of the books in the Whipple collections. The Head of the Department shall have discretion to delegate any or all of these responsibilities to the Curator of the Museum.

Board of History and Philosophy of Science

Constitution. **1.** The Board of History and Philosophy of Science shall consist of:

(*a*) the Head of the Department of History and Philosophy of Science;

(*b*) the Professors and Readers in the Department of History and Philosophy of Science;

(*c*) the Librarian and the Secretary of the Department of History and Philosophy of Science;

(*d*) the Curator of the Whipple Museum of the History of Science;

(*e*) four persons elected from among their own number by the University officers in the Department of History and Philosophy of Science and those persons whose contribution to the teaching programme of the Department is such that they have been recognized for this purpose by the Board of History and Philosophy of Science subject to the concurrence of the General Board;

(*f*) two persons appointed by the General Board; EPS.

(*g*) not more than five persons co-opted by the Board provided that in the case of a casual vacancy or vacancies in class (*b*) or class (*e*) an additional person or persons may be co-opted to serve until the end of the calendar year in which the vacancy or vacancies occurred;

(*h*) three persons elected in accordance with Regulation 3.

Appointments.

2. The election of members in class (*e*) shall be held in the Michaelmas Term of every year; the procedure for such an election shall be that prescribed in the Single Transferable Vote Regulations, except that the returning officer shall be the Chair of the Board or a deputy appointed by the Chair subject to the approval of the General Board. Members in class (*e*) shall serve for two years from 1 January following their election. Members in class (*f*) shall serve for two years from 1 January following their appointment. Co-opted members in class (*g*) shall serve until 31 December of the year in which they are co-opted or of the following year, as the Board shall determine at the time of their co-optation.

Student members of the Board.

3. The provisions for the election of members of Faculty Boards in class (*f*) and for the period for which such members shall serve, which are contained in the regulations for the constitution of the Faculty Boards and for the Classes of Faculty Board Membership, Elections, and Periods of Office, and in the rules made under those regulations, shall apply, *mutatis mutandis*, to the election and period of membership of members of the Board in class (*h*).

Chair and Secretary.

4. The Board shall elect annually one of their number as Chair of the Board, and a Secretary; provided that neither of the persons so elected shall be a Graduate Student or a person *in statu pupillari*.

Powers and duties.

5. Except so far as may be determined otherwise by Ordinance, the Board shall have the same powers and duties as are assigned by the General Regulations for the Constitution of the Faculty Boards to the Board of a Faculty organized in Departments.

Reserved business.

6. The provisions of Special Ordinance A (vii) 5 concerning reserved business shall apply as if the Board were a body constituted by Statute and any matter which, if the Board were a Faculty Board, would be reserved business under Regulation 11 of the General Regulations for the Constitution of the Faculty Boards shall also be reserved. These provisions shall apply to any member of the Board in class (*h*) who is not *in statu pupillari* as if he or she were a person *in statu pupillari*.

Curator and Assistant Curator of the Whipple Museum of the History of Science

Director.

1. There shall be a University office of Curator of the Whipple Museum of the History of Science, the holder of which shall also be entitled Director of the Museum.

Assistant Curator.

2. There shall be a University office of Assistant Curator of the Whipple Museum of the History of Science, the holder of which shall report to the Curator of the Museum.

Appointments and tenure.

3. Appointments and reappointments to the University offices of Curator and Assistant Curator of the Whipple Museum of the History of Science shall be made by the Appointments Committee for the Department of History and Philosophy of Science.

Duties.

4. The duties of the Curator shall be determined by the Board of History and Philosophy of Science and shall include the following:

(*a*) to assist the Head of the Department of History and Philosophy of Science in the preservation, augmentation, and display of the collections of the Museum, and in making them available for purposes of study and research;

(*b*) to undertake at the request of the Board of History and Philosophy of Science, without additional payment, such teaching as the Board may consider desirable, having regard to the due performance of her or his duties as Curator.

5. The duties of the Assistant Curator shall be determined by the Board of History and Philosophy of Science and shall include assisting the Curator in her or his duties under Regulation 4 above.

FACULTY OF HUMAN, SOCIAL, AND POLITICAL SCIENCE

Human, Social, and Political Science.

MUSEUM OF ARCHAEOLOGY AND ANTHROPOLOGY

Antiquarian Society.

1. Regulations for the use of the Museum shall be made in consultation with the Council of the Cambridge Antiquarian Society, members of the Society receiving, as far as practicable, special consideration.

Human, Social, and Political Science.

2. The alienation of books and other objects which have come into the possession of the University through the Cambridge Antiquarian Society shall require the sanction of the Council of the Society and the agreement of appropriate conditions between the Council of the Society and the University body directly responsible for the institution in which the objects are housed.

3. The Cambridge Antiquarian Society shall be allowed free of charge, for meetings and for occasional conferences, the use of a suitable room in the Museum of Archaeology and Anthropology or in some other University building.

Staff. **4.** There shall be the following University offices on the staff of the Museum of Archaeology and Anthropology:

(*a*) an office of Curator, the holder of which shall also be entitled Director of the Museum;

(*b*) such number of offices of Senior Assistant Curator or Assistant Curator as the General Board shall from time to time determine.

Curator and Director. **5.** Appointments and reappointments to the University office of Curator and Director of the Museum of Archaeology and Anthropology, which may be held concurrently with another University office, shall be made by the General Board on the advice of a committee specially constituted for the particular occasion.

Duties of Curator. **6.** The duties of the Curator shall be defined by the Faculty Board of Human, Social, and Political Science and shall include the following:

(*a*) to be responsible for the preservation, augmentation, labelling, and cataloguing of the collections; to display and label specimens in exhibition cases in such a manner as will be instructive to students and visitors, and to arrange that unexhibited specimens are readily available for research; and to assist those who desire to consult the collections;

(*b*) to give not more than twenty-four hours' teaching in each academical year for the Faculty, this teaching to include discussions and demonstrations in the Museum;

(*c*) to be the official Head of the Museum for all administrative purposes.

In the absence of the Curator the Faculty Board shall nominate a Senior Assistant Curator or an Assistant Curator to undertake the Curator's responsibilities under sub-paragraph (*c*) of this regulation.

Museum Committee. **7.** For the due performance of his or her duties, the Curator shall be responsible to the Faculty Board of Human, Social, and Political Science. The Faculty Board may delegate the administration of the Museum to a Museum Committee appointed by them for that purpose. A University officer on the staff of the Museum shall act as Secretary to the Museum Committee.

Appointments of other staff. **8.** Appointments and reappointments to an office of Senior Assistant Curator or Assistant Curator shall be made by the Appointments Committee for the Faculty of Human, Social, and Political Science, with the Curator of the Museum as an additional member for this purpose.

Duties. **9.** The duties of a Senior Assistant Curator or an Assistant Curator shall be defined by the Faculty Board of Human, Social, and Political Science and shall include the following:

(*a*) to assist the Curator in the duties specified in Regulation 6(*a*), and

(*b*) to give not more than twenty-four hours' teaching in each academical year for the Faculty, this teaching to include discussions and demonstrations in the Museum.

Hours of attendance. **10.** The hours of attendance in the Museum of members of the staff shall be determined by the Faculty Board.

Annual Report. **11.** The Faculty Board shall make an Annual Report on the Museum to the General Board.

Members of Faculty. **12.** The holders of University offices on the staff of the Museum shall be members of the Faculty of Human, Social, and Political Science under Regulation 1(*b*) of the Regulations for Faculty Membership.

McDonald Institute for Archaeological Research

Constitution and Management

1. The McDonald Institute for Archaeological Research shall be an institution within the Department of Archaeology and Anthropology.

Object. **2.** The object of the Institute shall be to further research into all aspects of the early human past, including the origins and development of the human species, the development of the human mind and its expression, and the variety of early human achievement, customs, and practice in every part of the world. The work of the Institute, which shall include archaeological fieldwork and excavation, shall be interdisciplinary in character and shall involve collaboration with the environmental and other

Human, Social, and Political Science.

sciences, and with disciplines relevant to the development of the human cognitive faculties, and shall be designed to lead to the collation and publication of data and conclusions. Research conducted by the Institute shall have primary (but not exclusive) reference to the Euro-Asian sector and shall involve co-operation and sharing of knowledge with similar bodies and organizations in all parts of the world.

3. The Institute shall be under the general control of a Managing Committee, which shall consist of: Managing Committee.

(*a*) the Disney Professor of Archaeology;
(*b*) the Director of the Institute, if not the Disney Professor;
(*c*) the George Pitt-Rivers Professor of Archaeological Science;
(*d*) the Deputy Director of the Institute;
(*e*) the Head of the Department of Archaeology and Anthropology, or his or her nominee;
(*f*) one person appointed by the General Board;
(*g*) two persons appointed by the Faculty Board of Human, Social, and Political Science, one of whom shall be a University officer in the Department of Archaeology and Anthropology and the other a University officer in the Faculty of Classics;
(*h*) two persons appointed by the D. M. C. McDonald Foundation.

Members in classes (*f*) and (*g*) shall be appointed in the Michaelmas Term to serve for three years from 1 January following their appointment and shall be eligible for reappointment. The D. M. C. McDonald Foundation shall have power to assign the right of appointment of members in class (*h*) either to a separate trust or to some official body or to the holder of a particular office.

4. The Managing Committee shall meet at least twice a year, and shall elect one of their own number as Chair for a period of three years at a time. The Director of the Institute shall act as Secretary of the Managing Committee. Chair and Secretary.

5. The Managing Committee shall make an Annual Report to the General Board on the work of the Institute and such other reports to the General Board as they think fit. Copies of all such reports shall at the same time be submitted to the D. M. C. McDonald Foundation or its nominated successors. Reports.

Staff of the Institute

1. There shall be a University office of Director of the McDonald Institute, which shall normally be held concurrently with the Disney Professorship of Archaeology. Director.

2. Appointments and reappointments to the Directorship shall be made by the General Board on the recommendation of the Managing Committee for the Institute, and shall be for a period or periods not exceeding five years at a time; provided that the General Board may, on the recommendation of the Managing Committee, require the Director to resign the Directorship with effect from the date on which a newly-elected holder of the Disney Professorship of Archaeology takes up the duties of that office, so that the latter may be appointed Director. Appointments and reappointments.

3. The Director shall be the administrative Head of the Institute, and shall be responsible for the direction of research in the Institute, subject to the overall control of the Managing Committee. Duties.

4. There shall be a University office of Deputy Director[1] of the Institute who shall act under the Director as the executive officer of the Institute The office of Deputy Director shall not normally be held concurrently with any other University office. Deputy Director.

5. Appointments and reappointments to the University office of Deputy Director of the Institute shall be made by the Managing Committee, subject to the approval of the General Board. Appointments and reappointments.

6. The duties of the Director and the Deputy Director of the Institute shall be determined by the Managing Committee, subject to the approval of the General Board. Duties.

7. The Director and the Deputy Director shall conform to such conditions of residence as may be determined by the Managing Committee, subject to the approval of the General Board. Residence.

Fellows of the Institute

1. There shall be such number of Fellows of the McDonald Institute as the Managing Committee may from time to time determine, subject to the approval of the General Board. Fellows.

2. Fellowships of the Institute shall be held by persons who have made or are making important contributions to research in archaeology, or who are pursuing advanced work in the subject. A Fellowship may be held concurrently with a University office.

[1] This is an office specified in the Schedule to Special Ordinance C (i) 1.

Human, Social, and Political Science.

Appointments and reappointments. **3.** Appointments and reappointments to Fellowships shall be made by the Managing Committee for periods not exceeding five years at a time.

Stipend. **4.** The stipend, if any, of a Fellow shall be determined by the Managing Committee, subject to the approval of the General Board.

Visiting Fellowships

Visiting Fellows. **1.** In order to enable scholars from outside Cambridge to take part in, and to contribute to, the work of the McDonald Institute there shall be Visiting Fellowships for persons who have made or are making important contributions to research in archaeology or who are pursuing advanced work in the subject.

Appointments and tenure. **2.** The maximum number of Visiting Fellows that there may be in the Institute at any one time shall be determined by the Managing Committee, subject to the approval of the General Board. Appointments and reappointments to Visiting Fellowships shall be made by the Managing Committee for periods not exceeding one year at a time.

Duties. **3.** A Visiting Fellow shall be required under the general supervision of the Managing Committee to take part in the research programme of the Institute.

Restrictions. **4.** Visiting Fellows shall not hold any University office during the tenure of their Fellowships.

Stipend. **5.** The stipend, if any, of a Visiting Fellow shall be determined by the Managing Committee, subject to the approval of the General Board.

Grants. **6.** Subject to the approval of the General Board the Managing Committee may make grants to Visiting Fellows to meet travelling or other expenses incurred in connection with their Fellowships.

D. M. McDonald Trust Fund

Title. **1.** The sums given to the University by Dr D. M. McDonald for the support of the McDonald Institute for Archaeological Research shall form a Fund called the D. M. McDonald Trust Fund.

Purpose. **2.** The Fund shall be held by the University upon trust for the furtherance of archaeological research within the McDonald Institute, in accordance with the objects of the Institute.

Administration. **3.** The Fund shall be administered by the Managing Committee for the Institute who shall regulate their own procedure. They may pay out of the Fund their own expenses and all other expenses, costs, and charges which they deem necessary in connection with the administration of the Fund.

Income. **4.** The first charge on the income of the Fund shall be the cost of carrying on the activities of the Institute, including the payment of the salaries of its staff, and the running costs of the Institute and the maintenance of its building. In this connection the Managing Committee may propose the establishment of University offices and assistant posts within the Institute, may provide equipment, and may fund Fellowships, Scholarships, and Studentships. If further income is available after meeting all the above mentioned costs, grants may also be approved by the Managing Committee to the D. M. McDonald Grants and Awards Fund[1] or to institutions or organizations in any part of the world having purposes similar to those of the Institute.

5. The Managing Committee shall decide from time to time what part of the Fund shall be available as income and what part shall be invested and used as capital, subject to the need to ensure that sufficient income shall be made available in every year to meet the running costs of the Institute and to maintain its building.

Investment Committee. **6.** The Managing Committee shall appoint an Investment Committee which shall consist of:

(*a*) one of the members of the Managing Committee in class (*h*);

(*b*) two other members of the Managing Committee;

(*c*) one person nominated by the Finance Committee of the Council;

(*d*) not more than two persons co-opted by the Investment Committee, provided that it shall not be obligatory for the Committee to co-opt any person or persons.

Investment advisers. **7.** The Managing Committee shall have power to appoint suitably qualified investment advisers or investment managers of the Fund, subject to the approval of the Finance Committee of the Council.

8. The Fund, or any part of it, may from time to time be invested in such manner as the Investment Committee shall think fit, in the name of the Chancellor, Masters, and Scholars of the University, and the Committee shall have power to vary or realize such investment at their discretion.

[1] See p. 880.

Human, Social, and Political Science.

Staff supported by the Fund.

9. All persons engaged on the staff of the Institute shall for all purposes be employees of the University but, except and in so far as they may be remunerated in respect of any other office or post in the University, their total emoluments shall be reimbursed by the D. M. McDonald Trust Fund

Department of Land Economy

Land Economy.

Independent of a Faculty.

1. The Department of Land Economy shall be a Department independent of any Faculty. The Department shall be controlled by the Board of Land Economy under the supervision of the General Board.

Appointments Committee.

2. Appointments and reappointments to a University office in the Department of Land Economy other than to an Assistantship in Research shall be made by an Appointments Committee for the Department consisting of the following persons:

(*a*) the Vice-Chancellor (or a duly appointed deputy) as Chair;

(*b*) the Head of the Department of Land Economy;

(*c*) three members of the Board of Land Economy appointed by that Board;

(*d*) two persons appointed by the General Board.

The Appointments Committee shall have the same powers and duties in respect of the Department as the Appointments Committee for a Faculty has by Statute or Ordinance in respect of a Faculty; and Special Ordinance C (x) 4 shall apply to the Committee as if it were the Appointments Committee for a Faculty.

Board of Land Economy

Constitution.

1. The Board of Land Economy shall consist of:

(*a*) the Head of the Department of Land Economy;

(*b*) the Directors of such Research Centres within the Department of Land Economy as approved by the Board of Land Economy;

(*c*) the Professors in the Department of Land Economy;

(*d*) the Secretary of the Degree Committee for the Department;

(*e*) six persons elected from among their own number by the Readers and other University officers in the Department of Land Economy and those members of the Regent House whose contribution to the teaching and research programme of the Department is such that they have been recognized by the Board;

(*f*) one person appointed by the Council;

(*g*) one person appointed by the General Board;

(*h*) one person appointed by each of the Faculty Boards of Earth Sciences and Geography, Economics, and Law;

(*i*) not more than two persons co-opted by the Board provided that in the case of a casual vacancy or vacancies in class (*e*) an additional person or persons may be co-opted to serve until the end of the calendar year in which the vacancy or vacancies occurred;

(*j*) three persons elected in accordance with Regulation 3.

2. The election of members in class (*e*) shall be held in the Michaelmas Term of every year; the procedure for such an election shall be that prescribed in the Single Transferable Vote Regulations except that the returning officer shall be the Chair of the Board or in the Chair's absence a deputy appointed by the Chair subject to the approval of the General Board. Members in class (*e*) shall serve for two years from 1 January following their election. Members in classes (*f*)–(*h*) shall serve for two years from 1 January following their appointment. Co-opted members in class (*i*) shall serve until 31 December of the year in which they are co-opted or of the following year as the Board shall determine at the time of their co-optation.

Student members of the Board.

3. The provisions for the election of members of Faculty Boards in class (*f*) and for the period for which such members shall serve, which are contained in the regulations for the constitution of the Faculty Boards and for the Classes of Faculty Board Membership, Elections, and Periods of Office, and in the rules made under those regulations, shall apply, *mutatis mutandis*, to the election and period of membership of members of the Board in class (*j*).

Chair and Secretary.

4. The Board shall elect annually one of their members as Chair of the Board, provided that the person so elected shall not be a Graduate Student or a person *in statu pupillari*. The Secretary of the Board shall be the Departmental Administrative Officer.

Land Economy.

Powers and duties.

5. Except so far as may be determined otherwise by Ordinance, the Board shall have the same powers and duties as are assigned by the General Regulations for the Constitution of the Faculty Boards to the Board of a Faculty organized in Departments. It shall also be their duty, under the supervision of the General Board, to exercise general control over the Department of Land Economy.

Reserved business.

6. The provisions of Special Ordinance A (vii) 5 concerning reserved business shall apply as if the Board were a body constituted by Statute and any matter which, if the Board were a Faculty Board, would be reserved business under Regulation 11 of the General Regulations for the Constitution of the Faculty Boards shall also be reserved. These provisions shall apply to any member of the Board in class (*j*) who is not *in statu pupillari* as if he or she were a person *in statu pupillari*.

Agricultural Economics Unit

General

1. Subject to the powers of the Board of Land Economy, the Agricultural Economics Unit shall be under the general control of the Head of the Department of Land Economy.

2. In accordance with such general arrangements as may be agreed upon between the Department for Environment, Food and Rural Affairs and the General Board, acting on behalf of the University, the Agricultural Economics Unit shall undertake investigations and provide specialist advice, as may be commissioned by the Ministry.

3. The Agricultural Economics Unit shall, in addition to the work commissioned by the Department for Environment, Food and Rural Affairs, promote and engage in research in agricultural economics.

Director of the Agricultural Economics Unit

Appointments.

1. Appointments and reappointments to the University office of Director of the Agricultural Economics Unit shall be made by the Appointments Committee for the Department of Land Economy, and two persons appointed by the General Board for the particular occasion.

Duties.

2. The duties of the Director of the Agricultural Economics Unit shall be to advance knowledge and to promote and direct research in Agricultural Economics, to give instruction to students, and to supervise the work of the Unit, subject to the powers of the Board of Land Economy and under the general control of the Head of the Department of Land Economy. Such teaching as the Director may give on behalf of the University other than the supervision of Graduate Students shall be given without additional remuneration as part of the duties of the office.

Residence.

3. The Director shall conform to such conditions of residence as may be determined by the Board with the approval of the General Board.

Restrictions.

4. The Director shall not be a Tutor, Assistant Tutor, Bursar, Assistant Bursar, or Steward of a College.

Cambridge Centre for Housing and Planning

General

1. Subject to the powers of the Board of Land Economy, the Cambridge Centre for Housing and Planning shall be under the general control of the Head of the Department of Land Economy.

2. The Centre shall promote and engage in research in the field of housing and planning.

Director of the Cambridge Centre for Housing and Planning

1. There shall be a University office of Director of the Cambridge Centre for Housing and Planning, which may be held concurrently with another University office.

Appointments and tenure.

2. If the office is held concurrently with another University office, appointments and reappointments to the office of Director shall be made by the Appointments Committee for the Department of Land Economy and shall be for a period or periods not exceeding five years at a time.

Duties.

3. The duties of the Director shall be:

(*a*) to promote and direct research in the field of housing and planning;

(*b*) to give instruction to students therein;

(*c*) subject to the powers of the Board of Land Economy and under the general control of the Head of the Department of Land Economy, to supervise the work of the Centre. Land Economy.

Such teaching as the Director may give on behalf of the University shall be given without additional remuneration as part of the duties of the office.

4. The Director shall conform to such conditions of residence as may be determined by the Board of Land Economy with the approval of the General Board. Residence.

5. The Director shall not be a Tutor, Assistant Tutor, Bursar, Assistant Bursar, or Steward of a College. Restrictions.

Faculty of Law

Law.

Committee of Management: Joint course in Law

Rescinded by Notice (Reporter, *2013–14, p. 119*)

Institute of Criminology

Management

1. The Institute of Criminology shall be a Department within the Faculty of Law.

2. The Institute shall be under the general control of a Committee of Management which shall consist of: Committee of Management.

(*a*) the Director of the Institute;

(*b*) the Wolfson Professor of Criminology;

(*c*) the Chair of the Faculty Board of Law;

(*d*) one person appointed by each of the following authorities: the Faculty Boards of Law, Business and Management, and Human, Social, and Political Science, the Strategic Committee for the Institute of Continuing Education, the Head of the Department of Psychiatry;

(*e*) three persons elected from among their own number by the University officers in the Institute;

(*f*) the Librarian of the Institute;

(*g*) not more than three persons co-opted by the Committee; provided that it shall not be obligatory for the Committee to co-opt any person or persons;

(*h*) two persons elected in accordance with Regulations 4 and 5 below.

3. Members in class (*d*) shall be appointed in the Michaelmas Term to serve for four years from 1 January following their appointment. An election of members in class (*e*) shall be held in the Michaelmas Term each year; members so elected shall serve for three years from 1 January following the election. The procedure for such an election shall be that prescribed in the Single Transferable Vote Regulations, except that the returning officer shall be the Director of the Institute or, in the absence of the Director, a duly appointed deputy, subject to the approval of the General Board. Members in class (*g*) shall serve until 31 December of the year in which they are co-opted or of the following year, as the Committee shall determine at the time of their co-optation.

4. Except as provided otherwise in these regulations, the provisions for the election and period of service of members of Faculty Boards in class (*f*) which are contained in the regulations for the constitution of the Faculty Boards and for the Classes of Faculty Board Membership, Elections, and Periods of Office, and in the rules made under those regulations, shall apply, *mutatis mutandis*, to the election and the period of service of members of the Committee of Management in class (*h*). Student members.

5. The scheme for the election of members of the Committee of Management in class (*h*) shall be as follows:[1] Scheme of election.

J. The members in class (*h*) shall be (i) one graduate student elected by and from among the graduate students pursuing a course of study in the Institute for the Ph.D. Degree, and (ii) one graduate student elected by and from among the graduate students pursuing a course of study in the Institute leading to the M.Phil. Degree. The returning officer for the election shall be the Director of the Institute.

6. The Committee shall elect annually one of their members as Chair, and a Secretary, provided that neither of the persons so elected shall be a Graduate Student or a person *in statu pupillari*. They may, subject to the approval of the General Board, pay a salary to the Secretary. Chair and Secretary.

[1] For Schemes A–H see p. 606.

Law.

Quorum. **7.** Six members of the Committee shall constitute a quorum.

Duties of the Committee. **8.** Subject to the powers of the Council, the General Board, and the Faculty Board of Law, the duties of the Committee shall be as follows:

(*a*) to promote teaching and research in Criminology and the publication of the results of such research;

(*b*) to co-operate with other institutions in the University in the encouragement of teaching and research in Criminology;

(*c*) to supervise the work of the Institute.

Reserved business. **9.** The provisions of Special Ordinance A (vii) 5 concerning reserved business shall apply as if the Committee were a body constituted by Statute and any matter which, if the Committee were a Faculty Board, would be reserved business under Regulation 11 of the General Regulations for the Constitution of the Faculty Boards shall also be reserved. These provisions shall apply to any member of the Committee in class (*h*) who is not *in statu pupillari* as if he or she were a person *in statu pupillari*.

Staff of the Institute of Criminology

1. There shall be the University office of Director of the Institute of Criminology[1] which shall be held concurrently with another University office for a period not exceeding five years, as determined by the General Board at the time of appointment. The Director shall be appointed by the General Board on the recommendation of the Management Committee.

Appointments. **2.** Appointments and reappointments to a University office of University Lecturer, Assistant Director of Research, or Senior Assistant in Research in the Institute shall be made by the Appointments Committee for the Faculty of Law as constituted for the particular office in accordance with Special Ordinance C (x) 2, or, if the General Board have determined that the duties of the office concern more than one Faculty or Department and have specified those Faculties or Departments, by an Appointments Committee constituted in accordance with Special Ordinance C (x) 3

3. The Director shall be the Head of the Department of the Institute of Criminology. Under the general control of the Committee of Management he or she shall carry out the duties specified for the Head of a Department in Statute A V 17.

Residence. **4.** The Director shall conform to such conditions of residence as may be determined by the Committee of Management with the approval of the General Board.

Restrictions. **5.** The Director shall not be a Tutor, Assistant Tutor, Bursar, Assistant Bursar, or Steward of a College.

Visiting Fellowships

Purpose and number. **1.** In order to enable scholars and experts from outside Cambridge to take part in and contribute to the work of the Institute of Criminology there shall be Visiting Fellowships for persons who are experienced in the administration of criminal justice or who have made important contributions to the criminological and allied disciplines. There shall not be more than four Visiting Fellows in the Institute at any one time.

Appointments and tenure. **2.** Appointments and reappointments to Visiting Fellowships shall be made by the Committee of Management of the Institute for periods not exceeding one year at a time.

Duties. **3.** A Visiting Fellow shall be required under the general supervision of the Committee of Management to take part in the teaching and research programme of the Institute.

Restrictions. **4.** Visiting Fellows shall not hold any University office during the tenure of their Fellowships. A Visiting Fellow who is not a member of the University at the time of appointment shall be required to become a member as soon as is conveniently possible thereafter.

Stipend. **5.** The stipend, if any, of a Visiting Fellow shall be determined by the Committee of Management with the approval of the General Board on the occasion of each appointment or reappointment.

Grants. **6.** Subject to the approval of the General Board, the Committee of Management may make grants to Visiting Fellows to meet travelling or other expenses incurred in connection with their Fellowships.

[1] This is an office specified in the Schedules to Special Ordinances C (i) 1 and C (vii) 1.

LAUTERPACHT RESEARCH CENTRE FOR INTERNATIONAL LAW

Law.

Management

Committee of Management.

1. The Lauterpacht Research Centre for International Law shall be an institution within the Faculty of Law and shall be under the general control of a Committee of Management which shall consist of:

(*a*) the Chair of the Faculty Board of Law and the Whewell Professor of International Law *ex officio*;

(*b*) the Director and the Deputy Director of the Centre;

(*c*) one person appointed by the General Board, three by the Faculty Board of Law, and one by the Faculty Board of Human, Social, and Political Science;

(*d*) not more than two additional persons co-opted at the discretion of the Committee.

2. Members in class (*c*) shall be appointed in the Michaelmas Term to serve for four years from 1 January following their appointment. Co-opted members in class (*d*) shall serve until 31 December of the year in which they are co-opted or of the year next following, as the Committee shall determine at the time of their co-optation.

Chair and Secretary.

3. The Faculty Board shall elect one of their number, other than the Director and the Deputy Director of the Centre, to be Chair of the Committee, to serve for four years from 1 January following his or her election. The Director shall serve as Secretary of the Committee.

Duties of the Committee.

4. Subject to the powers of the Council, the General Board, and the Faculty Board of Law, the duties of the Committee shall be as follows:

(*a*) to promote study and research in international law and to assist in the production of the *International Law Reports*;

(*b*) to co-operate with outside bodies in the encouragement of study and research in international law;

(*c*) to administer funds available to them for the purposes specified in (*a*) and (*b*) above, and to comply with any requirements of the General Board and of the Faculty Board of Law as regards the submission of reports, estimates, and accounts which shall be shown separately from the accounts of the Faculty;

(*d*) to supervise the work of the staff of the Research Centre.

Quorum.

5. Five members of the Committee shall form a quorum.

Finances.

6. The funds available to the Research Centre shall consist of donations including an annual donation from the Trustees of the *International Law Reports*.

Staff of the Research Centre

Director.

1. There shall be a University office of Director of the Research Centre, which may be held concurrently with another University office and shall be held on such terms and conditions as the General Board may from time to time determine.

Deputy Director.

2. There shall be a University office of Deputy Director of the Research Centre which shall be held concurrently with a University office in the Faculty of Law.

3. Appointments and reappointments to the office of Director shall be made by the General Board on the recommendation of the Faculty Board of Law. If the office is held concurrently with another University office, appointments and reappointments shall be made for such periods not exceeding four years at a time as shall be determined by the General Board on the recommendation of the Faculty Board.

4. Appointments and reappointments to the office of Deputy Director shall be made by the General Board on the recommendation of the Faculty Board of Law, and shall be for such periods not exceeding four years at a time as shall be determined by the General Board on the recommendation of the Faculty Board.

Duties.

5. Under the general control of the Committee of Management, the Director shall be the administrative Head of the Research Centre. The Director and the Deputy Director shall be responsible for the direction of study and research in the Centre.

Visiting Fellowships

Purpose.

1. In order to enable scholars to take part in and contribute to the work of the Research Centre there shall be Visiting Fellowships for persons who have made or are making important contributions to international law, or who are pursuing work in international law.

Law. Appointments and tenure. **2.** The maximum number of Visiting Fellows that there may be in the Research Centre at any one time shall be determined by the General Board. Appointments and reappointments to Visiting Fellowships shall be made by the Committee of Management of the Research Centre, subject to the approval of the Faculty Board of Law, for periods not exceeding two years at a time.

Duties. **3.** A Visiting Fellow shall be required under the general supervision of the Committee of Management to take part in the work of the Research Centre.

Restrictions. **4.** Visiting Fellows shall not hold any University office during the tenure of their Fellowships. A Visiting Fellow who is not a member of the University at the time of appointment shall be required to become a member as soon as is conveniently possible thereafter.

Stipend. **5.** The stipend, if any, of a Visiting Fellow shall be determined by the Committee of Management with the approval of the General Board on the occasion of each appointment or reappointment.

Management.

JUDGE INSTITUTE OF MANAGEMENT (JUDGE BUSINESS SCHOOL)

Amended by Notice (Reporter, *2013–14, p. 718*)

1. The Judge Institute of Management shall be a Department within the Faculty of Business and Management and shall have the title 'Judge Business School'. The Director of the Institute shall be the academic head of the School. The Institute shall be under the general control of the Faculty Board of Business and Management.

Advisory Board. **2.** There shall be an advisory board, which shall contain at least four persons who are not members of the Regent House and who have experience of business administration. It shall be the duty of the advisory board to advise the Director and the Faculty Board on policy for the future development of the Judge Business School in the University.

Staff of the Institute

Director. **1.** There shall be a University office of Director of the Institute which shall be held concurrently with another University office in the Institute.

Tenure. **2.** The Director of the Institute shall be appointed by the General Board on the recommendation of the Faculty Board of Business and Management. He or she shall be appointed for a period of five years and shall be eligible for reappointment for a further period of five years. The Director shall be the Head of the Department *ex officio*.

Director of M.B.A. course. **3.** There shall be a University office of Director of the M.B.A. course, which may be held concurrently with another University office.[1] The Director of the M.B.A. course shall be responsible to the Faculty Board of Business and Management for the planning, development, and administration of the course leading to the degree of M.B.A. Appointments and reappointments to the office of Director, if held concurrently with another University office, shall be for such period or periods not exceeding five years at a time as the Appointments Committee for the Faculty Board shall determine.

Careers Advisers. **4.** There shall be such number of Careers Advisers in the Institute as the General Board shall determine on the recommendation of the Faculty Board. Appointments and reappointments to the office of Careers Adviser shall be made in accordance with arrangements agreed from time to time by the appropriate authority.

CENTRE FOR BUSINESS RESEARCH

Management

Committee of Management. **1.** The Centre for Business Research shall be an interdisciplinary research institute within the Judge Business School and shall be under the general control of a Committee of Management, which shall consist of:

(*a*) the Director;
(*b*) the Assistant Directors;
(*c*) one person appointed by the General Board, who shall be Chair;

[1] This office is an office specified in the Schedule to Special Ordinance C (vii) 1.

(*d*) the Executive Director of Research in the Faculty of Economics, the Director of Judge Business School, the Heads of the Departments of Geography and Land Economy, and the Chairs of the Faculty Boards of Economics, Engineering, Human, Social, and Political Science, and Law, or in each case the elected representative of the Board; Management.

(*e*) not more than two persons co-opted at the discretion of the Committee.

2. The member in class (*c*) shall be appointed in the Michaelmas Term to serve for four years from 1 January following her or his appointment. Members in class (*e*) shall serve until 31 December of the year in which they are co-opted or of the following year, as the Committee shall determine at the time of their co-optation.

3. The Committee shall appoint annually one of their number to act as Secretary. Secretary.

4. The Committee shall meet at least once in each year. Five members present at a meeting shall constitute a quorum. Quorum.

5. The duties of the Committee shall be as follows: Duties of the Committee.

(*a*) to promote business research and the dissemination of the results of such research;

(*b*) to co-operate with outside bodies in the encouragement of business research;

(*c*) to administer funds allocated to them for the purposes specified in (*a*) and (*b*) above;

(*d*) to supervise the work of the staff of the Centre;

(*e*) to make an Annual Report to the Director of Judge Business School.

6. The Committee shall prepare annual estimates for submission to the Director of Judge Business School.

7. There shall be an Executive Committee, consisting of the Director, who shall be Chair, and the Assistant Directors. The Committee shall advise the Director on matters concerning the staffing, resources, and administration of the Centre, including the setting and revision of project budgets. The Committee may co-opt not more than three additional members to serve for such periods as they think fit. Executive Committee.

8. The Executive Committee shall meet at least once each term.

9. There shall be an Advisory Board consisting of: Advisory Board.

(*a*) the Director;

(*b*) two of the Assistant Directors elected by the Executive Committee;

(*c*) at least twelve persons appointed by the General Board on the recommendation of the Director. Members in classes (*b*) and (*c*) shall be elected or appointed in the Michaelmas Term to serve for four years from 1 January following their election or appointment. A member in classes (*b*) and (*c*) shall at the end of that period be eligible for re-election or reappointment, respectively, for one further period of four years, provided that the General Board may exceptionally allow a member to be eligible for a second further period of four years, after which two years shall elapse before he or she shall again be eligible for re-election or reappointment. The members in class (*c*) shall include at least nine persons who are not resident members of the University.

The General Board shall have power, after consulting the Director, to appoint two persons to attend meetings of the Advisory Board as observers.

10. The duties of the Advisory Board shall be: Duties of the Board.

(*a*) to advise the Director on lines of business research, their financial implications, and potential sources of funding for such research;

(*b*) to assist the Director in co-operation with outside bodies in furthering the Centre's programme of research;

(*c*) to receive reports of research conducted within the Centre and an annual statement of the Centre's financial position.

11. The Advisory Board shall elect one of their number, other than the Director, to act as Chair each year, and a Secretary. The Board shall meet at least twice in each year. Chair.

Staff of the Centre

1. There shall be a University office of Director of the Centre which may be held concurrently with another University office. Director of the Centre.

2. The Director of the Centre shall be appointed by the General Board on the recommendation of the Committee of Management of the Centre for Business Research. If held concurrently with another

Management. University office, appointments and reappointments to the office of Director shall be for such periods not exceeding five years at a time as the General Board may determine.

3. Under the general control of the Committee of Management, the Director shall be the administrative Head of the Centre and shall be responsible for the direction of research in the Centre.

Assist Directors. **4.** There shall be such number of University offices of Assistant Director of the Centre as the General Board may from time to time determine. The office of Assistant Director may be held concurrently with another University office.

5. If held concurrently with another University office, appointments and reappointments to a University office of Assistant Director of the Centre shall be made by the Committee of Management, subject to the approval of the General Board, and shall be for such periods as shall be determined by the General Board on the recommendation of the Committee.

6. The Assistant Directors shall be responsible to the Director for:

(*a*) the development and efficient conduct of groups of research projects allocated to them by the Director;

(*b*) the provision of annual progress reports to the Director on their groups of research projects.

7. During any absence of the Director, or when the office of Director is vacant, the General Board may, on the recommendation of the Committee of Management, appoint one of the Assistant Directors as Acting Director on such terms and conditions as the Board may determine.

Research Fellowships. **8.** There shall be such number of Junior Research Fellowships, Research Fellowships, and Senior Research Fellowships as shall be determined from time to time by the Committee of Management on the recommendation of the Director. Such Fellowships may be held concurrently with another University office.

Visiting Fellowships

1. In order to enable scholars from outside Cambridge to take part in and contribute to the work of the Centre there shall be Visiting Fellowships for persons who have made or are making important contributions to business research, or who are pursuing advanced work in the subject.

Appointments and tenure. **2.** Appointments and reappointments to Visiting Fellowships shall be made by the Director of the Centre for periods not exceeding one year at a time.

Stipend. **3.** The stipend, if any, of a Visiting Fellow shall be determined by the Director with the approval of the General Board on the occasion of each appointment or reappointment.

Research Affiliates

The Director may from time to time grant the status of Research Affiliate to persons (other than the salaried research staff of the Centre) who contribute to the Centre's work.

Cambridge Endowment for Research in Finance

Director

Appointments. **1.** Appointments and reappointments to the University office[1] of Director of the Cambridge Endowment for Research in Finance (CERF) shall be made by the General Board, on the advice of a committee specially constituted for the particular occasion.

Duties. **2.** The duties of the Director shall include:

(*a*) proposing research programmes that meet the objectives of CERF;

(*b*) monitoring and reporting on progress in meeting the objectives of CERF, and its constituent research projects;

(*c*) taking a leading role in generating funds for CERF;

(*d*) taking responsibility for operational, financial, and administrative management of CERF.

3. The Director shall be responsible to, and act for, the Managers of CERF in matters concerned with the general policy and intellectual development of CERF and its research programmes.

4. The office of Director may be held simultaneously with other offices in the University of Cambridge.

Residence. **5.** The Director shall be resident in the University during Full Term.

[1] This office is an office specified in the Schedule to Special Ordinance C (vii) 1.

Department of Physics

Physics.

Rayleigh Library

1. The Library at the Cavendish Laboratory shall be called the Rayleigh Library. Name.

2. Out of the sum received from the Committee of the Rayleigh Memorial Fund, the sum of £600 shall be separately invested in the name of the Chancellor, Masters, and Scholars of the University, and shall be called the Rayleigh Library Endowment Fund for Experimental Physics. Fund.

3. The income of the Fund shall be paid for the purposes of the Rayleigh Library to the Cavendish Professor of Physics, who shall keep an account thereof. Income.

4. A book-plate shall be prepared, and a copy of it placed in each book purchased out of the Fund. Book-plate.

Department of Physiology, Development, and Neuroscience

PDN.

Certain University offices in the Department of Physiology, Development, and Neuroscience

1. There shall be the offices of University Clinical Anatomist, University Clinical Veterinary Anatomist, and University Physiologist in the Department of Physiology, Development, and Neuroscience. The tenure of these offices shall be the same as that prescribed for a University Lecturer by Special Ordinance C (x) 5 and 6. Staff.

2. Appointment and reappointments to each office of University Clinical Anatomist and University Physiologist shall be made, in the manner prescribed by Special Ordinance C (x) 1, by the Appointments Committee for the Faculty of Biology. Appointments.

3. Appointment and reappointments to the office of University Clinical Veterinary Anatomist shall be made, in the manner prescribed by Special Ordinance C (x) 1, by an Appointments Committee constituted in accordance with Special Ordinance C (x) 3(*b*) for an office whose duties concern the Department of Physiology, Development, and Neuroscience and the Department of Veterinary Medicine.

4. The duties of each officer shall be to assist the Head of the Department of Physiology, Development, and Neuroscience in the work of the Department as directed by him or her throughout the year, save for a period or periods not exceeding a total of seven weeks in any one academical year as may be agreed between the officer and the Head of the Department. Duties.

5. Each officer shall undertake without additional payment such formal teaching as may be assigned to him or her by the Head of the Department, with the concurrence of the Faculty Board of Biology, being not less than 100 hours nor more than 200 hours of demonstrating in any one year, or an equivalent amount of other teaching.

6. None of the officers specified in Regulation 1 shall, without the leave of the General Board, engage in teaching other than teaching given on behalf of the University or a College or Colleges. The amount of teaching given on behalf of a College or Colleges shall not exceed six hours a week. Restrictions.

7. None of the officers specified in Regulation 1 shall, without the leave of the General Board, engage in private practice or other duties involving clinical responsibility.

Department of Plant Sciences

Plant Sciences.

Herbarium

1. There shall be the following University offices on the staff of the Herbarium: Staff.

(*a*) an office of Curator which shall be held concurrently with another University office in the Department of Plant Sciences;

(*b*) such number of offices of Senior Assistant Curator or Assistant Curator as the General Board shall from time to time determine.

2. Appointments and reappointments to the office of Curator of the Herbarium shall be made by the Appointments Committee for the Faculty of Biology. Appointment of Curator.

3. The Curator shall be responsible to the Head of the Department of Plant Sciences for the maintenance of the collection entrusted to his or her care, and for making it available for purposes of study and research. Duties of Curator.

4. The amount of teaching to be given by the Curator shall be determined by the Faculty Board of Biology after taking into account his or her curatorial duties. Teaching work.

Plant Sciences.

Stipend. **5.** The stipend of the Curator shall be his or her stipend as a University officer together with such payments for special responsibilities as Curator as may from time to time be approved by the General Board on the recommendation of the Faculty Board.

Appointments of other staff. **6.** Appointments and reappointments to a University office of Senior Assistant Curator or Assistant Curator of the Herbarium shall be made by the Appointments Committee for the Faculty of Biology, with the Curator of the Herbarium as an additional member for this purpose.

Duties. **7.** The duties of a Senior Assistant Curator or an Assistant Curator shall be determined by the General Board on the recommendation of the Faculty Board and shall include the following:

(*a*) to assist the Curator in the duties specified under Regulation 3 above;

(*b*) to undertake at the request of the Faculty Board, without additional payment, such teaching as the Faculty Board may consider desirable, having regard to his or her curatorial duties.

Members of Faculty. **8.** The holders of University offices on the staff of the Herbarium shall be members of the Faculty of Biology under Regulation 1(*b*) of the Regulations for Faculty Membership.

Veterinary Medicine.

Department of Veterinary Medicine

1. The short title of the Department shall be 'The Veterinary School'.

2. The Faculty Board of Veterinary Medicine shall designate as Dean of the Veterinary School an officer who holds an appointment in the Department.

3. The Faculty Board of Veterinary Medicine shall designate as Director of Teaching in the Department of Veterinary Medicine an officer who holds an appointment in the Department.

Certain University offices in the Department of Veterinary Medicine

Titles and number. **1.** (*a*) There shall be such number of University offices of University Pathologist, University Physician, University Surgeon, and University Equine Surgeon in the Department of Veterinary Medicine as the General Board may from time to time determine. The tenure of these offices shall be the same as that prescribed for a University Lecturer by Special Ordinance C (x) 5 and 6.

(*b*) There shall be such number of University offices of Resident in the Department of Veterinary Medicine as the General Board may from time to time determine. An office of Resident shall be tenable for three years, provided that

(i) in exceptional circumstances a Resident may be appointed for periods of not more than one year at a time;

(ii) no person shall hold the office of Resident for a total period exceeding five years;

(iii) any appointment to another office of Resident shall be regarded as a reappointment of the person concerned.

Duties. **2.** The duties of each officer shall be to assist the Head of the Department of Veterinary Medicine with the work of the Veterinary Hospital throughout the year save for such period or periods not exceeding six weeks in all in any one academical year as may be agreed by the Head of the Department.

3. Each officer shall undertake without additional payment such teaching as may be assigned to him or her by the Head of the Department of Veterinary Medicine, with the concurrence of the Faculty Board of Veterinary Medicine.

Restrictions. **4.** None of the officers specified in Regulation 1 shall, without the leave of the General Board, engage in teaching other than teaching on behalf of the University or a College or Colleges. The amount of teaching given on behalf of a College shall not exceed six hours a week.

5. The officers specified in Regulation 1 shall not, without the leave of the General Board, engage in private practice, but they may attend private patients in connection with their work in the Department of Veterinary Medicine, provided that any fees for such attendance are paid to a Clinical Research Fund which shall be administered according to arrangements approved by the Faculty Board of Veterinary Medicine.

Veterinary Students Register Veterinary Medicine.

Amended by Grace 1 of 29 January 2014

The Faculty Board and the Faculty Board of Biology shall maintain jointly through a Veterinary Fitness to Practise Committee a register of students who are deemed fit to practise veterinary medicine and consequently to be admitted as candidates for the Second Examination and the Final Examination for the degree of Bachelor of Veterinary Medicine A Veterinary Fitness to Practise Appeal Panel shall have the power on appeal from a student affected by a decision of the Veterinary Fitness to Practise Adjudication Panel to confirm, quash, amend, or refer back to the same, or a newly constituted, Veterinary Fitness to Practise Adjudication Panel the decision in question.

DEPARTMENT OF ZOOLOGY

Zoology.

MUSEUM OF ZOOLOGY

1. There shall be the following University offices on the staff of the Museum of Zoology: Staff.

(*a*) the office of Director;

(*b*) an office of Curator or Senior Assistant Curator or Assistant Curator, as the General Board shall determine from time to time, of Vertebrates;

(*c*) an office of Curator or Senior Assistant Curator or Assistant Curator, as the General Board shall determine from time to time, of Insects;

(*d*) either an office of Curator, Senior Assistant Curator, or an office of Assistant Curator, as the General Board shall determine from time to time;

(*e*) an office of Senior Assistant Curator or Assistant Curator, as the General Board shall determine from time to time, in Malacology (Watson).

The title of Strickland Curator, on the foundation of Miss Frances Strickland, may be granted by the Faculty Board of Biology, on the recommendation of the Head of the Department of Zoology, to a person holding a University office or an unestablished appointment on the staff of the Museum. A person to whom the title is granted shall hold it for such period as may be determined by the Faculty Board, subject to the approval of the General Board.

2. (*a*) The office of Director shall be held in conjunction with a Professorship in the Department of Zoology.

(*b*) An office of Curator shall be held in conjunction with another University office in the Department of Zoology.

(*c*) An office of Senior Assistant Curator or Assistant Curator shall not be tenable in conjunction with any other University office.

3. Appointments and reappointments to an office of Curator, Senior Assistant Curator, or Assistant Curator on the staff of the Museum shall be made by the Appointments Committee for the Faculty of Biology, with the Director as an additional member for this purpose. The tenure of a Curator shall be the same as that prescribed for a University Lecturer by Special Ordinance C (x) 5 and 6. In accordance with the express wishes of the founder of the Hugh Watson Fund, a holder of the office of Senior Assistant Curator or Assistant Curator in Malacology (Watson) shall be a graduate of a university. Appointments and tenure.

4. The Director shall be responsible to the Head of the Department of Zoology for the maintenance of the collections of the Museum, and for making them available for study and research. The Director shall also undertake such other duties in connection with the Museum as may be assigned to him or her by the Head of the Department or the Faculty Board of Biology. Duties.

5. It shall be the duty of the other members of the staff of the Museum to assist the Director in the duties specified in Regulation 4.

6. The hours of attendance in the Museum of members of the staff shall be determined by the Faculty Board of Biology on the recommendation of the Head of the Department of Zoology. Hours of attendance.

7. If a Curator holds a University Lectureship or a University Senior Lectureship, the performance of his or her duties in connection with the Museum shall be taken into account by the Faculty Board under Special Ordinance C (x) 10 in determining the amount of teaching that he or she is to undertake. Teaching work.

8. An Assistant Curator shall undertake at the request of the Faculty Board, without additional payment, such teaching in connection with the Department of Zoology as the Faculty Board may consider desirable, having regard to the due performance of his or her duties in the Museum.

Zoology.

Stipends. **9.** No stipend shall be attached to the offices of Director or Curator. The Director may receive such payments for administrative responsibility as may from time to time be approved by the General Board on the recommendation of the Faculty Board.

Members of Faculty. **10.** The holders of University offices on the staff of the Museum of Zoology shall be members of the Faculty of Biology under Regulation 1(*b*) of the Regulations for Faculty Membership.

Crotch Fund

Statute E XXXVII.

Endowments, 1904, p. 536

Income. **1.** The income of the Crotch Fund shall be placed at the disposal of the Director of the Museum of Zoology for the purchase of books or specimens for the Museum.

Reserve Fund. **2.** The unexpended income in any year shall be carried to a Reserve Fund.

3. The Reserve Fund may be used, at the discretion of the Director, for the purposes of Regulation 1 or for the purchase of cases for exhibiting specimens or for special work in connection with the Museum collections.

4. The Director shall make an annual report to the Faculty Board of Biology on the use of the Reserve Fund.

Balfour and Newton Libraries

In addition to the provisions of the regulations for Faculty, Departmental, and other Libraries the following special regulations shall apply to the Balfour Library and Endowment Fund and to the Newton Fund and Library.

Balfour Library and Endowment Fund

Library. **1.** The Balfour Library shall be under the charge of the Head of the Department of Zoology, and shall be housed in the Department of Zoology.

To whom open. **2.** The Library shall also be open to workers in the Department of Zoology who are not members of the University and to such other persons as have obtained the permission of the Head of the Department.

Fund. **3.** The income of the Balfour Library Endowment Fund shall be paid to the Head of the Department of Zoology, to be spent upon the upkeep of the Balfour Library or to be added to the capital of the Fund.

Alterations. **4.** These regulations shall be subject to alteration by Grace, provided that no change be made in the name of the Library or in that of the Fund, and that the Library continue to be the Departmental Library of the Department of Zoology.

Newton Fund and Library

Library. **1.** The Newton Library shall be under the charge of the Head of the Department of Zoology and shall be housed in the Department of Zoology.

To whom open. **2.** The Library shall also be open to workers in the Department of Zoology who are not members of the University and to such other persons as have obtained the permission of the Head of the Department.

Fund. **3.** The interest on the Fund bequeathed by the late Professor Newton shall be placed at the disposal of a Committee, consisting of the Head of the Department of Zoology, the Director of the Museum of Zoology, and the Strickland Curator, for keeping up and adding to the Newton Library.

Sub-departments.

SUB-DEPARTMENTS

GENERAL

Duties of Directors. **1.** The duties and responsibilities of the Director of a Sub-department shall be as follows:

(*a*) In all administrative and financial matters the Director shall be responsible to the Head of the Department.

(*b*) Within the first fortnight of the Easter Term the Director shall submit to the Head of the Department an estimate of the expenditure required in the ensuing financial year in his or her branch of the subject. After the estimate has been considered by the Head of the Department and the Finance Committee of the Council the Director shall have authority to expend sums not in excess of the amounts approved. All accounts shall be paid by the Head of the Department or by a person nominated by the Head under Statute A V 17, and all payments accounted for through the Departmental Account. A statement of the income and expenditure of each Sub-department shall be submitted at the end of each financial year to the General Board. Sub-departments.

(*c*) In each Sub-department those departmental demonstrators, assistants in research, and laboratory attendants whose stipends and wages are covered by the aforesaid estimates shall be recommended for appointment by the Director but their appointment shall rest with the Head of the Department.

(*d*) In each academical year the Director shall recommend to the Head of the Department the teaching programme to be given in his or her branch of the subject, for approval and transmission to the Faculty Board concerned.

(*e*) The Director shall be responsible to the Head of the Department for the direction of research in the Sub-department.

2. There shall be Sub-departments of the several Departments, as specified in Regulation 4.

3. Subject to the provisions of Regulation 4, the Director of each Sub-department shall be appointed by the General Board, on the recommendation of the relevant Faculty Board or other authority, for a period not exceeding five years at a time.

4. The Directors of the several Sub-departments shall be as follows: Directors.

Department	*Sub-department*
Geography	Scott Polar Research Institute The Director of the Scott Polar Research Institute.
Pure Mathematics and Mathematical Statistics	Statistical Laboratory A person appointed in accordance with Regulation 3.
Plant Sciences	Botanic Garden The Director of the Botanic Garden.
Zoology	Animal Behaviour A person appointed in accordance with Regulation 3.

5. During any period of absence from duty of the Director of a Sub-department, or during any period when there is a vacancy in an office whose holder is *ex officio* Director of a Sub-department, the General Board on the recommendation of the relevant Faculty Board or other authority shall have discretion to appoint a person to be Acting Director of that Sub-department. A person so appointed shall be recognized as Director of the Sub-department for all purposes. Acting Directors.

BOTANIC GARDEN

Botanic Garden.

Amended by Notices (Reporter*, 2013–14, pp. 9 and 619*)

1. The Botanic Garden shall be a Sub-department of the Department of Plant Sciences, and the Director of the Botanic Garden shall be the Director of that Sub-department. Sub-department.

2. There shall be a Syndicate called the Botanic Garden Syndicate, which, subject to the condition that no one shall be a member of the Syndicate who is not a member of the University, shall consist of: Syndicate.

(*a*) the Vice-Chancellor (or a duly appointed deputy) as Chair;

(*b*) the Head of the Department of Plant Sciences;

(*c*) eight members of the Senate, two appointed by the Council, two by the Faculty Board of Biology, and four by the General Board;

(*d*) not more than four persons co-opted by the Syndicate, provided that it shall not be obligatory for the Syndicate to co-opt any person or persons.

Members in classes (*c*) and (*d*) shall be appointed or co-opted in the Michaelmas Term to serve for four years from 1 January following their appointment or co-optation. The Director of the Botanic Garden shall act as Secretary to the Syndicate.

3. Six members of the Syndicate shall form a quorum. Quorum.

Botanic Garden.

Duties of Syndicate.

4. The duties of the Syndicate shall be:

(*a*) to determine the general policy of the Garden and to supervise its finances;

(*b*) to exercise a general supervision over the grounds, buildings, and collections;

(*c*) to advise the Director in matters relating to the amenities of the Garden;

(*d*) to inspect the Garden and its premises from time to time;

Annual Report.

(*e*) to make an Annual Report to the General Board on the condition of the Garden and its educational and research activities;

Rules of admission.

(*f*) subject to the provisions of Regulation 10, to make rules of admission to the Garden and to amend such rules from time to time as they may think fit.

Appointment of Director.

5. Except as may be otherwise provided by Statute or by Ordinances relating to a particular University office in the Department of Plant Sciences, appointments and reappointments to the University office[1] of Director of the Botanic Garden shall be made by the General Board, on the advice of a committee specially constituted for the particular occasion.

Duties of Director.

6. The duties of the Director shall include:

(*a*) the care of the Garden;

(*b*) the maintenance of the collections;

(*c*) provision for teaching and research;

(*d*) such teaching duties as the Faculty Board of Biology, in consultation with the Botanic Garden Syndicate, may consider desirable having regard to the Director's duties in the Garden.

The Director shall be responsible to, and shall act as executive officer of, the Botanic Garden Syndicate for matters connected with the general policy of the Garden and the maintenance of its amenities. The Director shall be an additional member of the Appointments Committee for any office in the Department of Plant Sciences the duties of which the General Board determine also concern the Garden.

Residence of Director.

7. The Director shall be resident in the University during Full Term and, subject to the proviso that the Syndicate shall have power to modify this requirement in any year, during not less than six weeks of the Long Vacation. The Director shall not be absent for more than two nights in any week during which he or she is required to reside without obtaining the permission of the Syndicate beforehand, if possible, or asking their approval upon return.

Fund.

8. The Fund of the Botanic Garden shall be a separate part of the Fund of the Department of Plant Sciences in the accounts of the Department.

Curator.

9. There shall be a University office of Curator of the Botanic Garden, the holder of which shall report to the Director of the Botanic Garden. Appointments and reappointments to the office shall be made by an Appointments Committee appointed by the Head of the Department of Plant Sciences, provided that the Appointments Committee shall include the Director of the Botanic Garden and a person appointed by the Botanic Garden Syndicate. The duties of the Curator shall be determined by the Syndicate and shall include assisting the Director in her or his duties under Regulation 6 above.

Hours of opening.

10. The Botanic Garden shall be open for not less than six hours on each weekday, except that on Christmas Day, Boxing Day, and on such other days as may appear necessary to the Syndicate, the Garden shall be closed.

Admission to the University Botanic Garden

Amended by Notice (Reporter, *2013–14, p. 250*)

Cambridge University Botanic Garden is private property. Visitors are welcome in accordance with the following rules made by the Botanic Garden Syndicate.

Rules of Admission

1. The Garden is open every day throughout the year except for the Christmas holiday period. There are two entrances, one in Bateman Street and one in Hills Road.

Times of opening and closing:

January, November, and December	10 a.m. – 4 p.m.
February, March, and October	10 a.m. – 5 p.m.
April–September	10 a.m. – 6 p.m.

[1] This office is an office specified in the Schedules to Special Ordinances C (i) 1 and C (vii) 1.

The Glasshouses and Cafe close half an hour before Garden closing time. The Botanic Garden Shop closes fifteen minutes before the Garden closing time. From time to time, parts of the Garden, including the Glasshouses, may be closed to the public for maintenance. The latest admission time is half an hour before the Garden closing time. Botanic Garden.

2. *Admission Charges*

A charge is made for admission. The charge for admission is determined by the Syndicate from time to time.

Language schools wishing to visit the Botanic Garden must book as a group visit at least a week in advance, through the Administration Office, and must complete the necessary documentation. They will be guided to suitable resources for use during their visit, for which a charge also will be made.

Waiving of admission charge

(i) General visits – No admission charge is made for the following categories of visitor:

- companions of disabled persons without whose assistance the disabled visitor would be unable to gain access to the Garden;
- all undergraduate and current graduate students of the University of Cambridge upon production of a valid University Card;
- children sixteen years and under visiting with family or friends (i.e. in a non-educational capacity) providing they are accompanied and closely supervised at all times by an adult;
- Friends and Corporate Friends of the Botanic Garden upon production of a valid Friends membership card
- visits by groups approved by the Botanic Garden as being 'therapeutic'.

(ii) Educational visits – Please note that charges are made for all Assisted Educational Visits.

No admission charge is made for the following groups providing the visit is pre-booked well in advance through the Education Office and the necessary documentation completed:

- groups from nurseries, home-schools, and colleges following the UK Department for Education's National Strategies or pursuing a UK curriculum qualification (e.g. GCSE, Baccalaureate, A Level);
- groups from further and higher educational institutions, horticulture colleges, and from organizations providing services for special needs persons, provided that the visit is approved as 'educational' by the Botanic Garden's Education Department.

All persons working in the Department of Plant Sciences, the Sainsbury Laboratory Cambridge University, and the Botanic Garden may apply to the Director for a card permitting free admission. An admission card is not transferable.

Bona fide researchers wishing to use the Garden or its facilities in connection with their work must contact the Director for permission to do so.

3. Cycles, including children's bicycles, tricycles, and scooters, must be left in the parking spaces provided for them near the entrances.

4. Children aged sixteen years and under must be accompanied by an adult at all times. Children are allowed on the Limestone Rock Garden or on the British Wild Plants area only under the close supervision of an adult.

5. No games, sports training, or jogging are allowed.

6. No radios or sound reproduction equipment, or musical instruments, may be played in the Garden by visitors.

7. A permit is required for commercial photography. Application should be made to the Administrator. A charge will normally be made for commercial photography.

8. Refreshments brought into the Garden by visitors may not be consumed in the cafe area.

9. Dogs are not admitted except guide dogs for the blind, hearing dogs for the deaf or assistance dogs.

10. Smoking is not allowed in any of the Garden's buildings.

11. Visitors may not handle or gather plant material unless permission has been obtained from the Director.

12. All groups intending to visit the Garden must book their visit at least a week in advance.

13. The Director, Curator or staff authorized by them shall exclude from the Garden any person who is considered to be guilty of misconduct.

14. The Director, Curator or staff authorized by them reserve the right to refuse admission.

Cory Fund

1. There shall be established a Cory Fund, into which shall be paid the sums received by the University under the will of Reginald Radcliffe Cory, of Trinity College, which provides that his bequest shall be used for the general interests of the Botanic Garden. Fund.

2. The Managers of the Fund shall be Managers.

(*a*) the Head of the Department of Plant Sciences as Chair, and the Director of the Finance Division (or a deputy);

(*b*) four members of the Senate appointed in the Michaelmas Term, two by the Council and two by the Faculty Board of Biology, to serve for four years from 1 January following their appointment.

3. The Director of the Botanic Garden shall act as Secretary to the Managers. Secretary.

Botanic Garden.

Annual and other Reports.

4. The Managers shall report to the General Board as occasion arises, and at least once in each academical year.

Polar Research.

Scott Polar Research Institute

Management

1. The Scott Polar Research Institute shall be a Sub-department of the Department of Geography.

2. The Institute, including its Museum and Archives, shall be under the general control of a Committee of Management which shall consist of:

(*a*) the Chair of the Council of the School of the Physical Sciences, who shall be Chair of the Committee;

(*b*) the Director of the Institute, who shall be Secretary of the Committee;

(*c*) the Head of the Department of Geography;

(*d*) two persons appointed by the Council of the School of the Physical Sciences;

(*e*) two persons appointed by the General Board after consultation with the Councils of the Schools of the Biological Sciences, the Humanities and Social Sciences, and Technology;

(*f*) not more than two persons co-opted by the Committee, provided that it shall not be obligatory for the Committee to co-opt any person or persons.

Members in classes (*d*) and (*e*) shall be appointed in the Michaelmas Term to serve for four years from 1 January following their appointment. Members in class (*f*) shall serve until 31 December of the year in which they are co-opted or of the following year, as the Committee shall determine at the time of their co-optation.

Meetings and quorum.

3. The Committee of Management shall meet at least once in each academical year. Five members of the Committee shall constitute a quorum.

4. Subject to the powers of the Council, the General Board, and the Faculty Board of Earth Sciences and Geography, the duties of the Committee shall be:

(*a*) to promote teaching and research in polar studies;

(*b*) to co-operate with outside bodies in the encouragement of research in polar studies;

(*c*) to assess the Institute's needs in respect of staffing and resources and report these to the Director;

(*d*) to make such reports to the Council of the School of the Physical Sciences and the General Board as those bodies may require.

Advisory Committee.

5. There shall be an Advisory Committee for the Institute, which shall consist of:

(*a*) one person appointed by the General Board on the nomination of the Council of the School of the Physical Sciences, who shall be Chair of the Committee;

(*b*) the Director of the Scott Polar Research Institute, who shall be Secretary of the Committee;

(*c*) the Director of the British Antarctic Survey;

(*d*) the Hydrographer of the Navy;

(*e*) the Head of the Polar Regions Section, Foreign and Commonwealth Office;

(*f*) the High Commissioner for Canada in the United Kingdom or a person appointed by the High Commissioner;

(*g*) two persons representative of industry appointed by the General Board on the nomination of the Committee of Management;

(*h*) one person appointed by the Royal Society;

(*i*) one person appointed by the Royal Geographical Society;

(*j*) not more than two persons co-opted by the Committee, provided that it shall not be obligatory for the Committee to co-opt any person or persons.

Members of the Committee in classes (*g*)–(*i*) shall be appointed in the Michaelmas Term to serve for four years from 1 January following their appointment. Members in class (*j*) shall serve until 31 December of the year in which they are co-opted or of the following year, as the Committee shall determine at the time of their co-optation.

6. The Advisory Committee shall meet not less than once in each academical year.

7. The duties of the Advisory Committee shall be to advise the Director of the Institute as to the most advantageous lines of education and research, and to promote co-operation with other bodies concerned with polar research.

Staff of the Institute

Polar Research.

1. There shall be a University office of Director of the Institute, which shall be held concurrently with another University office. Director.

2. The Director shall be appointed by the General Board on the recommendation of the Head of the Department of Geography and the Council of the School of the Physical Sciences, and shall be eligible for reappointment. Appointments and reappointments to the office of Director shall be for such periods not exceeding five years at a time as the General Board may determine on the recommendation of the Head of the Department of Geography and the Council of the School.

3. Under the general control of the Committee of Management, the Director shall be responsible for the direction of polar studies in the Institute and their encouragement generally in the University.

4. The Director shall conform to such conditions of residence as may be determined by the General Board after consultation with the Committee of Management.

Scott Polar Research Institute Endowment Funds

Scott Polar Research Institute Endowment Fund I

1. The sums received from the Captain Scott Memorial Polar Research Trust, the Pilgrim Trust, and the British Museum shall form a fund to be called the Scott Polar Research Institute Endowment Fund I. Fund.

2. The purpose of the Fund shall be to support the activities of the Scott Polar Research Institute. Purpose.

3. The Fund shall be administered by the Head of the Department of Geography and the Director of the Scott Polar Research Institute.

4. Any unspent income in a financial year may be added to the capital of the Fund, or accumulated for use as income in a future year, at the discretion of the administrators. Unexpended income.

Scott Polar Research Institute Endowment Fund II

1. The sums received as a result of the Scott Polar Research Institute Appeal shall form a fund to be called the Scott Polar Research Institute Endowment Fund II. Fund.

2. The income of the Fund shall be used to support the activities of the Library, Archives, and the Museum of the Scott Polar Research Institute. The first charge on the income of the Fund shall be the stipend, the national insurance and pension contributions, and associated indirect costs of staff appointed to develop the work of the Library, Archives, and Museum. Purpose.

3. The Fund shall be administered by a Board of Managers who shall be: Managers.

(*a*) The Director of the Scott Polar Research Institute as Chair;

(*b*) The Librarian of the Scott Polar Research Institute;

(*c*) The Head of the School of the Physical Sciences.

4. Any unspent income in a financial year shall either be added to the capital of the Fund, or accumulated for use as income in a future year, at the discretion of the Managers. Unexpended income.

OTHER INSTITUTIONS UNDER THE SUPERVISION OF THE GENERAL BOARD

Centre for Research in the Arts, Social Sciences, and Humanities

CRASSH.

Amended by Notice (Reporter, *2013–14, p. 777*)

Constitution

The Centre for Research in the Arts, Social Sciences, and Humanities (CRASSH) shall be an institution independent of any Faculty or Department but under the supervision of the General Board, and shall be within the School of Arts and Humanities.

Management Committee

1. The management of the Centre shall be the responsibility of a Management Committee, which shall consist of: Management Committee.

(*a*) the Director;

CRASSH.

(*b*) the Heads of the Schools of Arts and Humanities and of the Humanities and Social Sciences;

(*c*) six people appointed by the General Board, of whom three shall be appointed on the recommendation of the Council of the School of Arts and Humanities and three on the recommendation of the Council of the School of the Humanities and Social Sciences, and of whom one shall be appointed Chair by the Management Committee;

(*d*) two people, not members of the constituent Schools, co-opted at the discretion of the Committee.

2. Members in class (*c*) shall be appointed in the Michaelmas Term to serve for four years from 1 January following their appointment. A co-opted member in class (*d*) shall serve until 31 December of the year in which he or she is co-opted or of the following year, as the Committee shall decide at the time of co-optation.

Secretary. **3.** The Director, or failing whom the Deputy Director, shall serve as Secretary of the Committee.

4. The Committee shall meet at least once each term.

Duties of the Committee. **5.** Subject to the powers of the Council and the General Board, the duties of the Committee shall be to:

(*a*) promote research in the fields of the arts, humanities, and social sciences and the publication of the results of such research;

(*b*) co-operate with individuals and bodies inside the University to encourage research in the arts, humanities, and social sciences;

(*c*) administer funds allocated to them for the purposes specified in (*a*) and (*b*) above;

(*d*) supervise the work of the staff of the Centre;

(*e*) prepare annual estimates for submission to the General Board;

(*f*) make an Annual Report to the General Board.

Staff of the Centre

Director. **1.** There shall be a University office of Director of the Centre, which may be held concurrently with another University office and shall be held on such terms and conditions as the General Board may from time to time determine.

2. The Director shall be appointed by the General Board on the recommendation of the Management Committee.

Duties. **3.** Under the general control of the Management Committee the Director shall be the administrative Head of the Centre, and shall be responsible, subject to the advice of the Policy Committee and the approval of the Management Committee, for the choice of topics for the Centre's programmes.

Deputy Director. **4.** There shall be a University office of Deputy Director of the Centre which may be held concurrently with another University office. If held concurrently with another University office, appointments and reappointments to the office shall be made by the Management Committee for periods of not more than five years at a time, provided that no person may hold the office for a total period exceeding six years.

Duties. **5.** The duties of the Deputy Director shall be to assist the Director in all matters connected with the work of the Centre and to serve as Secretary of the Management Committee.

Biomedical Support Services.

University Biomedical Support Services

Staff of the University Biomedical Support Services

1. There shall be the University offices of Director, Deputy Director, and Assistant Director of University Biomedical Support Services in the School of the Biological Sciences.

Appointments. **2.** Appointments and reappointments to the office of Director of University Biomedical Support Services shall be made by an Appointments Committee consisting of the following:

(*a*) the Vice-Chancellor (or a duly appointed deputy) as Chair;

(*b*) the Chairs of the Councils of the Schools of the Biological Sciences and Clinical Medicine;

(*c*) the Head of the Department of Veterinary Medicine;

(*d*) three persons appointed by the Council of the School of the Biological Sciences, one after consultation with the Council of the School of Clinical Medicine and one after consultation with the Medical Research Council;

Biomedical Support Services.

(*e*) two persons appointed by the General Board.

Members in classes (*d*) and (*e*) shall be appointed in the Michaelmas Term to serve for two years from 1 January following their appointment.

3. Appointments and reappointments to the offices of Deputy Director and Assistant Director of University Biomedical Support Services shall be made by the Appointments Committee for the Director of University Biomedical Support Services, with the Director as an additional member for this purpose.

4. Appointments to the offices of Deputy Director and Assistant Director shall be subject to the same provisions as appointments to the office of Director.

5. The duties of the Director of University Biomedical Support Services shall be as follows: Duties.

(*a*) to ensure that the duties assigned to the holder of the certificate of designation for the University under the Animals (Scientific Procedures) Act 1986 are satisfactorily discharged;

(*b*) to give advice about the care of laboratory animals throughout the University;

(*c*) to undertake such other duties as the Council of the School of the Biological Sciences may from time to time determine.

The Director shall be responsible to the Chair of the Council of the School of the Biological Sciences.

6. The duties of the Deputy Director and the Assistant Director of University Biomedical Support Services shall be as follows:

(*a*) to ensure that the duties assigned to them as the named veterinary surgeons for the University under the Animals (Scientific Procedures) Act 1986 are satisfactorily discharged;

(*b*) to assist the Director in giving advice about the care of laboratory animals;

(*c*) to undertake such other duties as the Council of the School of the Biological Sciences may from time to time determine.

7. The Director, the Deputy Director, and the Assistant Director shall conform to such conditions of residence as may be determined by the General Board, after consultation with the Council of the School of the Biological Sciences. Residence.

UNIVERSITY OF CAMBRIDGE INSTITUTE FOR SUSTAINABILITY LEADERSHIP

CISL.

Amended by Notice (Reporter, *2013–14, p. 447*)

1. The University of Cambridge Institute for Sustainability Leadership shall be an institution under the supervision of the General Board, and shall be within the School of Technology.

2. A Management Board for the University of Cambridge Institute for Sustainability Leadership shall be responsible for the management of the Institute. The Management Board shall make an Annual Report to the Council of the School of Technology. Annual Report.

3. The Management Board for the University of Cambridge Institute for Sustainability Leadership shall consist of: Management Board.

(*a*) a member of the Regent House, appointed by the General Board, as Chair;

(*b*) a member of the Council of the School of Technology appointed by the Council of the School of Technology;

(*c*) the Director of the Institute, *ex officio*, who shall be Secretary of the Board;

(*d*) not more than six members of the Regent House appointed by the General Board on the nomination of the Council of the School of Technology;

(*e*) not more than three persons co-opted by the Board, provided that it shall not be obligatory for the Board to co-opt any person or persons.

4. Members in class (*d*) shall be appointed in the Michaelmas Term to serve for two years next following their appointment. Members in class (*e*) shall serve for two years from 1 January next following their co-optation. Appointment of members in classes (*d*) and (*e*) shall be staggered such that half of the Board membership is appointed each year.

5. The Management Board shall have authority

(*a*) to approve the Institute's strategy and business plans, in line with the Institute's mission;

(*b*) to establish advisory bodies including persons who are not resident members of the University, representing interests and activities associated with industry, business, and government.

6. There shall be a quorum of five members of the Board for the award of qualifications and for the proposal of changes to the constitutional arrangements of the Institute and its Management Board. Quorum.

CISL. Director.

7. There shall be a University office of Director of the University of Cambridge Institute for Sustainability Leadership. The Director shall be responsible to the Management Board for the conduct of the Institute.

Appointments Committee.

8. There shall be an Appointments Committee for the Cambridge Institute for Sustainability Leadership constituted as follows:

(*a*) the Vice-Chancellor (or a duly appointed deputy) as Chair;
(*b*) the Chair of the Management Board;
(*c*) three members of the Management Board appointed by the Board;
(*d*) two persons appointed by the General Board;
(*e*) (except for the appointment of the Director) the Director of the Institute.

Members in classes (*c*) and (*d*) shall be appointed in the Michaelmas Term of each calendar year of which the number is even, to serve for the two calendar years next ensuing. A member in class (*c*) who ceases to be a member of the Board shall thereupon cease to be a member of the Appointments Committee.

Gurdon Institute.

WELLCOME TRUST/CANCER RESEARCH UK GURDON INSTITUTE

Constitution

The Wellcome Trust/Cancer Research UK Gurdon Institute shall be an institution independent of any Faculty or Department but under the supervision of the General Board, and shall be within the School of the Biological Sciences.

Management

Committee of Management.

1. The Institute shall be under the general control of a Committee of Management which shall consist of:

(*a*) the Director of the Institute;
(*b*) the Deputy Director of the Institute;
(*c*) the Head of the Cancer Research UK section of the Institute;
(*d*) the Head of the Wellcome Trust section of the Institute;
(*e*) one person appointed by the General Board after consultation with Cancer Research UK;
(*f*) two persons appointed by the General Board after consultation with the Wellcome Trust;
(*g*) two persons appointed by the General Board, one of whom shall be appointed Chair of the Committee by the Board;
(*h*) two persons appointed by the Faculty Board of Biology and one person appointed by the Faculty Board of Clinical Medicine;
(*i*) not more than one additional person co-opted at the discretion of the Committee.

2. Members in classes (*e*)–(*h*) shall be appointed in the Michaelmas Term to serve for four years from 1 January following their appointment. The co-opted member in class (*i*) shall serve until 31 December of the year in which he or she is co-opted or of the year next following, as the Committee shall determine at the time of the member's co-optation.

3. The Director of the Institute shall serve as Secretary of the Committee.

Duties.

4. Subject to the powers of the Council, the General Board, and the Faculty Boards concerned, the duties of the Committee shall be as follows:

(*a*) to promote research in the fields of cancer and developmental biology and the publication of the results of such research;
(*b*) to co-operate with the Wellcome Trust and Cancer Research UK and with other institutions within the University in the encouragement of research in the fields of cancer and developmental biology;
(*c*) to administer funds allocated to them for the purposes specified in (*a*) and (*b*) above;
(*d*) to prepare annual estimates for submission to the General Board;
(*e*) to make an Annual Report to the General Board, the Wellcome Trust, and Cancer Research UK.

Administrative Committee.

5. There shall be an Institute Administrative Committee consisting of the Director of the Institute, who shall be Chair of the Committee, and the other principal investigators. The Committee may co-opt additional members for such periods as the Committee shall determine. The Committee shall be responsible for the internal allocation of space within the Institute, for advising the Wellcome Trust and Cancer Research UK, as appropriate, on the selection of new principal investigators, and for advising the Director on other matters concerning the administration of the Institute. Gurdon Institute.

Staff of the Institute

1. There shall be a University office of Director of the Institute, which may be held concurrently with another University office.

2. The Director of the Institute shall be appointed by the General Board on the recommendation of the Committee of Management. Appointments and reappointments to the office of Director shall be for such periods not exceeding five years at a time as shall be determined by the Board on the recommendation of the Committee. Director.

3. Under the general control of the Committee of Management, and subject to the powers of the Institute Administrative Committee, the Director of the Institute shall be the administrative Head of the Institute.

4. The duties of the Director of the Institute shall be determined by the Committee of Management, subject to the approval of the General Board. Duties.

5. The Director of the Institute shall conform to such conditions of residence as may be determined by the Committee of Management, subject to the approval of the General Board. Residence.

6. The Director of the Institute shall designate a member of the staff of the Institute as Deputy Director to serve for a period of one year at a time. The duties of the Deputy Director shall be determined by the Director. Deputy Director.

Visiting Fellowships

1. In order to enable scholars from outside Cambridge to take part in and contribute to the work of the Institute there shall be Visiting Fellowships for persons who have made or are making important contributions to research in the fields of cancer or developmental biology, or who are pursuing advanced work in either of these subjects.

2. Appointments and reappointments to Visiting Fellowships shall be made by the Director of the Institute for periods not exceeding three years at a time.

3. Visiting Fellows shall not hold any University office during the tenure of their Fellowships.

4. The stipend, if any, of a Visiting Fellow shall be determined by the Director of the Institute in consultation with the relevant sponsoring body and subject to the approval of the General Board on the occasion of each appointment or reappointment.

5. Subject to the approval of the General Board the Committee of Management may make grants to Visiting Fellows to meet travelling or other expenses incurred in connection with their Fellowships.

UNIVERSITY COMPUTING SERVICE

Rescinded by Grace 1 of 22 May 2013

INSTITUTE OF CONTINUING EDUCATION

Continuing Education.

1. There shall be an Institute of Continuing Education, which shall be an institution under the supervision of the General Board. There shall be a Strategic Committee for the Institute of Continuing Education which shall consist of: Strategic Committee.

(*a*) a member of the Regent House, appointed by the General Board, as Chair;

(*b*) six members appointed by the General Board on the nomination of the Councils of the Schools, to include a representative of each School;

(*c*) the Director of Continuing Education;

(*d*) three members of the academic staff of the Institute, elected in the Michaelmas Term by such staff to serve for three years from 1 January following their election;

(*e*) not more than four persons co-opted by the Committee, provided that it shall not be obligatory for the Committee to co-opt any person or persons.

Except as otherwise provided, members of the Committee shall be appointed in the Michaelmas Term to serve for four years from 1 January following their appointment. The Director of Continuing Education, or a University officer designated by the Director, shall be Secretary of the Committee.

Continuing Education.

Director of the Institute.

2. There shall be the University office of Director of Continuing Education. Appointments and reappointments to the office of Director shall be made by the General Board, on the advice of a committee specially constituted for the particular occasion. The duties of the Director shall be determined by the General Board on the advice of the Strategic Committee.

Other officers of the Institute.

3. There shall be such number of University offices of Senior Assistant Secretary, Assistant Secretary, and Junior Assistant Secretary (in Grades I, II, and III) as may be determined from time to time by the General Board on the recommendation of the Strategic Committee on the advice of the Director of Continuing Education. Appointments and reappointments to an office of Senior Assistant Secretary or Assistant Secretary or Junior Assistant Secretary shall be made in accordance with arrangements agreed by the General Board from time to time. The duties of each office shall be determined by the Strategic Committee on the advice of the Director of Continuing Education.

4. The office of Director may be held concurrently with another University office.

5. There shall be such number of University offices of Senior Staff Tutor and Tutor as may be determined from time to time by the General Board on the recommendation of the Strategic Committee on the advice of the Director of Continuing Education. The duties of the offices shall be determined by the Strategic Committee on the advice of the Director.

Appointments.

6. Appointments and reappointments to an office of University Lecturer or University Senior Lecturer or Senior Staff Tutor or Tutor in the Institute, shall be made by an Appointments Committee for the Institute constituted in accordance with Special Ordinance C (x) 2.

7. The Strategic Committee shall have the authority to make recommendations to the General Board for granting the title of Affiliated Lecturer to persons who make a substantial contribution to the Institute's teaching programmes.

8. The Strategic Committee may designate, for a period not exceeding five years at a time, one of the officers in the Institute as Deputy Director.

Madingley Hall.

9. The Strategic Committee shall be responsible to the General Board for the government of Madingley Hall. The General Board, on the advice of the Strategic Committee, shall designate a University officer as Warden of the Hall and may establish a committee for management of the Hall. The Warden shall be the principal officer in the Hall responsible under the direction of the Strategic Committee for the administration of the Hall and for presenting the annual accounts of the Hall to the Strategic Committee.

Payment to Warden.

10. The Warden shall be entitled to receive, in addition to the stipend of her or his University office, a pensionable payment for responsibility as Warden at an annual rate determined by the General Board after consultation with the Strategic Committee.

Duties of the Strategic Committee.

11. The duties of the Strategic Committee shall be:

(*a*) to determine academic policy for the Institute and the Hall and to report accordingly to the General Board;

(*b*) to make an annual report to the General Board;

(*c*) to act as an administering body in accordance with the Ordinances for the Master of Studies Degree;

(*d*) to act as an administering body in accordance with the Ordinances for Diplomas and Certificates open to non-members of the University;

(*e*) to co-operate with other University institutions and outside bodies in the development of continuing education;

(*f*) to establish such advisory bodies, representing interests and activities associated with continuing education, as it sees fit;

(*g*) to receive reports from the Director of the Institute and the Warden of the Hall on the deployment of funds allocated for the purposes set out in (*a*)–(*f*) above;

(*h*) to appoint managers, on the advice of the Director, to administer the following funds;

(i) the Churton Collins Prize Fund,[1]

(ii) the Hargood Memorial Fund,[1]

(iii) the James Stuart Endowment Fund.[1]

[1] The relevant regulations were last published in *Ordinances*, 1946, p. 22.

Centre for Applied Research in Educational Technologies

CARET.

1. The Centre for Applied Research in Educational Technologies shall be an institution independent of any Faculty or Department, within the University Library.

2. The Centre shall be under the general control of a Committee of Management, which shall consist of: Committee of Management.

(*a*) a member of the Regent House appointed by the Library Syndicate, who shall be Chair;
(*b*) the University Librarian;
(*c*) the Director of the University Computing Service *ex officio*;
(*d*) the Director of Continuing Education *ex officio*;
(*e*) one member of the Regent House appointed by each of the Councils of the Schools;
(*f*) not more than two members of the Regent House co-opted by the Committee.

Members in classes (*a*) and (*e*) shall be appointed in the Michaelmas Term to serve for four years from 1 January following their appointment. Members in class (*f*) shall be co-opted in the Michaelmas Term to serve for one year from 1 January following their co-optation.

3. Five members of the Committee shall form a quorum.

4. Subject to the powers of the Council, the General Board, and the Library Syndicate, the duties of the Committee of Management shall be: Duties.

(*a*) to determine the general policy of the Centre;
(*b*) to advise the Director on matters arising from the work of the Centre;
(*c*) to advise the Library Syndicate on matters relating to the activity of the Centre;
(*d*) to make an annual report to the Library Syndicate on matters related to the Centre;
(*e*) to receive reports of the Centre's activities.

Staff of the Centre

1. There shall be a University office of Director of the Centre, which shall be held on such terms and conditions as the General Board may from time to time determine after consultation with the Library Syndicate. Director.

2. The Director shall be the administrative Head of the Centre for Applied Research in Educational Technologies, and shall carry out such duties as may be determined by the General Board after consultation with the Library Syndicate. Duties.

3. There shall be such number of University offices of Assistant Director of the Centre as the General Board may from time to time determine, on the recommendation of the Library Syndicate. The duties of the Assistant Directors shall be to assist the Director in all matters connected with the work of the Centre. Assistant Director.

4. During any absence of the Director, or when the office of Director is vacant, the General Board may appoint an Acting Director on such terms and conditions as the Board may determine.

Fitzwilliam Museum

Fitzwilliam Museum.

Constitution

The Fitzwilliam Museum shall be an institution independent of any Faculty or Department but under the supervision of the General Board. It shall be under the general control of the Fitzwilliam Museum Syndicate.

Fitzwilliam Museum Syndicate

1. The Fitzwilliam Museum Syndicate shall consist of: Syndicate.

(*a*) the Vice-Chancellor (or a duly appointed deputy) as Chair;
(*b*) eight persons appointed by the General Board;
(*c*) the Head of the Department of History of Art;
(*d*) not more than four persons co-opted by the Syndicate, provided that it shall not be obligatory for the Syndicate to co-opt any person or persons.

Fitzwilliam Museum.

Members in class (*b*) shall be appointed in the Michaelmas Term to serve for four years from 1 January following their appointment. Co-opted members shall serve for one year from 1 January following their co-optation.

2. All meetings of the Syndicate shall be summoned by the Vice-Chancellor, and there shall be at least four meetings each year.

Quorum.

3. No business shall be transacted at any meeting unless at least four members be present, but in cases of emergency a smaller number may act, provided they be unanimous.

Duties.

4. It shall be the duty of the Syndicate:

(*a*) to supervise the management of the Museum;

(*b*) to make such arrangements as they may from time to time think desirable for the delivery of lectures or the holding of classes, meetings, exhibitions (with or without charge for admission as the Syndicate shall think fit), or other assemblies in the Museum;

(*c*) to appoint and dismiss the assistant staff subject to the regulations for employment by the University;

(*d*) to control the expenditure of all moneys devoted to the purposes of the Museum, and to present an annual statement of accounts to the Finance Committee of the Council;

(*e*) to decide, after consultation with the Director, when gifts or bequests are offered to the University for the Museum, or objects offered to the Museum for purchase, whether such offers shall be accepted or declined, or whether the question shall be referred to the University and on such other matters as the General Board may require;

(*f*) to report to the University at any time on any question on which they think the University ought to be consulted;

Annual Report.

(*g*) to make an Annual Report to the General Board upon any matters concerning the collections and the state of the buildings which in their opinion should be brought to the notice of the University;

(*h*) to be responsible in accordance with the regulations for the Hamilton Kerr Institute for the examination and certification of persons training in the Hamilton Kerr Institute.

Staff of the Fitzwilliam Museum

1. The staff of the Fitzwilliam Museum shall consist of the Director and Marlay Curator, the Assistant Directors, the Senior Keepers, the Keepers, the Senior Assistant Keepers, the Assistant Keepers, the Museum Assistants in Research, and the University assistants. The Fitzwilliam Museum Syndicate shall designate one of the Senior Keepers or Keepers as Librarian. The total number of University offices of Assistant Director, Senior Keeper, Keeper, Senior Assistant Keeper, Assistant Keeper, and Museum Assistant in Research and the number of offices in each of those categories shall be determined from time to time by the General Board. The number of University assistants shall be determined from time to time in accordance with the regulations for employment by the University.

Election of Director.

2. The Director shall be elected by a Board of Electors consisting of

(*a*) the Vice-Chancellor (or a duly appointed deputy);

(*b*) three persons appointed by the General Board of whom at least one shall be a person who at the time of his or her appointment is not resident in the University or officially connected with it;

(*c*) four persons appointed by the Fitzwilliam Museum Syndicate of whom three shall be persons who at the time of their appointment are members of that Syndicate, and the fourth shall be a person who at the time of his or her appointment is the Director of one of the following: the British Museum, the National Gallery, the Victoria and Albert Museum, the Wallace Collection, the Ashmolean Museum;

(*d*) one person appointed by the Faculty Board of Architecture and History of Art.

Members in classes (*b*)–(*d*) shall be appointed in the Michaelmas Term of each calendar year of which the number is even to serve for the four calendar years next ensuing.

The Registrary, or a deputy appointed by the Registrary, shall act as Secretary to the Board of Electors.

3. If an Elector is or becomes a candidate for the Directorship he or she shall be thereby disqualified from acting in the matter of that election and the remaining Electors shall have power to act. Fitzwilliam Museum.

4. If an appointment to the Board of Electors is made after the Electors have first met to consider a vacancy in the Directorship, the Elector so appointed shall not have any vote in the election of the Director, but his or her predecessor, if not a candidate for the Directorship, shall retain the right to vote in that election.

5. (*a*) When the Director is due under the Statutes and Ordinances to retire, the Vice-Chancellor shall report the fact to the General Board not later than the division of the Michaelmas Term in the academical year next before the year at the end of which the Director is due to retire.

(*b*) When the Vice-Chancellor knows that a vacancy has occurred or will occur in the Directorship otherwise than by the holder's becoming due under the Statutes and Ordinances to retire, he or she shall report the fact to the General Board at their next meeting.

6. Not later than the sixtieth day after the report under Regulation 5 of a vacancy or an expected vacancy in the Directorship, the Vice-Chancellor shall publish a Notice inviting applications to fill the vacancy; provided that the General Board shall have power to suspend the publication of such a Notice for any period not exceeding one year.

7. The Electors shall have power to act notwithstanding one or more vacancies in their number and shall have power to adjourn and generally to regulate their own procedure, provided that:

(*a*) no election shall be made earlier than the day following that on which the qualifications of the candidates have been considered in the first instance at a meeting of the Electors;

(*b*) no election shall be made unless two-thirds at least of the Electors (exclusive of any Elector disqualified by being a candidate) are present at the time of voting and a majority of those present vote in favour.

8. The Electors shall have power to enquire whether any person or persons other than those who have submitted applications would accept the office if offered, and to offer the office to a person who has not submitted an application, provided that such a person's qualifications have been considered at two meetings held on different days.

9. If, at the end of two years from the date of publication under Regulation 6 of the Notice inviting applications for the Directorship, the Electors have been unable to make an election, the Director shall be appointed by the Chancellor, or, if the office of Chancellor is vacant, by the High Steward.

10. The duties of the Director shall be: Duties of Director.

(*a*) to take charge of the collections and the library, to keep a register of all accessions to the collections, and to take measures under the sanction of the Syndicate that they be properly protected, kept in order, and exhibited;

(*b*) to exercise a general superintendence over the staff of the Museum, and to see that all rules laid down by the Syndicate are carried out;

(*c*) to undertake and superintend, under the sanction of the Syndicate, and with such assistance as they may think necessary, the formation of inventories and catalogues of the collections;

(*d*) to give, so far as is consistent with the performance of the above duties, assistance and guidance to persons visiting the Museum for purposes of study;

(*e*) to make inquiries and give advice respecting acquisitions for the Museum by purchase, donation, or bequest.

11. The Director shall be a member of the Faculty of Architecture and History of Art.

12. The Director shall be resident in the University during term and for four weeks in the Long Vacation, and shall normally be in attendance during Museum office hours. The Director shall not be absent for more than two nights in any week during Full Term without obtaining the permission of the Chair of the Syndicate. The Director shall nominate to the Syndicate a member of the staff of the Museum to act for the time being as his or her deputy during any period of absence from duty in circumstances not provided for by Statutes or Ordinance. Residence of the Director.

13. At the first meeting of the Syndicate in the Michaelmas Term of each year the Director shall make a report to the Syndicate on his or her residence and attendance during the preceding year. The report shall indicate the number of weeks during which the Director was resident in the University, and shall state whether he or she complied with the provisions of Regulation 12 concerning attendance at the Museum.

14. The Assistant Directors, the Senior Keepers, the Keepers, the Senior Assistant Keepers, the Assistant Keepers, and the Museum Assistants in Research (including the Librarian) shall give such Duties of other members of the staff.

Fitzwilliam Museum.

assistance in the work of the Museum as the Director may require. They shall be expected to attend (during each weekday) at such times as may be determined by the Syndicate.

Appointments Committee.

15. Appointments and reappointments to an office of Assistant Director, of Senior Keeper, of Keeper, of Senior Assistant Keeper, of Assistant Keeper, and of Museum Assistant in Research shall be made by an Appointments Committee consisting of the following persons:

(*a*) the Vice-Chancellor (or a duly appointed deputy) as Chair;
(*b*) the Chair of the Fitzwilliam Museum Syndicate;
(*c*) the Director of the Fitzwilliam Museum;
(*d*) two members of the Fitzwilliam Museum Syndicate appointed by the Syndicate;
(*e*) two persons appointed by the General Board.

Special Ordinance C (x) 4 shall apply to the Committee as if it were an Appointments Committee for a Faculty.

A Museum Assistant in Research shall not engage in teaching other than teaching given on behalf of the University or a College or Colleges. The amount of teaching given by a Museum Assistant in Research on behalf of a College or Colleges shall not exceed six hours a week.

Admission to the Fitzwilliam Museum

Galleries.

1. The galleries shall, unless the General Board on the recommendation of the Fitzwilliam Museum Syndicate determine otherwise, be open to the public on each weekday (with the exception of Mondays other than Bank Holidays and such other exceptions as are mentioned hereafter in these regulations) between the hours of 10 a.m. and 5 p.m., and on Sundays between noon and 5 p.m.

Exclusion.

2. The Syndicate shall have full authority to direct the exclusion of those persons whose admission appears to be undesirable.

Days of closing.

3. The Museum shall be closed on the following days: 24, 25, 26, and 31 December and 1 January and such other days as may appear necessary to the Syndicate.

Library and special collections.

4. The Syndicate shall from time to time make such rules as they think fit for the use of the library and for the inspection and study of the reserve and special collections.

Hamilton Kerr Institute

Purpose.

1. The Hamilton Kerr Institute shall be accommodated in the Mill House, Whittlesford, and shall be devoted to the conservation, and training in the conservation, of paintings.

2. The Institute shall be a Sub-department of the Fitzwilliam Museum.

3. There shall be the University office of Director of the Hamilton Kerr Institute and such number of University offices of Assistant to the Director of the Institute as the General Board shall from time to time determine.

Advisory Council.

4. There shall be an Advisory Council for the Hamilton Kerr Institute, whose duty it shall be to advise the Director of the Institute on the most advantageous lines of developing the work of the Institute, and to promote co-operation with other bodies concerned with the conservation of paintings. The Advisory Council shall consist of:

(*a*) the Chair of the Fitzwilliam Museum Syndicate, who shall be Chair of the Advisory Council;
(*b*) the Director of the Fitzwilliam Museum;
(*c*) two persons appointed by the General Board of the University;
(*d*) not less than four nor more than eight persons appointed by the Fitzwilliam Museum Syndicate, at least two of whom shall be Fellows of the International Institute for Conservation and at least one of whom shall be the holder of a University office in the Department of History of Art;
(*e*) not more than three persons co-opted by the Advisory Council, provided that it shall not be obligatory for the Council to co-opt any person or persons.

Members in classes (*c*) and (*d*) shall be appointed in the Michaelmas Term to serve for four years from 1 January next following their appointment. Members in class (*e*) shall serve until 31 December of the year in which they are co-opted, or of the following year, as the Council shall determine at the time of their co-optation.

The Advisory Council shall meet at least twice a year; five members shall constitute a quorum at any meeting. The Director of the Institute shall act as Secretary of the Council, and shall transmit a record of the Council's proceedings to the Fitzwilliam Museum Syndicate.

5. The holder of the office of Director of the Institute shall pursue study and research in the conservation of paintings, and shall supervise the work of the Institute under the general guidance of the Director of the Fitzwilliam Museum. **Fitzwilliam Museum.** Duties of Director.

6. The Director of the Institute shall be responsible in all administrative and financial matters to the Director of the Fitzwilliam Museum; shall submit to the Director of the Fitzwilliam Museum for approval by the General Board estimates of the expenditure of the Institute in the ensuing financial year; and shall recommend to the Director of the Fitzwilliam Museum for appointment such clerical and ancillary staff as are covered by those estimates and approved by the General Board.

7. Appointments and reappointments to the office of Director of the Institute shall be made by an Appointments Committee constituted for the purpose consisting of: Appointment and reappointment of Director.

(*a*) the Vice-Chancellor or a duly appointed deputy;
(*b*) the Director of the Fitzwilliam Museum;
(*c*) four persons nominated by the Fitzwilliam Museum Syndicate for appointment by the General Board;
(*d*) two persons appointed by the General Board.

One at least of the members in class (*c*) and one at least in class (*d*) shall be persons not in residence in the University or officially connected with it.

8. Appointments and reappointments to an office of Assistant to the Director of the Institute and to any other University office that may be established by Grace on the staff of the Institute shall be made by the Appointments Committee for the Fitzwilliam Museum, provided that for this purpose the Director of the Institute shall be an additional member of the Appointments Committee and that the Fitzwilliam Museum Syndicate may at their discretion appoint either one or two persons to serve as additional members of the Committee for a particular occasion. Appointments and reappointments to any other University office that may be established by Grace on the staff of the Institute shall, notwithstanding Regulation 15 for the staff of the Fitzwilliam Museum, be for such periods not exceeding five years at a time as the Committee shall determine. Staff of the Institute.

The duties of the holders of these offices shall be to assist the Director of the Institute in the prosecution of his or her duties.

9. Neither the Director nor any other University officer on the staff of the Institute shall be a Tutor, Assistant Tutor, Bursar, Assistant Bursar, or Steward of a College, nor shall they, without the permission of the General Board, give instruction on behalf of a College. Except as the General Board may otherwise determine, all fees received by the Director or any other University officer on the staff of the Institute for work or consultancy connected with the conservation of paintings shall be paid into the funds of the Institute. Restrictions.

10. The Director and any other University officer on the staff of the Institute shall be resident in the University during term and for four weeks in the Long Vacation. Residence.

11. The Fitzwilliam Museum Syndicate shall be empowered:

(*a*) to conduct and administer examinations of persons who are not members of the University but are undergoing training by the staff of the Institute, and for that purpose to fix fees, issue syllabuses, and appoint and pay examiners;
(*b*) to issue certificates and diplomas of the Institute to successful candidates.

HRH Prince Alwaleed Bin Talal Centre of Islamic Studies

Islamic Studies.

Management

1. The HRH Prince Alwaleed Bin Talal Centre of Islamic Studies shall be an institution under the supervision of the General Board and shall be under the general control of a Committee of Management which shall consist of: Committee of Management.

(*a*) the Chair of the Council of the School of Arts and Humanities who shall be Chair; Chair.
(*b*) a representative of the Department of Middle Eastern Studies;
(*c*) the Director of the Centre;
(*d*) no fewer than two other members appointed by the General Board including one on the recommendation of the Council of the School of the Humanities and Social Sciences and one on the recommendation of the Faculty Board of Asian and Middle Eastern Studies;
(*e*) up to three persons nominated by HRH Prince Alwaleed Bin Talal;

Islamic Studies.

(*f*) up to two additional persons co-opted at the discretion of the Committee, provided that it shall not be obligatory to co-opt any person.

2. Members in class (*d*) shall be appointed in the Michaelmas Term to serve from January following their appointment for two or four years as the General Board shall determine at their appointment.

3. Co-opted members in class (*f*) shall serve until 31 December of the year in which they are co-opted or of the following year as the Committee shall determine at the time of their co-optation.

Secretary. **4.** The Assistant Director of the Centre shall serve as Secretary of the Committee.

Duties. **5.** The duties of the Committee shall be as follows:

(*a*) to meet the aim of the Centre being to foster deeper understanding between the Muslim world and the West through the twin paths of high quality research and effective outreach;

(*b*) to meet the objectives of the Centre being:

(i) to create, on a self-sustaining basis, a world-class cadre of researchers at the postgraduate and postdoctoral levels by providing studentships and fellowships designed to feed into the next generation of academics as well as the public and private sectors;

(ii) to develop an energetic public outreach programme helping to ensure that public policy and debate is based on an informed understanding of Islam in today's societies;

(iii) to advance tolerance, mutual understanding, and cross-cultural dialogue between Islam and the West;

(iv) to act as an active partner with other national and international centres in promoting an informed understanding of Islam and Muslims in the contemporary world;

(v) to engage with Muslim organizations and members of the Muslim community in the United Kingdom and Europe;

(vi) to develop the activities of the Centre around the overarching theme of Islam in the Global Age and sub-themes of Islam in Europe and the United Kingdom, and Islam and the media, but so that the Centre should evolve over time (as approved by the General Board) to meet contemporary needs;

(*c*) in collaboration with the Faculty Boards concerned, to promote teaching in Islamic subjects, and to promote research in these subjects and the publication of the results of such research;

(*d*) to co-operate with outside bodies in the encouragement of teaching and research in Islamic subjects;

(*e*) to create programmes and communications accessible to the wider community which encourage informed discussion on contemporary issues in the study of Islamic subjects;

(*f*) to administer funds allocated to them for the purposes specified in (*a*) to (*e*) above;

(*g*) to manage the distribution of income from the HRH Prince Alwaleed Bin Talal Centre of Islamic Studies Fund between the activities of the Centre;

(*h*) to supervise the work of the staff of the Centre;

(*i*) to appoint at their discretion an advisory group comprising eminent persons who can assist in the development of the Centre and whose membership shall include representatives of HRH Prince Alwaleed Bin Talal.

6. The Committee of Management shall prepare annual estimates for submission to the General Board and shall submit written reports at least twice a year to HRH Prince Alwaleed Bin Talal.

7. The Committee shall have the right of reporting to the University.

Acting Director. **8.** During any period of absence from duty of the Director, the General Board on the recommendation of the Committee of Management shall have the discretion to appoint a person to be Acting Director. A person so appointed shall be recognized as Director of the Centre for all purposes.

Staff of the Centre

Director and Assistant Director. **9.** The Directorship and Assistant Directorship of the Centre shall each be held concurrently with a University office.

Tenure. **10.** The Director and Assistant Director shall be appointed by the General Board on the recommendation of the Committee of Management. The Director shall hold office for five years, and the Assistant Director shall hold office for four years. Each shall be eligible for reappointment.

Duties. **11.** Under the general control of the Committee of Management, the Director shall be the administrative Head of the Centre, and shall be responsible for the direction of Islamic studies in the Centre and their encouragement generally in the University.

Islamic Studies.

12. Appointments and reappointments to a University office in respect of the graduate staff of the Centre other than the offices of Director and Assistant Director shall be made by the Committee of Management but subject to the approval of the General Board. Appointments of graduate staff.

13. The duties of any graduate staff of the Centre other than the Director shall be determined by the Committee of Management, subject to approval by the General Board. Duties.

14. The Director and any other members of the graduate staff shall conform to such conditions of residence as may be determined by the Committee of Management with the approval of the General Board. Residence.

HRH Prince Alwaleed Bin Talal Visiting Fellowships

15. In order to enable scholars from outside Cambridge to take part in and contribute to the work of the HRH Prince Alwaleed Bin Talal Centre of Islamic Studies there shall be Visiting Fellowships for persons who are able to make important contributions to the objectives of the Centre. Purpose and definitions.

16. The maximum number of HRH Prince Alwaleed Bin Talal Visiting Fellowships that there may be in the Centre at any one time shall be determined by the Committee of Management of the Centre. Appointments and reappointments to Visiting Fellowships shall be made by the Committee of Management of the Centre for periods not exceeding one year at a time. Number, appointments, and tenure.

17. A Visiting Fellow shall be required under the general supervision of the Committee of Management to take part in the teaching and research programme of the Centre.

18. Visiting Fellows shall not hold any University office during the tenure of their Fellowships. A Visiting Fellow who is not a member of the University at the time of appointment shall be required to become a member as soon as is conveniently possible thereafter.

19. The stipend, if any, of a Visiting Fellow shall be determined by the Committee of Management with the approval of the General Board on the occasion of each appointment or reappointment.

20. Subject to the approval of the General Board the Committee of Management may make grants to Visiting Fellows to meet travelling or other expenses incurred in connection with their Fellowships.

HRH Prince Alwaleed Bin Talal Postdoctoral Fellowships

21. The Committee of Management shall decide upon the number of HRH Prince Alwaleed Bin Talal Postdoctoral Fellowships to be awarded each year always provided that at least one Fellowship is held in each year. Appointments to these Fellowships shall be made by the Committee of Management upon the recommendation of the Director of the HRH Prince Alwaleed Bin Talal Centre of Islamic Studies. Number and appointments.

22. The Fellowships shall be tenable for periods of up to five years. Tenure.

23. The annual stipend of a Fellow shall be within a range determined by the Committee of Management, to be approved from time to time by the General Board. Stipend.

24. Additional research support grants may also be awarded to HRH Prince Alwaleed Bin Talal Postdoctoral Fellows. Research support grants.

25. Subject to the approval of the General Board the Committee of Management may make grants to Postdoctoral Fellows to meet travelling or other expenses incurred in connection with their Fellowships.

HRH Prince Alwaleed Bin Talal Postgraduate Scholarships

26. The Committee of Management shall decide upon the number of HRH Prince Alwaleed Bin Talal Postgraduate Scholarships to be awarded each year, always provided that at least one Scholarship is held in each year. Number.

27. The Electors to an HRH Prince Alwaleed Bin Talal Scholarship shall be the Head of the Department of Middle Eastern Studies, the Director of the HRH Prince Alwaleed Bin Talal Centre of Islamic Studies, and the Assistant Director of the Centre provided that if the Director of the Centre and Head of the Department are the same person the Committee of Management shall appoint one other teaching officer in the Department of Middle Eastern Studies to serve for two years from 1 January following his or her appointment. Electors.

Islamic Studies. Who are eligible.

28. In order to be eligible for a Scholarship, a candidate must have been admitted, or be seeking admission, as a student studying towards the Ph.D. Degree in the field of Islamic studies, within the Department of Middle Eastern Studies.

Kettle's Yard.

KETTLE'S YARD COMMITTEE

1. Kettle's Yard shall be an institution independent of any Faculty or Department but under the supervision of the General Board. It shall be under the general control of the Kettle's Yard Committee.

Constitution.

2. The Kettle's Yard Committee shall consist of:

(*a*) the Vice-Chancellor (or a duly appointed deputy) as Chair;

(*b*) five members of the Senate appointed by the General Board in the Michaelmas Term to serve for five years from 1 January following their appointment, two being nominated by the Fitzwilliam Museum Syndicate and one by the Finance Committee of the Council;

(*c*) the Director of the Fitzwilliam Museum (or a deputy);

(*d*) the Chair of the Music Sub-committee;

(*e*) the Head of the Department of History of Art;

(*f*) one member of the University *in statu pupillari* appointed by the Council to serve for the academical year following that in which the appointment is made;

(*g*) not more than four persons co-opted by the Committee to serve until 31 December of the year in which they are co-opted or of the following year, as the Committee shall determine at the time of their co-optation.

Secretary.

3. The Secretary of the Committee shall be appointed by the Registrary.

Quorum.

4. Seven members of the Committee shall form a quorum, except when the Committee meets outside Full Term, when five members of the Committee shall form a quorum.

Music Sub-committee.

5. There shall be a Music Sub-committee, responsible to the Kettle's Yard Committee. The Sub-committee shall consist of:

(*a*) a Chair who shall be appointed by the Kettle's Yard Committee;

(*b*) one person appointed by the Eastern Arts Association;

(*c*) one member of the University *in statu pupillari* appointed by the Kettle's Yard Committee to serve for the academical year following that in which the appointment is made;

(*d*) not more than three persons co-opted by the Sub-committee in the Michaelmas Term to serve for two years from 1 January following their appointment.

Secretary of the Sub-committee.

6. The Secretary of the Kettle's Yard Committee shall act as secretary of the Music Sub-committee. There shall be a Music Secretary who may be paid an honorarium, the amount of which shall be approved by the Kettle's Yard Committee.

Honorary Curator.

7. An Honorary Curator of the Collection may be appointed by the members of the Kettle's Yard Committee in classes (*a*)–(*d*) and (*f*).

8. There shall be a University office of Director of Kettle's Yard and such number of University offices of Assistant to the Director as shall be determined from time to time by the General Board on the recommendation of the Kettle's Yard Committee. The Director shall be a member of the Faculty of Architecture and History of Art.

Appointments Committee.

9. Appointments and reappointments to the offices of Director and Assistant to the Director shall be made by an Appointments Committee consisting of:

(*a*) the Chair of the Kettle's Yard Committee as Chair;

(*b*) the Director of the Fitzwilliam Museum;

(*c*) two members appointed by the General Board;

(*d*) four members appointed by the Kettle's Yard Committee.

Members in classes (*c*) and (*d*) shall be appointed in the Michaelmas Term of each year of which the number is even, to serve for the two calendar years next ensuing.

10. The duties of the Director and the Assistants to the Director shall be determined by the Kettle's Yard Committee, subject to the approval of the General Board.

Purpose and duties of the Committee.

11. It shall be the main purpose of the Committee to ensure that the Kettle's Yard Collection is available not only to members of the University, especially those *in statu pupillari*, but also to the public, in such ways as to develop and improve the knowledge, understanding, enjoyment, and practice of the visual arts and to increase their general accessibility.

In particular the Committee shall have the following duties: Kettle's Yard.

(*a*) to supervise the maintenance and security of the Collection of paintings, bronzes, and other works of art at Kettle's Yard; to make such rules for admission to the Collection or for the loan of items from the Collection as may appear to them to be desirable; to arrange the programme of exhibitions to be held in the Exhibitions Gallery; and to make arrangements as they may from time to time think fit for holding meetings and other assemblies at Kettle's Yard;

(*b*) to administer the Kettle's Yard Fund and the Exhibitions Account;

(*c*) to decide whether to accept, decline, or refer to the General Board for decision, gifts, bequests, or objects offered for purchase, for the benefit of the Collection;

(*d*) to report to the General Board at any time on questions on which they think the General Board ought to be consulted;

(*e*) to report to the General Board annually in the Michaelmas Term on the condition of the Collection and the state of the buildings, and on the exhibitions, concerts, and other events held during the preceding academical year and on such other matters as the General Board may require;

(*f*) to consult with the Fitzwilliam Museum Syndicate from time to time regarding matters of mutual concern;

(*g*) to decide on the sale of any of the items in the Collection without impairing the general nature of the Collection, using the proceeds of any such sale for the benefit of the Collection.

12. The provisions of Special Ordinance A (vii) 5 concerning reserved business shall apply to the Kettle's Yard Committee and the Music Sub-committee as if these bodies were bodies constituted by Statute. Reserved business.

Language Centre

Language Centre.

The Language Centre shall be an institution independent of any Faculty or Department and within the School of Arts and Humanities.

Committee of Management

1. The Language Centre shall be under the general control of a Committee of Management, which shall consist of: Committee of Management.

(*a*) one person appointed by the General Board who shall be Chair, provided that the General Board shall have power to appoint as Chair a person who is already a member of the Committee in one of classes (*c*), (*d*), and (*f*);

(*b*) the Director of the Language Centre;

(*c*) two persons appointed by the Council of the School of Arts and Humanities; and five persons appointed by the General Board after consultation with the Council of the School of the Humanities and Social Sciences, the Council of the School of the Biological Sciences, the Council of the School of Clinical Medicine, the Council of the School of the Physical Sciences, and the Council of the School of Technology;

(*d*) one person appointed by the Senior Tutors' Committee;

(*e*) one member of the University *in statu pupillari*, appointed by Cambridge University Students Union;

(*f*) not more than two persons co-opted at the discretion of the Committee.

Members in classes (*a*), (*c*), and (*d*) shall be appointed in the Michaelmas Term to serve for four years from 1 January following their appointment. Members in class (*e*) shall be appointed in the Easter Term to serve for the academical year following their appointment. Members in class (*f*) shall serve until 31 December of the year in which they are co-opted.

2. Seven members of the Committee shall form a quorum.

3. Subject to the powers of the Council, the General Board, and the Council of the School of Arts and Humanities, the duties of the Committee of Management shall be: Duties.

(*a*) to determine the general policy of the Centre;

(*b*) to advise the Director in matters arising from the work of the Centre;

(*c*) to give guidance to the Director upon request on matters relating to language learning or teaching in the University;

(*d*) to assist the Director in promoting the teaching of modern languages;

Language Centre.

(*e*) to approve an Annual Report to the Council of the School on the work of the Centre prepared by the Director;

(*f*) to award certificates of proficiency in subjects approved by the General Board and listed in the Schedule to these regulations to those persons who have followed courses of the Language Centre and whose work on those courses has been assessed by criteria determined by the Language Centre.

4. The provisions of Special Ordinance A (vii) 5 concerning reserved business shall apply as if the Committee were a body constituted by Statute and any matter which, if the Committee were a Faculty Board, would be reserved business under Regulation 11 of the General Regulations for the Constitution of the Faculty Boards shall also be reserved.

Schedule of subjects approved for certificates of proficiency awarded by the Language Centre

Arabic Basic 1
Arabic Basic 2
Brazilian Portuguese Basic
Chinese Basic 1
Chinese Basic 2
French Basic
German Basic
Italian Basic
Russian Basic
Spanish Basic
Swahili Basic 1
Swahili Basic 2
Arabic Elementary 1
Mandarin Chinese Elementary 1
Mandarin Chinese Elementary 2
Brazilian Portuguese Intermediate 1
French Intermediate 1
German Intermediate 1
Italian Intermediate 1
Russian Intermediate 1
Spanish Intermediate 1
French Intermediate 2
German Intermediate 2
Italian Intermediate 2
Russian Intermediate 2
Spanish Intermediate 2

Staff of the Language Centre

Director and Deputy Director.

1. There shall be the University offices of Director and Deputy Director of the Language Centre.

2. Appointments and reappointments to the offices of Director and Deputy Director of the Centre shall be made by an Appointments Committee consisting of:

(*a*) the Vice-Chancellor (or a duly appointed deputy) as Chair;

(*b*) the Chair of the Committee of Management of the Centre;

(*c*) three members of the Committee of Management appointed by the Committee of Management;

(*d*) two persons appointed by the General Board.

Duties of Director.

3. The duties of the Director of the Language Centre shall be as follows:

(*a*) to be responsible to the Committee of Management for all aspects of the work of the Language Centre. He or she shall act as Secretary to the Committee of Management and shall also act as the executive officer of the Committee in respect of their responsibilities for the Language Centre;

(*b*) to perform, in relation to the Language Centre, the duties assigned to the Head of a Department by Statute A V 17(*b*) and (*c*);

(*c*) to arrange the provision of facilities for oral language teaching and examinations;

(*d*) to provide advice and assistance in matters relating to language teaching and learning;

(*e*) to be responsible for the direction of study and research in the field of language teaching and learning;

(*f*) to prepare and submit to the General Board, in accordance with arrangements determined by Ordinance, the annual estimates of the Department for consideration by the Board in accordance with Statute A V 1(*b*);

(*g*) to be responsible for the proper application of the funds available to the Department, and to ensure that the approved estimate of expenditure is not exceeded and that the accounts are correctly maintained.

Duties of Deputy Director.

4. The duties of the Deputy Director shall be to assist the Director in all matters connected with the work of the Centre.

Other offices.

5. There shall be such number of University offices of Language Adviser and Senior Language Adviser as the General Board shall approve on the recommendation of the Committee of Management.

6. Appointments and reappointments to an office of Language Adviser or Senior Language Adviser shall be made by the Committee of Management, excluding for this purpose the members in class (*e*), subject to the approval of the General Board.

7. The duties of the staff of the Centre shall be determined by the Director, subject to the approval of the General Board. Language Centre. Duties of other offices.

8. The Director and any other members of the staff of the Centre shall conform to such conditions of residence as may be determined by the General Board, after consultation with the Committee of Management. Residence.

University Library

Library.

Amended by Notice (Reporter, *2013–14, p. 29*)

Constitution

The University Library, the affiliated libraries, and the Centre for Applied Research in Educational Technologies shall jointly constitute an institution under the supervision of the General Board. The affiliated libraries shall be those listed in the Schedule to these regulations as may be amended by the General Board from time to time.

Library Syndicate

1. The Library Syndicate shall consist of: Library Syndicate.

(*a*) the Vice-Chancellor (or a duly appointed deputy), who shall be Chair;

(*b*) two persons appointed by the Council, who shall be appointed in the Michaelmas Term to serve for two years from 1 January following;

(*c*) eight persons appointed by the General Board, who shall be appointed in the Michaelmas Term to serve for four years from 1 January following;

(*d*) two persons elected from among their own number by the holders of University offices in the University Library, who shall be elected in the Michaelmas Term to serve for two years from 1 January following;

(*e*) not more than four persons co-opted by the Syndicate;

(*f*) not more than two members of the University *in statu pupillari* co-opted by the Syndicate.

Members in classes (*e*) and (*f*) shall serve until 31 December of the year following that in which they are co-opted, provided that if a member in class (*f*) ceases to be *in statu pupillari* he or she shall thereupon cease to be a member in that class.

2. All meetings of the Syndicate shall be summoned by the Vice-Chancellor; there shall be at least one and normally two meetings each term. Meetings.

3. No business shall be transacted at any meeting unless at least four members are present. Quorum.

4. Under the provisions of Special Ordinance A (vii) 5(iii), the appointment of members of the Board of Electors to the office of Librarian, the appointment of members of the Appointments Committee for the University Library, and the co-optation of members of the Syndicate in class (*e*) shall be reserved business. Reserved business.

5. (*a*) The Syndicate shall supervise the management of the University Library. Duties and powers.

(*b*) There shall be a Science Libraries Sub-syndicate, a Law and Criminology Libraries Sub-syndicate, and a Committee of Management for the Centre for Applied Research in Educational Technologies. There shall be a Medical Library Policy Advisory Group. Through the agency of the Sub-syndicates, the Policy Advisory Group, and the Committee of Management, the Syndicate shall supervise the management of the affiliated libraries and the Centre for Applied Research in Educational Technologies.

(*c*) The Syndicate shall supervise the custody and arrangement of the University Archives.

6. (*a*) The Syndicate shall do all such things as in their opinion are necessary or expedient for the regulation, security, and improvement of the University Library, the affiliated libraries, and the Centre for Applied Research in Educational Technologies. They shall exercise a general oversight over all matters relating to the administration, staffing, and financial resources of these libraries and the Centre for Applied Research in Educational Technologies, and shall be empowered to make recommendations to the General Board about the staff, accommodation, and equipment needed for their proper functioning.

(*b*) In the exercise of their power of making rules for the management of the Library, the Syndicate shall have power to approve, through the agency of the Sub-syndicates and Medical Library Policy Advisory Group, rules for the use of the affiliated libraries. In the case of the Central Science Library

Library.

these rules shall be consistent with the provisions of the agreement between the University and the Philosophical Society.

(*c*) The following affiliated libraries shall continue to receive printed material received under the Legal Deposit Libraries Act 2003 – the Betty and Gordon Moore Library, the Central Science Library, the Medical Library and the Squire Law Library.

Reports.

7. The Syndicate shall make an Annual Report to the General Board, and such other reports to the University as they shall think fit.

Science Libraries Sub-syndicate.

8. The Science Libraries Sub-syndicate shall consist of:

(*a*) four persons appointed by the Library Syndicate;

(*b*) two persons appointed by the Council of the Cambridge Philosophical Society;

(*c*) two persons appointed by the Council of the School of the Physical Sciences;

(*d*) two persons appointed by the Council of the School of Technology;

(*e*) two persons appointed by the Council of the School of the Biological Sciences;

(*f*) one person appointed by the Medical Library Policy Advisory Group;

(*g*) not more than three persons co-opted by the Sub-syndicate, provided that it shall not be obligatory to co-opt any person or persons;

(*h*) one member of the University *in statu pupillari*, normally a graduate, co-opted by the Sub-syndicate.

Members in classes (*a*)–(*f*) shall serve for four years from 1 January following their appointment. Members in classes (*g*) and (*h*) shall serve until 31 December of the year in which they are co-opted or of the following year, as the Sub-syndicate shall decide at the time of their co-optation, provided that if a member in class (*h*) ceases to be *in statu pupillari* he or she shall thereupon cease to be a member in that class.

Law and Criminology Libraries Sub-syndicate.

9. The Law and Criminology Libraries Sub-syndicate shall consist of:

(*a*) three persons appointed by the Library Syndicate (including one person from the Faculty of Law and one person from the Institute of Criminology);

(*b*) three persons appointed by the Faculty Board of Law (including one person from the Institute of Criminology);

(*c*) not more than two persons co-opted by the Sub-syndicate (one from the Faculty of Law and one from the Institute of Criminology), provided that it shall not be obligatory to co-opt any person or persons;

(*d*) not more than two members of the University *in statu pupillari* co-opted by the Sub-syndicate.

Members in classes (*a*) and (*b*) shall serve for four years from 1 January following their appointment. Members in classes (*c*) and (*d*) shall serve until 31 December of the year in which they are co-opted or of the following year, as the Sub-syndicate shall decide at the time of their co-optation, provided that if a member in class (*d*) ceases to be *in statu pupillari* he or she shall thereupon cease to be a member in that class.

Humanities and Social Sciences Libraries Sub-syndicate.

10. The Humanities and Social Sciences Libraries Sub-syndicate shall consist of:

(*a*) one person appointed by the Library Syndicate;

(*b*) one person appointed by each of the Faculty Boards of Economics, Education, and History;

(*c*) two persons appointed by the Faculty Board of Human, Social, and Political Science;

(*d*) one person appointed by each of the Boards of History and Philosophy of Science and Land Economy;

(*e*) not more than two persons co-opted by the Sub-syndicate, provided that it shall not be obligatory to co-opt any person or persons;

(*f*) not more than two members of the University *in statu pupillari* co-opted by the Sub-syndicate.

Members in classes (*a*)–(*d*) shall serve for four years from 1 January following their appointment. Members in classes (*e*) and (*f*) shall serve until 31 December of the year in which they are co-opted or of the following year, as the Sub-syndicate shall decide at the time of their co-optation, provided that if a member in class (*f*) ceases to be *in statu pupillari* he or she shall thereupon cease to be a member in that class.

Medical Library Policy Advisory Group.

11. The Medical Library Policy Advisory Group shall consist of:

(*a*) from the University of Cambridge:

the Director of Medical Education
the Secretary of the School of Clinical Medicine
the Director of the Cambridge Institute for Medical Research (or nominee)

Library.

the University Librarian
the Deputy University Librarian
the Head of the Medical and Science Libraries

(*b*) from the National Health Service:
a member of the Cambridge University Hospitals NHS Foundation Trust Board of Directors
Cambridge University Health partners Director of Postgraduate Education
the Director of Workforce and Leadership, East of England SHA
the NHS East of England Library Lead

(*c*) from the Medical Research Council:
the Head, Cambridge Medical Research Council Centre (or nominee)

(*d*) Co-optations:
up to three members to be co-opted by the *ex officio* members

Sub-syndicates and Policy Advisory Group.

12. (*a*) Each Sub-syndicate and the Medical Library Policy Advisory Group shall elect a Chair from among those of their own members who are members of the Library Syndicate. The Chair of each Sub-syndicate and Policy Advisory Group shall be a member of the Library Syndicate.

(*b*) No business shall be transacted at any meeting of a Sub-syndicate and Policy Advisory Group unless at least four members are present.

(*c*) The provisions of Special Ordinance A (vii) 5 concerning reserved business shall apply to each of the Sub-syndicates and Policy Advisory Group as if it were a body constituted by Statute; the election of the Chair and the co-optation of members of each Sub-syndicate shall also be reserved.

(*d*) The Librarian shall act as Secretary of each Sub-syndicate and Policy Advisory Group

Duties.

13. In respect of each of the affiliated libraries the relevant Sub-syndicate or Policy Advisory Group shall have the following duties:

(*a*) to co-ordinate policies between the University Library and the affiliated libraries;

(*b*) to submit recommendations to the Library Syndicate concerning the location in the affiliated library of library material received under the Legal Deposit Libraries Act (for those libraries where this is appropriate);

(*c*) on behalf of the Library Syndicate, and subject to their approval, to make rules for the use of the affiliated libraries;

(*d*) to oversee appropriate co-ordination of library services and resources in respect of teaching, learning, and research in connection with the relevant Faculties and Departments with which the libraries are associated.

Staff of the University Library and the affiliated libraries

Constitution.

1. The staff of the University Library, including for this purpose the affiliated libraries and the Centre for Applied Research in Educational Technologies, shall consist of the Librarian, the Deputy Librarian, the Director of the Centre for Applied Research in Educational Technologies, the Senior Under-Librarians, the Under-Librarians, the Assistant Under-Librarians, the Assistant Library Officers, the Graduate Trainees, the holders of such other offices as may be established in the Library from time to time, and the University assistants.

Designated offices.

2. (*a*) This staff shall include officers designated by the Library Syndicate, on the recommendation of the Librarian, as follows:

(i) two officers designated respectively Keeper of Manuscripts and University Archives and Deputy Keeper of the University Archives;

(ii) officers designated for duties in the affiliated libraries, who shall be responsible for the management of those libraries.

(*b*) In addition to the officers specified in sub-paragraph (*a*)(ii) above, the Library Syndicate, on the recommendation of the Librarian, may also designate other officers for duties in any of the affiliated libraries.

(*c*) The Library Syndicate may make appointments to such University offices of Curator as may be approved by the General Board, and may appoint such Honorary Keepers as they themselves think fit.

3. The number of University offices of Deputy Librarian, Director of Applied Research in Educational Technologies, Senior Under-Librarian, Under-Librarian, Assistant Under-Librarian, and Assistant Library Officer shall be determined from time to time by the General Board on the recommendation of the

Library. Library Syndicate. The number of University assistants shall be determined from time to time in accordance with the regulations for employment by the University.

4. Appointments and reappointments to a University office on the staff of the University Library, other than the office of Librarian or an office of Curator, shall be made in accordance with the arrangements agreed from time to time by the competent authority.

5. The Syndicate shall have power to appoint the Deputy Librarian to be Acting Librarian during any period of absence from duty of the Librarian, or during any period when there is a vacancy in the office of Librarian.

Librarian. **6**. It shall be the duty of the Librarian:

(*a*) subject to the direction of the Library Syndicate, to be responsible for the management and leadership of the University Library and the affiliated libraries;

(*b*) to perform, in relation to the University Library and the affiliated libraries, the duties assigned to the Head of a Department by A V 17(*b*) and (*c*);

(*c*) to act as the General Board's principal adviser on matters relating to libraries.

7. The holders of other University offices on the staff of the University Library and the affiliated libraries shall assist the Librarian and shall carry out their duties in accordance with such directions as may be issued from time to time by the Syndicate or the Sub-syndicate concerned, as the case may be.

Curators. **8**. The stipend, if any, of a Curator appointed under Regulation 2(*c*) shall be determined from time to time by the General Board on the recommendation of the Library Syndicate. The tenure of such an office and its duties shall be determined by the Syndicate.

Assistants. **9**. Subject to the approval of the Syndicate, the Librarian shall assign to the University assistants their several duties.

SCHEDULE

Amended by Notice (Reporter, *2013–14, p. 777*)

The affiliated libraries

SCHOOL OF ARTS AND HUMANITIES
Asian and Middle Eastern Studies Library
English Library
Pendlebury Library of Music
Philosophy Library

SCHOOL OF THE BIOLOGICAL SCIENCES
Central Science Library

SCHOOL OF CLINICAL MEDICINE
Medical Library

SCHOOL OF THE HUMANITIES AND SOCIAL SCIENCES
African Studies Library
Everton Library of Education
Haddon Library of Archaeology and Anthropology
Land Economy Library
Marshall Library of Economics
Radzinowicz Library of the Institute of Criminology
Seeley Historical Library
Social and Political Sciences Library
South Asian Studies Library
Squire Law Library
Whipple Library of the History and Philosophy of Science

SCHOOL OF THE PHYSICAL SCIENCES
Betty and Gordon Moore Library

Use of the University Library[1]

Opening and closing. **1.** Except on the days on which it is to be closed under Regulations 2 and 3, the Library shall be open for at least four hours on Saturdays and at least six hours on other days. Subject to this regulation the hours of opening may be determined from time to time by the Syndicate.

[1] Excluding the affiliated libraries listed in the Schedule to the regulations for staff of the University Library and the affiliated libraries.

Library.

2. The Library shall be closed on the following days:
Sundays throughout the year;
Christmas Eve and the following days up to and including the New Year public holiday;
Good Friday and the three following days;
the August Bank Holiday.

3. The Library shall be closed for the second full week (Monday to Saturday) of September, for the purpose of an annual inspection and the preparation of lists of missing books. No books shall be taken out of the Library during this period.

Admission.

4. The Library shall be open to all members of the University on the production of *either* a University Card, which has been registered by the University Library, *or* a valid Reader's Card, which shall be issued on request. Use of these cards shall be recorded, when readers enter and leave the Library, to provide statistical information on the use of the Library by different categories of user. These cards are not transferable and must be shown on request to any member of the Library staff in the proper discharge of her or his duties. In addition the Syndicate shall have power to determine by rules what other persons may be admitted and upon what terms. The Syndicate shall have absolute discretion to direct the exclusion, either indefinitely or for a specified period, of any person whose admission is considered prejudicial to the interests of the Library or its users.

Borrowing.

5. (1) Not more than ten volumes may be borrowed by the following persons: members of the Senate; University staff; Fellows of Colleges; honorary graduates of the University; Bachelors of Medicine and Bachelors of Surgery; students, other than Affiliated Students, who are graduates of this or any other university and who are following a course of study leading to a Tripos examination, or to a degree, diploma, or certificate of the University.[1] The Syndicate may grant permission for more than ten volumes to be borrowed if they are of the opinion that sufficient reasons have been advanced.

(2) Not more than five volumes may be borrowed by students who are graduates of any university and who are resident members of Ridley Hall, Westcott House, Westminster College, or Wesley House.

(3) Not more than five volumes may be borrowed by (*a*) undergraduates, and (*b*) Affiliated Students.

(4) Not more than five volumes may be borrowed, under such conditions as may from time to time be laid down by the Syndicate, by the following persons if they have been approved by the Syndicate on the recommendation of the Chair of the Faculty Board, Head of the Department, or Head of the College or Approved Society concerned:

(*a*) graduates of any university who for the time being are engaged in teaching, research, or administration in the University, or in a College or Approved Society, or in an institution connected with the University which has been recognized for this purpose by the General Board in consultation with the Syndicate;

(*b*) visiting scholars and others who for the time being have been allocated working facilities in a Faculty, Department, College, or Approved Society.

(5) In exceptional circumstances the Syndicate may grant to other persons the privilege of borrowing books under such conditions as they think fit.

6. (*a*) Any volume borrowed under Regulation 5(1), 5(4), or 5(5) shall be returned not later than eight weeks after the date of borrowing, provided that the Librarian shall have power to demand its return earlier.

(*b*) Any volume borrowed under Regulation 5(2) or 5(3) shall be returned not later than the fourteenth day after the date of borrowing, provided that the Librarian shall have power to demand its return earlier.

(*c*) Notwithstanding the provisions of Regulation 6(*b*), any volume borrowed under Regulation 5(3) between the Monday and Friday of the last week of either Michaelmas or Lent Full Term may be retained until the first day of the following Full Term, unless the Librarian has demanded its earlier return.

7. Any user of the Library who requires a volume that has been borrowed by another person may give notice to the Librarian that he or she requires the volume. The Librarian shall then notify the borrower that he or she is required to return the volume to the Library. The borrower shall comply with this requirement within seven days of the date of such notification.

[1] For the purposes of this regulation the term 'diploma or certificate of the University' does not apply to certificates of proficiency awarded by the Language Centre or to certificates and diplomas open to non-members of the University, except for those administered by the Institute of Continuing Education.

Library.

8. Volumes borrowed and returned shall be noted in the Library borrowing records by the Library staff in the presence of the borrowers or their representatives. When loans are renewed online the amendments to the Library borrowing records shall be recorded via the Library catalogue.

9. (*a*) No volume borrowed from the Library may be taken or sent outside the British Isles except with the written permission of the Syndicate.

(*b*) No volume borrowed from the Library may be used for commercial purposes except with the written permission of the Syndicate.

10. Any person who fails to return a volume in accordance with the provisions of Regulation 6 shall be liable to a fine. The level of the fines that may be levied under this regulation shall be determined from time to time by the Syndicate, subject to the provisions of Regulation 15.

11. A fine of not more than £175 may be imposed by the Syndicate on any person who removes a book or other item of library material from the Library without following the borrowing procedures laid down by the Syndicate, or who, having borrowed such a book or other item, is unable, without showing good reason, to return it, or who wilfully damages such a book or other item. The imposition of such a fine shall be without prejudice to the University's right to obtain, in addition, compensation for any loss or damage suffered by the University.

12. Manuscripts of special value or importance, other items of great rarity, and materials from collections to which special conditions apply, shall not be borrowed from the Library except with the approval of the Syndicate who shall specify the conditions and the period, which shall not exceed six months, of the loan.

13. Exercises and dissertations which are deposited in the Library by candidates for degrees shall be available for consultation, unless the Board of Graduate Studies or other comparable authority determine that a particular exercise or dissertation shall, for a specified period, be available only to the author or to those who have the author's written permission to consult the work. Exercises and dissertations shall not be borrowed.

Rules.

14. Rules made from time to time by the Syndicate shall be posted within the Library.

Penalties for infringement.

15. A fine of not more than £175 may be imposed by the Syndicate on any person who wilfully infringes any of these regulations or any rule made by the Syndicate. A person from whom any fine is due that has been imposed under these regulations shall not be admitted to the Library or allowed to borrow books until such fine has been paid.

Borrowing from the University Library:[1] Notice[2]

The General Board have announced that they have recognized the following institutions whose members may borrow books from the University Library under the conditions specified in Regulation 5(4)(*a*) of the regulations for the use of the University Library.

Biotechnology and Biological Sciences Research Council institutions

Babraham Institute
National Institute of Agricultural Botany
Institute of Plant Science Research
Statistics Group

Natural Environment Research Council institutions

British Antarctic Survey
Institute of Terrestrial Ecology

Other institutions

Animal Health Trust
BirdLife International
British Trust for Ornithology
Cambridge Group for History of Population and Social Structure
Commonwealth Bureau of Plant Breeding and Genetics
European Bioinformatics Institute
Fauna and Flora International
International Union for Conservation of Nature
Medical Research Council institutions in the Cambridge area

[1] Excluding the affiliated libraries listed in the Schedule to the regulations for staff of the University Library and the affiliated libraries.

[2] Amended by Notice (*Reporter*, 6356, 2013–14, p. 778).

Library.

Needham Research Institute
NHS Authorities and Trusts in the Cambridgeshire County Council area
Quadrant Research Foundation
Royal Society for the Protection of Birds
Strangeways Research Laboratory
TRAFFIC
Tropical Biology Association
Tyndale House Residential Centre for Biblical Research
UNEP World Conservation Monitoring Centre
Veterinary Investigation Centre
Wellcome Trust Sanger Institute
West Suffolk Hospital

Betty and Gordon Moore Library, Central Science Library, Medical Library, and Squire Law Library

1. Regulations 10, 11, and 15 of the regulations for the use of the University Library, relating to fines, shall apply also to the Betty and Gordon Moore Library, the Central Science Library, the Medical Library, and the Squire Law Library.

2. The rules made from time to time for the use of each of these libraries, in accordance with Regulations 6(*b*) and 12(*c*) of the regulations for the Library Syndicate, shall specify the arrangements for the opening and closing of the library, for admission to the library, and for borrowing from the library. Such rules shall be posted within the library concerned.

FACULTY, DEPARTMENTAL, AND OTHER LIBRARIES

Libraries.

Application.

The following regulations shall apply to all Faculty and Departmental Libraries (except the Squire Law Library) and to the libraries of the Centres of African Studies, Latin-American Studies, and South Asian Studies.

Authority responsible.

1. The authority responsible for the Library of a Faculty, Department, or other institution under the supervision of the General Board, shall be the Board, Syndicate, Committee, or other comparable body, provided that the responsibility may be delegated, wholly or in part, by the Faculty Board or other such body to the Head of a Department or other University officer or to a committee. Each authority shall be empowered to do such things in accordance with these regulations as are necessary for the management of the library, and in particular to authorize the purchase of books, provide a catalogue, and defray other expenses, from the funds at their disposal.

Library rules.

2. The authority responsible for a library shall make rules, in accordance with these regulations and subject to the approval of the General Board, for the use of the library, including rules for borrowing if it is decided to permit borrowing; and they shall display in the library a notice of all the rules.

Admission.

3. Unless the General Board on the application of the authority have agreed otherwise, the authority responsible for a library shall admit to it, in addition to those members of the University for whom it is primarily intended, any member of the Regent House or registered Graduate Student wishing to use it for purposes of scholarship or research. Other persons may be admitted at the authority's discretion. Borrowing may also be permitted at the authority's discretion, and may be restricted to such classes of user as the authority may decide.

Borrowing.

Acceptance of gifts.

4. The authority responsible for a library shall have power to accept gifts of books and other library material. The authority shall seek the approval of the General Board:

(*a*) if acceptance of the gift would involve additional expense falling on general University funds; or

(*b*) if any condition is imposed by the donor which would prevent the disposal of the books or other material that are found to be no longer required for the purposes of the Library.

Disposal of books, etc.

5. An authority responsible for a library wishing to dispose of any book, pamphlet, or periodical shall be at liberty to do so by sale or otherwise, provided that, before it is disposed of, it shall, unless the General Board agree otherwise, observe the procedure set out from time to time by the General Board which includes the requirement to offer such item to the Syndics of the University Library, for transfer to that library (including the dependent libraries), and to the authorities responsible for other libraries in the University. Before the authority disposes of any literary, historical, or scientific manuscript, paper, microform material, or other archive, it shall first be offered to the Syndics of the

Libraries. University Library or the Keeper of the University Archives for transfer to that library or to the University Archives as may be appropriate.

Periodicals. **6.** The authority responsible for a library shall, on first subscribing to any periodical, inform the Periodicals Department of the University Library of the placing of the subscription. The authority shall obtain the approval of the General Board before an existing subscription to a periodical is cancelled.

Mathematical Sciences.

Isaac Newton Institute for Mathematical Sciences

Constitution

The Isaac Newton Institute for Mathematical Sciences shall be an institution independent of any Faculty or Department but under the supervision of the General Board, and shall be within the School of the Physical Sciences.

Scientific Steering Committee

Constitution. **1.** There shall be a Scientific Steering Committee which, while taking into account its national and international responsibilities and its need for expertise across the mathematical sciences including multidisciplinary applications, shall consist of:

(*a*) the Director;

(*b*) four persons appointed by the General Board after consultation with the Engineering and Physical Sciences Research Council which will represent the views of other Research Councils in this process;

(*c*) two persons appointed by the General Board after consultation with the London Mathematical Society;

(*d*) six persons appointed by the General Board after consultation with the Councils of the Schools of the Physical Sciences, Technology, the Biological Sciences, Clinical Medicine, and the Humanities and Social Sciences, and those national scientific bodies listed in a Schedule to be approved from time to time by the General Board for this purpose;

(*e*) one additional person co-opted at the discretion of the Committee.

2. Members in classes (*b*), (*c*), and (*d*) shall serve for four years from 1 January following their appointment. A co-opted member in class (*e*) shall serve until 31 December of the year in which he or she is co-opted or of the year next following, as the Committee shall determine at the time of co-optation.

3. The General Board, in making their appointments to the Committee, shall ensure that at least seven of its members are not resident members of the University.

Chair. **4.** The Chair of the Committee shall be appointed by the General Board from among the members in classes (*b*), (*c*), and (*d*). The Chair shall be appointed for a period of not more than three years and shall be eligible for reappointment for a period or periods of not more than three years at a time.

Secretary. **5.** The Director of the Institute shall serve as Secretary of the Committee.

Meetings. **6.** The Committee shall meet at least once each year. Six members present at a meeting shall constitute a quorum.

Duties. **7.** The duty of the Committee shall be to advise the Director on all aspects of the scientific work and policy of the Institute.

Management Committee

Constitution. **1.** The management of the Institute shall be the responsibility of a Management Committee, which shall consist of:

(*a*) the Director;

(*b*) the Deputy Director;

(*c*) the Heads of the Departments of Applied Mathematics and Theoretical Physics and of Pure Mathematics and Mathematical Statistics;

(*d*) one person appointed by the General Board, who shall be Chair, provided that the General Board shall have power to appoint as Chair a person who is already a member of the Committee in one of classes (*c*), (*e*), and (*f*);

Mathematical Sciences.

(*e*) five persons appointed by the General Board, of whom one shall be appointed on the recommendation of the Council of the School of the Physical Sciences, one on the recommendation of the Council of the School of Technology, and one on the recommendation of the Faculty Board of Mathematics;
(*f*) one person appointed by St John's College and one person appointed by Trinity College;
(*g*) one person appointed by the Engineering and Physical Sciences Research Council;
(*h*) one additional person co-opted at the discretion of the Committee.

2. Members in classes (*d*)–(*g*) shall be appointed in the Michaelmas Term to serve for four years from 1 January following their appointment. A co-opted member in class (*h*) shall serve until 31 December of the year in which he or she is co-opted or of the year next following, as the Committee shall determine at the time of co-optation.

3. The General Board, in making their appointments to the Committee, shall ensure that at least two of its members are not resident members of the University.

4. The Director shall serve as Secretary of the Committee unless there is a Deputy Director, in which case the latter shall serve as Secretary of the Committee. Secretary.

5. The Committee shall meet at least once each term. Meetings.

6. Subject to the powers of the Council and the General Board, the duties of the Committee shall be as follows: Duties.

(*a*) to promote research in the field of the mathematical sciences and the publication of the results of such research;
(*b*) to co-operate with outside bodies in the encouragement of research in the mathematical sciences;
(*c*) to administer funds allocated to them for the purposes specified in (*a*) and (*b*) above;
(*d*) to supervise the work of the staff of the Institute;
(*e*) to prepare annual estimates for submission to the General Board;
(*f*) to make an Annual Report to the General Board and to the Councils of the Schools and the other bodies mentioned in Regulation 1(*e*), (*f*), and (*g*) above.

Staff of the Institute

1. There shall be a Director of the Institute who shall be the N. M. Rothschild & Sons Professor of Mathematical Sciences. Director.

2. Under the general control of the Management Committee the Director shall be the administrative Head of the Institute, and shall be responsible, subject to the advice of the Scientific Steering Committee and the approval of the Management Committee, for the choice of topics for the Institute's programmes. Duties of Director.

3. There shall be a University office of Deputy Director of the Institute, which may be held concurrently with another University office. Appointments and reappointments to the Deputy Directorship shall be made by the Management Committee. If the office is held concurrently with another University office, appointments and reappointments shall be made for periods of not more than five years at a time, provided that no person may hold the office for a total period exceeding six years. Deputy Director.

4. The duties of the Deputy Director shall be to assist the Director in all matters connected with the work of the Institute, to serve as Secretary of the Management Committee, to engage actively in research, and to carry out such teaching duties as may be required by the Head of the Department of Applied Mathematics and Theoretical Physics or of the Department of Pure Mathematics and Mathematical Statistics, as the Director agrees are compatible with the other duties of the office. Duties of Deputy Director.

Rothschild Visiting Professorships

1. The sum donated by N. M. Rothschild & Sons shall constitute a fund called the Rothschild Visiting Professorships Fund from which the stipend, travelling expenses, and subsistence allowance of Rothschild Visiting Professors and the travelling expenses and subsistence allowance of Rothschild Distinguished Visiting Fellows shall be paid. Fund.

2. A Rothschild Visiting Professor shall be elected under the authority of Special Ordinance C (vii) B.1(*c*)(iii) by the General Board on the recommendation of the Management Committee. The tenure of a Rothschild Visiting Professor shall normally be for a period of not more than six months but may, exceptionally, be for a period of not more than one year, and shall be determined by the General Board on the recommendation of the Management Committee on the occasion of each appointment. Election and tenure of Visiting Professor.

3. A Rothschild Distinguished Visiting Fellow shall be appointed by the Management Committee for a period of not more than six months, provided that the Management Committee may, exceptionally, make an appointment for one year. Distinguished Visiting Fellow.

Mathematical Sciences.

Duties. **4.** It shall be the duty of a Rothschild Visiting Professor and a Rothschild Distinguished Visiting Fellow to participate in the Institute's research programme.

Stipend. **5.** The stipend of a Rothschild Visiting Professor shall be determined by the General Board on the recommendation of the Management Committee.

Residence. **6.** A Rothschild Visiting Professor and a Rothschild Distinguished Visiting Fellow shall be required to reside in the University.

Other expenditure. **7.** After provision has been made in accordance with Regulations 1 and 5, such further payments may be made from the Fund in support of the work of a Rothschild Visiting Professor and a Rothschild Distinguished Visiting Fellow as may be approved by the Management Committee.

Visiting Fellowships

Purpose and definitions. **1.** In order to enable scholars from outside Cambridge to take part in and contribute to the work of the Institute, there shall be Visiting Fellowships for persons who have made or are making important contributions to research in mathematical sciences, or who are pursuing advanced work in the subject.

Appointments. **2.** Appointments and reappointments to Visiting Fellowships shall be made by the Director of the Institute for periods not exceeding one year at a time.

3. The stipend, if any, of a Visiting Fellow shall be determined by the Director with the approval of the General Board on the occasion of each appointment or reappointment.

Senior Fellowships

1. The Management Committee shall have power, subject to the approval of the General Board, to grant the title of Senior Fellow of the Institute to any person associated with the Institute (other than a member of the staff of the Institute) who has made or is making important contributions to research in mathematics.

2. A person to whom the title of Senior Fellow has been granted shall hold that title for not more than five years at a time. At the end of any such period the title may again be granted for a further period of not more than five years on each occasion.

Polymer Synthesis.

Melville Laboratory for Polymer Synthesis

Director

1. There shall be a University office of Director of the Melville Laboratory for Polymer Synthesis[1] in the Department of Chemistry.

Appointment. **2.** Appointments and reappointments to the office of Director of the Melville Laboratory for Polymer Synthesis shall be made by an Appointments Committee consisting of:

(*a*) the Vice-Chancellor, or a duly appointed deputy, as Chair;
(*b*) the Director of Industrial Liaison;
(*c*) the Head of the Department of Chemistry;
(*d*) two persons appointed by the Council of the School of the Physical Sciences;
(*e*) one person appointed by the Council of the School of Technology;
(*f*) three persons appointed by the General Board.

Members in classes (*d*), (*e*), and (*f*) shall be appointed in the Michaelmas Term of each year of which the number is even to serve for two years from 1 January following their appointment.

Duties. **3.** The duties of the Director shall be to engage in research in polymer synthesis and to manage the Melville Laboratory so as to promote polymer synthesis within the University, under the supervision of a Committee of Management consisting of:

Committee of Management.

(*a*) the Chair of the Council of the School of the Physical Sciences, who shall be Chair of the Committee;
(*b*) the Heads of the Departments of Engineering, Chemical Engineering and Biotechnology, Chemistry, Materials Science and Metallurgy, and Physics; provided that each Head may appoint a deputy to attend any meeting of the Committee;
(*c*) one member appointed by each of the sponsors of the Melville Laboratory, as defined in the agreement with the University;
(*d*) the Director of Industrial Liaison;

[1] This office is an office specified in the Schedules to Special Ordinances C (i) 1 and C (vii) 1.

(*e*) not more than three persons co-opted by the Committee to serve for two years from the date of their co-optation; Polymer Synthesis.

(*f*) the Director of the Melville Laboratory for Polymer Synthesis, who shall be Secretary of the Committee.

The Committee of Management shall meet at least twice in each academical year.

4. The provisions of Special Ordinance C (vii) A.10 that apply to a Professor shall also apply to the Director of the Melville Laboratory for Polymer Synthesis.

5. The Director shall conform to such conditions of residence as may be determined by the General Board, after consultation with the Committee of Management.

SAINSBURY LABORATORY

Sainsbury Laboratory.

Constitution

The Sainsbury Laboratory shall be an institution independent of any Faculty or Department but under the supervision of the General Board, and shall be within the School of the Biological Sciences.

Management

1. The Laboratory shall be under the general control of a Board of Management which shall consist of: Board of Management.

(*a*) four members appointed by the General Board;

(*b*) seven members appointed by the General Board, on the nomination of the Gatsby Charitable Foundation;

(*c*) the Director of the Laboratory, *ex officio*;

(*d*) two other senior members of the Laboratory appointed by the General Board on the nomination of the Management Board.

Members in classes (*a*), (*b*), and (*d*) shall be appointed in the Michaelmas Term to serve for four years from 1 January following their appointment. Among the members in classes (*a*) and (*b*) shall be not less than three scientists working in institutions overseas and one business person with a scientific background.

2. If any member in classes (*a*) and (*b*) misses two consecutive meetings her or his membership shall cease, unless the cause of the absence has been declared sufficient by the Board of Management. Condition of membership.

3. The Management Board shall elect a Chair from among the members in classes (*a*) and (*b*), to serve for three years from 1 January following election; the Chair shall be eligible for re-election for a further period of three years. Chair.

4. The Administrator of the Laboratory shall serve as Secretary of the Board. Secretary.

5. Subject to the powers of the Council, the General Board, the Council of the School of the Biological Sciences, and the Faculty Board of Biology, the general duties of the Board shall be: Duties of the Board.

(*a*) to promote research in plant development and plant diversity;

(*b*) to oversee the scientific progress of the Laboratory;

(*c*) to approve the distribution of funding in support of the Laboratory from the Gatsby Charitable Foundation;

(*d*) to prepare an Annual Report on the finances of the Laboratory for submission to the General Board and the Gatsby Charitable Foundation.

(*e*) to oversee the arrangements for the periodic review of the Laboratory, in accordance with agreements between the University and the Gatsby Charitable Foundation;

(*f*) to appoint, or reappoint, the scientific staff of the Laboratory, other than those who hold University offices.

6. The Chair, in consultation with the Director, shall submit an Annual Report on the scientific progress of the Laboratory to the General Board and the Gatsby Charitable Foundation. Annual Report.

Staff of the Laboratory

1. There shall be a University office of Director of the Laboratory which shall be held concurrently with a Professorship. Director.

2. The Director shall normally be appointed by the General Board for a term of five years and may be re-appointed for further periods, as determined by the General Board, on the advice of a Committee constituted for the particular occasion, in consultation with the Gatsby Charitable Foundation. Tenure.

Sainsbury Laboratory.

3. Subject to the duties of the Management Board, the Director shall be the administrative head of the Laboratory, and shall be responsible to the Management Board for the proper operation and management of the Laboratory and for ensuring the effective carrying out of the Laboratory's purpose and functions, including the direction of research in the Laboratory.

4. There shall be such other University offices in the Laboratory as the University, or the General Board, on the recommendation of the Management Board, may establish from time to time. Appointments to such offices shall be made in accordance with the relevant provisions of the Statutes and Ordinances.

Residence.

5. The staff of the Laboratory shall conform to such conditions of residence as may be determined by the Management Board, subject to the approval of the General Board.

Duties of the staff.

6. The duties of the staff of the Laboratory other than the Director, shall be determined by the Management Board subject to the approval of the General Board.

Acting Director.

7. During any period of absence from duty of the Director, the General Board, on the recommendation of the Management Board, shall have the authority to appoint a person to be Acting Director. A person so appointed shall be recognized as Director of the Laboratory for all purposes.

NOTICE BY THE GENERAL BOARD

University Research Ethics Committee

1. The General Board have agreed to establish a University Research Ethics Committee which shall consist of:

(*a*) the Chair of the Human Biology Research Ethics Committee;[1]
(*b*) the Chair of the Psychology Research Ethics Committee;
(*c*) a member of the Cambridge Local Research Ethics Committee;
(*d*) one person appointed by the General Board who shall be Chair, provided that the General Board shall have power to appoint as Chair a person who is already a member of the Committee in one of classes (*a*), (*b*), (*e*) or (*f*);
(*e*) two persons appointed by the General Board who shall not be resident members of the University;
(*f*) up to four persons appointed by the General Board on the nomination of the Councils of the Schools to ensure appropriate representation of areas of research involving human participants or personal data;
(*g*) one member of the University, *in statu pupillari*, appointed on the nomination of the Graduate Union;
(*h*) not more than two persons co-opted by the Committee, provided that it shall not be obligatory for the Committee to co-opt any person or persons.

2. The appointment of members in classes (*d*)–(*f*) shall be made in the Michaelmas Term for periods of four years from the following 1 January. Members shall be eligible for reappointment. Co-opted members shall serve until 31 December of the year in which they are co-opted or of the following year, as the Committee shall determine at the time of their co-optation. The Pro-Vice-Chancellor (Research), the Academic Secretary, the Director of the Research Services Division, and the Director of Human Resources shall have the right to attend meetings of the Committee. The Secretary of the Committee shall be the Academic Secretary or a duly appointed deputy.

3. Six members of the Committee shall constitute a quorum. The Committee shall:

(i) devise a University policy for approval by the General Board for the consideration and approval of research projects involving human participants or personal data, including the establishment of specialist sub-committees, where appropriate, to cover specific areas;
(ii) monitor the implementation of this policy, establish associated procedures, and recommend to the Board any changes that are considered necessary in the light of experience;
(iii) consider and decide on any application for approval of research involving human participation or personal data which is referred to the Committee by one of its sub-committees or by any other relevant body;
(iv) establish, implement, and keep under review a procedure for considering appeals against decisions made by sub-committees to withhold, suspend or withdraw approval of a research project which it considers to contravene University policies or procedures on research involving human participants or personal data;
(v) consider and advise on training provision for those involved in considering applications for research projects involving human participants or personal data and for those undertaking such research;
(vi) receive and consider annual reports from the ethics subject sub-committees;
(vii) report annually to the General Board on (i)–(v) above.

[1] The Human Biology Research Ethics Committee falls within the School of the Biological Sciences and considers applications from staff and students of the University for ethical approval of research programmes in fields within its scope involving human participants, except in the field of human psychology where applications are considered by the Psychology Research Ethics Committee. The Cambridge Local Research Ethics Committee normally considers applications from all departments within the Clinical School. It is an advisory committee to the Norfolk, Suffolk, and Cambridgeshire Strategic Health Authority and is independent of the NHS Trusts and the University.

CHAPTER X

INSTITUTIONS UNDER THE SUPERVISION OF THE COUNCIL

University Centre

Membership of the University Centre

1. The following shall be entitled to be members of the University Centre:

(*a*) members of the Regent House;

(*b*) University Officers and Fellows of Colleges;

(*c*) registered Graduate Students.

2. There shall be such other categories of membership as shall be determined from time to time by the Council.

3. The Registrary may, for good cause, suspend the membership of any member either for a limited period or indefinitely, provided that any suspension under this regulation is reported to the Council at the earliest opportunity and that such a member may appeal against the suspension, or against the period of suspension, to the Council, whose decision shall be final.

General Manager of the University Centre

1. There shall be the University office of General Manager of the University Centre, the holder of which may also be designated by the Council as University Catering Adviser. General Manager.

2. There shall be an Appointments Committee for the University Centre which shall consist of: Appointments Committee.

(*a*) The Vice-Chancellor (or a duly appointed deputy) as Chair;

(*b*) the Chair of the Standing Appointments Committee for the Central Administrative Offices;

(*c*) five members of the Regent House appointed by the Council, two on the Council's own nomination, one on the nomination of the Finance Committee, and two on the nomination of a member of the Council designated as the representative of the users of the University Centre.

The Registrary (or a deputy) shall act as Secretary of the Committee. Members in class (*c*) shall be appointed in the Michaelmas Term to serve for four years from 1 January following their appointment.

3. Appointments and reappointments to the University office of General Manager shall be made by the Appointments Committee for the University Centre. Appointments.

4. It shall be the duty of the General Manager to manage the University Centre and other catering and social facilities as agreed from time to time by the Council, in line with financial and other policy determined from time to time by the Council. The General Manager shall be accountable to the Council through the Registrary and shall: Duties.

(*a*) present an annual statement of accounts to the Finance Committee in the Michaelmas Term each year;

(*b*) make an Annual Report to the Council on the affairs of the Centre.

University Development and Alumni Relations

Amended by Grace 2 of 27 November 2013

University Development and Alumni Relations shall be an institution independent of any Faculty but under the supervision of the Council.

Executive Director of Development and Alumni Relations

1. Appointments and reappointments to the University office of Executive Director of Development and Alumni Relations shall be made by the Council, on the advice of a special committee appointed by the Council. Appointments.

2. The duties of the Director shall be to advise on, and assist with, specific appeals for funds and to initiate and develop fund-raising activities. Duties.

3. The Director shall conform to such conditions of residence as may be determined by the Council. Residence.

4. The Director shall not, without the consent of the Council, give instruction on behalf of a College. Restrictions.

University Farm

Director of the University Farm

Appointments.

1. Appointments and reappointments to the University office of Director of the University Farm shall be made by the Council on the recommendation of the Finance Committee.

Duties.

2. The Director shall be responsible to the Registrary or a University officer appointed by the Council. The duties of the Director shall be:

(*a*) under the general direction of the Management Committee for the University Farm, to supervise the work of the Farm and to ensure its efficient operation;

(*b*) to advance knowledge of the science of agriculture, and to promote and direct research in it.

3. The Director shall conform to such conditions of residence as may be determined by the Council.

4. The Director shall not be a Tutor, Assistant Tutor, Bursar, Assistant Bursar, or Steward of a College, and shall not, without the consent of the Council, give instruction on behalf of a College or Colleges for more than six hours a week.

University Information Services

The University Information Services shall be an institution independent of any Faculty or Department, but under the supervision of the Council, and under the general control of the Information Services Committee.

Staff of the University Information Services

Director.

1. There shall be a University office of Director of Information Services, who will be Head of the institution, and shall be accountable to the Vice-Chancellor for the satisfactory performance of the duties in Regulation 3.

Appointments Committee.

2. Appointments and reappointments to the University office of Director of Information Services shall be made by an Appointments Committee consisting of

(*a*) the Vice-Chancellor;

(*b*) three members appointed by the Information Services Committee;

(*c*) two members appointed by the Council;

(*d*) two members appointed by the General Board;

(*e*) the Registrary.

At least one of the members in class (*c*) or class (*d*) shall be not normally resident in the University. Members in classes (*b*), (*c*) and (*d*) shall be appointed in the Michaelmas Term to serve for two years from the 1 January following.

Duties of the Director.

3. The duties and responsibilities of the Director of Information Services shall be as follows:

(*a*) The Director shall be responsible to the Information Services Committee for all aspects of the work of the University Information Services. He or she shall act as the executive officer of the Committee.

(*b*) The Director shall perform, in relation to the University Information Services, the duties assigned to the Head of a Department by Statute A V 17(*b*) and (*c*).

(*c*) Such teaching as the Director may give on behalf of the University, other than the supervision of Graduate Students, shall be given without additional remuneration as part of the duties of the office.

Residence.

4. The Director shall conform to such conditions of residence as may be determined by the Information Services Committee with the approval of Council.

5. The Director shall not, without the consent of the Information Services Committee and Council, give instruction on behalf of a College.

Deputy and Assistant Directors.

6. There shall be such number of offices of Deputy Director, or Assistant Director, of Information Services as the Council may from time to time determine.

7. Appointments and reappointments to a University office of Deputy Director, or Assistant Director, of Information Services shall be made by an Appointments Committee comprising the Director of Information Services as Chair and three members of the Information Services Committee appointed by that Committee in the Michaelmas Term to serve for two years from 1 January following their appointment.

8. The duties of a Deputy Director, or Assistant Director, shall be determined by the Information Services Committee.

Wolfson Industrial Liaison Office

Constitution

The Wolfson Industrial Liaison Office shall be an institution within the University Offices, and shall be under the supervision of the Council.

Director of Industrial Liaison

1. Appointments and reappointments to the University office of Director of Industrial Liaison shall be made by the Standing Appointments Committee for the central administrative offices. Appointment

2. The duties of the Director shall be: Duties.

(*a*) to promote co-operation between the University and industry in general, including the provision of information to industry on research capabilities and opportunities for technology transfer;

(*b*) to advise and assist members of the University in identifying sources of industrial funding for their research, and in negotiating the terms and conditions of such funding, subject to the general academic policies of the University, with particular reference to the terms on which any research results might be commercially exploited;

(*c*) to advise and assist members of the University in seeking patent or other protection for the intellectual property arising out of their work and in pursuing commercial exploitation of that intellectual property on terms beneficial to the individual and the University;

(*d*) to endeavour to secure the commercial exploitation of inventions arising from work conducted in the University, and in particular to fulfil the obligations of the arrangements for exploitation of work funded by the Research Councils, in accordance with the agreement between the University and the Research Councils;

(*e*) to be responsible for all aspects of the work of the Wolfson Industrial Liaison Office, and to undertake such other duties as the Council may from time to time determine.

3. The Director shall conform to such conditions of residence as may be determined by the Council. Residence.

4. The Director shall not, without the consent of the Council, give instruction on behalf of a College. Restrictions.

CHAPTER XI

UNIVERSITY OFFICES AND GRANTS OF TITLE

GENERAL REGULATIONS FOR UNIVERSITY OFFICERS

1. Except as may be provided by Statute or by the Ordinances relating to the particular University office or category of office concerned:

Establishment of an office.

(*a*) A University office shall be established in a Faculty, Department, or other institution by the competent authority concerned.

Appointing bodies.

(*b*) Save as otherwise provided in Regulation 2 below every appointment or reappointment to a University office shall be made, unless prescribed otherwise, by the Appointments Committee for the Faculty, Department, or other institution concerned, which shall be constituted in accordance with Special Ordinance C (x) 2 or, if the General Board decide that the duties of a particular University office concern more than one institution and specify the institutions concerned, by a special Appointments Committee constituted in accordance with Special Ordinance C (x) 3. No person shall be appointed or reappointed a member of such an Appointments Committee, or of any other electing or appointing body whether prescribed by Ordinance or specially constituted by Grace for the purpose of appointment to a particular University office, who at the commencement of his or her period or further period of service, as the case may be, would have attained the age of seventy years.

Voting.

(*c*) Save as otherwise provided in Regulation 2 below every appointment or reappointment to a University office shall be made with the concurrence of the votes (which shall be given in person at a meeting) of at least

either (i) five members or two-thirds of the number of members present, whichever is the greater number, in the case of an Appointments Committee for a Faculty, Department, or other institution, constituted as in section (*b*) above (or of such an Appointments Committee together with an additional member or members as prescribed by Ordinance),

or (ii) five members or a majority of the members present, whichever is the greater number, in the case of any other electing or appointing body than an Appointments Committee as prescribed in subsection (i) of this section.

Appointments.

(*d*) Appointments to a University office shall be to the retiring age, subject to the satisfactory completion of a probationary period.

(*e*) The competent authority may waive the probationary period in a particular case.

(*f*) The competent authority may authorize the establishment of an office for a fixed term provided that there is objective justification for such authorization and shall decide what constitutes objective justification. Notwithstanding Regulation 1(*d*), the Appointments Committee may make an appointment for a term commensurate with the period for which the office has been established, subject to the satisfactory completion of a probationary period.

Probation.

(*g*) The period of probation for a University office shall be determined by the competent authority.

(*h*) The responsible person, as defined by Chapter III 1 of the Schedule to Statute C, shall decide whether or not the holder of a University office not included in the Schedule to Special Ordinance C (i) 1 has successfully completed the probationary period. If confirmation is not straightforward, the responsible person shall refer the matter to the relevant Appointments Committee, who will decide whether the officer's probationary period shall be extended or the appointment terminated.

Appeal against termination.

(*i*) An officer whose appointment has been terminated under section (*h*) above may appeal under the provisions of Chapter V of the Schedule to Statute C.

Restrictions.

(*j*) A University officer shall not undertake for remuneration during Full Term without the consent of the competent authority any teaching other than on behalf of the University or a College or Colleges or the delivery of occasional lectures.

(*k*) (i) If the duties of a University officer consist mainly of teaching and research, the amount of teaching which the officer shall be permitted to give on behalf of a College or Colleges shall not, except with the consent of the competent authority, exceed twelve hours a week or, if the officer is also a Tutor or Bursar or (unless in a particular case the competent authority shall decide otherwise) an Assistant Tutor or Assistant Bursar or Steward, eight hours a week, provided that the competent authority may on account of the nature of the subject or the circumstances of a particular case extend these amounts of teaching to fifteen and ten hours a week, respectively.

(ii) If the duties of a University officer consist mainly of work other than teaching and research,

(1) the officer shall be precluded from being a Tutor, Assistant Tutor, Bursar, Assistant Bursar, or Steward of a College, except with the consent of the competent authority, and

(2) the amount of teaching which the officer shall be permitted to give on behalf of a College or Colleges shall not, except with the consent of the competent authority, exceed six hours a week.

(*l*) The Board, Syndicate, or other body which is chiefly concerned with the duties of a particular officer, other than an officer specified in the Schedule to Special Ordinance C (i) 1, may direct the officer not to undertake work of any kind which lies outside the scope of his or her office, other than work on behalf of a College or Colleges as provided in section (*k*) above, or may limit the amount of such work; provided that an officer may appeal to the competent authority against such a decision of the Board, Syndicate, or other body, and that the decision of the competent authority shall be final.

(*m*) Unless the tenure of a University office is to the retiring age or is for a period prescribed by Ordinance or at the time of appointment, the employment of the person who holds it may be terminated at three months' notice (or such other period of notice as may in a particular case be provided by Ordinance or at the time of appointment). Termination of employment.

2. An appointment to a University office arising from a regrading review shall be made by the competent authority.

Professors' and Readers' Reports on Lectures and Teaching given

At the end of each academical year each Professor whose Professorship is governed by Statute C, and every Reader, shall make a complete report to the General Board on

(*a*) the number of lectures delivered during the year;

(*b*) the amount and kind of teaching given in addition to the lectures.

Emeritus Professors and Readers

A Professor or Reader who retires after reaching the age of sixty shall be granted the title of Emeritus Professor or Emeritus Reader, as the case may be. This regulation shall apply *mutatis mutandis* to the Vice-Chancellor,[1] the Registrary, the Librarian, the Director of the Fitzwilliam Museum, and on retirement. Grant of title.

Titles of Honorary Professor and Honorary Reader

1. The General Board, on the recommendation of a Faculty Board or comparable authority, may grant the title of Honorary Professor or Honorary Reader to a person who is not employed by the University but who is associated with the University and brings substantial benefit to it. Grant of title.

2. A person to whom the title of Honorary Professor or Honorary Reader has been granted shall hold that title for not more than five years at a time. At the end of any such period the title may again be granted for a further period of not more than five years at a time, provided that no person shall hold such a title after the end of the academical year in which he or she attains the age of sixty-seven years. A person who has reached the age of sixty-seven years and who has held the title of Honorary Professor or Honorary Reader for at least five years shall be granted the title of Emeritus Honorary Professor or Emeritus Honorary Reader.

Temporary Regulation

3. Any person who has been granted the title of Honorary Professor or Honorary Reader on or before 1 January 2007 shall be entitled to hold that title until the end of the academical year in which he or she attains the age of seventy years.

[1] This applies to any person who retires from the office of Vice-Chancellor after 1 October 1992.

Residence of University Officers

Residence.

1. Save as otherwise provided in Regulation 3 below, or in any special regulation for a particular office, every University officer in an institution under the supervision of the General Board shall reside in the University for the whole of each Full Term in each academical year, unless dispensed from discharging the duties of his or her office under the provisions of Special Ordinance C (i) 1 or 2. Every other University officer shall conform to such conditions of residence, if any, as may be specified in the regulations for the office concerned.

Definitions of residence.

2. A University officer shall be regarded as resident in the University when that officer

either (*a*) resides within five miles of Great St Mary's Church and is not habitually absent from home more than two nights in the week,

or (*b*) resides within twenty miles of Great St Mary's Church and is usually in Cambridge for a substantial part of the day,

or (*c*) has received from the General Board or from the Council, as appropriate, leave to reside farther than twenty miles from Great St Mary's Church, provided that the officer observes such conditions as the Board or the Council may require.

Substitution of residence.

3. The General Board may grant to any Professor or Reader leave to substitute for the residence required in any one term, or any part of it, residence for an equal time between 1 July and 31 August, provided that they are of opinion that such leave may be granted without prejudice to the interests of the University.

Officer holding Ely Canonry.

4. For the purpose of these regulations the official residence as Canon of Ely of a University officer who holds a residentiary Canonry of Ely shall be regarded as a place of residence within five miles of Great St Mary's Church.[1]

NOTICES BY THE COUNCIL AND THE GENERAL BOARD

Appointing arrangements for certain academic-related offices

1. *University offices covered by this Notice*

This Notice concerns the arrangements for making appointments and reappointments to the following:

- Offices in the Unified Administrative Service
- Offices of Secretaries, Assistant Secretaries, and Superintendents of Faculties, Departments, and other institutions not in the Unified Administrative Service
- Offices in the University Library and dependent libraries
- Offices of Librarians in Faculties and Departments
- Computer Officerships
- Technical Officerships and Senior Technical Officerships

The appointing provisions contained in the regulations for the offices referred to above require that appointments and reappointments shall be made in accordance with arrangements agreed from time to time by the competent authority. Set out below are the arrangements which shall apply until further notice.

2. *General*

Membership and constitution of the new appointing bodies

The appointing bodies may be constituted anew for each particular appointment. Members selected for appointing bodies should be in a grade of office or post at least equivalent to the officer to which appointment is being made.

Secretary

The Council and the General Board would expect the Secretary, where possible, to be the relevant institutional administrator.

Procedural advice

The relevant Personnel Consultant/Officer from the Human Resources Division will attend meetings as required to provide advice on procedures and legal aspects relating to the appointment and employment of individuals.

Documentation

There must be a formal agenda of business together with appropriate documentation, for example copies of applications, references, lists of candidates, and a record of the shortlisting process and outcome. There must also be formal Minutes recording the decisions. The Human Resources Division shall be notified of meetings of appointing bodies and of the outcomes of the meetings.

[1] See also p. 701.

Number of votes required for a valid decision

The number of members that must be present at a meeting and voting in favour shall be a majority of the members present or not less than three, whichever is the greater number.

Training

The Council and the General Board expect persons chairing appointing bodies to undertake training in their role before embarking on their duties. In due course, the Council and the General Board would expect all those who are likely to be members of such bodies to undertake such training.

3. *Offices in the Unified Administrative Service*

For the offices of Director, Deputy Director, Assistant Director, Principal Assistant Registrary, Senior Assistant Registrary, Principal Assistant Treasurer, Senior Assistant Treasurer:

- the Standing Appointments Committee of the Council.[1]

For offices in grades other than these:

- the Registrary,[2]
- the Head of the Division,
- an appropriate senior academic-related officer,
- a senior academic[3] with experience and interest in what the role of the office entails.

4. *Secretaries, Assistant Secretaries, and Superintendents of Faculties, Departments, and of other institutions*

- the Head of the institution or a deputy appointed by him or her (Chair and Convenor),
- the Academic Secretary, or a deputy appointed by him or her,
- a senior academic with experience and interest in what the role of the office entails
- a senior academic-related officer with knowledge and experience of the role of the office,
- up to two additional members may be co-opted by the Head of the institution.

Quorum: 4. Either the senior academic or academic-related officer must be from outside the institution.

5. *Offices in the University Library and dependent libraries*

For offices other than the University Librarian and the office of Curator:

- the University Librarian or a deputy appointed by him or her (Chair and Convenor),
- the Deputy Librarian responsible for staff and a member of the Senior Management Team,[4]
- the relevant University Library divisional/departmental Head,
- two academic members of the Library Syndicate. In the case of offices in one of the Dependent Libraries: one member of the Library Syndicate and one member of the relevant Sub-Syndicate.

Quorum: 4. One of whom must be one of the academic nominees.

6. *Librarians of Faculties, Departments, and other institutions*

- the Chair of the Faculty Board or Head of institution or a deputy appointed by him or her (Chair and Convenor),
- the University Librarian as the General Board's principal adviser on matters relating to Libraries or a deputy appointed by him or her,
- one Faculty/Departmental Librarian,
- two members of the relevant academic institution.

Quorum: 3. One of whom must be from outside the institution.

7. *Computer Officers*

For offices in the grades Computer Officer Grades I–IV, Senior Computer Officer, and Principal Computer Officer:

- the Head of the institution or a deputy appointed by him or her (Chair and Convenor),
- a senior academic with experience and interest in what the role of the office entails,
- the Director of Information Services or a deputy appointed by him or her,
- a senior academic-related officer with knowledge and experience of the role of the office,
- up to two additional members may be co-opted by the Head of the institution.

Quorum: 4. At least one of the members must be from outside the institution.

In any pre-committee selection arrangements, the Head of the institution should ensure that a Computer Officer (at the level of Grade I or above) is involved. If there is no such officer on the staff of the institution, the Head of the institution should ask the Director of Information Services to provide a senior member of his or her staff.

8. *Technical and Senior Technical Officers*

- the Head of the institution or a deputy appointed by him or her (Chair and Convenor),
- a senior academic with experience and interest in what the role of the office entails,
- a Senior Technical Officer with knowledge and experience of the role of the office,
- a senior academic-related officer with knowledge and experience of the role of the office,
- up to two additional members may be co-opted by the Head of the institution.

[1] See Regulations 6 and 7 of the regulations for the Unified Administrative Service, p. 699.

[2] The Registrary may be involved as a member at his/her discretion.

[3] Such a senior academic would normally be a member of the Council, General Board, or Finance Committee, or chair the Committee that oversees the work of the Division, or be the Head of the institution to which the officer or post-holder is to be assigned.

[4] In the case of appointment to the office of Deputy Librarian, these two members shall be replaced by up to three persons appointed by the Chair of the Library Syndicate, at least one of whom shall be from outside the University.

When an appointment or reappointment is to be made to an office whose holder will have responsibilities for the care of protected animals under the Animals (Scientific Procedures) Act 1986, the Committee shall include two additional members, appointed by the General Board – the holder of the designation certificate for the University and one of the persons appointed as the named veterinary surgeons for the University.

When an appointment or reappointment is to be made to an office whose holder will have responsibility for matters concerning safety in the University, the Head of the institution shall be as specified in the Schedule below. Two additional persons shall be appointed by the Health and Safety Executive Committee.

SCHEDULE

For an office established in:

An institution under the supervision of the General Board.	The Head of the institution concerned.
An institution under the supervision of the Council.	The Head of the institution concerned.
An institution under the supervision of the Unified Administrative Service.	*Either* the Registrary, if the officer appointed is to have responsibilities in a Council institution, *or* the Academic Secretary if the officer appointed is to have responsibilities in a General Board institution.

Quorum: 4. Either the academic or the Senior Technical Officer must be from outside the institution.

9. *Senior Assistant Secretaries, Assistant Secretaries, and Junior Assistant Secretaries of the Institute of Continuing Education*

- the Director of Continuing Education or a deputy appointed by him or her as Chair and Convener,
- the Academic Secretary or a deputy appointed by him or her,
- a senior academic with experience and interest in what the role of the office entails,
- a senior academic-related officer with knowledge and experience of the role of the office,
- up to two additional members to be co-opted at the discretion of the Director.

Quorum: 4. Either the senior academic or academic-related officer must be from outside the institution.

University maternity leave and other family-related leave policy

University maternity leave

Special factors relating to University officers

All women University officers shall be entitled to eighteen weeks' maternity leave with stipend and, in addition, up to thirty-four weeks' unpaid maternity leave. Since the statutory paid provision has been extended to thirty-nine weeks, payment of the standard rate of Statutory Maternity Pay or Maternity Allowance (included in the payment of full stipend for the initial eighteen weeks) will, for those eligible under statutory regulations, continue for the first twenty-one weeks of the unpaid leave provision under the University's maternity policy. (Under current legislation no woman may resume work earlier than two weeks after giving birth.)

Maternity leave should normally commence no earlier than the eleventh week before the expected date of childbirth. A University officer who intends to take maternity leave shall give notice of that fact by the fifteenth week before her expected week of childbirth, through the Personnel Consultant assigned to her institution, to the Registrary if she holds an office under the supervision of the Council, or to the Academic Secretary if she holds an office under the supervision of the General Board. Maternity leave will be granted under the provisions of Special Ordinance C (i) 2(*b*). Employer's contributions to USS will be continued for the period of paid leave; during any period of unpaid leave an officer may maintain her USS contributions by paying both the employee's and the employer's contributions. Stipend increments will accrue in the normal way during leave.

A term which includes maternity leave will be reckoned as a term of service for the purposes of Special Ordinance C (i) 1.

Further details, including new provisions aimed at improving communication, are contained in the policy statement which has been circulated to Heads of institutions and is available on the University's website (http://www.admin.cam.ac.uk/offices/hr/policy/maternity/).

University paternity leave provision

In the light of the right to paternity leave and pay under the Employment Act 2002, the Council and the General Board give notice of the existing, more favourable University paternity leave provision offered to eligible employees of up to two weeks on full pay, provided that satisfactory arrangements can be made to cover the absence at no additional cost to the University.

Leave of Absence under Special Ordinance C (i) 2(*a*) (sick leave)

1. Under the provisions of Special Ordinance C (i) 2(*a*), University officers may be dispensed from discharging the duties of their offices on account of illness for a period of up to six months without loss of stipend. This dispensation may be extended by the competent authority, who shall fix the amount of stipend (if any) payable.

Notification of incapacity for work on account of illness

2. All periods of incapacity for work on account of illness, including those that fall outside an academic term, shall be regarded as sick leave in accordance with Special Ordinance C (i) 2(*a*). In order to be granted sick leave, officers shall notify the head of their institution of the dates on which they are unable to work. Officers shall also provide either a completed self-certification form (blank copies available from the Human Resources Division) for absences of up to seven consecutive days, or a medical certificate (obtained from their GP or hospital, in the case of admission as an in-patient) for absences of seven days or more.

3. The dates on which sick leave is granted shall be recorded by the head of the institution and reported to the competent authority in order to determine the level of stipend (if any) payable.

4. The competent authority may seek informed consent from officers for information from their medical records to be made available in cases where the recurrence or continuation of an absence becomes a cause for concern.

Payment of stipend during sick leave

5. In determining the period for which leave with stipend will be granted, and the amount of stipend (if any) payable, the competent authority shall have regard to the following:

(*a*) The officer's length of continuous employment by the University.

(i) Officers employed from 1 January 2004 shall, during their first year of employment, normally receive their full stipend for the first eight weeks of any absence, followed by a corresponding period at half-pay, increasing to: twelve weeks after one year in employment; twenty weeks after three years in employment: and a maximum of twenty-six weeks after five years in employment.

(ii) With regard to officers employed prior to 1 January 2004, other than those in the first year of their employment by the University, the Council and the General Board have determined previously that they shall normally receive their full stipend for six months. Thereafter, following a review, a further period of leave at full pay may be granted, with the possibility of a limited period of leave being granted at a reduced rate of pay after twelve months.

(*b*) The number of days sick leave granted to the officer in the full year immediately prior to the date on which the current period of sick leave commences.

(*c*) Whether a period of four weeks has elapsed between the end of one period of sick leave and the start of another, in instances where there would otherwise be an increase in the period of leave granted with stipend as provided for in (*a*) above.

(*d*) The amount of any State Incapacity Benefit paid direct to the officer as a result of a continuing absence.

6. Where the period of incapacity for work exceeds the periods of sick leave with pay provided for in 5(*a*) above, the stipend would normally be discontinued. In exceptional circumstances the competent authority may extend the period for which leave is granted and the stipend (if any) payable, in variation of the provisions set out in 5(*a*) above, on the advice of the Human Resources Committee.

Entitlement to leave under Special Ordinance C (i) 1

7. The competent authority shall decide in each particular case whether the terms included within a period of sick leave are to be reckonable as terms of service for the purposes of Special Ordinance C (i) 1. As a general rule they shall regard sick leave of twenty-eight days or more during an academic term as normally precluding the officer from counting that term as reckonable as a term of service for the purposes of Special Ordinance C (i) 1.

Guidance

8. The Human Resources Committee will, from time to time, issue guidance[1] on implementing policy and procedures concerning sick leave and sick pay.

NOTICES BY THE GENERAL BOARD

LEAVE OF ABSENCE UNDER SPECIAL ORDINANCE C(i) 1 (SABBATICAL LEAVE)

1. Under the provisions of Special Ordinance C (i) 1, every University officer specified in the Schedule to Special Ordinance C (i) 1 is entitled to be dispensed from discharging the duties of his or her office during one term for every six terms of service, provided that the consent of the General Board is obtained, which consent shall not be unreasonably withheld. Such leave, commonly known as sabbatical leave, is normally granted as leave with stipend, subject to the conditions set out in paragraphs 6–8 below.

2. Applications for leave of absence in any term under Special Ordinance C (i) 1 should be sent, not later than the first week of the Full Term next but one preceding the period of the proposed leave, to the Academic Secretary and also to the Secretary of the Faculty Board or other body concerned.

Leave of absence in certain circumstances

3. In considering applications for leave under Special Ordinance C (i) 1, the General Board have agreed to adopt the following policy when it is known that the officer concerned will not, or may not, return to duty at the end of the period of leave applied for, or that the officer will return to duty for a short time only.

[1] This guidance has been circulated to Heads of institutions and is accessible on the Human Resources Division Web pages (www.admin.cam.ac.uk/offices/hr/).

4. (*a*) The Board will not normally allow an officer to take leave under Special Ordinance C (i) 1 for the whole or a part of the academical year at the end of which he or she is due to retire.

(*b*) The Board will normally regard as straightforward an application for leave under Special Ordinance C (i) 1

(i) if an officer applies for leave for the whole or a part of the year in which his or her current tenure is due to end, and if it is not known that the officer will be reappointed (or appointed to a different office);

or (ii) if an officer has submitted his or her resignation, to take effect *either* from the end of the period of the proposed leave *or* within a period of three terms from the beginning of the proposed leave.

5. Notwithstanding the general policy set out in paragraph 4 above, it is possible that, for special reasons, leave of absence may be granted in the circumstances referred to in paragraph 4(*a*), or that an application in the circumstances referred to in paragraph 4(*b*) may not be regarded as straightforward.

Payment of stipend during leave of absence

6. Under Special Ordinance C (i) 1 the General Board have power to fix the amount (if any) of the stipend payable to a University officer while on leave of absence under that section of the Special Ordinance. The General Board have agreed that normal pensionable stipend (and family allowances, where applicable) will be paid in full for any leave under Special Ordinance C (i) 1, provided that the officer observes the following conditions:

(*a*) a considerable portion of the leave shall be spent in study;

(*b*) the officer will give up all teaching, administrative, and examining duties for the University or for a College or Colleges, other than duties in connection with the supervision or examining of Graduate Students, or with acting as referee of applications for higher doctorates or College Fellowships;

(*c*) if, after taking account of any loss of normal sources of income and of income from any new sources, less any additional expenses associated with new activities, the officer is substantially better off than if he or she had not taken leave of absence, the officer shall forgo such part of the payment received from the University as will result in approximately the same financial state as if leave of absence had not been taken; and at the conclusion of the leave the officer shall inform the Academic Secretary whether he or she has decided to forgo any part of the payment received, and, if so, how much.

7. For the purpose of paragraph 6(*b*) above, the General Board do not regard examining for the Local Examinations Syndicate as falling under the head of examining for the University.

8. The General Board regard attendance at meetings of Boards, Syndicates, Committees, or other similar bodies of whatever name, as falling under the head of administrative duties for the purposes of these rules, and the undertaking referred to in paragraph 6(*b*) above therefore requires the officer either to resign from any such body or to secure exemption from attendance at its meetings during the period of leave of absence under Special Ordinance C (i) 1. In this connection, the General Board have decided that, to secure the proper working of Appointments Committees, it is necessary to require that an officer who is a member of an Appointments Committee and who has been granted leave of absence for a term or more shall tender his or her resignation as a member of the Appointments Committee.

Leave of Absence under Special Ordinance C (i) 2(*b*)

1. In addition to sabbatical leave, which is a statutory entitlement, Special Ordinance C (i) 2(*b*) gives the General Board discretion to grant leave of absence in other circumstances; such leave is normally granted as leave without stipend. For some years the Board have been willing to consider applications for leave without stipend for the purpose of secondment, when an officer intends to work for some other institution while on leave. Since 1987 the Board have also been willing to consider applications for leave without stipend for other purposes, in cases where officers are able to secure funds from outside sources to cover their stipends and wish to take extra leave, in addition to their regular entitlement to sabbatical leave, so as to carry out their research either in Cambridge or elsewhere. The Board's policy for granting leave without stipend under Special Ordinance C (i) 2(*b*) is set out below.

Secondment leave

2. Secondment leave may be granted to provide assistance for governments, or national agencies, or international agencies of which the United Kingdom is a member, or academic institutions or charitable organizations, or industrial or commercial concerns. Any request for the secondment of a University officer to any such body should be accompanied by a fully reasoned case, presented by the authorities of the body concerned, setting out the need for the assistance of the particular officer.

3. In considering such an application, the Board will take into account the possible academic benefits to the officer's institution, and will have in mind also the balance between the advantage to the outside body concerned of gaining the assistance of a University officer on the one hand and, on the other hand, the disadvantage to the University of losing that officer's services for the period of his or her secondment.

Leave for purposes other than secondment

4. The General Board wish to encourage University officers to obtain outside support which will allow them to pursue their research more effectively, either in Cambridge or elsewhere. They wish to stress, however, that the interests of the institution to which an officer belongs must not be neglected in favour of the interests of the individual officer. In considering such applications the Board will therefore have regard to maintaining a proper balance between the interests of the individual and those of his or her institution.

5. An officer must make a detailed case to the General Board on academic grounds in support of the application for leave. The application must be supported by the Faculty Board or other authority concerned, who will be required to show that the leave in question will be of direct benefit to the officer's institution.

6. The grant of leave must not involve the University in any additional cost.

7. While wishing to encourage University officers to seek outside funds for the support of their research, the Board are concerned to ensure that this policy is employed sparingly. The Board will normally expect that leave should be limited to a maximum of three years at any one time and that the total extent of such leave, whether taken in one or more periods, should be limited to a maximum of six years during the whole of an officer's academic career within the University.

8. The General Board will decide in each particular case whether the academical terms included within the period of leave are to be reckonable as terms of service for the purposes of Special Ordinance C (i) 1.

Savings accruing from the grant of leave without stipend

9. The allocation of savings that accrue from the grant of leave without stipend (after deductions have been made, where appropriate, for pension or National Insurance contributions and for certain central administrative costs) will be at the discretion of the Council of the relevant School. If the Council of the School so determines, savings may be allocated to, or accrue in the stipend account of, the Faculty, Department or other institution concerned. The cost of substitute teaching or full-time replacement required will be met from these savings.

PAYMENT OF PENSION CONTRIBUTIONS DURING LEAVE OF ABSENCE

1. Each case will be considered on its merits, and the general principles set out below will be subject to variation in the light of any special circumstances.

2. When an officer has been granted leave with stipend, the University will pay its share of the pension contributions on that stipend.

3. When the General Board under Special Ordinance C (i) 2(*a*) have extended a period of leave granted on account of illness to a date later than six months from the commencement of the officer's absence from duty, the University will continue to pay its share of the pension contributions on the officer's normal stipend, even if the General Board have fixed a stipend for the period of that extension less than the full University stipend, or given that extension without stipend.

4. When an officer has been given leave under Special Ordinance C (i) 1 (sabbatical leave) the University will pay its share of the pension contributions on the officer's normal stipend, even if the normal stipend is not received in full or at all from the University during the period of leave.

5. When an officer has been given leave in order to undertake national service, whether compulsory or voluntary, and the General Board have approved that service for the purpose of these rules, the University will pay its share of the pension contributions on the normal stipend even if the stipend is not received in full or at all during the period of leave.

6. If an officer applies for leave of absence under Special Ordinance C (i) 2(*b*) in order to undertake paid employment, other than national service, outside the University, it shall be a matter for consideration on each application whether the authority to whom the officer is being seconded shall be required, as a condition of the granting of the leave, to reimburse the University for the whole or part of the University's share of the pension contributions. As a rule the General Board will make it a condition of the granting of leave without stipend for this purpose that the authority to whom the officer is seconded shall reimburse the University for the whole of its share of the pension contributions on the normal stipend.

7. If an officer is given leave of absence under Special Ordinance C (i) 2(*b*) other than for the purposes mentioned in paragraphs 5 and 6, the University will usually maintain its share of the pension contributions on his or her normal stipend, even though there may be some deduction from that stipend on account of the leave.

8. If the Board under Special Ordinance C (i) 3 determine that any period (or part of a period) of leave is to be disregarded in reckoning the officer's limit of tenure, no stipend shall be payable for the period so disregarded and no pension contributions shall be payable by the University.

9. If the pension contributions payable by the University are maintained during the officer's period of leave, it shall be obligatory for the officer to maintain his or her contributions. If no pension contribution is payable by the University during the period of leave the officer may pay both the employee's and the employer's contribution if he or she wishes to do so.

10. For the purpose of these rules the normal stipend on which pension contributions are payable, if the University stipend has not been received in full by the officer during any period of leave, shall be the stipend that would have been received by the officer from the University had the officer not been granted leave, regard being had to any seniority increments that accrue during the period of leave, to supplementary payments (in accordance with the rules for such payments), and to any deduction on account of a Fellowship with dividend or a substantial College office. No seniority increments of stipend shall accrue during any period that is disregarded for the purpose of reckoning the tenure of an office.

STUDY LEAVE FOR HOLDERS OF CERTAIN UNIVERSITY OFFICES

The General Board have approved the following Schedule of offices whose holders may apply for study leave on the same conditions as are laid down in Special Ordinance C (i) 1 for University officers specified in the Schedule to Special Ordinance C (i) 1.

Faculty of Earth Sciences and Geography

Curator of the Sedgwick Museum.
Senior Assistant Curator of the Sedgwick Museum.
Assistant Curator of the Sedgwick Museum.

Faculty of Physics and Chemistry

John Couch Adams Astronomer.

Faculty of Human, Social, and Political Science

Director and Curator of the Museum of Archaeology and Anthropology.
Senior Assistant Curator of the Museum of Archaeology and Anthropology.
Assistant Curator of the Museum of Archaeology and Anthropology.

Faculty of Biology

Senior Assistant Curator in the Museum of Zoology.
Assistant Curator in the Museum of Zoology.

Faculty of Engineering

Superintendent of the Engineering Workshops.

Faculty of Clinical Medicine and other Faculties concerned

Clinical Lecturer.

Departments, etc., independent of any Faculty

Director of the Agricultural Economics Unit.
Director and Curator of the Whipple Museum of the History of Science.
Director of the Centre for Business Research.
Director of the Cambridge Endowment for Research in Finance.
Deputy Director of the Isaac Newton Institute of Mathematical Sciences

Application under Special Ordinances C (vii) A.10 and C (x) 11 for Permission to Undertake Certain Teaching

The General Board have to consider from time to time applications under Special Ordinances C (vii) A.10 and C (x) 11 from University officers specified in the Schedule to Special Ordinance C (i) 1 who wish to undertake for remuneration during Full Term regular teaching other than teaching given on behalf of the University or on behalf of a College or Colleges. The Board think that it may be convenient if they give notice of the procedure which they follow in considering such applications under these Special Ordinances.

Unless an application is for permission to undertake teaching for a very limited period in order to assist an institution which is in a temporary difficulty in providing instruction of a specialized kind, or for permission to accept a short-term appointment to a post as a visiting Professor or Lecturer, the General Board refer the application to the Faculty Board concerned and require evidence, before giving their consent, that it is to the advantage of the University that regular teaching at an institution outside the University should be undertaken by the officer concerned. Permission to undertake such regular teaching will be subject to review annually.

STIPENDS

Amended by Graces 1 of 20 November 2013, 1 of 15 January, and 6 of 16 July 2014

1. In Regulations 2 to 7 the term University staff shall apply to all University officers as described in the Statutes and Ordinances of the University and to all other persons employed by the University (except the Chancellor, the Vice-Chancellor, the High Steward, the Deputy High Steward, the Commissary, the Proctors, Pro-Proctors, Additional Pro-Proctors, and Special Pro-Proctor, the Orator, the Esquire Bedells, the University Organist, the University Marshal, the University Advocate, and the Deputy University Advocate; clinical staff, whose salaries are determined in accordance with national and local procedures for clinical staff; and persons in certain categories defined by the Council[1]).

2. The Cambridge general stipend and salary scale for University staff shall be as set out in Schedule I.

3. The grade structure set out in Schedule I shall apply to all University staff.

[1] The Council have defined the following categories of persons as excluded from these regulations:
(i) persons employed by Cambridge University Press or the Local Examinations Syndicate other than University officers;
(ii) the staff of the ADC Theatre;
(iii) estate workers on the Madingley Estate or persons other than University officers engaged in work on the University Farm.

4. A common grading methodology for determining the grades of University staff shall be approved by the University.[1]

5. (*a*) The stipends of the Vice-Chancellor, the Pro-Vice-Chancellors, the Pro-Proctors, Additional Pro-Proctors, and Special Pro-Proctor, the University Organist, and the University Marshal shall be determined by the Council.

(*b*) The stipends of the High Steward, the Deputy High Steward, the Commissary, the Proctors, the Orator, the Esquire Bedells, the University Advocate, and the Deputy University Advocate shall be determined by Grace.

(*c*) The grades for the holders of the offices of Professor, Reader, University Senior Lecturer, and University Lecturer shall be as follows:

Professor	Grade 12	points 68–100
Reader	Grade 11	point 63
University Senior Lecturer	Grade 10	points 59–63
University Lecturer	Grade 9	points 49–57

(*d*) The grades and stipends of all other University staff as defined in Regulation 1 shall be determined by the competent authority in accordance with procedures approved by that authority.

6. The competent authority, in accordance with procedures approved by the University, shall determine the initial place of the grade of the member of University staff concerned and any subsequent progression through the contribution part of a grade.

7. If a revision of the Cambridge general stipend and salary scale is approved at a time of a general revision of pay for University staff, the competent authority shall, if necessary, alter the salary of any member of the University staff in accordance with the objects and conditions of such general revision of pay.

Notes to Schedule I

Note 1: An asterisk(*) denotes a contribution point and progress through these is awarded on merit. A plus sign (+) denotes a spine point effective from 1 January 2014.

Note 2: Grade T is for staff who are studying for an approved qualification or undergoing 'in-service' training.

Note 3: On 1 January 2010 the first contribution points of Grades 2, 3, and 4 became service points.

Note 4: University Lecturers (ULs) and University Senior Lecturers (USLs) will be appointed to Grades 9 and 10 respectively.
ULs may progress through service points 1–9 of Grade 9.
USLs may progress through service points 1–3 and contribution points 4–5 of Grade 10.
Readers will only be appointed to point 2 in Grade 11 (point 63).
Research Associates and Senior Research Associates will be appointed to Grades 7 and 9 respectively.
Research Assistants are appointed to Grade 5.
The contribution points in Grades 9 and 11 do not apply to ULs and Readers. They apply to academic-related staff.
The professorial minimum will be point 68 in band 1 of Grade 12.

Note 5: For academic staff (other than Professors and USLs) contribution will be recognised through the promotions procedure as now and not by use of contribution points.
USLs will also have access to the Senior Academic Promotions procedure under which they may also be awarded contribution points 4–5 in Grade 10.

Note 6: Academic-related professorial-equivalent staff will be appointed on the contribution bands of Grade 12 according to the HERA points boundaries for each level.

Note 7: Specific arrangements will apply to progression in service-related points on some grades in compliance with the Memorandum of Understanding.

Note 8: Incremental progression through the service-related points occurs on the incremental date which will normally be on the anniversary of appointment or 1 April, 1 July, or 1 October respectively for staff engaged on terms and conditions for Manual, Clerical/Secretarial, and Technical Division appointments.

Note 9: Direct employees of the University appointed to Grade 1 will not be paid below spine point 6 with effect from 1 August 2014.

Note 10: Points 32 and 50 were aligned to the National Single Pay Spine for Higher Education Academic and Support Staff, as negotiated by the Universities and Colleges Employers Association on behalf of UK higher education employers, with effect from 1 January 2014.

[1] The grading methodology approved by Grace 3 of 27 July 2005 is the Higher Education Role Analysis scheme (HERA) with standard weightings (see the Human Resources Division's Web page (http://www.admin.cam.ac.uk/offices/hr/grading/hera.html)).

SCHEDULE I

Single Salary Spine as at 1 August 2014

	Point on scale	Grades																Point on scale	Single spine salary	
														12						
		T	1	2	3	4	5	6	7	8	9	10	11	Band 1	Band 2	Band 3	Band 4		From 1 August 2013	From 1 August 2014
	100																+	100	£169,947	£173,346
	99																+	99	£165,002	£168,302
	98																+	98	£160,199	£163,403
	97																+	97	£155,538	£158,649
	96																+	96	£151,011	£154,031
	95																+	95	£146,618	£149,550
	94																+	94	£142,351	£145,198
	93																+	93	£138,210	£140,974
	92																*	92	£134,189	£136,873
	91																*	91	£130,286	£132,892
	90																*	90	£126,496	£129,026
	89																*	89	£122,816	£125,272
	88															+	*	88	£119,244	£121,629
	87															+	*	87	£115,775	£118,091
	86															*		86	£112,405	£114,653
	85															*		85	£109,138	£111,321
Cambridge	84															*		84	£105,963	£108,082
extension to	83															*		83	£102,882	£104,940
national spine	82														+	*		82	£99,889	£101,887
	81														+	*		81	£96,984	£98,924
	80														*			80	£94,164	£96,047
	79														*			79	£91,425	£93,254
	78														*			78	£88,767	£90,542
	77														*			77	£86,187	£87,911
	76													+	*			76	£83,680	£85,354
	75													+	*			75	£81,247	£82,872
	74													*				74	£78,884	£80,462
	73													*				73	£76,592	£78,124
	72													*				72	£74,367	£75,854
	71													*				71	£72,204	£73,648
	70													*				70	£70,104	£71,506
	69													*				69	£68,067	£69,428
	68													*				68	£66,089	£67,411
	67												6*					67	£64,170	£65,453
	66												5*					66	£62,306	£63,552
	65												4*					65	£60,496	£61,706
	64											6*	3*					64	£58,738	£59,913
	63											5*	2*					63	£57,031	£58,172
	62											4*	1*					62	£55,375	£56,482
	61										13*	3						61	£53,765	£54,841
	60										12*	2						60	£52,204	£53,248
	59										11*	1						59	£50,688	£51,702
	58									14*	10*							58	£49,216	£50,200
	57									13*	9							57	£47,787	£48,743
	56									12*	8							56	£46,400	£47,328
	55									11	7							55	£45,053	£45,954
	54									10	6							54	£43,745	£44,620
	53									9	5							53	£42,476	£43,325
	52								14*	8	4							52	£41,242	£42,067
	51								13*	7	3							51	£40,046	£40,847
	50								12*	6	2							50	£38,907	£39,685
	49								11*	5	1							49	£37,756	£38,511
	48							12*	10	4								48	£36,661	£37,394
	47							11*	9	3								47	£35,597	£36,309
	46							10*	8	2								46	£34,565	£35,256
	45							9*	7	1								45	£33,562	£34,233
	44						11*	8*	6									44	£32,590	£33,242
	43						10*	7*	5									43	£31,644	£32,277
	42						9*	6	4									42	£30,728	£31,342
National	41						8*	5	3									41	£29,837	£30,434
spine	40						7*	4	2									40	£28,972	£29,552
(Framework	39						6*	3	1									39	£28,132	£28,695
Agreement)	38					10*	5	2										38	£27,318	£27,864
	37					9*	4	1										37	£26,527	£27,057
	36					8*	3											36	£25,759	£26,274
	35					7*	2											35	£25,013	£25,513
	34					6	1											34	£24,289	£24,775
	33				10*	5												33	£23,585	£24,057
	32				9*	4												32	£22,927	£23,386
	31				8*	3												31	£22,240	£22,685
	30				7*	2												30	£21,597	£22,029
	29				6	1												29	£20,972	£21,391
	28			10*	5													28	£20,374	£20,781
	27			9*	4													27	£19,802	£20,198
	26			8*	3													26	£19,247	£19,632
	25			7*	2													25	£18,708	£19,083
	24			6	1													24	£18,185	£18,549
	23			5														23	£17,678	£18,031
	22			4														22	£17,184	£17,528
	21		9*	3														21	£16,705	£17,039
	20		8*	2														20	£16,252	£16,577
	19		7*	1														19	£15,814	£16,131
	18		6*															18	£15,456	£15,765
	17		5															17	£15,054	£15,356
	16		4															16	£14,665	£14,959
	15		3															15	£14,344	£14,631
	14		2															14	£13,977	£14,257
	13		1															13	£13,621	£13,953
	12	T12																12	£13,272	£13,537
	11	T11																11	£12,936	£13,195
	10	T10																10	£12,611	£12,863
	9	T9																9	£12,295	£12,541
Trainees	8	T8																8	£11,988	£12,228
(steps 1-8	7	T7																7	£11,691	£11,925
no longer	6	T6																6	£11,400	£11,628
in use)	5	T5																5	£11,117	£11,339
	4	T4																4	£10,845	£11,062
	3	T3																3	£10,582	£10,794
	2	T2																2	£10,323	£10,529
	1	T1																1	£10,074	£10,275

SCHEDULE II

Amended by Notice (Reporter, *2013–14, p. 717)*

Stipends and scales of stipends for University offices in institutions under the supervision of the General Board: clinical appointments

The following stipends and scales of stipends are determined by the General Board:

For Clinical Lecturers on the equivalent of the NHS Specialist Registrar scales (pre-2009):
£31,301 by ten increments to £54,199

For Clinical Lecturers on the equivalent of the NHS Specialty Registrar scales (post-2009):
£31,838 by ten increments to £56,312

The offices of Associate Dean in the Faculty of Clinical Medicine, Director and Assistant Director of Studies in General Practice are part-time and stipends are determined by local agreement, with reference to the appropriate full-time Consultant salary.

The following is the basis for calculating rates of payment for clinical responsibility for University officers with honorary NHS contracts as Consultants:

New (2003) Consultant Contract:

If the integrated job plan and the honorary Consultant contract agreed with the NHS covers not less than ten Programmed Activities a week, the annual pensionable payment for clinical responsibility will amount to the difference between the officer's prime stipend and her or his notional place on the NHS full-time Consultant salary scale.

That scale is: £75,249, £77,605, £79,961, £82,318, £84,667, £90,263, £95,860, £101,451.

Pre-2003 Consultant Contract:

If the honorary Consultant contract agreed with the NHS covers not less than six NHS sessions a week, the annual pensionable payment for clinical responsibility will amount to the difference between the officer's prime stipend and her or his notional place on the NHS full-time Consultant salary scale.

That scale is: £62,478, £66,948, £71,419, £75,889, £80,988.

Payments Additional to Stipend

Amended by Grace 1 of 4 June 2014

1. The competent authority shall have the power to make pensionable additional payments and non-pensionable lump sum payments to University officers or to other persons approved by that authority as set out in Regulations 2–10 below. Heads of Departments.

2. The Head of each Department included in one of the Schedules 1–6 below shall be entitled, in addition to his or her stipend as a University officer, to a pensionable additional payment for administrative responsibility at an annual rate according to the following scale:

	Percentage of step 68 on the Cambridge general stipend and salary scale
Schedule 1	30%
Schedule 2	25%
Schedule 3	20%
Schedule 4	10%
Schedule 5	7.5%
Schedule 6	5%

3. The General Board shall have power to authorize pensionable payments to Deputy Heads of Departments, appointed in accordance with Regulation 5 of the regulations for Departments and Heads of Departments, as a proportion of the appropriate payment made under Regulation 1 to the Head of the Department.

4. The General Board shall have power to make alterations in the list of Departments in the Schedules as they may from time to time think fit.

5. The General Board shall have power, after consulting the Faculty Board concerned, to authorize a pensionable additional payment to a person who discharges any of the duties associated with the office of Chair or Secretary of the Board of a Faculty included in Schedule X, provided that the aggregate of the sums paid each year under this regulation in respect of any particular Faculty shall not exceed the payment made under Regulation 1 to the Head of a Department included in Schedule 3. Pensionable additional payment.

Pensionable payments for clinical responsibility.

6. A University officer who is medically qualified and who holds an honorary contract as a Consultant or a Senior Registrar or a Principal in General Practice in the National Health Service shall for the period of such a contract be entitled to receive, in addition to his or her stipend as a University officer, a pensionable additional payment for clinical responsibility at an annual rate according to a scale of payments determined by the General Board and published by Notice. The place of such an officer on the scale of payments shall be determined by a Joint Committee of the General Board and the Cambridge University Hospitals NHS Foundation Trust in relation to the weight of the officer's clinical responsibility as recognized by the grant of an honorary contract with the National Health Service and assessed not less than once each year by that Committee which shall consist of:

(*a*) the Regius Professor of Physic, as Chair;

(*b*) one person appointed by the Faculty Board of Clinical Medicine;

(*c*) two persons appointed by the General Board;

(*d*) two persons appointed by the Cambridge University Hospitals NHS Foundation Trust.

Non-pensionable payments.

In addition, the General Board shall have power, on the recommendation of the Faculty Board of Clinical Medicine, to approve a non-pensionable additional payment for extra clinical work which is undertaken, outside his or her normal duties, by the holder of an office of Clinical Lecturer or by some other person approved by the General Board.

7. The competent authority shall have power to authorize pensionable payments to officers temporarily carrying out the duties of a more senior post in addition to their appointment.

8. The competent authority shall have power, on the recommendation of the Faculty Board or other body concerned, to approve pensionable and non-pensionable additional payments to a University officer or to some other person approved by that authority, as published by Notice.

9. The competent authority shall have the power to establish procedures for, and authorize additional pensionable payments as market pay to any member of the University staff in accordance with a policy determined by the University. Market pay is a pensionable payment additional to stipend made for a defined period to reflect the fact that the market rate of pay for the individual concerned is higher than the stipend which would be awarded under the Ordinance relating to Stipends.

10. The General Board shall have the power to establish procedures for, and authorize, additional pensionable payments to be paid as Advanced Contribution Supplements to any University Lecturer, University Senior Lecturer, Reader or Professor. Advanced Contribution Supplements are pensionable payments that proleptically reward an expected future level of achievement.

11. The Council shall have the power to authorize pensionable payments additional to stipend to the Pro-Vice-Chancellor on whom the Vice-Chancellor confers the title of Senior Pro-Vice-Chancellor under Regulation 1 of the regulations for Pro-Vice-Chancellors.

SCHEDULE 1

Chemistry
Physics
Engineering

SCHEDULE 2

Applied Mathematics and Theoretical Physics
Archaeology and Anthropology
Biochemistry
Chemical Engineering and Biotechnology
Education
Judge Business School[1]
Materials Science and Metallurgy
Medicine
Oncology
Pathology
Physiology, Development, and Neuroscience
Public Health and Primary Care
Veterinary Medicine
Zoology

SCHEDULE 3

Astronomy (Institute)
Clinical Biochemistry
Clinical Neurosciences
Computer Laboratory
Earth Sciences
Genetics
Geography
Land Economy
Pharmacology
Plant Sciences
Psychology
Pure Mathematics and Mathematical Statistics

[1] Includes the Centre for Business Research.

SCHEDULE 4

Architecture
Haematology
Politics and International Studies
Psychiatry
Sociology

SCHEDULE 5

Cambridge Institute for Sustainability Leadership
East Asian Studies
French
German
History of Art
History and Philosophy of Science
Middle Eastern Studies
Paediatrics
Spanish and Portuguese
Surgery
Theoretical and Applied Linguistics

SCHEDULE 6

Anglo-Saxon, Norse, and Celtic
Italian
Medical Genetics
Obstetrics and Gynaecology
Radiology
Slavonic Studies

SCHEDULE X

Classics
Divinity
Economics
English
History
Law[1]
Modern and Medieval Languages
Music
Philosophy

NOTICE BY THE COUNCIL AND THE GENERAL BOARD

Additional Payments for Administrative Responsibility

1. Under the provisions of the regulations for payments additional to stipend for University Officers, as amended by Grace 5 of 12 June 2002, the competent authority shall have power, on the recommendation of the Faculty Board or other body concerned, to approve pensionable and non-pensionable additional administrative payments to a University officer or some other person approved by that authority.

Pensionable payments scheme

2. The competent authority will authorize pensionable additional payments on the recommendation of the administrative head of the institution to individuals carrying out additional roles with substantial responsibility, as specified under the regulations for payments additional to stipend.

3. These roles include formally appointed Heads and Deputy Heads of Departments falling within the scope of Schedules 1–6 to the regulations, Chairs or Secretaries of Faculty Boards not divided into Departments specified in Schedule X of the regulations, and all staff in receipt of an acting-up allowance or payment for temporary additional responsibility.

Payment arrangements

4. Payments to Heads, Deputy Heads, and Chairs or Secretaries of Faculty Boards not divided into Departments are charged against funds allocated to the relevant School. Acting-up allowances and additional responsibility payments made to a member of staff to cover for a vacant post or unpaid leave may be charged to the source of funding of the vacant post. In the case of other temporary cover, for example for paid sickness or maternity leave, the institution should apply for non-recurrent funding if the cost cannot be met from their own funds. All pensionable additional payments are made in monthly instalments with stipend or salary through the payroll.

Non-pensionable payments scheme

5. The competent authority will authorize non-pensionable additional payments on the recommendation of the administrative head of the institution to individuals temporarily carrying out additional duties or responsibilities on behalf of their Faculty or Department in addition to their usual role, as specified under the regulations for payments additional to stipend.

6. The criteria to be used to determine whether an additional payment is appropriate and will be approved by the competent authority are that:

(*a*) The work involved could not reasonably be regarded as falling within the member of staff's normal duties; and

[1] Includes the Institute of Criminology and the Lauterpacht Centre for International Law.

(*b*) The work is of a relatively long-term character or significant to the work of the institution concerned; and

(*c*) The work involves the member of staff in administrative duties which take up a significant amount of his or her time.

7. Roles for which a non-pensionable payment may be made include those for carrying out additional administrative duties[1] (either on an *ad hoc* basis or throughout the academical year) and those for taking on additional health and safety duties such as Departmental Safety Officer, Department Fire Safety Officer, Radiation Protection Supervisor, Biological Safety Officer, and Laser Safety Officer.

8. The payment to a member of staff should provide recompense for work that is carried out over and above duties that are required under the member of staff's contract of employment and should be commensurate with the weight of responsibility that is undertaken. The appropriate payment to be made should be determined by the institution by reference to and in comparison with the relevant payment made to the administrative head (and deputy head where relevant) of the institution concerned. For example, where the demand on the member of staff in terms of the amount of additional work, time, and responsibility is relatively small, the central bodies recommend that the payment should be no more than 15% of the appropriate headship rate laid down in the Schedules to the regulations; where the demand is moderate, the payment should be no more than 35% of the relevant headship payment and where the demand is high the payment should be no more than 75% of the relevant headship payment.

Payment arrangements

9. Funding for these payments is made through the annual resource allocation either to the Councils of the Schools, who disperse monies appropriately to Faculties and Departments within their scope, or to institutions under the direct supervision of the Council or General Board. Faculties, Departments, and other institutions are given the discretion to decide and recommend additional lump sum payments to their staff under the provisions of this scheme.

10. Applications from Faculties, Departments, and other institutions for additional payments to staff should be made each term using the relevant form, to be received by the Human Resources Division no later than the end of Full Term. On receipt of such forms the Human Resources Division would seek approval from the competent authority and implement the lump sum payments through the payroll, to take effect after the term in which the additional duty is carried out.

11. The Council of the Schools or institutions under the direct supervision of the Council or the General Board may bid for additional funds to meet the cost of payments they consider to be necessary by making a case to the competent authority. In addition to the use of central funds, Faculties, Departments, and other institutions may use their own resources to fund such payments.

12. *Ad hoc* payments for a single, substantial additional administrative duty should be funded through the relevant institution's resources and should be implemented using the relevant procedure recommended by the Finance Division. The payment would be approved by the competent authority and made through the monthly payroll.

13. *Ad hoc* payments for administration in connection with a contract between the University and an authority outside the University, to carry out research in University laboratories in the interest of outside bodies,[2] should be provided for in the contract and implemented using the relevant procedure recommended by the Finance Division. The payment will be approved by the relevant authority on receipt of a recommendation from the Head of the Department concerned and made through the monthly payroll.

OFFICIAL RESIDENCES

Rent and its assessment.

1. University officers or assistants who are required to occupy an official residence as a condition of their employment shall be liable to pay rent for the accommodation. The amount of the rent shall be assessed by the Estate Management and Building Service and shall be subject to revision at three-yearly intervals.

Rent reductions.

2. The rent assessed under Regulation 1 may be reduced by a sum calculated to take account of any duties arising from the occupation of the accommodation; this sum shall be assessed by the competent authority in the case of University officers and by the Assistant Staff Committee in the case of assistant staff, and shall be reassessed whenever the rent is revised or when there is any change in the duties arising from the occupation of the accommodation.

3. After any reduction in rent has been made under Regulation 2, the rent that remains payable shall be deducted from the salary of the person concerned.

Council Tax.

4. The occupation of an official residence shall be free of Council Tax, and shall be subject to such conditions as may be determined from time to time by the Finance Committee of the Council in consultation with the appropriate University body.

[1] This includes payment to Chairs of Examiners where an annual return is sent to the Board of Examinations.

[2] See p. 178.

SPECIAL REGULATIONS FOR UNIVERSITY OFFICERS

VICE-CHANCELLOR

Advisory Committee.

1. Not less than one year before the date on which the period of office of the Vice-Chancellor is expected to come to an end, or, in the event of a casual vacancy, as soon as possible after certain knowledge of the vacancy, the Council shall appoint an advisory committee to advise them on the choice of a person to be nominated for appointment to the office of Vice-Chancellor. The advisory committee shall consist of not less than eight persons, a majority of whom shall be resident members of the Regent House and at least two of whom shall be persons who are not resident members of the University. The committee shall propose a list of persons for consideration by the Council. The Council shall give public notice of the name of the person nominated and shall submit a Grace to the Regent House for the appointment of that person to the office of Vice-Chancellor.

Appointment.

Admission.

2. A Congregation of the Regent House for the formal admission of the Vice-Chancellor shall be held, as soon as conveniently may be after the Vice-Chancellor has entered upon office, on a day in term appointed by the Council. The Chancellor or, in the Chancellor's absence, the Proctors shall preside.

Procedure at Congregation.

3. At the Congregation the Senior Proctor shall ask the Vice-Chancellor, *Dabis fidem te bene et fideliter praestiturum (praestituram) omnia quae spectent ad officium procancellarii academiae Cantabrigiensis*? The Vice-Chancellor shall reply, *Ita do fidem*. The Senior Proctor shall then admit the Vice-Chancellor by saying, *Auctoritate nobis commissa admittimus te ad officium procancellarii hujus academiae, in nomine Patris, et Filii, et Spiritus Sancti.*[1] The Junior Proctor shall thereupon deliver to the Vice-Chancellor the insignia of the office. If a Grace has been submitted and approved for the admission of the Vice-Chancellor to the degree of Master of Arts under Statute B II 2(*a*) or a degree by incorporation under Statute B II 2(*b*), he or she shall be presented for that degree by the Registrary. Unless the Chancellor is present, the Vice-Chancellor shall then assume the presidency of the Congregation.

Residence.

4. Unless granted leave of absence under Special Ordinance C (i) 2, the Vice-Chancellor shall reside in the University during term-time and shall not without the consent of the Council be absent for more than eight weeks in each academical year.

Expenses.

5. The Vice-Chancellor shall be granted an allowance, of an amount determined by the Council, to meet the expenses arising out of the duties of the office. He or she may be granted a further allowance, of an amount determined by the Council, in respect of extraordinary expenses incurred through assumption of office.

Acceptance of benefactions.

6. The power of the University to accept benefactions is delegated to the Vice-Chancellor, provided that for any particular benefaction the Vice-Chancellor may request the Council to submit a Grace to the Regent House for its acceptance.

Designated officer.

7. The Vice-Chancellor shall be the designated officer for the University in accordance with the terms of the Financial Memorandum between the Higher Education Funding Council (England) and the University.

Reappointment.

8. Not more than one year before the end of his or her current term of office, and subject to the provisions of Statute C III 2, the Vice-Chancellor may be reappointed by the Regent House on the nomination of the Council.

PRO-VICE-CHANCELLORS

Amended by Grace 1 of 4 June 2014

1. The maximum number of offices of Pro-Vice-Chancellor shall be five. Although there shall not be an office of Senior Pro-Vice-Chancellor, the Vice-Chancellor may, after consultation with all of those appointed to the office of Pro-Vice-Chancellor, confer the title of Senior Pro-Vice-Chancellor on one of those appointed to the office of Pro-Vice-Chancellor, who shall take responsibility for leading and co-ordinating the work of the Pro-Vice-Chancellors.

[1] The Senior Proctor is authorized, at his or her discretion, to omit the words *in nomine Patris, et Filii, et Spiritus Sancti*.

Nominating Committee

Constitution.

2. The Nominating Committee for the office of Pro-Vice-Chancellor shall consist of:

(*a*) The Vice-Chancellor (or a duly appointed deputy) in the Chair, and the Vice-Chancellor elect (if any);

(*b*) a member of the Council in class (*a*);

(*c*) two other members of the Council;

(*d*) two members of the General Board in class (*b*), one nominated by the Board from among the members appointed by the Councils of the Schools of Arts and Humanities and the Humanities and Social Sciences, and one from among the members appointed by the other Councils of the Schools.

Members in classes (*b*), (*c*), and (*d*) shall be appointed by the Council in the Michaelmas Term to serve for two years from 1 January following their appointment. A member in any of these classes who ceases to be a member of the Council or the Board (as the case may be) shall cease to be a member of the Nominating Committee.

Secretary.

3. The Registrary (or a person appointed by the Registrary) shall act as Secretary of the Nominating Committee.

Stipend

4. The stipend for the office of Pro-Vice-Chancellor shall be determined by the Council. A Pro-Vice-Chancellor who is appointed on a part-time basis shall receive a *pro-rata* proportion of the full stipend for that office and shall, if he or she holds another University office concurrently, receive a correspondingly reduced *pro-rata* basic stipend for that other office plus any contribution payment, payment for clinical responsibility, or market supplement in full.

Proctors and Pro-Proctors

Form of certificate of residence for Proctor nominate.

1. The following form of certificate shall be used for the purpose of Special Ordinance C (iii) 3:

I hereby certify that *A.B.* of College has resided in the University during the major part of the three terms following, viz.

Witness my hand this day of
C.D., Master of College.

Seniority.

2. Of the two Proctors, one shall be designated Senior and the other Junior. The Proctor who first became a member of the Senate shall be Senior, provided that, if both became members on the same day, their seniority shall be determined in accordance with the regulations for the order of seniority of graduates.

Pro-Proctors.

Sched. to Special Ordinance C (iii) 1.

3. In the Easter Term each year two Pro-Proctors shall be appointed by Grace to hold office for the academical year next following. They shall be nominated for appointment by the Colleges according to the Cycle of Proctors, each College having the right to nominate a Pro-Proctor in the year next before that in which it has the right to nominate a Proctor. Such nominations shall be submitted in writing to the Vice-Chancellor not later than the last day of Full Lent Term each year.

Additional Pro-Proctors.

4. To assist the Proctors and Pro-Proctors in the maintenance of discipline, two additional Pro-Proctors, who shall be members of the Senate of not less than three years' standing, shall be appointed by Grace in the Easter Term of each year on the nomination of the Vice-Chancellor and of the Proctors designate and shall hold office for the academical year following their appointment.

5. The Vice-Chancellor, on the recommendation of the Proctors, may appoint additional Pro-Proctors to act on particular occasions.

Special Pro-Proctor.

6. The Vice-Chancellor shall have power to appoint a Special Pro-Proctor for motor vehicles who shall deal with the use of motor vehicles by members of the University *in statu pupillari* in accordance with regulations therefor.

7. Every breach by a person *in statu pupillari* of any of the regulations for motor vehicles shall be reported as soon as possible by the Special Pro-Proctor to the Tutor concerned.

Payments.

8. The payments to be made to the Proctors shall be determined from time to time by Grace as heretofore. The payments to be made to the Pro-Proctors, additional Pro-Proctors, and Special Pro-Proctor for motor vehicles shall be determined from time to time by the Council on the advice of the Finance Committee.

Constables

9. The Vice-Chancellor, on the nomination of the Proctors, shall appoint two Constables for each Proctor, Pro-Proctor, and Additional Pro-Proctor and one or two Constables to assist the Special Pro-Proctor for Motor Vehicles. The Vice-Chancellor shall have power to appoint additional Constables on the nomination of the Proctors.

10. The conditions of service and the payments to be made to persons appointed under Regulation 9 shall be determined from time to time by the Finance Committee of the Council on the recommendation of the Proctors. Conditions of service and payments.

University Advocate and Deputy University Advocates

1. The University Advocate shall hold office for four years, and shall be eligible for reappointment for a further period not exceeding two years. Tenure.

2. There shall be such number of University offices of Deputy University Advocate as the University shall from time to time determine on the recommendation of the Council. A Deputy University Advocate shall be appointed for two years in the first instance, and shall be eligible for reappointment for periods not exceeding two years at a time, subject to the requirement that he or she shall cease to hold office when a new University Advocate assumes office.

3. If the term of office of the University Advocate or of a Deputy University Advocate expires before the completion of any proceedings in which he or she has begun to act, he or she may continue to act for the remainder of those proceedings.

4. The University Advocate and any Deputy University Advocate shall have power to seek legal advice from sources outside the University at the expense of the University, up to a limit approved from time to time by the Council; subject to the provisions of Statute C, they may be represented in any proceedings by a barrister or solicitor or other suitably qualified person. Powers.

5. The stipend of the University Advocate shall be determined from time to time by Grace. There shall be no stipend attached to the office of Deputy University Advocate. Stipend.

6. In addition to the stipend attached to the office, the University Advocate shall be entitled to receive, in respect of any day on which he or she discharges the duties of the office, an additional non-pensionable payment at a rate determined from time to time by the Council and, in respect of part of a day, a proportionate amount of such payment. A Deputy University Advocate, and any person acting as University Advocate or Deputy University Advocate under the provisions of Regulation 3, shall be entitled to receive a similar payment in respect of any day or part of a day on which he or she carries out any of the duties of the Advocate.

Orator

The Orator shall keep such residence in the University as is necessary for the due discharge of the duties of the office. Without the permission of the Vice-Chancellor the Orator shall not be absent from any Congregation at which the title of a degree is to be conferred under Statute A II 14. He or she shall not be absent at any time for more than seven days in succession during Full Term without obtaining the permission of the Council beforehand, if possible, or asking their approval upon his or her return.

Unified Administrative Service (staff of the University Offices)

1. The staff of the University Offices shall form a Unified Administrative Service which shall be under the supervision of the Council and shall comprise the following Divisions: Divisions.

Academic Division (including the Planning and Resource Allocation Office)
Estate Management and Building Service
Finance Division
Human Resources Division
Research Services Division
Secretariat (including Legal Services)

2. Under the provisions of Statute C VI, the head of the Unified Administrative Service shall be the Registrary who, as such and under the direction of the Council, shall manage the University Offices Registrary's duties.

and their staff, budgets, space, and other resources provided to the Offices by the Council. It shall be the duty of the Registrary to ensure that arrangements for the quality assurance of the services provided by the Offices are presented to the Council and are implemented as agreed by the Council. The Registrary shall make such reports on the work of the University Offices to the Council as that body may require.

3. Within each Division of the Unified Administrative Service there shall be the University office of Director (or such other title as may be determined from time to time by the Council) who shall be head of the Division and whose duties shall include the management of the Division, under the overall responsibility of the Registrary.[1]

University offices.

4. Within the Unified Administrative Service there shall also be the following University offices, in such numbers as may be approved from time to time by the Council: Deputy Director, Assistant Director, Assistant Registrary and Assistant Treasurer (including the grades of Principal Assistant and Senior Assistant), Administrative Officer (in three grades, I, II, and III), Computer Officer (in six grades, Principal Computer Officer, Senior Computer Officer, and Officer I, II, III, and IV), and Advisory Officer (including the grade of Senior Advisory Officer).

The allocation of offices between the Divisions of the Unified Administrative Service shall be determined by the Council on the recommendation of the Registrary.

Duties.

5. The duties of the various offices and their conditions of service shall be determined by the Council.

Appointments and reappointments to senior offices.

6. Appointments and reappointments to the offices of Director, Deputy Director, Assistant Director, Principal Assistant Registrary, and Principal Assistant Treasurer shall be made by a Standing Appointments Committee which shall be a Committee of the Council. Every appointment or reappointment shall be made with the concurrence of the votes (which shall be given in person at the meeting) of at least five members of the Committee.

Standing Appointments Committee.

Membership of the Standing Appointments Committee shall consist of:

(*a*) the Vice-Chancellor (or a duly appointed deputy) as Chair;

(*b*) eight persons appointed by the Council (two on the nomination of the General Board, two on the nomination of the Finance Committee, and four on the Council's own nomination);

(*c*) the Registrary (or a deputy appointed by the Registrary) and the Director of the Division in which the appointment is to be made (except where it is the Director of the Division who is to be appointed or reappointed).

Any meeting of the Standing Appointments Committee must include members in classes (*a*) and (*c*) and four members to be selected by lot from among the members in panel (*b*).

A chair appointed by the Vice-Chancellor may appoint a deputy chair from among the members in class (*b*).

Members in class (*b*) shall be appointed in the Michaelmas Term to serve for two years from 1 January following their appointment. The Registrary, or a University officer designated by the Registrary, shall act as Secretary to the Committee.

Appointments and reappointments to other senior offices.

7. Appointments and reappointments to the offices of Senior Assistant Registrary and Senior Assistant Treasurer shall be made by the Standing Appointments Committee on the recommendation of an Appointing Committee, appointed by the Standing Appointments Committee, which shall consist of the Registrary (or a deputy appointed by the Registrary), the Director of the Division in which the appointment is to be made, an appropriate senior academic-related officer, a senior academic with experience and interest in what the role of the office entails, and a member of the Standing Appointments Committee in class (*b*).

The Standing Appointments Committee may reach their decision by circulation. Written reports of such appointments and reappointments shall be minuted at a subsequent meeting of that Committee.

Appointments and reappointments to other offices.

8. Appointments and reappointments to the offices of Assistant Registrary, Assistant Treasurer, Administrative Officer, Grades I, II, and III, Senior Advisory Officer, and Advisory Officer shall be made by the Registrary under procedures to be agreed from time to time with the Council.[2] Written reports of such appointments and reappointments shall be submitted to the Standing Appointments Committee.

[1] The Council have determined that the Director of the Academic Division shall have the title of Academic Secretary and the Director of the Secretariat shall have the title of Administrative Secretary.

[2] See p. 684.

9. Appointments and reappointments to the offices of Principal Computer Officer, Senior Computer Officer, Computer Officer, Grade I, within the Unified Administrative Service shall be made in accordance with the general regulations for the appointment of such officers.[1] Appointments and reappointments of Computer Officers.

10. The grades of the holders of various offices within the Unified Administrative Service shall be determined in accordance with procedures approved by the University. Grades.

11. Save as provided in Special Ordinance C (i) 2 the staff of the Unified Administrative Service shall be resident in the University during term-time, and shall not be absent for more than twelve weeks in the academical year; the Registrary and each Director, or a deputy appointed in his or her place, shall be resident throughout the year except during the periods when the University Offices are closed; and neither the Registrary nor the Directors shall be absent for more than two nights in any week during Full Term without obtaining beforehand, if possible, the permission of the Council or asking their approval on returning. Residence.

12. The University Offices shall be open throughout the year at such hours as may be approved from time to time by the Council except for such periods of closure at Christmas, Easter, and other public holidays as may be authorized by the Council.

Esquire Bedells

The Esquire Bedells shall be resident in the University during term. They shall so arrange that both of them shall be available at any time in term, and that one at least of them shall be available at any time in vacation, when their attendance on the Chancellor or the Vice-Chancellor is expected to be required.

University Organist

1. Appointments and reappointments to the University office of University Organist shall be made by the Council for such length of time, not exceeding five years, as the Council may fix at each appointment.

2. The University Organist shall be responsible for the music at such University services in Great St Mary's Church as the Vice-Chancellor may direct.

University Officer Holding a Residentiary Canonry of Ely Cathedral

Amended by Grace 1 of 27 November 2013

A University officer who is a member of the Faculty of Divinity and who is in Priest's Orders in the Church of England may hold a residentiary Canonry of Ely Cathedral. Not more than one University officer shall hold such a Canonry at any one time. The income, if any, of the Canonry held by such an officer, but not the annual value of the official residence of the Canonry, shall be reckoned as forming part of the stipend attached to such a person's University office. The University in making or amending regulations for the residence of University officers shall have regard to the obligations of such an officer to reside at Ely and to carry out other duties as Canon.

OFFICERS SPECIFIED IN THE SCHEDULE TO SPECIAL ORDINANCE C (i) 1

Professors and Professorships

Amended by Grace 1 of 27 November 2013

A Professor shall not undertake for remuneration during Full Term without the consent of the General Board any teaching other than teaching given on behalf of the University or a College or Colleges or the delivery of occasional lectures. The amount of teaching given by a Professor on behalf of a College or Colleges shall not, except with the consent of the General Board, exceed six hours a week, or if the Professor is also a Tutor or Bursar or an Assistant Tutor or Assistant Bursar or Steward, two hours a week.

In any Statute or Ordinance unless otherwise specified the term 'Professors' shall include Visiting Professors and the term 'Professorships' shall include Visiting Professorships.

[1] See p. 757.

After the title of each Professor there is printed the date of foundation of the Professorship and the name of the Faculty or Department to which it is assigned.

Stat. E XXXIII. *Lady Margaret's Professor of Divinity. 1502. Divinity*
Endowments, 1904, pp. 57–65[1]

Stat. E XXXII. *Regius Professor of Divinity. 1540. Divinity*
Endowments, 1904, pp. 153–64; for Jeremy Fund, p. 164; and, for Somersham Rectory Act, pp. 50–4

Stat. E XXXII. *Regius Professor of Civil Law. 1540. Law*
Endowments, 1904, pp. 153–4

Stat. E XXXII. *Regius Professor of Physic. 1540. Medicine*
Endowments, 1904, pp. 153–4

The Regius Professor of Physic shall not engage in private practice.

Stat. E XXXIII. *Regius Professor of Hebrew. 1540. Middle Eastern Studies*
Endowments, 1904, pp. 153–65

The duties of the Regius Professor of Hebrew shall include the interpretation of the Old Testament.

Stat. E VI. *Regius Professor of Greek. 1540. Classics*
Endowments, 1904, pp. 153–65

Sir Thomas Adams's Professor of Arabic. 1632. Middle Eastern Studies
Endowments, 1904, p. 172

Lucasian Professor of Mathematics. 1663. Applied Mathematics and Theoretical Physics
Endowments, 1904, p. 165

It shall be the duty of the Lucasian Professor to promote the study of some aspect of Applied Mathematics and Theoretical Physics by research and otherwise, and to conduct this work in the Department of Applied Mathematics and Theoretical Physics.

Knightbridge Professor of Philosophy. 1683. Philosophy
Endowments, 1904, p. 178

Professor of Music. 1684. Music
Endowments, 1904, p. 180

BP Professor of Chemistry. 1702. Chemistry
Endowments, 1904, p. 181

Stat. E XXVIII. *Plumian Professor of Astronomy and Experimental Philosophy. 1704. Institute of Astronomy*
Endowments, 1904, pp. 79–88

Professor of Anatomy. 1707. Physiology, Development, and Neuroscience
Endowments, 1904, pp. 182–3

1. The Professorship of Anatomy is not limited to Human Anatomy, but its scope includes also Vertebrate Anatomy and Embryology.

2. Histology, as distinguished from Microscopical Anatomy, shall continue to be taught in connection with Physiology.

Stat. E XXXII. *Regius Professor of History.*[2] *1724. History*
Endowments, 1904, pp. 183–92

Regius Professor of Botany.[3] *1724. Plant Sciences*
Endowments, 1904, pp. 194–5

Woodwardian Professor of Geology. 1728. Earth Sciences
Endowments, 1904, pp. 196–202

Stat. E XXXV. *Lowndean Professor of Astronomy and Geometry. 1749. Pure Mathematics and Mathematical Statistics*
Endowments, 1904, pp. 202–6

[1] See also p. 867.
[2] The title of the Professorship was amended by a Statute approved by Her Majesty in Council on 21 July 2010.
[3] By gracious permission of Her Majesty the Professorship was retitled by Instrument delivered to the University by Her Majesty on 19 November 2009.

It shall be the duty of the Lowndean Professor to promote the study of some aspect of Geometry by research and otherwise, and to conduct this work in the Department of Pure Mathematics and Mathematical Statistics.

Norris-Hulse Professor of Divinity. 1777, 1860. Divinity Stat. E VI, XIX, and XXXIII.
Endowments, 1904, pp. 104–21

Jacksonian Professor of Natural Philosophy. 1783. Physics
Endowments, 1904, pp. 206–16

It shall be the duty of the Jacksonian Professor to promote the study of some aspects of Physics by research and otherwise, and to conduct this work in the Department of Physics.

Downing Professor of the Laws of England. 1800. Law
Endowments, 1904, p. 217

Disney Professor of Archaeology. 1851. Archaeology and Anthropology
Endowments, 1904, pp. 222–5

Sadleirian Professor of Pure Mathematics. 1860. Pure Mathematics and Mathematical Statistics
Endowments, 1904, pp. 268–9

Professor of Political Economy. 1863. Economics
Endowments, 1904, pp. 225–6

Professor of Zoology. 1866. Zoology
Endowments, 1904, p. 226

Whewell Professor of International Law. 1867. Law Stat. E XX.
Endowments, 1904, pp. 136–40

Kennedy Professor of Latin. 1869. Classics
Endowments, 1904, pp. 234–40

Slade Professor of Fine Art. 1869. History of Art
Endowments, 1904, pp. 240–6; amended by Grace 11 of 16 July 2014

1. The election to the Professorship shall be conducted in accordance with the provisions of Special Ordinance C (vii) B.1; except that the Electors shall be empowered to make an election at any time not later than twelve months before the term or vacation in which a vacancy will occur. The Professor shall be elected for a period not exceeding three years to be determined by the Electors on each occasion.

2. Subject to the provisions of Special Ordinance C (vii) A.13 a present or past holder of the Professorship shall be re-eligible.

3. The Professor shall not be required to reside in the University.

4. It shall be the duty of the Professor to deliver annually in the University not fewer than twelve lectures on the History, Theory, and Practice of the Fine Arts, or of some section or sections of them; provided that, on the recommendation of the Head of the Department of History of Art and with the approval of the Faculty Board of Architecture and History of Art, the Professor may replace up to four of the lectures by an equivalent amount of teaching in the form of classes on a subject or subjects within that field. The lectures shall be given in Full Term and shall be open free of charge to all members of the University. If the Professor, in addition to delivering the aforementioned lectures, gives instruction at the request and on behalf of a Faculty Board, he or she shall receive such additional remuneration as may be approved by the General Board.

5. The Professor shall give at least a fortnight's public notice of the lectures.

6. After provision has been made for the payment of the stipend, national insurance, pension contributions, and associated indirect costs of the Professorship, the income of the Fund may be applied to promote the study of the fine arts in the University in such manner as may be recommended by the Faculty Board of Architecture and History of Art and approved by the General Board.

Cavendish Professor of Physics. 1871. Physics
Endowments, 1904, pp. 247–8

Professor of Engineering. 1875. Engineering
Endowments, 1904, p. 248

Elrington and Bosworth Professor of Anglo-Saxon. 1878. English
Endowments, 1904, pp. 228–33

Stat. E XXXIV. *Dixie Professor of Ecclesiastical History. 1882. History*
Endowments, 1904, pp. 248–9

Professor of Physiology. 1883. Physiology, Development, and Neuroscience
Endowments, 1904, p. 250

Professor of Pathology. 1883. Pathology
Endowments, 1904, pp. 251–2

Bertrand Russell Professor of Philosophy. 1896. Philosophy
Endowments, 1904, p. 252

1. The sums received towards the endowment of the Bertrand Russell Professorship of Philosophy shall form a fund called the Bertrand Russell Professorship of Philosophy Fund.

2. The Managers of the Fund shall be the Faculty Board of Philosophy who may delegate all or any of their functions concerning the Fund to a committee consisting of not less than three members appointed by the Board.

3. The first charge on the income of the Fund shall be the stipend, national insurance, pension contributions, and associated indirect costs of the Professor payable by the University.

4. After provision has been made in accordance with Regulation 3, the income of the Fund shall be applied by the Managers for the support of teaching or research in philosophy in the University.

5. Any unexpended income in a financial year may, at the discretion of the Managers, be either added to the capital of the Fund or accumulated for expenditure in any subsequent year in accordance with Regulation 4.

Professor of Ancient History. 1898. Classics
Endowments, 1904, p. 254

Quick Professor of Biology. 1906. Biochemistry, during the present tenure

Name and objects of Fund. **1.** The Fund shall be called the Frederick James Quick Fund and the income thereof shall be devoted to the promotion of study and research in the sciences of vegetable and animal biology.

Amount. **2.** The Fund shall consist of the residuary estate of the late Frederick James Quick (hereinafter called the Founder) bequeathed by him to the University of Cambridge for the purpose hereinbefore described and of any other moneys from time to time invested in accordance with Regulation 16(*e*) below.

Administrators. **3.** The Chancellor, Masters, and Scholars of the University shall be the persons authorized to hold and administer the principal of the Fund, and the receipt or receipts of the Vice-Chancellor of the University shall be a good discharge to the Trustees of the will of the Founder for all moneys therein acknowledged to be received.

Board of Managers. **4.** The administration of the income of the Fund shall be entrusted to a Board of Managers consisting of the Vice-Chancellor and six members of the Senate appointed by the Council, three on the nomination of the General Board and three on the nomination of the Faculty Board of Biology. Members shall be appointed in the Michaelmas Term to serve for six years from 1 January following their appointment.

Quorum. **5.** No resolution of the Managers shall be valid unless approved by at least four Managers at a meeting to which all the Managers have been summoned, save that a resolution circulated to and signed by all the Managers shall have the same validity as a resolution carried at a meeting.

Receipts and payments. **6.** The income of the Fund shall from time to time as and when received be placed to a separate account. Payments from this account shall be made as hereinafter provided. Statements showing the receipts and payments and the securities of which the Fund consists shall be published annually in the University Accounts.

Stipend of Professor. **7.** The Managers shall determine from time to time the sum which the Fund shall provide towards the stipend and pension contribution of the Quick Professor of Biology; such sum not being less than £1,000 nor more than nine-tenths of the income of the Fund.

8. (*a*) It shall be the duty of the Professor to undertake the study of some field of vegetable and animal biology, and generally to promote that branch of science by research and otherwise. He or she shall lecture in one term in each year on research in this branch of science. Duties.

(*b*) On each appointment of a Professor, the University shall determine to which Faculty or Department the Professorship shall be assigned. Assignment to Faculty or Department.

(*c*) The Professorship shall not be tenable with any other Professorship, Readership, or Lectureship in the University or elsewhere. Restriction.

9. A Quick Professor shall be elected by the General Board under the authority of Special Ordinance C (vii) B.1(*c*)(ii) in accordance with the procedure set out in Regulations 10–15.

10. (*a*) When a Quick Professor is due under Statutes and Ordinances to retire, the Vice-Chancellor shall report the fact to the Council and to the General Board in the Michaelmas Term, but not later than the division of that term, of the second academical year before the year at the end of which the Professor is due to retire.

(*b*) When the Vice-Chancellor knows that a vacancy has occurred or will occur in the Professorship otherwise than by the holder's becoming due under the Statutes and Ordinances to retire, he or she shall report the fact to the Council and the General Board at their next meetings.

11. Not later than the end of the eighteenth month after the Vice-Chancellor's report of a vacancy or of an expected vacancy in the Professorship the General Board shall determine the particular field to which candidature shall be limited or preference shall be given in considering candidates for the Professorship. For this purpose the Board shall consult appropriate Faculty Boards, Heads of Departments, and the Council of the School of the Biological Sciences on available accommodation and possible fields for the Professorship. They shall also consider whether they are themselves prepared to make provision for the development of some aspect of biology for which accommodation is not at the time available.

12. Not later than the end of the twelfth month after the General Board have determined the particular field to which candidature will be limited or preference will be given at the next election, the Vice-Chancellor shall publish a Notice inviting applications to fill the vacancy, and the General Board shall appoint a Committee, constituted on the same principles as a Board of Electors to a Professorship, of persons representative of the relevant branches of science to advise them in their choice.

13. If a member of the General Board is or becomes a candidate for the Professorship, he or she shall be disqualified from acting thereafter in the matter of that election to the Professorship, and the other members of the Board shall have power to act.

14. The General Board shall have power to enquire whether any person or persons other than those who have submitted applications would accept the Professorship if offered, and to offer the office to a person who has not submitted an application.

15. If at the end of two years from the date of publication of the Notice inviting applications for the Professorship the General Board have been unable to make an election they shall, after again consulting the appropriate bodies in accordance with Regulation 11,

either (*a*) determine that candidature shall be limited or preference shall be given to a different field from the field previously determined, so that the procedure under Regulation 12 may recommence,

or (*b*) publish a Notice discontinuing the Professorship for a specified period which shall neither be less than one year nor extend beyond the end of the seventh academical year following the date of publication under Regulation 12 of the Notice inviting applications.

16. The income of the Fund shall be applied from time to time as follows: Application of income.

(*a*) nine-tenths of the income in each year or such smaller sum as may be determined by the Managers shall be applied to the payment of the Quick Professor of Biology; Professor's stipend.

(*b*) from the balance of the income in each year a sum determined by the Managers shall be placed at the disposal of the Quick Professor of Biology to be used in providing assistance and in the general maintenance of the Professor's laboratory; Balance.

(*c*) subject to the provisions of the Founder's will the remainder (if any) of the income in each year shall be devoted, as the Managers shall from time to time direct, to the furtherance of original biological investigations conducted under the control of the Managers, and to the support and development of the study of vegetable and animal biology either by contributions towards the stipends of existing teaching posts or by the establishment of new teaching posts; Surplus.

Reserve fund. (*d*) if in any year any portion of the income be not expended, it shall be carried to a reserve fund, from which grants may be made for the same purposes as is provided by the last preceding regulation or which may be invested as provided in the next following regulation;

(*e*) any portion of the Fund, and any such reserve fund or any portion of it, may on the recommendation of the Board of Managers be invested from time to time.

How regulations may be altered. **17.** The foregoing regulations are subject to alteration by Grace; but unless this regulation is rescinded, no alteration in them shall be made except on the recommendation of the Board of Managers.

Professor of Astrophysics. 1909. Institute of Astronomy

The benefaction for the endowment of a Professorship of Astrophysics shall constitute a fund called the Astrophysics Professorship Fund. The stipend of the Professor and the pension contribution payable by the University thereon shall be the first charge on the Fund.

Schröder Professor of German. 1909. German and Dutch

1. The sum received from Messrs J. Henry Schröder and Company for the endowment of a Professorship of German in 1909, together with funds received for the same purpose in 2011 from the Schroder Foundation and Trinity College, shall form a fund to be called the Schröder Fund.

2. The Fund shall be administered by four Managers, who shall comprise:

(*a*) The Head of the Department of German and Dutch, who shall be Chair;

(*b*) The Schröder Professor of German;

(*c*) The Chair of the Faculty Board of Modern and Medieval Languages;

(*d*) The Head of the School of Arts and Humanities.

If two or more of these offices are held by the same person or if one or more of the named posts is vacant or its tenure has expired, the General Board shall appoint one or more additional Managers to ensure that there are always four Managers.

3. The first charge on the income of the Fund shall be the payment of the stipend, national insurance, pension contributions, and associated indirect costs of the Schröder Professor of German payable by the University.

4. After provision has been made in accordance with Regulation 3, income of the Fund may be applied for furtherance of teaching and research in German Studies, by the Schröder Professor, as the Managers may determine.

5. Any unexpended income in a financial year shall either be added to the capital of the Fund or accumulated for use as income in any one or more subsequent years, in such a manner as may be recommended by the Managers and approved by the General Board.

Stat. E XXXII. *King Edward VII Professor of English Literature. 1911. English*

1. The sum of £20,000 received from Sir Harold Harmsworth, Bart., for the endowment of a Professorship of English Literature shall be called the Harmsworth Fund.

2. The Professorship shall be called the King Edward VII Professorship of English Literature in memory of his late Majesty, in the year of whose death the endowment of the Professorship by Sir Harold Harmsworth, Bart., was accepted by the University.

3. It shall be the duty of the Professor to deliver courses of lectures on English Literature from the age of Chaucer onwards, and otherwise to promote the study in the University of the subject of English Literature. The Professor shall treat this subject on literary and critical rather than on philological and linguistic lines.

4. All appointments to the Professorship shall be made by the Crown.

5. The residence and duties of the Professor shall be governed by Special Ordinance C (vii) A.

6. The Professorship is assigned to the Faculty of English.

7. The income of the Harmsworth Fund, so far as it suffices, shall be applied in the following order:

(*a*) to the payment of the stipend of the Professor, which shall be not less than £800;

(*b*) to the pension contributions, if any, payable by the University in respect of the Professor's stipend;

(*c*) to the furtherance of the study of English Literature in the University in such manner as may be approved by Grace on the recommendation of the General Board.

8. With the exception of Regulations 2–5 and 8, these regulations shall be subject to alteration by Grace.

Stat. E XL. *Arthur Balfour Professor of Genetics. 1912. Genetics*

It shall be the duty of the Professor to promote by research and teaching the experimental study of heredity and of development by descent.

Serena Professor of Italian. 1919. Italian

1. The sum of £10,000 received from Mr Arthur Serena shall be called the Serena Benefaction; it shall form part of an Italian Fund, to which any further sums received for the endowment of the Chair shall be added.

2. If and whenever the income of the Italian Fund shall exceed the amount required for the payment of the stipend of the Professor, the excess of the income above that amount shall be employed for the furtherance of the study of Italian in the University in such manner as may be approved by Grace on the recommendation of the General Board after consultation with the Faculty Board of Modern and Medieval Languages.

Vere Harmsworth Professor of Imperial and Naval History.[1] *1919. History* Stat. E XXXVI

1. The sum of £20,000 received from Lord Rothermere for the endowment of a Vere Harmsworth Professorship of Naval[2] History shall be called the Vere Harmsworth Fund.

2. The Professorship shall be called the Vere Harmsworth Professorship of Imperial and Naval History, in memory of Lord Rothermere's son, Vere Harmsworth, who was killed while serving with the Hawke Battalion in the Royal Naval Division at the battle of the Ancre.

Drapers Professor of French. 1919. French

Francis Mond Professor of Aeronautical Engineering. 1919. Engineering

1. The sum of £20,000 received from Mr Emile Mond for the endowment of a Francis Mond Professorship of Aeronautical Engineering shall be called the Francis Mond Fund.

2. The Professorship shall be called the Francis Mond Professorship of Aeronautical Engineering in memory of Lieutenant Francis Mond of Peterhouse, who was killed in action while serving in the Royal Air Force.

3. Any part of the income of the Francis Mond Fund not paid as stipend to the Professor shall be transferred to the Departmental Fund for Engineering.

Professor of Physical Chemistry. 1920. Chemistry

Sir William Dunn Professor of Biochemistry. 1921. Biochemistry

Professor of the History of Political Thought. 1927. History

1. The sum of 150,000 dollars received from the Laura Spelman Rockefeller Memorial for the establishment of a Professorship of the History of Political Thought shall constitute a fund called the Political Thought Fund.

2. The Managers of the Fund shall be the Faculty Board of History who may delegate any or all of their functions under these regulations to a committee of no fewer than three persons not necessarily consisting wholly of members of the Board.

3. The first charge on the income of the Fund shall be the payment of the stipend, national insurance, and pension contributions of the Professor payable by the University.

4. The second charge on the income of the Fund shall be the payments determined by the Managers under Regulation 4 of the regulations for the John Seeley Lectureship in Political Thought.

5. After provision has been made in accordance with Regulations 3 and 4, the excess of the income above that amount may, at the discretion of the Managers, be applied for the furtherance of the study of political thought and its cognate disciplines in the University in such manner as the Managers may determine.

6. The Professor shall be a member of the Faculty Board of Human, Social, and Political Science.

7. Any part of the income of the Fund not expended in any year, and any income accruing during a vacancy in the Professorship, may in any subsequent year be expended in accordance with Regulations 3–5.

Rouse Ball Professor of Mathematics. 1927. Pure Mathematics and Mathematical Statistics

1. The sum received from the Trustees of the late Walter William Rouse Ball, Fellow of Trinity College, for the establishment of a Professorship or Readership in some branch or branches of Mathematics, the donor expressing a hope (but not making it in any way a condition) that it might be

[1] The Professorship will be discontinued from 1 October 2012 to 30 September 2015.
[2] The title of the Professorship was enlarged by a Statute approved by His Majesty in Council on 26 June 1933.

found practicable for such Professor or Reader to include in his or her lectures and treatment historical and philosophical aspects of the subject, shall constitute a fund called the Rouse Ball Professorship of Mathematics Fund, the income of which shall be applied to the maintenance of the Professorship.

2. It shall be the duty of the Rouse Ball Professor to promote the study of some aspect of Pure Mathematics by research and otherwise, and to conduct this work in the Department of Pure Mathematics and Mathematical Statistics.

Rouse Ball Professor of English Law. 1927. Law

The sum received from the Trustees of the late Walter William Rouse Ball, Fellow of Trinity College, for the establishment of a Professorship or Readership in some branch or branches of Modern English Law, the donor expressing a hope (but not making it in any way a condition) that it might be found practicable for such Professor or Reader to include in his or her lectures and treatment historical and philosophical aspects of the subject, shall constitute a fund called the Rouse Ball Professorship of English Law Fund, the income of which shall be applied to the maintenance of the Professorship.

Professor of Economic History. 1928. History

The Professor shall be a member of the Faculty Board of Economics.

Professor of Modern History. 1930. History

Laurence Professor of Ancient Philosophy. 1930. Classics

Laurence Professor of Classical Archaeology. 1930. Classics

Montague Burton Professor of Industrial Relations and Labour Economics.[1] *1931. Economics*

1. The shares transferred to the University by Mr Montague Burton shall constitute a fund called the Montague Burton Fund.

2. The income of the Fund shall be applied in the first instance to the maintenance of a Professorship called the Montague Burton Professorship of Industrial Relations and Labour Economics.

3. It shall be the duty of the Professor to study and give instruction upon the conditions of employment and the relations between employers and employed, with special reference to the causes of industrial disputes and the methods of promoting industrial peace.

4. If in any year during the continuance of the Professorship the income of the Fund, because of a vacancy in the Professorship or from any other cause, is more than sufficient to pay the stipend of the Professor and the pension contributions payable by the University thereon, the surplus shall be paid into a separate fund whence shall be defrayed such expenses as the Professor may incur in travelling abroad in order to investigate industrial relations and associated matters, including teaching and research in connection therewith, and in particular in order to keep in touch with the International Labour Organization.

Professor of Geography. 1931. Geography

Professor of Experimental Psychology. 1931. Psychology

Professor of Mineralogy and Petrology. 1931. Earth Sciences

Professorships on the John Humphrey Plummer Foundation: General Regulations

1. A John Humphrey Plummer Professor shall be elected by the General Board under the authority of Special Ordinance C (vii) B.1(*c*)(i) in accordance with the procedure set out in the following regulations.

2. (*a*) When a John Humphrey Plummer Professor is due under Statutes and Ordinances to retire, the Vice-Chancellor shall report the fact to the General Board in the Michaelmas Term, but not later than the division of that term, of the second academical year before the year at the end of which the Professor is due to retire.

(*b*) When the Vice-Chancellor knows that a vacancy has occurred or will occur in a John Humphrey Plummer Professorship otherwise than by the holder's becoming due under the Statutes and Ordinances to retire, he or she shall report the fact to the General Board at their next meeting.

[1] Retitled by Grace 2 of 7 March 2012.

3. When the Vice-Chancellor has reported that a vacancy has occurred or is expected to occur in a John Humphrey Plummer Professorship, the General Board shall consult the Councils of the Schools of the Biological Sciences, Clinical Medicine, the Physical Sciences, and Technology on whether it is desirable that the Professorship be continued, and if so, whether in the same or in a different subject.

4. When it has been decided whether the Professorship shall be continued, and if so, what shall be the subject of the Professor who will fill the vacancy, and a Professor is to be elected, the Vice-Chancellor shall publish a Notice inviting applications to fill the vacancy and the General Board shall appoint a Committee, constituted on the same principles as a Board of Electors to a Professorship, of persons representative of the relevant branches of science to advise them in their choice.

5. If a member of the General Board is or becomes a candidate for the Professorship, he or she shall be disqualified from acting thereafter in the matter of that election to the Professorship, and the other members of the Committee shall have power to act.

6. The General Board shall have power to enquire whether any person or persons other than those who have submitted applications would accept the Professorship if offered, and to offer the office to a person who has not submitted an application.

7. If at the end of two years from the date of publication of the Notice inviting applications for the Professorship the General Board have been unable to make an election, they shall, after again consulting the Councils of the relevant Schools,

either (*a*) propose that the Professorship be continued in a different subject;

or (*b*) publish a Notice temporarily discontinuing the Professorship for a specified period.

If under (*a*) the continuance of the Professorship in a different subject is approved by the University, the procedure for election shall recommence in accordance with Regulation 4. Any period specified in a Notice published under (*b*) shall neither be less than one year nor extend beyond the end of the seventh academical year following the date of publication under Regulation 4 of the Notice inviting applications.

Special Regulations

John Humphrey Plummer Professor of Theoretical Physics. 1993. Applied Mathematics and Theoretical Physics

John Humphrey Plummer Professor of Developmental Biology. 2001. Zoology

John Humphrey Plummer Professor of Chemical and Structural Biology. 2001. Chemistry

John Humphrey Plummer Professor of Physics of Materials. 2004. Physics

Scheme for the John Humphrey Plummer Foundation

In the matter of the charitable trust which is established under the Will and Codicils of the late John Humphrey Plummer proved on 26 February 1929 and which is subject to the Scheme for the John Humphrey Plummer Foundation approved by the Chancery Court of the County Palatine of Lancaster on 23 March 1931 and by Grace 2 of the Regent House of the University of Cambridge of 9 May 1931 ("the Charity")

And in the matter of the Charities Act 1993

The Charity Commissioners for England and Wales under the power given in the Charities Act 1993 hereby order that the following Scheme shall replace the said Will and Codicils and the said Scheme of the regulation of the Charity.

1. The trustee of the charity shall be [the body corporate known as] the Chancellor, Masters, and Scholars of the University of Cambridge ('the Trustee') which shall replace the existing trustees who shall retire and be discharged from the trusts of the Charity.

2. The property subject to the trusts of the Charity which is described in the schedule hereto [not reproduced] shall constitute a trust fund known as the John Humphrey Plummer Fund ('the Fund').

3. The income of the Fund shall be applied to advance education in Chemistry, Biochemistry, Physical Science, or such other allied subjects in the University as the Trustee shall in its discretion think fit, in particular by funding Professorships in those subjects and any excess of the income of the Fund over the amount required to meet this purpose may be applied to support the work of the holders of the said Professorships in such manner as the Trustee may think fit.

4. The name 'John Humphrey Plummer' shall be included in the title of each of the Professorships and the Charity and the Professorships shall be subject to the Statutes of the University.

5. The Trustee may from time to time make regulations governing the administration and application of the Fund, subject to the provisions of this Scheme and the Statutes of the University.

6. The Commissioners may decide any question put to them concerning:

(1) the interpretation of this Scheme; or

(2) the propriety or validity of anything done or intended to be done under it.
(Sealed by the Charity Commissioners on 4 April 2007.)

Goldsmiths' Professor of Materials Science.[1] *1931. Materials Science and Metallurgy*

1. It shall be the duty of the Professor to promote by teaching and research the study of the science and technology of materials.

2. The stipend of the Professor shall as far as possible be defrayed from the Goldsmiths' Fund.

William Wyse Professor of Social Anthropology. 1932. Archaeology and Anthropology

There shall be established in the University a William Wyse Professorship of Social Anthropology, partly supported by the Master, Fellows, and Scholars of Trinity College from money bequeathed by William Wyse, M.A., formerly Fellow and Honorary Fellow of the College.

Professor of Spanish. 1933. Spanish

The scope of the Professorship shall include, besides the language, literature, and history of Spain, the relations of the British Isles with Spain and with the Spanish-speaking countries of America.

Professor of Comparative Philology. 1937. Classics

Professor of Medieval History. 1937. History

Professor of Education. 1938. Education

Sched. to Special Ordinance G (i) 2.

Pitt Professor of American History and Institutions. 1944.

1. The Professor shall be elected annually by the General Board under the authority of Special Ordinance C (vii) B.1(*c*)(iii).

2. The tenure of the Professorship shall be one year.

3. The sum of £49,000 transferred from the funds of the University Press to the Chest shall constitute a Pitt Professorship Fund.

4. The stipend of the Professor shall be payable from this Fund and the balance of a year's income shall be available, at the discretion of the General Board, towards paying the travelling expenses of the Professor incurred by his or her appointment.

Professor of Electrical Engineering. 1944. Engineering

The first charge on the income of the Electrical Engineering Fund shall be the net cost to the University of the stipend and pension contributions of the Professor of Electrical Engineering.

Shell Professor of Chemical Engineering. 1945. Chemical Engineering and Biotechnology

Hopkinson and Imperial Chemical Industries Professor of Applied Thermodynamics. 1950. Engineering

1. The first charge on the income of the Hopkinson and Imperial Chemical Industries Fund shall be the net cost to the University of the stipend, and employers' contribution on account of superannuation and national insurance, of the Hopkinson and Imperial Chemical Industries Professor of Applied Thermodynamics, with the condition that for the purpose of this regulation the Hopkinson and Imperial Chemical Industries Income Reserve Fund shall not be treated as either income or capital of the Hopkinson and Imperial Chemical Industries Fund.

2. After provision has been made in accordance with Regulation 1 the remaining income of the Fund shall be applied from time to time, at the discretion of the Head of the Department of Engineering and subject to such conditions as he or she may think fit, for the purchase of equipment and for other needs associated with the study of heat engines.

Professor of Small Animal Surgery[2] *1950. Veterinary Medicine*

Smuts Professor of Commonwealth History. 1952. History

Professor of Medieval and Renaissance English. 1954. English

The Professor of Medieval and Renaissance English shall treat the subject on literary and critical rather than on philological and linguistic lines.

[1] Discontinued from 1 October 2014 until 30 September 2017 by Grace 6 of 17 July 2013.

[2] Retitled by Grace 1 of 12 June 2013. Previously entitled Professor of Comparative Oncology and Genetics and Professor of Veterinary Studies.

Wolfson Professor of Criminology. 1959. Institute of Criminology

1. The first charge on the income of the fund established from the benefaction in 1959 of the Isaac Wolfson Foundation shall be the net cost to the University of the stipend and employers' contribution on account of superannuation and national insurance of the Wolfson Professor of Criminology.

2. Any balance remaining of the annual income of the fund shall be applied to the support of the work, including the library, of the Institute of Criminology.

Professor of Manufacturing Engineering. 1960. Engineering

Sheild Professor of Pharmacology. 1961. Pharmacology

Professor of Mathematical Statistics. 1961. Pure Mathematics and Mathematical Statistics

Professor of Medicine. 1962. Medicine

Professor of Applied Mathematics. 1964. Applied Mathematics and Theoretical Physics

Frank Ramsey Professor of Economics.[1] *1965. Economics*

Professor of English. 1966 (Grace 2 of 1 December 1965). English

Professor of Modern Languages.[2] *1966. German and Dutch*

Professor of Engineering. 1966 (Grace 5 of 1 December 1965). Engineering

Sir Kirby Laing Professor of Civil Engineering.[3] *1966. Engineering*

Professor of Physics. 1966 (Grace 7 of 1 December 1965). Physics

Professor of Geophysics. 1966. Earth Sciences

Churchill Professor of Mathematics for Operational Research. 1966. Pure Mathematics and Mathematical Statistics

Joseph Needham Professor of Chinese History, Science, and Civilization.[4] *1966 East Asian Studies*

1. The sums of £1.25m received from The East Asian History of Science Foundation and £750,000 received from Trinity College, together with other sums donated for the same purpose, shall form a fund called the Joseph Needham Fund for Chinese History, Science, and Civilization.

2. The Managers of the Fund shall be the Head of the Department of East Asian Studies, the Joseph Needham Professor of Chinese History, Science, and Civilization and one other Manager appointed by the Faculty Board of Asian and Middle Eastern Studies for periods of five years, provided that, if two or more of these posts are held by the same person or if one or more of these posts is vacant or its tenure has expired, the Faculty Board of Asian and Middle Eastern Studies shall appoint one or more additional Managers so as to ensure that there are three Managers.

3. The income of the Fund shall be available for the payment of the stipend, national insurance, pension contributions, and associated indirect costs of the Joseph Needham Professor of Chinese History, Science, and Civilization.

4. After provision has been made in accordance with Regulation 3, the income of the Fund shall be applied for the support of teaching or research in some aspect of Chinese History, Science, and Civilization in such a manner as shall be approved by the General Board on the recommendation of the Managers.

5. Any unexpended income in a financial year may in any one or more subsequent years be expended in accordance with Regulations 3 and 4.

Mary Marshall and Arthur Walton Professor of the Physiology of Reproduction. 1967. Physiology, Development, and Neuroscience

Professor of Mathematical Physics. 1967. Applied Mathematics and Theoretical Physics

[1] Retitled by Grace 13 of 27 April 1994 for the tenure of the present holder and permanently retitled by Grace 1 of 12 January 2011.

[2] Suppressed by Grace 1 of 11 June 2014.

[3] Previously entitled Professor of Engineering (Grace 6 of 1 December 1965).

[4] Previously entitled Professor of Chinese.

Professor of Slavonic Studies. 1968. Slavonic Studies

Sched. to Special Ordinance G (i) 2.

Simón Bolívar Professor of Latin-American Studies. 1968.

1. The gift of 1,280,000 bolivares from the Venezuelan Government shall form a fund called the Simón Bolívar Professorship Fund.

2. The stipend of the Professor and charges associated therewith shall be payable from this Fund and any balance of the income shall be available, at the discretion of the General Board, towards paying the travelling expenses of the Professor incurred by his or her appointment and other expenses incurred in support of the Professor's work.

3. The Professor shall be elected by the General Board under the authority of Special Ordinance C (vii) B.1(*c*)(iii).

4. The tenure of the Professorship shall be one year, save that the General Board shall have power to make an election or elections for a shorter period if they so determine at the time of the election.

5. Any unexpended income in a financial year may in any one or more subsequent years be added to the capital of the Fund or applied in support of research or teaching in the field of Latin-American studies in such manner as may be approved by the General Board on the recommendation of the Committee of Management of the Centre of Latin-American Studies.

Professor of Chemistry. 1968. Physics and Chemistry

Geoffrey Moorhouse Gibson Professor of Chemistry. 1970. Chemistry

1. The sum of £2m received from Trinity College, trustees of the Geoffrey Moorhouse Gibson Fund which was created by Mrs Marjorie Gibson in memory of her husband, for research in Chemistry, shall form a fund called the Geoffrey Moorhouse Gibson Professorship of Chemistry Fund.

2. The Fund shall be administered by three Managers appointed by the Faculty Board of Physics and Chemistry, who shall include the Head of the Department of Chemistry (or the Deputy Head of the Department of Chemistry if the Head of the Department is the Geoffrey Moorhouse Gibson Professor), who shall be the Chair, the Geoffrey Moorhouse Gibson Professor of Chemistry, and one person appointed on the nomination of Trinity College.

3. If and whenever the income of the Fund shall exceed the amount required for the payment of the stipend, national insurance, pension contributions, and associated indirect costs of the Professor payable by the University, the excess of the income over that amount may be applied for the support of the work of the Professor in such manner as may be approved by the General Board on the recommendation of the Managers.

4. Any unexpended income in a financial year may in any subsequent year be expended in accordance with Regulation 3.

Professor of Architecture. 1970. Architecture

Professor of Economics. 1970. Economics

Rank Professor of Engineering. 1971. Engineering

1. The gift of £75,000 from the Rank Organization shall form a fund called the Rank Professorship Fund.

2. The first charge on the income of the Fund shall be the stipend of the Rank Professor.

3. In addition to his or her statutory duties under Special Ordinance C (vii) A, it shall be the duty of the Professor to undertake the study of acoustics in the University by teaching and research.

4. When a vacancy occurs in the Professorship the General Board shall consult the Rank Organization before they determine under Special Ordinance C (vii) A.2 whether to recommend that candidature at the next election shall be limited or preference given by the Electors to candidates whose work is connected with some particular subject or subjects falling within the scope of the title of the Professorship.

Sched. to Special Ordinance G (i) 2.

Arthur Goodhart Visiting Professor in Legal Science. 1971. Law

1. The benefaction from the Overbrook Foundation which was made to mark the eightieth birthday of Professor Arthur Lehman Goodhart shall form a fund called the Arthur Goodhart Fund.

2. The first charge on the income of the Fund shall be the cost of the stipend, national insurance, pension contributions, and family allowances, if any, of the Arthur Goodhart Visiting Professor in Legal Science.

3. After provision has been made in accordance with Regulation 2 the balance of the income of the Fund shall be applied to meet costs associated with the Professorship, including travel and the maintenance of the Professor's residence.

4. The Professor shall be elected by the General Board in accordance with Special Ordinance C (vii) B.1(*c*)(iii), on the advice of a Committee constituted on the same principles as a Board of Electors to a Professorship.

5. The Professor shall be elected for one year. In exceptional circumstances he or she shall be eligible for further election, provided that the tenure of the Chair by any one person shall not exceed two years in all.

Alexander Todd Visiting Professor of Chemistry. 1972. Physics and Chemistry

1. The sums donated to mark the retirement of Professor Alexander Todd in 1971 from the Professorship of Organic Chemistry shall constitute a fund called the Alexander Todd Visiting Professorship of Chemistry Fund.

2. The Managers of the Fund shall be the holder of the Professorship of Chemistry (1968), the holder of the Professorship of Chemistry (1970), the holder of the Unilever Professorship of Molecular Sciences Informatics (1999), the holder of the BP Professorship of Chemistry (1702), the holder of the Herchel Smith Professorship of Organic Chemistry (1988), the holder of the Professorship of Physical Chemistry (1920), the Director of the Melville Laboratory for Polymer Synthesis, and the Head of the Department of Chemistry.

3. An Alexander Todd Visiting Professor of Chemistry shall from time to time be elected under the authority of Special Ordinance C (vii) B.1(*c*)(iii) by the General Board, on the advice of the Managers of the Fund. The tenure of the Visiting Professor, during which he or she shall be in residence in Cambridge unless granted leave of absence by the General Board, shall not exceed three months and shall be determined by the General Board on the recommendation of the Managers.

4. If and whenever the income of the Fund shall exceed the amount required for the payment of the travelling expenses incurred by the Visiting Professor on his or her appointment and such emoluments as the General Board, on the recommendation of the Managers, shall determine at the time of the election, the excess of income over that amount may be applied in support of research or teaching in the field of organic chemistry in such manner as may be approved by the General Board on the recommendation of the Head of the Department of Chemistry.

5. Any unexpended income in a financial year may in any subsequent year be expended in accordance with Regulation 4.

Professor of Law. 1973. Law

Professor of Epidemiology and Medicine. 1975. Public Health and Primary Care

Professor of Obstetrics and Gynaecology.[1] *1975. Obstetrics and Gynaecology*

Professor of Clinical Biochemistry and Medicine. 1977. Clinical Biochemistry

Professor of Radiology. 1977. Radiology

Sheila Joan Smith Professor of Immunology.[2] *1977. Clinical Medicine*

1. The sum of US$650,000 received from the American Friends of Cambridge, representing a benefaction from Dr Herchel Smith for the endowment of a Professorship in the field of medical studies, shall form a fund called the Sheila Joan Smith Professorship Fund.

2. If and whenever the income of the Fund shall exceed the amount required for the payment of the stipend, national insurance, and pension contributions of the Professor payable by the University, the excess of the income over that amount may be applied to meet the cost of the work of the Professor in such manner as may be approved by the General Board on the recommendation of the Regius Professor of Physic.

3. Any unexpended income in a financial year may be expended in accordance with Regulation 2.

4. The Sheila Joan Smith Professorship of Immunology shall be limited to one tenure.

[1] Discontinued by Grace 6 of 17 May 2006 until such date as the Professorship of Obstetrics and Gynaecology (2000) becomes vacant.

[2] Re-established for one tenure by Grace 12 of 13 July 2011.

Professor of Paediatrics. 1978. Paediatrics

Professor of Mathematical Physics.[1] *1978. Applied Mathematics and Theoretical Physics*

Paul Mellon Professor of American History. 1980. History

1. A sum of US$1,000,000 received from the Andrew W. Mellon Foundation for the endowment of the Paul Mellon Professorship of American History shall constitute a fund to be called the Mellon Professorship Fund. For this purpose American history shall be defined as the history of the United States of America from its colonial beginnings.

2. If and whenever the income of the Fund shall exceed the amount required for the payment of the stipend, national insurance, and pension contributions of the Professor payable by the University, the excess of the income above that amount may be applied to meet the cost of the administrative, secretarial, research, and travelling expenses of the Professor in such manner as may be approved by the General Board on the recommendation of the Faculty Board of History.

3. Any unexpended income in a financial year shall be added to the capital of the Fund.

Herchel Smith Professor of Medicinal Chemistry. 1982. Clinical Medicine

1. A sum of US$1,000,000 received from the American Friends of Cambridge University for the endowment of a Herchel Smith Professorship of Medicinal Chemistry shall constitute a fund to be called the Herchel Smith Professorship of Medicinal Chemistry Fund.

2. If and whenever the income of the Fund shall exceed the amount required for the payment of the stipend, national insurance, and pension contributions of the Professor payable by the University, the excess of the income above that amount may be applied to meet the cost of the work of the Professor in such manner as may be approved by the General Board.

3. Any unexpended income in a financial year shall be added to the capital of the Fund.

Charles Darwin Professor of Animal Embryology.[2] *1982. School of the Biological Sciences*

The Charles Darwin Professorship of Animal Embryology shall be limited to one tenure.

Sched. to Special Ordinance G (i) 2.

Jawaharlal Nehru Visiting Professor. 1983.

1. Grants received for the establishment of a Jawaharlal Nehru Visiting Professorship shall form a fund to be called the Jawaharlal Nehru Fund.

2. The stipend of a Jawaharlal Nehru Visiting Professor and the charges associated therewith shall be payable from this Fund, together with such contribution towards the cost of the work of the Professor as may be approved by the General Board.

3. A Jawaharlal Nehru Visiting Professor shall be elected by the General Board under the authority of Special Ordinance C (vii) B.1(*c*)(iii). The field and title of a particular Professorship shall be determined by the Board on the occasion of each election. The Board shall appoint a special Committee to advise them on these questions and on the choice of the Professor.

4. The tenure of a Professorship shall be one year, except that, in exceptional cases, the tenure may be for a period not exceeding two years, provided that there is not more than one Professor in office at any time.

Professor of Japanese Studies. 1984. East Asian Studies

1. The sum of ¥217,500,000 received from Keidanren for the endowment of a Professorship of Japanese Studies shall form a fund to be called the Keidanren Fund.

2. If and whenever the income of the Fund shall exceed the amount required for the payment of the stipend, national insurance, and pension contributions of the Professor payable by the University, the excess of the income over that amount may be applied to meet the cost of the furtherance of Japanese Studies generally in the University, in such manner as may be approved by the General Board on the recommendation of the Professor of Japanese Studies in consultation with and with the agreement of the teaching officers in Japanese in the Department of East Asian Studies.

3. Any unexpended income of the Fund in a financial year may in any subsequent year be expended in accordance with Regulation 2.

[1] Discontinued from 1 October 2014 until 30 September 2019 by Grace 7 of 17 July 2013.
[2] Re-established for one tenure by Grace 3 of 19 October 2011.

Professor of Clinical Pharmacology. 1984. Medicine

The Professorship of Clinical Pharmacology shall be limited to one tenure.

Professor of Sociology. 1985. Sociology

Professor of Haematology. 1986. Haematology

KPMG Professor of Management Studies. 1986. Judge Business School

1. The sums received from Peat, Marwick, and Mitchell & Co. and their successors for the endowment of a Professorship of Management Studies shall form a fund called the KPMG Management Studies Fund.

2. The capital and the income of the Fund shall be available for the payment of the stipend, national insurance, and pension contributions of the Professor payable by the University.

3. After provision has been made in accordance with Regulation 2, the capital and income of the Fund may be applied in support of teaching or research in the general field of Management Studies in such manner as may be approved by the General Board on the recommendation of the Director of Judge Business School.

4. Any unexpended income of the Fund in a financial year may in any subsequent year be expended in accordance with Regulation 3.

Professor of Clinical Gerontology. 1987. Public Health and Primary Care

1. The sums received for the endowment of a Professorship of Clinical Gerontology shall form a fund called the Clinical Gerontology Fund.

2. If and whenever the income of the Fund shall exceed the amount required for the payment of the stipend, national insurance, pension contributions, and associated indirect costs of the Professor payable by the University, the excess of income above that amount may be applied in support of the work of the Professor in such manner as may be approved by the General Board on the recommendation of the Faculty Board of Clinical Medicine.

3. Any unexpended income in a financial year may be accumulated and may be expended in any subsequent year in accordance with Regulation 2.

Professor of Medicine. 1987. Medicine

Herchel Smith Professor of Organic Chemistry. 1988. Chemistry

1. A sum of US$1,050,000 received from the American Friends of Cambridge University for the endowment of a Herchel Smith Professorship of Organic Chemistry shall constitute a fund to be called the Herchel Smith Professorship of Organic Chemistry Fund.

2. If and whenever the income of the Fund shall exceed the amount required for the payment of the stipend, national insurance, and pension contributions of the Professor payable by the University, the excess of the income above that amount may be applied to meet the cost of the work of the Professor in such manner as may be approved by the General Board.

3. Any unexpended income in a financial year shall be added to the capital of the Fund.

Professor of Neurology. 1988. Clinical Neurosciences

The Professorship of Neurology shall be limited to one tenure.

Professor of English and Applied Linguistics. 1988. Theoretical and Applied Linguistics

Sir Alan Cottrell Professor of Materials Science.[1] *1988. Materials Science and Metallurgy*

It shall be the duty of the Professor to promote by teaching and research the study of the science and technology of materials.

Professor of Theoretical Geophysics. 1989. Applied Mathematics and Theoretical Physics

Professor of Aerothermal Technology.[2] *1989. Engineering*

The Professorship of Aerothermal Technology shall be limited to one tenure

[1] Retitled by Grace 5 of 18 July 2012.
[2] Re-established for one tenure by Grace 3 of 30 January 2013.

George Pitt-Rivers Professor of Archaeological Science. 1990. Archaeology and Anthropology

1. The sum of £1,100,000 received for the endowment of a Professorship of Archaeological Science shall form a fund called the George Pitt-Rivers Professorship of Archaeological Science Fund.

2. If and whenever the income of the Fund shall exceed the amount required for the payment of the stipend, national insurance, and pension contributions of the Professor payable by the University, the excess of the income over that amount may be applied in support of the work of the Professor in such manner as may be approved by the General Board on the recommendation of the Head of the Department of Archaeology and Anthropology.

3. Any unexpended income in a financial year may in any subsequent year be expended in accordance with Regulation 2.

Professor of Neurosurgery.[1] *1990. Clinical Neurosciences*

The Professorship of Neurosurgery shall be limited to one tenure.

Diageo Professor of Management Studies.[2] *1990. Judge Institute of Management*

1. The sums received from Guinness plc, and subsequently from Diageo plc, for the endowment of a Professorship of Management Studies shall form a fund called the Guinness Management Studies Fund.

2. If and whenever the income of the Fund shall exceed the amount required for the payment of the stipend, national insurance, and pension contributions of the Professor payable by the University, the excess of the income over that amount may be applied in support of the work of the Professor in such manner as may be approved by the General Board on the recommendation of the Director of the Judge Institute of Management. In the event of a vacancy in the Professorship the income may be applied in support of Management Studies in such manner as may be approved by the General Board on the recommendation of the Director of the Judge Institute of Management.

3. Any unexpended income of the Fund in a financial year may in any subsequent year be expended in accordance with Regulation 2.

Professor of the Mathematics of Systems. 1990. Pure Mathematics and Mathematical Statistics

The Professorship of the Mathematics of Systems shall be limited to one tenure.

Serono Professor of Molecular Endocrinology. 1990. Clinical Biochemistry

The Serono Professorship of Molecular Endocrinology shall be limited to one tenure.

Professor of Land Economy. 1991. Land Economy

The stipend, national insurance, and pension contributions of the Professor payable by the University shall be the first charge on the income of the Estate Management Development Fund.

Professor of Virology. 1991. Pathology

S. J. Berwin Professor of Corporate Law. 1991. Law

1. The sums received from S. J. Berwin and Co. in support of the endowment of an S. J. Berwin Professorship of Corporate Law shall form a fund called the S. J. Berwin Fund.

2. The first charge on the income of the Fund shall be the difference between the full cost of a University Lectureship and the amount required for the payment of the stipend, national insurance, and pension contributions of the S. J. Berwin Professor payable by the University.

3. After provision has been made in accordance with Regulation 2, the Fund may be used for such purposes as may be approved by the General Board on the recommendation of the Faculty Board of Law.

4. Any unexpended income of the Fund in a financial year may be either added to the capital of the Fund or accumulated for expenditure in accordance with Regulation 2 in future years, as the General Board shall determine.

GlaxoSmithKline Professor of Microbial Pathogenesis.[3] *1991. Medicine*

1. The sums received from Glaxo Holdings plc for the endowment of a GlaxoSmithKline Professorship of Microbial Pathogenesis shall form a fund called the Glaxo Fund.

[1] Re-established for one tenure by Grace 1 of 20 March 2013.
[2] Discontinued from 1 August 2013 by Grace 3 of 17 July 2013.
[3] Retitled by Grace 5 of 18 January 2012.

2. If and whenever the income of the Fund shall exceed the amount required for the payment of the stipend, national insurance, and pension contributions of the Professor payable by the University, the excess of the income over that amount may be applied in support of the work of the Professor in such manner as may be approved by the General Board on the recommendation of the Head of the Department to which the Professorship is assigned.

3. Any unexpended income of the Fund in a financial year may in any subsequent year be expended in accordance with Regulation 2.

Professor of Histopathology. 1992. Pathology

G. I. Taylor Professor of Fluid Mechanics.[1] *1992. Applied Mathematics and Theoretical Physics*

1. The sums given to the University in memory of Sir Geoffrey Ingram Taylor, formerly Royal Society Research Professor and Fellow of Trinity College, including the sum of £200,000 received under the will of Miss Gladys Davies, shall constitute a fund called the G. I. Taylor Memorial Fund.

2. If and whenever the income of the Fund shall exceed the amount required for the payment of the stipend, national insurance, and pension contributions of the Professor payable by the University, the excess of the income over that amount may be applied in support of the work of the Professor in such manner as may be approved by the General Board on the recommendation of the Head of the Department of Applied Mathematics and Theoretical Physics.

3. The Professor shall also be the G. I. Taylor Research Fellow in Fluid Mechanics during his or her tenure.

4. Any unexpended income in a financial year shall be added to the capital of the Fund.

Professor of Child and Adolescent Psychiatry. 1992. Psychiatry

The Professorship of Child and Adolescent Psychiatry shall be limited to one tenure.

BBV Foundation Visiting Professor.[2] *1992.*

Professor of Health Research and Development. 1992. Public Health and Primary Care Sched. to Special Ordinance G (i) 2.

The Professorship of Health Research and Development shall be limited to one tenure.

Professor of Neurophysiology. 1992. Physiology, Development, and Neuroscience

The Professorship of Neurophysiology shall be limited to one tenure.

Professor of Mechanical Engineering. 1993. Engineering

The Professorship of Mechanical Engineering shall be limited to one tenure.

John Wilfrid Linnett Visiting Professor of Chemistry. 1993. Chemistry

1. The sums donated in memory of Professor Jack Linnett, Vice-Chancellor from 1973 to 1975 and Professor of Physical Chemistry from 1965 to 1975, shall constitute a fund called the John Wilfrid Linnett Visiting Professorship of Chemistry Fund.

2. The Managers of the Fund shall be the holder of the Professorship of Chemistry (1968), the holder of the Professorship of Physical Chemistry (1920), the Head of the Department of Chemistry (if not the holder of one of those Professorships), the Master of Sidney Sussex College, and a representative appointed by the College.

3. A John Wilfrid Linnett Visiting Professor shall from time to time be elected by the General Board under the authority of Special Ordinance C (vii) B.1(*c*)(iii), on the advice of the Managers. The tenure of the Visiting Professor, during which he or she shall be in residence in Cambridge unless granted leave of absence by the General Board, shall not exceed three months and shall be determined by the General Board on the recommendation of the Managers.

4. If and whenever the income of the Fund shall exceed the amount required for the payment of the travelling expenses incurred by the Visiting Professor on his or her appointment and such emoluments as the General Board, on the recommendation of the Managers, shall determine at the time of the election, the excess of income over that amount may be applied in support of research or teaching in the fields of physical or theoretical chemistry in such manner as may be approved by the General Board on the recommendation of the Head of the Department of Chemistry.

[1] Discontinued from 1 October 2014 until 30 September 2017 by Grace 8 of 17 July 2013.
[2] See p. 771.

5. Any unexpended income in a financial year may in any subsequent year be expended in accordance with Regulation 4.

Professor of Geography. 1993. Geography

Herchel Smith Professor of Intellectual Property Law. 1993. Law

1. The sum of US$2m received from the American Friends of Cambridge University for the endowment of a Herchel Smith Professorship of Intellectual Property Law shall constitute a fund called the Herchel Smith Professorship of Intellectual Property Law Fund.

2. If and whenever the income of the Fund shall exceed the amount required for the payment of the stipend, national insurance, pension contributions, and associated indirect costs of the Professor payable by the University, the excess of the income above that amount may be applied to meet the cost of the work of the Professor and to further the study of Intellectual Property Law in the University in such manner as may be approved by the General Board on the recommendation of the Faculty Board of Law.

3. Any unexpended income of the Fund in a financial year may in any subsequent year be expended in accordance with Regulation 2.

Professor of Statistical Science. 1994. Pure Mathematics and Mathematical Statistics

Professor of Computer Science. 1994. Computer Laboratory

Professor of European Law. 1994. Law

Professor of Information Engineering. 1994. Engineering

Professor of Immunology. 1995. Pathology

Professor of Rheumatology. 1995. Medicine

The Professorship of Rheumatology shall be limited to one tenure.

Professor of Evolutionary Palaeobiology. 1995. Earth Sciences

The Professorship of Evolutionary Palaeobiology shall be limited to one tenure.

Professor of Behavioural Ecology. 1995. Zoology

The Professorship of Behavioural Ecology shall be limited to one tenure.

Royal Society Professor of Molecular Pharmacology. 1995. Pharmacology

The Royal Society Professorship of Molecular Pharmacology shall be limited to one tenure.

Marks & Spencer Professor of Farm Animal Health, Food Science, and Food Safety. 1996. Veterinary Medicine

1. The sums received from Marks and Spencer plc and a consortium of their suppliers for the endowment of a Professorship of Farm Animal Health, Food Science, and Food Safety shall constitute a fund called the Marks & Spencer Farm Animal Health Fund.

2. The income of the Fund shall be used for the payment of the stipend, national insurance, pension contributions, and associated indirect costs of the Professor payable by the University.

3. Any unexpected income in a financial year shall be added to the capital of the Fund.

Professor of Molecular Microbiology. 1996. Biochemistry

The Professorship of Molecular Microbiology shall be limited to one tenure.

Professor of Surgery. 1996. Surgery

Professor of Chemistry. 1996. Chemistry

The Professorship of Chemistry shall be limited to one tenure.

Professor of Computer Assisted Reasoning. 1996. Computer Laboratory

The Professorship of Computer Assisted Reasoning shall be limited to one tenure.

Professor of Econometrics. 1996. Economics

The Professorship of Econometrics shall be limited to one tenure.

Beckwith Professor of Management Studies. 1996. Judge Institute of Management

1. The sum of £1,000,000 received from Mr Peter Beckwith for the support of a Professorship of Management Studies shall form a fund called the Beckwith Management Studies Fund.

2. If and whenever the income of the Fund shall exceed the amount required for the payment of the stipend, national insurance, and pension contributions of the Professor payable by the University, the excess of the income over that amount may be applied to meet the cost of the work of the Professor in such manner as may be approved by the General Board on the recommendation of the Director of the Judge Institute of Management.

3. Any unexpended income in a financial year may be expended in accordance with Regulation 2.

Sir Patrick Sheehy Professor of International Relations. 1996. Politics and International Studies

1. The sums received from B.A.T. Industries plc for the endowment of a Professorship of International Relations shall constitute a fund called the Sir Patrick Sheehy International Relations Fund.

2. If and whenever the income of the Fund shall exceed the amount required for the payment of the stipend, national insurance, pension contributions, and associated indirect costs of the Professor payable by the University, the excess of the income over that amount may be applied in support of the work of the Professor in such manner as may be approved by the General Board on the recommendation of the Head of the Department of Politics and International Studies.

3. Any unexpended income in a financial year may in any subsequent year be expended in accordance with Regulation 2.

Professor of Medical Genetics. 1997. Medical Genetics

Hans Rausing Professor of History and Philosophy of Science. 1997. History and Philosophy of Science

Ursula Zoëllner Professor of Cancer Research. 1997. Oncology

1. The sums received from Dr F. A. Zoëllner for the endowment of a Professorship of Cancer Research shall constitute a fund called the Ursula Zoëllner Cancer Research Fund.

2. If and whenever the income of the Fund shall exceed the amount required for the payment of the stipend, national insurance, pension contributions, and associated indirect costs of the Professor payable by the University, the excess of the income over that amount may be applied in furtherance of work in clinical oncology in the Faculty of Clinical Medicine in such manner as may be approved by the General Board on the recommendation of the Faculty Board of Clinical Medicine.

3. Any unexpended income in a financial year may in any subsequent year be expended in accordance with Regulation 2.

Professor of Mechanical Engineering. 1997. Engineering

Professor of Computer Technology 1997. Computer Laboratory

Sinyi Professor of Chinese Management. 1997. Judge Institute of Management

1. The sum of £1,500,000 received from the Sinyi Foundation for the endowment of a Professorship of Chinese Management shall form a fund called the Sinyi Management Studies Fund.

2. If and whenever the income of the Fund shall exceed the amount required for the payment of the stipend, national insurance, pension contributions, and associated indirect costs of the Professor payable by the University, the excess of the income over that amount may be applied in support of the work of the Professor in such manner as may be approved by the General Board on the recommendation of the Director of the Judge Institute of Management.

3. Any unexpended income in a financial year may in any subsequent year be expended in accordance with Regulation 2.

Professor of Respiratory Medicine. 1997. Medicine

The Professorship of Respiratory Medicine shall be limited to one tenure.

Professor of Mechanics of Materials. 1997. Engineering

The Professorship of Mechanics of Materials shall be limited to one tenure.

Robert Sansom Professor of Computer Science. 1998. Computer Laboratory

1. The sums received from Dr Robert Sansom, of Emmanuel College, towards the endowment of a Professorship of Computer Science shall form a fund called the Robert Sansom Computer Science Fund.

2. If and whenever the income of the Fund shall exceed the amount required for the payment of the stipend, national insurance, pension contributions, and associated indirect costs of the Professor payable by the University, the excess of the income over that amount may be applied in support of the work of the Professor in such manner as may be approved by the General Board on the recommendation of the Faculty Board of Computer Science and Technology.

3. Any unexpended income in a financial year may in any subsequent year be expended in accordance with Regulation 2.

Professor of Endocrinology. 1998. Medicine

Dennis Gillings Professor of Health Management. 1998. Judge Institute of Management

1. The sum of £2,000,000 received from the Cambridge University Development Office in the United States for the endowment of a Dennis Gillings Professorship of Health Management shall form a fund called the Quintiles Health Management Fund.

2. If and whenever the income of the Fund shall exceed the amount required for the payment of the stipend, national insurance, pension contributions, and associated indirect costs of the Professor payable by the University, the excess of the income over that amount may be applied in support of the work of the Professor in such manner as may be approved by the General Board on the recommendation of the Director of the Judge Institute of Management.

3. Any unexpended income in a financial year may in any subsequent year be expended in accordance with Regulation 2.

Margaret Thatcher Professor of Enterprise Studies. 1998. Judge Institute of Management

1. The sum of £2,000,000 received from the Margaret Thatcher Foundation for the endowment of a Professorship of Enterprise Studies shall form a fund called the Margaret Thatcher Management Studies Fund.

2. If and whenever the income of the Fund shall exceed the amount required for the payment of the stipend, national insurance, pension contributions, and associated indirect costs of the Professor payable by the University, the excess of the income over that amount may be applied in support of the work of the Professor in such manner as may be approved by the General Board on the recommendation of the Director of Judge Institute of Management.

3. Any unexpended income in a financial year may in a subsequent year be expended in accordance with Regulation 2.

Professor of Paediatrics. 1998. Paediatrics

The Professorship of Paediatrics shall be limited to one tenure.

Professor of Fluid Mechanics. 1998. Applied Mathematics and Theoretical Physics

The Professorship of Fluid Mechanics shall be limited to one tenure.

Professor of Mathematical Physics. 1998. Applied Mathematics and Theoretical Physics

The Professorship of Mathematical Physics shall be limited to one tenure.

Professor of Theoretical Physics. 1998. Applied Mathematics and Theoretical Physics

The Professorship of Theoretical Physics shall be limited to one tenure.

Professor of Experimental Physics. 1998. Physics

The Professorship of Experimental Physics shall be limited to one tenure.

Professor of Psychiatry. 1998. Psychiatry

The Professorship of Psychiatry shall be limited to one tenure.

Unilever Professor of Molecular Sciences Informatics. 1999. Chemistry

1. The sum of £1,715,000 received from Unilever plc for the endowment of a Professorship of Molecular Sciences Informatics shall form a fund called the Unilever Molecular Sciences Informatics Fund.

2. If and whenever the income of the Fund shall exceed the amount required for the payment of the stipend, national insurance, pension contributions, and associated indirect costs of the Professor payable by the University, the excess of income over that amount may be applied in support of the work of the Professor in such manner as may be approved by the General Board on the recommendation of the Head of the Department of Chemistry.

3. Any unexpended income in a financial year may in any subsequent year be expended in accordance with Regulation 2.

Professor of Respiratory Biology.[1] *1999. Medicine*

The Professorship of Respiratory Biology shall be limited to one tenure.

BP Professor of Petroleum Science. 1999. Earth Sciences

Grosvenor Professor of Real Estate Finance. 1999. Land Economy

Schlumberger Professor of Complex Physical Systems. 1999. Applied Mathematics and Theoretical Physics

Professor of Haemato-oncology. 1999. Haematology

The Professorship of Haemato-oncology shall be limited to one tenure.

Professor of Chemical Engineering. 1999. Chemical Engineering and Biotechnology

Professor of Anaesthesia. 1999. Clinical Medicine

The Professorship of Anaesthesia shall be limited to one tenure.

Professor of Mathematical Biology. 1999. Plant Sciences

The Professorship of Mathematical Biology shall be limited to one tenure.

Professor of Human Population Biology and Health. 1999. Archaeology and Anthropology

The Professorship of Human Population Biology and Health shall be limited to one tenure.

Professor of Numerical Analysis of Differential Equations. 1999. Applied Mathematics and Theoretical Physics

The Professorship of Numerical Analysis of Differential Equations shall be limited to one tenure.

Professor of Physical Metallurgy. 1999. Materials Science and Metallurgy

The Professorship of Physical Metallurgy shall be limited to one tenure.

Professor of the Mechanics of Materials. 1999. Materials Science and Metallurgy

The Professorship of Mechanics of Materials shall be limited to one tenure.

Professor of Nanotechnology. 1999. Engineering

The Professorship of Nanotechnology shall be limited to one tenure.

Professor of Structural Dynamics. 1999. Engineering

The Professorship of Structural Dynamics shall be limited to one tenure.

Professor of Chemical Physics. 1999. Chemistry

The Professorship of Chemical Physics shall be limited to one tenure

Kuwait Professor of Number Theory and Algebra. 2000. Pure Mathematics and Mathematical Statistics

The Kuwait Professorship of Number Theory and Algebra shall be limited to one tenure.

Professor of Education. 2000. Education

Professor of Education.[2] *2000. Education*

Professor of Stroke Medicine.[3] *2000. Clinical Neurosciences*

The Professorship of Stroke Medicine shall be limited to one tenure.

[1] Re-established for one tenure by Grace 5 of 22 January 2014.
[2] Previously titled Professor of Educational Leadership.
[3] Re-established for one tenure by Grace 5 of 17 October 2012.

Professor of Linguistics. 2000. Theoretical and Applied Linguistics

Professor of Psychology in the Social Sciences. 2000. Psychology

Professor of Plant Ecology. 2000. Plant Sciences

Professor of Physical Geography. 2000. Geography

Professor of Human Geography. 2000. Geography

Professor of Public Health Medicine. 2000. Public Health and Primary Care
The Professorship of Public Health Medicine shall be limited to one tenure.

Professor of Nonlinear Mathematical Science. 2000. Applied Mathematics and Theoretical Physics
The Professorship of Nonlinear Mathematical Science shall be limited to one tenure.

Professor of Behavioural Science. 2000. Public Health and Primary Care
The Professorship of Behavioural Science shall be limited to one tenure.

Professor of Obstetrics and Gynaecology. 2000. Obstetrics and Gynaecology
The Professorship of Obstetrics and Gynaecology shall be limited to one tenure.

Professor of Psychiatry. 2000. Psychiatry

Professor of Clinical Oncology. 2000. Oncology
The Professorship of Clinical Oncology shall be limited to one tenure.

GKN Professor of Manufacturing Engineering. 2000. Engineering
The GKN Professorship of Manufacturing Engineering shall be limited to one tenure.

British Heart Foundation Professor of Cardiovascular Sciences. 2000. Medicine
The British Heart Foundation Professorship of Cardiovascular Sciences shall be limited to one tenure.

Professor of Intellectual History and English Literature. 2000. English
The Professorship of Intellectual History and English Literature shall be limited to one tenure.

Professor of Structural Biology. 2000. Biochemistry
The Professorship of Structural Biology shall be limited to one tenure.

Professor of Infectious Diseases. 2000. Medicine
The Professorship of Infectious Diseases shall be limited to one tenure.

Professor of History and Philosophy of the Sciences. 2000. History and Philosophy of Science
The Professorship of History and Philosophy of the Sciences shall be limited to one tenure.

Professor of Mediterranean History. 2000. History
The Professorship of Mediterranean History shall be limited to one tenure.

Professor of Tectonics. 2000. Earth Sciences
The Professorship of Tectonics shall be limited to one tenure.

Professor of Economic Geography. 2000. Geography
The Professorship of Economic Geography shall be limited to one tenure.

Professor of Astrophysical Fluid Dynamics. 2000. Applied Mathematics and Theoretical Physics
The Professorship of Astrophysical Fluid Dynamics shall be limited to one tenure.

Professor of Experimental Philosophy. 2000. Institute of Astronomy
The Professorship of Experimental Philosophy shall be limited to one tenure.

Professor of Astrophysics and Cosmology. 2000. Physics
The Professorship of Astrophysics and Cosmology shall be limited to one tenure.

Professor of Computational Physics. 2000. Physics

The Professorship of Computational Physics shall be limited to one tenure.

Professor of Biochemical Engineering. 2000. Chemical Engineering and Biotechnology

The Professorship of Biochemical Engineering shall be limited to one tenure.

Professor of Information Engineering. 2000. Engineering

The Professorship of Information Engineering shall be limited to one tenure.

Professor of Applied Thermodynamics. 2000. Engineering

The Professorship of Applied Thermodynamics shall be limited to one tenure.

N. M. Rothschild & Sons Professor of Mathematical Sciences. 2001.

1. The sums received from N. M. Rothschild & Sons for the endowment of a Professorship of Mathematical Sciences shall form a fund called the Rothschild Mathematical Sciences Fund.

2. The Professor shall be appointed to hold office for five years without possibility of reappointment. The General Board shall exercise their power of appointment under Special Ordinance C (vii) B.1(*c*)(iii), on the advice of a specially constituted Advisory Committee. The holder of the Professorship shall be Director of the Isaac Newton Institute for Mathematical Sciences, and shall vacate the Professorship on ceasing to hold the office of Director.

3. If and whenever the income of the Fund shall exceed the amount required for the payment of the stipend, national insurance, pension contributions, and associated indirect costs of the Professor payable by the University, the excess of the income over that amount may be applied in support of the work of the Professor in such manner as may be approved by the General Board on the recommendation of the Management Committee of the Isaac Newton Institute.

4. Any unexpended income in a financial year may be either added to the capital of the Fund or accumulated for expenditure in future years in accordance with Regulation 3, as the General Board shall determine.

Marconi Professor of Communications Systems. 2001. Computer Laboratory

1. The sum of £950,000 received from Marconi plc for the endowment of a Professorship of Communications Systems shall form a fund called the Marconi Communications Systems Fund.

2. The capital and the income of the Fund shall be available for the payment of the stipend, national insurance, pension contributions, and associated indirect costs of the Professor payable by the University.

3. After provision has been made in accordance with Regulation 2, the capital and income of the Fund may be applied in support of the work of the Professor in such manner as may be approved by the General Board on the recommendation of the Faculty Board of Computer Science and Technology.

4. Any unexpended income of the Fund in a financial year may be either added to the capital of the Fund or accumulated for expenditure in accordance with Regulation 3 in one or more subsequent years, as the General Board shall determine.

Professor of Oncological Pathology. 2001. Pathology

Professor of Cancer Research. 2001. Oncology

The Professorship of Cancer Research shall be limited to one tenure.

Professor of Cardiothoracic Surgery. 2001. Surgery

Professor of Clinical Magnetic Resonance Imaging. 2001. Radiology

The Professorship of Clinical Magnetic Resonance Imaging shall be limited to one tenure.

Adam Smith Professor of Corporate Governance.[1] *2001. Judge Institute of Management*

1. The sum of US$4m received from Mr D. Kozlowski and the Tyco Corporation for the endowment of a Professorship of Corporate Governance shall form a fund called the Adam Smith Corporate Governance Fund.

2. If and whenever the income of the Fund shall exceed the amount required for the payment of the stipend, national insurance, pension contributions, and associated indirect costs of the Professor payable by the University, the excess of the income over that amount may be applied in support of

[1] Retitled by Grace 3 of 12 October 2011.

the work of the Professor in such manner as may be approved by the General Board on the recommendation of the Director of the Judge Institute of Management.

3. Any unexpended income in a financial year may in any subsequent year be expended in accordance with Regulation 2.

Professor of English. 2001. English

Van Eck Professor of Engineering. 2001. Engineering

1. The sum of US$3.5m received from the will of Mr Fred van Eck for the endowment of a Professorship in the field of advanced science and technology, with an emphasis on high-speed communications, shall form a fund called the van Eck Fund.

2. If and whenever the income of the Fund shall exceed the amount required for the payment of the stipend, national insurance, pension contributions, and associated indirect costs of the Professor payable by the University, the excess of the income over that amount may be applied to support the work of the Professor in such manner as may be approved by the General Board on the recommendation of the Head of the Department of Engineering.

3. Any unexpended income of the Fund in a financial year may in any subsequent year be expended in accordance with Regulation 2.

Prince Philip Professor of Technology. 2001. Engineering

1. The Prince Philip Professorship of Technology shall be tenable by any person whose work falls within the scope of the disciplines represented within the School of Technology. The duties of the Professor shall be to undertake teaching and research in his or her subject and to promote the interests of technological disciplines in the University.

2. On the occasion of a vacancy in the Professorship the General Board shall consult the Council of the School of Technology, and the Faculty Boards or comparable authorities of institutions in the School, in accordance with Special Ordinance C (vii) B.17, about whether the Professorship should be filled and the questions relating to candidature for the Professorship specified therein.

3. The Professor shall be elected by a specially constituted Board of Electors under the provisions of Special Ordinance C (vii) B.5.

Professor of Mathematical Sciences. 2001. Applied Mathematics and Theoretical Physics

The Professorship of Mathematical Sciences shall be limited to one tenure.

Professor of Protein Crystallography. 2001. Haematology

The Professorship of Protein Crystallography shall be limited to one tenure.

Royal Society Napier Research Professor of Cancer Biology. 2001. Pathology

The Royal Society Napier Research Professorship of Cancer Biology shall be limited to one tenure for the period from 1 October 2001 to 30 September 2013.

Professor of English. 2001. English

The Professorship of English shall be limited to one tenure.

Professor of Developmental Psychopathology. 2001. Psychiatry

The Professorship of Developmental Psychopathology shall be limited to one tenure.

Professor of Microbiology. 2001. Pathology

The Professorship of Microbiology shall be limited to one tenure.

Professor of Molecular Membrane Biology. 2001. Clinical Biochemistry

The Professorship of Molecular Membrane Biology shall be limited to one tenure.

Professor of Cellular Pharmacology. 2001. Pharmacology

The Professorship of Cellular Pharmacology shall be limited to one tenure.

Professor of Sociology. 2001. Sociology

The Professorship of Sociology shall be limited to one tenure.

Professor of Ecological and Developmental Criminology. 2001. Institute of Criminology

The Professorship of Ecological and Developmental Criminology shall be limited to one tenure.

Professor of Mineralogy and Mineral Physics. 2001. Earth Sciences

The Professorship of Mineralogy and Mineral Physics shall be limited to one tenure.

Professor of Materials Science. 2001. Materials Science and Metallurgy

The Professorship of Materials Science shall be limited to one tenure.

Professor of Organic Chemistry. 2001. Chemistry

The Professorship of Organic Chemistry shall be limited to one tenure.

Professor of Ocean Physics. 2001. Applied Mathematics and Theoretical Physics

The Professorship of Ocean Physics shall be limited to one tenure.

Professor of Theoretical Physics. 2001. Physics

The Professorship of Theoretical Physics shall be limited to one tenure.

Professor of Algebraic Geometry. 2001. Pure Mathematics and Mathematical Statistics

The Professorship of Algebraic Geometry shall be limited to one tenure.

Professor of Theoretical Computer Science. 2001. Computer Laboratory

The Professorship of Theoretical Computer Science shall be limited to one tenure.

Professor of Electronics. 2001. Engineering

The Professorship of Electronics shall be limited to one tenure.

Professor of Engineering Design. 2001. Engineering

The Professorship of Engineering Design shall be limited to one tenure.

Hitachi Professor of Electron Device Physics. 2002. Department of Physics

1. The funds received from Hitachi Ltd towards the establishment of a Professorship of Electron Device Physics shall form a fund called the Hitachi Electron Device Physics Fund.

2. If and whenever the income of the Fund shall exceed the amount required for the payment of the stipend, national insurance, pension contributions, and associated indirect costs of the Professor payable by the University, the excess of the income over that amount may be applied in support of the work of the Professor and the Microelectronics Research Centre in such manner as may be approved by the General Board on the recommendation of the Head of the Department of Physics.

3. Any unexpended income in a financial year may in any subsequent year be expended in accordance with Regulation 2.

Professor of Experimental Combustion. 2002. Engineering

The Professorship of Experimental Combustion shall be limited to one tenure.

Leigh Trapnell Professor of Quantum Physics. 2002. Applied Mathematics and Theoretical Physics

1. The sums received from Mrs Hazel N. Trapnell in memory of her husband, Mr Roger Leigh Trapnell, formerly of King's College, towards the endowment of the Leigh Trapnell Professorship of Quantum Physics, shall form a fund called the Leigh Trapnell Professorship of Quantum Physics Fund.

2. The first charge on the Fund shall be the payment of the stipend, national insurance, pension contributions, and associated indirect costs of the Professor payable by the University.

3. After provision has been made in accordance with Regulation 2, the income of the Fund may be applied for the support of teaching or research in Quantum Physics in such manner as shall be approved by the General Board, on the recommendation of the Faculty Board of Mathematics.

4. Any unexpended income in a financial year may either be added to the capital of the Fund or accumulated for use as income in one or more subsequent years in accordance with Regulations 2 and 3, as the General Board, on the recommendation of the Faculty Board of Mathematics, may determine.

Merck Company Foundation Professor of Experimental Neurology. 2002. Clinical Neurosciences

The Merck Company Foundation Professorship of Experimental Neurology shall be limited to one tenure.

Professor of Accounting. 2002. Judge Institute of Management

Professor of Education. 2002. Education

The Professorship of Education shall be limited to one tenure.

Professor of Learning Disability Psychiatry. 2002. Psychiatry

The Professorship of Learning Disability Psychiatry shall be limited to one tenure.

Sandra Dawson Visiting Professor of Marketing, Strategy, and Innovation.[1] *2002. Judge Institute of Management*

1. The sum of £1m donated by Gianni and Joan Montezemolo shall constitute a fund called the Sandra Dawson Visiting Professorship of Marketing, Strategy, and Innovation Fund.

2. The Managers of the Fund shall be the Director of Judge Business School, *ex officio*, and three persons appointed by the Faculty Board of Business and Management, for periods of five years.

3. A Visiting Professor shall from time to time be elected by the General Board under the authority of Special Ordinance C (vii) B.1(*c*)(iii), on the advice of the Managers. The tenure of the Visiting Professor, during which he or she shall be in residence in Cambridge unless granted leave of absence by the General Board, shall not exceed three months and shall be determined by the General Board on the recommendation of the Managers.

4. If and whenever the income of the Fund shall exceed the amount required for the payment of the travelling expenses incurred by the Visiting Professor on his or her appointment, such emoluments as the General Board, on the recommendation of the Managers, shall determine at the time of the election, and the indirect costs to the University of the appointment, the excess of income over that amount may be applied in support of research or teaching in the fields of marketing, strategy, and innovation in such manner as may be approved by the General Board on the recommendations of the Director of the Judge Institute of Management.

5. Any unexpended income in a financial year may in any subsequent year be expended in accordance with Regulation 4.

Professor of Developmental Genetics. 2002. Genetics

The Professorship of Developmental Genetics shall be limited to one tenure.

Professor of Molecular Cell Biology. 2002. Clinical Biochemistry

The Professorship of Molecular Cell Biology shall be limited to one tenure.

Professor of Immunogenetics. 2002. Medical Genetics

The Professorship of Immunogenetics shall be limited to one tenure.

Royal Society Professor of Astronomy. 2002. Astronomy

The Royal Society Professorship of Astronomy shall be limited to one tenure.

Professor of Greek. 2002. Classics

The Professorship of Greek shall be limited to one tenure.

Professor of the History of Christianity. 2002. Divinity

The Professorship of the History of Christianity shall be limited to one tenure.

Professor of Modern Spanish Literature and Intellectual History. 2002. Spanish and Portuguese

The Professorship of Modern Spanish Literature and Intellectual History shall be limited to one tenure.

Professor of Perinatal Physiology. 2002. Physiology, Development, and Neuroscience

The Professorship of Perinatal Physiology shall be limited to one tenure.

Professor of Cell Physiology. 2002. Physiology, Development, and Neuroscience

The Professorship of Cell Physiology shall be limited to one tenure.

Professor of Clinical Neuropsychology. 2002. Psychiatry

The Professorship of Clinical Neuropsychology shall be limited to one tenure.

[1] Retitled by Grace 5 of 9 May 2013.

Professor of International History. 2002. History
The Professorship of International History shall be limited to one tenure.

Professor of History and Philosophy of Science. 2002. History and Philosophy of Science
The Professorship of History and Philosophy of Science shall be limited to one tenure.

Professor of Legal and Political Philosophy. 2002. Law
The Professorship of Legal and Political Philosophy shall be limited to one tenure.

Professor of Active Tectonics. 2002. Earth Sciences
The Professorship of Active Tectonics shall be limited to one tenure.

Professor of the Foundations of Mathematics. 2002. Pure Mathematics and Mathematical Statistics
The Professorship of the Foundations of Mathematics shall be limited to one tenure.

Professor of Observational Astronomy. 2002. Institute of Astronomy
The Professorship of Observational Astronomy shall be limited to one tenure.

Professor of Biological Chemistry. 2002. Chemistry
The Professorship of Biological Chemistry shall be limited to one tenure.

Professor of Physics. 2002. Physics
The Professorship of Physics shall be limited to one tenure.

Professor of Experimental Physics. 2002. Physics
The Professorship of Experimental Physics shall be limited to one tenure.

Professor of Computational Logic. 2002. Computer Laboratory
The Professorship of Computational Logic shall be limited to one tenure.

Professor of Applied Statistics and Signal Processing. 2002. Engineering
The Professorship of Applied Statistics and Signal Processing shall be limited to one tenure.

Professor of Photonics. 2002. Engineering
The Professorship of Photonics shall be limited to one tenure.

Professor of Control Engineering. 2002. Engineering
The Professorship of Control Engineering shall be limited to one tenure.

Professor of Information Engineering. 2002. Engineering
The Professorship of Information Engineering shall be limited to one tenure.

Professor of Environmental Systems Analysis. 2003. Geography

Professor of Plant Systematics and Evolution. 2003. Plant Sciences

Professor of Gastroenterology. 2003. Medicine

Professor of Metabolic Medicine. 2003. Medicine
The Professorship of Metabolic Medicine shall be limited to one tenure.

Professor of Developmental Neuroscience. 2003. Physiology, Development, and Neuroscience
The Professorship of Developmental Neuroscience shall be limited to one tenure.

Professor of Developmental Mechanick. 2003. Genetics
The Professorship of Developmental Mechanick shall be limited to one tenure.

Professor of Genetic Epidemiology. 2003. Public Health and Primary Care
The Professorship of Genetic Epidemiology shall be limited to one tenure.

Leverhulme Professor of Human Evolution. 2003. Archaeology and Anthropology
The Leverhulme Professorship of Human Evolution shall be limited to one tenure.

Professor of Sociology of Education. 2003. Education

The Professorship of Sociology of Education shall be limited to one tenure.

Professor of History of Science. 2003. History and Philosophy of Science

The Professorship of History of Science shall be limited to one tenure.

Professor of Public Law and Jurisprudence. 2003. Law

The Professorship of Public Law and Jurisprudence shall be limited to one tenure.

Professor of the History of International Relations. 2003. Politics and International Studies

The Professorship of the History of International Relations shall be limited to one tenure.

Professor of Applied Mathematics. 2003. Applied Mathematics and Theoretical Physics

The Professorship of Applied Mathematics shall be limited to one tenure.

Professor of Theoretical Physics. 2003. Applied Mathematics and Theoretical Physics

The Professorship of Theoretical Physics shall be limited to one tenure.

Professor of Mathematical Logic. 2003. Pure Mathematics and Mathematical Statistics

The Professorship of Mathematical Logic shall be limited to one tenure.

Professor of Algebra. 2003. Pure Mathematics and Mathematical Statistics

The Professorship of Algebra shall be limited to one tenure.

Professor of Theoretical and Computational Physics. 2003. Physics

The Professorship of Theoretical and Computational Physics shall be limited to one tenure.

Professor of High Energy Physics. 2003. Physics

The Professorship of High Energy Physics shall be limited to one tenure.

Professor of Analytical Biotechnology. 2003. Chemical Engineering and Biotechnology

The Professorship of Analytical Biotechnology shall be limited to one tenure.

Professor of Security Engineering. 2003. Computer Laboratory

The Professorship of Security Engineering shall be limited to one tenure.

Professor of Superconducting Engineering. 2003. Engineering

The Professorship of Superconducting Engineering shall be limited to one tenure.

Professor of Neurobiology. 2004. Zoology

The Professorship of Neurobiology shall be limited to one tenure.

Herchel Smith Professor of Pure Mathematics. 2004. Pure Mathematics and Mathematical Statistics

1. The sum received from the Trustees of the late Dr Herchel Smith for the establishment of a Professorship in some field or fields in Pure Mathematics shall form a fund called the Herchel Smith Pure Mathematics Fund.

2. The Fund shall be administered by three Managers appointed by the Faculty Board of Mathematics, who shall include the Head of the Department of Pure Mathematics and Mathematical Statistics, who shall be the Chair, the Herchel Smith Professor of Pure Mathematics, and the Chair of the Council of the School of the Physical Sciences.

3. The first charge on the income of the Fund shall be the stipend, national insurance, pension contributions, and associated indirect costs of the Professor payable by the University.

4. After provision has been made in accordance with Regulation 3, the Fund shall be applied for the support of teaching or research in Pure Mathematics in such manner as shall be approved by the General Board on the recommendation of the Managers.

5. Any unexpended income in a financial year may in any subsequent year be expended in accordance with Regulation 4.

Herchel Smith Professor of Molecular Genetics. 2004. Genetics

1. The sum received from the Trustees of the late Dr Herchel Smith for the establishment of a Professorship in some field or fields in Molecular Genetics shall form a fund called the Herchel Smith Molecular Genetics Fund.

2. The Managers of the Fund shall be three members appointed by the General Board on the recommendation of the Council of the School of the Biological Sciences, including the Herchel Smith Professor of Molecular Genetics and the Chair of the Council of the School of the Biological Sciences.

3. The first charge on the income of the Fund shall be the stipend, national insurance, pension contributions, and associated indirect costs of the Professor payable by the University.

4. After provision has been made in accordance with Regulation 3, the Fund shall be applied for the support of teaching or research in some aspect of Molecular Genetics in such manner as shall be approved by the General Board on the recommendation of the Managers.

5. Any unexpended income in a financial year may in any subsequent year be expended in accordance with Regulation 4.

Professor of Education. 2004. Education

Professor of Education. 2004. Education

Bernard Wolfe Professor of Health Neuroscience. 2004. Psychiatry[1]

Professor of Information Engineering. 2004. Engineering

Professor of Medical Physics. 2004. Physics

The Professorship of Medical Physics shall be limited to one tenure.

Herchel Smith Professor of Physics. 2004. Physics

1. The sum received from the Trustees of the late Dr Herchel Smith for the establishment of a Professorship in some field or fields in Physics shall form a fund called the Herchel Smith Physics Fund.

2. The Fund shall be administered by three Managers appointed by the Faculty Board of Physics and Chemistry, who shall include the Head of the Department of Physics, who shall be the Chair, the Herchel Smith Professor of Physics, and the Chair of the Council of the School of the Physical Sciences.

3. The first charge on the income of the Fund shall be the stipend, national insurance, pension contributions, and associated indirect costs of the Professor payable by the University.

4. After provision has been made in accordance with Regulation 3, the Fund shall be applied for the support of teaching or research in Physics in such manner as shall be approved by the General Board on the recommendation of the Managers.

5. Any unexpended income in a financial year may in any subsequent year be expended in accordance with Regulation 4.

Professor of Classics. 2004. Classics

The Professorship of Classics shall be limited to one tenure.

Professor of English Literature. 2004. English

The Professorship of English Literature shall be limited to one tenure.

Professor of History of Art. 2004. History of Art

The Professorship of History of Art shall be limited to one tenure.

Professor of Phonetics. 2004. Theoretical and Applied Linguistics

The Professorship of Phonetics shall be limited to one tenure.

Professor of Modern Chinese History. 2004. East Asian Studies

The Professorship of Modern Chinese History shall be limited to one tenure.

Professor of Parasitology. 2004. Pathology

The Professorship of Parasitology shall be limited to one tenure.

Professor of Molecular Biology. 2004. Physiology, Development, and Neuroscience

The Professorship of Molecular Biology shall be limited to one tenure.

[1] Assigned to the Department of Psychiatry for the tenure of the present holder.

Professor of Economic History. 2004. Economics

The Professorship of Economic History shall be limited to one tenure.

Professor of Theoretical and Mathematical Physics. 2004. Applied Mathematics and Theoretical Physics

The Professorship of Theoretical and Mathematical Physics shall be limited to one tenure.

Professor of Fluid Dynamics. 2004. Applied Mathematics and Theoretical Physics

The Professorship of Fluid Dynamics shall be limited to one tenure.

Professor of Theoretical Chemistry. 2004. Chemistry

The Professorship of Theoretical Chemistry shall be limited to one tenure.

Professor of Environment and Policy. 2004. Geography

The Professorship of Environment and Policy shall be limited to one tenure.

Professor of Device Materials. 2004. Materials Science and Metallurgy

The Professorship of Device Materials shall be limited to one tenure.

Professor of Combinatorial Mathematics. 2004. Pure Mathematics and Mathematical Statistics

The Professorship of Combinatorial Mathematics shall be limited to one tenure.

Professor of Computational Linguistics. 2004. Computer Laboratory

The Professorship of Computational Linguistics shall be limited to one tenure.

Professor of Computing. 2004. Computer Laboratory

The Professorship of Computing shall be limited to one tenure.

Professor of Engineering Design. 2004. Engineering

The Professorship of Engineering Design shall be limited to one tenure.

Herchel Smith Professor of Biochemistry. 2005. Biochemistry

1. The sum received from the Trustees of the late Dr Herchel Smith for the establishment of a Professorship in some field or fields in Biochemistry shall form a fund called the Herchel Smith Biochemistry Fund.

2. The Fund shall be administered by three Managers appointed by the Council of the School of the Biological Sciences, who shall include the Head of the Department of Biochemistry, who shall be the Chair, the Herchel Smith Professor of Biochemistry, and the Chair of the Council of the School of the Biological Sciences.

3. The first charge on the income of the Fund shall be the stipend, national insurance, pension contributions, and associated indirect costs of the Professor payable by the University.

4. After provision has been made in accordance with Regulation 3, the Fund shall be applied for the support of teaching or research in Biochemistry in such manner as shall be approved by the General Board on the recommendation of the Managers.

5. Any unexpended income in a financial year may in any subsequent year be expended in accordance with Regulation 4.

Professor of Family Research. 2005. Psychology

Professor of Sustainable Design. 2005. Architecture

The Professorship of Sustainable Design shall be limited to one tenure.

Sched. to Special Ordinance G (i) 2.

French Government Visiting Professor. 2005. French

1. A French Government Visiting Professor shall be elected annually under the authority of Special Ordinance C (vii) B.1(*c*)(iii) by the General Board, on the recommendation of an Advisory Committee, comprising the Chair of the Faculty Board of Modern and Medieval Languages, the Head of the Department of French, the Drapers Professor of French (if not one of the above), and two members appointed by the General Board.

2. The tenure of a French Government Visiting Professorship shall be for a period of not more than two terms, during which time he or she shall be in residence in Cambridge unless granted leave of absence by the General Board.

3. It shall be the duty of the French Government Visiting Professor to participate in the teaching programme of the Department of French.

Professor of Medical Oncology. 2005. Oncology

The Professorship of Medical Oncology shall be limited to one tenure.

Professor of Education 2005. Education

Professor of French Philology and Linguistics. 2005. Theoretical and Applied Linguistics

The Professorship of French Philology and Linguistics shall be limited to one tenure.

Professor of Historical Musicology. 2005. Music

The Professorship of Historical Musicology shall be limited to one tenure.

Professor of Medieval Music. 2005. Music

The Professorship of Medieval Music shall be limited to one tenure.

Professor of Biomedical Magnetic Resonance. 2005. Biochemistry

The Professorship of Biomedical Magnetic Resonance shall be limited to one tenure.

Professor of Plant and Microbial Biochemistry. 2005. Biochemistry

The Professorship of Plant and Microbial Biochemistry shall be limited to one tenure.

Professor of Comparative Cognition. 2005. Psychology

The Professorship of Comparative Cognition shall be limited to one tenure.

Professor of Molecular Genetics and Genomics. 2005. Pathology

The Professorship of Molecular Genetics and Genomics shall be limited to one tenure.

Professor of Signalling Pharmacology. 2005. Pharmacology

The Professorship of Signalling Pharmacology shall be limited to one tenure.

Professor of Nephrology. 2005. Medical Genetics

The Professorship of Nephrology shall be limited to one tenure.

Professor of Molecular Neurogenetics. 2005. Medical Genetics

The Professorship of Molecular Neurogenetics shall be limited to one tenure.

Professor of Immunology and Medicine. 2005. Medicine

The Professorship of Immunology and Medicine shall be limited to one tenure.

Professor of Molecular Virology. 2005. Medicine

The Professorship of Molecular Virology shall be limited to one tenure.

Professor of Economics and Game Theory. 2005. Economics

The Professorship of Economics and Game Theory shall be limited to one tenure.

Professor of Medieval English History. 2005. History

The Professorship of Medieval English History shall be limited to one tenure.

Professor of American Intellectual History. 2005. History

The Professorship of American Intellectual History shall be limited to one tenure.

Professor of Urban and Regional Economics. 2005. Land Economy

The Professorship of Urban and Regional Economics shall be limited to one tenure.

Professor of Company and Securities Law. 2005. Law

The Professorship of Company and Securities Law shall be limited to one tenure.

Professor of Public Law and Private International Law. 2005. Law

The Professorship of Public Law and Private International Law shall be limited to one tenure.

Professor of Empirical Sociology. 2005. Sociology

The Professorship of Empirical Sociology shall be limited to one tenure.

Professor of Theoretical Physics. 2005. Applied Mathematics and Theoretical Physics

The Professorship of Theoretical Physics shall be limited to one tenure.

Professor of Atmospheric Science. 2005. Chemistry

The Professorship of Atmospheric Science shall be limited to one tenure.

Professor of Mineral Physics. 2005. Earth Sciences

The Professorship of Mineral Physics shall be limited to one tenure.

Professor of Quaternary Palaeoenvironments. 2005. Geography

The Professorship of Quaternary Palaeoenvironments shall be limited to one tenure.

Professor of Physics. 2005. Physics

The Professorship of Physics shall be limited to one tenure.

Professor of Quantum Physics. 2005. Physics

The Professorship of Quantum Physics shall be limited to one tenure.

Professor of Experimental Quantum Physics. 2005. Physics

The Professorship of Experimental Quantum Physics shall be limited to one tenure.

Professor of Polymer Physics. 2005. Physics

The Professorship of Polymer Physics shall be limited to one tenure.

Professor of Particle Physics. 2005. Physics

The Professorship of Particle Physics shall be limited to one tenure.

Professor of Analytical Physics. 2005. Physics

The Professorship of Analytical Physics shall be limited to one tenure.

Professor of Pure Mathematics. 2005. Pure Mathematics and Mathematical Statistics

The Professorship of Pure Mathematics shall be limited to one tenure.

Professor of Computer Technology. 2005. Computer Laboratory

The Professorship of Computer Technology shall be limited to one tenure.

Professor of Engineering Tribology. 2005. Engineering

The Professorship of Engineering Tribology shall be limited to one tenure.

Professor of Rural Economy. 2005. Land Economy

The Professorship of Rural Economy shall be limited to one tenure.

Herchel Smith Professor of Molecular Biology. 2006. Physiology, Development, and Neuroscience

1. The sum received from the Trustees of the late Dr Herchel Smith for the establishment of a Professorship in some field or fields in Molecular Biology shall form a fund called the Herchel Smith Molecular Biology Fund.

2. The Fund shall be administered by three Managers appointed by the Council of the School of the Biological Sciences, who shall include the Head of the Department of Physiology, Development, and Neuroscience, who shall be the Chair, the Herchel Smith Professor of Molecular Biology, and the Chair of the Council of the School of the Biological Sciences.

3. The first charge on the income of the Fund shall be the stipend, national insurance, pension contributions, and associated indirect costs of the Professor payable by the University.

4. After provision has been made in accordance with Regulation 3, the Fund shall be applied for the support of teaching or research in Molecular Biology in such manner as shall be approved by the General Board on the recommendation of the Managers.

5. Any unexpended income in a financial year may in any subsequent year be expended in accordance with Regulation 4.

Sigrid Rausing Professor of Social Anthropology.[1] *2006. Archaeology and Anthropology*

1. The sum received from Dr Sigrid M. Rausing towards the endowment of the Sigrid Rausing Professorship of Social Anthropology shall form a fund called the Sigrid Rausing Fund.

2. If and whenever the income of the Fund exceeds the amount required for the payment of the stipend, national insurance, pension contributions, and associated indirect costs of the Professor payable by the University, the excess of the income over that amount shall be applied to support the work of the Professor in such a manner as may be approved by the General Board on the recommendation of the Head of the Department of Archaeology and Anthropology.

3. Any unexpended income in a financial year shall, in any subsequent year, be expended in accordance with Regulation 2.

Miriam Rothschild Professor of Conservation Biology. 2006. Zoology

1. The sum received from the Lisbet Rausing Charitable Fund for the endowment of a Professorship of Conservation Biology shall form a fund called the Miriam Rothschild Fund for Conservation Biology.

2. If and whenever the income of the Fund exceeds the amount required for the payment of the stipend, national insurance, pension contributions, and associated indirect costs of the Professor payable by the University, the excess of the income over that amount shall be applied to support the work of the Professor in such a manner as may be approved by the General Board on the recommendation of the Head of the Department of Zoology or that of any other Department or Faculty in which the Professorship is then held.

3. Any unexpended income in a financial year shall, in any subsequent year, be expended in accordance with Regulation 2.

4. On the occasion of a vacancy in the Professorship, the General Board shall consult the Council of the School of the Biological Sciences in accordance with Special Ordinance C (vii) B.17, as to whether the assignment or its field should be reviewed for the next tenure.

His Majesty Sultan Qaboos Bin Said Professor of Modern Arabic Studies. 2006. Middle Eastern Studies

1. The sum received from His Majesty Sultan Qaboos Bin Said for the endowment of a Professorship of Modern Arabic Studies shall form a fund called the His Majesty Sultan Qaboos Bin Said Fund.

2. If and whenever the income of the Fund shall exceed the amount required for the payment of the stipend, national insurance, pension contributions, and associated indirect costs of the Professor payable by the University, the excess of the income over that amount shall be applied to support the work of the Professor in such a manner as may be approved by the General Board on the recommendation of the Faculty Board of Asian and Middle Eastern Studies.

3. Any unexpended income in a financial year may in any subsequent year be expended in accordance with Regulation 2.

Professor of Molecular Immunology. 2006. Pathology

The Professorship of Molecular Immunology shall be limited to one tenure.

Professor of Stem Cell Biology. 2006. Biochemistry

The Professorship of Stem Cell Biology shall be limited to one tenure.

Professor of Applied Mathematics. 2006. Applied Mathematics and Theoretical Physics

Professor of Physics. 2006. Physics

Professor of Comparative Pathology.[2] *2006. Veterinary Medicine*

1. The sums accepted from the Ministry of Agriculture and Fisheries in accordance with Grace 3 of 16 February 1923 shall be separately invested and shall constitute a fund called the Professorship of Comparative Pathology Fund.

[1] Previously entitled Sigrid Rausing Professor of Collaborative Anthropology.
[2] Previously Professor of Veterinary Science.

2. If and whenever the income of the Fund shall exceed the amount required for the payment of this stipend, national insurance, pension contributions, and associated indirect costs of the Professor payable by the University, the excess of the income over that amount may be supplied in support of the work of the Professor in such manner as may be approved by the General Board on the recommendation of the Faculty Board of Veterinary Medicine.

3. Any unexpended income in a financial year may in any subsequent year be expended in accordance with Regulation 2.

Genzyme Professor of Experimental Medicine.[1] *2006. Medicine*

1. The sums received from the Board of Cambridge in America representing a donation from the Genzyme Corporation for the support of the Genzyme Professorship of Experimental Medicine shall form a fund called The Genzyme Experimental Medicine Fund.

2. If and whenever the income of the Fund exceeds the amount required for the payment of the stipend, national insurance, pension contributions, and associated indirect costs of the Professor payable by the University, the excess of the income over that amount shall be applied to support the work of the Professor in such a manner as may be approved by the Faculty Board of Clinical Medicine on the recommendation of the Head of the Department of Medicine.

3. Any unexpended income in a financial year shall, in any subsequent year, be expended in accordance with Regulation 2.

Professor of Historical Anthropology. 2006. Human, Social, and Political Science

1. The Professorship of Historical Anthropology shall be established for a single tenure with effect from 1 October 2006.

2. The Professor shall also hold the office of Director of the Museum of Archaeology and Anthropology during his tenure, and shall vacate the Professorship if he ceases to hold the latter office.

Professor of History of Medieval Art. 2006. History of Art

The Professorship of History of Medieval Art shall be limited to one tenure.

Professor of RNA Molecular Biology. 2006. Biochemistry

The Professorship of RNA Molecular Biology shall be limited to one tenure.

Professor of Cellular Neuroscience. 2006. Physiology, Development, and Neuroscience

The Professorship of Cellular Neuroscience shall be limited to one tenure.

Professor of Neuroscience. 2006. Physiology, Development, and Neuroscience

The Professorship of Neuroscience shall be limited to one tenure.

Professor of Vertebrate Palaeontology. 2006. Zoology

The Professorship of Vertebrate Palaeontology shall be limited to one tenure which shall be coterminous with the holding of the office of Senior Assistant Curator in the Museum of Zoology.

Professor of Econometric Theory and Economic Statistics. 2006. Economics

The Professorship of Econometric Theory and Economic Statistics shall be limited to one tenure.

Professor of International Law. 2006. Law

The Professorship of International Law shall be limited to one tenure.

Professor of Criminology and Criminal Justice. 2006. Institute of Criminology

The Professorship of Criminology and Criminal Justice shall be limited to one tenure.

Professor of Fluid Mechanics. 2006. Applied Mathematics and Theoretical Physics

The Professorship of Fluid Mechanics shall be limited to one tenure.

Professor of Theoretical Mineral Physics. 2006. Physics

The Professorship of Theoretical Mineral Physics shall be limited to one tenure.

[1] Re-established for one tenure by Grace 12 of 13 July 2011. The title of the Professorship shall be the Genzyme Professorship of Experimental Medicine for 21 months with effect from the date on which an appointment to the Professorship is next made.

Professor of Representation Theory. 2006. Pure Mathematics and Mathematical Statistics

The Professorship of Representation Theory shall be limited to one tenure.

Professor of Stochastic Analysis. 2006. Pure Mathematics and Mathematical Statistics

The Professorship of Stochastic Analysis shall be limited to one tenure.

Professor of Mechanical Engineering. 2006. Engineering

The Professorship of Mechanical Engineering shall be limited to one tenure.

Professor of Fluid Mechanics. 2006. Engineering

The Professorship of Fluid Mechanics shall be limited to one tenure.

Professor of Statistical Signal Processing. 2006. Engineering

The Professorship of Statistical Signal Processing shall be limited to one tenure.

Professor of Control Engineering. 2006. Engineering

The Professorship of Control Engineering shall be limited to one tenure.

Professor of Law. 2006. Law

The Professorship of Law shall be limited to one tenure.

Professor of Comparative Immunogenetics. 2006. Pathology

The Professorship of Comparative Immunogenetics shall be limited to one tenure.

Moran Professor of Conservation and Development. 2006. Geography

1. The sums received from the Board of Cambridge in America representing a donation from James and Jane Wilson for the support of the Moran Professorship of Conservation and Development shall form a fund called the Moran Conservation and Development Fund.

2. If and whenever the income of the Fund exceeds the amount required for the payment of the stipend, national insurance, pension contributions, and associated indirect costs of the Professor payable by the University, the excess of the income over that amount shall be applied to support the work of the Professor in such a manner as may be approved by the General Board on the recommendation of the Head of the Department of Geography or that of any other Department or Faculty in which the Professorship is then held.

3. Any unexpended income in a financial year shall, in any subsequent year, be expended in accordance with Regulation 2.

4. On the occasion of a vacancy in the Professorship, the General Board, in accordance with Special Ordinance C (vii) B.17, shall decide whether the assignment to a Faculty, Department or other institution, or its field, should be reviewed for the next tenure.

Professor of Systems Biology and Biochemistry. 2006. Biochemistry

The Professorship of Systems Biology and Biochemistry shall be limited to one tenure.

Winton Professor of the Public Understanding of Risk.[1] *2006. Pure Mathematics and Mathematical Statistics*

Professor of Politics.[2] *2007. Politics and International Studies*

Professor of Infectious Disease Informatics. 2007. Zoology

The Professorship of Infectious Disease Informatics shall be limited to one tenure.

Jawaharlal Nehru Professor of Indian Business and Enterprise. 2007. Judge Business School

1. The sum received from the High Commission of India for the endowment of a Jawaharlal Nehru Professorship of Indian Business and Enterprise shall form a fund called the Jawaharlal Nehru Fund for Indian Business and Enterprise.

2. If and whenever the income of the Fund shall exceed the amount required for the payment of the stipend, national insurance, pension contributions, and associated indirect costs of the Jawaharlal Nehru Professor of Indian Business and Enterprise payable by the University, the excess of the income

[1] See p. 1004.

[2] Suppressed by Grace 2 of 14 March 2012 on the retirement of the current holder.

above that amount may be applied to support the activities of the Professorship and for the study of Indian business and enterprise, in such a manner as shall be approved by the General Board on the recommendation of the Director of Judge Business School and after consultation with the donor.

3. Any unexpended income in any financial year may be accumulated as capital or expended in accordance with Regulation 2 in any one or more subsequent years as shall be determined by the General Board on the recommendation of the Director of Judge Business School.

Professor of Medical Genetics. 2007. Medical Genetics

The Professorship of Medical Genetics shall be limited to one tenure.

Li Ka Shing Professor of Oncology. 2007. Oncology

1. The sums received towards the endowment of the Li Ka Shing Professorship of Oncology shall form a fund called the Li Ka Shing Fund for Oncology.

2. If and whenever the income of the Fund exceeds the amount required for the payment of the stipend, national insurance, pension contributions, and associated indirect costs of the Professor payable by the University, the excess of the income over that amount shall be applied to support the research activities of the Professor in such a manner as may be approved by the General Board on the recommendation of the Chair of the Council of the School of Clinical Medicine.

3. Any unexpended income in a financial year shall, in any subsequent year, be expended in accordance with Regulation 2.

Prince Philip Professor of Ecology and Evolutionary Biology. 2007. Zoology

1. The sum set aside from the Chest to support the Prince Philip Professorship of Ecology and Evolutionary Biology shall form a fund designated the Prince Philip Fund for Ecology and Evolutionary Biology.

2. If and whenever the income of the Fund exceeds the amount required for the payment of the stipend, national insurance, pension contributions, and associated indirect costs of the Professor payable by the University, the excess of the income over that amount shall be applied to support the work of the Professor in such a manner as may be approved by the General Board on the recommendation of the Head of the Department of Zoology.

3. Any unexpended income in a financial year shall, in any subsequent year, be expended in accordance with Regulation 2.

Professor of Primary Care Research. 2007. Public Health and Primary Care

The Professorship of Primary Care Research shall be limited to one tenure.

Professor of Experimental Astrophysics. 2007. Physics

Sir Evelyn de Rothschild Professor of Finance. 2007. Judge Business School

The Sir Evelyn de Rothschild Professorship of Finance shall be limited to ten years from 1 October 2007.

Professor of Medieval French Literature. 2007. French

The Professorship of Medieval French Literature shall be limited to one tenure.

Professor of Philosophy. 2007. Philosophy

The Professorship of Philosophy shall be limited to one tenure.

Professor of Plant Biochemistry. 2007. Plant Sciences

The Professor of Plant Biochemistry shall be limited to one tenure.

Professor of Conservation Science. 2007. Zoology

The Professorship of Conservation Science shall be limited to one tenure.

Professor of Molecular Neurology. 2007. Clinical Neurosciences

The Professorship of Molecular Neurology shall be limited to one tenure.

Professorship of Cardiopulmonary Medicine. 2007. Medicine

The Professorship of Cardiopulmonary Medicine shall be limited to one tenure.

Professor of Economics. 2007. Economics

The Professorship of Economics shall be limited to one tenure.

Professor of French History. 2007. History

The Professorship of French History shall be limited to one tenure.

Professor of English Private Law. 2007. Law

The Professorship of English Private Law shall be limited to one tenure.

Professor of Psychology. 2007. Psychology

The Professorship of Psychology shall be limited to one tenure.

Professor of Theoretical Physics. 2007. Applied Mathematics and Theoretical Physics

The Professorship of Theoretical Physics shall be limited to one tenure.

Professor of Fluid Mechanics. 2007. Applied Mathematics and Theoretical Physics

The Professorship of Fluid Mechanics shall be limited to one tenure.

Professor of Observational Cosmology and Astrophysics. 2007. Institute of Astronomy

The Professorship of Observational Cosmology and Astrophysics shall be limited to one tenure.

Professor of Materials Chemistry. 2007. Chemistry

The Professorship of Materials Chemistry shall be limited to one tenure.

Professor of Biophysical Chemistry. 2007. Chemistry

The Professorship of Biophysical Chemistry shall be limited to one tenure

Professor of Materials Science. 2007. Materials Science and Metallurgy

The Professorship of Materials Science shall be limited to one tenure.

Professor of Theoretical Physics. 2007. Physics

The Professorship of Theoretical Physics shall be limited to one tenure.

Professor of Signal Processing. 2007. Engineering

The Professorship of Signal Processing shall be limited to one tenure.

Professor of Civil Engineering. 2007. Engineering

The Professorship of Civil Engineering shall be limited to one tenure.

Professor of Operations Research. 2007. Judge Business School

The Professorship of Operations Research shall be limited to one tenure.

Professor of Cancer Therapeutics. 2007. Oncology

The Professorship of Cancer Therapeutics shall be limited to one tenure.

Professor of Immunology and Cell Biology. 2007. Medicine

The Professorship of Immunology and Cell Biology shall be limited to one tenure.

Professor of Experimental Neuroscience. 2007. Clinical Neurosciences

The Professorship of Experimental Neuroscience shall be limited to one tenure.

Professor of Education. 2008. Education

Professor of Macroeconomics. 2008. Economics

The Professorship of Macroeconomics shall be limited to one tenure.

Alborada Professor of Equine and Farm Animal Science.[1] *2008. Veterinary Medicine*

1. The sums received from The Alborada Trust to support a Professorship of Equine and Farm Animal Science and for other purposes shall form a fund called the Alborada Fund for Equine and Farm Animal Science.

[1] The title of this Professorship shall be current to 30 September 2028.

2. The capital and the income of the Fund shall be available for the payment of the stipend, national insurance, and pension contributions of the Alborada Professor of Equine and Farm Animal Science, together with associated costs within the Department of Veterinary Medicine, payable by the University during the tenure of the Professorship.

3. After provision has been made in accordance with Regulation 2, the capital and the income of the Fund may be applied for the support of teaching or research in some aspect of Equine and Farm Animal Science in such a manner as shall be approved by the General Board on the recommendation of the Faculty Board of Veterinary Medicine.

4. As far as possible and except as permitted by The Alborada Trust, equal weight will be given to the areas of equine science and farm animal science in all aspects of the Professorship and in the use of the capital and income of the Fund for teaching and research.

5. Any unexpended income in a financial year may be expended in any one or more subsequent years in accordance with Regulations 2 and 3.

6. If at the end of the term of the Professorship any part of the capital or income of the Fund remains unspent, such unspent part shall be returned to The Alborada Trust for its general charitable purposes.

RAND Professor of Health Services Research.[1] *2008. Public Health and Primary Care*

The RAND Professorship of Health Services Research shall be limited to one tenure.

Professor of Nuclear Medicine. 2008. Radiology

The Professorship of Nuclear Medicine shall be limited to one tenure.

A. G. Leventis Professor of Greek Culture. 2008. Classics

1. The sum of £2.361m received from the A. G. Leventis Foundation for the endowment of an A. G. Leventis Professorship of Greek Culture, concerned with the study of Greek Culture before the Byzantine era, shall constitute a fund to be called the A. G. Leventis Fund for Greek Culture.

2. The Managers of the Fund shall be the Chair of the Faculty Board of Classics, the A. G. Leventis Professor of Greek Culture, and one other Manager appointed by the Faculty Board of Classics for periods of five years, provided that, if two or more of these posts are held by the same person or if one or more of these posts is vacant or its tenure has expired, the Faculty Board of Classics shall appoint one or more additional Managers so as to ensure that there are three Managers.

3. The first charge on the income and expendable capital of the Fund shall be the payment of the stipend, national insurance, pension contributions, and associated indirect costs of the A. G. Leventis Professorship of Greek Culture payable by the University.

4. After provision has been made in accordance with Regulation 3, the income of the Fund shall be applied for the support of teaching or research into periods of Greek culture before the Byzantine era in such a manner as shall be approved by the General Board on the recommendation of the Managers.

5. Any unexpended income in a financial year may, in any one or more subsequent years, be expended in accordance with Regulation 4.

Gorley Putt Professor of Poetry and Poetics. 2008. English

The Gorley Putt Professorship of Poetry and Poetics shall be limited to one tenure.

Professor of Persian History. 2008. Middle Eastern Studies

The Professorship of Persian History shall be limited to one tenure.

Professor of Matrix Biochemistry. 2008. Biochemistry

The Professorship of Matrix Biochemistry shall be limited to one tenure.

Professor of Reproductive Immunology. 2008. Pathology

The Professorship of Reproductive Immunology shall be limited to one tenure.

Professor of Developmental Biology. 2008. Physiology, Development, and Neuroscience

The Professorship of Developmental Biology shall be limited to one tenure.

[1] Retitled by Grace 3 of 16 October 2013.

Professor of Small Animal Medicine. 2008. Veterinary Medicine

The Professorship of Small Animal Medicine shall be limited to one tenure.

Professorship of Evolutionary Genetics. 2008. Zoology

The Professorship of Evolutionary Genetics shall be limited to one tenure.

Professor of Neuroradiology. 2008. Radiology

The Professorship of Neuroradiology shall be limited to one tenure.

Professor of Modern European History. 2008. History

The Professorship of Modern European History shall be limited to one tenure.

Professor of the History of European International Relations. 2008. Politics and International Studies

The Professorship of the History of European International Relations shall be limited to one tenure.

Professor of European Union and Employment Law. 2008. Law

The Professorship of European Union and Employment Law shall be limited to one tenure.

Professor of Cosmology. 2008. Applied Mathematics and Theoretical Physics

The Professorship of Cosmology shall be limited to one tenure.

Professor of Theoretical Astrophysics. 2008. Institute of Astronomy

The Professorship of Theoretical Astrophysics shall be limited to one tenure.

Professor of Chemical Physics. 2008. Chemistry

The Professorship of Chemical Physics shall be limited to one tenure.

Professor of Materials Science. 2008. Materials Science and Metallurgy

The Professorship of the Materials Science shall be limited to one tenure.

Professor of Experimental Particle Physics. 2008. Physics

The Professorship of Experimental Particle Physics shall be limited to one tenure.

Professor of Mathematics. 2008. Pure Mathematics and Mathematical Statistics

The Professorship of Mathematics shall be limited to one tenure.

Professor of Computational Engineering. 2008. Engineering

The Professorship of Computational Engineering shall be limited to one tenure.

Professor of Engineering. 2008. Engineering

The Professorship of Engineering shall be limited to one tenure.

Professor of Statistics in Biomedicine. 2008. Medical Genetics

The Professorship of Statistics in Biomedicine shall be limited to one tenure.

Tata Steel Professor of Metallurgy. 2008. Materials Science and Metallurgy

1. The sum of £2.084m received from Tata Steel UK Limited for the endowment of a Tata Steel Professorship of Metallurgy shall constitute a fund to be called the Tata Steel Fund for Metallurgy.

2. The Tata Steel Professorship of Metallurgy shall be concerned with the study of ferrous metallurgy.

3. Whenever the Tata Steel Professorship of Metallurgy is due to fall vacant for any reason, the General Board, following consultation with the Council of the School of the Physical Sciences, the Head of the Department of Materials Science and Metallurgy, and the donor, may recommend to the University that the particular field of the Professorship be concerned with the study of materials science and metallurgy in general.

4. The Managers of the Fund shall be the Head of the Department of Materials Science and Metallurgy, the Tata Steel Professor of Metallurgy, and one other Manager appointed by the Faculty Board of Physics and Chemistry for periods of five years, provided that, if two or more of these posts are held by the same person or if one or more of these posts is vacant or its tenure has expired, the Faculty Board of Physics and Chemistry shall appoint one or more additional Managers so as to ensure that there are three Managers.

5. The first charge on the income and expendable capital of the Fund shall be the payment of the stipend, national insurance, pension contributions, and associated indirect costs of the Tata Steel Professor of Metallurgy payable by the University.

6. After provision has been made in accordance with Regulation 5, the income of the Fund shall be applied for the support of teaching or research into ferrous metallurgy or, if (following a recommendation of the type referred to in Regulation 3) the subject matter of the Professorship has been changed, for the support of teaching or research in materials science and metallurgy generally, in each case in such a manner as shall be approved by the General Board on the recommendation of the Managers.

7. Any unexpended income in a financial year may in any one or more subsequent years be expended in accordance with Regulation 6.

Professor of Veterinary Diagnostic Pathology. 2009. Veterinary Medicine

Professor of Molecular Pathology. 2009. Pathology

The Professorship of Molecular Pathology shall be limited to one tenure.

Professor of Clinical Microbiology. 2009. Medicine

The Professorship of Clinical Microbiology shall be limited to one tenure.

Professor of Musical Performance Studies. 2009. Music

The Professorship of Musical Performance Studies shall be for the tenure of the current holder.

Professor of Philosophical Theology. 2009. Divinity

The Professorship of Philosophical Theology shall be limited to one tenure.

Professor of Cultural History and Aesthetics. 2009. English

The Professorship of Cultural History and Aesthetics shall be limited to one tenure.

Professor of Portuguese Literature and Culture. 2009. Spanish and Portuguese

The Professorship of Portuguese Literature and Culture shall be limited to one tenure.

Professor of Molecular and Cellular Biochemistry. 2009. Biochemistry

The Professorship of Molecular and Cellular Biochemistry shall be limited to one tenure.

Professor of Molecular Pharmacology. 2009. Pharmacology

The Professorship of Molecular Pharmacology shall be limited to one tenure.

Professor of Neurobiology. 2009. Physiology, Development, and Neuroscience

The Professorship of Neurobiology shall be limited to one tenure.

Professor of Reproductive Physiology. 2009. Physiology, Development, and Neuroscience

The Professorship of Reproductive Physiology shall be limited to one tenure.

Professor of Behavioural Neuroscience. 2009. Physiology, Development, and Neuroscience

The Professorship of Behavioural Neuroscience shall be limited to one tenure.

Professor of Structural and Molecular Biology. 2009. Clinical Biochemistry

The Professorship of Structural and Molecular Biology shall be limited to one tenure.

Professor of Molecular Nutrition and Metabolism. 2009. Clinical Biochemistry

The Professorship of Molecular Nutrition and Metabolism shall be limited to one tenure.

Professor of Modern Cultural History. 2009. History

The Professorship of Modern Cultural History shall be limited to one tenure.

Professor of Modern British History. 2009. History

The Professorship of Modern British History shall be limited to one tenure.

Professor of Comparative and Developmental Criminology. 2009. Institute of Criminology

The Professorship of Comparative and Developmental Criminology shall be limited to one tenure.

Professor of Astrophysics. 2009. Institute of Astronomy

The Professorship of Astrophysics shall be limited to one tenure.

Professor of Materials Science. 2009. Materials Science and Metallurgy

The Professorship of Materials Science shall be limited to one tenure.

Professor of Materials Science. 2009. Materials Science and Metallurgy

The Professorship of Materials Science shall be limited to one tenure.

Professor of High Energy Physics. 2009. Physics

The Professorship of High Energy Physics shall be limited to one tenure.

Professor of Physics. 2009. Physics

The Professorship of Physics shall be limited to one tenure.

Professor of Computer Vision and Pattern Recognition. 2009. Computer Laboratory

The Professorship of Computer Vision and Pattern Recognition shall be limited to one tenure.

Professor of Logic and Algorithms. 2009. Computer Laboratory

The Professorship of Logic and Algorithms shall be limited to one tenure.

Professor of Energy Technologies. 2009. Engineering

The Professorship of Energy Technologies shall be limited to one tenure.

Professor of Semiconductor Engineering. 2009. Engineering

The Professorship of Semiconductor Engineering shall be limited to one tenure.

Professor of Chemical Engineering. 2009. Chemical Engineering and Biotechnology

The Professorship of Chemical Engineering shall be limited to one tenure.

Professor of Transfusion Medicine. 2009. Haematology

The Professorship of Transfusion Medicine shall be limited to one tenure.

Diane Middlebrook and Carl Djerassi Visiting Professor of Gender Studies.[1] *2009. Politics and International Studies*

1. The Funding Sums identified in the Agreement between the University and Professor Carl Djerassi, together with any other monies received for the purpose, shall constitute a fund called the Diane Middlebrook and Carl Djerassi Fund of which the capital and the income shall be used to support the Diane Middlebrook and Carl Djerassi Visiting Professorship of Gender Studies.

2. The Managers of the Fund shall be the Committee of Management of the Gender Studies Fund.

3. A Visiting Professor shall from time to time be elected by the General Board under the authority of Special Ordinance C (vii) B.1(*c*)(iii), on the advice of the Managers. The tenure of the Visiting Professor, during which he or she shall be in residence in Cambridge, unless granted leave of absence by the General Board, shall not exceed two terms in one academical year and shall be determined by the General Board on the recommendation of the Managers.

4. The Managers shall ensure that the programme is sustained over the medium term and shall use the Fund to support no more than two Visiting Professors in any one academical year (which shall include payment of approved travelling expenses incurred by the Visiting Professor on her or his appointment, such emoluments as the General Board, on the recommendation of the Managers, shall determine at the time of the election, and the indirect costs to the University of the appointment).

5. Any unexpended sums in a financial year may in any subsequent year be expended in accordance with Regulation 4.

Professor of Pure Mathematics.[2] *2009. Pure Mathematics and Mathematical Statistics*

The Professorship of Pure Mathematics shall be limited to one tenure.

Professor of Ophthalmology. 2009. Clinical Neurosciences

The Professorship of Ophthalmology shall be limited to one tenure.

[1] Reassigned by Grace 6 of 30 July 2014.

[2] Re-established for one tenure by Grace 2 of 13 February 2013

British Heart Foundation Professor of Cardiovascular Medicine. 2010. Medicine

The British Heart Foundation Professorship of Cardiovascular Medicine shall be limited to one tenure.

Sir Arthur Marshall Visiting Professor of Sustainable Urban Design. 2010. Architecture

1. The sum of £900,000 donated by the D. G. Marshall of Cambridge Trust shall constitute a fund called the Sir Arthur Marshall Visiting Professorship of Sustainable Urban Design Fund.

2. The Managers of the Fund shall be the Head of the Department of Architecture, three persons appointed by the Faculty Board of Architecture and History of Art for periods of five years at a time, one of whom shall be on the nomination of the D. G. Marshall of Cambridge Trust, and one person appointed by Jesus College for periods of five years at a time.

3. A Visiting Professor shall from time to time be elected by the General Board under the authority of Special Ordinance C (vii) B.1(*c*)(iii), on the advice of the Managers. The tenure of the Visiting Professor, during which he or she shall be in residence in Cambridge unless granted leave of absence by the General Board, shall be determined by the General Board on the recommendation of the Managers.

4. If and whenever the income of the Fund shall exceed the amount required for the payment of the accommodation and travelling expenses incurred by the Visiting Professor on her or his appointment, such emoluments as the General Board, on the recommendation of the Managers, shall determine at the time of the election, and the indirect costs to the University of the appointment, the excess of income over that amount may be applied in support of research or teaching in the field of sustainable urban design in such manner as may be approved by the General Board on the recommendation of the Managers.

5. Any unexpended income in a financial year may in any subsequent year or years be expended in accordance with Regulation 4.

Visiting Professor of Architecture. 2010. Architecture

Amended by Grace 1 of 8 May 2014

1. Grants and other funds made available from time to time to support one or more Visiting Professorships of Architecture shall constitute a fund called the Visiting Professorships of Architecture Fund.

2. The Managers of the Fund shall be the Head of the Department of Architecture, the Head of the School of Arts and Humanities, and three persons appointed by the Faculty Board of Architecture and History of Art to serve for periods of five years.

3. One or more Visiting Professors of Architecture shall from time to time be elected under the authority of Part B 1 (*c*) (iii) of Special Ordinance C (vii) by the General Board on the recommendation of the Managers of the Fund. In each case, the tenure of the Visiting Professor, during which he or she shall be in residence in Cambridge, shall be determined by the General Board on the recommendation of the Managers.

4. The capital and income of the Fund shall be applied to meet the emoluments of the Visiting Professors, as determined by the General Board at the time of election, the Professors' travelling expenses, and the indirect costs to the University of their appointment.

5. Any unexpended income in a financial year may in any subsequent year or years be expended in accordance with Regulation 4.

Professor of Old Age Psychiatry. 2010. Psychiatry

The Professorship of Old Age Psychiatry shall be limited to one tenure.

Professor of Photonic Systems and Displays. 2010. Engineering

Sched. to Special Ordinance G (i) 2.

Pembroke Visiting Professor of International Finance. 2010. Judge Business School

1. The sum of £1.8m received by the University to establish a Pembroke Visiting Professorship of International Finance shall constitute a fund called the Pembroke Visiting Professor of International Finance Fund.

2. The Managers of the Fund shall be the Director of Judge Business School, two persons appointed by the Faculty Board of Business and Management for periods of five years at a time, and one person appointed by Pembroke College also for periods of five years at a time.

3. A Visiting Professor shall from time to time be elected by the General Board under the authority of Special Ordinance C (vii) B.1(*c*)(iii), on the advice of a Committee comprising the Director of Judge Business School, two persons appointed by the Faculty Board of Business and Management, the Master of Pembroke College or a duly appointed member of the College's Fellowship Committee, and one person appointed by the Governor of the Bank of England. Apart from the Director of Judge Business School and the Master of Pembroke College, appointments to the Committee shall be for periods not exceeding five years.

4. The tenure of the Visiting Professor, during which he or she shall be in residence in Cambridge unless granted leave of absence by the General Board, shall normally be for a period of not more than six months in one academical year, and shall be determined by the General Board on the recommendation of the Committee.

5. The first charge on the income of the Fund shall be such emoluments of the Professorship as the General Board, on the recommendation of the Managers, shall determine, together with all the indirect costs of the University associated with the Professorship and the travelling expenses incurred by the Visiting Professor at the start and end of her or his appointment.

6. The second charge on the income of the Fund shall be to support activities associated with the Visiting Professorship.

7. The third charge on the income of the Fund shall be to support research or teaching in the field of international finance.

8. Any unexpended income in any financial year may, at the discretion of the Managers, be accumulated and added to the capital of the Fund or be held as an income reserve and expended in any one or more subsequent years in accordance with Regulations 5 to 7 above.

Professor of Zoology. 2010. Zoology

1. The Professorship of Zoology shall be limited to one tenure.

2. The Professor shall be *ex officio* Director of the Museum of Zoology during his tenure of the Professorship.

BP Foundation McKenzie Professor of Earth Sciences.[1] *2010. Earth Sciences*

Humanitas Visiting Professors.[2] *2010.*

Professor of Medicine. 2010. Medicine Sched.to Special Ordinance G (i) 2.

The Professorship of Medicine shall be limited to one tenure for the period from 1 October 2010 to 30 September 2017.

Professor of Cellular Pathophysiology and Clinical Biochemistry. 2010. Clinical Biochemistry

The Professorship of Cellular Pathophysiology and Clinical Biochemistry shall be limited to one tenure.

Professor of Orthopaedic Surgery. 2010. Surgery

The Professorship of Orthopaedic Surgery shall be limited to one tenure.

Professor of Medieval English Literature and Palaeography. 2010. English

The Professorship of Medieval English Literature and Palaeography shall be limited to one tenure.

Professor of French Literature and the Visual Arts. 2010. French

The Professorship of French Literature and the Visual Arts shall be limited to one tenure.

Professor of Modern German and Comparative Culture. 2010. German and Dutch

The Professorship of Modern German and Comparative Culture shall be limited to one tenure

Professor of Linguistics and Philosophy of Language. 2010. Theoretical and Applied Linguistics

The Professorship of Linguistics and Philosophy of Language shall be limited to one tenure.

Professor of Plant Biochemistry and Cell Biology. 2010. Biochemistry

The Professorship of Plant Biochemistry and Cell Biology shall be limited to one tenure.

[1] See p. 771.
[2] See p. 854.

Professor of Structural Biology. 2010. Biochemistry

The Professorship of Structural Biology shall be limited to one tenure.

Professor of Cell and Cancer Biology. 2010. Pathology

The Professorship of Cell and Cancer Biology shall be limited to one tenure.

Professor of Mammalian Development and Stem Cell Biology. 2010. Physiology, Development, and Neuroscience

The Professorship of Mammalian Development and Stem Cell Biology shall be limited to one tenure.

Professor of Experimental Haematology. 2010. Haematology

The Professorship of Experimental Haematology shall be limited to one tenure.

Professor of History and Public Policy. 2010. History

The Professorship of History and Public Policy shall be limited to one tenure.

Professor of Criminology and Criminal Justice. 2010. Institute of Criminology

The Professorship of Criminology and Criminal Justice shall be limited to one tenure.

Professor of International Law and International Constitutional Studies. 2010. Politics and International Studies

The Professorship of International Law and International Constitutional Studies shall be limited to one tenure.

Professor of History and Philosophy of Science. 2010. History and Philosophy of Science

The Professorship of History and Philosophy of Science shall be limited to one tenure which shall be coterminous with the holding of the office of Curator and Director of the Whipple Museum of the History of Science.

Professor of Theoretical Physics. 2010. Applied Mathematics and Theoretical Physics

The Professorship of Theoretical Physics shall be limited to one tenure.

Professor of Molecular Biophysics. 2010. Chemistry

The Professorship of Molecular Biophysics shall be limited to one tenure.

Professor of Biophysics. 2010. Chemistry

The Professorship of Biophysics shall be limited to one tenure.

Professor of Inorganic Chemistry. 2010. Chemistry

The Professorship of Inorganic Chemistry shall be limited to one tenure.

Professor of Materials Science and Metallurgy. 2010. Materials Science and Metallurgy

The Professorship of Materials Science and Metallurgy shall be limited to one tenure.

Professor of Radio Astronomy. 2010. Physics

The Professorship of Radio Astronomy shall be limited to one tenure.

Professor of Graphics and Imaging. 2010. Computer Laboratory

The Professorship of Graphics and Imaging shall be limited to one tenure.

Professor of Aerodynamics. 2010. Engineering

The Professorship of Aerodynamics shall be limited to one tenure.

Professor of Materials Engineering. 2010. Engineering

The Professorship of Materials Engineering shall be limited to one tenure.

Professor of Industrial Information Engineering. 2010. Engineering

The Professorship of Industrial Information Engineering shall be limited to one tenure.

Professor of Cognitive Developmental Neuroscience. 2010. Psychology

The Professorship of Cognitive Developmental Neuroscience shall be limited to one tenure.

MRC Research Professor of Cognitive Psychology. 2010. Clinical Medicine

The MRC Research Professorship of Cognitive Psychology shall be limited to one tenure.

Professor of Plant Development. 2011. Sainsbury Laboratory

The Professorship of Plant Development shall be limited to one tenure.

Professor of Plant Development.[1] *2011. Sainsbury Laboratory*

The Professorship of Plant Development shall be limited to one tenure.

Professor of Demography. 2011. Geography

Laing O'Rourke Professor of Construction Engineering. 2011. Engineering

The Laing O'Rourke Professorship of Construction Engineering shall be limited to one tenure.

Professor of Stem Cell Medicine. 2011. Clinical Neurosciences

Assigned by Grace 2 of 15 January 2014

The Professorship of Stem Cell Medicine shall be limited to one tenure.

Sultan Qaboos Professor of Abrahamic Faiths and Shared Values. 2011. Divinity

1. The sum of £4.22m received from His Majesty Sultan Qaboos Bin Said to endow a Sultan Qaboos Professorship of Abrahamic Faiths and Shared Values shall form a fund called the Sultan Qaboos Fund for Abrahamic Faiths and Shared Values. The Managers of the Fund shall be:

(*a*) the Chair of the Faculty Board of Divinity, who shall be Chair;

(*b*) the Sultan Qaboos Professor of Abrahamic Faiths and Shared Values;

(*c*) one person appointed by the Council of the School of Arts and Humanities;

(*d*) one person appointed by the Faculty Board of Divinity on the nomination of His Majesty Sultan Qaboos Bin Said;

(*e*) at the discretion of the Board, one further person appointed by the Faculty Board of Divinity.

2. The Sultan Qaboos Professor of Abrahamic Faiths and Shared Values shall serve as Academic Director of the Cambridge Inter-Faith Programme in the Faculty of Divinity, and shall promote the study of the relationships between Judaism, Christianity, and Islam, and their relationship to other traditions and to the modern world.

3. The first charge on the income of the Fund shall be the stipend, national insurance, pension contributions, and associated indirect costs of the Sultan Qaboos Professor of Abrahamic Faiths and Shared Values payable by the University.

4. After provision has been made in accordance with Regulation 3, the income of the Fund shall be applied to support the activities of the Professorship and for the study of Abrahamic Faiths and Shared Values within the Faculty of Divinity in such manner as shall be approved by the General Board on the recommendation of the Managers.

5. Any unexpended income of the Fund in a financial year shall be either added to the capital of the Fund or retained for use as income in future years, as the Managers may determine.

Professor of Management Studies. 2011. Judge Business School

1. The Professorship of Management Studies shall be limited to one tenure.

2. The Professor shall be Director of Judge Business School for an initial period of six years in the first instance and shall be eligible for reappointment by the General Board for a further period of up to four years.

Professor of Molecular Physiology and Pathology. 2011. Physiology, Development, and Neuroscience

The Professorship of Molecular Physiology and Pathology shall be limited to one tenure.

Professor of Education. 2011. Education

Dyson Professor of Fluid Mechanics. 2011. Engineering

1. The sum of £1.4m received from Dyson Technology Limited to support a Dyson Professorship of Fluid Mechanics shall form a fund called the Dyson Fund for Fluid Mechanics.

2. The first charge on the capital and income of the Fund shall be the stipend, national insurance, pension contributions, and associated indirect costs of the Dyson Professor of Fluid Mechanics payable by the University.

[1] Retitled and re-established for one tenure by Grace 2 of 1 May 2013.

3. The Fund shall be administered by four Managers, who shall comprise:
(*a*) the Head of the Department of Engineering, who shall be Chair;
(*b*) the Dyson Professor of Fluid Mechanics;
(*c*) the Head of the School of Technology;
(*d*) a person appointed by the Faculty Board of Engineering.

4. After provision has been made in accordance with Regulation 2, the capital and the income of the Fund may be applied for the support of teaching or research in some aspect of Fluid Mechanics in such a manner as shall be approved by the General Board on the recommendation of the Faculty Board of Engineering.

Professor of Polymeric Materials Chemistry and Physics. 2011. Chemistry

The Professorship of Polymeric Materials Chemistry and Physics shall be limited to one tenure.

Professor of Medieval Music and Literature. 2011. English

The Professorship of Medieval Music and Literature shall be limited to one tenure.

Professor of Latin-American Literature. 2011. Spanish and Portuguese

The Professorship of Latin-American Literature shall be limited to one tenure.

Professor of Music and Science. 2011. Music

The Professorship of Music and Science shall be limited to one tenure.

Professor of Logic. 2011. Philosophy

The Professorship of Logic shall be limited to one tenure.

Professor of Molecular Biology. 2011. Biochemistry

The Professorship of Molecular Biology shall be limited to one tenure.

Professor of Molecular Pathology. 2011. Pathology

The Professorship of Molecular Pathology shall be limited to one tenure.

Professor in Developmental Cardiovascular Physiology and Medicine. 2011. Physiology, Development, and Neuroscience

The Professorship in Developmental Cardiovascular Physiology and Medicine shall be limited to one tenure.

Professorship of Metabolism and Medicine. 2011. Clinical Biochemistry

The Professorship of Metabolism and Medicine shall be limited to one tenure.

Professor of Clinical Neuroscience. 2011. Clinical Neurosciences

The Professorship of Clinical Neuroscience shall be limited to one tenure.

Professor of Molecular Haematology. 2011. Haematology

The Professorship of Molecular Haematology shall be limited to one tenure.

Professor of Molecular Haemostasis. 2011. Haematology

The Professorship of Molecular Haemostasis shall be limited to one tenure.

Professor of Human Genetics. 2011. Medical Genetics

The Professorship of Human Genetics shall be limited to one tenure.

Professor of Transplantation. 2011. Surgery

The Professorship of Transplantation shall be limited to one tenure.

Professor of Children's Poetry. 2011. Education

The Professorship of Children's Poetry shall be limited to one tenure.

Professor of Modern and Contemporary History. 2011. History

The Professorship of Modern and Contemporary History shall be limited to one tenure.

Professor of Civil Justice and Private Law. 2011. Law

The Professorship of Civil Justice and Private Law shall be limited to one tenure.

Professor of Private International Law. 2011. Law

The Professorship of Private International Law shall be limited to one tenure.

Professor of Theoretical Physics. 2011. Applied Mathematics and Theoretical Physics

The Professorship of Theoretical Physics shall be limited to one tenure.

Professor of Mathematical Physics. 2011. Pure Mathematics and Mathematical Statistics

The Professorship of Mathematical Physics shall be limited to one tenure.

Professor of Cosmology and Astrophysics. 2011. Institute of Astronomy

The Professorship of Cosmology and Astrophysics shall be limited to one tenure.

Professor of Theoretical Chemistry. 2011. Chemistry

The Professorship of Theoretical Chemistry shall be limited to one tenure.

Professor of Astrophysics. 2011. Physics

The Professorship of Astrophysics shall be limited to one tenure.

Professor of Information Systems and Innovation Studies. 2011. Judge Business School

The Professorship of Information Systems and Innovation Studies shall be limited to one tenure.

Professor of Computational Linguistics (2011). 2011. Computer Laboratory

The Professorship of Computational Linguistics (2011) shall be limited to one tenure.

Professor of Mathematical Foundations of Computer Science. 2011. Computer Laboratory

The Professorship of Mathematical Foundations of Computer Science shall be limited to one tenure.

Professor of Nanotechnology. 2011. Engineering

The Professorship of Nanotechnology shall be limited to one tenure.

Professor of Chemical Physics. 2011. Chemical Engineering and Biotechnology

The Professorship of Chemical Physics shall be limited to one tenure.

Professor of Molecular Biotechnology. 2011. Chemical Engineering and Biotechnology

The Professorship of Molecular Biotechnology shall be limited to one tenure.

Regius Professor of Engineering.[1] *2011. Engineering*

Professor of Medical Genetics and Genomic Medicine. 2011. Medical Genetics

The Professorship of Medical Genetics and Genomic Medicine shall be limited to one tenure.

Professor of Finance. 2012. Judge Business School

1. The Professorship of Finance shall be established for a single tenure from 1 October 2012.

2. The Professor shall also hold the office of Director of the Cambridge Endowment for Research in Finance during his or her tenure, and shall vacate the Professorship if he or she ceases to hold the latter office.

Chong Hua Professor of Chinese Development. 2012. Politics and International Studies

1. The sum received from Chong Hua Educational Foundation for the endowment of a Chong Hua Professorship of Chinese Development shall form a fund called The Chong Hua Fund for Chinese Development.

2. The Managers of the Fund shall be:

(*a*) The Chair of the Faculty Board of Human, Social, and Political Science who shall be Chair;
(*b*) the Chong Hua Professor of Chinese Development;
(*c*) the Head of the Department of Politics and International Studies;
(*d*) the Head of the School of the Humanities and Social Sciences;

[1] The title of the Professorship was amended by a Statute approved by Her Majesty in Council on 11 April 2012.

(*e*) such person as the Chong Hua Educational Foundation may nominate from time to time.

If any of these offices are held by the same person or if one or more of these posts is vacant or its tenure has expired, the Faculty of Human, Social, and Political Science shall appoint one or more additional Managers so as to ensure that there are always five Managers.

3. The first charge on the income of the Fund shall be the stipend, national insurance, pension contributions, and associated indirect costs of the Chong Hua Professor of Chinese Development payable by the University.

4. After provision has been made in accordance with Regulation 3, the income of the Fund may be applied for the support of the Professor or for the support of teaching or research in Chinese development as shall be approved by the General Board on the recommendation of the Managers.

5. Any unexpended income in a financial year shall be accumulated in accordance with the University's Statutes and Ordinances and may, in any subsequent year or years, be expended in accordance with Regulations 3 and 4, as the Managers shall determine, subject to the approval of the General Board.

Florence Nightingale Foundation Professor of Clinical Nursing Research. 2012. Public Health and Primary Care

Reassigned by Grace 2 of 12 March 2014

The Florence Nightingale Foundation Professorship of Clinical Nursing Research shall be limited to one tenure.

Professor of Statistics. 2012. Pure Mathematics and Mathematical Statistics

The Professorship of Statistics shall be limited to one tenure.

MRC Research Professor of Biostatistics. 2012. Clinical Medicine

The MRC Research Professorship of Biostatistics shall be limited to one tenure.

Professor of Sustainable Reaction Engineering. 2012. Chemical Engineering and Biotechnology

Professor of Politics. 2012. Politics and International Studies

Professor of Engineering. 2012. Engineering

Professor of Genetics. 2012. Genetics

Professor of General Practice. 2012. Public Health and Primary Care

The Professorship of General Practice shall be limited to one tenure.

Professor of Architecture and the Moving Image. 2012. Architecture

The Professorship of Architecture and the Moving Image shall be limited to one tenure.

Professor of Celtic. 2012. Anglo-Saxon, Norse, and Celtic

The Professorship of Celtic shall be limited to one tenure.

Professor of Medieval French and Occitan. 2012. French

The Professorship of Medieval French and Occitan shall be limited to one tenure.

Professor of Modern and Medieval German Studies. 2012. German and Dutch

The Professorship of Modern and Medieval German Studies shall be limited to one tenure.

Professor of Russian Literature and Cultural History. 2012. Slavonic Studies

The Professorship of Russian Literature and Cultural History shall be limited to one tenure.

Professor of Philosophy. 2012. Philosophy

The Professorship of Philosophy shall be limited to one tenure.

Professor of Cellular Biochemistry. 2012. Biochemistry

The Professorship of Cellular Biochemistry shall be limited to one tenure.

Professor of Cellular Dynamics. 2012. Biochemistry

The Professorship of Cellular Dynamics shall be limited to one tenure.

Professor of Molecular Neurobiology. 2012. Biochemistry
The Professorship of Molecular Neurobiology shall be limited to one tenure.

Professor of Endocrine Physiology. 2012. Clinical Biochemistry
The Professorship of Endocrine Physiology shall be limited to one tenure.

Professor of Neurological Genetics. 2012. Clinical Neurosciences
The Professorship of Neurological Genetics shall be limited to one tenure.

Professor of Reproductive Biology. 2012. Obstetrics and Gynaecology
The Professorship of Reproductive Biology shall be limited to one tenure.

Professor of Radiation Oncology. 2012. Oncology
The Professorship of Radiation Oncology shall be limited to one tenure.

Professor of Cancer Epidemiology. 2012. Public Health and Primary Care
The Professorship of Cancer Epidemiology shall be limited to one tenure.

Professor of Geoarchaeology. 2012. Archaeology and Anthropology
The Professorship of Geoarchaeology shall be limited to one tenure.

Professor of Developmental Psychology. 2012. Sociology
The Professorship of Developmental Psychology shall be limited to one tenure.

Professor of Sociology and Political Economy. 2012. Sociology
The Professorship of Sociology and Political Economy shall be limited to one tenure.

Professor of Regional and Applied Economics. 2012. Land Economy
The Professorship of Regional and Applied Economics shall be limited to one tenure.

Professor of Law and Legal History. 2012. Land Economy
The Professorship of Law and Legal History shall be limited to one tenure.

Professor of Volcanology. 2012. Geography
The Professorship of Volcanology shall be limited to one tenure.

Professor of Latin American Geography. 2012. Geography
The Professorship of Latin American Geography shall be limited to one tenure.

Professor of Geometry. 2012. Pure Mathematics and Mathematical Statistics
The Professorship of Geometry shall be limited to one tenure.

Professor of Astronomy. 2012. Institute of Astronomy
The Professorship of Astronomy shall be limited to one tenure.

Professor of Chemistry and Chemical Biology. 2012. Chemistry
The Professorship of Chemistry and Chemical Biology shall be limited to one tenure.

Professor of Chemistry. 2012. Chemistry
The Professorship of Chemistry shall be limited to one tenure.

Professor of Energy and Materials Science. 2012. Materials Science and Metallurgy
The Professorship of Energy and Materials Science shall be limited to one tenure.

Professor of Economics and Organization. 2012. Judge Business School
The Professorship of Economics and Organization shall be limited to one tenure.

Professor of Computer Science. 2012. Computer Laboratory
The Professorship of Computer Science shall be limited to one tenure.

Professor of Information Engineering. 2012. Engineering
The Professorship of Information Engineering shall be limited to one tenure.

Professor of Laser Engineering. 2012. Engineering

The Professorship of Laser Engineering shall be limited to one tenure.

Professor of Chemical Reaction Engineering. 2012. Chemical Engineering and Biotechnology

The Professorship of Chemical Reaction Engineering shall be limited to one tenure.

MRC Research Professor of Mitochondrial Medicine. 2012. Clinical Medicine

The MRC Research Professorship of Mitochondrial Medicine shall be limited to one tenure.

Harold Samuel Professor of Law and Environmental Policy. 2012. Land Economy

The Harold Samuel Professorship of Law and Environmental Policy shall be limited to one tenure.

Professor of Hypoxia Signalling and Cell Biology. 2012. Medicine

The Professorship of Hypoxia Signalling and Cell Biology shall be limited to one tenure.

Professor of Empirical Macroeconomics. 2013. Economics

The Professorship of Empirical Macroeconomics shall be limited to one tenure.

Professor of Experimental Psychology. 2013. Psychology

The Professorship of Experimental Psychology shall be limited to one tenure.

Professor of Philosophy. 2013. Philosophy

The Professorship of Philosophy shall be limited to one tenure.

Professor of Philosophy. 2013. Philosophy

The Professorship of Philosophy shall be limited to one tenure.

Professor of Neurorehabilitation. 2013. Clinical Neurosciences

The Professorship of Neurorehabilitation shall be limited to one tenure.

MRC Research Professor of Epidemiology. 2013. Clinical Medicine

The MRC Research Professorship of Epidemiology shall be limited to one tenure.

Royal Society Research Professor of Earth Sciences. 2013. Earth Sciences

The Royal Society Research Professorship of Earth Sciences shall be limited to one tenure.

Professor of International Education. 2013. Education

The Professorship of International Education shall be limited to one tenure.

John Harvard Professor in the Arts, Humanities, and Social Sciences. 2013. School of Arts and Humanities and School of the Humanities and Social Sciences

1. The sums received from the Board of Cambridge in America, representing donations from Mr Robert C. 'Peter' Milton and others, including a bequest from Dr Timothy Joyce, and Trinity College, to support a John Harvard Professorship in the Arts, Humanities, and Social Sciences, shall form a fund called the John Harvard Professorship Fund. The Fund may include other sums received from other bodies or persons for the same purpose.

2. The John Harvard Professorship in the Arts, Humanities, and Social Sciences shall be tenable concurrently with a Professorship in an institution in either the School of Arts and Humanities or the School of the Humanities and Social Sciences.

3. Each John Harvard Professor shall be elected for a tenure of up to five years under the authority of Special Ordinance C (vii) B.1(*c*)(iii) by the General Board, on the recommendation of an Advisory Committee including representatives of each of the Schools of Arts and Humanities and the Humanities and Social Sciences.

4. When a John Harvard Professor is to be elected, the Vice-Chancellor shall publish a Notice inviting applications from any Professor whose Professorship is established in an institution in the School of Arts and Humanities or the School of the Humanities and Social Sciences alternately.

5. In addition to her or his statutory duties under Statute C I and Special Ordinance C (vii) A, it shall be the duty of the Professor to undertake and promote research in the arts, humanities, or social sciences relevant to the present day.

6. The Managers of the John Harvard Professorship Fund shall be the Heads of the Schools of Arts and Humanities and the Humanities and Social Sciences.

7. The income of the Fund shall be applied for the following purposes:

(*a*) such contributions towards the stipend, national insurance, pension contributions, and associated indirect costs of the Professor payable by the University, during her or his period of tenure, as may be approved by the Managers;

(*b*) such payments in support of the research of the Professor as may be approved by the Managers.

8. Any unexpended income in any financial year may, at the discretion of the Managers, be accumulated and added to the capital of the Fund or be held as an income reserve and expended in any one or more subsequent years in accordance with Regulation 7 above.

Professor of Early Modern French Literature and Culture. 2013. French

The Professorship of Early Modern French Literature and Culture shall be limited to one tenure.

Professor of German Literature and Intellectual History. 2013. German and Dutch

The Professorship of German Literature and Intellectual History shall be limited to one tenure.

Professor of German History and Thought. 2013. German and Dutch

The Professorship of German History and Thought shall be limited to one tenure.

Professor of Italian and Romance Linguistics. 2013. Italian

The Professorship of Italian and Romance Linguistics shall be limited to one tenure.

Professor of Genome Biology. 2013. Genetics

The Professorship of Genome Biology shall be limited to one tenure.

Professor of Virus Pathogenesis. 2013. Pathology

The Professorship of Virus Pathogenesis shall be limited to one tenure.

Professor of Behavioural Neuroscience. 2013. Psychology

The Professorship of Behavioural Neuroscience shall be limited to one tenure.

Professor of Evolution and Behaviour. 2013. Zoology

The Professorship of Evolution and Behaviour shall be limited to one tenure.

Professor of Evolutionary Biology. 2013. Zoology

The Professorship of Evolutionary Biology shall be limited to one tenure.

Professor of Innate Immunity. 2013. Veterinary Medicine

The Professorship of Innate Immunity shall be limited to one tenure.

Professor of Brain Physics. 2013. Clinical Neurosciences

The Professorship of Brain Physics shall be limited to one tenure.

Professor of Therapeutics. 2013. Medicine

The Professorship of Therapeutics shall be limited to one tenure.

Professor of Economic Theory. 2013. Economics

The Professorship of Economic Theory shall be limited to one tenure.

Professor of Economics. 2013. Economics

The Professorship of Economics shall be limited to one tenure.

Professor of Early Modern European History. 2013. History

The Professorship of Early Modern European History shall be limited to one tenure.

Professor of Social Theory. 2013. Sociology

The Professorship of Social Theory shall be limited to one tenure.

Professor of Philosophy of Science. 2013. History and Philosophy of Science

The Professorship of Philosophy of Science shall be limited to one tenure.

Professor of Petrology. 2013. Earth Sciences

The Professorship of Petrology shall be limited to one tenure.

Professor of Cymatogeny. 2013. Earth Sciences

The Professorship of Cymatogeny shall be limited to one tenure.

Professor of Pacific Geography. 2013. Geography

The Professorship of Pacific Geography shall be limited to one tenure.

Professor of Applied Mathematics. 2013. Applied Mathematics and Theoretical Physics

The Professorship of Applied Mathematics shall be limited to one tenure.

Professor of Mathematical Astrophysics. 2013. Applied Mathematics and Theoretical Physics

The Professorship of Mathematical Astrophysics shall be limited to one tenure.

Professor of Theoretical Physics. 2013. Applied Mathematics and Theoretical Physics

The Professorship of Theoretical Physics shall be limited to one tenure.

Professor of Mathematical Sciences. 2013. Pure Mathematics and Mathematical Statistics

The Professorship of Mathematical Sciences shall be limited to one tenure.

Professor of Statistics. 2013. Pure Mathematics and Mathematical Statistics

The Professorship of Statistics shall be limited to one tenure.

Professor of Theoretical Chemistry. 2013. Chemistry

The Professorship of Theoretical Chemistry shall be limited to one tenure.

Professor of Chemistry and Chemical Biology. 2013. Chemistry

The Professorship of Chemistry and Chemical Biology shall be limited to one tenure.

Professor of Materials Physics. 2013. Materials Science and Metallurgy

The Professorship of Materials Physics shall be limited to one tenure.

Professor of Quantum Electronics. 2013. Physics

The Professorship of Quantum Electronics shall be limited to one tenure.

Professor of Innovation and Organization. 2013. Judge Business School

The Professorship of Innovation and Organization shall be limited to one tenure.

Professor of Information Engineering. 2013. Engineering

The Professorship of Information Engineering shall be limited to one tenure.

Professor of Civil Engineering. 2013. Engineering

The Professorship of Civil Engineering shall be limited to one tenure.

Professor of Mechanical Engineering. 2013. Engineering

The Professorship of Mechanical Engineering shall be limited to one tenure.

Professor of Photonic Engineering. 2013. Engineering

The Professorship of Photonic Engineering shall be limited to one tenure.

Professor of Neurotechnology. 2013. Chemical Engineering and Biotechnology

The Professorship of Neurotechnology shall be limited to one tenure.

Van Geest Professorship.[1] *2013. Clinical Neurosciences*

Grace 2 of 16 October 2013

The Van Geest Professorship shall be limited to one tenure.

[1] The title of the Professorship will be announced once the research interests of the person elected to the Professorship is known.

Professorship.[1] *2013. Clinical Neurosciences*

Grace 2 of 16 October 2013

The Professorship shall be limited to one tenure.

Stephen W. Hawking Professor of Cosmology 2014. Applied Mathematics and Theoretical Physics

Grace 1 of 22 January 2014

1. The gift of $2m from the Avery-Tsui Foundation to commemorate the scientific work of Professor S. W. Hawking, Emeritus Lucasian Professor of Mathematics, shall be used to establish the Stephen W. Hawking Professorship. The Professorship is assigned to the Department of Applied Mathematics and Theoretical Physics and the Professor shall be concerned with the study of cosmology which, for this purpose, shall include analysis as to the origins of matter and of the universe, theoretical cosmology and gravitation, and all other fields of academic scholarship as may from time to time be generally considered cosmology and theoretical physics.

2. The sums received from the Avery-Tsui Foundation for the endowment of the Stephen W. Hawking Professorship shall constitute a fund called the Avery Tsui Fund.

3. The income of the Fund shall be used for the payment of the stipend, national insurance, pension contributions, and associated indirect costs of the Professor (or of the post of Director of Research during such period as Emeritus Professor Stephen W. Hawking holds such post) payable by the University.

4. Any income not spent in a financial year may be added to the capital of the fund for a period of 21 years from receipt of the gift from the Avery-Tsui Foundation.

5. A Professor shall be elected in accordance with Special Ordinance C (vii) B.1(*c*)(iii) by the General Board on the advice of a committee which shall be established as if it were a Board of Electors constituted under Special Ordinance C (vii) B.4, but including the Master of Trinity Hall as an additional member. A Professor so elected shall hold the title of Stephen Hawking Professor for seven years in the first instance. The General Board, on the recommendation of a committee constituted for the purpose, shall have the power to extend that period for five years and, in an exceptional case, for a further five years.

6. A person who has held the Professorship for over eleven and a half years and who remains an employee of the University or who has retired under the Statutes or Ordinances may use the title of 'Stephen W. Hawking Professor Laureate' or 'Hawking Professor Laureate' and this title may be used in conjunction with any other title or titles.

Professor of Climate Change Economics and Policy. 2014. Land Economy

Grace 4 of 4 June 2014

The Professorship of Climate Change Economics and Policy shall be limited to one tenure.

Professor of Immunology and Infectious Diseases. 2014. Medicine

Grace 2 of 16 July 2014

The Professorship of Immunology and Infectious Diseases shall be limited to one tenure.

Royal Society Research Professor of Molecular Cancer Biology. 2014. Oncology

Grace 2 of 16 July 2014

The Royal Society Research Professorship of Molecular Cancer Biology shall be limited to one tenure.

Professor of History of Art. 2015. History of Art

Grace 4 of 22 January 2014

Expenses of non-resident Electors to Professorships

1. A non-resident Elector to a Professorship shall be entitled to reimbursement of his or her expenses in respect of any visit connected with an election to a Professorship up to a sum not exceeding the return railway fare between Cambridge and the Elector's normal place of residence or other place

[1] The title of the Professorship will be announced once the research interests of the person elected to the Professorship is known.

approved by the Finance Committee of the Council, together with a subsistence allowance in accordance with rates to be determined from time to time by the Finance Committee.

2. For the purposes of the preceding regulation a Committee appointed by the General Board to advise them in their choice of a person for election to any Professorship to which elections are made by the Board under the authority of Special Ordinance C (vii) B.1(*c*) shall be treated as a Board of Electors.

Readers and Readerships

Amended by Grace 1 of 27 November 2013

1. Save as provided in Regulation 4,

Appointments to Readership.

(*a*) every appointment to a Readership of which the work falls preponderantly within the scope of one Faculty or Department or other institution under the supervision of the General Board shall be made by a Committee consisting of the members of the Appointments Committee for the institution concerned and two persons appointed by the General Board for the particular occasion, unless a special appointing body has been constituted in the Report proposing the creation of the Readership;

(*b*) every appointment to a Readership of which the work does not fall preponderantly within the scope of any one Faculty or Department or other institution under the supervision of the General Board shall be made by a special appointing body constituted as follows: an Appointments Committee constituted in accordance with the provisions of Special Ordinance C (x) 3 and two persons appointed by the General Board for the particular occasion.

2. At least one member of every appointing body constituted under Regulation 1 shall be a person not resident in the University nor officially connected with it. A non-resident member of the Committee appointed for the occasion of an appointment to a Readership shall be entitled to reimbursement of his or her expenses in respect of any visit connected with such appointment to a Readership up to a sum not exceeding the return railway fare between Cambridge and the member's normal place of residence or other place approved by the Finance Committee of the Council, together with a subsistence allowance in accordance with rates to be determined from time to time by the Finance Committee.

3. Every appointment to a Readership under Regulations 1 and 2 shall require the attendance of at least two-thirds of the members of the appointing body and the concurrence of the votes of not fewer than five members.

4. When the creation of a Readership for a particular person is contemplated, the proposal shall be submitted to the University on the recommendation of the General Board in the form of a Grace authorizing the Board to appoint that person.

Restrictions.

5. The amount of instruction given by a Reader on behalf of a College or Colleges shall not, except with the consent of the General Board, exceed eight hours a week, or if the Reader is also a Tutor or Bursar or an Assistant Tutor or Assistant Bursar or Steward, four hours a week.

6. In any Statute or Ordinance the term 'Reader' shall not include the Sandars Readership in Bibliography.

In addition to Readerships created under Regulation 4 above for particular persons and other single-tenure Readerships, the following Readerships are established in the University:

Sir William Dunn Readership in Biochemistry (*1922*), assigned to the Department of Biochemistry.

Readership in Cell Biology (*2005*), assigned to the Department of Pathology.

Readership in Theoretical Econometrics (*2005*), assigned to the Faculty of Economics.

Readership in Economics (*2006*), assigned to the Faculty of Economics.

Readership in Economics (*2006*), assigned to the Faculty of Economics.

Readership in Education (*2006*), assigned to the Department of Education.

Readership in Education (*2006*), assigned to the Department of Education.

Readership in Physics (*2006*), assigned to the Department of Physics.

Readership in Physics (*2006*), assigned to the Department of Physics.

Readership in Pure Mathematics (2006), assigned to the Department of Pure Mathematics and Mathematical Statistics.

Readership in Social Anthropology (2006), assigned to the Department of Archaeology and Anthropology.

Readership in Sociology (2006), assigned to the Department of Sociology.

Readership in Human Resources and Organizational Behaviour (2007), assigned to Judge Business School.

Readership in Operations Management (2007), assigned to Judge Business School.

Readership in Economics (2010), assigned to the Faculty of Economics.

Readership in Pure Mathematics and Mathematical Statistics (2010), assigned to the Department of Pure Mathematics and Mathematical Statistics.

Readership in Real Estate and Housing Finance (2011), assigned to the Department of Land Economy.

Readership in Quantitative Sociology (2013), assigned to the Department of Sociology.

Readership in Operations Management (2013), assigned to Judge Business School.

Readership in Entrepreneurship (2013), assigned to Judge Business School.

Readership in Corporate Law (2014), assigned to the Faculty of Law

Grace 1 of 12 February 2014

University Senior Lecturers

Appointments and reappointments to the office of University Senior Lecturer shall be made by the Appointments Committee for the Faculty or Department or other institution concerned, in accordance with the provisions of Special Ordinance C (x) 2–6 for University Lecturers, provided that, where an appointment is made through promotion, the appointment shall be made by the General Board. Appointments.

Assistant Directors of Development Studies

1. There shall be such number of University offices[1] of Assistant Director of Development Studies as the General Board may from time to time determine. Number.

2. Appointments and reappointments to the University office of Assistant Director of Development Studies shall be made by an Appointments Committee consisting of: Appointments.

(*a*) the Vice-Chancellor (or a duly appointed deputy) as Chair;

(*b*) the Chair of the Faculty Board of Economics, and the Heads of the Departments of Archaeology and Anthropology and of Land Economy;

(*c*) the Chair of the Development Studies Committee;

(*d*) one person appointed by the Board of Land Economy;

(*e*) one person appointed by each of the Faculty Boards of Economics and of Human, Social, and Political Science;

(*f*) two persons appointed by the General Board.

The appointed members shall be appointed in the Michaelmas Term of each calendar year of which the number is even to serve for the two calendar years next ensuing.

3. The duties of an Assistant Director of Development Studies shall be determined by the General Board. Duties.

4. An Assistant Director of Development Studies shall not engage in teaching other than teaching given on behalf of the University or a College or Colleges. The amount of teaching given by an Assistant Director of Development Studies on behalf of a College or Colleges shall not exceed six hours a week, except with the specific approval of the General Board. Restrictions.

[1] These offices are offices specified in the Schedule to Special Ordinance C (i) 1.

Assistant Directors of Research and Senior Assistants in Research

Appointments. **1.** Appointments and reappointments to a University office[1] of Assistant Director of Research and to a University office[1] of Senior Assistant in Research shall be made by the Appointments Committee or other appointing body for the Faculty or other institution concerned.

Duties. **2.** The duties of an Assistant Director of Research or a Senior Assistant in Research (unless determined by Grace) shall be determined by the General Board after consulting the Faculty Board or other authority concerned; these duties shall normally relate to the periods of Full Term, but the General Board shall have power to reckon duties performed in vacation as if they were performed in Full Term.

Restrictions. **3.** Except with the leave of the General Board, Assistant Directors of Research and Senior Assistants in Research shall not engage in teaching other than teaching on behalf of the University or a College or Colleges. The amount of teaching given by an Assistant Director of Research or a Senior Assistant in Research on behalf of a College or Colleges shall not exceed six hours a week.

OFFICERS OTHER THAN THOSE SPECIFIED IN THE SCHEDULE TO SPECIAL ORDINANCE C (i) 1

Associate Lecturers

An Associate Lecturer shall conform to such conditions of residence as may be determined by the Faculty Board or other body concerned subject to the approval of the General Board.

Clinical Lecturers

Number. **1.** There shall be such number of University offices of Clinical Lecturer in each Faculty or Department as the General Board may from time to time determine on the recommendation of the Faculty Board or other body concerned.

Appointments. **2.** Appointments and reappointments to an office of Clinical Lecturer shall be made by an *ad hoc* Appointing Committee consisting of the members (excluding the Chair) of the Appointments Committee for the Faculty concerned and two (or, where the terms of the funding so require, up to four) persons appointed by the General Board on the nomination of the appropriate Health Authority or NHS Trust as additional members of the Committee for the purpose of the particular appointment or reappointment; provided that, if the Faculty concerned is a Faculty other than the Faculty of Clinical Medicine, there shall be two further members of the *ad hoc* Appointing Committee who shall be appointed by the General Board on the nomination of the Faculty Board of Clinical Medicine. The Regius Professor of Physic shall be Chair of the Committee.

Tenure. **3.** Appointments to a Clinical Lectureship shall be for four years excluding any period of leave approved by the General Board under Special Ordinance C (i) 2(*a*) and 2(*b*).

Eligibility. **4.** A Clinical Lecturer shall hold qualifications entitling him or her to be registered with the General Medical Council as a Medical Practitioner and shall hold an honorary appointment in the National Health Service.

Duties. **5.** The duties of a Clinical Lecturer, which shall include clinical responsibility in addition to teaching and research, shall be determined by the Faculty Board or other body concerned, subject to the approval of the General Board, and those duties shall apply throughout the year save for such period or periods not exceeding six weeks in all in any one academical year as may be agreed, if the Lecturer holds an office assigned to a Department, by the Head of the Department concerned or, if the Lecturer holds an office assigned to the Faculty of Clinical Medicine, by the Regius Professor of Physic.

Residence. **6.** A Clinical Lecturer shall conform to such conditions of residence as may be determined by the Faculty Board or other body concerned, with the approval of the General Board.

Restrictions. **7.** A Clinical Lecturer shall not be a Tutor, Assistant Tutor, Steward, Bursar, or Assistant Bursar of a College, nor shall a Clinical Lecturer undertake any teaching other than teaching given on behalf of the University or a College or Colleges or the Cambridge University Hospitals NHS Foundation Trust, or the delivery of occasional lectures. The amount of teaching given by a Clinical Lecturer on behalf of a College or Colleges shall not exceed six hours a week.

[1] These offices are offices specified in the Schedule to Special Ordinance C (i) 1.

Principal Computer Officers, Senior Computer Officers, and Computer Officers

1. There shall be University offices of Principal Computer Officer, Senior Computer Officer, and four grades of the University office of Computer Officer, Grades I, II, III, and IV. The stipend of the office of Principal Computer Officer, Senior Computer Officer, and the scale of stipends for each grade of Computer Officer, except where those offices are in the University Offices, shall be determined by the Council with the concurrence of the General Board. Offices and stipends.

2. The establishment and the duties of Principal Computer Officers, Senior Computer Officers, and Computer Officers in an institution shall be determined from time to time by the Council or by the General Board, as the case may be, on the recommendation of the authority concerned. Establishment and duties.

3. Appointments and reappointments to the offices of Principal Computer Officer, Senior Computer Officer, and Computer Officers in Grades I, II, III, and IV shall be made in accordance with arrangements agreed from time to time by the competent authority. Appointments and reappointments.

Senior Language Teaching Officers

1. There shall be such number of University offices of Senior Language Teaching Officer as the General Board shall approve on the recommendation of the Faculty Board concerned. Number.

2. Appointments and reappointments to an office of Senior Language Teaching Officer shall be made by the Appointments Committee for the Faculty concerned. Appointments.

3. The duties of a Senior Language Teaching Officer shall be determined by the Faculty Board concerned, subject to the approval of the General Board. Duties.

4. A Senior Language Teaching Officer shall not engage in teaching other than teaching given on behalf of the University or a College or Colleges. The amount of teaching given by a Senior Language Teaching Officer on behalf of a College or Colleges shall not exceed six hours a week. Restrictions.

Language Teaching Officers

1. The number of University offices of Language Teaching Officer shall be determined for each Faculty by the Faculty Board (or, if the Faculty is organized in Departments, for each Department by the Faculty Board on the recommendation of the Head of the Department concerned), subject to the approval of the General Board. Number.

2. Appointments and reappointments to an office of Language Teaching Officer shall be made by the Faculty Board concerned (or, if the Faculty is organized in Departments, by the Faculty Board on the recommendation of the Head of the Department concerned), subject to the approval of the General Board. Appointments.

3. The duties of a Language Teaching Officer shall be determined by the Faculty Board concerned, subject to the approval of the General Board. Duties.

4. A Language Teaching Officer shall not engage in teaching other than teaching given on behalf of the University or a College or Colleges. The amount of teaching given on behalf of a College or Colleges shall not exceed six hours a week. Restrictions.

Lectors in Languages

1. There shall be such number of University offices of Lector in Languages as the General Board shall determine. Number.

2. Appointments and reappointments to an office of Lector shall be made by the Head of the Department concerned, if the Faculty is organized in Departments, or, if the Faculty is not so organized, by the Faculty Board. Appointments.

3. A Lector shall be appointed in the first instance for one or two years, as may be decided by the appointing authority at the time of appointment. The tenure of a Lector may, subject to the approval of the General Board, be extended for one year at a time, provided that the total tenure shall not exceed five years. Tenure.

4. The stipend of a Lector shall be non-pensionable and shall be fixed by the Faculty Board subject to the approval of the General Board. Stipend.

Duties.

5. A Lector shall perform such teaching duties as are determined (*a*) by the Head of the Department, subject to the approval of the Faculty Board, if the Faculty is organized in Departments, or (*b*) if the Faculty is not so organized, by the Faculty Board. A Lector shall not undertake for remuneration any other teaching during Full Term without the permission of the Faculty Board.

LIBRARIANS OF CERTAIN FACULTIES, DEPARTMENTS, AND OTHER INSTITUTIONS

Appointments.

1. Appointments and reappointments to the University office of Librarian of a Faculty, Department, or other institution specified in Schedule I, Schedule II, or Schedule III to these regulations shall be made in accordance with the arrangements to be agreed from time to time by the competent authority.

Librarians: three grades.

2. There shall be three grades, Grades A, B, and C, in which an office of Librarian may be placed, and the grade of a particular such office shall be determined by the General Board after consultation with the Faculty Board or other body responsible for the management of the institution concerned. The scales of stipends of such offices of Librarian shall correspond with the scales of stipends of offices on the staff of the University Library as follows:

Stipends.

Scale for office in the Schedule	*Scale for office in the University Library*
Grade A	Under-Librarian
Grade B	Assistant Under-Librarian
Grade C	Assistant Library Officer

Duties.

3. The duties attached to an office of Librarian of a Faculty, Department, or other institution shall be determined by the General Board after consultation with the Faculty Board or other body responsible for the management of the institution concerned, and may include teaching on behalf of the University not exceeding twenty hours' lectures or equivalent teaching in any one year.

Member of Faculty.

4. Each Librarian of a Faculty, Department, or Sub-department within a Faculty shall be a member of the Faculty concerned under Regulation 1 (*b*) of the Regulations for Faculty Membership.

Other offices.

5. Where the special regulations for a particular University office provide that appointments and reappointments to the office shall be made by the Appointments Committee for Librarians, the above regulations shall apply to that office, subject to any modifications contained in the special regulations for the particular office.

6. The General Board shall have power to make alterations in the list of Faculties, Departments, and other institutions specified in the Schedules as they may from time to time think fit.

SCHEDULE I

Faculty of Asian and Middle Eastern Studies
Faculty of Classics
Faculty of Divinity
Faculty of Economics (Marshall Library)
Faculty of Education
Faculty of English
Faculty of History (Seeley Library)
Faculty of Human, Social, and Political Science
Faculty of Modern and Medieval Languages
Faculty of Music (Pendlebury Library)
Faculty of Philosophy

SCHEDULE II

Faculty of Architecture and History of Art

SCHEDULE III

Institute of Criminology
Department of Engineering
Department of Geography
Department of History and Philosophy of Science
Language Centre
Judge Institute of Management
Scott Polar Research Institute
Centre of South Asian Studies

SECRETARIES AND SUPERINTENDENTS OF FACULTIES, DEPARTMENTS, AND OTHER INSTITUTIONS UNDER THE SUPERVISION OF THE GENERAL BOARD

Appointments and reappointments.

1. Appointments and reappointments to the offices listed in Schedules I and II of these regulations shall be made in accordance with arrangements agreed from time to time by the competent authority.

Five grades.

2. There shall be five grades of the office of Secretary, Grades A, B, C*, C, and D. The grade of a particular office of Secretary shall be determined by the General Board after consultation with the Faculty Board or comparable authority concerned.

Stipends.

3. The scale of stipends of each grade of the office of Secretary of a Faculty, Department, or other institution shall be determined by the General Board.

Offices in Schedule II.

4. The scale of stipends of any of the offices specified in Schedule II shall be determined by the General Board after consultation with the Faculty Board or comparable authority concerned and, save for an office that is there marked with an asterisk, shall be the same as the scale of stipends of one of the five grades of the office of Secretary.

Duties.

5. The duties attached to an office of Secretary of an institution specified in Schedule I or to any of the offices specified in Schedule II shall be determined, apart from any duties determined by Ordinance, by the General Board after consultation with the Faculty Board or comparable authority concerned.

Member of Faculty.

6. The holder of a University office specified in Schedule I or II shall be a member of the Faculty concerned under Regulation 1 (*b*) of the Regulations for Faculty Membership.

7. The General Board shall have power to make alterations in the list of Faculties, Departments, and other institutions specified in the Schedules as they may from time to time think fit.

SCHEDULE I

University office of Secretary of a Faculty or Department or other institution

Applied Mathematics and Theoretical Physics
Archaeology and Anthropology
Astronomy
Chemical Engineering and Biotechnology
Chemistry
Computer Laboratory
Earth Sciences
Economics
Education
Engineering (Administration and Personnel)
Engineering (Finance)
Geography
History and Philosophy of Science
Judge Institute of Management
Language Laboratory
Materials Science and Metallurgy
Pathology
Pharmacology
Physics
Physiology, Development, and Neuroscience
Psychology
Pure Mathematics and Mathematical Statistics
Veterinary Medicine

SCHEDULE II

Other University offices governed by these regulations

Assistant Secretary of the School of Technology
Assistant Secretaries of the Department of Education
Assistant Secretaries of the Department of Engineering
Assistant Secretary of the Department of Chemistry
Assistant Secretary of the Department of Physics

Assistant Secretary of the Department of Veterinary Medicine
Assistant Secretary of the Institute of Astronomy
Assistant Secretary (Finance and Charged Services) of the University Computing Service
Superintendent of the Biochemical Laboratory
Assistant Superintendent of the Department of Pathology
*Director of Research (Administration and Development) in the Department of Engineering[1]
Administrator in the Clinical School
Administrator (Educational Services Manager) in the Judge Institute of Management
Assistant Administrator in the Clinical School
Public Health Aggregate Administrator in the Department of Public Health and Primary Care

Senior Technical Officers

Title and number. **1.** There shall be such number of University offices of Senior Technical Officer in each Faculty, Department, or other institution as the competent authority concerned shall from time to time determine.

Special titles. **2.** Special titles that have been given to certain holders of an office of Senior Technical Officer are specified in Schedule I appended to these regulations.

Appointments and reappointments. **3.** Appointments and reappointments to the office of Senior Technical Officer shall be made in accordance with arrangements agreed from time to time by the competent authority.

Duties. **4.** The duties of a Senior Technical Officer shall be determined by the competent authority after consultation with the Faculty Board or other body concerned.

Restrictions. **5.** A Senior Technical Officer shall not undertake for remuneration during Full Term without the consent of the competent authority any teaching other than teaching given on behalf of the University or a College or Colleges or the delivery of occasional lectures. The amount of teaching given by a Senior Technical Officer on behalf of a College or Colleges shall not exceed six hours a week.

Member of Faculty. **6.** A Senior Technical Officer shall, under Regulation 1 (*b*) of the Regulations for Faculty Membership, be a member of the Faculty, if any, in which his or her office is placed.

SCHEDULE I

Special Titles of Certain Holders of the Office of Senior Technical Officer

Prosector in Anatomy.

Technical Officers

Number. **1.** There shall be such number of University offices of Technical Officer in each Faculty, Department, or other institution as the competent authority concerned shall from time to time determine.

Appointments. **2.** Appointments and reappointments to the office of Technical Officer shall be made in accordance with arrangements agreed from time to time by the competent authority.

Duties. **3.** The duties of a Technical Officer shall be determined by the Faculty Board or other authority concerned, subject to the approval of the competent authority.

Restrictions. **4.** A Technical Officer shall not engage in teaching other than teaching given on behalf of the University or a College or Colleges. The amount of teaching given by a Technical Officer on behalf of a College or Colleges shall not exceed six hours a week.

GRANT OF TITLE

Affiliated Lecturers

1. Each Faculty Board or comparable authority shall have power, subject to the approval of the General Board, to grant the title of Affiliated Lecturer to any person who has been invited by the Faculty Board to give lectures or other instruction as part of the teaching programme of the Faculty under Regulation 7(*c*) of the General Regulations for the Constitution of Faculty Boards.

2. A person to whom the title of Affiliated Lecturer has been granted shall hold that title for not more than two years at a time. At the end of any such period the title may again be granted for a further period of not more than two years on each occasion.

[1] See Regulation 4.

CHAPTER XII

TRUSTS

ENDOWED UNIVERSITY LECTURESHIPS[1]

Amended by Grace 6 of 30 July 2014

1. Benefactions received by the University for the endowment of University teaching shall be applied to the payment of the stipends of University Lecturers in connection with the several Faculties as follows:

Fund	*Subject*	*Faculty or Department*
English Lectureship Fund	English	English
Gilbey Lectureship Fund	History and Economics of Agriculture	Land Economy
Sidgwick Memorial Fund	Philosophy	Philosophy
Girdlers' Lectureship Fund	Economics	Economics
Huddersfield Lectureship Fund	Special Pathology	Biology
Harding Fund	Zoology	Biology
Humphrey Owen Jones Lectureship Fund	Physical Chemistry	Physics and Chemistry
Sir Eustace Gurney's Benefaction	Forestry	Land Economy
Eric Yarrow Lectureship Fund	Assyriology	Archaeology and Anthropology
Modern Greek Fund	Modern Greek	Classics, and Modern and Medieval Languages
Japanese Studies Fund	Japanese Studies (Kawashima Lecturer) Modern Japanese Studies (Fuji Bank Lecturer)	East Asian Studies
Starbridge Lectureship Fund	Theology and Natural Science (Starbridge Lecturer)	Divinity
Dr William M. Scholl Lectureship Fund	Neurology (Dr William M. Scholl Lecturer)	Clinical Medicine
Kennedy Leigh Fund for Modern Hebrew	Modern Hebrew	Middle Eastern Studies
Sheikh Zayed Fund for Islamic Studies	Islamic Studies	Divinity
Ali Reza and Mohamed Soudavar Lectureship Fund	Persian Studies	Middle Eastern Studies
Herchel Smith Lectureship in Intellectual Property Law Fund	Intellectual Property Law	Law
Hibbitt Endowed Fund for Solid Mechanics	Solid Mechanics	Engineering
Herchel Smith Lectureships in Medicinal Chemistry Fund	Medicinal Chemistry	Any relevant Department in the School of Clinical Medicine or the Department of Chemistry
Gender Studies Fund	Gender Studies	Politics and International Studies
HRH Prince Alwaleed Bin Talal Fund	Islamic Studies	Middle Eastern Studies
David and Elaine Potter Fund for Governance and Human Rights	Governance and Human Rights	Politics and International Studies
Medieval Scandinavian History Fund	Medieval Scandinavian History	Anglo-Saxon, Norse, and Celtic
Polonsky–Coexist Fund for Jewish Studies	Jewish Studies (Polonsky–Coexist Lecturer)	Divinity

2. The Gilbey Lecturer shall deliver lectures on rural conservation and on the history and economics of agriculture. Gilbey.

3. An offer received from the Worshipful Company of Girdlers to renew their support of the teaching of Economics in the University by an annual grant of £120 was accepted by the Council of the Senate in April 1949. Girdlers.

[1] For endowed Professorships and Readerships see the regulations for Professors and Readers.

Humphrey Owen Jones.

4. If the Humphrey Owen Jones Lectureship Fund is in future united with any other fund making further provision for the teaching of Physical Chemistry in the University, the name Humphrey Owen Jones shall always form part of the title of the office. The interest of the Fund accruing during any vacancy shall be added to the principal sum and invested.

Eric Yarrow.

5. If in any year the income of the Eric Yarrow Lectureship Fund exceeds £500 but not £550, the excess over £500 may be used to pay the University's contribution in respect of the Lecturer under the Pension Scheme.

Lewis-Gibson.

6. The stipend and pension contributions of the Lewis-Gibson Lecturer shall be paid from the Modern Greek Fund. It shall be part of the duties of the Lecturer to give such instruction as the Faculty Board of Modern and Medieval Languages may require to provide for the teaching of students offering Modern Greek in the Modern and Medieval Languages Tripos.

Cayley and Stokes Lectureships.

7. Two of the University Lecturers in Mathematics shall bear the titles Cayley Lecturer and Stokes Lecturer respectively. When at any time there is no Lecturer bearing the title Cayley Lecturer or Stokes Lecturer, as the case may be, the General Board may, on the recommendation of the Faculty Board of Mathematics, confer the title on one of the University Lecturers in Mathematics.

Polonsky-Coexist Lectureships.

8. The Polonsky–Coexist Lecturer in Jewish Studies shall provide such teaching in Jewish Studies, with special reference to the relations with the other Abrahamic faiths, for students offering the relevant papers under the regulations for the Theological and Religious Studies Tripos, as determined by the Faculty Board of Divinity.

Vacancies.

9. When a Lectureship supported by a benefaction mentioned in Regulation 1 falls vacant, the Appointments Committee for the Faculty or Department with which the Lectureship is connected may transfer to it with his or her consent, if they think fit, an existing University Lecturer.

FUNDS, STUDENTSHIPS, PRIZES, LECTURESHIPS, ETC.

GENERAL REGULATIONS FOR AWARDS

Restriction of candidature: date of application.

1. Competition for any University Studentship, Scholarship, Exhibition, Prize, Medal, or other such award shall be restricted to candidates who are actual members of the University unless there is clear evidence of a contrary intention in the regulations or document governing the award. Whenever by any regulation for any award it is required that an application or an entry be submitted to the Registrary or to some other person by a certain date that regulation shall be interpreted as requiring that the application or entry shall be sent so as to reach the Registrary or other person not later than that date.

Honourable mention.

2. The Examiners are empowered to give honourable mention, in such form as they may think fit, to students who reach the standard of merit required for the award of an emolument though they fail to gain it in consequence of the superior merit of others; but honourable mention may not be given to a student who fails to reach such a standard.

3. If a University Studentship, Scholarship, Exhibition, Prize, Medal, or similar emolument is awarded, or honourable mention given, to a candidate who is a member of a House of Residence recognized by the University, the name of the House of Residence, if it is given in the candidate's entry for the emolument, shall be given in the announcement of the award in addition to the name of his or her College.

Standing and eligibility.

4. (*a*) For the purpose of these regulations an Affiliated Student shall be deemed to have kept by residence the three terms next preceding the term in which he or she first resides within the Precincts of the University, and to have been matriculated in the first of those terms.

(*b*) A person who possesses the status of Master of Arts or Bachelor of Arts shall not at any time be eligible for any University Prize, Scholarship, Studentship, or similar emolument for which only undergraduates are eligible. For the purposes of any regulation respecting the standing of candidates for other emoluments the term in which a person received the status of Master of Arts shall be counted as his or her twentieth term, and the term in which a person received the status of Bachelor of Arts shall be counted as his or her tenth term.

5. A candidate elected to any University emolument of which the tenure would normally begin at or shortly after the date of election may be permitted by the Council, for any reason which they may consider adequate, to postpone the commencement of tenure for such period as the Council may approve.

6. Subject to the decision of the Council in case of doubt, if payment of an instalment of the emolument of a Studentship, Scholarship, or similar award is conditional upon fulfilment of requirements which can normally be waived by Grace, and if the holder, by reason of deferment of commencement of tenure approved by the Council, has not satisfied those requirements during the whole, but has satisfied them during a part, of the period to which an instalment appertains, he or she shall receive a proportional part of the emolument.

Studentships and Scholarships

7. If the awarders of any University Studentship, Scholarship, or similar award learn that the holder has been elected to a Fellowship of a College, or has been awarded any other emolument for the support of research, or has been appointed to any office or employment in the University, they shall consider the case and may at their discretion reduce or withhold the emolument of the award. Restriction of tenure.

8. Subject to the provisions of any special regulations, the awarders of any University Studentship, Scholarship, or similar award may require that the whole or part of the emolument shall be used for one or more of the following purposes: Reduction or withholding of emoluments.

(*a*) the purchase of books or recordings;

(*b*) the purchase of equipment;

(*c*) travel abroad.

9. If payment of an instalment of the emolument of a Studentship or Scholarship is conditional upon the awarders' approval of a report from the holder, the awarders may delegate such approval to one or more of their number. Any such delegation shall be communicated by the awarders to the Treasurer, or to any other authority by whom payment is to be made. Where it is provided that such a report must be submitted before a prescribed time payment may nevertheless be authorized by the Council if the report is submitted after that time but is approved by the awarders. Continuation of payments.

Prizes and Medals

10. Candidates shall be required to state, generally in a preface to their submitted work, and specifically in notes, the sources from which their information is taken, the extent to which they have availed themselves of the work of others, or have received help and advice from a Director of Studies, Supervisor, or other person, and the portions of the submitted work which are claimed as original. Sources of information to be stated.

11. Candidates shall also be required to state in the preface what previous use (if any) has been made of the submitted work, or of any part of it, and whether it has been published in whole or in part; and a Graduate Student shall further be required to state whether and, if so, how, its subject appertains to his or her approved course of research or to work submitted for a degree of the University. Previous uses of work.

12. No work submitted for a University prize shall be considered which in the opinion of the Examiners or Adjudicators for that prize is substantially the same as work published by the candidate or used by the candidate elsewhere as a thesis for a degree or for a prize before coming into residence in the University; and if part of the work submitted has been so used, or if, in the case of a Graduate Student, the work submitted has already been submitted for a degree of the University, or closely appertains to work which has been so submitted, the Examiners or Adjudicators shall have power to take that circumstance into consideration in making their award.

13. Regulations 11 and 12 shall not apply to the Adams Prize, the Harness Prize, or the Raymond Horton-Smith Prize. Regulation 12 shall not apply to the Hare Prize, the Ellen McArthur Prize, the Gedge Prize, the Members' History Prize, the Sara Norton Prizes, the Prince Consort Prize, or the Thirlwall Prize. Exceptions.

Prize books

14. A prize-winner who is required or elects to lay out the whole or part of the value of a prize in the purchase of books, and who is required or desires to have the books stamped with the arms of the University, shall submit to the Registrary the title of each such book, together with a statement of its price and the cost of special binding if any. Applications.

15. The Registrary shall be authorized, after consultation with the Vice-Chancellor, to permit the arms of the University to be stamped on any book of which the title has been submitted in accordance with Regulation 14, and which the Vice-Chancellor has approved, and to issue for each such book a What may be permitted.

label recording the name and year of the prize and the name and College of the prize-winner; provided that permission shall not be given in respect of a book or books whose cost, including the cost of binding and stamping, exceeds the value of the prize.

Custody of the dies.

16. The custody of the dies to be used for stamping books under these regulations or under the special regulations for any prize shall be the responsibility of the Registrary.

Distribution of prizes and recitation of prize exercises

17. In each year, at a Congregation in the Easter Term selected for the purpose by the Vice-Chancellor, those prizes which are customarily distributed in the Senate-House shall be given by the Chancellor, or the Vice-Chancellor, to the several successful candidates; and at the same Congregation the successful candidate for the Chancellor's Medal for an English Poem shall recite his or her poem.

Deposit of prize exercises

18. Wherever the regulations for a prize or other award provide that a copy of the winning exercise shall be deposited in the University Library or in some other place, it shall be the responsibility of the author to ensure that the copy is bound or cased and identified by an inscription on the spine or cover in accordance with instructions given by the Registrary. The payment of the emolument shall be withheld until a copy of the exercise has been so deposited.

Investment of unexpended income

Unexpended income.

19. Except as otherwise provided in the regulations for a particular fund, any part of the income of a fund not expended in any year shall be accumulated by investment or otherwise, and any such accumulation shall, at the discretion of the Finance Committee of the Council after they have considered any recommendations that the Managers or other body responsible for the administration of the fund may wish to make, either be applied as income in subsequent years or be added to the capital of the fund.

Appointment of Awarders, etc.

20. Wherever the regulations for a Studentship, Scholarship, Exhibition, Prize, Medal, or other such award provide for Managers, Electors, Awarders, Examiners, or Adjudicators to be appointed by the Council or by the General Board on the nomination of another body, if it is necessary from whatever cause for such a nomination or appointment to be made after the date prescribed in the particular regulations, the Council or the General Board as the case may be (or, if the appointment cannot be considered by the appropriate body without undue delay, the Registrary) shall have power to appoint the person so nominated.

Deputies.

21. Subject to any provision of a trust binding on the University, the Council may appoint a member of the Regent House to act when there is a vacancy in a University office the holder of which is required *ex officio* by Ordinance to act as Examiner, Adjudicator, Elector, or Manager or in any other capacity in respect of a trust fund, or when the holder of such an office has been granted leave by the General Board under Special Ordinance C (i) 1 or 2. Such a member of the Regent House shall have the right to attend and vote at meetings, or to discharge other duties required by the Ordinance concerned, as if he or she held the University office specified therein.

SPECIAL REGULATIONS

2009 Computer Laboratory Research Students Fund

Title and Purpose.

1. There shall be a fund called the 2009 Computer Laboratory Research Students Fund. The aim of the Fund shall be the support of doctoral research students of the Computer Laboratory of the University of Cambridge.

Management Committee.

2. The Fund shall be managed by the Faculty Board of Computer Science and Technology, who may delegate any of their functions concerning the Fund to a Committee not necessarily composed wholly of members of the Board.

3. The income of the Fund shall be applied by the Managers to provide financial support to doctoral research students of the Computer Laboratory. The support may contribute towards the following: Application.

(i) a maintenance payment to a level determined from time to time by the Managers,
(ii) a payment to meet the student's University and College fees,
(iii) other costs such as additional training, equipment, travel expenses, conferences etc., according to the discretion of the Managers.

In considering a student for an award from the Fund the Managers shall have regard to evidence of academic merit.

4. In order to be eligible for support a candidate must have been accepted to follow a course of research towards the Ph.D. Degree in the Computer Laboratory and have been admitted, or be seeking admission by the Board of Graduate Studies as a registered Graduate Student in the University. If the candidate is not already a member of the University he or she shall become such by being matriculated before the end of the Michaelmas Term next after his or her acceptance as a doctoral student, provided that for good cause the Managers may allow matriculation to be deferred until a later date. Eligibility.

5. Recipients of an award may, at the discretion of the Managers and with the agreement of the individual donors, be designated as Named Students, and each such Studentship shall include reference to the name of a person or body that has contributed to the Fund. Named Students.

6. Any unexpended income may, at the discretion of the Managers, either be added to the capital of the Fund, or accumulated for use as income in any one or more subsequent years, or applied to the benefit of doctoral students in the Computer Laboratory more generally. Unexpended income.

7. In exceptional circumstances the Managers may use such part or parts of the capital of the Fund not earmarked for endowment purposes as they shall determine to support students as set out in Regulation 3 above.

AT&T Cambridge Laboratories Prize in Communications Engineering

1. The sum of £5,000 given to the University by AT&T Cambridge Laboratories shall form a fund called the AT&T Cambridge Laboratories Prize Fund, which shall be used to provide a prize called the AT&T Cambridge Laboratories Prize in Communications Engineering. Title and purpose.

2. The Prize shall be awarded annually by the Examiners for Part IIB of the Engineering Tripos to a candidate who achieves distinction in any area of electrical or information engineering in that Tripos, unless the Awarders are of the opinion that there is no candidate of sufficient merit to receive the Prize. How awarded.

3. The value of the Prize shall be the net annual income of the Fund. Value.

4. The Awarders shall be empowered to use accumulated income to provide an additional Prize or Prizes not exceeding such sum as shall be determined by the Faculty Board of Engineering within a range approved from time to time by the Council. Any unexpended income shall be added to the capital of the Fund. Accumulated income.

C. C. Abbott Fund

The money received from the bequest of the late Professor C. C. Abbott, of Gonville and Caius College, shall form a fund called the Abbott Fund the income of which shall be used for the supplementation of funds made available by the University to the Fitzwilliam Museum Syndicate to make purchases for the Museum. Title and purpose.

Adams Prize

Endowments, 1904, p. 393

1. The Adams Prize shall be awarded each year for achievements in research in any branch of the mathematical sciences, pure or applied, including astronomy. Prize.

2. The Prize shall be awarded by a Board of five Adjudicators, comprising: Adjudicators.

(*a*) two persons appointed by the Faculty Board of Mathematics;
(*b*) two persons appointed by the Council of St John's College;

(*c*) one person appointed by the Royal Society, who shall be a Fellow of the Society not resident in Cambridge.

Adjudicators shall be appointed in the Easter Term to serve for four years from 1 October following their appointment. The Faculty Board of Mathematics shall appoint one of the Adjudicators in class (*a*) to be Chair of the Adjudicators. Each Adjudicator shall receive from the Adams Prize Fund, unless there are no candidates, such sum as shall be determined by the Faculty Board of Mathematics within a range approved from time to time by the Council.

The Secretary of the Faculty Board of Mathematics shall act as Secretary to the Adjudicators.

Who may compete.

3. The Prize shall be open to any person who, on 31 October preceding the year in which the Prize is to be awarded,

(*a*) holds an appointment in the United Kingdom, either in a university or in some other institution; *and*

(*b*) is under forty years of age, provided that in exceptional circumstances the Adjudicators may relax this age limit.

Any question relating to eligibility shall be determined by the Adjudicators, whose decision shall be final.

Announcement of subject.

4. Not later than the last day of the Lent Term each year the Adjudicators shall give notice of the general area of research in which the Prize for the following calendar year is to be offered. The Adjudicators shall advertise the Prize widely within the United Kingdom and shall invite applications. Any person qualified under Regulation 3 who wishes to be a candidate for the Prize shall send to the Secretary to the Adjudicators, not later than 31 October next following, six copies of an application comprising a *curriculum vitae* and a list of publications, together with six copies of the work or works, either published or unpublished, which he or she wishes the Adjudicators to take into account.

5. The Adjudicators shall have power to obtain opinions from referees on the works submitted by candidates, and to authorize payment to a referee of such fee as they may determine in each particular case within a range approved from time to time by the Council.

Award.

6. The Prize shall be awarded not later than the last day of the Lent Term next following the closing date for applications.

Value.

7. The value of the Prize in any year shall be the income of the Prize Fund in the previous financial year, after meeting any expenses of advertising the Prize and of selecting the winner. The Prize shall be paid in three equal portions as follows:

(*a*) one-third to the prize-winner on the announcement of the award;

(*b*) one-third to the institution to which the prize-winner is affiliated at the time when the award is announced, to meet the expenses of his or her research;

(*c*) one-third to the prize-winner on the acceptance for publication within two years from the award of the Prize, by the editor of an internationally recognized journal, of a substantial original article (normally of at least twenty-five printed pages) of which the prize-winner is an author, surveying the general field of his or her research. In special circumstances the Adjudicators may allow an extension of the time period for acceptance of publication. If the prize-winner fails to satisfy this condition, or fails to apply for an extension within the time period, then the outstanding portion of the Prize shall be either added to the capital of the Fund or accumulated for use as income in subsequent years, as the Faculty Board of Mathematics shall determine.

When no Prize is awarded.

8. If in any year the Prize is not awarded the income for the year in question shall be either added to the capital of the Fund or accumulated for use as income in subsequent years, as the Faculty Board of Mathematics may determine.

9. These regulations may be amended from time to time by the University, subject to the consent of the Council of St John's College.

Aeronautical Research Fund

Grace 6 of 6 July 2005

The capital and the income of the Fund derived from the benefaction by Sir John Davenport Sidderley of £10,000 over a period of seven years ending in 1942, accepted by the University by Grace 1 of 22 October 1935, and now known as the Aeronautical Research Fund, shall be applied at the discretion of the Head of the Department of Engineering to support the general area of aeronautical research within that Department.

Alcuin Lectureship

1. The benefaction of the Right Hon. Sir Leon Brittan, of Trinity College, shall form a fund called the Alcuin Lecture Fund, the capital and the income of which shall be used to provide an annual lecture called the Alcuin Lecture. Fund.

2. The appointment of the Alcuin Lecturer shall be made annually by the Vice-Chancellor. The Lecturer shall deliver one lecture in the University on a subject concerning the relationship between the United Kingdom and European institutions. Lecturer.

Sidney Allen Prize

Grace 1 of 11 June 2008

1. The sum of £2,500 given to the University under Gift Aid arrangements by Professor P. H. Matthews, Emeritus Professor of Linguistics, in memory of Professor W. Sidney Allen, formerly Professor of Comparative Philology, shall form a fund, the income of which shall be used to provide a prize called the Sidney Allen Prize. The Prize shall be awarded for distinction in Linguistics where Linguistics is understood to include the study of language in general, and the study of the history and structure of specific languages or families of languages. Fund, prize, and purpose

2. The Prize shall be awarded annually by, jointly, the Chairs of Examiners for the Linguistics Tripos, and for Part II of the Modern and Medieval Languages Tripos, for a distinguished overall performance in Linguistics by a candidate for any Part II examination for the Linguistics Tripos or the Modern and Medieval Languages Tripos. How awarded.

3. To be eligible for consideration for the Prize a candidate shall have offered for examination at Part II at least three papers available in the Linguistics Tripos at Part IIA or Part IIB, or the Modern and Medieval Languages Tripos at Part II relating to the study of language in general, or the study of the history and structure of specific languages or families of languages. The Faculty Board of Modern and Medieval Languages shall announce from time to time the papers in the Triposes designated as meeting the requirements for the Prize. Who are eligible.

4. The value of the Prize shall be determined by the Examiners. Value.

5. If in any year the Prize is not awarded, the income for that year shall be added to the capital of the Fund. If not awarded.

Allen, Meek, and Read Fund for Research Scholarships

1. The investments representing the Allen, W. A. Meek, and Amy Mary Preston Read Funds shall form a fund known as the Allen, Meek, and Read Fund for Research Scholarships. Fund.

2. The income of the Fund shall be applied to the maintenance of such number of Allen, W. A. Meek, and Amy Mary Preston Read Scholars as shall be determined from time to time by the Board of Graduate Studies, who shall be the Electors to the Scholarships. Purpose.

3. It shall be the duty of a Scholar to undertake literary or scientific research. The Scholarships shall be open to graduates of the University and holders of the Certificate of Advanced Study in Mathematics who propose to undertake research as registered Graduate Students in any branch of study within the University, but the Electors shall give preference in awarding an Allen Scholarship to subjects in the arts, humanities, and social sciences, and shall give preference in awarding a Meek Scholarship to subjects in the biological and physical sciences, including mathematics, geography, technology, medicine, and veterinary medicine. Duties of Scholars.

4. Applications shall be made in such manner as may be provided for by the Board of Graduate Studies from time to time. Applications.

5. The tenure of a Scholarship shall not exceed three years and shall not extend beyond the Scholar's twelfth term of research as a registered Graduate Student. Tenure.

6. The value of a Scholarship shall be determined by the Electors within a range approved from time to time by the Council. Value.

7. The Electors may make grants to Scholars from any unexpended income accumulated in the Fund. Grants.

HRH Prince Alwaleed Bin Talal Fund

Grace 3 of 23 April 2008

Fund and purpose.

1. The sum of £8m received by the University from HRH Prince Alwaleed Bin Talal shall form a fund to be known as the HRH Prince Alwaleed Bin Talal Fund which shall be used to promote the study of Islam.

Administration Committee.

2. The administration of the Fund shall be under the control of a Committee consisting of the Chair of the Council of the School of Arts and Humanities who shall be Chair; the Chair of the Council of the School of the Humanities and Social Sciences; the Chair of the Faculty Board of Asian and Middle Eastern Studies; the Head of the Department of Middle Eastern Studies; and the Director of the HRH Prince Alwaleed Bin Talal Centre of Islamic Studies.

Application of Fund.

3. The expendable portion of the Fund shall be applied:

(i) to the payment of the stipend, national insurance, pension contributions, and associated indirect costs of a University Lecturer, to be known as the HRH Prince Alwaleed Bin Talal Lecturer in Islamic Studies, in the Department of Middle Eastern Studies, who shall be the Assistant Director of the HRH Prince Alwaleed Bin Talal Centre of Islamic Studies;

(ii) to support the activities of the HRH Prince Alwaleed Bin Talal Centre of Islamic Studies as the Committee of Management shall determine including making grants to the Director and Assistant Director of the Centre to meet travelling or other expenses incurred in connection with these activities;

(iii) to support such number of postdoctoral and visiting fellowships and postgraduate scholarships in Islamic Studies as the Committee of Management of the Centre shall determine;

(iv) to reimburse the University for any sums that it has made available from its own resources in order to underwrite the income available for the Centre during the first ten years of its life.

Unexpended income.

4. Any expendable portion of the Fund that is not applied under Regulation 3 in any financial year may be accumulated and expended in any one or more subsequent years.

Alterations.

5. The University shall have the power to alter these regulations by Grace on the recommendation of the Managers, subject to the approval of HRH Prince Alwaleed Bin Talal.

Anaesthesia Fund

Title.

1. The moneys given to the University by the Trustees of the Cambridge University Anaesthesia Trust shall form a fund called the Anaesthesia Fund.

Purpose.

2. The capital and income of the Fund shall be placed at the disposal of the Faculty Board of Clinical Medicine and shall be used for the purpose of promoting education and research in the University in the field of anaesthesia and related subjects.

Anglia Television Fund

Title.

1. The sum of £10,000 given to the University in 1975 by Anglia Television Limited to mark the election of Professor Glyn Daniel to the Disney Professorship of Archaeology shall form a fund called the Anglia Television Fund.

Purpose.

2. The income from the fund shall be applied

(*a*) to provide a prize, to be called the Anglia Prize, which shall be awarded by the Examiners for Part IIB of the Archaeological and Anthropological Tripos to the candidate for that Part who has shown the greatest distinction in the subject Archaeology;

(*b*) to further the training of archaeologists by the award of grants, at the discretion of the Disney Professor, for excavations, field classes, and visits organized by the Department of Archaeology and Anthropology.

Value of Prize.

3. The value of the Prize shall be such sum as shall be determined by the Disney Professor within a range approved from time to time by the Council.

Tom ap Rees Fund

Fund and purpose.

1. The sums subscribed in memory of Thomas ap Rees, Fellow of Gonville and Caius College and Professor of Botany, shall form a fund called the Tom ap Rees Fund, the income of which shall be used to make grants to students working in the Department of Plant Sciences, whether undergraduates or postgraduates, who are in need of financial assistance in connection with their studies.

2. The Managers of the Fund shall be the Head of the Department of Plant Sciences and two persons appointed by the Faculty Board of Biology in the Michaelmas Term to serve for four years from 1 January following their appointment. Managers.

3. Any unexpended income in a financial year shall be either added to the capital of the Fund or accumulated for use as income in future years, as the Managers may determine. Unexpended income.

Arberry Fund

1. The sum given to the University by Mrs Sarina Arberry in memory of her late husband, Arthur John Arberry, Sir Thomas Adams's Professor of Arabic from 1947 to 1969, shall form a fund called the Arberry Fund, the income of which shall be used to foster an interest in Arabic and Persian studies in English-speaking parts of the Commonwealth by means of a scholarship to be called the Professor A. J. Arberry Travelling Scholarship, which shall be used for the purpose of assisting students to visit an Arabic-speaking or Persian-speaking country. Name and purpose.

2. The Scholarship shall be restricted to students whose mother-tongue is English and who are citizens of the Commonwealth of Nations. Who are eligible.

3. The Awarders of the Scholarship shall be the Head of the Department of Middle Eastern Studies in consultation with and with the agreement of the teaching officers in the Department. Awarders.

4. The Scholarship shall be awarded to a student who has shown distinction in Arabic or in Persian or in Arabic and Persian in any Part of the Asian and Middle Eastern Studies Tripos, preference being given to a student who has shown distinction in both subjects. How awarded.

5. The Scholarship shall be awarded in 1973 and thereafter at intervals of not less than three years whenever a suitable candidate applies. When awarded.

6. A suitably qualified student who wishes to apply for the Scholarship shall send an application, together with details of his or her performance in the Tripos and a short description of the proposed travel, to the Registrary so as to arrive not later than the first day of General Admission to Degrees. Applications.

7. The value of the Scholarship shall be such sum not less than three years' income of the Fund as the Awarders may determine at the time of the award. Value.

8. The award shall be made not later than four weeks after the first day of General Admission to Degrees. Date of award.

9. The Scholar shall send a short report on his or her travel to the Awarders so as to reach them not later than the division of the term next following the term or vacation in which the travel is completed. Report on travel.

Department of Architecture Design Teaching Fund

Grace 2 of 5 November 2008

1. The moneys donated and covenanted in response to the appeal held by the Department of Architecture shall form a fund to be called the Department of Architecture Design Teaching Fund, the income and that portion of the capital that has not been specified as being permanent capital, shall be used to support the teaching of architectural design in the Department of Architecture. Title and purpose.

2. The Managers of the Fund shall be the Head of the Department of Architecture and two other members of the Department appointed by the Faculty Board of Architecture and History of Art for periods of four years at a time. Managers.

3. Any unexpended income of the Fund in a financial year may be either added to the capital of the Fund or accumulated for use as income in future years, as the Managers may determine.

4. After provision has been made in accordance with Regulation 1, the income of the Fund shall be applied from time to time, at the discretion of the Managers, to assist in any other way the promotion and encouragement of teaching in architectural design in the University. Additional income.

Armourers and Brasiers Prizes and Medal

1. The sum made available annually by the Armourers and Brasiers' Company shall be used to provide two prizes called the Armourers and Brasiers Prizes. Title and purpose.

2. The Prizes shall be awarded by the Examiners for the subject Materials Science and Metallurgy in the Natural Sciences Tripos, one by the Examiners for that subject in Part II for a distinguished How awarded.

performance in that examination and one by the Examiners for that subject in Part III for a distinguished performance in that examination.

Medal. **3.** The winner of the Prize for Part III shall also be awarded a medal provided by the Armourers and Brasiers' Company.

W. D. Armstrong Fund

Grace 6 of 17 December 2008

Title and purpose. **1.** The sum of £1.6m received by the University under the will of the late Dr W. D. Armstrong shall form a fund, to be entitled the W. D. Armstrong Fund, to encourage the application of Engineering in Medicine in the University.

Managers. **2.** The administration of the Fund shall be entrusted to a Committee of Managers consisting of:

(*a*) the Head of the School of Technology;
(*b*) the Head of the School of Clinical Medicine;
(*c*) the Head of the Department of Engineering;
(*d*) the Head of the Department of Medicine;
(*e*) the Head of the Department of Chemical Engineering and Biotechnology;
(*f*) one person appointed by the Council of the School of Clinical Medicine.

3. The member in class (*f*) shall be appointed in the Michaelmas Term to serve for three years from 1 January following her or his appointment. If one or more of the offices in classes (*a*)–(*f*) are held by the same person or if one or more of these offices is vacant or its tenure has expired, the Faculty Boards of Engineering and Clinical Medicine shall appoint one or more additional Managers so as to ensure that there are always six Managers.

4. The income, and under exceptional circumstances the capital, of the Fund shall be applied at the discretion of the Managers in accordance with Regulation 1.

Ashby Scholarship Fund

Fund and purpose. **1.** The sums donated by and in honour of Professor M. F. Ashby, CBE, FRS, FREng, formerly Professor of Engineering and Royal Society Research Professor, shall form a fund called the Ashby Scholarship Fund for the benefit of postgraduate students undertaking research in Mechanics and Materials and related areas in the Department of Engineering.

Scholarship. **2.** The income, and that part of the capital of the Fund not earmarked by the donors for endowment, shall be used for the provision of a Scholarship to be called the Ashby Scholarship in Mechanics and Materials.

Electors. **3.** The Electors to the Scholarship shall be the Head of the Department of Engineering, the Head of the relevant Division, and one member of staff of this Division who shall be appointed by the Faculty Board of Engineering in the Michaelmas Term to serve for four years from 1 January following her or his appointment.

Who are eligible. **4.** In order to be eligible for the Scholarship a candidate must have been admitted, or be seeking admission, as a registered Graduate Student for research towards the Ph.D. Degree in the Department of Engineering.

Tenure. **5.** The Scholarship shall be tenable for one year in the first instance, and may be renewed by the Electors for a second or third year but normally no longer.

Provisions. **6.** The Scholarship shall provide:

(*a*) a maintenance payment to be determined by the Electors,
(*b*) a payment to meet the Scholar's University and College fees,
(*c*) a contribution to other costs such as equipment and travel expenses according to the discretion of the Electors.

F. W. Aston Fund

Title. **1.** The money received from the bequest of the late Francis William Aston shall constitute a fund called the F. W. Aston Fund.

Application. **2.** The income of the Fund shall be applied, on the recommendation of the Cavendish Professor, to pay the expenses of members of the teaching staff and Graduate Students working in the Cavendish

Laboratory who wish to visit other laboratories or attend scientific conference in connection with their work.

BAE SYSTEMS NEVILL MOTT PRIZES

1. The sum made available annually by BAE SYSTEMS in recognition of the contribution to Semiconductor Physics made by Sir Nevill Mott, CH, FRS, formerly Cavendish Professor of Experimental Physics, shall be used to provide two BAE SYSTEMS Nevill Mott Prizes. Prizes.

2. The Prizes shall be awarded by the Examiners for the subject Experimental and Theoretical Physics in Part III of the Natural Sciences Tripos to the two candidates who acquit themselves with the greatest distinction in project work in that examination, one Prize being awarded for an experimental project and one Prize for a theoretical project. How awarded.

BBV FOUNDATION FUND

1. Grants received from the BBV Foundation, Bilbao, shall form a fund called the BBV Foundation Fund for the support of a BBV Foundation Visiting Professor or BBV Foundation Visiting Fellows. Fund and purpose.

2. The Fund shall be administered by a Board of Managers consisting of: Managers.

(*a*) the Vice-Chancellor (or a duly appointed deputy) as Chair;

(*b*) two persons appointed by the General Board on their own nomination;

(*c*) six persons appointed by the General Board, one on the recommendation of each of the following bodies: the Council of the School of the Biological Sciences, the Council of the School of Clinical Medicine, the Council of the School of the Humanities and Social Sciences, the Council of the School of the Physical Sciences, the Council of the School of Technology, and the Council of the School of Arts and Humanities;

(*d*) three persons appointed by the General Board on the recommendation of the BBV Foundation.

Managers in classes (*b*)–(*d*) shall be appointed in the Michaelmas Term to serve for four years from 1 January following their appointment.

3. A BBV Foundation Visiting Professor shall be elected from time to time by the General Board under the authority of Special Ordinance C (vii) B.1(*c*)(iii) and on the advice of the Managers. The title of a particular Professorship shall be determined by the Board on the occasion of each election. Visiting Professor

4. Elections to BBV Foundation Visiting Fellowships shall be made by the Managers subject to the approval of the General Board. Visiting Fellows.

5. The persons eligible to hold Visiting Professorships or Fellowships shall be scholars and scientists of Spanish nationality working anywhere in the world, and scholars and scientists not of Spanish nationality but working permanently in Spain. Who are eligible.

6. The tenure of a Visiting Professor or Fellow shall normally be for a period of not less than three months and not more than one year, as determined by the General Board on the occasion of each election. During the period of tenure a Visiting Professor or Fellow shall be required to reside in the University unless granted leave of absence by the General Board. Tenure.

7. The first charge on the Fund shall be the stipend and travelling expenses of persons elected to a Professorship or Fellowship and any costs incurred in the holding of the elections. The Managers may, subject to the approval of the General Board, authorize the payment of additional sums towards the expenses of a Professor or a Fellow. Any excess of income over expenditure shall be carried forward for use in a subsequent year. Emoluments.

8. No resolution of the Managers shall be valid unless approved by a majority consisting of at least four of their number at a meeting to which all the Managers have been summoned. Quorum.

BP FOUNDATION FUND FOR EARTH SCIENCES

Grace 3 of 16 June 2010

1. The sum of £4.15m received from the Board of Cambridge in America representing a donation from the BP Foundation to commemorate the scientific contributions of Professor Dan McKenzie, CH, FRS, Fellow of King's College and Emeritus Royal Society Professor of Earth Sciences, shall form a fund called the BP Foundation Fund for Earth Sciences. The purpose of the Fund shall be the support of research in the broad area of quantitative physical Earth Sciences. Fund and purpose.

Managers.

2. The Managers of the Fund shall be:

(*a*) the Head of the Department of Earth Sciences;

(*b*) the Head of the School of the Physical Sciences;

(*c*) three members, including one nominated by BP plc, appointed by the Faculty Board of Earth Sciences and Geography.

Managers in class (*c*) shall be appointed in the Michaelmas Term and serve for four years from 1 January following their appointment.

Professor.

3. The first charge on the Fund shall be the stipend, national insurance, pension contributions, and associated indirect costs payable by the University in respect of the BP Foundation McKenzie Professor of Earth Sciences and any other University offices and posts in the field of quantitative physical Earth Sciences as may be established from time to time by the University, or the General Board, as a charge on the Fund.

4. After provision has been made in accordance with Regulation 3, or during a vacancy in the Professorship, the income of the Fund may be applied at the discretion of the Managers for the support of research in quantitative physical Earth Sciences, including supporting the work of the Professor.

Unexpended income.

5. Any unexpended income of the Fund in a financial year may be either added to the capital of the Fund or accumulated for use as income in future years, as the Managers may determine.

BP Institute Fund

Title and purpose.

1. The sums received from British Petroleum plc for the support of work in Petroleum Science shall form a fund called the BP Institute Fund.

Managers.

2. The Fund shall be under the control of a Board of Managers who shall be:

(*a*) three persons appointed by the General Board, two of whom shall be appointed on the nomination of British Petroleum plc;

(*b*) the Heads of the Departments of Earth Sciences, of Applied Mathematics and Theoretical Physics, of Chemistry, of Engineering, and of Chemical Engineering and Biotechnology, or their representatives;

(*c*) the BP Professor of Petroleum Science;

(*d*) one person appointed by the Council of the School of the Physical Sciences and one by the Council of the School of Technology;

(*e*) not more than three persons co-opted at the discretion of the Managers.

Members of the Board of Managers in classes (*a*) and (*d*) shall be appointed in the Michaelmas Term to serve for four years from 1 January following their appointment. Members in class (*e*) shall serve until 31 December of the year in which they are co-opted or of the following year, as the Managers shall determine at the time of their co-optation.

3. The General Board shall appoint one of the Managers in class (*a*) to be Chair. The Managers shall elect one of their number to act as Secretary.

Duties.

4. The Managers shall be responsible for the administration of the Fund in support of teaching and research in Petroleum Science, for guiding the work of the Institute, and for encouraging collaboration with cognate Departments in the area of Petroleum Science.

Professor.

5. The first charge on the Fund shall be the stipend, national insurance, pension contributions, and associated indirect costs payable by the University in respect of the BP Professor of Petroleum Science, and of the holders of such other University offices and posts as may be established from time to time by the University or the General Board as a charge on the Fund.

6. After provision has been made in accordance with Regulation 5, the capital and the income of the Fund shall be applied at the discretion of the Managers for the support of work in Petroleum Science in the Institute.

Unexpended income.

7. Any unexpended income of the Fund in a financial year may be either added to the capital of the Fund or accumulated for use as income in future years, as the Managers may determine.

James Baird Fund

Fund and purpose.

1. The sum of £720,000 received under the will of Mrs A. D. Sennitt shall form a fund which, in accordance with the terms of the will, shall be called the James Baird Fund and shall be used to assist postgraduate students of the University in undertaking research in Medicine.

2. The Fund shall be administered by a Board of Managers consisting of: Managers.
(*a*) the Regius Professor of Physic;
(*b*) two persons appointed by the Faculty Board of Clinical Medicine;
(*c*) one person appointed by the Faculty Board of Biology.
Managers in classes (*b*) and (*c*) shall be appointed in the Michaelmas Term to serve for four years from 1 January following their appointment. The Managers shall elect annually one of their number as Chair. The Secretary of the Faculty Board of Clinical Medicine shall act as Secretary to the Managers.

3. The income of the Fund shall be used for the purpose specified in Regulation 1, by the award of grants or bursaries to postgraduate students of the University engaged in research in Medicine, or by the award of grants to the Faculty Board of Clinical Medicine for the assistance of such students in undertaking such research.

4. The foregoing regulations, except Regulation 1, shall be subject to alteration by Grace, provided that the regulations shall always be in accordance with the terms of Mrs Sennitt's will. Alteration of regulations.

George Peter Baker Prize in Medicine

Amended by Grace 12 of 24 April 2014

1. The sums given by George Peter Baker, M.D., of Trinity College, shall form a fund for the purpose of awarding a prize in Medicine to candidates for Part III of the Final M.B. Examination. Fund and purpose.

2. The title of the Prize shall be the George Peter Baker Prize in Medicine. Title.

3. A Prize shall be awarded each year to the candidate who achieves the highest combined score in the Single Best Answer Papers IA and IB and structured-answer components of Part III of the Final M.B. Examination held in that academical year. How awarded.

4. The value of the Prize shall be the annual income of the Fund. Value.

Stanley Baldwin Fund

1. The sum given to the University in memory of the Right Honourable Earl Baldwin of Bewdley, of Trinity College, sometime Chancellor of the University, by the Mary Kinross Charitable Trust shall form a fund for the encouragement of the study of British political history in the years 1919 to 1939. Fund and purpose.

2. The Faculty Board of History shall be the Managers of the Fund. The Faculty Board may delegate any or all of their functions under these regulations to a Committee not necessarily consisting wholly of members of the Faculty Board. Managers.

3. The first charge on the income of the Fund shall be the provision of one or two Stanley Baldwin Studentships, which may be awarded by the Managers to any Graduate Student pursuing or intending to pursue in the University a course of study or research in the field specified in Regulation 1. A Studentship shall be awarded for one year in the first instance and may be renewed for a period of one year at a time, subject to a maximum tenure of three years. Studentships.

4. The value of each Studentship shall be determined by the Managers within a range approved from time to time by the Council. Value.

5. Each year in the Michaelmas Term the Managers shall publish a Notice inviting applications for the Studentships, indicating the date by which applications shall be received. The names of the successful candidates shall be published not later than 30 June next following. Applications.

6. From any unexpended income accumulated in the Fund the Managers may make grants to Graduate Students working on the period specified in Regulation 1 to assist in meeting the expenses of research consistent with the object of the Fund. Grants from Fund.

Balfour Fund and Studentship

Endowments, 1904, pp. 347–50

1. The fund shall be called the Balfour Fund and shall be devoted to the furtherance of original research in Biology. Name and purpose.

2. The administration of the Fund shall be entrusted to three Managers, in conjunction with the Faculty Board of Biology, which Faculty Board is hereinafter called the Board. Appointments of Administration by Managers and Faculty Board of Biology.

Managers shall be made by the Board, and shall be for a period of five years in each case. Managers may be either members of the Board or not, and retiring Managers shall be re-eligible. All the powers of the Managers may be exercised by a majority of those present at a meeting, provided that two Managers at least be present.

3. The income accruing from the Fund shall be applied:

Balfour Studentship.

(*a*) to endow a Studentship, to be called the Balfour Studentship, the holder of which shall undertake original research in Biology, especially Animal Morphology;

(*b*) to further, by occasional grants of money, original research in the same subject.

Value of Studentship.

4. The annual value of the Studentship shall be determined for each year of the Student's tenure by the Board on the recommendation of the Managers and within a range approved from time to time by the Council.

Nomination to Board by Managers.

5. The Managers shall, when they decide that the income of the Fund in any year together with the accumulated income of the Fund is sufficient to enable a vacancy to be filled, nominate a person duly qualified in their opinion to the Board for election, and the Board shall, if they see fit, elect the person so nominated. The Managers shall give such notice of the vacancy or expected vacancy as they shall think desirable, and the Managers in nominating a person for election shall take into consideration the qualifications of all candidates whose names are sent in to them.

No examination.

6. The Studentship shall not be awarded by the result of a competitive examination.

7. Subject to the foregoing provision the Managers of the Board may take such steps as they may think fit to inquire into the qualifications of the candidates.

Not confined to members of the University.

8. Candidature for the Studentship shall be open, but the Student, if not a member of the University, must become such before the end of the term next after election and remain such during tenure.

Student to be devoted to biological research,

9. The Student during his or her tenure of the Studentship shall undertake original biological research, and shall not systematically follow any business or profession or engage in any educational or other work which in the opinion of those entrusted with the administration of the Fund would interfere with the Student's inquiries.

failing which may be removed,

10. If the Managers shall at any time learn that the Student is following any such business or profession, or has undertaken any such work, as would in their opinion interfere with the Student's inquiries, they shall at once call upon him or her to desist from the same, and if the Student shall refuse or neglect so to do they shall report the circumstances to the Board, and the Board may, if they think fit, remove such Student from the Studentship.

or for other causes.

If the Managers shall be of opinion that, through any other causes, such as confirmed ill health or want of diligence, the Student is not fulfilling and is not likely to fulfil the objects of the Studentship, they shall report accordingly to the Board, and the Board may, if they see fit, remove such Student from the Studentship.

Place and nature of studies:

11. The place and nature of the studies of the Student shall be subject to the approval of the Managers provided that the Student shall be bound to study within the University during at least three terms during the tenure of the Studentship unless the Managers shall, with the approval of the Board, dispense with this requirement for special reasons. The Managers shall take such steps as they may think necessary to satisfy themselves as to the diligence and progress of the Student and may require from the Student any reports or other information on the subject of his or her studies which they may think desirable.

diligence and progress.

Tenure.

12. The Studentship shall, subject as hereinbefore mentioned, be tenable for not more than three years; but it shall be lawful for the Managers (if they shall think fit) to nominate, and for the Board (if they shall think fit) to elect for a second period of not more than three years any Student whose work shall have been of such exceptional promise that it would, in the opinion of the Managers and of the Board, be clearly in the interests of biological research that such Student should continue to hold the Studentship for a second period of not more than three years.

Payment of stipend.

13. The stipend of the Student shall be paid in such manner as the Managers shall from time to time determine.

Unexpended income.

14. Any unexpended income accumulated in the Fund after providing for the Studentship and for any necessary expenses connected with the election may be used by the Managers with the approval of the Board to make grants for the purpose of furthering original research in Biology, especially Animal Morphology, either to the Balfour Student or to any other person engaged in research, subject to conditions made by the Managers with the approval of the Board.

15. These regulations, except Regulation 1, shall be subject to alteration by Grace provided that the main object of the Fund, that is to say the furtherance of original research in Biology, be adhered to. Alterations.

BALFOUR-BROWNE FUND

1. From the balance of the sum remaining from the bequest of £10,000 by Professor W. A. F. Balfour-Browne, of Gonville and Caius College, a Balfour-Browne Fund shall be established in the University for the advancement of the study of entomology. Title and purpose.

2. The Fund shall be administered by two Managers, who shall be University officers in the Faculty of Biology appointed by the Faculty Board, one on the nomination of the Head of the Department of Genetics and one on the nomination of the Head of the Department of Zoology. Managers shall be appointed in the Michaelmas Term to serve for two years from 1 January next following. Managers.

3. Any person working in the University, who need not be a member of the University, shall be eligible to apply for a grant from the Fund to support the study of entomology: provided that Grants.

(*a*) preference shall be given to persons *in statu pupillari*,

(*b*) preference shall be given to the support of studies in the field, especially in the United Kingdom,

(*c*) no grant shall be made to any registered Graduate Student if it would support work directly connected with his or her approved course of study or research.

4. In each Michaelmas Term the Managers shall announce the date or dates by which applications for grants from the Fund may be submitted.

5. Any unexpended income shall not be added to the capital of the Fund but shall be accumulated for use as income in subsequent years.

BARTLETT FUND AND PRIZE

1. The money given to the University by the Applied Probability Trust shall form a fund called the Bartlett Fund, in honour of Professor Maurice Stevenson Bartlett, M.A., of Queens' College, formerly University Lecturer in Mathematics, for the encouragement of study and research in mathematical statistics and applied probability. Fund and purpose.

2. The income of the Fund shall be used to provide a prize called the Bartlett Prize, which shall be awarded each year by the Examiners for the examination in Mathematics for the M.A.St. Degree and for Part III of the Mathematical Tripos to the candidate or candidates who have shown distinction in statistics in that examination. Prize.

3. The value of the Prize shall be such sum from the income of the Fund as shall be determined by the Director of the Statistical Laboratory within a range approved from time to time by the Council. Value.

BATTIE, BROWNE, CRAVEN, DAVIES, PITT, PORSON, AND WADDINGTON SCHOLARSHIPS (THE UNIVERSITY CLASSICAL SCHOLARSHIPS)

Stat. E VII and VIII.

Endowments, 1904, pp. 294, 96, 283, 300, 307, 121, 326

1. The Battie, Browne, Craven, Davies, Pitt, Porson, and Waddington Scholarships (the University Classical Scholarships) shall be divided into two groups, the first group consisting of the Craven, Pitt, and Waddington Scholarships, the second group consisting of the rest. Two groups.

2. The Scholarships shall be awarded on the performance of candidates in the examination for Part IB of the Classical Tripos. No candidate shall be awarded a Scholarship unless he or she has achieved a first-class aggregate mark in the papers specified in Regulation 18 for the Classical Tripos. How awarded.

3. Each Scholarship shall be of such value as shall be determined by the Faculty Board of Classics within a range approved from time to time by the Council; provided that Scholarships in the first group shall be of greater value than those in the second group. Value.

4. The Managers of the Battie, Browne, Davies, Pitt, Porson, and Waddington Funds shall be the Faculty Board of Classics, who shall have power to delegate any of their functions concerning the Funds to a Committee not necessarily consisting wholly of members of the Board. The Managers shall determine before the end of the Lent Term in each year what Scholarships are to be made available for award in that academical year. As far as possible, two Scholarships of the first group (including one Craven Scholarship) and two Scholarships of the second group shall be made available each year, as the income of the relevant Funds allows. Managers. Scholarships available.

Awarders. **5.** The Awarders for the Scholarships shall be the Examiners for Part IB of the Classical Tripos, who shall also act as Examiners and Awarders for the John Stewart of Rannoch Scholarships in Greek and Latin, and as Awarders for the Hallam Prize and the Henry Arthur Thomas Prizes. Each Awarder who is not a University officer shall out of one of the several Scholarship Funds be paid such sum as shall be determined by the Faculty Board of Classics within a range approved from time to time by the Council.

Announcement of awards. **6.** If two Scholarships are awarded in either group, the names of the award-winners shall be announced in order of merit and the Scholarships shall be assigned to them in the order of their foundation (*viz.* Craven, Pitt, Waddington in the first group; Battie, Browne, Davies, Porson in the second group); provided that, if the Scholars in a group are adjudged to be of equal merit, this shall be announced and the Scholarship senior in foundation shall be awarded to the Scholar whose name comes first in alphabetical order.

Tenure. **7.** A Scholarship shall be tenable for three years from 1 October preceding the date of the award. Each Scholar shall receive the emolument of his or her Scholarship in such instalments as shall be determined by the Council on the recommendation of the Faculty Board of Classics.

Grants. **8.** After the provision of the emoluments of the Scholarships, and after payment of any fees to Awarders under Regulation 5 above, any unexpended income accumulated in the several Funds may be applied at the discretion of the Faculty Board of Classics to provide grants for the furtherance of knowledge of the languages and civilizations of ancient Greece and Rome.

Mrs Claude Beddington Fund and Prizes

Title. **1.** The sum of £500 bequeathed to the University by the late Mrs Frances Ethel Beddington shall form a fund called the Mrs Claude Beddington Fund.

Application. **2.** One half of the income of the Fund shall be applied to provide a prize in English Literature, to be called the Mrs Claude Beddington English Literature Prize; the other half of the income of the Fund shall be applied to provide a prize in Modern Languages, to be called the Mrs Claude Beddington Modern Languages Prize.

English Literature Prize. **3.** The Mrs Claude Beddington English Literature Prize shall be awarded annually by the Examiners for Part II of the English Tripos to the undergraduate who has shown the greatest distinction in the examination for that Part, provided that he or she attains the standard of the first class.

Modern Languages Prize. **4.** The Mrs Claude Beddington Modern Languages Prize shall be awarded annually by the Examiners for Part II of the Modern and Medieval Languages Tripos to the undergraduate who has shown the greatest distinction in the examination for that Part, provided that he or she attains the standard of the first class.

Books to be purchased. **5.** The sum paid to each prize-winner shall be spent in the purchase of books selected by the prize-winner subject to the approval of the Vice-Chancellor.

Unexpended income. **6.** If in any year a Prize is not awarded, the unexpended income for that year shall be added to the capital of the Fund.

Bedford Travelling Grant in Geography

1. The benefaction of an anonymous donor shall form a fund, the income of which shall be applied to provide one or more annual travelling grants each of such value as may be determined from time to time by the Cambridge University Geographical Society with the approval of the Council, provided that their combined value shall not exceed the available income of the Fund. Any part of the income of the Fund not expended in any year or set aside for the award of an additional grant in a subsequent year shall be accumulated in the Fund for the purpose of establishing a prize from a date to be determined.

2. The rules governing the award of these grants, other than the rules governing its name and purpose, may be varied from time to time by the Cambridge University Geographical Society with the approval of the Council, provided that during the lifetime of the donor no alteration shall be made without the approval of the donor.

Theodore Chapin Beebe Fund

1. The sum bequeathed to the University by the late Mrs Ethel Haskins Beebe, of Boston, Massachusetts, shall at her request be known as the Gift of Theodore Chapin Beebe, and shall form a fund to be called the Theodore Chapin Beebe Fund. Name.

2. In accordance with the terms of Mrs Beebe's bequest the capital and income of the Fund shall be applied for such purposes in connection with medical instruction, research or experiments in the University as the Vice-Chancellor for the time being shall in his or her absolute discretion select. Application.

3. Any unapplied balance of the annual income of the Fund shall be added to the capital of the Fund. Unapplied income.

Bell, Abbott, and Barnes Funds

Stat. E II.

Endowments, 1904, pp. 301, 319, 332

1. Exhibitions or grants (or both) may be awarded from these Funds to candidates for the B.A. Degree needing assistance who have shown proficiency in their studies and who are recommended by their Tutors, provided that, if they are of standing for admission but have not been admitted to that degree, they are pursuing further study in the University to the satisfaction of the Awarders for the time being. Who are eligible.

2. The annual value of an Exhibition shall be such sum as shall be determined by the Awarders in a particular case within a range approved from time to time by the Council payable in equal instalments at the end of each term kept till the student is of standing for admission to the B.A. Degree. If the Awarders agree to continue an Exhibition after the holder has attained such standing, or if a Student is elected after attaining such standing, he or she shall receive a payment in respect of each of the next three terms kept or allowed, provided that no payment shall be made in respect of any term after the academical year following that in which an Exhibitioner became of standing for admission to the B.A. Degree. The Awarders may determine that the tenure of an Exhibition shall date from the beginning of the academical year in which the award is made. The value of a grant shall be determined by the Awarders within a range approved from time to time by the Council. Value.

3. Payment of the Exhibition shall be discontinued if the Awarders for the time being consider discontinuance desirable on account of a change in the financial circumstances of the student. Discontinuation.

4. The Awarders for the time being shall have power to deprive an Exhibitioner of the title and emoluments of the Exhibition for misconduct or for failure in industry or progress. Deprivation.

5. The Awarders shall be the Vice-Chancellor (or a duly appointed deputy) and four members of the Senate appointed by the Council in the Michaelmas Term to serve for two years from 1 January following their appointment. Before the division of the Lent Term in each year the Awarders shall elect one of themselves to act as their Secretary. Awarders.

6. Applications shall be made to the Secretary through Tutors before the division of each term. A Tutor shall furnish (*a*) a certificate that the applicant is a candidate for the B.A. Degree, (*b*) particulars as to the financial circumstances upon which the application is based, (*c*) a statement of the applicant's performance in his or her studies, (*d*) any particulars entitling the applicant to preference under Statute E II. The Tutor shall also undertake to inform the Secretary for the time being of any substantial change in the financial circumstances of an applicant to whom an Exhibition is awarded. Applications.

7. Awards shall be made as soon as convenient after the division of each term. When paid.

8. The Secretary shall be paid such sum as shall be determined by the Council, on the recommendation of the Awarders, which shall be charged on the Funds in such manner as the Treasurer may determine. Payment to Secretary.

9. Any part of the income of any of the Funds that is not expended in any year in accordance with the foregoing regulations shall be available for distribution on the recommendation of the Awarders in equal shares to Fitzwilliam College and to Murray Edwards College for the purpose of defraying the cost of awards made to members of those institutions who are candidates for the B.A. Degree and who are in need of financial assistance upon such conditions as their respective governing bodies shall from time to time determine. Unexpended income.

Bendall Sanskrit Exhibition

1. An Exhibition, called the Bendall Sanskrit Exhibition, shall be offered for competition in each year. Name.

2. Any member of the University, not being a Graduate Student, may be a candidate for first election to the Exhibition if at the time of the award twelve complete terms will not have passed since his or Who may compete.

her first term of residence, or if he or she will still be qualified to be a candidate for the Oriental Studies Tripos in the term of the award. Preference will be given to candidates who have obtained honours in the Classical Tripos, or who before the last date of entry for the Exhibition have been certified to the Registrary by the Chair of the Faculty Board of Asian and Middle Eastern Studies to possess a competent knowledge of Latin and Greek or of one of those languages.

3. Anyone to whom the Exhibition has been awarded may compete again if still a member of the University and not a Graduate Student, and if at the time of the award fifteen complete terms will not have passed since his or her first term of residence; but *ceteris paribus* a candidate for first election shall have the preference, and no one may be elected to the Exhibition a third time.

Names to Registrary. **4.** Candidates' names shall be sent by Tutors to the Registrary before 1 December of the academical year in which they are to compete.

Awarders. **5.** The Awarders shall be the Examiners in Sanskrit for the Oriental Studies Tripos.

Test papers. **6.** Candidates for first election shall be tested by the Sanskrit questions in Papers Sa. 1 and Sa. 2 of Part I of the Oriental Studies Tripos. A candidate for re-election, if also a candidate in Sanskrit for Part II of the Tripos, shall be tested by his or her work therein. Candidates for re-election who are not offering any paper in Sanskrit in the Tripos shall submit to the Awarders, through their Tutors, evidence of their study of Sanskrit since their first election.

Tenure. **7.** The period of tenure of the Exhibition shall be a year from the date of the award.

Value. **8.** The value of the Exhibition shall be such sum as shall be determined by the Faculty Board of Asian and Middle Eastern Studies within a range approved from time to time by the Council.

Unexpended income. **9.** Any unexpended income accumulated in the Fund may be used at the discretion of the Faculty Board of Asian and Middle Eastern Studies for the promotion and encouragement of the study of Sanskrit among undergraduate members of the University.

Bender Prize

Fund. **1.** The money received by the University under the will of the Reverend Alfred Philipp Bender, M.A., formerly of St John's College, shall be separately invested and shall constitute a fund called the Bender Fund.

Prize. **2.** There shall be a prize called the Bender Prize, which shall be awarded annually by the Examiners for the Asian and Middle Eastern Studies Tripos to the candidate who has shown the greatest distinction in Biblical Hebrew in Part II of that Tripos.

Value. **3.** The value of the Prize shall be such sum as shall be determined by the Faculty Board of Asian and Middle Eastern Studies within a range approved from time to time by the Council.

Unexpended income. **4.** Any unexpended income accumulated in the Fund may be used at the discretion of the Faculty Board of Asian and Middle Eastern Studies for the promotion and encouragement of the study of Biblical Hebrew in the University.

John Bennett Fund

Fund and purpose. **1.** The gift to the University by Mrs Mary Bennett in memory of her late husband, John Sloman Bennett, C.M.G., M.A., of Magdalene College, shall form a fund called the John Bennett Fund for the promotion of Middle Eastern historical studies.

Lecture. **2.** The first charge on the income of the Fund shall be the provision of a lecture, called the John Bennett Lecture, to be delivered from time to time.

Managers. **3.** The Fund shall be managed by the Head of the Department of Middle Eastern Studies in consultation with and with the agreement of the teaching officers in the Department, who shall appoint the Lecturer. So far as possible the Managers shall appoint a Lecturer at intervals of not more than three years.

Stipend of Lecturer. **4.** The stipend of the Lecturer shall be such sum as shall be determined by the Managers within a range approved from time to time by the Council.

Unexpended income. **5.** Any unexpended income accumulated in the Fund may be applied from time to time at the discretion of the Managers to meet:

(*a*) any expenses that may be incurred in connection with the Lecture;

(*b*) any other expenses of the teaching officers in the Department of Middle Eastern Studies related to historical studies, preference being given to expenses related to travel or the publication of research.

BENSON ENGLISH LIBRARY FUND

The income of the Fund derived from monies accruing to the Faculty of English from the unexpended balance of a legacy of Dr A. C. Benson, of Magdalene College, in 1925, and an appeal for the English Library made following the First World War, and now known as the Benson English Library Fund, shall, at the discretion of the Faculty Board of English, be expended to maintain a Library for the Faculty of English.

BERWIN LEIGHTON PAISNER PRIZE FOR INTERNATIONAL COMMERCIAL TAX

Grace 2 of 9 March 2011

1. The sum made available annually by Berwin Leighton Paisner LLP for the study of International Commercial Tax shall form a prize to be known as the Berwin Leighton Paisner Prize for International Commercial Tax which shall be awarded by the Examiners for the LL.M. Examination to the candidate who shows the greatest distinction in International Commercial Tax in Paper 2 of that examination. Title and purpose

2. The value of the Prize, provided there is a candidate of sufficient merit, shall be divided equally between the prize-winner and the Squire Law Library for the purpose of the purchase of books. Value.

BETHUNE-BAKER FUND

1. The sum bequeathed to the University by the late Professor J. F. Bethune-Baker, D.D., of Pembroke College, sometime Lady Margaret's Professor of Divinity, shall form a fund called the Bethune-Baker Fund. Name.

2. In accordance with the terms of Professor Bethune-Baker's bequest the annual income of the Fund shall be available to the Divinity Professors for the time being to be at their free disposal for the promotion of theological studies in the broadest sense of the word theological, preferentially but not necessarily among those men or women who are or have been members of the University of Cambridge. Purpose.

BEVAN FUND

The income of the Fund derived from the bequest of Professor Anthony Ashley Bevan, M.A., Lord Almoner's Professor of Arabic, 1893–1933, and Fellow of Trinity College, accepted by the University in 1933 by Grace 2 of 26 January 1934 and now known as the Bevan Fund, shall be applied at the discretion of the Library Syndicate for the benefit of the University Library.

BHAONAGAR MEDAL AND PRIZE

Endowments, 1904, p. 428

1. There shall be a medal called the Bhaonagar Medal.

2. The Medal shall be awarded annually by the Examiners for Part II of the Oriental Studies Tripos to that candidate for Part II of that Tripos who has in the judgement of the Examiners shown the greatest distinction in an Indian language or Indian languages in that examination, provided that his or her work is of sufficient merit. Purpose.

3. The winner of the Medal shall also be awarded a Prize, the value of which shall be such sum as shall be determined by the Faculty Board of Asian and Middle Eastern Studies within a range approved from time to time by the Council.

4. After provision has been made in accordance with Regulations 2 and 3 any unexpended income accumulated in the Fund may be used at the discretion of the Faculty Board of Asian and Middle Eastern Studies for the promotion and encouragement of the study of Indian languages in the University. Unexpended income.

Biffen Fund

Fund and purpose.

1. A portion of the sum received by the University under the will of Sir Rowland Harry Biffen, and accepted by Grace 1 of 29 October 1949, was allocated in accordance with the donor's wishes to the building of the Graham Robertson Room at the Fitzwilliam Museum. The residue shall form a fund to be called the Biffen Fund.

Income.

2. The income of the Fund shall be expended from time to time by the Fitzwilliam Museum Syndicate on the purchase of watercolours.

How spent.

3. Half of the annual income may be held in reserve for the purchase of works of unusual importance. The other half may be spent by the Director without seeking the prior consent of the Syndicate.

Carmen Blacker Prize for Japanese Studies

Fund and purpose.

1. The moneys subscribed by friends and former students of Carmen Blacker, formerly University Lecturer in Japanese and Fellow of Clare Hall, shall form a fund called the Carmen Blacker Fund for the encouragement of the study of Japanese culture in the University.

Managers.

2. The Fund shall be managed by the Head of the Department of East Asian Studies in consultation with and with the agreement of the teaching officers in Japanese in the Department.

Prize.

3. The first charge on the income of the Fund shall be the Carmen Blacker Prize, which shall be awarded annually by the Examiners for Part II of the Asian and Middle Eastern Studies Tripos for distinction in Japanese in that examination.

Value.

4. The value of the Prize shall be such sum as shall be determined by the Managers within a range approved from time to time by the Council.

Unexpended income.

5. Any unexpended income accumulated in the Fund may be used at the discretion of the Managers to purchase, for the Library of the Faculty of Asian and Middle Eastern Studies, books and other research material relating to (*a*) Japanese religion or (*b*) Japanese history, literature, and thought before 1945.

F. F. Blackman Memorial Fund

Title and purpose.

1. The gift to the University from Mrs Elsie Blackman, widow of the late F. F. Blackman, one time Fellow of St John's College and Reader in Botany, shall form a fund called the F. F. Blackman Memorial Fund, the income of which shall be used for the benefit of the subject Plant Physiology in the Department of Plant Sciences.

Managers.

2. The Fund shall be administered by two Managers who shall be:

(*a*) the Regius Professor of Botany,

(*b*) a member of the Department of Plant Sciences appointed by the General Board on the nomination of the Faculty Board of Biology.

Lecture.

3. The first charge on the income of the Fund shall be to meet the payment of an honorarium to and the expenses of a Lecturer who shall deliver a lecture to be called the F. F. Blackman Memorial Lecture in Plant Physiology. The Managers shall so far as is possible arrange for a lecture to be delivered at intervals of not more than three years. The Managers may make a grant from the Fund towards the cost of publishing the lecture.

Other uses of income.

4. After provision has been made in accordance with Regulation 3 any remaining income that is available may be used for such purposes associated with Plant Physiology as the Managers shall from time to time decide.

Dr E. J. Bles Fund

Purpose.

1. The whole of the available income of the Dr E. J. Bles Fund shall, in accordance with the terms of the will of the benefactor, be devoted to the promotion and furtherance of a branch of Biology as a pure science, and none of it shall be applied for the purpose of economical, technical, or medical biology.

Managers.

2. The Managers of the Fund shall be the Charles Darwin Professor of Animal Embryology, the Sir William Dunn Professor of Biochemistry, the John Humphrey Plummer Professor of Cell Biology, the Regius Professor of Botany, and the Professors of Physiology and Zoology.

3. The first charge on the income of the Fund shall be the cost of the stipend, national insurance, pension contributions, and family allowances, if any, of the Charles Darwin Professor of Animal Embryology. Professorship.

4. After provision has been made in accordance with Regulation 3 the remaining income of the Fund shall be applied as the Managers may from time to time decide towards meeting any expenditure directly connected with the Professor's work. Surplus income.

5. The General Board shall consult the Managers as to the subsequent application of the income of the Fund Review of regulations.

(*a*) when the Professorship of Animal Embryology lapses,

(*b*) during the academical year 1984–85 and at intervals of twenty-five years thereafter,

and effect shall be given to the result of such consultation provided always that the principal object of the Fund, as defined in Regulation 1, shall be maintained.

Bluegnome Molecular Genetic Pathology Fund

Grace 4 of 16 October 2013

1. The sum of £750,000 received by the University, via Cambridge Enterprise, from the sale of shares held on behalf of the Mammalian Molecular Genetics Group, Department of Pathology shall form a fund entitled the Bluegnome Molecular Genetic Pathology Fund. This title acknowledges the key role played by the Mammalian Molecular Genetics Group in the early development of Bluegnome Ltd. The income of the Fund shall be used solely for the benefit of the Department of Pathology and its purposes as provided for in Regulation 3 Title.

2. The Managers of the Fund shall comprise: Managers.

(*a*) the Head of the Department of Pathology or her or his deputy;

(*b*) the Head of the Division of Cellular and Molecular Pathology in the Department of Pathology or her or his deputy;

(*c*) three persons appointed by the Faculty Board of Biology in the Michaelmas Term to serve for a period of four years from 1 January following their appointment.

3. The income of the Fund shall be used as the Managers shall from time to time determine for any one or more of the following purposes: Purposes.

(*a*) the support of (i) posts, (ii) Research Fellowships, and (iii) Research Studentships, within the Department of Pathology;

(*b*) the repair and maintenance of equipment or purchase of new equipment in the Department; and

(*c*) the overall support and enhancement of the quality and breadth of (i) research implemented within the Department including provision of new (and improvement of existing) premises and facilities appropriate for such research; and (ii) research initiated or sponsored by the Department.

4. Any unexpended income of the Fund in any financial year may either be added to the capital of the Fund or accumulated for use as income in any one or more subsequent years, as determined by the Managers. Unexpended income.

5. The Managers may accept additional sums from time to time for the same purpose and add them to the capital of the Fund.

Boscawen Fund

1. The sum received under the will of the Hon. Mrs Pamela Sherek, sister of the Hon. Mildmay Thomas Boscawen, of Trinity College, shall form a fund called the Boscawen Fund. Fund.

2. The capital and the income of the Fund shall be at the disposal of the Fitzwilliam Museum Syndicate and shall be used for the purchase of works of art for the Fitzwilliam Museum, in particular works of sculpture and metalwork, and for the care of the Museum's collections. Purpose.

BOTANIC GARDEN ENDOWMENT FUND[1]

1. The Botanic Garden Endowment Fund shall consist of moneys given to the University for the benefit of the Botanic Garden.

2. The income of the Fund shall be employed by the General Board, after consulting the Botanic Garden Syndicate, to defray those costs of upkeep and maintenance which relate to the parts of the Garden that are regularly open to the public and which would otherwise be a charge on general University funds.

3. Any unexpended income shall be added to the capital of the Fund.

ISABELLE BOUHON FUND

Grace 1 of 27 January 2010

Title and purpose. **1.** The sums received by the University as memorial gifts from Mme Bouhon-Bustin, and others, shall form a fund, to be entitled the Isabelle Bouhon Fund, to promote the education and recognition of excellent researchers who are at an early stage of their academic careers in the University in the field of Regenerative Medicine or, if Regenerative Medicine is no longer an academic discipline, in the fields of cellular and developmental biology.

Managers. **2.** The administration of the Fund shall be entrusted to a Committee of Managers consisting of:

(*a*) the Head of the School of Clinical Medicine;

(*b*) three persons appointed by the Council of the School of Clinical Medicine, one on behalf of the donor and one to be active in the field of Regenerative Medicine or if it is no longer an academic discipline, in the fields of cellular and/or developmental biology;

(*c*) one person appointed by the Council of the School of the Biological Sciences.

The members in classes (*b*) and (*c*) shall be appointed in the Michaelmas Term to serve for three years from 1 January following their appointment. If one or more of the offices in classes (*a*)–(*c*) are held by the same person or if one or more of these offices is vacant or its tenure has expired, the Faculty Boards of Biology and Clinical Medicine shall appoint one or more additional Managers so as to ensure that there are always at least five Managers.

Application. **3.** The income, and under exceptional circumstances the capital, of the Fund shall be applied in such a manner as shall be approved by the Managers in accordance with Regulation 1, including payment of the expenses of visiting lecturers, seminar programmes, and grants to defray the expenses of Graduate Students and postdoctoral researchers when attending conferences or visiting or working in laboratories outside Cambridge, so as to promote the education and recognition of researchers at an early stage of their careers.

DEREK BREWER PRIZE

Grace 4 of 2 December 2009

Title. **1.** The sums subscribed in memory of Derek Brewer, Emeritus Professor of English, formerly Master of Emmanuel College, shall form a fund called the Derek Brewer Fund.

Prize. **2.** There shall be a Prize, called the Derek Brewer Prize, which shall be awarded annually by the Examiners for Part I of the English Tripos for an outstanding performance in Paper 1 (English literature and its contexts, 1300–1550) or Paper 10 (Early medieval literature and its contexts) in that examination.

Value and unexpended income. **3.** The value of the Prize shall be the annual income of the Fund. If in any year the Prize is not awarded, the unexpended income for that year shall be added to the capital of the Fund.

P.W. BRIAN FUND

Fund and purpose. **1.** The gift of Mrs Margaret Brian in memory of her husband Percy Wragg Brian, of Queens' College, Professor of Botany, shall form a fund the income of which shall be used to provide an award called the P. W. Brian Award in Botany.

How awarded. **2.** The Award shall be made each year before the end of the Long Vacation by the Head of the Department of Plant Sciences to a person who has achieved a distinguished performance in the

[1] By Grace 1 of 31 October 2007 the Maynard & Betham Fund and the Dr Walker's Rentcharge Fund were amalgamated in the Botanic Garden Endowment Fund.

execution of the research project in the subject Plant Sciences in Part II of the Natural Sciences Tripos and who intends to proceed to advanced study or research in any field of plant sciences.

3. The value of the Award shall be the income of the Fund. The sum paid shall be spent on the purchase of books or other materials selected by the winner of the Award, subject to the approval of the Head of the Department. Value.

4. If in any year no award is made the income for that year shall be added to the capital of the Fund. If not awarded.

British Petroleum Chemistry Fund

1. The sum of £1.5m received from British Petroleum plc for the support of work in Chemistry shall form a fund called the British Petroleum Chemistry Fund. The Managers of the Fund shall be: Fund and Managers.

(*a*) the Head of the Department of Chemistry, who shall be the Chair;

(*b*) the BP Professor of Chemistry;

(*c*) a person appointed by British Petroleum plc.

2. The first charge on the income of the Fund shall be the stipend, national insurance, and pension contributions of the BP Professor payable by the University. Professor.

3. After provision has been made in accordance with Regulation 2, the Fund shall be applied for the support of teaching or research in Chemistry within the Department of Chemistry in such manner as shall be approved by the General Board on the recommendation of the Managers. Teaching or research.

4. Any unexpended income of the Fund in a financial year may be expended in a subsequent year in accordance with Regulation 3. Unexpended income.

Jacob Bronowski Fund

1. The gift of Mrs Rita Bronowski, in memory of her husband, Jacob Bronowski, M.A., Ph.D., Honorary Fellow of Jesus College, shall form a Fund called the Jacob Bronowski Fund, the income of which shall be used to encourage the study of history and philosophy of science in the University. Title. Purpose.

2. There shall be a Jacob Bronowski Prize to be awarded annually by the Examiners appointed for the subject History and Philosophy of Science in Part II of the Natural Sciences Tripos to a candidate who has shown distinction in that examination. Prize.

3. The value of the Prize shall be the annual income of the Fund. Value.

4. If in any year the Prize is not awarded the income for that year shall be added to the capital of the Fund. If not awarded.

Broodbank Fund and Fellowships

1. The sum bequeathed to the University by the late Maud Mary Lady Broodbank shall form a fund called the Broodbank Fund, which shall be used for the purpose of providing the stipends, pension contributions, and expenses of one or more Broodbank Fellows, with the object of furthering research in Biochemistry or Biophysics with special reference to the principles and practice of food preservation. Name and purpose.

2. The Fund shall be administered and the Fellows elected by a Board of Managers, the members of which shall be the Heads of the Departments of Biochemistry, Plant Sciences, and Physiology, Development, and Neuroscience, the Secretary of the Biotechnology and Biological Sciences Research Council or his or her nominee, and one other person nominated by the Managers and appointed by the Council in the Michaelmas Term to serve for four years from 1 January following their appointment. Managers.

3. No resolution of the Managers shall be valid unless approved by at least six of them at a meeting to which they have all been summoned, save that a resolution circulated to and signed by all the Managers shall have the same validity as a resolution carried at a meeting. Quorum.

4. The Managers shall give not less than three months' notice of their intention to proceed to an election. Notice of election.

5. The Managers may elect to a Fellowship any person whose qualifications they consider suitable, whether a member of the University or not, and they may take such steps as they think fit to ascertain those qualifications. Who may be elected Fellows.

6. The tenure of a Fellowship shall be determined by the Managers. A Fellow shall be re-eligible but the tenure of a Fellowship shall not normally exceed three years in all. Tenure.

Duties of Fellows.

7. A Broodbank Fellow shall undertake full-time research in a subject approved by the Managers. The research work shall be carried out in Cambridge (unless in special circumstances the Managers have given leave for it to be carried out elsewhere) and shall be subject to such conditions as the Managers may impose.

Teaching work.

8. A Fellow may, with the permission of the Managers, undertake not more than six hours' teaching work a week for remuneration without suffering any deduction from the stipend of the Fellowship.

Stipend.

9. The annual stipend of a Fellow shall be such sum as may be determined by the Managers, within a range approved from time to time by the Council. The stipend shall be paid to the Fellow in quarterly instalments in advance.

Conditions.

10. The Managers may make the payment of the stipend of a Fellow, or of an instalment of the stipend, conditional on their approval of a report from the Fellow on the progress of his or her research. The Managers may delegate the consideration of a Fellow's report to one or more of themselves. Any such delegation shall be communicated by the Managers to the Treasurer.

The Managers may terminate the tenure of a Fellow at any time if, in their opinion, he or she is unfit to continue to hold the Fellowship.

11. A Fellow shall inform the Managers of the award of any other emolument or of his or her intention to undertake work other than work approved by the Managers in accordance with Regulations 7 and 8. On receiving such information the Managers shall consider whether a reduction should be made in the amount of the Fellow's stipend.

12. The Managers shall make grants from the Fund to cover the expenses incurred in the appointment and the work of the Fellows.

Unexpended income.

13. Any unexpended income accumulated in the Fund may be used at the discretion of the Managers for the furtherance of the object of the Fund.

14. These regulations, except Regulation 1, shall be subject to alteration by Grace on the recommendation of the Managers.

PETER BROOK AWARD

Fund and purpose.

1. The sum given to the University by Charles Peter Beynon Brook, M.A., FRCPsych, of Hughes Hall, formerly Associate Lecturer in the Faculty of Clinical Medicine, shall form a fund the income of which shall be used to provide an award called the Peter Brook Award. The purpose of the Award shall be to encourage students of clinical medicine in research in psychiatry or in the basic sciences associated with that branch of medicine.

Who are eligible.

2. The Award shall be open to any person who is pursuing, or has pursued, his or her clinical study in the University for the degrees of Bachelor of Medicine and Bachelor of Surgery, provided that no one shall be eligible to apply for the Award more than six months after being admitted to the degree of Bachelor of Surgery.

Submission of research material.

3. Candidates for the Award shall submit a piece of research which has already been completed or partially completed, or a detailed research proposal for a specific piece of research to be undertaken. The research shall concern the field of psychiatry or its associated basic science disciplines and, if already completed or partially completed, may have been undertaken by the candidate at any time since matriculation.

Notice.

4. In the Michaelmas Term each year the Professor of Psychiatry shall publish a notice giving the date by which, and the manner in which, applications are to be submitted.

Awarders.

5. The Awarders shall be the Professor of Psychiatry and at least one other person appointed by the Professor.

Value.

6. The value of the Award shall be the annual income of the Fund.

Unexpended income.

7. If in any year no award is made, the unexpended income shall be added to the capital of the Fund.

BROOKS FUND

Title and purpose.

1. The sum bequeathed to the University by the late Professor Frederick Tom Brooks shall constitute a fund called the Brooks Fund the purpose of which shall be to further original research in Botany.

Managers.

2. The Managers of the Fund shall be the Head of the Department of Plant Sciences, the Professors assigned to the Department, the Directors of Sub-departments in the Department, the person appointed by the Faculty Board of Biology as an Elector to the Frank Smart Studentship, and one other person appointed by the Faculty Board in the Michaelmas Term, on the nomination of the Head of the Department, to serve for four years from 1 January next following.

3. The Managers shall have discretion to apply the income of the Fund for the purpose described in Regulation 1, by making grants to the Department of Plant Sciences, or to research workers working in that Department or at some other place approved by the Head of the Department. Application of Fund.

4. In making grants to research workers the Managers shall give preference Who shall have preference.

(*a*) to persons who have been engaged in postgraduate research for not less than two years,

and (*b*) to persons who are investigating problems in Mycology, Bacteriology, Plant Pathology, Plant Physiology, or Plant Ecology.

BROTHERTON PRIZE

1. The Brotherton Prize shall be awarded by the Examiners for Part II of the Oriental Studies Tripos for distinction in South Asian Studies in that examination. If there are two candidates of equal merit, preference shall be given to a candidate showing distinction in Sanskrit. Prize.

2. The value of the Prize shall be such sum as shall be determined by the Faculty Board of Asian and Middle Eastern Studies within a range approved from time to time by the Council. Value.

3. The Faculty Board of Asian and Middle Eastern Studies shall be empowered, whenever the Brotherton Fund shows a sufficient balance, Grants.

(*a*) to make an additional grant to the winner of the Prize if, before the end of the next Michaelmas Term, they have received satisfactory assurance that he or she is engaged in some branch of advanced study or research in South Asian Studies, and is making good progress in the subject chosen;

(*b*) to make other grants for the furtherance of research in South Asian Studies.

4. Any unexpended income accumulated in the Fund may be used at the discretion of the Faculty Board of Asian and Middle Eastern Studies for the promotion and encouragement of South Asian Studies, with a preference for Sanskrit. Unexpended income.

BROWNE FUND AND MEDALS

Stat. E VIII.

Endowments, 1904, pp. 100–2

1. Four Medals on the foundation of Sir William Browne shall be offered for competition every year; one for a Greek Ode or Elegy, one for a Latin Ode or Elegy, one for a Greek Epigram, and one for a Latin Epigram. Four Medals.

2. Any resident undergraduate may be a candidate for any of Sir William Browne's Medals. Who may be candidates.

3. On or before 1 June in each year the Examiners shall announce subjects, and (if they think fit) metres and limits of length, for the poems; and exercises must be sent to the Secretary of the Faculty Board of Classics on or before 1 February in the following year. Announcement of subjects.

4. Each candidate shall send three copies of his or her exercise to the Secretary of the Faculty Board. The exercise shall be in a printed or typewritten form; it shall bear a motto but not the candidate's name, and shall be accompanied by a sealed envelope bearing the same motto outside and containing the candidate's name and College. Method of submitting exercises.

5. The Medals shall be awarded by three Examiners nominated by the Faculty Board of Classics and appointed by the General Board in the latter half of each Lent Term. The Examiners shall receive from the Browne Fund, unless no exercise is sent in, such amount as may be determined by the Faculty Board within a range approved from time to time by the Council. Examiners.

6. The cost of the Medals and their cases and the fees paid to the Examiners shall be the first charge on the Browne Fund. The second charge on the Fund shall be the provision of one or more Browne Scholarships. Any unexpended income accumulated in the Fund may be applied at the discretion of the Faculty Board of Classics to provide grants for the furtherance of knowledge of the languages and civilizations of ancient Greece and Rome. Application of income.

BROWNE MEMORIAL FUND

1. A fund shall be established in the University, called the Browne Memorial Fund, for the promotion of the study of the languages, literature, history, and religion of the Arabs, Persians, and Turks or other cognate Asiatic peoples, preferably by the purchase or acquisition for the University Library of books Name and purpose.

and manuscripts connected with those subjects, or by means of grants or endowments for the publication of texts, translations, or other books designed for this branch of study or for the teaching or investigation of those subjects.

Managers. **2.** The administration of the Fund shall be entrusted to five Managers, two of whom shall be appointed by the Council and three appointed by the Head of the Department of Middle Eastern Studies in consultation with and with the agreement of the teaching officers in the Department. The Managers shall be appointed in the Michaelmas Term to serve for four years from 1 January following their appointment.

All the powers of the Managers may be exercised by a majority of those present at a meeting duly summoned, provided that three Managers at least be present.

Grants. **3.** Grants from the income accruing from the capital of the Fund may be made by the Managers at their discretion for any of the specified purposes.

4. The Managers shall have power to expend for any special purpose such portion of the capital of the Fund as may be approved by the Finance Committee of the Council.

Accounts. **5.** The accounts of Managers shall be audited annually and published with the University Accounts.

Alterations by Grace. **6.** These regulations, except Regulation 1, shall be subject to alteration by Grace, provided that the object of the Fund, *viz.* the promotion of the study of the languages, literature, history, and religion of the Arabs, Persians, and Turks or other cognate Asiatic peoples, be adhered to.

7. Subject to the foregoing regulations it shall be lawful for the Managers from time to time to make and, if they see fit, to vary such by-laws as may seem to them expedient for regulating their own proceedings and the administration of the Fund.

E. G. BROWNE MEMORIAL RESEARCH STUDENTSHIP

Title. **1.** The E. G. Browne Memorial Research Studentship, of which the emolument was provided by the Iranian Government to mark the appreciation of the Iranian people of the contribution to Persian studies made by E. G. Browne, Sir Thomas Adams's Professor of Arabic from 1902 to 1926, shall be offered for competition in each year.

Value. **2.** The annual emolument of the Studentship shall be such sum as may be determined by the Managers of the Fund.

Electors. **3.** The Electors to the Studentship shall be the Degree Committee for the Faculty of Asian and Middle Eastern Studies. The Electors may delegate any of their functions under these regulations to a committee consisting of not less than three members of the Degree Committee.

Who are eligible. **4.** In order to be eligible for the Studentship a candidate must

(*a*) be a graduate of a university who has obtained honours in Persian or in Iranian;

(*b*) intend to undertake research in some branch of study connected with the Persian or Iranian language, or with Persian or Iranian literature, or with the history and civilization of Persia;

(*c*) have been admitted, or be seeking admission, as a registered Graduate Student of the University of Cambridge;

(*d*) normally not have attained the age of twenty-nine years on 1 April in the year of candidature.

Applications. **5.** Candidates must send their applications to the Registrary so as to arrive not later than the first day of General Admission to Degrees. Each application must be accompanied by evidence that the candidate satisfies the requirements of Regulation 4, and an outline of the research that he or she proposes to undertake.

Election. **6.** The election shall be made within four weeks following the first day of General Admission to Degrees.

Tenure. **7.** Tenure of the Studentship shall be for one year but, provided that he or she satisfies the requirements of Regulation 4(*d*), the Student may apply for re-election for a second year and for a third year. Tenure shall be conditional upon the Student being a registered Graduate Student of the University; if a Student ceases to be a registered Graduate Student his or her tenure of the Studentship shall thereupon lapse.

Unexpended income. **8.** Any unexpended income which may accumulate in the Fund shall be applied in the first instance at the discretion of the Electors either to the award of a second Studentship or to other awards in support of Graduate Students of the University carrying out research or study in Persian Studies. Any income remaining thereafter may be applied, at the discretion of the Faculty Board of Asian and Middle

Eastern Studies, to the encouragement of research in Persian Studies in the University in any other way which the Faculty Board may from time to time determine.

OSCAR BROWNING SOCIETY FUND

1. The sum donated to the University by the Oscar Browning Society for purposes connected with the Department of Education shall form a fund called the Oscar Browning Society Fund. Name and purpose.

2. The first charge on the income of the Fund shall be to provide an annual prize, called the Charles Fox Prize. The Prize shall be awarded by the Examiners for the Postgraduate Certificate in Education to the candidate who is adjudged by them to have shown the greatest distinction in the Certificate Examination. The value of the Prize shall be determined by the Head of the Department of Education within a range approved from time to time by the Council. Prize.

3. After provision has been made for the award of the Charles Fox Prize in accordance with Regulation 2, any unexpended income may be applied at the discretion of the Head of the Department of Education for any of the following purposes: Unexpended income.

(*a*) to pay to a person selected from time to time by the Head of the Department to give a lecture on a subject in the field of Education, which shall be entitled the Oscar Browning Society Lecture, an honorarium and any expenses incurred in giving the lecture;
(*b*) to give assistance to University officers in the Department in meeting the cost of their publications;
(*c*) to buy additional books or other materials for the library of the Department;
(*d*) for such other similar purposes as the Head of the Department of Education may determine.

MATTHEW BUNCOMBE PRIZE

1. The sums subscribed by Dr Teresa Clay and others in memory of Matthew Buncombe, M.A., Ph.D., of Trinity College, shall form a fund the income of which shall be used to provide a prize called the Matthew Buncombe Prize. Fund and Prize.

2. The Prize shall be awarded each year by the Degree Committee for the Faculty of Philosophy, on the recommendation of the Examiners for the examination in Philosophy for the M.Phil. Degree (one-year course), for the best overall performance in that examination. How awarded.

3. The Prize shall not be divided between more than two candidates.

4. The value of the Prize shall be the annual income of the Fund. Value.

5. If in any year the Prize is not awarded the income for that year shall be added to the capital of the Fund. If not awarded.

HARRY BUNNING FELLOWSHIP FUND

1. The sum of £101,593 bequeathed to the University by Mr Harry H. Bunning, of King's Lynn, shall form a fund called the Harry Bunning Fellowship Fund. Name.

2. The Managers of the Fund shall be the Head of the Department of Veterinary Medicine and four persons appointed by the Faculty Board of Veterinary Medicine, of whom two shall be on the nomination of the Faculty Board of Biology. Managers

3. No resolution of the Managers shall be valid unless passed by a majority of the Managers present at a meeting to which all the Managers have been summoned.

4. The income of the Fund shall be used to provide the stipend of a Harry Bunning Fellow who shall study the diagnosis and treatment of illness in cats and dogs in the furtherance of their welfare. The Harry Bunning Fellow shall be elected by the Managers, who may also authorize additional expenditure from the income of the Fund in support of the work of the Fellow. Fellowship.

5. The tenure of a Harry Bunning Fellow, which shall be determined by the Managers on the occasion of each election, shall be for a period not exceeding three years at a time. Tenure.

6. The stipend of a Harry Bunning Fellow shall be determined by the General Board on the recommendation of the Managers. Stipend.

Unexpended income.

7. Any unexpended income may be either added to the capital of the Fund or accumulated for use as income in future years, as the Managers may determine.

Stat. E XVIII.

Burney Prize and Studentship

Endowments, 1904, p. 390

1. The income of the Burney Fund, which is to be used for the furtherance of the study of the Philosophy of Religion (these words being interpreted so that they may include Christian Ethics and questions relating to the truth and evidence of the Christian Religion), shall be used to provide in each year a Burney Prize and a Burney Studentship.

Adjudicators and Electors.

2. The Adjudicators of the Prize and the Electors to the Studentship shall be the Norris-Hulse Professor of Divinity and two members of the Senate appointed by the General Board before the division of the Michaelmas Term, one on the nomination of the Faculty Board of Divinity and the other on the nomination of the Faculty Board of Philosophy, to serve until the end of the Michaelmas Term in the calendar year next following.

Second Prize or Studentship.

3. From any unexpended income which may have accumulated in the Fund the Electors may in any year award a second Prize, or a second Studentship, of such amount as they may think fit, or may at their discretion make grants for the promotion of the study of the Philosophy of Religion.

The Burney Prize

Value.

4. The value of the Burney Prize shall be such sum as shall be determined by the Adjudicators within a range approved from time to time by the Council.

5. Each of the appointed Adjudicators shall receive from the income of the Burney Fund such sum as shall be determined jointly by the Faculty Boards of Divinity and Philosophy within a range approved from time to time by the Council, except that no payment shall be made to the Adjudicators if no dissertations are referred to them under Regulation 7.

How awarded.

6. The Prize shall be awarded for a dissertation on a subject in the Philosophy of Religion submitted by a candidate for Part II of the Philosophy Tripos or by a candidate for Part IIB of the Theological and Religious Studies Tripos.

Dissertation.

7. At their final meeting of the year each of the two Boards of Examiners for the examinations specified in Regulation 6 shall identify the two best dissertations submitted by candidates for the examination concerned on subjects that fall within the field of the Philosophy of Religion. Each dissertation identified by the Examiners shall be referred to the Adjudicators, who shall award the Prize for the dissertation which in their opinion is most meritorious.

Preference for members of Christ's College.

8. If the dissertations submitted by two candidates are deemed by the Adjudicators to be of equal merit, and if one of the two is a member of Christ's College, the Prize shall be adjudged to that candidate.

Condition.

9. The Prize-winner shall ensure that a typewritten or printed copy of his or her dissertation is deposited in the University Library, and shall not receive the prize-money until this has been done.

The Burney Studentship

Value.

10. The annual value of the Burney Studentship shall be such sum as the Electors shall determine in each case after taking account of any other emolument that the Student may be receiving for study or research, provided that it shall not exceed an amount approved from time to time by the Council.

Who are eligible.

11. The Studentship shall be open to any member of the University, provided that on the day on which the election to the Studentship is made not more than seventeen terms have passed after his or her first term of residence. Candidates for the Studentship shall send their names to the Registrary not later than the division of the Lent Term, and the election to the Studentship shall be made before the end of the Lent Term.

Qualifications of candidates.

12. The Electors may take such steps as they think fit to enquire into the qualifications of the candidates for the Studentship, provided that it shall not be awarded by competitive examination. If the qualifications of two candidates appear to the Electors to be equal, and if one of the two is a member of Christ's College, that candidate shall be elected to the Studentship.

Tenure.

13. The Studentship shall be tenable for one year. A Student may be re-elected to it once.

14. It shall be the duty of the Student to undertake study or research in the Philosophy of Religion, according to a scheme proposed by the Student and approved by the Electors, provided that such scheme may be modified with the consent of the Electors. Duties of Student.

15. The Student shall not undertake without the sanction of the Electors during the tenure of the Studentship any other work to which remuneration is attached. Restriction.

RAYMOND BURTON FUND

1. The sum of £250,000 given to the University in 2001 by Mr Raymond Burton, of Trinity College, shall form a fund called the Raymond Burton Fund, which shall be used for the promotion and encouragement of the study of Economics in the University. Fund and purpose.

2. The Managers of the Fund shall be the Faculty Board of Economics, who may delegate any or all of their functions under these regulations to a committee not necessarily consisting wholly of members of the Board.

3. The income and capital of the Fund shall be used to provide awards known as Montague Burton Studentships in the Faculty of Economics. The Studentships shall be open to any person who is or is about to be registered as a Graduate Student in the University. Holders of the awards shall undertake advanced study or research in the Faculty of Economics, and may undertake such teaching assistant duties under the terms of the award as may be assigned to them by the Faculty Board. Who are eligible.

4. An award shall be tenable for one year in the first instance, and may be renewed by the Managers for a second or third year. Tenure.

5. The emolument paid to an award holder shall be determined by the Managers within a range approved from time to time by the Council.

6. After provision has been made, in accordance with the foregoing regulations, for at least one Montague Burton Studentship the balance of the annual income and any unexpended income accumulated in the Fund shall be available to the Faculty Board of Economics to be used for the encouragement of study or research in Economics.

7. Any unexpended income may be either added to the capital of the Fund or accumulated for use as income in subsequent years, as the Managers may determine. Unexpended income.

8. It shall be open to the University, on the recommendation of the Faculty Board of Economics, to alter these regulations from time to time, provided that the Fund shall be devoted to the encouragement of study or research in Economics.

GREGG BURY PRIZE

1. The bequest of the Reverend Robert Gregg Bury shall form a fund called the Gregg Bury Fund, the income of which shall be used to provide a Gregg Bury Prize which shall be awarded for a dissertation on a subject in the Philosophy of Religion. Dissertations shall be of not less than 10,000 words and not more than 20,000 words in length. Fund and purpose.

2. The value of the Gregg Bury Prize shall be such sum as shall be determined by the Adjudicators within a range approved from time to time by the Council. Value.

3. The Prize shall be open to any member of the University, provided that on the latest day for the submission of dissertations not more than eighteen complete terms have passed after the candidate's first term of residence, and provided that he or she has not previously been awarded the Burney Prize or the Gregg Bury Prize. Who are eligible.

4. The Adjudicators shall be the Adjudicators for the Burney Prize. Each of the appointed Adjudicators shall receive from the Gregg Bury Fund such sum as shall be determined jointly by the Faculty Boards of Divinity and Philosophy within a range approved from time to time by the Council, except that no payment shall be made to the Adjudicators if no entry is submitted for the Prize. Adjudicators.

5. Each candidate shall send the proposed subject of his or her dissertation to the Registrary so as to arrive not later than the division of the Lent Term. The Registrary shall submit the proposed subject to the Adjudicators and shall inform the candidate whether they approve the subject. Subject of dissertation.

6. The Prize-winner shall ensure that a typewritten or printed copy of his or her dissertation is deposited in the University Library, and shall not receive the prize-money until this has been done. Condition.

7. From any unexpended income which may have accumulated in the Fund the Adjudicators may at their discretion make grants for the promotion of the study of the Philosophy of Religion. Unexpended income.

J. P. T. Bury Fund

The income of the J. P. T. Bury Fund shall be applied at the discretion of the Library Syndicate to purchase rare French books published between 1814 and 1914. A book plate shall be affixed to each book so purchased recording that it was purchased through the Fund.

Montagu Butler Prize

Prize. **1.** The Prize shall be a prize in books. It shall be called the Montagu Butler Prize, and shall be awarded annually for the best original exercise in Latin Hexameter Verse.

Notice. **2.** On or before 1 June in each year the Examiners for the Browne Medals shall give public notice of the subject for the exercises, and all exercises must be sent to the Secretary of the Faculty Board of Classics on or before 1 February in the following year.

Length. **3.** No such exercise shall exceed in length 150 lines.

Candidates. **4.** Any resident undergraduate may be a candidate for the Montagu Butler Prize.

Submission of exercises. **5.** Each candidate shall send three copies of his or her exercise privately to the Secretary of the Faculty Board of Classics. Such copies shall not be in the handwriting of the candidate. They shall bear a motto but not the candidate's name, and shall be accompanied by a sealed envelope bearing the same motto outside and containing the candidate's name and College.

Award. **6.** The Prize shall be awarded by the Examiners for the Browne Medals who shall receive, unless no exercise is sent in, such amount from the income of the Prize Fund as may be determined by the Faculty Board of Classics within a range approved form time to time by the Council.

Copies of successful exercise. **7.** In every year in which the Prize is awarded, a copy of the successful exercise shall be sent to the Master of Trinity, to the University Library, to the Library of Trinity College, and to each of the Examiners for the year.

When no Prize is awarded. **8.** In any year in which the Prize is not awarded, the net proceeds of the Fund for that year shall be transferred to the funds of the University Library and shall be spent on the purchase of editions of the Latin poets, or on the purchase of books connected with the study of such poets, and every book so purchased shall contain a record that it was purchased from the proceeds of the Fund for the endowment of the Montagu Butler Prize.

Butterfield Studentship

Fund and purpose. **1.** The sum of £10,000 received under the will of Verena Nan Robertson McCririck shall form a fund called the McCririck Fund, which shall be used to assist students undertaking research in the field of Diabetes.

Studentship. **2.** The income of the Fund shall be used to provide a studentship each year called the Butterfield Studentship, in honour of Lord Butterfield of Stechford, M.D., formerly Regius Professor of Physic and Master of Downing College.

Eligibility. **3.** Candidature for the Studentship shall be open to any person who is, or is about to be, registered as a Graduate Student in the University, and who is undertaking, or proposes to undertake, research in the field of Diabetes.

Awarders. **4.** The Awarders of the Studentship shall be the Regius Professor of Physic, the Professor of Clinical Biochemistry, and one person appointed in the Michaelmas Term by the General Board on the recommendation of the Faculty Board of Clinical Medicine to serve for four years from 1 January following the appointment.

Tenure. **5.** The Studentship shall be tenable for one year in the first instance, and may be prolonged for a further period or periods of not more than one year at a time, subject to the Student's progress being deemed satisfactory by the Awarders.

Value. **6.** The value of the Studentship shall be the annual income of the Fund, provided that the Awarders may award a Studentship of lesser value if they think fit.

Notice. **7.** In the Michaelmas Term each year the Professor of Clinical Biochemistry shall publish a notice giving the date by which, and the manner in which, applications are to be submitted.

Unexpended income. **8.** Any unexpended income at the end of a financial year shall be added to the capital of the Fund.

CAMBRIDGE DISPLAY TECHNOLOGY CAVENDISH FUND

Rescinded by Grace 15 of 24 April 2014

CAMBRIDGE DISPLAY TECHNOLOGY MELVILLE FUND

1. The sum received for the benefit of the Department of Chemistry from the sale of part of the University's shareholding in Cambridge Display Technology Holdings plc shall form a fund called the Cambridge Display Technology Melville Fund. Title.

2. The Fund shall be administered by three Managers, who shall be the Director of the Melville Laboratory for Polymer Synthesis, the Head of the Department of Chemistry, and the BP Professor of Chemistry. Managers.

3. The capital and the income of the Fund shall be at the disposal of the Managers and shall be used for the support of research directed by the Director of the Melville Laboratory for Polymer Synthesis. Purpose.

CAMBRIDGE ENDOWMENT FOR RESEARCH IN FINANCE

1. The gift of $10m to the University from The Pyewacket Foundation shall form a fund to be called the Cambridge Endowment for Research in Finance, the income of which shall be devoted to the furtherance of research and study into all aspects of finance, financial institutions, and financial markets, and their relationship with the performance of the economy. Fund and purpose.

2. The Managers of the fund shall be: Managers.

(*a*) the Vice-Chancellor (or a duly appointed deputy) as Chair;

(*b*) the Director of Judge Business School;

(*c*) nine members (of whom one shall be a professor of finance external to the University) appointed by the Faculty Board of Business and Management;

(*d*) Weslie and William Janeway in their individual capacities or such persons as they may appoint as their successors.

Members in class (*c*) shall be appointed in the Michaelmas Term to serve for four years from 1 January following their appointment.

3. No business shall be transacted at any meeting of the Managers unless five members are present.

4. The fund, together with any subsequent gifts received for the fund from time to time, shall be administered by the Managers in accordance with the provisions of the agreement, dated 31 March 2001, between The Pyewacket Foundation and the University.

CAMBRIDGE QUARTERLY PRIZE

1. The sum of £1,600 given to the University by the Editors of *The Cambridge Quarterly* shall form a fund the income of which shall be used to provide a prize called the *Cambridge Quarterly* Prize.

2. The Prize shall be awarded each year by the Examiners for Part II of the English Tripos to the candidate who in that examination has submitted the best dissertation. How awarded.

3. If candidates of sufficient merit present themselves, it shall be open to the Examiners to award one or more additional *Cambridge Quarterly* Prizes. Additional Prizes.

4. The value of a *Cambridge Quarterly* Prize shall be such sum as shall be determined by the Faculty Board of English within a range approved from time to time by the Council, provided that (*a*) if two or more Prizes are awarded they shall be of equal value, and (*b*) the combined value of the Prizes awarded in any year shall not exceed the annual income of the fund. Value.

5. Any unexpended income may be either added to the capital of the fund or accumulated for use as income in future years, as the Faculty Board may determine. Unexpended income.

CAMBRIDGE UNIVERSITY MEDICAL SCHOOL CHARITABLE FUND FOR PUBLIC HEALTH

1. There shall be established within the University from a donation of £1m by the Trustees of the Cambridge University Medical School Charity a fund to be called the Cambridge University Medical School Charitable Fund for Public Health. Fund.

Purpose. **2.** The purpose of the Fund shall be to support the work of the School of Clinical Medicine's Institute of Public Health. The Fund may be applied for the benefit of the Department of Public Health and Primary Care within the School of Clinical Medicine, or for the benefit of any of the other constituent member organizations within the Institute, in any manner that the Managers shall in their absolute discretion determine.

3. It is intended that the income from the Fund shall be used regularly to support its stated purpose, but this shall not constrain its Managers from using some or all of its capital in order to fulfil that purpose if, having taken into account the consequential implications, it was deemed advantageous and appropriate so to do.

Managers. **4.** The Managers of the Fund shall consist of:

(*a*) the Regius Professor of Physic (who shall be Chair);

(*b*) the Director of the Institute of Public Health;

(*c*) the Regional Director of Public Health;

(*d*) the Head of the Department of Public Health and Primary Care;

(*e*) up to three members co-opted by the Managers in categories (*a*) to (*d*).

5. The Managers shall meet at intervals that they shall themselves determine, but this should be no less than at least once in each academical year.

Unapplied balance of income. **6.** Any unapplied balance of the annual income of the Fund shall be either added to the capital of the Fund or accumulated for use as income in one or more subsequent years, as the Managers of the Fund may determine.

Cambridge University Medical School Discretionary Fund

Fund. **1.** There shall be established within the University from a donation of £1m by the Trustees of the Cambridge University Medical School Charity a fund to be called the Cambridge University Medical School Discretionary Fund.

Purpose. **2.** The purpose of the Fund shall be to further the clinical, educational, and research needs of the School of Clinical Medicine. The Fund may be applied to further that purpose in any manner that the Regius Professor of Physic for the time being shall in his or her absolute discretion select.

3. It is intended that the income from the Fund shall be used regularly to support its stated purpose, but this shall not constrain the Regius Professor of Physic from using either some or all of its capital in order to fulfil that purpose if, having taken into account the consequential implications, it was deemed advantageous and appropriate so to do.

Unapplied balance of income. **4.** Any unapplied balance of the annual income of the Fund shall be either added to the capital of the Fund or accumulated for use as income in one or more subsequent years, as the Regius Professor of Physic may determine.

Maybud Sherwood Campbell Fund

Title. **1.** The bequest of Miss Maybud Sherwood Campbell, sometime Vice-President and Honorary Member of the Botanical Society of the British Isles, shall form a fund to be known as the Maybud Sherwood Campbell Fund.

Purpose. **2.** The income of the Fund shall be applied, at the discretion of the Head of the Department of Plant Sciences, to make grants to enable junior members of the staff of the Department of Plant Sciences working on European flowering plants to travel in Europe for the purpose of study or research.

Rosalie Canney Fund

Title and purpose. **1.** The sum of £1.46m received from the Trustees of the Cambridge Foundation shall form a fund, to be entitled the Rosalie Canney Fund, for the support of education, learning, and research in the University in the fields of Medicine and Psychology.

Managers. **2.** The administration of the Fund shall be entrusted to three Managers who shall be the Regius Professor of Physic, the Head of the Department of Psychology, and one Manager appointed by the

General Board. The income of the Fund shall be applied at the discretion of the Managers in accordance with Regulation 1.

Carus Prizes

Stat. E XXX.

Endowments, 1904, p. 397

1. The income of the Fund established in 1852 by friends of the Reverend William Carus, and augmented in 1853 and 1894, for the encouragement of the accurate study of the New Testament in Greek shall be used to provide one or more annual prizes to be called the Carus Greek Testament Prizes. The value of a Prize shall be such sum not exceeding the available income of the Fund as may be determined from time to time by the Faculty Board of Divinity with the approval of the Council. Name and purpose

2. Any member of the University may be a candidate for the Prizes provided that at the time of the examination Who may compete.

(*a*) he or she has kept five terms,

(*b*) if a graduate, he or she is of not more than ten years' standing from admission to a first degree, whether of this or another university;

and provided also that no previous winner of a Prize shall again be eligible as a candidate.

3. There shall be two Examiners appointed by the General Board on the nomination of the Faculty Board of Divinity. One shall be appointed in every year before the end of the Easter Term to hold office for the two following academical years. Examiners.

4. Each Examiner shall receive such sum yearly out of the income of the Fund as shall be determined by the Faculty Board of Divinity within a range approved from time to time by the Council, unless there be no candidate for the Prizes. All the other expenses of the examination shall likewise be paid out of the Fund.

5. The examination shall be held after the division and before the end of the Michaelmas Term, on a day of which notice shall be given by the Board of Examinations. The day shall not be any of the days on which an examination for another Divinity Prize or Scholarship is held. Date and nature of examination.

6. The names of candidates shall on or before 20 October next preceding the examination be sent by their Tutors to the Registrary, who shall forthwith communicate them to the Examiners.

7. The examination shall consist of two printed papers and shall be concluded in one day.

8. The examination shall embrace translation and questions on the criticism and interpretation of the New Testament in Greek with special reference to prescribed texts.

Central Electricity Generating Board Prize for Materials Science

1. The sum of £2,000 given to the University by the Central Electricity Generating Board shall form a fund called the Central Electricity Generating Board Prize Fund, which shall be used to provide a prize called the Central Electricity Generating Board Prize for Materials Science. Fund and purpose.

2. The Prize shall be awarded by the Examiners for Materials Science in Part II of the Natural Sciences Tripos for a distinguished performance in that examination. Prize: how awarded.

3. The value of the Prize shall be the net annual income of the Fund. Value.

Countess Martinengo Cesaresco's Bequest

1. The sum bequeathed to Gonville and Caius College by the Countess Martinengo Cesaresco shall constitute a fund called the Countess Martinengo Cesaresco fund. Name.

2. The Trustees of the Fund shall be the Master and Fellows of Gonville and Caius College. Trustees.

3. The income of the Fund shall be applied in the first instance to the maintenance of a Studentship called the Henry Carrington and Bentham Dumont Koe Studentship, which shall be awarded for the purpose of travel in lands where Greek is spoken, preferably in connection with the study of Greek literature. Purpose.

4. Subject to the foregoing provisions, the University shall have power to make regulations for carrying out the objects of the trust and to vary such regulations from time to time.

5. The Student shall undertake advanced study or research as specified in Regulation 3, according to a scheme to be approved by the Faculty Board of Classics. Such a scheme shall involve a travel or residence for not less than four months in lands where Greek is spoken.

Who are eligible. **6.** The Studentship shall be open to any person who is registered as a Graduate Student in the University, provided that at the date of the election not less than two complete terms have passed after the term of his or her admission as a Graduate Student.

Electors. **7.** The Electors to the Studentship shall be the Faculty Board of Classics, who may take such steps as they think fit to inquire into the qualifications of the candidates; provided that the studentship shall not be awarded on the result of a competitive examination.

Applications. **8.** Before the division of the Easter Term each year the Faculty Board shall give notice of the date by which and the manner in which applications for the Studentship are to be submitted. An election to the Studentship shall be held during the Michaelmas Term on a date to be determined by the Board.

Tenure. **9.** The Studentship shall be tenable from the date of the election until 30 September next following. A Student shall be eligible for re-election on not more than two occasions.

Emolument. **10.** The emolument of the Studentship shall be such sum, not exceeding the available income of the Fund, as shall be determined by the Faculty Board within a range approved from time to time by the Council. The emolument shall be paid in such instalments as the Board shall from time to time determine, provided that the Board may withhold payment of any instalment if they are not satisfied that the Student is pursuing his or her course of study with sufficient diligence.

Unexpended income. **11.** Any unexpended income which may accumulate in the Fund shall be applied at the discretion of the Faculty Board to make grants for travel in lands where Greek is spoken. Any member of the University who is a student of Classics shall be eligible to receive such a grant.

12. The Board may delegate any of their functions concerning the Studentship to a Committee not necessarily consisting wholly of members of the Board.

H. M. CHADWICK FUND

Name. **1.** The income received by the University under the will of Professor H. M. Chadwick shall form a fund to be called the H. M. Chadwick Fund.

Managers. **2.** The administration of the income of the Fund shall be entrusted to a Committee of Managers consisting of:

(*a*) three members appointed by the Faculty Board of English;
(*b*) one member appointed by the Faculty Board of Human, Social, and Political Science;
(*c*) one member appointed by the Faculty Board of Asian and Middle Eastern Studies; and
(*d*) two members appointed by the General Board.

Members of the Committee of Managers shall be appointed in the Michaelmas Term to serve for four years from 1 January following their appointment. The Committee of Managers shall meet at least once a year, as soon as possible after the annual meeting of the Managers of the Dame Bertha Phillpotts Memorial Fund.

Purpose. **3.** The income of the Fund shall be used for the provision of studentships, prizes, and grants to promote study and research in any subject listed in the Schedule to these regulations. The annual income shall be divided into two equal sections, one to be available for awards in subjects in category A as listed in the Schedule, and the other for awards in subjects in categories B, C, and D. At the end of each year, any unexpended income in either section shall, at the discretion of the Committee of Managers, either be added to the capital of the Fund or be applied as additional income in the following year in the same section.

Prizes. **4.** There shall be two Prizes, of a value to be determined by the Committee of Managers, within a range approved from time to time by the Council, which shall be offered annually to candidates for the Anglo-Saxon, Norse, and Celtic Tripos. The N. K. Chadwick Prize shall be awarded by the Examiners for Part I of the Tripos for the most outstanding performance in that examination. The H. M. Chadwick Prize shall be awarded by the Examiners for Part II of the Tripos for the most outstanding performance in that examination. If in any year either Prize is not awarded, the value of the Prize shall be added to the sum available in that year for other awards in subjects in category A.

Studentships. **5.** There shall be offered at least once every two years, in a subject or subjects in either or both of categories A and B, at least one H. M. Chadwick Studentship. The value of each Studentship shall be determined by the Committee of Managers within a range approved from time to time by the Council. Graduates or research students of any university in the United Kingdom or Eire shall be eligible for a Studentship, but preference shall be given to candidates who are graduates or Graduate Students of the University or applicants for admission as a Graduate Student. There shall be no competitive examination and no age limit. Each Studentship shall be tenable for one year in the first instance, and may be renewed and its value reviewed, subject to a maximum tenure of three years.

6. The Committee of Managers shall be empowered to make grants, including travel and subsistence, for attendance at conferences or courses, or for any other purpose which promotes study or research. Grants may be awarded to any member of the University in respect of any subject in category A, B, C, or D contained in the Schedule. Grants.

7. The award of studentships and grants shall in general require knowledge of the language or languages involved, but shall in general exclude studies of purely linguistic interest, biological anthropology, studies of primarily medical interest, archaeology relating to the Stone Age, or studies wholly concerned with material culture. Conditions.

8. In the Michaelmas Term the Committee of Managers shall publish a Notice inviting applications for the studentships and grants, and specifying the date by which and the manner in which applications shall be submitted. Notice of awards.

9. The regulations governing the Fund, other than this regulation, may be altered by Grace, provided that the name of the Fund shall not be changed. Alterations.

SCHEDULE

The subjects for which the studentships, prizes, and grants shall be available and the requirements to be observed in each subject are as follows:

A. The history, literature, thought, religion, sociology, antiquities, and art of any of the peoples of the British Isles or of the Scandinavian peoples before AD 1050, or of the Teutonic or the Celtic peoples collectively before AD 600.

B. The same subjects in relation to any people or peoples of the Near East primarily before 1000 BC.

C. The same subjects in relation to any modern primitive people or peoples in respect of their native culture.

D. Subjects included in the general history or comparative study of civilization, literature, thought, religion, sociology, or art, but subjects which are wholly or mainly concerned with Western Europe since AD 1050 or with the Classical periods of Greece and Rome or of India or with any other period of similarly advanced culture shall be excluded.

JOHN CHADWICK GREEK AND LATIN RESEARCH FUND

1. The sum given to the University by John Chadwick, Litt.D., Honorary Fellow of Downing College and formerly Reader in Greek Language, from the proceeds of the Antonio Feltrinelli Prize, awarded to him by the Accademia dei Lincei, Rome, shall form a fund called the John Chadwick Greek and Latin Research Fund, the purpose of which shall be the promotion of study and research in the Greek and Latin languages and in germane subjects. Name and purpose.

2. The Managers of the Fund shall be: Managers.

(*a*) the Professor of Comparative Philology,

(*b*) two persons appointed by the Faculty Board of Classics.

Managers in class (*b*) shall be appointed in the Michaelmas Term to serve for two years from 1 January following their appointment.

3. The income of the Fund shall be applied, at the discretion of the Managers, Application of Fund.

(*a*) to make grants to Graduate Students and other persons, including academic visitors to the University, who are engaged in advanced study or research in the subjects specified in Regulation 1;

(*b*) to assist in any other way the promotion of advanced study and research in the subjects specified in Regulation 1.

4. Any unexpended income in a financial year may be either added to the capital of the fund or accumulated for use as income in a future year, at the discretion of the Managers. Unexpended income.

NORA CHADWICK FUND

1. The sum bequeathed to the University by Mrs Nora Chadwick shall form a fund to be called the Nora Chadwick Fund. Title.

2. The income of the Fund shall be used, subject to the establishment by the University of a particular office for the purpose, to provide part or the whole of the cost of a Readership, to be known as the Nora Chadwick Readership in Celtic Studies, or of such University office assigned to the Purpose.

Department of Anglo-Saxon, Norse, and Celtic, other than a Professorship or Readership, as the General Board, on the recommendation of the Faculty Board of English, may determine; provided that the duties of the holder of the office shall consist mainly of teaching and research in Celtic studies.

Avik Chakravarty Memorial Fund for Physics

Grace 2 of 6 January 2010

Title and purpose. **1.** The sum given to the University by Mr Satyendra and Mrs Chhaya Chakravarty in memory of their son, Avik Chakravarty, shall form a fund called the Avik Chakravarty Memorial Fund for Physics. The income of the Fund shall be used for the purpose of supporting postgraduate students at the Cavendish Laboratory (Department of Physics) researching in one or more of the areas of luminescence phenomena, cavitation, control of friction between moving surfaces, explosive initiation and nano-science, or in other new innovative projects.

Managers. **2.** The Managers of the Fund shall be the Head of the Department of Physics and the Academic Secretary of the Department of Physics.

Unexpended income. **3.** Any unexpended income in a financial year may be expended in accordance with Regulation 1 in any one or more subsequent years.

Chamber Music Fund

Title and purpose. **1.** The sum of £10,000, the gift of an anonymous donor, for the promotion of an instrumental ensemble in the University to give chamber music concerts shall form a fund to be called the Chamber Music Fund.

Managers. **2.** The capital and income of the Fund shall be at the disposal of the Managers, who shall be the Professor of Music and two persons appointed by the Faculty Board of Music to serve for periods of two years at a time.

Powers of the Managers. **3.** The Managers shall be empowered to determine the remuneration and conditions of employment of musicians engaged as members of the instrumental ensemble, and to make all arrangements for the concerts subject to the approval of the Faculty Board.

Grace and Thomas C. H. Chan Scholarship Fund

Title and purpose. **1.** The sums received from Mr and Mrs Thomas C. H. Chan shall form a fund called the Grace and Thomas C. H. Chan Scholarship Fund. The capital and income of the Fund, together with other sums made available for the same purpose, shall be used for the purpose of providing scholarships for Ph.D. students starting doctoral research in any subject within the School of Arts and Humanities or the School of the Humanities and Social Sciences. Eligible students shall be resident or domiciled in the People's Republic of China. Priority shall be given to applicants from provinces or regions other than the Hong Kong Special Administrative Region.

Managers. **2.** The Managers of the Fund shall be (*a*) the Chair of the Council of the School of Arts and Humanities, or her or his nominee, (*b*) the Chair of the Council of the School of the Humanities and Social Sciences, or her or his nominee, and (*c*) the Secretary of the Board of Graduate Studies.

Scholarships. **3.** The first charge on the Fund shall be the provision of scholarships, called 'Grace and Thomas C. H. Chan Scholarships', for students from the People's Republic of China who are intending to undertake postgraduate study leading to a Ph.D. Degree of the University in any subject within the School of Arts and Humanities or the School of the Humanities and Social Sciences. Provided that candidates of sufficient merit present themselves, up to three Grace and Thomas C. H. Chan Scholarships shall be awarded in 2007, up to two awards per year for the next four years, and then one Scholarship per year until at least 2030.

Tenure. **4.** A Grace and Thomas C. H. Chan Scholarship shall normally be tenable for not more than three years from 1 October, 1 January, or 17 April following the date of the election.

5. A Grace and Thomas C. H. Chan Scholarship shall provide:

(*a*) a maintenance payment to be determined by the Managers,

(*b*) a payment to meet the student's University and College fees.

When no suitable candidates. **6.** If no suitable Ph.D. candidates present themselves in any particular year, the Fund may, at the discretion of the Managers, be used to support graduate students undertaking M.Phil. or equivalent one-year courses in the relevant Schools. If insufficient candidates present themselves in any year for either a three-year or one-year award, the award shall be held over until the following year.

7. Scholarships shall be awarded by a selection committee appointed by the Board of Managers. How awarded.

8. The Managers shall take such steps as are necessary to promote the Scholarship programme in ways it considers appropriate.

9. Recipients of a Scholarship shall be informed of the source of support and shall be offered the opportunity to make appropriate contact with the Donor.

10. The Managers shall provide the Donor with an annual report on the use made of the Fund together with a list of the Scholars supported and their areas of study. The University shall facilitate the provision to the Donor of annual reports on research undertaken by individual Scholars. Annual Reports.

Chancellor's Medals

Two for Proficiency in Classical Learning

Endowments, 1904, p. 370

1. Not more than two Chancellor's Medals for Proficiency in Classical Learning shall be awarded in each year to students qualified under Regulation 2 who have in that year obtained honours in Part II of the Classical Tripos, if the Awarders are satisfied that there are students whose attainments in the examination, considered in conjunction with their attainments in other University examinations, deserve such recognition. Who are eligible.

2. Eligibility for consideration for the award of Medals shall be restricted to students who have been elected to a University Classical Scholarship, or have been honourably mentioned by the Awarders for those Scholarships.

3. On or before the last weekday in April the Registrary shall send to the Chair of the Faculty Board of Classics particulars of the record in University examinations and prize competitions of any candidate for Part II of the Classical Tripos who is eligible under Regulation 2 for consideration for the award of a Medal.

4. The Awarders shall be the Chair of Examiners for Part II of the Classical Tripos and neither less than two nor more than four other persons appointed by the Faculty Board of Classics before the division of the Easter Term. These persons shall include a representative of the Awarders for University Scholarships in any year in which a candidate satisfied the requirement of Regulation 2. Awarders.

5. The names of the successful candidate or candidates shall be announced by the Awarders before the end of the Easter Term. Announcement of awards.

One for an English Poem

Endowments, 1904, p. 382

1. A resident undergraduate may be a candidate for the Chancellor's Medal for an English Poem in any year, if at the latest date on which exercises can be sent in not more than seven complete terms have passed after his or her first term of residence. Who may be candidates.

2. The Examiners shall be the King Edward VII Professor of English Literature and two additional Examiners appointed by the General Board in the Lent Term of each year on the nomination of the Council. Each of the two additional Examiners shall receive from the Chest, except in cases where no exercise is sent in, such amount as may be determined by the Faculty Board of English within a range approved from time to time by the Council. Examiners.

3. On or before 1 June in each year the Examiners shall publish a Notice inviting the submission of exercises for the Medal and may, if they think fit, announce a subject for the poem. The poem shall not exceed two hundred lines or such smaller number of lines as the Examiners may announce. All exercises must be sent to the Registrary so as to arrive not later than 1 February next following. Notice of subject and submission of exercises.

4. Each candidate shall send three copies of his or her exercise to the Registrary. The exercise shall be in a printed or typewritten form; it shall bear a motto but not the candidate's name, and shall be accompanied by a sealed envelope bearing the same motto outside and containing the candidate's name and College. Exercises: how to be sent in.

5. The successful candidate shall recite his or her poem in the Senate-House on the day fixed for the recitation of prize exercises, and shall deposit a printed or typewritten copy of the poem in the University Library. Exercises: when recited.

One for the encouragement of the study of English Law

Endowments, 1904, p. 398

The Chancellor's Medal for English Law shall be awarded by the Examiners for the LL.M. Examination for distinguished proficiency shown by a candidate in English Law and Legal History, provided that it shall not necessarily be awarded in each year but only in cases of exceptional merit, and that the candidate shall have taken the examination before fifteen complete terms have passed after his or her first term of residence. Before the end of the Easter Term each year the Faculty Board of Law shall announce which of the papers prescribed for the examination in the year next following are deemed to be papers in English Law and Legal History for this purpose.

1 Chancery Lane Prize in Law of Tort

Grace 1 of 30 January 2008

Fund and purpose. **1.** The sum made available annually by 1 Chancery Lane for the study of the Law of Tort shall be applied in equal amounts as follows:

(*a*) to provide a prize called the 1 Chancery Lane Prize in Law of Tort, which shall be awarded by the Examiners for Part IA or Part IB of the Law Tripos for distinction in the Law of Tort shown by performance in Paper 4 of the Law Tripos; and

(*b*) to fund the purchase of books, selected by the Chambers, for the Squire Law Library.

Unexpended income. **2.** If in any year the Prize is not awarded, the unexpended income for that year shall be applied for the purpose specified in paragraph 1(*b*) above.

Chaucer Reading Prize

Prize. **1.** The gift of Dr C. H. Page, of Sidney Sussex College, University Lecturer in English, shall form a fund the income of which shall be used to provide a prize called the Chaucer Reading Prize.

2. The Prize shall be offered for competition in each odd-numbered year and shall be open to all resident members of the University *in statu pupillari*.

Adjudicators. **3.** The Prize shall be awarded by two Adjudicators nominated by the Faculty Board of English before the division of the Lent Term of the year in which the Prize is to be offered.

Examination. **4.** The examination for the Prize shall consist of reading aloud a passage chosen by the candidate from the poetical works of Chaucer. A candidate's name shall be sent to the Registrary by his or her Tutor not less than fourteen days before the day of the examination, together with details of the passage chosen.

5. A winner of the Prize shall not be eligible to compete a second time.

Value. **6.** The value of the Prize shall be determined by the Faculty Board of English, within a range approved from time to time by the Council.

7. Any unexpended income in the Fund may be added to the capital of the Fund or accumulated for use as income in subsequent years, as the Faculty Board may determine.

Chemistry Endowment Fund

The Chemistry Endowment Fund shall be divided into six equal parts and distributed as follows:

Five parts to the Department of Chemistry.

One part to the Department of Materials Science and Metallurgy.

Chemistry Next Generation Fund

Title and purpose. **1.** The sums received from the Walters Kundert Charitable Trust and from Dr Philip Joseph Brown for the purpose of supporting research in any field of chemistry by persons of any age who are at an early stage of their academic careers in the Department of Chemistry shall form a fund called the Chemistry Next Generation Fund, which shall be used for that purpose. The Fund may include other sums received from other bodies or persons for the same purpose.

Managers. **2.** The Managers of the Fund shall be the Head of the Department of Chemistry, the Geoffrey Moorhouse Gibson Professor of Chemistry, the Professor of Physical Chemistry (1920), the Professor of Chemistry (1968), and the BP Professor of Chemistry (1702). If one Manager is both the Head of Department of Chemistry and one of the Professors named above, then in the event of a tied decision, that Manager will have a casting vote.

3. The capital and income of the Fund shall be used to provide unrestricted grants of £50,000 a year (or such lesser amount as the Managers may in their discretion award) to support the research in the Department of Chemistry of one or more Next Generation Fellows. The Managers shall determine the tenure of each Fellowship and may extend such tenure for one or more years provided that the maximum period of tenure shall be five years. In the event that any Next Generation Fellow ceases to be an employee of the University, his or her Next Generation Fellowship shall cease and any accompanying grant will also be terminated. Fellows. Tenure.

4. The Managers of the Fund shall be responsible for awarding Next Generation Fellowships. The titles of Fellowships awarded by the Managers may at the discretion of the Managers include reference to the names of persons or bodies which have contributed to the Fund, save that the Fellowships awarded shall include at least one Walters Kundert Next Generation Fellowship and at least one Philip and Patricia Brown Next Generation Fellowship. Fellowship titles.

5. Any unexpended income in a financial year may be accumulated and expended in any one or more subsequent years in accordance with Regulation 3. Unexpended income.

Children's Kidney Care Fund

Grace 1 of 27 October 2010

1. The sums donated for the furtherance of research into the prevention, diagnosis or treatment of children's urological and related disorders, and other sums donated for the same purpose, shall form a fund to be known as the Children's Kidney Care Fund. Title and purpose

2. The Managers of the Fund shall be: Managers.

(*a*) the Regius Professor of Physic;

(*b*) the Director of Medical Education in the Clinical School;

(*c*) three persons appointed by the Faculty Board of Clinical Medicine.

Managers in class (*c*) shall be appointed for a term of three years. The Secretary of the Faculty Board of Clinical Medicine shall act as Secretary to the Managers.

3. The Managers may at their discretion make grants from the Fund from both capital and income to any person engaged in research into the prevention, diagnosis or treatment of children's urological and related disorders in East Anglia. Grants.

4. The Managers may at their discretion seek the advice of independent assessors concerning the merits of an application to the Fund.

5. No resolution of the Managers shall be valid unless approved by at least three members at a meeting to which all the members have been summoned, provided that a resolution signed by all the members shall have the same validity as a resolution carried at a meeting.

6. Any unexpended income of the Fund may be either added to the capital of the Fund or accumulated for use as income in future years, as the Managers may determine. Unexpended income.

Chinese Studies Fund

1. The moneys donated to the University for the furtherance of Chinese Studies shall form a fund called the Chinese Studies Fund. Title and purpose.

2. The Fund shall be managed by the Head of the Department of East Asian Studies in consultation with and with the agreement of the teaching officers in Chinese in the Department. Managers.

3. The income of the Fund shall be applied at the discretion of the Managers Application of income.

(*a*) to provide an annual Prize to be called the Chinese Studies Prize, of a value determined by the Managers within a range approved from time to time by the Council, and to be awarded by the Examiners for any Part of the Asian and Middle Eastern Studies Tripos for distinguished work shown in the Chinese Studies papers;

(*b*) to advance Chinese Studies in the University by any other means (including the making of contributions towards the travelling expenses of members of the University, and towards the expenses of scholars in Chinese Studies when visiting the University).

Chuan Lyu Fellowship and Senior Visiting Scholarship Fund

Fund and purpose.

1. The sum received by the University from the Chuan Lyu Foundation shall form a fund, called the Chuan Lyu Fellowship and Senior Visiting Scholarship Fund, the income of which shall be used for the provision of Chuan Lyu Research Fellowships and Senior Visiting Scholarships for the support of teaching and research in Taiwanese Studies.

Managers.

2. The Managers of the Fund shall be:

(*a*) four persons appointed by the Head of the Department of East Asian Studies in consultation with and with the agreement of the teaching officers in Chinese in the Department, one of whom shall be a Professor in the field of Chinese Studies;

(*b*) one person appointed by the Chuan Lyu Foundation.

The Managers in class (*a*) shall be appointed in the Michaelmas Term to serve for one year from 1 January following their appointment.

Application of income.

3. The income of the Fund shall be applied at the discretion of the Managers

(*a*) to provide the stipend, national insurance, and pension contributions of a Chuan Lyu Research Fellow who shall engage in teaching and research in the field of Taiwanese Studies;

(*b*) to provide the subsistence allowance and travel costs of a Chuan Lyu Senior Visiting Scholar who shall offer lectures and engage in research in his or her area of expertise within the field of Taiwanese Studies.

4. The Managers of the Fund shall select the Chuan Lyu Research Fellow, taking account of the candidates' written research proposals. In considering any extension to the Fellow's original tenure, the Managers shall take account of progress made in the light of the original research proposal.

Tenure.

5. The Managers of the Fund shall have power to determine from time to time the period of tenure of the Chuan Lyu Research Fellowship and the stipend to be attached to each period of tenure, within a range approved from time to time by the General Board.

Termination of tenure.

6. The Managers of the Fund may terminate a Fellowship at any time if they are not satisfied that the Fellow is diligently fulfilling his or her duties.

7. The Managers of the Fund shall have power to determine from time to time the period of invitation of a Chuan Lyu Senior Visiting Scholar and the level of subsistence allowance to be offered.

Unexpended income.

8. Any unexpended income of the Fund in a financial year may be added either to the capital of the Fund or accumulated for use as income in subsequent years as the Managers may determine in support of the purposes of the Fund as set out in Regulation 1.

Chuan Lyu Lectureship Fund

Fund and purpose.

1. The sums given to the University by the Chuan Lyu Foundation of California shall form a fund called the Chuan Lyu Lectureship Fund. The first charge on the income of the Fund shall be the honorarium of a Chuan Lyu Lecturer.

Lecturer.

2. In the Easter Term of each year the Head of the Department of East Asian Studies in consultation with and with the agreement of the teaching officers in Chinese in the Department shall either appoint a Lecturer to hold office for the following academical year or defer the appointment for one year, provided that the appointment shall not be deferred for two successive years. In making the appointment the Faculty Board shall, if possible, select a scholar qualified to lecture on topics in the history and culture of the Taiwanese people.

Duties.

3. During his or her term of office the Lecturer shall give two lectures in Full Term dealing with some aspect of Chinese Studies, which shall be understood to include the culture and history of the Taiwanese people.

Honorarium.

4. The honorarium paid to the Lecturer shall be such sum as shall be determined by the Faculty Board within a range approved from time to time by the Council. In addition the Faculty Board may at their discretion defray from the income of the Fund any expenses of the Lecturer and any other expenses incurred in connection with the lectures.

Churchill Professorship of Mathematics for Operational Research Fund

Fund.

1. The sums received from the Esso Petroleum Company Limited for the endowment of a Professorship of Mathematics for Operational Research, in memory of Sir Winston Spencer Churchill, shall form a fund called the Churchill Professorship of Mathematics for Operational Research Fund.

2. The Fund shall be administered by three Managers appointed by the Faculty Board of Mathematics, who shall include the Director of the Statistical Laboratory, the Head of the Department of Pure Mathematics and Mathematical Statistics, and the Churchill Professor of Mathematics for Operational Research. Managers.

3. The first charge on the income of the Fund shall be the stipend, national insurance, and pension contributions of the Churchill Professor of Mathematics for Operational Research payable by the University. Application of income.

4. After provision has been made in accordance with Regulation 3, and after provision has also been made, in any year in which the election of a Professor is held, to meet the expenses incurred in holding the election, the income of the Fund shall be applied for the support of teaching or research in the Statistical Laboratory of the Department of Pure Mathematics and Mathematical Statistics in such manner as shall be approved by the General Board on the recommendation of the Managers.

5. Any unexpended income of the Fund in a financial year may be expended in a subsequent year in accordance with Regulation 4. Unexpended income.

Civil Engineers Fund

General

1. The moneys given to the University by the Institution of Civil Engineers shall form a fund called the Civil Engineers Fund, the first charge on which shall be the provision of prizes as follows:

(*a*) one Institution of Civil Engineers Prize for Management Studies;

(*b*) one Institution of Civil Engineers Roscoe Prize for Soil Mechanics;

(*c*) three Institution of Civil Engineers Baker Prizes for distinction in any subject of the Engineering Tripos.

The Prizes shall be awarded in accordance with the following special regulations

2. The Managers of the Fund shall be the Faculty Board of Engineering. Managers.

3. After provision has been made for the Prizes in accordance with the following special regulations, the balance of the income of the Fund shall be available to the Head of the Department of Engineering to use in such manner as he or she shall from time to time determine for the purpose of fostering among engineers the study of the economics of engineering projects, the organization and management of engineering works, and the relations of aesthetic considerations to engineering design and construction. Unexpended income.

Institution of Civil Engineers Prize for Management Studies

1. The Institution of Civil Engineers Prize for Management Studies shall be awarded each year by the Examiners for Part IIB of the Engineering Tripos to a candidate who achieves distinction in management studies in that examination.

2. The value of the Prize shall be determined from time to time by the Faculty Board of Engineering with the approval of the Council.

Civil Engineers Roscoe Prize for Soil Mechanics

1. The Institution of Civil Engineers Roscoe Prize for Soil Mechanics shall be awarded each year by the Examiners for Part IIB of the Engineering Tripos to a candidate who achieves distinction in the field of soil mechanics in that examination.

2. The value of the Prize shall be determined from time to time by the Faculty Board of Engineering with the approval of the Council.

Civil Engineers Baker Prizes

1. Two Institution of Civil Engineers Baker Prizes shall be awarded each year by the Examiners for Part IIA of the Engineering Tripos; one to each of two candidates who achieve distinction in any of the fields falling within the examination.

2. One Institution of Civil Engineers Baker Prize shall be awarded each year by the Examiners for Part IIB of the Engineering Tripos to a candidate who achieves distinction in any of the fields falling within the examination.

3. The value of each Prize shall be determined from time to time by the Faculty Board of Engineering with the approval of the Council.

B.R.D. Clarke Prize

Title. **1.** The sums received from Mrs B. R. D. Clarke in memory of her husband, Bruce Robert Duncan Clarke (1924–1998), M.A., LL.M., of Trinity College, shall form a fund called the B. R. D. Clarke Prize Fund.

Managers. **2.** The Managers of the Fund shall be the Faculty Board of Law, who may delegate any or all of their functions under these regulations to a committee consisting of not less than three persons, at least one of whom shall be a member of the Faculty Board.

How awarded. **3.** The Prize shall be awarded annually by the Examiners for the LL.M. Examination for the best overall performance in that examination.

Value. **4.** The value of the Prize shall be such sum as shall be determined by the Faculty Board of Law, within a range approved from time to time by the Council.

Unexpended income. **5.** At the discretion of the Faculty Board, any unexpended income in the Fund may be either added to the capital of the Fund or accumulated for use as income in a subsequent year.

David L. Clarke Lectureship

Fund. **1.** The sums subscribed in memory of David L. Clarke, formerly University Lecturer in Archaeology and Fellow of Peterhouse, shall form a fund called the David L. Clarke Fund.

Managers. **2.** The Managers of the Fund shall be:

(*a*) one person appointed by the Faculty Board of Human, Social, and Political Science, who shall be Chair;

(*b*) one person appointed by the Head of the Department of Archaeology and Anthropology;

(*c*) one person appointed by the Governing Body of Peterhouse.

Each Manager shall be appointed in the Michaelmas Term to serve for four years from 1 January next following.

Lecturer. **3.** A David L. Clarke Lecturer shall be appointed by the Managers in alternate years to hold office for two academical years. The duty of the Lecturer shall be to deliver in the University on a day in Full Term, on a date approved by the Managers, one lecture on new developments related to the method and theories of archaeology.

Honorarium. **4.** The honorarium to be paid to the Lecturer from the income of the Fund shall be determined by the Managers within a range approved from time to time by the Council. In addition, the Managers may from the income of the Fund pay expenses incurred by the Lecturer.

Faculty of Classics Appeal Fund 2000

Fund and purpose. **1.** The moneys donated and covenanted in response to the appeal held by the Faculty of Classics shall form a fund to be called the Faculty of Classics Appeal Fund 2000, the income of which shall be used to support the learning and teaching of the Greek and Latin languages in the University and the acquisition and development of resources for that purpose.

Managers. **2.** The Managers of the Fund shall be the Faculty Board of Classics.

Unexpended income. **3.** Any unexpended income of the Fund in a financial year may be either added to the capital of the Fund or accumulated for use as income in future years, as the Managers may determine.

Other uses of income. **4.** After provision has been made in accordance with Regulation 1, the income of the Fund shall be applied from time to time, at the discretion of the Managers, to assist in any other way the promotion and encouragement of classical studies in the University.

Clemoes Reading Prize

Prize. **1.** The bequest of Peter Alan Martin Clemoes, Fellow of Emmanuel College and Emeritus Elrington and Bosworth Professor of Anglo-Saxon, shall form a fund the income of which shall be used to provide a prize called the Clemoes Reading Prize.

2. The Prize shall be offered for competition each year and shall be open to all resident members of the University *in statu pupillari*.

3. The examination for the Prize shall consist of reading aloud a passage chosen by the candidate from poetry in one of the languages studied in the Department of Anglo-Saxon, Norse, and Celtic, namely: Old English, Old Norse, Medieval Welsh, Medieval Irish, Medieval Cornish, Medieval Breton, and Insular Latin. A candidate should send his or her name to the Secretary of the Department of Anglo-Saxon, Norse, and Celtic not later than the last Friday of Full Lent Term, together with details of the passage chosen. Examination.

4. The Prize shall be awarded by a panel of not less than two Adjudicators who shall be appointed each year on the nomination of the Head of the Department of Anglo-Saxon, Norse, and Celtic. Adjudicators shall be appointed in the Easter Term, after candidates' entries have been received. Adjudicators.

5. The examination shall be held not later than the division of the Easter Term.

6. A winner of the Prize shall not be eligible to compete a second time by offering a passage in the same language.

7. The value of the Prize shall be determined by the Head of the Department of Anglo-Saxon, Norse, and Celtic, within a range approved from time to time by the Council. Value.

8. If in any year the Prize is not awarded, the income for that year shall be added to the capital of the Fund.

Clifford Chance David Gottlieb Prize

1. The sum made available annually by Clifford Chance in memory of David Gottlieb, a Partner, shall be used to provide a prize, to be known as the Clifford Chance David Gottlieb Prize. Name.

2. The Prize shall be awarded annually by the Examiners for Part IB of the Law Tripos to the candidate who has shown the greatest distinction in the examination for that Part. How awarded.

3. Not less than £50 from the sum paid to each prize-winner shall be spent in the purchase of books selected by the prize-winner.

Clifford Chance C. J. Hamson Prizes

1. The sum made available annually by Clifford Chance in honour of C. J. Hamson, Fellow of Trinity College, Emeritus Professor of Comparative Law, shall be used to provide three Clifford Chance C. J. Hamson Prizes. Title.

2. The Prizes shall be awarded as follows: How awarded.

(*a*) one Prize shall be awarded by the Examiners for Part IB of the Law Tripos for a distinguished performance in Paper 10 (Law of contract) in that examination;

(*b*) one Prize shall be awarded by the Examiners for Part II of the Law Tripos for a distinguished performance in Paper 44 (Aspects of obligations) in that examination;

(*c*) one Prize shall be awarded by the Examiners for the LL.M. for distinction in Comparative Law shown by performance in that subject in the LL.M. Examination.

3. The value of each Prize shall be one-third of the sum made available in each year by Clifford Chance. Value.

Clifford Chance Prize in EU Law

1. The sum made available annually by Clifford Chance LLP for the study of EU Law shall be applied in equal amounts as follows: How awarded.

(*a*) to provide a prize called the Clifford Chance Prize in EU Law, which shall be awarded by the Examiners for Part IB or Part II of the Law Tripos for distinction in EU Law shown by performance in Paper 26 of the Law Tripos; and

(*b*) towards the purchase of books for the Squire Law Library.

2. If in any year the Prize is not awarded, the unexpended income for that year shall be applied for the purpose specified in paragraph 2(*b*) above. Unexpended income.

Cobbett Fund

Fund. **1.** The sum bequeathed to the University by Louis Cobbett, M.D., of Trinity College, formerly University Lecturer in Pathology, shall form a fund called the Cobbett Fund.

Purpose. **2.** The income of the Fund shall be applied from time to time at the discretion of the Professor of Pathology to promote research in Pathology.

Cockerell Fund

Title. **1.** The sums subscribed in honour of Sir Sydney Carlyle Cockerell, Director and Marlay Curator of the Fitzwilliam Museum from 1908 to 1937, shall form a fund to be called the Cockerell Fund.

Purpose. **2.** The income of the Fund shall be allocated by the Director to members of the Assistant Staff of the Museum in turn for foreign travel.

Dorothea Coke Fund

Title and purpose. **1.** The sum given to the University by Lt-Colonel B. E. Coke, M.A., of Clare College, in memory of his wife, Dorothea, shall form a fund called the Dorothea Coke Fund, the purpose of which shall be to promote the publication of original work on the early history of the Scandinavian countries.

Managers. **2.** The Managers of the Fund shall be the Managers of the Scandinavian Studies Fund.

Application of Fund. **3.** The capital and income of the Fund shall be used at the discretion of the Managers, and subject to such conditions as they may think fit, to aid the publication of books, memoirs, or articles, by British authors making original contributions to knowledge of the history and culture of Denmark, Iceland, Norway, and Sweden, before AD 1500.

Procedure. **4.** The Managers shall give not less than three months' notice of their intention to consider applications for assistance from the Fund.

5. Each applicant shall submit to the Managers on their request the manuscript of the work for which a grant is desired and shall furnish evidence that it has been accepted for publication subject to a contribution being paid by the author or on the author's behalf.

Referees. **6.** The Managers may appoint one or more referees to report to them on work submitted, and shall determine what fee, if any, shall be paid to each referee from the Fund.

Payment of grants. **7.** The names of successful applicants, together with the amounts awarded to them, shall be published in the *Reporter*; but a grant shall not be paid until the work for which it was made has been published.

Acknowledgements. **8.** The following note shall be printed in each published work for which a grant has been made:

The printing of this[1] .... *is made possible by a gift to the University of Cambridge in memory of Dorothea Coke, Skjaeret, 1951.*

Dennis Cole Fund

Title. **1.** The moneys received by the University under the will of Dennis Neligan Cole shall form a fund called the Dennis Cole Fund.

Purpose. **2.** The income of the fund shall be reserved for the Department of Paintings, Drawings, and Prints of the Fitzwilliam Museum and, under the terms of Mr Cole's will, may be allocated to any of the following purposes:

(*a*) the conservation of picture frames;

(*b*) travelling expenses incurred by members of the Department of Paintings, Drawings, and Prints in the course of their research into the collections:

(*c*) any purpose which may enhance the efficiency and pleasant use of the Department of Paintings, Drawings, and Prints and its collections.

Authorization of allocations. **3.** Allocations from the income of the Fund shall be authorized by the Director of the Fitzwilliam Museum on the recommendation of the Keeper of Paintings, Drawings, and Prints and reported to the Fitzwilliam Museum Syndicate.

[1] Insert appropriate description of the work.

WILLIAM GEORGE COLLINS ENDOWMENT FUND

Title.
1. The sum bequeathed to the University by the late William George Collins, a former Director of the Cambridge Instrument Company, shall form a fund to be called the William George Collins Endowment Fund.

Application.
2. The income of the Fund shall be used at the discretion of the Faculty Board of Engineering, and subject to such conditions as they may think fit,

(*a*) for making grants to members of the University who are engaged in research in the field of engineering in the Department of Engineering,

(*b*) for promoting and assisting research in the field of engineering by any other means,

provided always that, in accordance with the wishes of the benefactor, preference shall be given to research in the spheres of electrical engineering and mechanical engineering.

Publication of award.
3. In each year in which grants are made from the Fund the names of the persons to whom they have been awarded, but not the amounts of the grants, shall be published in the *Reporter*. Grants shall be payable in the manner determined by the Faculty Board of Engineering.

COMMONWEALTH LIBRARY FUND

Fund.
1. The moneys received from the Trustees of the fund to acquire the Royal Commonwealth Society Library for the nation shall form a fund called the Commonwealth Library Fund.

Purpose.
2. The capital and the income of the Fund shall be used for the cataloguing and digitization of material in the Royal Commonwealth Society Library and the Royal Commonwealth Society Archive, the production of online catalogue records for Commonwealth official publications in the University Library, and the provision of electronic access from the Royal Commonwealth Society's premises to the Royal Commonwealth Society Library at the University Library.

Annual report.
3. The Library Syndicate shall submit an annual report on their administration of the Fund to the Trustees until the capital and income of the Fund have been fully expended.

COMPARATIVE LAW ENDOWMENT FUND

Managers
1. The Managers of the Comparative Law Endowment Fund shall be the Faculty Board of Law, who may delegate any or all of their functions under these regulations to a committee not necessarily consisting wholly of members of the Board.

Income expenditure.
2. The income of the Fund shall be expended from time to time, as the Managers shall determine, for the general purposes of the Faculty of Law. It shall be open to the Managers to add any unexpended income in a financial year to the capital of the Fund.

CONNELL FUND

Grace 5 of 29 February 2012

1. The sum bequeathed to the University by Anthony Murdoch Connell for the purchase of books shall form a fund called the Connell Fund.

2. The income, and in exceptional cases the capital, of the Fund shall be applied at the discretion of the Library Syndicate for the purchase of books for the University Library to support the study of philosophy, psychology, sociology, and human relations.

3. Any unexpended income in a financial year may at the discretion of the Syndicate either be added to the capital of the Fund or accumulated for use as income in any one or more subsequent years.

CORBETT FUND AND PRIZE

Title and purpose.
1. The money received by the University under the will of Samuel Sterndale Corbett, B.A., of Christ's College, shall form a fund called the Corbett Fund, which shall be used for the promotion and encouragement of the study of classical Greek in the University.

Managers.
2. The Managers of the Fund shall be the Faculty Board of Classics, who may delegate any of their functions concerning the Fund to a Committee not necessarily composed wholly of members of the Board.

Prize.

3. There shall be a prize, called the Corbett Prize, which shall be awarded annually by the Examiners for Part IB of the Classical Tripos to a candidate who offers Paper 2 in that examination. The Prize shall be awarded on the performance of candidates in Paper 2 and in Paper 11 (if offered). In awarding the Prize, the Examiners shall have regard to the extent of each candidate's knowledge of Greek at the time of matriculation.

Value.

4. The provision of the Corbett Prize shall be the first charge on the income of the Fund. The value of the Prize shall be determined by the Managers, within a range approved from time to time by the Council.

Lecture.

5. The second charge on the income of the Fund shall be the provision of an annual lecture, to be called the Corbett Lecture.

Duties of Lecturer.

6. A Corbett Lecturer shall be appointed each year by the Faculty Board of Classics. It shall be the duty of the Lecturer to deliver one lecture in the University during Full Term, on a subject connected with ancient Greece.

Stipend.

7. The Lecturer shall receive as stipend such sum as shall be determined by the Managers within a range approved from time to time by the Council. In addition, the Managers may at their discretion pay any expenses of the Lecturer and any other expenses incurred in the holding of the Lecture.

Unexpended income.

8. Any unexpended income accumulated in the Fund may be applied from time to time at the discretion of the Managers

(*a*) to make grants to undergraduate members of the University who are students of Greek to enable them to travel in lands which were inhabited or colonized by the ancient Greeks;

(*b*) to make similar grants to Graduate Students and other postgraduate students in the Faculty of Classics;

(*c*) to assist in any other way the promotion and encouragement of the study of Greek in the University.

Sir Alan Cottrell Prize

Fund and Prize.

1. The sums subscribed on the occasion of his seventieth birthday to mark the many contributions in the field of physical metallurgy made by Sir Alan Cottrell, formerly Vice-Chancellor, Master of Jesus College, and Goldsmiths' Professor of Metallurgy, shall form a fund called the Sir Alan Cottrell Prize Fund, which shall be used to provide a prize called the Sir Alan Cottrell Prize for Materials Science.

How awarded.

2. The Prize shall be awarded by the Examiners for Part IB of the Natural Sciences Tripos for an outstanding performance in the subject Materials Science in that examination.

Value.

3. The value of the Prize shall be the annual income of the Fund.

If not awarded.

4. In any year in which the Prize is not awarded the income for that year shall be added to the capital of the Fund.

Sir Alan Cottrell Professorship of Materials Science Fund

Grace 2 of 6 March 2013

Fund and purpose.

1. The moneys received in response to the appeal held by the Department of Materials Science and Metallurgy to commemorate the scientific work of Professor Sir Alan Cottrell, FRS, former Goldsmiths' Professor of Metallurgy, sometime Vice-Chancellor and Master of Jesus College, shall form a fund to be called the Sir Alan Cottrell Professorship of Materials Science Fund, the income of which shall be used to support the research expenses of the Sir Alan Cottrell Professor of Materials Science.

Managers.

2. The Managers of the Fund shall be:

(*a*) the Head of the Department of Materials Science and Metallurgy;

(*b*) the Sir Alan Cottrell Professor of Materials Science;

(*c*) one person appointed by the Faculty Board of Physics and Chemistry.

If two or more of these offices are held by the same person or if one or more of the named posts is vacant or its tenure has expired, the General Board shall appoint one or more additional Managers to ensure that there are always three Managers. The Manager in class (*c*) shall be appointed for periods of five years at a time.

3. Any unexpended income in a financial year shall either be added to the capital of the Fund or held as an income reserve and expended in any one or more subsequent years in accordance with Regulation 1 above, as the Managers shall determine. Unexpended income.

ALAN COULSON PRIZE

1. The sum of $10,000 received from Dr A. S Coulson shall form a fund called the Alan Coulson Fund, the income of which shall be used to provide a prize called the Alan Coulson Prize in the history of British imperial expansion. Fund and Prize.

2. The Prize shall be awarded each year by the Examiners for Part II of the Historical Tripos to the candidate who in that examination has submitted the best dissertation on a topic in the field of British imperial expansion (including North American history before 1776), which shall be understood to cover such subjects as the discovery, conquest, settlement, and development of individual colonies, the motivation and philosophy of emigrants and colonists, and the role of public opinion in imperial expansion and development. How awarded.

3. The value of the Prize shall be the annual income of the Fund. If in any year the Prize is not awarded, the unexpended income for that year shall be added to the capital of the Fund. Value.

F. R. COWPER REED TRAVELLING GRANTS

1. The sums given and bequeathed by Mrs Cowper Reed shall form a fund called the F. R. Cowper Reed Fund, the purpose of which shall be to provide travelling grants for the furtherance of research in palaeontology. Name and purpose.

2. The Managers of the Fund shall be the Head of the Department of Earth Sciences, and two members of the Faculty of Earth Sciences and Geography one of whom shall be appointed by the Board of that Faculty in the Michaelmas Term of each year to serve for two years from 1 January next following. Managers.

3. The income of the Fund shall be applied from time to time, at the discretion of the Managers, and subject to such conditions as they may think fit, for the purpose of providing travelling grants to members of the University who desire to carry out research in palaeontology. Application.

CRAIG TAYLOR FUND

1. The income of the Craig Taylor Fund shall be used to provide one or more annual prizes, to be called the Craig Taylor Prizes, which shall be awarded by the Board of Examiners for Part IA, Part IB, or Part II of the Philosophy Tripos to the candidates who have shown the greatest distinction in any Part of the Philosophy Tripos, or in any component of any Part of the Tripos as the Faculty Board of Philosophy shall from time to time specify. Fund and prizes. How awarded.

2. It shall be open to the Faculty Board of Philosophy to specify more than one area in which a Craig Taylor Prize may be awarded in any given year.

3. In any year that a Prize is not awarded the income for that year shall be either added to the capital of the Fund or accumulated for use as income in future years, as the Faculty Board of Philosophy may determine. If not awarded.

BENEFACTION OF JOHN CRANE

Endowments, 1904, p. 565

1. The Distributors of Crane's Charity for the relief of poor sick scholars shall be: the Vice-Chancellor, the Master of Gonville and Caius College, the Regius Professors of Divinity, Civil Law, and Physic, and the Chief Apothecary. Distributors.

2. The Chief Apothecary shall be elected by the other Distributors before the end of the Michaelmas Term to serve for five years from 1 January next following. Apothecary.

3. The Distributors shall meet at least once in each academical year. Meeting of Distributors.

4. The Distributors shall give notice in the *Reporter* each year that they will consider applications from scholars, which shall be made by the Tutors of their respective Colleges.

Archbishop Cranmer Prize, Grants, and Studentships

Fund. **1.** The money received from the bequest of the Reverend Henry Sykes shall be separately invested and shall form a fund called the Henry Sykes Fund.

Prize. **2.** There shall be established in the University a prize called the Archbishop Cranmer Prize, to be awarded for an essay, the subject of which shall relate to the intention and result of the changes in doctrine, organization, and ritual within the Church of England between the years AD 1500 and 1700; also the bearing of these changes upon the political and economic, the national and international, the literary and social, the religious and home life of the English people.

3. The Prize shall be awarded each year in the Michaelmas Term.

Notice of award. **4.** The Faculty Board of History shall publish the conditions of the award in the course of the Michaelmas Term next preceding that in which the Prize is to be awarded.

Who may compete. **5.** Candidates for the Prize shall be members of the University and of not less than three years' standing from their first degree, whether of this or another university, at the time of the award.

Adjudicators. **6.** The Adjudicators of the Prize shall be the Faculty Board of History who shall appoint referees. Each referee shall receive such payment from the income of the Fund as may be determined by the Adjudicators within a range approved from time to time by the Council. The Adjudicators may, unless otherwise specified in these regulations, delegate any of their functions to a committee, consisting of not less than three persons, not all of whom shall necessarily be members of the Faculty of History or the Faculty Board.

Submission of essay. **7.** A student shall be required to submit the subject of his or her essay for the approval of the Adjudicators before the division of the term previous to the date fixed for the award; such approval must be obtained before the student is accepted as a candidate. A candidate who has successfully submitted a thesis for a University prize or for the degree of Ph.D. or M.Litt. must declare that the essay submitted for this Prize is not substantially identical with his or her previous thesis.

8. The essays shall be sent to the Registrary not later than 1 October in the year in which the Prize is to be awarded.

First charge. **9.** The provision of a Prize to the successful candidate shall be the first charge upon the Fund. The value of the Prize shall be determined by the Faculty Board of History within a range approved from time to time by the Council. Second charge. The cost of administration of the Prize and grants towards the expenses of publication of any essays that the Adjudicators think worthy of publication shall be the next charges upon the Fund; any remainder from the accumulated income or any part of it may at the discretion of the Adjudicators be awarded to the successful candidate as an addition to the Prize.

Application of unexpended income. **10.** After provision has been made for the award of a Prize in accordance with Regulation 9 any unexpended income accumulated in the Fund may be applied from time to time at the discretion of the Adjudicators for the following purposes:

(*a*) To make grants for the furtherance of research in English ecclesiastical history between 1500 and 1700 as to the intention and result of the changes in doctrine, organization, and ritual within the English Church between 1500 and 1700 and the bearing of these changes upon the political, economic, national, international, literary, social, religious, and home life of the English people. The Adjudicators shall determine the value of grants, within a range approved from time to time by the Council.

(*b*) To provide one or two Archbishop Cranmer Studentships the holders of which shall devote themselves to original research in English ecclesiastical history between 1500 and 1700 as to the intention and result of the changes in doctrine, organization, and ritual within the English Church between 1500 and 1700 and the bearing of these changes upon the political, economic, national, international, literary, social, religious, and home life of the English people. The Electors to the Studentships shall be the Adjudicators of the Prize who, on each occasion when they intend to proceed to an election, shall announce the date by which applications must be received and the manner in which they must be submitted. A Studentship shall be open to any person who is or is about to become registered as a Graduate Student in the University. The value of a Studentship shall be determined by the Adjudicators within a range approved from time to time by the Council. A Studentship shall be tenable for one year in the first instance, and may be renewed and its value reviewed, subject to a maximum tenure of three years.

11. If the income of the fund is materially augmented by the sale of published Prize essays beyond what is necessary to provide for the purposes specified in Regulations 6, 9, and 10 the Council may, on the advice of the Finance Committee, authorize grants to be made from the excess to the University Library or to the University Press.

12. Clause 5 of Mr Sykes's will (as printed in *Reporter*, 1927–28, pp. 634–5) shall be appended to each essay which is published wholly or in part at the expense of the Fund.

Crausaz Wordsworth Fund

Grace 1 of 1 December 2010

1. The sums of up to £250,000 given anonymously to the University from 2010 onwards shall form a fund called the Crausaz Wordsworth Fund, which shall be used for the promotion and encouragement of the study of philosophy in the University. Title and purpose.

2. The Managers of the Fund shall be the Faculty Board of Philosophy, who may delegate any or all of their functions under these regulations to a committee not necessarily consisting wholly of members of the Board. Managers.

3. The income of the Fund shall be used to provide awards known as Crausaz Wordsworth Studentships and Timothy Joyce Studentships in the Faculty of Philosophy. The Studentships shall be open to any person who is or is about to be registered as a Graduate Student in the University. Holders of the Crausaz Wordsworth Studentships shall undertake research in the Faculty of Philosophy leading to the award of a doctorate of Philosophy. Holders of the Timothy Joyce Studentships shall undertake advanced study in the Faculty of Philosophy leading to the award of a Master's Degree. Studentships.

4. A Crausaz Wordsworth Studentship shall be tenable for one year in the first instance, and may be renewed by the Managers for a second or third year, subject to satisfactory progress. A Timothy Joyce Studentship shall be tenable for one year.

5. The value of a Studentship shall be determined by the Managers within a range approved from time to time by the Council. Value.

6. After provision has been made, in accordance with the foregoing regulations, for at least one Crausaz Wordsworth Studentship and at least one Timothy Joyce Studentship, the balance of the annual income and any unexpended income accumulated in the Fund shall be available to the Faculty Board of Philosophy to be used for the encouragement of study or research in Philosophy.

7. Any unexpended income may be either added to the capital of the Fund or accumulated for use as income in subsequent years, as the Managers may determine. Unexpended income.

8. It shall be open to the University, on the recommendation of the Faculty Board of Philosophy, to alter these regulations from time to time, provided that the Fund shall be devoted to the encouragement of study or research in Philosophy. Alterations.

Craven Fund and Studentship

Endowments, 1904, p. 286 Stat. E VII.

1. The Managers of the Craven Fund shall be the Faculty Board of Classics.

2. There shall be a Craven Studentship, which shall be for the furtherance of research in the language, literature, history, philosophy, archaeology, and art of ancient Greece and Rome, and the comparative philology of the Indo-European languages. Studentship.

3. The holder of the Studentship shall undertake advanced study or research in one or more of the subjects specified in Regulation 2, according to a scheme to be approved by the Faculty Board. Such a scheme shall involve absence from Cambridge for not less than six months, unless the Board at their discretion waive this requirement. Purpose.

4. Candidature for the Studentship shall be open to any person who is or is about to be registered as a Graduate Student in the Faculty of Classics in the University. Election to and tenure of the Studentship shall lapse if the person elected does not become or ceases to be a registered Graduate Student. Who are eligible.

5. The Student shall be elected by the Faculty Board, who may take such steps as they think fit to inquire into the qualifications of the candidates; provided that the Studentship shall not be awarded on the results of a competitive examination. Electors.

6. Before the division of the Easter Term each year, the Board shall give notice of the date by which and the manner in which applications for the Studentship to be held in the next but one following Applications.

academical year are to be submitted. An election to the Studentship shall be held during the academical year prior to the Studentship's being taken up, on a date to be determined by the Board.

Tenure. **7.** The Studentship shall be tenable from the date on which the student comes into residence until 30 September of the calendar year next following. A Student shall be eligible for re-election on not more than two occasions.

Emolument. **8.** The emolument of the Studentship shall be such sum, not exceeding the available income of the Fund, as shall be determined by the Faculty Board within a range approved from time to time by the Council. The emolument shall be paid in such instalments as the Board shall from time to time determine, provided that the Board may withhold payment of any instalment if they are not satisfied that the Student is pursuing his or her course of study with sufficient diligence.

Balance of Fund. **9.** The balance of the Fund after payment of the emoluments of the Craven Student and the Craven Scholars, and of such fees as are to be paid to Examiners from the Fund, shall be devoted to the furtherance of research in the subjects specified in Regulation 2.

Grants. **10.** Grants for this purpose may be made by the Board, at their discretion, out of the income of the Fund, either to the Craven Student or to any other person engaged in such research, subject to any conditions they may think fit. Such grants may include payments towards the maintenance of the recipients.

11. The Board may delegate any of their functions concerning the Fund to a Committee not necessarily consisting wholly of members of the Board.

David Crighton Fund

Fund and purpose. **1.** The sums subscribed in memory of David Crighton, Professor of Applied Mathematics and Master of Jesus College, shall form a fund called the David Crighton Fund, the income of which shall be used to assist persons at an early stage of their careers who are undertaking research in Applied Mathematics in the fields of fluid mechanics, acoustics, waves, and vibration.

Managers. **2.** The Fund shall be administered by a Board of Managers consisting of:

(*a*) the Head of the Department of Applied Mathematics and Theoretical Physics (or a duly appointed deputy) as Chair;

(*b*) the Professor of Applied Mathematics;

(*c*) one person appointed by the Head of the Department of Applied Mathematics and Theoretical Physics;

(*d*) one person, who shall not normally be a member of the University, appointed by the Faculty Board of Mathematics.

The members appointed in classes (*c*) and (*d*) shall be appointed in the Michaelmas Term to serve for four years from 1 January following their appointment.

Fellowships. **3.** The income of the Fund shall be used to provide up to four David Crighton Fellowships, elected by the Managers, in the fields set out in Regulation 1 each year. The purpose of the Fellowships shall be to enable persons studying for a higher degree or working in the University to visit other institutions and persons studying for a higher degree or working in other institutions to visit the University. The tenure of the Fellowships shall be up to three months. The Managers shall give preference to candidates holding junior appointments (including Graduate Students).

Submission of applications. **4.** In the Michaelmas Term each year the Managers shall publish a notice giving the date by which, and the manner in which, applications are to be submitted.

Unexpended income. **5.** Any unexpended income in a financial year shall be either added to the capital of the Fund or accumulated for use as income in future years, as the Managers may determine.

Crosse Studentship

Stat. E X.

Name and purpose. **1.** The income of the Crosse Fund shall be used to provide a Studentship for the furtherance of the knowledge of the Holy Scriptures in Hebrew and Greek, Ecclesiastical History, and Christian Theology. The value of the Studentship shall be such sum, within a range determined from time to time by the Council, as the Electors shall determine in each case after taking account of any other emolument that the Student is receiving for study or research.

2. The Studentship shall be open to any person who is or is about to be registered as a Graduate Student in the University, provided that not more than four years have passed after the end of the calendar year in which he or she was first so registered. Who are eligible.

3. Elections to the Studentship shall be made by a body of Electors consisting of: Electors.

(*a*) the Regius Professor of Divinity, the Lady Margaret's Professor of Divinity, and the Norris-Hulse Professor of Divinity;

(*b*) three persons appointed by the Faculty Board of Divinity.

The Electors may take such steps as they think fit to inquire into the qualifications of the candidates, provided that the Studentship shall not be awarded by the result of a competitive examination.

4. The Student shall undertake a course of advanced study or research according to a scheme proposed by the Student and approved by the Electors, under the direction of a Supervisor appointed by the Electors. In the Easter Term each year the Supervisor shall submit a written report to the Electors on the work of the Student. Duties of Student.

5. The Studentship shall be tenable for one year in the first instance, and a Student shall be eligible for re-election thereafter for not more than three further years. Tenure.

6. The Electors shall give not less than three months' notice of their intention to proceed to an election. Notice of election.

7. The emolument of the Studentship shall be payable in such instalments as the Electors shall from time to time determine, provided that the Electors may terminate the Studentship or withhold payment of any instalment if they are not satisfied that the Student is pursuing his or her course of study with sufficient diligence. Payments.

8. From any unexpended income accumulated in the Fund the Electors may if they think fit in any year award one or more additional Studentships, of such amount as they think fit, or may make grants for the promotion and encouragement of studies in the fields specified in Regulation 1. Unexpended income.

Crowther-Beynon Fund

1. The sum bequeathed to the University by the late Vernon Bryan Crowther-Beynon, of Trinity College, shall form a fund called the Crowther-Beynon Fund. Title.

2. One-third of the income of the Fund shall be applied to the maintenance of the Museum of Archaeology and Anthropology. Maintenance of Museum.

3. The remaining two-thirds of the income of the Fund, and any accumulated balance, shall be retained as an endowment fund which, subject to the provisions of Regulation 4, shall be at the disposal of the Museum Committee for the following purposes: Endowment fund.

(*a*) the acquisition of new material for the Museum by purchase or by financing excavations or expeditions, at home or overseas, undertaken under the auspices of the Museum or by other organizations;

(*b*) making grants in aid of the publication of results of excavations or other research carried out under the auspices of the Museum;

(*c*) such other purposes connected with the Museum as the Museum Committee in consultation with the Faculty Board of Human, Social, and Political Science, may from time to time decide.

4. Proposals for expenditure from the endowment fund shall be included in the annual estimates submitted by the Faculty Board and such expenditure shall be subject to the approval of the General Board in accordance with Regulation 1 for the University Education Fund.

Cunliffe Fund

1. The moneys received by the University under the will of Leonard Daneham Cunliffe, and accepted by Grace 1 of 12 November 1937, shall be called the Cunliffe Fund. Title.

2. The income of the Fund, which may be allowed to accumulate, shall be expended from time to time by the Fitzwilliam Museum Syndicate on the purchase of works of art. Purpose.

3. Objects acquired from the Fund are to be displayed. Requirement.

Cuthbert Prize for Humanities in Medicine

1. The sum of £5,383 donated to the University by Susan Molyneux Warner and Andrew Calcutt in memory of their father Frederick Norton Cuthbert shall form a Fund for the purpose of awarding an annual prize for Humanities in Medicine. Fund and purpose.

Prize. **2.** The Prize shall be called the Cuthbert Prize for Humanities in Medicine and shall be awarded annually for an essay of approximately 3,000 words on a subject in the field of the interaction of the interests of the humanities with the concerns of Clinical Medicine.

Who are eligible. **3.** The Prize shall be open to any member of the University who is pursuing clinical study in Cambridge and is a candidate for Part III of the Final M.B. Examination. Entries for the Prize must be submitted to the Director of Medical Education before 1 February each year.

Adjudicators. **4.** The Prize shall be awarded by two Adjudicators appointed by the General Board on the nomination of the Faculty Board of Clinical Medicine.

Value. **5.** The value of the Prize shall be the income of the Fund for the financial year in which the award is made.

Unexpended income. **6.** If in any year the Prize is not awarded, the unexpended income shall be added to the capital of the Fund.

ROBERT DAGLISH FUND

Fund and purpose. **1.** The bequest of Mrs Inna Daglish in memory of her husband Robert Cyril Daglish, M.A., of Jesus College, shall form a fund for the encouragement of Russian studies.

Managers. **2.** The Managers of the Fund shall be the Head of the Department of Slavonic Studies (or a member of the Regent House appointed by the Head of the Department) as Chair, and two members of the academic staff of the Department of Slavonic Studies appointed by the Faculty Board of Modern and Medieval Languages in the Michaelmas Term to serve for two years from 1 January following their appointment.

Application of income. **3.** From the income of the Fund, or from any unexpended income accumulated in the Fund, the Managers may make grants or loans to undergraduate members of the University to assist them in travelling to or in Russia in connection with their studies in the University.

DANCKWERTS-PERGAMON PRIZE

Fund. **1.** The sum given to the University by Mr Robert Maxwell, M.C., Chairman of Pergamon Press, on behalf of *Chemical Engineering Science,* for the encouragement of the study of Chemical Engineering shall form a fund called the Danckwerts-Pergamon Fund, in commemoration of the late Peter Victor Danckwerts, G.C., M.A., formerly Fellow of Pembroke College and Shell Professor of Chemical Engineering.

Prize. **2.** The income of the Fund shall be used to provide a prize called the Danckwerts-Pergamon Prize, which shall be awarded in the Lent Term each year by the Head of the Department of Chemical Engineering and Biotechnology to that person among the successful candidates for the Ph.D. Degree who in the judgement of the Head of the Department has presented the best dissertation on a subject connected with Chemical Engineering.

Who are eligible. **3.** Those students shall be eligible for the Prize who have been approved by the Board of Graduate Studies for the award of the Ph.D. Degree under the regulations for Graduate Students during the preceding calendar year.

Value. **4.** The value of the Prize shall be the income of the Fund.

GLYN DANIEL AWARD

Fund and purpose. **1.** The gift of Mrs Ruth Daniel in memory of her husband Glyn Edmund Daniel, Litt.D., FBA, Fellow of St John's College, Disney Professor of Archaeology, shall form a fund the income of which shall be used to provide an award called the Glyn Daniel Award in Archaeology.

Award. **2.** The Award shall be made each year before the end of the Long Vacation by the Head of the Department of Archaeology and Anthropology or her or his deputy to a person who has achieved a distinguished performance in the subject Archaeology in Part IIB of the Archaeological and Anthropological Tripos and who intends to proceed to full-time advanced study or research in that subject.

Value. **3.** The value of the Award shall be the income of the Fund. The sum paid shall be spent on the purchase of books selected by the winner of the Award, subject to the approval of the Head of the Department.

Unexpended income. **4.** If in any year no award is made the income for that year shall be added to the capital of the Fund.

SURENDRANATH DASGUPTA FUND

1. The sum of £4,000 given to the University by Mrs Surama Dasgupta in memory of her husband, Surendranath Dasgupta, shall form a fund called the Surendranath Dasgupta Fund, the income of which shall be used for the advancement of the study of Indian philosophy in the University. Title and purpose.

2. The Managers of the Fund shall be the Faculty Board of Asian and Middle Eastern Studies who may delegate any of their functions concerning the Fund to a Committee not necessarily consisting wholly of members of the Board. Managers.

3. The first charge on the income of the Fund shall be to meet the payment of an honorarium to and the expenses of a Lecturer who shall be appointed from time to time by the Managers to deliver a course of at least three lectures, to be called the Surendranath Dasgupta Lectures, on Indian philosophy. The Managers may make a grant from the Fund towards the cost of publishing the lectures. Lecturer.

4. After provision has been made in accordance with Regulation 3, any unexpended income accumulated in the Fund may be used at the discretion of the Managers for any other purpose in conformity with the purpose for which the Fund has been established. Other uses of income.

DAVIES-JONES MEMORIAL FUND

Rescinded by Grace 3 of 27 November 2013

HENRY ROY DEAN PRIZE

1. The sums donated by the University officers in the Department of Pathology and others shall form a fund for the purpose of awarding a Prize in clinical pathology. Fund and purpose.

2. The title of the Prize shall be the Henry Roy Dean Prize. Title.

3. The Prize shall be open to any member of the University who is pursuing clinical study in Cambridge and has been entered as a candidate for Part I of the Final M.B. Examination. Who may compete.

4. The Prize shall be awarded on the results of a special examination to be held annually, and conducted by the Professor of Pathology and two Adjudicators appointed by the General Board on the nomination of the Professor. How awarded.

5. The value of the Prize shall be such sum, not exceeding the available income of the Fund, as may be determined by the Faculty Board of Clinical Medicine within a range approved from time to time by the Council. Value.

6. The Professor of Pathology shall publish a Notice of the Prize giving the date of the special examination and the last date by which entries shall be submitted, provided that such date for entries shall be not less than six weeks after the publication of the Notice. Notice.

DEBENHAM SCHOLARS FUND

Grace 1 of 16 January 2013

1. The sum bequeathed to the University by the late Barbara Debenham, daughter of Professor Frank Debenham OBE, sometime Professor of Geography at the University of Cambridge and Founder and first Director of the Scott Polar Research Institute, and other gifts received for the same purpose, shall form a fund called the Debenham Scholars Fund to support research in Polar Science. Title and purpose.

2. The Fund shall be administered by the Managers, who shall comprise: Managers.

(*a*) the Director of the Scott Polar Research Institute; and

(*b*) two persons who would normally be based in the Scott Polar Research Institute, appointed by the Faculty Board of Earth Sciences and Geography to serve for periods of five years at a time.

3. The income from the Fund shall be used to contribute to the fees, maintenance, and field research of postgraduate students at the Scott Polar Research Institute, to enable them to undertake scientific and other related research on polar topics. Scholarships supporting such research, in whole or in part, shall be advertised from time to time, and awarded on merit, by the Managers of the Fund. Use of income.

4. Acknowledgement of support from the Debenham Scholars Fund should be made in publications supported by an award. Acknowledgement of support.

de Fraine Fund

The income of the Fund derived from the bequest of Mr J. G. de Fraine, accepted by the University in 1965 and announced in the *Reporter* on 27 October 1965, shall be applied at the discretion of the Library Syndicate to purchase books and manuscripts in the field of music.

Odette de Mourgues Fund and Studentship

Fund and purpose.

1. The benefaction of Dorothy Coleman, Litt.D., of New Hall, in memory of Professor Odette de Mourgues, Litt.D., of Girton College, Professor of French, shall form a fund to be called the Odette de Mourgues Fund. The purpose of the Fund shall be the advancement of study and research in the French language or in French literature.

Studentship.

2. The income of the Fund shall be used to provide an Odette de Mourgues Studentship, the holder of which shall undertake advanced study or research on a subject in French language or literature.

Electors.

3. The Electors to the Studentship shall be the Drapers Professor of French and two persons appointed by the Faculty Board of Modern and Medieval Languages in the Michaelmas Term to hold office for two calendar years from 1 January following their appointment.

Who are eligible.

4. The Studentship shall be open to any person who is registered as a Graduate Student in the University, provided that at the date of the election not less than two complete terms have passed after the term of his or her admission as a Graduate Student.

Election.

5. Before the division of the Easter Term each year the Faculty Board shall give notice of the date by which and the manner in which applications for the Studentship are to be submitted. An election to the Studentship shall be held before the beginning of the Michaelmas Term.

Tenure.

6. The Studentship shall be tenable for one year from 1 October following the election.

Value.

7. The emolument of the Studentship shall be such sum, not exceeding the available income of the Fund, as shall be determined by the Electors within a range approved from time to time by the Council.

8. From the income of the Fund and from any unexpended income accumulated in the Fund, the Electors may make grants, either to the holder of the Studentship or to any other Graduate Student working in the field of French language or literature, for the purchase of books or equipment or towards the cost of visits, for the purpose of study, to lands where French is spoken.

Sir Evelyn de Rothschild Fund for Finance

Title.

1. The sum received from the Eranda Foundation to support a Professorship of Finance for a single tenure of ten years shall form a fund called the Sir Evelyn de Rothschild Fund for Finance.

Managers.

2. The Managers of the Fund shall be the Director of Judge Business School, the Sir Evelyn de Rothschild Professor of Finance for the time being, and one other Manager appointed by the Faculty Board of Business and Management for periods of five years provided that, if two of these offices are held by the same person or if one or more of these posts is vacant or its tenure has expired, the Faculty Board of Business and Management shall appoint one or more additional Managers so as to ensure that there are three Managers.

Professorship.

3. The capital and the income of the Fund shall be available for the payment of the stipend, national insurance, pension contributions, and associated indirect costs of the Sir Evelyn de Rothschild Professor of Finance payable by the University during the tenure of the Professor.

Teaching and research.

4. After provision has been made in accordance with Regulation 3, the capital and the income of the Fund shall be applied for the support of teaching or research in some aspect of Finance in such a manner as shall be approved by the General Board on the recommendation of the Managers.

Expiry of Professorship tenure.

5. In the event that there is capital or income of the Fund remaining after the expiry of the tenure of the Professor, the capital and income of the Fund shall be available for the purpose set out in Regulation 4.

Unexpended income.

6. Any unexpended income in a financial year may in any one or more subsequent year be expended in accordance with Regulations 3 and 4.

Archibald Denny Prizes

Awarders and subject.

1. Two Archibald Denny Prizes shall be awarded each year, one by the Examiners for Part IIA of the Engineering Tripos and one by the Examiners for Part IIB of that Tripos, to the candidates for those Parts who have shown the greatest distinction in the Theory of Structures.

2. The value of each Prize shall be such sum not exceeding half the available income of the Archibald Denny Fund as may be determined from time to time by the Faculty Board of Engineering with the approval of the Council. Value.

3. The University, on the recommendation of the Faculty Board of Engineering, may amend these regulations from time to time, provided that the Prizes shall always be called the Archibald Denny Prizes and shall always be devoted to the encouragement of the study of the Theory of Structures. Amendments.

HARRY DESAI FUND

Grace 2 of 11 November 2009

1. The sums given and bequeathed to the University by Mr Harry Desai, and other donations received for the same purpose, shall form a fund called the Harry Desai Fund, the income of which shall be used at least once a year to make one or more Harry Desai Research Awards to persons who are registered as candidates for the Ph.D. Degree with a preference for those engaged in research in teaching and education. Title and purpose.

2. The Managers of the Fund shall be the Board of Graduate Studies. The Managers may delegate any of their functions concerning the Fund to a Committee composed of members of the Board of Graduate Studies. Managers.

3. The Managers shall on each occasion when they invite applications give not less than three months' notice of their intention to make an award.

4. An award may be made to a person who has completed not less than four terms of research as a registered Graduate Student of the University, provided that he or she has shown a high aptitude for research and a devotion to study, and is in need of financial assistance. Award.

5. The value of each award shall be determined by the Managers within a range approved from time to time by the Council. Value.

DIVINITY (GERMAN LANGUAGE) FUND

1. The gift of an anonymous benefactor shall form a fund to be called the Divinity (German Language) Fund, for the encouragement of the study of the German language by members of the University pursuing or intending to pursue in the University a course of study or research in Divinity. Title and purpose

2. The Faculty Board of Divinity shall be the Managers of the Fund, and may appoint a committee, not necessarily consisting wholly of members of the Faculty Board, to perform any or all of the duties of the Managers under these regulations. Managers.

3. The income of the Fund shall be used, and any unexpended income accumulated in the Fund may be used, at the discretion of the Managers, for the encouragement, by way of grants or otherwise, of the study of the German language by members of the University pursuing or intending to pursue in the University a course of study or research in Divinity approved by the Managers. Application of income.

AUSTIN DOBSON FUND

1. The sum of £700, the bequest of the late Mrs M. E. Dobson in memory of her father Mr Austin Dobson, shall form a fund called the Austin Dobson Fund, the income from which shall be used to provide annually an Austin Dobson Prize for proficiency in the study of English literature. Title and purpose.

2. The Prize shall be awarded after account has been taken particularly of the extent to which work submitted for the Prize is distinguished by literary style and ability to appreciate the elements of excellence in good literature.

3. The Prize shall be awarded by the Examiners for Part II of the English Tripos for a distinguished performance in that examination in the papers on Practical Criticism and on Tragedy and in the dissertation that all candidates for the examination are required to offer. How awarded.

4. If candidates of sufficient merit present themselves, it shall be open to the Examiners to award one or more additional Austin Dobson Prizes. Additional awards.

5. The value of an Austin Dobson Prize shall be such sum as may be determined by the awarders within a range approved from time to time by the Council, provided that (*a*) if two or more Prizes are awarded they shall be of equal value, and (*b*) the combined value of the Prizes awarded in any year shall not exceed the annual income of the Fund. Value.

Unexpended income. **6.** Any unexpended income shall be added to the capital of the Fund.

Amendment. **7.** These regulations, other than Regulations 1 and 2 and this regulation, shall be subject to alteration by Grace, always provided that the main object of the Fund as described in Regulations 1 and 2 shall be adhered to.

DENIS DOOLEY PRIZE IN CLINICAL ANATOMY

1. The gift of Denis Dooley, FRCS, Her Majesty's Inspector of Anatomy, shall form a fund to be called the Clinical Anatomy Fund, for the encouragement of study and research in Clinical Anatomy.

Prize, subject, and value. **2.** The income of the Fund shall be used to provide a Denis Dooley Prize in Clinical Anatomy to be awarded annually for an essay on a subject in the field of Clinical Anatomy. The value of the Prize shall be the income of the Fund for the financial year in which the award is made.

Eligibility. **3.** The Prize shall be open to any person who is pursuing or has pursued a course of clinical study in the University for the degrees of Bachelor of Medicine and Bachelor of Surgery, provided that no one shall be eligible for the Prize if, on the date by which entries are to be submitted, more than five years have elapsed since he or she passed the Final M.B. Examination.

Notice of applications. **4.** In the Michaelmas Term the Regius Professor of Physic and the Professor of Anatomy shall give notice of the date by which and the manner in which candidates shall submit their entries for the Prize, and of any requirements relating to the subject, form, and length of an essay to be submitted for the Prize.

How awarded. **5.** The Prize shall be awarded by the Regius Professor of Physic and the Professor of Anatomy (or their deputies) who may at their discretion examine a candidate *viva voce*.

Joint submissions. **6.** The Prize may be awarded for an essay submitted jointly by two candidates. In comparing the merits of combined and independent work, the Adjudicators shall expect an appreciably higher standard for the former. In the case of an award made for a joint essay, the Prize shall be divided equally between the co-authors.

ANTHONY DORRELL PRIZE

Title. **1.** The gift to the University of Dr Jana Howlett, of Jesus College, University Lecturer in the Department of Slavonic Studies, in memory of her father Anthony Dorrell shall form a fund called the Anthony Dorrell Fund.

Prize. **2.** There shall be a prize, called the Anthony Dorrell Prize, which shall be awarded annually by the Examiners for Part IA of the Modern and Medieval Languages Tripos for an outstanding performance in Russian in that examination.

Value. **3.** The value of the Prize shall be the annual income of the Fund.

BRIAN DOUGLAS FUND

Title. **1.** The sum received under the will of Brian Kirkbride Douglas, Mus.B., of St John's College, shall form a fund called the Brian Douglas Fund.

Purpose. **2.** The income of the Fund shall be placed at the disposal of the Professor of Music, and shall be used for the promotion of the study of music in the University and for such other purposes connected with music in the Faculty of Music as the Professor of Music shall decide.

DREWITT PRIZE

Fund. **1.** The benefaction of Mr H. W. Drewitt shall form a fund the income of which shall be used to provide a prize called the Drewitt Prize.

How awarded. **2.** The Prize shall be awarded by the Examiners for Part IB of the Natural Sciences Tripos for an outstanding performance in the subject Ecology in that examination.

Unexpended income. **3.** If in any year the Prize is not awarded, the income for that year shall be added to the capital of the Fund.

GORDON DUFF FUND AND PRIZE

1. The sum bequeathed to the University by the late Edward Gordon Duff shall form a fund called the Gordon Duff Fund. Title.

2. The first charge on the Fund shall be to provide a Gordon Duff Prize for an essay on any one of the following subjects: bibliography, palaeography, typography, book-binding, book illustration, the science of books and manuscripts, and the arts relating thereto. Prize.

3. The Prize shall be open to all members of the University, and shall be offered for award annually. Public notice of the Prize shall be given by the Library Syndicate not later than the division of the Michaelmas Term. Who may compete.

4. The value of the Prize shall be such sum as shall be determined by the Library Syndicate within a range approved from time to time by the Council. Value.

5. Each candidate shall inform the Deputy Librarian of the University Library of the proposed subject of his or her essay not later than the last day of the Michaelmas Term. The Deputy Librarian of the University Library shall submit the proposed subject to the Library Syndicate and shall inform the candidate whether they approve the subject. Proposal of subjects.

6. Not more than two Adjudicators shall be appointed by the Library Syndicate at such time that in their selection the Syndicate may take account of the subjects approved for essays. In any year in which one or more essays are submitted each Adjudicator shall receive from the Fund such sum as may be determined by the Library Syndicate within a range approved from time to time by the Council. Adjudicators.

7. Essays shall be submitted to the Deputy Librarian of the University Library so as to arrive not later than the last day of the Lent Term. Each essay, which shall not exceed 10,000 words in length, shall be printed or typewritten. Submission of essays.

8. The Prize shall be awarded in the Easter Term. If essays of sufficient merit are submitted, it shall be open to the Adjudicators to award an additional Prize not exceeding in value such sum as shall be determined by the Library Syndicate within a range approved from time to time by the Council. If on any occasion there is no candidate of sufficient merit to deserve a Prize, the prize-money for that year shall be available for use as income in accordance with the provisions of Regulation 10. Award.

9. The Prize-winner shall ensure that a printed or typewritten copy of his or her essay is deposited in the University Library, and shall not receive the prize-money until this has been done. Condition.

10. After provision has been made for the Prize or Prizes, the income of the Fund shall be applied from time to time at the discretion of the Library Syndicate to purchase for the University Library old or rare manuscripts, printed books, and book-bindings, in the selection and purchase of which preference shall be given to those written, printed, executed, or produced before AD 1700. Use of income.

11. No part of the income of the Fund shall be available for the general expenses of the University Library. Restriction.

EAST MIDLAND REGIONAL EXAMINATIONS BOARD FUND (EMREB FUND)

1. The assets transferred to the University by the East Midland Regional Examinations Board (EMREB) shall form a fund called the EMREB Fund. Fund.

2. The capital and income of the EMREB Fund shall be at the disposal of the Local Examinations Syndicate for the following purposes: Purpose.

(*a*) to promote and develop the General Certificate of Secondary Education administered by the Midland Examining Group;

(*b*) to make payments to members of the staff of the EMREB whose employment is terminated by reason of redundancy or premature retirement;

(*c*) to provide relocation expenses for members of the staff of the EMREB who are transferred to Cambridge to work in the office of the Local Examinations Syndicate;

(*d*) to meet any costs which may fall on the University as a consequence of the transfer to the University of the assets and undertakings of the EMREB and the liabilities and commitments of the EMREB or its Governing Council.

Education Endowment Fund

The income of the fund derived in 1958 from funds accumulated from fees for the Certificate in Education and made available to the Faculty of Education (then the Department of Education) with the approval of the General Board, now known as the Education Endowment Fund, shall be applied, at the discretion of the Head of the Department of Education, for the benefit of students in the Faculty of Education.

Egyptology Endowment (Thompson Bequest) Fund

Grace 4 of 13 February 2013

Fund and purpose.

1. The sums bequeathed under the will of the late Sir Henry Francis Herbert Thompson towards the promotion in the University of the study of Egyptology, together with any other funds received for the purpose, shall form the Egyptology Endowment (Thompson Bequest) Fund.

Managers.

2. The Managers of the Fund shall be:

(*a*) the Chair of the Faculty Board of Human, Social, and Political Science who shall be Chair;

(*b*) the Head of the Department of Archaeology and Anthropology, or her/his deputy;

(*c*) two Officers of the Department of Archaeology and Anthropology appointed by the Faculty Board of Human, Social, and Political Science, on the nomination of the Head of the Department of Archaeology and Anthropology;

(*d*) the Head of the School of the Humanities and Social Sciences.

University Teaching Office.

3. The first charge on the income of the fund shall be the stipend, national insurance, pension contributions, and associated indirect costs of a University Teaching Office in Ancient Egyptian Language established from time to time by the General Board on the recommendation of the Managers and the Council of the School of the Humanities and Social Sciences.

4. After provision has been made in accordance with Regulation 3, the income of the Fund may be applied for the promotion of the study of Ancient Egypt through teaching or research as shall be approved by the General Board on the recommendation of the Managers.

Unexpended income.

5. Any unexpended income in a financial year shall be accumulated in accordance with the University's *Statutes and Ordinances* and may, in any subsequent year or years, be expended in accordance with Regulations 3 and 4, as the Managers shall determine, subject to the approval of the General Board.

Stat. E XLV.

Frank Edward Elmore Fund

Managers.

1. The Managers of the F. E. Elmore Fund shall be the Regius Professor of Physic (or a deputy appointed by the Regius Professor), who shall be Chair, and three persons appointed in the Michaelmas Term by the Faculty Board of Biology to serve for three years from 1 January following their appointment.

Studentships.

2. The first charge on the income of the Fund shall be the provision of such number of Elmore Medical Research Studentships as the Managers shall determine, the holders of which shall devote themselves to research in medicine or in some branch of the medical sciences at or from the University.[1] The value of any Studentship shall be determined by the Managers within a range approved from time to time by the Council. After provision has been made for payments to the Student or Students the Managers may from the income of the Fund make such grants as they consider appropriate in respect of expenses incurred in connection with the research undertaken by Students, for purposes associated with their work.

Unexpended income.

3. From unexpended income accumulated in the Fund the Managers may make grants for the support of study or research in the field of medical education or research within the University, and in particular within the School of Clinical Medicine or within the Faculty of Biology.

Engineering Endowment Fund

The moneys donated in response to an appeal made on behalf of the Department of Engineering, the details of which were announced in the *Reporter* of 23 January 1950 (p. 658), shall form a fund to be called the Engineering Endowment Fund, the income of which shall be expended, at the discretion of the Head of the Department of Engineering, for the general purposes of that Department.

[1] 'Research from the University' means research pursued elsewhere than at the University during the tenure of a Studentship.

Sixth Earl of Enniskillen Fund

1. The sum bequeathed to the University for the sole benefit of the University Library by Nancy Henderson Cole, Dowager Countess of Enniskillen, in memory of her late husband, David Lowry Cole, B.A., of Trinity College, Sixth Earl of Enniskillen, shall form a fund called the Sixth Earl of Enniskillen Fund. Title.

2. The income of the Fund shall be applied at the discretion of the Library Syndicate for the purchase of books for the University Library in any of the following subjects: history, military science, horticulture, dendrology, botany, zoology, agriculture, animal husbandry, wild animals, the natural world, outdoor sport, great paintings, great literature, great statesmen of the Western world, conservation, and finance. A book plate shall be affixed to each book so purchased recording that it was purchased from the Fund. Application of income.

3. Unexpended income shall not be added to the capital of the Fund but shall be accumulated for use as income in subsequent years. Unexpended income.

Keith Entwistle Memorial Fund

1. The sums subscribed in memory of Keith Entwistle, B.A., Vet.M.B., of Pembroke College, who died on 19 August 1959, shall form a Keith Entwistle Memorial Fund, for the encouragement of study and research in Veterinary Medicine. Fund and purpose.

2. The Fund shall be administered by five Managers, who shall be the Head of the Department of Veterinary Medicine, the Secretary of the Department of Veterinary Medicine, the Professor of Veterinary Clinical Studies, and the President and Secretary of the Cambridge University Veterinary Society. Managers.

3. The income of the Fund shall be applied to support a Keith Entwistle Memorial Lecture. The Lecturer shall be appointed each year by the Managers, and shall deliver one lecture in the Department of Veterinary Medicine. Lecture.

4. The Lecturer shall receive, from the income of the Fund, such sum as shall be determined by the Managers, within a range approved from time to time by the Council.

Erskine Chambers Prize for Company Law

1. The sum received annually from Erskine Chambers shall be applied in equal amounts as follows:

(*a*) to provide a prize called the Erskine Chambers Prize for Company Law, which shall be awarded annually by the Examiners for Part II of the Law Tripos, for the best first class performance in the Company Law paper in that examination; and Prize and how awarded.

(*b*) towards the purchase of books for the Squire Law Library.

2. If in any year the Prize is not awarded, the unexpended income for that year shall be applied for the purpose specified in paragraph 2(*b*) above. Unexpended income.

Estate Management Development Fund

By Grace 1 of 28 January 1956 the University accepted the offer made on behalf of Mr Harold Samuel, Chartered Surveyor, to provide an Estate Management Development Fund, to be held in trust for the furtherance in the University of research and study in estate management at the discretion of Managers.[1]

The terms of the Trust were specified in a letter, dated 24 October 1955, from Mr B. G. K. Allsop, Chartered Surveyor, to the Vice-Chancellor, which is reproduced below. By Grace 4 of 3 November 1962 the University suppressed the Department of Estate Management and dissolved the Board of Estate Management and established in their place a Department and a Board of Land Economy. When interpreting the terms of the Trust, references to the Department of Estate Management and to the Board of Estate Management shall therefore be deemed to be references respectively to the Department of Land Economy and the Board of Land Economy.

1. Mr Samuel is willing to enter into a covenant with the University to make seven annual payments of £35,700 (less income tax at the standard rate current at the date of payment) to provide a fund to be called the Cambridge University Estate Management Development Fund. This will produce a total of about £250,000.

[1] See Harold Samuel Studentships, p. 938.

2. The Fund shall be administered by Managers. There shall be four Managers, Mr Noël Dean, Mr E. P. Weller, Mr T. C. Thomas and myself. When I cease to be a Manager this number shall be increased to five as described below.

3. Upon the death or resignation of Mr Dean or Mr Weller they shall be succeeded respectively by the Head of the Department of Estate Management and the Chair of the Board of Estate Management, each *ex officio*, and upon the death or resignation of Mr Thomas or Mr Allsop they shall be succeeded respectively by a person nominated by the General Board of the Faculties and two persons nominated by the President of the Royal Institution of Chartered Surveyors, each appointed by the Board of Estate Management for a period of four years and to be eligible for reappointment.

4. The Managers shall regulate their own procedure, subject to the following provisions. They may pay out of the Fund their own expenses and all other expenses, costs, and charges which they deem necessary in connection with the administration of the Fund.

5. The Fund shall be held upon trust for the furtherance in the University of Cambridge of research and study in Estate Management at the discretion of the Managers. Without prejudice to the exercise of that discretion, or to the generality of the foregoing provisions, the objects for which it may be used shall include the establishment of offices and posts, scholarships, and research studentships, and the provision of buildings and equipment.

6. The Managers shall decide from time to time after consultation with the Board of Estate Management what part of the Fund shall be available as income and what part shall be invested and used as capital.

7. On the recommendation of the Board of Estate Management and subject to any approval required by the Statutes and Ordinances of the University, the Managers may from time to time authorize expenditure of income or capital from the Fund.

8. The Fund, or any part of it, may from time to time be invested in the name of the Chancellor, Masters, and Scholars of the University of Cambridge in such manner as the Managers shall think fit, and the Managers shall have power to vary or realize such investment at their discretion.

EVANS FUND

Title and purpose.

1. The capital and income of the Evans Fund, which was established under the will of the late Ivor Hugh Norman Evans, M.A., of Clare College, is held by the National Westminster Bank (hereinafter called the Trustees)[1] and is to be applied as the Advisory Committee specified in Regulation 2 shall from time to time think fit for the purpose of furthering research in anthropology and archaeology (broadly defined) in south-east Asia (preference being given to research in relation to Borneo, the Malay Peninsula, and Thailand), by making provision for:

(*a*) travelling Fellowships, which in accordance with the wishes of the benefactor shall be called Evans Fellowships;

(*b*) the cost of printing and publishing the results of the researches of students to whom Evans Fellowships have been awarded;

(*c*) meeting the cost of purchasing specimens and material for the Museum of Archaeology and Anthropology;

(*d*) the furtherance of the purpose of the Fund in any other way.

Advisory Committee.

2. In accordance with the wishes of the benefactor the Advisory Committee referred to in Regulation 1 shall consist of:

(*a*) the William Wyse Professor of Social Anthropology;

(*b*) the Disney Professor of Archaeology;

(*c*) one person appointed by the General Board;

(*d*) two persons appointed by the Faculty Board of Human, Social, and Political Science.

Members in classes (*c*) and (*d*) shall be appointed in the Michaelmas Term to serve for four years from 1 January following their appointment. The Faculty Board of Human, Social, and Political Science shall nominate one of the persons appointed by them to act as Secretary of the Committee.

Secretary.

Quorum.

3. No resolution of the Advisory Committee shall be valid unless it is approved by at least three members of the Committee at a meeting to which all the members have been summoned.

Eligibility for Fellowships.

4. A graduate of any university shall be eligible to apply for a Fellowship, provided that he or she intends to engage in research in relation to one or more areas of south-east Asia, and that the research shall contribute to the furtherance of the study of anthropology and archaeology in Cambridge.

Notice of election and applications.

5. The Advisory Committee shall give at least three months' notice of their intention to proceed to an election of Evans Fellows. The Committee shall be empowered to indicate in their Notice that for the election in a particular year preference will be given to candidates of a specified status or to

[1] Pursuant to a Deed of Retirement and Appointment of new Trustees dated 24 March 2009 the University has been appointed as sole Trustee in place of the bank.

candidates proposing schemes of travel and research relating to a specified area or topic. By a date to be announced by the Committee candidates shall send their applications to the Secretary of the Advisory Committee, together with an outline of their proposed scheme of travel and research.

6. Awards of Evans Fellowships shall be made not later than the end of Full Easter Term in each year. Awards.

7. The tenure of a Fellowship shall be for one or two years in the first instance as the Advisory Committee shall determine; candidates applying for election for an initial period of two years will be expected to be of postdoctoral status. A Fellow shall be eligible for re-election for a year at a time subject to a maximum tenure, save in exceptional circumstances, of three years in all; re-election shall be dependent on the receipt by the Advisory Committee by a specified date of a satisfactory report on the Fellow's diligence and progress in research during his or her tenure. Tenure.

8. An Evans Fellow shall engage in travel and research in accordance with a scheme approved by the Advisory Committee. The Committee may require a Fellow to publish the results of his or her research and shall be empowered to authorize a grant to meet the whole or part of the cost of printing and publication. Duties

9. The stipend of an Evans Fellow shall be such sum as may be determined by the Advisory Committee within a range approved by the Council on each occasion on which the Committee give notice of their intention to proceed to an election. Stipend.

10. The Advisory Committee shall be empowered to authorize the expenditure of capital and income of the Fund for the purchase of anthropological and archaeological specimens and other material for the Museum of Archaeology and Anthropology; and in any other way consistent with the purpose of the Fund as specified in Regulation 1. Other uses of the Fund.

11. These regulations, other than Regulation 1, and this regulation, may be amended from time to time by the University on the recommendation of the Advisory Committee with the approval of the Trustees. Alterations.

EVANS PRIZE FUND

Endowments, 1904, p. 407 **Stat. E XXX.**

1. The Evans Prize Fund shall be used to provide one or more annual prizes which shall be called the Evans Prizes. Any member of the University may be a candidate for the Prizes provided that at the time of the examination he or she (*a*) has kept five terms, (*b*) if a graduate, is of not more than ten years' standing from admission to a first degree, whether of this or another university; and provided also that no previous winner of a Prize shall again be eligible as a candidate. Who may compete.

2. The value of a Prize shall be such sum not exceeding the available income of the Fund as may be determined from time to time by the Faculty Board of Divinity with the approval of the Council.

3. The examination shall consist of two papers on selected Greek and Latin ecclesiastical writings earlier than AD 461. The papers shall contain passages for translation and interpretation, together with questions on the history of early Christian literature and doctrine in connection with the writings selected and the period to which they belong. Passages from other Greek and Latin ecclesiastical writings also may be set for translation and interpretation. Examination.

4. The examination shall be held after the division and before the end of the Michaelmas Term, on a day of which notice shall be given by the Board of Examinations. The day shall not be any of the days on which an examination for another Divinity Prize or Scholarship is held.

5. The names of candidates shall on or before 20 October next preceding the examination be sent by their Tutors to the Registrary, who shall forthwith communicate them to the Examiners. Names to Registrary.

6. The Faculty Board of Divinity shall select in each year the special ecclesiastical writings, and notice shall be given of the writings so selected before the end of the Michaelmas Term of the year preceding the examination. Subjects.

7. There shall be two Examiners appointed by the General Board on the nomination of the Faculty Board of Divinity. One shall be appointed in each year before the end of the Easter Term to hold office for the two following academical years. Each of the Examiners shall receive each year from the Fund such sum as shall be determined by the Faculty Board of Divinity within a range approved from time to time by the Council unless there be no candidate for the Prizes. All the other expenses of the examination shall likewise be paid out of the Fund. Examiners.

Eric Evans Fund

Fund. **1.** The benefaction received by the University from the Eric Evans Memorial Trust, established in memory of the late Eric Evans, B.A., of St Catharine's College, shall form a fund called the Eric Evans Fund, the income of which shall be used to provide assistance to members of the University, by means of scholarships, studentships, or grants, or in other ways, in connection with their participation in sport or physical recreation.

Managers. **2.** The Fund shall be administered by three Managers who shall be the Director of Physical Education and two other persons appointed by the Sports Syndicate in the Michaelmas Term to serve for three years from 1 January following their appointment.

Applications. **3.** A Notice inviting applications for assistance from the Fund shall be published from time to time at the discretion of the Managers.

Ulick Richardson Evans Research Fund

Title and purpose. **1.** The sum which, in accordance with the terms of the will of the late Ulick Richardson Evans, Sc.D., of King's College, sometime Reader in the Science of Metallic Corrosion, was received by the University from his Executors shall form a fund, to be called the Ulick Richardson Evans Research Fund, for the support of research in the University into metallic corrosion.

Application of income. **2.** The income of the Fund shall be applied as the Head of the Department of Materials Science and Metallurgy shall from time to time decide to further teaching and research in the study and the prevention of corrosion and oxidation of metals and in related fields, by one or more of the following means:

(*a*) establishing and maintaining research appointments,
(*b*) establishing a studentship,
(*c*) maintaining Graduate Students or research workers in the Department of Materials Science and Metallurgy,
(*d*) purchasing apparatus and equipment,

or by any other means consistent with the object of the Fund.

Evolution Education Trust Darwin Correspondence Fund

Grace 1 of 16 March 2011

Title. **1.** The sums received from the Evolution Education Trust shall form a fund known as the Evolution Education Trust Darwin Correspondence Fund.

Purpose. **2.** The income and capital of the Fund shall be used to support the University Library's Darwin Correspondence Project. Should the Darwin Correspondence Project cease to exist, the income and capital of the Fund shall be used to support activities related to the University Library's Darwin Collections as recommended by the Managers and approved by the Library Syndicate, following consultation with the Donor.

Managers. **3.** The Managers of the Fund shall be the University Librarian, the Head of the Department of History and Philosophy of Science, and two persons appointed by the Library Syndicate, one following a nomination by the Evolution Education Trust, for a period of five years at a time.

Unexpended income. **4.** Any unexpended income in any financial year may, at the discretion of the Managers, be accumulated and added to the capital of the Fund or be held as an income reserve and expended in any one or more subsequent years in accordance with Regulation 2 above.

ExxonMobil Chemical Engineering Prize

Prize. **1.** The sum made available annually by the Exxon Mobil Corporation shall be used to provide a prize in Chemical Engineering.

How awarded. **2.** The Prize shall be awarded annually by the Examiners for Part IIA of the Chemical Engineering Tripos to the candidate who has shown the greatest distinction in that examination.

Fairhaven Fund

Title. **1.** The sum of £30,000 given to the University by Lord Fairhaven to mark the centenary of the opening of the original Fitzwilliam Museum building shall form a fund to be called the Fairhaven Fund.

2. The income of the Fund shall be applied for the benefit of the Fitzwilliam Museum at the discretion of the Fitzwilliam Museum Syndicate for the purpose of purchasing paintings and drawings of the British School of landscape painting, particularly of the Norwich School. Purpose.

3. So far as is practicable the full income of the Fund shall be spent each year. Full income to be spent.

4. No living artist's work shall be purchased. Limitation.

ALISON FAIRLIE PRIZE IN FRENCH

1. The sums given to the University by a former student of Professor Alison Fairlie, formerly Professor of French and Fellow of Girton College, shall form a fund, the income of which shall be used to provide a prize in her memory called the Alison Fairlie Prize in French. Title and purpose.

2. The Prize shall be awarded annually by the Examiners in French for Part IA of the Modern and Medieval Languages Tripos for an outstanding performance in the examination for that subject. How awarded.

3. If in any year the Prize is not awarded, the income for that year shall be added to the capital of the Fund. If not awarded.

FALCON CHAMBERS PRIZE FOR LAND LAW

1. The sum made available annually by Falcon Chambers shall be used to provide a prize called the Falcon Chambers Prize for Land Law. Title.

2. The Prize shall be awarded by the Examiners for Part IB of the Law Tripos to the candidate who has shown the greatest distinction in the subject Land Law in that examination. How awarded.

ELLEN FARNELL FUND

Grace 6 of 18 January 2012

The sums derived from the will of Miss I. M. Silver shall form a fund to be called the Ellen Farnell Fund. The income derived from the Fund shall be applied to support medical research, at the discretion of the Regius Professor of Physic, in the following ways: Title and purpose.

(i) to support a Fellowship either full or part time in the Clinical School, which Fellowship shall bear the name of Ellen Farnell;

(ii) to provide a bed in Addenbrooke's Hospital, Cambridge, or in some other Hospital in which beds are under the authority of the University, for the study and investigation of some special disease;

(iii) to purchase necessary materials or apparatus for research.

The name of Ellen Farnell shall be attached to any bed, material, or apparatus supported by the Fund.

MARTIN C. FAULKES BELL FUND

Grace 1 of 28 January 2009

1. The sum of £350,000 received from Dr Martin C. Faulkes shall form a fund called the Martin C. Faulkes Bell Fund. Title.

2. The Fund shall be administered by three Managers, who shall comprise: Managers.

(*a*) The Vice-Chancellor (or a duly appointed deputy) who shall be Chair;

(*b*) The University Bellringer;

(*c*) one person nominated by the Parish of Great St Mary's.

3. The first charge on the capital and the income of the Bell Fund shall be a payment to the Parish of Great St Mary's Church to cover the costs of casting and installing a new ring of bells and the rehanging of existing bells (together the 'Bells') in Great St Mary's, the University Church, to commemorate the 800th anniversary of the University, together with such additional costs relating to or consequent upon such hanging or rehanging of the Bells as are agreed between the University and Dr Faulkes. Great St Mary's Church Bells.

4. After provision has been made in accordance with Regulation 3, the remaining capital and income of the Fund shall be used to provide grants towards the maintenance of the Bells from time to time as the Managers shall determine. Maintenance of the Bells.

John Fawcett Prize

Fund and purpose.

1. The sums subscribed in memory of Frederick John Fawcett, M.A., MRCP, FRCPath, Regional Postgraduate Dean and Consultant Pathologist, Peterborough District Hospital, shall form a fund called the John Fawcett Fund, the income of which shall be used to provide a prize called the John Fawcett Prize.

Prize: how awarded.

2. The Prize shall be awarded in the Michaelmas Term each year by the Regius Professor of Physic and the Director of Medical Education to a student pursuing clinical study in the University who has taken Part I of the Final M.B. Examination and who is judged by them to have given best evidence in his or her clinical work of qualities of personal understanding and the ability to communicate with patients and colleagues. In reaching their decision the Awarders shall take into account reports on the candidates received from clinical teachers in Cambridge and elsewhere.

Value.

3. The value of the Prize shall be the annual income of the Fund.

Unexpended income.

4. If in any year the Prize is not awarded, the unexpended income shall be added to the capital of the Fund.

E. G. Fearnsides Scholarship

Name and purpose.

1. This Scholarship, founded and endowed by the members of the Fearnsides family in memory of E. G. Fearnsides, M.A. (Trinity Hall), M.D., FRCP, who was drowned at Four Mile Bridge, Anglesey, on 26 June 1919, shall be called the E. G. Fearnsides Research Scholarship and shall be devoted to the encouragement of original clinical research on the organic diseases of the nervous system.

Management.

2. The administration of the Fund shall be entrusted to the Faculty Board of Clinical Medicine in consultation with the Faculty Board of Veterinary Medicine.

Delegation of functions.

3. The Faculty Board may delegate all or any of their functions concerning the Scholarship to a Committee not necessarily consisting wholly of members of the Board.

Postgraduate Medical Scholarship.

4. The Scholarship shall be called the E. G. Fearnsides Postgraduate Medical Scholarship, the holder of which shall undertake clinical research on the organic diseases of the nervous system. The value of the Scholarship may be determined by the Managers, within a range approved from time to time by the Council, after they have taken account of any other financial resources that may be available to the Student.

Qualifications of candidates.

5. The Faculty Board may take such steps as they may think fit to ascertain the qualifications of the candidates. Preference shall be given to graduates in Medicine or Veterinary Medicine.

Tenure.

6. The Scholarship shall be tenable for one, two, or three years as the Faculty Board shall in each case determine.

Conditions of research.

7. The conditions under which research is to be conducted and the place or places in which it is to be carried on shall be determined by the Faculty Board.

Notice of election.

8. Not less than one month's notice shall be given of an election.

Suspension of election.

9. If, after notice of a vacancy, there shall be, in the opinion of the Faculty Board, no suitable candidate for the Scholarship, it shall be lawful for the Faculty Board to suspend the election for a year, and if at the expiration of such time there shall, after notice of the vacancy given, be no suitable candidate as aforesaid, the election may again be suspended in the same way, and so until in the opinion of the Faculty Board there shall be a suitable candidate for the Scholarship.

Grants.

10. In any year, whether or not a Scholarship is awarded, the Managers may use such part of the available income as they shall determine to make grants to members of the University engaged in clinical research on the organic diseases of the nervous system towards meeting the cost of equipment and other expenses including travel expenses incurred by them in the course of their research.

11. These regulations, except Regulation 1, shall be subject to alteration by Grace, but in the lifetime of William G. Fearnsides only after consultation with him and so always that the principal object of the Fund, namely, the encouragement of clinical research on the organic diseases of the nervous system, may be attained.

Mary Feather Fund

Title and purpose.

1. The money received from the bequest of the late Miss Mary Feather shall form a fund called the Mary Feather Fund for the preservation of University buildings.

2. The income of the Fund shall be applied to the maintenance of the Senate-House.

DR GILLIAN FENN MEMORIAL FUND

1. The Fund given to the University by the Wolfson Foundation in memory of Dr Gillian Fenn, of Clare Hall, Senior Research Associate in the Faculty of Clinical Medicine, shall constitute a fund called the Dr Gillian Fenn Memorial Fund, which shall be used to fund a biennial lecture. Title and purpose.

2. The trustees of the Fund shall be the Regius Professor of Physic, the Director of Medical Education in the Clinical School, and the Secretary of the School of Clinical Medicine. Trustees.

FINGLAND FUND

The income of the Fund derived from the benefaction by Dr William Fingland, accepted by the University in 1958 and now known as the Fingland Fund, shall be applied at the discretion of the Library Syndicate to support the University Archives.

FITZPATRICK FUND

1. The bequest of £2,000 from Mrs Annie Rosa Fitzpatrick in memory of her husband, Dr T. C. Fitzpatrick, formerly President of Queens' College and University Lecturer in Physics, shall form a fund called the Fitzpatrick Fund. Title.

2. The income of the Fund shall be applied as the Cavendish Professor of Physics may from time to time decide to make grants to be called Fitzpatrick Grants for the purposes of Purposes.

(*a*) supplementing the emoluments which a Graduate Student in the Department of Physics is receiving from a Studentship, Scholarship, or other source but which the Professor considers to be inadequate,

(*b*) enabling a Graduate Student in the Department of Physics to continue research at the end of the period for which he or she was originally awarded an emolument if, in the opinion of the Professor, the particular project merits such support,

(*c*) defraying the expenses of Graduate Students in the Department of Physics when attending conferences or visiting or working in laboratories outside Cambridge.

FITZWILLIAM MUSEUM ENDOWMENT FUND

The income of the Fitzwilliam Museum Endowment Fund shall be used for the benefit of the Fitzwilliam Museum.

FORBES FUND

Grace 1 of 19 May 2010

1. The gift of £2m to the University from Dr Colin Forbes shall form a fund called the Forbes Fund. Title.

2. The capital and income of the Fund shall be applied for such purposes in the Sedgwick Museum of Earth Sciences as the Director and the Curators of the Museum and the Woodwardian Professor of Geology jointly shall from time to time decide. Purpose.

3. The Director of the Museum shall make an Annual Report on the outgoings of the Fund to the Faculty Board of Earth Sciences and Geography. Annual Report.

MAX FORBES FUND

1. The sum of £6,000 given to the University by Mrs E. M. Forbes in memory of her husband Lachlan Maxwell Forbes, of King's College, shall form a fund called the Max Forbes Fund. Title.

2. The income of the Fund shall be used, at the discretion of the Kettle's Yard Committee, for the promotion of concerts given by young musicians at Kettle's Yard. Purpose.

Ford of Britain Trust Fund

Title and purpose.

1. The benefaction of the Trustees of the Ford of Britain Trust shall form a fund to be called the Ford of Britain Trust Fund, which shall be used for the benefit of the Department of Engineering.

2. The income of the Fund shall be used at the discretion of the Degree Committee for the Faculty of Engineering, and subject to such conditions as they may think fit, for making grants to Graduate Students in the Department of Engineering.

Publication of awards.

3. The names of persons to whom grants have been awarded, but not the amounts of the grants, shall be published each year. Grants shall be payable in the manner determined by the Degree Committee for the Faculty of Engineering.

Ford Physiology Fund

Title and purpose.

1. The gift of $240,000 from the Ford Foundation shall form a fund called the Ford Physiology Fund, the income of which shall be applied to further the study and dissemination of knowledge of reproduction, especially those aspects that relate to the regulation of human fertility, by meeting the cost of one or more University offices in the Department of Physiology, Development, and Neuroscience.

Establishment of offices.

2. The University offices referred to in Regulation 1 shall be established by the General Board, after consultation with the Faculty Board of Biology. The whole cost of each office so established shall be met from the Ford Physiology Fund.

Surplus income.

3. After provision has been made in accordance with Regulations 1 and 2, any surplus income shall be applied as the General Board, on the recommendation of the Faculty Board of Biology, shall from time to time decide, to meet expenses associated with any office established under those regulations.

Foreign Travel Fund

Title.

1. The sum bequeathed to the University by the late George Walter Grabham, M.A., of St John's College, shall form the nucleus of a fund called the Foreign Travel Fund which shall be administered by the Council.

Purpose.

2. The income of the Fund shall be used to assist resident members of the Senate who have attained the age of fifty years to travel abroad with a view to extending their knowledge in any branch of learning with which their teaching or research is concerned.

Applications.

3. A Notice inviting applications for grants from the Fund shall be published from time to time at the discretion of the Council. Applications shall be submitted to the Registrary and shall be accompanied by a short statement of the nature and purpose of the travel proposed or undertaken.

Fortes Fund

Title.

1. The sums received from the publication of the *Cambridge Papers in Social Anthropology* shall constitute a fund called the Fortes Fund.

Managers.

2. The Managers of the Fund shall be the William Wyse Professor of Social Anthropology *ex officio* and one University officer in the Department of Archaeology and Anthropology appointed by the Faculty Board of Human, Social, and Political Science in the Michaelmas Term to serve for four years from 1 January next following, provided that if the person appointed by the Faculty Board ceases to be a University officer he or she shall not thereby cease to be a Manager.

Purpose.

3. The income of the Fund shall be used to make grants towards the expenses of publications in Social Anthropology by members of the University. Preference shall be given to applicants under the age of forty and to those with children under the age of ten years.

Foster Prize Fund

Title and purpose.

1. The sum of £6,570 given to the University by an anonymous donor, shall form a fund to be called the Foster Prize Fund, which shall be used for the award of two prizes annually to the persons who are judged to have given the best lectures to the Foster Club or successor organization in an academical year. One prize will be awarded for the best lecture given in the Michaelmas Term, and one for the best lecture given in the Lent Term.

2. The Prize shall be awarded by the Head of the Department of Physiology, Development, and Neuroscience on the recommendation of the Graduate Students and research and academic staff within the Department, provided that there is a lecture of sufficient merit. How awarded.

3. Any Graduate Student or postdoctoral Research Assistant or postdoctoral Research Associate in the Department shall be eligible for the Prize, provided that no previous winner may again be eligible as a candidate. Who are eligible.

4. The value of the Prizes shall be £250 or such larger sum as shall be determined by the Head of the Department within a range approved from time to time by the Council. Value.

5. The capital and the income of the Fund shall be applied to the award of the Prize.

MICHAEL FOSTER STUDENTSHIP IN PHYSIOLOGY

1. The sums given to the University by Jamieson Boyd Hurry, M.D., of St John's College, for the encouragement of research in Physiology shall form a fund called the Michael Foster Studentship Fund, the income of which shall be applied in the first instance to the maintenance of a studentship called the Michael Foster Studentship in Physiology. Name and object.

2. The Electors shall be the Professor of Physiology and two other members of the Regent House appointed in the Michaelmas Term, one by the Council and one by the Faculty Board of Biology, to serve for four years from 1 January following their appointment. Electors.

3. The Electors shall give not less than three months' notice of their intention to proceed to an election. Notice of election.

4. The Studentship shall be open to any person who is or is about to be registered as a Graduate Student in the University. Who are eligible.

5. The Studentship shall be tenable for one year. A Student shall be eligible for re-election on not more than two occasions. Tenure.

6. The value of the Studentship shall be such sum not exceeding the available income of the Fund as the Electors may determine in each case, after taking account of any other financial resources available to the Student. Value.

7. Students shall undertake research in the Department of Physiology, Development, and Neuroscience unless authorized by the Electors to work elsewhere. Conditions.

8. Any unexpended income accumulated in the Fund shall be applied at the discretion of the Electors for the encouragement of research in Physiology, either by the award of one or more additional Studentships or in such other ways as they may determine. Unexpended income.

9. These regulations, except Regulation 1, shall be subject to alteration by Grace, but so always that the principal object of the Fund, namely the encouragement of research in Physiology, shall be maintained.

T. R. C. FOX FUND

1. The moneys subscribed by friends and former students of the late T. R. C. Fox, Fellow of King's College and first Shell Professor of Chemical Engineering, shall form a fund called the T. R. C. Fox Fund, which shall be used to provide a T. R. C. Fox Prize. Title and purpose.

2. The value of the Prize shall be the annual income of the Fund. Value.

3. The Prize shall be awarded annually by the Examiners for Part IIB of the Chemical Engineering Tripos to the candidate who has shown the greatest distinction in the examination for that Part of the Tripos, provided that he or she attains the standard of the first class. How awarded.

FRAZER LECTURESHIP IN SOCIAL ANTHROPOLOGY

1. A Frazer Lectureship in Social Anthropology shall be founded, and the annual income of the Fund shall be assigned for a lecture to be delivered in rotation in the Universities of Oxford, Cambridge, Glasgow, and Liverpool. Name.

2. The administration of the Fund shall be placed in the hands of the Finance Committee of the Council; and in each academical year the Committee shall pay over the annual income to the university to which the Lectureship falls in that year. Administration.

Appointment. **3.** When the lecture falls to be delivered at Cambridge, the Lecturer shall be appointed by the Faculty Board of Human, Social, and Political Science.

Sir Bartle Frere's Memorial Fund

Name. **1.** The investments from time to time representing the amount paid over to the University by the Trustees of Sir Bartle Frere's Memorial Fund shall constitute a trust fund called the Bartle Frere Memorial Fund.

Purpose. **2.** The income of the Fund shall be used to promote study or research in any branch of knowledge relating to any part of the Commonwealth of Nations except the United Kingdom and countries in the Indian sub-continent.

Exhibitions. **3.** The Managers of the Fund shall be the Managers of the Mary Euphrasia Mosley Fund. In each year the Managers shall award one or more Bartle Frere Exhibitions before the end of the Easter Term if suitable candidates present themselves.

Tenure. **4.** The Exhibitions shall normally be tenable for one year, but may be prolonged for a second year at the discretion of the Managers. They shall be tenable with other emoluments.

Condition of tenure. **5.** A successful candidate, if not already a member of the University, must become such before the end of the first term of the ensuing academical year.

Applications. **6.** Candidates must submit their applications to the Registrary by a date specified by the Registrary with a statement of the course of study or research that they propose and with evidence of their qualifications.

Payments. **7.** The emolument of an Exhibition awarded to a member of the University shall be paid on the publication of the Notice of the award. If an Exhibition is awarded to a person who is not a member of the University, the emolument shall not be paid until the Exhibitioner has sent evidence that Regulation 5 has been satisfied.

Report of investigations. **8.** Each Exhibitioner shall send to the Registrary a short report of his or her investigations as soon as practicable after the year of tenure is ended, and in any publication of such investigations during this year shall make due acknowledgement of the Exhibition.

Hans Gadow Memorial Fund

Name and purpose. **1.** The income derived from Mrs C. M. Gadow's bequest to the University shall form a fund to be called the Hans Gadow Memorial Fund, the purpose of which shall be the promotion and advancement of the study of Vertebrate Zoology.

Managers. **2.** The Fund shall be administered by three Managers who shall be the Head of the Department of Zoology and two other persons appointed by the Faculty Board of Biology in the Michaelmas Term to serve for five years from 1 January following their appointment.

Application. **3.** The Fund shall be applied at the discretion of the Managers:

(*a*) to the payment of the fee and expenses of a lecturer to be called the Hans Gadow Lecturer,

(*b*) to the provision of payments in connection with the preservation or the study of the vertebrate fauna of Great Britain,

(*c*) to the provision of payments towards the cost of small biological expeditions approved by the Faculty Board of Biology,

(*d*) to such other purposes connected with the study of Vertebrate Zoology as may be approved from time to time by the Faculty Board of Biology.

Lecturer. **4.** The Hans Gadow Lecturer shall be appointed by the Managers to hold office for one year, but a Lecturer shall not necessarily be appointed every year. The Lecturer shall be required to give one or more lectures on a subject, approved by the Managers, on some aspect of Vertebrate Zoology. The lectures shall be called the Hans Gadow Memorial Lectures. The Managers may make a grant from the Fund towards the cost of publishing the lectures.

Isbel Fletcher Garden Fund and Scholarship

Title and purpose. **1.** The bequest to the University by the late Mrs Isbel Fletcher Garden shall form a fund to be called the Isbel Fletcher Garden Fund. The income of the Fund shall be used to provide a Scholarship, which shall be called the Isbel Fletcher Garden Scholarship, for the promotion of study or research in Archaeology or Astronomy.

2. The Fund shall be administered by four Managers who shall be: Managers.

(*a*) the Head of the Department of Archaeology and Anthropology or her or his deputy;

(*b*) the Director of the Institute of Astronomy;

(*c*) one person appointed by the Faculty Board of Human, Social, and Political Science;

(*d*) one person appointed by the Faculty Board of Physics and Chemistry.

Managers in classes (*c*) and (*d*) shall serve for three years from 1 October following their appointment.

How awarded. **3.** The Scholarship shall be awarded from time to time in Archaeology and Astronomy alternately, if there is a candidate of sufficient merit.

Applications. **4.** The Managers shall give at least six months' notice of their intention to proceed to an election. In such a notice they shall indicate the subject of the award, and the date by which, and the manner in which, applications are to be submitted.

5. If, after the publication of such a notice, there is no candidate of sufficient merit in the nominated subject, the Managers may at their discretion make arrangements for the award of the Scholarship in the other subject.

Who are eligible. **6.** The Scholarship shall be open to any person who is or is about to be registered as a Graduate Student in the University.

Tenure. **7.** The Scholarship shall be tenable for one, two, or three years in the first instance as the Managers shall determine; a Scholar shall be eligible for re-election, provided that the tenure of the Scholarship shall not normally exceed three years in total.

Stipend of Scholar. **8.** The annual stipend of a Scholar shall be such sum not exceeding the available income of the Fund as may be determined by the Managers, within a range approved from time to time by the Council, after they have taken account of any other financial resources that may be available to the Scholar.

Unexpended income. **9.** Any unexpended income may be either accumulated for use as income in subsequent years, or applied at the discretion of the Managers to make grants to the Scholar, during the tenure of his or her Scholarship, to meet additional costs arising from his or her course, including the cost of additional training, conferences, fieldwork, or other courses.

JOHN STANLEY GARDINER STUDENTSHIPS

Title and purpose. **1.** The sum bequeathed to the University by Professor John Stanley Gardiner shall constitute a fund called the John Stanley Gardiner Fund, the income of which shall be used for the furtherance of research in Zoology by the endowment of Studentships to be called John Stanley Gardiner Studentships.

Managers. **2.** The administration of the Fund shall be entrusted to three Managers in conjunction with the Faculty Board of Biology, which Faculty Board is hereinafter called the Board. The Managers, who may or may not be members of the Board, shall be appointed by the Board in the Michaelmas Term to serve for five years from 1 January following their appointment. All the powers of the Managers may be exercised by a majority of those present at a meeting, provided that two Managers at least be present.

Eligibility. **3.** The Studentships shall be open to any British subject or Commonwealth citizen who is ordinarily resident outside Europe but within the Commonwealth of Nations.

Method of election. **4.** Elections to Studentships shall be made in the manner provided for by the regulations for the Balfour Studentship, and Regulations 5–10 for that Studentship shall be applicable to them.

Duties of the Student. **5.** A Student who is not a member of the University must become such before the end of the term next after the election and must remain such during his or her tenure.

6. During the tenure of a Studentship a Student shall normally be required to undertake full-time study and research, but it shall be within the powers of the Managers to substitute for these requirements the obligation of a Student to undertake full-time study and training for research.

7. If the Managers shall be of opinion that through any cause a Student is not fulfilling and is not likely to fulfil the objects of the Studentship they shall report accordingly to the Board, and the Board may, if they see fit, remove such Student from the Studentship.

8. The Student shall study in the Department of Zoology unless otherwise authorized by the Managers. The Managers shall take such steps as they think necessary to satisfy themselves as to the diligence and progress of the Student and may require from the Student any reports or other information on the subject of his or her studies which they may think desirable.

Tenure.

9. The initial tenure of a Studentship shall be determined by the Managers but shall not exceed three years. A Student whose work shall have been of such exceptional promise that it would, in the opinion of the Managers and of the Board, be clearly in the interest of zoological research that he or she should continue to hold the Studentship for a second term of three years or for a part of such term, may be re-elected.

Value.

10. The value of a Studentship shall be the annual or accumulated income derived from the capital of the Fund or such smaller sum as may be determined by the Managers and paid to the Student in advance by equal quarterly instalments.

Robert Gardiner Memorial Scholarships

Two Funds.

1. The sums bequeathed to the University by Miss Susan Gardiner and Miss Margaret Gardiner shall be known as the Mary, Susan, and Margaret Gardiner Benefaction in memory of their brother Robert, and shall form two separate funds called the Susan Gardiner Fund and the Margaret Gardiner Fund.

Purpose.

2. The income of the benefaction shall be applied in assisting or enabling graduates or undergraduates of Trinity College, Dublin, or other Irish universities to proceed to the University of Cambridge for the purpose of undergraduate or postgraduate study by maintaining one or more scholarships to be called Robert Gardiner Memorial Scholarships.

Who are eligible.

3. A member of any Irish university shall be eligible for a Scholarship, but in the event of two or more candidates showing equal merit, the Electors shall have regard to the wishes of the foundresses that preference shall be given to gifted students of literature, to undergraduates or graduates of Trinity College, Dublin, and to the descendants of Irish landed proprietors.

Electors.

4. The Electors shall be the Vice-Chancellor and four members of the Senate appointed in the Michaelmas Term, two by the Council and two by the General Board, to serve for four years from 1 January following their appointment.

Notice of election.

5. If it is intended to make an election in any year, the Electors shall, not later than 30 November in the preceding year, give public notice of the date by which applications for a Scholarship shall be made. They shall at the same time take such steps as they think fit to inform the Provost, the Vice-Chancellor, or the President, as the case may be, of all Irish universities and university colleges, and invite them to nominate candidates.

Nomination of candidates.

6. A candidate must be nominated by the authorities of the university or university college of which he or she is a member. Each candidate shall submit to the Secretary of the Board of Graduate Studies, so as to arrive by the date of which notice has been given by the Electors in accordance with Regulation 5, evidence of character and qualifications together with a statement of his or her school and university record and some account of the course of study or research which he or she intends to pursue at Cambridge if elected. A candidate who wishes to claim preference on account of being descended from an Irish landed proprietor shall submit such evidence as he or she thinks fit in support of such claim.

Duties of Scholar.

7. Every Scholar who is not a member of the University shall become such before the end of the term next after the election unless allowed by the Electors to defer admission to the University till a later date, and shall remain a member of the University during tenure of the Scholarship.

8. Every Scholar shall be required to become a candidate for one of the Bachelor's Degrees specified in Statute B II 1(*a*), or for the degree of Master of Law, or for a Diploma, or to undertake whole-time study and training for research. No Scholar shall systematically follow any business or profession or engage in any educational or other work which in the opinion of the Electors would interfere in any way with his or her course of study.

Tenure.

9. A Scholarship shall be tenable for one year or two years or three years, as the Electors shall in each case determine.

Value.

10. The value of each Scholarship shall be determined by the Electors within a range approved from time to time by the Council.

Payments.

11. The Scholars shall be paid quarterly, the payment for each quarter being made in advance, but the Electors may withhold payment at any time if they are not satisfied with the diligence or progress of a Scholar.

12. A Robert Gardiner Memorial Scholarship shall not without the permission of the Electors be held with any other Scholarship or Studentship in the University, with any office in the University, or with a stipendiary Fellowship of a College. Restriction.

OLIVER GATTY FUND

1. The money given to the University in memory of Oliver Gatty, M.A., of St John's College, by his relatives and friends shall form a fund to be called the Oliver Gatty Fund, the income of which shall be used to support an Oliver Gatty Studentship in the fields of Biophysical and Colloid Science. Name and purpose.

2. The Student shall undertake whole-time study and training for research in the fields of Biophysical and Colloid Science.

3. The Electors shall be the Head of the Department of Biochemistry and the Director of the Wellcome/Cancer Research UK Gurdon Institute for the time being, and two persons appointed by the Council in the Michaelmas Term to serve for three years from 1 January following their appointment, one on the nomination of the Council of the School of the Biological Sciences and one on the nomination of the Council of the School of the Physical Sciences. Electors.

4. The Studentship shall be held in a Department determined by the Electors after satisfying themselves that the necessary facilities are available for the Student's work. Department.

5. The Studentship shall be open to graduates of all universities, preference being given to graduates of universities outside Great Britain. Who are eligible.

6. The Electors shall give not less than three months' notice of their intention to proceed to an election, and the election shall be made not later than 31 July. Notice of election.

7. The Electors shall take such steps as they may think fit to assess the candidates' capacities for training for research in the field of the Studentship.

8. The Studentship shall be tenable for one, two, three or four years, as determined by the Electors; a student elected for a shorter period may have her or his studentship extended provided that the total tenure of the Studentship shall not exceed four years. Tenure.

9. The Student, if not a member of the University, must become such as soon as practicable after his or her election.

10. The emolument of the Studentship shall be such sum not exceeding the available income of the Fund, within a range approved from time to time by the Council, as the Electors may determine after taking account of the Student's financial circumstances. The emolument shall be paid in such instalments as shall be determined by the Electors, provided that the Electors may withhold payment of any instalment if they are not satisfied that the Student is pursuing his or her course of study with sufficient diligence. Value.

11. Any unexpended income accumulated in the Fund may be used at the discretion of the Electors to assist the Student to meet travelling expenses or any other special expenses in connection with his or her research that may be approved by the Electors. Unexpended income.

GEDGE PRIZE

Endowments, 1904, p. 429

1. The Prize shall be called the Gedge Prize. It shall be offered for competition in every second year, and shall consist of the interest on the capital sum (£1,000) for the two years next preceding. How often awarded.

2. The Prize shall be awarded for the best original observations in Physiology or in any branch thereof, that is to say, in Histology, Physiological Chemistry, or Physiological Physics, the word Physiology being used in a wide sense. The observations must, however, be limited to research which has been conducted by the candidate since the commencement of his or her first term of residence. Subject.

3. A candidate for the Prize (who need not necessarily be a graduate of the University) shall be: Who may be candidates.

either (*a*) a member of the University who during six terms subsequent to the beginning of the term of his or her matriculation has studied in the University laboratories or attended University lectures and who at the time of the award of the Prize will be of not less than five years' and not more than seven years' standing from matriculation;

or (*b*) a Graduate Student who at the time of the award of the Prize will have been registered as a Graduate Student for not more than five years.

4. The Faculty Board of Biology shall cause a Notice of the conditions of the award to be inserted Conditions to be published in *Reporter*.

in the *Reporter* in the course of the Michaelmas Term next preceding that in which the Prize is to be awarded.

Examiners. **5.** The Examiners shall be the Professor of Physiology, and two persons nominated by the Faculty Board of Biology and appointed by the General Board. The persons so nominated shall be or shall have been engaged in the University in the teaching of Physiology or of any branch thereof. The Examiners shall be appointed before the end of the month of May previous to the term in which the Prize is to be awarded. Each of the Examiners nominated by the Faculty Board of Biology shall receive from the Chest, except in cases where no exercise is sent in, such amount as may be determined by the Faculty Board within a range approved from time to time by the Council. The Examiners shall have power to nominate an Assessor or Assessors (not exceeding three in number) for appointment by the General Board. Each Assessor so appointed shall receive from the Chest such sum as may be determined by the Faculty Board within a range approved from time to time by the Council. The number of Assessors so appointed shall not be more than the number of essays expected.

Assessors.

When essays must be sent in. **6.** Every candidate shall notify the subject of his or her essay to the Secretary of the Faculty Board of Biology before 1 May in the Easter Term preceding the award, and shall send the essay to the Registrary by 7 September. The Faculty Board of Biology shall decide whether the subject proposed falls within the scope of Regulation 2.

Essay may be presented as a lecture. **7.** The Examiners may require every candidate to deliver his or her essay in the form of a lecture and to demonstrate any experiments and researches mentioned therein.

When awarded. **8.** The Prize shall be awarded by the Examiners in the month of October of each year of which the number is even.

Report by Examiners to Faculty Board. **9.** The Examiners shall report to the Faculty Board of Biology whether any essay has been sent in and what, if any, award has been made. The Chair of the Faculty Board shall thereupon announce the decision of the Examiners.

If Prize not awarded. **10.** If in any year the Prize is not awarded, the interest on the capital sum for the two years next preceding shall be paid to the account of the Museum of Zoology.

Gender Studies Fund

Grace 1 of 12 March 2008; amended by Grace 6 of 30 July 2014

Fund. **1.** The sum of £1.1m received by the University to support teaching and research in Gender Studies, together with other sums received for the same purpose, shall form a fund called the Gender Studies Fund.

Committee of Management. **2.** The administration of the Fund shall be under the control of a Committee of Management consisting of:

(*a*) one person appointed by each of the Schools of Arts and Humanities, the Biological Sciences, Clinical Medicine, the Humanities and Social Sciences, the Physical Sciences, and Technology;

(*b*) the Head of the Department of Politics and International Studies;

(*c*) the Frankopan Director of the University of Cambridge Centre for Gender Studies (University Teaching Officer in Gender Studies);

(*d*) the Deputy Director of the University of Cambridge Centre for Gender Studies (University Teaching Officer in Gender Studies);

(*e*) one person who is not a resident member of the University appointed by the General Board to represent the national or international gender studies community;

(*f*) not more than two members co-opted by the Committee, provided that it shall not be obligatory for the Committee to co-opt any person or persons.

3. Members in classes (*a*) and (*e*) shall be appointed in the Michaelmas Term to serve for three years from 1 January following their appointment. Members in class (*f*) shall serve until 31 December of the year in which they are co-opted or of the year next following, as the Committee shall determine at the time of their co-optation.

4. The Committee shall elect one of their members other than the Director or Deputy Director of the Centre to be their Chair and to serve for three years from 1 January following the election.

5. The Committee shall meet at least three times a year.

University Lecturer. **6.** The first charge on the Fund shall be the stipend, national insurance, pension contributions, and associated indirect costs payable by the University in respect of the University Lecturer in Gender

Studies (Frankopan Director of the Cambridge Centre for Gender Studies) in the Department of Politics and International Studies.

7. Any unexpended income in a financial year, and such portion of the capital of the Fund as shall be determined by the Committee of Management, shall be applied, in any manner that the Committee shall determine, to support the study and teaching of Gender Studies in the University and to co-operate with outside bodies in the encouragement of gender research more generally. Unexpended income.

GENZYME FUND FOR CLINICAL NEUROSCIENCES

1. The sums to be received from the Board of Cambridge in America, representing a donation from the Genzyme Corporation, to support the study of Neuroimmunology shall form a fund to be called the Genzyme Fund for Clinical Neurosciences. Name and purpose.

2. The Managers of the Fund shall be: Managers.

(*a*) the Head of the Department of Clinical Neurosciences,

(*b*) one person appointed by the Council of the School of Clinical Medicine,

(*c*) one person appointed by the General Board.

The Managers in classes (*b*) and (*c*) shall be appointed in the Michaelmas Term for a period of three years from 1 January following their appointment.

3. The first charge on the Fund shall be the payment of the stipend, national insurance, pension contributions, and associated indirect costs payable by the University in respect of a University officer concerned with teaching and research in Neuroimmunology established in the Department of Clinical Neurosciences. University officer.

4. Any unexpended income of the Fund in any financial year may, at the discretion of the Managers, be either added to the capital of the Fund, or accumulated for use as income in any one or more subsequent years, or applied to support research in the Department of Clinical Neurosciences. Unexpended income.

5. In exceptional circumstances the Managers may, subject to the approval of the General Board, use such part or parts of the capital of the Fund as they shall determine to support the University officer referred to in Regulation 3 or for any other purpose as set out in Regulation 4 above.

GERMAN ENDOWMENT FUND

1. The income of the German Endowment Fund shall be used to support German studies in the University. Purpose.

2. The Managers of the Fund shall be the Head of the Department of German and Dutch and three other persons appointed by the Faculty Board of Modern and Medieval Languages in the Michaelmas Term to serve for four years from 1 January following their appointment. Managers.

3. The first charge on the income of the Fund in each year shall be to contribute towards the stipend of the Schröder Professor of German. Professorship.

4. In any year any unexpended income shall be applied for the support of German studies in the University in a manner to be determined by the Managers. It shall be open to the Managers to add the unexpended income to the capital of the Fund. Unexpended income.

ARNOLD GERSTENBERG FUND AND STUDENTSHIP

Stat. E XXVI.

Endowments, 1904, pp. 355–8

1. The income of the Arnold Gerstenberg Fund shall be applied to maintaining one or more Arnold Gerstenberg Studentships. Studentship.

2. There shall be a Board of Managers of the Fund, consisting of six persons appointed in the Michaelmas Term, two by the Faculty Board of Philosophy, two by the Board of History and Philosophy of Science, one by the Faculty Board of Physics and Chemistry, and one by the Faculty Board of Biology, to serve for six years from 1 January following their appointment. Managers.

3. A Studentship shall be open to any person who is or is about to become a member of the University *in statu pupillari* or a registered Graduate Student, provided that he or she has successfully completed a course of study in Natural Science at this or another university. All candidates shall declare their intention, if elected, of pursuing a course of philosophical study in the University to be approved by the Managers. Eligibility of candidates.

Applications. **4.** The date by which and the manner in which applications for Studentships shall be made shall be determined by the Managers. The Managers shall give not less than three months' notice of their intention to proceed to an election. In such notice they shall indicate the date by which applications shall be submitted. The Managers shall take such steps as they may think fit to assess the capacities of candidates for the study of philosophy.

Tenure. **5.** A Studentship shall be tenable for one academical year and unless otherwise determined by the Managers shall be tenable for the academical year next after the election of the Student. A Studentship may be extended by the Managers for a second or third academical year, provided that the Managers are satisfied with the Student's progress in philosophical study in the previous academical year.

Value of Studentship. **6.** A Student shall receive such emolument, within a range determined from time to time by the Council, as the Managers shall determine in each case after taking account of the Student's financial circumstances. If the tenure of a Studentship is extended beyond one year, the value of the emolument shall be reassessed each year. The Managers may for good cause delay, reduce, or withhold payment to a Student, and may for good cause deprive a Student of the Studentship.

Orlando Gibbons Fund

Fund. **1.** By Grace 14 of 3 February 1910 the University converted the sum raised by subscribers to the Orlando Gibbons Memorial into the Orlando Gibbons Fund.

Purpose. **2.** In accordance with the desire of the subscribers, the income of the Fund shall be paid annually to the Fitzwilliam Museum Syndicate to be laid out by them in increasing their collection of music, each book so bought to be distinguished by having the name of Orlando Gibbons stamped upon it or in it in such a way as the Syndicate may decide to be most suitable.

Gibson Spanish Scholarship

Amended by Grace 7 of 30 July 2014

Name. **1.** The amount of the benefaction of Mrs Gibson for the endowment of a Scholarship in Spanish Literature, together with any additional funds which may be available, shall form a fund to be called the Gibson Spanish Scholarship Fund.

Administration. **2.** The administration of the Fund shall be entrusted to four Electors who shall be the Head of the Department of Spanish and Portuguese and three persons appointed by the Faculty Board of Modern and Medieval Languages in the Michaelmas Term to serve for three years from 1 January following their appointment. Three Electors shall form a quorum.

Duties of Scholar. **3.** There shall be established a scholarship to be called the Gibson Spanish Scholarship. It shall be the duty of the Scholar to undertake advanced study or research in Spanish Literature, according to a scheme to be approved by the Electors.

Election. **4.** The Scholarship shall be offered in the Easter Term of every year and the Electors shall meet to consider the applications of candidates before the end of that term.

Tenure. **5.** The Scholarship shall be tenable for one, two, or three years, as determined by the Electors; a Scholar elected for one or two years shall be eligible for re-election, provided that the total tenure of the Scholarship shall not exceed three years.

Who are eligible. **6.** The Scholarship shall be open to any person who is, or is about to be, registered as a Graduate Student in the University. Election to and tenure of the Scholarship shall lapse if the person elected does not become or ceases to be a registered Graduate Student.

Form of applications. **7.** The Electors shall determine the form in which applications for the Studentship shall be made and the person to whom, and the date by which, they are to be submitted.

Qualifications of candidates. **8.** The Electors may take such steps as they may think fit to inquire into the qualifications of candidates, provided that the Scholarship shall not be awarded by competitive examination.

Stipend of Scholar. **9.** The stipend of the Scholar shall be such sum as shall be determined by the Electors within a range approved from time to time by the Council. The stipend shall be paid in such instalments as shall be determined by the Electors, provided that the Electors may withhold payment of any instalment if they are not satisfied that the Scholar is pursuing his or her course of study or research with sufficient diligence.

10. The Scholar shall not during the tenure of the Scholarship systematically follow any business or profession or engage in educational or other work which in the opinion of the Electors would in any way interfere with his or her course of research. Restrictions.

11. Any accumulated income of the Fund may be used from time to time at the discretion of the Electors and subject to such conditions as they may think fit Accumulated income.

(*a*) to provide the stipend of one or more additional Scholars;

(*b*) to make grants to Scholars to assist them in prosecuting their research.

12. These regulations shall be subject to alteration by Grace, provided that the income of the Fund shall always be devoted to the endowment of a scholarship for the encouragement of the study of Spanish Literature in the University, to be called the Gibson Spanish Scholarship.

GIRDLER FUND

1. The capital sum received under the terms of the will of Professor Ronald William Girdler, shall form a fund called the Girdler Fund. Title.

2. The Managers of the Fund shall be: Managers.

(*a*) the Head of the Department of Earth Sciences, and

(*b*) three persons appointed by the Departmental Committee of the Department of Earth Sciences.

Managers in class (*b*) shall be appointed in the Michaelmas Term to serve for four years from 1 January following their appointment.

3. The income of the Fund shall be applied to support, by way of grants, graduate students wishing to pursue research in Geophysics, the application of Physics to problems in the Earth Sciences, in the Department. Application of income.

4. Any unexpended income of the Fund in a financial year may be either added to the capital of the Fund or accumulated for use as income in future years, as the Managers shall determine. Unexpended income.

GLADSTONE MEMORIAL PRIZE

Endowments, 1904, p. 436[1]

1. The Gladstone Memorial Prize of £250, or such greater sum as shall be provided by the Gladstone Memorial Trustees, shall be offered each academical year. Value.

2. The Prize shall be awarded by three Adjudicators appointed by the General Board, who shall be paid by the Gladstone Memorial Trustees a sum approved by the Council. One Adjudicator shall be appointed each year by the Examiners for Part IIB of the Economics Tripos, one by the Examiners for Part II of the Historical Tripos, and one by the Examiners for Part IIB of the Social and Political Sciences Tripos.[2] Adjudicators.

3. At their final meeting of the year each of the Boards of Examiners for the Triposes referred to in Regulation 2 shall identify the one or two best dissertations submitted by candidates for the Part concerned. Each dissertation identified by the Examiners shall be referred to the Adjudicators, who shall award the Prize for the dissertation which in their opinion is most meritorious. How awarded.

GLAXO PHARMACOLOGY FUND

1. The sum paid to the University by Glaxo Group Research Limited in accordance with the agreement dated 17 February 1992 shall form a fund called the Glaxo Pharmacology Fund. Name.

2. The capital and the income of the Fund shall be applied for the support of research in the Department of Pharmacology, particularly but not exclusively in the fields of cardiovascular and gastro-intestinal pharmacology, in such manner as may be approved by the General Board on the recommendation of the Head of the Department. Purpose.

[1] This volume records that the Prize is to be awarded for proficiency in History, Political Science, and Economics or any of those subjects at the discretion of the University.

[2] See footnote on p. 424.

Glennie Prizes in Child Psychiatry

Fund and purpose. **1.** The sum of £3,000 donated to the University by Mrs E. M. Glennie, MBE, in memory of her husband Dr R. E. Glennie, first Consultant Child Psychiatrist to the United Cambridge Hospitals and East Anglian Regional Hospital Board, shall form a Fund for the purpose of awarding annual prizes in the field of child psychiatry.

Title. **2.** The Prizes shall be called the Glennie Prizes in Child Psychiatry.

Who may compete. **3.** The Prizes shall be open to any member of the University who is pursuing clinical study in Cambridge and is a candidate for the Final M.B. Examination.

How awarded. **4.** The Awarders of the Prizes shall be the Professor of Child and Adolescent Psychiatry and the University Lecturer in Child and Adolescent Psychiatry (or their deputies). A first Prize and a second Prize shall be awarded for the best and the next best annotated case history of a child with a psychosomatic illness seen during the clinical course leading to the Final M.B. Examination.

Value. **5.** The value of the first Prize shall be two-thirds of the income of the Fund for the financial year in which the award is made. The value of the second Prize shall be one-third of that income.

Notice. **6.** In the Michaelmas Term of each year the Awarders shall publish a Notice of the Prizes to be awarded in the calendar year next but one, giving details of the form in which the case reports should be presented, the particular areas of child psychiatry that may form the basis of the reports, and the dates by which and the person to whom the reports should be submitted.

Unexpended income. **7.** If in any year the second Prize or neither Prize is awarded, the unexpended income shall be added to the capital of the Fund.

Amendment. **8.** These regulations, other than Regulations 1 and 2 and this regulation, shall be subject to alteration by Grace.

Goldsmiths' Prize and Medal

Prize. **1.** The sum made available annually by the Goldsmiths' Company shall be used to provide a prize called the Goldsmiths' Prize.

How awarded. **2.** The Prize shall be awarded by the Examiners for Materials Science and Metallurgy in Part III of the Natural Sciences Tripos for a distinguished performance in that examination.

Medal. **3.** The prize-winner shall also be awarded a silver medal provided by the Goldsmiths' Company.

Gollan Fund

Fund and purpose. The sum received under the will of Mr D. H. L. Gollan, of Trinity College, shall form a fund called the Gollan Fund, which shall be placed at the disposal of the Head of the Department of Veterinary Medicine and shall be used to support the study of farm animals.

Gow Fund

Name and purpose. **1.** The sum received by the University under the will of A. S. F. Gow, M.A., Fellow of Trinity College, Emeritus Brereton Reader in Classics, shall form a fund to be called the Gow Fund. Two-thirds of that sum shall be invested as a purchase fund, the income of which shall be available for the purchase of works of art for the Fitzwilliam Museum, and one-third shall form a general fund the capital or income of which shall be available for any purpose of the Museum including the purchase of works of art or building work.

Managers. **2.** The Managers of the Fund shall be the Fitzwilliam Museum Syndicate.

Graham-Smith Fund

Name and purpose. **1.** The bequest of Dr G. S. Graham-Smith shall form a fund called the Graham-Smith Fund which shall in accordance with the terms of the will of the benefactor be used for any purpose connected with the Department of Pathology or for the use of any Department or other institution which may develop therefrom more especially if it is devoted to the science of bacteriology.

Managers. **2.** The Managers of the Fund shall be the Professor of Pathology and the Secretary of the School of the Biological Sciences. If the Managers fail to agree on the use of the Fund in any instance the matter shall be referred to the Regius Professor of Physic for a ruling.

3. The capital and income of the Fund shall be applied from time to time at the discretion of the Managers, and subject to such conditions as they may think fit, to any purpose consistent with Regulation 1. Application of Fund.

J.H. GRAY FUND

The income of the J. H. Gray Fund, which was established by a gift from the funds of the Cambridge University Rugby Union Football Club, shall be available to the Faculty Board of Classics to meet the expense of lectures, or courses of lectures, on subjects not adequately provided for by the University Education Fund. In accordance with the express wishes of the benefactor the Faculty Board shall have wide discretion in the use of the income, provided that it shall not be used to subvent lectures ordinarily included in the Lecture-list.

D. H. GREEN FUND

Grace 3 of 6 October 2010

1. The sum bequeathed to the University by Mrs Margaret Green in memory of her husband Professor Dennis Howard Green, sometime Schröder Professor of German and Fellow of Trinity College, together with other funds received for the same purpose, shall form a fund called the D. H. Green Fund, the income of which shall be used, subject to the provisions of Regulation 5, for the encouragement of medieval German studies, which for the purpose of these regulations shall be understood to mean the study of medieval German literature and the history of the German language in the medieval period. Name and purpose.

2. The Fund shall be administered by a Board of Managers consisting of: Board of Managers.

(*a*) the Schröder Professor of German;

(*b*) the holders of any other Professorships in German established in the Department of German and Dutch;

(*c*) three persons appointed by the Faculty Board of Modern and Medieval Languages in the Michaelmas Term to serve for three years from 1 January following their appointment, provided that the Faculty Board shall, as far as possible, appoint persons whose field of study falls within the field of medieval German studies.

3. The first charge on the income of the Fund shall be the provision of a Prize which shall be awarded annually by the Examiners for Part II of the Modern and Medieval Languages Tripos for an outstanding year abroad project or dissertation on a subject in medieval German language or literature submitted under Regulation 27(*b*) or (*c*) for the Modern and Medieval Languages Tripos. The value of the Prize shall be determined by the Managers, within a range approved from time to time by the Council. Prize.

4. After the provision of the Prize, or if the Prize is not awarded, the remaining income of the Fund shall be available for use by the Managers, at their discretion, for one or more of the following purposes, as listed:

(*a*) To provide a Studentship which may be awarded each year and which shall be open to any person who is or is about to be registered as a candidate for the Ph.D. Degree in the University. The Managers shall be the Electors to the Studentship; in making the award they shall take account of candidates' financial support from other sources. The value of the Studentship shall be determined by the Managers, within a range approved from time to time by the Council. It shall be the duty of the Student to undertake advanced study or research in medieval German studies. The Studentship shall be tenable for one year; a Student shall be eligible for re-election, provided that no one shall hold the Studentship for more than three years in total. Studentship.

(*b*) To provide an annual D. H. Green Lecture in medieval German Studies. Not later than the end of the Easter Term preceding the academical year in which a lecture is to be given, the Managers shall appoint a Lecturer who shall deliver in the University one lecture on a subject in medieval German studies, and shall, if possible, give one seminar in the Faculty of Modern and Medieval Languages on a similar subject. The stipend of the Lecturer shall be such sum as shall be determined by the Managers. In addition, the Managers may at their discretion pay any expenses of the Lecturer and any other expenses incurred in the holding of the Lecture. Lecture.

Book purchases. (*c*) To purchase books in the field of medieval German studies for the Beit German Library or the German section of the Students' Library of the Faculty of Modern and Medieval Languages, or for both these libraries.

Grants. (*d*) To make grants towards the cost of publication of works by members of the University in the field of medieval German studies.

(*e*) To assist in any other way the promotion and encouragement of medieval German studies in the University.

Unexpended income. **5.** At the discretion of the Managers, any unexpended income may be either accumulated in the Fund for use in future years or used for the promotion and encouragement of German studies at large in the University.

Alteration of regulations. **6.** These regulations, other than Regulations 1 and 5 and this regulation, shall be subject to alteration by Grace.

Mark Gregson Fund

Name and purpose. **1.** The sum subscribed in memory of Mark Stephen Gregson, B.A., of St John's College, shall form a fund called the Mark Gregson Fund, for the encouragement of study and research in archaeology.

Managers. **2.** The Managers of the Fund shall be the Head of the Department of Archaeology and Anthropology or her or his deputy and two University officers assigned to the Department, to be appointed in the Michaelmas Term by the Faculty Board of Human, Social, and Political Science to serve for two years from 1 January following their appointment.

Prize. **3.** The first charge on the income of the Fund shall be the provision of a prize called the Mark Gregson Prize, which shall be awarded annually by the Examiners for the Examination for Part IIA of the Archaeological and Anthropological Tripos to the candidate who has shown the greatest distinction in the subject Archaeology in that examination.

Value. **4.** The value of the Prize shall be such sum as shall be determined by the Managers, within a range approved from time to time by the Council.

Unexpended income. **5.** Any unexpended income accumulated in the Fund may be applied at the discretion of the Managers to assist members of the University *in statu pupillari* and registered Graduate Students in undertaking archaeological excavations or other archaeological fieldwork.

6. These regulations, except Regulation 1, shall be subject to alteration by Grace.

Gresham Prize in Pathology

Fund and purpose. **1.** The donation of £550 made in 1986 by Professor G. Austin Gresham, M.D., Sc.D., Fellow of Jesus College, shall form a fund called the Gresham Fund for the purpose of awarding a prize in Pathology.

Prize. **2.** The title of the Prize shall be the Gresham Prize in Pathology.

How awarded. **3.** The Prize shall be awarded each year to the candidate who achieves the highest score in the Final M.B. Part I Examinations in Pathology held in that academical year.

Value. **4.** The value of the Prize shall be the annual income of the Fund.

Unexpended income. **5.** If in any year the Prize is not awarded, the unexpended income shall be added to the capital of the Fund.

Catherine Grigoriou-Theocarakis Prize

Grace 1 of 28 October 2009

Title and purpose. **1.** The sum of £8,000 received from Dr Nikos Theocarakis, shall form a fund, the income of which shall be used to provide a prize called the Catherine Grigoriou-Theocarakis Prize for Excellence in Modern Greek Studies.

How awarded. **2.** The Prize shall be awarded by the Examiners for the Modern and Medieval Languages Tripos to the candidate who achieves the best overall result in Part IB or Part II of that Tripos, having taken one or more papers in Modern Greek.

Value. **3.** The value of the Prize shall be the annual income of the Fund.

Unexpended income. **4.** If in any year the Prize is not awarded, the income for that year shall be added to the capital of the Fund.

Grimshaw-Parkinson Fund

1. The investments representing that portion of the residuary estate of the late John Grimshaw wherein Sir John Parkinson released his life interest in favour of the University by Deed of Partition dated 2 August 1961 shall form a fund called the Grimshaw-Parkinson Fund. Title.

2. The regulations for the Fund which follow this regulation are based on directions contained in a codicil to the will of Sir John Parkinson and which in accordance with the terms of that codicil may be altered by Grace on the recommendation of the Managers in order to conform with the changing nature of medical practice and scientific investigation; provided always that the University shall adhere to the object of the bequest as described in the following extract from the will of John Grimshaw, that is to say 'furtherance of scientific education and/or scientific research of a character preferably but not necessarily medical and either by the provision of a scholarship or scholarships (resident or travelling) the establishment of a laboratory the purchase of instruments or apparatus or otherwise'. Purpose of bequest.

3. The Managers of the Fund shall be: Managers.

(*a*) the Regius Professor of Physic;

(*b*) a person appointed by the Vice-Chancellor;

(*c*) the President for the time being of the British Cardiac Society or a deputy appointed by the President;

(*d*) any other persons who may be appointed from time to time by the Faculty Board of Clinical Medicine.

4. The income of the Fund shall be applied to maintain one or more Grimshaw-Parkinson Studentships. It shall be the duty of a Grimshaw-Parkinson Student, under the general supervision of the Managers, to engage in research in the field of diseases of the heart and circulation preferably with a view to treatment. Application.

5. The Student shall be a registered medical practitioner or the holder of a medical degree, British or foreign, approved by the Managers, without restriction on nationality or sex. Eligibility.

G. C. Grindley Fund

1. The bequest of G. C. Grindley, M.A., formerly Fellow of University (now Wolfson) College, shall form a fund called the G. C. Grindley Fund the income of which shall be used in accordance with the terms of the will of the benefactor for the purpose of research into behaviour and its relation to mental processes and underlying physiological mechanisms. Title and purpose.

2. The Fund shall be administered by three Managers who shall be the Professor of Experimental Psychology and two other persons appointed in the Michaelmas Term, one by the Faculty Board of Biology and the other by the Council of the School of the Biological Sciences, each to serve for three years from 1 January following. Managers.

Grosvenor Fund

1. The sums received from the Westminster Foundation for the support of work in real estate finance within the Department of Land Economy shall form a fund called the Grosvenor Fund. Title and purpose.

2. The Fund shall be under the control of a Board of Managers who shall be: Managers.

(*a*) the Head of the Department of Land Economy as Chair;

(*b*) two persons appointed by the General Board, at least one of whom shall be appointed on the nomination of Grosvenor Group Holdings Ltd;

(*c*) the Grosvenor Professor of Real Estate Finance;

(*d*) not more than two persons co-opted at the discretion of the Managers.

Members in class (*b*) shall be appointed in the Michaelmas Term to serve for four years from 1 January following their appointment. Members in class (*d*) shall serve until 31 December of the year in which they are co-opted or of the following year, as the Managers shall decide at the time of their co-optation.

3. The first charge on the income of the Fund shall be the stipend, national insurance, pension contributions, and associated indirect costs payable by the University in respect of the Grosvenor Professor of Real Estate Finance. Professorship.

4. After provision has been made in accordance with Regulation 3, the income of the Fund shall be applied at the discretion of the Managers for the support of work in real estate finance for charitable and public benefit in the Department of Land Economy. Surplus income.

Unexpended income. **5.** Any unexpended income of the Fund in a financial year may be either added to the capital of the Fund or accumulated for use as income in future years, as the Managers shall determine.

Kurt Hahn Prizes

Prizes. **1.** The sum made available each year by the Trustees of the Kurt Hahn Trust shall be used to provide four Kurt Hahn Prizes.

How awarded. **2.** The Prizes shall be awarded as follows:

(*a*) one Prize shall be awarded by the Examiners for Part IA of the Modern and Medieval Languages Tripos for a distinguished performance in German (Option B) in that examination;

(*b*) one Prize shall be awarded by the Examiners for Part IB of the Modern and Medieval Languages Tripos for a distinguished performance in German in that examination;

(*c*) one Prize shall be awarded by the Examiners for Part II of the Modern and Medieval Languages Tripos for a distinguished performance by a candidate who has offered a majority of papers, including Paper C1, in German in that examination;

(*d*) one Prize shall be awarded by the Head of the Department of Engineering for a distinguished performance in German in an approved examination in that language taken by a candidate for Part IIB of the Engineering Tripos.

Value. **3.** The value of each Prize shall be one-quarter of the sum made available by the Trustees.

Andrew Hall Fund

Title and purpose. **1.** The sum subscribed in memory of Andrew Rodney Hall, of St Catharine's College, who was killed in a climbing accident in Norway in 1975, shall form a fund called the Andrew Hall Fund, for the encouragement of study and research in geography.

Managers. **2.** The Managers of the Fund shall be the Managers of the Philip Lake Fund II.

Prize. **3.** The income of the Fund shall be used to provide an Andrew Hall Prize to be awarded annually by the Examiners for Part IA of the Geographical Tripos to the best candidate in that examination. The value of the Prize shall be such sum as shall be determined by the Managers within a range approved from time to time by the Council.

4. These regulations, except Regulation 1, shall be subject to alteration by Grace.

John Hall Fund

Fund and purpose. **1.** The sum given to the University in 1977 by John Challice Hall, M.A., LL.B., of St John's College, shall form a fund called the John Hall Fund, the income of which shall be used for the promotion and encouragement of the study of Law in the University.

Managers. **2.** The Managers of the Fund shall be the Faculty Board of Law, who may delegate any or all of their functions under these regulations to a committee consisting of not less than three persons, at least one of whom shall be a member of the Faculty Board.

Prize. **3.** The first charge on the income of the Fund shall be the provision of a prize called the John Hall Prize, which shall be awarded annually for distinction in Family Law shown by performance in that subject in Part IB or Part II of the Law Tripos.

Value. **4.** The value of the Prize shall be such sum as shall be determined by the Faculty Board of Law within a range approved from time to time by the Council.

Unexpended income. **5.** After the provision of the John Hall Prize, the Managers shall have power to apply any unexpended income accumulated in the Fund:

(*a*) to provide lectures or other teaching in the Faculty of Law, supplementary to the teaching provided from the University Education Fund;

(*b*) to purchase books or other materials for the Squire Law Library;

(*c*) to make grants or payments related to any other educational or academic purpose of the Faculty of Law, and to attach to the award of any such grant or payment such conditions as they may think fit.

HALLAM FUND AND PRIZE

1. The sums given to the University by George Hanley Hallam, M.A., sometime Craven Scholar and Fellow of St John's College, shall be separately invested and shall form a fund called the Hallam Fund. Fund.

2. There shall be established in the University an annual prize, called the Hallam Prize, which shall be used for travel in Italy, including a visit to Rome. Prize.

3. The Prize shall be awarded annually by the Awarders for the University Classical Scholarships, and upon the papers set for Part IB of the Classical Tripos. Awarders.

4. The prize may be awarded together with one of the aforesaid Scholarships. In accordance with Mr Hallam's wish, women shall be eligible for the Prize. Who may compete.

5. The amount of the Prize shall be paid to the prize-winner, provided that an application through the Student's Tutor has been submitted before the proposed travel has taken place.

6. Except for grave cause approved by the Faculty Board of Classics, travel shall take place not later than the Long Vacation next after the thirteenth term from the student's first term of residence, and a brief report on the travel shall be sent to the Registrary, for communication to the Faculty Board, as soon as possible after the student's return. When to travel.

7. The value of the Prize shall be the income of the Fund for the financial year in which the award is made. Value.

HAMILTON PRIZE

1. The money given to the University by Mr J. W. O. Hamilton and accepted on 12 November 1937 shall form a fund called the Hamilton Fund, supporting a prize for research into radio and other forms of communication using electromagnetic radiation which shall be called the Hamilton Prize, founded in honour of James Clark Maxwell, late Fellow of Trinity College and first Cavendish Professor of Experimental Physics; with whose services to the science of wireless communication the donor has associated the names of Sir John Ambrose Fleming, M.A., Honorary Fellow of St John's College, and Sir Oliver Joseph Lodge, Hon. Sc.D. of the University. Fund and Prize.

2. The Prize shall be offered for competition in every year, and shall consist of the income of the Fund for the financial year preceding, after payment of the Examiners' fees. When offered.

3. The Prize shall be awarded for the best report embodying research carried out in the University on the theory or practice of the physics or engineering of any aspect of communication, propagation, or signal processing, associated with electromagnetic radiation or wave propagation. A report shall not exceed 5,000 words in length, excluding any appendices. Subject.

4. Members of the University who are or have been Graduate Students shall be eligible to compete for the prize, provided that: Who are eligible.

(*a*) not more than twelve terms of their course of research have been completed since admission as a Graduate Student;

(*b*) they have resided in Cambridge for not less than sixty days during the twelve months preceding the day on or before which dissertations are to be submitted.

5. No candidate who has already been awarded the Prize or part of it shall compete again.

6. Each candidate shall submit the title of his or her proposed report, together with a statement of its scope in not more than 300 words, to the Registrary not later than 15 September. The Registrary shall submit that information to the Secretaries of the Faculty Boards of Engineering and of Physics and Chemistry. Reports, which must be printed or typewritten, shall be submitted in duplicate to the Registrary not later than 31 October. Candidates may incorporate in their reports material already published, provided that the work was done in Cambridge, but they are expected to submit a connected account of their complete investigations. Submission of report.

7. The Examiners shall be two persons appointed by the General Board before the division of the Michaelmas Term, one on the nomination of the Faculty Board of Engineering and the other on the nomination of the Faculty Board of Physics and Chemistry. The award of the Prize shall be made not later than the first day of Full Lent Term. Each Examiner shall receive from the income of the Fund, unless no report is sent in, such sum as shall be determined jointly by the Faculty Boards of Engineering and of Physics and Chemistry within a range approved from time to time by the Council. Examiners.

8. The Prize may be awarded for a report submitted jointly by two candidates giving an account of the research which they have carried out in co-operation. In comparing the merits of combined and Division of Prize.

independent work, the Examiners shall expect an appreciably higher standard for the former. In the case of an award made for a joint report, the Prize shall be divided equally between the two co-authors.

Deposit of report. **9.** Each prize-winner shall present a copy of his or her report to the University Library.

10. The University shall have power to alter and amend these regulations from time to time by Grace, on the recommendation of the Faculty Boards of Engineering and of Physics and Chemistry, provided that the Prize shall always be associated with the four names mentioned in Regulation 1 and shall be devoted to the encouragement of radio research.

Stat. E V.

Hare Prize

Endowments, 1904, p. 401

Subject. **1.** The Hare Prize shall be offered annually for a dissertation on a subject, proposed by the candidate and approved by the Faculty Board of Classics, which falls within the scope of the Faculty of Classics.

Adjudicators. **2.** The Prize shall be awarded by not more than three Adjudicators, who shall be appointed by the General Board on the nomination of the Faculty Board of Classics not later than the division of the Easter Term. Each Adjudicator shall receive from the income of the Fund such sum as shall be determined by the Faculty Board of Classics within a range approved from time to time by the Council.

Who may compete. **3.** The Prize shall be open to any member of the University who has been approved by the Board of Graduate Studies for the award of the Ph.D. Degree during the calendar year next preceding the year of the award.

Dissertation. **4.** Not later than the fifth day of Full Lent Term, a candidate shall notify the Secretary of the Faculty Board of Classics of the title of the dissertation that he or she proposes to submit. The Secretary of the Faculty Board shall inform candidates of the approval or rejection of their titles. Candidates whose titles have been approved shall send their dissertations to the Secretary of the Faculty Board so as to arrive not later than the last day of the Lent Term. A dissertation shall not exceed 80,000 words in length.

Date of award. **5.** The Faculty Board of Classics shall select not more than three dissertations from among those submitted under Regulation 4, and shall refer them to the Adjudicators. The award shall be made not later than the division of the ensuing Michaelmas Term.

Value. **6.** The value of the Prize shall be the annual income of the Fund, after payments have been made to the Adjudicators.

7. The successful candidate shall deposit a copy of his or her dissertation in the Library of the Faculty of Classics.

8. If in any year the Prize is not awarded, the amount of the Prize for that year shall be added to the capital of the Fund.

Harkness Scholarship

Endowments, 1904, p. 337

Name. **1.** There shall be a Scholarship to be called the Harkness Scholarship, which shall be awarded annually for proficiency in Geology, including therein Palaeontology.

Who are eligible. **2.** Any member of the University shall be eligible to the Scholarship who has passed some final examination for the degree of Bachelor of Arts provided that on the day of election not more than three years have elapsed since 19 December next following the said final examination.

Managers. **3.** The Managers of the Fund shall be the Head of the Department of Earth Sciences and three University officers in the Department of Earth Sciences, appointed by the Faculty Board of Earth Sciences and Geography in the Michaelmas Term to serve for three years from 1 January following their appointment.

Electors. **4.** A Scholar shall be elected in the month of June each year by a Board of Electors consisting of the Managers and the Examiners in Geological Sciences for Part II of the Natural Sciences Tripos for that year and those for the preceding year. No business shall be transacted unless five members at least of the Board be present.

Names of candidates to be sent in. **5.** The names of candidates shall be made known to the Registrary not later than 31 May in each year.

6. In making the award the Electors shall have regard to proficiency in Geology, including therein Palaeontology, and to promise of future work. Qualifications.

7. The Electors shall have authority to take any steps they think advisable to enable them to ascertain the qualifications of the candidates; any necessary expenses incurred by them in so doing shall be charged to the Fund.

8. It shall be the duty of the Scholar during the academical year of tenure to undertake research in Geology or Palaeontology either in Cambridge or elsewhere under the direction of the Head of the Department of Earth Sciences or some person approved by the Head of the Department. Duty of Scholar.

9. The first charge on the income of the Fund shall be the stipend of the Scholar. The stipend shall be such sum as shall be determined by the Managers in each case, taking account of the other financial resources which may be available to the Scholar, within a range approved from time to time by the Council. The stipend shall be paid in two half-yearly instalments in advance. The second instalment shall not be paid unless the Managers are satisfied that the Scholar has been pursuing his or her studies with sufficient diligence. Stipend of Scholar.

10. The Managers may make grants from the balance of the annual income of the Fund to assist a Scholar during the year of his or her tenure, and from any unexpended income accumulated in the Fund to assist any former Scholar or Scholars in prosecuting geological or palaeontological researches, subject to a maximum total value of grants to any person determined by the Managers with the approval of the Council. No grant shall be paid to a former Scholar later than three years after the end of the academical year of his or her tenure, nor shall any grant be paid to a former Scholar unless he or she continues to undertake research in Geology or Palaeontology either in Cambridge or elsewhere under the direction of the Head of the Department of Earth Sciences or some person appointed by the Head of the Department. Grants from Fund.

HARNESS PRIZE

Stat. E XLI.

Endowments, 1904, p. 409

1. The Prize shall be offered annually. The value of the Prize shall be the annual income of the Fund after the expenses of the award have been met. Prize.

2. The Prize shall be given to the author of the best English essay on a subject connected with Shakespearian literature, such author being either an undergraduate or a postgraduate student. Subject, and who may compete.

3. The Prize shall be adjudged by two persons nominated by the Faculty Board of English for appointment in the Lent Term. Each Adjudicator shall receive from the income of the Fund, except when no essay is sent in, such amount as may be determined by the Faculty Board within a range approved from time to time by the Council. Adjudicators.

4. The Adjudicators shall select and announce a subject for the essay in the Michaelmas Term each year. A candidate who wishes to submit an essay on a subject connected with Shakespearian literature of his or her own choosing shall so inform the Registrary not later than the first day of the Full Lent Term next following the announcement; the Registrary shall submit the proposed subject to the Adjudicators and shall communicate the approval or rejection thereof to the candidate. Notice of subject.

5. An essay for the Prize shall meet the minimum and maximum word limits as prescribed by the Faculty Board of English in the Michaelmas Term each year. Each essay shall be printed or typewritten and, with a declaration of its length, shall be sent to the Registrary so as to arrive not later than 31 August in the calendar year next following the announcement of the selected subject. It shall bear a motto but not the candidate's name, and shall be accompanied by a sealed envelope bearing the same motto outside and containing the candidate's name and College. Essays.

6. The successful candidate shall send a printed or typewritten copy of his or her essay to the Vice-Chancellor, to each Adjudicator, to the University Library, and to the Library of Christ's College. Condition.

7. If on any occasion the Adjudicators shall be of opinion that no essay sent in is deserving of the Prize, the amount of the Prize for that occasion shall be added to the capital of the Fund.

8. The University shall have power to alter and determine from time to time, by Grace, the regulations respecting the persons by whom the subject of the essay shall be chosen and the Prize adjudged, and also the regulations respecting the intervals at which the Prize shall be offered and the times when the subject shall be announced and the essays sent in. Alterations.

HARNETT FUND

1. The bequest of Lt-Colonel W. L. Harnett shall form a fund called the Harnett Fund, which shall in accordance with the terms of the will of the benefactor be used for increasing medical knowledge and aiding medical research.

2. The capital and the income of the Fund shall be applied as the General Board shall from time to time determine after consultation with the Faculty Board of Clinical Medicine.

HARTREE AND CLERK MAXWELL PRIZES

Fund.

1. The sum bequeathed to the University by Douglas Rayner Hartree, M.A., Ph.D., of Christ's College, formerly John Humphrey Plummer Professor of Mathematical Physics, shall form a fund called the Hartree Fund.

Hartree Prize.

2. The income of the Fund shall be used to provide a prize called the Hartree Prize which shall be awarded annually by the Examiners for Part II of the Natural Sciences Tripos to the candidate who has shown the greatest distinction in Experimental and Theoretical Physics in that examination.

Clerk Maxwell Prize.

3. The Examiners shall be empowered at their discretion to award a Clerk Maxwell Prize to any winner of the Hartree Prize. The value of a Clerk Maxwell Prize shall be determined by the Cavendish Professor of Physics and the Head of the Department of Physics acting in conjunction; such a Prize shall be provided from the income of the Clerk Maxwell Memorial Fund, under Regulation 2(*c*) for that fund, and from the funds at the disposal of the Head of the Department of Physics.

HARTWELL FUND FOR ISLAMIC STUDIES

Title and purpose.

1. The sum given to the University by the Oakhill Group Ltd shall form a fund called the Hartwell Fund for Islamic Studies, the income of which shall be used for the advancement of Islamic Studies in the University.

Managers.

2. The Fund shall be administered by a Board of Managers, who shall be:

(*a*) the Vice-Chancellor (or a duly appointed deputy) as Chair;

(*b*) the Chair of the Faculty Board of Divinity;

(*c*) a member of the Faculty Board of Divinity appointed by that Board;

(*d*) two persons appointed by the Faculty Board of Divinity on the nomination of Hartwell plc.

Managers in class (*d*) shall be appointed in the Michaelmas Term to serve for four years from 1 January following their appointment.

3. The Managers shall meet at least once a year.

4. It shall be the duty of the Managers:

(*a*) to keep the financial position of the Fund under review;

(*b*) to decide on the future use of the Fund if the University should cease to be able to make provision for Islamic Studies in the Faculty of Divinity.

University office.

5. The first charge on the income of the Fund shall be payment of the stipend, national insurance, pension contributions, and associated indirect costs of the holder of a University office in the Faculty of Divinity concerned with teaching or research in Islamic Studies. In making appointments to such an office the appointing body shall be advised by an Assessor appointed by the Faculty Board of Divinity after consulting the Managers.

Unexpended income.

6. After provision has been made in accordance with Regulation 5, any unexpended income of the Fund may be applied by the Managers at their discretion for the advancement of Islamic Studies in the University.

7. These regulations may be amended by Grace, subject to the approval of the Oakhill Group Ltd.

WILLIAM HARVEY FUND

Title and purpose.

1. The moneys donated and covenanted by graduates of the University in Medicine shall form a fund to be called the William Harvey Fund. The income of the Fund but not the capital shall be applied at the discretion of the Managers, subject to any direction by the donors, for any of the following or similar purposes; making grants or loans to clinical medical students in cases of hardship; the purchase of special acquisitions for the Medical Library; the endowment of prizes, studentships, and scholarships; the provision of sports facilities and amenities for clinical medical students.

2. The Managers of the Fund shall be the Regius Professor of Physic, the Director of Medical Education, and two persons appointed by the Faculty Board of Clinical Medicine in the Michaelmas Term to serve for a period of four years from 1 January following the appointment. The Secretary of the Faculty Board of Clinical Medicine shall act as Secretary to the Managers. At least once in every academical year the Managers shall consult the appropriate representatives of the clinical students concerning the provision of funds for sports facilities and amenities and shall consider any proposals made by them on behalf of the clinical student body. Managers.

3. The Managers shall be empowered to receive donations, subscriptions, and other benefactions for the augmentation of the capital or income of the Fund as the Managers, in the absence of any direction by a donor, may decide. Augmentation of the Fund.

4. Any unexpended income at the end of a financial year shall be added to the capital of the Fund. Unexpended income.

William Harvey Studentships in Clinical Medicine

1. A sum to be determined in the Michaelmas Term each year by the Managers of the William Harvey Fund shall be set aside for the purpose of awarding annually a number of William Harvey Studentships in Clinical Medicine. The number and value of the Studentships shall be at the discretion of the Awarders within the total sum available. One of the Studentships shall be called the 'Cambridge Medical Graduates' Fund Studentship', three of the Studentships shall be called the 'Werner Jacobson Halley Stewart Scholarships', and one of the Studentships shall be called the 'Duncan Roland Studentship'. Name, purpose, and value.

2. The Awarders of the Studentships shall be the Regius Professor of Physic and the Director of Medical Education or their deputies appointed by the Faculty Board of Clinical Medicine. Awarders.

3. A William Harvey Studentship may be awarded to any student pursuing a course of clinical instruction in the University leading to the degrees of Bachelor of Medicine and Bachelor of Surgery. Werner Jacobson Halley Stewart Scholarships shall be awarded to students who are pursuing the M.B./Ph.D. course. Eligibility.

4. The Studentships shall normally be awarded in the Easter Term. When awarded.

Sylvia Haslam Prize in Ecology

1. The sum of £2,000 given to the University by Dr Sylvia Haslam, M.A., Ph.D., Sc.D., of Newnham College, shall form a fund called the Sylvia Haslam Prize Fund, which shall be used to provide a prize called the Sylvia Haslam Prize in Ecology. Title and purpose.

2. The Prize shall be awarded annually by the Head of the Department of Plant Sciences, the Professor of Plant Ecology, and the Examiners for the subject Plant Sciences in Part II of the Natural Sciences Tripos for an outstanding performance in ecology in the examination for that subject unless the Awarders are of the opinion that there is no candidate of sufficient merit to receive the Prize. How awarded.

3. The Prize shall consist of books, to the value of the annual income of the Fund, selected by the prize-winner subject to the approval of the Head of the Department of Plant Sciences. Value.

4. If in any year no award is made the income for that year shall be added to the capital of the Fund. If not awarded.

Stephen Hawking Endowment for Cosmological Research

1. The sum of US$1,845,000 received from the Board of Cambridge in America to honour the life and research of Stephen William Hawking, CH, CBE, Ph.D., FRS, Lucasian Professor of Mathematics, Fellow of Gonville and Caius College, shall form a fund to be known as the Stephen Hawking Endowment for Cosmological Research. Title.

2. The income and up to one-third of the capital of the Fund shall be used exclusively to assist, enhance, support, bolster, and sustain research, cosmological or otherwise, in the Department of Applied Mathematics and Theoretical Physics, as chosen by and approved by Professor Hawking personally during his lifetime. Thereafter, the Fund shall be administered by four Managers who shall be the Head of the Department of Applied Mathematics and Theoretical Physics, the Professor of Mathematical Physics (1967), and two Managers appointed by the Faculty Board of Mathematics. The Managers appointed by the Faculty Board shall each serve for four years from 1 January following his or her Purpose.

appointment. The Managers shall apply the income of the Fund to the support of scientific research and activity in the University which would further human understanding of the fundamental questions in cosmology and gravitation addressed by Professor Hawking, or to the support of research which they believe would have been of interest to Professor Hawking.

Stephen Hawking Trust Fund

Title and purpose.

1. The monies received by the University to perpetuate the intellectual legacy of Professor Stephen Hawking, Lucasian Professor of Mathematics, in the field of theoretical cosmology shall form a fund to be known as the Stephen Hawking Trust Fund.

2. The Fund may include both endowment and expendable capital contributed by donors. The expendable capital, and the income from the endowment shall be used to support the activities of a Centre for Theoretical Cosmology within the University, whose goals shall be:

(i) to promote research and postgraduate teaching in theoretical cosmology within the University;

(ii) to co-operate with outside bodies in the promotion of research and postgraduate teaching in theoretical cosmology internationally.

Managers.

3. The administration of the Fund shall be under the control of a Board of Managers consisting of:

(*a*) the Head of the Department of Applied Mathematics and Theoretical Physics, who shall serve as the Chair;

(*b*) the Professor of Mathematical Physics (1967);

(*c*) two Professors working in a relevant scientific discipline appointed by the Faculty Board of Mathematics;

(*d*) one additional University Teaching Officer in the Faculty of Mathematics co-opted by the Managers;

(*e*) Professor Stephen Hawking during his life-time;

(*f*) up to three distinguished persons external to the University appointed by the General Board on the recommendation of the Managers.

Tenure of Managers.

4. Members in classes (*c*) and (*f*) shall be appointed in the Michaelmas Term to serve for four years from 1 January following their appointment. Co-opted members in class (*d*) shall serve until 31 December of the year in which they are co-opted or of the year following, as the Managers shall determine at the time of their co-optation.

Director of the Centre for Theoretical Cosmology.

5. The Director of the Centre for Theoretical Cosmology shall be appointed by the General Board on the recommendation of the Managers. He or she shall hold office for four years, and shall be eligible for reappointment. The Director shall serve as Secretary to the Board.

6. The Directorship of the Centre shall be held concurrently with a University office in the Department of Applied Mathematics and Theoretical Physics.

7. The Board shall normally meet twice each academical year.

Unexpended income.

8. After provision has been made in accordance with Regulation 2 any unexpended income of the Fund may either be accumulated for use as income in future years or be applied by the Managers at their discretion for the following purposes:

(i) to support one or more Stephen Hawking Visiting Professors and/or Postdoctoral Fellows;

(ii) to support students accepted for the Certificate of Advanced Study in Mathematics or students approved for study towards the Ph.D. Degree within the field of theoretical physics in the Department of Applied Mathematics and Theoretical Physics by means of Stephen Hawking Studentships.

Scientific Advisory Board

Board members.

1. The Centre shall have an international Scientific Advisory Board, which shall consist of no fewer than four highly distinguished persons in relevant scientific disciplines appointed by the General Board on the recommendation of the Board of Managers.

Tenure of Board members.

2. Members of the Advisory Board shall be appointed in the Michaelmas Term to serve for four years from 1 January following their appointment.

3. The General Board, in making their appointments to the Advisory Board, shall ensure that not more than one of its members is a resident member of the University.

4. The Chair of the Advisory Board shall be appointed by the General Board for a period of not more than three years and shall be eligible for reappointment for a period or periods of not more than three years at a time. Chair.

5. The Director of the Centre shall serve as Secretary of the Advisory Board. Secretary.

6. The Advisory Board shall meet at least once every two years.

7. The duty of the Advisory Board shall be to advise the Director of the Centre on all aspects of the scientific programme and policy of the Centre. Advisory Board duty.

Stephen Hawking Visiting Professorships

1. One or more Stephen Hawking Visiting Professors shall be appointed by the General Board under the authority of Special Ordinance C (vii) B.1(*c*)(iii) on the recommendation of the Managers. The tenure of a Hawking Professor shall normally be for a period of not more than six months but may, exceptionally, be for a period of not more than one year. Tenure.

2. It shall be the duty of a Stephen Hawking Visiting Professor to participate in the teaching and research programme of the Centre for Theoretical Cosmology. Duty.

3. The stipend, travelling expenses, and subsistence allowance of a Stephen Hawking Visiting Professor shall be determined by the General Board on the recommendation of the Managers.

4. A Stephen Hawking Visiting Professor shall be required to reside in Cambridge unless granted leave of absence by the General Board. Residency

Stephen Hawking Postdoctoral Fellowships

1. The Managers shall decide upon the number of Stephen Hawking Postdoctoral Fellowships to be awarded each year. Appointments to these Fellowships shall be made upon the recommendation of the Director of the Centre for Theoretical Cosmology, in consultation with other Managers who are University Teaching Officers in the Department of Applied Mathematics and Theoretical Physics working in a relevant scientific discipline. Appointments.

2. The Fellowships shall be tenable for periods of up to five years. Tenure.

3. The annual stipend of a Fellow shall be within a range determined by the Managers, to be approved from time to time by the General Board. Stipend.

4. Additional research support grants may also be awarded to Stephen Hawking Postdoctoral Fellows. Research support grants.

Stephen Hawking Studentships

1. The Electors to a Stephen Hawking Studentship shall be the Head of the Department of Applied Mathematics and Theoretical Physics, the Director of the Centre of Theoretical Cosmology, and those Managers who are University Teaching Officers in the Department of Applied Mathematics and Theoretical Physics. Electors.

2. In order to be eligible for the Studentship, a candidate must have been admitted, or be seeking admission, as a student taking the Certificate of Advanced Study in Mathematics or as a student studying towards the Ph.D. Degree in the field of theoretical physics, within the Department of Applied Mathematics and Theoretical Physics. Eligibility.

DESMOND HAWKINS AWARD

1. The sum given to the University by Thomas Desmond Hawkins, M.A., FRCP, FRCR, of St John's College, formerly Clinical Dean of the School of Clinical Medicine, shall form a fund the income of which shall be used to provide an award called the Desmond Hawkins Award. The purpose of the Award shall be to assist students in financing a period of elective medical study abroad. Title and purpose.

2. The Award shall be open to any member of the University who is pursuing clinical studies in the University. Who are eligible.

3. In the Michaelmas Term of each year, the Director of Medical Education shall publish a Notice giving the date by which, and the manner in which, applications are to be submitted. Notice.

4. The Awarders shall be the Director and the Associate Dean. In making their decision, the Awarders shall have regard to the academic record of the candidates, their contribution to extra-curricular activities in the University generally, in the Clinical School, or in their College, and the How awarded.

nature of the proposed study. Preference shall be given to those who propose to study in a developing country.

Value. **5.** The value of the Award shall be the annual income of the Fund.

Unexpended income. **6.** If in any year no award is made, the income for that year shall be added to the capital of the Fund.

Stat. E XXX.

Hebrew Prizes

Endowments, 1904, p. 404

Object. **1.** The income of the money subscribed in 1865 and 1867 for the encouragement of the study of Hebrew in the University shall be used to provide prizes, which shall be awarded by the Examiners for the Theological and Religious Studies Tripos and the Advanced Diploma in Theology and Religious Studies, and by the Examiners in Theology and Religious Studies for the M.Phil. Degree.

Examinations on which prizes awarded. **2.** There shall be open for award annually one or more prizes to candidates for Parts IIA and IIB of the Theological and Religious Studies Tripos, and the Examination for the Advanced Diploma in Theology and Religious Studies, and one or more prizes to candidates for the Examination in Theology and Religious Studies for the M.Phil. Degree who acquit themselves with distinction in the Hebrew linguistic papers in those examinations.

Value. **3.** The value of a Prize shall be such sum not exceeding the available income of the Fund as may be determined from time to time by the Faculty Board of Divinity with the approval of the Council.

Margot Heinemann Prize

Fund. **1.** The sums subscribed in memory of Miss Margot Claire Heinemann, formerly Fellow of New Hall, shall form a Fund called the Margot Heinemann Fund.

Prize. **2.** There shall be a Prize, called the Margot Heinemann Prize, which shall be awarded annually by the Examiners for Part I of the English Tripos for an outstanding performance in Paper 5 (Shakespeare) in that examination.

Value. **3.** The value of the Prize shall be the annual income of the Fund. If in any year the Prize is not awarded, the unexpended income for that year shall be added to the capital of the Fund.

Heitland Fund

One-third of the residue of the estate of William Emerton Heitland, M.A., of St John's College, shall form a fund called the Heitland Fund, the capital and income of which shall be applied for such purposes in connection with the Fitzwilliam Museum as the Fitzwilliam Museum Syndicate shall in their absolute discretion think fit.

Heitland and William Aldis Wright Fund

Two-thirds of the residue of the estate of William Emerton Heitland, M.A., of St John's College, and the assets remaining on 11 January 1969 in the William Aldis Wright Pension Fund shall form a fund called the Heitland and William Aldis Wright Fund, the capital and income of which shall be applied from time to time for such purposes in connection with the University Library as the Library Syndicate shall in their absolute discretion think fit.

John and Margaret Henderson Memorial Prize

Fund and purpose. **1.** The sum of five thousand dollars received from Dr A. Comfort, M.A., M.B., B.Chir., of Trinity College, and Mrs Comfort shall form a fund for the purpose of awarding an annual prize in the field of Gerontology and Geriatrics.

Title. **2.** The title of the prize shall be the John and Margaret Henderson Memorial Prize, in memory of Mrs Comfort's parents.

Who may compete. **3.** The Prize shall be open to any member of the University who is pursuing clinical study in Cambridge for the degrees of Bachelor of Medicine and Bachelor of Surgery and has not yet taken Part III of the Final M.B. Examination.

4. The Prize shall be awarded for an essay or other written work of not more than 3,000 words on a subject in the field of either Gerontology or Geriatrics. The work shall be based on the candidate's actual experience in either or both of these fields, or shall concern proposals, based on that experience, for innovations in matters of care, teaching, or research. How awarded.

5. In the Michaelmas Term the General Board shall appoint two Adjudicators on the nomination of the Faculty Board of Clinical Medicine to serve for one year from 1 January following their appointment. The Adjudicators may at their discretion examine a candidate *viva voce*. Adjudicators.

6. The value of the Prize shall be the annual income of the Fund. If in any year there is no entry of sufficient merit to justify the award of a Prize of full value, the Adjudicators may at their discretion award a Prize of such lower value as they deem fit. Value.

7. Before the division of the Easter Term the Director of Medical Education shall publish a Notice giving the last date by which the work shall be submitted, provided that such date shall not be earlier than eight weeks after the publication of the Notice. Notice.

8. Any unexpended income shall be added to the capital of the Fund. Unexpended income.

Hibbitt Endowed Fund for Solid Mechanics

1. The sum of US$4m received from the Board of Cambridge in America, representing a donation from Dr David and Mrs Susan Hibbitt, shall form a fund called the Hibbitt Endowed Fund for Solid Mechanics. Title.

2. The stipend, national insurance, pension contributions, and associated indirect costs payable by the University in respect of a University Lecturer, to be known as the Hibbitt Lecturer in Solid Mechanics, shall be payable from the Fund. Lecturer.

3. Any unexpended income in a financial year shall be added to the capital of the fund. Unexpended income.

John Hickman Prize in Equine Studies

1. The sums subscribed in memory of Colonel John Hickman, of King's College, Emeritus Reader in Animal Surgery, who died on 2 January 2000, shall form a fund, to be called the John Hickman Fund, the income of which shall be used to provide a John Hickman Prize in Equine Studies. Fund and purpose.

2. The Managers of the Fund shall be the Head of the Department of Veterinary Medicine, the Deputy Head of that Department, the University Equine Surgeon, and the University Lecturer in Equine Medicine. Managers.

3. The Prize shall be awarded by the Examiners for Part III of the Final Veterinary Examination to the candidate who has obtained the highest recommendation on clinical rotations in equine studies during the final year and who has also obtained good marks in Section 1, Equine Studies, in that Examination. How awarded.

4. The value of the Prize shall be a sum determined by the Head of the Department of Veterinary Medicine, within a range approved from time to time by the Council. Value.

5. Any unexpended income of the Fund in a financial year may be added either to the capital of the Fund or accumulated for use as income in a subsequent year, as the Managers shall determine. Unexpended income.

Professor Dame Elizabeth Hill Fund

1. The sum given to the University by Dame Elizabeth Hill, of Girton College, Emeritus Professor of Slavonic Studies, shall form a fund called the Professor Dame Elizabeth Hill Fund for Postdoctoral Research, the income of which shall be used for the encouragement of advanced study and research in Slavonic Studies. Fund and purpose.

2. The Fund shall be administered by five Managers, who shall be: Managers.

(*a*) the Professor of Slavonic Studies;

(*b*) four persons appointed in the Michaelmas Term to serve for four years from 1 January following their appointment, one being appointed by each of the following bodies: the Faculty Boards of Asian and Middle Eastern Studies, History, and Modern and Medieval Languages, and the Board of History and Philosophy of Science.

3. The income of the Fund shall be used by the Managers to make grants for the support of advanced study or research in Slavonic Studies relating to the period before AD 1700, preference being given to Grants.

persons intending to undertake a substantial project in any of the following fields: palaeography; medieval hagiography or other literature; medieval art; the monastic tradition of the Orthodox Church; the biographical study of medieval Slav contributors to geography, historiography, or the history of science. Grants may be made to University officers or other persons employed by the University and to Fellows of Colleges in the University.

Notice. **4.** A notice inviting applications for grants shall be published from time to time at the discretion of the Managers.

Deposit. **5.** A recipient of a grant from the Fund shall deposit in the University Library a report on the work undertaken with the help of the grant and a copy of any publication resulting from it.

Unexpended income. **6.** Any unexpended income in a financial year may be either added to the capital of the Fund or accumulated for use as income in a future year, at the discretion of the Managers.

Martin Hinds Travel Fund

Fund and purpose. **1.** The benefaction of Mrs Pamela Hinds, Dr Patricia Crone, and others, in memory of George Martin Hinds, Fellow of Trinity Hall and University Lecturer in Arabic, shall form a fund called the Martin Hinds Travel Fund the income of which shall be used for the encouragement of study and research in Middle Eastern Studies.

Managers. **2.** The Fund shall be managed by the Head of the Department of Middle Eastern Studies in consultation with and with the agreement of the teaching officers in the Department.

Grants or loans. **3.** From the income of the Fund the Managers may make grants or loans to assist registered Graduate Students and other members of the University *in statu pupillari* with the cost of travel to, and residence in, the Islamic Middle East and North Africa, in order to permit them to pursue the study of the languages, culture, or history of those areas.

History Professorship Fund

Grace 7 of 2 December 2009

Title. **1.** The sum of £1m received from Trinity College to support a Professorship in the Faculty of History, together with other sums donated for the same purpose, shall form a fund called the History Professorship Fund.

Managers. **2.** The Managers of the Fund shall be the Faculty Board of History, who may delegate any or all of their functions under these regulations to a committee not necessarily consisting wholly of members of the Board.

Professorship. **3.** The first charge on the income of the Fund shall be the stipend, national insurance, pension contributions, and associated indirect costs payable by the University of the holder of a Professorship in the Faculty of History designated by the General Board on the recommendation of the Faculty Board of History.

4. On the occasion of a vacancy in the designated Professorship, the General Board, on the recommendation of the Faculty Board of History, may determine that the same or another Professorship in the Faculty shall be supported from the Fund.

5. After provision has been made in accordance with Regulation 3, the income of the Fund may be applied in support of the work of the Professor in such manner as may be approved by the General Board on the recommendation of the Managers.

Unexpended income. **6.** Any unexpended income of the Fund in a financial year may be either added to the capital of the Fund or accumulated for expenditure in accordance with Regulations 3 and 5 in one or more subsequent years, as the Managers shall determine.

Charles H. and Anna M. Hodgkins Memorial

Grace 1 of 11 March 2009

The sum of £147,000 received from the Board of Cambridge in America shall form a fund, to be entitled the Charles H. and Anna M. Hodgkins Memorial, the income of which shall be used to support fundamental research in the basic sciences appertaining to physiology, as shall be determined by the Head of the Department of Physiology, Development, and Neuroscience.

Ivy Rose Hood Memorial Bursary Fund

Grace 2 of 16 March 2011

1. The sums received from the Trustees of the Ivy Rose Hood Memorial Fund to support Bursaries for those studying courses administered by the Institute of Continuing Education shall form a fund known as the Ivy Rose Hood Memorial Bursary Fund. Title.

2. The Managers of the Fund shall be appointed by the Strategic Committee for the Institute of Continuing Education on the advice of the Director, who will also be responsible for selecting recipients of the Bursaries. Managers.

3. The Bursaries, to be known as the Ivy Rose Hood Memorial Bursaries, shall be awarded to cover in part or in full the fees of selected students studying for Diplomas and Certificates open to non-members of the University administered by the Institute of Continuing Education, or other programmes administered by the Institute as agreed by the Strategic Committee for the Institute. Bursaries.

4. In the event that no student is judged to be of sufficient merit, the Bursaries shall not be awarded.

5. The Bursaries shall be conferred at an event organized by the Institute of Continuing Education. Acceptance of a Bursary is subject to allowing the Institute of Continuing Education to publicize as appropriate the success of the candidate.

6. Any unexpended income of the Fund in a financial year shall be either added to the capital of the Fund or retained for use as income in future years, as the Managers may determine. Unexpended income.

Hort Memorial Fund

Endowments, 1904, p. 358

1. There shall be a fund in the University called the Hort Memorial Fund, which shall be devoted to the promotion of Biblical, Hellenistic, and Patristic research. Name and purpose.

2. The Managers of the Fund shall be the Faculty Board of Divinity, who may delegate some or all of their functions under these regulations to a committee not necessarily consisting wholly of members of the Board. Administration by Managers.

3. The income arising from the capital of the Fund shall be applied at the discretion of the Managers, and subject to such conditions as they may think fit, for the following purposes: Income.

(*a*) grants to any person engaged in Biblical, Hellenistic, or Patristic research; Grants.

(*b*) grants for the promotion of any undertaking connected with these departments of study.

4. The Managers shall be empowered to receive donations, subscriptions, and bequests for the augmentation of the capital of the Fund. Increase of capital.

5. These regulations, except Regulation 1 and this regulation, shall be subject to alteration by Grace, provided that the object of the Fund, *viz.* the promotion of Biblical, Hellenistic, and Patristic research, be adhered to. Alterations.

6. Subject to the foregoing regulations, it shall be lawful for the Managers from time to time to make and, if they see fit, to vary, such by-laws as may seem to them expedient for regulating their own proceedings and the administration of the Fund entrusted to their care. By-laws.

Raymond Horton-Smith Prize

Endowments, 1904, p. 434

1. The moneys given to the University by Richard Horton-Smith, M.A., Q.C., formerly Fellow of St John's College, and by his son Sir Percival Horton-Smith Hartley, C.V.O., M.D., formerly Fellow of the same College, and by Mrs A. G. Wornum, niece of Raymond Horton-Smith, shall form a fund to be called the Raymond Horton-Smith Fund, the income of which shall be used to provide a Raymond Horton-Smith Prize. Name.

2. The Prize shall be awarded annually by the M.D. Committee to that person among the candidates for the degree of Doctor of Medicine who shall in the judgement of the Committee have presented the best thesis or dissertation for the degree during the academical year. Awarded for best M.D. thesis or dissertation.

3. For their guidance in awarding the Prize for any year the M.D. Committee may consult one independent referee and may pay the referee such fee as shall be determined by the Faculty Board of Clinical Medicine within a range approved from time to time by the Council. Referee.

Value and nature of Prize.

4. The value of the Prize shall be the net annual income of the Fund after deducting any fee paid under the provisions of Regulation 3. Of the sum given to the prize-winner at least one book must be purchased with a cover suitable for embossing, the selection of which shall be with the prize-winner and the approval with the Vice-Chancellor. Any book so purchased shall be stamped with the arms of the University and with the Horton-Smith armorial bearings. Applications for the approval of books under this regulation shall be submitted to the Registrary in accordance with the general regulations for prize books.

Alterations.

5. The University shall have power to alter and amend these regulations from time to time by Grace, on the recommendation of the Vice-Chancellor, the Master of St John's College, the Regius Professor of Physic, and the Professor of Pathology, for the time being; provided that regard shall be had to the wishes of the founder that the name Raymond Horton-Smith shall always be used in connection with the Prize and that it shall be awarded for the encouragement of Medicine and Pathology.

Sir Albert Howard Travel Exhibition

Title.

1. The sum of £1,000, bequeathed to the University by the late Sir Albert Howard for the furtherance of botanical research, shall form a fund called the Sir Albert Howard Travel Exhibition.

Income.

2. The income of the Fund shall be used to provide an annual Travel Exhibition to be awarded to a candidate elected from among the students offering Plant Sciences in Part II of the Natural Sciences Tripos in the year of the award.

Candidates.

3. Every candidate shall apply to the Registrary not later than the seventh day of Full Easter Term, and shall submit a brief statement of the purpose and plan of the proposed travel.

Electors.

4. The Electors shall be the Regius Professor of Botany and the Examiners in Plant Sciences for Part II of the Natural Sciences Tripos in the year in which the award is made.

Date of award.

5. The Exhibition shall be awarded not later than 7 July, and the successful candidate shall normally be required to make use of the award before 1 October following. The Regius Professor of Botany shall have power to waive this requirement.

If not awarded.

6. If in any year the Electors are of opinion that none of the candidates is deserving of the Exhibition, no award shall be made in that year.

Unexpended income.

7. Any unexpended income accumulated in the Fund may be used by the Electors, in any subsequent year, to make grants to increase the value of an Exhibition.

Hughes Fund

Title and purpose.

1. A fund shall be established in the University, called the Hughes Fund in memory of Norman Francis Hughes, formerly University Lecturer in Geology and Fellow of Queens' College, which shall be for the sole benefit of the libraries in the Department of Earth Sciences, and any successor body to the libraries.

Managers.

2. The Managers of the Fund shall be the Head of the Department of Earth Sciences, and at least four persons appointed in the Michaelmas Term by the Departmental Committee of the Department of Earth Sciences to serve for three years from 1 January following their appointment, at least one of whom shall be a member of staff of the libraries in the Department, the other persons being members of the academic staff of the Department.

3. The income from the Fund shall be used solely for the purchase of printed (including books, journals, conference proceedings) and electronic materials (including access to journals and databases) for the libraries.

Unexpended income.

4. Unexpended income shall not be added to the capital of the Fund but shall be accumulated for use as income in subsequent years.

Stat. E VI.

Hulsean Fund

Endowments, 1904, p. 117

Division of income.

1. A stipend of £10.50 for the Preacher shall be a first charge on the income available under Statute E VI 3; the rest shall be divided into ten equal parts, eight of which parts shall be applied to the stipend of the Professor, one to the Prize, and one to the stipend of the Lecturer. Every second year after payment has been made to the Lecturer any unexpended income accumulated in the Fund shall be applied to the stipend of the Professor.

The Hulsean Preachership

2. The Preacher shall be elected each year before the end of the Lent Term for the ensuing academical year, and shall deliver in the University one sermon on the Truth and Excellence of Revealed Religion or the Evidence of Christianity.

The Hulsean Prize

3. The Prize shall be awarded for an essay on some subject, proposed by a candidate and approved by the Adjudicators, connected with the history of the Christian Religion. Prize.

4. The Adjudicators of the Prize shall be the Professors of Divinity. The Adjudicators shall be empowered to consult Assessors. Each Assessor shall receive such payment from the income of the Fund as may be determined from time to time by the Council on the recommendation of the Faculty Board of Divinity. Adjudicators.

5. Candidature shall be open to any member of the University to whom the Prize has not previously been awarded provided that on the latest date on which essays must be submitted to the Registrary Eligibility.

(*a*) eight complete terms at least or, if the candidate is an Affiliated Student, five complete terms at least have passed after his or her first term of residence;

(*b*) the candidate has not attained the age of twenty-seven years.

6. The subject proposed for an essay shall be sent by a candidate not later than 15 March in each year to the Registrary, who shall submit it to the Adjudicators and communicate its approval or rejection to the candidate. Each candidate shall submit his or her essay to the Registrary on or before 19 December in the year next following. Subject.

7. The prize-winner shall deposit a printed or typewritten copy of his or her essay in the University Library. Condition.

The Hulsean Lectureship

8. There shall be a Hulsean Lecturer, who shall be elected every second year to hold office for two years from 1 January next but one following the election and shall be capable of re-election after an interval of six years. Election, tenure, and income.

9. The Lecturer shall during the period of office deliver a course of lectures, not fewer than four nor more than eight in number, on some branch of Christian Theology, at such times and in such places as may be determined from time to time by the Electors. The Lecturer shall be required to deposit a printed or typewritten copy of the lectures in the University Library. Duties.

10. The Lecturer must be a graduate of Cambridge, or a graduate of some other university. Qualification.

11. Public notice of the election of the Lecturer shall be given in the first quarter of the Michaelmas Term of every second year, and the election shall take place before the end of that term. It shall be open to the Electors to invite any qualified person to undertake the office. Notice of election.

12. A Lecturer shall receive the income available for the stipend of the Lecturer for each of two years. The stipend accrued shall be paid to the Lecturer following deposition of the copy of the lectures as required under Regulation 9.

HUMANITARIAN TRUST FUND AND STUDENTSHIP

1. The benefaction of the Trustees of the Humanitarian Trust shall form a fund called the Humanitarian Trust Fund, the purpose of which shall be the advancement of the study of International Law. Name and purpose.

2. The capital of the Humanitarian Trust Fund shall be invested in the names of the Chancellor, Masters, and Scholars of the University of Cambridge. Investment.

3. The capital of the Fund shall be devoted to the maintenance in the University of Studentships, the object of which shall be to train Students for work in the field of International Law. The income of the Fund, both current and accumulated, shall be applied by the Faculty Board of Law, on the recommendation of the Whewell Professor of International Law, to the payment of administrative expenses not exceeding £40 a year, and otherwise to any purpose connected with the study and Capital and income.

development of International Law. Any income unexpended in any year shall be accumulated for use in this manner.

Tenure. **4.** One Studentship, which shall be called a Senior Studentship, shall be awarded once every two years provided that there is a candidate of sufficient merit. The Studentship shall be tenable for one year in the first instance, but the Electors may renew it for one further year.

Who are eligible. **5.** Candidates must produce evidence that they have obtained, or are likely to obtain, before the end of the academical year of their candidature a degree or diploma at a university or college in the Commonwealth of Nations, the United States of America, the Continent of Europe, the former Union of Soviet Socialist Republics, at the Hebrew University of Jerusalem, or at any other university or college approved by the Electors for the purpose of this regulation. They must also produce evidence of their fitness to engage in advanced study.

Restrictions. **6.** The Studentship shall not be tenable with a Commonwealth Fund Fellowship, or a College Fellowship or emolument of similar magnitude.

Value. **7.** The value of the Studentship shall be £1,000 a year or such greater sum as the Electors may determine from time to time; provided always that if a Student holds, or is elected to, another emolument, the value may be reduced by such amount as the Electors may determine. The emolument of the Studentship shall be paid in advance in three instalments, at the beginning of term.

Allowances for travel. **8.** The Electors may grant an allowance to cover in whole or in part the expenses of travel to and from Cambridge of a Student ordinarily resident overseas.

Termination of tenure. **9.** The Electors may terminate the tenure of a Student at any time if, in their opinion, he or she is unfit to continue to hold the Studentship.

Notice of award. **10.** The Secretary of the Faculty Board of Law shall advertise the Studentship, in each year in which an election is to be made, in such journals as the Whewell Professor may consider desirable.

Applications. **11.** Applications shall be required to reach the Secretary of the Faculty Board not later than 1 January.

Elections. **12.** Elections shall, if possible, be made before the division of the Lent Term, but the Electors shall not be debarred from making them at any other time.

Condition. **13.** Awards shall be subject to the Student being or becoming a member of the University.

14. The Student shall come into residence at the beginning of the Michaelmas Term following the election, subject to dispensation by the Electors for good cause.

Course of study. **15.** The Student shall pursue a course of study under the supervision of the Whewell Professor.

Restrictions **16.** The Student may not during his or her tenure be a candidate for the degree of LL.M. or for the Whewell Scholarship, but may be a candidate for a higher degree, or for a Postgraduate Diploma in International Law.

17. The Student shall keep terms by residence, provided that after one term of residence a student may be allowed by the Electors to reside elsewhere for a specified period, if it is in the interest of his or her work to do so.

Electors. **18.** The Electors shall be the Chair of the Faculty Board of Law (or a deputy designated by the Chair for the current year), the Whewell Professor of International Law (or a deputy designated by the Professor for the current year), and a person appointed by the Trustees of the Humanitarian Trust.

19. These regulations may be altered by the University with the agreement of the Trustees of the Humanitarian Trust.

Humanitas Visiting Professorships Fund

Grace 4 of 16 June 2010

Title. **1.** The sums received from the Institute for Strategic Dialogue, on behalf of benefactors associated with the Institute, towards the costs of the Humanitas Visiting Professorships shall form a fund called the Humanitas Visiting Professorships Fund.

Professors. **2.** A number of Humanitas Visiting Professors, focused on the arts, humanities, and social sciences, may be elected annually under the authority of Special Ordinance C (vii) B.1(*c*)(iii) by the General Board, on the recommendation of an Advisory Committee, comprising the Head of the School of Arts and Humanities and the Head of the School of the Humanities and Social Sciences (one of whom shall be Chair), the Director of the Centre for Research in the Arts, Social Sciences and Humanities, and up to two other persons co-opted by the Advisory Committee, to include a representative nominated by the Institute for Strategic Dialogue. The Advisory Committee shall also serve as the Management Committee of the Fund.

Management Committee.

3. The tenure of each Humanitas Visiting Professorship shall be for a minimum of two weeks in the year of the appointment and for a maximum of eight weeks. Tenure.

4. It shall be the duty of a Humanitas Visiting Professor to deliver up to three public lectures and to engage in a symposium in the field of the Visiting Professorship. Duties.

5. If and whenever the income of the Fund exceeds the amount required to defray the costs of the Visiting Professorships, the excess of the income over that amount may be retained for use in future years or shall be applied to support the goals of the scheme in such a manner as may be approved by the General Board on the recommendation of the Advisory Committee. Unexpended income.

Huppert Prize in Geophysics

1. The sum given to the University by Herbert Huppert, FRS, Fellow of King's College and Professor of Theoretical Geophysics, from the proceeds of the Arthur L. Day Prize awarded to him by the National Academy of Sciences, Washington, DC, shall form a fund, to be called the Huppert Prize Fund, the income of which shall be used to provide a Huppert Prize in Geophysics. Title and purpose.

2. The Adjudicators of the Prize shall be the Head of the Department of Applied Mathematics and Theoretical Physics, the Head of the Department of Earth Sciences, the Director of the Institute of Theoretical Geophysics, and the Professor of Active Tectonics. Adjudicators.

3. The Prize shall be awarded annually by the Adjudicators for the most imaginative and innovative written contribution to the field of geophysics by a resident undergraduate member of the University of Cambridge. How awarded.

4. The value of the Prize shall be such sum as shall be determined by the Adjudicators within a range approved from time to time by the Council. Value.

5. Public notice of the Prize shall be given by the Adjudicators not later than the division of the Michaelmas Term. The notice shall include the date by which and the manner in which candidates shall submit their entries for the Prize.

6. The Prize shall be awarded in the Easter Term. Condition.

7. One copy of the written work of the successful candidate shall be deposited in the Betty and Gordon Moore Library and one copy in the Library of the Department of Earth Sciences. Each Library shall maintain a consolidated record of all written works that have been awarded the Prize.

8. From any unexpended income which may have accumulated in the Fund the Adjudicators may in any year award a second Prize of such amount as they see fit. Unexpended income.

Ibn Battutah Fund

Grace 4 of 15 January 2014

1. The sums received from the Golden Web Foundation shall form a fund called the Ibn Battutah Fund. The income of the Fund, together with other sums made available for the same purpose, shall be used to provide studentships for Graduate Students in the arts and humanities, with a preference for supporting students in subject areas which align with the aim of the Golden Web Foundation to explore the shared heritage of humanity and the relationships between cultures and civilizations in the pre- or early modern period, as determined by the Managers of the Fund. Title and purpose.

2. The Managers of the Fund shall be: Managers.

(*a*) the Head of the School of Arts and Humanities or her or his deputy;

(*b*) the Head of the School of the Humanities and Social Sciences or her or his deputy; and

(*c*) the Secretary of the Board of Graduate Studies.

3. Studentships shall be awarded by a selection committee appointed by the Managers of the Fund. Award of studentships.

4. In order to be eligible for a studentship from the Fund a candidate must have been admitted, or be seeking admission, as a registered Graduate Student in the University.

5. If no suitable candidates present themselves in any year, the award shall be held over until the following year.

Industrial Management Endowment Fund

The income of the Industrial Management Endowment Fund shall be applied at the discretion of the Director of Judge Business School for the general purposes of teaching and research in the School

David James Fund

Grace 2 of 12 May 2010

Title and purpose.

1. The sum bequeathed to the University by the late David James, together with other funds received for the same purpose, shall form a fund called the David James Fund.

Managers.

2. The administration of the Fund shall be entrusted to three Managers, who shall be the Head of the Department of Pharmacology and two persons nominated by the Faculty Board of Biology.

3. The income and the capital of the Fund shall be available for:

Studentships.

(i) the provision of one or more studentships to be called David James Studentships for those undertaking postgraduate research degrees in the Department of Pharmacology;

(ii) the furtherance of research and teaching in the Department of Pharmacology.

Unexpended income.

4. Any unexpended income of the Fund in a financial year shall be either added to the capital of the Fund or retained for use as income in future years, as the Managers may determine.

Japanese Studies Fund

Name and purpose.

1. The sum of £750,000 received from Mr Kawashima Hiroshi, the similar sum received from Fuji Bank Limited, and other sums received for the support of Japanese Studies shall form a fund called the Japanese Studies Fund, the purpose of which shall be the furtherance of Japanese Studies generally in the University, in such manner as may be approved by the General Board on the recommendation of the Head of the Department of East Asian Studies in consultation with and with the agreement of the teaching officers in Japanese in the Department.

Lecturers.

2. The stipend, national insurance, and pension contributions payable by the University in respect of the Kawashima Lecturer in Japanese Studies and the Fuji Bank Lecturer in Modern Japanese Studies shall be payable from the Fund.

Unexpended income.

3. Any unexpended income of the Fund in a financial year may be either added to the capital of the Fund or accumulated for use as income in future years, as the General Board shall determine.

Jebb Fund

Name.

1. The money received by the University from the gift and bequest of Lady Jebb, widow of Sir Richard Claverhouse Jebb, Regius Professor of Greek and Representative of the University in Parliament, shall be separately invested and shall constitute a fund called the Jebb Fund.

The money received by the University under the will of Henry Ernest Cashmore for the purpose of research work shall be added to the capital of the Jebb Fund, but shall be accumulated separately.

Purpose.

2. The income of the Fund shall be used for the encouragement of Classical and other literary studies by the provision of Studentships in accordance with Regulations 5–13.

Electors.

3. The Electors to the Jebb Studentships shall be the King Edward VII Professor of English Literature, and four persons appointed in the Michaelmas Term by the Council, one on the nomination of the Faculty Board of Classics, one on the nomination of the Faculty Board of Modern and Medieval Languages, one on the nomination of the Senior Tutors' Committee, and one on the nomination of the General Board who shall be the Chair, to serve for three years from 1 January following their appointment.

Unexpended income.

4. Any unexpended income accumulated in the Fund shall be used

(*a*) to provide grants, at the discretion of the Electors after taking account of any other financial resources that may be available to the Student, not exceeding in any one case such amount as shall be determined from time to time by the Council on the recommendation of the Electors, to supplement the normal emoluments of Students who are in special need of such assistance, whether for buying necessary books, meeting expenses arising out of the studies of a Student, or otherwise carrying out the general purposes of the Studentships or for other objects germane to the purposes of the Fund;

(*b*) to provide travel grants, at the discretion of the Electors, subject to the same maximum as in section (*a*), to enable Students to visit countries relevant to their studies;

(*c*) for the award of grants to other persons engaged in the University in study or research in Classical or other literary studies.

Jebb Studentships

5. The annual income of the Fund shall be used to provide the emolument of three Jebb Studentships which shall be offered annually, one for the advanced study of some subject in the field of European literature from the time of the foundation of Constantinople to the birth of Dante, one for the advanced study of some subject in the field of European literature from the time of the birth of Dante onwards, and one for the advanced study of some subject in the field of European literature of any period. Purpose.

6. The maximum emolument of each Studentship shall be such amount as shall be determined from time to time by the Council on the recommendation of the Electors. Value.

7. If in any of the fields of study there be in any year no candidate whom the Electors deem of sufficient merit for the award of a Studentship, they may at their discretion award two Studentships for that year in one of the other fields of study. Fields of study.

8. Before the end of the Michaelmas Term in every year the Electors shall publish a Notice of the date by which and the manner in which applications for the Studentship shall be made, and the election to the Studentships shall take place not later than the end of the Long Vacation period of residence next following. Notice of election.

9. Any graduate of the University shall be eligible for a Studentship provided that on the first day of the Easter Term of the academical year in which the election is to take place he or she has not attained the age of twenty-six years. A Student may be re-elected for a year at a time, subject to a maximum tenure of four years in all. The age limit shall not apply to candidates for re-election. Eligibility and tenure.

10. A Studentship shall be tenable for the financial year next following the election or re-election, provided that in exceptional circumstances the Electors may postpone the tenure to a subsequent year.

11. The Electors may take such steps as they think fit to inquire into the qualifications of candidates, provided that the Studentships shall not be awarded on the result of a competitive examination.

12. It shall be the duty of each Student to undertake advanced study in connection with an author or authors of some literary problem within the limits prescribed in Regulation 5. A Student's proposed course of study shall be approved by the Electors, provided that such course may in special cases be altered or varied with the consent of the Electors. Duties of Student.

13. Every Student shall receive such stipend subject to Regulation 6 as the Electors shall determine in each case after taking account of any other financial resources that may be available to the Student. Payments.

JEREMIE PRIZES

Stat. E XXX.

Endowments, 1904, p. 408

1. The income of the Fund established by James Amiraux Jeremie in 1870 for the encouragement of a critical study of the Septuagint Version of the Old Testament and such other Hellenistic literature as may serve to illustrate the New Testament shall be used to provide two or more annual prizes, which shall be called the Jeremie Prizes. Any member of the University may be a candidate for the Prizes provided that at the time of the examination Prizes. Who may compete.

(*a*) he or she has kept five terms,

(*b*) if a graduate, he or she is of not more than ten years' standing from admission to a first degree, whether of this or another university.

The value of each Prize shall be such sum not exceeding the available income of the Fund as may be determined from time to time by the Faculty Board of Divinity with the approval of the Council.

2. One or more Prizes shall be offered for knowledge of the Septuagint Version of the Old Testament and one or more Prizes for knowledge of the Apocryphal Books and Pseudepigrapha, the works of Philo and Josephus, and other Hellenistic writings. A student to whom a Septuagint Prize has been awarded shall not again be eligible as a candidate for a Septuagint Prize, nor shall a student to whom a Hellenistic Prize has been awarded again be eligible as a candidate for a Hellenistic Prize.

3. The examination shall be held after the division and before the end of the Michaelmas Term, on a day of which notice shall be given by the Board of Examinations. The day shall not be any of the days on which an examination for another Divinity Prize or Scholarship is held. Examination.

4. No one shall be a candidate for both Prizes in one year.

5. The examination for each Prize shall consist of two printed papers and shall be concluded in one day. Printed papers.

Names to Registrary.

6. The names of candidates shall on or before 20 October be sent by their Tutors to the Registrary, who shall forthwith communicate them to the Examiners.

Examiners.

7. There shall be two Examiners for each examination, who shall be appointed by the General Board on the nomination of the Faculty Board of Divinity. One shall be appointed in each year before the division of the Easter Term to hold office for the two following academical years. Each of the Examiners shall receive each year from the Fund such sum, unless there be no candidate for the Prizes, as shall be determined by the Faculty Board of Divinity within a range approved from time to time by the Council. All the other expenses of the examination shall likewise be paid out of the Fund.

Subjects.

8. The Faculty Board of Divinity shall select as special subjects for examination in each year one or more books or portions of books taken, in the case of the Septuagint Prize, from each of the two classes (1) the Pentateuch and Historical Books, (2) the Prophets and Hagiographa; and in the case of the Hellenistic Prize, from each of the two classes (1) the Apocryphal Books and Pseudepigrapha, (2) the works of Philo and Josephus and other Hellenistic writings; and notice shall be given of the books or portions of books so selected in the Michaelmas Term of the year preceding the examination.

Nature of examination.

9. The examination shall be directed mainly, though not exclusively, to the selected books. It shall embrace translation and questions on the history, criticism, and interpretation of the books. In the case of a Septuagint Prize it shall include also questions on the relation of the Septuagint Version to the Hebrew original, and questions may be set to test the candidates' knowledge of the fragments of the other Greek versions.

C. H. W. Johns Memorial Fund and Studentship

Title and purpose.

1. The sum bequeathed to the University by Mrs A. S. Johns for the purpose of maintaining a postgraduate studentship in Assyriology shall form a fund called the C. H. W. Johns Memorial Fund. The studentship shall be called the C. H. W. Johns Studentship.

Managers.

2. The Board of Managers of the Fund shall be the Faculty Board of Asian and Middle Eastern Studies. The Board may delegate any of their functions concerning the Fund to a Committee which will include University Teaching Officers in Assyriology or cognate subjects.

Notice of election.

3. The Managers shall give not less than three months' notice of their intention to proceed to an election.

Who are eligible.

4. The Studentship may be held by any graduate who desires to undertake training for research in Assyriology. Candidates must produce evidence that they have obtained, or are likely to obtain before the end of the academical year of their candidature, a university degree. The Managers may take such steps as they think fit to ascertain the qualifications of candidates and their ability to undertake research.

Tenure.

5. The Managers shall elect a Student in the first instance for such period not exceeding three years as they shall think fit, and shall have power to re-elect a Student for any further period not exceeding three years if they are satisfied that his or her work is of sufficiently high standard to merit such an extension.

6. A Student who is not a member of the University must become such before the end of the term next after the election and must remain such during the tenure of the Studentship. If the Student is unable to become a member of the University before the end of the period prescribed in this regulation the Managers shall have power to extend that period.

Duties of the Student.

7. During the tenure of the Studentship a Student shall undertake whole-time study and training for research in Assyriology. The Managers may terminate a Studentship at any time if they are not satisfied that the Student is diligently pursuing his or her duties.

Stipend.

8. The stipend of the Studentship shall be the annual net income of the Fund and shall be paid to the Student by quarterly instalments in advance.

Unexpended income.

9. Any unexpended income accumulated in the Fund shall be used at the discretion of the Managers for the promotion of original research in, or the advancement of the study of, Assyriology in any or all of the following ways:

(*a*) to make grants to persons engaged in original research in Assyriology, who need not be members of the University;

(*b*) to help to finance excavation;

(*c*) to purchase specimens for the University of Cambridge;

(*d*) in any other way that the Managers may determine;

provided that all objects so purchased be labelled 'C. H. W. Johns Memorial Fund', and that all other benefits thus provided be acknowledged as arising from that Fund.

JONES FUND

1. The sum received by the University under the will of John Reginald Jones in 1963, and announced in the *Reporter* on 8 May 1963, shall be called the Jones Fund. Title.

2. The income of the Fund shall be expended from time to time by the Fitzwilliam Museum Syndicate on the purchase of pictures or other works of art not less than one hundred years old. Purpose.

GARETH JONES PRIZE

1. The moneys subscribed in honour of Gareth Jones, formerly Downing Professor of the Laws of England and Fellow of Trinity College, shall form a fund called the Gareth Jones Fund, the income of which shall be used to provide a prize called the Gareth Jones Prize. Fund and purpose.

2. The Prize shall be awarded by the Examiners for the LL.M. Examination to the candidate who has shown the greatest distinction in the subject Law of Restitution in that examination. How awarded.

JOWETT FUND

1. The sum bequeathed to the University by the late Walter Jowett shall form a fund called the Jowett Fund. Title.

2. The Fund shall be used, in accordance with the terms of the bequest, for the furtherance of research into diseases of animals, especially those transmissible to man and tropical diseases of domestic animals. Purpose.

3. The administration of the Fund shall be entrusted to five Managers, who shall be the Regius Professor of Physic, the Professor of Pathology, the Professor of Veterinary Science, the Professor of Veterinary Clinical Studies, and the Head of the Department of Veterinary Medicine. Managers.

4. Subject to the provisions of Regulation 2, the income and capital of the Fund shall be applied from time to time, at the discretion of the Managers and subject to such conditions as they may think fit, Application.

(*a*) to purchase equipment and apparatus;

(*b*) to make grants to persons who are conducting or who intend to conduct research in the University.

JUDGE MANAGEMENT EDUCATION TRUST M.B.A. PRIZE FOR MANAGEMENT ANALYSIS

1. The sum of £5,000 given to the University in 2004 by the Judge Management Education Trust shall form a fund, the income of which shall be used to provide a prize called the Judge Management Education Trust M.B.A. Prize for Management Analysis. Fund and purpose.

2. The Prize shall be awarded by the Director of the M.B.A. course for the best performance in Management Analysis in any one year. In awarding the Prize the Director shall take account of the reports of the teaching officer responsible for the delivery and assessment of the Management Analysis course or its successor course(s). How awarded.

3. The value of the Prize shall be determined by the Faculty Board of Business and Management, within a range approved from time to time by the Council. Value.

4. If in any year the Prize is not awarded, the income of the Fund for that year shall be added to the capital of the Fund. If not awarded.

RICHARD KAHN FUND

1. The sum of £65,000 given to the University in 1995 by Dr William Janeway, of Pembroke College, shall form a fund called the Richard Kahn Fund, in memory of Lord Kahn, formerly Professor of Economics, which shall be used for the promotion and encouragement of the study of Economics in the University. Fund and purpose.

Managers. **2.** The Managers of the Fund shall be the Faculty Board of Economics, who may delegate any or all of their functions under these regulations to a committee not necessarily consisting wholly of members of the Board.

Awards. **3.** The income and the capital of the Fund shall be used to provide awards known as Richard Kahn Research Studentships and Teaching Assistantships in the Faculty of Economics, which shall be open to any person who is or is about to be registered as a Graduate Student in the University, provided that, in accordance with the wishes of the benefactor, if two or more candidates are equally well qualified, preference shall be given to a candidate who is a citizen of the United States of America. Holders of the awards shall undertake advanced study or research in the Faculty of Economics; Teaching Assistants shall in addition undertake such teaching as may be assigned to them by the Faculty Board.

4. An award shall be tenable for one year in the first instance, and may be renewed by the Managers for a second or third year.

Value. **5.** The emolument paid to an award holder shall be determined by the Managers within a range approved from time to time by the Council.

Unexpended income. **6.** Any unexpended income may be either added to the capital of the Fund or accumulated for use as income in subsequent years, as the Managers may determine.

Kanthack Fund

Title and purpose. The sums accepted by the University in memory of Alfredo Antunes Kanthack, M.A., one time Fellow of King's College and Professor of Pathology, shall form a fund called the Kanthack Fund, the income of which shall be used for the benefit of the Department of Pathology.

Kaplanoff Fund

Title. **1.** The sum bequeathed to the University for the sole benefit of the University Library by Mark D. Kaplanoff, M.A., Ph.D., University Lecturer in History and Fellow of Pembroke College, shall form a fund called the Kaplanoff Fund.

Purpose. **2.** The income, and in exceptional cases the capital, of the Fund shall be applied at the discretion of the Library Syndicate for the purchase of materials for the University Library to support the study of American history.

Unexpended income. **3.** Unexpended income may at the discretion of the Syndicate either be added to the capital of the Fund or accumulated for use as income in subsequent years.

KAUST Fund for Biological Sciences

Grace 2 of 16 May 2012

Title. **1.** The benefaction from KAUST UK Ltd to support work in the School of the Biological Sciences, with a preference for biosciences and bioengineering, shall form a fund called the KAUST Fund for Biological Sciences.

Managers. **2.** The Managers of the Fund shall be the Head of the School of the Biological Sciences and two other Managers appointed by the Council of the School of the Biological Sciences for periods of five years.

Purpose. **3.** The Fund shall be applied for the following purposes in the School on the recommendation of the Managers and with the approval of the General Board:

(*a*) the payment of the stipend, national insurance, pension contributions, and associated indirect costs of the holders of such University offices as may be designated or established from time to time by the University or the General Board as a charge on the Fund,

(*b*) the funding of Ph.D. Studentships in the School of the Biological Sciences with a preference for bioscience and bioengineering,

(*c*) other purposes in the School of the Biological Sciences with a preference for the fields of bioscience and bioengineering.

4. In exceptional circumstances the capital may also be spent, on the recommendation of the Managers and with the approval of the General Board, for the purposes outlined in Regulation 3.

5. Any unexpended income of the Fund in a financial year may be added to the capital of the Fund; or retained for use as income in future years, as the Managers shall determine. Unexpended income.

KAVLI INSTITUTE FUND

1. The sums received from the Kavli Foundation for the support of work in Cosmology shall form a fund called the Kavli Institute Fund. Title and purpose.

2. The Fund shall be under the control of a Board of Managers who shall be: Managers.

(*a*) three persons appointed by the General Board, two of whom shall be appointed on the nomination of the Kavli Foundation;

(*b*) two persons appointed by the Council of the School of the Physical Sciences.

Members of the Board of Managers in classes (*a*) and (*b*) shall be appointed in the Michaelmas Term to serve for four years from 1 January following their appointment. The General Board shall appoint one of the Managers in class (*a*) to be Chair.

3. The Director of the Institute shall be appointed by the General Board on the recommendation of the Council of the School of the Physical Sciences and shall act as Secretary to the Board of Managers. Director.

4. The Managers shall be responsible for the administration of the Fund in support of research in Cosmology, for guiding the work of the Institute, and for encouraging collaboration with cognate Departments in the area of Cosmology.

5. The first charge on the Fund shall be the stipend, national insurance, and pension contributions payable by the University in respect of such number of Kavli Institute Fellows as the Managers shall so determine, and who shall be elected by the Managers of the Fund. Fellows.

6. A Fellowship shall be tenable for up to five years as the Managers shall determine. Tenure.

7. It shall be the duty of a Fellow to undertake full-time research in the field of Cosmology in the University of Cambridge. In any books, papers, or other publications containing the results of investigations carried out during the tenure of the Fellowship, the Fellow shall, where practicable, use the title 'Kavli Institute Fellow'. Duties of Fellows.

8. The annual stipend of a Fellow shall be such sum as shall be determined by the Managers, within a range approved from time to time by the General Board. Stipend.

9. After provision has been made in accordance with Regulation 5, the remaining income of the Fund shall be applied at the discretion of the Managers for the following purposes: Application of remaining income.

(i) to make such grants as they consider appropriate in respect of expenses incurred in connection with the research undertaken by a Kavli Institute Fellow,

(ii) to make grants in support of other research programmes in the Kavli Institute of Cosmology.

10. Any unexpended income of the Fund in a financial year may be either added to the capital of the Fund or accumulated for use as income in future years, as the Managers may determine. Unexpended income.

KAYE PRIZE

Stat. E XXX.

Endowments, 1904, p. 402

1. The Kaye Fund shall be used to provide a prize to be awarded every fourth year for a dissertation in English on some subject or question relating to ecclesiastical history up to the death of Gregory the Great, or Biblical studies which aid enquiry relating to the Scriptural authority for Christian doctrines, or which substantially advance the knowledge of Biblical history or of Biblical Hebrew and Greek. Prize.

2. The Prize shall be open to all graduates of the University and to all persons whose names are entered on the Register of Graduate Students, provided that on the last day appointed for sending in essays they are of not more than ten years' standing from admission to their first degree, whether of this or another university, and provided also that no previous prize-winner shall be eligible to compete. Who may compete.

3. The value of the Prize shall be such sum not exceeding the available income accumulated in the Fund as may be determined from time to time by the Faculty Board of Divinity with the approval of the Council. Value.

4. The Adjudicators of the Prize shall be two persons appointed by the General Board on the nomination of the Faculty Board of Divinity before the end of the Lent Term of the year preceding that in which a Prize is to be offered. Each Adjudicator shall receive from the Fund, unless no dissertation is sent in, such sum as shall be determined by the Faculty Board within a range approved by the Council. Adjudicators.

Notice of subject. **5.** In the Michaelmas Term in every fourth year the Registrary shall announce that a Kaye Prize is to be offered. On or before 19 December next following the announcement, each candidate shall give notice of the proposed subject of his or her dissertation to the Registrary, who shall submit it to the Adjudicators and shall communicate its approval or rejection to the candidate. Candidates shall send their dissertations to the Registrary so as to arrive on or before 15 November in the year next following the announcement.

Additional prizes. **6.** If dissertations of sufficient merit are submitted, it shall be open to the Adjudicators to award one or more additional Kaye Prizes not exceeding in value such sum as shall be determined by the Faculty Board of Divinity within a range approved from time to time by the Council.

Conditions. **7.** A prize-winner shall deposit two printed or typewritten copies of his or her dissertation in the Cathedral Library at Lincoln and one copy in the University Library.

THOMAS KEEPING FUND

Name. **1.** The benefaction of the late Mr T. J. H. H. Keeping shall form a fund called the Thomas Keeping Fund.

Purpose. **2.** The Fund shall be used to support research into the prevention and possible cure of such diseases as psoriasis, consumption, diabetes, and cancer.

Administration. **3.** The administration of the Fund shall be entrusted to two Managers who shall be the Regius Professor of Physic and the Professor of Pathology.

Application of Fund. **4.** Subject to the provisions of Regulation 2, the income or the capital of the Fund may be applied from time to time, at the discretion of the Managers and subject to such conditions as they may think fit, for the following purposes:

(*a*) to purchase equipment and apparatus;

(*b*) to make grants to persons who are conducting or who intend to conduct research under the direction of the Regius Professor of Physic.

ALEXANDER JAMES KEITH FUND AND STUDENTSHIPS

Title. **1.** The sum bequeathed to the University by the late Miss Christian Keith in memory of her brother, Alexander James Keith, student of Downing College, who was killed in the World War of 1914 to 1918, shall form a fund called the Alexander James Keith Fund.

Purpose. **2.** The income of the Fund shall be used to provide one or more Studentships for graduate studies in agriculture, which shall be called Alexander James Keith Studentships.

Electors. **3.** The Electors to the Studentships shall be three persons appointed by the Faculty Board of Biology in the Michaelmas Term to serve for three years from 1 January following their appointment.

Notice. **4.** Notice of an election shall be given by the Registrary, after consultation with the Electors, not later than the end of the Lent Term in any year.

Who are eligible. **5.** In order to be eligible for a Studentship a candidate must be a graduate or have been admitted as a Graduate Student by the Board of Graduate Studies and must intend to engage in graduate studies in agriculture. A Student who on election is not a member of the University shall be required to become a member of the University.

Value. **6.** The value of a Studentship shall be such sum not exceeding the available income of the Fund as may be determined by the Electors, within a range approved from time to time by the Council, after they have taken account of any other financial resources that may be available to the Student.

Duties. **7.** A Student shall undertake advanced study or research in agriculture.

Tenure. **8.** A Studentship shall be tenable for one year in the first instance. A Student may be re-elected for a second year and again for a third year but for no longer.

Unexpended income. **9.** Any unexpended income accumulated in the Fund may be applied from time to time by the Electors to make grants to Alexander James Keith Students and to other students engaged in research in agriculture in the Faculty of Biology towards meeting the cost of equipment and other expenses incurred by them in the course of their research.

The Vincent and Brigid Keown Memorial Prize for Medical Law

Grace 10 of 17 July 2013

1. The sum gifted annually by Professor John Keown, in memory of his late parents, shall form a prize for the study of Medical Law, to be known as The Vincent and Brigid Keown Memorial Prize for Medical Law. Prize.

2. The Prize shall be awarded by the Examiners for Part II of the Law Tripos to the candidate who shows the greatest distinction in the subject Medical Law in that examination. How awarded.

3. The value of the Prize, provided that there is a candidate of sufficient merit, shall be divided equally between the prize-winner and the Squire Law Library for the purchase of books. Value.

4. If in any year the Prize is not awarded, the unspent funds will be retained and awarded in a subsequent year. Unspent funds.

Kermode Prize

1. A donation of £1,000 by Dr Edwina Fairey, M.A., M.B., B.Chir., of Newnham College, in memory of her parents, Doris and Stanley Kermode, shall form a fund the income of which shall be used to provide a prize called the Kermode Prize in Obstetrics and Gynaecology. Prize.

2. The Prize shall be awarded not later than the first day of Full Michaelmas Term in each year by the Professor of Obstetrics and Gynaecology, or by a deputy appointed by the Professor, for distinction in Obstetrics and Gynaecology as shown by overall performance in those subjects in Part II of the Final M.B. Examination. How awarded.

3. The value of the Prize shall be such sum as may be determined by the Faculty Board of Clinical Medicine within a range approved from time to time by the Council. Value.

Sir Hamilton Kerr Trust Fund

1. The sum given to the University by Sir Hamilton Kerr, together with other sums received for the same purpose, shall form a fund to be called the Sir Hamilton Kerr Trust Fund. The first charge on the income of the Fund shall be the maintenance in good order as an extension of the Fitzwilliam Museum of the property known as the Mill House, Whittlesford, and the improvement or development of the property in whatever ways the Managers of the Fund may consider desirable. Title and purpose.

2. The balance of income shall be available to the Managers of the Fund for any purpose connected with the Mill House, Whittlesford, or connected with the Fitzwilliam Museum which they consider may be appropriately supported by the Fund.

3. The Managers of the Fund shall be the Fitzwilliam Museum Syndicate. They shall be responsible for approving expenditure from the income of the Fund and such part of the capital of the Fund as they may determine for the purposes set out in Regulations 1 and 2. Managers.

Hamilton Kerr Research Scientist Appeal Fund

1. The sums received as a result of an appeal to fund a research scientist at the Hamilton Kerr Institute shall form a fund to be called the Hamilton Kerr Research Scientist Appeal Fund the capital and income of which shall be applied towards the payment of the stipend, national insurance, pension contributions, and associated indirect costs of a research scientist in the Institute. Title of Appeal Fund.

2. Any unexpended income of the Fund in any financial year may, at the discretion of the Fitzwilliam Museum Syndicate, either be accumulated for use as income in any one or more subsequent years or applied to support the work of the Institute. Unexpended income.

Kettle's Yard Music Fund

1. The income of the Kettle's Yard Music Fund shall be used to support an annual series of concerts at Kettle's Yard. Purpose.

2. The Managers of the Fund shall be the Kettle's Yard Music Sub-committee. Managers.

3. Any unexpended income in a financial year shall be accumulated for use as income in future years. Unexpended income.

Kettle's Yard Travel Fund

Name and purpose. **1.** The sum of £8,000 shall form a fund which, in accordance with the wishes of the donor, shall be called the Kettle's Yard Travel Fund. The income of the Fund shall be devoted to making grants, to be called Brancusi Grants, towards the expenses of students of architecture or of history of art to enable them to travel abroad to study architecture or art, provided that, at the discretion of the Awarders, any income not so expended in any year may be used in that year for making grants for travel within the United Kingdom for the same purpose.

Awarders. **2.** The Awarders shall be the Professor of Architecture and two members of the Faculty of Architecture and History of Art appointed by the General Board before the division of the Lent Term in each year, one on the nomination of the Head of the Department of Architecture and one on the nomination of the Head of the Department of History of Art.

Eligibility for grants. **3.** Any member of the University who has graduated in architecture or in history of art at Cambridge or elsewhere shall be eligible for a grant from the Fund, but the Awarders shall give preference to candidates below the standing of Master of Arts.

Applications for grants. **4.** Applications for grants, accompanied by a short statement of the nature and purpose of the proposed travel, must be submitted to the Secretary of the Faculty Board of Architecture and History of Art so as to arrive not later than the division of the Lent Term.

Payment of grants. **5.** The names of students to whom grants have been awarded, but not the value of the grants, shall be published in the *Reporter*.

Duties of recipients of grants. **6.** Each recipient of a grant shall be required

(*a*) to make use of the grant before the end of the calendar year next following that in which the awards are announced, provided that the Professor of Architecture may waive this requirement;

(*b*) to send to the Professor of Architecture a short report on the result of his or her study as soon as is practicable after its completion.

Unexpended income. **7.** Any part of the income of the Fund not expended in any year shall be added to the capital of the Fund.

Keynes Fund for Applied Economics

Grace 2 of 28 September 2011

Title. **1.** The sums received by the University from an anonymous donor, and other sums received for the same purpose, shall form a fund called the Keynes Fund for Applied Economics.

Managers. **2.** The Managers of the Fund shall be:

(*a*) the Pro-Vice-Chancellor for Research as Chair;

(*b*) the Chair of the Faculty Board of Economics;

(*c*) two persons appointed by the Faculty Board of Economics, one of whom shall also serve as the Director of the Fund;

(*d*) one person appointed by the General Board on the nomination of the donor, or such a person as the donor may appoint as her or his successor;

(*e*) a Manager of the Cambridge Endowment for Research in Finance (in class (*d*) of the regulations for that Fund);

(*f*) one suitably qualified person who is not employed by the University, appointed by the General Board;

(*g*) one person co-opted by the other Managers.

If one of the named posts is vacant or its tenure has expired, the General Board shall appoint one or more additional Managers to ensure that there are always eight Managers. Managers in classes (*c*), (*f*), and (*g*) shall be appointed for periods of five years at a time.

Purpose. **3.** The income of the Fund shall be used to enable the Faculty of Economics to build on the legacy of J. M. Keynes in promoting innovative research and teaching that will help meet the need for practical solutions to economic problems including by way of funding seminars, lectures, Visiting Fellowship programmes, post-doctoral Fellowships, and Studentships.

4. No business shall be transacted at any meeting of the Managers unless at least five members are present.

Unexpended Income. **5.** Any unexpended income in a financial year shall either be added to the capital of the Fund or accumulated for use as income in any one or more subsequent years, as the Managers may determine.

6. The Fund shall be administered by the Managers in accordance with the provisions of the agreement with the donor dated 26 May 2011.

J. M. KEYNES FELLOWSHIPS IN FINANCIAL ECONOMICS

Grace 4 of 17 February 2010

1. The gift of £5m to the University from The Pyewacket Foundation shall form a fund to be called the J. M. Keynes Fellowships Fund the income of which shall be used for research into all aspects of finance, financial institutions, and financial markets, and their relationship with micro-economic behaviour and macro-economic performance, including public policy issues relating to financial markets. Title and purpose.

2. The Managers of the Fund shall be: Managers.

(*a*) The Vice-Chancellor (or a duly appointed Deputy) as Chair;

(*b*) one person appointed by each of the Faculty Boards of Business and Management, Economics, Law, and Mathematics;

(*c*) three persons, including two persons external to the University, appointed by the General Board;

(*d*) William Janeway in his personal capacity or such person as he may designate as his successor.

Members in classes (*b*) and (*c*) shall be appointed in the Michaelmas Term to serve for four years from 1 January following their appointment.

The Managers shall be responsible for the administration of the Fund, for the promotion of work in financial economics, and for encouraging collaboration between cognate Faculties and Departments in the areas specified in Regulation 1.

3. The first charge on the income of the Fund shall be the emoluments of such number of J. M. Keynes Fellows in Financial Economics as the Managers shall determine and shall be elected by the Managers of the Fund. The stipend of a Fellow shall be determined by the Managers within a range determined by the General Board. Fellows.

4. The duties of a Fellow shall be to further interdisciplinary research and study in the general area of financial economics, in accordance with Regulation 1, on the basis of a proposal approved by the Managers at the time of election. A Fellow shall give an annual lecture on her or his work during the tenure of the Fellowship and shall submit an annual report to the Managers on the activities subtended by the Fellowship. Duties.

5. A Fellowship shall be tenable for up to five years and shall not be renewable. Tenure.

6. After provision has been made in accordance with Regulation 3 the remaining income of the Fund may be applied at the discretion of the Managers for the following purposes Application of remaining income.

(i) to make grants as they consider appropriate in respect of expenses incurred in connection with the research undertaken by a Fellow,

(ii) to make grants in support of other research programmes in the fields specified in Regulation 1.

7. Any unexpended income of the Fund in a financial year may be either added to the capital of the Fund or accumulated for use as income in future years, as the Managers may determine. Unexpended income.

MILO KEYNES FUND

Grace 2 of 12 April 2012

1. The sum bequeathed to the University by the late Dr Milo Keynes, M.A., M.D., M.Chir., of Trinity College, shall form a Fund called the Milo Keynes Fund. Title.

2. The Managers of the Fund shall be the Regius Professor of Physic, the Professor of Surgery, and the Director of Medical Education in the Clinical School. Managers.

3. The income from the Fund shall be used for a Milo Keynes Prize or Prizes to be awarded at the absolute discretion of the Managers for the following purposes: Purpose.

(i) to encourage non-medically qualified persons to work in medical departments;

(ii) to help with the travel of medical postgraduates who are at an early stage of their academic career and who are not holding a tenured University post;

(iii) to reward an exceptional piece of research by a medical graduate who is at an early stage of her or his academic career and who is not holding a tenured University post.

4. Any unexpended income of the Fund in a financial year shall be either added to the capital of the Fund or retained for use as income in future years, as the Managers may determine. Unexpended Income.

Nita King Research Scholarship

Name and purpose.

1. The Scholarship, founded in memory of Miss Nita Madeline King, a member of a Voluntary Aid Detachment, who died in France of cerebrospinal fever in May 1917, and endowed by Mrs L. King, of Worthing, shall be called the Nita King Research Scholarship, and shall be devoted to the encouragement of original research in the aetiology, pathology, and prevention of fevers.

Board of Management.

2. The administration of the Fund shall be entrusted to a Board of Management consisting of the Regius Professor of Physic, the Professor of Pathology, and two persons appointed, one by the Faculty Board of Clinical Medicine and one by the Faculty Board of Veterinary Medicine, who shall be called the Managers of the Fund.

Quorum.

No resolution of the Managers shall be valid unless approved by at least two of these Managers at a meeting to which all the Managers have been summoned.

3. In case a deputy should be appointed to discharge the duties of any of the Managers aforesaid, such deputy shall for the purposes of these regulations take the place and exercise the powers of the Manager concerned during such time as he or she may be acting as such deputy.

Income of Fund.

4. The income of the Trust Fund shall be placed to a separate account, and applied from time to time to endow a Scholarship to be called the Nita King Research Scholarship, the holder of which shall undertake whole-time study and training for research in the aetiology, pathology, and prevention of fevers.

Qualifications of candidates.

5. The Scholarship shall not be awarded by the results of competitive examination, but the Managers may take such steps as they may think fit to ascertain the qualifications of the candidates, who shall be members of the University.

Value.

6. The Scholarship shall be of the annual value of £50 or such larger or smaller sum as the Fund may produce, and shall be paid to the Scholar by equal half-yearly payments, the payment for each half-year being made in advance.

Tenure.

7. The Managers shall elect in the first instance for such period not exceeding three years as they shall think fit, and shall have power to re-elect a Scholar for any further period not exceeding three years provided that a Scholar re-elected for a further period shall undertake original research.

Conditions of research.

8. The conditions under which the research is to be conducted and the place or places in which it is to be carried on shall be determined by the Professor of Pathology in consultation with the other Managers.

Notice of election.

9. Not less than one month's notice shall be given of an election. Elections shall in general be made as vacancies occur.

Suspension of election.

10. If, after notice of a vacancy, there shall be, in the opinion of the Managers, no suitable candidate for the Scholarship, it shall be lawful for the Managers to suspend the election for a time not greater than one year, and if at the expiration of such time there shall, after notice of the vacancy given, be no suitable candidate as aforesaid, the election may again be suspended in the same way, and so on until, in the opinion of the Managers, there shall be a suitable candidate for the Scholarship.

Unexpended income.

11. During any vacancy of the Scholarship the income shall be added to the Trust Fund.

Alterations.

12. These regulations, except Regulation 1, shall be subject to alteration by Grace.

Kuwait Foundation Fund

Title.

1. The sums received from the Kuwait Foundation for the Advancement of Sciences shall form a fund called the Kuwait Foundation Fund.

Managers.

2. The Fund shall be administered by a Board of Managers who shall be:

(*a*) the Sadleirian Professor of Pure Mathematics as Chair;

(*b*) the Head of the Department of Pure Mathematics and Mathematical Statistics;

(*c*) one person appointed by the General Board;

(*d*) one person appointed by the Faculty Board of Mathematics;

(*e*) two persons appointed by the Trustees of the Kuwait Foundation for the Advancement of Sciences.

Managers in classes (*c*)–(*e*) shall be appointed in the Michaelmas Term to serve for four years from 1 January following their appointment.

Professorship.

3. The first charge on the income of the Fund shall be the payment of the stipend, national insurance, pension contributions, and indirect costs of the Kuwait Professor of Number Theory and Algebra payable by the University.

4. If and whenever the income of the Fund shall exceed the amount required to meet the costs specified in Regulation 3, the excess of the income over that amount may be applied in support of the work of the Kuwait Professor of Number Theory and Algebra in such manner as may be approved by the General Board on the recommendation of the Managers.

5. After provision has been made in accordance with Regulation 3, and subject to the provisions of Regulation 4, the Fund shall be used at the discretion of the Managers for the following purposes: Junior Fellowship.

(*a*) to provide the stipend of a Kuwait Junior Fellowship for research in mathematics, which shall be tenable in the Department of Pure Mathematics and Mathematical Statistics;

(*b*) to provide lectures from time to time, to be called Kuwait Fund Lectures, on subjects in the field of number theory or algebra, and to pay a stipend to the lecturers;

(*c*) to support research in the field of number theory or algebra.

6. Elections to a Kuwait Junior Fellowship shall be made by the General Board on the recommendation of the Managers. Elections.

7. A Kuwait Junior Fellowship shall be tenable for not more than one year. The period of tenure and the stipend of the Fellow shall be determined by the General Board on the recommendation of the Managers in each particular case. Tenure.

8. Any unspent income in a financial year shall be either added to the capital of the Fund or accumulated for use as income in a future year, at the discretion of the Managers Unspent income.

KIRBY LAING FUND

Grace 1 of 7 November 2007

1. The sum of £1.2m received from the Kirby Laing Foundation together with other sums received for the same purpose shall form a fund called the Kirby Laing Fund. Title.

2. The Fund, which will be for the support of Christian Theology and New Testament Studies, shall be administered by four Managers, who shall comprise: Purpose and Managers.

(*a*) the Chair of the Faculty Board of Divinity, who shall be Chair;

(*b*) the Lady Margaret's Professor of Divinity;

(*c*) the Chair of the School of Arts and Humanities;

(*d*) a person nominated by the Kirby Laing Foundation for the time being, provided that, if no nominee is forthcoming, the Principal of Ridley Hall, Cambridge, shall serve as a Manager.

3. The first charge on the income of the Fund shall be the stipend, national insurance, pension contributions, and associated indirect costs of the Lady Margaret's Professor of Divinity payable by the University. Professorship.

4. Any unexpended income in a financial year may be used in any one or more subsequent years to support the research of the Professor or added to the capital of the Fund, as the Managers shall determine, subject to the approval of the General Board. Unexpended income.

KIRBY LAING FUND FOR CIVIL ENGINEERING

Grace 1 of 13 July 2011

1. The sum of £2m received from the Kirby Laing Foundation together with other sums received for the same purpose shall form a fund called the Kirby Laing Fund for Civil Engineering. Fund and purpose.

2. The Fund shall be administered by four Managers, who shall comprise: Managers.

(*a*) the Head of the Department of Engineering, who shall be Chair;

(*b*) the Sir Kirby Laing Professor of Civil Engineering;

(*c*) the Head of the School of Technology;

(*d*) a person nominated by the Kirby Laing Foundation and approved by the General Board.

3. The first charge on the income of the Fund shall be the stipend, national insurance, pension contributions, and associated indirect costs of the Sir Kirby Laing Professor of Civil Engineering payable by the University. Professorship.

4. If and whenever the income of the Fund shall exceed the amount required to meet the costs specified in Regulation 3, the excess of the income over that amount may be applied in support of research in the field of civil engineering in such manner as may be approved by the General Board on the recommendation of the Managers.

Unexpended income.

5. Any unexpended income in any financial year may, at the discretion of the Managers, be accumulated and added to the capital of the Fund or be held as an income reserve and expended in any one or more subsequent years in accordance with Regulations 3 and 4 above.

Philip Lake Bequest

Division of income.

The income derived from the bequest of Philip Lake shall be divided equally between two funds to be called Philip Lake Fund I and Philip Lake Fund II.

Philip Lake Fund I

Assignment.

1. Philip Lake Fund I shall be assigned to the Department of Earth Sciences.

Managers.

2. The Fund shall be administered by the Head of the Department of Earth Sciences *ex officio*, and by two other Managers, who shall be University officers in the Department of Earth Sciences, appointed by the Faculty Board of Earth Sciences and Geography during the Michaelmas Term of each year to serve for the ensuing calendar year. No resolution shall be valid unless it is approved by a majority of the Managers.

Application.

3. The Fund shall be applied at the discretion of the Managers for defraying the travelling expenses of students and University officers in the Department of Earth Sciences when engaged in geological studies.

Philip Lake Fund II

Assignment.

1. Philip Lake Fund II shall be assigned to the Department of Geography.

Managers.

2. The Fund shall be administered by the Head of the Department of Geography, and by two other Managers, who shall be members of the teaching staff of the Department of Geography, appointed by the Faculty Board of Earth Sciences and Geography in the Michaelmas Term of each year to serve for the ensuing calendar year. No resolution shall be valid unless it is approved by a majority of the Managers.

Prizes.

3. The first charge on Philip Lake Fund II shall be the provision of two Philip Lake Prizes in accordance with the regulations for those Prizes.

Grants.

4. After provision has been made for the two Philip Lake Prizes, the remaining income of the Fund shall be used at the discretion of the Managers for making grants to Graduate Students in the Department of Geography towards the cost of research or field-work, provided that preference shall be given to students who are following a course of research as candidates, or with a view to becoming candidates, for the Ph.D. Degree, and who have not yet completed nine terms of research.

Philip Lake Prizes

Prizes.

1. Two Prizes, to be called Philip Lake Prizes, shall be offered annually to candidates for the Geographical Tripos.

How awarded.

2. Philip Lake Prize I shall be awarded to the candidate who is adjudged by the Examiners for Part IB of the Geographical Tripos to have shown the greatest proficiency in that Part.

3. Philip Lake Prize II shall be awarded to the candidate who is adjudged by the Examiners for Part II of the Geographical Tripos to have shown the greatest proficiency in Physical Geography in that Part.

Value.

4. The Prizes shall be payable from the income of Philip Lake Fund II. The value of each Prize shall be £15 or such larger sum as may be determined each year by the Managers, within a range approved from time to time by the Council; provided that the combined value of the Prizes shall not exceed the annual income of the Fund.

Charles Lamb Prize

Name and purpose.

1. The sum bequeathed to the University by Charles George Lamb, Sc.D., of Clare College, shall form a fund called the Charles Lamb Fund for the encouragement of the study of electrical engineering.

2. The income of the Fund shall be applied to provide a prize to be called the Charles Lamb Prize.

Awarders.

3. The Awarders of the Prize shall be the Examiners for Part IIB of the Engineering Tripos.

4. The Prize shall be awarded annually to the candidate who shows the greatest proficiency in any area of electrical or information engineering in Part IIB of the Engineering Tripos, unless the Awarders are of the opinion that there is no candidate of sufficient merit to receive the Prize.

5. The value of the Prize shall be the net annual income of the Fund. Value.

6. The Awarders shall be empowered to use accumulated income to provide an additional Prize or Prizes not exceeding such sum as shall be determined by the Faculty Board of Engineering within a range approved from time to time by the Council. Any accumulated income in excess of such sum as shall be determined by the Finance Committee of the Council shall be added to the capital of the Fund. Unexpended income.

7. These regulations, except Regulations 1 and 2, shall be subject to alteration by Grace.

SIR WALTER LANGDON-BROWN PRIZE

1. The sum bequeathed to the University by Mr John Neville Brown in memory of his uncle, Sir Walter Langdon-Brown, of Corpus Christi College, formerly Regius Professor of Physic, shall form a fund called the Neville Brown Fund. Title.

2. The income of the Fund shall be used to provide a Prize called the Sir Walter Langdon-Brown Prize, which shall be awarded annually for a dissertation or thesis in any field of medicine, with preference given to a field related to endocrinology, metabolic medicine, or therapeutics, submitted in candidature for the M.D. Degree or the M.Chir. Degree.

3. The Prize shall be awarded by the Regius Professor of Physic, after consulting the M.D. Committee and the M.Chir. Committee. How awarded.

4. The value of the Prize shall be the annual income of the Fund.

5. If in any year the Prize is not awarded, the unexpended income shall be added to the capital of the Fund. Unexpended income.

SIR PERCEVAL MAITLAND LAURENCE'S BENEFACTION AND BEQUEST

Sir Perceval Maitland Laurence Fund I

1. The sum of £10,000, the benefaction of Sir Perceval Maitland Laurence, shall be invested separately in the name of the Chancellor, Masters, and Scholars of the University and shall be called the Sir Perceval Maitland Laurence Fund I. Fund.

2. One-half of the income of the Fund shall be transferred annually to the University Library General Fund. Purposes.

3. The other half of the income of the Fund shall be available to the Faculty of Classics to be used for the encouragement of classical study, especially that of Ancient History, and Greek and Roman Antiquities, in such manner as may be thought most advantageous by that Faculty.

Sir Perceval Maitland Laurence Fund II

4. The bequest of Sir Perceval Maitland Laurence shall be invested separately in the name of the Chancellor, Masters, and Scholars of the University and shall be called the Sir Perceval Maitland Laurence Fund II. Fund.

5. One-fifth of the income of the Fund shall be transferred annually to the University Library General Fund. Purposes.

6. Four-fifths of the income of the Fund shall be made available to the Faculty of Classics and shall be used in the first instance for the following purposes:

(*a*) to provide one-half of the cost of the stipends, national insurance, and pension contributions of the Laurence Professor of Ancient Philosophy, the Laurence Professor of Classical Archaeology, and the Professor of Comparative Philology, provided that not more than nine-tenths of that part of the income of the Fund available to the Faculty of Classics shall be used for that purpose;

(*b*) to provide £300 a year towards the cost of the Faculty Library in the Faculty of Classics;

(*c*) to provide £100 a year towards the University's subscription to the British School at Athens until the University shall otherwise determine;[1]

[1] The subscription is subject to the condition that the University shall have the right to appoint a representative to serve on the Managing Committee of the School. The representative shall be appointed in each Michaelmas Term on the nomination of the Faculty Board of Classics.

(*d*) to provide £85 a year towards the University's subscription to the British School at Rome until the University shall otherwise determine;

(*e*) to provide a sum annually for grants in aid of research which sum together with the sums specified in clauses (*b*), (*c*), and (*d*) shall amount to one-tenth of the income of the Fund available to the Faculty of Classics.

Sir Perceval Maitland Laurence Fund III

Fund and purpose.

7. After provision has been made for the charges detailed in Regulation 6(*a*)–(*e*), the residue of that portion of the income of the Sir Perceval Maitland Laurence Bequest assigned to the Faculty of Classics shall be transferred to a Reserve Fund known as the Sir Perceval Maitland Laurence Fund III to be used for the furtherance of classical studies in such ways as the Faculty Board of Classics shall from time to time determine.

Hersch Lauterpacht Fund

Title.

1. The sums of money subscribed in memory of the late Sir Hersch Lauterpacht shall form a fund called the Hersch Lauterpacht Fund.

Purpose.

2. The capital and income of the Fund shall be placed at the disposal of the Faculty Board of Law for the purpose of promoting the study of International Law in the University in any way in which the Faculty Board may from time to time determine.

Law Endowment Fund

Managers.

1. The Managers of the Law Endowment Fund shall be the Faculty Board of Law, who may delegate any or all of their functions under these regulations to a committee not necessarily consisting wholly of members of the Board.

Income expenditure.

2. The income of the Fund shall be expended from time to time, as the Managers shall determine, for the general purposes of the Faculty of Law. It shall be open to the Managers to add any unexpended income in a financial year to the capital of the Fund.

Stat. E XVI.

Le Bas Fund

Endowments, 1904, p. 395

Le Bas Prize

Prize.

1. A Le Bas Prize shall be offered in every year for an essay on a literary subject. The value of the Prize shall be £100 or such larger sum, not exceeding the annual income of the Fund, as the Council shall from time to time determine.

Who may compete.

2. Candidature for the Prize shall be open to any member of the University who is a graduate of this or another university and who will not have attained the age of thirty years on the day by which essays must be received by the Registrary.

Examiners.

3. One Examiner shall be appointed before the end of the Michaelmas Term in each year, on the nomination alternately of the Faculty Board of English and of the Faculty Board of History, to serve for two years from 1 January next following. Each Examiner shall receive from the income of the Fund, except when no essay is sent in, such amount as may be determined by the Faculty Boards of English and of History within a range approved from time to time by the Council.

4. If the Examiners in any year need assistance in making their award, they shall nominate one or more Assessors for appointment by the General Board. Each Assessor shall receive from the income of the Fund such amount as may be determined by the Faculty Boards of English and of History within a range approved from time to time by the Council.

Submission of essay.

5. In each year every candidate shall send the proposed subject of his or her essay to the Registrary so as to arrive not later than 14 February. The Registrary shall submit the subject to the Examiners and shall communicate its approval or rejection to the candidate. Essays shall be submitted to the Registrary so as to arrive not later than 30 June, and the award of the Prize shall be announced not later than 31 October.

6. Each essay shall be clearly written, or typewritten, or printed, and shall be prefixed by a declaration of its length, which shall not exceed 30,000 words and shall not be less than 15,000 words. An essay or dissertation for which any other University Prize has been awarded shall be inadmissible. Conditions.

7. The successful candidate shall deposit a printed or typewritten copy of his or her essay in the University Library.

Le Bas Research Studentships

1. The net income of the Le Bas Fund, after provision has been made in accordance with the regulations for the Le Bas Prize, shall be applied for the maintenance of one or more Le Bas Research Studentships for the furtherance of the study of literature. Title and purpose.

2. The Electors to the Studentships shall be the Board of Graduate Studies. Electors.

3. The Studentship shall be open to any person who is or is about to become registered as a Graduate Student in the University. Eligibility.

4. Applications shall be submitted to the Secretary of the Board of Graduate Studies. The date by which they must be received and the manner in which they must be submitted shall be announced in each year by the Board. Applications.

5. It shall be the duty of a Le Bas Research Student to undertake research with the object of furthering the study of literature. During the tenure of the Studentship a Student shall be subject, as far as they are applicable, to the provisions of the general regulations for admission as a Graduate Student, and of the regulations for the Ph.D., M.Sc., and M.Litt. Degrees, and for the M.Phil. Degree. Duties.

6. The tenure of the Studentship shall begin on 1 October following the Student's election and shall continue for one year or two years or three years as the Electors shall determine at the time of the election. A Student shall be re-eligible; provided that the tenure of a Studentship shall not exceed three years in all and shall be conditional upon the Student remaining on the Register of Graduate Students. Tenure.

7. The annual stipend of a Student shall be such sum not exceeding the available income of the Fund as may be determined by the Electors, within a range approved from time to time by the Council, after they have taken account of any other financial resources that may be available to the Student. Stipend.

8. The stipend shall be paid in such instalments as the Electors shall from time to time determine, provided that the Electors may withhold payment of any instalment if they are not satisfied that the Student is pursuing his or her research with sufficient diligence. Payments.

JERRY LEE FUND FOR EXPERIMENTAL CRIMINOLOGY

Grace 1 of 29 April 2009

1. The sums received from the Jerry Lee Foundation shall form a fund for the benefit of postgraduate students or postdoctoral research staff in the Institute of Criminology undertaking research in Experimental Criminology. Fund and purpose.

2. The Managers of the Fund shall be the Director of the Institute of Criminology (who shall be Chair), the Wolfson Professor of Criminology, and two persons with experience in Experimental Criminology appointed by the Committee of Management of the Institute of Criminology. Managers.

3. The capital and income of the Fund shall be applied at the discretion of the Managers:

(*a*) to provide the stipend, national insurance, and pension contributions of one or more Jerry Lee Fellows in Experimental Criminology who shall conduct research in the field of Experimental Criminology. The annual stipend of a Fellow shall be determined by the Managers. Fellowships.

(*b*) to provide one or more Jerry Lee Scholarships in Experimental Criminology for persons who are, or are about to be, registered for the Ph.D. Degree in the field of Experimental Criminology in the Institute of Criminology. Scholarships.

4. A Scholarship may provide

(*a*) a maintenance payment to be determined by the Managers,

(*b*) a payment to meet any University and/or College fees payable by the Scholar,

(*c*) a contribution to other costs such as equipment, travel expenses, according to the discretion of the Managers.

In determining the award the Managers shall take into account any other financial resources available to the Scholar.

5. After provision has been made for any Fellowships and Scholarships, the income of the Fund, and such portion of the capital as they may determine, shall be applied towards other costs related to experimental research in the Institute of Criminology at the discretion of the Managers.

Unexpended income. **6.** Any unexpended income of the Fund in a financial year may be accumulated and expended in any one or more subsequent years in accordance with Regulations 3 to 5, as may be determined by the Managers.

Dr S. T. Lee Public Policy Lecture Fund

Fund and purpose. **1.** The benefaction of Dr S. T. Lee, Honorary Fellow of Wolfson College, shall form a fund called the Dr S. T. Lee Public Policy Lecture Fund, the income of which shall be used to provide an annual lecture called the Dr S. T. Lee Public Policy Lecture.

Appointment of Lecturer. **2.** The appointment of the Dr S. T. Lee Public Policy Lecturer shall be made by the Vice-Chancellor each year on the advice of a committee comprising not more than five members of the Senate appointed by the Council in the Michaelmas Term to serve for four years from 1 January following their appointment.

Duties. **3.** The duty of the Lecturer shall be to deliver in the University during Full Term a lecture on some aspect or aspects of scientific, medical, or technological research and developments that are likely to have significant implications for public policy over the next decade, and should reflect on some of these policy implications.

Kennedy Leigh Fund for Modern Hebrew

Fund. **1.** The sums received from the Trustees of the Kennedy Leigh Charitable Trust towards the endowment of a University Lectureship in Modern Hebrew, to be entitled the Kennedy Leigh Lectureship, shall form a fund called the Kennedy Leigh Fund for Modern Hebrew.

Managers. **2.** The Fund shall be under the control of a Board of Managers, who shall be:

(*a*) the Regius Professor of Hebrew;

(*b*) two persons appointed by the Head of the Department of Middle Eastern Studies to serve for two years from 1 January following their appointment, one of whom shall be appointed after consultation with and with the agreement of the teaching officers in Hebrew in the Department and one in consultation with the Trustees of the Kennedy Leigh Charitable Trust.

Lecturer. **3.** The first charge on the income of the Fund shall be the stipend, national insurance, pension contributions, and associated indirect costs payable by the University in respect of the Kennedy Leigh Lecturer in Modern Hebrew.

Other purposes. **4.** After provision has been made in accordance with Regulation 3, the income of the Fund shall be applied at the discretion of the Managers for the encouragement of the study of Modern Hebrew in the University.

Unexpended income. **5.** Any unexpended income of the Fund in a financial year may be either added to the capital of the Fund or accumulated for use as income in future years, as the Managers may determine.

6. The University shall have power to alter these regulations by Grace on the recommendation of the Faculty Board of Asian and Middle Eastern Studies, subject to the approval of the Trustees of the Kennedy Leigh Charitable Trust.

Leverton Harris Fund

Fund. **1.** The moneys received by the University under the will of the Rt Hon. F. Leverton Harris in 1926, and announced in the *Reporter* on 7 December 1926, shall be called the Leverton Harris Fund.

Purpose. **2.** The income of the Fund shall be expended from time to time by the Director of the Fitzwilliam Museum on the purchase of works of art.

Stat. E XXXVIII.

Benn W. Levy Fund and Studentship

Name. **1.** The Fund shall be called the Benn W. Levy Fund, and shall be devoted to the furtherance of original research in Biochemistry.

Managers. **2.** The Managers of the Fund shall be

(*a*) the Sir William Dunn Professor of Biochemistry, who shall be Chair of the Managers;

(*b*) one person appointed by the Faculty Board of Clinical Medicine;

(*c*) one person appointed by the Faculty Board of Veterinary Medicine;

(*d*) two persons appointed by the Faculty Board of Biology;

(*e*) one person appointed by the Faculty Board of Physics and Chemistry.

Managers in classes (*b*)–(*e*) shall be appointed in the Michaelmas Term to serve for four years from 1 January following their appointment. No resolution of the Managers shall be valid unless approved by at least three of them at a meeting to which they have all been summoned, save that a resolution circulated to and signed by all the Managers shall have the same validity as a resolution carried at a meeting.

Studentship endowed.

3. The income of the present Trust Fund not exceeding £100 per annum shall from time to time as and when received be paid to the Managers and placed to a separate account, and shall be applied from time to time to endow a Studentship to be called the Benn W. Levy Studentship, the holder of which shall undertake original research in Biochemistry. Any income from the Trust Fund not applied for the purpose aforesaid or accruing during any vacancy in the Studentship shall be accumulated and added to the capital of the Fund,[1] and when such Trust Fund together with such accumulated income shall amount to £4,000[2] the full income of such Trust Fund and accumulated fund shall be applied for the purposes of the said Studentship; but the Managers shall have power at any time and from time to time to apply the accumulations or any part thereof to make good any deficiency in the income of £100 per annum in any year.

Increase of Fund.

4. The Managers shall give due notice of their intention to proceed to an election.

Who may be candidates.

5. The Studentship shall be open to members of the University of Cambridge who have been admitted to a degree. It shall not be awarded on the result of a competitive examination.

Emolument.

6. The emolument of the Studentship shall be determined by the Managers within a range approved from time to time by the Council.

Tenure.

7. The Studentship shall be tenable for such period as the Managers shall determine on the occasion of each election.

Unexpended income.

8. Any balance of the income of the Fund, after payment of the stipend of the Student, may be used by the Managers at their discretion

(*a*) to provide one or more additional Studentships;

(*b*) to make grants to the holder of a Studentship towards the expenses of his or her research.

Duties of the Student.

9. The Student during the tenure of the Studentship shall undertake original research in Biochemistry, and shall not systematically follow any business or profession, or engage in any educational or other work, which, in the opinion of those entrusted with the administration of the Fund, would seriously interfere with his or her inquiries. In any books, papers, or other publications containing the results of investigations carried out during the tenure of the Studentship, the Student shall, where practicable, use the title 'Benn W. Levy Student'.

Alterations.

10. These regulations, except Regulations 1, 3, 9, and this regulation shall be subject to alteration by Grace, always provided that the main object of the Fund, namely the furtherance of original research in Biochemistry, shall be adhered to.

Lewin Memorial Fund

Title and purpose.

1. The gift of Charles Lewin and Mrs Caroline Evans in memory of their father, Walpole S. Lewin, CBE, FRCS, Senior Neurological Surgeon to Addenbrooke's Hospital, and Fellow of Darwin College, together with other sums donated for the purpose shall form a fund, called the Lewin Memorial Fund, to provide a biennial Lewin Memorial Lecture.

Appointment of Lecturer.

2. The Lewin Memorial Lecturer shall be appointed by the Electors to the Lectureship in the Michaelmas Term of the academical year in which the Lecture is to be given. In appointing the Lecturer the Electors shall take into account the late W. S. Lewin's interests in head injuries and medical education, and any wishes expressed by his children.

Electors.

3. The Electors shall be the Regius Professor of Physic, the Senior Neurological Surgeon to Addenbrooke's Hospital, and one person distinguished in the field of neurological surgery or the neurosciences appointed by the Faculty Board of Clinical Medicine for a period of four years.

[1] But see also Statute E XXXVIII and Regulation 10.

[2] The Trust Fund together with accumulated income currently amounts to over £4,000.

Lecturer's honorarium and expenses. **4.** The Electors shall be empowered to make arrangements for the Lecture and to determine the honorarium and expenses to be paid to the Lecturer within the income of the Fund. Any unspent income shall be added to the capital of the Fund.

Lewin Prize Fund

Amended by Grace 13 of 24 April 2014

Fund and purpose. **1.** Donations of £1,000 from former colleagues of Walpole S. Lewin, CBE, FRCS, Senior Neurological Surgeon to Addenbrooke's Hospital and Fellow of Darwin College, shall form a fund called the Lewin Prize Fund for the purpose of awarding a prize in Surgery to candidates for Part III of the Final M.B. Examination.

Title. **2.** The title of the prize shall be the Lewin Prize in Medicine.

How awarded. **3.** The Prize shall be awarded each year to the candidate who achieves the second highest combined score in the Single Best Answer Papers IA and IB and structured-answer components of Part III of the Final M.B. Examination held in that academical year.

Value. **4.** The value of the Prize shall be the annual income of the Fund.

William Vaughan Lewis Fund and Prizes

Title and purpose. **1.** The sum subscribed in memory of William Vaughan Lewis, Fellow of Trinity College and University Lecturer in Geography, who was killed in a motor accident in the United States of America on 8 June 1961, shall form a fund called the William Vaughan Lewis Fund for the encouragement of study and research in geography.

Managers. **2.** The Managers of the Fund shall be the Head of the Department of Geography and three persons appointed by the Faculty Board of Earth Sciences and Geography from among the members of the Faculty who are not themselves eligible to receive an award under Regulation 4 of these regulations. The members appointed by the Faculty Board shall be appointed in the Michaelmas Term to serve for three years from 1 January following their appointment. No resolution shall be valid unless it is approved by three of the Managers.

Prizes. **3.** The first charge on the income of the Fund shall be the provision of one or more William Vaughan Lewis Prizes, which shall be of equal value and which shall be awarded annually to candidates for Part II of the Geographical Tripos who, in the opinion of the Examiners for that Part, have submitted outstanding dissertations on some geographical subject. The value of a William Vaughan Lewis Prize shall be such sum not exceeding the available income of the Fund as may be determined each year by the Managers, within a range approved from time to time by the Council.

Research grants. **4.** After provision has been made for the Prize or Prizes in accordance with Regulation 3 of these regulations, the remaining income of the Fund shall be at the disposal of the Managers to make grants from time to time as they may think fit for the encouragement of research in any branch of geography. A grant may be made to any member of the University who is of not less than one year's and not more than ten years' standing from his or her first degree, whether of this or another university.

Library Endowment Fund

The income of the Library Endowment Fund shall be expended for the general purposes of the University Library at the discretion of the Library Syndicate.

Dr Lightfoot's Scholarships and Prize

Endowments, 1904, p. 329

Fund. **1.** The sums given to the University in 1870 by the Reverend Joseph Barber Lightfoot, D.D., Hulsean Professor of Divinity, shall form a fund called the Lightfoot Fund.

Purpose. **2.** The income of the Fund shall be used for the encouragement of the study of History and more especially of Ecclesiastical History.

Managers. **3.** The Fund shall be administered by four Managers, namely the Dixie Professor of Ecclesiastical History and three persons appointed in the Michaelmas Term, one by the Faculty Board of Divinity and two by the Faculty Board of History, to serve for four years from 1 January following their appointment.

4. The first charge on the income of the Fund shall be the provision of one or more Lightfoot Scholarships, the holders of which shall devote themselves to the study of Ecclesiastical History. A Scholarship shall be open to any person who is or is about to be registered as a Graduate Student in the University. A Scholarship shall be tenable for one year in the first instance, and may be renewed by the Managers for a second or third year, provided that the Managers are satisfied with the Scholar's diligence and progress. Scholarships.

5. The Electors to the Scholarships shall be the Managers of the Fund. Before the end of each Michaelmas Term, the Managers shall publish a Notice giving details of the competition for Lightfoot Scholarships tenable from 1 October next following. Each candidate shall be required to submit a dissertation, of not less than 7,000 words and not more than 15,000 words in length, on a subject in Ecclesiastical History, which shall be chosen by the candidate and approved by the Managers. Each year the Managers may, if they see fit, appoint one or more referees who shall report to the Managers on the dissertations submitted. Each referee shall receive from the Fund such sum as shall be determined by the Managers within a range approved from time to time by the Council. A Manager may be appointed as a referee and shall not thereby cease to be a Manager. How awarded.

6. A Lightfoot Scholar shall receive such emolument, within a range determined from time to time by the Council, as the Managers shall determine after taking account of the Scholar's financial circumstances. Emolument.

7. The second charge on the Fund shall be the provision of a Lightfoot Prize for Ecclesiastical History, which shall be awarded annually by the Examiners for Part IIB of the Theological and Religious Studies Tripos for the best performance by a candidate for that examination in one or more papers of the examination designated for that purpose from time to time by the Faculty Board of Divinity.[1] For the purpose of making the award the Examiners shall be empowered (*a*) to take account either of an outstanding performance in a single paper or of the general level attained by a candidate in more than one of the papers designated, and (*b*) to consider as if it were a paper a dissertation submitted under Regulation 16 for the Tripos on an approved topic related to one of the designated papers. The value of the Prize shall be determined by the Managers within a range approved from time to time by the Council. Prize.

8. Any unexpended income in the Fund may be applied by the Managers for the purpose of furthering the study of History and more especially of Ecclesiastical History by making grants in aid of research to members of the University. Unexpended income.

9. The University shall have power to change these regulations, provided that the founder's object, namely the encouragement of the study of History and more especially Ecclesiastical History, be strictly respected. Power to change regulations.

Peter Lipton Fund

Grace 1 of 3 June 2009

1. Gifts to the University made in memory of Professor Peter Lipton, first Hans Rausing Professor of History and Philosophy of Science and Fellow of King's College, shall form a fund called the Peter Lipton Fund. Title.

2. The Managers of the Fund shall be: Managers.

(*a*) the Head of the Department of History and Philosophy of Science;
(*b*) the Chair of the Board of History and Philosophy of Science;
(*c*) the Secretary of the Department of History and Philosophy of Science;
(*d*) the Director and Curator of the Whipple Museum of the History of Science;
(*e*) three persons appointed by the Board of History and Philosophy of Science, who shall be appointed in the Michaelmas Term to serve for three years from 1 January following their appointment.

3. The income of the Fund shall be applied by the Managers to support research, teaching, and Purpose and application.

[1] For the examination to be held in 2006 and until further notice the Faculty Board of Divinity have designated the following papers for this purpose: Papers C4, D1, and D2 (provided that the only subjects eligible in Papers D1 and D2 are subjects in ecclesiastical history).

other academic activities in the Department of History and Philosophy of Science; applications may be made throughout the year and should be addressed to the Secretary of the Department of History and Philosophy of Science.

Unexpended income. **4.** Any unexpended income of the Fund in any financial year may either be added to the capital of the Fund or accumulated for use as income in any one or more subsequent years, as determined by the Managers.

Peter Lipton Lectureship Fund

Grace 1 of 9 March 2011

Title. **1.** The sums received from Dr A. L. Rausing and Professor Peter Baldwin, the Board of Cambridge in America, representing a donation from Mrs Lini Lipton, and Trinity College, to support a University Lectureship in memory of Peter Lipton, the first Hans Rausing Professor of History and Philosophy of Science, shall form a fund called the Peter Lipton Lectureship Fund.

Lectureship. **2.** The first charge on the income of the Fund shall be the stipend, national insurance, pension contributions, and associated indirect costs payable by the University in respect of a Peter Lipton Lectureship in History and Philosophy of Science in the Department of History and Philosophy of Science.

Committee of Management. **3.** The administration of the Fund shall be under the control of a Committee of Management consisting of:

(*a*) the Head of the Department of History and Philosophy of Science;
(*b*) the Secretary of the Board of History and Philosophy of Science;
(*c*) the Secretary of the Department of History and Philosophy of Science;
(*d*) the Director and Curator of the Whipple Museum of the History of Science;
(*e*) three persons appointed by the Board of History and Philosophy of Science in the Michaelmas Term to serve for three years from 1 January following their appointment.

Additional Managers. **4.** If one or more of the offices in classes (*b*)–(*d*) are held by the same person, or if one or more of these offices is vacant or its tenure has expired, the Board of History and Philosophy of Science shall appoint one or more additional Managers so as to ensure that there are always five Managers.

5. After provision has been made in accordance with Regulation 2, the income of the Fund may be applied for the support of teaching or research in the history and philosophy of science as shall be approved by the General Board on the recommendation of the Managers.

Unexpended income. **6.** Any unexpended income in a financial year shall either be added to the capital of the Fund or accumulated for use as income in any one or more subsequent years, as the Managers may determine.

Littleton Chambers Prize for Labour Law

Grace 1 of 24 March 2009

Fund and purpose. **1.** The sum made available annually by Littleton Chambers for the study of Labour Law shall be applied in equal amounts as follows:

(*a*) to provide a prize called the Littleton Chambers Prize for Labour Law, which shall be awarded by the Examiners for Part II of the Law Tripos for distinction in Labour Law shown by performance in Paper 41 of the Law Tripos; and
(*b*) to fund the purchase of books for the Squire Law Library.

Unexpended income. **2.** If in any year the Prize is not awarded, the unexpended income for that year shall be added to the capital of the Fund. If sufficient income has accumulated in the Fund, the Examiners may award more than one Prize in any year.

Michael Loewe Fund for Classical and Literary Chinese Studies

Grace 2 of 3 June 2009

Title and purpose. **1.** The moneys subscribed by friends and former students of Michael Loewe, formerly University Lecturer in Chinese Studies and Fellow of Clare Hall, shall form a fund called the Michael Loewe Fund for Classical and Literary Chinese Studies, which shall be used for the encouragement of classical Chinese studies in the University.

2. The Managers of the Fund shall be the Head of the Department of East Asian Studies and the teaching officers in Chinese in the Department. Managers.

3. The first charge on the income of the Fund shall be the Michael Loewe Prize, which shall be awarded annually for distinction in classical and literary Chinese shown by performance in those subjects in any Part of the Asian and Middle Eastern Studies Tripos. Prize.

4. The value of the Prize shall be such sum as shall be determined by the Managers within a range approved from time to time by the Council. Value.

5. Any further donations to the Fund shall either be added to the capital of the Fund or be made available as income as the Managers shall determine, taking into account the wishes of the donors.

6. Any unexpended income accumulated in the Fund may be used at the discretion of the Managers for the promotion of the study of classical Chinese and Chinese dynastic history, literature, religion, and thought. Unexpended income.

London Students Hardship Fund

1. The money received from the Trustees of the London Parochial Charities shall form a fund to be called the London Students Hardship Fund, the capital and income of which shall be applied to meet the needs of London undergraduates who encounter genuine hardship which is in no way due to improvidence on their part. Name and object.

2. The Fund shall be managed by the Loan Fund I Committee. Managers

3. Undergraduate students, who at the time of their application are domiciled in the Metropolitan Police District of London, shall be eligible to receive assistance from the Fund. Eligibility for assistance.

4. Applications for assistance from the Fund shall be sent by the students' Tutors to the Registrary. Applications.

5. The Managers may from time to time at their discretion make grants in furtherance of the object of the Fund as specified in Regulation 1; provided that no grant shall be made to assist a student during any period after he or she has ceased to be an undergraduate. Nature of assistance.

6. At the end of each academical year a report shall be submitted by the Managers to the Trustees of the London Parochial Charities giving details of the grants made during the year and of the circumstances of the recipients. Report to Trustees.

George Long Prizes

Stat. E XXII.

Endowments, 1904, p. 417

1. Six George Long Prizes shall be offered annually. Six Prizes.

2. Two Prizes shall be offered for distinguished proficiency in Roman Law shown by candidates offering the paper Civil law I in the Law Tripos, one for distinguished proficiency in Roman Law shown by a candidate offering the paper Civil law II in the Law Tripos, two for distinguished proficiency in Jurisprudence shown by candidates in Part IB or Part II of the Law Tripos, and one for distinguished proficiency in Roman Law or in Jurisprudence or in both those subjects shown by a candidate in the LL.M. Examination, who shall have taken the examination before fifteen complete terms have passed after his or her first term of residence. Subjects.

3. The value of each Prize shall be one-sixth of the income of the George Long Fund. Value.

Longsdon Trust Fund

Endowments, 1904, pp. 206–16

Four-fifths of the income of the Longsdon Trust Fund, which was established in 1783 under the will of the Reverend Richard Jackson, M.A., formerly of Trinity College, shall be applied to the maintenance of the Jacksonian Professorship of Natural Philosophy and one-fifth shall be applied to support the University Botanic Garden in such manner as the Director of the Botanic Garden shall determine.

Manuel Lopez-Rey Funds

The sums given to the University by Mrs Grace Lopez-Rey, in memory of her husband, Professor Manuel Lopez-Rey, shall form two funds, the Manuel Lopez-Rey Studentship Fund and the Manuel Lopez-Rey Prize Fund. Funds.

Manuel Lopez-Rey Studentship Fund

Title and purpose. **1.** The sum of £25,000 given by Mrs Lopez-Rey in November 1989 shall form a fund called the Manuel Lopez-Rey Studentship Fund for the encouragement of the study of Criminology.

Managers. **2.** The Managers of the Fund shall be the Committee of Management of the Institute of Criminology.

Studentship. **3.** The income of the Fund shall be used to provide a Manuel Lopez-Rey Studentship, the holder of which shall undertake advanced study or research in Criminology. A Studentship shall be open to any person who is or is about to be registered as a Graduate Student in the University, provided that the Managers may give preference to candidates who are citizens of countries in which, in the opinion of the Managers, there is a particular need for the development of the study of criminology.

4. The Electors to the Studentship shall be the Managers of the Fund. The Managers shall give due notice of their intention to proceed to an election.

Tenure. **5.** A Studentship shall be tenable for one year in the first instance, and may in exceptional circumstances be renewed by the Managers for a second or third year.

6. A Student shall receive such emolument, within a range determined from time to time by the Council, as the Managers shall determine after taking account of the Student's financial circumstances.

Unexpended income. **7.** At the discretion of the Managers, any unexpended income in the Fund may be either added to the capital of the Fund or accumulated for use as income in a subsequent year.

Manuel Lopez-Rey Prize Fund

Title and purpose. **1.** The sum of £2,000 given by Mrs Lopez-Rey in September 1991 shall form a fund, the income of which shall be used to provide a prize called the Manuel Lopez-Rey Graduate Prize in Criminology.

Prize. **2.** The Prize shall be awarded by the Examiners in Criminology for the degree of Master of Philosophy (one-year course) to the candidate who has achieved the most distinguished performance in the examination for that subject as prescribed either in Regulation 1 or in Regulation 2 of the special regulations for that examination.

Value. **3.** The value of the Prize shall be the annual income of the Fund.

4. If in any year the Prize is not awarded, the income for that year shall be added to the capital of the Fund.

MATT LOW FUND

Title and purpose. **1.** The sum given to the University by the North West Area Retail Fruit Trade Federation shall form a fund, called the Matt Low Fund, for the encouragement of research in the University into the production and storage of fruits and vegetables.

Application of income. **2.** The Managers of the Fund shall be the Regius Professor of Botany and the Professor of Genetics. The income of the Fund shall be applied at the discretion of the Managers in accordance with Regulation 1.

HEDLEY LUCAS FUND

Title and purpose. **1.** The sums bequeathed by Hedley Lucas, poet, and Mrs Gertrude Elaine Lucas, his wife, shall form a Hedley Lucas Fund, the purpose of which shall be to assist, by the award of scholarships or otherwise, members of the University who are preparing to enter the Christian Ministry.

Managers. **2.** The Managers of the Fund shall be the Faculty Board of Divinity, who may delegate some or all of their functions under these regulations to a committee not necessarily consisting wholly of members of the Board.

Scholarships. **3.** The income of the Fund shall be used to provide one or more Hedley Lucas Scholarships, to be held by members of the University preparing to enter the Christian Ministry. The Scholarships shall be awarded by the Managers, who shall give notice in the Michaelmas Term each year of their intention to offer the Scholarships.

4. The number of Scholarships to be awarded on each occasion, and the value of each Scholarship, shall be determined by the Managers, after taking account of the resources available to the candidates, within a range determined from time to time by the Council. A Scholarship shall be tenable for one, two, or three academical years, as determined by the Managers.

5. The Managers may make grants from any unexpended income accumulated in the Fund to Hedley Lucas Scholars, to assist them in preparing for the Christian Ministry. Grants.

LUNDGREN FUND

1. The sums bequeathed to the University by Beatrice Helen Worsley, Ph.D., of Newnham College, shall form a fund called the Lundgren Fund in honour of Helge Lundgren, the income of which shall be used at least once a year to make one or more Lundgren Research Awards to persons who are registered as candidates for the Ph.D. Degree provided that they are engaged in research in a scientific subject (which term shall be taken to include mathematics) and are not ordinarily resident in the United Kingdom. Title and purpose.

2. The Managers of the Fund shall be the Board of Graduate Studies. The Managers may delegate any of their functions concerning the Fund to a Committee composed of members of the Board of Graduate Studies. Managers.

3. The Managers shall on each occasion when they invite applications give not less than three months' notice of their intention to make an award. Notice of award.

4. An award may be made to a person who has completed four terms of research as a registered Graduate Student of the University, provided that he or she has shown a high aptitude for research and a devotion to study, and is in need of financial assistance. Who are eligible.

5. If in the opinion of the Managers two or more candidates appear to be equally deserving, preference shall be given to candidates who are working in the Computer Laboratory or whose research has been interrupted by national service or personal misfortune.

6. The value of each award shall be determined by the Managers within a range approved from time to time by the Council. Value.

ELLEN MCARTHUR FUND

Stat. E XLII.

1. The income of the Ellen McArthur Fund shall be used to further the study of Economic History. Purpose.

2. The Fund shall be administered by three Managers, namely, the Professor of Economic History and two persons appointed in the Michaelmas Term, one by the Faculty Board of Economics the other by the Faculty Board of History, to serve for four years from 1 January following their appointment. Managers.

3. Before the division of the Easter Term in each year the Professor of Economic History in consultation with the other Managers shall announce the offer of Prizes, which shall be called Ellen McArthur Prizes, for any work on Economic History which may be submitted to them, before a date specified in the Notice, by any graduate of the University or by any person who is registered as a Graduate Student in the University. Notice of Prizes.

4. Such number of Prizes shall be awarded as the work submitted may justify and the available income of the Fund permit. The value of each Prize shall be such sum as shall be determined by the Managers within a range approved from time to time by the Council. Number and value.

5. The Managers shall be empowered to appoint Assessors to report on work submitted, provided that all such appointments shall be reported to the General Board. Each Assessor, and any Manager who has been requested by his or her fellow Managers to report on work submitted, shall be paid from the Fund the fee that is paid under the regulations for the Ph.D., M.Sc., and M.Litt. Degrees to an Examiner who reports on a dissertation and takes part in an oral or other examination. Assessors.

6. The Managers shall be empowered to appoint a lecturer every year and shall be required to do so in each year of which the number is odd, provided always that they are satisfied that sufficient income is available to meet the cost. A lecturer appointed under this regulation shall be called the Ellen McArthur Lecturer and shall deliver in English a course of not less than four and not more than eight lectures on some aspect of Economic History. Lecturer.

7. The lectures shall be called the Ellen McArthur Lectures and they shall be delivered in Full Term during the academical year next but one following that in which the Lecturer is appointed.

8. The stipend to be offered to each Lecturer shall be such sum not exceeding half the estimated income of the Fund for one year as the Managers shall determine. Lecturer's stipend

Application of Fund.

9. After provision has been made in accordance with the foregoing Regulations 3–8 any unexpended income accumulated in the Fund shall be applied from time to time at the discretion of the Managers and subject to such conditions as they may think fit for the following purposes:

(*a*) To make grants towards the cost of publication of any work for which an Ellen McArthur Prize has been awarded or which has been commended by the Assessors for such a Prize, or towards the cost of publication of an Ellen McArthur Lecture or series of lectures. No such grant shall be paid until the material for which it has been awarded has been published. As a condition of making a grant the Managers may require any work or any lecture to be abridged or otherwise altered before publication.

(*b*) To reimburse an Ellen McArthur Lecturer for expenses incurred in connection with the performance of the duties of the office.

(*c*) To provide for not more than three Ellen McArthur Studentships the holders of which shall devote themselves to original research in Economic History. The Electors to the Studentships shall be the Managers of the Fund who, on each occasion when they intend to proceed to an election, shall announce the date by which applications must be received and the manner in which they must be submitted. A Studentship shall be open to any person who is or is about to become registered as a Graduate Student in the University. The tenure of a Studentship shall be for a period of not more than three years from 1 October following the election; a Studentship may be renewed, subject to a maximum tenure of three years. The stipend of a Student shall be such sum as may be determined by the Managers within a range approved from time to time by the Council.

(*d*) To make grants in aid of research in the University in Economic History.

(*e*) To further the study in the University of Economic History by any other means.

Annual Report.

10. The Managers shall make an Annual Report on their administration of the Fund to the General Board and to the Faculty Boards of Economics and of History.

Norman Maccoll Lectureship

Fund.

1. The bequest of Norman Maccoll, M.A., of Downing College, shall form a fund called the Norman Maccoll Lectureship Fund.

Lecturer.

2. A Norman Maccoll Lecturer shall be appointed from time to time by the Faculty Board of Modern and Medieval Languages. It shall be the duty of the Lecturer to deliver in the University one or more lectures on a subject in Hispanic or Portuguese studies. The Faculty Board shall seek to ensure that during a five-year period not fewer than five Norman Maccoll Lectures are delivered.

Stipend.

3. The first charge on the income of the Fund shall be the stipend of the Lecturer, which shall be such sum as shall be determined by the Faculty Board within a range approved from time to time by the Council. In addition, the Faculty Board may at their discretion pay any expenses of the Lecturer. If and whenever the income of the Fund shall exceed the amount required for the payment of the stipend and other expenses of the Lecturer, the excess of the income over that amount may be applied to pay any other expenses incurred in the holding of the lecture.

MacCurdy Library Fund

Title.

1. The sum bequeathed to the University under the will of the late Dr J. T. MacCurdy, formerly University Lecturer in Psychopathology and Fellow of Corpus Christi College, which was accepted by Grace 3 of 15 November 1947, shall form a fund known as the MacCurdy Library Fund.

Purpose.

2. The income of the Fund shall be used for the provision and maintenance of a Psychopathological Library in the University or for the provision and maintenance of a collection of Psychopathological works in some Library in the University in such manner as the Professor of Experimental Psychology shall direct.

D. M. McDonald Grants and Awards Fund

Title and purpose.

1. The sums given to the University by Dr D. M. McDonald, or by the D. M. C. McDonald Foundation or its successors, for the provision of grants or awards for fieldwork and research in archaeology, and any sums transferred for the same purpose from the D. M. McDonald Trust Fund by the Managing Committee for the McDonald Institute, shall form a fund called the D. M. McDonald Grants and Awards Fund.

2. The administration of the Fund shall be under the control of an Advisory Committee consisting of: Advisory Committee.

(*a*) the Disney Professor of Archaeology, or her or his deputy;
(*b*) the Director of the Institute, if not the Disney Professor;
(*c*) the George Pitt-Rivers Professor of Archaeological Science;
(*d*) the Deputy Director of the Institute;
(*e*) one person appointed by the General Board;
(*f*) two persons appointed by the Faculty Board of Human, Social, and Political Science, who shall be University officers in the Department of Archaeology and Anthropology;
(*g*) one member of a Faculty allied in its interests to archaeology, appointed by the General Board after consultation with the Department of Archaeology and Anthropology;
(*h*) two persons appointed by the D. M. C. McDonald Foundation.

Members in classes (*e*), (*f*), and (*g*) shall be appointed in the Michaelmas Term to serve for three years from 1 January following their appointment.

3. The income of the Fund shall be used to provide grants and awards for fieldwork and research in archaeology to Fellows of the McDonald Institute or to such other persons as the Advisory Committee shall determine. Grants and awards.

4. The Advisory Committee shall have power to regulate their own procedure and to approve rules governing the making of grants and awards. Procedure.

McLatchie Fund

1. The money received from the bequest of the late Dr John Drummond Pryde McLatchie shall form a fund called the McLatchie Fund. Title.

2. The capital and income of the Fund shall be applied as the Cavendish Professor may from time to time decide: Application of Fund.

(*a*) in defraying the expenses of persons working in the Cavendish Laboratory when attending conferences or visiting other laboratories outside Cambridge;
(*b*) in making grants to necessitous Graduate Students in the Cavendish Laboratory;
(*c*) in supporting for periods of less than six months persons engaged in research in the Cavendish Laboratory;
(*d*) in providing apparatus and books for the furtherance of teaching and research in the Cavendish Laboratory;
(*e*) in meeting or contributing to the cost of any major project which would be of lasting benefit to the Cavendish Laboratory.

3. Unexpended income shall not be added to the capital of the Fund but shall be accumulated for use as income in subsequent years. Unexpended income.

Arnold McNair Scholarship Fund

1. The sum bequeathed to the University by the late Sir Hersch Lauterpacht, M.A., LL.D., of Trinity College, formerly Whewell Professor of International Law, for the purpose of founding an Arnold McNair Scholarship in International Law, shall form a fund to be called the Arnold McNair Scholarship Fund. Title and purpose.

2. The Electors to the Scholarship shall be the Whewell Professor of International Law or a deputy appointed by the Whewell Professor and two other persons appointed by the Faculty Board of Law. Electors.

3. In the Michaelmas Term of each year the Secretary of the Faculty Board of Law shall publish a Notice announcing the offer of one or more Scholarships. Notice of vacancy.

4. The Scholarship shall be open to any member of the University who has kept at least eight terms[1] and who is a candidate for or has been classed in either Part IB or Part II of the Law Tripos in the year of application. Who are eligible.

[1] See also Regulation 4(*a*) of the general regulations, p. 762.

Names to Registrar.

5. Every candidate shall apply to the Secretary of the Faculty Board of Law not later than the day before the first day of General Admission to Degrees, and shall submit a statement of the nature of the further study or research that he or she proposes to undertake.

Election.

6. The election shall be held each year at some convenient date within four weeks following the first day of General Admission to Degrees. The Electors shall take whatever steps they deem advisable, whether by consultation with any Tripos Examiners or otherwise, to ascertain the merits of the candidates and their qualifications for pursuing further study or research in International Law. If the available income of the Fund is sufficient the Electors may elect a second Scholar.

Tenure.

7. The Scholarship shall be tenable for one year from 1 October following the election and shall not be renewable.

Duties of Scholar.

8. It shall be the duty of the Scholar to undertake study or research in International Law. A Scholar shall not, during the tenure of the Scholarship, follow any such business or profession or engage in any such educational or other work as in the opinion of the Electors would interfere with his or her study.

Stipend.

9. The amount of the stipend of the Scholarship shall be such sum within a range approved from time to time by the Council as the Electors shall determine in each case.

Payment of stipend.

10. The stipend of the Scholar shall be paid in equal half-yearly instalments in advance; provided that the Electors may withhold the whole or part of the second instalment if they are not satisfied that the Scholar is diligently pursuing his or her studies.

Regulations may be altered by Grace.

11. These regulations, other than Regulation 1 and this regulation, may be altered by Grace on the recommendation of the Whewell Professor of International Law and with the approval of the Faculty Board of Law.

Alasdair Charles Macpherson Fund

Name.

1. The sum bequeathed to the University by the Reverend Ranald Macpherson shall form a fund to be called the Alasdair Charles Macpherson Fund.

Managers.

2. The Managers of the Fund shall be the Faculty Board of Divinity. The Managers may delegate any of their functions concerning the Fund to a committee composed of members of the Faculty Board.

Application.

3. The income of the Fund shall be applied from time to time by the Managers, and subject to such conditions as they may think fit,

(*a*) to make grants in aid to deserving students,

(*b*) to make grants for research or travel,

(*c*) to purchase books for the Libraries of the Faculty of Divinity,

(*d*) for such other purposes as may be approved by the Managers.

Beneficiaries.

4. The beneficiaries of the Fund shall be those persons only who are or have been students in the Faculty of Divinity, and are of not more than ten years' standing from their first degree.

5. These regulations, except Regulations 1 and 4, shall be subject to alteration by Grace on the recommendation of the Faculty Board of Divinity with the concurrence of the Faculty of Divinity.

Maintenance Grants in Engineering Fund

The income of the Maintenance Grants in Engineering Fund shall be used, at the discretion of the Degree Committee for the Faculty of Engineering, to make grants to postgraduate students working in the Department of Engineering who are in need of financial assistance in connection with their studies in that Department.

Frederic William Maitland Memorial Fund

Name and object.

1. There shall be a fund in the University called the Frederic William Maitland Memorial Fund, which shall be devoted to the promotion of research and instruction in the History of Law and of Legal Language and Institutions.

Managers.

2. The administration of the Fund shall be entrusted to seven Managers. The Managers shall be the Vice-Chancellor and six other persons appointed, two by the Council, two by the Faculty Board of Law, and two by the Faculty Board of History. The Managers shall be appointed in the Michaelmas Term to serve for four years from 1 January following their appointment.

All the powers of the Managers may be exercised by a majority of those present at a meeting duly summoned, provided that three Managers at least be present. Quorum.

3. The income arising from the capital of the Fund shall be paid annually to the Managers, who shall also be empowered to receive subscriptions in augmentation of the annual income of the Fund. Out of the income thus accruing the Managers may at their discretion make grants to any person engaged in any research in the History of Law or of Legal Language or Institutions; or may make grants for the delivery of lectures, the publication of works, or the promotion of any other undertaking, connected with these departments of study; and they may attach to any grant such conditions as they may think fit. Employment of income.

4. The Managers shall be empowered to receive donations, subscriptions, and bequests for the augmentation of the capital of the Fund. Managers may augment capital of Fund.

5. The accounts of the Managers shall be audited annually and published with the University Accounts. Accounts.

6. These regulations, except Regulation 1 and this regulation, shall be subject to alteration by Grace provided that the object of the Fund, as defined in Regulation 1, be adhered to.

7. Subject to the foregoing regulation, it shall be lawful for the Managers from time to time to make and (if they see fit) to vary such by-laws as may seem to them expedient for regulating their own proceedings and the administration of the Fund entrusted to their care. By-laws.

PEREGRINE MAITLAND STUDENTSHIP

Stat. E XVII.

Endowments, 1904, pp. 386–8

1. The income of the Peregrine Maitland Fund, which is to be used to advance the study of subjects arising from or affecting the spread of the Christian Religion, the comparison of the Christian Religion with other religions, and the contact of Christian and other civilizations, shall be used to provide a Studentship in Comparative Religion, preference being given to candidates wishing to prepare themselves for missionary work. Purpose of Fund.

2. The Studentship shall be offered annually. The stipend of the Studentship shall be such sum as the Electors shall determine in each case, within a range approved from time to time by the Council. Stipend.

3. The Studentship shall be open to any graduate of the University or to any person who is or is about to be registered as a Graduate Student in the University. To whom available.

4. The Electors in each year shall be: Electors.

(*a*) the Professors of Divinity;

(*b*) one person appointed in the Michaelmas Term by the Faculty Board of Divinity.

5. Before the division of the Lent Term each year the Electors shall publish a Notice of the date by which, and the manner in which, applications are to be made. The election shall take place before the end of the Easter Term. Notice of award.

6. It shall be the duty of the Student to pursue a course of study approved by the Electors.

7. The Studentship shall be payable by equal half-yearly payments (each payment to be made in advance), provided as regards the second payment that the Electors be satisfied that the Student is diligently carrying out the scheme of study approved by them. Payment of emoluments.

8. The Electors shall for the purpose of the two preceding sections appoint one of their number to whom it shall be the duty of the Student to report from time to time on the progress of his or her scheme of study. Report of study.

9. From unexpended income accumulated in the Fund, the Electors may make grants to members of the University in aid of research in the subjects specified in Regulation 1. Unexpended income.

MANAGEMENT STUDIES IN ENGINEERING FUND

The income of the Management Studies in Engineering Fund shall be applied at the discretion of the Head of the Department of Engineering to further teaching and research in the general area of Management Studies within that Department.

Management Studies Project Prize

Grace 2 of 24 March 2010

Prize and purpose. **1.** Of the sum of £5,000 given to the University by Mr Neil Thomason, of St John's College, the capital and the income shall be used to provide an annual Prize to be shared equally between members of the three-person project team that delivers the best project presentation as part of the Management Studies Tripos.

Value. **2.** The value of each Prize shall be such sum as shall be determined by the Faculty Board of Business and Management within a range approved from time to time by the Council.

How awarded. **3.** The Prize shall be awarded by the Programme Director for the Management Studies Tripos to the team of three students that delivers the best project presentation, as measured by client.

Unexpended income. **4.** If in any year the Prize is not awarded, the income of the Fund for that year shall be added to the capital of the Fund.

Elizabeth Mann Fund

Fund. **1.** The sum received from the Cambridge University Fund for the Prevention of Disease (CAMPOD), representing a bequest to CAMPOD by Miss Elizabeth Hilary Frances Mann, M.A., of Girton College, shall form a fund called the Elizabeth Mann Fund.

Purpose. **2.** The Managers of the Fund shall be the CAMPOD Committee for the time being. The income of the Fund shall be available at the discretion of the Managers to support research in the Department of Pathology in furtherance of the understanding and prevention of disease.

Applications. **3.** The Managers shall invite applications from the Heads of the various Divisions within the Department of Pathology at such times and in such manner as they think fit.

Unexpended income. **4.** Any unexpended income at the end of a financial year may be accumulated for use as income in a subsequent year.

Stat. E XV. (1504)

The Lady Margaret's Preachership

Endowments, 1904, pp. 65–70

1. The appointment of the Preacher shall be announced in the Lent Term of the academical year next preceding the year in which the sermon is to be preached. The Preacher so appointed shall hold office until the first day of May in the year following his or her appointment.

2. Any member of the Senate shall be capable of being appointed.

3. The Preacher shall preach a sermon in the University Church at the Commemoration of Benefactors.

John Marks and Mulberry Trust Fund

Grace 2 of 13 June 2012

Title. **1.** The sum of £1m received from the charity formed and funded by John and Morwenna Marks and known as the Mulberry Trust, to support teaching and research in Christian Theology and to support the Regius Professorship of Divinity, together with other funds allocated for the same purpose out of a donation to the University from Trinity College, shall form a permanent endowment fund called the John Marks and Mulberry Trust Fund.

Purpose. **2.** The first charge on the income of the Fund shall be the stipend, national insurance, pension contributions, and associated indirect costs of the Regius Professor of Divinity payable by the University, provided that the work of the Professor at the time of her or his election to the Professorship is in the field of Christian Theology.

Managers. **3.** The Fund shall be administered by four Managers, who shall comprise:

(*a*) The Chair of the Faculty Board of Divinity, who shall be Chair

(*b*) The Regius Professor of Divinity

(*c*) The Head of the School of Arts and Humanities

(*d*) A person appointed by the Faculty Board of Divinity.

If two or more of these offices are held by the same person or if one or more of the named posts is vacant or its tenure has expired, the General Board shall appoint one or more additional Managers to ensure that there are always four Managers. The Manager in class (*d*) shall be appointed for periods of five years at a time.

4. If and whenever the income of the Fund shall exceed the amount required to meet the costs specified in Regulation 2, the excess of the income over that amount may be applied in support of teaching and research in Christian Theology in such manner as may be approved by the General Board on the recommendation of the Managers.

5. Any unexpended income in a financial year shall either be added to the capital of the Fund or held as an income reserve and expended in any one or more subsequent years in accordance with Regulations 2 and 4 above. Unexpended income.

MARLAY FUND

1. The moneys received by the University from the sale, authorized by Grace 2 of 15 February 1916, of works of art and books left to the University under the will of Charles Brinsley Marlay shall form a fund called the Marlay Fund. Fund.

2. The Managers of the Fund shall be the Fitzwilliam Museum Syndicate. Managers.

3. The income of the Fund shall be available at the discretion of the Syndicate for the purchase of equipment and works of art, and for general Museum purposes. Purpose.

MARR MEMORIAL FUND

1. The Fund given by subscribers in memory of John Edward Marr, Sc.D., Woodwardian Professor of Geology, shall be called the Marr Memorial Fund Name.

2. The Fund shall be used to provide grants for the study of Geology in the field. Purpose.

3. Grants shall be made only to members of the University. Who are eligible.

4. Preference shall be given to applicants who have obtained honours in Part IB of the Natural Sciences Tripos and who intend to pursue the study of Geology.

5. The Awarders in each year shall be: Awarders.

(*a*) the Head of the Department of Earth Sciences;

(*b*) a person appointed in the Michaelmas Term by the Faculty Board of Earth Sciences and Geography from among the University officers in the Department of Earth Sciences who have been appointed Examiners in Geology or Geological Sciences in the Natural Sciences Tripos for the current academical year, unless the Head of the Department of Earth Sciences is such an Examiner;

(*c*) one other person or, if the Head of the Department of Earth Sciences is such an Examiner, two other persons, appointed in the same manner from among the University officers in the Department of Earth Sciences.

6. Before the division of the Easter Term in each year the Head of the Department of Earth Sciences shall give notice of the sum which the Treasurer shall have certified to be at the Awarders' disposal, and shall invite applications for grants. The awards shall be made in June. Notice of awards.

7. The annual income of the Fund may be awarded each June, but if no award is made in any year, for lack of suitable candidates, two years' income may be awarded in the following June. If no award is made in two consecutive years, the unapplied income for one year shall be added to the capital of the Fund. Date of awards. Unapplied income.

8. The University may alter these regulations, provided that the Fund shall be associated with the name of Dr Marr and applied to the study of Geology in the field. Alterations.

ALFRED MARSHALL FUND AND LECTURESHIP

1. An Alfred Marshall Fund shall be created and an Alfred Marshall Lectureship shall be established in the Faculty of Economics. Fund.

2. Not later than the end of the Michaelmas Term of each academical year the Faculty Board of Economics shall either appoint a Lecturer to hold office during that academical year, or adjourn the appointment for a year; but the appointment shall not be adjourned for two successive years. Lecturer.

3. The Lecturer shall give in the year of office three lectures (or such other number as the Faculty Board may in any case approve) dealing with some development in Economics, or in Economic History, or in some kindred subject.

4. The lectures shall be given in Full Term.

5. The Lecturer shall deposit a copy of the text of the lectures in the Marshall Library.

Stipend. **6.** The Lecturer shall receive as stipend such sum as shall be determined by the Faculty Board of Economics within a range approved from time to time by the Council, and in addition the Faculty Board may at their discretion pay any expenses of the Lecturer, whether in travelling to and from Cambridge or in residing in Cambridge for the period of the lectures, from the surplus income of the Fund during the Lecturer's year of office or from any accumulated surplus of the Fund.

Suspension. **7.** The General Board may suspend the Alfred Marshall Lectureship at their discretion and apply the income of the Fund for general Faculty purposes should the financial situation appear to them to make such action desirable.

Kingsley Martin Memorial Fund

Title. **1.** The gift to the University by Miss Dorothy Woodman on behalf of the late Kingsley Martin shall form a fund called the Kingsley Martin Memorial Fund.

Purpose. **2.** The first charge on the income of the Fund shall be to provide for an annual lecture, to be called the Kingsley Martin Memorial Lecture, on a South Asian topic, preference being given to a topic relating to Burma. The lecture shall be delivered in Full Term.

Managers. **3.** The Managers of the Fund shall be the Committee of Management of the Centre of South Asian Studies.

Lecturer. **4.** A Lecturer shall be appointed by the Managers in each academical year, and shall deliver the Lecture by the end of the academical year following that in which he or she was appointed.

Stipend. **5.** The stipend of the Lecturer shall be such sum not exceeding the available income of the Fund as may be determined from time to time by the Managers with the approval of the Council.

Surplus income. **6.** Any unexpended income accumulated in the Fund shall be applied from time to time at the discretion of the Managers to meet:

(*a*) any expenses that may be incurred by the Lecturer in connection with the lecture;

(*b*) the general expenses of the Centre of South Asian Studies, preference being given to expenses related to the study of Burma.

Mason Prize for Biblical Hebrew

Endowments, 1904, p. 418

Prize. **1.** The Mason Prize for Biblical Hebrew shall be awarded annually to that candidate, or student qualified by standing to be a candidate, for Tyrwhitt's Hebrew Scholarships who shall be judged by the Examiners to have shown the greatest distinction in Biblical Hebrew in the examination for those Scholarships.

Value. **2.** The value of the Prize shall be such sum as shall be determined by the Faculty Board of Asian and Middle Eastern Studies within a range approved from time to time by the Council.

Unexpended income. **3.** Any unexpended income accumulated in the Fund may be used at the discretion of the Head of the Department of Middle Eastern Studies in consultation with and with the agreement of the teaching officers in Hebrew in the Department for the promotion and encouragement of the study of Biblical Hebrew.

4. A student who has once obtained the Prize shall be disqualified from competing for it a second time.

Regulations may be changed. **5.** It shall be competent for the University from time to time to make such changes in these regulations as shall be judged fit: provided always that the proceeds of the Fund be given for proficiency in the knowledge of Biblical Hebrew, and that the Prize be connected with the name of the Reverend P. H. Mason.

The MathWorks Studentship

1. The sums received from The MathWorks shall form a fund for the benefit of postgraduate students in the Department of Engineering undertaking research in Control Systems and related areas. Purpose.

2. The capital and income of the fund shall be used for the provision of a Studentship to be called The MathWorks Studentship in Engineering. Studentship.

3. The Electors to the Studentship shall be the Head of the Department of Engineering and two members of the staff of the Control Research Group in the Department, who shall be appointed by the Faculty Board of Engineering in the Michaelmas Term to serve for four years from 1 January following their appointment. Electors.

4. In order to be eligible for the Studentship a candidate must have been admitted, or be seeking admission, as a registered Graduate Student in the University.

5. The Studentship shall be tenable for one year in the first instance, and may be renewed by the Electors for a second or third year but for no longer. Tenure.

6. The Studentship shall provide Provisions.

(*a*) a maintenance payment to be determined by the Electors,
(*b*) a payment to meet the Student's University and College fees,
(*c*) a contribution to other costs such as equipment, travel expenses, etc., according to the discretion of the Electors.

MAVA Fondation Fund for Conservation Leadership

Grace 3 of 5 November 2008

1. The sum of £2.5m received by the University from the MAVA Fondation pour la Protection de la Nature Fund shall form a fund called the MAVA Fondation Fund for Conservation Leadership, the income and capital of which shall be used to support postgraduate study in Conservation Leadership and learning and research in Conservation in general. The currency of the Fund shall be eleven years from 1 October 2008 to 30 September 2019. Title and purpose.

2. The administration of the Fund shall be under the control of a Committee of Management consisting of: Managers.

(*a*) the Miriam Rothschild Professor of Conservation Biology;
(*b*) the Moran Professor of Conservation and Development;
(*c*) the Head of the Department of Geography;
(*d*) the person designated as Director of Research in Conservation Leadership;
(*e*) one person who is not a resident member of the University appointed by the General Board to represent the Cambridge Conservation Forum.

The member in class (*e*) shall be appointed by the General Board in the Michaelmas Term to serve for three years from 1 January following her or his appointment.

3. The capital and income of the Fund shall be used to support the design and delivery of a postgraduate course of study in Conservation Leadership, in any manner that the Managers shall determine, including the payment of the stipend, national insurance, pension contributions, and associated indirect costs payable by the University in respect of the Director of Research in Conservation Leadership. It may also be used, at the discretion of the Managers, to provide maintenance payments and payments to meet University and College fees and other costs, such as additional training, equipment, travel expenses, conferences, for students undertaking the course.

4. The MAVA Fondation may decide to apply any part of the capital or income of the donation that remains unspent, at the end of the programme, as the MAVA Fondation may determine, after agreement with the University, to support the study and teaching of conservation in the University and to co-operate with outside bodies in the encouragement of conservation learning or research more generally. Unspent income.

Clerk Maxwell Memorial Fund

1. The moneys received from Miss Frances Katherine Dunn shall form a fund called the Clerk Maxwell Memorial Fund, as a tribute to the memory of James Clerk Maxwell, the first Cavendish Professor of Experimental Physics. Title.

Application.

2. The capital and income of the Fund shall be applied as the Cavendish Professor of Physics may from time to time decide:

(*a*) to enable a Graduate Student in the Cavendish Laboratory to continue research at the end of the period for which he or she was originally awarded an emolument if in the opinion of the Professor the particular project merits such support;

(*b*) to defray the expenses of Graduate Students and other research workers in the Cavendish Laboratory when attending conferences or visiting or working in other laboratories outside Cambridge;

(*c*) to contribute to the cost of any project which, in the opinion of the Cavendish Professor, would be of lasting benefit to the Cavendish Laboratory and would appropriately commemorate the name and work of James Clerk Maxwell.

Stat. E XXXIX.

Clerk Maxwell Scholarship

Endowments, 1904, p. 340

Name and object.

1. The income of the Clerk Maxwell Fund shall be used to maintain one or more Clerk Maxwell Scholarships in connection with the Cavendish Laboratory, for the advancement by original research of Experimental Physics, especially Electricity, Magnetism, and Heat.

2. The person elected to the Scholarship shall be called the Clerk Maxwell Student in Experimental Physics.

Who are eligible.

3. Any member of the University who has been a student for one term or more in the Cavendish Laboratory shall be eligible for the Scholarship.

Electors.

4. The Electors to the Scholarship shall be the Cavendish Professor of Physics and the Lucasian Professor of Mathematics, and in case of any difference of opinion between them the final decision shall rest with the Master of Trinity College or with someone specially appointed by the Master for this purpose.

Deputy.

5. In case a deputy shall be appointed to discharge the duties of either of the two Professors aforesaid, such deputy shall, for all the purposes of these regulations, take the place and exercise the powers of the Professor concerned, during such time as he or she may be acting as such deputy.

Qualification of Scholar.

6. The Electors in electing the Scholar shall be guided by the promise shown by the candidates of capacity for original research in Experimental Physics, and shall take such steps as they may think desirable to enable them to form a judgement of such promise.

Duties of Scholar.

7. The Scholar so elected shall undertake under the direction of the Cavendish Professor original research in Experimental Physics within the University, but may carry on research elsewhere with the written permission of the Cavendish Professor.

Tenure.

8. The commencing date and duration of tenure of the Scholarship shall be determined by the Electors, and the holder shall be eligible for re-election, provided that a Scholar's total tenure of the Scholarship shall not exceed three years.

Stipend of Scholar.

9. The stipend of the Scholar shall be such sum not exceeding the available income of the Fund as may be determined by the Electors, within a range approved from time to time by the Council, after they have taken account of any other financial resources that may be available to the Scholar. The stipend shall be paid to the Scholar in equal quarterly instalments in advance.

10. The Scholar shall not during the tenure of the Scholarship systematically follow any business or profession or engage in any educational or other work which in the opinion of the Cavendish and Lucasian Professors would interfere with his or her duties as Scholar.

Scholar may be removed.

11. If the Cavendish Professor and the Lucasian Professor shall be of opinion that the Scholar by engaging in some business or occupation or from confirmed ill health or want of diligence, or from other causes, is not fulfilling the conditions of the Scholarship, they shall report their opinion to the Faculty Board of Physics and Chemistry, and the Board may then if they see fit remove the Scholar from the Scholarship.

Notice of election.

12. Not later than one month before the date at which in due course the Scholarship becomes vacant or immediately upon the occurrence of any casual vacancy the Cavendish Professor shall give such public notice thereof as the Electors may think desirable. The election shall be made as soon after the vacancy as is practicable, and the result communicated to the Vice-Chancellor for publication.

Unexpended income.

13. Any unexpended income accumulated in the Fund may be applied from time to time on the recommendation of the Cavendish Professor to meet travelling and other expenses consistent with the object of the Fund incurred by Clerk Maxwell Scholars or by other persons engaged in original research in Experimental Physics in the Cavendish Laboratory.

MAYHEW PRIZE

1. The Prize shall be called the Mayhew Prize. It shall be awarded annually and shall consist of the net annual income of the Fund. Prize.

2. The Prize shall be awarded to that candidate for Part III of the Mathematical Tripos who has in the judgement of the Examiners shown the greatest distinction in the subjects of Applied Mathematics, excluding Astronomy, in that examination, provided that his or her work in these subjects is of sufficient merit.

3. If in any year the Prize be not awarded the income for that year shall be added to the capital of the Fund. If not awarded

J. E. O. MAYNE FUND

1. The sum given to the University in 1969 by John Edwin Oakley Mayne, of Fitzwilliam College, shall form a fund, the object of which shall be to ensure the continuation of the work on metallic corrosion and in related fields which Ulick Richardson Evans, Sc.D., of King's College, sometime Reader in the Science of Metallic Corrosion, initiated in 1921. Title and object.

2. The income of the Fund shall be applied as the Head of the Department of Materials Science and Metallurgy shall from time to time decide to further teaching and research in the study and the prevention of corrosion and oxidation of metals and in related fields, by one or more of the following means: Application of income.

(*a*) establishing and maintaining any academic appointment,

(*b*) establishing a studentship,

(*c*) maintaining Graduate Students or research workers in the Department of Materials Science and Metallurgy,

(*d*) purchasing apparatus and equipment,

or by any other means consistent with the object of the Fund.

M.CHIR. DISTINCTION PRIZE

1. The income of the fund provided by an anonymous donor shall be used to provide a prize called the M.Chir. Distinction Prize, which shall be awarded annually for a thesis in the field of surgery, either clinical or in a relevant basic science, submitted in candidature for the M.Chir. Degree. Title and purpose.

2. The Prize shall be awarded by the Regius Professor of Physic, after consulting the M.Chir. Committee. How awarded.

3. Any thesis deemed to have reached Distinction standard shall be eligible for consideration for the Prize. If more than one candidate reaches this standard the Prize may be divided.

4. The value of the Prize shall be the annual income of the Fund. Value.

5. If in any year the Prize is not awarded, the unexpended income shall be added to the capital of the Fund. Unexpended income.

ETHEL MEASURES FELLOWSHIP IN VETERINARY MEDICINE FUND

1. The sum of £220,000 given to the University by the Trustees of the J. F. and E. A. Measures Charity shall form a fund called the Ethel Measures Fellowship in Veterinary Medicine Fund. Title.

2. The Managers of the Fund shall be the Chair of the Faculty Board of Veterinary Medicine, the Head of the Department of Veterinary Medicine, and the Dean of the Veterinary School, the Director of Research in the Department of Veterinary Medicine, and the Hospital Superintendent in the Department of Veterinary Medicine. Managers

3. No resolution of the Managers shall be valid unless passed by a majority of the Managers present at a meeting to which all the Managers have been summoned.

4. The income of the Fund shall be used to provide the whole or part of the stipend of an Ethel Measures Fellow in Veterinary Medicine who shall undertake advanced study or research in such Purpose.

specialist area of veterinary medicine as the Managers shall decide from time to time. With the consent of the General Board, the whole or part of the capital of the Fund may be used for the same purpose.

Election and tenure. **5.** An Ethel Measures Fellow shall be elected by the Managers, who may authorize additional expenditure from the income of the Fund in support of the work of the Fellow. The tenure of an Ethel Measures Fellow, which shall be determined by the Managers on the occasion of each election, shall be for a period not exceeding three years at a time.

Annual Report. **6.** The Managers shall advise the Trustees of the J. F. and E. A. Measures Charity of the election and the field of study of each Ethel Measures Fellow and shall provide the Trustees with an annual report on the work of the Fellow.

Stipend. **7.** The stipend of an Ethel Measures Fellow shall be determined by the General Board on the recommendation of the Managers.

Unexpended income. **8.** Any unexpended income in the Fund may be either added to the capital of the Fund or accumulated for use as income in future years, as the Managers may determine.

Medical Libraries Fund

Managers. **1.** The administration of the Medical Libraries Fund shall be entrusted to the Regius Professor of Physic and two other Managers who shall be appointed by the Faculty Board of Clinical Medicine in the Michaelmas Term to serve for two years from 1 January following their appointment. A retiring Manager other than one who is appointed to fill a casual vacancy shall not be immediately eligible for reappointment.

Purpose. **2.** The income of the Fund shall be used for the purchase of books and journals for the libraries of the Departments in the Faculties of Biology and of Clinical Medicine.

Application for grants. **3.** Application for grants from the income of the Fund for the purchase of books or journals shall be made annually by the Departments to the Secretary of the Faculty Board of Clinical Medicine, by 1 January in each academical year.

4. Grants shall be made mainly, but not exclusively, for the purchase of books which, because of expense or other reasons, could not be purchased out of Departmental funds.

Stat. E XLVII.

Medieval Scandinavian History Fund

Grace 5 of 5 November 2008

Title and purpose. **1.** The sums available under Statute E XLVII, together with other funds that may be donated for the same purpose, shall be used to establish a fund to support a University Lectureship in Medieval Scandinavian History in the Department of Anglo-Saxon, Norse, and Celtic.

Managers. **2.** The Managers of the Fund shall be the Faculty Board of English, who may delegate any of their functions concerning the Fund to a Committee not necessarily composed wholly of members of the Board.

Lecturer. **3.** The income of the Fund shall be used to contribute towards the stipend, national insurance, pension contributions, and associated indirect costs payable by the University in respect of the Lecturer in Medieval Scandinavian History.

Unexpended income. **4.** Any unexpended income of the Fund in a financial year may be either added to the capital of the Fund or accumulated for use as income in future years, as the Managers may determine.

Mellon Fellowship Fund

Title and purpose. **1.** The sum of US$250,000 received from the Andrew W. Mellon Foundation shall form a fund, called the Mellon Fellowship Fund, to be used for the provision of Mellon Research Fellowships and grants for the study of American history.

2. The administration of the Fund shall be entrusted to six Managers. The Managers shall be the Regius Professor of History, the Paul Mellon Professor of American History, the Chair of the Faculty Board of History, and three Managers appointed in the Michaelmas Term by the Faculty Board. The Pitt Professor of American History and Institutions shall be an additional Manager when that Professorship is assigned to the Faculty of History. The Managers appointed by the Faculty Board shall serve for four years from 1 January following their appointment. No resolution of the Managers for the election of a Research Fellow shall be valid unless passed by at least four of the Managers at a meeting to which all the Managers have been summoned, provided that

(*a*) if the Pitt Professor is a Manager, the number of votes required shall be increased by one;

(*b*) if either the Regius Professor or the Paul Mellon Professor is Chair of the Faculty Board, the number of votes required shall be reduced by one.

3. The first charge on the Fund shall be the stipends of one or more Mellon Research Fellows who shall engage in original research in American history which for this purpose shall be defined as the history of the United States of America from its colonial beginnings. Research Fellowships.

4. The Managers shall publish before the division of each Lent Term a Notice of the date by which applications for a Mellon Research Fellowship shall be submitted to them, and the manner in which such applications shall be made. The names of successful candidates shall be published not later than 30 June next following. Applications.

5. A Mellon Research Fellowship shall be tenable for a minimum period of one year, which may be extended by the Managers, provided that the tenure of a Fellowship shall not exceed four years in all. Tenure.

6. The stipend of a Mellon Research Fellow shall be determined by the General Board on the recommendation of the Managers. Stipend.

7. After provision has been made for the Mellon Research Fellowships the Managers shall be empowered to make grants to visiting scholars, Graduate Students, or other members of the University not *in statu pupillari*, for the furtherance of research in American history as defined in Regulation 3. Grants.

8. Any unexpended income may be added either to the capital of the Fund or accumulated for use as income in subsequent years as the Managers may determine. Unexpended income.

Paul Mellon Fund

1. The moneys received by the University under the will of Paul Mellon, Hon. K.B.E., M.A., Hon. LL.D., of Clare College, shall form a fund called the Paul Mellon Fund. Fund.

2. The Managers of the Fund shall be the Fitzwilliam Museum Syndicate. Managers.

3. The capital and income of the Fund shall be available, at the discretion of the Managers for any purpose of the Museum, including: Purpose.

(*a*) the provision of buildings, or the improvement of buildings;

(*b*) the preservation and maintenance of the collections including the employment of curatorial staff for that purpose.

Paul Mellon Discretionary Fund

1. The moneys received by the University at the discretion of the Executors of the will of Paul Mellon, Hon. K.B.E., M.A., Hon. LL.D. of Clare College shall form a fund called the Paul Mellon Discretionary Fund. Fund.

2. The Managers of the Fund shall be the Fitzwilliam Museum Syndicate, acting on the recommendations of the Director of the Museum with the concurrence of the Executors and their successors. Managers.

3. The income of the Fund shall be available for the following purposes: Purpose.

(*a*) the planning and implementation of temporary exhibitions at the Museum, especially those that draw upon the permanent collections of the University and the Colleges of the University;

(*b*) the production costs of publications for or by the Museum, especially those relating to its collections;

(*c*) educational programmes planned and implemented at the Museum, to encourage wider participation and appreciation of its collections; and

(*d*) refurbishing galleries used to display the permanent collection, to include such non-structural elements as wall coverings, display furniture, and light fittings, to ensure that high standards are maintained in the appearance of the galleries and the display of their contents.

Members' Classics Fund

Endowments, 1904, p. 373

1. The Managers of the Members' Classics Fund shall be the Faculty Board of Classics.

Purpose. **2.** The income of the Members' Classics Fund shall be applied to the provision of

(*a*) two or more Members' Classical Essay Prizes;

(*b*) two Members' Classical Translation Prizes;

(*c*) two Members' Classical Reading Prizes.

Awarders. **3.** The Essay Prizes shall be awarded by the Managers. The Translation Prizes and the Reading Prizes shall be awarded by three Adjudicators appointed by the General Board on the nomination of the Managers in each year before the division of the Michaelmas Term. Each Adjudicator shall receive from the income of the Fund such sum as shall be determined by the Managers with the approval of the Council.

Value of Prizes. **4.** The value of each Prize shall be such sum as shall be determined by the Adjudicators within a range approved from time to time by the Council.

Notice of competition. **5.** Before the end of the Michaelmas Term in every year the Adjudicators shall publish a Notice of the date by which and the manner in which entries for the Translation Prizes and the Reading Prizes shall be made, and of the dates by which the Prizes will be awarded.

Unexpended income. **6.** Any unexpended income accumulated in the Fund may be applied at the discretion of the Managers for the promotion and encouragement of the study of the languages and civilizations of ancient Greece and Rome.

Members' Classical Essay Prizes

Essay Prizes. Who may compete. **7.** Two or more Members' Classical Essay Prizes shall be awarded each year. One Prize shall be awarded for a thesis submitted by a candidate for Part II of the Classical Tripos, and one for a thesis submitted by a candidate for the examination in Classics for the M.Phil. Degree (one-year course).

8. The Examiners for Part II of the Classical Tripos and the Degree Committee for the Faculty of Classics shall each identify not more than three theses which in their opinion are worthy of a Prize from among those submitted in candidature for the examination with which they are concerned, and shall refer them to the Managers. It shall be open to the Managers to award not more than three Prizes to candidates for Part II of the Tripos and not more than three to candidates for the M.Phil. Degree.

Deposit of essay. **9.** Each prize-winner shall present a copy of his or her thesis to the library of the Faculty of Classics.

Members' Classical Translation Prizes

Translation Prizes. **10.** The Members' Classical Translation Prizes shall be offered each year for the translation of a passage or passages, set by the Examiners, of Greek or Latin verse into English verse in any style and form appropriate to the original. One Prize shall be offered for the translation of Greek verse and one for the translation of Latin verse.

Who may compete. **11.** The Prizes shall be open to all undergraduate students in residence.

Deposit of translation. **12.** Each prize-winner shall present a copy of his or her translation to the library of the Faculty of Classics.

Members' Classical Reading Prizes

Reading Prizes. **13.** The Members' Classical Reading Prizes shall be offered each year for the reading aloud of Greek or Latin. One Prize shall be offered for the reading of Greek, and the other for the reading of Latin.

14. The Prizes shall be open to all undergraduate students in residence.

Nature of competition. **15.** Each candidate shall be required to read aloud

(*a*) one set piece of verse and one set piece of prose, announced in advance,

(*b*) one set piece of verse, not announced in advance, and

(*c*) one piece of verse or prose chosen by the candidate.

Members' English Fund

Endowments, 1904, p. 373

1. The Managers of the Members' English Fund shall be the Faculty Board of English. The Faculty Board may appoint a committee, not necessarily consisting wholly of members of the Board, to discharge any of their functions under these regulations. Managers.

2. The first charge on the income of the Fund shall be the provision of the Members' English Prize, which shall be awarded each year for the best dissertation submitted for the M.Phil. Degree in the Faculty of English. Prize.

3. Candidates for the Prize shall be Graduate Students working under the supervision of the Degree Committee for the Faculty of English, who were admitted as Graduate Students with effect from a date not earlier than 1 August next but one preceding the academical year in which they compete for the Prize. Who may compete.

4. The Managers shall award the Prize not later than the end of the Full Easter Term next following. When awarded.

5. The value of the Prize shall be such sum as shall be determined by the Managers, within a range approved from time to time by the Council. Value.

6. After provision has been made for the award of the Members' English Prize, any unexpended income accumulated in the Fund may be applied by the Managers for the purpose of furthering the study of English and cognate subjects by making grants in aid of research to Graduate Students working under the supervision of the Degree Committee for the Faculty of English. Grants for research.

Members' History Fund

Endowments, 1904, p. 373

1. The Managers of the Members' History Fund shall be the Faculty Board of History. The Faculty Board may appoint a committee, not necessarily consisting wholly of members of the Board, to discharge any of their functions under these regulations. Managers.

2. The first charge on the income of the Fund shall be the provision of the Members' History Prize, which shall be awarded each year for the best dissertation on an historical subject. Prize.

3. The Prize shall be open to any member of the University who has been approved by the Board of Graduate Studies, on the recommendation of the Degree Committee for the Faculty of History, for the award of the M.Phil. Degree during the preceding academical year. Who may compete.

4. The Managers shall award the Prize not later than the end of the Full Easter Term next following. When awarded.

5. The value of the Prize shall be such sum as shall be determined by the Managers, within a range approved from time to time by the Council. Value.

6. After provision has been made for the award of the Members' History Prize, any unexpended income accumulated in the Fund may be applied by the Managers: Grants for research.

(*a*) to make grants in aid of research to Graduate Students working under the supervision of the Degree Committee for the Faculty of History;

(*b*) to promote in any other way the study of History in the University.

Charles Hesterman Merz Fund

1. The moneys given to the University in 1970 by Mrs Merz for the purpose of promoting teaching, study, and research in electrical engineering shall form a fund to be called the Charles Hesterman Merz Fund. Name and purpose.

2. The Managers of the Fund shall be the Faculty Board of Engineering. Managers.

3. The income of the Fund shall be used at the discretion of the Managers and subject to such conditions as they may think fit, Application.

(*a*) for making grants to members of the University who are citizens of the Commonwealth of Nations and who are engaged in teaching, study, or research in electrical engineering in the Faculty of Engineering;

(*b*) for promoting teaching, study, and research in the field of electrical engineering by any other means.

4. Grants from the Fund shall be called Charles Hesterman Merz Grants, and in each year the names of the persons to whom they have been awarded, but not the amounts of the grants, shall be published in the *Reporter*. Grants shall be payable in the manner determined by the Managers. Publication of grants.

T. H. Middleton Fund

Title. **1.** The sum received from an anonymous benefactor in 1947 to commemorate the work of the late Sir Thomas Hudson Middleton, Drapers Professor of Agriculture 1902–07, shall form a fund called the T. H. Middleton Fund.

Managers. **2.** The Fund shall be administered by three Managers who shall be:

(*a*) the Chair of the Degree Committee for the Faculty of Biology;

(*b*) the Regius Professor of Botany;

(*c*) one person appointed by the Faculty Board of Biology.

The Manager in class (*c*) shall be appointed in the Michaelmas Term to serve for three years from 1 January following his or her appointment. The Secretary of the Degree Committee for the Faculty of Biology shall act as Secretary to the Managers.

Application of income. **3.** The income of the Fund shall be applied by the Managers to make grants to enable Graduate Students working on subjects connected with agriculture to travel for the purpose of study or research.

Unexpended income. **4.** Any unexpended income in the Fund may be either added to the capital of the Fund or accumulated for use as income in future years, as the Managers may determine.

William Mills Library Acquisitions Fund

Grace 1 of 14 January 2009

Title. **1.** The sums subscribed in honour of William James Mills, M.A., of Emmanuel College, Librarian of the Scott Polar Research Institute from 1989 to 2004, shall form a William Mills Library Acquisitions Fund.

Purpose. **2.** The income of the Fund shall be applied for the purchase of books, periodicals, and maps, in any format, for the library of the Scott Polar Research Institute.

Managers. **3.** The Managers of the Fund shall be the Director and Librarian of the Institute and one person appointed by the Committee of Management of the Institute to serve for three years from 1 January following her or his appointment.

4. The Managers shall meet at least once a year to consider the needs of the Institute's library collections and to apply the Fund's income in furtherance of its objectives.

Unexpended income. **5.** Any unexpended income in a financial year may be added to the capital of the Fund, or accumulated for use as income in a future year in accordance with these regulations.

Graeme Minto Prize for Management Studies

Fund and purpose. **1.** The sum of £5,000 given to the University by Domino Printing Sciences plc shall form a fund called the Graeme Minto Fund for the encouragement of Management Studies in the University.

Prize. **2.** The Fund shall be used to provide a prize called the Graeme Minto Prize for Management Studies. The value of the Prize shall be such sum as shall be determined by the Faculty Board of Business and Management within a range approved from time to time by the Council.

How awarded. **3.** The Prize shall be awarded by the Examiners for the Management Studies Tripos for an outstanding performance in that examination.

Unexpended income. **4.** Any unexpended income may be used at the discretion of the Faculty Board of Business and Management for the promotion and encouragement of Management Studies in the University.

Professor Joseph Mitchell Cancer Research Fund

Name and purpose. **1.** The sums given and bequeathed to Professor J. S. Mitchell for the furtherance of research into human cancer, and received from him by the University, shall form a fund for that same purpose, to be called the Professor Joseph Mitchell Cancer Research Fund in recognition of his contribution to the treatment of cancer made while he held the Professorship of Radiotherapeutics and the Regius Professorship of Physic during the years 1946–76.

Managers. **2.** The Managers of the Fund shall be: (*a*) the Regius Professor of Physic; (*b*) two members appointed by the Faculty Board of Clinical Medicine; (*c*) one member appointed by the Faculty Board of Biology; and (*d*) two members appointed by the General Board. Managers in classes (*b*)–(*d*) shall be appointed in the Michaelmas Term to serve for four years from 1 January following their appointment.

The Managers shall elect annually one of their number as Chair. The Secretary of the Faculty Board of Clinical Medicine shall act as Secretary to the Managers.

3. The Managers may at their discretion make grants from the Fund to any person engaged in research in East Anglia which may, in the opinion of the Managers, contribute to the prevention, diagnosis, or treatment of human cancer; and they may attach to any grant such conditions as they may think fit. Grants.

4. The Managers shall be empowered to receive donations, subscriptions, and bequests for the augmentation of the income of the Fund. Augmentation of income.

5. The Managers may at their discretion seek the advice of independent assessors concerning the merits of any application to the Fund. Assessors.

6. No resolution of the Managers shall be valid unless approved by at least four members at a meeting to which all the members have been summoned, but a resolution signed by all the members shall have the same validity as a resolution carried at a meeting. Quorum.

Modern Hebrew Studies Fund

1. The sums received by the University for the promotion of the study of Modern Hebrew shall form a fund called the Modern Hebrew Studies Fund. Fund.

2. The Fund shall be under the control of a Board of Managers, who shall be: Managers.

(*a*) the Regius Professor of Hebrew;

(*b*) two persons appointed by the Head of the Department of Middle Eastern Studies in consultation with and with the agreement of the teaching officers in Hebrew in the Department to serve for two years from 1 January following their appointment, one of whom shall be a University officer engaged in teaching and research in Modern Hebrew.

3. The capital and the income of the Fund shall be applied at the discretion of the Managers for the encouragement of the study of Modern Hebrew in the University. Purpose.

4. Any unexpended income of the Fund in a financial year may be either added to the capital of the Fund or accumulated for use as income in future years, as the Managers may determine. Unexpended income.

Modern Jewish Studies Fund

1. The sum of $50,000 given to the University by the Righteous Persons Foundation shall form a fund called the Modern Jewish Studies Fund, which shall be used for the promotion and encouragement of the study of modern Jewish thought and history in the University. Title and purpose.

2. The Managers of the Fund shall be the Faculty Board of Divinity, who may delegate any or all of their functions under these regulations to a committee not necessarily consisting wholly of members of the Board. Managers.

3. The capital and the income of the Fund shall be applied, at the discretion of the Managers, Application of Fund.

(*a*) to meet the cost of lectures given by visiting Lecturers;

(*b*) to provide grants for Graduate Students working in the field of modern Jewish thought and history;

(*c*) to assist in any other way the promotion and encouragement of the study of modern Jewish thought and history in the University.

4. A visiting Lecturer shall be appointed by the Managers from time to time. It shall be the duty of the Lecturer to deliver one or more lectures in the University in Full Term on a subject or subjects connected with modern Jewish thought and history. Lecturer.

5. The stipend paid to a Lecturer shall be such sum as shall be determined by the Managers within a range approved from time to time by the Council. In addition the Managers may at their discretion pay any expenses incurred by the Lecturer or in connection with the Lecturer's visit. Stipend and expenses.

Rex Moir Fund

1. The sums given and bequeathed to the University by the late Sir Ernest Moir, Bart., shall form a fund called the Rex Moir Fund. Title.

2. The first charge on the income of the Fund shall be the provision of a Rex Moir Prize which shall be awarded annually by the Examiners for Part IB of the Engineering Tripos to the candidate Prize who has shown the greatest distinction in that examination. The value of the Prize shall be determined by the Faculty Board of Engineering within a range approved from time to time by the Council.

Grants. **3.** After provision has been made for the Rex Moir Prize, the remaining income of the Fund shall be used at the discretion of the Degree Committee for the Faculty of Engineering, and subject to such conditions as they may think fit, for making grants to postgraduate students and Graduate Students of the Department of Engineering.

Applicants for grants. **4.** Applications for grants shall be sent to the Secretary of the Degree Committee for the Faculty of Engineering so as to arrive on or before 1 July in each year. An applicant must

(*a*) have obtained an Honours Degree in a university of the United Kingdom or possess such other qualifications as may be approved by the Degree Committee,

(*b*) be or become a member of the University,

(*c*) forward with the application a full statement of his or her financial circumstances.

Periods covered by grants. **5.** Grants may be made for one, two, or three years, but no grant shall be tenable for more than three years in all.

Publication and payment of awards. **6.** The names of students to whom grants have been awarded, but not the amounts of the grants, shall be published each year. Grants shall be payable in the manner determined by the Degree Committee.

7. If at any time the Degree Committee are satisfied that a student is not diligently carrying out his or her work they shall have power to direct that any outstanding instalments of a grant shall be withheld.

P. A. Molteno Fund

Name. **1.** The sum of £3,000 bequeathed to the University by P. A. Molteno, M.A., LL.M., of Trinity College, shall constitute a fund called the P. A. Molteno Fund.

Purpose. **2.** The income of the Fund in any year and any accumulated income shall be at the disposal of the Head of the Department of Pathology for the purposes of research in Parasitology.

Mond Laboratory Endowment Fund

The income from sums that were made available to the University to endow the Mond Laboratory shall be used to support research in the Department of Physics.

Mordell Lectureship Fund

Title and purpose. **1.** The sum given to the University by Professor Louis Joel Mordell, of St John's College, and augmented by the gift of Professor Paul Erdős, shall form a fund called the Mordell Lectureship Fund. The first charge on the fund shall be the honorarium of a Mordell Lecturer.

Appointment. **2.** Not later than the division of the Lent Term in each year the Faculty Board of Mathematics on the nomination of the Head of the Department of Pure Mathematics and Mathematical Statistics shall either appoint a Lecturer to hold office for that academical year or defer the appointment until the following academical year; provided that the appointment shall not be deferred for two successive years. Before nominating a Lecturer the Head of the Department shall take into account any name that may have been suggested by any member of the Faculty of Mathematics.

Duties. **3.** During his or her term of office the Lecturer shall give one lecture in Full Term dealing with some aspect of or topic in pure mathematics.

Honorarium. **4.** The honorarium paid to the Lecturer shall be such sum as shall be determined by the Faculty Board within a range approved from time to time by the Council. In addition the Faculty Board may at their discretion pay any expenses incurred by the Lecturer.

Morien Morgan Prize

Title of Fund. **1.** The gift of Lady Morgan, widow of the late Sir Morien Morgan, FRS, Master of Downing College, shall form a fund called the Morien Morgan Fund.

Prize. **2.** The Morien Morgan Prize shall be awarded each year by the Examiners for Part IIB of the Engineering Tripos to the candidate who has shown the greatest distinction in aeronautical engineering, unless the Examiners are of the opinion that there is no candidate of sufficient merit to receive the Prize.

3. The value of the Prize shall be the annual income of the Fund. Value.

4. Any unexpended income shall be added to the capital of the Fund. Unexpended income.

5. The University, on the recommendation of the Faculty Board of Engineering, may amend these regulations from time to time, provided that the Prize shall always be devoted to the encouragement of the study of aeronautics. Alterations.

MORRELL FUND AND LECTURESHIP

1. The sum bequeathed to the University by the late Robert Selby Morrell, Sc.D., sometime Fellow of Gonville and Caius College, shall form a fund to be called the Morrell Fund, the object of which shall be the advancement of teaching and research in organic chemistry. Title of Fund.

2. The first charge on the income of the Fund shall be the cost of such stipend and travelling expenses as may be approved under Regulation 4 for a visiting lecturer. First charge on income.

3. The visiting lecturer, who shall be called the Morrell Lecturer, shall be appointed from time to time by the Faculty Board of Physics and Chemistry on the recommendation of the Head of the Department of Chemistry, advised by the BP Professor of Chemistry. Title of Lecturer and appointment.

4. The duties of the Lecturer shall be determined, at the time of appointment, by the General Board on the recommendation of the Head of the Department of Chemistry, provided that a Lecturer shall normally spend not less than three weeks in the Department of Chemistry and shall deliver at least four lectures consistent with the object of the Fund. Taking into account the duties so determined the stipend of the Lecturer and the allowance to be paid for travelling expenses shall be determined by the General Board at the same time and on the same recommendation. Duties, stipend, and allowances of the Lecturer.

5. Any unexpended income accumulated in the Fund may be used at the discretion of the Head of the Department of Chemistry, advised by the BP Professor of Chemistry, for the promotion of teaching or research in organic chemistry. Unexpended income.

ROGER MORRIS PRIZES IN MEDICINE AND SURGERY

Amended by Grace 14 of 24 April 2014

1. The sums given by Roger Brian Morris, M.A., Ph.D., of Clare College, shall form a fund for the purpose of awarding prizes in Medicine and in Surgery to candidates for Part III of the Final M.B. Examination. Fund and purpose.

2. The title of each Prize shall be the Roger Morris Prize in Clinical Medicine and Surgery. Titles.

3. The Prizes shall be awarded each year to the candidates who are judged by the Regius Professor of Physic to have shown the greatest distinction in the clinical aspects of the Final M.B. Part III Examinations held in that academical year. How awarded

4. The value of each Prize shall be one half of the annual income of the Fund. Value.

5. If in any year a Prize is not awarded the appropriate portion of the income for that year shall be added to the capital of the Fund. If not awarded.

BRITA MORTENSEN FUND

1. The moneys subscribed by the friends of Brita Mortensen, University Lecturer in Swedish, who died in 1958, shall form a fund called the Brita Mortensen Fund the income of which shall be used to provide grants to enable undergraduates of the University of Cambridge to visit Scandinavia in order to study the culture, literature, and arts of the Scandinavian countries. Name and purpose.

2. The Fund shall be administered by the Managers of the Scandinavian Studies Fund. Managers.

3. In the Michaelmas Term the Registrary shall publish a Notice inviting applications for grants from the Fund. Offer of grants.

4. Any candidate for the B.A. Degree shall be eligible to receive a grant from the Fund provided that he or she intends to make use of the grant before completing the examination requirements for that degree. Eligibility.

5. Applications must be submitted through a candidate's Tutor to the Registrary so as to arrive not later than 1 June, and must be accompanied by a description of the travel which the candidate proposes to undertake. Grants shall be awarded not later than the last day of the Easter Term and shall be payable on application to the Treasurer.

Mary Euphrasia Mosley Fund

Title. **1.** The sum bequeathed to the University by the late Mary Euphrasia Mosley shall form a fund to be called the Mary Euphrasia Mosley Fund.

Purposes. **2.** The annual income of the Fund shall be applied for the encouragement of travel to the countries of the Commonwealth of Nations for the promotion of study or research and for the maintenance of good relations between them.

Administration. **3.** The administration of the Fund shall be entrusted to a Board of Managers consisting of the Vice-Chancellor (or a duly appointed deputy), and four other persons appointed by the Council in the Michaelmas Term to serve for four years from 1 January following.

Awards. **4.** Awards from the Fund shall be confined to members of the University not of standing to become Masters of Arts, who shall undertake travel for the purposes mentioned in Regulation 2 above.

Application. **5.** By a date to be announced by the Managers each year before the division of the Lent Term, a candidate for an award shall apply to the Registrary, indicating the way in which he or she hopes to further the purposes of the Fund as described in Regulation 2 above, and providing such other evidence of his or her qualifications as the Managers may require.

Date. **6.** Awards shall be made each year not later than the end of the Easter Term.

Tenure. **7.** During the tenure of an award the holder shall undertake the scheme of travel approved by the Managers, provided that the scheme may be varied with the consent of the Managers.

Payment of awards. **8.** Awards shall be payable in one or more quarterly instalments, provided that the Managers shall not authorize any payment unless the holder of an award is pursuing, to their satisfaction, the purposes described in Regulation 2 above.

Alteration of regulations. **9.** The foregoing regulations except Regulations 2 and 4 shall be subject to alteration by Grace.

Mott Fund for Physics of the Environment

Title and purpose. **1.** The sum received from an anonymous benefactor by way of an endowment shall form a fund called the Mott Fund for Physics of the Environment in tribute to the memory of Sir Nevill Mott, CH, FRS, formerly Cavendish Professor of Physics. The income of the Fund shall be used for the purpose of providing Ph.D. studentships, bursaries, travel funds, and post-doctoral fellowships relating to research in Physics of the Environment in the Department of Physics. The Fund may include other sums received from other bodies or persons for the same purpose.

Managers. **2.** The Managers of the Fund shall be (*a*) the Head of the Department of Physics, (*b*) the Cavendish Professor of Physics, and (*c*) a person appointed by the General Board. If the Head of the Department of Physics and the Cavendish Professor are the same person, the Faculty Board of Physics and Chemistry shall appoint one other person as a Manager so as to ensure that there are three Managers. A person appointed by the General Board in class (*c*) shall be appointed for three years from 1 January of the year in which he or she is appointed.

Application of the income. **3.** After provision has been made out of the income of the Fund for the purpose of providing Ph.D. studentships, bursaries, travel funds, and post-doctoral fellowships relating to research in Physics of the Environment in the Department of Physics, the income of the Fund may be applied for the support of research in Physics of the Environment in the Department of Physics in such a manner as shall be approved by the Managers.

Unexpended income. **4.** Any unexpended income in a financial year may be expended in accordance with Regulations 1 and 3 in any one or more subsequent years.

Mott Publication Fund

Name and purpose. **1.** The royalties accruing from the Agreement between the Syndics of the Cambridge University Press and the Department of Physics (the Cavendish Laboratory) relating to two volumes of *The Physics of Metals* published in 1967 and 1975 in recognition of the work of Professor Sir Nevill Mott shall form a fund, called the Mott Publication Fund, which shall be used for the support of those engaged in research in the Cavendish Laboratory.

2. The Managers of the Fund shall be the Cavendish Professor of Physics and the Secretary of the Department of Physics. Managers

3. The capital and income of the Fund shall be applied by the Managers: Application of Fund.

(*a*) to enable Graduate Students and other research workers in the Cavendish Laboratory to acquire some knowledge of a foreign language;

(*b*) to contribute towards the expenses of Graduate Students and other research workers in the Cavendish Laboratory when attending conferences or visiting laboratories outside Cambridge.

THOMAS MULVEY EGYPTOLOGY FUND

1. The sums given to the University by Mrs M. Mulvey and by others, in memory of her husband Thomas Mulvey, shall form a fund called the Thomas Mulvey Egyptology Fund, the income of which shall be used to further the study of Egyptology by the provision of an annual prize to be called the Thomas Mulvey Egyptology Prize, and of grants for the promotion of Egyptology. Name and purpose.

Thomas Mulvey Egyptology Prize

2. The Prize shall be awarded by the Examiners for Part IIB of the Archaeological and Anthropological Tripos to a candidate taking two or more papers in Egyptology who has shown distinction in Egyptology papers in the examination in Archaeology for Part IIB of that Tripos. Prize.

3. The value of the Prize shall be such sum as shall be determined by the Faculty Board of Human, Social, and Political Science within a range approved from time to time by the Council. Value.

4. If in any year the Prize is not awarded the Committee established under Regulation 6 may make a grant from the income of the Fund of not more than the value of the Prize, for the purchase of books on the subject of Egyptology. If not awarded.

Thomas Mulvey Grants for Egyptology

5. In any year, after provision has been made for the award of the Thomas Mulvey Egyptology Prize or for any grant made under Regulation 4 grants may be made from the balance of the annual income and from any unexpended income accumulated in the Fund to assist persons carrying out or wishing to carry out fieldwork in Egyptology. Grants for fieldwork.

6. Grants shall be awarded by a Committee consisting of the Herbert Thompson Reader in Egyptology, together with four persons appointed by the Faculty Board of Human, Social, and Political Science in the Michaelmas Term to serve for four years from 1 January following their appointment. Awarders.

7. After the provision of any grants made under Regulation 5, the Committee may make further grants from the balance of the annual income and from any unexpended income accumulated in the Fund for the promotion of the study of Egyptology in the University.

8. Before the end of the Michaelmas Term in every year the Committee shall publish a Notice of the date by which and the manner in which applications for grants from the Fund shall be submitted. Notice of applications.

MUNBY FUND AND FELLOWSHIP

1. The money subscribed in memory of Alan Noel Latimer Munby, who died in 1974, shall form a fund called the Munby Fund, administered by the Library Syndicate, the income of which shall be used to provide the stipend of a Munby Fellowship for research in bibliographical studies tenable in the University Library. Name and purpose.

2. The holder of the Fellowship will be expected to undertake bibliographical research which shall directly or indirectly be of benefit to scholars using the collections of the University and Colleges of Cambridge. Duties of Fellow.

3. The Library Syndicate shall have power to determine from time to time the period of tenure of the Munby Fellowship, which shall normally be for one or two years, and the stipend to be attached to each period of tenure within a range approved from time to time by the Council. Tenure and stipend.

4. Any unexpended income of the Fund may be applied at the discretion of the Library Syndicate to meet expenses incurred by the Munby Fellow in carrying out his or her research.

Electors.

5. The Electors to the Munby Fellowship shall be the Librarian, *ex officio*, and not more than four other persons appointed from time to time by the Library Syndicate to serve for a period determined at the time of their appointment by the Syndicate. The Electors shall have discretion to seek the advice of appropriate bodies, including appropriate bodies overseas, before making an election.

Dispensation.

6. The Munby Fellow shall have no departmental or other staff duties and responsibilities within the University Library during his or her tenure of the Fellowship.

Margaret Munn-Rankin Fund for Assyriology

Title and purpose.

1. The sum bequeathed to the University by Miss Joan Margaret Munn-Rankin, M.A., of Newnham College, for the furtherance of study and research in Assyriology shall form a fund called the Margaret Munn-Rankin Fund for Assyriology.

Managers.

2. The Managers of the Fund shall be the Faculty Board of Human, Social, and Political Science. The Board may delegate any of their functions concerning the Fund to a Committee not necessarily consisting wholly of members of the Board.

Studentship.

3. The primary purpose of the Fund shall be to maintain a postgraduate studentship in Assyriology, which shall be called the Margaret Munn-Rankin Studentship in Assyriology.

Notice of election.

4. The Managers shall give not less than three months' notice of their intention to proceed to an election.

Who are eligible.

5. The Studentship may be held by any person who desires to undertake research or training for research in Assyriology. The Managers may take such steps as they think fit to ascertain the qualifications of candidates and their ability to undertake research.

Tenure.

6. The Managers shall elect a Student in the first instance for such period not exceeding three years as they shall think fit. They shall have power to re-elect a student for any further period not exceeding three years if they are satisfied that his or her work is of a sufficiently high standard to merit such an extension.

7. A Student who is not already a member of the University shall become such by being matriculated before the end of the term next after his or her election to the Studentship, provided that for good cause the Managers may allow a Student to defer matriculation until a later date.

Duties of the Student.

8. During the tenure of the Studentship a Student shall undertake full-time study or research in Assyriology. The Managers may terminate a Studentship at any time if they are not satisfied that the Student is diligently pursuing his or her studies.

Stipend.

9. The stipend of the Studentship shall be the annual net income of the Fund, which shall be paid to the Student by quarterly instalments in advance.

Application of income if Studentship vacant.

10. If at any time the Studentship is vacant, the income of the Fund for the period of the vacancy shall be employed as follows: three-quarters of the income of the Fund shall be appropriated in aid of the cost of the Eric Yarrow Lectureship in Assyriology, and one quarter shall be available to the Managers for the furtherance of study and research in Assyriology generally.

Unexpended income.

11. Any unexpended income of the Fund in a financial year may in any subsequent year be expended on the furtherance of study and research in Assyriology.

Edith Mary Pratt Musgrave Fund

Name.

1. The sum of £1,000, the benefaction of the late Edith Mary Pratt Musgrave, shall form a fund called the Edith Mary Pratt Musgrave Fund.

Purpose.

2. The Fund shall be used for the furtherance of research in the anatomy, physiology, or life-history of the *Alcyonaria*, corals, and related organisms.

Administration.

3. The administration of the Fund shall be entrusted to the Managers of the Balfour Fund.

Application of the Fund.

4. Subject to the provisions of Regulation 2 the Fund shall be applied from time to time, at the discretion of the Managers, and subject to such conditions as they may think fit, for the following purposes:

(*a*) to provide the emoluments of an Edith Mary Pratt Musgrave Research Studentship;

(*b*) to make grants for research.

Who are eligible for grants.

5. Awards from the Fund shall be made only to graduates of universities of the United Kingdom, British Dominions, and British Dependencies overseas, now working in or with the Department of

Zoology. In making awards the Managers shall give preference (*a*) to women graduates, and (*b*) to persons intending to carry out research in waters other than those surrounding the British Isles.

WALTER MYERS FUND

The income of the fund derived from the gift to the University of Mrs S. Churchill in memory of her brother Dr Walter Myers, M.A., M.B., B.Chir., of Gonville and Caius College, and now known as the Walter Myers Fund, shall be used to support the library of the Department of Pathology as the Head of the Department of Pathology shall determine. Title and purpose.

W. P. NAPIER FUND

1. The money received from the bequest of the late Walter Percy Napier shall constitute a fund, called the W. P. Napier Fund, for the endowment of teaching and research in the Cavendish Laboratory. Name and purpose.

2. The income of the Fund shall be applied as the Cavendish Professor may from time to time decide: Application of Fund.

(*a*) in defraying the expenses of small scientific conferences to be held in the Cavendish Laboratory and the expenses of persons working in the Cavendish Laboratory attending similar conferences outside Cambridge;

(*b*) in making grants to necessitous Graduate Students in the Cavendish Laboratory;

(*c*) in providing apparatus and books for the furtherance of teaching and research in the Cavendish Laboratory.

3. Unexpended income shall not be added to the capital of the Fund but shall be accumulated for use as income in subsequent years. Unexpended income.

NAPIER SHAW FUND

1. The money received from the bequest of the late Sir William Napier Shaw shall constitute a fund called the Napier Shaw Fund for the endowment of teaching and research in Meteorological Physics in the Cavendish Laboratory. Name and purpose.

2. The first charge on the Fund shall be the cost of the upkeep of the Napier Shaw Library. Application of Fund.

3. After provision has been made for the upkeep of the Napier Shaw Library in accordance with Regulation 2 the remaining income of the Fund shall be applied as the Cavendish Professor may from time to time decide:

(*a*) in making grants to necessitous Graduate Students working on meteorology in the Cavendish Laboratory;

(*b*) in defraying the expenses of small meteorological conferences to be held in the Cavendish Laboratory and the expenses of persons working in the Cavendish Laboratory attending similar conferences outside Cambridge;

(*c*) for the furtherance of teaching and research in Meteorological Physics in the Cavendish Laboratory.

SIR GEORGE NELSON PRIZE IN APPLIED MECHANICS

1. The gift of the English Electric Company Limited shall form a fund the income of which shall be used to provide a prize to be called the Sir George Nelson Prize in Applied Mechanics. Name.

2. Subject to the provisions of Regulation 3 the Prize shall be awarded annually by the Examiners for Part IIB of the Engineering Tripos to the candidate who has shown the greatest distinction in Applied Mechanics in that examination. How awarded.

3. If in any year no candidate be deemed worthy of the Prize the income for that year shall be added to the capital of the Fund. If not awarded.

Amendment of regulations.

4. It shall be open to the University, on the recommendation of the Faculty Board of Engineering, to alter these regulations from time to time provided that the income of the Fund shall always be used to encourage the study of Applied Mechanics.

Stat. E XXV.

Isaac Newton Fund and Studentships

Endowments, 1904, pp. 353–5

Objects of Fund.

1. The Isaac Newton Fund shall be used for the furtherance of advanced study and research in the subjects of astronomy (especially gravitational astronomy but also including the other branches of astronomy and astronomical physics) and those branches of physical optics which in the opinion of the Electors have a direct bearing on astronomy or astronomical techniques, by the maintenance of one or more studentships called Isaac Newton Studentships.

Electors.

2. The administration of the Fund shall be entrusted to five Electors who shall be two Professors of the University appointed by the Council, one member of the Regent House appointed by the Faculty Board of Mathematics, and two members of the Regent House appointed by the Faculty Board of Physics and Chemistry. Electors shall be appointed in the Michaelmas Term for four years from 1 January following their appointment.

Two Studentships.

3. The income of the Fund shall be primarily applicable to the maintenance of one or more Students, to be called Isaac Newton Students, whose duty it shall be to devote themselves to study and research in Astronomy (especially and including as aforesaid) and Physical Optics as aforesaid.

Eligibility for Studentships.

4. The Studentships shall be open to graduates of any university. Candidates shall normally be under the age of twenty-six years on 1 January next preceding the election. If a person who is not a member of the University is elected he or she shall become a member at the first opportunity.

Duties of Electors.

5. In every year there shall be a meeting of the Electors for the purpose of making elections. Three Electors shall form a quorum. Notice of an election shall be given before the end of Full Michaelmas Term and candidates shall be invited to send in their applications to the Registrary so as to arrive not later than the division of the Lent Term, together with such testimonials and other evidence of their qualifications and as to their proposed course of study or research as they may think fit. The Notice of an election shall include a list of subjects which the Electors consider to come within the meaning of the phrase 'those branches of physical optics which have a direct bearing on astronomy or astronomical techniques'.

6. The Electors shall take such steps as they think fit for ascertaining the intellectual qualification of the candidates, and for ascertaining the prospect that a candidate, if elected, will *bona fide* and with due diligence undertake study and research in accordance with these regulations.

Duty of Student.

7. It shall be the duty of a Student to undertake during the tenure of the Studentship study or research as aforesaid according to a course proposed by the Student and approved by the Electors, provided that such course may in special cases be altered or varied with the consent of the Electors. A Student's course of study or research shall be pursued at Cambridge under such conditions as to residence and otherwise as the Electors may determine, but the Electors may for special reasons direct or authorize the same to be pursued in any other place and under such conditions as they may think fit.

The Electors may allow a Student to break his or her tenure for a definite period without emolument for the purpose of study away from Cambridge and may allow the Student to complete his or her tenure with emolument on returning.

Election.

8. The meeting for election shall be held, and in the ordinary course one Student shall be elected, before the end of the second week of the Easter Term in each year, the Studentship to date from 1 October in the same year and to be tenable for up to three years.

If at any time the state of the Fund shall admit thereof, the Electors may elect to an additional Studentship or additional Studentships tenable for up to three years, or to prolong for an additional year the Studentship of any Student who in the opinion of the Electors shall have by diligent and successful carrying out of his or her course of study or research deserved the same; provided that no Student shall continue to hold a Studentship for longer than three years.

Elections to additional Studentships (if any) shall also be made at the annual election. But in any year, whatever be the number of vacancies, the Electors, if in their opinion there shall be no suitable candidate, shall not be bound to make any election. And the Electors may, if they think fit, defer an election to a subsequent meeting.

9. The annual emolument of the Student shall be such sum as shall be determined by the Electors within a range approved from time to time by the Council, provided that the income of the Fund shall be capable of bearing such charge, and shall be paid to the Student by equal half-yearly payments commencing immediately after the election of the Student and subject as regards each subsequent payment to the Electors being satisfied that the Student is diligently carrying out his or her course of study or research, but so nevertheless that if by illness or any other grave cause the Student shall have been prevented from thus carrying out the course of study or research, the Electors shall take account of the circumstances and shall be at liberty to make to the Student the full payment for the half-year. Emolument.

The Electors may in addition award a grant not exceeding such sum as shall be approved from time to time by the Council, provided that the income of the Fund is capable of bearing such a charge for fees, books, or other expenses incurred by the Student in the course of study or research. Such grants shall be paid in equal half-yearly instalments, and each payment shall be dependent on the approval by the Electors of a statement submitted by the Student.

10. If a Student shall in the opinion of the Electors fail in diligently carrying out the course of study or research, and if in consequence thereof they shall have withheld from the Student two successive half-years' payment of the Studentship, it shall be lawful for the Electors as from the expiration of the last of the same two half-years to remove the Student from the Studentship. Student may be removed.

11. Any unexpended income accumulated in the Fund may be applied by the Electors as follows: Unexpended income.

(*a*) in making up any deficiency in the income of the Fund for the purpose of paying the full amount of the Studentships;

(*b*) in providing any such additional Studentships or prolongations of Studentships as hereinbefore mentioned;

(*c*) in purchasing on the recommendation of the Electors any instruments or apparatus required by a Student in his or her course of study or research, provided that such instruments or apparatus shall be the property of the trust and shall remain at the disposal of the Electors and that the produce of the sale of any such instruments or apparatus shall be paid to the Fund and applied as income;

(*d*) in paying on the like recommendation any extraordinary expenses connected with the course of study or research of any Student;

(*e*) in making such investments by way of addition to the capital of the Fund as may be required to provide an income sufficient to meet the full amount of the expenses and the payments to the Electors and the Students.

Isaac Newton Institute Fund

1. The sum of £1m received from the Trustees of the Isaac Newton Trust for the benefit of the Isaac Newton Institute for Mathematical Sciences, together with other sums received for the same purpose, shall form a fund called the Isaac Newton Institute Fund. Title.

2. The income of the Fund shall be at the disposal of the Management Committee for the Isaac Newton Institute, and shall be applied by them, in such manner as may be approved by the General Board, for the support of the Institute and its activities. Application of income.

3. Any unexpended income in a financial year may be either added to the capital of the Fund or accumulated for use as income in a future year, as the Management Committee for the Institute may determine. Unexpended income.

Mau-sang Ng Prize

1. The sums subscribed in memory of Mau-sang Ng, formerly University Lecturer in Chinese Studies, shall form a fund called the Mau-sang Ng Prize Fund, the income of which shall be used to provide a Prize for Chinese Studies. Fund.

2. The Prize shall be awarded annually by the Examiners for Part IB of the Asian and Middle Eastern Studies Tripos for an outstanding performance in Chinese Studies in that examination. Prize.

3. The value of the Prize shall be such sum not exceeding the available income of the Fund as may be determined by the Faculty Board of Asian and Middle Eastern Studies, within a range approved from time to time by the Council.

4. In any year in which the Prize is not awarded the income for that year shall be added to the capital of the Fund.

Stat. E XLIV.

R. A. Nicholson Fund

Name and purpose.

1. The R. A. Nicholson Prize shall be awarded annually by the Examiners appointed to examine in Arabic and Persian in Part II of the Asian and Middle Eastern Studies Tripos for distinguished work in that examination in Arabic and Persian, or in one of those languages, preference being given to a candidate who has achieved distinction in both languages.

Value.

2. The value of the Prize shall be determined by the Faculty Board of Asian and Middle Eastern Studies, within a range approved from time to time by the Council.

Unexpended income.

3. Any unexpended income accumulated in the Fund may be used by the Faculty Board of Asian and Middle Eastern Studies for purposes connected with the advancement of study or research in the University in Arabic or Persian, or in both those languages.

Ralph Noble Prizes

Fund and Prizes.

1. The gift of Mrs Ralph Noble and her family, in memory of her husband Ralph Athelstane Noble, of King's College, shall form a fund called the Ralph Noble Fund, the income of which shall be used to provide three Ralph Noble Prizes each year.

How awarded.

2. The Prizes shall be awarded by the M.D. Committee for M.D. dissertations as follows:

(*a*) one or more Prizes may be awarded for a dissertation in any of the following fields: psychiatry, psychological medicine, neurology;

(*b*) one or more Prizes may be awarded for a dissertation on a subject of a clinical nature, preference being given to a subject in psychological medicine.

Value.

3. The value of each Prize shall be one-third of the annual income of the Fund.

Unexpended income.

4. If in any year fewer than three Prizes are awarded, the unexpended income shall be added to the capital of the Fund.

A. D. Nock Fund

The income of the Fund derived from the bequest of Arthur Darby Nock, M.A., Fellow of Clare College, 1923–30, University Lecturer in Classics, 1926–30, and Frothingham Professor of the History of Religion at Harvard University from 1930 until his death on 11 January 1963, accepted by the University in 1963 and announced in the *Reporter* on 24 July 1963, now known as the A. D. Nock Fund, shall be applied at the discretion of the Library Syndicate for the purpose of buying new or recent foreign books for the University Library.

Richard Norman Scholarship Fund

Grace 1 of 2 March 2011

Title and purpose.

1. The sums received from Mrs D. Norman in memory of her husband Richard Norman, formerly of King's College, shall form a fund for the benefit of postgraduate students in the Department of Engineering undertaking research in electrical engineering.

Managers.

2. The Managers of the Fund shall be the Head of the Department of Engineering (who shall be Chair), the Professor of Electrical Engineering, and one person appointed by the Faculty Board of Engineering in the Michaelmas Term to serve for four years from 1 January following her or his appointment.

Scholarship.

3. The income of the Fund, and such portion of the capital as they shall determine, shall be applied at the discretion of the Managers to provide one or more Richard Norman Scholarships in Electrical Engineering for persons who are, or are about to be, registered for the Ph.D. Degree in the field of electrical engineering in the Department of Engineering.

4. A Scholarship may provide

(*a*) a maintenance payment to be determined by the Managers,

(*b*) a payment to meet any University and/or College fees payable by the Scholar, (*c*) a contribution to other costs such as equipment, travel expenses, etc., according to the discretion of the Managers.

5. In determining the award the Managers shall take into account any other financial resources available to the Scholar.

Unexpended income.

6. Any unexpended income of the Fund in a financial year may be accumulated as capital or expended in any one or more subsequent years in accordance with Regulation 3 as may be determined by the Managers.

RONALD NORRISH FUND

Fund.

1. The royalties from the sale of *Photochemistry and Reaction Kinetics*, the copyright of which was assigned to the former Department of Physical Chemistry by the individual contributors and the editors, shall form a fund, to be called the Ronald Norrish Fund, the income of which shall be applied to provide an annual prize to an undergraduate for distinguished work in physical chemistry.

Prize.

2. The prize shall be called the Ronald Norrish Prize in Physical Chemistry and shall be awarded by the Head of the Department of Chemistry on the recommendation of the Professor of Physical Chemistry to a candidate for Part III of the Natural Sciences Tripos who achieves distinction in physical chemistry.

NORRISIAN PRIZE

Stat. E XIX.

Endowments, 1904, p. 112

Prize.

1. The Norrisian Prize shall be offered annually for an essay, of not less than 10,000 words and not more than 25,000 words in length, on a subject relating to Christian Doctrine or Systematic Theology.

Who may compete.

2. The Prize shall be open to all graduates of the University and to all persons whose names are entered on the Register of Graduate Students, provided that on the last day appointed for sending in essays they are of not more than thirteen years' standing from admission to their first degree, whether of this or another university, and provided also that no previous winner of the Prize shall be eligible to compete.

Adjudicators.

3. The Prize shall be adjudged by three Adjudicators, who shall be the Norris-Hulse Professor of Divinity and two members of the Regent House appointed by the General Board on the nomination of the Faculty Board of Divinity before the division of the Lent Term each year, to serve until the division of the Lent Term in the following year. Each appointed Adjudicator shall receive from the Norrisian Fund, unless no essay is sent in, such sum as shall be determined by the Faculty Board of Divinity within a range approved from time to time by the Council.

Subject.

4. Each candidate shall submit the proposed subject of his or her essay to the Registrary not later than the division of the Lent Term. The Registrary shall communicate the subject to the Adjudicators, and shall inform the candidate by the last day of Full Lent Term of its approval or rejection by them.

5. Candidates shall send their essays to the Registrary so as to arrive not later than 19 December.

Value.

6. The value of the Prize shall be such sum as shall be determined by the Faculty Board of Divinity within a range approved from time to time by the Council.

Conditions.

7. The prize-winner shall deposit a printed or typewritten copy of his or her essay in the University Library.

NORTH CAROLINA STATE UNIVERSITY FUND

Name and purpose.

1. The sum of £250, the gift of the Department of Engineering of the North Carolina State University, shall form a fund, to be called the North Carolina State University Fund, which shall be used to provide a North Carolina State University Prize.

Value.

2. The value of the Prize shall be the annual income of the Fund.

How awarded.

3. The Prize shall be awarded annually by the Examiners for Part IIB of the Chemical Engineering Tripos to a candidate for that Part of the Tripos who has shown distinction in the performance of original project work in the form of a theoretical or experimental investigation. The Prize shall not be awarded to the same candidate to whom the T. R. C. Fox Prize is awarded.

Sara Norton Prizes

Title and purpose.

1. The sum of 5,000 dollars bequeathed to the University by the late Sara Norton of Boston, Massachusetts, shall form a fund the income of which shall be used to provide two Sara Norton Prizes each year for essays on some aspect of the political history of the United States of America. There shall be one Senior Prize and one Junior Prize.

Who are eligible.

2. The Senior Prize shall be awarded for the best essay on some aspect of the political history of the United States of America. The Prize shall be open to any member of the University who has been approved by the Board of Graduate Studies for the award of the Ph.D. Degree during the calendar year next preceding the year of the award; provided that an essay submitted for the Prize shall not previously have been submitted for a prize, but may be an adaptation of the substantial piece of work undertaken by the candidate as a Graduate Student.

Notice.

3. Notice of the Senior Prize shall be given by the Registrary before the end of the Lent Term each year.

Adjudicators.

4. The Senior Prize shall be awarded by three Adjudicators appointed before the division of the Easter Term each year by the Faculty Board of History. Each Adjudicator shall receive from the income of the Fund, except in a year in which no essay is sent in, such sum as the Faculty Board with the approval of the Council shall from time to time determine.

Approval of subject.

5. A candidate for the Senior Prize shall submit the proposed subject of his or her essay to the Registrary so as to arrive not later than 31 May. The Registrary shall transmit the subjects submitted to the Adjudicators for their approval; the Adjudicators shall have power to modify or reject any subject, and shall communicate their decision to each candidate not later than 30 June.

Submission of essay.

6. An essay for the Senior Prize shall be sent to the Registrary so as to arrive not later than the last day of the Michaelmas Term following the Adjudicators' approval of the subject.

7. The Junior Prize shall be awarded by the Examiners for Part II of the Historical Tripos for a dissertation on some aspect of American political history submitted by a candidate for that examination.

Value.

8. The value of the Prizes shall be such sums not exceeding the available income of the Fund as may be determined from time to time by the Faculty Board of History with the approval of the Council.

Unexpended income.

9. Any unexpended income accumulated in the Fund may be applied from time to time at the discretion of the Faculty Board of History to make grants to further the study of the political history of the United States of America in any other way and subject to such conditions as the Faculty Board may think fit.

Norton Rose Fulbright Prize in Commercial Law[1]

1. The sum made available annually by Norton Rose Fulbright shall be used to provide a prize called the Norton Rose Fulbright Prize in Commercial Law.

How awarded.

2. The Prize shall be awarded by the Examiners for Part II of the Law Tripos to the candidate who has shown the greatest distinction in Commercial Law in Part II of the Tripos, provided that he or she has attained the standard of the first class in that subject.

Charles Oldham Scholarships

The Classical Scholarship

Title.

1. There shall be a Scholarship called the Charles Oldham Classical Scholarship, the holder of which shall undertake advanced study or research in connection with some classical author or authors, according to a scheme to be approved by the Faculty Board of Classics.

Who are eligible.

2. Candidature for the Scholarship shall be open to any person who is or is about to be registered as a Graduate Student in the Faculty of Classics in the University. Election to and tenure of the Scholarship shall lapse if the person elected does not become or ceases to be a registered Graduate Student.

Electors.

3. The Electors to the Scholarship shall be the Faculty Board of Classics, who may take such steps as they think fit to inquire into the qualifications of the candidates; provided that the Scholarship shall not be awarded on the result of a competitive examination.

[1] Retitled by Grace 6 of 3 July 2013.

4. Before the division of the Easter Term each year, the Board shall give notice of the date by which and the manner in which applications for the Scholarship to be held in the next but one following academical year are to be submitted. An election to the Scholarship shall be held during the academical year prior to the Scholarship's being taken up, on a date to be determined by the Board. Applications.

5. The Scholarship shall be tenable from the date on which the student comes into residence until 30 September of the calendar year next following. A Scholar shall be eligible for re-election on not more than two occasions. Tenure.

6. There shall be paid to the Charles Oldham Classical Scholarship Fund one half of the net annual income of the Oldham Bequest. The emolument of the Scholarship shall be such sum, not exceeding the available income of the Fund, as shall be determined by the Faculty Board within a range approved from time to time by the Council. The emolument shall be paid in such instalments as the Board shall from time to time determine, provided that the Board may withhold payment of any instalment if they are not satisfied that the Scholar is pursuing his or her course of study with sufficient diligence. Emolument.

7. Unexpended income shall be allowed to accumulate in the Fund and shall be applied to the furtherance of classical study or research in such manner as the Faculty Board shall from time to time determine. Unexpended income.

8. The Board may delegate any of their functions concerning the Scholarship to a Committee not necessarily consisting wholly of members of the Board.

The Shakespeare Scholarship

1. There shall be established a scholarship to be called the Charles Oldham Shakespeare Scholarship, which shall be awarded for knowledge of the works of William Shakespeare. Title.

2. One half of the net annual income of the Oldham Bequest shall be paid to the Charles Oldham Shakespeare Scholarship Fund. The annual value of the Scholarship shall be such sum as shall be determined by the Faculty Board of English within a range approved from time to time by the Council. Value.

3. The election of a Scholar, which shall be made by the Faculty Board of English, shall take place not later than the last day of July each year. Time of election.

4. The Scholar shall be required to undertake advanced study in connection with English literature.

5. The Scholarship shall be tenable for one year from 1 October next following the election, but a Scholar shall be eligible for re-election on not more than two occasions. Tenure.

6. The Board may take such steps as they think fit to inquire into the qualifications of candidates and their knowledge of William Shakespeare's works; provided that the Scholarship shall not be awarded on the result of a competitive examination. No competitive examination.

7. The Scholarship shall be open to any person Who are eligible.

(*a*) who is a member of the University *in statu pupillari*,

or

(*b*) who is, or is about to be, registered as a Graduate Student in the University.

8. The Faculty Board shall announce, not later than the end of the Michaelmas Term each year, the date by which, and the manner in which, applications are to be submitted. Applications.

9. The Scholar shall make a report at the end of the tenure of the award on the work carried out during the year of the award. Report.

10. From any unexpended income accumulated in the Fund the Faculty Board may make grants to Graduate Students to assist in meeting the expenses of research in English literature. Grants.

11. The Board may delegate any of their functions concerning the Scholarship to a Committee not necessarily consisting wholly of members of the Board.

Michelle Ong History Undergraduate Travel Fund

Grace 7 of 5 December 2012

1. The sum of £30,000 received from Michelle Ong shall form a Fund called the Michelle Ong History Undergraduate Travel Fund, the income of which shall be used to provide grants to undergraduate student members of the Faculty of History to cover travel and research expenses relating to their studies, with a preference for providing grants to students who would not otherwise have the opportunity to visit or access primary source materials, including libraries, archives, and collections across the UK and around the world. Title and purpose.

Managers. **2.** The Managers of the Fund will be appointed by the Faculty Board of History.

3. Awards shall be made by the Managers.

4. The value of the awards shall be determined by the Managers.

ERNEST OPPENHEIMER FUND

Title. **1.** The benefaction of the Rhokana Corporation Limited, the Nchanga Consolidated Copper Mines Limited, and the Rhodesia Broken Hill Development Company Limited, shall form a fund called the Ernest Oppenheimer Fund.

Purpose. **2.** The income of the Fund shall always be used for the support of teaching and research in surface chemistry and colloid science in such a manner as the University may consider best fitted to promote the advancement of knowledge in those subjects.

Committee of Management of the Ernest Oppenheimer Fund

1. There shall be a Committee of Management of the Ernest Oppenheimer Fund which shall consist of:

(*a*) the Chair, who shall be appointed by the General Board after consultation with the Council of the School of the Physical Sciences;

(*b*) two persons appointed by the General Board;

(*c*) two persons appointed by the Council of the School of the Physical Sciences;

(*d*) two persons appointed by the Council of the School of the Biological Sciences;

(*e*) one person appointed by the Council of the School of Technology.

2. Members of the Committee shall serve for periods to be determined by the General Board.

3. The Secretary of the School of the Physical Sciences shall be the Secretary of the Committee.

4. Subject to the powers of the Council and the General Board, the duty of the Committee shall be to administer the income of the Ernest Oppenheimer Fund for the support of teaching and research in surface chemistry and colloid science, including applications to metallurgical reactions.

ORD TRAVEL FUND

Name and purpose. **1.** The gift made to the University in 1959 by the Committee of the Cambridge University Madrigal Society in recognition of the work of Boris Ord, Fellow of King's College, formerly University Lecturer in Music and University Organist, who was the founder and for thirty-eight years conductor of the Society, shall form a fund called the Ord Travel Fund. The income of the Fund shall be used to provide grants to assist students of music to travel in Europe and in the Mediterranean countries of Africa and Asia, or exceptionally elsewhere, to enable them to increase their interest in and understanding of the art and practice of music, and to improve their knowledge of languages for the same purpose.

Who are eligible. **2.** Any member of the University shall be eligible to receive a grant from the Fund provided that he or she has spent at least two complete terms studying for a Part of the Music Tripos and that twelve complete terms have not passed after his or her first term of residence.

Awarders. **3.** The Awarders shall be the Faculty Board of Music.

Notice of awards. **4.** Before the division of the Michaelmas Term in each year the Secretary of the Faculty Board of Music shall publish a Notice inviting applications for grants from the Fund.

Applications for grants. **5.** Applications for grants, accompanied by a short description of the proposed travel, must be submitted through candidates' Tutors to the Secretary of the Faculty Board so as to arrive not later than the division of Lent Term.

Award. **6.** Grants shall be awarded not later than the last day of Full Lent Term.

Duties of recipients of grants. **7.** Not later than the division of the term next following the term or vacation in which the travel is completed, each recipient of a grant shall send to the Secretary of the Faculty Board of Music for transmission to the Awarders a short report on his or her travel.

ROBIN ORR LECTURESHIP

Fund. **1.** The sums subscribed in honour of Robert Kemsley Orr, Mus.D., Emeritus Professor of Music and Honorary Fellow of St John's and Pembroke Colleges, shall form a fund called the Robin Orr Lectureship Fund.

2. A Robin Orr Lecturer shall be appointed from time to time by the Faculty Board of Music. It shall be the duty of the Lecturer to deliver one lecture in the University during Full Term on a subject of general musical interest. Lecture.

3. The stipend of the Lecturer shall be such sum from the income of the Fund as shall be determined by the Faculty Board, within a range approved from time to time by the Council. In addition, the Faculty Board may at their discretion pay from the annual or the accumulated income of the Fund any expenses of the Lecturer and any other expenses incurred in the holding of the Lecture. Stipend.

Dorothea Oschinsky Fund

1. The sum bequeathed to the University for the purposes of the University Library by Dr Dorothea Oschinsky shall form a fund called the Dorothea Oschinsky Fund, the capital and the income of which shall be applied from time to time for such purposes in connection with the University Library as the Library Syndicate shall in their absolute discretion think fit. Fund and purpose

2. In exercising their discretion the Library Syndicate shall note the wish of the benefactor that the Fund should be used for the acquisition of medieval manuscripts or the advancement of research in medieval history. Wish of benefactor.

3. All disbursements made from the Fund shall be associated with the name of Dorothea Oschinsky. Recognition of benefactor.

PHSA Engage Mutual Health Fund

Grace 3 of 28 April 2011

1. The sum of £2m received from the Provincial Hospital Services Association for the endowment of a University Lectureship, to be entitled the PHSA Engage Mutual Health Lectureship, in the Department of Medicine, shall form a fund called the PHSA Engage Mutual Health Fund. Title and purpose.

2. The Managers of the Fund shall be: Managers.

(*a*) the Head of the Department of Medicine,

(*b*) one person appointed by the Council of the School of Clinical Medicine,

(*c*) one person appointed by the General Board.

The Managers in classes (*b*) and (*c*) shall be appointed in the Michaelmas Term for a period of three years from 1 January following their appointment. The Managers may co-opt up to two more Managers as required. Co-opted Managers shall be appointed in the Michaelmas Term to serve for three years from 1 January following their appointment.

3. The first charge on the Fund shall be the payment of the stipend, national insurance, pension contributions, and associated indirect costs payable by the University in respect of a University Lecturer, to be known as the PHSA Engage Mutual Health Lecturer, established in the Department of Medicine, whose research has a focus on diseases and illnesses predominantly associated with the elderly. University Lecturer.

4. The Lecturer shall be appointed by the Appointments Committee for the Faculty of Clinical Medicine in the manner prescribed by Special Ordinance C (x) 1.

5. Any unexpended income of the Fund in any financial year may, at the discretion of the Managers, be either Unexpended income.

(i) added to the capital of the Fund; or

(ii) accumulated for use as income in any one or more subsequent years; or

(iii) applied to support the work of the Lecturer, or applied for research in the Department of Medicine with a focus on diseases and illnesses predominantly associated with the elderly.

Paediatric Fund

1. There shall be established a Fund called the Paediatric Fund which shall consist of the sum bequeathed to the University by Mrs Ida Gandy and such further sums as may be added to the Fund from time to time from other sources. Name.

2. The Managers of the Fund shall be the Professor of Paediatrics and the Consultant Paediatricians on the staff of Addenbrooke's Hospital. The Secretary of the Clinical School or a deputy shall act as Secretary to the Managers. Managers.

3. The income of the Fund, together with any amount of the capital in excess of £100, shall be used to provide grants to further education and research in Paediatrics in Cambridge. Purpose.

Applications. **4.** Applications for grants from the Fund may be made at any time to the Secretary by any person working in the field of Paediatrics. For grants of more than £1,000 the agreement of all the Managers either at a meeting or in writing shall be required, but for grants of not more than £1,000 the agreement of a majority of the Managers so recorded or obtained shall be sufficient.

Paediatrics Prizes

Prizes. **1.** The sums made available annually by Cow and Gate Limited, by Fisons Limited, and by Pharmacia & Upjohn Limited shall be used to provide annual prizes in Paediatrics.

Titles. **2.** The titles of the prizes shall be the Cow and Gate Prize in Paediatrics, the Fisons Prize in Paediatrics, and the Pharmacia & Upjohn Prize in Paediatrics.

Who may compete. **3.** The Prizes shall be open to any member of the University who is pursuing his or her clinical studies in Cambridge and is a candidate for the Final M.B. Examination. A person to whom a Prize has been awarded shall not again be eligible as a candidate for the same prize.

How awarded. **4.** The Prizes shall be awarded by the Professor of Paediatrics and two Adjudicators appointed for each Prize in the Michaelmas Term by the General Board on the nomination of the Faculty Board of Clinical Medicine. The name of each prize-winner shall be communicated by the Professor of Paediatrics to the donors of the Prize.

Cow and Gate Prize and Fisons Prize

Notice. **5.** The Cow and Gate Prize and the Fisons Prize shall each be awarded for the best annotated case history or study in a particular area of Paediatrics. In the Michaelmas Term of each year the Professor of Paediatrics shall publish a notice of the Prizes to be awarded in the calendar year next following, giving the value of each prize and details of the form in which the case histories or studies are to be presented, the particular areas of Paediatrics that may form the basis of the presentations, and the dates by which and the person to whom they should be submitted.

Pharmacia & Upjohn Prize

6. The Pharmacia & Upjohn Prize shall be awarded for the best overall performance in the approved course of clinical instruction in Paediatrics for Part III of the Final M.B. Examination.

Suzy Paine Fund

Name and purpose. **1.** The gift of Mr C. C. Paine in memory of his wife Suzanne Helen Paine, of Clare and Girton Colleges, University Lecturer in the Faculty of Economics, shall form a fund called the Suzy Paine Fund, the purpose of which shall be the advancement of the study of Political Economy.

Managers. **2.** The Managers of the Fund shall be the Faculty Board of Economics, who may delegate some or all of their functions under these regulations to a Committee not necessarily consisting wholly of members of the Board.

Travel grants. **3.** The Managers may make grants from the income of the Fund to members of the University *in statu pupillari* who are or intend to be candidates for the Economics Tripos and to Graduate Students undertaking advanced study or research in Development and Asia in the University, with priority given to those who apply for travel costs and help towards conducting primary research in a country in Asia.

Parke-Davis Exchange Fellowship in Biomedical Sciences

Fund and purpose. **1.** The sum of $400,000 given to the University by the Warner-Lambert Company, for the support of a Parke-Davis Exchange Fellowship in Biomedical Sciences, shall form a fund called the Parke-Davis Exchange Fellowship Fund. The income of the Fund shall be used to provide Parke-Davis Exchange Fellowships, which shall be open to biomedical scientists working in Cambridge or in the United States of America or Canada.

Managers. **2.** The Fund shall be administered, and the Fellows elected, by a Board of Managers consisting of:

(*a*) the Regius Professor of Physic as Chair;

(*b*) the Head of the Department of Pharmacology;

(*c*) one person appointed by the Faculty Board of Biology;
(*d*) one person appointed by the Faculty Board of Clinical Medicine;
(*e*) one person appointed by the Warner-Lambert Company.

Managers in classes (*c*), (*d*), and (*e*) shall be appointed in the Michaelmas Term to serve for four years from 1 January following their appointment. The Secretary of the School of the Biological Sciences shall act as Secretary.

3. If candidates of sufficient merit present themselves, the Managers shall elect one or more Fellows each year. The purpose of the Fellowships shall be to enable persons working in Cambridge to visit institutions approved by the Managers in the United States of America or Canada and persons working in those countries to visit institutions in the University of Cambridge or Medical Research Council institutions (or other comparable institutions) associated with the University. A Fellow from Cambridge shall be a biomedical scientist working in the University or in a Medical Research Council institution in Cambridge; Graduate Students shall be eligible. A Fellow from the United States of America or Canada shall be a biomedical scientist holding a university appointment in one of those countries. Exchange Fellowship.

4. The Board of Managers shall invite nominations for candidature for the Parke-Davis Exchange Fellowships from the Faculty Boards of Biology and Clinical Medicine, and may, if they so determine, advertise the Fellowship. The Managers shall give preference to candidates holding junior appointments (including Graduate Students).

5. A Fellowship shall be tenable for not more than one year and shall not be renewable. Tenure

6. No resolution of the Managers shall be valid unless approved by at least three, or a majority, whichever is the greater, of the Managers. Quorum.

7. Any unexpended income may be either added to the capital of the Fund or accumulated for use as income in subsequent years as the Managers may determine. Unexpended income.

Clive Parry International Law Prize Fund

1. The sum received from the American Friends of Cambridge University shall form a fund called the Clive Parry International Law Prize Fund. Fund.

2. The income of the Fund shall be used to provide Clive Parry Prizes as follows: Prizes.

(*a*) one Prize to be awarded by the Examiners for Part IB of the Law Tripos for distinction in International Law shown by performance in that subject in Part IB of the Tripos;
(*b*) one Prize to be awarded by the Examiners for the LL.M. Examination for distinction in International Law shown by performance in not less than three subjects designated by the Faculty Board as subjects in International Law;
(*c*) one Prize to be awarded by the Examiners for the LL.M. Examination to a graduate of a university outside the British Isles who has offered not less than three subjects designated by the Faculty Board as subjects in International Law, and whose work in the examination the Examiners consider to be especially meritorious, after taking account of any linguistic disadvantage affecting the candidate's performance.

3. The value of each Prize shall be determined by the Faculty Board of Law within a range approved from time to time by the Council. Value of Prizes.

4. After provision has been made for the award of Clive Parry Prizes the annual income may also be used to make grants to successful candidates for the LL.M. Examination who, having taken International Law in that examination, wish to pursue some course of studies in international law. Such grants shall be made by a committee consisting of the Whewell Professor and two persons appointed by the Faculty Board of Law. Grants.

5. Any unexpended annual income shall be added to the capital of the Fund.

Tesni Parry Memorial Fund

1. The sum of £10,000, a gift to the University from Mrs Enfys Morris Chapman, shall form a fund to be called the Tesni Parry Memorial Fund. Title.

2. The Managers of the Fund shall be the Professor of Pathology, the Professor of Haematology, a Consultant Haematologist nominated by the Faculty Board of Clinical Medicine, and Mrs Enfys Morris Chapman or such person as she may appoint to represent her. Managers.

Object. **3.** The income of the Fund shall be applied in such manner as the Managers shall from time to time determine for the furtherance of research in the University into diseases of the blood with special reference to anaemia.

Regulations may be changed. **4.** The foregoing regulations shall be subject to alteration by Grace on the recommendation of the Managers, provided always that no alteration shall be made to them without the consent of Mrs Enfys Morris Chapman or such person as she may appoint to represent her.

Passingham Fund and Prize

Fund. **1.** The money received by the University under the will of Tremenheere John Passingham shall be separately invested and shall constitute a fund called the Passingham Fund.

Prize. **2.** There shall be a prize, called the Passingham Prize, which shall be open for award in each year by the Head of the Department of Psychology to a student who in the opinion of the Head of the Department has done work of sufficient merit in that year as a candidate for the Natural Sciences Tripos, Part II, either in Psychology or in Physiology and Psychology, or as a Graduate Student registered as a candidate for the degree of Ph.D. or M.Sc. in the Department of Psychology, provided that the Prize shall not be awarded to any student to whom it has been awarded on a previous occasion.

Value. **3.** The Prize shall consist of books to the value of the annual income of the Fund. If in any year the Prize is not awarded, the income of the Fund for that year shall be spent on the purchase of books for the library of the Department of Psychology.

Department of Pathology Centenary Fund and Studentship

Title. **1.** The moneys subscribed to the appeal held on the occasion of the centenary of the Department of Pathology in 1984 shall form a fund called the Department of Pathology Centenary Fund.

Managers. **2.** The Managers of the Fund shall be

(*a*) the Head of the Department of Pathology, and

(*b*) two University officers in the Department of Pathology appointed by the Faculty Board of Biology.

Managers in class (*b*) shall be appointed in the Michaelmas Term to serve for four years from 1 January following their appointment. The Secretary of the School of the Biological Sciences shall act as Secretary to the Managers.

Studentship. **3.** The income of the Fund shall be applied from time to time, at the discretion of the Managers, to provide a Studentship to be called the Department of Pathology Centenary Studentship, the holder of which shall undertake original research in Pathology. Any income from the Fund accruing during a vacancy in the Studentship shall be added to the capital of the Fund or retained as additional income, as the Managers may determine.

4. The Managers shall give due notice of their intention to proceed to an election.

5. The Managers may elect to a Studentship any person whom they consider suitable. A Student who on election is not a member of the University shall become such on taking up the Studentship.

Tenure. **6.** The Studentship shall be tenable for such period as the Managers shall determine on the occasion of each election.

Emolument. **7.** The emolument of the Studentship shall be determined by the Managers within a range approved from time to time by the Council.

Pathology Endowment Fund

The income of the Pathology Endowment Fund shall be used for the benefit of the Department of Pathology.

Pathology Prizes

Fund. **1.** The sum of £175, the gift of an anonymous donor, in memory of Dr Graham P. McCullagh, Dr A. Max Barrett, and Dr G. Fulton Roberts, shall form a fund to be called the Pathology Prize Fund.

Purpose. **2.** The capital and income of the Fund shall be at the disposal of the Professor of Pathology for the award, at the Professor's sole discretion, of prizes to candidates who have acquitted themselves with distinction in the subject Pathology in Part II of the Natural Sciences Tripos.

3. The Prizes shall consist of grants to assist the prize-winners to publish or communicate to learned societies the results of research that they have undertaken. Form of Prizes.

4. In accordance with the wishes of the benefactor each Prize awarded shall be named by the Professor after one or other of the three persons who are commemorated, according to the particular aspect of Pathology with which the prize-winner's work is chiefly concerned. If the work is chiefly concerned with experimental pathology the title of the Prize shall be the Graham McCullagh Memorial Prize; if it is chiefly concerned with morbid anatomy the title shall be the Max Barrett Memorial Prize; if it is chiefly concerned with immunology the title shall be the Fulton Roberts Memorial Prize. Titles of Prizes.

PERCEVAL FUND

1. The moneys received by the University under the will of Spencer George Perceval in 1922, and announced in the *Reporter* on 16 May 1922, shall be called the Perceval Fund. Fund.

2. The Managers of the Fund shall be the Fitzwilliam Museum Syndicate. Managers.

3. The income of the Fund shall be expended from time to time by the Syndicate on the purchase of letters, relics, or portraits of distinguished members of the University prior to the nineteenth century, or on other objects of art of the same class as the Perceval collections. Purpose

MICHAEL PERKINS FUND

1. The money received from the Reverend J. H. T. Perkins for the furtherance of the study of the natural history of animals shall form a fund called the Michael Perkins Fund. Fund.

2. The administration of the income of the Fund shall be entrusted to the Head of the Department of Zoology and two other Managers, who shall be appointed by the Faculty Board of Biology in the Michaelmas Term to serve for five years from 1 January following their appointment. All the powers of the Managers may be exercised by a majority of those present at a meeting, provided that two Managers at least be present. Managers.

3. The income of the Fund shall be applied: How income may be used.

(*a*) to the payment of a lecturer, to be called the Michael Perkins Lecturer;

(*b*) to the furtherance of the study of the natural history of animals by the occasional award, at the discretion of the Managers and subject to such conditions as they may think fit, of prizes or grants of money to young graduates of the University;

(*c*) to such other purposes as may from time to time be approved by the Faculty Board of Biology.

4. The Michael Perkins Lecturer shall be appointed by the Managers of the Michael Perkins Fund. The Lecturer shall hold office for one year, and shall be required to give one lecture on a subject, approved by the Managers, dealing with original investigation or interpretation of the natural history of animals. Lecturer.

DR AMANDA PERREAU-SAUSSINE DE EZCURRA LAW PRIZE FUND

Grace 4 of 31 July 2013; amended by Grace 1 of 29 May 2014

1. Income from the Dr Amanda Perreau-Saussine de Ezcurra Law Prize Fund shall be used to provide an Amanda Perreau-Saussine de Ezcurra Prize for the History and Philosophy of International Law. Fund.

2. The Managers of the Fund shall be the Faculty Board of Law. Managers.

3. The Prize shall be awarded annually by the Examiners for the LL.M. Examination for outstanding performance in: How awarded.

(*a*) the subject Foundations of International Law or such paper as the Faculty Board may announce;

or (*b*) an LL.M. thesis submitted in lieu of the written examination in that paper, so long as the Examiners consider that the thesis falls within the scope of the Prize's title;

or (*c*) a combination of (*a*) and (*b*).

4. The value of the Prize shall be determined by the Managers. Value.

5. Any unexpended income may at the discretion of the Managers be added to the capital of the Fund or accumulated for use as income in any one or more subsequent years or applied in support of the Squire Law Library. Unexpended income.

Prince Philip Scholarships Fund

Title and purpose.

1. The sums provided for scholarships by the Friends of Cambridge University in Hong Kong shall form a fund called the Prince Philip Scholarships Fund. The income of the Fund shall be applied to provide scholarships for students who are Hong Kong Permanent Identity Card holders at the time of application and have ordinarily resided in Hong Kong for a continuous period of not less than 7 years, in order that they may become matriculated members of the University following courses leading to a degree or other qualification of the University.

Managers.

2. The Fund shall be administered by a Board of Managers who shall consist of:

(*a*) the Vice-Chancellor, or a duly appointed deputy;

(*b*) two persons appointed by the Council;

(*c*) three persons appointed by the Friends of Cambridge University in Hong Kong.

Managers in classes (*b*) and (*c*) shall be appointed in the Michaelmas Term and shall serve for three years from 1 January following their appointment.

Undergraduate Scholarships.

3. The first charge on the Fund shall be the provision of scholarships, called Prince Philip Scholarships, for Hong Kong Permanent Identity Card holders at the time of application who have ordinarily resided in Hong Kong for a continuous period of not less than 7 years and who are intending to study for the B.A. Degree. Not fewer than three Prince Philip Scholarships shall be awarded in each year, provided that candidates of sufficient merit present themselves.

Graduate Scholarships.

4. Subject to the provisions of Regulations 1 and 3, any unexpended income of the Fund may be used by the Managers to provide scholarships, called Prince Philip Graduate Scholarships, for Hong Kong Permanent Identity Card holders at the time of application who have ordinarily resided in Hong Kong for a continuous period of not less than 7 years and who are intending to undertake postgraduate study leading to a degree or other qualification of the University.

How awarded.

5. Prince Philip Scholarships shall be awarded by a selection committee appointed by the Managers. Prince Philip Graduate Scholarships shall be awarded by the Managers.

Value.

6. The value of a Prince Philip Scholarship, and of a Prince Philip Graduate Scholarship, shall be determined by the Managers after taking account of the resources available to the holder.

Tenure.

7. A Prince Philip Scholarship or a Prince Philip Graduate Scholarship shall normally be tenable for not more than three years from 1 October following the date of the election.

Dame Bertha Phillpotts Memorial Fund

Name.

1. The Fund given by members and friends of Girton College in memory of Bertha Surtees Newall, Dame Commander of the Order of the British Empire, who before her marriage was Dame Bertha Surtees Phillpotts, shall be called the Dame Bertha Phillpotts Memorial Fund.

Purpose.

2. The income of the Fund shall be used primarily for the promotion of Old Norse and Icelandic studies, by means of a Scholarship of not less than £50, tenable for one year, or grants, including grants for travel. The Scholarship and the grants shall not be awarded upon a competitive examination but upon evidence of aptitude for advanced study or research, and shall be subject to such conditions as the Managers may think fit in each case.

Managers.

3. The Managers of the Fund shall be the Managers of the Scandinavian Studies Fund.

Notice of awards.

4. In the Michaelmas Term the Registrary shall publish a Notice inviting applications for the Scholarship or for grants.

Applications and awards.

5. An application must be submitted through the candidate's Tutor to the Registrary so as to arrive not later than 1 June, and must be accompanied by a statement of the course of study, research, or travel which the candidate proposes to undertake. The Managers shall make their awards before the end of June.

Grants for other purposes.

6. If in any year the sum at the Managers' disposal is in their opinion more than sufficient for the primary purposes of the Fund, they may make a grant or grants for the promotion of other linguistic, literary, or archaeological studies.

7. These regulations may be altered by Grace, save only that the Fund shall always be called the Dame Bertha Phillpotts Memorial Fund.

Philosophical Magazine Fund

The sum of £150 a year, the gift of Messrs Taylor and Francis Limited, of Red Lion Court, Fleet Street, London, EC4, shall form a fund, to be called the *Philosophical Magazine* Fund, which shall be applied at the discretion of the Cavendish Professor for the benefit of junior members of the teaching staff and research workers in the Department of Physics, particularly in connection with attendance at scientific conferences outside Cambridge.

PHILOSOPHY GRADUATE STUDENTS FUND

Grace 1 of 26 January 2011

1. The sums given to the University by Professor D. H. Mellor, Emeritus Professor of Philosophy (1896), and any later sums given for the same purpose, shall form a fund called the Philosophy Graduate Students Fund, which shall be used for the encouragement and support of the study of Philosophy in the University by Graduate Students. Title and purpose.

2. The Managers of the Fund shall be the Faculty Board of Philosophy, who may delegate any or all of their functions under these regulations to a committee of at least three persons, not necessarily consisting wholly of members of the Board. Managers.

3. The income of the Fund shall be used to provide awards to persons who are or are about to be registered as Graduate Students in the Faculty of Philosophy. Awards.

4. The Managers shall determine both the grounds for the selection of recipients of awards and the value of the awards made from the income of the Fund.

5. Any unexpended income may be either added to the capital of the Fund or accumulated for use as income in subsequent years, as the Managers may determine. Unexpended income.

6. It shall be open to the University, on the recommendation of the Faculty Board of Philosophy, to alter these regulations from time to time, provided that the Fund shall be devoted to the encouragement and support of the study of Philosophy. Alteration of regulations.

PIGOTT FUND FOR GRADUATE STUDENTSHIPS IN ARTS, HUMANITIES, AND SOCIAL SCIENCES

Grace 1 of 25 February 2009

1. The sum of £2m received from an allocation by the Board of Cambridge in America, representing a donation from Mr Mark Pigott, shall form an endowment fund called the Pigott Fund for Graduate Studentships in the Arts, Humanities, and Social Sciences. Title.

2. The Managers of the Fund shall be: Managers.

(*a*) the Head of the School of Arts and Humanities, or her or his nominee;

(*b*) the Head of the School of the Humanities and Social Sciences, or her or his nominee;

(*c*) the Head of the School of Physical Sciences or her or his nominee; and

(*d*) the Secretary of the Board of Graduate Studies.

3. The income of the Fund, together with other sums made available from any other source for the same purpose, shall be used to provide studentships for students from the United Kingdom or other member states of the European Union starting doctoral research in any subject within the fields of arts, humanities or social sciences. Studentships

4. Studentships shall be awarded by a selection committee appointed by the Managers. The same selection process shall apply to all applicant students, who shall be evaluated against the same criteria, with the best students being selected for studentships regardless of their nationality. The income of the Pigott Fund shall be allocated to fund studentships for UK nationals, provided there are sufficient other funds to finance studentships for those students selected by the Managers who are from other EU member states. If, at any time, there are insufficient other funds, the income of the Pigott Fund may be used for studentships for any of the selected students. How awarded.

5. Studentships funded by income from the Pigott Fund shall be known as Pigott Studentships with recipients of the studentships referred to as Pigott Students. Title of Studentships.

6. A Pigott Studentship shall normally be tenable for not more than three years from 1 October, 1 January, or 17 April following the date of selection. Tenure.

7. A Pigott Studentship shall provide:

(*a*) a maintenance payment to be determined by the Managers;

(*b*) a payment to meet the student's University and College fees.

8. The Managers shall take such steps as are necessary to promote the Studentship programme in ways it considers appropriate.

Annual report. **9.** The Managers shall provide the Donor with an annual report on the use made of the Fund together with a list of the students supported and their areas of study. The University shall facilitate the provision to the Donor of annual reports on research undertaken by individual students.

Unexpended income. **10.** Any unexpended income in a financial year shall either be added to the capital of the Fund or retained for use as income in future years, as the Managers may determine.

Alexander Pike Fund

Amended by Grace 2 of 29 May 2014

Fund. **1.** The sums subscribed in memory of Alexander Thomas Henry Paul Pike, of St John's College, formerly University Lecturer in Architecture, shall form a fund called the Alexander Pike Fund.

Prize: how awarded. **2.** The first charge on the income of the Fund shall be the provision of a prize called the Alexander Pike Prize. The Adjudicators for the Prize shall be the Head of Department of Architecture and two persons appointed by the General Board on the recommendations of the Faculty Board of Architecture and History of Art. The Prize shall be awarded annually by the Adjudicators to the graduate student of the Faculty, or group of such students making a joint submission, who in the judgement of the Adjudicators has or have submitted the best design, written work, or research on a subject connected with the philosophy and practice of sustainable design as part of their course-work in subjects for the degree of Master of Philosophy or for such other degree as determined by the Adjudicators.

Value. **3.** The value of the Prize shall be such sum as shall be determined by the Adjudicators within a range approved from time to time by the Council.

Second charge on Fund. **4.** After the provision of the Prize, or if for any reason the Prize is not awarded in any year, the second charge on the income of the Fund shall be the provision of an award, called the Alexander Pike Award, which may be made each year by the Adjudicators for the Prize to any member of the Faculty of Architecture and History of Art on the basis of a proposal related to the delivery of lectures, research, designs, exhibitions or publications dealing with the philosophy and practice of sustainable design, the value of which shall be determined by the Adjudicators within a range approved from time to time by the Council.

Unexpended income. **5.** Any unexpended income shall be added to the capital of the Fund.

Pinsent-Darwin Fund and Studentship

Title. **1.** The sum of £5,000 given to the University in 1924 by Mrs Pinsent and Sir Horace and the Honourable Lady Darwin, and the assets of the Darwin Trust, which was endowed by Miss Ruth Darwin in 1929 and was transferred to the University in 1959 by the Governors of that Trust, shall form a fund to be called the Pinsent-Darwin Fund.

Purpose. **2.** The income of the Fund shall be applied to endow a Studentship to be called the Pinsent-Darwin Studentship in Mental Pathology, the holder of which shall undertake original research into any problem which may have a bearing on mental defects, diseases, or disorders.

Managers. **3.** The administration of the income of the Fund shall be entrusted to ten Managers, namely: the Regius Professor of Physic, the Professor of Pathology, the Professor of Experimental Psychology, the Professor of Psychiatry, the University Lecturer in Psychopathology, a member of the Education Committee of the County of Cambridgeshire appointed by that Committee, and four persons appointed, one by the Faculty Board of Clinical Medicine, one by the Faculty Board of Biology, and two by the Managers themselves. The Managers shall be appointed in the Michaelmas Term to serve for four years from 1 January following their appointment.

Quorum. **4.** No resolution of the Managers shall be valid unless approved by at least three Managers at a meeting to which all the Managers have been summoned.

Unapplied income. **5.** Any part of the income of the Fund not expended in any year shall be accumulated by investment or otherwise, and any such accumulation shall be applied from time to time, at the discretion of the Managers, and subject to such conditions as they may think fit,

(*a*) to increase the value of the Studentship;

(*b*) to make grants to Students or to other persons for any special purpose;

(*c*) to make temporary provision for a second Studentship;

(*d*) in any other manner;

provided always that the principal object of the Fund, namely the encouragement of research into any problem which may have a bearing on mental defects, diseases, or disorders, is maintained.

6. In the event of further benefactions being offered to the University for the same or for similar objects, it shall be within the power of the University to add such benefactions either to the capital or to the accumulated income of the Fund. Further benefactions.

7. The Managers shall give due notice of their intention to proceed to an election or to make grants from the Fund. Notice of election, etc.

8. Candidature for the Studentship shall be open, but the Student, if not a member of the University, must become such before the end of the term next after election and remain such during tenure. The Managers may take such steps as they think fit to ascertain the qualifications of the candidates. Who are eligible.

9. The Studentship shall be tenable for such period not exceeding four years as the Managers shall determine at the time of the election. A Student who is appointed for less than four years in the first instance shall be re-eligible, provided that no Student shall hold the Studentship for more than four years in all. Tenure.

10. The Student, during the tenure of the Studentship, shall engage in original research. He or she shall be allowed to carry on educational or other work with the consent of the Managers. In any books, papers, or other publications in which the Student may publish the results of the investigations carried on during the tenure of Studentship, the Student shall, where practicable, use the title 'Pinsent-Darwin Student'. Duties of Student.

11. The research work shall be carried out in Cambridge, or elsewhere with the consent of the Managers, and shall be subject to such conditions as the Managers may impose.

12. The Managers may appoint one of their number, or some other person, to supervise the work of the Student, and may pay a fee for such supervision out of the income of the Fund.

13. It shall be the duty of the Student to write a statement of the work carried out during each year and to submit this to the Managers.

14. If the Managers shall be of opinion that, through any cause, the Student is not fulfilling and is not likely to fulfil the objects of the Studentship, they may, if they see fit, remove the Student from the Studentship.

15. The value of the Studentship shall be such sum as may be determined by the Managers, within a range approved by the Council, on each occasion on which the Managers give notice of their intention to proceed to an election. The stipend shall be paid to the Student in quarterly instalments in advance. Value.

Politics Professorship Fund

Grace 8 of 2 December 2009

1. The sum of £1m received from Trinity College to support a Professorship in the Faculty of Human, Social, and Political Science, together with other sums donated for the same purpose, shall form a fund called the Politics Professorship Fund. Title.

2. The Managers of the Fund shall be the Faculty Board of Human, Social, and Political Science, who may delegate any or all of their functions under these regulations to a committee not necessarily consisting wholly of members of the Board. Managers.

3. The first charge on the income of the Fund shall be the stipend, national insurance, pension contributions, and associated indirect costs payable by the University of the holder of a Professorship in the Faculty of Human, Social, and Political Science designated by the General Board on the recommendation of the Faculty Board of Human, Social, and Political Science. Professorship.

4. On the occasion of a vacancy in the designated Professorship, the General Board, on the recommendation of the Faculty Board of Human, Social, and Political Science, may determine that the same or another Professorship in the Faculty shall be supported from the Fund.

5. After provision has been made in accordance with Regulation 3, the income of the Fund may be applied in support of the work of the Professor in such manner as may be approved by the General Board on the recommendation of the Managers.

6. Any unexpended income of the Fund in a financial year may be either added to the capital of the Fund or accumulated for expenditure in accordance with Regulations 3 and 5 in one or more subsequent years, as the Managers shall determine. Unexpended income.

Polonsky–Coexist Fund for Jewish Studies

Grace 2 of 14 January 2009

Title and purpose.

1. The sums received by the University from the Polonsky Foundation and the Coexist Foundation to support teaching and research in Judaism, with special reference to the relations with the other Abrahamic faiths, namely Christianity and Islam, shall form a fund called the Polonsky–Coexist Fund for Jewish Studies.

Lectureship.

2. The first charge on the income of the Fund shall be the stipend, national insurance, pension contributions, and associated indirect costs payable by the University in respect of the Polonsky–Coexist Lectureship in Jewish Studies in the Faculty of Divinity.

Committee of Management.

3. The administration of the Fund shall be under the control of a Committee of Management consisting of:

(*a*) the Vice-Chancellor (or a duly appointed deputy) as Chair;

(*b*) one person appointed by the Council of the School of Arts and Humanities;

(*c*) the Chair of the Faculty Board of Divinity;

(*d*) two other persons appointed by the Faculty Board of Divinity.

4. The members in classes (*b*) and (*d*) shall be appointed in the Michaelmas Term to serve for three years from 1 January following their appointment. If one or more of the offices in classes (*b*)–(*d*) are held by the same person or if one or more of these offices is vacant or its tenure has expired, the Faculty Board of Divinity shall appoint one or more additional Managers so as to ensure that there are always five Managers.

5. After provision has been made in accordance with Regulation 2, the income of the Fund may be applied for the support of teaching or research in Jewish Studies in the University, with special reference to the relations between Judaism and the other Abrahamic faiths and more generally to support the study of the Abrahamic faiths and their inter-relations, as shall be approved by the General Board on the recommendation of the Managers.

Unexpended income.

6. Any unexpended income in a financial year shall either be added to the capital of the Fund or accumulated for use as income in any one or more subsequent years, as the Managers may determine.

Title.

Ronald Popperwell Memorial Fund

1. The sum subscribed in memory of Ronald George Popperwell, M.A., Ph.D., formerly University Lecturer in Norwegian and Fellow of Clare Hall, shall form a fund called the Ronald Popperwell Memorial Fund.

Purpose.

2. The income of the fund shall be used, at the discretion of the Faculty Board of Modern and Medieval Languages for the promotion of study, teaching, or research in Scandinavian studies in the University by means such as the provision of lectures or seminars, the purchase of books for the Faculty's library, or arranging commemorative events such as concerts.

3. All disbursements made from the Fund shall be associated with the name of Ronald Popperwell.

Stat. E VIII.

Porson Fund and Prize

Endowments, 1904, p. 121

Prize.

1. The Porson Prize is offered every year for the best translation of a set passage from an English poet into Greek verse. The value of the Prize shall be such sum as shall be determined by the Faculty Board of Classics within a range approved from time to time by the Council.

Who may be candidates.

2. Any resident undergraduate may be a candidate for the Prize.

Examiners.

3. The Prize shall be awarded by the Examiners for the Browne Medals who shall receive, unless no exercise is sent in, such amount from the income of the Porson Fund as may be determined by the Faculty Board within a range approved from time to time by the Council.

Subject: when notified and exercises sent in.

4. On or before 1 June in each year the Examiners shall give public notice of the subject, and all exercises for the Prize shall be sent to the Secretary of the Faculty Board of Classics not later than 1 February next following.

Exercises: how to be sent in.

5. Each candidate shall send three copies of his or her exercise to the Secretary of the Faculty Board. The exercise shall be in a printed or typewritten form; it shall bear a motto but not the candidate's name, and shall be accompanied by a sealed envelope bearing the same motto outside and containing the candidate's name and College.

6. The cost of the Prize and the fees paid to the Examiners shall be the first charge on the Porson Fund. The second charge on the Fund shall be the provision of one or more Porson Scholarships. Any unexpended income accumulated in the Fund may be applied at the discretion of the Faculty Board of Classics to provide grants for the furtherance of knowledge of the languages and civilizations of ancient Greece and Rome. Application of income.

Harry Porter Footlights Fund

Grace 1 of 19 November 2008

1. On the appointment of the University as trustees of the sum bequeathed for the purposes of the Footlights Dramatic Club by the late Dr Harry Culverwell Porter, the said sum shall form a fund called the Harry Porter Footlights Fund. Title.

2. The capital and the income of the Fund shall be available at the discretion of the Managers of the Fund for the support of the Footlights Dramatic Club or, should the Footlights Dramatic Club cease to exist, for the support of other clubs or societies of the University in the promotion of original plays and encouragement of the arts amongst the members of the University. Purpose.

3. The Managers of the Fund shall be the Senior Treasurer of the Footlights Dramatic Club, the Junior Proctor, and the Chair of the Theatre Syndicate. The Managers may co-opt one other person, being a member of the Senate, such person being preferably a past member of the Footlights Dramatic Club, to serve for one or two years at a time as the Managers shall determine at the time of the co-optation, provided it shall not be obligatory for the Managers to co-opt any person. Managers.

David and Elaine Potter Fund for Governance and Human Rights

Grace 2 of 16 July 2008

1. The sum of £2m received from the David and Elaine Potter Foundation for the endowment of a University Lectureship in Governance and Human Rights shall constitute a fund called the David and Elaine Potter Fund for Governance and Human Rights. Title and purpose.

2. The Managers of the Fund shall be the Faculty Board of Human, Social, and Political Science, who may delegate any of their functions concerning the Fund to a Committee not necessarily composed wholly of members of the Board. Managers.

3. The first charge on the income of the Fund shall be the stipend, national insurance, pension contributions, and associated indirect costs of the Lecturer payable by the University. Lecturer.

4. After provision has been made in accordance with Regulation 3, the income of the Fund shall be applied in support of the work of the Lecturer (or for the support of teaching or research in human rights and governance within the Faculty) in such manner as shall be approved by the General Board on the recommendation of the Managers.

5. Any unexpended income in a financial year may in any subsequent year be expended in accordance with Regulation 4. Unexpended income.

6. If the General Board are satisfied on the recommendation of the Faculty Board of Human, Social, and Political Science that funding the Lectureship as set out in Regulation 3 no longer provides a suitable and effective method of using the Fund, the University shall have power to resolve to hold the capital and income of the Fund on trust for the promotion of teaching and research in human rights and governance. Amendment of Fund.

Prendergast Fund and Studentship

Stat. E XXVII.

Endowments, 1904, pp. 352–3

1. The Prendergast Fund shall be devoted to the furtherance of study and research in the language, literature, history, philosophy, archaeology, and art of ancient Greece. Fund.

2. The Managers of the Fund shall be the Faculty Board of Classics. Managers.

3. The income of the Fund shall be applied in the first instance to the maintenance of a studentship to be called the Prendergast Studentship. Studentship.

4. Subject to the above-mentioned provisions, the University shall have power by Grace to make regulations for carrying out the objects of the Trust and to vary such regulations from time to time.

Purpose. **5.** The Student shall undertake advanced study or research in one or more of the subjects specified in Regulation 1, according to a scheme to be approved by the Faculty Board of Classics. Such a scheme shall involve absence from Cambridge for some considerable portion of the year, provided that the Board may for sufficient cause relax this requirement in special cases.

Who are eligible. **6.** Candidature for the Studentship shall be open to any person who is or is about to be registered as a Graduate Student in the Faculty of Classics in the University. Election to and tenure of the Studentship shall lapse if the person elected does not become or ceases to be a registered Graduate Student.

Electors. **7.** The Electors to the Studentship shall be the Faculty Board of Classics, who may take such steps as they think fit to inquire into the qualifications of the candidates; provided that the Studentship shall not be awarded on the result of a competitive examination.

Applications. **8.** Before the division of the Easter Term each year, the Board shall give notice of the date by which and the manner in which applications for the Studentship to be held in the next but one following academical year are to be submitted. An election to the Studentship shall be held during the academical year prior to the Studentship's being taken up, on a date to be determined by the Board.

Tenure. **9.** The Studentship shall be tenable from the date on which the student comes into residence until 30 September of the calendar year next following. A Student shall be eligible for re-election on not more than two occasions.

Emolument. **10.** The emolument of the Studentship shall be such sum, not exceeding the available income of the Fund, as shall be determined by the Faculty Board within a range approved from time to time by the Council. The emolument shall be paid in such instalments as the Board shall from time to time determine, provided that the Board may withhold payment of any instalment if they are not satisfied that the Student is pursuing his or her course of study with sufficient diligence.

Unexpended income. **11.** Any unexpended income accumulated in the Fund may be applied by the Board for making grants for the furtherance of study or research as aforesaid.

12. The Board may delegate any of their functions concerning the Fund to a Committee not necessarily consisting wholly of members of the Board.

A. J. Pressland Fund

Title. **1.** The sum bequeathed to the University by the late Arthur John Pressland, M.A., of St John's College, shall form a fund to be called the A. J. Pressland Fund.

Committee of Management. **2.** The administration of the Fund shall be entrusted to the Committee of Management of the Language Centre.

Purposes. **3.** The income of the Fund shall be used to provide instruction in modern languages without fee, primarily for science and medical students, and to provide bursaries to be called Pressland Bursaries for such students to attend language courses abroad. Not less than 20 per cent of the income of the Fund shall be used for bursaries.

Use of income. **4.** The members of the Committee of Management nominated by the Schools of Physical and Biological Sciences, and the School of Technology, shall have particular regard to the use of the Pressland Fund income.

Courses of instruction. **5.** The Committee of Management shall arrange a course or courses of instruction, according to the income available from the Fund, at least once in every academical year, preferably in the Long Vacation.

Languages to be taught. **6.** The languages to be taught in any particular course shall be decided by the Committee of Management in accordance with the needs of the Schools of the Physical and Biological Sciences and the School of Technology. Every course shall be advertised in the *Reporter* not later than the division of the term preceding the term or Long Vacation in which it is to be held. The Committee of Management shall have authority to restrict admission to the courses in the interests of effective teaching.

Gwynaeth Pretty Research Fund and Studentship

The Fund

1. The Trust Fund founded in memory of Miss Gwynaeth Pretty shall be called the Gwynaeth Pretty Research Fund and shall be devoted to the encouragement of research in the aetiology, pathology, or treatment of disease with particular, but not exclusive, reference to those diseases which cripple or disable in childhood or early life.
Name and purpose.

2. The administration of the income of the Fund shall be entrusted to the Professor of Pathology in conjunction with four other Managers. The other Managers shall be the Regius Professor of Physic, the Sir William Dunn Professor of Biochemistry, the Mistress of Girton College, and one other person who shall be nominated by the *ex officio* Managers and appointed by the Council in the Michaelmas Term to serve for three years from 1 January next following.
Managers.

3. No resolution of the Managers shall be valid unless approved by at least three Managers at a meeting to which all the Managers have been summoned, but a resolution signed by all the Managers shall have the same validity as a resolution carried at a meeting.
Quorum.

4. The income of the Trust Fund shall be applied from time to time for all or any of the following purposes:
Income.

(*a*) to endow a Studentship to be called the Gwynaeth Pretty Studentship, the holder of which shall undertake whole-time study and training for research in the aetiology, pathology, or treatment of disease with particular, but not exclusive, reference to those diseases which cripple or disable in childhood or early life;

(*b*) to further research in the aetiology, pathology, and treatment of disease by grants to defray the cost of research or to purchase apparatus or material necessary for such research.

5. If at any time there is insufficient money available in the Fund to carry out effectively the objects of the trust, it shall be lawful for the Managers to suspend the election to the Studentship and other expenditure under Regulation 4(*b*) in order that the income may accumulate.
Suspension of Studentship.

6. Additional moneys or securities may be accepted as additions to the Trust Fund or the Reserve Fund, and the names of any donor or donors thereto may by Grace be incorporated in the title of the Research Fund.

The Studentship

7. The Studentship shall be of an annual value to be determined from time to time by the Managers, and shall be tenable for three years. It shall not be awarded by competitive examination.
Value and tenure.

8. Candidature for the Studentship shall be open, but the Student, if not a member of the University, must become such before the end of the term next after election and remain such during tenure.
Who are eligible.

9. Three months before the date at which the Studentship would become vacant, or immediately upon the occurrence of any casual vacancy, the Professor of Pathology shall consult the other Managers, and if it shall seem desirable to hold an election to the Studentship, the Professor shall give public notice thereof inviting applications, and shall report upon the qualifications of all candidates whose names are sent in. The Managers shall consider the Professor's report and shall elect the person who is in their opinion best qualified.
Notice of vacancy.

10. The income of the Studentship shall be payable to the Student from the date of appointment, and shall be paid by equal quarterly payments, the payment for each quarter being made in advance.
Payments.

11. The place and nature of the studies of the Student shall be subject to the approval of the Professor of Pathology, provided that the Student shall be bound to study within the University unless the Managers shall dispense with this requirement for special reasons. The Managers shall take such steps as they may think necessary to satisfy themselves as to the diligence and progress of the Student, and may require from the Student any reports or other information on the subject of his or her studies which they may think desirable.
Nature of studies.

12. A Student during the tenure of the Studentship shall undertake whole-time study and training for research and shall not systematically follow any business or profession, but may, with the permission of the Managers, undertake a limited amount of teaching or demonstration for payment without suffering any deduction from the stipend of the Studentship, provided that such teaching or demonstration does not interfere with the Student's whole-time study and training for research.

Re-election. **13.** A Student whose work has been of such exceptional promise that it would, in the opinion of the Managers, be clearly in the interests of the objects of the trust that he or she should continue to hold the Studentship may be re-elected for a second period not exceeding three years, and during that period shall undertake original research. In such a case a vacancy shall not be announced.

14. A Student who has been re-elected for a second period may, with the permission of the Managers, undertake a limited amount of teaching or demonstration for payment without suffering any deduction from the stipend of the Studentship, provided that such teaching or demonstration does not interfere with the Student's research. In publishing the results of investigations carried out during the tenure of the Studentship such a Student shall, so far as is practicable, use the title 'Gwynaeth Pretty Research Student'.

15. The Managers may, for contravention of or failure to fulfil these regulations, remove a Student from the Studentship. If they consider that, through any other cause, such as confirmed ill health, want of diligence, or moral turpitude, the Student is not fulfilling and is not likely to fulfil the objects of the Studentship, the Managers may, if they see fit, remove the Student from the Studentship.

PricewaterhouseCoopers Prize in Economics

Prize. **1.** The sum made available annually by PricewaterhouseCoopers shall be used to provide a prize called the PricewaterhouseCoopers Prize in Economics.

How awarded. **2.** The prize shall be awarded by the Examiners for Part IIA of the Economics Tripos for an outstanding performance in that examination.

Prince Consort Prize and Thirlwall Prize

Endowments, 1904, pp. 419–22

Fund. **1.** The investments constituting the Prince Consort Prize Fund, the Thirlwall Prize Fund, and the Historical Essays Prize Fund shall form a single fund called the Prince Consort and Thirlwall Fund.

Managers. **2.** The Managers of the Fund shall be the Professors whose Professorships are assigned to the Faculty of History.

Prizes. **3.** The first charge on the income of the Fund shall be the provision of a prize for a dissertation involving original historical research.

4. The Prince Consort Prize shall be awarded in even-numbered years and the Thirlwall Prize in odd-numbered years. The value of each Prize shall be such sum, not exceeding half the income of the Fund, as shall be determined by the Managers within a range approved from time to time by the Council.

Medals. **5.** The second charge on the income of the Fund shall be the provision of a bronze medal, which shall be awarded to the winner of a Prize.

Notice of award. **6.** The Managers shall give notice of each Prize before the end of Full Michaelmas Term in the academical year next preceding the year in which it is to be awarded.

Who are eligible. **7.** The Prizes shall be open to all graduates of the University and to all persons whose names are entered on the Register of Graduate Students, provided that they have not attained the age of thirty years on the last day appointed for sending in dissertations, and provided also that no previous winner of either the Prince Consort Prize or the Thirlwall Prize shall be eligible to compete.

8. Each dissertation shall be on a subject selected by the candidate and approved by the Managers. Candidates shall submit the titles of their proposed subjects to the Registrary not later than 15 May in the academical year next preceding the award. The Registrary shall communicate the proposed subjects to the Managers.

Notice of subjects. **9.** Between 15 May and 15 July in each year the Regius Professor of History shall call a meeting of the Managers to consider the subjects submitted for dissertations and to elect two or more persons, at least one of whom shall be chosen from among the Managers, to act as Adjudicators for the ensuing academical year. Each Adjudicator shall receive from the Fund a payment equal to the fee that is paid under the regulations for the Ph.D., M.Sc., and M.Litt. Degrees to an Examiner who reports on a dissertation and takes part in an oral examination.

10. The Registrary shall communicate to each candidate the approval or rejection of his or her proposed subject by the Managers.

11. A dissertation shall not exceed 100,000 words in length. Each dissertation, with a declaration of its length, shall be sent to the Registrary in printed or typewritten form not later than 31 October. *Dissertations, when to be submitted.*

12. Each Prize shall be awarded not later than 1 March. In announcing the award the Adjudicators may also commend dissertations submitted by other candidates as deserving of publication.

13. The successful candidate shall deposit a printed or typewritten copy of his or her dissertation in the University Library.

14. Any unexpended income of the Fund shall be carried to a Reserve Fund, which shall be available for the purposes specified in Regulation 15. Any unexpended income of the Reserve Fund in any year shall be accumulated for use as income in subsequent years. *Reserve Fund.*

15. The Managers shall have power to use the Reserve Fund for the following purposes: *Application of Reserve Fund.*

(*a*) To make grants towards the cost of publication of any works for which a Prince Consort Prize or a Thirlwall Prize has been awarded or which have been commended by the Adjudicators.

(*b*) To provide one or more studentships, to be called Prince Consort Studentships or Thirlwall Studentships, the holders of which shall devote themselves to original research in History. The Electors to the Studentships shall be the Managers of the Fund who, on each occasion when they intend to proceed to an election, shall announce the date by which applications must be received and the manner in which they must be submitted. A Studentship shall be open to any person who is or is about to be registered as a Graduate Student in the University. A Studentship shall be awarded for one year in the first instance and may be renewed for a period of one year at a time, subject to a maximum tenure of three years. The stipend of a Student shall be such sum as shall be determined by the Managers within a range approved from time to time by the Council.

(*c*) To make grants to Graduate Students or to graduates of the University in aid of historical research.

(*d*) To further the study of History in the University by any other means.

Edward S. Prior Fund

1. The sum received from friends and pupils of Edward Schröder Prior, Slade Professor of Fine Art from 1915 to 1932, shall constitute a trust fund called the Edward S. Prior Fund. *Fund*

2. In each year there shall be a prize, called the Edward S. Prior Prize, the value of which shall be the annual income of the Fund. *Prize*

3. Candidates for the Prize shall be students of Architecture who have completed the studio-work for Parts Ib and II of the Architecture Tripos. *Who may compete.*

4. In the Michaelmas Term of each year the Registrary shall publish a Notice to competitors for the Prize. *Notice of award.*

5. Each candidate shall submit a portfolio of drawings which he or she has made since becoming a candidate for the Architecture Tripos, and the Prize shall be awarded to the candidate whose drawings show the best understanding of building construction and of the use of materials. *Submission of work*

6. The portfolios shall be sent to the Secretary of the Faculty Board of Architecture and History of Art not later than the first day of the examination for Part II of the Architecture Tripos in the year in which the Prize is to be awarded.

7. The Prize shall be awarded by three honorary Awarders nominated by the Faculty Board before the division of the Easter Term and appointed by the General Board. It shall be awarded before the end of the Easter Term. *Awarders.*

L. P. Pugh Medal

1. The sums subscribed in memory of Leslie Penrys Pugh, of Magdalene College, formerly Professor of Veterinary Clinical Studies, shall form a fund called the L. P. Pugh Fund, the income of which shall be used to provide a medal for distinguished work in clinical veterinary medicine. *Fund and purpose.*

2. The Medal shall be awarded each year by the Head of the Department of Veterinary Medicine for distinction in veterinary studies as shown by performance in all three Parts of the Final Veterinary Examination. *Award of Medal.*

Gorley Putt Fund and Lectureship

Managers. **1.** The sum bequeathed to the University by Samuel Gorley Putt, M.A., Fellow of Christ's College, shall form a fund called the Gorley Putt Fund. The Managers of the Fund shall be the Faculty Board of English.

Lecturer. **2.** The first charge on the income of the Fund shall be the stipend and, as appropriate, the national insurance and pension contributions of a Gorley Putt Lecturer in English Literary History. On the occasion of each appointment the Managers shall determine, having regard to the income of the Fund and the needs of the Faculty of English, and after taking account of the requirements of Regulation 6 below, whether the Gorley Putt Lectureship is to be a visiting Lectureship, to be held for such period as the Managers shall specify, or a University office established in the Faculty of English.

Appointments. **3.** If the Managers determine that the Gorley Putt Lectureship is to be a visiting Lectureship, the Lecturer shall be appointed by a Committee specially constituted for the purpose, which shall consist of:

(*a*) the Chair of the Faculty Board of English;

(*b*) three persons appointed by the Faculty Board;

(*c*) one person appointed by the governing body of Christ's College.

It shall be the duty of the Lecturer to give one or more lectures, as determined by the Managers, in English Literary History.

4. If the Managers determine that the Gorley Putt Lectureship is to be a University office, they shall further determine, after consulting the General Board, whether the tenure of the office is to be the same as that prescribed by Special Ordinance C (x) 5 and 6 for a University Lecturer. Appointments and reappointments to such an office shall be made by the Appointments Committee for the Faculty of English, with one person appointed by the governing body of Christ's College as an additional member for this purpose. The Lectureship shall be placed in the Schedule to Special Ordinance C (i) 1 for the tenure of the person appointed.

Stipend. **5.** (*a*) The stipend of a Gorley Putt Lecturer appointed under Regulation 3 shall be such sum as shall be determined by the Managers on the occasion of each election, subject to the approval of the General Board; in addition, the Managers may at their discretion pay any expenses of the Lecturer.

(*b*) A Gorley Putt Lecturer appointed under Regulation 4 shall receive the same stipend as a University Lecturer.

Christ's College. **6.** When an appointment of a Gorley Putt Lecturer has been made either under Regulation 3 or under Regulation 4, the Managers shall inform the governing body of Christ's College. If the Lecturer is either elected to a Fellowship of Christ's College or appointed to some other position in the College, there shall be paid to the College from the income of the Fund such annual sum during the tenure of the Lecturer as shall be agreed between the governing body of the College and the General Board, to meet the cost of maintaining the Fellowship or other post, as the case may be.

Qualcomm European Research Studentship Fund in Technology

Grace 2 of 25 February 2009

Title and purpose. **1.** The sum received from an allocation by the Board of Cambridge in America, representing a donation from Qualcomm Inc, shall form a fund called the Qualcomm European Research Studentship Fund in Technology. The purpose of the Fund shall be the support of doctoral research students of the Computer Laboratory, Judge Business School, and the Department of Engineering, who are citizens of countries in the European Union. The term of the Fund shall be from 28 February 2009 to 28 February 2019.

Managers. **2.** The Fund shall be managed by the Council of the School of Technology, who may delegate any of their functions concerning the Fund to a Committee not necessarily composed wholly of members of the Council of the School.

Doctoral research students. **3.** The capital and the income of the Fund shall be applied by the Managers to provide financial support to doctoral research students of the Computer Laboratory, Judge Business School, and the Department of Engineering who are citizens of countries in the European Union. The support may contribute towards the following:

(i) a maintenance payment to a level determined from time to time by the Managers,

(ii) a payment to meet the student's University and College fees,

(iii) other costs such as additional training, equipment, travel expenses, conferences, etc., according to the discretion of the Managers.

4. In considering a student for an award from the Fund the Managers shall have regard to evidence of academic merit.

5. In order to be eligible for support a candidate must have been accepted to follow a course of research towards the Ph.D. Degree in the Computer Laboratory, Judge Business School or Department of Engineering and have been admitted, or be seeking admission by the Board of Graduate Studies as a registered Graduate Student in the University. If the candidate is not already a member of the University he or she shall become such by being matriculated before the end of the Michaelmas Term next after her or his acceptance as a doctoral student, provided that for good cause the Managers may allow a recipient of an award to defer matriculation until a later date. Who are eligible.

6. Recipients of awards shall be known as Qualcomm Scholars. Qualcomm Scholars.

7. Any unexpended income may, at the discretion of the Managers, either be added to the capital of the Fund, or retained for use as income in any one or more subsequent years, or applied to the benefit of doctoral students in the Computer Laboratory, Judge Business School or Department of Engineering more generally. Unexpended income.

8. The University will apply any part of the capital or income of the Fund that remains unspent, at the end of the term of the Fund, to the benefit of doctoral students in the Computer Laboratory, Judge Business School or Department of Engineering, at the discretion of the Managers

QUILLER-COUCH AND T. R. HENN FUND

1. The sums given to the University in memory of Sir Arthur Quiller-Couch, King Edward VII Professor of English Literature, and T. R. Henn, Reader in Anglo-Irish Literature, shall form a fund, called the Quiller-Couch and T. R. Henn Fund, for the encouragement of creative work of a literary kind in the Faculty of English. Name and purpose.

2. The first charge on the income of the Fund shall be the provision of a Quiller-Couch Prize and a T. R. Henn Prize. Prizes.

3. The T. R. Henn Prize shall be awarded annually by the Examiners for Part I of the English Tripos, to the author of an original composition, or compositions, of a creative nature, who is also a candidate for Part I of the English Tripos in the year in question, and the Quiller-Couch Prize shall be awarded annually by the Examiners for Part II of the English Tripos to the author of an original composition, or compositions, of a creative nature, who is also a candidate for Part II of the English Tripos in the year in question. Each Prize shall be awarded to the author whose work is adjudged to be the most outstanding among the compositions submitted for the Prize concerned, save that, if candidates of sufficient merit present themselves, one or more additional T. R. Henn and Quiller-Couch Prizes may be awarded. How awarded.

4. The Examiners for Parts I and II of the English Tripos may make such rules from time to time as may be necessary to govern the award of Prizes under Regulation 3.

5. The value of each Prize shall be such sum as shall be determined by the Faculty Board of English within a range approved from time to time by the Council. Value.

6. Any unexpended income accumulated in the Fund may be applied to provide grants to undergraduate students in the Faculty at the discretion of a Committee appointed by the Faculty Board, for the furtherance of the purpose for which the Fund was established. Unexpended income.

RIBA (ANDERSON AND WEBB) SCHOLARSHIP FOR ARCHITECTURE

1. The Scholarship offered to the University by the Council of the Royal Institute of British Architects, for the advancement of the study of architecture within the University, shall be called the RIBA (Anderson and Webb) Scholarship. Name.

2. The Scholarship shall be awarded by the Faculty Board of Architecture and History of Art, who shall publish the conditions of candidature and tenure and any changes that they may make therein from time to time, and shall give due notice of vacancies of the Scholarship as they occur. Conditions.

RA JONG-YIL FUND

Grace 1 of 24 February 2010

Title and purpose. **1.** The sums given to the University by Ra Jong-Yil, of Seoul, Republic of Korea, and others shall form a fund called the Ra Jong-Yil Fund. The first charge on the income of the Fund shall be the honorarium of a Ra Jong-Yil Lecturer.

Managers. **2.** The Managers of the Fund shall be the Head of the Department of East Asian Studies and the teaching officers in the Department.

Lecture. **3.** In the Easter Term of each year the Managers shall appoint a person to give the annual Ra Jong-Yil Lecture. In making the appointment the Managers shall, if possible, select a scholar qualified to lecture on a topic related to the history, politics, and culture of Korea.

Honorarium. **4.** The honorarium paid to the Lecturer shall be such sum as shall be determined by the Managers within a range approved from time to time by the Council. In addition the Managers may at their discretion defray from the income of the Fund any expenses of the Lecturer and any other expenses incurred in connection with the lecture.

Unexpended income. **5.** Any unexpended income of the Fund in a financial year may be either added to the capital of the Fund or accumulated for use as income in future years, as the Managers may determine.

RABBINICS FUND

1. The Fund collected by Dr Salaman shall be called the Rabbinics Fund and shall be devoted to the furtherance of teaching, study, and research in Rabbinics and cognate subjects.

2. So long as a Readership in Rabbinics is maintained by the University the income of the Fund shall be applied towards the payment of the stipend of the Reader.

SIR LEON RADZINOWICZ CRIMINOLOGICAL FUND

Title. **1.** The money received by the University from the bequest of the late Sir Leon Radzinowicz, of Trinity College, the first holder of the Wolfson Professorship of Criminology (1959–73), shall form a fund to be known as the Sir Leon Radzinowicz Criminological Fund.

Purpose. **2.** The income of the Fund shall be used to provide a Nigel Walker Prize and a Sir Leon Radzinowicz Visiting Fellowship.

Managers. **3.** The Managers of the Fund shall be the Committee of Management of the Institute of Criminology.

If not awarded or elected. **4.** In any year that the Prize is not awarded or a Fellow is not elected, the income of the Fund may be added to the capital of the Fund or accumulated for use as income in future years, as the Director of the Institute shall determine.

Nigel Walker Prize

1. A Nigel Walker Prize shall be offered annually, in recognition of the contribution to the work of the University by Nigel Walker, of King's College, second holder of the Wolfson Professorship of Criminology (1973–84).

Assessors. Value. **2.** The Prize shall be awarded by Assessors appointed each year by the Managers of the Sir Leon Radzinowicz Criminological Fund. The value of the Prize shall be at the discretion of the Managers of the Fund.

How awarded. **3.** The Prize shall be awarded, at the discretion of the Assessors, for an outstanding written contribution to the field of criminology by a member of the University of Cambridge.

4. No person may be awarded the Prize on more than one occasion.

Conditions. **5.** The written work of the successful candidate shall be deposited in the Radzinowicz Library of Criminology, and the Library shall maintain a consolidated record of all written works that have been awarded the Prize.

Sir Leon Radzinowicz Visiting Fellowship

1. Not more frequently than every second year, the Managers of the Sir Leon Radzinowicz Criminological Fund may elect a Sir Leon Radzinowicz Visiting Fellow.

Duties. **2.** It shall be the duty of the Sir Leon Radzinowicz Visiting Fellow to prepare, deliver, and discuss at least two public lectures, to be known as the Radzinowicz Lectures, on topics to be agreed with the

Managers. The lectures shall be within the field of public policy in relation to crime and criminal justice.

3. In electing each Sir Leon Radzinowicz Visiting Fellow, the Managers shall take into account the wish of Sir Leon Radzinowicz that holders of the Fellowship should normally be persons who have served with distinction in Government, the Judiciary, Parliament, or other public office in the United Kingdom or elsewhere. Requirements for election.

4. No person shall be elected to the Sir Leon Radzinowicz Visiting Fellowship on more than one occasion.

5. The emolument to be provided to each Fellow shall be decided by the Managers at the time of each election. Emolument.

6. Copies of the text of the Radzinowicz Lectures shall on each occasion be deposited in the Radzinowicz Library of Criminology, and the Library shall maintain a consolidated record of all such Lectures. Conditions.

J. Arthur Ramsay Fund

1. The royalties accruing from the publication in 1977 of a book entitled *Transport of Ions and Water in Animals* in honour of Professor J. A. Ramsay shall form a fund, called the J. Arthur Ramsay Fund, which shall be devoted to the furtherance of education and research in Experimental Zoology in the Department of Zoology. Title and purpose.

2. The Managers of the Fund shall be the Head of the Department of Zoology and two of the University officers in the Department of Zoology who shall be appointed by the Head of the Department in the Michaelmas Term to serve for two years from 1 January following their appointment. Managers.

3. The income arising from the capital of the Fund shall be applied at the discretion of the Managers, and subject to such conditions as the Managers may think fit, to make grants as follows: Grants.

(*a*) to assist registered Graduate Students pursuing a course of research in the Department of Zoology to visit laboratories outside the University in connection with their research;

(*b*) to assist persons, admitted as Graduate Students to pursue a course of research in the Department of Zoology, to participate before coming into residence in experimental research under the supervision of a person normally working within the Department or to visit laboratories outside the University in connection with their research;

(*c*) to assist candidates for Part II of the Natural Sciences Tripos intending to offer the subject Zoology to participate, in one or more of the three vacations in the twelve months preceding the Tripos Examination, in experimental research under the supervision of a person normally working within the Department.

4. The preceding regulations may be altered by Grace provided that the object of the Fund as defined in Regulation 1 is adhered to.

Rapson Fund and Scholarship

1. The bequest to the University by the late Professor E. J. Rapson, M.A., formerly Professor of Sanskrit and Fellow of St John's College, shall form a fund to be called the Rapson Fund. The income of the Fund shall be applied to provide the emolument of a scholarship to be called the Rapson Scholarship, for the promotion of study or research in Indian Studies or Iranian Studies. Title and purpose.

2. The Scholarship shall be open to any person who is, or is about to be, registered as a Graduate Student in the University, provided that he or she (*a*) has successfully completed a course of study in Classics or Oriental Studies at this or another university, and (*b*) intends to follow a course of study or research in a subject falling within the field of Indian Studies or Iranian Studies. Eligibility.

3. Applications for the Scholarship shall be sent to the Registrary so as to arrive not later than the division of the Lent Term. Applications.

4. The Scholar shall be elected by the Faculty Board of Asian and Middle Eastern Studies, who shall be the Managers of the Fund. When there are two or more applications of equal merit the Managers shall give preference to a candidate whose interests are wholly or mainly concerned with the study of the Sanskrit, Pali, or Avestan languages. Election.

5. The name of the successful candidate shall be published not later than 31 July in each year.

Tenure. **6.** The Scholarship shall be tenable for one year, but the Managers may renew it for the year next following and for the year next but one following the year of the original tenure. In exceptional circumstances the Managers may postpone the tenure to a subsequent year.

Duties of Scholar. **7.** It shall be the duty of the Scholar to undertake study or research in the University in accordance with any conditions which the Managers shall impose.

Value of Scholarship, and payment of emolument. **8.** The first charge on the income of the Fund shall be the stipend of the Scholar. The stipend shall be such sum as shall be determined by the Managers in each case, taking account of the other financial resources which may be available to the Scholar, within a range approved from time to time by the Council. The stipend shall be paid in two half-yearly instalments in advance. The second instalment shall not be paid unless the Managers are satisfied that the Scholar has been pursuing his or her studies with sufficient diligence.

Unexpended income. **9.** Any unexpended income accumulated in the Fund may be applied at the discretion of the Managers to make grants to students engaged in study or research in Indian Studies and Iranian Studies; or to make grants for any other purpose which in their opinion will promote study or research in those subjects in the University.

Managers may delegate functions. **10.** The Managers may delegate any of their functions under these regulations to a Committee consisting of not less than three members not all of whom shall necessarily be members of the Faculty Board of Asian and Middle Eastern Studies.

Hans Rausing Fund

Fund. **1.** The gift to the University made by Professor Lisbet Rausing Koerner, in honour of her father Hans Rausing on the occasion of his seventieth birthday, shall form a fund called the Hans Rausing Fund.

Lecturer. **2.** A Hans Rausing Lecturer shall be appointed from time to time by the Board of History and Philosophy of Science. It shall be the duty of the Lecturer to deliver one lecture in the University during Full Term on a subject in the history of technology and industry.

Stipend. **3.** The stipend of the Lecturer shall be such sum from the income of the Fund as shall be determined by the Board of History and Philosophy of Science, within a range approved from time to time by the Council. In addition, the Board may at their discretion pay from the annual or the accumulated income of the Fund any expenses of the Lecturer and any expenses incurred in the holding of the Lecture.

Rausing Fund for History and Philosophy of Science

Fund and purpose. **1.** The sum of £2m, received from Dr L. Rausing, for the support of work in History and Philosophy of Science, shall form a fund called the Rausing Fund for History and Philosophy of Science. The Managers of the Fund shall be:

Managers.

(*a*) the Head of the Department of History and Philosophy of Science;

(*b*) the Secretary of the Board of History and Philosophy of Science;

(*c*) the Secretary of the Department of History and Philosophy of Science;

(*d*) the Curator of the Whipple Museum of the History of Science;

(*e*) three persons appointed by the Board of History and Philosophy of Science, who shall be appointed in the Michaelmas Term to serve for three years from 1 January following their appointment.

University Lectureship. **2.** The first charge on the income of the Fund shall be the stipend, national insurance, pension contributions, and associated indirect costs of a University Lectureship in the History and Philosophy of Science. On the occasion of each appointment, the field of candidature, which shall exclude the History of Medicine, shall be determined by the Board of History and Philosophy of Science.

3. After provision has been made in accordance with Regulation 2, the Fund shall be applied for the support of teaching or research within the Department of History and Philosophy of Science, but excluding expenditure on buildings, in such manner as shall be approved by the General Board on the recommendation of the Managers.

Unexpended income. **4.** Any unexpended income of the Fund in a financial year may be expended in a subsequent year in accordance with Regulation 3.

RAWLINSON FUND

The gift of the freehold premises No. 14 King's Parade, and the bequest of £1,500, made by the Rt Hon. Dr J. F. P. Rawlinson, KC, to the University forms the capital of a fund named the Rawlinson Fund. Any credit balance in the Rawlinson Fund at the end of each financial year is transferred to the Special Purposes Fund.

ALBERT RECKITT FUND

1. The benefaction of the late Mr A. L. Reckitt shall form a fund to be called the Albert Reckitt Fund. Name.

2. The income from the Fund shall be used for promoting study and research in the University in History and Philosophy of Science. Application.

3. The Board of History and Philosophy of Science shall be responsible for the management of the Fund. Management.

SIR ROBERT REDE'S LECTURESHIP

Stat. E XIV. (1524)

Endowments, 1904, pp. 261–8

1. The appointment of Sir Robert Rede's Lecturer shall be made annually by the Vice-Chancellor.

2. The Lecturer shall deliver one lecture in Full Term within one year of appointment, the time and place of delivery being fixed on each occasion by the Vice-Chancellor.

JENNIFER REDHEAD PRIZE

Grace 1 of 8 December 2010

1. The gift of Professor Michael Redhead, Emeritus Professor of History and Philosophy of Science, in memory of his wife, Jennifer Redhead, shall form a fund called the Jennifer Redhead Fund, the income of which shall be used to encourage the study of history and philosophy of science in the University. Title and purpose.

2. There shall be a Jennifer Redhead Prize to be awarded annually by the Examiners for the examination in History, Philosophy, and Sociology of Science, Technology, and Medicine for the M.Phil. Degree for an outstanding performance on the essay components of that examination. Prize.

3. The value of the Prize shall be the annual income of the Fund. Value.

4. If in any year the Prize is not awarded, the income for that year shall be added to the capital of the Fund. If not awarded.

HENRY REITLINGER FUND

1. The moneys received by the University under the will of Henry Scipio Reitlinger, M.A., of King's College, shall form a fund called the Henry Reitlinger Fund. Fund.

2. The Managers of the Fund shall be the Fitzwilliam Museum Syndicate. Managers.

3. The capital and the income of the Fund shall be applied, at the discretion of the Managers, and in accordance with the provisions of Mr Reitlinger's will as varied by two Schemes of the Charity Commissioners dated 4 January 1995 and 3 September 1996, for the maintenance and the augmentation of the collection of works of art bequeathed to the University by Mr Reitlinger, by one or more of the following means: Purpose.

(*a*) the provision of buildings to hold the collection, or the improvement of buildings in which the collection is held, including the means of display of the collection;

(*b*) the preservation and maintenance of the collection, including the employment of curatorial staff for that purpose;

(*c*) the purchase of objects to be added to the collection.

RESEARCH STUDENTS AMENITIES FUND

1. The Research Students Amenities Fund shall consist of the capital representing a portion (allocated by the Council in 1963 in accordance with the wishes of the benefactor) of an anonymous benefaction made in 1962 to assist in implementing the recommendations concerning the establishment of a Fund

University Centre which were put forward by the Syndicate under the Chairmanship of Lord Bridges on the relationship between the University and the Colleges.

Purpose. **2.** In accordance with the wishes of the benefactor, the income of the Fund shall be available for the purpose of 'providing amenities for research students which would not otherwise be available'. Applications for grants from the Fund shall be determined by the University Council after consideration by the Managers.

Managers. **3.** The Managers shall be:

(*a*) the Vice-Chancellor (or a duly appointed deputy);

(*b*) a member of the Regent House who has been appointed as Patron of the Graduate Union;

(*c*) one member of the Regent House appointed by the University Council in the Michaelmas Term to serve for three years from 1 January next following;

(*d*) the President of the Graduate Union;

(*e*) the member of the University Council in class (*d*) elected by graduate students;

(*f*) one registered Graduate Student elected by the Council of the Graduate Union in the Michaelmas Term to serve for one year from 1 January next following.

Ricardo Prize

Prize. **1.** The Prize shall be called the Ricardo Prize in Thermodynamics. It shall be offered for competition annually, and shall consist of the net annual income of the Prize Fund.

Examiners. **2.** Subject to Regulation 3 below, the award shall be made by the Examiners for the Engineering Tripos to the candidate who achieves the greatest distinction in Thermodynamics in Part IIB of that Tripos.

3. It shall be open to the Examiners in any year to declare that no work of sufficient merit has been submitted.

Unexpended income. **4.** Any unexpended income accumulated in the Fund may be used to award an additional Prize or Prizes not exceeding such sum as may be determined by the Faculty Board of Engineering within a range approved from time to time by the Council. If the unexpended income accumulated in the Fund at any time exceeds £50 the excess shall be added to the capital of the Fund.

Alterations. Proviso. **5.** It shall be open to the University on the recommendation of the Faculty Board of Engineering to alter these regulations from time to time, subject to the conditions that the Prize shall always be called the Ricardo Prize and shall be devoted to the encouragement of the study of Thermodynamics.

Richards Fund

Purpose. **1.** The gift by Dr Audrey Richards shall form a fund which shall be called the Richards Fund, the income of which shall be used to provide financial support for field research in Social Anthropology.

Managers. **2.** The Managers of the Fund shall be the Head of the Department of Archaeology and Anthropology or her or his deputy and two University officers in that Department appointed in the Michaelmas Term by the Faculty Board of Human, Social, and Political Science to serve for a period of three years from 1 January following their appointment.

Eligibility. **3.** Expenditure from the Fund shall be incurred at the discretion of the Managers to award Studentships or grants to Graduate Students registered for a course of research in the Department of Archaeology and Anthropology as candidates, or with a view to becoming candidates, for the Ph.D., M.Sc., or M.Litt. Degree.

Applications and awards. **4.** Applications for assistance from the Fund in any academical year shall be submitted to the Head of the Department not later than the last day of the Lent Term. The Managers shall have discretion whether to award the applicant a Studentship for a period of not more than one year or a grant to support his or her research. The stipend of a Student shall be such sum as shall be determined by the Managers within a range approved from time to time by the Council, and shall be payable in equal half-yearly instalments (each payment to be made in advance), provided as regards the second payment that the Managers be satisfied that the Student is diligently carrying out his or her course of research.

David Richards Fund and Travel Scholarships

Title and purpose. **1.** The sum bequeathed to the University by the late Miss K. Richards shall form a fund to be called the David Richards Fund, the income of which shall be used to provide annually a number of David Richards Travel Scholarships.

2. The Scholarships shall be open to British-born students who are reading either for Part IB or for the Preliminary Examination for Part II of the Geographical Tripos. Who are eligible.

3. The name of a candidate, together with a concise statement of the purpose and plan of the proposed travel, shall be sent by the candidate's Tutor so as to reach the Registrary not later than the end of the second week of Full Easter Term. Application for awards.

4. The Awarders shall be the Managers of Philip Lake Fund II. Awarders.

5. The number of Scholarships to be awarded and the value of each shall be determined in each year by the Awarders. If in any year the Awarders are of the opinion that none of the candidates is deserving of a Scholarship, no award shall be made in that year. Number and value of Scholarships.

6. The Scholarships shall be awarded not later than the last day of May, and the names of the successful candidates and the values of the awards shall be communicated by the Awarders to the Registrary by the first day of June. The names, but not the values of the awards, shall be published in the *Reporter*. Date of award.

7. The emolument of a Scholar shall be paid, upon his or her Tutor's application, in the term preceding the vacation in which the Scholar intends to travel. Payments.

8. Travel shall normally take place not later than the Long Vacation in the year following the year of the award, but the Head of the Department of Geography may, upon application by the Scholar's Tutor, allow it to take place at a later date. Date of travel.

9. These regulations may be altered by Grace, provided always that the Fund shall be called the David Richards Fund and shall be used to provide a Scholarship or Scholarships to be awarded at the end of their first year of residence to British-born students who are reading for the Geographical Tripos. Regulations may be altered.

RIDGEWAY-VENN TRAVEL FUND

1. The sum bequeathed to the University by Professor Sir William Ridgeway, formerly Disney Professor of Archaeology, and by his daughter, Mrs Lucy Venn, shall form a fund to be called the Ridgeway-Venn Travel Fund. Title.

2. The first charge on the income of the Fund shall be the maintenance and repair of the sundial bequeathed to the University by Professor Sir William Ridgeway. First charge.

3. After provision has been made for the maintenance and repair of the sundial in accordance with Regulation 2 the remaining income of the Fund shall be used to provide one or more Ridgeway-Venn Travel Studentships to help students of archaeology or anthropology to advance knowledge in their subjects, preference being given alternately to a student of archaeology and a student of anthropology; provided that no Studentship shall be offered in any year in which less than £50 is available in the Fund for that purpose. Studentships.

4. The Awarders shall be the Faculty Board of Human, Social, and Political Science. They may delegate any of their functions relating to the award to a committee consisting of members of the Board. Awarders.

5. A Notice inviting applications for Studentships shall be published by the Awarders before 31 January. Notice of award.

6. Any member of the University *in statu pupillari* shall be eligible provided that: Eligibility.

either (*a*) on the day on which the travel is due to begin the student will have completed the requirements for the B.A. Degree having obtained honours in at least one Part of the Archaeological and Anthropological Tripos; and provided that the student intends to complete the travel before the end of the academical year next following that in which he or she completed the requirements for the B.A. Degree;

or (*b*) on the day on which the travel is due to begin the student has been a Graduate Student for not more than one year, working under the supervision of the Degree Committee for the Faculty of Human, Social, and Political Science; and provided that the student intends to complete the travel before the end of the academical year next following that in which he or she was admitted as a Graduate Student.

7. Applications, accompanied by the dates and a short description of the nature and purpose of the proposed travel, must be submitted through the candidate's Tutor to the Registrary so as to arrive not later than the last day of Full Lent Term. Applications.

8. Studentships shall be awarded not later than 1 May and the emolument shall be payable on application to the Treasurer. Date of award.

Duty of Student.

9. Not later than the division of the term next following the term or vacation in which the travel is completed, each Ridgeway-Venn Student shall send to the Registrary for transmission to the Awarders a short report on his or her travel.

Ritchie-Ginsburg Fund

Fund.

1. The proceeds from the sale of coins from the collection of Dr C. D. Ginsburg given to the University by his grand-daughter, Miss J. M. Ritchie in 1964, and announced in the *Reporter* on 11 March 1964, shall form a fund to be called, in accordance with her wishes, the Ritchie-Ginsburg Fund.

Purpose.

2. The income of the Fund shall be expended from time to time by the Fitzwilliam Museum Syndicate on the purchase of coins.

Rivers Lectureship in Social Anthropology

Name.

1. A Lectureship in Social Anthropology, to be called the Rivers Lectureship in memory of Dr W. H. R. Rivers, FRS, sometime Fellow of St John's College, shall be established in the University.

Managers.

2. The Managers of the Rivers Lectureship Fund shall be:

(*a*) the William Wyse Professor of Social Anthropology (or a duly appointed deputy), who shall be Chair;

(*b*) one person appointed by the Faculty Board of Human, Social, and Political Science in the Michaelmas Term to serve for four years from 1 January next following;

(*c*) one person appointed by the Council of St John's College to serve for four years from 1 January next following;

(*d*) one University officer, not being a Professor or a Reader, in the Department of Archaeology and Anthropology, appointed by the Faculty Board of Human, Social, and Political Science to serve for two years from 1 January next following.

Appointment and duties.

3. A Rivers Lecturer may be appointed by the Managers in respect of any year in which the Frazer Lecture is not to be delivered in the University. The duty of the Lecturer shall be to deliver in the University on some day in Full Term one lecture on a subject in Social Anthropology, in its relation to other fields of study.

Stipend and expenses.

4. The stipend of the Lecturer shall be such sum within the income of the Fund as shall be determined by the Managers within a range approved from time to time by the Council. The Managers may from unexpended income, including unexpended income accumulated in the Fund, pay the cost of publishing the lecture and any expenses incurred by the Lecturer.

A. W. Rymer Roberts Fund

Title.

1. The sum of £1,000 bequeathed to the University by Arthur William Rymer Roberts, M.A., of Trinity College, shall form a fund to be called the A. W. Rymer Roberts Fund.

2. The income of the Fund shall be at the disposal of the Head of the Department of Pathology for the promotion of research in Parasitology.

B. B. Roberts Fund

Title.

1. The sum bequeathed to the University for the purposes of the Scott Polar Research Institute by the late Dr B. B. Roberts, CMG, of Churchill College, shall form a fund called the B. B. Roberts Fund.

Purpose.

2. The annual income of the Fund and any unexpended income accumulated in the Fund shall be used at the discretion of the Managers of the Fund for the purposes of the Scott Polar Research Institute, primarily for the support of research work in that Institute and for the provision of facilities for such research.

Managers.

3. The Managers of the Fund shall be the Director of the Scott Polar Research Institute, and two persons appointed in the Michaelmas Term by the General Board on the nomination of the Committee for the Scott Polar Research Institute, to serve for three years from 1 January following their appointment.

D. W. Roberts Prize Fund

1. The sums given to the University in memory of D. W. Roberts, formerly University Lecturer in Architecture, shall form a fund for the award annually of a prize in architecture called the David Wyn Roberts Memorial Prize. Fund and purpose.

2. The value of the Prize shall be the annual income of the Fund. Value.

3. The Prize shall be awarded each year before the end of the Easter Term by the Examiners for Part II of the Architecture Tripos to the candidate who in the thesis submitted under the regulations for that Part of the Tripos achieves the greatest distinction. How awarded.

4. In any year in which the Prize is not awarded the income for that year shall be added to the capital of the Fund. If no award.

Rose Book-Collecting Prize

1. The donation of James H. Marrow and Emily Rose, given in honour of Daniel and Joanna Rose, shall form a fund, the income of which shall be used to provide a prize to be called the Rose Book-Collecting Prize. Name and title.

2. The Prize shall be offered for competition each year and shall be open either to all resident undergraduate and graduate students in the University, or to resident undergraduate and graduate students in alternate years, at the discretion of the Library Syndicate. Who are eligible.

3. The purpose of the Prize shall be to encourage students to assemble coherent collections of books, which can be on any topic, from any period, or of any genre. The entry for the Prize shall consist of the submission of a list of the books collected and entered for the Prize, together with an essay explaining the theme and significance of the collection. Purpose.

4. The competition, together with detailed rules for participation, shall be announced by the Library Syndicate during the Michaelmas Term each year. Entries shall be submitted to the University Librarian so as to arrive not later than the first day of Full Lent Term and the Prize shall be awarded in the Easter Term. Competition rules.

5. The competition shall be judged by a panel of not less than two Adjudicators who shall be appointed each year by the Library Syndicate. Adjudicators.

6. The value of the Prize shall be a minimum of £500, but this sum shall be reviewed from time to time by the Library Syndicate. If on any occasion there is no entry of sufficient merit to deserve a prize, the unexpended income of the fund for that year shall either be available for use in future years or added to the capital of the fund as the Library Syndicate may determine. Value.

7. A winner of the Prize shall not be eligible to compete a second time by offering the same collection for consideration. Restriction.

Holland Rose Studentship

1. The Studentship founded by Dr John Holland Rose, sometime Vere Harmsworth Professor of Naval History, for the purpose of encouraging the study of the recent history and present problems of the British Empire, shall be called the Holland Rose Studentship and shall be applied also for the purpose of encouraging the study of the recent history and present problems of the Commonwealth. Name and purpose.

2. The first charge on the income of the Fund shall be to provide for the Holland Rose Studentship. Studentship.

3. The Electors to the Studentship shall be three Professors assigned to the Faculty of History appointed by the Faculty Board of History not later than the division of the Easter Term in each year, provided that, if they will be available to act, the Board shall always appoint the Vere Harmsworth Professor of Imperial and Naval History and the Smuts Professor of Commonwealth History. The Electors shall have power to co-opt not more than two additional Electors. Electors.

If the Vere Harmsworth Professor of Imperial and Naval History is an Elector he or she shall be Chair *ex officio*; otherwise, the Electors shall elect one of themselves to be Chair.

4. Any person who satisfies the following conditions may be a candidate for the Studentship: Who are eligible.

(*a*) a candidate shall be a citizen of a Commonwealth country, or of a country which was in membership of the British Empire or Commonwealth in 1932;

(*b*) a candidate shall have graduated in any university with high honours in History, or in some other subject held by the Electors to be relevant to the subject of study proposed by the candidate;

(*c*) a candidate *either* shall have received his or her first degree at any university not earlier than the academical year next but three preceding that in which he or she submits an application for the Studentship, *or* shall have been registered as a Graduate Student for not more than nine terms on the date by which applications are to be sent in;

(*d*) a candidate shall submit to the Electors evidence of his or her competence for historical or other relevant studies;

(*e*) a candidate shall promise, if elected, to undertake during the tenure of the Studentship continuous and full-time study of some subject connected with the general history or constitutional, social, or cultural development of the British Empire since 1815, of the Commonwealth, or of the present problems of the Commonwealth, such subject to be approved by the Electors.

5. Preference shall be given to a student who intends to prepare for a career in the service of the Commonwealth or of any Commonwealth country.

Tenure. **6.** The Studentship shall be tenable for one academical year, but a Student in the first year of tenure may compete for re-election for a second year.

Stipend. **7.** The stipend of the Studentship shall be such sum as shall be determined by the Electors within a range approved from time to time by the Council. In determining the sum the Electors shall take into consideration the financial circumstances of the successful candidate. The stipend shall be paid in half-yearly instalments in advance; provided that the Electors may withhold the second instalment if they are not satisfied that the Student has been pursuing his or her studies with sufficient diligence.

Notice of election. **8.** The Studentship shall be offered for competition in the Easter Term of each academical year. The Chair of the Faculty Board of History shall issue a Notice to candidates before the division of each such term; candidates shall send in their applications before the end of Full Term, and the award shall be made before the end of June.

Beginning of tenure. **9.** Tenure of the Studentship shall begin with the academical year after election; provided that the Electors may at or after an election allow a Student to postpone the beginning of tenure for not more than one year.

Condition of tenure. **10.** The Student, if not a member of the University, must become such before the end of the term next after election and remain such during tenure. In making his gift of the Studentship the donor expressed the hope that the candidate elected might become a member of Christ's College, if not already a member of a College, and if approved by the College; also that he or she might remain a member of the College during the tenure of the Studentship.

Second Studentship. **11.** If in any year the Electors consider that a second Studentship should be awarded they may make such an award, and the provisions of Regulations 3–10 shall apply to the second Studentship and its holder.

Unexpended income. **12.** After provision has been made for the Studentship or for Studentships in accordance with the foregoing Regulations 1–11 any unexpended income accumulated in the Fund may be applied from time to time at the discretion of the Electors and subject to such conditions as they may think fit for the purposes of making grants to Graduate Students in the University for the encouragement of study in any of the fields specified in Regulation 4(*d*).

13. These regulations may be altered by Grace, provided that Dr Rose's gift shall always be used to maintain a Studentship for the furtherance of the studies mentioned in Regulation 1.

Archibald Douglas Ross Fund

From the sum bequeathed by Archibald Douglas Ross, M.A., of St John's College, a fund shall be established in the University called the Archibald Douglas Ross Fund, which shall be designated a General Purpose Fund.

Henry Ling Roth Research Fund

Name. **1.** The sum bequeathed to the University by Alfred Bernard Roth shall constitute a fund called the Henry Ling Roth Research Fund.

Purpose. **2.** The income of the Fund shall be applied for the maintenance of Henry Ling Roth Scholarships to aid research in Ethnology and the publication of the results of such research.

Tenure and value. **3.** A Scholarship or Scholarships shall be offered from time to time at the discretion of the William Wyse Professor of Social Anthropology and shall be awarded by the Professor. A Scholarship shall be of such value as may be determined by the William Wyse Professor, subject to the approval of the Finance Committee of the Council, and shall be tenable for such period, not exceeding three years, as the Professor may determine in each case.

4. Any member of the University who is working or has worked in the Faculty of Human, Social, and Political Science shall be eligible for the award of a Scholarship. Who are eligible.

ROUSE BALL LECTURESHIP

1. The sum accepted by the University in 1922 from Walter William Rouse Ball, Fellow of Trinity College, shall be separately invested and shall constitute a fund called the Rouse Ball Lectureship Fund. The first charge on the income of the Fund shall be the stipend of a Rouse Ball Lecturer. Name.

2. There shall be established in the University a Rouse Ball Lectureship.

3. In the Michaelmas Term of each year the Faculty Board of Mathematics shall either appoint a Lecturer to hold office during the current academical year, or adjourn the appointment for a year; but the appointment shall not be adjourned in two successive years. Appointment.

4. The Lecturer shall give in the year of office a lecture dealing either with some particular development of Mathematics, or with some application of Mathematics to science. Duties.

5. The lecture shall be given in Full Term, and shall normally be given in the Easter Term.

6. The stipend of the Lecturer shall be such sum as shall be determined by the Faculty Board within a range approved from time to time by the Council. In addition the Faculty Board may pay from the annual or the accumulated income of the Fund any expenses incurred by the Lecturer. Stipend and expenses.

ROUSE BALL LIBRARY FUND

The income of the Fund derived from the bequest of £10,000 by Walter William Rouse Ball, M.A., Fellow of Trinity College, accepted by the University in 1927 by Grace 1 of 14 July 1927 and now known as the Rouse Ball Library Fund, shall be applied at the discretion of the Library Syndicate for the benefit of, or towards the expenses of maintaining, the University Library.

ROYAL AERONAUTICAL SOCIETY PRIZE IN AERONAUTICS

1. The Royal Aeronautical Society Prize in Aeronautics shall be offered for competition annually. Prize.

2. The value of the Prize shall be such sum as shall be made available for the purpose by the Royal Aeronautical Society. Value.

3. The Prize shall be awarded by the Examiners for Part IIB of the Engineering Tripos to the candidate who in that examination achieves the greatest distinction in aeronautics. How awarded.

4. If in any year the Prize is not awarded, the prize-money shall be retained by the University to form the next award. If not awarded.

5. These regulations may be altered by Grace provided that the Prize shall always be called the Royal Aeronautical Society Prize in Aeronautics and shall be offered for competition annually. Amendment.

BETHA WOLFERSTAN RYLANDS PRIZE

1. The sum of £1,000, the gift of G. H. W. Rylands, M.A., Hon. Litt.D., Fellow of King's College, University Lecturer in English, in memory of his mother Betha Wolferstan Rylands, shall form a fund called the Betha Wolferstan Rylands Fund, the income of which shall be used to provide a Betha Wolferstan Rylands Prize. Title.

2. The Prize shall be awarded annually by the Examiners for Part I of the English Tripos to a candidate who achieves distinction in that examination. Prize.

3. The value of the Prize shall be the annual income of the Fund which shall be paid to the prize-winner not later than 30 June in each year. Value.

4. The prize-winner shall use the prize-money *either* towards meeting the cost of some form of travel *or* for the purchase of books *or* for both purposes, and shall send to the Secretary of the Faculty Board of English as soon as is practicable a short statement of the way in which the prize-money has been used. Duties of prize-winner.

If not awarded. **5.** If in any year no candidate is deemed worthy of the Prize the income for that year shall be added to the capital of the Fund.

G. H. W. Rylands Fund

Name. **1.** The sum given to the University by G. H. W. Rylands, M.A., Hon. Litt.D., Fellow of King's College, shall form a fund to be called the G. H. W. Rylands Fund.

Purpose. **2.** The income of the Fund shall be expended from time to time by the Fitzwilliam Museum Syndicate on the purchase, or a contribution towards the purchase, of objets d'art to be added to the collections in the Fitzwilliam Museum; for this purpose objets d'art shall be deemed to include china, glass, silver, furniture (preferably European and before 1850), and drawings.

Unexpended income. **3.** Unexpended income shall not be added to the capital of the Fund, but shall be accumulated for use as income in subsequent years.

Raymond and Beverly Sackler Benefactions

Sackler Fund for Medical Sciences

Fund and purpose. **1.** The sum of £1.2m, the benefaction of the Raymond and Beverly Sackler Foundation, shall form a fund called the Sackler Fund for Medical Sciences, the income of which shall be used for the support of postgraduate teaching and research in medicine and for the encouragement and enhancement of clinical and basic medical research in the University and in other institutions connected with the University.

2. The Fund shall be administered by the Faculty Board of Clinical Medicine, in accordance with the provisions of the Deed of Gift, dated 8 December 1990, between the Sackler Foundation and the University. The Faculty Board shall report each year to the Trustees of the Sackler Foundation on the operation of the Fund.

Sackler Fund for Astronomy

Fund and purpose. **1.** The sum of £250,000, the benefaction of the Raymond and Beverly Sackler Foundation, shall form a fund called the Sackler Fund for Astronomy, the income of which shall be used to provide grants for the support of Visiting Fellows at the Institute of Astronomy.

Managers. **2.** The Managers of the Fund shall be:

(*a*) the Director of the Institute of Astronomy;

(*b*) two persons appointed by the Faculty Board of Physics and Chemistry from among the astronomers employed by the University, of whom at least one shall be the holder of a Professorship and at least one shall be the holder of an appointment in the Institute of Astronomy;

(*c*) a representative of the Sackler Foundation.

Annual report. **3.** The Fund shall be administered by the Managers in accordance with the provisions of the Deed of Gift, dated 12 November 1992, between the Sackler Foundation and the University. The Managers shall report each year to the Trustees of the Sackler Foundation on the operation of the Fund.

Sackler Distinguished Lectures Fund

Fund and purpose. **1.** The sum of $45,000, the benefaction of the Raymond and Beverly Sackler Foundation, shall form a fund called the Sackler Distinguished Lectures Fund, the income of which shall be used to provide lectures by distinguished scholars and scientists on subjects within the field of the medical sciences.

2. The Fund shall be administered by the Faculty Board of Clinical Medicine, in accordance with the agreement, dated 8 October 1993, between the Sackler Foundation and the University.

Endowment Fund of the Regius Professor of Physic

Fund and purpose. **1.** The two sums of £200,000, the benefaction of Dr Raymond R. Sackler, K.B.E., and Mrs Beverly Sackler, made by gifts from the Raymond and Beverly Sackler Foundation, shall form a fund called the Endowment Fund of the Regius Professor of Physic, the income of which shall be applied for the support of research in the School of Clinical Medicine.

2. The Fund shall be administered by the Regius Professor of Physic, in accordance with the agreements, dated 7 May 1996 and 23 December 1996, between the Raymond and Beverly Sackler Foundation and the University.

Raymond and Beverly Sackler Fund for the Physics of Medicine

Grace 1 of 3 November 2010

1. The sum of £2m given to the University by the Raymond and Beverly Sackler Foundation shall form a fund to be held in perpetuity as the Raymond and Beverly Sackler Fund for the Physics of Medicine. Name.

2. The purpose of the Fund shall be the promotion and support of a programme of activity under the auspices of the Raymond and Beverly Sackler Research Centre in the Physics of Medicine located within the Centre for Physics of Medicine in the Department of Physics. Purpose.

3. The Managers of the Fund shall be: Managers.

(*a*) the Head of the Department of Physics;

(*b*) the Herchel Smith Professor of Physics of Medicine;

(*c*) the Director of the Centre for Physics of Medicine;

(*d*) one person appointed by the School of Clinical Medicine;

(*e*) one person appointed by the General Board on the joint nomination of the Heads of the Schools of Clinical Medicine and the Physical Sciences.

Managers in classes (*d*) and (*e*) shall be appointed in the Michaelmas Term to serve for three years from 1 January following their appointment. Should either one person hold more than one of the positions named at (*a*), (*b*) or (*c*), or any of these positions be vacant, a further Manager shall be appointed by the General Board, on the nomination of the Council of the School of the Physical Sciences, so that the number of Managers shall always be five.

4. The income of the Fund shall be used to promote and encourage research in the Physics of Medicine by: Application.

(*a*) initiating studies into innovative new research ideas in the Physics of Medicine;

(*b*) supporting student training and exchanges of staff at all levels in the field of Physics of Medicine, including international exchanges, internal secondments to the Centre for Physics of Medicine, summer schools, and enabling persons studying or working in other institutions to visit the University;

(*c*) providing Graduate Studentships in the Physics of Medicine which may be awarded to any persons who are or are about to be registered as a candidate for the Ph.D. Degree in the University;

(*d*) furthering scientific discussion and exchange both among persons carrying out research in the field of Physics of Medicine in the University through seminars, early stage project development, international exchanges, and collaboration;

(*e*) supporting carcinoid research as set out in (*a*)–(*d*) above;

(*f*) any other means as may be agreed by the Managers.

5. Any unexpended income may be either added to the capital of the Fund or accumulated for use as income in subsequent years, as the Managers may determine. Unexpended income.

F. S. SALISBURY FUND

1. The gifts of Frederick Stimpson Salisbury, M.A., of Christ's College, shall form a fund called the F. S. Salisbury Fund. Name.

2. The Managers of the Fund shall be the Faculty Board of Classics. The Managers may appoint a Committee, composed of the Laurence Professor of Classical Archaeology, the Professor of Ancient History, and not less than two other members of the Faculty Board of Classics, to discharge any of their functions concerning the Fund. Applications for grants from the Fund shall be made to the Secretary of the Faculty Board of Classics. Managers.

3. The income of the Fund shall be applied from time to time at the discretion of the Managers, and subject to such conditions as they may think fit, in making grants to assist members of the University *in statu pupillari* engaged in excavations on Roman sites in Britain. Purpose.

Unexpended income.

4. Unexpended income shall not be added to the capital of the Fund, but shall be accumulated for use as income in subsequent years.

HAROLD SAMUEL STUDENTSHIPS

Name and purpose.

1. The Harold Samuel Studentships shall be for the encouragement of research in economic, legal, or social matters relating to the use, tenure, or development of land.

Number.

2. Within the limit of the funds provided for the purpose by the Managers of the Estate Management Development Fund the number of Studentships to be offered annually shall be determined by the Board of Land Economy.

Announcement of awards.

3. Not later than 30 November in the calendar year preceding that in which an election is to be held the Board of Land Economy shall announce the number of Studentships offered, and the date by which, and the manner in which, applications for a Studentship are to be made.

Electors.

4. The Electors to the Studentships shall be the Board of Land Economy, or a committee appointed by that Board.

5. Elections shall take place not later than the end of the Long Vacation period of residence in any year.

Value.

6. The annual value of a Studentship shall be such sum as may be determined by the Board in consultation with the Managers subject to a maximum approved from time to time by the Council. In addition the Student shall receive from the Fund such sum as may be approved by the Board to meet University and College fees. In deciding the amount to be paid to each Student the Board shall take into account any financial assistance which he or she is receiving from any other sources.

Eligibility and condition of tenure.

7. Candidature for the Studentships shall be open, but tenure shall be conditional upon the Student being a registered Graduate Student of the University. If the holder ceases to be a registered Graduate Student his or her tenure of the Studentship shall thereupon lapse.

Duties of Student.

8. The Student shall be required to pursue to the satisfaction of the Board a course of training in research approved by them.

Tenure.

9. Subject to the provisions of Regulation 7, a Studentship shall be tenable for two years, and may at the discretion of the Board be extended for one more year.

Payments.

10. Payments to Students shall be made by quarterly instalments in advance, provided that the Board may at any time withhold payment if in their opinion the Student has not been pursuing his or her studies with sufficient diligence.

SANDARS READERSHIP IN BIBLIOGRAPHY

Endowments, 1904, pp. 275–6

The duties of the Reader are described in the following extract from a codicil to the will of Mr Sandars:

I bequeath to the University of Cambridge in its corporate capacity the sum of £2,000 free of duty

Election.

And I direct that this sum be invested and that the Income arising therefrom be paid to a Reader in Bibliography such Reader to be elected in the first instance and on each vacancy by the Vice-Chancellor the Master of Trinity College Cambridge when not holding the office of Vice-Chancellor and the other persons for the time being composing the Syndicate of the University Library and such Reader may be appointed for such a period as the elective body shall think fit and specify and shall be subject to removal by such elective body at their discretion.

Duties.

And I declare that the duty of such Reader shall be to deliver one or more lectures annually or if the elective body shall so determine biennially in some suitable place and on a day and hour to be determined by the Vice-Chancellor for the time being that the lecture shall be delivered during Term and shall embrace the subjects of Bibliography Palaeography Typography Bookbinding Book Illustration the science of Books and Manuscripts and the Arts relating thereto

It is my wish subject to the discretion of the elective body for the time being that the lectures be based on and be illustrated by examples contained in the University Library or the College Libraries at Cambridge

And I direct that it be a condition of the tenure of the office of Reader that the Reader deliver a written or printed copy of each lecture to the University Library and also to the British Museum Library.

And I declare that in all matters relating to the administration of this Bequest which may have to be determined by the elective body the votes of a majority shall be sufficient to determine the same.

Stat. E XLVI.

SANDYS FUND AND STUDENTSHIP

Fund and purpose.

1. The Sandys Fund shall be devoted primarily to the furtherance of study and research in the languages, literature, history, archaeology, and art of ancient Greece and Rome and the comparative philology of the Indo-European languages.

2. The Trustees of the Fund shall be the Master, Fellows, and Scholars of St John's College. Trustees.

3. The income of the Fund shall be applied in the first instance to the maintenance of a Sandys Studentship, the holder of which shall undertake advanced study or research in one or more of the subjects specified in Regulation 1, according to a scheme to be approved by the Electors. Such a scheme shall involve residence for a large part of the year at a university or other place of learning outside the British Isles. Studentship.

4. The Studentship shall be open Who are eligible.

(*a*) to any graduate of the University who at the date of the election is of not less than three and not more than nine terms' standing from admission to his or her first degree; *or*

(*b*) to any person who is registered as a Graduate Student in the University, provided that at the date of the election not less than two complete terms have passed after the term of his or her admission as a Graduate Student.

5. Before the division of the Easter Term each year the Faculty Board shall give notice of the date by which and the manner in which applications for the Studentship are to be submitted. An election to the Studentship shall be held during the Michaelmas Term on a date to be determined by the Board. Applications.

6. The Electors to the Studentship shall be the Classical Lecturers of St John's College, the Regius Professor of Greek, the Kennedy Professor of Latin, the Professor of Ancient History, the Laurence Professor of Classical Archaeology, and the Professor of Comparative Philology. The Electors may take such steps as they think fit to inquire into the qualifications of the candidates; provided that the Studentship shall not be awarded on the result of a competitive examination. Electors.

7. The Studentship shall be tenable from the date of the election until 30 September next following. A Student shall be eligible for re-election on not more than two occasions. Tenure.

8. The emolument of the Studentship shall be such sum, not exceeding the available income of the Fund, as shall be determined by the Faculty Board within a range approved from time to time by the Council. The emolument shall be paid in such instalments as the Board shall from time to time determine, provided that the Board may withhold payment of any instalment if they are not satisfied that the Student is pursuing his or her course of study with sufficient diligence. Emolument.

9. Any unexpended income of the Fund in a financial year shall be applied by the Trustees for the benefit of the Library of St John's College. Unexpended income.

10. These regulations, except Regulations 1 and 9, shall be subject to alteration by Grace.

Dr F. Sanger Fund

Grace 3 of 28 September 2011

1. The sum of £23,500 received by the University from the trustees of the Max Perutz Fund out of donations made at the time of Dr Fred Sanger's retirement from his post at the MRC Laboratory of Molecular Biology to support attendance at conferences by young scientists shall form a fund called the Dr F. Sanger Fund. This benefaction is in recognition of the many years that Dr Sanger was associated with the Department of Biochemistry. Name and purpose.

2. The Managers of the Fund shall be the Head of the Department of Biochemistry, the Administrative Officer of the Department of Biochemistry, and the Chair of the Postgraduate Committee in the Department. Managers.

3. The income of the Fund shall be used to offer financial support to Graduate Students in the Department to assist with travel to scientific conferences, if they have no other funding for this purpose from any Studentship, Scholarship, or other source. To be eligible for support from the Fund, students must be presenting a poster or giving a talk at the conference. Graduate Students in the first year of their studies will not be eligible. Who are eligible.

4. Any unexpended income in a financial year shall be either added to the capital of the Fund or accumulated for use as income in future years, as the Managers may determine. Unexpended Income.

Scandinavian Studies Fund

1. The Scandinavian Studies Fund shall be administered by Managers who shall also act as the Electors to the Scandinavian Studentship. Administration.

2. The Managers shall be: Managers.

(*a*) the Head of the Department of Anglo-Saxon, Norse, and Celtic;

(*b*) three persons appointed by the General Board;

(*c*) two persons appointed by the Faculty Board of Modern and Medieval Languages, one of whom shall be a University officer engaged in teaching and research in the area of Scandinavian Studies;

(*d*) one University officer from the Department of Anglo-Saxon, Norse, and Celtic, appointed by the Faculty Board of English.

3. Managers in classes (*b*)–(*d*) shall be appointed in the Michaelmas Term to serve for three years from 1 January following their appointment.

Income. **4.** The income of the Fund in any year may be applied as follows:

(*a*) to provide the emolument of the Scandinavian Student;

(*b*) to meet the cost of the Wallenberg Prize;

(*c*) subject to the foregoing two prior charges, and with the approval of the Managers, to contribute towards the cost of such teaching in Scandinavian subjects as may be arranged by the Faculty Board of Modern and Medieval Languages with the approval of the General Board.

Unexpended income. **5.** Any unexpended income accumulated in the Fund may be used by the Managers to make grants to students for the furtherance of study connected with Scandinavian countries, or grants for any other purpose which they may approve as being in the interests of Scandinavian studies and Scandinavian teaching in the University of Cambridge.

Scandinavian Studentship

Who are eligible. **6.** There shall be established from the Fund for the promotion of Scandinavian Studies a Studentship to be called the Scandinavian Studentship, which shall be open to members of the University.

Duties of Student. **7.** It shall be the duty of the Student to pursue in a Scandinavian country, and in the first instance preferably in Sweden, advanced study or research in the languages, literature, philosophy, history, economic conditions, art, or archaeology of Sweden, Denmark, Norway, or Iceland.

Election. **8.** The election of the Student shall be made annually in June.

Tenure. **9.** The Studentship shall be tenable for one year; but a Student shall be eligible for re-election on not more than two occasions.

Standing of candidates. **10.** At the date of the election candidates for election or re-election to the Studentship shall have passed some final examination for the degree of Bachelor of Arts and not more than twenty-four terms shall have elapsed since the end of their first term of residence.

11. An application for election must be submitted through the candidate's Tutor to the Registrary so as to arrive not later than 1 June, and must be accompanied by a statement of the course of advanced study or research which the candidate proposes to undertake if elected. Such course shall involve residence in a Scandinavian country or Scandinavian countries for not less than three months. The course proposed may be varied with the consent of the Managers.

12. The Managers shall have authority to take any steps that they think advisable to enable them to ascertain the qualifications of the candidates: provided that the Studentship shall not be awarded by competitive examination.

Value. **13.** The Student shall receive a stipend of £50, which shall be paid not later than the thirtieth day following the election, and such additional stipend, subject to a maximum approved from time to time by the Council, as may be determined by the Managers after taking account of any other financial resources that may be available to the Student. The additional stipend shall be paid to the Student in two equal instalments not later than the first day of the Full Michaelmas Term and of the Full Lent Term following the election; provided that the second instalment shall not be paid until the Managers have received from the Student a report on his or her work for the past half-year and have informed the Treasurer that they have approved the same.

Restriction. **14.** The Scandinavian Studentship shall not be tenable concurrently with the Tennant Studentship.

Schiff Foundation

Name and purpose. **1.** The income of the Schiff Foundation shall be used to provide one or more studentships, which shall be called George and Lilian Schiff Studentships, to enable suitably qualified persons to undertake advanced study or research in the University in physics, engineering, or related sciences.

Managers. **2.** The Fund shall be administered by five Managers who shall be:

(*a*) the Vice-Chancellor, or a duly appointed deputy, as Chair;

(*b*) the Head of the Department of Physics or a deputy;
(*c*) the Head of the Department of Engineering or a deputy;
(*d*) one person appointed by the Council;
(*e*) one person appointed by the General Board.

Managers in classes (*d*) and (*e*) shall be appointed in the Michaelmas Term to serve for four years from 1 January following their appointment.

3. Studentships shall be open to any person who is or is about to be registered as a Graduate Student in the University, or who has been or is about to be admitted to some other full-time postgraduate course in the University, provided that preference shall be given to candidates who are British Nationals and who are, in the opinion of the Managers, in financial need. Studentships.

4. The Managers shall make regulations under the Trust Deed of the Schiff Foundation regarding the procedure for advertising Studentships, for selecting suitable candidates, and for the tenure of Studentships. A Student shall be eligible for re-election, provided that the tenure of a Studentship shall not normally exceed three years in all.

5. The annual stipend of a Student shall be such sum not exceeding the available income of the Foundation as may be determined by the Managers, within a range approved from time to time by the Council, after they have taken account of any other financial resources that may be available to the Student. The Managers may make grants additional to stipend to any Student during the tenure of his or her Studentship, to meet additional costs arising from his or her course, including the cost of additional training, conferences, or other courses. Stipend.

6. The stipend shall be paid quarterly in advance, provided that the Managers may withhold any instalment if they are not satisfied that the Student is pursuing his or her research with sufficient diligence.

7. Any unexpended income may be either added to the capital of the Foundation or accumulated for use as income in subsequent years, as the Managers may determine. Unexpended income.

8. When the holder of a Studentship or a person who formerly held a Studentship has been approved for, and has been admitted to, the Ph.D. Degree, the Managers may arrange for the presentation to him or her of a Certificate of Fellowship. Such a person shall thereafter be entitled to be known as a George and Lilian Schiff Fellow. Fellowships.

9. The Managers may from time to time make Special Awards to holders or former holders of Studentships who in their opinion have submitted work of outstanding merit as candidates for the Ph.D. Degree. Not more than one Special Award shall be made in any calendar year, provided that the Council, on the recommendation of the Managers, may approve the waiver of this restriction. The value of a Special Award shall be determined by the Managers and shall not exceed the sum estimated by the Managers to be twice the current value of a full-cost studentship covering University and College fees, together with all reasonable living expenses, for a student undertaking a course of research for the Ph.D. Degree. Special Awards.

Schlumberger Complex Physical Systems Fund

1. The sums received from Schlumberger Ltd for the support of work on multi-scale modelling shall form a fund called the Schlumberger Complex Physical Systems Fund. Title and purpose.

2. The Fund shall be under the control of a Board of Managers who shall be: Managers.

(*a*) the Head of the Department of Applied Mathematics and Theoretical Physics as Chair;
(*b*) three persons appointed by the General Board, one of whom shall be appointed on the nomination of Schlumberger Cambridge Research;
(*c*) the Schlumberger Professor of Complex Physical Systems;
(*d*) one person appointed by the Faculty Board of Mathematics;
(*e*) not more than two persons co-opted at the discretion of the Managers.

Managers in classes (*b*) and (*d*) shall be appointed in the Michaelmas Term to serve for four years from 1 January following their appointment. Members in class (*e*) shall serve until 31 December of the year in which they are co-opted or of the following year, as the Managers shall decide at the time of their co-optation.

3. The first charge on the income of the Fund shall be the stipend, national insurance, pension contributions, and associated indirect costs payable by the University in respect of the Schlumberger Professor.

Professor of Complex Physical Systems and of the holders of such posts as may be established by the General Board as a charge on the Fund.

4. After provision has been made in accordance with Regulation 3, the income of the Fund shall be applied at the discretion of the Managers for the support of work in multi-scale modelling in the Department of Applied Mathematics and Theoretical Physics.

Unexpended income. **5.** Any unexpended income of the Fund in a financial year may be either added to the capital of the Fund or accumulated for use as income in future years, as the Managers shall determine.

Stat. E XXX.

Scholefield Prizes

Endowments, 1904, p. 400

Name and purpose. **1.** The income of the Fund subscribed by friends of James Scholefield, Regius Professor of Greek, who died in 1853, for the encouragement of the critical study of the Holy Scriptures shall be used to provide prizes, which shall be called the Scholefield Prizes.

Prizes. **2.** There shall be one or more Junior Prizes and one or more Senior Prizes. The value of a Prize shall be such sum not exceeding the available income of the Fund as may be determined from time to time by the Faculty Board of Divinity with the approval of the Council. The Awarders shall be for the Junior Prizes the Examiners for Parts IIA and IIB of the Theological and Religious Studies Tripos, and the Advanced Diploma in Theology and Religious Studies, and for the Senior Prizes the Examiners for the Examination in Theology and Religious Studies for the M.Phil. Degree.

3. The Junior Prizes shall be open to candidates for Parts IIA and IIB of the Theological and Religious Studies Tripos and the Advanced Diploma in Theology and Religious Studies, and the Senior Prizes shall be open to candidates offering a dissertation on the critical study of the Holy Scriptures, including the New Testament in Greek, in the Examination in Theology and Religious Studies for the M.Phil. Degree.

Value. **4.** In the Michaelmas Term of each year the Faculty Board of Divinity shall specify the number and the value of the prizes which they intend to offer, and the papers in each Part of the Tripos or in the examination for the Diploma on which the candidates' knowledge of the Holy Scriptures, including the New Testament in Greek, shall be tested.

Dr William M. Scholl Lectureship Fund

Title. **1.** The sum of $1,500,000, to be received from the Scholl Foundation over a period of three years for the endowment of a University Lectureship in Neurology, entitled the Dr William M. Scholl Lectureship, shall form a fund called the Dr William M. Scholl Lectureship Fund.

Application of income. **2.** The stipend, national insurance, and pension contributions payable by the University in respect of the Dr William M. Scholl Lecturer in Neurology shall be payable from the Fund.

3. If and when the income of the Fund shall exceed the amount required for the payment of the stipend, national insurance, pension contributions, and associated indirect costs of the Dr William M. Scholl Lecturer payable by the University, the excess of the income over that amount may be applied in support of the work of the Lecturer in such manner as may be approved by the General Board on the recommendation of the Faculty Board of Clinical Medicine.

Unexpended income. **4.** Any unexpended income of the Fund in a financial year may in any subsequent year be expended in accordance with Regulation 3.

Schroders Book Fund for Japanese Studies

The sums given to the University by Schroder Investment Management Limited shall form a fund called the Schroders Book Fund for Japanese Studies. The income of the Fund shall be used at the discretion of the Head of the Department of East Asian Studies in consultation with and with the agreement of the teaching officers in Japanese in the Department to purchase books and other materials on Japanese subjects for the library of the Faculty of Asian and Middle Eastern Studies.

A.W. Scott Fund

1. The money received from the bequest of Professor A. W. Scott for the furtherance of Physical Science shall constitute a fund called the A. W. Scott Fund. Name.

2. A short course of lectures, to be called the Scott Lectures, shall be delivered each year in the Department of Physics. The Lecturer, who shall be called the Scott Lecturer, shall be appointed by the Faculty Board of Physics and Chemistry, and shall be paid from the income of the A. W. Scott Fund such sum as the Faculty Board shall from time to time determine. Lecturer.

3. The Head of the Department of Physics may, from that part of the income of the fund which remains each year after the payment to the Lecturer has been made,

(*a*) make grants to registered Graduate Students working in the Department of Physics, and Grants.

(*b*) defray the expenses of scientific conferences to be held in the Department. Conferences.

4. The remaining income of the Fund shall be paid into the funds available to the Department of Physics for general purposes. Remaining income.

Scott Polar Scholarship Fund

Grace 2 of 1 February 2012

1. The Scott Polar Scholarship Fund was established at the centenary of the year in which Captain R. F. Scott and his four companions reached the South Pole and perished on their return journey, to mark their achievements and the scientific legacy of Scott's Discovery and Terra Nova expeditions to Antarctica. Fund.

2. The income from the Fund shall be used to contribute to the fees, maintenance, and field research of postgraduate students at the Scott Polar Research Institute, to enable them to undertake scientific and other related research on polar topics. Scholarships supporting such research, in whole or in part, shall be advertised from time to time by the Managers of the Fund. Application of income.

3. The Managers of the Fund shall be the Director of the Scott Polar Research Institute and two persons, who would normally be based in the Scott Polar Research Institute, appointed by the Faculty Board of Earth Sciences and Geography to serve for periods of four years at a time. Managers.

Seatonian Prize

Stat. E XI.

Endowments, 1904, p. 369

1. There shall be offered in each year a Seatonian Prize for a poem on a subject conducive to the honour of the Supreme Being and the recommendation of virtue. Prize.

2. The Prize shall be awarded by three Examiners who shall be appointed in the Lent Term of each year, two on the nomination of the Faculty Board of Divinity and one on the nomination of the Faculty Board of English. Each Examiner shall receive from the Seatonian Fund, unless no exercise is sent in, such amount as may be determined by the Faculty Boards within a range approved from time to time by the Council. Examiners.

3. The Prize shall be open for competition among all members of the Senate and all persons who are possessors of the status of Master of Arts. Who may be candidates.

4. In the course of the Michaelmas Term next following their appointment the Examiners shall give public notice of a subject for the Prize, and all exercises for the Prize shall be sent to the Registrary not later than 30 September next following. Subject, when to be announced.

5. Each candidate shall send three copies of his or her exercise to the Registrary. The exercise shall be in a printed or typewritten form; it shall bear a motto but not the candidate's name, and shall be accompanied by a sealed envelope bearing the same motto outside and containing the candidate's name and College. Exercises to Registrary.

6. The successful candidate shall receive the net income of the Seatonian Fund after payment of the Examiners. Value of Prize.

7. The successful candidate shall deposit a printed or typewritten copy of his or her poem in the University Library. Condition.

Sedgwick Prize

Endowments, 1904, p. 404

Prize. **1.** A prize, called the Sedgwick Prize, shall be given every second year for the best essay on some subject in Geology or the kindred sciences.

Who may compete. **2.** The Prize shall be open to all University officers and Fellows of Colleges, and to other persons employed by the University to carry out research in the Faculty of Earth Sciences and Geography, who have resided sixty days during the twelve months preceding the day on or before which the essays are to be sent in.

Submission of essays. **3.** The essays shall be sent to the Registrary on or before 1 October 2007; and so on every second year. Each essay shall be clearly written, or printed, or typewritten. It is open to candidates to incorporate in their essays material which they have already published, but they are expected to submit a connected presentation of their complete investigations.

Value. **4.** The successful candidate shall receive two years' net income of the Fund, or, if no essay be thought worthy of a Prize, this amount shall be added to the capital of the Fund.

Examiners. **5.** The Examiners shall be the Woodwardian Professor of Geology, and two persons appointed by the General Board on the nomination of the Faculty Board of Earth Sciences and Geography. Each of the Examiners appointed by the General Board shall receive such sum from the income of the Prize Fund, except where no essay is sent in, as shall be determined by the Faculty Board of Earth Sciences and Geography within a range approved from time to time by the Council.

6. If an Examiner is prevented by illness or other cause from examining, a deputy shall be appointed by the General Board on the nomination of the Faculty Board of Earth Sciences and Geography.

7. The Examiners appointed in the Michaelmas Term 2006 shall hold office until the end of the Lent Term 2008, that is to say, until the award has been made. The new Examiners shall be appointed in the Michaelmas Term 2007, and they shall then, in consultation with the outgoing Examiners, select a subject for the essays on which the award is to be made in the Lent Term 2010; and so on every second year.

8. The Examiners appointed in the Michaelmas Term 2006 shall award the Prize some time in the Lent Term 2008, and at the same time the Woodwardian Professor of Geology shall announce the subject for the next essay; and so on every second year.

9. The University shall have power to alter and amend this scheme from time to time by Grace, on the recommendation of the Faculty Board of Earth Sciences and Geography.

Sedgwick Rough Fund

Title. **1.** The gift of Major W. Sedgwick Rough, a great-nephew of Professor Adam Sedgwick in whose memory the Sedgwick Museum of Geology (now the Sedgwick Museum of Earth Sciences) was erected, shall form a fund called the Sedgwick Rough Fund.

Application. **2.** The capital and income of the Fund shall be applied for such purposes in the Sedgwick Museum of Earth Sciences as the Director and the Curators of the Museum, jointly, with the concurrence of the Woodwardian Professor of Geology shall from time to time decide.

John Robert Seeley Lectureship in Political Thought

Title. **1.** There shall be a biennial course of lectures called the John Robert Seeley Lectures in Political Thought which shall be delivered by a distinguished scholar from outside the University in each year the number of which is odd.

Managers. **2.** The lecturer shall be appointed by the Managers of the Political Thought Fund at least two years before he or she is required to deliver the lectures.

Lectures. **3.** The lecturer shall deliver in English a course of no fewer than four nor more than six lectures in Full Term during one academical year.

Stipend. **4.** The stipend paid to the lecturer shall be determined by the Managers of the Political Thought Fund.

5. The lecturer shall also receive reimbursement in respect of such travelling and subsistence expenses as may be approved by the Managers.

6. The Managers may at their discretion defray from the income of the Fund any other expenses incurred in connection with the lectures.

SEELEY MEDAL

Endowments, 1904, p. 363

1. The Medal shall be called the Seeley Medal. Name.

2. The Medal may be awarded in each year to a candidate for the Thirlwall or Prince Consort Prize, as the case may be, for that year whose dissertation in the judgement of the Adjudicators is worthy of the Thirlwall or Prince Consort Prize. How awarded.

3. These regulations, except Regulation 1, shall be subject to alteration by Grace on the recommendation of the Faculty Board of History: provided that in all cases regard be given to the object of the subscribers to commemorate Sir John Seeley.

ALKIS SERAPHIM MEMORIAL FUND

1. The gift of Mr and Mrs G. M. Seraphim in memory of their son, Alkis Seraphim, of Selwyn College, shall form a fund, called the Alkis Seraphim Memorial Fund, to provide an annual Alkis Seraphim Memorial Lecture on a subject in biochemistry. Title and purpose.

2. The Alkis Seraphim Memorial Lecturer shall be appointed by the Electors to the Lectureship in the Michaelmas Term of the academical year in which the Lecture is to be given. Appointment of Lecturer.

3. The Electors shall be the Sir William Dunn Professor of Biochemistry and one person appointed in the Michaelmas Term by the University officers in the Department of Biochemistry from among their own number to serve for a period of three years from 1 January next following. Electors.

4. The Electors shall be empowered to make arrangements for the Lecture and to determine the honorarium and expenses to be paid to the Lecturer within the income of the Fund. Lecturer's honorarium and expenses.

SEVEN PILLARS STUDENTSHIP FUND

1. The donation received from the Seven Pillars of Wisdom Trust and any other sums which may be contributed by that Trust or otherwise for the same purpose shall constitute a fund, called The Seven Pillars Studentship Fund, for the advancement of classical learning in accordance with these regulations. Title and purpose.

2. The Managers of the Fund shall be the Faculty Board of Classics, who may delegate any of their functions concerning the Fund to a Committee not necessarily composed wholly of members of the Board. Managers.

3. The income of the Fund shall be used to provide one or more annual Studentships to be known as Seven Pillars Studentships open to persons registered or intending to be registered for the M.Phil. Degree in the Faculty of Classics. Who are eligible.

4. The Studentships shall be for the furtherance of research in accordance with the regulations governing the M.Phil. Degree in any of the subject areas within the Faculty of Classics. In the case of one or more candidates for the Studentships being of equal merit in the opinion of the Managers, preference shall be given to a candidate electing to work in the field of Art or Archaeology. Subject areas.

5. The Managers shall take such steps as they think fit to enquire into the qualifications of the candidates, provided that no Studentship shall be awarded on the result of a competitive examination. Qualifications of candidates.

6. Any candidate for the M.Phil. Degree in the Faculty of Classics will be deemed to be an applicant for the Studentships. An election will be held at a date to be determined by the Faculty Board no later than 30 September immediately preceding the first term of study. The name of each successful candidate will be published in the *Reporter*. Application, election, and notification.

7. Each Studentship shall be tenable from the date of the commencement of the Michaelmas Term next following the date of the election until 30 September next following such date. No student shall be eligible for re-election. Tenure.

8. The emolument of the Studentship shall be such sum, not exceeding the available income of the Fund, as shall be determined by the Managers within a range approved from time to time by the Council. The emolument shall be paid in such instalments as the Managers shall from time to time Emolument.

determine, provided that the Managers may withhold payment of any instalment if they are not satisfied that a Student is pursuing his or her course of study with sufficient diligence.

Unexpended income.

9. Any unexpended income of the Fund in any year (whether because there is no candidate in that year who merits an award, or for any other reason) shall be carried forward for expenditure in subsequent years.

10. These regulations may be amended by Grace, so long as the main object of the Fund, as defined in Regulations 1, 3, and 4 above, shall always be kept in view.

David Sexton Fund

Fund and purpose.

1. The investments representing the sums given by his family and friends in memory of David James Sexton, of Emmanuel College, research student in the Scott Polar Research Institute, who was killed on 16 August 1989 on South Inyl'chek Glacier in the Tien Shan Mountains, at that time part of the Soviet Union, shall form a fund called the David Sexton Fund, for the advancement of the study of scientific and environmental aspects of polar and mountainous regions and the conservation of such areas.

Application of income.

2. The income of the Fund and any unexpended income accumulated in the Fund shall be available at the discretion of the Director of the Scott Polar Research Institute for the purchase of books on topics relevant to the fields mentioned in Regulation 1 for the library of the Institute.

Marmaduke Sheild Fund

Fund and purpose.

1. The sum bequeathed to the University by the late Arthur Marmaduke Sheild, of Downing College, who died on 4 August 1922, shall form a fund called the Marmaduke Sheild Fund which shall be applied in accordance with the wishes of the donor as stated in his will as follows:

> I GIVE the remainder of my residuary trust fund...to the Medical School of the University of Cambridge to be applied as follows:
>
> FIRST for the foundation of a Scholarship in Human Anatomy of the value of One hundred pounds to be called the Marmaduke Sheild Scholarship and
>
> SECONDLY for the general purposes and benefit of the said Medical School and the terms and conditions of such Scholarship and the general purposes for which the remainder of the residuary trust fund is to be applied shall be determined in such manner in every respect as the Board of Medical Studies of Cambridge University shall direct.

For the purpose of fulfilling those conditions the 'Medical School of the University of Cambridge' shall be deemed to consist of the Faculties of Biology and Clinical Medicine.

Managers.

2. The Managers of the Fund shall be (*a*) the Chair of the Faculty Board of Biology, (*b*) the Chair of the Faculty Board of Clinical Medicine, (*c*) two members appointed by the Faculty Board of Biology, (*d*) two members appointed by the Faculty Board of Clinical Medicine. The members in classes (*c*) and (*d*) shall be appointed to serve for three years from 1 January following their appointment. The Chair of the Managers shall be alternately the member in class (*a*) and the member in class (*b*), each for one year at a time. The Secretary of the School of the Biological Sciences shall act as Secretary to the Managers.

Application of income.

3. After provision has been made for the Marmaduke Sheild Scholarship, the income of the Fund shall be applied from time to time at the discretion of the Managers and, subject to such conditions as they may decide, for any purpose consistent with the benefactor's wishes as indicated in Regulation 1.

4. Any proposal by the Managers to spend the capital of the Fund shall require the approval of both the Faculty Board of Biology and the Faculty Board of Clinical Medicine.

5. No resolution of the Managers shall be valid unless approved by at least three of their number.

Grants.

6. Applications for grants from the Fund shall be submitted to the Secretary to the Managers through the Head of the appropriate Department.

Marmaduke Sheild Scholarship

Name.

1. There shall be established from the bequest of Arthur Marmaduke Sheild a Marmaduke Sheild Scholarship in Human Anatomy.

Who are eligible.

2. The persons eligible to the Scholarship shall be such undergraduates of not more than three years' standing from matriculation, and such Bachelors of Arts of not more than four years' standing from matriculation, as have passed or gained exemption from the Second M.B. Examination, and have also obtained honours in Part IB of the Medical and Veterinary Sciences Tripos with Anatomy as one of their subjects.

3. The Head of the Department of Physiology, Development, and Neuroscience shall publish a Notice to candidates in the Michaelmas Term of each year. The names of candidates shall be sent before 6 July to the Registrary for transmission to the Head of the Department. The award shall be made after the publication of the results of the aforesaid examinations. Notice of award.

4. The Awarders shall be the Regius Professor of Physic, the Head of the Department of Physiology, Development, and Neuroscience or a member of the academic staff of the Department appointed by the Head of the Department, and a third person appointed by the Faculty Board of Biology not later than the end of the Easter Term in each year. Awarders

5. The Awarders shall take into consideration not only the candidates' performance in examinations in Anatomy, but also reports by the staff of the Department of Physiology, Development, and Neuroscience on their general ability and performance as students of Anatomy, as well in practical as in theoretical work.

6. The Scholarship shall be tenable for one year. The period of tenure shall begin on 1 October following the award unless the Awarders otherwise determine. A Scholar may be re-elected for a second year and for this purpose shall be exempt from the rules of standing contained in Regulation 2. Tenure.

7. The emolument of the Scholarship shall be a sum determined by the Faculty Board of Biology in consultation with the Faculty Board of Clinical Medicine, within a range approved from time to time by the Council. Value.

8. A Scholar who has not already obtained honours in Part II of the Natural Sciences Tripos shall be a candidate for that examination in Anatomy in the first year of the tenure of the Scholarship unless he or she is over the standing for such candidature. A Scholar who has obtained honours as aforesaid before the election, or is over the standing for such candidature, shall undertake a course of research in Human Anatomy approved by the Head of the Department of Physiology, Development, and Neuroscience, and shall pursue it under the supervision of the Head or of a person appointed by the Head for this purpose from among the academic staff of the Department. Duties of Scholar.

9. If in any year the Awarders consider that a second Scholarship should be awarded they may make such an award, and the provisions of Regulations 1–8 shall apply to the second Scholarship and to its holder.

Shell Fund for Chemical Engineering

1. The gifts to the University from the Shell Group of Oil Companies for the furtherance of Chemical Engineering shall form a fund to be called the Shell Fund for Chemical Engineering. Name and purpose.

2. The administration of the Fund shall be entrusted to five Managers. The Managers shall be: Managers.

(*a*) the Head of the Department of Chemical Engineering and Biotechnology who shall be Chair,

(*b*) the Secretary of the Chemical Engineering and Biotechnology Syndicate who shall act as Secretary to the Managers,

(*c*) a person appointed by the Shell Group of Oil Companies (or a deputy),

(*d*) two members of the Regent House appointed by the Chemical Engineering and Biotechnology Syndicate.

The Managers in classes (*c*) and (*d*) shall be appointed in the Michaelmas Term to serve for three years from 1 January following their appointment.

3. The Fund shall be used to defray the expenses of visiting scholars invited to Cambridge by the Managers, or to support research in the Department of Chemical Engineering and Biotechnology, or for any purpose which in the opinion of the Managers will help towards the development of the study of Chemical Engineering at Cambridge. Application.

4. The Managers shall meet in the Michaelmas Term of each year and at other times as they think fit. No resolution of the Managers shall be valid unless approved by at least three of their number. Meetings and quorum.

5. The Managers shall report to the Chemical Engineering and Biotechnology Syndicate in the Lent Term of each year on the administration of the Fund during the previous academical year. Annual report.

6. Subject to the foregoing regulations the Managers may make supplementary regulations for their own proceedings and administration of the Fund. Proceedings.

Shore Fund for Language Teaching

Name. **1.** The sum received from an anonymous donor by way of endowment shall form a fund called the Shore Fund for Language Teaching.

Managers. **2.** The Managers of the Fund shall be the Faculty Board of Classics, who may delegate any of their functions concerning the Fund to a Committee not necessarily composed wholly of members of the Board.

Senior Language Teaching Officer. **3.** The first charge on the income of the Fund shall be to contribute towards the stipend, national insurance, pension contributions, and associated indirect costs of a Senior Language Teaching Officer payable by the University.

4. After provision has been made in accordance with Regulation 3, the Fund shall be applied for the support of language teaching in the Faculty of Classics in such a manner as shall be approved by the Managers.

Unexpended income. **5.** Any unexpended income in a financial year may be expended in accordance with Regulation 4 in any one or more subsequent years.

Kathleen Madge Short Cancer Fund

1. The sum bequeathed to the University by Harold George Short, in memory of his wife Kathleen Madge Short, shall form a fund called the Kathleen Madge Short Cancer Fund, the capital and the income of which shall be used for the support of research in human cancer.

2. The Fund shall be administered by the Head of the Department of Oncology, in consultation with the Regius Professor of Physic.

Norman Douglas Simpson Memorial Fund

Name. **1.** The gift to the University by Dr William T. Stearn and Mr Patrick Brenan as Executors of Norman Douglas Simpson, M.A., of Trinity College, shall form a fund called the Norman Douglas Simpson Memorial Fund.

Purpose. **2.** The annual income of the Fund shall be used to purchase for the Norman Douglas Simpson Collection of publications on the plants of the British Isles any books or pamphlets not already in that collection which record the occurrence or distribution of plants in the British Isles, particularly those relating to regions, counties, or some smaller areas. The books or pamphlets so purchased shall normally be ones published during the financial year. The acquisition of such a book or pamphlet through the Fund shall be indicated by the insertion of a special book-plate or stamp.

3. The balance of the income in any financial year may be used for the repair and binding of books of the Collection.

Managers. **4.** The Managers of the Fund shall be the Regius Professor of Botany and the Curator of the Herbarium in the Department of Plant Sciences.

Report. **5.** A report on expenditure from the Fund during the preceding financial year shall be sent by the Regius Professor of Botany to the Keeper of Botany, British Museum (Natural History) and to the Keeper of the Herbarium, Royal Botanic Gardens, Kew.

Sims Fund and Scholarship

Name. **1.** The moneys provided by Mrs Agnes Marian Sims shall form the capital of a fund to be called the Sims Fund.

Managers. **2.** The administration of the income of the Fund shall be entrusted to seven Managers. The Managers shall be the Vice-Chancellor (or a duly appointed deputy) who shall be Chair, and six members of the Senate, two appointed by the Faculty Board of Physics and Chemistry, two by the Faculty Board of Mathematics, and two by the Faculty Board of Clinical Medicine. Managers shall be appointed in the Michaelmas Term to serve for four years from 1 January following their appointment.

Quorum. **3.** The Managers shall meet at such times as they shall think fit. No resolution shall be valid unless it has been approved by a majority of the Managers. If a resolution is proposed for approval otherwise than at a meeting any Manager may request that it should be considered at a meeting of the Managers, and such resolution shall be so considered. If the votes of the Managers are equally divided, the Chair shall have a second or casting vote.

Purpose. **4.** The income of the Fund shall be applied to endow a Scholarship to be called the Sims Scholarship, which shall be awarded for outstanding merit and promise in the subjects Physics, Chemistry, Mathematics, and Medicine, or in one of these subjects.

Value. **5.** The annual value of the Scholarship shall be fixed by the Managers at the time of inviting applications for a Scholarship within the net annual income of the Fund.

Tenure. **6.** Except as hereinafter provided, the Scholarship shall be tenable for three years.

Election. **7.** Scholars shall be elected by the Managers on the recommendation, in rotation, of the Degree Committees for the Faculties of Physics and Chemistry, Mathematics, and Clinical Medicine. The Degree Committee concerned with a particular election shall personally interview those candidates whom they consider to be most deserving of election, and shall take into consideration the personal qualifications as well as the academic record of such candidates.

Who are eligible. **8.** The Scholarship shall be open to members of the University of Cambridge who have been admitted to a degree, provided that every candidate shall

either (*a*) have been born in Great Britain or, so long as Northern Ireland remains in the United Kingdom, in Northern Ireland;

or (*b*) be the child of parents who were themselves British subjects at the date of his or her birth.

Notice of election. **9.** Before the division of the Lent Term in each year in which a Scholarship is to be offered, the Managers shall publish a Notice of the date by which, and the manner in which, applications for the Scholarship are to be made, and the Secretary of the Board of Graduate Studies shall inform the Degree Committee concerned accordingly. The election to the Scholarship shall take place before the end of the Long Vacation period of residence next following the publication of the Notice.

Duties of Scholar. **10.** It shall be the duty of the Scholar to pursue a course of study or research approved by the Managers, under the direction of a Supervisor appointed by them. The Scholar shall be required at the end of each year's tenure of the Scholarship to furnish the Managers with a report upon his or her work certified by the Supervisor.

11. The Scholar shall pursue the course of study or research at any institution in Great Britain which has been approved for this purpose by the Managers, provided that the Managers shall have discretion to give the Scholar leave to work outside Great Britain during part of the tenure of the Scholarship. If the institution approved by the Managers be a general hospital in London, that institution shall, if possible, be St Bartholomew's Hospital.

12. During the tenure of the Scholarship the Scholar shall not, without the permission of the Managers, hold any position of emolument other than a Fellowship, Studentship, Scholarship, or Exhibition at one of the Colleges.

Payments. **13.** The emolument of the Scholarship shall be paid by half-yearly instalments in advance, but the Managers may terminate a Scholarship at any time if they are satisfied that the holder is not diligently carrying out his or her course of study or research. Upon the Scholarship being so terminated, the Managers shall have power to provide for the payment of a solatium if in all the circumstances they consider this desirable.

Unexpended income. **14.** After provision has been made for the Scholarship in accordance with Regulations 4 and 5, any unexpended annual income or income accumulated in the Fund may be applied, at the discretion of the Managers, to

(*a*) award a second Scholarship under similar conditions; *or*

(*b*) extend the tenure of an existing Scholarship for a fourth year or part of a fourth year; *or*

(*c*) award grants, on the recommendation of the Degree Committee concerned, to Graduate Students who show outstanding merit and promise in any of the subjects prescribed in Regulation 4 but are ineligible for a Scholarship by not being graduates of the University; these grants shall be subject to such conditions as the Managers may think fit.

Powers of Managers. **15.** If the Managers shall at any time be of opinion that it is not expedient to apply the income of the Fund in accordance with these regulations, the University shall have power on the recommendation of the Managers to apply the capital or the income of the Fund, or any part thereof, for the encouragement of education or research work in Great Britain in such manner as it may in its absolute discretion direct, but so that limited periods of educational or research work outside Great Britain shall not be excluded.

Oreste and Florence Sinanide Fund and Scholarship

Name and purpose.

1. The sum received by the University under the will of Dr Oreste Sinanide shall form a fund called the Oreste and Florence Sinanide Fund, the income of which shall be used to provide a scholarship called the Oreste and Florence Sinanide Scholarship. It shall be the duty of the Oreste and Florence Sinanide Scholar, under the general supervision of the Managers, to engage in research directed to the mitigation of the diseases of the circulation related to other systems.

Managers.

2. The Managers of the Fund shall be:

(*a*) the Regius Professor of Physic;

(*b*) the Director of Medical Education;

(*c*) the person appointed by the Vice-Chancellor as a Manager of the Grimshaw-Parkinson Fund;

(*d*) any other persons who may be appointed from time to time by the Faculty Board of Clinical Medicine.

Scholarship.

3. The income of the Fund shall be applied to maintain a Scholarship which shall be awarded once every three years and shall be tenable for three years.

Eligibility.

4. The Scholarship shall be open to any member of the University who holds one or more of the degrees of M.B., B.Chir., M.Chir., and M.D.

Notice of award.

5. Not less than six months before the date on which the Scholarship is due to become vacant, or as soon as possible after the occurrence of any casual vacancy, the Managers shall announce the offer of the Scholarship and shall publish details, in accordance with these regulations, regarding the manner in which applications are to be made, the qualifications of candidates, and the duties, tenure, and value of the Scholarship.

Unexpended income.

6. If in any year the Scholarship is vacant, the unexpended income shall be added to the capital of the Fund.

Morgan Sindall Prize

Amended by Grace 3 of 29 May 2014

Prize.

1. The sum received by the University from William Sindall plc shall form a fund called the Morgan Sindall Prize Fund, the income of which shall be used to provide a Morgan Sindall Prize. The value of the Prize shall be the annual income of the Fund.

Adjudicators.

2. The Prize shall be awarded by three Adjudicators who shall be the Head of the Department of Architecture and two persons appointed by the General Board on the nomination of the Faculty Board of Architecture and History of Art, one of whom shall be a person with knowledge or experience of the building industry.

How awarded.

3. At their final meeting of the year the Examiners for the degree of Master of Philosophy in subjects for that degree or for such other degree as determined by the Adjudicators shall identify the three best designs submitted by graduate students for those examinations as part of their studio-work. These designs shall be referred to the Adjudicators, who shall award the Prize for the design which in their opinion gives the best evidence of attention to the mode of construction, the selection and use of materials, and the likely behaviour of the building fabric over a period of time.

Manmohan Singh Bursary Fund

Grace 3 of 14 January 2009

Title.

1. The sums received by the University from the Eranda Foundation and Bharti Airtel Limited at the request of the Bharti Foundation, and other donations received for the same purpose, shall form a fund to be known as the Manmohan Singh Bursary Fund.

Bursaries.

2. The income of the Fund, and that portion of the capital that has not been specified as permanent capital by the donor or donors, shall be applied only to provide one or more bursaries, to be called Manmohan Singh Bursaries, for persons only of Indian citizenship who demonstrate financial need in order that they may follow courses leading to a degree or other qualification of the University.

3. A person who is not already a member of the University shall become such by being matriculated before the end of the term next after her or his receipt of a Bursary provided that for good cause the Managers may allow a recipient to defer matriculation until a later date.

4. The Fund shall be administered by four Managers who shall be: Managers.
(*a*) the Vice-Chancellor, or a duly appointed deputy, as Chair;
(*b*) three persons appointed by the Council.
Managers in class (*b*) shall serve for three years from 1 October following their appointment.

5. Any unexpended income, in any one year, may be retained and used as income in subsequent years. Unexpended income.

SISMEY FUND

The income of the Sismey Fund shall be at the disposal of the Faculty Board of Veterinary Medicine for the award of prizes in connection with the Department of Veterinary Medicine under such conditions as the Faculty Board may from time to time determine.

QUENTIN SKINNER PRIZE FUND

Grace 5 of 3 December 2008

1. The sum of £12,800 received from Professor Quentin Skinner, FBA, Regius Professor of Modern History Emeritus, shall form a fund, the income of which shall be used to provide a prize called the Quentin Skinner Prize in History. Title and purpose.

2. The Prize shall be awarded by the relevant Sub-Committee of the Degree Committee of the Faculty of History for the best performance in the examination in Political Thought and Intellectual History for the M.Phil. Degree. Prize.

3. The value of the Prize shall be the annual income of the Fund. Value.

4. If in any year the Prize is not awarded, the income for that year shall be added to the capital of the Fund.

CHARLES SLATER FUND

1. The sum bequeathed to the University by the late Charles Slater, M.A., M.B., of St John's College, 'for purposes in any way connected with the teaching of or research work in medical science or any other science ancillary to medicine', shall form a fund to be called the Charles Slater Fund. Name and purpose.

2. The income of the Fund shall be applied for the furtherance of teaching and research in medical science.

3. The Managers of the Fund shall be (*a*) the Chair of the Faculty Board of Biology, (*b*) the Chair of the Faculty Board of Clinical Medicine, (*c*) two members appointed by the Faculty Board of Biology, (*d*) two members appointed by the Faculty Board of Clinical Medicine, (*e*) one member appointed by the Faculty Board of Veterinary Medicine. The members in classes (*c*), (*d*), and (*e*) shall be appointed to serve for three years from 1 January following their appointment. The Chair of the Managers shall be alternately the member in class (*a*) and the member in class (*b*), each for one year at a time. The Secretary of the School of the Biological Sciences shall act as Secretary to the Managers. Managers. Exercises.

4. No resolution of the Managers shall be valid unless approved by at least four of their number Quorum.

5. The Managers may make grants to University officers or other persons, preference being given to graduates in Medicine, towards the expenses of research, or of travel undertaken in connection with research, or of travel undertaken to study methods of teaching, in Medicine or in any science ancillary to Medicine. Grants.

6. Applications for grants from the Fund shall be submitted to the Secretary to the Managers through the Head of the appropriate Department. Applications.

ELIOT SLATER PRIZE IN PSYCHIATRY

1. The sums made available by the Department of Psychiatry, from donations received, shall form a Fund for the provision of an annual prize for an essay on a subject in the field of psychiatry. Fund and purpose.

2. The title of the Prize shall be the Eliot Slater Prize in Psychiatry, in honour of E. T. O. Slater, M.D., of St John's College. Title.

Who may compete. **3.** The Prize shall be open to any member of the University who is undertaking clinical study in Cambridge and who was a candidate for Part I of the Final M.B. Examination at the last occasion on which an examination for that Part was held.

How awarded. **4.** The Prize shall be awarded by the Professor of Psychiatry and two Adjudicators appointed by the General Board on the nomination of the Faculty Board of Clinical Medicine, who may, at their discretion, examine a candidate *viva voce*.

Value. **5.** The value of the Prize shall be the annual income of the Fund.

Notice. **6.** In the Michaelmas Term of each year the Professor of Psychiatry shall publish a Notice of the Prize, giving

(*a*) the particular area of psychiatry within which the subject of a candidate's essay should fall;

(*b*) the last date by which essays are to be sent in;

provided that such date for entries shall be not less than six weeks after the publication of the Notice.

If not awarded. **7.** In any year in which the Prize is not awarded the income for that year shall be added to the capital of the Fund.

Slaughter and May Prize

Title. **1.** The sum made available annually by Slaughter and May shall be used to provide a Slaughter and May Prize.

How awarded. **2.** The Prize shall be awarded annually by the Examiners for Part II of the Law Tripos to the candidate who has shown the greatest distinction in the examination for that Part.

Frank Smart Studentship in Botany

Name. **1.** The Studentship shall be called the Frank Smart University Studentship in Botany, and shall be devoted to the encouragement of research in Botany.

Value. **2.** The stipend of the Frank Smart University Student in Botany shall be £50, or such larger sum not exceeding the balance of the annual income of the Fund as the Electors shall determine in each case after taking account of any other financial resources that may be available to the Student.

Who are eligible. **3.** There shall be eligible for the Studentship

(*a*) graduates of the University, provided that not more than eighteen complete terms have elapsed after their first term of residence;

(*b*) Graduate Students, not being graduates of the University, provided that not more than nine complete terms have elapsed after their first term of actual residence.

Electors. **4.** The Electors to the Studentship shall be the Master of Gonville and Caius College, the Regius Professor of Botany, and a person appointed by the Faculty Board of Biology in the Michaelmas Term to serve for two years from 1 January next following.

Duties. **5.** The successful candidate shall undertake research in Botany in the University.

Conditions. **6.** The conditions under which the research is to be conducted, and the place or places in which it is to be carried on, shall be determined by the Regius Professor of Botany.

Tenure. **7.** The Studentship shall be tenable for one, two, or three years, as shall be determined by the Electors; a student elected for one or two years may be re-elected, subject to a maximum tenure of three years in total. The Electors shall have power to terminate the tenure of a Student if they are not satisfied with the Student's progress in research.

Notice of appointment. **8.** Due notice that an appointment is to be made shall in each case be given. Appointments shall ordinarily be made as vacancies arise.

Vacancy. **9.** During any vacancy of the Studentship, the income shall be added to the capital of the Fund.

10. No member of Gonville and Caius College, provided that he or she is otherwise qualified, shall be debarred from being appointed to the Studentship by reason of having held or at the time of the election holding the Frank Smart Studentship in Botany founded in the aforenamed College.

Unexpended income. **11.** Any unexpended income accumulated in the Fund shall be applied at the discretion of the Electors for the encouragement of research in Botany in such ways as they shall from time to time determine.

Proviso. **12.** These regulations, except Regulation 1, shall be subject to alteration by Grace, but so always that the principal object of the Fund, namely, the encouragement of research in Botany, shall be maintained.

Frank Smart Prizes

1. The annual income of the Frank Smart Prize Fund shall be used to provide a Frank Smart Prize for Botany and a Frank Smart Prize for Zoology. Title.

2. The value of each Prize shall be half the annual income of the Fund. Value.

3. The Prizes shall be awarded by a Board consisting of the Regius Professor of Botany, the Professor of Zoology, and the Examiners in Plant Sciences and Zoology for the Natural Sciences Tripos of the year in which the award is made. By whom awarded.

No business shall be transacted unless three members of the Board be present.

4. The Prize for Botany shall be awarded in June of each year to that member of the University who, having passed Part IB of the Natural Sciences Tripos and not being of more than ten terms' standing, is in the opinion of the Board most proficient in the Science of Botany. The Prize for Zoology shall be awarded in June of each year to that member of the University who, having passed Part II of the Natural Sciences Tripos and not being of more than thirteen terms' standing, is in the opinion of the Board most proficient in the Science of Zoology. For proficiency in Botany and Zoology.

5. Neither Prize shall be awarded more than once to the same candidate. Proviso.

6. In case no person be deemed worthy of one of the Prizes the sum available for that Prize shall be added to the capital of the Fund. If no award.

7. These regulations shall be subject to alteration by Grace, but so always that the principal object of the Fund, namely, the encouragement of the study of Botany and Zoology in the University, shall be maintained. Regulations may be altered.

Adam Smith Prize Endowment Fund

1. Two Adam Smith Prizes shall be awarded annually by the Examiners for Part IIB of the Economics Tripos, as follows: Prizes.

(*a*) the Adam Smith Prize shall be awarded for the best overall performance in Part IIB;

(*b*) the Adam Smith Dissertation Prize shall be awarded for the best dissertation submitted by a candidate for Part IIB.

2. The value of each Prize shall be one quarter of the annual income of the Fund. Value.

3. In awarding the Prizes the Examiners shall be governed chiefly by the quality of the work done, and shall have regard to the candidates' constructive ability and their grasp of scientific principles rather than to the erudition displayed.

4. After provision has been made, in accordance with the foregoing regulations, for the award of Adam Smith Prizes, the balance of the annual income and any unexpended income accumulated in the Fund shall be applied from time to time at the discretion of the Faculty Board of Economics, on the recommendation of a committee of Managers consisting of the Chair and the Secretary for the time being of the Degree Committee for the Faculty of Economics and one other person appointed for a period of three years from 1 January by the Faculty Board of Economics, for the purpose of making grants to registered Graduate Students who are following a course of research in Economics and are in need of financial assistance. In considering a student for the award of a grant from the Fund, the Board and the Managers shall have regard to evidence not only of financial hardship but also of academic merit. Grants.

5. It shall be open to the University, on the recommendation of the Faculty Board of Economics, to alter these regulations from time to time provided that Amendment of regulations.

(*a*) the Fund shall be devoted to the encouragement of study or research in Economics;

(*b*) any Prize provided from the Fund shall be entitled an Adam Smith Prize and shall be awarded in accordance with the provisions of Regulation 3.

Herbert Smith Prize in the Conflict of Laws

1. The sum made available annually by Messrs Herbert Smith shall be used to provide a prize called the Herbert Smith Prize in the Conflict of Laws. Prize.

2. The Prize shall be awarded by the Examiners for Part II of the Law Tripos to the candidate who has shown the greatest distinction in the subject Conflict of Laws in that examination. How awarded.

Herchel Smith Fellowship Fund

Title and purpose. **1.** The sum of £17.25m bequeathed to the University by the late Dr Herchel Smith to support postdoctoral research at Cambridge shall form a fund called the Herchel Smith Fellowship Fund. The income from the Fund shall be used for the purpose of providing the stipends, national insurance, pension contributions, and indirect costs of such number of Herchel Smith Fellows as shall be determined from time to time by the Managers of the Fund, such expenses incurred by the Fellows as may be approved by the Managers, and expenses connected with the administration of the Fund.

Managers. **2.** The Fund shall be administered, and the Fellows elected, by a Board of Managers consisting of:

(*a*) one person each appointed by the Schools of the Biological Sciences and the Physical Sciences;

(*b*) two persons appointed by the General Board, one of whom shall be Chair.

Notice of election and application. **3.** The Managers shall give not less than three months' notice of their intention to proceed to an election. They shall be empowered to indicate in their Notice that for election in any particular year preference will be given to candidates working in a specific field or fields. If in any year, whatever the number of vacancies, in the Managers' opinion there are no suitable candidates, they shall not be bound to make an election.

4. A graduate of any university, but normally excepting the Universities of Cambridge and Harvard, who is of postdoctoral or equivalent status shall be eligible to apply for a Fellowship provided that a Fellow shall have been awarded his or her Ph.D. Degree, or equivalent, not more than three years before the date on which tenure of the Fellowship will commence.

Tenure. **5.** The Fellowship shall be tenable for at least two but not more than three years and shall not be renewable.

Duties. **6.** It shall be the duty of a Fellow to undertake full-time research in a subject approved by the Managers within the fields of Pure Mathematics, Physics, Organic Chemistry, Biochemistry, or Molecular Biology, or in related fields in the Experimental Natural Sciences (but excluding the History and Philosophy of Science). The research work shall be carried out in Cambridge (unless in special circumstances the Managers give leave for it to be carried out elsewhere) and shall be subject to such conditions as the Managers may impose. In any books, papers, or other publications containing the results of investigations carried out during the tenure of the Fellowship, the Fellow shall, where practicable, use the title 'Herchel Smith Fellow'.

Teaching work. **7.** A Fellow may, with the permission of the Managers, undertake not more than six hours' teaching work a week for remuneration without suffering any deduction from the stipend of the Fellowship.

Stipend. **8.** The annual stipend of a Fellow shall be such sum as shall be determined by the Managers, within a range approved from time to time by the Council.

Grants. **9.** The Managers shall make grants from the Fund to cover the expenses incurred in the appointment of the Fellows. They shall also be empowered to make grants for purposes in support of a Fellow's research, provided that the income of the Fund is capable of bearing such a charge.

Stipend conditions. **10.** The Managers may make the payment of the stipend of a Fellow, or of an instalment of the stipend, conditional on their approval of a report from the Fellow on the progress of his or her research. The Managers may delegate the consideration of a Fellow's report to one or more of themselves. The Managers may terminate the tenure of a Fellow at any time if, in their opinion, he or she is unfit to continue to hold the Fellowship.

11. A Fellow shall inform the Managers of the award of any other emolument or his or her intention to undertake work other than work approved by the Managers in accordance with Regulations 6 and 7. On receiving such information the Managers shall consider whether a reduction should be made in the amount of the Fellow's stipend.

Unexpended income. **12.** After provision has been made for the Fellowships in accordance with Regulations 1 and 9, any unexpended income of the Fund in a financial year may, at the discretion of the Managers:

(*a*) be added to the capital of the Fund;

(*b*) be accumulated for use as income in subsequent years;

(*c*) be used to promote research in the University in one or more of the fields specified in Regulation 6.

Annual report. **13.** The Managers shall make an annual report on their administration of the Fund to the General Board.

HERCHEL SMITH LABORATORY OF MEDICINAL CHEMISTRY FUND

1. The sums received from the American Friends of Cambridge University for the benefit of the Herchel Smith Laboratory of Medicinal Chemistry shall form a fund called the Endowment Fund for maintenance and refurbishment of the Herchel Smith Laboratory of Medicinal Chemistry, the short title of which shall be the Herchel Smith Laboratory of Medicinal Chemistry Fund. Fund.

2. The income of the fund shall be applied to the maintenance and refurbishment of the Herchel Smith Laboratory of Medicinal Chemistry in such manner as may be approved by the Herchel Smith Professor of Medicinal Chemistry. Purpose.

3. Any unexpended income in a financial year shall be accumulated for use as income in a subsequent year. Unexpended income.

HERCHEL SMITH LECTURESHIP IN INTELLECTUAL PROPERTY LAW FUND

1. The sum of US$2,500,000 bequeathed to the University by Dr Herchel Smith for the endowment of a University Lectureship in Intellectual Property Law shall form a fund called the Herchel Smith Lectureship in Intellectual Property Law Fund. Title and purpose.

2. The first charge on the income of the Fund shall be the stipend, national insurance, pension contributions, and associated indirect costs of the Lecturer payable by the University. Lectureships.

3. After provision has been made in accordance with Regulation 2, the income of the Fund shall be applied to support teaching or research in Intellectual Property Law within the Faculty of Law in such manner as shall be approved by the General Board on the recommendation of the Faculty Board of Law.

4. Any unexpended income in a financial year shall be added to the capital of the Fund. Unexpended income.

HERCHEL SMITH LECTURESHIPS IN MEDICINAL CHEMISTRY FUND

1. The sums of US$1,000,000 bequeathed to the University by Dr Herchel Smith to supplement his previous donation in 1982 for the endowment of a University office in Medicinal Chemistry, and of $2,350,000 for the endowment of a University Lectureship in Medicinal Chemistry, shall form a fund called the Herchel Smith Lectureships in Medicinal Chemistry Fund. Title.

2. The first charge on the income of the Fund shall be the stipends, national insurance, pension contributions, and associated indirect costs of two Herchel Smith Lecturers in Medicinal Chemistry payable by the University. Lectureships.

3. From time to time, the General Board, after consultation with the Faculty Boards of Clinical Medicine, and Physics and Chemistry, may establish an office for a single tenure in place of one of the Lectureships. During any period that such an office is held, the first charge on the income of the Fund shall be as set out in Regulation 2 above, save that references to such a Herchel Smith Lecturer in Medicinal Chemistry shall be treated as references to the office established under this regulation.

4. Any unexpended income in a financial year shall be added to the capital of the Fund. Unexpended income.

HERCHEL SMITH MEDICINAL CHEMISTRY FELLOWSHIP AND STUDENTSHIP FUND

1. The sums donated and bequeathed to the University by Dr Herchel Smith to support postdoctoral and postgraduate research in the field of medicinal chemistry at Cambridge shall form a fund called the Herchel Smith Medicinal Chemistry Fellowship and Studentship Fund. Title.

2. The Managers of the Fund shall be: Managers.

(*a*) one person each appointed by the Councils of the Schools of the Physical Sciences and Clinical Medicine;

(*b*) the Herchel Smith Professor of Medicinal Chemistry.

The Managers in class (*a*) shall be appointed in the Michaelmas Term for a period of three years from 1 January following their appointment.

3. The income of the Fund shall be applied at the discretion of the Managers:

(*a*) to provide the stipend, national insurance, and pension contributions of a Herchel Smith Fellow who shall conduct research in the field of medicinal chemistry for at least one year. The Fellowship shall be tenable for not more than two years. The annual stipend of the Fellow shall be determined by the Managers; Fellow.

Studentships. (*b*) to provide Studentships for persons who are, or are about to be, registered for the Ph.D. Degree in the field of medicinal chemistry. A Studentship shall be tenable for one year in the first instance and a Student may be eligible for re-election thereafter for not more than three further years.

4. In the Michaelmas Term each year the Managers shall publish a notice giving the date by which, and the manner in which, applications are to be submitted.

5. In any books, papers, or other publications containing the results of investigations carried out during the tenure of a Fellowship or Studentship, the title of Herchel Smith Fellow or Student shall be used wherever practicable.

Unexpended income. **6.** Any unexpended income in a financial year shall either be added to the capital of the Fund or accumulated for use as income in future years, as the Managers may determine.

HERCHEL SMITH RESEARCH STUDENTSHIP AND RESEARCH FELLOWSHIP FUND

Grace 2 of 5 March 2008

Title and Purpose. **1.** The sums received from Harvard University, in accordance with the bequest of the late Dr Herchel Smith, shall form a fund called the Herchel Smith Research Studentship and Research Fellowship Fund, which shall be used for the promotion and encouragement of research in Biochemistry, Molecular Biology, and Organic Chemistry, and related fields.

Committee of Managers. **2.** The Fund shall be managed by a Committee of Managers which shall comprise five persons appointed by the General Board after consultation with the Councils of the Schools of the Biological Sciences and of the Physical Sciences. Members of the Committee shall serve for four years from 1 January following their appointment.

Committee's duties. **3.** The Committee shall meet at least once a year and shall meet periodically with a Harvard University Herchel Smith Advisory Committee to determine the field or fields in which awards shall be made and other matters of common interest which further the intentions of Dr Herchel Smith in seeking to enhance collaboration between the University and Harvard University.

Who is Eligible. **4.** The Fund shall be used to provide support for such number of Herchel Smith Research Studentships and Herchel Smith Research Fellowships in the University as the Committee shall determine. In order to be eligible for a Studentship, a candidate must have been accepted to follow a course of research within the field(s) in which the Studentships have been advertised and have been admitted, or be seeking admission, by the Board of Graduate Studies as a registered Graduate Student of the University. In the case of Fellows, not more than three years shall have elapsed between the date of completion of a Ph.D. Degree at either the University or Harvard University and the date of appointment.

Value. **5.** The value of Studentships and Fellowships shall be determined by the Committee in consultation with the Harvard University Herchel Smith Advisory Committee, after taking account in the case of Studentships of any other financial resources that may be available. The stipend received by a Student shall normally comprise University and College fees, a sum for maintenance, and a contribution to departmental expenses.

Tenure. **6.** A Studentship or Fellowship shall be tenable for one or more years, as the Committee shall determine in each case; a Studentship may, at the discretion of the Committee, be extended.

Grants. **7.** The Managers shall make grants from the Fund to cover the expenses incurred of any colloquia, conference or other arrangement with Harvard University which supports Herchel Smith Research Students and Fellows in the furtherance of their research and the administration costs of making the awards.

8. In any books, papers, or other publications containing the results of investigations carried out during the tenure of a Studentship, or Fellowship, the title 'Herchel Smith Research Student' or 'Herchel Smith Research Fellow' shall be used wherever practicable.

Unexpended income. **9.** Any unexpended income in a financial year may be accumulated and expended in any one or more subsequent years in accordance with Regulations 4 and 7.

SHEILA JOAN SMITH RESEARCH FUND

Title. **1.** The benefaction to the University by Dr Herchel Smith of Pennsylvania shall form a fund to be known as the Sheila Joan Smith Research Fund.

Purpose. **2.** The income of the Fund shall be applied for such purposes in connection with medical studies and clinical research in the University as the Regius Professor of Physic for the time being shall in his or her absolute discretion select.

Unexpended income.

3. Any unapplied balance of the annual income of the Fund shall be either added to the capital of the Fund or accumulated for use as income in a subsequent year, as the Regius Professor of Physic may determine.

Smith-Knight Prizes and Rayleigh-Knight Prizes

Endowments, 1904, p. 93

Stat. E XXVIII and XXIX.

Prizes.

1. There shall be a Mathematical Essay Prize Fund, to which shall be paid the annual income of the Smith Prize Fund (being that portion of the Smith Fund which under the terms of Statute E XXVIII 2(*b*) is to be used to provide prizes in mathematics and its applications), the Rayleigh Prize Fund, and the J. T. Knight Prize Fund. The income of the Mathematical Essay Prize Fund shall be used to provide one or more Smith-Knight Prizes and one or more Rayleigh-Knight Prizes each year for essays on any subject in mathematics and its applications.

Eligibility.

2. The Prizes shall be open to:

(*a*) any student who is a Bachelor of Arts of the University, if at the latest date for the submission of essays at least three, but not more than five, complete terms have passed since the term of the student's admission as a Graduate Student other than as a candidate for the M.Phil. Degree or for a Diploma or, if the student is not a Graduate Student, since he or she last obtained honours in an Honours Examination or was approved for the M.Phil. Degree or for a Diploma;

(*b*) any member of the University who, not being a Bachelor of Arts, has been admitted as a Graduate Student other than as a candidate for the M.Phil. Degree or for a Diploma, if at the latest date for the submission of essays at least three, but not more than five, complete terms have passed since the term of his or her admission.

Adjudicators.

3. The Adjudicators of the Prizes shall be the Professors assigned to the Faculty of Mathematics or to a Department within the Faculty. The Faculty Board of Mathematics shall have power to appoint a deputy for an Adjudicator who is unable to serve, provided that they shall publish the appointment in the *Reporter* and that the deputy shall continue to serve until the end of the academical year in which he or she is appointed.

4. Candidates shall send their essays to the Secretary of the Faculty Board of Mathematics not later than the first day of Full Lent Term. Each candidate shall state in a preface to the essay what portion thereof is claimed as original.

Announcement of Prizes.

5. The Adjudicators shall publish a single list of the candidates whose essays they judge to be of distinction, giving the title of each candidate's essay. The list shall be arranged in groups; in each group the candidates shall be of equal merit. In grouping the candidates, the Adjudicators may take into account relevant experience gained by any candidate before the first of the terms which are required by Regulation 2 to have elapsed since the candidate obtained honours in an Honours Examination, or was approved for the M.Phil. Degree or for a Diploma, or was admitted as a Graduate Student other than as a candidate for the M.Phil. Degree or for a Diploma, as the case may be.

Standard.

6. The standard required for a Smith-Knight Prize shall be higher than the standard required for a Rayleigh-Knight Prize.

Value of Prizes.

7. The Smith-Knight Prizes in any year need not be of equal value, and the Rayleigh-Knight Prizes in any year need not be of equal value. The value of a Smith-Knight Prize in any year shall not exceed half the income of the Smith Prize Fund in that year, and the value of a Rayleigh-Knight Prize in any year shall not exceed the value of a Smith-Knight Prize in that year.

8. The Prizes shall be awarded before the end of the Easter Term.

Unexpended income.

9. Any unexpended income of the Mathematical Essay Prize Fund shall be accumulated in the Fund and shall be available for use as income in a subsequent year.

Smith System Engineering Prize

Title.

1. The sum made available annually by Smith System Engineering Limited shall be used to provide a prize called the Smith System Engineering Prize for Physics.

How awarded.

2. The Prize shall be awarded by the Examiners for Part IA of the Natural Sciences Tripos for an outstanding performance in the subject Physics in that examination.

Smuts Memorial Fund

Purpose. **1.** The income of the Smuts Memorial Fund, created in memory of Jan Christiaan Smuts, sometime Chancellor of the University, shall be devoted to the advancement of Commonwealth Studies.

Professorship. **2.** The first charge on the income of the Fund shall be the cost of the stipend, national insurance, pension contributions, and family allowances, if any, of the Smuts Professor of Commonwealth History. For this purpose there shall be paid each year to the University Education Fund the interest derived from that part of the capital of the Fund which was represented on 1 August 1966 by 68,000 Amalgamated Fund units and this payment shall be deemed to meet in full the first charge on the income of the Fund. Readership. The second charge on the income of the Fund shall be the cost of the stipend, national insurance, pension contributions, and family allowances, if any, of any person holding a Smuts Readership. Lectureship. The third charge on the income of the Fund shall be the cost of a lecture or course of lectures to be delivered by a Smuts Memorial Lecturer appointed from time to time, on such conditions as they may think fit, by the Board of Managers of the Fund.

Board of Managers. **3.** The Managers of the Fund, all of whom shall be members of the Regent House, shall be:

(*a*) the Vice-Chancellor (or a duly appointed deputy) as Chair;

(*b*) two persons appointed by the Council;

(*c*) two persons appointed by the General Board;

(*d*) one person appointed by each of the Faculty Boards of Asian and Middle Eastern Studies, Economics, English, History, Human, Social, and Political Science, and Law;

(*e*) one person, being a University officer in the Department of Geography, appointed by the Faculty Board of Earth Sciences and Geography;

(*f*) two persons co-opted by the Managers, provided that it shall not be obligatory for the Managers to co-opt any person.

Managers in classes (*b*)–(*e*) shall be appointed in the Michaelmas Term to serve for four years from 1 January following their appointment. Managers in class (*f*) shall serve until 31 December of the year in which they are co-opted or of the following year, as the Board of Managers shall determine at the time of their co-optation.

Powers and duties of the Managers. **4.** The Board of Managers shall have the right of reporting to the University.

5. It shall be the duty of the Board of Managers to make recommendations from time to time for the advancement of Commonwealth Studies in the widest sense of the term.

6. After provision has been made in accordance with Regulation 2, the remaining income of the Fund shall be applied from time to time, at the discretion of the Board of Managers, and subject to such conditions as they may think fit, for the advancement of Commonwealth Studies in the University

Visiting Fellowships. (*a*) by the offer in any academical year of one or more Smuts Visiting Research Fellowships, which shall be tenable for one year by a member of the staff of another university, or by any other persons whom the Managers consider suitably qualified provided that such a Fellowship shall not be awarded to an officer of this University;

Studentships. (*b*) by the offer in any academical year of one or more Smuts Studentships, which shall be tenable by members of the University of Cambridge *in statu pupillari* to enable them to pursue their studies at a university or at some other institution approved by the Managers in some part of the Commonwealth other than the Student's country of origin;

(*c*) by purchase of books and periodicals for libraries of the University;

(*d*) by providing travel grants;

(*e*) by any other means;

provided that the Board of Managers shall report annually to the University in the Michaelmas Term on the disbursements made under this regulation in the preceding financial year.

Sir Edward Snelson Fund

Grace 4 of 25 April 2012

Title. **1.** The sums given by Ms Sheila McCullagh, in memory of her cousin Sir Edward Snelson, shall form a Fund to be known as the Sir Edward Snelson Fund.

Bursaries. **2.** The income of the Fund shall be applied to provide one or more bursaries, to be called Sir Edward Snelson Bursaries, for persons, who demonstrate financial need, to assist them in meeting the costs of an undergraduate course leading to a degree of the University in any subject within the School of Arts and Humanities or the School of the Humanities and Social Sciences.

3. The Fund shall be managed by the General Board. Managers.

4. Any unexpended income in a financial year shall either be added to the capital of the Fund or accumulated for use as income in any one or more subsequent years, as the General Board may determine. Unexpended Income.

Robert M. Somers Prize

1. The sums subscribed in memory of Robert Milton Somers, of Clare Hall, shall form a fund called the Robert M. Somers Prize Fund, the income of which shall be used to provide a Prize for Chinese Studies. Fund and purpose.

2. The Prize shall be awarded annually by the Examiners for Part II of the Oriental Studies Tripos for an outstanding performance in Chinese Studies in that examination. How awarded.

3. The value of the Prize shall be such sum not exceeding the available income of the Fund as may be determined by the Faculty Board of Asian and Middle Eastern Studies, within a range approved from time to time by the Council. Value.

4. In any year in which the Prize is not awarded the income for that year shall be added to the capital of the Fund. Unexpended income.

Ali Reza and Mohamed Soudavar Fund for Persian Studies

1. The sums received from Mr Freydoun Soudavar shall form a fund called the Ali Reza and Mohamed Soudavar Fund for Persian Studies, in memory of his sons Ali Reza and Mohamed. Fund.

2. The Fund shall be under the control of a Board of Managers who shall be three teaching officers in the Department of Middle Eastern Studies appointed by the Head of the Department in consultation with and with the agreement of the teaching officers in the Department to serve for two years from 1 January following their appointment, one of whom shall be appointed on the nomination of Mr Freydoun Soudavar or his duly authorized representative. Managers.

3. The capital and the income of the Fund may be applied at the discretion of the Managers for the promotion and encouragement of Persian Studies in the University, by such means as the Managers shall think fit. Purpose.

4. Any unexpended income of the Fund in a financial year may be either added to the capital of the Fund or accumulated for use as income in future years, as the Managers shall determine. Unexpended income.

Ali Reza and Mohamed Soudavar Lectureship Fund

1. The sum received from the Azerila Foundation for the endowment of a Lectureship in Persian Studies shall form a fund called the Ali Reza and Mohamed Soudavar Lectureship Fund. Fund.

2. The Fund shall be under the control of a Board of Managers who shall be three teaching officers in the Department of Middle Eastern Studies appointed by the Head of the Department in consultation with and with the agreement of the teaching officers in the Department to serve for two years from 1 January following their appointment, one of whom shall be appointed on the nomination of the Trustees of the Azerila Foundation. Managers

3. The income of the Fund shall be used for the payment of the stipend, national insurance, pension contributions, and associated indirect costs payable by the University in respect of a Lecturer in Persian Studies. Lecturer.

4. Any unexpended income of the Fund in a financial year may be either added to the capital of the Fund or accumulated for use as income in future years, as the Managers may determine. Unexpended income.

D. E. B. Soulby Fund

1. The sum bequeathed to the University by Mr D. E. B. Soulby for the purposes of supporting research with an emphasis on either Geology or Zoology or Botany shall form a fund called the D. E. B. Soulby Fund. Fund.

Managers. **2.** The Managers of the Fund shall be the Heads of the Departments of Earth Sciences and Plant Sciences.

Purpose. **3.** The income of the Fund shall be applied at the discretion of the Managers for the promotion of research in quaternary science.

Spärck Needham Fund

Grace 2 of 9 January 2008

Title. **1.** The moneys received by the University under the will of Professor Karen Ida Boalth Spärck Needham shall form a fund called the Spärck Needham Fund.

Managers. **2.** The Managers of the Fund shall be the Fitzwilliam Museum Syndicate.

Purpose. **3.** The income of the Fund shall be available at the discretion of the Syndicate to support the preservation and management of the Museum's digital assets, and for general Museum purposes.

Spencer Fund

Fund. **1.** The sum of £2,000 given to the University by Mrs Barman in memory of her father, Leonard James Spencer, Sc.D., of Sidney Sussex College, formerly Keeper of Minerals in the British Museum of Natural History, President of the Mineralogical Society and for fifty-five years editor of the *Mineralogical Magazine*, shall form a fund called the Spencer Fund.

Purpose. **2.** The income of the Fund shall be applied from time to time at the discretion of the Head of the Department of Earth Sciences in defraying the travelling expenses of undergraduate members of the University and Graduate Students who are working in the Department of Earth Sciences when they are engaged on mineralogical or petrological research in the field.

Ron Spratling Fund

The income of the Ron Spratling Fund shall be at the disposal of the Faculty Board of Veterinary Medicine for the award of a prize in memory of Frederick Ronald Spratling, M.A., FRCVS, formerly University Lecturer in the Department of Veterinary Clinical Studies and Fellow of Wolfson College. The conditions for the award of the prize shall be determined by the Faculty Board from time to time.

Squire Law Library Appeal Fund

Grace 1 of 16 July 2008

Title. **1.** The moneys donated in response to the appeal held by the Faculty of Law shall form a fund to be called the Squire Law Library Appeal Fund.

Purpose. **2.** The income, and in exceptional cases the capital, of the Fund shall be used for purchasing and maintaining resources and facilities for the Squire Law Library.

Managers. **3.** The Committee of Managers of the Fund shall represent the Faculty of Law and Cambridge University Library and shall consist of:

(*a*) the Chair of the Law Library Sub-Syndicate who shall be Chair;

(*b*) the Chair of the Faculty Board of Law;

(*c*) one member of the Faculty of Law appointed by the Faculty Board of Law to serve for a period of four years from 1 January following her or his appointment;

(*d*) the University Librarian;

(*e*) the Squire Law Librarian.

Unexpended income. **4.** Any unexpended income of the Fund in a financial year may be either added to the capital of the Fund or accumulated for use as income in future years, as the Managers may determine.

Stat. E XLIII.

Rebecca Flower Squire Fund

Endowments, 1904, p. 146

Object. **1.** The income of the Rebecca Flower Squire Fund shall be applied (*a*) in accordance with Regulations 3–8 of these regulations to provide Squire Scholarships in Law, one half (or as near as may be) of which shall be called Rebecca Flower Squire Scholarships and the other half James William Squire

Scholarships, (*b*) in accordance with Regulations 9–13 of these regulations to provide Squire Postgraduate Studentships in Law, and (*c*) in accordance with Regulation 14 of these regulations to make grants on grounds of financial hardship to Scholars and other persons engaged in the study of law.

Managers.

2. The Managers of the Fund shall be the Faculty Board of Law, who may delegate any of their functions under these regulations to a Committee consisting of not less than three members at least one of whom shall be a member of the Faculty Board.

Rebecca Flower Squire Scholarships and James William Squire Scholarships in Law

Notice of Scholarships.

3. The Managers shall publish not later than the division of the Lent Term in each year a Notice inviting applications for Scholarships.

Who are eligible for Scholarships.

4. Any student who is qualified under Statute E XLIII 2(*a*) shall be eligible for election to a Scholarship.

Applications for Scholarships.

5. Applications for Scholarships shall be made on forms which may be obtained from the Secretary of the Faculty Board of Law and which must be completed and returned to the Secretary, through candidates' Tutors, so as to arrive not later than the division of the Michaelmas Term.

Elections and announcement of awards.

6. The Managers shall at their discretion elect into Scholarships those candidates whom they consider to have shown outstanding merit or promise in school or university examinations. They may require candidates to attend for interview. If in the opinion of the Managers two or more candidates show equal merit, preference as prescribed in Statute E XLIII 2(*b*) shall be given to the Founder's kin and to candidates born within the parish of St Mary Newington, London. The Managers shall announce elections to Scholarships not later than 30 November.

Value.

7. The value of a Scholarship shall be such sum, within a range approved from time to time by the Council, as the Managers may determine in each particular case after taking into account any other financial resources that may be available to the Scholar.

Tenure.

8. The tenure of a Scholarship, which shall at all times be subject to the Scholar becoming or continuing to be a resident member of the University, shall begin on 1 October and shall be for one year in the first instance. The Managers may re-elect a Scholar annually until the end of the academical year in which he or she becomes of standing to proceed to the B.A. Degree and for one year thereafter, provided that on each occasion they are satisfied that the Scholar's conduct, diligence, and financial circumstances justify the re-election; a Scholar who is of exceptional ability and who intends to engage in research in law, may be re-elected for a further year. A Scholar who was first elected after proceeding to the B.A. Degree may be re-elected for a second year, but for no longer. At any re-election the Managers may vary the emolument of the Scholar.

Squire Postgraduate Studentships in Law

Notice of Postgraduate Studentships.

9. The Managers shall publish not later than the division of the Lent Term in each year a Notice giving the date by which, and the manner in which, applications for Postgraduate Studentships are to be submitted.

Who are eligible for Studentships.

10. Any person who intends to engage in research in law and has been admitted, or is seeking admission, as a registered Graduate Student of the University of Cambridge and who is qualified under Statute E XLIII 2(*a*) shall be eligible for election to a Studentship.

Elections and announcement of awards

11. The Managers shall at their discretion elect into Studentships those candidates intending to engage in research in law whom they consider to show outstanding merit or promise. They may require candidates to attend for interview. If in the opinion of the Managers two or more candidates show equal merit, preference as prescribed in Statute E XLIII 2(*b*) shall be given to the Founder's kin and to candidates born within the parish of St Mary Newington, London. The Managers shall announce elections not later than 30 September. Election to and tenure of the Scholarship shall lapse if the person elected does not become or ceases to be a registered Graduate Student.

Value.

12. The value of a Studentship shall be such sum, within a range approved from time to time by the Council, as the Managers may determine in each particular case after taking into account any other financial resources that may be available to the Student.

Tenure.

13. The tenure of a Studentship shall begin on 1 October and shall be for one year in the first instance. The Managers may re-elect a Student for one or two years, but for no longer. At any re-election the Managers may vary the emolument of the Student.

Grants. **14.** An application for a grant from the Fund may be made at any time on grounds of financial hardship by a Scholar or a Postgraduate Student or by any other person who is qualified under Statute E XLIII 3. Such an application shall be made on a form which may be obtained from the Secretary of the Faculty Board of Law and which must be completed and returned to the Secretary through the applicant's Tutor. The value of a grant shall be determined by the Managers for each particular applicant, subject to an upper limit to be determined from time to time by the Council.

William Barclay Squire Fund

Two Prizes. **1.** The sums given to the University by Mrs J. A. Fuller-Maitland and Mrs F. L. Nicholson in memory of their brother William Barclay Squire shall form a fund called the William Barclay Squire Fund the income of which shall be used to further antiquarian research in music by the provision of annual prizes to be called the William Barclay Squire Prize and the William Barclay Squire Essay Prize, and of grants to Graduate Students.

Unexpended income. **2.** Any unexpended income accumulated in the Fund may be applied from time to time by the Faculty Board of Music and subject to such conditions as they may think fit for the purpose of furthering research in the history of music.

William Barclay Squire Prize

Prize. **3.** The Prize shall be awarded each year by the Examiners for Part II of the Music Tripos to a candidate who has shown distinction in any two papers which in the judgement of the Examiners are to be regarded as on subjects in the history of music.

Value. **4.** The value of the Prize shall be such sum as shall be determined by the Faculty Board of Music within a range approved from time to time by the Council.

William Barclay Squire Essay Prize

Prize. **5.** The William Barclay Squire Essay Prize shall be awarded for the best course-work essay and/or dissertation in the examination for the degree of Master of Philosophy (one-year course) which, in the judgement of the Degree Committee for the Faculty of Music, is on a subject connected with the history of music.

Who are eligible. **6.** The Prize shall be open to any registered Graduate Student under the supervision of the Degree Committee for the Faculty of Music.

Value. **7.** The value of the Prize shall be such sum as shall be determined by the Faculty Board of Music within a range approved from time to time by the Council.

Grants to Graduate Students

Grants. **8.** In any year, after provision has been made for the award of the William Barclay Squire Prize and the William Barclay Squire Essay Prize, the Degree Committee for the Faculty of Music may make grants from the annual income of the Fund towards the expenses of Graduate Students under their supervision who are pursuing or about to pursue research on topics in the history of music.

9. Applications for grants shall be submitted to the Secretary of the Degree Committee by Graduate Students through their Supervisors so as to arrive by 1 July each year.

Stat. E XXIII.

Stanton Lectureship in the Philosophy of Religion

Endowments, 1904, pp. 625–6

Name. **1.** The income of the Stanton Fund shall be used for the provision of lectures in the Philosophy of Religion. For this purpose there shall be a Lectureship called the Stanton Lectureship in the Philosophy of Religion, and the Lecturer shall be called the Stanton Lecturer in the Philosophy of Religion. The Lectureship shall not be deemed a University Lectureship and may, subject to the provisions of Special Ordinances C (vii) A.10 and C (x) 11, be held concurrently with a University office.

Electors. **2.** The Lecturer shall be appointed by a Board of Electors consisting of:

(*a*) the Vice-Chancellor;

(*b*) five other persons, one appointed by the General Board, three by the Faculty Board of Divinity, and one by the Faculty Board of Philosophy.

Members in class (*b*) shall be appointed in the Michaelmas Term to serve for three years from 1 January following their appointment. No appointment of a Lecturer shall be made at any meeting at which less than four members of the Board are present.

3. The Lecturer shall hold office for such period not exceeding three academical years as shall be determined by the Electors, and shall deliver in each year during the tenure of the Lectureship not less than four and not more than eight lectures, the number to be determined by the Electors. Tenure and duties.

4. Before the division of the Easter Term preceding each year of his or her tenure of office the Lecturer shall submit to the Faculty Boards of Divinity and Philosophy a statement of the term or terms in which he or she proposes to lecture during the ensuing academical year, and of the subjects to be treated in the lectures.

5. The stipend of the Lecturer shall be such sum as shall be determined by the Electors on the occasion of each election, subject to the approval of the General Board. Any balance of the net income of the Stanton Fund shall be applied to the teaching of the philosophy of religion in the University, at the discretion of the Electors and subject to the approval of the General Board. Stipend.

STARBRIDGE LECTURESHIP FUND

1. The sum of £800,000, to be received from Mrs Susan Howatch over a period of four years for the endowment of a University Lectureship in Theology and Natural Science, entitled the Starbridge Lectureship, and any subsequent sum received for the same purpose, shall form a fund to be called the Starbridge Lectureship Fund. Title and purpose.

2. The stipend, national insurance, and pension contributions payable by the University in respect of the Starbridge Lecturer in Theology and Natural Science shall be payable from the Fund. Lecturer.

3. If and when the income of the Fund shall exceed the amount required for the payment of the stipend, national insurance, pension contributions, and associated indirect costs of the Starbridge Lecturer payable by the University, the excess of the income over that amount may be applied in support of the work of the Starbridge Lecturer in such manner as may be approved by the General Board on the recommendation of the Faculty Board of Divinity.

4. Any unexpended income of the Fund in a financial year may in any subsequent year be expended in accordance with Regulation 3. Unexpended income.

STEEL THEOLOGICAL STUDENTSHIPS

1. The Managers of the Steel Theological Studentships shall be the Regius Professor of Divinity and two members of the Faculty of Divinity appointed by the Faculty Board of Divinity in the Michaelmas Term to hold office for two years from 1 January following their appointment. Managers.

2. Before the end of the Michaelmas Term each year the Managers shall give notice of the date by which and the manner in which application for Studentships shall be made. Notice.

3. The Managers shall inform the Professors of Divinity of the names and financial circumstances of candidates whom they recommend for nomination by the Professors for Studentships in accordance with Clause 3 sub-clause (1) of the Scheme. The University's power of awarding Studentships shall be exercised by the Faculty Board of Divinity. Selection and nomination for Studentship.

4. The Managers, after taking into consideration his or her financial circumstances, shall determine for each Student whom the Professors nominate the value of the Studentship within a range approved from time to time by the Council. Each Studentship shall be tenable for one year in the first instance, and may be renewed with its value reviewed, subject to a maximum tenure of three years. Value and tenure.

5. On the recommendation of the Managers the Professors of Divinity may nominate to the Faculty Board of Divinity persons qualified under Clause 3 sub-clause (1) of the Scheme to whom grants of an amount determined by the Managers may be awarded. The Managers, the Professors, and the Faculty Board shall take into account the financial circumstances of the candidates. Grants.

Extract from a Scheme established by Order dated 14 October 1970 of the Secretary of State for Education and Science under Section 18 of the Charities Act 1960:

The Foundation

1. In this Scheme the expression 'the Foundation' means the Foundation called The Steel Theological Studentships, in the University of Cambridge, founded and now regulated by Deed Poll dated 19th July 1890 under the hand and seal of Esther Steel.

Trustee and Administration of Foundation

2. The Foundation and its endowment (including the particulars specified in the Schedule to this Scheme) shall be administered in accordance with the provisions of this Scheme by The Chancellor, Masters and Scholars of the University of Cambridge (hereinafter called "the Trustee") as the Trustee of the Foundation.

Application of Income

3. (1) After the payment of any expenses of administration, the net yearly income of the Foundation shall be applied by the Trustee in the award of Studentships, Bursaries, Maintenance Allowances or other Grants to members of the University of Cambridge who:

(*a*) are preparing for Holy Orders in the Church of England;
(*b*) have completed the examination requirements of the said University for the degree of Bachelor of Arts;
(*c*) are resident in the said University or in any College or Hall therein;
(*d*) have been nominated for an award by the Professors of Divinity, for the time being, in the said University; and
(*e*) are, in the opinion of such Professors as aforesaid, in need of financial assistance.

(2) Within the limits prescribed by this Scheme, the Trustee shall have full power to make rules for the award of Studentships, Bursaries, Maintenance Allowances or other Grants, including rules as to the value and period of tenure of the awards, and the qualifications, and method of ascertainment and selection, of beneficiaries.

Surplus Cash

4. Any sum of cash at any time belonging to the Foundation and not needed as a balance for working purposes shall be invested and any such investments may, unless appropriated by the Trustee as an addition to the capital of the Foundation, be realized at any time and the proceeds of such realization applied as income of the Foundation for the purposes specified in Clause 3 of this Scheme.

Questions under Scheme

5. If any question arises as to the construction of this Scheme, or as to the regularity or the validity of any acts done or about to be done under this Scheme, it shall be determined by the Secretary of State for Education and Science, upon such application made to him for the purpose as he thinks sufficient, and such determination shall be binding on the Trustee and all persons claiming under the Foundation.

(*Clauses 6 and 7 of the Scheme and its Schedule are not reproduced here.*)

Leslie Stephen Lectureship

Name. **1.** A Lectureship shall be established in the University to be called the Leslie Stephen Lectureship.

Electors. **2.** The Lecturer shall be elected in the Michaelmas Term of every year of which the number is even by the Vice-Chancellor (or a duly appointed deputy), the Master of Trinity Hall, the Knightbridge Professor of Philosophy, the Regius Professor of History, and the King Edward VII Professor of English Literature.

Duties. **3.** It shall be the duty of the Lecturer to deliver one lecture on some day in Full Term within two calendar years of her or his election. The lecture shall be delivered in the Senate-House or in some other University building or in Trinity Hall.

Subject. **4.** The lecture shall be on some literary subject, including therein criticism, biography, and ethics.

Date and place of delivery. **5.** Subject to Regulation 3, the date of the lecture and the place of its delivery shall be fixed by the Vice-Chancellor.

6. The stipend of the Lecturer shall be the aggregate of the income of the endowment fund for the financial year in which the lecture is given and that of the year immediately preceding it, less any expenses associated with the lecture.

Proviso. **7.** These regulations shall be subject to alteration by Grace provided that the name of Leslie Stephen be always connected with the foundation and that the income arising therefrom be appropriated to some academical object of a literary character.

Stevenson Prizes

Fund. **1.** The sum of £2,000 bequeathed to the University by the late Claude Maberly Stevenson, M.D., of St John's College, shall form a fund called the Stevenson Fund, for the purpose of providing one or more annual postgraduate prizes in Economics which shall be called Stevenson Prizes.

Prizes. **2.** At least one and no more than four Stevenson Prizes shall be awarded each year by the Degree Committee for the Faculty of Economics for distinction shown by candidates in the examination for the degree of Master of Philosophy in Economics.

Value.

3. The value of a Prize shall be such sum as shall be determined by the Faculty Board of Economics within a range approved from time to time by the Council.

4. In awarding the Prizes the Degree Committee shall be governed chiefly by the quality of the work done, and shall have regard to the candidates' constructive ability and their grasp of scientific principles rather than to the erudition displayed.

Unexpended income.

5. After provision has been made, in accordance with the foregoing regulations, for the award of Stevenson Prizes, the balance of the annual income and any unexpended income accumulated in the Fund shall be available to the Faculty Board of Economics to be used for the encouragement of study or research in Economics.

Amendment of regulations.

6. It shall be open to the University, on the recommendation of the Faculty Board of Economics, to alter these regulations from time to time provided that

(*a*) any Prize provided from the Fund shall be entitled a Stevenson Prize;

(*b*) at least one Stevenson Prize shall be offered annually as a postgraduate prize in Economics.

The John Stewart of Rannoch Hebrew Fund and Scholarships

Stat. E III.

Endowments, 1904, p. 335

Managers.

1. The John Stewart of Rannoch Hebrew Fund shall be managed by the Head of the Department of Middle Eastern Studies in consultation with and with the agreement of the teaching officers in Hebrew in the Department.

Scholarships.

2. The first charge on the income of the Fund shall be provision, if there are candidates of sufficient merit, for the award in each year of at least two Scholarships in Hebrew. The Scholarships shall be awarded on the results of a competitive examination.

Examination.

3. The examination shall consist of three papers namely (*a*) passages from specified books of the Old Testament for translation from Hebrew into English and questions arising out of the passages set; (*b*) passages from unspecified books of the Old Testament for translation from Hebrew into English and questions arising out of the passages set, and passages for pointing; (*c*) passages for translation from English into Hebrew, together with questions on grammar and syntax. The specified books shall be selected from time to time by the Faculty Board of Asian and Middle Eastern Studies.

Date of examination.

4. The examination shall begin on the first day of Full Easter Term.

Eligibility and entries.

5. Candidature shall be open to any student resident in the University, provided that at the time of the examination not more than nine complete terms will have passed after his or her first term of residence. The names of candidates shall be sent to the Registrary so as to arrive not later than 25 January preceding the examination. A student who wishes to claim preference under Regulation 7 shall submit at the same time a certificate of his or her place of birth.

Examiners.

6. The examination shall be conducted by two Examiners appointed not later than the division of the Lent Term on the nomination of the Managers. Each Examiner shall receive from the Fund, unless there are no candidates, such amount as may be determined by the Managers within a range approved from time to time by the Council. All other expenses of the examination shall be defrayed out of the Fund.

Awards.

7. At every award of Scholarships the Examiners shall publish an order of merit of the candidates who have distinguished themselves in the examination. If two or more candidates show equal proficiency preference shall be given to natives of the counties of Wilts, Somerset, or Gloucester, including the city and county of Bristol.

Tenure.

8. A Scholarship shall be tenable for three years from 1 October preceding the award.

Value.

9. The annual value of each Scholarship shall be such sum as shall be determined by the Managers within a range approved from time to time by the Council.

Payment of emolument.

10. Each Scholar shall receive the emolument of his or her Scholarship in such instalments as shall be determined by the Council on the recommendation of the Managers.

Unexpended income.

11. After provision has been made for the Scholarships in accordance with Regulation 2 any unexpended income accumulated in the Fund shall be applied from time to time, at the discretion of the Managers and subject to such conditions as they may think fit,

(*a*) to make grants to Scholars or other persons engaged in the study of Hebrew;

(*b*) to make purchases of books and other material;

(*c*) to assist in any other way the promotion and encouragement of the study of Hebrew in the University.

Recognition of benefactor. All disbursements that are made from the Fund under this regulation shall be published in the *Reporter* and shall be associated with the name of John Stewart of Rannoch.

Stat. E III.

THE JOHN STEWART OF RANNOCH GREEK AND LATIN FUND AND SCHOLARSHIPS

Endowments, 1904, p. 335

Managers. **1.** The Managers of the John Stewart of Rannoch Greek and Latin Fund shall be the Faculty Board of Classics.

Scholarships. **2.** The first charge on the income of the Fund shall be provision, if there are candidates of sufficient merit, for the award in each year of at least four Scholarships in Greek and Latin.

How awarded. **3.** The Scholarships shall be awarded on the performance of the candidates for Part IB of the Classical Tripos; provided that

(*a*) no candidate shall be awarded a Scholarship unless he or she has attained a first-class aggregate mark in the papers in translation from Greek and Latin into English;

(*b*) a candidate who has not been placed in the first class in the examination as a whole shall not be awarded a Scholarship unless in the view of the Awarders the circumstances are exceptional.

Awarders. **4.** The Examiners for Part IB of the Classical Tripos shall be the Awarders for the Scholarships.

Awards. **5.** At every award of Scholarships the Awarders shall publish an order of merit of the candidates who have distinguished themselves in the examination. If two or more candidates show equal proficiency preference shall be given to natives of the counties of Wilts, Somerset, or Gloucester, including the city and county of Bristol.

Tenure. **6.** A Scholarship shall be tenable for three years from 1 October preceding the award. A Scholarship shall not be tenable with a Battie, Browne, Craven, Davies, Pitt, Porson, or Waddington Scholarship.

Value. **7.** The annual value of each Scholarship shall be such sum as shall be determined by the Managers within a range approved from time to time by the Council. In addition the Awarders shall be empowered to award to each Scholar a prize or prizes of books, the value of which shall not exceed such sum as shall be determined by the Managers within a range approved from time to time by the Council.

Payment of emolument. **8.** Each Scholar shall receive the emolument of his or her Scholarship in such instalments as shall be determined by the Council on the recommendation of the Managers.

Unexpended income. **9.** After provision has been made for the Scholarships in accordance with Regulation 2 any unexpended income accumulated in the Fund shall be applied from time to time, at the discretion of the Managers and subject to such conditions as they may think fit,

(*a*) to make grants to Scholars or other persons engaged in the study of Greek and Latin;

(*b*) to make purchases of books and other material;

(*c*) to assist in any other way the promotion and encouragement of the study of Greek and Latin in the University.

Recognition of benefactor. All disbursements that are made from the Fund under this regulation shall be published in the *Reporter* and shall be associated with the name of John Stewart of Rannoch.

Stat. E III.

THE JOHN STEWART OF RANNOCH SACRED MUSIC FUND AND SCHOLARSHIPS

Endowments, 1904, p. 335

Managers. **1.** The Managers of the John Stewart of Rannoch Sacred Music Fund shall be the Faculty Board of Music.

Scholarships. **2.** The first charge on the income of the Fund shall be provision, if there are candidates of sufficient merit, for the award in each year of at least two Scholarships in Sacred Music. The Scholarships shall be awarded on the results of a competitive examination.

Examination. **3.** The scheme of examination shall consist of:

(*a*) a dissertation of not less than 5,000 words and not more than 10,000 words on a topic in the field of sacred music proposed by the candidate and approved by the Managers;

(*b*) a *viva voce* examination on the dissertation, which may also include ear-tests, keyboard-tests, and such other tests as the Examiners deem to be desirable.

Eligibility and entries. **4.** Candidature shall be open to any student resident in the University, provided that at the time of the examination not more than twelve complete terms will have passed after his or her first term of residence. Each candidate shall send the proposed subject of his or her dissertation to the Secretary of the Faculty Board of Music not later than the end of the third quarter of the Michaelmas Term; a candidate who wishes to claim preference under Regulation 7 shall submit at the same time a certificate of his or her place of birth. The Secretary of the Faculty Board shall communicate each candidate's proposed subject to the Managers, and shall inform the candidate not later than the last day of the Michaelmas Term of its approval or rejection by them.

5. Candidates shall send their dissertations to the Secretary of the Faculty Board so as to arrive not later than the last day of Full Lent Term; each dissertation shall be accompanied by a statement certifying that it is the candidate's own original work. The *viva voce* examination shall be held in the Easter Term, not later than the division of term.

Examiners. **6.** The examination shall be conducted by two Examiners appointed in the Michaelmas Term on the nomination of the Managers. Each Examiner shall receive from the Fund, unless there are no candidates, such amount as may be determined by the Managers within a range approved from time to time by the Council. In addition to the foregoing payments, an external Examiner as defined in the regulations for payments to Examiners and Assessors shall receive a payment of such sum, unless there are no candidates, as shall be determined by the Managers within a range approved from time to time by the Council. All other expenses of the examination shall be defrayed out of the Fund.

Awards. **7.** If two or more candidates show equal proficiency preference shall be given to natives of the counties of Wilts, Somerset, or Gloucester, including the city and county of Bristol.

Tenure. **8.** A Scholarship shall be tenable for three years from 1 October preceding the award. The Managers shall be empowered to renew the tenure for a fourth year, but for no longer.

9. The annual value of each Scholarship shall be such sum as shall be determined by the Managers within a range approved from time to time by the Council.

Payment of emolument. **10.** At the end of the Easter Term in which the election is held, each newly elected Scholar shall be entitled to receive one year's emolument of the Scholarship. In succeeding years the emolument shall be paid in equal termly instalments, provided that no payment shall be made in respect of any term unless the Scholar has kept the term or has pursued a course of study or research approved by the Managers.

Unexpended income. **11.** After provision has been made for the Scholarships in accordance with Regulation 2 any unexpended income accumulated in the Fund shall be applied from time to time, at the discretion of the Managers and subject to such conditions as they may think fit,

(*a*) to make grants to Scholars or other persons engaged in the study of Sacred Music;
(*b*) to defray, in whole or in part, expenses incurred by Graduate Students in pursuing research projects in Sacred Music;
(*c*) to make purchases of books, musical instruments, and other material for the Faculty of Music;
(*d*) to assist in any other way the promotion and encouragement of the study of Sacred Music in the University.

Recognition of benefactor. All disbursements that are made from the Fund under this regulation shall be published in the *Reporter* and shall be associated with the name of John Stewart of Rannoch.

Grants from the Fund. **12.** Applications for grants under Regulation 11 may be sent to the Secretary of the Faculty Board of Music at any time. They must be accompanied by a full explanatory statement for the guidance of the Managers.

GRAHAM STOREY FUND

Fund. **1.** The sum bequeathed to the University by Dr Graham Storey, Emeritus Reader in English Literature and Fellow of Trinity Hall, and augmented by gifts in his memory from the Governing Body of Trinity Hall, shall form a fund called the Graham Storey Fund.

Managers. **2.** The Managers of the Fund shall be the Faculty Board of English, who may delegate any or all of their functions under these regulations to a committee not necessarily consisting wholly of members of the Board.

Lecture. **3.** The first charge on the income of this Fund shall be to meet the payment of an honorarium to and the expenses of a Lecturer who shall be appointed biennially by the Managers to deliver a lecture on an English novelist, to be called the Graham Storey Lecture.

4. After provision has been made in accordance with Regulation 3 any additional income of the Fund in a financial year may, at the discretion of the Managers, be applied to further the study of English Literature in the University.

Unexpended income. **5.** Any unexpended income of the Fund in a financial year may be either added to the capital of the Fund or accumulated for use as income in future years, as the Managers may determine.

Strauss Fund

Name. **1.** The sum of £10,000 made available by the Executors of the estate of Samuel George Strauss shall form a fund to be called the Strauss Fund. The capital of the Fund may be augmented from time to time by further donations or bequests.

Purpose. **2.** The income of the Fund shall be available at the sole discretion of the Head of the Department of Pathology for the purchase of books or periodicals for the library of the Department.

Unexpended income. **3.** Any unexpended income shall be added to the capital of the Fund.

Study of Religion Fund

Fund and purpose. **1.** The gift of an anonymous benefactor shall form a fund to be called the Study of Religion Fund, the income of which shall be used for the advancement of the Study of Religion, with special reference to Implicit Religion.

Managers. **2.** The Fund shall be under the control of a Board of Managers who shall be:

(*a*) the Vice-Chancellor (or a duly appointed deputy) as Chair;

(*b*) the Chair of the Faculty Board of Divinity;

(*c*) a member of the Faculty Board of Divinity appointed by that Board;

(*d*) two members appointed by the Faculty Board of Divinity for periods not exceeding three years at a time.

3. The Managers shall meet at least once a year.

Duties. **4.** It shall be the duty of the Managers:

(*a*) to keep the financial position of the Fund under review;

(*b*) to make recommendations on the future use of the endowment, if the University or the Faculty cease to be able to make provision for the study of Implicit Religion.

University office in Faculty of Divinity. **5.** The first charge on the income of the Fund shall be the payment of the stipend, national insurance, pension contributions, and associated indirect costs of the holder of a University office in the Faculty of Divinity concerned with teaching and research in Implicit Religion. In making appointments to such an office the appointing body shall be advised by an Assessor appointed by the Faculty Board of Divinity after consulting the Managers.

6. After provision has been made in accordance with Regulation 5, the income of the Fund may be applied at the discretion of the Managers for the encouragement of the Study of Religion in the University, with special reference to Implicit Religion.

Unexpended income. **7.** Any unexpended income of the Fund in a financial year may be either added to the capital of the Fund or accumulated for use as income in future years, as the Managers may determine.

Department of Surgery Prize

Prize. **1.** There shall be offered annually a Department of Surgery Prize for a dissertation on a subject of the candidate's choice related to surgery.

Value. **2.** The value of the Prize shall be the annual income of the Department of Surgery Prize Fund.

Who are eligible. **3.** Any person who has pursued clinical study in the University for the degrees of Bachelor of Medicine and Bachelor of Surgery may enter for the Prize, provided that no dissertation shall be eligible for the award of the Prize if it is submitted more than two years after the candidate has passed the Final M.B. Examination.

Dissertation. **4.** A dissertation shall not exceed 5,000 words in length (excluding tables and diagrams), and its subject may be restricted either to experimental or to clinical surgery.

Notice of submission. **5.** In each year the Professor of Surgery shall, before the end of the Michaelmas Term, give notice of the date in the following calendar year by which and the manner in which dissertations should be submitted.

6. The Prize shall be awarded by the Regius Professor of Physic and the Professor of Surgery (or their deputies) who may at their discretion examine a candidate *viva voce*. Awarders.

Sweet and Maxwell Prize

The Sweet and Maxwell Prize, which was established to commemorate over one hundred and seventy years' connection with law publishing of the Maxwell family, shall be awarded each year in June by the Examiners for Part IA of the Law Tripos to the candidate for that examination who shows the greatest distinction in the examination; provided that an Affiliated Student holding a degree in Law of another university shall not be eligible for the award of a Prize.

C. T. Taylor Fund and Studentships

1. The sum given to the University by Mr V. T. Taylor in memory of his father, Cuthbert Tuke Taylor, M.A., of Trinity College, shall form a fund called the C. T. Taylor Fund. Fund.

2. The income of the Fund shall be used to provide one or more Studentships, which shall be called C. T. Taylor Studentships, for persons who are not ordinarily resident in the United Kingdom to enable them to undertake advanced study or research at Cambridge in science, including Engineering, Mathematics, Geography, and Land Economy, but excluding medical research. Studentships.

3. The Fund shall be administered by four Managers who shall be: Managers.

(*a*) the Vice-Chancellor or a duly appointed deputy, as Chair;

(*b*) three persons appointed by the Council.

Managers in class (*b*) shall serve for three years from 1 October following their appointment.

4. Subject to the provisions of Regulation 2, the Studentships shall be open to any person who is or is about to become registered as a Graduate Student in the University. If two or more candidates are equally well qualified, preference shall be given to a candidate from Australia, Canada, New Zealand, or the United States of America. Eligibility

5. The Managers shall give at least three months' notice of their intention to proceed to an election. They shall be empowered to indicate in their notice that for the election in a particular year preference will be given to candidates working in a specified field. Notice of election.

6. The tenure of a Studentship shall be determined by the Managers on the occasion of each election. A Student shall be eligible for re-election, provided that the tenure of a Studentship shall not normally exceed three years in all. Tenure.

7. The annual stipend of a Student shall be such sum not exceeding the available income of the Fund as may be determined by the Managers, within a range approved from time to time by the Council, after they have taken account of any other financial resources that may be available to the Student. Stipend.

8. The stipend shall be paid quarterly in advance, provided that the Managers may withhold any instalment if they are not satisfied that the Student is pursuing his or her research with sufficient diligence.

9. Any unexpended income may be either added to the capital of the Fund or accumulated for use as income in subsequent years, as the Managers may determine. Unexpended income.

Teape Prize

1. The sum received by the University from the Trustees of the Teape Fund shall form a fund called the Teape Prize Fund. Title.

2. The income of the Fund shall be used to provide a prize called the Teape Prize, in memory of William Marshall Teape, M.A., B.D., of St John's College, which shall be awarded by the Examiners for Parts IIA and IIB of the Theological and Religious Studies Tripos for distinction in the study of religions of India, as shown by performance either in a dissertation or in a paper on the study or the comparative study of religions in that examination. Purpose.

3. The value of the Prize shall be determined by the Faculty Board of Divinity within a range approved from time to time by the Council. Value.

4. Any unexpended income in a financial year shall be added to the capital of the Fund. Unexpended income.

RICHARD TENCH FUND

Title. **1.** The sum received under the will of Richard T. Tench of Portland, Oregon, shall form a fund called the Richard Tench Fund.

Purpose. **2.** The income of the Fund shall be used towards meeting the additional costs that the University has incurred following the General Board's agreement in 2001 to extend the hours during which the University Library shall remain open to include Saturday afternoons.

TENNANT FUND AND STUDENTSHIP

Name. **1.** The benefaction of an anonymous donor in memory of Mr W. A. Tennant, sometime chairman of C. Tennant, Sons and Company, Limited, London, shall form a fund called the Tennant Fund.

Purpose. **2.** The income of the Fund shall be applied to provide the emoluments of a Studentship to be called the Tennant Studentship, the holder of which shall undertake advanced study or research in Norway.

Managers. **3.** The Managers of the Fund shall be the Managers of the Scandinavian Studies Fund.

4. The Managers, other than the *ex officio* Managers, shall be appointed to serve for three years from 1 January following their appointment.

Quorum. **5.** No resolution of the Managers shall be valid unless approved by at least three Managers at a meeting to which all the Managers have been summoned.

Who are eligible. **6.** The Studentship shall be open to members of the University who shall at the date of the election have passed some final examination for the degree of Bachelor of Arts, provided that at the same date not more than twenty-four terms shall have elapsed since the end of their first term of residence. A Tennant Student, provided that he or she is otherwise qualified, may be a candidate for the Studentship on a second occasion, but the Studentship shall never be held for more than two years in all. It shall not be tenable concurrently with the Scandinavian Studentship.

Applications. **7.** An application for election must be submitted through the candidate's Tutor to the Registrary so as to arrive not later than 1 June, and must be accompanied by a statement of the course of advanced study or research which the candidate proposes to undertake. The course proposed, which may be varied with the consent of the Managers, shall involve residency in Norway for not less than three months.

8. The Managers shall have authority to take any steps that they think advisable to ascertain the qualifications of the candidates, provided that the Studentship shall not be awarded by competitive examination.

Election and tenure. **9.** The election of the Student shall be made annually in June, and shall be for a period of one year.

Value. **10.** The Student shall receive a stipend of £50, which shall be paid not later than the thirtieth day following the election, and such additional stipend within the annual income of the Fund as the Managers shall determine in each case after taking account of any other financial resources that may be available to the Student. The additional stipend shall be paid to the Student in two equal instalments not later than the first day of the Full Michaelmas Term and of the Full Lent Term following the election; provided that the second instalment shall not be paid till the Managers have received from the Student a report on his or her work for the past half-year.

Grants. **11.** Any income of the Fund not used for the emoluments of the Studentship may at the discretion of the Managers be used in making grants to students or University officers or other persons employed by the University or Fellows of Colleges in the University for the furtherance of studies in Norway.

12. These regulations shall be subject to alteration by the University, provided that the income of the Fund shall always be devoted to the endowment of a Studentship, called the Tennant Studentship, for the encouragement of studies in Norway by students of the University.

THALMANN BEQUEST

Funds. **1.** The investments representing the bequest to the University by Rene Hugo Thalmann for the provision of scholarships shall be divided equally to form two funds to be known as the Thalmann Overseas Fund and the Thalmann European Fund.

Thalmann Overseas Fund. **2.** The income of the Thalmann Overseas Fund and any unexpended income accumulated in the Fund shall be available for expenditure by the Trustees of the Cambridge Commonwealth, European and International Trust for the provision of scholarships tenable in the University by students resident in or educated in countries overseas. In accordance with the wishes of the benefactor, the Trustees, with the approval of the Council, may authorize expenditure of the whole or part of the capital of the Thalmann Overseas Fund on the provision of such scholarships.

Thalmann European Fund.

3. The income of the Thalmann European Fund and any unexpended income accumulated in the Fund shall be available for expenditure by the Council for the provision of scholarships tenable in the University by students resident in or educated in European countries. The Council may delegate their functions under this regulation to a Committee.

4. In accordance with the wishes of the benefactor the Council may authorize expenditure of the whole or part of the capital of the Thalmann European Fund on the provision of scholarships tenable in the University by students resident in or educated in European countries.

THEOLOGICAL STUDIES FUND

Stat. E, XXX.

Administration.

1. The Theological Studies Fund, established in accordance with Statute E XXX 9 shall be administered by the Faculty Board of Divinity, who may delegate some or all of their functions under these regulations to a committee not necessarily consisting wholly of members of the Board.

Prizes.

2. The first charge on the Fund shall be the provision of prizes for distinguished work submitted by candidates for the Theological and Religious Studies Tripos, for the examination in Theology and Religious Studies for the M.Phil. Degree, or for the examination for the Advanced Diploma in Theology and Religious Studies.

How awarded.

3. The Examiners for Parts IIA and IIB of the Theological and Religious Studies Tripos, the Examiners for the examination in Theology and Religious Studies for the M.Phil. Degree, and the Examiners for the Advanced Diploma in Theology and Religious Studies shall have power to award prizes, to be called Theological Studies Prizes, for a distinguished performance in any part of the examination with which they are concerned. The value of a Prize shall be such sum not exceeding the available income of the Fund as may be determined by the Faculty Board within a range approved from time to time by the Council.

Other applications of Fund.

4. After provision has been made for the award of Theological Studies Prizes in accordance with Regulations 2 and 3, any unexpended income or capital of the Fund may be applied, at the discretion of the Faculty Board:

(*a*) to provide grants to enable students who are in need of financial assistance to engage in the study of theology in the University or elsewhere;

(*b*) to provide lectures on theological subjects in the University with special (but not exclusive) reference to the fields of study associated with the Carus, Evans, Hebrew, Jeremie, Kaye, Scholefield, and George Williams Prizes;

(*c*) to purchase books for the library of the Faculty of Divinity;

(*d*) to assist in any other way the promotion and encouragement of theological studies in the University.

Grants.

5. Any student engaged in the study of theology in the University may apply for a grant under Regulation 4(*a*). Before the end of the Michaelmas Term each year the Faculty Board shall give public notice of the date by which, and the manner in which, applications for grants are to be made. Each application shall be accompanied by a statement of the applicant's financial circumstances. No grant shall be paid to any student until four terms have passed after his or her first term of residence.

6. Grants made under Regulation 4(*a*) shall be payable either in full or in instalments, as determined by the Faculty Board. Instalments shall be paid in advance, provided that the Board may postpone or disallow any payment if they are of the opinion that a student is not diligently pursuing his or her course of theological study.

Visiting lecturers.

7. The Faculty Board shall have power to appoint from time to time a visiting lecturer who shall deliver during Full Term one or more lectures on a subject or subjects in theological studies. A visiting lecturer shall receive such stipend as may be approved by the General Board on the recommendation of the Faculty Board, together with such payment for expenses as shall be determined by the General Board on the same recommendation.

Barnard Randolph Fund.

8. The income and accumulated income of the Barnard Randolph Fund may be applied, at the discretion of the Faculty Board or of any Committee appointed under Regulation 1, for the provision of one or more Barnard Randolph Exhibitions to be held by graduates of the University in need of financial assistance to enable them to study theology in the University, and for the provision of grants to enable students in need of financial assistance to engage in the study of theology in the University or elsewhere.

J. M. THODAY FUND

Fund and purpose. **1.** The sums subscribed to mark the retirement in 1983 of John Marion Thoday, Sc.D., of Emmanuel College, from the Arthur Balfour Professorship of Genetics, shall form a fund called the J. M. Thoday Fund for the encouragement of the study of Genetics in the University.

Prize. **2.** The Fund shall be used to provide a J. M. Thoday Prize for Genetics. The value of the Prize shall be the annual income of the Fund.

How awarded. **3.** The Prize shall be awarded each year by the Examiners for Genetics in Part II of the Natural Sciences Tripos to the candidate who shows the greatest distinction in the subject Genetics in that examination.

HENRY ARTHUR THOMAS FUND

Name and purpose. **1.** The money received from the bequest of the late Henry Arthur Thomas shall constitute a fund, called the Henry Arthur Thomas Fund, for the advancement of classical learning.

Who are eligible. **2.** The income of the Fund shall be used to provide Scholarships open to all members of the University.

Administration. **3.** The income of the Fund shall be administered by the Faculty Board of Classics, who may delegate any of their functions concerning the Fund to a Committee not necessarily composed wholly of members of the Board.

4. Subject to the foregoing provisions the University shall have power, on the recommendation of the Faculty Board of Classics, to make regulations for carrying out the objects of the Fund, and to vary such regulations from time to time.[1]

5. The income of the Fund shall be used to support:

(*a*) one Henry Arthur Thomas Studentship;

(*b*) Henry Arthur Thomas Prizes;

(*c*) Henry Arthur Thomas Travel Exhibitions.

Unexpended income. **6.** Any unexpended income accumulated in the Fund shall be applied from time to time at the discretion of the Faculty Board of Classics and subject to such conditions as they may think fit for

(*a*) the provision of Travel Exhibitions in accordance with the provisions of Regulations 15–19 of these regulations;

(*b*) the advancement of classical learning by any other means.

Henry Arthur Thomas Studentship

Purpose. **7.** There shall be a Henry Arthur Thomas Studentship, which shall be for the furtherance of research in the archaeology, art, history, language, law, literature, and philosophy of ancient Greece and Rome, and the comparative philology of the Indo-European languages.

8. The holder of the Studentship shall undertake advanced study or research in one or more of the subjects specified in Regulation 7, according to a scheme to be approved by the Faculty Board of Classics.

Who are eligible. **9.** Candidature for the Studentship shall be open to any person who is or is about to be registered as a Graduate Student in the Faculty of Classics in the University. Election to and tenure of the Studentship shall lapse if the person elected does not become or ceases to be a registered Graduate Student.

Electors. **10.** The Electors to the Studentship shall be the Faculty Board of Classics, who may take such steps as they think fit to inquire into the qualifications of the candidates; provided that the Studentship shall not be awarded on the result of a competitive examination.

Applications. **11.** Before the division of the Easter Term each year, the Board shall give notice of the date by which and the manner in which applications for the Studentship to be held in the next but one following

[1] Regulations 5–24 are subject to variation by Grace.

academical year are to be submitted. An election to the Studentship shall be held during the academical year prior to the Studentship's being taken up, on a date to be determined by the Board.

12. The Studentship shall be tenable from the date on which the student comes into residence until 30 September of the calendar year next following. A Student shall be eligible for re-election on not more than two occasions. Tenure.

13. The emolument of the Studentship shall be such sum, not exceeding the available income of the Fund, as shall be determined by the Faculty Board within a range approved from time to time by the Council. The emolument shall be paid in such instalments as the Board shall from time to time determine, provided that the Board may withhold payment of any instalment if they are not satisfied that the Student is pursuing his or her course of study with sufficient diligence. Emolument

Henry Arthur Thomas Prizes

14. The Examiners for Part IB of the Classical Tripos shall be empowered at their discretion to award to winners of University Classical Scholarships and other candidates Henry Arthur Thomas Prizes of books, which shall be charged on the income of the Henry Arthur Thomas Fund. These Prizes shall be of such value as shall be determined by the Faculty Board of Classics within a range approved from time to time by the Council.

Henry Arthur Thomas Travel Exhibitions

15. Henry Arthur Thomas Travel Exhibitions shall be awarded each year to enable students to travel in Greece and Italy and other lands bordering on the Mediterranean. Purpose.

16. Three Awarders shall be appointed annually in the Lent Term by the Faculty Board of Classics. Awarders.

17. The Faculty Board shall inform the Awarders of the total sum that has been made available in accordance with Regulation 5(*c*) for the award of Travel Exhibitions. The number and the value of the awards shall be determined each year by the Awarders. Number and value of awards.

18. A student shall be eligible for a Travel Exhibition if his or her performance in any of the following examinations is, in the opinion of the Awarders, of sufficient merit: Who are eligible.

(i) the Preliminary Examination for Part II of the Classical Tripos;

(ii) Part IA or Part IB or Part II of the Classical Tripos;

(iii) the examination in classical Greek or in classical Latin either in Part IA or in Part IB of the Modern and Medieval Languages Tripos;

provided that

(*a*) the student has not previously been awarded a Henry Arthur Thomas Travel Exhibition,

and (*b*) not more than twelve complete terms have passed after his or her first term of residence.

19. As soon as convenient after the publication of the class-lists for the examinations specified in Regulation 18 and in any case not later than 30 June, the Awarders shall forward to the Registrary the names of those students to whom Exhibitions have been awarded and the value of the awards. The names shall be published forthwith in the *Reporter*. Awards.

20. Travel shall normally take place not later than the Long Vacation in the year following the year of the award, but the Faculty Board of Classics may, on the application of the Exhibitioner's Tutor, allow it to take place at a later date.

Henry Arthur Thomas Research Facilitation Fund

21. The sums available to the Faculty Board of Classics on 1 January 2005 from the unexpended income accumulated in the Henry Arthur Thomas, Battie, Browne, Craven, Davies, Oldham, Porson, Waddington, and Winter Warr Funds, shall be invested separately in the name of the Chancellor, Masters, and Scholars of the University and shall be called the Henry Arthur Thomas Research Facilitation Fund. Name.

22. The Managers of the Fund shall be the Faculty Board of Classics who may delegate all or any of their functions concerning the Fund to a committee consisting of not less than three members appointed by the Board. Managers.

23. The income of the Fund shall be applied at the discretion of the Faculty Board to support the research activities of registered Graduate Students and University officers in the Faculty. Purpose.

Unexpended income.

24. Any unexpended income of the Fund in a financial year may be either added to the capital of the Fund or accumulated for use as income in future years, as the Managers may determine.

Sir J. J. Thomson Fund

Name and purpose.

The sum of £1,000 bequeathed to the University for the benefit of the Cavendish Laboratory by Sir Joseph John Thomson, formerly Cavendish Professor and Master of Trinity College, shall be separately invested and shall constitute a fund called the Sir J. J. Thomson Fund, the income of which shall be put at the disposal of the Cavendish Professor to use as he or she thinks fit in accordance with the terms of the bequest.

Tiarks German Scholarship Fund

Name of Fund.

1. The amount of the benefaction of Mr Henry F. Tiarks for the endowment of one or more Scholarships for the encouragement of the study of German in the University, together with any additional funds which may be available, shall form a fund to be called the Tiarks German Scholarship Fund.

Electors.

2. The administration of the Fund shall be entrusted to a Board of Electors. The Electors shall be the Head of the Department of German and Dutch, and three persons appointed by the Faculty Board of Modern and Medieval Languages in the Michaelmas Term to serve for three years from 1 January following their appointment. All the powers of the Electors may be exercised by a majority of those present at a meeting duly summoned, provided that three Electors at least be present. No Elector shall have more than one vote, except that the Elector in the chair shall have a casting vote.

Awards.

3. The income of the Fund shall be used to provide the following awards, the holders of which shall undertake advanced study or research in German language or literature, under the direction of the Head of the Department of German and Dutch, according to a scheme to be approved by the Electors:

(*a*) one or more Scholarships called Tiarks German Scholarships;

(*b*) one or more Bursaries called Tiarks Bursaries.

Eligibility.

4. Tiarks German Scholarships and Tiarks Bursaries shall be open to any person who is, or is about to be, registered as a Graduate Student in the University.

Election.

5. Before the division of the Easter Term each year the Electors shall give notice of the date by which and the manner in which applications for awards are to be submitted. An election shall be held not earlier than the Monday following the last day of General Admission to Degrees. The Electors may take such steps as they think fit to enquire into the qualifications of candidates, provided that the awards shall not be made on the results of a competitive examination.

Tenure.

6. Tiarks German Scholarships and Tiarks Bursaries shall be tenable for one year, normally from 1 October following the election. A Tiarks German Scholar shall spend some considerable portion, to be determined by the Electors, of the year in Germany or some other German-speaking country, provided that the Electors may at their discretion relax this condition. A Tiarks German Scholar shall be eligible for re-election on not more than two occasions; a Tiarks Bursar shall be eligible for re-election on not more than one occasion.

Stipend.

7. The stipend of a Tiarks German Scholarship or a Tiarks Bursary shall be such sum within a range approved from time to time by the Council as shall be determined by the Electors in each case after taking account of any other financial resources that may be available to the holder; provided that the maximum value of a Scholarship shall be greater than the maximum value of a Bursary. The stipend shall be paid in two half-yearly instalments in advance, provided that the Electors may withhold the second instalment if they are not satisfied that a Scholar or Bursar has been pursuing his or her studies with sufficient diligence.

Unexpended income.

8. Any income accumulated in the Fund may be applied at the discretion of the Electors

(*a*) for the award of grants to Tiarks Scholars and Bursars;

(*b*) for the award of grants to other persons engaged in study or research in German language or literature in the University, provided that they are not candidates for the B.A. Degree;

(*c*) for the encouragement of the study of German in the University by any other means.

Regulations may be changed.

9. These regulations shall be subject to alteration by Grace, provided that the first charge on the income of the Fund shall always be the maintenance of one or more Scholarships for the encouragement of the study of German in the University, to be called the Tiarks German Scholarships.

Tiarks Prize

1. The sum made available each year by the Electors for the Tiarks German Scholarship Fund shall be used to provide a prize to be called the Tiarks Prize. Prize.

2. The Prize shall be awarded by the Examiners in German for Part IA of the Modern and Medieval Languages Tripos, for a distinguished performance in German in that examination, to a candidate who was studying German *ab initio*. How awarded.

J. B. TREND FUND

Amended by Grace 8 of 30 July 2014

1. The moneys subscribed in response to an appeal for contributions to a fund to commemorate the late Professor J. B. Trend, Litt.D., of Christ's College, Professor of Spanish, shall form a fund called the J. B. Trend Fund the income of which shall be used to provide grants to enable undergraduates and registered Graduate Students of the University of Cambridge to visit Spanish and Portuguese speaking countries in order to study the language, literature, history, or music, of the countries of their choice. Name and purpose.

2. The Fund shall be administered by the Electors to the Gibson Spanish Scholarship. Managers.

3. Any candidate for the B.A. Degree and any registered Graduate Student shall be eligible to receive a grant from the Fund provided that he or she intends to make use of the grant before completing the examination requirements for the B.A. Degree or before submitting a dissertation, as the case may be. Eligibility.

4. An application for a grant accompanied by a short description of the proposed travel must be submitted through the candidate's Director of Studies or Supervisor in the case of a Graduate Student to such person as may be designated by the Electors to receive applications so as to arrive not later than a date in Full Easter Term of which notice has been given by the Electors in the previous Michaelmas Term. Applications.

5. Grants shall be awarded not later than the last day of the Easter Term. Awards.

GEORGE MACAULAY TREVELYAN FUND AND LECTURESHIP

1. The income of the George Macaulay Trevelyan Fund shall be applied to meet the cost of lectures on historical subjects. Fund and purpose.

2. The first charge on the income of the Fund shall be the provision of a biennial course of lectures to be called the George Macaulay Trevelyan Lectures. G. M. Trevelyan Lectures.

3. A George Macaulay Trevelyan Lecturer shall be appointed in the Michaelmas Term of each year the number of which is even. It shall be the duty of the Lecturer to deliver in English a course of not less than six nor more than eight lectures in Full Term during the academical year next but one following that in which the appointment is made.

4. The Electors to the George Macaulay Trevelyan Lectureship shall be the Regius Professor of History, the Chair of the Faculty Board of History, and three other persons appointed by the Faculty Board of History in the Lent Term of each year the number of which is even to serve for two years from 1 April following their appointment. Electors.

5. The stipend to be offered to each George Macaulay Trevelyan Lecturer shall be such sum not exceeding the estimated income of the Fund for two years as may be determined by the Faculty Board of History on the recommendation of the Electors. Stipend.

6. Unexpended income in the Fund, after provision has been made for the stipend of the George Macaulay Trevelyan Lecturer, may be applied by the Faculty Board of History, on the recommendation of the Electors, for any of the following purposes: Unexpended income.

(*a*) to provide one or more additional lectures, to be called Trevelyan Lectures, on historical subjects, and to pay a stipend to the lecturer or lecturers;

(*b*) to pay the expenses of the George Macaulay Trevelyan Lecturer, or of any lecturer who delivers a Trevelyan Lecture;

(*c*) to meet any other expenses incurred in connection with the George Macaulay Trevelyan Lectures or a Trevelyan Lecture;

(*d*) to assist with the cost of publishing the George Macaulay Trevelyan Lectures or a Trevelyan Lecture.

Trophoblast Research Fund

Grace 3 of 31 October 2007

Fund and purpose.

1. The sum of £5m received by the University from the Board of Cambridge in America shall form a fund to be known as the Trophoblast Research Fund, which shall be used to perpetuate the study of placental biology, with special reference to the trophoblast.

Centre for Trophoblast Research.

2. The Fund, together with any further donations received for the same purpose, shall form an endowment to support a Centre for Trophoblast Research within the School of Biological Sciences. In each financial year for a five-year period covering the financial years 2007–08 to 2011–12, the income of the Fund, and up to 5% of the capital of the Fund at the start of the financial year, shall be available to support the activities of the Centre. Any unexpended income of the Fund in any financial year may be accumulated and expended in any one or more subsequent years. After the financial year 2011–12, only the income of the Fund, including accumulated income, shall be available to support the Centre.

Unexpended income.

3. The goals of the Centre shall be:

(i) to promote research and teaching in placental biology within the University and affiliated institutes through Next Generation Research Fellowships, Studentships, seminars, workshops, and infrastructural support;

(ii) to co-operate with outside bodies in the promotion of research and teaching in placental biology internationally through Visiting Scholarships, travel awards, and research meetings;

(iii) to foster research into placental biology by any other means.

Board of Managers.

4. The administration of the Fund shall be under the control of a Board of Managers consisting of:

(*a*) the Head of the Department of Physiology, Development, and Neuroscience;

(*b*) four persons working in relevant scientific disciplines, of whom at least three shall be members of the Regent House, appointed by the Council of the School of the Biological Sciences.

5. Members in class (*b*) shall be appointed in the Michaelmas Term to serve from 1 January following their appointment for two or four years as the Council of the School of the Biological Sciences shall determine at their appointment.

Director of the Centre.

6. The Board of Managers shall elect one of their members, being a member of the Regent House, to serve as Director of the Centre, subject to the approval of the General Board. He or she shall hold office for four years, and shall be eligible for reappointment for a further term of four years.

7. The Director shall be the administrative head of the Centre, and shall be advised by the Scientific Advisory Board and the Board of Managers.

8. The Board shall normally meet twice each academical year.

Scientific Advisory Board

Members of the Advisory Board.

1. The Centre shall have an international Scientific Advisory Board, which shall consist of no fewer than four highly distinguished persons in relevant scientific disciplines appointed by the Council of the School of the Biological Sciences on the recommendation of the Board of Managers.

2. Members of the Advisory Board shall be appointed in the Michaelmas Term to serve for four years from 1 January following their appointment.

3. The Council of the School of the Biological Sciences, in making their appointments to the Advisory Board, shall ensure that not more than one of its members is a resident member of the University.

Chair.

4. The Chair of the Advisory Board shall be appointed by the Council of the School of the Biological Sciences for a period of not more than three years and shall be eligible for reappointment for a period or periods of not more than three years at a time.

Secretary.

5. The Director of the Centre shall serve as Secretary of the Advisory Board.

6. The Advisory Board shall meet at least once every two years.

Advisory Board duty.

7. The duty of the Advisory Board shall be to advise the Director of the Centre on all aspects of the scientific programme, policy, and future directions of the Centre.

Visiting Scholars

1. In order to enable scholars from outside Cambridge to take part in and contribute to the work of the Centre there shall be Visiting Scholarships for persons who are pursuing advanced work in placental biology.

2. Appointments of Visiting Scholars shall be made by the Director of the Centre in consultation with at least two of the Managers. Appointments.

3. Visiting Scholars shall be required under the general supervision of the Director to take part in the teaching and research programme of the Centre. Requirements.

4. The Director may make grants to Visiting Scholars to meet travelling or other expenses incurred in connection with their appointment. Grants.

Next Generation Fellowships

1. In order to enable innovative research to be pursued, at all levels in the Centre, a number of Next Generation Fellowships may be awarded.

2. The Managers shall decide upon the number of Next Generation Fellows to be funded each year. The Director of the Centre shall be responsible for awarding the Fellowships, in consultation with the Managers. Number of Fellows.

3. A Fellowship shall be tenable for one or more years at a time, and may be renewed by the Managers for up to a total of five years. Tenure.

4. The value of each Fellowship shall be determined by the Managers, taking into account other sources of research funding available to the Fellow. Value.

Studentships

1. The Electors to a Studentship shall be the Managers. Electors.

2. In order to be eligible for a Studentship, a candidate must have been admitted, or be seeking admission, as a student studying towards the Ph.D. Degree in reproductive biology within the School of Biological Sciences. Eligibility for Studentship.

3. The Studentship shall provide Provisions of the Studentship.

(*a*) a maintenance payment, in line with that provided to postgraduate students by the Wellcome Trust and determined from time to time by the Managers, for a period of up to no more than four years,

(*b*) a payment to meet the Student's University and College fees,

(*c*) a contribution to other costs such as equipment, consumables, travel expenses, and other costs according to the discretion of the Managers to be in accordance with the prevailing norms offered by the relevant Research Councils.

NIGEL TROWER FUND

1. The sum of £5,000 given to the University by Mr and Mrs David Trower in memory of their son Nigel David Trower, M.A., Vet.M.B., MRCVS, of Pembroke College, together with other sums subscribed for the purpose, shall form a fund called the Nigel Trower Fund. Fund.

2. The Managers of the Fund shall be the Head of the Department of Veterinary Medicine and three persons appointed by the Faculty Board of Veterinary Medicine. Managers.

3. No resolution of the Managers shall be valid unless passed by a majority of the Managers present at a meeting to which all the Managers have been summoned. Quorum.

4. The income of the Fund shall be used to provide an award called the Nigel Trower Award, to enable a Resident on the staff of the Clinical Studies Division of the Veterinary School to undertake a course of professional training outside the University. Purpose.

5. In the Michaelmas Term each year the Managers shall publish a Notice giving the date by which, and the manner in which, applications are to be submitted. Notice.

6. The value of the award shall be such sum, not exceeding the available income of the Fund, as may be determined by the Managers in each individual case. Value.

7. The Managers shall advise Mr and Mrs Trower of the award made each year.

8. On completion of the course of training, the award-winner shall submit to the Managers and to Mr and Mrs Trower a brief report on the training undertaken.

Unexpended income. **9.** Any unexpended income of the Fund may be either added to the capital of the Fund or accumulated for use as income in subsequent years, as the Managers shall determine.

Tudor Studentships in Financial Econometrics

Title and purpose. **1.** The sum of £120,000 given to the University by the Tudor Investment Corporation shall form a fund, which shall be used to provide awards known as Tudor Studentships in Financial Econometrics in the Faculty of Economics.

Managers. **2.** The Managers of the Fund shall be the Chair and the Secretary of the Degree Committee for the Faculty of Economics, and one person appointed by the Faculty Board of Economics in the Michaelmas Term to serve for three years from 1 January following the appointment.

Studentships. **3.** The income of the Fund shall be used to provide awards known as Tudor Studentships in Financial Econometrics in the Faculty of Economics, which shall be open to any person who is or is about to be registered as a Graduate Student in the University. Holders of the awards shall undertake advanced study or research in the Faculty of Economics.

Tenure. **4.** An award shall be tenable for one year in the first instance, and may be renewed by the Managers for a second or third year.

5. The emolument paid to an award holder shall be determined by the Managers within a range approved from time to time by the Council.

Unexpended income. **6.** Any unexpended income may be either added to the capital of the Fund or accumulated for use as income in subsequent years, as the Managers may determine.

H. A. Turner Prize

Prize. **1.** The sum of £3,000 bequeathed to the University by the late Professor H. A. Turner shall form a fund called the Turner Fund, for the purpose of providing an annual prize in Economics, which shall be called the H. A. Turner Prize in Labour Studies.

How awarded. **2.** The Prize shall be awarded each year by the Examiners for Part IIA of the Economics Tripos to the candidate who achieves the best mark in Paper 7 (Labour) in that examination.

Value. **3.** The value of the Prize shall be such sum as shall be determined by the Faculty Board of Economics within a range approved from time to time by the Council.

Unexpended income. **4.** After provision has been made, in accordance with the foregoing regulations, for the award of the Prize, the balance of the annual income shall be added to the capital of the Fund.

Turner and Newall Fellowships

Name and purpose. **1.** The gifts from Turner and Newall Limited to the University shall form a fund called the Turner and Newall Fund which shall be used for the purpose of providing the stipends and pension contributions of Turner and Newall Fellows, such expenses incurred by Fellows as may be approved by the General Board, and expenses connected with the administration of the Fund.

Administration. **2.** The Fund shall be administered and the Fellows elected by the General Board.

Notice of election. **3.** The General Board shall give not less than three months' notice of their intention to proceed to an election.

Qualifications. **4.** The General Board may elect to a Fellowship a person whose qualifications they consider suitable, whether a member of the University or not, and they may take such steps as they think fit to ascertain those qualifications. A Fellow who on election is not a member of the University shall be required to obtain admission as a member of the University.

Value. **5.** The annual stipend of a Fellow shall be determined by the General Board with the approval of the Council.

Tenure. **6.** The tenure of a Turner and Newall Fellowship shall be determined by the General Board, but no tenure shall exceed five years in all.

Duties of Fellows. **7.** Turner and Newall Fellows shall engage in original research in Engineering, Chemical Engineering, Inorganic Chemistry, Physical Chemistry, Metallurgy, or Physics (or in any allied science which the University may suggest and which Turner and Newall Limited may agree has some direct relation to the manufacturing interest of Turner and Newall Limited). The subject of each Fellow's research shall be approved by the General Board. The research work shall be carried out in Cambridge, or elsewhere with the General Board's consent, and shall be subject to such conditions as the General Board may impose.

8. As part of their duties Fellows shall engage in University teaching, the amount of such teaching being determined in each case by the General Board on the recommendation of the Head of the Department in which the Fellow is working. Any teaching undertaken for a College or Colleges shall require the approval of the General Board.

9. The General Board may make the payment of the stipend of a Fellowship, or of an instalment of the stipend, conditional on their approval of a report from the Fellow on the progress of his or her research. Conditions.

10. A Turner and Newall Fellowship shall not be held together with a stipendiary Fellowship of a College, or with any University Studentship or Scholarship, or with any University office. Restrictions.

11. A Fellow who has been awarded any other emolument for research or who proposes to undertake any work other than work approved by the General Board in accordance with Regulations 7 and 8 shall so inform the General Board. On receiving such information the General Board shall consider whether a reduction should be made in the amount of the Fellow's stipend.

TYRWHITT'S HEBREW SCHOLARSHIPS

Endowments, 1904, p. 309

1. There shall be four scholarships called Tyrwhitt's Hebrew Scholarships. Name.

2. The Scholarships shall be open to any member of the University provided that at the time of the examination not more than nineteen complete terms have passed after his or her first term of residence. Who are eligible.

3. The Electors to these Scholarships shall be the Regius Professor of Hebrew and two persons nominated by the Head of the Department of Middle Eastern Studies in consultation with and with the agreement of the teaching officers in Hebrew in the Department, and appointed by the General Board in each year before the division of the Lent Term; and these Electors shall conduct the examination. Electors.

4. The examination for these Scholarships shall commence in each year on the second Tuesday in May; and persons intending to be candidates shall send in their names to the Registrary on or before 25 January. Examination.

5. The Scholarships shall be tenable for two years from the time of the election. If candidates of sufficient merit present themselves two Scholars shall be elected in each year. The annual stipend of the Scholars shall be determined by the Electors within a range approved from time to time by the Council, provided that the candidate first in order of merit shall receive a higher stipend than the candidate second in order of merit. In case of equality of merit the stipend of the two Scholars shall be equal, and shall be determined in the same way. Should it appear to the majority of the Electors that none of the candidates deserves a Scholarship within the range determined by the Council, they may elect one Scholar, with a stipend lower than the minimum of the range. Two Scholars. Value of Scholarship.

6. No one who has been elected to a Scholarship shall be allowed to compete again. One tenure only.

7. The Electors shall also have power in each year to award out of the surplus of the benefaction, provided that this will allow of their so doing, a single gratuity to a candidate who, although not elected to a Scholarship, shall have performed with credit in the examination. The value of the gratuity shall be determined by the Electors, but it shall be less than the minimum of the range approved by the Council in accordance with Regulation 5. Benefaction.

8. Each Elector appointed by the General Board shall, if required to set papers for the examination, receive such fee as shall be determined by the Faculty Board of Asian and Middle Eastern Studies within a range approved from time to time by the Council. Payments to Electors.

9. Any unexpended income accumulated in the Fund may be expended at the discretion of the Head of the Department of Middle Eastern Studies, in consultation with and with the agreement of the teaching officers in Hebrew in the Department, in the promotion and encouragement of Hebrew studies. Unexpended income.

Aramaic.

10. Notwithstanding the name of these Scholarships, it shall be competent for the Electors to set simple passages for translation from Aramaic into English, together with questions arising out of the same.

Stat. E IV.

Tyson Fund

Endowments, 1904, p. 427

Medal and prize.

1. The Tyson Fund shall be applied to the annual award of a medal to be called the Tyson Medal and to be accompanied by a prize in money, consisting of the balance of the net annual income of the fund for the year.

For proficiency in Part III of the Mathematical Tripos.

2. The Medal shall be of bronze, and shall be awarded annually to that candidate for Part III of the Mathematical Tripos who has in the judgement of the Examiners shown the greatest distinction in Astronomy in that examination, provided that his or her work in this subject be of sufficient merit.

3. It shall be in the power of the Examiners, if they think fit, to award two or more Medals and to divide the Prize between two or more candidates.

If not awarded.

4. If in any year the Medal shall not be awarded, the income for that year shall be added to the capital of the Fund.

UAC of Nigeria Travel Fund

Fund.

1. The sum given to the University by UAC of Nigeria plc shall form a fund called the UAC of Nigeria Travel Fund.

Administration.

2. The Fund shall be administered by the Committee of Management of the Centre of African Studies, who may delegate any of their functions under these regulations to a sub-committee not necessarily composed wholly of members of the Committee.

Grants.

3. The income of the Fund shall be applied to provide grants to enable Graduate Students to visit African countries, especially Nigeria, for the purpose of study or research, or for other purposes approved by the Committee of Management.

Unexpended income.

4. Any unexpended income shall be added to the capital of the Fund.

Ukrainian Studies Endowment Fund

Grace 2 of 3 November 2010; amended by Grace 2 of 23 October 2013

Title and purpose.

1. The income of the Ukrainian Studies Endowment Fund shall be applied for the benefit of teaching and research in the field of Ukrainian Studies.

Managers.

2. The Managers of the Fund shall be the Chair of the Faculty Board of Modern and Medieval Languages, the Head of the Department of Slavonic Studies, and one other person appointed by the Faculty Board of Modern and Medieval Languages in the Michaelmas Term to serve for five years from 1 January following her or his appointment provided that, if the Chair of the Faculty Board of Modern and Medieval Languages is an officer in the Department of Slavonic Studies, the Faculty Board shall instead appoint one additional Manager who is not in that Department. The Managers may co-opt up to two more Managers as required. Co-opted Managers shall serve until 31 December of the year following that in which they are co-opted.

University Lectureships.

3. The first charge on the income of the Fund shall be the stipend, national insurance, pension contributions, and associated indirect costs of a University Lectureship in Ukrainian Studies and a University Lectureship in pre-Modern East Slav Culture, payable by the University; the second charge shall be the stipend, national insurance, pension contributions, and associated indirect costs of a language-teaching post in Ukrainian payable by the University; and the third charge shall be the support of teaching and research in, and public understanding of, the history, languages, and cultures of Ukraine, at the discretion of the Managers.

4. After provision has been made in accordance with Regulation 3, the income of the Fund shall be applied to support related activities in the Department of Slavonic Studies, at the discretion of the Managers.

Unexpended income.

5. Any unexpended income of the Fund in a financial year shall be either added to the capital of the Fund or retained for use as income in future years, as the Managers may determine.

UKRAINIAN STUDIES FUND

Grace 3 of 9 January 2008

1. The capital and income of the Ukrainian Studies Fund shall be applied for the benefit of teaching and research in the field of Ukrainian Studies as shall be determined by the Managers of the Fund. Fund and purpose.

2. The Managers of the Fund shall be the Chair of the Faculty Board of Modern and Medieval Languages, the Head of the Department of Slavonic Studies, and one other person appointed by the Faculty Board of Modern and Medieval Languages in the Michaelmas Term to serve for five years from 1 January following his or her appointment provided that, if the Chair of the Faculty Board of Modern and Medieval Languages is an officer in the Department of Slavonic Studies, the Faculty Board shall instead appoint one additional Manager who is not in that Department. The Managers may co-opt up to two more Managers as required. Co-opted Managers shall serve until 31 December of the year following that in which they are co-opted. Managers.

EDWARD ULLENDORFF SEMITIC PHILOLOGY LECTURE FUND

Grace 1 of 11 July 2012

1. The benefaction received from Mrs Dina Ullendorff, in memory of Professor Edward Ullendorff, shall form a Fund called the Edward Ullendorff Semitic Philology Lecture Fund. The income from the Fund shall be used to provide an annual lecture called the Edward Ullendorff Semitic Philology Lecture. Fund and purpose.

2. The Fund shall be administered by a Board of Managers who shall be the Regius Professor of Hebrew and two other persons from among the teaching officers in the Department of Middle Eastern Studies appointed by the Head of the Department of Middle Eastern Studies. Managers.

3. If the Regius Professorship of Hebrew is vacant, the Head of the Department of Middle Eastern Studies shall appoint an additional Manager to ensure that there are always three Managers.

4. The appointment of the Edward Ullendorff Lecturer shall be made annually by the Managers. The Edward Ullendorff Lecture will be delivered once per year during term. Lecturer.

5. Any unexpended income may either be added to the capital of the Fund or accumulated for use as income in future years or be applied for the benefit of study in the Department of Middle Eastern Studies in the field of Semitic Philology as the Managers may determine. Unexpended income.

UNILEVER PRIZE FOR PHYSICAL CHEMISTRY

1. The sum given to the Department of Chemistry by Unilever plc shall form a fund the income of which shall be used to provide an annual prize called the Unilever Prize for Physical Chemistry. Prize.

2. The Prize shall be awarded by the Head of the Department of Chemistry on the recommendation of the Professor of Physical Chemistry to a candidate who offers Chemistry in Part III of the Natural Sciences Tripos, for distinction in practical work in Physical Chemistry. How awarded.

3. The value of the Prize shall be the annual income of the Fund. Value.

4. If in any year the Prize is not awarded, the unexpended income for that year shall be added to the capital of the Fund. Unexpended income.

VAN GEEST FOUNDATION FUND

1. The sum of £4,160,000 received from the John and Lucille van Geest Foundation for the endowment of a University Lectureship to be entitled the John van Geest Lectureship and a Gussy Marlowe Clinician Ph.D. Fellowship, both in Brain Repair, in the Department of Clinical Neurosciences, shall form a fund called the Van Geest Foundation Fund. Fund and purpose.

2. The Managers of the Fund shall be the Chair of the John van Geest Centre for Brain Repair, the Head of the Department of Clinical Neurosciences, and a representative nominated by the Faculty Board of Clinical Medicine. The Managers may co-opt up to two more Managers as required. Co-opted Managers shall be appointed in the Michaelmas Term to serve for four years from 1 January following their appointment. Managers.

3. If and whenever the income of the Fund exceeds the amount required for the payment of the stipend, national insurance, pension contributions, and associated indirect costs of the John van Geest Application of surplus income.

Lectureship and the provision of the Gussy Marlowe Clinician Ph.D. Fellowship, the surplus shall be applied to support:

(i) the work of the Lecturer;

(ii) the work of the Fellow; and/or

(iii) research in the Department of Clinical Neurosciences

in such a manner as may be approved by the General Board of the Faculties on the recommendation of the Managers.

Appointments. **4.** (*a*) The Lecturer shall be appointed by the Appointments Committee for the Faculty of Clinical Medicine in the manner prescribed by Special Ordinance C (x) 1.

(*b*) The Fellow shall be selected on the recommendation of the Graduate Committee of the Department of Clinical Neurosciences, and approved by the Managers. The Fellowship may be awarded to non-clinicians and to candidates who already have a higher degree with the approval of the Managers.

Unexpended income. **5.** Any unexpended income of the Fund in a financial year may, in any one or more subsequent years, be expended in accordance with Regulation 3 or added to the capital of the Fund.

Van Geest Foundation Fund for Brain Repair and Neuroscience

Grace 1 of 3 August 2011

Fund and title. **1.** The £500,000 benefaction received from the John and Lucille van Geest Foundation, shall form a fund to be entitled the Van Geest Foundation Fund for Brain Repair and Neuroscience, the income of which shall be used to support teaching and research in the School of Clinical Medicine, with a preference for brain repair and neuroscience; the Fund shall include any future benefactions received from the John and Lucille van Geest Foundation by way of additions thereto.

Managers. **2.** The Managers of the Fund shall be the Head of the School of Clinical Medicine, the Head of the Department of Clinical Neurosciences, and one other Manager appointed by the Council of the School of Clinical Medicine for periods of five years.

Purposes. **3.** The income of the Fund shall be applied for the following purposes in the School of Clinical Medicine, with a preference for the fields of brain repair and neuroscience:

(*a*) research purposes (including the funding of equipment and other capital items) in the School;

(*b*) the funding of graduate studentships in the School;

(*c*) the payment of the stipend, national insurance, pension contributions, and associated indirect costs of the holders of such named posts in the School as may be designated or established from time to time by the University or the General Board as a charge on the Fund.

4. In exceptional circumstances the capital of the Fund may also be spent, on the recommendation of the Managers and with the approval of the General Board, for the purposes outlined in Regulation 3 or to provide additional or new laboratory space needed for the furtherance of such purposes.

Unexpended income. **5.** Any unexpended income of the Fund in a financial year may be added to the capital of the Fund; or retained for use as income in future years, as the Managers shall determine.

Ver Heyden de Lancey Fund

Fund. **1.** The sum accumulated from the donations of the de Lancey and de la Hanty Foundation shall form a fund called the Ver Heyden de Lancey Fund, for the promotion of medico-legal studies in the University.

Managers. **2.** The Managers of the Fund shall be three persons appointed in the Michaelmas Term to serve for two years from 1 January following their appointment, as follows: one appointed by the General Board, who shall be Chair, one by the Faculty Board of Clinical Medicine, and one by the Faculty Board of Law.

Purpose. **3.** The income of the Fund may be used, at the discretion of the Managers, to promote medico-legal studies in the University by providing lectures on medico-legal subjects (to be known as Baron de Lancey Lectures), or to purchase books and journals for the University on such subjects.

Unexpended income. **4.** Any unexpended income accumulated in the Fund shall be available for use by the Managers for the purposes specified in Regulation 3.

George and Marie Vergottis Fund

1. The sums bequeathed to the University by Mrs Marie Vergottis shall form a fund to be known as the George and Marie Vergottis Fund. Title.

2. The income of the fund shall be applied to provide one or more scholarships to be called George and Marie Vergottis Scholarships for persons of Greek citizenship in order that they may follow courses leading to a degree or other qualification of the University. Purpose and eligibility.

3. A Scholar who is not already a member of the University shall become such by being matriculated before the end of the term next after her or his election to the Scholarship, provided that for good cause the Managers may allow a Scholar to defer matriculation until a later date.

4. The Fund shall be administered by four Managers who shall be: Managers.

(*a*) the Vice-Chancellor or a duly appointed deputy, as Chair;

(*b*) three persons appointed by the Council.

Managers in class (*b*) shall serve for three years from 1 October following their appointment.

5. The Managers shall give at least six months' notice of their intention to award a Scholarship.

6. A Scholarship shall be tenable for one, two, three, or four years, as the Managers shall in each case determine; a Scholarship may, at the discretion of the Managers, be extended by one or two or three years, provided that the total tenure of the Scholarship shall not exceed four years. Tenure.

7. The value of each Scholarship shall be determined by the Managers, within a range approved from time to time by the Council, after taking account of the Scholar's financial circumstances. Value.

8. Any unexpended income accumulated in the Fund may be either accumulated for use as income in subsequent years, or used at the discretion of the Managers to assist a Scholar to meet travelling expenses or any other special expenses in connection with his or her course of study or research, as the Managers may determine. Unexpended income.

3 Verulam Buildings Prizes

1. The sum made available annually by 3 Verulam Buildings shall be used to provide two prizes called 3 Verulam Buildings Prizes. Title.

2. The Prizes shall be awarded by the Examiners for Part II of the Law Tripos and by the Examiners for the LL.M., as follows: How awarded.

(*a*) one Prize shall be awarded to the candidate who has shown the greatest distinction in the subject Equity;

(*b*) one Prize shall be awarded to the candidate who has shown the greatest distinction in the subject International Commercial Litigation.

3. The value of each Prize shall be one-half of the sum made available in each year by 3 Verulam Buildings. Value.

Vice-Chancellor's Endowment Fund

Grace 4 of 23 April 2008

1. The sum of £5m received from an anonymous donor for the benefit of the University in general shall form a fund called the Vice-Chancellor's Endowment Fund. The Fund may include other sums received from other bodies or persons for the same purpose. Fund.

2. The Managers of the Fund shall be the Vice-Chancellor, the Pro-Vice-Chancellor for Planning and Resources, a member of the Council in class (*e*) appointed by the Council, and the Registrary. Managers.

3. The income of the Fund shall be available for the benefit of the University in fulfilment of its mission to contribute to society through the pursuit of education, learning, and research at the highest international levels of excellence. Purpose.

4. Any unexpended income in a financial year may in any one or more subsequent years be expended in accordance with Regulation 3 or added to the permanent capital as the Managers shall determine. Unexpended income.

Wace Medal

The Wace Medal, which was established as a memorial to the late A. J. B. Wace, Laurence Professor of Classical Archaeology from 1934 to 1944, shall be awarded each year by the Examiners for Part II of the Classical Tripos for a distinguished performance in Classical Archaeology in that examination.

In any year in which no award is made by the Examiners for Part II of the Classical Tripos, the Degree Committee for the Faculty of Classics may award the Medal, after taking account of the reports of the Examiners on the performance of candidates in the examination in Classics for the M.Phil. Degree (one-year course), to the candidate who in that examination has submitted the best thesis on a subject which in the judgement of the Degree Committee is to be regarded as a subject in Classical Archaeology. No person shall be awarded the Medal more than once.

E. C. S. Wade Prizes

Fund. **1.** The sums given to the University by J. W. N. Petty, M.A., LL.M., of Gonville and Caius and Wolfson Colleges, shall form a fund called the E. C. S. Wade Prizes Fund, in memory of the late Emlyn Capel Stewart Wade, LL.D., Fellow of Gonville and Caius College, formerly Downing Professor of the Laws of England.

Prizes. **2.** The income of the Fund shall be used to provide two prizes, called the E. C. S. Wade Prize in Constitutional Law and the E. C. S. Wade Prize in Administrative Law. The Prize in Constitutional Law shall be awarded for distinguished proficiency in that subject shown by a candidate for Part IA or Part IB of the Law Tripos. The Prize in Administrative Law shall be awarded for distinguished proficiency in that subject shown by a candidate for Part IB or Part II of the Law Tripos.

Value. **3.** The value of each Prize shall be half the annual income of the Fund.

Unexpended income. **4.** If in any year either Prize is not awarded, the unexpended income shall be added to the capital of the Fund.

Sir William Wade Prize for Civil Liberties and Human Rights

Grace 4 of 7 March 2012

1. The sum of £20,000 bequeathed by Mr Joseph Petty shall form a fund called The Sir William Wade Fund in memory of Professor Sir William Wade.

2. The income of the Fund shall be used to provide a prize called The Sir William Wade Prize to be awarded annually by the Examiners for the LL.M. Examination to the candidate who has shown the greatest distinction in Civil Liberties and Human Rights in that subject in the LL.M. Examination provided a candidate of sufficient merit presents his or her self.

3. The value of the prize, provided there is a candidate of sufficient merit, shall be divided between the prize-winner and the Squire Law Library.

4. If, in any year, the Prize is not awarded, the unexpended income shall be added to the capital of the Fund.

Wakefield Book Fund for Criminology

Fund. **1.** The sum given to the University by Mrs Priscilla Mitchell (née Wakefield) for the encouragement of teaching and research in Criminology shall form a fund called the Wakefield Book Fund for Criminology.

Purpose. **2.** The income of the Fund shall be used at the discretion of the Committee of Management of the Institute of Criminology to purchase books and other materials for the Radzinowicz Library of Criminology within the Institute.

Unexpended income. **3.** At the discretion of the Committee of Management, any unexpended income in the Fund may be either added to the capital of the Fund or accumulated for use as income in a subsequent year.

Wakefield Fund and Scholarships

Title. **1.** The benefaction of Mrs Priscilla Mitchell (née Wakefield) shall form a fund called the Wakefield Scholarship Fund, in memory of Mrs Mitchell's brother, Captain Edward Roger Wakefield, and also in recognition of the historic work of her forebears Edward Gibbon Wakefield, Daniel Bell Wakefield, William Hayward Wakefield, and Arthur Wakefield in the development of New Zealand, South Australia, and Canada.

Scholarships. **2.** The income of the Fund shall be used to provide one or more scholarships which shall be called Wakefield Scholarships.

3. It shall be the duty of a Wakefield Scholar to pursue a course of advanced study or research in Criminology in the University.

4. The Fund shall be administered by four Managers, who shall be: Managers.

(*a*) the Director of the Institute of Criminology;

(*b*) three persons appointed by the Committee of Management of the Institute of Criminology, of whom not more than one shall be a member of the staff of the Institute.

Managers in class (*b*) shall be appointed in the Michaelmas Term and shall serve for three years from 1 January following their appointment.

5. The Scholarships shall be open to any person who was born in Australia, Canada, or New Zealand, or who has been educated in one of those countries, and who is, or is about to become, registered as a Graduate Student in the University. If two or more candidates born or educated in Australia are equally well qualified, preference shall be given to a candidate who was born or educated in South Australia. Who are eligible.

6. The tenure of a Scholarship shall be determined by the Managers on the occasion of each election. A Scholar shall be eligible for re-election, provided that the tenure of a Scholarship shall not normally exceed three years in all. Tenure.

7. The annual value of a Scholarship shall be such sum not exceeding the available income of the Fund as may be determined by the Managers, within a range approved from time to time by the Council, after they have taken account of any other financial resources that may be available to the Scholar. Value.

8. Any unexpended income may be either added to the capital of the Fund or accumulated for use as income in subsequent years, as the Managers may determine. Unexpended income.

WALDMANN FUND

Grace 3 of 4 February 2009

1. The sum of £1.2m received by the University, via Cambridge University Technical Services Ltd, in connection with income arising from the commercial exploitation of the antibody CAMPATH 1 shall form a fund entitled the Waldmann Fund. This title recognizes the work of Professor Herman Waldmann (leader of a research group in the Department of Pathology in the University of Cambridge which also included Dr Michael Clark, Dr Geoff Hale, and Dr Stephen Cobbold), in developing CAMPATH 1 for use in therapy of human diseases. The income derived from the Fund shall be used solely for the benefit of the Department of Pathology and its purposes. Title.

2. The Managers of the Fund shall comprise both the Head of the Department of Pathology for the time being and the Professor of Immunology (being the Head of the Division of Immunology) in the Department of Pathology for the time being and three persons appointed by the Faculty Board of Biology in the Michaelmas Term to serve for a period of four years from 1 January following their appointment. In the event of the Head of Department of Pathology or the Professor of Immunology at any stage being unable or unwilling to serve as Managers a replacement shall be appointed by the General Board on the recommendation of the Faculty Board of Biology, to hold office for four years or until such time as the new incumbent is elected to the relevant office. Managers.

3. The income of the Fund shall be used as the Managers shall from time to time determine for any one or more of the following purposes, namely: Purposes.

(i) the support of research studentships within the Department of Pathology;

(ii) the repair and maintenance of existing equipment or purchase of new equipment in the Department; and

(iii) the overall support and enhancement of the quality and breadth of (*a*) research implemented within the Department including provision of new (and improvement of existing) premises and facilities appropriate for such research; and (*b*) research initiated or sponsored by the Department.

4. Any unexpended income of the Fund in any financial year may either be added to the capital of the Fund or accumulated for use as income in any one or more subsequent years, as determined by the Managers. Unexpended income.

5. The Managers may accept additional sums from time to time for the same purpose and add them to the capital of the Fund.

6. All powers and discretions conferred on the Managers by this Grace, general law, and statute shall be exercised by a decision of a majority consisting of at least three Managers, who shall include the Head of Department of Pathology or the Professor of Immunology, present and voting at any meeting.

Stat. E IX.

John Lucas Walker Fund and Studentship

Endowments, 1904, pp. 350–1

General regulations

Administration.

1. The administration of the Fund shall be entrusted to the Professor of Pathology in the University of Cambridge, in conjunction with a Board consisting of three Managers.

The Regius Professor of Physic in the University of Cambridge, the Professor of Physiology in the University of Cambridge, and the President of the Royal College of Physicians of London, shall be the Managers.

No resolution of the Managers shall be valid unless approved by at least two Managers, at a meeting to which all the Managers have been summoned, save that a resolution circulated to and signed by all the Managers shall have the same validity as a resolution carried at a meeting.

2. In case a deputy shall be appointed to discharge the duties of any of the three Professors aforesaid, such deputy shall, for all the purposes of these regulations, take the place and exercise the powers of the Professor concerned while acting as deputy.

3. The income of the Fund shall be applied from time to time as follows:

(*a*) to provide one or more Studentships to be called John Lucas Walker Studentships the holders of which shall be either Senior Students, who shall devote themselves to original research in Pathology, or Junior Students, who shall devote themselves to whole-time study and training for research in Pathology;

(*b*) after provision has been made for at least one Studentship, to further original research in Pathology by Exhibitions, Prizes, or grants, at Cambridge or in London.

The Studentship

Studentship.

4. The value of a Senior Studentship and the value of a Junior Studentship shall be such sums as may be determined by the Managers, within ranges approved by the Council, on each occasion on which the Managers give notice of their intention to proceed to an election.

Notice of vacancy.

5. Three months before the date at which, in due course, the Studentship would become vacant, or immediately upon the occurrence of any casual vacancy, the Professor of Pathology shall give such public notice thereof as the Managers may think desirable; and the Professor of Pathology shall report to the Managers upon the qualifications of all candidates whose names are sent in. The Professor of Pathology shall at the same time nominate one of the candidates as the person best qualified, in his or her opinion, for election, and the Managers shall either elect the person so nominated, or such other of the candidates as the three Managers may unanimously agree to elect.

Nomination and election.

6. The nomination and election shall be made so that the newly elected Student may be able to enter upon the Studentship as soon as the vacancy occurs, or as soon as is practicable.

7. The Studentship shall not be awarded upon the result of a competitive examination.

8. Subject to the foregoing provisions, the Professor of Pathology or the Managers may take such steps as they may think fit to ascertain the qualifications of the candidates.

9. Candidature for the Studentship shall be open, but the Student, if not a member of the University, must become such before the end of the term next after election and remain such during tenure.

Condition of tenure.

10. A Student during the tenure of the Studentship shall, if a Senior Student, undertake original research in Pathology, or, if a Junior Student, undertake whole-time study and training for research in Pathology, and shall not systematically follow any business or profession, or engage in any educational or other work, which in the opinion of those entrusted with the administration of the Fund would interfere with his or her inquiries. In publishing the results of investigation carried on during his or her tenure a Student shall, so far as is practicable, use the title 'John Lucas Walker Student'.

11. If the Professor of Pathology shall at any time learn that the Student is following any such business or profession, or has undertaken any such work as will in the opinion of such Professor interfere with his or her inquiries, the Professor shall at once call the Student to desist from the same, and if the Student shall refuse or neglect so to do, the Professor shall report the circumstances to the Managers, and the Managers may, if they think fit, remove such Student from the Studentship.

If the Professor of Pathology shall be of opinion that, through any other causes, such as confirmed ill health or want of diligence, the Student is not fulfilling and is not likely to fulfil the objects of the Studentship, he or she shall report accordingly to the Managers, and the Managers may, if they see fit, remove such Student from the Studentship.

12. The place and nature of the studies of the Student shall be subject to the approval of the Professor of Pathology, provided that the Student shall be bound to study within the University during at least three terms of the tenure of the Studentship, unless the Professor of Pathology shall, with the approval of the Managers, dispense with this requirement for special reasons. The Professor of Pathology and the Managers shall take such steps as they may think necessary to satisfy themselves as to the diligence and progress of the Student, and may require from the Student any reports or other information on the subject of his or her studies which they may think desirable. Studies of Student to be approved.

13. The Studentship shall, subject as hereinbefore mentioned, be tenable for three years, at the end of which time a fresh nomination and election shall take place; but it shall be lawful for the Professor of Pathology, if he or she shall think fit, to recommend, and for the Managers, if they shall think fit, to elect, for a second period not exceeding two years, any Student whose labours during the period of holding the Studentship shall have been of such exceptional promise that it would, in the opinion of the Professor of Pathology and of the Managers, be clearly in the interests of pathological research that such Student should continue to hold the Studentship for such further period. Length of tenure.

14. The income of the Studentship shall be payable to such Student from the date of his or her appointment, and shall be paid to the Student by equal quarterly payments, the payment for each quarter being made in advance. Suspension of election.

15. If, after due notice of a vacancy, there shall be, in the opinion of the Managers, no suitable candidate for the Studentship, it shall be lawful for the Professor of Pathology, with the approval of the Managers, to suspend the election for a time not greater than one year, and if at the expiration of such time there shall, after notice of the vacancy given, be no suitable candidate as aforesaid, the election may be again suspended in the same way, and so on until, in the opinion of the Managers, there shall be a suitable candidate for the Studentship.

Exhibitions and Prizes

16. Exhibitions or Prizes may from time to time be awarded by the Managers to any person in respect of an essay, discovery, or meritorious service connected with or conducing to the science of Pathology. Exhibitions and Prizes.

17. No Exhibition or Prize shall exceed the value of £50, and not more than £50 shall be expended in any one year in such Exhibitions or Prizes.

18. No Exhibition or Prize shall be awarded to any person during the tenure by such person of the John Lucas Walker Studentship.

19. The recipient of an Exhibition or Prize shall not necessarily be or become a member of the University.

Balance of income

20. The balance of the income of the Trust Fund, after providing for the Studentship, Exhibitions, and any Prizes which may have been awarded, and for any necessary expenses connected with the management and application of the Trust Fund, may be devoted to the furtherance of original research in Pathology. Appropriation of balance of income.

21. Grants for this purpose may be made by the Managers on the recommendation of the Professor of Pathology, either to the John Lucas Walker Student or to any other person engaged in such research, subject to any conditions made by the Professor of Pathology with the approval of the Managers. The recipient of a grant shall not necessarily be or become a member of the University. Grants.

22. If on any occasion the Professor of Pathology shall recommend, and the Managers shall be of opinion, that a second John Lucas Walker Student should be appointed, and if the funds at the disposal of the Managers will admit of such appointment, such second Student may be appointed in the manner aforesaid; such Studentship shall be tenable for such period not exceeding three years, and shall be of Second Student.

such annual value, not exceeding £400, as the Professor of Pathology, with the approval of the Managers, may determine.

Robert Walker Prize in Surgery

Fund and purpose. **1.** The sums subscribed in memory of Robert George Walker, M.A., of Trinity College, University Lecturer in Animal Surgery, who died on 23 November 1980, shall form a fund called the Robert Walker Surgery Fund, for the encouragement of study and research in Veterinary Medicine.

Prize. **2.** The Prize shall be awarded by the Examiners for Part III of the Final Veterinary Examination to the candidate who has obtained the highest recommendation on clinical rotations in Small Animal Surgery during the final year and who has also obtained good marks in Small Animal Surgery in that Examination.

Value. **3.** The value of the Prize shall be the income of the Fund.

Wallenberg Prize

Name. **1.** A prize, to be called the Wallenberg Prize, shall be offered annually for an essay on some subject chosen by the candidate and approved by the Managers of the Scandinavian Studies Fund, and connected with the language, literature, history, or civilization of one or more of the Scandinavian peoples.

Managers and subject.

Value. **2.** The value of the Prize shall be such sum as shall be determined by the Managers within a range approved from time to time by the Council. The sum shall be paid from the income of the Scandinavian Studies Fund.

Who may compete. **3.** The competition shall be open to any member of the University, provided that at the time by which essays are to be sent in not more than nine complete terms have passed since the candidate's admission to her or his first degree (if any) at this or at any other university.

Referees. **4.** The Managers may nominate, for appointment by the General Board, one or more referees to report to them upon the essays sent in, and shall determine, subject to the approval of the Council, what fee shall be paid to each referee out of the income of the Scandinavian Studies Fund. The Prize shall be awarded by the Managers.

5. A winner of the Prize may not compete again.

Notice. **6.** The Managers shall publish a Notice of the Prize by the first day of Full Lent Term of each year and the essays shall be sent to the Registrary by the first day of Full Easter Term. The subject proposed by the candidate shall be communicated to the Registrary, with a view to its approval by the Managers, not later than the division of the Lent Term.

Walston Fund

The income of the fund derived from the gift of Sir Charles and Lady Waldstein, accepted by the University in 1911 by Grace 1 of 23 November 1911, and now known as the Walston Fund, shall be applied at the discretion of the Faculty Board of Architecture and History of Art for the advancement of Architectural Studies and the wider teaching of Art History.

Walston Studentship

Trustees. **1.** The Trustees of the Walston Benefaction shall be the Vice-Chancellor, the Chair of the Managing Committee of the British School at Athens, and the President of the Royal Institute of British Architects.

Purpose. **2.** There shall be a Walston Studentship, the purpose of which shall be the furtherance of classical archaeology by facilitating for Cambridge students of archaeology or architecture visits to Greek lands. The Student shall undertake advanced study or research in classical archaeology, or in the art or architecture of ancient Greece, according to a scheme to be approved by the Faculty Board of Classics. Such a scheme shall normally involve travel or residence in Greek lands for a period of not less than three months.

Who are eligible. **3.** The Studentship shall be open to any person who is registered as a Graduate Student in the University, provided that at the date of the election not less than two complete terms have passed after the term of his or her admission as a Graduate Student.

4. The Electors to the Studentship shall be the Faculty Board of Classics, who may take such steps as they think fit to inquire into the qualifications of the candidates; provided that the Studentship shall not be awarded on the result of a competitive examination. Electors.

5. Before the division of the Easter Term each year the Faculty Board shall give notice of the date by which and the manner in which applications for the Studentship are to be submitted. An election to the Studentship shall be held during the Michaelmas Term on a date to be determined by the Board. Applications.

6. The Studentship shall be tenable from the date of the election until 30 September next following. A Student shall be eligible for re-election on not more than two occasions. Tenure.

7. The emolument of the Studentship shall be such sum, not exceeding the available income of the Fund, as shall be determined by the Faculty Board within a range approved from time to time by the Council. The emolument shall be paid in such instalments as the Board shall from time to time determine, provided that the Board may withhold payment of any instalment if they are not satisfied that the Student is pursuing his or her course of study with sufficient diligence. Emolument.

8. Any unexpended income accumulated in the Fund shall be applied from time to time at the discretion of the Faculty Board in any way consistent with the purposes of the Walston Benefaction as defined in Regulation 2. Unexpended income.

9. At the end of his or her tenure the Student shall submit a report on the work undertaken to the Secretary of the Faculty Board, who shall furnish a copy of the report to the Hon. Oliver Walston or to such representative as he may name. Report.

10. Subject to the foregoing regulations, and to any additional regulations not inconsistent with them which may be at any time approved by Grace, it shall be lawful for the Trustees from time to time to make, and if they see fit to vary, such by-laws as seem to them expedient for regulating their own proceedings and the administration of the benefaction entrusted to their care.

Peter Warnock Fund

1. The Fund given by Mr and Mrs H. E. Warnock in memory of their son Peter Warnock, B.A., of Downing College, shall be called the Peter Warnock Fund. Name.

2. Grants from the Fund shall be made annually by the Regius Professor of Botany at his or her discretion to one or more research workers in the Botany School who were born in the United Kingdom of Great Britain and Northern Ireland, to enable them to have a holiday which they could not otherwise afford. Preference shall be given to research workers under the standing of M.A. or Ph.D. Purpose.

3. If in any year no grant is made, the accumulated income may be used for grants in the following year or years, at the absolute discretion of the Regius Professor of Botany. Accumulated income.

George Charles Winter Warr Scholarship

1. There shall be a Scholarship for classical research called the George Charles Winter Warr Scholarship. Title.

2. Candidature for the Scholarship shall be open to any person who is or is about to be registered as a Graduate Student in the Faculty of Classics in the University. Election to and tenure of the Scholarship shall lapse if the person elected does not become or ceases to be a registered Graduate Student. Who are eligible.

3. The Electors to the Scholarship shall be the Faculty Board of Classics, who may take such steps as they think fit to inquire into the qualifications of the candidates; provided that the Scholarship shall not be awarded on the result of a competitive examination. Electors.

4. Before the division of the Easter Term each year, the Board shall give notice of the date by which and the manner in which applications for the Scholarship to be held in the next but one following academical year are to be submitted. An election to the Scholarship shall be held during the academical year prior to the Scholarship's being taken up, on a date to be determined by the Board. Applications.

5. The Scholarship shall be tenable from the date on which the student comes into residence until 30 September of the calendar year next following. A Scholar shall be eligible for re-election on not more than two occasions. Tenure.

6. The emolument of the Scholarship shall be such sum, not exceeding the available income of the Fund, as shall be determined by the Faculty Board within a range approved from time to time by the Council. The emolument shall be paid in such instalments as the Board shall from time to time Emolument.

determine, provided that the Board may withhold payment of any instalment if they are not satisfied that the Scholar is pursuing his or her course of study with sufficient diligence.

Unexpended income.

7. From any unexpended income accumulated in the Fund the Board may make grants for the furtherance of classical study or research.

8. The Board may delegate any of their functions concerning the Scholarship and the aforesaid grants to a Committee not necessarily consisting wholly of members of the Board.

9. These regulations, except Regulation 1, shall be subject to alteration by Grace.

Hugh Watson Fund

Title and purpose.

1. The sum bequeathed to the University by the late Hugh Watson, M.A., of Trinity College, shall form a fund called the Hugh Watson Fund, the income of which shall be used for the promotion of the study of malacology.

Application of Fund.

2. The first charge on the income of the Fund shall be the cost of the stipend, national insurance, and pension contributions of the holder of the University office of Assistant Curator in Malacology (Watson) in the Department of Zoology. After provision has been made for the Assistant Curator the remaining income of the Fund shall be used for the maintenance and enrichment of the molluscan collections and for the promotion of malacological interests, as the Faculty Board of Biology may from time to time decide on the recommendation of the Head of the Department of Zoology in consultation with the Director of the Museum of Zoology.

3. These regulations, except Regulation 1, may be altered by Grace provided always that the main purpose of the Fund, that is to say the promotion of the study of malacology, is adhered to.

Hanne and Torkel Weis-Fogh Fund

Name.

1. In memory of the distinguished scientific work of Professor Torkel Weis-Fogh in the fields of zoology and zoophysiology in Denmark and in England there shall be established a fund which shall be called the Hanne and Torkel Weis-Fogh Fund.

Capital.

2. The capital of the Fund shall consist in the first instance of the sums bequeathed to the University from the estate in England of Hanne and Torkel Weis-Fogh.

Purpose.

3. The object of the Fund shall be to further research in the fields of zoology and zoophysiology, at the Departments of Zoology and Zoophysiology of the Universities of Copenhagen and Aarhus in Denmark and at the Department of Zoology of this University, so as to improve the sum of communicable knowledge in those fields.

Managers.

4. The income of the Fund shall be administered by a Committee of Managers consisting of two persons appointed by the General Board and one person appointed by the Faculty Board of Biology who shall be a University officer in the Department of Zoology but need not be a member of the Faculty Board. The Managers shall be appointed in the Michaelmas Term to serve for five years from 1 January following their appointment.

Grants.

5. Subject to the provisions of Regulation 3, the income shall be applied to make grants

(*a*) to promote research in the fields of zoology and zoophysiology in the Departments of the Universities specified in that regulation;

(*b*) to promote exchange of those engaged in research (including students) between those on the one hand in either of the Departments of the two Danish Universities and those on the other hand in the Department of Zoology of this University;

(*c*) to assist students in any of those Universities who wish to conduct research in zoology or zoophysiology.

Applications.

6. Applications for a grant for any of the purposes specified in Regulation 5 shall be submitted to the Committee of Managers (i) by the University of Copenhagen or the University of Aarhus on behalf of any person or persons working therein, and (ii) by any person working in this University. In any year the income, after meeting any necessary expenses arising from the management of the Fund, shall be divided into two equal parts, of which the first shall be available for distribution to successful applicants under (i) and the second to successful applicants under (ii). Any unexpended income of either part shall be accumulated separately and shall be available for expenditure together with the corresponding part of the income in any subsequent year.

7. Any recipient of a grant from the Fund under Regulation 5 may be required as a condition of the grant to furnish the Treasurer of this University with such details of expenditure from the grant as the Treasurer may require, and to submit to the Managers at their request a report upon the research undertaken with its assistance. Conditions.

West Midlands Examinations Board Fund (WMEB Fund)

1. The assets transferred to the University by the West Midlands Examinations Board shall form a fund called the WMEB Fund.

2. The capital and income of the Fund shall be at the disposal of the Local Examinations Syndicate for the following purposes:

(*a*) to promote and develop examinations administered by Oxford Cambridge and RSA Examinations (OCR);

(*b*) to provide annually one or more bursaries or prizes for students resident and educated in the West Midlands area;

(*c*) to provide annually one or more bursaries for teachers in service in the West Midlands area to enable them to undertake a period of study leave or research with the Local Examinations Syndicate or OCR into some aspect of educational development, particularly learning and assessment.

3. The Local Examinations Syndicate may make such rules from time to time as may be necessary to govern the award of bursaries and prizes under Regulation 2(*b*) and (*c*).

Whalley Prize

1. The gift of Geoffrey Peter Cubbin, M.A., Ph.D., of King's College, University Lecturer in German, shall form a fund known as the Whalley Fund. Title of Fund.

2. There shall be a Whalley Prize which shall be awarded to qualified candidates. The University may from time to time define further the qualifications of candidates, but such qualifications shall always include the demonstration of a direct reading knowledge of one or more of the following languages: Medieval Welsh, Gothic, Old Church Slavonic, Medieval Irish, Occitan. Eligibility.

3. The Whalley Prize shall be awarded each year by, jointly, the Chairs of Examiners for Part II of the Linguistics Tripos and for Part II of the Modern and Medieval Languages Tripos to the student who has shown the greatest distinction in the examination for Part II of the Linguistics Tripos or Part II of the Modern and Medieval Languages Tripos, provided that such student is a qualified candidate for the purpose of Regulation 4. Award.

4. A qualified candidate shall be one who demonstrates a direct reading knowledge of the languages specified in Regulation 2 in her or his answers to one or more of those papers which the Faculty Board of Modern and Medieval Languages shall from time to time announce that they have specified for the purpose from among the papers that may be offered in Part II of the Linguistics Tripos and Part II of the Modern and Medieval Languages Tripos.

5. The value of the Prize shall be the income of the Fund. Value.

6. The University may, in Dr Cubbin's lifetime with his consent, or after his death, determine that the Fund should be known as the Geoffrey Cubbin Fund, and the Prize established by Regulation 2 as the Geoffrey Cubbin Prize. Change of title of Fund and Prize.

7. Regulations 1 and 2 and this regulation shall be amended only in accordance with Regulation 6. The remaining regulations shall be subject to amendment by Grace. Amendment of regulations.

Whewell Trust Fund and Whewell Scholarships

Endowments, 1904, pp. 136–40

Application of the Whewell Trust Fund

Stat. E XX.

1. The Whewell Trust Fund consists of the sum paid each year to the University by Trinity College in pursuance of Statute E XX. Fund.

2. There shall be a first charge on the Fund of the sum of £300 to be paid in each year to the Chest towards the stipend of the Whewell Professor of International Law. First charge.

Second charge. **3.** There shall be a second charge on the Fund of the sum of £200 (or so much thereof as is available) to be paid in each year to a fund called the Whewell Scholarship Fund, which shall be used for the provision of Whewell Scholarships in International Law, and otherwise as hereinafter provided.

Excess income. **4.** If in any year the net income of the Trust Fund exceeds £500, the excess up to a maximum of £200 shall be paid to the Chest towards the stipend of the Whewell Professor.

5. If in any year the net income of the Trust Fund exceeds £700, the excess shall be paid to the Whewell Scholarship Fund.

Unapplied income. **6.** Any part of the Whewell Scholarship Fund which is not paid to Scholars in any year shall be at the disposal of the Electors either for payments to Scholars in subsequent years or for investment with a view to making provision for such payments or for the furtherance in any other manner of the study of International Law: provided that any payment authorized by the Electors for purposes other than the emolument of Scholars shall require the consent of the Faculty Board of Law.

The Whewell Scholarships

7. There shall be offered in each year at least one Whewell Scholarship in International Law.

Eligibility. **8.** The competition for Scholarships shall be open to any member of the University who is a candidate for the LL.M. Examination in the year of candidature for the Scholarships, or who satisfied the Examiners in the LL.M. Examination in the year next preceding the year of candidature, provided that no one who has been awarded a Scholarship shall compete on a second occasion.

Value. **9.** The Electors may award one or more Scholarships, each of such value as they may determine, provided that (*a*) the value of a Scholarship shall not exceed such sum as shall be determined by the Faculty Board of Law within a range approved from time to time by the Council, and (*b*) the aggregate value of the Scholarships awarded at any one election shall not exceed the amount fixed for that election by the Finance Committee of the Council.

Tenure. **10.** A Scholarship shall be tenable for one year from 1 October next following the election. During the year of tenure a Scholar shall have the rights defined in Statute E XX in regard to membership of Trinity College and the occupation of chambers in Whewell's Courts.

Electors. **11.** The Electors shall be the Whewell Professor (or a deputy nominated by the Whewell Professor and appointed by the General Board) as Chair, and two other Electors appointed annually by the General Board in the Lent Term on the nomination of the Faculty Board of Law. The Electors shall conduct the examination.

Examination. **12.** The examination shall comprise not less than three of the papers in International Law which have been prescribed by the Faculty Board of Law for the LL.M. Examination, a fourth paper chosen by the candidate from among all the papers prescribed for that examination, and a paper on problems and disputed points in International Law.

The Faculty Board of Law shall announce in the Michaelmas Term each year the papers to be set in the examination, and the date by which, and the manner in which, applications are to be submitted.

The Electors shall make to the Faculty Board of Law any representations which they may consider desirable from time to time with regard to the subjects and date of the examination.

WHIPPLE MUSEUM OF THE HISTORY OF SCIENCE CONSERVATION FUND

Grace 3 of 14 November 2012

Fund and title. **1.** The gifts received from the grandchildren and other family members of the late Mr Robert Stewart Whipple, and other gifts received for the same purpose, shall form a fund called the Whipple Museum of the History of Science Conservation Fund.

Purpose. **2.** The income of the Fund shall be used to support conservation of the collections of the Whipple Museum of the History of Science including the provision of resources to obtain specialist conservation advice and support.

Management. **3.** The Board of History and Philosophy of Science shall be responsible for the management of the Fund.

Unexpended income. **4.** Any unexpended income in a financial year may be: (*a*) added to the capital of the Fund; (*b*) applied under the purposes specified in Regulation 2; or (*c*) applied in support of the Whipple Museum of the History of Science with the prior consent of the descendants of Mr Robert Stewart Whipple who are recognised by the University at the date of the Grace to establish the Fund.

R.S. WHIPPLE FUND

1. The sums given and bequeathed to the University by Mr R. S. Whipple shall form a fund called the R. S. Whipple Fund. Name.

2. The income of the Fund shall be used for the purchase of instruments, models, or books for the Whipple Museum of the History of Science, but not for the purchase of equipment or for the part-payment of running expenses of the Museum. Application.

3. The Board of History and Philosophy of Science shall be responsible for the management of the Fund. Management.

SIR LIONEL WHITBY MEDAL AND PRIZE

1. The Sir Lionel Whitby Medal and Prize shall be awarded annually by the M.D. Committee for an M.D. thesis, which in their opinion is of exceptional merit, and which deals with investigation carried out in the laboratory, preference being given to a haematological subject; provided that if in any year the M.D. Committee declare that no thesis of sufficient merit has been submitted no Medal or Prize shall be awarded in that year.

2. The sum available for the Prize shall be determined by the M.D. Committee within a range approved from time to time by the Council.

SIR LIONEL WHITBY MEMORIAL FUND

1. A gift of £3,500, the sum of voluntary contributions made by American servicemen and other American citizens stationed in the United Kingdom, and presented to the University on the recommendation of the medical staff and patients of the 7,510th United States Air Force Hospital, Wimpole Park, shall form a fund to be called the Sir Lionel Whitby Memorial Fund. Title.

2. The income of the Fund shall be at the disposal of the Head of the Department of Pathology to be applied from time to time, at his or her discretion, for the purpose of assisting the work of the Department of Pathology. Application.

TIM WHITMORE GEOGRAPHY AND ZOOLOGY FUNDS

The income derived from the donation of £100,000 received from Mrs Wendy Whitmore in memory of her husband Dr Timothy Charles Whitmore, formerly of St John's College and the Department of Geography, shall be divided equally between two funds to be called the Tim Whitmore Geography Fund and the Tim Whitmore Zoology Fund.

Tim Whitmore Geography Fund

1. The Tim Whitmore Geography Fund shall be administered by the Managers of the Philip Lake Fund II. Managers.

2. The income of the Fund shall be used at the discretion of the Managers for making grants to Graduate Students in the Department of Geography towards the cost of travel, fieldwork, or research in the fields of conservation and sustainable development. Application of Fund.

3. Any unexpended income of the Fund in a financial year shall be accumulated for use as income in future years. Unexpended income.

Tim Whitmore Zoology Fund

1. The Managers of the Tim Whitmore Zoology Fund shall be the Head of the Department of Zoology and two of the University officers in the Department of Zoology who shall be appointed by the Head of the Department in the Michaelmas Term to serve for two years from 1 January following their appointment. Managers.

2. The income of the Fund shall be used at the discretion of the Managers to support the training of Graduate Students in the Department of Zoology, particularly those from developing countries, working in conservation science or in the sustainable use of biological resources. Application of Fund.

3. Any unexpended income of the Fund in a financial year shall be accumulated for use as income in future years. Unexpended income.

H. B. and Dorothy A. Whittington Fund

Name and purpose.

1. The capital sum given to the University by Professor Harry Blackmore Whittington, Emeritus Woodwardian Professor of Geology in the University, shall form a fund called the H. B. and Dorothy A. Whittington Fund, which shall be used for the promotion and encouragement of palaeontology in the Department of Earth Sciences.

Managers.

2. The Managers of the Fund shall be the Woodwardian Professor of Geology, the Director of the Sedgwick Museum of Earth Sciences, and one or two persons pursuing palaeontological research in the Department of Earth Sciences appointed from time to time by the Head of the Department.

Grants.

3. The income of the Fund shall be applied

(*a*) to support, by way of grants, graduate and postdoctoral students engaged in palaeontological research in the Department;

(*b*) provided that the accumulated income of the Fund becomes sufficient, to support a graduate student undertaking advanced study or research in palaeontology in the Department by means of a Harry and Dorothy Whittington Studentship. The Managers shall publish a Notice inviting applications for the Studentship which shall provide:

(i) a maintenance payment to be determined by the Managers,

(ii) a payment to meet the student's University and College fees.

4. After provision has been made in accordance with Regulation 3, any remaining income of the Fund shall be applied, at the discretion of the Managers, to support other persons engaged in palaeontological research in the Department, or persons visiting the Department for periods of less than six months who wish to pursue a specific piece of palaeontological research that will have at least some involvement with collections of the Sedgwick Museum.

Unexpended income.

5. Any unexpended income of the Fund in a financial year may be either added to the capital of the Fund or accumulated for use as income in future years, as the Managers shall determine.

Restrictions.

6. The Fund shall not be available for stipends, nor may it be used for expenditure connected with the Sedgwick Museum other than as specified in Regulations 3 and 4.

Whittle Lab Studentship Fund

Title and purpose.

1. The sum of £410,000 received by the University, via Cambridge University Technical Services Ltd, from the sale of software created by Professor J. D. Denton, FREng, FRS, formerly Professor of Turbomachinery Aerodynamics, Fellow of Trinity Hall, shall form a fund, entitled the Whittle Lab Studentship Fund, for the benefit of postgraduate students working at the Whittle Laboratory in the Department of Engineering.

2. Any further income received by the University from the sale of Professor Denton's software shall be added to the Fund.

Studentship.

3. The capital and income of the Fund shall be used for the provision of a studentship to be called the Whittle Lab Studentship.

Electors.

4. The Electors to the Studentship shall normally be all the University teaching officers at the Whittle Laboratory.

Who are eligible.

5. In order to be eligible for the Studentship a candidate must have been admitted or be seeking admission as a registered Graduate Student in the University and normally with the intention of being based at the Whittle Laboratory.

Tenure.

6. The Studentship shall be tenable for one year in the first instance. It may be renewed by the Electors for a second or third year but may not normally be used to support a Student beyond her or his third year of research.

7. No more than one such Studentship may be allocated at any one time.

Provisions.

8. The Studentship shall provide

(*a*) a maintenance payment to be determined by the Electors, but normally at no more than the then current Engineering and Physical Sciences Research Council rate, or equivalent;

(*b*) a payment to cover all or part of the Student's University and College fees.

9. In the event that the Whittle Laboratory ceases to be a centre for research on turbomachinery the Studentship may be used to support other Graduate Students in the Department of Engineering. In this instance it should normally be allocated by the Head of the Division most closely related to the study of turbomachinery.

Peter Whittle Fund

Grace 2 of 27 October 2010

Name.
1. The sums given to the University by Dr Roland Tegeder and the Goldman Sachs Group Inc., and any later sums similarly given, shall form a fund called the Peter Whittle Fund, in honour of the research and scholarship of Peter Whittle, Churchill Professor of Mathematics for Operational Research from 1967 to 1994.

Purpose.
2. The purpose of the Fund shall be to support advanced research in mathematics, particularly at the intersections between established mathematical research fields, and between mathematics and other sciences.

Managers.
3. The Managers of the Fund shall be the Churchill Professor of Mathematics for Operational Research; the Professor of Mathematical Statistics; and the Director of the Statistical Laboratory. Should either a single individual hold more than one of these positions or any of the positions be vacant, a further Manager or Managers shall be appointed by the Board of the Faculty of Mathematics from among its senior members, on the nomination of the existing Managers, so that the number of Managers shall always be three.

Annual seminar.
4. The first charge on the Fund shall be an annual mathematics research seminar named in honour of Peter Whittle, which shall be held at the discretion of the Managers at either the University of Cambridge or a comparable university in New Zealand. The Managers shall appoint annually an individual of professorial standing in the field of mathematics, who shall be responsible for conducting the Seminar.

Grants.
5. After provision has been made in accordance with Regulation 4, the capital and the income of the Fund shall be applied at the discretion of the Managers for the support of innovative research in mathematics conducted by individuals in the University of Cambridge. Grants made from the Fund shall honour the name of Peter Whittle.

Unexpended income.
6. Any unexpended income of the Fund in a financial year may be either added to the capital of the Fund or accumulated for use as income in future years, as the Managers may determine.

Power to rescind regulations.
7. If the General Board are satisfied on the recommendation of the Faculty Board of Mathematics that the sum remaining in the Fund after a period of ten years from the date of establishment of the Fund is inadequate for the continuance of its activities, the University shall have the power to rescind these regulations and any sum remaining shall be disbursed in accordance with Regulation 2.

Gordon Wigan Fund

Name.
1. The sum bequeathed to the University by the late Gordon Taylor Bentinck Wigan, M.A., of Trinity College, shall form a fund to be called the Gordon Wigan Fund.

Application of income.
2. The annual income of the Gordon Wigan Fund shall be applied for the purpose of promoting and encouraging scientific education or research or scientific education and research in the University of Cambridge, as to two-fifths thereof in such manner as the Faculty Board of Physics and Chemistry may from time to time determine, as to two-fifths thereof in such manner as the Council of the School of the Biological Sciences may from time to time determine, and as to one-fifth thereof in such manner, for the benefit of the subjects Mineralogy and Geology, as the Faculty Board of Earth Sciences and Geography may from time to time determine.

Restriction on use of income.
3. No part of the income of the Fund shall be applied to a specified purpose for a longer period than five years, but renewals of any such application may be made for periods not exceeding five years at a time.

Proviso.
4. The foregoing regulations shall be subject to alteration by Grace provided that the regulations shall always be in accordance with the provisions of Mr Wigan's will.[1]

Anthony Wilkin Studentship in Ethnology and Archaeology

Name.
1. The Studentship shall be called the Anthony Wilkin Studentship in Ethnology and Archaeology, and shall be devoted to the encouragement of research in these subjects.

Income.
2. No Student shall be appointed nor shall a grant be made out of the Fund under Regulation 9 unless there shall have accrued to the Fund an amount of at least £100.

[1] An extract from the will was printed in *Reporter*, 31 January 1935, p. 520.

Date of election.

3. Subject to the preceding regulation a Student may be appointed whenever the Faculty Board of Human, Social, and Political Science think fit, provided that a candidate of sufficient merit shall apply. Not less than four weeks before the latest day for the receipt of applications the Faculty Board shall give public notice in the *Reporter* of their intention to make an appointment.

Who are eligible.

4. Members of the University shall be eligible for the Studentship, preference being given *ceteris paribus* to candidates who have obtained honours in the Archaeological and Anthropological Tripos or have been approved for the award of the degree of Master of Philosophy having followed a course under the supervision of the Degree Committee for the Faculty of Human, Social, and Political Science.

Electors.

5. The appointment to the Studentship shall be made by the Faculty Board of Human, Social, and Political Science.

Conditions.

6. The Student shall undertake research in Ethnology or Anthropology or Archaeology under the direction of an honorary Supervisor, appointed for the purpose by the Faculty Board; the Supervisor shall determine the conditions under which the research is to be conducted and shall generally keep in touch with the work of the Student.

Income.

7. The stipend of the Student shall be £100 or such larger amount as shall be determined by the Faculty Board within a range approved from time to time by the Council. The stipend shall be paid in two equal instalments, the first within one month of the election, and the second six months after the first, provided that at the time of the second payment the Student's Supervisor is satisfied that the Student is diligently carrying out his or her course of research. If the Supervisor is not so satisfied, he or she shall inform the Faculty Board through the Secretary, and they shall have power to withhold the payment of the second instalment.

Designation of Student.

8. In any books, papers, or other publications in which the Student may publish the results of the investigations carried on during the tenure of the Studentship, the Student shall use the title 'Anthony Wilkin Student'.

9. The Faculty Board shall further have the right to make grants to members of the University desiring to pursue research in Ethnology or Anthropology or Archaeology, provided that by so doing they shall not reduce the amount in the Fund below £100. Recipients of such grants shall make due acknowledgement in any publication resulting therefrom. The value of such grants shall be determined by the Faculty Board within a range approved from time to time by the Council.

10. Applications for the Studentship or for a grant from the funds of the trust shall be made to the Secretary of the Faculty Board of Human, Social, and Political Science. They should contain full particulars of the applicant's qualifications and of the work proposed.

Proviso.

11. These regulations, except Regulation 1, shall be subject to alteration by Grace, but so always that the principal object of the Fund, namely, the furtherance of ethnological and archaeological research, preferably by fieldwork among the more primitive peoples, and in other lands than Greece, Italy, or Egypt, shall be maintained.

Professor Sir David Williams Fund

Grace 2 of 26 May 2011

Title.

1. The sum subscribed in memory of Sir David Williams, Emeritus Rouse Ball Professor of English Law, Vice-Chancellor, 1989–96, and President of Wolfson College, 1980–92, shall form a fund to be known as the Professor Sir David Williams Fund.

Managers.

2. The Managers of the Fund shall be the Faculty Board of Law, who may delegate any or all of their functions under these regulations to a committee consisting of not less than three persons, at least one of whom shall be a member of the Faculty Board.

Purpose.

3. The Managers may apply the income and capital of the Fund for the following purposes:

(*a*) to support the teaching and research of Public Law in the University of Cambridge;

(*b*) to support travel costs and other exceptional academic expenses by graduate students in the Faculty of Law;

(*c*) to purchase books or other materials for the Squire Law Library;

(*d*) to make grants or payments related to any other educational or academic purpose of the Faculty of Law, and to attach to the award of any such grant or payment such conditions as they may think fit.

GEORGE WILLIAMS PRIZE

Stat. E XXX.

Endowments, 1904, p. 418

Title.

1. A George Williams Prize shall be offered each year for an essay on some subject, proposed by the candidate and approved by the Adjudicators, connected with liturgical study. The value of the Prize shall be such sum as shall be determined by the Faculty Board of Divinity within a range approved from time to time by the Council.

Who may compete.

2. Any member of the University may be a candidate for the Prize provided that at the time of the examination

(*a*) he or she has kept five terms,

(*b*) if a graduate, he or she is of not more than ten years' standing from admission to a first degree, whether of this or another university;

and provided also that no previous winner of the Prize shall again be eligible as a candidate.

Adjudicators.

3. The Faculty Board of Divinity shall appoint as Adjudicators not more than three nor less than two members of the Senate one of whom shall be a Professor chosen from among the three Professors of Divinity and the Dixie Professor of Ecclesiastical History. The Adjudicators shall be appointed in the Michaelmas Term to serve for eighteen months from 1 January following their appointment. Except in a year in which no essay is submitted each Adjudicator shall receive from the income of the Fund such sum as shall be determined by the Faculty Board of Divinity within a range approved from time to time by the Council.

Submission of subjects and essays.

4. Each candidate shall submit the proposed subject of his or her essay to the Registrary not later than 1 February. The Registrary shall communicate the subject to the Adjudicators, and shall inform the candidate by the last day of Full Lent Term of its approval or rejection by them. Candidates shall send their essays to the Registrary so as to arrive not later than 19 December.

Conditions

5. The prize-winner shall deposit a printed or typewritten copy of his or her essay in the University Library.

Unexpended income.

6. Any unexpended income accumulated in the Fund shall be transferred to the Theological Studies Fund in accordance with the provisions of Statute E XXX 9.

GLANVILLE WILLIAMS PRIZE

Prize.

1. The sum received from Mrs Lorna Williams and Dr Rendel Williams in memory of Glanville Llewelyn Williams, LL.D., (Hon.) Litt.D., Honorary Fellow of Jesus College and Emeritus Rouse Ball Professor of English Law, shall form a fund called the Glanville Williams Fund, the income of which shall be used to provide a Glanville Williams Prize for Criminal Law.

How awarded.

2. The Prize shall be awarded by the Examiners for Part IA or Part II of the Law Tripos for distinction in Criminal Law shown by performance in Paper 3 in that examination.

Value.

3. The value of the Prize shall be such sum as shall be determined by the Faculty Board of Law within a range approved from time to time by the Council.

Unexpended income.

4. Any unexpended income in a financial year shall be added to the capital of the Fund.

FREDERICK WILLIAMSON MEMORIAL FUND

Fund and purpose.

1. The sums given and bequeathed to the University by Mrs Margaret D. Williamson in memory of her husband, the late Frederick Williamson, B.A., of Emmanuel College, shall form a fund called the Frederick Williamson Memorial Fund, the income of which shall be used:

(*a*) for the purpose of furthering research relating to the peoples of Tibet, Bhutan, Sikkim, and neighbouring Himalayan areas, their society, religion, and material culture; and

(*b*) for the development of the Williamson Collection in the Museum of Archaeology and Anthropology.

Managers.

2. The Fund shall be administered by a Board of Managers consisting of:

(*a*) the Curator of the Museum of Archaeology and Anthropology, who shall act as Secretary;

(*b*) two persons appointed by the Faculty Board of Human, Social, and Political Science, one of whom shall be a person engaged in the study of Social Anthropology;

(*c*) one person appointed by the Faculty Board of Asian and Middle Eastern Studies;

(*d*) one person appointed by Emmanuel College.

Managers in classes (*b*), (*c*), and (*d*) shall be appointed in the Michaelmas Term to serve for four years from 1 January following their appointment.

Application of Fund.

3. Subject to the provisions of Regulation 1, the income of the Fund shall be applied from time to time, at the discretion of the Managers and subject to such conditions as they may think fit, for the following purposes:

(*a*) to make grants to persons engaged in advanced study or research;

(*b*) to make provision for one or more Fellowships, which shall be named Williamson Fellowships;

(*c*) to purchase specimens and material for the Museum of Archaeology and Anthropology;

(*d*) to further in any other way the purposes of the Fund as specified in Regulation 1.

The Fund shall not be applied to the regular maintenance of the Museum of Archaeology and Anthropology.

Notice.

4. Before the end of the Michaelmas Term each year the Managers shall publish a Notice inviting applications for Fellowships, or for grants from the Fund, or for both.

Fellowships.

5. The Managers may elect to a Fellowship any person whose qualifications they consider suitable, whether such person is a member of the University or not. A Fellow shall undertake research in a subject approved by the Managers.

Tenure.

6. The tenure of a Fellowship shall be determined by the Managers on the occasion of each election. A Fellow shall be eligible for re-election, provided that the tenure of a Fellowship shall not normally exceed three years in all.

Stipend.

7. The stipend of a Fellow shall be determined by the General Board on the recommendation of the Managers on the occasion of each election.

Raymond and Edith Williamson Fund

Name and purpose.

1. The sums received under the wills of Raymond Williamson, of Clare College, formerly Reader in Morbid Histology, and Edith Ethel Williamson, his wife, shall form a fund called the Raymond and Edith Williamson Fund for History and Philosophy of Science, the income of which shall be used to further the study of the history of the biological sciences, including medicine.

Managers.

2. The Managers of the Fund shall be:

(*a*) the Head of the Department of History and Philosophy of Science;

(*b*) the Chair of the Board of History and Philosophy of Science;

(*c*) the Secretary of the Department of History and Philosophy of Science;

(*d*) the Curator of the Whipple Museum of the History of Science;

(*e*) three persons appointed by the Board of History and Philosophy of Science, who shall be appointed in the Michaelmas Term to serve for three years from 1 January following their appointment.

Studentships.

3. The first charge on the income of the Fund shall be the provision of one or more studentships, to be known as Williamson Studentships, which shall be open to any person who is, or is about to be, registered as a Graduate Student in the University, and who intends to undertake advanced study or research in the history of the biological sciences, including medicine.

4. The Managers shall give not less than three months' notice of their intention to proceed to an election. A Studentship shall be tenable for one year in the first instance. A Student shall be eligible for re-election, provided that the tenure of a Studentship shall not normally exceed three years in all.

Emolument.

5. The emolument of a Studentship shall be such sum not exceeding the available income of the Fund as may be determined by the Managers, within a range approved from time to time by the Council, after they have taken account of any other financial resources that may be available to the Student.

6. The emolument shall be paid quarterly in advance, provided that the Managers may withhold any instalment if they are not satisfied that the Student is pursuing his or her course of study or research with sufficient diligence.

Support of research.

7. After the provision of a Studentship or Studentships in accordance with Regulation 3, the income of the Fund shall be applied at the discretion of the Managers for the support of research in the history of the biological sciences, including medicine, by such means as they may think fit.

Unexpended income.

8. Any unexpended income in a financial year may be either added to the capital of the Fund or accumulated for use as income in future years, as the Managers may determine.

Edward Wilson Memorial Funds

The income derived from the royalties arising from publication in 1966 of the Antarctic diaries of Dr Edward Adrian Wilson, B.A., M.B., of Gonville and Caius College, who died with Captain Robert Falcon Scott on the return from the South Pole in 1912, together with additional funds received for the same purposes, shall form two funds to be called the Edward Wilson Memorial Funds (I) and (II). Titles.

Edward Wilson Memorial Fund (I)

1. The income of the Edward Wilson Memorial Fund (I) shall provide grants to persons wishing to undertake fieldwork or expeditions in polar regions. Purpose.

2. The Managers of the Fund shall be the Director of the Scott Polar Research Institute and two persons appointed by the Committee of Management of the Institute for periods of three years at a time. Managers.

3. The Managers shall invite applications for grants from the Fund, and shall meet annually to consider those applications and award grants consistent with the purpose of the Fund. Application for grants.

4. In making awards, the Managers shall consider fieldwork or expeditions which have a strong emphasis on *either (i) scientific work, particularly projects in biology, ecology, or natural history, and more particularly ornithology; or* (ii) polar artwork, particularly painting of landscapes and wildlife.

5. All recipients of grants from the Fund shall undertake to provide a report to the Managers upon completion of their expedition or fieldwork. The report shall be lodged in the Library of the Institute. Recipients shall also undertake to donate copies of any research or publications resulting from the expedition or fieldwork to the Library of the Institute, or original examples of artwork to the Institute archives, as appropriate. Condition of award.

6. Unspent income in a financial year may be added to the capital of the Fund, or accumulated for use as income in a future year in accordance with these regulations. Unexpended income.

Edward Wilson Memorial Fund (II)

1. The income of the Edward Wilson Memorial Fund (II) shall be used to contribute towards the costs of the curation, maintenance, and increase of the polar art collections of the Scott Polar Research Institute. Purpose.

2. The Managers of the Fund shall be the Director of the Institute and two persons appointed by the Committee of Management of the Institute for periods of three years at a time. Managers.

3. The Managers shall meet at least once a year to consider the needs of the Institute's art collections and to apply the Fund's income in furtherance of its objects.

4. Any unexpended income in a financial year may be added to the capital of the Fund, or accumulated for use as income in a future year in accordance with these regulations. Unexpended income.

Judith E. Wilson Fund

1. The sums given and bequeathed to the University by Miss Judith E. Wilson shall form a fund to be called the Judith E. Wilson Fund, the income of which shall be used to encourage the study of literature and especially of literature relating to drama and poetry. Title and purpose.

2. The Managers of the Fund shall be the Faculty Board of English, who may delegate any or all of their functions under these regulations to a committee not necessarily consisting wholly of members of the Board. Managers.

3. The first charge on the income of the Fund shall be to provide the stipend and employers' pension and national insurance contributions of a Professor of or Reader or University Senior Lecturer or University Lecturer in Poetry and Drama in the Faculty of English. The second charge on the income of the Fund shall be to provide for one or more lectures in drama or poetry which shall be entitled the Judith E. Wilson Lectures on Drama and Poetry. The third charge on the income of the Fund shall be to support activities associated with the drama studio in the Faculty of English. The Managers may at their discretion pay any expenses incurred in the administration of the Fund or in connection with the Lectures. Charges on income of Fund.

4. The Professor of or Reader or University Senior Lecturer or University Lecturer in Poetry and Drama shall perform the duties appropriate to the office as defined in the Statutes and Ordinances of Duties of appointee.

the University, and in particular shall encourage the study of drama and poetry with emphasis on contemporary dramatic works.

5. A Judith E. Wilson Lecturer shall be some distinguished exponent of poetry or drama (including poets, dramatists, actors, or directors) appointed by the Faculty Board of English. The lectures shall be given at a time and place to be announced by the Faculty Board of English and shall be open without fee to all persons interested.

Honorarium. **6.** A Judith E. Wilson Lecturer shall receive an honorarium of such sum as shall be approved by the General Board on the recommendation of the Faculty Board of English and reimbursement in respect of such travelling and subsistence expenses as may be approved by the General Board on the recommendation of the Faculty Board of English.

Unexpended income. **7.** After provision has been made in accordance with Regulation 3, the remaining income and any unexpended income accumulated in the Fund may be applied from time to time, at the discretion of the Faculty Board of English and subject to such conditions as they may think fit, for the purpose of furthering the study of literature, especially of literature relating to drama and poetry, with particular emphasis on contemporary practices:

Visiting Fellowships. (*a*) by the appointment of not more than two Judith E. Wilson Visiting Fellows in any academical year; such Fellowships may be held by any persons whom the Faculty Board consider suitably qualified, provided that

(1) no University officer shall be eligible for appointment;

(2) no one who has held a Judith E. Wilson Visiting Fellowship shall be eligible for reappointment until a year has elapsed since the expiry of his or her previous tenure;

(3) in any academical year if two Judith E. Wilson Visiting Fellowships are appointed one shall be in Drama and one in Poetry;

(*b*) by any other means.

Tenure. **8.** The tenure of a Judith E. Wilson Visiting Fellowship shall be determined by the Faculty Board.

Wilson-Barkworth Fund

The income of the Fund derived from the bequest of Arthur Bromby Wilson-Barkworth, B.A., LL.D., of Jesus College, accepted by the University in 1929 by Grace 1 of 11 May 1929 and now known as the Wilson-Barkworth Fund, shall be applied at the discretion of the Library Syndicate for 'the purchase of original manuscripts or copies thereof or any other documents or books which it may be desirable to acquire for the University Library and particularly any manuscripts, documents, or books illustrating or bearing upon the local history of England and more especially of the East Riding of Yorkshire'.

Stat. E XXXI.

Wiltshire Prize

Endowments, 1904, p. 435

Name and purpose. **1.** The income of the Wiltshire Fund shall be used to provide one or more annual prizes, to be called Wiltshire Prizes, for proficiency in the sciences of Geology and Mineralogy.

Value. **2.** The value of a Wiltshire Prize shall be the annual income of the Wiltshire Fund.

Awarders. **3.** The Awarders shall be the Woodwardian Professor of Geology, the Professor of Mineralogy and Petrology, and the Examiners in Geological Sciences A and B for Part IB of the Natural Sciences Tripos in the year in which the award is made. Quorum. No business shall be transacted at any meeting unless three Awarders are present.

How awarded. **4.** A Wiltshire Prize shall be awarded in June of each year to a student who has obtained honours in Part IB of the Natural Sciences Tripos in the year in which the award is made, who offered the subjects Geological Sciences A and B, and who, in the opinion of the Awarders, has achieved distinction in the sciences of Geology and Mineralogy. More than one Prize. If sufficient income has accumulated in the Fund the Awarders may award more than one Prize in any year.

John Winbolt Prize

Endowments, 1904, p. 624

Name. **1.** A prize to be called the John Winbolt Prize shall be offered for competition annually, and shall consist of the net annual income of the John Winbolt Fund.

By whom awarded. **2.** The award shall be made by the Head of the Department of Engineering and an Adjudicator appointed by the General Board on the nomination of the Faculty Board of Engineering in the Easter

Term of each year in which entries for the Prize are sent in. The Adjudicator appointed by the General Board shall receive from the income of the Fund, except in cases where no entry is sent in, such amount as may be determined by the Faculty Board within a range approved from time to time by the Council.

3. The Prize shall be awarded for a paper on some subject selected by the candidate and related to the profession of a civil engineer. The paper shall have been accepted for publication in an established professional or learned journal. Entries (limited to one paper per candidate) shall be submitted to the Registrary so as to arrive not later than 1 May. Conditions.

4. Candidates must be graduates of the University or registered Graduate Students under the supervision of the Degree Committee for the Faculty of Engineering, and must be under the age of twenty-eight years on the date by which entries are to be sent in, provided that the following shall not be eligible to compete:

(*a*) a person whose name was entered on the Register of Graduate Students more than four years before the date by which entries are to be sent in;

(*b*) a person who holds the Ph.D. Degree, or who is qualified to proceed to that degree.

5. No person shall be eligible to whom the Prize has already been awarded. Proviso.

6. In any year the award may be made for an entry (limited to one paper) submitted jointly by two candidates giving an account of research that they have carried out in co-operation. In comparing the merits of combined and independent work an appreciably higher standard is to be exacted for the former. In the case of an award being made for a joint paper the Prize shall be divided equally between the two candidates concerned. Joint candidature.

7. It shall be open to the Awarders in any year to declare that no entry has been submitted of sufficient merit. From the unexpended income accumulated in the Fund an additional Prize or Prizes not exceeding in value such sum as shall be determined by the Faculty Board within a range approved from time to time by the Council may be awarded in any year in which the Awarders so decide. Unexpended income.

8. It shall be open to the University, on the recommendation of the Faculty Board of Engineering, to alter these regulations from time to time subject to the conditions that the Prize shall always be called the John Winbolt Prize and shall be devoted to the encouragement of study or research in subjects related to the profession of a civil engineer. For the purpose of these regulations all the subjects prescribed in Parts IIA and IIB of the Engineering Tripos shall be deemed to be subjects related to the profession of a civil engineer. Regulations may be altered. Proviso.

9. In every year in which the Prize is awarded, each successful candidate shall present a copy of his or her entry to the University Library.

Winchester Reading Prizes

Endowments, 1904, p. 406

1. The sum given to the University in 1867 by John Noble shall form a fund the income of which shall be used to provide two prizes called the Winchester Reading Prizes. Fund and prizes.

2. The Prizes shall be offered for competition each year and shall be open to all resident members of the University *in statu pupillari*. Who may compete.

3. The Prizes shall be adjudged by two Examiners nominated by the Faculty Board of English. Before the division of the Lent Term each year the Faculty Board shall nominate one Examiner for appointment to serve for two years. Examiners.

4. The examination for the Prizes shall be held in the Easter Term each year on a day appointed by the Faculty Board. The names of candidates shall be sent to the Registrary by their Tutors not less than fourteen days before the day of the examination. Date of examination.

5. The examination shall be confined to reading, in public, passages: Subjects of examination.

(*a*) of classical English prose and poetry;

(*b*) of the Old and the New Testament and the English liturgy;

(*c*) of a work or portion of a work of some standard English divine, to be announced by the Examiners at the conclusion of the preceding year's examination.

6. The Examiners shall be at liberty to institute a preliminary trial in all or any of the foregoing subjects, and to admit only such candidates to the examination as shall have satisfied them in that trial. Preliminary trial.

7. The sum available for the Prizes shall be determined by the Faculty Board within a range approved from time to time by the Council. The Examiners shall have discretion, if candidates of Value of prizes.

sufficient merit present themselves, to award *either* a First Prize and a Second Prize *or* two Prizes of equal value.

Payments to Examiners.

8. Each Examiner shall receive from the income of the Fund such sum as the Faculty Board may determine within a range approved from time to time by the Council. Any expenses incurred in conducting the examination shall be defrayed from the income of the Fund.

9. The winner of a Prize shall not be eligible to compete a second time.

Other uses of Fund.

10. After provision has been made for the award of the Prizes in accordance with Regulations 7 and 8, the remaining income of the Fund shall be applied by the Faculty Board for the purpose of promoting elocution or good reading among the students of the University. The Faculty Board may delegate their functions under this regulation to a committee not necessarily consisting wholly of members of the Board.

Unexpended income.

11. Any unexpended income in the Fund may be added to the capital of the Fund or accumulated for use as income in subsequent years, as the Faculty Board may determine.

Power of alteration; proviso.

12. The University shall have power from time to time, by Grace, to vary and alter the foregoing regulations as to the method of conducting the examination and awarding the prizes, and to make such new rules as may be necessary for rendering the Prizes efficient in promoting elocution or good reading among the students of the University: provided, however, in compliance with the wish of the donor, that the reading of the Old and New Testament, the English liturgy, and a work or portion of a work of some standard English divine, shall under all circumstances form part of the examination.

Winton Fund for the Physics of Sustainability

Grace 2 of 17 November 2010

Name.

1. The sum of £20m given to the University by the Trustees of the David Harding Foundation shall form a fund called the Winton Fund for the Physics of Sustainability.

Purpose.

2. The purpose of the Fund shall be the promotion and support of a programme of innovative fundamental research in physics and other associated fields called the Winton Programme for the Physics of Sustainability which shall be designed to help meet the need for sustainable use of natural resources including in particular energy generation and use.

Managers.

3. The Managers of the Fund, who shall also be the Committee of Management of the Winton Programme for the Physics of Sustainability, shall be:

(*a*) the Head of the Department of Physics;
(*b*) the Cavendish Professor of Physics;
(*c*) the Pro-Vice-Chancellor with responsibility for research;
(*d*) one suitably qualified person who is not employed by the University, appointed by the General Board on the nomination of the Council of the School of the Physical Sciences for a period of five years;
(*e*) one person appointed by the General Board on the nomination of the donor for a period of five years.

Should either a single person hold more than one of the positions named at (*a*), (*b*), and (*c*), or any of these positions be vacant, a further Manager or Managers shall be appointed by the General Board, on the nomination of the Council of the School of the Physical Sciences, so that the number of Managers shall always be five. The Head of the School of the Physical Sciences and the Director of the Programme, if not otherwise Managers of the Fund, shall have the right of attendance at meetings of the Managers in a non-voting capacity.

Director.

4. The Director of the Programme, who shall be a University officer, shall be appointed by the General Board on the nomination of the Council of the School of the Physical Sciences. He or she shall hold office for three years, and shall be eligible for reappointment for one or more further terms of three years. The position of Director shall not be held concurrently with the office of Head of the Department of Physics.

5. The Director shall be the scientific and administrative head of the Programme, and shall be advised by an Advisory Board and the Managers of the Fund.

Application.

6. The income and capital of the Fund shall be used to promote and encourage innovative fundamental research in physics and other associated fields both within the University and in collaboration with other suitable partner institutions, through:

(*a*) the creation and support of awards and fellowships designed to attract outstanding scientific researchers from around the world;

(*b*) the payment of the costs, including the associated indirect costs of the University, of such University offices and posts as may be established, in accordance with the relevant provisions of the Statutes and Ordinances, from time to time, on the recommendation of the Managers, as a charge on the Fund;
(*c*) the support of innovative research with the potential to attract additional funding from other sources;
(*d*) the provision of shared experimental equipment and infrastructure;
(*e*) outreach work to promote the discoveries and achievements enabled by the Fund and the public policy opportunities thereby presented;
(*f*) other means as may be agreed by the Managers.

7. Any unexpended income may be either added to the capital of the Fund or accumulated for use as income in subsequent years, as the Managers may determine. Unexpended income.

8. Any proposal to release capital from the Fund to the value of £2m or more in any one year shall be agreed unanimously by all the Managers and notified to the General Board. Release of capital.

Advisory Board

1. There shall be an International Advisory Board for the Programme, which shall consist of no fewer than eight distinguished persons in relevant disciplines. Board members.

2. The Chair of the Advisory Board, who shall not be a Manager of the Fund or a beneficiary of the Fund, shall be appointed by the General Board on the nomination of the Managers of the Fund for periods of not more than four years at a time. Chair.

3. Six members of the Advisory Board shall be appointed by the Managers of the Fund and the Chair of the Advisory Board in the Michaelmas Term to serve for periods of up to four years at a time as shall be determined by the Managers. One member of the Advisory Board shall be appointed by the Chair of the Advisory Board on the nomination of the Trustees of the David Harding Foundation. Tenure.

4. The General Board, the Managers of the Fund, and the Chair of the Advisory Board, in making their appointments to the Board, shall ensure that at least one of its members is not a resident member of the University and that at least one member shall be a senior resident member of the University. Board members residency.

5. The Advisory Board shall meet at least once every year with the Managers of the Fund and the Director of the Programme.

6. The duty of the Advisory Board shall be to advise the Managers and Director on the future strategic direction of the Programme and to review the use and effectiveness made of the Fund. Board's duties.

Winton Research Fellowships

1. In order to enable outstanding post-doctoral scholars to take part in and contribute to the work of the Programme there shall be Research Fellowships for persons who are pursuing advanced work in physics and other associated fields that will help meet the need for sustainable use of natural resources including in particular energy generation and use. Fellowship requirements.

2. Appointments of Winton Research Fellowships shall be made by the Director of the Programme in consultation with at least two of the Managers. Appointments.

3. A Research Fellowship shall be tenable for one or more years at a time, and may be renewed by the Managers for up to a total of five years. Tenure.

4. The value of each Research Fellowship shall be determined by the Managers, taking into account other sources of research funding available to the Fellow. Value.

Winton Studentships

1. The Electors to a Winton Studentship shall be the Managers. Electors.

2. In order to be eligible for a Studentship, a candidate must have been admitted, or be seeking admission, as a student studying towards the Ph.D. Degree in the broad area of sustainability normally within the School of the Physical Sciences. Eligibility.

3. In the Michaelmas Term each year the Managers shall publish a notice giving the date by which, and the manner in which, applications are to be submitted. Publication of application date.

Studentship.

4. The Studentship shall provide

(*a*) a maintenance payment, determined from time to time by the Managers, for a period of up to no more than four years,

(*b*) a payment to assist in meeting the Student's University and College fees,

(*c*) a contribution to other costs such as equipment, consumables, travel expenses, and other costs according to the discretion of the Managers to be in accordance with the prevailing norms offered by the relevant Research Councils.

Winton Fund for the Public Understanding of Risk

Fund and Professorship.

1. The sum received from the Winton Charitable Foundation for the endowment of a Professorship of the Public Understanding of Risk shall form a fund called the Winton Fund for the Public Understanding of Risk.

Managers.

2. The Fund shall be administered by three Managers who shall be the Head of the Department of Pure Mathematics and Mathematical Statistics, the Director of the Statistical Laboratory, and the Winton Professor of the Public Understanding of Risk, provided that, if two or more of these posts are held by the same person or if one or more of these posts is vacant, the Faculty Board of Mathematics shall appoint one or more additional Managers so as to ensure that there are three Managers.

Application of income.

3. The first charge on the income of the Fund shall be the stipend, national insurance, pension contributions, and associated indirect costs of the Professor payable by the University.

Other applications.

4. After provision has been made in accordance with Regulation 3, the income of the Fund may be applied to support the activities of the Professorship in such a manner as shall be approved by the General Board on the recommendation of the Managers.

Unexpended income.

5. Any unexpended income for a financial year may (i) be accumulated and added to the capital of the Fund, or (ii) be held as an income reserve and, in any one or more subsequent years, expended in accordance with Regulations 3 and 4, or (iii) be used to promote teaching and research in mathematics including, in particular, the public understanding of risk and mathematics in such a manner as shall be approved by the General Board on the recommendation of the Managers.

Insufficient income.

6. If in any year the income of the Fund is insufficient to meet the expenses set out in Regulations 3 and 4, the Managers with the approval of the Faculty Board of Mathematics may use all or such part or parts of the capital of the Fund as they shall determine for or towards such expenses.

Alternative use of the Fund.

7. If the General Board are satisfied on the recommendation of the Faculty Board of Mathematics that funding the Professorship as set out in Regulations 3 and 4 no longer provides a suitable and effective method of using the Fund, the University shall have power to resolve to hold the capital and income of the Fund on trust for the promotion of teaching and research in mathematics including, in particular, the public understanding of risk and mathematics.

Neil Wiseman Fund

Title.

1. The sums subscribed in memory of Neil Ernest Wiseman, Reader in Computer Graphics and Fellow of Wolfson College, shall form a fund called the Neil Wiseman Fund.

Purpose.

2. The income and the capital of the Fund, and any accumulated unspent income, shall be placed at the disposal of the Head of the Computer Laboratory and shall be used for the support of Graduate Students working in the Computer Laboratory.

Wishart Fund

Title.

1. The sum bequeathed to the University by the late Mrs Olive Wishart shall form a fund called the Wishart Fund.

Purpose.

2. The annual income of the Fund and any unexpended income accumulated in the Fund shall be used to provide a prize or prizes called the John Wishart Prize or Prizes in memory of John Wishart, of Clare College, formerly Reader in Statistics and Director of the Statistical Laboratory. The Prize or Prizes shall be awarded each year by the Examiners for the examination in Mathematics for the M.A.St. Degree and for Part III of the Mathematical Tripos to the candidate or candidates who have shown distinction in statistics in that examination.

3. The value of a John Wishart Prize shall be determined by the Faculty Board of Mathematics within a range approved from time to time by the Council. Value.

4. The foregoing regulations, other than Regulation 1 and this regulation, shall be subject to alteration by Grace on the recommendation of the Faculty Board of Mathematics to enable all or part of the resources of the Fund to be used for a purpose similar to that specified in Regulation 2. Power to change regulations.

BERNARD WOLFE HEALTH NEUROSCIENCE FUND

1. The benefaction of £3.7m from the Woco Foundation for the support of work in health neuroscience shall form a fund called the Bernard Wolfe Health Neuroscience Fund to be held in perpetuity. Title and purpose.

2. The first charge on the income of the Fund shall be the stipend, national insurance, and pension contributions, payable by the University in respect of the Bernard Wolfe Professor of Health Neuroscience, together with an annual provision in respect of recruitment expenses. Professorship.

3. The second charge on the income of the Fund shall be such share of the University's central overheads attributed to the School of Clinical Medicine as is fair and appropriate to be borne by the Fund in support of the Professorship.

4. From time to time the General Board, on the recommendation of the Faculty Board of Clinical Medicine, may establish an office for a single tenure in place of the Professorship. During any period that such an office is held the first and second charges on the income of the Fund shall be as set out in Regulations 2 and 3 above, save that references to the Bernard Wolfe Professor of Health Neuroscience shall be treated as references to the office established under this regulation. Establishment of an office in place of Professorship.

5. After provision has been made in accordance with Regulations 2 to 4, the income of the Fund shall be applied to meet the cost of such secretarial assistance, research assistance, office supplies, and equipment, (in that order), as the Professor or holder of the office mentioned in Regulation 4 may in his or her unfettered discretion require.

6. Any unexpended income of the Fund in a financial year shall be Unexpended income.

(*a*) added to the unexpendable capital of the Fund; or

(*b*) applied in support of the work of the Professor or the holder of the office mentioned in Regulation 4; or

(*c*) accumulated for use as income in future years (in the order of priorities mentioned in these regulations);

as the General Board, on the recommendation of the Faculty Board of Clinical Medicine, shall determine, provided that no unexpended income shall be applied in accordance with paragraph (*b*) and no income accumulated in accordance with paragraph (*c*) shall be used unless the General Board are satisfied that, after applying reasonably prudent assumptions, the unexpendable capital of the Fund is sufficient to generate income to support the primary purpose of the Fund, as set out in Regulations 2 to 4, in perpetuity.

7. Pending the appointment of the first Bernard Wolfe Professor for Health Neuroscience or (if earlier) the appointment of the first holder of the office mentioned in Regulation 4, the income of the Fund may be applied in support of such research in Health Neuroscience as the Woco Foundation may approve in writing, provided that the General Board are satisfied that, after applying reasonably prudent assumptions, the unexpendable capital of the Fund is sufficient to generate income to support the primary purpose of the Fund, as set out in Regulations 2 to 4, in perpetuity.

8. The Faculty Board of Clinical Medicine shall make an annual report to the Woco Foundation on the financial position of the Fund, the work supported by it, and the detailed expenditures by the Fund under Regulations 2 to 7 for that work. Annual report.

WOLFSON FUND FOR INDUSTRIAL CO-OPERATION

1. The sums made available by the Wolfson Foundation shall form a fund called the Wolfson Fund for Industrial Co-operation. Title.

2. The first charge on the Fund shall be the cost of maintaining a Directorship of Industrial Liaison. Director of Industrial Liaison.

3. Subject to the first charge being met in accordance with Regulation 2, the capital and income of the Fund shall be applied for the purpose of advancing co-operation between members of the University and industry in such manner as the General Board shall from time to time determine.

T. B. Wood Prize

Title. **1.** The sum given by the Indian Tea Association shall be separately invested, and the income from the Fund shall be used to provide the T. B. Wood Prize.

How awarded. **2.** The Prize shall be awarded by the Examiners for the subject Plant Sciences in Part II of the Natural Sciences Tripos for an outstanding performance in the examination for that subject.

3. If no candidate be deemed worthy of the Prize the income for that year shall be added to the capital of the Fund.

Wood-Legh Prize

Fund. **1.** The sum bequeathed to the University by Kathleen Louise Wood-Legh, Litt.D., formerly Fellow of Lucy Cavendish Collegiate Society (now Lucy Cavendish College), in gratitude to the Faculty of History, shall form a fund called the Wood-Legh Fund.

Prize. **2.** The income of the Fund shall be used to provide a prize called the Wood-Legh Prize, which shall be awarded each year by the Degree Committee for the Faculty of History, on the recommendation of the Examiners for the Examination in Medieval History for the M.Phil. Degree (one-year course), to the candidate who in that examination has submitted the best dissertation.

Value. **3.** The value of the Prize shall be the annual income of the Fund.

4. If in any year the Prize is not awarded, the income for that year shall be added to the capital of the Fund.

H.E. Woodman Fund and Prize

Title. **1.** The sum of £300, the gift of Mrs L. Woodman in memory of her late husband, H. E. Woodman, M.A., Reader in Animal Nutrition, shall form a fund called the H. E. Woodman Fund, the income from which shall be used to provide an H. E. Woodman Prize.

Awarders and purpose. **2.** The Awarders of the Prize shall be the Regius Professor of Botany and the Professor of Genetics. The Prize shall be awarded in the Lent Term each year to that person among the successful candidates for the degree of Ph.D. or M.Phil. who in the judgement of the Awarders has presented the best dissertation on a subject connected with the chemistry of foods.

Who are eligible. **3.** Those students shall be eligible for the Prize who have been approved by the Board of Graduate Studies during the preceding calendar year either for the award of the Ph.D. Degree under the regulations for Graduate Students or for the award of the M.Phil. Degree.

Value. **4.** The value of the Prize shall be the income of the Fund. If in any year the Prize is not awarded the income for that year shall be added to the capital of the Fund.

Wordsworth Fund and Studentships

Title. **1.** The benefaction of the late William Nicholson shall form a fund called the Wordsworth Fund in memory of the late Right Reverend Christopher Wordsworth, D.D., Lord Bishop of Lincoln, and of his services to the Church especially as Headmaster of Harrow School.

Purpose. **2.** The income of the Fund shall be used to maintain one or more Wordsworth Studentships for the purpose of enabling students educated at the University of Cambridge who have taken honours and who intend to take Holy Orders in the Church of England to continue in residence at Cambridge for a period of not less than twelve months in order to study Divinity.

Electors. **3.** The Electors to the Studentships shall be the Regius Professor of Divinity and two members of the Faculty of Divinity appointed by the Faculty Board of Divinity in the Michaelmas Term to hold office for two years from 1 January following their appointment.

Notice of election. **4.** The Electors shall give not less than three months' notice of their intention to proceed to an election.

Who are eligible. **5.** A Studentship may be held by any member of the University provided that not less than five terms have passed after his or her first term of residence, and provided also that he or she

(*a*) has obtained honours in at least one Honours Examination;

(*b*) has declared in writing to the Electors that he or she (i) intends to take, or has taken, Holy Orders in the Church of England, and (ii) if elected, will reside in the University for at least one year from the date of taking up the Studentship and will *either* (1) take at least one Part of the Theological and Religious Studies Tripos, or the Examination in Theology and Religious Studies for the M.Phil. Degree, or the Advanced Diploma in Theology and Religious Studies, as the Electors may require, *or* (2) engage in some form of research in theology approved by the Electors.

6. Any eligible person may apply for a Studentship provided that three terms have passed after his or her first term of residence. Each application must be accompanied by Applications.

(*a*) a record of the candidate's previous education;

(*b*) the declaration required by Regulation 5(*b*);

(*c*) a full account of the candidate's pecuniary circumstances including details of any assistance expected from other sources.

7. The election shall be held not later than 30 September. If two or more candidates are of equal merit, the Electors shall give preference to persons who have been educated for not less than two years at Harrow School or at Winchester College. Elections.

8. A Studentship shall be tenable for twelve months from 1 October following or next but one following the election. A Student shall be eligible for re-election, provided that no one shall hold the Studentship for more than four years in total. Tenure.

9. The value of a Studentship shall be such sum as shall be determined in each particular case by the Electors, within a range approved from time to time by the Council. In determining the value of a Studentship the Electors shall take into account the pecuniary circumstances of the holder. Value.

10. The emolument of a Studentship shall be paid in half-yearly instalments in advance; provided that the Electors may withhold the whole or part of the second instalment if they are not satisfied that the Student is diligently pursuing his or her studies. Payment of emolument.

11. These regulations, other than Regulations 1 and 2 and this regulation, may be changed by Grace subject to the approval of the Lord Archbishop of Canterbury. Alterations.

Donald Wort Fund I

1. The sum bequeathed to the University by the late Donald Arthur Wort, M.A., of Hughes Hall and Corpus Christi College, shall form a fund called the Donald Wort Fund, which shall be used for the advancement of the study of music in the University and for such other purposes connected with music in the University as the Faculty Board of Music shall from time to time decide. Fund and purpose.

2. The first charge on the income of the Fund shall be the provision of three Donald Wort Prizes, as follows: Prizes.

(*a*) one Prize shall be awarded to the candidate who is adjudged by the Examiners for Part IA of the Music Tripos to have shown the greatest proficiency in that examination;

(*b*) one Prize shall be awarded to the candidate who is adjudged by the Examiners for Part IB of the Music Tripos to have shown the greatest proficiency in that examination;

(*c*) one Prize shall be awarded to the candidate who is adjudged by the Examiners for Part II of the Music Tripos to have shown the greatest proficiency in the Test of Performance in that examination.

3. The value of the Prizes shall be determined by the Faculty Board of Music within a range approved from time to time by the Council. Value.

4. After provision has been made for Donald Wort Prizes in accordance with Regulation 2, any unexpended income accumulated in the Fund shall be applied at the discretion of the Faculty Board of Music: Unexpended income.

(*a*) to enable distinguished scholars to visit the Faculty of Music from time to time in order to give lectures and engage in other work of benefit to the Faculty;

(*b*) to purchase books for the library of the Faculty of Music;

(*c*) to assist in any other way the advancement of the study of music in the University;

(*d*) to make grants for purposes connected with music in the University.

Donald Wort Fund II

Fund and purpose.

1. The sum given to the University by the Trustees of the late Donald Arthur Wort, M.A., of Hughes Hall and Corpus Christi College, shall form a fund called the Donald Wort Fund II, the income of which shall be used for the support of music making in the University.

Managers.

2. The Managers of the Fund shall be the Faculty Board of Music, who may delegate some or all of their functions under these regulations to a Committee not necessarily consisting wholly of members of the Board.

Application of income.

3. The income of the Fund shall be applied at the discretion of the Managers to facilitate music making in the University by any or all of the following means:

(*a*) by the provision of group coaching in instrumental playing or in singing for members of the University *in statu pupillari*;

(*b*) by the provision of grants to support concerts or other musical events arranged by the Faculty Board of Music or by University or College musical societies, or by groups of individuals;

(*c*) by such other means as the Managers may think fit.

Unexpended income.

4. Any unexpended income may be either added to the capital of the Fund or accumulated for use as income in future years, as the Managers may determine.

Stat. E XIII.

Worts Travelling Scholars Fund

At disposal of General Board.

1. The Worts Travelling Scholars Fund shall be at the disposal of the General Board for making grants for the promotion or encouragement of investigations in countries outside Great Britain respecting the religion, learning, law, politics, customs, manner and rarities, natural or artificial, of those countries, or for purposes of geographical discovery or of antiquarian or scientific research in such countries, subject to any conditions as to publication of the results of investigations which may be laid down at the time of the making of the grant.

Who may receive grants.

2. Grants shall be confined to members of the University. They may be made without regard to the standing of the applicant.[1]

Method of payment.

3. Each grant shall be paid on the application of the person concerned or of a person designated for the purpose, in the financial year in which it is approved after a Notice of the grants made for that year has appeared in the *Reporter*.

Reports of investigations.

4. Each recipient of a grant shall send to the Registrary a short report of his or her investigations as soon as practicable after returning to this country.

Wrenbury Scholarship Fund[2]

Deed Poll sealed on 5 August 1974 under Grace 3 of 24 July 1974

Deed Poll.

This declaration of the trusts of the Wrenbury Scholarship Fund is made by The Chancellor Masters and Scholars of the University of Cambridge (hereinafter called 'the University') with the consent and approval of the Right Honourable John Burton Baron Wrenbury (hereinafter called 'Lord Wrenbury').

Whereas this Deed is supplemental to an Indenture (hereinafter called 'the Principal Deed') dated the 22nd day of March 1918 and made between Henry Burton the first Baron Wrenbury (hereinafter called 'the first Baron'), Robert Burton Buckley, Albert Charles Clauson and Bryan Burton Buckley of the one part and the University of the other part whereby certain trusts were declared for the endowment and advancement of the study of Political Economy, is also supplemental to a Deed Poll dated the 5th day of May 1928 and made by the first Baron and the University whereby other trusts for the same object were substituted for the trusts declared by the Principal Deed, and is also supplemental to a Deed Poll dated the 2nd day of July 1949 (hereinafter called 'the Principal Deed Poll') and made by Lord Wrenbury and the University whereby other trusts for the same object are substituted for the trusts declared by the Principal Deed and by the said Deed Poll dated the 5th day of May 1928.

And whereas in the opinion of the University it has now become desirable that other trusts for the original object should be substituted for those declared by the Principal Deed Poll.

And whereas the Trust Fund constituted by the investments and cash specified in the Schedule to the Principal Deed is now represented by the investments specified in the Schedule hereto.

Now this deed witnesseth as follows:

[1] Although Regulation 2 allows grants to be made without regard to the standing of the applicant the General Board have given notice that they will give preference to candidates below the standing of Master of Arts.

[2] Supplemental Deed Poll and regulations substituted for the trusts declared by the Principal Deed Poll (see *Ordinances*, 1973, p. 797), as amended by Grace 7 of 12 December 1973.

1. In exercise of the Power for this purpose conferred upon the University by Clause 16 of the Principal Deed Poll and of every or any other power enabling the University in this behalf and with the consent and approval of Lord Wrenbury testified by his joining in and executing this Deed the University hereby revokes and determines the trusts substituted by the Principal Deed Poll and hereby declares that in lieu thereof the Trust Fund shall be held upon the trusts and subject to the powers and provisions hereinafter contained.

2. There shall be maintained in the University of Cambridge a Wrenbury Scholarship Fund, the income of which shall be used for the study of economics and political economy, by the provision of Wrenbury Scholarships in Political Economy, or otherwise.

3. The University may from time to time make regulations for the Fund.[1]

4. Clauses 2 and 3 of this deed shall have effect as though they were a Statute of the University of Cambridge made under the provisions of the Universities of Oxford and Cambridge Act 1923, save that they shall only be amended by the procedure set out in clause 5. Without prejudice to the generality of the foregoing, Statutes E, I, F, IV, and K, 5 of the Statutes of the University of Cambridge[2] shall apply to clauses 2 and 3 of this deed as though they were a Statute of the University.

5. If at any time in the opinion of the University the purposes for the time being directed for the appropriation of the Trust Fund shall cease to be the most useful or the manner for the time being directed for its appropriation to such purposes shall cease to be the most useful and appropriate the University may by Deed Poll under their Common Seal but only with the consent in writing of the person if any who being *sui juris* and competent shall for the time being be the holder of the Barony now held by Lord Wrenbury of Old Castle determine the trusts for the time being declared and declare such other trusts being trusts for the encouragement of the study of Economics or any other branch of study as they think fit. Variation by Deed Poll.

The Schedule hereinbefore referred to
3934 units in the University Amalgamated Fund.

APPENDIX

THE WRENBURY SCHOLARSHIP FUND

1. The Managers of the Wrenbury Scholarship Fund shall be the Faculty Board of Economics. Managers.

2. The Faculty Board shall have power to delegate some or all of their functions under these regulations to a committee not necessarily consisting wholly or partly of members of the Faculty Board.

3. The income of the Fund shall be applied to provide such number of Scholarships called Wrenbury Scholarships in Political Economy as shall be determined by the Managers from time to time subject to a maximum approved from time to time by the Council. Scholarships.

4. The value of a Scholarship shall be such sum within a range approved from time to time by the Council as shall be determined by the Managers, after they have taken account of any other financial resources that may be available to the Scholar. Value.

5. The Scholarships shall be tenable for one year from 1 October following the election, or from such date as the Managers may determine. Tenure.

6. The emoluments of the Scholarship shall be paid in two half-yearly instalments in advance. The second instalment of the emolument shall not be paid unless the Scholar has satisfied the Managers that he or she has pursued with sufficient diligence a course of study and training for research approved by them. Emoluments.

7. The Scholarships shall be open to any member of the University who is or is about to be registered as a Graduate Student working under the supervision of the Degree Committee for the Faculty of Economics. It shall be the duty of a Scholar to undertake during the tenure of the Scholarship a course of full-time study and training for research in some branch of economics or political economy, or economic history subsequent to the year 1800. A Scholar shall not during the tenure of the Scholarship follow any business or profession, or engage in any other work which in the opinion of the Managers would interfere with his or her course of study and training for research, provided that the Managers may specifically permit a Scholar to hold a Teaching Assistantship in the Faculty of Economics. Eligibility.

8. The Managers may for good cause delay, reduce, or withhold any payment to be made to a Scholar, and they may for good cause deprive a Scholar of the Scholarship.

9. The date by which and the manner in which application for the Scholarships shall be made shall be determined by the Managers. Before the end of the Michaelmas Term in each year the Managers shall publish a Notice of the date and manner which they have determined, and they shall also indicate the date by which they expect to proceed to an election. Notice of election.

[1] See Appendix to this Deed Poll.
[2] Now Statutes A IX 1, E I, and Regulation 19 of the regulations for Funds, Studentships, Prizes, Lectureships, etc.

Unexpended income.

10. Unexpended income may be either added to the capital of the Fund or accumulated for use as income in future years, as the Managers may determine.

Wright Studentship

Object.

1. The object of the Wright Studentship shall be to encourage the study of the Arabic language and literature and of subjects closely connected therewith.

Electors.

2. The Electors to the Studentship shall be the Degree Committee for the Faculty of Asian and Middle Eastern Studies.

Who are eligible.

3. The Studentship shall be open to any member of the University who has been admitted to a degree.

Election.

4. The election should be made annually during the first half of the Lent Term.

5. Notice that an election is to take place shall be given by the Electors by the beginning of the Michaelmas Term preceding the election.

Applications.

6. Applications shall be sent to the Registrary by the end of the Michaelmas Term preceding the election and shall be accompanied by a statement of the course of research which the candidate proposes to undertake together with such evidence of her or his qualifications as the candidate may wish to submit.

Tenure.

7. The Studentship shall be tenable for one year, but a Student may be re-elected for a second year and again for a third year, but for no longer. In exceptional circumstances the Electors may postpone the tenure to a subsequent year.

Value.

8. The value of the Studentship shall be such sum as shall be determined by the Electors within a range approved from time to time by the Council. The payments shall be made in two half-yearly instalments in advance, provided that the Electors may withhold the second instalment if they are not satisfied that the Student has been pursuing his or her course with sufficient diligence.

Unexpended income.

9. Any unexpended income accumulated in the Fund shall be applied in the first instance at the discretion of the Electors to the award of a second Graduate Studentship. Any income remaining thereafter may be applied, at the discretion of the Head of the Department of Middle Eastern Studies in consultation with and with the agreement of the teaching officers in Arabic in the Department, to provide Scholarships for undergraduate members of the University or to the promotion of the study of Arabic in the University in any other way which they may from time to time determine.

Wright Rogers Scholarship Fund

Title.

1. The sum bequeathed to the University by the late Mrs E. M. B. Wright Rogers with the main purpose of founding, in memory of her husband Herbert Edwin Wright Rogers, two Wright Rogers Law Scholarships for proficiency in the study of the Laws of England shall form a fund called the Wright Rogers Scholarship Fund.

Electors.

2. The Electors to the Scholarships shall be the Faculty Board of Law, who may delegate any of their functions under these regulations to a Committee consisting of not less than three members of whom at least one shall be a member of the Faculty Board.

Notice.

3. The Registrary shall publish a Notice before the end of the Lent Term of each year announcing the offer of two Scholarships.

Who are eligible.

4. Any person who has successfully completed a degree-bearing course of study in any university or polytechnic in the United Kingdom and who has spent at least one year in the study of law shall be eligible for a Scholarship.

Applications.

5. Candidates shall send their applications, accompanied by an outline of their career and of their proposed course of study at Cambridge, to the Secretary of the Faculty Board of Law so as to arrive not later than 1 August. Every candidate shall request two persons each to send a written assessment of his or her qualifications to the Secretary of the Faculty Board of Law so as to arrive by the same date.

Election.

6. An election shall be held not later than 30 September in each year.

Tenure.

7. The tenure of a Scholarship shall be for one year from 1 October following the election, and shall be conditional upon the Scholar being or becoming a member of the University. A Scholar shall be eligible for re-election for a second year and again for a third year but for no longer.

8. It shall be the duty of a Scholar, under the direction of the Electors, to undertake study or research in the University relating to the Laws of England. Duty of Scholar.

9. The value of a Scholarship shall be such sum, within a range approved from time to time by the Council, as the Electors may determine after taking into account any other financial resources that may be available to the Scholar. Value.

10. Any unexpended income accumulated in the Fund may be applied, at the discretion of the Electors, for the furtherance of the study of the Laws of England Surplus income.

(*a*) in making grants to Wright Rogers Law Scholars and to other graduate students in the Faculty of Law who are in need of financial assistance;

(*b*) in meeting expenses of legal research;

(*c*) in such other manner as the Faculty Board of Law may from time to time determine.

Yasuda Trust and Banking Company Fund

1. The benefaction of the Yasuda Trust and Banking Company Limited, on the occasion of the fifteenth anniversary of the opening of the Company's operations in London, shall form a fund for the advancement of Japanese Studies in the University. Fund and purpose.

2. The Managers of the Fund shall be the Professor of Japanese Studies, the Head of the Department of East Asian Studies, and the teaching officers in Japanese in the Department. Managers.

3. The capital and the income of the Fund shall be used to provide postgraduate Scholarships and postdoctoral Fellowships in Japanese Studies tenable in the University, and to make grants to meet expenses incurred or to be incurred by the holders of these awards. Each year the Managers shall give public notice of the competition for awards. Candidature shall not be restricted to members of the University, but a person appointed to a Scholarship or a Fellowship shall become a member of the University before his or her tenure begins. Scholarships and Fellowships.

4. The tenure of the awards shall be determined by the Managers. The value of the awards and of any grants made in respect of expenses incurred or to be incurred by award holders shall be determined by the Managers within ranges approved from time to time by the Council. Tenure and value.

5. The Managers shall seek to make at least one appointment of a Scholar or a Fellow in each year during the currency of the Fund, and shall seek to expend the capital and the income of the Fund during such period. At least one appointment each year.

6. Any surplus income or capital may be applied by the Managers, with the approval of the Council, for the support of Japanese Studies in the University. Surplus income or capital.

Ghulam Yazdani Essay Prize Fund

1. The sum of £1,000 donated to the University by Mrs G. Yazdani shall form a fund to be called the Ghulam Yazdani Essay Prize Fund, the income of which shall be used for the purpose of awarding a Ghulam Yazdani Essay Prize for Ancient Deccan History and Archaeology. Name and purpose.

2. The Managers of the Fund shall be three persons appointed by the Faculty Board of Asian and Middle Eastern Studies in the Michaelmas Term to serve for three years from 1 January following their appointment. Managers.

3. The Managers shall award the Prize for the best essay submitted by any member of the University *in statu pupillari* on a topic approved by the Managers in the field of Ancient Deccan history and archaeology. The Managers shall publish a Notice annually of the manner in which and the dates by which topics shall be proposed and essays submitted. Prize.

4. The value of the Prize shall be the annual income of the Fund. Value.

5. If in any year the Prize is not awarded, the income shall be accumulated in the Fund and may be used from time to time by the Managers to make grants for the general advancement of Indian archaeology. Grants.

Yorke Prizes

Stat. E XXI.

1. One or more Yorke Prizes shall be offered annually for an essay on a legal subject (including the history, analysis, administration, and reform of law). Prizes.

2. The Prizes shall be open to any graduate of the University or any person who is or has been registered as a Graduate Student in the University, provided that at the date by which essays are to be submitted Who may compete.

(*a*) if the candidate has been approved by the Board of Graduate Studies for the degree of Ph.D. or M.Litt. under the regulations for the Ph.D., M.Sc., and M.Litt. Degrees, not more than four years have passed after the date of such approval;

(*b*) if the candidate has not been so approved, not more than ten years have passed after the date of his or her admission to a first degree, whether of this or another university.

Selection of subject. **3.** Each candidate shall obtain the approval of the Faculty Board of Law for the proposed subject of his or her essay.

Submission of essay. **4.** Essays shall be submitted to the Secretary of the Faculty Board of Law so as to arrive not later than the last day of the Michaelmas Term. Each essay shall be printed or typewritten, shall be presented in bound form, and shall be of not less than 30,000 words nor more than 100,000 words in length; provided that the Faculty Board may remit any of these requirements on application by a candidate.

Referees. **5.** The Board shall have power to refer each essay to one or more referees for report. Each referee shall receive such fee as the Board shall determine within a range approved from time to time by the Council.

Awards. **6.** The Board shall determine the awards and their decision shall be final.

7. The Board shall have power:

(*a*) to award one or more Yorke Prizes, each of such value as they shall determine within a range approved from time to time by the Council;

(*b*) to make awards to candidates whose essays, although meritorious, have not gained the award of a Yorke Prize;

(*c*) to make grants to assist an author to publish his or her Yorke Prize essay.

8. A successful candidate shall deposit one copy of his or her essay in the Squire Law Library.

9. The Prize shall be paid as soon as the copy of the essay has been deposited in accordance with Regulation 8.

Other uses of income. **10.** The Board shall also have power:

(*a*) to award Studentships or Scholarships or make grants to any persons engaged in research in law;

(*b*) to make grants for the delivery of lectures;

(*c*) to make grants for the publication of works (in addition to assisting the author to publish a Prize essay under Regulation 7(*c*));

(*d*) to make grants for the promotion of any other undertaking connected with the study of law;

and to attach to the award of any such Studentship, Scholarship, or grant such conditions as they may think fit.

11. There shall be charged on the income of the Fund, or on any accumulation of unexpended income, any amounts payable under Regulations 5, 7, and 10.

Committee. **12.** The Faculty Board of Law may delegate any of their functions concerning the Yorke Prizes and Fund to a Committee not necessarily consisting wholly of members of the Board.

Olga Youhotsky, Catherine Matthews, and Irene Gore Fund and Prize

Title. **1.** The gift to the University of Mrs Catherine Matthews and Dr Irene Gore in memory of their mother Mrs Olga Youhotsky, and the gift of Dr Gore in memory of Mrs Matthews, shall form a fund called the Olga Youhotsky, Catherine Matthews, and Irene Gore Fund.

Prize. **2.** There shall be a prize, called the Olga Youhotsky, Catherine Matthews, and Irene Gore Prize, which shall be awarded annually by the Examiners for Part II of the Modern and Medieval Languages Tripos for an outstanding performance in Russian in that examination.

Value. **3.** The value of the Prize shall be the annual income of the Fund.

Thomas Young Medal

Name and purpose. **1.** The Thomas Young Medal shall be awarded to a candidate who in Part IIB of the Archaeological and Anthropological Tripos has shown outstanding distinction in any branch of oriental archaeology.

Awarders. **2.** The Awarders shall meet in June of each year in which a candidate offers a branch of oriental archaeology in either of the examinations specified in Regulation 1.

3. The Awarders in any year shall be

(*a*) The Herbert Thompson Reader in Egyptology;

(*b*) not more than six persons appointed by the Faculty Board of Human, Social, and Political Science.

Quorum. **4.** No business shall be conducted at a meeting unless at least three Awarders are present.

SHEIKH ZAYED FUND FOR ISLAMIC STUDIES

1. The sums received from the Sheikh Zayed Foundation of Abu Dhabi for the promotion and encouragement of Islamic Studies in the University shall form a fund called the Sheikh Zayed Fund for Islamic Studies. Name and purpose.

2. The Fund shall be under the control of a Board of Managers who shall be: Managers.

(*a*) the Vice-Chancellor (or a duly appointed deputy) as Chair;

(*b*) the Chair of the Faculty Board of Divinity;

(*c*) a member of the Faculty Board of Divinity appointed by that Board;

(*d*) two persons appointed by the Trustees of the Sheikh Zayed Foundation.

3. The first charge on the income of the Fund shall be the stipend, national insurance, pension contributions, and associated indirect costs payable by the University in respect of a University office established in the Faculty of Divinity which shall be associated with the name of Sheikh Zayed. University office.

4. The second charge on the income of the Fund shall be the provision of a prize called the Sheikh Zayed Prize for Islamic Studies, which shall be awarded by the Examiners for Parts IIA and IIB of the Theological and Religious Studies Tripos for distinction in Islamic Studies as shown by performance in one or more papers of the examination designated for that purpose by the Faculty Board of Divinity.[1] The value of the Prize shall be determined by the Managers, within a range approved from time to time by the Council. Prize.

5. After provision has been made in accordance with Regulations 3 and 4, the income of the Fund shall be applied at the discretion of the Managers for the encouragement of Islamic Studies in the University.

6. Any unexpended income of the Fund in a financial year may be either added to the capital of the Fund or accumulated for use as income in future years, as the Managers may determine. Unexpended income.

7. The University shall have power to alter these regulations by Grace on the recommendation of the Faculty Board of Divinity, subject to the approval of the Trustees of the Sheikh Zayed Foundation.

ZOOLOGY FUND FOR OUTSTANDING CONTRIBUTION

Grace 3 of 19 January 2011

1. The sums subscribed in honour of former Professors in the Department of Zoology to recognize excellence in performance or outstanding contribution shall form a fund to be called the Zoology Fund for Outstanding Contribution. Title and purpose.

2. The capital and income of the Fund shall be at the disposal of the Head of the Department of Zoology to reward, at her or his sole discretion, one or more students, teaching, research, and support staff in the Department who have acquitted themselves with distinction in their study or work. Who are eligible.

[1] The Faculty Board of Divinity have designated the following papers for this purpose until further notice: Paper C1.D; Paper C9, in any year in which a subject in Islamic Studies has been prescribed as one of the subjects for this paper.

CHAPTER XIII

FINANCE AND PROPERTY

FINANCIAL MATTERS

Amended by Grace 1 of 27 November 2013

Duties. **1.** It shall be the duty of the Council, acting through the Finance Committee:

(*a*) to collect the contributions for University purposes due from the several Colleges under the provisions of Statute G II;

(*b*) to publish the accounts of the several Colleges;

Property and securities. **2.** The Finance Committee shall have authority under the Council to exercise the powers of the University under Statute A II 3–5, subject to Regulations 5 and 6 below and subject to the following restrictions:

(*a*) approval by Grace of the Regent House shall be required for the sale or transfer of any real or leasehold property belonging to the University, or for the grant of a lease on behalf of the University for a period of sixty years or more, if in the judgement of the Council such a sale or lease would deprive the University of the use of lands or buildings which are of present or prospective use to the University;

(*b*) all investments capable of registration shall be registered in the name of the Chancellor, Masters, and Scholars of the University of Cambridge or of nominees appointed by resolution of the Finance Committee;

(*c*) all certificates for securities shall be deposited for safe custody at a bank or other recognized financial institution, which shall be approved by resolution of the Finance Committee;

(*d*) all purchases and sales of bearer bonds or securities transferable by mere delivery or by delivery and endorsement shall be conducted through bankers approved for the purpose by resolution of the Finance Committee;

(*e*) approval by Grace of the Regent House shall be required for the grant of security for any loan, and the terms of any loan so secured shall provide for the repayment of the loan within fifty years or less either by annual instalment or otherwise.

Bankers. **3.** Barclays Bank plc shall be Bankers to the University until further order.

Financial year. **4.** The financial year of the University shall end on 31 July.

5. Regulations 2–4 shall not apply to the finance and property of the University Press, which shall be governed by Statute J and by the regulations for the Press Syndicate made under that Statute and Regulation 2 shall not apply in connection with the management, development, and stewardship of the North West Cambridge Estate which is the responsibility of the West and North West Cambridge Estates Syndicate, which shall be governed by regulations for that Syndicate made under Statute A VI 1.

6. In order to facilitate the management of investments under the control of the University the Council may at any time and from time to time resolve that all or any part of the endowments or other funds of the University and of the funds of any specific trust for purposes connected with the University of which the University is trustee (hereinafter called the constituent funds) be treated as one amalgamated fund invested for the rateable benefit of the constituent funds and to and upon any such resolution the following provisions shall apply:

(*a*) an investment shall not be brought into an amalgamated fund upon its first constitution or upon any change of investment unless it is an authorized investment for all the constituent funds;

(*b*) an amalgamated fund shall be held on behalf of the constituent funds in shares as nearly as may conveniently be proportionate to their respective capital values upon the first constitution of the amalgamated fund; such shares shall be fixed by resolution of the Council on the recommendation of the Finance Committee of the Council;

(*c*) the Council, on the recommendation of the Finance Committee of the Council, may at any time increase any amalgamated fund by adding thereto new constituent funds and upon any such increase shall fix the share of such new constituent funds in the resulting amalgamated fund;

(*d*) the Council may at any time wind up any amalgamated fund and divide the investments thereof between the constituent funds in proportion to their respective shares therein or may bring all or any of the shares into a new or other amalgamated fund in accordance with the provisions of this regulation;

(*e*) the Council may appropriate and distribute for expenditure as much of the fair value of any amalgamated fund as prescribed by Ordinance as it considers in its absolute discretion is prudent having regard to the total return achieved and reasonably to be expected in the long term of the amalgamated fund and distribute in proportion to the constituent funds at the time of the distribution.

7. The Council, the Finance Committee, and the General Board shall jointly issue regulations for the financial and operational management of University sites and buildings.

8. The Buildings Committee shall be a joint committee of the Council and the General Board. It shall be the duty of the Buildings Committee: Buildings Committee.

(*a*) within the terms of sites and buildings approved by the Council, the Finance Committee, and the General Board from time to time

(i) to consider and give technical approvals for building proposals submitted to them in accordance with regulations for sites and buildings approved by the Council, the Finance Committee, and the General Board;

(ii) to consider and give such approvals as it thinks fit for the delegation of responsibility for maintenance and building work; and

(iii) to oversee applications for planning approvals on University land;

(*b*) to maintain general oversight over the technical aspects of the erection of any new building or the alteration of any existing building;

(*c*) to advise on the annual budget needed in the Building Maintenance Fund. Building Maintenance Fund.

(*d*) to perform such other duties as the Council and General Board may from time to time direct.

NOTICES BY THE COUNCIL

Ethical guidelines on the acceptance of benefactions

1. Under Regulation 6 of the regulations for the Vice-Chancellor[1] the Regent House has delegated the acceptance of benefactions to the Vice-Chancellor. In exercising this responsibility, the Vice-Chancellor will seek the advice of the Advisory Committee on Benefactions and External and Legal Affairs of the Council for all benefactions over £1m, or that are likely to give rise to significant public interest.

2. Charity law places certain constraints on charities, and in recommending acceptance of any benefaction the Advisory Committee shall make available to the Vice-Chancellor information under the following headings:

(*a*) Are the purposes of the benefaction compatible with the purpose of the University as defined in its Statutes?

(*b*) Do the purposes of the benefaction fall within the University's mission and strategic plan?

(*c*) What additional costs or burdens, if any, would acceptance of the benefaction create for the University?

(*d*) Is there published evidence that the proposed benefaction arises in whole or in part from activity that

- evaded taxation?
- violated international conventions that bear on human rights?
- limited freedom of inquiry?
- suppressed or falsified academic research?

In the case of unproven allegations of criminality against a potential donor, no account shall be taken of mere rumour, but care will be exercised in accepting any benefaction, or continuing negotiations towards a possible benefaction, where there is a risk of significant damage to the University's reputation.

(*e*) Is there evidence that the proposed benefaction, or any of its terms, will

- require action that is illegal?
- limit freedom of inquiry?
- suppress or falsify academic research?
- create unacceptable conflicts of interest for the University?

(*f*) Is there evidence that acceptance of the proposed benefaction or compliance with any of its terms will damage the University's reputation, including deterring other benefactors?

Although benefactions which are uncontroversial and which are worth less than £1m may not be subject to detailed scrutiny by the Advisory Committee, acceptance will nevertheless be considered explicitly against these ethical guidelines.

3. All members of the University involved in fundraising are encouraged to consult Development and Alumni Relations at an early stage in their discussions with a potential benefactor. Development and Alumni Relations can advise on the use of these guidelines, and consultation will also reduce the risk of unco-ordinated approaches to a single potential donor; spread familiarity with the process for accepting benefactions; and may allow an early warning of anyone unknowingly approaching a potential benefactor whose donation is not likely to be acceptable.

[1] See p. 697.

Financial Regulations

Adopted and approved on 28 May 2012 by the Council after consultation with the Finance Committee

A. Preliminary

Terms in capitals are defined in Schedule 2 where necessary to aid interpretation.

The Council is responsible for the supervision and management of University resources and finances. The purpose of these Regulations is to provide sound arrangements for internal financial management, accounting and control, promote best value for money, and fulfil the University's legal and financial obligations.

1. Scope

1.1. These Regulations apply to
- all University Income and Business;
- all Staff; and
- all Departments and University subsidiary companies but not Cambridge University Press and Cambridge Assessment.

2. Ethical Principles

2.1. University Business shall be conducted in accordance with the Nolan Principles: selflessness, integrity, objectivity, accountability, openness, honesty, and leadership.

2.2. Staff must ensure that

(*a*) neither their conduct of University Business; nor

(*b*) the conduct of any person or organization entering into any contract or arrangement with the University contravenes the Bribery Act 2010. (See Financial Regulation 20.)

There are four offences under the Bribery Act:
- Bribing another person;
- being Bribed;
- Bribing a foreign public official; and
- failure to prevent Bribery.

Staff must not use their authority or office for personal gain and must always seek to uphold and enhance the standing of the University.

2.3. Staff must declare to their Head of Department any personal interest, which may affect any University Business and act in accordance with the instructions given as to management of any conflict.

2.4. Staff must seek written permission from their Head of Department before accepting gifts or hospitality directly or indirectly from suppliers, other than low value items such as a gift worth less than £25 or hospitality worth less than £50. Receipt of gifts or hospitality must not influence or appear to influence the choice of supplier or prejudice the University's reputation. If in doubt, gifts and hospitality must be refused. Excessive or lavish gifts or hospitality may constitute Bribery.

2.5. Where Heads of Department have a conflict of interest or wish to accept gifts or hospitality (other than low value items) they must seek the advice of the body or person to whom they are responsible, for example Head of School, management board or General Board, and act as advised.

3. Staff Responsibilities

3.1. Staff shall, irrespective of sources of funding,
- comply with these Regulations and Statutes, Ordinances, and University policies;
- take all necessary advice;
- assess and manage risks (including to health and safety) entailed in University Business they transact;
- safeguard University property and Income for which they are responsible;
- use University resources economically, efficiently, effectively, and secure value for money;
- ensure compliance with all obligations in contracts relevant to them entered into by or on behalf of the University; and
- comply with the University's legal, financial, administrative, and other obligations including to HEFCE, HM Revenue and Customs, and other government authorities.

3.2. Non-observance of these Regulations may result in disciplinary action.

B. Heads of Department

4. Definition and Responsibility

4.1. 'Head of Department' means any of the following: the Head of a Department or a Faculty not organized in Departments, Secretaries of Faculty Boards, Head of a Centre, Institute, or other body under the supervision of the General Board or Council, and Head of a Division within the Unified Administrative Service. 'Department' is interpreted accordingly.

4.2. Heads of Department shall ensure
- proper allocation of funds;
- sound financial control, authorizations, and separation of duties;

- that accounts are correctly maintained;
- that funds available for spending are not exceeded;
- that these Regulations are publicized and observed within their Department; and
- that all information and explanations required by the University's internal or external auditors are provided promptly.

5. Departmental Management

5.1. Heads of Department may designate in writing one or more people to execute specified tasks for and subject to the supervision of the Head of Department. The Head of Department remains responsible.

C. Contract Execution and Commencement

6. Authority to Sign Contracts

6.1. Subject to Regulations 6.2, 6.3, and 18.4, Heads of Departments have authority to sign contracts in the course of the ordinary business of their Department in respect only of available funds for which they are responsible.

6.2. Contracts for the purchase, lease, or licence of land or property or for the erection, demolition, substantial repair, or alteration of buildings must be referred to EM and are subject to the Sites and Buildings Regulations (see further Regulation 32 and Explanatory Note in Section M). The Director of EM or the Registrary shall approve and sign all such contracts, provided all approvals required under Statutes, Ordinances, and the Sites and Buildings Regulations have been given.

6.3. The Head of the Research Operations Office shall approve and sign all contracts relating to sponsored research activity.

6.4. Subject to Regulations 6.2 and 6.3, the following persons have authority to sign contracts affecting more than one Department:

- the Vice-Chancellor;
- a Pro-Vice-Chancellor;
- the Chair of the Faculty Board or Head of School where all the Departments affected are in that Faculty or School;
- the Registrary;
- the Director of Finance; and
- the Head of Procurement Services.

7. Sealing

7.1. The following persons have authority to authorize affixing of the University's seal, where any necessary approvals are in place:

- the Vice-Chancellor;
- a Pro-Vice-Chancellor;
- the Registrary;
- the Director of Finance; and
- (for assignment of University intellectual property) the Head of the Research Operations Office.

8. Documentation, Liability, and Performance

8.1. The person having authority to execute a contract is responsible for its safekeeping. If required, the Registrary will keep the documentation for contracts affecting more than one Department.

8.2. Departments are responsible for meeting obligations and for all costs or losses arising from contracts entered into by or for them.

8.3. Contract performance shall not begin before

- all necessary approvals have been obtained; and
- the contract has been executed or the person having authority to execute the contract gives prior written consent, which consent shall normally be given only if key terms have been agreed and the risks created by delay outweigh the risk of proceeding prior to full contractual agreement.

D. Income and Expenditure

9. Accounting and Other Records

9.1. Heads of Department shall

- maintain financial records as specified in *Statutes and Ordinances*;
- certify whether annual statements of account (which are distributed by the Finance Division) are true and fair and that responsibilities under these Regulations have been discharged during the year; and
- properly record all transactions in CUFS and any other financial system, the use of which has been authorized by the Director of Finance.

9.2. Staff must comply with the Finance Division CUFS user policy.

9.3. Record-keeping must comply with the Data Protection Act 1998. The University is subject to the Freedom of Information Act 2000 and members of the public may request copies of University documents. Advice on these matters must be obtained from the University's Data Protection and Freedom of Information Officer.

10. Cash and Banking

10.1. All University Income must be paid promptly into a bank account in the name of the University (and into no other account) and be accounted for in CUFS. All University expenditure must be paid from a University bank account and be accounted for in CUFS.

10.2. Departments and Staff have no authority to open bank accounts (whether in the UK or abroad) for any University activities without the prior written consent of the Director of Finance.

10.3. Where possible, Departments shall separate duties for receiving and recording University Income. Where this is not possible, regular independent checks shall be made.

10.4. The Financial Procedures Manual lays out further financial requirements including in respect of cash, petty cash, banking, credit card, and related matters.

11. Management of Expenditure

11.1. Heads of Departments are authorized to incur expenditure not exceeding the limits of funds available to the Department. They are responsible for ensuring that monitoring and control arrangements are adequate to prevent over-commitment of expenditure and that all funds under their control are used only for the purposes for which they are allocated. The Head of Department (or budget holder where authorized by the Head of Department) shall approve expenditure.

11.2. The Financial Procedures Manual lays out further financial requirements including in respect of Travel, subsistence, and entertainment and related matters.

12. Supplying Goods or Services including Research

12.1. Heads of Departments must establish procedures to ensure that

- all supplies of goods and services are authorized and are supplied as agreed;
- trading accounts are managed to break even or achieve a surplus;
- all relevant risks to the University are considered and managed, there are adequate credit control procedures, and supplies are made only where the credit risks are acceptable;
- the University's standard terms and conditions are where possible applied;
- invoices other than for sponsored research funding (see Regulation 13.3) are raised
  - in the name of the University of Cambridge showing the University's VAT number;
  - through CUFS unless prior written consent is given by the Director of Finance; and
  - wherever possible in sterling for settlement in sterling (any exchange risk lies with the Department for invoices in a currency other than sterling);
- the liability for all taxation is established and tax is charged and accounted for as appropriate;
- except for research contracts, which are subject to Regulation 13, the full economic cost to the University is recovered, unless the advice of the Taxation Section is sought and it is appropriate to do otherwise having regard to the particular circumstances (see further Regulation 29);
- best value is obtained for sale of any goods to external bodies or to staff (and the Taxation Section consulted about VAT and tax implications);
- sales to staff or their families below the cost incurred by the Department in providing the benefit (including where no charge is made) are recorded and reported as a taxable benefit at the end of the tax year;
- where payment for goods is received in cash, the sum does not exceed the cash equivalent of €15,000 (for any single transaction (per the Money Laundering Regulations 2007)).

12.2. With the exception of research grants claims, Departments are responsible for debt collection in respect of invoices issued to third parties. Advice must be sought from the Director of Finance where legal action to recover monies is considered.

12.3. Uncollectible debts, including in respect of sponsored research activity, will be an expense against the Department. The following authorities exist to write off bad debts or for part settlement, where all reasonable steps have been taken to recover them:

- Debtors up to £10,000 – Head of Department
- Debtors of between £10,000 and £25,000 – Director of Finance
- Debtors over £25,000 – Finance Committee

The Taxation Section must be informed of all write-offs (including partial write-offs) of VAT invoices, as the VAT may be reclaimable.

13. Research Grants

13.1. Staff shall send grant applications and proposals for research contracts to the Research Operations Office for approval before their submission in accordance with Research Office policy.

13.2. Heads of Department shall ensure there are appropriate arrangements

(*a*) in conjunction with the Research Office to

- cost grant applications and proposals on the basis of the full economic costs of the research; and
- recover charges for facilities and overheads in accordance with and at the rates specified in University policy or record the extent and justification for subsidizing the cost where in exceptional cases Head of Department agrees not to apply University policy for recovery rates; and

(*b*) ensure that research which is funded is conducted to meet the funding terms and conditions.

13.3. The Research Office shall raise all invoices for sponsored research funding.

13.4. All research grant or contract income and expenditure, from whatever source of funds, must be notified to the Research Office and no part of this income may be transferred into donation accounts or other special funds, other than funding remaining unspent at the end of the research which the funder has agreed the Department may retain.

13.5. Heads of Department shall ensure that expenditure on research activity complies with these Regulations. Financial control and record-keeping shall also comply with any additional Research Council or other funder's requirements.

13.6. The Research Office shall ensure all grants are closed on a timely basis and without residual balances.

14. Donation Accounts and Trust Funds

14.1. Donations belong to the University, not to an individual, and must be paid into a donation account in accordance with Regulation 10.1. Donations must be requested and received exclusively for charitable purposes. Receipt which improperly influences any decisions made by or on behalf of the University may constitute Bribery. Acceptance of donations must be made in accordance with the Ethical Guidelines for the Acceptance of Benefactions.

14.2. Heads of Department must ensure that

- donation accounts and trust funds are maintained in credit;
- funds are applied for the public benefit for charitable, educational, or research purposes only; and
- any Ordinances or regulations governing the receipt of donations and the conduct of individual accounts are followed.

14.3. University trust funds are governed by regulations set out in *Statutes and Ordinances*. Trust fund managers shall ensure that funds are used for proper purposes in accordance with the rules of the specific fund and the University's general charitable purposes.

14.4. Transfers of donated funds to other institutions can only be to other charitable bodies and must always be approved by the Head of Department and be in accordance with the terms of the gift and the University's general charitable purposes. Transfers shall not be made until the receiving institution has confirmed in writing that the terms of the gift will be observed. Where the transfer relates to the Head of Department's research the Director of Finance's prior written consent must be obtained.

14.5. Donations cannot be transferred to individuals, except where the individual is the donor and the University is unable to meet the terms of the original gift.

E. Investment and Borrowing

15. The Cambridge University Endowment Fund ('CUEF')

15.1. The University's Chief Investment Officer is responsible for all CUEF investment management activities. The Chief Investment Officer appoints and monitors external investment managers.

15.2. No Department or trust of the University may invest in any securities or other investments (including land and buildings) without the prior approval of the Finance Committee.

15.3. Acquisition of land is also subject to the Sites and Buildings Regulations (see para 32.1 below).

16. Investment in the CUEF and Deposit Account

16.1. Surplus funds (only) may be invested in the CUEF and Deposit Account. The Director of Finance is responsible for approving all new and any changes in CUEF holdings. Deposit Account eligibility rules and interest rates are published by the Director of Finance from time to time.

17. Borrowing, Guarantees, and Loans

17.1. Departments must not borrow money outside the University.

17.2. No guarantees or letters of comfort may be issued except with the prior written consent of the Director of Finance.

17.3. No Department may make a loan including to staff or (outside the normal course of business) extend credit arrangements without the Director of Finance's prior written consent.

F. Purchasing

18. Obtaining Goods, Services, or Construction Works

18.1. Expenditure of £2,000,000 or above on capital items (inclusive of VAT) requires the consent of the Planning and Resources Committee.

18.2. Value for money in purchasing is normally demonstrated through competition The table in Schedule 1 sets out the minimum competition requirement when obtaining goods, services, or construction works for all Departments; the only flexibility for a Department being set out in Financial Regulation 18.3. These requirements apply to all expenditure irrespective of the source of funding (including spending of grant monies and Leasing). If there is any reason to believe that offers which have been received are not competitive, further offers must be obtained. A Department must not enter into separate contracts, nor apply the Total Value calculation separately to contracts, with the intention of avoiding the application of these Regulations.

18.3. Prior written consent not to follow the competition procedures may be granted

(*a*) for construction and Construction Related Procurement by

- the Director of EM where the Total Value is less than the EU Threshold; and
- the Registrary where it is at or exceeds the EU Threshold;

(*b*) for other procurement by

- the Head of Department where the Total Value is £50,000 or less and the Director of Finance where the Total Value exceeds £50,000 by recording the reasons on Procurement Services' online dispensation form;
- for any procurement where the Director of Finance has issued a general consent (irrespective of the Total Value).

Schedule 1 sets out non-exhaustive examples of circumstances where dispensation might be appropriate. Notwithstanding the grant of a dispensation, all the other requirements of Financial Regulations must be met, including Regulations 18.5 to 18.9 inclusive.

18.4. (*a*) Departments must seek all necessary advice.

(*b*) The Head of Department's *prior* written consent is needed for one or more payments in advance in relation to any contract totalling £10,000 or less.

(*c*) The Director of Finance's advice and prior written consent is needed for:

- procurement (other than construction) where the Total Value exceeds £100,000 (advice only);
- procurement where the Total Value exceeds £50,000 and supplier terms are used (advice only);
- all Leasing[1] irrespective of the Total Value (except where a Leasing Framework Contract is used – see the definitions in Schedule 2); a cost benefit analysis shall be submitted where consent is required;
- payments in advance exceeding £10,000; and
- payment under early settlement terms exceeding £250,000.

(*d*) The Director of EM's advice is needed for procurement falling within Regulation 6.3.

18.5. All purchasing shall be based on a specification drafted after consultation with anticipated users and assessment of the risks associated with the procurement. The Procurement Procedures provide further guidance on purchasing.

18.6. Goods and services may be purchased externally only if

- they are required for the achievement of financial, academic, or organizational plans;
- they are not reasonably available elsewhere within the University; and
- the source, sufficiency, and terms of the funding have been checked and confirmed.

18.7. Heads of Department must establish levels of authorization and segregation of duties for contracts where the Total Value exceeds £500 for:

- short listing and acceptance of tenders;
- ordering and inspection of goods and services; and
- payment.

Where payment duties cannot be segregated, transactions must be independently checked on a regular basis.

18.8. Orders must state the nature, quantity, and price of goods and services to be provided and where possible apply the University's terms and conditions. Copies of orders must be kept securely. Where an order is placed through CUFS, the electronic record suffices.

18.9. Official orders must be produced in a form approved by the Director of Finance for all purchases above £100 or any lower threshold set by the Head of Department.

18.10. Where equipment is to be loaned to the University free or at a discount, advice must be taken, the principles of Regulation 18 observed and an agreement put in place, including to regulate the University's responsibilities and rights at the end of the loan.

19. Receipt of Goods or Services, Payments for services to individuals

19.1. All goods and services must be checked promptly on receipt to ensure that they accord with order requirements and suppliers advised promptly about any discrepancies. Copies of signed delivery notes must be retained. If deliveries have to be acknowledged prior to checking, endorse the delivery note 'Goods received unchecked'.

19.2. Invoices must be checked and not authorized for payment until the goods or services have been checked, unless authority is in place to pay in advance (see Regulation 18.4).

19.3. Payments to individuals must comply with Regulation 31.6.

19.4. Heads of Department shall establish arrangements for monitoring and regular appraisal of purchasing activity to ensure that best value for money is secured for current and future purchases.

G. Bribery and Fraud

20. Bribery, Fraud, and Irregularity

20.1. Heads of Department shall implement procedures as required under the University's policy against Bribery and Corruption, including to prevent Fraud. Any member of staff shall report immediately in writing any suspicion of Bribery, Fraud or other irregularity to the Registrary and the Director of Finance. The Registrary is the lead officer under the University's policy against Bribery and Corruption.

[1] Leasing, as defined in Schedule 2, does not include pure finance leases, which are a form of borrowing which Departments must not do (Regulation 17.1).

20.2. The Director of Finance will advise the University's internal auditors and if necessary the University Security Adviser and police, and report to the Audit Committee and the Vice-Chancellor any Fraud or irregularity which has any of the following characteristics:

- exceeds £10,000
- is unusual or complex
- public interest is likely.

20.3. Any member of Staff who has reasonable grounds for believing there is serious malpractice within the institution (see Human Resources Division website, Policies and Procedures; Public Disclosure by University Employees: Whistleblowing Policy) should raise their concerns using the specified procedure.

H. Corporate Requirements

21. Taxation

21.1. Heads of Departments shall ensure that their Department accounts correctly for VAT and where appropriate corporation tax. Where there is any doubt as to the correct VAT or tax treatment of a transaction, the Taxation Section must be consulted.

21.2. Heads of Departments shall ensure that any taxable benefits paid to individuals are reported to the Finance Division for inclusion in P11D returns.

22. Legal Advice and Proceedings

22.1. The Council's Advisory Committee on Benefactions and External and Legal Affairs and the Registrary have authority to take legal advice and to conduct legal proceedings. Departments shall not take any action to initiate or defend legal proceedings or obtain external legal advice without first involving the Legal Services Office, which will seek consent from the Registrary or Advisory Committee as necessary. The Legal Services Office should be contacted immediately if legal proceedings are threatened or served on any part of the University or any University subsidiary company. See also Regulation 23.3 and 23.4.

23. Insurance

23.1. Departments must comply with the insurance requirements set out in Financial Procedures and on the Insurance Section web pages.

23.2. Contents whether owned, borrowed, or hired must be valued, recorded, and notified to insurers. Departments should regularly review the value of contents held and notify the Insurance Section of

- departmental moves;
- the acquisition and disposal of high value items (exceeding £1,000,000); and
- temporary removal from University premises (where the single article exceeds £50,000 or the total exceeds £100,000).

23.3. Departments must take all necessary steps to prevent losses and accidents and ensure that the Insurance Officer is advised immediately of any new unusual or significant risk. Liabilities should not be accepted on behalf of the University without careful consideration. Any liabilities not covered by insurance will fall on the Department.

23.4. Third party claims must be passed immediately to the Insurance Section without comment to the third party to ensure that the University's legal position and insurance policies are not compromised.

24. Overseas Activity

24.1. No Department may enter into any arrangements for activity outside the United Kingdom, unless the Director of Finance gives prior written consent, where this activity involves either or both setting up any establishment and employing individuals overseas. In giving such consent, the Director of Finance shall seek advice from the Legal Services Office and the Taxation Section. The Director may require that external advice is procured at the expense of the Department seeking to enter into such arrangements. Consent shall not be deemed to override the need to obtain any other approval from University bodies including the General Board.

I. Commercial Activity

25. New Income Generation or Trading Activity

25.1. Apart from core teaching, research, and the organization of conferences, when a new income-generating or trading activity is set up (whether in the UK or abroad), the Head of Department must consult the Taxation Section beforehand to consider the VAT implications and whether the activity constitutes trading which might be subject to Corporation Tax.

25.2. The Director of Finance may direct that transactions be undertaken through a University subsidiary company.

26. University Companies

26.1. No University company may be formed or shares taken in any company (whether in the UK or abroad) for any purpose without advice from the Director of Finance and the prior approval of the Finance Committee, except when done through the Investment Office for investment purposes or by Cambridge Enterprise in relation to the exploitation of intellectual property.

26.2. University subsidiary companies shall enter into and keep under review a memorandum of understanding with the University. Each company shall operate in accordance with such memorandum and within the framework provided by these Regulations, including the provisions regarding procurement, and any additional procedural requirements imposed by their boards.

27. University Embedded Companies

27.1. Heads of Department and EM shall maintain departmental and corporate registers of Embedded Companies.
27.2. Heads of Department shall in respect of Embedded Companies

- undertake financial and space cost benefit analysis for all new and (periodically for) existing Embedded Companies;
- comply with Regulation 29;
- take into account University policies (including the University's Guidelines for Establishing and Working with Embedded Companies);
- ensure that Embedded Companies comply with health and safety requirements;
- put in place appropriate contractual arrangements to govern the relationship between the University and the company;
- obtain evidence of Public Liability and employer's insurance annually; and
- identify, and deal appropriately with, conflicts of interest.

28. Consultancy and Private Activity

28.1. When engaging in consultancy or other commercial activity in a private capacity, Staff must not hold themselves out as acting on behalf of the University, use University headed stationery nor (except in accordance with Regulation 29) use any University premises, facilities or resources.

28.2. The University accepts no responsibility for any work done, advice given, or activity undertaken by Staff in a private capacity. Staff are reminded of the need to take out professional indemnity insurance for such work, advice, and activity and that they are responsible for all liabilities arising including as to tax. Staff who conduct work through Cambridge University Technical Services Limited are insured under the University's insurance policies.

29. Non-University Activities – Use of Premises, Facilities, etc.

29.1. Unless the Head of Department gives prior written consent and an appropriate contractual agreement with the University is put in place, non-University activities may not be carried out on University premises nor University facilities or resources used for such activities. Care is needed to avoid breaching any obligation of the University to a third party (for example in relation to use of computing facilities and software).

29.2. Heads of Department shall ensure that appropriate charges are made for the use of University premises, facilities, or resources for non-University purposes (see Regulation 12).

29.3. The Director of EM must be consulted before making any arrangement (including leases or licences) for the use of any University space for non-University purposes. See also Regulation 27.

30. Intellectual Property

30.1. Intellectual property generated through University activities is governed by the Intellectual Property Ordinance graced on 12 December 2005.

J. STAFFING

31. Salaries and Staff Appointments

31.1. All University employees shall have a properly authorized letter of appointment in the form approved by or under the authority of the Human Resources Committee. For the avoidance of doubt the term 'employees' includes temporary and casual workers.

31.2. The source of available funding to support the posts or post shall be identified before a member of staff is given a contract of employment.

31.3. The only payments which may be made to University employees are those in accordance with approved University salary scales and such other payments as have been specifically approved by the Human Resources Committee. Rules on expenses reimbursement are set out in the Financial Procedures Manual.

31.4. Heads of Departments must provide the Payroll Section with and keep up to date a list (signed by the Head of Department) of persons authorized to sign salary documents for departmental staff paid through the payroll. Where the proposed signatory is not a University employee the approval of the Director of Finance is also required.

31.5. For all new employees the Head of Department or other authorized signatory shall ensure that the person is legally eligible to work in the UK. The Payroll Section will not add a non-EU citizen to the payroll unless it is clear that any necessary work permit has been obtained or that the immigration status of the person concerned does not require the University to seek permission for the specific employment proposed.

31.6. Individuals may not be paid as suppliers through CUFS unless the Taxation Section has given prior written consent.

K. PROPERTY

32. Property

32.1. The University's real property is governed by *Statutes and Ordinances* including the Sites and Buildings Regulations.

32.2. Departments may not acquire or dispose of real property without taking the advice of the Directors of Finance and of EM. See further Regulation 2.

32.3. The University's Taxation Section must be consulted about VAT and the tax implications of property acquisitions, disposals, and usage.

33. Stores and Equipment

33.1. Stores and equipment shall be dealt with as set out in the Financial Procedures Manual. Assets bought with University Income irrespective of the source of funding remain the property of the University until sold or destroyed, unless contracts with external sponsors specify otherwise.

33.2. Fixed asset registers must be maintained (with a minimum requirement for all items costing more than £2,000).

33.3. Heads of Departments shall keep full, proper, and correct records of stock. A full stock take must be performed annually between 1 June and 31 July in addition to any regular interim stock takes.

L. AUTHORITY

34. Council Delegations and Directions

34.1. The Council hereby gives all delegations and directions contemplated by these Regulations.

35. Revision

35.1. Every three years, or more frequently if appropriate, the Director of Finance shall arrange for these Regulations to be reviewed and for proposed changes to be submitted to the Finance Committee for onward recommendation to Council and adoption by Council Notice.

M. EXPLANATORY NOTE

- The University endeavours to conduct University Business in accordance with the Nolan Principles:[1]
- The Council is the principal executive body and policy making body of the University. The Council has general responsibility for administration, planning of work, management of resources, and general supervision of finances including of all University institutions other than the University Press.[2] It has the authority to take legal advice and conduct proceedings on behalf of the University.[3] The Council and its Finance Committee exercise the University's powers of investment subject to certain restrictions.[4] The Council has responsibilities in relation to the care, management, and maintenance of property.[5]
- The Vice-Chancellor has the customary rights and duties of the office[6] and is the designated officer responsible under the University Financial Memorandum with HEFCE and to the Public Accounts Committee.
- Pro-Vice-Chancellors perform duties as prescribed by *Statutes and Ordinances*, the Council, or the Vice-Chancellor.[7]
- Heads of University Departments and Secretaries of Faculty Boards have financial responsibility under *Statutes and Ordinances,* and are accountable for the proper application of funds.[8] Heads of other institutions are similarly responsible under particular provisions of *Statutes and Ordinances.*
- Acting Heads of Department may be appointed during a vacancy and count as Head of Department. The General Board appoints Deputy Heads and defines their duties and powers.[9]
- The Registrary is the principal administrative officer of the University under the direction of the Council and is the head of the Unified Administrative Service.[10]
- The University Offices form the Unified Administrative Service under the supervision of the Council and are organized in Divisions.[11]
- Special Ordinance A (vii) 4 provides for delegation by any University body to any committee or University officer (including in relation to finance) subject to *Statutes and Ordinances.*

[1] See the University's Corporate Governance Statement, annexed to the University's Annual Reports and Financial Statements.

[2] Statute A IV 1 and Statute F I 1(*a*). See also Ordinances, Ch I, Special Regulations for Syndicates, Local Examinations Syndicate, and Press Syndicate.

[3] Ordinances, Ch I, The Council, Legal Powers.

[4] Statute A II 8 and Ordinances, Ch XIII, Financial Matters, paragraph 2.

[5] Statute F II 2–3.

[6] Statute C III 3.

[7] Statute C III 17.

[8] Statute A V 17(*c*) and Regulation 8 of the General Regulations for the Constitution of the Faculty Boards.

[9] Ordinances, Ch IX, Departments and Heads of Department, paragraphs 4 and 5.

[10] Statute C VI 1.

[11] Ordinances, Chapter XI, Special Regulations for University Officers, Unified Administrative Service, paragraphs 1 and 2.

- The Audit Committee has responsibilities under *Statutes and Ordinances*. The University's internal and external auditors have unrestricted access to all records, assets, personnel, and premises and the right to obtain such information and explanations as they consider necessary. HEFCE, HM Revenue and Customs, and others may also have the right to audit University Business.
- The purpose of the EU Public Procurement Directives and implementing UK Regulations is to encourage competitive tendering for public contracts throughout the European Union. The Council, on the advice of their Finance Committee, declared the University to be outside their scope in December 2003. It reviews and confirms this status annually. The Council intends that the University's procurement procedures should continue to follow the good practice set out in the Regulations.
- In addition to compliance with Financial Regulations Staff must also comply with the requirements of *Statutes and Ordinances* and Sites and Building Regulations.
- Ethical guidance on acceptance of donations and the provisions for acceptance of donations by or with the authority of the Vice-Chancellor are set out in Ordinances.[1]
- The Council may from time to time determine procedures for the financial regulation and conduct of the West and North West Cambridge Syndicate after consultation with the Chair of the Syndicate.[2]

Schedule 1 – Competition Procedures

Total Value (before VAT)	**Procedure for inviting offers**		
	Framework Contracts	**Marketplace**	**Other purchases**
< £1,000	follow procedures recommended by Procurement Services for the contract	Only the price from the marketplace is required	Written price confirmation
£1,000–£25,000			Three Written Quotes
> £25,000–£50,000		Three Written Quotes or three Written Proposals, depending on complexity, risk, and value of the purchase (see the guidance in Procurement Procedures)	
> £50,000		Three Tender Submissions	
> £100,000	Procurement services must be consulted/involved and agree the most appropriate procurement method		
EU Thresholds (updated biennially) as at January 2012 > £173,934 (goods and services) > £4,348,350 (works)	EU Tenders managed through Procurement Services		

In particular the contract value must be calculated per the definition of Total Value.

Notes

1. Competition procedures are applicable unless a dispensation has been granted in accordance with Regulation 18.3.

Non-exhaustive examples of when a dispensation might be appropriate include:

- Sole source supply necessary in the following circumstances:
  - Technical compatibility, e.g. upgrade to an existing solution or purchase of additional goods which must be compatible with existing goods
  - Protection of technical rights
  - Single provider (membership of a professional institute/proprietary training)
  - Purchase of or repairs to goods or materials, including machinery or plant, available only as proprietary or patented articles
  - The work to be executed or the goods/services to be supplied constitute an extension of an existing contract where a change of supplier would cause:
    - Disproportionate technical difficulties
    - Diseconomies, or
    - Significant disruption
- Other reasons might include:
  - A one-off, unique opportunity which offers significant value
  - Extreme urgency, which was unforeseeable and is not attributable to the requester and which precludes the invitation of quotations or tenders.

2. The expectation is that, where the required goods are available, purchases up to £25,000 will be made via the Marketplace or under a Framework Contract. Other offers should not be sought, unless better value can be

[1] Ordinances, Ch XIII, Council Notice: Ethical Guidelines on the Acceptance of Benefactions.
[2] Ordinances, Ch I, West and North West Cambridge Estates Syndicate, paragraph 9.

achieved elsewhere, in which case Procurement Services must be notified so that any price discrepancies and inclusion of the supplier on the Marketplace can be explored.

Schedule 2 – Definition, Advice, and Guidance

Definitions and Interpretation

Bribery	As defined in the University's Policy against Bribery and Corruption
Certifying	Completion of Procurement Services' online dispensation form
Construction Related Procurement	The procurement of goods or services which could not be procured separately from the construction or alteration of a building (for example lift maintenance, the procurement and installation of equipment including air conditioning are not Construction Related Procurement)
CUEF	The Cambridge University Endowment Fund in which the main University endowments are pooled
CUFS	Cambridge University Financial System
Department, Head of Department	As defined in Regulation 4.1
Deposit Account	A University-wide facility that allows Departments to invest surpluses
EM	The University's Estate Management Service
Embedded Company	A company occupying University premises or whose employees' normal place of work is on University premises, other than as temporary visitors or to provide services to the University
EU Threshold	A threshold from time to time in force above which a public contract must be let in accordance with public procurement legislation
Framework Contract	Any framework contracts approved by Procurement Services
Fraud	As defined in the University's Policy against Bribery and Corruption
HEFCE	The Higher Education Funding Council for England
Investment Board	The board which manages for the University the investment of the CUEF
Leasing	A third party (including a supplier or a finance company) makes available for the University's use assets owned by the third party (ownership never vests in the University), for which a rental payment is made for a period of use; as distinct from an arrangement which amounts to borrowing to fund the possible acquisition of assets
Marketplace	Any supplier catalogue or process for obtaining offers which is made available electronically through CUFS
Nolan Principles	The seven principles identified by the Committee on Standards in Public Life
PCI	Payment Card Industry Data Security Standards
Planning and Resources Committee	Planning and Resources Committee of the Council and the General Board
Procurement Services	The University's Procurement Services section of the Finance Division
Procurement Procedures	The guidance and model documents on procurement in the Financial Procedures Manual or published on the Procurement Services web pages
Proposals	Bona fide, comparable Written bids submitted by a specified date (the Procurement Procedures provide sample documentation)
Quotes	Bona fide, comparable Written quotations (the Procurement Procedures provide sample documentation)
Research Office	The University's Research Operations Office
Staff	All employees, including temporary and casual workers, irrespective of whether their appointment specifically includes financial responsibilities and however their employment is financed together with anyone else who has any responsibility for the administration, management, or expenditure of any University Income or conducts any University Business
Tender Submissions	Formal tender documents submitted by suppliers in response to an Invitation to Tender
Total Value	The contract value or estimated value as follows: (*a*) fixed period contract: the total price to be paid or which might be paid during the whole of the period; (*b*) recurrent transactions for the same type of item: the aggregated value of those transactions in the coming 12 months; (*c*) uncertain duration: monthly payment x 48; (*d*) feasibility studies: value of the follow-on scheme; (*e*) the aggregated value of separate contracts meeting a single requirement.
University	The Chancellor, Masters, and Scholars of the University of Cambridge
University Business	University business which has a financial impact
University Income	All monies, regardless of source or purpose, which are due or paid to the University or made available to individuals because of their association with the University, including donations
Written	In writing, including submission by fax or mail

Terms are to be understood as used in *Statutes and Ordinances*, unless the context of the Regulation requires otherwise.

Words preceding 'include', 'includes', 'including', and 'included' shall be construed without limitation by the words which follow those words.

Further Guidance is contained in
- the Financial Procedures Manual
- the web pages of:
  - Finance Division (including Procurement Services and Insurance)
  - Research Office
  - Human Resources Division
  - Registrary's Office (Data Protection and Freedom of Information)
  - University Information Services
  - Legal Services Office and
  - Cambridge Enterprise (for Cambridge University Technical Services Limited)

NOTICE BY THE COUNCIL, FINANCE COMMITTEE, AND THE GENERAL BOARD

SITES AND BUILDINGS REGULATIONS

Adopted and approved on 21 July 2014 by Order of the Council, Finance Committee, and the General Board, following approval of Grace 5 of 21 May 2014.

Distributed by the Registrary to all Heads of Department.

Terms beginning with capital letters are defined in Schedule 5 where necessary to aid interpretation.

1. Scope and responsibilities

1.1 The Council, Finance Committee, and General Board have responsibilities in relation to University land and buildings.[1] These regulations are issued as part of the discharge of those responsibilities and to facilitate compliance with Statutes and Ordinances. In particular these regulations seek to set out in one place the arrangements for management of University land, buildings, and capital projects from a technical, operational, and financial perspective.

1.2 A Grace is required for the disposal of land of present or prospective use to the University;[2] and for substantial alteration of an existing University building (understood as involving aesthetic as well as financial considerations), the erection of a new University building or the demolition of an existing University building.[3] Disposal of land means the sale or transfer of any freehold or leasehold property or the grant of a lease for more than 60 years.[4]

1.3 These regulations apply to all University land and buildings owned or leased or to be acquired by the University and related capital and maintenance expenditure. The regulations must be followed by all Staff; all Departments and University subsidiary companies but not Cambridge University Press except where specifically provided (the Press is governed by its own Statute and Ordinances) or in general Cambridge Assessment (see further Schedule 2).

1.4 Compliance with these regulations does not remove any requirement to comply with the University's Financial Regulations issued by the Council.

1.5 Committee and other responsibilities in relation to land and buildings are set out diagrammatically in Schedule 1 and summarized in Schedule 2.

1.6 Breach of these regulations may result in disciplinary action and will be reported to the Registrary, who will then report to the appropriate committee.

2. Approvals and contract execution

2.1 Projects which relate to land and buildings require Expenditure Approvals and in some cases Specific Operational Approvals. The Expenditure Approvals are set out in Schedule 3 and the Specific Operational Approvals in Schedule 4.

2.2 Compliance with Schedule 3 satisfies the requirement in Financial Regulations for Capital Approval.[5]

2.3 Heads of Department (see definition in Schedule 5) shall

(*a*) take all necessary advice and

(*b*) for projects involving their Department secure the approvals required by these regulations before any contractual commitment is given.

2.4 Subject to the issue of Expenditure and Specific Operational Approvals, the Head of Estate Management shall approve and sign all contracts for the purchase, lease or licence of land or property or for the erection,

[1] Statutes A IV 1, F I 1(*a*), F II 2–3, and Regulation 2 of the regulations for Financial Matters.

[2] Regulation 2(*a*) of the regulations for Financial Matters.

[3] Statute F II 3.

[4] Regulation 2(*a*) of the regulations for Financial Matters.

[5] Financial Regulation 18.1.

demolition, substantial repair or alteration of buildings. Financial Regulation 7.1 governs who may authorize the affixing the University's seal.

2.5 Financial Regulation 8.3 governs when contract performance may begin.

3. Authorities and review

3.1 The Council, Finance Committee, and General Board hereby give all delegations and directions contemplated by these regulations.

3.2 Chairs of committees shall have delegated authority to act for their committees between meetings in urgent, minor or straightforward cases, reporting in full to the next committee meeting.

3.3 All decisions made under delegation shall be reported back to the responsible committee, which may call the matter back for further consideration.[1]

3.4 Every three years, or more frequently if appropriate, the Registrary shall arrange for these regulations to be reviewed and for proposed changes to be submitted to the Council, Finance Committee, and the General Board and adoption by their joint Notice.

Schedule 1 – Committee structure diagram

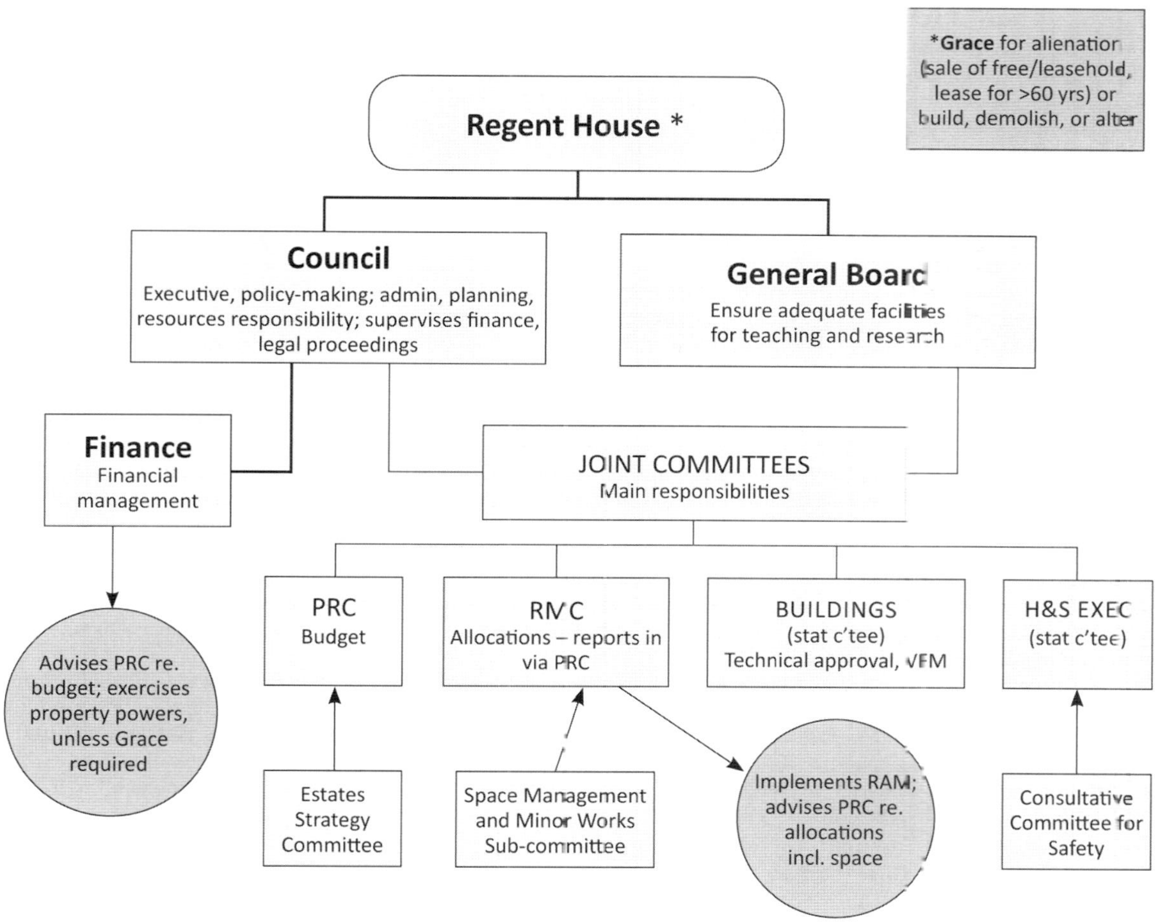

Schedule 2 – Committee and other responsibilities

1. The Council

1.1 The Council[2] is the principal executive and policy making body of the University, responsible for administration, planning, resources, and supervision of finances.[3] The Council delegates business to its standing and occasional committees.[4] The committees dealing with finance, planning and resources are the Finance Committee and the Planning and Resources Committee (PRC).[5]

[1] Special Ordinance A (vii) 4(*b*): delegation does not relieve the delegating body of responsibility.

[2] https://www.governance.cam.ac.uk/committees/council/.

[3] Statutes A IV 1, F I 1(*a*), F II 2–3, and Regulation 2 of the regulations for Financial Matters. See also the special regulations for Syndicates, the Local Examinations Syndicate, and the Press Syndicate.

[4] Statute A IV 7(*b*).

[5] The Consultative Report of the Council in March 2004 (see http://www.admin.cam.ac.uk/reporter/2003-04/weekly/5955/11.html at para 1(*a*)).

1.2 The Council has the primary responsibility for determining if the sale or transfer of freehold or leasehold land or the grant of a lease for 60 years or more would deprive the University of the use of land or buildings which are of present or prospective use to the University (defined in Schedule 5 to these regulations as "PPU Land"). If so its disposal requires a Grace.[1] For the purposes of ongoing management, PPU Land is divided into the Operational and the Non-Operational Estate (both as defined in Schedule 5).

1.3 The Council lays down the scheme of Expenditure and Specific Operational Approvals set out in Schedules 3 and 4.

1.4 The Council and Finance Committee delegate the overall management of the Operational Estate to PRC and the Buildings Committee, which report back to the Council.

1.5 The General Board is responsible for ensuring there are adequate resources for teaching and research.[2]

2. Council Committees

2.1 The Finance Committee and Audit Committee are standing committees of the Council.[3] The Council from time to time establishes further standing or occasional committees.[4]

2.2 The *Finance Committee* is responsible under the Council for financial management and stewardship of all assets and land, whether PPU Land or land held for investment. The Finance Committee itself oversees the management of the Non-Operational Estate, which is managed and maintained on a self-funding basis. The Non-Operational Estate includes land held for investment. The Finance Committee's remit includes overview of the University's accounts (and accounting policies, practices, and systems), consideration of management accounts and investment management, and the custody of tangible and intangible University assets. It reports to the Council as necessary and advises PRC about the budgetary envelope predicted prudently to be available to the University for both capital and recurrent expenditure. It is responsible with the Council for investment.[5]

2.3 All borrowing requires Finance Committee approval.

3. Joint Council and General Board Committees

3.1 The *Planning and Resources Committee* (PRC)[6] is a joint committee of the Council and General Board, reporting to both bodies. It is responsible for advice to the central bodies about major strategic matters and for the conduct, subject to the responsibilities of the Council and the General Board, of the higher-level planning and resource management of the University including, with advice from the Finance Committee, proposing the University budget to the Council and the General Board.

3.2 PRC provides the financial oversight for the management of the Operational Estate and approves the estate plans for the management of PPU Land. It ensures the provision of funding for acquisition of land and work in relation to land.

3.3 PRC gives Funding Approvals (see Schedule 3).

3.4 The *Estates Strategy Committee* is a sub-committee of the PRC which advises on the strategic management of the Operational and Non-Operational Estate. In doing so it takes account of the estate plans for Cambridge University Press and Cambridge Assessment.[7]

3.5 The *Buildings Committee*[8] is a sub-committee of the PRC. It gives Technical Approvals where the Total Cost exceeds £1m. It reviews retrospectively the Technical Approvals given by the Space Management and Minor Works Sub-Committee, giving advice where necessary about how to approach future decisions. Estate Management advises and conducts the operational work for Buildings Committee with the assistance of Finance Division and the Planning and Resource Allocations Office (PRAO).

3.6 The Buildings Committee advises PRC on the annual budget needed in the Building Maintenance Fund for the maintenance of the Operational Estate. It gives Technical Approvals (see Schedule 3) and technical advice on the management of the Operational Estate. The cost of maintaining the Operational Estate is chargeable to the Buildings Maintenance Fund or, if the body giving the Funding Approval determines (see Schedule 3), to departmental or other funds.[9] The Buildings Committee has power to delegate maintenance responsibility.[10]

[1] Regulation 2(*a*) of the regulations for Financial Matters.

[2] Statute A V 1(*c*)(ii).

[3] Statute A IV 7(*a*).

[4] Statute A IV 7(*b*).

[5] Statutes A IV 7–10 and A II 3–8, Regulation 2 of the regulations for Financial Matters, the Consultative Report of the Council in March 2004 (see http://www.admin.cam.ac.uk/reporter/2003-04/weekly/5955/11.html at para 8(*b*)).

[6] See http://www.admin.cam.ac.uk/cam-only/committee/prc/. The PRC is a joint committee of the Council and General Board, serviced by the Planning and Resource Allocation Office (PRAO). See the Council Consultative Committee report in March 2004 at http://www.admin.cam.ac.uk/reporter/2003-04/weekly/5955/11.html at para 6, 8(*a*), 10(*a*), and 19.

[7] See Grace 5 of 21 May 2014.

[8] The Consultative Report of the Council identifies the Buildings Committee as responsible for advising the PRC about executive matters relating to the operational estate and the buildings programme, including buildings maintenance, within budgets and estate plans approved by the central bodies on the recommendation of the PRC. It is a joint committee of the Council and General Board serviced by the Planning and Resource Allocation Office (PRAO), with business prepared by the Director of Estate Management. See http://www.admin.cam.ac.uk/reporter/2003-04/weekly/5955/11.html at para 8 and 10(*c*). See also Grace 1 of 9 February 2005, and Regulation 9 of the Sites and Buildings regulations (1994 as amended in 2005), confirmed by these regulations.

[9] Regulations for Buildings Maintenance Funds; and Regulation 9 of the Sites and Buildings regulations (1994 as amended in 2005), re-confirmed by these regulations.

[10] Regulations 9 and 10 (1994 as amended in 2005). The delegation is confirmed by these regulations.

3.7 The Buildings Committee oversees applications for planning approvals for the Operational Estate and is consulted by Cambridge University Press and Cambridge Assessment about planning applications for premises and land in the city of Cambridge.[1] Planning Applications which it considers are inconsistent with the University's long-term estate strategy and agreed principles and policies for planning and design may be referred to the Estates Strategy Committee before any approval is given.

3.8 The *Space Management and Minor Works Sub-committee* (SMMWS) is a sub-committee of the Resource Management Committee[2] to which it reports, reporting for information to the Buildings Committee. It gives Technical Approvals where the Total Cost is £50,000 to £1m, reporting these decisions retrospectively to the Buildings Committee. It makes funding recommendations to the Resource Management Committee (RMC) where the Total Cost is between £50,000 and £1m in parallel with the application to RMC for Funding Approval.[3] It makes proposals about allocation of University space.

3.9 The *Resource Management Committee* (RMC)[4] is a joint committee of the Council and General Board and reports in to those committees via PRC. RMC deals with the detailed work of resource allocation.[5]

3.10 RMC gives Funding Approvals (see Schedule 3).

3.11 RMC[6] allocates space, dealing with the detailed work on resource allocation, following a proposal by the SMMWS. The PRAO allocates space less than 100 square metres under RMC supervision. As part of its space allocation remit, RMC approves proposals to share University space, including with Embedded Companies.

3.12 The *Health and Safety Executive Committee*[7] is a joint committee of the Council and General Board. It is advised by the Consultative Committee for Safety. The Consultative Committee receives and considers the annual University Fire Report from Estate Management. The report then goes to the Health and Safety Executive Committee for consideration.

3.13 The *Environmental Strategy Committee*[8] is a joint committee of the Council and General Board and reports in to those committees via PRC. It is responsible for monitoring and enhancing the University's environmental management system.

4. Financial planning process

4.1 RMC and PRC propose the budget parameters, which are approved by the Finance Committee. RMC then constructs the budget for PRC approval. The budget then goes to Council with advice from the Finance Committee, prior to being Graced.

5. Other bodies and committees

5.1 The *Press Syndicate* is responsible for the management of the finance, property, and affairs of Cambridge University Press, except if Statutes and Ordinances expressly or by necessary implication provide otherwise.[9] Cambridge University Press will consult the Buildings Committee and if necessary the Estates Strategy Committee about any significant planning applications to be made in respect of any premises or land in the city of Cambridge.[10]

5.2 A Grace is not required for the sale or transfer of freehold or leasehold land by Cambridge University Press or for the grant of a lease of more than 60 years or for the erection of a new building or for the demolition or substantial alteration of an existing building.[11] However the Press Syndicate have undertaken not to dispose, without the approval of the University, of the Pitt Building or of any property acquired from the University and specially designated by agreement between the Press Syndicate and the Council at the time of acquisition. The Press Syndicate have also undertaken to offer the Council the first option to acquire, at prevailing market price,

[1] Previously Regulation 11(*a*) of the Sites and Buildings regulations (1994 as amended in 2005), delegation confirmed by these regulations in relation to the Operational Estate.

[2] The Council Consultative Report of March 2004 confirmed, for the time being, the (predecessor) Minor Works Review Group as a technical review and implementation group, reporting to the Buildings Committee but suggested it would be reconstituted as a sub-committee of the Buildings Committee – see http://www.admin.cam.ac.uk/reporter/2003-04/weekly/5955/11.html, para 1(*f*) and 8(*d*). The combining of the Minor Works Sub-Committee and the then Space Management Advisory Group into the Space Management and Minor Works Sub-Committee of the Resource Management Committee was approved by Grace 5 of 21 May 2014 (see the Report, *Reporter*, 6344, 2013–14, p. 467).

[3] See Schedule 3.

[4] See http://www.admin.cam.ac.uk/cam-only/committee/rmc/.

[5] See further the RMC terms of reference on the RMC website and the Consultative Report of the Council in March 2004 – see http://www.admin.cam.ac.uk/reporter/2003-04/weekly/5955/11.html at para 1(*e*) and 16 and RMC terms of reference at http://www.admin.cam.ac.uk/cam-only/committee/rmc/terms.pdf.

[6] Regulation 5 of the Sites and Buildings regulations (1994 as amended in 2005) described as a Council responsibility the assignment of buildings to faculties, departments and other institutions or bodies. This task has been delegated to RMC.

[7] See Regulations 3 and 4 of the regulations for the Health and Safety Executive Committee and http://www.admin.cam.ac.uk/cam-only/committee/safety/. See also the Council Notice of 26 April 2010 which revised the membership of the Consultative Committee for Safety.

[8] See http://www.admin.cam.ac.uk/cam-only/committee/environment/terms/. The Buildings Committee confirmed the organization, terms of reference and constitution of the Committee for Environmental Management on 21 June 2000, see http://www.admin.cam.ac.uk/cam-only/committee/environment/constitution/.

[9] Statute J; Regulation 3 of the regulations for the Press Syndicate; Regulation 5 of the regulations for Financial Managers; Financial Regulation 1; see also Regulations 1 and 11 of the Sites and Buildings regulations (1994 as amended in 2005), re-confirmed in these regulations. The Council has power to limit the Press's powers and may reclaim control – see Statute J 5 and 13.

[10] Regulation 11 of the Sites and Buildings regulations (1994 as amended in 2005), continued in the current regulation.

[11] Statute J 3 and Regulation 5 of the regulations for Financial Matters.

any property in Cambridge which is to be disposed of by the Syndicate, such option if not taken up to lapse fourteen days after the offer.[1] Cambridge University Press will share its estate plan and co-operate with the Estates Strategy Committee in strategic decisions affecting its estate.[2]

5.3 The Local Examinations Syndicate provides the oversight of *Cambridge Assessment*, including in relation to the management of property assigned to Cambridge Assessment subject to the following requirements:

- A Grace is required for the disposal of land.[3]
- The Local Examinations Syndicate shall offer the Council the first option to acquire, at prevailing market price, any property in Cambridge which is to be disposed of by the Syndicate, such option if not taken up to lapse fourteen days after the offer.
- Cambridge Assessment shall seek the prior written consent of the Finance Committee before contracting for any land or building acquisition or borrowing for capital purposes above £15m. Cambridge Assessment will share its estate plan and co-operate with the Estates Strategy Committee in strategic decisions affecting its estate.[2]
- Cambridge Assessment shall consult the Buildings Committee about any significant planning applications to be made in respect of any premises or land in the city of Cambridge.

6. Unified Administrative Service (UAS)

6.1 The *Estate Management* Division of the UAS undertakes the technical management of the Operational and Non-Operational Estate (but not investment land within the CUEF), including the following:

- preparing the draft estate plans (estate strategy and its implementation) for approval of PRC, the Council, and the General Board, including the categorization of land not held as part of PPU Land;
- undertaking all planned maintenance, drawing on the Building Maintenance Fund, and all unplanned maintenance (under the supervision of and reporting to the Buildings Committee);
- providing monitoring, guidance, and training for Departments on fire safety; checking fire equipment; managing the Fire Team; reporting annually on fire safety to the Consultative Committee for Safety;[4]
- planning and managing University property and facilities;
- advising on security matters and responding to incidents;[5]
- securing planning permission as required;
- procuring University building work;
- managing University and private rented residential accommodation for University use;
- operating the University Centre and other catering outlets around the University;
- advising on the drafting and negotiation of licences and leases for the approved sharing of space; and
- managing the University Farm.

6.2 Following the issue of a Funding Approval for building work, the Finance Division conducts final due diligence checks including as to the sources and reliability of funding. The building warrant (being the formal authority to spend) is issued

- by the Director of Estate Management for maintenance work,
- by the Deputy Director of Finance for other building work up to and including £100,000,
- by the Pro-Vice-Chancellor for Planning and Resources for other building work above £100,000.

6.3 *PRAO* is a unit within the Academic Division. Among other responsibilities it gives Funding Approvals and, under RMC supervision, allocates space less than 100 square metres. PRAO services PRC, RMC, the Buildings Committee, and the SMMWS.

7. Schools and Departments

7.1 *Schools* are responsible for resource allocation within the parameters set by the annual budget report.

7.2 *Heads of Department*

The definition in the Financial Regulations from time to time in force[6] is adopted for the purposes of these regulations. At the time of adoption of these regulations this means: "the head of a department or a faculty not organized in departments, secretaries of faculties, head of a centre, institute or other body under the supervision of the General Board or Council and head of a division within the Unified Administrative Service". "Department" is interpreted accordingly.

Heads of Department are responsible, in respect of buildings assigned to the Department, for

- identifying and reporting to Estate Management the need for any unplanned maintenance;
- cleaning;
- observance of safety, security and fire precautions in line with advice and guidance from Estate Management;[7]
- maintenance only where specifically delegated by Buildings Committee (see Schedule 4); and

[1] Footnote to Regulation 3(*c*) of the regulations for the Press Syndicate.

[2] See the recommendations of the Report approved by Grace 5 of 21 May 2014 (*Reporter*, 6344, 2013–14, p. 467).

[3] See Regulation 1.2

[4] Previously the Buildings Committee had overall responsibility for the taking of measures for the safety of premises (including fire precautions) – see Regulation 9(*a*) and (*b*) of the Sites and Buildings regulations (1994 as amended in 2005).

[5] Previously the Buildings Committee had overall responsibility for the taking of measures for the safety and security of the premises in consultation with the bodies concerned – see Regulation 9(*a*) and (*b*) of the Sites and Buildings regulations (1994 as amended in 2005).

[6] See Financial Regulation 4.1.

[7] Previously Schedule 1 paragraph 1(*c*) of the Sites and Buildings regulations (1994 as amended in 2005), delegation confirmed by these regulations. Security obligations not previously itemized.

- undertaking a cost and space analysis for any Embedded Company, securing a Specific Operational Approval to share space with the company (see Schedule 5) and ensuring contractual arrangements are put in place between the company and the University and that the company complies with health and safety legislation and University policies.[1]

8. The Investment Office

8.1 The Investment Office buys and sells and arranges the technical management of land and buildings held for investment purposes within the CUEF, under the oversight of the Investment Board, reporting to the Council via the Finance Committee.

9. The Land Fund

9.1 All payments of premium for the lease of land and receipts from the sale of land (other than land held for investment purposes) shall be credited to the Land Fund. The capital and the income of the Fund may be used (*a*) to purchase sites which are suitable for development for University purposes, and (*b*) to meet the cost of planning and providing the infrastructure for the development of sites in University ownership, including costs relating to the requirements of Town and Country Planning legislation.[2]

[1] Regulations for Financial Matters, Financial Regulation 26.
[2] Regulations for Financial Matters, regulations for the Land Fund.

Schedule 3 – Expenditure Approvals, required for: (i) all building work, including refurbishment and re-structuring, and (ii) maintenance, where delegation has been approved pursuant to Schedule 4*

*Where any delegation has been approved pursuant to Schedule 4, the Department will act in place of Estate Management

Total Cost	**Head of Department**	**Estate Management***	**PRAO**	**SMMWS**	**Buildings Com-mittee**	**RMC**	**PRC**
Total Cost of less than £50k unless Buildings Committee has approved a Minor Works Expenditure Approval Exemption	Provides Brief Business Case to PRAO.	Estate Management prepares the budget for PRAO and gives Technical Approval.	PRAO checks funding availability. Provided Estate Management agrees PRAO issues the Funding Approval.				
Total Cost is £50k to £1m.	Provides Brief Business Case to PRAO.	Estate Management checks value for money and prepares the budget for SMMWS.	PRAO checks funding availability and consults Estate Management. Reports to SMMWS.	Receives Estate Management and PRAO advice. Makes a funding recommendation to RMC. Gives the Technical Approval which is then reported to Buildings Committee.		Funding Approval.	
Total Cost is >£1m to <£2m.	Provides Brief Business Case to PRAO.	Estate Management checks value for money and prepares the budget for Buildings Committee.	PRAO reviews and recommends to Buildings Committee business need (academic or administrative need and value for money).		Technical Approval.		Funding Approval.
Total Cost is £2m or above (Capital Projects Process).	**Registers** the project with PRC at the outset. The Chair of PRC has power to register small, straightforward projects. **Prepares the Concept Paper**. When the Concept Paper is approved, **prepares full business case** including the confirmation/ revision of the Concept Paper and business plan and the provision of estimates.	Estate Management checks value for money and prepares the budget for Buildings Committee.	PRAO assists Department working with Estate Management.		Technical Approval.		**Approves Concept Paper** before proceeding further and **determines** how the preparation of the full business case is to be funded. **Funding Approval**.

Schedule 4 – Specific Operational Approvals

Subject	Approval or determination by	Other requirements
Alienation of land		
Determination whether land is PPU Land.[1]	Finance Committee. In straightforward cases the determination can be made by the Director of Finance (on advice of the Director of Estate Management) and reported to the Finance Committee.	PRC advises the Finance Committee. Estate Management provide technical advice.
Approval for sale or transfer or grant of a lease for more than 60 years of land which is PPU Land.[2]	Regent House (Grace).	Report from Council to Regent House.
Approval for sale or transfer or grant of a lease for more than 60 years of land which is not PPU Land.[2]	Finance Committee.	
Approval for grant of a lease of PPU Land for less than 60 years.[2]	Finance Committee.	
Use of Land Fund (receipts from sale or lease of land other than land held for investment purposes).[3]	Finance Committee.	
Alteration or change of use		
Consideration of whether a repair or alteration is substantial and, if not substantial what publicity is appropriate.[4]	The body which gives the Technical Approval (SMMWS or Buildings Committee depending on project Total Cost).	
Preliminary approval of proposals for substantial repair or alteration (prior to seeking a Grace).[5]	PRC gives the Funding Approval. Buildings Committee gives the Technical Approval.	
Approval for substantial alteration of an existing University building.[6]	Regent House (Grace).	Consult the Directors of Estate Management and Finance and the Taxation Section. Execution of contract documents is done by the Director of Estate Management.[7]
Approval for change of use.[8]	RMC.	Estate Management advises

[1] Regulation 2(*a*) of the regulations for Financial Matters: A Grace is required for a sale or lease of more than 60 years if in the judgement of the Council this would deprive the University of the use of lands or buildings which are of present or prospective use to the University.

[2] Regulation 2(*a*) of the regulations for Financial Matters.

[3] Premiums from the lease of land and receipts from the sale of land (other than land held for investment purposes) are credited to the Land Fund and are subject to the requirements of the regulations for the Land Fund.

[4] Delegation from Council: i.e. is it substantial for the purpose of Statute F II 3.

[5] Delegation from Council to PRC and (per previous Regulation 8 of the Sites and Buildings regulations (1994 as amended in 2005)) to Buildings Committee, re-confirmed by these regulations.

[6] Statute F II 3.

[7] Financial Regulations 6.2. Regulation 2.4 of these regulations.

[8] Delegation by Council in line with previous Regulation 6 of the Sites and Buildings regulations (1994 as amended in 2005).

Subject	Approval or determination by	Other requirements
Erection or demolition of a building		
Approval for the erection of a new University building or for the demolition of an existing University building.[1]	Regent House (Grace).	Consult the Directors of Estate Management and Finance and the Taxation Section. The Director of Estate Management signs the contract documents.[2]
Maintenance		
Setting the annual budget for the Building Maintenance Fund.	PRC – Financial Approval Buildings Committee – Technical Approval.	
Delegation of maintenance (for the execution of one or more maintenance projects).	Buildings Committee.	When considering a request until further notice to delegate maintenance, Committee shall set any appropriate thresholds and conditions and shall have regard to the following: (*a*) The extent of delegation to be given (scope and Total Cost delegated). (*b*) Legal, regulatory, and insurance issues. (*c*) Levels of necessary expertise (technical, health and safety, purchasing, etc.). (*d*) Value for money. (*e*) Conditions to be imposed in addition to those in Financial Regulations. A list shall be published on the Estate Management website setting out delegations made.[3]
Minor works expenditure approval exemption		
Exemption from need to seek an Expenditure Approval for work not exceeding £50,000.	Buildings Committee.	When considering a request for exemption until further notice from the need to seek an Expenditure Approval for work where the Total Cost does not exceed £50,000, Committee shall set any appropriate thresholds and conditions and shall have regard to the following: (*a*) The extent of permission to be given (scope and Total Cost permitted). (*b*) Legal, regulatory, and insurance issues. (*c*) Levels of necessary expertise (technical, health and safety, purchasing, etc.). (*d*) Value for money. (*e*) Conditions to be imposed in addition to those in Financial Regulations. A list shall be published on the Estate Management website setting out delegations made.

[1] Statute F II 3.
[2] Financial Regulation 6.2. Regulation 2.4 of these regulations.
[3] Statute F II 2–3; Statute J; confirmation of delegation by Council in line with previous Regulations 1, 7, and 9 of the Sites and Buildings regulations (1994 as amended in 2005).

Subject	Approval or determination by	Other requirements
Permission to carry out minor works		
Permission to carry out minor works.	Buildings Committee.	When considering a request for permission until further notice to carry out minor works, Committee shall set any appropriate thresholds and conditions and shall have regard to the following: (*a*) The extent of permission to be given (Total Cost permitted). (*b*) Legal, regulatory, and insurance issues. (*c*) Levels of necessary expertise (technical, health and safety, purchasing, etc.). (*d*) Value for money. (*e*) Conditions to be imposed in addition to those in Financial Regulations including requirements to consult EM and/or not to do certain specified work. A list shall be published on the Estate Management website setting out delegations made.
Permission to carry out emergency work		
Permission to carry out Emergency work without seeking an expenditure approval.	Buildings Committee.	When considering a request for permission until further notice to carry out emergency work as it arises, Committee shall set any appropriate thresholds and conditions and shall have regard to the following: (*a*) The extent of permission to be given (Total Cost permitted). (*b*) Legal, regulatory, and insurance issues. (*c*) Levels of necessary expertise (technical, health and safety, purchasing, etc.). (*d*) Value for money. (*e*) Conditions to be imposed in addition to those in Financial Regulations including requirements to consult EM and/or not to do certain specified work. A list shall be published on the Estate Management website setting out delegations made.
Acquisition of land		
Approval for acquisition of property (freehold leasehold or any building) anywhere in the world to form part of PPU Land whether for value or not.[1]	Finance Committee.	PRC advises Finance Committee as necessary.
Borrowing		
Prior approval required.	Finance Committee.	

[1] New requirement of the Council under its supervisory jurisdiction.

Subject	Approval or determination by	Other requirements
Allocation of space		
Allocation of space. Approval for sharing University space with any third party, including an Embedded Company, and whether by way of lease, licence or any other formal or informal arrangement. A change to the net usable area of the building. A change of use.[1]	RMC.	Consult the SMMWS, which considers and puts proposals to RMC. Consult Estate Management about the terms of any arrangement with a third party. Execution of contract documents is done by the Director of Estate Management.[2]

Schedule 5 – Definitions and guidance

'Brief Business Case'	A paper setting out the academic or administrative need, value for money, and funding source and confirming that, where the Department belongs to a School, the Head of School approves the project.
'Buildings Maintenance Fund'	The fund referred to in Ordinance Ch. XIII, 'University Funds, Special Regulations, Buildings Maintenance Funds'.
'Cambridge Assessment'	The operational arm of the Local Examinations Syndicate.
'Capital Approval'	The approval required (under these Regulations) for capital projects where the Cost of works is £2m or above and (under Financial Regulations) expenditure on capital items (inclusive of VAT), is £2m or above.
'Concept Paper'	A paper setting out the academic or administrative case, value for money and preliminary costings.
'CUEF'	Cambridge University Endowment Fund.
'Department', 'Head of Department'	As defined in Financial Regulations.
'Embedded Company'	A company occupying University premises or whose employees' normal place of work is on University premises, other than as temporary visitors or to provide services to the University.
'Emergency Work'[3]	If an unforeseen Maintenance event causes damage, the minimum work immediately necessary to preserve property and address health and safety risks.
'Estate Management'	The University's Estate Management Service.
'Expenditure Approval'	An approval in accordance with Schedule 3.
'Funding Approval'	Authority given to Finance Division to issue a building warrant.
'Financial Regulations'	The University's Financial Regulations (an Order of Council set out in Ordinances).
'Investment Board'	The board which manages for the University the investment of the Cambridge University Endowment Fund (CUEF).
'Investment Office'	The officer group which provides technical management for the Investment Board.

[1] Delegation by Council in line with previous Regulation 5 of the Sites and Buildings regulations (1994 as amended in 2005).
[2] Financial Regulation 26. Regulation 2.4 of these regulations.
[3] Emergency Work conducted by Estate Management is authorized as part of the approval of the Buildings Maintenance Fund which includes an allocation for emergency work.

'Maintenance'	The repair, refreshment or renewal of what already exists to enable the facilities to function as originally intended, as distinct from Refurbishment and Restructuring; Maintenance does not change the scope, capacity or structure of any facility, nor does it add or remove any facility; it has the sense of continuance and preservation.
'Minor Works Expenditure Approval Exemption'	Buildings Committee approval for a Department to proceed with work (not to exceed £50,000) without seeking an Expenditure Approval.
'Non-Operational Estate'	Land and buildings held for the general purposes of the University (e.g. residences) and land and property that could be needed in the foreseeable future for the Operational Estate. It is managed on a self-funded basis and remits income to the Chest.
'Operational Estate'	Land and buildings currently used for teaching and research or for administrative and other support functions, including the University Farm, and retention of specialist use and 'churn' space but excluding land used by Cambridge University Press and Cambridge Assessment (the Local Examinations Syndicate).
'PPU Land'	Freehold or leasehold land where the sale or transfer or the grant of lease for sixty years or more would deprive the University of the use of land or buildings which are of present or prospective use to the University.
'PRC'	Planning and Resources Committee of the Council and the General Board.
'PRAO'	Planning and Resource Allocation Office.
'Refurbishment'	Upgrading what exists
'Restructuring'	Changing what exists.
'RMC'	Resource Management Committee.
'SMMWS'	Space Management and Minor Works Committee.
'Specific Operational Approval'	An approval in accordance with Schedule 4.
'Staff'	All employees irrespective of whether their appointment specifically includes responsibilities for land and buildings and however their employment is financed together with anyone else who has any responsibility for the management or Maintenance of or expenditure on any University land or buildings.
'Technical Approval'	Confirmation that the proposed budget and specification for building work meet the operational, quality and technical needs and provide value for money.
'Total Cost'	The total cost or estimated total cost to bring a project to completion, including without limitation all design work, VAT, constructions costs and planning advice.
'University'	The Chancellor, Masters, and Scholars of the University of Cambridge.

Terms are to be understood as used in Statutes and Ordinances, unless the context of the regulation requires otherwise. Words preceding 'include', 'includes', 'including', and 'included' shall be construed without limitation by the words which follow those words.

If in doubt, consult Estate Management or PRAO. Further written guidance is contained in the Finance Committee, PRC, RMC, and Estate Management[1] web pages.

[1] http://www.admin.cam.ac.uk/offices/em/, http://www.admin.cam.ac.uk/cam-only/offices/em/estate/.

AUDIT COMMITTEE

Amended by Grace 1 of 27 November 2013

Duties.

1. The Audit Committee shall meet at least twice in each financial year. It shall be the duty of the Committee:

(*a*) to keep under review the effectiveness of the University's internal systems of financial and other control;

(*b*) to advise the Council on matters relating to the external and internal auditors, including their appointment, the provision by the auditors of any additional services outside the scope of their regular responsibilities, the remuneration of the auditors, and any questions relating to the resignation or dismissal of auditors;

(*c*) to ensure that sufficient resources are made available for internal audit;

(*d*) to approve proposals for internal audit put forward by the internal auditors;

(*e*) to review annually with the external auditors the nature and scope of the external audit;

(*f*) to consider any reports submitted by the auditors, both external and internal;

(*g*) to monitor the implementation of any recommendations made by the internal auditors;

(*h*) to satisfy themselves that satisfactory arrangements are adopted throughout the University for promoting economy, efficiency, effectiveness, and risk management;

(*i*) to establish appropriate performance measures and to monitor annually the performance and effectiveness of the external and internal auditors;

(*j*) to consider, in consultation with the external auditors, (i) any financial statements annexed to the abstract of accounts, including the auditors' report, and (ii) any statement provided by the Council on the governance of the University;

(*k*) to ensure that all significant losses are properly investigated and that the internal and external auditors, and where appropriate the Higher Education Funding Council for England, are informed;

(*l*) to oversee the University's policy on fraud and irregularity, and to ensure that they are informed of any action taken under that policy;

(*m*) to make an annual report to the Council, the Vice-Chancellor, and the Higher Education Funding Council for England;

(*n*) to receive reports from the National Audit Office and the Higher Education Funding Council for England, and to advise the Council thereon;

(*o*) to forward minutes of their meetings to the Council.

INTELLECTUAL PROPERTY RIGHTS

General

Who the regulations apply to.

1. The following regulations apply to all University officers, as described in the Statutes and Ordinances of the University, and to all other persons employed by the University. The term 'University staff' in these regulations denotes all the above persons. The provisions of these regulations may also concern visitors to the University, and to associates and students of it, by virtue of Regulations 12, 13, and 14.

Non Disclosure Agreement.

2. Nothing in these regulations shall override the requirement for employees and students to keep confidential: material the disclosure of which would be inconsistent with their duties under professional codes; material that is decreed to be confidential by a relevant ethics committee; or material that is obtained under the terms of a Non Disclosure Agreement. Moreover, nothing in these regulations shall override agreements that students or the University, on behalf of, and with the knowledge of, University staff or students, have entered into with third parties as a condition of sponsorship or research funding.

Definitions

3. In the following regulations, the following definitions shall apply:

'creator': a person who invents, devises, designs, develops, breeds, works out, discovers, conceives, performs, produces, translates or expresses;

'creates': invents, devises, designs, develops, breeds, works out, discovers, conceives, performs, produces, translates or expresses;

'relevant creator': a creator eligible to be named in an application for registerable rights, for example inventors in the case of a patent; or any creator in the case of nonregisterable rights.

Freedom to make research public

4. University staff are entitled to decide that the results of any research undertaken by them in the course of their employment by the University shall be published or disseminated to other persons to use or disclose as they wish in accordance with normal academic practice.

However, if University staff decide that the results of their research should be commercialized, they should be aware that, in respect of patents and similar rights in inventions and new technology, protection for and subsequent commercialization of such inventions may be jeopardized if information about the inventions is made available to the public anywhere in the world before all relevant applications for protection have been lodged. Any statement, oral or written, which is made to another person or persons who are under no obligation to keep the information confidential will negate the validity of a patent for the invention in many countries. Prior disclosure.

Initial entitlement to intellectual property rights

5. Where intellectual property rights arise, or the right to apply for such rights arises, from the results of activities undertaken by University staff in the course of their employment by the University, the initial entitlement to those rights shall be as provided in the following regulations. Research undertaken by University staff in the course of their employment by the University shall include all research conducted under the obligation to do so, expressed or implied, in their terms of employment. The time when, and the place where, particular research results are reached or achieved shall be factors to be taken into consideration in assessing whether the research is in the course of employment. Where a person external to the University consults a University staff member for advice, that advice will normally be regarded as private and therefore as forming no part of her or his obligations in the course of employment by the University.

6. The University shall have the initial right to apply throughout the world for a patent for an invention, for another right in novel technology such as a utility model or petty patent, for a plant variety right or plant patent, and for a registered design for a product, any trade mark registration associated with another registerable right belonging to the University, or any other type of intellectual property that is dependent on registration, deposit, or grant at the time that these regulations are approved. The University or its delegated nominee, currently the University's wholly owned subsidiary, Cambridge University Technical Services Ltd (CUTS), will become the proprietor of any intellectual property right that is in consequence granted or registered. A University staff member who is the relevant creator shall be named as such in the application.

7. Other intellectual property rights, arising from the activities of University staff in the course of their employment by the University, which exist without the need for any formal application at the time these regulations are approved, belong to the University staff member who creates the results subject to any third party rights which he or she may have previously agreed. This applies in particular to copyright and moral rights in literary, dramatic, musical, and artistic works; copyright in software, notwithstanding that there may also be patentable results embodied in the software; copyright arising from authorship of a database; performers' rights; unregistered design rights; and rights over information (such as trade secrets and confidential know-how).

8. The University shall own any registered trademark which would associate the University with the exploitation of a product or service. Notwithstanding Regulation 7, the University shall own copyright, database rights, and other unregistered rights arising from the activities of University staff in the course of their employment by the University in (*a*) subject matter created for the administrative or managerial purposes of the University, including advice to students other than teaching materials; (*b*) subject matter such as examination papers and library catalogues; and (*c*) any other subject matter commissioned by the University, such as special reports on its policy or management. For the purposes of this regulation, works commissioned by Cambridge University Press in the course of its business shall not be regarded as such commissioned subject matter. Registered trademark ownership.

9. Material or other subject matter that is developed in the University of which the copyright is owned by the University, including any that may fall under Regulation 8, may be released under Open

Open Source arrangements.

Source or similar arrangements on the authority of the Head of Department in which the material is created. The Head of Department may delegate such authority within a Department without restriction. (When material is derived from material acquired under Open Source arrangements that require any distribution of derived material to be under the same arrangements, no authority to distribute need be sought.)

10. The law accords rights against exploitation of certain products by third parties to creators who organize their production; these include sound recordings, films, broadcasts, published works (in respect of their typographical arrangement) and databases (in respect of extraction and utilization of their content). These rights over products are additional to, and do not affect, copyrights and performers' rights of the kind referred to in Regulation 7 that protect works and performances included in the products. In any case where, because the University is the investor or co-investor in such products, it acquires these rights by operation of law, the University:

(*a*) by virtue of these regulations grants licence to these rights to each creator free of charge or other obligation; and

(*b*) undertakes, on the joint request of all who contributed to the creation of the product, to assign these rights to those persons free of charge or other obligation on the latters' part.

11. The party initially entitled to an intellectual property right by virtue of Regulations 6–8, whether the University or a University staff member, may deal with the right by assignment, licence, waiver, or other dealing entered into before or after creation of the subject-matter of the right, so far as is permitted by law. The University may elect to assign its intellectual property rights in appropriate cases to a nominee company.

College Teaching Officers and Research Fellows.

12. The University shall require College Teaching Officers and College Research Fellows working on University research projects to agree to be bound by the regulations in the same manner as University staff or by such other terms as may be agreed in the circumstances. It shall be for the relevant College to agree with the University what share (if any) in the portion of net revenue accorded to central funds under Regulation 25 shall instead be allotted to the College.

13. It shall be the responsibility of a University staff member to ensure that visitors or other non-University employees, working on a University project for which the University staff member is named as principal investigator, do not compromise the University's intellectual property obligations to third parties with respect to that project. University staff members named as principal investigators on research grants and contracts should consider whether visitors or other non-University employees should be asked to enter into agreements in order to achieve this.

Students.

14. The entitlement to intellectual property rights in material created by a student shall rest with the student, with the following exceptions:

(*a*) Where a student is sponsored by a third party, a condition of sponsorship may be that the sponsor may own any intellectual property developed during the period of sponsorship. Sponsored students are, therefore, advised to check the terms of their sponsorship agreement.

(*b*) Where a student is working on a sponsored project as part of his or her course-work or research, the sponsor may own any intellectual property that the student develops. This will be specified in the research contract and the supervisor or Department should inform students if this is the case as early as possible in the admissions process and in any case prior to the start of their research.

(*c*) Where a student is working in collaboration with others in a manner that gives rise to joint creation of intellectual property, or interdependent intellectual property, the student may be required to assign intellectual property to the University or place the results in the public domain without restriction. He or she will be treated in the same way as University staff under these regulations. If this case is likely to arise, students should be so informed at the offer of admission where practical, and in any case prior to the start of their research.

A student who believes that clause (*c*) above has been inappropriately applied may make an application to the University Technology Referee under Regulation 15.

A sponsorship agreement may also place a requirement on the student and his or her examiners to undertake to keep results confidential while steps are being taken to protect intellectual property or to establish exploitation arrangements. The student may also be required to submit the dissertation to the sponsor for scrutiny before submitting it for examination. Any confidentiality agreement whose purpose is to delay public disclosure for the purpose of protection should usually not have effect for longer than three months from the time the sponsor is notified of intent to publish. When the University obtains an assignment of student-created intellectual property, it undertakes to provide the student with a share in such financial returns from the exploitation as there may be on the same basis as that applying to University staff by virtue of Regulation 25.

15. Where a dispute occurs between the University and a University staff member, a person referred to in Regulation 12 or a student, or between staff members, a person referred to in Regulation 12 and/or a student, as to the application of these regulations or the terms of the agreement on which they should enter, or on which they have already agreed to proceed, concerning the commercial exploitation of any intellectual property rights, or the subject matter to which such rights relate, the dispute shall, at the request of either, be referred to a University Technology Referee in accordance with Regulations 32–39. Disputes.

Scope of application

16. These regulations shall apply to all intellectual property rights relating to subject-matter created on or after 12 December 2005 save to the extent that a University staff member has, before that date, entered into an explicit arrangement to the contrary with the University or the University has previously entered into an agreement with a third party relating to those rights. Intellectual property rights in subject-matter invented, devised, made, or created before that date shall be governed by the previous agreements, rules, policies, and notifications of the University which affect them. In all other respects the present regulations shall replace and supersede the policy set out in the General Board Notice[1] on commercial exploitation of inventions funded by Research Councils, and that approved by Grace 6 of 21 March 2001. Effective date.

Interpretation

17. In these regulations, references to acts to be done by or in relation to the University in the exercise of any right or power, or in fulfilment of any duty or responsibility, are to acts done by or on behalf of the Council or by a duly designated officer and to directions given by the Council.

ADMINISTRATION OF THE UNIVERSITY'S INTELLECTUAL PROPERTY PROVISIONS

General

18. If University staff decide that the results of their activities should be the subject of commercial exploitation, and that the rights to those results are reasonably capable of including rights to which the University is initially entitled by virtue of Regulation 6, they must notify the University, through the Research Services Division, and the relevant Chair of Faculty Board, or Head of Department or other institution and provide the University with full disclosure of the relevant results in order that the steps referred to in Regulations 19–24 may take place. University staff shall assist the Research Services Division to take reasonable steps to determine who all the creators of the subject matter are and whether any agreements govern the ownership or exploitation of the subject matter. The Research Services Division shall ensure that students' supervisors or contract researchers' line managers are aware of the intention to exploit commercially. Commercial exploitation.

19. The University staff shall discuss with Cambridge Enterprise the path for exploitation, with the aim of reaching agreement on confidentiality, whether a patent application should be filed, and whether a company should be formed to exploit the technology. Cambridge Enterprise.

20. If Cambridge Enterprise, with the agreement of the University staff member(s), decides that a patent or other form of intellectual property right requiring registration should be applied for in respect of one or more countries in the world, it may exercise its entitlement to do so in the University's name, or in the name of its designated nominee, in accordance with Regulation 6. In respect of any such application, all inventors shall be included in any application that requires them to be named.

21. The relevant creator of the subject matter, or creators acting jointly, may decide that they do not wish it to be exploited through Cambridge Enterprise and then may require the University to assign the rights referred to in Regulations 6 and 20. If not in contravention of any agreement governing ownership or exploitation of the subject-matter, this assignment may be to the creators for a fixed Assignment of rights.

[1] *Reporter*, 1986–87, p. 440, dated 26 February 1987.

percentage of royalty income in the case where the creators decide to license or assign the rights to a third party; or under negotiated licence/equity terms when the creators are forming a company to exploit the rights. In the last-mentioned case, the guiding principle shall be that a fixed percentage of the rights attributed, on a fair and reasonable basis, to intellectual property, often referred to as inventors' rights, shall be assigned to the University. Any assignment by the University shall be conditional on the repayment of any funds expended by Cambridge Enterprise on protection of the subject-matter. If the creators cannot reach agreement, Cambridge Enterprise shall make a decision, against which any party may make application to the Technology Referee. The fixed percentages referred to in this regulation are set out in the Schedule attached to these regulations.

The determination of whether such an assignment is or is not contrary to any agreement shall be made by the Research Services Division within 30 days of being supplied with all relevant information. Any determination may be the subject of a reference in accordance with Regulations 32–39.

Decision to pursue application.

22. In the case where the creators do wish to commercialize through Cambridge Enterprise, Cambridge Enterprise shall decide, within 30 days, or such longer time as it and the University staff may agree to, of receiving notification of sufficiently detailed research results, whether to make any application, in the UK or elsewhere, of the type referred to in Regulations 6 and 20. If it does, it must inform the University staff who have notified the results and it must make and prosecute the application with all reasonable diligence.

Decision not to pursue application.

23. If Cambridge Enterprise decides not to pursue an application, to withdraw an application, or not to maintain a granted or registered right, it must forthwith inform the University staff who have created the subject-matter of its decision. The University shall seek to determine with those persons the future course of action with financial arrangements as in Regulation 21.

24. During the period following receipt of notification of the research results from a University staff member, Cambridge Enterprise shall consider with her or him how commercial exploitation of the results shall or may be pursued, having regard to all reasonable proposals for that exploitation made by the staff member. Cambridge Enterprise and the University staff member shall keep each other informed and shall co-operate fully in order to achieve an agreed outcome. Where a University staff member is entitled to intellectual property rights under Regulation 7 over information in subject matter or other material and those rights are relevant to the exploitation of the University's rights under Regulation 6, the staff member may agree to assign or license her or his intellectual property rights either to the University, to the University's designated nominee, or to a third party in furtherance of such arrangements for exploitation as may be reached.[1]

Net revenue shared.

25. Where the University or its designated nominee receives licensing income from the commercialization of intellectual property rights by virtue of Regulation 6, or by virtue of any assignment to the University or nominee of a University staff member's intellectual property rights under Regulation 7, whether in association with the exploitation of the University's rights under Regulation 6 or by virtue of Regulation 27, any direct costs, as defined in the Schedule to these regulations, shall be deducted and the net revenue shall be shared between the relevant creators of the material or other subject matter (here referred to together as 'inventors') protected by intellectual property rights, her or his Department, Faculty or other institution, and the University as specified in the Schedule to these regulations.

Where University staff together contribute to the creation of intellectual property that is subsequently exploited, the distribution of the inventors' share of revenue shall be a matter for those staff members to determine, referring the matter if necessary in accordance with Regulation 15. They shall notify Cambridge Enterprise of the resulting arrangements. If the staff members do not reach an agreement, Cambridge Enterprise shall refer the matter, by application, to the Technology Referee under Regulation 33.

A royalty sharing arrangement under this regulation shall continue in effect after the person concerned ceases to be a University staff member or to hold a position or status which makes the regulation applicable. Upon the death of such a person, her or his share under this regulation shall continue to be payable to her or his estate or a nominee thereof.

Confidentiality.

26. During any period in which Cambridge Enterprise, with the agreement of the University staff concerned, is considering whether to make an intellectual property application or applications that entail keeping the subject-matter from being available to the public beforehand, Cambridge Enterprise

[1] See the explanatory note on p. 1045.

shall, and other parties should, keep the research results confidential until those applications have been made and are therefore no longer in jeopardy from any prior publication. If a University staff member decides to make the relevant results public before the applications have been made, he or she must be aware that those applications are likely to fail and shall inform Cambridge Enterprise as soon as possible.

Where a University staff member is solely entitled to intellectual property rights under Regulation 7

27. Where a University staff member is entitled to any intellectual property right in accordance with Regulation 7, he or she may seek the assistance of Cambridge Enterprise in arranging exploitation of the rights, for instance by agreeing a fee for management by the University's designated nominee, or by assigning the rights to the nominee in return for use of the University's name, arms, or trade marks and then adopting the revenue-sharing arrangement described in Regulation 25.

External sponsorship

28. An agreement may be reached by the University with an external sponsor of research or a third party, under which, in return for the agreed level of funding or sponsorship for research, transfer of materials, or other collaboration, the third party or the University shall be entitled to the intellectual property rights relating to the results of the research, or the third party shall be entitled to an assignment of those rights or the right to apply for them, or a licence of or other interest in any such rights that the University may subsequently own. So far, however, as such intellectual property rights consist of copyright or other informal rights referred to in Regulations 7 and 10, this provision applies only where it is explicitly stated that such rights are included in the agreement. University staff, in agreeing to conduct research under such an agreement shall be deemed to have agreed to comply with the terms of the agreement. In particular the University staff shall execute any assignment of intellectual property required by the agreement and abide by any confidentiality conditions specified in the agreement. Such agreements shall designate the person to whom University staff must notify relevant research results and the period within which the notification must be given. Standard terms for these undertakings may be included in the Model Research Collaboration Agreement that is available from the Research Services Division.

Specific exceptions concerning copyright and database right

29. Where the University participates in, or establishes, a specific project to organize teaching or other dissemination of knowledge, otherwise than to its own students, or a project to set up and maintain a database it may require that intellectual property rights arising in relation to material incorporated into the project or arising from it be assigned or licensed to it as part of an agreement for the management of the project. If such a requirement exists it shall be made and agreement sought before the project is begun.

30. In relation to teaching materials prepared by a University staff member for use in the teaching primarily of the University's students, unless the Faculty Board or other body responsible for teaching has agreed explicitly to the contrary, the University shall have a non-exclusive, royalty-free, perpetual licence to use the material for teaching in the University. Teaching materials.

Use of the University's name, arms, and trade and service marks

31. The University is solely entitled to use its name and arms, and to trade marks, service marks, corporate names, and domain names in which either appears, where the use of the name, shield, or mark is such as to suggest that the University is engaged in, or is connected with, or sponsors, the activities. In appropriate circumstances the Council or a duly authorized officer may, subject to such conditions as may be determined in a particular case, permit a University staff member wishing to commercialize her or his intellectual property rights under Regulation 7 or 21 to use the name, arms, or mark for commercial activities with which they are or will be associated.

ADJUDICATION AND APPEAL

University Technology Referees.

32. The Council shall maintain a panel of persons to serve as University Technology Referees. Such persons need not be members of the University. One member of the panel shall be designated by the Council as Chair of the panel. The Council may appoint a Deputy Chair to serve if the Chair is not able or willing to act in a particular case. A Secretary of the Panel of University Technology Referees shall be appointed in accordance with Regulation 39. The identity of the members of the Panel of University Technology Referees, its Chair, and Secretary shall be published in the *Reporter*.

The Council shall also maintain a panel of persons to serve on a Technology Appeal Tribunal in accordance with Regulation 35.

33. If a dispute arises as to the interpretation of these regulations:

(*a*) the University staff member, or a person referred to under Regulation 12 or the student concerned, or a duly authorized person representing the University, hereinafter the 'applicant', shall send written notice to the Secretary of the Panel of Referees of the facts of the dispute within thirty days of the dispute arising, and shall at the same time send the same material to the other parties to the dispute;

(*b*) any other party to the dispute may submit comments on the applicant's submission to the Secretary within fourteen days of receipt of the submission;

(*c*) the Secretary shall notify the Chair (or Deputy Chair) who shall act herself or himself or shall designate a member of the panel to act as the Referee in a particular case; the Secretary shall notify the applicant and other parties to the dispute of this appointment;

(*d*) the Referee shall consider the material submitted by the applicant and other parties to the dispute;

(*e*) at her or his discretion the Referee may hold a hearing at which all parties to the dispute shall normally be entitled to be present and to be represented. The Referee may also request evidence be given in writing, or by way of oral hearing, by any other member of the University staff, College Teaching Officer, College Research Fellow, or student, as the Referee sees fit;

(*f*) following consideration and hearing the Referee shall issue a written adjudication, to be communicated to the Registrary, and the parties to the dispute. Such adjudication shall include recommendations as to the resolution of the matter in dispute. The Referee shall make reasonable efforts to issue this adjudication within 45 days of the original application to the Secretary of the Panel of Referees;

(*g*) the Chair, or the Referee if a Referee has been appointed, may dismiss summarily a complaint which, in her or his opinion, is trivial, vexatious, or out of time.

34. Any participating party aggrieved by the Referee's adjudication may, within thirty days of notification of the adjudication, appeal to the Technology Appeal Tribunal. Such appeal shall be made in writing to the Clerk of the Tribunal, and shall include full documentation. A copy of such papers shall be sent by the appellant to those mentioned in Regulation 33(*a*).

Technology Appeal Tribunal.

35. The Technology Appeal Tribunal shall consist of:

(*a*) a legally qualified Chair, designated by the Registrary to serve in a particular case from a panel of Chairs to be maintained by the Council;

(*b*) *either*

(i) (when the referral does not involve a student) two members of the Regent House, designated by the Registrary from a panel of members of the Tribunal to be maintained by the Council;

or

(ii) (when the referral does involve a student), two members of the Regent House, one designated by the Registrary from a panel of members of the Tribunal to be maintained by the Council, the other nominated by the Senior Tutors' Committee,

(*c*) (when the referral involves a student) a student chosen from a panel of members of the University *in statu pupillari* appointed by the Council under the procedure used to choose a student member of the Court of Discipline.[1]

No person shall serve on the Tribunal if he or she has previously served as Chair, Deputy Chair, or Referee in the initial reference of the particular case or is subject to a conflict of interest.

36. The Chair of the Tribunal for the particular case shall determine whether the proceedings shall be dealt with on the basis of written representations, or at an oral hearing, or both, provided that the Chair shall normally determine that an oral hearing shall take place if one of the parties requests it.

[1] See p. 214.

37. The decision of the Tribunal shall be notified in writing to the parties, and to the Registrary.

38. The Chair of the Panel of Referees and the Chair of the Tribunal may from time to time make procedural rules about the respective procedures, either of general application, or in respect of a particular case. A decision of the Tribunal in a particular case shall bind the parties, subject to any rights which a member of the academic staff has under the Schedule to Statute C, to any disciplinary proceedings brought by the University under Statute D and the Schedule to Statute C, to any review proceedings before the Commissary under Statute A IX 3–10, to any legal proceedings, and in respect of students, to any relevant student complaints or adjudication procedures.

39. The Registrary shall designate a person to act as Secretary of the Panel of Referees, and as Clerk of the Tribunal.

SCHEDULE

Royalty income

In the following, net royalty refers to royalty income less expenditure on:

(*a*) all reasonable expenses paid outside the University and Cambridge Enterprise, including patent agent fees, for the filing, prosecution and maintenance of intellectual property rights;
(*b*) all reasonable external legal fees incurred in the commercialization of the intellectual property;
(*c*) all reasonable external legal fees expended on litigation;
(*d*) all reasonable expenditure on insurance relating to the maintenance and enforcement of intellectual property rights;
(*e*) any revenue due to third parties, for example sponsors; and
(*f*) any other expenditure that is agreed with the inventors.

Where Cambridge Enterprise is involved in exploitation, the share of revenues from net royalties shall be as follows.

Net Income	*Inventors (jointly)*	*Department*	*Cambridge Enterprise*
First £100,000	90%	5%	5%
Next £100,000	60%	20%	20%
Above £200,000	34%	33%	33%

Where Cambridge Enterprise is not involved in exploitation, the share of revenues from net royalties shall be as follows.

Net Income	*Inventors (jointly)*	*Department*	*Central Funds*
First £50,000	100%	0%	0%
Above £50,000	85%	7.5%	7.5%

Where the inventors form a company under Regulation 21, that is, without the involvement of Cambridge Enterprise, the fixed percentage of inventors' rights referred to therein shall be 15%.

Thresholds in these schedules shall be index linked from 12 December 2005 using the Retail Prices Index.

Share of equity in new businesses

The share of equity in new businesses shall be negotiated on a case by case basis having due regard of the contribution of creators to the business beyond the creation of IPR and of any funding that is made available by the University or Cambridge Enterprise.

Explanatory Note to Regulation 24

The Council in its Notice (*Reporter*, 2008–09, p. 335) in response to the Board of Scrutiny's Thirteenth Report agreed to the Board's Recommendation 8 that it should publish an explanatory note to Regulation 24 for Intellectual Property Rights in *Statutes and Ordinances*. It accordingly attaches below the comments on the scope of Regulation 24 made by the Technology Appeal Tribunal after a hearing held on 1 May 2007. The full text of the Tribunal's decision is available at http://www.admin.cam.ac.uk/offices/secretariat/ipr/ipr_appeal.pdf.

The scope of Regulation 24:

5. Regulation 24 commences as follows;

'During the period following receipt of notification of the research results from a University staff member, Cambridge Enterprise shall consider with her or him how commercial exploitation of the results shall or may be pursued, having regard to all reasonable proposals for that exploitation made by the staff member. Cambridge Enterprise and the University staff member shall keep each other informed and shall co-operate fully in order to achieve an agreed outcome.'

6. In his written submissions to the Tribunal, [the appellant] said 'there has to be an agreed outcome and co-operation between the University staff member and CE and this has to be based upon the wishes of the creator of the intellectual property'. This was developed during the course of oral submissions before us. It was argued that if there was no agreement on a particular issue there was no 'agreed outcome' as referred to by Regulation 24. In

the absence of agreement, the matter had to go to the Referee for determination. We do not accept this argument except in as much as there should normally be reasonable opportunity for the Referee to become involved if appropriate. In our view, when the Regulations refer to CE [Cambridge Enterprise] and the staff member co-operating 'in order to achieve an agreed outcome' it means that those parties must co-operate with the objective of achieving an agreed outcome. It is not dependent upon an agreement being achieved and it does not bestow on the staff member a veto. The Regulations mandate a process, not an outcome. Furthermore, where CE and the relevant staff member have agreed a particular outcome, for example an agreement for exploitation between CE and a third party, Regulation 24 does not give the staff member a right to be consulted on, or a veto over, every commercial decision to be made within the scope of that agreement. Were it otherwise it would become difficult to run any normal commercial arrangement with third parties. Indeed we think that were staff members to have such wide-ranging powers, it could be a significant disincentive to third parties who might otherwise be tempted to invest in the results of Cambridge research. We do not believe the Regulations should be read that way. That would be to the long term disadvantage of both the University and its staff.

7. In our view, Regulation 24 requires CE and the staff member to enter into bona fide discussions with the aim of achieving an agreed outcome. The views of the originator of the research are to be given great weight. The Regulation requires the member of staff and CE to keep each other informed and to co-operate fully. The word 'fully' clearly governs the obligation on the parties to co-operate. Whilst, as a matter of grammar, it may not also govern their obligation to keep each other informed, in our view full co-operation involves not just bona fide discussion but also an obligation to keep each other fully informed of any significant factor which can be or is likely to be taken into account in determining how the research is to be exploited. Full co-operation involves the parties being on as near an equal footing as possible as far as knowledge of relevant facts is concerned. Furthermore such disclosure must be done at a time which gives the disclosee a reasonable opportunity to make a proper assessment, to respond and, where suitable, to make counter-proposals. Save in cases of necessary urgency, the disclosee must also be informed sufficiently in advance to enable him or her to properly consider the implications of what is being proposed by CE, to formulate and properly present a response. We emphasise that the obligation of disclosure only applies to significant factors. It does not mean that the parties are obliged to disclose trivial matters to each other.

8. We accept that situations may arise where full disclosure may not be possible. For example it may not always be possible where defence related research is involved. Similarly, occasions may arise where disclosure of some information may put the discloser at significant risk of being in breach of a legal obligation to some third party. In such cases, the discloser must indicate to the other party the nature of the restraint. Once again this must be done in sufficient time to allow the disclosee to express informed views on the claimed restriction and to suggest ways in which it can be avoided or its effect minimised. For example, if commercially sensitive information is involved, the disclosee may be able to suggest a reasonable compromise whereby the information is disclosed to an independent third party acting on her or his behalf who can express views to the disclosee without the need to disclose the confidential information to her or him.

9. In addition to this, we believe that Regulation 24 obliges both CE and members of staff to avoid, wherever possible, entering into arrangements which would hinder their ability to comply with their duty to make full disclosure of relevant information. A party should take reasonable steps to ensure that third parties do not impose restraints on the disclosure of relevant information or, where such restraints are unavoidable, that they are no more extensive than necessary.

10. In any case where there is a reference to the Referee under the Regulations and it appears that significant relevant information has been withheld from one of the parties by the other, the onus is on the withholding party to demonstrate that the information was not significant, that there was a binding obligation not to disclose it or that no reasonable alternative mechanism could have been put in place which would have allowed the disclosee or someone acting on her or his behalf to have access to all or some of the information.

UNIVERSITY FUNDS

GENERAL REGULATIONS

In addition to the several funds prescribed by Statute there shall be a University Education Fund, a Buildings Maintenance Fund, a Quinquennial Equalization Fund, a Land Fund, and such other funds as may be prescribed by Ordinance or as the Council shall from time to time determine.

Distribution from the Amalgamated Fund

1. The appropriation and distribution for expenditure of the fair value of any Amalgamated Fund under Regulation 6(*e*) of the regulations for financial matters shall be determined as set out in Regulation 2. The Council, on the advice of the Finance Committee, may from time to time recommend amendment of the formula set out in Regulation 2 to the Regent House for approval by Grace.

2. The sum distributed to each unit shall be calculated according to the following formula:

$$(PYD \times 0.7) + (0.0425 \times BMV \times 0.3)$$

where:

(i) PYD for 2005–06 is 110.5p uplifted by an inflation factor taken as the retail prices index of June 2005 plus one per cent and, for the year 2006–07 and subsequent years, is the previous year's distribution per unit in the Amalgamated Fund uplifted by an inflation factor taken as the retail prices index of June of the previous financial year plus one per cent or such other inflation factor as the Council may from time to time determine.

(ii) BMV is the capital value of one unit in the Amalgamated Fund taken as the mean of the starting capital values of the most recent six half-years, including the first half-year of the current financial year (i.e. the closing value of the Fund on 31 July of that year, plus the two previous 31 July closing values and three previous 31 January closing values).

FUNDS OF FACULTIES, DEPARTMENTS, AND OTHER INSTITUTIONS

1. Separate accounts shall be maintained for each Faculty, Department, and other institution in such manner as may be prescribed by the Finance Committee of the Council in consultation with the Council or the General Board as the case may be. Accounts.

2. An officer who is required, by or under Statute or Ordinance, to be responsible for the proper application of funds at the disposal of a Faculty, Department, or other institution shall, at the end of each financial year, certify that the statement of the account for which he or she is responsible is correct and that the funds have been properly applied. Responsible officer.

3. Any balance in the funds of a Faculty, Department, or other institution at the end of a financial year shall be available for the purposes of the particular Faculty, Department, or other institution. Balances.

FUNDS ALLOCATED TO THE COUNCIL

In each year an allocation from the Chest to the Council shall be approved by Grace. The Council shall be empowered to approve grants for recurrent and non-recurrent expenditure from this allocation to the funds of institutions under the supervision of the Council and to such other University funds (other than the University Education Fund and the Travelling Expenses Fund) as they may consider appropriate.

ESTIMATES

1. During the Lent Term in each year Faculty Boards and comparable authorities, and Heads of Departments and other institutions, shall prepare estimates of expenditure for the ensuing financial year. Such estimates shall be submitted either to the Council, in the case of institutions under the supervision of the Council, or to the General Board, in the case of institutions under the supervision of the Board, for consideration by those bodies. Submission.

2. Estimates submitted in accordance with Regulation 1 shall be transmitted, when approved by the Council or the General Board, as the case may be, to the Finance Committee of the Council.

3. In the first half of the Easter Term, or as soon as possible thereafter, the Finance Committee shall submit to the Council a statement of the receipts of the Chest and payments from the Chest during the preceding financial year, a revised estimate of the corresponding figures for the current financial year, and an estimate of the corresponding figures for the ensuing financial year.

4. Before the end of the Easter Term or as soon as possible thereafter, the Council shall publish a Report on the financial position of the Chest, recommending allocations for the ensuing financial year to: Allocations Report.

(*a*) the General Board for the University Education Fund;

(*b*) the Council for all other purposes save those specified in other recommendations contained in the Report.

Accounts

1. The Council shall publish an annual abstract of the accounts of the University, signed by the Vice-Chancellor and a University officer designated for the purpose by the Council.

2. The Council shall also publish an abstract of each of the following accounts: the accounts of the Local Examinations Syndicate, the accounts of the University Farm, the accounts of the Contributory Pension Fund, the accounts of the Colleges Fund, and the accounts of any amalgamated fund established by the Council under the provisions of Regulation 6(*e*) of the regulations for financial matters.

SPECIAL REGULATIONS

Buildings Maintenance Fund

The Buildings Maintenance Fund shall be at the disposal of the Council for the performance of their duties relating to the care and maintenance of University buildings. The Council, on the advice of the Buildings Committee, shall from time to time make allocations to the Fund of amounts within their total allocation as approved by Grace.

Colleges Fund

Purpose. **1.** The Colleges Fund maintained under Statute G II 18 shall be used to make grants to Colleges for either recurrent or non-recurrent purposes.

Committee. **2.** The Fund shall be managed by a Committee consisting of:

(*a*) the Vice-Chancellor (or a duly appointed deputy) who shall be Chair;

(*b*) one person appointed by the Council on the nomination of the Finance Committee;

(*c*) one person appointed by the Council on their own nomination;

(*d*) two persons appointed by the Colleges.

Members in classes (*b*)–(*d*) shall be appointed to serve for six years.

Secretary. **3.** The Secretary of the Committee shall be the Registrary or a University officer designated for the purpose by the Council.

Grants. **4.** The Committee shall meet annually to consider representations from Colleges. The Committee shall have discretion to make grants to Colleges from time to time according to their needs and the resources of the Fund. Grants may be either single or recurrent for such period of years as the Committee may decide. All grants shall be reported by the Committee to the Council, who shall publish them to the University.

General Purpose Funds

Title. **1.** Funds which have been established from benefactions made to the University for general or unspecified purposes shall be known as General Purpose Funds and shall consist, as long as any balance remains in the Fund concerned, of the Davy, Harrison, Kirkpatrick, Watkins, and Wightman Funds and such others as may be so designated by the University from time to time.[1]

How used. **2.** The income or capital of any Fund specified in Regulation 1 shall be placed at the disposal of the Council to be used as the Council think fit provided that a statement is published in the *Reporter* on any expenditure therefrom.

Land Fund

Purpose. All payments of premium for the lease of land and receipts from the sale of land (other than land held for investment purposes) shall be credited to the Land Fund. The capital and the income of the Fund may be used (*a*) to purchase sites which are suitable for development for University purposes, and (*b*) to meet the cost of planning and providing the infrastructure for the development of sites in University ownership, including costs relating to the requirements of Town and Country Planning legislation.

[1] By Grace 2 of 12 October 2005, the Archibald Douglas Ross Fund was designated a General Purpose Fund.

Loan Fund I

1. Loan Fund I shall be administered by a Committee consisting of: Committee.

(*a*) the Vice-Chancellor (or a duly appointed deputy) as Chair;

(*b*) two members of the Regent House appointed by the Council on the nomination of the Council's Finance Committee;

(*c*) two members of the Regent House appointed by the Council on their own nomination.

Members in classes (*b*) and (*c*) shall serve for two years from 1 January next following their appointment.

2. The Committee shall meet not less than once in each term.

3. Applications for loans shall be sent to the Registrary by Tutors of Colleges. Applications.

4. Applications on behalf of students in their first year of residence shall be considered only in very exceptional circumstances. Condition under which loans may be granted.

5. Loans shall not be granted unless in the opinion of the Committee the applicant's College is already giving him or her as much assistance as may reasonably be expected.

6. Loans shall be free of interest. The recipient shall sign an undertaking to repay the loan, and in proper cases the recipient's parent or guardian shall be associated with the undertaking. The Committee shall determine, and shall have power to relax, the conditions of repayment.

Loan Fund II

1. In order to help University officers and University assistants who have, or have had, insufficient capital to buy, build, or extend houses, loans shall be offered from Loan Fund II, at a variable rate of interest equal to the standard rate charged by the Cambridge Building Society. Purpose.

2. Subject to an upper limit of £100,000 in each case, loans may be offered of an amount up to the full value of the house as assessed by the Estate Management and Building Service reduced by the amount borrowed on first mortgage from a Bank, Building Society, or Insurance Company approved by the Finance Committee of the Council, provided that in each case the Committee are satisfied that the maximum advance on first mortgage has in fact been obtained. Conditions.

3. A loan shall be secured by a second charge on the house.

4. Conditions of eligibility for loans, for the award of loans, and for their repayment shall be determined by the Finance Committee, who shall have power to exercise discretion in exceptional circumstances. Eligibility and repayment.

5. The granting of loans under these regulations shall be subject to review by the Finance Committee of the Council in 1998–99 and at intervals of five years thereafter.

Pension Fund II[1]

Pension Fund II shall be used by the Council on the recommendation of the Managing Committee of the Pension Scheme for the following purposes: Purpose.

(*a*) to make grants or advances to assistants in needy cases,

(*b*) to meet cases of necessity relating to dependants of assistants who have died in the service of the University.

Quinquennial Equalization Fund

The surplus income of the Chest shall be transferred at the end of the financial year to the Quinquennial Equalization Fund which shall be used to make good any deficiency of income in a year in which the authorized expenditure of the Chest exceeds the income. Purpose.

[1] For Pension Fund I, see the regulations for FSSU, which were last published in *Ordinances*, 1979, p. 109.

Research Maintenance Grants Fund[1]

Conditions.

1. Applications for grants from the Research Maintenance Grants Fund may be made by Tutors of Colleges on behalf of students who fulfil the following conditions:

(*a*) they must have proceeded, or have qualified or be about to qualify to proceed, to a Bachelor's Degree[2] after having completed not less than nine terms of residence (including any allowed), and they must make application not later than the end of the academical year next but one following that in which they qualified to proceed to that degree;

(*b*) they must be or be about to become registered Graduate Students admitted by the Board of Graduate Studies to follow a course of research as candidates, or with a view to becoming candidates, for the Ph.D. Degree.[3]

Value.

2. The annual value of any grant shall be fixed by the Board of Graduate Studies after consideration of the value of other awards which the applicant may have received. Alterations of the value of these awards and particulars of new awards received after the grant has been fixed must be notified to the Board by the holder and the Board may vary the amount of a grant on account of any such alterations or new awards.

Payments.

3. Grants shall be paid quarterly in advance to the holders, subject after the third payment to a certificate that the holder is pursuing research to the satisfaction of the Supervisor appointed by the Degree Committee concerned.

Periods covered by grants.

4. A grant to a Graduate Student shall be made ordinarily for a period of two years and shall be renewable for a further year, but no grant shall be tenable for more than three years in all. The holder of a grant who ceases to be a registered Graduate Student following a course of research as a candidate, or with a view to becoming a candidate, for the Ph.D. Degree shall thereby cease to be qualified to receive any further instalments of the grant.

Applications.

5. Applications for grants shall be submitted to the Secretary of the Board of Graduate Studies. The Board shall publish from time to time a notice of the dates by which such applications must be received.

Names to be published.

6. The names of students to whom the Board of Graduate Studies have awarded Research Maintenance Grants shall be published in the *Reporter*, but no statement of the amount of the grant made to any individual recipient shall be published.

Strategic Planning Reserve Fund

The Strategic Planning Reserve Fund shall consist of such sums as the University may from time to time transfer to it on the recommendation of the Council. The Fund shall be at the disposal of the Council, to be used for such strategic purposes as the Council may consider appropriate. A list of allocations from the Fund shall be published annually in the *Reporter*.

Student Housing Fund

Purpose.

1. The Student Housing Fund shall be used to make grants to Colleges or to the University for the provision of accommodation for members of the University *in statu pupillari*.

Committee of Management.

2. The Fund shall be under the control of a Committee of Management consisting of

(*a*) the Vice-Chancellor (or a duly appointed deputy) who shall be Chair;

(*b*) two persons appointed by the Council;

(*c*) one person appointed by the Council on the nomination of the Buildings Committee;

(*d*) three persons appointed by the Colleges Committee.

Members in classes (*b*)–(*d*) shall be appointed in the Michaelmas Term to serve for six years from 1 January following their appointment.

[1] Research Maintenance Grants are currently suspended. Students should apply to their Faculty or Department for nomination for Domestic Research Studentships.

[2] For the purposes of this regulation the term 'Bachelor's Degree' shall be taken to mean a Bachelor's Degree of this University (see Statute A X 2(*d*)).

[3] Under this regulation persons, otherwise eligible, who have applied initially for admission as Graduate Students registered for the Ph.D. Degree but who have been required by the Board of Graduate Studies and the Degree Committee concerned to register for the M.Phil. Degree in the first instance as a condition of possible subsequent registration for a research degree, or who, having so applied for admission, have been admitted by the Board of Graduate Studies as Graduate Students not at first registered for any qualification, will be eligible to apply for grants from the Research Maintenance Grants Fund.

3. The Secretary of the Committee shall be the Registrary or a University officer designated for the purpose by the Council. Secretary.

4. The Committee of Management shall meet at least once in each financial year to consider representations from Colleges or from the Council. The Committee shall have discretion to make grants to Colleges or to the University from time to time according to their needs and the resources of the Fund. Grants may be either single or recurrent for such period of years as the Committee may determine. All grants shall be reported by the Committee to the Council, who shall publish them to the University.

UNIVERSITY EDUCATION FUND

1. In each year an allocation from the Chest to the General Board for the University Education Fund shall be approved by Grace. The General Board shall be empowered to approve grants for recurrent and for non-recurrent expenditure from the University Education Fund to the funds of Faculties, Departments, and other institutions under the supervision of the General Board, and to the Travelling Expenses Fund. Allocation to, and grants from, Fund.

2. The Finance Committee of the Council in consultation with the General Board shall be empowered to adjust the allocation to the Fund from the Chest in any year on account of differences between actual and estimated expenditure of the institutions under the supervision of the General Board on pensionable stipends, wages, pensions, national insurance contributions, family allowances, and other personal emoluments, except where the savings have arisen from deciding to suppress or not to fill any office or post with a view to applying the savings to new developments of a recurrent nature or for other General Board purposes. Any balance in the Fund at the end of the financial year after such adjustment, if any, has been made shall remain in the Fund. Adjustments of allocation. Balance.

3. When a deficit has arisen in the accounts of one or more institutions under the supervision of the General Board the General Board may make non-recurrent grants from the Fund to meet the whole or part of the deficit. Grants for deficits.

CHAPTER XIV

COLLEGES

FELLOWSHIP OF A COLLEGE

Amended by Grace 1 of 27 November 2013

In any Statute or Ordinance unless otherwise specified, the term 'Fellowship of a College' shall mean any Fellowship of a College other than an Honorary Fellowship, and the term 'Fellow of a College' shall mean the holder of such a Fellowship.

COLLEGE ACCOUNTS

1. The accounts prepared annually by each College and the report of its Auditors submitted under the provision of Statute G III shall conform to the Recommended Cambridge College Accounts set out in the Schedule below, provided that a College which has not given notice under Statute G III 6 that it will use the Recommended Cambridge College Accounts shall prepare its accounts in the form that was required by Statute G III on 1 October 2002.

2. The form of the Recommended Cambridge College Accounts shall be determined from time to time by the University on the recommendation of the Finance Committee, made after considering the advice of the Inter-Collegiate Committee on College Accounts.

3. The index referred to in the Schedule to Statute G II in relation to College contributions under Statute G II 16 shall be the Higher Education Pay and Prices Index (all).

SCHEDULE

RECOMMENDED CAMBRIDGE COLLEGE ACCOUNTS (RCCA)

This document is intended to be read in conjunction with the HE/FE SORP available from the Universities UK website: http://www.universitiesuk.ac.uk/highereducation/Documents/2007/SORP.pdf.

Reference and Administrative Details

Name of College

Address

Charity Registration number

Charity Trustees[1] (Members of the Governing Body or Council)

Senior officers
- Head of House:
- Senior Tutor:
- Senior Bursar:
- Other:

Principal advisers
- Auditors:
- Bankers:
- Property Managers:

[1] The names of the trustees who served ***at any time during the year*** are to be given.

- Investment Managers:
- Legal Advisers:

Operating and Financial Review

The format and content of the Operating and Financial Review (which may also be called the Trustees' Report or Report of the Governing Body) is not prescribed by the SORP. However, this review must provide an overview of the College's finances and operations and follow best practice. Specifically, the OFR should provide a comprehensive and balanced analysis, consistent with the size and complexity of the College, covering:

(*a*) *the development, performance, and operation of the business and operation of the College during the financial year;*
(*b*) *the position of the College at the end of the year;*
(*c*) *the main trends and factors underlying the development, performance and position of the College and its academic performance during the financial year; and*
(*d*) *the main trends and factors which are likely to affect the College's future development, performance and position.*

The following headings may provide a useful guide:

Introduction

Scope of the financial statements

Aims and objectives of the College

Public benefit

Funding

Achievements and performance

Financial review

Maintenance of buildings

Capital expenditure

Endowment and investment performance

Staff costs and pensions

Reserves policy

Principal risks and uncertainties

Plans for the future

Corporate Governance

Paragraph 24(b) of the SORP requires the inclusion of a statement of corporate governance. The following is shown for guidance only.

1. The following statement is provided by the Trustees [Governing Body/Council] to enable readers of the financial statements to obtain a better understanding of the arrangements in the College for the management of its resources and for audit.
2. The College is a registered charity (registered number 1234567) and subject to regulation by the Charity Commission for England and Wales. The members of the [Governing Body/Council] are the charity trustees and are responsible for ensuring compliance with charity law.
3. The Trustees are [Governing Body/Council is] advised in carrying out its duties by a number of Committees. [Set out details]
4. The principal officers of the College are [insert titles].
5. It is the duty of the [insert name of Committee] to keep under review the effectiveness of the College's internal systems of financial and other controls; to advise the Trustees [Governing Body/Council] on the appointment of external [and internal] auditors; to consider reports submitted by the auditors, [both external and internal]; to monitor the implementation of recommendations made by the auditors; to make an annual report to the Trustees [Governing Body/Council]. Membership of the [insert name of Committee] includes ......
6. There are Registers of Interests of Trustees [Members of the Governing Body/Council], the Finance Committee and Audit Committee, and of the senior administrative officers. Declarations of interest are made systematically at meetings.
7. The College's Trustees [Members of the Governing Body/Council] during the year ended 30 June [20..] are set out on page 1.

Statement of Internal Control

Paragraph 24(b) of the SORP also requires the inclusion of a statement of internal control.

The following statement is by way of example only.

1. The Trustees are [Governing Body/Council is] responsible for maintaining a sound system of internal control that supports the achievement of policy, aims, and objectives while safeguarding the public and other funds and assets for which the Governing Body is responsible, in accordance with the College's Statutes.
2. The system of internal control is designed to manage rather than eliminate the risk of failure to achieve policies, aims, and objectives; it therefore provides reasonable but not absolute assurance of effectiveness.
3. The system of internal control is designed to identify the principal risks to the achievement of policies, aims and objectives, to evaluate the nature and extent of those risks and to manage them efficiently, effectively, and economically. This process was in place for the year ended 30 June [20..] and up to the date of approval of the financial statements.
4. The Trustees are [Governing Body/Council is] responsible for reviewing the effectiveness of the system of internal control. The following processes have been established:

5. The Trustees' [Governing Body's/Council's] review of the effectiveness of the system of internal control is informed by the work of the various Committees, Bursar, and College officers, who have responsibility for the development and maintenance of the internal control framework, and by comments made by the external auditors in their management letter and other reports.

Alternatively, the statement may be included in the Operating and Financial Review (OFR) or the Statement of Corporate Governance.

Responsibilities of the Trustees [Governing Body]

The Trustees are [Governing Body/Council is] responsible for preparing the Annual Report and financial statements in accordance with applicable law and United Kingdom Accounting Standards (United Kingdom Generally Accepted Accounting Practice).

The College's Statutes and the Statutes and Ordinances of the University of Cambridge require the Governing Body to prepare financial statements for each financial year which give a true and fair view of the state of affairs of the College and of the surplus or deficit of the College for that period. In preparing these financial statements, the Trustees are [Governing Body/Council is] required to:

- select suitable accounting policies and then apply them consistently;
- make judgements and estimates that are reasonable and prudent;
- state whether applicable accounting standards have been followed, subject to any material departures disclosed and explained in the financial statements; and
- prepare the financial statements on the going concern basis unless it is inappropriate to presume that the College will continue in operation[1].

The Trustees are [Governing Body/Council is] responsible for keeping accounting records which disclose with reasonable accuracy at any time the financial position of the College and enable them to ensure that the financial statements comply with the Statutes of the University of Cambridge. They are also responsible for safeguarding the assets of the College and hence for taking reasonable steps for the prevention and detection of fraud and other irregularities.

[The Trustees are [Governing Body/Council is] responsible for the maintenance and integrity of the corporate and financial information included on the College's website. Legislation in the United Kingdom governing the preparation and dissemination of financial statements may differ from legislation in other jurisdictions[2].]

Alternatively, this statement may be included in the Operating and Financial Review (OFR) or the Statement of Corporate Governance.

[1] If no separate statement on the going concern is made by the Trustees/Governing Body/Council.

[2] Where the financial statements are published on the internet.

Independent Auditors' Report to the Trustees [Governing Body/Council] of Cambridge College

We have audited the financial statements of [name of College] for the year ended .... which comprise the [consolidated*] income and expenditure account, the [consolidated*] statement of total recognised gains and losses, the [consolidated and College*] balance sheet[s*], the [consolidated*] cash flow statement and related notes. The financial reporting framework that has been applied in their preparation is applicable law and United Kingdom Accounting Standards (United Kingdom Generally Accepted Accounting Practice).

This report is made solely to the College's Trustees [Governing Body/Council], as a body, in accordance with the College's Statutes, and the Statutes of the University of Cambridge. Our audit work has been undertaken so that we might state to the College's Trustees [Governing Body/Council] those matters we are required to state to them in an auditors' report and for no other purpose. To the fullest extent permitted by law, we do not accept or assume responsibility to anyone other than the College and the College's Trustees [Governing Body/Council] as a body, for our audit work, for this report, or for the opinions we have formed.

Respective responsibilities of the trustees [Governing Body/Council] and auditors

As explained more fully in the Trustees' [Governing Body's/Council's] Responsibilities Statement [set out [on page ...]], the Trustees are [Governing Body/Council is] responsible for the preparation of financial statements which give a true and fair view.

We have been appointed as auditors under section 43 of the Charities Act 1993 and report in accordance with regulations made under section 44 of that Act. Our responsibility is to audit and express an opinion on the financial statements in accordance with applicable law and International Standards on Auditing (UK and Ireland). Those standards require us to comply with the Auditing Practices Board's [APB's] Ethical Standards for Auditors.

Scope of the audit of financial statements

An audit involves obtaining evidence about the amounts and disclosures in the financial statements sufficient to give reasonable assurance that the financial statements are free from material misstatement, whether caused by fraud or error. This includes an assessment of: whether the accounting policies are appropriate to the College's circumstances and have been consistently applied and adequately disclosed; the reasonableness of significant accounting estimates made by the trustees [Governing Body/Council]; and the overall presentation of the financial statements. In addition, we read all the financial information in the [*describe the annual report*] to identify material inconsistencies with the audited financial statements. If we become aware of any apparent material misstatements or inconsistencies we consider the implications for our report.

Opinion on financial statements

In our opinion:

- the financial statements give a true and fair view of the state of the [group's and the*] College's affairs as at .... and of [its*] [the group's*] income and expenditure for the year then ended;
- the financial statements have been properly prepared in accordance with United Kingdom Generally Accepted Accounting Practice;
- the financial statements have been prepared in accordance with the requirements of the Charities Act 1993, the College's Statutes, and the Statutes of the University of Cambridge;
- the contribution due from the College to the University has been correctly computed as advised in the provisional assessment by the University of Cambridge and in accordance with the provisions of Statute G II, of the University of Cambridge.

* Delete if not applicable.

Matters on which we are required to report by exception

We have nothing to report in respect of the following matters where the Charities Act 1993 requires us to report to you if, in our opinion:

- the information given in the Trustees' [Governing Body's/Council's] Annual Report is inconsistent in any material respect with the financial statements; or
- sufficient accounting records have not been kept; or
- the financial statements are not in agreement with the accounting records and returns; or
- we have not received all the information and explanations we require for our audit.

Name and address of firm

Chartered Accountants and Statutory Auditors

Date:

[Name of firm] is eligible to act as an auditor in terms of section 1212 of the Companies Act 2006.

Statement of Principal Accounting Policies

Basis of preparation

The financial statements have been prepared in accordance with the provisions of the Statutes of the College and of the University of Cambridge and applicable United Kingdom accounting standards. In addition, the financial statements comply with the Statement of Recommended Practice: Accounting for Further and Higher Education (the SORP).

The income and expenditure account includes activity analysis in order to demonstrate that the College is satisfying its obligations to the University of Cambridge with regard to the use of public funds. The analysis required by the SORP is set out in note 7.

Basis of accounting

The financial statements have been prepared under the historical cost convention, modified in respect of the treatment of investments [and certain operational properties] which are included at valuation.

Basis of consolidation

The consolidated financial statements include the College and its subsidiary undertakings. Details of the subsidiary undertakings included are set out in note xx. Intra-group balances are eliminated on consolidation.

The consolidated financial statements do not include the activities of student societies [as these are separate bodies in which the College has no financial interest and over whose policy decisions it has no control].

Recognition of income

Academic fees

Academic fees are recognised in the period to which they relate and include all fees chargeable to students or their sponsors. [The costs of any fees waived or written off by the College are included as expenditure.]

Restricted grant income

Grants received for restricted purposes are recognised as income to the extent that relevant expenditure has been incurred.

Income from research grants

[Income from research grants, contracts and other services rendered is included to the extent of the completion of the contract or service concerned.]

Donations and benefactions

Charitable donations are recognised on receipt or where there is certainty of future receipt and the value can be measured reliably. The accounting treatment of a donation depends on the nature and extent of restrictions specified by the donor. Donations with no substantial restrictions are recognised as income in the income and expenditure account. Donations which are to be retained for the future benefit of the College, and other donations with substantially restricted purposes, other than for the acquisition or construction of tangible fixed assets, are recognised in the statement of total recognised gains and losses as new endowments.

Capital grants and donations

Grants and donations are received for the purposes of funding the acquisition and construction of tangible fixed assets. In the case of depreciable assets these are credited to deferred capital grants when the related capital expenditure is incurred and released to income over the estimated useful life of the respective assets in line with the depreciation policy. Grants and donations of, or for the acquisition of, freehold land or heritage assets, which are non-depreciable assets, are credited to the income and expenditure account in the year of acquisition.

Other income

Income is received from a range of activities including residences, catering conferences, and other services rendered.

Endowment and investment income

All investment income is credited to the Income and Expenditure Account in the period in which it is earned. Income from restricted endowments not expended in accordance with the restrictions of the endowment is transferred from the Income and Expenditure Account to restricted endowments.

[*Total return*

Where the Total Return basis of accounting for investment returns has been adopted, Colleges should include an explanation of the basis of the calculation.]

Foreign currency translation

Transactions denominated in foreign currencies are recorded at the rate of exchange ruling at the date of the transactions. Monetary assets and liabilities denominated in foreign currencies are translated into sterling at year end rates or, where there are forward foreign exchange contracts, at contract rates. The resulting exchange differences are dealt with in the determination of the income and expenditure for the financial year.

Statement of Principal Accounting Policies (continued)

Tangible fixed assets

Land and buildings

Land and buildings are stated at [cost] [or] [valuation]. Where buildings have been revalued, they are valued on the basis of their depreciated replacement cost. [The valuation on [date] was carried out by [name of firm, Chartered Surveyors.] Freehold buildings are depreciated on a straight line basis over their expected useful economic life of x years. Freehold land is not depreciated. [Leasehold land and buildings are amortised over 50 years, or, if shorter, the period of the lease.]

Where land and buildings are acquired with the aid of specific bequests or donations they are capitalised and depreciated as above. [The related benefactions are credited to a deferred capital account and are released to the Income and Expenditure Account over the expected useful economic life of the related asset on a basis consistent with the depreciation policy.] [The related benefactions are credited to permanent capital.]

Finance costs which are directly attributable to the construction of buildings are [not] capitalised as part of the cost of those assets.

A review for impairment of a fixed asset is carried out if events or changes in circumstances indicate that the carrying amount of the fixed asset may not be recoverable.

Buildings under construction are valued at cost, based on the value of architects' certificates and other direct costs incurred. They are not depreciated until they are brought into use.

[Land held specifically for development, investment, and subsequent sale is included in current assets at the lower of cost and net realisable value.]

[The cost of additions to operational property shown in the balance sheet includes the cost of land.]

Maintenance of premises

[The College has a [five year] [other period] rolling maintenance plan which is reviewed on an annual basis.] The cost of routine maintenance is [charged to the Income and Expenditure Account as it is incurred] [capitalised and depreciated over the expected useful economic life of the asset concerned]. [The College also sets aside sums on a regular basis to meet major maintenance costs which occur on an irregular basis. These are disclosed as designated funds.]

Equipment

Furniture, fittings, and equipment [is written off in the year of acquisition] [costing less than [£x] per individual item or group of related items is written off in the year of acquisition. All other assets are capitalised and depreciated over their expected useful life as follows:

Furniture and fittings	[10%] per annum
Motor vehicles and general equipment	[20%] per annum
Computer equipment	[25%] per annum].

[Where equipment is acquired with the aid of specific bequests or donations it is capitalised and depreciated as above. [The related benefactions are credited to a deferred capital account and are released to the Income and Expenditure Account over the expected useful economic life of the related asset on a basis consistent with the depreciation policy.] [The related benefactions are credited to permanent capital.]]

Leased assets

Fixed assets held under finance leases and the related lease obligations are recorded in the Balance Sheet at the fair value of the leased assets at the inception of the lease. The excesses of lease payments over recorded lease obligations are treated as finance charges which are amortised over each lease term to give a constant rate of charge on the remaining balance of the obligations. Rental costs under operating leases are charged to expenditure in equal amounts over the periods of the leases.

Heritage assets

The College holds and conserves a number of collections, exhibits, artefacts and other assets of historical, artistic or scientific importance. In accordance with FRS 15 and FRS 30 (Heritage assets) heritage assets acquired before 1 July 1999 have not been capitalised since reliable estimates of cost or value are not available on a cost-benefit basis. Acquisitions since 1 July 1999 have been capitalised at cost or, in the case of donated assets, at expert valuation on receipt. Heritage assets are not depreciated since their long economic life and high residual value mean that any depreciation would not be material.

Investments

Fixed asset investment and endowment assets are included in the balance sheet at market value, except for investments in subsidiary undertakings which are stated in the College's balance sheet at cost and eliminated on consolidation. Investments that are not listed on a recognised stock exchange are carried at historical cost less any provision for impairment in their value.

Stocks

Stocks are stated at the lower of cost and net realisable value after making provision for slow moving and obsolete items.

Provisions

Provisions are recognised when the College has a present legal or constructive obligation as a result of a past event, it is probable that a transfer of economic benefits will be required to settle the obligation, and a reliable estimate can be made of the amount of the obligation.

Statement of Principal Accounting Policies (continued)

Taxation

The College is a registered charity (number 1234567) and also a charity within the meaning of Section 506 (1) of the Taxes Act 1988. Accordingly, the College is exempt from taxation in respect of income or capital gains received within the categories covered by Section 505 of the Taxes Act 1988 or Section 256 of the Taxation of Chargeable Gains Act 1992 to the extent that such income or gains are applied to exclusively charitable purposes.

The College receives no similar exemption in respect of Value Added Tax.

Contribution under Statute G II

The College is liable to be assessed for Contribution under the provisions of Statute G II of the University of Cambridge. Contribution is used to fund grants to Colleges from the Colleges Fund. The College may from time to time be eligible for such grants. The liability for the year is as advised to the College by the University based on an assessable amount derived from the value of the College's assets as at the end of the previous financial year.

Pension costs

The College participates in the Universities Superannuation Scheme (USS), a defined benefit scheme which is externally funded and contracted out of the State Second Pension (S2P). The assets of the scheme are held in a separate trustee administered fund. Because of the mutual nature of the scheme, the College is unable to identify its share of the underlying assets and liabilities of the scheme on a consistent and reasonable basis and therefore, as required by FRS 17 'Retirement Benefits', accounts for the scheme as if it were a defined contribution scheme. As a result, the amount charged to the Income and Expenditure Account represents the contributions payable to the scheme in respect of the accounting period.

[A similar note of accounting policy is required in respect of any other scheme in which the College participates, e.g. CCFPS.]

Consolidated Income and Expenditure Account

For the year ended 30 June [20..]

		Current year	Previous year
	Note	£	£
Income			
Academic fees and charges	1		
Residences, catering, and conferences	2		
Endowment and investment income	3		
Donations	4		
Total income			
Expenditure			
Education	5		
Residences, catering, and conferences	6		
Other expenditure			
Total expenditure	7		
Surplus/(deficit) on continuing operations before Contribution under Statute G II			
Contribution under Statute G II			
Surplus/(deficit) on continuing operations after Contribution under Statute G II			
Surplus/(deficit) for the year transferred to accumulated income in endowment funds	20		
Surplus/(deficit) for the year retained within general reserves			

All items dealt with in arriving at the surplus/(deficit) for [current year] and [previous year] relate to continuing operations.

Note of Historical Cost Surpluses and Deficits

For the year ended 30 June [20..]

		Current year	Previous year
	Note	£	£
Surplus/(deficit) on continuing operations			
Difference between historical cost depreciation and the actual charge for the period calculated on the revalued amount	21		
Realisation of gains/(losses) on disposal of fixed asset investments	21		
Historical cost surplus/(deficit) for the year			

This note will only apply to those Colleges that have adopted a policy of revaluation with regard to tangible fixed assets.

The notes on pages xx to xx form part of these accounts.

Consolidated Statement of Total Recognised Gains and Losses

For the year ended 30 June [20..]

		Restricted Funds	Unrestricted Funds	Current year Total Funds	Previous year Total Funds
	Note	**£**	**£**	**£**	**£**
Surplus/(deficit) on Income and Expenditure Account					
Unspent endowment fund income					
Increase/(decrease) in market value of investments					
Endowment assets	20				
Fixed asset investments	21				
Unrealised surplus on revaluation of fixed assets	9				
New endowments	20				
Capital grant from Colleges Fund					
Transfers					
Actuarial gain/(loss) in respect of pension schemes	28				
Total recognised gains/(losses) relating to the year					
Reconciliation					
Opening reserves and endowments					
Total recognised gains/(losses) for the year					
Closing reserves and endowments					

The notes on pages xx to xx form part of these accounts.

Consolidated Balance Sheet as at 30 June [20..]

				Current year	**Previous year**
				Group	**Group**
	Note			**£**	**£**
Fixed assets					
Tangible assets	9				
Investments	10				
Endowment assets	11				
Current assets					
Stocks and work in progress	12				
Debtors	13				
Cash at bank and in hand	14				
Creditors: amounts falling due within one year	15				
Net current assets					
Creditors: amounts falling due after more than one year	16				
Provision for liabilities and charges	17				
Net assets excluding pension asset/(liability)					
Net pension asset/(liability)	18				
Net assets including pension asset/(liability)					
Represented by:					
		Restricted funds	**Unrestricted funds**	**Current year Total**	**Previous year Total**
Deferred capital grants	19				
Endowments					
Expendable endowments	20				
Permanent endowments	20				
Reserves					
General reserves excluding pension reserve	21				
Pension reserve	21				
Operational property revaluation reserve	21				
Fixed asset investment revaluation reserve	21				
Total funds					

[Where the Group and College figures are materially different, separate balance sheets for each must be produced.]

The financial statements were approved by the Trustees [Governing Body/Council] on [insert date] and signed on its behalf by:

The notes on pages xx to xx form part of these accounts.

Consolidated Cash Flow Statement

For the year ended 30 June [20..]

		Current year	Previous year
	Note	£	£
Net cash inflow from operating activities	23		
Returns on investments and servicing of finance	24		
Capital expenditure and financial investment	24		
Cash inflow/(outflow) before management of liquid resources			
Management of liquid resources			
Increase/(decrease) in short term deposits			
Financing	24		
Bank loan drawn down in year			
Loan repayment in year			
Increase/(decrease) in cash in the year			
Reconciliation in net cash flow to movement in net funds			
Increase/(decrease) in cash in the year			
New bank loan			
Cash inflow/(outflow) from liquid resources			
Change in net funds			
Net funds at beginning of year			
Net funds at end of year	25		

The notes on pages xx to xx form part of these accounts.

Notes to the Accounts

For the year ended 30 June [20..]

1	**Academic fees and charges**	**Current year**	**Previous year**
		£	**£**
	Colleges fees:		
	Fee income paid on behalf of undergraduates at the Publicly-funded Undergraduate rate (per capita fee £……..)		
	Privately-funded undergraduate fee income (per capita fee (£……..)		
	Fee income received at the Graduate fee rate (per capita fee £……..)		
	Other income		
	Total		

2	**Income from residences, catering and conferences**		**Current year**	**Previous year**
			£	**£**
	Accommodation	College members		
		Conferences		
	Catering	College members		
		Conferences		
	Total			

3	**Endowment and investment income**	**Current year**	**Previous year**
		£	**£**
3a	**Analysis**		
	[Total return contribution (see note 3b)]		
	Income from:		
	Land and buildings		
	Quoted securities		
	Fixed interest securities		
	Income from short-term investments		
	Other interest receivable		
	Total		
3b	**Summary of total return**		
	Income from:		
	Land and buildings		
	Quoted and other securities and cash		
	Gains/(losses) on endowment assets:		
	Land and buildings		
	Quoted and other securities and cash		
	Investment management costs (see note 3c)		
	Total return for year		
	Total return transferred to Income and Expenditure Account (see note 3a)		
	Unapplied total return for year included within statement of total recognised gains and losses (see note 22)		

Notes to the Accounts (continued)

For the year ended 30 June [20..]

3c	**Investment management costs**	**Current year**	**Previous year**
		£	£
	Land and buildings		
	Quoted securities – equities		
	Fixed interest securities		
	Other investments		
	Cash		
	Total		

4	**Donations**	**Current year**	**Previous year**
		£	£
	Unrestricted donations		
	Restricted donations		
	Released from deferred capital grants (see note 19)		
	Total		

5	**Education expenditure**	**Current year**	**Previous year**
		£	£
	Teaching		
	Tutorial		
	Admissions		
	Research		
	Scholarships and awards		
	Other educational facilities		
	Total		

6	**Residences, catering and conferences expenditure**		**Current year**	**Previous year**
			£	£
	Accommodation	College members		
		Conferences		
	Catering	College members		
		Conferences		
	Total			

7a	**Analysis of [current year's] expenditure by activity**				
		Staff costs (note 8)	**Other operating expenses**	**Depreciation**	**Total**
		£	£	£	£
	Education				
	Residences, catering and conferences				
	Other				
	Totals				

Expenditure includes fundraising costs of £xx,xxx. This expenditure [includes] [does not include] the costs of alumni relations.

Notes to the Accounts (continued)

For the year ended 30 June [20..]

7b	**Analysis of [previous year's] expenditure by activity**				
		Staff costs (note 8)	**Other operating expenses**	**Depreciation**	**Total**
		£	**£**	**£**	**£**
	Education				
	Residences, catering and conferences				
	Other				
	Totals				

Expenditure includes fundraising costs of £xx,xxx. This expenditure [includes] [does not include] the costs of alumni relations.

7c	**Auditors' remuneration**		
		Current year	**Previous year**
		£	**£**
	Other operating expenses include:		
	Audit fees payable to the College's external auditors		
	Other fees payable to the College's external auditors		
	[Audit fees payable to other firms]		

8	**Staff costs**					
	Group	**College Fellows**	**Other academic**	**Non-academic**	**Current year Total**	**Previous year Total**
		£	**£**	**£**	**£**	**£**
	Staff costs:					
	Emoluments					
	Social security costs					
	Other pension costs					
	Average staff numbers (full-time equivalents):					
	Academic ([numbers in Governing Body][numbers of stipendiary staff])					
	Non-academic (full time equiv.)					
	Total					

[The Governing Body comprises xx Fellows, of which the xx declared above are stipendiary.] [Of the xx Fellows declared above, xx are stipendiary.]

The number of officers and employees of the College, including Head of House, who received emoluments in the following ranges was:

					Current year Total	**Previous year Total**
	£100,001 – £110,000					
	£110,001 – £120,000					

*(Continuing in bands of £10,000 until the highest combined stipend and other taxable benefits is reached)**

* *(or, if relevant)*
No officer or employee of the College, including the Head of House, received emoluments of over £100,000.

Notes to the Accounts (continued)

For the year ended 30 June [20..]

9	**Tangible fixed assets**						
	Group	**Land and buildings**	**Assets in construction**	**Equipment**	**Heritage assets**	**Current year Total**	**Previous year Total**
		£	**£**	**£**	**£**	**£**	**£**
	Cost or valuation						
	At beginning of year						
	Additions at cost						
	Transfers						
	Disposals						
	At end of year						
	Depreciation						
	At beginning of year						
	Charge for the year						
	Eliminated on disposals						
	Written back on revaluation						
	At end of year						
	Net book value						
	At end of year						
	At beginning of year						
	College						
	Cost or valuation						
	At beginning of year						
	Additions at cost						
	Transfers						
	Disposals						
	At end of year						
	Depreciation						
	At beginning of year						
	Charge for the year						
	Eliminated on disposals						
	Written back on revaluation						
	At end of year						
	Net book value						
	At end of year						
	At beginning of year						

The insured value of freehold land and buildings as at 30 June [current year] was £xx,xxx,xxx ([previous year]: £xx,xxx,xxx).

The net book value of tangible fixed assets includes an amount of £xxx,xxx ([previous year]: £xxx,xxx) in respect of assets held under finance leases. The depreciation charge on these assets for the year was £xx,xxx ([previous year]: £xx,xxx).

The cost to the group of freehold buildings and assets in construction consists of the costs incurred by the College less the surplus recorded in the accounts of XYZ Limited, a subsidiary undertaking, and eliminated on consolidation.

Notes to the Accounts (continued)

For the year ended 30 June [20..]

9	**Tangible fixed assets (continued)**

Heritage assets

The College holds and conserves certain collections, artefacts and other assets of historical, artistic or scientific importance.

As stated in the statement of principal accounting policies, heritage assets acquired since [insert date] have been capitalised. However, the majority of assets held in the College's collections were acquired prior to this date. As reliable estimates of cost or valuation are not available for these on a cost-benefit basis, they have not been capitalised. As a result the total included in the balance sheet is partial.
Amounts for the current and previous four years were as follows:

		Current year	**[Each of previous four years]**			
		£	**£**	**£**	**£**	**£**
	Acquisitions purchased with specific donations					
	Acquisitions purchased with College funds					
	Total cost of acquisitions purchased					
	Value of acquisitions by donation					
	Total acquisitions capitalised					

10	**Fixed asset investments**				
		Group	**Group**	**College**	**College**
		Current year	**Previous year**	**Current year**	**Previous year**
		£	**£**	**£**	**£**
	Balance at beginning of year				
	Additions				
	Disposals				
	Appreciation/(depreciation)				
	Increase/(decrease) in cash balances held at fund managers				
	Balance at end of year				
	Represented by:				
	Property				
	Quoted securities – equities				
	Fixed interest securities				
	Investments in subsidiary undertakings				
	Cash in hand and at investment managers				
	Other investments				

Notes to the Accounts (continued)

For the year ended 30 June [20..]

11	Endowment assets				
		Group	**Group**	**College**	**College**
		Current year	**Previous year**	**Current year**	**Previous year**
		£	**£**	**£**	**£**
	Long-term investments:				
	Property				
	Quoted securities – equities				
	Fixed interest securities				
	Cash in hand and at investment managers				
	Other investments				
	Bank balances				

Notes 9 and 10 above may need to be adapted to include Endowment Assets (e.g. where investments are managed as a single pool) in which case the figures in note 11 should be suitably cross-referenced. In either case, Endowment Assets must always be shown separately on the face of the balance sheet.

12	Stocks and work in progress				
		Group	**Group**	**College**	**College**
		Current year	**Previous year**	**Current year**	**Previous year**
		£	**£**	**£**	**£**
	Goods for resale				
	Work in progress				
	Other stocks				

13	Debtors				
		Group	**Group**	**College**	**College**
		Current year	**Previous year**	**Current year**	**Previous year**
		£	**£**	**£**	**£**
	Members of the College				
	Amounts due from subsidiary undertakings				
	Other debtors				
	Prepayments and accrued income				

14	Cash and bank balances				
		Group	**Group**	**College**	**College**
		Current year	**Previous year**	**Current year**	**Previous year**
		£	**£**	**£**	**£**
	Short-term money market investments				
	Bank deposits				
	Current accounts				
	Cash in hand				

Notes to the Accounts (continued)

For the year ended 30 June [20..]

15	**Creditors: amounts falling due within one year**				
		Group	**Group**	**College**	**College**
		Current year	**Previous year**	**Current year**	**Previous year**
		£	**£**	**£**	**£**
	Bank overdraft				
	Trade creditors				
	Members of the College				
	Amounts due to subsidiary undertakings				
	University fees				
	Contribution to Colleges Fund				
	Other creditors (e.g. VAT)				
	Accruals and deferred income				

16	**Creditors: amounts falling due after more than one year**				
		Group	**Group**	**College**	**College**
		Current year	**Previous year**	**Current year**	**Previous year**
		£	**£**	**£**	**£**
	Bank loans				
	Obligations under finance leases				

17	**Provisions for liabilities and charges**				
		Group	**Group**	**College**	**College**
		Current year	**Previous year**	**Current year**	**Previous year**
		£	**£**	**£**	**£**
	Balance at beginning of year				
	Charge to Income and Expenditure Account				
	Utilised in year				
	Balance at end of year				

18	**Pension liabilities**				
		Group	**Group**	**College**	**College**
		Current year	**Previous year**	**Current year**	**Previous year**
		£	**£**	**£**	**£**
	Balance at beginning of year				
	Movement in year:				
	Current service cost including life assurance				
	Contributions				
	Other finance (income)/cost				
	Actuarial loss/(gain) recognised in statement of total recognised gains and losses				
	Balance at end of year				

Notes to the Accounts (continued)

For the year ended 30 June [20..]

19	**Deferred capital grants**				
				Current year	**Previous year**
	Group and College	**Grants**	**Donations**	**Total**	**Total**
		£	£	£	£
	Balance at beginning of year:				
	Buildings				
	Equipment				
	Grants and donations received:				
	Buildings				
	Equipment				
	Released to Income and Expenditure Account:				
	Buildings				
	Equipment				
	Balances at end of year:				
	Buildings				
	Equipment				

20	**Endowments**						
	Group	**Unrestricted Permanent**	**Restricted Permanent**	**Total Permanent**	**Restricted Expendable**	**Current year Total**	**Previous year Total**
		£	£	£	£	£	£
	Balance at beginning of year:						
	Capital						
	Unspent income						
	New endowments received						
	Income receivable from endowment asset investments						
	Expenditure						
	Net transfer (to)/from income and expenditure account						
	Increase/(decrease) in market value of investments						
	Balance at end of year						
	Comprising:						
	Capital						
	Unspent income						
	Representing						
	Fellowship Funds						
	Scholarship Funds						
	Prize Funds						
	Hardship Funds						
	Bursary Funds						
	Travel Grant Funds						
	Other Funds						
	General endowments						
	Group total						

Notes to the Accounts (continued)

For the year ended 30 June [20..]

20	**Endowments (continued)**						
	College	**Unrestricted Permanent**	**Restricted Permanent**	**Total Permanent**	**Restricted Expendable**	**Current year Total**	**Previous year Total**
		£	**£**	**£**	**£**	**£**	**£**
	Balance at beginning of year:						
	Capital						
	Unspent income						
	New endowments received						
	Income receivable from endowment asset investments						
	Expenditure						
	Net transfer (to)/from income and expenditure account						
	Increase/(decrease) in market value of investments						
	Balance at end of year						
	Comprising:						
	Capital						
	Unspent income						
	Representing						
	Fellowship Funds						
	Scholarship Funds						
	Prize Funds						
	Hardship Funds						
	Bursary Funds						
	Travel Grant Funds						
	Other Funds						
	General endowments						
	College total						

Notes to the Accounts (continued)

For the year ended 30 June [20..]

21	**Reserves**					
	Group	**General reserves**	**Operational property revaluation reserve**	**Fixed asset investment revaluation reserve**	**Current year Total**	**Previous year Total**
			£	£	£	£
	Balance at beginning of year					
	Surplus retained for the year					
	Actuarial gain/(loss)					
	Transfer in respect of depreciation on revalued operational properties					
	Transfer in respect of disposals of fixed asset investments					
	Increase/(decrease) in market value of investments					
	Balance at end of year					
	College					
	Balance at beginning of year					
	Surplus retained for the year					
	Actuarial gain/(loss)					
	Transfer in respect of depreciation on revalued operational properties					
	Transfer in respect of disposals of fixed asset investments					
	Increase/(decrease) in market value of investments					
	Balance at end of year					

22	**Memorandum of Unapplied Total Return**			
	Included within reserves the following amounts represent the Unapplied Total Return of the College:			
			Current year	**Previous year**
			£	£
	Unapplied Total Return at beginning of year			
	Unapplied Total Return for year (see note 3b)			
	Unapplied Total Return at end of year			

Notes to the Accounts (continued)

For the year ended 30 June [20..]

23	**Reconciliation of consolidated operating surplus to net cash inflow from operating activities**		
		Current year	**Previous year**
		£	**£**
	Surplus/(deficit) on continuing operations before donations of heritage assets		
	Depreciation of tangible fixed assets		
	Surplus on disposal of tangible fixed assets		
	Deferred capital grants released to income		
	Investment income		
	Interest payable		
	Pension costs less contributions payable		
	Decrease/(increase) in stocks		
	Decrease/(increase) in debtors		
	Increase in creditors		
	Net cash inflow from operating activities		

24	**Cash flows**		
		Current year	**Previous year**
		£	**£**
	Returns on investments and servicing of finance		
	Endowment and investment income received		
	Interest paid		
	Net cash inflow from returns on income and servicing of finance		
	Capital expenditure and financial investment		
	Purchase of tangible fixed assets		
	Donations for buildings and other deferred capital grants received		
	Proceeds of disposal of tangible fixed assets		
	Net purchase of long-term investments		
	New endowments received		
	Net cash outflow from capital expenditure and financial investment		
	Financing		
	Bank loan acquired		
	Repayment of long-term loan		
	Net cash inflow from financing		

25	**Analysis of cash and bank balances**			
		At beginning of year	**Cash flows**	**At end of year**
		£	**£**	**£**
	Bank overdrafts			
	Cash at bank and in hand			
	Net Funds			

Notes to the Accounts (continued)

For the year ended 30 June [20..]

26	**Capital commitments**		
		Current year	**Previous year**
		£	**£**
	Capital commitments at 30 June [20..] are as follows:		
	Authorised and contracted		
	Authorised but not yet contracted for		
	Commitments under finance leases entered into but not yet provided for in the financial statements		

27	**Financial commitments**		
	At 30 June [20..] the College had annual commitments under non-cancellable operating leases as follows:		
		Current year	**Previous year**
		£	**£**
	Land and buildings:		
	Expiring within one year		
	Expiring between two and five years		
	Expiring in over five years		
	Other		
	Expiring within one year		
	Expiring between two and five years		
	Expiring in over five years		

28 Pension schemes

The College participates in three defined benefit schemes, the Universities Superannuation Scheme (USS), the Cambridge Colleges Federated Pension Scheme (CCFPS) and the Church of England Funded Pensions Scheme, as follows:

Universities Superannuation Scheme

The College participates in the Universities Superannuation Scheme (USS), a defined benefit scheme which is contracted out of the State Second Pension (S2P). The assets of the scheme are held in a separate fund administered by the trustee, Universities Superannuation Scheme Limited.
Insert specimen wording provided by USS.

Cambridge Colleges Federated Pension Scheme

Insert the disclosures required by FRS 17, provided by the scheme actuary.

Other pension schemes

Insert the disclosures required by FRS 17, provided by the pension provider or scheme actuary.

The total pension cost, after personal health insurance contributions, for the year to 30 June [20..] (see note x) was as follows:

	Year to 30 June	**Previous year to 30 June**
USS: Contributions	xx,xxx	xx,xxx
CCFPS: Charged to income and expenditure account	xxx,xxx	xxx,xxx
Other Pension Schemes: Contributions	xx,xxx	xx,xxx
	xxx,xxx	xxx,xxx

Notes to the Accounts (continued)

For the year ended 30 June [20..]

29 Principal subsidiary and associated undertakings and other significant investments

Give details where relevant.

30 Contingent Liabilities

Give details where relevant.

31 Related Party Transactions

Owing to the nature of the College's operations and the composition of the Governing Body it is inevitable that transactions will take place with organisations in which a member of the Governing Body may have an interest. All transactions involving organisations in which a member of the Governing Body may have an interest are conducted at arm's length and in accordance with the College's normal procedures.

[Transactions totalling £xx,xxx relating to .... took place with .... Limited, a company in which the College has a majority interest. There were no amounts outstanding at the balance sheet date.]

COLLEGES: MATRICULATION AND PRESENTATION OF CANDIDATES FOR CERTAIN DEGREES

HUGHES HALL

1. Hughes Hall shall be empowered to present for matriculation, to enter as a candidate for any examination leading to the degree of B.A., Mus.B., B.Ed., and B.Th., and to present as a candidate for the degree, a student who (*a*) has attained the age of twenty-one years or (*b*) is entitled to be, or has been, approved as an Affiliated Student.

2. Except as provided in Regulation 1 and except in so far as the Council upon application from Hughes Hall shall have waived, in respect of a particular student, one or more of the following restrictions, Hughes Hall shall not:

(*a*) present for matriculation any student who does not hold the status of Bachelor of Arts or of Master of Arts in the University;

(*b*) enter a student as a candidate for any examination leading to the B.A. Degree or the B.Ed. Degree (otherwise than for a Tripos Examination as a candidate not for honours), or for the Mus.B. Examination, or for an examination leading to the B.Th. Degree;

(*c*) present a candidate for the degree of B.A., Mus.B., B.Ed., or B.Th.

LUCY CAVENDISH COLLEGE

1. Lucy Cavendish College shall be empowered to present for matriculation, to enter as a candidate for any examination leading to the degree of B.A., Mus.B., B.Ed., or B.Th., and to present as a candidate for the degree, a student who (*a*) has attained the age of twenty-one years or (*b*) is entitled to be, or has been, approved as an Affiliated Student.

2. Except as provided in Regulation 1 and except in so far as the Council upon application from the College shall have waived, in respect of a particular student, one or more of the following restrictions, Lucy Cavendish College shall not:

(*a*) present for matriculation any student who does not hold the status of Bachelor of Arts or of Master of Arts in the University;

(*b*) enter a student as a candidate for any examination leading to the B.A. Degree or the B.Ed. Degree (otherwise than for a Tripos Examination as a candidate not for honours), or for the Mus.B. Examination, or for an examination leading to the B.Th. Degree;

(*c*) present a candidate for the degree of B.A., Mus.B., B.Ed., or B.Th.

ST EDMUND'S COLLEGE

1. St Edmund's College shall be empowered to present for matriculation, to enter as a candidate for any examination leading to the degree of B.A., Mus.B., or B.Th., and to present as a candidate for the degree, a student who (*a*) has attained the age of twenty-one years or (*b*) is entitled to be, or has been, approved as an Affiliated Student.

2. Except as provided in Regulation 1 and except in so far as the Council upon application from the College shall have waived, in respect of a particular student, one or more of the following restrictions, St Edmund's College shall not:

(*a*) present for matriculation any student who does not hold the status of Bachelor of Arts or of Master of Arts in the University;

(*b*) enter a student as a candidate for any examination leading to the B.A. Degree (otherwise than for a Tripos Examination as a candidate not for honours), or for the Mus.B. Examination, or for an examination leading to the B.Th. Degree;

(*c*) present a candidate for the degree of B.A., Mus.B., or B.Th.

WOLFSON COLLEGE

1. Wolfson College shall be empowered to present for matriculation, and to present as a candidate for the degree of B.A., or Mus.B., or B.Ed., a person who (*a*) has attained the age of twenty-one years or (*b*) is entitled to be, or has been, approved as an Affiliated Student.

2. Except as provided in Regulation 1 and except in so far as the Council upon application from the College shall have waived, in respect of a particular person, one or more of the following restrictions, Wolfson College shall not:

(*a*) present for matriculation any person who does not hold the status of Bachelor of Arts or of Master of Arts in the University;

(*b*) present a candidate for the degree of B.A., or Mus.B., or B.Ed.

CHAPTER XV

INSTITUTIONS RECOGNIZED UNDER STATUTE G I

APPROVED FOUNDATIONS[1]

APPROVED SOCIETIES[1]

[1] There are currently no institutions in this category.

APPENDIX I: PROCEDURES AND GUIDELINES

NOTICE BY THE COUNCIL

Procedure for handling claims for the transfer of stewardship of human remains

The Council, after consultation with relevant institutions within the University, has drawn up a Procedure for handling claims for the transfer of stewardship of human remains.

In October 2005 the Department for Media, Culture and Sport published *Guidance for the Care of Human Remains in Museums*. This non-statutory document provides guidance, and best practice, on the care of human remains, for museums and other institutions in England, Wales, and Northern Ireland, which hold human remains in permanent collections. That Guidance recommended that such institutions prepare and publish a clear process for the handling of claims for the return of human remains. The Council recognizes the need for the University, in common with institutions housing collections which include human remains, to have such a process in place. It expects all institutions in the University to follow the Procedure set out below. A copy of the Procedure will also be available on the University's website at http://www.admin.cam.ac.uk/offices/secretariat/.

Procedure for handling claims for the transfer of stewardship of human remains

1. **Making a request or enquiry**

1.1 Requests or enquiries relating to the transfer of stewardship of human remains in the University's collections should be submitted in writing to:

The Registrary
The Old Schools
Trinity Lane
Cambridge
CB2 1TN

1.2 The Registrary shall take responsibility for dealing with the request or enquiry and shall act as the point of contact in respect of such request or enquiry. The Registrary may appoint a delegate to act in her or his place under this procedure, and any reference to the Registrary in this procedure shall be deemed to include a reference to any such delegate.

1.3 The Registrary will openly engage and enter into constructive dialogue with anyone making a request or enquiry. Every attempt will be made to achieve a resolution by informal means through consultation with those with responsibility for the University collection in which the human remains are located, and where appropriate by mediation.

2. **Making a claim**

2.1 In the event that it is not possible informally to resolve a request for the transfer of stewardship of human remains, a formal claim for the transfer of such stewardship should be submitted in writing to the Registrary at the above address and should include as much supporting information as possible, including information about:

- the identity of the individual(s) or community making the claim and any intermediary or representative;
- the specific human remains being claimed;
- the connection between the claimant(s) and the human remains in question;
- the basis for the claim and the reason for making it;
- the wishes of the claimant(s) for the future of the remains; and
- any information in the possession of the claimant(s) regarding other potential claims in respect of the same human remains.

2.2 The Registrary will formally acknowledge the claim in writing and provide an indication of how long it is likely to take for a decision to be made.

2.3 The Registrary will consider the information provided by the claimant(s) and may gather further information as necessary, either from the claimant(s), or from other sources, including from the national government of the country from which the claimant(s) originate. The Registrary shall also invite those with responsibility for the University collection in which the human remains are located to provide a response to the claim, together with any material which they consider to be relevant to the claim, including expert evidence.

2.4 The Registrary may take such steps as may be deemed necessary to advertise or give notice of any request or claim for the transfer of stewardship of human remains with a view to ensuring that any competing claims to the same remains are brought to the attention of the University.

3. **Human Remains Advisory Panel**

3.1 The information provided by the claimant(s) and by those responsible for the relevant University collection, as well as any other information gathered by the Registrary shall be presented to a Human Remains Advisory Panel, which shall be established in accordance with Annex I.

3.2 The Panel shall consider the information presented to it and, taking into account the criteria set out in Annex II, which are derived from the Department for Media, Culture and Sport's *Guidance for the Care of Human Remains in Museums*, the Panel shall give advice and make recommendations to the University Council regarding the claim. The Panel shall submit its advice and recommendations to the Council in the form of a full written report of all the relevant facts, factors, and evidence.

3.3 The Panel may itself seek additional information or evidence as appropriate from any persons in order to assist it in determining its advice and recommendations to the University Council, including independent advice from experts on ethical, scientific, legal, and political issues.

4. **Decision**

4.1 Based upon the advice and recommendations contained in the Panel's report, the University Council shall make a decision regarding the claim.

4.2 Once a decision has been made it shall be formally minuted. The Registrary shall promptly inform the claimant(s) of the decision and the reasons for it.

4.3 The claimant(s) shall be allowed time to respond. It is possible that further discussions may continue. If a request for the transfer of stewardship of human remains is declined, this shall not preclude future dialogue or communication between parties.

5. **Costs**

5.1 The costs of administrative support for the Panel, together with any approved costs of any independent expert or third party who is commissioned to provide evidence at the reasonable request of the Panel, shall be met out of central University funds. Claimants shall meet their own costs.

6. **Review**

6.1 The efficacy of this procedure shall be regularly reviewed by the University Council and this procedure shall be revised as deemed necessary or appropriate in the light of feedback and comment from interested parties.

ANNEX I

1. A Human Remains Advisory Panel shall be established to give advice and make recommendations to the University Council regarding claims for the transfer of stewardship of human remains held in the University's collections.
2. There shall be three members of the Panel.
3. The members of the Panel will be appointed by the University Council on the recommendation of the Advisory Committee on Committee Membership and External Nominations. One member of the Panel shall be appointed as Chair of the Panel. The Panel shall have a sufficient and appropriate range of expertise amongst its members to enable it properly and fairly to perform its functions.
4. Members of the Panel shall be appointed in their own right, not as representatives of any interests or institutions.
5. Members will be appointed for an initial term of up to five years. Terms of appointment may be renewed.
6. The Registrary shall appoint the Secretary of the Panel.
7. The Panel may set procedures regulating its own activities, including procedures for the summary resolution of a claim by one or more members of the Panel. The Panel may at its discretion hear oral evidence or submissions from the parties involved and may at its discretion allow the parties to be represented at such a hearing.
8. The activities of the Panel shall be reviewed by the University Council every three years.

ANNEX II

A. The status of those making the request and continuity with remains

Genealogical descendants: If individuals can demonstrate a direct and close genealogical link to the human remains, their wishes would generally be given very strong weight. However, consideration should be given as to whether they are the only people in this category and if they are not, whether there was any risk of harm to others in this category if the request being made were granted.

There may be exceptional cases where remains would not be returned to genealogical descendants. However, it is expected that in the majority of cases they would be, or that consent would be required from the descendants for any further use by the University.

In practice, individuals who died more than 100 years ago may have many descendants from more than one community, so genealogical descent alone may not be the only criteria considered.

In such cases, the University will need to assess the range of potential claimants and gauge how the interests of these individuals might be balanced with any other relevant considerations. The ethical principles will help to guide the University through these cases. The principles of avoiding harm (to the particular individuals concerned) and solidarity (seeking co-operation and consensus) are likely to be particularly important here.

Cultural community of origin: The concept of a community can be a difficult one to define. The assumption is that human society is characterized by the creation of communities that individuals feel a part of and which take on a collective set of values, often identified by particular cultural behaviour. It is often far less easy to identify which particular cultural community, or part of a community, has the greatest authority in any particular instance.

When considering claims based on cultural links, the University will need to take care to verify that the group it is dealing with is the only potential claimant, or that, if it is not, the other potential claimants support them. For overseas claims, where there may be doubt on this, advice should generally be sought from the national government concerned. It might also be normal to look for precedents for how a community has acted in the past.

For a community to be recognized and their claim considered it would generally be expected that continuity of belief, customs or language could be demonstrated between the claimants and the community from which the remains originate. Cultures evolve and change through time but these changes can normally be recorded and demonstrated. The relationship between the location of the claimant community and the origin of the remains might also be a consideration.

It would be unusual to accept a claim for return from a group who did not either occupy the land from which the remains came, practice the same religious beliefs, share the same culture or language, or could not demonstrate why this was no longer the case.

The University will need to be assured that a sufficient link does exist and that the group they are dealing with has sufficient authority to make a community claim.

A clear demonstration of a continuity of association between the claimant and the remains will be of great importance in dealing with any claim.

The country of origin: In some cases a nation may make a claim for remains, either on behalf of a particular community or for all of its nationals. Such a claim would be considered along similar lines to claims based on cultural community.

B. The cultural, spiritual, and religious significance of the remains

Where claims are made it would be expected, but not essential, for the claimant group to show that human remains and their treatment have a cultural, religious or spiritual significance to their community. The claim may be being made purely on cultural, spiritual or religious grounds. The claimant group may show that remains were removed without the permission of their community, or at least outside its laws and normal practices. Further the claimant may show that the correct 'laying to rest' of remains is of religious or spiritual importance.

The remains might also be of a particular cultural significance to a community, for example as being from an important family or representing war dead, or victims of a particular event, such as a massacre.

Demonstration through some or all of the ways above, of strong continuous cultural, spiritual or religious significance of particular human remains, will add weight to a claim. This is particularly so in cases where there is clearly a risk of harm to the individuals or communities concerned, for example, where the continued holding of the remains by the University perpetuates a strong feeling of grief amongst claimants.

C. The age of the remains

The vast majority of claims that have been made for return have concerned the remains of overseas people who died within the last 100 to 300 years. This corresponds most closely to the period when expansion took place by European powers with its subsequent effect on Indigenous peoples – a period that does not go back further than 500 years. It is also the period in which it is more likely for a close genealogical link to be made between the living and the dead.

Archaeological and historical study has shown that it is very difficult to demonstrate clear genealogical, cultural or ethnic continuity far into the past, although there are exceptions to this. For these reasons it is considered that claims are unlikely to be successful for any remains over 300 years old, and are unlikely to be considered for remains over 500 years old, except where a very close and continuous geographical, religious, spiritual, and cultural link can be demonstrated. Some cultures put more emphasis on association with land that has a cultural, spiritual or religious importance and less on relative age. In such cases, the chronological age of the remains may be less significant.

D. How the remains were originally removed and acquired

There are many cases of human remains being removed and studied without dispute. There are other instances, particularly during the 19th and early 20th century, of remains being removed against the will of individuals, families, and communities.

E. The status of the remains within the University/legal status of institution

The University should be sure of the exact legal status of the remains within its collections and that it has the right to make decisions over their fate.

The University should identify the remains being claimed and then ascertain why they are being held and how they have been, and are likely to be, used:

1. Are the remains fully documented and the information about them publicly available?
2. Do they have continued, reasonably foreseeable, research potential?
3. Do they form part of a documented access strategy?
4. Are they curated according to the very highest standards?
5. Are they curated in such a way as their long-term preservation is assured?
6. Can the long-term security of the remains be guaranteed within the University?

F. The scientific, educational, and historical value of the remains to the University and the public

Many human remains have undoubted potential to further the knowledge and understanding of humanity through research, study, and display. In considering a request for return of human remains, the University should carefully assess their value and reasonably foreseeable potential for research, teaching, and display and should ensure that specialists with appropriate knowledge and experience have assessed this.

If the remains do have value for research, teaching, and display, the University should decide whether this can override other factors, particularly such as the wishes and feelings of genealogical descendants or cultural communities.

G. How the remains have been used in the past

In considering the future of remains, consideration may be given to what use they had been put in the past. Evidence of extensive previous research use would normally support an argument for scientific value.

H. The future of the remains if returned

The care of remains, if returned, also requires consideration. Some requests might require re-burial or removal from the public arena, whereas some claimants may be prepared to keep the remains in such a way that future research, teaching or even display is possible.

I. Records of the remains

Whether a record of the remains exists, or can be made before return, might be a factor in making a decision.

J. Other options

There may be more than two options when a claim is made. The University should explore further alternatives if this helps in reaching a consensus. For example, it may be possible that remains would stay in the relevant University collection, but a claimant group would gain a level of control over their future use.

K. Policy of the country of origin

Some nation states have developed domestic legislation or policy to govern claims for the return of remains. The University would normally expect to be aware of any policies of the national government from which a claim originated. It is worth considering how a claim would be resolved if made in the country from which the claimants originate, as well as the expectations of the claimant based on the practice in their country of origin.

L. Precedent

Claims will generally be dealt with on a case-by-case basis However, it would be expected that the University would review past cases of claims made to it, or claims of a similar kind made to other collections and their outcomes, as well as giving some thought to the impact of any decision on future claims.

INDEX TO THE STATUTES AND ORDINANCES

(2014)

Proper names of persons are indexed under their surnames

D

F

G

H

K

L

Q

R

S

V

W